INDEX OF ECONOMIC ARTICLES
In Journals and Collective Volumes

Index of
Economic Articles

IN JOURNALS AND COLLECTIVE VOLUMES

Volume XXVI · 1984

Part One—Subject Index

Prepared under the auspices of

THE JOURNAL OF ECONOMIC LITERATURE

of the

AMERICAN ECONOMIC ASSOCIATION

JOHN PENCAVEL

Managing Editor

MOSES ABRAMOVITZ

Associate Editor

DRUCILLA EKWURZEL

Associate Editor

ASATOSHI MAESHIRO

Editorial Consultant

MARY KAY AKERMAN

Assistant Editor

NASHVILLE, TENNESSEE
AMERICAN ECONOMIC ASSOCIATION
1987

Student Classifiers: A'Amer Farooqi; Nayyer Hussain; Edgar L. Zamalloa, and Lorena M. Zamalloa.

Library of Congress Catalog Card Number: 61–8020
International Standard Book Number: 0–917290–15–1
International Standard Serial Number: 0536–647X
Printed in the United States of America

TABLE OF CONTENTS

INTRODUCTORY DISCUSSION

This volume of the *Index* lists, both by subject category and by author, articles in major economic journals and in collective volumes published during the year 1984. The articles listed include all articles published in English or with English summaries in the journals and books listed below (p. x). Part one includes the Subject Index of Articles in Journals and Collective Volumes, and Part Two consists of an alphabetical Author Index of all the articles indexed in Part One.

Relationship to JEL

This *Index* is prepared largely as an adjunct to the bibliographic activities of the *Journal of Economic Literature (JEL)*. Economies of joint production are pursued throughout the production process. Journals included are those indexed in the *JEL* quarterly; collective volumes are selected from the annotated 1984 books; the classification system is a more detailed version of the *JEL* system.

Journals Included

The 293 journals listed represent, in general, those journals that we believe will be most helpful to research workers and teachers of economics. These journals are listed below on p. x.

Generally, articles, notes, communications, comments, replies, rejoinders, as well as papers and formal discussions in proceedings and review articles have been indexed. There are some exceptions; only articles in English or with English summaries are included—this practice results in a slightly reduced coverage compared with the *JEL* quarterly. Articles lacking author identification are omitted, as are articles without economic content. Identical articles appearing in two different journals in 1984 are listed from both sources. The journal issues included usually fall within a single volume. When a volume of a journal overlaps two calendar years, for example, Fall 1983 to Summer 1984, we include the issues from the two volumes relating to 1984 as best we can determine.

Collective Volumes

The collective volumes consist of the following:
1. *Festschriften*
2. Conference publications with individual papers
3. Collected essays, original, by one or more authors
4. Collected essays, reprinted, by one or more authors
5. Proceedings volumes
6. Books of readings

All original articles in English are indexed with the exception of unsigned articles or articles without economic content. Reprinted articles are included on the basis that a researcher would be interested in knowing about another source of the article. The original publication dates are shown in italics on the citations of reprinted articles. Excerpts are not included. The same article appearing for the first time in different collective volumes in the same year is cited from both publications.

In the article citation, reference to the book in which the article appears is by author or editor of the volume. If the same person or persons wrote or edited more than one book included in the 1984 *Index*, it is indicated by a I or II appearing in both the source given in the article citation and the bibliographic reference in the book listing. If the same person wrote one book and edited another in 1984, the specification of "ed" in the reference indicates which book is being cited.

The collective volumes are listed alphabetically by author or editor beginning on p. xvi and include a full bibliographic reference. If there is more than one edition, the publisher cited is the one on the copy the *JEL* received, usually the American publisher.

Arrangement

The *Index* consists of two parts:
1. A Subject Index in which the articles are arranged by subject.
2. An Author Index.

Part One—Subject Index

In Part One, all articles are listed alphabetically by first author under each 4-digit subject category. Joint authors are listed up to three; beyond that, only the first author is listed, followed by *et al*.

There is one exception to the alphabetical author arrangement. In the 0322 category, a subdivision of **History of Thought** entitled **Individuals,** the arrangement is first alphabetical by the individual discussed in the article and then alphabetical by the article's author.

Articles with empirical content or discussing a particular geographic area carry a geographic descriptor (see discussion below).

Classification System

The classification system is an expansion of the 3-digit classification system used in the *Journal of Economic Literature* to a 4-digit system with slightly over 300 subcategories. The classification system, itself, is shown beginning on p. xxxiii (Part One). In most cases the classification heading is self-explanatory; however, in some cases notes have been added to clarify the coverage or indicate alternative subject classifications. The basic approach in classification is from the point of view of the researcher rather than the teacher; course content does not necessarily coincide with subfields of our classification system. In all cases where there are two or more 4-digit classifications under a 3-digit category, there is a zero classification; in most instances this is labeled "General." The zero or general category has been used both as an inclusive and a residual category. For example, an article discussing *all* aspects of international trade theory appears in the general category. There are also some articles that do not fall in any of the individual subcategories, and these, too, are classified in the general or zero category.

The criterion used in the classifying process is whether persons interested in this topic would wish to have the article drawn to their attention. With the advent of the online ECONOMIC LITERATURE INDEX on DIALOG, the interpretation of "interest" has broadened slightly to include cross-classifications that indicate the subject matter, particularly in such categories as industry studies or occupational designations. Over half of the articles are classified in more than one subcategory. From time to time, we find it desirable to add subject classifications as particular topics become prominent or to change subject headings to make them more descriptive of the contents of the category. This year we have added the following categories:

Additions: 0229, Microeconomics of Intertemporal Choice. 0239, Macroeconomics of Intertemporal Choice. 0250 has been broken down into: 0250, General; 0251, Social Choice Theory; and 0252, Social Choice Studies: Voting, Committees, etc. 1310 has been broken down into 1310, General, and 1312, Economic Fluctuations: Theory. 4410 has also been broken down into: 4410, General, and 4411, International Investment and Long-term Capital Movements: Theory. (1313, Economic Fluctuations: Studies, and 4412, International Investments and Long-term Capital Movements; Studies, have been categories in earlier *Indexes*.) 6000, General, has been added. 6130 has been changed to 6130, Regulation of Public Utilities, and the 6131 and 6132 categories have been dropped. 6190, Economics of Regulation, now includes articles formerly classified in 6130 and 6132. 6313 now includes articles on communication equipment formerly found in 6314, which now includes only articles on transportation equipment.

Geographic Descriptors

Geographic descriptors appear in brackets at the end of any article entry in the Subject Index where the article cites data from or refers to a particular country or area. Research workers interested in these countries thus are made aware of the empirical content in the article. The descriptors used are countries or broader areas, such as southeast Asia (S. E. Asia); articles referring to cities or regions within a country are classified under the country. In general, the country name is written out in full with some adaptations and abbreviations, *e.g.*, U.S. is used for United States, U.K. for United Kingdom, and U.S.S.R. for Union of Soviet Socialist Republics. Abbreviations include: W. for West, E. for East, S. for South, N. for North. A shortened name such as W. Germany is used rather than the correct, but longer, Federal Republic of Germany. When broader regions are used as descriptors, the article may or may not refer to the full unit. For example, OECD has been used at times when most, but not all, of the OECD member countries are referred to.

Index volumes prior to 1979 sometimes did not include geographic descriptors on articles listed under subject categories 1210, 1211, 1220, 1221, 1230, 1240, and 1241, involving general or comparative economic country studies. In the 1979 *Index* and later volumes, these articles carry geographic descriptors in order to facilitate online identification in the Economic Literature Index on DIALOG. Because the descriptor fields are limited to five, very general descriptors, such as LDCs (developing countries) and MDCs (developed countries), are often used on articles.

The fact that an article carries a geographic descriptor does not necessarily preclude its being primarily theoretical in nature. Any theoretical article drawing on empirical data to demonstrate its findings will carry a geographic descriptor.

Topical Guide to the Classification System

At the end of Part One there is an alphabetical listing of standard economic terms and concepts. References are to the appropriate 4-digit classification numbers, not to page numbers.

Part Two—Author Index

Part two consists of an alphabetical Author Index in which citations appear under each author (up to three) of an article. Wherever possible the full first name and middle initial or middle name(s) are used. Wherever it could be definitely ascertained, articles by the same person are grouped together with only one listing of the name. Authors' first names and initials are listed differently in various journals and books; for example, an individual may be identified as John L. Smith, J. L. Smith, or John Smith. Thus, despite our best efforts, we were left in doubt in several instances. Joint authors are listed up to three; beyond that, only the first author is listed, followed by *et al.* Under each author, articles are listed alphabetically. Names carrying prefixes are alphabetized according to the first *capitalized* letter, with occasional exceptions following national practices. Thus, van Arkadie would appear under A and D'Alabro under D.

LIST OF JOURNALS INDEXED 1984

Accounting Review, Vol. 59.

Acta Oeconomica, Vol. 32; Vol. 33.

L'Actualité Economique, Vol. 60.

African Economic History, No. 13, 1984.

Agricultural Economics Research, Vol. 36.

American Economic Review, Vol. 74.
Includes American Economic Association Papers and Proceedings of the annual meeting in 74(2).

American Economist, Vol. 28.

American Historical Review, Vol. 89.

American Journal of Agricultural Economics, Vol. 66.
Title changed from Journal of Farm Economics in 1968.

American Journal of Economics and Sociology, Vol. 43.

American Political Science Review, Vol. 78.

American Real Estate and Urban Economics Association Journal, Vol. 12.

Annales de l'INSEE, Issue nos. 53–56.

Annals of Public and Co-operative Economy, Vol. 55.

Annals of Regional Science, Vol. 18, Issue no. 3.

Antitrust Bulletin, Vol. 29.

Applied Economics, Vol. 16.

ACES Bulletin (Association for Comparative Economic Studies Bulletin), Vol. 26.

Atlantic Economic Journal, Vol. 12.

Aussenwirtschaft, Vol. 39.

Australian Bulletin of Labour, Vol. 10, Issue nos. 2–4, Supplement; Vol. 11, Issue no. 1.

Australian Economic History Review, Vol. 24.
Title changed from Business Archives and History in 1967; prior to 1962 entitled Bulletin of the Business Archives Council of Australia.

Australian Economic Papers, Vol. 23.

Australian Economic Review, Issue nos. 65–68.

Australian Journal of Agricultural Economics, Vol. 28.

Australian Tax Forum, Vol. 1.

Banca Nazionale del Lavoro—Quarterly Review, Issue nos. 148–151.

Bancaria, Vol. 40.

Bangladesh Development Studies, Vol. 12.

Bell Journal of Economics.
See Rand Journal of Economics.

British Journal of Industrial Relations, Vol. 22.

British Review of Economic Issues, Vol. 6

Brookings Papers on Economic Activity, Issue nos. 1–2, 1984.

Bulletin of Economic Research, Vol. 36.
Title changed from Yorkshire Bulletin of Economic and Social Research in 1971.

Bulletin of Indonesian Economic Studies, Vol. 20.

Bulletin for International Fiscal Documentation, Vol. 38.

Business Economics, Vol. 19.

Business History Review, Vol. 58.
Title changed from Bulletin of the Business Historical Society in 1954.

Cahiers Économiques de Bruxelles, Issue nos. 101–104.

Cambridge Journal of Economics, Vol. 8.

Canadian Journal of Agricultural Economics, Vol. 32.

Canadian Journal of Development Studies, Vol. 5.

Canadian Journal of Economics, Vol. 17.

Canadian Public Policy, Vol. 10.

Carnegie–Rochester Conference Series on Public Policy, Vols. 20–21.
Vols. 1–17 were listed as supplements to the Journal of Monetary Economics.

Cato Journal, Vol. 4. Issue nos. 1–2.

Cepal Review, Issue nos. 22–24.

Challenge, Vol. 26, Issue no. 6; Vol. 27, Issue nos. 1–5.

Chinese Economic Studies, Vol. 17, Issue nos. 2–4; Vol. 18, Issue no. 1.

Conflict Management and Peace Science, Vol. 7, Issue no. 2; Vol. 8, Issue no. 1.
Title changed from Journal of Peace Science in 1979–80.

Consommation, Vol. 31.

Contemporary Policy Issues, Issue nos. 4–6, 1984; Vol. 3, Issue no. 1.

Cuadernos de Economia, Vol. 21.

Czechoslovak Economic Digest, Issue nos. 1–8, 1984.

Czechoslovak Economic Papers, Issue no. 22, 1984.

Demography, Vol. 21.

Desarrollo Económico, Vol. 23, Issue no. 92; Vol. 24, Issue nos. 93–95.

Eastern Economic Journal, Vol. 10.

Eastern European Economics, Vol. 22, Issue no. 3–4; Vol. 23, Issue nos. 1–2.

Econometric Reviews, Vol. 3.

Econometrica, Vol. 52.

Economia (Portuguese Catholic University), Vol. 8.

Economia Internazionale, Vol. 37.

Economia e Lavoro, Vol. 18.

Economía et Política, Vol. 1.

Economic Analysis and Workers' Management, Vol. 18.

Economic Computation and Economic Cybernetics Studies and Research, Vol. 19.
Title changed from Studii şi Cercetări Economicè in 1974. Changed from issue numbers to volume numbers in 1978.

Economic Development and Cultural Change, Vol. 32, Issue nos. 2–4; Vol. 33, Issue no. 1.

Economic Forum, Vol. 5, Issue no. 1.
Title changed from Intermountain Economic Review in 1979.

Economic Geography, Vol. 60.

Economic History Review, Vol. 37.

Economic Inquiry, Vol. 22.
Title changed from Western Economic Journal in 1974.

Economic Journal, Vol. 94, Issue nos. 373–376, Supplement.

Economic Notes, Issue nos. 1–3, 1984.

Economic Record, Vol. 60.

Economic and Social Review, Vol. 15, Issue nos. 2–4; Vol. 16, Issue no. 1.

Economic Studies Quarterly, Vol. 35.

Economica, Vol. 51.
Title changed from Economica, N.S. in 1974.

Económica, Vol. 30.

Economics of Education Review, Vol. 3.

Économie Appliquée, Vol. 37.

Économies et Sociétés, Vol. 18.

De Economist, Vol. 132.

Ekonomiska Samfundets Tidskrift, Vol. 37.

Empirica, Vol. 11.

Empirical Economics, Vol. 9.

Energy Economics, Vol. 6.

Energy Journal, Vol. 5.

European Economic Review, Vols. 24–26.

European Review of Agricultural Economics, Vol. 11.

Explorations in Economic History, Vol. 21.
Title changed from Explorations in Entrepreneurial History in 1969–70.

Federal Reserve Bank of Dallas Economic Review, January, March, May, July, September, November, 1984.

Federal Reserve Bank of Minneapolis Quarterly Review, Vol. 8.

Federal Reserve Bank of New York Quarterly Review, Vol. 9.

Federal Reserve Bank of Richmond Economic Review, Vol. 70.

Federal Reserve Bank of San Francisco Economic Review, Issue nos. 1–4, 1984.

Federal Reserve Bank of St. Louis Review, Vol. 66.

Journal of Economic Issues, Vol. 18.

Journal of Economic Literature, Vol. 22.

Journal of Economic Studies, Vol. 11.

Journal of Economic Theory, Vols. 32–34.

Journal of Economics and Business, Vol. 36.
Title changed from **Economics and Business Bulletin** in 1972–73.

Journal of Energy and Development, Vol. 9, Issue no. 2; Vol. 10, Issue no. 1.

Journal of Environmental Economics and Management, Vol. 11.

Journal of European Economic History, Vol. 13, Special Issue.

Journal of Finance, Vol. 39.

Journal of Financial Economics, Vol. 13.

Journal of Financial and Quantitative Analysis, Vol. 19.

Journal of Financial Research, Vol. 7.

Journal of Futures Markets, Vol. 4.

Journal of Health Economics, Vol. 3.

Journal of Human Resources, Vol. 19.

Journal of Industrial Economics, Vol. 32, Issue nos. 3–4; Vol. 33, Issue nos. 1–2.

Journal of International Business Studies, Vol. 15, Issue no. 1.

Journal of International Economics, Vols. 16–17.

Journal of International Money and Finance, Vol. 3.

Journal of Labor Economics, Vol. 2.

Journal of Labor Research, Vol. 5.

Journal of Law and Economics, Vol. 27.

Journal of Macroeconomics, Vol. 6.

Journal of Mathematical Economics, Vol. 13.

Journal of Monetary Economics, Vols. 13–14.

Journal of Money, Credit and Banking, Vol. 16.

Journal of Policy Analysis and Management, Vol. 3, Issue nos. 2–4; Vol. 4, Issue no. 1.

Journal of Policy Modeling, Vol. 6.

Journal of Political Economy, Vol. 92.

Journal of Portfolio Management, Vol. 10, Issue nos. 2–4; Vol. 11, Issue no. 1.

Journal of Post Keynesian Economics, Vol. 6, Issue nos. 2–4; Vol. 7, Issue no. 1.

Journal of Public Economics, Vols. 23–25.

Journal of Regional Science, Vol. 24.

Journal of Research in Islamic Economics, Vol. 1, Issue no. 2; Vol. 2, Issue no. 1.

Journal of Risk and Insurance, Vol. 51.

Journal of the Royal Statistical Society, Series A, Vol. 147.

Journal for Studies in Economics and Econometrics, Issue nos. 18–20, 1984.

Journal of Transport Economics and Policy, Vol. 18.

Journal of Urban Economics, Vols. 15–16.

Journal of World Trade Law, Vol. 18.

Kansantaloudellinen Aikakauskirja, Vol. 80.

Kobe Economic and Business Review, Vol. 30.

Kobe University Economic Review, Issue no. 30, 1984.

Konjunkturpolitik, Vol. 30.

Kredit und Kapital, Vol. 17.

Kyklos, Vol. 37.

Kyoto University Economic Review, Vol. 54.

Labor History, Vol. 25.

Land Economics, Vol. 60.

Law and Contemporary Problems, Vol. 47.

Liiketaloudellinen Aikakauskirja, Vol. 33.

Lloyds Bank Review, Issue nos. 151–152, 1984.

Logistics and Transportation Review, Vol. 20.

Malayan Economic Review.
See **Singapore Economic Review.**

Managerial and Decision Economics, Vol. 5.

Manchester School of Economics and Social Studies, Vol. 52.
Title changed from **The Manchester School** in 1939; prior to 1932 entitled **The Manchester School of Economics, Commerce and Administration.**

Margin, Vol. 16, Issue nos. 2–4; Vol. 17, Issue no. 1.

Review of Marketing and Agricultural Economics, Vol. 52.

Review of Public Data Use, Vol. 12.

Review of Radical Political Economics, Vol. 16.

Review of Regional Studies, Vol. 14.

Review of Social Economy, Vol. 42.

Revue d'Economie Industrielle, Issue nos. 28–30, 1984.

Revue d'Economie Politique, Vol. 94.

Revue Économique, Vol. 35.

Rivista Internazionale di Scienze Economiche e Commerciali, Vol. 31.

Scandinavian Economic History Review, Vol. 32.

Scandinavian Journal of Economics, Vol. 86.
Title changed from **Swedish Journal of Economics** in 1976; prior to 1965 entitled **Ekonomisk Tidskrift.**

Schweizerische Zeitschrift für Volkswirtschaft und Statistik, Vol. 120.

Science and Society, Vol. 48.

Scottish Journal of Political Economy, Vol. 31.

Singapore Economic Review, Vol. 29.
Title changed from **Malayan Economic Review** in 1983.

Sloan Management Review, Vol. 25, Issue nos. 2–4; Vol. 26, Issue no. 1.

Social and Economic Studies, Vol. 33.

Social Research, Vol. 51, Issue no. 1–2.

Social Science Quarterly, Vol. 65.

South African Journal of Economics, Vol. 52.

Southern Economic Journal, Vol. 50, Issue nos. 3–4; Vol. 51, Issue nos. 1–2.

Southern Journal of Agricultural Economics, Vol. 16.

Soviet and Eastern European Foreign Trade, Vol. 20.

Statistica, Vol. 44.

Statistical Journal, Vol. 2.

Studi Economici, Vol. 39, Issue no. 22.

Survey of Current Business, Vol. 64.

Tijdschrift Voor Economie en Management, Vol. 29.
Title changed from **Tijdschrift voor Economie** in 1975.

Urban Studies, Vol. 21.

Water Resources Research, Vol. 20.

Weltwirtschaftliches Archiv, Vol. 120.

World Development, Vol. 12.

World Economy, Vol. 7.

Yale Journal on Regulation, Vol. 1, Issue no. 2; Vol. 2, Issue no. 1.

Yale Law Journal, Vol. 93, Issue nos. 3, 5–8; Vol. 94, Issue no. 2.

Zeitschrift für Betriebswirtschaft, Vol. 54, Issue no. 1.

Zeitschrift für die gesamte Staatswissenschaft, Vol. 140.

Zeitschrift für Nationalökonomie, Vol. 44, Supplement.

Zeitschrift für Wirtschafts-und Socialwissenschaften, Vol. 104.

LIST OF COLLECTIVE VOLUMES INDEXED 1984

AARON, HENRY J. AND BURTLESS, GARY, eds. *Retirement and Economic Behavior.* Studies in Social Economics series. Washington, D.C.: Brookings Institution, 1984.

ACHILLI, MICHELE AND KHALDI, MOHAMED, eds. *The Role of the Arab Development Funds in the World Economy.* New York: St. Martin's Press in association with ICEI, Institute for International Economic Cooperation, Milan, 1984.

ADAMS, DALE W.; GRAHAM, DOUGLAS H. AND VON PISCHKE, J. D., eds. *Undermining Rural Development with Cheap Credit.* Westview Special Studies in Social, Political and Economic Development series. Boulder, Colo., and London: Westview Press, 1984.

ADDO, HERB, ed. *Transforming the World-Economy? Nine Critical Essays on the New International Economic Order.* London; Sydney and Toronto: Hodder and Stoughton in Association with the United Nations University and Boulder, Colo.: Westview Press, 1984.

AGMON, TAMIR; HAWKINS, ROBERT G. AND LEVICH, RICHARD M., eds. *The Future of the International Monetary System.* Lexington, Mass., and Toronto: Heath, Lexington Books, 1984.

AHMAD, YUSUF J.; DASGUPTA, PARTHA AND MALER, KARL-GORAN, eds. *Environmental Decision-making. Volume 2.* United Nations Environment Programme Studies series. London; Sydney and Toronto: Hodder and Stoughton, 1984.

AKERLOF, GEORGE A. *An Economic Theorist's Book of Tales: Essays that Entertain the Consequences of New Assumptions in Economic Theory.* Cambridge; New York and Sydney: Cambridge University Press, 1984.

ALBERT, BILL AND GRAVES, ADRIAN, eds. *Crisis and Change in the International Sugar Economy, 1860–1914.* Edinburgh and Norwich: ISC Press, 1984.

ALM, ALVIN L. AND WEIMER, ROBERT J., eds. *Oil Shock: Policy Response and Implementation.* Cambridge, Mass.: Harper & Row, Ballinger, 1984.

ALPEROVITZ, GAR AND SKURSKI, ROGER, eds. *American Economic Policy: Problems and Prospects.* Notre Dame: University of Notre Dame Press, 1984.

AMIN, SAMIR, ed. *Human Resources, Employment and Development. Volume 5. Developing Countries: Proceedings of the Sixth World Congress of the International Economic Association Held in Mexico City, 1980.* New York: St. Martin's Press, 1984.

ANCOT, J. P., ed. *Analysing the Structure of Econometric Models.* Advanced Studies in Theoretical and Applied Econometrics series, vol. 2. The Hague; Boston and Lancaster: Nijhoff; distributed in the U.S. and Canada by Kluwer Boston, Hingham, Mass., 1984.

ANDERSON, RONALD W., ed. *The Industrial Organization of Futures Markets.* Lexington, Mass., and Toronto: Heath, Lexington Books, 1984.

ANDERSSON, AKE E.; ISARD, WALTER AND PUU, TONU, eds. *Regional and Industrial Development Theories, Models and Empirical Evidence.* Studies in Regional Science and Urban Economics series, vol. 11. Amsterdam; New York and Oxford: North-Holland; distributed in the U.S. by Elsevier Science, New York, 1984.

AOKI, MASAHIKO, ed. *The Economic Analysis of the Japanese Firm.* Contributions to Economic Analysis series, no. 151. New York; Amsterdam and Oxford: North-Holland; distributed in the U.S. and Canada by Elsevier Science, New York. 1984

ARROW, KENNETH J. *Collected Papers of Kenneth J. Arrow. Volume 3. Individual Choice under Certainty and Uncertainty.* Cambridge, Mass.: Harvard University Press, Belknap Press, 1984.

ARROW, KENNETH J. *Collected Papers of Kenneth J. Arrow. Volume 4. The Economics of Information* Cambridge, Mass.: Harvard University Press, Belknap Press, 1984.

ASPE, PEDRO AND SIGMUND, PAUL E., eds. *The Political Economy of Income Distribution in Mexico.* The Political Economy of Income Distribution in Developing Countries series, no. 4. New York and London: Holmes & Meier, 1984.

AUGUSZTINOVICS, MARIA, ed. *Long-term Models at Work.* Translated from the Hungarian by GYÖRGY HAJDU. Translation revised by PAUL G. HARE. Budapest: Akadémiai Kiadó, 1984.

AVULA, XAVIER J. R., ET AL. *Mathematical Modelling in Science and Technology: The Fourth*

International Conference, Zurich, Switzerland, August 1983. New York; Oxford; Toronto and Sydney: Pergammon Press, 1984.

AYOUB, ANTOINE, ed. *The International Oil Market Ten Years after the 1973 Crisis: Evaluation and Prospects.* Groupe de Recherche en Économie de l'Énergie et des Ressources Naturelles (GREEN), no. 6. Quebec: Laval University Press, 1984.

BAHRENBERG, GERHARD; FISCHER, MANFRED M., AND NIJKAMP, PETER. *Recent Developments in Spatial Data Analysis: Methodology, Measurement, Models.* Aldershot, Hampshire, and Brookfield, Vt.: Gower, 1984.

BALL, TERENCE AND FARR, JAMES, eds. *After Marx.* Cambridge; New York and Sydney: Cambridge University Press, 1984.

BAMBERG, GUNTER AND SPREMANN, KLAUS, eds. *Risk and Capital: Proceedings of the 2nd Summer Workshop on Risk and Capital Held at the University of Ulm, West Germany, June 20–24, 1983.* Lecture Notes in Economics and Mathematical Systems, no. 227. New York; Berlin and Tokyo: Springer, 1984.

BANCA D'ITALIA. *Italian Credit Structures: Efficiency, Competition and Controls.* London: Euromoney, 1984.

BARNES, CAROLYN; ENSMINGER, JEAN AND O'KEEFE, PHIL, eds. *Wood, Energy and Households: Perspectives on Rural Kenya.* Energy, Environment, and Development in Africa series, no. 6. Stockholm: Royal Swedish Academy of Sciences, Beijer Institute and The Scandinavian Institute of African Studies, 1984.

BARRY, NORMAN, ET AL. *Hayek's "Serfdom" revisited: Essays by Economists, Philosophers and Political Scientists on "The Road to Serfdom" after 40 years.* Hobart Paperback series, no. 18. London: Institute of Economic Affairs; distributed in North America by Transatlantic Arts, Albuquerque, N.M., 1984.

BAUER, P. T. *Reality and Rhetoric: Studies in the Economics of Development.* Cambridge, Mass.: Harvard University Press, 1984.

BAUM, VLADIMIR, ET AL. *Energy Planning in Developing Countries.* Oxford; New York; Toronto and Melbourne: Oxford University Press in Cooperation with the United Nations, 1984.

BAUMGARTNER, THOMAS AND BURNS, TOM R., eds. *Transitions to Alternative Energy Systems: Entrepreneurs, New Technologies, and Social Change.* Boulder, Colo., and London: Westview Press, 1984.

BAWDEN, D. LEE, ed. *The Social Contract Revisited: Aims and Outcomes of President Reagan's Social Welfare Policy.* The Changing Domestic Priorities series. Washington, D.C.: Urban Institute Press, 1984.

BECKER, WILLIAM H. AND WELLS, SAMUEL F., JR., eds. *Economics and World Power: An Assessment of American Diplomacy since 1789.* Political Economy of International Change series. New York and Guildford, Surrey: Columbia University Press, 1984.

[BECKMANN, MARTIN J.] *Operations Research and Economic Theory: Essays in Honor of Martin J. Beckmann.* Edited by H. HAUPTMANN; W. KRELLE AND K. C. MOSLER. New York; Heidelberg and Tokyo: Springer, 1984.

BEHREND, HILDE. *Problems of Labour and Inflation.* London; Sydney and Dover, N.H.: Croom Helm, 1984.

BENGTSSON, TOMMY; FRIDLIZIUS, GUNNAR AND OHLSSON, ROLF, eds. *Pre-industrial Population Change: The Mortality Decline and Short-term Population Movements.* Stockholm: Almqvist and Wiksell International, 1984.

BENJAMIN, ROGER AND KUDRLE, ROBERT T. *The Industrial Future of the Pacific Basin.* Foreword by HARLAN CLEVELAND. Pacific Basin Project series, no. 2. Boulder, Colo., and London: Westview Press in cooperation with the Hubert H. Humphrey Institute of Public Affairs, University of Minnesota, 1984.

BHAGWATI, JAGDISH N. AND RUGGIE, JOHN GERARD, eds. *Power, Passions and Purpose: Prospects for North–South Negotiations.* Cambridge and London: MIT Press, 1984.

BIGMAN, DAVID AND TAYA, TEIZO, eds. *Floating Exchange Rates and the State of World Trade Payments.* Cambridge, Mass.: Harper & Row, Ballinger, 1984.

CAMPBELL, COLIN D., ed. *Controlling the Cost of Social Security*. An American Enterprise Institute Book. Lexington, Mass., and Toronto: Heath, Lexington Books, 1984.

CARR, JAMES H., ed. *Crisis and Constraint in Municipal Finance: Local Fiscal Prospects in a Period of Uncertainty*. New Brunswick, N.J.: Center for Urban Policy Research, Rutgers University, 1984.

CAVACO SILVA, ANIBAL A., ed. *Economic and Social Partnership and Incomes Policy*. Lisbon: Portuguese Catholic University, 1984.

CAVES, RICHARD E. AND KRAUSE, LAWRENCE B., eds. *The Australian Economy: A View from the North*. Washington, D.C.: Brookings Institution, 1984.

[CHENERY, HOLLIS B.] *Economic Structure and Performance. Essays in Honor of Hollis B. Chenery*. Edited by MOSHE SYRQUIN, LANCE TAYLOR AND LARRY E. WESTPHAL. Orlando; London; Toronto and Sydney: Harcourt Brace Jovanovich, Academic Press, 1984.

CLOWER, ROBERT W. *Money and Markets: Essays by Robert W. Clower*. Edited by DONALD A. WALKER. Cambridge; New York and Sydney: Cambridge University Press, 1984.

COCKLE, PAUL, ed. *Public Expenditure Policy, 1984–85*. New York: St. Martin's Press, 1984.

COHEN, S. I., ET AL., eds. *The Modelling of Socio-Economic Planning Processes*. Aldershot, Hampshire, and Brookfield, Vt.: Gower, 1984.

COLANDER, DAVID C., ed. *Neoclassical Political Economy: The Analysis of Rent-seeking and DUP Activities*. Cambridge, Mass.: Harper & Row, Ballinger, 1984.

COLES, JAMES S., ed. *Technological Innovation in the '80s*. American Assembly, Columbia University series. Englewood Cliffs, N.J.: Prentice-Hall, Spectrum Books, 1984.

COLLARD, D. A., ET AL., eds. *Economic Theory and Hicksian Themes*. Oxford; New York; Toronto and Delhi: Oxford University Press, Clarendon Press, 1984.

COLLINS, EILEEN L. AND TANNER, LUCRETIA DEWEY, eds. *American Jobs and the Changing Industrial Base*. Cambridge, Mass.: Harper & Row, Ballinger, 1984.

CONKLIN, DAVID W.; BENNETT, JALYNN H. AND COURCHENE, THOMAS J., eds. *Pensions Today and Tomorrow: Background Studies*. Special Research Report series. Toronto: Ontario Economic Council; distributed by Ontario Government Bookstore, 1984.

CORDOVA, EFREN, ed. *Industrial Relations in Latin America: A Study of the Parties Involved, the Theory and Practice of Their Interactions and Procedures in Disputes, with Special Reference to the Private Sector*. New York; Eastbourne, U.K.; Toronto and Tokyo: Praeger, 1984.

CREEDY, J. AND O'BRIEN, D. P., eds. *Economic Analysis in Historical Perspective*. Butterworths Advanced Economics Texts. London; Boston; Singapore and Toronto: Butterworths, 1984.

CSIKOS-NAGY, BELA; HAGUE, DOUGLAS AND HALL, GRAHAM, eds. *The Economics of Relative Prices: Proceedings of a Conference Held by the International Economic Association in Athens, Greece*. New York: St. Martin's Press, 1984.

CZINKOTA, MICHAEL R., ed. *Export Controls: Building Reasonable Commercial Ties with Political Adversaries*. In cooperation with SCOT MARCIEL. New York; Eastbourne, England; Toronto and Sydney: Praeger, 1984.

DARITY, WILLIAM, JR., ed. *Labor Economics: Modern Views*. Recent Economic Thought Series. Boston; The Hague and Lancaster: Kluwer-Nijhoff, 1984.

DEAN, EDWIN, ed. *Education and Economic Productivity*. Cambridge, Mass.: Harper & Row, Ballinger, 1984.

DESAI, MEGHNAD; RUDOLPH, SUSANNE HOEBER AND RUDRA, ASHOK, eds. *Agrarian Power and Agricultural Productivity in South Asia*. Berkeley and London: University of California Press, 1984.

DESPONTIN, M.; NIJKAMP, P. AND SPRONK, J., eds. *Macro-economic Planning with Conflicting Goals: Proceedings of a Workshop Held at the Vrije Universiteit of Brussels, Belgium, December 10, 1982*. Lecture Notes in Economics and Mathematical Systems, vol. 230. New York; Berlin and Tokyo: Springer, 1984.

DIJKSTRA, THEO K., ed. *Misspecification Analysis: Proceedings of a Workshop Held in Groningen, The Netherlands, December 15–16, 1983*. Lecture Notes in Economics and Mathematical Systems, no. 237. New York; Berlin and Tokyo: Springer, 1984.

DOUGLASS, GORDON K., ed. *Agricultural Sustainability in a Changing World Order.* Westview Special Studies in Agriculture, Science and Policy. Boulder, Colo.: Westview Press, 1984.

DOWNEN, ROBERT L. AND DICKSON, BRUCE J., eds. *The Emerging Pacific Community: A Regional Perspective.* CSIS Significant Issues series, vol. 6, no. 2. Boulder, Colo., and London: Westview Press in cooperation with the Center for Strategic and International Studies, Georgetown University, Washington, D.C., 1984.

DOWNS, ANTHONY AND BRADBURY, KATHARINE L., eds. *Energy Costs, Urban Development, and Housing.* Washington, D.C.: Brookings Institution, 1984.

DRISCOLL, ROBERT E. AND BEHRMAN, JACK N., eds. *National Industrial Policies.* Cambridge, Mass.: Oelgeschlager, Gunn & Hain, 1984.

DUSEK, E. RALPH, ET AL., eds. *American Psychological Association's Guide to Research Support.* Second edition. Washington, D.C.: American Psychological Association, Scientific Affairs Office, [1981] 1984.

EADS, GEORGE C. AND FIX, MICHAEL, eds. *The Reagan Regulatory Strategy: An Assessment.* Changing Domestic Priorities series. Washington, D.C.: Urban Institute Press, 1984.

EICHER, CARL K. AND STAATZ, JOHN M., eds. *Agricultural Development in the Third World.* Johns Hopkins Studies in Development series. Baltimore and London: Johns Hopkins University Press, 1984.

ELLMAN, MICHAEL. *Collectivisation, Convergence and Capitalism: Political Economy in a Divided World.* Studies in Political Economy. London; Orlando; Sydney and Tokyo: Harcourt Brace Jovanovich, Academic Press, 1984.

EMERSON, MICHAEL, ed. *Europe's Stagflation.* Oxford; New York; Toronto and Hong Kong: Oxford University Press, Clarendon Press, 1984.

EMERSON, ROBERT D., ed. *Seasonal Agricultural Labor Markets in the United States.* Ames: Iowa State University Press, 1984.

ENGELS, WOLFRAM AND POHL, HANS, eds. *German Yearbook on Business History 1983.* Translated by EILEEN MARTIN. New York; Berlin and Tokyo: Springer, 1984.

EUCKEN, WALTER AND BOHM, FRANZ, eds. *ORDO: Jahrbuch für die ordnung von Wirtschaft und Gesellschaft.* Band 35. Stuttgart and New York: Fischer, 1984.

FARLOW, STANLEY J., ed. *Self-organizing Methods in Modeling: GMDH Type Algorithms.* Statistics: Textbooks and Monographs series, vol. 54. New York and Basel; Dekker, 1984.

[FARMER, B. H.] *Understanding Green Revolutions: Agrarian Change and Development Planning in South Asia: Essays in Honour of B. H. Farmer.* Edited by TIM P. BAYLISS-SMITH AND SUDHIR WANMALI. Cambridge; New York; and Sydney: Cambridge University Press, 1984.

FEDERAL HOME LOAN BANK OF SAN FRANCISCO. *Identification and Control of Risk in the Thrift Industry: Proceedings of the Ninth Annual Conference, December 8–9, 1983, San Francisco, California.* San Francisco: Author, 1984.

FEDERAL RESERVE BANK OF ATLANTA. *Payments in the Financial Services Industry of the 1980s: Conference Proceedings.* Westport, Conn., and London: Greenwood Press, Quorum Books, 1984.

FEDERAL RESERVE BANK OF BOSTON. *The International Monetary System: Forty Years after Bretton Woods: Proceedings of a Conference Held at Bretton Woods, New Hampshire, May 1984.* The Federal Reserve Bank of Boston Conference series, no. 28. Boston: author, 1984.

FEINBERG, RICHARD E. AND KALLAB, VALERIANA, eds. *Adjustment Crisis in the Third World.* Overseas Development Council, U.S.–Third World Policy Perspectives series, no 1. New Brunswick, N.J., and London: Transaction Books, 1984.

FEINBERG, RICHARD E. AND KALLAB, VALERIANA, eds. *Uncertain Future: Commercial Banks and the Third World.* Overseas Development Council series, U.S.–Third World Policy Perspectives, no. 2. New Brunswick, N.J., and London: Transaction Books, 1984.

FELLNER, WILLIAM, ed. *Essays in Contemporary Economic Problems: Disinflation.* AEI Annual Series on Contemporary Economic Problems, no. 7. Washington and London: American Enterprise Institute for Public Policy Research, 1984.

[FERBER, ROBERT] *The Collection and Analysis of Economic and Consumer Behavior Data: In*

Memory of Robert Ferber. Edited by SEYMOUR SUDMAN AND MARY A. SPAETH. Champaign: Bureau of Economic and Business Research and Survey Research Laboratory, University of Illinois, 1984.

FOSTER, JOHN BELLAMY AND SZLAJFER, HENRYK, eds. *The Faltering Economy: The Problem of Accumulation under Monopoly Capitalism.* New York: Monthly Review Press, 1984.

FOSTER, J. RHOADS, ET AL., eds. *Regulatory Reform: The State of the Regulatory Art: Emerging Concepts and Procedures.* Washington, D.C.: Institute for Study of Regulation, 1984.

FOX, ELEANOR M. AND HALVERSON, JAMES T., eds. *Antitrust Policy in Transition: The Convergence of Law and Economics.* Chicago: American Bar Association, Section of Antitrust Law, 1984.

FRANK, ANDRE GUNDER. *Critique and Anti-critique: Essays on Dependence and Reformism.* New York; Eastborne, England; Toronto and Tokyo: Praeger, 1984.

FRANSMAN, MARTIN AND KING, KENNETH, eds. *Technological Capability in the Third World.* New York: St. Martin's Press, 1984.

FRENKEL, JACOB A. AND MUSSA, MICHAEL L., eds. *The World Economic System: Performance and Prospects.* Foreword by RAND V. ARASKOG. ITT Key Issues Lecture series. Dover, Mass.: Auburn House, 1984.

FRIED, EDWARD R. AND TREZISE, PHILIP H., eds. *U.S.–Canadian Economic Relations: Next Steps? Papers Presented at a Conference at the Brookings Institution Chaired by Bruce K. MacLaury on April 10, 1984.* Brookings Dialogues on Public Policy. Washington, D.C.: Brookings Institution, 1984.

FRIEDHEIM, ROBERT L., ET AL. *Japan and the New Ocean Regime.* Westview Special Studies in Ocean Science and Policy. Boulder, Colo., and London: Westview Press, 1984.

FUSFELD, HERBERT I. AND HAKLISCH, CARMELA S., eds. *University–Industry Research Interactions.* Technology Policy and Economic Growth series. New York; Oxford; Toronto and Sydney: Pergamon Press in cooperation with The Center for Science and Technology Policy, Graduate School of Business Administration, New York University, 1984.

GEISLER, CHARLES C. AND POPPER, FRANK J., eds. *Land Reform, American Style.* Totowa, N.J.: Littlefield, Adams; Rowman & Allanheld, 1984.

GHOSH, PRADIP K., ed. *Appropriate Technology in Third World Development.* Foreword by GAMANI COREA. International Development Resource Books, no. 14. Westport Conn., and London: Greenwood Press, 1984.

GHOSH, PRADIP K., ed. *Developing Latin America: A Modernization Perspective.* Foreword by GAMANI COREA. International Development Resource Books, no. 19. Westport, Conn., and London: Greenwood Press, 1984.

GHOSH, PRADIP K., ed. *Developing South Asia: A Modernization Perspective.* Foreword by GAMANI COREA. International Development Resource Books, no. 18. Westport, Conn., and London: Greenwood Press, 1984.

GHOSH, PRADIP K., ed. *Development Co-operation and Third World Development.* Foreword by GAMANI COREA. International Development Resource Books, no. 15. Westport, Conn., and London: Greenwood Press, 1984.

GHOSH, PRADIP K., ed. *Development Policy and Planning: A Third World Perspective.* Foreword by GAMANI COREA. International Development Resource Books, no. 8. Westport, Conn., and London: Greenwood Press, 1984.

GHOSH, PRADIP K., ed. *Disarmament and Development: A Global Perspective.* Foreword by GAMANI COREA. International Development Resource Books, no. 17. Westport, Conn., and London: Greenwood Press, 1984.

GHOSH, PRADIP K., ed. *Economic Integration and Third World Development.* Foreword by GAMANI COREA. International Development Resource Books, no. 12. Westport, Conn., and London: Greenwood Press, 1984.

GHOSH, PRADIP K., ed. *Economic Policy and Planning in Third World Development.* Foreword by GAMANI COREA. International Development Resource Books, no. 7. Westport, Conn., and London: Greenwood Press, 1984.

GORDON, SUZANNE AND McFADDEN, DAVE, eds. *Economic Conversion: Revitalizing America's Economy.* Cambridge, Mass.: Harper & Row, Ballinger, 1984.

GOUREVITCH, PETER, ET AL. *Unions and Economic Crisis: Britain, West Germany and Sweden.* Harvard Center for European Studies Project on European Trade Union Responses to Economic Crisis, vol. 2. London; Boston and Sydney: Allen & Unwin, 1984.

GRAUER, M. AND WIERZBICKI, A. P., eds. *Interactive Decision Analysis: Proceedings of an International Workshop.* Lecture Notes in Economics and Mathematical Systems, no. 229. New York; Berlin and Tokyo: Springer, 1984.

GRIFFITHS, BRIAN AND WOOD, GEOFFREY E., eds. *Monetarism in the United Kingdom.* New York: St. Martin's Press, 1984.

GRILICHES, ZVI, ed. *R&D, Patents, and Productivity.* NBER Conference Report. Chicago and London: University of Chicago Press, 1984.

GRILICHES, ZVI AND INTRILIGATOR, MICHAEL D., eds. *Handbook of Econometrics.* Volume II. Handbooks in Economics series, book 2. Amsterdam; New York and Oxford: North-Holland; distributed in the U.S. and Canada by Elsevier Science, New York, 1984.

GROTH, ALEXANDER J. AND WADE, LARRY L., eds. *Comparative Resource Allocation: Politics, Performance, and Policy Priorities.* Sage Yearbooks in Politics and Public Policy, vol. 13. Beverly Hills; London and New Delhi: Sage, 1984.

GRUBER, JOSEF, ed. *Multicollinearity and Biased Estimation: Proceedings of a Conference at the University of Hagen, September 8–10, 1980.* Applied Statistics and Econometrics series, no. 27. Göttingen, West Germany: Vandenhoeck & Ruprecht, 1984.

GUARDUCCI, ANNALISA, ed. *Agriculture as a Factor in the Modifying of the Environment: A Five-Century Survey (1200–1700). Acts of the 11th "Settimana di studio" (25th–30th April 1979).* Instituto Internazionale di Storia Economica "F. Datini", Pubblicazioni Serie II, Atti delle "Settimane di studio" e altri Convegni. Florence, Italy: Le Monnier, 1984.

HAGEN, OLE AND WENSTOP, FRED, eds. *Progress in Utility and Risk Theory.* Theory and Decision Library, vol. 42. Dordrecht; Boston and Lancaster: Reidel; distributed in U.S. and Canada by Kluwer Academic, Hingham, Mass., 1984.

HAHN, FRANK. *Equilibrium and Macroeconomics.* Cambridge, Mass.: MIT Press and Oxford: Blackwell, 1984.

HAMMER, G. AND PALLASCHKE, D., eds. *Selected Topics in Operations Research and Mathematical Economics: Proceedings of the 8th Symposium on Operations Research Held at the University of Karlsruhe, West Germany, August 22–25, 1983.* Lecture Notes in Economics and Mathematical Systems, vol. 226. New York; Berlin and Tokyo: Springer, 1984.

HANSON, ROYCE, ed. *Perspectives on Urban Infrastructure.* Washington, D.C.: National Academy Press, 1984.

HANUSCH, HORST, ed. *Public Finance and the Quest for Efficiency: Proceedings of the 38th Congress of the International Institute of Public Finance, Copenhagen, 1982.* Detroit: Wayne State University Press, 1984.

HARBERGER, ARNOLD C., ed. *World Economic Growth.* San Francisco: ICS Press, 1984.

HARDING, HARRY, ed. *China's Foreign Relations in the 1980s.* New Haven and London: Yale University Press in cooperation with The Asia Society, New York, 1984.

HARRISS, JOHN AND MOORE, MICK, eds. *Development and the Rural–Urban Divide.* London and Totowa, N.J.: Cass, 1984.

HAUSMAN, DANIEL M., ed. *The Philosophy of Economics: An Anthology.* Cambridge; New York and Sydney: Cambridge University Press, 1984.

HAVEMAN, ROBERT H.; HALBERSTADT, VICTOR AND BURKHAUSER, RICHARD V. *Public Policy toward Disabled Workers: Cross-national Analyses of Economic Impacts.* Ithaca, N.Y., and London: Cornell University Press, 1984.

HAWDON, DAVID, ed. *The Energy Crisis Ten Years After.* New York: St. Martin's Press; London and Canberra: Croom Helm, 1984.

VON HAYEK, FRIEDRICH A. *The Essence of Hayek.* Edited by CHIAKI NISHIYAMA AND KURT R. LEUBE. Foreword by W. GLENN CAMPBELL. Stanford, Calif.: Hoover Institution Press, 1984. (I)

JACKALL, ROBERT AND LEVIN, HENRY M., eds. *Worker Cooperatives in America*. Berkeley, Calif.
and London: University of California Press, 1984.

JACKSON, MARVIN R. AND WOODSON, JAMES D., JR., eds. *New Horizons in East–West Economic
and Business Relations*. East European Monographs series, no. 156. Boulder, Colo.: East European Monographs; distributed by Columbia University Press, New York, 1984.

JACQUEMIN, ALEXIS, ed. *European Industry: Public Policy and Corporate Strategy*. Oxford; New
York; Toronto and Delhi: Oxford University Press, Clarendon Press, 1984.

JOLLY, RICHARD AND CORNIA, GIOVANNI ANDREA, eds. *The Impact of World Recession on Children*.
Oxford; New York; Toronto and Sydney: Pergamon Press, 1984.

JONES, RICHARD C., ed. *Patterns of Undocumented Migration: Mexico and the United States*.
Totowa, N.J.: Littlefield, Adams; Rowman & Allanheld, 1984.

JONES, RONALD W. AND KENEN, PETER, eds. *Handbook of International Economics*. Volume 1.
Handbooks in Economics series, no. 3. New York; Amsterdam and Oxford: North-Holland;
distributed in the U.S. and Canada by Elsevier Science, New York, 1984.

JORGE, ANTONIO; SALAZAR-CARRILLO, JORGE AND SANCHEZ, ENRIQUE P. *Trade, Debt and Growth
in Latin America*. New York; Oxford; Toronto and Sydney: Pergamon Press, 1984.

JUSSAWALLA, MEHEROO AND EBENFIELD, HELENE, eds. *Communication and Information Economics:
New Perspectives*. Foreword by KENNETH E. BOULDING. Information Research and Resource
Reports, vol. 5. New York; Amsterdam and Oxford: North-Holland; distributed in North America
by Elsevier Science, New York, 1984.

KADANE, JOSEPH B., ed. *Robustness of Bayesian Analyses*. Studies in Bayesian Econometrics series,
vol. 4. Amsterdam; New York and Oxford: North-Holland; distributed in the U.S. by Elsevier
Science, New York, 1984.

KAPLINSKY, RAPHAEL, ed. *Third World Industrialisation in the 1980s: Open Economies in a Closing
World*. London and Totowa, N.J.: Cass, 1984.

KATES, DON B., JR., ed. *Firearms and Violence: Issues of Public Policy*. Foreword by JOHN KAPLAN.
Pacific Studies in Public Policy. San Francisco: Pacific Institute for Public Policy Research and
Cambridge, Mass.: Harper & Row, Ballinger, 1984.

KAYNAK, ERDENER, ed. *International Marketing Management*. New York; Eastbourne, England;
Toronto and Sydney: Praeger, 1984.

KAYNAK, ERDENER AND SAVITT, RONALD, eds. *Comparative Marketing Systems*. New York: Praeger,
1984.

KEMP, M. C. AND LONG, N. V., eds. *Essays in the Economics of Exhaustible Resources*. Contributions to Economic Analysis series, no. 150. Amsterdam; New York and Oxford: North-Holland;
distributed by Elsevier Science, New York, 1984.

KENDRICK, JOHN W., ed. *International Comparisons of Productivity and Causes of the Slowdown*.
Cambridge, Mass.: Harper & Row, Ballinger and Washington D.C.: American Enterprise Institute, 1984.

KESSLER, DENIS AND ULLMO, PIERRE-ANTOINE, eds. *Savings and Development: Proceedings of a
Colloquium Held in Paris: 28, 29 and 30 May 1984*. Paris: Economica, 1984.

KIERZKOWSKI, HENRYK, ed. *Monopolistic Competition and International Trade*. Oxford; New York;
Toronto and Delhi: Oxford University Press, Clarendon Press, 1984.

KILLICK, TONY, ed. *The IMF and Stabilization: Developing Country Experiences*. New York: St.
Martin's Press, 1984. (I)

KILLICK, TONY, ed. *The Quest for Economic Stabilization: The IMF and the Third World*. New
York: St. Martin's Press, 1984. (II)

KINDLEBERGER, CHARLES P. *Multinational Excursions*. Cambridge, Mass., and London: MIT Press,
1984.

KINDRA, G. S., ed. *Marketing in Developing Countries*. New York: St. Martin's Press, 1984.

KOROPECKYJ, I. S., ed. *Selected Contributions of Ukrainian Scholars to Economics*. Harvard Ukrainian Research Institute Sources and Documents series. Cambridge, Mass.: Harvard Ukranian
Research Institute; distributed by Harvard University Press, 1984.

ior. Foreign Policy Issues; a Foreign Policy Research Institute series. New York; Eastbourne, England; Toronto and Sydney: Praeger, 1984.

McDONALD, TERRENCE J. AND WARD, SALLY K., eds. *The Politics of Urban Fiscal Policy.* New Approaches to Social Science History, vol. 5. Beverly Hills; London and New Delhi: Sage in cooperation with the Social Science History Association, 1984.

McKENZIE, RICHARD B., ed. *Constitutional Economics: Containing the Economic Powers of Government.* Lexington, Mass., and Toronto: Heath, Lexington Books, 1984. (I)

McKENZIE, RICHARD B., ed. *Plant Closings: Public or Private Choices?* Revised edition. Washington, D.C.: Cato Institute, [1982] 1984. (II)

McKINLAY, JOHN B., ed. *Issues in the Political Economy of Health Care.* Contemporary Issues in Health, Medicine, and Social Policy series. New York and London: Tavistock, 1984.

McLURE, CHARLES E., JR., ed. *The State Corporation Income Tax: Issues in Worldwide Unitary Combination.* Stanford, Calif.: Hoover Institution Press, Stanford University, 1984.

MERLINI, CESARE, ed. *Economic Summits and Western Decision-making.* New York: St. Martin's Press and London and Canberra: Croom Helm in association with the European Institute of Public Administration, 1984.

MEYER, JOHN R. AND OSTER, CLINTON V., JR., eds. *Deregulation and the New Airline Entrepreneurs.* With MARNI CLIPPINGER ET AL. MIT Press series on the Regulation of Economic Activity, no. 9. Cambridge and London: MIT Press, 1984.

MIKKELSEN, ARNE, ET AL. *Economic Growth in a Nordic Perspective.* Copenhagen: Danish Economic Council and the Institute for Future Studies in cooperation with institutes at Helsinki, Bergen, and Stockholm, 1984.

MILLER, TRUDI C., ed. *Public Sector Performance: A Conceptual Turning Point.* Baltimore and London: Johns Hopkins University Press, 1984.

MILLS, GREGORY B. AND PALMER, JOHN L., eds. *Federal Budget Policy in the 1980s.* Changing Domestic Priorities series. Washington, D.C.: Urban Institute Press, 1984.

MIYAWAKI, NAGASADA, ed. *Problems of Advanced Economies: Proceedings of the Third Conference on New Problems of Advanced Societies, Tokyo, Japan, November 1982.* Studies in Contemporary Economics series, no. 10. New York; Berlin and Tokyo: Springer, 1984.

MOON, MARILYN, ed. *Economic Transfers in the United States.* Studies in Income and Wealth, vol. 49. Chicago and London: University of Chicago Press, 1984.

MOORE, JOHN H., ed. *To Promote Prosperity: U.S. Domestic Policy in the mid-1980s.* Foreword by W. GLENN CAMPBELL. Stanford: Hoover Institution Press, 1984.

MOREHOUSE, THOMAS A., ed. *Alaskan Resources Development: Issues of the 1980s.* Boulder, Colo.: Westview Press, 1984.

MORTON, HENRY W. AND STUART, ROBERT C., eds. *The Contemporary Soviet City.* Armonk, N.Y.: Sharpe, 1984.

MUNASINGHE, MOHAN AND RUNGTA, SHYAM, eds. *Costing and Pricing Electricity in Developing Countries: Proceedings of the Asian Development Bank Regional Power Utility Tariff Symposium, August 1982.* Manila: Asian Development Bank, 1984.

MUNS, JOAQUIN, ed. *Adjustment, Conditionality, and International Financing: Papers Presented at the Seminar on "The Role of the International Monetary Fund in the Adjustment Process" Held in Viña del Mar, Chile, April 5–8, 1983.* Washington, D.C.: International Monetary Fund, 1984.

MUNSLOW, B. AND FINCH, H., eds. *Proletarianisation in the Third World: Studies in the Creation of a Labour Force under Dependent Capitalism.* London; Sydney and Dover, N.H.: Croom Helm, 1984.

MURPHY, ANTOIN E., ed. *Economists and the Irish Economy from the Eighteenth Century to the Present Day.* Dublin: Irish Academic Press in association with Hermathena, Trinity College, Dublin, 1984.

NAKAGAWA, KEIICHIRO AND MORIKAWA, HIDEMASA, eds. *Japanese Yearbook on Business Industry: 1984.* No. 1. Tokyo: Japan Business History Institute, 1984.

NAYLOR, THOMAS H. AND THOMAS, CELIA, eds. *Optimization Models for Strategic Planning.* Studies

PECHMAN, JOSEPH A., ed. *Options for Tax Reform: Papers Presented at a Conference at the Brookings Institution on April 23–24, 1984.* Brookings Dialogues on Public Policy. Washington, D.C.: Brookings Institute and Morristown, N.J.: Financial Executives Research Foundation, 1984.

PICKERING, J. F. AND COCKERILL, T. A. J., eds. *The Economic Management of the Firm.* Oxford: Allan and Totowa, N.J.: Barnes & Noble Books, 1984.

PIERRE, ANDREW J., ed. *Unemployment and Growth in the Western Economies.* Introduction by ROBERT D. HORMATS. Europe–America series, no. 2. New York: Council on Foreign Relations, 1984.

PITFIELD, D. E., ed. *Discrete Choice Models in Regional Science.* London Papers in Regional Science series, no. 14. London: Pion; distributed in the U.S. by Methuen, New York, 1984.

VAN DER PLOEG, FREDERICK, ed. *Mathematical Methods in Economics.* Wiley Interscience publication. Handbook of Applicable Mathematics Guidebooks series, no. 6. Chichester, England; New York; Brisbane and Toronto: Wiley, 1984.

POOLE, MICHAEL, ET AL. *Industrial Relations in the Future: Trends and Possibilities in Britain over the Next Decade.* London; Boston and Melbourne: Routledge and Kegan Paul, 1984.

PORTER, PAUL R. AND SWEET, DAVID C., eds. *Rebuilding America's Cities: Roads to Recovery.* New Brunswick, N.J.: Center for Urban Policy Research, Rutgers University, 1984.

PREMCHAND, A. AND BURKHEAD, JESSE, eds. *Comparative International Budgeting and Finance.* New Brunswick, N.J., and London: Transaction Books, 1984.

PURDEN, CHRISTINE, ed. *Selected Income Tax Aspects of the Purchase and Sale of a Business: Corporate Management Tax Conference, 1984.* Toronto: Canadian Tax Foundation, 1984.

RABA, ANDRAS AND SCHENK, KARL-ERNST, eds. *Organization and Interaction Patterns in Hungarian Industry.* Ökonomische Studien, no. 35. Stuttgart and New York: Fischer, 1984.

RAMANADHAM, V. V., ed. *Public Enterprise and the Developing World.* London and Sydney: Croom Helm, 1984.

[REYNOLDS, LLOYD G.] *Comparative Development Perspectives: Essays in Honor of Lloyd G. Reynolds.* Edited by GUSTAV RANIS, ET AL. Westview Replica Edition. Boulder, Colo.: Westview Press in cooperation with the Economic Growth Center, Yale University, 1984.

RICHARDS, P. J. AND THOMSON, A. M., eds. *Basic Needs and the Urban Poor: The Provision of Communal Services.* London; Sydney and Dover, N.H.: Croom Helm, 1984.

RICHARDSON, JACQUES, ed. *Models of Reality: Shaping Thought and Action.* Mt. Airy, Md.: Lomond Books in cooperation with UNESCO, 1984.

ROBSON, R. THAYNE, ed. *Employment and Training R&D: Lessons Learned and Future Directions: Conference Proceedings of the National Council on Employment Policy.* Kalamazoo, Mich.: W. E. Upjohn Institute for Employment Research, 1984.

ROSA, JEAN-JACQUES, ed. *The Economics of Trade Unions: New Directions.* Boston Studies in Applied Economics. Series on Labor and Employment. Boston; Dordrecht and Lancaster, England: Kluwer-Nijhoff; distributed in North America by Kluwer Boston, Hingham, Mass., 1984.

SALAZAR-CARILLO, JORGE AND TIRADO DE ALONSO, IRMA, eds. *Latin American External Debt and Economic Growth.* IESCARIBE Research Summaries series, no. 1. Miami: Florida International University for the Institutes of Economic and Social Research of the Caribbean Basin, 1984.

SALAZAR-CARRILLO, JORGE AND TIRADO DE ALONSO, IRMA, eds. *Trade, Debt, and Development in the Caribbean Basin.* IESCARIBE Research Summaries series, no. 2. Miami: Florida International University for the Institutes of Economic and Social Research of the Caribbean Basin, 1984.

SAMETZ, ARNOLD W., ed. *The Emerging Financial Industry: Implications for Insurance Products, Portfolios, and Planning.* Lexington Books/Salomon Brothers Center series on Financial Institutions and Markets. Lexington, Mass., and Toronto: Heath, Lexington Books, 1984.

SAMUELS, WARREN J., ed. *Research in the History of Economic Thought and Methodology.* Volume 2. A Research Annual. Greenwich, Conn., and London: JAI Press, 1984.

SANDFORD, CEDRIC AND BRADBURY, MALCOLM, eds. *Case Studies in Economics.* Second edition. London and New York: Longman, [1971] 1984.

born, West Germany, June 1–June 3, 1983. Studies in Contemporary Economics. New York; Berlin and Tokyo: Springer, 1984.

STOREY, GARY G.; SCHMITZ, ANDREW AND SARRIS, ALEXANDER H., eds. *International Agricultural Trade: Advanced Readings in Price Formation, Market Structure, and Price Instability.* Westview Replica Editions. Boulder, Colo., and London: Westview Press, 1984.

STRANGE, SUSAN, ed. *Paths to International Political Economy.* London; Boston and Sydney: Allen & Unwin, 1984.

SYLOS-LABINI, PAOLO. *The Forces of Economic Growth and Decline.* Cambridge and London: The MIT Press, 1984.

TABB, WILLIAM K. AND SAWERS, LARRY, eds. *Marxism and the Metropolis: New Perspectives in Urban Political Economy.* Second edition. New York and Oxford: Oxford University Press, [1978] 1984.

TANZI, VITO, ed. *Taxation, Inflation, and Interest Rates.* Washington, D.C.: International Monetary Fund, 1984.

THAMBIPILLAI, PUSHPA, ed. *Southeast Asian Affairs 1984.* Singapore: Institute of Southeast Asian Studies, 1984.

THOMPSON, FRED, ed. *Regulatory Regimes in Conflict: Problems of Regulation in a Continental Perspective.* Lanham, Md., and London: University Press of America, 1984.

TRENT, JOHN AND LAMY, PAUL, eds. *Global Crises and the Social Sciences: North American Perspectives.* Ottawa: University of Ottawa Press and UNESCO, 1984.

ULLRICH, ROBERT A., ed. *The American Work Force: Labor and Employment in the 1980s.* Foreword by RAND V. ARASKOG. ITT Key Issues Lecture series. Dover, Mass.: Auburn House, 1984.

UNITED NATIONS CONFERENCE ON TRADE AND DEVELOPMENT. *Trends, Policies and Prospects in Trade among Countries Having Different Economic and Social Systems: Selected Studies.* New York and Geneva: United Nations, 1984.

UNITED NATIONS DEPARTMENT OF TECHNICAL CO-OPERATION FOR DEVELOPMENT. *Performance Evaluation of Public Enterprises in Developing Countries: Criteria and Institutions.* New York: Author, 1984.

UTRECHT, ERNST, ed. *Fiji: Client State of Australasia?* Sydney: Transnational Corporations Research Project, University of Sydney, 1984.

WACHTER, MICHAEL L. AND WACHTER, SUSAN M., eds. *Removing Obstacles to Economic Growth.* Philadelphia; University of Pennsylvania Press, 1984.

WANDER, W. THOMAS; HEBERT, F. TED AND COPELAND, GARY W., eds. *Congressional Budgeting: Politics, Process, and Power.* Baltimore and London: Johns Hopkins University Press, 1984.

WARD, ROBIN AND JENKINS, RICHARD, eds. *Ethnic Communities in Business: Strategies for Economic Survival.* Comparative Ethnic and Race Relations series. Cambridge; New York and Melbourne: Cambridge University Press, 1984.

WARNER, MALCOLM, ed. *Microprocessors, Manpower and Society: A Comparative, Cross-national Approach.* New York: St. Martin's Press, 1984.

WAUGH, FREDERICK V. *Selected Writings on Agricultural Policy and Economic Analysis.* Edited by JAMES P. HOUCK AND MARTIN E. ABEL. Minneapolis: University of Minnesota Press, 1984.

WEICHER, JOHN C., ed. *Maintaining the Safety Net: Income Redistribution Programs in the Reagan Administration.* AEI Studies in Public Policy, no. 401. Washington, D.C., and London: American Enterprise Institute for Public Policy Research, 1984.

WEISS, CHARLES AND JEQUIER, NICOLAS, eds. *Technology, Finance, and Development: An Analysis of the World Bank as a Technological Institution.* Lexington, Mass., and Toronto: Heath, Lexington Books, 1984.

WESSON, ROBERT, ed. *Politics, Policies, and Economic Development in Latin America.* Hoover Press Publication no. 306. Stanford, Calif.: Hoover Institution Press, Stanford University, 1984.

WEST, LOUIS JOLYON, ed. *Alcoholism and Related Problems: Issues for the American Public.* The American Assembly, Columbia University series. Englewood Cliffs, N.J.: Prentice-Hall, Spectrum, 1984.

WESTALL, OLIVER M., ed. *The Historian and the Business of Insurance*. Manchester, England, and Dover, N.H.: Manchester University Press, 1984.

WHYNES, DAVID K., ed. *What Is Political Economy? Eight Perspectives*. Oxford and New York: Blackwell, 1984.

WIARDA, HOWARD J. *In Search of Policy: The United States and Latin America*. AEI Studies in Foreign Policy, no. 396. Washington, D.C., and London: American Enterprise Institute for Public Policy Research, 1984.

WIARDA, HOWARD J., ed. *Rift and Revolution: The Central American Imbroglio*. AEI Studies in Foreign Policy, no. 394. Washington, D.C., and London: American Enterprise Institute for Public Policy Research, 1984.

WILES, PETER AND ROUTH, GUY, eds. *Economics in Disarray*. Oxford and New York: Blackwell, 1984.

WINDMULLER, JOHN P. AND GLADSTONE, ALAN, eds. *Employers Associations and Industrial Relations: A Comparative Study*. New York; Toronto and Oxford: Oxford University Press, Clarendon Press, 1984.

WOOD, W. D. AND KUMAR, PRADEEP, eds. *The Current Industrial Relations Scene in Canada, 1984*. Kingston, Ontario: Queen's University, Industrial Relations Centre, 1984.

WYNN, MARTIN, ed. *Housing in Europe*. New York: St. Martin's Press and London and Canberra: Croom Helm, 1984.

ZAREMBKA, PAUL, ed. *Research in Political Economy. Volume 7*. A Research Annual. Greenwich, Conn., and London: JAI Press, 1984.

ZARTMAN, I. WILLIAM AND DELGADO, CHRISTOPHER L., eds. *The Political Economy of Ivory Coast*. A SAIS Study on Africa. New York; Eastbourne, U.K.; Toronto and Tokyo: Praeger, 1984.

ZELLNER, ARNOLD. *Basic Issues in Econometrics*. Chicago and London: University of Chicago Press, 1984.

ZIMBALIST, ANDREW, ed. *Comparative Economic Systems: An Assessment of Knowledge, Theory and Method*. Recent Economic Thought series. Boston; The Hague and Lancaster: Kluwer-Nijhoff, 1984.

CLASSIFICATION SYSTEM

Editor's note: Notes on the *Classification System* further clarify the subject matter covered under specific categories or point out specific topics included. They also may contain cross references to other categories. In addition, the *Topical Guide* at the end of this volume provides an index to classification numbers appropriate for specific topics. Please note that "General" categories may include *both* detailed articles covering all subcategories and very general articles falling into no subcategory.

For studies of particular countries, as distinct from discussions of a
system, see category 120.

Includes articles discussing or critiquing capitalist systems. Also includes articles on the cooperative as a system
in predominantly market economies. Articles on mixed
enterprise systems and nontheoretical articles on entrepreneurship also appear here (for theoretical articles on
entrepreneurship and profits, see 0224).

Articles discussing socialist or communist systems generally or in a specific country are included here. For theory,
see the 027 category and for planning, see the 113 category.
Studies of particular communist or socialist countries or
of particular sectors in the countries will be found in
either the country division (124 subcategories) or the appropriate subject category for the article. For example,
an article dealing with agriculture in the Soviet Union
would be classified in one of the 710 subcategories.

For development theory see 1120; for empirical studies of an individual
country, see category 120, or for primarily historical studies, 040.

Does not include theory and analyses of productivity, which
appear in 2260.

Subject Index of Articles
in Current Periodicals and Collective Volumes

Abbreviated titles for journals are the same as those used in the *Journal of Economic Literature*. Full titles of journals may be found on pages x–xv.

Books have been identified by author or editor (noted *ed.*). In rare cases where two books by the same author appear, volumes are distinguished by I or II after the name. In some cases there appear two books by the same person, once as author, once as editor. These may be distinguished by *ed.* noted for the edited volume. Full titles and bibliographic references for books may be found on pages xvi–xxxii.

Geographic Descriptors when appropriate appear in brackets at the end of the article citation.

000 General Economics; Theory; History; Systems

010 GENERAL ECONOMICS

011 General Economics

0110 General

Arndt, Heinz W. Introduction to Economics. *Singapore Econ. Rev.*, October 1984, 29(2), pp. 3–10.

Ascah, Louis. Sommes-nous tous des néo-keynésiens à la Friedman–Phelps–Lucas maintenant? (Are We All Neo-Keynesians a là Friedman–Phelps–Lucas Now? With English summary.) *L'Actual. Econ.*, March 1984, 60(1), pp. 132–35.

Bennett, John. Bibliography, 1982. *Brit. J. Ind. Relat.*, July 1984, 22(2), pp. 218–64.

Broder, Josef M. and Ziemer, Rod F. Assessment of Journals Used by Agricultural Economists at Land-Grant Universities. *Southern J. Agr. Econ.*, July 1984, 16(1), pp. 167–72. [G: U.S.]

Caves, Richard E. Harry Johnson as a Social Scientist. *J. Polit. Econ.*, August 1984, 92(4), pp. 642–58.

Cicarelli, James and Spizman, Lawrence. The Production of Economic Knowledge. *Quart. Rev. Econ. Bus.*, Summer 1984, 24(2), pp. 41–50. [G: U.S.]

Davis, Paul and Papanek, Gustav F. Faculty Ratings of Major Economics Departments by Citations. *Amer. Econ. Rev.*, March 1984, 74(1), pp. 225–30. [G: U.S.]

Dublin, Thomas. The Merrimack Valley Textile Museum—An Appreciation. *Labor Hist.*, Spring 1984, 25(2), pp. 240–42. [G: U.S.]

Frey, Bruno S., et al. Consensus and Dissension among Economists: An Empirical Inquiry. *Amer. Econ. Rev.*, December 1984, 74(5), pp. 986–94. [G: U.S.; France; Austria; Germany; Switzerland]

Gilreath, James. Labor History Sources in the Library of Congress Rare Book and Special Collections Division. *Labor Hist.*, Spring 1984, 25(2), pp. 243–51. [G: U.S.]

Graves, Philip E.; Marchand, James and Thompson, Randall. Economics Departmental Rankings: Reply and Errata [Economics Departmental Rankings: Research Incentives, Constraints, and Efficiency]. *Amer. Econ. Rev.*, September 1984, 74(4), pp. 834–36. [G: U.S.]

Hägerstrand, Torsten. Presence and Absence: A Look at Conceptual Choices and Bodily Necessities. *Reg. Stud.*, October 1984, 18(5), pp. 373–79.

Harcourt, Geoffrey C. Reflections on the Development of Economics as a Discipline. *Hist. Polit. Econ.*, Winter 1984, 16(4), pp. 489–517.

Hargreaves-Heap, Shaun and Hollis, Martin. Bread and Circumstances: The Need for Political Economy. In *Whynes, D. K., ed.*, 1984, pp. 7–30.

Hausman, Daniel M. The Philosophy of Economics: Introduction. In *Hausman, D. M., ed.*, 1984, pp. 1–50.

Havlicek, Joseph, Jr. The Southern Agricultural Economics Association: Past, Present, and Future. *Southern J. Agr. Econ.*, July 1984, 16(1), pp. 1–5. [G: U.S.]

Heilbroner, Robert L. Economics and Political Economy: Marx, Keynes, and Schumpeter. *J. Econ. Issues*, September 1984, 18(3), pp. 681–95.

Heilbroner, Robert L. Is Economic Theory Possible? *Soc. Res.*, Spring & Summer 1984, 51(1&2), pp. 437–59.

Henderson, John P. Malthus and the *Edinburgh Review*. In *Samuels, W. J., ed.*, 1984, pp. 107–24.

Hill, Lewis E. and Owen, Donald W. The Humane and Human: Rejoinder [An Assault on the Citadel: Is a Constructive Synthesis Feasible?]. *J. Econ. Issues*, September 1984, 18(3), pp. 908–09.

Hirsch, Barry T., et al. Economics Departmental Rankings: Comment [Economics Departmental Rankings: Research Incentives, Constraints, and Efficiency]. *Amer. Econ. Rev.*, September 1984, 74(4), pp. 822–26. [G: U.S.]

Hogan, Timothy D. Economics Departmental Rankings: Comment [Economics Departmental Rankings: Research Incentives, Constraints, and Efficiency]. *Amer. Econ. Rev.*, September 1984, 74(4), pp. 827–33. [G: U.S.]

Kane, Edward J. Why Journal Editors Should

Encourage the Replication of Applied Econometric Research. *Quart. J. Bus. Econ.*, Winter 1984, *23*(1), pp. 3–8.

Kaufman, George G. Rankings of Finance Departments by Faculty Representation on Editorial Boards of Professional Journals: A Note. *J. Finance*, September 1984, *39*(4), pp. 1189–97.

Liebowitz, S. J. and Palmer, John P. Assessing the Relative Impacts of Economic Journals. *J. Econ. Lit.*, March 1984, *22*(1), pp. 77–88.

Lissner, Will. Scientific Journals—Are They 'Unreadable'? *Amer. J. Econ. Soc.*, January 1984, *43*(1), pp. 123–24.

Longawa, Vicky M. Harry G. Johnson: A Bibliography. *J. Polit. Econ.*, August 1984, *92*(4), pp. 659–711.

McCormick, Gordon H. Strategic Considerations in the Development of Economic Thought. In *McCormick, G. H. and Bissell, R. E., eds.*, 1984, pp. 3–25.

Michwitz, Gösta. Ekonomiska Samfundets Profil. (The Profile of the Economic Society. With English summary.) *Ekon. Samfundets Tidskr.*, 1984, *37*(3), pp. 143–51. **[G: Finland]**

Mittelstaedt, Robert A. and Zorn, Thomas S. Econometric Replication: Lessons from the Experimental Sciences. *Quart. J. Bus. Econ.*, Winter 1984, *23*(1), pp. 9–15.

Morikawa, Hidemasa. Report of the Long-term Trends of the Business History Society of Japan. In *Nakagawa, K. and Morikawa, H., eds.*, 1984, pp. 131–49. **[G: Japan]**

Munroe, Trevor. Caribbean Politics and the Faculty of Social Sciences. *Soc. Econ. Stud.*, March 1984, *33*(1), pp. 59–81.
[G: Caribbean]

Neale, Walter C. The Humane and the Human: Assaulting Petr (with a Swipe at Hill and Owen) [An Assault on the Citadel: Is a Constructive Synthesis Feasible?]. *J. Econ. Issues*, September 1984, *18*(3), pp. 903–07.

Olson, Mancur. Why Nations Rise and Fall. *Challenge*, March/April 1984, *27*(1), pp. 15–23.

Petr, Jerry L. An Assault on the Citadel: Is a Constructive Synthesis Feasible? *J. Econ. Issues*, June 1984, *18*(2), pp. 589–97.

Petr, Jerry L. Rejoinder to Neale [An Assault on the Citadel: Is a Constructive Synthesis Feasible?]. *J. Econ. Issues*, September 1984, *18*(3), pp. 907–08.

Reder, Melvin W. Chicago Economics: Permanence and Change. In *Caldwell, B. J., ed.*, 1984, *1982*, pp. 360–97.

Reder, Melvin W. Complete Bibliography of the Works of Melvin W. Reder. *J. Lab. Econ.*, April 1984, *2*(2), pp. 151–53.

Rock, James M. A Reason for Ranking Recent Articles: The Case of Macromonetary Articles. *Amer. Econ.*, Spring 1984, *28*(1), pp. 80–85.
[G: U.S.]

Rugina, Anghel N. The Future Belongs to a Social Economy of Human Solidarity: A New Orientation in Theory and Practice. *Int. J. Soc. Econ.*, 1984, *11*(1/2), pp. 49–82.

Salda, Anne C. M. The International Monetary Fund, 1983: A Selected Bibliography. *Int. Monet. Fund Staff Pap.*, Supplement, December 1984, *31*, pp. 763–809.

Seth, K. G. Non-economic Factors in Economic Analysis. *Indian Econ. J.*, April–June 1984, *31*(4), pp. 53–61.

Shafey, Erfan. Islamic Economics as a Social Science: Some Methodological Issues: Comment. *J. Res. Islamic Econ.*, Summer 1984, *2*(1), pp. 55–56.

Sherman, Howard J. Contemporary Radical Economics. *J. Econ. Educ.*, Fall 1984, *15*(4), pp. 265–74.

Soldofsky, Robert M. Age and Productivity of University Faculties: A Case Study. *Econ. Educ. Rev.*, 1984, *3*(4), pp. 289–98.
[G: U.S.]

Spaeth, Mary A. Bibliography of the Publications of Robert Ferber. In *[Ferber, R.]*, 1984, pp. 393–406.

Spiegel, Uriel and Templeman, Joseph. The Ethics of Suboptimal Resource Allocation in Academe: A Note. *Amer. Econ.*, Fall 1984, *28*(2), pp. 81–83.

Stanfield, J. R. Social Reform and Economic Policy. *J. Econ. Issues*, March 1984, *18*(1), pp. 19–44.

Steindl, Josef. Reflections on the Present State of Economics. *Banca Naz. Lavoro Quart. Rev.*, March 1984, (148), pp. 3–14.

Stigler, George J. Economics—The Imperial Science? *Scand. J. Econ.*, 1984, *86*(3), pp. 301–13.

Tauer, Loren W. and Tauer, Janelle R. Ranking Doctoral Programs by *Journal* Contributions of Recent Graduates. *Amer. J. Agr. Econ.*, May 1984, *66*(2), pp. 170–72. **[G: U.S.]**

Thompson, N. W. The Attitude to Political Economy of Writers in the Working-class Press, 1816–1834. In *Samuels, W. J., ed.*, 1984, pp. 21–45.

Tuomainen, Eero. Kansantaloudellisen Yhdistyksen vaiheita. (The Finnish Economic Association 1884–1984. With English summary.) *Kansant. Aikak.*, 1984, *80*(1), pp. 4–6.
[G: Finland]

Varian, Hal R. Gerard Debreu's Contributions to Economics. *Scand. J. Econ.*, 1984, *86*(1), pp. 4–16.

Weiner, Paul; Carstensen, Fred and Golden, John. Recent Publication Performance in Economics: An Abstract Approach. *Quart. Rev. Econ. Bus.*, Spring 1984, *24*(1), pp. 93–98.
[G: U.S.]

You, Poh Seng. Fond Memories. *Singapore Econ. Rev.*, October 1984, *29*(2), pp. 148–54.

0112 Role of Economics; Role of Economists

Bauer, P. T. Further Reflections on the State of Economics. In *Bauer, P. T.*, 1984, pp. 152–63.

Baumol, William J. On My Attitudes: Sociopolitical and Methodological. *Amer. Econ.*, Spring 1984, *28*(1), pp. 5–9.

Baxter, William F. Comments [The Role of Eco-

4

nomic Analysis in the Antitrust Division before and after the Establishment of the Economic Policy Office: A Lawyer's View] [Pigeonholes in antitrust]. *Antitrust Bull.*, Spring 1984, 29(1), pp. 147–50.

Becattini, Giacomo. L'economista e l'ambiente. (The Economist and the Environment. With English summary.) *Giorn. Econ.*, March–April 1984, 43(3–4), pp. 145–59.

Bhagwati, Jagdish N. Development Economics: What Have We Learned? *METU*, 1984, 11(1–2), pp. 49–69.

Boulding, Kenneth E. How Do Things Go from Bad to Better? The Contribution of Economics. In *Boulding, K. E., ed.*, 1984, pp. 1–14.

Caldwell, Bruce J. and Coats, A. W. The Rhetoric of Economists: A Comment. *J. Econ. Lit.*, June 1984, 22(2), pp. 575–78.

Fanning, Ronan. Economists and Governments: Ireland 1922–52. In *Murphy, A. E., ed.*, 1984, pp. 138–56. **[G: Ireland]**

Ganssman, Heiner. Political Economics and Social Action. *Eastern Econ. J.*, April-June 1984, 10(2), pp. 129–37.

Genovese, Frank C. An Economics Classic and Plutology: The 'Science of Wealth' Reminds Economists That Their Goal Should Be Well-being for All. *Amer. J. Econ. Soc.*, October 1984, 43(4), pp. 455–67.

Giersch, Herbert and Heimenz, Ulrich. Past Trends and Present Needs in Research on Economic Development. *METU*, 1984, 11(1–2), pp. 41–48.

Gilad, Benjamin; Kaish, Stanley and Loeb, Peter D. From Economic Behavior to Behavioral Economics: The Behavioral Uprising in Economics. *J. Behav. Econ.*, Winter 1984, 13(2), pp. 3–24.

Gilad, Benjamin; Kaish, Stanley and Loeb, Peter D. From Economic Behavior to Behavioral Economics: The Behavioral Uprising in Economics. *J. Behav. Econ.*, Summer 1984, 13(1), pp. 1–22.

Gordon, Wendell C. The Role of Institutional Economics. *J. Econ. Issues*, June 1984, 18(2), pp. 369–81.

Goulbourne, Harry. The Social Sciences and Caribbean Society: Conclusion: Some Challenges for the Future. *Soc. Econ. Stud.*, June 1984, 33(2), pp. 157–67.

Hahn, Frank H. Economic Theory and Policy. In *Hahn, F.*, 1984, pp. 327–49.

Hamilton, David. Economics: Science or Legend? *J. Econ. Issues*, June 1984, 18(2), pp. 565–72.

Harris, Robert G. The Values of Economic Theory in Management Education. *Amer. Econ. Rev.*, May 1984, 74(2), pp. 122–26.

Hart, Oliver. The Wider World and Economic Methodology: Comment. In *Wiles, P. and Routh, G., eds.*, 1984, pp. 47–50.

Hay, George A. Pigeonholes in Antitrust. *Antitrust Bull.*, Spring 1984, 29(1), pp. 133–45.

von Hayek, Friedrich A. The Pretence of Knowledge. In *von Hayek, F. A. (I)*, 1984, 1975, pp. 266–77.

von Hayek, Friedrich A. The Use of Knowledge

in Society. In *von Hayek, F. A. (I)*, 1984, 1945, pp. 211–24.

Hennipman, P. Normative or Positive: Mishan's Half-Way House. *De Economist*, 1984, 132(1), pp. 86–99.

Jäckel, Hans. Twenty Annual Reports of the German Council of Economic Experts: A Short Survey. *Z. ges. Staatswiss.*, June 1984, 140(2), pp. 380–86. **[G: W. Germany]**

Kauper, Thomas E. The Role of Economic Analysis in the Antitrust Division before and after the Establishment of the Economic Policy Office: A Lawyer's View. *Antitrust Bull.*, Spring 1984, 29(1), pp. 111–32.

Khosro, A. M. Economists and Indian Development. *Indian Econ. J.*, July–Sept. 1984, 32(1), pp. 1–36. **[G: India]**

Klein, Philip A. Economic Policy and the Obligations of the Economist. *J. Econ. Issues*, June 1984, 18(2), pp. 537–46.

Knight, Frank. Economics and Human Action. In *Hausman, D. M., ed.*, 1984, 1935, pp. 141–48.

Martellaro, Joseph A. Business and Economics as Pre-law Majors. *Soc. Econ. Stud.*, December 1984, 33(4), pp. 125–49. **[G: U.S.]**

McCloskey, Donald N. Reply [The Rhetoric of Economics]. *J. Econ. Lit.*, June 1984, 22(2), pp. 579–80.

McCloskey, Donald N. The Rhetoric of Economics. In *Caldwell, B. J., ed.*, 1984, 1983, pp. 320–56.

McCracken, Paul W. Has Macro-Theory Failed Economic Policy? *Southern Econ. J.*, October 1984, 51(2), pp. 319–29. **[G: U.S.]**

Mishan, E. J. The Implications of Alternative Foundations for Welfare Economics. *De Economist*, 1984, 132(1), pp. 75–85.

Neild, Robert. The Wider World and Economic Methodology. In *Wiles, P. and Routh, G., eds.*, 1984, pp. 37–46.

Nelson, James R. and Doeksen, Gerald A. Agricultural Economists in Rural Development: Responsibilities, Opportunities, Risks, and Payoffs. *Southern J. Agr. Econ.*, July 1984, 16(1), pp. 41–47. **[G: U.S.]**

Owen, Bruce M. Comments [The Role of Economic Analysis in the Antitrust Division before and after the Establishment of the Economic Policy Office: A Lawyer's View] [Pigeonholes in Antitrust]. *Antitrust Bull.*, Spring 1984, 29(1), pp. 151–52.

Parker, William N. A Comment on the Papers: Personal Reflections and Some Diagrams. In *Parker, W. N.*, 1984, pp. 238–55.

Peacock, Alan. The Political Economy of Strukturpolitik: A Tribute to the German Council of Economic Experts. *Z. ges. Staatswiss.*, June 1984, 140(2), pp. 364–70. **[G: Germany]**

Petr, Jerry L. Fundamentals of an Institutionalist Perspective on Economic Policy. *J. Econ. Issues*, March 1984, 18(1), pp. 1–17.

Rätzer, Ernst. Institutionelle Ursachen der geringen ökonomischen Forschungsaktivität im deutschsprachigen Raum. (Institutional Causes of the Low Economic Research Activity in Ger-

man Speaking Countries. With English summary. *Kyklos*, 1984, *37*(2), pp. 223–46.
[G: Germany; Switzerland; Austria]

Rosen, George. Development Economics: Some Thoughts on Its Past and Its Future. *METU*, 1984, *11*(1–2), pp. 21–28.

Samuels, Warren J. Galbraith on Economics as a System of Professional Belief. *J. Post Keynesian Econ.*, Fall 1984, *7*(1), pp. 61–76.

Schumpeter, Joseph A. The Meaning of Rationality in the Social Sciences. *Z. ges. Staatswiss.*, December 1984, *140*(4), pp. 577–93.

Şenses, Fikret. Development Economics at a Crossroad. *METU*, 1984, *11*(1–2), pp. 109–50.

Smirnov, A. D. Definitions of the Subject Matter of Political Economy. In *Smirnov, A. D.; Golosov, V. V. and Maximova, V. F., eds.,* 1984, pp. 25–34.

Stein, Herbert. Bricks without Straw: Making Economic Policy out of Economics. *Contemp. Policy Issue*, Fall 1984-85, *3*(1), pp. 1–14.
[G: U.S.]

Streeten, Paul. Development Economics in Retrospect and Prospect. *METU*, 1984, *11*(1–2), pp. 29–39.

Sufrin, Sidney C. A Quadrant of Views. *Rivista Int. Sci. Econ. Com.*, April 1984, *31*(4), pp. 289–304.

Teece, David J. and Winter, Sidney G. The Limits of Neoclassical Theory in Management Education. *Amer. Econ. Rev.*, May 1984, *74*(2), pp. 116–21.

Thirlwall, A. P. In Praise of Development Economics. *METU*, 1984, *11*(1–2), pp. 93–107.

Tinbergen, Jan. My Life Philosophy. *Amer. Econ.*, Fall 1984, *28*(2), pp. 5–8.

Tullock, Gordon. How to Do Well While Doing Good!! In *Colander, D. C., ed.,* 1984, pp. 229–40.

Verdier, James M. Advising Congressional Decision-Makers: Guidelines for Economists. *J. Policy Anal. Manage.*, Spring 1984, *3*(3), pp. 421–38.
[G: U.S.]

Wallich, Henry C. The German Council of Economic Advisers in an American Perspective. *Z. ges. Staatswiss.*, June 1984, *140*(2), pp. 355–63.
[G: U.S.; Germany]

Waris, Klaus. Ekonomistit talouspolitiikkaa ideoimassa. (The Role of Economists in the Making of Economic Policy. With English summary.) *Kansant. Aikak.*, 1984, *80*(1), pp. 7–16.
[G: Finland]

White, Lawrence H. Comments [The Role of Economic Analysis in the Antitrust Division before and after the Establishment of the Economic Policy Office: A Lawyer's View] [Pigeonholes in Antitrust]. *Antitrust Bull.*, Spring 1984, *29*(1), pp. 153–57.

Williamson, Oliver E. Pretrial Uses of Economists: On the Use of "Incentive Logic" to Screen Predation. *Antitrust Bull.*, Fall 1984, *29*(3), pp. 475–500.
[G: U.S.]

0113 Relation of Economics to Other Disciplines

Acham, Karl. Schumpeter—The Sociologist. In *Seidl, C., ed.,* 1984, pp. 155–72.

Akerlof, George A. and Dickens, William T. The Economic Consequences of Cognitive Dissonance. In *Akerlof, G. A., 1984, 1982,* pp. 123–44.

Arrow, Kenneth J. Homogeneous Systems in Mathematical Economics: A Comment. In *Arrow, K. J., vol. 3, 1984, 1950,* pp. 1–4.

Arrow, Kenneth J. Risk Perception in Psychology and Economics. In *Arrow, K. J., vol. 3, 1984, 1982,* pp. 261–70.

Bourdieu, Pierre. Réponses aux économistes. (With English summary.) *Écon. Soc.*, October 1984, *18*(10), pp. 23–32.

Bronsard, Camille. Economie et anthropologie sociale. Sur l'existence d'un contrat social implicite. (Economics and Social Anthropology [On the Existence of an Implicit Social Contract]. With English summary.) *Écon. Appl.*, 1984, *37*(3–4), pp. 645–85.

Coleman, James S. Introducing Social Structure into Economic Analysis. *Amer. Econ. Rev.*, May 1984, *74*(2), pp. 84–88.

Domenach, Jean-Marie. Epistemologia e autonomia. (Epistemology and Autonomy. With English summary.) *Rivista Int. Sci. Econ. Com.*, January 1984, *31*(1), pp. 5–13.

Fox, Karl A. Behavior Settings and Eco-behavioral Science: A New Arena for Mathematical Social Science Permitting a Richer and More Coherent View of Human Activities in Social Systems, Part I: Concepts, Measurements, and Linkages to Economic Data Systems, Time-Allocation Matrices, and Social System Accounts. *Math. Soc. Sci.*, April 1984, *7*(2), pp. 117–38.
[G: U.S.]

Fox, Karl A. Behavior Settings and Eco-behavioral Science: A New Arena for Mathematical Social Science Permitting a Richer and More Coherent View of Human Activities in Social Systems, Part II: Relationships to Established Disciplines, and Needs for Mathematical Development. *Math. Soc. Sci.*, April 1984, *7*(2), pp. 139–65.
[G: U.S.]

Frank, Andre Gunder. On Theoretical Issues in Economic Anthropology. In *Frank, A. G., 1984, 1970,* pp. 42–57.

Gilad, Benjamin; Kaish, Stanley and Loeb, Peter D. From Economic Behavior to Behavioral Economics: The Behavioral Uprising in Economics. *J. Behav. Econ.*, Summer 1984, *13*(1), pp. 1–22.

Gilad, Benjamin; Kaish, Stanley and Loeb, Peter D. From Economic Behavior to Behavioral Economics: The Behavioral Uprising in Economics. *J. Behav. Econ.*, Winter 1984, *13*(2), pp. 3–24.

Greene, J. Edward. Challenges and Responses in Social Science Research in the English-speaking Caribbean. *Soc. Econ. Stud.*, March 1984, *33*(1), pp. 9–46.
[G: Caribbean]

Hackman, J. Richard. Psychological Contributions to Organizational Productivity: A Commentary. In *Brief, A. P., ed.,* 1984, pp. 207–26.

Hill, Bruce M. The Robust Bayesian Viewpoint:

Comment. In *Kadane, J. B., ed.*, 1984, pp. 134–35.

Labeyrie, Vincent. Contraintes écologiques, équilibres et activités humaines. (Ecological Constraints, Equilibrium, and Human Activities. With English summary.) *Écon. Appl.*, 1984, *37*(2), pp. 243–77.

Little, Graham R. Social Models: Blueprints or Processes? In *Richardson, J., ed.*, 1984, pp. 101–11.

Mäkinen, Vesa. Tulevaisuudentutkimusperspektiivi taloustieteissä. (Futurology and Economics. With English summary.) *Liiketaloudellinen Aikak.*, 1984, *33*(2), pp. 218–27.

Mănescu, Manea. Cybernetics and Social Progress. *Econ. Computat. Cybern. Stud. Res.*, 1984, *19*(1), pp. 5–11.

March, James G. and Olsen, Johan P. The New Institutionalism: Organizational Factors in Political Life. *Amer. Polit. Sci. Rev.*, September 1984, *78*(3), pp. 734–49.

Matthews, R. C. O. Darwinism and Economic Change. In *Collard, D. A., et al., eds.*, 1984, pp. 91–117.

Mirowski, Philip. Physics and the 'Marginalist Revolution.' *Cambridge J. Econ.*, December 1984, *8*(4), pp. 361–79.

Namiki, Nobuyoshi. Fundamental Causes of Difficulties in the Contemporary World. In *Miyawaki, N., ed.*, 1984, pp. 287–99.

Niculescu-Mizil, E. Genetics and the Conditioned Reflex in the Cybernetic Economic-Social Systems. *Econ. Computat. Cybern. Stud. Res.*, 1984, *19*(1), pp. 25–30.

Offe, Claus. 'Ungovernability': The Renaissance of Conservative Theories of Crisis. In *Offe, C.*, 1984, *1979*, pp. 65–87.

Prewitt, Kenneth. Social Science and the Third World: Constraints on the United States. In *Trent, J. and Lamy, P., eds.*, 1984, pp. 33–43.

Schumpeter, Joseph A. The Meaning of Rationality in the Social Sciences. *Z. ges. Staatswiss.*, December 1984, *140*(4), pp. 577–93.

Sen, Amartya. Rights and Capabilities. In *Sen, A.*, 1984, pp. 307–24.

Singer, Eleanor. Public Reactions to Some Ethical Issues of Social Research: Attitudes and Behavior. *J. Cons. Res.*, June 1984, *11*(1), pp. 501–09. [G: U.S.]

Soedjatmoko. The Social Sciences and Global Transformation. In *Trent, J. and Lamy, P., eds.*, 1984, pp. 17–32.

Stigler, George J. Economics—The Imperial Science? *Scand. J. Econ.*, 1984, *86*(3), pp. 301–13.

Tamanoï, Yoshiro; Tsuchida, Atsushi and Murota, Takeshi. Towards an Entropic Theory of Economy and Ecology: Beyond the Mechanistic Equilibrium Approach. *Écon. Appl.*, 1984, *37*(2), pp. 279–94.

Thistle, Paul D. Psychological Learning Theory and Economic Behavior. *J. Behav. Econ.*, Summer 1984, *13*(1), pp. 67–100.

Tinbergen, Jan. Alternative Optimal Social Orders. *Pakistan Devel. Rev.*, Spring 1984, *23*(1), pp. 1–7.

Trent, John. The Social Sciences in Canada in the Eighties: The Unloved Middle Brother Syndrome. In *Trent, J. and Lamy, P., eds.*, 1984, pp. 45–95.

Ursel, Laurent. Impérialisme de la science économique et néo-libéralisme. (With English summary.) *Écon. Soc.*, October 1984, *18*(10), pp. 33–59.

Weiss, Howard M. Contributions of Social Psychology to Productivity. In *Brief, A. P., ed.*, 1984, pp. 143–73.

0114 Relation of Economics to Social Values

Akerlof, George A. Loyalty Filters. In *Akerlof, G. A.*, 1984, *1983*, pp. 175–91.

Barry, Norman P. Ideas versus Interests: The Classical Liberal Dilemma. In *Barry, N., et al.*, 1984, pp. 43–64.

Bauer, P. T. Ecclesiastical Economics: Envy Legitimized. In *Bauer, P. T.*, 1984, pp. 73–89.

Baumol, William J. On My Attitudes: Sociopolitical and Methodological. *Amer. Econ.*, Spring 1984, *28*(1), pp. 5–9.

Briefs, Henry W. Solidarity within the Firm: Principles, Concepts and Reflections. *Rev. Soc. Econ.*, December 1984, *42*(3), pp. 295–317.

Buchanan, James M. The Ethical Limits of Taxation. *Scand. J. Econ.*, 1984, *86*(2), pp. 102–14.

Collard, David. The Welfare State, Economics and Morality. In *Boulding, K. E., ed.*, 1984, pp. 174–90.

Danner, Peter L. The Moral Foundations of Community. *Rev. Soc. Econ.*, December 1984, *42*(3), pp. 231–52.

Ditz, G. W. The Calvinism in Adam Smith. *Tijdschrift Econ. Manage.*, 1984, *29*(2), pp. 233–54.

Dorn, James A. Planning America: Government or the Market? Introduction. *Cato J.*, Fall 1984, *4*(2), pp. 365–80. [G: U.S.]

Flew, Antony. The Concept of Human Betterment. In *Boulding, K. E., ed.*, 1984, pp. 132–50.

Ganssman, Heiner. Political Economics and Social Action. *Eastern Econ. J.*, April-June 1984, *10*(2), pp. 129–37.

Gissurarson, Hannes H. 'The Only Truly Progressive Policy...' In *Barry, N., et al.*, 1984, pp. 1–23.

Gray, John. The Road to Serfdom: Forty Years On. In *Barry, N., et al.*, 1984, pp. 25–42.

Hart, John. Land Reform and the Church. In *Geisler, C. C. and Popper, F. J., eds.*, 1984, pp. 73–87. [G: U.S.]

von Hayek, Friedrich A. The Origins and Effects of Our Morals: A Problem for Science. In *von Hayek, F. A. (I)*, 1984, pp. 318–30.

von Hayek, Friedrich A. The Principles of a Liberal Social Order. In *von Hayek, F. A. (I)*, 1984, *1966*, pp. 363–81.

von Hayek, Friedrich A. Whither Democracy? In *von Hayek, F. A. (I)*, 1984, pp. 352–62.

Hennipman, P. Normative or Positive: Mishan's Half-Way House. *De Economist*, 1984, *132*(1), pp. 86–99.

Hickerson, Steven R. Complexity and the Meaning of Freedom: The Instrumentalist View. *Amer. J. Econ. Soc.*, October 1984, *43*(4), pp. 435–42.

Higgins, Benjamin. Jan Boeke and the Doctrine of 'The Little Push.' *Bull. Indonesian Econ. Stud.*, December 1984, *20*(3), pp. 55–69.
[G: Indonesia]

Hill, Lewis E. A Comment on Solidarity within the Firm [Solidarity within the Firm: Principles, Concepts and Reflections] [Industrial Justice in a Practical Sense]. *Rev. Soc. Econ.*, December 1984, *42*(3), pp. 328–29.

Horn, Walter. Libertarianism and Private Property in Land: The Positions of Rothbard and Nozick, Critically Examined, Are Disputed. *Amer. J. Econ. Soc.*, July 1984, *43*(3), pp. 341–55.

Inada, Kenneth K. Toward an Organismic Society. In *Miyawaki, N., ed.*, 1984, pp. 279–86.

Ito, Shuntaro. Turning Points of Civilization and the Role of Japan Today. In *Miyawaki, N., ed.*, 1984, pp. 89–99.
[G: Japan]

Jensen, Hans E. Some Aspects of the Social Economics of John Maynard Keynes. *Int. J. Soc. Econ.*, 1984, *11*(3/4), pp. 72–91.

Klappholz, Kurt. Value Judgments and Economics. In *Hausman, D. M., ed.*, 1984, *1964*, pp. 276–92.

Kolm, Serge-Christophe. Théorie de la réciprocité et du choix des systèmes économiques. (Theory of Reciprocity and the Choice of Economic Systems. With English summary.) *Revue Écon.*, September 1984, *35*(5), pp. 871–910.

Leite, Celso Barroso. Social Solutions for Economic Problems. *Int. J. Soc. Econ.*, 1984, *11*(3/4), pp. 108–13.
[G: Brazil]

Lichtenstein, Peter M. Some Theoretical Coordinates of Radical Liberalism. *Amer. J. Econ. Soc.*, July 1984, *43*(3), pp. 333–39.

Lieske, Joel. The Salvation of American Cities. In *Porter, P. R. and Sweet, D. C., eds.*, 1984, pp. 71–92.
[G: U.S.]

Macpherson, C. B. Democracy: Utopian and Scientific. In *Ball, T. and Farr, J., eds.*, 1984, pp. 141–53.

Malliaris, A. G. Economic Stabilization, Social Issues and the Role of Government. *Rev. Soc. Econ.*, October 1984, *42*(2), pp. 117–29.
[G: U.S.]

McCain, Roger A. Social Economy and Community. *Int. J. Soc. Econ.*, 1984, *11*(1/2), pp. 89–99.

McKee, Arnold F. Market Failure and the Place of Government in Social Economy. *Rev. Soc. Econ.*, April 1984, *42*(1), pp. 1–15.

McKee, Arnold F. Social Economy and the Theory of Consumer Behaviour. *Int. J. Soc. Econ.*, 1984, *11*(3/4), pp. 45–61.

McPherson, Michael S. Limits on Self-seeking: The Role of Morality in Economic Life. In *Colander, D. C., ed.*, 1984, pp. 71–85.

Mishan, E. J. The Implications of Alternative Foundations for Welfare Economics. *De Economist*, 1984, *132*(1), pp. 75–85.

Miyawaki, Nagasada. Problems of Advanced Economics. In *Miyawaki, N., ed.*, 1984, pp. 4–13.

Mubyarto. Social and Economic Justice. *Bull. Indonesian Econ. Stud.*, December 1984, *20*(3), pp. 36–54.
[G: Indonesia]

Namiki, Nobuyoshi. Fundamental Causes of Difficulties in the Contemporary World. In *Miyawaki, N., ed.*, 1984, pp. 287–99.

Samuels, Warren J. Economics and Theology: The Fundamental Common Problem. *Econ. Forum*, Summer 1984, *15*(1), pp. 1–7.

Schelling, Thomas C. Economic Reasoning and the Ethics of Policy. In *Schelling, T. C.*, 1984, pp. 1–26.

Schelling, Thomas C. Ethics, Law, and the Exercise of Self-Command. In *Schelling, T. C.*, 1984, pp. 83–112.

Schumpeter, Joseph A. Science and Ideology. In *Hausman, D. M., ed.*, 1984, *1949*, pp. 260–75.

Seldon, Arthur. Recollections: Before and After the Road to Serfdom: Reflections on Hayek in 1935, 1944, 1960, 1982. In *Barry, N., et al.*, 1984, pp. xiii–xxxii.

Sen, Amartya. Ethical Issues in Income Distribution: National and International. In *Sen, A.*, 1984, *1981*, pp. 277–306.

Sen, Amartya. Rights and Capabilities. In *Sen, A.*, 1984, pp. 307–24.

Shearmur, Jeremy. Hayek and the Wisdom of the Age. In *Barry, N., et al.*, 1984, pp. 65–85.

Singer, Eleanor. Public Reactions to Some Ethical Issues of Social Research: Attitudes and Behavior. *J. Cons. Res.*, June 1984, *11*(1), pp. 501–09.
[G: U.S.]

Smith, Vardaman R. Marx's Social Ontology, His Critical Method and Contemporary Social Economics. *Rev. Soc. Econ.*, October 1984, *42*(2), pp. 143–69.

Stanfield, J. R. Social Reform and Economic Policy. *J. Econ. Issues*, March 1984, *18*(1), pp. 19–44.

Thanawala, Kishor. George Rohrlich's Social Economics. *Int. J. Soc. Econ.*, 1984, *11*(1/2), pp. 83–88.

Tiemstra, John P. The Moral Foundations of Community: Comment. *Rev. Soc. Econ.*, December 1984, *42*(3), pp. 257–59.

Tilman, Rick. Dewey's Liberalism versus Veblen's Radicalism: A Reappraisal of the Unity of Progressive Social Thought. *J. Econ. Issues*, September 1984, *18*(3), pp. 745–69.
[G: U.S.]

Tinbergen, Jan. My Life Philosophy. *Amer. Econ.*, Fall 1984, *28*(2), pp. 5–8.

Vaughn, Karen I. The Constitution of Liberty from an Evolutionary Perspective. In *Barry, N., et al.*, 1984, pp. 117–42.

Waters, William R. Development of Solidarist Economics in the U.S. *Int. J. Soc. Econ.*, 1984, *11*(1/2), pp. 100–116.
[G: U.S.]

Wilkinson, Bruce W. The Catholic Bishops and Canadian Public Policy: A Comment. *Can. Public Policy*, March 1984, *10*(1), pp. 88–91.
[G: Canada]

Williams, John R. Religion, Ethics and Development: An Analysis of the Sarvodaya Shramadana Movement of Sri Lanka. *Can. J. Devel. Stud.*, 1984, *5*(1), pp. 157–67.
[G: Sri Lanka]

Worland, Stephen T. Prospects for Creative Synthesis. *Rev. Soc. Econ.*, December 1984, *42*(3), pp. 417–23.

0115 Methods Used by Economists

Arrow, Kenneth J. Homogeneous Systems in Mathematical Economics: A Comment. In *Arrow, K. J., vol. 3*, 1984, *1950*, pp. 1–4.

Hicks, John R. Methods of Dynamic Analysis. In *Hicks, J.*, 1984, *1956*, pp. 200–215.

Hill, Bruce M. The Robust Bayesian Viewpoint: Comment. In *Kadane, J. B., ed.*, 1984, pp. 134–35.

Marschak, Jacob. On Econometric Tools. In *Hausman, D. M., ed.*, 1984, *1969*, pp. 294–99.

Morishima, Michio. The Good and Bad Uses of Mathematics. In *Wiles, P. and Routh, G., eds.*, 1984, pp. 51–73.

Zellner, Arnold. Perspectives on Mathematical Models in the Social Sciences. In *Zellner, A.*, 1984, pp. 12–25.

012 Teaching of Economics

0120 Teaching of Economics

Adelberg, Arthur H. and Razek, Joseph R. The Cloze Procedure: A Methodology for Determining the Understandability of Accounting Textbooks. *Accounting Rev.*, January 1984, *59*(1), pp. 109–22.
[G: U.S.]

Allison, Elisabeth. Otto Eckstein: Contributions in Education. *Rev. Econ. Statist.*, November 1984, *66*(4), pp. 543–46.

Amernic, Joel H. and Beechy, Thomas H. Accounting Students' Performance and Cognitive Complexity: Some Empirical Evidence. *Accounting Rev.*, April 1984, *59*(2), pp. 300–313.

Arens, Alvin A. and Ward, D. Dewey. The Use of a Systems Understanding Aid in the Accounting Curriculum. *Accounting Rev.*, January 1984, *59*(1), pp. 98–108.
[G: U.S.]

Arndt, Heinz W. Introduction to Economics. *Singapore Econ. Rev.*, October 1984, *29*(2), pp. 3–10.

Arnold, Donald F. and Geiselhart, Thomas J. Practitioners' Views on Five-Year Educational Requirements for CPAs. *Accounting Rev.*, April 1984, *59*(2), pp. 314–24.
[G: U.S.]

Ashton, Robert H. Integrating Research and Teaching in Auditing: Fifteen Cases on Judgment and Decision Making. *Accounting Rev.*, January 1984, *59*(1), pp. 78–97.

Bach, George L. and Kelley, Allen C. Improving the Teaching of Economics: Achievements and

Aspirations. *Amer. Econ. Rev.*, May 1984, *74*(2), pp. 12–18.

Ball, Donald A. and McCulloch, Wendell H., Jr. International Business Education Programs in American Schools: How They Are Ranked by Members of the Academy of International Business. *J. Int. Bus. Stud.*, Spring/Summer 1984, *15*(1), pp. 175–80.

Beckford, George L. The Struggle for a Relevant Economics. *Soc. Econ. Stud.*, March 1984, *33*(1), pp. 47–57.
[G: Trinidad and Tobago; Jamaica]

Bogan, Elizabeth C. The Use of Interactive Video in Teaching Microeconomics: A Note. *J. Econ. Educ.*, Fall 1984, *15*(4), pp. 329–30.
[G: U.S.]

Bonello, Frank J.; Swartz, Thomas R. and Davisson, William I. Freshman–Sophomore Learning Differentials: A Comment. *J. Econ. Educ.*, Summer 1984, *15*(3), pp. 205–10.
[G: U.S.]

Boyes, William J.; Happel, Stephen K. and Hogan, Timothy D. Publish or Perish: Fact or Fiction? *J. Econ. Educ.*, Spring 1984, *15*(2), pp. 136–41.
[G: U.S.; Canada]

Buckles, Stephen and Freeman, Vera. A Longitudinal Analysis of a Developmental Economics Education Program. *J. Econ. Educ.*, Winter 1984, *15*(1), pp. 5–10.

Chizmar, John F., Jr. and McCarney, Bernard J. An Evaluation of a "Trade Offs" Implementation Using Canonical Estimation of Joint Educational Production Functions. *J. Econ. Educ.*, Winter 1984, *15*(1), pp. 11–20.

Chizmar, John F., Jr. and Zak, Thomas A. Canonical Estimation of Joint Educational Production Functions. *Econ. Educ. Rev.*, 1984, *3*(1), pp. 37–43.
[G: U.S.]

Cyert, Richard M. Economic Education in Our Schools: A Renewed Mission. *J. Econ. Educ.*, Fall 1984, *15*(4), pp. 261–64.
[G: U.S.]

Dalgaard, Bruce R.; Lewis, Darrell R. and Boyer, Carol M. Cost and Effectiveness Considerations in the Use of Computer-assisted Instruction in Economics. *J. Econ. Educ.*, Fall 1984, *15*(4), pp. 309–23.
[G: U.S.]

Dockweiler, Raymond C. and Willis, Carl G. On the Use of Entry Requirements for Undergraduate Accounting Programs. *Accounting Rev.*, July 1984, *59*(3), pp. 496–504.
[G: U.S.]

Edmonds, Thomas P. On the Benefits of Cumulative Exams: An Experimental Study. *Accounting Rev.*, October 1984, *59*(4), pp. 660–68.
[G: U.S.]

Fels, Rendigs. Student Papers on Macroeconomic Policy. *J. Econ. Educ.*, Summer 1984, *15*(3), pp. 237–38.
[G: U.S.]

Ferber, Marianne A. Suggestions for Improving the Classroom Climate for Women in the Introductory Economics Course: A Review Article. *J. Econ. Educ.*, Spring 1984, *15*(2), pp. 160–68.
[G: U.S.]

Finlay, P. N. and King, M. New Approaches to Teaching Mathematical Modelling to Management Students. In *Avula, X. J. R., et al.*, 1984, pp. 942–47.

Hansen, W. Lee. Teaching the Concept of Demand: Another Approach. *J. Econ. Educ.*, Spring 1984, *15*(2), pp. 148–56. [G: U.S.]

Harris, Robert G. The Values of Economic Theory in Management Education. *Amer. Econ. Rev.*, May 1984, *74*(2), pp. 122–26.

Henderson, James P. "Just Notions of Political Economy"— George Pryme, the First Professor of Political Economy at Cambridge. In *Samuels, W. J., ed.*, 1984, pp. 1–20.

Hodgin, Robert F. Information Theory and Attitude Formation in Economic Education. *J. Econ. Educ.*, Summer 1984, *15*(3), pp. 191–96. [G: U.S.]

Karpoff, Jonathan M. Barter Trading as a Microeconomics Teaching Device. *J. Econ. Educ.*, Summer 1984, *15*(3), pp. 226–36. [G: U.S.]

Kaufman, George G. The Academic Preparation of Economists Employed by Commercial and Investment Banks: A Note. *J. Money, Credit, Banking*, August 1984, *16*(3), pp. 351–59.

Klein, Ronald D. Adding International Business to the Core Program via the Simulation Game. *J. Int. Bus. Stud.*, Spring/Summer 1984, *15*(1), pp. 151–59.

Kozmetsky, George. Creative and Innovative Management: A New Academic Frontier. In *[Kozmetsky, G.]*, 1984, pp. 3–25.

Kuhn, Robert Lawrence. Creative and Innovative Management—A Challenge to Academia. In *[Kozmetsky, G.]*, 1984, pp. 27–37.

Luker, William A. DEEP Revisited. *J. Econ. Educ.*, Spring 1984, *15*(2), pp. 111–18. [G: U.S.]

Lumsden, Keith and Scott, Alex. How to Maximize Golden Opinions. *Appl. Econ.*, October 1984, *16*(5), pp. 647–54. [G: U.K.]

Mann, Harvey. A Worksheet for Demonstrating the Articulation of Financial Statements. *Accounting Rev.*, October 1984, *59*(4), pp. 669–73.

McConnell, Campbell R. and Sosin, Kim H. Some Determinants of Student Attitudes toward Large Classes. *J. Econ. Educ.*, Summer 1984, *15*(3), pp. 181–90. [G: U.S.]

McNown, Robert F. and Hunt, Gary L. An Econometrics Laboratory. *J. Econ. Educ.*, Winter 1984, *15*(1), pp. 71–76.

Moscardini, A. O. and Cross, M. Issues Involved in the Design of a Mathematical Modelling Course. In *Avula, X. J. R., et al.*, 1984, pp. 954–63.

Mulligan, James G. A Cost Function for Computer-assisted Programmed Instruction. *J. Econ. Educ.*, Fall 1984, *15*(4), pp. 275–81.

Nelson, Jon P. and Lynch, Kathleen A. Grade Inflation, Real Income, Simultaneity, and Teaching Evaluations. *J. Econ. Educ.*, Winter 1984, *15*(1), pp. 21–37.

Perlman, Morris. What to Teach to Undergraduates: Comment. In *Wiles, P. and Routh, G., eds.*, 1984, pp. 249–59.

Pulley, Lawrence B. and Dolbear, F. Trenery. Computer Simulation Exercises for Economics Statistics. *J. Econ. Educ.*, Winter 1984, *15*(1), pp. 77–87.

Ray, A. K. Curriculum Development in Mathe-

matical Modelling. In *Avula, X. J. R., et al.*, 1984, pp. 948–53.

Rhodes, Edwardo L. and Cerveny, Robert P. Interactive Video as an Economic Teaching Supplement. *J. Econ. Educ.*, Fall 1984, *15*(4), pp. 325–28. [G: U.S.]

Richardson, J. David. A Modified Examination Format. *J. Econ. Educ.*, Spring 1984, *15*(2), pp. 157–59. [G: U.S.]

Rider, Christine. Reevaluating Economic Education: Principles of Economics Texts. *Rev. Radical Polit. Econ.*, Summer & Fall 1984, *16*(2&3), pp. 167–79.

Routh, Guy. What to Teach to Undergraduates. In *Wiles, P. and Routh, G., eds.*, 1984, pp. 240–48.

Samuels, Warren J. Institutional Economics. *J. Econ. Educ.*, Summer 1984, *15*(3), pp. 211–16.

Schenk, Robert and Silvia, John E. Why Has CAI Not Been More Successful in Economic Education: A Note. *J. Econ. Educ.*, Summer 1984, *15*(3), pp. 239–42. [G: U.S.]

Schober, Howard M. The Effects of Inservice Training on Participating Teachers and Students in Their Economics Classes. *J. Econ. Educ.*, Fall 1984, *15*(4), pp. 282–95. [G: U.S.]

Siegfried, John J. and Raymond, Jennie E. A Profile of Senior Economics Majors in the United States. *Amer. Econ. Rev.*, May 1984, *74*(2), pp. 19–25. [G: U.S.]

Soper, John C. and Brenneke, Judith Staley. DEEP Revisited: Another Reply. *J. Econ. Educ.*, Spring 1984, *15*(2), pp. 123. [G: U.S.]

Spirer, Herbert F. and Jaffe, A. J. Misuses of Statistics: Lessons for Statisticians, Non-Statisticians, Students and Teachers. *Amer. J. Econ. Soc.*, April 1984, *43*(2), pp. 205–16.

Tauer, Loren W. and Tauer, Janelle R. Ranking Doctoral Programs by *Journal* Contributions of Recent Graduates. *Amer. J. Agr. Econ.*, May 1984, *66*(2), pp. 170–72. [G: U.S.]

Teece, David J. and Winter, Sidney G. The Limits of Neoclassical Theory in Management Education. *Amer. Econ. Rev.*, May 1984, *74*(2), pp. 116–21.

Turnovsky, Stephen J. Rational Expectations and the Theory of Macroeconomic Policy: An Exposition of Some of the Issues. *J. Econ. Educ.*, Winter 1984, *15*(1), pp. 55–69.

Van Iwaarden, John L. Mathematical Modelling in a Differential Equations Course. In *Avula, X. J. R., et al.*, 1984, pp. 964–67.

Walstad, William B. The Relative Effectiveness of Economics Instruction for Teachers and College Students. *J. Econ. Educ.*, Fall 1984, *15*(4), pp. 297–308. [G: U.S.]

Walstad, William B. and Soper, John C. DEEP Revisited: A Reply. *J. Econ. Educ.*, Spring 1984, *15*(2), pp. 119–22. [G: U.S.]

Wetzstein, Michael E.; Broder, Josef M. and Wilson, Gene. Bayesian Inference and Student Evaluations of Teachers and Courses. *J. Econ. Educ.*, Winter 1984, *15*(1), pp. 40–45.

Zarenda, H. and Rees, D. Economics Education in South Africa—An Output Analysis. *S. Afr. J. Econ.*, June 1984, *52*(2), pp. 188–207.
[G: S. Africa]

020 GENERAL ECONOMIC THEORY

0200 General Economic Theory

Addison, John T.; Burton, John and Torrance, Thomas S. Causation, Social Science and Sir John Hicks. *Oxford Econ. Pap.*, March 1984, *36*(1), pp. 1–11.

Addleson, Mark S. General Equilibrium and 'Competition': On Competition as Strategy. *S. Afr. J. Econ.*, June 1984, *52*(2), pp. 156–71.

Addleson, Mark S. Robbins's *Essay* in Retrospect: On Subjectivism and an "Economics of Choice." *Rivista Int. Sci. Econ. Com.*, June 1984, *31*(6), pp. 506–23.

Akerlof, George A. An Economic Theorist's Book of Tales: Introduction. In *Akerlof, G. A.*, 1984, pp. 1–6.

Arrow, Kenneth J. Homogeneous Systems in Mathematical Economics: A Comment. In *Arrow, K. J.*, vol. 3, 1984, *1950*, pp. 1–4.

Arrow, Kenneth J. Limited Knowledge and Economic Analysis. In *Arrow, K. J.*, vol. 4, 1984, *1974*, pp. 153–66.

Asimakopulos, Athanasios. Joan Robinson and Economic Theory. *Banca Naz. Lavoro Quart. Rev.*, December 1984, (151), pp. 381–409.

Asimakopulos, Athanasios. Joan Robinson et la théorie économique. (Joan Robinson and Economic Theory. With English summary.) *L'Actual. Econ.*, December 1984, *60*(4), pp. 521–52.

Bausor, Randall. Toward a Historically Dynamic Economics: Examples and Illustrations. *J. Post Keynesian Econ.*, Spring 1984, *6*(3), pp. 360–76.

Bhagwati, Jagdish N. Splintering and Disembodiment of Services and Developing Nations. *World Econ.*, June 1984, *7*(2), pp. 133–43.
[G: LDCs; U.K.; U.S.]

Blaug, Mark. Our Methodological Crisis: Comment 2. In *Wiles, P. and Routh, G.*, eds., 1984, pp. 30–36.

Blaug, Mark. The Methodology of Economics: Conclusions. In *Caldwell, B. J.*, ed., 1984, *1980*, pp. 308–19.

Boland, Lawrence A. On the Futility of Criticizing the Neoclassical Maximization Hypothesis. In *Caldwell, B. J.*, ed., 1984, *1981*, pp. 246–51.

Boland, Lawrence A. The Neoclassical Maximization Hypothesis: Reply. In *Caldwell, B. J.*, ed., 1984, *1984*, pp. 256–58.

Bose, Arun. Modern Marxian Political Economy. In *Whynes, D. K.*, ed., 1984, pp. 90–115.

Brochier, Hubert. La valeur heuristique du paradigme économique. (With English summary.) *Écon. Soc.*, October 1984, *18*(10), pp. 3–21.

Bruter, Claude P. Catastrophes locales en économie. (Local Catastrophes in Economy. With English summary.) *Écon. Appl.*, 1984, *37*(1), pp. 123–41.

Caldwell, Bruce J. The Neoclassical Maximization Hypothesis: Comment. In *Caldwell, B. J.*, ed., 1984, *1983*, pp. 252–55.

Carvalho, Fernando. On the Concept of Time in Shacklean and Sraffian Economics. *J. Post Keynesian Econ.*, Winter 1983-84, *6*(2), pp. 265–80.

Coase, Ronald H. The New Institutional Economics. *Z. ges. Staatswiss.*, March 1984, *140*(1), pp. 229–31.

Collard, David. The Ascent of High Theory: A View from the Foothills. *Oxford Econ. Pap.*, Supplement November 1984, *36*, pp. 1–12.

Collard, David. The Ascent of High Theory: A View from the Foothills. In *Collard, D. A.*, et al., eds., 1984, pp. 1–12.

Coujard, J. L. Equilibre—Crises—Reproduction. (Equilibrium—Crisis—Reproduction. With English summary.) *Écon. Appl.*, 1984, *37*(2), pp. 347–61.

Culbertson, John M. The New Potential of Evolutionary–Institutional Economics. *J. Econ. Issues*, June 1984, *18*(2), pp. 611–18.

Day, Richard H. Disequilibrium Economic Dynamics: A Post-Schumpeterian Contribution. *J. Econ. Behav. Organ.*, March 1984, *5*(1), pp. 57–76.

De Vroey, Michel. La procédure de socialisation et le statut des échangistes dans trois représentations théoriques du marché. (With English summary.) *Écon. Soc.*, October 1984, *18*(10), pp. 129–50.

Debreu, Gerard. Economic Theory in the Mathematical Mode. *Amer. Econ. Rev.*, June 1984, *74*(3), pp. 267–78.

DiLorenzo, Thomas J. The Domain of Rent-seeking Behavior: Private or Public Choice? *Int. Rev. Law Econ.*, December 1984, *4*(2), pp. 185–97.

Dixit, Avinash and Grossman, Gene M. Directly Unproductive Prophet-seeking Activities. *Amer. Econ. Rev.*, December 1984, *74*(5), pp. 1087–88.

Dow, Sheila C. Methodology and the Analysis of a Monetary Economy. *Écon. Soc.*, April 1984, *18*(4), pp. 7–35.

Dow, Sheila C. Substantive Mountains and Methodological Molehills: A Rejoinder [Weintraub and Wiles: The Methodological Basis of Policy Conflict]. In *Caldwell, B. J.*, ed., 1984, *1982*, pp. 433–37.

Fox, Karl A. Behavior Settings and Eco-behavioral Science: A New Arena for Mathematical Social Science Permitting a Richer and More Coherent View of Human Activities in Social Systems, Part II: Relationships to Established Disciplines, and Needs for Mathematical Development. *Math. Soc. Sci.*, April 1984, *7*(2), pp. 139–65.
[G: U.S.]

Fox, Karl A. Behavior Settings and Eco-behavioral Science: A New Arena for Mathematical Social Science Permitting a Richer and More Coherent View of Human Activities in Social Systems, Part I: Concepts, Measurements, and Linkages to Economic Data Systems, Time-Allocation Matrices, and Social System Accounts.

Math. Soc. Sci., April 1984, 7(2), pp. 117–38. [G: U.S.]

Furubotn, Eirik G. and Richter, Rudolf. The New Institutional Economics: Symposium June 6–10, 1983, Mettlach/Saar. *Z. ges. Staatswiss.*, March 1984, *140*(1), pp. 1–6.

Gilad, Benjamin; Kaish, Stanley and Loeb, Peter D. From Economic Behavior to Behavioral Economics: The Behavioral Uprising in Economics. *J. Behav. Econ.*, Summer 1984, *13*(1), pp. 1–22.

Görün, Fikret. Iktisatta rasyonellik aksiyomunun yeri üzerine. (On the Rationality Axiom of Economics. With English summary.) *METU*, 1984, *11*(3–4), pp. 347–68.

Hahn, Frank H. Economic Theory and Keynes' Insights. *Empirica*, 1984, *11*(1), pp. 7–22.

Hahn, Frank H. Economic Theory and Policy. In *Hahn, F.*, 1984, pp. 327–49.

Hahn, Frank H. Equilibrium and Macroeconomics: Introduction. In *Hahn, F.*, 1984, pp. 1–19.

Hahn, Frank H. On the Notion of Equilibrium in Economics. In *Hahn, F.*, 1984, *1974*, pp. 43–71.

Hahn, Frank H. Reflections on the Invisible Hand. In *Hahn, F.*, 1984, *1982*, pp. 111–33.

Hahn, Frank H. The Neo-Ricardians. In *Hahn, F.*, 1984, *1982*, pp. 353–86.

Hammond, Peter J. Schumpeter and the Economic Problems of Today. In *Seidl, C.*, *ed.*, 1984, pp. 3–13.

Hargreaves-Heap, Shaun and Hollis, Martin. Bread and Circumstances: The Need for Political Economy. In *Whynes, D. K.*, *ed.*, 1984, pp. 7–30.

Hart, Oliver. The Wider World and Economic Methodology: Comment. In *Wiles, P. and Routh, G.*, *eds.*, 1984, pp. 47–50.

Hax, Herbert. The Economics of Governance: Framework and Implications: Comment. *Z. ges. Staatswiss.*, March 1984, *140*(1), pp. 227–28.

von Hayek, Friedrich A. Competition as a Discovery Procedure. In *von Hayek, F. A. (I)*, 1984, *1969*, pp. 254–65.

von Hayek, Friedrich A. The Use of Knowledge in Society. In *von Hayek, F. A. (I)*, 1984, *1945*, pp. 211–24.

Heilbroner, Robert L. Is Economic Theory Possible? *Soc. Res.*, Spring & Summer 1984, *51*(1&2), pp. 437–59.

Helm, Dieter. The Economics of John Hicks: Introduction. In *Hicks, J.*, 1984, pp. 1–20.

Helmstädter, Ernst. Sättigung: Ein Phänomen und kein Begriff. (Saturation: A Phenomenon and Not a Concept. With English summary.) *Ifo-Studien*, 1984, *30*(3), pp. 243–47.

Henry, John F. On Equilibrium. *J. Post Keynesian Econ.*, Winter 1983-84, *6*(2), pp. 214–29.

Hicks, John R. Methods of Dynamic Analysis. In *Hicks, J.*, 1984, *1956*, pp. 200–215.

Hicks, John R. The "New Causality": An Explanation. *Oxford Econ. Pap.*, March 1984, *36*(1), pp. 12–15.

Hicks, John R. Time in Economics. In *Hicks, J.*, 1984, *1976*, pp. 263–80.

Hill, Lewis E. and Owen, Donald W. The Humane and Human: Rejoinder [An Assault on the Citadel: Is a Constructive Synthesis Feasible?]. *J. Econ. Issues*, September 1984, *18*(3), pp. 908–09.

Hollis, Martin. In Defence of Two Demons: Comment 1 [Our Methodological Crisis]. In *Wiles, P. and Routh, G.*, *eds.*, 1984, pp. 22–29.

Honkapohja, Seppo. Rationaaliset odotukset kansantaloustieteessä: johdanto kirjallisuuteen. (Rational Expectations in Economics: An Introduction to the Literature. With English summary.) *Kansant. Aikak.*, 1984, *80*(4), pp. 362–82.

Hurwicz, Leonid. Economic Planning and the Knowledge Problem: A Comment. *Cato J.*, Fall 1984, *4*(2), pp. 419–25.

Hutchison, Terence W. Our Methodological Crisis. In *Wiles, P. and Routh, G.*, *eds.*, 1984, pp. 1–21.

Hutchison, Terence W. Positivism Enters Economic Methodology. In *Caldwell, B. J.*, *ed.*, 1984, *1960*, pp. 3–94.

Hutchison, Terence W. Professor Machlup on Verification in Economics [The Problem of Verification in Economics]. In *Caldwell, B. J.*, *ed.*, 1984, *1956*, pp. 118–25.

Kirzner, Israel M. Economic Planning and the Knowledge Problem. *Cato J.*, Fall 1984, *4*(2), pp. 407–18.

Koropeckyj, I. S. Academic Economics in the Nineteenth-Century Ukraine. In *Koropeckyj, I. S.*, *ed.*, 1984, pp. 163–222. [G: U.S.S.R.]

Leibenstein, Harvey. A Branch of Economics is Missing: Micro-Micro Theory. In *Caldwell, B. J.*, *ed.*, 1984, *1979*, pp. 398–423.

Machlup, Fritz. Professor Samuelson on Theory and Realism. In *Caldwell, B. J.*, *ed.*, 1984, *1964*, pp. 194–97.

Machlup, Fritz. Rejoinder to a Reluctant Ultra-Empiricist [The Problem of Verification in Economics]. In *Caldwell, B. J.*, *ed.*, 1984, *1956*, pp. 125–35.

Machlup, Fritz. The Southern Economic Journal: The Problem of Verification in Economics. In *Caldwell, B. J.*, *ed.*, 1984, *1955*, pp. 97–117.

Matthaei, Julie. Rethinking Scarcity: Neoclassicism, NeoMalthusianism, and NeoMarxism. *Rev. Radical Polit. Econ.*, Summer & Fall 1984, *16*(2&3), pp. 81–94.

Matthews, R. C. O. Darwinism and Economic Change. In *Collard, D. A.*, *et al.*, *eds.*, 1984, pp. 91–117.

Matthews, R. C. O. Darwinsim and Economic Change. *Oxford Econ. Pap.*, Supplement November 1984, *36*, pp. 91–117.

Mongin, Philippe. Modèle rationnel ou modèle économique de la rationalité? (Is the Economic Model of Rationality the Model of Rational Choice? With English summary.) *Revue Écon.*, January 1984, *35*(1), pp. 9–63.

Morishima, Michio. The Good and Bad Uses of Mathematics. In *Wiles, P. and Routh, G.*, *eds.*, 1984, pp. 51–73.

Munier, Bertrand. Quelques critiques de la rationalité économique dans l'incertain. (Some Criticisms of Economic Rationality under Uncertainty. With English summary.) *Revue Écon.*, January 1984, *35*(1), pp. 65–86.

Neale, Walter C. The Humane and the Human: Assaulting Petr (with a Swipe at Hill and Owen) [An Assault on the Citadel: Is a Constructive Synthesis Feasible?]. *J. Econ. Issues*, September 1984, *18*(3), pp. 903–07.

Neild, Robert. The Wider World and Economic Methodology. In *Wiles, P. and Routh, G., eds.*, 1984, pp. 37–46.

Petr, Jerry L. An Assault on the Citadel: Is a Constructive Synthesis Feasible? *J. Econ. Issues*, June 1984, *18*(2), pp. 589–97.

Petr, Jerry L. Rejoinder to Neale [An Assault on the Citadel: Is a Constructive Synthesis Feasible?]. *J. Econ. Issues*, September 1984, *18*(3), pp. 907–08.

Ponstein, J. Dualizing Optimization Problems in Mathematical Economics. *J. Math. Econ.*, December 1984, *13*(3), pp. 255–72.

Puu, Tönu. On the Art of Successful Analogy Formation: Martin Beckmann's Continuous Model of Economic Space. In *[Beckmann, M. J.]*, 1984, pp. 175–79.

Quadrio Curzio, Alberto and Scazzieri, Roberto. Sui momenti costitutivi dell'economia politica. (On the Founding Principles of Political Economy. With English summary.) *Giorn. Econ.*, January–February 1984, *43*(1–2), pp. 37–76.

Rima, Ingrid H. Balogh's Assessment of Conventional Economics. *J. Post Keynesian Econ.*, Summer 1984, *6*(4), pp. 630–33.

Rohrlich, George F. Community—The Submerged Component of Economic Theorizing. *Rev. Soc. Econ.*, December 1984, *42*(3), pp. 221–30.

Royer, D. and Ritschard, G. Qualitative Structural Analysis: Game or Science? In *Ancot, J. P., ed.*, 1984, pp. 3–13.

Samuels, Warren J. Galbraith on Economics as a System of Professional Belief. *J. Post Keynesian Econ.*, Fall 1984, *7*(1), pp. 61–76.

Samuelson, Paul A. Theory and Realism: A Reply [Professor Samuelson on Theory and Realism]. In *Caldwell, B. J., ed.*, 1984, *1964*, pp. 197–200.

Sato, Ryuzo; Nôno, Takayuki and Mimura, Fumitake. Hidden Symmetries: Lie Groups and Economic Conservation Laws. In *[Beckmann, M. J.]*, 1984, pp. 35–54.

Scitovsky, Tibor. Lerner's Contribution to Economics. *J. Econ. Lit.*, December 1984, *22*(4), pp. 1547–71.

Shackle, G. L. S. Comment on the Papers by Randall Bausor and Malcolm Rutherford [Toward a Historically Dynamic Economics: Examples and Illustrations] [Rational Expectations and Keynesian Uncertainty: A Critique]. *J. Post Keynesian Econ.*, Spring 1984, *6*(3), pp. 388–93.

Silk, Leonard. Getting Back to the Real World. *J. Post Keynesian Econ.*, Spring 1984, *6*(3), pp. 483–85.

Simon, Herbert A. On the Behavioral and Rational Foundations of Economic Dynamics. *J. Econ. Behav. Organ.*, March 1984, *5*(1), pp. 35–55.

Smolinski, Leon. Slutsky and Metaeconomics. In *Koropeckyj, I. S., ed.*, 1984, pp. 60–70.

Spear, Stephen E. Sufficient Conditions for the Existence of Sunspot Equilibria. *J. Econ. Theory*, December 1984, *34*(2), pp. 360–70.

Swoboda, Peter. Schumpeter's Entrepreneur in Modern Economic Theory. In *Seidl, C., ed.*, 1984, pp. 17–29.

Ursel, Laurent. Impérialisme de la science économique et néo-libéralisme. (With English summary.) *Écon. Soc.*, October 1984, *18*(10), pp. 33–59.

Varian, Hal R. Gerard Debreu's Contributions to Economics. *Scand. J. Econ.*, 1984, *86*(1), pp. 4–16.

Weintraub, E. Roy. Substantive Mountains and Methodological Molehills: Comment [Weintraub and Wiles: The Methodological Basis of Policy Conflict]. In *Caldwell, B. J., ed.*, 1984, *1982*, pp. 424–32.

von Weizsäcker, Carl Christian. Rights and Relations in Modern Economic Theory. *J. Econ. Behav. Organ.*, June 1984, *5*(2), pp. 133–57.

Wessel, Robert H. A Re-Examination of Opportunity Costs. *Rivista Int. Sci. Econ. Com.*, January 1984, *31*(1), pp. 21–39.

Whynes, David K. What Is Political Economy? Concluding Comments. In *Whynes, D. K., ed.*, 1984, pp. 209–16.

Wible, James R. Towards a Process Conception of Rationality in Economics and Science. *Rev. Soc. Econ.*, October 1984, *42*(2), pp. 89–104.

Wiggins, Steven N. Organizational Structures and Economic Efficiency: Comment. *Z. ges. Staatswiss.*, March 1984, *140*(1), pp. 224–26.

Wiles, Peter. Economics in Disarray: Epilogue: The Role of Theory. In *Wiles, P. and Routh, G., eds.*, 1984, pp. 293–325.

Williamson, Oliver E. The Economics of Governance: Framework and Implications. *Z. ges. Staatswiss.*, March 1984, *140*(1), pp. 195–223.

Zellner, Arnold. Causality and Econometrics. In *Zellner, A.*, 1984, *1979*, pp. 35–74.

021 General Equilibrium and Disequilibrium Theory

0210 General Equilibrium and Disequilibrium Theory

Addleson, Mark S. General Equilibrium and 'Competition': On Competition as Strategy. *S. Afr. J. Econ.*, June 1984, *52*(2), pp. 156–71.

Alkan, Ahmet. No Equilibrium in Infinite Economies: Two Examples. *J. Econ. Theory*, October 1984, *34*(1), pp. 180–86.

Allen, Beth. Equilibria in Which Prices Convey Information: The Finite Case. In *Boyer, M. and Kihlstrom, R. E., eds.*, 1984, pp. 63–92.

Armstrong, Thomas E. and Richter, Marcel K. The Core–Walras Equivalence. *J. Econ. Theory*, June 1984, *33*(1), pp. 116–51.

Bell, Clive and Srinivasan, T. N. On the Uses and Abuses of Economywide Models in Development Policy Analysis. In *[Chenery, H. B.]*, 1984, pp. 451–76.

Bester, Helmut. Core and Equilibrium in Incomplete Markets. *Z. Nationalökon.*, 1984, *44*(3), pp. 255–66.

Bester, Helmut. Increasing Risk and Equilibrium under Uncertainty. *J. Econ. Theory*, August 1984, *33*(2), pp. 378–86.

Blume, Lawrence E. and Easley, David. Rational Expectations Equilibrium: An Alternative Approach. *J. Econ. Theory*, October 1984, *34*(1), pp. 116–29.

Border, Kim C. A Core Existence Theorem for Games without Ordered Preferences. *Econometrica*, November 1984, *52*(6), pp. 1537–42.

Bronsard, Camille. Economie et anthropologie sociale. Sur l'existence d'un contrat social implicite. (Economics and Social Anthropology [On the Existence of an Implicit Social Contract]. With English summary.) *Écon. Appl.*, 1984, *37*(3–4), pp. 645–85.

Campbell, Donald E. Enforcement of Resource Allocation Mechanisms and Second Best Industrial Policy. *J. Econ. Theory*, December 1984, *34*(2), pp. 319–41.

Chenault, Larry A. A Note on the Stability Limitations in "A Stable Price Adjustment Process." *Quart. J. Econ.*, May 1984, *99*(2), pp. 385–86.

Cheng, Hsueh-Cheng. On the Generic Existence of Fully Revealing Price Equilibria [Rational Expectations Equilibrium: Generic Existence and the Information Revealed by Prices]. *J. Econ. Theory*, April 1984, *32*(2), pp. 351–58.

Clower, Robert W. A Reconsideration of the Microfoundations of Monetary Theory. In *Clower, R. W.*, 1984, *1967*, pp. 81–89.

Clower, Robert W. Reflections on the Keynesian Perplex. In *Clower, R. W.*, 1984, *1975*, pp. 187–208.

Clower, Robert W. Say's Principle, What It Means and Doesn't Mean. In *Clower, R. W.*, 1984, *1973*, pp. 145–65.

Clower, Robert W. The Coordination of Economic Activities: A Keynesian Perspective. In *Clower, R. W.*, 1984, *1975*, pp. 209–17.

Clower, Robert W. The Keynesian Counter-Revolution: A Theoretical Appraisal. In *Clower, R. W.*, 1984, *1965*, pp. 34–58.

Dasgupta, Dipankar. The Hawkins–Simon Theorem: An Input–Output Analytic Approach. *Indian Econ. Rev.*, July-Dec. 1984, *19*(2), pp. 171–83.

Debreu, Gerard. Economic Theory in the Mathematical Mode. *Scand. J. Econ.*, 1984, *86*(4), pp. 393–410.

Dehez, Pierre and Drèze, Jacques H. On Supply-Constrained Equilibria. *J. Econ. Theory*, June 1984, *33*(1), pp. 172–82.

Delbono, Flavio. Teorema delle contrazioni ed esistenza di un equilibrio nei modelli di Drèze e di Benassy. (With English summary.) *Econ. Polít.*, August 1984, *1*(2), pp. 243–60.

Diamond, Peter A. Money in Search Equilibrium. *Econometrica*, January 1984, *52*(1), pp. 1–20.

Donaldson, John B. and Mehra, Rajnish. Comparative Dynamics of an Equilibrium Intertemporal Asset Pricing Model. *Rev. Econ. Stud.*, July 1984, *51*(3), pp. 491–508.

Dubey, Pradeep and Neyman, Abraham. Payoffs in Nonatomic Economies: An Axiomatic Approach. *Econometrica*, September 1984, *52*(5), pp. 1129–50.

Dutta, Bhaskar. Effectivity Functions and Acceptable Game Forms. *Econometrica*, September 1984, *52*(5), pp. 1151–66.

Eckalbar, John C. Money, Barter, and Convergence to the Competitive Allocation: Menger's Problem. *J. Econ. Theory*, April 1984, *32*(2), pp. 201–11.

Emmons, David W. Existence of Lindahl Equilibria in Measure Theoretic Economies without Ordered Preferences. *J. Econ. Theory*, December 1984, *34*(2), pp. 342–59.

Feltenstein, Andrew. Money and Bonds in a Disaggregated Open Economy. In *Scarf, H. E. and Shoven, J. B.*, eds., 1984, pp. 209–42.

Ferretti, Mario. Il "vizio paretiano." Note critiche sul principio d'interdipendenza economica generale. (The "Paretian Vice": Critical Notes on the Principal of General Economic Interdependence and Other Related Problems. With English summary.) *Giorn. Econ.*, March–April 1984, *43*(3–4), pp. 191–212.

Forsythe, Robert and Suchanek, Gerry L. Collective Decision Mechanisms and Efficient Stock Market Allocations: Existence of a Participation Equilibrium. *Int. Econ. Rev.*, February 1984, *25*(1), pp. 21–43.

Gay, Antonio. Verso una concezione dinamica della teoria dell'equilibrio economico generale: le prospettive ed il senso dell'uso dell'analisi globale. (With English summary.) *Econ. Polít.*, August 1984, *1*(2), pp. 271–309.

Geanakoplos, John D. Utility Functions for Debreu's 'Excess Demands.' *J. Math. Econ.*, April 1984, *13*(1), pp. 1–9.

Geanakoplos, John D. and Polemarchakis, Herakles M. Intertemporally Separable, Overlapping-Generations Economies. *J. Econ. Theory*, December 1984, *34*(2), pp. 207–15.

Ginsburgh, Victor and Robinson, Sherman. Equilibrium and Prices in Multisector Models. In *[Chenery, H. B.]*, 1984, pp. 429–50.

Ginsburgh, Victor and Waelbroeck, Jean. Free Trade and Tariff-ridden International Equilibria: Formulation and Computation. In *Andersson, Å. E.; Isard, W. and Puu, T.*, eds., 1984, pp. 133–56.

Gorman, W. M. Le Chatelier and General Equilibrium. In *[Pearce, I. F.]*, 1984, pp. 1–18.

Gozzi, Giancarlo. Posizioni di lungo periodo e stabilità. (With English summary.) *Econ. Polít.*, December 1984, *1*(3), pp. 407–27.

Green, Edward J. Continuum and Finite-Player Noncooperative Models of Competition. *Econometrica*, July 1984, *52*(4), pp. 975–93.

Greenberg, Joseph and Shitovitz, Benyamin. Aumann–Shapley Prices as a Scarf Social Equilibrium. *J. Econ. Theory*, December 1984, *34*(2), pp. 380–82.

Hahn, Frank H. General Equilibrium Theory. In *Hahn, F.*, 1984, *1981*, pp. 72–87.

Hahn, Frank H. Keynesian Economics and General Equilibrium Theory: Reflections on Some Current Debates. In *Hahn, F.*, 1984, *1977*, pp. 175–94.

Hahn, Frank H. On Some Problems of Proving the Existence of Equilibrium in a Monetary Economy. In *Hahn, F.*, 1984, pp. 147–57.

Hahn, Frank H. Some Adjustment Problems. In *Hahn, F.*, 1984, *1970*, pp. 88–110.

Hahn, Frank H. The Winter of our Discontent. In *Hahn, F.*, 1984, *1973*, pp. 134–44.

Hahn, Frank H. Why I Am Not a Monetarist. In *Hahn, F.*, 1984, pp. 307–26.

Hands, Douglas W. The Role of Crucial Counterexamples in the Growth of Economic Knowledge: Two Case Studies in the Recent History of Economic Thought. *Hist. Polit. Econ.*, Spring 1984, *16*(1), pp. 59–67.

Hausman, Daniel M. Are General Equilibrium Theories Explanatory? In *Hausman, D. M., ed.*, 1984, *1981*, pp. 344–59.

von Hayek, Friedrich A. On 'Neutral Money.' In *von Hayek, F. A. (II)*, 1984, *1933*, pp. 159–62.

Henn, Rudolf and Kischka, Peter. Tatonnement Processes with Set-Valued Excess-Demand. In *[Beckmann, M. J.]*, 1984, pp. 15–22.

James, John A. The Use of General Equilibrium Analysis in Economic History. *Exploration Econ. Hist.*, July 1984, *21*(3), pp. 231–53. [G: U.S.]

Jones, Larry E. A Competitive Model of Commodity Differentiation. *Econometrica*, March 1984, *52*(2), pp. 507–30.

Joyce, Patrick. The Walrasian *tâtonnement* Mechanism and Information. *Rand J. Econ.*, Autumn 1984, *15*(3), pp. 416–25.

Kamiya, Kazuya. On the Existence and Uniqueness of General Equilibrium Prices. *Int. Econ. Rev.*, February 1984, *25*(1), pp. 79–83.

Kantorovich, L. V. and Makarov, V. L. Prices and Production Efficiency. *Matekon*, Fall 1984, *21*(1), pp. 3–27.

Karmann, Alexander J. Space–Time Economies under Free Mobility: Competitive Equilibria and Efficiency. *Reg. Sci. Urban Econ.*, August 1984, *14*(3), pp. 303–15.

Katzner, Donald W. Capital and Walrasian Equilibrium. In *[Pearce, I. F.]*, 1984, pp. 123–48.

Kehoe, Timothy J. Computing All of the Equilibria of Economies with Two Factors of Production. *J. Math. Econ.*, December 1984, *13*(3), pp. 207–23.

Kehoe, Timothy J. and Levine, David K. Intertemporal Separability in Overlapping-Generations Models. *J. Econ. Theory*, December 1984, *34*(2), pp. 216–26.

Kehoe, Timothy J. and Levine, David K. Regularity in Overlapping Generations Exchange Economies. *J. Math. Econ.*, April 1984, *13*(1), pp. 69–93.

Keiding, Hans. Existence of Economic Equilib-

rium: New Results and Open Problems. In *Hammer, G. and Pallaschke, D., eds.*, 1984, pp. 223–42.

Khan, M. Ali. A Remark on the Existence of Equilibria in Markets without Ordered Preferences and with a Riesz Space of Commodities. *J. Math. Econ.*, October 1984, *13*(2), pp. 165–69.

Khan, M. Ali and Vohra, Rajiv. Equilibrium in Abstract Economies without Ordered Preferences and with a Measure Space of Agents. *J. Math. Econ.*, October 1984, *13*(2), pp. 133–42.

Kim, K. H. and Roush, F. W. Stability of Command Economies. *Math. Soc. Sci.*, June 1984, *7*(3), pp. 267–74.

Koda, Keiichi. A Note on the Existence of Monetary Equilibria in Overlapping Generations Models with Storage. *J. Econ. Theory*, December 1984, *34*(2), pp. 388–95.

Kohn, Robert E. Total Satiation and Competitive Equilibrium. *S. Afr. J. Econ.*, March 1984, *52*(1), pp. 69–74.

van der Laan, Gerard. Supply-constrained Fixed Price Equilibria in Monetary Economies. *J. Math. Econ.*, October 1984, *13*(2), pp. 171–87.

Laffont, Jean-Jacques. Information imparfaite et rationalité collective. (Collective Rationality under Incomplete Information. With English summary.) *Revue Écon.*, January 1984, *35*(1), pp. 163–76.

Lau, Lawrence J. Numerical Specification of Applied General Equilibrium Models: Estimation, Calibration, and Data: Comments. In *Scarf, H. E. and Shoven, J. B., eds.*, 1984, pp. 127–37. [G: U.S.; U.K.]

Lucas, Robert E., Jr. and Stokey, Nancy L. Optimal Growth with Many Consumers. *J. Econ. Theory*, February 1984, *32*(1), pp. 139–71.

Madden, Paul J. Existence of Drèze Equilibrium under Set-Up Costs. *J. Econ. Theory*, August 1984, *33*(2), pp. 275–88.

Magill, Michael J. P. Understanding Futures Markets. *Empirica*, 1984, *11*(2), pp. 125–45.

Mansur, Ahsan Habib and Whalley, John. Numerical Specification of Applied General Equilibrium Models: Estimation, Calibration, and Data. In *Scarf, H. E. and Shoven, J. B., eds.*, 1984, pp. 69–127. [G: U.S.; U.K.]

Mantel, Rolf R. Economia Matemática, su evolución histórica y estado actual. (Mathematical Economics, Its Historical Evolution and Present State. With English summary.) *Económica*, May-December 1984, *30*(2–3), pp. 203–15.

Marzi, Graziella. Aggregazione ed efficienza produttiva: un'analisi delle distorsioni. (Aggregation and Productive Efficiency: An Analysis of Biases. With English summary.) *Rivista Int. Sci. Econ. Com.*, January 1984, *31*(1), pp. 49–68. [G: Italy]

Mas-Colell, Andreu. On a Thorem of Schmeidler. *J. Math. Econ.*, December 1984, *13*(3), pp. 201–06.

Maskin, Eric S. and Tirole, Jean. On the Efficiency of Fixed Price Equilibrium. *J. Econ. Theory*, April 1984, *32*(2), pp. 317–27.

Mazzoleni, Piera and Montesano, Aldo. General Competitive Equilibrium of the Spatial Economy. *Reg. Sci. Urban Econ.*, August 1984, *14*(3), pp. 285–302.

McKinnon, Ronald I. Money and Bonds in a Disaggregated Open Economy: Modeling Structural Adjustment: Micro and Macro Elements in a General Equilibrium Framework: Comments. In *Scarf, H. E. and Shoven, J. B., eds.*, 1984, pp. 271–74.

Medvegyev, Péter. A General Existence Theorem for von Neumann Economic Growth Models. *Econometrica*, July 1984, *52*(4), pp. 963–74.

Nabeya, Seiji. Examples on Core and Equilibria in Coalition Production Economies. *Econ. Stud. Quart.*, August 1984, *35*(2), pp. 181–89.

Obstfeld, Maurice. Multiple Stable Equilibria in an Optimizing Perfect-Foresight Model. *Econometrica*, January 1984, *52*(1), pp. 223–28.

Ostroy, Joseph M. A Reformulation of the Marginal Productivity Theory of Distribution. *Econometrica*, May 1984, *52*(3), pp. 599–630.

Ostroy, Joseph M. On the Existence of Walrasian Equilibrium in Large-Square Economies. *J. Math. Econ.*, October 1984, *13*(2), pp. 143–63.

Ponstein, J. Mirrored Pairs of Optimization Problems: A Comment. *Economica*, February 1984, *51*(201), pp. 97.

Prescott, Edward C. and Townsend, Robert M. General Competitive Analysis in an Economy with Private Information. *Int. Econ. Rev.*, February 1984, *25*(1), pp. 1–20.

Prescott, Edward C. and Townsend, Robert M. Pareto Optima and Competitive Equilibria with Adverse Selection and Moral Hazard. *Econometrica*, January 1984, *52*(1), pp. 21–45.

ten Raa, Thijs. An Alternative to Debreu's Dated and Located Commodities (or the Economy as an Onion). In *Ancot, J. P., ed.*, 1984, pp. 247–55.

Reichelstein, Stefan. A Note on Allocations Attainable through Nash Equilibria. *J. Econ. Theory*, April 1984, *32*(2), pp. 384–90.

Rhee, Jeong J. and Miranowski, John A. Determination of Income, Production, and Employment under Pollution Control: An Input–Output Approach. *Rev. Econ. Statist.*, February 1984, *66*(1), pp. 146–50.

Robinson, Sherman and Tyson, Laura D'Andrea. Modeling Structural Adjustment: Micro and Macro Elements in a General Equilibrium Framework. In *Scarf, H. E. and Shoven, J. B., eds.*, 1984, pp. 243–71.

Rodano, Giorgio. Walrasian Equilibrium and Rational Expectations: A Difficult Coexistence. *Metroecon.*, February 1984, *36*(1), pp. 25–46.

Rotheim, Roy J. Contingent Contracts and Uncertain Economies [On the Nature of Production and Contracts in an Arrow–Debreu Economy]. *J. Post Keynesian Econ.*, Summer 1984, *6*(4), pp. 637–39.

Rothengatter, Werner. Quantity Rationing of Economic Transactions in a Risky Environ-

ment. In *Bamberg, G. and Spremann, K., eds.*, 1984, pp. 243–70.

Scafuri, Allen J. and Yannelis, Nicholas C. Non-symmetric Cardinal Value Allocations. *Econometrica*, November 1984, *52*(6), pp. 1365–68.

Scarf, Herbert E. The Computation of Equilibrium Prices. In *Scarf, H. E. and Shoven, J. B., eds.*, 1984, pp. 1–49.

Schofield, Norman J. Social Equilibrium and Cycles on Compact Sets. *J. Econ. Theory*, June 1984, *33*(1), pp. 59–71.

Shaffer, Sherrill. Production and Contingent Contracts: Comment [On the Nature of Production and Contracts in an Arrow–Debreu Economy]. *J. Post Keynesian Econ.*, Summer 1984, *6*(4), pp. 634–36.

Shoven, John B. and Whalley, John. Applied General-Equilibrium Models of Taxation and International Trade: An Introduction and Survey. *J. Econ. Lit.*, September 1984, *22*(3), pp. 1007–51.

Simon, Leo K. Bertrand, the Cournot Paradigm and the Theory of Perfect Competition. *Rev. Econ. Stud.*, April 1984, *51*(2), pp. 209–30.

Simons, S. Minimaximin Results with Applications to Economic Equilibrium. *J. Math. Econ.*, December 1984, *13*(3), pp. 289–303.

Smith, Bruce D. Money, Nonconvex Preferences, and the Existence of Equilibrium: A Note. *J. Econ. Theory*, April 1984, *32*(2), pp. 359–66.

Svensson, Lars E. O. Walrasian and Marshallian Stability. *J. Econ. Theory*, December 1984, *34*(2), pp. 371–79.

Svensson, Lars-Gunnar. Competitive Equilibria with Indivisible Goods. *Z. Nationalökon.*, 1984, *44*(4), pp. 373–86.

Svensson, Lars-Gunnar. The Existence of Budget-Constrained Pareto-Efficient Allocations. *J. Econ. Theory*, April 1984, *32*(2), pp. 346–50.

Takekuma, Shin-Ichi. A New Concept of Equilibrium for a Private Ownership Economy with Profit-Making Firms. *Hitotsubashi J. Econ.*, June 1984, *25*(1), pp. 93–104.

Todd, Michael J. Efficient Methods of Computing Economic Equilibria. In *Scarf, H. E. and Shoven, J. B., eds.*, 1984, pp. 51–68.

Toussaint, Sabine. On the Existence of Equilibria in Economies with Infinitely Many Commodities and without Ordered Preferences. *J. Econ. Theory*, June 1984, *33*(1), pp. 98–115.

Varian, Hal R. Gerard Debreu's Contributions to Economics. *Scand. J. Econ.*, 1984, *86*(1), pp. 4–16.

Vind, Karl. Erratum [Equilibrium with Coordination]. *J. Math. Econ.*, October 1984, *13*(2), pp. 195.

Vohra, Rajiv. Local Public Goods and Average Cost Pricing. *J. Math. Econ.*, April 1984, *13*(1), pp. 51–67.

Wako, Jun. A Note on the Strong Core of a Market with Indivisible Goods. *J. Math. Econ.*, October 1984, *13*(2), pp. 189–94.

Walker, Donald A. Is Walras's Theory of General Equilibrium a Normative Scheme? *Hist. Polit. Econ.*, Fall 1984, *16*(3), pp. 445–69.

Walker, Mark. A Simple Auctioneerless Mechanism with Walrasian Properties. *J. Econ. Theory*, February 1984, *32*(1), pp. 111–27.

Wang, Leonard F. S. Olech's Theorem and the Global Stability of Walrasian Price Adjustment with Positivity Constraint. *Rivista Int. Sci. Econ. Com.*, April 1984, *31*(4), pp. 338–45.

Weddepohl, Claus. General Equilibrium Theory. In *van der Ploeg, F., ed.*, 1984, pp. 331–69.

Weinrich, Gerd. On the Theory of Effective Demand under Stochastic Rationing. *J. Econ. Theory*, October 1984, *34*(1), pp. 95–115.

Wooders, Myrna Holtz and Zame, William R. Approximate Cores of Large Games. *Econometrica*, November 1984, *52*(6), pp. 1327–50.

Yamazaki, Akira. The Critical Set of a Demand Correspondence in the Price Space and the Weak Axiom of Revealed Preference. *Hitotsubashi J. Econ.*, December 1984, *25*(2), pp. 137–44.

Yamazaki, Akira. Walras Degrees and Probability of a Blocking Coalition at Pareto Allocations. *J. Math. Econ.*, October 1984, *13*(2), pp. 105–21.

Yannelis, Nicholas C. and Prabhakar, N. D. Erratum [Existence of Maximal Elements and Equilibria in Linear Topological Spaces]. *J. Math. Econ.*, December 1984, *13*(3), p. 305.

Yano, Makoto. Competitive Equilibria on Turnpikes in a McKenzie Economy, I: A Neighborhood Turnpike Theorem. *Int. Econ. Rev.*, October 1984, *25*(3), pp. 695–717.

Yano, Makoto. The Turnpike of Dynamic General Equilibrium Paths and Its Insensitivity to Initial Conditions. *J. Math. Econ.*, December 1984, *13*(3), pp. 235–54.

022 Microeconomic Theory

0220 General

Abraham-Frois, G. and Berrebi, E. Le probleme de la transformation: Solution(s). *Econometrica*, September 1984, *52*(5), p. 1315.

Akerlof, George A. A Theory of Social Custom, of Which Unemployment May Be One Consequence. In *Akerlof, G. A.*, 1984, 1980, pp. 69–99.

Akerlof, George A. The Economics of Caste and of the Rat Race and Other Woeful Tales. In *Akerlof, G. A.*, 1984, 1976, pp. 23–44.

Arnott, Richard; Davidson, Russell and Pines, David. Unanticipated Shocks and the Maintenance and Replacement of Durable Goods. *J. Econ. Dynam. Control*, October 1984, *8*(1), pp. 99–115.

Arrow, Kenneth J. Information and Economic Behavior. In *Arrow, K. J., vol. 4*, 1984, 1973, pp. 136–52.

Barberá, Salvador; Barrett, C. Richard and Pattanaik, Prasanta K. On Some Axioms for Ranking Sets of Alternatives. *J. Econ. Theory*, August 1984, *33*(2), pp. 301–08.

Borglin, Anders and Keiding, Hans. Efficiency in One-Sector, Discrete-Time, Infinite-Horizon Models. *J. Econ. Theory*, June 1984, *33*(1), pp. 183–96.

Bowles, Roger. Theory of the Firm. In *Sandford, C. and Bradbury, M., eds.*, 1984, pp. 66–92. **[G: Belgium; U.K.]**

Brandt, Karl. Das neoklassische Marktmodell und die Wettbewerbstheorie. (The Neoclassical Market Model and the Theory of Competition. With English summary.) *Jahr. Nationalökon. Statist.*, March 1984, *199*(2), pp. 97–122.

Brown, Thomas C. The Concept of Value in Resource Allocation. *Land Econ.*, August 1984, *60*(3), pp. 231–46.

Chasse, John Dennis. Marshall, the Human Agent and Economic Growth: Wants and Activities Revisited. *Hist. Polit. Econ.*, Fall 1984, *16*(3), pp. 381–404.

Cohen, Michael D. and Axelrod, Robert. Coping with Complexity: The Adaptive Value of Changing Utility. *Amer. Econ. Rev.*, March 1984, *74*(1), pp. 30–42.

Coleman, James S. Introducing Social Structure into Economic Analysis. *Amer. Econ. Rev.*, May 1984, *74*(2), pp. 84–88.

Cooper, Russell and Ross, Thomas W. Prices, Product Qualities and Asymmetric Information: The Competitive Case. *Rev. Econ. Stud.*, April 1984, *51*(2), pp. 197–207.

Field, Alexander James. Microeconomics, Norms, and Rationality. *Econ. Develop. Cult. Change*, July 1984, *32*(4), pp. 683–711.

Freixas, Xavier and Kihlstrom, Richard E. Risk Aversion and Information Demand. In *Boyer, M. and Kihlstrom, R. E., eds.*, 1984, pp. 93–104.

Freixas, Xavier and Laffont, Jean-Jacques. On the Irreversibility Effect. In *Boyer, M. and Kihlstrom, R. E., eds.*, 1984, pp. 105–14.

Fukuba, Yo and Ito, Komayuki. The So-Called Expected Utility Theory Is Inadequate. *Math. Soc. Sci.*, February 1984, *7*(1), pp. 1–12.

George, David. Meta-Preferences: Reconsidering Contemporary Notions of Free Choice. *Int. J. Soc. Econ.*, 1984, *11*(3/4), pp. 92–107.

Giffin, Phillip E. and Hutchinson, E. Bruce. A Metaphysical Notion: The Symmetry between Consumer and Producer Demand. *J. Post Keynesian Econ.*, Fall 1984, *7*(1), pp. 134–36.

Gilad, Benjamin; Kaish, Stanley and Loeb, Peter D. From Economic Behavior to Behavioral Economics: The Behavioral Uprising in Economics. *J. Behav. Econ.*, Winter 1984, *13*(2), pp. 3–24.

Gill, Flora. The Costs of Adjustment and the Invisible Hand; with Special Reference to the Labour Market. *Écon. Appl.*, 1984, *37*(3–4), pp. 523–41.

Goldman, M. Barry; Leland, Hayne E. and Sibley, David S. Optimal Nonuniform Prices. *Rev. Econ. Stud.*, April 1984, *51*(2), pp. 305–19.

Gorman, W. M. Le Chatelier and General Equilibrium. In *[Pearce, I. F.]*, 1984, pp. 1–18.

Harris, Milton. Comment on "Pricing a Product Line." *J. Bus.*, Part 2, January 1984, *57*(1), pp. S109–10.

Hauser, John R. Pricing Theory and the Role of Marketing Science [Pricing Research in Marketing: The State of the Art]. *J. Bus.*, Part 2, January 1984, *57*(1), pp. S65–71.

Henocq, Christophe and Kempf, Hubert. Agrégation quasi parfaite par convergence. (Quasiperfect Aggregation and the Convergence Approach. With English summary.) *Revue Écon.*, September 1984, *35*(5), pp. 911–27.

Hey, John D. Decision Under Uncertainty. In *van der Ploeg, F., ed.*, 1984, pp. 433–55.

Hillier, Brian and Malcomson, James M. Dynamic Inconsistency, Rational Expectations, and Optimal Government Policy. *Econometrica*, November 1984, *52*(6), pp. 1437–51.

Hirschman, Albert O. Against Parsimony: Three Easy Ways of Complicating Some Categories of Economic Discourse. *Amer. Econ. Rev.*, May 1984, *74*(2), pp. 89–96.

Holzman, Ron. A Note on the Redundancy of an Axiom in the Pattanaik-Peleg Characterization of the Lexicographic Maximin Extension. *Soc. Choice Welfare*, August 1984, *1*(2), pp. 123–25.

Joyce, Patrick. The Walrasian *tâtonnement* Mechanism and Information. *Rand J. Econ.*, Autumn 1984, *15*(3), pp. 416–25.

Kubin, Ingrid. Equilibrium and Stability Analysis in the Classical Framework. *Metroecon.*, February 1984, *36*(1), pp. 47–64.

Leibenstein, Harvey. A Branch of Economics is Missing: Micro-Micro Theory. In *Caldwell, B. J., ed.*, 1984, *1979*, pp. 398–423.

Loasby, Brian J. Hypothesis and Paradigm in the Theory of the Firm. In *Caldwell, B. J., ed.*, 1984, *1971*, pp. 261–83.

Nagle, Thomas. Economic Foundations for Pricing. *J. Bus.*, Part 2, January 1984, *57*(1), pp. S3–26.

Narasimhan, Chakravarthi. Comments on "Economic Foundations for Pricing." *J. Bus.*, Part 2, January 1984, *57*(1), pp. S27–34.

O'Keeffe, Mary; Viscusi, W. Kip and Zeckhauser, Richard J. Economic Contests: Comparative Reward Schemes. *J. Lab. Econ.*, January 1984, *2*(1), pp. 27–56.

Oren, Shmuel S. Comments on "Pricing Research in Marketing: The State of the Art." *J. Bus.*, Part 2, January 1984, *57*(1), pp. S61–64.

Oren, Shmuel S.; Smith, Stephen and Wilson, Robert B. Pricing a Product Line. *J. Bus.*, Part 2, January 1984, *57*(1), pp. S73–99.

Orosel, Gerhard. Profitable Speculation and Price Stability. *Jahr. Nationalökon. Statist.*, November 1984, *199*(6), pp. 485–501.

Pattanaik, Prasanta K. and Peleg, Bezalel. An Axiomatic Characterization of the Lexicographic Maximin Extension of an Ordering over a Set to the Power Set. *Soc. Choice Welfare*, August 1984, *1*(2), pp. 113–22.

Pfouts, Ralph W. Method and Applied Microeconomics. *Atlantic Econ. J.*, September 1984, *12*(3), pp. 16–19.

Rao, Vithala R. Pricing Research in Marketing: The State of the Art. *J. Bus.*, Part 2, January 1984, *57*(1), pp. S39–60.

Raviv, Artur. Comments on "Economic Founda-tions for Pricing." *J. Bus.*, Part 2, January 1984, *57*(1), pp. S35–38.

Rosenberg, Alexander. On the Interanimation of Micro and Macroeconomics. In *Hausman, D. M., ed.*, 1984, *1976*, pp. 324–43.

Roth, Alvin E. Misrepresentation and Stability in the Marriage Problem. *J. Econ. Theory*, December 1984, *34*(2), pp. 383–87.

Sato, Ryuzo and Tsutsui, Shunichi. Technical Progress, the Schumpeterian Hypothesis, and Market Structure. *Z. Nationalökon.*, Supplement 1984, pp. 1–37.

Semmler, Willi. On the Classical Theory of Competition, Value and Prices of Production. *Australian Econ. Pap.*, June 1984, *23*(42), pp. 130–50.

Shavell, Steven. The Design of Contracts and Remedies for Breach. *Quart. J. Econ.*, February 1984, *99*(1), pp. 121–48.

Shugan, Steven M. Comments on "Pricing a Product Line." *J. Bus.*, Part 2, January 1984, *57*(1), pp. S101–07.

Simmons, P. Multivariate Risk Premia with a Stochastic Objective. *Econ. J.*, 1984 Supplement, *94*, pp. 124–32.

Spear, Stephen E. Sufficient Conditions for the Existence of Sunspot Equilibria. *J. Econ. Theory*, December 1984, *34*(2), pp. 360–70.

Stahl, Dale O., II. Cardinal vs. Characteristic Indices of Preference for Applied Welfare Economics. *Public Finance Quart.*, October 1984, *12*(4), pp. 473–86.

Svensson, Lars E. O. Walrasian and Marshallian Stability. *J. Econ. Theory*, December 1984, *34*(2), pp. 371–79.

Takekuma, Shin-Ichi. On Duality Theory for the Continuous Time Model of Capital Accumulation. *Hitotsubashi J. Econ.*, December 1984, *25*(2), pp. 145–54.

Thistle, Paul D. Psychological Learning Theory and Economic Behavior. *J. Behav. Econ.*, Summer 1984, *13*(1), pp. 67–100.

Walker, Mark. A Simple Auctioneerless Mechanism with Walrasian Properties. *J. Econ. Theory*, February 1984, *32*(1), pp. 111–27.

Weibull, Jörgen W. Continuous Linear Representations of Preference Orderings in Vector Spaces. In *[Beckmann, M. J.]*, 1984, pp. 291–305.

Weinrich, Gerd. On the Theory of Effective Demand under Stochastic Rationing. *J. Econ. Theory*, October 1984, *34*(1), pp. 95–115.

von Weizsäcker, Carl Christian. The Costs of Substitution. *Econometrica*, September 1984, *52*(5), pp. 1085–1116.

Williams, Steven R. Implementing a Generic Smooth Function. *J. Math. Econ.*, December 1984, *13*(3), pp. 273–88.

Wright, Brian D. and Williams, Jeffrey C. The Welfare Effects of the Introduction of Storage. *Quart. J. Econ.*, February 1984, *99*(1), pp. 169–92.

0222 Theory of the Household (consumer demand)

Adams, Roy D. The Slutsky Equation for Club Goods-per-Member and the Aggregate Demand for Club Goods. *Public Finance*, 1984, *39*(2), pp. 182–90.

Afriat, S. N. The True Index. In *[Pearce, I. F.]*, 1984, pp. 37–56.

Agenor, Pierre-Richard. Income Uncertainty and the Propensity to Consume: A Note. *Indian Econ. J.*, July–Sept. 1984, *32*(1), pp. 115–16.

Allais, Maurice. The Foundations of the Theory of Utility and Risk: Some Central Points of the Discussions at the Oslo Conference. In *Hagen, O. and Wenstop, F., eds.*, 1984, pp. 3–131.

Anttila, Mai and Möller, Kristian. Conjoint Analysis Models in Explaining Consumer Price Utility Structures. *Liiketaloudellinen Aikak.*, 1984, *33*(4), pp. 379–404. **[G: Finland]**

Arrow, Kenneth J. Additive Logarithmic Demand Functions and the Slutsky Relations. In *Arrow, K. J., vol. 3*, 1984, *1961*, pp. 109–16.

Arrow, Kenneth J. Alternative Approaches to the Theory of Choice in Risk-Taking Situations. In *Arrow, K. J., vol. 3*, 1984, *1951*, pp. 5–41.

Arrow, Kenneth J. Exposition of the Theory of Choice under Uncertainty. In *Arrow, K. J., vol. 3*, 1984, *1971*, pp. 172–208.

Arrow, Kenneth J. Permanent and Transitory Substitution Effects in Health Insurance Experiments. *J. Lab. Econ.*, April 1984, *2*(2), pp. 259–67.

Arrow, Kenneth J. Rational Choice Functions and Orderings. In *Arrow, K. J., vol. 3*, 1984, *1959*, pp. 100–08.

Arrow, Kenneth J. The Determination of Many-Commodity Preference Scales by Two-Commodity Comparisons. In *Arrow, K. J., vol. 3*, 1984, *1952*, pp. 42–54.

Arrow, Kenneth J. The Use of Unbounded Utility Functions in Expected-Utility Maximization: Response. In *Arrow, K. J., vol. 3*, 1984, *1974*, pp. 209–11.

Arrow, Kenneth J. The Value of and Demand for Information. In *Arrow, K. J., vol. 4*, 1984, *1971*, pp. 106–14.

Arrow, Kenneth J. Utilities, Attitudes, Choices: A Review Note. In *Arrow, K. J., vol. 3*, 1984, *1958*, pp. 55–84.

Arrow, Kenneth J. Utility and Expectation in Economic Behavior. In *Arrow, K. J., vol. 3*, 1984, *1963*, pp. 117–46.

Barmish, B. Ross. A New Approach to the Incorporation of Attributes into Consumer Theory. *J. Econ. Theory*, February 1984, *32*(1), pp. 93–110.

Basu, Kaushik. Fuzzy Revealed Preference Theory. *J. Econ. Theory*, April 1984, *32*(2), pp. 212–27.

Beckmann, Martin J. Risk and Saving. In *Bamberg, G. and Spremann, K., eds.*, 1984, pp. 5–12.

Berliant, Marcus. A Characterization of the Demand for Land. *J. Econ. Theory*, August 1984, *33*(2), pp. 289–300.

Bernanke, Ben S. Permanent Income, Liquidity, and Expenditure on Automobiles: Evidence from Panel Data. *Quart. J. Econ.*, August 1984, *99*(3), pp. 587–614. **[G: U.S.]**

Bernard, Georges. Utility and Risk Preference Functions. In *Hagen, O. and Wenstop, F., eds.*, 1984, pp. 135–43.

Bernardo, John J. A Heuristic Model to Predict Brand Switching in Consumer Choice. *J. Behav. Econ.*, Winter 1984, *13*(2), pp. 25–51.

Berninghaus, Siegfried. A General Existence Theorem for Equilibrium Price Dispersions. *Info. Econ. Policy*, 1984, *1*(3), pp. 239–66.

Blackorby, Charles; Donaldson, David and Moloney, David. Consumer's Surplus and Welfare Change in a Simple Dynamic Model. *Rev. Econ. Stud.*, January 1984, *51*(1), pp. 171–76.

Blundell, Richard and Ray, Ranjan. Testing for Linear Engel Curves and Additively Separable Preferences Using a New Flexible Demand System. *Econ. J.*, December 1984, *94*(376), pp. 800–811. **[G: U.K.]**

Borooah, Vani K. Theory of the Household. In *van der Ploeg, F., ed.*, 1984, pp. 315–30.

Bouyssou, Denis. Decision-Aid and Expected Utility Theory: A Critical Survey. In *Hagen, O. and Wenstop, F., eds.*, 1984, pp. 181–216.

Bowden, Roger. A Note on the "Bottom-up" Approach to Measuring Compensating Variations. *Metroecon.*, February 1984, *36*(1), pp. 65–76.

Brubaker, Earl R. Demand Disclosures and Conditions on Exclusion: An Experiment. *Econ. J.*, September 1984, *94*(375), pp. 536–53. **[G: U.S.]**

Bruter, Claude P. Catastrophes locales en économie. (Local Catastrophes in Economy. With English summary.) *Écon. Appl.*, 1984, *37*(1), pp. 123–41.

Buiter, Willem H. and Carmichael, Jeffrey. Government Debt: Comment [Government Debt in an Overlapping-Generations Model with Bequests and Gifts]. *Amer. Econ. Rev.*, September 1984, *74*(4), pp. 762–65. **[G: U.S.]**

Burbidge, John B. Government Debt: Reply [Government Debt in an Overlapping-Generations Model with Bequests and Gifts]. *Amer. Econ. Rev.*, September 1984, *74*(4), pp. 766–67. **[G: U.S.]**

Carlson, John A. and McAfee, R. Preston. Joint Search for Several Goods [The Theory of Search for Several Goods]. *J. Econ. Theory*, April 1984, *32*(2), pp. 337–45.

Cha, Dong-deuck and Saklas, James G. Integration of Choice Set Reduction in Behavioral Choice Travel Demand Models. In *Avula, X. J. R., et al.*, 1984, pp. 853–59.

Chavas, Jean-Paul. The Theory of Mixed Demand Functions. *Europ. Econ. Rev.*, April 1984, *24*(3), pp. 321–44.

Cooter, Robert and Rappoport, Peter. Were the Ordinalists Wrong about Welfare Economics? *J. Econ. Lit.*, June 1984, *22*(2), pp. 507–30.

Cremer, Jacques. On the Economics of Repeat

Buying. *Rand J. Econ.*, Autumn 1984, *15*(3), pp. 396–403.

Daboni, L. On the Axiomatic Treatment of the Utility Theory. *Metroecon.*, June-Oct. 1984, *36*(2–3), pp. 203–09.

Dalal, S. R.; Lee, J. C. and Sabavala, D. J. Prediction of Individual Buying Behavior: A Poisson–Bernoulli Model with Arbitrary Heterogeneity. *Marketing Sci.*, Fall 1984, *3*(4), pp. 352–67. [G: U.S.]

Dierker, Egbert; Dierker, Hildegard and Trockel, Walter. Price-dispersed Preferences and C^1 Mean Demand. *J. Math. Econ.*, April 1984, *13*(1), pp. 11–42.

Diewert, W. Erwin and Edlefsen, Lee E. Consumption Theorems in Terms of Over and Under Compensation Revisited. *Int. Econ. Rev.*, June 1984, *25*(2), pp. 379–85.

Dobbs, Ian M. and Hill, Martyn B. Technical Innovation and the Demand for Goods. *Scot. J. Polit. Econ.*, June 1984, *31*(2), pp. 147–56.

Dwyer, Gerald P., Jr. and Lindsay, Cotton M. Robert Giffen and the Irish Potato. *Amer. Econ. Rev.*, March 1984, *74*(1), pp. 188–92. [G: Ireland]

Economides, Nicholas S. The Principle of Minimum Differentiation Revisited. *Europ. Econ. Rev.*, April 1984, *24*(3), pp. 345–68.

Edmonds, Radcliffe G., Jr. A Theoretical Basis for Hedonic Regression: A Research Primer. *Amer. Real Estate Urban Econ. Assoc. J.*, Spring 1984, *12*(1), pp. 72–85.

Egidi, Massimo and Gilibert, Giorgio. La teoria oggettiva dei prezzi. (With English summary.) *Econ. Polít.*, April 1984, *1*(1), pp. 43–61.

Elías, Víctor J. Una nota sobre la elasticidad del ahorro con respecto a la tasa de interés. (With English summary.) *Cuadernos Econ.*, April 1984, *21*(62), pp. 83–89.

Fishburn, Peter C. Dominance in SSB Utility Theory. *J. Econ. Theory*, October 1984, *34*(1), pp. 130–48.

Fishburn, Peter C. SSB Utility Theory and Decision-making under Uncertainty. *Math. Soc. Sci.*, December 1984, *8*(3), pp. 253–85.

Fishburn, Peter C. SSB Utility Theory: An Economic Perspective. *Math. Soc. Sci.*, August 1984, *8*(1), pp. 63–94.

Folbre, Nancy R. Market Opportunities, Genetic Endowments, and Intrafamily Resource Distribution: Comment. *Amer. Econ. Rev.*, June 1984, *74*(3), pp. 518–20. [G: India]

Freeman, A. Myrick, III. The Sign and Size of Option Value. *Land Econ.*, February 1984, *60*(1), pp. 1–13.

Fuchs-Seliger, Susanne. An Application of Helly's Theorem to Preference-Generated Choice Correspondences. *Int. Econ. Rev.*, February 1984, *25*(1), pp. 71–77.

Fukuba, Yo; Tabata, Yoshio and Sakagami, Yoshitaka. Notes on Measurement and Approximation (I). (In Japanese. With English summary.) *Osaka Econ. Pap.*, December 1984, *34*(2–3), pp. 275–82.

Geanakoplos, John D. Utility Functions for De-

breau's 'Excess Demands.' *J. Math. Econ.*, April 1984, *13*(1), pp. 1–9.

Glazer, A. The Client Relationship and a "Just" Price. *Amer. Econ. Rev.*, December 1984, *74*(5), pp. 1089–95.

Graham, John W. Why Is Consumption Out of Labor Income Greater Than Consumption Out of Nonlabor Income? *Quart. J. Bus. Econ.*, Summer 1984, *23*(3), pp. 59–69.

Grossman, Sanford J. and Weiss, Laurence. Saving and Insurance. In *Boyer, M. and Kihlstrom, R. E., eds.*, 1984, pp. 303–11.

Gunning, J. Patrick. Marriage Law and Human Capital Investment: A Comment. *Southern Econ. J.*, October 1984, *51*(2), pp. 594–97.

Hagen, Ole. Neo-Cardinalism. In *Hagen, O. and Wenstop, F., eds.*, 1984, pp. 145–64.

Hagen, Ole. Relativity in Decision Theory. In *Hagen, O. and Wenstop, F., eds.*, 1984, pp. 237–49.

Hanemann, W. Michael. Discrete/Continuous Models of Consumer Demand. *Econometrica*, May 1984, *52*(3), pp. 541–61.

von Hayek, Friedrich A. Marginal Utility and Economic Calculation: A Review. In *von Hayek, F. A. (II)*, 1984, *1925*, pp. 183–89.

Hey, John D. Optimal Consumption When Income Follows a Markov Process. *Bull. Econ. Res.*, November 1984, *36*(2), pp. 109–18.

Hey, John D. The Economics of Optimism and Pessimism: A Definition and Some Applications. *Kyklos*, 1984, *37*(2), pp. 181–205.

Hicks, John R. Valuation of Social Income—The Utility Approach [The Measurement of Real Income]. In *Hicks, J.*, 1984, *1958*, pp. 57–95.

Hicks, John R. and Allen, Roy. A Reconsideration of the Theory of Value. In *Hicks, J.*, 1984, *1934*, pp. 24–48.

High, Jack. Knowledge, Maximizing, and Conjecture: A Critical Analysis of Search Theory. *J. Post Keynesian Econ.*, Winter 1983-84, *6*(2), pp. 252–64.

Holler, M. J. A Collective Choice Approach to Individual Decision Making. In *Holler, M. J., ed.*, 1984, pp. 338–44.

Jackson, Laurence Fraser. Hierarchic Demand and the Engel Curve for Variety. *Rev. Econ. Statist.*, February 1984, *66*(1), pp. 8–15. [G: U.S.]

Jehle, Geoffrey A. Individual Welfare and the Demand for Financial Instruments. *Southern Econ. J.*, July 1984, *51*(1), pp. 116–34. [G: U.S.]

Jerison, Michael. Aggregation and Pairwise Aggregation of Demand When the Distribution of Income Is Fixed. *J. Econ. Theory*, June 1984, *33*(1), pp. 1–31.

Kallberg, Jerry G. and Ziemba, William T. Misspecifications in Portfolio Selection Problems. In *Bamberg, G. and Spremann, K., eds.*, 1984, pp. 74–87.

Kaneko, Mamoru. On Interpersonal Utility Comparisons. *Soc. Choice Welfare*, October 1984, *1*(3), pp. 165–75.

Keasey, Kevin. Regret Theory and Information:

A Note. *Econ. J.*, September 1984, *94*(375), pp. 645–48.

Kiefer, Nicholas M. Microeconometric Evidence on the Neoclassical Model of Demand. *J. Econometrics*, July 1984, *25*(3), pp. 285–302.
[G: Belgium]

Kihlstrom, Richard E.; Mirman, Leonard J. and Postlewaite, Andrew. Experimental Consumption and the "Rothschild Effect." In *Boyer, M. and Kihlstrom, R. E., eds.*, 1984, pp. 279–302.

Kingston, Geoffrey H. Microeconomic Justification of the Hoarding Function. *Int. Econ. Rev.*, June 1984, *25*(2), pp. 385–89.

Knetsch, Jack L. and Sinden, J. A. Willingness to Pay and Compensation Demanded: Experimental Evidence of an Unexpected Disparity in Measures of Value. *Quart. J. Econ.*, August 1984, *99*(3), pp. 507–21.

Knowles, Glenn J. Some Econometric Problems in the Measurement of Utility. *Amer. J. Agr. Econ.*, November 1984, *66*(4), pp. 505–10.

Kohn, Robert E. Total Satiation and Competitive Equilibrium. *S. Afr. J. Econ.*, March 1984, *52*(1), pp. 69–74.

Koskela, Erkki and Virén, Matti. Credit Rationing and Consumer Intertemporal Choice. *Oxford Econ. Pap.*, June 1984, *36*(2), pp. 241–47.

Krelle, Wilhelm. Remarks to Professor Allais' Contributions to the Theory of Expected Utility and Related Subjects. In *Hagen, O. and Wenstop, F., eds.*, 1984, pp. 173–80.

Krzysztofowicz, Roman. Prediction, Measurement, and Error of Utility: A Reply. In *Hagen, O. and Wenstop, F., eds.*, 1984, pp. 165–70.

Kurz, Mordecai. Capital Accumulation and the Characteristics of Private Inter-Generational Transfers. *Economica*, February 1984, *51*(201), pp. 1–22. [G: U.S.]

Kushman, John E. A Simple Derivation of Roy's Identity and Further Results. *Atlantic Econ. J.*, September 1984, *12*(3), pp. 78.

Levy, Haim and Levy, Azriel. Multivariate Decision-Making. *J. Econ. Theory*, February 1984, *32*(1), pp. 36–51.

Lindenberg, Siegwart. Preference versus Constraints: A Commentary on von Weizsäcker's 'The Influence of Property Rights on Tastes.' *Z. ges. Staatswiss.*, March 1984, *140*(1), pp. 96–103.

Lloyd, P. J. Marriages and Mergers: Super-additivity of Functions. *Singapore Econ. Rev.*, October 1984, *29*(2), pp. 83–92.

Longley, Paul A. Discrete Choice Modelling and Complex Spatial Choice: An Overview. In *Bahrenberg, G.; Fischer, M. M., and Nijkamp, P.*, 1984, pp. 375–91.

Loomes, Graham and Sugden, Robert. Regret Theory and Information: A Reply. *Econ. J.*, September 1984, *94*(375), pp. 649–50.

Loomes, Graham and Sugden, Robert. The Importance of What Might Have Been. In *Hagen, O. and Wenstop, F., eds.*, 1984, pp. 219–35.

Machina, Mark J. Temporal Risk and the Nature of Induced Preferences. *J. Econ. Theory*, August 1984, *33*(2), pp. 199–231.

Mak, King-tim. Notes on Separable Preferences. *J. Econ. Theory*, August 1984, *33*(2), pp. 309–21.

Marshall, John M. Gambles and the Shadow Price of Death. *Amer. Econ. Rev.*, March 1984, *74*(1), pp. 73–86.

McKee, Arnold F. Social Economy and the Theory of Consumer Behaviour. *Int. J. Soc. Econ.*, 1984, *11*(3/4), pp. 45–61.

de Meza, David and Dickinson, Paul T. Risk Preferences and Transaction Costs. *J. Econ. Behav. Organ.*, June 1984, *5*(2), pp. 223–36.

Michener, Ron. Permanent Income in General Equilibrium. *J. Monet. Econ.*, May 1984, *13*(3), pp. 297–305.

Montesano, Aldo. Sono i prezzi indici di scarsità relativa? (With English summary.) *Econ. Polít.*, April 1984, *1*(1), pp. 9–41.

Morey, Edward R. Confuser Surplus. *Amer. Econ. Rev.*, March 1984, *74*(1), pp. 163–73.

Nagatani, Hiroaki. Algorithms for the Hicksian Measures of Consumer's Surplus: Professor Houthakker Revaluated. (In Japanese. With English summary.) *Osaka Econ. Pap.*, December 1984, *34*(2–3), pp. 135–46.

Nairay, Alain. Asymptotic Behavior and Optimal Properties of a Consumption–Investment Model with Variable Time Preference. *J. Econ. Dynam. Control*, September 1984, *7*(3), pp. 283–313.

Ng, Yew-Kwang. Expected Subjective Utility: Is the Neumann–Morgenstern Utility the Same as the Neoclassical's? *Soc. Choice Welfare*, October 1984, *1*(3), pp. 177–86.

Nielsen, Lars Tyge. Unbounded Expected Utility and Continuity. *Math. Soc. Sci.*, December 1984, *8*(3), pp. 201–16.

Pallaschke, Diethard. On the Construction of Utility Functions Which Correspond to Homogeneous Demand Systems. In *[Beckmann, M. J.]*, 1984, pp. 75–81.

Parrinello, Sergio. Adaptive Preferences and the Theory of Demand. *J. Post Keynesian Econ.*, Summer 1984, *6*(4), pp. 551–60.

Phlips, Louis and Spinnewyn, Frans. True Indexes and Rational Habit Formation. *Europ. Econ. Rev.*, March 1984, *24*(2), pp. 209–23.
[G: U.S.]

Polemarchakis, Herakles M. and Rose, D. Another Proposition on the Recoverability of Cardinal Utility. *J. Econ. Theory*, October 1984, *34*(1), pp. 164–68.

Polemarchakis, Herakles M. and Selden, L. On the Recoverability of Risk and Time Preferences from Consumption and Asset Demands. *Europ. Econ. Rev.*, October–November 1984, *26*(1–2), pp. 115–33.

Pope, Robin. The Utility of Gambling and of Outcomes: Inconsistent First Approximations. In *Hagen, O. and Wenstop, F., eds.*, 1984, pp. 251–73.

Pressacco, Flavio. A Life Cycle Model of Life Insurance Purchases. *Metroecon.*, June-Oct. 1984, *36*(2–3), pp. 227–38.

Quizon, Jaime B.; Binswanger, Hans P. and Machina, Mark J. Attitudes toward Risk: Further Remarks. *Econ. J.*, March 1984, *94*(373), pp. 144–48. **[G: India]**

Rosenzweig, Mark R. and Schultz, T. Paul. Market Opportunities, Genetic Endowments, and Intrafamily Resource Distribution: Reply. *Amer. Econ. Rev.*, June 1984, *74*(3), pp. 521–22. **[G: India]**

Roy, C. R. Consumer Behaviour under Partial Rationing. *Margin*, July 1984, *16*(4), pp. 48–63. **[G: India]**

Roy, Subroto. Considerations on Utility, Benevolence, and Taxation. *Hist. Polit. Econ.*, Fall 1984, *16*(3), pp. 349–62.

Samuelson, Paul A. and Sato, Ryuzo. Unattainability of Integrability and Definiteness Conditions in the General Case of Demand for Money and Goods. *Amer. Econ. Rev.*, September 1984, *74*(4), pp. 588–604.

Sattinger, Michael. Value of an Additional Firm in Monopolistic Competition. *Rev. Econ. Stud.*, April 1984, *51*(2), pp. 321–32.

Scapparone, Paolo. Rappresentazione di una relazione di preferenza per mezzo di funzioni di utilità. (With English summary.) *Econ. Polit.*, August 1984, *1*(2), pp. 261–69.

Schelling, Thomas C. Self-Command in Practice, in Policy, and in a Theory of Rational Choice. *Amer. Econ. Rev.*, May 1984, *74*(2), pp. 1–11.

Sen, Amartya. Economics and the Family. In *Sen, A.*, 1984, *1983*, pp. 369–85.

Sen, Amartya. The Welfare Basis of Real Income Comparisons. In *Sen, A.*, 1984, *1979*, pp. 389–451.

Seo, Fumiko and Sakawa, Masatoshi. Fuzzy Assessment of Multiattribute Utility Functions. In *Grauer, M. and Wierzbicki, A. P., eds.*, 1984, pp. 97–104.

Shaffer, Sherrill. Regulation and Risk Preferences. *J. Ind. Econ.*, March 1984, *32*(3), pp. 349–57.

Shah, Anup R. Intergenerational Distribution of Wealth in the Presence of Credit Rationing. *Metroecon.*, February 1984, *36*(1), pp. 97–109.

Silberberg, Eugene and Walker, Donald A. A Modern Analysis of Giffen's Paradox. *Int. Econ. Rev.*, October 1984, *25*(3), pp. 687–94.

Simmons, P. A Complement to Pearce on Complements. In *[Pearce, I. F.]*, 1984, pp. 19–36.

Smith, Terence R. and Lundberg, C. G. Psychological Foundations of Individual Choice Behaviour and a New Class of Decision Making Models. In *Bahrenberg, G.; Fischer, M. M., and Nijkamp, P.*, 1984, pp. 355–73.

Sobel, Joel. Non-linear Prices and Price-taking Behavior. *J. Econ. Behav. Organ.*, September–December 1984, *5*(3–4), pp. 387–96.

Sonis, M. Dynamic Choice of Alternatives, Innovation Diffusion, and Ecological Dynamics of the Volterra-Lotka Model. In *Pitfield, D. E., ed.*, 1984, pp. 29–43.

Sotomayor, Marlida A. de Oliveira. On Income Fluctuations and Capital Gains. *J. Econ. Theory*, February 1984, *32*(1), pp. 14–35.

Stahl, Dale O., II. Monotonic Variations of Consumer Surplus and Comparative Performance

Results. *Southern Econ. J.*, October 1984, *51*(2), pp. 503–20.

Stoker, Thomas M. Exact Aggregation and Generalized Slutsky Conditions. *J. Econ. Theory*, August 1984, *33*(2), pp. 368–77.

Takayama, Akira. Consumer's Surplus, Path Independence, Compensating and Equivalent Variation. *Z. ges. Staatswiss.*, December 1984, *140*(4), pp. 594–625.

Timmermans, H. J. P. Decision Models for Predicting Preferences among Multiattribute Choice Alternatives. In *Bahrenberg, G.; Fischer, M. M., and Nijkamp, P.*, 1984, pp. 337–54.

Tishler, Asher and Zilcha, Itzhak. A Model of the Household's Demand for Durables and Energy. *Scand. J. Econ.*, 1984, *86*(4), pp. 411–22.

Tonks, Ian. A Bayesian Approach to the Production of Information with a Linear Utility Function. *Rev. Econ. Stud.*, July 1984, *51*(3), pp. 521–27.

Trockel, Walter. On the Uniqueness of Individual Demand at Almost Every Price System. *J. Econ. Theory*, August 1984, *33*(2), pp. 397–99.

Verstegen, Bernard H. J. Aspirations, Reference Groups, and the Consumer. *De Economist*, 1984, *132*(3), pp. 300–325.

Walker, Joe. A Note on Income and Substitution Effects in Dieting. *Eastern Econ. J.*, July-September 1984, *10*(3), pp. 323–24.

Waugh, Frederick V. Consumer Aspects of Price Instability. In *Waugh, F. V.*, 1984, *1966*, pp. 127–31.

Waugh, Frederick V. Does the Consumer Benefit from Price Instability? In *Waugh, F. V.*, 1984, *1944*, pp. 27–39.

von Weizsäcker, Carl Christian. The Influence of Property Rights on Tastes. *Z. ges. Staatswiss.*, March 1984, *140*(1), pp. 90–95.

Wolinsky, Asher. Product Differentiation with Imperfect Information. *Rev. Econ. Stud.*, January 1984, *51*(1), pp. 53–61.

Yamazaki, Akira. The Critical Set of a Demand Correspondence in the Price Space and the Weak Axiom of Revealed Preference. *Hitotsubashi J. Econ.*, December 1984, *25*(2), pp. 137–44.

0223 Theory of Production

Abel, Andrew B. The Effects of Uncertainty on Investment and the Expected Long-Run Capital Stock. *J. Econ. Dynam. Control*, February 1984, *7*(1), pp. 39–53.

Afxentiou, Panayotis C. The Envelope Curve and Market Structure: A Pedagogical Note. *Econ. Notes*, 1984, (3), pp. 31–46.

Aiginger, K. Economic Rational Expectations and their Influence on Production and Inventory Decisions. In *Oppenländer, K. H. and Poser, G., eds.*, 1984, pp. 541–97. **[G: Japan; Austria]**

Akerlof, George A. Gift Exchange and Efficiency-Wage Theory: Four Views. *Amer. Econ. Rev.*, May 1984, *74*(2), pp. 79–83.

Albarracén, Jesus. Constant Returns and Uniform Profit Rates: Two False Assumptions. In *Mandel, E. and Freeman, A., eds.*, 1984, pp. 177–209.

Alchian, Armen A. Specificity, Specialization, and Coalitions. *Z. ges. Staatswiss.*, March 1984, *140*(1), pp. 34–49.

Allen, Franklin. Reputation and Product Quality. *Rand J. Econ.*, Autumn 1984, *15*(3), pp. 311–27.

Andersen, Peder and Sutinen, Jon G. Stochastic Bioeconomics: A Review of Basic Methods and Results. *Marine Resource Econ.*, 1984, *1*(2), pp. 117–36.

Appelbaum, Elie and Ullah, Aman. An Empirical Test of the Risk Aversion Hypothesis. *Pakistan J. Appl. Econ.*, Summer 1984, *3*(1), pp. 57–64.   **[G: U.S.]**

Arrow, Kenneth J. Vertical Integration and Communication. In *Arrow, K. J., vol. 4*, 1984, *1975*, pp. 185–96.

Artus, Patrick. Capacité de production, demande de facteurs et incertitude sur la demande. (Production Capacity, Factor Demand and Demand Uncertainty. With English summary.) *Ann. INSEE*, January–March 1984, (53), pp. 3–29.   **[G: France]**

Artus, Patrick and Muet, Pierre-Alain. Un panorama des développements récents de l'économétrie de l'investissement. (A Survey of Recent Developments in the Econometrics of Investment. With English summary.) *Revue Écon.*, September 1984, *35*(5), pp. 791–830.   **[G: Japan; France; U.K.; U.S.; Germany]**

Auerbach, Alan J. Taxes, Firm Financial Policy and the Cost of Capital: An Empirical Analysis. *J. Public Econ.*, February/March 1984, *23*(1/2), pp. 27–57.   **[G: U.S.]**

d'Autume, Antoine and Michel, Philippe. Évaluation du capital en présence de contraintes anticipées sur les achats de biens d'investissement. (Capital Evaluation with Expected Constraints on Purchases of Investment Goods. With English summary.) *Ann. INSEE*, April–June 1984, (54), pp. 101–15.

Balcer, Yves and Lippman, Steven A. Technological Expectations and Adoption of Improved Technology. *J. Econ. Theory*, December 1984, *34*(2), pp. 292–318.

Baldone, Salvatore. From Surrogate to Pseudo Production Functions. *Cambridge J. Econ.*, September 1984, *8*(3), pp. 271–88.

Bamberg, Günter. The Impacts of Variance Reducing Strategies in Dyopolistic Capital Markets. In *Bamberg, G. and Spremann, K., eds.*, 1984, pp. 15–32.

Barron, John M.; Loewenstein, Mark A. and Black, Dan A. On Recalls, Layoffs, Variable Hours, and Labor Adjustment Costs. *J. Econ. Dynam. Control*, December 1984, *8*(3), pp. 265–75.

Baumol, William J. Toward a Theory of Public Enterprise. *Atlantic Econ. J.*, March 1984, *12*(1), pp. 12–19.

Beato, Paulina and Mas-Colell, Andreu. The Marginal Cost Pricing Rule as a Regulation Mechanism in Mixed Markets. In *Marchand, M.; Pestieau, P. and Tulkens, H., eds.*, 1984, pp. 81–100.

Ben-Ner, Avner. Labor-managed and Participatory Firms: A Note. *J. Econ. Issues*, December 1984, *18*(4), pp. 1189–95.

Ben-Ner, Avner. On the Stability of the Cooperative Type of Organization. *J. Compar. Econ.*, September 1984, *8*(3), pp. 247–60.

Benhabib, Jess and Nishimura, Kazuo. Cyclical Input Demands and the Adjustment Cost Theory of the Firm. In *Goodwin, R. M.; Krüger, M. and Vercelli, A., eds.*, 1984, pp. 73–85.

Benson, Bruce L. Spatial Price Theory and an Efficient Congestion Toll Established by the Free Market. *Econ. Inquiry*, April 1984, *22*(2), pp. 244–52.

Berninghaus, Siegfried. A General Existence Theorem for Equilibrium Price Dispersions. *Info. Econ. Policy*, 1984, *1*(3), pp. 239–66.

Blackorby, Charles and Schworm, William. The Structure of Economies with Aggregate Measures of Capital: A Complete Characterization. *Rev. Econ. Stud.*, October 1984, *51*(4), pp. 633–50.

Bohnet, Armin. Effizienz und Preise—zwei zentrale Kategorien in der Wirtschaftsordnungstheorie. (With English summary.) In *Bohnet, A., ed.*, 1984, pp. 121–51.

Bonin, John P. Membership and Employment in an Egalitarian Cooperative. *Economica*, August 1984, *51*(203), pp. 295–305.

Borooah, Vani K. Theory of the Firm. In *van der Ploeg, F., ed.*, 1984, pp. 289–314.

Bös, Dieter and Tillmann, Georg. Cost-Axiomatic versus Welfare-Maximizing Marginal Cost Pricing. In *Marchand, M.; Pestieau, P. and Tulkens, H., eds.*, 1984, pp. 101–17.

Boulier, Bryan L. What Lies behind Verdoorn's Law? *Oxford Econ. Pap.*, June 1984, *36*(2), pp. 259–67.

Braeutigam, Ronald R. and Quirk, James P. Demand Uncertainty and the Regulated Firm. *Int. Econ. Rev.*, February 1984, *25*(1), pp. 45–60.

Brander, James A. and Eaton, Jonathan. Product Line Rivalry. *Amer. Econ. Rev.*, June 1984, *74*(3), pp. 323–34.

Braulke, Michael. The Firm in Short-run Industry Equilibrium: Comment. *Amer. Econ. Rev.*, September 1984, *74*(4), pp. 750–53.

Brick, Ivan E. and Jagpal, Harsharanjeet S. Utility Theory, Value Maximization and the Quality Decision under Uncertainty. *Int. Econ. Rev.*, June 1984, *25*(2), pp. 369–77.

Britto, Ronald. The Simultaneous Determination of Spot and Futures Prices in a Simple Model with Production Risk. *Quart. J. Econ.*, May 1984, *99*(2), pp. 351–65

Brockway, George P. Kaldor's "Best" Choice [Allyn Young on Increasing Returns]. *J. Post Keynesian Econ.*, Spring 1984, *6*(3), pp. 481–82.

Brunner, Johann K. Decision-Making in a Multiproduct Firm: A Comment. *Managerial Dec. Econ.*, March 1984, *5*(1), pp. 58–59.

Buchanan, James M. and Tollison, Robert D. The Homogenization of Heterogeneous Inputs: Reply. *Amer. Econ. Rev.*, September 1984, *74*(4), pp. 808.

Calvo, Guillermo A. and Thoumi, Francisco E. Demand Fluctuations, Inventories and Capacity Utilization. *Southern Econ. J.*, January 1984, *50*(3), pp. 743–54.

Carmichael, H. Lorne. Reputations in the Labor Market. *Amer. Econ. Rev.*, September 1984, *74*(4), pp. 713–25.

Carson, R. The Optimal Size of the Competitive Firm. *J. Econ. Bus.*, February 1984, *36*(1), pp. 15–28.

Chambers, Robert G. A Note on Separability of the Indirect Production Function and Measures of Substitution. *Southern Econ. J.*, April 1984, *50*(4), pp. 1189–91.

Chiappori, Pierre-André. Sélection naturelle et rationalité absolue des entreprises. (Natural Selection and Substantive Rationality of Business Firms. With English summary.) *Revue Écon.*, January 1984, *35*(1), pp. 87–107.

Chillemi, Ottorino. Un modello per l'analisi della produzione di capitale umano specifico. (A Model for the Analysis of the Production of Specific Human Capital. With English summary.) *Rivista Int. Sci. Econ. Com.*, December 1984, *31*(12), pp. 1201–20.

Clarke, Harry R. The Separability of Production and Location Decisions: Comment. *Amer. Econ. Rev.*, June 1984, *74*(3), pp. 528–30.

Clarke, Richard N. Scale Economies, Entry, and Welfare. *J. Econ. Bus.*, May 1984, *36*(2), pp. 161–76.

Cohen, Avi J. The Methodological Resolution of the Cambridge Controversies. *J. Post Keynesian Econ.*, Summer 1984, *6*(4), pp. 614–29.

Considine, Timothy J. and Mount, Timothy D. The Use of Linear Logit Models for Dynamic Input Demand Systems. *Rev. Econ. Statist.*, August 1984, *66*(3), pp. 434–43. **[G: U.S.]**

Crain, W. Mark; Shughart, William F., II and Tollison, Robert D. The Convergence of Satisficing to Marginalism: An Empirical Test. *J. Econ. Behav. Organ.*, September–December 1984, *5*(3–4), pp. 375–85. **[G: U.S.]**

Crampes, Claude. Choix des inputs et règles de gestion face à une demande aléatoire. (With English summary.) *Revue Écon. Polit.*, July–August 1984, *94*(4), pp. 465–84.

Dalal, Ardeshir J. A Simple Proof of the Concavity of the Transformation Curve. *Atlantic Econ. J.*, July 1984, *12*(2), pp. 67.

Daughety, Andrew F. Stochastically Separable Production Functions: Reply [Stochastic Production and Cost]. *Southern Econ. J.*, January 1984, *50*(3), pp. 904–05.

De Bondt, Raymond R. and Goovaerts, Marc J. The Effectiveness of Temporary Marginal Cost Subsidies. *Int. J. Ind. Organ.*, September 1984, *2*(3), pp. 235–49.

Dechert, W. Davis. Has the Averch–Johnson Effect Been Theoretically Justified? *J. Econ. Dynam. Control*, October 1984, *8*(1), pp. 1–17.

Donaldson, David and Eaton, B. Curtis. Person-Specific Costs of Production: Hours of Work, Rates of Pay, Labour Contracts. *Can. J. Econ.*, August 1984, *17*(3), pp. 441–49.

Dormont, Brigitte. Productivité-croissance quelle relation a moyen-long terme? Un rapprochement des modèles de Brechling et de Kaldor–Verdoorn. (Productivity and Growth: What Is the Long-Run Relationship? Bringing Together Brechling's and Kaldor–Verdoorn's Models. With English summary.) *Revue Écon.*, May 1984, *35*(3), pp. 447–78. **[G: France; W. Germany]**

Duménil, Gérard and Lévy, Dominique. The Unifying Formalism of Domination: Value, Price, Distribution, and Growth in Joint Production. *Z. Nationalökon.*, 1984, *44*(4), pp. 349–71.

Edwards, J. S. S. and Keen, Michael J. Wealth Maximization and the Cost of Capital: A Comment. *Quart. J. Econ.*, February 1984, *99*(1), pp. 211–14.

Eichenbaum, Martin S. Rational Expectations and the Smoothing Properties of Inventories of Finished Goods. *J. Monet. Econ.*, July 1984, *14*(1), pp. 71–96. **[G: U.S.]**

Enos, J. L. Public Policy in an Economy with Different Types of Agents. *Greek Econ. Rev.*, December 1984, *6*(3), pp. 424–52.

Evans, David S. and Heckman, James J. A Test for Subadditivity of the Cost Function with an Application to the Bell System. *Amer. Econ. Rev.*, September 1984, *74*(4), pp. 615–23.

Faith, Roger L.; Higgins, Richard S. and Tollison, Robert D. Managerial Rents and Outside Recruitment in the Coasian Firm. *Amer. Econ. Rev.*, September 1984, *74*(4), pp. 660–72. **[G: U.S.]**

Färe, Rolf. The Dual Measurement of Efficiency. *Z. Nationalökon.*, 1984, *44*(3), pp. 283–88.

Färe, Rolf. The Existence of Plant Capacity. *Int. Econ. Rev.*, February 1984, *25*(1), pp. 209–13.

Farjoun, Emmanuel. The Production of Commodities by Means of What? In *Mandel, E. and Freeman, A.,* eds., 1984, pp. 11–41.

Farmer, Roger E. A. Unemployment, Bankruptcy and Asymmetric Information. *Manchester Sch. Econ. Soc. Stud.*, September 1984, *52*(3), pp. 284–91.

Fehr, Ernst. Workers' Management and Capitalism in a Nutshell. *Econ. Anal. Worker's Manage.*, 1984, *18*(4), pp. 319–31.

Fershtman, Chaim and Muller, Eitan. Capital Accumulation Games of Infinite Duration. *J. Econ. Theory*, August 1984, *33*(2), pp. 322–39.

Finsinger, Jörg and Kraft, Kornelius. Markup Pricing and Firm Decisions. *Z. ges. Staatswiss.*, September 1984, *140*(3), pp. 500–509. **[G: Germany]**

Finsinger, Jörg and Pauly, Mark V. Reserve Levels and Reserve Requirements for Profit-maximizing Insurance Firms. In *Bamberg, G. and Spremann, K.,* eds., 1984, pp. 160–80.

Fishelson, Gideon. Constraints on Transactions in the Futures Markets for Output and Inputs.

J. Econ. Bus., December 1984, *36*(4), pp. 415–20.

Forsythe, Robert and Suchanek, Gerry L. Collective Decision Mechanisms and Efficient Stock Market Allocations: Existence of a Participation Equilibrium. *Int. Econ. Rev.*, February 1984, *25*(1), pp. 21–43.

Fraser, R. W. Demand Fluctuations, Inventories and Flexibility. *Australian Econ. Pap.*, June 1984, *23*(42), pp. 105–11.

French, Kenneth R. and McCormick, Robert E. Sealed Bids, Sunk Costs, and the Process of Competition. *J. Bus.*, October 1984, *57*(4), pp. 417–41.

Furubotn, Eirik G. and Wiggins, Steven N. Plant Closings, Worker Reallocation Costs and Efficiency Gains to Labor Representation on Boards of Directors. *Z. ges. Staatswiss.*, March 1984, *140*(1), pp. 176–92. **[G: U.S.]**

Fusfeld, Daniel R. Labor-managed and Participatory Firms: Reply. *J. Econ. Issues*, December 1984, *18*(4), pp. 1195–98.

Galeotti, Marzio. Recent Developments in Investment Theory. *Giorn. Econ.*, May–June 1984, *43*(5–6), pp. 393–415.

Garrod, Peter V. and Miklius, Walter. Owner-Operators, Demand Fluctuations and the Choice of Technology. *J. Transp. Econ. Policy*, September 1984, *18*(3), pp. 293–302. **[G: U.S.]**

Gegax, Douglas and Tschirhart, John T. An Analysis of Interfirm Cooperation: Theory and Evidence from Electric Power Pools. *Southern Econ. J.*, April 1984, *50*(4), pp. 1077–97. **[G: U.S.]**

Getzen, Thomas E. A "Brand Name Firm" Theory of Medical Group Practice. *J. Ind. Econ.*, December 1984, *33*(2), pp. 199–215. **[G: U.S.]**

Gibbons, Joel C. The Optimal Durability of Fixed Capital When Demand Is Uncertain. *J. Bus.*, July 1984, *57*(3), pp. 389–403. **[G: U.S.]**

Gozzi, Giancarlo. Posizioni di lungo periodo e stabilità. (With English summary.) *Econ. Polít.*, December 1984, *1*(3), pp. 407–27.

Greenwald, Bruce C.; Stiglitz, Joseph E. and Weiss, Andrew. Informational Imperfections in the Capital Market and Macroeconomic Fluctuations. *Amer. Econ. Rev.*, May 1984, *74*(2), pp. 194–99.

Grinols, Earl L. Competition and Optimal Departures from Stock Market Value Maximization by Firms. *J. Econ. Dynam. Control*, December 1984, *8*(3), pp. 277–89.

Gronchi, Sandro. On Karmel's Criterion for Optimal Truncation. *Econ. Notes*, 1984, (3), pp. 21–30.

Grout, Paul A. Investment and Wages in the Absence of Binding Contracts: A Nash Bargaining Approach. *Econometrica*, March 1984, *52*(2), pp. 449–60.

Guesnerie, Roger and Laffont, Jean-Jacques. A Complete Solution to a Class of Principal–Agent Problems with an Application to the Control of a Self-managed Firm. *J. Public Econ.*, December 1984, *25*(3), pp. 329–69.

Guesnerie, Roger and Laffont, Jean-Jacques. Indirect Public Control of Self-Managed Monopolies. *J. Compar. Econ.*, June 1984, *8*(2), pp. 139–58.

Gunning, J. Patrick. The Homogenization of Heterogeneous Inputs: Comment. *Amer. Econ. Rev.*, September 1984, *74*(4), pp. 805–07.

Hall, Robert E. and Lazear, Edward P. The Excess Sensitivity of Layoffs and Quits to Demand. *J. Lab. Econ.*, April 1984, *2*(2), pp. 233–57.

Hansson, Ingemar. Determinants of Investment Volatility. *Z. Nationalökon.*, 1984, *44*(1), pp. 11–26.

Hart, Oliver. The Firm as a Collection of Human Resources: Comment. In *Wiles, P. and Routh, G., eds.*, 1984, pp. 207–10.

Hart, Robert A. Worksharing and Factor Prices. *Europ. Econ. Rev.*, March 1984, *24*(2), pp. 165–88. **[G: OECD]**

Hawawini, Gabriel. Uncertainty and the Production Decisions of Owner-Managed and Labor-Managed Firms. *Oxford Econ. Pap.*, March 1984, *36*(1), pp. 119–30.

Heiner, Ronald A. The Firm in Short-run Industry Equilibrium: Further Comment. *Amer. Econ. Rev.*, September 1984, *74*(4), pp. 754.

Hellwig, Klaus. Corporate Planning and Capital Maintenance. In *Bamberg, G. and Spremann, K., eds.*, 1984, pp. 198–202.

Hey, John D. The Economics of Optimism and Pessimism: A Definition and Some Applications. *Kyklos*, 1984, *37*(2), pp. 181–205.

Hiebert, L. Dean. Producer Preference for Price Stability. *Amer. J. Agr. Econ.*, February 1984, *66*(1), pp. 88–90.

Hill, Stephen. Decision-Making in a Multiproduct Firm: A Reply. *Managerial Dec. Econ.*, March 1984, *5*(1), pp. 60–62.

Holländer, Heinz. A Further Note on Sraffa's Negative Quantities of Allegedly Embodied Labour. *Econ. J.*, March 1984, *94*(373), pp. 155–57.

Hsu, Song-ken and Mai, Chao-cheng. Production Location and Random Input Price. *Reg. Sci. Urban Econ.*, February 1984, *14*(1), pp. 45–62.

van Hulle, C. Unanimous Investment Decisions: A Note on the Hirshleifer Paradigm. *Tijdschrift Econ. Manage.*, 1984, *29*(4), pp. 529–38.

Hurter, Arthur P., Jr.; Martinich, Joseph S. and Venta, Enrique R. The Separability of Production and Location Decisions: Reply. *Amer. Econ. Rev.*, June 1984, *74*(3), pp. 531–32.

Inoue, Tadashi. On the Shape of the Production Possibility Frontier with More Commodities than Primary Factors. *Int. Econ. Rev.*, June 1984, *25*(2), pp. 409–24.

Ireland, Norman J. Codetermination, Wage Bargaining and the Horizon Problem. *Z. Nationalökon.*, 1984, *44*(1), pp. 1–10.

Ireland, Norman J. and Law, Peter J. On the Labour-Managed Firm with Homothetic Technology. *Econ. Anal. Worker's Manage.*, 1984, *18*(1), pp. 1–13.

Iwai, Katsuhito. Schumpeterian Dynamics: An Evolutionary Model of Innovation and Imitation. *J. Econ. Behav. Organ.*, June 1984, 5(2), pp. 159–90. **[G: U.S.]**

Johnson, Dennis A. Opportunity Cost: A Pedagogical Note. *Southern Econ. J.*, January 1984, 50(3), pp. 866–70.

Kahana, Nava and Paroush, Jacob. A Multi-factor Labor-managed Firm under Price Uncertainty. *Eastern Econ. J.*, January-March 1984, 10(1), pp. 23–29.

Katz, Eliakim. The Firm and Price Hedging in an Imperfect Market. *Int. Econ. Rev.*, February 1984, 25(1), pp. 215–19.

Katzner, Donald W. Capital and Walrasian Equilibrium. In *[Pearce, I. F.]*, 1984, pp. 123–48.

Kihlstrom, Richard E. and Riordan, Michael H. Advertising as a Signal. *J. Polit. Econ.*, June 1984, 92(3), pp. 427–50.

Kim, Kyoo H. A Modified Minkowski Theorem and Applications: Comment. *Atlantic Econ. J.*, March 1984, 12(1), pp. 118.

Kohn, Robert E. Industry Isoquants when the Number of Firms Is a Variable. *Rivista Int. Sci. Econ. Com.*, March 1984, 31(3), pp. 257–63.

Kokkelenberg, Edward C. The Specification and Estimation of Interrelated Factor Demands under Uncertainty. *J. Econ. Dynam. Control*, September 1984, 7(3), pp. 181–207. **[G: U.S.]**

Kooiman, P. Smoothing the Aggregate Fix-Price Model and the Use of Business Survey Data. *Econ. J.*, December 1984, 94(376), pp. 899–913. **[G: Netherlands]**

Kuenne, Robert E. Economic Decision Making in a Poisson Demand Space. In *Andersson, Å. E.; Isard, W. and Puu, T., eds.*, 1984, pp. 331–46.

Lächler, Ulrich. On Optimal Factor Proportions in a Competitive Firm under Factor and Output Price Uncertainty. *Z. Nationalökon.*, 1984, 44(2), pp. 117–30.

Langston, Robert H. A New Approach to the Relation between Prices and Values. In *Mandel, E. and Freeman, A., eds.*, 1984, pp. 1–10.

Lee, Frederic S. The Marginalist Controversy and the Demise of Full Cost Pricing. *J. Econ. Issues*, December 1984, 18(4), pp. 1107–32.

Lee, Frederic S. Whatever Happened to the Full-Cost Principle (USA)? In *Wiles, P. and Routh, G., eds.*, 1984, pp. 233–39.

Lehmijoki, Ulla. Notes on Quasi-Convexity of the Cost Function. *Scand. J. Econ.*, 1984, 86(3), pp. 385–89.

Lichtenstein, Peter M. Economic Democracy: The Rawls–Vanek–Sraffa Connection. *Rev. Soc. Econ.*, October 1984, 42(2), pp. 170–81.

Lloyd, P. J. Marriages and Mergers: Super-additivity of Functions. *Singapore Econ. Rev.*, October 1984, 29(2), pp. 83–92.

Loasby, Brian J. Hypothesis and Paradigm in the Theory of the Firm. In *Caldwell, B. J., ed.*, 1984, 1971, pp. 261–83.

Loasby, Brian J. Organisational Control and Performance. In *Pickering, J. F. and Cockerill, T. A. J., eds.*, 1984, pp. 72–100.

Maccini, Louis J. The Interrelationship between

Price and Output Decisions and Investment Decisions: Microfoundations and Aggregate Implications. *J. Monet. Econ.*, January 1984, 13(1), pp. 41–65.

Mai, Chao-cheng. Demand Function and Location Theory of the Firm under Price Uncertainty. *Urban Stud.*, November 1984, 21(4), pp. 459–64.

Mai, Chao-cheng and Shieh, Yeung-Nan. Transport Rates Structure, Optimum Location, and Theory of Production: Reexamination. *J. Urban Econ.*, September 1984, 16(2), pp. 225–31.

Mai, Chao-cheng and Shih, Jun-ji. Output Effect of the Labour-managed Firm under Price Discrimination. *Econ. J.*, December 1984, 94(376), pp. 931–35.

Malgrange, Pierre and Villa, Pierre. Comportement d'investissement avec coûts d'adjustements et contraintes quantitatives. (Investment Behavior with Adjustment Costs and Quantitative Constraints. With English summary.) *Ann. INSEE*, January–March 1984, (53), pp. 31–61.

Manes, Rene P.; Shoumaker, Francoise and Silhan, Peter A. Demand Relationships and Pricing Decisions for Related Products. *Managerial Dec. Econ.*, June 1984, 5(2), pp. 120–22.

Mann, Barbara S. Capital Heterogeneity, Capital Utilization, and the Demand for Shiftworkers. *Can. J. Econ.*, August 1984, 17(3), pp. 450–70.

Marangoni, Giandemetrio. Prezzi positivi e merce tipo nel modello di produzione congiunta di Piero Sraffa. (Positive Prices and Standard Commodity in Piero Sraffa's Model of Joint Production. With English summary.) *Rivista Int. Sci. Econ. Com.*, December 1984, 31(12), pp. 1186–1200.

Marchand, Maurice; Pestieau, Pierre and Tulkens, Henry. The Performance of Public Enterprises: Normative, Positive and Empirical Issues. In *Marchand, M.; Pestieau, P. and Tulkens, H., eds.*, 1984, pp. 3–42.

Marcus, Alan J. and Modest, David M. Futures Markets and Production Decisions. *J. Polit. Econ.*, June 1984, 92(3), pp. 409–26. **[G: U.S.]**

Martin, Robert E. Stochastic Input Supply: Theory and Evidence. *Appl. Econ.*, June 1984, 16(3), pp. 343–54. **[G: U.S.]**

Maruyama, Shigeru. Wage Stickiness and Unemployment Due to the Part of Firms. *Econ. Stud. Quart.*, December 1984, 35(3), pp. 206–15.

McNulty, Paul J. On the Nature and Theory of Economic Organization: The Role of the Firm Reconsidered. *Hist. Polit. Econ.*, Summer 1984, 16(2), pp. 233–53.

de Meza, David. Private Disclosure: Is Honesty Enough? *Europ. Econ. Rev.*, March 1984, 24(2), pp. 203–07.

Mills, David E. Demand Fluctuations and Endogenous Firm Flexibility. *J. Ind. Econ.*, September 1984, 33(1), pp. 55–71.

Mirucki, Jean. Vérification des conditions d'efficacité dans les décisions de production à partir de l'hypothèse Averch-Johnson: étude de cas. (With English summary.) *Rev. Econ. Ind.*, 4th Trimester 1984, (30), pp. 60–76.

[G: Canada]

Mitchell, Thomas M. A Functional Equation Approach to the Theory of Production, Technical Change, and Invariance. *Z. Nationalökon.*, 1984, 44(2), pp. 177–87.

Mitra, Tapan and Ray, Debraj. Dynamic Optimization on a Non-convex Feasible Set: Some General Results for Non-smooth Technologies. *Z. Nationalökon.*, 1984, 44(2), pp. 151–75.

Miyazaki, Hajime. Internal Bargaining, Labor Contracts, and a Marshallian Theory of the Firm. *Amer. Econ. Rev.*, June 1984, 74(3), pp. 381–93.

Miyazaki, Hajime. On Success and Dissolution of the Labor-Managed Firm in the Capitalist Economy. *J. Polit. Econ.*, October 1984, 92(5), pp. 909–31.

Mosler, Karl Clemens. Location Theory of the Firm Facing Uncertain Prices and Transport Rates. In *[Beckmann, M. J.]*, 1984, pp. 163–74.

Moss, Scott J. The History of the Theory of the Firm from Marshall to Robinson and Chamberlin: The Source of Positivism in Economics. *Economica*, August 1984, 51(203), pp. 307–18.

Muysken, Joan. Overhead Labour and Bounded Substitutability. *De Economist*, 1984, 132(4), pp. 440–50.

Neggers, Joseph and Ingólfsson, Ketill. Estimates of the Horizon in Mathematical Models of Marketing. *Math. Soc. Sci.*, April 1984, 7(2), pp. 199–204.

Nguyen, Dung. Adjustment Costs and Theory of Investment under Uncertainty. *J. Econ. Bus.*, August 1984, 36(3), pp. 307–21.

Odagiri, Hiroyuki. The Firm as a Collection of Human Resources. In *Wiles, P. and Routh, G., eds.*, 1984, pp. 190–206.

Özol, Cengiz. Parable and Realism in Production Theory: The Surrogate Wage Function. *Can. J. Econ.*, May 1984, 17(2), pp. 353–68.

Pagano, Ugo. Welfare, Productivity, and Self-management. *Econ. Notes*, 1984, (3), pp. 5–20.

Persky, A. L. Stochastically Separable Production Functions: Comment [Stochastic Production and Cost]. *Southern Econ. J.*, January 1984, 50(3), pp. 902–03.

Picot, Arnold. Specificity, Specialization, and Coalitions: Comment. *Z. ges. Staatswiss.*, March 1984, 140(1), pp. 50–53.

Punzo, Lionello F. and Velupillai, Kumaraswamy. Multisectoral Models and Joint Production. In *van der Ploeg, F., ed.*, 1984, pp. 57–92.

Putterman, Louis. On Some Recent Explanations of Why Capital Hires Labor. *Econ. Inquiry*, April 1984, 22(2), pp. 171–87.

Quiggin, John and Bui-Lan, Anh. The Use of Cross-Sectional Estimates of Profit Functions for Tests of Relative Efficiency: A Critical Review. *Australian J. Agr. Econ.*, April 1984, 28(1), pp. 44–55.

Raymon, Neil. Changing Input Costs in Competitive Markets with Variable Quality. *J. Econ. Bus.*, December 1984, 36(4), pp. 403–13.

Rees, Ray. A Positive Theory of the Public Enterprise. In *Marchand, M.; Pestieau, P. and Tulkens, H., eds.*, 1984, pp. 179–91.

Robinson, Austin. Whatever Happened to the Full-Cost Principle (UK)? Comment. In *Wiles, P. and Routh, G., eds.*, 1984, pp. 222–32.

Romero, Hector Guillén. Marx, Sraffa and the Neo-Classicals in Context. In *Mandel, E. and Freeman, A., eds.*, 1984, pp. 85–113.

Rossana, Robert J. A Model of the Demand for Investment in Inventories of Finished Goods and Employment. *Int. Econ. Rev.*, October 1984, 25(3), pp. 731–41.

Sampson, Anthony A. The Demand for Capital Goods by the Quantity Constrained Firm. *Oxford Econ. Pap.*, June 1984, 36(2), pp. 232–40.

Sandelin, Bo. Några "oneoklassiska" resultati neoklassisk investeringsteori. (Some "Non-Neoclassical" Results in Neoclassical Investment Theory. With English summary.) *Ekon. Samfundets Tidskr.*, 1984, 37(2), pp. 89–102.

Sav, G. Thomas. The Engineering Approach to Economic Production Functions Revisited: An Application to Solar Processes. *J. Ind. Econ.*, September 1984, 33(1), pp. 21–35. [G: U.S.]

Savran, Sungur. The Negation of 'Negative Values.' In *Mandel, E. and Freeman, A., eds.*, 1984, pp. 211–19.

Schankerman, Mark and Nadiri, M. Ishaq. Investment in R&D, Costs of Adjustment, and Expectations. In *Griliches, Z., ed.*, 1984, pp. 315–38. [G: U.S.]

Scherer, Frederic M. Measuring Surplus Attributable to Differentiated Products: Reply. *J. Ind. Econ.*, September 1984, 33(1), pp. 133.

Scherer, Frederic M. Research and Development Resource Allocation under Rivalry. In *Scherer, F. M.*, 1984, pp. 83–119.

Scherer, Frederic M. The Microeconomics of Decision Making for Innovation. In *Scherer, F. M.*, 1984, pp. 120–29.

Scherer, Frederic M. The Welfare Economics of Product Variety: An Application to the Ready-to-Eat Cereals Industry. In *Scherer, F. M.*, 1984, 1979, pp. 142–67. [G: U.S.]

Schlicht, Ekkehart. Plant Closings, Worker Reallocation Costs and Efficiency Gains to Labor Representation on Board of Directors: Comment. *Z. ges. Staatswiss.*, March 1984, 140(1), pp. 193–94.

Schmidt, Peter J. and Lin, Tsai-Fen. Simple Tests of Alternative Specifications in Stochastic Frontier Models. *J. Econometrics*, March 1984, 24(3), pp. 349–61.

Schutte, David Peter. Optimal Inventories and Equilibrium Price Behavior. *J. Econ. Theory*, June 1984, 33(1), pp. 46–58.

Sen, Amartya. On Some Debates in Capital Theory. In *Sen, A.*, 1984, 1974, pp. 162–71.

Sertel, Murat R. and Steinherr, Alfred. Information, Incentives, and the Design of Efficient

Institutions. *Z. ges. Staatswiss.*, June 1984, *140*(2), pp. 233–46.

Sessa, Carmen. Sobre la versión stock de la teoría de la producción. (On the Version Stock of Production Theory. With English summary.) *Económica*, January-April 1984, *30*(1), pp. 119–27.

Shaffer, Sherrill. Regulation and Risk Preferences. *J. Ind. Econ.*, March 1984, *32*(3), pp. 349–57.

Shaffer, Sherrill. Scale Economies in Multiproduct Firms. *Bull. Econ. Res.*, May 1984, *36*(1), pp. 51–58. [G: U.S.]

Shaffer, Sherrill. Selective Cost-reducing Innovation. *Rev. Ind. Organ.*, Fall 1984, *1*(3), pp. 240–45.

Shaked, Avner and Sutton, John. Involuntary Unemployment as a Perfect Equilibrium in a Bargaining Model. *Econometrica*, November 1984, *52*(6), pp. 1351–64.

Shieh, Yeung-Nan and Mai, Chao-cheng. Location and the Theory of Production: Clarifications and Extensions. *Reg. Sci. Urban Econ.*, May 1984, *14*(2), pp. 199–218.

Shumway, C. Richard; Pope, Rulon D. and Nash, Elizabeth K. Allocatable Fixed Inputs and Jointness in Agricultural Production: Implications for Economic Modeling. *Amer. J. Agr. Econ.*, February 1984, *66*(1), pp. 72–78.

Smith, Stephen C. Does Employment Matter to the Labour-managed Firm? Some Theory and an Empirical Illustration. *Econ. Anal. Worker's Manage.*, 1984, *18*(4), pp. 303–18. [G: U.S.; Italy]

Soete, Luc and Turner, Roy. Technology Diffusion and the Rate of Technical Change. *Econ. J.*, September 1984, *94*(375), pp. 612–23.

Spremann, Klaus. A Firm in Statu Nascendi—Initial and Final Shareholders. In *Bamberg, G. and Spremann, K.*, eds., 1984, pp. 103–21.

Stewart, Geoff. Labour-managed Firms and Monopsony Power. *Int. J. Ind. Organ.*, March 1984, *2*(1), pp. 63–74.

Stowe, John D. and Ingene, Charles A. Microeconomic Influences on Operating Leverage. *J. Econ. Bus.*, May 1984, *36*(2), pp. 233–41.

Tawada, Makoto and Abe, Kenzo. Production Possibilities and International Trade with a Public Intermediate Good. *Can. J. Econ.*, May 1984, *17*(2), pp. 232–48.

Taylor, C. Robert. Stochastic Dynamic Duality: Theory and Empirical Applicability. *Amer. J. Agr. Econ.*, August 1984, *66*(3), pp. 351–57.

Todd, Douglas. Productive Performance in the Firm: The Economic Approach. In *Pickering, J. F. and Cockerill, T. A. J.*, eds., 1984, pp. 101–31. [G: Ireland]

Toker, Mehmet Ayhan. A Note on the 'Negative' Quantities of Embodied Labour. *Econ. J.*, March 1984, *94*(373), pp. 149–54.

Varian, Hal R. The Nonparametric Approach to Production Analysis. *Econometrica*, May 1984, *52*(3), pp. 579–97.

Vickers, Douglas. The Uncertainty about Uncertainty: A Paradigmatic Comment on *Professor*

Weiss' Theory of the Firm: Capital Markets, Output, and the Demand for Inputs under Uncertainty. *Eastern Econ. J.*, January-March 1984, *10*(1), pp. 71–77.

Waldman, Michael. Job Assignments, Signalling, and Efficiency. *Rand J. Econ.*, Summer 1984, *15*(2), pp. 255–67.

Waldman, Michael. Worker Allocation, Hierarchies and the Wage Distribution. *Rev. Econ. Stud.*, January 1984, *51*(1), pp. 95–109.

Wang, Leonard F. S. and Bowles, David. Demand Uncertainty, Risk Aversion and the Labour-Managed Firm. *J. Econ. Stud.*, 1984, *11*(1), pp. 49–54.

Weiss, Andrew and Landau, Henry J. Wages, Hiring Standards, and Firm Size. *J. Lab. Econ.*, October 1984, *2*(4), pp. 477–99. [G: U.S.]

Weiss, Nitzan. Capital Markets, Output, and the Demand for Inputs under Uncertainty. *Eastern Econ. J.*, January-March 1984, *10*(1), pp. 51–69.

Weiss, Nitzan. Reply to a Paradigmatic Comment: Capital Markets, Output, and the Demand for Inputs under Uncertainty. *Eastern Econ. J.*, January-March 1984, *10*(1), pp. 79–85.

Wildasin, David E. The *q* Theory of Investment with Many Capital Goods. *Amer. Econ. Rev.*, March 1984, *74*(1), pp. 203–10.

Wildman, Steven S. A Note on Measuring Surplus Attributable to Differentiated Products. *J. Ind. Econ.*, September 1984, *33*(1), pp. 123–32.

Wiles, Peter. Whatever Happened to the Full-Cost Principle (UK)? In *Wiles, P. and Routh, G.*, eds., 1984, pp. 211–21.

Williams, Edward E. and Findlay, M. Chapman, III. Corporate Governance: A Problem of Hierarchies and Self Interest. *Amer. J. Econ. Soc.*, January 1984, *43*(1), pp. 19–36.

Wolfstetter, Elmar; Brown, Murray and Meran, Georg. Optimal Employment and Risk Sharing in Illyria: The Labor Managed Firm Reconsidered. *Z. ges. Staatswiss.*, December 1984, *140*(4), pp. 655–68.

Wolken, John D. and Navratil, Frank J. The Valuation of Subsidies in Kind and Their Effects on Costs. *J. Econ. Bus.*, May 1984, *36*(2), pp. 217–32. [G: U.S.]

Wong, Robert E. and Fan, Yiu-Kwan. Capital Accumulation and Financing Programs in a Neoclassical Investment Model. *Atlantic Econ. J.*, July 1984, *12*(2), pp. 3–11.

Wright, Brian D. The Effects of Price Uncertainty on the Factor Choices of the Competitive Firm. *Southern Econ. J.*, October 1984, *51*(2), pp. 443–55.

Ylä-Liedenpohja, Jouko. On Investment Incentives and Allocational Implications of Corporate Income Taxation. *Liiketaloudellinen Aikak.*, 1984, *33*(3), pp. 264–302. [G: Finland]

Zieschang, Kimberly D. An Extended Farrell Technical Efficiency Measure. *J. Econ. Theory*, August 1984, *33*(2), pp. 387–96.

Zorn, Thomas S. The Allocative Effect of Nonbinding Price Controls. *Econ. Inquiry*, January 1984, *22*(1), pp. 136–41.

0224 Theory of Factor Distribution and Distributive Shares

Albarracén, Jesus. Constant Returns and Uniform Profit Rates: Two False Assumptions. In *Mandel, E. and Freeman, A.*, eds., 1984, pp. 177–209.

Antipova, O. N. and Golosov, V. V. Ideas of Profit and Interest. In *Smirnov, A. D.; Golosov, V. V. and Maximova, V. F.*, eds., 1984, pp. 88–109.

Bennett, John. A Model of Income Distribution in a Revenue-sharing Firm. *J. Compar. Econ.*, September 1984, 8(3), pp. 237–46.

Bird, Ronald. On Recent Misinterpretations of Pareto's Theory of Rent. *Indian Econ. J.*, April–June 1984, 31(4), pp. 25–34.

Dobb, Maurice. A Note on Distribution and the Price Mark-Up. In *Foster, J. B. and Szlajfer, H.*, eds., 1984, 1973, pp. 85–90.

Duménil, Gérard and Lévy, Dominique. The Unifying Formalism of Domination: Value, Price, Distribution, and Growth in Joint Production. *Z. Nationalökon.*, 1984, 44(4), pp. 349–71.

Farjoun, Emmanuel. The Production of Commodities by Means of What? In *Mandel, E. and Freeman, A.*, eds., 1984, pp. 11–41.

Freeman, Alan. The Logic of the Transformation Problem. In *Mandel, E. and Freeman, A.*, eds., 1984, pp. 221–64.

Funke, Michael. Technikwahl und Profitrate. Ein kritischer Überblick über die augenblickliche Diskussion zum "Gesetz vom tendenziellen Fall der Profitrate." (With English summary.) *Z. Wirtschaft. Sozialwissen.*, 1984, 104(3), pp. 307–25.

Garagnani, Pierangelo. On Some Illusory Instances of "Marginal Products." *Metroecon.*, June-Oct. 1984, 36(2–3), pp. 143–60.

Gibson, Bill. Profit and Rent in a Classical Theory of Exhaustible and Renewable Resources. *Z. Nationalökon.*, 1984, 44(2), pp. 131–49.

Giussani, Paulo. Labour-Power: The Missing Commodity. In *Mandel, E. and Freeman, A.*, eds., 1984, pp. 115–40.

von Hayek, Friedrich A. Some Remarks on the Problem of Imputation. In *von Hayek, F. A. (II)*, 1984, 1926, pp. 33–54.

Karpikov, E. I. and Pikin, A. S. Bourgeois and Reformist Agrarian Conceptions. In *Smirnov, A. D.; Golosov, V. V. and Maximova, V. F.*, eds., 1984, pp. 110–17.

Kubin, Ingrid. Equilibrium and Stability Analysis in the Classical Framework. *Metroecon.*, February 1984, 36(1), pp. 47–64.

Langston, Robert H. A New Approach to the Relation between Prices and Values. In *Mandel, E. and Freeman, A.*, eds., 1984, pp. 1–10.

Mandel, Ernest. Gold, Money and the Transformation Problem. In *Mandel, E. and Freeman, A.*, eds., 1984, pp. 141–63.

Münker, Horst. Reallohn und Marktmacht. (Real Wages and Market Power. With English summary.) *Jahr. Nationalökon. Statist.*, March 1984, 199(2), pp. 123–44.

Murrell, Peter. Incentives and Income under Market Socialism. *J. Compar. Econ.*, September 1984, 8(3), pp. 261–76.

Nairay, Alain. Asymptotic Behavior and Optimal Properties of a Consumption–Investment Model with Variable Time Preference. *J. Econ. Dynam. Control*, September 1984, 7(3), pp. 283–313.

Ostroy, Joseph M. A Reformulation of the Marginal Productivity Theory of Distribution. *Econometrica*, May 1984, 52(3), pp. 599–630.

Romero, Hector Guillén. Marx, Sraffa and the Neo-Classicals in Context. In *Mandel, E. and Freeman, A.*, eds., 1984, pp. 85–113.

Salama, Pierre. Value and Price of Production: A Differential Approach. In *Mandel, E. and Freeman, A.*, eds., 1984, pp. 165–76.

Samuelson, Larry. Returns to Scale and Wicksell's Missing Equation: A Note. *Hist. Polit. Econ.*, Winter 1984, 16(4), pp. 577–82.

Saposnik, Rubin. Efficiency and Equality in a Simple Neoclassical Economy. *Southern Econ. J.*, October 1984, 51(2), pp. 588–93.

Sattinger, Michael. Factor Pricing in the Assignment Problem. *Scand. J. Econ.*, 1984, 86(1), pp. 17–34.

Shaikh, Anwar. The Transformation from Marx to Sraffa. In *Mandel, E. and Freeman, A.*, eds., 1984, pp. 43–84.

Steedman, Ian. Natural Prices, Differential Profit Rates and the Classical Competitive Process. *Manchester Sch. Econ. Soc. Stud.*, June 1984, 52(2), pp. 123–40.

Waldman, Michael. Worker Allocation, Hierarchies and the Wage Distribution. *Rev. Econ. Stud.*, January 1984, 51(1), pp. 95–109.

0225 Theory of Firm and Industry under Competitive Market Structure

Afxentiou, Panayotis C. The Envelope Curve and Market Structure: A Pedagogical Note. *Econ. Notes*, 1984, (3), pp. 31–46.

Allen, Franklin. Reputation and Product Quality. *Rand J. Econ.*, Autumn 1984, 15(3), pp. 311–27.

Beuthe, Michel; Eeckhoudt, Louis and Lefoll, Jean. Production Uncertainty and the Market Equilibrium of the Competitive Firm. *Europ. Econ. Rev.*, October–November 1984, 26(1–2), pp. 1–11.

Borooah, Vani K. Theory of the Firm. In *van der Ploeg, F.*, ed., 1984, pp. 289–314.

Bryant, John. Sunk Cost, "Contestable" Markets, and Long-Term Contracts. *Public Finance Quart.*, July 1984, 12(3), pp. 385–87.

Chilton, John. The Pricing of Durable Exhaustible Resources: Comment. *Quart. J. Econ.*, August 1984, 99(3), pp. 629–37.

Copes, Parzival. The Market as an Open Access Commons: A Neglected Aspect of Excess Capacity. *De Economist*, 1984, 132(1), pp. 49–60.

Cox, James C. and Isaac, R. Mark. In Search of the Winner's Curse. *Econ. Inquiry*, October 1984, 22(4), pp. 579–92.

Cugno, Franco and Montrucchio, Luigi. Teorema della ragnatela, aspettative adattive e dinamiche caotiche. (Cobweb Theorem, Adaptive Expectations and Chaotic Dynamics. With English summary.) *Rivista Int. Sci. Econ. Com.*, August 1984, *31*(8), pp. 713–24.

Daniel, Coldwell, III. Competition, Imperfect Competition, and Dynamic Market Processes. *Amer. J. Econ. Soc.*, July 1984, *43*(3), pp. 301–12.

Eriksson, Göran. Growth, Entry and Exit of Firms. *Scand. J. Econ.*, 1984, *86*(1), pp. 52–67.

Hahn, Robert W. Market Power and Transferable Property Rights. *Quart. J. Econ.*, November 1984, *99*(4), pp. 753–65.

Katz, Eliakim. The Optimal Location of the Competitive Firm under Price Uncertainty. *J. Urban Econ.*, July 1984, *16*(1), pp. 65–75.

Kemp, Murray C. and Long, Ngo Van. The Efficiency of Competitive Markets in a Context of Exhaustible Resources. In *Kemp, M. C. and Long, N. V., eds.*, 1984, *1982*, pp. 219–25.

Lächler, Ulrich. On Optimal Factor Proportions in a Competitive Firm under Factor and Output Price Uncertainty. *Z. Nationalökon.*, 1984, *44*(2), pp. 117–30.

Metcalfe, J. S. Technological Innovation and the Competitive Process. *Greek Econ. Rev.*, December 1984, *6*(3), pp. 287–316.

Mills, David E. Demand Fluctuations and Endogenous Firm Flexibility. *J. Ind. Econ.*, September 1984, *33*(1), pp. 55–71.

Mirman, Leonard J. and Spulber, Daniel F. Uncertainty and Markets for Renewable Resources. *J. Econ. Dynam. Control*, December 1984, *8*(3), pp. 239–64.

Perry, Martin K. Vertical Equilibrium in a Competitive Input Market. *Int. J. Ind. Organ.*, June 1984, *2*(2), pp. 159–70.

Pfouts, Ralph W. Modelling Non-price Competition and Market Share. In *Avula, X. J. R., et al.*, 1984, pp. 795–98.

Raymon, Neil. Changing Input Costs in Competitive Markets with Variable Quality. *J. Econ. Bus.*, December 1984, *36*(4), pp. 403–13.

Salama, Pierre. Value and Price of Production: A Differential Approach. In *Mandel, E. and Freeman, A., eds.*, 1984, pp. 165–76.

Simon, Leo K. Bertrand, the Cournot Paradigm and the Theory of Perfect Competition. *Rev. Econ. Stud.*, April 1984, *51*(2), pp. 209–30.

Waugh, Frederick V. Cobweb Models. In *Waugh, F. V.*, 1984, *1964*, pp. 88–106.

0226 Theory of Firm and Industry under Imperfectly Competitive Market Structures

Afxentiou, Panayotis C. The Envelope Curve and Market Structure: A Pedagogical Note. *Econ. Notes*, 1984, (3), pp. 31–46.

Akerlof, George A. The Market for "Lemons": Quality Uncertainty and the Market Mechanism. In *Akerlof, G. A.*, 1984, *1970*, pp. 7–22. **[G: India]**

Alberts, William W. Do Oligopolists Earn "Non-competitive" Rates of Return? *Amer. Econ. Rev.*, September 1984, *74*(4), pp. 624–32.

Anderson, Ronald W. and Sundaresan, Mahadevan. Futures Markets and Monopoly. In *Anderson, R. W., ed.*, 1984, pp. 75–105.

Aoki, Masahiko. Risk-sharing in the Corporate Group. In *Aoki, M., ed.*, 1984, pp. 259–64.

Baldani, Jeffrey and Masson, Robert T. Economies of Scale, Strategic Advertising and Fully Credible Entry Deterrence. *Rev. Ind. Organ.*, Fall 1984, *1*(3), pp. 190–205.

Baron, David P. and Besanko, David. Regulation and Information in a Continuing Relationship. *Info. Econ. Policy*, 1984, *1*(3), pp. 267–302.

Baron, David P. and Besanko, David. Regulation, Asymmetric Information, and Auditing. *Rand J. Econ.*, Winter 1984, *15*(4), pp. 447–70.

Beato, Paulina and Mas-Colell, Andreu. The Marginal Cost Pricing Rule as a Regulation Mechanism in Mixed Markets. In *Marchand, M.; Pestieau, P. and Tulkens, H., eds.*, 1984, pp. 81–100.

Bennett, John. Alternative Price and Quantity Controls for Regulation under Uncertainty. *Z. Nationalökon.*, 1984, *44*(2), pp. 103–15.

Benoit, Jean-Pierre. Financially Constrained Entry in a Game with Incomplete Information. *Rand J. Econ.*, Winter 1984, *15*(4), pp. 490–99.

Benson, Bruce L. On the Ability of Spatial Competitors to Price Discriminate. *J. Ind. Econ.*, December 1984, *33*(2), pp. 251–55.

Benson, Bruce L. Spatial Competition with Free Entry, Chamberlinian Tangencies, and Social Efficiency. *J. Urban Econ.*, May 1984, *15*(3), pp. 270–86.

Benson, Bruce L. The Level of Average Production Cost Chosen by a Multiplant Spatial Monopolist. *Reg. Sci. Urban Econ.*, February 1984, *14*(1), pp. 37–44.

Bental, Benjamin and Spiegel, Menahem. Horizontal Product Differentiation, Prices and Quantity Selection of a Multi-product Monopolist. *Int. J. Ind. Organ.*, June 1984, *2*(2), pp. 99–104.

Bernheim, B. Douglas. Strategic Deterrence of Sequential Entry into an Industry. *Rand J. Econ.*, Spring 1984, *15*(1), pp. 1–11.

Bhattacharya, Gautam. Learning and the Behavior of Potential Entrants. *Rand J. Econ.*, Summer 1984, *15*(2), pp. 281–89.

Blair, Roger D. and Cheng, Leonard. On Dumping. *Southern Econ. J.*, January 1984, *50*(3), pp. 857–65.

Bond, Eric W. and Samuelson, Larry. Durable Good Monopolies with Rational Expectations and Replacement Sales. *Rand J. Econ.*, Autumn 1984, *15*(3), pp. 336–45.

Borooah, Vani K. Theory of the Firm. In *van der Ploeg, F., ed.*, 1984, pp. 289–314.

Bös, Dieter; Tillmann, Georg and Zimmermann, Hans-Georg. Bureaucratic Public Enterprises. *Z. Nationalökon.*, Supplement 1984, pp. 127–76. **[G: U.K.]**

Bowes, Marianne. Profit-Maximizing vs. Optimal

Behavior in a Spatial Setting: Summary and Extensions. *Southern Econ. J.*, January 1984, *50*(3), pp. 680–89.

Boyer, Marcel; Kihlstrom, Richard E. and Laffont, Jean-Jacques. Market Determinants of Misleading Advertising. In *Boyer, M. and Kihlstrom, R. E., eds.*, 1984, pp. 241–70.

Boyer, Marcel and Moreaux, Michel. Equilibres de duopole et variations conjecturales rationnelles. (Duopoly Equilibria and Rational Conjectural Variations. With English summary.) *Can. J. Econ.*, February 1984, *17*(1), pp. 111–25.

Brander, James A. and Eaton, Jonathan. Product Line Rivalry. *Amer. Econ. Rev.*, June 1984, *74*(3), pp. 323–34.

Brander, James A. and Spencer, Barbara J. Tariff Protection and Imperfect Competition. In *Kierzkowski, H., ed.*, 1984, pp. 194–206.

Bruni, Franco. Monopolistic Competition, Fixed Real Wages and Aggregate Supply. *Rivista Int. Sci. Econ. Com.*, December 1984, *31*(12), pp. 1168–85.

Bryant, John. Sunk Cost, "Contestable" Markets, and Long-Term Contracts. *Public Finance Quart.*, July 1984, *12*(3), pp. 385–87.

Calem, Paul S. and Spulber, Daniel F. Multiproduct Two Part Tariffs. *Int. J. Ind. Organ.*, June 1984, *2*(2), pp. 105–15.

Casarosa, Carlo. Il prezzo minimo nel duopolio di Edgeworth. (With English summary.) *Econ. Polit.*, April 1984, *1*(1), pp. 63–78.

Casey, William L., Jr. and Kaushik, Surendra K. The Improper Derivation of Marginal Revenue in Kinky Oligopoly Models: A Reply [The Kinked-Demand Model of Oligopoly: Textbook Departures from the Original Sweezy Model]. *Amer. Econ.*, Fall 1984, *28*(2), pp. 89.

Casson, Mark. The Theory of Vertical Integration: A Survey and Synthesis. *J. Econ. Stud.*, 1984, *11*(2), pp. 3–43.

Chichilnisky, Graciela and Heal, Geoffrey. Patterns of Power: Bargaining and Incentives in Two-Person Games. *J. Public Econ.*, April 1984, *23*(3), pp. 333–49.

Chilton, John. The Pricing of Durable Exhaustible Resources: Comment. *Quart. J. Econ.*, August 1984, *99*(3), pp. 629–37.

Chung, Kwang S. Forward Integration by a Monopolist: Some Extensions. *Southern Econ. J.*, January 1984, *50*(3), pp. 690–710.

Clarke, Darral G. and Dolan, Robert J. A Simulation Analysis of Alternative Pricing Strategies for Dynamic Environments. *J. Bus.*, Part 2, January 1984, *57*(1), pp. S179–200.

Clarke, R. A Note on Revenue-maximising Oligopoly. *J. Econ. Stud.*, 1984, *11*(3), pp. 62–65.

Clarke, Richard N. Scale Economies, Entry, and Welfare. *J. Econ. Bus.*, May 1984, *36*(2), pp. 161–76.

Comanor, William S. and Frech, H. E., III. Strategic Behavior and Antitrust Analysis. *Amer. Econ. Rev.*, May 1984, *74*(2), pp. 372–76.

Conlisk, John; Gerstner, Eitan and Sobel, Joel. Cyclic Pricing by a Durable Goods Monopolist.

Quart. J. Econ., August 1984, *99*(3), pp. 489–505.

Cooper, Russell. On Allocative Distortions in Problems of Self-Selection. *Rand J. Econ.*, Winter 1984, *15*(4), pp. 568–77.

Corcoran, William J. Long-Run Equilibrium and Total Expenditures in Rent-Seeking. *Public Choice*, 1984, *43*(1), pp. 89–94.

Coughlin, Peter J. Changes in Marginal Revenue and Related Elasticities. *Southern Econ. J.*, October 1984, *51*(2), pp. 568–73.

Cremer, Jacques. On the Economics of Repeat Buying. *Rand J. Econ.*, Autumn 1984, *15*(3), pp. 396–403.

Daniel, Coldwell, III. Competition, Imperfect Competition, and Dynamic Market Processes. *Amer. J. Econ. Soc.*, July 1984, *43*(3), pp. 301–12.

Dansby, Robert E. and Conrad, Cecilia A. Commodity Bundling. *Amer. Econ. Rev.*, May 1984, *74*(2), pp. 377–81.

Danziger, Leif. Stochastic Inflation and the Optimal Policy of Price Adjustment. *Econ. Inquiry*, January 1984, *22*(1), pp. 98–108.

Daughety, Andrew F. Regulation and Industrial Organization. *J. Polit. Econ.*, October 1984, *92*(5), pp. 932–53.

Davidson, Carl and Deneckere, Raymond. Horizontal Mergers and Collusive Behavior. *Int. J. Ind. Organ.*, June 1984, *2*(2), pp. 117–32.

DeCanio, Stephen J. Delivered Pricing and Multiple Basing Point Equilibria: A Reevaluation. *Quart. J. Econ.*, May 1984, *99*(2), pp. 329–49.

Demsetz, Harold. Purchasing Monopoly. In *Colander,D.C.,ed.*,1984,pp.101–13.

Dickens, William T. Occupational Safety and Health Regulation and Economic Theory. In *Darity, W., Jr.,ed.*,1984,pp.133–73.   **[G: U.S.]**

DiLorenzo, Thomas J. Corporate Management, Property Rights and the X-istence of X-inefficiency: Reply. *Southern Econ. J.*, April 1984, *50*(4), pp. 1209–13.

Dixit, Avinash. Growth and Terms of Trade under Imperfect Competition. In *Kierzkowski, H., ed.*, 1984, pp. 109–23.

Dobb, Maurice. A Note on Distribution and the Price Mark-Up. In *Foster, J. B. and Szlajfer, H., eds.*, 1984, *1973*, pp. 85–90.

Dohner, Robert S. Export Pricing, Flexible Exchange Rates, and Divergence in the Prices of Traded Goods. *J. Int. Econ.*, February 1984, *16*(1/2), pp. 79–101.

Donnenfeld, Shabtai. Domestic Price Regulation and the Exporting Monopolist. *Oxford Econ. Pap.*, June 1984, *36*(2), pp. 285–87.

Donsimoni, Marie-Paule; Geroski, Paul A. and Jacquemin, Alexis. Concentration Indices and Market Power: Two Views. *J. Ind. Econ.*, June 1984, *32*(4), pp. 419–34.

Dowell, Richard. Asset Salvageability and the Potential for Trade Restraint through Merger. *Rand J. Econ.*, Winter 1984, *15*(4), pp. 537–45.

Drèze, Jacques H. Second-best Analysis with Markets in Disequilibrium: Public Sector Pricing in a Keynesian Regime. In *Marchand, M.; Pestieau, P. and Tulkens, H., eds.*, 1984, pp. 45–79.

Drèze, Jacques H. and Sheshinski, Eytan. On Industry Equilibrium under Uncertainty. *J. Econ. Theory*, June 1984, 33(1), pp. 88–97.

Eaton, Jonathan and Kierzkowski, Henryk. Oligopolistic Competition, Product Variety, and International Trade. In *Kierzkowski, H., ed.*, 1984, pp. 69–83.

Eaton, Jonathan and Kierzkowski, Henryk. Oligopolistic Competition, Product Variety, Entry Deterrence, and Technology Transfer. *Rand J. Econ.*, Spring 1984, 15(1), pp. 99–107.

Economides, Nicholas S. The Principle of Minimum Differentiation Revisited. *Europ. Econ. Rev.*, April 1984, 24(3), pp. 345–68.

Endres, Alfred. Optimale Produktvariation. (Optimal Product Variation. With English summary.) *Jahr. Nationalökon. Statist.*, November 1984, 199(6), pp. 557–74.

Farber, Stephen C. Cyclical Price Flexibility: A Test of Administered Pricing. *J. Ind. Econ.*, June 1984, 32(4), pp. 465–76. [G: U.S.]

Feinberg, Robert M. Mutual Forebearance as an Extension of Oligopoly Theory. *J. Econ. Bus.*, May 1984, 36(2), pp. 243–49.

Feldman, David H. and Tower, Edward. Profitable Destabilizing Speculation as Intertemporal Price Discrimination. *Amer. Econ.*, Fall 1984, 28(2), pp. 60–63.

Fershtman, Chaim. Goodwill and Market Shares in Oligopoly. *Economica*, August 1984, 51(203), pp. 271–81.

Findlay, Ronald and Wellisz, Stanislaw. Toward a Model of Endogenous Rent-Seeking. In *Colander, D. C., ed.*, 1984, pp. 89–100.

Fine, Ben and Murfin, Andy. The Political Economy of Monopoly and Competition: A Critique of Monopoly and Stagnation Theory. *Int. J. Ind. Organ.*, June 1984, 2(2), pp. 133–46.

Formby, John P. and Smith, W. James. Collusion, Entry, and Market Shares. *Rev. Ind. Organ.*, Spring 1984, 1(1), pp. 15–25.

Frantz, Roger S. Corporate Management, Property Rights and the X-istence of X-inefficiency: Comment. *Southern Econ. J.*, April 1984, 50(4), pp. 1204–08.

Fried, Dov. Incentives for Information Production and Disclosure in a Duopolistic Environment. *Quart. J. Econ.*, May 1984, 99(2), pp. 367–81.

Friedman, James W. Comments on "A Simulation Analysis of Alternative Pricing Strategies for Dynamic Environments." *J. Bus.*, Part 2, January 1984, 57(1), pp. S201–04.

Fudenberg, Drew and Tirole, Jean. The Fat-Cat Effect, the Puppy-Dog Ploy, and the Lean and Hungry Look. *Amer. Econ. Rev.*, May 1984, 74(2), pp. 361–66.

Gal-Or, Esther. Price Dispersion with Uncertain Demand. *Int. Econ. Rev.*, June 1984, 25(2), pp. 441–57.

Gallini, Nancy T. Deterrence by Market Sharing: A Strategic Incentive for Licensing. *Amer.*

Econ. Rev., December 1984, 74(5), pp. 931–41.

Geroski, Paul A. The Incidence of Entry in Three Oligopoly Models. *Economica*, August 1984, 51(203), pp. 283–93.

Geroski, Paul A. and Jacquemin, Alexis. Dominant Firms and Their Alleged Decline. *Int. J. Ind. Organ.*, March 1984, 2(1), pp. 1–27.

Ghemawat, Pankaj. Capacity Expansion in the Titanium Dioxide Industry. *J. Ind. Econ.*, December 1984, 33(2), pp. 145–63. [G: U.S.]

Gilbert, Richard J. and Harris, Richard G. Competition with Lumpy Investment. *Rand J. Econ.*, Summer 1984, 15(2), pp. 197–212.

Gilbert, Richard J. and Newbery, David M. G. Uncertain Innovation and the Persistence of Monopoly: Comment. *Amer. Econ. Rev.*, March 1984, 74(1), pp. 238–42.

Glazer, A. The Client Relationship and a "Just" Price. *Amer. Econ. Rev.*, December 1984, 74(5), pp. 1089–95.

Golosov, V. V.; Matveev, V. P. and Korneeva, K. G. The Interpretation of Monopoly Capitalism. In *Smirnov, A. D.; Golosov, V. V. and Maximova, V. F., eds.*, 1984, pp. 137–70.

Gorham, Abby H. Imperfect Price Adjustment, Controlled Price and Multimarket Rationing Models: Their Potential Application to the Modelling of Trade in King and Tanner Crab Products. In *Avula, X. J. R., et al.*, 1984, pp. 837–43.

Gould, John P. Comments on "Firm-Specific Differentiation and Competition among Multiproduct Firms." *J. Bus.*, Part 2, January 1984, 57(1), pp. S173–77.

Gravelle, Hugh S. E. Bargaining and Efficiency in Public and Private Sector Firms. In *Marchand, M.; Pestieau, P. and Tulkens, H., eds.*, 1984, pp. 193–220.

Green, Edward J. and Porter, Robert H. Noncooperative Collusion under Imperfect Price Information. *Econometrica*, January 1984, 52(1), pp. 87–100.

Grossman, Gene M. and Shapiro, Carl. Informative Advertising with Differentiated Products. *Rev. Econ. Stud.*, January 1984, 51(1), pp. 63–81.

Hahn, Robert W. Market Power and Transferable Property Rights. *Quart. J. Econ.*, November 1984, 99(4), pp. 753–65.

Hall, William P. The Learning Curve, Demand Growth, and Market Concentration. *Int. J. Ind. Organ.*, June 1984, 2(2), pp. 147–57.

Hanjoul, Pierre and Thisse, Jacques-François. The Location of a Firm on a Network. In *Hughes Hallet, A.J., ed.*, 1984, pp. 289–326.

Harrington, Joseph E., Jr. Noncooperative Behavior by a Cartel as an Entry-deterring Signal. *Rand J. Econ.*, Autumn 1984, 15(3), pp. 426–33.

Hayes, James. Futures Markets and Monopoly Comment. In *Anderson, R. W., ed.*, 1984, pp. 109–12.

Helpman, Elhanan. Increasing Returns, Imperfect Markets, and Trade Theory. In *Jones, R. W. and Kenen, P., eds.*, 1984, pp. 325–65.

Helpman, Elhanan and Razin, Assaf. Increasing Returns, Monopolistic Competition, and Factor Movements: A Welfare Analysis. In *Kierzkowski, H., ed., 1984, 1983*, pp. 124–36.

Hillman, Arye L. Preemptive Rent Seeking and the Social Cost of Monopoly Power. *Int. J. Ind. Organ.*, September 1984, *2*(3), pp. 277–81.

Hillman, Arye L. and Katz, Eliakim. Risk-Averse Rent Seekers and the Social Cost of Monopoly Power. *Econ. J.*, March 1984, *94*(373), pp. 104–10.

Hollander, Abraham. Market Structure and Performance in Intellectual Property: The Case of Copyright Collectives. *Int. J. Ind. Organ.*, September 1984, *2*(3), pp. 199–216.

Honkapohja, Seppo. On the Design of Bilateral Contracts. *Europ. Econ. Rev.*, October–November 1984, *26*(1–2), pp. 55–71.

Horowitz, Ira. Market Growth, Demand Uncertainty, and Potential Entry. *Quart. Rev. Econ. Bus.*, Summer 1984, *24*(2), pp. 33–40.

Horowitz, Ira. On the Use and Nonuse of Entry Deterrents. *J. Econ. Bus.*, December 1984, *36*(4), pp. 371–89.

Howroyd, T. D. and Russell, A. M. Cournot Oligopoly Models with Time Delays. *J. Math. Econ.*, October 1984, *13*(2), pp. 97–103.

Hwang, Hong. Intra-Industry Trade and Oligopoly: A Conjectural Variations Approach. *Can. J. Econ.*, February 1984, *17*(1), pp. 126–37.

Ireland, Norman J. Dual Equilibria and Discontinuous Response in Monopolistic Competition with Two Classes of Consumers. *Rand J. Econ.*, Autumn 1984, *15*(3), pp. 377–84.

Jeuland, Abel. Comments on "Gaussian Demand and Commodity Bundling." *J. Bus.*, Part 2, January 1984, *57*(1), pp. S231–34.

Kalish, Shlomo. Comments on "A Simulation Analysis of Alternative Pricing Strategies in a Dynamic Environment." *J. Bus.*, Part 2, January 1984, *57*(1), pp. S205–09.

Kamien, Morton I. and Tauman, Yair. The Private Value of a Patent: A Game Theoretic Analysis. *Z. Nationalökon.*, Supplement 1984, pp. 93–118.

Karp, Larry. Optimality and Consistency in a Differential Game with Non-renewable Resources. *J. Econ. Dynam. Control*, October 1984, *8*(1), pp. 73–97.

Katsoulacos, Y. Product Innovation and Employment. *Europ. Econ. Rev.*, October–November 1984, *26*(1–2), pp. 83–108.

Katz, Michael L. Firm-Specific Differentiation and Competition among Multiproduct Firms. *J. Bus.*, Part 2, January 1984, *57*(1), pp. S149–66.

Katz, Michael L. Nonuniform Pricing with Unobservable Numbers of Purchases. *Rev. Econ. Stud.*, July 1984, *51*(3), pp. 461–70.

Katz, Michael L. Price Discrimination and Monopolistic Competition. *Econometrica*, November 1984, *52*(6), pp. 1453–71.

Kihlstrom, Richard E. and Mirman, Leonard J. Market Experience and Accurate Price Expectations. In *Boyer, M. and Kihlstrom, R. E., eds.*, 1984, pp. 271–78.

Koutsoyiannis, Anna. Goals of Oligopolistic Firms: An Empirical Test of Competing Hypotheses. *Southern Econ. J.*, October 1984, *51*(2), pp. 540–67.   [G: U.S.]

Krugman, Paul R. Import Protection as Export Promotion: International Competition in the Presence of Oligopoly and Economics of Scale. In *Kierzkowski, H., ed.*, 1984, pp. 180–93.

Kudrle, Robert Thomas. Excise Tax Incidence in Limit Price Oligopoly. *Public Finance*, 1984, *39*(3), pp. 321–46.

Kwoka, John E., Jr. Output and Allocative Efficiency under Second-Degree Price Discrimination. *Econ. Inquiry*, April 1984, *22*(2), pp. 282–86.

La Croix, Sumner J. Marketing, Price Discrimination, and Welfare: Reply. *Southern Econ. J.*, January 1984, *50*(3), pp. 900–901.   [G: U.S.]

LaFrance, Jeffrey T.; Schmitz, Andrew and Zilberman, David. Small Leading Firms. *Econ. Rec.*, June 1984, *60*(169), pp. 160–64.

Lambson, Val Eugene. Self-enforcing Collusion in Large Dynamic Markets. *J. Econ. Theory*, December 1984, *34*(2), pp. 282–91.

Lancaster, Kelvin. Protection and Product Differentiation. In *Kierzkowski, H., ed.*, 1984, pp. 137–56.

Lee, Frederic S. Full Cost Pricing: A New Wine in a New Bottle. *Australian Econ. Pap.*, June 1984, *23*(42), pp. 151–66.

Lee, Frederic S. Whatever Happened to the Full-Cost Principle (USA)? In *Wiles, P. and Routh, G., eds.*, 1984, pp. 233–39.

Lee, Li Way. Franchising and Interbrand Competition. *Southern Econ. J.*, July 1984, *51*(1), pp. 219–34.   [G: U.S.]

Levedahl, J. William. Marketing, Price Discrimination, and Welfare: Comment. *Southern Econ. J.*, January 1984, *50*(3), pp. 886–91.   [G: U.S.]

Lindsay, Cotton M. and Feigenbaum, Bernard. Rationing by Waiting Lists. *Amer. Econ. Rev.*, June 1984, *74*(3), pp. 404–17.   [G: U.K.]

Lombardi, Waldo John. A Note on the Improper Derivation of Marginal Revenue in Kinky Oligopoly Models [The Kinked-Demand Model of Oligopoly: Textbook Departures from the Original Sweezy Model]. *Amer. Econ.*, Fall 1984, *28*(2), pp. 87–88.

Long, John B., Jr. Comments on "Gaussian Demand and Commodity Bundling." *J. Bus.*, Part 2, January 1984, *57*(1), pp. S235–46.

Lyons, Bruce R. The Pattern of International Trade in Differentiated Products: An Incentive for the Existence of Multinational Firms. In *Kierzkowski, H., ed.*, 1984, pp. 157–79.

MacMinn, Richard D.; Morgan, George Emir, III and Smith, Stephen D. Forward Market Equilibrium. *Southern Econ. J.*, July 1984, *51*(1), pp. 41–58.

Mai, Chao-cheng. Location and the Theory of the Imperfectly Competitive Firm under Demand

Uncertainty. *Southern Econ. J.*, April 1984, *50*(4), pp. 1160–70.

Marchand, Maurice; Pestieau, Pierre and Tulkens, Henry. The Performance of Public Enterprises: Normative, Positive and Empirical Issues. In *Marchand, M.; Pestieau, P. and Tulkens, H., eds.*, 1984, pp. 3–42.

Martin, Stephen. A Bainsian Interpretation of Von Weisäcker's Model of Scale Economies [A Welfare Analysis of Barriers to Entry]. *Southern Econ. J.*, April 1984, *50*(4), pp. 1192–95.

Mas-Colell, Andreu. The Profit Motive in the Theory of Monopolistic Competition. *Z. Nationalökon.*, Supplement 1984, pp. 119–26.

Maskin, Eric S. and Riley, John G. Monopoly with Incomplete Information. *Rand J. Econ.*, Summer 1984, *15*(2), pp. 171–96.

Mathewson, G. F. and Winter, R. A. An Economic Theory of Vertical Restraints. *Rand J. Econ.*, Spring 1984, *15*(1), pp. 27–38.

McCormick, Robert E.; Shughart, William F., II and Tollison, Robert D. The Disinterest in Deregulation. *Amer. Econ. Rev.*, December 1984, *74*(5), pp. 1075–79.

McKinney, Scott. Public Good Producers and Spillovers: An Analysis of Duopoly Behavior. *Public Finance Quart.*, January 1984, *12*(1), pp. 97–116.

McLennan, Andrew. Price Dispersion and Incomplete Learning in the Long Run. *J. Econ. Dynam. Control*, September 1984, *7*(3), pp. 331–47.

McMillan, John. Collusion, Competition, and Conjectures. *Can. J. Econ.*, November 1984, *17*(4), pp. 788–805.

McMillan, John and Sinn, Hans-Werner. Oligopolistic Extraction of a Common-Property Resource: Dynamic Equilibria. In *Kemp, M. C. and Long, N. V., eds.*, 1984, pp. 199–214.

McNulty, Paul J. On the Nature and Theory of Economic Organization: The Role of the Firm Reconsidered. *Hist. Polit. Econ.*, Summer 1984, *16*(2), pp. 233–53.

Mejstřík, Michal. Economic Effects of Export and Their Dependence on the Quality of Products. *Czech. Econ. Pap.*, 1984, (22), pp. 57–82. [G: Czechoslovakia]

Moorthy, K. Sridhar. Comments on "Firm-Specific Differentiation and Competition among Multiproduct Firms." *J. Bus.*, Part 2, January 1984, *57*(1), pp. S167–71.

Moorthy, K. Sridhar. Market Segmentation, Self-Selection, and Product Line Design. *Marketing Sci.*, Fall 1984, *3*(4), pp. 288–307.

Moulin, Hervé. Dominance Solvability and Cournot Stability. *Math. Soc. Sci.*, February 1984, *7*(1), pp. 83–102.

Moussavian, Mohammed and Samuelson, Larry. On the Extraction of an Exhaustible Resource by a Monopoly. *J. Environ. Econ. Manage.*, June 1984, *11*(2), pp. 139–46.

Münker, Horst. Reallohn und Marktmacht. (Real Wages and Market Power. With English summary.) *Jahr. Nationalökon. Statist.*, March 1984, *199*(2), pp. 123–44.

Myers, Samuel L., Jr. Labor Economics, Preferences, and the Rationality Assumption: A Comment on Blau, Dickens, and Malveaux. In *Darity, W., Jr., ed.*, 1984, pp. 257–68. [G: U.S.]

Neary, Hugh M. Labor-managed Cournot Oligopoly and Industry Output: A Comment. *J. Compar. Econ.*, September 1984, *8*(3), pp. 322–27.

Nelson, Carl H. and McCarl, Bruce A. Including Imperfect Competition in Spatial Equilibrium Models. *Can. J. Agr. Econ.*, March 1984, *32*(1), pp. 55–70.

Newbery, David M. G. Commodity Price Stabilization in Imperfectly Competitive Markets. In *Storey, G. G.; Schmitz, A. and Sarris, A. H., eds.*, 1984, pp. 261–84.

Newbery, David M. G. The Economics of Oil. In *van der Ploeg, F., ed.*, 1984, pp. 519–67.

Nguyen, Dung. Product Diversification and Demand Uncertainty. *Southern Econ. J.*, October 1984, *51*(2), pp. 330–40.

Nielsen, Lars Tyge. Risk Sensitivity in Bargaining with More than Two Participants. *J. Econ. Theory*, April 1984, *32*(2), pp. 371–76.

Novshek, William. Finding All *n*-Firm Cournot Equilibria. *Int. Econ. Rev.*, February 1984, *25*(1), pp. 61–70.

Nti, Kofi O. and Shubik, Martin. Noncooperative Exchange Using Money and Broker–Dealers. *Math. Soc. Sci.*, February 1984, *7*(1), pp. 59–82.

Ohta, Hiroshi. Agglomeration and Competition. *Reg. Sci. Urban Econ.*, February 1984, *14*(1), pp. 1–17.

Ohta, Hiroshi. On the Neutrality of Freight in Monopoly Spatial Pricing. *J. Reg. Sci.*, August 1984, *24*(3), pp. 359–71.

Perri, Timothy J. The Social Loss from Private Monopoly and Optimal Antitrust Enforcement. *Rev. Ind. Organ.*, Winter 1984, *1*(4), pp. 276–88.

Perry, Martin K. Scale Economies, Imperfect Competition, and Public Policy. *J. Ind. Econ.*, March 1984, *32*(3), pp. 313–33.

Perry, Motty. Sustainable Positive Profit Multiple-Price Strategies in Contestable Markets. *J. Econ. Theory*, April 1984, *32*(2), pp. 246–65.

Peters, Michael. Bertrand Equilibrium with Capacity Constraints and Restricted Mobility. *Econometrica*, September 1984, *52*(5), pp. 1117–27.

Peters, Michael. Restrictions on Price Advertising. *J. Polit. Econ.*, June 1984, *92*(3), pp. 472–85.

Pfouts, Ralph W. Modelling Non-price Competition and Market Share. In *Avula, X. J. R., et al.*, 1984, pp. 795–98.

ten Raa, Thijs. Resolution of Conjectures on the Sustainability of Natural Monopoly. *Rand J. Econ.*, Spring 1984, *15*(1), pp. 135–41.

Reinganum, Jennifer F. Uncertain Innovation and the Persistence of Monopoly: Reply. *Amer. Econ. Rev.*, March 1984, *74*(1), pp. 243–46.

Reynolds, Peter John. An Empirical Analysis of the Degree of Monopoly Theory of Distribution. *Bull. Econ. Res.*, May 1984, *36*(1), pp. 59–84. **[G: U.K.]**

Riordan, Michael H. Uncertainty, Asymmetric Information and Bilateral Contracts. *Rev. Econ. Stud.*, January 1984, *51*(1), pp. 83–93.

Roberts, Mark J. Testing Oligopolistic Behavior. *Int. J. Ind. Organ.*, December 1984, *2*(4), pp. 367–83. **[G: U.S.]**

Robinson, Austin. Whatever Happened to the Full-Cost Principle (UK)? Comment. In *Wiles, P. and Routh, G., eds.*, 1984, pp. 222–32.

Robson, Arthur J. and McMillan, John. Dynamic Duopoly under Demand Uncertainty. *Can. J. Econ.*, November 1984, *17*(4), pp. 695–98.

Rogerson, William P. A Note on the Incentive for a Monopolist to Increase Fixed Costs as a Barrier to Entry. *Quart. J. Econ.*, May 1984, *99*(2), pp. 399–402.

Rosenthal, Robert W. Futures Markets and Monopoly: Comment. In *Anderson, R. W., ed.*, 1984, pp. 107–08.

Sattinger, Michael. Value of an Additional Firm in Monopolistic Competition. *Rev. Econ. Stud.*, April 1984, *51*(2), pp. 321–32.

Scharfstein, David. A Policy to Prevent Rational Test-Market Predation. *Rand J. Econ.*, Summer 1984, *15*(2), pp. 229–43.

Schmalensee, Richard. Gaussian Demand and Commodity Bundling. *J. Bus.*, Part 2, January 1984, *57*(1), pp. S211–30.

Schutte, David Peter. Optimal Inventories and Equilibrium Price Behavior. *J. Econ. Theory*, June 1984, *33*(1), pp. 46–58.

Scott, Frank A., Jr. Uncertain Input Prices, Profit Risk, and the Rate-of-Return Regulated Firm: Reply. *Land Econ.*, November 1984, *60*(4), pp. 411–13.

Seldon, Zena A. and Seldon, James R. Natural Monopolies versus Desirable Monopolies and Regulation in the Public Interest: Two Quibbles and a Policy Note. *Quart. J. Bus. Econ.*, Spring 1984, *23*(2), pp. 58–71.

Selten, Reinhard. Are Cartel Laws Bad for Business? In *[Beckmann, M. J.]*, 1984, pp. 85–117.

Shaked, Avner and Sutton, John. Natural Oligopolies and International Trade. In *Kierzkowski, H., ed.*, 1984, pp. 34–50.

Shepherd, William G. "Contestability" vs. Competition. *Amer. Econ. Rev.*, September 1984, *74*(4), pp. 572–87.

Simon, Julian L. and Rice, Edward M. The Theory of Price-Changing and Monopoly Power. *J. Post Keynesian Econ.*, Winter 1983-84, *6*(2), pp. 198–213.

Simon, Leo K. Bertrand, the Cournot Paradigm and the Theory of Perfect Competition. *Rev. Econ. Stud.*, April 1984, *51*(2), pp. 209–30.

Singh, Nirvikar and Vives, Xavier. Price and Quantity Competition in a Differentiated Duopoly. *Rand J. Econ.*, Winter 1984, *15*(4), pp. 546–54.

Sinn, Hans-Werner. Common Property Resources, Storage Facilities and Ownership Structures: A Cournot Model of the Oil Market. *Economica*, August 1984, *51*(203), pp. 235–52.

Skinner, A. S. and MacLennan, M. C. Oligopoly and the Theory of the Firm. In *Creedy, J. and O'Brien, D. P., eds.*, 1984, pp. 117–51.

Sobel, Joel. Non-linear Prices and Price-taking Behavior. *J. Econ. Behav. Organ.*, September–December 1984, *5*(3–4), pp. 387–96.

Sobel, Joel. The Timing of Sales. *Rev. Econ. Stud.*, July 1984, *51*(3), pp. 353–68.

Spulber, Daniel F. Competition and Multiplant Monopoly with Spatial Nonlinear Pricing. *Int. Econ. Rev.*, June 1984, *25*(2), pp. 425–39.

Spulber, Daniel F. Nonlinear Pricing, Advertising and Welfare. *Southern Econ. J.*, April 1984, *50*(4), pp. 1025–35.

Spulber, Daniel F. Scale Economies and Existence of Sustainable Monopoly Prices. *J. Econ. Theory*, October 1984, *34*(1), pp. 149–63.

Stark, A. W. Uncertain Input Prices, Profit Risk, and the Rate-of-Return Regulated Firm: Comment. *Land Econ.*, November 1984, *60*(4), pp. 404–07.

Stegemann, Klaus. The Social Costs of Monopoly in an Open Economy. *Can. J. Econ.*, November 1984, *17*(4), pp. 718–30.

Stiglitz, Joseph E. Price Rigidities and Market Structure. *Amer. Econ. Rev.*, May 1984, *74*(2), pp. 350–55.

Sweeney, George. Marketing, Price Discrimination, and Welfare: Comment. *Southern Econ. J.*, January 1984, *50*(3), pp. 892–99.

Sweezy, Paul M. Competition and Monopoly. In *Foster, J. B. and Szlajfer, H., eds.*, 1984, pp. 27–40.

Sylos-Labini, Paolo. The Theory of Prices in Oligopoly and the Theory of Growth. In *Sylos-Labini, P.*, 1984, *1971*, pp. 123–45. **[G: U.K.; U.S.]**

Thompson, Gerald L. and Teng, Jinn-Tsair. Optimal Pricing and Advertising Policies for New Product Oligopoly Models. *Marketing Sci.*, Spring 1984, *3*(2), pp. 148–68.

Tullock, Gordon. Long-Run Equilibrium and Total Expenditures in Rent-Seeking: A Comment. *Public Choice*, 1984, *43*(1), pp. 95–97.

Turnbull, Geoffrey K. Uncertain Input Prices, Profit Risk, and the Rate-of-Return Regulated Firm: Comment. *Land Econ.*, November 1984, *60*(4), pp. 408–10.

Ursprung, Heinrich W. Schumpeterian Entrepreneurs and Catastrophe Theory or a New Chapter to the Foundations of Economic Analysis. *Z. Nationalökon.*, Supplement 1984, pp. 39–69.

Vind, Karl. Erratum [Equilibrium with Coordination]. *J. Math. Econ.*, October 1984, *13*(2), pp. 195.

Vives, Xavier. Duopoly Information Equilibrium: Cournot and Bertrand. *J. Econ. Theory*, October 1984, *34*(1), pp. 71–94.

Wahlroos, Björn. Monopoly Welfare Losses under Uncertainty. *Southern Econ. J.*, October 1984, *51*(2), pp. 429–42. **[G: Finland; U.S.]**

Ware, Roger. Lumpy Investment in a Growing Differentiated Market. *Economica*, November 1984, *51*(204), pp. 377–91.

Wernerfelt, Birger. Consumers with Differing

Reaction Speeds, Scale Advantages and Industry Structure. *Europ. Econ. Rev.*, March 1984, *24*(2), pp. 257–70.

West, Douglas S. and Von Hohenbalken, Balder. Spatial Predation in a Canadian Retail Oligopoly. *J. Reg. Sci.*, August 1984, *24*(3), pp. 415–29. [G: Canada]

Whitten, David O. A Flat-kinked Demand Function for Oligopolistic Sellers of Homogeneous Products. *Rev. Ind. Organ.*, Fall 1984, *1*(3), pp. 206–15.

Wiles, Peter. Whatever Happened to the Full-Cost Principle (UK)? In *Wiles, P. and Routh, G., eds.*, 1984, pp. 211–21.

Winston, Wayne. The Effect of Uncertainty and Instability on Dynamic Economic Models with an Application to Cournot Oligopoly. *J. Econ. Dynam. Control*, May 1984, *7*(2), pp. 171–79.

Wolinsky, Asher. Product Differentiation with Imperfect Information. *Rev. Econ. Stud.*, January 1984, *51*(1), pp. 53–61.

Woodbury, Stephen A. Occupational Safety and Health Regulation and Economic Theory: Comment. In *Darity, W., Jr., ed.*, 1984, pp. 269–78.

Young, Leslie and Schmitz, Andrew. Storage under a Cartel. In *Storey, G. G.; Schmitz, A. and Sarris, A. H., eds.*, 1984, pp. 285–303.

0227 Theory of Auction Markets

Brannman, Lance; Klein, J. Douglass and Weiss, Leonard W. Concentration and Winning Bids in Auctions. *Antitrust Bull.*, Spring 1984, *29*(1), pp. 27–31.

Coursey, Don and Smith, Vernon L. Experimental Tests of an Allocation Mechanism for Private, Public or Externality Goods. *Scand. J. Econ.*, 1984, *86*(4), pp. 468–84.

Cox, James C. and Isaac, R. Mark. In Search of the Winner's Curse. *Econ. Inquiry*, October 1984, *22*(4), pp. 579–92.

Cox, James C.; Smith, Vernon L. and Walker, James M. Theory and Behavior of Multiple Unit Discriminative Auctions. *J. Finance*, September 1984, *39*(4), pp. 983–1010.

French, Kenneth R. and McCormick, Robert E. Sealed Bids, Sunk Costs, and the Process of Competition. *J. Bus.*, October 1984, *57*(4), pp. 417–41.

Friedman, Daniel. On the Efficiency of Experimental Double Auction Markets. *Amer. Econ. Rev.*, March 1984, *74*(1), pp. 60–72.

Ketcham, Jon; Smith, Vernon L. and Williams, Arlington W. A Comparison of Posted-Offer and Double-Auction Pricing Institutions. *Rev. Econ. Stud.*, October 1984, *51*(4), pp. 595–614.

Maskin, Eric S. and Riley, John G. Optimal Auctions with Risk Averse Buyers. *Econometrica*, November 1984, *52*(6), pp. 1473–1518.

Matthews, Steven A. Information Acquisition in Discriminatory Auctions. In *Boyer, M. and Kihlstrom, R. E., eds.*, 1984, pp. 181–207.

Matthews, Steven A. On the Implementability of Reduced Form Auctions. *Econometrica*, November 1984, *52*(6), pp. 1519–22.

Moore, John. Global Incentive Constraints in Auction Design. *Econometrica*, November 1984, *52*(6), pp. 1523–35.

Shepherd, William G. Discussion of "Concentration and Winning Bids in Auctions." *Antitrust Bull.*, Spring 1984, *29*(1), pp. 89–100.

Townsend, Robert M. Theories of Contract Design and Market Organization: Conceptual Bases for Understanding Futures Markets. In *Anderson, R. W., ed.*, 1984, pp. 275–306.

Williams, Arlington W. and Smith, Vernon L. Cyclical Double-Auction Markets with and without Speculators. *J. Bus.*, Part 1, January 1984, *57*(1), pp. 1–33.

0228 Agent Theory

Arrow, Kenneth J. The Economics of Moral Hazard: Further Comment. In *Arrow, K. J., vol. 4*, 1984, *1968*, pp. 103–05.

Barry, Christopher B. and Starks, Laura T. Investment Management and Risk Sharing with Multiple Managers. *J. Finance*, June 1984, *39*(2), pp. 477–91.

Demski, Joel S.; Patell, James M. and Wolfson, Mark A. Decentralized Choice of Monitoring Systems. *Accounting Rev.*, January 1984, *59*(1), pp. 16–34.

Demski, Joel S. and Sappington, David. Optimal Incentive Contracts with Multiple Agents. *J. Econ. Theory*, June 1984, *33*(1), pp. 152–71.

Dye, Ronald A. The Trouble with Tournaments. *Econ. Inquiry*, January 1984, *22*(1), pp. 147–49.

Enos, J. L. Public Policy in an Economy with Different Types of Agents. *Greek Econ. Rev.*, December 1984, *6*(3), pp. 424–52.

Eswaran, Mukesh and Kotwal, Ashok. The Moral Hazard of Budget-breaking. *Rand J. Econ.*, Winter 1984, *15*(4), pp. 578–81.

Farmer, Roger E. A. Unemployment, Bankruptcy and Asymmetric Information. *Manchester Sch. Econ. Soc. Stud.*, September 1984, *52*(3), pp. 284–91.

Fellingham, John C.; Kwon, Young K. and Newman, D. Paul. *Ex ante* Randomization in Agency Models. *Rand J. Econ.*, Summer 1984, *15*(2), pp. 290–301.

Guesnerie, Roger and Laffont, Jean-Jacques. A Complete Solution to a Class of Principal–Agent Problems with an Application to the Control of a Self-managed Firm. *J. Public Econ.*, December 1984, *25*(3), pp. 329–69.

Holmström, Bengt. On the Theory of Delegation. In *Boyer, M. and Kihlstrom, R. E., eds.*, 1984, pp. 115–41.

Katz, Eliakim and Paroush, Jacob. Royalty vs. Partnership Agreement in the Creative Arts. *Atlantic Econ. J.*, July 1984, *12*(2), pp. 41–46.

Lambert, Richard A. Income Smoothing as Rational Equilibrium Behavior. *Accounting Rev.*, October 1984, *59*(4), pp. 604–18.

MacDonald, Glenn M. New Directions in the Economic Theory of Agency. *Can. J. Econ.*, August 1984, *17*(3), pp. 415–40.

Martin, Donald L. The Agency Problem in a Nonproprietary Theory of Union Behavior. **In** *Rosa, J.-J., ed.*, 1984, pp. 191–220.

Maskin, Eric S. and Riley, John G. Monopoly with Incomplete Information. *Rand J. Econ.*, Summer 1984, *15*(2), pp. 171–96.

Mookherjee, Dilip. Optimal Incentive Schemes with Many Agents. *Rev. Econ. Stud.*, July 1984, *51*(3), pp. 433–46.

Nickerson, David and Sandler, Todd. Intertemporal Incentive Allocation in Simple Hierarchies. *Math. Soc. Sci.*, February 1984, *7*(1), pp. 33–57.

Prescott, Edward C. and Townsend, Robert M. Pareto Optima and Competitive Equilibria with Adverse Selection and Moral Hazard. *Econometrica*, January 1984, *52*(1), pp. 21–45.

Ramakrishnan, Ram T. S. and Thakor, Anjan V. The Valuation of Assets under Moral Hazard. *J. Finance*, March 1984, *39*(1), pp. 229–38.

Sappington, David. Incentive Contracting with Asymmetric and Imperfect Precontractual Knowledge. *J. Econ. Theory*, October 1984, *34*(1), pp. 52–70.

Sykes, Alan O. The Economics of Vicarious Liability. *Yale Law J.*, June 1984, *93*(7), pp. 1231–280.

Walkling, Ralph A. and Long, Michael S. Agency Theory, Managerial Welfare, and Takeover Bid Resistance. *Rand J. Econ.*, Spring 1984, *15*(1), pp. 54–68. **[G: U.S.]**

0229 Microeconomics of Intertemporal Choice

Ahn, Kookshin. Optimal Foreign Borrowing and Altruism in an Overlapping Generations Model. *J. Econ. Devel.*, December 1984, *9*(2), pp. 171–90.

Buiter, Willem H. and Carmichael, Jeffrey. Government Debt: Comment [Government Debt in an Overlapping-Generations Model with Bequests and Gifts]. *Amer. Econ. Rev.*, September 1984, *74*(4), pp. 762–65. **[G: U.S.]**

Burbidge, John B. Government Debt: Reply [Government Debt in an Overlapping-Generations Model with Bequests and Gifts]. *Amer. Econ. Rev.*, September 1984, *74*(4), pp. 766–67. **[G: U.S.]**

Denton, Frank T. and Spencer, Byron G. The Time Path of the Economy as the Population Moves towards a Stationary State. **In** *Steinmann, G., ed.*, 1984, pp. 109–31.

Donaldson, John B. and Mehra, Rajnish. Comparative Dynamics of an Equilibrium Intertemporal Asset Pricing Model. *Rev. Econ. Stud.*, July 1984, *51*(3), pp. 491–508.

Dow, Gregory K. Myopia, Amnesia, and Consistent Intertemporal Choice. *Math. Soc. Sci.*, October 1984, *8*(2), pp. 95–109.

Geanakoplos, John D. and Polemarchakis, Herakles M. Intertemporally Separable, Overlapping-Generations Economies. *J. Econ. Theory*, December 1984, *34*(2), pp. 207–15.

Kehoe, Timothy J. and Levine, David K. Intertemporal Separability in Overlapping-Generations Models. *J. Econ. Theory*, December 1984, *34*(2), pp. 216–26.

Koskela, Erkki and Virén, Matti. Credit Rationing and Consumer Intertemporal Choice. *Oxford Econ. Pap.*, June 1984, *36*(2), pp. 241–47.

Kurz, Mordecai. Capital Accumulation and the Characteristics of Private Inter-Generational Transfers. *Economica*, February 1984, *51*(201), pp. 1–22. **[G: U.S.]**

Parsons, Donald O. On the Economics of Intergenerational Control. *Population Devel. Rev.*, March 1984, *10*(1), pp. 41–54.

Spremann, Klaus. Intergenerational Contracts and Their Decomposition. *Z. Nationalökon.*, 1984, *44*(3), pp. 237–53.

Watson, Harry S. A Note on the Effects of Taxation on Charitable Giving over the Life Cycle and Beyond. *Quart. J. Econ.*, August 1984, *99*(3), pp. 639–47.

023 Macroeconomic Theory

0230 General

Adachi, Hideyuki. On the Economic Implications of the Growth of the Non-market Sector. *Oxford Econ. Pap.*, November 1984, *36*(3), pp. 418–37. **[G: LDCs]**

Ahtiala, Pekka. A Synthesis of the Macroeconomic Approaches to Exchange Rate Determination. *Europ. Econ. Rev.*, March 1984, *24*(2), pp. 117–36.

Allsbrook, O. O. Inflationary Recession and Saving Ratios. *S. Afr. J. Econ.*, March 1984, *52*(1), pp. 63–68.

Arestis, Philip and Driver, Ciaran. The Policy Implications of Post Keynesianism. *J. Econ. Issues*, December 1984, *18*(4), pp. 1093–1105.

Ascah, Louis. Sommes-nous tous des néo-keynésiens à la Friedman–Phelps–Lucas maintenant? (Are We All Neo-Keynesians a là Friedman–Phelps–Lucas Now? With English summary.) *L'Actual. Econ.*, March 1984, *60*(1), pp. 132–35.

Asimakopulos, Athanasios. The General Theory and Its Marshallian Microfoundations. *Metroecon.*, June-Oct. 1984, *36*(2–3), pp. 161–75.

Atesoglu, H. Sonmez and Dutkowsky, Donald H. Rational Expectations, Fatality, and Keynesian Models. *Quart. J. Bus. Econ.*, Summer 1984, *23*(3), pp. 18–28.

Bagella, Michele. Note sul concetto di disoccupazione involuntaria. (Some Notes on the Concept of Involuntary Unemployment. With English summary.) *Giorn. Econ.*, March–April 1984, *43*(3–4), pp. 213–36.

Baldassarri, Mario. Optimal "Mix" of Government Expenditure and Optimal Growth Path for an Open Economy within a Three Targets–Three Guns Framework. *Econ. Notes*, 1984, (2), pp. 5–24.

Barro, Robert J. Rational Expectations and Macroeconomics in 1984. *Amer. Econ. Rev.*, May 1984, *74*(2), pp. 179–82.

Barro, Robert J. and King, Robert G. Time-separable Preferences and Intertemporal-Substitution Models of Business Cycles. *Quart. J. Econ.*, November 1984, *99*(4), pp. 817–39.

Bean, Charles R. Optimal Wage Bargains. *Economica*, May 1984, *51*(202), pp. 141–49.

Begg, David K. H. and Haque, Md Badrul. A Nominal Interest Rate Rule and Price Level Indeterminacy Reconsidered. *Greek Econ. Rev.*, April 1984, *6*(1), pp. 31–46.

Belongia, Michael T. Money Growth Variability and GNP. *Fed. Res. Bank St. Louis Rev.*, April 1984, *66*(4), pp. 23–31. [G: U.S.]

Benavie, Arthur. Imported Inflation and Monetary-Fiscal Policy under a Flexible Exchange Rate. *Atlantic Econ. J.*, March 1984, *12*(1), pp. 41–49.

Benninga, Simon and Protopapadakis, Aris. The Neutrality of the Real Equilibrium under Alternative Financing of Government Expenditures. *J. Monet. Econ.*, September 1984, *14*(2), pp. 183–208.

Bhandari, Jagdeep S. Wage Contracting and Aggregate Adjustment in an Open Economy. *Aussenwirtschaft*, December 1984, *39*(4), pp. 335–56.

Blake, David. Complete Systems Methods of Estimating Models with Rational and Adaptive Expectations: A Case Study. *Europ. Econ. Rev.*, March 1984, *24*(2), pp. 137–50. [G: U.S.]

Blanchard, Olivier J. Current and Anticipated Deficits, Interest Rates and Economic Activity. *Europ. Econ. Rev.*, June 1984, *25*(1), pp. 7–27. [G: EEC; U.S.]

Blanchard, Olivier J. and Dornbusch, Rudiger. U.S. Deficits, the Dollar and Europe. *Banca Naz. Lavoro Quart. Rev.*, March 1984, (148), pp. 89–113. [G: U.S.; OECD]

Blinder, Alan S. and Mankiw, N. Gregory. Aggregation and Stabilization Policy in a Multi-Contract Economy. *J. Monet. Econ.*, January 1984, *13*(1), pp. 67–86.

Blomqvist, Hans C. On the Sources and Macroeconomic Implications of Nonuniform and Uncertain Price Expectations. *Weltwirtsch. Arch.*, 1984, *120*(2), pp. 366–75.

Blomqvist, Hans C. Stagflation—inget mysterium. (Stagflation Is No Mystery. With English summary.) *Ekon. Samfundets Tidskr.*, 1984, *37*(1), pp. 45–50. [G: Finland]

Bodkin, Ronald G. and Arroja, Pedro. A Simulation Study of the Solow–Stiglitz Model of Aggregative Income Distribution. *Metroecon.*, February 1984, *36*(1), pp. 1–23.

Bohanon, Cecil E. and Van Cott, T. Norman. Shapiro on Marginal Tax Rates and Aggregate Labor Supply: A Comment. *Quart. J. Bus. Econ.*, Spring 1984, *23*(2), pp. 15–19.

Boitani, Andrea. Two Views on Oligopoly and Stagnation. *Econ. Notes*, 1984, (3), pp. 128–54.

Booth, Alan. Defining a "Keynesian Revolution" [The "Keynesian Revolution" in Economic Policy-Making]. *Econ. Hist. Rev., 2nd Ser.*, May 1984, *37*(2), pp. 263–67. [G: U.K.]

Bortis, Heinrich. Employment in a Capitalist Economy. *J. Post Keynesian Econ.*, Summer 1984, *6*(4), pp. 590–604.

Bowles, David C. and Wang, Leonard F. S. The

Efficacy of Bond-financed Fiscal Policy Revisited. *Rivista Int. Sci. Econ. Com.*, October–November 1984, *31*(10–11), pp. 1006–16.

Brandsma, Andries S. and Hughes Hallett, Andrew J. The Structure of Rational Expectations Behaviour in Economics: An Empirical View. In *Ancot, J. P., ed.*, 1984, pp. 143–72. [G: Netherlands]

Brown-Collier, Elba and Smith, William Doyle. The Wealth Effect: Pigou, Patinkin and Supply-Side Economics. *Eastern Econ. J.*, October-December 1984, *10*(4), pp. 380–88.

Brown, Elba K. Review of Social Economy: The Neoclassical and Post-Keynesian Research Programs: The Methodological Issues. In *Caldwell, B. J., ed.*, 1984, *1981*, pp. 438–59.

Broze, L. and Szafarz, A. On Linear Models with Rational Expectations which Admit a Unique Solution. *Europ. Econ. Rev.*, February 1984, *24*(1), pp. 103–11.

Brunner, Karl. Hat der Monetarismus versagt? (Has Monetarism Failed? With English summary.) *Kredit Kapital*, 1984, *17*(1), pp. 18–63.

Brunner, Karl and Meltzer, Allan H. Essays on Macroeconomic Implications of Financial and Labor Markets and Political Processes. *Carnegie-Rochester Conf. Ser. Public Policy*, Autumn 1984, *21*, pp. 1–8.

Buiter, Willem H. Granger-Causality and Policy Effectiveness. *Economica*, May 1984, *51*(202), pp. 151–62.

Buiter, Willem H. Saddlepoint Problems in Continuous Time Rational Expectations Models: A General Method and Some Macroeconomic Examples. *Econometrica*, May 1984, *52*(3), pp. 665–80.

Bukh, E. M.; Alexandrov, L. A. and Lebedev, V. N. Interpretations of Reproduction. In *Smirnov, A. D.; Golosov, V. V. and Maximova, V. F., eds.*, 1984, pp. 118–36.

Bureau, D.; Miqueu, D. and Norotte, M. The Disequilibrium Theory in Macroeconomic Models: A Small-Scale Model. In *Ancot, J. P., ed.*, 1984, pp. 173–94.

Canterbery, E. Ray. Galbraith, Sraffa, Kalecki and Supra-surplus Capitalism. *J. Post Keynesian Econ.*, Fall 1984, *7*(1), pp. 77–90.

Canto, Victor A.; Joines, Douglas H. and Webb, Robert I. Taxation, Rational Expectations, and the Neutrality of Money. *J. Macroecon.*, Winter 1984, *6*(1), pp. 69–78.

Caprara, Ugo. Opinioni e teorie di John Maynard Keynes nella interpretazione di un economista aziendale. (Opinions and Theories of John Maynard Keynes: An Interpretation by a Business Economist. With English summary.) *Bancaria*, March 1984, *40*(3), pp. 256–65.

Casarosa, Carlo. The Microfoundations of Keynes's Aggregate Supply and Expected Demand Analysis: A Reply. *Econ. J.*, December 1984, *94*(376), pp. 941–45.

Chamouton, Thierry and Piatecki, Cyrille. Anticipations rationnelles et théorie économique. (With English summary.) *Revue Écon. Polit.*, November–December 1984, *94*(6), pp. 754–72.

Chand, Sheetal K. A Keynesian Fiscal Policy and the New Classical Macroeconomics. *J. Post Keynesian Econ.*, Summer 1984, *6*(4), pp. 509–22.

Chernomas, Robert. Keynes on Post-scarcity Society. *J. Econ. Issues*, December 1984, *18*(4), pp. 1007–26.

Chiappori, Pierre-André and Mongin, Philippe. Un modèle de politique monétaire avec aléas stratégiques. (A Model of Monetary Policy with Strategic Uncertainty. With English summary.) *Revue Écon.*, September 1984, *35*(5), pp. 831–69.

Clower, Robert W. Keynes and the Classics: A Dynamical Perspective. In *Clower, R. W.*, 1984, *1960*, pp. 21–26.

Clower, Robert W. Money and Markets. In *Clower, R. W.*, 1984, pp. 259–72.

Clower, Robert W. Reflections on the Keynesian Perplex. In *Clower, R. W.*, 1984, *1975*, pp. 187–208.

Clower, Robert W. Say's Principle, What It Means and Doesn't Mean. In *Clower, R. W.*, 1984, *1973*, pp. 145–65.

Clower, Robert W. The Coordination of Economic Activities: A Keynesian Perspective. In *Clower, R. W.*, 1984, *1975*, pp. 209–17.

Clower, Robert W. The Keynesian Counter-Revolution: A Theoretical Appraisal. In *Clower, R. W.*, 1984, *1965*, pp. 34–58.

Cobham, David. Convergence, Divergence and Realignment in British Macroeconomics. *Banca Naz. Lavoro Quart. Rev.*, June 1984, (149), pp. 159–76. [G: U.K.]

Colander, David C. Galbraith and the Theory of Price Control. *J. Post Keynesian Econ.*, Fall 1984, *7*(1), pp. 30–42.

Colander, David C. Was Keynes a Keynesian or a Lernerian? *J. Econ. Lit.*, December 1984, *22*(4), pp. 1572–75.

Colander, David C. and Olson, Mancur. Coalitions and Macroeconomics. In *Colander, D. C.*, ed., 1984, pp. 115–28. [G: U.S.]

Cooley, Thomas F.; LeRoy, Stephen F. and Raymon, Neil. Econometric Policy Evaluation: Note. *Amer. Econ. Rev.*, June 1984, *74*(3), pp. 467–70.

Corden, W. M. Booming Sector and Dutch Disease Economics: Survey and Consolidation. *Oxford Econ. Pap.*, November 1984, *36*(3), pp. 359–80.

Cross, Rod. Friedman and Phelps on the Natural Rate of Unemployment. *Atlantic Econ. J.*, July 1984, *12*(2), pp. 47–53.

Cross, Rod. Monetarism and Duhem's Thesis: Reply to Comments. In *Wiles, P. and Routh, G.*, eds., 1984, pp. 111–20.

Cross, Rod. Monetarism and Duhem's Thesis. In *Wiles, P. and Routh, G.*, eds., 1984, pp. 78–99.

Cross, Rod. The Duhem-Quine Thesis, Lakatos and the Appraisal of Theories in Macroeconomics. In *Caldwell, B. J.*, ed., 1984, *1982*, pp. 284–304.

Currie, David and Levine, Paul. Stochastic Macroeconomic Policy Simulations for a Small Open Economy. In *van der Ploeg, F.*, ed., 1984, pp. 217–48.

D'Adda, Carlo. Recenti sviluppi nella teoria monetaria. (With English summary.) *Econ. Polít.*, December 1984, *1*(3), pp. 429–56.

Danthine, Jean-Pierre and Donaldson, John B. Investment, Stability and Taxation in a Long-Run Macroeconomic Model. *J. Econ. Dynam. Control*, May 1984, *7*(2), pp. 79–110.

Danthine, Jean-Pierre and Peytrignet, Michel. Complement to 'Rationing Macro-economics: A Graphic Exposition': Aggregate Demand and Supply. *Europ. Econ. Rev.*, October–November 1984, *26*(1–2), pp. 203–08.

Davidson, Paul. Reviving Keynes's Revolution. *J. Post Keynesian Econ.*, Summer 1984, *6*(4), pp. 561–75.

Delbono, Flavio. Teorema delle contrazioni ed esistenza di un equilibrio nei modelli di Drèze e di Benassy. (With English summary.) *Econ. Polít.*, August 1984, *1*(2), pp. 243–60.

Demery, David. Aggregate Demand, Rational Expectations and Real Output: Some New Evidence for the U.K., 1963.2–1982.2. *Econ. J.*, December 1984, *94*(376), pp. 847–62. [G: U.K.]

Dow, Sheila C. Methodology and the Analysis of a Monetary Economy. *Écon. Soc.*, April 1984, *18*(4), pp. 7–35.

Drabicki, John Z. and Takayama, Akira. Money, National Debt, and Economic Growth. *J. Econ. Theory*, August 1984, *33*(2), pp. 356–67.

Driskill, Robert A. and McCafferty, Stephen. The Workings of a Commodity Money System in an Incomplete Information Macro Model. *J. Macroecon.*, Spring 1984, *6*(2), pp. 139–57.

Duesenberry, James S. A Critique of Rational Expectations Theory. *Kobe Univ. Econ.*, 1984, (30), pp. 1–13.

Eckstein, Otto; Mosser, Patricia and Cebry, Michael. The DRI Market Expectations Model. *Rev. Econ. Statist.*, May 1984, *66*(2), pp. 181–91. [G: U.S.]

Eichhorn, Wolfgang and Buhl, Hans Ulrich. Optimal Growth Policies for Resource-Dependent Open Economies. In *Hammer, G. and Pallaschke, D.*, eds., 1984, pp. 175–87.

Eichner, Alfred S. Joan Robinson's Legacy. *Challenge*, May/June 1984, *27*(2), pp. 42–46.

Enders, Klaus. The Dutch Disease or Problems of a Sectoral Boom. *Z. Wirtschaft. Sozialwissen.*, 1984, *104*(1), pp. 1–20.

Engel, Charles M. and Frankel, Jeffrey A. The Secular Inflation Term in Open-Economy Phillips Curves. *Europ. Econ. Rev.*, March 1984, *24*(2), pp. 161–64.

Entov, R. M. The "Rule" and Fall of the Phillips Curve. *Prob. Econ.*, February 1984, *26*(10), pp. 3–36.

Farmer, Roger E. A. A New Theory of Aggregate Supply. *Amer. Econ. Rev.*, December 1984, *74*(5), pp. 920–30.

Farmer, Roger E. A. Bursting Bubbles: On the Rationality of Hyperinflations in Optimizing

Models. *J. Monet. Econ.*, July 1984, *14*(1), pp. 29–35.

Fazzari, Steve M. and Minsky, Hyman P. Domestic Monetary Policy: If Not Monetarism, What? *J. Econ. Issues*, March 1984, *18*(1), pp. 101–16.

Felix, David. The Impotence of Macroeconomic Policy Activism: A Critical Appraisal of the New Classical Macroeconomics. *J. Econ. Issues*, September 1984, *18*(3), pp. 825–59.
[G: OECD]

Fender, John. Sectoral and Macroeconomic Effects in a Two Good Open Economy with an Intermediate Input. *Bull. Econ. Res.*, May 1984, *36*(1), pp. 9–32.

Ferrari, Francesco. Stabilità macroeconomica e vincolo di bilancio pubblico. (Macroeconomic Stability and Government's Budget Restraint. With English summary.) *Econ. Int.*, August–November 1984, *37*(3–4), pp. 288–307.

Fethke, Gary C. and Policano, Andrew J. Wage Contingencies, the Patterns of Negotiation and Aggregate Implications of Alternative Contract Structures. *J. Monet. Econ.*, September 1984, *14*(2), pp. 151–70.

Fischer, Stanley and Merton, Robert C. Macroeconomics and Finance: The Role of the Stock Market. *Carnegie-Rochester Conf. Ser. Public Policy*, Autumn 1984, *21*, pp. 57–108.

Fitoussi, Jean-Paul. Développements récents de la théorie macroéconomique: un bilan critique. (With English summary.) *Revue Écon. Polit.*, November–December 1984, *94*(6), pp. 717–53.

Fourgeaud, Claude; Gourieroux, Christian and Pradel, Jacqueline. Modèles à anticipations rationnelles: apprentissage par régression. (Models with Rational Expectations: Learning by Regression. With English summary.) *Ann. INSEE*, April–June 1984, (54), pp. 63–77.

Fourgeaud, Claude; Lenclud, Bernard and Picard, Pierre. Calcul économique prix fictifs et contrainte extérieure. (Cost–Benefit Analysis, Shadow Prices and Foreign Trade Constraint. With English summary.) *Revue Écon.*, May 1984, *35*(3), pp. 425–45.

Fraser, R. W. Demand Uncertainty and Unemployment. *Oxford Econ. Pap.*, March 1984, *36*(1), pp. 27–36.

Frazer, William J., Jr. "The Economics of Supply and Demand" and Friedman. *Econ. Notes*, 1984, (3), pp. 47–73.

Freeman, Richard T. Information Structure and the Transmission of Inflationary Expectations. *Math. Soc. Sci.*, October 1984, *8*(2), pp. 169–93.

Friedman, Benjamin M. Lessons from the 1979–82 Monetary Policy Experiment. *Amer. Econ. Rev.*, May 1984, *74*(2), pp. 382–87.
[G: U.S.]

Garrison, Charles B. Friedman versus Keynes on the Theory of Employment. *J. Post Keynesian Econ.*, Fall 1984, *7*(1), pp. 114–27.

Garrison, Roger W. Time and Money: The Universals of Macroeconomic Theorizing. *J. Macroecon.*, Spring 1984, *6*(2), pp. 197–213.

Gray, Jo Anna. Dynamic Instability in Rational Expectations Models: An Attempt to Clarify. *Int. Econ. Rev.*, February 1984, *25*(1), pp. 93–122.

Groenewegen, John and van Paridon, Kees. *John Groenwegen and Kees van Paridon:* Conference of the Dutch Study Circle on Post-Keynesian Economics on "International Keynesianism," September 1983. *J. Econ. Issues*, March 1984, *18*(1), pp. 315–23.
[G: Global]

Groenewold, Nicolaas. The Effects of Fiscal Policy in a Two-Period Model. *J. Macroecon.*, Winter 1984, *6*(1), pp. 23–41.

Gylfason, Thorvaldur and Lindbeck, Assar. Competing Wage Claims, Cost Inflation, and Capacity Utilization. *Europ. Econ. Rev.*, February 1984, *24*(1), pp. 1–21.

Hafer, R. W. The Money-GNP Link: Assessing Alternative Transaction Measures. *Fed. Res. Bank St. Louis Rev.*, March 1984, *66*(3), pp. 19–27.
[G: U.S.]

Hahn, Frank H. Economic Theory and Keynes' Insights. *Empirica*, 1984, *11*(1), pp. 7–22.

Hahn, Frank H. Expectations and Equilibrium. In *Hahn, F.*, 1984, *1952*, pp. 23–42.

Hahn, Frank H. Keynesian Economics and General Equilibrium Theory: Reflections on Some Current Debates. In *Hahn, F.*, 1984, *1977*, pp. 175–94.

Hahn, Frank H. Monetarism and Economic Theory. In *Hahn, F.*, 1984, *1980*, pp. 283–306.

Hahn, Frank H. On Some Problems of Proving the Existence of Equilibrium in a Monetary Economy. In *Hahn, F.*, 1984, pp. 147–57.

Hahn, Frank H. Wages and Employment. *Oxford Econ. Pap.*, Supplement November 1984, *36*, pp. 47–58.

Hahn, Frank H. Wages and Employment. In *Collard, D. A., et al., eds.*, 1984, pp. 47–58.

Hahn, Frank H. Why I Am Not a Monetarist. In *Hahn, F.*, 1984, pp. 307–26.

Halevi, Joseph. Structure économique et demande effective. (Economic Structure and Effective Demand. With English summary.) *Écon. Appl.*, 1984, *37*(1), pp. 201–13.

Hartropp, Andrew and Heathfield, David. Monetarism and Duhem's Thesis: Comment. In *Wiles, P. and Routh, G., eds.*, 1984, pp. 105–10.

Hayakawa, Hiroaki. Balance Sheet Identity and Walras' Law. *J. Econ. Theory*, October 1984, *34*(1), pp. 187–202.

von Hayek, Friedrich A. The Exchange Value of Money: A Review. In *von Hayek, F. A. (II)*, 1984, pp. 190–94.

von Hayek, Friedrich A. The Keynes Centenary: The Austrian Critique. In *von Hayek, F. A. (I)*, 1984, *1983*, pp. 43–50.

Heckman, James J. Comments on the Ashenfelter and Kydland Papers [Macroeconomic Analyses and Microeconomic Analyses of Labor Supply] [Labor-Force Heterogeneity and the Business Cycle]. *Carnegie-Rochester Conf. Ser. Public Policy*, Autumn 1984, *21*, pp. 209–24.

Hénin, Pierre-Yves and Zylberberg, André. Sur

la compatibilité à long terme d'un adjustement partiel des prix avec l'hypothèse de prévisions rationnelles. *Revue Écon. Polit.*, November–December 1984, *94*(6), pp. 792–807.

Henocq, Christophe and Kempf, Hubert. Agrégation quasi parfaite par convergence. (Quasi-perfect Aggregation and the Convergence Approach. With English summary.) *Revue Écon.*, September 1984, *35*(5), pp. 911–27.

Henry, Jacques. Théorie, modèles et interprétation des résultats théoriques. (Theories, Models, and Interpretations of Theoretical Results. With English summary.) *Écon. Soc.*, April 1984, *18*(4), pp. 119–45.

Henry, S. G. B. Real Wage Implications of Wage Inflation Models. *Bull. Econ. Res.*, November 1984, *36*(2), pp. 119–42. **[G: U.K.]**

Hersoug, Tor. Can Tax Cuts Beat the Phillips-Curve? *Europ. Econ. Rev.*, April 1984, *24*(3), pp. 369–81.

Hicks, John R. IS–LM—An Explanation. In *Hicks, J.*, 1984, *1980*, pp. 216–29.

Hicks, John R. Mr. Keynes and the Classics. In *Hicks, J.*, 1984, *1937*, pp. 186–99.

Hirschhorn, Eric. Rational Expectations and the Effects of Government Debt. *J. Monet. Econ.*, July 1984, *14*(1), pp. 55–70. **[G: U.S.]**

Holly, Sean and Corker, R. Optimal Feedback and Feedforward Stabilisation of Exchange Rates, Money, Prices and Output under Rational Expectations. In *Hughes Hallet, A.J., ed.*, 1984, pp. 33–60. **[G: U.K.]**

Hoover, Kevin D. Two Types of Monetarism. *J. Econ. Lit.*, March 1984, *22*(1), pp. 58–76.

Horne, Jocelyn and McDonald, Ian M. Rational Expectations, Gradual Price Adjustment and Monetary Policy in Australia. *Australian Econ. Pap.*, June 1984, *23*(42), pp. 79–90. **[G: Australia]**

Hosios, Arthur J. A Welfare Analysis of Employment Contracts with and without Asymmetric Information. *Rev. Econ. Stud.*, July 1984, *51*(3), pp. 471–89.

Howitt, Peter. Information and Coordination: A Review Article. *Econ. Inquiry*, July 1984, *22*(3), pp. 429–46.

Hwang, Been Kwei and Yu, Eden S.-H. Wealth Effects, IS-LM Stability and the Efficacy of Economic Policies. *J. Macroecon.*, Spring 1984, *6*(2), pp. 229–34.

Ize, Alain. Disequilibrium Theories, Imperfect Competition and Income Distribution: A Fix-Price Analysis. *Oxford Econ. Pap.*, June 1984, *36*(2), pp. 248–58.

Jaeger, Klaus. Persistenz und zyklische Schwankungen der Unterbeschäftigung in Gleichgewichtsmodellen mit rationalen Erwartungen. (Persistence and Cyclical Movements of Unemployment in Equilibrium Models with Rational Expectations. With English summary.) *Z. Wirtschaft. Sozialwissen.*, 1984, *104*(6), pp. 645–73.

Jeong, Ki-Jun. The Relation between Two Different Notions of Direct and Indirect Input Requirements. *J. Macroecon.*, Fall 1984, *6*(4), pp. 473–76.

Karacaoglu, Girol. Absence of Gross Substitution in Portfolios and Demand for Finance: Some Macroeconomic Implications. *J. Post Keynesian Econ.*, Summer 1984, *6*(4), pp. 576–89.

Karp, Larry and Havenner, Arthur. Toward the Resurrection of Optimal Macroeconomic Policies. In *Hughes Hallet, A.J., ed.*, 1984, pp. 23–32.

King, Robert G. and Trehan, Bharat. Money: Endogeneity and Neutrality. *J. Monet. Econ.*, November 1984, *14*(3), pp. 385–93.

Klamer, Arjo. Levels of Discourse in New Classical Economics. *Hist. Polit. Econ.*, Summer 1984, *16*(2), pp. 263–90.

Klausinger, Hansjörg. Fristigkeitsaspekte in der Theorie der Stabilisierungspolitik. (Maturity Aspects in the Theory of Stabilization Policy. With English summary.) *Kredit Kapital*, 1984, *17*(2), pp. 180–98.

Klein, Philip A. Economic Policy and the Obligations of the Economist. *J. Econ. Issues*, June 1984, *18*(2), pp. 537–46.

Knoester, Anthonie. Theoretical Principles of the Buffer Mechanism, Monetary Quasi-Equilibrium and Its Spillover Effects. *Kredit Kapital*, 1984, *17*(2), pp. 243–60.

Kormendi, Roger C. and Meguire, Philip G. Cross-Regime Evidence of Macroeconomic Rationality. *J. Polit. Econ.*, October 1984, *92*(5), pp. 875–908. **[G: Selected Countries]**

Krasker, William S. Heterogeneous Expectations and Capital Intensity in an Overlapping-Generations Model. *J. Macroecon.*, Fall 1984, *6*(4), pp. 433–46.

Kromphardt, Jürgen. Die Phillips-Kurve bei informierter Erwartungsbildung. Eine keynesianische Alternative zur Theorie der natürlichen Arbeitslosenquote. (Informed Expectations and the Phillips Curve. With English summary.) *Z. Wirtschaft. Sozialwissen.*, 1984, *104*(6), pp. 631–44.

Kubin, Ingrid. Equilibrium and Stability Analysis in the Classical Framework. *Metroecon.*, February 1984, *36*(1), pp. 47–64.

Lachmann, Werner. Kann die staatliche Kreditaufnahme im Ausland ein "Crowding-out" verhindern? (Does Public Borrowing Abroad Prevent Crowding-out Effects? With English summary.) *Jahr. Nationalökon. Statist.*, November 1984, *199*(6), pp. 522–36.

Laidler, David. Harry Johnson as a Macroeconomist. *J. Polit. Econ.*, August 1984, *92*(4), pp. 592–615.

Laumas, G. S. and McMillin, W. D. Anticipated Fiscal Policy and Real Output. *Rev. Econ. Statist.*, August 1984, *66*(3), pp. 468–71. **[G: U.S.]**

Lavoie, Marc. Un modèle post-keynésian d'économie monétaire fondé sur la théorie du circuit. (A Post-Keynesian Model of a Money Economy, Based upon the Theory of the Circuit. With English summary.) *Écon. Soc.*, April 1984, *18*(4), pp. 233–58.

Le Van, Cuong. Specification of the Import Function and the Determination of Short and Long Term Equilibria in a Macroeconometric

023 Macroeconomic Theory

Model. In *Ancot, J. P., ed.*, 1984, pp. 229–45.

Leijonhufvud, Axel. Hicks on Time and Money. *Oxford Econ. Pap.*, Supplement November 1984, *36*, pp. 26–46.

Leijonhufvud, Axel. Hicks on Time and Money. In *Collard, D. A., et al., eds.*, 1984, pp. 26–46.

Levi-Jakšić, Maja and Jakšić, Miomir. A Systems Approach to the Multiplier Principle. *Econ. Anal. Worker's Manage.*, 1984, *18*(4), pp. 371–78.

Lianos, Theodore P. A Graphical Exposition of a Post Keynesian Model. *J. Post Keynesian Econ.*, Winter 1983-84, *6*(2), pp. 313–23.

Lucas, Robert E., Jr. Money in a Theory of Finance. *Carnegie-Rochester Conf. Ser. Public Policy*, Autumn 1984, *21*, pp. 9–45.

Lybeck, Johan A. and Carlsson, Evert. From Small to Large: A Systematic Comparison of Gradually More Complex Econometric Models. *Europ. Econ. Rev.*, February 1984, *24*(1), pp. 83–101.

Madden, Paul J. Existence of Drèze Equilibrium under Set-Up Costs. *J. Econ. Theory*, August 1984, *33*(2), pp. 275–88.

Maddock, Rodney. Rational Expectations Macrotheory: A Lakatosian Case Study in Program Adjustment. *Hist. Polit. Econ.*, Summer 1984, *16*(2), pp. 291–309.

Malinvaud, E. Current and Anticipated Deficits, Interest Rates and Economic Activity: Comments. *Europ. Econ. Rev.*, June 1984, *25*(1), pp. 29–32.   [G: EEC; U.S.]

Marglin, Stephen A. Growth, Distribution, and Inflation: A Centennial Synthesis. *Cambridge J. Econ.*, June 1984, *8*(2), pp. 115–44.

Marion, Nancy Peregrim and Svensson, Lars E. O. Adjustment to Expected and Unexpected Oil Price Changes. *Can. J. Econ.*, February 1984, *17*(1), pp. 15–31.

Marris, Stephen N. Current and Anticipated Deficits, Interest Rates and Economic Activity: Comments. *Europ. Econ. Rev.*, June 1984, *25*(1), pp. 33–36. [G: U.S.; Japan; Germany; U.K.]

Martinengo, G. Notes on Financial Instability and Effective Demand. *Metroecon.*, June-Oct. 1984, *36*(2–3), pp. 176–201.

Mattesini, Fabrizio. The Wicksell Connection: A Variation on the Theme. *Econ. Notes*, 1984, (2), pp. 121–38.

Mattoscio, Niccola. Intertemporal Coordination and Interest Rates in Neoclassic and Keynesian Models: Problems and Perspectives. (In Italian. With English summary.) *Giorn. Econ.*, September–October 1984, *43*(9–10), pp. 651–69.

Mayer, Thomas. The Government Budget Constraint and Standard Macrotheory. *J. Monet. Econ.*, May 1984, *13*(3), pp. 371–79.

McCallum, Bennett T. A Linearized Version of Lucas's Neutrality Model. *Can. J. Econ.*, February 1984, *17*(1), pp. 138–45.

McCallum, Bennett T. Macroeconomics and Finance: The Role of the Stock Market: A Comment. *Carnegie-Rochester Conf. Ser. Public Policy*, Autumn 1984, *21*, pp. 109–15.

McCallum, Bennett T. On Low-Frequency Estimates of Long-Run Relationships in Macroeconomics. *J. Monet. Econ.*, July 1984, *14*(1), pp. 3–14.

McCormick, Brian J. Monetarism and Duhem's Thesis: Comment. In *Wiles, P. and Routh, G., eds.*, 1984, pp. 100–104.

McCracken, Paul W. Has Macro-Theory Failed Economic Policy? *Southern Econ. J.*, October 1984, *51*(2), pp. 319–29.   [G: U.S.]

McMahon, Michael R. An Appraisal of the New Classical Macroeconomics. *J. Macroecon.*, Summer 1984, *6*(3), pp. 335–46.

McMahon, Michael R. Expectations and Knowledge Assumptions in Some Popular Macroeconomic Models. *Atlantic Econ. J.*, July 1984, *12*(2), pp. 68.

Meltzer, Allan H. Keynes's Labor Market: A Reply. *J. Post Keynesian Econ.*, Summer 1984, *6*(4), pp. 532–39.

Miatto, Giorgio. Il dibattito sulla teoria di Keynes: controversie teoriche e alternative concrete di politica economica. (Debate on Keynes' Theory: Theoretic Controversies and Actual Alternatives of Political Economy. With English summary.) *Econ. Lavoro*, Apr.-June 1984, *18*(2), pp. 61–84.

Micwitz, Gösta. Vad var felet med keynesianismen? (What Went Wrong with Keynesian Economics? With English summary.) *Ekon. Samfundets Tidskr.*, 1984, *37*(4), pp. 235–36.

Miller, Edward M. Extension of the Economics of Keynes to the United States. *Southern Econ. J.*, January 1984, *50*(3), pp. 781–801.

Minsky, Hyman P. and Ferri, Piero. Prices, Employment, and Profits. *J. Post Keynesian Econ.*, Summer 1984, *6*(4), pp. 489–99.

Mistri, Maurizio. Su di un caso di variabilità del saggio di interesse reale in condizioni di inflazione con ipotesi di aspettative razionali. (On a Case of Variability of the Real Interest Rate in Conditions of Inflation under Hypothesis of Rational Expectations. With English summary.) *Giorn. Econ.*, March–April 1984, *43*(3–4), pp. 261–70.

von Natzmer, Wulfheinrich and Reim, O. Wirtschaftspolitik und Konjunktur in einem modifizierten ISLM-Modell. (Economic Policy and the Business Cycle in a Modified ISLM Model. With English summary.) *Kredit Kapital*, 1984, *17*(3), pp. 371–95.

Neary, J. Peter and van Wijnbergen, Sweder. Can an Oil Discovery Lead to a Recession? A Comment. *Econ. J.*, June 1984, *94*(374), pp. 390–95.   [G: U.K.]

Neck, Reinhard. Keynesian and Monetarist Models of Unemployment and Inflation: A Simulation Study for Austria. *Empirica*, 1984, *11*(1), pp. 23–45.   [G: Austria]

Nielsen, Peter Erling. Nyere pengeteori—en oversigt. (Recent Trends in Monetary Theory—A Survey Article. With English summary.) *Nationaløkon. Tidsskr.*, 1984, *122*(1), pp. 1–29.

Nishijima, Shoji. Indexing Policies and Macroeconomic Stability in Brazil: Rational Expectation Model. *Kobe Econ. Bus. Rev.*, 1984, *30*, pp. 73–86. **[G: Brazil]**

O'Driscoll, Gerald P., Jr. Expectations and Monetary Regimes. *Fed. Res. Bank Dallas Econ. Rev.*, September 1984, pp. 1–11.

Ogata, Toshio. A View of Uncertainty and Finance: A Micro Foundation in a Shifting Equilibrium Model. *Écon. Soc.*, April 1984, *18*(4), pp. 147–64.

Olson, Mancur. Beyond Keynesianism and Monetarism. *Econ. Inquiry*, July 1984, *22*(3), pp. 297–322.

Olson, Mancur. Microeconomic Incentives and Macroeconomic Decline. *Weltwirtsch. Arch.*, 1984, *120*(4), pp. 631–45. **[G: W. Europe; U.S.]**

Olson, Mancur. Why Nations Rise and Fall. *Challenge*, March/April 1984, *27*(1), pp. 15–23.

Osborne, M. J. A Note on the Presentations of IS-LM Analysis. *Indian Econ. J.*, July–Sept. 1984, *32*(1), pp. 107–14.

Padoa Schioppa, Fiorella. Public Expenditure in a Flexi-price Model. *Public Finance*, 1984, *39*(1), pp. 133–48.

Parkins, Michael. On *Core Inflation* by Otto Eckstein: A Review Essay. *J. Monet. Econ.*, September 1984, *14*(2), pp. 251–64. **[G: U.S.]**

Patinkin, Don. Keynes and Economics Today. *Amer. Econ. Rev.*, May 1984, *74*(2), pp. 97–102.

Peiwel, George R. Equilibrium Business Cycle Theory and the Real World: Part I. *Economia (Portugal)*, May 1984, *8*(2), pp. 333–60.

Pellanda, Anna. Keynes' Theory of the Rate of Interest and Its Links with the Mercantilist Theory of Money and Fisher's Theory of Income. *Rivista Int. Sci. Econ. Com.*, March 1984, *31*(3), pp. 220–40.

Perry, George L. Reflections on Macroeconomics. *Amer. Econ. Rev.*, May 1984, *74*(2), pp. 401–07.

Persson, Torsten and Svensson, Lars E. O. Misperceptions, Rigidity and Welfare. *Europ. Econ. Rev.*, August 1984, *25*(3), pp. 387–99.

Pesaran, M. H. Macroeconomic Policy in an Oil-exporting Economy with Foreign Exchange Controls. *Economica*, August 1984, *51*(203), pp. 253–70.

Pesaran, M. H. The New Classical Macroeconomics: A Critical Exposition. In *van der Ploeg, F.*, ed., 1984, pp. 195–215.

Peterson, Wallace C. Economic Stabilization and Inflation. *J. Econ. Issues*, March 1984, *18*(1), pp. 69–100. **[G: U.S.]**

Piacentini, Paolo. The Real Wage/Employment Relationship in the Short-Run in Flex-Price and Fix-Price Markets. *Econ. Notes*, 1984, (1), pp. 87–108.

Piersanti, Giovanni. Tasso naturale di disoccupazione, aspettative razionali e incertezza sul tasso di inflazione: alcune evidenze empiriche per l'Italia. (Natural Rate of Unemployment, Rational Expectations and Inflation Uncertainty: Some Empirical Evidence for Italy.

With English summary.) *Giorn. Econ.*, May–June 1984, *43*(5–6), pp. 369–92. **[G: Italy]**

van der Ploeg, Frederick. The Principle of Political-Economic Assignment. *J. Macroecon.*, Summer 1984, *6*(3), pp. 283–94.

Plosser, Charles I. Money in a Theory of Finance: Some Observations. *Carnegie-Rochester Conf. Ser. Public Policy*, Autumn 1984, *21*, pp. 47–55.

Ramb, Bernd-Thomas. Ineffektivität der Wirtschaftspolitik bei "rationalen Erwartungen"? Eine unkorrekte, aber auch modellspezifische Behauptung. (Ineffectiveness of Economic Policy under "Rational Expectations"? An Incorrect but Also Model-Specific Assertion. With English summary.) *Kredit Kapital*, 1984, *17*(2), pp. 165–79.

Rhodes, James R. Walras' Law and Clower's Inequality. *Australian Econ. Pap.*, June 1984, *23*(42), pp. 112–22.

Rima, Ingrid H. Involuntary Unemployment and the Respecified Labor Supply Curve. *J. Post Keynesian Econ.*, Summer 1984, *6*(4), pp. 540–50.

Roberts, David L. How Consistent Was Keynes' Theory of Effective Demand? *Econ. Inquiry*, January 1984, *22*(1), pp. 45–56.

Robinson, William D. Government Bonds and Unstable Growth Paths. *Quart. J. Bus. Econ.*, Summer 1984, *23*(3), pp. 36–58. **[G: U.S.]**

Rodano, Giorgio. Walrasian Equilibrium and Rational Expectations: A Difficult Coexistence. *Metroecon.*, February 1984, *36*(1), pp. 25–46.

Rødseth, Asbjørn. Progressive Taxes and Automatic Stabilization in an Open Economy. *J. Macroecon.*, Summer 1984, *6*(3), pp. 265–82.

Roger, Colin. Erratum [Neo-Walrasian Macroeconomics Microfoundations and Pseudo-Production Models]. *Australian Econ. Pap.*, June 1984, *23*(42), pp. 167.

Rogers, C. and Morgenrood, P. The St Louis Equation and the South African Economy: Some Preliminary Results. *S. Afr. J. Econ.*, June 1984, *52*(2), pp. 172–87. **[G: S. Africa]**

Rohwedder, Jürgen and Herberg, Horst. Effects of Exogenous Nominal Wage Increases: The Purchasing Power Argument vs. the Production Cost Argument. *Z. Wirtschaft. Sozialwissen.*, 1984, *104*(6), pp. 585–601.

Rosenberg, Alexander. On the Interanimation of Micro and Macroeconomics. In *Hausman, D. M.*, ed., 1984, *1976*, pp. 324–43.

Rotemberg, Julio J. Interpreting the Statistical Failures of Some Rational Expectations Macroeconomic Models. *Amer. Econ. Rev.*, May 1984, *74*(2), pp. 188–93. **[G: U.S.]**

Rothengatter, Werner. Quantity Rationing of Economic Transactions in a Risky Environment. In *Bamberg, G. and Spremann, K., eds.*, 1984, pp. 243–70.

Rouzaud, Catherine. Les modèles à générations successives et la monnaie: une présentation introductive. (Overlapping Generations Models and Money: An Introduction. With English summary.) *Écon. Appl.*, 1984, *37*(3–4), pp. 565–91.

Rutherford, Malcolm H. Rational Expectations and Keynesian Uncertainty: A Critique. *J. Post Keynesian Econ.*, Spring 1984, *6*(3), pp. 377–87.

Saint-Étienne, Christian. De l'importance réelle de l'hypothèse de la rationalitè des anticipations. (With English summary.) *Revue Écon. Polit.*, November–December 1984, *94*(6), pp. 773–91.

Sampson, Anthony A. Real Balances, Relative Prices and the Marshall–Lerner Conditions in an Open Model Temporary Equilibrium with Rationing. *Bull. Econ. Res.*, May 1984, *36*(1), pp. 33–49.

Samuelson, Paul A. Evaluating Reaganomics. *Challenge,* November/December 1984, *27*(5), pp. 4–11.   [G: U.S.]

Samuelson, Paul A. Evaluation of Reaganomics as Scientific Macroeconomics. *Economia (Portugal),* October 1984, *8*(3), pp. 453–69.
[G: U.S.]

Sargent, Thomas J. Autoregressions, Expectations, and Advice. *Amer. Econ. Rev.*, May 1984, *74*(2), pp. 408–15.

Scheele, Erwin. Perioden-Gleichgewicht und zeitliche Entwicklung in einem *IS/LM*-Modell mit Finanzierungsrestriktion der Investitionen und Bilanzrestriktion der Unternehmen. (Temporary Equilibrium and Intrinsic Dynamics of an *IS/LM* Model with a Financial Constraint for Investment and a Balance Sheet Restraint for Firms. With English summary.) *Z. Wirtschaft. Sozialwissen.*, 1984, *104*(4), pp. 339–68.

Seccareccia, Mario S. The Fundamental Macroeconomic Link between Investment Activity, the Structure of Employment and Price Changes: A Theoretical and Empirical Analysis. *Écon. Soc.*, April 1984, *18*(4), pp. 165–219.   [G: Canada]

Seidl, Christian. Schumpeter versus Keynes: Supply-side Economics or Demand Management? In *Seidl, C., ed.*, 1984, pp. 139–51.

Sen, Amartya. The Welfare Basis of Real Income Comparisons. In *Sen, A.*, 1984, *1979*, pp. 389–451.

Shackle, G. L. S. Comment on the Papers by Randall Bausor and Malcolm Rutherford [Toward a Historically Dynamic Economics: Examples and Illustrations] [Rational Expectations and Keynesian Uncertainty: A Critique]. *J. Post Keynesian Econ.*, Spring 1984, *6*(3), pp. 388–93.

Shackle, G. L. S. The Romantic Mountain and the Classic Lake: Alan Coddington's *Keynesian Economics. J. Post Keynesian Econ.*, Winter 1983-84, *6*(2), pp. 241–51.

Shah, Anup R. Crowding Out, Capital Accumulation, the Stock Market, and Money-financed Fiscal Policy. *J. Money, Credit, Banking*, Part 1 November 1984, *16*(4), pp. 461–73.

Shaller, Douglas R. On the Missing Equation: Comment. *J. Macroecon.*, Winter 1984, *6*(1), pp. 97–102.

Sheikh, Munir A. An analysis of Some Possible Causes for the Absence or Presence of the Neu-

trality and Homogeneity Properties in Large Macroeconomic Models. *Empirical Econ.*, 1984, *9*(2), pp. 113–30.   [G: Canada]

Shupp, F. R. Macroeconomic Theory and Policy. In *van der Ploeg, F., ed.*, 1984, pp. 165–94.

Sinn, Hans-Werner. Rationale Erwartungen, Rationierung und Rezession—Braucht keynesianische Politik dumme Bürger? (Rational Expectations, Rationing, and Recession—Does Keynesian Policy Need Dull Citizens? With English summary.) *Jahr. Nationalökon. Statist.*, March 1984, *199*(2), pp. 158–78.
[G: W. Germany]

Smithin, John Nicholas. Medio and Musu's Keynesian Analysis of Money Wage Changes: A Comment [Changes in Money Wages and Employment in a Keynesian Analysis]. *Econ. Notes*, 1984, (3), pp. 167–71.

Sneessens, Henri R. Rationing Macroeconomics: A Graphical Exposition. *Europ. Econ. Rev.*, October–November 1984, *26*(1–2), pp. 187–201.

Snower, Dennis J. Rational Expectations, Nonlinearities, and the Effectiveness of Monetary Policy. *Oxford Econ. Pap.*, June 1984, *36*(2), pp. 177–99.

Solow, Robert M. Mr. Hicks and the Classics. *Oxford Econ. Pap.*, Supplement November 1984, *36*, pp. 13–25.

Solow, Robert M. Mr. Hicks and the Classics. In *Collard, D. A., et al., eds.*, 1984, pp. 13–25.

Sørensen, Peter Birch. Er statens budgetunderskud rentedrivende? (The Effects of Government Budget Deficits on Interest Rates. With English summary.) *Nationaløkon. Tidsskr.*, 1984, *122*(1), pp. 41–55.

Sørensen, Peter Birch. Countercyclical versus Passive Monetary Policy in a Medium-run Macro Model. *Scand. J. Econ.*, 1984, *86*(4), pp. 452–67.

Spear, Stephen E. Sufficient Conditions for the Existence of Sunspot Equilibria. *J. Econ. Theory*, December 1984, *34*(2), pp. 360–70.

Startz, Richard. Prelude to Macroeconomics. *Amer. Econ. Rev.*, December 1984, *74*(5), pp. 881–92.

Steindl, Josef. On Maturity in Capitalist Economies. In *Foster, J. B. and Szlajfer, H., eds.*, 1984, *1966*, pp. 167–78.

Stemp, Peter J. and Turnovsky, Stephen J. Equilibrium, Stability, and Deficit Financing in a Simple Nonlinear Monetary Model under Perfect Foresight. *J. Macroecon.*, Fall 1984, *6*(4), pp. 377–97.

Stemp, Peter J. and Turnovsky, Stephen J. Optimal Stabilisation Policies under Perfect Foresight. In *Hughes Hallet, A.J., ed.*, 1984, pp. 3–22.

Struthers, John J. Rational Expectations: A Promising Research Program or a Case of Monetarist Fundamentalism? *J. Econ. Issues*, December 1984, *18*(4), pp. 1133–54.

Strydom, P. D. F. The New Keynesian Approach to Economic Policy. *S. Afr. J. Econ.*, September 1984, *52*(3), pp. 282–95.

Sundaresan, Mahadevan. Consumption and Equilibrium Interest Rates in Stochastic Production Economies. *J. Finance*, March 1984, *39*(1), pp. 77–92.

Svensson, Lars-Gunnar and Weibull, Jörgen W. Stability and Efficiency from a Neo-Keynesian Viewpoint. *J. Econ. Dynam. Control*, September 1984, *7*(3), pp. 349–62.

Sylos-Labini, Paolo. Keynes's *General Theory* and the Great Depression. In *Sylos-Labini, P.*, 1984, pp. 227–43. [G: U.S.]

Thalenhorst, Jobst and Wenig, Alois. F. A. Hayek's "Prices and Production" Re-Analyzed. *Jahr. Nationalökon. Statist.*, May 1984, *199*(3), pp. 213–36.

Thornton, Daniel L. The Government Budget Constraint with Endogenous Money. *J. Macroecon.*, Winter 1984, *6*(1), pp. 57–67.

Tomlinson, J. D. A "Keynesian Revolution" in Economic Policy-Making? *Econ. Hist. Rev.*, 2nd Ser., May 1984, *37*(2), pp. 258–62. [G: U.K.]

Torr, Christopher S. W. Expectations and the New Classical Economics. *Australian Econ. Pap.*, December 1984, *23*(43), pp. 197–205.

Torr, Christopher S.W. The Microfoundations of Keynes's Aggregate Supply and Expected Demand Analysis: A Comment. *Econ. J.*, December 1984, *94*(376), pp. 936–40.

Torr, Christopher S. W. The Principle of Effective Demand versus Effective Demand Failure. *S. Afr. J. Econ.*, December 1984, *52*(4), pp. 409–12.

Tosato, Domenico. Sostituzione tra capitale e lavoro e teoria del processo cumulativo di Wicksell. (With English summary.) *Econ. Polit.*, August 1984, *1*(2), pp. 167–95.

Tuchscherer, Thomas. Meltzer on Keynes's Labor Market Theory: A Review of the *General Theory*'s Second Chapter. *J. Post Keynesian Econ.*, Summer 1984, *6*(4), pp. 523–31.

Turnovsky, Stephen J. Rational Expectations and the Theory of Macroeconomic Policy: An Exposition of Some of the Issues. *J. Econ. Educ.*, Winter 1984, *15*(1), pp. 55–69.

Turnovsky, Stephen J. and Miller, Marcus H. The Effects of Government Expenditure on the Term Structure of Interest Rates. *J. Money, Credit, Banking*, February 1984, *16*(1), pp. 16–33.

Turnovsky, Stephen J. and Wohar, Mark E. Monetarism and the Aggregate Economy: Some Longer-Run Evidence. *Rev. Econ. Statist.*, November 1984, *66*(4), pp. 619–29. [G: U.S.]

Usher, Dan. An Elephantine Theory of Depressions. *J. Macroecon.*, Fall 1984, *6*(4), pp. 477–80.

Vicarelli, F. Stagflation in the Seventies: A Relative Prices Theoretical Approach. *Metroecon.*, June-Oct. 1984, *36*(2–3), pp. 127–41. [G: OECD]

Visco, Ignazio. On Linear Models with Rational Expectations: An Addendum. *Europ. Econ. Rev.*, February 1984, *24*(1), pp. 113–15.

Wallace, Myles S. Economic Stabilization as a Public Good: What Does It Mean? *J. Post Keynesian Econ.*, Winter 1983-84, *6*(2), pp. 295–302.

Watson, Mark W. and Kraft, Dennis F. Testing the Interpretation of Indices in a Macroeconomic Index Model. *J. Monet. Econ.*, March 1984, *13*(2), pp. 165–81. [G: U.S.]

Wedlin, A. Expectations Formation and Revision in Economics. *Metroecon.*, June-Oct. 1984, *36*(2–3), pp. 211–25.

Weinrich, Gerd. L'effetto dei mutamenti del salario in uno stato di sottoccupazione keynesiana con razionamento stocastico. (The Effect of Wage Rate Changes in a Keynesian State of Underemployment with Stochastic Rationing. With English summary.) *Giorn. Econ.*, July–August 1984, *43*(7–8), pp. 531–46.

Weinrich, Gerd. Les effets du changement du taux de salaire dans un état de chômage keynésien avec rationnement stochastique. (The Effect of Wage Rate Changes in a State of Keynesian Unemployment with Stochastic Rationing. With English summary.) *L'Actual. Econ.*, December 1984, *60*(4), pp. 452–70.

Weinrich, Gerd. On the Theory of Effective Demand under Stochastic Rationing. *J. Econ. Theory*, October 1984, *34*(1), pp. 95–115.

Weisman, Dennis L. Tobin on Keynes: A Suggested Interpretation. *J. Post Keynesian Econ.*, Spring 1984, *6*(3), pp. 411–20.

Wernerfelt, Birger. Stagflation, New Products, and Speculation. *J. Macroecon.*, Summer 1984, *6*(3), pp. 295–309.

Wisley, Thomas O. The Effectiveness of Fiscal Policy under a Consumption Tax. *Quart. Rev. Econ. Bus.*, Spring 1984, *24*(1), pp. 33–41.

Wren-Lewis, Simon. A Note on Nominal Government Expenditure Targets. *J. Macroecon.*, Winter 1984, *6*(1), pp. 89–95.

Yoshikawa, Hiroshi. Demand–Supply Constraints and Inventory Stock in Macroeconomic Analysis. *Econ. Stud. Quart.*, December 1984, *35*(3), pp. 193–205. [G: Japan]

0232 Theory of Aggregate Demand: Consumption

Bliss, Christopher. Notes on the Keynes–Ramsey Rule. In *[Pearce, I. F.]*, 1984, pp. 93–104.

Brown-Collier, Elba and Smith, William Doyle. The Wealth Effect: Pigou, Patinkin and Supply-Side Economics. *Eastern Econ. J.*, October-December 1984, *10*(4), pp. 380–88.

Davis, E. P. The Consumption Function in Macroeconomic Models: A Comparative Study. *Appl. Econ.*, December 1984, *16*(6), pp. 799–838. [G: U.K.]

Evans, Owen J. Empirical Tests of the Life Cycle Hypothesis: Comment. *Amer. Econ. Rev.*, March 1984, *74*(1), pp. 254–57. [G: U.S.]

Evans, Robert A. The Aggregate Consumption Function. In *van der Ploeg, F., ed.*, 1984, pp. 95–120.

Gazioglou, Shaziye. Alternative Theories of the Consumption Function: The Case of Turkey. *Greek Econ. Rev.*, August 1984, *6*(2), pp. 203–32. [G: Turkey]

Goacher, D. J. National Savings, Fiscal Policy and Macroeconomic Stability. *Oxford Econ. Pap.*, March 1984, *36*(1), pp. 16–26.

Green, Francis. A Critique of the Neo-Fisherian Consumption Function. *Rev. Radical Polit. Econ.*, Summer & Fall 1984, *16*(2&3), pp. 95–114. **[G: U.S.]**

Hey, John D. Optimal Consumption When Income Follows a Markov Process. *Bull. Econ. Res.*, November 1984, *36*(2), pp. 109–18.

Horioka, Charles Yuji. The Applicability of the Life-Cycle Hypothesis of Saving to Japan. *Kyoto Univ. Econ. Rev.*, October 1984, *54*(2), pp. 31–56. **[G: Japan]**

Jerison, Michael. Aggregation and Pairwise Aggregation of Demand When the Distribution of Income Is Fixed. *J. Econ. Theory*, June 1984, *33*(1), pp. 1–31.

Kalecki, Michal. The Problem of Effective Demand with Tugan-Baranovski and Rosa Luxemburg. In *Foster, J. B. and Szlajfer, H., eds.*, 1984, *1971*, pp. 151–58.

Kessler, Denis. Foreign Indebtedness, Savings and Growth in Developing Countries. In *Kessler, D. and Ullmo, P.-A., eds.*, 1984, pp. 351–63.

Khan, M. Fahim. Macro Consumption Function in an Islamic Framework. *J. Res. Islamic Econ.*, Winter 1984, *1*(2), pp. 1–24.

Kingston, Geoffrey H. Microeconomic Justification of the Hoarding Function. *Int. Econ. Rev.*, June 1984, *25*(2), pp. 385–89.

Koskela, Erkki and Virén, Matti. Credit Rationing and Consumer Intertemporal Choice. *Oxford Econ. Pap.*, June 1984, *36*(2), pp. 241–47.

Kurz, Mordecai. Capital Accumulation and the Characteristics of Private Inter-Generational Transfers. *Economica*, February 1984, *51*(201), pp. 1–22. **[G: U.S.]**

Lawson, Tony. Generalized Adaptive Expectations. In *van der Ploeg, F., ed.*, 1984, pp. 121–29.

Markose, Sheri M. Non-separability of Consumption and Portfolio Choice with a Precautionary Demand for Money. *Greek Econ. Rev.*, August 1984, *6*(2), pp. 171–202.

Michener, Ron. Permanent Income in General Equilibrium. *J. Monet. Econ.*, May 1984, *13*(3), pp. 297–305.

Mückl, Wolfgang J. Über den Einfluss von parametrischen Änderungen der Sparneigung auf die Gewinnquote und den Kapitalkoeffizienten. (Changes in Thriftiness and Their Effect on Profits Share and Capital Coefficient. With English summary.) *Jahr. Nationalökon. Statist.*, January 1984, *199*(1), pp. 76–87.

Ng, Yew-Kwang. The Response of Aggregate Demand to Income, Money Supply, and Price Level. *J. Macroecon.*, Summer 1984, *6*(3), pp. 357–63.

Parrinello, Sergio. Adaptive Preferences and the Theory of Demand. *J. Post Keynesian Econ.*, Summer 1984, *6*(4), pp. 551–60.

Patterson, K. D. Some Properties of Consumption Functions with Integral Correction Mechanisms. *Manchester Sch. Econ. Soc. Stud.*, December 1984, *52*(4), pp. 347–62. **[G: U.K.]**

Pesaran, M. H. and Evans, Robert A. Inflation, Capital Gains and U.K. Personal Savings: 1953–1981. *Econ. J.*, June 1984, *94*(374), pp. 237–57. **[G: U.K.]**

Sen, Amartya. Optimum Savings, Technical Choice and the Shadow Price of Labour. In *Sen, A., 1984, 1968*, pp. 207–23.

Sen, Amartya. Terminal Capital and Optimum Savings. In *Sen, A., 1984, 1967*, pp. 147–61.

Serow, William J. The Impact of Population Change on Consumption. In *Steinmann, G., ed.*, 1984, pp. 168–78.

Sheffrin, Steven M. The Dispersion Hypothesis in Macroeconomics. *Rev. Econ. Statist.*, August 1984, *66*(3), pp. 482–85. **[G: U.S.]**

Stoker, Thomas M. Exact Aggregation and Generalized Slutsky Conditions. *J. Econ. Theory*, August 1984, *33*(2), pp. 368–77.

Sylos-Labini, Paolo. The Problem of Effective Demand. In *Foster, J. B. and Szlajfer, H., eds.*, 1984, *1962*, pp. 134–50.

Tagel-Din, Seif E. I. Macro-consumption Function in an Islamic Framework. *J. Res. Islamic Econ.*, Summer 1984, *2*(1), pp. 57–62.

Teekens, R. Aspiration Level, Consumption Possibilities and Transaction Behaviour in the Case of a Basic Needs Commodity: An Illustration. In *Cohen, S. I., et al., eds.*, 1984, pp. 267–87.

Varian, Hal R. Social Indifference Curves and Aggregate Demand. *Quart. J. Econ.*, August 1984, *99*(3), pp. 403–14.

White, Betsy Buttrill. Empirical Tests of the Life Cycle Hypothesis: Reply. *Amer. Econ. Rev.*, March 1984, *74*(1), pp. 258–59. **[G: U.S.]**

Wickens, M. R. and Molana, H. Stochastic Life Cycle Theory with Varying Interest Rates and Prices. *Econ. J.*, 1984 Supplement, *94*, pp. 133–47. **[G: U.K.]**

0233 Theory of Aggregate Demand: Investment

Adachi, Hideyuki. Investment, Replacement and Depreciation Funds. *Kobe Univ. Econ.*, 1984, (30), pp. 47–63. **[G: Japan]**

Artus, Patrick and Muet, Pierre-Alain. Un panorama des développements récents de l'économétrie de l'investissement. (A Survey of Recent Developments in the Econometrics of Investment. With English summary.) *Revue Écon.*, September 1984, *35*(5), pp. 791–830. **[G: Japan; France; U.K.; U.S.; Germany]**

d'Autume, Antoine and Michel, Philippe. Évaluation du capital en présence de contraintes anticipées sur les achats de biens d'investissement. (Capital Evaluation with Expected Constraints on Purchases of Investment Goods. With English summary.) *Ann. INSEE*, April–June 1984, (54), pp. 101–15.

Bowles, David; Wallace, Myles S. and Wang, Leonard F. S. Crowding Out: A New Perspective. *Econ. Notes*, 1984, (2), pp. 85–89.

Clower, Robert W. On the Invariance of Demand

for Cash and Other Assets. In *Clower, R. W.*, 1984, *1960*, pp. 138–44.

Driehuis, Wim. Macroeconomic Investment and Employment Functions. In *van der Ploeg, F., ed.*, 1984, pp. 131–61.

Eichenbaum, Martin S. Rational Expectations and the Smoothing Properties of Inventories of Finished Goods. *J. Monet. Econ.*, July 1984, *14*(1), pp. 71–96. **[G: U.S.]**

Fiorito, Riccardo. Multisectoral Inventory Cycles under Different Expectations and Technologies. *Econ. Notes*, 1984, (1), pp. 109–20. **[G: Italy]**

Fischer, Stanley and Merton, Robert C. Macroeconomics and Finance: The Role of the Stock Market. *Carnegie-Rochester Conf. Ser. Public Policy*, Autumn 1984, *21*, pp. 57–108.

Fortune, J. Neill. Inventory Accumulation and Expectations of Real Income, Inflation and Interest Rates. *Appl. Econ.*, June 1984, *16*(3), pp. 411–19. **[G: U.S.]**

Galeotti, Marzio. Recent Developments in Investment Theory. *Giorn. Econ.*, May–June 1984, *43*(5–6), pp. 393–415.

Hosek, William R. and Zahn, Frank. Real Rates of Return and Aggregate Investment. *Southern Econ. J.*, July 1984, *51*(1), pp. 157–65. **[G: U.S.]**

Hulten, Charles R. Tax Policy and the Investment Decision. *Amer. Econ. Rev.*, May 1984, *74*(2), pp. 236–41. **[G: U.S.]**

Kračun, Davorin. Aktivizacijska doba investicij v Jugoslaviji—Metodologija in izračun. (Maturation Period of Investment in Yugoslavia—Methodology and Computation. With English summary.) *Econ. Anal. Worker's Manage.*, 1984, *18*(3), pp. 201–16. **[G: Yugoslavia]**

Maccini, Louis J. and Rossana, Robert J. Joint Production, Quasi-Fixed Factors of Production, and Investement in Finished Goods Inventories. *J. Money, Credit, Banking*, May 1984, *16*(2), pp. 218–36. **[G: U.S.]**

Malgrange, Pierre and Villa, Pierre. Comportement d'investissement avec coûts d'adjustements et contraintes quantitatives. (Investment Behavior with Adjustment Costs and Quantitative Constraints. With English summary.) *Ann. INSEE*, January–March 1984, (53), pp. 31–61.

McCallum, Bennett T. Macroeconomics and Finance: The Role of the Stock Market: A Comment. *Carnegie-Rochester Conf. Ser. Public Policy*, Autumn 1984, *21*, pp. 109–15.

von Natzmer, Wulfheinrich and Reim, O. Wirtschaftspolitik und Konjunktur in einem modifizierten ISLM-Modell. (Economic Policy and the Business Cycle in a Modified ISLM Model. With English summary.) *Kredit Kapital*, 1984, *17*(3), pp. 371–95.

Ng, Yew-Kwang. The Response of Aggregate Demand to Income, Money Supply, and Price Level. *J. Macroecon.*, Summer 1984, *6*(3), pp. 357–63.

Okishio, Nobuo. The Decision of New Investment, Technique and Rate of Utilization. *Kobe Univ. Econ.*, 1984, (30), pp. 15–32.

Potestio, Paola. Investment in Some Neoclassical

Models of Capital Accumulation. *Econ. Appl.*, 1984, *37*(3–4), pp. 543–63.

Sampson, Anthony A. The Demand for Capital Goods by the Quantity Constrained Firm. *Oxford Econ. Pap.*, June 1984, *36*(2), pp. 232–40.

Sardoni, Claudio. Some Ties of Kalecki to the 1926 "Sraffian Manifesto." *J. Post Keynesian Econ.*, Spring 1984, *6*(3), pp. 458–65.

Seccareccia, Mario S. The Fundamental Macroeconomic Link between Investment Activity, the Structure of Employment and Price Changes: A Theoretical and Empirical Analysis. *Econ. Soc.*, April 1984, *18*(4), pp. 165–219. **[G: Canada]**

Sen, Amartya. Optimum Savings, Technical Choice and the Shadow Price of Labour. In *Sen, A.*, 1984, *1968*, pp. 207–23.

Sheffrin, Steven M. The Dispersion Hypothesis in Macroeconomics. *Rev. Econ. Statist.*, August 1984, *66*(3), pp. 482–85. **[G: U.S.]**

Sylos-Labini, Paolo. On the Concept of the Optimum Rate of Profit. In *Sylos-Labini, P.*, 1984, *1981*, pp. 211–25. **[G: U.S.]**

Teschner, Manfred. Sparen, Investieren und Wirtschaftswachstum. (Saving, Investment and Economic Growth. With English summary.) *Konjunkturpolitik*, 1984, *30*(4), pp. 233–58.

Trivedi, Pravin K. Adjustment Costs and Production Smoothing: Some Econometric Implications. *Manchester Sch. Econ. Soc. Stud.*, March 1984, *52*(1), pp. 1–13.

Wildasin, David E. The *q* Theory of Investment with Many Capital Goods. *Amer. Econ. Rev.*, March 1984, *74*(1), pp. 203–10.

Yoshikawa, Hiroshi. Demand–Supply Constraints and Inventory Stock in Macroeconomic Analysis. *Econ. Stud. Quart.*, December 1984, *35*(3), pp. 193–205. **[G: Japan]**

0234 Theory of Aggregate Supply

Aizenman, Joshua. Optimal Wage Re-Negotiation in a Closed and Open Economy. *J. Monet. Econ.*, March 1984, *13*(2), pp. 251–62.

Ashenfelter, Orley C. Macroeconomic Analyses and Microeconomic Analyses of Labor Supply. *Carnegie-Rochester Conf. Ser. Public Policy*, Autumn 1984, *21*, pp. 117–55. **[G: U.S.; U.K.; Canada]**

d'Autume, Antoine and Michel, Philippe. Évaluation du capital en présence de contraintes anticipées sur les achats de biens d'investissement. (Capital Evaluation with Expected Constraints on Purchases of Investment Goods. With English summary.) *Ann. INSEE*, April–June 1984, (54), pp. 101–15.

Baldone, Salvatore. From Surrogate to Pseudo Production Functions. *Cambridge J. Econ.*, September 1984, *8*(3), pp. 271–88.

Baldone, Salvatore. Integrazione verticale, struttura temporale dei processi produttivi e transizione fra le tecniche. (With English summary.) *Econ. Polít.*, April 1984, *1*(1), pp. 79–105.

Baldry, J. C. Wage Indexation in a Two-Sector Economy: A Generalisation. *Australian Econ. Pap.*, December 1984, *23*(43), pp. 219–34.

Balducci, Renato and Denicolò, Vincenzo. Quando i lavortori risparmiano: sovraccumulazione del capitale ed eutanasia dei capitalisti. (With English summary.) *Econ. Polít.*, December 1984, *1*(3), pp. 361–406.

Bhandari, Jagdeep S. and Turnovsky, Stephen J. Materials Price Increases and Aggregate Adjustment in an Open Economy: A Stochastic Approach. *Europ. Econ. Rev.*, July 1984, *25*(2), pp. 151–82.

Blackorby, Charles and Schworm, William. The Structure of Economies with Aggregate Measures of Capital: A Complete Characterization. *Rev. Econ. Stud.*, October 1984, *51*(4), pp. 633–50.

Bosi, Paolo and Stagni, Anna. Domanda di fattori e sostituibilità nell'industria italiana: una verifica dell'ipotesi "putty–clay." (With English summary.) *Econ. Polít.*, August 1984, *1*(2), pp. 197–241. [G: Italy]

Boulier, Bryan L. What Lies behind Verdoorn's Law? *Oxford Econ. Pap.*, June 1984, *36*(2), pp. 259–67.

Brockway, George P. Kaldor's "Best" Choice [Allyn Young on Increasing Returns]. *J. Post Keynesian Econ.*, Spring 1984, *6*(3), pp. 481–82.

Bruni, Franco. Monopolistic Competition, Fixed Real Wages and Aggregate Supply. *Rivista Int. Sci. Econ. Com.*, December 1984, *31*(12), pp. 1168–85.

Bull, Clive and Frydman, Roman. A Reply [The Derivation and Interpretation of the Lucas Supply Function]. *J. Money, Credit, Banking*, August 1984, *16*(3), pp. 377–79.

Burgess, David F. Energy Prices, Capital Formation, and Potential GNP. *Energy J.*, April 1984, *5*(2), pp. 1–27. [G: U.S.]

Carling, Alan. Value and Strategy. *Sci. Soc.*, Summer 1984, *48*(2), pp. 129–60.

Cohen, Avi J. The Methodological Resolution of the Cambridge Controversies. *J. Post Keynesian Econ.*, Summer 1984, *6*(4), pp. 614–29.

Collier, Paul and Pemberton, James. Unemployment, Information, and Job Competition. *Greek Econ. Rev.*, April 1984, *6*(1), pp. 121–40.

Drèze, Jacques H. Second-best Analysis with Markets in Disequilibrium: Public Sector Pricing in a Keynesian Regime. In *Marchand, M.; Pestieau, P. and Tulkens, H., eds.*, 1984, pp. 45–79.

Driehuis, Wim. Macroeconomic Investment and Employment Functions. In *van der Ploeg, F., ed.*, 1984, pp. 131–61.

Eckstein, Otto. Foundations of Aggregate Supply Price. *Amer. Econ. Rev.*, May 1984, *74*(2), pp. 216–20. [G: U.S.]

Egidi, Massimo and Gilibert, Giorgio. La teoria oggettiva dei prezzi. (With English summary.) *Econ. Polít.*, April 1984, *1*(1), pp. 43–61.

Farmer, Roger E. A. A New Theory of Aggregate Supply. *Amer. Econ. Rev.*, December 1984, *74*(5), pp. 920–30.

Ferro, Angelo. Fondamenti teorici ed origini storiche della politica dell'offerta. (Theoretical Fundamentals and Historical Origins of Supply-Side Policy. With English summary.) *Bancaria*, January 1984, *40*(1), pp. 12–18.

Francesco, Farina. "Inefficient" Equilibrium in V. Lutz's Two-Sector Model: A Critique. *Econ. Notes*, 1984, (2), pp. 25–50.

Froyen, Richard T. and Waud, Roger N. The Changing Relationship between Aggregate Price and Output: The British Experience. *Economica*, February 1984, *51*(201), pp. 53–67. [G: U.K.]

Galeotti, Marzio. On the Micro-foundations of the Lucas Supply Function. *Econ. Notes*, 1984, (3), pp. 115–27.

Gallaway, Lowell E. The Nature of Equilibrium in a Simple Marxian Economy. *Rivista Int. Sci. Econ. Com.*, February 1984, *31*(2), pp. 126–30.

Georgescu-Roegen, Nicholas. Feasible Recipes versus Viable Technologies. *Atlantic Econ. J.*, March 1984, *12*(1), pp. 20–31.

Giussani, Paulo. Labour-Power: The Missing Commodity. In *Mandel, E. and Freeman, A., eds.*, 1984, pp. 115–40.

Gordon, Robert J. Supply Shocks and Monetary Policy Revisited. *Amer. Econ. Rev.*, May 1984, *74*(2), pp. 38–43.

Gozzi, Giancarlo. Posizioni di lungo periodo e stabilità. (With English summary.) *Econ. Polít.*, December 1984, *1*(3), pp. 407–27.

Hamada, Koichi and Kurosaka, Yoshio. The Relationship between Production and Unemployment in Japan: Okun's Law in Comparative Perspective. *Europ. Econ. Rev.*, June 1984, *25*(1), pp. 71–94. [G: U.S.; Japan]

Haraf, William S. The Relationship between Production and Unemployment in Japan: Okun's Law in Comparative Perspective: Comments. *Europ. Econ. Rev.*, June 1984, *25*(1), pp. 95–98. [G: U.S.; Japan]

von Hayek, Friedrich A. Capital Consumption. In *von Hayek, F. A. (II)*, 1984, *1932*, pp. 136–58.

von Hayek, Friedrich A. Technical Progress and Excess Capacity. In *von Hayek, F. A. (II)*, 1984, *1936*, pp. 163–80.

Heckman, James J. Comments on the Ashenfelter and Kydland Papers [Macroeconomic Analyses and Microeconomic Analyses of Labor Supply] [Labor-Force Heterogeneity and the Business Cycle]. *Carnegie-Rochester Conf. Ser. Public Policy*, Autumn 1984, *21*, pp. 209–24.

Holländer, Heinz. A Further Note on Sraffa's Negative Quantities of Allegedly Embodied Labour. *Econ. J.*, March 1984, *94*(373), pp. 155–57.

Kalecki, Michal. The Marxian Equations of Reproduction and Modern Economics. In *Foster, J. B. and Szlajfer, H., eds.*, 1984, *1968*, pp. 159–66.

Kemp, Murray C.; Long, Ngo Van and Shimomura, Kazuo. The Problem of Survival: A Closed Economy. In *Kemp, M. C. and Long, N. V., eds.*, 1984, pp. 13–26.

Kierzkowski, Henryk. Trade Unions, Wage Relativities and Employment. *Australian Econ. Pap.*, June 1984, 23(42), pp. 91–104.

Kimbrough, Kent P. The Derivation and Interpretation of the Lucas Supply Function: A Comment. *J. Money, Credit, Banking*, August 1984, 16(3), pp. 367–77.

Kohn, Meir. The Inflation Tax and the Value of Equity. *Can. J. Econ.*, May 1984, 17(2), pp. 312–26.

Kohn, Robert E. Industry Isoquants when the Number of Firms Is a Variable. *Rivista Int. Sci. Econ. Com.*, March 1984, 31(3), pp. 257–63.

Koizumi, Susumu. Wage–Employment Contract and Okun's Law. (In Japanese. With English summary.) *Osaka Econ. Pap.*, December 1984, 34(2–3), pp. 27–35. **[G: Japan; U.S.]**

Kydland, Finn E. A Clarification: Using the Growth Model to Account for Fluctuations: Reply [Labor-Force Heterogeneity and the Business Cycle]. *Carnegie-Rochester Conf. Ser. Public Policy*, Autumn 1984, 21, pp. 225–30.

Kydland, Finn E. Labor-Force Heterogeneity and the Business Cycle. *Carnegie-Rochester Conf. Ser. Public Policy*, Autumn 1984, 21, pp. 173–208.

Leiderman, Leonardo. On the Monetary-Macro Dynamics of Colombia and Mexico. *J. Devel. Econ.*, January–February 1984, 14(1–2), pp. 183–201. **[G: Colombia; Mexico]**

Lewis, Philip E. T. and Makepeace, Gerald H. The Estimation of a Disequilibrium Real Wage Equation for Britain. *J. Macroecon.*, Fall 1984, 6(4), pp. 399–410. **[G: U.K.]**

Lubrano, Michel and Sneessens, Henri R. Un modèle de production CES–Léontief pour l'industrie française. (A Léontief–CES Production Model for the French Industry. With English summary.) *Ann. INSEE*, April–June 1984, (54), pp. 3–30. **[G: France]**

Maccini, Louis J. The Interrelationship between Price and Output Decisions and Investment Decisions: Microfoundations and Aggregate Implications. *J. Monet. Econ.*, January 1984, 13(1), pp. 41–65.

Mairesse, Jacques. The Relationship between Production and Unemployment in Japan: Okun's Law in Comparative Perspective: Comments. *Europ. Econ. Rev.*, June 1984, 25(1), pp. 99–105. **[G: U.S.; Japan; EEC]**

Mandel, Ernest. Gold, Money and the Transformation Problem. In *Mandel, E. and Freeman, A., eds.*, 1984, pp. 141–63.

Marangoni, Giandemetrio. Prezzi positivi e merce tipo nel modello di produzione congiunta di Piero Sraffa. (Positive Prices and Standard Commodity in Piero Sraffa's Model of Joint Production. With English summary.) *Rivista Int. Sci. Econ. Com.*, December 1984, 31(12), pp. 1186–1200.

McDonald, Ian M. Anti-stagflationary Tax Cuts and the Problem of Investment. *Econ. Rec.*, September 1984, 60(170), pp. 284–93.

Meacci, Ferdinando. L'analisi del capitale nella teoria dello sviluppo economico di J. A. Schumpeter. (The Analysis of Capital in Schumpeter's

Theory of Economic Development. With English summary.) *Rivista Int. Sci. Econ. Com.*, February 1984, 31(2), pp. 131–46.

Mirochnichenko, V. L. and Parinov, S. I. Analyzing Economic Growth Using Spline Macroeconomic Production Functions. *Matekon*, Winter 1984–85, 21(2), pp. 68–89. **[G: U.S.S.R.]**

Mitchell, Douglas W. Macro Effects of Interest-sensitive Aggregate Supply. *J. Macroecon.*, Winter 1984, 6(1), pp. 43–56.

Mückl, Wolfgang J. Über den Einfluss von parametrischen Änderungen der Sparneigung auf die Gewinnquote und den Kapitalkoeffizienten. (Changes in Thriftiness and Their Effect on Profits Share and Capital Coefficient. With English summary.) *Jahr. Nationalökon. Statist.*, January 1984, 199(1), pp. 76–87.

Muysken, Joan. Overhead Labour and Bounded Substitutability. *De Economist*, 1984, 132(4), pp. 440–50.

Nakatani, Takeshi. Technical Change and the Rate of Profit: Considering Fixed Capital. *Kobe Univ. Econ.*, 1984, (30), pp. 65–78.

Oi, Walter Y. A Comment on the Ashenfelter Analysis of Labor Market Fluctuations [Macroeconomic Analyses and Microeconomic Analyses of Labor Supply]. *Carnegie-Rochester Conf. Ser. Public Policy*, Autumn 1984, 21, pp. 157–72. **[G: U.S.; U.K.; Canada]**

Pemberton, James. Equilibrium Unemployment and the Long-run Phillips Curve in a Partially Unionized Economy. *Manchester Sch. Econ. Soc. Stud.*, December 1984, 52(4), pp. 402–16.

Reinwald, Thomas P. Aggregate Supply Once More: A Rejoinder [A Note on the Treatment of Aggregate Supply in Some Textbooks]. *Amer. Econ.*, Fall 1984, 28(2), pp. 84–86.

Roger, Colin. Erratum [Neo-Walrasian Macroeconomics Microfoundations and Pseudo-Production Models]. *Australian Econ. Pap.*, June 1984, 23(42), pp. 167.

Rohwedder, Jürgen and Herberg, Horst. Effects of Exogenous Nominal Wage Increases: The Purchasing Power Argument vs. the Production Cost Argument. *Z. Wirtschaft. Sozialwissen.*, 1984, 104(6), pp. 585–601.

Sawyer, Malcolm C. The Surprise Supply Function: A Critique. *Brit. Rev. Econ. Issues*, Autumn 1984, 6(15), pp. 1–21.

Scarth, William M. Adjustment Costs and Aggregate Supply Theory. *Can. J. Econ.*, November 1984, 17(4), pp. 847–54.

Sen, Amartya. On Some Debates in Capital Theory. In *Sen, A.*, 1984, 1974, pp. 162–71.

Seton, F. Relative Prices Across Space and Time—The Production of Commodities by Means of Commodities and Factors. In *Csikós-Nagy, B.; Hague, D. and Hall, G., eds.*, 1984, pp. 24–45.

Shaked, Avner and Sutton, John. Involuntary Unemployment as a Perfect Equilibrium in a Bargaining Model. *Econometrica*, November 1984, 52(6), pp. 1351–64.

Sheehey, Edmund J. Money and Output in Latin America: Some Tests of a Rational Expectations

Approach. *J. Devel. Econ.*, January–February 1984, *14*(1–2), pp. 203–18.
[G: Latin America]

Simon, Julian L. and Steinmann, Gunter. The Economic Implications of Learning-by-Doing for Population Size and Growth. *Europ. Econ. Rev.*, October–November 1984, *26*(1–2), pp. 167–85.

Stanfield, Ron. A Revision of the Economic Surplus Concept. In *Foster, J. B. and Szlajfer, H., eds.*, 1984, *1974*, pp. 251–61. [G: U.S.]

Sylos-Labini, Paolo. Factors Affecting Changes in Productivity. *J. Post Keynesian Econ.*, Winter 1983-84, *6*(2), pp. 161–79. [G: Italy; U.S.]

Szlajfer, Henryk. Economic Surplus and Surplus Value Under Monopoly Capitalism. In *Foster, J. B. and Szlajfer, H., eds.*, 1984, *1983*, pp. 262–93.

Toker, Mehmet Ayhan. A Note on the 'Negative' Quantities of Embodied Labour. *Econ. J.*, March 1984, *94*(373), pp. 149–54.

Trivedi, Pravin K. Adjustment Costs and Production Smoothing: Some Econometric Implications. *Manchester Sch. Econ. Soc. Stud.*, March 1984, *52*(1), pp. 1–13.

Ueda, Kazuo. Supply Shocks and the Interdependence of Macroeconomic Stability under Flexible Exchange Rates. *Europ. Econ. Rev.*, July 1984, *25*(2), pp. 253–77. [G: Japan; Germany]

Uri, Noel D. The Impact of Technical Change on the Aggregate Production Function. *Appl. Econ.*, August 1984, *16*(4), pp. 555–67. [G: U.S.]

Viñals, Jose M. Energy–Capital Substitutions, Wage Flexibility and Aggregate Output Supply. *Europ. Econ. Rev.*, October–November 1984, *26*(1–2), pp. 229–45. [G: U.S.; Europe]

Westphal, Larry E. and Cremer, Jacques. "The Independence of Investment Decisions" Revisited. In *[Chenery, H. B.]*, 1984, pp. 543–72.

van Wijnbergen, Sweder. The 'Dutch Disease': A Disease after All? *Econ. J.*, March 1984, *94*(373), pp. 41–55.

Zamagni, Stefano. Ricardo and Hayek Effects in a Fixwage Model of Traverse. In *Collard, D. A., et al., eds.*, 1984, pp. 135–51.

Zamagni, Stefano. Ricardo and Hayek Effects in a Fixwage Model of Traverse. *Oxford Econ. Pap.*, Supplement November 1984, *36*, pp. 135–51.

0235 Theory of Aggregate Distribution

Ahmad, Ausaf. A Macro Model of Distribution in an Islamic Economy. *J. Res. Islamic Econ.*, Summer 1984, *2*(1), pp. 1–20.

Antipova, O. N. and Golosov, V. V. Ideas of Profit and Interest. In *Smirnov, A. D.; Golosov, V. V. and Maximova, V. F., eds.*, 1984, pp. 88–109.

Baldone, Salvatore. From Surrogate to Pseudo Production Functions. *Cambridge J. Econ.*, September 1984, *8*(3), pp. 271–88.

Balducci, Renato and Denicolò, Vincenzo. Quando i lavortori risparmiano: sovraccumula-

zione del capitale ed eutanasia dei capitalisti. (With English summary.) *Econ. Polít.*, December 1984, *1*(3), pp. 361–406.

Bandyopadhyay, Pradeep. Value and Post-Sraffa Marxian Analysis. *Sci. Soc.*, Winter 1984-1985, *48*(4), pp. 433–48.

Barnes, Trevor. Theories of Agricultural Rent within the Surplus Approach. *Int. Reg. Sci. Rev.*, November 1984, *9*(2), pp. 125–40.

Bodkin, Ronald G. and Arroja, Pedro. A Simulation Study of the Solow–Stiglitz Model of Aggregative Income Distribution. *Metroecon.*, February 1984, *36*(1), pp. 1–23.

Bowles, Samuel. Class Alliances and Surplus Labor Time. In *[Chenery, H. B.]*, 1984, pp. 103–14.

Brush, Brian C. and Crane, Steven E. Wage Share, Market Power and Unionism: Some Contrary U.S. Evidence. *Manchester Sch. Econ. Soc. Stud.*, December 1984, *52*(4), pp. 417–24. [G: U.S.]

Burmeister, Edwin. Sraffa, Labor Theories of Value, and the Economics of Real Wage Rate Determination. *J. Polit. Econ.*, June 1984, *92*(3), pp. 508–26.

Carling, Alan. Observations on the Labor Theory of Value. *Sci. Soc.*, Winter 1984-1985, *48*(4), pp. 407–18.

Carling, Alan. Value and Strategy. *Sci. Soc.*, Summer 1984, *48*(2), pp. 129–60.

Chishti, Salim. Theory of Profit: The Islamic Viewpoint: Comment. *J. Res. Islamic Econ.*, Summer 1984, *2*(1), pp. 49–51.

Costrell, Robert M. Equilibrium Unemployment and Excess Capacity in Steady-State and Growth Cycles. *Economica*, February 1984, *51*(201), pp. 69–82.

Dobb, Maurice. A Note on Distribution and the Price Mark-Up. In *Foster, J. B. and Szlajfer, H., eds.*, 1984, *1973*, pp. 85–90.

Duménil, Gérard. The So-Called "Transformation Problem" Revisited: A Brief Comment. *J. Econ. Theory*, August 1984, *33*(2), pp. 340–48.

Dutt, Amitava Krishna. Stagnation, Income Distribution and Monopoly Power. *Cambridge J. Econ.*, March 1984, *8*(1), pp. 25–40. [G: India]

Egidi, Massimo and Gilibert, Giorgio. La teoria oggettiva dei prezzi. (With English summary.) *Econ. Polít.*, April 1984, *1*(1), pp. 43–61.

Flaschel, Peter. The So-Called "Transformation Problem" Revisited: A Comment. *J. Econ. Theory*, August 1984, *33*(2), pp. 349–51.

Flaschel, Peter. The Standard Commodity and the Theory of Income Distribution—A Critical Note. *Australian Econ. Pap.*, June 1984, *23*(42), pp. 123–29.

Foster, John Bellamy. Investment and Capitalist Maturity. In *Foster, J. B. and Szlajfer, H., eds.*, 1984, pp. 57–73.

Freeman, Alan. The Logic of the Transformation Problem. In *Mandel, E. and Freeman, A., eds.*, 1984, pp. 221–64.

Funke, Michael. Technikwahl und Profitrate. Ein kritischer Überblick über die augenblickliche

Diskussion zum "Gesetz vom tendenziellen Fall der Profitrate." (With English summary.) *Z. Wirtschaft. Sozialwissen.*, 1984, *104*(3), pp. 307–25.

Gallaway, Lowell E. The Nature of Equilibrium in a Simple Marxian Economy. *Rivista Int. Sci. Econ. Com.*, February 1984, *31*(2), pp. 126–30.

Garagnani, Pierangelo. On Some Illusory Instances of "Marginal Products." *Metroecon.*, June-Oct. 1984, *36*(2–3), pp. 143–60.

Garegnani, Pierangelo. Value and Distribution in the Classical Economists and Marx. *Oxford Econ. Pap.*, June 1984, *36*(2), pp. 291–325.

Goleva, A. P. and Goleva, Yu. P. Definitions of Capital and Surplus Value. In *Smirnov, A. D.; Golosov, V. V. and Maximova, V. F.*, *eds.*, 1984, pp. 60–70.

Hagemann, Harald and Jeck, Albert. Lowe and the Marx–Fel'dman–Dobb Model: Structural Analysis of a Growing Economy. *Eastern Econ. J.*, April-June 1984, *10*(2), pp. 169–86.

Hart, Robert A. Worksharing and Factor Prices. *Europ. Econ. Rev.*, March 1984, *24*(2), pp. 165–88.   [G: OECD]

von Hayek, Friedrich A. Capital Consumption. In *von Hayek, F. A. (II)*, 1984, *1932*, pp. 136–58.

von Hayek, Friedrich A. Some Remarks on the Problem of Imputation. In *von Hayek, F. A. (II)*, 1984, *1926*, pp. 33–54.

Himmelweit, Susan. Value Relations and Divisions within the Working Class. *Sci. Soc.*, Fall 1984, *48*(3), pp. 323–43.   [G: Global]

Kalecki, Michal. Class Struggle and the Distribution of National Income. In *Foster, J. B. and Szlajfer, H.*, *eds.*, 1984, *1971*, pp. 77–84.

Karpikov, E. I. and Pikin, A. S. Bourgeois and Reformist Agrarian Conceptions. In *Smirnov, A. D.; Golosov, V. V. and Maximova, V. F.*, *eds.*, 1984, pp. 110–17.

Kohn, Meir. The Inflation Tax and the Value of Equity. *Can. J. Econ.*, May 1984, *17*(2), pp. 312–26.

Kubin, Ingrid. Equilibrium and Stability Analysis in the Classical Framework. *Metroecon.*, February 1984, *36*(1), pp. 47–64.

Laibman, David. Value: A Dialog in One Act. *Sci. Soc.*, Winter 1984-1985, *48*(4), pp. 449–65.

Lenel, Hans Otto. Ein dritter Weg? Zu Ota Šiks "Hummaner Wirtschaftsdemokratie." (With English Summary.) In *Eucken, W. and Böhm, F.*, *eds.*, 1984, pp. 179–230.

Lipietz, Alain. The So-Called "Transformation Problem" Revisited: A Brief Reply to Brief Comments. *J. Econ. Theory*, August 1984, *33*(2), pp. 352–55.

Manzar, A. M. Theory of Profit: The Islamic Viewpoint: Comment. *J. Res. Islamic Econ.*, Summer 1984, *2*(1), pp. 53–54.

Meacci, Ferdinando. L'analisi del capitale nella teoria dello sviluppo economico di J. A. Schumpeter. (The Analysis of Capital in Schumpeter's Theory of Economic Development. With En-

glish summary.) *Rivista Int. Sci. Econ. Com.*, February 1984, *31*(2), pp. 131–46.

Mikhalkina, T. Y.; Lebedev, V. N. and Maryganova, E. A. Western Views of Wages and Unemployment. In *Smirnov, A. D.; Golosov, V. V. and Maximova, V. F.*, *eds.*, 1984, pp. 71–87.

Mohun, Simon. Abstract Labor and Its Value-Form. *Sci. Soc.*, Winter 1984-1985, *48*(4), pp. 388–406.

Morris, Jacob. Profit Rates and Capital Formation in American Monopoly Capitalism. In *Foster, J. B. and Szlajfer, H.*, *eds.*, 1984, *1979*, pp. 217–35.

Pohjola, Matti. Threats and Bargaining in Capitalism: A Differential Game View. *J. Econ. Dynam. Control*, December 1984, *8*(3), pp. 291–302.

Potestio, Paola. Investment in Some Neoclassical Models of Capital Accumulation. *Écon. Appl.*, 1984, *37*(3–4), pp. 543–63.

Sampson, Anthony A. Unemployment and the Distribution of Income. *Australian Econ. Pap.*, December 1984, *23*(43), pp. 249–58.

Schmitt-Rink, Gerhard. Population Growth and Income Distribution. In *Steinmann, G.*, *ed.*, 1984, pp. 59–67.

Scott, Maurice. Maintaining Capital Intact. *Oxford Econ. Pap.*, Supplement November 1984, *36*, pp. 59–73.

Scott, Maurice. Maintaining Capital Intact. In *Collard, D. A.*, *et al.*, *eds.*, 1984, pp. 59–73.

Sekine, Thomas T. An Uno School Seminar on the Theory of Value. *Sci. Soc.*, Winter 1984-1985, *48*(4), pp. 419–32.

Sen, Amartya. On Some Debates in Capital Theory. In *Sen, A.*, 1984, *1974*, pp. 162–71.

Sen, Amartya. Terminal Capital and Optimum Savings. In *Sen, A.*, 1984, *1967*, pp. 147–61.

Steedman, Ian. Natural Prices, Differential Profit Rates and the Classical Competitive Process. *Manchester Sch. Econ. Soc. Stud.*, June 1984, *52*(2), pp. 123–40.

Sweezy, Paul M. Some Problems in the Theory of Capital Accumulation. In *Foster, J. B. and Szlajfer, H.*, *eds.*, 1984, *1973*, pp. 41–56.

Sylos-Labini, Paolo. On the Concept of the Optimum Rate of Profit. In *Sylos-Labini, P.*, 1984, *1981*, pp. 211–25.   [G: U.S.]

Sylos-Labini, Paolo. Prices and Income Distribution in the Manufacturing Industry. In *Sylos-Labini, P.*, 1984, *1979*, pp. 185–209.
          [G: Italy; U.S.; U.K.; W. Germany; Argentina]

Wolff, Richard D.; Callari, Antonino and Roberts, Bruce. A Marxian Alternative to the Traditional "Transformation Problem." *Rev. Radical Polit. Econ.*, Summer & Fall 1984, *16*(2&3), pp. 115–35.

Wolff, Richard D.; Roberts, Bruce and Callari, Antonino. Unsnarling the Tangle: A Rejoinder [Marx's (Not Ricardo's) "Transformation Problem": A Radical Reconceptualization]. *Hist. Polit. Econ.*, Fall 1984, *16*(3), pp. 431–36.

Wolfson, Murray. Weaving a Tangled Web: The

Transformation of Values into Prices. *Hist. Polit. Econ.*, Fall 1984, *16*(3), pp. 423–30.

0239 Macroeconomics of Intertemporal Choice

Buiter, Willem H. and Carmichael, Jeffrey. Government Debt: Comment [Government Debt in an Overlapping-Generations Model with Bequests and Gifts]. *Amer. Econ. Rev.*, September 1984, *74*(4), pp. 762–65. **[G: U.S.]**

Burbidge, John B. Government Debt: Reply [Government Debt in an Overlapping-Generations Model with Bequests and Gifts]. *Amer. Econ. Rev.*, September 1984, *74*(4), pp. 766–67. **[G: U.S.]**

Costabile, Lilia. Preferenze intertemporali, risparmi e investimenti. Note su due approcci alternativi. (With English summary.) *Econ. Polit.*, December 1984, *1*(3), pp. 335–59.

von Hayek, Friedrich A. Intertemporal Price Equilibrium and Movements in the Value of Money. In *von Hayek, F. A. (II)*, 1984, *1928*, pp. 71–117.

Kehoe, Timothy J. and Levine, David K. Intertemporal Separability in Overlapping-Generations Models. *J. Econ. Theory*, December 1984, *34*(2), pp. 216–26.

Kehoe, Timothy J. and Levine, David K. Regularity in Overlapping Generations Exchange Economies. *J. Math. Econ.*, April 1984, *13*(1), pp. 69–93.

Koda, Keiichi. A Note on the Existence of Monetary Equilibria in Overlapping Generations Models with Storage. *J. Econ. Theory*, December 1984, *34*(2), pp. 388–95.

Kurz, Mordecai. Capital Accumulation and the Characteristics of Private Inter-Generational Transfers. *Economica*, February 1984, *51*(201), pp. 1–22. **[G: U.S.]**

Laitner, John P. Transition Time Paths for Overlapping-Generations Models. *J. Econ. Dynam. Control*, May 1984, 7(2), pp. 111–29. **[G: U.S.]**

Sen, Amartya. Isolation, Assurance and the Social Rate of Discount. In *Sen, A.*, 1984, *1967*, pp. 135–46.

Sen, Amartya. On Optimizing the Rate of Saving. In *Sen, A.*, 1984, *1961*, pp. 113–34.

Sen, Amartya. Optimum Savings, Technical Choice and the Shadow Price of Labour. In *Sen, A.*, 1984, *1968*, pp. 207–23.

Sen, Amartya. Terminal Capital and Optimum Savings. In *Sen, A.*, 1984, *1967*, pp. 147–61.

Straub, Martin and Wenig, Alois. Human Fertility and the Distribution of Wealth. In *Steinmann, G., ed.*, 1984, pp. 68–86.

024 Welfare Theory

0240 General

Basu, Kaushik. Fuzzy Revealed Preference Theory. *J. Econ. Theory*, April 1984, 32(2), pp. 212–27.

Basu, Kaushik. The Right to Give up Rights. *Economica*, November 1984, *51*(204), pp. 413–22.

Bhagwati, Jagdish N.; Brecher, Richard A. and Hatta, Tatsuo. The Paradoxes of Immiserizing Growth and Donor-enriching "Recipient-immiserizing" Transfers: A Tale of Two Literatures. *Weltwirtsch. Arch.*, 1984, *120*(2), pp. 228–43.

Blackorby, Charles and Donaldson, David. Ethical Social Index Numbers and the Measurement of Effective Tax/Benefit Progressivity. *Can. J. Econ.*, November 1984, *17*(4), pp. 683–94.

Blackorby, Charles and Donaldson, David. Social Criteria for Evaluating Population Change. *J. Public Econ.*, November 1984, *25*(1/2), pp. 13–33.

Blackorby, Charles; Donaldson, David and Moloney, David. Consumer's Surplus and Welfare Change in a Simple Dynamic Model. *Rev. Econ. Stud.*, January 1984, *51*(1), pp. 171–76.

Bliss, Christopher and Nalebuff, Barry. Dragonslaying and Ballroom Dancing: The Private Supply of a Public Good. *J. Public Econ.*, November 1984, *25*(1/2), pp. 1–12.

Bockstael, Nancy E. The Welfare Implications of Minimum Quality Standards. *Amer. J. Agr. Econ.*, November 1984, *66*(4), pp. 466–71.

Bohm, Peter. Revealing Demand for an Actual Public Good. *J. Public Econ.*, July 1984, *24*(2), pp. 135–51. **[G: Sweden]**

Bowden, Roger. A Note on the "Bottom-up" Approach to Measuring Compensating Variations. *Metroecon.*, February 1984, *36*(1), pp. 65–76.

Broome, John. Uncertainty and Fairness. *Econ. J.*, September 1984, *94*(375), pp. 624–32.

Brown, Thomas C. The Concept of Value in Resource Allocation. *Land Econ.*, August 1984, *60*(3), pp. 231–46.

Brubaker, Earl R. Demand Disclosures and Conditions on Exclusion: An Experiment. *Econ. J.*, September 1984, *94*(375), pp. 536–53. **[G: U.S.]**

Buchanan, James M. The Ethical Limits of Taxation. *Scand. J. Econ.*, 1984, *86*(2), pp. 102–14.

Calvert, Randall L. and Wilson, Rick K. Comment on van de Kragt, Orbell, and Dawes [The Minimal Contributing Set as a Solution to Public Goods Problems]. *Amer. Polit. Sci. Rev.*, June 1984, *78*(2), pp. 496–97.

Collard, David. The Welfare State, Economics and Morality. In *Boulding, K. E., ed.*, 1984, pp. 174–90.

Cornes, Richard and Sandler, Todd. Easy Riders, Joint Production, and Public Goods. *Econ. J.*, September 1984, *94*(375), pp. 580–98.

Cornes, Richard and Sandler, Todd. The Theory of Public Goods: Non-Nash Behaviour. *J. Public Econ.*, April 1984, *23*(3), pp. 367–79.

Cox, Gary W. Non-collegial Simple Games and the Nowhere Denseness of the Set of Preference Profiles Having a Core. *Soc. Choice Welfare*, August 1984, *1*(2), pp. 159–64.

Creedy, John. Public Finance. In *Creedy, J. and O'Brien, D. P., eds.*, 1984, pp. 84–116.

Culyer, Anthony J. The Quest for Efficiency in the Public Sector: Economists versus Dr. Pangloss (or Why Conservative Economists Are Not Nearly Conservative Enough). In *Hanusch, H., ed.*, 1984, pp. 39–48.

Demsetz, Harold. Purchasing Monopoly. In *Colander, D. C., ed.*, 1984, pp. 101–13.

Desai, Meghnad. A General Theory of Poverty? A Review Article. *Indian Econ. Rev.*, July–Dec. 1984, *19*(2), pp. 157–69. **[G: India]**

Ebert, Udo. Exact Welfare Measures and Economic Index Numbers. *Z. Nationalökon.*, 1984, *44*(1), pp. 27–38.

Ebert, Udo. Measures of Distance between Income Distributions. *J. Econ. Theory*, April 1984, *32*(2), pp. 266–74.

Foster, James E.; Greer, Joel and Thorbecke, Erik. A Class of Decomposable Poverty Measures. *Econometrica*, May 1984, *52*(3), pp. 761–66. **[G: Kenya]**

Fountain, John. A Production Theory Perspective on Collective Choice Theory. *Quart. J. Econ.*, November 1984, *99*(4), pp. 673–91.

Fraser, Clive D. Optimal Compensation for Potential Fatality. *J. Public Econ.*, April 1984, *23*(3), pp. 307–32.

Giorgi, Giovanni Maria. A Methodological Survey of Recent Studies for the Measurement of Inequality of Economic Welfare Carried Out by Some Italian Statisticians. *Econ. Notes*, 1984, (1), pp. 146–58.

Hahn, Frank H. Some Adjustment Problems. In *Hahn, F.*, 1984, *1970*, pp. 88–110.

Hamada, Koichi and Iwata, Kazumasa. National Income, Terms of Trade and Economic Welfare. *Econ. J.*, December 1984, *94*(376), pp. 752–71. **[G: Japan]**

Hamlin, Alan P. Public Choice, Markets and Utilitarianism. In *Whynes, D. K., ed.*, 1984, pp. 116–38.

Hanusch, Horst. Public Finance and the Quest for Efficiency. In *Hanusch, H., ed.*, 1984, pp. 1–9.

Hébert, R. F. and Ekelund, Robert B., Jr. Welfare Economics. In *Creedy, J. and O'Brien, D. P., eds.*, 1984, pp. 46–83.

Hempenius, A. L. Relative Income Position, Individual and Social Income Satisfaction, and Income Inequality. *De Economist*, 1984, *132*(4), pp. 468–78.

Hennipman, P. Normative or Positive: Mishan's Half-Way House. *De Economist*, 1984, *132*(1), pp. 86–99.

Hennipman, P. The Nature of Welfare Economics: A Final Note. *De Economist*, 1984, *132*(2), pp. 238.

Hickerson, Steven R. Complexity and the Meaning of Freedom: The Instrumentalist View. *Amer. J. Econ. Soc.*, October 1984, *43*(4), pp. 435–42.

Hicks, John R. Preference and Welfare. In *Hicks, J.*, 1984, pp. 145–63.

Hicks, John R. The Foundations of Welfare Economics. In *Hicks, J.*, 1984, *1939*, pp. 126–44.

Hicks, John R. Valuation of Social Income—The Utility Approach [The Measurement of Real Income]. In *Hicks, J.*, 1984, *1958*, pp. 57–95.

Hillman, Arye L. and Katz, Eliakim. Risk-Averse Rent Seekers and the Social Cost of Monopoly Power. *Econ. J.*, March 1984, *94*(373), pp. 104–10.

Holler, M. J. A Public Good Power Index. In *Holler, M. J., ed.*, 1984, pp. 51–59.

Hoy, Michael. The Impact of Imperfectly Categorizing Risks on Income Inequality and Social Welfare. *Can. J. Econ.*, August 1984, *17*(3), pp. 557–68.

Isaac, R. Mark; Walker, James M. and Thomas, Susan H. Divergent Evidence on Free Riding: An Experimental Examination of Possible Explanations. *Public Choice*, 1984, *43*(2), pp. 113–49.

Jehle, Geoffrey A. Individual Welfare and the Demand for Financial Instruments. *Southern Econ. J.*, July 1984, *51*(1), pp. 116–34. **[G: U.S.]**

Jorgenson, Dale W. and Slesnick, Daniel T. Aggregate Consumer Behaviour and the Measurement of Inequality. *Rev. Econ. Stud.*, July 1984, *51*(3), pp. 369–92. **[G: U.S.]**

Kakwani, Nanak. The Relative Deprivation Curve and Its Applications. *J. Bus. Econ. Statist.*, October 1984, *2*(4), pp. 384–94. **[G: Australia]**

Kakwani, Nanak. The Relative Deprivation Curve and Its Applications: Reply. *J. Bus. Econ. Statist.*, October 1984, *2*(4), pp. 400–405. **[G: Australia]**

Kanbur, S. M. Ravi. The Measurement and Decomposition of Inequality and Poverty. In *van der Ploeg, F., ed.*, 1984, pp. 403–32.

Kaneko, Mamoru. On Interpersonal Utility Comparisons. *Soc. Choice Welfare*, October 1984, *1*(3), pp. 165–75.

Kaneko, Mamoru. Reformulation of the Nash Social Welfare Function for a Continuum of Individuals. *Soc. Choice Welfare*, 1984, *1*(1), pp. 33–43.

Kemp, Murray C. On the Applicability and Implementability of the (Finite) Compensation Principle. *Kobe Econ. Bus. Rev.*, 1984, *30*, pp. 17–22.

Kim, Oliver and Walker, Mark. The Free Rider Problem: Experimental Evidence. *Public Choice*, 1984, *43*(1), pp. 3–24.

Knetsch, Jack L. and Sinden, J. A. Willingness to Pay and Compensation Demanded: Experimental Evidence of an Unexpected Disparity in Measures of Value. *Quart. J. Econ.*, August 1984, *99*(3), pp. 507–21.

Kolm, Serge-Christophe. Théorie de la réciprocité et du choix des systèmes économiques. (Theory of Reciprocity and the Choice of Economic Systems. With English summary.) *Revue Écon.*, September 1984, *35*(5), pp. 871–910.

Lockwood, Ben. Social Choice, Interpersonal Comparability and Welfare Economics. In *van der Ploeg, F., ed.*, 1984, pp. 371–400.

Marchand, Maurice; Pestieau, Pierre and Tulkens, Henry. The Performance of Public Enterprises: Normative, Positive and Empirical Issues. In *Marchand, M.; Pestieau, P. and Tulkens, H., eds.*, 1984, pp. 3–42.

Marchand, Maurice; Pestieau, Pierre and Weymark, John A. Discount Rates for Public Enterprises in the Presence of Alternative Financial Constraints: A Correction. *Z. Nationalökon.*, 1984, 44(3), pp. 289–91.

Markandya, Anil. The Welfare Measurement of Changes in Economic Mobility. *Economica,* November 1984, 51(204), pp. 457–71. [G: U.K.]

McKee, Arnold F. Beauchamp and Donaldson on Economic Justice [The Ethical Foundations of Economic Justice] [What Justice Demands]. *Rev. Soc. Econ.*, April 1984, 42(1), pp. 63–66.

McKee, Michael and West, Edwin G. Do Second-Best Considerations Affect Policy Decisions? *Public Finance,* 1984, 39(2), pp. 246–60.

McKinney, Scott. Public Good Producers and Spillovers: An Analysis of Duopoly Behavior. *Public Finance Quart.*, January 1984, 12(1), pp. 97–116.

Mendell, Marguerite. Social Determinants of Economic Activity: The Economy of Transfer. *J. Econ. Issues,* June 1984, 18(2), pp. 401–10.

Mishan, E. J. The Implications of Alternative Foundations for Welfare Economics. *De Economist,* 1984, 132(1), pp. 75–85.

Mishan, E. J. Welfare Criteria: Concluding Comments. *De Economist,* 1984, 132(2), pp. 234–38.

Møller, Flemming. Social cost–benefit analyse. (Social Cost–Benefit Analysis. With English summary.) *Nationaløkon. Tidsskr.*, 1984, 122(2), pp. 180–200. [G: Denmark]

Nagatani, Hiroaki. Algorithms for the Hicksian Measures of Consumer's Surplus: Professor Houthakker Revaluated. (In Japanese. With English summary.) *Osaka Econ. Pap.*, December 1984, 34(2–3), pp. 135–46.

Ng, Yew-Kwang. Expected Subjective Utility: Is the Neumann–Morgenstern Utility the Same as the Neoclassical's? *Soc. Choice Welfare,* October 1984, 1(3), pp. 177–86.

Nitzan, Shmuel I. and Pattanaik, Prasanta K. Median-based Extensions of an Ordering over a Set to the Power Set: An Axiomatic Characterization. *J. Econ. Theory,* December 1984, 34(2), pp. 252–61.

Novos, Ian E. and Waldman, Michael. The Effects of Increased Copyright Protection: An Analytic Approach. *J. Polit. Econ.*, April 1984, 92(2), pp. 236–46.

Okuguchi, Koji. Utility Function, Group Size, and the Aggregate Provision of a Pure Public Good. *Public Choice,* 1984, 42(3), pp. 247–55.

Palfrey, Thomas R. and Rosenthal, Howard. Participation and the Provision of Discrete Public Goods: A Strategic Analysis. *J. Public Econ.*, July 1984, 24(2), pp. 171–93.

Perri, Timothy J. The Social Loss from Private Monopoly and Optimal Antitrust Enforcement. *Rev. Ind. Organ.*, Winter 1984, 1(4), pp. 276–88.

Posner, Richard A. Wealth Maximization and Judicial Decision-making. *Int. Rev. Law Econ.*, December 1984, 4(2), pp. 131–35. [G: U.S.]

Recktenwald, Horst Claus. The Public Waste Syndrome: A Comprehensive Theory of Government Failures. In *Hanusch, H., ed.*, 1984, pp. 11–26.

van Rompuy, Paul and de Bruyne, Guido. A General Framework for Analysing the Stability of Fiscal Federalism. In *Despontin, M.; Nijkamp, P. and Spronk, J., eds.*, 1984, pp. 141–53.

Rosen, Sherwin. The Relative Deprivation Curve and Its Applications. *J. Bus. Econ. Statist.*, October 1984, 2(4), pp. 395–97. [G: Australia]

Ross, Thomas W. Uncovering Regulators' Social Welfare Weights. *Rand J. Econ.*, Spring 1984, 15(1), pp. 152–55.

Roy, Subroto. Considerations on Utility, Benevolence, and Taxation. *Hist. Polit. Econ.*, Fall 1984, 16(3), pp. 349–62.

Ryscavage, Paul and Lamas, Enrique. The Relative Deprivation Curve and Its Applications: Comment. *J. Bus. Econ. Statist.*, October 1984, 2(4), pp. 398–99. [G: Australia]

Samuels, Warren J. and Mercuro, Nicholas. Posnerian Law and Economics on the Bench. *Int. Rev. Law Econ.*, December 1984, 4(2), pp. 107–30. [G: U.S.]

Schelling, Thomas C. Economic Reasoning and the Ethics of Policy. In *Schelling, T. C.*, 1984, pp. 1–26.

Schelling, Thomas C. Strategic Analysis and Social Problems. In *Schelling, T. C.*, 1984, pp. 195–212.

Schmalensee, Richard. Imperfect Information and the Equitability of Competitive Prices. *Quart. J. Econ.*, August 1984, 99(3), pp. 441–60.

Schmidt-Sørensen, Jan Beyer. Velfærdskriteriernes paradoksproblemer. (The Paradoxes of Welfare Criteria. With English summary.) *Nationaløkon. Tidsskr.*, 1984, 122(2), pp. 161–79.

Schofield, Norman J. Bargaining over Public Goods. In *Holler, M. J., ed.*, 1984, pp. 33–50.

Seldon, Arthur. Enhancement of Public Sector Efficiency by Micro-economic Control of Public Supply. In *Hanusch, H., ed.*, 1984, pp. 155–65.

Sen, Amartya. Ingredients of Famine Analysis: Availability and Entitlements. In *Sen, A.*, 1984, 1981, pp. 452–84. [G: India; Bangladesh]

Sen, Amartya. Isolation, Assurance and the Social Rate of Discount. In *Sen, A.*, 1984, 1967, pp. 135–46.

Sen, Amartya. Poor, Relatively Speaking. In *Sen, A.*, 1984, pp. 325–45.

Sen, Amartya. The Living Standard. In *Collard, D. A., et al., eds.*, 1984, pp. 74–90.

Sen, Amartya. The Living Standard. *Oxford Econ. Pap.*, Supplement November 1984, 36, pp. 74–90.

Sen, Amartya. The Welfare Basis of Real Income Comparisons. In *Sen, A.*, 1984, 1979, pp. 389–451.

Silvestre, Joaquim. Voluntariness and Efficiency

in the Provision of Public Goods. *J. Public Econ.*, July 1984, *24*(2), pp. 249–56.

Stahl, Dale O., II. Cardinal vs. Characteristic Indices of Preference for Applied Welfare Economics. *Public Finance Quart.*, October 1984, *12*(4), pp. 473–86.

Stahl, Dale O., II. Monotonic Variations of Consumer Surplus and Comparative Performance Results. *Southern Econ. J.*, October 1984, *51*(2), pp. 503–20.

Subrahmanyam, Marti G. and Swirski, Moises. The Public Investment Decision under Uncertainty: A Mean-Variance Synthesis. In *Marchand, M.; Pestieau, P. and Tulkens, H., eds.*, 1984, pp. 119–55.

Sugden, Robert. Reciprocity: The Supply of Public Goods through Voluntary Contributions. *Econ. J.*, December 1984, *94*(376), pp. 772–87.

Sugden, Robert. Voluntary Organisations and the Welfare State. In *Le Grand, J. and Robinson, R., eds.*, 1984, pp. 70–89.

Takayama, Akira. Consumer's Surplus, Path Independence, Compensating and Equivalent Variation. *Z. ges. Staatswiss.*, December 1984, *140*(4), pp. 594–625.

Tesfatsion, Leigh. Welfare Implications of Net Social Security Wealth. *J. Public Econ.*, June 1984, *24*(1), pp. 1–27.

Tinbergen, Jan. Alternative Optimal Social Orders. *Pakistan Devel. Rev.*, Spring 1984, *23*(1), pp. 1–7.

Tinbergen, Jan. On Collective and Part-Collective Goods. *De Economist*, 1984, *132*(2), pp. 171–82.

Ulen, Thomas S. The Efficiency of Specific Performance: Toward a Unified Theory of Contract Remedies. *Mich. Law Rev.*, November 1984, *83*(2), pp. 341–403. **[G: U.S.]**

Varian, Hal R. Social Indifference Curves and Aggregate Demand. *Quart. J. Econ.*, August 1984, *99*(3), pp. 403–14.

Violi, Roberto. Un'interpretazione del contratto sociale in termini di "nucleo" di un meta-gioco. (An Interpretation of the Social Contract in Terms of "Nucleus" of a Meta-Game. With English summary.) *Rivista Int. Sci. Econ. Com.*, May 1984, *31*(5), pp. 395–416.

Vlach, Milan. Levitin-Miljutin-Osmolovskii Conditions for Local Pareto Optimality. In *Grauer, M. and Wierzbicki, A. P., eds.*, 1984, pp. 91–96.

Walker, Alan. The Political Economy of Privatisation. In *Le Grand, J. and Robinson, R., eds.*, 1984, pp. 19–44.

Waugh, Frederick V. Does the Consumer Benefit from Price Instability? In *Waugh, F. V.*, 1984, *1944*, pp. 27–39.

Waugh, Frederick V. Market Prorates and Social Welfare. In *Waugh, F. V.*, 1984, *1938*, pp. 132–45.

Weymark, John A. Arrow's Theorem with Social Quasi-Orderings. *Public Choice*, 1984, *42*(3), pp. 235–46.

Wildasin, David E. On Public Good Provision

with Distortionary Taxation. *Econ. Inquiry*, April 1984, *22*(2), pp. 227–43.

Wright, Brian D. and Williams, Jeffrey C. The Welfare Effects of the Introduction of Storage. *Quart. J. Econ.*, February 1984, *99*(1), pp. 169–92.

Yaari, M. E. and Bar-Hillel, M. On Dividing Justly. *Soc. Choice Welfare*, 1984, *1*(1), pp. 1–24.

Yunker, James A. Objective Information and Social Consensus: Some Empirical Evidence on the Relative Importance of Objective and Subjective Determinants of Social Judgment. *Amer. J. Econ. Soc.*, October 1984, *43*(4), pp. 413–26.

0242 Allocative Efficiency Including Theory of Cost/Benefit

Arrow, Kenneth J. Allocation of Resources in Large Teams. In *Arrow, K. J., vol. 4*, 1984, *1979*, pp. 233–61.

Arrow, Kenneth J. The Property Rights Doctrine and Demand Revelation under Incomplete Information. In *Arrow, K. J., vol. 4*, 1984, *1979*, pp. 216–32.

Bandyopadhyay, Taradas. On the Frontier between Possibility and Impossibility Theorems in Social Choice. *J. Econ. Theory*, February 1984, *32*(1), pp. 52–66.

Bennett, John. Alternative Price and Quantity Controls for Regulation under Uncertainty. *Z. Nationalökon.*, 1984, *44*(2), pp. 103–15.

Benson, Bruce L. Rent Seeking from a Property Rights Perspective. *Southern Econ. J.*, October 1984, *51*(2), pp. 388–400.

Benson, Bruce L. Spatial Price Theory and an Efficient Congestion Toll Established by the Free Market. *Econ. Inquiry*, April 1984, *22*(2), pp. 244–52.

Bester, Helmut. Increasing Risk and Equilibrium under Uncertainty. *J. Econ. Theory*, August 1984, *33*(2), pp. 378–86.

Bliss, Christopher. Notes on the Keynes–Ramsey Rule. In *[Pearce, I. F.]*, 1984, pp. 93–104.

Blume, Lawrence E.; Rubinfeld, Daniel L. and Shapiro, Perry. The Taking of Land: When Should Compensation Be Paid? *Quart. J. Econ.*, February 1984, *99*(1), pp. 71–92.

Bohnet, Armin. Effizienz und Preise—zwei zentrale Kategorien in der Wirtschaftsordnungstheorie. (With English summary.) In *Bohnet, A., ed.*, 1984, pp. 121–51.

Borch, Karl. Equilibrium Premiums in an Insurance Market. *J. Risk Ins.*, September 1984, *51*(3), pp. 468–76.

Borglin, Anders and Keiding, Hans. Efficiency in One-Sector, Discrete-Time, Infinite-Horizon Models. *J. Econ. Theory*, June 1984, *33*(1), pp. 183–96.

Boyer, Marcel and Dionne, Georges. Sécurité routière: efficacité, subvention et réglementation. (Road Security: Efficiency, Subsidies, Regulation. With English summary.) *L'Actual. Econ.*, June 1984, *60*(2), pp. 200–222.

Breeden, Douglas T. Futures Markets and Commodity Options: Hedging and Optimality in Incomplete Markets. *J. Econ. Theory*, April 1984, *32*(2), pp. 275–300.

Brent, Robert J. A Three-Objective Social Welfare Function for Cost–Benefit Analysis. *Appl. Econ.*, June 1984, *16*(3), pp. 369–78.
[G: U.K.]

Brent, Robert J. Use of Distributional Weights in Cost–Benefit Analysis: A Survey of Schools. *Public Finance Quart.*, April 1984, *12*(2), pp. 213–30.

Bucovetsky, Sam. On the Use of Distributional Waits. *Can. J. Econ.*, November 1984, *17*(4), pp. 699–717.

Campbell, Donald E. Enforcement of Resource Allocation Mechanisms and Second Best Industrial Policy. *J. Econ. Theory*, December 1984, *34*(2), pp. 319–41.

Clark, Simon. Informational and Performance Properties of a Class of Iterative Planning Procedures. *Rev. Econ. Stud.*, October 1984, *51*(4), pp. 615–31.

Coleman, Jules L. The Foundations of Constitutional Economics. In *McKenzie, R. B., ed. (I)*, 1984, pp. 141–55.

Copes, Parzival. The Market as an Open Access Commons: A Neglected Aspect of Excess Capacity. *De Economist*, 1984, *132*(1), pp. 49–60.

Corcoran, William J. Long-Run Equilibrium and Total Expenditures in Rent-Seeking. *Public Choice*, 1984, *43*(1), pp. 89–94.

Demange, Gabrielle. Implementing Efficient Egalitarian Equivalent Allocations. *Econometrica*, September 1984, *52*(5), pp. 1167–77.

Demski, Joel S. and Sappington, David. Optimal Incentive Contracts with Multiple Agents. *J. Econ. Theory*, June 1984, *33*(1), pp. 152–71.

Diewert, W. Erwin. The Measurement of Deadweight Loss in an Open Economy. *Economica*, February 1984, *51*(201), pp. 23–42.

Dominique, C. René. Choosing the Appropriate Project Appraisal Method for a Labour Surplus Economy. *Industry Devel.*, 1984, (10), pp. 1–37.

Drèze, Jacques H. Second-best Analysis with Markets in Disequilibrium: Public Sector Pricing in a Keynesian Regime. In *Marchand, M.; Pestieau, P. and Tulkens, H., eds.*, 1984, pp. 45–79.

Drèze, Jacques H. and Sheshinski, Eytan. On Industry Equilibrium under Uncertainty. *J. Econ. Theory*, June 1984, *33*(1), pp. 88–97.

Farber, Stephen C. Pareto-Optimal Effluent Taxation and Market Structure in the Presence of Uncertain Demand and Detection. *J. Ind. Econ.*, September 1984, *33*(1), pp. 105–11.

Fourgeaud, Claude; Lenclud, Bernard and Picard, Pierre. Calcul économique prix fictifs et contrainte extérieure. (Cost–Benefit Analysis, Shadow Prices and Foreign Trade Constraint. With English summary.) *Revue Écon.*, May 1984, *35*(3), pp. 425–45.

Freeman, A. Myrick, III. On the Tactics of Bene-

fit Estimation under Executive Order 12291. In *Smith, V. K., ed.*, 1984, pp. 167–86.
[G: U.S.]

Geanakoplos, John D. and Polemarchakis, Herakles M. Intertemporally Separable, Overlapping-Generations Economies. *J. Econ. Theory*, December 1984, *34*(2), pp. 207–15.

Goldman, M. Barry; Leland, Hayne E. and Sibley, David S. Optimal Nonuniform Prices. *Rev. Econ. Stud.*, April 1984, *51*(2), pp. 305–19.

Graham, Daniel A. Cost–Benefit Analysis under Uncertainty: Reply. *Amer. Econ. Rev.*, December 1984, *74*(5), pp. 1100–102.

Greenberg, Joseph and Shitovitz, Benyamin. Aumann–Shapley Prices as a Scarf Social Equilibrium. *J. Econ. Theory*, December 1984, *34*(2), pp. 380–82.

Harberger, Arnold C. Basic Needs versus Distributional Weights in Social Cost–Benefit Analysis. *Econ. Develop. Cult. Change*, April 1984, *32*(3), pp. 455–74.

Horn, Henrik. Product Diversity, Trade and Welfare. In *Kierzkowski, H., ed.*, 1984, pp. 51–68.

Hosios, Arthur J. A Welfare Analysis of Employment Contracts with and without Asymmetric Information. *Rev. Econ. Stud.*, July 1984, *51*(3), pp. 471–89.

Huberman, Gur. Capital Asset Pricing in an Overlapping Generations Model. *J. Econ. Theory*, August 1984, *33*(2), pp. 232–48.

Hung, Nguyen Manh; Kemp, Murray C. and Long, Ngo Van. On the Transition from an Exhaustible Resource-Stock to an Inexhaustible Substitute. In *Kemp, M. C. and Long, N. V., eds.*, 1984, pp. 105–22.

Keenan, Donald C. and Keenan, Taewon K. First and Second-Best Pricing with Uncertain Demand. *Southern Econ. J.*, July 1984, *51*(1), pp. 80–88.

Kemp, Murray C. and Long, Ngo Van. On the Development of a Substitute for an Exhaustible Natural Resource. In *Kemp, M. C. and Long, N. V., eds.*, 1984, *1982*, pp. 123–43.

Kemp, Murray C. and Long, Ngo Van. The Efficiency of Competitive Markets in a Context of Exhaustible Resources. In *Kemp, M. C. and Long, N. V., eds.*, 1984, *1982*, pp. 219–25.

Kemp, Murray C. and Long, Ngo Van. Towards a More General Theory of the Order of Exploitation of Non-renewable Resource-Deposits. In *Kemp, M. C. and Long, N. V., eds.*, 1984, pp. 39–74.

Kula, Erhun. Derivation of Social Time Preference Rates for the United States and Canada. *Quart. J. Econ.*, November 1984, *99*(4), pp. 873–82.
[G: U.S.; Canada]

Kurz, Mordecai. Capital Accumulation and the Characteristics of Private Inter-Generational Transfers. *Economica*, February 1984, *51*(201), pp. 1–22.
[G: U.S.]

La Croix, Sumner J. Marketing, Price Discrimination, and Welfare: Reply. *Southern Econ. J.*, January 1984, *50*(3), pp. 900–901.
[G: U.S.]

Laffont, Jean-Jacques. Information imparfaite et

rationalité collective. (Collective Rationality under Incomplete Information. With English summary.) *Revue Écon.*, January 1984, *35*(1), pp. 163–76.

Laffont, Jean-Jacques and Maskin, Eric S. A Second-Best Approach to Incentive Compatibility. In *Boyer, M. and Kihlstrom, R. E., eds.*, 1984, pp. 143–54.

Lane, John and Leininger, Wolfgang. Differentiable Nash Equilibria in Altruistic Economies. *Z. Nationalökon.*, 1984, *44*(4), pp. 329–47.

Levedahl, J. William. Marketing, Price Discrimination, and Welfare: Comment. *Southern Econ. J.*, January 1984, *50*(3), pp. 886–91. [G: U.S.]

Lucas, Robert E. B. On the Theory of DRC Criteria. *J. Devel. Econ.*, April 1984, *14*(3), pp. 407–17.

Mäler, Karl-Göran. Cost–Benefit Analysis: The Basic Facts. In *Ahmad, Y. J.; Dasgupta, P. and Mäler, K.-G., eds.*, 1984, pp. 1–20.

Manne, Henry G. Antitrust and Economic Analysis of Law: Comments. *Z. ges. Staatswiss.*, March 1984, *140*(1), pp. 172–75. [G: U.S.]

Mantel, Rolf R. Substitutability and the Welfare Effects of Endowment Increases. *J. Int. Econ.*, November 1984, *17*(3/4), pp. 325–34.

Marchand, Maurice; Mintz, J. and Pestieau, Pierre. Shadow Pricing of Labour and Capital in an Economy with Unemployed Labour. *Europ. Econ. Rev.*, July 1984, *25*(2), pp. 239–52.

Maskin, Eric S. and Tirole, Jean. On the Efficiency of Fixed Price Equilibrium. *J. Econ. Theory*, April 1984, *32*(2), pp. 317–27.

Masson, Robert T. and Shaanan, Joseph. Social Costs of Oligopoly and the Value of Competition. *Econ. J.*, September 1984, *94*(375), pp. 520–35. [G: U.S.]

Mendelsohn, Robert and Strang, William J. Cost–Benefit Analysis under Uncertainty: Comment. *Amer. Econ. Rev.*, December 1984, *74*(5), pp. 1096–99.

Mitra, Tapan and Ray, Debraj. Dynamic Optimization on a Non-convex Feasible Set: Some General Results for Non-smooth Technologies. *Z. Nationalökon.*, 1984, *44*(2), pp. 151–75.

Mitsui, Toshihide. A Simple Stochastic Adjustment Process. *Econometrica*, September 1984, *52*(5), pp. 1317–19.

Mohammad, Sharif and Whalley, John. Rent Seeking in India: Its Costs and Policy Significance. *Kyklos*, 1984, *37*(3), pp. 387–413. [G: India]

Möschel, Wernhard. Antitrust and Economic Analysis of Law. *Z. ges. Staatswiss.*, March 1984, *140*(1), pp. 156–71.

Moulin, Hervé. The Conditional Auction Mechanism for Sharing a Surplus. *Rev. Econ. Stud.*, January 1984, *51*(1), pp. 157–70.

Murrell, Peter and Miller, Jeffrey B. The Applicability of Information-revealing Incentive Schemes in Economic Organizations. *J. Compar. Econ.*, September 1984, *8*(3), pp. 277–89.

Nairay, Alain. Asymptotic Behavior and Optimal Properties of a Consumption–Investment Model with Variable Time Preference. *J. Econ. Dynam. Control*, September 1984, *7*(3), pp. 283–313.

Nas, Tevfik. The World Price Methodology for Shadow Pricing: Theory and Practice. *METU*, 1984, *11*(3–4), pp. 295–306.

Ng, Yew-Kwang. Quasi-Pareto Social Improvements. *Amer. Econ. Rev.*, December 1984, *74*(5), pp. 1033–50.

Nickerson, David and Sandler, Todd. Intertemporal Incentive Allocation in Simple Hierarchies. *Math. Soc. Sci.*, February 1984, *7*(1), pp. 33–57.

Ostroy, Joseph M. A Reformulation of the Marginal Productivity Theory of Distribution. *Econometrica*, May 1984, *52*(3), pp. 599–630.

Packel, E. W. Power Structure and Cardinality Restrictions for Paretian Social Choice Rules. *Soc. Choice Welfare*, August 1984, *1*(2), pp. 105–11.

Peled, Dan. Stationary Pareto Optimality of Stochastic Asset Equilibria with Overlapping Generations. *J. Econ. Theory*, December 1984, *34*(2), pp. 396–403.

Pohjola, Matti. Union Rivalry and Economic Growth: A Differential Game Approach. *Scand. J. Econ.*, 1984, *86*(3), pp. 365–70.

Prescott, Edward C. and Townsend, Robert M. General Competitive Analysis in an Economy with Private Information. *Int. Econ. Rev.*, February 1984, *25*(1), pp. 1–20.

Prescott, Edward C. and Townsend, Robert M. Pareto Optima and Competitive Equilibria with Adverse Selection and Moral Hazard. *Econometrica*, January 1984, *52*(1), pp. 21–45.

Reichelstein, Stefan. Incentive Compatibility and Informational Requirements. *J. Econ. Theory*, October 1984, *34*(1), pp. 32–51.

Runge, Carlisle Ford. Economic Criteria and "Net Social Risk" in the Analysis of Environmental Regulation. In *Smith, V. K., ed.*, 1984, pp. 187–202. [G: U.S.]

Saposnik, Rubin. Efficiency and Equality in a Simple Neoclassical Economy. *Southern Econ. J.*, October 1984, *51*(2), pp. 588–93.

Scherer, Frederic M. Measuring Surplus Attributable to Differentiated Products: Reply. *J. Ind. Econ.*, September 1984, *33*(1), pp. 133.

Sen, Amartya. Approaches to the Choice of Discount Rates for Social Benefit–Cost Analysis. In *Sen, A.*, 1984, 1982, pp. 172–203.

Sen, Amartya. Control Areas and Accounting Prices: An Approach to Economic Evaluation. In *Sen, A.*, 1984, 1972, pp. 224–41.

Shimomura, Kazuo. The Optimal Order of Exploitation of Deposits of a Renewable Resource. In *Kemp, M. C. and Long, N. V., eds.*, 1984, pp. 75–104.

Smith, V. Kerry. A Bound for Option Value. *Land Econ.*, August 1984, *60*(3), pp. 292–96.

Søndergaard, Jørgen. Some Remarks on Anomalies in the Theory of Externalities. *Public Finance*, 1984, *39*(2), pp. 281–91.

Spremann, Klaus. Intergenerational Contracts

and Their Decomposition. *Z. Nationalökon.*, 1984, *44*(3), pp. 237–53.

Stiglitz, Joseph E. Information, Screening, and Welfare. In *Boyer, M. and Kihlstrom, R. E., eds.*, 1984, pp. 209–39.

Streit, Manfred E. The Shadow Economy: A Challenge to the Welfare State? In *Eucken, W. and Böhm, F., eds.*, 1984, pp. 109–19.

Summers, Robert S. The Foundations of Constitutional Economics: Comment. In *McKenzie, R. B., ed. (I)*, 1984, pp. 157–60.

Svensson, Lars-Gunnar. The Existence of Budget-Constrained Pareto-Efficient Allocations. *J. Econ. Theory*, April 1984, *32*(2), pp. 346–50.

Svensson, Lars-Gunnar and Weibull, Jörgen W. Stability and Efficiency from a Neo-Keynesian Viewpoint. *J. Econ. Dynam. Control*, September 1984, *7*(3), pp. 349–62.

Sweeney, George. Marketing, Price Discrimination, and Welfare: Comment. *Southern Econ. J.*, January 1984, *50*(3), pp. 892–99.

Thomson, William. Monotonicity, Stability, and Egalitarianism. *Math. Soc. Sci.*, August 1984, *8*(1), pp. 15–28.

Thomson, William. The Manipulability of Resource Allocation Mechanisms. *Rev. Econ. Stud.*, July 1984, *51*(3), pp. 447–60.

Thomson, William. Truncated Egalitarian Solutions. *Soc. Choice Welfare*, 1984, *1*(1), pp. 25–32.

Toumanoff, Peter G. A Positive Analysis of the Theory of Market Failure. *Kyklos*, 1984, *37*(4), pp. 529–41.

Townsend, Robert M. Theories of Contract Design and Market Organization: Conceptual Bases for Understanding Futures Markets. In *Anderson, R. W., ed.*, 1984, pp. 275–306.

Truchon, Michel. Nonmyopic Strategic Behavior in the MDP Planning Procedure. *Econometrica*, September 1984, *52*(5), pp. 1179–89.

Tullock, Gordon. Long-Run Equilibrium and Total Expenditures in Rent-Seeking: A Comment. *Public Choice*, 1984, *43*(1), pp. 95–97.

Vaubel, Roland. The Government's Money Monopoly: Externalities or Natural Monopoly? *Kyklos*, 1984, *37*(1), pp. 27–58. [G: Selected OECD]

Wahlroos, Björn. Monopoly Welfare Losses under Uncertainty. *Southern Econ. J.*, October 1984, *51*(2), pp. 429–42. [G: Finland; U.S.]

Wildman, Steven S. A Note on Measuring Surplus Attributable to Differentiated Products. *J. Ind. Econ.*, September 1984, *33*(1), pp. 123–32.

Williams, Steven R. Implementing a Generic Smooth Function. *J. Math. Econ.*, December 1984, *13*(3), pp. 273–88.

Yamazaki, Akira. Walras Degrees and Probability of a Blocking Coalition at Pareto Allocations. *J. Math. Econ.*, October 1984, *13*(2), pp. 105–21.

Zorn, Thomas S. The Allocative Effect of Nonbinding Price Controls. *Econ. Inquiry*, January 1984, *22*(1), pp. 136–41.

0243 Redistribution Analyses

Andic, Fuat M. and Andic, Suphan. The Politics of Redistribution in a Democracy. *Int. J. Soc. Econ.*, 1984, *11*(1/2), pp. 3–13.

Brambilla, Francesco. Povertà e ricchezza. (Poverty and Wealth. With English summary.) *Giorn. Econ.*, Nov.-Dec. 1984, *43*(11–12), pp. 801–50. [G: Italy]

Brock, William A. and Magee, Stephen P. The Invisible Foot and the Waste of Nations: Redistribution and Economic Growth. In *Colander, D. C., ed.*, 1984, pp. 177–85.

Broome, John. Uncertainty and Fairness. *Econ. J.*, September 1984, *94*(375), pp. 624–32.

Browning, Edgar K. and Johnson, William R. The Trade-Off between Equality and Efficiency. *J. Polit. Econ.*, April 1984, *92*(2), pp. 175–203. [G: U.S.]

Buchanan, James M. The Political Economy of the Welfare State. In *Buchanan, J. M. and Tollison, R. D., eds.*, 1984, pp. 174–93.

Deutsch, Joseph. Philanthropic Motives and Contribution Policy: A Note. *Public Choice*, 1984, *44*(3), pp. 501–05.

Eichhorn, Wolfgang; Funke, Helmut and Richter, Wolfram F. Tax Progression and Inequality of Income Distribution. *J. Math. Econ.*, October 1984, *13*(2), pp. 127–31.

Fishburn, Peter C. and Willig, Robert D. Transfer Principles in Income Redistribution. *J. Public Econ.*, December 1984, *25*(3), pp. 323–28.

Freeman, Katherine B. The Significance of Motivational Variables in International Public Welfare Expenditures. *Econ. Develop. Cult. Change*, July 1984, *32*(4), pp. 725–48. [G: OECD]

Guesnerie, Roger and Roberts, Kevin. Effective Policy Tools and Quantity Controls. *Econometrica*, January 1984, *52*(1), pp. 59–86.

Hamermesh, Daniel S. The Role of Time in the Measurement of Transfers and Well-Being: Comment. In *Moon, M., ed.*, 1984, pp. 234–38. [G: U.S.]

Le Grand, Julian. Optimal Taxation, the Compensation Principle and the Measurement of Changes in Economic Welfare. *J. Public Econ.*, July 1984, *24*(2), pp. 241–47.

Long, Ngo Van and Sinn, Hans-Werner. Optimal Taxation and Economic Depreciation: A General Equilibrium Model with Capital and an Exhaustible Resource. In *Kemp, M. C. and Long, N. V., eds.*, 1984, pp. 227–46.

Lütkenhorst, Wilfried. Zur Relevanz neuerer Gerechtigkeits-theorien für die Wirtschaftspolitik. Grundsätzliche Betrachtungen am Beispiel einer grundbedürfnisorientierten Entwicklungspolitik. (On the Relevance of Recent Theories of Justice for Economic Policy. With Special Emphasis on Basic Needs Oriented Development Policy. With English summary.) *Z. Wirtschaft. Sozialwissen.*, 1984, *104*(2), pp. 131–49.

Morgan, James N. The Role of Time in the Measurement of Transfers and Well-Being. In *Moon, M., ed.*, 1984, pp. 199–234. [G: U.S.]

Offe, Claus. Some Contradictions of the Modern Welfare State. In *Offe, C.*, 1984, *1981*, pp. 147–61.

Osborne, Martin J. Why Do Some Goods Bear Higher Taxes than Others? *J. Econ. Theory*, April 1984, *32*(2), pp. 301–16.

Ravallion, Martin. How Much Is a Transfer Payment Worth to a Rural Worker? *Oxford Econ. Pap.*, November 1984, *36*(3), pp. 478–89. [G: LDCs]

Roberts, Kevin. The Theoretical Limits of Redistribution. *Rev. Econ. Stud.*, April 1984, *51*(2), pp. 177–95.

Roberts, Russell D. A Positive Model of Private Charity and Public Transfers. *J. Polit. Econ.*, February 1984, *92*(1), pp. 136–48. [G: U.S.]

Seidman, Laurence S. The Welfare Economics of Taxes: A Three-Class Disposable Income Growth Model. *Public Finance Quart.*, January 1984, *12*(1), pp. 3–26.

Sen, Amartya. Ethical Issues in Income Distribution: National and International. In *Sen, A.*, 1984, *1981*, pp. 277–306.

Steinberg, Richard. A Comment on Motives Underlying Individual Contributions to Charity. *Atlantic Econ. J.*, July 1984, *12*(2), pp. 61–64.

Stutzer, Michael J. Variable Rate Subsidies: The Inefficiency of In-Kind Transfers Revisited. *Public Finance Quart.*, January 1984, *12*(1), pp. 77–95. [G: U.S.]

Wickström, Bengt-Arne. Economic Justice and Economic Power: An Inquiry into Distributive Justice and Political Stability. *Public Choice*, 1984, *43*(3), pp. 225–49.

0244 Externalities

Arnold, Volker. Umweltschutz als international öffentliches Gut: Komparative Kostenvorteile und Verhandlungsgewinne. (Environmental Protection as an International Public Good: Comparative Advantage, and Gains from Bargaining. With English summary.) *Z. Wirtschaft. Sozialwissen.*, 1984, *104*(2), pp. 111–29.

Atkinson, Scott E. and Tietenberg, T. H. Approaches for Reaching Ambient Standards in Non-Attainment Areas: Financial Burden and Efficiency Considerations. *Land Econ.*, May 1984, *60*(2), pp. 148–59. [G: U.S.]

Baumol, William J. and Mills, Edwin S. Incentives for Solving Social Problems. *Challenge*, November/December 1984, *27*(5), pp. 47–53.

Bowles, Roger. Property and the Legal System. In *Whynes, D. K., ed.*, 1984, pp. 187–208.

Buchanan, James M. The Coase Theorem and the Theory of the State. In *Buchanan, J. M. and Tollison, R. D., eds.*, 1984, *1973*, pp. 159–73.

Dorfman, Robert. On Optimal Congestion. *J. Environ. Econ. Manage.*, June 1984, *11*(2), pp. 91–106.

Forster, Bruce A. The Backward Incidence of Pollution Control: A Dual Approach. *J. Environ. Econ. Manage.*, March 1984, *11*(1), pp. 14–17.

Freeman, A. Myrick, III. Depletable Externalities and Pigouvian Taxation. *J. Environ. Econ. Manage.*, June 1984, *11*(2), pp. 173–79.

Godard, Olivier. Autonomie socio-économique et externalisation de l'environnement: la théorie néo-classique mise en perspective. (Socio-economic Autonomy and the Externalization of the Environment: The Neo-classical Theory in Perspective. With English summary.) *Écon. Appl.*, 1984, *37*(2), pp. 315–45.

Kjeldsen-Kragh, Søren. Mål og midler i miljøpolitikken. (Ends of Means in Environmental Policy. With English summary.) *Nationaløkon. Tidsskr.*, 1984, *122*(2), pp. 213–27.

Koenig, Evan F. Uncertainty and Pollution: The Role of Indirect Taxation. *J. Public Econ.*, June 1984, *24*(1), pp. 111–22.

Lindenberg, Siegwart. Preference versus Constraints: A Commentary on von Weizsäcker's 'The Influence of Property Rights on Tastes.' *Z. ges. Staatswiss.*, March 1984, *140*(1), pp. 96–103.

Martin, Lawrence W. The Optimal Magnitude and Enforcement of Evadable Pigovian Charges. *Public Finance*, 1984, *39*(3), pp. 347–58.

Massey, Stephen J. Justice Rehnquist's Theory of Property. *Yale Law J.*, January 1984, *93*(3), pp. 541–60.

Oates, Wallace E. and Strassmann, Diana L. Effluent Fees and Market Structure. *J. Public Econ.*, June 1984, *24*(1), pp. 29–46.

Oehsen, Johann Hermann. Ein erweitertes umweltökonomisches Standardmodell. (An Extended Standard Model of Environmental Economics. With English summary.) *Jahr. Nationalökon. Statist.*, January 1984, *199*(1), pp. 49–64.

Opaluch, James J. Dynamic Aspects of Effluent Taxation under Uncertainty. *J. Environ. Econ. Manage.*, March 1984, *11*(1), pp. 1–13.

Søndergaard, Jørgen. Some Remarks on Anomalies in the Theory of Externalities. *Public Finance*, 1984, *39*(2), pp. 281–91.

Teubal, Morris and Steinmueller, Edward. The Introduction of a Major New Technology—Externalities and Government Policy. In *Csikós-Nagy, B.; Hague, D. and Hall, G., eds.*, 1984, pp. 117–39.

von Weizsäcker, Carl Christian. The Influence of Property Rights on Tastes. *Z. ges. Staatswiss.*, March 1984, *140*(1), pp. 90–95.

Yohe, Gary W. Comparative Results in Pollution Control. *Amer. Econ.*, Spring 1984, *28*(1), pp. 10–17.

025 Social Choice

0250 General

Adelman, Irma and Hihn, Jairus M. Analysis of Contemporary Latin American Political History: An Application of the Use of Catastrophe Theory. In *Cohen, S. I., et al., eds.*, 1984, pp. 221–49. [G: Latin America]

Anderson, Gary M. and Tollison, Robert D. A Rent-Seeking Explanation of the British Factory Acts. In *Colander, D. C., ed.*, 1984, pp. 187–201. **[G: U.K.]**

Aronson, J. Richard and Schwartz, Eli. Public Sector Performance: A Public Finance Perspective. In *Miller, T. C., ed.*, 1984, pp. 193–223. **[G: U.S.]**

Arrow, Kenneth J. The Property Rights Doctrine and Demand Revelation under Incomplete Information. In *Arrow, K. J., vol. 4*, 1984, *1979*, pp. 216–32.

Bailey, Elizabeth E. A Comment on the Papers by Theodore Keeler and Barry Weingast [Theories of Regulation and the Deregulation Movement] [The Congressional–Bureaucratic System: A Principal–Agent Perspective (with Application to the SEC)]. *Public Choice*, 1984, *44*(1), pp. 197–200. **[G: U.S.]**

Bennett, James T. Privatizing Municipal Services. In *Giersch, H., ed.*, 1984, pp. 44–57.

Bennett, James T. and DiLorenzo, Thomas J. Political Entrepreneurship and Reform of the Rent-Seeking Society. In *Colander, D. C., ed.*, 1984, pp. 217–27. **[G: U.S.]**

Bhagwati, Jagdish N.; Brecher, Richard A. and Srinivasan, T. N. DUP Activities and Economic Theory. *Europ. Econ. Rev.*, April 1984, *24*(3), pp. 291–307.

Bhagwati, Jagdish N.; Brecher, Richard A. and Srinivasan, T. N. DUP Activities and Economic Theory. In *Colander, D. C., ed.*, 1984, pp. 17–32.

Boyd, John H. The Use of Inputs by the Federal Reserve System: Comment. *Amer. Econ. Rev.*, December 1984, *74*(5), pp. 1114–17.

Brennan, Geoffrey and Buchanan, James M. The Normative Purpose of Economic "Science": Rediscovery of an Eighteenth-Century Method. In *Buchanan, J. M. and Tollison, R. D., eds.*, 1984, pp. 382–94.

Buchanan, James M. Constitutional Restrictions on the Power of Government. In *Buchanan, J. M. and Tollison, R. D., eds.*, 1984, pp. 439–52.

Burton, John. The Economic Analysis of the Trade Union as a Political Institution. In *Rosa, J.-J., ed.*, 1984, pp. 123–54.

Colander, David C. Neoclassical Political Economy: The Analysis of Rent-Seeking and DUP Activities: Introduction. In *Colander, D. C., ed.*, 1984, pp. 1–13.

Colander, David C. and Olson, Mancur. Coalitions and Macroeconomics. In *Colander, D. C., ed.*, 1984, pp. 115–28. **[G: U.S.]**

Deutsch, Joseph. Philanthropic Motives and Contribution Policy: A Note. *Public Choice*, 1984, *44*(3), pp. 501–05.

Faith, Roger L. and Buchanan, James M. Towards a Theory of Yes–No Voting. In *Buchanan, J. M. and Tollison, R. D., eds.*, 1984, *1981*, pp. 90–104.

Findlay, Ronald and Wellisz, Stanislaw. Toward a Model of Endogenous Rent-Seeking. In *Colander, D. C., ed.*, 1984, pp. 89–100.

Frey, Bruno S. Modelling Politico–Economic Relationships. In *Whynes, D. K., ed.*, 1984, pp. 141–61.

Hamlin, Alan P. Public Choice, Markets and Utilitarianism. In *Whynes, D. K., ed.*, 1984, pp. 116–38.

Kalt, Joseph P. and Zupan, Mark A. Capture and Ideology in the Economic Theory of Politics. *Amer. Econ. Rev.*, June 1984, *74*(3), pp. 279–300. **[G: U.S.]**

Kirsch, Guy. The Role of Elected Representatives in Parliamentary Forms of Government. In *Hanusch, H., ed.*, 1984, pp. 175–86.

Koford, Kenneth J. and Colander, David C. Taming the Rent-Seeker. In *Colander, D. C., ed.*, 1984, pp. 205–16.

Larkey, Patrick D.; Stolp, Chandler and Winer, Mark D. Why Does Government Grow? In *Miller, T. C., ed.*, 1984, pp. 65–101. **[G: OECD]**

Lassila, Jaakko. Industripolitik—reglering versus marknadskrafter. (With English summary.) *Nationaløkon. Tidsskr.*, 1984, *122*(3), pp. 347–56. **[G: Nordic Countries]**

Leibenstein, Harvey. Motivations and Constraints in the Supply-Cost of Government Services: A Game Theoretic Analysis. In *Hanusch, H., ed.*, 1984, pp. 223–40.

Lipset, Seymour Martin. The Economy, Elections, and Public Opinion. In *Moore, J. H., ed.*, 1984, pp. 393–429. **[G: U.S.]**

Lockwood, Ben. Social Choice, Interpersonal Comparability and Welfare Economics. In *van der Ploeg, F., ed.*, 1984, pp. 371–400.

Magee, Stephen P. Endogenous Tariff Theory: A Survey. In *Colander, D. C., ed.*, 1984, pp. 41–51.

Most, Benjamin A. Latin America: The Case of Argentina. In *Groth, A. J. and Wade, L. L., eds.*, 1984, pp. 181–211. **[G: Argentina]**

Mueller, Dennis C. Public Choice: A Survey. In *Buchanan, J. M. and Tollison, R. D., eds.*, 1984, *1976*, pp. 23–67.

Mueller, Dennis C. Voting by Veto and Majority Rule. In *Hanusch, H., ed.*, 1984, pp. 69–86.

North, Douglass C. Three Approaches to the Study of Institutions. In *Colander, D. C., ed.*, 1984, pp. 33–40.

Offe, Claus. Social Policy and the Theory of the State. In *Offe, C.*, 1984, pp. 88–118.

Ostrom, Vincent. Why Governments Fail: An Inquiry into the Use of Instruments of Evil to Do Good. In *Buchanan, J. M. and Tollison, R. D., eds.*, 1984, pp. 422–35.

Pommerehne, Werner W. and Schneider, Friedrich. Identification of Individual Preferences for Government Activity from Voting Behavior. In *Hanusch, H., ed.*, 1984, pp. 109–26. **[G: Switzerland]**

Pryor, Frederic L. Rent-Seeking and the Growth and Fluctuations of Nations: Empirical Tests of Some Recent Hypotheses. In *Colander, D. C., ed.*, 1984, pp. 155–75. **[G: Selected Countries]**

Ranade, Ravindra R. Rationality of Social Preferences under the Majority Rule and Tie Breaking Mechanisms. *Indian Econ. Rev.*, July-Dec. 1984, *19*(2), pp. 203–11.

Rapping, Leonard A. Economic Change, Bureaucracy, and the Innovative Process. In *Alperovitz, G. and Skurski, R., eds.*, 1984, pp. 56–75. **[G: U.S.]**

Romer, David. The Theory of Social Custom: A Modification and Some Extensions. *Quart. J. Econ.*, November 1984, 99(4), pp. 717–27.

Romer, Thomas; Rosenthal, Howard and Ladha, Krishna. If at First You Don't Succeed: Budgeting by a Sequence of Referenda. In *Hanusch, H., ed.*, 1984, pp. 87–108. **[G: U.S.]**

Samuels, Warren J. and Mercuro, Nicholas. A Critique of Rent-Seeking Theory. In *Colander, D. C., ed.*, 1984, pp. 55–70.

Schelling, Thomas C. Strategic Analysis and Social Problems. In *Schelling, T. C.*, 1984, pp. 195–212.

Shibata, Hirofumi. Economics of Representative Democracy: A Model of Skewed Representation. In *Hanusch, H., ed.*, 1984, pp. 51–67.

Thompson, Frederick and Stanbury, W. T. The Comparative Politics of Regulation: A Contingency Theory of the Function of Interest Groups in the Legislative Process. In *Thompson, F., ed.*, 1984, pp. 81–102. **[G: Canada; U.S.]**

Tullock, Gordon. How to Do Well While Doing Good!! In *Colander, D. C., ed.*, 1984, pp. 229–40.

Tullock, Gordon. The Backward Society: Static Inefficiency, Rent Seeking, and the Rule of Law. In *Buchanan, J. M. and Tollison, R. D., eds.*, 1984, pp. 224–37. **[G: W. Europe; U.S.]**

Wagner, Richard E. Boom and Bust: The Political Economy of Economic Disorder. In *Buchanan, J. M. and Tollison, R. D., eds.*, 1984, pp. 238–72.

Wellisz, Stanislaw and Findlay, Ronald. Protection and Rent-Seeking in Developing Countries. In *Colander, D. C., ed.*, 1984, pp. 141–53. **[G: LDCs]**

Wickström, Bengt-Arne. Economic Justice and Economic Power: An Inquiry into Distributive Justice and Political Stability. *Public Choice*, 1984, 43(3), pp. 225–49.

0251 Social Choice Theory

Bandyopadhyay, Taradas. On the Frontier between Possibility and Impossibility Theorems in Social Choice. *J. Econ. Theory*, February 1984, 32(1), pp. 52–66.

Barberá, Salvador; Barrett, C. Richard and Pattanaik, Prasanta K. On Some Axioms for Ranking Sets of Alternatives. *J. Econ. Theory*, August 1984, 33(2), pp. 301–08.

Basu, Kaushik. The Right to Give up Rights. *Economica*, November 1984, 51(204), pp. 413–22.

Bennett, E. A New Approach to Predicting Coalition Formation and Payoff Distribution in Characteristic Function Games. In *Holler, M. J., ed.*, 1984, pp. 60–80.

Bennett, James T. and DiLorenzo, Thomas J. The Political Economy of Political Philosophy: Discretionary Spending by Senators on Staff.

In *Buchanan, J. M. and Tollison, R. D., eds.*, 1984, 1982, pp. 275–86. **[G: U.S.]**

Bernholz, Peter. A General Social Dilemma: Profitable Exchange and Intransitive Group Preferences. In *Holler, M. J., ed.*, 1984, 1980, pp. 197–215.

Bernholz, Peter. A General Social Dilemma: Profitable Exchange and Intransitive Group Preferences. In *Buchanan, J. M. and Tollison, R. D., eds.*, 1984, 1980, pp. 361–81.

Bjurulf, B. and Berg, S. A Combinatorial and Probabilistic Analysis of Voting Blocs: With Application to Multiparty Systems. In *Holler, M. J., ed.*, 1984, pp. 175–94. **[G: Sweden]**

Blackorby, Charles and Donaldson, David. Social Criteria for Evaluating Population Change. *J. Public Econ.*, November 1984, 25(1/2), pp. 13–33.

Blackorby, Charles; Donaldson, David and Weymark, John A. Social Choice with Interpersonal Utility Comparisons: A Diagrammatic Introduction. *Int. Econ. Rev.*, June 1984, 25(2), pp. 327–56.

Border, Kim C. An Impossibility Theorem for Spatial Models. *Public Choice*, 1984, 43(3), pp. 293–305.

Boute, S. Subjective Policy Distance Theory. In *Holler, M. J., ed.*, 1984, pp. 113–26.

Brambilla, Francesco. Povertà e ricchezza. (Poverty and Wealth. With English summary.) *Giorn. Econ.*, Nov.-Dec. 1984, 43(11–12), pp. 801–50. **[G: Italy]**

Brennan, Geoffrey. Elements of a Fiscal Politics: Public Choice and Public Finance. *Australian Econ. Rev.*, 3rd Quarter 1984, (67), pp. 62–72.

Brent, Robert J. A Three-Objective Social Welfare Function for Cost–Benefit Analysis. *Appl. Econ.*, June 1984, 16(3), pp. 369–78. **[G: U.K.]**

Brubaker, Earl R. Demand Disclosures and Conditions on Exclusion: An Experiment. *Econ. J.*, September 1984, 94(375), pp. 536–53. **[G: U.S.]**

Buchanan, James M. Politics without Romance: A Sketch of Positive Public Choice Theory and Its Normative Implications. In *Buchanan, J. M. and Tollison, R. D., eds.*, 1984, pp. 11–22.

Buchanan, James M. The Coase Theorem and the Theory of the State. In *Buchanan, J. M. and Tollison, R. D., eds.*, 1984, 1973, pp. 159–73.

Buchanan, James M. The Political Economy of the Welfare State. In *Buchanan, J. M. and Tollison, R. D., eds.*, 1984, pp. 174–93.

Buchanan, James M. and Lee, Dwight R. Tax Rates and Tax Revenues in Political Equilibrium: Some Simple Analytics. In *Buchanan, J. M. and Tollison, R. D., eds.* 1984, 1982, pp. 194–205.

Chapman, Randall G. and Palda, Kristian S. Assessing the Influence of Campaign Expenditures on Voting Behavior with a Comprehensive Electoral Market Model. *Marketing Sci.*, Summer 1984, *3*(3), pp. 207–26. [G: Canada]

Chichilnisky, Graciela and Heal, Geoffrey. Patterns of Power: Bargaining and Incentives in Two-Person Games. *J. Public Econ.*, April 1984, *23*(3), pp. 333–49.

Collins, D. J. Elements of a Fiscal Politics: Public Choice and Public Finance: Comment. *Australian Econ. Rev.*, 3rd Quarter 1984, (67), pp. 77–78.

Cox, Gary W. Non-collegial Simple Games and the Nowhere Denseness of the Set of Preference Profiles Having a Core. *Soc. Choice Welfare*, August 1984, *1*(2), pp. 159–64.

Cox, Gary W. and McKelvey, Richard D. A Ham Sandwich Theorem for General Measures. *Soc. Choice Welfare*, 1984, *1*(1), pp. 75–83.

Crain, W. Mark and McCormick, Robert E. Regulators as an Interest Group. In *Buchanan, J. M. and Tollison, R. D., eds.*, 1984, pp. 287–304. [G: U.S.]

Dutta, Bhaskar. Effectivity Functions and Acceptable Game Forms. *Econometrica*, September 1984, *52*(5), pp. 1151–66.

Ekelund, Robert B., Jr. and Tollison, Robert D. A Rent-Seeking Theory of French Mercantilism. In *Buchanan, J. M. and Tollison, R. D., eds.*, 1984, pp. 206–23. [G: France]

Faith, Roger L. and Buchanan, James M. Towards a Theory of Yes–No Voting. In *Buchanan, J. M. and Tollison, R. D., eds.*, 1984, 1981, pp. 90–104.

Fountain, John. A Production Theory Perspective on Collective Choice Theory. *Quart. J. Econ.*, November 1984, *99*(4), pp. 673–91.

Freixas, Xavier. A Cardinal Approach to Straightforward Probabilistic Mechanisms. *J. Econ. Theory*, December 1984, *34*(2), pp. 227–51.

Frey, Bruno S. Politico-Economic Models and Cycles. In *Buchanan, J. M. and Tollison, R.D., eds.*, 1984, pp. 305–22. [G: U.S.; U.K.; W. Germany]

Grofman, Bernard. The General Irrelevance of the Zero Sum Assumption in the Legislative Context. In *Holler, M. J., ed.*, 1984, pp. 99–112.

Grossman, N. B. Party Distances and Coalition Governments: A New Model. In *Holler, M. J., ed.*, 1984, pp. 127–36.

Hart, S. and Kurz, Mordecai. Stable Coalition Structures. In *Holler, M. J., ed.*, 1984, pp. 235–58.

Hoffman, Elizabeth and Packel, E. W. A Stochastic Model of Coalition Formation with Exogenous Costs: Theory and Experiments. In *Holler, M. J., ed.*, 1984, pp. 283–94.

Holler, M. J. A Collective Choice Approach to Individual Decision Making. In *Holler, M. J., ed.*, 1984, pp. 338–44.

Holler, M. J. A Public Good Power Index. In *Holler, M. J., ed.*, 1984, pp. 51–59.

Holler, M. J. On the Theory of Coalition Formation. In *Holler, M. J., ed.*, 1984, pp. 3–5.

Holzman, Ron. A Note on the Redundancy of an Axiom in the Pattanaik-Peleg Characteriza-

tion of the Lexicographic Maximin Extension. *Soc. Choice Welfare*, August 1984, *1*(2), pp. 123–25.

Janowitz, M. F. On the Semilattice of Weak Orders of a Set. *Math. Soc. Sci.*, December 1984, *8*(3), pp. 229–39.

Kaneko, Mamoru. Reformulation of the Nash Social Welfare Function for a Continuum of Individuals. *Soc. Choice Welfare*, 1984, *1*(1), pp. 33–43.

Kelsey, David. Acyclic Choice without the Pareto Principle. *Rev. Econ. Stud.*, October 1984, *51*(4), pp. 693–99.

Kelsey, David. The Structure of Social Decision Functions. *Math. Soc. Sci.*, December 1984, *8*(3), pp. 241–52.

Kim, K. H. and Roush, F. W. Nonmanipulability in Two Dimensions. *Math. Soc. Sci.*, August 1984, *8*(1), pp. 29–43.

Kim, Oliver and Walker, Mark. The Free Rider Problem: Experimental Evidence. *Public Choice*, 1984, *43*(1), pp. 3–24.

Kliemt, H. and Schauenberg, B. Coalitions and Hierarchies: Some Observations on the Fundamentals of Human Cooperation. In *Holler, M. J., ed.*, 1984, pp. 9–32.

de Koster, M. B. M. and Paelinck, J. H. P. A Hypergraph Approach to Conflict. *Conflict Manage. Peace Sci.*, Spring 1984, *7*(2), pp. 55–69.

Laffont, Jean-Jacques and Maskin, Eric S. A Second-Best Approach to Incentive Compatibility. In *Boyer, M. and Kihlstrom, R. E., eds.*, 1984, pp. 143–54.

Leclerc, B. Efficient and Binary Consensus Functions on Transitively Valued Relations. *Math. Soc. Sci.*, August 1984, *8*(1), pp. 45–61.

Mason, T. David. Individual Participation in Collective Racial Violence: A Rational Choice Synthesis. *Amer. Polit. Sci. Rev.*, December 1984, *78*(4), pp. 1040–56.

McKee, Arnold F. Beauchamp and Donaldson on Economic Justice [The Ethical Foundations of Economic Justice] [What Justice Demands]. *Rev. Soc. Econ.*, April 1984, *42*(1), pp. 63–66.

de Mesquita, B. Bueno and Niemi, Richard G. A Dynamic, Multiple-Goal Theory of Coalition Formation. In *Holler, M. J., ed.*, 1984, pp. 81–95. [G: Selected Countries]

Mestelman, Stuart. The Social Choice of Alternative Corrective Devices. *Public Choice*, 1984, *42*(1), pp. 55–71.

Miller, N. R. Coalition Formation and Political Outcomes: A Critical Note. In *Holler, M. J., ed.*, 1984, pp. 259–65.

Mitchell, William C. Schumpeter and Public Choice, Part I: Precursor to Public Choice? *Public Choice*, 1984, *42*(1), pp. 73–88.

Mitchell, William C. Schumpeter and Public Choice, Part II: Democracy and the Demise of Capitalism: The Missing Chapter in Schumpeter. *Public Choice*, 1984, *42*(2), pp. 161–74.

Moorhouse, John C. Is Tullock Correct about Sunday Closing Laws? *Public Choice*, 1984, *42*(2), pp. 197–203. [G: U.S.]

Moulin, Hervé. Generalized Condorcet-Winners for Single Peaked and Single-Plateau Preferences. *Soc. Choice Welfare*, August 1984, *1*(2), pp. 127–47.

Mueller, Dennis C. Voting by Veto. In *Buchanan, J. M. and Tollison, R. D., eds.*, 1984, 1978, pp. 395–412.

Mueller, Dennis C.; Tollison, Robert D. and Willett, Thomas D. On Equalizing the Distribution of Political Income. In *Buchanan, J. M. and Tollison, R. D., eds.*, 1984, 1974, pp. 413–21.

Nitzan, Shmuel I. and Paroush, Jacob. Potential Variability of Decisional Skills in Uncertain Dichotomous Choice Situations. *Math. Soc. Sci.*, December 1984, *8*(3), pp. 217–27.

Owen, Guillermo and Grofman, Bernard. Coalitions and Power in Political Situations. In *Holler, M. J., ed.*, 1984, pp. 137–44.

Packel, E. W. Power Structure and Cardinality Restrictions for Paretian Social Choice Rules. *Soc. Choice Welfare*, August 1984, *1*(2), pp. 105–11.

Reichelstein, Stefan. A Note on Allocations Attainable through Nash Equilibria. *J. Econ. Theory*, April 1984, *32*(2), pp. 384–90.

Reichelstein, Stefan. Incentive Compatibility and Informational Requirements. *J. Econ. Theory*, October 1984, *34*(1), pp. 32–51.

Richelson, Jeffrey T. Social Choice and the Status Quo. *Public Choice*, 1984, *42*(3), pp. 225–34.

Rietveld, Piet. Public Choice Theory and Qualitative Discrete Multicriteria Decision Methods. In *Bahrenberg, G.; Fischer, M. M., and Nijkamp, P.*, 1984, pp. 409–26.

River, Douglas. Comment on Goodin [Voting through the Looking Glass]. *Amer. Polit. Sci. Rev.*, June 1984, *78*(2), pp. 502–04.

Romer, Thomas and Rosenthal, Howard. Political Resource Allocation, Controlled Agendas, and the Status Quo. In *Buchanan, J. M. and Tollison, R. D., eds.*, 1984, 1978, pp. 105–20.

Roth, Alvin E. Stable Coalition Formation: Aspects of a Dynamic Theory. In *Holler, M. J., ed.*, 1984, pp. 228–34.

Rubinstein, Ariel. The Single Profile Analogues to Multi Profile Theorems: Mathematical Logic's Approach. *Int. Econ. Rev.*, October 1984, *25*(3), pp. 719–30.

Saposnik, Rubin. A Power Rule for Social Choice. *Soc. Choice Welfare*, August 1984, *1*(2), pp. 97–103.

Schofield, Norman J. Bargaining over Public Goods. In *Holler, M. J., ed.*, 1984, pp. 33–50.

Schofield, Norman J. Classification Theorem for Smooth Social Choice on a Manifold. *Soc. Choice Welfare*, October 1984, *1*(3), pp. 187–210.

Schofield, Norman J. Social Equilibrium and Cycles on Compact Sets. *J. Econ. Theory*, June 1984, *33*(1), pp. 59–71.

Seidl, Christian. Asymmetric Information and the Dynamics of Coalition Formation Observations on Some Unsolved Problems. In *Holler, M. J., ed.*, 1984, pp. 216–27.

Shapley, Lloyd and Grofman, Bernard. Optimizing Group Judgmental Accuracy in the Presence of Interdependencies. *Public Choice*, 1984, *43*(3), pp. 329–43.

Sugden, Robert. Reciprocity: The Supply of Public Goods through Voluntary Contributions. *Econ. J.*, December 1984, *94*(376), pp. 772–87.

Taylor, Lance. Social Choice Theory and the World in Which We Live: Review Article. *Cambridge J. Econ.*, June 1984, *8*(2), pp. 189–96.

Tideman, T. Nicolaus and Tullock, Gordon. A New and Superior Process for Making Social Choices. In *Buchanan, J. M. and Tollison, R. D., eds.*, 1984, 1976, pp. 121–33.

Tollison, Robert D. and Willett, Thomas D. An Economic Theory of Mutually Advantageous Issue Linkages in International Negotiations. In *Buchanan, J. M. and Tollison, R. D., eds.*, 1984, pp. 134–55.

Violi, Roberto. Un'interpretazione del contratto sociale in termini di "nucleo" di un meta-gioco. (An Interpretation of the Social Contract in Terms of "Nucleus" of a Meta-Game. With English summary.) *Rivista Int. Sci. Econ. Com.*, May 1984, *31*(5), pp. 395–416.

Walker, Martin. Risk Attitudes, Value-restricted Preferences, and Public Choice over Lotteries and Information Systems. *Accounting Rev.*, April 1984, *59*(2), pp. 278–86.

Walsh, Cliff. Elements of a Fiscal Politics: Public Choice and Public Finance: Comment. *Australian Econ. Rev.*, 3rd Quarter 1984, (67), pp. 73–76.

Weymark, John A. Arrow's Theorem with Social Quasi-Orderings. *Public Choice*, 1984, *42*(3), pp. 235–46.

Wilson, Robert B. A Note on Revelation of Information for Joint Production. *Soc. Choice Welfare*, 1984, *1*(1), pp. 69–73.

van Winden, Franz. Towards a Dynamic Theory of Cabinet Formation. In *Holler, M. J., ed.*, 1984, pp. 145–59.

Wittman, Donald. *A Priori* Probabilities of Coalition Formation and Power Measurement. In *Holler, M. J., ed.*, 1984, pp. 163–74.

Yaari, M. E. and Bar-Hillel, M. On Dividing Justly. *Soc. Choice Welfare*, 1984, *1*(1), pp. 1–24.

Yunker, James A. Objective Information and Social Consensus: Some Empirical Evidence on the Relative Importance of Objective and Subjective Determinants of Social Judgment. *Amer. J. Econ. Soc.*, October 1984, *43*(4), pp. 413–26.

0252 Social Choice Studies: Voting, Committees, etc.

Adams, Roy D. The Slutsky Equation for Club Goods-per-Member and the Aggregate Demand for Club Goods. *Public Finance*, 1984, *39*(2), pp. 182–90.

Adelman, Irma and Hihn, Jairus M. Crisis Politics in Developing Countries. *Econ. Develop.*

Cult. Change, October 1984, *33*(1), pp. 1–22.
[G: LDCs]

Alexis, Marcus. Politics and Economics. *Rev. Black Polit. Econ.*, Summer–Fall 1984, *13*(1–2), pp. 9–24. [G: U.S.]

Alexis, Marcus. Politics and Economics: Rejoinder. *Rev. Black Polit. Econ.*, Summer–Fall 1984, *13*(1–2), pp. 27–29. [G: U.S.]

Alperovich, Gershon. The Economics of Choice in the Allocation of Intergovernmental Grants to Local Authorities. *Public Choice*, 1984, *44*(2), pp. 285–96. [G: Israel]

Amar, Akhil Reed. Choosing Representatives by Lottery Voting. *Yale Law J.*, June 1984, *93*(7), pp. 1283–308.

Ancot, Jean Pierre and Hughes Hallett, Andrew J. Establishing Public Preferences for Coalition Government: An Empirical Study in Economic Planning Behaviour. *De Economist*, 1984, *132*(2), pp. 153–70. [G: Netherlands]

Anderson, S. and Glazer, A. Public Opinion and Regulatory Behavior. *Public Choice*, 1984, *43*(2), pp. 187–94. [G: U.S.]

Arcelus, Francisco J. Forecasting the Partisan Composition of the House as a Function of Seniority. *Math. Soc. Sci.*, February 1984, *7*(1), pp. 103–09.

Arndt, Heinz W. The Role of Political Leadership in Economic Development. *Can. J. Devel. Stud.*, 1984, *5*(1), pp. 51–63.

Austen-Smith, David. The Pure Theory of Large Two-Candidate Elections: A Comment. *Public Choice*, 1984, *44*(1), pp. 43–47.

Austen-Smith, David. Two-Party Competition with Many Constituencies. *Math. Soc. Sci.*, April 1984, *7*(2), pp. 177–98.

Badelt, Christoph. Freiwilligengruppen als Problem der ökonomischen Klubtheorie. (A Club Theoretical View of Volunteer Groups. With English summary.) *Kyklos*, 1984, *37*(1), pp. 59–81.

Barberá, Salvador and Pattanaik, Prasanta K. Extending an Order on a Set to the Power Set: Some Remarks on Kannai and Peleg's Approach. *J. Econ. Theory*, February 1984, *32*(1), pp. 185–91.

Beck, Nathaniel. Comment on Hibbs [Political Parties and Macroeconomic Policy]. *Amer. Polit. Sci. Rev.*, June 1984, *78*(2), pp. 499–502. [G: N. America; W. Europe]

Behn, Robert D. and Vaupel, James W. The Wasted Vote Fallacy. *J. Policy Anal. Manage.*, Summer 1984, *3*(4), pp. 607–12.

Bennett, James T. and DiLorenzo, Thomas J. The Political Economy of Political Philosophy: Reply. *Amer. Econ. Rev.*, June 1984, *74*(3), pp. 526–27. [G: U.S.]

Bennett, R. J. A Bureaucratic Model of Local Government Tax and Expenditure Decisions. *Appl. Econ.*, April 1984, *16*(2), pp. 257–68. [G: U.K.]

Benson, Bruce L. Rent Seeking from a Property Rights Perspective. *Southern Econ. J.*, October 1984, *51*(2), pp. 388–400.

Berglas, Eitan. and Pines, David. Resource Constraint, Replicability and Mixed Clubs: A Reply

[Clubs, Local Public Goods and Transportation Models: A Synthesis]. *J. Public Econ.*, April 1984, *23*(3), pp. 391–97.

Bernardo, José M. Monitoring the 1982 Spanish Socialist Victory: A Bayesian Analysis. *J. Amer. Statist. Assoc.*, September 1984, *79*(387), pp. 510–15. [G: Spain]

Bernholz, Peter. Median Voter Theorem, Instability of Outcomes in Non-Oligarchic Societies and Constitutional Reform: A Commentary on Rowley's 'The Relevance of the Median Voter Theorem.' *Z. ges. Staatswiss.*, March 1984, *140*(1), pp. 127–35.

Bhagwati, Jagdish N.; Brecher, Richard A. and Srinivasan, T. N. DUP Activities and Economic Theory. *Europ. Econ. Rev.*, April 1984, *24*(3), pp. 291–307.

Black, Harold. Politics and Economics: Comments. *Rev. Black Polit. Econ.*, Summer–Fall 1984, *13*(1–2), pp. 25–27. [G: U.S.]

Bös, Dieter; Tillmann, Georg and Zimmermann, Hans-Georg. Bureaucratic Public Enterprises. *Z. Nationalökon.*, Supplement 1984, pp. 127–76. [G: U.K.]

Brams, Steven J. and Fishburn, Peter C. Proportional Representation in Variable-Size Legislatures. *Soc. Choice Welfare*, October 1984, *1*(3), pp. 211–29. [G: U.K.]

Breton, Albert. An Analysis of Constitutional Change, Canada, 1980–82. *Public Choice*, 1984, *44*(1), pp. 251–72. [G: Canada]

Buchanan, Cathy and Prior, Elizabeth W. Bureaucrats and Babies: Government Regulation of the Supply of Genetic Material. *Econ. Rec.*, September 1984, *60*(170), pp. 222–30.

Buchanan, James M. Sources of Opposition to Constitutional Reform. In *McKenzie, R. B., ed. (I)*, 1984, pp. 21–34.

Carter, John R. Early Projections and Voter Turnout in the 1980 Presidential Election. *Public Choice*, 1984, *43*(2), pp. 195–202. [G: U.S.]

Cebula, Richard J. and Murphy, Dennis R. The Electoral College and Voter Participation Rates: Reply. *Public Choice*, 1984, *43*(1), pp. 101–02. [G: U.S.]

Chaffee, Wilber A. The Political Economy of Revolution and Democracy: Toward a Theory of Latin American Politics. *Amer. J. Econ. Soc.*, October 1984, *43*(4), pp. 385–98. [G: Latin America]

Coakley, John and Ó Néill, Gerald. Chance in Preferential Voting Systems: An Unacceptable Element in Irish Electoral Law? *Econ. Soc. Rev.*, October 1984, *16*(1), pp. 1–18. [G: Ireland]

Cobb, Steven A. and Hagemann, Robert P. The Political Economy of Political Philosophy: Comment. *Amer. Econ. Rev.*, June 1984, *74*(3), pp. 523–25. [G: U.S.]

Congleton, Roger D. Committees and Rent-seeking Effort. *J. Public Econ.*, November 1984, *25*(1/2), pp. 197–209.

Conybeare, John. Politicians and Protection: Tariffs and Elections in Australia. *Public Choice*, 1984, *43*(2), pp. 203–09. [G: Australia]

Copeland, Gary W. Changes in the House of Representatives after the Passage of the Budget Act of 1974. In *Wander, W. T.; Hebert, F. T. and Copeland, G. W., eds.*, 1984, pp. 51–77. [G: U.S.]

Coughlin, Peter J. Davis–Hinich Conditions and Median Outcomes in Probabilistic Voting Models. *J. Econ. Theory*, October 1984, *34*(1), pp. 1–12.

Coughlin, Peter J. Expectations about Voter Choices: A Comment [The Pure Theory of Large Two-Candidate Elections]. *Public Choice*, 1984, *44*(1), pp. 49–59.

Coughlin, Peter J. and Hinich, Melvin J. Necessary and Sufficient Conditions for Single-Peakedness in Public Economic Models. *J. Public Econ.*, November 1984, *25*(1/2), pp. 161–79.

Courchene, Thomas J. The Political Economy of Canadian Constitution-Making: The Canadian Economic-Union Issue. *Public Choice*, 1984, *44*(1), pp. 201–49. [G: Canada]

Cox, Gary W. Electoral Equilibrium in Double Member Districts. *Public Choice*, 1984, *44*(3), pp. 443–51.

Cox, Gary W.; McCubbins, M. D. and Sullivan, Teresa A. Policy Choice as an Electoral Investment. *Soc. Choice Welfare*, October 1984, *1*(3), pp. 231–42.

Cullis, John G. and Jones, Philip R. The Economic Theory of Bureaucracy, X-Inefficiency and Wagner's Law: A Note. *Public Finance*, 1984, *39*(2), pp. 191–201.

Davidson, James Dale. The Limits of Constitutional Determinism. In *McKenzie, R. B., ed. (I)*, 1984, pp. 61–87.

Delorme, Robert. A New View on the Economic Theory of the State: A Case Study of France. *J. Econ. Issues*, September 1984, *18*(3), pp. 715–44. [G: France]

Diba, Behzad and Feldman, Allan M. Utility Functions for Public Outputs and Majority Voting. *J. Public Econ.*, November 1984, *25*(1/2), pp. 235–43.

DiLorenzo, Thomas J. The Domain of Rent-seeking Behavior: Private or Public Choice? *Int. Rev. Law Econ.*, December 1984, *4*(2), pp. 185–97.

Dudley, Leonard and Montmarquette, Claude. The Effects of Non-clearing Labor Markets on the Demand for Public Spending. *Econ. Inquiry*, April 1984, *22*(2), pp. 151–70. [G: Selected Countries]

Dunne, John Paul; Pashardes, Panos and Smith, Ronald P. Needs, Costs and Bureaucracy: The Allocation of Public Consumption in the UK. *Econ. J.*, March 1984, *94*(373), pp. 1–15. [G: U.K.]

Eavey, Cheryl L. and Miller, Gary J. Bureaucratic Agenda Control: Imposition or Bargaining? *Amer. Polit. Sci. Rev.*, September 1984, *78*(3), pp. 719–33.

Ellwood, John W. Budget Reforms and Interchamber Relations. In *Wander, W. T.; Hebert, F. T. and Copeland, G. W., eds.*, 1984, pp. 100–132. [G: U.S.]

Enelow, James M. A New Theory of Congres-

sional Compromise. *Amer. Polit. Sci. Rev.*, September 1984, *78*(3), pp. 708–18.

Epple, Dennis; Filimon, Radu and Romer, Thomas. Equilibrium among Local Jurisdictions: Toward an Integrated Treatment of Voting and Residential Choice. *J. Public Econ.*, August 1984, *24*(3), pp. 281–308.

Feld, Scott L. and Grofman, Bernard. The Accuracy of Group Majority Decisions in Groups with Added Members. *Public Choice*, 1984, *42*(3), pp. 273–85.

Ferejohn, J. A.; McKelvey, Richard D. and Packel, E. W. Limiting Distributions for Continuous State Markov Voting Models. *Soc. Choice Welfare*, 1984, *1*(1), pp. 45–67.

Fishburn, Peter C. Comment on the Kannai–Peleg Impossibility Theorem for Extending Orders [A Note on the Extension of an Order on a Set to the Power Set]. *J. Econ. Theory*, February 1984, *32*(1), pp. 176–79.

Fishburn, Peter C. Probabilistic Social Choice Based on Simple Voting Comparisons. *Rev. Econ. Stud.*, October 1984, *51*(4), pp. 683–92.

Fishburn, Peter C. and Brams, Steven J. Manipulability of Voting by Sincere Truncation of Preferences. *Public Choice*, 1984, *44*(3), pp. 397–410.

Fishburn, Peter C. and Gehrlein, W. V. Powers of Subgroups in Voting Bodies. *Soc. Choice Welfare*, August 1984, *1*(2), pp. 85–95.

Flowers, Marilyn R. and Danzon, Patricia M. Separation of the Redistributive and Allocative Functions of Government: A Public Choice Perspective. *J. Public Econ.*, August 1984, *24*(3), pp. 373–80.

Forte, Francesco. Controlling the Productivity of Bureaucratic Behavior. *Atlantic Econ. J.*, March 1984, *12*(1), pp. 32–40.

Foster, Carroll B. The Performance of Rational Voter Models in Recent Presidential Elections. *Amer. Polit. Sci. Rev.*, September 1984, *78*(3), pp. 678–90.

Frey, Bruno S. The Function of Governments and Intergovernmental Organizations in the International Resource Transfer—The Case of the World Bank. *Weltwirtsch. Arch.*, 1984, *120*(4), pp. 702–19. [G: Global]

Frohlich, Norman and Oppenheimer, Joe. Post Election Redistributive Strategies of Representatives: A Partial Theory of the Politics of Redistribution. *Public Choice*, 1984, *42*(2), pp. 113–31.

Gifford, Adam, Jr. and Kenney, Roy W. Socialism and the Revenue Maximizing Leviathan. *Public Choice*, 1984, *42*(1), pp. 101–06.

Gist, John R. and Hill, R. Carter. Political and Economic Influences on the Bureaucratic Allocation of Federal Funds: The Case of Urban Development Action Grants. *J. Urban Econ.*, September 1984, *16*(2), pp. 158–72. [G: U.S.]

Gitelman, Zvi. Working the Soviet System: Citizens and Urban Bureaucracies. In *Morton, H. W. and Stuart, R. C., eds.*, 1984, pp. 221–43. [G: U.S.S.R.]

Greene, Kenneth V. Sequential Referenda and

Bureaucratic Man. *Public Choice*, 1984, *43*(1), pp. 77–82. [G: U.S.]

Hamlin, Alan P. Constitutional Control of Processes and Their Outcomes. *Public Choice*, 1984, *42*(2), pp. 133–45.

Hammond, P. Brett. The Energy Model Muddle. *Policy Sci.*, February 1984, *16*(3), pp. 227–43.

Hansson, Ingemar and Stuart, Charles E. Voting Competitions with Interested Politicians: Platforms Do Not Converge to the Preferences of the Median Voter. *Public Choice*, 1984, *44*(3), pp. 431–41.

Haurin, Donald R. and Gill, H. Leroy. The Spatial Distribution of Public Services: A Structural Model of Voting, Educational Production, and the Government's Allocation of Educational Inputs. *Public Choice*, 1984, *44*(3), pp. 481–500. [G: U.S.]

Heiner, Ronald A. and Packard, Dennis J. A Uniqueness Result for Extending Orders; with Application to Collective Choice as Inconsistency Resolution [A Note on the Extension of an Order on a Set to the Power Set]. *J. Econ. Theory*, February 1984, *32*(1), pp. 180–84.

Hillman, Arye L. Declining Industries and Political-Support Protectionist Motives: Errata. *Amer. Econ. Rev.*, March 1984, *74*(1), pp. 260.

Hillman, Arye L. Preemptive Rent Seeking and the Social Cost of Monopoly Power. *Int. J. Ind. Organ.*, September 1984, *2*(3), pp. 277–81.

Holzman, Ron. An Extension of Fishburn's Theorem on Extending Orders [A Note on the Extension of an Order on a Set to the Power Set]. *J. Econ. Theory*, February 1984, *32*(1), pp. 192–96.

Johnson, Bruce E. From Analyst to Negotiator: The OMB's New Role. *J. Policy Anal. Manage.*, Summer 1984, *3*(4), pp. 501–15. [G: U.S.]

Kalt, Joseph P. The Congressional–Bureaucratic System: A Principal–Agent Perspective (with Applications to the SEC): A Comment. *Public Choice*, 1984, *44*(1), pp. 193–95. [G: U.S.]

Kannai, Yakar and Peleg, Bezalel. A Note on the Extension of an Order on a Set to the Power Set. *J. Econ. Theory*, February 1984, *32*(1), pp. 172–75.

Katz, Amoz. Can a Party Represent Its Constituency? *Public Choice*, 1984, *44*(3), pp. 453–56.

Kau, James B. and Rubin, Paul H. Economic and Ideological Factors in Congressional Voting: The 1980 Election. *Public Choice*, 1984, *44*(2), pp. 385–88. [G: U.S.]

Keiding, Hans. Heights of Representative Systems: A Proof of Fishburn's Conjecture. *Soc. Choice Welfare*, August 1984, *1*(2), pp. 149–58.

Keim, Gerald D.; Zeithaml, Carl P. and Baysinger, Barry D. New Directions for Corporate Political Strategy. *Sloan Manage. Rev.*, Spring 1984, *25*(3), pp. 53–62. [G: U.S.]

Keller, Robert R. and May, Ann Mari. The Presidential Political Business Cycle of 1972. *J. Econ. Hist.*, June 1984, *44*(2), pp. 265–71. [G: U.S.]

Kelly, Jerry S. Simple Majority Voting Isn't Special. *Math. Soc. Sci.*, February 1984, *7*(1), pp. 13–20.

Kelly, Jerry S. The Sertel and Van der Bellen Problems. *Math. Soc. Sci.*, December 1984, *8*(3), pp. 287–90.

Kenyon, Daphne A. Preference Revelation and Supply Response in the Arena of Local Government. *Public Choice*, 1984, *42*(2), pp. 147–60. [G: U.S.]

Kilgour, D. Marc and Levesque, Terrence J. The Canadian Constitutional Amending Formula: Bargaining in the Past and the Future. *Public Choice*, 1984, *44*(3), pp. 457–80. [G: Canada]

Kirchgässner, Gebhard. On the Theory of Optimal Government Behaviour. *J. Econ. Dynam. Control*, November 1984, *8*(2), pp. 167–95. [G: U.S.]

Koehler, David H. Ordinal Preference Games: An Analysis of Legislative Coalition Formation without Transferable Utility. *Amer. Polit. Sci. Rev.*, September 1984, *78*(3), pp. 750–63.

Kramer, Gerald H. Reply [The Ecological Fallacy Revisited: Aggregate- versus Individual-Level Findings on Economics and Elections, and Sociotropic Voting]. *Amer. Polit. Sci. Rev.*, September 1984, *78*(3), pp. 791–92. [G: U.S.]

Kramer, Gerald H. and McKelvey, Richard D. The Relationship between the Generalized Median and Minimax Sets: A Correction [Limiting Distributions for Continuous State Markov Voting Models]. *Soc. Choice Welfare*, October 1984, *1*(3), pp. 243–44.

Laband, David N. Economics and Overthrows: Private Wants vs. Public Goods. *Atlantic Econ. J.*, September 1984, *12*(3), pp. 79.

Laband, David N. Is There a Relationship between Economic Conditions and Political Structure? *Public Choice*, 1984, *42*(1), pp. 25–37. [G: Global]

Lächler, Ulrich. The Political Business Cycle under Rational Voting Behavior. *Public Choice*, 1984, *44*(3), pp. 411–30.

Lecaillon, Jacques. Disparités de revenus et stratégie politique. (With English summary.) *Revue Écon. Polit.*, July–August 1984, *94*(4), pp. 433–45. [G: France]

Ledyard, John O. The Pure Theory of Large Two-Candidate Elections. *Public Choice*, 1984, *44*(1), pp. 7–41.

LeLoup, Lance T. Appropriations Politics in Congress: The House Appropriations Committee and the Executive Agencies. *Public Budg. Finance*, Winter 1984, *4*(4), pp. 78–98. [G: U.S.]

LeLoup, Lance T. The Impact of Budget Reform on the Senate. In *Wander, W. T.; Hebert, F. T. and Copeland, G. W., eds.*, 1984, pp. 78–99. [G: U.S.]

Levesque, Terrence J. Measuring State Power in Presidential Elections. *Public Choice*, 1984, *42*(3), pp. 295–310. [G: U.S.]

Levy, David M. Towards a Neoaristotelean Theory of Politics: A Positive Account of 'Fairness.' *Public Choice*, 1984, *42*(1), pp. 39–54.

Lewis, Gordon H. The Taichman–Young Knot Unravelled [The Day Care Tangle]. *J. Policy Anal. Manage.*, Fall 1984, *4*(1), pp. 119–20. [G: U.S.]

Lichbach, Mark. An Economic Theory of Governability: Choosing Policy and Optimizing Performance. *Public Choice*, 1984, *44*(2), pp. 307–37.

Lichtenstein, Peter M. Economic Democracy: The Rawls–Vanek–Sraffa Connection. *Rev. Soc. Econ.*, October 1984, *42*(2), pp. 170–81.

Maloney, Michael T.; McCormick, Robert E. and Tollison, Robert D. Economic Regulation, Competitive Governments, and Specialized Resources. *J. Law Econ.*, October 1984, *27*(2), pp. 329–38. [G: U.S.]

March, James G. and Olsen, Johan P. The New Institutionalism: Organizational Factors in Political Life. *Amer. Polit. Sci. Rev.*, September 1984, *78*(3), pp. 734–49.

Marvel, Mary K. Sunset: An Early Evaluation. *Public Choice*, 1984, *42*(2), pp. 193–96. [G: U.S.]

Mayer, Wolfgang. Endogenous Tariff Formation. *Amer. Econ. Rev.*, December 1984, *74*(5), pp. 970–85.

McClelland, Peter D. The Presidential Political Business Cycle of 1972: Discussion. *J. Econ. Hist.*, June 1984, *44*(2), pp. 273–76. [G: U.S.]

McCormick, Robert E. and Tollison, Robert D. Legislatures as Unions. In *Buchanan, J. M. and Tollison, R. D., eds.*, 1984, *1978*, pp. 323–37. [G: U.S.]

McDonald, Terrence J. San Francisco: Socioeconomic Change, Political Culture, and Fiscal Politics, 1870–1906. In *McDonald, T. J. and Ward, S. K., eds.*, 1984, pp. 39–67. [G: U.S.]

McGuire, Robert A. and Ohsfeldt, Robert L. Economic Interests and the American Constitution: A Quantitative Rehabilitation of Charles A. Beard. *J. Econ. Hist.*, June 1984, *44*(2), pp. 509–19. [G: U.S.]

McKee, Michael and West, Edwin G. Do Second-Best Considerations Affect Policy Decisions? *Public Finance*, 1984, *39*(2), pp. 246–60.

McKelvey, Richard D. and Ordeshook, Peter C. Rational Expectations in Elections: Some Experimental Results Based on a Multidimensional Model. *Public Choice*, 1984, *44*(1), pp. 61–102.

McKenzie, Richard B. Constitutional Economics: Introduction. In *McKenzie, R. B., ed. (I)*, 1984, pp. 1–18.

McMeekin, Gordon C. Delegation and Symmetry Approaches to Committee Decision Problems. *Atlantic Econ. J.*, December 1984, *12*(4), pp. 64–65.

Mehay, Stephen L. The Effect of Governmental Structure on Special District Expenditures. *Public Choice*, 1984, *44*(2), pp. 339–48. [G: U.S.]

Meyer, Marshall W. and Solomon, Kenneth A. Risk Management in Local Communities. *Policy Sci.*, February 1984, *16*(3), pp. 245–65.

Midlarsky, Manus I. Political Stability of Two-Party and Multiparty Systems: Probabilistic Bases for the Comparison of Party Systems. *Amer. Polit. Sci. Rev.*, December 1984, *78*(4), pp. 929–51. [G: U.S.; Selected Countries]

Miller, James C., III; Shughart, William F., II and Tollison, Robert D. A Note on Centralized Regulatory Review. *Public Choice*, 1984, *43*(1), pp. 83–88.

Mohammad, Sharif and Whalley, John. Rent Seeking in India: Its Costs and Policy Significance. *Kyklos*, 1984, *37*(3), pp. 387–413. [G: India]

Moulin, Hervé. The Conditional Auction Mechanism for Sharing a Surplus. *Rev. Econ. Stud.*, January 1984, *51*(1), pp. 157–70.

Mueller, Dennis C. Interest Groups, Redistribution and Political Stability. *Economia (Portugal)*, January 1984, *8*(1), pp. 67–80.

Munger, Michael C. On the Mutuality of Interest between Bureaus and High Demand Review Committees: The Case of Joint Production. *Public Choice*, 1984, *43*(2), pp. 211–15.

Munley, Vincent G. Has the Median Voter Found a Ballot Box That He Can Control? *Econ. Inquiry*, July 1984, *22*(3), pp. 323–36. [G: U.S.]

Muramatsu, Michio and Krauss, Ellis S. Bureaucrats and Politicians in Policymaking: The Case of Japan. *Amer. Polit. Sci. Rev.*, March 1984, *78*(1), pp. 126–46. [G: Japan]

Murrell, Peter. An Examination of the Factors Affecting the Formation of Interest Groups in OECD Countries. *Public Choice*, 1984, *43*(2), pp. 151–71. [G: OECD]

Nachmias, David. Are Federal Bureaucrats Conservative? A Modest Test of a Popular Image. *Soc. Sci. Quart.*, December 1984, *65*(4), pp. 1080–87.

Nellor, David C. L. Public Bureau Budgets and Jurisdiction Size: An Empirical Note. *Public Choice*, 1984, *42*(2), pp. 175–83. [G: U.S.]

Niemi, Richard G. The Problem of Strategic Behavior under Approval Voting. *Amer. Polit. Sci. Rev.*, December 1984, *78*(4), pp. 952–58.

Nitzan, Shmuel I. and Paroush, Jacob. Are Qualified Majority Rules Special? *Public Choice*, 1984, *42*(3), pp. 257–72.

Nitzan, Shmuel I. and Pattanaik, Prasanta K. Median-based Extensions of an Ordering over a Set to the Power Set: An Axiomatic Characterization. *J. Econ. Theory*, December 1984, *34*(2), pp. 252–61.

Offe, Claus. Competitive Party Democracy and the Keynesian Welfare State. In *Offe, C.*, 1984, pp. 179–206.

Offe, Claus. Political Culture and Social Democratic Administration. In *Offe, C.*, 1984, pp. 207–19.

Offe, Claus. The Separation of Form and Content in Liberal Democracy. In *Offe, C.*, 1984, *1980*, pp. 162–78.

Olson, Mancur. Microeconomic Incentives and Macroeconomic Decline. *Weltwirtsch. Arch.*, 1984, *120*(4), pp. 631–45. [G: W. Europe; U.S.]

Olson, Mancur. The Limits of Constitutional Determinism: Comment. In *McKenzie, R. B., ed. (I),* 1984, pp. 89–94.

Osborne, Martin J. Why Do Some Goods Bear Higher Taxes than Others? *J. Econ. Theory,* April 1984, *32*(2), pp. 301–16.

Ostrosky, Anthony L. The Electoral College and Voter Participation Rates: A Comment. *Public Choice,* 1984, *43*(1), pp. 99–100.   [G: U.S.]

Owen, Guillermo and Crofman, Bernard. To Vote or Not to Vote: The Paradox of Nonvoting. *Public Choice,* 1984, *42*(3), pp. 311–25.

Palfrey, Thomas R. Spatial Equilibrium with Entry. *Rev. Econ. Stud.,* January 1984, *51*(1), pp. 139–56.

Pattanaik, Prasanta K. and Peleg, Bezalel. An Axiomatic Characterization of the Lexicographic Maximin Extension of an Ordering over a Set to the Power Set. *Soc. Choice Welfare,* August 1984, *1*(2), pp. 113–22.

Pauly, Mark V.; Kunreuther, Howard and Vaupel, James W. Public Protection against Misperceived Risks: Insights from Positive Political Economy. *Public Choice,* 1984, *43*(1), pp. 45–64.

Peltzman, Sam. Constituent Interest and Congressional Voting. *J. Law Econ.,* April 1984, *27*(1), pp. 181–210.   [G: U.S.]

Pitney, John J., Jr. Bile Barrel Politics: Siting Unwanted Facilities *J. Policy Anal. Manage.,* Spring 1984, *3*(3), pp. 446–48.   [G: U.S.]

van der Ploeg, Frederick. Government Ideology and Re-election Efforts. *Oxford Econ. Pap.,* June 1984, *36*(2), pp. 213–31.

van der Ploeg, Frederick. The Principle of Political-Economic Assignment. *J. Macroecon.,* Summer 1984, *6*(3), pp. 283–94.

Primeaux, Walter J., Jr., et al. Determinants of Regulatory Policies toward Competition in the Electric Utility Industry. *Public Choice,* 1984, *43*(2), pp. 173–86.   [G: U.S.]

ten Raa, Thijs. The Interest Function Approach. *De Economist,* 1984, *132*(4), pp. 479–90.

Rae, Douglas W. Sources of Opposition to Constitutional Reform: Comment. In *McKenzie, R. B., ed. (I),* 1984, pp. 35–37.

Rapping, Leonard A. Bureaucracy, the Corporation, and Economic Policy. *J. Post Keynesian Econ.,* Spring 1984, *6*(3), pp. 337–53.
    [G: U.S.]

Raymon, Neil and Stuart, Charles E. Short-Run Politicians and Long-Run Tax Revenue: An Empirical Assessment. *Scand. J. Econ.,* 1984, *86*(3), pp. 314–25.   [G: U.S.]

Rowley, Charles K. The Relevance of the Median Voter Theorem. *Z. ges. Staatswiss.,* March 1984, *140*(1), pp. 104–26.   [G: U.S.]

Rubin, Irene S. Marasmus or Recovery? The Effects of Cutbacks in Federal Agencies. *Soc. Sci. Quart.,* March 1984, *65*(1), pp. 74–88.
    [G: U.S.]

Rustem, Berc and Velupillai, Kumaraswamy. Cooperation between Politicians and Econometricians and the Search for Optimal Economic Policy. *J. Policy Modeling,* August 1984, *6*(3), pp. 341–50.

Salisbury, Robert H. Interest Representation: The Dominance of Institutions. *Amer. Polit. Sci. Rev.,* March 1984, *78*(1), pp. 64–76.
    [G: U.S.]

Samuelson, Larry. Electoral Equilibria with Restricted Strategies. *Public Choice,* 1984, *43*(3), pp. 307–27.

Sandler, Todd and Tschirhart, John T. Mixed Clubs: Further Observations [Clubs, Local Public Goods and Transportation Models: A Synthesis]. *J. Public Econ.,* April 1984, *23*(3), pp. 381–89.

Schelling, Thomas C. Command and Control. In *Schelling, T. C.,* 1984, pp. 27–56.

Schofield, Norman J. Political Fragmentation and the Stability of Coalition Governments in Western Europe. In *Holler, M. J., ed.,* 1984, pp. 297–319.

Scicchitano, Michael J. Comment on Kramer [The Ecological Fallacy Revisited: Aggregate-versus Individual-Level Findings on Economics and Elections, and Sociotropic Voting]. *Amer. Polit. Sci. Rev.,* September 1984, *78*(3), pp. 790–91.   [G: U.S.]

Sen, Manimay. Strategy-Proofness of a Class of Borda Rules. *Public Choice,* 1984, *43*(3), pp. 251–85.

Senior Nello, Susan. An Application of Public Choice Theory to the Question of CAP Reform. *Europ. Rev. Agr. Econ.,* 1984, *11*(3), pp. 261–83.   [G: EEC]

Shepsle, Kenneth A. and Weingast, Barry R. Political Solutions to Market Problems. *Amer. Polit. Sci. Rev.,* June 1984, *78*(2), pp. 417–34.

Shughart, William F., II and Tollison, Robert D. The Use of Inputs by the Federal Reserve System: Reply. *Amer. Econ. Rev.,* December 1984, *74*(5), pp. 1121–23.

Simmons, Randy T. and Mitchell, William C. Politics and the New Resource Economics. *Contemp. Policy Issue,* March 1984, (5), pp. 1–13.

Skaggs, Neil T. A Theory of the Bureaucratic Value of Federal Reserve Operating Procedures. *Public Choice,* 1984, *43*(1), pp. 65–76.
    [G: U.S.]

Smith, Richard A. Advocacy, Interpretation, and Influence in the U.S. Congress. *Amer. Polit. Sci. Rev.,* March 1984, *78*(1), pp. 44–63.

Sonntag, Niels and Featherstone, Kevin. Looking towards the 1984 European Elections: Problems of Political Integration. *J. Common Market Stud.,* March 1984, *22*(3), pp. 269–82.
    [G: U.K.; France; Italy; W. Germany]

Sproule-Jones, Mark. On the Analysis of Constitutional Change in Canada: Comments [The Political Economy of Canadian Constitution-Making: The Canadian Economic-Union Issue] [An Analysis of Constitutional Change, Canada, 1980–82]. *Public Choice,* 1984, *44*(1), pp. 279–83.   [G: Canada]

Strong, John S. The Use of Inputs by the Federal Reserve System: Comment. *Amer. Econ. Rev.,* December 1984, *74*(5), pp. 1118–20.

Stubblebine, Wm. Craig. Practical Problems of

Constitutional Reform. In *McKenzie, R. B., ed. (I)*, 1984, pp. 213–23. **[G: U.S.]**

Sugden, Robert. Free Association and the Theory of Proportional Representation. *Amer. Polit. Sci. Rev.*, March 1984, *78*(1), pp. 31–43.

Swaney, James A. The Future Be Damned: Economists' Optimism and Nuclear Proliferation. *J. Econ. Issues*, June 1984, *18*(2), pp. 527–36.

Taichman, Ettie and Young, Dennis R. A Knot in the Day Care Tangle. *J. Policy Anal. Manage.*, Fall 1984, *4*(1), pp. 117–19. **[G: U.S.]**

Toma, Eugenia Froedge and Toma, Mark. Constitutional Tax Constraints within a Classical Model of Leviathan. *Hist. Polit. Econ.*, Spring 1984, *16*(1), pp. 89–105.

Tullock, Gordon. A (Partial) Rehabilitation of the Public Interest Theory. *Public Choice*, 1984, *42*(1), pp. 89–99.

Vaughn, Karen I. Constitutional Economics: Themes and Reflections. In *McKenzie, R. B., ed. (I)*, 1984, pp. 239–45.

Walker, Alan. The Political Economy of Privatisation. In *Le Grand, J. and Robinson, R., eds.*, 1984, pp. 19–44.

Wallace, Myles S. and Warner, John T. Fed Policy and Presidential Elections. *J. Macroecon.*, Winter 1984, *6*(1), pp. 79–88. **[G: U.S.]**

Warren, Ronald S., Jr. Maximizing Models of Legislative Choice. *Public Choice*, 1984, *42*(3), pp. 287–94.

Weede, Erich. Democracy, Creeping Socialism, and Ideological Socialism in Rent-seeking Societies. *Public Choice*, 1984, *44*(2), pp. 349–66. **[G: OECD; Israel]**

Weingast, Barry R. The Congressional–Bureaucratic System: A Principal–Agent Perspective (with Application to the SEC). *Public Choice*, 1984, *44*(1), pp. 147–91. **[G: U.S.]**

Werner, Josua. Marktwirtschaftliche Koordination und gesellschaftliche Entscheidungsprozesse. (Market Economy Coordination and Political Decision Processes. With English summary.) *Schweiz. Z. Volkswirtsch. Statist.*, June 1984, *120*(2), pp. 169–89.

Weymark, John A. Majority-Rule Directions of Income Tax Reform and Second-Best Optimality. *Scand. J. Econ.*, 1984, *86*(2), pp. 194–213.

van Winden, Franz. The Interest Function Approach: A Reply. *De Economist*, 1984, *132*(4), pp. 491–96.

Winer, Stanley. A Comment on the Papers by Thomas Courchene and Albert Breton [The Political Economy of Canadian Constitution-Making: The Canadian Economic-Union Issue] [An Analysis of Constitutional Change, Canada, 1980–82]. *Public Choice*, 1984, *44*(1), pp. 273–78. **[G: Canada]**

Wittman, Donald. Multi-Candidate Equilibria. *Public Choice*, 1984, *43*(3), pp. 287–91.

Wollmann, Hellmutt. Policy Analysis: Some Observations on the West German Scene. *Policy Sci.*, May 1984, *17*(1), pp. 27–47. **[G: W. Germany]**

Yandle, Bruce. Intertwined Interests, Rent Seeking, and Regulation. *Soc. Sci. Quart.*, December 1984, *65*(4), pp. 1002–12.

Yandle, Bruce. The Wages of Regulation. *J. Lab. Res.*, Fall 1984, *5*(4), pp. 435–39.

Yang, Chin-Wei and Dennis, Enid. Elasticities and Rent Control Revisited. *Atlantic Econ. J.*, December 1984, *12*(4), pp. 59–61.

026 Economics of Uncertainty and Information; Game Theory and Bargaining Theory

0260 General

Arrow, Kenneth J. Risk Perception in Psychology and Economics. In *Arrow, K. J., vol. 3, 1984, 1982*, pp. 261–70.

Samuelson, William F. Bargaining under Asymmetric Information. *Econometrica*, July 1984, *52*(4), pp. 995–1005.

Seidl, Christian. Asymmetric Information and the Dynamics of Coalition Formation Observations on Some Unsolved Problems. In *Holler, M. J., ed.*, 1984, pp. 216–27.

0261 Theory of Uncertainty and Information

Akerlof, George A. The Economics of Caste and of the Rat Race and Other Woeful Tales. In *Akerlof, G. A., 1984, 1976*, pp. 23–44.

Akerlof, George A. The Market for "Lemons": Quality Uncertainty and the Market Mechanism. In *Akerlof, G. A., 1984, 1970*, pp. 7–22. **[G: India]**

Allais, Maurice. The Foundations of the Theory of Utility and Risk: Some Central Points of the Discussions at the Oslo Conference. In *Hagen, O. and Wenstop, F., eds.*, 1984, pp. 3–131.

Allen, Beth. Convergence of σ-Fields and Applications to Mathematical Economics. In *Hammer, G. and Pallaschke, D., eds.*, 1984, pp. 161–74.

Allen, Beth. Equilibria in Which Prices Convey Information: The Finite Case. In *Boyer, M. and Kihlstrom, R. E., eds.*, 1984, pp. 63–92.

Arai, Kazuhiro. Expected-Utility-Maximizing Search. *Hitotsubashi J. Econ.*, June 1984, *25*(1), pp. 71–92.

Arrow, Kenneth J. Allocation of Resources in Large Teams. In *Arrow, K. J., vol. 4, 1984, 1979*, pp. 233–61.

Arrow, Kenneth J. Alternative Approaches to the Theory of Choice in Risk-Taking Situations. In *Arrow, K. J., vol. 3, 1984, 1951*, pp. 5–41.

Arrow, Kenneth J. Exposition of the Theory of Choice under Uncertainty. In *Arrow, K. J., vol. 3, 1984, 1971*, pp. 172–208.

Arrow, Kenneth J. Information and Economic Behavior. In *Arrow, K. J., vol. 4, 1984, 1973*, pp. 136–52.

Arrow, Kenneth J. Insurance, Risk, and Resource Allocation. In *Arrow, K. J., vol. 4, 1984, 1965*, pp. 77–86.

Arrow, Kenneth J. On the Agenda of Organizations. In *Arrow, K. J., vol. 4, 1984, 1974*, pp. 167–84.

Arrow, Kenneth J. Risk Allocation and Information: Some Recent Theoretical Developments.

In *Arrow, K. J., vol. 4*, 1984, *1978*, pp. 197–215.

Arrow, Kenneth J. Statistics and Economic Policy. In *Arrow, K. J., vol. 4*, 1984, *1957*, pp. 43–54.

Arrow, Kenneth J. The Economics of Moral Hazard: Further Comment. In *Arrow, K. J., vol. 4*, 1984, *1968*, pp. 103–05.

Arrow, Kenneth J. The Theory of Risk Aversion. In *Arrow, K. J., vol. 3*, 1984, *1965*, pp. 147–71.

Arrow, Kenneth J. The Value of and Demand for Information. In *Arrow, K. J., vol. 4*, 1984, *1971*, pp. 106–14.

Arrow, Kenneth J. Vertical Integration and Communication. In *Arrow, K. J., vol. 4*, 1984, *1975*, pp. 185–96.

Arrow, Kenneth J.; Blackwell, D. and Girshick, M. A. Bayes and Minimax Solutions of Sequential Decision Problems. In *Arrow, K. J., vol. 4*, 1984, *1949*, pp. 1–37.

Barberá, Salvador; Barrett, C. Richard and Pattanaik, Prasanta K. On Some Axioms for Ranking Sets of Alternatives. *J. Econ. Theory*, August 1984, *33*(2), pp. 301–08.

Baron, David P. and Besanko, David. Regulation and Information in a Continuing Relationship. *Info. Econ. Policy*, 1984, *1*(3), pp. 267–302.

Bausor, Randall. Toward a Historically Dynamic Economics: Examples and Illustrations. *J. Post Keynesian Econ.*, Spring 1984, *6*(3), pp. 360–76.

Bebchuk, Lucian Arye. Litigation and Settlement under Imperfect Information. *Rand J. Econ.*, Autumn 1984, *15*(3), pp. 404–15.

Beckmann, Martin J. Risk and Saving. In *Bamberg, G. and Spremann, K., eds.*, 1984, pp. 5–12.

Bernard, Georges. Utility and Risk Preference Functions. In *Hagen, O. and Wenstop, F., eds.*, 1984, pp. 135–43.

Berninghaus, Siegfried. A General Existence Theorem for Equilibrium Price Dispersions. *Info. Econ. Policy*, 1984, *1*(3), pp. 239–66.

Bernstein, Peter L. The Surprises of Risk. *J. Portfol. Manage.*, Summer 1984, *10*(4), pp. 4.

Bester, Helmut. Increasing Risk and Equilibrium under Uncertainty. *J. Econ. Theory*, August 1984, *33*(2), pp. 378–86.

Blume, Lawrence E. and Easley, David. Rational Expectations Equilibrium: An Alternative Approach. *J. Econ. Theory*, October 1984, *34*(1), pp. 116–29.

Borch, Karl. Equilibrium Premiums in an Insurance Market. *J. Risk Ins.*, September 1984, *51*(3), pp. 468–76.

Borch, Karl. Premiums in a Competitive Insurance Market. *J. Banking Finance*, September 1984, *8*(3), pp. 431–41.

Bouyssou, Denis. Decision-Aid and Expected Utility Theory: A Critical Survey. In *Hagen, O. and Wenstop, F., eds.*, 1984, pp. 181–216.

Boyer, Marcel and Kihlstrom, Richard E. Bayesian Models in Economic Theory: Introduction. In *Boyer, M. and Kihlstrom, R. E., eds.*, 1984, pp. 1–12.

Brennan, Michael J. and Kraus, Allan. Notes on Costless Financial Signalling. In *Bamberg, G. and Spremann, K., eds.*, 1984, pp. 33–51.

Brick, Ivan E. and Jagpal, Harsharanjeet S. Utility Theory, Value Maximization and the Quality Decision under Uncertainty. *Int. Econ. Rev.*, June 1984, *25*(2), pp. 369–77.

Buccola, Steven T. and Subaei, Abdelbagi. Mean-Gini Analysis, Stochastic Efficiency and Weak Risk Aversion. *Australian J. Agr. Econ.*, August/December 1984, *28*(2–3), pp. 77–86.

Carlson, John A. and McAfee, R. Preston. Joint Search for Several Goods [The Theory of Search for Several Goods]. *J. Econ. Theory*, April 1984, *32*(2), pp. 337–45.

Charnes, A., et al. An MDI Model and an Algorithm for Composite Hypotheses Testing and Estimation in Marketing. *Marketing Sci.*, Winter 1984, *3*(1), pp. 55–72.

Cheng, Hsueh-Cheng. On the Generic Existence of Fully Revealing Price Equilibria [Rational Expectations Equilibrium: Generic Existence and the Information Revealed by Prices]. *J. Econ. Theory*, April 1984, *32*(2), pp. 351–58.

Cooper, Russell. On Allocative Distortions in Problems of Self-Selection. *Rand J. Econ.*, Winter 1984, *15*(4), pp. 568–77.

Cooper, Russell and Ross, Thomas W. Prices, Product Qualities and Asymmetric Information: The Competitive Case. *Rev. Econ. Stud.*, April 1984, *51*(2), pp. 197–207.

Crampes, Claude. Choix des inputs et règles de gestion face à une demande aléatoire. (With English summary.) *Revue Écon. Polit.*, July–August 1984, *94*(4), pp. 465–84.

Currie, David and Levine, Paul. Exchange Rate and Price Level Volatility under Partial Information. *Greek Econ. Rev.*, August 1984, *6*(2), pp. 149–70.

Daboni, L. On the Axiomatic Treatment of the Utility Theory. *Metroecon.*, June-Oct. 1984, *36*(2–3), pp. 203–09.

Demski, Joel S. and Sappington, David. Optimal Incentive Contracts with Multiple Agents. *J. Econ. Theory*, June 1984, *33*(1), pp. 152–71.

Denneberg, Dieter. Elements of Finance under Risk, an Average Deviation Approach to Risk. *Écon. Appl.*, 1984, *37*(1), pp. 165–99.

Dionne, Georges. Search and Insurance. *Int. Econ. Rev.*, June 1984, *25*(2), pp. 357–67.

Dow, Gregory K. Myopia, Amnesia, and Consistent Intertemporal Choice. *Math. Soc. Sci.*, October 1984, *8*(2), pp. 95–109.

Dubey, Pradeep and Kaneko, Mamoru. Information Patterns and Nash Equilibria in Extensive Games: I. *Math. Soc. Sci.*, October 1984, *8*(2), pp. 111–39.

Feldman, David H. and Tower, Edward. Profitable Destabilizing Speculation as Intertemporal Price Discrimination. *Amer. Econ.*, Fall 1984, *28*(2), pp. 60–63.

Fellingham, John C.; Kwon, Young K. and Newman, D. Paul. *Ex ante* Randomization in Agency Models. *Rand J. Econ.*, Summer 1984, *15*(2), pp. 290–301.

Fischoff, Baruch; Watson, Stephen R. and Hope,

Chris. Defining Risk. *Policy Sci.*, October 1984, *17*(2), pp. 123–39.

Fishburn, Peter C. Dominance in SSB Utility Theory. *J. Econ. Theory*, October 1984, *34*(1), pp. 130–48.

Fishburn, Peter C. SSB Utility Theory and Decision-making under Uncertainty. *Math. Soc. Sci.*, December 1984, *8*(3), pp. 253–85.

Fishburn, Peter C. SSB Utility Theory: An Economic Perspective. *Math. Soc. Sci.*, August 1984, *8*(1), pp. 63–94.

Freeman, Richard T. Information Structure and the Transmission of Inflationary Expectations. *Math. Soc. Sci.*, October 1984, *8*(2), pp. 169–93.

Freixas, Xavier and Kihlstrom, Richard E. Risk Aversion and Information Demand. In *Boyer, M. and Kihlstrom, R. E., eds.*, 1984, pp. 93–104.

Freixas, Xavier and Laffont, Jean-Jacques. On the Irreversibility Effect. In *Boyer, M. and Kihlstrom, R. E., eds.*, 1984, pp. 105–14.

Fried, Dov. Incentives for Information Production and Disclosure in a Duopolistic Environment. *Quart. J. Econ.*, May 1984, *99*(2), pp. 367–81.

Friedman, Daniel. On the Efficiency of Experimental Double Auction Markets. *Amer. Econ. Rev.*, March 1984, *74*(1), pp. 60–72.

Fukuba, Yo and Ito, Komayuki. The So-Called Expected Utility Theory Is Inadequate. *Math. Soc. Sci.*, February 1984, *7*(1), pp. 1–12.

Fukuba, Yo; Tabata, Yoshio and Sakagami, Yoshitaka. Notes on Measurement and Approximation (I). (In Japanese. With English summary.) *Osaka Econ. Pap.*, December 1984, *34*(2–3), pp. 275–82.

Gehm, Fred. Techniques for Making Decisions under Uncertainty. *J. Futures Markets*, Spring 1984, *4*(1), pp. 65–73.

Green, Edward J. On the Difficulty of Eliciting Summary Information. *J. Econ. Theory*, April 1984, *32*(2), pp. 228–45.

Grossman, Sanford J. and Weiss, Laurence. Saving and Insurance. In *Boyer, M. and Kihlstrom, R. E., eds.*, 1984, pp. 303–11.

Guesnerie, Roger and Laffont, Jean-Jacques. The Government Control of Public Firms and the Economics of Incomplete Information: An Introduction. In *Marchand, M.; Pestieau, P. and Tulkens, H., eds.*, 1984, pp. 159–78.

Hagen, Ole. Relativity in Decision Theory. In *Hagen, O. and Wenstop, F., eds.*, 1984, pp. 237–49.

Hagerty, Michael R. and Aaker, David A. A Normative Model of Consumer Information Processing. *Marketing Sci.*, Summer 1984, *3*(3), pp. 227–46.

Hess, James D. Imperfect Information and Credit Rationing: Comment. *Quart. J. Econ.*, November 1984, *99*(4), pp. 865–68.

Hey, John D. Decision Under Uncertainty. In *van der Ploeg, F., ed.*, 1984, pp. 433–55.

Hey, John D. The Economics of Optimism and Pessimism: A Definition and Some Applications. *Kyklos*, 1984, *37*(2), pp. 181–205.

High, Jack. Knowledge, Maximizing, and Conjecture: A Critical Analysis of Search Theory. *J. Post Keynesian Econ.*, Winter 1983-84, *6*(2), pp. 252–64.

Hosios, Arthur J. A Welfare Analysis of Employment Contracts with and without Asymmetric Information. *Rev. Econ. Stud.*, July 1984, *51*(3), pp. 471–89.

Howitt, Peter. Information and Coordination: A Review Article. *Econ. Inquiry*, July 1984, *22*(3), pp. 429–46.

Hoy, Michael. The Impact of Imperfectly Categorizing Risks on Income Inequality and Social Welfare. *Can. J. Econ.*, August 1984, *17*(3), pp. 557–68.

Huberman, Gur. Capital Asset Pricing in an Overlapping Generations Model. *J. Econ. Theory*, August 1984, *33*(2), pp. 232–48.

Hughes Hallett, A. J. Optimal Stockpiling in a High-Risk Commodity Market: The Case of Copper. *J. Econ. Dynam. Control*, November 1984, *8*(2), pp. 211–38.   [G: Global]

Jaffee, Dwight M. and Russell, Thomas. Imperfect Information, Uncertainty, and Credit Rationing: A Reply. *Quart. J. Econ.*, November 1984, *99*(4), pp. 869–72.

Jones, Robert A. and Ostroy, Joseph M. Flexibility and Uncertainty. *Rev. Econ. Stud.*, January 1984, *51*(1), pp. 13–32.

Joyce, Patrick. The Walrasian *tâtonnement* Mechanism and Information. *Rand J. Econ.*, Autumn 1984, *15*(3), pp. 416–25.

Jüttner, D. Johannes. Information and Futures Trading—Some Missing Facts and Consequences [Informationsaktivitäten und Preisbildungsprozesse auf Terminkontraktmärkten]. *Jahr. Nationalökon. Statist.*, September 1984, *199*(5), pp. 460–63.

Kallberg, Jerry G. and Ziemba, William T. Misspecifications in Portfolio Selection Problems. In *Bamberg, G. and Spremann, K., eds.*, 1984, pp. 74–87.

Katz, Barbara Goody and Owen, Joel. Disequilibrium Theory, Waiting Costs, and Saving Behavior in Centrally Planned Economies: A Queueing-Theoretic Approach. *J. Compar. Econ.*, September 1984, *8*(3), pp. 301–21.

Katz, Michael L. Nonuniform Pricing with Unobservable Numbers of Purchases. *Rev. Econ. Stud.*, July 1984, *51*(3), pp. 461–70.

Keasey, Kevin. Regret Theory and Information: A Note. *Econ. J.*, September 1984, *94*(375), pp. 645–48.

Kihlstrom, Richard E. A "Bayesian" Exposition of Blackwell's Theorem on the Comparison of Experiments. In *Boyer, M. and Kihlstrom, R. E., eds.*, 1984, pp. 13–31.

Kihlstrom, Richard E. A Simple Example of the Radner–Stiglitz Nonconcavity in the Value of Information. In *Boyer, M. and Kihlstrom, R. E., eds.*, 1984, pp. 53–61.

Kihlstrom, Richard E. and Mirman, Leonard J. Market Experience and Accurate Price Expectations. In *Boyer, M. and Kihlstrom, R. E., eds.*, 1984, pp. 271–78.

Kihlstrom, Richard E.; Mirman, Leonard J. and

Postlewaite, Andrew. Experimental Consumption and the "Rothschild Effect." In *Boyer, M. and Kihlstrom, R. E., eds.*, 1984, pp. 279–302.

Krelle, Wilhelm. Remarks to Professor Allais' Contributions to the Theory of Expected Utility and Related Subjects. In *Hagen, O. and Wenstop, F., eds.*, 1984, pp. 173–80.

Kroll, Yoram. The Analysis of Risky Investment: A State-Contingent Approach. *J. Banking Finance*, December 1984, *8*(4), pp. 509–24.

Krzysztofowicz, Roman. Prediction, Measurement, and Error of Utility: A Reply. In *Hagen, O. and Wenstop, F., eds.*, 1984, pp. 165–70.

Laffont, Jean-Jacques. Information imparfaite et rationalité collective. (Collective Rationality under Incomplete Information. With English summary.) *Revue Écon.*, January 1984, *35*(1), pp. 163–76.

Lamberton, D. M. The Emergence of Information Economics. In *Jussawalla, M. and Ebenfield, H., eds.*, 1984, pp. 7–22.

Langlois, Richard N. Internal Organization in a Dynamic Context: Some Theoretical Considerations. In *Jussawalla, M. and Ebenfield, H., eds.*, 1984, pp. 23–49.

Leitzinger, Jeffrey J. and Stiglitz, Joseph E. Information Externalities in Oil and Gas Leasing. *Contemp. Policy Issue*, March 1984, (5), pp. 44–57. [G: U.S.]

Levy, Haim and Levy, Azriel. Multivariate Decision-Making. *J. Econ. Theory*, February 1984, *32*(1), pp. 36–51.

Loomes, Graham and Sugden, Robert. Regret Theory and Information: A Reply. *Econ. J.*, September 1984, *94*(375), pp. 649–50.

Loomes, Graham and Sugden, Robert. The Importance of What Might Have Been. In *Hagen, O. and Wenstop, F., eds.*, 1984, pp. 219–35.

Machina, Mark J. Temporal Risk and the Nature of Induced Preferences. *J. Econ. Theory*, August 1984, *33*(2), pp. 199–231.

Maskin, Eric S. and Riley, John G. Monopoly with Incomplete Information. *Rand J. Econ.*, Summer 1984, *15*(2), pp. 171–96.

Maskin, Eric S. and Riley, John G. Optimal Auctions with Risk Averse Buyers. *Econometrica*, November 1984, *52*(6), pp. 1473–1518.

Matthews, Steven A. Information Acquisition in Discriminatory Auctions. In *Boyer, M. and Kihlstrom, R. E., eds.*, 1984, pp. 181–207.

Matthews, Steven A. On the Implementability of Reduced Form Auctions. *Econometrica*, November 1984, *52*(6), pp. 1519–22.

McLennan, Andrew. Price Dispersion and Incomplete Learning in the Long Run. *J. Econ. Dynam. Control*, September 1984, *7*(3), pp. 331–47.

de Meza, David. Private Disclosure: Is Honesty Enough? *Europ. Econ. Rev.*, March 1984, *24*(2), pp. 203–07.

de Meza, David and Dickinson, Paul T. Risk Preferences and Transaction Costs. *J. Econ. Behav. Organ.*, June 1984, *5*(2), pp. 223–36.

Moore, John. Global Incentive Constraints in Auction Design. *Econometrica*, November 1984, *52*(6), pp. 1523–35.

Mosler, Karl Clemens. Increasing Multivariate Risk: Some Definitions. In *Bamberg, G. and Spremann, K., eds.*, 1984, pp. 88–102.

Murrell, Peter and Miller, Jeffrey B. The Applicability of Information-revealing Incentive Schemes in Economic Organizations. *J. Compar. Econ.*, September 1984, *8*(3), pp. 277–89.

Ng, Yew-Kwang. Expected Subjective Utility: Is the Neumann–Morgenstern Utility the Same as the Neoclassical's? *Soc. Choice Welfare*, October 1984, *1*(3), pp. 177–86.

Nielsen, Lars Tyge. Common Knowledge, Communication, and Convergence of Beliefs. *Math. Soc. Sci.*, August 1984, *8*(1), pp. 1–14.

Nielsen, Lars Tyge. Unbounded Expected Utility and Continuity. *Math. Soc. Sci.*, December 1984, *8*(3), pp. 201–16.

Nijkamp, Peter. Information Systems: A General Introduction. In *Nijkamp, P. and Rietveld, P., eds.*, 1984, pp. 3–33.

Nitzan, Shmuel I. and Paroush, Jacob. Potential Variability of Decisional Skills in Uncertain Dichotomous Choice Situations. *Math. Soc. Sci.*, December 1984, *8*(3), pp. 217–27.

Ohlson, James A. The Structure of Asset Prices and Socially Useless/Useful Information. *J. Finance*, December 1984, *39*(5), pp. 1417–35.

Orosel, Gerhard. Profitable Speculation and Price Stability. *Jahr. Nationalökon. Statist.*, November 1984, *199*(6), pp. 485–501.

Peled, Dan. Stationary Pareto Optimality of Stochastic Asset Equilibria with Overlapping Generations. *J. Econ. Theory*, December 1984, *34*(2), pp. 396–403.

Pikkemaat, G. F. A Dynamic Model of an Informationally Disaggregate Economy. In *Avula, X. J. R., et al.*, 1984, pp. 789–94.

van der Ploeg, Frederick. Economic Policy Rules for Risk-Sensitive Decision Making. *Z. Nationalökon.*, 1984, *44*(3), pp. 207–35.

Polemarchakis, Herakles M. and Rose, D. Another Proposition on the Recoverability of Cardinal Utility. *J. Econ. Theory*, October 1984, *34*(1), pp. 164–68.

Pope, Robin. The Utility of Gambling and of Outcomes: Inconsistent First Approximations. In *Hagen, O. and Wenstop, F., eds.*, 1984, pp. 251–73.

Prescott, Edward C. and Townsend, Robert M. General Competitive Analysis in an Economy with Private Information. *Int. Econ. Rev.*, February 1984, *25*(1), pp. 1–20.

Prescott, Edward C. and Townsend, Robert M. Pareto Optima and Competitive Equilibria with Adverse Selection and Moral Hazard. *Econometrica*, January 1984, *52*(1), pp. 21–45.

Quizon, Jaime B.; Binswanger, Hans P. and Machina, Mark J. Attitudes toward Risk: Further Remarks. *Econ. J.*, March 1984, *94*(373), pp. 144–48. [G: India]

Radner, Roy and Stiglitz, Joseph E. A Nonconcavity in the Value of Information. In *Boyer, M. and Kihlstrom, R. E., eds.*, 1984, pp. 33–52.

Ramakrishnan, Ram T. S. and Thakor, Anjan

V. Information Reliability and a Theory of Financial Intermediation. *Rev. Econ. Stud.*, July 1984, *51*(3), pp. 415–32.

Ray, Debraj. Intertemporal Borrowing to Sustain Exogenous Consumption Standards under Uncertainty. *J. Econ. Theory*, June 1984, *33*(1), pp. 72–87.

Reichelstein, Stefan. Incentive Compatibility and Informational Requirements. *J. Econ. Theory*, October 1984, *34*(1), pp. 32–51.

Rietveld, Piet. Public Choice Theory and Qualitative Discrete Multicriteria Decision Methods. In *Bahrenberg, G.; Fischer, M. M., and Nijkamp, P.,* 1984, pp. 409–26.

Riordan, Michael H. Uncertainty, Asymmetric Information and Bilateral Contracts. *Rev. Econ. Stud.*, January 1984, *51*(1), pp. 83–93.

Rosenthal, Robert W. and Weiss, Andrew. Mixed-Strategy Equilibrium in a Market with Asymmetric Information. *Rev. Econ. Stud.*, April 1984, *51*(2), pp. 333–42.

Roth, Alvin E. Stability and Polarization of Interests in Job Matching. *Econometrica*, January 1984, *52*(1), pp. 47–57.

Rothengatter, Werner. Quantity Rationing of Economic Transactions in a Risky Environment. In *Bamberg, G. and Spremann, K., eds.,* 1984, pp. 243–70.

Rutherford, Malcolm H. Rational Expectations and Keynesian Uncertainty: A Critique. *J. Post Keynesian Econ.*, Spring 1984, *6*(3), pp. 377–87.

Saari, Donald G. A Method for Constructing Message Systems for Smooth Performance Functions. *J. Econ. Theory*, August 1984, *33*(2), pp. 249–74.

Sappington, David. Incentive Contracting with Asymmetric and Imperfect Precontractual Knowledge. *J. Econ. Theory*, October 1984, *34*(1), pp. 52–70.

Schmalensee, Richard. Imperfect Information and the Equitability of Competitive Prices. *Quart. J. Econ.*, August 1984, *99*(3), pp. 441–60.

Sertel, Murat R. and Steinherr, Alfred. Information, Incentives, and the Design of Efficient Institutions. *Z. ges. Staatswiss.*, June 1984, *140*(2), pp. 233–46.

Shackle, G. L. S. Comment on the Papers by Randall Bausor and Malcolm Rutherford [Toward a Historically Dynamic Economics: Examples and Illustrations] [Rational Expectations and Keynesian Uncertainty: A Critique]. *J. Post Keynesian Econ.*, Spring 1984, *6*(3), pp. 388–93.

Shaffer, Sherrill. Regulation and Risk Preferences. *J. Ind. Econ.*, March 1984, *32*(3), pp. 349–57.

Shavell, Steven. The Design of Contracts and Remedies for Breach. *Quart. J. Econ.*, February 1984, *99*(1), pp. 121–48.

Shefrin, Hersh M. Inferior Forecasters, Cycles, and the Efficient-Markets Hypothesis: A Comment [Market 'Efficiency' in a Market with Heterogeneous Information]. *J. Polit. Econ.*, February 1984, *92*(1), pp. 156–61.

Shubik, Martin. On the Value of Market Information and Rational Expectations. In *[Beckmann, M. J.],* 1984, pp. 119–34.

Stiglitz, Joseph E. Information, Screening, and Welfare. In *Boyer, M. and Kihlstrom, R. E., eds.,* 1984, pp. 209–39.

Streit, Manfred E. Information Processing in Futures Market—An Essay on Adequate Abstraction. *Jahr. Nationalökon. Statist.*, September 1984, *199*(5), pp. 385–400.

Tisdell, Clem A. Slanting Advice and Biasing Recommendations for Welfare Gains in an Imperfect World. *Info. Econ. Policy*, 1984, *1*(3), pp. 229–37.

Tonks, Ian. A Bayesian Approach to the Production of Information with a Linear Utility Function. *Rev. Econ. Stud.*, July 1984, *51*(3), pp. 521–27.

Tsutsui, Yoshiro. Credit Rationing and Competitive Loan Markets: A Comment on the Jaffee–Russell Model. *Econ. Stud. Quart.*, December 1984, *35*(3), pp. 269–76.

Vandell, Kerry D. Imperfect Information, Uncertainty, and Credit Rationing: Comment and Extension. *Quart. J. Econ.*, November 1984, *99*(4), pp. 841–63.

Vives, Xavier. Duopoly Information Equilibrium: Cournot and Bertrand. *J. Econ. Theory*, October 1984, *34*(1), pp. 71–94.

Walker, Martin. Risk Attitudes, Value-restricted Preferences, and Public Choice over Lotteries and Information Systems. *Accounting Rev.*, April 1984, *59*(2), pp. 278–86.

Wedlin, A. Expectations Formation and Revision in Economics. *Metroecon.*, June-Oct. 1984, *36*(2–3), pp. 211–25.

Weinrich, Gerd. On the Theory of Effective Demand under Stochastic Rationing. *J. Econ. Theory*, October 1984, *34*(1), pp. 95–115.

Weisman, Dennis L. Tobin on Keynes: A Suggested Interpretation. *J. Post Keynesian Econ.*, Spring 1984, *6*(3), pp. 411–20.

von Weizsäcker, Carl Christian. The Costs of Substitution. *Econometrica*, September 1984, *52*(5), pp. 1085–1116.

Wilson, Robert B. A Note on Revelation of Information for Joint Production. *Soc. Choice Welfare*, 1984, *1*(1), pp. 69–73.

Winston, Wayne. The Effect of Uncertainty and Instability on Dynamic Economic Models with an Application to Cournot Oligopoly. *J. Econ. Dynam. Control*, May 1984, *7*(2), pp. 171–79.

Wright, Brian D. The Effects of Price Uncertainty on the Factor Choices of the Competitive Firm. *Southern Econ. J.*, October 1984, *51*(2), pp. 443–55.

Zilcha, Itzhak. Risk-Aversely Efficient Random Variables: Characterization and an Application to Growth under Uncertainty. *J. Econ. Theory*, April 1984, *32*(2), pp. 328–36.

0262 Game Theory and Bargaining Theory

Abreu, Dilip and Pearce, David G. On the Inconsistency of Certain Axioms on Solution Concepts for Non-cooperative Games. *J. Econ. Theory*, October 1984, *34*(1), pp. 169–74.

Arrow, Kenneth J. The Property Rights Doctrine and Demand Revelation under Incomplete Information. In *Arrow, K. J., vol. 4, 1984, 1979,* pp. 216–32.

Bamberg, Günter. The Impacts of Variance Reducing Strategies in Dyopolistic Capital Markets. In *Bamberg, G. and Spremann, K., eds.,* 1984, pp. 15–32.

Bennett, E. A New Approach to Predicting Coalition Formation and Payoff Distribution in Characteristic Function Games. In *Holler, M. J., ed.,* 1984, pp. 60–80.

Benoit, Jean-Pierre. Financially Constrained Entry in a Game with Incomplete Information. *Rand J. Econ.,* Winter 1984, *15*(4), pp. 490–99.

Berheim, B. Douglas. Rationalizable Strategic Behavior. *Econometrica,* July 1984, *52*(4), pp. 1007–28.

Bjurulf, B. and Berg, S. A Combinatorial and Probabilistic Analysis of Voting Blocs: With Application to Multiparty Systems. In *Holler, M. J., ed.,* 1984, pp. 175–94.   [G: Sweden]

Border, Kim C. A Core Existence Theorem for Games without Ordered Preferences. *Econometrica,* November 1984, *52*(6), pp. 1537–42.

Brams, Steven J.; Davis, Morton D. and Straffin, Philip D., Jr. Comment on Wagner [The Theory of Games and the Problem of International Cooperation]. *Amer. Polit. Sci. Rev.,* June 1984, *78*(2), pp. 495–96.

Brandsma, Andries S. and Hughes Hallett, Andrew J. Economic Conflict and the Solution of Dynamic Games. *Europ. Econ. Rev.,* October–November 1984, *26*(1–2), pp. 13–32.
[G: U.S.]

Cegielski, A. Silent Duel with Accuracies Less than 1. In *Hammer, G. and Pallaschke, D., eds.,* 1984, pp. 245–51.

Chichilnisky, Graciela. Manipulation and Repeated Games in Futures Markets. In *Anderson, R. W., ed.,* 1984, pp. 193–214.

Chichilnisky, Graciela and Heal, Geoffrey. Patterns of Power: Bargaining and Incentives in Two-Person Games. *J. Public Econ.,* April 1984, *23*(3), pp. 333–49.

Cox, Gary W. Non-collegial Simple Games and the Nowhere Denseness of the Set of Preference Profiles Having a Core. *Soc. Choice Welfare,* August 1984, *1*(2), pp. 159–64.

Cramton, Peter C. Bargaining with Incomplete Information: An Infinite-Horizon Model with Two-Sided Uncertainty. *Rev. Econ. Stud.,* October 1984, *51*(4), pp. 579–93.

d'Alcantara, Gonzalez. A Game Theoretic Approach of Macroeconomic Simulations for the Study of Conflicting Goals. In *Despontin, M.; Nijkamp, P. and Spronk, J., eds.,* 1984, pp. 125–40.   [G: Belgium]

Demange, Gabrielle. Implementing Efficient Egalitarian Equivalent Allocations. *Econometrica,* September 1984, *52*(5), pp. 1167–77.

Driessen, T. S. H. and Tijs, S. H. Extensions and Modifications of the τ-Value for Cooperative Games. In *Hammer, G. and Pallaschke, D., eds.,* 1984, pp. 252–61.

Dubey, Pradeep and Kaneko, Mamoru. Information Patterns and Nash Equilibria in Extensive Games: I. *Math. Soc. Sci.,* October 1984, *8*(2), pp. 111–39.

Dutta, Bhaskar. Effectivity Functions and Acceptable Game Forms. *Econometrica,* September 1984, *52*(5), pp. 1151–66.

Dwyer, F. Robert. Are Two Better than One? Bargaining Behavior and Outcomes in an Asymmetrical Power Relationship. *J. Cons. Res.,* September 1984, *11*(2), pp. 680–93.

Economides, Nicholas S. The Principle of Minimum Differentiation Revisited. *Europ. Econ. Rev.,* April 1984, *24*(3), pp. 345–68.

Enos, J. L. Public Policy in an Economy with Different Types of Agents. *Greek Econ. Rev.,* December 1984, *6*(3), pp. 424–52.

Fershtman, Chaim and Muller, Eitan. Capital Accumulation Games of Infinite Duration. *J. Econ. Theory,* August 1984, *33*(2), pp. 322–39.

Field, Alexander James. Microeconomics, Norms, and Rationality. *Econ. Develop. Cult. Change,* July 1984, *32*(4), pp. 683–711.

Forgó, Ferenc. A Game–Theoretic Approach for Multicriteria Decision Making. In *Grauer, M. and Wierzbicki, A. P., eds.,* 1984, pp. 41–46.

Green, Edward J. Continuum and Finite-Player Noncooperative Models of Competition. *Econometrica,* July 1984, *52*(4), pp. 975–93.

Green, Edward J. and Porter, Robert H. Noncooperative Collusion under Imperfect Price Information. *Econometrica,* January 1984, *52*(1), pp. 87–100.

Güth, Werner and Stephan, Jürgen. Equilibrium Selection in the One Seller and Many Buyers-Game. *Z. Nationalökon.,* 1984, *44*(3), pp. 267–81.

Hart, S. and Kurz, Mordecai. Stable Coalition Structures. In *Holler, M. J., ed.,* 1984, pp. 235–58.

Herz, John. Comment on Wagner [The Theory of Games and the Problem of International Cooperation]. *Amer. Polit. Sci. Rev.,* June 1984, *78*(2), pp. 495.

Hoffman, Elizabeth and Packel, E. W. A Stochastic Model of Coalition Formation with Exogenous Costs: Theory and Experiments. In *Holler, M. J., ed.,* 1984, pp. 283–94.

Honkapohja, Seppo. On the Design of Bilateral Contracts. *Europ. Econ. Rev.,* October–November 1984, *26*(1–2), pp. 55–71.

Hughes Hallett, Andrew J. Non-cooperative Strategies for Dynamic Policy Games and the Problem of Time Inconsistency. *Oxford Econ. Pap.,* November 1984, *36*(3), pp. 381–99.

Kamien, Morton I. and Tauman, Yair. The Private Value of a Patent: A Game Theoretic Analysis. *Z. Nationalökon.,* Supplement 1984, pp. 93–118.

Kaufer, Erich. On the Economics of Conventions and Institutions: An Exploratory Essay: Comment. *Z. ges. Staatswiss.,* March 1984, *140*(1), pp. 87–89.

Kihlstrom, Richard E. Manipulation and Repeated Games in Futures Markets: Comment. In *Anderson, R. W., ed.*, 1984, pp. 215–24.

Kliemt, H. and Schauenberg, B. Coalitions and Hierarchies: Some Observations on the Fundamentals of Human Cooperation. In *Holler, M. J., ed.*, 1984, pp. 9–32.

Koehler, David H. Ordinal Preference Games: An Analysis of Legislative Coalition Formation without Transferable Utility. *Amer. Polit. Sci. Rev.*, September 1984, *78*(3), pp. 750–63.

Lambson, Val Eugene. Self-enforcing Collusion in Large Dynamic Markets. *J. Econ. Theory*, December 1984, *34*(2), pp. 282–91.

Lane, John and Leininger, Wolfgang. Differentiable Nash Equilibria in Altruistic Economies. *Z. Nationalökon.*, 1984, *44*(4), pp. 329–47.

Leibenstein, Harvey. Motivations and Constraints in the Supply-Cost of Government Services: A Game Theoretic Analysis. In *Hanusch, H., ed.*, 1984, pp. 223–40.

Leibenstein, Harvey. On the Economics of Conventions and Institutions: An Exploratory Essay. *Z. ges. Staatswiss.*, March 1984, *140*(1), pp. 74–86.

Majeski, Stephen J. Arms Races as Iterated Prisoner's Dilemma Games. *Math. Soc. Sci.*, June 1984, *7*(3), pp. 253–66.

Mas-Colell, Andreu. On a Thorem of Schmeidler. *J. Math. Econ.*, December 1984, *13*(3), pp. 201–06.

de Mesquita, B. Bueno and Niemi, Richard G. A Dynamic, Multiple-Goal Theory of Coalition Formation. In *Holler, M. J., ed.*, 1984, pp. 81–95.   [G: Selected Countries]

Michener, H. A.; Clancy, P. D. and Yuen, K. Do Outcomes of *N*-Person Sidepayment Games Fall in the Core? In *Holler, M. J., ed.*, 1984, pp. 269–82.

Michener, H. A., et al. A Test of the Core Solution in Finite Strategy Non-sidepayment Games. *Math. Soc. Sci.*, October 1984, *8*(2), pp. 141–68.

Miller, N. R. Coalition Formation and Political Outcomes: A Critical Note. In *Holler, M. J., ed.*, 1984, pp. 259–65.

Mookherjee, Dilip. Optimal Incentive Schemes with Many Agents. *Rev. Econ. Stud.*, July 1984, *51*(3), pp. 433–46.

Moulin, Hervé. Comportement stratégique et communication conflictuelle: le cas non coopératif. (Strategic Behaviour and Conflictual Communication: The Non-Cooperative Case. With English summary.) *Revue Écon.*, January 1984, *35*(1), pp. 109–45.

Moulin, Hervé. Dominance Solvability and Cournot Stability. *Math. Soc. Sci.*, February 1984, *7*(1), pp. 83–102.

Moulin, Hervé. Implementing the Kalai–Smorodinsky Bargaining Solution. *J. Econ. Theory*, June 1984, *33*(1), pp. 32–45.

Moulin, Hervé. The Conditional Auction Mechanism for Sharing a Surplus. *Rev. Econ. Stud.*, January 1984, *51*(1), pp. 157–70.

Myerson, Roger B. Two-Person Bargaining Problems with Incomplete Information. *Econometrica*, March 1984, *52*(2), pp. 461–87.

Nielsen, Lars Tyge. Risk Sensitivity in Bargaining with More than Two Participants. *J. Econ. Theory*, April 1984, *32*(2), pp. 371–76.

Nti, Kofi O. and Shubik, Martin. Noncooperative Exchange Using Money and Broker–Dealers. *Math. Soc. Sci.*, February 1984, *7*(1), pp. 59–82.

Orbell, John M.; Schwartz-Shea, Peregrine and Simmons, Randy T. Do Cooperators Exit More Readily than Defectors? *Amer. Polit. Sci. Rev.*, March 1984, *78*(1), pp. 147–62.

Osborne, Martin J. Capitalist–Worker Conflict and Involuntary Unemployment. *Rev. Econ. Stud.*, January 1984, *51*(1), pp. 111–27.

Palfrey, Thomas R. Spatial Equilibrium with Entry. *Rev. Econ. Stud.*, January 1984, *51*(1), pp. 139–56.

Palfrey, Thomas R. and Rosenthal, Howard. Participation and the Provision of Discrete Public Goods: A Strategic Analysis. *J. Public Econ.*, July 1984, *24*(2), pp. 171–93.

Panayotopoulos, A. and Yannacopoulos, N. Bargaining and the Negotiation Set. *Rivista Int. Sci. Econ. Com.*, January 1984, *31*(1), pp. 40–48.

Parthasarathy, T.; Tijs, S. H. and Vrieze, O. J. Stochastic Games with State Independent Transitions and Separable Rewards. In *Hammer, G. and Pallaschke, D., eds.*, 1984, pp. 262–71.

Pearce, David G. Rationalizable Strategic Behavior and the Problem of Perfection. *Econometrica*, July 1984, *52*(4), pp. 1029–50.

Peleg, Bezalel. Core Stability and Duality of Effectivity Functions. In *Hammer, G. and Pallaschke, D., eds.*, 1984, pp. 272–87.

Pohjola, Matti. Threats and Bargaining in Capitalism: A Differential Game View. *J. Econ. Dynam. Control*, December 1984, *8*(3), pp. 291–302.

Ray, Debraj. Intertemporal Borrowing to Sustain Exogenous Consumption Standards under Uncertainty. *J. Econ. Theory*, June 1984, *33*(1), pp. 72–87.

Reichelstein, Stefan. A Note on Allocations Attainable through Nash Equilibria. *J. Econ. Theory*, April 1984, *32*(2), pp. 384–90.

Rochford, Sharon C. Symmetrically Pairwise-bargained Allocations in an Assignment Market. *J. Econ. Theory*, December 1984, *34*(2), pp. 262–81.

Roth, Alvin E. Misrepresentation and Stability in the Marriage Problem. *J. Econ. Theory*, December 1984, *34*(2), pp. 383–87.

Roth, Alvin E. The Evolution of the Labor Market for Medical Interns and Residents: A Case Study in Game Theory. *J. Polit. Econ.*, December 1984, *92*(6), pp. 991–1016.   [G: U.S.]

Schelling, Thomas C. What Is Game Theory? In *Schelling, T. C.*, 1984, pp. 213–42.

Schofield, Norman J. Bargaining over Public Goods. In *Holler, M. J., ed.*, 1984, pp. 33–50.

Selten, Reinhard. Are Cartel Laws Bad for Business? In *[Beckmann, M. J.]*, 1984, pp. 85–117.

Shaked, Avner and Sutton, John. Involuntary Unemployment as a Perfect Equilibrium in a Bargaining Model. *Econometrica*, November 1984, *52*(6), pp. 1351–64.

Shubik, Martin. On the Value of Market Information and Rational Expectations. In *[Beckmann, M. J.]*, 1984, pp. 119–34.

Simon, Leo K. Bertrand, the Cournot Paradigm and the Theory of Perfect Competition. *Rev. Econ. Stud.*, April 1984, *51*(2), pp. 209–30.

Thomson, William. Monotonicity, Stability, and Egalitarianism. *Math. Soc. Sci.*, August 1984, *8*(1), pp. 15–28.

Thomson, William. The Manipulability of Resource Allocation Mechanisms. *Rev. Econ. Stud.*, July 1984, *51*(3), pp. 447–60.

Thomson, William. Truncated Egalitarian Solutions. *Soc. Choice Welfare*, 1984, *1*(1), pp. 25–32.

Tomasini, Luigi M. A Game Theoretic Approach to the Marschak Optimal Incentives Problem. *Econ. Notes*, 1984, (3), pp. 104–14.

Violi, Roberto. Un'interpretazione del contratto sociale in termini di "nucleo" di un meta-gioco. (An Interpretation of the Social Contract in Terms of "Nucleus" of a Meta-Game. With English summary.) *Rivista Int. Sci. Econ. Com.*, May 1984, *31*(5), pp. 395–416.

Wallmeier, E. A Procedure for Computing the f-Nucleolus of a Cooperative Game. In *Hammer, G. and Pallaschke, D., eds.*, 1984, pp. 288–96.

Wernerfelt, Birger. Consumers with Differing Reaction Speeds, Scale Advantages and Industry Structure. *Europ. Econ. Rev.*, March 1984, *24*(2), pp. 257–70.

Winkler, G. Michael. The Reduced Sets: A New Solution Concept for Cooperative Games and Other Decision Problems. *Z. Nationalökon.*, 1984, *44*(4), pp. 309–27.

Wittman, Donald. *A Priori* Probabilities of Coalition Formation and Power Measurement. In *Holler, M. J., ed.*, 1984, pp. 163–74.

Wooders, Myrna Holtz and Zame, William R. Approximate Cores of Large Games. *Econometrica*, November 1984, *52*(6), pp. 1327–50.

de Zeeuw, Aart J. Policy Evaluation with Conflicting Goals for a Linked Two Country Model. In *Despontin, M.; Nijkamp, P. and Spronk, J., eds.*, 1984, pp. 99–124.
[G: W. Germany; Netherlands]

027 Economics of Centrally Planned Economies

0270 General

Abalkin, L. Theoretical Questions Regarding the Structure of the Economy. *Prob. Econ.*, March 1984, *26*(11), pp. 73–91. [G: U.S.S.R.]

Babic, Stojan. The Problem of Choosing Indicators of Efficiency in the Yugoslav Economic System, 1976–1980. *Eastern Europ. Econ.*, Winter 1984–85, *23*(2), pp. 43–70.
[G: Yugoslavia]

Bunich, P. G. Only Efficiency Will Triumph over

Scarcity. *Prob. Econ.*, January 1984, *26*(9), pp. 26–43. [G: U.S.S.R.]

Chander, Parkash. On Material Balances When There Are Capacity Limitations. *J. Compar. Econ.*, June 1984, *8*(2), pp. 159–67.

Constantinescu, N. N. Objective and Subjective, Stability and Dynamism in the Functioning Mechanism of the Socialist Economy. *Econ. Computat. Cybern. Stud. Res.*, 1984, *19*(2), pp. 11–17.

Csikós-Nagy, Béla. The Role of the Law of Values in Socialist Economy. *Eastern Europ. Econ.*, Spring–Summer 1984, *22*(3–4), pp. 102–21.
[G: Hungary; CMEA]

Dai, Yuanchen. Methods to Appraise Economic Efficiency. *Chinese Econ. Stud.*, Summer 1984, *17*(4), pp. 72–80. [G: China]

Dániel, Zsuzsa. A Model for Analyzing Desired and Realizable Changes in Housing. *Matekon*, Summer 1984, *20*(4), pp. 3–47.
[G: Hungary]

Ericson, Richard E. The "Second Economy" and Resource Allocation under Central Planning. *J. Compar. Econ.*, March 1984, *8*(1), pp. 1–24.

Fedorenko, N., et al. The Theory and Practice of Assessing the Effectiveness of Economic Measures. *Prob. Econ.*, September 1984, *27*(5), pp. 3–22. [G: U.S.S.R.]

Gorodetskii, A. and Gorodetskii, D. Planned Proportionality and the Mechanism of Supply and Demand. *Prob. Econ.*, May 1984, *27*(1), pp. 79–93. [G: U.S.S.R.]

Jovanovic, Aleksandar. Struktura sistema društvene proizvodnje i organizacija planiranja. (Structure of Social Production System and the Organization of Planning. With English summary.) *Econ. Anal. Worker's Manage.*, 1984, *18*(3), pp. 217–39.

Kantorovich, L. V. and Makarov, V. L. Prices and Production Efficiency. In *Csikós-Nagy, B.; Hague, D. and Hall, G., eds.*, 1984, pp. 3–23.

Kantorovich, L. V. and Makarov, V. L. Prices and Production Efficiency. *Matekon*, Fall 1984, *21*(1), pp. 3–27.

Kostecki, Michel M. Can Tariff Be Effective under Central Planning? *Econ. Int.*, February–May 1984, *37*(1–2), pp. 94–107.

Krasovskii, V. The Economic Effectiveness of Production and Capital Investments. *Prob. Econ.*, July 1984, *27*(3), pp. 41–60. [G: U.S.S.R.]

Kuboniwa, Masaaki. Stepwise Aggregation for Material Balances. *J. Compar. Econ.*, March 1984, *8*(1), pp. 41–53. [G: U.S.S.R.]

Kumm, K. The Subsistence Fund and the Reproduction of Labor Power. *Prob. Econ.*, April 1984, *26*(12), pp. 44–53. [G: U.S.S.R.]

Lisitsian, N. Commodity and Money Circulation and Bank Credit (Problems of Theory and Management). *Prob. Econ.*, December 1984, *27*(8), pp. 40–54. [G: U.S.S.R.]

Makarov, V. L. The Introduction of Nontechnical Innovations. *Prob. Econ.*, August 1984, *27*(4), pp. 64–77. [G: U.S.S.R.]

Mihalek, Jozef. Economy: Looking Ahead to the

New Century. *Czech. Econ. Digest.*, June 1984, (4), pp. 25–33.

Okólski, Marek and Winiecki, Jan. Structural Change and Adaptation: On Reintegrating Planned Economies into the World Economy. *Konjunkturpolitik*, 1984, *30*(2/3), pp. 148–69. **[G: Europe]**

Paseta, Vesna. Dinimički model jugoslovenske privrede na bazi matrice rasta. (Dynamic Model of Yugoslav Economy on the Growth Matrix Basis. With English summary.) *Econ. Anal. Worker's Manage.*, 1984, *18*(3), pp. 241–57. **[G: Yugoslavia]**

Peng, Tian. A Rational Economic Structure Is the Precondition for Healthy Development of the National Economy. *Chinese Econ. Stud.*, Summer 1984, *17*(4), pp. 10–15. **[G: China]**

Poliak, A. Economic Problems in the Utilization of Materials. *Prob. Econ.*, April 1984, *26*(12), pp. 25–43. **[G: U.S.S.R.]**

Rous, Jan and Hejl, Lubomir. Contributions to the Evaluation and Stimulation of Effectiveness in External Economic Relations. *Soviet E. Europ. Foreign Trade*, Winter 1984-85, *20*(4), pp. 77–105. **[G: Czechoslovakia]**

Ryszkiewicz, Alicja. Norms of Distribution and Protection and Restrictions on Exports and Imports in the Central Plan. *Soviet E. Europ. Foreign Trade*, Spring 1984, *20*(1), pp. 36–56.

Simon, András. The Role of Prices and Supply in Shortage. *Acta Oecon.*, 1984, *33*(3–4), pp. 321–35.

Yue, Ping. Stress the Effect of Consumption on Production. *Chinese Econ. Stud.*, Summer 1984, *17*(4), pp. 3–9. **[G: China]**

Zhang, Zhuoyuan. In Stressing Economic Results Attention Must Be Paid to the Law of Value. *Chinese Econ. Stud.*, Spring 1984, *17*(3), pp. 68–75. **[G: China]**

0271 Microeconomic Theory

Badea-Dincă, N., et al. Problems Deriving from the Directives of the XIIIth Congress of the Romanian Communist Party Concerning the Problems of Economic Efficiency in Introducing Information Systems for Processes Management. *Econ. Computat. Cybern. Stud. Res.*, 1984, *19*(4), pp. 13–20. **[G: Romania]**

Ben-Ner, Avner. Labor-managed and Participatory Firms: A Note. *J. Econ. Issues*, December 1984, *18*(4), pp. 1189–95.

Bennett, John. A Model of Income Distribution in a Revenue-sharing Firm. *J. Compar. Econ.*, September 1984, *8*(3), pp. 237–46.

Bunich, P. G. Economic Stimulation of High Final Results. *Prob. Econ.*, November 1984, *27*(7), pp. 3–25. **[G: U.S.S.R.]**

Cholewicka-Gozdźik, Krystyna. The Reform of the Price System in Poland. Its Assumptions and First Results. In *Bohnet, A., ed.*, 1984, pp. 97–117.

Csikós-Nagy, Béla. Die Rolle der Preise in den verschiedenen Modellvarianten der sozialistischen Planwirtschaft. (With English summary.) In *Bohnet, A., ed.*, 1984, pp. 19–40.

Donaldson, David and Neary, Hugh M. Decentralized Control of a Socialist Industry. *Can. J. Econ.*, February 1984, *17*(1), pp. 99–110.

Esterin, Saul. Self-Management and Capitalism Compared: A Review of M. R. Sertel's, *Workers and Incentives*. *Econ. Anal. Worker's Manage.*, 1984, *18*(1), pp. 103–07.

Fusfeld, Daniel R. Labor-managed and Participatory Firms: Reply. *J. Econ. Issues*, December 1984, *18*(4), pp. 1195–98.

Gay, David E. R. Microeconomic Theory and the Centralized Socialist Firm. *Rivista Int. Sci. Econ. Com.*, March 1984, *31*(3), pp. 264–74.

Glushkov, N. Planned Price Formation (Theoretical and Practical Questions). *Prob. Econ.*, October 1984, *27*(6), pp. 3–23. **[G: U.S.S.R.]**

Granick, David. Central Physical Planning, Incentives and Job Rights. In *Zimbalist, A., ed.*, 1984, pp. 133–57. **[G: U.S.; U.S.S.R.]**

Gu, Shutang and Yang, Yuchuan. A Further Inquiry into Value Determination and the Law of Value. *Chinese Econ. Stud.*, Fall 1984, *18*(1), pp. 59–76.

Gu, Shutang and Yang, Yuchuan. The Transformed Form of Value under the Socialist System. *Chinese Econ. Stud.*, Fall 1984, *18*(1), pp. 44–58.

Guesnerie, Roger and Laffont, Jean-Jacques. Indirect Public Control of Self-Managed Monopolies. *J. Compar. Econ.*, June 1984, *8*(2), pp. 139–58.

Gui, Benedetto. Basque versus Illyrian Labor-managed Firms: The Problem of Property Rights. *J. Compar. Econ.*, June 1984, *8*(2), pp. 168–81. **[G: Spain; Yugoslavia]**

Haffner, Friedrich. Theorie und Praxis der Preisbildung in der Sowjetunion und in der DDR. (With English summary.) In *Bohnet, A., ed.*, 1984, pp. 41–67.

Hawawini, Gabriel. Uncertainty and the Production Decisions of Owner-Managed and Labor-Managed Firms. *Oxford Econ. Pap.*, March 1984, *36*(1), pp. 119–30.

Ireland, Norman J. and Law, Peter J. On the Labour-Managed Firm with Homothetic Technology. *Econ. Anal. Worker's Manage.*, 1984, *18*(1), pp. 1–13.

Ji, Zhenghzhi. The Profit in Planned Prices Should Be Formulated in Accordance with a Composite Profit Index. *Chinese Econ. Stud.*, Fall 1984, *18*(1), pp. 14–33. **[G: China]**

Kahana, Nava and Paroush, Jacob. A Multi-factor Labor-managed Firm under Price Uncertainty. *Eastern Econ. J.*, January-March 1984, *10*(1), pp. 23–29.

Katz, Barbara Goody and Owen, Joel. Disequilibrium Theory, Waiting Costs, and Saving Behavior in Centrally Planned Economies: A Queueing-Theoretic Approach. *J. Compar. Econ.*, September 1984, *8*(3), pp. 301–21.

Koont, Sinan and Zimbalist, Andrew. Incentives and Elicitation Schemes: A Critique and an Extension. In *Zimbalist, A., ed.*, 1984, pp. 159–75.

Kornai, János. Adjustment to Price and Quantity Signals in a Socialist Economy. In *Csikós-Nagy,*

B.; Hague, D. and Hall, G., eds., 1984, pp. 60–77.

Kornai, János and Matits, Ágnes. Softness of the Budget Constraint—An Analysis Relying on Data of Firms. *Acta Oecon.*, 1984, 32(3–4), pp. 223–49. [G: Hungary]

Kurashvili, B. P. The Fate of Branch Management. *Prob. Econ.*, August 1984, 27(4), pp. 3–28. [G: U.S.S.R.]

Li, Zili. Again on "Standard Output": A Further Inquiry into the Distribution Form of United Production with Remuneration Calculated According to the Standard Output. *Chinese Econ. Stud.*, Spring 1984, 17(3), pp. 3–17. [G: China]

Liberman, E. G. and Khaikin, V. P. A Simpler, More Accurate Method of Calculating Profitability. *Prob. Econ.*, March 1984, 26(11), pp. 40–52. [G: U.S.S.R.]

Lipiński, Jan and Mujżl, Jan. Price Formation, Market Structure, Economic System of Enterprises. *In Bohnet, A., ed.*, 1984, pp. 153–81. [G: Poland]

Liu, Chao-Nan. Managerial Objectives and Equilibrium Outputs in the Socialist Firm: Reply. *J. Compar. Econ.*, September 1984, 8(3), pp. 333–34.

Miliukov, A. New Aspects of the Cost-accounting Independence and Responsibility of Enterprises. *Prob. Econ.*, October 1984, 27(6), pp. 39–53. [G: U.S.S.R.]

Murrell, Peter. Incentives and Income under Market Socialism. *J. Compar. Econ.*, September 1984, 8(3), pp. 261–76.

Murrell, Peter and Miller, Jeffrey B. The Applicability of Information-revealing Incentive Schemes in Economic Organizations. *J. Compar. Econ.*, September 1984, 8(3), pp. 277–89.

Nagy, Tamás. Das System "weltmarktorientierter" Preise in Ungarn. (With English summary.) *In Bohnet, A., ed.*, 1984, pp. 69–95. [G: Hungary]

Neary, Hugh M. Labor-managed Cournot Oligopoly and Industry Output: A Comment. *J. Compar. Econ.*, September 1984, 8(3), pp. 322–27.

Pagano, Ugo. Welfare, Productivity, and Self-management. *Econ. Notes*, 1984, (3), pp. 5–20.

Pomanskii, A. B. On the Convergence of Processes for Coordinating Economic Interests. *Matekon*, Spring 1984, 20(3), pp. 22–38.

Pomanskii, A. B. and Rusakov, V. P. On One Approach to Modeling Consumer Demand. *Matekon*, Summer 1984, 20(4), pp. 81–96.

Rozenova, L. The Price and Effectiveness of Machine-building Output. *Prob. Econ.*, November 1984, 27(7), pp. 44–60. [G: U.S.S.R.]

Sertel, Murat R. and Steinherr, Alfred. Information, Incentives, and the Design of Efficient Institutions. *Z. ges. Staatswiss.*, June 1984, 140(2), pp. 233–46.

Smith, Stephen C. Does Employment Matter to the Labour-managed Firm? Some Theory and

an Empirical Illustration. *Econ. Anal. Worker's Manage.*, 1984, 18(4), pp. 303–18. [G: U.S.; Italy]

Stewart, Geoff. Labour-managed Firms and Monopsony Power. *Int. J. Ind. Organ.*, March 1984, 2(1), pp. 63–74.

Taga, Leonore Shever. Managerial Objectives and Equilibrium Output in the Socialist Firm: A Comment. *J. Compar. Econ.*, September 1984, 8(3), pp. 328–32.

Val'tukh, K. K. Input–Output and the Theory of Value. *Matekon*, Fall 1984, 21(1), pp. 72–86.

Wang, Leonard F. S. and Bowles, David. Demand Uncertainty, Risk Aversion and the Labour-Managed Firm. *J. Econ. Stud.*, 1984, 11(1), pp. 49–54.

Zalai, Ernö. Economic Reform, Allocative Efficiency, and Terms of Trade. *Acta Oecon.*, 1984, 33(3–4), pp. 255–71.

0272 Macroeconomic Theory

Boot, Pieter. Industrial Cycles in the German Democratic Republic and Professor Wiles' Thesis [Are There Any Communist Cycles?]. *ACES Bull.*, Spring 1984, 26(1), pp. 1–26. [G: E. Germany]

Erdös, Tibor. The Development of Investment Purchasing Power: Theoretical Questions. *Acta Oecon.*, 1984, 33(1–2), pp. 105–26. [G: Hungary]

Gardner, Roy J. Power and Taxes in a One-Party State: The USSR, 1925–1929. *Int. Econ. Rev.*, October 1984, 25(3), pp. 743–55. [G: U.S.S.R.]

Gedeon, Shirley J. Monetary Control and Inflation in Market-Based Socialism. *ACES Bull.*, Spring 1984, 26(1), pp. 27–42.

Goldman, Josef and Kouba, Karel. Terms of Trade, Adjustment Processes, and the Economic Mechanism (A Quantitative Approach). *Acta Oecon.*, 1984, 32(1–2), pp. 137–60. [G: CMEA]

Gorbunov, E. Investment Problems in the Intensification of Social Production. *Prob. Econ.*, August 1984, 27(4), pp. 46–63. [G: U.S.S.R.]

Kersten, G. Tendencies in a Shortage Economy [*Economics of Shortage*]. *Acta Oecon.*, 1984, 32(3–4), pp. 375–89.

Medaiskis, T. I. and Raiatskas, R. L. On Overcoming the Switching Problem in Optimizing Macroeconomic Models. *Matekon*, Summer 1984, 20(4), pp. 48–63.

Mednitskii, V. G. On Using Aggregated Variables in Mathematical Economics. *Matekon*, Fall 1984, 21(1), pp. 54–71.

Mirochnichenko, V. L. and Parinov, S. I. Analyzing Economic Growth Using Spline Macroeconomic Production Functions. *Matekon*, Winter 1984–85, 21(2), pp. 68–89. [G: U.S.S.R.]

Novikov, O. Stimulating the Growth of the Effectiveness of Capital Investments. *Prob. Econ.*, February 1984, 26(10), pp. 37–49. [G: U.S.S.R.]

Poliak, A. The Assessment of Material Resources. *Prob. Econ.*, December 1984, 27(8), pp. 71–88. [G: U.S.S.R.]

Sah, Raaj Kumar and Stiglitz, Joseph E. The Economics of Price Scissors. *Amer. Econ. Rev.*, March 1984, *74*(1), pp. 125–38.

Sitarian, Stepan. Economic Norms and Limits. *Prob. Econ.*, January 1984, *26*(9), pp. 44–63.
[G: U.S.S.R.]

Sitaryan, Stepan and Sichev, Nickolai. Strengthening the Role of Finances in a Planned Economy. In *Hanusch, H., ed.*, 1984, pp. 27–37.
[G: U.S.S.R.]

Soós, Károly A. A Propos the Explanation of Shortage Phenomena: Volume of Demand and Structural Inelasticity. *Acta Oecon.*, 1984, *33*(3–4), pp. 305–20.

030 HISTORY OF THOUGHT; METHODOLOGY

031 History of Economic Thought

0310 General

Beinsen, Lutz. Schumpeter as an Historian of Economic Doctrine. In *Seidl, C., ed.*, 1984, pp. 173–86.

Chipman, J. S. Balance of Payments Theory. In *Creedy, J. and O'Brien, D. P., eds.*, 1984, pp. 186–217.

Clower, Robert W. Reflections on the Keynesian Perplex. In *Clower, R. W.*, 1984, *1975*, pp. 187–208.

Creedy, John. Public Finance. In *Creedy, J. and O'Brien, D. P., eds.*, 1984, pp. 84–116.

Foster, John Bellamy and Szlajfer, Henryk. The Faltering Economy: Introduction. In *Foster, J. B. and Szlajfer, H., eds.*, 1984, pp. 7–22.

Georgescu-Roegen, Nicholas. Are There Minds that Think above Their Time? The Case of Herman Heinrich Gossen. *Rivista Int. Sci. Econ. Com.*, December 1984, *31*(12), pp. 1141–61.

Harcourt, Geoffrey C. Reflections on the Development of Economics as a Discipline. *Hist. Polit. Econ.*, Winter 1984, *16*(4), pp. 489–517.

Hébert, R. F. and Ekelund, Robert B., Jr. Welfare Economics. In *Creedy, J. and O'Brien, D. P., eds.*, 1984, pp. 46–83.

Lallement, Jérôme. Histoire de la pensée ou archéologie du savoir? (With English summary.) *Écon. Soc.*, October 1984, *18*(10), pp. 61–93.

O'Brien, D. P. Monetary Economics. In *Creedy, J. and O'Brien, D. P., eds.*, 1984, pp. 3–45.

Quadrio Curzio, Alberto and Scazzieri, Roberto. Sui momenti costitutivi dell'economia politica. (On the Founding Principles of Political Economy. With English summary.) *Giorn. Econ.*, January–February 1984, *43*(1–2), pp. 37–76.

Rima, Ingrid H. Balogh's Assessment of Conventional Economics. *J. Post Keynesian Econ.*, Summer 1984, *6*(4), pp. 630–33.

0311 Ancient, Medieval

Worland, Stephen T. Aristotle and the Neoclassical Tradition: The Shifting Ground of Complementarity. *Hist. Polit. Econ.*, Spring 1984, *16*(1), pp. 107–34.

0312 Preclassical Except Mercantilist

Faccarello, Gilbert. Quelques réflexions sur l'équilibre économique chez P. de Boisguilbert. (Some Considerations on the Concept of Economic Equilibrium in Boisguilbert's Writings. With English summary.) *Écon. Soc.*, March 1984, *18*(3), pp. 35–62.

Giacometti, Jacques. Langage et monnaie chez Locke et Turgot. (Language and Money: Locke and Turgot. With English summary.) *Écon. Soc.*, March 1984, *18*(3), pp. 119–37.

von Hayek, Friedrich A. Dr. Bernard Mandeville. In *von Hayek, F. A. (I)*, 1984, *1967*, pp. 176–94.

Masson, Bernard. La notion de production en relation avec la constitution des classes chez F. Quesnay. (François Quesnay's Concept of Production as Related to the Constitution of Classes. With English summary.) *Écon. Soc.*, March 1984, *18*(3), pp. 161–74.

Ravix, Joël and Romani, Paul-Marie. L'idée de progrès comme fondement des analyses économiques de Turgot. (The Idea of Progress as the Basis of Turgot's Economic Thought. With English summary.) *Écon. Soc.*, March 1984, *18*(3), pp. 97–118.

Spengler, Joseph J. Boisguilbert's Economic Views Vis-à-Vis Those of Contemporary *Réformateurs*. *Hist. Polit. Econ.*, Spring 1984, *16*(1), pp. 69–88.

Steiner, Philippe. Locke et Quesnay: une conception politique de l'économie. (Locke and Quesnay: A Political Conception of Political Economy. With English summary.) *Écon. Soc.*, March 1984, *18*(3), pp. 139–59.

0313 Mercantilist

Anderson, Gary M. and Tollison, Robert D. Sir James Steuart as the Apotheosis of Mercantilism and His Relation to Adam Smith. *Southern Econ. J.*, October 1984, *51*(2), pp. 456–68.

Arena, Richard. Valeur intrinsèque, production et échange chez Richard Cantillon. (Intrinsic Value, Production, and Exchange in the Writings of Richard Cantillon. With English summary.) *Écon. Soc.*, March 1984, *18*(3), pp. 63–96.

Pellanda, Anna. Keynes' Theory of the Rate of Interest and Its Links with the Mercantilist Theory of Money and Fisher's Theory of Income. *Rivista Int. Sci. Econ. Com.*, March 1984, *31*(3), pp. 220–40.

0314 Classical

Black, R. D. Collison. The Irish Dissenters and Nineteenth-Century Political Economy. In *Murphy, A. E., ed.*, 1984, pp. 120–37.

Bordo, Michael D. The Gold Standard: The Traditional Approach. In *Bordo, M. D. and Schwartz, A. J., eds.*, 1984, pp. 23–113.

Caire, Guy. Un ou deux Mathus? (One or Two Malthus? With English summary.) *Revue Écon.*, July 1984, *35*(4), pp. 623–33.

Chiodi, Guglielmo and Messori, Marcello. Marx's Analysis of the Relationship between the Rate of Interest and the Rate of Profits: A Comment. *Cambridge J. Econ.*, March 1984, 8(1), pp. 93–97.

Cirillo, Renato. Economists and Social Reformers on Land Ownership and Economic Rents. *Rivista Int. Sci. Econ. Com.*, March 1984, 31(3), pp. 241–56.

Clower, Robert W. A Reconsideration of the Microfoundations of Monetary Theory. In *Clower, R. W.*, 1984, 1967, pp. 81–89.

Clower, Robert W. Say's Principle, What It Means and Doesn't Mean. In *Clower, R. W.*, 1984, 1973, pp. 145–65.

Cooter, Robert and Rappoport, Peter. Were the Ordinalists Wrong about Welfare Economics? *J. Econ. Lit.*, June 1984, 22(2), pp. 507–30.

De Vroey, Michel. La procédure de socialisation et le statut des échangistes dans trois représentations théoriques du marché. (With English summary.) *Écon. Soc.*, October 1984, 18(10), pp. 129–50.

Euzent, Patricia J. and Martin, Thomas L. Classical Roots of the Emerging Theory of Rent Seeking: The Contribution of Jean-Baptiste Say. *Hist. Polit. Econ.*, Summer 1984, 16(2), pp. 255–62.

Garegnani, Pierangelo. Value and Distribution in the Classical Economists and Marx. *Oxford Econ. Pap.*, June 1984, 36(2), pp. 291–325.

Guthrie, William G. Selective Rediscovery of Economic Ideas: What Keynes Found in Malthus. *Southern Econ. J.*, January 1984, 50(3), pp. 771–80.

Hamouda, O. F. On the Notion of Short-run and Long-run: Marshall, Ricardo and Equilibrium Theories. *Brit. Rev. Econ. Issues*, Spring 1984, 6(14), pp. 55–82.

Harley, C. Knick. The Gold Standard: The Traditional Approach: Comment. In *Bordo, M. D. and Schwartz, A. J.*, eds., 1984, pp. 113–17.

Harpham, Edward J. Natural Law and Early Liberal Economic Thought: A Reconsideration of Locke's Theories of Value. *Soc. Sci. Quart.*, December 1984, 65(4), pp. 966–74.

Henderson, John P. The Political Economy Club: Robert Torrens and the Decline of Ricardo's Influence. In *Samuels, W. J.*, ed., 1984, pp. 77–105.

Hicks, John R. Mr. Keynes and the Classics. In *Hicks, J.*, 1984, 1937, pp. 186–99.

Hollander, Samuel. 'Dynamic Equilibrium' with Constant Wages: J. S. Mill's Malthusian Analysis of the Secular Wage Path. *Kyklos*, 1984, 37(2), pp. 247–65.

Hollander, Samuel. J. S. Mill on "Derived Demand" and the Wage-Fund Theory Recantation. *Eastern Econ. J.*, January-March 1984, 10(1), pp. 87–98.

Hollander, Samuel. Marx and Malthusianism: Marx's Secular Path of Wages. *Amer. Econ. Rev.*, March 1984, 74(1), pp. 139–51.

Hollander, Samuel. The Wage Path in Classical Growth Models: Ricardo, Malthus and Mill.

Oxford Econ. Pap., June 1984, 36(2), pp. 200–212.

Johnson, L. E. Ricardo's Labor Theory of the Determinant of Value. *Atlantic Econ. J.*, March 1984, 12(1), pp. 50–59.

Kindleberger, Charles P. Was Adam Smith a Monetarist or a Keynesian? *Bus. Econ.*, January 1984, 19(1), pp. 5–12.

Kriesler, Peter. On Dobb's Interpretation of Jevons on Ricardo. *Cambridge J. Econ.*, December 1984, 8(4), pp. 403–05.

Laidler, David. Misconceptions about the Real-Bills Doctrine: A Comment [The Real-Bills Doctrine versus the Quantity Theory: A Reconsideration]. *J. Polit. Econ.*, February 1984, 92(1), pp. 149–55.

Lowe, Adolph. The Classical Theory of Economic Growth. *Soc. Res.*, Spring & Summer 1984, 51(1&2), pp. 111–42.

Moore, Mick. Political Economy and the Rural–Urban Divide, 1767–1981. In *Harriss, J. and Moore, M.*, eds., 1984, pp. 5–27.

Nell, Edward. Structure and Behavior in Classical and Neo-Classical Theory. *Eastern Econ. J.*, April-June 1984, 10(2), pp. 139–55.

Panico, C. Interest Costs, Profit and Pricing: A Reply [Marx's Analysis of the Relationship between the Rate of Interest and the Rate of Profits]. *Cambridge J. Econ.*, March 1984, 8(1), pp. 99–104.

Peach, Terry. David Ricardo's Early Treatment of Profitability: A New Interpretation. *Econ. J.*, December 1984, 94(376), pp. 733–51.

Platteau, Jean-Philippe. Malthus et le sous-développement ou le problème de la cohérence d'une théorie. (Malthus and the Problem of Underdevelopment: One or Two Theories? With English summary.) *Revue Écon.*, July 1984, 35(4), pp. 635–66.

Rankin, Steve. The Wage Basket in Ricardo's *Essay on Profits*. *Cambridge J. Econ.*, March 1984, 8(1), pp. 83–86.

Semmler, Willi. On the Classical Theory of Competition, Value and Prices of Production. *Australian Econ. Pap.*, June 1984, 23(42), pp. 130–50.

Sen, Amartya. The Living Standard. *Oxford Econ. Pap.*, Supplement November 1984, 36, pp. 74–90.

Sen, Amartya. The Living Standard. In *Collard, D. A., et al.*, eds., 1984, pp. 74–90.

Steedman, Ian. Natural Prices, Differential Profit Rates and the Classical Competitive Process. *Manchester Sch. Econ. Soc. Stud.*, June 1984, 52(2), pp. 123–40.

Steiner, Philippe. Locke et Quesnay: une conception politique de l'économie. (Locke and Quesnay: A Political Conception of Political Economy. With English summary.) *Écon. Soc.*, March 1984, 18(3), pp. 139–59.

Sylos-Labini, Paolo. Competition and Economic Growth in Adam Smith. In *Sylos-Labini, P.*, 1984, pp. 3–36. **[G: U.K.]**

Toma, Eugenia Froedge and Toma, Mark. Constitutional Tax Constraints within a Classical

Model of Leviathan. *Hist. Polit. Econ.*, Spring 1984, *16*(1), pp. 89–105.

0315 Austrian, Marshallian, Neoclassical

Addleson, Mark S. Robbins's *Essay* in Retrospect: On Subjectivism and an "Economics of Choice." *Rivista Int. Sci. Econ. Com.*, June 1984, *31*(6), pp. 506–23.

Baldone, Salvatore. Integrazione verticale, struttura temporale dei processi produttivi e transizione fra le tecniche. (With English summary.) *Econ. Polit.*, April 1984, *1*(1), pp. 79–105.

Barry, Norman P. The 'Austrian' Perspective. In *Whynes, D. K., ed.*, 1984, pp. 33–58.

Bloomfield, Arthur I. Effect of Growth on the Terms of Trade: Some Earlier Views. *Economica*, May 1984, *51*(202), pp. 187–93.

Bordo, Michael D. The Gold Standard: The Traditional Approach. In *Bordo, M. D. and Schwartz, A. J., eds.*, 1984, pp. 23–113.

Brown, Elba K. Review of Social Economy: The Neoclassical and Post-Keynesian Research Programs: The Methodological Issues. In *Caldwell, B. J., ed.*, 1984, *1981*, pp. 438–59.

Chasse, John Dennis. Marshall, the Human Agent and Economic Growth: Wants and Activities Revisited. *Hist. Polit. Econ.*, Fall 1984, *16*(3), pp. 381–404.

Clark, David. Confronting the Linear Imperialism of the Austrians: Lowe's Contribution to Capital and Growth Theory. *Eastern Econ. J.*, April-June 1984, *10*(2), pp. 107–27.

Clower, Robert W. Classical Monetary Theory Revisited. In *Clower, R. W.*, 1984, *1963*, pp. 27–33.

Cooter, Robert and Rappoport, Peter. Were the Ordinalists Wrong about Welfare Economics? *J. Econ. Lit.*, June 1984, *22*(2), pp. 507–30.

Darnell, A. C. Economic Statistics and Econometrics. In *Creedy, J. and O'Brien, D. P., eds.*, 1984, pp. 152–85.

De Vroey, Michel. La procédure de socialisation et le statut des échangistes dans trois représentations théoriques du marché. (With English summary.) *Écon. Soc.*, October 1984, *18*(10), pp. 129–50.

Dugger, William M. Methodological Differences Between Institutional and Neoclassical Economics. In *Hausman, D. M., ed.*, 1984, *1979*, pp. 312–22.

Endres, A. M. Institutional Elements in Carl Menger's Theory of Demand: A Comment [Carl Menger and *Homo Oeconomicus*: Some Thoughts on Austrian Theory and Methodology]. *J. Econ. Issues*, September 1984, *18*(3), pp. 897–902.

Fulton, G. Research Programmes in Economics. *Hist. Polit. Econ.*, Summer 1984, *16*(2), pp. 187–205.

Hamouda, O. F. On the Notion of Short-run and Long-run: Marshall, Ricardo and Equilibrium Theories. *Brit. Rev. Econ. Issues*, Spring 1984, *6*(14), pp. 55–82.

Harley, C. Knick. The Gold Standard: The Traditional Approach: Comment. In *Bordo, M. D. and Schwartz, A. J., eds.*, 1984, pp. 113–17.

von Hayek, Friedrich A. Marginal Utility and Economic Calculation: A Review. In *von Hayek, F. A. (II)*, 1984, *1925*, pp. 183–89.

von Hayek, Friedrich A. On the Problem of the Theory of Interest. In *von Hayek, F. A. (II)*, 1984, *1927*, pp. 55–70.

von Hayek, Friedrich A. Some Remarks on the Problem of Imputation. In *von Hayek, F. A. (II)*, 1984, *1926*, pp. 33–54.

von Hayek, Friedrich A. The Place of Menger's *Grundsätze* in the History of Economic Thought. In *von Hayek, F. A. (I)*, 1984, *1973*, pp. 195–207.

Hutchison, Terence W. Mr. White on Jevons: A Rejoinder [Jevons in Australia: A Reassessment]. *Manchester Sch. Econ. Soc. Stud.*, March 1984, *52*(1), pp. 73–74.

Kogan, A. M.; Maximova, V. E. and Golosov, V. V. The Treatment of Value and Money. In *Smirnov, A. D.; Golosov, V. V. and Maximova, V. F., eds.*, 1984, pp. 35–59.

Lee, Frederic S. The Marginalist Controversy and the Demise of Full Cost Pricing. *J. Econ. Issues*, December 1984, *18*(4), pp. 1107–32.

Mirowski, Philip. Macroeconomic Instability and the "Natural" Processes in Early Neoclassical Economics. *J. Econ. Hist.*, June 1984, *44*(2), pp. 345–54. [G: U.K.]

Mirowski, Philip. Physics and the 'Marginalist Revolution.' *Cambridge J. Econ.*, December 1984, *8*(4), pp. 361–79.

Moss, Scott J. The History of the Theory of the Firm from Marshall to Robinson and Chamberlin: The Source of Positivism in Economics. *Economica*, August 1984, *51*(203), pp. 307–18.

Nell, Edward. Structure and Behavior in Classical and Neo-Classical Theory. *Eastern Econ. J.*, April-June 1984, *10*(2), pp. 139–55.

Nishiyama, Chiaki. The Essence of Hayek: Introduction. In *von Hayek, F. A. (I)*, 1984, pp. xxxvii–lxviii.

Petridis, Anastasios. Trade Unions and the Theory of Competition. *Eastern Econ. J.*, July-September 1984, *10*(3), pp. 295–314.

Potestio, Paola. Investment in Some Neoclassical Models of Capital Accumulation. *Écon. Appl.*, 1984, *37*(3–4), pp. 543–63.

Powers, Charles H. Sociopolitical Determinants of Economic Cycles: Vilfredo Pareto's Final Statement. *Soc. Sci. Quart.*, December 1984, *65*(4), pp. 988–1001.

Pujol, Michèle A. Gender and Class in Marshall's *Principles of Economics*. *Cambridge J. Econ.*, September 1984, *8*(3), pp. 217–34.

Roy, Subroto. Considerations on Utility, Benevolence, and Taxation. *Hist. Polit. Econ.*, Fall 1984, *16*(3), pp. 349–62.

Scott, Maurice. Maintaining Capital Intact. *Oxford Econ. Pap.*, Supplement November 1984, *36*, pp. 59–73.

Scott, Maurice. Maintaining Capital Intact. In *Collard, D. A., et al., eds.*, 1984, pp. 59–73.

Shaikh, Anwar. The Transformation from Marx to Sraffa. In *Mandel, E. and Freeman, A., eds.*, 1984, pp. 43–84.

Skinner, A. S. and MacLennan, M. C. Oligopoly

and the Theory of the Firm. In *Creedy, J. and O'Brien, D. P., eds.*, 1984, pp. 117–51.

Thomas, Mark. Discussion [Keynes and Protection] [Macroeconomic Instability and the "Natural" Processes in Early Neoclassical Economics]. *J. Econ. Hist.*, June 1984, *44*(2), pp. 375–79.   [G: U.K.]

Tosato, Domenico. Sostituzione tra capitale e lavoro e teoria del processo cumulativo di Wicksell. (With English summary.) *Econ. Polít.*, August 1984, *1*(2), pp. 167–95.

Veblen, Thorstein. The Limitations of Marginal Utility. In *Hausman, D. M., ed.*, 1984, *1909*, pp. 173–86.

Walker, Donald A. Walras and His Critics on the Maximum Utility of New Capital Goods. *Hist. Polit. Econ.*, Winter 1984, *16*(4), pp. 529–54.

White, Michael. Jevons in Australia: Response. *Manchester Sch. Econ. Soc. Stud.*, March 1984, *52*(1), pp. 70–72.

Worland, Stephen T. Aristotle and the Neoclassical Tradition: The Shifting Ground of Complementarity. *Hist. Polit. Econ.*, Spring 1984, *16*(1), pp. 107–34.

Yeager, Leland B. Henry George and Austrian Economics. *Hist. Polit. Econ.*, Summer 1984, *16*(2), pp. 157–74.

0316 General Equilibrium until 1945

Clower, Robert W. Classical Monetary Theory Revisited. In *Clower, R. W.*, 1984, *1963*, pp. 27–33.

Hamouda, O. F. On the Notion of Short-run and Long-run: Marshall, Ricardo and Equilibrium Theories. *Brit. Rev. Econ. Issues*, Spring 1984, *6*(14), pp. 55–82.

Hands, Douglas W. The Role of Crucial Counterexamples in the Growth of Economic Knowledge: Two Case Studies in the Recent History of Economic Thought. *Hist. Polit. Econ.*, Spring 1984, *16*(1), pp. 59–67.

Mantel, Rolf R. Economía Matemática, su evolución histórica y estado actual. (Mathematical Economics, Its Historical Evolution and Present State. With English summary.) *Económica*, May-December 1984, *30*(2–3), pp. 203–15.

Walker, Donald A. Is Walras's Theory of General Equilibrium a Normative Scheme? *Hist. Polit. Econ.*, Fall 1984, *16*(3), pp. 445–69.

0317 Socialist and Marxian until 1945

Bose, Arun. Modern Marxian Political Economy. In *Whynes, D. K., ed.*, 1984, pp. 90–115.

Bronfenbrenner, Martin and Woflson, Murray. Marxian Macrodynamics and the Harrod Growth Model. *Hist. Polit. Econ.*, Summer 1984, *16*(2), pp. 175–86.

Burris, Val. The Politics of Marxist Crisis Theory. In *Zarembka, P., ed.*, 1984, pp. 237–67.

Claeys, Gregory. Engels' *Outlines of a Critique of Political Economy* (1843) and the Origins of the Marxist Critique of Capitalism. *Hist. Polit. Econ.*, Summer 1984, *16*(2), pp. 207–32.

Dillard, Dudley. Keynes and Marx: A Centennial Appraisal. *J. Post Keynesian Econ.*, Spring 1984, *6*(3), pp. 421–32.

Elster, Jon. Historical Materialism and Economic Backwardness. In *Ball, T. and Farr, J., eds.*, 1984, pp. 36–58.

Foster, John Bellamy. Investment and Capitalist Maturity. In *Foster, J. B. and Szlajfer, H., eds.*, 1984, pp. 57–73.

Foster, John Bellamy. Marxian Economics and the State. In *Foster, J. B. and Szlajfer, H., eds.*, 1984, *1982*, pp. 325–49.

Frank, Andre Gunder. On Some Questionable Questions about Marxist Theory and International Capital Flows [Marxist Theory and International Capital Flows]. In *Frank, A. G.*, 1984, *1976*, pp. 82–86.

Frank, Andre Gunder. Real Marxism Is Marxist Realism. In *Frank, A. G.*, 1984, *1983*, pp. 279–89.

Grafstein, Robert. Philosophical Issues in the Study of Historical Materialism. *Soc. Sci. Quart.*, December 1984, *65*(4), pp. 955–60.

Gurley, John G. Some Elements of a Marxist Theory of Socialist Economic Development. In *[Chenery, H. B.]*, 1984, pp. 115–31.

Hagemann, Harald and Jeck, Albert. Lowe and the Marx–Fel'dman–Dobb Model: Structural Analysis of a Growing Economy. *Eastern Econ. J.*, April-June 1984, *10*(2), pp. 169–86.

Himka, John-Paul. Roman Rosdolsky's Reconsideration of the Traditional Marxist Debate on the Schemes of Reproduction on New Methodological Grounds: Comments. In *Koropeckyj, I. S., ed.*, 1984, pp. 135–47.

Hunt, E. K. The Social Scientific Basis of Socialism. *Econ. Forum*, Summer 1984, *15*(1), pp. 9–16.

Hunt, E. K. Was Marx a Utopian Socialist? *Sci. Soc.*, Spring 1984, *48*(1), pp. 90–97.

Kalecki, Michal. The Marxian Equations of Reproduction and Modern Economics. In *Foster, J. B. and Szlajfer, H., eds.*, 1984, *1968*, pp. 159–66.

Kalecki, Michal. The Problem of Effective Demand with Tugan-Baranovski and Rosa Luxemburg. In *Foster, J. B. and Szlajfer, H., eds.*, 1984, *1971*, pp. 151–58.

Mandel, Ernest. Ricardo, Marx, Sraffa: Introduction. In *Mandel, E. and Freeman, A., eds.*, 1984, pp. ix–xvi.

Noble, James. Marxian Functionalism. In *Ball, T. and Farr, J., eds.*, 1984, pp. 105–19.

Pachter, Henry. The Idea of Progress in Marxism. In *Pachter, H.*, 1984, *1974*, pp. 65–85.

Pachter, Henry. The Right to be Lazy. In *Pachter, H.*, 1984, *1956*, pp. 3–15.

Paris, R. Mariátegui et Gramsci: quelques prolégomènes à une étude contrastive de la diffusion du marxisme. (Mariátegui and Gramsci. With English summary.) *Écon. Soc.*, July–August 1984, *18*(7–8), pp. 183–221.

Petrella, Frank. Henry George's Theory of State's Agenda: The Origins of His Ideas on Economic Policy in Adam Smith's Moral Theory. *Amer. J. Econ. Soc.*, July 1984, *43*(3), pp. 269–86.

Shaikh, Anwar. The Transformation from Marx to Sraffa. In *Mandel, E. and Freeman, A., eds.,* 1984, pp. 43–84.

Shaw, William H. Marxism, Revolution, and Rationality. In *Ball, T. and Farr, J., eds.,* 1984, pp. 12–35.

Smith, Steven B. Historical Materialism Reconsidered. *Soc. Sci. Quart.,* December 1984, *65*(4), pp. 961–65.

Smith, Vardaman R. Marx's Social Ontology, His Critical Method and Contemporary Social Economics. *Rev. Soc. Econ.,* October 1984, *42*(2), pp. 143–69.

Sweezy, Paul M. Competition and Monopoly. In *Foster, J. B. and Szlajfer, H., eds.,* 1984, pp. 27–40.

Sweezy, Paul M. Marxian Value Theory and Crises. In *Foster, J. B. and Szlajfer, H., eds.,* 1984, *1979,* pp. 236–50.

Sweezy, Paul M. Some Problems in the Theory of Capital Accumulation. In *Foster, J. B. and Szlajfer, H., eds.,* 1984, *1973,* pp. 41–56.

Szlajfer, Henryk. Waste, Marxian Theory, and Monopoly Capital: Toward a New Synthesis. In *Foster, J. B. and Szlajfer, H., eds.,* 1984, pp. 297–321.

Turban, Manfred A. Roman Rosdolsky's Reconsideration of the Traditional Marxist Debate on the Schemes of Reproduction on New Methodological Grounds. In *Koropeckyj, I. S., ed.,* 1984, pp. 91–134.

Van Parijs, Philippe. Marxism's Central Puzzle. In *Ball, T. and Farr, J., eds.,* 1984, pp. 88–104.

0318 Historical and Institutional

Adams, John. Galbraith on Economic Development. *J. Post Keynesian Econ.,* Fall 1984, *7*(1), pp. 91–102.

Coase, Ronald H. The New Institutional Economics. *Z. ges. Staatswiss.,* March 1984, *140*(1), pp. 229–31.

Culbertson, John M. The New Potential of Evolutionary–Institutional Economics. *J. Econ. Issues,* June 1984, *18*(2), pp. 611–18.

Dugger, William M. Methodological Differences Between Institutional and Neoclassical Economics. In *Hausman, D. M., ed.,* 1984, *1979,* pp. 312–22.

Dugger, William M. Veblen and Kropotkin on Human Evolution. *J. Econ. Issues,* December 1984, *18*(4), pp. 971–85.

Dyer, Alan W. The Habit of Work: A Theoretical Exploration. *J. Econ. Issues,* June 1984, *18*(2), pp. 557–64.

Elliott, John E. The Institutionalist School of Political Economy. In *Whynes, D. K., ed.,* 1984, pp. 59–89.

Furubotn, Eirik G. and Richter, Rudolf. The New Institutional Economics: Symposium June 6–10, 1983, Mettlach/Saar. *Z. ges. Staatswiss.,* March 1984, *140*(1), pp. 1–6.

Galbraith, James K. Galbraith and the Theory of the Corporation. *J. Post Keynesian Econ.,* Fall 1984, *7*(1), pp. 43–60.

Ghosh, Syamal K. On the Validity of Veblen's Criticisms of Economic Orthodoxy: An Analysis of His Positions in the Light of Current Conditions and Economic Thought. *Amer. J. Econ. Soc.,* April 1984, *43*(2), pp. 235–46.

Gordon, Wendell C. The Role of Institutional Economics. *J. Econ. Issues,* June 1984, *18*(2), pp. 369–81.

Gowdy, John M. Marx and Resource Scarcity: An Institutionalist Approach. *J. Econ. Issues,* June 1984, *18*(2), pp. 393–400.

Greenwood, Daphne. The Economic Significance of "Woman's Place" in Society: A New-Institutionalist View. *J. Econ. Issues,* September 1984, *18*(3), pp. 663–80. **[G: U.S.]**

Gruchy, Allan G. Neo-Institutionalism, Neo-Marxism, and Neo-Keynesianism: An Evaluation. *J. Econ. Issues,* June 1984, *18*(2), pp. 547–56.

Hill, Lewis E. and Owen, Donald W. The Instrumental Philosophy of Economic History and the Institutionalist Theory of Normative Value. *J. Econ. Issues,* June 1984, *18*(2), pp. 581–87.

Hutchison, Terence W. Institutionalist Economics Old and New. *Z. ges. Staatswiss.,* March 1984, *140*(1), pp. 20–29.

Jennings, Ann and Shuklian, Steve. Marx, Dewey and Instrumentalism. *Econ. Forum,* Summer 1984, *15*(1), pp. 89–101.

Kaufer, Erich. On the Economics of Conventions and Institutions: An Exploratory Essay: Comment. *Z. ges. Staatswiss.,* March 1984, *140*(1), pp. 87–89.

Leathers, Charles G. Liberation Theology, the New Religious Political Right, and Veblen's Ambivalent View of Christianity. *J. Econ. Issues,* December 1984, *18*(4), pp. 1155–75.

Leibenstein, Harvey. On the Economics of Conventions and Institutions: An Exploratory Essay *Z. ges. Staatswiss.,* March 1984, *140*(1), pp. 74–86.

Littlechild, Stephen C. German *"Ordnungspolitik"* as Institutional Choice. *Z. ges. Staatswiss.,* March 1984, *140*(1), pp. 71–73. **[G: Germany; U.S.; U.K.]**

North, Douglass C. Transaction Costs, Institutions, and Economic History. *Z. ges. Staatswiss.,* March 1984, *140*(1), pp. 7–17.

Petr, Jerry L. Fundamentals of an Institutionalist Perspective on Economic Policy. *J. Econ. Issues,* March 1984, *18*(1), pp. 1–17.

Petridis, Anastasios. Trade Unions and the Theory of Competition. *Eastern Econ. J.,* July-September 1984, *10*(3), pp. 295–314.

Pollard, Sidney. Transaction Costs, Institutions, and Economic History: Comment. *Z. ges. Staatswiss.,* March 1984, *140*(1), pp. 18–19.

Ranson, Baldwin. A Commentary on Lux, Lutz, and Petr [Creative vs. Mechanical Evolution: A Commentary on Petr]. *J. Econ. Issues,* September 1984, *18*(3), pp. 895–97. **[G: U.S.]**

Rutherford, Malcolm H. Thorstein Veblen and the Processes of Institutional Change. *Hist. Polit. Econ.,* Fall 1984, *16*(3), pp. 331–48.

Samuels, Warren J. Institutional Economics. *J.*

031 History of Economic Thought

Econ. Educ., Summer 1984, *15*(3), pp. 211–16.

Samuels, Warren J. On the Nature and Existence of Economic Coercion: The Correspondence of Robert Lee Hale and Thomas Nixon Carver. *J. Econ. Issues*, December 1984, *18*(4), pp. 1027–48.

Schmidtchen, Dieter. German *"Ordnungspolitik"* as Institutional Choice. *Z. ges. Staatswiss.*, March 1984, *140*(1), pp. 54–70.
[G: Germany]

Sturgeon, James I. Induction and Instrumentalism in Institutional Thought. *J. Econ. Issues*, June 1984, *18*(2), pp. 599–609.

Tilman, Rick and Simich, J. L. On the Use and Abuse of Thorstein Veblen in Modern American Sociology, II: Daniel Bell and the 'Utopianizing' of Veblen's Contribution and Its Integration by Robert Merton and C. W. Mills. *Amer. J. Econ. Soc.*, January 1984, *43*(1), pp. 103–14.

Veblen, Thorstein. The Limitations of Marginal Utility. In *Hausman, D. M., ed.*, 1984, *1909*, pp. 173–86.

Wegehenkel, Lothar. Institutional Economics Old and New: Comment. *Z. ges. Staatswiss.*, March 1984, *140*(1), pp. 30–33.

032 History of Economic Thought (continued)

0321 Other Schools Since 1800

Arndt, Heinz W. Political Economy. *Econ. Rec.*, September 1984, *60*(170), pp. 266–73.

Bernal, Richard L.; Figueroa, Mark and Witter, Michael. Caribbean Economic Thought: The Critical Tradition. *Soc. Econ. Stud.*, June 1984, *33*(2), pp. 5–96. [G: Caribbean]

Black, R. D. Collison. The Irish Dissenters and Nineteenth-Century Political Economy. In *Murphy, A. E., ed.*, 1984, pp. 120–37.

Bordo, Michael D. The Gold Standard: The Traditional Approach. In *Bordo, M. D. and Schwartz, A. J., eds.*, 1984, pp. 23–113.

Gruchy, Allan G. Neo-Institutionalism, Neo-Marxism, and Neo-Keynesianism: An Evaluation. *J. Econ. Issues*, June 1984, *18*(2), pp. 547–56.

Harley, C. Knick. The Gold Standard: The Traditional Approach: Comment. In *Bordo, M. D. and Schwartz, A. J., eds.*, 1984, pp. 113–17.

Schmitz, Wolfgang. Economic and Social Partnership and Incomes Policy and the Social Doctrine of the Church. In *Cavaco Silva, A. A., ed.*, 1984, pp. 195–217.

0322 Individuals

Angell, James

Lee, Joong-Koon and Wellington, Donald C. Angell and the Stable Money Rule. *J. Polit. Econ.*, October 1984, *92*(5), pp. 972–78.
[G: U.S.]

Aristotle

Worland, Stephen T. Aristotle and the Neoclassical Tradition: The Shifting Ground of Complementarity. *Hist. Polit. Econ.*, Spring 1984, *16*(1), pp. 107–34.

Bagehot, Walter

Humphrey, Thomas M. and Keleher, Robert E. The Lender of Last Resort: A Historical Perspective [International Debt, Bank Failures, and the Money Supply: The Thirties and the Eighties]. *Cato J.*, Spring/Summer 1984, *4*(1), pp. 275–318. [G: U.K.]

Meiselman, David I. The Lender of Last Resort and a Money Supply Rule [International Debt, Bank Failures, and the Money Supply: The Thirties and the Eighties]. *Cato J.*, Spring/Summer 1984, *4*(1), pp. 319–21. [G: U.K.]

Bauer, Otto

Bronfenbrenner, Martin and Wolfson, Murray. Marxian Macrodynamics and the Harrod Growth Model. *Hist. Polit. Econ.*, Summer 1984, *16*(2), pp. 175–86.

Baumol, William J.

Baumol, William J. On My Attitudes: Sociopolitical and Methodological. *Amer. Econ.*, Spring 1984, *28*(1), pp. 5–9.

de Beauvoir, Simone

Greenwood, Daphne. The Economic Significance of "Woman's Place" in Society: A New-Institutionalist View. *J. Econ. Issues*, September 1984, *18*(3), pp. 663–80.
[G: U.S.]

Bellamy, Edward

Cugno, Franco and Ferrero, Mario. Individual Incentives by Adjusting Work Hours: Bellamy's Egalitarian Economy. *J. Compar. Econ.*, June 1984, *8*(2), pp. 182–206.

Samuels, Warren J. A Centenary Reconsideration of Bellamy's *Looking Backward*. *Amer. J. Econ. Soc.*, April 1984, *43*(2), pp. 129–48.

von Böhm-Bawerk, Eugen

Lederer, Emil. Social Control vs. Economic Law: An Old Dogma and a New Situation. *Soc. Res.*, Spring & Summer 1984, *51*(1&2), pp. 91–110.

von Weizsäcker, Carl Christian. Rights and Relations in Modern Economic Theory. *J. Econ. Behav. Organ.*, June 1984, *5*(2), pp. 133–57.

de Boisguilbert, Pierre

Faccarello, Gilbert. Quelques réflexions sur l'équilibre économique chez P. de Boisguilbert. (Some Considerations on the Concept of Economic Equilibrium in Boisguilbert's Writings. With English summary.) *Écon. Soc.*, March 1984, *18*(3), pp. 35–62.

Spengler, Joseph J. Boisguilbert's Economic Views Vis-à-Vis Those of Contemporary *Réformateurs*. *Hist. Polit. Econ.*, Spring 1984, *16*(1), pp. 69–88.

von Bortkiewicz, Ladislaus

Walker, Donald A. Walras and His Critics on the Maximum Utility of New Capital Goods. *Hist. Polit. Econ.*, Winter 1984, *16*(4), pp. 529–54.

Cairnes, John Elliot

Boylan, T. A. and Foley, T. P. John Elliot Cairnes, John Stuart Mill and Ireland: Some Problems for Political Economy. In *Murphy, A. E., ed.*, 1984, pp. 96–119.

Cantillon, Richard

Arena, Richard. Valeur intrinsèque, production et échange chez Richard Cantillon. (Intrinsic Value, Production, and Exchange in the Writings of Richard Cantillon. With English summary.) *Écon. Soc.*, March 1984, *18*(3), pp. 63–96.

Murphy, Antoin E. Richard Cantillon—an Irish Banker in Paris. In *Murphy, A. E., ed.*, 1984, pp. 45–74.   [G: France]

Carver, Thomas Nixon

Samuels, Warren J. On the Nature and Existence of Economic Coercion: The Correspondence of Robert Lee Hale and Thomas Nixon Carver. *J. Econ. Issues*, December 1984, *18*(4), pp. 1027–48.

Chadwick, Edwin

Price, Edward O., III. The Political Economy of Sir Edwin Chadwick: An Appraisal. *Soc. Sci. Quart.*, December 1984, *65*(4), pp. 975–87.

von Charasoff, Georg

Egidi, Massimo and Gilibert, Giorgio. La teoria oggettiva dei prezzi. (With English summary.) *Econ. Polít.*, April 1984, *1*(1), pp. 43–61.

Clower, Robert W.

Walker, Donald A. Money and Markets: Introduction. In *Clower, R. W.*, 1984, pp. 1–18.

Debreu, Gerard

Varian, Hal R. Gerard Debreu's Contributions to Economics. *Scand. J. Econ.*, 1984, *86*(1), pp. 4–16.

Dewey, John

Jennings, Ann and Shuklian, Steve. Marx, Dewey and Instrumentalism. *Econ. Forum*, Summer 1984, *15*(1), pp. 89–101.

Tilman, Rick. Dewey's Liberalism versus Veblen's Radicalism: A Reappraisal of the Unity of Progressive Social Thought. *J. Econ. Issues*, September 1984, *18*(3), pp. 745–69.   [G: U.S.]

Dobb, Maurice

Ellman, Michael. Dobb and the Crisis. In *Ellman, M.*, 1984, *1981*, pp. 273–88.

Halevi, Joseph. Lowe, Dobb and Hicks. *Eastern Econ. J.*, April-June 1984, *10*(2), pp. 157–67.

Eckstein, Otto

Allison, Elisabeth. Otto Eckstein: Contributions in Education. *Rev. Econ. Statist.*, November 1984, *66*(4), pp. 543–46.

Marron, Donald B. Otto Eckstein and the Founding of Data Resources, Inc. *Rev. Econ. Statist.*, November 1984, *66*(4), pp. 537–42.

Parkins, Michael. On *Core Inflation* by Otto Eckstein: A Review Essay. *J. Monet. Econ.*, September 1984, *14*(2), pp. 251–64.   [G: U.S.]

Wilson, Thomas A. Otto Eckstein: Applied Economist par Excellence. *Rev. Econ. Statist.*, November 1984, *66*(4), pp. 531–36.

Edgeworth, Francis Y.

Casarosa, Carlo. Il prezzo minimo nel duopolio di Edgeworth. (With English summary.) *Econ. Polít.*, April 1984, *1*(1), pp. 63–78.

Creedy, John. Edgeworth: Utilitarianism and Arbitration. *Hist. Polit. Econ.*, Winter 1984, *16*(4), pp. 609–18.

Hicks, John R. Francis Ysidro Edgeworth. In *Murphy, A. E., ed.*, 1984, pp. 157–74.

Walker, Donald A. Walras and His Critics on the Maximum Utility of New Capital Goods. *Hist. Polit. Econ.*, Winter 1984, *16*(4), pp. 529–54.

Einaudi, Luigi

D'Aroma, Antonio. Luigi Einaudi, "Giornale degli Economisti" and the "Bocconi" University. (In Italian. With English summary.) *Giorn. Econ.*, September–October 1984, *43*(9–10), pp. 587–618.

Engels, Friedrich

Claeys, Gregory. Engels' *Outlines of a Critique of Political Economy* (1843) and the Origins of the Marxist Critique of Capitalism. *Hist. Polit. Econ.*, Summer 1984, *16*(2), pp. 207–32.

Ferber, Robert

Grunwald, Joseph. The Collection and Analysis of Economic and Consumer Behavior Data: Introduction and Overview. In *[Ferber, R.]*, 1984, pp. 1–16.

Spaeth, Mary A. Bibliography of the Publications of Robert Ferber. In *[Ferber, R.]*, 1984, pp. 393–406.

Friedman, Milton

Breit, William. Galbraith and Friedman: Two Versions of Economic Reality. *J. Post Keynesian Econ.*, Fall 1984, *7*(1), pp. 18–29.

Clower, Robert W. Monetary History and Positive Economics. In *Clower, R. W.*, 1984, *1964*, pp. 59–77.

Garrison, Charles B. Friedman versus Keynes on the Theory of Employment. *J. Post Keynesian Econ.*, Fall 1984, *7*(1), pp. 114–27.

Hahn, Frank H. Professor Friedman's Views on Money. In *Hahn, F.*, 1984, *1971*, pp. 259–82.

Helm, Dieter. Predictions and Causes: A Comparison of Friedman and Hicks on Method. *Oxford Econ. Pap.*, Supplement November 1984, *36*, pp. 118–34.

Helm, Dieter. Predictions and Causes: A Comparison of Friedman and Hicks on Method. In *Collard, D. A., et al., eds.*, 1984, pp. 118–34.

Hill, Martyn B. Friedman's Framework for Economic Stability and the Government Budget Constraint: A Comment. *Manches-*

ter Sch. Econ. Soc. Stud., March 1984, *52*(1), pp. 75–78.

Scarth, William M. Friedman's Framework for Economic Stability: A Reply. *Manchester Sch. Econ. Soc. Stud.*, March 1984, *52*(1), pp. 79–83.

Galbraith, John Kenneth

Adams, John. Galbraith on Economic Development. *J. Post Keynesian Econ.*, Fall 1984, *7*(1), pp. 91–102.

Breit, William. Galbraith and Friedman: Two Versions of Economic Reality. *J. Post Keynesian Econ.*, Fall 1984, *7*(1), pp. 18–29.

Canterbery, E. Ray. Galbraith, Sraffa, Kalecki and Supra-surplus Capitalism. *J. Post Keynesian Econ.*, Fall 1984, *7*(1), pp. 77–90.

Colander, David C. Galbraith and the Theory of Price Control. *J. Post Keynesian Econ.*, Fall 1984, *7*(1), pp. 30–42.

Galbraith, James K. Galbraith and the Theory of the Corporation. *J. Post Keynesian Econ.*, Fall 1984, *7*(1), pp. 43–60.

Greenwood, Daphne. The Economic Significance of "Woman's Place" in Society: A New-Institutionalist View. *J. Econ. Issues*, September 1984, *18*(3), pp. 663–80.
[G: U.S.]

Samuels, Warren J. Galbraith on Economics as a System of Professional Belief. *J. Post Keynesian Econ.*, Fall 1984, *7*(1), pp. 61–76.

Schlesinger, Arthur, Jr. The Political Galbraith. *J. Post Keynesian Econ.*, Fall 1984, *7*(1), pp. 7–17.

George, Henry

Ferro, Angelo. Fondamenti teorici ed origini storiche della politica dell'offerta. (Theoretical Fundamentals and Historical Origins of Supply-Side Policy. With English summary.) *Bancaria*, January 1984, *40*(1), pp. 12–18.

Genovese, Frank C. An Economics Classic and Plutology: The 'Science of Wealth' Reminds Economists That Their Goal Should Be Well-being for All. *Amer. J. Econ. Soc.*, October 1984, *43*(4), pp. 455–67.

Genovese, Frank C. Why Everyone Should Read George's 'Progress and Poverty': On the Classic's Centenary, the Specialists Find This 19th Century Best Seller Still Very Timely. *Amer. J. Econ. Soc.*, January 1984, *43*(1), pp. 115–21.

Petrella, Frank. Henry George's Theory of State's Agenda: The Origins of His Ideas on Economic Policy in Adam Smith's Moral Theory. *Amer. J. Econ. Soc.*, July 1984, *43*(3), pp. 269–86.

Yandle, Bruce. Henry George, His Advocates and Adversaries: Together, Friend and Foe of His American Philosophy Helped to Develop Modern Economic Theory (Review). *Amer. J. Econ. Soc.*, January 1984, *43*(1), pp. 125–27.

Yeager, Leland B. Henry George and Austrian

Economics. *Hist. Polit. Econ.*, Summer 1984, *16*(2), pp. 157–74.

Giffen, Robert

Dwyer, Gerald P., Jr. and Lindsay, Cotton M. Robert Giffen and the Irish Potato. *Amer. Econ. Rev.*, March 1984, *74*(1), pp. 188–92. [G: Ireland]

Gossen, Herman Heinrich

Bruschke, Heinrich Hermann, et al. On Translating Gossen's Classic *Entwickelung*. *Rivista Int. Sci. Econ. Com.*, December 1984, *31*(12), pp. 1162–67.

Georgescu-Roegen, Nicholas. Are There Minds that Think above Their Time? The Case of Herman Heinrich Gossen. *Rivista Int. Sci. Econ. Com.*, December 1984, *31*(12), pp. 1141–61.

Gramsci, Antonio

Paris, R. Mariátegui et Gramsci: quelques prolégomènes à une étude contrastive de la diffusion du marxisme. (Mariátegui and Gramsci. With English summary.) *Écon. Soc.*, July–August 1984, *18*(7–8), pp. 183–221.

Hahn, Frank

Minsky, Hyman P. Frank Hahn's *Money and Inflation:* A Review Article. *J. Post Keynesian Econ.*, Spring 1984, *6*(3), pp. 449–57.

Hale, Robert Lee

Samuels, Warren J. On the Nature and Existence of Economic Coercion: The Correspondence of Robert Lee Hale and Thomas Nixon Carver. *J. Econ. Issues*, December 1984, *18*(4), pp. 1027–48.

von Hayek, Friedrich A.

Gissurarson, Hannes H. 'The Only Truly Progressive Policy...' In *Barry, N., et al.*, 1984, pp. 1–23.

Gray, John. The Road to Serfdom: Forty Years On. In *Barry, N., et al.*, 1984, pp. 25–42.

Leube, Kurt R. Friedrich August von Hayek: A Biographical Introduction. In *von Hayek, F. A. (I)*, 1984, pp. xvii–xxxvi.

Nishiyama, Chiaki. The Essence of Hayek: Introduction. In *von Hayek, F. A. (I)*, 1984, pp. xxxvii–lxviii.

Scott, Maurice. Maintaining Capital Intact. *Oxford Econ. Pap.*, Supp. Nov. 1984, *36*, pp. 59–73.

Scott, Maurice. Maintaining Capital Intact. In *Collard, D. A., et al., eds.*, 1984, pp. 59–73.

Seldon, Arthur. Recollections: Before and After the Road to Serfdom: Reflections on Hayek in 1935, 1944, 1960, 1982. In *Barry, N., et al.*, 1984, pp. xiii–xxxii.

Shearmur, Jeremy. Hayek and the Wisdom of the Age. In *Barry, N., et al.*, 1984, pp. 65–85.

Thalenhorst, Jobst and Wenig, Alois. F. A. Hayek's "Prices and Production" Re-Analyzed. *Jahr. Nationalökon. Statist.*, May 1984, *199*(3), pp. 213–36.

Vaughn, Karen I. The Constitution of Liberty from an Evolutionary Perspective. In *Barry, N., et al.*, 1984, pp. 117–42.

Hicks, John R.

Addison, John T.; Burton, John and Torrance, Thomas S. Causation, Social Science and Sir John Hicks. *Oxford Econ. Pap.*, March 1984, *36*(1), pp. 1–11.

Collard, David. The Ascent of High Theory: A View from the Foothills. In *Collard, D. A., et al., eds.*, 1984, pp. 1–12.

Collard, David. The Ascent of High Theory: A View from the Foothills. *Oxford Econ. Pap.*, Supplement November 1984, *36*, pp. 1–12.

Halevi, Joseph. Lowe, Dobb and Hicks. *Eastern Econ. J.*, April-June 1984, *10*(2), pp. 157–67.

Helm, Dieter. Predictions and Causes: A Comparison of Friedman and Hicks on Method. *Oxford Econ. Pap.*, Supplement November 1984, *36*, pp. 118–34.

Helm, Dieter. Predictions and Causes: A Comparison of Friedman and Hicks on Method. In *Collard, D. A., et al., eds.*, 1984, pp. 118–34.

Helm, Dieter. The Economics of John Hicks: Introduction. In *Hicks, J.*, 1984, pp. 1–20.

Hicks, John R. The Formation of an Economist. In *Hicks, J.*, 1984, *1979*, pp. 281–90.

Leijonhufvud, Axel. Hicks on Time and Money. In *Collard, D. A., et al., eds.*, 1984, pp. 26–46.

Leijonhufvud, Axel. Hicks on Time and Money. *Oxford Econ. Pap.*, Supplement November 1984, *36*, pp. 26–46.

Scott, Maurice. Maintaining Capital Intact. *Oxford Econ. Pap.*, Supplement November 1984, *36*, pp. 59–73.

Scott, Maurice. Maintaining Capital Intact. In *Collard, D. A., et al., eds.*, 1984, pp. 59–73.

Sen, Amartya. The Living Standard. *Oxford Econ. Pap.*, Supplement November 1984, *36*, pp. 74–90.

Sen, Amartya. The Living Standard. In *Collard, D. A., et al., eds.*, 1984, pp. 74–90.

Solow, Robert M. Mr. Hicks and the Classics. *Oxford Econ. Pap.*, Supplement November 1984, *36*, pp. 13–25.

Solow, Robert M. Mr. Hicks and the Classics. In *Collard, D. A., et al., eds.*, 1984, pp. 13–25.

Irwin, Richard D.

Davidson, Alexander N. Richard D. Irwin. *J. Behav. Econ.*, Summer 1984, *13*(1), pp. 117–34. [G: U.S.]

Jevons, William Stanley

Hutchison, Terence W. Mr. White on Jevons: A Rejoinder [Jevons in Australia: A Reassessment]. *Manchester Sch. Econ. Soc. Stud.*, March 1984, *52*(1), pp. 73–74.

Mirowski, Philip. Macroeconomic Instability and the "Natural" Processes in Early Neoclassical Economics. *J. Econ. Hist.*, June 1984, *44*(2), pp. 345–54. [G: U.K.]

Thomas, Mark. Discussion [Keynes and Protection] [Macroeconomic Instability and the "Natural" Processes in Early Neoclassical Economics]. *J. Econ. Hist.*, June 1984, *44*(2), pp. 375–79. [G: U.K.]

White, Michael. Jevons in Australia: Response. *Manchester Sch. Econ. Soc. Stud.*, March 1984, *52*(1), pp. 70–72.

Johnson, Harry G.

Caves, Richard E. Harry Johnson as a Social Scientist. *J. Polit. Econ.*, August 1984, *92*(4), pp. 642–58.

Corden, W. M. Harry Johnson's Contributions to International Trade Theory. *J. Polit. Econ.*, August 1984, *92*(4), pp. 567–91.

Harberger, Arnold C. and Wall, David. Harry G. Johnson as a Development Economist. *J. Polit. Econ.*, August 1984, *92*(4), pp. 616–41.

Laidler, David. Harry Johnson as a Macroeconomist. *J. Polit. Econ.*, August 1984, *92*(4), pp. 592–615.

Longawa, Vicky M. Harry G. Johnson: A Bibliography. *J. Polit. Econ.*, August 1984, *92*(4), pp. 659–711.

Kalecki, Michal

Boitani, Andrea. Two Views on Oligopoly and Stagnation. *Econ. Notes*, 1984, (3), pp. 128–54.

Canterbery, E. Ray. Galbraith, Sraffa, Kalecki and Supra-surplus Capitalism. *J. Post Keynesian Econ.*, Fall 1984, *7*(1), pp. 77–90.

Sardoni, Claudio. Some Ties of Kalecki to the 1926 "Sraffian Manifesto." *J. Post Keynesian Econ.*, Spring 1984, *6*(3), pp. 458–65.

Keynes, John Maynard

Arena, Richard. Monnaie, production et actifs financiers dans une perspective keynésienne: quelques éléments d'interprétation. (Money Production and Financial Assets within a Keynesian Framework: Some Results for an Interpretation. With English summary.) *Écon. Soc.*, April 1984, *18*(4), pp. 259–82.

Aschheim, Joseph and Tavlas, George S. The Monetary Thought–Ideology Nexus: Simons versus Keynes. *Banca Naz. Lavoro Quart. Rev.*, June 1984, (149), pp. 177–96.

Bagella, Michele. Note sul concetto di disoccupazione involontaria. (Some Notes on the Concept of Involuntary Unemployment. With English summary.) *Giorn. Econ.*, March–April 1984, *43*(3–4), pp. 213–36.

Booth, Alan. Defining a "Keynesian Revolution" [The "Keynesian Revolution" in Economic Policy-Making]. *Econ. Hist. Rev.*, 2nd Ser., May 1984, *37*(2), pp. 263–67. [G: U.K.]

Caprara, Ugo. Opinioni e teorie di John Maynard Keynes nella interpretazione di un economista aziendale. (Opinions and Theories of John Maynard Keynes: An Interpretation by a Business Economist. With English summary.) *Bancaria*, March 1984, *40*(3), pp. 256–65.

Chernomas, Robert. Keynes on Post-scarcity Society. *J. Econ. Issues*, December 1984, *18*(4), pp. 1007–26.

Colander, David C. Was Keynes a Keynesian or a Lernerian? *J. Econ. Lit.*, December 1984, *22*(4), pp. 1572–75.

Davidson, Paul. Reviving Keynes's Revolution. *J. Post Keynesian Econ.*, Summer 1984, *6*(4), pp. 561–75.

Dillard, Dudley. Keynes and Marx: A Centennial Appraisal. *J. Post Keynesian Econ.*, Spring 1984, *6*(3), pp. 421–32.

Eichengreen, Barry. Keynes and Protection. *J. Econ. Hist.*, June 1984, *44*(2), pp. 363–73. [G: U.K.]

Galbraith, John Kenneth. Keynes, Roosevelt, and the Complementary Revolutions. *Challenge*, January/February 1984, *26*(6), pp. 4–8. [G: U.S.]

Garrison, Charles B. Friedman versus Keynes on the Theory of Employment. *J. Post Keynesian Econ.*, Fall 1984, *7*(1), pp. 114–27.

Giovannetti, Giorgia. The Role of the Rate of Interest: From Wicksell to Keynes' Treatise on Money. *Econ. Notes*, 1984, (1), pp. 66–86.

Gold, Joseph [Sir]. Keynes on Legal Problems of International Organization. In *Gold, J.*, 1984, *1981*, pp. 841–61.

Graziani, Augusto. The Debate on Keynes' Finance Motive. *Econ. Notes*, 1984, (1), pp. 5–34.

Guthrie, William G. Selective Rediscovery of Economic Ideas: What Keynes Found in Malthus. *Southern Econ. J.*, January 1984, *50*(3), pp. 771–80.

Halevi, Joseph. Structure économique et demande effective. (Economic Structure and Effective Demand. With English summary.) *Écon. Appl.*, 1984, *37*(1), pp. 201–13.

von Hayek, Friedrich A. The Keynes Centenary: The Austrian Critique. In *von Hayek, F. A. (I)*, 1984, *1983*, pp. 43–50.

Heilbroner, Robert L. Economics and Political Economy: Marx, Keynes, and Schumpeter. *J. Econ. Issues*, September 1984, *18*(3), pp. 681–95.

Heilbrun, James. Keynes and the Economics of the Arts. *J. Cult. Econ.*, December 1984, *8*(2), pp. 37–49.

Heinsohn, Gunnar and Steiger, Otto. "Marx and Keynes—Private Property and Money." *Écon. Soc.*, April 1984, *18*(4), pp. 37–71.

Hicks, John R. Mr. Keynes and the Classics. In *Hicks, J.*, 1984, *1937*, pp. 186–99.

Jensen, Hans E. Some Aspects of the Social Economics of John Maynard Keynes. *Int. J. Soc. Econ.*, 1984, *11*(3/4), pp. 72–91.

Kosmicke, Ralph. The Contradiction between Keynes and the EMH. *J. Portfol. Manage.*, Fall 1984, *11*(1), pp. 41–43.

Kregel, Jan A. Monetary Production Economics and Monetary Policy. *Écon. Soc.*, April 1984, *18*(4), pp. 221–32.

Lavoie, Marc. Le Québec de 1944 et John Maynard Keynes. (Quebec in 1944 and John Maynard Keynes. With English summary.) *L'Actual. Econ.*, December 1984, *60*(4), pp. 553–55.

Liang, Ming-Yih. Keynes's Errors in the Liquidity Preference versus Loanable Funds Controversy. *J. Macroecon.*, Spring 1984, *6*(2), pp. 215–27.

Meltzer, Allan H. Keynes's Labor Market: A Reply. *J. Post Keynesian Econ.*, Summer 1984, *6*(4), pp. 532–39.

Miller, Edward M. Extension of the Economics of Keynes to the United States. *Southern Econ. J.*, January 1984, *50*(3), pp. 781–801.

Moore, Basil J. Keynes and the Endogeneity of the Money Stock. *Stud. Econ.*, 1984, *39*(22), pp. 23–69.

Mukund, Kanakalatha. Keynes on Indian Economic Problems and Policies: A Historical Appraisal. *Indian Econ. J.*, July–Sept. 1984, *32*(1), pp. 37–48. [G: India]

Patinkin, Don. Keynes and Economics Today. *Amer. Econ. Rev.*, May 1984, *74*(2), pp. 97–102.

Roberts, David L. How Consistent Was Keynes' Theory of Effective Demand? *Econ. Inquiry*, January 1984, *22*(1), pp. 45–56.

Seidl, Christian. Schumpeter versus Keynes: Supply-side Economics or Demand Management? In *Seidl, C., ed.*, 1984, pp. 139–51.

Shackle, G. L. S. The Romantic Mountain and the Classic Lake: Alan Coddington's *Keynesian Economics*. *J. Post Keynesian Econ.*, Winter 1983-84, *6*(2), pp. 241–51.

Spahn, H.-Peter. Marx–Schumpeter–Keynes: Drei Fragmente über Geld, Zins und Profit. (Marx–Schumpeter–Keynes: Three Approaches to Money, Interest, and Profit. With English summary.) *Jahr. Nationalökon. Statist.*, May 1984, *199*(3), pp. 237–55.

Sylos-Labini, Paolo. Keynes's *General Theory* and the Great Depression. In *Sylos-Labini, P.*, 1984, pp. 227–43. [G: U.S.]

Sylos-Labini, Paolo. New Aspects of the Cyclical Development of the Economy. *Banca Naz. Lavoro Quart. Rev.*, March 1984, (148), pp. 15–31. [G: Italy]

Thomas, Mark. Discussion [Keynes and Protection] [Macroeconomic Instability and the "Natural" Processes in Early Neoclassical Economics]. *J. Econ. Hist.*, June 1984, *44*(2), pp. 375–79. [G: U.K.]

Tomlinson, J. D. A "Keynesian Revolution" in Economic Policy-Making? *Econ. Hist. Rev., 2nd Ser.*, May 1984, *37*(2), pp. 258–62. [G: U.K.]

Tuchscherer, Thomas. Meltzer on Keynes's Labor Market Theory: A Review of the *General Theory*'s Second Chapter. *J. Post Keynesian Econ.*, Summer 1984, *6*(4), pp. 523–31.

Weisman, Dennis L. Tobin on Keynes: A Suggested Interpretation. *J. Post Keynesian Econ.*, Spring 1984, *6*(3), pp. 411–20.

Kropotkin, Peter

Dugger, William M. Veblen and Kropotkin on Human Evolution. *J. Econ. Issues*, December 1984, *18*(4), pp. 971–85.

Latané, Henry A.

Trent, Robert H. and Kemp, Robert S. The Writings of Henry A. Latané: A Compilation and Analysis. *J. Finan. Res.*, Summer 1984, *7*(2), pp. 161–74.

Lenin, Vladimir Illyich

Lindsey, Charles W. Lenin's Theory of Imperialism: A Reply. *Rev. Radical Polit. Econ.*, Summer & Fall 1984, *16*(2&3), pp. 221–25.

Obrinsky, Mark. Lindsey's Lenin and the Problem of Imperialism [Lenin's Theory of Imperialism]. *Rev. Radical Polit. Econ.*, Summer & Fall 1984, *16*(2&3), pp. 211–19.

Lerner, Abba P.

Colander, David C. Was Keynes a Keynesian or a Lernerian? *J. Econ. Lit.*, December 1984, *22*(4), pp. 1572–75.

Scitovsky, Tibor. Lerner's Contribution to Economics. *J. Econ. Lit.*, December 1984, *22*(4), pp. 1547–71.

Locke, John

Giacometti, Jacques. Langage et monnaie chez Locke et Turgot. (Language and Money: Locke and Turgot. With English summary.) *Écon. Soc.*, March 1984, *18*(3), pp. 119–37.

Harpham, Edward J. Natural Law and Early Liberal Economic Thought: A Reconsideration of Locke's Theories of Value. *Soc. Sci. Quart.*, December 1984, *65*(4), pp. 966–74.

Steiner, Philippe. Locke et Quesnay: une conception politique de l'économie. (Locke and Quesnay: A Political Conception of Political Economy. With English summary.) *Écon. Soc.*, March 1984, *18*(3), pp. 139–59.

Longfield, Mountifort

Black, R. D. Collison. The Irish Dissenters and Nineteenth-Century Political Economy. In *Murphy, A. E., ed.*, 1984, pp. 120–37.

Murphy, Antoin E. Mountifort Longfield's Appointment to the Chair of Political Economy in Trinity College, Dublin, 1832. In *Murphy, A. E., ed.*, 1984, pp. 13–24.

Lowe, Adolph

Clark, David. Confronting the Linear Imperialism of the Austrians: Lowe's Contribution to Capital and Growth Theory. *Eastern Econ. J.*, April-June 1984, *10*(2), pp. 107–27.

Ganssman, Heiner. Political Economics and Social Action. *Eastern Econ. J.*, April-June 1984, *10*(2), pp. 129–37.

Hagemann, Harald and Jeck, Albert. Lowe and the Marx–Fel'dman–Dobb Model: Structural Analysis of a Growing Economy. *Eastern Econ. J.*, April-June 1984, *10*(2), pp. 169–86.

Halevi, Joseph. Lowe, Dobb and Hicks. *East-ern Econ. J.*, April-June 1984, *10*(2), pp. 157–67.

Kurz, Heinz D. Ricardo and Lowe on Machinery. *Eastern Econ. J.*, April-June 1984, *10*(2), pp. 211–29.

McFarlane, Bruce. Economic Planning and Adolph Lowe's Economic Perspective. *Eastern Econ. J.*, April-June 1984, *10*(2), pp. 187–202. [G: China]

Nell, Edward. Structure and Behavior in Classical and Neo-Classical Theory. *Eastern Econ. J.*, April-June 1984, *10*(2), pp. 139–55.

Rima, Ingrid H. Adolph Lowe at Ninety One: An Appreciation. *Eastern Econ. J.*, April-June 1984, *10*(2), pp. 105–06.

Luxemburg, Rosa

Bronfenbrenner, Martin and Wolfson, Murray. Marxian Macrodynamics and the Harrod Growth Model. *Hist. Polit. Econ.*, Summer 1984, *16*(2), pp. 175–86.

Mackeprang, Edvard P.

Kærgaard, Niels. The Earliest History of Econometrics: Some Neglected Danish Contributions. *Hist. Polit. Econ.*, Fall 1984, *16*(3), pp. 437–44.

Malthus, Thomas Robert

Caire, Guy. Un ou deux Mathus? (One or Two Malthus? With English summary.) *Revue Écon.*, July 1984, *35*(4), pp. 623–33.

Guthrie, William G. Selective Rediscovery of Economic Ideas: What Keynes Found in Malthus. *Southern Econ. J.*, January 1984, *50*(3), pp. 771–80.

Harvey-Phillips, Michael B. Malthus' Theodicy: The Intellectual Background of His Contribution to Political Economy. *Hist. Polit. Econ.*, Winter 1984, *16*(4), pp. 591–608.

Henderson, John P. Malthus and the *Edinburgh Review*. In *Samuels, W. J., ed.*, 1984, pp. 107–24.

Hollander, Samuel. 'Dynamic Equilibrium' with Constant Wages: J. S. Mill's Malthusian Analysis of the Secular Wage Path. *Kyklos*, 1984, *37*(2), pp. 247–65.

Hollander, Samuel. The Wage Path in Classical Growth Models: Ricardo, Malthus and Mill. *Oxford Econ. Pap.*, June 1984, *36*(2), pp. 200–212.

Ó Gráda, Cormac. Malthus and the Pre-famine Economy. In *Murphy, A. E., ed.*, 1984, pp. 75–95. [G: Ireland]

Platteau, Jean-Philippe. Malthus et le sous-développement ou le problème de la cohérence d'une théorie. (Malthus and the Problem of Underdevelopment: One or Two Theories? With English summary.) *Revue Écon.*, July 1984, *35*(4), pp. 635–66.

Rashid, Salim. Malthus' Theology: An Overlooked Letter and Some Comments. *Hist. Polit. Econ.*, Spring 1984, *16*(1), pp. 135–38.

Mandeville, Bernard
  von Hayek, Friedrich A. Dr. Bernard Mande-
    ville. In *von Hayek, F. A. (I)*, 1984, *1967*,
    pp. 176–94.
Mariátegui, J. C.
  Paris, R. Mariátegui et Gramsci: quelques pro-
    légomènes à une étude contrastive de la
    diffusion du marxisme. (Mariátegui and
    Gramsci. With English summary.) *Écon.
    Soc.*, July–August 1984, *18*(7–8), pp. 183–
    221.
Marshall, Alfred
  Chasse, John Dennis. Marshall, the Human
    Agent and Economic Growth: Wants and
    Activities Revisited. *Hist. Polit. Econ.*, Fall
    1984, *16*(3), pp. 381–404.
  Coase, Ronald H. Alfred Marshall's Mother
    and Father. *Hist. Polit. Econ.*, Winter 1984,
    16(4), pp. 519–27.
  Hamouda, O. F. On the Notion of Short-run
    and Long-run: Marshall, Ricardo and Equi-
    librium Theories. *Brit. Rev. Econ. Issues*,
    Spring 1984, *6*(14), pp. 55–82.
Marshall, T. H.
  Reisman, David. T. H. Marshall on the Middle
    Ground. In *Boulding, K. E., ed.*, 1984, pp.
    151–73.
Marx, Karl
  Arnon, Arie. Marx's Theory of Money: The
    Formative Years. *Hist. Polit. Econ.*, Winter
    1984, *16*(4), pp. 555–75.
  Ball, Terence and Farr, James. After Marx:
    Introduction. In *Ball, T. and Farr, J., eds.*,
    1984, pp. 1–6.
  Ball, Terence and Farr, James. History and
    Revolution. In *Ball, T. and Farr, J., eds.*,
    1984, pp. 7–11.
  Ball, Terence and Farr, James. Methodology
    and Criticism. In *Ball, T. and Farr, J., eds.*,
    1984, pp. 213–16.
  Bandyopadhyay, Pradeep. Value and Post-
    Sraffa Marxian Analysis. *Sci. Soc.*, Winter
    1984-1985, *48*(4), pp. 433–48.
  Barnes, Trevor. Theories of Agricultural Rent
    within the Surplus Approach. *Int. Reg. Sci.
    Rev.*, November 1984, *9*(2), pp. 125–40.
  Carling, Alan. Observations on the Labor The-
    ory of Value. *Sci. Soc.*, Winter 1984-1985,
    48(4), pp. 407–18.
  Carling, Alan. Value and Strategy. *Sci. Soc.*,
    Summer 1984, *48*(2), pp. 129–60.
  Carver, Terrell. Marxism as Method. In *Ball,
    T. and Farr, J., eds.*, 1984, pp. 261–79.
  Cayatte, Jean-Louis. Travail simple et travail
    complexe chez Marx. (Simple Labour and
    Complex Labour According to Marx. With
    English summary.) *Revue Écon.*, March
    1984, *35*(2), pp. 221–45.
  Chiodi, Guglielmo and Messori, Marcello.
    Marx's Analysis of the Relationship between
    the Rate of Interest and the Rate of Profits:
    A Comment. *Cambridge J. Econ.*, March
    1984, *8*(1), pp. 93–97.
  Dillard, Dudley. Keynes and Marx: A Centen-
    nial Appraisal. *J. Post Keynesian Econ.*,
    Spring 1984, *6*(3), pp. 421–32.

DiQuattro, Arthur. A Note on the Dispensibil-
  ity of the Labor Theory of Value [The Ontol-
  ogy of Abstract Labor] [Marx's Concept of
  Human Nature and the Labor Theory of
  Value]. *Rev. Radical Polit. Econ.*, Summer
  & Fall 1984, *16*(2&3), pp. 199–203.
Ditz, G. W. The Calvinism in Adam Smith.
  Tijdschrift Econ. Manage., 1984, *29*(2), pp.
  233–54.
Dos Santos Ferreira, Rodolphe. Analyse et
  dialectique dans la pensée marxienne (à pro-
  pos de la loi de la baisse tendancielle du
  taux de profit). (With English summary.)
  Écon. Soc., October 1984, *18*(10), pp. 95–
  128.
Duménil, Gérard. The So-Called "Transforma-
  tion Problem" Revisited: A Brief Comment.
  J. Econ. Theory, August 1984, *33*(2), pp.
  340–48.
Elliott, John E. Karl Marx's Theory of Socio-
  Institutional Transformation in Late-Stage
  Capitalism. *J. Econ. Issues*, June 1984,
  18(2), pp. 383–91.
Elster, Jon. Historical Materialism and Eco-
  nomic Backwardness. In *Ball, T. and Farr,
  J., eds.*, 1984, pp. 36–58.
Farr, James. Marx and Positivism. In *Ball,
  T. and Farr, J., eds.*, 1984, pp. 217–34.
Fischer, Norman. A Response to Arthur Di-
  Quattro's "A Note on the Dispensability of
  the Labor Theory of Value" [The Ontology
  of Abstract Labor]. *Rev. Radical Polit.
  Econ.*, Summer & Fall 1984, *16*(2&3), pp.
  205–10.
Flaschel, Peter. The So-Called "Transforma-
  tion Problem" Revisited: A Comment. *J.
  Econ. Theory*, August 1984, *33*(2), pp. 349–
  51.
Garegnani, Pierangelo. Value and Distribu-
  tion in the Classical Economists and Marx.
  Oxford Econ. Pap., June 1984, *36*(2), pp.
  291–325.
Gibson, Roland. Marx and Logic as Social
  Function. *Int. J. Soc. Econ.*, 1984, *11*(6),
  pp. 3–43.
Gowdy, John M. Marx and Resource Scarcity:
  An Institutionalist Approach. *J. Econ. Is-
  sues*, June 1984, *18*(2), pp. 393–400.
Grafstein, Robert. Philosophical Issues in the
  Study of Historical Materialism. *Soc. Sci.
  Quart.*, December 1984, *65*(4), pp. 955–60.
Greenwood, Daphne. The Economic Signifi-
  cance of "Woman's Place" in Society: A
  New-Institutionalist View. *J. Econ. Issues*,
  September 1984, *18*(3), pp. 663–80.
                                    [G: U.S.]
Gurley, John G. Marx's Contributions and
  Their Relevance Today. *Amer. Econ. Rev.*,
  May 1984, *74*(2), pp. 110–15.
Heilbroner, Robert L. Economics and Political
  Economy: Marx, Keynes, and Schumpeter.
  J. Econ. Issues, September 1984, *18*(3), pp.
  681–95.
Heinsohn, Gunnar and Steiger, Otto. "Marx
  and Keynes—Private Property and Money."
  Écon. Soc., April 1984, *18*(4), pp. 37–71.

Hollander, Samuel. Marx and Malthusianism: Marx's Secular Path of Wages. *Amer. Econ. Rev.*, March 1984, *74*(1), pp. 139–51.

Hunt, E. K. The Relation between Theory and History in the Writings of Karl Marx. *Atlantic Econ. J.*, December 1984, *12*(4), pp. 1–8.

Hunt, E. K. The Social Scientific Basis of Socialism. *Econ. Forum*, Summer 1984, *15*(1), pp. 9–16.

Hunt, E. K. Was Marx a Utopian Socialist? *Sci. Soc.*, Spring 1984, *48*(1), pp. 90–97.

Janover, L. and Rubel, M. Matériaux pour un lexique de Marx: Révolution, I. (Material for a Marx Lexicon: Revolution I. With English summary.) *Écon. Soc.*, July–August 1984, *18*(7–8), pp. 15–55.

Jennings, Ann and Shuklian, Steve. Marx, Dewey and Instrumentalism. *Econ. Forum*, Summer 1984, *15*(1), pp. 89–101.

Laibman, David. Value: A Dialog in One Act. *Sci. Soc.*, Winter 1984-1985, *48*(4), pp. 449–65.

Lipietz, Alain. The So-Called "Transformation Problem" Revisited: A Brief Reply to Brief Comments. *J. Econ. Theory*, August 1984, *33*(2), pp. 352–55.

Mattick, Paul, Jr. Marx and Idea of a Social Science. *Écon. Soc.*, July–August 1984, *18*(7–8), pp. 147–81.

Mattick, Paul, Jr. Théorie et réalité. (Theory and Reality. With English summary.) *Écon. Soc.*, July–August 1984, *18*(7–8), pp. 93–146.

Miller, Richard W. Producing Change: Work, Technology, and Power in Marx's Theory of History. In *Ball, T. and Farr, J., eds.*, 1984, pp. 59–87.

Mohun, Simon. Abstract Labor and Its Value-Form. *Sci. Soc.*, Winter 1984-1985, *48*(4), pp. 388–406.

Pachter, Henry. Marx and the Jews. In *Pachter, H.*, 1984, *1979*, pp. 219–55.

Panico, C. Interest Costs, Profit and Pricing: A Reply [Marx's Analysis of the Relationship between the Rate of Interest and the Rate of Profits]. *Cambridge J. Econ.*, March 1984, *8*(1), pp. 99–104.

Rubel, M. Avant-propos (Quel bilan?). (Preface: Which Inventory? With English summary.) *Écon. Soc.*, July–August 1984, *18*(7–8), pp. 3–13.

Rubel, M. Gloses en marge d'un abécédaire apologétique du bolchevisme. (Marginal Notes on an Apologetic Treatise of Bolchevism. With English summary.) *Écon. Soc.*, July–August 1984, *18*(7–8), pp. 243–67.

Rubel, M. Pour une étiologie de l'aliénation politique: Marx à l'école de Spinoza. (Contribution to an Aetiology of Political Alienation. With English summary.) *Écon. Soc.*, July–August 1984, *18*(7–8), pp. 223–41.

Schrader, F. E. Marxens Abstraktionskritik: Differenzierung und Funktionswandel 1843–1858. (Marx's Critique of Abstraction. With English summary.) *Écon. Soc.*, July–August 1984, *18*(7–8), pp. 57–92.

Sekine, Thomas T. An Uno School Seminar on the Theory of Value. *Sci. Soc.*, Winter 1984-1985, *48*(4), pp. 419–32.

Semmler, Willi. Marx and Schumpeter on Competition, Transient Surplus Profit and Technical Change. *Écon. Appl.*, 1984, *37*(3–4), pp. 419–55.

Shaw, William H. Marxism, Revolution, and Rationality. In *Ball, T. and Farr, J., eds.*, 1984, pp. 12–35.

Smith, Steven B. Considerations in Marx's Base and Superstructure. *Soc. Sci. Quart.*, December 1984, *65*(4), pp. 940–54.

Smith, Steven B. Historical Materialism Reconsidered. *Soc. Sci. Quart.*, December 1984, *65*(4), pp. 961–65.

Smith, Vardaman R. Marx's Social Ontology, His Critical Method and Contemporary Social Economics. *Rev. Soc. Econ.*, October 1984, *42*(2), pp. 143–69.

Spahn, H.-Peter. Marx—Schumpeter—Keynes: Drei Fragmente über Geld, Zins und Profit. (Marx—Schumpeter—Keynes: Three Approaches to Money, Interest, and Profit. With English summary.) *Jahr. Nationalökon. Statist.*, May 1984, *199*(3), pp. 237–55.

Sylos-Labini, Paolo. The Problem of Economic Growth in Marx and Schumpeter. In *Sylos-Labini, P.*, 1984, *1983*, pp. 37–78.

Wolff, Richard D.; Callari, Antonino and Roberts, Bruce. A Marxian Alternative to the Traditional "Transformation Problem." *Rev. Radical Polit. Econ.*, Summer/Fall 1984, *16*(2/3), pp. 115–35.

Wolff, Richard D.; Roberts, Bruce and Callari, Antonino. Unsnarling the Tangle: A Rejoinder [Marx's (Not Ricardo's) "Transformation Problem": A Radical Reconceptualization]. *Hist. Polit. Econ.*, Fall 1984, *16*(3), pp. 431–36.

Wolfson, Murray. Weaving a Tangled Web: The Transformation of Values into Prices. *Hist. Polit. Econ.*, Fall 1984, *16*(3), pp. 423–30.

Menger, Carl

Endres, A. M. Institutional Elements in Carl Menger's Theory of Demand: A Comment [Carl Menger and *Homo Oeconomicus*: Some Thoughts on Austrian Theory and Methodology]. *J. Econ. Issues*, September 1984, *18*(3), pp. 897–902.

von Hayek, Friedrich A. The Place of Menger's *Grundsätze* in the History of Economic Thought. In *von Hayek, F. A. (I)*, 1984, *1973*, pp. 195–207.

Mill, James

McAlpin, Michelle Burge. Economic Policy and the True Believer: The Use of Ricardian Rent Theory in the Bombay Survey and Settlement System. *J. Econ. Hist.*, June 1984, *44*(2), pp. 421–27. **[G: India]**

Mill, John Stuart

Boylan, T. A. and Foley, T. P. John Elliot Cairnes, John Stuart Mill and Ireland: Some Problems for Political Economy. In *Murphy, A. E., ed.*, 1984, pp. 96–119.

Ferro, Angelo. Fondamenti teorici ed origini storiche della politica dell'offerta. (Theoretical Fundamentals and Historical Origins of Supply-Side Policy. With English summary.) *Bancaria*, January 1984, *40*(1), pp. 12–18.

Hollander, Samuel. 'Dynamic Equilibrium' with Constant Wages: J. S. Mill's Malthusian Analysis of the Secular Wage Path. *Kyklos*, 1984, *37*(2), pp. 247–65.

Hollander, Samuel. J. S. Mill on "Derived Demand" and the Wage-Fund Theory Recantation. *Eastern Econ. J.*, January-March 1984, *10*(1), pp. 87–98.

Hollander, Samuel. The Wage Path in Classical Growth Models: Ricardo, Malthus and Mill. *Oxford Econ. Pap.*, June 1984, *36*(2), pp. 200–212.

de Schweinitz, Karl, Jr. John Stuart Mill and India. In *Samuels, W. J., ed.*, 1984, pp. 47–61.

Millar, John

Bowles, Paul. John Millar, the Four-Stages Theory, and Women's Position in Society. *Hist. Polit. Econ.*, Winter 1984, *16*(4), pp. 619–38.

von Mises, Ludwig

Caldwell, Bruce J. Praxeology and Its Critics: An Appraisal. *Hist. Polit. Econ.*, Fall 1984, *16*(3), pp. 363–79.

Nemchinov, Vasily Sergeevich

Nemchinova, M. B. The Scientific Work of Vasily Sergeevich Nemchinov (on the 90th Anniversary of His Birth). *Matekon*, Winter 1984–85, *21*(2), pp. 3–25.

Notestein, Frank Wallace

Ryder, Norman B. Frank Wallace Notestein (1902–1983). *Population Stud.*, March 1984, *38*(1), pp. 5–20.

Offe, Claus

Keane, John. Contradictions of the Welfare State: Introduction. In *Offe, C.*, 1984, pp. 11–34.

Pagani, Angelo

Aniasi, Aldo. L'impegno politico e sociale di Angelo Pagani. (The Political and Social Engagement of Angelo Pagani. With English summary.) *Giorn. Econ.*, Nov.-Dec. 1984, *43*(11–12), pp. 795–800.

Cavalieri, Ugo. Il contributo di Angelo Pagani alla gerontologia. (The Contribution of Angelo Pagani to Gerontology. With English summary.) *Giorn. Econ.*, Nov.-Dec. 1984, *43*(11–12), pp. 759–61.

Gasparini, Innocenzo. Considerazioni sul ruolo dell'imprenditorialità. (Remarks on the Role of Entrepreneurship. With English summary.) *Giorn. Econ.*, Nov.-Dec. 1984, *43*(11–12), pp. 851–60.

Treves, Renato. In ricordo di un amico. (In Memory of a Friend. With English summary.) *Giorn. Econ.*, Nov.-Dec. 1984, *43*(11–12), pp. 739–42.

Palander, Tord F.

Beckmann, Martin J. Reflections on Palander's "Beiträge Zur Standortstheorie" In *Andersson, Å. E.; Isard, W. and Puu, T., eds.*, 1984, pp. 31–40.

Puu, Tönu. Tord F. Palander: 1902–1972. In *Andersson, Å. E.; Isard, W. and Puu, T., eds.*, 1984, pp. xv–xvii.

Pareto, Vilfredo

Powers, Charles H. Sociopolitical Determinants of Economic Cycles: Vilfredo Pareto's Final Statement. *Soc. Sci. Quart.*, December 1984, *65*(4), pp. 988–1001.

Penny, David H.

McCawley, Peter. David Penny: An Appreciation. *Bull. Indonesian Econ. Stud.*, April 1984, *20*(1), pp. 117–29.

Pesch, Heinrich

Briefs, Henry W. Solidarity within the Firm: Principles, Concepts and Reflections. *Rev. Soc. Econ.*, December 1984, *42*(3), pp. 295–317.

Hill, Lewis E. A Comment on Solidarity within the Firm [Solidarity within the Firm: Principles, Concepts and Reflections] [Industrial Justice in a Practical Sense]. *Rev. Soc. Econ.*, December 1984, *42*(3), pp. 328–29.

Mueller, Franz H. Heinrich Pesch, SJ, 1854–1926: Social Economist in a Cassock. *Int. J. Soc. Econ.*, 1984, *11*(5), pp. 62–65.

Phillips, Willard

Thompson, James H. Willard Phillips: A Neglected American Economist. *Hist. Polit. Econ.*, Fall 1984, *16*(3), pp. 405–21.

Pigou, A. C.

Bagella, Michele. Note sul concetto di disoccupazione involontaria. (Some Notes on the Concept of Involuntary Unemployment. With English summary.) *Giorn. Econ.*, March–April 1984, *43*(3–4), pp. 213–36.

Scott, Maurice. Maintaining Capital Intact. *Oxford Econ. Pap.*, Supplement November 1984, *36*, pp. 59–73.

Scott, Maurice. Maintaining Capital Intact. In *Collard, D. A., et al., eds.*, 1984, pp. 59–73.

Sen, Amartya. The Living Standard. *Oxford Econ. Pap.*, Supp. Nov. 1984, *36*, pp. 74–90.

Pryme, George

Henderson, James P. "Just Notions of Political Economy"— George Pryme, the First Professor of Political Economy at Cambridge. In *Samuels, W. J., ed.*, 1984, pp. 1–20.

Ptukha, Mykhailo V.

Clem, Ralph S. An Assessment of the Work of the Demographer M. V. Ptukha. In *Koropeckyj, I. S., ed.*, 1984, pp. 71–90.

Quesnay, Francois

Garegnani, Pierangelo. Value and Distribution in the Classical Economists and Marx. *Oxford Econ. Pap.*, June 1984, *36*(2), pp. 291–325.

Masson, Bernard. La notion de production en

relation avec la constitution des classes chez F. Quesnay. (François Quesnay's Concept of Production as Related to the Constitution of Classes. With English summary.) *Écon. Soc.*, March 1984, *18*(3), pp. 161–74.

Steiner, Philippe. Locke et Quesnay: une conception politique de l'économie. (Locke and Quesnay: A Political Conception of Political Economy. With English summary.) *Écon. Soc.*, March 1984, *18*(3), pp. 139–59.

Reder, Melvin W.

Lazear, Edward P. Some Reflections on Melvin W. Reder. *J. Lab. Econ.*, April 1984, *2*(2), pp. 145–50.

Ricardo, David

Barnes, Trevor. Theories of Agricultural Rent within the Surplus Approach. *Int. Reg. Sci. Rev.*, November 1984, *9*(2), pp. 125–40.

Ferro, Angelo. Fondamenti teorici ed origini storiche della politica dell'offerta. (Theoretical Fundamentals and Historical Origins of Supply-Side Policy. With English summary.) *Bancaria*, January 1984, *40*(1), pp. 12–18.

Garegnani, Pierangelo. Value and Distribution in the Classical Economists and Marx. *Oxford Econ. Pap.*, June 1984, *36*(2), pp. 291–325.

Hamouda, O. F. On the Notion of Short-run and Long-run: Marshall, Ricardo and Equilibrium Theories. *Brit. Rev. Econ. Issues*, Spring 1984, *6*(14), pp. 55–82.

Henderson, John P. Ricardo and the Provident Institutions. In *Samuels, W. J., ed.*, 1984, pp. 65–76.   [G: U.K.]

Henderson, John P. The Political Economy Club: Robert Torrens and the Decline of Ricardo's Influence. In *Samuels, W. J., ed.*, 1984, pp. 77–105.

Hollander, Samuel. The Wage Path in Classical Growth Models: Ricardo, Malthus and Mill. *Oxford Econ. Pap.*, June 1984, *36*(2), pp. 200–212.

Johnson, L. E. Ricardo's Labor Theory of the Determinant of Value. *Atlantic Econ. J.*, March 1984, *12*(1), pp. 50–59.

Kriesler, Peter. On Dobb's Interpretation of Jevons on Ricardo. *Cambridge J. Econ.*, December 1984, *8*(4), pp. 403–05.

Kurz, Heinz D. Ricardo and Lowe on Machinery. *Eastern Econ. J.*, April-June 1984, *10*(2), pp. 211–29.

Peach, Terry. David Ricardo's Early Treatment of Profitability: A New Interpretation. *Econ. J.*, December 1984, *94*(376), pp. 733–51.

Rankin, Steve. The Wage Basket in Ricardo's *Essay on Profits*. *Cambridge J. Econ.*, March 1984, *8*(1), pp. 83–86.

Wolff, Richard D.; Callari, Antonino and Roberts, Bruce. A Marxian Alternative to the Traditional "Transformation Problem." *Rev. Radical Polit. Econ.*, Summer/Fall 1984, *16*(2/3), pp. 115–35.

Robbins, Lionel

Addleson, Mark S. Robbins's *Essay* in Retrospect: On Subjectivism and an "Economics of Choice." *Rivista Int. Sci. Econ. Com.*, June 1984, *31*(6), pp. 506–23.

Robertson, Dennis Holme

Giovannetti, Giorgia. The Role of the Rate of Interest: From Wicksell to Keynes' Treatise on Money. *Econ. Notes*, 1984, (1), pp. 66–86.

Presley, J. R. D. H. Robertson: Some Restoration. *J. Post Keynesian Econ.*, Winter 1983–84, *6*(2), pp. 230–40.

Robinson, Joan

Asimakopulos, Athanasios. Joan Robinson and Economic Theory. *Banca Naz. Lavoro Quart. Rev.*, December 1984, (151), pp. 381–409.

Asimakopulos, Athanasios. Joan Robinson et la théorie économique. (Joan Robinson and Economic Theory. With English summary.) *L'Actual. Econ.*, December 1984, *60*(4), pp. 521–52.

Eichner, Alfred S. Joan Robinson's Legacy. *Challenge*, May/June 1984, *27*(2), pp. 42–46.

Harcourt, Geoffrey C. The End of an Era: Joan Robinson (1903–83) and Piero Sraffa (1898–1983). *J. Post Keynesian Econ.*, Spring 1984, *6*(3), pp. 466–69.

Rohrlich, George

Thanawala, Kishor. George Rohrlich's Social Economics. *Int. J. Soc. Econ.*, 1984, *11*(1/2), pp. 83–88.

Rosdolsky, Roman

Himka, John-Paul. Roman Rosdolsky's Reconsideration of the Traditional Marxist Debate on the Schemes of Reproduction on New Methodological Grounds: Comments. In *Koropeckyj, I. S., ed.*, 1984, pp. 135–47.

Turban, Manfred A. Roman Rosdolsky's Reconsideration of the Traditional Marxist Debate on the Schemes of Reproduction on New Methodological Grounds. In *Koropeckyj, I. S., ed.*, 1984, pp. 91–134.

Rostow, Walter W.

Supple, Barry. Revisiting Rostow. *Econ. Hist. Rev., 2nd Ser.*, February 1984, *37*(1), pp. 107–14.

Rothbarth, Erwin

Cuyvers, Ludo. Erwin Rothbarth's Life and Work. *J. Post Keynesian Econ.*, Winter 1983-84, *6*(2), pp. 305–12.

Say, Jean-Baptiste

Clower, Robert W. Say's Principle, What It Means and Doesn't Mean. In *Clower, R. W.*, 1984, *1973*, pp. 145–65.

Euzent, Patricia J. and Martin, Thomas L. Classical Roots of the Emerging Theory of Rent Seeking: The Contribution of Jean-Baptiste Say. *Hist. Polit. Econ.*, Summer 1984, *16*(2), pp. 255–62.

Schumpeter, Joseph Alois

Acham, Karl. Schumpeter—The Sociologist. In *Seidl, C., ed.*, 1984, pp. 155–72.

Beinsen, Lutz. Schumpeter as an Historian of

Economic Doctrine. In *Seidl, C., ed.*, 1984, pp. 173–86.

Breton, Yves. La théorie schumpétérienne de l'entrepreneur ou le problème de la connaissance économique. (Schumpeter's Theory of the Entrepreneur or the Problem of Economic Knowledge. With English summary.) *Revue Écon.*, March 1984, *35*(2), pp. 247–66.

Dahmén, Erik. Schumpeterian Dynamics: Some Methodological Notes. *J. Econ. Behav. Organ.*, March 1984, *5*(1), pp. 25–34.

Fellner, William. Currents and Countercurrents in Political and Economic Thought. *Carnegie-Rochester Conf. Ser. Public Policy*, Autumn 1984, *21*, pp. 231–52.

Giersch, Herbert. The Age of Schumpeter. *Amer. Econ. Rev.*, May 1984, *74*(2), pp. 103–09.

Hammond, Peter J. Is Entrepreneurship Obsolescent? In *Seidl, C., ed.*, 1984, pp. 31–43.

Hammond, Peter J. Must Monopoly Power Accompany Innovation? In *Seidl, C., ed.*, 1984, pp. 45–56.

Hammond, Peter J. Schumpeter and the Economic Problems of Today. In *Seidl, C., ed.*, 1984, pp. 3–13.

Hammond, Peter J. What to Do about Business Cycles? In *Seidl, C., ed.*, 1984, pp. 59–75.

Heilbroner, Robert L. Economics and Political Economy: Marx, Keynes, and Schumpeter. *J. Econ. Issues*, September 1984, *18*(3), pp. 681–95.

Meacci, Ferdinando. L'analisi del capitale nella teoria dello sviluppo economico di J. A. Schumpeter. (The Analysis of Capital in Schumpeter's Theory of Economic Development. With English summary.) *Rivista Int. Sci. Econ. Com.*, February 1984, *31*(2), pp. 131–46.

Mitchell, William C. Schumpeter and Public Choice, Part II: Democracy and the Demise of Capitalism: The Missing Chapter in Schumpeter. *Public Choice*, 1984, *42*(2), pp. 161–74.

Mitchell, William C. Schumpeter and Public Choice, Part I: Precursor to Public Choice? *Public Choice*, 1984, *42*(1), pp. 73–88.

Santarelli, Enrico. L'influsso dell'analisi schumpeteriana della funzione imprenditoriale e del credito nel pensiero economico italiano tra le due guerre. (The Influence of Schumepeterian Analysis of the Entrepreneurial Function and of the Banking Function on Italian Economic Thought in the Period between the Two Wars. With English summary.) *Giorn. Econ.*, July–August 1984, *43*(7–8), pp. 507–29. [G: Italy]

Schachner-Blazizek, Peter. The Current Relevance of Schumpeter's Theory of the Decay of Capitalism. In *Seidl, C., ed.*, 1984, pp. 111–21.

Schwartz, Anna J. Currents and Countercurrents in Political and Economic Thought:

A Comment. *Carnegie-Rochester Conf. Ser. Public Policy*, Autumn 1984, *21*, pp. 253–58.

Seidl, Christian. Joseph Alois Schumpeter: Character, Life and Particulars of His Graz Period. In *Seidl, C., ed.*, 1984, pp. 187–205.

Seidl, Christian. Schumpeter versus Keynes: Supply-side Economics or Demand Management? In *Seidl, C., ed.*, 1984, pp. 139–51.

Seidl, Christian. The Tax State in Crisis: Can Schumpeterian Public Finance Claim Modern Relevance? In *Seidl, C., ed.*, 1984, pp. 89–109.

Semmler, Willi. Marx and Schumpeter on Competition, Transient Surplus Profit and Technical Change. *Écon. Appl.*, 1984, *37*(3–4), pp. 419–55.

Spahn, H.-Peter. Marx—Schumpeter—Keynes: Drei Fragmente über Geld, Zins und Profit. (Marx—Schumpeter—Keynes: Three Approaches to Money, Interest, and Profit. With English summary.) *Jahr. Nationalökon. Statist.*, May 1984, *199*(3), pp. 237–55.

Swoboda, Peter. Schumpeter's Entrepreneur in Modern Economic Theory. In *Seidl, C., ed.*, 1984, pp. 17–29.

Sylos-Labini, Paolo. New Aspects of the Cyclical Development of the Economy. *Banca Naz. Lavoro Quart. Rev.*, March 1984, (148), pp. 15–31. [G: Italy]

Sylos-Labini, Paolo. The Problem of Economic Growth in Marx and Schumpeter. In *Sylos-Labini, P.*, 1984, *1983*, pp. 37–78.

Tichy, Gunther. Schumpeter's Business Cycle Theory: Its Importance for Our Time. In *Seidl, C., ed.*, 1984, pp. 77–88.

Tichy, Gunther. Schumpeter's Monetary Theory—An Unjustly Neglected Part of His Work. In *Seidl, C., ed.*, 1984, pp. 125–38.

Schwartz, Anna J.

Clower, Robert W. Monetary History and Positive Economics. In *Clower, R. W.*, 1984, *1964*, pp. 59–77.

Shackle, G. L. S.

Carvalho, Fernando. On the Concept of Time in Shacklean and Sraffian Economics. *J. Post Keynesian Econ.*, Winter 1983-84, *6*(2), pp. 265–80.

Shann, Edward Owen Giblin

Stone, J. O. 1929 and All That . . . . *Australian Econ. Rev.*, 3rd Quarter 1984, (67), pp. 18–31. [G: Australia]

Simons, Henry

Aschheim, Joseph and Tavlas, George S. The Monetary Thought–Ideology Nexus: Simons versus Keynes. *Banca Naz. Lavoro Quart. Rev.*, June 1984, (149), pp. 177–96.

Bernholz, Peter. Henry Simons and Chicago Liberalism: A Review Article. *Z. ges. Staatswiss.*, June 1984, *140*(2), pp. 387–90.

Slutsky, Eugene

Smolinski, Leon. Slutsky and Metaeconomics. In *Koropeckyj, I. S., ed.*, 1984, pp. 60–70.

Smith, Adam
Anderson, Gary M. and Tollison, Robert D. Sir James Steuart as the Apotheosis of Mercantilism and His Relation to Adam Smith. *Southern Econ. J.*, October 1984, *51*(2), pp. 456–68.

Baumol, William J. Toward a Theory of Public Enterprise. *Atlantic Econ. J.*, March 1984, *12*(1), pp. 12–19.

Ditz, G. W. The Calvinism in Adam Smith. *Tijdschrift Econ. Manage.*, 1984, *29*(2), pp. 233–54.

Dow, Alexander. The Hauteur of Adam Smith: An Unpublished Letter from James Anderson of Monkshill. *Scot. J. Polit. Econ.*, November 1984, *31*(3), pp. 284–85.

Ferro, Angelo. Fondamenti teorici ed origini storiche della politica dell'offerta. (Theoretical Fundamentals and Historical Origins of Supply-Side Policy. With English summary.) *Bancaria*, January 1984, *40*(1), pp. 12–18.

Harpham, Edward J. Liberalism, Civic Humanism, and the Case of Adam Smith. *Amer. Polit. Sci. Rev.*, September 1984, *78*(3), pp. 764–74.

Kindleberger, Charles P. Was Adam Smith a Monetarist or a Keynesian? *Bus. Econ.*, January 1984, *19*(1), pp. 5–12.

Sen, Amartya. The Living Standard. *Oxford Econ. Pap.*, Supplement November 1984, *36*, pp. 74–90.

Sen, Amartya. The Living Standard. In *Collard, D. A., et al., eds.*, 1984, pp. 74–90.

Sraffa, Piero
Albani, Paolo. Teoria economica e linguaggio scientifico. Elementi per uno studio sul rapporto Sraffa–Wittgenstein. (With English summary.) *Econ. Polit.*, April 1984, *1*(1), pp. 107–42.

Bandyopadhyay, Pradeep. Value and Post-Sraffa Marxian Analysis. *Sci. Soc.*, Winter 1984-1985, *48*(4), pp. 433–48.

Canterbery, E. Ray. Galbraith, Sraffa, Kalecki and Supra-surplus Capitalism. *J. Post Keynesian Econ.*, Fall 1984, *7*(1), pp. 77–90.

Carvalho, Fernando. On the Concept of Time in Shacklean and Sraffian Economics. *J. Post Keynesian Econ.*, Winter 1983-84, *6*(2), pp. 265–80.

Eatwell, John. Piero Sraffa: Seminal Economic Theorist. *Sci. Soc.*, Summer 1984, *48*(2), pp. 211–16.

Garegnani, Pierangelo. Piero Sraffa. *Cambridge J. Econ.*, March 1984, *8*(1), pp. 1–2.

Garegnani, Pierangelo. Value and Distribution in the Classical Economists and Marx. *Oxford Econ. Pap.*, June 1984, *36*(2), pp. 291–325.

Harcourt, Geoffrey C. The End of an Era: Joan Robinson (1903–83) and Piero Sraffa (1898–1983). *J. Post Keynesian Econ.*, Spring 1984, *6*(3), pp. 466–69.

Kaldor, Nicholas. Piero Sraffa. *Cambridge J. Econ.*, March 1984, *8*(1), pp. 2–5.

Napolitano, Giorgio. The "Secret Life" of a Great Intellectual. *Sci. Soc.*, Summer 1984, *48*(2), pp. 216–19.

Porta, Pier Luigi. Piero Sraffa (1898–1983). *Rivista Int. Sci. Econ. Com.*, January 1984, *31*(1), pp. 14–20.

Sardoni, Claudio. Some Ties of Kalecki to the 1926 "Sraffian Manifesto." *J. Post Keynesian Econ.*, Spring 1984, *6*(3), pp. 458–65.

Steuart, James
Anderson, Gary M. and Tollison, Robert D. Sir James Steuart as the Apotheosis of Mercantilism and His Relation to Adam Smith. *Southern Econ. J.*, October 1984, *51*(2), pp. 456–68.

Thornton, Henry
Humphrey, Thomas M. and Keleher, Robert E. The Lender of Last Resort: A Historical Perspective. [International Debt, Bank Failures, and the Money Supply: The Thirties and the Eighties]. *Cato J.*, Spring/Summer 1984, *4*(1), pp. 275–318. [G: U.K.]

Meiselman, David I. The Lender of Last Resort and a Money Supply Rule [International Debt, Bank Failures, and the Money Supply: The Thirties and the Eighties]. *Cato J.*, Spring/Summer 1984, *4*(1), pp. 319–21. [G: U.K.]

von Thünen, Johann H.
von Böventer, Edwin. The von Thünen-Hotelling Rule: On Johann Heinrich von Thünen's Model of General Economic Interdependence in Space and Time. In *[Beckmann, M. J.]*, 1984, pp. 137–49.

Tinbergen, Jan
Bos, Henk C. Jan Tinbergen: A Profile. *J. Policy Modeling*, May 1984, *6*(2), pp. 151–58.

Tinbergen, Jan. My Life Philosophy. *Amer. Econ.*, Fall 1984, *28*(2), pp. 5–8.

Tooke, Thomas
Arnon, Arie. The Transformation in Thomas Tooke's Monetary Theory Reconsidered. *Hist. Polit. Econ.*, Summer 1984, *16*(2), pp. 311–26.

Tuhan-Baranovsky, Mykhailo
Amato, Sergio. Tuhan-Baranovsky's Theories of Markets, Accumulation and Industrialization: Their Influence on the Development of Economic Thought and Modern Historiographic Research. In *Koropeckyj, I. S., ed.*, 1984, pp. 1–59.

Turgot, A. R. J.
Giacometti, Jacques. Langage et monnaie chez Locke et Turgot. (Language and Money: Locke and Turgot. With English summary.) *Écon. Soc.*, March 1984, *18*(3), pp. 119–37.

Ravix, Joël and Romani, Paul-Marie. L'idée de progrès comme fondement des analyses économiques de Turgot. (The Idea of Progress as the Basis of Turgot's Economic Thought. With English summary.) *Écon. Soc.*, March 1984, *18*(3), pp. 97–118.

Usher, Abbot Payson
Parker, William N. A. P. Usher: An Appreciative Essay. In *Parker, W. N.*, 1984, *1956*, pp. 257–66.
Veblen, Thorstein
Dugger, William M. Veblen and Kropotkin on Human Evolution. *J. Econ. Issues*, December 1984, *18*(4), pp. 971–85.
Ghosh, Syamal K. On the Validity of Veblen's Criticisms of Economic Orthodoxy: An Analysis of His Positions in the Light of Current Conditions and Economic Thought. *Amer. J. Econ. Soc.*, April 1984, *43*(2), pp. 235–46.
Greenwood, Daphne. The Economic Significance of "Woman's Place" in Society: A New-Institutionalist View. *J. Econ. Issues*, September 1984, *18*(3), pp. 663–80. [G: U.S.]
Leathers, Charles G. Liberation Theology, the New Religious Political Right, and Veblen's Ambivalent View of Christianity. *J. Econ. Issues*, December 1984, *18*(4), pp. 1155–75.
Rutherford, Malcolm H. Thorstein Veblen and the Processes of Institutional Change. *Hist. Polit. Econ.*, Fall 1984, *16*(3), pp. 331–48.
Tilman, Rick. Dewey's Liberalism versus Veblen's Radicalism: A Reappraisal of the Unity of Progressive Social Thought. *J. Econ. Issues*, September 1984, *18*(3), pp. 745–69. [G: U.S.]
Tilman, Rick and Simich, J. L. On the Use and Abuse of Thorstein Veblen in Modern American Sociology, II: Daniel Bell and the 'Utopianizing' of Veblen's Contribution and Its Integration by Robert Merton and C. W. Mills. *Amer. J. Econ. Soc.*, January 1984, *43*(1), pp. 103–14.
Walker, E. Ronald
Cain, Neville. The Propagation of Keynesian Thinking in Australia: E. R. Walker 1933–36. *Econ. Rec.*, December 1984, *60*(171), pp. 366–80. [G: Australia]
Walras, Auguste
Jaffé, William. The Antecedents and Early Life of Léon Walras. *Hist. Polit. Econ.*, Spring 1984, *16*(1), pp. 1–57.
Yamashita, Hiroshi. Economic Theory of Auguste Walras. (In Japanese. With English summary.) *Osaka Econ. Pap.*, December 1984, *34*(2–3), pp. 110–24.
Walras, Léon
Cirillo, Renato. Léon Walras and Social Justice. *Amer. J. Econ. Soc.*, January 1984, *43*(1), pp. 53–60.
Jaffé, William. The Antecedents and Early Life of Léon Walras. *Hist. Polit. Econ.*, Spring 1984, *16*(1), pp. 1–57.
Walker, Donald A. Is Walras's Theory of General Equilibrium a Normative Scheme? *Hist. Polit. Econ.*, Fall 1984, *16*(3), pp. 445–69.
Walker, Donald A. Walras and His Critics on the Maximum Utility of New Capital Goods.

Hist. Polit. Econ., Winter 1984, *16*(4), pp. 529–54.
Warming, Jens
Kærgaard, Niels. The Earliest History of Econometrics: Some Neglected Danish Contributions. *Hist. Polit. Econ.*, Fall 1984, *16*(3), pp. 437–44.
Waugh, Frederick V.
Houck, James P. and Abel, Martin E. Selected Writings on Agricultural Policy and Economic Analysis: Introduction. In *Waugh, F. V.*, 1984, pp. ix–xiii.
Wicksell, Knut
Giovannetti, Giorgia. The Role of the Rate of Interest: From Wicksell to Keynes' Treatise on Money. *Econ. Notes*, 1984, (1), pp. 66–86.
Samuelson, Larry. Returns to Scale and Wicksell's Missing Equation: A Note. *Hist. Polit. Econ.*, Winter 1984, *16*(4), pp. 577–82.
Wittgenstein, Ludwig
Albani, Paolo. Teoria economica e linguaggio scientifico. Elementi per uno studio sul rapporto Sraffa–Wittgenstein. (With English summary.) *Econ. Polít.*, April 1984, *1*(1), pp. 107–42.
Young, Allyn
Brockway, George P. Kaldor's "Best" Choice [Allyn Young on Increasing Returns]. *J. Post Keynesian Econ.*, Spring 1984, *6*(3), pp. 481–82.
Zijlstra, Jelle
de Roos, F. Jelle Zijlstra: A Versatile Economist. *De Economist*, 1984, *132*(1), pp. 1–22.

0329 Other Special Topics

Arnon, Arie. Marx's Theory of Money: The Formative Years. *Hist. Polit. Econ.*, Winter 1984, *16*(4), pp. 555–75.
Aschheim, Joseph and Tavlas, George S. The Monetary Thought–Ideology Nexus: Simons versus Keynes. *Banca Naz. Lavoro Quart. Rev.*, June 1984, (149), pp. 177–96.
Bagella, Michele. Note sul concetto di disoccupazione involontaria. (Some Notes on the Concept of Involuntary Unemployment. With English summary.) *Giorn. Econ.*, March–April 1984, *43*(3–4), pp. 213–36.
Bernal, Richard L.; Figueroa, Mark and Witter, Michael. Caribbean Economic Thought: The Critical Tradition. *Soc. Econ. Stud.*, June 1984, *33*(2), pp. 5–96. [G: Caribbean]
Bernholz, Peter. Henry Simons and Chicago Liberalism: A Review Article. *Z. ges. Staatswiss.*, June 1984, *140*(2), pp. 387–90.
Bird, Ronald. On Recent Misinterpretations of Pareto's Theory of Rent. *Indian Econ. J.*, April–June 1984, *31*(4), pp. 25–34.
Bloomfield, Arthur I. Effect of Growth on the Terms of Trade: Some Earlier Views. *Economica*, May 1984, *51*(202), pp. 187–93.
von Böventer, Edwin. The von Thünen-Hotelling Rule: On Johann Heinrich von Thünen's Model of General Economic Interdependence in

Space and Time. In *[Beckmann, M. J.]*, 1984, pp. 137–49.

Bowles, Paul. John Millar, the Four-Stages Theory, and Women's Position in Society. *Hist. Polit. Econ.*, Winter 1984, *16*(4), pp. 619–38.

Breit, William. Galbraith and Friedman: Two Versions of Economic Reality. *J. Post Keynesian Econ.*, Fall 1984, *7*(1), pp. 18–29.

Carling, Alan. Value and Strategy. *Sci. Soc.*, Summer 1984, *48*(2), pp. 129–60.

Clark, David. Confronting the Linear Imperialism of the Austrians: Lowe's Contribution to Capital and Growth Theory. *Eastern Econ. J.*, April-June 1984, *10*(2), pp. 107–27.

Cooter, Robert and Rappoport, Peter. Were the Ordinalists Wrong about Welfare Economics? *J. Econ. Lit.*, June 1984, *22*(2), pp. 507–30.

Creedy, John. Edgeworth: Utilitarianism and Arbitration. *Hist. Polit. Econ.*, Winter 1984, *16*(4), pp. 609–18.

Debreu, Gerard. Economic Theory in the Mathematical Mode. *Scand. J. Econ.*, 1984, *86*(4), pp. 393–410.

Dore, M. H. I. and Kaser, Michael C. The Millions of Equations Debate: Seventy Years after Barone. *Atlantic Econ. J.*, September 1984, *12*(3), pp. 30–44.

Etner, François. L'ancien régime et le calcul économique. (The "Ancien Regime" and the Cost–Benefit Analysis. With English summary.) *Écon. Soc.*, March 1984, *18*(3), pp. 175–98.

Gasparini, Innocenzo. Considerazioni sul ruolo dell'imprenditorialità. (Remarks on the Role of Entrepreneurship. With English summary.) *Giorn. Econ.*, Nov.-Dec. 1984, *43*(11–12), pp. 851–60.

Genovese, Frank C. An Economics Classic and Plutology: The 'Science of Wealth' Reminds Economists That Their Goal Should Be Well-being for All. *Amer. J. Econ. Soc.*, October 1984, *43*(4), pp. 455–67.

Giersch, Herbert. The Age of Schumpeter. *Amer. Econ. Rev.*, May 1984, *74*(2), pp. 103–09.

Giovannetti, Giorgia. The Role of the Rate of Interest: From Wicksell to Keynes' Treatise on Money. *Econ. Notes*, 1984, (1), pp. 66–86.

Greenwood, Daphne. The Economic Significance of "Woman's Place" in Society: A New-Institutionalist View. *J. Econ. Issues*, September 1984, *18*(3), pp. 663–80. [G: U.S.]

Hamouda, O. F. On the Notion of Short-run and Long-run: Marshall, Ricardo and Equilibrium Theories. *Brit. Rev. Econ. Issues*, Spring 1984, *6*(14), pp. 55–82.

Harpham, Edward J. Liberalism, Civic Humanism, and the Case of Adam Smith. *Amer. Polit. Sci. Rev.*, September 1984, *78*(3), pp. 764–74.

Heinsohn, Gunnar and Steiger, Otto. "Marx and Keynes—Private Property and Money." *Écon. Soc.*, April 1984, *18*(4), pp. 37–71.

Herman, James. Monetarism: A Paradoxical Counter-revolution. *Hist. Polit. Econ.*, Winter 1984, *16*(4), pp. 583–90.

Hickerson, Steven R. Complexity and the Meaning of Freedom: The Classical Liberal View.

Amer. J. Econ. Soc., January 1984, *43*(1), pp. 91–101.

Hollander, Samuel. 'Dynamic Equilibrium' with Constant Wages: J. S. Mill's Malthusian Analysis of the Secular Wage Path. *Kyklos*, 1984, *37*(2), pp. 247–65.

Humphrey, Thomas M. Algebraic Quantity Equations before Fisher and Pigou. *Fed. Res. Bank Richmond Econ. Rev.*, Sept./Oct. 1984, *70*(5), pp. 13–22.

Humphrey, Thomas M. On Nonneutral Relative Price Effects in Monetarist Thought: Some Austrian Misconceptions. *Fed. Res. Bank Richmond Econ. Rev.*, May/June 1984, *70*(3), pp. 13–19.

Jennings, Ann and Shuklian, Steve. Marx, Dewey and Instrumentalism. *Econ. Forum*, Summer 1984, *15*(1), pp. 89–101.

Joël, Marie-Ève. L'économie de l'assistance dans la période prérévolutionnaire. (The Economics of Assistance during the Prerevolutionary Period. With English summary.) *Écon. Soc.*, March 1984, *18*(3), pp. 199–231. [G: France]

Kærgaard, Niels. The Earliest History of Econometrics: Some Neglected Danish Contributions. *Hist. Polit. Econ.*, Fall 1984, *16*(3), pp. 437–44.

Koropeckyj, I. S. Academic Economics in the Nineteenth-Century Ukraine. In *Koropeckyj, I. S., ed.*, 1984, pp. 163–222. [G: U.S.S.R.]

Koropeckyj, I. S. Selected Contributions of Ukrainian Scholars to Economics: Introduction. In *Koropeckyj, I. S., ed.*, 1984, pp. vii–xiv. [G: U.S.S.R.]

Maddock, Rodney. Rational Expectations Macrotheory: A Lakatosian Case Study in Program Adjustment. *Hist. Polit. Econ.*, Summer 1984, *16*(2), pp. 291–309.

McCain, Roger A. Social Economy and Community. *Int. J. Soc. Econ.*, 1984, *11*(1/2), pp. 89–99.

McCormick, Gordon H. Strategic Considerations in the Development of Economic Thought. In *McCormick, G. H. and Bissell, R. E., eds.*, 1984, pp. 3–25.

Meacci, Ferdinando. L'analisi del capitale nella teoria dello sviluppo economico di J. A. Schumpeter. (The Analysis of Capital in Schumpeter's Theory of Economic Development. With English summary.) *Rivista Int. Sci. Econ. Com.*, February 1984, *31*(2), pp. 131–46.

Moss, Scott J. The History of the Theory of the Firm from Marshall to Robinson and Chamberlin: The Source of Positivism in Economics. *Economica*, August 1984, *51*(203), pp. 307–18.

Patinkin, Don. Keynes and Economics Today. *Amer. Econ. Rev.*, May 1984, *74*(2), pp. 97–102.

Reder, Melvin W. Chicago Economics: Permanence and Change. In *Caldwell, B. J., ed.*, 1984, *1982*, pp. 360–97.

Roger, Colin. Erratum [Neo-Walrasian Macroeconomics Microfoundations and Pseudo-Production Models]. *Australian Econ. Pap.*, June 1984, *23*(42), pp. 167.

Santarelli, Enrico. L'influsso dell'analisi schumpeteriana della funzione imprenditoriale e del credito nel pensiero economico italiano tra le due guerre. (The Influence of Schumepeterian Analysis of the Entrepreneurial Function and of the Banking Function on Italian Economic Thought in the Period between the Two Wars. With English summary.) *Giorn. Econ.*, July–August 1984, *43*(7–8), pp. 507–29. **[G: Italy]**

Sardoni, Claudio. Some Ties of Kalecki to the 1926 "Sraffian Manifesto." *J. Post Keynesian Econ.*, Spring 1984, *6*(3), pp. 458–65.

Sherman, Howard J. Contemporary Radical Economics. *J. Econ. Educ.*, Fall 1984, *15*(4), pp. 265–74.

Silberberg, Eugene and Walker, Donald A. A Modern Analysis of Giffen's Paradox. *Int. Econ. Rev.*, October 1984, *25*(3), pp. 687–94.

Spahn, H.-Peter. Marx–Schumpeter–Keynes: Drei Fragmente über Geld, Zins und Profit. (Marx–Schumpeter–Keynes: Three Approaches to Money, Interest, and Profit. With English summary.) *Jahr. Nationalökon. Statist.*, May 1984, *199*(3), pp. 237–55.

Vercelli, Alessandro. Fluctuations and Growth: Keynes, Schumpeter, Marx and the Structural Instability of Capitalism. In *Goodwin, R. M.; Krüger, M. and Vercelli, A., eds.*, 1984, pp. 209–31.

Waters, William R. Development of Solidarist Economics in the U.S. *Int. J. Soc. Econ.*, 1984, *11*(1/2), pp. 100–116. **[G: U.S.]**

Yeager, Leland B. The Image of the Gold Standard. In *Bordo, M. D. and Schwartz, A. J., eds.*, 1984, pp. 651–69.

036 Economic Methodology

0360 Economic Methodology

Addison, John T.; Burton, John and Torrance, Thomas S. Causation, Social Science and Sir John Hicks. *Oxford Econ. Pap.*, March 1984, *36*(1), pp. 1–11.

Addleson, Mark S. Robbins's *Essay* in Retrospect: On Subjectivism and an "Economics of Choice." *Rivista Int. Sci. Econ. Com.*, June 1984, *31*(6), pp. 506–23.

Akerlof, George A. An Economic Theorist's Book of Tales: Introduction. In *Akerlof, G. A.*, 1984, pp. 1–6.

Arndt, Heinz W. Political Economy. *Econ. Rec.*, September 1984, *60*(170), pp. 266–73.

Ball, Terence and Farr, James. Methodology and Criticism. In *Ball, T. and Farr, J., eds.*, 1984, pp. 213–16.

Barry, Norman P. The 'Austrian' Perspective. In *Whynes, D. K., ed.*, 1984, pp. 33–58.

Blaug, Mark. Our Methodological Crisis: Comment 2. In *Wiles, P. and Routh, G., eds.*, 1984, pp. 30–36.

Blaug, Mark. The Methodology of Economics: Conclusions. In *Caldwell, B. J., ed.*, 1984, *1980*, pp. 308–19.

Boland, Lawrence A. A Critique of Friedman's Critics. In *Caldwell, B. J., ed.*, 1984, *1979*, pp. 205–24.

Boland, Lawrence A. Methodology: Reply [An Essay on the Foundations of Friedman's Methodology]. *Amer. Econ. Rev.*, September 1984, *74*(4), pp. 795–97.

Boland, Lawrence A. On the Futility of Criticizing the Neoclassical Maximization Hypothesis. In *Caldwell, B. J., ed.*, 1984, *1981*, pp. 246–51.

Boland, Lawrence A. On the State of Economic Methodology. In *Samuels, W. J., ed.*, 1984, pp. 173–77.

Boland, Lawrence A. The Neoclassical Maximization Hypothesis: Reply. In *Caldwell, B. J., ed.*, 1984, *1984*, pp. 256–58.

Bourdieu, Pierre. Réponses aux économistes. (With English summary.) *Écon. Soc.*, October 1984, *18*(10), pp. 23–32.

Brandis, Royall. On the Current State of Methodology in Economics. In *Samuels, W. J., ed.*, 1984, pp. 151–60.

Brennan, Geoffrey and Buchanan, James M. The Normative Purpose of Economic "Science": Rediscovery of an Eighteenth-Century Method. In *Buchanan, J. M. and Tollison, R. D., eds.*, 1984, pp. 382–94.

Brennan, Timothy J. Is Economics Methodologically Special? In *Samuels, W. J., ed.*, 1984, pp. 127–40.

Breton, Yves. La théorie schumpétérienne de l'entrepreneur ou le problème de la connaissance économique. (Schumpeter's Theory of the Entrepreneur or the Problem of Economic Knowledge. With English summary.) *Revue Écon.*, March 1984, *35*(2), pp. 247–66.

Brochier, Hubert. La valeur heuristique du paradigme économique. (With English summary.) *Écon. Soc.*, October 1984, *18*(10), pp. 3–21.

Brown, Elba K. Review of Social Economy: The Neoclassical and Post-Keynesian Research Programs: The Methodological Issues. In *Caldwell, B. J., ed.*, 1984, *1981*, pp. 438–59.

Caldwell, Bruce J. A Critique of Friedman's Methodological Instrumentalism. In *Caldwell, B. J., ed.*, 1984, *1980*, pp. 225–33.

Caldwell, Bruce J. Economic Methodology in the Postpositivist Era. In *Samuels, W. J., ed.*, 1984, pp. 195–205.

Caldwell, Bruce J. Praxeology and Its Critics: An Appraisal. *Hist. Polit. Econ.*, Fall 1984, *16*(3), pp. 363–79.

Caldwell, Bruce J. The Neoclassical Maximization Hypothesis: Comment. In *Caldwell, B. J., ed.*, 1984, *1983*, pp. 252–55.

Caldwell, Bruce J. and Coats, A. W. The Rhetoric of Economists: A Comment. *J. Econ. Lit.*, June 1984, *22*(2), pp. 575–78.

Carver, Terrell. Marxism as Method. In *Ball, T. and Farr, J., eds.*, 1984, pp. 261–79.

Clower, Robert W. Monetary History and Positive Economics. In *Clower, R. W.*, 1984, *1964*, pp. 59–77.

Coats, A. W. The Sociology of Knowledge and the History of Economics. In *Samuels, W. J., ed.*, 1984, pp. 211–34.

Cohen, Avi J. The Methodological Resolution of

the Cambridge Controversies. *J. Post Keynesian Econ.*, Summer 1984, *6*(4), pp. 614–29.

Coleman, James S. Introducing Social Structure into Economic Analysis. *Amer. Econ. Rev.*, May 1984, *74*(2), pp. 84–88.

Cross, Rod. Methodology in Economics [A Review Article]. *Scot. J. Polit. Econ.*, February 1984, *31*(1), pp. 100–110.

Cross, Rod. Monetarism and Duhem's Thesis: Reply to Comments. In *Wiles, P. and Routh, G., eds.*, 1984, pp. 111–20.

Cross, Rod. Monetarism and Duhem's Thesis. In *Wiles, P. and Routh, G., eds.*, 1984, pp. 78–99.

Cross, Rod. The Duhem-Quine Thesis, Lakatos and the Appraisal of Theories in Macroeconomics. In *Caldwell, B. J., ed.*, 1984, *1982*, pp. 284–304.

Culbertson, John M. The New Potential of Evolutionary–Institutional Economics. *J. Econ. Issues*, June 1984, *18*(2), pp. 611–18.

Dahmén, Erik. Schumpeterian Dynamics: Some Methodological Notes. *J. Econ. Behav. Organ.*, March 1984, *5*(1), pp. 25–34.

Debreu, Gerard. Economic Theory in the Mathematical Mode. *Amer. Econ. Rev.*, June 1984, *74*(3), pp. 267–78.

Debreu, Gerard. Economic Theory in the Mathematical Mode. *Scand. J. Econ.*, 1984, *86*(4), pp. 393–410.

Dos Santos Ferreira, Rodolphe. Analyse et dialectique dans la pensée marxienne (à propos de la loi de la baisse tendancielle du taux de profit). (With English summary.) *Écon. Soc.*, October 1984, *18*(10), pp. 95–128.

Dow, Sheila C. Methodology and the Analysis of a Monetary Economy. *Écon. Soc.*, April 1984, *18*(4), pp. 7–35.

Dow, Sheila C. Substantive Mountains and Methodological Molehills: A Rejoinder [Weintraub and Wiles: The Methodological Basis of Policy Conflict]. In *Caldwell, B. J., ed.*, 1984, *1982*, pp. 433–37.

Dow, Sheila C. and Earl, Peter E. Methodology and Orthodox Monetary Policy. *Écon. Appl.*, 1984, *37*(1), pp. 143–63. **[G: U.K.]**

Dugger, William M. Methodological Differences Between Institutional and Neoclassical Economics. In *Hausman, D. M., ed.*, 1984, *1979*, pp. 312–22.

Dugger, William M. Veblen and Kropotkin on Human Evolution. *J. Econ. Issues*, December 1984, *18*(4), pp. 971–85.

Elliott, John E. The Institutionalist School of Political Economy. In *Whynes, D. K., ed.*, 1984, pp. 59–89.

Endres, A. M. Institutional Elements in Carl Menger's Theory of Demand: A Comment [Carl Menger and *Homo Oeconomicus*: Some Thoughts on Austrian Theory and Methodology]. *J. Econ. Issues*, September 1984, *18*(3), pp. 897–902.

Farr, James. Marx and Positivism. In *Ball, T. and Farr, J., eds.*, 1984, pp. 217–34.

Frazer, William J., Jr. Methodology: Reply [An Essay on the Foundations of Friedman's Meth-odology]. *Amer. Econ. Rev.*, September 1984, *74*(4), pp. 793–94.

Friedman, Milton. The Methodology of Positive Economics. In *Caldwell, B. J., ed.*, 1984, *1953*, pp. 138–78.

Friedman, Milton. The Methodology of Positive Economics. In *Hausman, D. M., ed.*, 1984, *1953*, pp. 210–44.

Fulton, G. Research Programmes in Economics. *Hist. Polit. Econ.*, Summer 1984, *16*(2), pp. 187–205.

Gibson, Roland. Marx and Logic as Social Function. *Int. J. Soc. Econ.*, 1984, *11*(6), pp. 3–43.

Gilad, Benjamin; Kaish, Stanley and Loeb, Peter D. From Economic Behavior to Behavioral Economics: The Behavioral Uprising in Economics. *J. Behav. Econ.*, Summer 1984, *13*(1), pp. 1–22.

Gorman, Terence. Towards a Better Economic Methodology? In *Wiles, P. and Routh, G., eds.*, 1984, pp. 260–88.

Görün, Fikret. Iktisatta rasyonellik aksiyomunun yeri üzerine. (On the Rationality Axiom of Economics. With English summary.) *METU*, 1984, *11*(3–4), pp. 347–68.

Grafstein, Robert. Philosophical Issues in the Study of Historical Materialism. *Soc. Sci. Quart.*, December 1984, *65*(4), pp. 955–60.

Gruchy, Allan G. Neo-Institutionalism, Neo-Marxism, and Neo-Keynesianism: An Evaluation. *J. Econ. Issues*, June 1984, *18*(2), pp. 547–56.

Guthrie, William G. Methodological Diversity: Recognition, Responses, and Implications. In *Samuels, W. J., ed.*, 1984, pp. 141–49.

Guthrie, William G. Selective Rediscovery of Economic Ideas: What Keynes Found in Malthus. *Southern Econ. J.*, January 1984, *50*(3), pp. 771–80.

Hägerstrand, Torsten. Presence and Absence: A Look at Conceptual Choices and Bodily Necessities. *Reg. Stud.*, October 1984, *18*(5), pp. 373–79.

Hahn, Frank H. The Winter of our Discontent. In *Hahn, F.*, 1984, *1973*, pp. 134–44.

Hamlin, Alan P. Public Choice, Markets and Utilitarianism. In *Whynes, D. K., ed.*, 1984, pp. 116–38.

Hands, Douglas W. The Role of Crucial Counterexamples in the Growth of Economic Knowledge: Two Case Studies in the Recent History of Economic Thought. *Hist. Polit. Econ.*, Spring 1984, *16*(1), pp. 59–67.

Hargreaves-Heap, Shaun and Hollis, Martin. Bread and Circumstances: The Need for Political Economy. In *Whynes, D. K., ed.*, 1984, pp. 7–30.

Hart, Oliver. The Wider World and Economic Methodology: Comment. In *Wiles, P. and Routh, G., eds.*, 1984, pp. 47–50.

Hartropp, Andrew and Heathfield, David. Monetarism and Duhem's Thesis: Comment. In *Wiles, P. and Routh, G., eds.*, 1984, pp. 105–10.

Hausman, Daniel M. The Philosophy of Economics: Introduction. **In** *Hausman, D. M., ed.*, 1984, pp. 1–50.

von Hayek, Friedrich A. Competition as a Discovery Procedure. **In** *von Hayek, F. A. (I)*, 1984, *1969*, pp. 254–65.

von Hayek, Friedrich A. The Pretence of Knowledge. **In** *von Hayek, F. A. (I)*, 1984, *1975*, pp. 266–77.

Helm, Dieter. Predictions and Causes: A Comparison of Friedman and Hicks on Method. **In** *Collard, D. A., et al., eds.*, 1984, pp. 118–34.

Helm, Dieter. Predictions and Causes: A Comparison of Friedman and Hicks on Method. *Oxford Econ. Pap.*, Supplement November 1984, *36*, pp. 118–34.

Hicks, John R. 'Revolutions' in Economics. **In** *Hicks, J.*, 1984, *1976*, pp. 244–56.

Hicks, John R. The "New Causality": An Explanation. *Oxford Econ. Pap.*, March 1984, *36*(1), pp. 12–15.

Hicks, John R. Time in Economics. **In** *Hicks, J.*, 1984, *1976*, pp. 263–80.

Hill, Lewis E. and Owen, Donald W. The Instrumental Philosophy of Economic History and the Institutionalist Theory of Normative Value. *J. Econ. Issues*, June 1984, *18*(2), pp. 581–87.

Hirsch, Abraham and de Marchi, Neil. Methodology: A Comment on Frazer and Boland, I [An Essay on the Foundations of Friedman's Methodology]. *Amer. Econ. Rev.*, September 1984, *74*(4), pp. 782–88.

Hirschman, Albert O. Against Parsimony: Three Easy Ways of Complicating Some Categories of Economic Discourse. *Amer. Econ. Rev.*, May 1984, *74*(2), pp. 89–96.

Hollis, Martin. In Defence of Two Demons: Comment 1 [Our Methodological Crisis]. **In** *Wiles, P. and Routh, G., eds.*, 1984, pp. 22–29.

Hoover, Kevin D. Methodology: A Comment on Frazer and Boland, II [An Essay on the Foundations of Friedman's Methodology]. *Amer. Econ. Rev.*, September 1984, *74*(4), pp. 789–92.

Hunt, E. K. The Relation between Theory and History in the Writings of Karl Marx. *Atlantic Econ. J.*, December 1984, *12*(4), pp. 1–8.

Hunt, E. K. The Social Scientific Basis of Socialism. *Econ. Forum*, Summer 1984, *15*(1), pp. 9–16.

Hutchison, Terence W. Institutionalist Economics Old and New. *Z. ges. Staatswiss.*, March 1984, *140*(1), pp. 20–29.

Hutchison, Terence W. On Verification in Economics. **In** *Hausman, D. M., ed.*, 1984, *1956*, pp. 188–97.

Hutchison, Terence W. Our Methodological Crisis. **In** *Wiles, P. and Routh, G., eds.*, 1984, pp. 1–21.

Hutchison, Terence W. Positivism Enters Economic Methodology. **In** *Caldwell, B. J., ed.*, 1984, *1960*, pp. 3–94.

Hutchison, Terence W. Professor Machlup on Verification in Economics [The Problem of Verification in Economics]. **In** *Caldwell, B. J., ed.*, 1984, *1956*, pp. 118–25.

Klamer, Arjo. Levels of Discourse in New Classical Economics. *Hist. Polit. Econ.*, Summer 1984, *16*(2), pp. 263–90.

Klappholz, Kurt. Value Judgments and Economics. **In** *Hausman, D. M., ed.*, 1984, *1964*, pp. 276–92.

Knight, Frank. Economics and Human Action. **In** *Hausman, D. M., ed.*, 1984, *1935*, pp. 141–48.

Lallement, Jérôme. Histoire de la pensée ou archéologie du savoir? (With English summary.) *Écon. Soc.*, October 1984, *18*(10), pp. 61–93.

Leamer, Edward E. Let's Take the Con out of Econometrics. **In** *Caldwell, B. J., ed.*, 1984, *1983*, pp. 460–72. [G: U.S.]

Levy, David M. Towards a Neoaristotelean Theory of Politics: A Positive Account of 'Fairness.' *Public Choice*, 1984, *42*(1), pp. 39–54.

Loasby, Brian J. Hypothesis and Paradigm in the Theory of the Firm. **In** *Caldwell, B. J., ed.*, 1984, *1971*, pp. 261–83.

Loasby, Brian J. On Scientific Method. *J. Post Keynesian Econ.*, Spring 1984, *6*(3), pp. 394–410.

Machlup, Fritz. On Indirect Verification [Rejoiner to a Reluctant Ultra-Empiricist]. **In** *Hausman, D. M., ed.*, 1984, *1956*, pp. 198–209.

Machlup, Fritz. Professor Samuelson on Theory and Realism. **In** *Caldwell, B. J., ed.*, 1984, *1964*, pp. 194–97.

Machlup, Fritz. Rejoinder to a Reluctant Ultra-Empiricist [The Problem of Verification in Economics]. **In** *Caldwell, B. J., ed.*, 1984, *1956*, pp. 125–35.

Machlup, Fritz. The Southern Economic Journal: The Problem of Verification in Economics. **In** *Caldwell, B. J., ed.*, 1984, *1955*, pp. 97–117.

Maddock, Rodney. Rational Expectations Macrotheory: A Lakatosian Case Study in Program Adjustment. *Hist. Polit. Econ.*, Summer 1984, *16*(2), pp. 291–309.

Mäkinen, Vesa. Tulevaisuudentutkimusperspektiivi taloustieteissä. (Futurology and Economics. With English summary.) *Liiketaloudellinen Aikak.*, 1984, *33*(2), pp. 218–27.

Mattick, Paul, Jr. Marx and Idea of a Social Science. *Écon. Soc.*, July–August 1984, *18*(7–8), pp. 147–81.

Mattick, Paul, Jr. Théorie et réalité. (Theory and Reality. With English summary.) *Écon. Soc.*, July–August 1984, *18*(7–8), pp. 93–146.

McCloskey, Donald N. Reply [The Rhetoric of Economics]. *J. Econ. Lit.*, June 1984, *22*(2), pp. 579–80.

McCloskey, Donald N. The Rhetoric of Economics. **In** *Caldwell, B. J., ed.*, 1984, *1983*, pp. 320–56.

McCormick, Brian J. Monetarism and Duhem's Thesis: Comment. **In** *Wiles, P. and Routh, G., eds.*, 1984, pp. 100–104.

Morishima, Michio. Towards a Better Economic Methodology? A Reply. **In** *Wiles, P. and Routh, G., eds.*, 1984, pp. 74–77.

Musgrave, Alan. 'Unreal Assumptions' in Economic Theory: The F-Twist Untwisted. **In** *Caldwell, B. J., ed.*, 1984, *1981*, pp. 234–44.

Nagel, Ernest. Assumptions in Economic Theory. In *Caldwell, B. J., ed.*, 1984, *1963*, pp. 179–87.

Neild, Robert. The Wider World and Economic Methodology. In *Wiles, P. and Routh, G., eds.*, 1984, pp. 37–46.

Nell, Edward. Structure and Behavior in Classical and Neo-Classical Theory. *Eastern Econ. J.*, April-June 1984, *10*(2), pp. 139–55.

Paris, R. Mariátegui et Gramsci: quelques prolégomènes à une étude contrastive de la diffusion du marxisme. (Mariátegui and Gramsci. With English summary.) *Écon. Soc.*, July–August 1984, *18*(7–8), pp. 183–221.

Petr, Jerry L. Fundamentals of an Institutionalist Perspective on Economic Policy. *J. Econ. Issues*, March 1984, *18*(1), pp. 1–17.

Pfouts, Ralph W. Method and Applied Microeconomics. *Atlantic Econ. J.*, September 1984, *12*(3), pp. 16–19.

Quadrio Curzio, Alberto and Scazzieri, Roberto. Sui momenti costitutivi dell'economia politica. (On the Founding Principles of Political Economy. With English summary.) *Giorn. Econ.*, January–February 1984, *43*(1–2), pp. 37–76.

Rosenberg, Alexander. On the Interanimation of Micro and Macroeconomics. In *Hausman, D. M., ed.*, 1984, *1976*, pp. 324–43.

Samuels, Warren J. Comments on McCloskey on Methodology and Rhetoric. In *Samuels, W. J., ed.*, 1984, pp. 207–10.

Samuels, Warren J. Galbraith on Economics as a System of Professional Belief. *J. Post Keynesian Econ.*, Fall 1984, *7*(1), pp. 61–76.

Samuelson, Paul A. Realism of Assumptions and Descriptivism. In *Caldwell, B. J., ed.*, 1984, *1964*, pp. 188–93.

Samuelson, Paul A. Theory and Realism: A Reply [Professor Samuelson on Theory and Realism]. In *Caldwell, B. J., ed.*, 1984, *1964*, pp. 197–200.

Schrader, F. E. Marxens Abstraktionskritik: Differenzierung und Funktionswandel 1843–1858. (Marx's Critique of Abstraction. With English summary.) *Écon. Soc.*, July–August 1984, *18*(7–8), pp. 57–92.

Schumpeter, Joseph Alois. Science and Ideology. In *Hausman, D. M., ed.*, 1984, *1949*, pp. 260–75.

Schumpeter, Joseph Alois. The Meaning of Rationality in the Social Sciences. *Z. ges. Staatswiss.*, December 1984, *140*(4), pp. 577–93.

Sherman, Howard J. Contemporary Radical Economics. *J. Econ. Educ.*, Fall 1984, *15*(4), pp. 265–74.

Simon, Herbert A. Testability and Approximation [Problems of Methodology -- Discussion]. In *Hausman, D. M., ed.*, 1984, *1963*, pp. 245–48.

Smith, Steven B. Considerations in Marx's Base and Superstructure. *Soc. Sci. Quart.*, December 1984, *65*(4), pp. 940–54.

Smith, Steven B. Historical Materialism Reconsidered. *Soc. Sci. Quart.*, December 1984, *65*(4), pp. 961–65.

Smith, Vardaman R. Marx's Social Ontology, His Critical Method and Contemporary Social Economics. *Rev. Soc. Econ.*, October 1984, *42*(2), pp. 143–69.

Stewart, Ian M. T. Views of Economic Ignorance. In *Samuels, W. J., ed.*, 1984, pp. 161–72.

Sturgeon, James I. Induction and Instrumentalism in Institutional Thought. *J. Econ. Issues*, June 1984, *18*(2), pp. 599–609.

Sufrin, Sidney C. A Quadrant of Views. *Rivista Int. Sci. Econ. Com.*, April 1984, *31*(4), pp. 289–304.

Termini, Valeria. A Note on Hicks's 'Contemporaneous Causality.' *Cambridge J. Econ.*, March 1984, *8*(1), pp. 87–92.

Toumanoff, Peter G. A Positive Analysis of the Theory of Market Failure. *Kyklos*, 1984, *37*(4), pp. 529–41.

Ursel, Laurent. Impérialisme de la science économique et néo-libéralisme. (With English summary.) *Écon. Soc.*, October 1984, *18*(10), pp. 33–59.

Veblen, Thorstein. The Limitations of Marginal Utility. In *Hausman, D. M., ed.*, 1984, *1909*, pp. 173–86.

Weber, Max. Objectivity and Understanding in Economics. In *Hausman, D. M., ed.*, 1984, *1949*, pp. 99–112.

Wegehenkel, Lothar. Institutional Economics Old and New: Comment. *Z. ges. Staatswiss.*, March 1984, *140*(1), pp. 30–33.

Weintraub, E. Roy. Substantive Mountains and Methodological Molehills: Comment [Weintraub and Wiles: The Methodological Basis of Policy Conflict]. In *Caldwell, B. J., ed.*, 1984, *1982*, pp. 424–32.

von Weizsäcker, Carl Christian. Rights and Relations in Modern Economic Theory. *J. Econ. Behav. Organ.*, June 1984, *5*(2), pp. 133–57.

Whynes, David K. International Political Economy. In *Whynes, D. K., ed.*, 1984, pp. 162–86.

Whynes, David K. What Is Political Economy? Concluding Comments. In *Whynes, D. K., ed.*, 1984, pp. 209–16.

Wible, James R. The Instrumentalisms of Dewey and Friedman. *J. Econ. Issues*, December 1984, *18*(4), pp. 1049–70.

Wible, James R. Towards a Process Conception of Rationality in Economics and Science. *Rev. Soc. Econ.*, October 1984, *42*(2), pp. 89–104.

Wilber, Charles K. and Hoksbergen, Roland. Current Thinking on the Role of Value Judgments in Economic Science: A Survey. In *Samuels, W. J., ed.*, 1984, pp. 179–94.

Wiles, Peter. Economics in Disarray: Epilogue: The Role of Theory. In *Wiles, P. and Routh, G., eds.*, 1984, pp. 293–325.

Wiles, Peter. Towards a Better Economic Methodology? A Reply. In *Wiles, P. and Routh, G., eds.*, 1984, pp. 289–92.

Williams, Rhonda M. The Methodology and Practice of Modern Labor Economics: A Critique. In *Darity, W., Jr., ed.*, 1984, pp. 23–51.

Winrich, Joseph Steven. Self-reference and the Incomplete Structure of Neoclassical Economics. *J. Econ. Issues*, December 1984, *18*(4), pp. 987–1005.

Zellner, Arnold. Philosophy and Objectives of Econometrics. In *Zellner, A.*, 1984, *1981*, pp. 3–11.

040 ECONOMIC HISTORY

041 Economic History: General

0410 General

Adelman, Irma and Morris, Cynthia Taft. Patterns of Economic Growth, 1850–1914, or Chenery–Syrquin in Historical Perspective. In *[Chenery, H. B.]*, 1984, pp. 45–74.

Bernstein, Edward M. Reflections on Bretton Woods. In *Fed. Res. Bank Boston*, 1984, pp. 15–20.

Carlsson, Bo. The Development and Use of Machine Tools in Historical Perspective. *J. Econ. Behav. Organ.*, March 1984, *5*(1), pp. 91–114.

van Creveld, Martin. The Origins and Development of Mobilization Warfare. In *McCormick, G. H. and Bissell, R. E., eds.*, 1984, pp. 26–43.

Geary, Frank. The Cause of the Industrial Revolution and 'Single-Factor' Arguments: An Assessment. *J. Europ. Econ. Hist.*, Spring 1984, *13*(1), pp. 167–73.

Hara, Terushi. The Works of Japanese Business Historians in 1982: Business History of Foreign Countries. In *Nakagawa, K. and Morikawa, H., eds.*, 1984, pp. 160–70.

Maurer, John H. Economics, Strategy, and War in Historical Perspective. In *McCormick, G. H. and Bissell, R. E., eds.*, 1984, pp. 59–83.

McNeill, William H. Human Migration in Historical Perspective. *Population Devel. Rev.*, March 1984, *10*(1), pp. 1–18. [G: Global]

Mokyr, Joel. Disparities, Gaps, and Abysses: Review Article. *Econ. Develop. Cult. Change*, October 1984, *33*(1), pp. 173–77. [G: Global]

Parker, William N. Capitalistic Organization and National Response: Social Dynamics in the Age of Schumpeter. *J. Econ. Behav. Organ.*, March 1984, *5*(1), pp. 3–23. [G: U.S.; Germany; France; England]

Parker, William N. What Historians Must Explain. In *Parker, W. N.*, 1984, pp. 3–11.

Wightman, David. Paths to International Political Economy: Why Economic History? In *Strange, S., ed.*, 1984, pp. 23–32.

0411 Development of the Discipline

Fenoaltea, Stefano. Slavery and Supervision in Comparative Perspective: A Model. *J. Econ. Hist.*, September 1984, *44*(3), pp. 635–68. [G: U.S.; U.K.; Italy; Latin America]

Goldsmith, James L. The Agrarian History of Preindustrial France: Where Do We Go from Here? *J. Europ. Econ. Hist.*, Spring 1984, *13*(1), pp. 175–99. [G: France]

Gottlieb, Roger S. Feudalism and Historical Materialism: A Critique and a Synthesis. *Sci. Soc.*, Spring 1984, *48*(1), pp. 1–37. [G: U.S.]

Hannah, Leslie. Entrepreneurs and the Social Sciences. *Economica*, August 1984, *51*(203), pp. 219–34. [G: U.K.]

Hill, Lewis E. and Owen, Donald W. The Instrumental Philosophy of Economic History and the Institutionalist Theory of Normative Value. *J. Econ. Issues*, June 1984, *18*(2), pp. 581–87.

Hunt, E. K. The Relation between Theory and History in the Writings of Karl Marx. *Atlantic Econ. J.*, December 1984, *12*(4), pp. 1–8.

James, John A. The Use of General Equilibrium Analysis in Economic History. *Exploration Econ. Hist.*, July 1984, *21*(3), pp. 231–53. [G: U.S.]

Jones, F. Stuart. The New Economic History and the Industrial Revolution. *S. Afr. J. Econ.*, June 1984, *52*(2), pp. 113–32. [G: U.K.]

Miller, Harold. The American Bureau of Industrial Research and the Origins of the "Wisconsin School" of Labor History. *Labor Hist.*, Spring 1984, *25*(2), pp. 165–88.

North, Douglass C. Government and the Cost of Exchange in History. *J. Econ. Hist.*, June 1984, *44*(2), pp. 255–64.

North, Douglass C. Transaction Costs, Institutions, and Economic History. *Z. ges. Staatswiss.*, March 1984, *140*(1), pp. 7–17.

Pollard, Sidney. Transaction Costs, Institutions, and Economic History: Comment. *Z. ges. Staatswiss.*, March 1984, *140*(1), pp. 18–19.

Théré, Christine. Éléments d'une sociologie des auteurs économiques de langue française (1715–1776). (Material for a Social Study of Economic Authors [1715–1776]. With English summary.) *Écon. Soc.*, March 1984, *18*(3), pp. 11–33. [G: France]

0412 Comparative Intercountry or Intertemporal Economic History

Barro, Robert J. Some Evidence on the Real Price of Gold, Its Costs of Production, and Commodity Prices: Comment. In *Bordo, M. D. and Schwartz, A. J., eds.*, 1984, pp. 644–46. [G: U.S.; U.S.S.R.; S. Africa; Australia]

Baumol, William J. and Oates, Wallace E. Long-run Trends in Environmental Quality. In *Simon, J. L. and Kahn, H., eds.*, 1984, pp. 439–75. [G: U.S.; Selected Countries]

Ben-Shachar, Ari Y. Demand versus Supply in the Industrial Revolution: A Comment. *J. Econ. Hist.*, September 1984, *44*(3), pp. 801–05. [G: U.K.]

Bissell, Richard E. The Importance of the Economic Base to National Security. In *McCormick, G. H. and Bissell, R. E., eds.*, 1984, pp. 87–104. [G: OECD; U.S.S.R.]

Boserup, Ester. Demographic Pressure, Growth and Productivity in an Historical Perspective. In *Amin, S., ed.*, 1984, pp. 20–32. [G: OECD; U.S.S.R.; LDCs]

Chandler, Alfred D., Jr. The Emergence of Managerial Capitalism. *Bus. Hist. Rev.*, Winter 1984, *58*(4), pp. 473–503. [G: U.S.; U.K.; Germany; Japan]

Clark, Colin. Is There a Long Cycle? *Banca Naz.*

Lavoro Quart. Rev., September 1984, (150), pp. 307–20. [G: U.S.; U.K.; Japan; Sweden]

Coale, Ansley J. The Demographic Transition. *Pakistan Devel. Rev.*, Winter 1984, 23(4), pp. 531–52. [G: OECD; LDCs]

Connolly, Michael B. The Gold Standard and the Transmission of Business Cycles, 1833–1932: Comment. In Bordo, M. D. and Schwartz, A. J., eds., 1984, pp. 507–11. [G: U.S.; U.K.]

Crafts, N. F. R. Patterns of Development in Nineteenth Century Europe. *Oxford Econ. Pap.*, November 1984, 36(3), pp. 438–58. [G: Europe]

Díaz-Alejandro, Carlos F. No Less than One Hundred Years of Argentine Economic History Plus Some Comparisons. In [Reynolds, L. G.], 1984, pp. 328–61. [G: Argentina; Australia; Brazil]

Easton, Stephen T. Real Output and the Gold Standard Years, 1830–1913. In Bordo, M. D. and Schwartz, A. J., eds., 1984, pp. 513–38. [G: OECD]

Friedman, Milton. The Success of Purchasing Power Parity: Historical Evidence and Its Implications for Macroeconomics: Comment. In Bordo, M. D. and Schwartz, A. J., eds., 1984, pp. 157–62. [G: U.S.; U.K.; Canada]

Goldsmith, Raymond W. The Stability of the Ratio of Nonfinancial Debt to Income. *Banca Naz. Lavoro Quart. Rev.*, September 1984, (150), pp. 285–305.

von Hayek, Friedrich A. The Fate of the Gold Standard. In von Hayek, F. A. (II), 1984, 1932, pp. 118–35. [G: U.K.; U.S.]

Huffman, Wallace E. and Lothian, James R. The Gold Standard and the Transmission of Business Cycles, 1833–1932. In Bordo, M. D. and Schwartz, A. J., eds., 1984, pp. 455–507. [G: U.S.; U.K.]

Inoue, Tadakatsu. A Comparison of the Emergence of Multinational Manufacturing by U.S., European, and Japanese Firms. In Okochi, A. and Inoue, T., eds., 1984, pp. 3–20. [G: Europe; Japan; U.S.]

Kindleberger, Charles P. Financial Institutions and Economic Development: A Comparison of Great Britain and France in the Eighteenth and Nineteenth Centuries. *Exploration Econ. Hist.*, April 1984, 21(2), pp. 103–24. [G: U.K.; France]

Laaksonen, Seppo. Palkkojen kehitys ja palkkapoliittinen keskustelu 1900-luvulla. (Development of Wages and Salaries and Wage Policy Discussion in Finland in the 20th Century. With English summary.) *Kansant. Aikak.*, 1984, 80(1), pp. 34–65. [G: Finland]

Laibman, David. Modes of Production and Theories of Transition. *Sci. Soc.*, Fall 1984, 48(3), pp. 257–94.

Lipsey, Robert E. The Success of Purchasing Power Prity: Historical Evidence and Its Implications for Macroeconomics: Comment. In Bordo, M. D. and Schwartz, A. J., eds., 1984, pp. 151–56. [G: U.S.; U.K.; Canada]

Maddison, Angus. Origins and Impact of the Wel-

fare State, 1883–1983. *Banca Naz. Lavoro Quart. Rev.*, March 1984, (148), pp. 55–87. [G: Selected OECD]

McCloskey, Donald N. and Zecher, J. Richard. The Success of Purchasing Power Parity: Historical Evidence and Its Implications for Macroeconomics. In Bordo, M. D. and Schwartz, A. J., eds., 1984, pp. 121–50. [G: U.S.; U.K.; Canada]

Mokyr, Joel. Demand versus Supply in the Industrial Revolution: A Reply. *J. Econ. Hist.*, September 1984, 44(3), pp. 806–09. [G: U.K.]

Mowery, David C. Firm Structure, Government Policy, and the Organization of Industrial Research: Great Britain and the United States, 1900–1950. *Bus. Hist. Rev.*, Winter 1984, 58(4), pp. 504–31. [G: U.S.; U.K.]

Nakagawa, Keiichiro. A Comparison of the Emergence of Multinational Manufacturing by U.S., European, and Japanese Firms: Japanese Firms' Foreign Direct Investment in the U.S.: Comments. In Okochi, A. and Inoue, T., eds., 1984, pp. 61–63. [G: Europe; Japan; U.S.]

Rockoff, Hugh. Some Evidence on the Real Price of Gold, Its Costs of Production, and Commodity Prices. In Bordo, M. D. and Schwartz, A. J., eds., 1984, pp. 613–44. [G: U.S.; S. Africa; Australia; U.S.S.R.]

Rockoff, Hugh. Some Evidence on the Real Price of Gold, Its Costs of Production, and Commodity Prices: Reply. In Bordo, M. D. and Schwartz, A. J., eds., 1984, pp. 646–48. [G: U.S.; U.S.S.R.; S. Africa; Australia]

Streeten, Paul. Technology Gaps between Rich and Poor Countries. In Ghosh, P. K., ed., no. 3, 1984, 1972, pp. 7–26. [G: MDCs]

Sugiyama, Kazuo. Business Finance in Japanese Business History. In Nakagawa, K. and Morikawa, H., eds., 1984, pp. 24–46. [G: U.K.; U.S.; W. Germany; Japan]

Sylos-Labini, Paolo. The Theory of Prices in Oligopoly and the Theory of Growth. In Sylos-Labini, P., 1984, 1971, pp. 123–45. [G: U.K.; U.S.]

Wood, Geoffrey E. Real Output and the Gold Standard Years, 1830–1913: Comment. In Bordo, M. D. and Schwartz, A. J., eds., 1984, pp. 538–44. [G: OECD]

042 Economic History: United States and Canada

0420 General

Abbott, Carl. Planning for the Home Front in Seattle and Portland, 1940–45. In Lotchin, R. W., ed., 1984, pp. 163–89. [G: U.S.]

Ahlburg, Dennis A. and Schapiro, Morton Owen. The Social Cost of Economic Decline: Some Earlier Evidence. *J. Post Keynesian Econ.*, Winter 1983-84, 6(2), pp. 303–04. [G: U.S.]

Ashton, Patrick J. Urbanization and the Dynamics of Suburban Development under Capitalism. In Tabb, W. K. and Sawers, L., eds., 1984, pp. 54–81.

Barth, Gunther. Urbanization in the American West—A Review Article. *Bus. Hist. Rev.*, Summer 1984, *58*(2), pp. 263–67.   [G: U.S.]

Bordo, Michael D. The Gold Standard: Myths and Realities. In *Siegel, B. N., ed.*, 1984, pp. 197–237.   [G: U.K.; U.S.]

Cassese, Sabino. The Long Life of the Financial Institutions Set Up in the Thirties. *J. Europ. Econ. Hist.*, Special Issue 1984, *13*(2), pp. 273–94.   [G: OECD]

Clark, Truman A. Violations of the Gold Points, 1890–1908. *J. Polit. Econ.*, October 1984, *92*(5), pp. 791–823.   [G: U.S.; U.K.]

Condran, Gretchen A. An Evaluation of Estimates of Underenumeration in the Census and the Age Pattern of Mortality, Philadelphia, 1880. *Demography*, February 1984, *21*(1), pp. 53–69.   [G: U.S.]

Davidson, Alexander N. Richard D. Irwin. *J. Behav. Econ.*, Summer 1984, *13*(1), pp. 117–34.   [G: U.S.]

DeCanio, Stephen J. Expectations and Business Confidence during the Great Depression. In *Siegel, B. N., ed.*, 1984, pp. 157–75.
   [G: U.S.]

Denison, Edward F. Productivity Analysis Through Growth Accounting. In *Brief, A. P., ed.*, 1984, pp. 7–55.   [G: U.S.; OECD]

Douty, H. M. A Century of Wage Statistics: The BLS Contribution. *Mon. Lab. Rev.*, November 1984, *107*(11), pp. 16–28.   [G: U.S.]

Dutton, John M.; Thomas, Annie and Butler, John E. The History of Progress Functions as a Managerial Technology. *Bus. Hist. Rev.*, Summer 1984, *58*(2), pp. 204–33.   [G: U.S.]

Eichengreen, Barry. Mortgage Interest Rates in the Populist Era. *Amer. Econ. Rev.*, December 1984, *74*(5), pp. 995–1015.   [G: U.S.]

Field, Alexander James. A New Interpretation of the Onset of the Great Depression. *J. Econ. Hist.*, June 1984, *44*(2), pp. 489–98.
   [G: U.S.]

Field, Alexander James. Asset Exchanges and the Transactions Demand for Money, 1919–29. *Amer. Econ. Rev.*, March 1984, *74*(1), pp. 43–59.   [G: U.S.]

Field, James A., Jr. 1789–1820: All Œconomists, All Diplomats. In *Becker, W. H. and Wells, S. F., Jr., eds.*, 1984, pp. 1–54.   [G: U.S.]

Foster, John Bellamy. The Limits of U.S. Capitalism: Surplus Capacity and Capacity Surplus. In *Foster, J. B. and Szlajfer, H., eds.*, 1984, pp. 198–213.   [G: U.S.]

Gitelman, H. M. Management's Crisis of Confidence and the Origin of the National Industrial Conference Board, 1914–1916. *Bus. Hist. Rev.*, Summer 1984, *58*(2), pp. 153–77.
   [G: U.S.]

Gordon, David M. Capitalist Development and the History of American Cities. In *Tabb, W. K. and Sawers, L., eds.*, 1984, pp. 21–53.
   [G: U.S.]

Gordon, David M.; Weisskopf, Thomas E. and Bowles, Samuel. Long-term Growth and the Cyclical Restoration of Profitability. In *Good-*

win, R. M.; Krüger, M. and Vercelli, A., eds., 1984, pp. 86–102.   [G: U.S.]

Higgs, Robert. Accumulation of Property by Southern Blacks before World War I: Reply. *Amer. Econ. Rev.*, September 1984, *74*(4), pp. 777–81.   [G: U.S.]

Hopkins, George W. From Naval Pauper to Naval Power: The Development of Charleston's Metropolitan-Military Complex. In *Lotchin, R. W., ed.*, 1984, pp. 1–34.   [G: U.S.]

Hughes, Jonathan R. T. Stagnation without 'Flation: The 1930s Again. In *Siegel, B. N., ed.*, 1984, pp. 137–56.   [G: U.S.]

Johnson, David R. The Failed Experiment: Military Aviation and Urban Development in San Antonio, 1910–40. In *Lotchin, R. W., ed.*, 1984, pp. 89–108.   [G: U.S.]

Jones, Alice Hanson. Wealth and Growth of the Thirteen Colonies: Some Implications. *J. Econ. Hist.*, June 1984, *44*(2), pp. 239–54.
   [G: U.S.]

Kindleberger, Charles P. Banking and Industry between the Two Wars: An International Comparison. *J. Europ. Econ. Hist.*, Special Issue 1984, *13*(2), pp. 7–28.   [G: U.S.; Europe]

Kindleberger, Charles P. Origins of U.S. Direct Investment in France. In *Kindleberger, C. P.*, 1984, *1974*, pp. 118–54.   [G: France; U.S.]

Littlefield, Douglas R. The Potomac Company: A Misadventure in Financing an Early American Internal Improvement Project. *Bus. Hist. Rev.*, Winter 1984, *58*(4), pp. 562–85.
   [G: U.S.]

Mahoney, Thomas A. Growth Accounting and Productivity: Comments. In *Brief, A. P., ed.*, 1984, pp. 56–67.   [G: U.S.; OECD]

Margo, Robert A. Accumulation of Property by Southern Blacks before World War I: Comment and Further Evidence. *Amer. Econ. Rev.*, September 1984, *74*(4), pp. 768–76.
   [G: U.S.]

Markusen, Ann R. Class and Urban Social Expenditure: A Marxist Theory of Metropolitan Government. In *Tabb, W. K. and Sawers, L., eds.*, 1984, pp. 82–100.

Martin, Albro. Introductory Essay: Transportation and the Evolution of the American Economic Republic. *Bus. Hist. Rev.*, Spring 1984, *58*(1), pp. 1–13.   [G: U.S.]

McCraw, Thomas K. The Public and Private Spheres in Historical Perspective. In *Brooks, H.; Liebman, L. and Schelling, C. S., eds.*, 1984, pp. 31–60.   [G: U.S.]

McDonald, Terrence J. San Francisco: Socioeconomic Change, Political Culture, and Fiscal Politics, 1870–1906. In *McDonald, T. J. and Ward, S. K., eds.*, 1984, pp. 39–67.
   [G: U.S.]

Menchik, Paul L. Is the Family Wealth Squandered? A Test of the Merry-Widow Model. *J. Econ. Hist.*, September 1984, *44*(3), pp. 835–38.   [G: U.S.]

Minsky, Hyman P. Banking and Industry between the Two Wars: The United States. *J. Europ. Econ. Hist.*, Special Issue 1984, *13*(2), pp. 235–72.   [G: U.S.]

Modell, John. The Politics of Urban Fiscal Policy: Afterword. **In** *McDonald, T. J. and Ward, S. K., eds.,* 1984, pp. 161–74.

Monkkonen, Eric H. The Politics of Municipal Indebtedness and Default, 1850–1936. **In** *McDonald, T. J. and Ward, S. K., eds.,* 1984, pp. 125–59. [G: U.S.]

Mowery, David C. Firm Structure, Government Policy, and the Organization of Industrial Research: Great Britain and the United States, 1900–1950. *Bus. Hist. Rev.,* Winter 1984, *58*(4), pp. 504–31. [G: U.S.; U.K.]

Oshima, Harry T. The Growth of U.S. Factor Productivity: The Significance of New Technologies in the Early Decades of the Twentieth Century. *J. Econ. Hist.,* March 1984, *44*(1), pp. 161–70. [G: U.S.]

Owen, Wilfred. The Evolution of the Urban Infrastructure in the Nineteenth and Twentieth Centuries: Discussion. **In** *Hanson, R., ed.,* 1984, pp. 60–62. [G: U.S.]

Parker, William N. Capitalistic Organization and National Response: Social Dynamics in the Age of Schumpeter. *J. Econ. Behav. Organ.,* March 1984, *5*(1), pp. 3–23. [G: U.S.; Germany; France; England]

Parker, William N. The Response Mechanism in the Twentieth Century. **In** *Parker, W. N.,* 1984, *1984,* pp. 214–37.

Pletcher, David M. 1861–1898: Economic Growth and Diplomatic Adjustment. **In** *Becker, W. H. and Wells, S. F., Jr., eds.,* 1984, pp. 119–71. [G: U.S.]

Redish, Angela. Why Was Specie Scarce in Colonial Economies? An Analysis of the Canadian Currency, 1796–1830. *J. Econ. Hist.,* September 1984, *44*(3), pp. 713–28. [G: Canada]

Reynolds, Alan. Gold and Economic Boom: Five Case Studies, 1792–1926. **In** *Siegel, B. N., ed.,* 1984, pp. 249–68. [G: France; U.K.; U.S.]

Riefler, Roger F. Development of the U.S. Urban System: A Review Article. *J. Econ. Hist.,* March 1984, *44*(1), pp. 179–84. [G: U.S.]

Roberts, Russell D. A Positive Model of Private Charity and Public Transfers. *J. Polit. Econ.,* February 1984, *92*(1), pp. 136–48. [G: U.S.]

Sawers, Larry. The Political Economy of Urban Transportation: An Interpretive Essay. **In** *Tabb, W. K. and Sawers, L., eds.,* 1984, pp. 223–54. [G: U.S.]

Schurr, S. H. Energy, Economic Growth, and Human Welfare. **In** *Brookes, L. G. and Motamen, H., eds.,* 1984, *1978,* pp. 362–70. [G: U.S.]

Silver, Christopher. Norfolk and the Navy: The Evolution of City–Federal Relations, 1917–46. **In** *Lotchin, R. W., ed.,* 1984, pp. 109–33. [G: U.S.]

Stock, James H. Real Estate Mortgages, Foreclosures, and Midwestern Agrarian Unrest, 1865–1920. *J. Econ. Hist.,* March 1984, *44*(1), pp. 89–105. [G: U.S.]

Sylos-Labini, Paolo. Keynes's *General Theory* and the Great Depression. **In** *Sylos-Labini, P.,* 1984, pp. 227–43. [G: U.S.]

Sylos-Labini, Paolo. On the Concept of the Optimum Rate of Profit. **In** *Sylos-Labini, P.,* 1984, *1981,* pp. 211–25. [G: U.S.]

Tarr, Joel A. The Evolution of the Urban Infrastructure in the Nineteenth and Twentieth Centuries. **In** *Hanson, R., ed.,* 1984, pp. 4–60. [G: U.S.]

Tobier, Emanuel. Setting Municipal Priorities: The Setting: Population. **In** *Brecher, C. and Horton, R. D., eds.,* 1984, pp. 19–42. [G: U.S.]

Tolnay, Stewart E. and Guest, Avery M. American Family Building Strategies in 1900: Stopping or Spacing. *Demography,* February 1984, *21*(1), pp. 9–18. [G: U.S.]

Vaubel, Roland. International Debt, Bank Failures, and the Money Supply: The Thirties and the Eighties. *Cato J.,* Spring/Summer 1984, *4*(1), pp. 249–67. [G: U.S.]

Vinovskis, Maris A. Historical Perspectives on Rural Development and Human Fertility in Nineteenth-Century America. **In** *Schutjer, W. A. and Stokes, C. S., eds.,* 1984, pp. 77–96. [G: U.S.]

Ward, W. Peter and Ward, Patricia C. Infant Birth Weight and Nutrition in Industrializing Montreal. *Amer. Hist. Rev.,* April 1984, *89*(2), pp. 324–45. [G: Canada]

Waugh, Frederick V. The Marginal Utility of Money in the United States from 1917 to 1921 and from 1922 to 1932. **In** *Waugh, F. V.,* 1984, *1935,* pp. 3–26. [G: U.S.]

Weinberg, Edgar. BLS and the Economy: A Centennial Timetable. *Mon. Lab. Rev.,* November 1984, *107*(11), pp. 29–37. [G: U.S.]

White, Eugene Nelson. A Reinterpretation of the Banking Crisis of 1930. *J. Econ. Hist.,* March 1984, *44*(1), pp. 119–38. [G: U.S.]

White, Lawrence H. Bank Failures and Monetary Policy [International Debt, Bank Failures, and the Money Supply: The Thirties and the Eighties]. *Cato J.,* Spring/Summer 1984, *4*(1), pp. 269–74. [G: U.S.]

Wickins, Peter L. The Economics of Privateering: Capital Dispersal in the American War of Independence. *J. Europ. Econ. Hist.,* Fall 1984, *13*(2), pp. 375–95. [G: U.S.]

Wolman, Abel. The Evolution of the Urban Infrastructure in the Nineteenth and Twentieth Centuries: Discussion. **In** *Hanson, R., ed.,* 1984, pp. 62–64. [G: U.S.]

Yang, Donghyu. Notes on the Wealth Distribution of Farm Households in the United States, 1860: A New Look at Two Manuscript Census Samples. *Exploration Econ. Hist.,* January 1984, *21*(1), pp. 88–102. [G: U.S.]

0421 History of Product Prices and Markets

Armstrong, Christopher and Nelles, H. V. A Curious Capital Flow: Canadian Investment in Mexico, 1902–1910. *Bus. Hist. Rev.,* Summer 1984, *58*(2), pp. 178–203. [G: Canada; Mexico]

Aukrust, Odd. 1980-årenes okonomi sammenlignet med 1930-årenes—tallenes tale. (With English summary.) *Nationaløkon. Tidsskr.*, 1984, *122*(3), pp. 313–32.   [G: U.S.; W. Europe; Nordic Countries]

Bernstein, Michael A. and Wilentz, Sean. Marketing, Commerce, and Capitalism in Rural Massachusetts [The Market and Massachusetts Farmers, 1750–1855]. *J. Econ. Hist.*, March 1984, *44*(1), pp. 171–73.   [G: U.S.]

Bessler, David A. Additional Evidence on Money and Prices: U.S. Data, 1870–1913. *Exploration Econ. Hist.*, April 1984, *21*(2), pp. 125–32.   [G: U.S.]

Bils, Mark. Tariff Protection and Production in the Early U.S. Cotton Textile Industry. *J. Econ. Hist.*, December 1984, *44*(4), pp. 1033–45.   [G: U.S.]

Carlos, Ann M. Steel Rails versus Iron Rails: Evidence from Canada. *Exploration Econ. Hist.*, April 1984, *21*(2), pp. 169–75.   [G: Canada]

Caves, Richard E.; Fortunato, Michael and Ghemawat, Pankaj. The Decline of Dominant Firms, 1905–1929. *Quart. J. Econ.*, August 1984, *99*(3), pp. 523–46.   [G: U.S.]

Cohen, Avi J. Technological Change as Historical Process: The Case of the U.S. Pulp and Paper Industry, 1915–1940. *J. Econ. Hist.*, September 1984, *44*(3), pp. 775–99.   [G: U.S.]

Cuenca Esteban, Javier. Trends and Cycles in U.S. Trade with Spain and the Spanish Empire, 1790–1819. *J. Econ. Hist.*, June 1984, *44*(2), pp. 521–43.   [G: U.S.; Spain]

Doucet, Michael and Weaver, John. The North American Shelter Business, 1860–1920: A Study of a Canadian Real Estate and Property Management Agency. *Bus. Hist. Rev.*, Summer 1984, *58*(2), pp. 234–62.   [G: Canada]

Dow, Alexander. Finance and Foreign Control in Canadian Base Metal Mining, 1918–55 *Econ. Hist. Rev.*, 2nd Ser., February 1984, *37*(1), pp. 54–67.   [G: Canada]

Frieburger, William. War Prosperity and Hunger: The New York Food Riots of 1917. *Labor Hist.*, Spring 1984, *25*(2), pp. 217–39.   [G: U.S.]

Gilbert, Geoffrey. Maritime Enterprise in the New Republic: Investment in Baltimore Shipping, 1789–1793. *Bus. Hist. Rev.*, Spring 1984, *58*(1), pp. 14–29.   [G: U.S.]

Jones, Derek C. American Producer Cooperatives and Employee-Owned Firms: A Historical Perspective. In *Jackall, R. and Levin, H. M., eds.*, 1984, pp. 37–56.   [G: U.S.]

Lewis, Frank D. and Robinson, David R. The Timing of Railway Construction on the Canadian Prairies. *Can. J. Econ.*, May 1984, *17*(2), pp. 340–52.   [G: Canada]

Libecap, Gary D. and Wiggins, Steven N. Contractual Responses to the Common Pool: Prorationing of Crude Oil Production. *Amer. Econ. Rev.*, March 1984, *74*(1), pp. 87–98.   [G: U.S.]

MacDonald, Ronald. The Monetary Approach to the Exchange Rate and the 1920s' Experience with Floating Exchange Rates. *J. Econ. Stud.*, 1984, *11*(3), pp. 14–25.   [G: U.S.; U.K.; France]

Mongar, Tom. Monopoly Pricing and Stagnation. *Econ. Forum*, Summer 1984, *15*(1), pp. 63–87.   [G: U.S.]

Painter, David S. Oil and the Marshall Plan. *Bus. Hist. Rev.*, Autumn 1984, *58*(3), pp. 359–83.   [G: U.S.; W. Europe]

Perkins, Edwin J. Langdon Cheves and the Panic of 1819: A Reassessment. *J. Econ. Hist.*, June 1984, *44*(2), pp. 455–61.   [G: U.S.]

Rolnick, Arthur J. and Weber, Warren E. The Causes of Free Bank Failures: A Detailed Examination. *J. Monet. Econ.*, November 1984, *14*(3), pp. 267–91.   [G: U.S.]

Rothenberg, Winifred B. Markets, Values and Capitalism: A Discourse on Method [The Market and Massachusetts Farmers, 1750–1855]. *J. Econ. Hist.*, March 1984, *44*(1), pp. 174–78.   [G: U.S.]

Shughart, William F., II and Tollison, Robert D. The Random Character of Merger Activity. *Rand J. Econ.*, Winter 1984, *15*(4), pp. 500–509.   [G: U.S.]

Smith, Bruce D. Money and Inflation in Colonial Massachusetts. *Fed. Res. Bank Minn. Rev.*, Winter 1984, *8*(1), pp. 1–14.   [G: U.S.]

Sokoloff, Kenneth L. Was the Transition from the Artisanal Shop to the Nonmechanized Factory Associated with Gains in Efficiency? Evidence from the U.S. Manufacturing Censuses of 1820 and 1850. *Exploration Econ. Hist.*, October 1984, *21*(4), pp. 351–82.   [G: U.S.]

Sushka, Marie Elizabeth and Barrett, W. Brian. Banking Structure and the National Capital Market, 1869–1914. *J. Econ. Hist.*, June 1984, *44*(2), pp. 463–77.   [G: U.S.]

Usselman, Steven W. Air Brakes for Freight Trains: Technological Innovation in the American Railroad Industry, 1869–1900. *Bus. Hist. Rev.*, Spring 1984, *58*(1), pp. 30–50.   [G: U.S.]

Van Fenstermaker, J.; Filer, John E. and Herren, Robert Stanley. Money Statistics of New England, 1785–1837. *J. Econ. Hist.*, June 1984, *44*(2), pp. 441–53.   [G: U.S.]

Waugh, Frederick V. Factors Influencing the Price of New Jersey Potatoes on the New York Market. In *Waugh, F. V.*, 1984, *1923*, pp. 385–408.   [G: U.S.]

Waugh, Frederick V. Reserve Stocks of Farm Products. In *Waugh, F. V.*, 1984, *1967*, pp. 198–247.   [G: U.S.]

Waugh, Frederick V. and Ogren, Kenneth E. An Interpretation of Changes in Agricultural Marketing Costs. In *Waugh, F. V.*, 1984, *1961*, pp. 183–97.   [G: U.S.]

Williams, Jeffrey C. Fractional Reserve Banking in Grain. *J. Money, Credit, Banking*, Part 1 November 1984, *16*(4), pp. 488–96.   [G: U.S.]

Wright, Gavin. Rethinking the Postbellum Southern Political Economy: A Review Essay. *Bus. Hist. Rev.*, Autumn 1984, *58*(3), pp. 409–16. [G: U.S.]

0422 History of Factor Prices and Markets

Almaguer, Tomás. Racial Domination and Class Conflict in Capitalist Agriculture: The Oxnard Sugar Beet Workers' Strike of 1903. *Labor Hist.*, Summer 1984, *25*(3), pp. 325–50. [G: U.S.]

Alston, Lee J.; Datta, Samar K. and Nugent, Jeffrey B. Tenancy Choice in a Competitive Framework with Transactions Costs. *J. Polit. Econ.*, December 1984, *92*(6), pp. 1121–33. [G: U.S.]

Armstrong, Thomas F. The Transformation of Work: Turpentine Workers in Coastal Georgia, 1865–1901. *Labor Hist.*, Fall 1984, *25*(4), pp. 518–32. [G: U.S.]

Aukrust, Odd. 1980-årenes okonomi sammenlignet med 1930-årenes—tallenes tale. (With English summary.) *Nationaløkon. Tidsskr.*, 1984, *122*(3), pp. 313–32. [G: U.S.; W. Europe; Nordic Countries]

Baillie, Richard T. and Bailey, Ralph W. International Currency Speculation, Market Stability and Efficiency in the 1920s: A Time Series Approach. *J. Macroecon.*, Spring 1984, *6*(2), pp. 127–37. [G: Belgium; France; Netherlands; U.S.; Germany]

Beatty, Bess. Textile Labor in the North Carolina Piedmont: Mill Owner Images and Mill Worker Response, 1830–1900. *Labor Hist.*, Fall 1984, *25*(4), pp. 485–503. [G: U.S.]

Beechert, Ed. Labour Relations in the Hawaiian Sugar Industry, 1850–1937. In *Albert, B. and Graves, A., eds.*, 1984, pp. 281–92. [G: U.S.]

Berch, Bettina. 'The Sphinx in the Household': A New Look at the History of Household Workers. *Rev. Radical Polit. Econ.*, Spring 1984, *16*(1), pp. 105–20. [G: U.S.]

Bernstein, Michael A. A Reassessment of Investment Failure in the Interwar American Economy. *J. Econ. Hist.*, June 1984, *44*(2), pp. 479–88. [G: U.S.]

Biles, Roger. Ed Crump versus the Unions: The Labor Movement in Memphis during the 1930s. *Labor Hist.*, Fall 1984, *25*(4), pp. 533–52. [G: U.S.]

Boughton, James M. and Wicker, Elmus R. A Reply [The Behavior of the Currency–Deposit Ratio during the Great Depression]. *J. Money, Credit, Banking*, August 1984, *16*(3), pp. 366–67. [G: U.S.]

Bukowczyk, John J. The Transformation of Working-Class Ethnicity: Corporate Control, Americanization, and the Polish Immigrant Middle Class in Bayonne, New Jersey, 1915–1925. *Labor Hist.*, Winter 1984, *25*(1), pp. 53–82. [G: U.S.]

Clark, Gregory. Authority and Efficiency: The Labor Market and the Managerial Revolution of the Late Nineteenth Century. *J. Econ. Hist.*, December 1984, *44*(4), pp. 1069–83. [G: U.S.; U.K.]

Cohn, Raymond L. Mortality on Immigrant Voyages to New York, 1836–1853. *J. Econ. Hist.*, June 1984, *44*(2), pp. 289–300. [G: U.S.]

Davis, Kingsley. Wives and Work: The Sex Role Revolution and Its Consequences. *Population Devel. Rev.*, September 1984, *10*(3), pp. 397–417. [G: U.S.; U.K.; Sweden]

Dickman, Howard. Exclusive Representation and American Industrial Democracy: An Historical Reappraisal. *J. Lab. Res.*, Fall 1984, *5*(4), pp. 325–50. [G: U.S.]

Dublin, Thomas. The Merrimack Valley Textile Museum—An Appreciation. *Labor Hist.*, Spring 1984, *25*(2), pp. 240–42. [G: U.S.]

Eichengreen, Barry. Experience and the Male–Female Earnings Gap in the 1890s. *J. Econ. Hist.*, September 1984, *44*(3), pp. 822–34. [G: U.S.]

Ekirch, A. Roger. Great Britain's Secret Convict Trade to America, 1783–84. *Amer. Hist. Rev.*, December 1984, *89*(5), pp. 1285–91. [G: U.S.]

Fenoaltea, Stefano. Slavery and Supervision in Comparative Perspective: A Model. *J. Econ. Hist.*, September 1984, *44*(3), pp. 635–68. [G: U.S.; U.K.; Italy; Latin America]

Fishback, Price. Segregation in Job Hierarchies: West Virginia Coal Mining, 1906–1932. *J. Econ. Hist.*, September 1984, *44*(3), pp. 755–74. [G: U.S.]

Foster, James C. Western Miners and Silicosis: "The Scourge of the Underground Toiler," 1890–1943. *Ind. Lab. Relat. Rev.*, April 1984, *37*(3), pp. 371–85. [G: U.S.]

Fraser, Steve. From the "New Unionism" to the New Deal. *Labor Hist.*, Summer 1984, *25*(3), pp. 405–30. [G: U.S.]

Galenson, David W. The Rise and Fall of Indentured Servitude in the Americas: An Economic Analysis. *J. Econ. Hist.*, March 1984, *44*(1), pp. 1–26. [G: Caribbean; Latin America; U.S.]

Gilreath, James. Labor History Sources in the Library of Congress Rare Book and Special Collections Division. *Labor Hist.*, Spring 1984, *25*(2), pp. 243–51. [G: U.S.]

Gitelman, H. M. Being of Two Minds: American Employers Confront the Labor Problem, 1915–1919. *Labor Hist.*, Spring 1984, *25*(2), pp. 189–216. [G: U.S.]

Goldin, Claudia. The Historical Evolution of Female Earnings Functions and Occupations. *Exploration Econ. Hist.*, January 1984, *21*(1), pp. 1–27. [G: U.S.]

Goldin, Claudia and Sokoloff, Kenneth L. The Relative Productivity Hypothesis of Industrialization: The American Case, 1820 to 1850. *Quart. J. Econ.*, August 1984, *99*(3), pp. 461–87. [G: U.S.]

Hine, William C. Black Organized Labor in Reconstructed Charleston. *Labor Hist.*, Fall 1984, *25*(4), pp. 504–17. [G: U.S.]

Hunnicutt, Benjamin Kline. The End of Shorter Hours. *Labor Hist.*, Summer 1984, *25*(3), pp. 373–404. [G: U.S.]

Inoki, Takenori. Japanese Emigration to Hawaii and North America in 1890s. (In Japanese. With English summary.) *Osaka Econ. Pap.*, December 1984, *34*(2–3), pp. 239–47. [G: Japan; U.S.]

Jacobson, Cardell K. Internal Colonialism and Native Americans: Indian Labor in the United States from 1871 to World War II. *Soc. Sci. Quart.*, March 1984, *65*(1), pp. 158–71. [G: U.S.]

Jacoby, Sanford M. The Development of Internal Labor Markets in American Manufacturing Firms. In *Osterman, P., ed.*, 1984, pp. 23–69. [G: U.S.]

James, John A. The Use of General Equilibrium Analysis in Economic History. *Exploration Econ. Hist.*, July 1984, *21*(3), pp. 231–53. [G: U.S.]

Jones, Derek C. American Producer Cooperatives and Employee-Owned Firms: A Historical Perspective. In *Jackall, R. and Levin, H. M., eds.*, 1984, pp. 37–56. [G: U.S.]

Kau, James B. and Sirmans, C. F. Changes in Urban Land Values: 1836–1970. *J. Urban Econ.*, January 1984, *15*(1), pp. 18–25. [G: U.S.]

Kearl, James R. and Pope, Clayne L. Mobility and Distribution. *Rev. Econ. Statist.*, May 1984, *66*(2), pp. 192–99. [G: U.S.]

Lane, A. T. American Trade Unions, Mass Immigration and the Literacy Test: 1900–1917. *Labor Hist.*, Winter 1984, *25*(1), pp. 5–25. [G: U.S.]

Levine, Bruce C. Immigrant Workers, "Equal Rights," and Anti-Slavery: The Germans of Newark, New Jersey. *Labor Hist.*, Winter 1984, *25*(1), pp. 26–52. [G: U.S.]

Magdoff, Harry. A Note on Inflation. In *Foster, J. B. and Szlajfer, H., eds.*, 1984, 1973, pp. 118–23. [G: U.S.]

Margo, Robert A. "Teacher Salaries in Black and White": The South in 1910. *Exploration Econ. Hist.*, July 1984, *21*(3), pp. 306–26. [G: U.S.]

May, Martha. The "Good Managers": Married Working Class Women and Family Budget Studies, 1895–1915. *Labor Hist.*, Summer 1984, *25*(3), pp. 351–72. [G: U.S.]

McHugh, Cathy L. Earning in the Post-Bellum Southern Cotton Textile Industry: A Case Study. *Exploration Econ. Hist.*, January 1984, *21*(1), pp. 28–39. [G: U.S.]

McKay, R. Reynolds. The Impact of the Great Depression on Immigrant Mexican Labor: Repatriation of the Bridgeport, Texas, Coal Miners. *Soc. Sci. Quart.*, June 1984, *65*(2), pp. 354–63. [G: U.S.; Mexico]

Miller, Harold. The American Bureau of Industrial Research and the Origins of the "Wisconsin School" of Labor History. *Labor Hist.*, Spring 1984, *25*(2), pp. 165–88.

Murayama, Yuzo. Contractors, Collusion, and Competition: Japanese Immigrant Railroad Laborers in the Pacific Northwest, 1898–1911. *Exploration Econ. Hist.*, July 1984, *21*(3), pp. 290–305. [G: Japan; U.S.]

Nemirow, Martin. Short-Time Compensation: Some Policy Considerations. In *MaCoy, R. and Morand, M. J., eds.*, 1984, pp. 158–82. [G: U.S.; W. Germany]

Neumann, George R. and Rissman, Ellen R. Where Have All the Union Members Gone? *J. Lab. Econ.*, April 1984, *2*(2), pp. 175–92. [G: U.S.]

Nolan, Peter and Edwards, P. K. Homogenise, Divide and Rule: An Essay on *Segmented Work, Divided Workers*: Review Article. *Cambridge J. Econ.*, June 1984, *8*(2), pp. 197–215. [G: U.S.]

Norton, Mary Beth. The Evolution of White Women's Experience in Early America. *Amer. Hist. Rev.*, June 1984, *89*(3), pp. 593–619. [G: U.S.]

Oestreicher, Richard. A Note on Knights of Labor Membership Statistics. *Labor Hist.*, Winter 1984, *25*(1), pp. 102–08. [G: U.S.]

Pencavel, John H. and Hartsog, Catherine E. A Reconsideration of the Effects of Unionism on Relative Wages and Employment in the United States, 1920–1980. *J. Lab. Econ.*, April 1984, *2*(2), pp. 193–232. [G: U.S.]

Perlman, Mark. Collective Bargaining and Industrial Relations: The Past, the Present, and the Future. In *Fellner, W., ed.*, 1984, pp. 287–322. [G: U.S.]

Roth, Alvin E. The Evolution of the Labor Market for Medical Interns and Residents: A Case Study in Game Theory. *J. Polit. Econ.*, December 1984, *92*(6), pp. 991–1016. [G: U.S.]

Shapiro, Herbert. The Impact of the Aptheker Thesis: A Retrospective View of *American Negro Slave Revolts*. *Sci. Soc.*, Spring 1984, *48*(1), pp. 52–73. [G: U.S.]

Skeels, Jack W. Determinants of Strikes: Reply [The Economic and Organizational Basis of Early United States Strikes, 1900–1948]. *Ind. Lab. Relat. Rev.*, January 1984, *37*(2), pp. 272–75. [G: U.S.]

Smith, James P. Race and Human Capital. *Amer. Econ. Rev.*, September 1984, *74*(4), pp. 685–98. [G: U.S.]

Sokoloff, Kenneth L. Investment in Fixed and Working Capital during Early Industrialization: Evidence from U.S. Manufacturing Firms. *J. Econ. Hist.*, June 1984, *44*(2), pp. 545–56. [G: U.S.]

Soltow, Lee. Wealth Inequality in the United States in 1798 and 1860. *Rev. Econ. Statist.*, August 1984, *66*(3), pp. 444–51. [G: U.S.]

Trescott, Paul B. The Behavior of the Currency–Deposit Ratio during the Great Depression: A Comment. *J. Money, Credit, Banking*, August 1984, *16*(3), pp. 362–65. [G: U.S.]

Turbin, Carole. Reconceptualizing Family, Work, and Labor Organizing: Working Women in Troy, 1860–1890. *Rev. Radical Polit. Econ.*, Spring 1984, *16*(1), pp. 1–16. [G: U.S.]

Woolf, Arthur G. Electricity, Productivity, and Labor Saving: American Manufacturing, 1900–1929. *Exploration Econ. Hist.*, April 1984, 21(2), pp. 176–91.   [G: U.S.]

0423 History of Public Economic Policy, all levels

Alston, Lee J. Farm Foreclosure Moratorium Legislation: A Lesson from the Past. *Amer. Econ. Rev.*, June 1984, 74(3), pp. 445–57.   [G: U.S.]

Alston, Lee J. and Schapiro, Morton Owen. Inheritance Laws across Colonies: Causes and Consequences. *J. Econ. Hist.*, June 1984, 44(2), pp. 277–87.   [G: U.S.]

Becker, William H. 1899–1920: America Adjusts to World Power. In *Becker, W. H. and Wells, S. F., Jr., eds.*, 1984, pp. 173–223. [G: U.S.]

Benjamin, Robert L. Cook. From Waterways to Waterfronts: Public Investment for Cities, 1815–1980. In *Bingham, R. D. and Blair, J. P., eds.*, 1984, pp. 23–45.   [G: U.S.]

Bennett, James T. and DiLorenzo, Thomas J. Political Entrepreneurship and Reform of the Rent-Seeking Society. In *Colander, D. C., ed.*, 1984, pp. 217–27.   [G: U.S.]

Bernstein, Michael A. A Reassessment of Investment Failure in the Interwar American Economy. *J. Econ. Hist.*, June 1984, 44(2), pp. 479–88.   [G: U.S.]

Brauer, Kinley J. 1821–1860: Economics and the Diplomacy of American Expansionism. In *Becker, W. H. and Wells, S. F., Jr., eds.*, 1984, pp. 55–118.   [G: U.S.]

Brown, M. Craig and Halaby, Charles N. Bosses, Reform, and the Socioeconomic Bases of Urban Expenditure, 1890–1940. In *McDonald, T. J. and Ward, S. K., eds.*, 1984, pp. 69–99.   [G: U.S.]

Clements, Kendrick A. Herbert Hoover and Conservation, 1921–33. *Amer. Hist. Rev.*, February 1984, 89(1), pp. 67–88.   [G: U.S.]

Dowdle, Barney. Why Have We Retained the Federal Lands? An Alternative Hypothesis. In *Brubaker, S., ed.*, 1984, pp. 61–73.   [G: U.S.]

Dugger, William M. The Nature of Capital Accumulation and Technological Progress in the Modern Economy. *J. Econ. Issues*, September 1984, 18(3), pp. 799–823.   [G: U.S.]

Epstein, Gerald and Ferguson, Thomas. Monetary Policy, Loan Liquidation, and Industrial Conflict: The Federal Reserve and the Open Market Operations of 1932. *J. Econ. Hist.*, December 1984, 44(4), pp. 957–83.   [G: U.S.]

Fairbanks, Robert B. and Miller, Zane L. The Martial Metropolis: Housing, Planning, and Race in Cincinnati, 1940–55. In *Lotchin, R. W., ed.*, 1984, pp. 191–222.   [G: U.S.]

Freedman, Charles. Canada and the Interwar Gold Standard, 1920–35: Monetary Policy without a Central Bank: Comment. In *Bordo, M. D. and Schwartz, A. J., eds.*, 1984, pp. 303–08.   [G: U.S.; Canada]

Friedman, Milton. Monetary Policy for the 1980s. In *Moore, J. H., ed.*, 1984, pp. 23–60.   [G: U.S.]

Galbraith, John Kenneth. Keynes, Roosevelt, and the Complementary Revolutions. *Challenge*, January/February 1984, 26(6), pp. 4–8.   [G: U.S.]

Gates, Paul W. The Federal Lands: Why We Retained Them. In *Brubaker, S., ed.*, 1984, pp. 35–60.   [G: U.S.]

Geisler, Charles C. A History of Land Reform in the United States: Old Wine, New Battles. In *Geisler, C. C. and Popper, F. J., eds.*, 1984, pp. 7–31.   [G: U.S.]

Geisler, Charles C. and Popper, Frank J. Land Reform, American Style: Introduction. In *Geisler, C. C. and Popper, F. J., eds.*, 1984, pp. 3–6.

Hannon, Joan Underhill. Poverty in the Antebellum Northeast: The View from New York State's Poor Relief Rolls. *J. Econ. Hist.*, December 1984, 44(4), pp. 1007–32.   [G: U.S.]

Hannon, Joan Underhill. The Generosity of Antebellum Poor Relief. *J. Econ. Hist.*, September 1984, 44(3), pp. 810–21.   [G: U.S.]

Hathaway, Robert M. 1933–1945: Economic Diplomacy in a Time of Crisis. In *Becker, W. H. and Wells, S. F., Jr., eds.*, 1984, pp. 277–331.   [G: U.S.]

Hornig, Donald F. The Role of Government in Scientific Innovation. In *Coles, J. S., ed.*, 1984, pp. 30–55.   [G: U.S.]

Hunnicutt, Benjamin Kline. The End of Shorter Hours. *Labor Hist.*, Summer 1984, 25(3), pp. 373–404.   [G: U.S.]

Hurst, J. Willard. Public Power and Market Power. In *Sherman, M., ed.*, 1984, pp. 23–37.   [G: U.S.]

James, John A. Public Debt Management Policy and Nineteenth-Century American Economic Growth. *Exploration Econ. Hist.*, April 1984, 21(2), pp. 192–217.   [G: U.S.]

Jones, Derek C. and Schneider, Donald J. Self-Help Production Cooperatives: Government-Administered Cooperatives during the Depression. In *Jackall, R. and Levin, H. M., eds.*, 1984, pp. 57–84.   [G: U.S.]

Kagin, Donald H. Monetary Aspects of the Treasury Notes of the War of 1812. *J. Econ. Hist.*, March 1984, 44(1), pp. 69–88.   [G: U.S.]

Keller, Robert R. A Macroeconomic History of Supply-Side Fiscal Policies in the 1920s. *Rev. Soc. Econ.*, October 1984, 42(2), pp. 130–42.   [G: U.S.]

Keran, Michael W. Velocity and Inflation Expectations: 1922–1983. *Fed. Res. Bank San Francisco Econ. Rev.*, Summer 1984, (3), pp. 40–55.   [G: U.S.]

La Croix, Sumner J. and Roumasset, James. An Economic Theory of Political Change in Premissionary Hawaii. *Exploration Econ. Hist.*, April 1984, 21(2), pp. 151–68.   [G: U.S.]

Lee, David D. Herbert Hoover and the Development of Commercial Aviation, 1921–1926. *Bus. Hist. Rev.*, Spring 1984, *58*(1), pp. 78–102. **[G: U.S.]**

Leffler, Melvyn P. 1921–1932: Expansionist Impulses and Domestic Constraints. In *Becker, W. H. and Wells, S. F., Jr., eds.*, 1984, pp. 225–75. **[G: U.S.]**

Leshy, John D. Sharing Federal Multiple-Use Lands: Historic Lessons and Speculations for the Future. In *Brubaker, S., ed.*, 1984, pp. 235–73. **[G: U.S.]**

Libecap, Gary D. The Political Allocation of Mineral Rights: A Re-Evaluation of Teapot Dome. *J. Econ. Hist.*, June 1984, *44*(2), pp. 381–91. **[G: U.S.]**

Lux, Guillermo. Ancient Aspirations: A Mexican-American View of Land Reform. In *Geisler, C. C. and Popper, F. J., eds.*, 1984, pp. 188–205. **[G: U.S.]**

McCarthy, F. Ward, Jr. The Evolution of the Bank Regulatory Structure: A Reappraisal. *Fed. Res. Bank Richmond Econ. Rev.*, Mar./Apr. 1984, *70*(2), pp. 3–21. **[G: U.S.]**

McCracken, Paul W. Has Macro-Theory Failed Economic Policy? *Southern Econ. J.*, October 1984, *51*(2), pp. 319–29. **[G: U.S.]**

McDougall, Harold A. Land Reform and the Struggle for Black Liberation: From Reconstruction to Remote Claims. In *Geisler, C. C. and Popper, F. J., eds.*, 1984, pp. 172–87. **[G: U.S.]**

McDowall, David and Loftin, Colin. Conflict, Crime, and Budgetary Constraint: Police Strength in Detroit, 1927–1976. In *McDonald, T. J. and Ward, S. K., eds.*, 1984, pp. 101–24. **[G: U.S.]**

McGuire, Robert A. and Ohsfeldt, Robert L. Economic Interests and the American Constitution: A Quantitative Rehabilitation of Charles A. Beard. *J. Econ. Hist.*, June 1984, *44*(2), pp. 509–19. **[G: U.S.]**

Merkel, Philip L. The Origins of an Expanded Federal Court Jurisdiction: Railroad Development and the Ascendancy of the Federal Judiciary. *Bus. Hist. Rev.*, Autumn 1984, *58*(3), pp. 336–58. **[G: U.S.]**

Mitch, David. Underinvestment in Literacy? The Potential Contribution of Government Involvement in Elementary Education to Economic Growth in Nineteenth-Century England. *J. Econ. Hist.*, June 1984, *44*(2), pp. 557–66. **[G: U.K.]**

Montias, John Michael. Public Support for the Performing Arts in Western Europe and the United States: History and Analysis. In *[Reynolds, L. G.]*, 1984, pp. 409–44. **[G: U.S.; W. Europe]**

Ortiz, Roxanne Dunbar. Land Reform and Indian Survival in the United States. In *Geisler, C. C. and Popper, F. J., eds.*, 1984, pp. 151–71. **[G: U.S.]**

Painter, David S. Oil and the Marshall Plan. *Bus. Hist. Rev.*, Autumn 1984, *58*(3), pp. 359–83. **[G: U.S.; W. Europe]**

Peden, G. C. The "Treasury View" on Public Works and Employment in the Interwar Pe-

riod. *Econ. Hist. Rev., 2nd Ser.*, May 1984, *37*(2), pp. 167–81. **[G: U.S.]**

Perkins, Edwin J. Langdon Cheves and the Panic of 1819: A Reassessment. *J. Econ. Hist.*, June 1984, *44*(2), pp. 455–61. **[G: U.S.]**

Racette, Daniel and Bergeron, Pierre. La Grande dépression américaine et la neutralité de la monnaie: un test économétrique. (U.S. Great Depression and the Neutrality Hypothesis: An Econometric Test. With English summary.) *L'Actual. Econ.*, September 1984, *60*(3), pp. 280–307. **[G: U.S.]**

Renaghan, Thomas M. Distributional Effects of Federal Tax Policy 1929–1939. *Exploration Econ. Hist.*, January 1984, *21*(1), pp. 40–63. **[G: U.S.]**

Rich, Georg. Canada without a Central Bank: Operation of the Price-Specie-Flow Mechanism, 1872–1913. In *Bordo, M. D. and Schwartz, A. J., eds.*, 1984, pp. 547–75. **[G: Canada]**

Roistacher, Elizabeth and Tobier, Emanuel. Setting Municipal Priorities: Service Delivery: Housing Policy. In *Brecher, C. and Horton, R. D., eds.*, 1984, pp. 446–81. **[G: U.S.]**

Rosner, David and Markowitz, Gerald. Safety and Health on the Job as a Class Issue: The Workers' Health Bureau of America in the 1920s. *Sci. Soc.*, Winter 1984-1985, *48*(4), pp. 464–82. **[G: U.S.]**

Rothbard, Murray N. The Federal Reserve as a Cartelization Device: The Early Years, 1913–1930. In *Siegel, B. N., ed.*, 1984, pp. 89–136. **[G: U.S.]**

Seely, Bruce E. Engineers and Government–Business Cooperation: Highway Standards and the Bureau of Public Roads, 1900–1940. *Bus. Hist. Rev.*, Spring 1984, *58*(1), pp. 51–77. **[G: U.S.]**

Shearer, Ronald A. and Clark, Carolyn. Canada and the Interwar Gold Standard, 1920–35: Monetary Policy without a Central Bank. In *Bordo, M. D. and Schwartz, A. J., eds.*, 1984, pp. 277–302. **[G: U.S.; Canada]**

Silcox, Clark R. Unfair Methods of Competition: The Courts Revive Proof of Injury to Competition in Antitrust Cases under Section 5 of the FTC Act. *Antitrust Bull.*, Fall 1984, *29*(3), pp. 423–74. **[G: U.S.]**

Temin, Peter. Canada without a Central Bank: Operation of the Price-Specie-Flow Mechanism, 1872–1913: Comment. In *Bordo, M. D. and Schwartz, A. J., eds.*, 1984, pp. 576–81. **[G: Canada]**

Timberlake, Richard H., Jr. The Central Banking Role of Clearinghouse Associations. *J. Money, Credit, Banking*, February 1984, *16*(1), pp. 1–15. **[G: U.S.]**

Wallis, John Joseph. The Birth of the Old Federalism: Financing the New Deal, 1932–1940. *J. Econ. Hist.*, March 1984, *44*(1), pp. 139–59. **[G: U.S.]**

Wander, W. Thomas. The Politics of Congressional Budget Reform. In *Wander, W. T.; Hebert, F. T. and Copeland, G. W., eds.*, 1984, pp. 3–30. **[G: U.S.]**

Williamson, John B. Old Age Relief Policy Prior

to 1900: The Trend Toward Restrictiveness. *Amer. J. Econ. Soc.*, July 1984, *43*(3), pp. 369–84. [G: U.S.]

043 Economic History: Ancient and Medieval (until 1453)

0430 General

Gissel, Svend. Village and Environment. Case: Danish Isles in the Later Middle Ages. In *Guarducci, A., ed.*, 1984, pp. 297–310. [G: Scandinavia]

Gottlieb, Roger S. Feudalism and Historical Materialism: A Critique and a Synthesis. *Sci. Soc.*, Spring 1984, *48*(1), pp. 1–37. [G: U.S.]

McNeill, William H. Human Migration in Historical Perspective. *Population Devel. Rev.*, March 1984, *10*(1), pp. 1–18. [G: Global]

Witney, K. P. The Economic Position of Husbandmen at the time of Domesday Book: A Kentish Perspective. *Econ. Hist. Rev.*, *2nd Ser.*, February 1984, *37*(1), pp. 23–34. [G: U.K.]

0431 History of Product Prices and Markets

Goldsmith, Raymond W. An Estimate of the Size and Structure of the National Product of the Early Roman Empire. *Rev. Income Wealth*, September 1984, *30*(3), pp. 263–88. [G: Italy]

Kamiki, Tetsuo. Transportation of Goods on the Inland Sea of Japan in the Middle of the Fifteenth Century. *Kobe Univ. Econ.*, 1984, (30), pp. 33–45. [G: Japan]

McCloskey, Donald N. and Nash, John. Corn at Interest: The Extent and Cost of Grain Storage in Medieval England. *Amer. Econ. Rev.*, March 1984, *74*(1), pp. 174–87. [G: U.K.]

Pryor, J. H. Commenda: The Operation of the Contract in Long Distance Commerce at Marseilles during the Thirteenth Century. *J. Europ. Econ. Hist.*, Fall 1984, *13*(2), pp. 397–440. [G: France]

0432 History of Factor Prices and Markets

Boswell, John Eastburn. *Expositio* and *Oblatio*: The Abandonment of Children and the Ancient and Medieval Family. *Amer. Hist. Rev.*, February 1984, *89*(1), pp. 10–33.

Kamiki, Tetsuo. Transportation of Goods on the Inland Sea of Japan in the Middle of the Fifteenth Century. *Kobe Univ. Econ.*, 1984, (30), pp. 33–45. [G: Japan]

044 Economic History: Europe

0440 General

Anderson, Otto. The Decline in Danish Mortality before 1850 and Its Economic and Social Background. In *Bengtsson, T.; Fridlizius, G. and Ohlsson, R., eds.*, 1984, pp. 115–26. [G: Denmark]

Ben-Shachar, Ari Y. Demand versus Supply in the Industrial Revolution: A Comment. *J. Econ. Hist.*, September 1984, *44*(3), pp. 801–05. [G: U.K.]

Bengtsson, Tommy. Harvest Fluctuations and Demographic Response: Southern Sweden 1751–1859. In *Bengtsson, T.; Fridlizius, G. and Ohlsson, R., eds.*, 1984, pp. 329–55. [G: Sweden]

Benjamin, Daniel K. and Kochin, Levis A. War, Prices, and Interest Rates: A Martial Solution to Gibson's Paradox. In *Bordo, M. D. and Schwartz, A. J., eds.*, 1984, pp. 587–604. [G: U.K.]

Berend, Ivan T. Balkan Economic Development. *Econ. Hist. Rev.*, *2nd Ser.*, May 1984, *37*(2), pp. 268–73. [G: Balkans]

Bordo, Michael D. The Gold Standard: Myths and Realities. In *Siegel, B. N., ed.*, 1984, pp. 197–237. [G: U.K.; U.S.]

Bouvier, Jean. The French Banks, Inflation and the Economic Crisis, 1919–1939. *J. Europ. Econ. Hist.*, Special Issue 1984, *13*(2), pp. 29–80. [G: France]

Breen, Richard. Population Trends in Late Nineteenth and Early Twentieth Century Ireland: A Local Study. *Econ. Soc. Rev.*, January 1984, *15*(2), pp. 95–108. [G: Ireland]

Bridbury, A. R. Late Medieval Urban Prosperity: A Rejoinder [English Provincial Towns in the Later Middle Ages]. *Econ. Hist. Rev.*, *2nd Ser.*, November 1984, *37*(4), pp. 555–56. [G: U.K.]

Broadberry, S. N. The North European Depression of the 1920s. *Scand. Econ. Hist. Rev.*, 1984, *32*(3), pp. 159–67. [G: U.S.; Sweden; Norway; Denmark]

Cagan, Phillip. War, Prices, and Interest Rates: A Martial Solution to Gibson's Paradox: Comment. In *Bordo, M. D. and Schwartz, A. J., eds.*, 1984, pp. 604–10. [G: U.K.]

Caroselli, M. R. Aspects of the Economic History of the Roman "Campagna" in the Modern and Contemporary World. *J. Europ. Econ. Hist.*, September–December 1984, *13*(3), pp. 591–98. [G: Italy]

Cassese, Sabino. The Long Life of the Financial Institutions Set Up in the Thirties. *J. Europ. Econ. Hist.*, Special Issue 1984, *13*(2), pp. 273–94. [G: OECD]

Ciocca, Pierluigi and Toniolo, Gianni. Industry and Finance in Italy, 1918–1940. *J. Europ. Econ. Hist.*, Special Issue 1984, *13*(2), pp. 113–36. [G: Italy]

Clark, Truman A. Violations of the Gold Points, 1890–1908. *J. Polit. Econ.*, October 1984, *92*(5), pp. 791–823. [G: U.S.; U.K.]

Claydon, Tim; Liebenau, Jonathan and Ville, Simon. List of Publications on the Economic and Social History of Great Britain and Ireland: Published in 1983. *Econ. Hist. Rev.*, *2nd Ser.*, November 1984, *37*(4), pp. 563–608. [G: U.K.; Ireland]

Corsini, Carlo A. Structural Changes in Infant Mortality in Tuscany from the 18th to the 19th

Century. In *Bengtsson, T.; Fridlizius, G. and Ohlsson, R., eds.*, 1984, pp. 127–50.
[G: Italy]

Crafts, N. F. R. Economic Growth in France and Britain, 1830–1910: A Review of the Evidence. *J. Econ. Hist.*, March 1984, *44*(1), pp. 49–67.
[G: France; U.K.]

Crafts, N. F. R. Patterns of Development in Nineteenth Century Europe. *Oxford Econ. Pap.*, November 1984, *36*(3), pp. 438–58.
[G: Europe]

Cullen, L. M. Landlords, Bankers and Merchants: The Early Irish Banking World, 1700–1820. In *Murphy, A. E., ed.*, 1984, pp. 25–44.
[G: Ireland]

Davis, Lance. Discussion [The Decline of the British Economy: An Institutional Perspective] [Structural Transformation and the Demand for New Labor in Advanced Economies: Interwar Britain]. *J. Econ. Hist.*, June 1984, *44*(2), pp. 596–99.
[G: U.K.]

Dimsdale, N. H. Employment and Real Wages in the Inter-war Period. *Nat. Inst. Econ. Rev.*, November 1984, (110), pp. 94–103.
[G: U.K.]

Edelstein, Michael. Discussion [The Decline of the British Economy: An Institutional Perspective] [Structural Transformation and the Demand for New Labor in Advanced Economies: Interwar Britain]. *J. Econ. Hist.*, June 1984, *44*(2), pp. 599–602.
[G: U.K.]

Elbaum, Bernard and Lazonick, William. The Decline of the British Economy: An Institutional Perspective. *J. Econ. Hist.*, June 1984, *44*(2), pp. 567–83.
[G: U.K.]

Ellman, Michael. Did the Agricultural Surplus Provide the Resources for the Increase in Investment in the USSR 1928–32? In *Ellman, M.*, 1984, *1975*, pp. 27–53.
[G: U.S.S.R.]

Fanning, Ronan. Economists and Governments: Ireland 1922–52. In *Murphy, A. E., ed.*, 1984, pp. 138–56.
[G: Ireland]

Fridlizius, Gunnar. The Mortality Decline in the First Phase of the Demographic Transition: Swedish Experiences. In *Bengtsson, T.; Fridlizius, G. and Ohlsson, R., eds.*, 1984, pp. 71–114.
[G: Sweden]

Friedlander, Dov. Erratum [Demographic Responses and Socioeconomic Structure: Population Processes in England and Wales in the Nineteenth Century]. *Demography*, May 1984, *21*(2), pp. 270.
[G: U.K.]

Gissel, Svend. Village and Environment. Case: Danish Isles in the Later Middle Ages. In *Guarducci, A., ed.*, 1984, pp. 297–310.
[G: Scandinavia]

Goldsmith, James L. The Agrarian History of Preindustrial France: Where Do We Go from Here? *J. Europ. Econ. Hist.*, Spring 1984, *13*(1), pp. 175–99.
[G: France]

Goubert, Jean-Pierre. Public Hygiene and Mortality Decline in France in the 19th Century. In *Bengtsson, T.; Fridlizius, G. and Ohlsson, R., eds.*, 1984, pp. 151–59.
[G: France]

Greaves, C. Desmond. Connolly and Easter Week: A Rejoinder. *Sci. Soc.*, Summer 1984, *48*(2), pp. 220–23.
[G: Ireland]

Grigg, David B. The Agricultural Revolution in Western Europe. In *[Farmer, B. H.]*, 1984, pp. 1–17.
[G: W. Europe]

Hardach, Gerd. Banking and Industry in Germany in the Interwar Period, 1919–1939. *J. Europ. Econ. Hist.*, Special Issue 1984, *13*(2), pp. 203–34.
[G: Germany]

Henderson, John P. Ricardo and the Provident Institutions. In *Samuels, W. J., ed.*, 1984, pp. 65–76.
[G: U.K.]

Hjerppe, Riitta; Peltonen, Matti and Pihkala, Erkki. Investment in Finland, 1860–1979. *Scand. Econ. Hist. Rev.*, 1984, *32*(1), pp. 42–59.
[G: Finland]

Imhof, Arthur E. The Amazing Simultaneousness of the Big Differences and the Boom in the 19th Century—Some Facts and Hypotheses about Infant Mortality in Germany, 18th to 20th Century. In *Bengtsson, T.; Fridlizius, G. and Ohlsson, R., eds.*, 1984, pp. 191–222.
[G: Germany]

James, Harold. The Causes of the German Banking Crisis of 1931. *Econ. Hist. Rev., 2nd Ser.*, February 1984, *37*(1), pp. 68–87.
[G: Germany]

Jenkins, Richard. Ethnicity and the Rise of Capitalism in Ulster. In *Ward, R. and Jenkins, R., eds.*, 1984, pp. 57–72.
[G: U.K.]

Jones, E. L. Subculture and Market: Review Article. *Econ. Develop. Cult. Change*, July 1984, *32*(4), pp. 873–79.
[G: U.K.]

Jones, F. Stuart. The New Economic History and the Industrial Revolution. *S. Afr. J. Econ.*, June 1984, *52*(2), pp. 113–32.
[G: U.K.]

Jonsson, Ulf. Population Growth and Agrarian Economic and Social Structure: Some Swedish Examples. In *Bengtsson, T.; Fridlizius, G. and Ohlsson, R., eds.*, 1984, pp. 223–34.
[G: Sweden]

Joshi, P. C. Conflicting Pulls of Productivity and Employment: Contemporary Choices in the Light of Historical Experience. In *Ngo, M., ed., vol. 2*, 1984, pp. 797–814.
[G: India; Japan; U.K.]

Kaukiainen, Yrjö. Harvest Fluctuations and Mortality in Agrarian Finland (1810–1870). In *Bengtsson, T.; Fridlizius, G. and Ohlsson, R., eds.*, 1984, pp. 235–54.
[G: Finland]

Kerridge, Eric. Landowners and Farmers in England during the 'Price Revolution' in the Sixteenth and Seventeenth Centuries. In *Guarducci, A., ed.*, 1984, pp. 219–54.
[G: U.K.]

Kindleberger, Charles P. Banking and Industry between the Two Wars: An International Comparison. *J. Europ. Econ. Hist.*, Special Issue 1984, *13*(2), pp. 7–28.
[G: U.S.; Europe]

Kindleberger, Charles P. Financial Institutions and Economic Development: A Comparison of Great Britain and France in the Eighteenth and Nineteenth Centuries. *Exploration Econ. Hist.*, April 1984, *21*(2), pp. 103–24.
[G: U.K.; France]

Kindleberger, Charles P. Origins of U.S. Direct

Investment in France. In *Kindleberger, C. P.*, 1984, *1974*, pp. 118–54. **[G: France; U.S.]**

Lee, W. Robert. Mortality Levels and Agrarian Reform in Early 19th Century Prussia: Some Regional Evidence. In *Bengtsson, T.; Fridlizius, G. and Ohlsson, R.*, eds., 1984, pp. 161–90. **[G: Germany]**

Lorenzen, Gunter. The Kuznets Curve: Evidence from Prussia Revisited. *Weltwirtsch. Arch.*, 1984, *120*(4), pp. 764–81. **[G: Prussia]**

Matoušek, Jirí. The Agrarian Policy of the Communist Party of Czechoslovakia and Thirty-Five Years of the Development of Socialism in the Countryside. *Czech. Econ. Digest.*, November 1984, (7), pp. 29–55.
[G: Czechoslovakia]

Mingay, Gordon E. The Revolution in Eighteenth-Century Farming Practice. In *Guarducci, A.*, ed., 1984, pp. 621–37. **[G: U.K.]**

Mokyr, Joel. And Thou, Happy Austria? A Review Essay. *J. Econ. Hist.*, December 1984, *44*(4), pp. 1094–99. **[G: Austria; Hungary]**

Mokyr, Joel. Demand versus Supply in the Industrial Revolution: A Reply. *J. Econ. Hist.*, September 1984, *44*(3), pp. 806–09. **[G: U.K.]**

Mowery, David C. Firm Structure, Government Policy, and the Organization of Industrial Research: Great Britain and the United States, 1900–1950. *Bus. Hist. Rev.*, Winter 1984, *58*(4), pp. 504–31. **[G: U.S.; U.K.]**

Murphy, Antoin E. Richard Cantillon—an Irish Banker in Paris. In *Murphy, A. E.*, ed., 1984, pp. 45–74. **[G: France]**

Nötel, Rudolf. Money, Banking and Industry in Interwar Austria and Hungary. *J. Europ. Econ. Hist.*, Special Issue 1984, *13*(2), pp. 137–202.
[G: Austria; Hungary]

Ó Gráda, Cormac. Malthus and the Pre-famine Economy. In *Murphy, A. E.*, ed., 1984, pp. 75–95. **[G: Ireland]**

Ohlsson, Rolf and Bengtsson, Tommy. Population and Economic Fluctuations in Sweden 1749–1914. In *Bengtsson, T.; Fridlizius, G. and Ohlsson, R.*, eds., 1984, pp. 277–97.
[G: Sweden]

Palmer, Robin. The Rise of the Britalian Culture Entrepreneur. In *Ward, R. and Jenkins, R.*, eds., 1984, pp. 89–104. **[G: U.K.]**

Pamuk, Şevket. The Ottoman Empire in the "Great Depression" of 1873–1896. *J. Econ. Hist.*, March 1984, *44*(1), pp. 107–18.
[G: Middle East; S. Europe; Turkey]

Parker, William N. A Comment on the Papers: Personal Reflections and Some Diagrams. In *Parker, W. N.*, 1984, pp. 238–55.

Parker, William N. Capitalistic Organization and National Response: Social Dynamics in the Age of Schumpeter. *J. Econ. Behav. Organ.*, March 1984, *5*(1), pp. 3–23. **[G: U.S.; Germany; France; England]**

Parker, William N. Communication Techniques and Social Organization in the World Economy. In *Parker, W. N.*, 1984, *1982*, pp. 150–63.

Parker, William N. Europe-Centered Development: Its Natural Logic. In *Parker, W. N.*, 1984, *1961*, pp. 141–49.

Parker, William N. Opportunity Sequences in European History. In *Parker, W. N.*, 1984, *1982*, pp. 191–213.

Parker, William N. The Historians' Reviews of the Terrain. In *Parker, W. N.*, 1984, pp. 164–88.

Parker, William N. The Interruption of Expansion. In *Parker, W. N.*, 1984, *1957*, pp. 57–75. **[G: Europe]**

Parker, William N. The Pre-History of the Nineteenth Century. In *Parker, W. N.*, 1984, *1979*, pp. 15–54.

Parker, William N. The Response Mechanism in the Twentieth Century. In *Parker, W. N.*, 1984, *1984*, pp. 214–37.

Perrenoud, Alfred. Mortality Decline in Its Secular Setting. In *Bengtsson, T.; Fridlizius, G. and Ohlsson, R.*, eds., 1984, pp. 41–69.
[G: France; Sweden; Norway; Switzerland]

Pollins, Harold. The Development of Jewish Business in the United Kingdom. In *Ward, R. and Jenkins, R.*, eds., 1984, pp. 73–88. **[G: U.K.]**

Price, Roger. Recent Work on the Economic History of Nineteenth-Century France. *Econ. Hist. Rev.*, 2nd Ser., August 1984, *37*(3), pp. 417–34. **[G: France]**

Redmond, John. The Sterling Overvaluation in 1925: A Multilateral Approach. *Econ. Hist. Rev.*, 2nd Ser., November 1984, *37*(4), pp. 520–32. **[G: U.K.]**

Reynolds, Alan. Gold and Economic Boom: Five Case Studies, 1792–1926. In *Siegel, B. N.*, ed., 1984, pp. 249–68. **[G: France; U.K.; U.S.]**

Richards, Toni. Weather, Nutrition and the Economy: The Analysis of Short Run Fluctuations in Births, Deaths and Marriages, France 1740–1909. In *Bengtsson, T.; Fridlizius, G. and Ohlsson, R.*, eds., 1984, pp. 357–89.
[G: France]

Riley, James C. The Dutch Economy after 1650: Decline or Growth? *J. Europ. Econ. Hist.*, September–December 1984, *13*(3), pp. 521–69. **[G: Netherlands]**

Rubel, M. Avant-propos (Quel bilan?). (Preface: Which Inventory? With English summary.) *Écon. Soc.*, July–August 1984, *18*(7–8), pp. 3–13.

Sakai, Akihiro. Literacy in Modern England: A Survey of the Studies on the Ability to Sign. *Osaka Econ. Pap.*, March 1984, *33*(3–4), pp. 95–122. **[G: U.K.]**

Schofield, Roger. Population Growth in the Century after 1750: The Role of Mortality Decline. In *Bengtsson, T.; Fridlizius, G. and Ohlsson, R.*, eds., 1984, pp. 17–39. **[G: U.K.; Sweden; France]**

Shaffer, Harry G. Soviet Economic Performance Under the Plan. In *Shaffer, H. G.*, ed., 1984, pp. 328–44. **[G: U.S.S.R.]**

Smith, Louis P. F. British Policy on Building Societies. *Irish Banking Rev.*, December 1984, pp. 52–68. **[G: U.K.; Ireland]**

Smith, Woodruff D. The Function of Commercial Centers in the Modernization of European

Capitalism: Amsterdam as an Information Exchange in the Seventeenth Century. *J. Econ. Hist.*, December 1984, *44*(4), pp. 985–1005.
[G: Netherlands; Europe]

Söderberg, Johan. A Long-Term Perspective on Regional Economic Development in Sweden, Ca. 1550–1914. *Scand. Econ. Hist. Rev.*, 1984, *32*(1), pp. 1–16. [G: Sweden]

Söderberg, Johan. Interrelationships between Short-term Economic and Demographic Fluctuations in a Period of Crisis: South-eastern Sweden 1866–1872. In *Bengtsson, T.; Fridlizius, G. and Ohlsson, R., eds.*, 1984, pp. 255–76. [G: Sweden]

Thirsk, Joan. The Agricultural 'Economic' and Social Background to the Diffusion of New Crops: 1500–1700. In *Guarducci, A., ed.*, 1984, pp. 749–53. [G: U.K.]

Thompson, N. W. The Attitude to Political Economy of Writers in the Working-class Press, 1816–1834. In *Samuels, W. J., ed.*, 1984, pp. 21–45.

Tittler, Robert. Late Medieval Urban Prosperity: Comment [English Provincial Towns in the Later Middle Ages]. *Econ. Hist. Rev., 2nd Ser.*, November 1984, *37*(4), pp. 551–54. [G: U.K.]

Tortella, Gabriel and Palafox, Jordi. Banking and Industry in Spain, 1918–1936. *J. Europ. Econ. Hist.*, Special Issue 1984, *13*(2), pp. 81–111. [G: Spain]

Weir, David R. Life under Pressure: France and England, 1670–1870. *J. Econ. Hist.*, March 1984, *44*(1), pp. 27–47. [G: U.K.; France]

Williamson, Jeffrey G. British Mortality and the Value of Life, 1781–1931 *Population Stud.*, March 1984, *38*(1), pp. 157–72. [G: U.K.]

Williamson, Jeffrey G. Why Was British Growth So Slow during the Industrial Revolution? *J. Econ. Hist.*, September 1984, *44*(3), pp. 687–712. [G: U.K.]

Worswick, G. David N. The Sources of Recovery in UK in the 1930s. *Nat. Inst. Econ. Rev.*, November 1984, (110), pp. 85–93. [G: U.K.]

Worswick, G. David N. Two Great Recessions: The 1980s and the 1930s in Britain. *Scot. J. Polit. Econ.*, November 1984, *31*(3), pp. 209–28. [G: U.K.; U.S.]

0441 History of Product Prices and Markets

Anes, Gonzalo. Prices in 16th Century Spain—An Analysis of Inflation. In *Csikós-Nagy, B.; Hague, D. and Hall, G., eds.*, 1984, pp. 205–13.

Aukrust, Odd. 1980-årenes okonomi sammenlignet med 1930-årenes—tallenes tale. (With English summary.) *Nationaløkon. Tidsskr.*, 1984, *122*(3), pp. 313–32. [G: U.S.; W. Europe; Nordic Countries]

Benedict, Philip. Rouen's Foreign Trade during the Era of the Religious Wars (1560–1600). *J. Europ. Econ. Hist.*, Spring 1984, *13*(1), pp. 29–74. [G: France]

Björklund, Jörgen. From the Gulf of Bothnia to the White Sea—Swedish Direct Investments

in the Sawmill Industry of Tsarist Russia. *Scand. Econ. Hist. Rev.*, 1984, *32*(1), pp. 17–41. [G: Sweden; U.S.S.R.]

Bourguignon, François and Levy-Leboyer, M. An Econometric Model of France during the 19th Century. *Europ. Econ. Rev.*, June 1984, *25*(1), pp. 107–41. [G: France]

Butt, John. Life Assurance in War and Depression: The Standard Life Assurance Company and Its Environment, 1914–39. In *Westall, O. M., ed.*, 1984, pp. 155–72. [G: U.K.]

Chalmin, Ph. G. The Important Trends in Sugar Diplomacy before 1914. In *Albert, B. and Graves, A., eds.*, 1984, pp. 9–19. [G: Global]

Chapman, S. D. Hogg Robinson: The Rise of a Lloyd's Broker. In *Westall, O. M., ed.*, 1984, pp. 173–89. [G: U.K.]

Collins, James B. The Role of Atlantic France in the Baltic Trade: Dutch Traders and Polish Grain at Nantes, 1625–1675. *J. Europ. Econ. Hist.*, Fall 1984, *13*(2), pp. 239–89. [G: France]

Cuenca Esteban, Javier. Trends and Cycles in U.S. Trade with Spain and the Spanish Empire, 1790–1819. *J. Econ. Hist.*, June 1984, *44*(2), pp. 521–43. [G: U.S.; Spain]

Dewey, Peter E. British Farming Profits and Government Policy during the First World War. *Econ. Hist. Rev., 2nd Ser.*, August 1984, *37*(3), pp. 373–90. [G: U.K.]

Dwyer, Gerald P., Jr. and Lindsay, Cotton M. Robert Giffen and the Irish Potato. *Amer. Econ. Rev.*, March 1984, *74*(1), pp. 188–92. [G: Ireland]

Ellman, Michael. Fifty Years of Collectivised Soviet Agriculture, 1929–79. In *Ellman, M.*, 1984, pp. 58–71. [G: U.S.S.R.]

Feldenkirchen, Wilfried. Capital Raised and its Use by German Mechanical Engineering Firms in the 19th and Early 20th Centuries. In *Engels, W. and Pohl, H., eds.*, 1984, pp. 19–55. [G: W. Germany]

Gordon, Robert J. An Econometric Model of France during the 19th Century: Comments. *Europ. Econ. Rev.*, June 1984, *25*(1), pp. 143–46. [G: France]

Hannah, Leslie. Entrepreneurs and the Social Sciences. *Economica*, August 1984, *51*(203), pp. 219–34. [G: U.K.]

Hausman, William J. Cheap Coals or Limitation of the Vend? The London Coal Trade, 1770–1845. *J. Econ. Hist.*, June 1984, *44*(2), pp. 321–28. [G: U.K.]

Hausman, William J. Market Power in the London Coal Trade: The Limitation of the Vend, 1770–1845. *Exploration Econ. Hist.*, October 1984, *21*(4), pp. 383–405. [G: U.K.]

Hausman, William J. Profitability of English Colliers in the Eighteenth Century: Reply to a Reappraisal. *Bus. Hist. Rev.*, Spring 1984, *58*(1), pp. 121–25. [G: U.K.]

Heim, Carol E. Limits to Intervention: The Bank of England and Industrial Diversification in the

Depressed Areas. *Econ. Hist. Rev., 2nd Ser.,* November 1984, *37*(4), pp. 533–50.
[G: U.K.]

Henderson, William O. Die Manufaktur in Deutschland im 18. Jahrhundert. (Manufactories in Germany in the Eighteenth Century. With English summary.) *Jahr. Nationalökon. Statist.,* November 1984, *199*(6), pp. 586–602.
[G: Germany]

Herranen, Timo and Myllyntaus, Timo. Effects of the First World War on the Engineering Industries of Estonia and Finland. *Scand. Econ. Hist. Rev.,* 1984, *32*(3), pp. 121–42.
[G: U.S.S.R.; Finland]

Horsman, Andrew. Money, Banking and Inflation. In *Sandford, C. and Bradbury, M., eds.,* 1984, pp. 164–87. [G: Germany; U.S.]

Huang, Roger D. Exchange Rate and Relative Monetary Expansions: The Case of Simultaneous Hyperinflation and Rational Expectations. *Europ. Econ. Rev.,* March 1984, *24*(2), pp. 189–95. [G: Poland; Germany]

Huang, Roger D. Tests of Variance Bounds Implied by Cagan's Hyperinflation Model. *Int. Econ. Rev.,* October 1984, *25*(3), pp. 545–61.
[G: Germany]

Jenkins, D. T. The Practice of Insurance Against Fire, 1750–1840, and Historical Research. In *Westall, O. M., ed.,* 1984, pp. 9–38.
[G: U.K.]

Jones, Charles A. Competition and Structural Change in the Buenos Aires Fire Insurance Market: The Local Board of Agents, 1875–1921. In *Westall, O. M., ed.,* 1984, pp. 114–29. [G: Argentina; U.K.]

Jones, Geoffrey. The Expansion of British Multinational Manufacturing, 1890–1939. In *Okochi, A. and Inoue, T., eds.,* 1984, pp. 125–53.
[G: U.K.]

Jones, Geoffrey. The Growth and Performance of British Multinational Firms before 1939: The Case of Dunlop. *Econ. Hist. Rev., 2nd Ser.,* February 1984, *37*(1), pp. 35–53. [G: U.K.]

Junge, Georg. Purchasing Power Parity in the 1920s and the 1970s: A Note. *Europ. Econ. Rev.,* October–November 1984, *26*(1–2), pp. 73–82. [G: Switzerland]

Klíma, Arnošt. Glassmaking Industry and Trade in Bohemia in the XVIIth and XVIIIth Centuries. *J. Europ. Econ. Hist.,* September–December 1984, *13*(3), pp. 499–520.
[G: Czechoslovakia]

Kostrowicka, Irena. Changes in Agricultural Productivity in the Kingdom of Poland in the XIXth and Early XXth Centuries. *J. Europ. Econ. Hist.,* Spring 1984, *13*(1), pp. 75–97.
[G: Poland]

Larsen, Hans Kryger and Nilsson, Carl-Axel. Consumption and Production of Bicycles in Denmark, 1890–1980. *Scand. Econ. Hist. Rev.,* 1984, *32*(3), pp. 143–58. [G: Denmark]

MacDonald, Ronald. The Monetary Approach to the Exchange Rate and the 1920s' Experience with Floating Exchange Rates. *J. Econ. Stud.,* 1984, *11*(3), pp. 14–25. [G: U.S.; U.K.; France]

Mate, Mavis. Agrarian Economy after the Black Death: The Manors of Canterbury Cathedral Priory, 1348–91. *Econ. Hist. Rev., 2nd Ser.,* August 1984, *37*(3), pp. 341–54. [G: U.K.]

McGregor, Patrick. The Impact of the Blight upon the Pre-Famine Rural Economy in Ireland. *Econ. Soc. Rev.,* July 1984, *15*(4), pp. 289–303. [G: U.K.]

Metz, Rainer. Zur empirischen Evidenz "langer Wellen." (On the Empirical Evidence of "Long Waves." With English summary.) *Kyklos,* 1984, *37*(2), pp. 266–90. [G: U.K.; France; Germany]

Millward, Robert. The Early Stages of European Industrialization: Economic Organization under Serfdom. *Exploration Econ. Hist.,* October 1984, *21*(4), pp. 406–28. [G: U.S.S.R.; E. Europe]

Milward, Alan S. Restriction of Supply as a Strategic Choice. In *McCormick, G. H. and Bissell, R. E., eds.,* 1984, pp. 44–58. [G: Japan; Germany; U.K.]

Mirowski, Philip. Macroeconomic Instability and the "Natural" Processes in Early Neoclassical Economics. *J. Econ. Hist.,* June 1984, *44*(2), pp. 345–54. [G: U.K.]

de Montbrial, Thierry. An Econometric Model of France during the 19th Century: Comments. *Europ. Econ. Rev.,* June 1984, *25*(1), pp. 147–48. [G: France]

Munting, Roger. The Russian Beet Sugar Industry in the XIXth Century. *J. Europ. Econ. Hist.,* Fall 1984, *13*(2), pp. 291–309.
[G: U.S.S.R.]

Munting, Roger. The State and the Beet Sugar Industry in Russia before 1914. In *Albert, B. and Graves, A., eds.,* 1984, pp. 21–28.
[G: U.S.S.R.]

Murota, Takeshi. Heat Economy of the Water Planet Earth: An Entropic Analysis and the Water–Soil Matrix Theory. *Hitotsubashi J. Econ.,* December 1984, *25*(2), pp. 161–72.
[G: U.K.; Japan]

Nicholas, Stephen J. The Overseas Marketing Performance of British Industry, 1870–1914. *Econ. Hist. Rev., 2nd Ser.,* November 1984, *37*(4), pp. 489–506. [G: U.K.]

North, Michael. A Small Baltic Port in the Early Modern Period: The Port of Elbing in the Sixteenth and Seventeenth Century. *J. Europ. Econ. Hist.,* Spring 1984, *13*(1), pp. 117–27.
[G: Poland]

Ó Gráda, Cormac. Irish Agricultural Output before and after the Famine. *J. Europ. Econ. Hist.,* Spring 1984, *13*(1), pp. 149–65.
[G: Ireland]

Ó Gráda, Cormac. Technical Change in the Mid-Ninteenth Century British Cotton Industry: A Note. *J. Europ. Econ. Hist.,* Fall 1984, *13*(2), pp. 345–52. [G: U.K.]

Overton, Mark. Agricultural Productivity in Eighteenth-Century England: Some Further Speculation. *Econ. Hist. Rev., 2nd Ser.,* May 1984, *37*(2), pp. 244–51. [G: U.K.]

Painter, David S. Oil and the Marshall Plan. *Bus. Hist. Rev.*, Autumn 1984, *58*(3), pp. 359–83.
[G: U.S.; W. Europe]

Palairet, Michael. Beet Sugar and Peasant Economy in the Balkans before 1914. In *Albert, B. and Graves, A., eds.*, 1984, pp. 47–57.
[G: Bulgaria; Yugoslavia]

Palmer, Sarah. The Indemnity in the London Marine Insurance Market, 1824–50. In *Westall, O. M., ed.*, 1984, pp. 74–94.
[G: U.K.]

Parker, William N. Kartelle und Konzerne: The German Coal Syndicate under the Steel Mills' Domination. In *Parker, W. N.*, 1984, *1954*, pp. 103–24.
[G: Germany]

Parker, William N. Law and Enterprise: Ore-Mining on Two Sides of the Franco–German Border [National States and National Development: French and German Ore-Mining in the Late Nineteenth Century]. In *Parker, W. N.*, 1984, *1959*, pp. 91–102.
[G: France; Germany]

Peña, Daniel and Sánchez-Albornoz, Nicolás. Wheat Prices in Spain, 1857–1890: An Application of the Box–Jenkins Methodology. *J. Europ. Econ. Hist.*, Fall 1984, *13*(2), pp. 353–73.
[G: Spain]

Perkins, John A. The Political Economy of Sugar Beet in Imperial Germany. In *Albert, B. and Graves, A., eds.*, 1984, pp. 31–45.
[G: Germany]

Reece, B. F. The Price Adjustment Mechanism in Glasgow's Rental Housing Market, 1871–1913: The Claim of "Sticky" Rents Re-assessed. *Scot. J. Polit. Econ.*, November 1984, *31*(3), pp. 286–93.
[G: U.K.]

Ryan, Roger. The Norwich Union and the British Fire Insurance Market in the Early Nineteenth Century. In *Westall, O. M., ed.*, 1984, pp. 39–73.
[G: U.K.]

Sales, Hubert. La recherche-développement dans la stratégie des grandes entreprises chimiques de l'entre-deux-guerres: Du Pont de Nemours, Imperial chemical industries, I. G. Farben. (With English summary.) *Revue Écon. Polit.*, July–August 1984, *94*(4), pp. 446–64.
[G: Germany]

Saxonhouse, Gary R. and Wright, Gavin. New Evidence on the Stubborn English Mule and the Cotton Industry, 1878–1920. *Econ. Hist. Rev.*, 2nd Ser., November 1984, *37*(4), pp. 507–19.
[G: U.K.]

Scherer, Frederic M. Invention and Innovation in the Watt–Boulton Steam Engine Venture. In *Scherer, F. M.*, 1984, pp. 8–31.
[G: Europe]

Sullivan, Richard J. Measurement of English Farming Technological Change, 1523–1900. *Exploration Econ. Hist.*, July 1984, *21*(3), pp. 270–89.
[G: U.K.]

Supple, Barry. Insurance in British History. In *Westall, O. M., ed.*, 1984, pp. 1–8.
[G: U.K.]

Thomas, Mark. Discussion [Keynes and Protection] [Macroeconomic Instability and the "Natural" Processes in Early Neoclassical Econom-

ics]. *J. Econ. Hist.*, June 1984, *44*(2), pp. 375–79.
[G: U.K.]

Treble, J. H. The Record of the Standard Life Assurance Company in the Life Insurance Market of the United Kingdom, 1850–64. In *Westall, O. M., ed.*, 1984, pp. 95–113.
[G: U.K.]

Turner, Michael. Agricultural Productivity in Eighteenth-Century England: Further Strains of Speculation. *Econ. Hist. Rev.*, 2nd Ser., May 1984, *37*(2), pp. 252–57.
[G: U.K.]

Ville, Simon. Note: Size and Profitability of English Colliers in the Eighteenth Century—A Reappraisal. *Bus. Hist. Rev.*, Spring 1984, *58*(1), pp. 103–20.
[G: U.K.]

Webb, Steven B. The Supply of Money and Reichsbank Financing of Government and Corporate Debt in Germany, 1919–1923. *J. Econ. Hist.*, June 1984, *44*(2), pp. 499–507.
[G: Germany]

Wessel, Horst A. A Review of the New Literature on Business History and Biography. In *Engels, W. and Pohl, H., eds.*, 1984, pp. 119–53.
[G: W. Germany]

Wessel, Horst A. The German Feeble Current Cable Association (DSV)—Background, Foundation and Early Years (1876–1917.) In *Engels, W. and Pohl, H., eds.*, 1984, pp. 57–75.
[G: W. Germany]

Westall, Oliver M. David and Goliath: The Fire Offices Committee and Non-tariff Competition, 1898–1907. In *Westall, O. M., ed.*, 1984, pp. 130–54.
[G: U.K.]

0442 History of Factor Prices and Markets

Amelang, James S. Barristers and Judges in Early Modern Barcelona: The Rise of a Legal Elite. *Amer. Hist. Rev.*, December 1984, *89*(5), pp. 1264–84.
[G: Spain]

Anderson, Gary M. and Tollison, Robert D. A Rent-Seeking Explanation of the British Factory Acts. In *Colander, D. C., ed.*, 1984, pp. 187–201.
[G: U.K.]

Aukrust, Odd. 1980-årenes økonomi sammenlignet med 1930-årenes—tallenes tale. (With English summary.) *Nasjonaløkon. Tidsskr.*, 1984, *122*(3), pp. 313–32.
[G: U.S.; W. Europe; Nordic Countries]

Baillie, Richard T. and Bailey, Ralph W. International Currency Speculation, Market Stability and Efficiency in the 1920s: A Time Series Approach. *J. Macroecon.*, Spring 1984, *6*(2), pp. 127–37.
[G: Belgium; France; Netherlands; U.S.; Germany]

Beckett, J. V. The Pattern of Landownership in England and Wales, 1660–1880. *Econ. Hist. Rev.*, 2nd Ser., February 1984, *37*(1), pp. 1–22.
[G: U.K.]

Björklund, Jörgen. From the Gulf of Bothnia to the White Sea—Swedish Direct Investments in the Sawmill Industry of Tsarist Russia. *Scand. Econ. Hist. Rev.*, 1984, *32*(1), pp. 17–41.
[G: Sweden; U.S.S.R.]

Bourguignon, François and Levy-Leboyer, M. An Econometric Model of France during the

19th Century. *Europ. Econ. Rev.*, June 1984, 25(1), pp. 107–41. **[G: France]**

Chapman, John. The Chronology of English Enclosure. *Econ. Hist. Rev.*, 2nd Ser., November 1984, 37(4), pp. 557–59. **[G: U.K.]**

Clark, Gregory. Authority and Efficiency: The Labor Market and the Managerial Revolution of the Late Nineteenth Century. *J. Econ. Hist.*, December 1984, 44(4), pp. 1069–83. **[G: U.S.; U.K.]**

Crafts, N. F. R. A Time Series Study of Fertility in England and Wales, 1877–1938. *J. Europ. Econ. Hist.*, September–December 1984, 13(3), pp. 571–90. **[G: U.K.]**

Davis, Kingsley. Wives and Work: The Sex Role Revolution and Its Consequences. *Population Devel. Rev.*, September 1984, 10(3), pp. 397–417. **[G: U.S.; U.K.; Sweden]**

Davis, Lance. Discussion [The Decline of the British Economy: An Institutional Perspective] [Structural Transformation and the Demand for New Labor in Advanced Economies: Interwar Britain]. *J. Econ. Hist.*, June 1984, 44(2), pp. 596–99. **[G: U.K.]**

Desai, Meghnad. An Econometric Model of the Share of Wages in National Income: UK 1855–1965. In *Goodwin, R. M.; Krüger, M. and Vercelli, A., eds.*, 1984, pp. 253–77. **[G: U.K.]**

Domar, Evsey D. and Machina, Mark J. On the Profitability of Russian Serfdom. *J. Econ. Hist.*, December 1984, 44(4), pp. 919–55. **[G: U.S.S.R.]**

Dumnov, D. and Dmitrichev, I. From the History of Studying Family Budgets. *Prob. Econ.*, August 1984, 27(4), pp. 78–85. **[G: U.S.S.R.]**

Eckstein, Zvi; Schultz, T. Paul and Wolpin, Kenneth I. Short-run Fluctuations in Fertility and Mortality in Pre-industrial Sweden. *Europ. Econ. Rev.*, December 1984, 26(3), pp. 295–317. **[G: Sweden]**

Ellman, Michael. On a Mistake of Preobrazhensky and Stalin. In *Ellman, M.*, 1984, pp. 54–57. **[G: U.S.S.R.; China]**

Evans, E. W. and Wiseman, N. C. Education, Training and Economic Performance: British Economists' Views, 1868–1939. *J. Europ. Econ. Hist.*, Spring 1984, 13(1), pp. 129–48. **[G: U.K.]**

Fenoaltea, Stefano. Slavery and Supervision in Comparative Perspective: A Model. *J. Econ. Hist.*, September 1984, 44(3), pp. 635–68. **[G: U.S.; U.K.; Italy; Latin America]**

Flinn, M. W. English Workers' Living Standards during the Industrial Revolution: A Comment. *Econ. Hist. Rev.*, 2nd Ser., February 1984, 37(1), pp. 88–92. **[G: U.K.]**

Fridlizius, Gunnar and Ohlsson, Rolf. Mortality Patterns in Sweden 1751–1802—A Regional Analysis. In *Bengtsson, T.; Fridlizius, G. and Ohlsson, R., eds.*, 1984, pp. 299–328. **[G: Sweden]**

Gordon, Robert J. An Econometric Model of France during the 19th Century: Comments. *Europ. Econ. Rev.*, June 1984, 25(1), pp. 143–46. **[G: France]**

Heim, Carol E. Structural Transformation and the

Demand for New Labor in Advanced Economies: Interwar Britain. *J. Econ. Hist.*, June 1984, 44(2), pp. 585–95. **[G: U.K.]**

Hobsbawm, E. J. Artisan or Labour Aristocrat? *Econ. Hist. Rev.*, 2nd Ser., August 1984, 37(3), pp. 355–72. **[G: U.K.]**

Hoffman, Philip T. The Economic Theory of Sharecropping in Early Modern France. *J. Econ. Hist.*, June 1984, 44(2), pp. 309–19. **[G: France]**

Joël, Marie-Ève. L'économie de l'assistance dans la période prérévolutionnaire. (The Economics of Assistance during the Prerevolutionary Period. With English summary.) *Écon. Soc.*, March 1984, 18(3), pp. 199–231. **[G: France]**

Lazonick, William. Rings and Mules in Britain: Reply [Factor Costs and the Diffusion of Ring Spinning in Britain Prior to World War I]. *Quart. J. Econ.*, May 1984, 99(2), pp. 393–98. **[G: U.K.]**

Lewchuk, Wayne A. The Role of the British Government in the Spread of Scientific Management and Fordism in the Interwar Years. *J. Econ. Hist.*, June 1984, 44(2), pp. 355–61. **[G: U.K.]**

Lindert, Peter H. and Williamson, Jeffrey G. Reply [English Workers' Living Standards during the Industrial Revolution: A New Look]. *Econ. Hist. Rev.*, 2nd Ser., February 1984, 37(1), pp. 93–94. **[G: U.K.]**

Lorenz, Edward H. Two Patterns of Development: The Labour Process in the British and French Shipbuilding Industries 1880 to 1930. *J. Europ. Econ. Hist.*, September–December 1984, 13(3), pp. 599–634. **[G: U.K.; France]**

MacKinnon, Mary and Johnson, Paul. The Case against Productive Whipping. *Exploration Econ. Hist.*, April 1984, 21(2), pp. 218–23. **[G: U.K.]**

Mantelli, Roberto. The Sale of Crown Lands in Spain in the Early Modern Era: Review Article. *J. Europ. Econ. Hist.*, Spring 1984, 13(1), pp. 201–05. **[G: Spain]**

Mate, Mavis. Agrarian Economy after the Black Death: The Manors of Canterbury Cathedral Priory, 1348–91. *Econ. Hist. Rev.*, 2nd Ser., August 1984, 37(3), pp. 341–54. **[G: U.K.]**

Matossian, Mary Kilbourne. Mold Poisoning and Population Growth in England and France, 1750–1850. *J. Econ. Hist.*, September 1984, 44(3), pp. 669–86. **[G: U.K.; France]**

Maurice, Marc; Sellier, François and Silvestre, Jean-Jacques. The Search for a Societal Effect in the Production of Company Hierarchy: A Comparison of France and Germany. In *Osterman, P., ed.*, 1984, pp. 231–70. **[G: W. Germany; France]**

McGregor, Patrick. The Impact of the Blight upon the Pre-Famine Rural Economy in Ireland. *Econ. Soc. Rev.*, July 1984, 15(4), pp. 289–303. **[G: U.K.]**

Mielke, James H., et al. Historical Epidemiology of Smallpox in Åland, Finland: 1751–1890. *Demography*, August 1984, 21(3), pp. 271–95. **[G: Finland]**

Millward, Robert. The Early Stages of European

Industrialization: Economic Organization under Serfdom. *Exploration Econ. Hist.*, October 1984, *21*(4), pp. 406–28.　　　**[G: U.S.S.R.; E. Europe]**

Mokyr, Joel and Ó Gráda, Cormac. New Developments in Irish Population History, 1700–1850. *Econ. Hist. Rev., 2nd Ser.*, November 1984, *37*(4), pp. 473–88. **[G: Ireland; France; U.K.]**

de Montbrial, Thierry. An Econometric Model of France during the 19th Century: Comments. *Europ. Econ. Rev.*, June 1984, *25*(1), pp. 147–48.　　　**[G: France]**

Morgan, V. and MacAfee, W. Irish Population in the Pre-Famine Period: Evidence from County Antrim. *Econ. Hist. Rev., 2nd Ser.*, May 1984, *37*(2), pp. 182–96.　**[G: Ireland]**

Moss, Bernard H. Workers and Communists in France. *Sci. Soc.*, Fall 1984, *48*(3), pp. 350–57.　　　**[G: France]**

Nardinelli, Clark. The Productivity of Corporal Punishment: A Reply. *Exploration Econ. Hist.*, April 1984, *21*(2), pp. 224–28.　**[G: U.K.]**

Parker, William N. The Organization of Rapid Expansion. In *Parker, W. N.*, 1984, pp. 76–91.　　　**[G: W. Europe]**

Sandberg, Lars G. The Remembrance of Things Past: Rings and Mules Revisited [Factor Costs and the Diffusion of Ring Spinning in Britain Prior to World War I]. *Quart. J. Econ.*, May 1984, *99*(2), pp. 387–92.　**[G: U.K.]**

Sapsford, David. The Determinants of Trade Union Growth in the Republic of Ireland: An Econometric Investigation. *Econ. Soc. Rev.*, July 1984, *15*(4), pp. 305–23.　**[G: U.K.]**

Schäfer, Hermann. Italian Migrant Workers in Germany, 1890–1914. In *Engels, W. and Pohl, H., eds.*, 1984, pp. 77–94. **[G: W. Germany]**

Shammas, Carole. The Eighteenth-Century English Diet and Economic Change. *Exploration Econ. Hist.*, July 1984, *21*(3), pp. 254–69.　　　**[G: U.K.]**

Toumanoff, Peter G. Some Effects of Land Tenure Reforms on Russian Agricultural Productivity, 1901–1913. *Econ. Develop. Cult. Change*, July 1984, *32*(4), pp. 861–72.　**[G: U.S.S.R.]**

Wellington, Donald C. The English Poor Law: A Negative Income Tax. *Atlantic Econ. J.*, December 1984, *12*(4), pp. 46–50.　**[G: U.K.]**

Wessel, Horst A. A Review of the New Literature on Business History and Biography. In *Engels, W. and Pohl, H., eds.*, 1984, pp. 119–53.　　　**[G: W. Germany]**

Wilson, C. Natural Fertility in Pre-Industrial England, 1600–1799. *Population Stud.*, July 1984, *38*(2), pp. 225–40.　**[G: U.K.]**

Wordie, J. R. The Chronology of English Enclosure: A Reply. *Econ. Hist. Rev., 2nd Ser.*, November 1984, *37*(4), pp. 560–62.　**[G: U.K.]**

Wright, J. F. Real Wage Resistance: Eighty Years of the British Cost of Living. *Oxford Econ. Pap.*, Supplement November 1984, *36*, pp. 152–67.　　　**[G: U.K.]**

Wright, J. F. Real Wage Resistance: Eighty Years of the British Cost of Living. In *Collard, D. A., et al., eds.*, 1984, pp. 152–67.
　　　[G: U.K.]

0443 History of Public Economic Policy, all levels

Anderson, Gary M. and Tollison, Robert D. A Rent-Seeking Explanation of the British Factory Acts. In *Colander, D. C., ed.*, 1984, pp. 187–201.　　　**[G: U.K.]**

Bähre, Inge Lore. Economic Development and Banking Supervision from 1934 to Today. In *Engels, W. and Pohl, H., eds.*, 1984, pp. 95–106.　　　**[G: W. Germany]**

Bandera, V. N. Capital Accumulation and Growth in a Mixed Socialist Economy: The Case of Soviet NEP. *J. Europ. Econ. Hist.*, Spring 1984, *13*(1), pp. 7–27.　**[G: U.S.S.R.]**

Booth, Alan. Defining a "Keynesian Revolution" [The "Keynesian Revolution" in Economic Policy-Making]. *Econ. Hist. Rev., 2nd Ser.*, May 1984, *37*(2), pp. 263–67.　**[G: U.K.]**

Borchardt, Knut. Could and Should Germany Have Followed Great Britain in Leaving the Gold Standard? *J. Europ. Econ. Hist.*, September–December 1984, *13*(3), pp. 471–97.
　　　[G: Germany]

Broadberry, S. N. Fiscal Policy in Britain during the 1930s [The Constant Employment Budget Balance and British Budgetary Policy, 1929–39]. *Econ. Hist. Rev., 2nd Ser.*, February 1984, *37*(1), pp. 95–102.　**[G: U.K.]**

Chalmin, Ph. G. The Important Trends in Sugar Diplomacy before 1914. In *Albert, B. and Graves, A., eds.*, 1984, pp. 9–19.
　　　[G: Global]

Chapman, John. The Chronology of English Enclosure. *Econ. Hist. Rev., 2nd Ser.*, November 1984, *37*(4), pp. 557–59.　**[G: U.K.]**

Delorme, Robert. A New View on the Economic Theory of the State: A Case Study of France. *J. Econ. Issues*, September 1984, *18*(3), pp. 715–44.　　　**[G: France]**

Delson, Roberta M. Sugar Production for the Nineteenth Century British Market: Rethinking the Roles of Brazil and the British West Indies. In *Albert, B. and Graves, A., eds.*, 1984, pp. 59–80.　**[G: Brazil; Caribbean; U.K.]**

Dewey, Peter E. British Farming Profits and Government Policy during the First World War. *Econ. Hist. Rev., 2nd Ser.*, August 1984, 37(3), pp. 373–90.　　　**[G: U.K.]**

Dornbusch, Rudiger and Frenkel, Jacob A. The Gold Standard and the Bank of England in the Crisis of 1847. In *Bordo, M. D. and Schwartz, A. J., eds.*, 1984, pp. 233–64.　**[G: U.K.]**

Dornbusch, Rudiger and Frenkel, Jacob A. The Gold Standard Crisis of 1847. *J. Int. Econ.*, February 1984, *16*(1/2), pp. 1–27. **[G: U.K.]**

Dutton, John C., Jr. The Bank of England and the Rules of the Game under the International Gold Standard: New Evidence. In *Bordo, M. D. and Schwartz, A. J., eds.*, 1984, pp. 173–95.　　　**[G: U.K.]**

Dutton, John C., Jr. The Bank of England and

the Rules of the Game under the International Gold Standard: New Evidence: Reply. In *Bordo, M. D. and Schwartz, A. J., eds.*, 1984, pp. 199–202. [G: U.K.]

Eichengreen, Barry. Central Bank Cooperation under the Interwar Gold Standard. *Exploration Econ. Hist.*, January 1984, *21*(1), pp. 64–87. [G: France; U.K.]

Eichengreen, Barry. Keynes and Protection. *J. Econ. Hist.*, June 1984, *44*(2), pp. 363–73. [G: U.K.]

Ekelund, Robert B., Jr. and Tollison, Robert D. A Rent-Seeking Theory of French Mercantilism. In *Buchanan, J. M. and Tollison, R. D., eds.*, 1984, pp. 206–23. [G: France]

Fleisig, Heywood. Operations of the German Central Bank and the Rules of the Game, 1879–1913: Comment. In *Bordo, M. D. and Schwartz, A. J., eds.*, 1984, pp. 349–58. [G: Germany]

Fratianni, Michele and Spinelli, Franco. Italy in the Gold Standard Period, 1861–1914. In *Bordo, M. D. and Schwartz, A. J., eds.*, 1984, pp. 405–41. [G: Italy]

Freudenberger, Herman; Mather, Frances J. and Nardinelli, Clark. A New Look at the Early Factory Labor Force. *J. Econ. Hist.*, December 1984, *44*(4), pp. 1085–90. [G: U.K.]

Gardner, Roy J. Power and Taxes in a One-Party State: The USSR, 1925–1929. *Int. Econ. Rev.*, October 1984, *25*(3), pp. 743–55. [G: U.S.S.R.]

Geiger, Reed. Planning the French Canals: The "Becquey Plan" of 1820–1822. *J. Econ. Hist.*, June 1984, *44*(2), pp. 329–39. [G: France]

Goodhart, Charles A. E. Bank of England Operations, 1893–1913: Comment. In *Bordo, M. D. and Schwartz, A. J., eds.*, 1984, pp. 222–27. [G: U.K.]

Gustafsson, Björn. Macroeconomic Performance, Old Age Security and the Rate of Social Assistance Recipients in Sweden. *Europ. Econ. Rev.*, December 1984, *26*(3), pp. 319–38. [G: Sweden]

Hafter, Daryl M. The Business of Invention in the Paris Industrial Exposition of 1806. *Bus. Hist. Rev.*, Autumn 1984, *58*(3), pp. 317–35. [G: France]

Hausman, William J. Cheap Coals or Limitation of the Vend? The London Coal Trade, 1770–1845. *J. Econ. Hist.*, June 1984, *44*(2), pp. 321–28. [G: U.K.]

Heim, Carol E. Limits to Intervention: The Bank of England and Industrial Diversification in the Depressed Areas. *Econ. Hist. Rev., 2nd Ser.*, November 1984, *37*(4), pp. 533–50. [G: U.K.]

Henderson, William O. Die Manufaktur in Deutschland im 18. Jahrhundert. (Manufactories in Germany in the Eighteenth Century. With English summary.) *Jahr. Nationalökon. Statist.*, November 1984, *199*(6), pp. 586–602. [G: Germany]

Hicks, John R. Lineamenti storici dei metodi di controllo della moneta. (Methods of Monetary Control. With English summary.) *Bancaria*, November 1984, *40*(11), pp. 1069–75. [G: U.K.]

Hughes, Jonathan R. T. The Gold Standard and the Bank of England in the Crisis of 1847: Comment. In *Bordo, M. D. and Schwartz, A. J., eds.*, 1984, pp. 264–71. [G: U.K.]

Humphrey, Thomas M. and Keleher, Robert E. The Lender of Last Resort: A Historical Perspective [International Debt, Bank Failures, and the Money Supply: The Thirties and the Eighties]. *Cato J.*, Spring/Summer 1984, *4*(1), pp. 275–318. [G: U.K.]

Johnson, Paul. Self-Help versus State Help: Old Age Pensions and Personal Savings in Great Britain, 1906–1937. *Exploration Econ. Hist.*, October 1984, *21*(4), pp. 329–50. [G: U.K.]

Jonung, Lars. Swedish Experience under the Classical Gold Standard, 1873–1914. In *Bordo, M. D. and Schwartz, A. J., eds.*, 1984, pp. 361–99. [G: Sweden]

Lewchuk, Wayne A. The Role of the British Government in the Spread of Scientific Management and Fordism in the Interwar Years. *J. Econ. Hist.*, June 1984, *44*(2), pp. 355–61. [G: U.K.]

Lindert, Peter H. Swedish Experience under the Classical Gold Standard, 1873–1914: Comment. In *Bordo, M. D. and Schwartz, A. J., eds.*, 1984, pp. 399–404. [G: Sweden]

Lynch, Frances M. B. Resolving the Paradox of the Monnet Plan: National and International Planning in French Reconstruction. *Econ. Hist. Rev., 2nd Ser.*, May 1984, *37*(2), pp. 229–43. [G: France]

McGouldrick, Paul. Operations of the German Central Bank and the Rules of the Game, 1879–1913. In *Bordo, M. D. and Schwartz, A. J., eds.*, 1984, pp. 311–49. [G: Germany]

Meiselman, David I. The Lender of Last Resort and a Money Supply Rule [International Debt, Bank Failures, and the Money Supply: The Thirties and the Eighties]. *Cato J.*, Spring/Summer 1984, *4*(1), pp. 319–21. [G: U.K.]

Middleton, Roger. The Measurement of Fiscal Influence in Britain in the 1930s [The Constant Employment Budget Balance and British Budgetary Policy, 1929–39]. *Econ. Hist. Rev., 2nd Ser.*, February 1984, *37*(1), pp. 103–06. [G: U.K.]

Moggridge, Donald E. The Bank of England and the Rules of the Game under the International Gold Standard: New Evidence: Comment. In *Bordo, M. D. and Schwartz, A. J., eds.*, 1984, pp. 195–99. [G: U.K.]

Mokyr, Joel. Discussion [The Economic Theory of Sharecropping in Early Modern France] [Cheap Coals or Limitation of the Vend? The London Coal Trade, 1770–1845]. *J. Econ. Hist.*, June 1984, *44*(2), pp. 341–43. [G: U.K.; France]

Montias, John Michael. Public Support for the Performing Arts in Western Europe and the United States: History and Analysis. In *[Reynolds, L. G.]*, 1984, pp. 409–44. [G: U.S.; W. Europe]

Munting, Roger. The State and the Beet Sugar Industry in Russia before 1914. In *Albert, B. and Graves, A., eds.*, 1984, pp. 21–28. **[G: U.S.S.R.]**

Neale, Walter C. The Evolution of Colonial Institutions: An Argument Illustrated from the Economic History of British Central Africa. *J. Econ. Issues*, December 1984, *18*(4), pp. 1177–87. **[G: U.K.; Zimbabwe; Zambia; Malawi]**

Peacock, A. E. The Successful Prosecution of the Factory Acts, 1833–55. *Econ. Hist. Rev., 2nd Ser.*, May 1984, *37*(2), pp. 197–210. **[G: U.K.]**

Perkins, John A. Fiscal Policy and Economic Development in XIXth Century Germany. *J. Europ. Econ. Hist.*, Fall 1984, *13*(2), pp. 311–44. **[G: Germany]**

Perkins, John A. The Political Economy of Sugar Beet in Imperial Germany. In *Albert, B. and Graves, A., eds.*, 1984, pp. 31–45. **[G: Germany]**

Péteri, György. The Inflation-Proof Gold Standard: The Foreign Policy of *Riksbankschefen.* Victor Moll and the Origin of the Swedish Ban on Gold Imports in 1924. *J. Europ. Econ. Hist.*, September–December 1984, *13*(3), pp. 635–63. **[G: Sweden]**

Pippenger, John. Bank of England Operations, 1893–1913. In *Bordo, M. D. and Schwartz, A. J., eds.*, 1984, pp. 203–22. **[G: U.K.]**

Rooth, T. J. T. Limits of Leverage: The Anglo–Danish Trade Agreements of 1933. *Econ. Hist. Rev., 2nd Ser.*, May 1984, *37*(2), pp. 211–28. **[G: U.K.; Denmark]**

Santoni, G. J. A Private Central Bank: Some Olde English Lessons. *Fed. Res. Bank St. Louis Rev.*, April 1984, *66*(4), pp. 12–22. **[G: U.K.]**

Schwartz, Anna J. A Retrospective on the Classical Gold Standard, 1821–1931: Introduction. In *Bordo, M. D. and Schwartz, A. J., eds.*, 1984, pp. 1–20. **[G: U.K.]**

Smith, Roger. Housing in Europe: Great Britain. In *Wynn, M., ed.*, 1984, pp. 75–120. **[G: U.K.]**

Sylla, Richard E. Italy in the Gold Standard Period, 1861–1914: Comment. In *Bordo, M. D. and Schwartz, A. J., eds.*, 1984, pp. 442–46. **[G: Italy]**

Thomas, Mark. Discussion [Keynes and Protection] [Macroeconomic Instability and the "Natural" Processes in Early Neoclassical Economics]. *J. Econ. Hist.*, June 1984, *44*(2), pp. 375–79. **[G: U.K.]**

Tomlinson, J. D. A "Keynesian Revolution" in Economic Policy-Making? *Econ. Hist. Rev., 2nd Ser.*, May 1984, *37*(2), pp. 258–62. **[G: U.K.]**

Toumanoff, Peter G. Some Effects of Land Tenure Reforms on Russian Agricultural Productivity, 1901–1913. *Econ. Develop. Cult. Change*, July 1984, *32*(4), pp. 861–72. **[G: U.S.S.R.]**

Trebilcock, Michael. Restrictive Covenants in the Sale of a Business: An Economic Perspective. *Int. Rev. Law Econ.*, December 1984, *4*(2), pp. 137–61. **[G: U.K.; U.S.; Canada]**

Webb, Steven B. The Supply of Money and Reichsbank Financing of Government and Corporate Debt in Germany, 1919–1923. *J. Econ. Hist.*, June 1984, *44*(2), pp. 499–507. **[G: Germany]**

Wellington, Donald C. The English Poor Law: A Negative Income Tax. *Atlantic Econ. J.*, December 1984, *12*(4), pp. 46–50. **[G: U.K.]**

Wood, John H. The Search for a Monetary Policy Rule in an Uncertain World. *Fed. Res. Bank Dallas Econ. Rev.*, September 1984, pp. 13–23. **[G: U.S.; U.K.]**

Wordie, J. R. The Chronology of English Enclosure: A Reply. *Econ. Hist. Rev., 2nd Ser.*, November 1984, *37*(4), pp. 560–62. **[G: U.K.]**

Wynn, Martin. Housing in Europe: Spain. In *Wynn, M., ed.*, 1984, pp. 121–54. **[G: Spain]**

045 Economic History: Asia

0450 General

Ahmed, Feroz. Transformation of Agrarian Structures in Pakistan: The Punjab: A Preliminary Analysis. In *Ngo, M., ed., vol. 2*, 1984, pp. 606–39. **[G: Pakistan]**

Asajima, Shoichi. Flow-of-Funds Analysis of the Sumitomo Zaibatsu. In *Nakagawa, K. and Morikawa, H., eds.*, 1984, pp. 72–103. **[G: Japan]**

Ellman, Michael. On a Mistake of Preobrazhensky and Stalin. In *Ellman, M.*, 1984, pp. 54–57. **[G: U.S.S.R.; China]**

Harada, Toshimaru. "Murameisaichō" in Ōmi Province Written during Tokugawa Era. (In Japanese. With English summary.) *Osaka Econ. Pap.*, December 1984, *34*(2–3), pp. 322–27. **[G: Japan]**

Joshi, P. C. Conflicting Pulls of Productivity and Employment: Contemporary Choices in the Light of Historical Experience. In *Ngo, M., ed., vol. 2*, 1984, pp. 797–814. **[G: India; Japan; U.K.]**

Ludden, David. South Asia Cambridged in Economic Perspective: A Review Article. *J. Econ. Hist.*, December 1984, *44*(4), pp. 1091–93. **[G: S. Asia]**

Miyamoto, Matao and Hiroyama, Kensuke. The Retreat from Diversification and the Desire for Specialization in Kōnoike: Late Meiji to Early Shōwa. In *Nakagawa, K. and Morikawa, H., eds.*, 1984, pp. 104–30. **[G: Japan]**

Mukund, Kanakalatha. Keynes on Indian Economic Problems and Policies: A Historical Appraisal. *Indian Econ. J.*, July–Sept. 1984, *32*(1), pp. 37–48. **[G: India]**

Nagasawa, Yasuaki. The Works of Japanese Business Historians in 1982: Business History of Japan. In *Nakagawa, K. and Morikawa, H., eds.*, 1984, pp. 150–59.

Pamuk, Şevket. The Ottoman Empire in the "Great Depression" of 1873–1896. *J. Econ. Hist.*, March 1984, *44*(1), pp. 107–18. **[G: Middle East; S. Europe; Turkey]**

Patrick, Hugh. Japanese Financial Development in Historical Perspective, 1868–1980. In *[Reynolds, L. G.]*, 1984, pp. 302–27. **[G: Japan]**

Prasad, Pradhan H. Changing Class Relations in India's Agriculture: A Statistical Appraisal. In *Ngo, M., ed., vol. 2*, 1984, pp. 567–605. [G: India]

Reid, Anthony. The Pre-colonial Economy of Indonesia. *Bull. Indonesian Econ. Stud.*, August 1984, *20*(2), pp. 151–67. [G: Indonesia]

Watanabe, Hisashi. A History of the Process Leading to the Formation of Fuji Electric. In *Nakagawa, K. and Morikawa, H., eds.*, 1984, pp. 47–71. [G: Japan]

Yano, Yuko. Energy and Economic Development in Japan. In *Baum, V., et al.*, 1984, pp. 134–45. [G: Japan]

Yui, Tsunehiko. The Development of the Organizational Structure of Top Management in Meiji Japan. In *Nakagawa, K. and Morikawa, H., eds.*, 1984, pp. 1–23. [G: Japan]

0451 History of Product Prices and Markets

Alderman, Harold. Attributing Technological Bias to Public Goods. *J. Devel. Econ.*, April 1984, *14*(3), pp. 375–93. [G: Japan]

Attwood, Donald W. Capital and the Transformation of Agrarian Class Systems: Sugar Production in India. In *Desai, M.; Rudolph, S. H. and Rudra, A., eds.*, 1984, pp. 20–50. [G: India]

Chaudhuri, B. B. Rural Power Structure and Agricultural Productivity in Eastern India, 1757–1947. In *Desai, M.; Rudolph, S. H. and Rudra, A., eds.*, 1984, pp. 100–70. [G: India]

Hiroyama, Kensuke. Human Factors and the Acquisition of Capital in a National Bank—A Case of the 13th National Bank in Osaka: 1888–1897. (In Japanese. With English summary.) *Osaka Econ. Pap.*, December 1984, *34*(2–3), pp. 362–93. [G: Japan]

Kiyokawa, Yukihiko. The Diffusion of New Technologies in the Japanese Sericulture Industry: The Case of the Hybrid Silkworm. *Hitotsubashi J. Econ.*, June 1984, *25*(1), pp. 31–59. [G: Japan]

Larkin, John A. The International Face of the Philippine Sugar Industry, 1836–1920. *Philippine Rev. Econ. Bus.*, Mar./June 1984, *21*(1/2), pp. 39–58. [G: Philippines]

Ludden, David. Productive Power in Agriculture: A Survey of Work on the Local History of British India. In *Desai, M.; Rudolph, S. H. and Rudra, A., eds.*, 1984, pp. 51–99. [G: India]

Milward, Alan S. Restriction of Supply as a Strategic Choice. In *McCormick, G. H. and Bissell, R. E., eds.*, 1984, pp. 44–58. [G: Japan; Germany; U.K.]

Miyamoto, Matao. Family Companies in the Early Showa Era—Its Position and Performance. (In Japanese. With English summary.) *Osaka Econ. Pap.*, December 1984, *34*(2–3), pp. 328–44. [G: Japan]

Murota, Takeshi. Heat Economy of the Water Planet Earth: An Entropic Analysis and the Water–Soil Matrix Theory. *Hitotsubashi J. Econ.*, December 1984, *25*(2), pp. 161–72. [G: U.K.; Japan]

Pray, Carl E. The Impact of Agricultural Research in British India. *J. Econ. Hist.*, June 1984, *44*(2), pp. 429–40. [G: India]

Shimotani, Masahiro. Formation of "New Zaibatsu" in Prewar Japan: Case Study on Nisso Konzern. *Kyoto Univ. Econ. Rev.*, April 1984, *54*(1), pp. 40–59. [G: Japan]

Tucker, Richard P. The Historical Context of Social Forestry in the Kumaon Himalayas. *J. Devel. Areas*, April 1984, *18*(3), pp. 341–55. [G: India]

Udagawa, Masaru. The Contribution of Sogo Shosha to the Multinationalization of Japanese Industrial Enterprises in Historical Perspective: Comments. In *Okochi, A. and Inoue, T., eds.*, 1984, pp. 93–94. [G: Japan]

Yang, Tien-yi. Foreign Business Activities and the Chinese Response, 1842–1937. In *Okochi, A. and Inoue, T., eds.*, 1984, pp. 215–57. [G: China]

Yasumuro, Ken'ichi. The Contribution of Sogo Shosha to the Multinationalization of Japanese Industrial Enterprises in Historical Perspective. In *Okochi, A. and Inoue, T., eds.*, 1984, pp. 65–92. [G: Japan]

0452 History of Factor Prices and Markets

Coale, Ansley J. Fertility in Prerevolutionary Rural China: In Defense of a Reassessment. *Population Devel. Rev.*, September 1984, *10*(3), pp. 471–80. [G: China]

Inoki, Takenori. Japanese Emigration to Hawaii and North America in 1890s. (In Japanese. With English summary.) *Osaka Econ. Pap.*, December 1984, *34*(2–3), pp. 239–47. [G: Japan; U.S.]

Mookerjee, Rajen. The Demand for Money in Colonial India: A Secular Perspective. *Indian Econ. J.*, July–Sept. 1984, *32*(1), pp. 49–60. [G: India]

Murray, Martin J. The Development of Capitalism and the Making of the Working Class in Colonial Indochina, 1870–1940. In *Munslow, B. and Finch, H., eds.*, 1984, pp. 216–33. [G: Indochina]

Newman, Richard. Vanguard of the Proletariat? Communists and Unions in Shanghai and Bombay, 1927–1929. In *Munslow, B. and Finch, H., eds.*, 1984, pp. 272–98. [G: China; India]

Sakudō, Yōtarō. Labor Management Practices and Philosophy of a Spinning Company in the Early Showa Period—Riemon Uno and Toyobo Himeji Factory. (In Japanese. With English summary.) *Osaka Econ. Pap.*, December 1984, *34*(2–3), pp. 345–61. [G: Japan]

Sugiyama, Kazuo. Business Finance in Japanese Business History. In *Nakagawa, K. and Morikawa, H., eds.*, 1984, pp. 24–46. [G: U.K.; U.S.; W. Germany; Japan]

Whittaker, William. Migration and Agrarian Change in Garhwal District, Uttar Pradesh. In *[Farmer, B. H.]*, 1984, pp. 109–35. [G: India]

Wolf, Arthur P. Fertility in Prerevolutionary Rural China. *Population Devel. Rev.*, September 1984, *10*(3), pp. 443–70. [G: China]

0453 History of Public Economic Policy, all levels

Duus, Peter. The Reaction of Japanese Big Business to a State-controlled Economy in the 1930s. *Rivista Int. Sci. Econ. Com.*, September 1984, *31*(9), pp. 819–32. [G: Japan]

McAlpin, Michelle Burge. Economic Policy and the True Believer: The Use of Ricardian Rent Theory in the Bombay Survey and Settlement System. *J. Econ. Hist.*, June 1984, *44*(2), pp. 421–27. [G: India]

Silagi, Michael. Land Reform in Kiaochow, China: From 1898 to 1914 the Menace of Disastrous Land Speculation Was Averted by Taxation. *Amer. J. Econ. Soc.*, April 1984, *43*(2), pp. 167–78. [G: China]

046 Economic History: Africa

0460 General

Alpers, Edward A. State, Merchant Capital, and Gender Relations in Southern Mozambique to the End of the Nineteenth Century: Some Tentative Hypotheses. *African Econ. Hist.*, 1984, (13), pp. 23–55. [G: Mozambique]

Choate, Stephen. Agricultural Development and Government Policy in Settler Economies: A Comment. *Econ. Hist. Rev., 2nd Ser.*, August 1984, *37*(3), pp. 409–13. [G: Rhodesia]

Mandala, Elias. Capitalism, Kinship and Gender in the Lower Tchiri (Shire) Valley of Malawi, 1860–1960: An Alterntive Theoretical Framework. *African Econ. Hist.*, 1984, (13), pp. 137–69.

Mosley, Paul. Agricultural Development and Government Policy: A Reply. *Econ. Hist. Rev., 2nd Ser.*, August 1984, *37*(3), pp. 414–16. [G: Rhodesia]

Taylor, Elizabeth. Peasants or Proletarians? The Transformation of Agrarian Production Relations in Egypt. In *Munslow, B. and Finch, H., eds.*, 1984, pp. 164–88. [G: Egypt]

0461 History of Product Prices and Markets

Clarence-Smith, W. G. The Sugar and Rum Industries in the Portuguese Empire, 1850–1914. In *Albert, B. and Graves, A., eds.*, 1984, pp. 227–35. [G: Africa]

Dyer, Mark. Export Production in Western Libya, 1750–1793. *African Econ. Hist.*, 1984, (13), pp. 117–36. [G: Libya]

Lovejoy, Paul E. Commercial Sectors in the Economy of the Nineteenth-Century Central Sudan: The Trans-Saharan Trade and the Desert-Side Salt Trade. *African Econ. Hist.*, 1984, (13), pp. 85–116. [G: Sudan]

Owen, Roger. The Egyptian Sugar Industry, 1870–1914: From State to Private Ownership and from Export Orientation to Production for the Local Market. In *Albert, B. and Graves, A., eds.*, 1984, pp. 217–25. [G: Egypt]

Richardson, Peter. The Natal Sugar Industry in the Nineteenth Century. In *Albert, B. and Graves, A., eds.*, 1984, pp. 237–58. [G: S. Africa]

Richardson, Peter and Van Helten, Jean-Jacques. The Development of the South African Gold-Mining Industry, 1895–1918. *Econ. Hist. Rev., 2nd Ser.*, August 1984, *37*(3), pp. 319–40. [G: S. Africa]

0462 History of Factor Prices and Markets

Crisp, Jeff. The Labour Question in the Gold Coast, 1870–1906. In *Munslow, B. and Finch, H., eds.*, 1984, pp. 18–41. [G: Ghana]

Eltis, David. Mortality and Voyage Length in the Middle Passage: New Evidence from the Nineteenth Century. *J. Econ. Hist.*, June 1984, *44*(2), pp. 301–08. [G: Africa]

Lovejoy, Paul E. Commercial Sectors in the Economy of the Nineteenth-Century Central Sudan: The Trans-Saharan Trade and the Desert-Side Salt Trade. *African Econ. Hist.*, 1984, (13), pp. 85–116. [G: Sudan]

Munslow, Barry. Proletarianisation in Mozambique. In *Munslow, B. and Finch, H., eds.*, 1984, pp. 77–98. [G: Mozambique]

O'Brien, Jay. The Political Economy of Semi-Proletarianisation under Colonialism: Sudan 1925–50. In *Munslow, B. and Finch, H., eds.*, 1984, pp. 121–47. [G: Sudan]

Parpart, Jane L. The "Labor Aristocracy" Debate in Africa: The Copperbelt Case, 1924–1967. *African Econ. Hist.*, 1984, (13), pp. 171–91. [G: Africa]

0463 History of Public Economic Policy, all levels

Neale, Walter C. The Evolution of Colonial Institutions: An Argument Illustrated from the Economic History of British Central Africa. *J. Econ. Issues*, December 1984, *18*(4), pp. 1177–87. [G: U.K.; Zimbabwe; Zambia; Malawi]

047 Economic History: Latin America and Caribbean

0470 General

Bernholz, Peter. Inflation, Over-indebtedness, Crisis and Consolidation: Argentina and the Baring Crisis (1884–1900). *Z. ges. Staatswiss.*, December 1984, *140*(4), pp. 669–84. [G: Argentina]

Burns, E. Bradford. The Modernization of Underdevelopment: El Salvador, 1858–1931. *J. Devel. Areas*, April 1984, *18*(3), pp. 293–316. [G: El Salvador]

Cortés Douglas, Hernán. Lecciones del Pasado Recesiones Económicas en Chile: 1926–1982. (With English summary.) *Cuadernos Econ.*, August 1984, *21*(63), pp. 137–68. [G: Chile]

Díaz-Alejandro, Carlos F. No Less than One Hundred Years of Argentine Economic History Plus Some Comparisons. In *[Reynolds, L. G.]*, 1984, pp. 328–61. [G: Argentina; Australia; Brazil]

Guy, Donna J. Dependency, the Credit Market, and Argentine Industrialization, 1860–1940. *Bus. Hist. Rev.*, Winter 1984, *58*(4), pp. 532–61. [G: Argentina]

Wessman, James W. Sugar and Demography: Population Dynamics in the Spanish Antilles During the Nineteenth and Twentieth Centuries. In *Albert, B. and Graves, A., eds.*, 1984, pp. 95–108. [G: Cuba; Puerto Rico]

0471 History of Product Prices and Markets

Armstrong, Christopher and Nelles, H. V. A Curious Capital Flow: Canadian Investment in Mexico, 1902–1910. *Bus. Hist. Rev.*, Summer 1984, *58*(2), pp. 178–203. [G: Canada; Mexico]

Delson, Roberta M. Sugar Production for the Nineteenth Century British Market: Rethinking the Roles of Brazil and the British West Indies. In *Albert, B. and Graves, A., eds.*, 1984, pp. 59–80. [G: Brazil; Caribbean; U.K.]

Donghi, Tulio Halperin. Canción de otoño en primavera: previsiones sobre la crisis de la agricultura cerealera argentina (1894–1930). (With English summary.) *Desarrollo Econ.*, October–December 1984, *24*(95), pp. 367–86. [G: Argentina]

Feuer, Carl Henry. Better Must Come: Sugar and Jamaica in the 20th Century. *Soc. Econ. Stud.*, December 1984, *33*(4), pp. 1–49. [G: Jamaica]

Gelman, Jorge Daniel. Natural Economies or Money Economies? Silver Production and Monetary Circulation in Spanish America (Late XVI–Early XVII Centuries). *J. Europ. Econ. Hist.*, Spring 1984, *13*(1), pp. 99–115. [G: Bolivia; Argentina; Paraguay]

Guy, Donna J. Sugar Industries at the Periphery of the World Market: Argentina, 1860–1914. In *Albert, B. and Graves, A., eds.*, 1984, pp. 147–62. [G: Argentina]

Haraksingh, Kusha. Labour, Technology and the Sugar Estates in Trinidad, 1870–1914. In *Albert, B. and Graves, A., eds.*, 1984, pp. 133–45. [G: Trinidad]

Jones, Charles A. Competition and Structural Change in the Buenos Aires Fire Insurance Market: The Local Board of Agents, 1875–1921. In *Westall, O. M., ed.*, 1984, pp. 114–29. [G: Argentina; U.K.]

Kronish, Rich and Mericle, Kenneth S. The Development of the Latin American Motor Vehicle Industry, 1900-1980: A Class Analysis. In *Kronish, R. and Mericle, K. S., eds.*, 1984, pp. 261–306. [G: Latin America]

Mattei, Andres A. Ramos. The Growth of the Puerto Rican Sugar Industry under North American Domination: 1899–1910. In *Albert, B. and Graves, A., eds.*, 1984, pp. 121–31. [G: Puerto Rico]

O'Connell, Arturo. La Argentina en la Depresión: los problemas de una economía abierta. (With English summary.) *Desarrollo Econ.*, January–March 1984, *23*(92), pp. 479–514. [G: Argentina]

Schnakenbourg, Christian. From Sugar Estate to Central Factory: The Industrial Revolution in the Caribbean (1840–1905). In *Albert, B. and Graves, A., eds.*, 1984, pp. 83–93. [G: Caribbean]

Warman, Arturo. The Cauldron of the Revolution: Agrarian Capitalism and Sugar Industry in Morelos, Mexico, 1880–1910. In *Albert, B. and Graves, A., eds.*, 1984, pp. 165–79. [G: Mexico]

0472 History of Factor Prices and Markets

Albert, Bill. The Creation of a Proletariat on Peru's Coastal Sugar Plantations: 1880–1920. In *Munslow, B. and Finch, H., eds.*, 1984, pp. 99–120. [G: Peru]

Albert, Bill. The Labour Force on Peru's Sugar Plantations 1820–1930: A Survey. In *Albert, B. and Graves, A., eds.*, 1984, pp. 199–215. [G: Peru]

Engerman, Stanley L. Economic Change and Contract Labor in the British Caribbean: The End of Slavery and the Adjustment to Emancipation. *Exploration Econ. Hist.*, April 1984, *21*(2), pp. 133–50. [G: British W. Indies; Caribbean]

Fenoaltea, Stefano. Slavery and Supervision in Comparative Perspective: A Model. *J. Econ. Hist.*, September 1984, *44*(3), pp. 635–68. [G: U.S.; U.K.; Italy; Latin America]

Fernández, Manuel A. British Nitrate Companies and the Emergence of Chile's Proletariat, 1880–1914. In *Munslow, B. and Finch, H., eds.*, 1984, pp. 42–76. [G: Chile]

Galenson, David W. The Rise and Fall of Indentured Servitude in the Americas: An Economic Analysis. *J. Econ. Hist.*, March 1984, *44*(1), pp. 1–26. [G: Caribbean; Latin America; U.S.]

Haraksingh, Kusha. Labour, Technology and the Sugar Estates in Trinidad, 1870–1914. In *Albert, B. and Graves, A., eds.*, 1984, pp. 133–45. [G: Trinidad]

Haworth, Nigel. Proletarianisation in the World Order: The Peruvian Experience. In *Munslow, B. and Finch, H., eds.*, 1984, pp. 234–54. [G: Peru]

Lundahl, Mats. Defense and Distribution: Agricultural Policy in Haiti during the Reign of Jean-Jacques Dessalines, 1804–1806. *Scand. Econ. Hist. Rev.*, 1984, *32*(2), pp. 77–103. [G: Haiti]

McKay, R. Reynolds. The Impact of the Great Depression on Immigrant Mexican Labor: Repatriation of the Bridgeport, Texas, Coal Miners. *Soc. Sci. Quart.*, June 1984, *65*(2), pp. 354–63. [G: U.S.; Mexico]

Munck, Ronaldo. The Formation and Development of the Working Class in Argentina, 1857–1919. In *Munslow, B. and Finch, H., eds.*, 1984, pp. 255–71. [G: Argentina]

Olwig, Karen Fog. 'Witnesses in Spite of Themselves': Reconstructing Afro-Caribbean Culture in the Danish W. Indian Archives. *Scand. Econ. Hist. Rev.*, 1984, *32*(2), pp. 61–76. [G: Danish W. Indies; Caribbean]

Scott, Rebecca J. The Transformation of Sugar

Production in Cuba after Emancipation, 1880–1900: Planters, Colonos and Former Slaves. In *Albert, B. and Graves, A., eds.*, 1984, pp. 111–19. [G: Cuba]

Warman, Arturo. The Cauldron of the Revolution: Agrarian Capitalism and Sugar Industry in Morelos, Mexico, 1880–1910. In *Albert, B. and Graves, A., eds.*, 1984, pp. 165–79. [G: Mexico]

0473 History of Public Economic Policy, all levels

Amaral, Samuel. El empréstito de Londres de 1824. (With English summary.) *Desarrollo Econ.*, January-March 1984, *23*(92), pp. 559–88. [G: Argentina]

Aspe, Pedro and Beristain, Javier. The Evolution of Income Distribution Policies during The Post-Revolutionary Period in Mexico. In *Aspe, P. and Sigmund, P. E., eds.*, 1984, pp. 15–29. [G: Mexico]

Gaudio, Ricardo and Pilone, Jorge. Estado y relaciones laborales en el período previo al surgimiento del peronismo, 1935–1943. (With English summary.) *Desarrollo Econ.*, July–September 1984, *24*(94), pp. 235–73. [G: Argentina]

Guy, Donna J. Sugar Industries at the Periphery of the World Market: Argentina, 1860–1914. In *Albert, B. and Graves, A., eds.*, 1984, pp. 147–62. [G: Argentina]

Horowitz, Joel. Ideologías sindicales y políticas estatales en la Argentina, 1930–1943. (With English summary.) *Desarrollo Econ.*, July–September 1984, *24*(94), pp. 275–96. [G: Argentina]

Llach, Juan Jose. El Plan Pinedo de 1940, su significado histórico y los orígenes de la economía política del peronismo. (With English summary.) *Desarrollo Econ.*, January-March 1984, *23*(92), pp. 515–58. [G: Argentina]

Lundahl, Mats. Defense and Distribution: Agricultural Policy in Haiti during the Reign of Jean-Jacques Dessalines, 1804–1806. *Scand. Econ. Hist. Rev.*, 1984, *32*(2), pp. 77–103. [G: Haiti]

Thalmann, Emilio Lozoya. Social Security, Health, and Social Solidarity in Mexico. In *Aspe, P. and Sigmund, P. E., eds.*, 1984, pp. 397–437. [G: Mexico]

048 Economic History: Oceania

0480 General

Díaz-Alejandro, Carlos F. No Less than One Hundred Years of Argentine Economic History Plus Some Comparisons. In *[Reynolds, L. G.]*, 1984, pp. 328–61. [G: Argentina; Australia; Brazil]

Helliwell, John F. Natural Resources and the Australian Economy. In *Caves, R. E. and Krause, L. B., eds.*, 1984, pp. 81–126. [G: Australia]

Maddock, Rodney and McLean, Ian. Supply-Side Shocks: The Case of Australian Gold. *J. Econ. Hist.*, December 1984, *44*(4), pp. 1047–67. [G: Australia]

McDonald, Ian M. Trying to Understand Stagflation. *Australian Econ. Rev.*, 3rd Quarter 1984, (67), pp. 32–56. [G: Australia]

Pope, David. Rostow's Kondratieff Cycle in Australia. *J. Econ. Hist.*, September 1984, *44*(3), pp. 729–53. [G: Australia]

Treadgold, Malcolm L. Growth, Structural Change, and Distribution in a Very Small Economy: A Case Study of Norfolk Island. *J. Devel. Areas*, October 1984, *19*(1), pp. 35–58. [G: Australia]

0481 History of Product Prices and Markets

Blainey, Geoffrey. The History of Multinational Factories in Australia. In *Okochi, A. and Inoue, T., eds.*, 1984, pp. 183–210. [G: Australia]

Giles, David E. A. and Hampton, Peter. Regional Production Relationships during the Industrialization of New Zealand, 1935–1948. *J. Reg. Sci.*, November 1984, *24*(4), pp. 519–33. [G: New Zealand]

Graves, Adrian. Crisis and Change in the Queensland Sugar Industry, 1862–1906. In *Albert, B. and Graves, A., eds.*, 1984, pp. 261–79. [G: Australia]

Snooks, G. D. Growth and Productivity Change in the Australian Mechanical Engineering Industry, 1910–1940. *Australian Econ. Hist. Rev.*, March 1984, *24*(1), pp. 53–70. [G: Australia]

Stanton, J. Protection, Market Structure, and Firm Behaviour: Inefficiency in the Early Australian Tyre Industry. *Australian Econ. Hist. Rev.*, September 1984, *24*(2), pp. 91–114. [G: Australia]

Statham, Pamela. The Role of the Commissariat in Early West Australian Economic Development. *Australian Econ. Hist. Rev.*, March 1984, *24*(1), pp. 20–33. [G: Australia]

Tsokhas, K. 'A Touch of Midas': The Rise of Western Mining Corporation, 1945–1975. *Australian Econ. Hist. Rev.*, September 1984, *24*(2), pp. 132–49. [G: Australia]

Yuzawa, Takeshi. The History of Multinational Factories in Australia: Comments. In *Okochi, A. and Inoue, T., eds.*, 1984, pp. 211–13. [G: Australia]

0482 History of Factor Prices and Markets

Brosnan, Peter. Australian Net Interstate Migration: 1911 to 1961. *Australian Econ. Hist. Rev.*, September 1984, *24*(2), pp. 150–72. [G: Australia]

Graves, Adrian. Crisis and Change in the Queensland Sugar Industry, 1862–1906. In *Albert, B. and Graves, A., eds.*, 1984, pp. 261–79. [G: Australia]

Nichol, W. The Medical Profession in New South Wales, 1788–1850. *Australian Econ. Hist. Rev.*, September 1984, *24*(2), pp. 115–31. [G: Australia]

Pope, David. Some Factors Inhibiting Australian Immigration in the 1920s. *Australian Econ. Hist. Rev.*, March 1984, *24*(1), pp. 34–52. [G: Australia]

0483 History of Public Economic Policy, all levels

Stanton, J. Protection, Market Structure, and Firm Behaviour: Inefficiency in the Early Australian Tyre Industry. *Australian Econ. Hist. Rev.*, September 1984, *24*(2), pp. 91–114.
[G: Australia]

Statham, Pamela. The Role of the Commissariat in Early West Australian Economic Development. *Australian Econ. Hist. Rev.*, March 1984, *24*(1), pp. 20–33. [G: Australia]

Stutchbury, Michael. The Playford Legend and the Industrialization of South Australia. *Australian Econ. Hist. Rev.*, March 1984, *24*(1), pp. 1–19. [G: Australia]

050 ECONOMIC SYSTEMS

0500 General

Balassa, Bela. Prices, Incentives, and Economic Growth. *Weltwirtsch. Arch.*, 1984, *120*(4), pp. 611–30. [G: Global]

Cugno, Franco and Ferrero, Mario. Individual Incentives by Adjusting Work Hours: Bellamy's Egalitarian Economy. *J. Compar. Econ.*, June 1984, *8*(2), pp. 182–206.

Desai, Meghnad. A General Theory of Poverty? A Review Article. *Indian Econ. Rev.*, July-Dec. 1984, *19*(2), pp. 157–69. [G: India]

Ellman, Michael. Against Convergence. In *Ellman, M.*, 1984, *1980*, pp. 291–310.

Gissurarson, Hannes H. 'The Only Truly Progressive Policy...' In *Barry, N., et al.*, 1984, pp. 1–23.

Gottlieb, Roger S. Feudalism and Historical Materialism: A Critique and a Synthesis. *Sci. Soc.*, Spring 1984, *48*(1), pp. 1–37. [G: U.S.]

Gray, John. The Road to Serfdom: Forty Years On. In *Barry, N., et al.*, 1984, pp. 25–42.

Groth, Alexander J.; Wade, Larry L. and Wiggins, Alvin D. Classifying the World's Political Systems: A Resource-Allocation Approach. In *Groth, A. J. and Wade, L. L., eds.*, 1984, pp. 19–40.

Gurley, John G. Marx's Contributions and Their Relevance Today. *Amer. Econ. Rev.*, May 1984, *74*(2), pp. 110–15.

Kersten, G. Tendencies in a Shortage Economy [*Economics of Shortage*]. *Acta Oecon.*, 1984, *32*(3–4), pp. 375–89.

Ruttan, Vernon W. and Hayami, Yujiro. Toward a Theory of Induced Institutional Innovation. *J. Devel. Stud.*, July 1984, *20*(4), pp. 203–23.
[G: Philippines]

Seldon, Arthur. Recollections: Before and After the Road to Serfdom: Reflections on Hayek in 1935, 1944, 1960, 1982. In *Barry, N., et al.*, 1984, pp. xiii–xxxii.

Shearmur, Jeremy. Hayek and the Wisdom of the Age. In *Barry, N., et al.*, 1984, pp. 65–85.

Zimbalist, Andrew. Introduction: Reflections on the State of the Art of Comparative Economics. In *Zimbalist, A., ed.*, 1984, pp. 1–14.

Zinam, Oleg. Economic Controls, Quality of Life, and Human Dignity. *Rivista Int. Sci. Econ. Com.*, February 1984, *31*(2), pp. 97–108.

051 Capitalist Economic Systems: Market Economies

0510 Capitalist Economic Systems: Market Economies

Abouchar, Alan. The Firm in Abyssinia: Capitalism, Socialism, and Economic Development in Ethiopia. *ACES Bull.*, Winter 1984, *26*(4), pp. 25–42. [G: Ethiopia]

Acham, Karl. Schumpeter—The Sociologist. In *Seidl, C., ed.*, 1984, pp. 155–72.

Adams, John. Foreign Economic Policy: Challenges of the 1980s. *J. Econ. Issues*, March 1984, *18*(1), pp. 275–94. [G: U.S.]

Alchian, Armen A. Specificity, Specialization, and Coalitions. *Z. ges. Staatswiss.*, March 1984, *140*(1), pp. 34–49.

Andic, Fuat M. and Andic, Suphan. The Politics of Redistribution in a Democracy. *Int. J. Soc. Econ.*, 1984, *11*(1/2), pp. 3–13.

Balducci, Renato; Candela, G. and Ricci, G. A Generalization of R. Goodwin Model with Rational Behavior of Economic Agents. In *Goodwin, R. M.; Krüger, M. and Vercelli, A., eds.*, 1984, pp. 47–66.

Bandyopadhyay, Pradeep. The State, Private Capital and Housing in the Paris Region. *Sci. Soc.*, Summer 1984, *48*(2), pp. 161–91.
[G: France]

Bandyopadhyay, Pradeep. Value and Post-Sraffa Marxian Analysis. *Sci. Soc.*, Winter 1984-1985, *48*(4), pp. 433–48.

Barone, Charles A. Reply [Dependency, Marxist Theory, and Salvaging the Idea of Capitalism in South Korea]. *Rev. Radical Polit. Econ.*, Summer & Fall 1984, *16*(2&3), pp. 195–97.
[G: S. Korea]

Barrère, Christian; Kebabdjian, Gérard and Weinstein, Olivier. L'accumulation intensive, norme de lecture du capitalisme? (Intensive Accumulation, the Key to Understanding Modern Capitalism? With English summary.) *Revue Écon.*, May 1984, *35*(3), pp. 479–506.

Barták, Vlastislav. Treatment of the Economic Maladies of Capitalism. *Czech. Econ. Digest.*, June 1984, (4), pp. 90–101. [G: U.S.; EEC; Japan]

Ben-Ner, Avner. Labor-managed and Participatory Firms: A Note. *J. Econ. Issues*, December 1984, *18*(4), pp. 1189–95.

Ben-Ner, Avner. On the Stability of the Cooperative Type of Organization. *J. Compar. Econ.*, September 1984, *8*(3), pp. 247–60.

Bernholz, Peter. The Political Economy of Growth [Review Article]. *Kyklos*, 1984, *37*(2), pp. 291–94. [G: Selected OECD]

Bernstein, Michael A. and Wilentz, Sean. Marketing, Commerce, and Capitalism in Rural Massachusetts [The Market and Massachusetts Farmers, 1750–1855]. *J. Econ. Hist.*, March 1984, *44*(1), pp. 171–73. [G: U.S.]

Black, Jennifer Ann. The Path to a "Sane Society," A Note. *Amer. Econ.*, Fall 1984, *28*(2), pp. 76–80.

Blinder, Alan S. The Keynesian Restoration. *Challenge*, May/June 1984, *27*(2), pp. 26–34. [G: U.S.]

Boitani, Andrea. Two Views on Oligopoly and Stagnation. *Econ. Notes*, 1984, (3), pp. 128–54.

Bonin, John P. Membership and Employment in an Egalitarian Cooperative. *Economica*, August 1984, *51*(203), pp. 295–305.

Booth, Douglas E. and Fortis, Louis C. Building a Cooperative Economy: A Strategy for Community Based Economic Development. *Rev. Soc. Econ.*, December 1984, *42*(3), pp. 339–59.

Bowles, Roger. Property and the Legal System. In *Whynes, D. K., ed.*, 1984, pp. 187–208.

Bowles, Samuel. Class Alliances and Surplus Labor Time. In *[Chenery, H. B.]*, 1984, pp. 103–14.

Breit, William. Galbraith and Friedman: Two Versions of Economic Reality. *J. Post Keynesian Econ.*, Fall 1984, *7*(1), pp. 18–29.

Breton, Yves. La théorie schumpétérienne de l'entrepreneur ou le problème de la connaissance économique. (Schumpeter's Theory of the Entrepreneur or the Problem of Economic Knowledge. With English summary.) *Revue Écon.*, March 1984, *35*(2), pp. 247–66.

Bruyn, Severyn T. The Community Self-Study: Worker Self-Management versus the New Class. *Rev. Soc. Econ.*, December 1984, *42*(3), pp. 388–412.

Bryceson, Deborah Fahy and Vuorela, Ulla. Outside the Domestic Labor Debate: Towards a Theory of Modes of Human Reproduction. *Rev. Radical Polit. Econ.*, Summer & Fall 1984, *16*(2&3), pp. 137–66. [G: Global]

Burton, John. The Instability of the 'Middle Way.' In *Barry, N., et al.*, 1984, pp. 87–115.

Buxbaum, Richard M. Federalism and Company Law. *Mich. Law Rev.*, April–May 1984, *82*(5 & 6), pp. 1163–81. [G: U.S.]

Caballero, José María. Unequal Pricing and Unequal Exchange between the Peasant and Capitalist Economies. *Cambridge J. Econ.*, December 1984, *8*(4), pp. 347–59.

Cameron, David R. Social Democracy, Corporatism, Labour Quiescence and the Representation of Economic Interest in Advanced Capitalist Society. In *Goldthorpe, J. H., ed.*, 1984, pp. 143–78. [G: OECD]

Carling, Alan. Observations on the Labor Theory of Value. *Sci. Soc.*, Winter 1984-1985, *48*(4), pp. 407–18.

Carling, Alan. Value and Strategy. *Sci. Soc.*, Summer 1984, *48*(2), pp. 129–60.

Caswell, Julie A. An Institutional Perspective on Corporate Control and the Network of Interlocking Directorates. *J. Econ. Issues*, June 1984, *18*(2), pp. 619–26.

Cavalli, Alessandro. Giovani, politica sociale e "Welfare State." (Young People, Social Policy and Welfare State. With English summary.)

Giorn. Econ., Nov.-Dec. 1984, *43*(11–12), pp. 861–66.

Chandler, Alfred D., Jr. The Emergence of Managerial Capitalism. *Bus. Hist. Rev.*, Winter 1984, *58*(4), pp. 473–503. [G: U.S.; U.K.; Germany; Japan]

Christians, Friedrich Wilhelm. Entrepreneurs and Society. In *Engels, W. and Pohl, H., eds.*, 1984, pp. 1–10. [G: W. Germany]

Chrystal, K. Alec. Dutch Disease or Monetarist Medicine? The British Economy under Mrs. Thatcher. *Fed. Res. Bank St. Louis Rev.*, May 1984, *66*(5), pp. 27–37. [G: U.K.]

Chyba, Antonín. The Problem of Raw Material and Energy Supplies in Today's World. *Czech. Econ. Digest.*, March 1984, (2), pp. 50–68. [G: Global]

Cirillo, Renato. Léon Walras and Social Justice. *Amer. J. Econ. Soc.*, January 1984, *43*(1), pp. 53–60.

Ciscel, David H. Galbraith's Planning System as a Substitute for Market Theory. *J. Econ. Issues*, June 1984, *18*(2), pp. 411–18.

Cornforth, Chris. The Role of Local Co-operative Development Agencies in Promoting Worker Co-operatives. *Ann. Pub. Co-op. Econ.*, July–September 1984, *55*(3), pp. 253–79. [G: U.K.]

Culbertson, John M. The New Potential of Evolutionary–Institutional Economics. *J. Econ. Issues*, June 1984, *18*(2), pp. 611–18.

Dahmén, Erik. Ekonomi i omvandling Utländska och finländska erfarenheter. (A Changing Economy: Foreign and Finnish Experience. With English summary.) *Ekon. Samfundets Tidskr.*, 1984, *37*(1), pp. 23–44. [G: MDCs; Finland]

Dahmén, Erik. Industriens villkor nu och på 1930-talet. (With English summary.) *Nationaløkon. Tidsskr.*, 1984, *122*(3), pp. 333–46. [G: Nordic Countries]

Danner, Peter L. The Moral Foundations of Community. *Rev. Soc. Econ.*, December 1984, *42*(3), pp. 231–52.

Deloche, Régis. Aménagement infrastructurel du territoire et politique de concurrence. (With English summary.) *Revue Écon. Polit.*, January–February 1984, *94*(1), pp. 92–115. [G: France]

Dorn, James A. Planning America: Government or the Market? Introduction. *Cato J.*, Fall 1984, *4*(2), pp. 365–80. [G: U.S.]

Dos Santos, Theotonio. Theory of Development, Dependence and Social Change. In *Ngo, M., ed., vol. 2*, 1984, pp. 862–81. [G: LDCs]

Dugger, William M. Human Liberation: Workplace Reform as the Next Step in Social Evolution. *Int. J. Soc. Econ.*, 1984, *11*(5), pp. 29–39.

Dugger, William M. The Nature of Capital Accumulation and Technological Progress in the Modern Economy. *J. Econ. Issues*, September 1984, *18*(3), pp. 799–823. [G: U.S.]

Dupuis, Xavier; Greffe, Xavier and Pflieger, Sylvie. Quel mode de développement pour l'Économie Sociale? (Which Way of Development for the Social Economy Sector? With English summary.) *Consommation*, April–June 1984, *31*(2), pp. 3–21. **[G: France]**

Dyer, Alan W. The Habit of Work: A Theoretical Exploration. *J. Econ. Issues*, June 1984, *18*(2), pp. 557–64.

Edelstein, Michael. Discussion [The Decline of the British Economy: An Institutional Perspective] [Structural Transformation and the Demand for New Labor in Advanced Economies: Interwar Britain]. *J. Econ. Hist.*, June 1984, *44*(2), pp. 599–602. **[G: U.K.]**

Elbaum, Bernard and Lazonick, William. The Decline of the British Economy: An Institutional Perspective. *J. Econ. Hist.*, June 1984, *44*(2), pp. 567–83. **[G: U.K.]**

Ellerman, David P. Entrepreneurship in the Mondragon Cooperatives. *Rev. Soc. Econ.*, December 1984, *42*(3), pp. 272–94.
[G: Spain]

Ellerman, David P. Theory of Legal Structure: Worker Cooperatives. *J. Econ. Issues*, September 1984, *18*(3), pp. 861–91. **[G: U.S.; Yugoslavia; Spain]**

Ellerman, David P. Workers' Cooperatives: The Question of Legal Structure. In *Jackall, R. and Levin, H. M., eds.*, 1984, pp. 257–74.
[G: U.S.]

Elliott, John E. Karl Marx's Theory of Socio-Institutional Transformation in Late-Stage Capitalism. *J. Econ. Issues*, June 1984, *18*(2), pp. 383–91.

Elliott, John E. Recapitulation and Prospects: Worker Ownership and Self-Government. *Rev. Soc. Econ.*, December 1984, *42*(3), pp. 433–38.

Ellman, Michael. The Crisis of the Welfare State—The Dutch Experience. In *Boulding, K. E., ed.*, 1984, pp. 191–211.
[G: Netherlands; OECD]

Engellau, Patrik. The Self-Destruction of Affluence. In *Miyawaki, N., ed.*, 1984, pp. 198–206. **[G: MDCs]**

Entov, R. M. The "Rule" and Fall of the Phillips Curve. *Prob. Econ.*, February 1984, *26*(10), pp. 3–36.

Esping-Andersen, Gösta and Korpi, Walter. Social Policy as Class Politics in Post-war Capitalism: Scandinavia, Austria, and Germany. In *Goldthorpe, J. H., ed.*, 1984, pp. 179–208.
[G: Scandinavia; Austria; Germany]

Esterin, Saul. Self-Management and Capitalism Compared: A Review of M. R. Sertel's, *Workers and Incentives*. *Econ. Anal. Worker's Manage.*, 1984, *18*(1), pp. 103–07.

Eyer, Joe. Capitalism, Health, and Illness. In *McKinlay, J. B., ed.*, 1984, pp. 23–59.

Fehr, Ernst. Workers' Management and Capitalism in a Nutshell. *Econ. Anal. Worker's Manage.*, 1984, *18*(4), pp. 319–31.

Fellner, William. Currents and Countercurrents in Political and Economic Thought. *Carnegie-Rochester Conf. Ser. Public Policy*, Autumn 1984, *21*, pp. 231–52.

Figura, Ivan. Crisis of the Concepts of the De-

fence of Neo-Colonialism. *Czech. Econ. Digest.*, June 1984, (4), pp. 68–89. **[G: Global]**

Fine, Ben and Murfin, Andy. The Political Economy of Monopoly and Competition: A Critique of Monopoly and Stagnation Theory. *Int. J. Ind. Organ.*, June 1984, *2*(2), pp. 133–46.

Ford, G. W. The Democratization of Work in Australia. *Econ. Anal. Worker's Manage.*, 1984, *18*(1), pp. 77–102. **[G: Australia]**

Foster, John Bellamy. Marxian Economics and the State. In *Foster, J. B. and Szlajfer, H., eds.*, 1984, *1982*, pp. 325–49.

Foster, John Bellamy. The Limits of U.S. Capitalism: Surplus Capacity and Capacity Surplus. In *Foster, J. B. and Szlajfer, H., eds.*, 1984, pp. 198–213. **[G: U.S.]**

Foster, John Bellamy and Szlajfer, Henryk. The Faltering Economy: Introduction. In *Foster, J. B. and Szlajfer, H., eds.*, 1984, pp. 7–22.

Frank, Andre Gunder. Even Heretics Remain Bound by Traditional Thought in Formulating Their Heresies. In *Frank, A. G.*, 1984, *1970*, pp. 87–103.

Frank, Andre Gunder. On "Feudal" Modes, Models and Methods of Escaping Capitalist Reality. In *Frank, A. G.*, 1984, *1973*, pp. 58–61.

Fröbel, Folker. The Current Development of the World-Economy: Reproduction of Labour and Accumulation of Capital on a World Scale. In *Addo, H., ed.*, 1984, pp. 51–118. **[G: Global]**

Furubotn, Eirik G. and Richter, Rudolf. The New Institutional Economics: Symposium June 6–10, 1983, Mettlach/Saar. *Z. ges. Staatswiss.*, March 1984, *140*(1), pp. 1–6.

Fusfeld, Daniel R. Labor-managed and Participatory Firms: Reply. *J. Econ. Issues*, December 1984, *18*(4), pp. 1195–98.

Galbraith, James K. Galbraith and the Theory of the Corporation. *J. Post Keynesian Econ.*, Fall 1984, *7*(1), pp. 43–60.

Gamson, Zelda F. and Levin, Henry M. Obstacles to the Survival of Democratic Workplaces. In *Jackall, R. and Levin, H. M., eds.*, 1984, pp. 219–44. **[G: U.S.]**

George, David. Worker Self-Management versus the New Class: A Response. *Rev. Soc. Econ.*, December 1984, *42*(3), pp. 413–16.

Gibson, Roland. Marx and Logic as Social Function. *Int. J. Soc. Econ.*, 1984, *11*(6), pp. 3–43.

Giersch, Herbert. The Age of Schumpeter. *Amer. Econ. Rev.*, May 1984, *74*(2), pp. 103–09.

Gilbert, Alan and Ward, Peter. Community Action by the Urban Poor: Democratic Involvement, Community Self-Help or a Means of Social Control? *World Devel.*, August 1984, *12*(8), pp. 769–82. **[G: Colombia; Mexico; Venezuela]**

Gilpin, Robert. Structural Constraints on Economic Leverage: Market-Type Systems. In *McCormick, G. H. and Bissell, R. E., eds.*, 1984, pp. 105–28.

Glavanis, Pandeli. State and Labour in Libya. In *Lawless, R. and Findlay, A., eds.*, 1984, pp. 120–49. **[G: Libya]**

Goldthorpe, John H. Order and Conflict in Contemporary Capitalism: Introduction. In *Goldthorpe, J. H., ed.*, 1984, pp. 1–14.

Goldthorpe, John H. The End of Convergence: Corporatist and Dualist Tendencies in Modern Western Societies. In *Goldthorpe, J. H., ed.*, 1984, pp. 315–43.

Goleva, A. P. and Goleva, Yu. P. Definitions of Capital and Surplus Value. In *Smirnov, A. D.; Golosov, V. V. and Maximova, V. F., eds.*, 1984, pp. 60–70.

Golosov, V. V.; Matveev, V. P. and Korneeva, K. G. The Interpretation of Monopoly Capitalism. In *Smirnov, A. D.; Golosov, V. V. and Maximova, V. F., eds.*, 1984, pp. 137–70.

Gordon, David M. Capitalist Development and the History of American Cities. In *Tabb, W. K. and Sawers, L., eds.*, 1984, pp. 21–53.
[G: U.S.]

Gordon, Wendell C. The Role of Institutional Economics. *J. Econ. Issues*, June 1984, *18*(2), pp. 369–81.

Greenberg, Edward S. Producer Cooperatives and Democratic Theory: The Case of the Plywood Firms. In *Jackall, R. and Levin, H. M., eds.*, 1984, pp. 171–214. [G: U.S.]

Greffe, Xavier. Etat-providence et économie non officielle: liaisons possibles et impossibles. (The Relationship between Welfare State and Informal Economy. With English summary.) *Revue Écon.*, July 1984, *35*(4), pp. 667–89.

Gruchy, Allan G. Neo-Institutionalism, Neo-Marxism, and Neo-Keynesianism: An Evaluation. *J. Econ. Issues*, June 1984, *18*(2), pp. 547–56.

Gruenberg, Gladys W. Prospects: Solidarity within the Firm. *Rev. Soc. Econ.*, December 1984, *42*(3), pp. 424–26.

Gui, Benedetto. Basque versus Illyrian Labor-managed Firms: The Problem of Property Rights. *J. Compar. Econ.*, June 1984, *8*(2), pp. 168–81. [G: Spain; Yugoslavia]

Guttmann, Robert. Stagflation and Credit–Money in the U.S.A. *Brit. Rev. Econ. Issues*, Autumn 1984, *6*(15), pp. 79–119. [G: U.S.]

Habermas, Jürgen. What Does a Crisis Mean Today? Legitimation Problems in Late Capitalism. *Soc. Res.*, Spring & Summer 1984, *51*(1&2), pp. 39–64.

Hahn, Frank H. Reflections on the Invisible Hand. In *Hahn, F.*, 1984, *1982*, pp. 111–33.

Hammond, Peter J. Is Entrepreneurship Obsolescent? In *Seidl, C., ed.*, 1984, pp. 31–43.

Hanson, Charles and Rathkey, Paul. Industrial Democracy: A Post-Bullock Shopfloor View. *Brit. J. Ind. Relat.*, July 1984, *22*(2), pp. 154–68. [G: U.K.]

Hart-Landsberg, Martin. Capitalism and Third World Economic Development: A Critical Look at the South Korean "Miracle" [Dependency, Marxist Theory, and Salvaging the Idea of Capitalism in South Korea]. *Rev. Radical Polit. Econ.*, Summer & Fall 1984, *16*(2&3), pp. 181–93. [G: S. Korea]

Hart-Landsberg, Martin and Lembcke, Jerry. Class Struggle and Economic Transformation. *Rev. Radical Polit. Econ.*, Winter 1984, *16*(4), pp. 14–31.

Hasanuzzaman, S. M. Definition of Islamic Economics. *J. Res. Islamic Econ.*, Winter 1984, *1*(2), pp. 51–53.

Hauschildt, Jürgen. Opportunities for New Entrepreneurship in Old Firms. In *Giersch, H., ed.*, 1984, pp. 249–56.

von Hayek, Friedrich A. The Principles of a Liberal Social Order. In *von Hayek, F. A. (I)*, 1984, *1966*, pp. 363–81.

von Hayek, Friedrich A. Whither Democracy? In *von Hayek, F. A. (I)*, 1984, pp. 352–62.

Heinsohn, Gunnar and Steiger, Otto. "Marx and Keynes—Private Property and Money." *Écon. Soc.*, April 1984, *18*(4), pp. 37–71.

Hentze, Joachim. Die Stellung des Menschen in der sozialistischen Arbeitsökonomie. (With English summary.) *Z. Betriebswirtshaft*, January 1984, *54*(1), pp. 63–77.

Himmelweit, Susan. The Real Dualism of Sex and Class. *Rev. Radical Polit. Econ.*, Spring 1984, *16*(1), pp. 167–83.

Himmelweit, Susan. Value Relations and Divisions within the Working Class. *Sci. Soc.*, Fall 1984, *48*(3), pp. 323–43. [G: Global]

Honko, Jaakko. Challenges of Future Changes for Management and Management Development. *Liiketaloudellinen Aikak.*, 1984, *33*(3), pp. 239–52.

Horn, Walter. Libertarianism and Private Property in Land: The Positions of Rothbard and Nozick, Critically Examined, Are Disputed. *Amer. J. Econ. Soc.*, July 1984, *43*(3), pp. 341–55.

Inose, Hiroshi. Challenges for Policy of Network Oriented Society: A Japanese View. *Info. Econ. Policy*, 1984, *1*(4), pp. 369–79.
[G: Japan]

Ize, Alain. Disequilibrium Theories, Imperfect Competition and Income Distribution: A Fix-Price Analysis. *Oxford Econ. Pap.*, June 1984, *36*(2), pp. 248–58.

Jackall, Robert and Crain, Joyce. The Shape of the Small Worker Cooperative Movement. In *Jackall, R. and Levin, H. M., eds.*, 1984, pp. 88–108. [G: U.S.]

Jackall, Robert and Levin, Henry M. The Prospects for Worker Cooperatives in the United States. In *Jackall, R. and Levin, H. M., eds.*, 1984, pp. 277–90. [G: U.S.]

Jackall, Robert and Levin, Henry M. Work in America and the Cooperative Movement. In *Jackall, R. and Levin, H. M., eds.*, 1984, pp. 3–15. [G: U.S.]

Janover, L. Du capitalisme libéral au capitalisme libéré. (From Liberal to Liberated Capitalism. With English summary.) *Écon. Soc.*, July–August 1984, *18*(7–8), pp. 317–28.

Jenkins, Richard. Ethnicity and the Rise of Capitalism in Ulster. In *Ward, R. and Jenkins, R., eds.*, 1984, pp. 57–72. [G: U.K.]

Jones, Derek C. American Producer Cooperatives and Employee-Owned Firms: A Historical Perspective. In *Jackall, R. and Levin, H. M., eds.*, 1984, pp. 37–56. [G: U.S.]

Karpikov, E. I. and Pikin, A. S. Bourgeois and Reformist Agrarian Conceptions. In *Smirnov, A. D.; Golosov, V. V. and Maximova, V. F., eds.*, 1984, pp. 110–17.

Keane, John. Contradictions of the Welfare State: Introduction. In *Offe, C.*, 1984, pp. 11–34.

Keohane, Robert O. The World Political Economy and the Crisis of Embedded Liberalism. In *Goldthorpe, J. H., ed.*, 1984, pp. 15–38.

Khan, M. Akram. Islamic Economics: Nature and Need. *J. Res. Islamic Econ.*, Winter 1984, *1*(2), pp. 55–61.

Khan, M. Fahim. Macro Consumption Function in an Islamic Framework. *J. Res. Islamic Econ.*, Winter 1984, *1*(2), pp. 1–24.

Kienbaum, Gerhard. Opportunities for New Entrepreneurship in Old Firms: Comment. In *Giersch, H., ed.*, 1984, pp. 257–60.

Kindleberger, Charles P. Book Review: Magdoff, The Age of Imperialism. In *Kindleberger, C. P.*, 1984, *1971*, pp. 177–79.

Kirsch, Guy. Social Structure of Developed Societies—Review of the Government's Role. In *Miyawaki, N., ed.*, 1984, pp. 169–78.

Klein, Rudolf. Privatization and the Welfare State. *Lloyds Bank Rev.*, January 1984, (151), pp. 12–29. [G: U.K.]

Kogan, A. M.; Maximova, V. E. and Golosov, V. V. The Treatment of Value and Money. In *Smirnov, A. D.; Golosov, V. V. and Maximova, V. F., eds.*, 1984, pp. 35–59.

Kolm, Serge-Christophe. Théorie de la réciprocité et du choix des systèmes économiques. (Theory of Reciprocity and the Choice of Economic Systems. With English summary.) *Revue Écon.*, September 1984, *35*(5), pp. 871–910.

Laibman, David. Modes of Production and Theories of Transition. *Sci. Soc.*, Fall 1984, *48*(3), pp. 257–94.

Laibman, David. Value: A Dialog in One Act. *Sci. Soc.*, Winter 1984-1985, *48*(4), pp. 449–65.

Lassila, Jaakko. Industripolitik—reglering versus marknadskrafter. (With English summary.) *Nationaløkon. Tidsskr.*, 1984, *122*(3), pp. 347–56. [G: Nordic Countries]

Leathers, Charles G. Thatcher–Reagan Conservatism and Schumpeter's Prognosis for Capitalism. *Rev. Soc. Econ.*, April 1984, *42*(1), pp. 16–31.

Lederer, Emil. Social Control vs. Economic Law: An Old Dogma and a New Situation. *Soc. Res.*, Spring & Summer 1984, *51*(1&2), pp. 91–110.

Lehmbruch, Gerhard. Concertation and the Structure of Corporatist Networks. In *Goldthorpe, J. H., ed.*, 1984, pp. 60–80. [G: OECD]

Leite, Celso Barroso. Social Solutions for Economic Problems. *Int. J. Soc. Econ.*, 1984, *11*(3/4), pp. 108–13. [G: Brazil]

Lenel, Hans Otto. Ein dritter Weg? Zu Ota Šiks "Hummaner Wirtschaftsdemokratie." (With English Summary.) In *Eucken, W. and Böhm, F., eds.*, 1984, pp. 179–230.

Lévai, Imre. Capitalist International Trade: The Contradiction of Equality and Reciprocity. In *Ngo, M., ed., vol. 1*, 1984, pp. 68–78. [G: LDCs; MDCs]

Levin, Henry M. Employment and Productivity of Producer Cooperatives. In *Jackall, R. and Levin, H. M., eds.*, 1984, pp. 16–31. [G: Spain]

Levin, Henry M. ESOPs and the Financing of Worker Cooperatives. In *Jackall, R. and Levin, H. M., eds.*, 1984, pp. 245–56. [G: U.S.]

Lill, J. Lloyd, Jr. Cooperative Ventures in the United States. *Rev. Soc. Econ.*, December 1984, *42*(3), pp. 376–87. [G: U.S.]

Littlechild, Stephen C. German "Ordnungspolitik" as Institutional Choice. *Z. ges. Staatswiss.*, March 1984, *140*(1), pp. 71–73. [G: Germany; U.S.; U.K.]

Loasby, Brian J. Entrepreneurs and Organisation. *J. Econ. Stud.*, 1984, *11*(2), pp. 75–88.

Lowe, Adolph. The Classical Theory of Economic Growth. *Soc. Res.*, Spring & Summer 1984, *51*(1&2), pp. 111–42.

MacEwan, Arthur. Interdependence and Instability: Do the Levels of Output in the Advanced Capitalist Countries Increasingly Move Up and Down Together? *Rev. Radical Polit. Econ.*, Summer & Fall 1984, *16*(2&3), pp. 57–79. [G: Selected OECD]

Macpherson, C. B. Democracy: Utopian and Scientific. In *Ball, T. and Farr, J., eds.*, 1984, pp. 141–53.

Maddison, Angus. Origins and Impact of the Welfare State, 1883–1983. *Banca Naz. Lavoro Quart. Rev.*, March 1984, (148), pp. 55–87. [G: Selected OECD]

Magallona, Merlin M. The Export of Free-Enterprise Capitalism: The Politics of TNCs. In *Ngo, M., ed., vol. 1*, 1984, pp. 124–42. [G: LDCs]

Maier, Charles S. Preconditions for Corporatism. In *Goldthorpe, J. H., ed.*, 1984, pp. 39–59.

Manley, John F. Pluralism and Class: A Rejoinder [Neopluralism: A Class Analysis of Pluralism I and Pluralism II]. *Amer. Polit. Sci. Rev.*, December 1984, *78*(4), pp. 1071–73. [G: U.S.]

Mann, Michael. Capitalism and Militarism. In *Shaw, M., ed.*, 1984, pp. 25–46.

Manzar, A. M. Theory of Profit: The Islamic Viewpoint: Comment. *J. Res. Islamic Econ.*, Summer 1984, *2*(1), pp. 53–54.

Marée, Michel and Saive, Marie-Anne. Economie sociale et renouveau coopératif: définition, financement, enjeux. (Social Economy and Co-operative Renewal: Definition, Financing, Issues. With English summary.) *Ann. Pub. Co-op. Econ.*, January–March 1984, *55*(1), pp. 33–69. [G: France; Belgium]

Massey, Stephen J. Justice Rehnquist's Theory of Property. *Yale Law J.*, January 1984, *93*(3), pp. 541–60.

Matthaei, Julie. Rethinking Scarcity: Neoclassicism, NeoMalthusianism, and NeoMarxism. *Rev. Radical Polit. Econ.*, Summer & Fall 1984, *16*(2&3), pp. 81–94.

Mattick, Paul, Jr. Théorie et réalité. (Theory and Reality. With English summary.) *Écon. Soc.*, July–August 1984, *18*(7–8), pp. 93–146.

McCormack, Thelma. Culture and the State. *Can. Public Policy,* September 1984, *10*(3), pp. 267–77.

McCullagh, Ciaran. Entrepreneurship and Development: An Alternative Perspective. *Econ. Soc. Rev.,* January 1984, *15*(2), pp. 109–24. **[G: Selected Countries]**

McFarlane, Bruce. Western Strategies in the Asia–Pacific Region. In *Ngo, M., ed., vol. 1,* 1984, pp. 259–72. **[G: Asia; OECD]**

McKee, Arnold F. Market Failure and the Place of Government in Social Economy. *Rev. Soc. Econ.,* April 1984, *42*(1), pp. 1–15.

Mendell, Marguerite. Social Determinants of Economic Activity: The Economy of Transfer. *J. Econ. Issues,* June 1984, *18*(2), pp. 401–10.

Miyawaki, Nagasada. Problems of Advanced Economics. In *Miyawaki, N., ed.,* 1984, pp. 4–13.

Miyazaki, Hajime. On Success and Dissolution of the Labor-Managed Firm in the Capitalist Economy. *J. Polit. Econ.,* October 1984, *92*(5), pp. 909–31.

Moghadam, Val. Iran: Development, Revolution, and the Problem of Analysis. *Rev. Radical Polit. Econ.,* Summer & Fall 1984, *16*(2&3), pp. 227–40. **[G: Iran]**

Mohun, Simon. Abstract Labor and Its Value-Form. *Sci. Soc.,* Winter 1984-1985, *48*(4), pp. 388–406.

Mollner, Terry. Mondragon: A Third Way. *Rev. Soc. Econ.,* December 1984, *42*(3), pp. 260–71. **[G: Spain]**

Mongar, Tom. Monopoly Pricing and Stagnation. *Econ. Forum,* Summer 1984, *15*(1), pp. 63–87. **[G: U.S.]**

Morris, Jacob. Profit Rates and Capital Formation in American Monopoly Capitalism. In *Foster, J. B. and Szlajfer, H., eds.,* 1984, *1979,* pp. 217–35.

Murray, Martin J. The Development of Capitalism and the Making of the Working Class in Colonial Indochina, 1870–1940. In *Munslow, B. and Finch, H., eds.,* 1984, pp. 216–33. **[G: Indochina]**

Nakatani, Iwao. Growth and Distribution Policy of the Firm and Workers' Morale. (In Japanese. With English summary.) *Osaka Econ. Pap.,* December 1984, *34*(2–3), pp. 189–202.

Navarro, Vicente. The Crisis of the International Capitalist Order and Its Implications on the Welfare State. In *McKinlay, J. B., ed.,* 1984, pp. 107–40. **[G: U.S.]**

Nelson, Richard R. Incentives for Entrepreneurship and Supporting Institutions. *Weltwirtsch. Arch.,* 1984, *120*(4), pp. 646–61. **[G: U.S.]**

Nevitte, Neil Gibbins, Roger. Neoconservatism: Canadian Variations on an Ideological Theme? *Can. Public Policy,* December 1984, *10*(4), pp. 384–94. **[G: Canada]**

Nickerson, Gary W. Political Economy and Policy in the 1980's: Introduction. *Rev. Radical Polit. Econ.,* Winter 1984, *16*(4), pp. iv–ix.

Nolan, Peter and Edwards, P. K. Homogenise, Divide and Rule: An Essay on *Segmented Work, Divided Workers:* Review Article. *Cambridge J. Econ.,* June 1984, *8*(2), pp. 197–215. **[G: U.S.]**

North, Douglass C. Transaction Costs, Institutions, and Economic History. *Z. ges. Staatswiss.,* March 1984, *140*(1), pp. 7–17.

Novek, Joel. The Mechanization of Work: Paradise or Purgatory? *Challenge,* September/October 1984, *27*(4), pp. 43–48. **[G: U.S.; Global]**

O'Toole, James. The Mixed (Up) American Economy. *Ann. Pub. Co-op. Econ.,* Oct.–Dec. 1984, *55*(4), pp. 383–93. **[G: U.S.]**

Offe, Claus. 'Crises of Crisis Management': Elements of a Political Crisis Theory. In *Offe, C.,* 1984, *1973,* pp. 35–64.

Offe, Claus. 'Ungovernability': The Renaissance of Conservative Theories of Crisis. In *Offe, C.,* 1984, *1979,* pp. 65–87.

Offe, Claus. Competitive Party Democracy and the Keynesian Welfare State. In *Offe, C.,* 1984, pp. 179–206.

Offe, Claus. Legitimacy versus Efficiency. In *Offe, C.,* 1984, pp. 130–46.

Offe, Claus. Political Culture and Social Democratic Administration. In *Offe, C.,* 1984, pp. 207–19.

Offe, Claus. Reflections on the Welfare State and the Future of Socialism [An Interview]. In *Offe, C.,* 1984, pp. 252–99.

Offe, Claus. Social Policy and the Theory of the State. In *Offe, C.,* 1984, pp. 88–118.

Offe, Claus. Some Contradictions of the Modern Welfare State. In *Offe, C.,* 1984, *1981,* pp. 147–61.

Offe, Claus. The Separation of Form and Content in Liberal Democracy. In *Offe, C.,* 1984, *1980,* pp. 162–78.

Offe, Claus. Theses on the Theory of the State. In *Offe, C.,* 1984, *1976,* pp. 119–29.

Onitsuka, Yusuke. Economic Growth and Social Welfare Policy in the 1980s. In *Miyawaki, N., ed.,* 1984, pp. 220–27.

Osborne, Martin J. Capitalist–Worker Conflict and Involuntary Unemployment. *Rev. Econ. Stud.,* January 1984, *51*(1), pp. 111–27.

Pachter, Henry. Three Economic Models: Capitalism, the Welfare State, and Socialism. In *Pachter, H.,* 1984, pp. 16–35.

Palmer, Robin. The Rise of the Britalian Culture Entrepreneur. In *Ward, R. and Jenkins, R., eds.,* 1984, pp. 89–104. **[G: U.K.]**

Parker, William N. Capitalistic Organization and National Response: Social Dynamics in the Age of Schumpeter. *J. Econ. Behav. Organ.,* March 1984, *5*(1), pp. 3–23. **[G: U.S.; Germany; France; England]**

Parson, Don. Politics beyond the Point of Production: Class Struggle and Regional Underdevelopment in Northern Ireland. *Rev. Radical Polit. Econ.,* Summer & Fall 1984, *16*(2&3), pp. 29–56. **[G: U.K.]**

Peet, Richard. Class Struggle, the Relocation of Employment, and Economic Crisis. *Sci. Soc.,* Spring 1984, *48*(1), pp. 38–51. **[G: U.S.]**

Picot, Arnold. Specificity, Specialization, and Coalitions: Comment. *Z. ges. Staatswiss.*, March 1984, *140*(1), pp. 50–53.

van der Ploeg, Frederick. Implications of Workers' Savings for Economic Growth and the Class Struggle. In *Goodwin, R. M.; Krüger, M. and Vercelli, A., eds.*, 1984, pp. 1–13.

Pohjola, Matti. Threats and Bargaining in Capitalism: A Differential Game View. *J. Econ. Dynam. Control*, December 1984, *8*(3), pp. 291–302.

Pollard, Sidney. Transaction Costs, Institutions, and Economic History: Comment. *Z. ges. Staatswiss.*, March 1984, *140*(1), pp. 18–19.

Power, Marilyn. Unity and Division among Women: Feminist Theories of Gender and Class in Capitalist Society. *Econ. Forum*, Summer 1984, *15*(1), pp. 39–62. **[G: U.S.]**

Prebisch, Raúl. The Global Crisis of Capitalism and Its Theoretical Background. *Cepal Rev.*, April 1984, (22), pp. 159–78. **[G: Global]**

Preston, Larry M. Freedom, Markets, and Voluntary Exchange. *Amer. Polit. Sci. Rev.*, December 1984, *78*(4), pp. 959–70.

Przeworski, Adam and Wallerstein, Michael. Reply [The Structure of Class Conflict in Democratic Capitalist Societies]. *Amer. Polit. Sci. Rev.*, September 1984, *78*(3), pp. 787–90.

Pugh, Cedric. Public Policy, Welfare and the Singaporean Economy. *Ann. Pub. Co-op. Econ.*, Oct.–Dec. 1984, *55*(4), pp. 433–55.
[G: Singapore]

Putník, Jiří. The Position of Developing Countries in Present-Day International Economic Relations. *Czech. Econ. Digest.*, June 1984, (4), pp. 48–67. **[G: LDCs]**

Ranson, Baldwin. A Commentary on Lux, Lutz, and Petr [Creative vs. Mechanical Evolution: A Commentary on Petr]. *J. Econ. Issues*, September 1984, *18*(3), pp. 895–97. **[G: U.S.]**

Reati, Angelo. Taux de profit et composition organique du capital dans le cycle long de l'après-guerre: le cas de l'industrie du Royaume-Uni de 1959 à 1981. (With English summary.) *Cah. Écon. Bruxelles*, Fourth Trimester 1984, (104), pp. 547–609. **[G: U.K.]**

Reynolds, R. Larry. The Regulatory Matrix and Rigidity in the Economic System. *J. Econ. Issues*, June 1984, *18*(2), pp. 627–31.

Roemer, John E. Exploitation, Class, and Property Relations. In *Ball, T. and Farr, J., eds.*, 1984, pp. 184–211.

Rosenberg, Nathan and Frischtak, Claudio R. Technological Innovation and Long Waves. *Cambridge J. Econ.*, March 1984, *8*(1), pp. 7–24.

Rothenberg, Winifred B. Markets, Values and Capitalism: A Discourse on Method [The Market and Massachusetts Farmers, 1750–1855]. *J. Econ. Hist.*, March 1984, *44*(1), pp. 174–78. **[G: U.S.]**

Rugina, Anghel N. The Future Belongs to a Social Economy of Human Solidarity: A New Orientation in Theory and Practice. *Int. J. Soc. Econ.*, 1984, *11*(1/2), pp. 49–82.

Rus, Veljko. The Future of Industrial Democracy. *Int. Soc. Sci. J.*, 1984, *36*(2), pp. 233–54.

Ryndina, M. N. The Main Features of Contemporary Western Political Economy, Right-wing Socialist Theories, and Revisionism. In *Smirnov, A. D.; Golosov, V. V. and Maximova, V. F., eds.*, 1984, pp. 12–24.

Sabel, Charles F. Industrial Reorganization and Social Democracy in Austria. *Ind. Relat.*, Fall 1984, *23*(3), pp. 344–61. **[G: Austria]**

Samuels, Warren J. A Centenary Reconsideration of Bellamy's *Looking Backward*. *Amer. J. Econ. Soc.*, April 1984, *43*(2), pp. 129–48.

Sandkull, Bengt. Using New Technology to Erode Economic and Industrial Democracy: The Case of Sweden. *Econ. Anal. Worker's Manage.*, 1984, *18*(3), pp. 287–96. **[G: Sweden]**

Santarelli, Enrico. L'influsso dell'analisi schumpeteriana della funzione imprenditoriale e del credito nel pensiero economico italiano tra le due guerre. (The Influence of Schumepeterian Analysis of the Entrepreneurial Function and of the Banking Function on Italian Economic Thought in the Period between the Two Wars. With English summary.) *Giorn. Econ.*, July–August 1984, *43*(7–8), pp. 507–29. **[G: Italy]**

Sawers, Larry. New Perspectives on the Urban Political Economy. In *Tabb, W. K. and Sawers, L., eds.*, 1984, pp. 3–17.

Schachner-Blazizek, Peter. The Current Relevance of Schumpeter's Theory of the Decay of Capitalism. In *Seidl, C., ed.*, 1984, pp. 111–21.

Schmidtchen, Dieter. German *"Ordnungspolitik"* as Institutional Choice. *Z. ges. Staatswiss.*, March 1984, *140*(1), pp. 54–70.
[G: Germany]

Schott, Kerry. Investment, Order and Conflict in a Simple Dynamic Model of Capitalism. In *Goldthorpe, J. H., ed.*, 1984, pp. 81–97.

Schwartz, Anna J. Currents and Countercurrents in Political and Economic Thought: A Comment. *Carnegie-Rochester Conf. Ser. Public Policy*, Autumn 1984, *21*, pp. 253–58.

Seidl, Christian. Schumpeter versus Keynes: Supply-side Economics or Demand Management? In *Seidl, C., ed.*, 1984, pp. 139–51.

Sekine, Thomas T. An Uno School Seminar on the Theory of Value. *Sci. Soc.*, Winter 1984-1985, *48*(4), pp. 419–32.

Semmler, Willi. Marx and Schumpeter on Competition, Transient Surplus Profit and Technical Change. *Écon. Appl.*, 1984, *37*(3–4), pp. 419–55.

Sen, Amartya. Labour Allocation in a Cooperative Enterprise. In *Sen, A.*, 1984, *1966*, pp. 72–89.

Sen, Amartya. The Profit Motive. In *Sen, A.*, 1984, *1983*, pp. 90–110.

Sengenberger, Werner. West German Employment Policy: Restoring Worker Competition. *Ind. Relat.*, Fall 1984, *23*(3), pp. 323–43.
[G: W. Germany]

Sertel, Murat R. and Steinherr, Alfred. Information, Incentives, and the Design of Efficient Institutions. *Z. ges. Staatswiss.*, June 1984, *140*(2), pp. 233–46.

Shackleton, J. R. Privatization: The Case Examined. *Nat. Westminster Bank Quart. Rev.*, May 1984, pp. 59–73. [G: U.K.]

Shafey, Erfan. Islamic Economics as a Social Science: Some Methodological Issues: Comment. *J. Res. Islamic Econ.*, Summer 1984, 2(1), pp. 55–56.

Shalev, Michael. Labor, State, and Crisis: An Israeli Case Study. *Ind. Relat.*, Fall 1984, 23(3), pp. 362–86. [G: Israel]

Shaw, Martin. War, Imperialism and the State System: A Critique of Orthodox Marxism for the 1980s. In *Shaw, M., ed.*, 1984, pp. 47–70.

Sheppard, Eric. Value and Exploitation in a Capitalist Space Economy. *Int. Reg. Sci. Rev.*, November 1984, 9(2), pp. 97–107.

Shepsle, Kenneth A. and Weingast, Barry R. Political Solutions to Market Problems. *Amer. Polit. Sci. Rev.*, June 1984, 78(2), pp. 417–34.

Sherman, Howard J. Inflation, Unemployment, and the Contemporary Business Cycle. In *Foster, J. B. and Szlajfer, H., eds.*, 1984, *1979*, pp. 91–117. [G: U.S.]

Simpson, David. Technology, Communications, Economics and Progress. In *Boulding, K. E., ed.*, 1984, pp. 58–70.

Smith, Stephen C. Does Employment Matter to the Labour-managed Firm? Some Theory and an Empirical Illustration. *Econ. Anal. Worker's Manage.*, 1984, 18(4), pp. 303–18. [G: U.S.; Italy]

Smith, Woodruff D. The Function of Commercial Centers in the Modernization of European Capitalism: Amsterdam as an Information Exchange in the Seventeenth Century. *J. Econ. Hist.*, December 1984, 44(4), pp. 985–1005. [G: Netherlands; Europe]

Solo, Robert A. Industrial Policy. *J. Econ. Issues*, September 1984, 18(3), pp. 697–714. [G: U.S.]

Sorvina, G. N. The Role of the State in the System of State Monopoly Capitalism. In *Smirnov, A. D.; Golosov, V. V. and Maximova, V. F., eds.*, 1984, pp. 171–79.

Soulas de Russel, D. J. M. Anforderungsgerechter ausbildungsgänge im internationalen genossenschaftsbereich. (Design of Training Schemes to Support Co-operative Action at the International Level. With English summary.) *Ann. Pub. Co-op. Econ.*, July–September 1984, 55(3), pp. 309–13. [G: W. Germany; LDCs]

Spinrad, William. Work Democracy: An Overview. *Int. Soc. Sci. J.*, 1984, 36(2), pp. 195–215.

Stewart, James B. Building a Cooperative Economy: Lessons from the Black Experience. *Rev. Soc. Econ.*, December 1984, 42(3), pp. 360–68. [G: U.S.]

Stigler, George J. Gioie e dolori del capitalismo moderno. (The Pleasures and Pains of Modern Capitalism. With English summary.) *Mondo Aperto*, January-February 1984, 38(1), pp. 1–11. [G: U.S.]

Streeck, Wolfgang. Neo-Corporatist Industrial Relations and the Economic Crisis in West Germany. In *Goldthorpe, J. H., ed.*, 1984, pp. 291–314. [G: W. Germany]

Sundaram, Jomo Kwame and Woon, Toh Kin. Malaysia: The New Economic Policy (NEP) In *Ngo, M., ed., vol. 1*, 1984, pp. 453–78. [G: Malaysia]

Sunkel, Osvaldo. Past, Present and Future of the International Economic Crisis. *Cepal Rev.*, April 1984, (22), pp. 81–105. [G: Latin America; OECD]

Sweezy, Paul M. Competition and Monopoly. In *Foster, J. B. and Szlajfer, H., eds.*, 1984, pp. 27–40.

Swoboda, Peter. Schumpeter's Entrepreneur in Modern Economic Theory. In *Seidl, C., ed.*, 1984, pp. 17–29.

Szlajfer, Henryk. Economic Surplus and Surplus Value Under Monopoly Capitalism. In *Foster, J. B. and Szlajfer, H., eds.*, 1984, *1983*, pp. 262–93.

Szymanski, Al. Productivity Growth and Capitalist Stagnation. *Sci. Soc.*, Fall 1984, 48(3), pp. 295–322. [G: U.S.; Japan; W. Europe]

Tabb, William K. Economic Democracy and Regional Restructuring: An Internationalization Perspective. In *Sawers, L. and Tabb, W. K., eds.*, 1984, pp. 403–16. [G: U.S.]

Tagel-Din, Seif E. I. Macro-consumption Function in an Islamic Framework. *J. Res. Islamic Econ.*, Summer 1984, 2(1), pp. 57–62.

Thanawala, Kishor. Solidarity: Reflections and Prospects. *Rev. Soc. Econ.*, December 1984, 42(3), pp. 427–32.

Tiemstra, John P. The Moral Foundations of Community: Comment. *Rev. Soc. Econ.*, December 1984, 42(3), pp. 257–59.

Tinbergen, Jan. Alternative Optimal Social Orders. *Pakistan Devel. Rev.*, Spring 1984, 23(1), pp. 1–7.

Trebing, Harry M. Public Control of Enterprise: Neoclassical Assault and Neoinstitutional Reform: Remarks upon Receipt of the Veblens–Commons Award. *J. Econ. Issues*, June 1984, 18(2), pp. 353–68.

Tsebelis, George. Comment on Przeworski and Wallerstein [The Structure of Class Conflict in Democratic Capitalist Societies]. *Amer. Polit. Sci. Rev.*, September 1984, 78(3), pp. 785–87.

Velez, Jorge Child. Unjust International Economic Relations. *Can. J. Devel. Stud.*, 1984, 5(2), pp. 303–08.

Vercelli, Alessandro. Fluctuations and Growth: Keynes, Schumpeter, Marx and the Structural Instability of Capitalism. In *Goodwin, R. M.; Krüger, M. and Vercelli, A., eds.*, 1984, pp. 209–31.

Waters, William R. Development of Solidarist Economics in the U.S. *Int. J. Soc. Econ.*, 1984, 11(1/2), pp. 100–116. [G: U.S.]

Weede, Erich. Democracy, Creeping Socialism, and Ideological Socialism in Rent-seeking Societies. *Public Choice*, 1984, 44(2), pp. 349–66. [G: OECD; Israel]

Weitzman, Martin L. The Case for a Share Economy. *Challenge*, November/December 1984, 27(5), pp. 34–40. [G: U.S.]

von Weizsäcker, Carl Christian. Rights and Relations in Modern Economic Theory. *J. Econ. Behav. Organ.*, June 1984, 5(2), pp. 133–57.

Werner, Josua. Marktwirtschaftliche Koordination und gesellschaftliche Entscheidungsprozesse. (Market Economy Coordination and Political Decision Processes. With English summary.) *Schweiz. Z. Volkswirtsch. Statist.*, June 1984, 120(2), pp. 169–89.

Wickins, Peter L. The Economics of Privateering: Capital Dispersal in the American War of Independence. *J. Europ. Econ. Hist.*, Fall 1984, 13(2), pp. 375–95. [G: U.S.]

Wilmoth, David. Regional Economic Policy and the New Corporatism. In *Sawers, L. and Tabb, W. K., eds.*, 1984, pp. 235–58. [G: U.S.]

Wisman, Jon D. From Capital–Labor Strife to Community. *Rev. Soc. Econ.*, December 1984, 42(3), pp. 369–75.

Wolff, Goetz. Reindustrialization: A Debate among Capitalists. In *Sawers, L. and Tabb, W. K., eds.*, 1984, pp. 259–68.

Wolff, Richard D.; Callari, Antonino and Roberts, Bruce. A Marxian Alternative to the Traditional "Transformation Problem." *Rev. Radical Polit. Econ.*, Summer & Fall 1984, 16(2&3), pp. 115–35.

Woodworth, Warner. Cooperative Movements in the U.S.A.: The Third Stage. *Ann. Pub. Co-op. Econ.*, July–September 1984, 55(3), pp. 239–51. [G: U.S.]

Worland, Stephen T. Prospects for Creative Synthesis. *Rev. Soc. Econ.*, December 1984, 42(3), pp. 417–23.

Yoshihara, Kunio. Indigenous Entrepreneurs in the ASEAN Countries. *Singapore Econ. Rev.*, October 1984, 29(2), pp. 132–47.
[G: ASEAN]

052 Socialist and Communist Economic Systems

0520 Socialist and Communist Economic Systems

Abalkin, L. Theoretical Questions Regarding the Structure of the Economy. *Prob. Econ.*, March 1984, 26(11), pp. 73–91. [G: U.S.S.R.]

Alexandrov, L. A.; Volkov, F. M. and Mokrov, G. G. Western Economists on the Patterns of Socialist Extended Reproduction. In *Smirnov, A. D.; Golosov, V. V. and Maximova, V. F., eds.*, 1984, pp. 293–305.

Asztalos, László Gy.; Bokros, Lajos and Surányi, György. Reform and Financial Institutional System in Hungary. *Acta Oecon.*, 1984, 32(3–4), pp. 251–68. [G: Hungary]

Auerbach, Paul. On the Theory of Social Democracy. *Brit. Rev. Econ. Issues*, Spring 1984, 6(14), pp. 83–92. [G: U.S.S.R.; China; U.K.]

Babic, Stojan. The Problem of Choosing Indicators of Efficiency in the Yugoslav Economic System, 1976–1980. *Eastern Europ. Econ.*, Winter 1984–85, 23(2), pp. 43–70.
[G: Yugoslavia]

Babkina, Z. Employment under Socialism and Its Bourgeois Interpretations. *Prob. Econ.*, April 1984, 26(12), pp. 54–74. [G: U.S.S.R.]

Balázsy, Sándor. Reform and Property: Reflections on Tamás Bauer's Article. *Eastern Europ. Econ.*, Spring–Summer 1984, 22(3–4), pp. 88–101. [G: Hungary; CMEA]

Bandera, V. N. Capital Accumulation and Growth in a Mixed Socialist Economy: The Case of Soviet NEP. *J. Europ. Econ. Hist.*, Spring 1984, 13(1), pp. 7–27. [G: U.S.S.R.]

Bauer, Tamás. The Second Economic Reform and Ownership Relations: Some Considerations for the Further Development of the New Economic Mechanism. *Eastern Europ. Econ.*, Spring–Summer 1984, 22(3–4), pp. 33–87.
[G: CMEA; Hungary]

Belousov, R. A. Democratic Centralism and Economic Independence. *Prob. Econ.*, November 1984, 27(7), pp. 26–43. [G: U.S.S.R.]

Bennett, John. A Model of Income Distribution in a Revenue-sharing Firm. *J. Compar. Econ.*, September 1984, 8(3), pp. 237–46.

Bergson, Abram. Income Inequality under Soviet Socialism. *J. Econ. Lit.*, September 1984, 22(3), pp. 1052–99. [G: U.S.S.R.]

Berliner, Joseph S. Managing the Soviet Economy: Alternative Models. In *Hoffmann, E. P., ed.*, 1984, pp. 49–56. [G: U.S.S.R.]

Berliner, Joseph S. Planning and Management. In *Hoffmann, E. P. and Laird, R. F., eds.*, 1984, 1983, pp. 467–509. [G: U.S.S.R.]

Birman, A. M. Tons, Pieces, Rubles. *Prob. Econ.*, July 1984, 27(3), pp. 22–40. [G: U.S.S.R.]

Brada, Josef C. and Montias, John Michael. Industrial Policy in Eastern Europe: A Three-Country Comparison. *J. Compar. Econ.*, December 1984, 8(4), pp. 377–419.
[G: Czechoslovakia; Poland; Hungary]

Bronfenbrenner, Martin. China since Mao: A Great Leap Backward? *Atlantic Econ. J.*, March 1984, 12(1), pp. 1–11. [G: China]

Bulgaru, M. National-Economy Indicators System Model. *Econ. Computat. Cybern. Stud. Res.*, 1984, 19(2), pp. 19–36.

Cholewicka-Gozdzik, Krystyna. The Reform of the Price System in Poland. Its Assumptions and First Results. In *Bohnet, A., ed.*, 1984, pp. 97–117.

Chyba, Antonín. The Problem of Raw Material and Energy Supplies in Today's World. *Czech. Econ. Digest.*, March 1984, (2), pp. 50–68.
[G: Global]

Ciucur, D. and Popescu, C. Compatibility and Equilibrium in the Development of the National Economy. *Econ. Computat. Cybern. Stud. Res.*, 1984, 19(2), pp. 93–99.
[G: Romania]

Conn, David. The Evaluation of Centrally Planned Economic Systems: *Methodological Precepts*. In *Zimbalist, A., ed.*, 1984, pp. 15–46.

Constantinescu, N. N. Objective and Subjective, Stability and Dynamism in the Functioning Mechanism of the Socialist Economy. *Econ.*

Computat. Cybern. Stud. Res., 1984, *19*(2), pp. 11–17.

Csaba, Laszlo COMECON Perspectives for the 1980's. *Écon. Soc.*, February 1984, *18*(2), pp. 5–44. **[G: CMEA]**

Csikós-Nagy, Béla. Die Rolle der Preise in den verschiedenen Modellvarianten der sozialistischen Planwirtschaft. (With English summary.) In *Bohnet, A., ed.*, 1984, pp. 19–40.

Csikós-Nagy, Béla. Further Development of the Hungarian Price System. *Acta Oecon.*, 1984, *32*(1–2), pp. 21–37. **[G: Hungary]**

Csikós-Nagy, Béla. The Role of the Law of Values in Socialist Economy. *Eastern Europ. Econ.*, Spring–Summer 1984, *22*(3–4), pp. 102–21.
[G: Hungary; CMEA]

Culbertson, William Patterson, Jr. and Amacher, Ryan C. Inflation in the Planned Economies: Reply [Inflation in the Planned Economies: Some Estimates for Eastern Europe]. *Southern Econ. J.*, October 1984, *51*(2), pp. 613–14.
[G: E. Europe]

Donaldson, David and Neary, Hugh M. Decentralized Control of a Socialist Industry. *Can. J. Econ.*, February 1984, *17*(1), pp. 99–110.

Dore, M. H. I. and Kaser, Michael C. The Millions of Equations Debate: Seventy Years after Barone. *Atlantic Econ. J.*, September 1984, *12*(3), pp. 30–44.

Dostovalov, Y. L. Notions of the Distribution of Material Wealth and Incomes under Socialism. In *Smirnov, A. D.; Golosov, V. V. and Maximova, V. F., eds.*, 1984, pp. 263–71.

Du, Runsheng. New Developments in the Contracting System of United Production and the Cooperative Economy in the Countryside. *Chinese Econ. Stud.*, Summer 1984, *17*(4), pp. 16–39. **[G: China]**

Dugger, William M. Human Liberation: Workplace Reform as the Next Step in Social Evolution. *Int. J. Soc. Econ.*, 1984, *11*(5), pp. 29–39.

Durgin, Frank. *USSR in Crisis: The Failure of an Economic System:* Review Article. *ACES Bull.*, Summer–Fall 1984, *26*(2–3), pp. 99–110.
[G: U.S.S.R.]

Durgin, Frank. The USSR in Crisis: A Reply to a Reply. *ACES Bull.*, Winter 1984, *26*(4), pp. 55–64. **[G: U.S.S.R.]**

Elliott, John E. Contending Perspectives on the Nature of Soviet Economic Society. *Int. J. Soc. Econ.*, 1984, *11*(5), pp. 40–61. **[G: U.S.S.R.]**

Ellman, Michael. Agricultural Productivity under Socialism. In *Ellman, M., 1984, 1981*, pp. 198–214. **[G: China; U.S.S.R.]**

Ellman, Michael. Collectivisation, Convergence and Capitalism: Introduction. In *Ellman, M.,* 1984, pp. 1–23.

Ellman, Michael. Full Employment—Lessons from State Socialism. In *Ellman, M.*, 1984, *1979*, pp. 149–73. **[G: E. Europe; U.S.S.R.; China]**

Ellman, Michael. Seven Theses on Kosyginism. In *Ellman, M.*, 1984, *1977*, pp. 75–96.
[G: U.S.S.R.]

Ericson, Richard E. The "Second Economy" and

Resource Allocation under Central Planning. *J. Compar. Econ.*, March 1984, *8*(1), pp. 1–24.

Falus-Szikra, Katalin. Distribution According to Work and Reform in Hungary. *Acta Oecon.*, 1984, *33*(1–2), pp. 1–16. **[G: Hungary]**

Farrell, John P. Inflation in the Planned Economies: Comment [Inflation in the Planned Economies: Some Estimates for Eastern Europe]. *Southern Econ. J.*, October 1984, *51*(2), pp. 603–12. **[G: E. Europe]**

Fingerland, Jaroslav. CMEA Looks ahead Realistically and with Optimism. *Czech. Econ. Digest.*, May 1984, (3), pp. 55–62. **[G: CMEA]**

Frank, Andre Gunder. The Political Economy of the Economic Policy of the Communist Party of Chile. In *Frank, A. G.*, 1984, pp. 155–60.
[G: Chile]

Goldman, Marshall I. *USSR in Crisis: The Failure of an Economic System:* Review Article: Reply. *ACES Bull.*, Summer–Fall 1984, *26*(2–3), pp. 111–16. **[G: U.S.S.R.]**

Goldman, Marshall I. Reply to a Reply to a Reply [The USSR in Crisis]. *ACES Bull.*, Winter 1984, *26*(4), pp. 69–71. **[G: U.S.S.R.]**

Granick, David. Central Physical Planning, Incentives and Job Rights. In *Zimbalist, A., ed.*, 1984, pp. 133–57. **[G: U.S.; U.S.S.R.]**

Gray, Kenneth R. The USSR in Crisis: Comment. *ACES Bull.*, Winter 1984, *26*(4), pp. 65–67.
[G: U.S.S.R.]

Graziani, Giovanni. Des multinationales à l'Est? (With English summary.) *Rev. Econ. Ind.*, 2nd Trimester 1984, (28), pp. 36–58. **[G: CMEA]**

Gu, Shutang and Yang, Yuchuan. A Further Inquiry into Value Determination and the Law of Value. *Chinese Econ. Stud.*, Fall 1984, *18*(1), pp. 59–76.

Gu, Shutang and Yang, Yuchuan. The Transformed Form of Value under the Socialist System. *Chinese Econ. Stud.*, Fall 1984, *18*(1), pp. 44–58.

Gudac, Toma. Pricing and Exchange Rates in Planned Economies. *Finance Develop.*, September 1984, *21*(3), pp. 40–43.

Gui, Benedetto. Basque versus Illyrian Labor-managed Firms: The Problem of Property Rights. *J. Compar. Econ.*, June 1984, *8*(2), pp. 168–81. **[G: Spain; Yugoslavia]**

Gvishiani, D. and Mil'ner, B. Organizational Reserves of Management. *Prob. Econ.*, August 1984, *27*(4), pp. 29–45. **[G: U.S.S.R.]**

Haffner, Friedrich. Theorie und Praxis der Preisbildung in der Sowjetunion und in der DDR. (With English summary.) In *Bohnet, A., ed.*, 1984, pp. 41–67.

Hart-Landsberg, Martin and Lembcke, Jerry. Class Struggle and Economic Transformation. *Rev. Radical Polit. Econ.*, Winter 1984, *16*(4), pp. 14–31.

Havasi, Ferenc. Further Development of the System of Economic Control and Management in Hungary. *Acta Oecon.*, 1984, *32*(3–4), pp. 199–221. **[G: Hungary]**

von Hayek, Friedrich A. Two Pages of Fiction:

The Impossibility of Socialist Calculation. In *von Hayek, F. A. (I), 1984, 1982*, pp. 53–61.

Hazard, John N. Socialism and Federation. *Mich. Law Rev.*, April–May 1984, *82*(5 & 6), pp. 1182–94. [G: U.S.S.R.]

Hentze, Joachim. Die Stellung des Menschen in der sozialistischen Arbeitsökonomie. (With English summary.) *Z. Betriebswirtshaft*, January 1984, *54*(1), pp. 63–77.

Horvat, Branko. The Economic System and Stabilization. *Eastern Europ. Econ.*, Fall 1984, *23*(1), pp. 66–105. [G: Yugoslavia]

Horvat, Branko. Two Widespread Ideological Deviations in Contemporary Yugoslav Society. *Eastern Europ. Econ.*, Fall 1984, *23*(1), 45–57. [G: Yugoslavia]

Horvat, Branko. Work and Power: The Prospects for the Disalienation of Work. *Econ. Anal. Worker's Manage.*, 1984, *18*(4), pp. 365–69.

Hradecký, Stanislav. Structural Changes and International Socialist Economic Integration. *Czech. Econ. Digest.*, February 1984, (1), pp. 70–83. [G: CMEA]

Janover, L. Pour une critique matérialiste de l'idéologie antitotalitaire. (Elements for a Materialist Critique of Antitotalitarianism Ideology. With English summary.) *Écon. Soc.*, July–August 1984, *18*(7–8), pp. 269–315.

Ji, Zhenghzhi. The Profit in Planned Prices Should Be Formulated in Accordance with a Composite Profit Index. *Chinese Econ. Stud.*, Fall 1984, *18*(1), pp. 14–33. [G: China]

Kaltakhchian, N. M. Interpretations of Planned and Balanced Development of the Socialist Economy. In *Smirnov, A. D.; Golosov, V. V. and Maximova, V. F., eds.*, 1984, pp. 243–52.

Kaltakhchian, N. M. and Golosov, V. V. Non-Marxian Conceptions of the Development of the World Socialist Economic System. In *Smirnov, A. D.; Golosov, V. V. and Maximova, V. F., eds.*, 1984, pp. 306–23.

Karagedov, R. G. On the Organizational Structure of Industrial Management. *Prob. Econ.*, April 1984, *26*(12), pp. 3–24. [G: U.S.S.R.]

Kaser, Michael C. Human Betterment in a Planned Economy—The Case of the Soviet Union. In *Boulding, K. E., ed.*, 1984, pp. 71–86. [G: U.S.S.R.]

Katsenelinboigen, Aron J. Some Notes on Vertical and Horizontal Economic Mechanisms. In *Andersson, Å. E.; Isard, W. and Puu, T., eds.*, 1984, pp. 383–405.

Khavina, S. A. Non-Marxian Ideas of Money-exchange Relations. In *Smirnov, A. D.; Golosov, V. V. and Maximova, V. F., eds.*, 1984, pp. 253–62.

Knaack, Ruud. Dynamic Comparative Economics: Lessons from Socialist Planning. In *Zimbalist, A., ed.*, 1984, pp. 109–32.

Koont, Sinan and Zimbalist, Andrew. Incentives and Elicitation Schemes: A Critique and an Extension. In *Zimbalist, A., ed.*, 1984, pp. 159–75.

Kornai, János. Adjustment to Price and Quantity Signals in a Socialist Economy. In *Csikós-Nagy,*

B.; Hague, D. and Hall, G., eds., 1984, pp. 60–77.

Kornai, János. Some Properties of the Eastern European Growth Pattern. In *Cohen, S. I., et al., eds.*, 1984, *1981*, pp. 13–23.

Kornai, János and Matits, Ágnes. Softness of the Budget Constraint—An Analysis Relying on Data of Firms. *Acta Oecon.*, 1984, *32*(3–4), pp. 223–49. [G: Hungary]

Kosterina, T. M. and Pashkovskaya, M. V. Capitalist Views on Socialist Property. In *Smirnov, A. D.; Golosov, V. V. and Maximova, V. F., eds.*, 1984, pp. 225–32.

Köves, András. On New Trends in International Industrial Development and the Division of Labour. *Acta Oecon.*, 1984, *33*(1–2), pp. 147–53. [G: Hungary]

Krasovskii, V. The Economic Effectiveness of Production and Capital Investments. *Prob. Econ.*, July 1984, *27*(3), pp. 41–60. [G: U.S.S.R.]

Kumm, K. The Subsistence Fund and the Reproduction of Labor Power. *Prob. Econ.*, April 1984, *26*(12), pp. 44–53. [G: U.S.S.R.]

Kurashvili, B. P. The Fate of Branch Management. *Prob. Econ.*, August 1984, *27*(4), pp. 3–28. [G: U.S.S.R.]

Laaksonen, Oiva. Participation down and up the Line: Comparative Industrial Democracy Trends in China and Europe. *Int. Soc. Sci. J.*, 1984, *36*(2), pp. 299–318. [G: China]

Laki, Mihály. The Enterprise Crisis. *Acta Oecon.*, 1984, *32*(1–2), pp. 113–24. [G: Hungary]

Laky, Teréz. Small Enterprises in Hungary—Myth and Reality. *Acta Oecon.*, 1984, *32*(1–2), pp. 39–63. [G: Hungary]

Laski, Kazimierz. Das Inflationsproblem und Warenmängel in den sozialistischen Ländern. (With English summary.) In *Bohnet, A., ed.*, 1984, pp. 183–202.

Levine, Herbert S. Structural Constraints on Economic Leverage: Command-Type Systems. In *McCormick, G. H. and Bissell, R. E., eds.*, 1984, pp. 129–47.

Li, Zili. Again on "Standard Output": A Further Inquiry into the Distribution Form of United Production with Remuneration Calculated According to the Standard Output. *Chinese Econ. Stud.*, Spring 1984, *17*(3), pp. 3–17. [G: China]

Ligay, G. A. Notions of the Economic Laws of Socialism and Economic Interests. In *Smirnov, A. D.; Golosov, V. V. and Maximova, V. F., eds.*, 1984, pp. 233–42.

Lipiński, Jan and Mujżel, Jan. Price Formation, Market Structure, Economic System of Enterprises. In *Bohnet, A., ed.*, 1984, pp. 153–81. [G: Poland]

Ma, Hong. Strengthen Planned Economy and Improve Planning Work. *Chinese Econ. Stud.*, Spring 1984, *17*(3), pp. 27–32. [G: China]

Mandle, J. R. Strategies of Change in Paternalistic Socialism: The Case of China. *Int. J. Soc. Econ.*, 1984, *11*(3/4), pp. 3–11. [G: China]

Mănescu, Manea. Grandiose Prospects in the Multilateral Development of Socialist Romania. *Econ. Computat. Cybern. Stud. Res.*, 1984, *19*(3), pp. 5–8. **[G: Romania]**

Marrese, Michael and Mitchell, Janet L. Kornai's Resource-Constrained Economy: A Survey and an Appraisal. *J. Compar. Econ.*, March 1984, *8*(1), pp. 74–84.

Matoušek, Jirí. The Agrarian Policy of the Communist Party of Czechoslovakia and Thirty-Five Years of the Development of Socialism in the Countryside. *Czech. Econ. Digest.*, November 1984, (7), pp. 29–55.
[G: Czechoslovakia]

Mihalek, Jozef. Economy: Looking Ahead to the New Century. *Czech. Econ. Digest.*, June 1984, (4), pp. 25–33.

Milenkovitch, Deborah Duff. Is Market Socialism Efficient? In *Zimbalist, A., ed.*, 1984, pp. 65–107.

Minaeva, M. V. and Radaeva, K. M. Non-Marxian Notions of Price and Profit under Socialism. In *Smirnov, A. D.; Golosov, V. V. and Maximova, V. F., eds.*, 1984, pp. 282–92.

Mun, Kin-chok. Marketing in the PRC. In *Kaynak, E. and Savitt, R., eds.*, 1984, pp. 247–60. **[G: China]**

Nagy, Tamás. Das System "weltmarktorientierter" Preise in Ungarn. (With English summary.) In *Bohnet, A., ed.*, 1984, pp. 69–95.
[G: Hungary]

Nasilowski, Mieczyslaw. Planning: Bureaucratic or Socialized? *Kansant. Aikak.*, 1984, *80*(3), pp. 316–20.

Nove, Alec. The Soviet Economy: Problems and Prospects. In *Hoffmann, E. P. and Laird, R. F., eds.*, 1984, *1980*, pp. 447–65.
[G: U.S.S.R.]

Offe, Claus. European Socialism and the Role of the State. In *Offe, C.*, 1984, pp. 239–51.

Offe, Claus. Reflections on the Welfare State and the Future of Socialism [An Interview]. In *Offe, C.*, 1984, pp. 252–99.

Okólski, Marek and Winiecki, Jan. Structural Change and Adaptation: On Reintegrating Planned Economies into the World Economy. *Konjunkturpolitik*, 1984, *30*(2/3), pp. 148–69.
[G: Europe]

Pachter, Henry. Confessions of an Old-Timer: Aphorisms on Socialism. In *Pachter, H.*, 1984, *1958*, pp. 317–31.

Pachter, Henry. Freedom, Authority, Participation. In *Pachter, H.*, 1984, *1978*, pp. 36–64.

Pachter, Henry. Three Economic Models: Capitalism, the Welfare State, and Socialism. In *Pachter, H.*, 1984, pp. 16–35.

Peng, Tian. A Rational Economic Structure Is the Precondition for Healthy Development of the National Economy. *Chinese Econ. Stud.*, Summer 1984, *17*(4), pp. 10–15. **[G: China]**

Poliak, A. Economic Problems in the Utilization of Materials. *Prob. Econ.*, April 1984, *26*(12), pp. 25–43. **[G: U.S.S.R.]**

Popovic, Mihailo V. Causes of Economic and Sociopolitical Instability in Yugoslavia. *Eastern Europ. Econ.*, Fall 1984, *23*(1), pp. 5–16.
[G: Yugoslavia]

Průcha, Václav. 35th Anniversary of the Council

for Mutual Economic Assistance. *Czech. Econ. Digest.*, May 1984, (3), pp. 47–54.
[G: CMEA]

Prybyla, Jan S. China's Special Economic Zones. *ACES Bull.*, Winter 1984, *26*(4), pp. 1–23.
[G: China]

Pulai, Miklós and Vissi, Ferenc. Tasks and Problems in Developing the Hungarian Economic Control and Management System. *Acta Oecon.*, 1984, *33*(3–4), pp. 221–36.
[G: Hungary]

Putník, Jiří. The Position of Developing Countries in Present-Day International Economic Relations. *Czech. Econ. Digest.*, June 1984, (4), pp. 48–67. **[G: LDCs]**

Putterman, Louis. Tanzanian and African Socialism: Comment. *World Devel.*, April 1984, *12*(4), pp. 461–64. **[G: Tanzania]**

Radaeva, K. M. Non-Marxian Conceptions of Management Accounting. In *Smirnov, A. D.; Golosov, V. V. and Maximova, V. F., eds.*, 1984, pp. 272–81.

Révész, Gábor. Enterprise Business Partnerships (VGMK) in Hungary—A Case Study. *Acta Oecon.*, 1984, *33*(3–4), pp. 337–59.
[G: Hungary]

Ross, Anthony Clunies. Feasible Socialism: Review Article. *J. Econ. Stud.*, 1984, *11*(3), pp. 66–70.

Rugina, Anghel N. The Future Belongs to a Social Economy of Human Solidarity: A New Orientation in Theory and Practice. *Int. J. Soc. Econ.*, 1984, *11*(1/2), pp. 49–82.

Rus, Veljko. Long-run, Medium-term, and Short-run Social Conditions for Coming Out of the Crisis. *Eastern Europ. Econ.*, Fall 1984, *23*(1), pp. 17–44. **[G: Yugoslavia]**

Sabolčík, Michal. Rationalization of the Price System in the Years 1984–1985. *Czech. Econ. Digest.*, September 1984, (6), pp. 35–55.
[G: Czechoslovakia]

Samli, A. Coskun. Comparative Marketing Systems in Eastern Europe: An Illustration of Marketing Evolution. In *Kaynak, E. and Savitt, R., eds.*, 1984, pp. 217–32. **[G: E. Europe]**

Schenk, Karl-Ernst and Wass von Czege, Andreas. Industrial Organization and Interfirm Co-operation in a Regime of Central Regulation—The Hungarian Case. In *Rába, A. and Schenk, K.-E., eds.*, 1984, pp. 1–32.
[G: Hungary]

Sen, Amartya. Labour Allocation in a Cooperative Enterprise. In *Sen, A.*, 1984, *1966*, pp. 72–89.

Shchagina, M. F. and Mikhalkina, T. Y. Non-Marxian Views of the Establishment of Socialist Society. In *Smirnov, A. D.; Golosov, V. V. and Maximova, V. F., eds.*, 1984, pp. 215–24.

Siline, Anatole. The New Role of Workers' Collectives in the USSR. *Int. Lab. Rev.*, November–December 1984, *123*(6), pp. 743–52.
[G: U.S.S.R.]

Sitaryan, Stepan and Sichev, Nickolai. Strengthening the Role of Finances in a Planned Economy. In *Hanusch, H., ed.*, 1984, pp. 27–37.
[G: U.S.S.R.]

Sláma, Jiří. Empirische Prüfung der Wirkung der Reformen in den planwirtschaftlichen Ländern. (An Empirical Analysis of the Effects of Economic Reforms in Countries with Planned Economy. With English summary.) *Jahr. Nationalökon. Statist.*, November 1984, *199*(6), pp. 537–56. **[G: Yugoslavia; Czechoslovakia]**

Soós, Károly A. A Propos the Explanation of Shortage Phenomena: Volume of Demand and Structural Inelasticity. *Acta Oecon.*, 1984, *33*(3–4), pp. 305–20.

Svirchevskii, V. and Nikol'skii, D. Developing the Brigade Form of Organizing and Stimulating Industrial Labor. *Prob. Econ.*, September 1984, *27*(5), pp. 85–90. **[G: U.S.S.R.]**

Szamuely, László. The Second Wave of the Economic Mechanism Debate and the 1968 Reform in Hungary. *Acta Oecon.*, 1984, *33*(1–2), pp. 43–67. **[G: Hungary]**

Tardos, Márton. A Development Program for Economic Control and Organization in Hungary. *Eastern Europ. Econ.*, Spring–Summer 1984, *22*(3–4), pp. 3–32. **[G: Hungary]**

Tian, Jiyun. Problems in the "Substitution of Taxes for Profits" in State-Run Enterprises. *Chinese Econ. Stud.*, Winter 1983–84, *17*(2), pp. 68–77. **[G: China]**

Tomášek, Přemysl. Egalitarianism Is Harmful. *Czech. Econ. Digest.*, June 1984, (4), pp. 3–13. **[G: Czechoslovakia]**

Vikent'ev, A. On Rates of Economic Growth in the Present Stage. *Prob. Econ.*, September 1984, *27*(5), pp. 23–43. **[G: CMEA]**

Wachtel, Howard M. Self-Management Proposals in Poland: 1981. *Econ. Anal. Worker's Manage.*, 1984, *18*(2), pp. 141–49. **[G: Poland]**

Waters, William R. Development of Solidarist Economics in the U.S. *Int. J. Soc. Econ.*, 1984, *11*(1/2), pp. 100–116. **[G: U.S.]**

Weede, Erich. Democracy, Creeping Socialism, and Ideological Socialism in Rent-seeking Societies. *Public Choice*, 1984, *44*(2), pp. 349–66. **[G: OECD; Israel]**

White, Gordon. Developmental States and Socialist Industrialisation in the Third World. *J. Devel. Stud.*, October 1984, *21*(1), pp. 97–120. **[G: Selected Global]**

Xu, Dixin, et al. China's Search for Economic Growth. *Australian Bull. Lab.*, September 1984, *10*(4), pp. 196–210. **[G: China]**

Xue, Muqiao. China: The Law of Value, Adjustment and Price Policy. In *Ngo, M., ed., vol. 1*, 1984, pp. 505–22. **[G: China]**

Xue, Muqiao. An Inquiry into the Problems Concerning the Reform of the Economic System. *Chinese Econ. Stud.*, Winter 1983–84, *17*(2), pp. 3–30. **[G: China]**

Yu, Guangyuan. The Key Lies in Enhancing Economic Efficiency. *Chinese Econ. Stud.*, Summer 1984, *17*(4), pp. 99–109. **[G: China]**

Zagoria, Donald S. China's Quiet Revolution. *Foreign Aff.*, Spring 1984, *62*(4), pp. 879–904. **[G: China]**

Zhang, Chunsheng and Song, Dahan. Separation of Government Administration from Commune Management Is a Need of Rural Economic De-velopment and of Building Political Power. *Chinese Econ. Stud.*, Spring 1984, *17*(3), pp. 76–83. **[G: China]**

Zhang, Zhuoyuan. In Stressing Economic Results Attention Must Be Paid to the Law of Value. *Chinese Econ. Stud.*, Spring 1984, *17*(3), pp. 68–75. **[G: China]**

053 Comparative Economic Systems

0530 Comparative Economic Systems

Bauer, P. T. Market Order and State Planning in Economic Development. In *Bauer, P. T.*, 1984, pp. 19–37.

Csizmadia, Magdolna, Jr.; Ehrlich, Éva and Pártos, Gyula. The Effects of Recession on Infrastructure. *Acta Oecon.*, 1984, *32*(3–4), pp. 317–42. **[G: Selected Countries]**

Drabek, Zdenek. A Comparison of Technology in Centrally Planned and Market-Type Economies. *Europ. Econ. Rev.*, August 1984, *25*(3), pp. 293–318. **[G: Czechoslovakia; Austria]**

Groth, Alexander J.; Wade, Larry L. and Wiggins, Alvin D. Classifying the World's Political Systems: A Resource-Allocation Approach. In *Groth, A. J. and Wade, L. L., eds.*, 1984, pp. 19–40.

Karlsson, Lars-Erik. Planning for Self-Management: A Swedish View. *Econ. Anal. Worker's Manage.*, 1984, *18*(1), pp. 15–34.

Knaack, Ruud. Dynamic Comparative Economics: Lessons from Socialist Planning. In *Zimbalist, A., ed.*, 1984, pp. 109–32.

Laibman, David. Modes of Production and Theories of Transition. *Sci. Soc.*, Fall 1984, *48*(3), pp. 257–94.

Marrese, Michael and Mitchell, Janet L. Kornai's Resource-Constrained Economy: A Survey and an Appraisal. *J. Compar. Econ.*, March 1984, *8*(1), pp. 74–84.

Martellaro, Joseph A. China's Two Economies and the USA Factor. *Rivista Int. Sci. Econ. Com.*, September 1984, *31*(9), pp. 875–97. **[G: China; Taiwan]**

Milenkovitch, Deborah Duff. The Incentive to Innovate under Alternative Property Rights: A Comment. *Cato J.*, Fall 1984, *4*(2), pp. 447–55. **[G: Japan; U.S.S.R.; U.S.]**

Miller, Jeffrey B. The Big Nail and Other Stories: Product Quality Control in the Soviet Union. *ACES Bull.*, Spring 1984, *26*(1), pp. 43–57. **[G: U.S.S.R.]**

Murrell, Peter. Incentives and Income under Market Socialism. *J. Compar. Econ.*, September 1984, *8*(3), pp. 261–76.

Nove, Alec. Some Observations on Intersystem Comparisons. In *Zimbalist, A., ed.*, 1984, pp. 47–64.

Pejovich, Steve. The Incentive to Innovate under Alternative Property Rights. *Cato J.*, Fall 1984, *4*(2), pp. 427–46. **[G: Yugoslavia]**

Pryor, Frederic L. Interpretations of Public Expenditure Trends in East and West. In *[Reynolds, L. G.]*, 1984, pp. 362–88. **[G: CMEA; OECD]**

Rába, András. Restriction and Adjustment. *Acta Oecon.*, 1984, 33(1–2), pp. 69–87.
[G: Hungary]

Rao, V. K. R. V. and Joshi, P. C. India's Socialist Experience in a Mixed Economy. In *Ngo, M., ed., vol. 1*, 1984, pp. 341–54. [G: India]

Stuart, Edward F. The PQLI as a Measure of Comparative Economic Performance. *ACES Bull.*, Winter 1984, 26(4), pp. 43–53.
[G: Global]

Wiedemann, Paul. Comparing the Process of Socio-economic Development in Market and Non-market Economies: The EEC and CMEA. *Cambridge J. Econ.*, December 1984, 8(4), pp. 311–30. [G: EEC; CMEA]

Wiedemann, Paul. Economic Fluctuations and Income Distribution: A Comparative Study. *ACES Bull.*, Spring 1984, 26(1), pp. 59–76.
[G: U.S.; U.K.; Yugoslavia; Bulgaria]

Yunker, James A. The Distribution of Lifetime Capital Property Income under Capitalism and Market Socialism. *ACES Bull.*, Summer–Fall 1984, 26(2–3), pp. 77–97.

100 Economic Growth; Development; Planning; Fluctuations

110 ECONOMIC GROWTH; DEVELOPMENT; AND PLANNING THEORY AND POLICY

111 Economic Growth Theory and Models

1110 Growth Theories

Adachi, Hideyuki. Investment, Replacement and Depreciation Funds. *Kobe Univ. Econ.*, 1984, (30), pp. 47–63. [G: Japan]

Adelman, Irma and Levy, Amnon. The Equalizing Role of Human Resource Intensive Growth Strategies: A Theoretical Model. *J. Policy Modeling*, May 1984, 6(2), pp. 271–87.

Amendola, Mario. Towards a Dynamic Analysis of the "Traverse." *Eastern Econ. J.*, April–June 1984, 10(2), pp. 203–10.

Bernholz, Peter. The Political Economy of Growth [Review Article]. *Kyklos*, 1984, 37(2), pp. 291–94. [G: Selected OECD]

Brock, William A. and Magee, Stephen P. The Invisible Foot and the Waste of Nations: Redistribution and Economic Growth. In *Colander, D. C., ed.*, 1984, pp. 177–85.

Bronfenbrenner, Martin and Woflson, Murray. Marxian Macrodynamics and the Harrod Growth Model. *Hist. Polit. Econ.*, Summer 1984, 16(2), pp. 175–86.

Buhl, Hans Ulrich. A Discrete Model of Optimal Economic Growth. *J. Macroecon.*, Fall 1984, 6(4), pp. 447–56.

Buiter, Willem H. and Carmichael, Jeffrey. Government Debt: Comment [Government Debt in an Overlapping-Generations Model with Bequests and Gifts]. *Amer. Econ. Rev.*, September 1984, 74(4), pp. 762–65. [G: U.S.]

Burbidge, John B. Government Debt: Reply [Government Debt in an Overlapping-Generations Model with Bequests and Gifts]. *Amer. Econ. Rev.*, September 1984, 74(4), pp. 766–67. [G: U.S.]

Cigno, Alessandro. Further Implications of Learning by Doing: The Effect of Population on Per-Capita Income. *Bull. Econ. Res.*, November 1984, 36(2), pp. 97–108.

Eliasson, Gunnar. Micro Heterogeneity of Firms and the Stability of Industrial Growth. *J. Econ. Behav. Organ.*, September–December 1984, 5(3–4), pp. 249–74. [G: Sweden]

Garagnani, Pierangelo. On Some Illusory Instances of "Marginal Products." *Metroecon.*, June–Oct. 1984, 36(2–3), pp. 143–60.

Hagemann, Harald and Jeck, Albert. Lowe and the Marx–Fel'dman–Dobb Model: Structural Analysis of a Growing Economy. *Eastern Econ. J.*, April–June 1984, 10(2), pp. 169–86.

Hahn, Frank H. Expectations and Equilibrium. In *Hahn, F.*, 1984, 1952, pp. 23–42.

Halevi, Joseph. Lowe, Dobb and Hicks. *Eastern Econ. J.*, April–June 1984, 10(2), pp. 157–67.

Halevi, Joseph. Lowe, Dobb and Hicks. *Eastern Econ. J.*, April–June 1984, 10(2), pp. 157–67.

Hori, Hajime. Competitive Price Paths of an Exhaustible Resource with Increasing Extraction Costs. *J. Econ. Dynam. Control*, October 1984, 8(1), pp. 19–32.

Kurz, Heinz D. Ricardo and Lowe on Machinery. *Eastern Econ. J.*, April–June 1984, 10(2), pp. 211–29.

Lane, John and Leininger, Wolfgang. Differentiable Nash Equilibria in Altruistic Economies. *Z. Nationalökon.*, 1984, 44(4), pp. 329–47.

Langmantel, Erich. Die Beschäftigungswirkungen sättigungsbedingten Strukturwandels—Eine Analyse anhand von Pasinettis "Structural Change and Economic Growth." (Employment Effects of Structural Change Induced by Saturation of Markets—An Analysis on the Basis of Pasinetti's "Structural Change and Economic Growth." With English summary.) *Ifo-Studien*, 1984, 30(3), pp. 231–41.

Lowe, Adolph. The Classical Theory of Economic Growth. *Soc. Res.*, Spring & Summer 1984, 51(1&2), pp. 111–42.

Lucas, Robert E., Jr. and Stokey, Nancy L. Optimal Growth with Many Consumers. *J. Econ. Theory*, February 1984, 32(1), pp. 139–71.

Matthews, R. C. O. Darwinism and Economic Change. In *Collard, D. A., et al., eds.*, 1984, pp. 91–117.

Matthews, R. C. O. Darwinsim and Economic Change. *Oxford Econ. Pap.*, Supplement November 1984, 36, pp. 91–117.

Mellor, John W. Agricultural Development and the Intersectoral Transfer of Resources. In *Eicher, C. K. and Staatz, J. M., eds.*, 1984, 1973, pp. 136–46. [G: Taiwan]

Mincer, Jacob. Human Capital and Economic Growth. *Econ. Educ. Rev.*, 1984, 3(3), pp. 195–205.

van der Ploeg, Frederick. Macro-Dynamic Theories of Economic Growth and Fluctuations. In *van der Ploeg, F., ed.*, 1984, pp. 249–85.

Ryndina, M. N. Theories of Economic Growth. In *Smirnov, A. D.; Golosov, V. V. and Maximova, V. F., eds.*, 1984, pp. 180–89.

Sen, Amartya. On Optimizing the Rate of Saving. In *Sen, A.*, 1984, *1961*, pp. 113–34.

Sen, Amartya. On Some Debates in Capital Theory. In *Sen, A.*, 1984, *1974*, pp. 162–71.

Sen, Amartya. Terminal Capital and Optimum Savings. In *Sen, A.*, 1984, *1967*, pp. 147–61.

Simon, Julian L. Research on Population and Productivity Growth. In *Steinmann, G., ed.*, 1984, pp. 50–57.

Simon, Julian L. and Steinmann, Gunter. The Economic Implications of Learning-by-Doing for Population Size and Growth. *Europ. Econ. Rev.*, October–November 1984, *26*(1–2), pp. 167–85.

Steindl, Josef. Stagnation Theory and Stagnation Policy. In *Foster, J. B. and Szlajfer, H., eds.*, 1984, *1979*, pp. 179–97. [G: U.S.]

Sylos-Labini, Paolo. Competition and Economic Growth in Adam Smith. In *Sylos-Labini, P.*, 1984, pp. 3–36. [G: U.K.]

Sylos-Labini, Paolo. Introduction: Innovations, Market Structures, Income Distribution, and the Process of Economic Growth. In *Sylos-Labini, P.*, 1984, *1976*, pp. vii–xiv.

Sylos-Labini, Paolo. Technological Change under Contemporary Conditions: An Economist's View. In *Sylos-Labini, P.*, 1984, *1981*, pp. 81–99.

Sylos-Labini, Paolo. The Problem of Economic Growth in Marx and Schumpeter. In *Sylos-Labini, P.*, 1984, *1983*, pp. 37–78.

Sylos-Labini, Paolo. The Theory of Prices in Oligopoly and the Theory of Growth. In *Sylos-Labini, P.*, 1984, *1971*, pp. 123–45. [G: U.K.; U.S.]

Takekuma, Shin-Ichi. On Duality Theory for the Continuous Time Model of Capital Accumulation. *Hitotsubashi J. Econ.*, December 1984, *25*(2), pp. 145–54.

Teschner, Manfred. Sparen, Investieren und Wirtschaftswachstum. (Saving, Investment and Economic Growth. With English summary.) *Konjunkturpolitik*, 1984, *30*(4), pp. 233–58.

Zamagni, Stefano. Ricardo and Hayek Effects in a Fixwage Model of Traverse. *Oxford Econ. Pap.*, Supplement November 1984, *36*, pp. 135–51.

Zamagni, Stefano. Ricardo and Hayek Effects in a Fixwage Model of Traverse. In *Collard, D. A., et al., eds.*, 1984, pp. 135–51.

1112 One and Two Sector Growth Models and Related Topics

Bacha, Edmar L. Growth with Limited Supplies of Foreign Exchange: A Reappraisal of the Two-Gap Model. In *[Chenery, H. B.]*, 1984, pp. 263–80.

Balducci, Renato; Candela, G. and Ricci, G. A Generalization of R. Goodwin Model with Rational Behavior of Economic Agents. In *Goodwin, R. M.; Krüger, M. and Vercelli, A., eds.*, 1984, pp. 47–66.

Burgstaller, A. and Saavedra-Rivano, Neantro. Capital Mobility and Growth in a North–South Model. *J. Devel. Econ.*, May–June–August 1984, *15*(1,2,3), pp. 213–37.

Cigno, Alessandro. Consumption vs. Procreation in Economic Growth. In *Steinmann, G., ed.*, 1984, pp. 2–28.

Dana, R. A. and Malgrange, Pierre. The Dynamics of a Discrete Version of a Growth Cycle Model. In *Ancot, J. P., ed.*, 1984, pp. 115–42.

Danthine, Jean-Pierre and Donaldson, John B. Investment, Stability and Taxation in a Long-Run Macroeconomic Model. *J. Econ. Dynam. Control*, May 1984, *7*(2), pp. 79–110.

Dechert, W. Davis. Does Optimal Growth Preclude Chaos? A Theorem on Monotonicity. *Z. Nationalökon.*, 1984, *44*(1), pp. 57–61.

Falkinger, Josef. Grenzen der innovatorischen Anpassung: Ein skeptisches Wachstumsmodell. (Limits of Innovational Capacity: A Sceptical Growth Model. With English summary.) *Jahr. Nationalökon. Statist.*, July 1984, *199*(4), pp. 321–33.

Flaschel, Peter. Some Stability Properties of Goodwin's Growth Cycle: A Critical Elaboration. *Z. Nationalökon.*, 1984, *44*(1), pp. 63–69.

Krelle, Wilhelm. Waves of Entrepreneurial Activity Induced by Transfer of Information and Valuation. *Z. Nationalökon.*, Supplement 1984, pp. 71–92.

Laitner, John P. Resource Extraction Costs and Competitive Steady-State Growth. *Int. Econ. Rev.*, June 1984, *25*(2), pp. 297–314.

Laitner, John P. Transition Time Paths for Overlapping-Generations Models. *J. Econ. Dynam. Control*, May 1984, *7*(2), pp. 111–29. [G: U.S.]

Neal, Larry. Slowing Population Growth and Investment Demand: The West German Case. In *Steinmann, G., ed.*, 1984, pp. 179–202. [G: W. Germany]

van der Ploeg, Frederick. Implications of Workers' Savings for Economic Growth and the Class Struggle. In *Goodwin, R. M.; Krüger, M. and Vercelli, A., eds.*, 1984, pp. 1–13.

Potestio, Paola. Investment in Some Neoclassical Models of Capital Accumulation. *Écon. Appl.*, 1984, *37*(3–4), pp. 543–63.

Reetz, Norbert. Österreichische Kapitaltheorie, neoklassisches Wachstum und Konjunktur. (Austrian Capital Theory, Neoclassical Growth, and Business Cycles. With English summary.) *Schweiz. Z. Volkswirtsch. Statist.*, March 1984, *120*(1), pp. 1–30.

Schmitt-Rink, Gerhard. Population Growth and Income Distribution. In *Steinmann, G., ed.*, 1984, pp. 59–67.

Steinmann, Gunter. A Model of the History of Demographic-Economic Growth. In *Steinmann, G., ed.*, 1984, pp. 29–49.

Thio, K. B. T. Cyclical and Structural Aspects of Unemployment and Growth in a Nonlinear Model of Cyclical Growth. In *Goodwin, R. M.; Krüger, M. and Vercelli, A., eds.*, 1984, pp. 127–45.

Tosato, Domenico. Sostituzione tra capitale e lavoro e teoria del processo cumulativo di Wicksell. (With English summary.) *Econ. Polít.*, August 1984, *1*(2), pp. 167–95.

Weaver, James H.; Jameson, Kenneth P. and Blue, Richard N. Growth and Equity: Can They Be Happy Together? An Analysis of Seven Models and Their Critics. In *Ghosh, P. K., ed., no. 13, 1984, 1978*, pp. 146–57.

1113 Multisector Growth Models and Related Topics

Drabicki, John Z. and Takayama, Akira. Money, National Debt, and Economic Growth. *J. Econ. Theory*, August 1984, *33*(2), pp. 356–67.

Findlay, Ronald. Growth and Development in Trade Models. In *Jones, R. W. and Kenen, P., eds., 1984*, pp. 185–236.

Goodwin, R. M. Disaggregating Models of Fluctuating Growth. In *Goodwin, R. M.; Krüger, M. and Vercelli, A., eds., 1984*, pp. 67–72.

Hahn, Frank H. Some Adjustment Problems. In *Hahn, F., 1984, 1970*, pp. 88–110.

Judita, Samuel. Monotonicity Properties of Optimal Trajectories for a Family of Stochastic Economic Growth Models. *Econ. Computat. Cybern. Stud. Res.*, 1984, *19*(3), pp. 21–34.

Klacek, Jan and Nešporová, Alena. Economic Growth in Czechoslovakia—Application of the CES Production Function. *Czech. Econ. Pap.*, 1984, (22), pp. 83–100.   [G: Czechoslovakia]

Krelle, Wilhelm. Economic Growth with Exhaustible Resources and Environmental Protection. *Z. ges. Staatswiss.*, September 1984, *140*(3), pp. 399–429.

Medvegyev, Péter. A General Existence Theorem for von Neumann Economic Growth Models. *Econometrica*, July 1984, *52*(4), pp. 963–74.

Persson, Håkan. A Way of Modelling Investment in a Multisectoral Model. *Reg. Sci. Urban Econ.*, August 1984, *14*(3), pp. 331–43.

Yano, Makoto. Competitive Equilibria on Turnpikes in a McKenzie Economy, I: A Neighborhood Turnpike Theorem. *Int. Econ. Rev.*, October 1984, *25*(3), pp. 695–717.

Yano, Makoto. The Primal Route to the Turnpike and Asymptotic Stability. *J. Math. Econ.*, December 1984, *13*(3), pp. 225–34.

Yano, Makoto. The Turnpike of Dynamic General Equilibrium Paths and Its Insensitivity to Initial Conditions. *J. Math. Econ.*, December 1984, *13*(3), pp. 235–54.

Zilcha, Itzhak. Risk-Aversely Efficient Random Variables: Characterization and an Application to Growth under Uncertainty. *J. Econ. Theory*, April 1984, *32*(2), pp. 328–36.

1114 Monetary Growth Models

Clower, Robert W. Is There an Optimal Money Supply? In *Clower, R. W., 1984, 1970*, pp. 128–37.

Costabile, Lilia. Preferenze intertemporali, risparmi e investimenti. Note su due approcci alternativi. (With English summary.) *Econ. Polít.*, December 1984, *1*(3), pp. 335–59.

Di Matteo, M. Alternative Monetary Policies in a Classical Growth Cycle. In *Goodwin, R. M.; Krüger, M. and Vercelli, A., eds., 1984*, pp. 14–24.

Drabicki, John Z. and Takayama, Akira. The Stability of a Neoclassical Monetary Growth Model. *Econ. Stud. Quart.*, December 1984, *35*(3), pp. 262–68.

Hahn, Frank H. On Money and Growth. In *Hahn, F., 1984, 1969*, pp. 195–213.

Hayakawa, Hiroaki. A Dynamic Generalization of the Tobin Model. *J. Econ. Dynam. Control*, September 1984, *7*(3), pp. 209–31.

Shieh, Yeung-Nan. On Monetary Expansion, Terms of Trade and Economic Growth. *Econ. Rec.*, June 1984, *60*(169), pp. 128–32.

Srivastava, N. N. Integration of Monetary and Growth Theories. In *Singh, A. K.; Papola, T. S. and Mathur, R. S., eds., 1984*, pp. 442–60.

112 Economic Development Models and Theories

1120 Economic Development Models and Theories

Adachi, Hideyuki. On the Economic Implications of the Growth of the Non-market Sector. *Oxford Econ. Pap.*, November 1984, *36*(3), pp. 418–37.   [G: LDCs]

Adams, John. Galbraith on Economic Development. *J. Post Keynesian Econ.*, Fall 1984, *7*(1), pp. 91–102.

Adelman, Irma. Beyond Export-led Growth. *World Devel.*, September 1984, *12*(9), pp. 937–49.   [G: S. Korea]

Adelman, Irma. Development Strategies and the Size Distribution of World Income. *METU*, 1984, *11*(1–2), pp. 177–93.   [G: LDCs]

Adelman, Irma and Hihn, Jairus M. Crisis Politics in Developing Countries. *Econ. Develop. Cult. Change*, October 1984, *33*(1), pp. 1–22.   [G: LDCs]

Adelman, Irma and Levy, Amnon. The Equalizing Role of Human Resource Intensive Growth Strategies: A Theoretical Model. *J. Policy Modeling*, May 1984, *6*(2), pp. 271–87.

Adelman, Irma and Morris, Cynthia Taft. Patterns of Economic Growth, 1850–1914, or Chenery–Syrquin in Historical Perspective. In *[Chenery, H. B.], 1984*, pp. 45–74.

Agarwala, Ramgopal. Price Distortions and Growth. *Finance Develop.*, March 1984, *21*(1), pp. 33–37.   [G: LDCs]

Agmon, Tamir; Lessard, Donald R. and Paddock, James L. Appropriate Financing for Petroleum Development in Developing Countries. *Energy J.*, July 1984, *5*(3), pp. 27–40.

Ahn, Kookshin. Optimal Foreign Borrowing and Altruism in an Overlapping Generations Model. *J. Econ. Devel.*, December 1984, *9*(2), pp. 171–90.

Alam, M. Shahid. Import Substitution Growth:

A Simple Intersectoral Analysis. *Philippine Econ. J.*, Winter 1984, *23*(1), pp. 157–60.

Alam, M. Shahid. Import Substitution Growth: A Simple Intersection Analysis. *Pakistan J. Appl. Econ.*, Winter 1984, *3*(2), pp. 157–60.

Allam, Mohamed N. and Marks, David H. Irrigated Agricultural Expansion Planning in Developing Countries: Income Redistribution Objective. *Water Resources Res.*, July 1984, *20*(7), pp. 767–74.

Allam, Mohamed N. and Marks, David H. Irrigated Agricultural Expansion Planning in Developing Countries: Resilient System Design. *Water Resources Res.*, July 1984, *20*(7), pp. 775–84.

Amin, Samir. A Note on the Concept of Delinking. *METU*, 1984, *11*(1–2), pp. 225–32.

Amin, Samir. Human Resources, Employment and Development: Introduction. In *Amin, S., ed.*, 1984, pp. viii–xxiii.

Anker, Richard and Farooq, Ghazi M. Population and Socio-economic Development: The New Perspective. In *Ghosh, P. K., ed., no. 5*, 1984, *1978*, pp. 265–79.

Arndt, Heinz W. The Role of Political Leadership in Economic Development. *Can. J. Devel. Stud.*, 1984, *5*(1), pp. 51–63.

Aziz, Sartaj. Rural Development—Some Essential Prerequisites. *Int. Lab. Rev.*, May–June 1984, *123*(3), pp. 277–85. **[G: LDCs]**

Bacha, Edmar L. Growth with Limited Supplies of Foreign Exchange: A Reappraisal of the Two-Gap Model. In *[Chenery, H. B.]*, 1984, pp. 263–80.

Baer, Werner. Industrialization in Latin America: Successes and Failures. *J. Econ. Educ.*, Spring 1984, *15*(2), pp. 124–35. **[G: Latin America]**

Baer, Werner. Semi-industrialization and Semi-development: The Legacy of Import-Substitution on Development Problems and on Development Economics. *METU*, 1984, *11*(1–2), pp. 151–62. **[G: LDCs]**

Balassa, Bela. Adjustment Policies in Developing Countries: A Reassessment. *World Devel.*, September 1984, *12*(9), pp. 955–72. **[G: LDCs]**

Bar-El, Raphael. Rural Industrialization Objectives: The Income–Employment Conflict. *World Devel.*, February 1984, *12*(2), pp. 129–40. **[G: Brazil]**

Bardhan, Pranab K. and Kletzer, Kenneth M. Quality Variations and the Choice between Foreign and Indigenous Goods or Technology. *J. Devel. Econ.*, April 1984, *14*(3), pp. 323–30. **[G: LDCs]**

Barone, Charles A. Reply [Dependency, Marxist Theory, and Salvaging the Idea of Capitalism in South Korea]. *Rev. Radical Polit. Econ.*, Summer & Fall 1984, *16*(2&3), pp. 195–97. **[G: S. Korea]**

Bauer, P. T. Collective Self-reliance as Development Strategy. In *Ghosh, P. K., ed., no. 8*, 1984, *1977*, pp. 266–76.

Bauer, P. T. Market Order and State Planning in Economic Development. In *Bauer, P. T.*, 1984, pp. 19–37.

Bauer, P. T. Remembrance of Studies Past: Retracing First Steps. In *Bauer, P. T.*, 1984, pp. 1–18. **[G: S.E. Asia; W. Africa]**

Bauer, P. T. Substance and Method in Development Economics: A Commentary on the Views of Professor Stern. In *Bauer, P. T.*, 1984, pp. 140–51.

Beckford, George L. Induced Innovation Model of Agricultural Development: Comment. In *Eicher, C. K. and Staatz, J. M., eds.*, 1984, *1972*, pp. 75–81.

Bell, Clive and Srinivasan, T. N. On the Uses and Abuses of Economywide Models in Development Policy Analysis. In *[Chenery, H. B.]*, 1984, pp. 451–76.

Bell, Martin; Ross-Larson, Bruce and Westphal, Larry E. Assessing the Performance of Infant Industries. *J. Devel. Econ.*, September–October 1984, *16*(1–2), pp. 101–28. **[G: LDCs]**

Bequele, Assefa and Freedman, David H. Employment and Basic Needs: An Overview. In *Ghosh, P. K., ed., no. 13*, 1984, *1979*, pp. 188–204.

Berlage, L. Commodity Price Stabilization by Buffer Stocks and by Export Quotas. *Tijdschrift Econ. Manage.*, 1984, *29*(3), pp. 437–48. **[G: LDCs]**

Bernal, Richard L.; Figueroa, Mark and Witter, Michael. Caribbean Economic Thought: The Critical Tradition. *Soc. Econ. Stud.*, June 1984, *33*(2), pp. 5–96. **[G: Caribbean]**

Berry, Albert. Income Distribution Trends in Labor Surplus Economies. In *[Reynolds, L. G.]*, 1984, pp. 182–200. **[G: LDCs]**

Berry, Albert and Sabot, R. H. Unemployment and Economic Development. *Econ. Develop. Cult. Change*, October 1984, *33*(1), pp. 99–116. **[G: LDCs]**

Bhagwati, Jagdish N. Development Economics: What Have We Learned? *METU*, 1984, *11*(1–2), pp. 49–69.

Bills, David B. and Haller, Archibald O. Socioeconomic Development and Social Stratification: Reassessing the Brazilian Case. *J. Devel. Areas*, October 1984, *19*(1), pp. 59–69. **[G: Brazil]**

Birdsall, Nancy. Analytical Approaches to the Relationship of Population Growth and Development. In *Ghosh, P. K., ed., no. 5*, 1984, *1977*, pp. 177–220.

Black, Philip A. The 'Demonstration Effect' and Labour Unemployment in Developing Countries. *J. Stud. Econ. Econometrics*, March 1984, (19), pp. 31–40. **[G: LDCs]**

Blejer, Mario I. and Khan, Mohsin S. Government Policy and Private Investment in Developing Countries. *Int. Monet. Fund Staff Pap.*, June 1984, *31*(2), pp. 379–403. **[G: LDCs]**

Bolin, Meb. An Institutionalist Perspective on Economic Development. *J. Econ. Issues*, June 1984, *18*(2), pp. 643–50.

Bor, Walter. Planning and Development in Developing Countries. In *Ghosh, P. K., ed., no. 8*, 1984, *1982*, pp. 40–47.

Bornschier, Volker. Multinational Corporations, Economic Policy and National Development in the World System. In *Ghosh, P. K., ed.*, *no. 11*, 1984, *1980*, pp. 30–46.

Bose, Arun. Agrarian Reform, International Trade and Development. In *Ngo, M., ed., vol. 2*, 1984, pp. 765–84.

Bourguignon, François and Leibovich, José. Offre et demande dans le processus de développement: un modèle agrégé de déséquilibre appliqué à la Colombie. (Supply and Demand in the Development Process: An Applied Aggregate Disequilibrium Model for Colombia. With English summary.) *Ann. INSEE*, July–December 1984, (55/56), pp. 223–44. **[G: Colombia]**

Bruton, Henry J. Development as a Searching and Learning Process. *METU*, 1984, *11*(1–2), pp. 71–79. **[G: LDCs]**

Bruton, Henry J. Economic Development with Unlimited Supplies of Foreign Exchange. In *[Reynolds, L. G.]*, 1984, pp. 124–44. **[G: LDCs]**

Buffie, Edward F. Financial Repression, the New Structuralists, and Stabilization Policy in Semi-Industrialized Economies. *J. Devel. Econ.*, April 1984, *14*(3), pp. 305–22. **[G: LDCs]**

Buffie, Edward F. The Macroeconomics of Trade Liberalization. *J. Int. Econ.*, August 1984, *17*(1/2), pp. 121–37. **[G: LDCs]**

Bugliarello, George. Technology and Economic Development. *Metroecon.*, February 1984, *36*(1), pp. 111–19. **[G: Global]**

Burgstaller, A. and Saavedra-Rivano, Neantro. Capital Mobility and Growth in a North–South Model. *J. Devel. Econ.*, May–June–August 1984, *15*(1,2,3), pp. 213–37.

Caballero, José María. Unequal Pricing and Unequal Exchange between the Peasant and Capitalist Economies. *Cambridge J. Econ.*, December 1984, *8*(4), pp. 347–59.

Calderón-Rossell, Jorge R. Optimal Financial Structure of Finance Companies in a Regulated Environment of a Developing Country. *J. Banking Finance*, September 1984, *8*(3), pp. 443–57. **[G: LDCs]**

Callier, Philippe. Growth of Developing Countries and World Interest Rates. *J. Macroecon.*, Fall 1984, *6*(4), pp. 465–71. **[G: LDCs]**

Cantarelli, Davide and Bressan, Franco. Diseguaglianze regionali e sviluppo economico: un'analisi econometrica "internazionale." (Regional Inequalities and Economic Development: An "International" Econometric Analysis. With English summary.) *Giorn. Econ.*, March–April 1984, *43*(3–4), pp. 161–89. **[G: Global]**

Chaudhuri, T. Datta and Khan, M. Ali. Educated Unemployed, Educational Subsidies, and Growth. *Pakistan Devel. Rev.*, Summer-Autumn 1984, *23*(2&3), pp. 395–409.

Chenery, Hollis B. The Evolution of Development Planning. *J. Policy Modeling*, May 1984, *6*(2), pp. 159–74.

Chenery, Hollis B. Poverty and Progress—Choices for the Developing World. In *Ghosh, P. K., ed., no. 13*, 1984, *1980*, pp. 75–84.

Chichilnisky, Graciela. Basic Needs, Exhaustible Resources and Growth in a North–South Con-

text. In *Ghosh, P. K., ed., no. 13*, 1984, *1982*, pp. 158–72.

Chichilnisky, Graciela. Necesidades básicas, recursos no renovables y crecimiento en el contexto de las relaciones Norte–Sur. (With English summary.) *Desarrollo Econ.*, July–September 1984, *24*(94), pp. 171–85.

Chichilnisky, Graciela. North–South Trade and Export-led Policies [Terms of Trade and Domestic Distribution: Export-led Growth with Abundant Labour]. *J. Devel. Econ.*, May–June–August 1984, *15*(1,2,3), pp. 131–60. **[G: U.K.; Sri Lanka]**

Chichilnisky, Graciela. Terms of Trade, Domestic Distribution and Export-led Growth: A Rejoinder to Rejoinders. *J. Devel. Econ.*, May–June–August 1984, *15*(1,2,3), pp. 177–84.

Chiswick, Carmel U. The Impact of Education Policy on Economic Development: Quantity, Quality, and Earnings of Labor. *Econ. Educ. Rev.*, 1984, *3*(2), pp. 121–30.

Ciucur, D. and Popescu, C. Compatibility and Equilibrium in the Development of the National Economy. *Econ. Computat. Cybern. Stud. Res.*, 1984, *19*(2), pp. 93–99. **[G: Romania]**

Clapp, John M. and Richardson, Harry W. Technological Change in Information-processing Industries and Regional Income Differentials in Developing Countries. *Int. Reg. Sci. Rev.*, December 1984, *9*(3), pp. 241–56. **[G: LDCs]**

Cohen, Alvin. Review Article: The Macroeconomic versus the Microeconomic Approach to Development: The Futility of Development Efforts as a Function of Institutional Inertia. *Econ. Develop. Cult. Change*, January 1984, *32*(2), pp. 423–30. **[G: LDCs]**

Cohen, S. I. Towards Social Group Approaches in Economic Models. In *Cohen, S. I., et al., eds.*, 1984, pp. 27–58.

Cole, Sam. Methods of Analysis for Long-term Development Issues. In *Ghosh, P. K., ed., no. 8*, 1984, *1981*, pp. 221–39.

Collier, Paul and Lal, Deepak. Why Poor People Get Rich: Kenya, 1960–79. *World Devel.*, October 1984, *12*(10), pp. 1007–18. **[G: Kenya]**

Cornelisse, Peter A. Towards an Analysis of Markets in Developing Countries. In *Cohen, S. I., et al., eds.*, 1984, pp. 253–65.

Dell, Sidney. Basic Needs or Comprehensive Development: Should UNDP Have a Development Strategy? In *Ghosh, P. K., ed., no. 13*, 1984, *1978*, pp. 115–45.

Dervis, Kemal and Page, John M., Jr. Industrial Policy in Developing Countries. *J. Compar. Econ.*, December 1984, *8*(4), pp. 436–51. **[G: LDCs]**

Desai, Meghnad. A General Theory of Poverty? A Review Article. *Indian Econ. Rev.*, July–Dec. 1984, *19*(2), pp. 157–69. **[G: India]**

Dholakia, Nikhilesh. Marketing in Less Developed Countries: Its Nature and Prospects. In *Kindra, G. S., ed.*, 1984, pp. 10–28. **[G: LDCs]**

Dholakia, Nikhilesh and Dholakia, Ruby Roy. Missing Links: Marketing and the Newer Theories of Development. **In** *Kindra, G. S., ed.,* 1984, pp. 57–75. **[G: LDCs]**

Di Filippo, Armando. Social Use of the Surplus, Accumulation, Distribution, and Employment. *Cepal Rev.,* 1984, (24), pp. 117–34. **[G: Latin America]**

Dixit, Avinash. Growth and Terms of Trade under Imperfect Competition. **In** *Kierzkowski, H., ed.,* 1984, pp. 109–23.

Dixon, William J. Trade Concentration, Economic Growth, and the Provision of Basic Human Needs. *Soc. Sci. Quart.,* September 1984, 65(3), pp. 761–74. **[G: LDCs]**

Djokanovic, Timohir. Choice of Type of Industrialisation in Developing Countries. **In** *Amin, S., ed.,* 1984, pp. 173–85.

Dominique, C. René. Choosing the Appropriate Project Appraisal Method for a Labour Surplus Economy. *Industry Devel.,* 1984, (10), pp. 1–37.

Dos Santos, Theotonio. The Structure of Dependence. **In** *Seligson, M. A., ed.,* 1984, 1970, pp. 95–104.

Dos Santos, Theotonio. Theory of Development, Dependence and Social Change. **In** *Ngo, M., ed., vol. 2,* 1984, pp. 862–81. **[G: LDCs]**

Dostovalov, Y. L. and Allpatov, S. B. The Interpretation of Neocolonialism and the Economies of Developing Countries. **In** *Smirnov, A. D.; Golosov, V. V. and Maximova, V. F., eds.,* 1984, pp. 190–214.

Dutt, Amitava Krishna. Rent, Income Distribution and Growth in an Underdeveloped Agrarian Economy. *J. Devel. Econ.,* May–June–August 1984, 15(1,2,3), pp. 185–211.
[G: LDCs]

Dutt, Amitava Krishna. Stagnation, Income Distribution and Monopoly Power. *Cambridge J. Econ.,* March 1984, 8(1), pp. 25–40.
[G: India]

Edwards, Sebastian. Domestic Policies and Foreign Resource Requirements: Comment. *Quart. J. Econ.,* February 1984, 99(1), pp. 201–06.

Eicher, Carl K. and Staatz, John M. Agricultural Growth and the Transformation of Rural Institutions: Introduction. **In** *Eicher, C. K. and Staatz, J. M., eds.,* 1984, pp. 255–62.

Ellis, Frank. Relative Agricultural Prices and the Urban Bias Model: A Comparative Analysis of Tanzania and Fiji. *J. Devel. Stud.,* April 1984, 20(3), pp. 28–51. **[G: Tanzania; Fiji]**

Emmerij, Louis. Basic Needs and Employment-oriented Strategies Reconsidered. **In** *Amin, S., ed.,* 1984, pp. 147–69.

Enders, Klaus. Strukturelle Konsequenzen eines Rohstoffbooms in einem Industrieland: De-Industrialisierungstheorie und norwegische Erfahrungen. (Structural Consequences of a Resource Boom in an Industrialized Economy: De-industrialization Theory and Norwegian Experience. With English summary.) *Konjunkturpolitik,* 1984, 30(6), pp. 328–47.
[G: Norway]

Enos, J. L. Public Policy in an Economy with

Different Types of Agents. *Greek Econ. Rev.,* December 1984, 6(3), pp. 424–52.

Etemad, Hamid. Is Marketing the Catalyst in the Economic Development Process? **In** *Kindra, G. S., ed.,* 1984, pp. 29–56. **[G: LDCs]**

Evans, David and Alizadeh, Parvin. Trade, Industrialisation, and the Visible Hand. *J. Devel. Stud.,* October 1984, 21(1), pp. 22–46.
[G: S. Korea; Taiwan]

Ewing, A. F. The Assault on Development Economics: Consequences for Intergovernmental Co-operation. *J. World Trade Law,* May–June 1984, 18(3), pp. 187–205.

Faini, Riccardo. Increasing Returns, Non-Traded Inputs and Regional Development. *Econ. J.,* June 1984, 94(374), pp. 308–23.

Falvey, Rodney E. and Fried, Harold O. Sectoral Trading Arrangements. *Int. Econ. Rev.,* October 1984, 25(3), pp. 671–85.

Farooq, Ghazi M. Population, Human Resources and Development Planning: Towards an Integrated Approach. **In** *Ghosh, P. K., ed., no. 5,* 1984, 1981, pp. 161–76.

Ferrer, Ricardo D. Society, Politics, and Economic Development: Some Exploratory Notes. *Philippine Rev. Econ. Bus.,* Mar./June 1984, 21(1/2), pp. 1–38. **[G: LDCs]**

Fields, Gary S. Employment, Income Distribution and Economic Growth in Seven Small Open Economies. *Econ. J.,* March 1984, 94(373), pp. 74–83. **[G: Selected LDCs]**

Findlay, Ronald. A Comment on 'North–South Trade and Export-led Policies' [Terms of Trade and Domestic Distribution: Export-led Growth with Abundant Labour]. *J. Devel. Econ.,* May–June–August 1984, 15(1,2,3), pp. 161–67.

Findlay, Ronald. Growth and Development in Trade Models. **In** *Jones, R. W. and Kenen, P., eds.,* 1984, pp. 185–236.

Fishlow, Albert. Summary Comment on Adelman, Balassa and Streeten [Beyond Export-Led Growth] [Adjustment Policies in Developing Countries: A Reassessment] [Basic Needs: Some Unsettled Questions]. *World Devel.,* September 1984, 12(9), pp. 979–82.

Frank, Andre Gunder. Real Marxism Is Marxist Realism. **In** *Frank, A. G.,* 1984, 1983, pp. 279–89.

Frank, Andre Gunder. [Dependence is Dead, Long Live Dependence and the Class Struggle:] An Answer to Critics. **In** *Frank, A. G.,* 1984, 1977, pp. 245–78. **[G: Latin America]**

Frank, Andre Gunder. Science and Underdevelopment in the Third World. **In** *Frank, A. G.,* 1984, 1968, pp. 6–19.

Frank, Andre Gunder. What Is the Scientific Value of the Study of the Development of Underdevelopment? None!! **In** *Frank, A. G.,* 1984, pp. 3–5.

Frank, Andre Gunder and Shah, Said Ahmad. Introduction, Contents, and Requiem for a Reader on Underdevelopment. **In** *Frank, A. G.,* 1984, pp. 293–322.

Fransman, Martin. Technological Capability in the Third World: An Overview and Introduction to Some of the Issues Raised in This Book.

In *Fransman, M. and King, K., eds.*, 1984, pp. 3–30. **[G: LDCs]**

Fritz, Richard G. Time Series Evidence of the Causal Relationship between Financial Deepening and Economic Development. *J. Econ. Devel.*, July 1984, *9*(1), pp. 91–111. **[G: Philippines]**

Galtung, Johan. Grand Designs on a Collison Course. In *Ghosh, P. K., ed., no. 9*, 1984, *1978*, pp. 59–65.

Galtung, Johan. Grand Designs on a Collision Course. In *Ghosh, P. K., ed., no. 13*, 1984, *1978*, pp. 108–14.

Gaude, J.; Phan-Thuy, N. and Van Kempen, C. Evaluation of Special Public Works Programmes: Some Policy Conclusions. *Int. Lab. Rev.*, March-April 1984, *123*(2), pp. 203–19. **[G: Selected Countries]**

Giersch, Herbert and Heimenz, Ulrich. Past Trends and Present Needs in Research on Economic Development. *METU*, 1984, *11*(1–2), pp. 41–48.

van Ginneken, Wouter and Baron, Christopher. Appropriate Products, Employment and Technology: Introduction. In *van Ginneken, W. and Baron, C., eds.*, 1984, pp. 1–13.

Ginsburgh, Victor and Robinson, Sherman. Equilibrium and Prices in Multisector Models. In *[Chenery, H. B.]*, 1984, pp. 429–50.

Glezakos, Constantine. Inflation and Growth: A Reconsideration of the Evidence from the LDCs. In *Ghosh, P. K., ed., no. 7*, 1984, *1978*, pp. 163–75. **[G: LDCs]**

Goldin, Claudia and Sokoloff, Kenneth L. The Relative Productivity Hypothesis of Industrialization: The American Case, 1820 to 1850. *Quart. J. Econ.*, August 1984, *99*(3), pp. 461–87. **[G: U.S.]**

Gómez M., G. L. Modelling the Economic Development by Means of Impulsive Control Techniques. In *Avula, X. J. R., et al.*, 1984, pp. 802–06.

Gordon, Wendell C. The Implementation of Economic Development. *J. Econ. Issues*, March 1984, *18*(1), pp. 295–313. **[G: Global]**

Goulet, Denis. Can Values Shape Third World Technology Policy? In *Ghosh, P. K., ed., no. 3*, 1984, *1979*, pp. 50–74.

Graaff, Jan. Economic Theory and the Economy of Palanpur: A Review Article. *Oxford Econ. Pap.*, November 1984, *36*(3), pp. 327–35. **[G: India]**

Graciarena, Jorge. The Basic Needs Strategy as an Option: Its Possibilities in the Latin American Context. In *Ghosh, P. K., ed., no. 13*, 1984, *1979*, pp. 245–66. **[G: Latin America]**

Graves, Philip E. and Sexton, Robert Louis. Overurbanization and Its Relation to Economic Growth for Less Developed Countries. In *Ghosh, P. K., ed., no. 2*, 1984, *1979*, pp. 160–66.

Griffin, Keith and James, Jeffrey. Managing the Transition to Egalitarian Development. In *Amin, S., ed.*, 1984, pp. 97–115.

Gunning, Jan Willem. Comparative Statics, Stability and Optimal Trade Policy [Terms of Trade and Domestic Distribution: Export-led Growth with Abundant Labour]. *J. Devel. Econ.*, May–June–August 1984, *15*(1,2,3), pp. 169–72.

Gunning, Jan Willem. Export-led Growth with Abundant Labour: A Defense of Orthodoxy. *J. Devel. Econ.*, May–June–August 1984, *15*(1,2,3), pp. 97–103.

Gupta, Kanhaya L. Financial Liberalization and Economic Growth: Some Simulation Results. *J. Econ. Devel.*, December 1984, *9*(2), pp. 25–43. **[G: Latin America; S.E. Asia]**

Gupta, Manash Ranjan. The Productivity of Workers' Consumption and the Choice of Techniques: A Comment. *Indian Econ. Rev.*, July-Dec. 1984, *19*(2), pp. 241–42.

Gupta, Sanjeev and Togan, Sübidey. Who Benefits from the Adjustment Process in Developing Countries? A Test on India, Kenya, and Turkey. *J. Policy Modeling*, February 1984, *6*(1), pp. 95–109. **[G: India; Kenya; Turkey]**

Gupta, Suraj B. The Productivity of Workers' Consumption and the Choice of Techniques: A Reply. *Indian Econ. Rev.*, July-Dec. 1984, *19*(2), pp. 243–45.

Gurley, John G. Some Elements of a Marxist Theory of Socialist Economic Development. In *[Chenery, H. B.]*, 1984, pp. 115–31.

Halevi, Joseph. Lowe, Dobb and Hicks. *Eastern Econ. J.*, April-June 1984, *10*(2), pp. 157–67.

Halevi, Joseph. Lowe, Dobb and Hicks. *Eastern Econ. J.*, April-June 1984, *10*(2), pp. 157–67.

Harberger, Arnold C. Basic Needs versus Distributional Weights in Social Cost–Benefit Analysis. *Econ. Develop. Cult. Change*, April 1984, *32*(3), pp. 455–74.

Harberger, Arnold C. and Wall, David. Harry G. Johnson as a Development Economist. *J. Polit. Econ.*, August 1984, *92*(4), pp. 616–41.

Hardaker, J. Brian; Anderson, Jock R. and Dillon, John L. Perspectives on Assessing the Impacts of Improved Agricultural Technologies in Developing Countries. *Australian J. Agr. Econ.*, August/December 1984, *28*(2–3), pp. 87–108. **[G: LDCs]**

Harriss, John C. and Moore, Mick. Development and the Rural–Urban Divide: Introduction. In *Harriss, J. and Moore, M., eds.*, 1984, pp. 1–4.

Hart-Landsberg, Martin. Capitalism and Third World Economic Development: A Critical Look at the South Korean "Miracle" [Dependency, Marxist Theory, and Salvaging the Idea of Capitalism in South Korea]. *Rev. Radical Polit. Econ.*, Summer & Fall 1984, *16*(2&3), pp. 181–93. **[G: S. Korea]**

Hasan, Parvez. Adjustment to External Shocks. *Finance Develop.*, December 1984, *21*(4), pp. 14–17. **[G: E. Asia]**

Hayami, Yujiro and Ruttan, Vernon W. The Green Revolution: Inducement and Distribution. *Pakistan Devel. Rev.*, Spring 1984, *23*(1), pp. 37–63. **[G: Asia]**

Heal, Geoffrey and McLeod, Darryl. Gains from Trade, Stability and Profits: A Comment on Chichilnisky's 'Terms of Trade and Domestic

Distribution: Export-led Growth with Abundant Labour.' *J. Devel. Econ.*, May–June–August 1984, *15*(1,2,3), pp. 117–30.

Hicks, Norman L. Is There a Tradeoff Between Growth and Basic Needs? In *Ghosh, P. K., ed., no. 13, 1984, 1980*, pp. 216–25.

Hicks, Norman L. Is There a Tradeoff Between Growth and Basic Needs? In *Seligson, M. A., ed., 1984, 1980*, pp. 338–47. **[G: LDCs]**

Higgins, Benjamin. Jan Boeke and the Doctrine of 'The Little Push.' *Bull. Indonesian Econ. Stud.*, December 1984, *20*(3), pp. 55–69. **[G: Indonesia]**

Hoy, Don R. and Bélisle, François J. Environmental Protection and Economic Development in Guatemala's Western Highlands. *J. Devel. Areas*, January 1984, *18*(2), pp. 161–76. **[G: Guatemala]**

Hughes, Helen. Industrialization and Development: A Stocktaking. In *Ghosh, P. K., ed., no. 1, 1984, 1978*, pp. 5–29.

Hughes, Helen. Industrializing Small Countries. *Industry Devel.*, 1984, (12), pp. 89–99.

Hui, Lim Mah. Industrial Development in Malaysia and the Dependency Debate. In *Ngo, M., ed., vol. 1, 1984*, pp. 357–77. **[G: Malaysia]**

Iglesias, Enrique V. Development and Equity: The Challenge of the 1980s. In *Ghosh, P. K., ed., no. 8, 1984, 1981*, pp. 313–72. **[G: Latin America]**

Islam, Nurul. Development Strategy in the Poor Countries. In *Ghosh, P. K., ed., no. 8, 1984, 1975*, pp. 48–57.

Islam, Shafiqul. Devaluation, Stabilization Policies and the Developing Countries: A Macroeconomic Analysis. *J. Devel. Econ.*, January–February 1984, *14*(1–2), pp. 37–60.

Jackman, Robert W. Dependence on Foreign Investment and Economic Growth in the Third World. In *Seligson, M. A., ed., 1984, 1982*, pp. 211–31. **[G: LDCs]**

Johnson, Omotunde E. G. On Growth and Inflation in Developing Countries. *Int. Monet. Fund Staff Pap.*, December 1984, *31*(4), pp. 636–60. **[G: LDCs]**

Kamenetzky, Mario. The Socio-economic Iceberg and the Design of Policies for Scientific and Technological Development. In *Ghosh, P. K., ed., no. 3, 1984*, pp. 239–54.

Kaplinsky, Raphael. The International Context for Industrialisation in the Coming Decade. *J. Devel. Stud.*, October 1984, *21*(1), pp. 75–96.

Katz, Jorge M. Domestic Technological Innovations and Dynamic Comparative Advantage: Further Reflections on a Comparative Case-Study Program. *J. Devel. Econ.*, September–October 1984, *16*(1–2), pp. 13–37. **[G: Latin America]**

Kavoussi, Rostam M. Export Expansion and Economic Growth: Further Empirical Evidence. *J. Devel. Econ.*, January–February 1984, *14*(1–2), pp. 241–50. **[G: LDCs]**

Kawanabe, Noboru. Urban Traditional Sector and Rural–Urban Migration in LDCs. (In Japanese. With English summary.) *Osaka Econ. Pap.*, December 1984, *34*(2–3), pp. 248–60. **[G: LDCs]**

Kelley, Allen C. and Williamson, Jeffrey G. Population Growth, Industrial Revolutions, and the Urban Transition. *Population Devel. Rev.*, September 1984, *10*(3), pp. 419–41. **[G: LDCs]**

Khan, Ghulam Ishaq. First Annual General Meeting of the Pakistan Society of Development Economists: Inaugural Address. *Pakistan Devel. Rev.*, Summer-Autumn 1984, *23*(2&3), pp. 105–17. **[G: Pakistan]**

Killick, Tony. Political Processes and the Modelling of Development Strategies: A Critical Approach. In *Cohen, S. I., et al., eds., 1984*, pp. 211–19.

Killick, Tony. Review Article: Development Economics. *J. Econ. Stud.*, 1984, *11*(1), pp. 55–62.

Kim, Kwan S. and Turrubiate, Gerardo. Structures of Foreign Trade and Income Distribution: The Case of Mexico. *J. Devel. Econ.*, December 1984, *16*(3), pp. 263–78. **[G: Mexico]**

Kobrin, Stephen J. Multinational Corporations, Sociocultural Dependence, and Industrialization: Need Satisfaction or Want Creation? In *Ghosh, P. K., ed., no. 11, 1984, 1979*, pp. 195–218. **[G: LDCs; U.S.]**

Kogut, Edy Luiz and Langoni, Carlos Geraldo. Population Growth, Income Distribution and Economic Development. In *Ghosh, P. K., ed., no. 5, 1984, 1975*, pp. 147–60. **[G: Latin America; U.S.]**

Krueger, Anne O. Debt Problems of Developing Countries. *METU*, 1984, *11*(3–4), pp. 249–61. **[G: LDCs]**

Krueger, Anne O. and Tuncer, Baran. An Empirical Test of the Infant Industry Argument: Reply. *Amer. Econ. Rev.*, December 1984, *74*(5), pp. 1112–13. **[G: Turkey]**

Lahiri, A. K. Non-luxurious Money, Secular Behaviour of Velocity and Implications for Development Planning. *Indian Econ. J.*, July–Sept. 1984, *32*(1), pp. 94–99.

Lall, Sanjaya. Transnationals and the Third World: Changing Perceptions. *Nat. Westminster Bank Quart. Rev.*, May 1984, pp. 2–16. **[G: OECD]**

LaPorte, Robert, Jr. Administering Development. In *Burki, S. J. and LaPorte, R., Jr., eds., 1984*, pp. 239–70. **[G: Pakistan]**

Laumas, Prem S. and Williams, Martin. Urbanization and Economic Development. *Eastern Econ. J.*, July-September 1984, *10*(3), pp. 325–32. **[G: Global]**

Lecaillon, Jacques and Germidis, Dimitrios. Income Differentials and the Dynamics of Development. In *Ghosh, P. K., ed., no. 7, 1984, 1976*, pp. 176–94. **[G: Africa]**

Leff, Nathaniel H. Externalities, Information Costs, and Social Benefit–Cost Analysis for Economic Development: An Example from Telecommunications. *Econ. Develop. Cult. Change*, January 1984, *32*(2), pp. 255–76. **[G: LDCs]**

Leff, Nathaniel H. Social Benefit–Cost Analysis and Telecommunications Investment in Developing Countries. *Info. Econ. Policy*, 1984, *1*(3), pp. 217–27. **[G: LDCs]**

Leonard, David K. Disintegrating Agricultural Development. *Food Res. Inst. Stud.*, 1984, *19*(2), pp. 177–86. **[G: Kenya]**

Leontief, Wassily. Population Growth and Economic Development: Illustrative Projections. In *Ghosh, P. K., ed., no. 5*, 1984, *1979*, pp. 221–46. **[G: Global]**

Lewis, Stephen R., Jr. Development Problems of the Mineral-Rich Countries. In *[Chenery, H. B.]*, 1984, pp. 157–77.

Lewis, W. Arthur. The State of Development Theory. *Amer. Econ. Rev.*, March 1984, *74*(1), pp. 1–10.

Lim, Chong-Yah. The Causes of Development. *Singapore Econ. Rev.*, October 1984, *29*(2), pp. 63–82.

Lindbeck, Assar. The International Economic Environment and Industrialization Possibilities in Developing Countries. *Industry Devel.*, 1984, (12), pp. 9–42.

Lipschitz, Leslie. Domestic Credit and Exchange Rates in Developing Countries: Some Policy Experiments with Korean Data. *Int. Monet. Fund Staff Pap.*, December 1984, *31*(4), pp. 595–635. **[G: Korea]**

Lipton, Michael. Urban Bias Revisited. In *Harriss, J. and Moore, M., eds.*, 1984, pp. 139–66.

Lipton, Michael. Urban Bias Revisited. *J. Devel. Stud.*, April 1984, *20*(3), pp. 139–66. **[G: LDCs]**

Llach, Juan Jose. El Plan Pinedo de 1940, su significado histórico y los orígenes de la economía política del peronismo. (With English summary.) *Desarrollo Econ.*, January-March 1984, *23*(92), pp. 515–58. **[G: Argentina]**

Lorenzen, Gunter. The Kuznets Curve: Evidence from Prussia Revisited. *Weltwirtsch. Arch.*, 1984, *120*(4), pp. 764–81. **[G: Prussia]**

Love, James. External Market Conditions, Competitiveness, Diversification, and LDCs' Exports. *J. Devel. Econ.*, December 1984, *16*(3), pp. 279–91. **[G: LDCs]**

Lucas, Robert E. B. An Empirical Test of the Infant Industry Argument: Comment. *Amer. Econ. Rev.*, December 1984, *74*(5), pp. 1110–11. **[G: Turkey]**

Lütkenhorst, Wilfried. Zur Relevanz neuerer Gerechtigkeits-theorien für die Wirtschaftspolitik. Grundsätzliche Betrachtungen am Beispiel einer grundbedürfnisorientierten Entwicklungspolitik. (On the Relevance of Recent Theories of Justice for Economic Policy. With Special Emphasis on Basic Needs Oriented Development Policy. With English summary.) *Z. Wirtschaft. Sozialwissen.*, 1984, *104*(2), pp. 131–49.

Mac Bean, A. I. Export Instability and Economic Growth. *METU*, 1984, *11*(1–2), pp. 195–205. **[G: LDCs]**

Maizels, Alfred. A Conceptual Framework for Analysis of Primary Commodity Markets. *World Devel.*, January 1984, *12*(1), pp. 25–41. **[G: Global]**

Manh-Lan, Ngo. Unreal Growth: Introduction. In *Ngo, M., ed., vol. 1*, 1984, pp. xxi–xxx. **[G: Asian LDCs]**

Manne, Alan S. and Preckel, Paul V. North–South Trade, Capital Flows, and Economic Growth: An Almost Neoclassical Model. In *[Chenery, H. B.]*, 1984, pp. 409–27.

Marshall, Susan E. Politics and Female Status in North Africa: A Reconsideration of Development Theory. *Econ. Develop. Cult. Change*, April 1984, *32*(3), pp. 499–524. **[G: Tunisia; Egypt; Morocco; Libya; Algeria]**

Martin, Ricardo and Selowsky, Marcelo. Energy Prices, Substitution, and Optimal Borrowing in the Short Run: An Analysis of Adjustment in Oil Importing Developing Countries. *J. Devel. Econ.*, April 1984, *14*(3), pp. 331–50. **[G: LDCs]**

Mason, Edward S. The Chenery Analysis and Some Other Considerations. In *[Chenery, H. B.]*, 1984, pp. 3–21. **[G: Egypt; S. Korea]**

Massad, Carlos and Zahler, Roberto. The Adjustment Process in the 1980s: The Need for a Global Approach. *Cepal Rev.*, 1984, (23), pp. 83–105. **[G: Latin America]**

Mathur, Gautam. Employment and Manpower Generation. In *Amin, S., ed.*, 1984, pp. 67–93.

McCullagh, Ciaran. Entrepreneurship and Development: An Alternative Perspective. *Econ. Soc. Rev.*, January 1984, *15*(2), pp. 109–24. **[G: Selected Countries]**

McIntosh, James. An Oligopsonistic Model of Wage Determination in Agrarian Societies. *Econ. J.*, September 1984, *94*(375), pp. 569–79. **[G: LDCs]**

McNicoll, Geoffrey. Consequences of Rapid Population Growth: An Overview and Assessment. *Population Devel. Rev.*, June 1984, *10*(2), pp. 177–240. **[G: Global]**

Mellor, John W. Agricultural Development and the Intersectoral Transfer of Resources. In *Eicher, C. K. and Staatz, J. M., eds.*, 1984, *1973*, pp. 136–46. **[G: Taiwan]**

Mellor, John W. and Johnston, Bruce F. The World Food Equation: Interrelations among Development, Employment, and Food Consumption. *J. Econ. Lit.*, June 1984, *22*(2), pp. 53–74. **[G: Global]**

Milenkovitch, Deborah Duff. The Incentive to Innovate under Alternative Property Rights: A Comment. *Cato J.*, Fall 1984, *4*(2), pp. 447–55. **[G: Japan; U.S.S.R.; U.S.]**

Mochizuki, Kazuhiko. A New Dichotomy in Development Economics—Formal–Informal Sector Analysis. (In Japanese. With English summary.) *Osaka Econ. Pap.*, December 1984, *34*(2–3), pp. 261–74. **[G: LDCs]**

Mohan, Rakesh. The Effect of Population Growth, the Pattern of Demand and of Technology on the Process of Urbanization. *J. Urban Econ.*, March 1984, *15*(2), pp. 125–56. **[G: India]**

Mokyr, Joel. Disparities, Gaps, and Abysses: Review Article. *Econ. Develop. Cult. Change*, October 1984, *33*(1), pp. 173–77. **[G: Global]**

Moore, Mick. Political Economy and the Rural–Urban Divide, 1767–1981. In *Harriss, J. and Moore, M., eds.*, 1984, pp. 5–27.

Moore, Mick. Political Economy and the Rural–Urban Divide, 1767–1981. *J. Devel. Stud.*, April 1984, *20*(3), pp. 5–27. **[G: LDCs]**

Morris, Cynthia Taft. The Measurement of Economic Development: Quo Vadis? In *[Reynolds, L. G.]*, 1984, pp. 145–81. **[G: LDCs]**

Myint, Hla. Inward and Outward-Looking Countries Revisited: The Case of Indonesia. *Bull. Indonesian Econ. Stud.*, August 1984, *20*(2), pp. 39–52. **[G: Indonesia]**

Naqvi, Syed Nawab Haider. Development Economists in "Emperor's Clothes"? *Pakistan Devel. Rev.*, Summer-Autumn 1984, *23*(2&3), pp. 121–44.

Narayana, D. L. Population Growth and Economic Growth. *Indian Econ. J.*, Oct.–Dec. 1984, *32*(2), pp. 1–40.

Neffa, Julio César. Enfoques alternativos para el análisis del empleo en los países en vías de desarrollo. (Alternative Focusing for the Analysis of Employment in Developing Countries. With English summary.) *Económica*, January-April 1984, *30*(1), pp. 3–33. **[G: Latin America]**

Nelson, Joan M. The Political Economy of Stabilization: Commitment, Capacity, and Public Response. *World Devel.*, October 1984, *12*(10), pp. 983–1006. **[G: Ghana; Zambia; Kenya; Sri Lanka; Jamaica]**

Nishimizu, Mieko and Robinson, Sherman. Trade Policies and Productivity Change in Semi-industrialized Countries. *J. Devel. Econ.*, September–October 1984, *16*(1–2), pp. 177–206. **[G: S. Korea; Turkey; Yugoslavia; Japan]**

Nixson, Frederick. Economic Development: Utopian Ideal or Historical Process? *METU*, 1984, *11*(1–2), pp. 81–92.

Nolan, Peter and White, Gordon. Urban Bias, Rural Bias or State Bias? Urban–Rural Relations in Post-Revolutionary China. *J. Devel. Stud.*, April 1984, *20*(3), pp. 52–81. **[G: China]**

Norgaard, Richard B. Coevolutionary Agricultural Development. *Econ. Develop. Cult. Change*, April 1984, *32*(3), pp. 525–46.

Norgaard, Richard B. Coevolutionary Development Potential. *Land Econ.*, May 1984, *60*(2), pp. 160–73.

Nunez del Prado, Arturo. The Transnational Corporations in a New Planning Process. In *Ghosh, P. K., ed., no. 11*, 1984, *1981*, pp. 273–93. **[G: Latin America]**

O.E.C.D. Development's Place on the Policy Agenda. In *Ghosh, P. K., ed., no. 8*, 1984, *1979*, pp. 253–65.

Ohlin, Goran. A New Case for Personal Savings in Development Policy? In *Kessler, D. and Ullmo, P.-A., eds.*, 1984, pp. 79–83.

Öniş, Ziya. Inflation and Economic Growth: A Critical Assessment of the Forced Saving Thesis. *METU*, 1984, *11*(3–4), pp. 285–93.

Oshima, Harry T. Towards a Model of Monsoon Asian Economic Growth. *Singapore Econ. Rev.*, October 1984, *29*(2), pp. 93–110. **[G: Asia]**

Pajestka, Józef. Some Basic Premises for Development: The Eastern European Experience. In *Ngo, M., ed., vol. 2*, 1984, pp. 830–44. **[G: E. Europe]**

Patel, Surendra J. L'èra del Terzo Mondo. (The Third World Age. With English summary.) *Mondo Aperto*, June–August 1984, *38*(3–4), pp. 149–61. **[G: LDCs]**

Patterson, Orlando. The Realities of Intervention in Alienated Cultures: A Jamaican Case Study. In *Brooks, H.; Liebman, L. and Schelling, C. S., eds.*, 1984, pp. 131–52. **[G: Jamaica]**

Pejovich, Steve. The Incentive to Innovate under Alternative Property Rights. *Cato J.*, Fall 1984, *4*(2), pp. 427–46. **[G: Yugoslavia]**

Perkins, John A. Fiscal Policy and Economic Development in XIXth Century Germany. *J. Europ. Econ. Hist.*, Fall 1984, *13*(2), pp. 311–44. **[G: Germany]**

Platteau, Jean-Philippe. Malthus et le sous-développement ou le problème de la cohérence d'une théorie. (Malthus and the Problem of Underdevelopment: One or Two Theories? With English summary.) *Revue Écon.*, July 1984, *35*(4), pp. 635–66.

Portes, Alejandro and Benton, Lauren. Industrial Development and Labor Absorption: A Reinterpretation. *Population Devel. Rev.*, December 1984, *10*(4), pp. 589–611. **[G: Latin America]**

Prasad, Kamta. Planning in India: Some Basic Issues Relating to Operational and Strategic Aspects. *Indian Econ. J.*, April–June 1984, *31*(4), pp. 1–24. **[G: India]**

Putník, Jiří. The Position of Developing Countries in Present-Day International Economic Relations. *Czech. Econ. Digest.*, June 1984, (4), pp. 48–67. **[G: LDCs]**

Qadir, Asghar. Educated Unemployed, Educational Subsidies, and Growth: Comment. *Pakistan Devel. Rev.*, Summer-Autumn 1984, *23*(2&3), pp. 411–12.

Quibria, M. G. Domestic Policies and Foreign Resource Requirements: A Reply. *Quart. J. Econ.*, February 1984, *99*(1), pp. 207–09.

Raj, K. N. Linkages in Industrialization and Development Strategy: Some Basic Issues. In *Ghosh, P. K., ed., no. 1*, 1984, *1975*, pp. 65–84. **[G: India; Brazil; China]**

Ranis, Gustav. Typology in Development Theory: Retrospective and Prospects. In *[Chenery, H. B.]*, 1984, pp. 23–44. **[G: Kenya; Mexico; Taiwan]**

Ranney, Susan I. Terms of Trade and Domestic Distribution: A Comment. *J. Devel. Econ.*, May–June–August 1984, *15*(1,2,3), pp. 89–96.

Ravallion, Martin. How Much Is a Transfer Payment Worth to a Rural Worker? *Oxford Econ. Pap.*, November 1984, *36*(3), pp. 478–89. **[G: LDCs]**

Redclift, M. R. 'Urban Bias' and Rural Poverty:

A Latin American Perspective. *J. Devel. Stud.*, April 1984, *20*(3), pp. 123–38. [G: Mexico; Brazil]

Renard, Robrecht. Rural-to-Urban Migration and the Shadow Wage in LDCs. *Europ. Econ. Rev.*, April 1984, *24*(3), pp. 401–07. [G: LDCs]

Reutlinger, Shlomo. Project Food Aid and Equitable Growth: Income–Transfer Efficiency First! *World Devel.*, September 1984, *12*(9), pp. 901–11. [G: Egypt; India; Pakistan]

Riedel, James. Trade as the Engine of Growth in Developing Countries, Revisited. *Econ. J.*, March 1984, *94*(373), pp. 56–73.

Rist, Gilbert. Relations Interculturelles et Pratiques du *Développement*. (With English summary.) *Can. J. Devel. Stud.*, 1984, *5*(2), pp. 233–42.

Robinson, Warren and Schutjer, Wayne A. Agricultural Development and Demographic Change: A Generalization of the Boserup Model. *Econ. Develop. Cult. Change*, January 1984, *32*(2), pp. 355–66. [G: LDCs]

Rosen, George. Development Economics: Some Thoughts on Its Past and Its Future. *METU*, 1984, *11*(1–2), pp. 21–28.

Rothgeb, John M., Jr. Investment Penetration in Manufacturing and Extraction and External Public Debt in Third World States. *World Devel.*, November–December 1984, *12*(11–12), pp. 1063–75. [G: LDCs]

Rubinson, Richard. The World-Economy and the Distribution of Income Within States: A Cross-National Study. In *Seligson, M. A., ed.*, 1984, *1976*, pp. 156–86. [G: Selected Countries]

Rush, H. J. Sources of Technology in Development. In *Ghosh, P. K., ed., no. 3*, 1984, *1981*, pp. 35–49.

Rushton, Gerard. Use of Location-Allocation Models for Improving the Geographical Accessibility of Rural Services in Developing Countries. *Int. Reg. Sci. Rev.*, December 1984, *9*(3), pp. 217–40. [G: LDCs]

Ruttan, Vernon W. Integrated Rural Development Programmes: A Historical Perspective. *World Devel.*, April 1984, *12*(4), pp. 393–401. [G: LDCs]

Ruttan, Vernon W. Models of Agricultural Development. In *Eicher, C. K. and Staatz, J. M., eds.*, 1984, *1980*, pp. 38–45.

Ruttan, Vernon W. and Hayami, Yujiro. Induced Innovation Model of Agricultural Development. In *Eicher, C. K. and Staatz, J. M., eds.*, 1984, *1972*, pp. 59–74.

Ruttan, Vernon W. and Hayami, Yujiro. Toward a Theory of Induced Institutional Innovation. *J. Devel. Stud.*, July 1984, *20*(4), pp. 203–23. [G: Philippines]

Saavedra-Rivano, Neantro. Terms of Trade and Domestic Distribution: A Comment. *J. Devel. Econ.*, May–June–August 1984, *15*(1,2,3), pp. 105–10.

Sabato, Jorge A. Technological Development in Latin America and the Caribbean. In *Ghosh, P. K., ed., no. 3*, 1984, *1980*, pp. 352–70. [G: Latin America; Caribbean]

Sachs, Ignacy and Laski, Kazimierz. Industrial Development Strategy. In *Ghosh, P. K., ed., no. 1*, 1984, *1970*, pp. 184–203.

Sah, Raaj Kumar and Stiglitz, Joseph E. The Economics of Price Scissors. *Amer. Econ. Rev.*, March 1984, *74*(1), pp. 125–38.

Santiago, Carlos E. and Thorbecke, Erik. Regional and Technological Dualism: A Dual–Dual Development Framework Applied to Puerto Rico. *J. Devel. Stud.*, July 1984, *20*(4), pp. 271–89. [G: Puerto Rico]

Savane, Landing. Problems of Scientific and Technological Development in Black Africa. In *Ghosh, P. K., ed., no. 3*, 1984, *1973*, pp. 371–79. [G: Africa]

Schmitz, Hubert. Industrialisation Strategies in Less Developed Countries: Some Lessons of Historical Experience. *J. Devel. Stud.*, October 1984, *21*(1), pp. 1–21. [G: LDCs]

Schmitz, Hubert. Industrialisation Strategies in Less Developed Countries: Some Lessons of Historical Experience. In *Kaplinsky, R., ed.*, 1984, pp. 1–21.

Schwefel, Detlef. Basic Needs, Planning and Policies. In *Ghosh, P. K., ed., no. 13*, 1984, *1979*, pp. 205–15.

Scitovsky, Tibor. Beyond Export-Led Growth: Comment. *World Devel.*, September 1984, *12*(9), pp. 953–54.

Seers, Dudley. The Meaning of Development. In *Ghosh, P. K., ed., no. 8*, 1984, *1977*, pp. 7–16.

Seers, Dudley. The Meaning of Development. In *Ghosh, P. K., ed., no. 7*, 1984, *1977*, pp. 7–16.

Seligson, Mitchell A. Inequality in a Global Perspective: Directions for Further Research. In *Seligson, M. A., ed.*, 1984, pp. 397–408. [G: Global]

Sen, Amartya. Development: Which Way Now? In *Sen, A.*, 1984, *1983*, pp. 485–508. [G: LDCs]

Sen, Amartya. Employment, Institutions and Technology: Some Policy Issues. In *Sen, A.*, 1984, *1975*, pp. 242–73. [G: LDCs]

Sen, Amartya. Goods and People. In *Sen, A.*, 1984, *1983*, pp. 509–32.

Sen, Amartya. Peasants and Dualism with or without Surplus Labour. In *Sen, A.*, 1984, *1966*, pp. 37–72.

Sen, Amartya. Resources, Values and Development: Introduction. In *Sen, A.*, 1984, pp. 1–34.

Şenses, Fikret. Development Economics at a Crossroad. *METU*, 1984, *11*(1–2), pp. 109–50.

Siggel, Eckhard. On the Nature of Technology Shelves Facing Less Developed Countries: Some Hypotheses and Case Studies. *J. Devel. Areas*, January 1984, *18*(2), pp. 227–45. [G: Zaire; U.K.; Canada]

Simmons, Ozzie G. Population Policy Analysis and Development Planning. *J. Devel. Areas*, July 1984, *18*(4), pp. 433–48. [G: LDCs]

Singer, Hans W. Appropriate Technology for a Basic Human Needs Strategy. In *Ghosh, P. K., ed., no. 13*, 1984, *1977*, pp. 226–31.

Singer, Hans W. Industrialisation: Where Do We Stand? Where Are We Going? *METU*, 1984, *11*(1–2), pp. 163–75. **[G: LDCs]**

Smith, M. G. Some Future Directions for Social Research in the Commonwealth Caribbean. *Soc. Econ. Stud.*, June 1984, *33*(2), pp. 123–55. **[G: Caribbean]**

Soza, Hector. The Industrialization Debate in Latin America. In *Ghosh, P. K., ed., no. 1*, 1984, *1981*, pp. 309–29. **[G: Latin America]**

Spinanger, Dean. Objectives and Impact of Economic Activity Zones—Some Evidence from Asia. *Weltwirtsch. Arch.*, 1984, *120*(1), pp. 64–89. **[G: Asia]**

Srinivasan, T. N. Development, Poverty, and Basic Human Needs: Some Issues. In *Ghosh, P. K., ed., no. 13*, 1984, *1977*, pp. 7–28. **[G: LDCs]**

Srinivasan, T. N. and Bhagwati, Jagdish N. A Rejoinder [Terms of Trade and Domestic Distribution: Export-led Growth with Abundant Labour]. *J. Devel. Econ.*, May–June–August 1984, *15*(1,2,3), pp. 173–75.

Srinivasan, T. N. and Bhagwati, Jagdish N. On Transfer Paradoxes and Immiserizing Growth: Part II [Terms of Trade and Domestic Distribution: Export-led Growth with Abundant Labour]. *J. Devel. Econ.*, May–June–August 1984, *15*(1,2,3), pp. 111–15.

Staatz, John M. and Eicher, Carl K. Agricultural Development Ideas in Historical Perspective. In *Eicher, C. K. and Staatz, J. M., eds.*, 1984, pp. 3–30.

Streeten, Paul. Basic Needs: Some Unsettled Questions. *World Devel.*, September 1984, *12*(9), pp. 973–78.

Streeten, Paul. Development Economics in Retrospect and Prospect. *METU*, 1984, *11*(1–2), pp. 29–39.

Streeten, Paul. The Distinctive Features of a Basic Needs Approach to Development. In *Ghosh, P. K., ed., no. 13*, 1984, *1977*, pp. 29–40.

Sunkel, Osvaldo. Past, Present and Future of the International Economic Crisis. *Cepal Rev.*, April 1984, (22), pp. 81–105. **[G: Latin America; OECD]**

Sutcliffe, Robert B. Industry and Underdevelopment Re-examined. *J. Devel. Stud.*, October 1984, *21*(1), pp. 121–33.

Sutcliffe, Robert B. Comments by R. B. Sutcliffe on the Reader on Underdevelopment. In *Frank, A. G.*, 1984, pp. 323–25.

Sutcliffe, Robert B. Industry and Underdevelopment Re-examined. In *Kaplinsky, R., ed.*, 1984, pp. 121–33.

Svejnar, Jan and Smith, Stephen C. The Economics of Joint Ventures in Less Developed Countries. *Quart. J. Econ.*, February 1984, *99*(1), pp. 149–67.

Szentes, Tamas. The Structural Defects of Periphery Economies. In *Amin, S., ed.*, 1984, pp. 33–51.

Teitel, Simón. Technology Creation in Semi-industrial Economies. *J. Devel. Econ.*, September–October 1984, *16*(1–2), pp. 39–61. **[G: Latin America]**

Teitel, Simón and Westphal, Larry E. Symposium on Technological Change and Industrial Development: Editors' Introduction. *J. Devel. Econ.*, September–October 1984, *16*(1–2), pp. 1–11.

Thirlwall, A. P. In Praise of Development Economics. *METU*, 1984, *11*(1–2), pp. 93–107.

Tinbergen, Jan. Development Modelling: The State of the Art. In *Cohen, S. I., et al., eds.*, 1984, *1980*, pp. 3–12.

Tinbergen, Jan. Lessons and Prospects. *METU*, 1984, *11*(1–2), pp. 11–19.

Tisdell, Clem A. and Fairbairn, T'eo Ian. Labor Supply Constraints on Industrialization, and Production Deficiencies in Traditional Sharing Societies. *J. Econ. Devel.*, December 1984, *9*(2), pp. 7–23. **[G: LDCs]**

Tisdell, Clem A. and Fairbairn, T'eo Ian. Subsistence Economies and Unsustainable Development and Trade: Some Simple Theory. *J. Devel. Stud.*, January 1984, *20*(2), pp. 227–41. **[G: S. Pacific]**

Todaro, Michael P. Intergenerational Income-Fertility Linkages in Developing Countries: A Conceptual Framework. In *[Reynolds, L. G.]*, 1984, pp. 42–62. **[G: LDCs]**

Trak, Ayse Bugra. A Decade of Dependency and Two Controversial Books. *Rev. Radical Polit. Econ.*, Summer & Fall 1984, *16*(2&3), pp. 241–47.

Velez, Jorge Child. Unjust International Economic Relations. *Can. J. Devel. Stud.*, 1984, *5*(2), pp. 303–08.

Volkov, Mai. Third World Countries: Problems of Economic Development and Ways of Solving Them. In *Ghosh, P. K., ed., no. 7*, 1984, *1977*, pp. 408–12.

Von Witzke, Harald. Poverty, Agriculture, and Economic Development: A Survey. *Europ. Rev. Agr. Econ.*, 1984, *11*(4), pp. 439–53.

Wachtel, Paul. Observations on Saving by Individuals in Developing Countries. In *Kessler, D. and Ullmo, P.-A., eds.*, 1984, pp. 17–26.

Waelbroeck, Jean Capital, Foreign Exchange, and Growth: The Two-Gap and Labor-Income-Floor Views. In *[Chenery, H. B.]*, 1984, pp. 281–94.

Watanabe, Susumu. Institutional Factors, Government Policies and Appropriate Technologies. In *Ghosh, P. K., ed., no. 14*, 1984, *1980*, pp. 142–62.

Weaver, James H.; Jameson, Kenneth P. and Blue, Richard N. Growth and Equity: Can They Be Happy Together? An Analysis of Seven Models and Their Critics. In *Ghosh, P. K., ed., no. 13*, 1984, *1978*, pp. 146–57.

Weede, Erich and Tiefenbach, Horst. Some Recent Explanations of Income Inequality. In *Seligson, M. A., ed.*, 1984, *1981*, pp. 232–55. **[G: Selected Countries]**

Weisskopf, Thomas E. Self-Reliance and Development Strategy. In *Ngo, M., ed., vol. 2*, 1984, pp. 845–61. **[G: LDCs]**

Wells, Miriam J. and Climo, Jacob. Parallel Process in the World System: Intermediate Agencies and Local Factionalism in the United States and Mexico. *J. Devel. Stud.*, January 1984, *20*(2), pp. 151–70. [G: Mexico; U.S.]

Wesson, Robert. Politics, Policies, & Economic Development in Latin America: Introduction. In *Wesson, R., ed.*, 1984, pp. xi–xvii.

White, Gordon. Developmental States and Socialist Industrialisation in the Third World. *J. Devel. Stud.*, October 1984, *21*(1), pp. 97–120. [G: Selected Global]

van Wijnbergen, Sweder. Oil Price Shocks and the Current Account: An Analysis of Short Run Adjustment Measures. *Weltwirtsch. Arch.*, 1984, *120*(3), pp. 460–80. [G: OPEC; LDCs]

Winegarden, Calman R. Income Redistribution versus Accelerated Economic Growth: A Comparison of Demographic Effects. *Oxford Bull. Econ. Statist.*, August 1984, *46*(3), pp. 255–71. [G: LDCs]

Wolfe, Marshall. Participation: The View from Above. *Cepal Rev.*, 1984, (23), pp. 155–79.

Yeats, Alexander J. On the Analysis of Tariff Escalation: Is There a Methodological Bias against the Interest of Developing Countries? *J. Devel. Econ.*, May–June–August 1984, *15*(1,2,3), pp. 77–88. [G: LDCs]

Yu, Guangyuan. A Scientific Study of China's Strategy of Economic and Social Development. *Chinese Econ. Stud.*, Winter 1983–84, *17*(2), pp. 78–87. [G: China]

Zalacain, Fernando. Puerto Rico: An Experiment in Growth with a Maximum Degree of Openness. *Atlantic Econ. J.*, September 1984, *12*(3), pp. 11–16. [G: Puerto Rico]

113 Economic Planning Theory and Policy

1130 Economic Planning Theory and Policy

Ancot, Jean Pierre and Hughes Hallett, Andrew J. Establishing Public Preferences for Coalition Government: An Empirical Study in Economic Planning Behaviour. *De Economist*, 1984, *132*(2), pp. 153–70. [G: Netherlands]

Arrow, Kenneth J. Statistical Requirements for Greek Economic Planning. In *Arrow, K. J., vol. 4*, 1984, *1965*, pp. 87–102.

Balázsy, Sándor. Reform and Property: Reflections on Tamás Bauer's Article. *Eastern Europ. Econ.*, Spring–Summer 1984, *22*(3–4), pp. 88–101. [G: Hungary; CMEA]

Batey, Peter W. J. Information for Long-Term Planning of Regional Development. In *Nijkamp, P. and Rietveld, P., eds.*, 1984, pp. 63–79. [G: W. Germany]

Bauer, P. T. Market Order and State Planning in Economic Development. In *Bauer, P. T.*, 1984, pp. 19–37.

Bauer, Tamás. The Second Economic Reform and Ownership Relations: Some Considerations for the Further Development of the New Economic Mechanism. *Eastern Europ. Econ.*, Spring–Summer 1984, *22*(3–4), pp. 33–87. [G: CMEA; Hungary]

Belousov, R. A. Democratic Centralism and Economic Independence. *Prob. Econ.*, November 1984, *27*(7), pp. 26–43. [G: U.S.S.R.]

Brown, Peter J. B. Monitoring and Regional Information Systems under Uncertainty. In *Nijkamp, P. and Rietveld, P., eds.*, 1984, pp. 81–100.

Bunich, P. G. Economic Stimulation of High Final Results. *Prob. Econ.*, November 1984, *27*(7), pp. 3–25. [G: U.S.S.R.]

Bunich, P. G. Only Efficiency Will Triumph over Scarcity. *Prob. Econ.*, January 1984, *26*(9), pp. 26–43. [G: U.S.S.R.]

Carter, Charles [Sir]. Proposals for Plan: An Outside View. *Irish Banking Rev.*, September 1984, pp. 3–12. [G: Ireland]

Cassetti, Mario. La coordinazione delle decisioni di investimento in un modello di programmazione a due livelli. (The Coordination of the Investment Decision in a Two-Level Programming Model. With English summary.) *Giorn. Econ.*, March–April 1984, *43*(3–4), pp. 237–60.

Catinat, Michel and Maurice, Joël. Analyse quantitative de la stratégie macro-économique du IXᵉ Plan. (A Quantitative Analysis of the IXth Plan: Macroeconomic Strategy. With English summary.) *Revue Écon.*, November 1984, *35*(6), pp. 1007–90. [G: France]

Celasun, Merih. Piyasa ekonomilerinde plânlama: 1970'lerin Dış şoklarinin Etkisinde Yeni Sorunlar ve Eğilimler. (Planning in Market Economies. With English summary.) *METU*, 1984, *11*(3–4), pp. 325–45. [G: LDCs]

Chenery, Hollis B. The Evolution of Development Planning. *J. Policy Modeling*, May 1984, *6*(2), pp. 159–74.

Csikós-Nagy, Béla. The Role of the Law of Values in Socialist Economy. *Eastern Europ. Econ.*, Spring–Summer 1984, *22*(3–4), pp. 102–21. [G: Hungary; CMEA]

Deng, Huansong. On the Duality of Price Subsidy and the Path to Its Reform. *Chinese Econ. Stud.*, Fall 1984, *18*(1), pp. 3–13. [G: China]

Dhesi, Autar S. and Ghuman, B. S. Aspects of Financing State Plans (With Special Reference to Punjab). *Margin*, April 1984, *16*(3), pp. 31–43. [G: India]

Drozd, Antonin. Information Systems for Integrated Regional Planning and Policy Making in Czechoslovakia. In *Nijkamp, P. and Rietveld, P., eds.*, 1984, pp. 375–87.

Dujnic, P.; Issaev, B. and Slimak, D. Regional Information Systems in Centrally Planned Economies. In *Nijkamp, P. and Rietveld, P., eds.*, 1984, pp. 121–38.

Ellman, Michael. Economic Reform in Chinese Industry. In *Ellman, M.*, 1984, *1981*, pp. 215–41. [G: China]

van Est, Jan; Scheurwater, Jan and Voogd, Henk. Information Systems for Integrated Regional Planning and Policy Making in the Netherlands. In *Nijkamp, P. and Rietveld, P., eds.*, 1984, pp. 353–73.

van Est, Jan and de Vroege, Frans. Disaggregate Spatial Information Systems: The Use of Geocoding in Regional Planning. In *Nijkamp, P. and Rietveld, P., eds.*, 1984, pp. 251–61.

Farooq, Ghazi M. Population, Human Resources and Development Planning: Towards an Integrated Approach. In *Ghosh, P. K., ed., no. 5*, 1984, *1981*, pp. 161–76.

Fedorenko, N., et al. The Theory and Practice of Assessing the Effectiveness of Economic Measures. *Prob. Econ.*, September 1984, 27(5), pp. 3–22.   [G: U.S.S.R.]

Garnick, Daniel H. Information Systems for Integrated Regional Planning and Policy Making in the United States. In *Nijkamp, P. and Rietveld, P., eds.*, 1984, pp. 335–51.

Gilbert, Gary G. Investment Planning for Latin American Economic Integration. In *Ghosh, P. K., ed., no. 12*, 1984, *1973*, pp. 177–89.
                                [G: Latin America]

Glushkov, N. Planned Price Formation (Theoretical and Practical Questions). *Prob. Econ.*, October 1984, 27(6), pp. 3–23.   [G: U.S.S.R.]

Gruchy, Allan G. Uncertainty, Indicative Planning, and Industrial Policy. *J. Econ. Issues*, March 1984, 18(1), pp. 159–80.   [G: U.S.]

Guteland, G. and Nygren, O. Information Systems for Integrated Regional Planning and Policy Making in Sweden. In *Nijkamp, P. and Rietveld, P., eds.*, 1984, pp. 297–317.

Hinloopen, Edwin and Nijkamp, Peter. Information Systems and Uncertainty in Planning. In *Nijkamp, P. and Rietveld, P., eds.*, 1984, pp. 101–19.

Hinloopen, Edwin; Nijkamp, Peter and Rietveld, Piet. International Comparison of Regional Planning and Information Systems. In *Nijkamp, P. and Rietveld, P., eds.*, 1984, pp. 411–26.   [G: Europe; U.S.]

Janhunen, Olli. Information Systems for Integrated Regional Planning and Policy Making in Finland. In *Nijkamp, P. and Rietveld, P., eds.*, 1984, pp. 389–409.

Janza, Vladimír. The Role of the Plan in the System of Plan-based Management. *Czech. Econ. Digest.*, November 1984, (7), pp. 56–83.
                                [G: Czechoslovakia]

Ji, Chongwei. China's Utilization of Foreign Funds and Relevant Policies. *Chinese Econ. Stud.*, Winter 1983–84, 17(2), pp. 37–49.
                                [G: China]

Ji, Zhenghzhi. The Profit in Planned Prices Should Be Formulated in Accordance with a Composite Profit Index. *Chinese Econ. Stud.*, Fall 1984, 18(1), pp. 14–33.   [G: China]

Join-Lambert, Marie-Thérèse. La planification sociale dans le IXe Plan. (Social Planning in the IXth Plan. With English summary.) *Revue Écon.*, November 1984, 35(6), pp. 1147–72.
                                [G: France]

Jovanovic, Aleksandar. Struktura sistema društvene proizvodnje i organizacija planiranja. (Structure of Social Production System and the Organization of Planning. With English summary.) *Econ. Anal. Worker's Manage.*, 1984, 18(3), pp. 217–39.

Kaltakhchian, N. M. Interpretations of Planned and Balanced Development of the Socialist

Economy. In *Smirnov, A. D.; Golosov, V. V. and Maximova, V. F., eds.*, 1984, pp. 243–52.

von Känel, Siegfried. On the Problem of the Controllability of Economic Systems. *Econ. Computat. Cybern. Stud. Res.*, 1984, 19(1), pp. 75–82.

Karadimova, Raina and Petrov, Ilia. Data Base Design for Working out the Plan for Capital Investments in the State Planning Committee of the People's Republic of Bulgaria. *Econ. Computat. Cybern. Stud. Res.*, 1984, 19(3), pp. 83–89.   [G: Bulgaria]

Karlsson, Lars-Erik. Planning for Self-Management: A Swedish View. *Econ. Anal. Worker's Manage.*, 1984, 18(1), pp. 15–34.

Katsenelinboigen, Aron J. Some Notes on Vertical and Horizontal Economic Mechanisms. In *Andersson, Å. E.; Isard, W. and Puu, T., eds.*, 1984, pp. 383–405.

Kuboniwa, Masaaki. Stepwise Aggregation for Material Balances. *J. Compar. Econ.*, March 1984, 8(1), pp. 41–53.   [G: U.S.S.R.]

Malmygin, I. The Balance of Workplaces and Manpower. *Prob. Econ.*, July 1984, 27(3), pp. 80–93.   [G: U.S.S.R.]

Matějka, Ladislav. Importance of the Complex of Measures for Intensification of the Czechoslovak National Economy. *Czech. Econ. Digest.*, February 1984, (1), pp. 26–50.
                                [G: Czechoslovakia]

McFarlane, Bruce. Economic Planning and Adolph Lowe's Economic Perspective. *Eastern Econ. J.*, April-June 1984, 10(2), pp. 187–202.
                                [G: China]

Muguet, Jean. Information Systems for Integrated Regional Planning and Policy Making in France. In *Nijkamp, P. and Rietveld, P., eds.*, 1984, pp. 319–33.

Nasilowski, Mieczyslaw. Planning: Bureaucratic or Socialized? *Kansant. Aikak.*, 1984, 80(3), pp. 316–20.

Poliak, A. The Assessment of Material Resources. *Prob. Econ.*, December 1984, 27(8), pp. 71–88.   [G: U.S.S.R.]

Prasad, Kamta. Planning in India: Some Basic Issues Relating to Operational and Strategic Aspects. *Indian Econ. J.*, April–June 1984, 31(4), pp. 1–24.   [G: India]

Rao, V. K. R. V. Some Reminiscences and Suggestions on Planning. In *Singh, A. K.; Papola, T. S. and Mathur, R. S., eds.*, 1984, pp. 141–47.   [G: India]

Schwefel, Detlef. Basic Needs, Planning and Policies. In *Ghosh, P. K., ed., no. 13*, 1984, *1979*, pp. 205–15.

Shaffer, Harry G. Soviet Economic Performance Under the Plan. In *Shaffer, H. G., ed.*, 1984, pp. 328–44.   [G: U.S.S.R.]

Sun, Yefang. To Raise Production Four-Fold in Two Decades Is Not Only Politically Probable but Technologically Feasible. *Chinese Econ. Stud.*, Winter 1983–84, 17(2), pp. 50–67.
                                [G: China]

Szamuely, László. The Second Wave of the Economic Mechanism Debate and the 1968 Reform in Hungary. *Acta Oecon.*, 1984, *33*(1–2), pp. 43–67. **[G: Hungary]**

Taddei, Dominique. Le IXe Plan: de la rigueur a une politique de l'offre. (The French IXth Plan: From Rigor to a Supply Policy. With English summary.) *Revue Écon.*, November 1984, *35*(6), pp. 1239–60. **[G: France]**

Tardos, Márton. A Development Program for Economic Control and Organization in Hungary. *Eastern Europ. Econ.*, Spring–Summer 1984, *22*(3–4), pp. 3–32. **[G: Hungary]**

Wang, Bingquian. On Several Problems Involving Financial Work. *Chinese Econ. Stud.*, Summer 1984, *17*(4), pp. 81–98. **[G: China]**

Xu, Dixin, et al. China's Search for Economic Growth. *Australian Bull. Lab.*, September 1984, *10*(4), pp. 196–210. **[G: China]**

Xue, Muqiao. An Inquiry into the Problems Concerning the Reform of the Economic System. *Chinese Econ. Stud.*, Winter 1983–84, *17*(2), pp. 3–30. **[G: China]**

Yu, Guangyuan. A Scientific Study of China's Strategy of Economic and Social Development. *Chinese Econ. Stud.*, Winter 1983–84, *17*(2), pp. 78–87. **[G: China]**

Zala, Julia. Hungary: How to Live with Slow-Growth Conditions: Adaptations of Economic Conditions and Management. *Eastern Europ. Econ.*, Spring–Summer 1984, *22*(3–4), pp. 122–53. **[G: Hungary]**

1132 Economic Planning Theory

Ács, Magda. Long-term Models at Work: Comparison with the Past. In *Augusztinovics, M., ed.*, 1984, pp. 284–318. **[G: Hungary]**

Augusztinovics, Mária. On Long-term Planning. In *Augusztinovics, M., ed.*, 1984, pp. 13–27. **[G: Hungary]**

Augusztinovics, Mária. Quantitative Synthesis in Long-term Planning. In *Augusztinovics, M., ed.*, 1984, pp. 43–85.

Augusztinovics, Mária. The Planning Process. In *Augusztinovics, M., ed.*, 1984, pp. 28–42. **[G: Hungary]**

Bánhidi, Ferenc. Price Model—Price Computations. In *Augusztinovics, M., ed.*, 1984, pp. 246–83. **[G: Hungary]**

Bennett, John. Alternative Price and Quantity Controls for Regulation under Uncertainty. *Z. Nationalökon.*, 1984, *44*(2), pp. 103–15.

Berliner, Joseph S. Managing the Soviet Economy: Alternative Models. In *Hoffmann, E. P., ed.*, 1984, pp. 49–56. **[G: U.S.S.R.]**

Bod, Péter. The DYNAMIC Model and Its Functioning. In *Augusztinovics, M., ed.*, 1984, pp. 153–89. **[G: Hungary]**

Boda, György. Input–Output Analysis. In *Augusztinovics, M., ed.*, 1984, pp. 215–45. **[G: Hungary]**

Cella, Guido. The Input–Output Measurement of Interindustry Linkages. *Oxford Bull. Econ. Statist.*, February 1984, *46*(1), pp. 73–84.

Chander, Parkash. On Material Balances When There Are Capacity Limitations. *J. Compar. Econ.*, June 1984, *8*(2), pp. 159–67.

Clark, Simon. Informational and Performance Properties of a Class of Iterative Planning Procedures. *Rev. Econ. Stud.*, October 1984, *51*(4), pp. 615–31.

Csikós-Nagy, Béla. Die Rolle der Preise in den verschiedenen Modellvarianten der sozialistischen Planwirtschaft. (With English summary.) In *Bohnet, A., ed.*, 1984, pp. 19–40.

Dore, M. H. I. and Kaser, Michael C. The Millions of Equations Debate: Seventy Years after Barone. *Atlantic Econ. J.*, September 1984, *12*(3), pp. 30–44.

Ellman, Michael. Investment Planning in the State Socialist Countries and its Relevance for Reindustrialisation. In *Ellman, M.*, 1984, *1980*, pp. 174–97. **[G: E. Europe]**

Fashola, M. A. A Policy Model for Nigeria Featuring Price Formation. In *Cohen, S. I., et al., eds.*, 1984, pp. 289–311. **[G: Nigeria]**

Faur, Tivadar. The LAG Model and Its Functioning. In *Augusztinovics, M., ed.*, 1984, pp. 190–214. **[G: Hungary]**

Goudard, Daniel. Nouvelles avancées dans le calcul économique public. (Improvements in Public Choice Analysis. With English summary.) *Revue Écon.*, November 1984, *35*(6), pp. 1173–1212. **[G: France]**

Granick, David. Central Physical Planning, Incentives and Job Rights. In *Zimbalist, A., ed.*, 1984, pp. 133–57. **[G: U.S.; U.S.S.R.]**

Grauer, Manfred and Zalai, Ernö. A Reference Point Approach to Nonlinear Macroeconomic Multiobjective Models. In *Despontin, M.; Nijkamp, P. and Spronk, J., eds.*, 1984, pp. 73–96.

Haraszti, Katalin. Long-term Models at Work: Comparison with Other Countries. In *Augusztinovics, M., ed.*, 1984, pp. 319–48. **[G: Hungary; U.S.; W. Europe]**

Holmström, Bengt. On the Theory of Delegation. In *Boyer, M. and Kihlstrom, R. E., eds.*, 1984, pp. 115–41.

Hurwicz, Leonid. Economic Planning and the Knowledge Problem: A Comment. *Cato J.*, Fall 1984, *4*(2), pp. 419–25.

Kantorovich, L. V. and Makarov, V. L. Prices and Production Efficiency. In *Csikós-Nagy, B.; Hague, D. and Hall, G., eds.*, 1984, pp. 3–23.

Kirzner, Israel M. Economic Planning and the Knowledge Problem. *Cato J.*, Fall 1984, *4*(2), pp. 407–18.

Knaack, Ruud. Dynamic Comparative Economics: Lessons from Socialist Planning. In *Zimbalist, A., ed.*, 1984, pp. 109–32.

Krekó, Ildikó. Operation of the WHERE Model. In *Augusztinovics, M., ed.*, 1984, pp. 117–52. **[G: Hungary]**

Krekó, Ildikó. The WHERE Model. In *Augusztinovics, M., ed.*, 1984, pp. 86–116.

Krekó, Ildikó; Bod, Péter and Faur, Tivadar. Formal Description of the Planning Models. In *Augusztinovics, M., ed.*, 1984, pp. 354–75. **[G: Hungary]**

Laski, Kazimierz. Das Inflationsproblem und Warenmängel in den sozialistischen Ländern.

(With English summary.) In *Bohnet, A., ed.*, 1984, pp. 183–202.

Medaiskis, T. I. and Raiatskas, R. L. On Overcoming the Switching Problem in Optimizing Macroeconomic Models. *Matekon,* Summer 1984, *20*(4), pp. 48–63.

Pehartz, Ferenc and Székely, Béla. The Computerized Planning System. In *Augusztinovics, M., ed.*, 1984, pp. 349–53. **[G: Hungary]**

Perminov, S. B. Evaluating the Quality of a Plan Using Computer Simulations of the Implementation Process. *Matekon,* Summer 1984, *20*(4), pp. 97–115.

Sen, Amartya. Control Areas and Accounting Prices: An Approach to Economic Evaluation. In *Sen, A.*, 1984, *1972*, pp. 224–41.

Sitarian, Stepan. Economic Norms and Limits. *Prob. Econ.,* January 1984, *26*(9), pp. 44–63. **[G: U.S.S.R.]**

Tondini, Giovanni. Further Discussion on Controllability and the Theory of Economic Policy [On a Generalization of Tinbergen's Condition in the Theory of Policy to Dynamic Models]. *J. Public Econ.,* June 1984, *24*(1), pp. 123–25.

1136 Economic Planning Policy

Alagh, Yoginder K.; Kashyap, S. P. and Murty, G. V. S. N. Policy Modelling for Planning in India. In *Cohen, S. I., et al., eds.*, 1984, pp. 59–88. **[G: India]**

Bacon, Peter. National Planning. *Irish Banking Rev.,* June 1984, pp. 3–11. **[G: Ireland]**

Bandera, V. N. Capital Accumulation and Growth in a Mixed Socialist Economy: The Case of Soviet NEP. *J. Europ. Econ. Hist.,* Spring 1984, *13*(1), pp. 7–27. **[G: U.S.S.R.]**

Berliner, Joseph S. Planning and Management. In *Hoffmann, E. P. and Laird, R. F., eds.*, 1984, *1983*, pp. 467–509. **[G: U.S.S.R.]**

Bienaymé, Alain. Les choix économiques du IXe Plan. (The Economic Choices of the IXth Plan. With English summary.) *Revue Écon.,* November 1984, *35*(6), pp. 1261–88. **[G: France]**

Black, William. The National Plan—A Northern Perspective. *Irish Banking Rev.,* December 1984, pp. 4–9. **[G: Ireland]**

Cave, Martin. French Planning Reforms, 1981–1984. *ACES Bull.,* Summer–Fall 1984, *26*(2–3), pp. 29–38. **[G: France]**

Csikós-Nagy, Béla. Further Development of the Hungarian Price System. *Acta Oecon.,* 1984, *32*(1–2), pp. 21–37. **[G: Hungary]**

Cuddy, Michael P. Building on Reality 1985–1987: A Comment. *Irish Banking Rev.,* December 1984, pp. 10–15. **[G: Ireland]**

Durkan, Joe. The National Plan. *Irish Banking Rev.,* December 1984, pp. 16–19. **[G: Ireland]**

Faluvégi, Lajos. Economic Efficiency, Control and Management. *Acta Oecon.,* 1984, *33*(3–4), pp. 201–20. **[G: Hungary]**

Frank, Andre Gunder. The Political Economy of the Economic Policy of the Communist Party of Chile. In *Frank, A. G.*, 1984, pp. 155–60. **[G: Chile]**

Geary, Patrick T. The National Plan: An Appraisal. *Irish Banking Rev.,* December 1984, pp. 20–24. **[G: Ireland]**

Horn, R. V. Social Indicators for Development Planning and Analysis. In *Ghosh, P. K., ed., no. 8*, 1984, *1975*, pp. 166–91. **[G: LDCs]**

Husain, Tariq. Potential for Irrigated Agricultural Development in Pakistan. In *Burki, S. J. and LaPorte, R., Jr., eds.*, 1984, pp. 45–83. **[G: Pakistan]**

Ionescu, Nicolae. Coordination of Economic Development Plans among the CMEA Member Countries. *Soviet E. Europ. Foreign Trade,* Spring 1984, *20*(1), pp. 27–35. **[G: CMEA]**

Jakeš, Miloš. Fulfilment of the Program of the 16th Congress of the Communist Party of Czechoslovakia. *Czech. Econ. Digest.,* December 1984, (8), pp. 63–95. **[G: Czechoslovakia]**

Lakdawala, D. T. Plan Finances in a Federal Economy. In *Singh, A. K.; Papola, T. S. and Mathur, R. S., eds.*, 1984, pp. 363–402. **[G: India]**

Li, Xuezeng and Yang, Shengming. Raise Economic Efficiency and Accelerate the Growth of National Income. *Chinese Econ. Stud.,* Winter 1983–84, *17*(2), pp. 88–92. **[G: China]**

Liu, Tai-Ying and Chan, Yie-Lang. Industrial Policy and Strategies In the Republic of China. In *Driscoll, R. E. and Behrman, J. N., eds.*, 1984, pp. 137–49. **[G: Republic of China]**

Lohani, Prakash C. Nepal's Economy in Retrospect and Its Prospects for the 1980s. In *Ghosh, P. K., ed., no. 18*, 1984, *1980*, pp. 179–238. **[G: Nepal]**

Lynch, Frances M. B. Resolving the Paradox of the Monnet Plan: National and International Planning in French Reconstruction. *Econ. Hist. Rev., 2nd Ser.,* May 1984, *37*(2), pp. 229–43. **[G: France]**

Malkin, Daniel. Mutations industrielles et IXe Plan. (Industrial Mutations and the IXth Plan. With English summary.) *Revue Écon.,* November 1984, *35*(6), pp. 1091–145. **[G: France]**

Marsden, Keith. Progressive Technologies for Developing Countries. In *Ghosh, P. K., ed., no. 3*, 1984, *1970*, pp. 292–324. **[G: Japan; Middle East]**

McAleese, Dermot. Building on Reality 1985–1987: A Commentary. *Irish Banking Rev.,* December 1984, pp. 25–29. **[G: Ireland]**

McDonell, Michael. Recent Developments in Medium-term Planning and Policy Implementation in Ireland. *Econ. Lavoro,* Oct.-Dec. 1984, *18*(4), pp. 85–90. **[G: Ireland]**

O'Mahony, David. How Should the Plan Be Interpreted? *Irish Banking Rev.,* December 1984, pp. 30–36. **[G: Ireland]**

Orlov, Ia. The Demand of the Population and Tasks of Production and Trade. *Prob. Econ.,* June 1984, *27*(2), pp. 3–19. **[G: U.S.S.R.]**

Potáč, Svatopluk. State Plan of Economic and Social Development for 1984. *Czech. Econ. Digest.,* May 1984, (3), pp. 3–18. **[G: Czechoslovakia]**

Pulai, Miklós and Vissi, Ferenc. Tasks and Prob-

lems in Developing the Hungarian Economic Control and Management System. *Acta Oecon.*, 1984, *33*(3–4), pp. 221–36.
[G: Hungary]

Rao, M. V. S. Socio-economic Indicators for Development Planning. In *Ghosh, P. K., ed., no. 8, 1984, 1976,* pp. 192–220. [G: India]

Ruiz Dueñas, Jorge. Public Enterprise and Planning in Mexico. *Ann. Pub. Co-op. Econ.*, January–March 1984, *55*(1), pp. 91–107.
[G: Mexico]

Sabolčík, Michal. Rationalization of the Price System in the Years 1984–1985. *Czech. Econ. Digest.*, September 1984, (6), pp. 35–55.
[G: Czechoslovakia]

Simmons, Ozzie G. Population Policy Analysis and Development Planning. *J. Devel. Areas,* July 1984, *18*(4), pp. 433–48. [G: LDCs]

Singh, A. K. Planning in a Mixed Economy: The Indian Experience. In *Singh, A. K.; Papola, T. S. and Mathur, R. S., eds.,* 1984, pp. 148–64. [G: India]

Skolka, Jiri. Use of Input–Output Models in the Preparation of Price Reform in China. *Industry Devel.*, 1984, (10), pp. 61–73. [G: China]

Soják, Zbyněk. Intensification of the Economy—A Strategic Task of the Economic Policy of the Party. *Czech. Econ. Digest.*, February 1984, (1), pp. 3–25. [G: Czechoslovakia]

Tin, Maung Maung Than. Burma in 1983: From Recovery to Growth? In *Thambipillai, P., ed.,* 1984, pp. 89–122. [G: Burma]

Tomášek, Přemysl. Egalitarianism Is Harmful. *Czech. Econ. Digest.*, June 1984, (4), pp. 3–13. [G: Czechoslovakia]

Wanmali, Sudhir. Rural-based Models for Rural Development: The Indian Experience. In *[Farmer, B. H.],* 1984, pp. 253–69.
[G: India]

Zotov, M. Intensification of the Investment Process. *Prob. Econ.*, October 1984, *27*(6), pp. 24–38. [G: U.S.S.R.]

114 Economics of War, Defense, and Disarmament

1140 Economics of War, Defense, and Disarmament

Abbott, Carl. Planning for the Home Front in Seattle and Portland, 1940–45. In *Lotchin, R. W., ed.,* 1984, pp. 163–89. [G: U.S.]

Adams, Gordon. Undoing the Iron Triangle: Conversion and the "Black Box" of Politics. In *Gordon, S. and McFadden, D., eds.,* 1984, pp. 147–63. [G: U.S.]

Awokoya, Stephen Oluwole. The Failure to Disarm: Main Obstacle to Development? In *Ghosh, P. K., ed., no. 17,* 1984, *1975,* pp. 168–83.

Ball, Nicole. Measuring Third World Security Expenditure: A Research Note. *World Devel.*, February 1984, *12*(2), pp. 157–64.
[G: LDCs]

Ball, Nicole and Leitenberg, Milton. Disarmament and Development: Their Interrelation-

ship. In *Ghosh, P. K., ed., no. 17,* 1984, *1979,* pp. 28–47.

Benjamin, Daniel K. and Kochin, Levis A. War, Prices, and Interest Rates: A Martial Solution to Gibson's Paradox. In *Bordo, M. D. and Schwartz, A. J., eds.,* 1984, pp. 587–604.
[G: U.K.]

Benoit, Emile. Growth Effects of Defense in Developing Countries. In *Ghosh, P. K., ed., no. 17, 1984, 1972,* pp. 135–49. [G: LDCs]

Bertram, Christoph. Arms Control and Technological Change. In *Ghosh, P. K., ed., no. 17,* 1984, *1981,* pp. 120–34.

Bigman, David and Weksler, Itzhak. Emergency Stocks: A Theoretical Analysis and an Illustration for Israel. *J. Policy Modeling,* February 1984, *6*(1), pp. 81–94. [G: Israel]

Bissell, Richard E. The Importance of the Economic Base to National Security. In *McCormick, G. H. and Bissell, R. E., eds.,* 1984, pp. 87–104. [G: OECD; U.S.S.R.]

Blechman, Barry M. and Fried, Edward R. Disarmament and Development: Some Specific Proposals. In *Ghosh, P. K., ed., no. 17,* 1984, *1977,* pp. 189–205.

Boulding, Kenneth E. Sources of Reasonable Hope for the Future. *Amer. Econ. Rev.,* May 1984, *74*(2), pp. 221–25. [G: Global]

Bracken, Paul. Mobilization Dynamics in the Nuclear Age. In *McCormick, G. H. and Bissell, R. E., eds.,* 1984, pp. 229–48.

Brams, Steven J.; Davis, Morton D. and Straffin, Philip D., Jr. Comment on Wagner [The Theory of Games and the Problem of International Cooperation]. *Amer. Polit. Sci. Rev.,* June 1984, *78*(2), pp. 495–96.

Brouthers, Lance. Comment on Russett [Defense Expenditures and National Well-Being]. *Amer. Polit. Sci. Rev.,* March 1984, *78*(1), pp. 202–04.

Cagan, Phillip. War, Prices, and Interest Rates: A Martial Solution to Gibson's Paradox: Comment. In *Bordo, M. D. and Schwartz, A. J., eds.,* 1984, pp. 604–10. [G: U.K.]

Carroll, Gene. How to Get Labor Involved. In *Gordon, S. and McFadden, D., eds.,* 1984, pp. 219–30. [G: U.S.]

Casetti, Emilio. The Military Power Potential of Nations: A Model and Some Measures. *Conflict Manage. Peace Sci.,* Spring 1984, *7*(2), pp. 25–31. [G: U.S.; U.S.S.R.; China; Japan]

Cole, Sam. Disarmament in the Context of a New International Economic Order. In *Ghosh, P. K., ed., no. 17,* 1984, *1979,* pp. 206–14.

Compa, Lance. Labor and the Military—A History. In *Gordon, S. and McFadden, D., eds.,* 1984, pp. 33–43. [G: U.S.]

van Creveld, Martin. The Origins and Development of Mobilization Warfare. In *McCormick, G. H. and Bissell, R. E., eds.,* 1984, pp. 26–43.

Deger, Saadet and Sen, Somnath. Optimal Control and Differential Game Models of Military Expenditure in Less Developed Countries. *J. Econ. Dynam. Control,* May 1984, *7*(2), pp. 153–69. [G: LDCs]

Domke, William K. Waste, Weapons, and Resolve: Defense Posture and Politics in the Defense Budget. *Policy Sci.*, March 1984, *16*(4), pp. 371–90. [G: U.S.]

Dumas, Lloyd J. Making Peace Possible: The Legislative Approach to Economic Conversion. In *Gordon, S. and McFadden, D., eds.*, 1984, pp. 67–85. [G: U.S.]

Dunne, John Paul and Smith, Ronald P. The Economic Consequences of Reduced UK Military Expenditure. *Cambridge J. Econ.*, September 1984, *8*(3), pp. 297–310. [G: U.K.]

Eichenberg, Richard C. The Expenditure and Revenue Effects of Defense Spending in the Federal Republic of Germany. *Policy Sci.*, March 1984, *16*(4), pp. 391–411.
[G: W. Germany]

Eichner, Alfred S. Budgeting for Peace and Growth. *Challenge*, January/February 1984, *26*(6), pp. 9–20. [G: U.S.]

Enns, John H.; Nelson, Gary R. and Warner, John T. Retention and Retirement: The Case of the U.S. Military. *Policy Sci.*, October 1984, *17*(2), pp. 101–21. [G: U.S.]

Faini, Riccardo; Annez, Patricia and Taylor, Lance. Defense Spending, Economic Structure, and Growth: Evidence among Countries and Over Time. *Econ. Develop. Cult. Change*, April 1984, *32*(3), pp. 487–98. [G: India; Global]

Fairbanks, Robert B. and Miller, Zane L. The Martial Metropolis: Housing, Planning, and Race in Cincinnati, 1940–55. In *Lotchin, R. W., ed.*, 1984, pp. 191–222. [G: U.S.]

Fischer, Dietrich. Weapons Technology and the Intensity of Arms Races. *Conflict Manage. Peace Sci.*, Fall 1984, *8*(1), pp. 49–69.

Fontenot, Gregory. Junction City–Fort Riley: A Case of Symbiosis. In *Lotchin, R. W., ed.*, 1984, pp. 35–60. [G: U.S.]

Freedenberg, Paul. High Technology and the Export Administration Act. In *Czinkota, M. R., ed.*, 1984, pp. 169–76. [G: U.S.]

Frieburger, William. War Prosperity and Hunger: The New York Food Riots of 1917. *Labor Hist.*, Spring 1984, *25*(2), pp. 217–39.
[G: U.S.]

Galal, Essam. Dynamics of the Arms Race: A Third World View. In *Ghosh, P. K., ed., no. 17*, 1984, *1982*, pp. 48–59.

Galbraith, Karl D. and Wakefield, Joseph C. National Defense Spending: A Review of Appropriations and Real Purchases. *Surv. Curr. Bus.*, November 1984, *64*(11), pp. 11–16.
[G: U.S.]

Gansler, Jacques S. Defense: A "Demonstration Case" for Industrial Strategy. *Challenge*, January/February 1984, *26*(6), pp. 58–61.
[G: U.S.]

Gilpin, Robert. Structural Constraints on Economic Leverage: Market-Type Systems. In *McCormick, G. H. and Bissell, R. E., eds.*, 1984, pp. 105–28.

Gold, David. Conversion and Industrial Policy. In *Gordon, S. and McFadden, D., eds.*, 1984, pp. 191–203. [G: U.S.]

Gordon, Suzanne and McFadden, Dave. Economic Conversion: Revitalizing America's Economy: Introduction. In *Gordon, S. and McFadden, D., eds.*, 1984, pp. xiii–xxi.

Greenwood, David. Public Expenditure Policy, 1984–85: Defence. In *Cockle, P., ed.*, 1984, pp. 172–92. [G: U.K.]

Hale, Robert F. The Defense Budget: Comment. In *Mills, G. B. and Palmer, J. L., eds.*, 1984, pp. 116–19. [G: U.S.; U.S.S.R.]

Herranen, Timo and Myllyntaus, Timo. Effects of the First World War on the Engineering Industries of Estonia and Finland. *Scand. Econ. Hist. Rev.*, 1984, *32*(3), pp. 121–42.
[G: U.S.S.R.; Finland]

Herz, John. Comment on Wagner [The Theory of Games and the Problem of International Cooperation]. *Amer. Polit. Sci. Rev.*, June 1984, *78*(2), pp. 495.

Holloway, David. War, Militarism, and the Soviet State. In *Hoffmann, E. P. and Laird, R. F., eds.*, 1984, *1980*, pp. 359–91. [G: U.S.S.R.]

Holzman, Franklyn D. Myths That Drive the Arms Race. *Challenge*, September/October 1984, *27*(4), pp. 32–36. [G: U.S.S.R.; NATO; U.S.]

Hopkins, George W. From Naval Pauper to Naval Power: The Development of Charleston's Metropolitan-Military Complex. In *Lotchin, R. W., ed.*, 1984, pp. 1–34. [G: U.S.]

Hufbauer, Gary Clyde and Schott, Jeffrey J. Economic Sanctions: An Often Used and Occasionally Effective Tool of Foreign Policy. In *Czinkota, M. R., ed.*, 1984, pp. 18–33.
[G: Global]

Jackson, Kenneth T. The City Loses the Sword: The Decline of Major Military Activity in the New York Metropolitan Region. In *Lotchin, R. W., ed.*, 1984, pp. 151–62. [G: U.S.]

James, Patrick and Wilkenfeld, Jonathan. Structural Factors and International Crisis Behavior. *Conflict Manage. Peace Sci.*, Spring 1984, *7*(2), pp. 33–53.

Johnson, David R. The Failed Experiment: Military Aviation and Urban Development in San Antonio, 1910–40. In *Lotchin, R. W., ed.*, 1984, pp. 89–108. [G: U.S.]

Kirby, Stephen and Cox, Andrew. Defence Budgeting and Accountability in Britain and America: Executive Innovation and Legislative Response in the 1970s. In *Shaw, M., ed.*, 1984, pp. 217–57. [G: U.K.; U.S.]

Knorr, Klaus. Economic Relations as an Instrument of National Power. In *McCormick, G. H. and Bissell, R. E., eds.*, 1984, pp. 183–207.

Laird, Robbin F. Soviet Arms Trade with the Noncommunist Third World. In *Hoffmann, E. P., ed.*, 1984, pp. 196–213. [G: U.S.S.R.; LDCs]

Lambeth, Benjamin S. and Lewis, Kevin N. Economic Targeting in Modern Warfare. In *McCormick, G. H. and Bissell, R. E., eds.*, 1984, pp. 249–69. [G: U.S.; U.S.S.R.]

Levine, Herbert S. Structural Constraints on Economic Leverage: Command-Type Systems. In

McCormick, G. H. and Bissell, R. E., eds., 1984, pp. 129–47.

Lock, Peter and Wulf, Herbert. Consequences of the Transfer of Military-Oriented Technology on the Development Process. In *Ghosh, P. K., ed., no. 17, 1984, 1977*, pp. 104–19. [G: LDCs]

Lotchin, Roger W. The Martial Metropolis: Conclusion. In *Lotchin, R. W., ed.*, 1984, pp. 223–32. [G: U.S.]

Lotchin, Roger W. The Martial Metropolis: Introduction. In *Lotchin, R. W., ed.*, 1984, pp. x–xiii. [G: U.S.]

Majeski, Stephen J. Arms Races as Iterated Prisoner's Dilemma Games. *Math. Soc. Sci.*, June 1984, 7(3), pp. 253–66.

Mann, Michael. Capitalism and Militarism. In *Shaw, M., ed.*, 1984, pp. 25–46.

Maurer, John H. Economics, Strategy, and War in Historical Perspective. In *McCormick, G. H. and Bissell, R. E., eds.*, 1984, pp. 59–83.

McNamara, Robert S. Development and the Arms Race. In *Ghosh, P. K., ed., no. 17, 1984, 1982*, pp. 16–20.

Milward, Alan S. Restriction of Supply as a Strategic Choice. In *McCormick, G. H. and Bissell, R. E., eds.*, 1984, pp. 44–58. [G: Japan; Germany; U.K.]

Murdoch, James C. and Sandler, Todd. Complementarity, Free Riding, and the Military Expenditures of NATO Allies. *J. Public Econ.*, November 1984, 25(1/2), pp. 83–101. [G: W. Europe; U.S.]

Naru, Saleem M. Khan. Pakistan–U.S. Relations: Strategies of Growthmanship. In *Ngo, M., ed., vol. 1*, 1984, pp. 188–204. [G: Pakistan; U.S.]

Ohiorhenuan, John F. E. The Political Economy of Military Rule in Nigeria. *Rev. Radical Polit. Econ.*, Summer & Fall 1984, 16(2&3), pp. 1–27. [G: Nigeria]

Pirie, Robert B. The Defense Budget: Comment. In *Mills, G. B. and Palmer, J. L., eds.*, 1984, pp. 111–15. [G: U.S.; U.S.S.R.]

Prina, L. Edgar. Why Defense Costs So Much: The Rationale for a $300 Billion Budget. *Policy Rev.*, Spring 1984, (28), pp. 80–84. [G: U.S.]

Reimers, Niels. The Government-Industry-University Interface: Improving the Innovative Process. In *Coles, J. S., ed.*, 1984, pp. 109–48. [G: U.S.]

Rogalski, Michel and Yakubovich, Carlos. Strategies for Reconversion of Armaments Industry. In *Ghosh, P. K., ed., no. 17, 1984, 1982*, pp. 260–68. [G: U.S.]

Roling, Bert. Peace Research. In *Ghosh, P. K., ed., no. 17*, 1984, pp. 282–96.

Rossano, Geoffrey. Suburbia Armed: Nassau County Development and the Rise of the Aerospace Industry, 1909–60. In *Lotchin, R. W., ed.*, 1984, pp. 61–87. [G: U.S.]

Sandler, Todd and Forbes, John F. Burden Sharing, Strategy, and the Design of NATO. In *Buchanan, J. M. and Tollison, R. D., eds.*, 1984, 1980, pp. 338–57. [G: OECD]

Schelling, Thomas C. A Framework for the Evaluation of Arms Proposals. In *Schelling, T. C.*, 1984, pp. 243–67.

Schelling, Thomas C. The Strategy of Inflicting Costs. In *Schelling, T. C.*, 1984, pp. 268–90.

Schelling, Thomas C. Thinking about Nuclear Terrorism. In *Schelling, T. C.*, 1984, pp. 309–27.

Schelling, Thomas C. Who Will Have the Bomb? In *Schelling, T. C.*, 1984, pp. 291–308.

Schiesl, Martin J. Airplanes to Aerospace: Defense Spending and Economic Growth in the Los Angeles Region, 1945–60. In *Lotchin, R. W., ed.*, 1984, pp. 135–49. [G: U.S.]

Shaw, Martin. War, Imperialism and the State System: A Critique of Orthodox Marxism for the 1980s. In *Shaw, M., ed.*, 1984, pp. 47–70.

Silver, Christopher. Norfolk and the Navy: The Evolution of City–Federal Relations, 1917–46. In *Lotchin, R. W., ed.*, 1984, pp. 109–33. [G: U.S.]

Smith, Dan. The Political Economy of British Defence Policy. In *Shaw, M., ed.*, 1984, pp. 195–216. [G: U.K.]

Stubbing, Richard A. The Defense Budget. In *Mills, G. B. and Palmer, J. L., eds.*, 1984, pp. 81–110. [G: U.S.; U.S.S.R.]

Swaney, James A. The Future Be Damned: Economists' Optimism and Nuclear Proliferation. *J. Econ. Issues*, June 1984, 18(2), pp. 527–36.

Thore, Sten; Kozmetsky, George and Burtis, Michelle. Effects of Defense Spending on the Texas Economy: An Example of Concave Programming. *J. Policy Modeling*, November 1984, 6(4), pp. 573–86. [G: U.S.]

Thorsson, Inga. The Arms Race and Development: A Competitive Relationship. In *Ghosh, P. K., ed., no. 17, 1984, 1982*, pp. 21–27.

Vidal, J. E. Appréciation des conséquences écologiques et économiques de la défoliation chimique au Viêt Nam. (Evaluation of the Economic and Ecological Consequences of Chemical Defoliation in Viet Nam. With English summary.) *Écon. Appl.*, 1984, 37(2), pp. 393–403. [G: Vietnam]

Vitaliano, Donald F. Defense Spending and Inflation: An Empirical Analysis. *Quart. Rev. Econ. Bus.*, Spring 1984, 24(1), pp. 22–32. [G: U.S.]

Wakefield, Joseph C. and Ziemer, Richard C. Federal Fiscal Programs. *Surv. Curr. Bus.*, February 1984, 64(2), pp. 9–21. [G: U.S.]

Ward, Michael Don. Differential Paths to Parity: A Study of the Contemporary Arms Race. *Amer. Polit. Sci. Rev.*, June 1984, 78(2), pp. 297–317. [G: U.S.; U.S.S.R.]

Ward, Michael Don. The Political Economy of Arms Races and International Tension. *Conflict Manage. Peace Sci.*, Spring 1984, 7(2), pp. 1–23. [G: U.S.; U.S.S.R.]

Weinrod, W. Bruce. National Security Dimensions of International Trade. In *Czinkota, M. R., ed.*, 1984, pp. 192–203. [G: U.S.]

Williamson, Jeffrey G. Why Was British Growth So Slow during the Industrial Revolution? *J.*

Econ. Hist., September 1984, *44*(3), pp. 687–712. **[G: U.K.]**

Wionczek, Miguel S. The Emergence of Military Industries in the South: Longer-Term Implications. *Industry Devel.*, 1984, (12), pp. 115–20. **[G: LDCs]**

Yudken, Joel S. Conversion in the Aerospace Industry: The McDonnell Douglas Project. In *Gordon, S. and McFadden, D., eds.*, 1984, pp. 130–43. **[G: U.S.]**

120 COUNTRY STUDIES

121 Economic Studies of Developing Countries

1210 General

Balassa, Bela. Adjustment Policies in Developing Countries: A Reassessment. *World Devel.*, September 1984, *12*(9), pp. 955–72.
[G: LDCs]

Balassa, Bela and Stoutjesdijk, Ardy. Economic Integration Among Developing Countries. In *Ghosh, P. K., ed., no. 12*, 1984, *1978*, pp. 33–50. **[G: LDCs]**

Bauer, P. T. Remembrance of Studies Past: Retracing First Steps. In *Bauer, P. T.*, 1984, pp. 1–18. **[G: S.E. Asia; W. Africa]**

Blejer, Mario I. and Khan, Mohsin S. Government Policy and Private Investment in Developing Countries. *Int. Monet. Fund Staff Pap.*, June 1984, *31*(2), pp. 379–403. **[G: LDCs]**

Bollino, C. Andrea and Klein, Lawrence R. World Recovery Strategies in the 1980s: Is World Recovery Synonymous to LDC Recovery? *J. Policy Modeling*, May 1984, *6*(2), pp. 175–207. **[G: Global]**

Bruton, Henry J. Development as a Searching and Learning Process. *METU*, 1984, *11*(1–2), pp. 71–79. **[G: LDCs]**

Callier, Philippe. Growth of Developing Countries and World Interest Rates. *J. Macroecon.*, Fall 1984, *6*(4), pp. 465–71. **[G: LDCs]**

Chenery, Hollis B. Poverty and Progress—Choices for the Developing World. In *Ghosh, P. K., ed., no. 13*, 1984, *1980*, pp. 75–84.

Chenery, Hollis B. The Alleviation of Poverty. In *Trent, J. and Lamy, P., eds.*, 1984, pp. 99–111. **[G: LDCs]**

Cohen, Michael A. Cities in Developing Countries: 1975–2000. In *Ghosh, P. K., ed., no. 2*, 1984, *1976*, pp. 27–35. **[G: LDCs]**

Cox, Robert W. The Alleviation of Poverty: Comment. In *Trent, J. and Lamy, P., eds.*, 1984, pp. 113–18. **[G: LDCs]**

DeLorme, Charles D., Jr.; Terza, Joseph and Wood, Norman J. Inflation and Political Unrest in Developing Nations. *Econ. Notes*, 1984, (2), pp. 76–84. **[G: LDCs]**

Elkan, Peter G. Measuring the Impact of Economic Integration Among Developing Countries. In *Ghosh, P. K., ed., no. 12*, 1984, *1975*, pp. 190–202. **[G: Central America; E. Africa]**

Emmanuel, Arghiri. The Multinational Corporations and Inequality of Development. In *Ghosh, P. K., ed., no. 11*, 1984, *1976*, pp. 92–113.

Ferrer, Ricardo D. Society, Politics, and Economic Development: Some Exploratory Notes. *Philippine Rev. Econ. Bus.*, Mar./June 1984, *21*(1/2), pp. 1–38. **[G: LDCs]**

Fields, Gary S. Employment, Income Distribution and Economic Growth in Seven Small Open Economies. *Econ. J.*, March 1984, *94*(373), pp. 74–83. **[G: Selected LDCs]**

Frank, Andre Gunder. Economic Crisis, Export Promotion and Political Repression in the Third World. In *Ngo, M., ed., vol. 1*, 1984, pp. 54–67. **[G: LDCs; S. Korea]**

Galbis, Vicente. Ministate Economies. *Finance Develop.*, June 1984, *21*(2), pp. 36–39. **[G: Selected LDCs]**

Glezakos, Constantine. Export Instability and Economic Growth: Reply. *Econ. Develop. Cult. Change*, April 1984, *32*(3), pp. 615–23. **[G: LDCs; MDCs]**

Glezakos, Constantine. Inflation and Growth: A Reconsideration of the Evidence from the LDCs. In *Ghosh, P. K., ed., no. 7*, 1984, *1978*, pp. 163–75. **[G: LDCs]**

Greenaway, David. A Statistical Analysis of Fiscal Dependence on Trade Taxes and Economic Development. *Public Finance*, 1984, *39*(1), pp. 70–89. **[G: Global]**

Hicks, Norman L. A Model of Trade and Growth for the Developing World. In *Ghosh, P. K., ed., no. 16*, 1984, *1976*, pp. 92–110. **[G: LDCs]**

Johnson, Omotunde E. G. On Growth and Inflation in Developing Countries. *Int. Monet. Fund Staff Pap.*, December 1984, *31*(4), pp. 636–60. **[G: LDCs]**

Kobrin, Stephen J. Multinational Corporations, Sociocultural Dependence, and Industrialization: Need Satisfaction or Want Creation? In *Ghosh, P. K., ed., no. 11*, 1984, *1979*, pp. 195–218. **[G: LDCs; U.S.]**

Krueger, Anne O. The Developing Countries' Role in the World Economy. In *Frenkel, J. A. and Mussa, M. L., eds.*, 1984, pp. 63–83. **[G: LDCs]**

Legarda, Benito. Small Island Economies. *Finance Develop.*, June 1984, *21*(2), pp. 42–43.

Manh-Lan, Ngo. Unreal Growth: Introduction. In *Ngo, M., ed., vol. 1*, 1984, pp. xxi–xxx. **[G: Asian LDCs]**

Meltzer, Allan H. The International Debt Problem. *Cato J.*, Spring/Summer 1984, *4*(1), pp. 63–69. **[G: LDCs]**

Munasinghe, Mohan. Energy Strategies for Oil Importing Developing Countries. *Natural Res. J.*, April 1984, *24*(2), pp. 351–68. **[G: LDCs]**

Palloix, Christian. Crisis and Third World Industrialization. In *Ngo, M., ed., vol. 1*, 1984, pp. 33–53. **[G: LDCs; MDCs]**

Papanek, Hanna. The Alleviation of Poverty: Comment. In *Trent, J. and Lamy, P., eds.*, 1984, pp. 119–29. **[G: LDCs]**

Preston, Samuel H. Urban Growth in Developing Countries—A Demographic Appraisal. In

Ghosh, P. K., ed., no. 2, 1984, 1979, pp. 36–56. **[G: LDCs]**

Ragazzi, Giorgio. LDCs Debt and Net Financial Transfers: The Search for Equilibrium between Stocks and Flows. *Giorn. Econ.,* May–June 1984, *43*(5–6), pp. 359–67. **[G: LDCs]**

Rothgeb, John M., Jr. Investment Penetration in Manufacturing and Extraction and External Public Debt in Third World States. *World Devel.,* November–December 1984, *12*(11–12), pp. 1063–75. **[G: LDCs]**

Savvides, Andreas. Export Instability and Economic Growth: Some New Evidence. *Econ. Develop. Cult. Change,* April 1984, *32*(3), pp. 607–14. **[G: LDCs; MDCs]**

Schmitz, Hubert. Industrialisation Strategies in Less Developed Countries: Some Lessons of Historical Experience. *J. Devel. Stud.,* October 1984, *21*(1), pp. 1–21. **[G: LDCs]**

Singh, Ajit. The Interrupted Industrial Revolution of the Third World: Prospects and Policies for Resumption. *Industry Devel.,* 1984, (12), pp. 43–68. **[G: LDCs]**

Sutcliffe, Robert B. Industry and Underdevelopment Re-examined. *J. Devel. Stud.,* October 1984, *21*(1), pp. 121–33.

Sutcliffe, Robert B. Industry and Underdevelopment Re-examined. In *Kaplinsky, R., ed.,* 1984, pp. 121–33.

Tinbergen, Jan. Lessons and Prospects. *METU,* 1984, *11*(1–2), pp. 11–19.

Ullmo, Pierre-Antoine. Financial Crisis and Development Strategy. In *Kessler, D. and Ullmo, P.-A., eds.,* 1984, pp. 269–80. **[G: LDCs]**

Vaitsos, Constantine V. Strategic Choices in the Commercialization of Technology: The Point of View of Developing Countries. In *Ghosh, P. K., ed., no. 3, 1984, 1973,* pp. 273–91. **[G: LDCs]**

Wai, U. Tun. Some Economic Concepts and Policy Issues in Developing Countries. In *Ghosh, P. K., ed., no. 7, 1984, 1980,* pp. 154–62. **[G: LDCs]**

Wilmots-Vandendaele, André. Les perspectives économiques des pays en voie de développement non exportateurs de pétrole. L'amélioration des perspectives dans le domaine de l'énergie. (With English summary.) *Revue Écon. Polit.,* September–October 1984, *94*(5), pp. 602–14. **[G: LDCs]**

Zerby, J. A. and Khan, M. H. A Comparison of Multivariate Methods for Indexing Socioeconomic Development. *Singapore Econ. Rev.,* April 1984, *29*(1), pp. 47–66. **[G: LDCs]**

1211 Comparative Country Studies

Altimir, Oscar. Poverty, Income Distribution and Child Welfare in Latin America: A Comparison of Pre- and Post-recession Data. In *Jolly, R. and Cornia, G. A., eds.,* 1984, pp. 91–112. **[G: Latin America]**

Balassa, Bela. Adjustment to External Shocks in Developing Countries. In *Csikós-Nagy, B.; Hague, D. and Hall, G., eds.,* 1984, pp. 352–84. **[G: LDCs]**

Benoit, Emile. Growth Effects of Defense in Developing Countries. In *Ghosh, P. K., ed., no. 17, 1984, 1972,* pp. 135–49. **[G: LDCs]**

Bos, Henk C. The Role of Industry and Industrial Policies in the Third Development Decade. In *Ghosh, P. K., ed., no. 1, 1984, 1978,* pp. 30–49. **[G: LDCs]**

Clark, George J. International Indebtedness: Economic Development. In *Hewlett, S. A.; Kaufman, H. and Kenen, P. B., eds.,* 1984, pp. 61–76. **[G: LDCs]**

Cornia, Giovanni Andrea. A Survey of Cross-sectional and Time-series Literature on Factors Affecting Child Welfare. In *Jolly, R. and Cornia, G. A., eds.,* 1984, pp. 17–32. **[G: LDCs]**

Hopkins, Mike and van der Hoeven, Rolf. Economic and Social Factors in Development: A Socioeconomic Framework for Basic Needs Planning. In *Cohen, S. I., et al., eds.,* 1984, pp. 161–95. **[G: Brazil; India; Kenya]**

Lambert, Denis-Clair. Amérique Latine: un indicateur synthétique de développement. (With English summary.) *Can. J. Devel. Stud.,* 1984, *5*(1), pp. 25–50. **[G: Latin America]**

Mason, Edward S. The Chenery Analysis and Some Other Considerations. In *[Chenery, H. B.],* 1984, pp. 3–21. **[G: Egypt; S. Korea]**

Parikh, Ashok and Shah, C. H. Poverty, Growth and Policy Options. *Can. J. Devel. Stud.,* 1984, *5*(2), pp. 257–72. **[G: Kenya; Taiwan; Sri Lanka]**

Perasso, Giancarlo. Sviluppo economico e qualità della vita: un confronto fra i paesi OPEC e altri paesi in via di sviluppo. (Economic Development and Quality of Life: A Comparison between OPEC Countries and Other Developing Countries. With English summary.) *Rivista Int. Sci. Econ. Com.,* June 1984, *31*(6), pp. 558–75. **[G: LDCs]**

Ramanadham, V. V. Public Enterprise in Developing Countries: The Development Context. In *Ramanadham, V. V., ed.,* 1984, pp. 1–13. **[G: Selected LDCs]**

Ranis, Gustav. Typology in Development Theory: Retrospective and Prospects. In *[Chenery, H. B.],* 1984, pp. 23–44. **[G: Kenya; Mexico; Taiwan]**

Srinivasan, T. N. Development, Poverty, and Basic Human Needs: Some Issues. In *Ghosh, P. K., ed., no. 13, 1984, 1977,* pp. 7–28. **[G: LDCs]**

Zerby, J. A. and Khan, M. H. A Comparison of Multivariate Methods for Indexing Socioeconomic Development. *Singapore Econ. Rev.,* April 1984, *29*(1), pp. 47–66. **[G: LDCs]**

1213 European Countries

Baklanoff, Eric N. Changing Systems: The Portuguese Revolution and the Public Enterprise Sector. *ACES Bull.,* Summer–Fall 1984, *26*(2–3), pp. 63–76. **[G: Portugal]**

Balassa, Bela. Medium-term Economic Policies for Portugal. *Economia (Portugal),* October 1984, *8*(3), pp. 543–67. **[G: Portugal]**

Baysan, Tercan. Some Economic Aspects of Turkey's Accession to the EC: Resource Shifts, Comparative Advantage, and Static Gains. *J. Common Market Stud.*, September 1984, 23(1), pp. 15–34. **[G: Turkey; EEC]**

Brera, Paolo. Self-Management and Economic Development: Jugoslavia's Growth Patterns in the Seventies and Their Crisis in the Eighties. *Rivista Int. Sci. Econ. Com.*, January 1984, 31(1), pp. 77–96. **[G: Yugoslavia]**

Deimezis, Nikitas. Quelques réflexions sur l'utilisation des modèles économétriques dans les économies semi-industrailisées. (With English summary.) *Cah. Écon. Bruxelles*, Fourth Trimester 1984, (104), pp. 610–46. **[G: Greece]**

Ledić Michèle. Debt Analysis and Debt-Related Issues: The Case of Yugoslavia. *Econ. Anal. Worker's Manage.*, 1984, 18(1), pp. 35–64. **[G: Yugoslavia]**

Paseta, Vesna. Dinimički model jugoslovenske privrede na bazi matrice rasta. (Dynamic Model of Yugoslav Economy on the Growth Matrix Basis. With English summary.) *Econ. Anal. Worker's Manage.*, 1984, 18(3), pp. 241–57. **[G: Yugoslavia]**

Sláma, Jiří. Empirische Prüfung der Wirkung der Reformen in den planwirtschaftlichen Ländern. (An Empirical Analysis of the Effects of Economic Reforms in Countries with Planned Economy. With English summary.) *Jahr. Nationalökon. Statist.*, November 1984, 199(6), pp. 537–56. **[G: Yugoslavia; Czechoslovakia]**

Tortella, Gabriel and Palafox, Jordi. Banking and Industry in Spain, 1918–1936. *J. Europ. Econ. Hist.*, Special Issue 1984, 13(2), pp. 81–111. **[G: Spain]**

1214 Asian Countries

Adelman, Irma. Beyond Export-led Growth. *World Devel.*, September 1984, 12(9), pp. 937–49. **[G: S. Korea]**

Ali, M. Shaukat. Employment Expansion—Import Substitution or Export Promotion? A General Equilibrium Study of Pakistan. *Indian Econ. J.*, January–March 1984, 31(3), pp. 53–61. **[G: Pakistan]**

Bandyopadhyay, T. and Ghatak, S. Errata [Some Remarks on Agricultural Backwardness under Semi-feudalism]. *Indian Econ. Rev.*, January–June 1984, 19(1), pp. 157. **[G: India]**

Baqai, Moinuddin. Pakistan's Development Pattern and Prospects. In *Ghosh, P. K., ed., no. 18*, 1984, 1980, pp. 52–97. **[G: Pakistan]**

Barone, Charles A. Reply [Dependency, Marxist Theory, and Salvaging the Idea of Capitalism in South Korea]. *Rev. Radical Polit. Econ.*, Summer & Fall 1984, 16(2&3), pp. 195–97. **[G: S. Korea]**

Benjamin, Roger; Kudrle, Robert Thomas and McCoy, Jennifer. The Dynamics of Economic Change in the Pacific Basin. In *Benjamin, R. and Kudrle, R. T.*, 1984, pp. 1–11.

Booth, Anne. Survey of Recent Developments. *Bull. Indonesian Econ. Stud.*, December 1984, 20(3), pp. 1–35. **[G: Indonesia]**

Burki, Shahid Javed. A Historical Perspective on

Development. In *Burki, S. J. and LaPorte, R., Jr., eds.*, 1984, pp. 15–41. **[G: Pakistan]**

Burki, Shahid Javed and LaPorte, Robert, Jr. Pakistan's Development Priorities: Future Choices. In *Burki, S. J. and LaPorte, R., Jr., eds.*, 1984, pp. 353–72. **[G: Pakistan]**

Burki, Shahid Javed and LaPorte, Robert, Jr. Pakistan's Development Priorities: The Political and Social Environment for Development. In *Burki, S. J. and LaPorte, R., Jr., eds.*, 1984, pp. 3–14. **[G: Pakistan]**

Chang, Parris H. The Future of Hong Kong. In *Downen, R. L. and Dickson, B. J., eds.*, 1984, pp. 209–19. **[G: Hong Kong]**

Cho, Lee-Jay. The Industrial Future of the Pacific Basin: Conclusion. In *Benjamin, R. and Kudrle, R. T.*, 1984, pp. 237–47.

Cole, S. and Meagher, G. A. Growth and Income Distribution in India: A General Equilibrium Analysis. In *Cohen, S. I., et al., eds.*, 1984, pp. 315–48. **[G: Sri Lanka; India]**

Constantino, Renato. Nationalist Perspectives in Asia. In *Ngo, M., ed., vol. 2*, 1984, pp. 817–29. **[G: Philippines]**

Davis, Kingsley. Asia's Cities: Problems and Options. In *Ghosh, P. K., ed., no. 2*, 1984, 1975, pp. 236–52. **[G: LDCs]**

Econ. Soc. Comm. for Asia and the Pacific. Prospects for the Economic Development of Bangladesh in the 1980s. In *Ghosh, P. K., ed., no. 18*, 1984, 1980, pp. 98–122. **[G: Bangladesh]**

Estanislao, Jesus P. A Perspective on Our Economic Crisis. *Philippine Econ. J.*, Winter 1984, 23(1), pp. 12–22. **[G: Philippines]**

Evans, David and Alizadeh, Parvin. Trade, Industrialisation, and the Visible Hand. *J. Devel. Stud.*, October 1984, 21(1), pp. 22–46. **[G: S. Korea; Taiwan]**

Fan, Liang-Shing. The Influence of Japan on Taiwan's Economy as a Newly Industrialized Country. *Rivista Int. Sci. Econ. Com.*, September 1984, 31(9), pp. 898–909. **[G: Taiwan]**

Fischer, Stanley. The Economy of Israel. *Carnegie-Rochester Conf. Ser. Public Policy*, Spring 1984, 20, pp. 7–52. **[G: Israel]**

Frenkel, Jacob A. Comments on the Economy of Israel. *Carnegie-Rochester Conf. Ser. Public Policy*, Spring 1984, 20, pp. 57–67. **[G: Israel]**

Gillis, Malcolm. Episodes in Indonesian Economic Growth. In *Harberger, A. C., ed.*, 1984, pp. 231–64. **[G: Indonesia]**

Grais, W. Aggregate Demand and Macro-economic Imbalances in Thailand: Simulations with the SIAM 1 Model. In *Cohen, S. I., et al., eds.*, 1984, pp. 349–79. **[G: Thailand]**

Habir, Ahmad D. Indonesia in 1983: Searching for Efficiency. In *Thambipillai, P., ed.*, 1984, pp. 125–36. **[G: Indonesia]**

Halliday, Jon. Japan and the Two Unfinished Reunifications: Korea and China. In *Ngo, M., ed., vol. 1*, 1984, pp. 231–58. **[G: E. Asia]**

Hart-Landsberg, Martin. Capitalism and Third World Economic Development: A Critical

Look at the South Korean "Miracle" [Dependency, Marxist Theory, and Salvaging the Idea of Capitalism in South Korea]. *Rev. Radical Polit. Econ.*, Summer & Fall 1984, *16*(2&3), pp. 181–93. **[G: S. Korea]**

Hasan, Parvez. Adjustment to External Shocks. *Finance Develop.*, December 1984, *21*(4), pp. 14–17. **[G: E. Asia]**

Hewavitharana, B. New Patterns of Developments for Sri Lanka. In *Ghosh, P. K., ed., no. 18*, 1984, *1980*, pp. 123–78.
[G: Sri Lanka]

Heyzer, Noeleen. The Merging of State with Foreign Investment: Building a Technocratic Elite in Singapore. In *Ngo, M., ed., vol. 1*, 1984, pp. 404–26. **[G: Singapore]**

Hiemenz, Ulrich. Structural Change in Manufacturing: Issues and Perspectives for Developing Asian Countries. In *Benjamin, R. and Kudrle, R. T.*, 1984, pp. 13–34. **[G: S.E. Asia; U.S.]**

Hill, Hal. Survey of Recent Developments. *Bull. Indonesian Econ. Stud.*, August 1984, *20*(2), pp. 1–38. **[G: Indonesia]**

Holub, A. Mongolia: Modernizing the Industrial Structure. In *Ngo, M., ed., vol. 1*, 1984, pp. 536–61. **[G: Mongolia]**

Kabir, M. An Anatomy of Inflation in Bangladesh. *J. Econ. Devel.*, December 1984, *9*(2), pp. 121–43. **[G: Bangladesh]**

Kao, Charles H. C. and Liu, Ben-chieh. Socioeconomic Advance in the Republic of China (Taiwan): An Intertemporal Analysis of Its Quality of Life Indicators. *Amer. J. Econ. Soc.*, October 1984, *43*(4), pp. 399–412. **[G: Taiwan]**

Khader, Bichara. The Afro–Arab Alliance: an Economic Strategy for the 1980s. In *Achilli, M. and Khaldi, M., eds.*, 1984, pp. 155–93.
[G: OECD; Arab Countries; LDCs]

Khan, Ghulam Ishaq. First Annual General Meeting of the Pakistan Society of Development Economists: Inaugural Address. *Pakistan Devel. Rev.*, Summer-Autumn 1984, *23*(2&3), pp. 105–17. **[G: Pakistan]**

Kintanar, Agustin, Jr. Economic Developments in Southeast Asia in 1983: An Overview. In *Thambipillai, P., ed.*, 1984, pp. 18–32.
[G: S.E. Asia]

Koo, Hagen. The Political Economy of Income Distribution in South Korea: The Impact of the State's Industrialization Policy. *World Devel.*, October 1984, *12*(10), pp. 1029–37.
[G: S. Korea]

Krishnamurty, K.; Saibaba, P. and Kazmi, N. A. Inflation and Growth: A Model for India. *Indian Econ. Rev.*, January–June 1984, *19*(1), pp. 16–111. **[G: India]**

Kugai, Saburo. The Big-Power Game in East Asia: U.S.–Japan Relations. In *Ngo, M., ed., vol. 1*, 1984, pp. 205–16. **[G: E. Asia; Japan; U.S.]**

Kuznets, Paul W. Economic Development, Export Structure, and Shifting Comparative Advantage in the Pacific Basin Region. In *Benjamin, R. and Kudrle, R. T.*, 1984, pp. 35–58.
[G: Selected Countries]

Lau, Lawrence J. Taiwan's Economic Miracle:

Lessons in Economic Development: Comments. In *Harberger, A. C., ed.*, 1984, pp. 327–31. **[G: Taiwan]**

Liang, Kuo-shu and Liang, Ching-ing Hou. Trade, Technology Transfers, and Risks of Protectionism: The Experience of the Republic of China. In *Downen, R. L. and Dickson, B. J., eds.*, 1984, pp. 145–59. **[G: Taiwan]**

Lim, Chong-Yah. Economic Development of Singapore since Self-government in 1959. In *Boulding, K. E., ed.*, 1984, pp. 105–31.
[G: Singapore]

Lohani, Prakash C. Nepal's Economy in Retrospect and Its Prospects for the 1980s. In *Ghosh, P. K., ed., no. 18*, 1984, *1980*, pp. 179–238.
[G: Nepal]

Martellaro, Joseph A. China's Two Economies and the USA Factor. *Rivista Int. Sci. Econ. Com.*, September 1984, *31*(9), pp. 875–97.
[G: China; Taiwan]

Maton, J. and Joos, M. A Simplified Dynamic SAM Model of Malaysia: The Effects of Technical Progress, Capital Accumulation and Income Distribution on Employment. In *Cohen, S. I., et al., eds.*, 1984, pp. 381–405.
[G: Malaysia]

Mellor, John W. Agricultural Development and the Intersectoral Transfer of Resources. In *Eicher, C. K. and Staatz, J. M., eds.*, 1984, *1973*, pp. 136–46. **[G: Taiwan]**

Moghadam, Val. Iran: Development, Revolution, and the Problem of Analysis. *Rev. Radical Polit. Econ.*, Summer & Fall 1984, *16*(2&3), pp. 227–40. **[G: Iran]**

Moles, Jerry A. and Riker, James V. Hope, Ideas, and Our Only Alternative—Ourselves and Our Values: National Heritage and the Future of Sri Lanka Agriculture. In *Douglass, G. K., ed.*, 1984, pp. 239–70. **[G: Sri Lanka]**

Moore, Mick. Categorizing Space: Urban–Rural or Core-Periphery in Sri Lanka. *J. Devel. Stud.*, April 1984, *20*(3), pp. 102–22.
[G: Sri Lanka]

Myint, Hla. Inward and Outward-Looking Countries Revisited: The Case of Indonesia. *Bull. Indonesian Econ. Stud.*, August 1984, *20*(2), pp. 39–52. **[G: Indonesia]**

Naya, Seiji. Effects of External Shocks on the Balance of Payments, Policy Responses and Debt Problems of Asian Developing Countries. *Philippine Econ. J.*, Winter 1984, *23*(1), pp. 23–49. **[G: Asia]**

Ng, Shui Meng. Vietnam in 1983: Keeping a Delicate Balance. In *Thambipillai, P., ed.*, 1984, pp. 343–68. **[G: Vietnam]**

Oshima, Harry T. Towards a Model of Monsoon Asian Economic Growth. *Singapore Econ. Rev.*, October 1984, *29*(2), pp. 93–110.
[G: Asia]

Paauw, Douglas S. Economic Growth, Employment, and Productivity: Prospects for Indonesia. *Singapore Econ. Rev.*, October 1984, *29*(2), pp. 111–25. **[G: Indonesia]**

Pandit, V. Macroeconomic Adjustments in a Developing Economy: A Medium Term Model

of Outputs and Prices in India. *Indian Econ. Rev.*, January–June 1984, *19*(1), pp. 112–56.
[G: India]

Parkin, Michael. The Economy of Israel: A Comment. *Carnegie-Rochester Conf. Ser. Public Policy*, Spring 1984, *20*, pp. 53–56.
[G: Israel]

Pugh, Cedric. Public Policy, Welfare and the Singaporean Economy. *Ann. Pub. Co-op. Econ.*, Oct.–Dec. 1984, *55*(4), pp. 433–55.
[G: Singapore]

Rao, V. K. R. V. and Joshi, P. C. India's Socialist Experience in a Mixed Economy. In *Ngo, M., ed., vol. 1*, 1984, pp. 341–54. [G: India]

Rosendale, Phyllis. Survey of Recent Developments. *Bull. Indonesian Econ. Stud.*, April 1984, *20*(1), pp. 1–29. [G: Indonesia]

Roy, Ajit. Monopoly Capital and Prospects of Social Change. In *Ngo, M., ed., vol. 1*, 1984, pp. 277–94. [G: India]

Shalev, Michael. Labor, State, and Crisis: An Israeli Case Study. *Ind. Relat.*, Fall 1984, *23*(3), pp. 362–86. [G: Israel]

Simkin, Colin. Does Money Matter in Singapore? *Singapore Econ. Rev.*, April 1984, *29*(1), pp. 1–15. [G: Singapore]

Sundaram, Jomo Kwame and Woon, Toh Kin. Malaysia: The New Economic Policy (NEP) In *Ngo, M., ed., vol. 1*, 1984, pp. 453–78.
[G: Malaysia]

Sunoo, Harold Hakwon. The Transnational Development of South Korea. In *Ngo, M., ed., vol. 1*, 1984, pp. 427–50. [G: S. Korea]

Sutton, Mary. The IMF and Stabilisation: Indonesia, 1966–70. In *Killick, Tony, ed. (I)*, 1984, pp. 68–114. [G: Indonesia]

Tin, Maung Maung Than. Burma in 1983: From Recovery to Growth? In *Thambipillai, P., ed.*, 1984, pp. 89–122. [G: Burma]

Tsiang, S. C. Taiwan's Economic Miracle: Lessons in Economic Development. In *Harberger, A. C., ed.*, 1984, pp. 301–25. [G: Taiwan]

Utrecht, Ernst. Structural Distortions in Indonesia's Economic Development. In *Ngo, M., ed., vol. 1*, 1984, pp. 378–403. [G: Indonesia]

Vaidyanathan, A. Indian Economic Performance and Prospects. In *Ghosh, P. K., ed., no. 18*, 1984, *1980*, pp. 9–51. [G: India]

Wiboonchutikula, Paitoon. The Growth of Thailand in a Changing World Economy: Past Performance and Current Outlook. In *Thambipillai, P., ed.*, 1984, pp. 326–39. [G: Thailand]

Williams, John R. Religion, Ethics and Development: An Analysis of the Sarvodaya Shramadana Movement of Sri Lanka. *Can. J. Devel. Stud.*, 1984, *5*(1), pp. 157–67.
[G: Sri Lanka]

1215 African Countries

Abouchar, Alan. The Firm in Abyssinia: Capitalism, Socialism, and Economic Development in Ethiopia. *ACES Bull.*, Winter 1984, *26*(4), pp. 25–42. [G: Ethiopia]

Acharya, Shankar. Development Perspectives and Priorities in Sub-Saharan Africa. In *Ghosh, P. K., ed., no. 8*, 1984, *1981*, pp. 291–301.
[G: Sub-Saharan Africa]

Ansu, Yaw. Ghana, 1950–1980: Missed Opportunities: Comments. In *Harberger, A. C., ed.*, 1984, pp. 227–30. [G: Ghana]

Balassa, Bela. Adjustment Policies and Development Strategies in Sub-Saharan Africa, 1973–1978. In *[Chenery, H. B.]*, 1984, pp. 317–40.
[G: Africa]

Balassa, Bela. External Shocks and Policy Responses in Sub-Saharan Africa, 1973–78. *Finance Develop.*, March 1984, *21*(1), pp. 10–12. [G: Sub-Saharan Africa]

Barker, F. S. The Macro-economic Consequences of the Drought. *J. Stud. Econ. Econometrics*, July 1984, (20), pp. 17–27. [G: S. Africa]

Bauer, P. T. and Yamey, B. S. Black Africa: The Living Legacy of Dying Colonialism. In *Bauer, P. T.*, 1984, *1983*, pp. 90–105. [G: Africa]

Bauer, P. T. and Yamey, B. S. Industrialization and Development: The Nigerian Experience. In *Bauer, P. T.*, 1984, pp. 106–27.
[G: Nigeria]

Birks, Stace and Sinclair, Clive. Libya: Problems of a Rentier State. In *Lawless, R. and Findlay, A., eds.*, 1984, pp. 241–75. [G: Libya]

Brejon de Lavargnée, Nicolas. Un réexamen de la dominance économique: théorie et application au cas du Maroc. *Revue Écon. Polit.*, January–February 1984, *94*(1), pp. 116–37.
[G: Morocco]

Burdette, Marcia M. The Political Economy of African Foreign Policy: Zambia. In *Shaw, T. M. and Aluko, O., eds.*, 1984, pp. 319–47.
[G: Zambia]

Calika, Nur. Somalia's Adjustment Experience, 1981–83. *Finance Develop.*, March 1984, *21*(1), pp. 8. [G: Somalia]

Carr, David W. Difficulty of Restoring Economic Viability with Lopsided Development: The Mauritanian Case. *J. Devel. Areas*, April 1984, *18*(3), pp. 373–86. [G: Mauritania]

Chazan, Naomi. The Political Economy of African Foreign Policy: Ghana. In *Shaw, T. M. and Aluko, O., eds.*, 1984, pp. 94–121.
[G: Ghana]

Clapham, Christopher. The Political Economy of African Foreign Policy: Ethiopia. In *Shaw, T. M. and Aluko, O., eds.*, 1984, pp. 79–93.
[G: Ethiopia]

Clark, Paul G. Step-by-Step Liberalization of a Controlled Economy: Experience in Egypt. In *[Chenery, H. B.]*, 1984, pp. 179–203.
[G: Egypt]

Clausen, A. W. Toward Sustained Development: A Joint Program of Action for Sub-Saharan Africa. *Finance Develop.*, December 1984, *21*(4), pp. 29–30. [G: Sub-Saharan Africa]

Collier, Paul and Lal, Deepak. Why Poor People Get Rich: Kenya, 1960–79. *World Devel.*, October 1984, *12*(10), pp. 1007–18. [G: Kenya]

Curry, Robert L., Jr. Problems in Acquiring Mineral Revenues for Financing Economic Development: A Case Study of Zambia during 1970–

78. *Amer. J. Econ. Soc.*, January 1984, *43*(1), pp. 37–52. [G: Zambia]

Daddieh, Cyril Kofie. The Political Economy of African Foreign Policy: Ivory Coast. In *Shaw, T. M. and Aluko, O., eds.*, 1984, pp. 122–44. [G: Ivory Coast]

Due, John F. and Due, Jean M. The Challenges Faced by Four African Economies: Zimbabwe, Zambia, Tanzania, and the Sudan. *J. Econ. Devel.*, December 1984, *9*(2), pp. 67–86. [G: Zimbabwe; Zambia; Tanzania; Sudan]

El Shibly, Mekki. Foreign Capital Inflow, Domestic Savings and Economic Growth: The Experience of the Sudan (1960/61–1974/75). *J. Econ. Devel.*, July 1984, *9*(1), pp. 125–45. [G: Sudan]

Ellis, Frank. Relative Agricultural Prices and the Urban Bias Model: A Comparative Analysis of Tanzania and Fiji. *J. Devel. Stud.*, April 1984, *20*(3), pp. 28–51. [G: Tanzania; Fiji]

Findlay, Allan. Tunisia: The Vicissitudes of Economic Development. In *Lawless, R. and Findlay, A., eds.*, 1984, pp. 217–40. [G: Tunisia]

Findlay, Anne M. The Moroccan Economy in the 1970s. In *Lawless, R. and Findlay, A., eds.*, 1984, pp. 191–216. [G: Morocco]

Fredland, R. A. OCAM: One Scene in the Drama of West African Development. In *Mazzeo, D., ed.*, 1984, pp. 103–30. [G: W. Africa]

Frolich, Alan. Lesotho. In *O'Keefe, P. and Munslow, B., eds., Part I*, 1984, pp. 135–70. [G: Lesotho]

Glavanis, Pandeli. State and Labour in Libya. In *Lawless, R. and Findlay, A., eds.*, 1984, pp. 120–49. [G: Libya]

Good, Ken. The Political Economy of African Foreign Policy: Zimbabwe. In *Shaw, T. M. and Aluko, O., eds.*, 1984, pp. 348–71. [G: Zimbabwe]

Green, Reginald Herbold and Singer, Hans W. Sub-Saharan Africa in Depression: The Impact on the Welfare of Children. *World Devel.*, March 1984, *12*(3), pp. 283–95. [G: Nigeria; Zambia; Tanzania]

Green, Reginald Herbold and Singer, Hans W. Sub-Saharan Africa in Depression: The Impact on the Welfare of Children. In *Jolly, R. and Cornia, G. A., eds.*, 1984, pp. 113–25. [G: Sub-Saharan Africa]

Guillaumont, Sylviane. La situation monétaire et finacière des États africains de la zone franc. (With English summary.) *Revue Écon. Polit.*, September–October 1984, *94*(5), pp. 592–601. [G: Africa]

Higgott, Richard A. The Political Economy of African Foreign Policy: Niger. In *Shaw, T. M. and Aluko, O., eds.*, 1984, pp. 165–89. [G: Niger]

Hugon, Ph. Crise économique et vulnérabilité externe en Afrique sub-saharienne. (Economic Crisis and External Vulnerability in Sub-Saharian Africa. With English summary.) *Écon. Soc.*, June 1984, *18*(6), pp. 159–94. [G: Sub-Saharan Africa]

Johns, David H. The Political Economy of African Foreign Policy: Tanzania. In *Shaw, T. M. and Aluko, O., eds.*, 1984, pp. 263–82. [G: Tanzania]

Khader, Bichara. The Afro–Arab Alliance: an Economic Strategy for the 1980s. In *Achilli, M. and Khaldi, M., eds.*, 1984, pp. 155–93. [G: OECD; Arab Countries; LDCs]

Khapoya, Vincent B. The Political Economy of African Foreign Policy: Kenya. In *Shaw, T. M. and Aluko, O., eds.*, 1984, pp. 145–64. [G: Kenya]

Killick, Tony. The IMF and Stabilisation: Kenya, 1975–81. In *Killick, Tony, ed. (I)*, 1984, pp. 164–216. [G: Kenya]

Kostiuk, Nadia. The Political Economy of African Foreign Policy: Botswana. In *Shaw, T. M. and Aluko, O., eds.*, 1984, pp. 60–78. [G: Botswana]

Lawless, Richard I. Algeria: The Contradictions of Rapid Industrialisation. In *Lawless, R. and Findlay, A., eds.*, 1984, pp. 153–90. [G: Algeria]

Lele, Uma. Tanzania: Phoenix or Icarus? In *Harberger, A. C., ed.*, 1984, pp. 159–95. [G: Tanzania]

Levy, Victor. The Savings Gap and the Productivity of Foreign Aid to a Developing Economy: Egypt. *J. Devel. Areas*, October 1984, *19*(1), pp. 21–34. [G: Egypt]

Lundahl, Mats. Economic Effects of a Trade and Investment Boycott against South Africa. *Scand. J. Econ.*, 1984, *86*(1), pp. 68–83. [G: S. Africa]

Michel, Gilles and Noel, Michel. The Ivorian Economy and Alternative Trade Regimes. In *Zartman, I. W. and Delgado, C. L., eds.*, 1984, pp. 77–114. [G: Ivory Coast]

Munslow, Barry. Mozambique. In *O'Keefe, P. and Munslow, B., eds., Part II*, 1984, pp. 5–47. [G: Mozambique]

Ohiorhenuan, John F. E. The Political Economy of Military Rule in Nigeria. *Rev. Radical Polit. Econ.*, Summer & Fall 1984, *16*(2&3), pp. 1–27. [G: Nigeria]

Ojo, Olatunde J. B. The Political Economy of African Foreign Policy: Nigeria. In *Shaw, T. M. and Aluko, O., eds.*, 1984, pp. 190–220. [G: Nigeria]

Omo-Fadaka, Jimoh. The Tanzanian Way of Effective Development. In *Ghosh, P. K., ed., no. 8*, 1984, *1973*, pp. 302–12. [G: Tanzania]

Putterman, Louis. Tanzanian and African Socialism: Comment. *World Devel.*, April 1984, *12*(4), pp. 461–64. [G: Tanzania]

Richards, Alan. Ten Years of Infitah: Class, Rent, and Policy Stasis in Egypt: Review Article. *J. Devel. Stud.*, July 1984, *20*(4), pp. 323–38. [G: Egypt]

Roemer, Michael. Ghana, 1950–1980: Missed Opportunities. In *Harberger, A. C., ed.*, 1984, pp. 201–25. [G: Ghana]

Rothchild, Donald. Middle Africa: Hegemonial Exchange and Resource Allocation. In *Groth, A. J. and Wade, L. L., eds.*, 1984, pp. 151–80. [G: Africa]

Schatzberg, Michael G. The Political Economy

of African Foreign Policy: Zaire. In *Shaw, T. M. and Aluko, O., eds.*, 1984, pp. 283–318. [G: Zaire]

Shahi, M. A.; Khawja, N. and Contogiannis, E. A Model of the Nigerian Foreign Trade Sector. *J. Stud. Econ. Econometrics*, January 1984, (18), pp. 48–65. [G: Nigeria]

Shaw, Timothy M. Conclusion: The Future of a Political Economy of African Foreign Policy. In *Shaw, T. M. and Aluko, O., eds.*, 1984, pp. 372–79. [G: Sub-Saharan Africa]

Shaw, Timothy M. and Aluko, Olajide. Introduction: Towards a Political Economy of African Foreign Policy. In *Shaw, T. M. and Aluko, O., eds.*, 1984, pp. 1–24. [G: Sub-Saharan Africa]

Sluglett, Peter and Farouk-Sluglett, Marion. Modern Morocco: Political Immobilism, Economic Dependence. In *Lawless, R. and Findlay, A., eds.*, 1984, pp. 50–100. [G: Morocco]

Soremekun, Fola. The Political Economy of African Foreign Policy: Angola. In *Shaw, T. M. and Aluko, O., eds.*, 1984, pp. 25–59. [G: Angola]

Southall, Roger J. The Political Economy of African Foreign Policy: South Africa. In *Shaw, T. M. and Aluko, O., eds.*, 1984, pp. 221–62. [G: S. Africa]

Svendsen, Knud Erik. Tanzania: Phoenix or Icarus?: Comments. In *Harberger, A. C., ed.*, 1984, pp. 197–99. [G: Tanzania]

Wassermann, Ursula. The Economic Situation in Africa. *J. World Trade Law*, November:December 1984, *18*(6), pp. 555–62. [G: Africa]

Wheeler, David. Sources of Stagnation in Sub-Saharan Africa. *World Devel.*, January 1984, *12*(1), pp. 1–23. [G: Sub-Saharan Africa]

Wright, Sanford. Struggling against Apartheid: The Use of Economic Sanctions on South Africa. *Rev. Black Polit. Econ.*, Winter 1984–85, *13*(3), pp. 37–47. [G: S. Africa]

Zartman, I. William and Delgado, Christopher L. The Political Economy of Ivory Coast: Introduction. In *Zartman, I. W. and Delgado, C. L., eds.*, 1984, pp. 1–20. [G: Ivory Coast]

Zulu, Justin B. and Nsouli, Saleh M. Adjustment Programs in Africa. *Finance Develop.*, March 1984, *21*(1), pp. 5–7, 9. [G: Africa]

1216 Latin American and Caribbean Countries

Adelman, Irma and Hihn, Jairus M. Analysis of Contemporary Latin American Political History: An Application of the Use of Catastrophe Theory. In *Cohen, S. I., et al., eds.*, 1984, pp. 221–49. [G: Latin America]

Alameda, José I. and Mann, Arthur J. Technology Dependency and Energy Substitutability in a Small, Open, and Petroleum-importing Developing Economy: The Case of Puerto Rico. *J. Econ. Devel.*, July 1984, *9*(1), pp. 147–66. [G: Puerto Rico]

Altimir, Oscar. Poverty, Income Distribution and Child Welfare in Latin America: A Comparison

of Pre- and Post-Recession Data. *World Devel.*, March 1984, *12*(3), pp. 261–82. [G: Chile; Colombia; Costa Rica; Panama; Venezuela]

Baer, Werner. Brazil: Political Determinants of Development. In *Wesson, R., ed.*, 1984, pp. 53–73. [G: Brazil]

Baer, Werner. Industrialization in Latin America: Successes and Failures. *J. Econ. Educ.*, Spring 1984, *15*(2), pp. 124–35. [G: Latin America]

Baer, Werner and Birch, Melissa H. Expansion of the Economic Frontier: Paraguayan Growth in the 1970s. *World Devel.*, August 1984, *12*(8), pp. 783–98. [G: Paraguay]

Bagley, Bruce Michael. Colombia: National Front and Economic Development. In *Wesson, R., ed.*, 1984, pp. 124–60. [G: Colombia]

Baklanoff, Eric N. and Brannon, Jeffery T. Forward and Backward Linkages in a Plantation Economy: Imigrant Entrepreneurship and Industrial Development in Yucatan, Mexico. *J. Devel. Areas*, October 1984, *19*(1), pp. 83–94. [G: Mexico]

Behrens, Alfredo. Energy and Output Implications of Income Redistribution in Brazil. *Energy Econ.*, April 1984, *6*(2), pp. 110–16. [G: Brazil]

Bernal, Richard L. Economic Growth and External Debt of Jamaica. In *Salazar-Carillo, J. and Tirado de Alonso, I., eds., no. 1*, 1984, pp. 1–27. [G: Jamaica]

Bills, David B. and Haller, Archibald O. Socioeconomic Development and Social Stratification: Reassessing the Brazilian Case. *J. Devel. Areas*, October 1984, *19*(1), pp. 59–69. [G: Brazil]

Bolin, William H. Central America: Real Economic Help Is Workable Now. *Foreign Aff.*, Summer 1984, *62*(5), pp. 1095–1106. [G: Central America]

Bonfiglioli, Alberto. Universal Science, Appropriate Technology and Underdevelopment—A Reprise of the Latin American Case. In *Ghosh, P. K., ed., no. 14*, 1984, *1981*, pp. 248–65. [G: Latin America]

Bonnick, Gladstone G. Jamaica: Liberalization to Centralization, and Back? In *Harberger, A. C., ed.*, 1984, pp. 265–91. [G: Jamaica]

Booth, John A. "Trickle-Up" Income Redistribution and Development in Central America During the 1960s and 1970s. In *Seligson, M. A., ed.*, 1984, pp. 351–65. [G: Central America]

Bourguignon, François and Leibovich, José. Offre et demande dans le processus de développement: un modèle agrégé de déséquilibre appliqué à la Colombie. (Supply and Demand in the Development Process: An Applied Aggregate Disequilibrium Model for Colombia. With English summary.) *Ann. INSEE*, July–December 1984, (55/56), pp. 223–44. [G: Colombia]

Bourne, Compton and Joefield-Napier, Wallace. Export Performance and Prospects for the Commonwealth Caribbean. In *Jorge, A.; Salazar-Carrillo, J. and Sanchez, E. P.*, 1984, pp. 47–59. [G: Caribbean]

Bourne, Compton and Joefield-Napier, Wallace.

Export Performance and Prospects for the Commonwealth Caribbean. In *Salazar-Carrillo, J. and Tirado de Alonso, I., eds., no. 2*, 1984, pp. 1–26. [G: Caribbean]

Briones, Rodrigo K. The Chilean Malaise. *Challenge*, March/April 1984, *27*(1), pp. 57–60. [G: Chile]

Brun, J. Ricardo Ramirez and Díaz, Ernesta Guizar. Employment and Development: The Mexican Case. In *Amin, S., ed.*, 1984, pp. 3–19. [G: Mexico]

Burns, E. Bradford. The Modernization of Underdevelopment: El Salvador, 1858–1931. *J. Devel. Areas*, April 1984, *18*(3), pp. 293–316. [G: El Salvador]

Cason, Jeffrey. Allende's Chile and the Professional-Managerial Class. *Econ. Forum*, Summer 1984, *15*(1), pp. 103–24. [G: Chile]

Cernea, Michael M. Can Local Participation Help Development? *Finance Develop.*, December 1984, *21*(4), pp. 41–44. [G: Mexico]

Chalumeau, Jean-Luc. La situation économique du Brésil. (With English summary.) *Revue Écon. Polit.*, September–October 1984, *94*(5), pp. 615–19. [G: Brazil]

Connolly, Michael B. Jamaica: Liberalization to Centralization, and Back? Comments. In *Harberger, A. C., ed.*, 1984, pp. 293–99. [G: Jamaica]

Cortés Douglas, Hernán. Lecciones del Pasado Recesiones Económicas en Chile: 1926–1982. (With English summary.) *Cuadernos Econ.*, August 1984, *21*(63), pp. 137–68. [G: Chile]

Couriel, Alberto. Poverty and Underemployment in Latin America. *Cepal Rev.*, 1984, (24), pp. 39–62. [G: Latin America]

Crist, Raymond E. Development and Agrarian Land Reform in Venezuela's Pioneer Zone: Social Progress along the Llano-Andes Border in a Half Century of Political Advance. *Amer. J. Econ. Soc.*, April 1984, *43*(2), pp. 149–58. [G: Venezuela]

Diaz-Alejandro, Carlos F. Latin American Debt: I Don't Think We Are in Kansas Anymore. *Brookings Pap. Econ. Act.*, 1984, (2), pp. 335–89. [G: Latin America]

Díaz-Alejandro, Carlos F. The 1940s in Latin America. In *[Chenery, H. B.]*, 1984, pp. 341–62. [G: Latin America]

Díaz, Francisco Gil. Mexico's Path from Stability to Inflation. In *Harberger, A. C., ed.*, 1984, pp. 333–76. [G: Mexico]

Díaz, Rámon. Uruguay's Erratic Growth. In *Harberger, A. C., ed.*, 1984, pp. 377–402. [G: Uruguay]

Dick, Hermann, et al. Stabilisation Strategies in Primary Commodity Exporting Countries: A Case Study of Chile. *J. Devel. Econ.*, May–June–August 1984, *15*(1,2,3), pp. 47–75. [G: Chile]

Duncan, W. Raymond. Jamaica: Alternative Approaches. In *Wesson, R., ed.*, 1984, pp. 188–212. [G: Jamaica]

Edwards, Sebastian. Coffee, Money, and Inflation in Colombia. *World Devel.*, November–December 1984, *12*(11–12), pp. 1107–17. [G: Colombia]

Feinberg, Richard E. The Kissinger Commission Report: A Critique. *World Devel.*, August 1984, *12*(8), pp. 867–76. [G: U.S.; Central America]

Feuer, Carl Henry. Better Must Come: Sugar and Jamaica in the 20th Century. *Soc. Econ. Stud.*, December 1984, *33*(4), pp. 1–49. [G: Jamaica]

Fishlow, Albert. Reciprocal Trade Growth: The Latin American Integration Experience. In *[Chenery, H. B.]*, 1984, pp. 235–60. [G: Latin America]

Foxley, Alejandro and Raczynski, Dagmar. Vulnerable Groups in Recessionary Situations: The Case of Children and the Young in Chile. *World Devel.*, March 1984, *12*(3), pp. 223–46. [G: Chile]

Frankenhoff, Charles A. and Giulini, Lorenzo T. Environment and Development: The Caribbean Region. In *Ghosh, P. K., ed., no. 5, 1984, 1975*, pp. 363–73. [G: Caribbean]

Glade, William. Mexico: Party-Led Development. In *Wesson, R., ed.*, 1984, pp. 94–123. [G: Mexico]

Gonçalves, Reinaldo. Brazil and Mexico: The IMF Stabilization Programmes and Banks' Rescheduling. *Econ. Int.*, February–May 1984, *37*(1–2), pp. 76–93. [G: Brazil; Mexico]

Griffith-Jones, Stephany and Rodriguez, Ennio. Private International Finance and Industrialisation of LDCs. *J. Devel. Stud.*, October 1984, *21*(1), pp. 47–74. [G: Brazil; Chile]

Gutierrez, Francisco de Paula. A Comment on Central America. In *Jorge, A.; Salazar-Carrillo, J. and Sanchez, E. P.*, 1984, pp. 41–45. [G: Central America]

Guy, Donna J. Dependency, the Credit Market, and Argentine Industrialization, 1860–1940. *Bus. Hist. Rev.*, Winter 1984, *58*(4), pp. 532–61. [G: Argentina]

Harberger, Arnold C. La Crisis Cambiaria Chilena de 1982. (With English summary.) *Cuadernos Econ.*, August 1984, *21*(63), pp. 123–36. [G: Chile]

Hirschman, Albert O. Grassroots Development in Latin America. *Challenge*, September/October 1984, *27*(4), pp. 4–9. [G: Latin America]

Iglesias, Enrique V. A Preliminary Overview of the Latin American Economy during 1983. *Cepal Rev.*, April 1984, (22), pp. 7–38. [G: Latin America]

Iglesias, Enrique V. Development and Equity: The Challenge of the 1980s. In *Ghosh, P. K., ed., no. 8, 1984, 1981*, pp. 313–72. [G: Latin America]

Iglesias, Enrique V. Latin America: Crisis and Development Options. *Cepal Rev.*, 1984, (23), pp. 7–28. [G: Latin America]

de Janvry, Alain. The Political Economy of Rural Development in Latin America: An Interpretation. In *Eicher, C. K. and Staatz, J. M., eds.*, 1984, 1975, pp. 82–95. [G: Latin America]

Katzman, Martin T. The Land and People of

Northeast Brazil: Is Geography a Useful Guide to Development Policy? Review Article. *Econ. Develop. Cult. Change*, April 1984, *32*(3), pp. 633–38.   [G: Brazil]

Krugman, Paul R. Latin American Debt: I Don't Think We Are in Kansas Anymore: Comment. *Brookings Pap. Econ. Act.*, 1984, (2), pp. 390–93.   [G: Latin America]

LaFeber, Walter. The Reagan Administration and Revolutions in Central America. *Polit. Sci. Quart.*, Spring 1984, *99*(1), pp. 1–25.   [G: Central America]

Lagos, Ricardo and Tokman, Víctor E. Monetarism, Employment and Social Stratification. *World Devel.*, January 1984, *12*(1), pp. 43–65.   [G: Argentina; Chile]

Lambert, Denis-Clair. Amérique Latine: un indicateur synthétique de développement. (With English summary.) *Can. J. Devel. Stud.*, 1984, *5*(1), pp. 25–50.   [G: Latin America]

Langoni, Carlos Geraldo. Country Debt Problems: The Brazilian Case. *Cato J.*, Spring/Summer 1984, *4*(1), pp. 343–53.   [G: Brazil]

Llach, Juan Jose. El Plan Pinedo de 1940, su significado histórico y los orígenes de la economía política del peronismo. (With English summary.) *Desarrollo Econ.*, January-March 1984, *23*(92), pp. 515–58.   [G: Argentina]

Looney, Robert E. Mexican Optimism and Economic Reality: An Analysis of the Mexican Industrial Development Plan. *Rivista Int. Sci. Econ. Com.*, May 1984, *31*(5), pp. 432–51.   [G: Mexico]

Lopes, Francisco L. and Modiano, Eduardo M. Indexación, shock externo y nivel de actividad: notas sobre el caso brasileño. (With English summary.) *Desarrollo Econ.*, April–June 1984, *24*(93), pp. 71–84.   [G: Brazil]

Macedo, Roberto. Brazilian Children and the Economic Crisis: Evidence from the State of São Paulo. *World Devel.*, March 1984, *12*(3), pp. 203–21.   [G: Brazil]

Macedo, Roberto. Brazilian Children and the Economic Crisis: Evidence from the State of São Paulo. In *Jolly, R. and Cornia, G. A., eds.*, 1984, pp. 33–51.   [G: Brazil]

Mann, Arthur J. and Sánchez, Carlos E. Monetarism, Economic Reform and Socio-Economic Consequences: Argentina, 1976–1982. *Int. J. Soc. Econ.*, 1984, *11*(3/4), pp. 12–28.   [G: Argentina]

Martz, John D. Venezuela: Democratic Politics of Petroleum. In *Wesson, R., ed.*, 1984, pp. 161–87.   [G: Venezuela]

Merrick, Thomas W. Population, Development, and Planning in Brazil. In *Ghosh, P. K., ed., no. 5*, 1984, *1976*, pp. 343–62.   [G: Brazil]

O'Connell, Arturo. La Argentina en la Depresión: los problemas de una economía abierta. (With English summary.) *Desarrollo Econ.*, January-March 1984, *23*(92), pp. 479–514.   [G: Argentina]

Palmer, David Scott. Peru: Military and Civilian Political Economy. In *Wesson, R., ed.*, 1984, pp. 74–93.   [G: Peru]

Palmer, Ransford W. Problems of Development in Beautiful Countries: Introduction. In *Palmer, R. W.*, 1984, pp. xiii–xvii.

Palmer, Ransford W. The Eastern Caribbean: Problems of Peripheral Development. In *Palmer, R. W.*, 1984, pp. 49–58.   [G: E. Caribbean]

Pinto, Aníbal. Metropolization and Tertiarization: Structural Distortions in Latin American Development. *Cepal Rev.*, 1984, (24), pp. 17–38.   [G: Latin America]

Redclift, M. R. 'Urban Bias' and Rural Poverty: A Latin American Perspective. *J. Devel. Stud.*, April 1984, *20*(3), pp. 123–38.   [G: Mexico; Brazil]

Rodríguez, Carlos Alfredo. Inflación, salario real y tipo real de cambio. (With English summary.) *Cuadernos Econ.*, December 1984, *21*(64), pp. 247–61.   [G: Argentina]

Rosende, Francisco and Bengolea, J. Manuel. Teoría de los ciclos y la Crisis Económica actual. (With English summary.) *Cuadernos Econ.*, August 1984, *21*(63), pp. 207–26.   [G: Chile]

Rosende, Francisco and Toso, Roberto. Una explicación para la tasa de interés real en Chile en el período, 1975–1983. (With English summary.) *Cuadernos Econ.*, April 1984, *21*(62), pp. 25–36.   [G: Chile]

Rosett, Claudia. Economic Paralysis in El Salvador: What the Guerillas Don't Destroy, Central Planning Does. *Policy Rev.*, Fall 1984, (30), pp. 44–47.   [G: El Salvador]

Sachs, I. Internationalisation de l'économie ou développement endogène? les enjeux de la crise au Brésil. (Internationalization of the Economy or Endogenous Development? The Challengers of the Brazilian Crisis. With English summary.) *Écon. Soc.*, June 1984, *18*(6), pp. 195–220.   [G: Brazil]

Sachs, Jeffrey D. Latin American Debt: I Don't Think We Are in Kansas Anymore: Comment. *Brookings Pap. Econ. Act.*, 1984, (2), pp. 393–401.   [G: Latin America]

Santiago, Carlos E. and Thorbecke, Erik. Regional and Technological Dualism: A Dual–Dual Development Framework Applied to Puerto Rico. *J. Devel. Stud.*, July 1984, *20*(4), pp. 271–89.   [G: Puerto Rico]

Sawyer, W. Charles and Sprinkle, Richard L. Caribbean Basin Economic Recovery Act: Export Expansion Effects. *J. World Trade Law*, September–October 1984, *18*(5), pp. 429–36.   [G: U.S.; Caribbean]

Schuh, G. Edward. The Political Economy of Rural Development in Latin America: Comment. In *Eicher, C. K. and Staatz, J. M., eds.*, 1984, pp. 96–109.   [G: Latin America]

Sharpley, Jennifer. The IMF and Stabilisation: Jamaica, 1972–80. In *Killick, Tony, ed. (I)*, 1984, pp. 115–63.   [G: Jamaica]

Sigmund, Paul E. Chile: Free-Market Authoritarianism. In *Wesson, R., ed.*, 1984, pp. 1–13.   [G: Chile]

Soza, Hector. The Industrialization Debate in Latin America. In *Ghosh, P. K., ed., no. 1*, 1984, *1981*, pp. 309–29.   [G: Latin America]

Sunkel, Osvaldo. Past, Present and Future of the International Economic Crisis. *Cepal Rev.*, April 1984, (22), pp. 81–105.
[G: Latin America; OECD]

Sutton, Mary. Structuralism: The Latin American Record and the New Critique. In *Killick, Tony, ed. (1)*, 1984, pp. 19–67. [G: Chile; Peru]

Tirado de Alonso, Irma. Economic Growth and International Trade in the Caribbean Basin. In *Jorge, A.; Salazar-Carrillo, J. and Sanchez, E. P.*, 1984, pp. 25–35. [G: Latin America; Caribbean Basin]

Tirado de Alonso, Irma. Economic Growth and International Trade in the Caribbean Basin. In *Salazar-Carrillo, J. and Tirado de Alonso, I., eds., no. 2*, 1984, pp. 1–7.
[G: Caribbean Basin]

Truett, Dale B. and Truett, Lila J. The Maquiladoras: Prospects for Mexico. *J. Econ. Devel.*, December 1984, 9(2), pp. 45–66.
[G: Mexico]

de Vries, Barend A. Exports in the New World Environment: The Case of Latin America. In *Ghosh, P. K., ed., no. 16*, 1984, 1977, pp. 333–76. [G: Latin America]

Weinstein, Martin. Uruguay: Military Rule and Economic Failure. In *Wesson, R., ed.*, 1984, pp. 38–52. [G: Uruguay]

Wesson, Robert. Costa Rica: Problems of Social Democracy. In *Wesson, R., ed.*, 1984, pp. 213–33. [G: Costa Rica]

Wesson, Robert. Politics, Policies, & Economic Development in Latin America: Conclusion. In *Wesson, R., ed.*, 1984, pp. 235–45.

Wiarda, Howard J. Changing Realities and U.S. Policy in the Caribbean Basin: An Overview. In *Wiarda, H. J.*, 1984, pp. 57–101.
[G: Caribbean]

Wogart, Jan Peter and Marques, Jose Siverio. Trade Liberalization, Tariff Redundancy and Inflation: A Methodological Exploration Applied to Argentina. *Weltwirtsch. Arch.*, 1984, 120(1), pp. 18–39. [G: Argentina]

Woolcock, Joseph. Class Conflict and Class Reproduction: An Historical Analysis of the Jamaican Educational Reforms of 1957 and 1962. *Soc. Econ. Stud.*, December 1984, 33(4), pp. 51–99. [G: Jamaica]

Wynia, Gary W. Argentina: The Frustration of Ungovernability. In *Wesson, R., ed.*, 1984, pp. 14–37. [G: Argentina]

Wynia, Gary W. Setting the Stage for Rebellion: Economics and Politics in Central America's Past. In *Wiarda, H. J., ed.*, 1984, pp. 53–69.
[G: Central America]

Wynia, Gary W. The Roots of Central American Revolution. *Challenge*, May/June 1984, 27(2), pp. 18–25. [G: Central America]

Zalacain, Fernando. Puerto Rico: An Experiment in Growth with a Maximum Degree of Openness. *Atlantic Econ. J.*, September 1984, 12(3), pp. 11–16. [G: Puerto Rico]

1217 Oceanic Countries

Ellis, Frank. Relative Agricultural Prices and the Urban Bias Model: A Comparative Analysis of

Tanzania and Fiji. *J. Devel. Stud.*, April 1984, 20(3), pp. 28–51. [G: Tanzania; Fiji]

Utrecht, Ernst. Fiji: A Client State. In *Utrecht, E., ed.*, 1984, pp. 3–65. [G: Fiji]

122 Economic Studies of Developed Countries

1220 General

Balassa, Bela. The Economic Consequences of Social Policies in the Industrial Countries. *Weltwirtsch. Arch.*, 1984, 120(2), pp. 213–27.
[G: U.S.; EEC]

Dahmén, Erik. Ekonomi i omvandling Utländska och finländska erfarenheter. (A Changing Economy: Foreign and Finnish Experience. With English summary.) *Ekon. Samfundets Tidskr.*, 1984, 37(1), pp. 23–44. [G: MDCs; Finland]

Freedman, David. Employment and Unemployment in the 1980s: Economic Dilemmas and Socio-political Challenges. *Int. Lab. Rev.*, September–October 1984, 123(5), pp. 557–68.
[G: OECD]

Williams, Shirley. Unemployment and Economic Strains in the Western Alliance. In *Pierre, A. J., ed.*, 1984, pp. 113–42. [G: OECD]

1221 Comparative Country Studies

Aukrust, Odd. 1980-årenes okonomi sammenlignet med 1930-årenes—tallenes tale. (With English summary.) *Nationaløkon. Tidsskr.*, 1984, 122(3), pp. 313–32. [G: U.S.; W. Europe; Nordic Countries]

Curzon-Price, Victoria. Europe: Renaissance or Decline? *Aussenwirtschaft*, December 1984, 39(4), pp. 383–98. [G: EEC]

Easton, Stephen T. Real Output and the Gold Standard Years, 1830–1913. In *Bordo, M. D. and Schwartz, A. J., eds.*, 1984, pp. 513–38.
[G: OECD]

Felix, David. The Impotence of Macroeconomic Policy Activism: A Critical Appraisal of the New Classical Macroeconomics. *J. Econ. Issues*, September 1984, 18(3), pp. 825–59.
[G: OECD]

Friedman, Charles S. International Comparison of Tax Rates and Their Effects on National Incomes: Comment. In *Kendrick, J. W., ed.*, 1984, pp. 227–33. [G: OECD]

Hughes, Barry. Is There a Macroeconomic World of One Simple Model? *Econ. Rec.*, June 1984, 60(169), pp. 186–89. [G: OECD]

Kindleberger, Charles P. Financial Institutions and Economic Development: A Comparison of Great Britain and France in the Eighteenth and Nineteenth Centuries. *Exploration Econ. Hist.*, April 1984, 21(2), pp. 103–24.
[G: U.K.; France]

Kumar, Pradeep. The Economy: Summary Outline. In *Wood, W. D. and Kumar, P., eds.*, 1984, pp. 3–37. [G: Canada; U.S.]

MacEwan, Arthur. Interdependence and Instability: Do the Levels of Output in the Advanced Capitalist Countries Increasingly Move

Up and Down Together? *Rev. Radical Polit. Econ.*, Summer & Fall 1984, *16*(2&3), pp. 57–79. **[G: Selected OECD]**

Maddison, Angus. Comparative Analysis of the Productivity Situation in the Advanced Capitalist Countries. In *Kendrick, J. W., ed.*, 1984, pp. 59–92. **[G: OECD]**

McAleese, Dermot. Regional Disequilibria. *Economia (Portugal)*, January 1984, *8*(1), pp. 19–41. **[G: EEC]**

McDonald, Daina. The International Economy in 1984 and 1985. *Australian Econ. Rev.*, 1st Quarter 1984, (65), pp. 5–23. **[G: OECD]**

McMahon, Walter W. Comparative Analysis of the Productivity Situation in the Advanced Capitalist Countries: Comment. In *Kendrick, J. W., ed.*, 1984, pp. 93–108. **[G: OECD]**

Miyawaki, Nagasada. Direction of the Civilized Societies of Today Viewed on the Basis of Anomie Indexes. In *Miyawaki, N., ed.*, 1984, pp. 14–43. **[G: OECD]**

Moore, Geoffrey H. and Cullity, John P. Trends and Cycles in Productivity, Unit Costs, and Prices: An International Perspective. In *Kendrick, J. W., ed.*, 1984, pp. 157–90. **[G: OECD]**

Norton, W. E. and McDonald, Robin. Is There a Macroeconomic World of One Simple Model? Reply. *Econ. Rec.*, June 1984, *60*(169), pp. 190–91.

Olson, Mancur. Ideology and Economic Growth. In *Hulten, C. R. and Sawhill, I. V., eds.*, 1984, pp. 229–51. **[G: OECD]**

Rose, Richard and Karran, Terence. Inertia or Incrementalism? A Long-term View of the Growth of Government. In *Groth, A. J. and Wade, L. L., eds.*, 1984, pp. 43–71. **[G: OECD]**

Tobin, James. Unemployment in the 1980s: Macroeconomic Diagnosis and Prescription. In *Pierre, A. J., ed.*, 1984, pp. 79–112. **[G: OECD]**

Tolley, George S. and Shear, William B. International Comparison of Tax Rates and Their Effects on National Incomes. In *Kendrick, J. W., ed.*, 1984, pp. 197–225. **[G: OECD]**

Waldorf, William H. Trends and Cycles in Productivity, Unit Costs, and Prices: An International Perspective: Comment. In *Kendrick, J. W., ed.*, 1984, pp. 191–95. **[G: OECD]**

Wood, Geoffrey E. Real Output and the Gold Standard Years, 1830–1913: Comment. In *Bordo, M. D. and Schwartz, A. J., eds.*, 1984, pp. 538–44. **[G: OECD]**

1223 European Countries

Bacon, Peter. National Planning. *Irish Banking Rev.*, June 1984, pp. 3–11. **[G: Ireland]**

Barker, Kate; Britton, Andrew J. C. and Major, Robin. Macroeconomic Policy in France and Britain. *Nat. Inst. Econ. Rev.*, November 1984, (110), pp. 68–84. **[G: U.K.; France]**

Beckerman, Wilfred. Economic Policy and Performance in Britain since World War II. In *Harberger, A. C., ed.*, 1984, pp. 13–33. **[G: U.K.]**

Bossier, F.; Biolley, T. and Vandamme, L. Cumulated Costs and Import Contents in the Belgium Input–Output Tables of 1965, 1970 and 1975. *Cah. Écon. Bruxelles*, 1st Trimester 1984, (101), pp. 125–67. **[G: Belgium]**

Bouvier, Jean. The French Banks, Inflation and the Economic Crisis, 1919–1939. *J. Europ. Econ. Hist.*, Special Issue 1984, *13*(2), pp. 29–80. **[G: France]**

Bruno, Michael. Stagflation in the EC Countries 1973–1981: A Cross-sectional View. In *Emerson, M., ed.*, 1984, pp. 33–56. **[G: EEC]**

Budd, Alan P. Macroeconomic Aspects of the 1984 Budget. *Fisc. Stud.*, May 1984, *5*(2), pp. 8–16. **[G: U.K.]**

Butschek, Felix. Kontrollierte Inflation—ein missglücktes Experiment? *Empirica*, 1984, *11*(1), pp. 59–80. **[G: Austria]**

Chrystal, K. Alec. Dutch Disease or Monetarist Medicine? The British Economy under Mrs. Thatcher. *Fed. Res. Bank St. Louis Rev.*, May 1984, *66*(5), pp. 27–37. **[G: U.K.]**

Ciocca, Pierluigi and Toniolo, Gianni. Industry and Finance in Italy, 1918–1940. *J. Europ. Econ. Hist.*, Special Issue 1984, *13*(2), pp. 113–36. **[G: Italy]**

Deschamps, Robert. Chômage et inflation en Belgique pendant la crise: la politique économique et ses effets. (With English summary.) *Revue Écon. Polit.*, September–October 1984, *94*(5), pp. 581–91. **[G: Belgium]**

van Driel, Gerald, et al. Objectives and Potentials of the Dutch Economy in the Eighties. In *Despontin, M.; Nijkamp, P. and Spronk, J., eds.*, 1984, pp. 55–72. **[G: Netherlands]**

von Furstenberg, George M. A Step Ahead: 1983/84 Report of the German Council of Economic Experts. *Z. ges. Staatswiss.*, June 1984, *140*(2), pp. 371–79. **[G: W. Germany]**

Hardach, Gerd. Banking and Industry in Germany in the Interwar Period, 1919–1939. *J. Europ. Econ. Hist.*, Special Issue 1984, *13*(2), pp. 203–34. **[G: Germany]**

den Hartog, Hans. Empirical Vintage Models for the Netherlands: A Review in Outline. *De Economist*, 1984, *132*(3), pp. 326–49. **[G: Netherlands]**

Jäckel, Hans. Twenty Annual Reports of the German Council of Economic Experts: A Short Survey. *Z. ges. Staatswiss.*, June 1984, *140*(2), pp. 380–86. **[G: W. Germany]**

Jakobsson, Ulf. Economic Growth in Sweden. In *Harberger, A. C., ed.*, 1984, pp. 59–94. **[G: Sweden]**

Kestens, P.; Thys-Clement, F. and Van Regemorter, D. Diagnostic de la situation économique de la Belgique à horizon 1990. (With English summary.) *Cah. Écon. Bruxelles*, 1st Trimester 1984, (101), pp. 105–24. **[G: Belgium]**

Kreye, Otto. Western Europe's Economic and Social Development and the Rationality and Reality of a New International Economic Order. In *Addo, H., ed.*, 1984, pp. 119–37. **[G: W. Europe]**

Laidler, David. Economic Policy and Performance in Britain since World War II: Comments. In *Harberger, A. C., ed.*, 1984, pp. 35–39. **[G: U.K.]**

Laursen, Karsten. Dansk økonomi på længere sigt. (Long Term Perspectives in the Danish Economy. With English summary.) *Nationaløkon. Tidsskr.*, 1984, *122*(1), pp. 115–23. **[G: Denmark]**

Morishima, Michio and Prosperetti, Luigi. An Input–Output Analysis of the De-Industrialisation of the U.K. Economy, 1963–1973. *Banca Naz. Lavoro Quart. Rev.*, March 1984, (148), pp. 33–54. **[G: U.K.]**

Nötel, Rudolf. Money, Banking and Industry in Interwar Austria and Hungary. *J. Europ. Econ. Hist.*, Special Issue 1984, *13*(2), pp. 137–202. **[G: Austria; Hungary]**

O'Riordan, William K. A Wasted Decade. *Irish Banking Rev.*, March 1984, pp. 43–54. **[G: Ireland]**

Parson, Don. Politics beyond the Point of Production: Class Struggle and Regional Underdevelopment in Northern Ireland. *Rev. Radical Polit. Econ.*, Summer & Fall 1984, *16*(2&3), pp. 29–56. **[G: U.K.]**

Pekkala, Ahti. Vuoden 1985 tulo- ja menoarvioesitys. (The Budget for 1985. With English summary.) *Kansant. Aikak.*, 1984, *80*(4), pp. 349–55. **[G: Finland; OECD]**

Riley, James C. The Dutch Economy after 1650: Decline or Growth? *J. Europ. Econ. Hist.*, September–December 1984, *13*(3), pp. 521–69. **[G: Netherlands]**

Sabel, Charles F. Industrial Reorganization and Social Democracy in Austria. *Ind. Relat.*, Fall 1984, *23*(3), pp. 344–61. **[G: Austria]**

Saini, Krishan G. Economic Policy Management in Italy. *Rev. Econ. Cond. Italy*, Sept.–Dec. 1984, (3), pp. 345–63. **[G: Italy]**

Salemi, Michael K. Real Economic Activity in Switzerland. *Schweiz. Z. Volkswirtsch. Statist.*, December 1984, *120*(4), pp. 521–46. **[G: Switzerland]**

Sandkull, Bengt. Using New Technology to Erode Economic and Industrial Democracy: The Case of Sweden. *Econ. Anal. Worker's Manage.*, 1984, *18*(3), pp. 287–96. **[G: Sweden]**

Soullié, Janine. La situation économique récente du Royaume-Uni. (With English summary.) *Revue Écon. Polit.*, September–October 1984, *94*(5), pp. 562–70. **[G: U.K.]**

Spencer, Peter D. The Effect of Oil Discoveries on the British Economy—Theoretical Ambiguities and the Consistent Expectations Simulation Approach. *Econ. J.*, September 1984, *94*(375), pp. 633–44. **[G: U.K.]**

Taddei, Dominique. Le IXᵉ Plan: de la rigueur a une politique de l'offre. (The French IXth Plan: From Rigor to a Supply Policy. With English summary.) *Revue Écon.*, November 1984, *35*(6), pp. 1239–60. **[G: France]**

Tichy, Gunther. Strategy and Implementation of Employment Policy in Austria: Successful Experiments with Unconventional Assignment of Instruments to Goals. *Kyklos*, 1984, *37*(3), pp. 363–86. **[G: Austria]**

Walsh, Brendan M. Employment and Competitiveness in the European Community. *World Econ.*, March 1984, *7*(1), pp. 47–62. **[G: EEC; U.S.]**

Wiedemann, Paul. Comparing the Process of Socio-economic Development in Market and Non-market Economies: The EEC and CMEA. *Cambridge J. Econ.*, December 1984, *8*(4), pp. 311–30. **[G: EEC; CMEA]**

Wolter, Frank. From Economic Miracle to Stagnation: On the German Disease. In *Harberger, A. C., ed.*, 1984, pp. 95–121. **[G: W. Germany]**

Worswick, G. David N. The Sources of Recovery in UK in the 1930s. *Nat. Inst. Econ. Rev.*, November 1984, (110), pp. 85–93. **[G: U.K.]**

Worswick, G. David N. Two Great Recessions: The 1980s and the 1930s in Britain. *Scot. J. Polit. Econ.*, November 1984, *31*(3), pp. 209–28. **[G: U.K.; U.S.]**

1224 Asian Countries

Brown, J. A. C. and Helou, A. The Fiscal Policy of Japan since 1970. *Oxford Bull. Econ. Statist.*, May 1984, *46*(2), pp. 89–124. **[G: Japan]**

Fodella, Gianni. Il giappone e l'estasia verso l'egemonia economica mondiale. (Japan's Economic role in East Asia. With English summary.) *Rivista Int. Sci. Econ. Com.*, September 1984, *31*(9), pp. 809–11. **[G: Japan]**

Fouquin, Michel. Qu'est-ce qui arrêtera le Japon? (With English summary.) *Revue Écon. Polit.*, September–October 1984, *94*(5), pp. 555–61. **[G: Japan]**

Hamada, Koichi and Kurosaka, Yoshio. The Relationship between Production and Unemployment in Japan: Okun's Law in Comparative Perspective. *Europ. Econ. Rev.*, June 1984, *25*(1), pp. 71–94. **[G: U.S.; Japan]**

Haraf, William S. Japanese Macroeconomic Performance since 1970: Comments. *Carnegie-Rochester Conf. Ser. Public Policy*, Spring 1984, *20*, pp. 115–20. **[G: Japan]**

Haraf, William S. The Relationship between Production and Unemployment in Japan: Okun's Law in Comparative Perspective: Comments. *Europ. Econ. Rev.*, June 1984, *25*(1), pp. 95–98. **[G: U.S.; Japan]**

Komiya, Ryutaro and Yasui, Kazuo. Japan's Macroeconomic Performance since the First Oil Crisis: Review and Appraisal. *Carnegie-Rochester Conf. Ser. Public Policy*, Spring 1984, *20*, pp. 69–114. **[G: Japan]**

Kosai, Yutaka. Japan's Growth Problem. In *Harberger, A. C., ed.*, 1984, pp. 41–58. **[G: Japan]**

Mairesse, Jacques. The Relationship between Production and Unemployment in Japan: Okun's Law in Comparative Perspective: Comments. *Europ. Econ. Rev.*, June 1984, *25*(1), pp. 99–105. **[G: U.S.; Japan; EEC]**

Pugel, Thomas A. Japan's Industrial Policy: Instruments, Trends, and Effects. *J. Compar. Econ.*, December 1984, *8*(4), pp. 420–35. **[G: Japan]**

Scharpf, Fritz W. Economic and Institutional Constraints of Full-Employment Strategies: Sweden, Austria, and Western Germany, 1973–1982. In *Goldthorpe, J. H., ed.,* 1984, pp. 257–90. **[G: Sweden; Austria; W. Germany]**

1227 Oceanic Countries

Caves, Richard E. and Krause, Lawrence B. The Australian Economy: A View from the North: Conclusions. In *Caves, R. E. and Krause, L. B., eds.,* 1984, pp. 391–402.
[G: Australia]

Caves, Richard E. and Krause, Lawrence B. The Australian Economy: A View from the North: Introduction. In *Caves, R. E. and Krause, L. B., eds.,* 1984, pp. 1–23. **[G: Australia]**

Dixon, Peter B. and McDonald, Daina. Developments in Output, Employment, Prices, Wages, and Profits: Australia, 1983–84 and 1984–85. *Australian Econ. Rev.,* 4th Quarter 1984, (68), pp. 3–17. **[G: Australia]**

Dornbusch, Rudiger and Fischer, Stanley. The Australian Macroeconomy. In *Caves, R. E. and Krause, L. B., eds.,* 1984, pp. 25–79.
[G: Australia]

Helliwell, John F. Natural Resources and the Australian Economy. In *Caves, R. E. and Krause, L. B., eds.,* 1984, pp. 81–126. **[G: Australia]**

Horne, Jocelyn. Trying to Understand Stagflation: Comment. *Australian Econ. Rev.,* 3rd Quarter 1984, (67), pp. 57–58. **[G: Australia]**

Karunaratne, Neil Dias. Planning for the Australian Information Economy. *Info. Econ. Policy,* 1984, *1*(4), pp. 345–67. **[G: Australia]**

Kenyon, Peter D. Trying to Understand Stagflation: Comment. *Australian Econ. Rev.,* 3rd Quarter 1984, (67), pp. 59–61. **[G: Australia]**

McDonald, Ian M. Trying to Understand Stagflation. *Australian Econ. Rev.,* 3rd Quarter 1984, (67), pp. 32–56. **[G: Australia]**

Stone, J. O. 1929 and All That . . . . *Australian Econ. Rev.,* 3rd Quarter 1984, (67), pp. 18–31. **[G: Australia]**

Stutchbury, Michael. The Playford Legend and the Industrialization of South Australia. *Australian Econ. Hist. Rev.,* March 1984, *24*(1), pp. 1–19. **[G: Australia]**

Treadgold, Malcolm L. Growth, Structural Change, and Distribution in a Very Small Economy: A Case Study of Norfolk Island. *J. Devel. Areas,* October 1984, *19*(1), pp. 35–58.
[G: Australia]

1228 North American Countries

Bartel, Richard D. Structural Change and Policy Response in an Interdependent World. In *Alperovitz, G. and Skurski, R., eds.,* 1984, pp. 15–39. **[G: U.S.]**

Boskin, Michael J. U.S. Stabilization Policy: Lessons from the Past Decade: Comments. In *Harberger, A. C., ed.,* 1984, pp. 151–56.
[G: U.S.]

Clark, Peter K. Unemployment and Potential Output in the 1980s: Comment. *Brookings Pap. Econ. Act.,* 1984, (2), pp. 565–67.
[G: U.S.]

Danziger, Sheldon, et al. Reviewing Reagan's Economic Program. *Challenge,* January/February 1984, *26*(6), pp. 42–50. **[G: U.S.]**

Evans, M. K. The Use of Judgement in Econometric Forecasting. In *Oppenländer, K. H. and Poser, G., eds.,* 1984, pp. 3–45. **[G: U.S.]**

Gordon, Robert J. U.S. Stabilization Policy: Lessons from the Past Decade. In *Harberger, A. C., ed.,* 1984, pp. 123–49. **[G: U.S.]**

Gordon, Robert J. Unemployment and Potential Output in the 1980s. *Brookings Pap. Econ. Act.,* 1984, (2), pp. 537–64. **[G: U.S.]**

Janácková, Stanislava. The Theoretical Basis and the Aims of "Reaganomics"—Proclamations and Reality. *Czech. Econ. Digest.,* November 1984, (7), pp. 84–106. **[G: U.S.]**

Kendrick, John W. The Implications of Growth Accounting Models. In *Hulten, C. R. and Sawhill, I. V., eds.,* 1984, pp. 19–43. **[G: U.S.]**

Kitova, G. A. and Kuznetsova, T. E. The Modified Version of an Aggregated Econometric Model of the USA. *Matekon,* Spring 1984, *20*(3), pp. 74–98. **[G: U.S.]**

Kumar, Pradeep. The Economy: Summary Outline. In *Wood, W. D. and Kumar, P., eds.,* 1984, pp. 3–37. **[G: Canada; U.S.]**

McNees, Stephen K. Economic Growth: How Much Is Too Much? *New Eng. Econ. Rev.,* January–February 1984, pp. 15–22. **[G: U.S.]**

McNees, Stephen K. The Current Expansion in Historical Perspective. *New Eng. Econ. Rev.,* November–December 1984, pp. 5–11.
[G: U.S.]

Minsky, Hyman P. Banking and Industry between the Two Wars: The United States. *J. Europ. Econ. Hist.,* Special Issue 1984, *13*(2), pp. 235–72. **[G: U.S.]**

Motley, Brian. How Soon Will the U.S. Reach Full Employment? An Assessment Based on Okun's Law. *Fed. Res. Bank San Francisco Econ. Rev.,* Summer 1984, (3), pp. 26–39.
[G: U.S.]

O'Toole, James. The Mixed (Up) American Economy. *Ann. Pub. Co-op. Econ.,* Oct.–Dec. 1984, *55*(4), pp. 383–93. **[G: U.S.]**

Palmer, John L. and Sawhill, Isabel V. The Reagan Record: Overview. In *Palmer, J. L. and Sawhill, I. V., eds.,* 1984, pp. 1–30.
[G: U.S.]

Pollard, Robert A. and Wells, Samuel F., Jr. 1945–1960: The Era of American Economic Hegemony. In *Becker, W. H. and Wells, S. F., Jr., eds.,* 1984, pp. 333–90. **[G: U.S.]**

Sawhill, Isabel V. Can We Salvage the 1980s? *Challenge,* September/October 1984, *27*(4), pp. 18–24. **[G: U.S.]**

Sawhill, Isabel V. and Stone, Charles F. The Economy: The Key to Success. In *Palmer, J. L. and Sawhill, I. V., eds.,* 1984, pp. 69–105.
[G: U.S.]

Turner, Brian and Williams, Lynn R. Economic Policy in a Global Economy: The Future of American Industry. In *Hewlett, S. A.; Kauf-*

man, H. and Kenen, P. B., eds., 1984, pp. 181–98. [G: U.S.]

Walsh, Brendan M. Employment and Competitiveness in the European Community. *World Econ.,* March 1984, 7(1), pp. 47–62. [G: EEC; U.S.]

Weinberg, Edgar. BLS and the Economy: A Centennial Timetable. *Mon. Lab. Rev.,* November 1984, 107(11), pp. 29–37. [G: U.S.]

123 Comparative Studies of Developing, Developed, and/or Centrally Planned Economies

1230 Comparative Studies of Developing, Developed, and/or Centrally Planned Economies

Adelman, Irma and Morris, Cynthia Taft. Patterns of Economic Growth, 1850–1914, or Chenery–Syrquin in Historical Perspective. In *[Chenery, H. B.],* 1984, pp. 45–74.

Artus, Patrick and Avouyi-Dovi, S. Une estimation comparative de modèles avec rationnement quantitatif pour la France et les Etats-Unis. (Comparative Estimation for France and the United States of Models with Quantity Rationing. With English summary.) *Écon. Appl.,* 1984, 37(3–4), pp. 489–522. [G: France; U.S.]

Behrman, Jere R. The Importance of Supply and Demand Variations in Earnings Instability: Comment. *Econ. Develop. Cult. Change,* October 1984, 33(1), pp. 167–70.

Bhagwati, Jagdish N. Why Are Services Cheaper in the Poor Countries? *Econ. J.,* June 1984, 94(374), pp. 279–86.

Bird, Roger. International Financial Disorder. In *Jorge, A.; Salazar-Carrillo, J. and Sanchez, E. P.,* 1984, pp. 105–20. [G: Global]

Bornschier, Volker. Multinational Corporations, Economic Policy and National Development in the World System. In *Ghosh, P. K., ed., no. 11,* 1984, 1980, pp. 30–46.

Boserup, Ester. Demographic Pressure, Growth and Productivity in an Historical Perspective. In *Amin, S., ed.,* 1984, pp. 20–32. [G: OECD; U.S.S.R.; LDCs]

Bruno, Michael. Petrodollars and the Different Growth Performance of Industrial and Middle-Income Countries in the 1970s. In *[Chenery, H. B.],* 1984, pp. 363–90. [G: OECD; MDCs]

Cantarelli, Davide and Bressan, Franco. Diseguaglianze regionali e sviluppo economico: un'analisi econometrica "internazionale." (Regional Inequalities and Economic Development: An "International" Econometric Analysis. With English summary.) *Giorn. Econ.,* March–April 1984, 43(3–4), pp. 161–89. [G: Global]

Christensen, Laurits R. The Diffusion of Economic Growth in the World Economy, 1950–80: Comment. In *Kendrick, J. W., ed.,* 1984, pp. 153–56. [G: Global]

Chung, In-Uk and Jung, W. S. The Currency Ratio with Inflation and Economic Growth. *J. Econ. Devel.,* July 1984, 9(1), pp. 77–90.

Coale, Ansley J. The Demographic Transition. *Pakistan Devel. Rev.,* Winter 1984, 23(4), pp. 531–52. [G: OECD; LDCs]

Crafts, N. F. R. Patterns of Development in Nineteenth Century Europe. *Oxford Econ. Pap.,* November 1984, 36(3), pp. 438–58. [G: Europe]

Csizmadia, Magdolna, Jr.; Ehrlich, Éva and Pártos, Gyula. The Effects of Recession on Infrastructure. *Acta Oecon.,* 1984, 32(3–4), pp. 317–42. [G: Selected Countries]

Culbertson, William Patterson, Jr. and Amacher, Ryan C. Inflation in the Planned Economies: Reply [Inflation in the Planned Economies: Some Estimates for Eastern Europe]. *Southern Econ. J.,* October 1984, 51(2), pp. 613–14. [G: E. Europe]

Drechsler, Laszlo. International Comparisons of Real Product and of Purchasing Power Parities. A Review of the Development of the Methodology. *Econ. Int.,* August–November 1984, 37(3–4), pp. 280–87. [G: Global]

Farrell, John P. Inflation in the Planned Economies: Comment [Inflation in the Planned Economies: Some Estimates for Eastern Europe]. *Southern Econ. J.,* October 1984, 51(2), pp. 603–12. [G: E. Europe]

Frey, Bruno S. and Weck-Hanneman, Hannelore. The Hidden Economy as an 'Unobserved' Variable. *Europ. Econ. Rev.,* October–November 1984, 26(1–2), pp. 33–53. [G: OECD]

Gaudard, Gaston; Caille, Pierre and Donzé, Laurent. La transformation de l'inégalité économique internationale. (The Change of International Economic Equality. With English summary.) *Schweiz. Z. Volkswirtsch. Statist.,* June 1984, 120(2), pp. 141–67. [G: Global]

Glezakos, Constantine. Export Instability and Economic Growth: Reply. *Econ. Develop. Cult. Change,* April 1984, 32(3), pp. 615–23. [G: LDCs; MDCs]

Goldsmith, Raymond W. National Balance Sheets as Tools of International Economic Comparisons. In *[Reynolds, L. G.],* 1984, pp. 280–301. [G: Selected Countries]

Goldsmith, Raymond W. The Stability of the Ratio of Nonfinancial Debt to Income. *Banca Naz. Lavoro Quart. Rev.,* September 1984, (150), pp. 285–305.

Haraszti, Katalin. Long-term Models at Work: Comparison with Other Countries. In *Augusztinovics, M., ed.,* 1984, pp. 319–48. [G: Hungary; U.S.; W. Europe]

Harberger, Arnold C. Economic Policy and Economic Growth. In *Harberger, A. C., ed.,* 1984, pp. 427–66. [G: MDCs; LDCs]

Harberger, Arnold C. World Economic Growth: Introduction. In *Harberger, A. C., ed.,* 1984, pp. 3–9.

Heller, H. Robert, et al. Economic Outlook. *Contemp. Policy Issue,* Fall 1984-85, 3(1), pp. 15–52. [G: Global]

Keren, Michael and Weinblatt, J. A Geometrical

Approach to Real Income Comparisons: A Comment on Samuelson's 'Analytical Notes on International Real-Income Measures.' *Econ. J.*, June 1984, *94*(374), pp. 258–64.

Kogut, Edy Luiz and Langoni, Carlos Geraldo. Population Growth, Income Distribution and Economic Development. In *Ghosh, P. K., ed., no. 5*, 1984, *1975*, pp. 147–60. **[G: Latin America; U.S.]**

Kravis, Irving B. and Lipsey, Robert E. The Diffusion of Economic Growth in the World Economy, 1950–80. In *Kendrick, J. W., ed.*, 1984, pp. 109–51. **[G: Global]**

Krueger, Anne O. Comparative Advantage and Development Policy 20 Years Later. In *[Chenery, H. B.]*, 1984, pp. 135–56. **[G: LDCs; MDCs]**

Leff, Nathaniel H. Dependency Rates and Savings: Another Look [Dependency Rates and Aggregate Savings: A New International Cross-Section Study]. *Amer. Econ. Rev.*, March 1984, *74*(1), pp. 231–33. **[G: LDCs; MCDs]**

Lempérière, J. La restructuration des échanges internationaux. (The Restructuring of Trade. With English summary.) *Écon. Soc.*, June 1984, *18*(6), pp. 21–58. **[G: Global]**

Leontief, Wassily. Population Growth and Economic Development: Illustrative Projections. In *Ghosh, P. K., ed., no. 5*, 1984, *1979*, pp. 221–46. **[G: Global]**

Lipietz, Alain. Le fordisme périphérique étranglé par le monétarisme central. (Peripheral Fordism Choked by Central Monetarism. With English summary.) *L'Actual. Econ.*, March 1984, *60*(1), pp. 72–94. **[G: Global]**

Madeuf, B. and Ominami, C. Nouvelle D.I.T. et Keynésianisme planétaire: la fin des illusions. (New International Division of Labour and Worldwide Keynesianism: The End of the Illusions. With English summary.) *Écon. Soc.*, June 1984, *18*(6), pp. 81–98. **[G: Global]**

Marczewski, Jean. Le concept de coût macroéconomique et son utilité. (The Concept of Macroeconomic Cost and Its Utility. With English summary.) *Écon. Appl.*, 1984, *37*(3–4), pp. 457–88. **[G: France; W. Germany]**

Marsden, Keith. Global Development Strategies and the Poor: Alternative Scenarios. In *Ghosh, P. K., ed., no. 8*, 1984, *1978*, pp. 58–83. **[G: Global]**

Marsden, Keith. Progressive Technologies for Developing Countries. In *Ghosh, P. K., ed., no. 3*, 1984, *1970*, pp. 292–324. **[G: Japan; Middle East]**

Mokyr, Joel. Disparities, Gaps, and Abysses: Review Article. *Econ. Develop. Cult. Change*, October 1984, *33*(1), pp. 173–77. **[G: Global]**

Morrisson, Christian. Income Distribution in East European and Western Countries. *J. Compar. Econ.*, June 1984, *8*(2), pp. 121–38. **[G: Europe; Canada; U.S.]**

Murray, David. The Importance of Supply and Demand Variations in Earnings Instability: Reply. *Econ. Develop. Cult. Change*, October 1984, *33*(1), pp. 171–72.

Okólski, Marek and Winiecki, Jan. Structural

Change and Adaptation: On Reintegrating Planned Economies into the World Economy. *Konjunkturpolitik*, 1984, *30*(2/3), pp. 148–69. **[G: Europe]**

Ortona, Guido. Qualche dato e qualche ipotesi sulla relazione fra tasso di inflazione e livello di sviluppo nei paesi OCDE. (Inflation Rate and Development Level: Some Data and Some Hypotheses for OECD Countries. With English summary.) *Econ. Lavoro*, July-Sept. 1984, *18*(3), pp. 23–46. **[G: Global]**

Pryor, Frederic L. A Quantitative Study of the Structure and Behavior of Consumption and Prices in Different Economic Systems. In *Bohnet, A., ed.*, 1984, pp. 213–46. **[G: Selected Countries]**

Psacharopoulos, George. The Contribution of Education to Economic Growth: International Comparisons. In *Kendrick, J. W., ed.*, 1984, pp. 335–55. **[G: Selected Countries]**

Raj, K. N. The Causes and Consequences of World Recession. In *Jolly, R. and Cornia, G. A., eds.*, 1984, pp. 7–15. **[G: MDCs; LDCs]**

Ram, Rati. Dependency Rates and Savings: Reply. *Amer. Econ. Rev.*, March 1984, *74*(1), pp. 234–37. **[G: LDCs; MCDs]**

Ram, Rati. Further International Evidence on Inflation–Output Trade-offs. *Can. J. Econ.*, August 1984, *17*(3), pp. 523–40. **[G: Global]**

Ram, Rati. Market Opportunities, Intrafamily Resource Allocation, and Sex-Specific Survival Rates: An Intercountry Extension. *Amer. Econ. Rev.*, December 1984, *74*(5), pp. 1080–86. **[G: U.S.; OECD; LDCs]**

Ram, Rati. Population Increase, Economic Growth, Educational Inequality, and Income Distribution: Some Recent Evidence. *J. Devel. Econ.*, April 1984, *14*(3), pp. 419–28.

Samuelson, Paul A. Second Thoughts on Analytical Income Comparisons. *Econ. J.*, June 1984, *94*(374), pp. 267–78.

Savvides, Andreas. Export Instability and Economic Growth: Some New Evidence. *Econ. Develop. Cult. Change*, April 1984, *32*(3), pp. 607–14. **[G: LDCs; MDCs]**

Schultz, Theodore W. A Comment on Education and Economic Growth. In *Kendrick, J. W., ed.*, 1984, pp. 357–60. **[G: Selected Countries]**

Sheehan, Glen and Hopkins, Mike. Meeting Basic Needs: An Examination of the World Situation in 1970. In *Ghosh, P. K., ed., no. 13*, 1984, *1978*, pp. 85–107.

Shen, T. Y. The Estimation of X-Inefficiency in Eighteen Countries. *Rev. Econ. Statist.*, February 1984, *66*(1), pp. 98–104. **[G: Selected Countries]**

Singer, Hans W. Success Stories of the 1970s: Some Correlations. *World Devel.*, September 1984, *12*(9), pp. 951–52.

Sinha, Radha. Culture and Economy: Human Betterment in India and Japan. In *Boulding, K. E., ed.*, 1984, pp. 87–104. **[G: India; Japan; OECD]**

Streeten, Paul. Technology Gaps between Rich

and Poor Countries. In *Ghosh, P. K., ed., no. 3, 1984, 1972,* pp. 7–26. [G: MDCs]

Stuart, Robert C. Wheat Yields in Socialist and Capitalist Economic Systems: A Statistical Comparison. *ACES Bull.,* Spring 1984, *26*(1), pp. 77–85.

Summers, Robert and Heston, Alan. Improved International Comparisons of Real Product and Its Composition: 1950–1980. *Rev. Income Wealth,* June 1984, *30*(2), pp. 207–62.
[G: Global]

Swamy, Subramanian. Samuelson's Analytical Notes on International Real-Income Measures: A Comment. *Econ. J.,* June 1984, *94*(374), pp. 265–66.

Syrquin, Moshe. Resource Reallocation and Productivity Growth. In *[Chenery, H. B.],* 1984, pp. 75–101. [G: OECD; LDCs; Hungary]

Szarvas, Péter. Capital Formation in Hungary in International Comparison. *Acta Oecon.,* 1984, *32*(3–4), pp. 303–16. [G: Selected Countries]

Szilágyi, György. International Comparisons—Types and Methods. *Statist. J.,* December 1984, *2*(4), pp. 345–55.

Szilágyi, György. Procedures for Updating the Results of International Comparisons. *Rev. Income Wealth,* June 1984, *30*(2), pp. 153–65.
[G: Europe; U.S.]

124 Economic Studies of Centrally Planned Economies

1240 General

White, Gordon. Developmental States and Socialist Industrialisation in the Third World. In *Kaplinsky, R., ed.,* 1984, pp. 97–120.
[G: E. Europe; China; LDCs]

Brada, Josef C. and Montias, John Michael. Industrial Policy in Eastern Europe: A Three-Country Comparison. *J. Compar. Econ.,* December 1984, *8*(4), pp. 377–419.
[G: Czechoslovakia; Poland; Hungary]

White, Gordon. Developmental States and Socialist Industrialisation in the Third World. *J. Devel. Stud.,* October 1984, *21*(1), pp. 97–120.
[G: Selected Global]

1243 European Countries

Balázsy, Sándor. Reform and Property: Reflections on Tamás Bauer's Article. *Eastern Europ. Econ.,* Spring–Summer 1984, *22*(3–4), pp. 88–101. [G: Hungary; CMEA]

Bálek, Alexej. The Problems and Reserves of the Czechoslovak Economy. *Czech. Econ. Pap.,* 1984, (22), pp. 7–23. [G: Czechoslovakia]

Bandera, V. N. Capital Accumulation and Growth in a Mixed Socialist Economy: The Case of Soviet NEP. *J. Europ. Econ. Hist.,* Spring 1984, *13*(1), pp. 7–27. [G: U.S.S.R.]

Bauer, Tamás. The Second Economic Reform and Ownership Relations: Some Considerations for the Further Development of the New Economic Mechanism. *Eastern Europ. Econ.,* Spring–Summer 1984, *22*(3–4), pp. 33–87.
[G: CMEA; Hungary]

Bélyácz, Iván. Investment Policy and Structural Transformation in Hungary. *Acta Oecon.,* 1984, *33*(3–4), pp. 273–91. [G: Hungary]

Brada, Josef C.; Jackson, Marvin R. and King, Arthur E. The Romanian Balance of Payments Crisis: An Econometric Study of its Causes and Cures. In *Jackson, M. R. and Woodson, J. D., Jr., eds.,* 1984, pp. 23–53. [G: Romania]

Durgin, Frank. USSR in Crisis: The Failure of an Economic System: Review Article. *ACES Bull.,* Summer–Fall 1984, *26*(2–3), pp. 99–110.
[G: U.S.S.R.]

Durgin, Frank. The USSR in Crisis: A Reply to a Reply. *ACES Bull.,* Winter 1984, *26*(4), pp. 55–64. [G: U.S.S.R.]

Elliott, John E. Contending Perspectives on the Nature of Soviet Economic Society. *Int. J. Soc. Econ.,* 1984, *11*(5), pp. 40–61. [G: U.S.S.R.]

Ellman, Michael. Did the Agricultural Surplus Provide the Resources for the Increase in Investment in the USSR 1928–32? In *Ellman, M.,* 1984, *1975,* pp. 27–53. [G: U.S.S.R.]

Ellman, Michael. Did Soviet Economic Growth End in 1978? In *Ellman, M.,* 1984, *1982,* pp. 135–45. [G: U.S.S.R.]

Ellman, Michael. Seven Theses on Kosyginism. In *Ellman, M.,* 1984, *1977,* pp. 75–96.
[G: U.S.S.R.]

Faluvégi, Lajos. Economic Efficiency, Control and Management. *Acta Oecon.,* 1984, *33*(3–4), pp. 201–20. [G: Hungary]

Goldman, Marshall I. USSR in Crisis: The Failure of an Economic System: Review Article: Reply. *ACES Bull.,* Summer–Fall 1984, *26*(2–3), pp. 111–16. [G: U.S.S.R.]

Goldman, Marshall I. Reply to a Reply to a Reply [The USSR in Crisis]. *ACES Bull.,* Winter 1984, *26*(4), pp. 69–71. [G: U.S.S.R.]

Goldman, Marshall I. The Failure of Soviet Leadership. *Challenge,* May/June 1984, *27*(2), pp. 4–10. [G: U.S.S.R.]

Granberg, A. G. The Economic Interaction of Soviet Republics. *Prob. Econ.,* January 1984, *26*(9), pp. 3–25. [G: U.S.S.R.]

Gray, Kenneth R. The USSR in Crisis: Comment. *ACES Bull.,* Winter 1984, *26*(4), pp. 65–67.
[G: U.S.S.R.]

Havasi, Ferenc. Further Development of the System of Economic Control and Management in Hungary. *Acta Oecon.,* 1984, *32*(3–4), pp. 199–221. [G: Hungary]

Houston, David B. Poland's Economic Crisis. *Eastern Econ. J.,* October-December 1984, *10*(4), pp. 441–54. [G: Poland]

Jakeš, Miloš. Fulfilment of the Program of the 16th Congress of the Communist Party of Czechoslovakia. *Czech. Econ. Digest.,* December 1984, (8), pp. 63–95.
[G: Czechoslovakia]

Kádár, Béla. The External Economic Framework and the Conditions of Accelerating Hungarian Growth. *Acta Oecon.,* 1984, *33*(1–2), pp. 89–104. [G: Hungary]

Kaser, Michael C. Human Betterment in a Planned Economy—The Case of the Soviet

Union. In *Boulding, K. E., ed.*, 1984, pp. 71–86. **[G: U.S.S.R.]**

Kemme, David M. and Crane, Keith. The Polish Economic Collapse: Contributing Factors and Economic Costs. *J. Compar. Econ.*, March 1984, *8*(1), pp. 25–40. **[G: Poland]**

Kheinman, S. The Production and Scientific Potential of the USSR. *Prob. Econ.*, February 1984, *26*(10), pp. 50–67. **[G: U.S.S.R.]**

Köves, András. On New Trends in International Industrial Development and the Division of Labour. *Acta Oecon.*, 1984, *33*(1–2), pp. 147–53. **[G: Hungary]**

Lackó, Mária. Behavioral Rules in the Distribution of Sectoral Investments in Hungary, 1951–1980. *J. Compar. Econ.*, September 1984, *8*(3), pp. 290–300. **[G: Hungary]**

Loginov, V. P. Trends and Factors in the Intensification of the Economy. *Prob. Econ.*, March 1984, *26*(11), pp. 27–39. **[G: U.S.S.R.]**

Mănescu, Manea. Forty Years of Outstanding Successes in the Socio-economic Development of Romania, 1944–1984. *Econ. Computat. Cybern. Stud. Res.*, 1984, *19*(2), pp. 5–10. **[G: Romania]**

Mănescu, Manea. President Nicolae Ceauşescu's Report—A Revolutionary Scientific Construction of Genius—An Ample Programme for Romania's Development on New Peaks of Progress and Civilization. *Econ. Computat. Cybern. Stud. Res.*, 1984, *19*(4), pp. 7–12. **[G: Romania]**

Martinka, Karol. The 40th Anniversary of the Slovak National Uprising and the Socio-economic Development of Slovakia. *Czech. Econ. Digest.*, December 1984, (8), pp. 96–124. **[G: Czechoslovakia]**

Matějka, Ladislav. Importance of the Complex of Measures for Intensification of the Czechoslovak National Economy. *Czech. Econ. Digest.*, February 1984, (1), pp. 26–50. **[G: Czechoslovakia]**

Mirochnichenko, V. L. and Parinov, S. I. Analyzing Economic Growth Using Spline Macroeconomic Production Functions. *Matekon*, Winter 1984–85, *21*(2), pp. 68–89. **[G: U.S.S.R.]**

Nechemias, Carol and Bahry, Donna. The Soviet Union: Consumer Sector. In *Groth, A. J. and Wade, L. L., eds.*, 1984, pp. 101–26. **[G: U.S.S.R.]**

Nyers, Rezso and Tardos, Márton. The Necessity for Consolidation of the Economy and the Possibility of Development in Hungary. *Acta Oecon.*, 1984, *32*(1–2), pp. 1–19. **[G: Hungary]**

Pajestka, Józef. Some Basic Premises for Development: The Eastern European Experience. In *Ngo, M., ed., vol. 2*, 1984, pp. 830–44. **[G: E. Europe]**

Rába, András. Restriction and Adjustment. *Acta Oecon.*, 1984, *33*(1–2), pp. 69–87. **[G: Hungary]**

Rowen, Henry S. Central Intelligence Agency Briefing on the Soviet Economy. In *Hoffmann, E. P. and Laird, R. F., eds.*, 1984, pp. 417–46. **[G: U.S.S.R.]**

Rowen, Henry S. The Soviet Economy. In *Hoffmann, E. P., ed.*, 1984, *1982*, pp. 32–48. **[G: U.S.S.R.]**

Rowen, Henry S. The Soviet Economy: Strengths and Weaknesses. In *Shaffer, H. G., ed.*, 1984, *1982*, pp. 349–69. **[G: U.S.S.R.]**

Ruble, Blair A. Muddling Through. In *Hoffmann, E. P. and Laird, R. F., eds.*, 1984, pp. 903–14. **[G: U.S.S.R.]**

Shaffer, Harry G. Soviet Economic Performance Under the Plan. In *Shaffer, H. G., ed.*, 1984, pp. 328–44. **[G: U.S.S.R.]**

Siline, Anatole. The New Role of Workers' Collectives in the USSR. *Int. Lab. Rev.*, November–December 1984, *123*(6), pp. 743–52. **[G: U.S.S.R.]**

Smyshliaeva, L. Improving the Structure of Reproduction of Capital Investments. *Prob. Econ.*, July 1984, *27*(3), pp. 61–79. **[G: U.S.S.R.]**

Soják, Zbyněk. Intensification of the Economy—A Strategic Task of the Economic Policy of the Party. *Czech. Econ. Digest.*, February 1984, (1), pp. 3–25. **[G: Czechoslovakia]**

Tardos, Márton. A Development Program for Economic Control and Organization in Hungary. *Eastern Europ. Econ.*, Spring–Summer 1984, *22*(3–4), pp. 3–32. **[G: Hungary]**

Wiedemann, Paul. Comparing the Process of Socio-economic Development in Market and Non-market Economies: The EEC and CMEA. *Cambridge J. Econ.*, December 1984, *8*(4), pp. 311–30. **[G: EEC; CMEA]**

Zala, Julia. Hungary: How to Live with Slow-Growth Conditions: Adaptations of Economic Conditions and Management. *Eastern Europ. Econ.*, Spring–Summer 1984, *22*(3–4), pp. 122–53. **[G: Hungary]**

Zala, Julia. Protection of the Price Level and a Dynamic Economy. *Acta Oecon.*, 1984, *33*(3–4), pp. 237–54. **[G: Hungary]**

1244 Asian Countries

Bronfenbrenner, Martin. China since Mao: A Great Leap Backward? *Atlantic Econ. J.*, March 1984, *12*(1), pp. 1–11. **[G: China]**

Deng, Huansong. On the Duality of Price Subsidy and the Path to Its Reform. *Chinese Econ. Stud.*, Fall 1984, *18*(1), pp. 3–13. **[G: China]**

Kueh, Yak-Yeow. China's New Agricultural-Policy Program: Major Economic Consequences, 1979–1983. *J. Compar. Econ.*, December 1984, *8*(4), pp. 353–75. **[G: China]**

Mandle, J. R. Strategies of Change in Paternalistic Socialism: The Case of China. *Int. J. Soc. Econ.*, 1984, *11*(3/4), pp. 3–11. **[G: China]**

Martellaro, Joseph A. China's Two Economies and the USA Factor. *Rivista Int. Sci. Econ. Com.*, September 1984, *31*(9), pp. 875–97. **[G: China; Taiwan]**

Naya, Seiji. Effects of External Shocks on the Balance of Payments, Policy Responses and Debt Problems of Asian Developing Countries. *Philippine Econ. J.*, Winter 1984, *23*(1), pp. 23–49. **[G: Asia]**

Nolan, Peter and White, Gordon. Urban Bias, Rural Bias or State Bias? Urban–Rural Relations in Post-Revolutionary China. *J. Devel. Stud.*, April 1984, *20*(3), pp. 52–81.
[G: China]

Reynolds, Bruce. China in the International Economy. In *Harding, H., ed.*, 1984, pp. 71–106.
[G: China]

Sun, Yefang. To Raise Production Four-Fold in Two Decades Is Not Only Politically Probable but Technologically Feasible. *Chinese Econ. Stud.*, Winter 1983–84, *17*(2), pp. 50–67.
[G: China]

Zagoria, Donald S. China's Quiet Revolution. *Foreign Aff.*, Spring 1984, *62*(4), pp. 879–904.
[G: China]

1246 Latin American and Caribbean Countries

Gutierrez Muniz, José A., et al. The Recent Worldwide Economic Crisis and the Welfare of Children: The Case of Cuba. *World Devel.*, March 1984, *12*(3), pp. 247–60.   [G: Cuba]

130 ECONOMIC FLUCTUATIONS; FORECASTING; STABILIZATION; AND INFLATION

131 Economic Fluctuations

1310 Economic Fluctuations: General

Chu, Ke-young and Morrison, Thomas K. The 1981–82 Recession and Non-Oil Primary Commodity Prices. *Int. Monet. Fund Staff Pap.*, March 1984, *31*(1), pp. 93–140.

Coombs, R. W. Long-term Trends in Automation. In *Marstrand, P., ed.*, 1984, pp. 146–62.
[G: U.K.; MDCs]

DeCanio, Stephen J. Expectations and Business Confidence during the Great Depression. In *Siegel, B. N., ed.*, 1984, pp. 157–75.
[G: U.S.]

Freeman, Christopher. Keynes or Kondratiev? How Can We Get Back to Full Employment? In *Marstrand, P., ed.*, 1984, pp. 103–23.
[G: U.K.]

Frey, Bruno S. Politico-Economic Models and Cycles. In *Buchanan, J. M. and Tollison, R. D., eds.*, 1984, pp. 305–22.   [G: U.S.; U.K.; W. Germany]

van der Ploeg, Frederick. Government Ideology and Re-election Efforts. *Oxford Econ. Pap.*, June 1984, *36*(2), pp. 213–31.

Steinmann, Gunter. A Model of the History of Demographic-Economic Growth. In *Steinmann, G., ed.*, 1984, pp. 29–49.

Tsuru, Tsuyoshi. S. Bowles *et al.* on Stagflation: A Commentary. *Hitotsubashi J. Econ.*, December 1984, *25*(2), pp. 173–82.   [G: U.S.]

Wagner, Richard E. Boom and Bust: The Political Economy of Economic Disorder. In *Buchanan, J. M. and Tollison, R. D., eds.*, 1984, pp. 238–72.

Wainhouse, Charles E. Empirical Evidence for Hayek's Theory of Economic Fluctuations. In *Siegel, B. N., ed.*, 1984, pp. 37–71.
[G: U.S.]

Yaun, P. J. Econometric and Empirical Evidence on the Relationship between Survey Data and Official Data and its Relevance for Monitoring the Business Cycle. In *Oppenländer, K. H. and Poser, G., eds.*, 1984, pp. 47–66.
[G: U.K.]

1312 Economic Fluctuations: Theory

Balducci, Renato; Candela, G. and Ricci, G. A Generalization of R. Goodwin Model with Rational Behavior of Economic Agents. In *Goodwin, R. M.; Krüger, M. and Vercelli, A., eds.*, 1984, pp. 47–66.

Barro, Robert J. and King, Robert G. Time-separable Preferences and Intertemporal-Substitution Models of Business Cycles. *Quart. J. Econ.*, November 1984, *99*(4), pp. 817–39.

Benassy, Jean-Pascal. A Non-Walrasian Model of the Business Cycle. *J. Econ. Behav. Organ.*, March 1984, *5*(1), pp. 77–89.

Boitani, Andrea. Two Views on Oligopoly and Stagnation. *Econ. Notes*, 1984, (3), pp. 128–54.

Boshoff, C. H. Structural Bottlenecks and a Shift in Economic Theory: Its Implication for Monitoring Business Cycles in South Africa. *J. Stud. Econ. Econometrics*, March 1984, (19), pp. 19–30.   [G: S. Africa]

Bukh, E. M.; Alexandrov, L. A. and Lebedev, V. N. Interpretations of Reproduction. In *Smirnov, A. D.; Golosov, V. V. and Maximova, V. F., eds.*, 1984, pp. 118–36.

Checchi, Daniele. Some Notes Regarding Goodwin's Model "A Growth Cycle." *Econ. Notes*, 1984, (1), pp. 121–35.

Cigno, Alessandro. Consumption vs. Procreation in Economic Growth. In *Steinmann, G., ed.*, 1984, pp. 2–28.

Coppe, A. The "Long Wave" Is Not a Wave. *Tijdschrift Econ. Manage.*, 1984, *29*(3), pp. 337–49.   [G: U.S.; W. Germany]

Costrell, Robert M. Equilibrium Unemployment and Excess Capacity in Steady-State and Growth Cycles. *Economica*, February 1984, *51*(201), pp. 69–82.

Cugno, Franco and Montrucchio, Luigi. Some New Techniques for Modelling Nonlinear Economic Fluctuations: A Brief Survey. In *Goodwin, R. M.; Krüger, M. and Vercelli, A., eds.*, 1984, pp. 146–65.

Cugno, Franco and Montrucchio, Luigi. Teorema della ragnatela, aspettative adattive e dinamiche caotiche. (Cobweb Theorem, Adaptive Expectations and Chaotic Dynamics. With English summary.) *Rivista Int. Sci. Econ. Com.*, August 1984, *31*(8), pp. 713–24.

Demery, David and Duck, Nigel W. Inventories and Monetary Growth in the Business Cycle: Some Theoretical Considerations and Empirical Results for the U.K. *Manchester Sch. Econ. Soc. Stud.*, December 1984, *52*(4), pp. 363–79.   [G: U.K.]

Eichenbaum, Martin S. Rational Expectations and the Smoothing Properties of Inventories of Finished Goods. *J. Monet. Econ.*, July 1984, *14*(1), pp. 71–96. **[G: U.S.]**

Farmer, Roger E. A. A New Theory of Aggregate Supply. *Amer. Econ. Rev.*, December 1984, *74*(5), pp. 920–30.

Fellner, William. Monetary and Fiscal Policy in a Disinflationary Process: Justified and Unjustified Misgivings about Budget Deficits. In *Fellner, W., ed.*, 1984, pp. 55–86. **[G: U.S.]**

Fine, Ben and Murfin, Andy. The Political Economy of Monopoly and Competition: A Critique of Monopoly and Stagnation Theory. *Int. J. Ind. Organ.*, June 1984, *2*(2), pp. 133–46.

Fiorito, Riccardo. Multisectoral Inventory Cycles under Different Expectations and Technologies. *Econ. Notes*, 1984, (1), pp. 109–20. **[G: Italy]**

Flaschel, Peter. Some Stability Properties of Goodwin's Growth Cycle: A Critical Elaboration. *Z. Nationalökon.*, 1984, *44*(1), pp. 63–69.

Gabisch, Guenter. Nonlinear Models of Business Cycle Theory. In *Hammer, G. and Pallaschke, D., eds.*, 1984, pp. 205–22.

Glombowski, Jörg and Krüger, Michael. Unemployment Insurance and Cyclical Growth. In *Goodwin, R. M.; Krüger, M. and Vercelli, A., eds.*, 1984, pp. 25–46.

Goodwin, R. M. Disaggregating Models of Fluctuating Growth. In *Goodwin, R. M.; Krüger, M. and Vercelli, A., eds.*, 1984, pp. 67–72.

Gordon, Robert J. Using Monetary Control to Dampen the Business Cycle: A New Set of First Principles. In *Wachter, M. L. and Wachter, S. M., eds.*, 1984, pp. 302–36. **[G: U.S.]**

Greenwald, Bruce C.; Stiglitz, Joseph E. and Weiss, Andrew. Informational Imperfections in the Capital Market and Macroeconomic Fluctuations. *Amer. Econ. Rev.*, May 1984, *74*(2), pp. 194–99.

Hammond, Peter J. What to Do about Business Cycles? In *Seidl, C., ed.*, 1984, pp. 59–75.

Heckman, James J. Comments on the Ashenfelter and Kydland Papers [Macroeconomic Analyses and Microeconomic Analyses of Labor Supply] [Labor-Force Heterogeneity and the Business Cycle]. *Carnegie-Rochester Conf. Ser. Public Policy*, Autumn 1984, *21*, pp. 209–24.

Hunt, Lacy H. Using Monetary Control to Dampen the Business Cycle: A New Set of First Principles: Comment. In *Wachter, M. L. and Wachter, S. M., eds.*, 1984, pp. 341–44. **[G: U.S.]**

Jaeger, Klaus. Persistenz und zyklische Schwankungen der Unterbeschäftigung in Gleichgewichtsmodellen mit rationalen Erwartungen. (Persistence and Cyclical Movements of Unemployment in Equilibrium Models with Rational Expectations. With English summary.) *Z. Wirtschaft. Sozialwissen.*, 1984, *104*(6), pp. 645–73.

Kalecki, Michal. The Mechanism of the Business

Upswing. In *Foster, J. B. and Szlajfer, H., eds.*, 1984, *1966*, pp. 127–33.

King, Robert G. and Plosser, Charles I. Money, Credit, and Prices in a Real Business Cycle. *Amer. Econ. Rev.*, June 1984, *74*(3), pp. 363–80. **[G: U.S.]**

Krelle, Wilhelm. Waves of Entrepreneurial Activity Induced by Transfer of Information and Valuation. *Z. Nationalökon.*, Supplement 1984, pp. 71–92.

Kydland, Finn E. A Clarification: Using the Growth Model to Account for Fluctuations: Reply [Labor-Force Heterogeneity and the Business Cycle]. *Carnegie-Rochester Conf. Ser. Public Policy*, Autumn 1984, *21*, pp. 225–30.

Kydland, Finn E. Labor-Force Heterogeneity and the Business Cycle. *Carnegie-Rochester Conf. Ser. Public Policy*, Autumn 1984, *21*, pp. 173–208.

Lächler, Ulrich. The Political Business Cycle under Rational Voting Behavior. *Public Choice*, 1984, *44*(3), pp. 411–30.

Lenel, Hans Otto. Ein dritter Weg? Zu Ota Šiks "Hummaner Wirtschaftsdemokratie." (With English Summary.) In *Eucken, W. and Böhm, F., eds.*, 1984, pp. 179–230.

Martinengo, G. Notes on Financial Instability and Effective Demand. *Metroecon.*, June-Oct. 1984, *36*(2–3), pp. 176–201.

Medio, A. Synergetics and Dynamic Economic Models. In *Goodwin, R. M.; Krüger, M. and Vercelli, A., eds.*, 1984, pp. 166–91.

Möller, Hans. "Wirtschaftliche Sättigung" im Lichte der ökonomischen Theorie. ("Economic Glut" in the Light of Economic Theory. With English summary.) *Ifo-Studien*, 1984, *30*(3), pp. 171–92. **[G: W. Germany]**

Montgomery, Edward. Aggregate Dynamics and Staggered Contracts: A Test of the Importance of Spillover Effects: A Note. *J. Money, Credit, Banking*, Part 1 November 1984, *16*(4), pp. 505–14. **[G: U.S.]**

von Natzmer, Wulfheinrich and Reim, O. Wirtschaftspolitik und Konjunktur in einem modifizierten ISLM-Modell. (Economic Policy and the Business Cycle in a Modified ISLM Model. With English summary.) *Kredit Kapital*, 1984, *17*(3), pp. 371–95.

Peiwel, George R. Equilibrium Business Cycle Theory and the Real World: Part I. *Economia (Portugal)*, May 1984, *8*(2), pp. 333–60.

van der Ploeg, Frederick. Macro-Dynamic Theories of Economic Growth and Fluctuations. In *van der Ploeg, F., ed.*, 1984, pp. 249–85.

Poole, William. Government Deficit and Business Cycle: Comment. In *Wachter, M. L. and Wachter, S. M., eds.*, 1984, pp. 346–49. **[G: U.S.]**

Powers, Charles H. Sociopolitical Determinants of Economic Cycles: Vilfredo Pareto's Final Statement. *Soc. Sci. Quart.*, December 1984, *65*(4), pp. 988–1001.

Presley, J. R. D. H. Robertson: Some Restoration. *J. Post Keynesian Econ.*, Winter 1983-84, *6*(2), pp. 230–40.

Ramsey, James B. and Alexander, Albert. The

Econometric Approach to Business-Cycle Analysis Reconsidered. *J. Macroecon.*, Summer 1984, *6*(3), pp. 347–55.

Reetz, Norbert. Österreichische Kapitaltheorie, neoklassisches Wachstum und Konjunktur. (Austrian Capital Theory, Neoclassical Growth, and Business Cycles. With English summary.) *Schweiz. Z. Volkswirtsch. Statist.*, March 1984, *120*(1), pp. 1–30.

Rosenberg, Nathan and Frischtak, Claudio R. Technological Innovation and Long Waves. *Cambridge J. Econ.*, March 1984, *8*(1), pp. 7–24.

Saint-Étienne, Christian. De l'importance réelle de l'hypothèse de la rationalitè des anticipations. (With English summary.) *Revue Écon. Polit.*, November–December 1984, *94*(6), pp. 773–91.

Silverberg, Gerald. Embodied Technical Progress in a Dynamic Economic Model: The Self-Organization Paradigm. In *Goodwin, R. M.; Krüger, M. and Vercelli, A., eds.*, 1984, pp. 192–208.

Simon, Herbert A. On the Behavioral and Rational Foundations of Economic Dynamics. *J. Econ. Behav. Organ.*, March 1984, *5*(1), pp. 35–55.

Sørensen, Peter Birch. Countercyclical versus Passive Monetary Policy in a Medium-run Macro Model. *Scand. J. Econ.*, 1984, *86*(4), pp. 452–67.

Sylos-Labini, Paolo. Keynes's *General Theory* and the Great Depression. In *Sylos-Labini, P.*, 1984, pp. 227–43. [G: U.S.]

Sylos-Labini, Paolo. New Aspects of the Cyclical Development of the Economy. *Banca Naz. Lavoro Quart. Rev.*, March 1984, (148), pp. 15–31. [G: Italy]

Thio, K. B. T. Cyclical and Structural Aspects of Unemployment and Growth in a Nonlinear Model of Cyclical Growth. In *Goodwin, R. M.; Krüger, M. and Vercelli, A., eds.*, 1984, pp. 127–45.

Tichy, Gunther. Schumpeter's Business Cycle Theory: Its Importance for Our Time. In *Seidl, C., ed.*, 1984, pp. 77–88.

Vercelli, Alessandro. Fluctuations and Growth: Keynes, Schumpeter, Marx and the Structural Instability of Capitalism. In *Goodwin, R. M.; Krüger, M. and Vercelli, A., eds.*, 1984, pp. 209–31.

Vicarelli, F. Stagflation in the Seventies: A Relative Prices Theoretical Approach. *Metroecon.*, June-Oct. 1984, *36*(2–3), pp. 127–41. [G: OECD]

Wentzler, Nancy A. Inflation, Expectations, and Cyclical Aggravations. *Atlantic Econ. J.*, December 1984, *12*(4), pp. 51–54.

Wood, J. Stuart. Some Refinements in Austrian Trade-Cycle Theory. *Managerial Dec. Econ.*, September 1984, *5*(3), pp. 141–49.

Yellen, Janet L. Efficiency Wage Models of Unemployment. *Amer. Econ. Rev.*, May 1984, *74*(2), pp. 200–205.

1313 Economic Fluctuations: Studies

Allen, Larry and Price, Don. Variations in the Flow of Credit from Regional Financial Institutions as a Source of Cyclical Instability in the Regional Economy: An Application of Causal Analysis. *Reg. Sci. Persp.*, 1984, *14*(2), pp. 3–14. [G: U.S.]

Aukrust, Odd. 1980-årenes okonomi sammenlignet med 1930-årenes—tallenes tale. (With English summary.) *Nationaløkon. Tidsskr.*, 1984, *122*(3), pp. 313–32. [G: U.S.; W. Europe; Nordic Countries]

Baba, M.; Nomura, N. and Tahara, S. Major Features of New Business Cycle Indicators in Japan. In *Oppenländer, K. H. and Poser, G., eds.*, 1984, pp. 605–20. [G: Japan]

Bieshaar, Hans and Kleinknecht, Alfred. Kondratieff Long Waves in Aggregate Output? An Econometric Test. *Konjunkturpolitik*, 1984, *30*(5), pp. 279–303. [G: OECD]

Blanchard, Olivier J. and Summers, Lawrence H. Perspectives on High World Real Interest Rates. *Brookings Pap. Econ. Act.*, 1984, (2), pp. 273–324. [G: U.S.; W. Europe; Japan]

Blinder, Alan S. Perspectives on High World Real Interest Rates: Comment. *Brookings Pap. Econ. Act.*, 1984, (2), pp. 325–33. [G: U.S.; W. Europe; Japan]

Blomqvist, Hans C. Stagflation—inget mysterium. (Stagflation Is No Mystery. With English summary.) *Ekon. Samfundets Tidskr.*, 1984, *37*(1), pp. 45–50. [G: Finland]

Boehm, Ernst A. Money Wages, Consumer Prices, and Causality in Australia. *Econ. Rec.*, September 1984, *60*(170), pp. 236–51. [G: Australia]

Boehm, Ernst A. and Moore, Geoffrey H. New Economic Indicators for Australia, 1949–84. *Australian Econ. Rev.*, 4th Quarter 1984, (68), pp. 34–56. [G: Australia]

Bollino, C. Andrea and Klein, Lawrence R. World Recovery Strategies in the 1980s: Is World Recovery Synonymous to LDC Recovery? *J. Policy Modeling*, May 1984, *6*(2), pp. 175–207. [G: Global]

Boltho, Andrea. Economic Policy and Performance in Europe since the Second Oil Shock. In *Emerson, M., ed.*, 1984, pp. 10–32. [G: W. Europe]

Boot, Pieter. Industrial Cycles in the German Democratic Republic and Professor Wiles' Thesis [Are There Any Communist Cycles?]. *ACES Bull.*, Spring 1984, *26*(1), pp. 1–26. [G: E. Germany]

Boskin, Michael J. U.S. Stabilization Policy: Lessons from the Past Decade: Comments. In *Harberger, A. C., ed.*, 1984, pp. 151–56. [G: U.S.]

Brada, Josef C. The Political Business Cycle and Investment Fluctuations in France. *Rivista Int. Sci. Econ. Com.*, April 1984, *31*(4), pp. 305–11. [G: France]

Broadberry, S. N. The North European Depression of the 1920s. *Scand. Econ. Hist. Rev.*, 1984, *32*(3), pp. 159–67.   [G: U.S.; Sweden; Norway; Denmark]

Bruno, Michael. Stagflation in the EC Countries 1973–1981: A Cross-sectional View. In *Emerson, M., ed.*, 1984, pp. 33–56.   [G: EEC]

Burbidge, John B. and Harrison, Alan. Testing for the Effects of Oil-Price Rises Using Vector Autoregressions. *Int. Econ. Rev.*, June 1984, *25*(2), pp. 459–84.   [G: U.S.; Japan; W. Germany; U.K.; Canada]

Cagan, Phillip. Monetary Policy and Subduing Inflation. In *Fellner, W., ed.*, 1984, pp. 21–53.   [G: U.S.]

Chand, Sheetal K. A Keynesian Fiscal Policy and the New Classical Macroeconomics. *J. Post Keynesian Econ.*, Summer 1984, *6*(4), pp. 509–22.

Chand, Sheetal K. The Stabilizing Role of Fiscal Policy. *Finance Develop.*, March 1984, *21*(1), pp. 38–41.   [G: LDCs; U.S.]

Checchi, Daniele. Una teoria del ciclo economico: esposizione e confronto con le analisi esistenti sul caso italiano. (The Economic Cycle Theory: An Exposition and a Comparison with Other Analyses on the Italian Case. With English summary.) *Giorn. Econ.*, January–February 1984, *43*(1–2), pp. 103–22.   [G: Italy]

Ciampi, Carlo Azeglio. Politica di bilancio, politica dei redditi e stabilità monetaria, presupposti di una crescita stabile. (Budget Policy, Incomes Policy and Monetary Stability as Prerequisites for Stable Growth. With English summary.) *Bancaria*, March 1984, *40*(3), pp. 241–55.   [G: Italy]

Cifarelli, Giulio. Una interpretazione macrorazionale del ciclo. (A Macrorational Interpretation of Cycle. With English summary.) *Giorn. Econ.*, May–June 1984, *43*(5–6), pp. 345–58.   [G: Italy]

Clark, Colin. Is There a Long Cycle? *Banca Naz. Lavoro Quart. Rev.*, September 1984, (150), pp. 307–20.   [G: U.S.; U.K.; Japan; Sweden]

Clark, Peter K. Productivity and Profits in the 1980s: Are They Really Improving? *Brookings Pap. Econ. Act.*, 1984, (1), pp. 133–67.   [G: U.S.]

Clauss, Franz Joachim. Über die Konjunkturabhängigkeit der statistischen Produktivität. (On the Cyclical Dependence of Productivity as Measured Statistically. With English summary.) *Ifo-Studien*, 1984, *30*(4), pp. 273–305.   [G: U.S.]

Connolly, Michael B. The Gold Standard and the Transmission of Business Cycles, 1833–1932: Comment. In *Bordo, M. D. and Schwartz, A. J., eds.*, 1984, pp. 507–11.   [G: U.S.; U.K.]

Cortés Douglas, Hernán. Lecciones del Pasado Recesiones Económicas en Chile: 1926–1982. (With English summary.) *Cuadernos Econ.*, August 1984, *21*(63), pp. 137–68.   [G: Chile]

Cripps, Francis and Ward, Terry. Erratum [European Recession and Problems of Recovery]. *Cambridge J. Econ.*, March 1984, *8*(1), pp. 115.   [G: W. Europe]

Csizmadia, Magdolna, Jr.; Ehrlich, Éva and Pártos, Gyula. The Effects of Recession on Infrastructure. *Acta Oecon.*, 1984, *32*(3–4), pp. 317–42.   [G: Selected Countries]

Devilliers, M. The Use of Business Surveys in Short-term Forecasts: The French Experience. In *Oppenländer, K. H. and Poser, G., eds.*, 1984, pp. 135–60.   [G: France]

Ducos, Gilbert and Laffont, Jean-Jacques. Stock et déséquilibre: une analyse comparative et internationale. (Inventories and Disequilibrium: A Comparative International Analysis. With English summary.) *Ann. INSEE*, July–December 1984, (55/56), pp. 183–202.   [G: U.S.; France; Canada; Japan]

Early, John F.; Schmidt, Mary Lynn and Mosimann, Thomas J. Inflation and the Business Cycle during the Postwar Period. *Mon. Lab. Rev.*, November 1984, *107*(11), pp. 3–7.   [G: U.S.]

Eliasson, Gunnar. Micro Heterogeneity of Firms and the Stability of Industrial Growth. *J. Econ. Behav. Organ.*, September–December 1984, *5*(3–4), pp. 249–74.   [G: Sweden]

Entov, R. M. Cyclical Factors behind the Movement of Prices. In *Nikitin, S. M., ed.*, 1984, pp. 126–78.   [G: U.S.]

Farber, Stephen C. Cyclical Price Flexibility: A Test of Administered Pricing. *J. Ind. Econ.*, June 1984, *32*(4), pp. 465–76.   [G: U.S.]

Foss, Murray F. Corporate Liquidity under Stagflation and Disinflation. In *Fellner, W., ed.*, 1984, pp. 205–45.   [G: U.S.]

Friedman, Milton. Monetary Policy for the 1980s. In *Moore, J. H., ed.*, 1984, pp. 23–60.   [G: U.S.]

Galbraith, James K. The Case for Rapid Growth. *Challenge*, March/April 1984, *27*(1), pp. 10–14.   [G: U.S.]

Gandolfo, G. and Padoan, P. C. Cyclical Growth in a Nonlinear Macrodynamic Model of the Italian Economy. In *Goodwin, R. M.; Krüger, M. and Vercelli, A., eds.*, 1984, pp. 232–52.   [G: Italy]

Goedhuys, D. W. The Business Cycle and Public Policy. *S. Afr. J. Econ.*, June 1984, *52*(2), pp. 133–45.   [G: S. Africa]

Gordon, David M.; Weisskopf, Thomas E. and Bowles, Samuel. Long-term Growth and the Cyclical Restoration of Profitability. In *Goodwin, R. M.; Krüger, M. and Vercelli, A., eds.*, 1984, pp. 86–102.   [G: U.S.]

Gordon, Robert J. Productivity and Profits in the 1980s: Are They Really Improving? Comments. *Brookings Pap. Econ. Act.*, 1984, (1), pp. 168–72.   [G: U.S.]

Gordon, Robert J. U.S. Stabilization Policy: Lessons from the Past Decade. In *Harberger, A. C., ed.*, 1984, pp. 123–49.   [G: U.S.]

Gramlich, Edward M. and Laren, Deborah S. How Widespread Are Income Losses in a Recession? In *Bawden, D. L., ed.*, 1984, pp. 157–80.   [G: U.S.]

Grilli, Enzo R. and Yang, Maw-Cheng. Real and Monetary Determinants of Non-Oil Primary Commodity Price Movements. In *Storey,*

G. G.; Schmitz, A. and Sarris, A. H., eds., 1984, pp. 3–44. [G: Global]

Guglielmi, Jean-Louis. Mutations techniques. Formation du capital et monnaie. Essai sur une nouvelle révolution industrielle: 1952–1983. (With English summary.) Revue Écon. Polit., March–April 1984, 94(2), pp. 181–201.
[G: OECD]

Haberler, Gottfried. The International Monetary System in the World Recession. In Fellner, W., ed., 1984, pp. 87–129. [G: OECD]

Helliwell, John F. Stagflation and Productivity Decline in Canada, 1974–82. Can. J. Econ., May 1984, 17(2), pp. 191–216. [G: Canada]

Henschel, Rudolf. Ursachen der Beschäftigungskrise im Meinungsspektrum der Gewerkschaften. (The Spectrum of Opinions on the Causes of the Employment Crisis in the German Trade Union Movement. With English summary.) Konjunkturpolitik, 1984, 30(2/3), pp. 73–92.
[G: W. Germany]

Houston, David B. Poland's Economic Crisis. Eastern Econ. J., October-December 1984, 10(4), pp. 441–54. [G: Poland]

Howland, Marie. Age of Capital and Regional Business Cycles. Growth Change, April 1984, 15(2), pp. 29–37. [G: U.S.]

Huffman, Wallace E. and Lothian, James R. The Gold Standard and the Transmission of Business Cycles, 1833–1932. In Bordo, M. D. and Schwartz, A. J., eds., 1984, pp. 455–507.
[G: U.S.; U.K.]

Hughes, Jonathan R. T. Stagnation without 'Flation: The 1930s Again. In Siegel, B. N., ed., 1984, pp. 137–56. [G: U.S.]

Jasinowski, Jerry J. In Search of an Optimistic Scenario for the 1980s: Comment. In Wachter, M. L. and Wachter, S. M., eds., 1984, pp. 419–24. [G: Global; U.S.]

Keeley, Michael C. Cyclical Unemployment and Employment: Effects of Labor Force Entry and Exit. Fed. Res. Bank San Francisco Econ. Rev., Summer 1984, (3), pp. 5–25. [G: U.S.]

Keller, Robert R. and May, Ann Mari. The Presidential Political Business Cycle of 1972. J. Econ. Hist., June 1984, 44(2), pp. 265–71.
[G: U.S.]

Kirchgässner, Gebhard. On the Theory of Optimal Government Behaviour. J. Econ. Dynam. Control, November 1984, 8(2), pp. 167–95.
[G: U.S.]

Klein, Philip A. Improving Forecasts with Survey Indicators: An Empirical Test. In Oppenländer, K. H. and Poser, G., eds., 1984, pp. 193–233. [G: Italy; W. Germany; U.K.; France]

Krämer, Walter and Neusser, Klaus. The Emergence of Countercyclical U.S. Fertility: Note. Amer. Econ. Rev., March 1984, 74(1), pp. 201–02. [G: U.S.]

Lahiri, Kajal and Zaporowski, Mark. A Note on the Variability of Real Interest Rates, Business Cycles, and the Livingston Data. J. Banking Finance, September 1984, 8(3), pp. 483–90.
[G: U.S.]

Lawrence, Colin. The Role of Information and

the International Business Cycle. J. Int. Econ., August 1984, 17(1/2), pp. 101–20.

Lecaillon, Jacques. Disparités de revenus et stratégie politique. (With English summary.) Revue Écon. Polit., July–August 1984, 94(4), pp. 433–45. [G: France]

MacEwan, Arthur. Interdependence and Instability: Do the Levels of Output in the Advanced Capitalist Countries Increasingly Move Up and Down Together? Rev. Radical Polit. Econ., Summer & Fall 1984, 16(2&3), pp. 57–79. [G: Selected OECD]

McClelland, Peter D. The Presidential Political Business Cycle of 1972: Discussion. J. Econ. Hist., June 1984, 44(2), pp. 273–76.
[G: U.S.]

McNees, Stephen K. The Current Expansion in Historical Perspective. New Eng. Econ. Rev., November–December 1984, pp. 5–11.
[G: U.S.]

Merrick, John J., Jr. The Anticipated Real Interest Rate, Capital Utilization and the Cyclical Pattern of Real Wages. J. Monet. Econ., January 1984, 13(1), pp. 17–30. [G: U.S.]

Metz, Rainer. Zur empirischen Evidenz "langer Wellen." (On the Empirical Evidence of "Long Waves." With English summary.) Kyklos, 1984, 37(2), pp. 266–90. [G: U.K.; France; Germany]

Minsky, Hyman P. Banking and Industry between the Two Wars: The United States. J. Europ. Econ. Hist., Special Issue 1984, 13(2), pp. 235–72. [G: U.S.]

Mongar, Tom. Monopoly Pricing and Stagnation. Econ. Forum, Summer 1984, 15(1), pp. 63–87. [G: U.S.]

Moore, Geoffrey H. and Cullity, John P. Trends and Cycles in Productivity, Unit Costs, and Prices: An International Perspective. In Kendrick, J. W., ed., 1984, pp. 157–90.
[G: OECD]

Neftçi, Salih N. Are Economic Time Series Asymmetric over the Business Cycle? J. Polit. Econ., April 1984, 92(2), pp. 307–28. [G: U.S.]

O'Connell, Arturo. La Argentina en la Depresión: los problemas de una economía abierta. (With English summary.) Desarrollo Econ., January-March 1984, 23(92), pp. 479–514.
[G: Argentina]

Ostry, Sylvia. OECD Economic Outlook: How We Got Here and Where We're Headed. J. Bus. Econ. Statist., April 1984, 2(2), pp. 105–09. [G: OECD]

Pope, David. Rostow's Kondratieff Cycle in Australia. J. Econ. Hist., September 1984, 44(3), pp. 729–53. [G: Australia]

Popkin, Joel. The Business Cycle at Various Stages of Process. J. Bus. Econ. Statist., July 1984, 2(3), pp. 215–23. [G: U.S.]

Pryor, Frederic L. Rent-Seeking and the Growth and Fluctuations of Nations: Empirical Tests of Some Recent Hypotheses. In Colander, D. C., ed., 1984, pp. 155–75.
[G: Selected Countries]

Raj, K. N. The Causes and Consequences of

World Recession. *World Devel.*, March 1984, *12*(3), pp. 177–85. **[G: Global]**

Reati, Angelo. Taux de profit et composition organique du capital dans le cycle long de l'après-guerre: le cas de l'industrie du Royaume-Uni de 1959 à 1981. (With English summary.) *Cah. Écon. Bruxelles*, Fourth Trimester 1984, (104), pp. 547–609. **[G: U.K.]**

Reinhard, Michael. Sättigung, privater Verbrauch und Konsumgüterinnovation—Das Beispiel der Informationstechnik. (Saturation, Private Consumption, and Consumer Good Innovation—The Example of Information Technology. With English summary.) *Ifo-Studien*, 1984, *30*(3), pp. 209–29. **[G: W. Germany]**

Reynolds, Alan. Gold and Economic Boom: Five Case Studies, 1792–1926. In *Siegel, B. N., ed.*, 1984, pp. 249–68. **[G: France; U.K.; U.S.]**

Rich, Georg. Canada without a Central Bank: Operation of the Price-Specie-Flow Mechanism, 1872–1913. In *Bordo, M. D. and Schwartz, A. J., eds.*, 1984, pp. 547–75. **[G: Canada]**

Rosende, Francisco and Bengolea, J. Manuel. Teoría de los ciclos y la Crisis Económica actual. (With English summary.) *Cuadernos Econ.*, August 1984, *21*(63), pp. 207–26. **[G: Chile]**

Schultze, Charles L. Productivity and Profits in the 1980s: Are They Really Improving? Comments. *Brookings Pap. Econ. Act.*, 1984, (1), pp. 172–79. **[G: U.S.]**

Sellekaerts, Willy and Sellekaerts, Brigitte H. Technical Change, Capital Formation, and Capacity Unemployment in the United States. *Eastern Econ. J.*, July–September 1984, *10*(3), pp. 231–41. **[G: U.S.]**

Sherman, Howard J. Inflation, Unemployment, and the Contemporary Business Cycle. In *Foster, J. B. and Szlajfer, H., eds.*, 1984, *1979*, pp. 91–117. **[G: U.S.]**

Slater, Courtenay. The Impact of Recession on Profits and Employee Compensation. *Bus. Econ.*, October 1984, *19*(5), pp. 18–25. **[G: U.S.]**

Smit, E. V. D. M. and Kotze, D. A Psychological Profile of the South African Business Cycle Based on Qualitative Data. *J. Stud. Econ. Econometrics*, July 1984, (20), pp. 7–16. **[G: S. Africa]**

Spencer, Peter D. The Effect of Oil Discoveries on the British Economy—Theoretical Ambiguities and the Consistent Expectations Simulation Approach. *Econ. J.*, September 1984, *94*(375), pp. 633–44. **[G: U.K.]**

Sulock, Joseph M. and Sabo, William A. The U.S. Political Business Cycle: An Update of Supportive Evidence. *Atlantic Econ. J.*, December 1984, *12*(4), pp. 68. **[G: U.S.]**

Temin, Peter. Canada without a Central Bank: Operation of the Price-Specie-Flow Mechanism, 1872–1913: Comment. In *Bordo, M. D. and Schwartz, A. J., eds.*, 1984, pp. 576–81. **[G: Canada]**

Tobin, James. Impasse of the 1980s: Locomotives Who Can't or Won't. *World Econ.*, March 1984, *7*(1), pp. 5–21. **[G: OECD]**

Whitman, Marina v. N. Persistent Unemployment: Economic Policy Perspectives in the United States and Western Europe. In *Pierre, A. J., ed.*, 1984, pp. 14–52. **[G: U.S.; W. Europe]**

Wiedemann, Paul. Economic Fluctuations and Income Distribution: A Comparative Study. *ACES Bull.*, Spring 1984, *26*(1), pp. 59–76. **[G: U.S.; U.K.; Yugoslavia; Bulgaria]**

Worswick, G. David N. Two Great Recessions: The 1980s and the 1930s in Britain. *Scot. J. Polit. Econ.*, November 1984, *31*(3), pp. 209–28. **[G: U.K.; U.S.]**

Zarnowitz, V. Business Cycle Analysis and Expectational Survey Data. In *Oppenländer, K. H. and Poser, G., eds.*, 1984, pp. 93–133. **[G: U.S.]**

132 Forecasting; Econometric Models

1320 General

Bell, Clive and Srinivasan, T. N. On the Uses and Abuses of Economywide Models in Development Policy Analysis. In *[Chenery, H. B.]*, 1984, pp. 451–76.

Britton, Andrew J. C. Uncertainty, Forecasting and Budget Changes. *Nat. Inst. Econ. Rev.*, February 1984, (107), pp. 60–62. **[G: U.K.]**

Bureau, D.; Miqueu, D. and Norotte, M. The Disequilibrium Theory in Macroeconomic Models: A Small-Scale Model. In *Ancot, J. P., ed.*, 1984, pp. 173–94.

Cole, Sam. Methods of Analysis for Long-term Development Issues. In *Ghosh, P. K., ed., no. 8*, 1984, *1981*, pp. 221–39.

Daub, Mervin. Some Reflections on the Importance of Forecasting to Policy-making. *Can. Public Policy*, December 1984, *10*(4), pp. 377–83.

Gass, Saul I. and Parikh, Shailendra C. On the Determinants of Credible Analysis. In *Avula, X. J. R., et al.*, 1984, pp. 975–80.

Ginsburgh, Victor and Waelbroeck, Jean. Planning Models and General Equilibrium Activity Analysis. In *Scarf, H. E. and Shoven, J. B., eds.*, 1984, pp. 415–39. **[G: India]**

Kendrick, David. Style in Multisectoral Modelling. In *Hughes Hallet, A.J., ed.*, 1984, pp. 329–60. **[G: U.S.]**

Khan, Rahat Nabi. Uses and Limitations of Models in Policy Planning and Evaluation. In *Richardson, J., ed.*, 1984, pp. 231–45. **[G: India; U.K.]**

Kieschnick, Robert L., Jr. State Energy Modeling and Planning: The Current Texas Experience. In *Lev, B., et al., eds.*, 1984, pp. 311–16. **[G: U.S.]**

Murphy, Frederic H., et al. An Introduction to the Intermediate Future Forecasting System. In *Lev, B., et al., eds.*, 1984, pp. 255–64.

Nijkamp, Peter and Spronk, Jaap. Perspectives of Macroeconomic Conflict Analysis. In *Despontin, M.; Nijkamp, P. and Spronk, J., eds.*, 1984, pp. 283–94.

Richardson, John M., Jr. Global Modeling in the

1980s. In *Richardson, J., ed.*, 1984, pp. 115–29.

Silverberg, Gerald. Embodied Technical Progress in a Dynamic Economic Model: The Self-Organization Paradigm. In *Goodwin, R. M.; Krüger, M. and Vercelli, A., eds.*, 1984, pp. 192–208.

Stern, Robert M. Planning Models and General Equilibrium Activity Analysis: Comments. In *Scarf, H. E. and Shoven, J. B., eds.*, 1984, pp. 439–45.   **[G: India]**

Taylor, Lance; Sarkar, Hiren and Rattsø, Jørn. Macroeconomic Adjustment in a Computable General Equilibrium Model for India. In *[Chenery, H. B.]*, 1984, pp. 493–514.
[G: India]

Thorbecke, Erik. The Modelling of Socio-economic Planning Processes: Overview and Conclusions. In *Cohen, S. I., et al., eds.*, 1984, pp. 445–60.

1322 General Forecasts and Models

Ács, Magda. Long-term Models at Work: Comparison with the Past. In *Augusztinovics, M., ed.*, 1984, pp. 284–318.   **[G: Hungary]**

Ahmed, Ehsan and Johannes, James M. St. Louis Equation Restrictions and Criticisms Revisited: A Note. *J. Money, Credit, Banking*, Part 1 November 1984, *16*(4), pp. 514–20.
[G: U.S.]

Apostolakis, Bobby E. A Translogarithmic Cost Function Approach: Greece, 1953–1977. *Empirical Econ.*, 1984, *9*(4), pp. 247–62.
[G: Greece]

Arestis, Philip and Karakitsos, E. The Impact of Fiscal Policy in the UK: Evidence from Two Macroeconomic Models. *Appl. Econ.*, October 1984, *16*(5), pp. 729–47.   **[G: U.K.]**

Artis, M. J., et al. The Effects of Economic Policy, 1979–82. *Nat. Inst. Econ. Rev.*, May 1984, (108), pp. 54–67.   **[G: U.K.]**

Artus, Patrick and Avouyi-Dovi, S. Une estimation comparative de modèles avec rationnement quantitatif pour la France et les Etats-Unis. (Comparative Estimation for France and the United States of Models with Quantity Rationing. With English summary.) *Écon. Appl.*, 1984, *37*(3–4), pp. 489–522.   **[G: France; U.S.]**

Artus, Patrick; Laroque, Guy and Michel, Gilles. Estimation of a Quarterly Macroeconomic Model with Quantity Rationing. *Econometrica*, November 1984, *52*(6), pp. 1387–1414.
[G: France]

Bergmann, Barbara R. and Bennett, Robert L. Macroeconomic Models on Microfoundations: Data Requirements. *Rev. Public Data Use*, June 1984, *12*(2), pp. 91–96.

Bianchi, Carlo; Brillet, Jean-Louis and Calzolari, Giorgio. Analyse et mesure de l'incertitude en prévision d'un modèle économétrique. Application au modèle mini-DMS. (Analysis and Measurement of the Uncertainty in Mini-DMS Model for the French Economy. With English summary.) *Ann. INSEE*, April–June 1984, (54), pp. 31–62.   **[G: France]**

Bod, Péter. The DYNAMIC Model and Its Functioning. In *Augusztinovics, M., ed.*, 1984, pp. 153–89.   **[G: Hungary]**

Bollino, C. Andrea and Klein, Lawrence R. World Recovery Strategies in the 1980s: Is World Recovery Synonymous to LDC Recovery? *J. Policy Modeling*, May 1984, *6*(2), pp. 175–207.   **[G: Global]**

Borges, Antonio M. and Goulder, Lawrence H. Decomposing the Impact of Higher Energy Prices on Long-term Growth. In *Scarf, H. E. and Shoven, J. B., eds.*, 1984, pp. 319–62.
[G: U.S.]

Bourguignon, François and Leibovich, José. Offre et demande dans le processus de développement: un modèle agrégé de déséquilibre appliqué à la Colombie. (Supply and Demand in the Development Process: An Applied Aggregate Disequilibrium Model for Colombia. With English summary.) *Ann. INSEE*, July–December 1984, (55/56), pp. 223–44. **[G: Colombia]**

Brada, Josef C.; Jackson, Marvin R. and King, Arthur E. The Romanian Balance of Payments Crisis: An Econometric Study of its Causes and Cures. In *Jackson, M. R. and Woodson, J. D., Jr., eds.*, 1984, pp. 23–53.   **[G: Romania]**

Brandsma, Andries S. and Hughes Hallett, Andrew J. The Structure of Rational Expectations Behaviour in Economics: An Empirical View. In *Ancot, J. P., ed.*, 1984, pp. 143–72.
[G: Netherlands]

Brooks, Stephen H. Macroeconometric Models: Theory and Practice—A Summary. *Bus. Econ.*, October 1984, *19*(5), pp. 9–17.   **[G: U.S.]**

Budd, Alan P. and Holly, Sean. Short-term Models and Long-term Problems. In *[Pearce, I. F.]*, 1984, pp. 213–35.   **[G: U.K.]**

Burgess, David F. Energy Prices, Capital Formation, and Potential GNP. *Energy J.*, April 1984, *5*(2), pp. 1–27.   **[G: U.S.]**

Chan-Lee, James H. and Kato, Hiromi. A Comparison of Simulation Properties of National Econometric Models. *OECD Econ. Stud.*, Spring 1984, (2), pp. 109–50.   **[G: OECD]**

Choucri, Nazli and Lahiri, Supriya. Short-Run Energy–Economy Interactions in Egypt. *World Devel.*, August 1984, *12*(8), pp. 799–820.   **[G: Egypt]**

Chowdhury, Anisuzzaman. Integration of Input–Output and Macroeconometric Models—A Review of Alternative Methodologies. *Singapore Econ. Rev.*, April 1984, *29*(1), pp. 97–115.

Cifarelli, Giulio. Una interpretazione macrorazionale del ciclo. (A Macrorational Interpretation of Cycle. With English summary.) *Giorn. Econ.*, May–June 1984, *43*(5–6), pp. 345–58.
[G: Italy]

Cockle, Paul. Public Expenditure Policy, 1984–85: The Economic Context. In *Cockle, P., ed.*, 1984, pp. 40–62.   **[G: U.K.]**

Cockle, Paul. Public Expenditure Policy, 1984–85: Alternative Scenarios. In *Cockle, P., ed.*, 1984, pp. 63–76.   **[G: U.K.]**

Cole, S. and Meagher, G. A. Growth and Income Distribution in India: A General Equilibrium

Analysis. In *Cohen, S. I., et al., eds.*, 1984, pp. 315–48. **[G: Sri Lanka; India]**

Cooley, Thomas F. Forecasting and Conditional Projection Using Realistic Prior Distributions: Comment. *Econometric Rev.*, 1984, *3*(1), pp. 101–04. **[G: U.S.]**

d'Alcantara, Gonzalez. A Game Theoretic Approach of Macroeconomic Simulations for the Study of Conflicting Goals. In *Despontin, M.; Nijkamp, P. and Spronk, J., eds.*, 1984, pp. 125–40. **[G: Belgium]**

Darby, Jane. Fiscal Policy and Interest Rates. *Nat. Inst. Econ. Rev.*, August 1984, (109), pp. 38–44. **[G: U.K.]**

Deimezis, Nikitas. Quelques réflexions sur l'utilisation des modèles économétriques dans les économies semi-industrailisées. (With English summary.) *Cah. Écon. Bruxelles*, Fourth Trimester 1984, (104), pp. 610–46. **[G: Greece]**

Deleau, Michel; Le Van, Cuong and Malgrange, Pierre. The Uncertainty Frontier as a Global Approach to the Efficient Stabilisation of Economic Systems: Experiments with the Micro-DMS Model. In *Hughes Hallet, A.J., ed.*, 1984, pp. 97–117. **[G: France]**

Devilliers, M. The Use of Business Surveys in Short-term Forecasts: The French Experience. In *Oppenländer, K. H. and Poser, G., eds.*, 1984, pp. 135–60. **[G: France]**

Dixon, Peter B.; McDonald, Daina and Meagher, G. A. Prospects for the Australian Economy, 1983–84 and 1984–85. *Australian Econ. Rev.*, 2nd Quarter 1984, (66), pp. 3–25. **[G: Australia]**

Dixon, Peter B.; Parmenter, B. R. and Rimmer, Russell J. Extending the ORANI Model of the Australian Economy: Adding Foreign Investment to a Miniature Version. In *Scarf, H. E. and Shoven, J. B., eds.*, 1984, pp. 485–533. **[G: Australia]**

Doan, Thomas; Litterman, Robert B. and Sims, Christopher. Forecasting and Conditional Projection Using Realistic Prior Distributions: Reply. *Econometric Rev.*, 1984, *3*(1), pp. 131–44. **[G: U.S.]**

Doan, Thomas; Litterman, Robert B. and Sims, Christopher. Forecasting and Conditional Projection Using Realistic Prior Distributions. *Econometric Rev.*, 1984, *3*(1), pp. 1–100. **[G: U.S.]**

Dramais, A. Use of Business Survey Data into a Short-term Prediction Model. In *Oppenländer, K. H. and Poser, G., eds.*, 1984, pp. 621–60. **[G: EEC]**

van Driel, Gerald, et al. Objectives and Potentials of the Dutch Economy in the Eighties. In *Despontin, M.; Nijkamp, P. and Spronk, J., eds.*, 1984, pp. 55–72. **[G: Netherlands]**

Eckstein, Otto; Mosser, Patricia and Cebry, Michael. The DRI Market Expectations Model. *Rev. Econ. Statist.*, May 1984, *66*(2), pp. 181–91. **[G: U.S.]**

Evans, M. K. The Use of Judgement in Econometric Forecasting. In *Oppenländer, K. H. and Poser, G., eds.*, 1984, pp. 3–45. **[G: U.S.]**

Fashola, M. A. A Policy Model for Nigeria Featur-

ing Price Formation. In *Cohen, S. I., et al., eds.*, 1984, pp. 289–311. **[G: Nigeria]**

Faur, Tivadar. The LAG Model and Its Functioning. In *Augusztinovics, M., ed.*, 1984, pp. 190–214. **[G: Hungary]**

Feltenstein, Andrew. Money and Bonds in a Disaggregated Open Economy. In *Scarf, H. E. and Shoven, J. B., eds.*, 1984, pp. 209–42.

Fischer, Stanley. The Economy of Israel. *Carnegie-Rochester Conf. Ser. Public Policy*, Spring 1984, *20*, pp. 7–52. **[G: Israel]**

Frenkel, Jacob A. Comments on the Economy of Israel. *Carnegie-Rochester Conf. Ser. Public Policy*, Spring 1984, *20*, pp. 57–67. **[G: Israel]**

Frenzel, Bill. In Search of an Optimistic Scenario for the 1980s: Comment. In *Wachter, M. L. and Wachter, S. M., eds.*, 1984, pp. 427–30. **[G: Global; U.S.]**

Gaburro, Giuseppe. A Preliminary Experiment for an Optimal Control Model of the Italian Economy. *Metroecon.*, June-Oct. 1984, *36*(2–3), pp. 239–58. **[G: Italy]**

Gandolfo, G. and Padoan, P. C. Cyclical Growth in a Nonlinear Macrodynamic Model of the Italian Economy. In *Goodwin, R. M.; Krüger, M. and Vercelli, A., eds.*, 1984, pp. 232–52. **[G: Italy]**

Garbely, M. and Gilli, M. Two Approaches in Reading Model Interdependencies. In *Ancot, J. P., ed.*, 1984, pp. 15–33. **[G: U.S.]**

Geweke, John F. Forecasting and Conditional Projection Using Realistic Prior Distributions: Comment. *Econometric Rev.*, 1984, *3*(1), pp. 105–12. **[G: U.S.]**

Grais, W. Aggregate Demand and Macro-economic Imbalances in Thailand: Simulations with the SIAM 1 Model. In *Cohen, S. I., et al., eds.*, 1984, pp. 349–79. **[G: Thailand]**

Grauer, Manfred and Zalai, Ernö. A Reference Point Approach to Nonlinear Macroeconomic Multiobjective Models. In *Despontin, M.; Nijkamp, P. and Spronk, J., eds.*, 1984, pp. 73–96.

Hafkamp, Wim and Nijkamp, Peter. An Operational Multi-component Multi-actor Policy Model for Economic-Environmental Scenarios. In *Despontin, M.; Nijkamp, P. and Spronk, J., eds.*, 1984, pp. 157–82. **[G: Netherlands]**

Helliwell, John F. Stagflation and Productivity Decline in Canada, 1974–82. *Can. J. Econ.*, May 1984, *17*(2), pp. 191–216. **[G: Canada]**

Hickman, Bert G. and Klein, Lawrence R. Wage–Price Behavior in the National Models of Project LINK. *Amer. Econ. Rev.*, May 1984, *74*(2), pp. 150–54. **[G: OECD]**

Hillier, Grant H. and Giles, David E. A. Estimation in Equilibrium Models Involving Discretionary Policy Instrument Choice. *Australian Econ. Pap.*, December 1984, *23*(43), pp. 179–96. **[G: Australia]**

Hoehn, James G.; Gruben, William C. and Fomby, Thomas B. Time Series Forecasting Models of the Texas Economy: A Comparison. *Fed. Res. Bank Dallas Econ. Rev.*, May 1984, pp. 11–23. **[G: U.S.]**

Hopkins, Mike and van der Hoeven, Rolf. Economic and Social Factors in Development: A Socioeconomic Framework for Basic Needs Planning. In *Cohen, S. I., et al., eds.*, 1984, pp. 161–95. [G: Brazil; India; Kenya]

Jahnke, Wilfried. Gesamtwirtschaftliche Wirkungen öffentlicher Nachfrageimpulse. Eine Auseinandersetzung mit kritischen Anmerkungen zu einer Untersuchung der Deutschen Bundesbank. (Macroeconomic Effects of Government Expediture: A Reply to Critical Comments on a Study of the Deutsche Bundesbank. With English summary.) *Konjunkturpolitik*, 1984, *30*(1), pp. 45–60. [G: W. Germany]

Jasinowski, Jerry J. In Search of an Optimistic Scenario for the 1980s: Comment. In *Wachter, M. L. and Wachter, S. M., eds.*, 1984, pp. 419–24. [G: Global; U.S.]

Kendrick, John W. Long-Term Economic Projection: Stronger U.S. Growth Ahead. *Southern Econ. J.*, April 1984, *50*(4), pp. 945–64. [G: U.S.]

Kestens, P.; Thys-Clement, F. and Van Regemorter, D. Diagnostic de la situation économique de la Belgique à horizon 1990. (With English summary.) *Cah. Écon. Bruxelles*, 1st Trimester 1984, (101), pp. 105–24. [G: Belgium]

Kirchgässner, Gebhard. Wie gut sind die Prognosen der Arbeitsgemeinschaft wirtschaftswissenschaftlicher Forschungsinstitute in der Bundesrepublik Deutschland? (How Good Are the Forecasts of the "Arbeitsgemeinschaft wirtschaftswissenschaftlicher Forschungsinstitute" in the Federal Republic of Germany? With English summary.) *Weltwirtsch. Arch.*, 1984, *120*(2), pp. 279–300. [G: W. Germany]

Kitova, G. A. and Kuznetsova, T. E. The Modified Version of an Aggregated Econometric Model of the USA. *Matekon*, Spring 1984, *20*(3), pp. 74–98. [G: U.S.]

Klein, Lawrence R. In Search of an Optimistic Scenario for the 1980s. In *Wachter, M. L. and Wachter, S. M., eds.*, 1984, pp. 390–412. [G: Global]

Klein, Lawrence R. Money in the Wharton Quarterly Model: A Reply. *J. Money, Credit, Banking*, February 1984, *16*(1), pp. 76–79. [G: U.S.]

Klein, Lawrence R.; Fardoust, S. and Filatov, V. Endogenous Exchange Rate in the Medium Term: A Weak Law of Purchasing Power Parity for the LINK System. In *[Pearce, I. F.]*, 1984, pp. 171–90. [G: OECD]

Krekó, Ildikó. Operation of the WHERE Model. In *Augusztinovics, M., ed.*, 1984, pp. 117–52. [G: Hungary]

Krishnamurty, K. and Pandit, V. Macroeconometric Modelling of the Indian Economy: An Overview. *Indian Econ. Rev.*, January–June 1984, *19*(1), pp. 1–15. [G: India]

Krishnamurty, K.; Saibaba, P. and Kazmi, N. A. Inflation and Growth: A Model for India. *Indian Econ. Rev.*, January–June 1984, *19*(1), pp. 16–111. [G: India]

Kuprianov, Anatoli and Lupoletti, William. The

Economic Outlook for Fifth District States in 1984: Forecasts from Vector Autoregression Models. *Fed. Res. Bank Richmond Econ. Rev.*, Jan./Feb. 1984, *70*(1), pp. 12–23. [G: U.S.]

Lambert, Jean-Pierre; Lubrano, Michel and Sneessens, Henri R. Emploi et chômage en France de 1955 à 1982: un modèle macroéconomique annuel avec rationnement. (Employment and Unemployment in France: An Annual Macroeconomic Model with Rationing. With English summary.) *Ann. INSEE*, July–December 1984, (55/56), pp. 39–76. [G: France]

Lau, Lawrence J. Numerical Specification of Applied General Equilibrium Models: Estimation, Calibration, and Data: Comments. In *Scarf, H. E. and Shoven, J. B., eds.*, 1984, pp. 127–37. [G: U.S.; U.K.]

Leontief, Wassily. Population Growth and Economic Development: Illustrative Projections. In *Ghosh, P. K., ed., no. 5*, 1984, *1979*, pp. 221–46. [G: Global]

Litterman, Robert B. Above-Average National Growth in 1985 and 1986. *Fed. Res. Bank Minn. Rev.*, Fall 1984, *8*(4), pp. 3–7. [G: U.S.]

Litterman, Robert B. Forecasting and Policy Analysis with Bayesian Vector Autoregression Models. *Fed. Res. Bank Minn. Rev.*, Fall 1984, *8*(4), pp. 30–41. [G: U.S.]

Llewellyn, John and Arai, Haruhito. International Aspects of Forecasting Accuracy. *OECD Econ. Stud.*, Autumn 1984, (3), pp. 73–117. [G: OECD]

Looney, Robert E. Inflation and Oil Based Development: Failure of the Monetarist Model in Saudi Arabia. *Rivista Int. Sci. Econ. Com.*, October–November 1984, *31*(10–11), pp. 1100–20. [G: Saudi Arabia]

Lubrano, Michel and Sneessens, Henri R. Un modèle de production CES–Léontief pour l'industrie française. (A Léontief–CES Production Model for the French Industry. With English summary.) *Ann. INSEE*, April–June 1984, (54), pp. 3–30. [G: France]

Lybeck, Johan A., et al. A Comparison of the Dynamic Properties of Five Nordic Macroeconometric Models. *Scand. J. Econ.*, 1984, *86*(1), pp. 35–51. [G: Sweden; Finland; Norway]

Macura, M. and Popović, B. BACHUE—Yugoslavia: Background Structure and Utilisation. In *Cohen, S. I., et al., eds.*, 1984, pp. 107–38.

Malinvaud, E. Forecasting and Conditional Projection Using Realistic Prior Distributions: Comment. *Econometric Rev.*, 1984, *3*(1), pp. 113–17. [G: U.S.]

Manne, Alan S. Decomposing the Impact of Higher Energy Prices on Long-term Growth: Comments. In *Scarf, H. E. and Shoven, J. B., eds.*, 1984, pp. 362–65. [G: U.S.]

Mannermaa, Kauko and Leppä, August. KESSUmalli ja sen käyttö keskipitkän ajan ennustamisessa ja suunnittelussa. (The KESSU Model of the Finnish Economy and Its Use in Medium-

Term Forecasting and Planning. With English summary.) *Kansant. Aikak.*, 1984, *80*(3), pp. 277–90.   [G: Finland]

Mansur, Ahsan Habib and Whalley, John. Numerical Specification of Applied General Equilibrium Models: Estimation, Calibration, and Data. In *Scarf, H. E. and Shoven, J. B., eds.*, 1984, pp. 69–127.   [G: U.S.; U.K.]

Maton, J. and Joos, M. A Simplified Dynamic SAM Model of Malaysia: The Effects of Technical Progress, Capital Accumulation and Income Distribution on Employment. In *Cohen, S. I., et al., eds.*, 1984, pp. 381–405.
[G: Malaysia]

Melino, Angelo. Forecasting and Conditional Projection Using Realistic Prior Distributions: Comment. *Econometric Rev.*, 1984, *3*(1), pp. 119–23.   [G: U.S.]

Mercenier, Jean and Waelbroeck, Jean. The Sensitivity of Developing Countries to External Shocks in an Interdependent World. *J. Policy Modeling*, May 1984, *6*(2), pp. 209–35.
[G: OECD; LDCs]

Mosley, Paul and Cracknell, Richard. Endogenous Government Policy in a Model of the UK Economy. *Appl. Econ.*, October 1984, *16*(5), pp. 633–45.   [G: U.K.]

Naggl, W. The Anticipations Model: A Short-term Forecasting Model Based on Anticipations Data. In *Oppenländer, K. H. and Poser, G., eds.*, 1984, pp. 161–91.   [G: W. Germany]

Naqvi, Syed Nawab Haider; Ahmed, Ather Maqsood and Khan, Ashfaque H. Possibilities of Regional Trade Expansion: A Link Model for Pakistan, India, Bangladesh, and Sri Lanka. *Pakistan Devel. Rev.*, Spring 1984, *23*(1), pp. 9–35.   [G: Pakistan; India; Bangladesh; Sri Lanka]

Nasseh, Ali Reza and Elyasiani, Elyas. Energy Price Shocks, Aggregate Supply Displacement, and Macroeconomic Activity. *Eastern Econ. J.*, October-December 1984, *10*(4), pp. 468–87.   [G: U.S.]

Neese, J. W. and Pindyck, Robert S. Behavioural Assumptions in Decentralised Stabilisation Policies. In *Hughes Hallet, A.J., ed.*, 1984, pp. 251–70.   [G: U.S.]

Newbold, Paul. Forecasting and Conditional Projection Using Realistic Prior Distributions: Comment. *Econometric Rev.*, 1984, *3*(1), pp. 125–30.   [G: U.S.]

Paleologos, John M. The Dynamic Impacts of Fiscal and Monetary Policy on an Aggregate Macroeconomic Model of the Greek Economy—Some Policy Experiments. *Public Finance*, 1984, *39*(2), pp. 261–80.   [G: Greece]

Pandit, V. Macroeconomic Adjustments in a Developing Economy: A Medium Term Model of Outputs and Prices in India. *Indian Econ. Rev.*, January–June 1984, *19*(1), pp. 112–56.
[G: India]

Parkin, Michael. The Economy of Israel: A Comment. *Carnegie-Rochester Conf. Ser. Public Policy*, Spring 1984, *20*, pp. 53–56.
[G: Israel]

Paseta, Vesna. Dinimički model jugoslovenske

privrede na bazi matrice rasta. (Dynamic Model of Yugoslav Economy on the Growth Matrix Basis. With English summary.) *Econ. Anal. Worker's Manage.*, 1984, *18*(3), pp. 241–57.   [G: Yugoslavia]

Robinson, Sherman. A General Equilibrium Model for the Mexican Economy: Comments. In *Scarf, H. E. and Shoven, J. B., eds.*, 1984, pp. 482–84.   [G: Mexico]

Sandblom, C. L. and Banasik, J. L. Optimizing Economic Policy with Sliding Windows. *Appl. Econ.*, February 1984, *16*(1), pp. 45–56.
[G: Canada]

Sandblom, C. L. and Eiselt, H. A. Controlling an Econometric Model Using Different Coefficient Sets. In *Hughes Hallet, A.J., ed.*, 1984, pp. 85–95.

Serra-Puche, Jaime. A General Equilibrium Model for the Mexican Economy. In *Scarf, H. E. and Shoven, J. B., eds.*, 1984, pp. 447–82.   [G: Mexico]

Sheikh, Munir A. An analysis of Some Possible Causes for the Absence or Presence of the Neutrality and Homogeneity Properties in Large Macroeconomic Models. *Empirical Econ.*, 1984, *9*(2), pp. 113–30.   [G: Canada]

Shishido, Shuntaro. A Multisector Approach to Global Econometric Modeling, with Special Reference to Heavy Industries. In *[Chenery, H. B.]*, 1984, pp. 391–405.   [G: OECD; LDCs]

Spencer, Grant H. and Duggan, K. G. On the Structural Sensitivity of Short Term Output-Inflation Tradeoffs. *Appl. Econ.*, February 1984, *16*(1), pp. 81–98.   [G: New Zealand]

Webb, Roy H. Forecasts 1984. *Fed. Res. Bank Richmond Econ. Rev.*, Jan./Feb. 1984, *70*(1), pp. 24–26.   [G: U.S.]

Webb, Roy H. Vector Autoregressions as a Tool for Forecast Evaluation. *Fed. Res. Bank Richmond Econ. Rev.*, Jan./Feb. 1984, *70*(1), pp. 3–11.   [G: U.S.]

Weintraub, Robert E. Money in the Wharton Quarterly Model: A Rejoinder. *J. Money, Credit, Banking*, February 1984, *16*(1), pp. 79–80.   [G: U.S.]

Weintraub, Robert E. Money in the Wharton Quarterly Model: A Comment. *J. Money, Credit, Banking*, February 1984, *16*(1), pp. 69–75.   [G: U.S.]

Welfe, Wladyslaw. Multicollinearity and Iterative Estimation Procedure. In *Gruber, J., ed.*, 1984, pp. 92–124.   [G: Poland]

Whalley, John. Extending the ORANI Model of the Australian Economy: Adding Foreign Investment to a Miniature Version: Comments. In *Scarf, H. E. and Shoven, J. B., eds.*, 1984, pp. 533–38.   [G: Australia]

Zarnowitz, V. Business Cycle Analysis and Expectational Survey Data. In *Oppenländer, K. H. and Poser, G., eds.*, 1984, pp. 93–133.
[G: U.S.]

de Zeeuw, Aart J. Policy Evaluation with Conflicting Goals for a Linked Two Country Model.

In *Despontin, M.; Nijkamp, P. and Spronk, J., eds.*, 1984, pp. 99–124.
[G: W. Germany; Netherlands]

Zellner, Arnold and Peck, Stephen C. Simulation Experiments with a Quarterly Macroeconometric Model of the U.S. Economy. In *Zellner, A.*, 1984, *1973*, pp. 141–57. [G: U.S.]

Zwick, Burton. Economic Projections. In *Shadow Open Market Committee*, 1984, pp. 45–50.
[G: U.S.]

1323 Specific Forecasts and Models

Adam, M. C.; Thys-Clement, F. and Van Regemorter, D. La modélisation des intermédiaires fianciers non monétaires en Belgique: méthodologie et premiers résultats. (With English summary.) *Cah. Écon. Bruxelles*, 2nd Trimester 1984, (102), pp. 202–42. [G: Belgium]

Ajinkya, Bipin B. and Gift, Michael J. Corporate Managers' Earnings Forecasts and Symmetrical Adjustments of Market Expectations. *J. Acc. Res.*, Autumn 1984, *22*(2), pp. 425–44.
[G: U.S.]

Alagh, Yoginder K.; Kashyap, S. P. and Murty, G. V. S. N. Policy Modelling for Planning in India. In *Cohen, S. I., et al., eds.*, 1984, pp. 59–88. [G: India]

Anderson, Gordon J. and Hendry, David F. An Econometric Model of United Kingdom Building Societies. *Oxford Bull. Econ. Statist.*, August 1984, *46*(3), pp. 185–210. [G: U.K.]

Andrikopoulos, Andreas A.; Brox, James A. and Gamaletsos, Theodore. Forecasting Canadian Consumption Using the Dynamic Generalized Linear Expenditure System (DGLES). *Appl. Econ.*, December 1984, *16*(6), pp. 839–53.
[G: Canada]

Arestis, Philip and Driver, Ciaran. A Comparison of the Monetary–Financial Blocks of Two Post-Keynesian Short-Period Models. *Brit. Rev. Econ. Issues*, Autumn 1984, *6*(15), pp. 53–78.
[G: U.K.]

Artus, Patrick and Muet, Pierre-Alain. Un panorama des développements récents de l'économétrie de l'investissement. (A Survey of Recent Developments in the Econometrics of Investment. With English summary.) *Revue Écon.*, September 1984, *35*(5), pp. 791–830.
[G: Japan; France; U.K.; U.S.; Germany]

Aschheim, Joseph and Tavlas, George S. The Simultaneity Problem in Forecasting Inflation. *Atlantic Econ. J.*, September 1984, *12*(3), pp. 20–29. [G: U.S.]

Aurikko, Esko. Exchange Rate Policies Simulated by Means of a Disequilibrium Model of the Finnish Economy. *J. Policy Modeling*, November 1984, *6*(4), pp. 531–54. [G: Finland]

Baba, M.; Nomura, N. and Tahara, S. Major Features of New Business Cycle Indicators in Japan. In *Oppenländer, K. H. and Poser, G., eds.*, 1984, pp. 605–20. [G: Japan]

Bahl, Roy and Schroeder, Larry. The Role of Multi-year Forecasting in the Annual Budgeting Process for Local Governments. *Public Budg. Finance*, Spring 1984, *4*(1), pp. 3–13.
[G: U.S.]

Ban, Kanemi and Nakamura, Jirou. A Simplified Japan–U.S. Energy Linkage Model. *Osaka Econ. Pap.*, March 1984, *33*(3–4), pp. 81–94.
[G: Japan; U.S.]

Bemmaor, Albert. Durée de vie des biens durables: modèles et tests. (Life Duration for Consumer Durables: Models and Tests. With English summary.) *Consommation*, July–September 1984, *31*(3), pp. 51–73.

Berndt, Ernst R. The Role of Energy in Productivity Growth: Comment. In *Kendrick, J. W., ed.*, 1984, pp. 325–34. [G: U.S.]

Blackburn, Joseph and Clancy, Kevin. An Empirical Comparison of Awareness Forecasting Models of New Product Introduction: Comment. *Marketing Sci.*, Summer 1984, *3*(3), pp. 198–201. [G: U.S.]

Botha, J. P. The Wharton Annual and Industry Forecasting Model Predictions and ARIMA Type Model Predictions. *J. Stud. Econ. Econometrics*, January 1984, (18), pp. 5–14.

Bourdon, F.; Bourdon, J. and Hallak, J. The EDFOREM Model: A Case Study of Thailand. In *Cohen, S. I., et al., eds.*, 1984, pp. 139–59. [G: Thailand]

Brooks, Robert E. The Tenrac Gas Pipeline Competition Model. In *Lev, B., et al., eds.*, 1984, pp. 337–54.

Carlevaro, Fabrizio and Spierer, Charles. Nouvelles perspectives d'évolution de la demande d'énergie en Suisse jusqu'à l'an 2000. (New Prospects for Swiss Energy Demand until the Year 2000. With English summary.) *Schweiz. Z. Volkswirtsch. Statist.*, December 1984, *120*(4), pp. 483–520. [G: Switzerland]

Centre for World Food Studies. A Computable General Equilibrium Model for Thailand with Emphasis on the Agricultural Sector. In *Cohen, S. I., et al., eds.*, 1984, pp. 407–43.
[G: Thailand]

Claycamp, H. J.; Dodson, Joe A., Jr. and Doughty, N. An Empirical Comparison of Awareness Forecasting Models of New Product Introduction: Comment. *Marketing Sci.*, Summer 1984, *3*(3), pp. 201–02. [G: U.S.]

Collins, William A.; Hopwood, William S. and McKeown, James C. The Predictability of Interim Earnings over Alternative Quarters. *J. Acc. Res.*, Autumn 1984, *22*(2), pp. 467–79.
[G: U.S.]

Craine, Roger and Havenner, Arthur. Choosing a Monetary Instrument: The Case of Supply-Side Shocks: Reply. *J. Econ. Dynam. Control*, September 1984, *7*(3), pp. 381–82. [G: U.S.]

Davis, E. P. The Consumption Function in Macroeconomic Models: A Comparative Study. *Appl. Econ.*, December 1984, *16*(6), pp. 799–838. [G: U.K.]

Decaestecker, J. P. and Mouillart, M. Rationing and Aggregation in a Multi-level Model of Household Behaviour: The S.A.B.I.N.E. Model. In *Ancot, J. P., ed.*, 1984, pp. 63–86.
[G: France]

Decaluwe, Bernard. Le modèle scandinave et l'économie canadienne. (The Scandinavian Model and the Canadian Economy. With English summary.) *L'Actual. Econ.*, June 1984, *60*(2), pp. 164–85. **[G: Canada]**

Demeny, Paul. A Perspective on Long-Term Population Growth. *Population Devel. Rev.*, March 1984, *10*(1), pp. 103–26. **[G: Global]**

Desai, Meghnad; Keil, Manfred and Wadhwani, Sushil. Incomes Policy in a Political Environment: A Structural Model for the U.K. 1961–1980. In *Hughes Hallet, A.J.*, ed., 1984, pp. 121–44. **[G: U.K.]**

Desai, Meghnad. An Econometric Model of the Share of Wages in National Income: UK 1855–1965. In *Goodwin, R. M.; Krüger, M. and Vercelli, A.*, eds., 1984, pp. 253–77. **[G: U.K.]**

Dixon, Bruce L. and Chen, Wu-Hsiung. Endogenous versus Exogenous Price Targets for Commodity Market Stabilisation. In *Hughes Hallet, A.J.*, ed., 1984, pp. 181–207. **[G: Taiwan]**

Dodson, Joe A., Jr. An Empirical Comparison of Awareness Forecasting Models of New Product Introduction: Comment. *Marketing Sci.*, Summer 1984, *3*(3), pp. 202. **[G: U.S.]**

Dormayer, H.-J. and Lindlbauer, J. D. Sectoral Indicators by Use of Survey Data. In *Oppenländer, K. H. and Poser, G.*, eds., 1984, pp. 467–98. **[G: W. Germany]**

Duan, Naihua, et al. Choosing between the Sample-Selection Model and the Multi-part Model. *J. Bus. Econ. Statist.*, July 1984, *2*(3), pp. 283–89. **[G: U.S.]**

Fase, Martin M. G. The Monetary Sector of the Netherlands in 50 Equations. A Quarterly Model for the Netherlands (1970–1979). In *Ancot, J. P.*, ed., 1984, pp. 195–228. **[G: Netherlands]**

Felderer, Bernhard. Population and Per-capita Income in Simulation Models. In *Steinmann, G.*, ed., 1984, pp. 132–46. **[G: W. Germany]**

Fishe, Raymond P. H. On Testing Hypotheses Using the Livingston Price Expectations Data: A Note. *J. Money, Credit, Banking*, Part 1 November 1984, *16*(4), pp. 520–27. **[G: U.S.]**

Forman, Leonard; Groves, Miles and Eichner, Alfred S. The Monetary–Financial Block of a Post-Keynesian Short-Period Model. *Brit. Rev. Econ. Issues*, Autumn 1984, *6*(15), pp. 23–52. **[G: U.S.]**

Fullerton, Don; Henderson, Yolanda Kodrzycki and Shoven, John B. A Comparison of Methodologies in Empirical General Equilibrium Models of Taxation. In *Scarf, H. E. and Shoven, J. B.*, eds., 1984, pp. 367–410. **[G: OECD; Mexico]**

Gholamnezhad, H. Energy Conservation: A Policy Model for the United States. In *Avula, X. J. R., et al.*, 1984, pp. 969–74. **[G: U.S.]**

Golanty, John L. Clarification of the Tracker Methodology and Limitations [An Empirical Comparison of Awareness Forecasting Models of New Product Introduction]. *Marketing Sci.*, Summer 1984, *3*(3), pp. 203. **[G: U.S.]**

Goudie, Andrew W. and Meeks, G. Individual Economic Agents in a Macroeconomic Model:

UK Companies in Cambridge MDM. *J. Policy Modeling*, August 1984, *6*(3), pp. 289–309. **[G: U.K.]**

Green, David Jay. A Small Scale, Partial Equilibrium Model of Natural Gas Markets: Responses to Alternative Deregulation Scenarios and Oil Price Changes. *Southern Econ. J.*, April 1984, *50*(4), pp. 1112–30. **[G: U.S.]**

Hafer, R. W. Comparing Time-Series and Survey Forecasts of Weekly Changes in Money: A Methodological Note. *J. Finance*, September 1984, *39*(4), pp. 1207–13. **[G: U.S.]**

Hamilton, K. E.; Hoffman, R. B. and Sande, G. T. Energy Modelling in SERF: The Socio-Economic-Resource Framework. In *Lev, B., et al.*, eds., 1984, pp. 233–53. **[G: Canada]**

Harris, Curtis C., Jr.; McConnell, Virginia D. and Cumberland, John H. A Model for Forecasting the Economic and Environmental Impact of Energy Policy. *Energy Econ.*, July 1984, *6*(3), pp. 167–76. **[G: U.S.]**

Hay, Joel W. and Olsen, Randall J. Let Them Eat Cake: A Note on Comparing Alternative Models of the Demand for Medical Care. *J. Bus. Econ. Statist.*, July 1984, *2*(3), pp. 279–82. **[G: U.S.]**

Hendry, David F. Econometric Modelling of House Prices in the United Kingdom. In *Hendry, D. F. and Wallis, K. F.*, eds., 1984, pp. 211–52. **[G: U.K.]**

Henin, Roushdi A. Alternative Population Projections for Kenya, 1969–89. In *Ominde, S. H.*, ed., 1984, pp. 78–90. **[G: Kenya]**

Heri, Erwin W. Zur Prognostizierbarkeit von Wechselkursänderungen. Ein empirischer Vergleich verschiedener Prognosefunktionen. (Forecasting Exchange Rate Changes: An Empirical Comparison of Different Models. With English summary.) *Z. Wirtschaft. Sozialwissen.*, 1984, *104*(4), pp. 369–88. **[G: U.S.; U.K.; Germany; Switzerland]**

Hicks, Norman L. A Model of Trade and Growth for the Developing World. In *Ghosh, P. K.*, ed., no. 16, 1984, *1976*, pp. 92–110. **[G: LDCs]**

Howrey, E. Philip. Data Revision, Reconstruction, and Prediction: An Application to Inventory Investment. *Rev. Econ. Statist.*, August 1984, *66*(3), pp. 386–93. **[G: U.S.]**

Ikeda, Saburo. Nonlinear Prediction Models for River Flows and Typhoon Precipitation by Self-Organizing Methods. In *Farlow, S. J.*, ed., 1984, pp. 149–67. **[G: Japan]**

Jansen, Dennis W. Choosing a Monetary Instrument: The Case of Supply-Side Shocks: Comment. *J. Econ. Dynam. Control*, September 1984, *7*(3), pp. 377–79. **[G: U.S.]**

Johannes, James M. and Rasche, Robert H. Recent Behavior of the M1—Adjusted Monetary Base Multiplier and Forecasts for Early 1984. In *Shadow Open Market Committee*, 1984, pp. 51–55. **[G: U.S.]**

Jordan, Jerry L. Monetary Policy Options and the Outlook—1984. In *Shadow Open Market Committee*, 1984, pp. 39–43. **[G: U.S.]**

Jorgenson, Dale W. Econometric Methods for

Applied General Equilibrium Analysis. **In** *Scarf, H. E. and Shoven, J. B., eds.*, 1984, pp. 139–203. [G: U.S.]

Jorgenson, Dale W. The Role of Energy in Productivity Growth. **In** *Kendrick, J. W., ed.*, 1984, pp. 279–323. [G: U.S.]

Keen, Howard, Jr. Composite Models Reduce Forecast Errors: The Case of New Automobile Sales, 1979–1983. *Bus. Econ.*, July 1984, *19*(4), pp. 47–50. [G: U.S.]

King, Michael J. and Scott, Michael J. Forecasting Electricity Demand with an End-Use/Econometric Model. **In** *Lev, B., et al., eds.*, 1984, pp. 151–64. [G: U.S.]

Krekó, Ildikó; Bod, Péter and Faur, Tivadar. Formal Description of the Planning Models. **In** *Augusztinovics, M., ed.*, 1984, pp. 354–75. [G: Hungary]

Le Van, Cuong. Specification of the Import Function and the Determination of Short and Long Term Equilibria in a Macroeconometric Model. **In** *Ancot, J. P., ed.*, 1984, pp. 229–45.

Lebow, William M., et al. Forecasting Applications of GMDH in Agricultural and Meteorological Time Series. **In** *Farlow, S. J., ed.*, 1984, pp. 121–47. [G: Canada]

Leu, Robert E. Medical Technology Assessment in Terms of Improved Life Quality. **In** *Lindgren, B., ed.*, 1984, pp. 97–121. [G: Switzerland]

Levin, Nissan; Tishler, Asher and Zahavi, Jacob. A Model for Planning Investments in the Energy Sector in the Medium Range. **In** *Lev, B., et al., eds.*, 1984, pp. 285–308. [G: Israel]

Lobo, Gerald J. and Nair, R. D. Predictions of Annual Earnings Using Quarterly Earnings, Annual Earnings, and Dividend Payout Ratios. *Managerial Dec. Econ.*, December 1984, *5*(4), pp. 228–33. [G: U.S.]

Lorek, Kenneth S. and Bathke, Allen W., Jr. A Time-Series Analysis of Nonseasonal Quarterly Earnings Data. *J. Acc. Res.*, Spring 1984, *22*(1), pp. 369–79. [G: U.S.]

MacKinnon, James G. Econometric Methods for Applied General Equilibrium Analysis: Comments. **In** *Scarf, H. E. and Shoven, J. B., eds.*, 1984, pp. 203–07. [G: U.S.]

Mahajan, Vijay; Muller, Eitan and Sharma, Subhash. An Empirical Comparison of Awareness Forecasting Models of New Product Introduction. *Marketing Sci.*, Summer 1984, *3*(3), pp. 179–97. [G: U.S.]

Mahajan, Vijay; Muller, Eitan and Sharma, Subhash. Reflections on Awareness Forecasting Models of New Product Introduction: Rejoinder. *Marketing Sci.*, Summer 1984, *3*(3), pp. 205–06. [G: U.S.]

Marwah, Kanta and Bodkin, Ronald G. A Model of the Canadian Global Exchange Rate: A Test of the 1970s. *J. Policy Modeling*, November 1984, *6*(4), pp. 455–83. [G: Canada]

McCutchen, William W., Jr. The Use of Box Jenkins Techniques for Forecasting U.S. Merchandise Exports: An Update and Extension.

Quart. J. Bus. Econ., Autumn 1984, *23*(4), pp. 64–75. [G: U.S.]

Meese, Richard A. and Geweke, John F. A Comparison of Autoregressive Univariate Forecasting Procedures for Macroeconomic Time Series. *J. Bus. Econ. Statist.*, July 1984, *2*(3), pp. 191–200. [G: U.S.; Japan; U.K.]

Meganck, B. and Maes, G. Experience in Belgium with Business Surveys in Trade: Elements of Forecasting the Evolution of Private Consumption. **In** *Oppenländer, K. H. and Poser, G., eds.*, 1984, pp. 309–42. [G: Belgium]

Mensah, Yaw M. An Examination of the Stationarity of Multivariate Bankruptcy Prediction Models: A Methodological Study. *J. Acc. Res.*, Spring 1984, *22*(1), pp. 380–95.

Mieszkowski, Peter. A Comparison of Methodologies in Empirical General Equilibrium Models of Taxation: Comments. **In** *Scarf, H. E. and Shoven, J. B., eds.*, 1984, pp. 410–14.

Moon, Marilyn and Sawhill, Isabel V. Family Incomes: Gainers and Losers. **In** *Palmer, J. L. and Sawhill, I. V., eds.*, 1984, pp. 317–46. [G: U.S.]

Murfin, Andy and Ormerod, Paul. The Forward Rate for the U.S. Dollar and the Efficient Markets Hypothesis, 1978–1983. *Manchester Sch. Econ. Soc. Stud.*, September 1984, *52*(3), pp. 292–99. [G: U.S.]

Newton, John R. and Sepulveda, Victor. The Puerto Rico Revenue Projection Model: An Econometric Approach. *Rev. Reg. Stud.*, Fall 1984, *14*(3), pp. 17–24. [G: Puerto Rico]

Nickell, Stephen J. An Investigation of the Determinants of Manufacturing Employment in the United Kingdom. *Rev. Econ. Stud.*, October 1984, *51*(4), pp. 529–57. [G: U.K.]

Nickell, Stephen J. The Modelling of Wages and Employment. **In** *Hendry, D. F. and Wallis, K. F., eds.*, 1984, pp. 13–35.

Norrie, Kenneth H. and Percy, Michael B. Sustained Harvest Fluctuations and Economic Change: A General Equilibrium Analysis. **In** *Bengtsson, T.; Fridlizius, G. and Ohlsson, R., eds.*, 1984, pp. 391–418.

Öhlén, S. L. Plans and Attitudes from the Survey of Consumer Buying Expectations in Forecasting the Total Private Consumption. **In** *Oppenländer, K. H. and Poser, G., eds.*, 1984, pp. 243–79. [G: Sweden]

Ottenwaelter, B. and Vuong, Quang H. An Empirical Analysis of Backlog, Inventory, Production, and Price Adjustments: An Application of Recursive Systems of Log-Linear Models. *J. Bus. Econ. Statist.*, July 1984, *2*(3), pp. 224–34. [G: France]

Perlman, Mark. The Role of Population Projections for the Year 2000. **In** *Simon, J. L. and Kahn, H., eds.*, 1984, pp. 50–66. [G: Global]

Pomanskii, A. B. and Rusakov, V. P. On One Approach to Modeling Consumer Demand. *Matekon*, Summer 1984, *20*(4), pp. 81–96.

Price, Jeffrey P. Coal Supply Models: The State of the Art. **In** *Lev, B., et al., eds.*, 1984, pp. 3–20. [G: U.S.]

Pringle, Lewis G.; Wilson, R. Dale and Brody, Edward I. Issues in Comparing the Awareness Component of New Product Models. *Marketing Sci.*, Summer 1984, *3*(3), pp. 203–05. [G: U.S.]

Promboin, Ronald L. Energy Shocks and the U.S. Economy: How Much Has OPEC Helped Recently? *Bus. Econ.*, July 1984, *19*(4), pp. 34–39. [G: U.S.]

Radharamanan, R.; Camargo, M. E. and Sortica, G. B. System Identification and Analysis of Inflation in Brazil. In *Avula, X. J. R., et al.*, 1984, pp. 822–27. [G: Brazil]

Ray, George F. Relative Prices—Methods and Constraints in Forecasting: Some Empirical Considerations. In *Csikós-Nagy, B.; Hague, D. and Hall, G., eds.*, 1984, pp. 89–111. [G: OECD]

Rotemberg, Julio J. Interpreting the Statistical Failures of Some Rational Expectations Macroeconomic Models. *Amer. Econ. Rev.*, May 1984, *74*(2), pp. 188–93. [G: U.S.]

Sargan, J. Denis. Wages and Prices in the United Kindgom: A Study in Econometric Methodology. In *Hendry, D. F. and Wallis, K. F., eds.*, 1984, pp. 275–314. [G: U.K.]

Scott, Donald E. and Hutchinson, Charles E. An Application of the GMDH Algorithm to Economic Modeling. In *Farlow, S. J., ed.*, 1984, pp. 243–55. [G: U.S.]

Secrest, T. J. Economic and Energy End-Use Assessment. In *Lev, B., et al., eds.*, 1984, pp. 185–200. [G: U.S.]

Smit, E. V. D. M. and Kotze, D. A Psychological Profile of the South African Business Cycle Based on Qualitative Data. *J. Stud. Econ. Econometrics*, July 1984, (20), pp. 7–16. [G: S. Africa]

Spanos, Aris. Liquidity as a Latent Variable—An Application of the MIMIC Model. *Oxford Bull. Econ. Statist.*, May 1984, *46*(2), pp. 125–43. [G: U.K.]

Spreen, Thomas H. and Arnade, Carlos A. Use of Forecasts in Decisionmaking: The Case of Stocker Cattle in Florida. *Southern J. Agr. Econ.*, July 1984, *16*(1), pp. 145–50. [G: U.S.]

Strom, David. Opportunities for Cogeneration in Commercial Buildings. In *Lev, B., et al., eds.*, 1984, pp. 201–12. [G: U.S.]

Wachter, Michael L. Unemployment in the American Economy: Types, Causes, and Outlooks for the 1980's. In *Ullrich, R. A., ed.*, 1984, pp. 1–24. [G: U.S.]

Weistroffer, H. Roland. Modelling the Demand for Construction. *J. Stud. Econ. Econometrics*, January 1984, (18), pp. 36–47. [G: S. Africa]

Welch, Paul R. A Generalized Distributed Lag Model for Predicting Quarterly Earnings. *J. Acc. Res.*, Autumn 1984, *22*(2), pp. 744–57. [G: U.S.]

Westoby, Richard and Pearce, David W. Single Equation Models for the Projection of Energy Demand in the United Kingdom, 1954–80. *Scot. J. Polit. Econ.*, November 1984, *31*(3), pp. 229–54. [G: U.K.]

Yano, Yuko. Energy and Economic Development in Japan. In *Baum, V., et al.*, 1984, pp. 134–45. [G: Japan]

Yaun, P. J. Econometric and Empirical Evidence on the Relationship between Survey Data and Official Data and its Relevance for Monitoring the Business Cycle. In *Oppenländer, K. H. and Poser, G., eds.*, 1984, pp. 47–66. [G: U.K.]

Zweifel, Peter. Drugs as an Ambulatory Care Technology: Costs and Benefits to the Insurer. In *Lindgren, B., ed.*, 1984, pp. 37–65. [G: Switzerland]

1324 Forecasting and Econometric Models: Theory and Methodology

Ahking, Francis W. The Predictive Performance of the Time-Series Model and the Regression Model of the Income Velocity of Money: Evidence from Five EEC Countries. *J. Banking Finance*, September 1984, *8*(3), pp. 389–415. [G: Italy; U.K.; France; W. Germany; Netherlands]

Armstrong, J. S. Recent Trends in Forecasting Methods. In *Oppenländer, K. H. and Poser, G., eds.*, 1984, pp. 67–83.

Augusztinovics, Mária. Quantitative Synthesis in Long-term Planning. In *Augusztinovics, M., ed.*, 1984, pp. 43–85.

Bernstein, Peter L. Surprising the Smoothies. *J. Portfol. Manage.*, Fall 1984, *11*(1), pp. 7–11.

Billeter-Frey, Ernst P. Wirtschaftsprognosen im Lichte der Systemtheorie. (Economic Forecasting Based on System Theory. With English summary.) *Jahr. Nationalökon. Statist.*, September 1984, *199*(5), pp. 433–44. [G: U.S.]

Botha, J. P. The Wharton Annual and Industry Forecasting Model Predictions and ARIMA Type Model Predictions. *J. Stud. Econ. Econometrics*, January 1984, (18), pp. 5–14.

Boutillier, M. Reading Macroeconomic Models and Building Causal Structures. In *Ancot, J. P., ed.*, 1984, pp. 35–48.

Brooks, Stephen H. Macroeconometric Models: Theory and Practice—A Summary. *Bus. Econ.*, October 1984, *19*(5), pp. 9–17. [G: U.S.]

Broze, L. and Szafarz, A. On Linear Models with Rational Expectations which Admit a Unique Solution. *Europ. Econ. Rev.*, February 1984, *24*(1), pp. 103–11.

Budd, Alan P. and Holly, Sean. Short-term Models and Long-term Problems. In *[Pearce, I. F.]*, 1984, pp. 213–35. [G: U.K.]

Burgstahler, David. An Application of the Bootstrap Method to the Analysis of Squared, Standardized Market Model Prediction Errors: Discussion. *J. Acc. Res.*, Supplement 1984, *22*, pp. 55–58. [G: U.S.]

Casti, John. On the Theory of Models and the Modelling of Natural Phenomena. In *Bahrenberg, G.; Fischer, M. M., and Nijkamp, P.*, 1984, pp. 73–92.

Charney, Alberta H. and Taylor, Carol A. Decomposition of Ex Ante State Model Forecasting Errors. *J. Reg. Sci.*, May 1984, *24*(2), pp. 229–47. [G: U.S.]

Cooley, Thomas F. Forecasting and Conditional Projection Using Realistic Prior Distributions: Comment. *Econometric Rev.*, 1984, *3*(1), pp. 101–04.   [G: U.S.]

Doan, Thomas; Litterman, Robert B. and Sims, Christopher. Forecasting and Conditional Projection Using Realistic Prior Distributions. *Econometric Rev.*, 1984, *3*(1), pp. 1–100.   [G: U.S.]

Doan, Thomas; Litterman, Robert B. and Sims, Christopher. Forecasting and Conditional Projection Using Realistic Prior Distributions: Reply. *Econometric Rev.*, 1984, *3*(1), pp. 131–44.   [G: U.S.]

Evans, M. K. The Use of Judgement in Econometric Forecasting. In *Oppenländer, K. H. and Poser, G., eds.*, 1984, pp. 3–45.   [G: U.S.]

Forrester, Jay W. Information Sources for Modeling the National Economy. In *Richardson, J., ed.*, 1984, pp. 167–84.   [G: U.S.]

Garbely, M. and Gilli, M. Two Approaches in Reading Model Interdependencies. In *Ancot, J. P., ed.*, 1984, pp. 15–33.   [G: U.S.]

Geweke, John F. Forecasting and Conditional Projection Using Realistic Prior Distributions: Comment. *Econometric Rev.*, 1984, *3*(1), pp. 105–12.   [G: U.S.]

Greenberg, Ralph. Adaptive Estimation: An Alternative to the Traditional Stationarity Assumption. *J. Acc. Res.*, Autumn 1984, *22*(2), pp. 719–30.   [G: U.S.]

Hall, S. G. Confidence Intervals. *Nat. Inst. Econ. Rev.*, August 1984, (109), pp. 33–37.
                                    [G: U.K.]

Hauer, J. Towards Multilevel Analysis: General and Theoretical Considerations. In *Bahrenberg, G.; Fischer, M. M., and Nijkamp, P.*, 1984, pp. 117–30.

Keller, A. A. Semi-reduced Forms of Econometric Models. In *Ancot, J. P., ed.*, 1984, pp. 89–113.

Klein, Philip A. Improving Forecasts with Survey Indicators: An Empirical Test. In *Oppenländer, K. H. and Poser, G., eds.*, 1984, pp. 193–233.   [G: Italy; W. Germany; U.K.; France]

Krekó, Ildikó. The WHERE Model. In *Augusztinovics, M., ed.*, 1984, pp. 86–116.

Leahey, Cary. Linking Business Decisions to Macroeconomic Models. *Bus. Econ.*, October 1984, *19*(5), pp. 49–56.   [G: U.S.]

Lütkepohl, Helmut. Forecasting Contemporaneously Aggregated Vector ARMA Processes. *J. Bus. Econ. Statist.*, July 1984, *2*(3), pp. 201–14.   [G: U.S.]

Lybeck, Johan A. and Carlsson, Evert. From Small to Large: A Systematic Comparison of Gradually More Complex Econometric Models. *Europ. Econ. Rev.*, February 1984, *24*(1), pp. 83–101.

Malinvaud, E. Forecasting and Conditional Projection Using Realistic Prior Distributions: Comment. *Econometric Rev.*, 1984, *3*(1), pp. 113–17.   [G: U.S.]

Marais, M. Laurentius. An Application of the Bootstrap Method to the Analysis of Squared, Standardized Market Model Prediction Errors.

J. Acc. Res., Supplement 1984, *22*, pp. 34–54.   [G: U.S.]

McCarl, Bruce A. Model Validation: An Overview with Some Emphasis on Risk Models. *Rev. Marketing Agr. Econ.*, December 1984, *52*(3), pp. 153–73.

Meadows, Dennis. On Modeling, Limits and Understanding. In *Richardson, J., ed.*, 1984, pp. 161–65.

Meese, Richard A. and Geweke, John F. A Comparison of Autoregressive Univariate Forecasting Procedures for Macroeconomic Time Series. *J. Bus. Econ. Statist.*, July 1984, *2*(3), pp. 191–200.   [G: U.S.; Japan; U.K.]

Melino, Angelo. Forecasting and Conditional Projection Using Realistic Prior Distributions: Comment. *Econometric Rev.*, 1984, *3*(1), pp. 119–23.   [G: U.S.]

Narasimham, Gorti V. L. Estimation and Prediction of Time-Varying Parameter Economic Models. In *Avula, X. J. R., et al.*, 1984, pp. 784–88.   [G: U.S.]

Newbold, Paul. Forecasting and Conditional Projection Using Realistic Prior Distributions: Comment. *Econometric Rev.*, 1984, *3*(1), pp. 125–30.   [G: U.S.]

Patterson, K. D. and Ryding, J. Dynamic Time Series Models with Growth Effects Constrained to Zero. *Econ. J.*, March 1984, *94*(373), pp. 137–43.

Rietveld, Piet. The Use of Qualitative Information in Macro-Economic Policy Analysis. In *Despontin, M.; Nijkamp, P. and Spronk, J., eds.*, 1984, pp. 264–80.

Sandee, J.; Don, F. J. H. and van den Berg, P. J. C. M. Adjustment of Projections to Recent Observations. *Europ. Econ. Rev.*, October–November 1984, *26*(1–2), pp. 153–66.

Shoven, John B. and Whalley, John. Applied General-Equilibrium Models of Taxation and International Trade: An Introduction and Survey. *J. Econ. Lit.*, September 1984, *22*(3), pp. 1007–51.

Todd, Richard M. Improving Economic Forecasting with Bayesian Vector Autoregression. *Fed. Res. Bank Minn. Rev.*, Fall 1984, *8*(4), pp. 18–29.   [G: U.S.]

Visco, Ignazio. On Linear Models with Rational Expectations: An Addendum. *Europ. Econ. Rev.*, February 1984, *24*(1), pp. 113–15.

Wallis, Kenneth F. Comparing Time-Series and Nonlinear Model-based Forecasts. *Oxford Bull. Econ. Statist.*, November 1984, *46*(4), pp. 383–89.

Webb, Roy H. Vector Autoregressions as a Tool for Forecast Evaluation. *Fed. Res. Bank Richmond Econ. Rev.*, Jan./Feb. 1984, *70*(1), pp. 3–11.   [G: U.S.]

Weller, Barry R. and Wellington, John. Alternate Estimation Criteria and Measures of Forecast Accuracy. *J. Macroecon.*, Spring 1984, *6*(2), pp. 235–38.   [G: U.S.]

Willekens, F. J. and Shah, M. R. A Note on Log-Linear Modelling of Rates and Proportions. In *Bahrenberg, G.; Fischer, M. M., and Nijkamp, P.*, 1984, pp. 253–69.

Zellner, Arnold. Statistical Analysis of Econometric Models. In *Zellner, A.*, 1984, *1979*, pp. 83–119.

133 General Outlook and Stabilization Theories and Policies

1330 General Outlook

Adams, F. Gerard. Perspectives on Latin America and the World Economic Outlook. In *Jorge, A.; Salazar-Carrillo, J. and Sanchez, E. P.*, 1984, pp. 7–10.

Amin, Samir. Human Resources, Employment and Development: Introduction. In *Amin, S., ed.*, 1984, pp. viii–xxiii.

Amirizadeh, Hossain and Todd, Richard M. More Growth Ahead for Ninth District States. *Fed. Res. Bank Minn. Rev.*, Fall 1984, *8*(4), pp. 8–17.   [G: U.S.]

Anderson, Martin. An Economic Bill of Rights. In *Moore, J. H., ed.*, 1984, pp. 1–22.   [G: U.S.]

Angelis, Ivan. A Forecast of the External Conditions for the Development of the Czechoslovak National Economy (The Outlook until the Year 2000). *Czech. Econ. Pap.*, 1984, (22), pp. 43–56.   [G: Czechoslovakia]

Ansu, Yaw. Ghana, 1950–1980: Missed Opportunities: Comments. In *Harberger, A. C., ed.*, 1984, pp. 227–30.   [G: Ghana]

Aubrey, Agnès. La conjoncture de l'économie allemande des années 80. (With English summary.) *Revue Écon. Polit.*, September–October 1984, *94*(5), pp. 571–80.   [G: Germany]

Balassa, Bela. Prices, Incentives, and Economic Growth. *Weltwirtsch. Arch.*, 1984, *120*(4), pp. 611–30.   [G: Global]

Bartel, Richard D. Structural Change and Policy Response in an Interdependent World. In *Alperovitz, G. and Skurski, R., eds.*, 1984, pp. 15–39.   [G: U.S.]

Blanchard, Olivier J. and Dornbusch, Rudiger. U.S. Deficits, the Dollar and Europe. *Banca Naz. Lavoro Quart. Rev.*, March 1984, (148), pp. 89–113.   [G: U.S.; OECD]

Bolin, William H. Central America: Real Economic Help Is Workable Now. *Foreign Aff.*, Summer 1984, *62*(5), pp. 1095–1106.   [G: Central America]

Bollino, C. Andrea and Klein, Lawrence R. World Recovery Strategies in the 1980s: Is World Recovery Synonymous to LDC Recovery? *J. Policy Modeling*, May 1984, *6*(2), pp. 175–207.   [G: Global]

Bos, Henk C. The Role of Industry and Industrial Policies in the Third Development Decade. In *Ghosh, P. K., ed., no. 1*, 1984, *1978*, pp. 30–49.   [G: LDCs]

Boshoff, C. H. Structural Bottlenecks and a Shift in Economic Theory: Its Implication for Monitoring Business Cycles in South Africa. *J. Stud. Econ. Econometrics*, March 1984, (19), pp. 19–30.   [G: S. Africa]

Boussemart, Jean-Michel. États-Unis, une conjoncture économique bonne mais de graves déséquilibres financiers. (With English summary.) *Revue Écon. Polit.*, September–October 1984, *94*(5), pp. 544–54.   [G: U.S.]

Bradford, Colin I., Jr. World Economic Outlook and the Prospects for U.S. Exports to Latin America. In *Jorge, A.; Salazar-Carrillo, J. and Sanchez, E. P.*, 1984, pp. 121–25.   [G: Global]

Briones, Rodrigo K. The Chilean Malaise. *Challenge*, March/April 1984, *27*(1), pp. 57–60.   [G: Chile]

Britton, Andrew J. C. The Budget and the Economic Strategy. *Fisc. Stud.*, May 1984, *5*(2), pp. 1–7.   [G: U.K.]

Brunner, Karl. Resolving the Debt Problem: Some Policy Considerations [U.S. Macroeconomic Policy and Third World Debt]. *Cato J.*, Spring/Summer 1984, *4*(1), pp. 97–103.   [G: U.S.; LDCs]

Carnoy, Martin and Shearer, Derek. Towards a Democratic Alternative: Neo-liberals vs. Economic Democrats. In *Alperovitz, G. and Skurski, R., eds.*, 1984, pp. 167–89.   [G: U.S.]

Chalumeau, Jean-Luc. La situation économique du Brésil. (With English summary.) *Revue Écon. Polit.*, September–October 1984, *94*(5), pp. 615–19.   [G: Brazil]

Ciampi, Carlo Azeglio. Progressi e difficoltà nel cammino verso la stabilità e lo sviluppo. (Difficulties in Progress towards Stability and Growth. With English summary.) *Bancaria*, August 1984, *40*(8), pp. 713–20.   [G: Italy]

Co, Nemesio. Crisis Management Directions for the Export Sector. *Philippine Econ. J.*, Winter 1984, *23*(1), pp. 66–71.   [G: Philippines]

Cohen, Jacob. International Implications of U.S. Macroeconomic Policy. *Singapore Econ. Rev.*, October 1984, *29*(2), pp. 11–26.   [G: OECD]

Cooper, Richard N. The United States and the World Economy. In *Frenkel, J. A. and Mussa, M. L., eds.*, 1984, pp. 1–21.   [G: U.S.; Global]

Coussy, J. Intégration ou déconnexion du nord et du sud sous l'impact de la crise: introduction. (North and South under the Impact of the Crisis: Linking or Delinking? Introduction. With English summary.) *Écon. Soc.*, June 1984, *18*(6), pp. 3–17.

Cranston, Alan. The Economic Policy Failure of the Past and A Policy Agenda for the Future. In *Wachter, M. L. and Wachter, S. M., eds.*, 1984, pp. 15–19.   [G: U.S.]

Csaba, Laszlo. COMECON Perspectives for the 1980's. *Écon. Soc.*, February 1984, *18*(2), pp. 5–44.   [G: CMEA]

Cuddy, Michael P. Building on Reality 1985–1987: A Comment. *Irish Banking Rev.*, December 1984, pp. 10–15.   [G: Ireland]

Danzin, Andre. Are Science and Technology Leading to a New Pattern of Development? In *Ghosh, P. K., ed., no. 3*, 1984, *1979*, pp. 182–94.

Daub, Mervin. Some Reflections on the Importance of Forecasting to Policy-making. *Can.*

Public Policy, December 1984, *10*(4), pp. 377–83.

Davidson, Paul. The Conventional Wisdom on Deficits Is Wrong. *Challenge*, November/December 1984, *27*(5), pp. 54–56.   [G: U.S.]

Dixon, Peter B.; McDonald, Daina and Meagher, G. A. Prospects for the Australian Economy, 1983–84 and 1984–85. *Australian Econ. Rev.*, 2nd Quarter 1984, (66), pp. 3–25.   [G: Australia]

Dugger, William M. The Nature of Capital Accumulation and Technological Progress in the Modern Economy. *J. Econ. Issues*, September 1984, *18*(3), pp. 799–823.   [G: U.S.]

Earle, John S. and Kniesner, Thomas J. Did Reaganomics Shift the Phillips Curve? *Indian Econ. Rev.*, July-Dec. 1984, *19*(2), pp. 235–40.   [G: U.S.]

Ellman, Michael. Albania's Economy Today and Tomorrow. *World Econ.*, September 1984, *7*(3), pp. 333–40.   [G: Albania]

Emerson, Michael. "Europe: The Case for Unsustainable Growth": A Comment. *J. Common Market Stud.*, December 1984, *23*(2), pp. 169–73.   [G: Europe]

Estanislao, Jesus P. A Perspective on Our Economic Crisis. *Philippine Econ. J.*, Winter 1984, *23*(1), pp. 12–22.   [G: Philippines]

Fellner, William. Currents and Countercurrents in Political and Economic Thought. *Carnegie-Rochester Conf. Ser. Public Policy*, Autumn 1984, *21*, pp. 231–52.

Fiedler, Edgar R. Stagflation: Our Pernicious Social Disease—That Our Antibiotics Can't Cure. *Bus. Econ.*, January 1984, *19*(1), pp. 13–23.   [G: U.S.]

Fodella, Gianni. Il giappone e l'estasia verso l'egemonia economica mondiale. (Japan's Economic role in East Asia. With English summary.) *Rivista Int. Sci. Econ. Com.*, September 1984, *31*(9), pp. 809–11.   [G: Japan]

Frank, Andre Gunder. After Reaganomics and Thatcherism, What? From Keynesian Demand Management via Supply-side Economics to Corporate State Planning and 1984. In *Frank, A. G.*, 1984, *1981*, pp. 189–207.   [G: U.S.; U.K.]

Frank, Andre Gunder. Policy Ad Hockery: Unemployment and World Crisis of Economic Policy Formation. In *Frank, A. G.*, 1984, *1983*, pp. 230–42.

Frank, Andre Gunder and Wheelwright, Ted. The Theories of Milton Friedman on Chile: Equilibrium on the Point of a Bayonet [Interview]. In *Frank, A. G.*, 1984, *1977*, pp. 125–36.   [G: Chile]

Fröbel, Folker. The Current Development of the World-Economy: Reproduction of Labour and Accumulation of Capital on a World Scale. In *Addo, H.*, ed., 1984, pp. 51–118. [G: Global]

Galbraith, James K. The Case for Rapid Growth. *Challenge*, March/April 1984, *27*(1), pp. 10–14.   [G: U.S.]

Gollas, Manuel. Mexico's Perspectives under a Three-Year Agreement with the IMF: Remarks. In *Jorge, A.; Salazar-Carrillo, J. and Sanchez, E. P.*, 1984, pp. 69–70.   [G: Mexico]

Gonçalves, Reinaldo. Brazil and Mexico: The IMF Stabilization Programmes and Banks' Rescheduling. *Econ. Int.*, February–May 1984, *37*(1–2), pp. 76–93.   [G: Brazil; Mexico]

Greenspan, Alan. Removing Structural Barriers to Growth. In *Wachter, M. L. and Wachter, S. M.*, eds., 1984, pp. 10–14.   [G: U.S.]

Guglielmi, Jean-Louis. Rythmes d'essor de la conjoncture et disparités des structures. (With English summary.) *Revue Écon. Polit.*, September–October 1984, *94*(5), pp. 535–43.   [G: OECD]

Gupta, Sanjeev and Togan, Sübidey. Who Benefits from the Adjustment Process in Developing Countries? A Test on India, Kenya, and Turkey. *J. Policy Modeling*, February 1984, *6*(1), pp. 95–109.   [G: India; Kenya; Turkey]

Heller, H. Robert, et al. Economic Outlook. *Contemp. Policy Issue*, Fall 1984-85, *3*(1), pp. 15–52.   [G: Global]

Hewlett, Sylvia Ann. Overview and Policy Options. In *Hewlett, S. A.; Kaufman, H. and Kenen, P. B.*, eds., 1984, pp. 199–221.

Hill, Hal. Survey of Recent Developments. *Bull. Indonesian Econ. Stud.*, August 1984, *20*(2), pp. 1–38.   [G: Indonesia]

Hulten, Charles R. and Sawhill, Isabel V. The Legacy of Reaganomics: An Overview. In *Hulten, C. R. and Sawhill, I. V.*, eds., 1984, pp. 1–17.   [G: U.S.]

Iglesias, Enrique V. A Preliminary Overview of the Latin American Economy during 1983. *Cepal Rev.*, April 1984, (22), pp. 7–38.   [G: Latin America]

Iglesias, Enrique V. Latin America: Crisis and Development Options. *Cepal Rev.*, 1984, (23), pp. 7–28.   [G: Latin America]

Jakobsson, Ulf. Economic Growth in Sweden. In *Harberger, A. C.*, ed., 1984, pp. 59–94.   [G: Sweden]

Janeway, Eliot. Inflation or Deflation: Which Is It? *Challenge*, November/December 1984, *27*(5), pp. 26–33.   [G: U.S.]

Jones, Reginald H. Responses to the Slowdown in Growth. In *Wachter, M. L. and Wachter, S. M.*, eds., 1984, pp. 3–9.   [G: U.S.]

Jordan, Jerry L. Economic Policy Priorities for the Mid–1980s. *Bus. Econ.*, July 1984, *19*(4), pp. 5–12.   [G: U.S.]

Jorgensen-Dahl, Arnfinn. Southeast Asia in 1983: Approaching a Turning Point? In *Thambipillai, P.*, ed., 1984, pp. 3–17.   [G: S.E. Asia]

Kendrick, John W. U.S. Economic Policy and Productivity Growth. *Cato J.*, Fall 1984, *4*(2), pp. 387–400.   [G: U.S.]

Kenyon, Peter D. and Nowak, Margaret J. Public Policy for Sustainable Growth: Overview. *Australian Econ. Rev.*, 3rd Quarter 1984, (67), pp. 4–6.

Keohane, Robert O. The World Political Economy and the Crisis of Embedded Liberalism. In *Goldthorpe, J. H.*, ed., 1984, pp. 15–38.

Khane, Abd-El Rahman. The Importance of the

External Environment for Industrial Development in Developing Countries. *Industry Devel.*, 1984, (12), pp. 1–7. [G: LDCs]

Killick, Tony. The Impact of Fund Stabilisation Programmes. In *Killick, Tony, ed. (II),* 1984, pp. 227–69. [G: LDCs]

Killick, Tony, et al. Towards a Real Economy Approach. In *Killick, Tony, ed. (II),* 1984, pp. 270–320. [G: LDCs]

Kissinger, Henry A. Foreign Policy and Economics. In *Wachter, M. L. and Wachter, S. M., eds.,* 1984, pp. 447–56. [G: U.S.]

Kornai, János. Some Properties of the Eastern European Growth Pattern. In *Cohen, S. I., et al., eds.,* 1984, *1981,* pp. 13–23.

Kosai, Yutaka. Japan's Growth Problem. In *Harberger, A. C., ed.,* 1984, pp. 41–58.
[G: Japan]

Kouri, Pentti J. K. Europe in the World Economy. *Economia (Portugal),* January 1984, *8*(1), pp. 7–17. [G: Global]

Kuprianov, Anatoli and Lupoletti, William. The Economic Outlook for Fifth District States in 1984: Forecasts from Vector Autoregression Models. *Fed. Res. Bank Richmond Econ. Rev.,* Jan./Feb. 1984, *70*(1), pp. 12–23. [G: U.S.]

Lara, Juan. Mexico's Perspectives under a Three-Year Agreement with the IMF. In *Jorge, A.; Salazar-Carrillo, J. and Sanchez, E. P.,* 1984, pp. 61–68. [G: Mexico]

Lee, Lai To. Singapore's Continuous Search for Quality. In *Thambipillai, P., ed.,* 1984, pp. 279–93. [G: Singapore]

Lele, Uma. Tanzania: Phoenix or Icarus? In *Harberger, A. C., ed.,* 1984, pp. 159–95.
[G: Tanzania]

Litterman, Robert B. Above-Average National Growth in 1985 and 1986. *Fed. Res. Bank Minn. Rev.,* Fall 1984, *8*(4), pp. 3–7.
[G: U.S.]

Lortie, Pierre. Fostering Economic Growth. *Can. Public Policy,* June 1984, *10*(2), pp. 225–30.
[G: Canada]

MacGregor, Ian. The Need for a Long-term Perspective in Government-Business Relations. In *Wachter, M. L. and Wachter, S. M., eds.,* 1984, pp. 34–37. [G: U.S.]

Madeuf, B. and Ominami, C. Nouvelle D.I.T. et Keynésianisme planétaire: la fin des illusions. (New International Division of Labour and Worldwide Keynesianism: The End of the Illusions. With English summary.) *Écon. Soc.,* June 1984, *18*(6), pp. 81–98. [G: Global]

Mănescu, Manea. President Nicolae Ceauşescu's Report—A Revolutionary Scientific Construction of Genius—An Ample Programme for Romania's Development on New Peaks of Progress and Civilization. *Econ. Computat. Cybern. Stud. Res.,* 1984, *19*(4), pp. 7–12.
[G: Romania]

Maramba, Felix K., Jr. The State of Domestic Essential Industries Today. *Philippine Econ. J.,* Winter 1984, *23*(1), pp. 60–65.
[G: Philippines]

Meyerson, Adam. Better Off Than Four Years

Ago? *Policy Rev.,* Summer 1984, (29), pp. 41–42. [G: U.S.]

Möller, Hans. "Wirtschaftliche Sättigung" im Lichte der ökonomischen Theorie. ("Economic Glut" in the Light of Economic Theory. With English summary.) *Ifo-Studien,* 1984, *30*(3), pp. 171–92. [G: W. Germany]

Moncarz, Raul. The Economic Outlook for Latin America and the IMF. In *Jorge, A.; Salazar-Carrillo, J. and Sanchez, E. P.,* 1984, pp. 21–23. [G: Latin America]

Motono, Moriyuki. World Trade Issues Require More than a Piecemeal Approach. *World Econ.,* September 1984, *7*(3), pp. 229–39.
[G: Global]

Mussa, Michael. U.S. Macroeconomic Policy and Third World Debt. *Cato J.,* Spring/Summer 1984, *4*(1), pp. 81–95. [G: U.S.; LDCs]

Neil, Herbert E., Jr. Marginal Shifts in Economic Policy with a Mondale Presidency. *Bus. Econ.,* July 1984, *19*(4), pp. 5, 13–17. [G: U.S.]

Nevitte, Neil Gibbins, Roger. Neoconservatism: Canadian Variations on an Ideological Theme? *Can. Public Policy,* December 1984, *10*(4), pp. 384–94. [G: Canada]

Nickerson, Gary W. Political Economy and Policy in the 1980's: Introduction. *Rev. Radical Polit. Econ.,* Winter 1984, *16*(4), pp. iv–ix.

Nielsen, Niels Christian. AEndrede manovremuligheder for den okonomiske politik. (With English summary.) *Nationaløkon. Tidsskr.,* 1984, *122*(3), pp. 357–70. [G: OECD]

Niskanen, William A. A "Supply-Side" Industrial Policy. *Cato J.,* Fall 1984, *4*(2), pp. 381–86.
[G: U.S.]

Nordhaus, William D. Reaganomics and Economic Growth: A Summing Up. In *Hulten, C. R. and Sawhill, I. V., eds.,* 1984, pp. 253–61. [G: U.S.]

Nyers, Rezso and Tardos, Márton. The Necessity for Consolidation of the Economy and the Possibility of Development in Hungary. *Acta Oecon.,* 1984, *32*(1–2), pp. 1–19.
[G: Hungary]

O'Riordan, William K. A Wasted Decade. *Irish Banking Rev.,* March 1984, pp. 43–54.
[G: Ireland]

Ong, Michael. Malaysia in 1983: On the Road to Greater Malaysia. In *Thambipillai, P., ed.,* 1984, pp. 197–230. [G: Malaysia]

Oppenländer, Karl Heinrich. Reicht die Arbeit für alle? Zur Entwicklung von Wirtschaft und Arbeitsmarkt in den achtziger Jahren. (Is There Enough Work for Everyone? On the Economy and the Labour Market in the 1980s. With English summary.) *Ifo-Studien,* 1984, *30*(3), pp. 193–207. [G: W. Germany]

Ostry, Sylvia. OECD Economic Outlook: How We Got Here and Where We're Headed. *J. Bus. Econ. Statist.,* April 1984, *2*(2), pp. 105–09. [G: OECD]

Ostry, Sylvia. The World Economy in 1983: Marking Time. *Foreign Aff.,* 1984, *62*(3), pp. 533–60. [G: Global]

Owen, Henry. The World Economy: The Dollar

and the Summit. *Foreign Aff.*, Winter 1984/ 85, *63*(2), pp. 344–59. [G: OECD]

Palmer, John L. and Sawhill, Isabel V. The Reagan Record: Overview. In *Palmer, J. L. and Sawhill, I. V., eds.*, 1984, pp. 1–30. [G: U.S.]

Palmer, Ransford W. Problems of Development in Beautiful Countries: Introduction. In *Palmer, R. W.*, 1984, pp. xiii–xvii.

Parker, William N. The Response Mechanism in the Twentieth Century. In *Parker, W. N.*, 1984, *1984*, pp. 214–37.

Parkin, Michael. The United Kingdom: Political Economy and Macroeconomics: A Comment. *Carnegie-Rochester Conf. Ser. Public Policy*, Autumn 1984, *21*, pp. 281–93. [G: U.K.]

Peterson, Peter G. The Government Debt-Imposed Ceiling on Economic Growth. In *Wachter, M. L. and Wachter, S. M., eds.*, 1984, pp. 20–27. [G: U.S.]

Petridis, Anastasios. Prospects for the Australian Economy in 1984. *Econ. Rec.*, March 1984, *60*(168), pp. 1–15. [G: Australia]

Plassard, Jacques. Le rééquilibrage de l'économie française a commencé au deuxième trimestre 1983. (With English summary.) *Revue Écon. Polit.*, September–October 1984, *94*(5), pp. 620–28. [G: France]

Popovic, Mihailo V. Causes of Economic and Sociopolitical Instability in Yugoslavia. *Eastern Europ. Econ.*, Fall 1984, *23*(1), pp. 5–16. [G: Yugoslavia]

Pugh, Cedric. Public Policy, Welfare and the Singaporean Economy. *Ann. Pub. Co-op. Econ.*, Oct.–Dec. 1984, *55*(4), pp. 433–55. [G: Singapore]

Reynolds, Alan. How Supply-Side Triumphed. *Challenge*, November/December 1984, *27*(5), pp. 12–18. [G: U.S.]

Riley, Cristopher. The Medium Term Policy Framework in the UK. *Econ. Lavoro*, Oct.-Dec. 1984, *18*(4), pp. 79–83. [G: U.K.]

Rivlin, Alice M. Out of the Trenches: A Public Policy Paradox. *J. Policy Anal. Manage.*, Fall 1984, *4*(1), pp. 17–22. [G: U.S.]

Roberts, Paul Craig. Supply-Side Economics, Growth, and Liberty. In *Moore, J. H., ed.*, 1984, pp. 73–89. [G: U.S.]

Roemer, Michael. Ghana, 1950–1980: Missed Opportunities. In *Harberger, A. C., ed.*, 1984, pp. 201–25. [G: Ghana]

Romero-Barceló, Carlos. Economic Challenges in Puerto Rico and the Caribbean Community. *Atlantic Econ. J.*, September 1984, *12*(3), pp. 1–3. [G: Puerto Rico]

del Rosario, Ramon R., Jr. Crisis Management in Financial Institutions. *Philippine Econ. J.*, Winter 1984, *23*(1), pp. 72–78. [G: Philippines]

Rürup, Bert and Seidler, Hanns. Das vergessene Stabilitätsgesetz. (The German Law for Stability and Growth—Forgotten but Not Obsolete. With English summary.) *Konjunkturpolitik*, 1984, *30*(5), pp. 259–78. [G: W. Germany]

Rus, Veljko. Long-run, Medium-term, and Short-run Social Conditions for Coming Out of the Crisis. *Eastern Europ. Econ.*, Fall 1984, *23*(1), pp. 17–44. [G: Yugoslavia]

Saini, Krishan G. Economic Policy Management in Italy. *Rev. Econ. Cond. Italy*, Sept.–Dec. 1984, (3), pp. 345–63. [G: Italy]

Sakamoto, Masahiro. Scenarios for the 21st Century and Reconstruction of the International Order—The Economic Aspect. In *Miyawaki, N., ed.*, 1984, pp. 139–47. [G: Selected Countries]

Samuelson, Paul A. Evaluating Reaganomics. *Challenge*, November/December 1984, *27*(5), pp. 4–11. [G: U.S.]

Samuelson, Paul A. Evaluation of Reaganomics as Scientific Macroeconomics. *Economia (Portugal)*, October 1984, *8*(3), pp. 453–69. [G: U.S.]

Sawhill, Isabel V. Can We Salvage the 1980s? *Challenge*, September/October 1984, *27*(4), pp. 18–24. [G: U.S.]

Sawhill, Isabel V. and Stone, Charles F. The Economy: The Key to Success. In *Palmer, J. L. and Sawhill, I. V., eds.*, 1984, pp. 69–105. [G: U.S.]

Sawyer, W. Charles and Sprinkle, Richard L. Caribbean Basin Economic Recovery Act: Export Expansion Effects. *J. World Trade Law*, September–October 1984, *18*(5), pp. 429–36. [G: U.S.; Caribbean]

Schwartz, Anna J. Currents and Countercurrents in Political and Economic Thought: A Comment. *Carnegie-Rochester Conf. Ser. Public Policy*, Autumn 1984, *21*, pp. 253–58.

Sicat, Gerardo P. The Philippines in 1983: Economic Crisis in Perspective. In *Thambipillai, P., ed.*, 1984, pp. 249–65. [G: Philippines]

Simonsen, Palle. Okonomisk politik og styring af den offentlige sektor. (With English summary.) *Nationaløkon. Tidsskr.*, 1984, *122*(3), pp. 307–12. [G: Denmark]

Skurski, Roger. The Need for New Directions and a Progressive Response. In *Alperovitz, G. and Skurski, R., eds.*, 1984, pp. 1–14.

Smith, M. G. Some Future Directions for Social Research in the Commonwealth Caribbean. *Soc. Econ. Stud.*, June 1984, *33*(2), pp. 123–55. [G: Caribbean]

Soullié, Janine. La situation économique récente du Royaume-Uni. (With English summary.) *Revue Écon. Polit.*, September–October 1984, *94*(5), pp. 562–70. [G: U.K.]

Stein, Herbert. Bricks without Straw: Making Economic Policy out of Economics. *Contemp. Policy Issue*, Fall 1984-85, *3*(1), pp. 1–14. [G: U.S.]

Stuart-Fox, Martin. Laos in 1983: A Time of Consolidation. In *Thambipillai, P., ed.*, 1984, pp. 179–94. [G: Laos]

Summers, Lawrence H. The Long-term Effects of Current Macroeconomic Policies. In *Hulten, C. R. and Sawhill, I. V., eds.*, 1984, pp. 179–98. [G: U.S.]

Svendsen, Knud Erik. Tanzania: Phoenix or Icarus?: Comments. In *Harberger, A. C., ed.*, 1984, pp. 197–99. [G: Tanzania]

Tobin, James. Impasse of the 1980s: Locomotives

Who Can't or Won't. *World Econ.*, March 1984, 7(1), pp. 5–21. [G: OECD]

Tomassini, Luciano. The International Scene and Latin America's External Debt. *Cepal Rev.*, 1984, (24), pp. 135–46. [G: Latin America]

Vogel, Ezra F. Japanese and American Societies in the 1980s. In *Miyawaki, N., ed.*, 1984, pp. 49–57. [G: U.S.; Japan]

Volcker, Paul A. Facing Up to the Twin Deficits. *Challenge*, March/April 1984, 27(1), pp. 4–9. [G: U.S.]

Volcker, Paul A. Statement to the Joint Economic Committee, February 9, 1984. *Fed. Res. Bull.*, February 1984, 70(2), pp. 105–07. [G: U.S.]

Volcker, Paul A. Statement to the U.S. Congress Joint Economic Committee, July 30, 1984. *Fed. Res. Bull.*, August 1984, 70(8), pp. 632–36. [G: U.S.]

Volcker, Paul A. Statement to the U.S. House Committee on Banking, Finance, and Urban Affairs, February 7, 1984. *Fed. Res. Bull.*, February 1984, 70(2), pp. 96–102. [G: U.S.]

Volcker, Paul A. Statement to the U.S. Senate Committee on Banking, Housing, and Urban Affairs, July 25, 1984. *Fed. Res. Bull.*, August 1984, 70(8), pp. 626–32. [G: U.S.]

Volcker, Paul A. Statement to the U.S. Senate Committee on the Budget, February 29, 1984. *Fed. Res. Bull.*, March 1984, 70(3), pp. 206–10. [G: U.S.]

Walters, Alan A. The United Kingdom: Political Economy and Macroeconomics. *Carnegie-Rochester Conf. Ser. Public Policy*, Autumn 1984, 21, pp. 259–79. [G: U.K.]

Wolf, Martin. Sustained Economic Growth—Prospect or Mirage? *World Econ.*, September 1984, 7(3), pp. 313–31. [G: Global]

1331 Stabilization Theories and Policies

Alperovitz, Gar. Government Deficit and Business Cycle: Comment. In *Wachter, M. L. and Wachter, S. M., eds.*, 1984, pp. 337–41. [G: U.S.]

Anderson, Robert; Ando, Albert and Enzler, Jared. Interaction between Fiscal and Monetary Policy and the Real Rate of Interest. *Amer. Econ. Rev.*, May 1984, 74(2), pp. 55–60. [G: U.S.]

Annable, James. The Free Market Needs Help: Incomes Policy. *Challenge*, May/June 1984, 27(2), pp. 59–61. [G: U.S.]

Arce, Horacio. The Trade Liberalization Policy of Argentina: Its Impact on Latin American Integration. In *Núñez del Arco, J.; Margain, E. and Cherol, R., eds.*, 1984, pp. 280–314. [G: Argentina]

Arestis, Philip and Driver, Ciaran. The Policy Implications of Post Keynesianism. *J. Econ. Issues*, December 1984, 18(4), pp. 1093–1105. [G: U.K.]

Arndt, Sven W. The External Effects of U.S. Disinflation. In *Fellner, W., ed.*, 1984, pp. 131–53. [G: OECD; U.S.]

Artis, M. J., et al. The Effects of Economic Policy, 1979–82. *Nat. Inst. Econ. Rev.*, May 1984, (108), pp. 54–67. [G: U.K.]

Balassa, Bela. Medium-term Economic Policies for Portugal. *Economia (Portugal)*, October 1984, 8(3), pp. 543–67. [G: Portugal]

Baldassarri, Mario. Optimal "Mix" of Government Expenditure and Optimal Growth Path for an Open Economy within a Three Targets–Three Guns Framework. *Econ. Notes*, 1984, (2), pp. 5–24.

Balfi, Paulo. Sui limiti della politica economica. (On the Limitations of Economic Policy. With English summary.) *Bancaria*, January 1984, 40(1), pp. 9–11. [G: Italy]

Barker, Kate; Britton, Andrew J. C. and Major, Robin. Macroeconomic Policy in France and Britain. *Nat. Inst. Econ. Rev.*, November 1984, (110), pp. 68–84. [G: U.K.; France]

Barre, Raymond. National versus International Solutions for Unemployment. In *Pierre, A. J., ed.*, 1984, pp. 53–78. [G: U.S.; W. Europe]

Barth, Michael C. and Berk, Edwin. Oil Supply Shocks and Macroeconomic Policy: Economic Response: Administrative Options and Analytical Framework. In *Alm, A. L. and Weimer, R. J., eds.*, 1984, pp. 129–43. [G: U.S.]

Baum, C. F. The Evaluation of Historical Policy via Optimal Control Techniques. In *Hughes Hallet, A.J., ed.*, 1984, pp. 165–77. [G: U.S.]

Beckerman, Wilfred. Economic Policy and Performance in Britain since World War II. In *Harberger, A. C., ed.*, 1984, pp. 13–33. [G: U.K.]

Bird, Graham. Relationships, Resource Uses and the Conditionality Debate. In *Killick, Tony, ed. (II)*, 1984, pp. 145–82. [G: LDCs]

Blanchard, Olivier J. A Reexamination of the Theory of Automatic Stabilizers: Income Stability and Economic Efficiency under Alternative Tax Schemes: Comments. *Carnegie-Rochester Conf. Ser. Public Policy*, Spring 1984, 20, pp. 207–08.

Blanchard, Olivier J. Macroeconomic Policy Coordination among the Industrial Economies: Comments. *Brookings Pap. Econ. Act.*, 1984, (1), pp. 65–68. [G: U.S.; W. Germany; Japan]

Blinder, Alan S. Reaganomics and Growth: The Message in the Models. In *Hulten, C. R. and Sawhill, I. V., eds.*, 1984, pp. 199–227. [G: U.S.]

Blinder, Alan S. The Keynesian Restoration. *Challenge*, May/June 1984, 27(2), pp. 26–34. [G: U.S.]

Blinder, Alan S. and Mankiw, N. Gregory. Aggregation and Stabilization Policy in a Multi-Contract Economy. *J. Monet. Econ.*, January 1984, 13(1), pp. 67–86.

Boloña, Carlos. The Role of Economy-Wide Prices in the Adjustment Process: Comment. In *Muns, J., ed.*, 1984, pp. 110–12. [G: LDCs]

Boltho, Andrea. Economic Policy and Performance in Europe since the Second Oil Shock. In *Emerson, M., ed.*, 1984, pp. 10–32. [G: W. Europe]

Bonnick, Gladstone G. Jamaica: Liberalization to

Centralization, and Back? In *Harberger, A. C., ed.*, 1984, pp. 265–91.   [G: Jamaica]

Boskin, Michael J. U.S. Stabilization Policy: Lessons from the Past Decade: Comments. In *Harberger, A. C., ed.*, 1984, pp. 151–56.

[G: U.S.]

Brewer, H. L. Regional Economic Stabilization: An Efficient Diversification Approach. *Rev. Reg. Stud.*, Winter 1984, *14*(1), pp. 8–21.

[G: U.S.]

Britton, Andrew J. C. Uncertainty, Forecasting and Budget Changes. *Nat. Inst. Econ. Rev.*, February 1984, (107), pp. 60–62.   [G: U.K.]

Britton, Andrew J. C. Full Employment as a Policy Objective. *Nat. Inst. Econ. Rev.*, August 1984, (109), pp. 78–84.   [G: U.K.]

Buffie, Edward F. Financial Repression, the New Structuralists, and Stabilization Policy in Semi-Industrialized Economies. *J. Devel. Econ.*, April 1984, *14*(3), pp. 305–22.   [G: LDCs]

Buiter, Willem H. Comment: Some Unpleasant Monetarist Arithmetic. In *Griffiths, B. and Wood, G. E., eds.*, 1984, pp. 42–60.

[G: U.K.]

Buiter, Willem H. Granger-Causality and Policy Effectiveness. *Economica*, May 1984, *51*(202), pp. 151–62.

Buiter, Willem H. and Gersovitz, Mark. Controllability and the Theory of Economic Policy: A Further Note. *J. Public Econ.*, June 1984, *24*(1), pp. 127–29.

Burns, Leland S. and Grebler, Leo. Is Public Construction Countercyclical? *Land Econ.*, November 1984, *60*(4), pp. 367–77.

[G: U.S.]

Butschek, Felix. Kontrollierte Inflation—ein missglücktes Experiment? *Empirica*, 1984, *11*(1), pp. 59–80.   [G: Austria]

Cagan, Phillip and Fellner, William. The Cost of Disinflation, Credibility, and the Deceleration of Wages 1982–1983. In *Fellner, W., ed.*, 1984, pp. 7–19.   [G: U.S.]

Calleo, David P. Since 1961: American Power in a New World Economy. In *Becker, W. H. and Wells, S. F., Jr., eds.*, 1984, pp. 391–457.

[G: U.S.]

Calmfors, Lars. Stabilization Policy and Wage Formation in Economies with Strong Trade Unions. In *Emerson, M., ed.*, 1984, pp. 89–121.   [G: Scandinavia; Belgium; Austria; Netherlands]

Chiang, Alpha C. and Fei, John C. H. Growth Epochs and Compensatory Fiscal Policy. *Singapore Econ. Rev.*, October 1984, *29*(2), pp. 38–62.   [G: U.S.]

Christiano, Lawrence J. A Reexamination of the Theory of Automatic Stabilizers: Reply. *Carnegie-Rochester Conf. Ser. Public Policy*, Spring 1984, *20*, pp. 209–10.

Christiano, Lawrence J. A Reexamination of the Theory of Automatic Stabilizers. *Carnegie-Rochester Conf. Ser. Public Policy*, Spring 1984, *20*, pp. 147–206.

Ciampi, Carlo Azeglio. Politica di bilancio, politica dei redditi e stabilità monetaria, presupposti di una crescita stabile. (Budget Policy, Incomes Policy and Monetary Stability as Prerequisites for Stable Growth. With English summary.) *Bancaria*, March 1984, *40*(3), pp. 241–55.   [G: Italy]

Cobham, David. French Macro-Economic Policy under President Mitterrand: An Assessment. *Nat. Westminster Bank Quart. Rev.*, February 1984, pp. 41–51.   [G: France]

Colander, David C. Was Keynes a Keynesian or a Lernerian? *J. Econ. Lit.*, December 1984, *22*(4), pp. 1572–75.

Conci, Paolo and Ferrarese, Giulio. Coordinamento internazionale delle politiche economiche. Indispensabile o superfluo? (With English summary.) *Econ. Int.*, August–November 1984, *37*(3–4), pp. 255–67.   [G: U.S.; W. Germany; Japan]

Congdon, Tim G. A Comment: The problem of Debt Interest Seen in Historical Perspective [Some Unpleasant Monetarist Arithmetic]. In *Griffiths, B. and Wood, G. E., eds.*, 1984, pp. 67–71.

Connolly, Michael B. Jamaica: Liberalization to Centralization, and Back? Comments. In *Harberger, A. C., ed.*, 1984, pp. 293–99.

[G: Jamaica]

Cooley, Thomas F.; LeRoy, Stephen F. and Raymon, Neil. Econometric Policy Evaluation: Note. *Amer. Econ. Rev.*, June 1984, *74*(3), pp. 467–70.

Corden, W. M. Macroeconomic Targets and Instruments for a Small Open Economy. *Singapore Econ. Rev.*, October 1984, *29*(2), pp. 27–37.

Cossiga, Giovanni. The Budget in the Italian Economic Crisis. *Rev. Econ. Cond. Italy*, February 1984, (1), pp. 91–106.   [G: Italy]

Cripps, Francis and Ward, Terry. Erratum [European Recession and Problems of Recovery]. *Cambridge J. Econ.*, March 1984, *8*(1), pp. 115.   [G: W. Europe]

Currie, David and Levine, Paul. Stochastic Macroeconomic Policy Simulations for a Small Open Economy. In *van der Ploeg, F., ed.*, 1984, pp. 217–48.

d'Alcantara, Gonzalez. A Game Theoretic Approach of Macroeconomic Simulations for the Study of Conflicting Goals. In *Despontin, M.; Nijkamp, P. and Spronk, J., eds.*, 1984, pp. 125–40.   [G: Belgium]

Danziger, Sheldon, et al. Reviewing Reagan's Economic Program. *Challenge*, January/February 1984, *26*(6), pp. 42–50.   [G: U.S.]

Darrat, Ali F. The Dominant Influence of Fiscal Actions in Developing Countries. *Eastern Econ. J.*, July-September 1984, *10*(3), pp. 271–84.   [G: Brazil; Chile; Mexico; Peru; Venezuela]

Deleau, Michel; Le Van, Cuong and Malgrange, Pierre. Stabilisation efficace des systèmes économiques en présence d'incertitude: expérimentation avec une maquette du modèle DMS. (The Uncertainty Frontier as a Global Approach to the Efficient Stabilization of Economic Systems: An Experimentation with the

Micro-DMS Model. With English summary.) *Revue Écon.*, May 1984, *35*(3), pp. 507–36.

Deleau, Michel; Le Van, Cuong and Malgrange, Pierre. The Uncertainty Frontier as a Global Approach to the Efficient Stabilisation of Economic Systems: Experiments with the Micro-DMS Model. In *Hughes Hallet, A. J., ed.*, 1984, pp. 97–117. [G: France]

Demery, David. Aggregate Demand, Rational Expectations and Real Output: Some New Evidence for the U.K., 1963.2–1982.2. *Econ. J.*, December 1984, *94*(376), pp. 847–62. [G: U.K.]

Deschamps, Robert. Chômage et inflation en Belgique pendant la crise: la politique économique et ses effets. (With English summary.) *Revue Écon. Polit.*, September–October 1984, *94*(5), pp. 581–91. [G: Belgium]

Díaz, Francisco Gil. Mexico's Path from Stability to Inflation. In *Harberger, A. C., ed.*, 1984, pp. 333–76. [G: Mexico]

Díaz, Rámon. Uruguay's Erratic Growth. In *Harberger, A. C., ed.*, 1984, pp. 377–402. [G: Uruguay]

Dick, Hermann, et al. Stabilisation Strategies in Primary Commodity Exporting Countries: A Case Study of Chile. *J. Devel. Econ.*, May–June–August 1984, *15*(1,2,3), pp. 47–75. [G: Chile]

Dornbusch, Rudiger. U.S. Monetary and Fiscal Policy, the Dollar and the International Financial System. In *Frenkel, J. A. and Mussa, M. L., eds.*, 1984, pp. 23–48. [G: U.S.; OECD; Latin America]

Dornbusch, Rudiger and Fischer, Stanley. The Australian Macroeconomy. In *Caves, R. E. and Krause, L. B., eds.*, 1984, pp. 25–79. [G: Australia]

Edgar, Robert. Government Deficit and Business Cycle: Comment. In *Wachter, M. L. and Wachter, S. M., eds.*, 1984, pp. 350–51. [G: U.S.]

Emerson, Michael. The European Stagflation Disease in International Perspective and Some Possible Therapy. In *Emerson, M., ed.*, 1984, pp. 195–228. [G: N. Europe; OECD]

Farnleitner, Johannes. Introdução às Formas de Concertação Social: Comment. In *Cavaco Silva, A. A., ed.*, 1984, pp. 175–77. [G: Austria]

Felix, David. The Impotence of Macroeconomic Policy Activism: A Critical Appraisal of the New Classical Macroeconomics. *J. Econ. Issues*, September 1984, *18*(3), pp. 825–59. [G: OECD]

Fellner, William. Monetary and Fiscal Policy in a Disinflationary Process: Justified and Unjustified Misgivings about Budget Deficits. In *Fellner, W., ed.*, 1984, pp. 55–86. [G: U.S.]

Fendt, Roberto, Jr. Trade Prospects for Brazil after the Devaluation. In *Jorge, A.; Salazar-Carrillo, J. and Sanchez, E. P.*, 1984, pp. 93–96. [G: Brazil]

Ferro, Angelo. Strumentazione fiscale e monetaria nella politica dell 'offerta. (The Use of Fiscal and Monetary Tools in Supply-Side Policy.

With English summary.) *Bancaria*, October 1984, *40*(10), pp. 957–64.

Fischer, Stanley. The Economy of Israel. *Carnegie-Rochester Conf. Ser. Public Policy*, Spring 1984, *20*, pp. 7–52. [G: Israel]

Frank, Andre Gunder and Fuentes, Marta. Critique of the Finance Minister's 1970 Report to the Congress of Chile. In *Frank, A. G.*, 1984, pp. 137–54. [G: Chile]

Frenkel, Jacob A. Comments on the Economy of Israel. *Carnegie-Rochester Conf. Ser. Public Policy*, Spring 1984, *20*, pp. 57–67. [G: Israel]

Gaburro, Giuseppe. A Preliminary Experiment for an Optimal Control Model of the Italian Economy. *Metroecon.*, June-Oct. 1984, *36*(2–3), pp. 239–58. [G: Italy]

Galbis, Vicente. Ministate Economies. *Finance Develop.*, June 1984, *21*(2), pp. 36–39. [G: Selected LDCs]

Garavello, Oscar and Mauri, Arnaldo. Savings Policies and Exchange Rate Variations in the Context of a Stabilization Program of an Oil-Importing LDC. In *Kessler, D. and Ullmo, P.-A., eds.*, 1984, pp. 311–22.

Ghosh, S.; Gilbert, C. L. and Hughes Hallett, Andrew J. Simple and Optimal Control Rules for Stabilising Commodity Markets. In *Hughes Hallet, A.J., ed.*, 1984, pp. 209–48.

Gilbert, Richard J. and Mork, Knut Anton. Will Oil Markets Tighten Again? A Survey of Policies to Manage Possible Oil Supply Disruptions. *J. Policy Modeling*, February 1984, *6*(1), pp. 111–42. [G: U.S.]

Gillis, Malcolm. Episodes in Indonesian Economic Growth. In *Harberger, A. C., ed.*, 1984, pp. 231–64. [G: Indonesia]

Goedhuys, D. W. The Business Cycle and Public Policy. *S. Afr. J. Econ.*, June 1984, *52*(2), pp. 133–45. [G: S. Africa]

Goldman, Josef and Kouba, Karel. Terms of Trade, Adjustment Processes, and the Economic Mechanism (A Quantitative Approach). *Acta Oecon.*, 1984, *32*(1–2), pp. 137–60. [G: CMEA]

Goodfriend, Marvin. Income Stability and Economic Efficiency under Alternative Tax Schemes: A Comment. *Carnegie-Rochester Conf. Ser. Public Policy*, Spring 1984, *20*, pp. 143–46. [G: U.S.]

Gordon, Kathryn M. and Rausser, Gordon C. Country Hedging for Real Income Stabilization: A Case Study of South Korea and Egypt. *J. Futures Markets*, Winter 1984, *4*(4), pp. 449–64. [G: S. Korea]

Gordon, Robert J. U.S. Stabilization Policy: Lessons from the Past Decade. In *Harberger, A. C., ed.*, 1984, pp. 123–49. [G: U.S.]

Gordon, Robert J. Using Monetary Control to Dampen the Business Cycle: A New Set of First Principles. In *Wachter, M. L. and Wachter, S. M., eds.*, 1984, pp. 302–36. [G: U.S.]

Griffin, Keith and James, Jeffrey. Managing the Transition to Egalitarian Development. In *Amin, S., ed.*, 1984, pp. 97–115.

Griffiths, Brian and Wood, Geoffrey E. Monetarism in the United Kingdom. In *Griffiths, B. and Wood, G. E., eds.*, 1984, pp. 3–12. [G: U.K.]

Ground, Richard Lynn. Orthodox Adjustment Programmes in Latin America: A Critical Look at the Policies of the International Monetary Fund. *Cepal Rev.*, 1984, (23), pp. 45–82. [G: Latin America]

Guess, George and Koford, Kenneth J. Inflation, Recession, and the Federal Budget Deficit (or, Blaming Economic Problems on a Statistical Mirage). *Policy Sci.*, December 1984, *17*(4), pp. 385–402. [G: OECD]

Haraf, William S. Japanese Macroeconomic Performance since 1970: Comments. *Carnegie-Rochester Conf. Ser. Public Policy*, Spring 1984, *20*, pp. 115–20. [G: Japan]

Harberger, Arnold C. Economic Policy and Economic Growth. In *Harberger, A. C., ed.*, 1984, pp. 427–66. [G: MDCs; LDCs]

Harkness, Jon. Optimal Oil Pricing in a Small Open Economy: A Macro-economic Perspective. *Can. J. Econ.*, November 1984, *17*(4), pp. 762–73.

Harris, Donald J. The Strategy of Macroeconomic Policy and Black Americans: Comments. *Rev. Black Polit. Econ.*, Summer–Fall 1984, *13*(1–2), pp. 56–59. [G: U.S.]

von Hayek, Friedrich A. The Fate of the Gold Standard. In *von Hayek, F. A. (II)*, 1984, *1932*, pp. 118–35. [G: U.K.; U.S.]

Hillier, Brian and Malcomson, James M. Dynamic Inconsistency, Rational Expectations, and Optimal Government Policy. *Econometrica*, November 1984, *52*(6), pp. 1437–51.

Holly, Sean and Corker, R. Optimal Feedback and Feedforward Stabilisation of Exchange Rates, Money, Prices and Output under Rational Expectations. In *Hughes Hallet, A. J., ed.*, 1984, pp. 33–60. [G: U.K.]

Hormats, Robert D. Unemployment and Growth in the Western Economies: Introduction. In *Pierre, A. J., ed.*, 1984, pp. 1–13.

Hughes Hallett, Andrew J. Non-cooperative Strategies for Dynamic Policy Games and the Problem of Time Inconsistency. *Oxford Econ. Pap.*, November 1984, *36*(3), pp. 381–99.

Hunt, Lacy H. Using Monetary Control to Dampen the Business Cycle: A New Set of First Principles: Comment. In *Wachter, M. L. and Wachter, S. M., eds.*, 1984, pp. 341–44. [G: U.S.]

Hwang, Been Kwei and Yu, Eden S.-H. Wealth Effects, IS-LM Stability and the Efficacy of Economic Policies. *J. Macroecon.*, Spring 1984, *6*(2), pp. 229–34.

Janácková, Stanislava. The Theoretical Basis and the Aims of "Reaganomics"—Proclamations and Reality. *Czech. Econ. Digest.*, November 1984, (7), pp. 84–106. [G: U.S.]

Johnson, Ronald. The Strategy of Macroeconomic Policy and Black Americans. *Rev. Black Polit. Econ.*, Summer–Fall 1984, *13*(1–2), pp. 51–55. [G: U.S.]

Karp, Larry and Havenner, Arthur. Toward the

Resurrection of Optimal Macroeconomic Policies. In *Hughes Hallet, A.J., ed.*, 1984, pp. 23–32.

Karunaratne, Neil Dias. Short-term Stabilization and Long-term Development of Fiji in 1983. In *Utrecht, E., ed.*, 1984, pp. 309–15. [G: Fiji]

Kaufman, Henry. Complexities of U.S. Stabilization Policies in an International Context. In *Hewlett, S. A.; Kaufman, H. and Kenen, P. B., eds.*, 1984, pp. 1–12. [G: U.S.]

Kenen, Peter B. Beyond Recovery: Challenges to U.S. Economic Policy in the 1980s. In *Hewlett, S. A.; Kaufman, H. and Kenen, P. B., eds.*, 1984, pp. 13–25. [G: U.S.]

Killick, Tony. IMF Stabilisation Programmes. In *Killick, Tony, ed. (II)*, 1984, pp. 183–226.

Killick, Tony. The IMF and Stabilisation: Kenya, 1975–81. In *Killick, Tony, ed. (I)*, 1984, pp. 164–216. [G: Kenya]

Klausinger, Hansjörg. Fristigkeitsaspekte in der Theorie der Stabilisierungspolitik. (Maturity Aspects in the Theory of Stabilization Policy. With English summary.) *Kredit Kapital*, 1984, *17*(2), pp. 180–98.

Komiya, Ryutaro and Yasui, Kazuo. Japan's Macroeconomic Performance since the First Oil Crisis: Review and Appraisal. *Carnegie-Rochester Conf. Ser. Public Policy*, Spring 1984, *20*, pp. 69–114. [G: Japan]

Krueger, Anne O. Problems of Liberalization. In *Harberger, A. C., ed.*, 1984, pp. 403–23.

Lächler, Ulrich. Stabilization Policy in an Open-Economy Equilibrium Model. *Weltwirtsch. Arch.*, 1984, *120*(3), pp. 403–23.

Lai, Ching-chong and Chen, Chau-nan. Flexible Exchange Rates, Tight Money Effects, and Macroeconomic Policy. *J. Post Keynesian Econ.*, Fall 1984, *7*(1), pp. 128–33.

Laidler, David. Economic Policy and Performance in Britain since World War II: Comments. In *Harberger, A. C., ed.*, 1984, pp. 35–39. [G: U.K.]

León, Carlos Amat Y. Fiscal Deficits and Balance of Payments Disequilibrium in IMF Adjustment Programs: Comment. In *Muns, J., ed.*, 1984, pp. 137–40. [G: LDCs; Peru]

Levin, Jay H. Non-sterilization, Pegged Exchange Rates, and Stabilization Policy. *Metroecon.*, February 1984, *36*(1), pp. 77–96.

Lipschitz, Leslie. Domestic Credit and Exchange Rates in Developing Countries: Some Policy Experiments with Korean Data. *Int. Monet. Fund Staff Pap.*, December 1984, *31*(4), pp. 595–635. [G: Korea]

Lipschitz, Leslie and Schadler, Susan M. Relative Prices, Real Wages, and Macroeconomic Policies: Some Evidence from Manufacturing in Japan and the United Kingdom. *Int. Monet. Fund Staff Pap.*, June 1984, *31*(2), pp. 303–38. [G: Japan; U.K.]

Lopes, Francisco L. and Modiano, Eduardo M. Indexación, shock externo y nivel de actividad: notas sobre el caso brasileño. (With English summary.) *Desarrollo Econ.*, April–June 1984, *24*(93), pp. 71–84. [G: Brazil]

Loser, Claudio M. The Role of Economy-Wide Prices in the Adjustment Process. In *Muns, J., ed.*, 1984, pp. 84–109. [G: LDCs]

Maciejowski, J. M. and Vines, David. Decoupled Control of a Macroeconomic Model Using Frequency-Domain Methods. *J. Econ. Dynam. Control*, February 1984, 7(1), pp. 55–77.

Makinen, Gail E. The Greek Stabilization of 1944–46. *Amer. Econ. Rev.*, December 1984, 74(5), pp. 1067–74. [G: Greece]

Malan, Pedro S. and Wells, John R. 'Structural' Models of Inflation and Balance of Payments Disequilibria in Semi-industrialised Economies—Some Implications for Stabilisation and Growth Policies. In *Csikós-Nagy, B.; Hague, D. and Hall, G., eds.*, 1984, pp. 391–408.

Malliaris, A. G. Economic Stabilization, Social Issues and the Role of Government. *Rev. Soc. Econ.*, October 1984, 42(2), pp. 117–29. [G: U.S.]

Marion, Nancy Peregrim. Exchange Rate Regimes: The Problem of Rate Swings. In *Hewlett, S. A.; Kaufman, H. and Kenen, P. B., eds.*, 1984, pp. 77–95.

Marris, Stephen N. Macroeconomic Policy Coordination among the Industrial Economies: Comments. *Brookings Pap. Econ. Act., 1984*, (1), pp. 68–71. [G: U.S.; W. Germany; Japan]

Marris, Stephen N. Why the Dollar Won't Come Down. *Challenge*, November/December 1984, 27(5), pp. 19–25. [G: U.S.]

Masera, Rainer S. Monetary Policy and Budget Policy: Blend or Dichotomy? In *Masera, R. S. and Triffin, R., eds.*, 1984, pp. 196–223. [G: Italy; OECD]

McCracken, Paul W. Has Macro-Theory Failed Economic Policy? *Southern Econ. J.*, October 1984, 51(2), pp. 319–29. [G: U.S.]

McDonald, Ian M. Anti-stagflationary Tax Cuts and the Problem of Investment. *Econ. Rec.*, September 1984, 60(170), pp. 284–93.

McEntee, Gerald W. Government Deficit and Business Cycle: Comment. In *Wachter, M. L. and Wachter, S. M., eds.*, 1984, pp. 344–46. [G: U.S.]

Meade, J. E. Structural Changes in the Rate of Interest and the Rate of Foreign Exchange to Preserve Equilibrium in the Balance of Payments and the Budget Balance. *Oxford Econ. Pap.*, March 1984, 36(1), pp. 52–66.

Meltzer, Allan H. The Fight Against Inflation: A Comment [Some Unpleasant Monetarist Arithmetic]. In *Griffiths, B. and Wood, G. E., eds.*, 1984, pp. 61–66.

Miatto, Giorgio. Il dibattito sulla teoria di Keynes: controversie teoriche e alternative concrete di politica economica. (Debate on Keynes' Theory: Theoretic Controversies and Actual Alternatives of Political Economy. With English summary.) *Econ. Lavoro*, Apr.-June 1984, 18(2), pp. 61–84.

Michalski, Wolfgang. The Need for Positive Adjustment Policies in the 1980's. In *Miyawaki, N., ed.*, 1984, pp. 207–19.

Micwitz, Gösta. Vad var felet med keynesianismen? (What Went Wrong with Keynesian Economics? With English summary.) *Ekon. Samfundets Tidskr.*, 1984, 37(4), pp. 235–36.

Miller, Marcus H. Government, Unions and Stagflation in the UK. *Nat. Inst. Econ. Rev.*, August 1984, (109), pp. 68–72. [G: U.K.]

Miller, Preston J. Income Stability and Economic Efficiency under Alternative Tax Schemes. *Carnegie-Rochester Conf. Ser. Public Policy*, Spring 1984, 20, pp. 121–41. [G: U.S.]

Mosley, Paul and Cracknell, Richard. Endogenous Government Policy in a Model of the UK Economy. *Appl. Econ.*, October 1984, 16(5), pp. 633–45. [G: U.K.]

Neese, J. W. and Pindyck, Robert S. Behavioural Assumptions in Decentralised Stabilisation Policies. In *Hughes Hallet, A.J., ed.*, 1984, pp. 251–70. [G: U.S.]

Nelson, Joan M. The Political Economy of Stabilization: Commitment, Capacity, and Public Response. *World Devel.*, October 1984, 12(10), pp. 983–1006. [G: Ghana; Zambia; Kenya; Sri Lanka; Jamaica]

Nelson, Joan M. The Politics of Stabilization. In *Feinberg, R. E. and Kallab, V., eds., no. 1*, 1984, pp. 99–118. [G: LDCs]

Nishijima, Shoji. Indexing Policies and Macroeconomic Stability in Brazil: Rational Expectation Model. *Kobe Econ. Bus. Rev.*, 1984, 30, pp. 73–86. [G: Brazil]

Ogawa, Kazuo. On the Substitutability of Public Stocks for Private Stocks under Rational Expectations. *Kobe Univ. Econ.*, 1984, (30), pp. 79–96.

Oudiz, Gilles and Sachs, Jeffrey D. Macroeconomic Policy Coordination among the Industrial Economies. *Brookings Pap. Econ. Act.*, 1984, (1), pp. 1–64. [G: U.S.; W. Germany; Japan]

Parkin, Michael. The Economy of Israel: A Comment. *Carnegie-Rochester Conf. Ser. Public Policy*, Spring 1984, 20, pp. 53–56. [G: Israel]

Pelkmans, Jacques. Collective Management and Economic Cooperation. In *Merlini, C., ed.*, 1984, pp. 89–136. [G: OECD]

Pesaran, M. H. Macroeconomic Policy in an Oil-exporting Economy with Foreign Exchange Controls. *Economica*, August 1984, 51(203), pp. 253–70.

Pesaran, M. H. The New Classical Macroeconomics: A Critical Exposition. In *van der Ploeg, F., ed.*, 1984, pp. 195–215.

Peterson, Wallace C. Economic Stabilization and Inflation. *J. Econ. Issues*, March 1984, 18(1), pp. 69–100. [G: U.S.]

Petkovski, Djordjija B. Stability Analysis of Large Scale Economic Systems Which Have a Multi-Time Scale Property. In *Hughes Hallet, A. J., ed.*, 1984, pp. 271–88.

Pikoulakis, Emmanuel. Fiscal and Monetary Policies in a Flexible Exchange Rate Model with Full Employment and Static Expectations. In *Black, J. and Dorrance, G. S., eds.*, 1984, pp. 167–86.

Pindyck, Robert S. and Rotemberg, Julio J. Energy Shocks and the Macroeconomy. In *Alm, A. L. and Weimer, R. J.*, eds., 1984, pp. 97–120. **[G: U.S.]**

van der Ploeg, Frederick. Economic Policy Rules for Risk-Sensitive Decision Making. *Z. Nationalökon.*, 1984, *44*(3), pp. 207–35.

van der Ploeg, Frederick. Government Ideology and Re-election Efforts. *Oxford Econ. Pap.*, June 1984, *36*(2), pp. 213–31.

Poole, William. Government Deficit and Business Cycle: Comment. In *Wachter, M. L. and Wachter, S. M.*, eds., 1984, pp. 346–49. **[G: U.S.]**

Potter, Stephen and Feiner, Michael. Macroeconomic Policies and Exchange Rates. *OECD Econ. Stud.*, Autumn 1984, (3), pp. 119–44. **[G: OECD]**

Pultz, Niels. Inflation og stabiliseringspolitik i Argentina 1970–81. (Inflation and Stabilization Policy in Argentina, 1970–81. With English summary.) *Nationaløkon. Tidsskr.*, 1984, *122*(2), pp. 283–97. **[G: Argentina]**

Rába, András. Restriction and Adjustment. *Acta Oecon.*, 1984, *33*(1–2), pp. 69–87. **[G: Hungary]**

Ramb, Bernd-Thomas. Ineffektivität der Wirtschaftspolitik bei "rationalen Erwartungen"? Eine unkerrekte, aber auch modellspezifische Behauptung. (Ineffectiveness of Economic Policy under "Rational Expectations"? An Incorrect but Also Model-Specific Assertion. With English summary.) *Kredit Kapital*, 1984, *17*(2), pp. 165–79.

Rapping, Leonard A. Economic Change, Bureaucracy, and the Innovative Process. In *Alperovitz, G. and Skurski, R.*, eds., 1984, pp. 56–75. **[G: U.S.]**

Rehn, Gösta. Intorução às Formas de Concertação Social: Comment. In *Cavaco Silva, A. A.*, ed., 1984, pp. 165–73.

Ristic, Žarko. Društvena potrošnja i ekonomska stabilizacija—Efekti na interni ekvilibrijum. (Social Consumption and Economic Stabilization—The Effects on Internal Equilibrium. With English summary.) *Econ. Anal. Worker's Manage.*, 1984, *18*(2), pp. 151–70. **[G: Yugoslavia]**

Rodríguez, Carlos Alfredo. The Role of Economy-Wide Prices in the Adjustment Process: Comment. In *Muns, J.*, ed., 1984, pp. 113–16. **[G: LDCs]**

Rødseth, Asbjørn. Progressive Taxes and Automatic Stabilization in an Open Economy. *J. Macroecon.*, Summer 1984, *6*(3), pp. 265–82.

Rothengatter, Werner. The Dynamics of Financial Adjustments in an Open Economy and the Effects of Stabilization Policy. *Z. ges. Staatswiss.*, June 1984, *140*(2), pp. 308–29.

Saint-Étienne, Christian. De l'importance réelle de l'hypothèse de la rationalitè des anticipations. (With English summary.) *Revue Écon. Polit.*, November–December 1984, *94*(6), pp. 773–91.

Sandblom, C. L. and Eiselt, H. A. Controlling an Econometric Model Using Different Coeffi-

cient Sets. In *Hughes Hallet, A.J.*, ed., 1984, pp. 85–95.

Sargent, Thomas J. and Wallace, Neil. Some Unpleasant Monetarist Arithmetic. In *Griffiths, B. and Wood, G. E.*, eds., 1984, pp. 15–41.

Scharpf, Fritz W. Economic and Institutional Constraints of Full-Employment Strategies: Sweden, Austria, and Western Germany, 1973–1982. In *Goldthorpe, J. H.*, ed., 1984, pp. 257–90. **[G: Sweden; Austria; W. Germany]**

Shafer, Jeffrey R. Stabilization Policies in Open Economies. *Amer. Econ. Rev.*, May 1984, *74*(2), pp. 305–10.

Shalit, Haim. Does It Pay to Stabilise the Price of Vegetables? An Empirical Evaluation of Agricultural Price Policies. *Europ. Rev. Agr. Econ.*, 1984, *11*(1), pp. 1–16. **[G: Israel]**

Sharpley, Jennifer. The IMF and Stabilisation: Jamaica, 1972–80. In *Killick, Tony*, ed. (*I*), 1984, pp. 115–63. **[G: Jamaica]**

Sharpley, Jennifer. The Potential of Domestic Stabilisation Measures in Developing Countries. In *Killick, Tony*, ed. (*II*), 1984, pp. 55–85. **[G: LDCs]**

Shupp, F. R. Macroeconomic Theory and Policy. In *van der Ploeg, F.*, ed., 1984, pp. 165–94.

Siegel, Barry N. Money in Crisis: Introduction. In *Siegel, B. N.*, ed., 1984, pp. 1–16. **[G: U.S.]**

Spencer, Grant H. and Duggan, K. G. On the Structural Sensitivity of Short Term Output-Inflation Tradeoffs. *Appl. Econ.*, February 1984, *16*(1), pp. 81–98. **[G: New Zealand]**

Starbatty, Joachim. Zur Rollenverteilung in der Konjunkturpolitik. (With English Summary.) In *Eucken, W. and Böhm, F.*, eds., 1984, pp. 151–66. **[G: W. Germany]**

Steindl, Josef. On Maturity in Capitalist Economies. In *Foster, J. B. and Szlajfer, H.*, eds., 1984, *1966*, pp. 167–78.

Steindl, Josef. Stagnation Theory and Stagnation Policy. In *Foster, J. B. and Szlajfer, H.*, eds., 1984, *1979*, pp. 179–97. **[G: U.S.]**

Stemp, Peter J. and Turnovsky, Stephen J. Equilibrium, Stability, and Deficit Financing in a Simple Nonlinear Monetary Model under Perfect Foresight. *J. Macroecon.*, Fall 1984, *6*(4), pp. 377–97.

Stemp, Peter J. and Turnovsky, Stephen J. Optimal Stabilisation Policies under Perfect Foresight. In *Hughes Hallet, A.J.*, ed., 1984, pp. 3–22.

Street, James H. Values in Conflict: Developing Countries as Social Laboratories. *J. Econ. Issues*, June 1984, *18*(2), pp. 633–41. **[G: Mexico; Argentina; Chile; Uruguay; Brazil]**

Struthers, John J. Rational Expectations: A Promising Research Program or a Case of Monetarist Fundamentalism? *J. Econ. Issues*, December 1984, *18*(4), pp. 1133–54.

Strydom, P. D. F. The New Keynesian Approach to Economic Policy. *S. Afr. J. Econ.*, September 1984, *52*(3), pp. 282–95.

Summers, Lawrence H. The Long-term Effects

of Current Macroeconomic Policies. In *Hulten, C. R. and Sawhill, I. V., eds.*, 1984, pp. 179–98. [G: U.S.]

Sutton, Mary. Structuralism: The Latin American Record and the New Critique. In *Killick, Tony, ed. (I)*, 1984, pp. 19–67. [G: Chile; Peru]

Sutton, Mary. The IMF and Stabilisation: Indonesia, 1966–70. In *Killick, Tony, ed. (I)*, 1984, pp. 68–114. [G: Indonesia]

Sweeney, Richard James. Anticipate Countercyclical Monetary Policy. *Econ. Inquiry*, January 1984, 22(1), pp. 28–36.

Tabata, Yoshio and Sawaki, Katsushige. Optimal Exercise Policies for an American Call Option. (In Japanese. With English summary.) *Osaka Econ. Pap.*, December 1984, 34(2–3), pp. 283–89.

Taddei, Dominique. Le IXe Plan: de la rigueur a une politique de l'offre. (The French IXth Plan: From Rigor to a Supply Policy. With English summary.) *Revue Écon.*, November 1984, 35(6), pp. 1239–60. [G: France]

Tanzi, Vito and Blejer, Mario I. Fiscal Deficits and Balance of Payments Disequilibrium in IMF Adjustment Programs. In *Muns, J., ed.*, 1984, pp. 117–36. [G: LDCs]

Taylor, Lance. IMF Conditionality: Incomplete Theory, Policy Malpractice. *METU*, 1984, 11(1–2), pp. 233–47. [G: LDCs]

Taylor, Lance. Mexico's Adjustment in the 1980s: Look Back Before Leaping Ahead. In *Feinberg, R. E. and Kallab, V., eds., no. 1*, 1984, pp. 147–58. [G: Mexico]

Tichy, Gunther. Strategy and Implementation of Employment Policy in Austria: Successful Experiments with Unconventional Assignment of Instruments to Goals. *Kyklos*, 1984, 37(3), pp. 363–86. [G: Austria]

Tobin, James. Unemployment in the 1980s: Macroeconomic Diagnosis and Prescription. In *Pierre, A. J., ed.*, 1984, pp. 79–112. [G: OECD]

Tondini, Giovanni. Further Discussion on Controllability and the Theory of Economic Policy [On a Generalization of Tinbergen's Condition in the Theory of Policy to Dynamic Models]. *J. Public Econ.*, June 1984, 24(1), pp. 123–25.

Turner, Brian and Williams, Lynn R. Economic Policy in a Global Economy: The Future of American Industry. In *Hewlett, S. A.; Kaufman, H. and Kenen, P. B., eds.*, 1984, pp. 181–98. [G: U.S.]

Turnovsky, Stephen J. and Wohar, Mark E. Monetarism and the Aggregate Economy: Some Longer-Run Evidence. *Rev. Econ. Statist.*, November 1984, 66(4), pp. 619–29. [G: U.S.]

Usoskin, V. M. "Demand Management" within the System of Anti-inflation Measures Employed by the Bourgeois State. In *Nikitin, S. M., ed.*, 1984, pp. 179–96. [G: OECD]

Wagner, Richard E. Boom and Bust: The Political Economy of Economic Disorder. In *Buchanan, J. M. and Tollison, R. D., eds.*, 1984, pp. 238–72.

Wallace, Myles S. Economic Stabilization as a Public Good: What Does It Mean? *J. Post Keynesian Econ.*, Winter 1983-84, 6(2), pp. 295–302.

Wallich, Henry C. The German Council of Economic Advisers in an American Perspective. *Z. ges. Staatswiss.*, June 1984, 140(2), pp. 355–63. [G: U.S.; Germany]

Wesson, Robert. Politics, Policies, & Economic Development in Latin America: Introduction. In *Wesson, R., ed.*, 1984, pp. xi–xvii.

Whitman, Marina v.N. Persistent Unemployment: Economic Policy Perspectives in the United States and Western Europe. In *Pierre, A. J., ed.*, 1984, pp. 14–52. [G: U.S.; W. Europe]

Williams, Shirley. Unemployment and Economic Strains in the Western Alliance. In *Pierre, A. J., ed.*, 1984, pp. 113–42. [G: OECD]

Witte, Willard E. Macroeconomic Stability and the Short Run Federal Reserve Reaction Function, 1969–1979. *Econ. Inquiry*, October 1984, 22(4), pp. 571–78. [G: U.S.]

Wohltmann, Hans-Werner and Krömer, Wolfgang. Sufficient Conditions for Dynamic Path Controllability of Economic Systems. *J. Econ. Dynam. Control*, September 1984, 7(3), pp. 315–30.

Woo, Wing T. Macroeconomic Policy Coordination among the Industrial Economies: Comments. *Brookings Pap. Econ. Act.*, 1984, (1), pp. 71–74. [G: U.S.]

1332 Wage and Price Controls

Barcella, Mary L. In Defense of Price Controls for "Old" Natural Gas. *Bus. Econ.*, July 1984, 19(4), pp. 24–33. [G: U.S.]

Brunetta, Renato and Pozzana, Roberto. La politica dei redditi nei paesi industrializzati: strategie alternative di controllo e sviluppo. (Income Policies in Industrialized Countries: Alternative Strategies for Control and Growth. With English summary.) *Econ. Lavoro*, Apr.-June 1984, 18(2), pp. 31–60. [G: OECD]

Burdjhalov, F. E. Incomes Policy in the System of State-Monopoly Action against Inflation. In *Nikitin, S. M., ed.*, 1984, pp. 197–208. [G: OECD]

Chaloupek, Gunter. The Regulation of Inflation in Western Countries and the Degree of Neocorporatism: Comment. In *Cavaco Silva, A. A., ed.*, 1984, pp. 75–78. [G: OECD]

Colander, David C. Galbraith and the Theory of Price Control. *J. Post Keynesian Econ.*, Fall 1984, 7(1), pp. 30–42.

Cornelisse, Peter A. Towards an Analysis of Markets in Developing Countries. In *Cohen, S. I., et al., eds.*, 1984, pp. 253–65.

Cukierman, Alex and Leiderman, Leonardo. Price Controls and the Variability of Relative Prices. *J. Money, Credit, Banking*, August 1984, 16(3), pp. 271–84. [G: Israel]

Danziger, Leif. Stochastic Inflation and Wage Indexation. *Scand. J. Econ.*, 1984, 86(3), pp. 326–36.

Deng, Huansong. On the Duality of Price Subsidy and the Path to Its Reform. *Chinese Econ. Stud.*, Fall 1984, *18*(1), pp. 3–13. [G: China]

Desai, Meghnad; Keil, Manfred and Wadhwani, Sushil. Incomes Policy in a Political Environment: A Structural Model for the U.K. 1961–1980. In *Hughes Hallet, A.J., ed.*, 1984, pp. 121–44. [G: U.K.]

Grubb, D.; Layard, R. and Symons, J. Wages, Unemployment, and Incomes Policies. In *Emerson, M., ed.*, 1984, pp. 57–88. [G: OECD]

Herrmann, Roland and Schmitz, Peter Michael. Stabilizing Producers' Revenue by Fixing Agricultural Prices within the EC? *Europ. Rev. Agr. Econ.*, 1984, *11*(4), pp. 395–414. [G: EEC]

Kanbur, S. M. Ravi. How to Analyse Commodity Price Stabilization? A Review Article. *Oxford Econ. Pap.*, November 1984, *36*(3), pp. 336–58. [G: LDCs]

Koch, Walter A. S. Negative Einkommensteuern und Konjunkturpolitik. (Negative Income Taxes and Stabilization Policy. With English summary.) *Konjunkturpolitik*, 1984, *30*(6), pp. 348–73. [G: U.S.]

Kunnas, Heikki J. Hinta- ja kilpailuvalvonta inflaation torjunnan osana. (Price and Competition Controls for Anti-Inflationary Policy. With English summary.) *Kansant. Aikak.*, 1984, *80*(1), pp. 17–27. [G: Finland]

Laaksonen, Seppo. Palkkojen kehitys ja palkkapoliittinen keskustelu 1900-luvulla. (Development of Wages and Salaries and Wage Policy Discussion in Finland in the 20th Century. With English summary.) *Kansant. Aikak.*, 1984, *80*(1), pp. 34–65. [G: Finland]

Mayer, Thomas. Fervent Hopes vs. Dismal Reality. *Challenge*, March/April 1984, *27*(1), pp. 49–52. [G: U.S.]

Mitchell, Daniel J. B. The Australian Labor Market. In *Caves, R. E. and Krause, L. B., eds.*, 1984, pp. 127–93. [G: Australia]

Perlman, Mark. Collective Bargaining and Industrial Relations: The Past, the Present, and the Future. In *Fellner, W., ed.*, 1984, pp. 287–322. [G: U.S.]

Schmitz, Wolfgang. Economic and Social Partnership and Incomes Policy and the Social Doctrine of the Church. In *Cavaco Silva, A. A., ed.*, 1984, pp. 195–217.

Sinai, Allen. Buying Time for a TIP. *Challenge*, March/April 1984, *27*(1), pp. 55–57. [G: U.S.]

Tarantelli, Ezio. The Regulation of Inflation in Western Countries and the Degree of Neocorporatism. In *Cavaco Silva, A. A., ed.*, 1984, pp. 27–66. [G: OECD]

Tinbergen, Jan. The Future of Incomes Policies. In *[Chenery, H. B.]*, 1984, pp. 205–15. [G: U.S.; Netherlands]

Tobin, James. A Social Compact for Restraint. *Challenge*, March/April 1984, *27*(1), pp. 52–54. [G: U.S.]

Wilton, David A. An Evaluation of Wage and Price Controls in Canada. *Can. Public Policy*, June 1984, *10*(2), pp. 167–76. [G: Canada]

Zorn, Thomas S. The Allocative Effect of Nonbinding Price Controls. *Econ. Inquiry*, January 1984, *22*(1), pp. 136–41.

134 Inflation and Deflation

1340 General

Afridi, Usman; Qadir, Asghar and Zaki, Javed. Effects of Dual Sector Inflation across Income Levels in Pakistan. *Pakistan Devel. Rev.*, Summer-Autumn 1984, *23*(2&3), pp. 381–90. [G: Pakistan]

Anes, Gonzalo. Prices in 16th Century Spain—An Analysis of Inflation. In *Csikós-Nagy, B.; Hague, D. and Hall, G., eds.*, 1984, pp. 205–13.

Arndt, Heinz W. and Sundrum, R. M. Devaluation and Inflation: The 1978 Experience. *Bull. Indonesian Econ. Stud.*, April 1984, *20*(1), pp. 83–97. [G: Indonesia]

Aspe, Pedro and Blanco, Herminio. Macroeconomic Uncertainty and Employment: The Case of Mexico. In *Aspe, P. and Sigmund, P. E., eds.*, 1984, pp. 187–202. [G: Mexico]

Behrend, Hilde. Inflation and Attitudes to Pay Increases: The Major Issues. In *Behrend, H.*, 1984, pp. 206–17.

Behrend, Hilde. Problems of Labour and Inflation: Concluding Comments. In *Behrend, H.*, 1984, pp. 224–43.

Behrend, Hilde. Research into Inflation and Conceptions of Earnings. In *Behrend, H.*, 1984, pp. 178–90. [G: U.K.]

Behrend, Hilde. Research into Public Attitudes and the Attitudes of the Public to Inflation. In *Behrend, H.*, 1984, pp. 191–205. [G: U.K.]

Behrend, Hilde and Gould, Elisabeth. Bridging the Communications Gap with the Ordinary Citizen. In *Behrend, H.*, 1984, pp. 218–23. [G: U.K.]

Ben-Zion, Uri. Recent Literature on the Impact of Taxation and Inflation on Interest Rates. In *Tanzi, V., ed.*, 1984, pp. 69–98. [G: U.S.; OECD]

Ben-Zion, Uri. Recent Literature on the Impact of Taxation and Inflation on the International Financial Market. In *Tanzi, V., ed.*, 1984, pp. 99–109.

Boadway, Robin; Bruce, Neil and Mintz, Jack. Taxation, Inflation, and the Effective Marginal Tax Rate on Capital in Canada. *Can. J. Econ.*, February 1984, *17*(1), pp. 62–79. [G: Canada]

Bomhoff, Eduard J. North Sea Oil and Manufacturing Output: Comment. In *Griffiths, B. and Wood, G. E., eds.*, 1984, pp. 200–04. [G: U.K.; Selected Countries]

Bruno, Michael. Stagflation in the EC Countries 1973–1981: A Cross-sectional View. In *Emerson, M., ed.*, 1984, pp. 33–56. [G: EEC]

Cagan, Phillip. Monetary Policy and Subduing Inflation. In *Fellner, W., ed.*, 1984, pp. 21–53. [G: U.S.]

Cameron, David R. Social Democracy, Corporatism, Labour Quiescence and the Representation of Economic Interest in Advanced Capitalist Society. In *Goldthorpe, J. H., ed.*, 1984, pp. 143–78. [G: OECD]

Chaloupek, Gunter. The Regulation of Inflation in Western Countries and the Degree of Neocorporatism: Comment. In *Cavaco Silva, A. A., ed.*, 1984, pp. 75–78. [G: OECD]

Conine, Thomas E., Jr. and Tamarkin, Maurry. On the Theory of Inflation and Optimal Investment Policy: Equilibrium Considerations. *Southern Econ. J.*, January 1984, *50*(3), pp. 755–60.

Csikós-Nagy, Béla. The Economics of Relative Prices: Introduction. In *Csikós-Nagy, B.; Hague, D. and Hall, G., eds.*, 1984, pp. xii–xv.

Demidova, L. S. Price Rises for Services and Inflation. In *Nikitin, S. M., ed.*, 1984, pp. 74–92. [G: U.S.]

Earle, John S. and Kniesner, Thomas J. Inflation, Unemployment and the Reagan Administration. *Bus. Econ.*, October 1984, *19*(5), pp. 26–33. [G: U.S.]

Ellman, Michael. The Control of Inflation? Errors in the Interpretation of CPE Data. In *Ellman, M.*, 1984, *1981*, pp. 130–34. [G: E. Europe]

Entov, R. M. Cyclical Factors behind the Movement of Prices. In *Nikitin, S. M., ed.*, 1984, pp. 126–78. [G: U.S.]

Evans, George and Gulamani, Riyaz. Tests for Rationality of the Carlson–Parkin Inflation Expectations Data. *Oxford Bull. Econ. Statist.*, February 1984, *46*(1), pp. 1–19. [G: U.K.]

Faxén, Karl O. Risk Management. In *[Kozmetsky, G.]*, 1984, pp. 155–75. [G: U.S.; Sweden]

Fiedler, Edgar R. Stagflation: Our Pernicious Social Disease—That Our Antibiotics Can't Cure. *Bus. Econ.*, January 1984, *19*(1), pp. 13–23. [G: U.S.]

Fogler, H. Russell. Bond Portfolio Immunization, Inflation, and the Fisher Equation. *J. Risk Ins.*, June 1984, *51*(2), pp. 244–64.

Friedman, Milton. Financial Futures Markets and Tabular Standards. *J. Polit. Econ.*, February 1984, *92*(1), pp. 165–67.

Glezakos, Constantine. Inflation and Growth: A Reconsideration of the Evidence from the LDCs. In *Ghosh, P. K., ed., no. 7*, 1984, *1978*, pp. 163–75. [G: LDCs]

Grishin, I. V. Inflation and the Intensification of the Socio-economic Contradictions of Capitalism. In *Nikitin, S. M., ed.*, 1984, pp. 225–38. [G: OECD]

Haraf, William S. Japanese Macroeconomic Performance since 1970: Comments. *Carnegie-Rochester Conf. Ser. Public Policy*, Spring 1984, *20*, pp. 115–20. [G: Japan]

Horsman, Andrew. Money, Banking and Inflation. In *Sandford, C. and Bradbury, M., eds.*, 1984, pp. 164–87. [G: Germany; U.S.]

IMF Fiscal Affairs Department. Interest Rates and Tax Treatment of Interest Income and Expense. In *Tanzi, V., ed.*, 1984, pp. 3–66. [G: OECD]

Katz, Menachem. Inflation, Taxation, and the Rate of Interest in Eight Industrial Countries, 1961–82. In *Tanzi, V., ed.*, 1984, pp. 172–203. [G: OECD]

Kay, John A. North Sea Oil and Manufacturing Output. In *Griffiths, B. and Wood, G. E., eds.*, 1984, pp. 185–99. [G: U.K.; Selected Countries]

Khan, Shahrukh Rafi. Effects of Dual Sector Inflation across Income Levels in Pakistan: Comment. *Pakistan Devel. Rev.*, Summer-Autumn 1984, *23*(2&3), pp. 391–92. [G: Pakistan]

Killick, Tony and Sharpley, Jennifer. Extent, Causes and Consequences of Disequilibria in Developing Countries. In *Killick, Tony, ed. (II)*, 1984, pp. 15–54. [G: LDCs; MDCs]

Koenig, Linda M. Recent Developments in the World Economy and in Non-Oil Developing Countries of the Western Hemisphere. In *Muns, J., ed.*, 1984, pp. 16–29. [G: OECD; LDCs; Latin America]

Komiya, Ryutaro and Yasui, Kazuo. Japan's Macroeconomic Performance since the First Oil Crisis: Review and Appraisal. *Carnegie-Rochester Conf. Ser. Public Policy*, Spring 1984, *20*, pp. 69–114. [G: Japan]

Magdoff, Harry. A Note on Inflation. In *Foster, J. B. and Szlajfer, H., eds.*, 1984, *1973*, pp. 118–23. [G: U.S.]

Makin, John H. and Tanzi, Vito. Level and Volatility of U.S. Interest Rates: Roles of Expected Inflation, Real Rates, and Taxes. In *Tanzi, V., ed.*, 1984, pp. 110–42. [G: U.S.]

Makinen, Gail E. The Greek Stabilization of 1944–46. *Amer. Econ. Rev.*, December 1984, *74*(5), pp. 1067–74. [G: Greece]

Markham, Jesse. Inflation and the Wage-Price Issue: A Reappraisal. In *[Reynolds, L. G.]*, 1984, pp. 227–44. [G: U.S.]

Mayer, Thomas. Fervent Hopes vs. Dismal Reality. *Challenge*, March/April 1984, *27*(1), pp. 49–52. [G: U.S.]

Metwally, Mokhtar M. and Tamaschke, H. U. The Effect of Inflation on the Patterns of Consumption. *Indian Econ. J.*, July–Sept. 1984, *32*(1), pp. 81–93. [G: Europe; Japan; U.S.]

Minford, Patrick. North Sea Oil and Manufacturing Output: Comment. In *Griffiths, B. and Wood, G. E., eds.*, 1984, pp. 205–10. [G: U.K.; Selected Countries]

Modigliani, Franco. I problemi di indicizzazione nel finanziamento dell'edilizia abitativa. Il progetto MIT di mutuo ipotecario per i giovani. (The Inflation Proof Mortgage [IPM]. The Mortgage for the Young. With English summary.) *Bancaria*, July 1984, *40*(7), pp. 607–17. [G: Italy]

Mosley, Paul. The Behaviour of the Macro-economy. In *Sandford, C. and Bradbury, M., eds.*, 1984, pp. 145–63. [G: U.K.]

Murty, G. V. S. N. Inflation and Relative Prices in India. *Indian Econ. J.*, July–Sept. 1984, *32*(1), pp. 72–80. [G: India]

Naslund, Bertil. Uncertainty and the Need for Innovation in Management Techniques and Methods. In *[Kozmetsky, G.]*, 1984, pp. 177–80. [G: Sweden]

Nevile, J. W. and Warren, Neil A. Inflation and

Personal Income Distribution in Australia. *Australian Econ. Rev.*, 1st Quarter 1984, (65), pp. 26–33. **[G: Australia]**

Nikitin, S. M. and Tulin, I. V. Prices on the World Capitalist Market and Inflation. In *Nikitin, S. M., ed.*, 1984, pp. 93–107. **[G: Global]**

Nikitin, S. M. and Usoskin, V. M. Bourgeois Political Economy and New Trends in Anti-inflationary Policy. In *Nikitin, S. M., ed.*, 1984, pp. 209–24.

Nikitin, S. M., et al. Big Companies and Inflation. In *Nikitin, S. M., ed.*, 1984, pp. 49–73. **[G: U.S.]**

Nikitin, S. M., et al. Inflation Today: Essence and Causes. In *Nikitin, S. M., ed.*, 1984, pp. 7–24. **[G: OECD]**

Postiaux, Jean-Marie. La maîtrise de l'inflation aux Etats-Unis, une condition nécessaire pour un scénario de redressement économique—L'exemple de l'Allemagne, de la France et de la Belgique—1984–1986. (With English summary.) *Cah. Écon. Bruxelles*, 3rd Trimester 1984, (103), pp. 419–39. **[G: Germany; France; Belgium]**

Radharamanan, R.; Camargo, M. E. and Sortica, G. B. System Identification and Analysis of Inflation in Brazil. In *Avula, X. J. R., et al.*, 1984, pp. 822–27. **[G: Brazil]**

Sherman, Howard J. Inflation, Unemployment, and the Contemporary Business Cycle. In *Foster, J. B. and Szlajfer, H., eds.*, 1984, *1979*, pp. 91–117. **[G: U.S.]**

Sinai, Allen. Buying Time for a TIP. *Challenge*, March/April 1984, *27*(1), pp. 55–57. **[G: U.S.]**

Smith, Bruce D. Money and Inflation in Colonial Massachusetts. *Fed. Res. Bank Minn. Rev.*, Winter 1984, *8*(1), pp. 1–14. **[G: U.S.]**

Smyslov, D. V. The Crisis in the Modern Monetary System of Capitalism and Inflation. In *Nikitin, S. M., ed.*, 1984, pp. 108–25. **[G: OECD]**

Stockton, David. Perspectives on the Recent Behavior of Inflation. *Fed. Res. Bull.*, June 1984, *70*(6), pp. 483–91. **[G: U.S.]**

Tanzi, Vito. Inflation and the Incidence of Income Taxes on Interest Income in the United States, 1972–81. In *Tanzi, V., ed.*, 1984, pp. 143–58. **[G: U.S.]**

Tanzi, Vito. Inflationary Expectations, Taxes, and the Demand for Money in the United States. In *Tanzi, V., ed.*, 1984, pp. 159–71. **[G: U.S.]**

Tarantelli, Ezio. The Regulation of Inflation in Western Countries and the Degree of Neocorporatism. In *Cavaco Silva, A. A., ed.*, 1984, pp. 27–66. **[G: OECD]**

Thore, Sten. Uncertainty and the Opportunities for Innovation and Investment. In *[Kozmetsky, G.]*, 1984, pp. 181–83. **[G: U.S.; Sweden]**

Tobin, James. A Social Compact for Restraint. *Challenge*, March/April 1984, *27*(1), pp. 52–54. **[G: U.S.]**

Tsuru, Tsuyoshi. S. Bowles *et al.* on Stagflation: A Commentary. *Hitotsubashi J. Econ.*, December 1984, *25*(2), pp. 173–82. **[G: U.S.]**

Usoskin, V. M. "Demand Management" within the System of Anti-inflation Measures Employed by the Bourgeois State. In *Nikitin, S. M., ed.*, 1984, pp. 179–96. **[G: OECD]**

Usoskin, V. M. Monetary and Budgetary Factors behind Inflation. In *Nikitin, S. M., ed.*, 1984, pp. 25–48. **[G: OECD]**

Vernon, Jack. Interest on Checking Deposits and the Inflation Tax. *Atlantic Econ. J.*, July 1984, *12*(2), pp. 72–73. **[G: U.S.]**

Virén, Matti. Inflation, Relative Prices and Household Saving Behavior. *Empirical Econ.*, 1984, *9*(3), pp. 183–97. **[G: OECD]**

Weicher, John C. Disinflation in the Housing Market. In *Fellner, W., ed.*, 1984, pp. 155–204. **[G: U.S.]**

Wiles, Peter. Price Indices under Suppressed Inflation; and an Alternative Approach to Economic Measurement. In *Bohnet, A., ed.*, 1984, pp. 203–11.

Wood, J. Stuart. Capital Formation in the United States and the Question of a Capital Shortage. In *Siegel, B. N., ed.*, 1984, pp. 73–86. **[G: U.S.]**

Woodham, Douglas M. Potential Output Growth and the Long-Term Inflation Outlook. *Fed. Res. Bank New York Quart. Rev.*, Summer 1984, *9*(2), pp. 16–23. **[G: U.S.]**

1342 Inflation Theories; Studies Illustrating Inflation Theories

Addison, John T. Trade Unions, Corporatism, and Inflation. *J. Lab. Res.*, Winter 1984, *5*(1), pp. 39–62.

Addison, John T. and Burton, John. The Sociopolitical Analysis of Inflation. *Weltwirtsch. Arch.*, 1984, *120*(1), pp. 90–120. **[G: U.S.; U.K.]**

Ahmad, Jaleel. Inflationary Expectations and Transmission of Inflation under Floating Exchange Rates. *Weltwirtsch. Arch.*, 1984, *120*(3), pp. 424–35.

Allen, Kathryn E. The Phillips Curve Controversy and Orthodox Visions of the Labor Market. In *Darity, W., Jr., ed.*, 1984, pp. 219–37.

Allsbrook, O. O. Inflationary Recession and Saving Ratios. *S. Afr. J. Econ.*, March 1984, *52*(1), pp. 63–68.

Aschheim, Joseph and Tavlas, George S. The Simultaneity Problem in Forecasting Inflation. *Atlantic Econ. J.*, September 1984, *12*(3), pp. 20–29. **[G: U.S.]**

Baldry, J. C. Wage Indexation in a Two-Sector Economy: A Generalisation. *Australian Econ. Pap.*, December 1984, *23*(43), pp. 219–34.

Baltensperger, Ernst. Inflation und Staatliche Budgetpolitik. (Inflation and Government Debt Financing. With English summary.) *Z. Wirtschaft. Sozialwissen.*, 1984, *104*(6), pp. 675–93.

Bartoli, Gloria. An Assessment of the Scandinavian Model of Inflation. *Econ. Int.*, August–November 1984, *37*(3–4), pp. 215–35. **[G: Sweden]**

Batchelor, Roy A. A Natural Interpretation of the

Present Unemployment. In *Griffiths, B. and Wood, G. E., eds.*, 1984, pp. 139–71.
[G: U.K.; U.S.; EEC]

Benavie, Arthur. Imported Inflation and Monetary-Fiscal Policy under a Flexible Exchange Rate. *Atlantic Econ. J.*, March 1984, *12*(1), pp. 41–49.

Berg, Ivar. Unemployment, Productivity, and Inflation: Misgivings About the Sapient Orthodoxy. In *Brief, A. P., ed.*, 1984, pp. 71–89.

Bernholz, Peter. Inflation, Over-indebtedness, Crisis and Consolidation: Argentina and the Baring Crisis (1884–1900). *Z. ges. Staatswiss.*, December 1984, *140*(4), pp. 669–84.
[G: Argentina]

Bessler, David A. Additional Evidence on Money and Prices: U.S. Data, 1870–1913. *Exploration Econ. Hist.*, April 1984, *21*(2), pp. 125–32.
[G: U.S.]

Bhandari, Jagdeep S. A Computational Stochastic Equilibrium Model of Oil-importing Economies. *Weltwirtsch. Arch.*, 1984, *120*(2), pp. 301–28.

Bhatia, D. P. Impact of Taxes, Budgetary Deficit & Money Supply on Prices. *Margin*, January 1984, *16*(2), pp. 95–102. [G: India]

Biacabe, Pierre. La politique monétaire en France. (With English summary.) *Revue Écon. Polit.*, September–October 1984, *94*(5), pp. 639–48. [G: France]

Blake, David. Complete Systems Methods of Estimating Models with Rational and Adaptive Expectations: A Case Study. *Europ. Econ. Rev.*, March 1984, *24*(2), pp. 137–50.
[G: U.S.]

Blanchard, Olivier J. The Lucas Critique and the Volcker Deflation. *Amer. Econ. Rev.*, May 1984, *74*(2), pp. 211–15. [G: U.S.]

Blomqvist, Hans C. On the Sources and Macroeconomic Implications of Nonuniform and Uncertain Price Expectations. *Weltwirtsch. Arch.*, 1984, *120*(2), pp. 366–75.

Boehm, Ernst A. Money Wages, Consumer Prices, and Causality in Australia. *Econ. Rec.*, September 1984, *60*(170), pp. 236–51.
[G: Australia]

Bossons, John. Indexed Bonds as an Instrument of Pension Reform. In *Conklin, D. W.; Bennett, J. H. and Courchene, T. J., eds.*, 1984, pp. 327–59. [G: Canada]

Bouvier, Jean. The French Banks, Inflation and the Economic Crisis, 1919–1939. *J. Europ. Econ. Hist.*, Special Issue 1984, *13*(2), pp. 29–80. [G: France]

Browne, F. X. The International Transmission of Inflation to a Small Open Economy under Fixed Exchange Rates and Highly Interest-sensitive Capital Flows: An Empirical Analysis. *Europ. Econ. Rev.*, July 1984, *25*(2), pp. 187–212.

Buiter, Willem H. Comment: Some Unpleasant Monetarist Arithmetic. In *Griffiths, B. and Wood, G. E., eds.*, 1984, pp. 42–60.
[G: U.K.]

Bulkley, George. Does Inflation Uncertainty In-

crease with the Level of Inflation? *Europ. Econ. Rev.*, July 1984, *25*(2), pp. 213–21.
[G: U.K.]

Butschek, Felix. Kontrollierte Inflation—ein missglücktes Experiment? *Empirica*, 1984, *11*(1), pp. 59–80. [G: Austria]

Cagan, Phillip and Fellner, William. The Cost of Disinflation, Credibility, and the Deceleration of Wages 1982–1983. In *Fellner, W., ed.*, 1984, pp. 7–19. [G: U.S.]

Canto, Victor A.; Joines, Douglas H. and Webb, Robert I. Taxation, Rational Expectations, and the Neutrality of Money. *J. Macroecon.*, Winter 1984, *6*(1), pp. 69–78.

Carr, Jack L. and Smith, Lawrence B. Housing Finance Contracts and the Nonneutrality of Inflation. *Housing Finance Rev.*, January 1984, *3*(1), pp. 39–49. [G: U.S.]

Chiappori, Pierre-André and Mongin, Philippe. Un modèle de politique monétaire avec aléas stratégiques. (A Model of Monetary Policy with Strategic Uncertainty. With English summary.) *Revue Écon.*, September 1984, *35*(5), pp. 831–69.

Cifarelli, Giulio. Una interpretazione macrorazionale del ciclo. (A Macrorational Interpretation of Cycle. With English summary.) *Giorn. Econ.*, May–June 1984, *43*(5–6), pp. 345–58.
[G: Italy]

Clower, Robert W. A Reconsideration of the Theory of Inflation. In *Clower, R. W.*, 1984, *1976*, pp. 218–30.

Clower, Robert W. The Genesis and Control of Inflation. In *Clower, R. W.*, 1984, *1979*, pp. 242–55.

Colander, David C. Galbraith and the Theory of Price Control. *J. Post Keynesian Econ.*, Fall 1984, *7*(1), pp. 30–42.

Congdon, Tim G. A Comment: The problem of Debt Interest Seen in Historical Perspective [Some Unpleasant Monetarist Arithmetic]. In *Griffiths, B. and Wood, G. E., eds.*, 1984, pp. 67–71.

Cooley, Thomas F.; LeRoy, Stephen F. and Raymon, Neil. Econometric Policy Evaluation: Note. *Amer. Econ. Rev.*, June 1984, *74*(3), pp. 467–70.

Costa, José. Government Budget Deficits, Money Supply, and Inflation in Portugal. *Economia (Portugal)*, January 1984, *8*(1), pp. 97–116.
[G: Portugal]

Cross, Rod. Friedman and Phelps on the Natural Rate of Unemployment. *Atlantic Econ. J.*, July 1984, *12*(2), pp. 47–53.

Cukierman, Alex and Leiderman, Leonardo. Price Controls and the Variability of Relative Prices. *J. Money, Credit, Banking*, August 1984, *16*(3), pp. 271–84. [G: Israel]

Culbertson, William Patterson, Jr. and Amacher, Ryan C. Inflation in the Planned Economies: Reply [Inflation in the Planned Economies: Some Estimates for Eastern Europe]. *Southern Econ. J.*, October 1984, *51*(2), pp. 613–14.
[G: E. Europe]

Danziger, Leif. Stochastic Inflation and Wage Indexation. *Scand. J. Econ.*, 1984, *86*(3), pp. 326–36.

Danziger, Leif. Stochastic Inflation and the Optimal Policy of Price Adjustment. *Econ. Inquiry*, January 1984, *22*(1), pp. 98–108.

Darvat, Ali F. The Inflationary Process in Greece: An Empirical Investigation. *Econ. Int.*, August–November 1984, *37*(3–4), pp. 268–79. [G: Greece]

De Vroey, Michel. Inflation: A Non-monetarist Monetary Interpretation. *Cambridge J. Econ.*, December 1984, *8*(4), pp. 381–99.

Debonneuil, Michèle and Sterdyniak, Henri. La boucle prix-salaires dans l'inflation. (Inflation and Wage–Price Feed-Back. With English summary.) *Revue Écon.*, March 1984, *35*(2), pp. 267–311.

DeLorme, Charles D., Jr.; Terza, Joseph and Wood, Norman J. Inflation and Political Unrest in Developing Nations. *Econ. Notes*, 1984, (2), pp. 76–84. [G: LDCs]

Demery, David. Aggregate Demand, Rational Expectations and Real Output: Some New Evidence for the U.K., 1963.2–1982.2. *Econ. J.*, December 1984, *94*(376), pp. 847–62. [G: U.K.]

Desai, Meghnad. Wages, Prices and Unemployment a Quarter Century after the Phillips Curve. In *Hendry, D. F. and Wallis, K. F.*, eds., 1984, pp. 253–73.

Dollery, B. E. Market Structure and Inflation in South Africa: A Test of the Administered Price Hypothesis. *S. Afr. J. Econ.*, December 1984, *52*(4), pp. 345–58. [G: S. Africa]

Dwyer, Gerald P., Jr. Inflation and Government Deficits: A Reply. *Econ. Inquiry*, October 1984, *22*(4), pp. 597–601. [G: U.S.]

Earle, John S. and Kniesner, Thomas J. Did Reaganomics Shift the Phillips Curve? *Indian Econ. Rev.*, July-Dec. 1984, *19*(2), pp. 235–40. [G: U.S.]

Early, John F.; Schmidt, Mary Lynn and Mosimann, Thomas J. Inflation and the Business Cycle during the Postwar Period. *Mon. Lab. Rev.*, November 1984, *107*(11), pp. 3–7. [G: U.S.]

Edwards, Sebastian. Coffee, Money, and Inflation in Colombia. *World Devel.*, November–December 1984, *12*(11–12), pp. 1107–17. [G: Colombia]

Engle, Charles M. and Frankel, Jeffrey A. The Secular Inflation Term in Open-Economy Phillips Curves. *Europ. Econ. Rev.*, March 1984, *24*(2), pp. 161–64.

Engle, Robert F.; Granger, Clive W. J. and Kraft, Dennis F. Combining Competing Forecasts of Inflation Using a Bivariate ARCH Model. *J. Econ. Dynam. Control*, November 1984, *8*(2), pp. 151–65. [G: U.S.]

Entov, R. M. The "Rule" and Fall of the Phillips Curve. *Prob. Econ.*, February 1984, *26*(10), pp. 3–36.

Fama, Eugene F. and Gibbons, Michael R. A Comparison of Inflation Forecasts. *J. Monet. Econ.*, May 1984, *13*(3), pp. 327–48. [G: U.S.]

Farmer, Roger E. A. Bursting Bubbles: On the Rationality of Hyperinflations in Optimizing Models. *J. Monet. Econ.*, July 1984, *14*(1), pp. 29–35.

Farrell, John P. Inflation in the Planned Economies: Comment [Inflation in the Planned Economies: Some Estimates for Eastern Europe]. *Southern Econ. J.*, October 1984, *51*(2), pp. 603–12. [G: E. Europe]

Feldman, Robert A. The Impact of the Recent Strength of the Dollar on the U.S. Merchandise Trade Balance: Some "First-Round" Effects and Feedbacks from Exchange Rate Induced Changes in U.S.-Relative Inflation. *J. Policy Modeling*, February 1984, *6*(1), pp. 29–44. [G: U.S.]

Fethke, Gary C. and Policano, Andrew J. Cyclical Implications of Indexing the Minimum Wage. *J. Macroecon.*, Winter 1984, *6*(1), pp. 1–21. [G: U.S.]

Flaschel, Peter. The Inflation-based 'Natural' Rate of Unemployment and the Conflict Over Income Distribution. In *Goodwin, R. M.; Krüger, M. and Vercelli, A.*, eds., 1984, pp. 103–26.

Flood, Robert P. and Garber, Peter M. Gold Monetization and Gold Discipline. *J. Polit. Econ.*, February 1984, *92*(1), pp. 90–107.

Flood, Robert P.; Garber, Peter M. and Scott, Louis O. Multi-country Tests for Price Level Bubbles. *J. Econ. Dynam. Control*, December 1984, *8*(3), pp. 329–40. [G: Germany; Hungary; Poland]

Fornasari, Franco. The Basic Rate of Inflation in Italy. *Rev. Econ. Cond. Italy*, February 1984, (1), pp. 59–88. [G: Italy]

Fourie, F. C. v. N. Industriële Konsentrasie en Inflasie in Suid-Afrika 1972–1979. *S. Afr. J. Econ.*, December 1984, *52*(4), pp. 359–76. [G: S. Africa]

Franz, Wolfgang. Inflation und interindustrielle Lohnstruktur. (Inflation and the Interindustrial Wage Structure. With English summary.) *Ifo-Studien*, 1984, *30*(2), pp. 81–106. [G: Germany]

Franz, Wolfgang. Wohin treibt die Phillipskurve? Theoretische und empirische Überlegungen zur inflationsstabilen Arbeitslosenquote in der Bundesrepublik Deutschland. (The Shift of the Phillips Curve. Theoretical and Empirical Considerations about the Non-accelerating Inflation Rate of Unemployment for the Federal Republic of Germany. With English summary.) *Z. Wirtschaft. Sozialwissen.*, 1984, *104*(6), pp. 603–29. [G: W. Germany]

Freeman, Richard T. Information Structure and the Transmission of Inflationary Expectations. *Math. Soc. Sci.*, October 1984, *8*(2), pp. 169–93.

Frenkel, Roberto. Salarios industriales e inflación. El período 1976–82. (With English summary.) *Desarrollo Econ.*, October–December 1984, *24*(95), pp. 387–414. [G: Argentina]

Froyen, Richard T. and Waud, Roger N. The Changing Relationship between Aggregate Price and Output: The British Experience.

Economica, February 1984, *51*(201), pp. 53–67. [G: U.K.]

Galbraith, James K. The Case for Rapid Growth. *Challenge*, March/April 1984, *27*(1), pp. 10–14. [G: U.S.]

Garrison, Roger W. Deficits and Inflation: A Comment. *Econ. Inquiry*, October 1984, *22*(4), pp. 593–96. [G: U.S.]

Gedeon, Shirley J. Monetary Control and Inflation in Market-Based Socialism. *ACES Bull.*, Spring 1984, *26*(1), pp. 27–42.

Giannola, Giuseppina. Il "potere sindacale" ed i modelli di "inflazione salariale": un'analisi statistica dell'esperienza italiana per il periodo 1951–1977. (Trade-union Power and the Models of "Wage Inflation": A Statistical Analysis for Italy, 1951–1977. With English summary.) *Econ. Lavoro*, Apr.-June 1984, *18*(2), pp. 105–18. [G: Italy]

Glezakos, Constantine and Nugent, Jeffrey B. Price Instability and Inflation: The Latin American Case. *World Devel.*, July 1984, *12*(7), pp. 755–58. [G: Latin America]

Goldstein, Henry N. and Haynes, Stephen E. A Critical Appraisal of McKinnon's World Money Supply Hypothesis [Currency Substitution and Instability in the World Dollar Standard]. *Amer. Econ. Rev.*, March 1984, *74*(1), pp. 217–24. [G: U.S.]

Granziol, M. J. General Price Level Instability and the Variability of Relative Prices in Switzerland. *Empirical Econ.*, 1984, *9*(1), pp. 1–13. [G: Switzerland]

Guess, George and Koford, Kenneth J. Inflation, Recession, and the Federal Budget Deficit (or, Blaming Economic Problems on a Statistical Mirage). *Policy Sci.*, December 1984, *17*(4), pp. 385–402. [G: OECD]

Guttmann, Robert. Stagflation and Credit–Money in the U.S.A. *Brit. Rev. Econ. Issues*, Autumn 1984, *6*(15), pp. 79–119. [G: U.S.]

Gylfason, Thorvaldur and Lindbeck, Assar. Competing Wage Claims, Cost Inflation, and Capacity Utilization. *Europ. Econ. Rev.*, February 1984, *24*(1), pp. 1–21.

Hafer, R. W. Examining the Recent Behavior of Inflation. *Fed. Res. Bank St. Louis Rev.*, August/September 1984, *66*(7), pp. 29–37. [G: U.S.]

Hasbrouck, Joel. Stock Returns, Inflation, and Economic Activity: The Survey Evidence. *J. Finance*, December 1984, *39*(5), pp. 1293–1310. [G: U.S.]

von Hayek, Friedrich A. Inflation, the Misdirection of Labour, and Unemployment. In *von Hayek, F. A. (I)*, 1984, *1975*, pp. 3–17.

Helman, Héctor; Roiter, Daniel and Yoguel, Gabriel. Inflación, variación de precios relativos e inflexibilidad de precios. (With English summary.) *Desarrollo Econ.*, October–December 1984, *24*(95), pp. 415–30. [G: Argentina]

Hénin, Pierre-Yves and Zylberberg, André. Sur la compatibilité à long terme d'un adjustement partiel des prix avec l'hypothèse de prévisions rationnelles. *Revue Écon. Polit.*, November–December 1984, *94*(6), pp. 792–807.

Henry, S. G. B. Real Wage Implications of Wage Inflation Models. *Bull. Econ. Res.*, November 1984, *36*(2), pp. 119–42. [G: U.K.]

Hersoug, Tor. Can Tax Cuts Beat the Phillips-Curve? *Europ. Econ. Rev.*, April 1984, *24*(3), pp. 369–81.

Hetzel, Robert L. The Behavior of the M1 Demand Function in the Early 1980s. *Fed. Res. Bank Richmond Econ. Rev.*, Nov./Dec. 1984, *70*(6), pp. 20–29. [G: U.S.]

Hill, Peter. Inflation, Holding Gains and Saving. *OECD Econ. Stud.*, Spring 1984, (2), pp. 151–64.

Holland, A. Steven. Does Higher Inflation Lead to More Uncertain Inflation? *Fed. Res. Bank St. Louis Rev.*, February 1984, *66*(2), pp. 15–26. [G: U.S.]

Horne, Jocelyn. Trying to Understand Stagflation: Comment. *Australian Econ. Rev.*, 3rd Quarter 1984, (67), pp. 57–58. [G: Australia]

Huang, Roger D. Tests of Variance Bounds Implied by Cagan's Hyperinflation Model. *Int. Econ. Rev.*, October 1984, *25*(3), pp. 545–61. [G: Germany]

Huber, Gérard. Inflation and Nominal Tax System in an Open Economy. *Europ. Econ. Rev.*, February 1984, *24*(1), pp. 23–37.

Hughes, Barry. Is There a Macroeconomic World of One Simple Model? *Econ. Rec.*, June 1984, *60*(169), pp. 186–89. [G: OECD]

Ihori, Toshihiro. Welfare Implications of Indexing Capital Income Taxation. *Econ. Stud. Quart.*, April 1984, *35*(1), pp. 21–30.

Johnson, Omotunde E. G. On Growth and Inflation in Developing Countries. *Int. Monet. Fund Staff Pap.*, December 1984, *31*(4), pp. 636–60. [G: LDCs]

Kabir, M. An Anatomy of Inflation in Bangladesh. *J. Econ. Devel.*, December 1984, *9*(2), pp. 121–43. [G: Bangladesh]

Katsimbris, George M. and Miller, Stephen M. The Over-Time Relationship between Inflation and Its Variability Once Again: A Rejoinder. *Kyklos*, 1984, *37*(1), pp. 110–12. [G: OECD]

Kawasaki, S.; Gahlen, D. and Buck, Andrew J. The Variability of Relative Price Expectations, the Rate of Inflation and the Phillips Curve. In *Oppenländer, K. H. and Poser, G., eds.*, 1984, pp. 499–539. [G: W. Germany]

Kelly, William A., Jr. and Miles, James A. Darby and Fisher: Resolution of a Paradox. *Financial Rev.*, March 1984, *19*(1), pp. 103–10.

Kenyon, Peter D. Trying to Understand Stagflation: Comment. *Australian Econ. Rev.*, 3rd Quarter 1984, (67), pp. 59–61. [G: Australia]

Kohn, Meir. The Inflation Tax and the Value of Equity. *Can. J. Econ.*, May 1984, *17*(2), pp. 312–26.

Kopcke, Richard W. Inflation and the Choice of "Monetary" Guidelines. *New Eng. Econ. Rev.*, January–February 1984, pp. 5–14. [G: U.S.]

Kormendi, Roger C. and Meguire, Philip G. Cross-Regime Evidence of Macroeconomic Rationality. *J. Polit. Econ.*, October 1984, *92*(5), pp. 875–908. [G: Selected Countries]

Krishnamurty, K.; Saibaba, P. and Kazmi,

N. A. Inflation and Growth: A Model for India. *Indian Econ. Rev.*, January–June 1984, *19*(1), pp. 16–111. **[G: India]**

Kromphardt, Jürgen. Die Phillips-Kurve bei informierter Erwartungsbildung. Eine keynesianische Alternative zur Theorie der natürlichen Arbeitslosenquote. (Informed Expectations and the Phillips Curve. With English summary.) *Z. Wirtschaft. Sozialwissen.*, 1984, *104*(6), pp. 631–44.

Lahiri, Kajal and Zaporowski, Mark. A Note on the Variability of Real Interest Rates, Business Cycles, and the Livingston Data. *J. Banking Finance*, September 1984, *8*(3), pp. 483–90. **[G: U.S.]**

Laski, Kazimierz. Das Inflationsproblem und Warenmängel in den sozialistischen Ländern. (With English summary.) In *Bohnet, A., ed.*, 1984, pp. 183–202.

Lecaldano Sasso La Terza, Edoardo. Il prodotto interno lordo a prezzi correnti come obiettivo di politica economica. (Gross Domestic Product at Current Prices as an Economic Policy Objective. With English summary.) *Bancaria*, February 1984, *40*(2), pp. 159–65. **[G: Italy]**

de Leeuw, Frank and McKelvey, Michael J. Price Expectations of Business Firms: Bias in the Short and Long Run. *Amer. Econ. Rev.*, March 1984, *74*(1), pp. 99–110. **[G: U.S.]**

Leiderman, Leonardo. On the Monetary-Macro Dynamics of Colombia and Mexico. *J. Devel. Econ.*, January–February 1984, *14*(1–2), pp. 183–201. **[G: Colombia; Mexico]**

Leijonhufvud, Axel. Inflation and Economic Performance. In *Siegel, B. N., ed.*, 1984, pp. 19–36.

LeRoy, Stephen F. Nominal Prices and Interest Rates in General Equilibrium: Money Shocks. *J. Bus.*, April 1984, *57*(2), pp. 177–95.

LeRoy, Stephen F. Nominal Prices and Interest Rates in General Equilibrium: Endowment Shocks. *J. Bus.*, April 1984, *57*(2), pp. 197–213.

Liviatan, Nissan. Tight Money and Inflation. *J. Monet. Econ.*, January 1984, *13*(1), pp. 5–15.

Looney, Robert E. Inflation and Oil Based Development: Failure of the Monetarist Model in Saudi Arabia. *Rivista Int. Sci. Econ. Com.*, October–November 1984, *31*(10–11), pp. 1100–20. **[G: Saudi Arabia]**

Loranger, Jean-Guy. La théorie qualitative de la monnaie: quelques résultats économétriques pour l'ensemble de l'économie canadienne. (The Qualitative Theory of Money: Some Econometrical Results for the Whole Canadian Economy. With English summary.) *Écon. Soc.*, April 1984, *18*(4), pp. 283–310. **[G: Canada]**

Malan, Pedro S. and Wells, John R. 'Structural' Models of Inflation and Balance of Payments Disequilibria in Semi-industrialised Economies—Some Implications for Stabilisation and Growth Policies. In *Csikós-Nagy, B.; Hague, D. and Hall, G., eds.*, 1984, pp. 391–408.

Mann, Arthur J. and Sánchez, Carlos E. Monetarism, Economic Reform and Socio-Economic Consequences: Argentina, 1976–1982. *Int. J. Soc. Econ.*, 1984, *11*(3/4), pp. 12–28. **[G: Argentina]**

Marston, Richard C. Real Wages and the Terms of Trade: Alternative Indexation Rules for an Open Economy. *J. Money, Credit, Banking*, August 1984, *16*(3), pp. 285–301.

Matolcsy, Z. P. The Micro Effects of Inflation on Corporate Taxation and Profitability: Some Empirical Evidence for Seventeen Industry Groups. *Econ. Rec.*, December 1984, *60*(171), pp. 356–65. **[G: Australia]**

Maynard, Geoffrey W. A Natural Interpretation of The Present Unemployment: Comment. In *Griffiths, B. and Wood, G. E., eds.*, 1984, pp. 172–75. **[G: U.K.; U.S.; EEC]**

McCallum, Bennett T. Are Bond-Financed Deficits Inflationary? A Ricardian Analysis. *J. Polit. Econ.*, February 1984, *92*(1), pp. 123–35.

McCallum, Bennett T. On Low-Frequency Estimates of Long-Run Relationships in Macroeconomics. *J. Monet. Econ.*, July 1984, *14*(1), pp. 3–14.

McDonald, Ian M. Anti-stagflationary Tax Cuts and the Problem of Investment. *Econ. Rec.*, September 1984, *60*(170), pp. 284–93.

McDonald, Ian M. Trying to Understand Stagflation. *Australian Econ. Rev.*, 3rd Quarter 1984, (67), pp. 32–56. **[G: Australia]**

McKenna, Edward J. and Zannoni, Diane C. Comment on Stein and Weintraub: "The Acceleration of Inflation." *J. Post Keynesian Econ.*, Spring 1984, *6*(3), pp. 470–78. **[G: U.S.]**

Melnick, Rafi and Sokoler, Meir. The Government's Revenue from Money Creation and the Inflationary Effects of a Decline in the Rate of Growth of G.N.P. *J. Monet. Econ.*, March 1984, *13*(2), pp. 225–36. **[G: Selected OECD; Israel; Argentina]**

Meltzer, Allan H. The Fight Against Inflation: A Comment [Some Unpleasant Monetarist Arithmetic]. In *Griffiths, B. and Wood, G. E., eds.*, 1984, pp. 61–66.

Mengarelli, Gianluigi. "New Inflation" in Italy and the Other Industrialized Countries. *Rev. Econ. Cond. Italy*, February 1984, (1), pp. 31–58. **[G: EEC; OECD; Italy]**

Meyer, W. N. Structuralist and Sociological Views on the Inflation Problem. *J. Stud. Econ. Econometrics*, March 1984, (19), pp. 5–18. **[G: S. Africa]**

Mikhalkina, T. Y.; Lebedev, V. N. and Maryganova, E. A. Western Views of Wages and Unemployment. In *Smirnov, A. D.; Golosov, V. V. and Maximova, V. F., eds.*, 1984, pp. 71–87.

Miller, Marcus H. Government, Unions and Stagflation in the UK. *Nat. Inst. Econ. Rev.*, August 1984, (109), pp. 68–72. **[G: U.K.]**

Minsky, Hyman P. Frank Hahn's *Money and Inflation*: A Review Article. *J. Post Keynesian Econ.*, Spring 1984, *6*(3), pp. 449–57.

Minsky, Hyman P. and Ferri, Piero. Prices, Employment, and Profits. *J. Post Keynesian Econ.*, Summer 1984, *6*(4), pp. 489–99.

Mistri, Maurizio. Su di un caso di variabilità del saggio di interesse reale in condizioni di inflazione con ipotesi di aspettative razionali. (On a Case of Variability of the Real Interest Rate in Conditions of Inflation under Hypothesis of Rational Expectations. With English summary.) *Giorn. Econ.*, March–April 1984, *43*(3–4), pp. 261–70.

Moore, Basil J. and Stuttman, Stephen L. A Causality Analysis of the Determinants of Money Growth. *Brit. Rev. Econ. Issues*, Spring 1984, *6*(14), pp. 1–25. **[G: U.S.]**

Mori, Nobuhiro. The Oil Crises and the Phillips Curve. *Osaka Econ. Pap.*, March 1984, *33*(3–4), pp. 123–34. **[G: Japan]**

Nasseh, Ali Reza and Elyasiani, Elyas. Energy Price Shocks in the 1970s: Impact in Industrialized Economies. *Energy Econ.*, October 1984, *6*(4), pp. 231–44. **[G: U.S.; U.K.; Canada; Germany; France]**

Nickell, Stephen J. Discussants' Comments on: A Natural Interpretation of the Present Unemployment, by Roy A. Batchelor, presented at the City University Conference on Monetarism in the United Kingdom, September 1981. In *Griffiths, B. and Wood, G. E., eds.*, 1984, pp. 176–81. **[G: U.K.; U.S.; EEC]**

Nishijima, Shoji. Indexing Policies and Macroeconomic Stability in Brazil: Rational Expectation Model. *Kobe Econ. Bus. Rev.*, 1984, *30*, pp. 73–86. **[G: Brazil]**

Norton, W. E. and McDonald, Robin. Is There a Macroeconomic World of One Simple Model? Reply. *Econ. Rec.*, June 1984, *60*(169), pp. 190–91.

Nugent, Jeffrey B. and Glezakos, Constantine. The Over-Time Relationship between Inflation and Its Variability Once Again. *Kyklos*, 1984, *37*(1), pp. 104–09. **[G: OECD]**

Öniş, Ziya. Inflation and Economic Growth: A Critical Assessment of the Forced Saving Thesis. *METU*, 1984, *11*(3–4), pp. 285–93.

Opromolla, Paolo. Indicizzazione saliare a punto unico e a punto variabile: un'analisis teorica. (Wage Indexation at a Single and Fixed Point, and at a Flexible Point: A Theoretical Analysis. With English summary.) *Giorn. Econ.*, July–August 1984, *43*(7–8), pp. 547–61.

Ortona, Guido. Qualche dato e qualche ipotesi sulla relazione fra tasso di inflazione e livello di sviluppo nei paesi OCDE. (Inflation Rate and Development Level: Some Data and Some Hypotheses for OECD Countries. With English summary.) *Econ. Lavoro*, July-Sept. 1984, *18*(3), pp. 23–46. **[G: Global]**

Paldam, Martin. Ved Phillipskurvens sølvbryllup—Hvad ved vi om løndannelsen? (At the Silver Wedding of the Phillips Curve—What Have We Learned about Wage Formation? With English summary.) *Nationaløkon. Tidsskr.*, 1984, *122*(1), pp. 133–51. **[G: OECD; U.S.]**

Palermio, Giovanni. Alcune considerazioni su disavanzo pubblico, inflazione e tasso di sviluppo dell'economia. (Reflections on the Public Sector Deficit, Inflation and Economic Growth

Rate. With English summary.) *Bancaria*, March 1984, *40*(3), pp. 272–78.

Papadia, Francesco. Estimates of Ex Ante Real Rates of Interest in the EEC Countries and in the United States, 1973–82: A Note. *J. Money, Credit, Banking*, August 1984, *16*(3), pp. 335–44. **[G: EEC; U.S.]**

Parikh, Ashok. Causality between Money and Prices in Indonesia. *Empirical Econ.*, 1984, *9*(4), pp. 217–32. **[G: Indonesia]**

Parkins, Michael. On *Core Inflation* by Otto Eckstein: A Review Essay. *J. Monet. Econ.*, September 1984, *14*(2), pp. 251–64. **[G: U.S.]**

Pemberton, James. The Long Run Phillips Curve and the Government Budget Constraint. *Scot. J. Polit. Econ.*, November 1984, *31*(3), pp. 255–64.

Peterson, Wallace C. Economic Stabilization and Inflation. *J. Econ. Issues*, March 1984, *18*(1), pp. 69–100. **[G: U.S.]**

Piersanti, Giovanni. Tasso naturale di disoccupazione, aspettative razionali e incertezza sul tasso di inflazione: alcune evidenze empiriche per l'Italia. (Natural Rate of Unemployment, Rational Expectations and Inflation Uncertainty: Some Empirical Evidence for Italy. With English summary.) *Giorn. Econ.*, May–June 1984, *43*(5–6), pp. 369–92. **[G: Italy]**

Prebisch, Raúl. The Global Crisis of Capitalism and Its Theoretical Background. *Cepal Rev.*, April 1984, (22), pp. 159–78. **[G: Global]**

Pultz, Niels. Inflation og stabiliseringspolitik i Argentina 1970–81. (Inflation and Stabilization Policy in Argentina, 1970–81. With English summary.) *Nationaløkon. Tidsskr.*, 1984, *122*(2), pp. 283–97. **[G: Argentina]**

Ram, Rati. Causal Ordering across Inflation and Productivity Growth in the Post-war United States. *Rev. Econ. Statist.*, August 1984, *66*(3), pp. 472–77. **[G: U.S.]**

Ram, Rati. Further International Evidence on Inflation–Output Trade-offs. *Can. J. Econ.*, August 1984, *17*(3), pp. 523–40. **[G: Global]**

Rodríguez, Carlos Alfredo. Inflación, salario real y tipo real de cambio. (With English summary.) *Cuadernos Econ.*, December 1984, *21*(64), pp. 247–61. **[G: Argentina]**

Rodríguez, Carlos Alfredo. La Estrategia de Estabilización con Tipo de Cambio Flexible y Politica Monetaria Activa. (With English summary.) *Cuadernos Econ.*, August 1984, *21*(63), pp. 103–21.

Rødseth, Asbjørn. Progressive Taxes and Automatic Stabilization in an Open Economy. *J. Macroecon.*, Summer 1984, *6*(3), pp. 265–82.

Rosner, Peter, et al. Lohnbestimmung, aussenwirtschaftliche Stabilität und internationale Stagnation. (Wage Determination, External Economic Stability and International Stagnation. With English summary.) *Jahr. Nationalökon. Statist.*, May 1984, *199*(3), pp. 193–212. **[G: Global]**

Rovelli, Riccardo. Expected Inflation and the Real Interest Rate: A Survey of Current Issues. *Giorn. Econ.*, September–October 1984, *43*(9–10), pp. 671–97.

Saini, Krishan G. Can Monetary Growth Explain Inflation in India? *Indian Econ. J.*, July–Sept. 1984, *32*(1), pp. 61–71. **[G: India]**

Salvatore, Dominick. Oil Import Costs and Domestic Inflation in Industrial Countries. *Atlantic Econ. J.*, July 1984, *12*(2), pp. 75.

Salvatore, Dominick. Petroleum Prices, Exchange Rates, and Domestic Inflation in Developing Nations. *Weltwirtsch. Arch.*, 1984, *120*(3), pp. 580–89. **[G: LDCs]**

Sarantis, Nicholas C. Foreign Influences, Exchange Rates, Expectations and Price Inflation in a Developing Economy: The Case of Greece. *J. Devel. Econ.*, January–February 1984, *14*(1–2), pp. 1–18. **[G: Greece]**

Sargent, Thomas J. and Wallace, Neil. Some Unpleasant Monetarist Arithmetic. In *Griffiths, B. and Wood, G. E., eds.*, 1984, pp. 15–41.

Scanagatta, Giovanni. Tasso di interesse e aspettative di inflazione: aspetti teorici ed empirici. (Interest Rates and Inflationary Expectations: Theoretical and Empirical Aspects. With English summary.) *Bancaria*, January 1984, *40*(1), pp. 19–28. **[G: U.S.]**

Schilirò, Daniele. A Note on Eatwell, Llewellyn and Tarling Wage Inflation Model. *Rivista Int. Sci. Econ. Com.*, April 1984, *31*(4), pp. 329–37. **[G: MDCs]**

Schultze, Charles L. Cross-Country and Cross-Temporal Differences in Inflation Responsiveness. *Amer. Econ. Rev.*, May 1984, *74*(2), pp. 160–65. **[G: OECD]**

Seaks, Terry G. Selden's Model of Inflation: A Reexamination [Monetary Growth and the Long-run Rate of Inflation]. *J. Macroecon.*, Winter 1984, *6*(1), pp. 103–07. **[G: U.S.; Canada; Belgium; Netherlands]**

Seccareccia, Mario S. The Fundamental Macroeconomic Link between Investment Activity, the Structure of Employment and Price Changes: A Theoretical and Empirical Analysis. *Écon. Soc.*, April 1984, *18*(4), pp. 165–219. **[G: Canada]**

Selden, Richard T. The Lag from Money to Prices [Monetary Growth and the Long-run Rate of Inflation]. *J. Macroecon.*, Winter 1984, *6*(1), pp. 109–11. **[G: U.S.; Canada]**

Sellekaerts, Willy and Sellekaerts, Brigitte H. Both Anticipated and Unanticipated Inflation Determine Relative Price Variability. *J. Post Keynesian Econ.*, Summer 1984, *6*(4), pp. 500–508.

Sharma, Ramlal. Causality between Money and Price Level in India. *Indian Econ. Rev.*, July–Dec. 1984, *19*(2), pp. 213–21. **[G: India]**

Simkin, Colin. Does Money Matter in Singapore? *Singapore Econ. Rev.*, April 1984, *29*(1), pp. 1–15. **[G: Singapore]**

Spencer, Grant H. and Duggan, K. G. On the Structural Sensitivity of Short Term Output-Inflation Tradeoffs. *Appl. Econ.*, February 1984, *16*(1), pp. 81–98. **[G: New Zealand]**

Stein, Jerome L. Reply to McKenna and Zannoni: "The Acceleration of Inflation." *J. Post Keynesian Econ.*, Spring 1984, *6*(3), pp. 779–80. **[G: U.S.]**

Stemp, Peter J. and Turnovsky, Stephen J. Optimal Stabilisation Policies under Perfect Foresight. In *Hughes Hallet, A.J., ed.*, 1984, pp. 3–22.

Stenius, Marianne. Hur genereras inflationsförväntningarna? En kommentar. (The Inflation Expectation Generating Process: Comment. With English summary.) *Ekon. Samfundets Tidskr.*, 1984, *37*(3), pp. 205–11. **[G: Finland]**

Struth, Friedrich K. Modelling Expectations Formation with Parameter-Adaptive Filters: An Empirical Application to the Livingston Forecasts. *Oxford Bull. Econ. Statist.*, August 1984, *46*(3), pp. 211–39. **[G: U.S.]**

Sylos-Labini, Paolo. Prices and Income Distribution in the Manufacturing Industry. In *Sylos-Labini, P.*, 1984, *1979*, pp. 185–209. **[G: Italy; U.S.; U.K.; W. Germany; Argentina]**

Sylos-Labini, Paolo. Rigid Prices, Flexible Prices, and Inflation. In *Sylos-Labini, P.*, 1984, *1982*, pp. 147–82.

Tabellini, Guido. Why Do We Observe So Little Indexation? An Answer from the Theory of Insurance. *Giorn. Econ.*, May–June 1984, *43*(5–6), pp. 417–31.

Tavlas, George S. The Price Equation and Excess Demand: A Reappraisal. *Appl. Econ.*, December 1984, *16*(6), pp. 935–44. **[G: U.K.]**

Taylor, John B. Recent Changes in Macro Policy and Its Effects: Some Time-Series Evidence. *Amer. Econ. Rev.*, May 1984, *74*(2), pp. 206–10. **[G: U.S.]**

Tobin, James. Impasse of the 1980s: Locomotives Who Can't or Won't. *World Econ.*, March 1984, *7*(1), pp. 5–21. **[G: OECD]**

VanderHoff, James. A 'Rational' Explanation for 'Irrational' Forecasts of Inflation. *J. Monet. Econ.*, May 1984, *13*(3), pp. 387–92. **[G: U.S.]**

Vartia, Pentti L. I. and Mankinen, Reijo. Perceived and Expected Price Changes in Finland. *Weltwirtsch. Arch.*, 1984, *120*(1), pp. 121–32. **[G: Finland]**

Vicarelli, F. Stagflation in the Seventies: A Relative Prices Theoretical Approach. *Metroecon.*, June-Oct. 1984, *36*(2–3), pp. 127–41. **[G: OECD]**

Virén, Matti. Expected Inflation and Interest Rates: Some Cross-Country Evidence. *Liiketaloudellinen Aikak.*, 1984, *33*(4), pp. 433–45. **[G: OECD]**

Vitaliano, Donald F. Defense Spending and Inflation: An Empirical Analysis. *Quart. Rev. Econ. Bus.*, Spring 1984, *24*(1), pp. 22–32. **[G: U.S.]**

Wallace, Myles S. World Money or Domestic Money: Which Predicts U.S. Inflation Best? *J. Int. Money Finance*, August 1984, *3*(2), pp. 241–44. **[G: U.S.]**

Warr, Peter G. Exchange Rate Protection in Indonesia. *Bull. Indonesian Econ. Stud.*, August 1984, *20*(2), pp. 53–89. **[G: Indonesia]**

Wentzler, Nancy A. Inflation, Expectations, and

Cyclical Aggravations. *Atlantic Econ. J.*, December 1984, *12*(4), pp. 51–54.

van Wijnbergen, Sweder. Oil Price Shocks and the Current Account: An Analysis of Short Run Adjustment Measures. *Weltwirtsch. Arch.*, 1984, *120*(3), pp. 460–80. **[G: OPEC; LDCs]**

Wogart, Jan Peter and Marques, Jose Siverio. Trade Liberalization, Tariff Redundancy and Inflation: A Methodological Exploration Applied to Argentina. *Weltwirtsch. Arch.*, 1984, *120*(1), pp. 18–39. **[G: Argentina]**

Wolters, Jürgen. Preiserwartungen des Ifo-Konjunkturtestes und die tatsächliche Preisentwicklung. (Price Expectations in the IFO-Business Test and the Development of Prices—An Empirical Study. With English summary.) *Ifo-Studien*, 1984, *30*(1), pp. 29–61.
[G: W. Germany]

Wren-Lewis, Simon. Omitted Variables in Equations Relating Prices to Money. *Appl. Econ.*, August 1984, *16*(4), pp. 483–96. **[G: U.K.]**

Zala, Julia. Protection of the Price Level and a Dynamic Economy. *Acta Oecon.*, 1984, *33*(3–4), pp. 237–54. **[G: Hungary]**

200 Quantitative Economic Methods and Data

210 ECONOMETRIC, STATISTICAL, AND MATHEMATICAL METHODS, AND MODELS

211 Econometric and Statistical Methods and Models

2110 General

Arrow, Kenneth J. Decision Theory and the Choice of a Level of Significance for the *t*-Test. In *Arrow, K. J., vol. 4*, 1984, *1960*, pp. 66–76.

Arrow, Kenneth J.; Barankin, E. W. and Blackwell, D. Admissible Points of Convex Sets. In *Arrow, K. J., vol. 4*, 1984, *1953*, pp. 38–42.

Barbu, G. A New Fast Method for Computer Generation of Gamma and Beta Random Variables by Transformation of Uniform Variables. *Econ. Computat. Cybern. Stud. Res.*, 1984, *19*(3), pp. 69–81.

Bernardo, José M. Monitoring the 1982 Spanish Socialist Victory: A Bayesian Analysis. *J. Amer. Statist. Assoc.*, September 1984, *79*(387), pp. 510–15. **[G: Spain]**

Bilgen, Semih and Deligönül, Z. Şeyda. Yenileme kuraminda volterra denkleminin çözümü için bir yöntem. (A Method of Solution for the Volterra Equation for the Renewal Theory. With English summary.) *METU*, 1984, *11*(3–4), pp. 369–90.

Bock, M. E.; Judge, G. G. and Yancey, T. A. A Simple Form for the Inverse Moments of Non-Central ψ^2 and F Random Variables and Certain Confluent Hypergeometric Functions. *J. Econometrics*, May/June 1984, *25*(1/2), pp. 217–34.

Breusch, Trevor S. Tests of Specification in Econometrics: Comment. *Econometric Rev.*, 1984, *3*(2), pp. 243–51.

Cameron, Murray A. Choosing a Symmetrizing Power Transformation. *J. Amer. Statist. Assoc.*, March 1984, *79*(385), pp. 107–09.

Chesher, Andrew D. Testing for Neglected Heterogeneity. *Econometrica*, July 1984, *52*(4), pp. 865–72.

Cuthbert, J. R. Proportion Analysis on Cell Data: Distortions Due to Variations in Cell Sizes. *Urban Stud.*, February 1984, *21*(1), pp. 83–88. **[G: U.K.]**

Darnell, A. C. Economic Statistics and Econometrics. In *Creedy, J. and O'Brien, D. P., eds.*, 1984, pp. 152–85.

Draper, Norman R. The Box–Wetz Criterion versus R^2. *J. Roy. Statist. Soc.*, Part 1, 1984, *147*(1), pp. 100–103.

Ebert, Udo. Measures of Distance between Income Distributions. *J. Econ. Theory*, April 1984, *32*(2), pp. 266–74.

Faden, Arnold M. The Foundations of Probability. In *[Beckmann, M. J.]*, 1984, pp. 195–213.

Frosini, Benito V. Concentration, Dispersion and Spread: An Insight into Their Relationship. *Statistica*, July–September 1984, *44*(3), pp. 373–94.

Gerbing, David W. and Anderson, James C. On the Meaning of Within-Factor Correlated Measurement Errors. *J. Cons. Res.*, June 1984, *11*(1), pp. 572–80.

Goldstein, Harvey. Present Position and Potential Developments: Some Personal Views: Statistics in the Social Sciences. *J. Roy. Statist. Soc.*, 1984, *147*(2), pp. 260–67.

Hausman, Jerry A. Tests of Specification in Econometrics: Comment. *Econometric Rev.*, 1984, *3*(2), pp. 253–55.

Hendry, David F. Monte Carlo Experimentation in Econometrics. In *Griliches, Z. and Intriligator, M. D., eds.*, 1984, pp. 939–76.

Johnston, R. J. Quantitative Ecological Analysis in Human Geography: An Evaluation of Four Problem Areas. In *Bahrenberg, G.; Fischer, M. M., and Nijkamp, P.*, 1984, pp. 131–41.

Kakwani, Nanak. The Relative Deprivation Curve and Its Applications: Reply. *J. Bus. Econ. Statist.*, October 1984, *2*(4), pp. 400–405.
[G: Australia]

Kakwani, Nanak. The Relative Deprivation Curve and Its Applications. *J. Bus. Econ. Statist.*, October 1984, *2*(4), pp. 384–94.
[G: Australia]

Kanbur, S. M. Ravi. The Measurement and Decomposition of Inequality and Poverty. In *van der Ploeg, F., ed.*, 1984, pp. 403–32.

Kariya, Takeaki; Sinha, Bimal K. and Subramanyam, Kasala. First, Second and Third Order Efficiencies of the Estimators for a Common Mean. *Hitotsubashi J. Econ.*, June 1984, *25*(1), pp. 61–69.

Kingman, J. F. C. Present Position and Potential Developments: Some Personal Views: Probability and Random Processes. *J. Roy. Statist. Soc.*, 1984, *147*(2), pp. 233–44.

Knowles, Glenn J. Some Econometric Problems in the Measurement of Utility. *Amer. J. Agr. Econ.*, November 1984, *66*(4), pp. 505–10.

Krieger, Abba M. and Gastwirth, Joseph L. Interpolation from Grouped Data for Unimodal Densities. *Econometrica*, March 1984, *52*(2), pp. 419–26.

Lancaster, Tony. The Covariance Matrix of the Information Matrix Test. *Econometrica*, July 1984, *52*(4), pp. 1051–53.

Leamer, Edward E. Let's Take the Con out of Econometrics. In *Caldwell, B. J., ed., 1984, 1983*, pp. 460–72.   [G: U.S.]

Lee, Lung-Fei. Tests of Specification in Econometrics: Comment. *Econometric Rev.*, 1984, *3*(2), pp. 257–59.

MacKinnon, James G. Econometric Methods for Applied General Equilibrium Analysis: Comments. In *Scarf, H. E. and Shoven, J. B., eds.,* 1984, pp. 203–07.   [G: U.S.]

Marschak, Jacob. On Econometric Tools. In *Hausman, D. M., ed., 1984, 1969*, pp. 294–99.

McDonald, James B. Some Generalized Functions for the Size Distribution of Income. *Econometrica*, May 1984, *52*(3), pp. 647–63.   [G: U.S.]

McNown, Robert F. and Hunt, Gary L. An Econometrics Laboratory. *J. Econ. Educ.*, Winter 1984, *15*(1), pp. 71–76.

Mittelstaedt, Robert A. and Zorn, Thomas S. Econometric Replication: Lessons from the Experimental Sciences. *Quart. J. Bus. Econ.*, Winter 1984, *23*(1), pp. 9–15.

Mizon, Grayham E. The Encompassing Approach in Econometrics. In *Hendry, D. F. and Wallis, K. F., eds.,* 1984, pp. 135–72.

Moore, Peter G. Present Position and Potential Developments: Some Personal Views: Statistics in Business and Commerce. *J. Roy. Statist. Soc.*, 1984, *147*(2), pp. 268–77.

Onukogu, Ike B. An Analysis of Variance of Nominal Data. *Statistica*, January–March 1984, *44*(1), pp. 87–96.

Pope, Rulon D. and Ziemer, Rod F. Stochastic Efficiency, Normality, and Sampling Errors in Agricultural Risk Analysis. *Amer. J. Agr. Econ.*, February 1984, *66*(1), pp. 31–40.

Pulley, Lawrence B. and Dolbear, F. Trenery. Computer Simulation Exercises for Economics Statistics. *J. Econ. Educ.*, Winter 1984, *15*(1), pp. 77–87.

Ravallion, Martin and Van de Walle, Dominique. Measuring Ex-Ante Information: What the Newspapers Said during the 1974 Famine in Bangladesh. *Rev. Public Data Use*, October 1984, *12*(3), pp. 169–84.   [G: Bangladesh]

Rodgers, Willard L. An Evaluation of Statistical Matching. *J. Bus. Econ. Statist.*, January 1984, *2*(1), pp. 91–102.

Rosen, Sherwin. The Relative Deprivation Curve and Its Applications. *J. Bus. Econ. Statist.*, October 1984, *2*(4), pp. 395–97.

          [G: Australia]

Ruud, Paul A. Tests of Specification in Econometrics. *Econometric Rev.*, 1984, *3*(2), pp. 211–42.

Ruud, Paul A. Tests of Specification in Econometrics: Reply. *Econometric Rev.*, 1984, *3*(2), pp. 269–76.

Ryscavage, Paul and Lamas, Enrique. The Relative Deprivation Curve and Its Applications: Comment. *J. Bus. Econ. Statist.*, October 1984, *2*(4), pp. 398–99.   [G: Australia]

Schmitz, Norbert. Asymptotic Optimality of Differentiated SPRT's for Composite Hypotheses. In *[Beckmann, M. J.],* 1984, pp. 267–74.

Sirvanci, Mete and Yang, Grace. Estimation of the Wiebull Parameters under Type I Censoring. *J. Amer. Statist. Assoc.*, March 1984, *79*(385), pp. 183–87.

Spirer, Herbert F. and Jaffe, A. J. Misuses of Statistics: Lessons for Statisticians, Non-Statisticians, Students and Teachers. *Amer. J. Econ. Soc.*, April 1984, *43*(2), pp. 205–16.

Stoker, Thomas M. Completeness, Distribution Restrictions, and the Form of Aggregate Functions. *Econometrica*, July 1984, *52*(4), pp. 887–907.

White, Halbert. Maximum Likelihood Estimation of Misspecified Dynamic Models. In *Dijkstra, T. K., ed.,* 1984, pp. 1–19.

White, Halbert. Tests of Specification in Econometrics: Comment. *Econometric Rev.*, 1984, *3*(2), pp. 261–67.

Zellner, Arnold. Basic Issues in Econometrics: Introduction. In *Zellner, A.,* 1984, pp. ix–xxi.

Zellner, Arnold. Basic Issues in Econometrics, Past and Present. In *Zellner, A., 1984, 1982*, pp. 26–34.

Zellner, Arnold. Causality and Econometrics. In *Zellner, A., 1984, 1979*, pp. 35–74.

Zellner, Arnold. Estimation of Functions of Population Means and Regression Coefficients Including Structural Coefficients: A Minimum Expected Loss (MELO) Approach. In *Zellner, A., 1984, 1978*, pp. 238–68.

Zellner, Arnold. Philosophy and Objectives of Econometrics. In *Zellner, A., 1984, 1981*, pp. 3–11.

Zellner, Arnold. Statistical Analysis of Econometric Models. In *Zellner, A., 1984, 1979*, pp. 83–119.

Zenga, Michele. Proposta per un indice di concentrazione basato sui rapporti fra quantili di popolazione e quantili di reddito. (A Proposal for a Concentration Index Based on the Ratios between the Quantiles of Population and the Quantiles of Income. With English summary.) *Giorn. Econ.*, May–June 1984, *43*(5–6), pp. 301–26.   [G: U.K.; Sweden; Italy]

2112 Inferential Problems in Simultaneous Equation Systems

Aigner, Dennis J., et al. Latent Variable Models in Econometrics. In *Griliches, Z. and Intriligator, M. D., eds.,* 1984, pp. 1323–93.

Baltagi, Badi H. A Monte Carlo Study for Pooling Time Series of Cross-Section Data in the Simultaneous Equations Model. *Int. Econ. Rev.*, October 1984, *25*(3), pp. 603–24.

Bekker, Paul; Kapteyn, Arie and Wansbeek, Tom. Measurement Error and Endogeneity in Regression: Bounds for ML and 2SLS Estimates. In *Dijkstra, T. K., ed.*, 1984, pp. 85–103.

ter Berg, Peter and Harkema, Rins. Bayesian Limited-Information Analysis of Nonlinear Simultaneous Equations Systems. *J. Econometrics*, March 1984, *24*(3), pp. 379–95.
[G: Netherlands]

Bergstrom, A. R. Continuous Time Stochastic Models and Issues of Aggregation Over Time. In *Griliches, Z. and Intriligator, M. D., eds.*, 1984, pp. 1146–1212.

Binkley, James K. and Nelson, Glenn. Impacts of Alternative Degrees of Freedom Corrections in Two and Three Stage Least Squares. *J. Econometrics*, March 1984, *24*(3), pp. 223–33.

Brown, Bryan W. and Mariano, Roberto S. Residual-Based Procedures for Prediction and Estimation in a Nonlinear Simultaneous System. *Econometrica*, March 1984, *52*(2), pp. 321–43.

Chamberlain, Gary. Panel Data. In *Griliches, Z. and Intriligator, M. D., eds.*, 1984, pp. 1248–1318. [G: U.S.]

Chow, Gregory C. Random and Changing Coefficient Models. In *Griliches, Z. and Intriligator, M. D., eds.*, 1984, pp. 1214–45.

Dawid, A. P. Causal Inference from Messy Data: Comment [On the Nature and Discovery of Structure]. *J. Amer. Statist. Assoc.*, March 1984, *79*(385), pp. 22–24.

Demidenko, E. Z. The Identification of Econometric Models Which Are Linear with Lags or Non-linear. *Matekon*, Fall 1984, *21*(1), pp. 87–102.

Dijkstra, Theo K. Misspecification and the Choice of Estimators, a Heuristic Approach. In *Dijkstra, T. K., ed.*, 1984, pp. 37–55.

Dwivedi, T. D. and Srivastava, Virendra K. Exact Finite Sample Properties of Double k-Class Estimators in Simultaneous Equations. *J. Econometrics*, July 1984, *25*(3), pp. 263–83.

Engle, Robert F. Wald, Likelihood Ratio, and Lagrange Multiplier Tests in Econometrics. In *Griliches, Z. and Intriligator, M. D., eds.*, 1984, pp. 776–826.

Fisher, Franklin M. The Place of Least Squares in Econometrics: Comment. In *Waugh, F. V.*, 1984, *1962*, pp. 435–37.

Freedman, David A. and Peters, Stephen C. Bootstrapping a Regression Equation: Some Empirical Results. *J. Amer. Statist. Assoc.*, March 1984, *79*(385), pp. 97–106. [G: U.S.]

Freedman, David A. and Peters, Stephen C. Bootstrapping an Econometric Model: Some Empirical Results. *J. Bus. Econ. Statist.*, April 1984, *2*(2), pp. 150–58.

Frisch, Ragnar and Waugh, Frederick V. Partial Time Regressions as Compared with Individual Trends. In *Waugh, F. V.*, 1984, *1933*, pp. 409–23.

Garen, John. The Returns to Schooling: A Selectivity Bias Approach with a Continuous Choice Variable. *Econometrica*, September 1984, *52*(5), pp. 1199–1218. [G: U.S.]

Geweke, John F. Inference and Causality in Economic Time Series Models. In *Griliches, Z. and Intriligator, M. D., eds.*, 1984, pp. 1102–1144.

Geweke, John F. The Indispensable Art of Econometrics: Comment [On the Nature and Discovery of Structure]. *J. Amer. Statist. Assoc.*, March 1984, *79*(385), pp. 25–26.

Godfrey, L. G. On the Uses of Misspecification Checks and Tests of Non-Nested Hypotheses in Emperical Econometrics. *Econ. J.*, 1984 Supplement, *94*, pp. 69–81.

Gourieroux, Christian; Laffont, Jean-Jacques and Monfort, Alain. Econométrie des modèles d'équilibre avec rationnement: une mise à jour. (Disequilibrium Econometrics: Recent Developments. With English summary.) *Ann. INSEE*, July–December 1984, (55/56), pp. 5–38.

Hendry, David F. Monte Carlo Experimentation in Econometrics. In *Griliches, Z. and Intriligator, M. D., eds.*, 1984, pp. 939–76.

Hillier, Grant H. and Giles, David E. A. Estimation in Equilibrium Models Involving Discretionary Policy Instrument Choice. *Australian Econ. Pap.*, December 1984, *23*(43), pp. 179–96. [G: Australia]

Hillier, Grant H.; Kinal, Terrence W. and Srivastava, Virendra K. On the Moments of Ordinary Least Squares and Instrumental Variables Estimators in a General Structural Equation. *Econometrica*, January 1984, *52*(1), pp. 185–202.

Knight, John L. Asymptotic Distribution of Dynamic Multipliers in Dynamic Autoregressive Models. *Econometrica*, January 1984, *52*(1), pp. 217–22.

McFadden, Daniel L. Econometric Analysis of Qualitative Response Models. In *Griliches, Z. and Intriligator, M. D., eds.*, 1984, pp. 1396–1457.

Morimune, Kimio and Tsukuda, Yoshihiko. Asymptotic Expansions of the Distributions of the Structural Variance Estimators in a Simultaneous Equations System. *J. Econometrics*, March 1984, *24*(3), pp. 279–92.

Morimune, Kimio and Tsukuda, Yoshihiko. Testing a Subset of Coefficients in a Structural Equation. *Econometrica*, March 1984, *52*(2), pp. 427–48.

Pagan, Adrian R. and Nicholls, Desmond F. Estimating Predictions, Prediction Errors and Their Standard Deviations Using Constructed Variables. *J. Econometrics*, March 1984, *24*(3), pp. 293–310.

Phillips, Peter C. B. The Exact Distribution of LIML: I. *Int. Econ. Rev.*, February 1984, *25*(1), pp. 249–61.

Phillips, Peter C. B. The Exact Distribution of Exogenous Variable Coefficient Estimators. *J. Econometrics*, December 1984, *26*(3), pp. 387–98.

Polasek, Wolfgang. Multivariate Regression Systems. In *Kadane, J. B., ed.*, 1984, pp. 231–309. [G: U.S.]

Pollock, D. S. G. Two Reduced-Form Approaches to the Derivation of the Maximum-Likelihood

Estimators for Simultaneous-Equation Systems. *J. Econometrics*, March 1984, *24*(3), pp. 331–47.

van Praag, Bernard M. S. and Koster, Jan T. A. Specification in Simultaneous Linear Equations Models: The Relation between a Priori Specifications and Resulting Estimators. **In** *Dijkstra, T. K., ed.*, 1984, pp. 71–84.

Pratt, J. W. and Schlaifer, Robert. On the Nature and Discovery of Structure. *J. Amer. Statist. Assoc.*, March 1984, *79*(385), pp. 9–21.

Pratt, J. W. and Schlaifer, Robert. On the Nature and Discovery of Structure: Rejoinder. *J. Amer. Statist. Assoc.*, March 1984, *79*(385), pp. 29–33.

Prucha, Ingmar R. On the Asymptotic Efficiency of Feasible Aitken Estimators for Seemingly Unrelated Regression Models with Error Components. *Econometrica*, January 1984, *52*(1), pp. 203–07.

Prucha, Ingmar R. and Kelejian, Harry H. The Structure of Simultaneous Equation Estimators: A Generalization towards Nonnormal Disturbances. *Econometrica*, May 1984, *52*(3), pp. 721–36.

Richard, Jean-François. Classical and Bayesian Inference in Incomplete Simultaneous Equation Models. **In** *Hendry, D. F. and Wallis, K. F., eds.*, 1984, pp. 61–102.

Rosenbaum, Paul R. and Rubin, Donald B. Estimating the Effects Caused by Treatments: Comment [On the Nature and Discovery of Structure]. *J. Amer. Statist. Assoc.*, March 1984, *79*(385), pp. 26–28.

Rothenberg, Thomas J. Approximating the Distributions of Econometric Estimators and Test Statistics. **In** *Griliches, Z. and Intriligator, M. D., eds.*, 1984, pp. 882–935.

Srivastava, Virendra K. and Srivastava, Anil K. Improved Estimation in a Two Equation Seemingly Unrelated Regression Model. *Statistica*, July–September 1984, *44*(3), pp. 417–22.

Stapleton, David C. Errors-in-Variables in Demand Systems. *J. Econometrics*, December 1984, *26*(3), pp. 255–70. [G: U.K.]

Waugh, Frederick V. The Place of Least Squares in Econometrics. **In** *Waugh, F. V.*, 1984, *1961*, pp. 424–34.

Waugh, Frederick V. The Place of Least Squares in Econometrics: Further Comment. **In** *Waugh, F. V.*, 1984, *1962*, pp. 438–39.

White, Halbert and Domowitz, Ian. Nonlinear Regression with Dependent Observations. *Econometrica*, January 1984, *52*(1), pp. 143–61.

2113 Distributed Lags and Serially Correlated Disturbance Terms; Inferential Problems in Single Equation Models

Aigner, Dennis J., et al. Latent Variable Models in Econometrics. **In** *Griliches, Z. and Intriligator, M. D., eds.*, 1984, pp. 1323–93.

Ali, Mukhtar M. and Giaccotto, Carmelo. A Study of Several New and Existing Tests for Heteroscedasticity in the General Linear Model. *J. Econometrics*, December 1984, *26*(3), pp. 355–73.

Amemiya, Takeshi. Tobit Models: A Survey. *J. Econometrics*, January/February 1984, *24*(1/2), pp. 3–61.

Anas, Alex and Moses, Leon N. Qualitative Choice and the Blending of Discrete Alternatives. *Rev. Econ. Statist.*, November 1984, *66*(4), pp. 547–55. [G: S. Korea]

Ashley, Richard. A Simple Test for Regression Parameter Instability. *Econ. Inquiry*, April 1984, *22*(2), pp. 253–68.

Atkinson, A. C. and McCullagh, P. Graphical Methods for Assessing Logistic Regression Models: Comment. *J. Amer. Statist. Assoc.*, March 1984, *79*(385), pp. 72.

Baltagi, Badi H. A Monte Carlo Study for Pooling Time Series of Cross-Section Data in the Simultaneous Equations Model. *Int. Econ. Rev.*, October 1984, *25*(3), pp. 603–24.

Baltagi, Badi H. and Griffin, James M. Short and Long Run Effects in Pooled Models. *Int. Econ. Rev.*, October 1984, *25*(3), pp. 631–45.

Barron, Andrew R. Predicted Squared Error: A Criterion for Automatic Model Selection. **In** *Farlow, S. J., ed.*, 1984, pp. 87–103.

Bekker, Paul; Kapteyn, Arie and Wansbeek, Tom. Measurement Error and Endogeneity in Regression: Bounds for ML and 2SLS Estimates. **In** *Dijkstra, T. K., ed.*, 1984, pp. 85–103.

Bera, Anil K.; Jarque, Carlos M. and Lee, Lung-Fei. Testing the Normality Assumption in Limited Dependent Variable Models. *Int. Econ. Rev.*, October 1984, *25*(3), pp. 563–78. [G: Mexico]

Berger, James O. and Berliner, L. M. Bayesian Input in Stein Estimation and a New Minimax Empirical Bayes Estimator. *J. Econometrics*, May/June 1984, *25*(1/2), pp. 87–108.

Bickel, Peter J. Adaptive Estimation of Non-linear Regression Models: Comment. *Econometric Rev.*, 1984, *3*(2), pp. 195–98.

Bickel, Peter J. The Analysis of Transformed Data: Comment. *J. Amer. Statist. Assoc.*, June 1984, *79*(386), pp. 315–16.

Bierens, Herman J. Model Specification Testing of Time Series Regressions. *J. Econometrics*, December 1984, *26*(3), pp. 323–53.

Bierens, Herman J. Testing Parameter Constancy of Linear Regressions. **In** *Dijkstra, T. K., ed.*, 1984, pp. 104–17.

Blackley, Paul R.; Follain, James R., Jr. and Ondrich, Jan. Box–Cox Estimation of Hedonic Models: How Serious Is the Iterative OLS Variance Bias? *Rev. Econ. Statist.*, May 1984, *66*(2), pp. 348–53. [G: U.S.]

Bock, M. E.; Judge, G. G. and Yancey, T. A. A Simple Form for the Inverse Moments of Non-Central ψ^2 and F Random Variables and Certain Confluent Hypergeometric Functions. *J. Econometrics*, May/June 1984, *25*(1/2), pp. 217–34.

Bohrer, R. and Yancey, T. A. Algorithms for Numerical Evaluation of Stein-Like and Limited-

Translation Estimators. *J. Econometrics*, May/June 1984, *25*(1/2), pp. 235–39.

Buse, A. Tests for Additive Heteroskedasticity: Goldfeld and Quandt Revisited. *Empirical Econ.*, 1984, *9*(4), pp. 199–216.

Butler, Ronald W. The Significance Attained by the Best-Fitting Regressor Variable. *J. Amer. Statist. Assoc.*, June 1984, *79*(386), pp. 341–48.

Carroll, Raymond J. and Ruppert, David. Power Transformation When Fitting Theoretical Models to Data. *J. Amer. Statist. Assoc.*, June 1984, *79*(386), pp. 321–28.

Carroll, Raymond J. and Ruppert, David. The Analysis of Transformed Data: Comment. *J. Amer. Statist. Assoc.*, June 1984, *79*(386), pp. 312–13.

Chamberlain, Gary. Adaptive Estimation of Nonlinear Regression Models: Comment. *Econometric Rev.*, 1984, *3*(2), pp. 199–202.

Chamberlain, Gary. Panel Data. In *Griliches, Z. and Intriligator, M. D., eds.*, 1984, pp. 1248–1318. [G: U.S.]

Chang, Y. C. A Truncated Maximum Likelihood Estimator of a Constrained Bivariate Linear Regression Coefficient. *J. Amer. Statist. Assoc.*, June 1984, *79*(386), pp. 454–58.

Chesher, Andrew D. Improving the Efficiency of Probit Estimators. *Rev. Econ. Statist.*, August 1984, *66*(3), pp. 523–27.

Chow, Gregory C. Random and Changing Coefficient Models. In *Griliches, Z. and Intriligator, M. D., eds.*, 1984, pp. 1214–45.

Christensen, Ronald. A Note on Ordinary Least Squares Methods for Two-Stage Sampling. *J. Amer. Statist. Assoc.*, September 1984, *79*(387), pp. 720–21.

Chung, Ching-Fan and Goldberger, Arthur S. Proportional Projections in Limited Dependent Variable Models. *Econometrica*, March 1984, *52*(2), pp. 531–34.

Cox, D. R. Present Position and Potential Developments: Some Personal Views: Design of Experiments and Regression. *J. Roy. Statist. Soc.*, 1984, *147*(2), pp. 306–15.

Dadkhah, Kamran M. Confidence Interval for Predictions from a Logarithmic Model. *Rev. Econ. Statist.*, August 1984, *66*(3), pp. 527–28.

Davidson, Russell and MacKinnon, James G. Convenient Specification Tests for Logit and Probit Models. *J. Econometrics*, July 1984, *25*(3), pp. 241–62.

Davidson, Russell and MacKinnon, James G. Model Specification Tests Based on Artificial Linear Regressions. *Int. Econ. Rev.*, June 1984, *25*(2), pp. 485–502.

Davies, Richard B. and Crouchley, Robert. Calibrating Longitudinal Models of Residential Mobility and Migration: An Assessment of a Non-Parametric Marginal Likelihood Approach. *Reg. Sci. Urban Econ.*, May 1984, *14*(2), pp. 231–47. [G: U.S.]

Dawid, A. P. Causal Inference from Messy Data: Comment [On the Nature and Discovery of Structure]. *J. Amer. Statist. Assoc.*, March 1984, *79*(385), pp. 22–24.

Derrick, Frederick W. Interpretation of Dummy Variables in Semilogarithmic Equations: Small Sample Implications. *Southern Econ. J.*, April 1984, *50*(4), pp. 1185–88.

Doksum Kjell A. The Transformation Controversy: Comment [The Analysis of Transformed Data]. *J. Amer. Statist. Assoc.*, June 1984, *79*(386), pp. 316–19.

Duncan, Gregory M. Adaptive Estimation of Non-linear Regression Models: Comment. *Econometric Rev.*, 1984, *3*(2), pp. 203–08.

Efron, Bradley. Comparing Non-nested Linear Models. *J. Amer. Statist. Assoc.*, December 1984, *79*(388), pp. 791–803.

Engle, Robert F. Wald, Likelihood Ratio, and Lagrange Multiplier Tests in Econometrics. In *Griliches, Z. and Intriligator, M. D., eds.*, 1984, pp. 776–826.

Erlat, Haluk. Testing for Structural Change under Heteroscedasticity: A Note. *Manchester Sch. Econ. Soc. Stud.*, December 1984, *52*(4), pp. 380–90.

Evans, G. B. A. and Savin, N. E. Testing for Unit Roots: 2. *Econometrica*, September 1984, *52*(5), pp. 1241–69.

Ferrari, Guido. Stima del modello trasformato di Koyck generato da ipotesi di aspettative economiche con disturbi AR (p) ed MA (q). (Estimating Koyck Model Generated by Economic Expectations Hypotheses with AR (p) and MA (q) Disturbances. With English summary.) *Statistica*, July–September 1984, *44*(3), pp. 501–11.

Fienberg, Stephen E. and Gong, Gail D. Graphical Methods for Assessing Logistic Regression Models: Comment. *J. Amer. Statist. Assoc.*, March 1984, *79*(385), pp. 72–77.

Folmer, H. and Nijkamp, Peter. Linear Structural Equation Models with Latent Variables and Spatial Correlation. In *Bahrenberg, G.; Fischer, M. M., and Nijkamp, P.*, 1984, pp. 163–70.

Fourgeaud, Claude; Gourieroux, Christian and Pradel, Jacqueline. Some Theoretical Results for Generalized Ridge Regression Estimators. *J. Econometrics*, May/June 1984, *25*(1/2), pp. 191–203.

Gallant, A. Ronald and Golub, Gene H. Imposing Curvature Restrictions on Flexible Functional Forms. *J. Econometrics*, December 1984, *26*(3), pp. 295–321. [G: U.S.]

Geweke, John F. The Indispensable Art of Econometrics: Comment [On the Nature and Discovery of Structure]. *J. Amer. Statist. Assoc.*, March 1984, *79*(385), pp. 25–26.

Ghali, Moheb A. and Snow, Marcellus S. A Generalized Test for Four Types of Regression Specification Error. In *Avula, X. J. R., et al.*, 1984, pp. 778–83.

Godfrey, L. G. On the Uses of Misspecification Checks and Tests of Non-Nested Hypotheses in Emperical Econometrics. *Econ. J.*, 1984 Supplement, *94*, pp. 69–81.

Gori, Enrico. Asymptotic Properties of Nonlinear

Least Squares Estimators When the Parameters Are Subject to Equality Constraints. *Statistica*, October–December 1984, *44*(4), pp. 699–708.

Gourieroux, Christian; Monfort, Alain and Trognon, Alain. Pseudo Maximum Likelihood Methods: Theory. *Econometrica*, May 1984, *52*(3), pp. 681–700.

Gourieroux, Christian; Monfort, Alain and Trognon, Alain. Pseudo Maximum Likelihood Methods: Applications to Poisson Models. *Econometrica*, May 1984, *52*(3), pp. 701–20.

Gourieroux, Christian and Trognon, Alain. Specifications Pre-Test Estimator. *J. Econometrics*, May/June 1984, *25*(1/2), pp. 15–27.

Greene, William H. Reverse Regression: The Algebra of Discrimination [Reverse Regression, Fairness, and Employment Discrimination]. *J. Bus. Econ. Statist.*, April 1984, *2*(2), pp. 117–20.   [G: U.S.]

Greenlees, John S. and Zieschang, Kimberly D. Grouping Tests for Misspecification: An Application to Housing Demand. *J. Bus. Econ. Statist.*, April 1984, *2*(2), pp. 159–69.   [G: U.S.]

Gregory, Allan W. and McCurdy, Thomas H. Testing the Unbiasedness Hypothesis in the Forward Foreign Exchange Market: A Specification Analysis. *J. Int. Money Finance*, December 1984, *3*(3), pp. 357–68.   [G: Canada; U.S.]

Griffiths, W. E. and Beesley, P. A. A. The Small-Sample Properties of Some Preliminary Test Estimators in a Linear Model with Autocorrelated Errors. *J. Econometrics*, May/June 1984, *25*(1/2), pp. 49–61.

Hall, Bronwyn H. Software for the Computation of Tobit Model Estimates. *J. Econometrics*, January/February 1984, *24*(1/2), pp. 215–22.

Hanemann, W. Michael. Discrete/Continuous Models of Consumer Demand. *Econometrica*, May 1984, *52*(3), pp. 541–61.

Hasenkamp, Georg. Fehlende Beobachtungen in autoregressiven Verhaltensgleichungen. (Missing Observations in Autoregressive Equations. With English summary.) *Z. Wirtschaft. Sozialwissen.*, 1984, *104*(1), pp. 21–28.

Hastie, Trevor J. Graphical Methods for Assessing Logistic Regression Models: Comment. *J. Amer. Statist. Assoc.*, March 1984, *79*(385), pp. 77–78.

Hausman, Jerry A. and McFadden, Daniel L. Specification Tests for the Multinomial Logit Model. *Econometrica*, September 1984, *52*(5), pp. 1219–40.

Healy, M. J. R. The Use of R^2 as a Measure of Goodness of Fit. *J. Roy. Statist. Soc.*, 1984, *147*(4), pp. 608–09.

Heckman, James J. The x^2 Goodness of Fit Statistic for Models with Parameters Estimated from Microdata. *Econometrica*, November 1984, *52*(6), pp. 1543–47.

Heckman, James J. and Singer, Burton. A Method for Minimizing the Impact of Distributional Assumptions in Econometric Models for Duration Data. *Econometrica*, March 1984, *52*(2), pp. 271–320.

Heckman, James J. and Singer, Burton. Econometric Duration Analysis. *J. Econometrics*, January/February 1984, *24*(1/2), pp. 63–132.

Heckman, James J. and Singer, Burton. The Identifiability of the Proportional Hazard Model. *Rev. Econ. Stud.*, April 1984, *51*(2), pp. 231–41.

Hendry, David F. Monte Carlo Experimentation in Econometrics. In *Griliches, Z. and Intriligator, M. D., eds.*, 1984, pp. 939–76.

Hendry, David F.; Pagan, Adrian R. and Sargan, J. Denis. Dynamic Specification. In *Griliches, Z. and Intriligator, M. D., eds.*, 1984, pp. 1025–1100.

Hill, R. Carter and Ziemer, R. F. The Risk of General Stein-Like Estimators in the Presence of Multicollinearity. *J. Econometrics*, May/June 1984, *25*(1/2), pp. 205–16.

Hinich, Melvin J. and Weber, Warren E. A Method for Estimating Distributed Lags When Observations Are Randomly Missing. *J. Amer. Statist. Assoc.*, June 1984, *79*(386), pp. 368–73.

Hinkley, David V. The Analysis of Transformed Data: Rejoinder. *J. Amer. Statist. Assoc.*, June 1984, *79*(386), pp. 319–20.

Hinkley, David V. and Runger, G. The Analysis of Transformed Data. *J. Amer. Statist. Assoc.*, June 1984, *79*(386), pp. 302–09.

Hoffman, Dennis L.; Low, Stuart A. and Schlagenhauf, Don E. Tests of Rationality, Neutrality and Market Efficiency: A Monte Carlo Analysis of Alternative Test Statistics. *J. Monet. Econ.*, November 1984, *14*(3), pp. 339–63.

Honda, Yuzo and Ohtani, Kazuhiro. Improving the Size of the Theil's Compatibility Test in Mixed Regression. *Econ. Stud. Quart.*, December 1984, *35*(3), pp. 253–61.

Huang, Cliff J. Estimation of Stochastic Frontier Production Function and Technical Inefficiency via the EM Algorithm. *Southern Econ. J.*, January 1984, *50*(3), pp. 847–56.   [G: India]

Hubert, L. J., et al. Nonparametric Tests for Directional Data. In *Bahrenberg, G.; Fischer, M. M., and Nijkamp, P.*, 1984, pp. 171–89.

Ilmakunnas, Pekka and Tsurumi, Hiroki. Testing for Parameter Shifts in a Regression Model with Two Regimes of Autocorrelated Errors. *Econ. Stud. Quart.*, April 1984, *35*(1), pp. 46–56.

Johnson, Richard A. The Analysis of Transformed Data: Comment. *J. Amer. Statist. Assoc.*, June 1984, *79*(386), pp. 314–15.

Judge, G. G., et al. The Non-Optimality of the Inequality Restricted Estimator under Squared Error Loss. *J. Econometrics*, May/June 1984, *25*(1/2), pp. 165–77.

Kackar, Raghu N. and Harville, David A. Approximations for Standard Errors of Estimators of Fixed and Random Effects in Mixed Linear Models. *J. Amer. Statist. Assoc.*, December 1984, *79*(388), pp. 853–62.

Kiefer, Nicholas M. A Simple Test for Heterogeneity in Exponential Models of Duration.

J. Lab. Econ., October 1984, *2*(4), pp. 539–49. **[G: U.S.]**

Kiefer, Nicholas M. and Skoog, Gary R. Local Asymptotic Specification Error Analysis. *Econometrica*, July 1984, *52*(4), pp. 873–85.

Kinal, Terrence W. and Lahiri, Kajal. A Note on "Selection of Regressors." *Int. Econ. Rev.*, October 1984, *25*(3), pp. 625–29.

King, M. L. and Giles, David E. A. Autocorrelation Pre-Testing in the Linear Model: Estimation, Testing and Prediction. *J. Econometrics*, May/June 1984, *25*(1/2), pp. 35–48.

King, Maxwell L. A New Test for Fourth-Order Autoregressive Disturbances. *J. Econometrics*, March 1984, *24*(3), pp. 269–77.

Klepper, Steven and Leamer, Edward E. Consistent Sets of Estimates for Regressions with Errors in All Variables. *Econometrica*, January 1984, *52*(1), pp. 163–83.

Kloek, Teun. Dynamic Adjustment When the Target Is Nonstationary. *Int. Econ. Rev.*, June 1984, *25*(2), pp. 315–26.

Kockläuner, Gerhard. Multicollinearity in Equality Constrained Linear Models. In *Gruber, J., ed.*, 1984, pp. 86–91.

Landwehr, James M.; Pregibon, Daryl and Shoemaker, Anne C. Graphical Methods for Assessing Logistic Regression Models: Rejoinder. *J. Amer. Statist. Assoc.*, March 1984, *79*(385), pp. 81–83.

Landwehr, James M.; Pregibon, Daryl and Shoemaker, Anne C. Graphical Methods for Assessing Logistic Regression Models. *J. Amer. Statist. Assoc.*, March 1984, *79*(385), pp. 61–71.

Layson, Stephen K. and Seaks, Terry G. Estimation and Testing for Functional Form in First Difference Models. *Rev. Econ. Statist.*, May 1984, *66*(2), pp. 338–43.

Leamer, Edward E. Global Sensitivity Results for Generalized Least Squares Estimates. *J. Amer. Statist. Assoc.*, December 1984, *79*(388), pp. 867–70.

Lee, Lung-Fei. Maximum Likelihood Estimation and a Specification Test for Non-Normal Distributional Assumption for the Accelerated Failure Time Models. *J. Econometrics*, January/February 1984, *24*(1/2), pp. 159–79.

Lee, Lung-Fei. Tests for the Bivariate Normal Distribution in Econometric Models with Selectivity. *Econometrica*, July 1984, *52*(4), pp. 843–63.

Lee, Lung-Fei and Porter, Robert H. Switching Regression Models with Imperfect Sample Separation Information—With an Application on Cartel Stability. *Econometrica*, March 1984, *52*(2), pp. 391–418. **[G: U.S.]**

de Leeuw, Jan. Discrete Normal Linear Regression Models. In *Dijkstra, T. K., ed.*, 1984, pp. 56–70.

Lin, Tsai-Fen and Schmidt, Peter J. A Test of the Tobit Specification against an Alternative Suggested by Cragg. *Rev. Econ. Statist.*, February 1984, *66*(1), pp. 174–77.

Lütkepohl, Helmut. The Optimality of Rational Distributed Lags: A Comment. *Int. Econ. Rev.*, June 1984, *25*(2), pp. 503–06.

Malone, James M., II. Regression Without Models: Directions in the Search for Structure. In *Farlow, S. J., ed.*, 1984, pp. 67–86.

Mandy, D. M. The Moments of a Pre-Test Estimator under Possible Heteroscedasticity. *J. Econometrics*, May/June 1984, *25*(1/2), pp. 29–33.

Manski, Charles F. Adaptive Estimation of Nonlinear Regression Models: Reply. *Econometric Rev.*, 1984, *3*(2), pp. 209–10.

Manski, Charles F. Adaptive Estimation of Nonlinear Regression Models. *Econometric Rev.*, 1984, *3*(2), pp. 145–94.

McFadden, Daniel L. Econometric Analysis of Qualitative Response Models. In *Griliches, Z. and Intriligator, M. D., eds.*, 1984, pp. 1396–1457.

Messer, Karen and White, Halbert. A Note on Computing the Heteroskedasticity Consistent Covariance Matrix Using Instrumental Variable Techniques. *Oxford Bull. Econ. Statist.*, May 1984, *46*(2), pp. 181–84.

Miller, Alan J. Selection of Subsets of Regression Variables. *J. Roy. Statist. Soc.*, 1984, *147*(3), pp. 389–410.

Miller, Stephen E.; Capps, Oral, Jr. and Wells, Gary J. Confidence Intervals for Elasticities and Flexibilities from Linear Equations. *Amer. J. Agr. Econ.*, August 1984, *66*(3), pp. 392–96. **[G: U.S.]**

Minford, Patrick and Peel, David A. Testing for Unbiasedness and Efficiency under Incomplete Current Information. *Bull. Econ. Res.*, May 1984, *36*(1), pp. 1–7.

Mittelhammer, R. C. Restricted Least Squares, Pre-Test, OLS and Stein Rule Estimators: Risk Comparisons under Model Misspecification. *J. Econometrics*, May/June 1984, *25*(1/2), pp. 151–64.

Morey, M. J. The Statistical Implications of Preliminary Specification Error Testing. *J. Econometrics*, May/June 1984, *25*(1/2), pp. 63–72.

Nelson, Charles R. and Kang, Heejoon. Pitfalls in the Use of Time as an Explanatory Variable in Regression. *J. Bus. Econ. Statist.*, January 1984, *2*(1), pp. 73–82.

Nelson, Forrest D. Efficiency of the Two-Step Estimator for Models with Endogenous Sample Selection. *J. Econometrics*, January/February 1984, *24*(1/2), pp. 181–96.

Nenna, Enrico. Estensione della trasformata di Helmert al caso della regressione lineare semplice. (An Extension of Helmert's Transformation to Linear Regression. With English summary.) *Statistica*, January–March 1984, *44*(1), pp. 79–86.

Nordberg, Leif. Hushållsbudgetunder-sökningarna i ekonomisk analys. (Household Surveys in Economic Analysis. With English summary.) *Ekon. Samfundets Tidskr.*, 1984, *37*(3), pp. 191–203. **[G: Finland; Norway]**

Ohtani, Kazuhiro and Honda, Yuzo. Small Sample Properties of the Mixed Regression Estimator. *J. Econometrics*, December 1984, *26*(3), pp. 375–85.

Paarsch, Harry J. A Monte Carlo Comparison

of Estimators for Censored Regression Models. *J. Econometrics*, January/February 1984, 24(1/2), pp. 197–213.

Pagan, Adrian R. Econometric Issues in the Analysis of Regressions with Generated Regressors. *Int. Econ. Rev.*, February 1984, 25(1), pp. 221–47.

Pagan, Adrian R. Model Evaluation by Variable Addition. In *Hendry, D. F. and Wallis, K. F., eds.*, 1984, pp. 103–33.

Pagan, Adrian R. and Nicholls, Desmond F. Estimating Predictions, Prediction Errors and Their Standard Deviations Using Constructed Variables. *J. Econometrics*, March 1984, 24(3), pp. 293–310.

Pakes, Ariel and Griliches, Zvi. Estimating Distributed Lags in Short Panels with an Application to the Specification of Depreciation Patterns and Capital Stock Constructs. *Rev. Econ. Stud.*, April 1984, 51(2), pp. 243–62.
[G: U.S.]

Palm, Franz C. and Nijman, Theo E. Missing Observations in the Dynamic Regression Model. *Econometrica*, November 1984, 52(6), pp. 1415–35.

Palm, Franz C.; Vogelvang, Engbert and Kodde, David A. Efficient Estimation of the Geometric Distributed Lag Model: Some Monte Carlo Results on Small Sample Properties. *Int. Econ. Rev.*, October 1984, 25(3), pp. 579–601.

Peña, Daniel and Ruiz-Castillo, Javier. Robust Methods of Building Regression Models—An Application to the Housing Sector. *J. Bus. Econ. Statist.*, January 1984, 2(1), pp. 10–20.
[G: Spain]

Peters, Stephen C. and Freedman, David A. Some Notes on the Bootstrap in Regression Problems. *J. Bus. Econ. Statist.*, October 1984, 2(4), pp. 406–09.

Phillips, Peter C. B. The Exact Distribution of the Stein-Rule Estimator. *J. Econometrics*, May/June 1984, 25(1/2), pp. 123–31.

Picard, Richard R. and Cook, R. Dennis. Cross-Validation of Regression Models. *J. Amer. Statist. Assoc.*, September 1984, 79(387), pp. 575–83.

Polasek, Wolfgang. Regression Diagnostics for General Linear Regression Models. *J. Amer. Statist. Assoc.*, June 1984, 79(386), pp. 336–40.

Powell, James L. Least Absolute Deviations Estimation for the Censored Regression Model. *J. Econometrics*, July 1984, 25(3), pp. 303–25.

Pratt, J. W. and Schlaifer, Robert. On the Nature and Discovery of Structure: Rejoinder. *J. Amer. Statist. Assoc.*, March 1984, 79(385), pp. 29–33.

Pratt, J. W. and Schlaifer, Robert. On the Nature and Discovery of Structure. *J. Amer. Statist. Assoc.*, March 1984, 79(385), pp. 9–21.

Prucha, Ingmar R. On the Asymptotic Efficiency of Feasible Aitken Estimators for Seemingly Unrelated Regression Models with Error Components. *Econometrica*, January 1984, 52(1), pp. 203–07.

Randles, Ronald H. On Tests Applied to Residu-

als. *J. Amer. Statist. Assoc.*, June 1984, 79(386), pp. 349–54.

Reinsel, Gregory. Estimation and Prediction in a Multivariate Random Effects Generalized Linear Model. *J. Amer. Statist. Assoc.*, June 1984, 79(386), pp. 406–14.

Rinne, Horst. A Method of Choosing Additional Sets of Observations in Multiple Linear Regression Models to Overcome Multicollinearity. In *Gruber, J., ed.*, 1984, pp. 25–44.

Roehrig, C. S. Optimal Critical Regions for Pre-Test Estimators Using a Bayes Risk Criterion. *J. Econometrics*, May/June 1984, 25(1/2), pp. 3–14.

Rosenbaum, Paul R. and Rubin, Donald B. Estimating the Effects Caused by Treatments: Comment [On the Nature and Discovery of Structure]. *J. Amer. Statist. Assoc.*, March 1984, 79(385), pp. 26–28.

Rothenberg, Thomas J. Approximate Normality of Generalized Least Squares Estimates. *Econometrica*, July 1984, 52(4), pp. 811–25.

Rothenberg, Thomas J. Approximating the Distributions of Econometric Estimators and Test Statistics. In *Griliches, Z. and Intriligator, M. D., eds.*, 1984, pp. 882–935.

Rothenberg, Thomas J. Hypothesis Testing in Linear Models When the Error Covariance Matrix Is Nonscalar. *Econometrica*, July 1984, 52(4), pp. 827–42.

Rousseeuw, Peter J. Least Median of Squares Regression. *J. Amer. Statist. Assoc.*, December 1984, 79(388), pp. 871–80.

Rubin, Donald B. Assessing the Fit of Logistic Regressions Using the Implied Discriminant Analysis: Comment [Graphical Methods for Assessing Logistic Regression Models]. *J. Amer. Statist. Assoc.*, March 1984, 79(385), pp. 79–80.

Rubin, Donald B. Distinguishing between the Scale of the Estimand and the Transformation to Normality: Comment [The Analysis of Transformed Data]. *J. Amer. Statist. Assoc.*, June 1984, 79(386), pp. 309–12.

Sadamichi, Hiroshi. Efficiency of the Least Squares Estimators in Linear Models with Idempotent Covariance Matrix of the Error Terms. *Kobe Econ. Bus. Rev.*, 1984, 30, pp. 55–60.

Satchell, Stephen Ellwood. Approximation to the Finite Sample Distribution for Nonstable First Order Stochastic Difference Equations. *Econometrica*, September 1984, 52(5), pp. 1271–89.

Savin, N. E. Multiple Hypothesis Testing. In *Griliches, Z. and Intriligator, M. D., eds.*, 1984, pp. 828–79.

Schmidt, Peter J. and Lin, Tsai-Fen. Simple Tests of Alternative Specifications in Stochastic Frontier Models. *J. Econometrics*, March 1984, 24(3), pp. 349–61.

Silverman, B. W. A Fast and Efficient Cross-Validation Method for Smoothing Parameter Choice in Spline Regression. *J. Amer. Statist. Assoc.*, September 1984, 79(387), pp. 584–89.

Smith, Richard J. A Note on Likelihood Ratio Tests for the Independence between a Subset of Stochastic Regressors and Disturbances. *Int. Econ. Rev.*, February 1984, *25*(1), pp. 263–69.

Spitzer, John J. Variance Estimates in Models with the Box–Cox Transformation: Implications for Estimations and Hypothesis Testing. *Rev. Econ. Statist.*, November 1984, *66*(4), pp. 645–52.

Srivastava, Virendra K. and Srivastava, Anil K. Improved Estimation in a Two Equation Seemingly Unrelated Regression Model. *Statistica*, July–September 1984, *44*(3), pp. 417–22.

Stapleton, David C. and Young, Douglas J. Censored Normal Regression with Measurement Error on the Dependent Variable. *Econometrica*, May 1984, *52*(3), pp. 737–60.

Steerneman, Ton. Prediction Performance and the Number of Variables in Multivariate Linear Regression. In *Dijkstra, T. K., ed.*, 1984, pp. 118–29.

Suits, Daniel B. Dummy Variables: Mechanics v. Interpretation. *Rev. Econ. Statist.*, February 1984, *66*(1), pp. 177–80. **[G: U.S.]**

Šujan, Ivan. Methods for Solving the Problem of Multicollinearity in Econometric Models: A Survey. In *Gruber, J., ed.*, 1984, pp. 45–85.

Swanson, David A. and Tedrow, Lucky M. Improving the Measurement of Temporal Change in Regression Models Used for County Population Estimates. *Demography*, August 1984, *21*(3), pp. 373–81. **[G: U.S.]**

Treble, John G. Correcting for Heteroscedasticity in Regressions Where the Dependent Variable Is a Logarithm: A Warning Note. *Appl. Econ.*, April 1984, *16*(2), pp. 159–61.

Trenkler, Götz. On the Performance of Biased Estimators in the Linear Regression Model with Correlated or Heteroscedastic Errors. *J. Econometrics*, May/June 1984, *25*(1/2), pp. 179–90.

Trenkler, Götz. Some Further Remarks on Multicollinearity and the Minimax Conditions of the Bock Stein-Like Estimator. *Econometrica*, July 1984, *52*(4), pp. 1067–69.

Tritchler, David. An Algorithm for Exact Logistic Regression. *J. Amer. Statist. Assoc.*, September 1984, *79*(387), pp. 709–11.

Trivedi, Pravin K. Uncertain Prior Information and Distributed Lag Analysis. In *Hendry, D. F. and Wallis, K. F., eds.*, 1984, pp. 173–210.

Tsurumi, Hiroki. On Jayatissa's Test of Constancy of Regressions under Heteroscedasticity and Some Alternative Test Procedures. *Econ. Stud. Quart.*, April 1984, *35*(1), pp. 57–62.

Ullah, Aman; Carter, R. A. L. and Srivastava, Virendra K. The Sampling Distribution of Shrinkage Estimators and Their *F*-Ratios in the Regression Model. *J. Econometrics*, May/June 1984, *25*(1/2), pp. 109–22.

Ullah, Aman and Zinde-Walsh, Victoria. On the Robustness of LM, LR, and W Tests in Regression Models. *Econometrica*, July 1984, *52*(4), pp. 1055–66.

Verbeek, Albert. The Geometry of Model Selection in Regression. In *Dijkstra, T. K., ed.*, 1984, pp. 20–36.

Waldman, Donald M. Properties of Technical Efficiency Estimators in the Stochastic Frontier Model. *J. Econometrics*, July 1984, *25*(3), pp. 353–64.

Watts, Geof and Quiggin, John. A Note on the Use of a Logarithmic Time Trend. *Rev. Marketing Agr. Econ.*, August 1984, *52*(2), pp. 91–99. **[G: Australia]**

Waugh, Frederick V. Choice of the Dependent Variable in Regression Analysis. In *Waugh, F. V.*, 1984, *1943*, pp. 272–76.

Waugh, Frederick V. Regressions between Sets of Variables. In *Waugh, F. V.*, 1984, *1942*, pp. 251–71. **[G: U.S.; Canada]**

Waugh, Frederick V. The Computation of Partial Correlation Coefficients. In *Waugh, F. V.*, 1984, *1946*, pp. 277–80.

Weiss, Andrew A. Systematic Sampling and Temporal Aggregation in Time Series Models. *J. Econometrics*, December 1984, *26*(3), pp. 271–81.

Welfe, Wladyslaw. Multicollinearity and Iterative Estimation Procedure. In *Gruber, J., ed.*, 1984, pp. 92–124. **[G: Poland]**

White, Halbert and Domowitz, Ian. Nonlinear Regression with Dependent Observations. *Econometrica*, January 1984, *52*(1), pp. 143–61.

Xekalaki, Evdokia. Linear Regression and the Yule Distribution. *J. Econometrics*, March 1984, *24*(3), pp. 397–403.

Yancey, T. A.; Judge, G. G. and Miyazaki, S. Some Improved Estimators in the Case of Possible Heteroscedasticity. *J. Econometrics*, May/June 1984, *25*(1/2), pp. 133–50.

Zaman, A. Avoiding Model Selection by the Use of Shrinkage Techniques. *J. Econometrics*, May/June 1984, *25*(1/2), pp. 73–85.

Zelias, Aleksander. Some Remarks on Criteria for the Selection of Regressors in Econometric Models. In *Gruber, J., ed.*, 1984, pp. 11–24.

Zellner, Arnold. Bayesian and Non-Bayesian Analysis of the Regression Model with Multivariate Student-*t* Error Terms. In *Zellner, A.*, 1984, *1976*, pp. 225–37.

Zellner, Arnold. Bayesian and Non-Bayesian Analysis of the Log-Normal Distribution and Log-Normal Regression. In *Zellner, A.*, 1984, *1971*, pp. 216–24.

Zellner, Arnold. Jeffreys-Bayes Posterior Odds Ratio and the Akaike Information Criterion for Discriminating between Models. In *Zellner, A.*, 1984, *1978*, pp. 269–74.

Zellner, Arnold and Rossi, Peter E. Bayesian Analysis of Dichotomous Quantal Response Models. *J. Econometrics*, July 1984, *25*(3), pp. 365–93.

2114 Multivariate Analysis, Statistical Information Theory, and Other Special Inferential Problems; Queuing Theory; Markov Chains

Arrow, Kenneth J. On Partitioning a Sample with Binary-Type Questions in Lieu of Collecting Observations. In *Arrow, K. J., vol. 4*, 1984, *1981*, pp. 262–80.

Bonney, G. E. and Kissling, G. E. On the Inverse of a Patterned Covariance Matrix. *J. Amer. Statist. Assoc.*, September 1984, 79(387), pp. 722–23.

Chamberlain, Gary. Panel Data. In *Griliches, Z. and Intriligator, M. D., eds.*, 1984, pp. 1248–1318. [G: U.S.]

Chhikara, Raj S. and McKeon, Jim. Linear Discriminant Analysis with Misallocation in Training Samples. *J. Amer. Statist. Assoc.*, December 1984, 79(388), pp. 899–906.

Flury, Bernhard N. Common Principal Components in *k* Groups. *J. Amer. Statist. Assoc.*, December 1984, 79(388), pp. 892–98.

Frydman, Halina. Maximum Likelihood Estimation in the Mover–Stayer Model. *J. Amer. Statist. Assoc.*, September 1984, 79(387), pp. 632–38.

Hausman, Jerry A.; Hall, Bronwyn H. and Griliches, Zvi. Econometric Models for Count Data with an Application to the Patents–R&D Relationship. *Econometrica*, July 1984, 52(4), pp. 909–38. [G: U.S.]

Ionescu, C. and Petrovici, V. Estimating Redundancy between Two Groups of Dependent Files. *Econ. Computat. Cybern. Stud. Res.*, 1984, 19(4), pp. 27–30.

Jones, Kelvyn. Graphical Methods for Exploring Relationships. In *Bahrenberg, G.; Fischer, M. M., and Nijkamp, P.*, 1984, pp. 215–27.

Kariya, Takeaki; Sinha, Bimal K. and Krishnaiah, P. K. On Multivariate Left Orthogonal Invariant Distributions. *Hitotsubashi J. Econ.*, December 1984, 25(2), pp. 155–59.

Kelton, Christina M. L. and Kelton, W. David. Markov Process Models: A General Framework for Estimation and Inference in the Absence of State Transition Data. In *Avula, X. J. R., et al.*, 1984, pp. 299–304.

Kelton, W. David and Kelton, Christina M. L. Hypothesis Tests for Markov Process Models Estimated from Aggregate Frequency Data. *J. Amer. Statist. Assoc.*, December 1984, 79(388), pp. 922–28.

Marais, M. Laurentius; Patell, James M. and Wolfson, Mark A. The Experimental Design of Classification Models: An Application of Recursive Partitioning and Bootstrapping to Commercial Bank Loan Classifications. *J. Acc. Res.*, Supplement 1984, 22, pp. 87–114. [G: U.S.]

Marksjö, Bertil. Simple Aggregation and Disaggregation Subject to Minimal Information Loss and Other Criteria. *Reg. Sci. Urban Econ.*, August 1984, 14(3), pp. 465–78.

Newman, John L. and McCulloch, Charles E. A Hazard Rate Approach to the Timing of Births. *Econometrica*, July 1984, 52(4), pp. 939–61. [G: Costa Rica]

Olsen, Chris. The Experimental Design of Classification Models: An Application of Recursive Partitioning and Bootstrapping to Commercial Bank Loan Classifications: Discussion. *J. Acc. Res.*, Supplement 1984, 22, pp. 115–18. [G: U.S.]

Poulsen, Carsten Stig. Analyse af konjunkturbarometret for industrien. (Latent Structure Analysis Applied to Danish Data. With English summary.) *Nationaløkon. Tidsskr.*, 1984, 122(2), pp. 266–82. [G: Denmark]

Rizzi, Alfredo. Some Mathematical Properties of Cluster Methods. *Econ. Notes*, 1984, (2), pp. 139–55. [G: Italy]

Sibson, Robin. Present Position and Potential Developments: Some Personal Views: Multivariate Analysis. *J. Roy. Statist. Soc.*, 1984, 147(2), pp. 198–207.

Staroverov, O. V. Markov Models of Mobility. *Matekon*, Spring 1984, 20(3), pp. 3–21.

Waugh, Frederick V. Factor Analysis: Some Basic Principles and an Application. In *Waugh, F. V.*, 1984, 1962, pp. 349–52. [G: U.S.]

2115 Bayesian Statistics and Bayesian Econometrics

Arrow, Kenneth J. Alternative Approaches to the Theory of Choice in Risk-Taking Situations. In *Arrow, K. J., vol. 3*, 1984, 1951, pp. 5–41.

Arrow, Kenneth J.; Blackwell, D. and Girshick, M. A. Bayes and Minimax Solutions of Sequential Decision Problems. In *Arrow, K. J., vol. 4*, 1984, 1949, pp. 1–37.

ter Berg, Peter and Harkema, Rins. Bayesian Limited-Information Analysis of Nonlinear Simultaneous Equations Systems. *J. Econometrics*, March 1984, 24(3), pp. 379–95. [G: Netherlands]

Berger, James O. The Robust Bayesian Viewpoint. In *Kadane, J. B., ed.*, 1984, pp. 64–124.

Berger, James O. The Robust Bayesian Viewpoint: Reply. In *Kadane, J. B., ed.*, 1984, pp. 139–44.

Berger, James O. and Berliner, L. M. Bayesian Input in Stein Estimation and a New Minimax Empirical Bayes Estimator. *J. Econometrics*, May/June 1984, 25(1/2), pp. 87–108.

Brown, Lawrence D. The Robust Bayesian Viewpoint: Comment. In *Kadane, J. B., ed.*, 1984, pp. 126–33.

Chuang, David T. Further Theory of Stable Decisions. In *Kadane, J. B., ed.*, 1984, pp. 166–228.

Edwards, Ward; Lindman, Harold and Savage, Leonard J. Bayesian Statistical Inference for Psychological Research. In *Kadane, J. B., ed.*, 1984, pp. 2–62.

Hill, Bruce M. The Robust Bayesian Viewpoint: Comment. In *Kadane, J. B., ed.*, 1984, pp. 134–35.

Judge, G. G., et al. The Non-Optimality of the Inequality Restricted Estimator under Squared Error Loss. *J. Econometrics*, May/June 1984, 25(1/2), pp. 165–77.

Kadane, Joseph B. The Robust Bayesian Viewpoint: Comment. In *Kadane, J. B., ed.*, 1984, pp. 136.

Kadane, Joseph B. and Chuang, David T. Stable Decision Problems. In *Kadane, J. B., ed.*, 1984, pp. 146–63.

Kihlstrom, Richard E. A "Bayesian" Exposition of Blackwell's Theorem on the Comparison of

Experiments. In *Boyer, M. and Kihlstrom, R. E.*, eds., 1984, pp. 13–31.

Klein, Roger W. and Brown, Stephen J. Model Selection When There Is "Minimal" Prior Information. *Econometrica*, September 1984, 52(5), pp. 1291–1312.

Lindley, Dennis V. The Robust Bayesian Viewpoint: Comment. In *Kadane, J. B.*, ed., 1984, pp. 137–38.

de Meza, David and Dickinson, Paul T. Risk Preferences and Transaction Costs. *J. Econ. Behav. Organ.*, June 1984, 5(2), pp. 223–36.

Mouchart, Michel and Rolin, Jean-Marie. A Note on Conditional Independence with Statistical Applications. *Statistica*, October–December 1984, 44(4), pp. 557–84.

Richard, Jean-François. Classical and Bayesian Inference in Incomplete Simultaneous Equation Models. In *Hendry, D. F. and Wallis, K. F.*, eds., 1984, pp. 61–102.

Shamseldin, Adel A. and Press, S. James. Bayesian Parameter and Reliability Estimation for a Bivariate Exponential Distribution: Parallel Sampling. *J. Econometrics*, March 1984, 24(3), pp. 363–78.

Shiller, Robert J. Smoothness Priors and Nonlinear Regression. *J. Amer. Statist. Assoc.*, September 1984, 79(387), pp. 609–15. [G: U.S.]

Smith, A. F. M. Present Position and Potential Developments: Some Personal Views: Bayesian Statistics. *J. Roy. Statist. Soc.*, 1984, 147(2), pp. 245–59.

Smouse, Evan P. A Note on Bayesian Least Squares Inference for Finite Population Models. *J. Amer. Statist. Assoc.*, June 1984, 79(386), pp. 390–92.

Waugh, Dan F. and Waugh, Frederick V. On Probabilities in Bridge. In *Waugh, F. V.*, 1953, 1984, pp. 294–302.

West, Mike. Bayesian Aggregation. *J. Roy. Statist. Soc.*, 1984, 147(4), pp. 600–607.

Zellner, Arnold. Bayesian and Non-Bayesian Analysis of the Log-Normal Distribution and Log-Normal Regression. In *Zellner, A.*, 1984, 1971, pp. 216–24.

Zellner, Arnold. Estimation of Functions of Population Means and Regression Coefficients Including Structural Coefficients: A Minimum Expected Loss (MELO) Approach. In *Zellner, A.*, 1984, 1978, pp. 238–68.

Zellner, Arnold. Is Jeffreys a "Necessarist"? In *Zellner, A.*, 1984, 1982, pp. 75–80.

Zellner, Arnold. Jeffreys-Bayes Posterior Odds Ratio and the Akaike Information Criterion for Discriminating between Models. In *Zellner, A.*, 1984, 1978, pp. 269–74.

Zellner, Arnold. Maximal Data Information Prior Distributions. In *Zellner, A.*, 1984, 1977, pp. 201–15.

Zellner, Arnold. Posterior Odds Ratios for Regression Hypotheses: General Considerations and Some Specific Results. In *Zellner, A.*, 1984, 1981, pp. 275–305.

Zellner, Arnold. Statistical Analysis of Econometric Models. In *Zellner, A.*, 1984, 1979, pp. 83–119.

Zellner, Arnold. The Bayesian Approach and Alternatives in Econometrics. In *Zellner, A.*, 1984, 1971, pp. 187–200.

Zellner, Arnold. The Current State of Bayesian Econometrics. In *Zellner, A.*, 1984, 1983, pp. 306–21.

Zellner, Arnold and Rossi, Peter E. Bayesian Analysis of Dichotomous Quantal Response Models. *J. Econometrics*, July 1984, 25(3), pp. 365–93.

2116 Time Series and Spectral Analysis

Akaike, Hirotugu. Issues Involved with the Seasonal Adjustment of Economic Time Series: Comment. *J. Bus. Econ. Statist.*, October 1984, 2(4), pp. 321–22.

Ali, Mukhtar M. Distributions of the Sample Autocorrelations When Observations Are from a Stationary Autoregressive-Moving-Average Process. *J. Bus. Econ. Statist.*, July 1984, 2(3), pp. 271–78.

Ansley, Craig F. and Wecker, William E. Issues Involved with the Seasonal Adjustment of Economic Time Series: Comment: On Dips in the Spectrum of a Seasonally Adjusted Time Series. *J. Bus. Econ. Statist.*, October 1984, 2(4), pp. 323–24.

Azzalini, Adelchi. A Markov Process with Beta Marginal Distribution. *Statistica*, April–June 1984, 44(2), pp. 241–43.

Bell, William R. and Hillmer, Steven C. Issues Involved with the Seasonal Adjustment of Economic Time Series. *J. Bus. Econ. Statist.*, October 1984, 2(4), pp. 291–320. [G: U.S.]

Bell, William R. and Hillmer, Steven C. Issues Involved with the Seasonal Adjustment of Time Series: Reply. *J. Bus. Econ. Statist.*, October 1984, 2(4), pp. 343–49.

Bergstrom, A. R. Continuous Time Stochastic Models and Issues of Aggregation Over Time. In *Griliches, Z. and Intriligator, M. D.*, eds., 1984, pp. 1146–1212.

Bessler, David A. and Kling, J. L. A Note on Tests of Granger Causality. *Appl. Econ.*, June 1984, 16(3), pp. 335–42. [G: U.S.]

Bierens, Herman J. Model Specification Testing of Time Series Regressions. *J. Econometrics*, December 1984, 26(3), pp. 323–53.

Burman, J. Peter. Issues Involved with the Seasonal Adjustment of Economic Time Series: Comment. *J. Bus. Econ. Statist.*, October 1984, 2(4), pp. 325–27.

Burridge, Peter and Wallis, Kenneth F. Unobserved-Components Models for Seasonal Adjustment Filters. *J. Bus. Econ. Statist.*, October 1984, 2(4), pp. 350–59.

Cartwright, Phillip A. A Note on Using State-Dependent Models with a Time-Dependent Variance. *J. Bus. Econ. Statist.*, October 1984, 2(4), pp. 410–13. [G: U.S.]

Conway, Roger K., et al. The Impossibility of Causality Testing. *Agr. Econ. Res.*, Summer 1984, 36(3), pp. 1–19.

Cooley, Thomas F. Forecasting and Conditional Projection Using Realistic Prior Distributions:

Comment. *Econometric Rev.*, 1984, *3*(1), pp. 101–04. [G: U.S.]

Corduas, Marcella. Distanza tra modelli: problemi metodologici ed indici statistici. (On Distance between Models: Methodological Problems and Statistical Indices. With English summary.) *Statistica*, July–September 1984, *44*(3), pp. 513–24.

Dagli, C. Ates and Taylor, John B. Estimation and Solution of Linear Rational Expectations Models Using a Polynomial Matrix Factorization. *J. Econ. Dynam. Control*, December 1984, *8*(3), pp. 341–48.

Dagum, Estela Bee and Laniel, Normand J. D. Issues Involved with the Seasonal Adjustment of Economic Time Series: Comment. *J. Bus. Econ. Statist.*, October 1984, *2*(4), pp. 328–32.

Dagum, Estela Bee and Morry, Marietta. Basic Issues on the Seasonal Adjustment of the Canadian Consumer Price Index. *J. Bus. Econ. Statist.*, July 1984, *2*(3), pp. 250–59. [G: Canada]

Davies, Neville and Petruccelli, Joseph D. On the Use of the General Partial Autocorrelation Function for Order Determination in ARMA(p,q) Processes. *J. Amer. Statist. Assoc.*, June 1984, *79*(386), pp. 374–77.

Dawid, A. P. Present Position and Potential Developments: Some Personal Views: Statistical Theory. The Prequential Approach. *J. Roy. Statist. Soc.*, 1984, *147*(2), pp. 278–92.

Dickey, D. A.; Hasza, D. P. and Fuller, W. A. Testing for Unit Roots in Seasonal Time Series. *J. Amer. Statist. Assoc.*, June 1984, *79*(386), pp. 355–67.

Doan, Thomas; Litterman, Robert B. and Sims, Christopher. Forecasting and Conditional Projection Using Realistic Prior Distributions: Reply. *Econometric Rev.*, 1984, *3*(1), pp. 131–44. [G: U.S.]

Doan, Thomas; Litterman, Robert B. and Sims, Christopher. Forecasting and Conditional Projection Using Realistic Prior Distributions. *Econometric Rev.*, 1984, *3*(1), pp. 1–100. [G: U.S.]

Dufour, Jean-Marie. Unbiasedness of Predictions from Estimated Autoregressions When the True Order Is Unknown. *Econometrica*, January 1984, *52*(1), pp. 209–15.

Durbin, J. Present Position and Potential Developments: Some Personal Views: Time Series Analysis. *J. Roy. Statist. Soc.*, 1984, *147*(2), pp. 161–73.

Eberts, Ronald W. and Steece, B. M. A Test for Granger-Causality in a Multivariate ARMA Model. *Empirical Econ.*, 1984, *9*(1), pp. 51–58.

Engle, Robert F.; Granger, Clive W. J. and Kraft, Dennis F. Combining Competing Forecasts of Inflation Using a Bivariate ARCH Model. *J. Econ. Dynam. Control*, November 1984, *8*(2), pp. 151–65. [G: U.S.]

Faliva, Mario. Trend-Cycle Estimation in Economic Time Series by Filtering Methods. *Sta-*

tistica, October–December 1984, *44*(4), pp. 601–17.

Fase, Martin M. G. Issues Involved with the Seasonal Adjustment of Economic Time Series: Comment. *J. Bus. Econ. Statist.*, October 1984, *2*(4), pp. 333–34.

Ferrari, Guido. Stima del modello trasformato di Koyck generato da ipotesi di aspettative economiche con disturbi AR (p) ed MA (q). (Estimating Koyck Model Generated by Economic Expectations Hypotheses with AR (p) and MA (q) Disturbances. With English summary.) *Statistica*, July–September 1984, *44*(3), pp. 501–11.

Gebski, Val and McNeil, Don. A Refined Method of Robust Smoothing. *J. Amer. Statist. Assoc.*, September 1984, *79*(387), pp. 616–23. [G: Australia]

Geweke, John F. Forecasting and Conditional Projection Using Realistic Prior Distributions: Comment. *Econometric Rev.*, 1984, *3*(1), pp. 105–12. [G: U.S.]

Geweke, John F. Inference and Causality in Economic Time Series Models. In *Griliches, Z. and Intriligator, M. D., eds.*, 1984, pp. 1102–1144.

Geweke, John F. Measures of Conditional Linear Dependence and Feedback between Time Series. *J. Amer. Statist. Assoc.*, December 1984, *79*(388), pp. 907–15. [G: U.S.]

Granger, Clive W. J. Issues Involved with the Seasonal Adjustment of Economic Time Series: Comment. *J. Bus. Econ. Statist.*, October 1984, *2*(4), pp. 335–36.

Granger, Clive W. J. and Watson, Mark W. Time Series and Spectral Methods in Econometrics. In *Griliches, Z. and Intriligator, M. D., eds.*, 1984, pp. 980–1022.

Griffiths, W. E. and Beesley, P. A. A. The Small-Sample Properties of Some Preliminary Test Estimators in a Linear Model with Autocorrelated Errors. *J. Econometrics*, May/June 1984, *25*(1/2), pp. 49–61.

Hall, S. G. On the Solution of High Order, Symmetric, Difference Equations. *Oxford Bull. Econ. Statist.*, February 1984, *46*(1), pp. 85–88.

Harvey, Andrew C. Dynamic Models, the Prediction Error Decomposition and State Space. In *Hendry, D. F. and Wallis, K. F., eds.*, 1984, pp. 37–59.

Harvey, Andrew C. and Pierse, R. G. Estimating Missing Observations in Economic Time Series. *J. Amer. Statist. Assoc.*, March 1984, *79*(385), pp. 125–31.

Hasenkamp, Georg. Fehlende Beobachtungen in autoregressiven Verhaltensgleichungen. (Missing Observations in Autoregressive Equations. With English summary.) *Z. Wirtschaft. Sozialwissen.*, 1984, *104*(1), pp. 21–28.

Hendry, David F. Present Position and Potential Developments: Some Personal Views: Time-Series Econometrics. *J. Roy. Statist. Soc.*, 1984, *147*(2), pp. 327–39.

Hendry, David F.; Pagan, Adrian R. and Sargan, J. Denis. Dynamic Specification. In *Griliches,*

Z. and Intriligator, M. D., eds., 1984, pp. 1025–1100.

Kitagawa, Genshiro and Gersch, Will. A Smoothness Priors—State Space Modeling of Time Series with Trend and Seasonality. *J. Amer. Statist. Assoc.*, June 1984, *79*(386), pp. 378–89.

Kollintzas, Tryphon E. and Husted, Steven L. Distributed Lags and Intermediate Good Imports. *J. Econ. Dynam. Control*, December 1984, *8*(3), pp. 303–27.

Levin, D. and Sidi, A. An Autoregressive Model with Varying Coefficients with Application to Prediction. In *Avula, X. J. R., et al.*, 1984, pp. 58–61.

Lütkepohl, Helmut. Forecasting Contemporaneously Aggregated Vector ARMA Processes. *J. Bus. Econ. Statist.*, July 1984, *2*(3), pp. 201–14. **[G: U.S.]**

Lütkepohl, Helmut. Linear Transformations of Vector ARMA Processes. *J. Econometrics*, December 1984, *26*(3), pp. 283–93.

Malinvaud, E. Forecasting and Conditional Projection Using Realistic Prior Distributions: Comment. *Econometric Rev.*, 1984, *3*(1), pp. 113–17. **[G: U.S.]**

Maravall, Agustin. Issues Involved with the Seasonal Adjustment of Economic Time Series: Comment. *J. Bus. Econ. Statist.*, October 1984, *2*(4), pp. 337–39.

McCallum, Bennett T. On Low-Frequency Estimates of Long-Run Relationships in Macroeconomics. *J. Monet. Econ.*, July 1984, *14*(1), pp. 3–14.

McKenzie, Sandra K. Concurrent Seasonal Adjustment with Census X-11. *J. Bus. Econ. Statist.*, July 1984, *2*(3), pp. 235–49. **[G: U.S.]**

Meese, Richard A. and Geweke, John F. A Comparison of Autoregressive Univariate Forecasting Procedures for Macroeconomic Time Series. *J. Bus. Econ. Statist.*, July 1984, *2*(3), pp. 191–200. **[G: U.S.; Japan; U.K.]**

Melino, Angelo. Forecasting and Conditional Projection Using Realistic Prior Distributions: Comment. *Econometric Rev.*, 1984, *3*(1), pp. 119–23. **[G: U.S.]**

Mezrich, J. J.; Frysinger, S. and Slivjanovski, R. Dynamic Representation of Multivariate Time Series Data. *J. Amer. Statist. Assoc.*, March 1984, *79*(385), pp. 34–40.

Morton, M. J. and Gray, H. L. The G-Spectral Estimator. *J. Amer. Statist. Assoc.*, September 1984, *79*(387), pp. 692–701.

Narasimham, Gorti V. L. Estimation and Prediction of Time-Varying Parameter Economic Models. In *Avula, X. J. R., et al.*, 1984, pp. 784–88. **[G: U.S.]**

Neftçi, Salih N. Are Economic Time Series Asymmetric over the Business Cycle? *J. Polit. Econ.*, April 1984, *92*(2), pp. 307–28. **[G: U.S.]**

Nelson, Charles R. and Kang, Heejoon. Pitfalls in the Use of Time as an Explanatory Variable in Regression. *J. Bus. Econ. Statist.*, January 1984, *2*(1), pp. 73–82.

das Neves, João César. Filtro de Kalman: Uma apresentação sumária. (With English summary.) *Economia (Portugal)*, October 1984, *8*(3), pp. 527–42.

Newbold, Paul. Forecasting and Conditional Projection Using Realistic Prior Distributions: Comment. *Econometric Rev.*, 1984, *3*(1), pp. 125–30. **[G: U.S.]**

Newbold, Paul and Thury, Gerhard. Seasonal Adjustment of Austrian Labour Force Series. *Empirica*, 1984, *11*(2), pp. 147–204. **[G: Austria]**

Nourney, Martin. Seasonal Adjustment by Frequency Determined Filter Procedures. *Statist. J.*, April 1984, *2*(2), pp. 161–68.

Osborn, Denise R. Causality Testing and Its Implications for Dynamic Econometric Models. *Econ. J.*, 1984 Supplement, *94*, pp. 82–96. **[G: Canada]**

Palm, Franz C. and Nijman, Theo E. Missing Observations in the Dynamic Regression Model. *Econometrica*, November 1984, *52*(6), pp. 1415–35.

Penm, Jack H. W. and Terrell, Richard D. Multivariate Subset Autoregressive Modelling with Zero Constraints for Detecting 'Overall Causality.' *J. Econometrics*, March 1984, *24*(3), pp. 311–30. **[G: Canada]**

Piccolo, Domenico. Una topologia per la classe dei processi ARIMA. (A Topology for the Class of ARIMA Processes. With English summary.) *Statistica*, January–March 1984, *44*(1), pp. 47–59.

Pierce, David A. Issues Involved with the Seasonal Adjustment of Time Series: Comment: Seasonal Adjustment—Models, Assumptions, and Criteria. *J. Bus. Econ. Statist.*, October 1984, *2*(4), pp. 340–42.

Pierce, David A.; Grupe, Michael R. and Cleveland, William P. Seasonal Adjustment of the Weekly Monetary Aggregates: A Model-based Approach. *J. Bus. Econ. Statist.*, July 1984, *2*(3), pp. 260–70. **[G: U.S.]**

Prosperetti, Luigi. Procedure ottimali di destagionalizzazione e di stima del trend. Alcuni esperimenti con gli indice della produzione industriale. (Optimal Seasonal Adjustment and Trend Estimation: Some Experiments with Industrial Production Indexes. With English summary.) *Statistica*, April–June 1984, *44*(2), pp. 219–33. **[G: Italy]**

Raveh, Adi. Comments on Some Properties of X-11. *Rev. Econ. Statist.*, May 1984, *66*(2), pp. 343–48. **[G: U.S.]**

Solo, Victor. The Order of Differencing in ARIMA Models. *J. Amer. Statist. Assoc.*, December 1984, *79*(388), pp. 916–21.

Tanaka, Katsuto and Maekawa, Koichi. The Sampling Distributions of the Predictor for an Autoregressive Model under Misspecifications. *J. Econometrics*, July 1984, *25*(3), pp. 327–51.

Tsay, Ruey S. Regression Models with Time Series Errors. *J. Amer. Statist. Assoc.*, March 1984, *79*(385), pp. 118–24.

Tsay, Ruey S. and Tiao, George C. Consistent Estimates of Autoregressive Parameters and Extended Sample Autocorrelation Function for Stationary and Nonstationary ARMA Models.

J. Amer. Statist. Assoc., March 1984, 79(385), pp. 84–96.

Vitale, Cosimo. Definizione ed uso delle matrici di auto-cross covarianze inverse. (Definition and Use of the Inverse Auto-Cross Covariance Matrices. With English summary.) *Statistica,* July–September 1984, *44*(3), pp. 395–416.

Wallis, Kenneth F. Comparing Time-Series and Nonlinear Model-based Forecasts. *Oxford Bull. Econ. Statist.,* November 1984, *46*(4), pp. 383–89.

Watson, Mark W. and Kraft, Dennis F. Testing the Interpretation of Indices in a Macroeconomic Index Model. *J. Monet. Econ.,* March 1984, *13*(2), pp. 165–81.   [G: U.S.]

Weiss, Andrew A. Systematic Sampling and Temporal Aggregation in Time Series Models. *J. Econometrics,* December 1984, *26*(3), pp. 271–81.

Weiss, Andrew A. and Andersen, A. P. Estimating Time Series Models Using the Relevant Forecast Evaluation Criterion. *J. Roy. Statist. Soc.,* 1984, *147*(3), pp. 484–87.

White, Halbert and Domowitz, Ian. Nonlinear Regression with Dependent Observations. *Econometrica,* January 1984, *52*(1), pp. 143–61.

Zellner, Arnold. Retrospect and Prospect: Summarization of the 1976 NBER-Census Conference on Seasonal Analysis of Economic Time Series. In *Zellner, A.,* 1984, *1978,* pp. 158–68.

Zellner, Arnold. Time Series Analysis and Econometric Model Construction. In *Zellner, A.,* 1984, *1975,* pp. 120–40.

2117 Survey Methods; Sampling Methods

Bailar, Barbara A. Nonresponse: What It Is and What We Do about It. *Statist. J.,* December 1984, *2*(4), pp. 381–92.   [G: U.S.]

Bell, Ralph. Item Nonresponse in Telephone Surveys: An Analysis of Who Fails to Report Income. *Soc. Sci. Quart.,* March 1984, *65*(1), pp. 207–15.   [G: U.S.]

Burt, Vicki L. and Cohen, Steven B. A Comparison of Methods to Approximate Standard Errors for Complex Survey Data. *Rev. Public Data Use,* October 1984, *12*(3), pp. 159–68.   [G: U.S.]

Godfrey, James; Roshwalb, Alan and Wright, Roger L. Model-based Stratification in Inventory Cost Estimation. *J. Bus. Econ. Statist.,* January 1984, *2*(1), pp. 1–9.   [G: U.S.]

Kersten, H. M. P. and Bethlehem, J. G. Exploring and Reducing the Nonresponse Bias by Asking the Basic Question. *Statist. J.,* December 1984, *2*(4), pp. 369–80. [G: Netherlands]

Nordberg, Leif. Hushållsbudgetundersökningarna i ekonomisk analys. (Household Surveys in Economic Analysis. With English summary.) *Ekon. Samfundets Tidskr.,* 1984, *37*(3), pp. 191–203.

[G: Finland; Norway]

Norwood, Janet L. and Early, John F. A Century of Methodological Progress at the U.S. Bureau of Labor Statistics. *J. Amer. Statist. Assoc.,* December 1984, *79*(388), pp. 748–61.

[G: U.S.]

Pokropp, Fritz. Optimale Korrekturen bei Kontrollerhebungen auf Doppel-Stichproben. (Optimal Corrections with Controlled Survey Methods in Double Sampling. With English summary.) *Jahr. Nationalökon. Statist.,* September 1984, *199*(5), pp. 445–59.

Ronning, Gerd. Welche Informationen enthält die Antwortkategorie "unverändert" in Tendenzbefragungen? (What Kind of Information Does the Category 'No Change' Contain in Business Tendency Surveys? With English summary.) *Ifo-Studien,* 1984, *30*(4), pp. 261–71.

Smith, Stanley K. and Mandell, Marylou. A Comparison of Population Estimation Methods: Housing Unit versus Component II, Ratio Correlation, and Administrative Records. *J. Amer. Statist. Assoc.,* June 1984, *79*(386), pp. 282–89.   [G: U.S.]

Smith, T. M. F. Present Position and Potential Developments: Some Personal Views: Sample Surveys. *J. Roy. Statist. Soc.,* 1984, *147*(2), pp. 208–21.

Stem, Donald E., Jr. and Steinhorst, R. Kirk. Telephone Interview and Mail Questionnaire Applications of the Randomized Response Model. *J. Amer. Statist. Assoc.,* September 1984, *79*(387), pp. 555–64.

Strecker, Heinrich; Wiegert, Rolf and Kafka, Knut. Practical Determination of a Response Variance on the Basis of Survey Models with Re-Enumerations. *Jahr. Nationalökon. Statist.,* January 1984, *199*(1), pp. 1–31.

[G: Belgium]

Thatcher, A. R. Topic of Public Interest: The 1981 Census of Population in England and Wales. *J. Roy. Statist. Soc.,* 1984, *147*(2), pp. 222–32.   [G: U.K.]

2118 Theory of Index Numbers and Aggregation

Afriat, S. N. The True Index. In *[Pearce, I. F.],* 1984, pp. 37–56.

Ershov, E. B. Aggregation Analysis of Systems of Linear Equations, Input–Output Models, and Econometric Models. *Matekon,* Fall 1984, *21*(1), pp. 28–53.   [G: U.S.S.R.]

Fuchs-Seliger, Susanne. A Logical Foundation of the Cost of Living Index. In *[Beckmann, M. J.],* 1984, pp. 65–74.

Hansen, Bent and Lucas, Edward F. On the Accuracy of Index Numbers. *Rev. Income Wealth,* March 1984, *30*(1), pp. 25–38.   [G: Egypt]

Keren, Michael and Weinblatt, J. A Geometrical Approach to Real Income Comparisons: A Comment on Samuelson's 'Analytical Notes on International Real-Income Measures.' *Econ. J.,* June 1984, *94*(374), pp. 258–64.

Khamis, Salem H. On Aggregation Methods for International Comparisons. *Rev. Income Wealth,* June 1984, *30*(2), pp. 185–205.

Kott, Phillip S. A Superpopulation Theory Approach to the Design of Price Index Estimators

with Small Sampling Biases. *J. Bus. Econ. Statist.*, January 1984, *2*(1), pp. 83–90.
[G: U.S.]

Mark, Jonathan H. and Goldberg, Michael A. Alternative Housing Price Indices: An Evaluation. *Amer. Real Estate Urban Econ. Assoc. J.*, Spring 1984, *12*(1), pp. 30–49.
[G: Canada]

Marksjö, Bertil. Simple Aggregation and Disaggregation Subject to Minimal Information Loss and Other Criteria. *Reg. Sci. Urban Econ.*, August 1984, *14*(3), pp. 465–78.

Mednitskii, V. G. On Using Aggregated Variables in Mathematical Economics. *Matekon*, Fall 1984, *21*(1), pp. 54–71.

Samuelson, Paul A. Second Thoughts on Analytical Income Comparisons. *Econ. J.*, June 1984, *94*(374), pp. 267–78.

Sen, Amartya. The Welfare Basis of Real Income Comparisons. In *Sen, A.*, 1984, *1979*, pp. 389–451.

Shorrocks, Anthony F. Inequality Decomposition by Population Subgroups. *Econometrica*, November 1984, *52*(6), pp. 1369–85.

Stoker, Thomas M. Completeness, Distribution Restrictions, and the Form of Aggregate Functions. *Econometrica*, July 1984, *52*(4), pp. 887–907.

Swamy, Subramanian. Samuelson's Analytical Notes on International Real-Income Measures: A Comment. *Econ. J.*, June 1984, *94*(374), pp. 265–66.

Vartia, Yrjö O. and Vartia, Pentti L. I. Descriptive Index Number Theory and the Bank of Finland Currency Index. *Scand. J. Econ.*, 1984, *86*(3), pp. 352–64. [G: Finland]

2119 Experimental Design; Social Experiments

Cox, D. R. Present Position and Potential Developments: Some Personal Views: Design of Experiments and Regression. *J. Roy. Statist. Soc.*, 1984, *147*(2), pp. 306–15.

Praet, Peter and Vuchelen, Jozef. The Integration of Consumer Survey Results in the Modelling of Private Consumption in Italy. *Econ. Notes*, 1984, (3), pp. 74–85. [G: Italy]

212 Construction, Analysis, and Use of Econometric Models

2120 Construction, Analysis, and Use of Econometric Models

Agbeyegbe, Terence D. The Exact Discrete Analog to a Closed Linear Mixed-Order System. *J. Econ. Dynam. Control*, September 1984, *7*(3), pp. 363–75.

Aigner, Dennis J. and Leamer, Edward E. Estimation of Time-of-Use Pricing Response in the Absence of Experimental Data: An Application of the Methodology of Data Transferability. *J. Econometrics*, September/October 1984, *26*(1/2), pp. 205–27. [G: U.S.]

Anas, Alex and Moses, Leon N. Qualitative Choice and the Blending of Discrete Alterna-

tives. *Rev. Econ. Statist.*, November 1984, *66*(4), pp. 547–55. [G: S. Korea]

Andersen, Peder and Sutinen, Jon G. Stochastic Bioeconomics: A Review of Basic Methods and Results. *Marine Resource Econ.*, 1984, *1*(2), pp. 117–36.

Aracil, Javier. Qualitative Methods in Social Systems Modelling. In *Avula, X. J. R., et al.*, 1984, pp. 125–32.

Artus, Patrick. Analyse du marché des biens dans les secteurs industriels. (An Analysis of the Disequilibrium on the Markets for Manufactured Goods. With English summary.) *Ann. INSEE*, July–December 1984, (55/56), pp. 77–107. [G: France]

Artus, Patrick. Capacité de production, demande de facteurs et incertitude sur la demande. (Production Capacity, Factor Demand and Demand Uncertainty. With English summary.) *Ann. INSEE*, January–March 1984, (53), pp. 3–29. [G: France]

Artus, Patrick and Avouyi-Dovi, S. Une estimation comparative de modèles avec rationnement quantitatif pour la France et les Etats-Unis. (Comparative Estimation for France and the United States of Models with Quantity Rationing. With English summary.) *Econ. Appl.*, 1984, *37*(3–4), pp. 489–522. [G: France; U.S.]

Artus, Patrick; Laroque, Guy and Michel, Gilles. Estimation of a Quarterly Macroeconomic Model with Quantity Rationing. *Econometrica*, November 1984, *52*(6), pp. 1387–1414.
[G: France]

Artus, Patrick and Muet, Pierre-Alain. Un panorama des développements récents de l'économétrie de l'investissement. (A Survey of Recent Developments in the Econometrics of Investment. With English summary.) *Revue Écon.*, September 1984, *35*(5), pp. 791–830.
[G: Japan; France; U.K.; U.S.; Germany]

Atkinson, Anthony B. and Jenkins, S. P. The Steady-State Assumption and the Estimation of Distributional and Related Models. *J. Human Res.*, Summer 1984, *19*(3), pp. 358–76.
[G: U.S.]

Auray, J. P. and Duru, G. Structural Analysis, Hierarchical Functions and Weak Structures. In *Ancot, J. P., ed.*, 1984, pp. 49–62.

Balasko, Yves. The Size of Dynamic Econometric Models. *Econometrica*, January 1984, *52*(1), pp. 123–41.

Barnett, William A. On the Flexibility of the Rotterdam Model: A First Empirical Look. *Europ. Econ. Rev.*, April 1984, *24*(3), pp. 285–89.

Barron, Andrew R. Predicted Squared Error: A Criterion for Automatic Model Selection. In *Farlow, S. J., ed.*, 1984, pp. 87–103.

Barron, Roger L., et al. Adaptive Learning Networks: Development and Application in the United States of Algorithms Related to GMDH. In *Farlow, S. J., ed.*, 1984, pp. 25–65.

Batts, John and Dowling, J. M. The Stability of the Demand-for-Money Function in the

United Kingdom: 1880–1975. *Quart. Rev. Econ. Bus.*, Autumn 1984, *24*(3), pp. 37–48.
[G: U.K.]

Baum, C. F. The Evaluation of Historical Policy via Optimal Control Techniques. In *Hughes Hallet, A.J., ed.*, 1984, pp. 165–77.
[G: U.S.]

Bera, Anil K.; Jarque, Carlos M. and Lee, Lung-Fei. Testing the Normality Assumption in Limited Dependent Variable Models. *Int. Econ. Rev.*, October 1984, *25*(3), pp. 563–78.
[G: Mexico]

Berzeg, Korhan. A Note on Statistical Approaches to Shift-Share Analysis. *J. Reg. Sci.*, May 1984, *24*(2), pp. 277–85.

Bhandari, Jagdeep S. A Computational Stochastic Equilibrium Model of Oil-importing Economies. *Weltwirtsch. Arch.*, 1984, *120*(2), pp. 301–28.

Bianchi, Carlo; Brillet, Jean-Louis and Calzolari, Giorgio. Analyse et mesure de l'incertitude en prévision d'un modèle économétrique. Application au modèle mini-DMS. (Analysis and Measurement of the Uncertainty in Mini-DMS Model for the French Economy. With English summary.) *Ann. INSEE*, April–June 1984, (54), pp. 31–62.
[G: France]

Bierens, Herman J. Model Specification Testing of Time Series Regressions. *J. Econometrics*, December 1984, *26*(3), pp. 323–53.

Billeter-Frey, Ernst P. Wirtschaftsprognosen im Lichte der Systemtheorie. (Economic Forecasting Based on System Theory. With English summary.) *Jahr. Nationalökon. Statist.*, September 1984, *199*(5), pp. 433–44. [G: U.S.]

Blake, David. Complete Systems Methods of Estimating Models with Rational and Adaptive Expectations: A Case Study. *Europ. Econ. Rev.*, March 1984, *24*(2), pp. 137–50.
[G: U.S.]

Bouissou, Michel-Benoît; Laffont, Jean-Jacques and Vuong, Quang H. Économétrie du déséquilibre sur données microéconomiques. (Econometrics of Disequilibrium with Microeconomic Data. With English summary.) *Ann. INSEE*, July–December 1984, (55/56), pp. 109–51.
[G: France]

Boutillier, M. Reading Macroeconomic Models and Building Causal Structures. In *Ancot, J. P., ed.*, 1984, pp. 35–48.

Brandsma, Andries S. and Hughes Hallett, Andrew J. Economic Conflict and the Solution of Dynamic Games. *Europ. Econ. Rev.*, October–November 1984, *26*(1–2), pp. 13–32.
[G: U.S.]

Brandsma, Andries S. and Hughes Hallett, Andrew J. The Structure of Rational Expectations Behaviour in Economics: An Empirical View. In *Ancot, J. P., ed.*, 1984, pp. 143–72.
[G: Netherlands]

Breusch, Trevor S. Tests of Specification in Econometrics: Comment. *Econometric Rev.*, 1984, *3*(2), pp. 243–51.

Bronsard, Camille and Salvas-Bronsard, Lise. On Price Exogeneity in Complete Demand Systems. *J. Econometrics*, March 1984, *24*(3), pp. 235–47. [G: U.S.; Canada]

Brown, Bryan W. and Mariano, Roberto S. Residual-Based Procedures for Prediction and Estimation in a Nonlinear Simultaneous System. *Econometrica*, March 1984, *52*(2), pp. 321–43.

Broze, L. and Szafarz, A. On Linear Models with Rational Expectations which Admit a Unique Solution. *Europ. Econ. Rev.*, February 1984, *24*(1), pp. 103–11.

Buiter, Willem H. Granger-Causality and Policy Effectiveness. *Economica*, May 1984, *51*(202), pp. 151–62.

Buiter, Willem H. Saddlepoint Problems in Continuous Time Rational Expectations Models: A General Method and Some Macroeconomic Examples. *Econometrica*, May 1984, *52*(3), pp. 665–80.

Buiter, Willem H. and Gersovitz, Mark. Controllability and the Theory of Economic Policy: A Further Note. *J. Public Econ.*, June 1984, *24*(1), pp. 127–29.

Bulgaru, M. National-Economy Indicators System Model. *Econ. Computat. Cybern. Stud. Res.*, 1984, *19*(2), pp. 19–36.

Bureau, D.; Miqueu, D. and Norotte, M. The Disequilibrium Theory in Macroeconomic Models: A Small-Scale Model. In *Ancot, J. P., ed.*, 1984, pp. 173–94.

Byron, R. P. On the Flexibility of the Rotterdam Model. *Europ. Econ. Rev.*, April 1984, *24*(3), pp. 273–83.

Catinat, Michel. Fondement microéconomique par le déséquilibre des équations d'importation et d'exportation. (Microeconomic Foundation via Disequilibrium: Import and Export Equations. With English summary.) *Ann. INSEE*, July–December 1984, (55/56), pp. 153–81.
[G: France]

Cha, Dong-deuck and Saklas, James G. Integration of Choice Set Reduction in Behavioral Choice Travel Demand Models. In *Avula, X. J. R., et al.*, 1984, pp. 853–59.

Considine, Timothy J. and Mount, Timothy D. The Use of Linear Logit Models for Dynamic Input Demand Systems. *Rev. Econ. Statist.*, August 1984, *66*(3), pp. 434–43. [G: U.S.]

Cooley, Thomas F. Forecasting and Conditional Projection Using Realistic Prior Distributions: Comment. *Econometric Rev.*, 1984, *3*(1), pp. 101–04. [G: U.S.]

Cordonnier, J. L.; Lesourd, J. B. and Ruiz, J. M. Substitutions in the French Food Industry from a Translog Cost Function Model. In *Avula, X. J. R., et al.*, 1984, pp. 833–36.
[G: France]

Dagli, C. Ates and Taylor, John B. Estimation and Solution of Linear Rational Expectations Models Using a Polynomial Matrix Factorization. *J. Econ. Dynam. Control*, December 1984, *8*(3), pp. 341–48.

Dana, R. A. and Malgrange, Pierre. The Dynamics of a Discrete Version of a Growth Cycle Model. In *Ancot, J. P., ed.*, 1984, pp. 115–42.

Deaton, Angus and Irish, Margaret. Statistical

Models for Zero Expenditures in Household Budgets. *J. Public Econ.*, February/March 1984, *23*(1/2), pp. 59–80. **[G: U.K.]**

Deleau, Michel; Le Van, Cuong and Malgrange, Pierre. Stabilisation efficace des systèmes économiques en présence d'incertitude: expérimentation avec une maquette du modèle DMS. (The Uncertainty Frontier as a Global Approach to the Efficient Stabilization of Economic Systems: An Experimentation with the Micro-DMS Model. With English summary.) *Revue Écon.*, May 1984, *35*(3), pp. 507–36.

Despontin, Marc; Nijkamp, Peter and Spronk, Jaap. Conflict Analysis in Macroeconomic Planning Models. In *Despontin, M.; Nijkamp, P. and Spronk, J., eds.*, 1984, pp. 1–19.

Dixon, Bruce L.; Batte, Marvin T. and Sonka, Steven T. Random Coefficients Estimation of Average Total Product Costs for Multiproduct Firms. *J. Bus. Econ. Statist.*, October 1984, *2*(4), pp. 360–66. **[G: U.S.]**

Doan, Thomas; Litterman, Robert B. and Sims, Christopher. Forecasting and Conditional Projection Using Realistic Prior Distributions: Reply. *Econometric Rev.*, 1984, *3*(1), pp. 131–44. **[G: U.S.]**

Doan, Thomas; Litterman, Robert B. and Sims, Christopher. Forecasting and Conditional Projection Using Realistic Prior Distributions. *Econometric Rev.*, 1984, *3*(1), pp. 1–100. **[G: U.S.]**

Ducos, Gilbert and Laffont, Jean-Jacques. Stock et déséquilibre: une analyse comparative et internationale. (Inventories and Disequilibrium: A Comparative International Analysis. With English summary.) *Ann. INSEE*, July–December 1984, (55/56), pp. 183–202. **[G: U.S.; France; Canada; Japan]**

Edmonds, Radcliffe G., Jr. A Theoretical Basis for Hedonic Regression: A Research Primer. *Amer. Real Estate Urban Econ. Assoc. J.*, Spring 1984, *12*(1), pp. 72–85.

Engle, Robert F.; Granger, Clive W. J. and Kraft, Dennis F. Combining Competing Forecasts of Inflation Using a Bivariate ARCH Model. *J. Econ. Dynam. Control*, November 1984, *8*(2), pp. 151–65. **[G: U.S.]**

Erickson, Elizabeth and House, Robert. Multiple Objective Policy Analysis: A Factor Analysis and Tradeoff Approach Applied to the Agricultural Sector of the Dominican Republic. *J. Policy Modeling*, August 1984, *6*(3), pp. 369–87. **[G: Dominican Republic]**

Ershov, E. B. Aggregation Analysis of Systems of Linear Equations, Input–Output Models, and Econometric Models. *Matekon*, Fall 1984, *21*(1), pp. 28–53. **[G: U.S.S.R.]**

Farlow, Stanley J. The GMDH Algorithm. In *Farlow, S. J., ed.*, 1984, pp. 1–24.

Feltenstein, Andrew. Money and Bonds in a Disaggregated Open Economy. In *Scarf, H. E. and Shoven, J. B., eds.*, 1984, pp. 209–42.

Fourgeaud, Claude; Gourieroux, Christian and Pradel, Jacqueline. Modèles à anticipations rationnelles: apprentissage par régression. (Models with Rational Expectations: Learning by

Regression. With English summary.) *Ann. INSEE*, April–June 1984, (54), pp. 63–77.

Freedman, David A. and Peters, Stephen C. Bootstrapping an Econometric Model: Some Empirical Results. *J. Bus. Econ. Statist.*, April 1984, *2*(2), pp. 150–58.

Friedmann, Ralph. Multiperiod Prediction from Dynamic Models with Autocorrelated Errors Conditional on Feedback Rules for the Future Policy Variables. In *Hughes Hallet, A.J., ed.*, 1984, pp. 145–63.

Fullerton, Don; Henderson, Yolanda Kodrzycki and Shoven, John B. A Comparison of Methodologies in Empirical General Equilibrium Models of Taxation. In *Scarf, H. E. and Shoven, J. B., eds.*, 1984, pp. 367–410. **[G: OECD; Mexico]**

Gallant, A. Ronald. The Fourier Flexible Form. *Amer. J. Agr. Econ.*, May 1984, *66*(2), pp. 204–08.

Gallant, A. Ronald and Golub, Gene H. Imposing Curvature Restrictions on Flexible Functional Forms. *J. Econometrics*, December 1984, *26*(3), pp. 295–321. **[G: U.S.]**

Garbely, M. and Gilli, M. Two Approaches in Reading Model Interdependencies. In *Ancot, J. P., ed.*, 1984, pp. 15–33. **[G: U.S.]**

Garen, John. The Returns to Schooling: A Selectivity Bias Approach with a Continuous Choice Variable. *Econometrica*, September 1984, *52*(5), pp. 1199–1218. **[G: U.S.]**

Gelovani, Viktor A. An Interactive Modeling System as a Tool for Analyzing Complex Socioeconomic Problems. In *Richardson, J., ed.*, 1984, pp. 75–86.

Geweke, John F. Forecasting and Conditional Projection Using Realistic Prior Distributions: Comment. *Econometric Rev.*, 1984, *3*(1), pp. 105–12. **[G: U.S.]**

Ginsburgh, Victor and Waelbroeck, Jean. Free Trade and Tariff-ridden International Equilibria: Formulation and Computation. In *Andersson, Å. E.; Isard, W. and Puu, T., eds.*, 1984, pp. 133–56.

Ginsburgh, Victor and Waelbroeck, Jean. Planning Models and General Equilibrium Activity Analysis. In *Scarf, H. E. and Shoven, J. B., eds.*, 1984, pp. 415–39. **[G: India]**

Gómez M., G. L. Modelling the Economic Development by Means of Impulsive Control Techniques. In *Avula, X. J. R., et al.*, 1984, pp. 802–06.

Goodhardt, G. J.; Ehrenberg, A. S. C. and Chatfield, C. The Dirichlet: A Comprehensive Model of Buying Behaviour. *J. Roy. Statist. Soc.*, 1984, *147*(5), pp. 621–43. **[G: U.K.]**

Gorham, Abby H. Imperfect Price Adjustment, Controlled Price and Multimarket Rationing Models: Their Potential Application to the Modelling of Trade in King and Tanner Crab Products. In *Avula, X. J. R., et al.*, 1984, pp. 837–43.

Goudie, Andrew W. and Meeks, G. Individual Economic Agents in a Macroeconomic Model:

UK Companies in Cambridge MDM. *J. Policy Modeling*, August 1984, *6*(3), pp. 289–309.
[G: U.K.]

Gourieroux, Christian; Laffont, Jean-Jacques and Monfort, Alain. Econométrie des modèles d'équilibre avec rationnement: une mise à jour. (Disequilibrium Econometrics: Recent Developments. With English summary.) *Ann. INSEE*, July–December 1984, (55/56), pp. 5–38.

Gregory, Allan W. A Systems Approach to Simultaneity and the Demand for Money in Canada. *Southern Econ. J.*, October 1984, *51*(2), pp. 401–18. [G: Canada]

Haining, Robert P. Testing a Spatial Interacting-Markets Hypothesis. *Rev. Econ. Statist.*, November 1984, *66*(4), pp. 576–83. [G: U.K.]

Halperin, W. C. and Gale, N. Towards Behavioural Models of Spatial Choice: Some Recent Developments. In *Pitfield, D. E., ed.*, 1984, pp. 9–28.

Harvey, Andrew C. Dynamic Models, the Prediction Error Decomposition and State Space. In *Hendry, D. F. and Wallis, K. F., eds.*, 1984, pp. 37–59.

Hausman, Jerry A. Tests of Specification in Econometrics: Comment. *Econometric Rev.*, 1984, *3*(2), pp. 253–55.

Hausman, Jerry A.; Hall, Bronwyn H. and Griliches, Zvi. Econometric Models for Count Data with an Application to the Patents–R&D Relationship. *Econometrica*, July 1984, *52*(4), pp. 909–38. [G: U.S.]

Hensher, David A. and Louviere, J. J. Towards an Approach to Forecasting Attendance at Unique Events Using a Discrete Choice Model and Experimental Design Data. In *Pitfield, D. E., ed.*, 1984, pp. 67–87. [G: Australia]

Hey, John D. Optimal Consumption When Income Follows a Markov Process. *Bull. Econ. Res.*, November 1984, *36*(2), pp. 109–18.

Hillier, Grant H. and Giles, David E. A. Estimation in Equilibrium Models Involving Discretionary Policy Instrument Choice. *Australian Econ. Pap.*, December 1984, *23*(43), pp. 179–96. [G: Australia]

Hughes Hallett, Andrew J. Non-cooperative Strategies for Dynamic Policy Games and the Problem of Time Inconsistency. *Oxford Econ. Pap.*, November 1984, *36*(3), pp. 381–99.

Imhoff, Evert. Estimation of Demand Systems Using Both Time Series and Cross Section Data. *De Economist*, 1984, *132*(4), pp. 419–39. [G: Netherlands]

Jorgenson, Dale W. Econometric Methods for Applied General Equilibrium Analysis. In *Scarf, H. E. and Shoven, J. B., eds.*, 1984, pp. 139–203. [G: U.S.]

Jusélius, Katarina. Empirisk formulering av dynamiska ekonomiska modeller. (Empirical Formulation of Dynamic, Economic Models. With English summary.) *Ekon. Samfundets Tidskr.*, 1984, *37*(2), pp. 117–21.

Kalaba, Robert E. and Tishler, Asher. Automatic Derivative Evaluation in the Optimization of Nonlinear Models. *Rev. Econ. Statist.*, November 1984, *66*(4), pp. 653–60.

von Känel, Siegfried. On the Problem of the Controllability of Economic Systems. *Econ. Computat. Cybern. Stud. Res.*, 1984, *19*(1), pp. 75–82.

Keller, A. A. Semi-reduced Forms of Econometric Models. In *Ancot, J. P., ed.*, 1984, pp. 89–113.

Kemp, Murray C.; Leonard, Daniel and Long, Ngo Van. Three Pitfalls in the Construction of Family-based Models of Population Growth. *Europ. Econ. Rev.*, August 1984, *25*(3), pp. 345–54.

Kendrick, David. Style in Multisectoral Modelling. In *Hughes Hallet, A.J., ed.*, 1984, pp. 329–60. [G: U.S.]

Kinal, Terrence W. and Lahiri, Kajal. A Note on "Selection of Regressors." *Int. Econ. Rev.*, October 1984, *25*(3), pp. 625–29.

King, Gordon A. Estimating Functional Forms with Special Reference to Agriculture: Discussion. *Amer. J. Agr. Econ.*, May 1984, *66*(2), pp. 221–22.

Klein, Roger W. and Brown, Stephen J. Model Selection When There Is "Minimal" Prior Information. *Econometrica*, September 1984, *52*(5), pp. 1291–1312.

Kloek, Teun. Dynamic Adjustment When the Target Is Nonstationary. *Int. Econ. Rev.*, June 1984, *25*(2), pp. 315–26.

Knight, John L. Asymptotic Distribution of Dynamic Multipliers in Dynamic Autoregressive Models. *Econometrica*, January 1984, *52*(1), pp. 217–22.

Knowles, Glenn J. Some Econometric Problems in the Measurement of Utility. *Amer. J. Agr. Econ.*, November 1984, *66*(4), pp. 505–10.

Kokkelenberg, Edward C. The Specification and Estimation of Interrelated Factor Demands under Uncertainty. *J. Econ. Dynam. Control*, September 1984, *7*(3), pp. 181–207.
[G: U.S.]

Kollintzas, Tryphon E. and Husted, Steven L. Distributed Lags and Intermediate Good Imports. *J. Econ. Dynam. Control*, December 1984, *8*(3), pp. 303–27.

Kunstman, A. Controlling a Linear Dynamic System According to Asymmetric Preferences. *J. Econ. Dynam. Control*, September 1984, *7*(3), pp. 261–81.

Lee, Lung-Fei. Tests of Specification in Econometrics: Comment. *Econometric Rev.*, 1984, *3*(2), pp. 257–59.

Litterman, Robert B. Forecasting and Policy Analysis with Bayesian Vector Autoregression Models. *Fed. Res. Bank Minn. Rev.*, Fall 1984, *8*(4), pp. 30–41. [G: U.S.]

Lybeck, Johan A. and Carlsson, Evert. From Small to Large: A Systematic Comparison of Gradually More Complex Econometric Models. *Europ. Econ. Rev.*, February 1984, *24*(1), pp. 83–101.

Maciejowski, J. M. and Vines, David. Decoupled Control of a Macroeconomic Model Using Frequency-Domain Methods. *J. Econ. Dynam. Control*, February 1984, *7*(1), pp. 55–77.

Malinvaud, E. Forecasting and Conditional Projection Using Realistic Prior Distributions: Comment. *Econometric Rev.*, 1984, *3*(1), pp. 113–17. **[G: U.S.]**

Malone, James M., II. Regression Without Models: Directions in the Search for Structure. In *Farlow, S. J., ed.*, 1984, pp. 67–86.

Mazurik, V. Hierarchical Model-Oriented System Organization. In *Grauer, M. and Wierzbicki, A. P., eds.*, 1984, pp. 77–81.

McFadden, Daniel L. Econometric Analysis of Qualitative Response Models. In *Griliches, Z. and Intriligator, M. D., eds.*, 1984, pp. 1396–1457.

McKenzie, George and Thomas, Stephen. The Econometric Modelling of Aggregate Consumer Behaviour. *Europ. Econ. Rev.*, August 1984, *25*(3), pp. 355–72.

McKinnon, Ronald I. Money and Bonds in a Disaggregated Open Economy: Modeling Structural Adjustment: Micro and Macro Elements in a General Equilibrium Framework: Comments. In *Scarf, H. E. and Shoven, J. B., eds.*, 1984, pp. 271–74.

Medio, A. Synergetics and Dynamic Economic Models. In *Goodwin, R. M.; Krüger, M. and Vercelli, A., eds.*, 1984, pp. 166–91.

Melino, Angelo. Forecasting and Conditional Projection Using Realistic Prior Distributions: Comment. *Econometric Rev.*, 1984, *3*(1), pp. 119–23. **[G: U.S.]**

Mendelsohn, Robert. Estimating the Structural Equations of Implicit Markets and Household Production Functions. *Rev. Econ. Statist.*, November 1984, *66*(4), pp. 673–77.

Mieszkowski, Peter. A Comparison of Methodologies in Empirical General Equilibrium Models of Taxation: Comments. In *Scarf, H. E. and Shoven, J. B., eds.*, 1984, pp. 410–14.

Minford, Patrick and Peel, David A. Testing for Unbiasedness and Efficiency under Incomplete Current Information. *Bull. Econ. Res.*, May 1984, *36*(1), pp. 1–7.

Mizon, Grayham E. The Encompassing Approach in Econometrics. In *Hendry, D. F. and Wallis, K. F., eds.*, 1984, pp. 135–72.

Morey, Edward R. The Choice of Ski Areas: Estimation of a Generalized CES Preference Ordering with Characteristics. *Rev. Econ. Statist.*, November 1984, *66*(4), pp. 584–90. **[G: U.S.]**

Narasimham, Gorti V. L. Estimation and Prediction of Time-Varying Parameter Economic Models. In *Avula, X. J. R., et al.*, 1984, pp. 784–88. **[G: U.S.]**

Neck, Reinhard. Dynamische Simulation und optimale Kontrolle ökonomischer Systeme: Ein Methodenvergleich. (Dynamic Simulation and Optimal Control of Economic Systems: A Comparison of Methods. With English summary.) *Jahr. Nationalökon. Statist.*, May 1984, *199*(3), pp. 256–74.

Newbold, Paul. Forecasting and Conditional Projection Using Realistic Prior Distributions: Comment. *Econometric Rev.*, 1984, *3*(1), pp. 125–30. **[G: U.S.]**

Nickell, Stephen J. An Investigation of the Deter-

minants of Manufacturing Employment in the United Kingdom. *Rev. Econ. Stud.*, October 1984, *51*(4), pp. 529–57. **[G: U.K.]**

Nijkamp, Peter and Spronk, Jaap. Perspectives of Macroeconomic Conflict Analysis. In *Despontin, M.; Nijkamp, P. and Spronk, J., eds.*, 1984, pp. 283–94.

Norman, Alfred Lorn. Alternative Algorithms for the MacRae OLCV Strategy. *J. Econ. Dynam. Control*, February 1984, *7*(1), pp. 21–37.

Norman, Alfred Lorn. Information Structure and Stochastic Control Performance. *J. Econ. Dynam. Control*, November 1984, *8*(2), pp. 137–49.

Osborn, Denise R. Causality Testing and Its Implications for Dynamic Econometric Models. *Econ. J.*, 1984 Supplement, *94*, pp. 82–96. **[G: Canada]**

Pagan, Adrian R. Model Evaluation by Variable Addition. In *Hendry, D. F. and Wallis, K. F., eds.*, 1984, pp. 103–33.

Pallaschke, Diethard. On the Construction of Utility Functions Which Correspond to Homogeneous Demand Systems. In *[Beckmann, M. J.]*, 1984, pp. 75–81.

Patterson, K. D. and Ryding, J. Dynamic Time Series Models with Growth Effects Constrained to Zero. *Econ. J.*, March 1984, *94*(373), pp. 137–43.

Pawlowski, Zbigniew. Basic Concepts of Discriminatory Prediction. In *Gruber, J., ed.*, 1984, pp. 125–39.

Penm, Jack H. W. and Terrell, Richard D. Multivariate Subset Autoregressive Modelling with Zero Constraints for Detecting 'Overall Causality.' *J. Econometrics*, March 1984, *24*(3), pp. 311–30. **[G: Canada]**

Petkovski, Djordjija B. Stability Analysis of Large Scale Economic Systems Which Have a Multi-Time Scale Property. In *Hughes Hallet, A.J., ed.*, 1984, pp. 271–88.

Picard, Richard R. and Cook, R. Dennis. Cross-Validation of Regression Models. *J. Amer. Statist. Assoc.*, September 1984, *79*(387), pp. 575–83.

Pierce, David A.; Grupe, Michael R. and Cleveland, William P. Seasonal Adjustment of the Weekly Monetary Aggregates: A Model-based Approach. *J. Bus. Econ. Statist.*, July 1984, *2*(3), pp. 260–70. **[G: U.S.]**

Pikkemaat, G. F. A Dynamic Model of an Informationally Disaggregate Economy. In *Avula, X. J. R., et al.*, 1984, pp. 789–94.

van der Ploeg, Frederick. Economic Policy Rules for Risk-Sensitive Decision Making. *Z. Nationalökon.*, 1984, *44*(3), pp. 207–35.

Pollak, Robert A.; Sickles, Robin C. and Wales, Terence J. The CES-Translog: Specification and Estimation of a New Cost Function. *Rev. Econ. Statist.*, November 1984, *66*(4), pp. 602–07. **[G: U.S.]**

Pope, Rulon D. Estimating Functional Forms with Special Reference to Agriculture: Discussion. *Amer. J. Agr. Econ.*, May 1984, *66*(2), pp. 223–24.

Portes, Richard, et al. Estimation de la taille des

erreurs de planification. (Estimation of the Possible Size of Plan Errors. With English summary.) *Ann. INSEE*, July–December 1984, (55/56), pp. 245–55. **[G: Poland]**

Quiggin, John and Bui-Lan, Anh. The Use of Cross-Sectional Estimates of Profit Functions for Tests of Relative Efficiency: A Critical Review. *Australian J. Agr. Econ.*, April 1984, 28(1), pp. 44–55.

Richardson, Jacques G. A Primer of Model Systems. In *Richardson, J., ed.*, 1984, pp. 3–18.

Rietveld, Piet. The Use of Qualitative Information in Macro-Economic Policy Analysis. In *Despontin, M.; Nijkamp, P. and Spronk, J., eds.*, 1984, pp. 264–80.

Robinson, Sherman and Tyson, Laura D'Andrea. Modeling Structural Adjustment: Micro and Macro Elements in a General Equilibrium Framework. In *Scarf, H. E. and Shoven, J. B., eds.*, 1984, pp. 243–71.

Rossi, Nicola. The Estimation of Product Supply and Input Demand by the Differential Approach. *Amer. J. Agr. Econ.*, August 1984, 66(3), pp. 368–75. **[G: Italy]**

Royer, D. and Ritschard, G. Qualitative Structural Analysis: Game or Science? In *Ancot, J. P., ed.*, 1984, pp. 3–13.

Rustem, Berc and Velupillai, Kumaraswamy. Cooperation between Politicians and Econometricians and the Search for Optimal Economic Policy. *J. Policy Modeling*, August 1984, 6(3), pp. 341–50.

Ruud, Paul A. Tests of Specification in Econometrics. *Econometric Rev.*, 1984, 3(2), pp. 211–42.

Ruud, Paul A. Tests of Specification in Econometrics: Reply. *Econometric Rev.*, 1984, 3(2), pp. 269–76.

Sandblom, C. L. and Banasik, J. L. Optimizing Economic Policy with Sliding Windows. *Appl. Econ.*, February 1984, 16(1), pp. 45–56. **[G: Canada]**

Sandblom, C. L. and Eiselt, H. A. Controlling an Econometric Model Using Different Coefficient Sets. In *Hughes Hallet, A.J., ed.*, 1984, pp. 85–95.

Sandee, J.; Don, F. J. H. and van den Berg, P. J. C. M. Adjustment of Projections to Recent Observations. *Europ. Econ. Rev.*, October–November 1984, 26(1–2), pp. 153–66.

Sargan, J. Denis. Wages and Prices in the United Kindgom: A Study in Econometric Methodology. In *Hendry, D. F. and Wallis, K. F., eds.*, 1984, pp. 275–314. **[G: U.K.]**

Sargent, Thomas J. Autoregressions, Expectations, and Advice. *Amer. Econ. Rev.*, May 1984, 74(2), pp. 408–15.

Scarf, Herbert E. The Computation of Equilibrium Prices. In *Scarf, H. E. and Shoven, J. B., eds.*, 1984, pp. 1–49.

Schmidt, Peter J. and Lin, Tsai-Fen. Simple Tests of Alternative Specifications in Stochastic Frontier Models. *J. Econometrics*, March 1984, 24(3), pp. 349–61.

Schmidt, Peter J. and Sickles, Robin C. Produc-

tion Frontiers and Panel Data. *J. Bus. Econ. Statist.*, October 1984, 2(4), pp. 367–74. **[G: U.S.]**

Schönfeld, Peter. Dynamic Linear Models with Rational Expectations of Current Endogenous Variables. In *[Beckmann, M. J.]*, 1984, pp. 275–90.

Scott, Donald E. and Hutchinson, Charles E. An Application of the GMDH Algorithm to Economic Modeling. In *Farlow, S. J., ed.*, 1984, pp. 243–55. **[G: U.S.]**

Sendov, Blagovest. Some Principles of Mathematical Modeling. In *Richardson, J., ed.*, 1984, pp. 65–70.

Sheikh, Munir A. An analysis of Some Possible Causes for the Absence or Presence of the Neutrality and Homogeneity Properties in Large Macroeconomic Models. *Empirical Econ.*, 1984, 9(2), pp. 113–30. **[G: Canada]**

Shmueli, A. and Tapiero, Charles S. Adaptive Econometric Forecasting by an Approximate Filtering-Smoothing Algorithm: The Case of the Israeli Meat Sector. In *Hughes Hallet, A.J., ed.*, 1984, pp. 63–84. **[G: Israel]**

Shonkwiler, J. S. and Taylor, Timothy G. The Implications of Estimating Market Demand Curves by Least Squares Regression. *Europ. Rev. Agr. Econ.*, 1984, 11(1), pp. 107–18. **[G: U.S.]**

Sonis, M. Dynamic Choice of Alternatives, Innovation Diffusion, and Ecological Dynamics of the Volterra-Lotka Model. In *Pitfield, D. E., ed.*, 1984, pp. 29–43.

Spanos, Aris. Liquidity as a Latent Variable—An Application of the MIMIC Model. *Oxford Bull. Econ. Statist.*, May 1984, 46(2), pp. 125–43. **[G: U.K.]**

Stapleton, David C. Errors-in-Variables in Demand Systems. *J. Econometrics*, December 1984, 26(3), pp. 255–70. **[G: U.K.]**

Stephanedes, Y. J. and Kumar, V. Comparative Evaluation of Intercity Demand Models. In *Pitfield, D. E., ed.*, 1984, pp. 114–21. **[G: U.S.]**

Stern, Robert M. Planning Models and General Equilibrium Activity Analysis: Comments. In *Scarf, H. E. and Shoven, J. B., eds.*, 1984, pp. 439–45. **[G: India]**

Stoker, Thomas M. Completeness, Distribution Restrictions, and the Form of Aggregate Functions. *Econometrica*, July 1984, 52(4), pp. 887–907.

Struth, Friedrich K. Modelling Expectations Formation with Parameter-Adaptive Filters: An Empirical Application to the Livingston Forecasts. *Oxford Bull. Econ. Statist.*, August 1984, 46(3), pp. 211–39. **[G: U.S.]**

Šujan, Ivan. Methods for Solving the Problem of Multicollinearity in Econometric Models: A Survey. In *Gruber, J., ed.*, 1984, pp. 45–85.

Tamura, Hiroyuki and Kondo, Tadashi. On Revised Algorithms of GMDH with Applications. In *Farlow, S. J., ed.*, 1984, pp. 225–41.

Taylor, C. Robert. Stochastic Dynamic Duality: Theory and Empirical Applicability. *Amer. J. Agr. Econ.*, August 1984, 66(3), pp. 351–57.

Timmermans, H. J. P. Discrete Choice Models versus Decompositional Multiattribute Preference Models: A Comparative Analysis of Model Performance in the Context of Spatial Shopping-Behaviour. In *Pitfield, D. E., ed.*, 1984, pp. 88–101. **[G: Netherlands]**

Todd, Michael J. Efficient Methods of Computing Economic Equilibria. In *Scarf, H. E. and Shoven, J. B., eds.*, 1984, pp. 51–68.

Todd, Richard M. Improving Economic Forecasting with Bayesian Vector Autoregression. *Fed. Res. Bank Minn. Rev.*, Fall 1984, *8*(4), pp. 18–29. **[G: U.S.]**

Tondini, Giovanni. Further Discussion on Controllability and the Theory of Economic Policy [On a Generalization of Tinbergen's Condition in the Theory of Policy to Dynamic Models]. *J. Public Econ.*, June 1984, *24*(1), pp. 123–25.

Varian, Hal R. The Nonparametric Approach to Production Analysis. *Econometrica*, May 1984, *52*(3), pp. 579–97.

Várlaki, P. and Veres, S. On Measures of Nonlinearity for Dynamic Stochastic Systems. In *Avula, X. J. R., et al.*, 1984, pp. 143–48.

Visco, Ignazio. On Linear Models with Rational Expectations: An Addendum. *Europ. Econ. Rev.*, February 1984, *24*(1), pp. 113–15.

Waldman, Donald M. Properties of Technical Efficiency Estimators in the Stochastic Frontier Model. *J. Econometrics*, July 1984, *25*(3), pp. 353–64.

Wallis, Kenneth F. Comparing Time-Series and Nonlinear Model-based Forecasts. *Oxford Bull. Econ. Statist.*, November 1984, *46*(4), pp. 383–89.

Watson, Mark W. and Kraft, Dennis F. Testing the Interpretation of Indices in a Macroeconomic Index Model. *J. Monet. Econ.*, March 1984, *13*(2), pp. 165–81. **[G: U.S.]**

Watts, Geof and Quiggin, John. A Note on the Use of a Logarithmic Time Trend. *Rev. Marketing Agr. Econ.*, August 1984, *52*(2), pp. 91–99. **[G: Australia]**

Weale, Martin R. Linear Economic Models. In *van der Ploeg, F., ed.*, 1984, pp. 37–56.

Weaver, Robert D. Caveats on the Application of the Fourier Flexible Form: Discussion. *Amer. J. Agr. Econ.*, May 1984, *66*(2), pp. 209–10.

White, Halbert. Tests of Specification in Econometrics: Comment. *Econometric Rev.*, 1984, *3*(2), pp. 261–67.

Wibe, Sören A. Engineering Production Functions: A Survey. *Economica*, November 1984, *51*(204), pp. 401–11.

Wohltmann, Hans-Werner and Krömer, Wolfgang. Sufficient Conditions for Dynamic Path Controllability of Economic Systems. *J. Econ. Dynam. Control*, September 1984, *7*(3), pp. 315–30.

Wrigley, N. and Dunn, R. Diagnostics and Resistant Fits in Logit Choice Models. In *Pitfield, D. E., ed.*, 1984, pp. 44–66. **[G: U.K.]**

Zellner, Arnold. Basic Issues in Econometrics, Past and Present. In *Zellner, A.*, 1984, *1982*, pp. 26–34.

Zellner, Arnold. Perspectives on Mathematical Models in the Social Sciences. In *Zellner, A.*, 1984, pp. 12–25.

Zellner, Arnold. Statistical Analysis of Econometric Models. In *Zellner, A.*, 1984, *1979*, pp. 83–119.

Zellner, Arnold. The Quality of Quantitative Economic Policymaking When Targets and Costs of Change Are Misspecified. In *Zellner, A.*, 1984, *1973*, pp. 169–83.

Zellner, Arnold. Time Series Analysis and Econometric Model Construction. In *Zellner, A.*, 1984, *1975*, pp. 120–40.

Ziemer, Rod F. Reporting Econometric Results: Believe It or Not? *Land Econ.*, February 1984, *60*(1), pp. 122–27.

213 Mathematical Methods and Models

2130 General

Allen, Beth. Convergence of σ-Fields and Applications to Mathematical Economics. In *Hammer, G. and Pallaschke, D., eds.*, 1984, pp. 161–74.

Aracil, Javier. Qualitative Methods in Social Systems Modelling. In *Avula, X. J. R., et al.*, 1984, pp. 125–32.

Arrow, Kenneth J. Homogeneous Systems in Mathematical Economics: A Comment. In *Arrow, K. J., vol. 3*, 1984, *1950*, pp. 1–4.

Arrow, Kenneth J.; Barankin, E. W. and Blackwell, D. Admissible Points of Convex Sets. In *Arrow, K. J., vol. 4*, 1984, *1953*, pp. 38–42.

Auray, J. P. and Duru, G. Structural Analysis, Hierarchical Functions and Weak Structures. In *Ancot, J. P., ed.*, 1984, pp. 49–62.

Bischoff, Eberhard E. A Posteriori Trade-Off Analysis in Reference Point Approaches. In *Grauer, M. and Wierzbicki, A. P., eds.*, 1984, pp. 139–45.

Brunner, Johann K. Zur Funktion mathematischer Modelle in der Nationalökonomie. Anmerkungen zu einem Konfliktmodell von H. W. Holub. (On the role of Mathematical Models in Economics: Remarks on a Conflict-Model of H. W. Holub. With English summary.) *Jahr. Nationalökon. Statist.*, July 1984, *199*(4), pp. 308–20.

Dreyfus, Stuart E. Mathematical Modeling and Long Range Planning. In *Avula, X. J. R., et al.*, 1984, pp. 37–43.

Finlay, P. N. and King, M. New Approaches to Teaching Mathematical Modelling to Management Students. In *Avula, X. J. R., et al.*, 1984, pp. 942–47.

Fukuba, Yo; Tabata, Yoshio and Sakagami, Yoshitaka. Notes on Measurement and Approximation (I). (In Japanese. With English summary.) *Osaka Econ. Pap.*, December 1984, *34*(2–3), pp. 275–82.

Gelovani, Viktor A. An Interactive Modeling System as a Tool for Analyzing Complex Socioeconomic Problems. In *Richardson, J., ed.*, 1984, pp. 75–86.

Gustman, Alan L. Modeling Individuals' Behavior: Evaluation of a Policymaker's Tool. *J. Policy Anal. Manage.*, Winter 1984, *3*(2), pp. 191–205. [G: U.S.]

Jacobsen, Edward. On Logic, Axioms, Theorems, Paradoxes and Proofs. In *Richardson, J., ed.*, 1984, pp. 71–73.

Kim, Kyoo H. A Modified Minkowski Theorem and Applications: Comment. *Atlantic Econ. J.*, March 1984, *12*(1), pp. 118.

Kushnirsky, F. I. Selected Contributions of Kiev Scholars to Mathematical Economics. In *Koropeckyj, I. S., ed.*, 1984, pp. 148–62.

Leroux, Alain. Other Determinental Conditions for Concavity and Quasi-concavity. *J. Math. Econ.*, April 1984, *13*(1), pp. 43–49.

Mantel, Rolf R. Economia Matemática, su evolución histórica y estado actual. (Mathematical Economics, Its Historical Evolution and Present State. With English summary.) *Económica*, May-December 1984, *30*(2–3), pp. 203–15.

Medio, A. Synergetics and Dynamic Economic Models. In *Goodwin, R. M.; Krüger, M. and Vercelli, A., eds.*, 1984, pp. 166–91.

Morishima, Michio. The Good and Bad Uses of Mathematics. In *Wiles, P. and Routh, G., eds.*, 1984, pp. 51–73.

Moscardini, A. O. and Cross, M. Issues Involved in the Design of a Mathematical Modelling Course. In *Avula, X. J. R., et al.*, 1984, pp. 954–63.

Nabeya, Seiji. On the Maximum Number of Balancing Subsets. *J. Math. Econ.*, October 1984, *13*(2), pp. 123–26.

van der Ploeg, Frederick. Mathematical Methods in Economics: Introduction. In *van der Ploeg, F., ed.*, 1984, pp. 1–6.

Ray, A. K. Curriculum Development in Mathematical Modelling. In *Avula, X. J. R., et al.*, 1984, pp. 948–53.

Richardson, Jacques G. A Primer of Model Systems. In *Richardson, J., ed.*, 1984, pp. 3–18.

Sendov, Blagovest. Some Principles of Mathematical Modeling. In *Richardson, J., ed.*, 1984, pp. 65–70.

Ursprung, Heinrich W. Schumpeterian Entrepreneurs and Catastrophe Theory or a New Chapter to the Foundations of Economic Analysis. *Z. Nationalökon.*, Supplement 1984, pp. 39–69.

Vajda, S. Actuarial Mathematics. In *van der Ploeg, F., ed.*, 1984, pp. 457–76.

Van Iwaarden, John L. Mathematical Modelling in a Differential Equations Course. In *Avula, X. J. R., et al.*, 1984, pp. 964–67.

Weibull, Jörgen W. Continuous Linear Representations of Preference Orderings in Vector Spaces. In *[Beckmann, M. J.]*, 1984, pp. 291–305.

Wohltmann, Hans-Werner. A Note on Aoki's Conditions for Path Controllability of Continuous-Time Dynamic Economic Systems. *Rev. Econ. Stud.*, April 1984, *51*(2), pp. 343–49.

Zellner, Arnold. Perspectives on Mathematical Models in the Social Sciences. In *Zellner, A.*, 1984, pp. 12–25.

2132 Optimization Techniques

Carlsson, Christer. Handling Conflicts in Fuzzy Multiple-Criteria Optimization. In *Grauer, M. and Wierzbicki, A. P., eds.*, 1984, pp. 31–40.

Guddat, Jürgen and Wendler, Klaus. On Dialogue Algorithms for Linear and Nonlinear Vector Optimization from the Point of View of Parametric Optimization. In *Grauer, M. and Wierzbicki, A. P., eds.*, 1984, pp. 123–31.

Hughes Hallett, Andrew J. Non-cooperative Strategies for Dynamic Policy Games and the Problem of Time Inconsistency. *Oxford Econ. Pap.*, November 1984, *36*(3), pp. 381–99.

Katz, Eliakim. A Rule for Signing the Effect of Uncertainty in an Optimization Problem with Two Control Variables. *J. Econ. Dynam. Control*, October 1984, *8*(1), pp. 65–71.

Katz, Eliakim. On Variability under Certainty. *Europ. Econ. Rev.*, October–November 1984, *26*(1–2), pp. 109–13.

Kim, K. V., et al. An Efficient Algorithm for Computing Derivatives and Extremal Problems. *Matekon*, Winter 1984–85, *21*(2), pp. 49–67.

Knobloch, H. W. On the Principle of "Internal Modelling" in Linear Control Theory. In *Hammer, G. and Pallaschke, D., eds.*, 1984, pp. 131–51.

Korte, Bernhard and Schrader, Rainer. Can the Ellipsoid Method Be Efficient? In *[Beckmann, M. J.]*, 1984, pp. 337–43.

Kushnirsky, F. I. Selected Contributions of Kiev Scholars to Mathematical Economics. In *Koropeckyj, I. S., ed.*, 1984, pp. 148–62.

Martić, Ljubomir. Characterization of Complete Efficiency in a Special Problem of Multicriterion Hyperbolic Programming. *Econ. Anal. Worker's Manage.*, 1984, *18*(2), pp. 171–74.

Mazurik, V. Hierarchical Model-Oriented System Organization. In *Grauer, M. and Wierzbicki, A. P., eds.*, 1984, pp. 77–81.

Medaiskis, T. I. and Raiatskas, R. L. On Overcoming the Switching Problem in Optimizing Macroeconomic Models. *Matekon*, Summer 1984, *20*(4), pp. 48–63.

Mitra, Tapan and Ray, Debraj. Dynamic Optimization on a Non-convex Feasible Set: Some General Results for Non-smooth Technologies. *Z. Nationalökon.*, 1984, *44*(2), pp. 151–75.

Nakayama, Hirotaka and Sawaragi, Yoshikazu. Satisficing Trade-Off Method for Multiobjective Programming. In *Grauer, M. and Wierzbicki, A. P., eds.*, 1984, pp. 113–22.

Norman, Alfred Lorn. Information Structure and Stochastic Control Performance. *J. Econ. Dynam. Control*, November 1984, *8*(2), pp. 137–49.

Petkovski, Djordjija B. Stability Analysis of Large Scale Economic Systems Which Have a Multi-Time Scale Property. In *Hughes Hallet, A.J., ed.*, 1984, pp. 271–88.

van der Ploeg, Frederick. Economic Policy Rules for Risk-Sensitive Decision Making. *Z. Nationalökon.*, 1984, *44*(3), pp. 207–35.

Ponstein, J. Dualizing Optimization Problems in

Mathematical Economics. *J. Math. Econ.*, December 1984, *13*(3), pp. 255–72.

Ponstein, J. Mirrored Pairs of Optimization Problems: A Comment. *Economica*, February 1984, *51*(201), pp. 97.

Seierstad, Atle. Sufficient Conditions in Free Final Time Optimal Control Problems: A Comment. *J. Econ. Theory*, April 1984, *32*(2), pp. 367–70.

Serafini, Paolo. Dual Relaxation and Branch-and-Bound Techniques for Multiobjective Optimization. In *Grauer, M. and Wierzbicki, A. P., eds.*, 1984, pp. 84–90.

Simmons, P. Multivariate Risk Premia with a Stochastic Objective. *Econ. J.*, 1984 Supplement, *94*, pp. 124–32.

Tarvainen, Kyösti. On the Implementation of the Interactive Surrogate Worth Trade-Off (ISWT) Method. In *Grauer, M. and Wierzbicki, A. P., eds.*, 1984, pp. 154–61.

Vijverberg, Wim P. M. Discrete Choices in Continuous Time as a Dynamic Programming Problem. *Amer. Econ.*, Fall 1984, *28*(2), pp. 9–17.

Vlach, Milan. Levitin-Miljutin-Osmolovskii Conditions for Local Pareto Optimality. In *Grauer, M. and Wierzbicki, A. P., eds.*, 1984, pp. 91–96.

2133 Existence and Stability Conditions of Equilibrium

Dasgupta, Dipankar. The Hawkins–Simon Theorem: An Input–Output Analytic Approach. *Indian Econ. Rev.*, July-Dec. 1984, *19*(2), pp. 171–83.

Keiding, Hans. Existence of Economic Equilibrium: New Results and Open Problems. In *Hammer, G. and Pallaschke, D., eds.*, 1984, pp. 223–42.

Lüthi, H.-J. On Equilibrium Programming. In *Avula, X. J. R., et al.*, 1984, pp. 87–91.

ten Raa, Thijs. Fixed Points of Compositions. *Europ. Econ. Rev.*, October–November 1984, *26*(1–2), pp. 209–12.

2134 Computational Techniques

Allgower, Eugene L. and Schmidt, Phillip H. Piecewise Linear Approximation of Solution Manifolds for Nonlinear Systems of Equations. In *Hammer, G. and Pallaschke, D., eds.*, 1984, pp. 339–47.

Barron, Roger L., et al. Adaptive Learning Networks: Development and Application in the United States of Algorithms Related to GMDH. In *Farlow, S. J., ed.*, 1984, pp. 25–65.

Bilgen, Semih and Deligönül, Z. Şeyda. Yenileme kuraminda volterra denkleminin çözümü için bir yöntem. (A Method of Solution for the Volterra Equation for the Renewal Theory. With English summary.) *METU*, 1984, *11*(3–4), pp. 369–90.

Buiter, Willem H. Saddlepoint Problems in Continuous Time Rational Expectations Models:

A General Method and Some Macroeconomic Examples. *Econometrica*, May 1984, *52*(3), pp. 665–80.

Dwyer, Paul S. and Waugh, Frederick V. On Errors in Matrix Inversion. In *Waugh, F. V.*, 1984, *1953*, pp. 303–33.

Farlow, Stanley J. The GMDH Algorithm. In *Farlow, S. J., ed.*, 1984, pp. 1–24.

Friesz, Terry L.; Harker, Patrick T. and Tobin, Roger L. Alternative Algorithms for the General Network Spatial Price Equilibrium Problem. *J. Reg. Sci.*, November 1984, *24*(4), pp. 475–507.

Gabasov, R. and Kirillova, F. M. New Algorithms and Results of Numerical Experiments for Solution of Mathematical Programming and Optimal Control Problems. In *Hammer, G. and Pallaschke, D., eds.*, 1984, pp. 440–56.

Guddat, Jürgen and Wendler, Klaus. On Dialogue Algorithms for Linear and Nonlinear Vector Optimization from the Point of View of Parametric Optimization. In *Grauer, M. and Wierzbicki, A. P., eds.*, 1984, pp. 123–31.

Hall, S. G. On the Solution of High Order, Symmetric, Difference Equations. *Oxford Bull. Econ. Statist.*, February 1984, *46*(1), pp. 85–88.

Houska, R. V. Using Stochastic Optimal Control to Find Shortest Paths in Networks. In *Avula, X. J. R., et al.*, 1984, pp. 295–98.

Kalaba, Robert E. and Tishler, Asher. Automatic Derivative Evaluation in the Optimization of Nonlinear Models. *Rev. Econ. Statist.*, November 1984, *66*(4), pp. 653–60.

Kim, K. V., et al. An Efficient Algorithm for Computing Derivatives and Extremal Problems. *Matekon*, Winter 1984–85, *21*(2), pp. 49–67.

Korhonen, Pekka and Laakso, Jukka. A Visual Interactive Method for Solving the Multiple-Criteria Problem. In *Grauer, M. and Wierzbicki, A. P., eds.*, 1984, pp. 146–53.

Lau, Lawrence J. Numerical Specification of Applied General Equilibrium Models: Estimation, Calibration, and Data: Comments. In *Scarf, H. E. and Shoven, J. B., eds.*, 1984, pp. 127–37.   [G: U.S.; U.K.]

Mansur, Ahsan Habib and Whalley, John. Numerical Specification of Applied General Equilibrium Models: Estimation, Calibration, and Data. In *Scarf, H. E. and Shoven, J. B., eds.*, 1984, pp. 69–127.   [G: U.S.; U.K.]

Marksjö, Bertil. Simple Aggregation and Disaggregation Subject to Minimal Information Loss and Other Criteria. *Reg. Sci. Urban Econ.*, August 1984, *14*(3), pp. 465–78.

Norman, Alfred Lorn. Alternative Algorithms for the MacRae OLCV Strategy. *J. Econ. Dynam. Control*, February 1984, *7*(1), pp. 21–37.

Pang, Jong-Shi. Solution of the General Multicommodity Spatial Equilibrium Problem by Variational and Complementarity Methods. *J. Reg. Sci.*, August 1984, *24*(3), pp. 403–14.

van der Ploeg, Frederick. Generalized Least Squares Methods for Balancing Large Systems and Tables of National Accounts. *Rev. Public Data Use*, March 1984, *12*(1), pp. 17–33. [G: U.K.]

Scarf, Herbert E. The Computation of Equilibrium Prices. In *Scarf, H. E. and Shoven, J. B., eds.*, 1984, pp. 1–49.

Soong, Tsai C. Some Useful Formulas for Multivariable Interpolation and Integration. In *Avula, X. J. R., et al.*, 1984, pp. 424–29.

Ştefănescu, Maria Viorica. Mathematical Basis of Total Hierarchical Clustering. *Econ. Computat. Cybern. Stud. Res.*, 1984, *19*(4), pp. 55–60.

Stone, Richard [Sir]. Accounting Matrices in Economics and Demography. In *van der Ploeg, F., ed.*, 1984, pp. 9–36.

Tamura, Hiroyuki and Kondo, Tadashi. On Revised Algorithms of GMDH with Applications. In *Farlow, S. J., ed.*, 1984, pp. 225–41.

Todd, Michael J. Efficient Methods of Computing Economic Equilibria. In *Scarf, H. E. and Shoven, J. B., eds.*, 1984, pp. 51–68.

Uebe, Götz. Computational Problems in Economics. In *[Beckmann, M. J.]*, 1984, pp. 365–75.

Wallmeier, E. A Procedure for Computing the f-Nucleolus of a Cooperative Game. In *Hammer, G. and Pallaschke, D., eds.*, 1984, pp. 288–96.

Waugh, Frederick V. Inversion of the Leontief Matrix by Power Series. In *Waugh, F. V., 1984, 1950*, pp. 281–93.

Waugh, Frederick V. and Abel, Martin E. On Fractional Powers of a Matrix. In *Waugh, F. V., 1984, 1967*, pp. 378–81.

Waugh, Frederick V. and Maxfield, Margaret W. Side-and-Diagonal Numbers. In *Waugh, F. V., 1984, 1967*, pp. 368–77.

Wendell, Richard E. and Peterson, Elmor L. A Dual Approach for Obtaining Lower Bounds to the Weber Problem. *J. Reg. Sci.*, May 1984, *24*(2), pp. 219–28.

2135 Construction, Analysis, and Use of Mathematical Programming Models

Allgower, Eugene L. and Schmidt, Phillip H. Piecewise Linear Approximation of Solution Manifolds for Nonlinear Systems of Equations. In *Hammer, G. and Pallaschke, D., eds.*, 1984, pp. 339–47.

Bartmann, Dieter. Reduction of State Space in Dynamic Programming with Integrated Forecasting. In *[Beckmann, M. J.]*, 1984, pp. 183–93.

Batten, David F. Adaptive Learning and Multistage Compromises for Multilevel Decision Making in Macroeconomic Systems. In *Despontin, M.; Nijkamp, P. and Spronk, J., eds.*, 1984, pp. 23–53. [G: Australia]

Cassetti, Mario. La coordinazione delle decisioni di investimento in un modello di programmazione a due livelli. (The Coordination of the Investment Decision in a Two-Level Programming Model. With English summary.) *Giorn. Econ.*, March–April 1984, *43*(3–4), pp. 237–60.

Corley, H. W. Maximizations with Respect to Cones in Mathematical Modelling. In *Avula, X. J. R., et al.*, 1984, pp. 196–201.

Dandy, G. C.; McBean, Edward A. and Hutchinson, B. G. A Model for Constrained Optimum Water Pricing and Capacity Expansion. *Water Resources Res.*, May 1984, *20*(5), pp. 511–20.

Despontin, Marc; Nijkamp, Peter and Spronk, Jaap. Conflict Analysis in Macroeconomic Planning Models. In *Despontin, M.; Nijkamp, P. and Spronk, J., eds.*, 1984, pp. 1–19.

Duţă, L. D. and Fabian, Cs. Solving Cutting-Stock Problems through the Monte-Carlo Method. *Econ. Computat. Cybern. Stud. Res.*, 1984, *19*(3), pp. 35–54.

Farlow, Stanley J. Searching for Structure: the GMDH Algorithm. In *Avula, X. J. R., et al.*, 1984, pp. 66–70.

Gabasov, R. and Kirillova, F. M. New Algorithms and Results of Numerical Experiments for Solution of Mathematical Programming and Optimal Control Problems. In *Hammer, G. and Pallaschke, D., eds.*, 1984, pp. 440–56.

Gaitsgori, V. G. and Pervozvanskii, A. A. The Perturbation Method in Mathematical Programming Problems. *Matekon*, Spring 1984, *20*(3), pp. 39–58.

Grauer, Manfred and Zalai, Ernö. A Reference Point Approach to Nonlinear Macroeconomic Multiobjective Models. In *Despontin, M.; Nijkamp, P. and Spronk, J., eds.*, 1984, pp. 73–96.

Hammer, Gerald. Greedy Solutions for General Set Covering Problems. In *[Beckmann, M. J.]*, 1984, pp. 321–26.

Harrigan, Frank and Buchanan, Iain. A Quadratic Programming Approach to Input–Output Estimation and Simulation. *J. Reg. Sci.*, August 1984, *24*(3), pp. 339–58. [G: U.K.; U.S.]

Heinhold, Michael. The German Nonlinear Income Tax Scale in Linear Programming Models—Linear Approximations and Error Analysis. In *[Beckmann, M. J.]*, 1984, pp. 327–35. [G: W. Germany]

Hirshfeld, David S. An Overview of Mathematical Programming for Strategic Planning. In *Naylor, T. H. and Thomas, C., eds.*, 1984, pp. 121–37.

Houska, R. V. Using Stochastic Optimal Control to Find Shortest Paths in Networks. In *Avula, X. J. R., et al.*, 1984, pp. 295–98.

Knobloch, H. W. On the Principle of "Internal Modelling" in Linear Control Theory. In *Hammer, G. and Pallaschke, D., eds.*, 1984, pp. 131–51.

Martić, Ljubomir. Characterization of Complete Efficiency in a Special Problem of Multicriterion Hyperbolic Programming. *Econ. Anal. Worker's Manage.*, 1984, *18*(2), pp. 171–74.

Mednitskii, V. G. On Using Aggregated Variables in Mathematical Economics. *Matekon*, Fall 1984, *21*(1), pp. 54–71.

Punzo, Lionello F. and Velupillai, Kumaraswamy. Multisectoral Models and Joint Production. In *van der Ploeg, F., ed.*, 1984, pp. 57–92.

Ritter, Klaus. A Dual Quadratic Programming Algorithm. In *[Beckmann, M. J.]*, 1984, pp. 345–63.

Sakawa, Masatoshi. Interactive Fuzzy Decision Making for Multiobjective Nonlinear Programming Problems. In *Grauer, M. and Wierzbicki, A. P., eds.*, 1984, pp. 105–12.

Steuer, Ralph E. Operating Considerations Pertaining to the Interactive Weighted Tchebycheff Procedure. In *Grauer, M. and Wierzbicki, A. P., eds.*, 1984, pp. 132–38.

Stoica, M. and Angheluţă, G. An Application of the Problem of Three-Dimensional Allocation. *Econ. Computat. Cybern. Stud. Res.*, 1984, *19*(4), pp. 61–66.

Sweeney, Dennis J. A Practical Evaluation of the Potential of Mixed Integer Programming as a Strategic Planning Tool. In *Naylor, T. H. and Thomas, C., eds.*, 1984, pp. 111–20.

Sysło, Maciej M. On Two Problems Related to the Traveling Salesman Problem on Halin Graphs. In *Hammer, G. and Pallaschke, D., eds.*, 1984, pp. 325–35.

Taylor, C. Robert. Stochastic Dynamic Duality: Theory and Empirical Applicability. *Amer. J. Agr. Econ.*, August 1984, *66*(3), pp. 351–57.

Thore, Sten; Kozmetsky, George and Burtis, Michelle. Effects of Defense Spending on the Texas Economy: An Example of Concave Programming. *J. Policy Modeling*, November 1984, *6*(4), pp. 573–86.   [G: U.S.]

Waugh, Frederick V. Alligation, Forerunner of Linear Programming. In *Waugh, F. V.*, 1984, *1958*, pp. 334–48.

Westphal, Larry E. and Cremer, Jacques. "The Independence of Investment Decisions" Revisited. In *[Chenery, H. B.]*, 1984, pp. 543–72.

Zionts, Stanley and Wallenius, Jyrki. Recent Developments in Our Approach to Multiple-Criteria Decision Making. In *Grauer, M. and Wierzbicki, A. P., eds.*, 1984, pp. 54–62.

214 Computer Programs

2140 Computer Programs

Barbu, G. A New Fast Method for Computer Generation of Gamma and Beta Random Variables by Transformation of Uniform Variables. *Econ. Computat. Cybern. Stud. Res.*, 1984, *19*(3), pp. 69–81.

Brown, J. A. C. and Mazzarino, G. Drawing the Lorenz Curve and Calculating the Gini Concentration Index from Grouped Data by Computer. *Oxford Bull. Econ. Statist.*, August 1984, *46*(3), pp. 273–78.   [G: U.K.]

Farlow, Stanley J. A FORTRAN Program for the GMDH Algorithm. In *Farlow, S. J., ed.*, 1984, pp. 277–89.

Hall, Bronwyn H. Software for the Computation of Tobit Model Estimates. *J. Econometrics*, January/February 1984, *24*(1/2), pp. 215–22.

Jordan, Jeffrey L. and Brooks, Rusty. IO/EAM: An Input–Output Economic Assessment Model. *Southern J. Agr. Econ.*, December 1984, *16*(2), pp. 145–49.

Kalaba, Robert E. and Tishler, Asher. Automatic Derivative Evaluation in the Optimization of Nonlinear Models. *Rev. Econ. Statist.*, November 1984, *66*(4), pp. 653–60.

Laughlin, David H. A Microcomputer Linear Programming Package: An Alternative to Mainframes. *Southern J. Agr. Econ.*, July 1984, *16*(1), pp. 183–86.

Mażbic-Kulma, Barbara. Methods of Determining Systems of Time-Table Arranging with Predetermined Area. In *Hammer, G. and Pallaschke, D., eds.*, 1984, pp. 457–64.

Prager, Michael H. An SAS Program for Simplified GMDH Models. In *Farlow, S. J., ed.*, 1984, pp. 291–315.

Tice, Thomas F. and Kletke, Marilyn G. Reliability of Linear Programming Software: An Experience with the IBM Mathematical Programming System Series. *Amer. J. Agr. Econ.*, February 1984, *66*(1), pp. 104–07.

Văduva, I., et al. Future of Electronic Computer Programming. *Econ. Computat. Cybern. Stud. Res.*, 1984, *19*(2), pp. 37–48.

Wierzbicki, A. Interactive Decision Analysis and Interpretative Computer Intelligence. In *Grauer, M. and Wierzbicki, A. P., eds.*, 1984, pp. 2–19.

215 Experimental Economic Methods

2150 Experimental Economic Methods

Brubaker, Earl R. Demand Disclosures and Conditions on Exclusion: An Experiment. *Econ. J.*, September 1984, *94*(375), pp. 536–53.
[G: U.S.]

Coursey, Don and Smith, Vernon L. Experimental Tests of an Allocation Mechanism for Private, Public or Externality Goods. *Scand. J. Econ.*, 1984, *86*(4), pp. 468–84.

Kim, Oliver and Walker, Mark. The Free Rider Problem: Experimental Evidence. *Public Choice*, 1984, *43*(1), pp. 3–24.

Michener, H. A.; Clancy, P. D. and Yuen, K. Do Outcomes of *N*-Person Sidepayment Games Fall in the Core? In *Holler, M. J., ed.*, 1984, pp. 269–82.

220 ECONOMIC AND SOCIAL STATISTICAL DATA AND ANALYSIS

2200 General

Arrow, Kenneth J. Statistical Requirements for Greek Economic Planning. In *Arrow, K. J., vol. 4*, 1984, *1965*, pp. 87–102.

Arrow, Kenneth J. Statistics and Economic Policy. In *Arrow, K. J., vol. 4*, 1984, *1957*, pp. 43–54.

Boreham, John [Sir]. Present Position and Potential Developments: Some Personal Views: Official Statistics. *J. Roy. Statist. Soc.*, 1984, *147*(2), pp. 174–85.   [G: U.K.]

Camus, B., et al. The French Unified System of Business Statistics. *Statist. J.*, April 1984, *2*(2), pp. 149–59.   [G: France]

Centre for World Food Studies. A Computable General Equilibrium Model for Thailand with Emphasis on the Agricultural Sector. In *Cohen, S. I., et al., eds.*, 1984, pp. 407–43. [G: Thailand]

Clark, Cynthia Z. F. and Coffey, Jerry L. How Many People Can Keep a Secret? Data Interchange within a Decentralized System. *Rev. Public Data Use*, December 1984, *12*(4), pp. 271–77. [G: U.S.]

Cole, S. and Meagher, G. A. Growth and Income Distribution in India: A General Equilibrium Analysis. In *Cohen, S. I., et al., eds.*, 1984, pp. 315–48. [G: Sri Lanka; India]

David, Elizabeth L. and Peskin, Henry M. The USGS National Water Use Data System: An Optimal Data Base? *Rev. Public Data Use*, June 1984, *12*(2), pp. 97–105. [G: U.S.]

Defourny, Jacques and Thorbecke, Erik. Structural Path Analysis and Multiplier Decomposition within a Social Accounting Matrix Framework. *Econ. J.*, March 1984, *94*(373), pp. 111–36. [G: S. Korea]

Duncan, Joseph W. Disclosure and Confidentiality Issues in the Federal Statistical Environment: Comments [How Many People Can Keep a Secret? Data Interchange within a Decentralized System]. *Rev. Public Data Use*, December 1984, *12*(4), pp. 317–20. [G: U.S.]

Grais, W. Aggregate Demand and Macro-economic Imbalances in Thailand: Simulations with the SIAM 1 Model. In *Cohen, S. I., et al., eds.*, 1984, pp. 349–79. [G: Thailand]

Huang, Hai. Problems in the Reform of Statistical Work. *Chinese Econ. Stud.*, Spring 1984, *17*(3), pp. 61–67. [G: China]

Karunatilake, H. N. S. Main Socio-economic Statistical Series of South Asian Countries: A Critical Survey. *Int. Soc. Sci. J.*, 1984, *36*(2), pp. 369–402. [G: LDCs]

Katz, Arnold; Teuter, Klaus and Sidel, Philip. Comparison of Alternative Ways of Deriving Panel Data from the Annual Demographic Files of the Current Population Survey. *Rev. Public Data Use*, March 1984, *12*(1), pp. 35–44. [G: U.S.]

Keyfitz, Nathan. Is the Census Good Enough? *J. Policy Anal. Manage.*, Summer 1984, *3*(4), pp. 597–603.

Kincannon, C. L. Disclosure and Confidentiality Issues in the Federal Statistical Environment: Comment [How Many People Can Keep a Secret? Data Interchange within a Decentralized System]. *Rev. Public Data Use*, December 1984, *12*(4), pp. 321–24. [G: U.S.]

Kumar, Pradeep. The Current Industrial Relations Scene in Canada, 1984: Technical Notes. In *Wood, W. D. and Kumar, P., eds.*, 1984, pp. 483–97. [G: Canada]

Laganier, Jean. The Possible Impact of National Accounts and Balances on the Development of Frameworks for Environment Statistics. *Statist. J.*, January 1984, *2*(1), pp. 43–61.

Maton, J. and Joos, M. A Simplified Dynamic SAM Model of Malaysia: The Effects of Techni-cal Progress, Capital Accumulation and Income Distribution on Employment. In *Cohen, S. I., et al., eds.*, 1984, pp. 381–405. [G: Malaysia]

McDonald, Daina. The International Economy in 1984 and 1985. *Australian Econ. Rev.*, 1st Quarter 1984, (65), pp. 5–23. [G: OECD]

Mellor, John W. and Johnston, Bruce F. The World Food Equation: Interrelations among Development, Employment, and Food Consumption. *J. Econ. Lit.*, June 1984, *22*(2), pp. 53–74. [G: Global]

Norwood, Janet L. and Early, John F. A Century of Methodological Progress at the U.S. Bureau of Labor Statistics. *J. Amer. Statist. Assoc.*, December 1984, *79*(388), pp. 748–61. [G: U.S.]

Pearson, Robert W. The Changing Fortunes of the U.S. Statistical System, 1980–1985. *Rev. Public Data Use*, December 1984, *12*(4), pp. 245–69. [G: U.S.]

Peskin, Henry M. and David, Elizabeth L. Theory of an Optimal Data Base. *Rev. Public Data Use*, March 1984, *12*(1), pp. 45–53.

Quelennec, M. The Business Statistics System in France and Consistency between Sources. *Statist. J.*, April 1984, *2*(2), pp. 137–48. [G: France]

Scheuren, Fritz; Schwartz, Otto and Kilss, Beth. Erratum [Statistics from Individual Income Tax Returns: Quality Issues and Budget Cut Impact]. *Rev. Public Data Use*, June 1984, *12*(2), pp. 157. [G: U.S.]

Scheuren, Fritz; Schwartz, Otto and Kilss, Beth. Statistics from Individual Income Tax Returns: Quality Issues and Budget Cut Impact. *Rev. Public Data Use*, March 1984, *12*(1), pp. 55–67. [G: U.S.]

Spirer, Herbert F. and Jaffe, A. J. Misuses of Statistics: Lessons for Statisticians, Non-Statisticians, Students and Teachers. *Amer. J. Econ. Soc.*, April 1984, *43*(2), pp. 205–16.

Spruill, Nancy L. The Confidentiality and Analytic Usefulness of Masked Business Microdata. *Rev. Public Data Use*, December 1984, *12*(4), pp. 307–14. [G: U.S.]

Stone, Richard [Sir]. Accounting Matrices in Economics and Demography. In *van der Ploeg, F., ed.*, 1984, pp. 9–36.

Szilágyi, György. International Comparisons—Types and Methods. *Statist. J.*, December 1984, *2*(4), pp. 345–55.

Thorbecke, Erik. The Modelling of Socio-economic Planning Processes: Overview and Conclusions. In *Cohen, S. I., et al., eds.*, 1984, pp. 445–60.

Vaughan, Denton R.; Whiteman, T. Cameron and Lininger, Charles A. The Quality of Income and Program Data in the 1979 ISDP Research Panel: Some Preliminary Findings. *Rev. Public Data Use*, June 1984, *12*(2), pp. 107–31. [G: U.S.]

Walker, Paul C. The Value of the Canadian Census of Agriculture. *Can. J. Agr. Econ.*, March 1984, *32*(1), pp. 163–74. [G: Canada]

Weale, Martin R. Quantity and Price Effects in

an Analysis of World Trade Based on an Accounting Matrix. *Rev. Income Wealth*, March 1984, *30*(1), pp. 85–117. [G: Global]

Wilson, Oliver H. and Smith, William J. Access to Tax Records for Statistical Purposes. *Rev. Public Data Use*, December 1984, *12*(4), pp. 295–305. [G: U.S.]

221 National Income Accounting

2210 National Income Accounting Theory and Procedures

Arndt, Heinz W. Measuring Trade in Financial Services. *Banca Naz. Lavoro Quart. Rev.*, June 1984, (149), pp. 197–213.

Arya, P. L. Measuring Economic Growth—A Critique of the Views of Fell and Greenfield. *Rev. Income Wealth*, September 1984, *30*(3), pp. 377–82.

Barker, Terry; van der Ploeg, Frederick and Weale, Martin R. A Balanced System of National Accounts for the United Kingdom. *Rev. Income Wealth*, December 1984, *30*(4), pp. 461–85. [G: U.K.]

Britton, Andrew J. C. and Savage, David. The Three Measures of GDP. *Nat. Inst. Econ. Rev.*, February 1984, (107), pp. 54–59. [G: U.K.]

Budd, Edward C.; Radner, Daniel B. and Whiteman, T. Cameron. An Accounting Framework for Transfer Payments and Its Implications for the Size Distribution of Income. In *Moon, M., ed.*, 1984, pp. 37–83. [G: U.S.]

Buiter, Willem H. A Comprehensive Balance Sheet and Permanent Income Accounting Framework for the Public Sector: Theory and Applications. In *Masera, R. S. and Triffin, R., eds.*, 1984, pp. 153–95. [G: EEC; U.S.]

Dean, Peter. National Income and Output. In *Sandford, C. and Bradbury, M., eds.*, 1984, pp. 117–44. [G: Nigeria; U.K.]

Di Fonzo, Tommaso; Rettore, Enrico and Trivellato, Ugo. Stime preliminari e revisioni degli aggregati di contabilità nazionale a prezzi correnti. (Provisional and Revised Estimates of Italian National Accounts Aggregates at Current Prices. With English summary.) *Statistica*, October–December 1984, *44*(4), pp. 649–73. [G: Italy]

Drechsler, Laszlo. International Comparisons of Real Product and of Purchasing Power Parities. A Review of the Development of the Methodology. *Econ. Int.*, August–November 1984, *37*(3–4), pp. 280–87. [G: Global]

Eisner, Robert. Transfers in a Total Incomes System of Accounts. In *Moon, M., ed.*, 1984, pp. 9–35. [G: U.S.]

Feige, Edgar L. Macroeconomics and the Unobserved Sector. In *Block, W. and Walker, M., eds.*, 1984, pp. 21–37. [G: U.S.; U.K.]

Hamermesh, Daniel S. The Role of Time in the Measurement of Transfers and Well-Being: Comment. In *Moon, M., ed.*, 1984, pp. 234–38. [G: U.S.]

Hicks, John R. Valuation of Social Income—The

Cost Approach. In *Hicks, J.*, 1984, *1981*, pp. 96–121.

Hicks, John R. Valuation of Social Income—The Utility Approach [The Measurement of Real Income]. In *Hicks, J.*, 1984, *1958*, pp. 57–95.

Lampman, Robert. An Accounting Framework for Transfer Payments and Its Implications for the Size Distribution of Income: Comment. In *Moon, M., ed.*, 1984, pp. 83–86. [G: U.S.]

Lavrač, Ivo. Micro Payments Flows as a Data Source for the National Accounts. *Econ. Anal. Worker's Manage.*, 1984, *18*(2), pp. 175–78. [G: Yugoslavia]

Marczewski, Jean. Le concept de coût macroéconomique et son utilité. (The Concept of Macroeconomic Cost and Its Utility. With English summary.) *Écon. Appl.*, 1984, *37*(3–4), pp. 457–88. [G: France; W. Germany]

Mishan, E. J. GNP—Measurement or Mirage? *Nat. Westminster Bank Quart. Rev.*, November 1984, pp. 2–13.

Morgan, James N. The Role of Time in the Measurement of Transfers and Well-Being. In *Moon, M., ed.*, 1984, pp. 199–234. [G: U.S.]

van der Ploeg, Frederick. Generalized Least Squares Methods for Balancing Large Systems and Tables of National Accounts. *Rev. Public Data Use*, March 1984, *12*(1), pp. 17–33. [G: U.K.]

Postner, Harry H. New Developments towards Resolving the Company–Establishment Problem. *Rev. Income Wealth*, December 1984, *30*(4), pp. 429–59.

Scott, Maurice. Maintaining Capital Intact. *Oxford Econ. Pap.*, Supplement November 1984, *36*, pp. 59–73.

Scott, Maurice. Maintaining Capital Intact. In *Collard, D. A., et al., eds.*, 1984, pp. 59–73.

Stanfield, Ron. A Revision of the Economic Surplus Concept. In *Foster, J. B. and Szlajfer, H., eds.*, 1984, *1974*, pp. 251–61. [G: U.S.]

Stone, Richard [Sir]. Balancing the National Accounts: The Adjustment of Initial Estimates—A Neglected Stage in Measurement. In *[Pearce, I. F.]*, 1984, pp. 191–212. [G: U.K.]

Streit, Manfred E. The Shadow Economy: A Challenge to the Welfare State? In *Eucken, W. and Böhm, F., eds.*, 1984, pp. 109–19.

Sunga, Preetom S. An Alternative to the Current Treatment of Interest as Transfer in the United Nations and Canadian Systems of National Accounts. *Rev. Income Wealth*, December 1984, *30*(4), pp. 385–402. [G: Canada]

2212 National Income Accounts

Acharya, Shankar. The Underground Economy in the United States: Comment. *Int. Monet. Fund Staff Pap.*, December 1984, *31*(4), pp. 742–46. [G: U.S.]

Albach, Horst. The Rate of Return in German Manufacturing Industry: Measurement and Policy Implications. In *Holland, D. M., ed.*, 1984, pp. 273–311. [G: W. Germany]

Amemiya, Takeshi. Tobit Models: A Survey. *J.*

Econometrics, January/February 1984, *24*(1/2), pp. 3–61.

Auerbach, Alan J. Investment, Taxation, and Growth. In *Wachter, M. L. and Wachter, S. M., eds.,* 1984, pp. 224–50. [G: U.S.]

Bach, Christopher L. U.S. International Transactions, Fourth Quarter and Year 1983. *Surv. Curr. Bus.,* March 1984, *64*(3), pp. 38–66. [G: U.S.]

Baer, Werner and Birch, Melissa H. Expansion of the Economic Frontier: Paraguayan Growth in the 1970s. *World Devel.,* August 1984, *12*(8), pp. 783–98. [G: Paraguay]

Barker, Terry; van der Ploeg, Frederick and Weale, Martin R. A Balanced System of National Accounts for the United Kingdom. *Rev. Income Wealth,* December 1984, *30*(4), pp. 461–85. [G: U.K.]

Bayer, Kurt. Profitability in Austrian Industrial Corporations. In *Holland, D. M., ed.,* 1984, pp. 421–64. [G: Austria]

Beeman, William J. How Bad Are the Large Deficits? Comment. In *Mills, G. B. and Palmer, J. L., eds.,* 1984, pp. 74–78. [G: U.S.]

Bélyácz, Iván. Investment Policy and Structural Transformation in Hungary. *Acta Oecon.,* 1984, *33*(3–4), pp. 273–91. [G: Hungary]

Benoit, J. Pierre V. International Interest Rates, External Indebtedness of Developing Countries and Foreign Aid. In *Kessler, D. and Ullmo, P.-A., eds.,* 1984, pp. 241–67. [G: LDCs; MDCs]

Bequele, Assefa and van der Hoeven, Rolf. Poverty and Inequality in Sub-Saharan Africa. In *Ghosh, P. K., ed., no. 13,* 1984, *1980,* pp. 232–44. [G: Sub-Saharan Africa]

Blejer, Mario I. and Khan, Mohsin S. Private Investment in Developing Countries. *Finance Develop.,* June 1984, *21*(2), pp. 26–29. [G: Selected LDCs]

Bourguignon, François and Levy-Leboyer, M. An Econometric Model of France during the 19th Century. *Europ. Econ. Rev.,* June 1984, *25*(1), pp. 107–41. [G: France]

Boyle, G. E. In Search of Ireland's Black Economy. *Irish Banking Rev.,* March 1984, pp. 32–42. [G: Ireland]

Brox, James A. A Note on Capacity Utilization, Productivity, and the Canadian Output Gap. *Empirical Econ.,* 1984, *9*(3), pp. 131–38. [G: Canada]

Carson, Carol S. The Underground Economy: An Introduction. *Surv. Curr. Bus.,* May 1984, *64*(5), pp. 21–37. [G: OECD]

Carson, Carol S. The Underground Economy: An Introduction. *Surv. Curr. Bus.,* July 1984, *64*(7), pp. 106–18. [G: U.S.]

Cartaxo, Rui. Equaçoes input–output para os preços da procura final. (With English summary.) *Economia (Portugal),* May 1984, *8*(2), pp. 381–94. [G: Portugal]

Carter, Michael. Issues in the Hidden Economy—A Survey. *Econ. Rec.,* September 1984, *60*(170), pp. 209–21. [G: Australia; U.K.]

Clark, Peter K. Unemployment and Potential Output in the 1980s: Comment. *Brookings Pap. Econ. Act.,* 1984, (2), pp. 565–67. [G: U.S.]

Curzon-Price, Victoria. Europe: Renaissance or Decline? *Aussenwirtschaft,* December 1984, *39*(4), pp. 383–98. [G: EEC]

Dawkins, Peter and Sloan, Judith. The Australian Labour Market, September 1984. *Australian Bull. Lab.,* September 1984, *10*(4), pp. 179–95. [G: Australia]

Dean, Peter. National Income and Output. In *Sandford, C. and Bradbury, M., eds.,* 1984, pp. 117–44. [G: Nigeria; U.K.]

Denison, Edward F. Accounting for Slower Economic Growth: An Update. In *Kendrick, J. W., ed.,* 1984, pp. 1–45. [G: U.S.]

Desai, Meghnad. An Econometric Model of the Share of Wages in National Income: UK 1855–1965. In *Goodwin, R. M.; Krüger, M. and Vercelli, A., eds.,* 1984, pp. 253–77. [G: U.K.]

Di Fonzo, Tommaso; Rettore, Enrico and Trivellato, Ugo. Stime preliminari e revisioni degli aggregati di contabilità nazionale a prezzi correnti. (Provisional and Revised Estimates of Italian National Accounts Aggregates at Current Prices. With English summary.) *Statistica,* October–December 1984, *44*(4), pp. 649–73. [G: Italy]

DiLullo, Anthony J. U.S. International Transactions, Third Quarter, 1984. *Surv. Curr. Bus.,* December 1984, *64*(12), pp. 41–64. [G: U.S.]

Dixon, Peter B. and McDonald, Daina. Developments in Output, Employment, Prices, Wages, and Profits: Australia, 1983–84 and 1984–85. *Australian Econ. Rev.,* 4th Quarter 1984, (68), pp. 3–17. [G: Australia]

Donahoe, Gerald F. The National Income and Product Accounts: Preliminary Revised Estimates, 1977. *Surv. Curr. Bus.,* May 1984, *64*(5), pp. 38–41. [G: U.S.]

Douty, H. M. A Century of Wage Statistics: The BLS Contribution. *Mon. Lab. Rev.,* November 1984, *107*(11), pp. 16–28. [G: U.S.]

Drechsler, Laszlo. Recent Developments in the National Accounting System of Hungary. *Statist. J.,* August 1984, *2*(3), pp. 243–53. [G: Hungary]

Easton, Stephen T. Real Output and the Gold Standard Years, 1830–1913. In *Bordo, M. D. and Schwartz, A. J., eds.,* 1984, pp. 513–38. [G: OECD]

Ellman, Michael. Investment Planning in the State Socialist Countries and its Relevance for Reindustrialisation. In *Ellman, M.,* 1984, *1980,* pp. 174–97. [G: E. Europe]

Ellman, Michael. Natural Gas, Restructuring and Re-industrialisation: The Dutch Experience of Industrial Policy. In *Ellman, M.,* 1984, *1981,* pp. 253–72. [G: Netherlands]

Felderer, Bernhard. Population and Per-capita Income in Simulation Models. In *Steinmann, G., ed.,* 1984, pp. 132–46. [G: W. Germany]

Frey, Bruno S. Schattenwirtschaft und Wirtschaftspolitik. (Shadow Economy and Eco-

nomic Policy. With English summary.) *Kredit Kapital*, 1984, *17*(1), pp. 102–19.
[G: Selected OECD]

Frey, Bruno S. and Pommerehne, Werner W. The Hidden Economy: State and Prospects for Measurement. *Rev. Income Wealth*, March 1984, *30*(1), pp. 1–23. [G: OECD]

Frey, Bruno S. and Weck-Hanneman, Hannelore. The Hidden Economy as an 'Unobserved' Variable. *Europ. Econ. Rev.*, October–November 1984, *26*(1–2), pp. 33–53. [G: OECD]

Friedman, Benjamin M. Managing the U.S. Government Deficit in the 1980s. In *Wachter, M. L. and Wachter, S. M., eds.*, 1984, pp. 265–301. [G: U.S.]

Gaudin, Jocelyne and Schiray, Michel. L'économie cachée en France: état du débat et bilan des travaux. (The Hidden Economy in France: A State of the Art Review. With English summary.) *Revue Écon.*, July 1984, *35*(4), pp. 691–731. [G: France]

Goldsmith, Raymond W. An Estimate of the Size and Structure of the National Product of the Early Roman Empire. *Rev. Income Wealth*, September 1984, *30*(3), pp. 263–88.
[G: Italy]

Goldsmith, Raymond W. The Stability of the Ratio of Nonfinancial Debt to Income. *Banca Naz. Lavoro Quart. Rev.*, September 1984, (150), pp. 285–305.

Gordon, Robert J. An Econometric Model of France during the 19th Century: Comments. *Europ. Econ. Rev.*, June 1984, *25*(1), pp. 143–46. [G: France]

Gordon, Robert J. Unemployment and Potential Output in the 1980s. *Brookings Pap. Econ. Act.*, 1984, (2), pp. 537–64. [G: U.S.]

Goudreau, Karen; Oberheu, Howard and Vaughan, Denton R. An Assessment of the Quality of Survey Reports of Income from the Aid to Families with Dependent Children (AFDC) Program. *J. Bus. Econ. Statist.*, April 1984, *2*(2), pp. 179–86. [G: U.S.]

Gramlich, Edward M. How Bad Are the Large Deficits? In *Mills, G. B. and Palmer, J. L., eds.*, 1984, pp. 43–68. [G: U.S.]

Haveman, Robert H. How Bad Are the Large Deficits? Comment. In *Mills, G. B. and Palmer, J. L., eds.*, 1984, pp. 69–73.
[G: U.S.]

Hjerppe, Riitta; Peltonen, Matti and Pihkala, Erkki. Investment in Finland, 1860–1979. *Scand. Econ. Hist. Rev.*, 1984, *32*(1), pp. 42–59. [G: Finland]

Holland, Daniel M. Measuring and Combatting Income Tax Evasion. In *Hanusch, H., ed.*, 1984, pp. 329–48. [G: U.S.]

Holland, Daniel M. Measuring Profitability and Capital Costs: Introduction and Summary. In *Holland, D. M., ed.*, 1984, pp. 1–42.
[G: OECD; Finland]

Holland, Daniel M. and Myers, Stewart C. Trends in Corporate Profitability and Capital Costs in the United States. In *Holland, D. M., ed.*, 1984, pp. 43–115. [G: U.S.]

Howenstine, Ned G. U.S. Direct Investment

Abroad in 1983. *Surv. Curr. Bus.*, August 1984, *64*(8), pp. 18–40. [G: U.S.]

Howrey, E. Philip. Data Revision, Reconstruction, and Prediction: An Application to Inventory Investment. *Rev. Econ. Statist.*, August 1984, *66*(3), pp. 386–93. [G: U.S.]

Khamis, Salem H. On Aggregation Methods for International Comparisons. *Rev. Income Wealth*, June 1984, *30*(2), pp. 185–205.

King, Mervyn A. and Mairesse, Jacques. Profitability in Britain and France 1956–1975: A Comparative Study. In *Holland, D. M., ed.*, 1984, pp. 221–71. [G: U.K.; France]

Klovland, Jan Tore. Tax Evasion and the Demand for Currency in Norway and Sweden. Is There a Hidden Relationship? *Scand. J. Econ.*, 1984, *86*(4), pp. 423–39. [G: Norway; Sweden]

Koizumi, Susumu. Wage–Employment Contract and Okun's Law. (In Japanese. With English summary.) *Osaka Econ. Pap.*, December 1984, *34*(2–3), pp. 27–35. [G: Japan; U.S.]

Koskenkylä, Heikki. Rates of Return, Cost of Capital, and Valuation Rates in Finnish Manufacturing 1960–1980. In *Holland, D. M., ed.*, 1984, pp. 387–419. [G: Finland]

Kozlow, Ralph. Capital Expenditures by Majority-Owned Foreign Affiliates of U.S. Companies, 1984. *Surv. Curr. Bus.*, March 1984, *64*(3), pp. 32–37. [G: U.S.]

Kravis, Irving B. Comparative Studies of National Incomes and Prices. *J. Econ. Lit.*, March 1984, *22*(1), pp. 1–39. [G: Selected Countries]

Landefeld, J. Steven and Seskin, Eugene P. Plant and Equipment Expenditures, First and Second Quarters and Second Half of 1984. *Surv. Curr. Bus.*, March 1984, *64*(3), pp. 26–31.
[G: U.S.]

de Leeuw, Frank. Conflicting Measures of Private Saving. *Surv. Curr. Bus.*, November 1984, *64*(11), pp. 17–23. [G: U.S.]

Lejeune, Guy. De B.N.P. schattingen: groeivoeten en statistische aanpassingen. (With English summary.) *Cah. Écon. Bruxelles*, 3rd Trimester 1984, (103), pp. 485–507. [G: Belgium]

Locker, Hugo Krijnse and Faerber, H. D. Space and Time Comparisons of Purchasing Power Parities and Real Values. *Rev. Income Wealth*, March 1984, *30*(1), pp. 53–83. [G: EEC]

Marczewski, Jean. Le concept de coût macroéconomique et son utilité. (The Concept of Macroeconomic Cost and Its Utility. With English summary.) *Écon. Appl.*, 1984, *37*(3–4), pp. 457–88. [G: France; W. Germany]

Marris, Robin. Comparing the Incomes of Nations: A Critique of the International Comparison Project. *J. Econ. Lit.*, March 1984, *22*(1), pp. 40–57.

Martin, Frank D.; Landefeld, J. Steven and Peskin, Janice. The Value of Services Provided by the Stock of Government-owned Fixed Capital in the United States, 1948–79. *Rev. Income Wealth*, September 1984, *30*(3), pp. 331–49.
[G: U.S.]

Matthews, K. G. P. The GDP Residual Error and the Black Economy: A Note. *Appl. Econ.*, June 1984, *16*(3), pp. 443–48. [G: U.K.]

McDonald, Richard J. The "Underground Economy" and BLS Statistical Data. *Mon. Lab. Rev.*, January 1984, *107*(1), pp. 4–18.
[G: U.S.]

McKenzie, Sandra K. Concurrent Seasonal Adjustment with Census X-11. *J. Bus. Econ. Statist.*, July 1984, *2*(3), pp. 235–49. [G: U.S.]

de Montbrial, Thierry. An Econometric Model of France during the 19th Century: Comments. *Europ. Econ. Rev.*, June 1984, *25*(1), pp. 147–48. [G: France]

Mosley, Paul. The Behaviour of the Macro-economy. In *Sandford, C. and Bradbury, M., eds.*, 1984, pp. 145–63. [G: U.K.]

Murphy, Robert G. Capital Mobility and the Relationship between Saving and Investment Rates in OECD Countries. *J. Int. Money Finance*, December 1984, *3*(3), pp. 327–42.
[G: OECD]

Neal, Larry. Slowing Population Growth and Investment Demand: The West German Case. In *Steinmann, G., ed.*, 1984, pp. 179–202.
[G: W. Germany]

Nechemias, Carol and Bahry, Donna. The Soviet Union: Consumer Sector. In *Groth, A. J. and Wade, L. L., eds.*, 1984, pp. 101–26.
[G: U.S.S.R.]

Nelson, Charles R. A Benchmark for the Accuracy of Econometric Forecasts of GNP. *Bus. Econ.*, April 1984, *19*(3), pp. 52–58. [G: U.S.]

Norsworthy, J. R. Capital Input Measurement: Options and Inaccuracies. In *Intn'l. Productivity Symp.*, 1984, pp. 73–94. [G: U.S.]

Onofri, Paolo and Stagni, Anna. Rate of Profit and Return on Financial Assets in Italian Industry 1951–1981. In *Holland, D. M., ed.*, 1984, pp. 465–80. [G: Italy]

Park, Thae S. Personal Income and Adjusted Gross Income, 1980-82. *Surv. Curr. Bus.*, April 1984, *64*(4), pp. 53–55. [G: U.S.]

Parker, Robert P. Improved Adjustments for Misreporting of Tax Return Information Used to Estimate the National Income and Product Accounts, 1977. *Surv. Curr. Bus.*, June 1984, *64*(6), pp. 17–25. [G: U.S.]

Pommerehne, Werner W. and Frey, Bruno S. L'économie souterraine: problèmes de mesure et résultats quantitatifs. (With English summary.) *Revue Écon. Polit.*, May–June 1984, *94*(3), pp. 375–98. [G: U.S.; EEC; Canada]

Porter, Richard D. and Bayer, Amanda S. A Monetary Perspective on Underground Economic Activity in the United States. *Fed. Res. Bull.*, March 1984, *70*(3), pp. 177–90.
[G: U.S.]

Pryor, Frederic L. A Quantitative Study of the Structure and Behavior of Consumption and Prices in Different Economic Systems. In *Bohnet, A., ed.*, 1984, pp. 213–46.
[G: Selected Countries]

Reuter, Peter. The Economic Significance of Illegal Markets in the United States: Some Observations. *Econ. Lavoro*, Jan.-Mar. 1984, *18*(1), pp. 135–42. [G: U.S.]

Ricketts, Martin. On the Simple Macroeconomics of Tax Evasion: An Elaboration of the Peacock-Shaw Approach. *Public Finance*, 1984, *39*(3), pp. 420–24.

Rose, Richard and Karran, Terence. Inertia or Incrementalism? A Long-term View of the Growth of Government. In *Groth, A. J. and Wade, L. L., eds.*, 1984, pp. 43–71.
[G: OECD]

Russo, William J., Jr. and Rutledge, Gary L. Plant and Equipment Expenditures by Business for Pollution Abatement, 1983 and Planned 1984. *Surv. Curr. Bus.*, June 1984, *64*(6), pp. 31–34. [G: U.S.]

Sahling, Leonard and Akhtar, M. A. What Is Behind the Capital Spending Boom? *Fed. Res. Bank New York Quart. Rev.*, Winter 1984–85, *9*(4), pp. 19–30. [G: U.S.]

Salemi, Michael K. Real Economic Activity in Switzerland. *Schweiz. Z. Volkswirtsch. Statist.*, December 1984, *120*(4), pp. 521–46.
[G: Switzerland]

Schwerin, Don S. Historic Compromise and Pluralist Decline? Profits and Capital in the Nordic Countries. In *Goldthorpe, J. H., ed.*, 1984, pp. 231–56. [G: OECD]

Seskin, Eugene P. Plant and Equipment Expenditures: Quarters of 1984, First and Second Quarters of 1985, Year 1985. *Surv. Curr. Bus.*, December 1984, *64*(12), pp. 23–25. [G: U.S.]

Seskin, Eugene P. Plant and Equipment Expenditures, the Four Quarters of 1984. *Surv. Curr. Bus.*, September 1984, *64*(9), pp. 24–27.
[G: U.S.]

Seskin, Eugene P. and Landefeld, J. Steven. Plant and Equipment Expenditures, the Four Quarters of 1984. *Surv. Curr. Bus.*, June 1984, *64*(6), pp. 26–30. [G: U.S.]

Seskin, Eugene P. and Landefeld, J. Steven. Plant and Equipment Expenditures, 1984. *Surv. Curr. Bus.*, January 1984, *64*(1), pp. 26–29. [G: U.S.]

Singh, A. K. Planning in a Mixed Economy: The Indian Experience. In *Singh, A. K.; Papola, T. S. and Mathur, R. S., eds.*, 1984, pp. 148–64. [G: India]

Slater, Courtenay. The Impact of Recession on Profits and Employee Compensation. *Bus. Econ.*, October 1984, *19*(5), pp. 18–25.
[G: U.S.]

Smyshliaeva, L. Improving the Structure of Reproduction of Capital Investments. *Prob. Econ.*, July 1984, *27*(3), pp. 61–79.
[G: U.S.S.R.]

Summers, Robert and Heston, Alan. Improved International Comparisons of Real Product and Its Composition: 1950–1980. *Rev. Income Wealth*, June 1984, *30*(2), pp. 207–62.
[G: Global]

Szarvas, Péter. Capital Formation in Hungary in International Comparison. *Acta Oecon.*, 1984, *32*(3–4), pp. 303–16. [G: Selected Countries]

Szilágyi, György. Procedures for Updating the Results of International Comparisons. *Rev. Income Wealth*, June 1984, *30*(2), pp. 153–65.
[G: Europe; U.S.]

Tanzi, Vito. The Underground Economy in the United States: Comment. *Int. Monet. Fund*

Staff Pap., December 1984, *31*(4), pp. 747–50. [G: U.S.]

Tarasofsky, Abraham. Aggregate Rates of Return in Canada. In *Holland, D. M., ed.*, 1984, pp. 313–44. [G: Canada]

Waelbroeck, Jean. The Logic of EC Commercial and Industrial Policy Making. In *Jacquemin, A., ed.*, 1984, pp. 99–144. [G: EEC]

Wakasugi, Takaaki, et al. Measuring the Profitability of the Nonfinancial Corporate Sector in Japan. In *Holland, D. M., ed.*, 1984, pp. 345–86. [G: Japan]

Weck, Hannelore and Frey, Bruno S. Tax Financing and the Shadow Economy. In *Hanusch, H., ed.*, 1984, pp. 313–27. [G: OECD]

Williams, Norman P. United Kingdom Industrial Sectors' Rates of Return. In *Holland, D. M., ed.*, 1984, pp. 177–219. [G: U.K.]

Williamson, Jeffrey G. Why Was British Growth So Slow during the Industrial Revolution? *J. Econ. Hist.*, September 1984, *44*(3), pp. 687–712. [G: U.K.]

Wolff, Edward N. Accounting for Slower Economic Growth: An Update: Comment. In *Kendrick, J. W., ed.*, 1984, pp. 47–58. [G: U.S.]

Wood, Geoffrey E. Real Output and the Gold Standard Years, 1830–1913: Comment. In *Bordo, M. D. and Schwartz, A. J., eds.*, 1984, pp. 538–44. [G: OECD]

Woodham, Douglas M. Potential Output Growth and the Long-Term Inflation Outlook. *Fed. Res. Bank New York Quart. Rev.*, Summer 1984, *9*(2), pp. 16–23. [G: U.S.]

Wynia, Gary W. Argentina: The Frustration of Ungovernability. In *Wesson, R., ed.*, 1984, pp. 14–37. [G: Argentina]

Yu, Eden S.-H. and Hwang, Been Kwei. The Relationship between Energy and GNP: Further Results. *Energy Econ.*, July 1984, *6*(3), pp. 186–90. [G: U.S.]

Yunker, James A. The Distribution of Lifetime Capital Property Income under Capitalism and Market Socialism. *ACES Bull.*, Summer–Fall 1984, *26*(2–3), pp. 77–97.

2213 Income Distribution

Adelman, Irma. Development Strategies and the Size Distribution of World Income. *METU*, 1984, *11*(1–2), pp. 177–93. [G: LDCs]

Adelman, Irma and Levy, Amnon. Decomposing Theil's Income of Income Inequality into Between and Within Components: A Note. *Rev. Income Wealth*, March 1984, *30*(1), pp. 119–21. [G: Israel]

Agarwala, Ramgopal. Price Distortions and Growth. *Finance Develop.*, March 1984, *21*(1), pp. 33–37. [G: LDCs]

Alam, M. Shahid. Consumption and Employment Effects of Income Redistribution in Pakistan: Comment. *Pakistan Devel. Rev.*, Summer-Autumn 1984, *23*(2&3), pp. 361–63. [G: Pakistan]

Altimir, Oscar. Poverty, Income Distribution and Child Welfare in Latin America: A Comparison

of Pre- and Post-Recession Data. *World Devel.*, March 1984, *12*(3), pp. 261–82. [G: Chile; Colombia; Costa Rica; Panama; Venezuela]

Aspe, Pedro and Beristain, Javier. The Evolution of Income Distribution Policies during The Post-Revolutionary Period in Mexico. In *Aspe, P. and Sigmund, P. E., eds.*, 1984, pp. 15–29. [G: Mexico]

Aspe, Pedro and Beristain, Javier. Toward a First Estimate of the Evolution of Inequality in Mexico. In *Aspe, P. and Sigmund, P. E., eds.*, 1984, pp. 31–57. [G: Mexico]

Avery, Robert B.; Elliehausen, Gregory E. and Canner, Glenn B. Survey of Consumer Finances, 1983. *Fed. Res. Bull.*, September 1984, *70*(9), pp. 679–92. [G: U.S.]

van Batenburg, Paul and Tinbergen, Jan. Income Distribution: A Correction and a Generalization. *Weltwirtsch. Arch.*, 1984, *120*(2), pp. 361–65.

Behrens, Alfredo. Energy and Output Implications of Income Redistribution in Brazil. *Energy Econ.*, April 1984, *6*(2), pp. 110–16. [G: Brazil]

Bell, Ralph. Item Nonresponse in Telephone Surveys: An Analysis of Who Fails to Report Income. *Soc. Sci. Quart.*, March 1984, *65*(1), pp. 207–15. [G: U.S.]

Bergson, Abram. Income Inequality under Soviet Socialism. *J. Econ. Lit.*, September 1984, *22*(3), pp. 1052–99. [G: U.S.S.R.]

Berry, Albert. Income Distribution Trends in Labor Surplus Economies. In *[Reynolds, L. G.]*, 1984, pp. 182–200. [G: LDCs]

Betson, David and van der Gaag, Jacques. Working Married Women and the Distribution of Income. *J. Human Res.*, Fall 1984, *19*(4), pp. 532–43. [G: U.S.]

Betson, David and Haveman, Robert H. The Role of Income Transfers in Reducing Inequality between and within Regions. In *Moon, M., ed.*, 1984, pp. 283–322. [G: U.S.]

Booth, John A. "Trickle-Up" Income Redistribution and Development in Central America During the 1960s and 1970s. In *Seligson, M. A., ed.*, 1984, pp. 351–65. [G: Central America]

Brown, J. A. C. and Mazzarino, G. Drawing the Lorenz Curve and Calculating the Gini Concentration Index from Grouped Data by Computer. *Oxford Bull. Econ. Statist.*, August 1984, *46*(3), pp. 273–78. [G: U.K.]

Budd, Edward C.; Radner, Daniel B. and Whiteman, T. Cameron. An Accounting Framework for Transfer Payments and Its Implications for the Size Distribution of Income. In *Moon, M., ed.*, 1984, pp. 37–83. [G: U.S.]

Burkett, John P. Capitalistic and Market Socialistic Distribution of Lifetime Capital Property: Comment. *Atlantic Econ. J.*, December 1984, *12*(4), pp. 73.

Cheema, Aftab Ahmad and Malik, Muhammad Hussain. Consumption and Employment Effects of Income Redistribution in Pakistan. *Pakistan Devel. Rev.*, Summer-Autumn 1984, *23*(2&3), pp. 347–59. [G: Pakistan]

Conlisk, John. Four Invalid Propositions about Equality, Efficiency, and Intergenerational Transfers through Schooling. *J. Human Res.*, Winter 1984, *19*(1), pp. 3–21.

Cowell, Frank A. The Structure of American Income Inequality. *Rev. Income Wealth*, September 1984, *30*(3), pp. 351–75. [G: U.S.]

Creedy, John and Gemmell, Norman. Income Redistribution through Taxes and Transfers in Britain. *Scot. J. Polit. Econ.*, February 1984, *31*(1), pp. 44–59. [G: U.K.]

Danziger, Sheldon, et al. Income Transfers and the Economic Status of the Elderly. In *Moon, M., ed.*, 1984, pp. 239–76. [G: U.S.]

DaVanzo, Julie and Kusnic, Michael. Regional Income Differences and the Definition of Income: The Case of Malaysia. *Int. Reg. Sci. Rev.*, September 1984, *9*(1), pp. 59–73. [G: Malaysia]

David, Martin and Menchik, Paul L. Nonearned Income, Income Instability, and Inequality: A Life-Cycle Interpretation. In *[Ferber, R.]*, 1984, pp. 53–73. [G: U.S.]

Dawkins, Peter and Sloan, Judith. The Australian Labour Market, June 1984. *Australian Bull. Lab.*, June 1984, *10*(3), pp. 113–33. [G: Australia]

Denslow, David A., Jr. and Tyler, William. Perspectives on Poverty and Income Inequality in Brazil. *World Devel.*, October 1984, *12*(10), pp. 1019–28. [G: Brazil]

Dieguez, Héctor L. and Petrecolla, Alberto. Income Distribution in Greater Buenos Aires. In *[Ferber, R.]*, 1984, pp. 123–44. [G: Argentina]

Dostovalov, Y. L. Notions of the Distribution of Material Wealth and Incomes under Socialism. In *Smirnov, A. D.; Golosov, V. V. and Maximova, V. F., eds.*, 1984, pp. 263–71.

Downes, E. Beverly. Tanzania (1969) In *van Ginneken, W. and Park, J., eds.*, 1984, pp. 145–49. [G: Tanzania]

Ebert, Udo. Measures of Distance between Income Distributions. *J. Econ. Theory*, April 1984, *32*(2), pp. 266–74.

Ellman, Michael. Income Distribution in the USSR. In *Ellman, M.*, 1984, pp. 112–29. [G: U.S.S.R.]

Ellman, Michael. The Distribution of Earnings under Brezhnev. In *Ellman, M.*, 1984, *1980*, pp. 108–11. [G: U.S.S.R.]

Fields, Gary S. Employment, Income Distribution and Economic Growth in Seven Small Open Economies. *Econ. J.*, March 1984, *94*(373), pp. 74–83. [G: Selected LDCs]

Figueroa, Adolfo. The Distribution Problem in Different Sociopolitical and Economic Contexts: Peru, 1950–1980. In *[Ferber, R.]*, 1984, pp. 145–67. [G: Peru]

Fisch, Oscar. Regional Income Inequality and Economic Development. *Reg. Sci. Urban Econ.*, February 1984, *14*(1), pp. 89–111. [G: U.S.]

Friedenberg, Howard and Bretzfelder, Robert. Regional Shifts in Personal Income by Industrial Component, 1959–83. *Surv. Curr. Bus.*, November 1984, *64*(11), pp. 28–36. [G: U.S.]

Fry, Vanessa C. Inequality in Family Earnings. *Fisc. Stud.*, August 1984, *5*(3), pp. 54–61. [G: U.K.]

Furtan, W. H. and Clark, J. S. An Application of the New Household Economics to Explaining Farm Income Distributions. *Can. J. Agr. Econ.*, March 1984, *32*(1), pp. 151–62. [G: Canada]

van Ginneken, Wouter. Denmark (1976) In *van Ginneken, W. and Park, J., eds.*, 1984, pp. 33–39. [G: Denmark]

van Ginneken, Wouter. Federal Republic of Germany (1974) In *van Ginneken, W. and Park, J., eds.*, 1984, pp. 65–68. [G: W. Germany]

van Ginneken, Wouter. France (1975) In *van Ginneken, W. and Park, J., eds.*, 1984, pp. 59–63. [G: France]

van Ginneken, Wouter. Ireland (1973) In *van Ginneken, W. and Park, J., eds.*, 1984, pp. 83–88. [G: Ireland]

van Ginneken, Wouter. Mexico (1968) In *van Ginneken, W. and Park, J., eds.*, 1984, pp. 95–99. [G: Mexico]

van Ginneken, Wouter. Spain (1973–74) In *van Ginneken, W. and Park, J., eds.*, 1984, pp. 125–30. [G: Spain]

van Ginneken, Wouter. Sweden (1979) In *van Ginneken, W. and Park, J., eds.*, 1984, pp. 139–44. [G: Sweden]

van Ginneken, Wouter. United Kingdom (1979) In *van Ginneken, W. and Park, J., eds.*, 1984, pp. 157–61. [G: U.K.]

Giorgi, Giovanni Maria. A Methodological Survey of Recent Studies for the Measurement of Inequality of Economic Welfare Carried Out by Some Italian Statisticians. *Econ. Notes*, 1984, (1), pp. 146–58.

Gottschalk, Peter. The Role of Income Transfers in Reducing Inequality between and within Regions: Comment. In *Moon, M., ed.*, 1984, pp. 322–26. [G: U.S.]

Gupta, Gir S. and Singh, Ram D. Income Inequality across Nations over Time: How Much and Why. *Southern Econ. J.*, July 1984, *51*(1), pp. 250–57. [G: LDCs; OECD]

Gupta, Manash Ranjan. Functional Form for Estimating the Lorenz Curve. *Econometrica*, September 1984, *52*(5), pp. 1313–14.

Heroles, Jesús F. Reyes. The Distribution of Labor Income in Mexico. In *Aspe, P. and Sigmund, P. E., eds.*, 1984, pp. 129–86. [G: Mexico]

van der Hoeven, Rolf. Zambia (1976) In *van Ginneken, W. and Park, J., eds.*, 1984, pp. 169–74. [G: Zambia]

Ingberg, Mikael. Eläkkeet ja tulonjako. (Pensions and Redistribution. With English summary.) *Kansant. Aikak.*, 1984, *80*(2), pp. 141–62. [G: Finland]

Kakwani, Nanak. The Relative Deprivation Curve and Its Applications: Reply. *J. Bus. Econ. Statist.*, October 1984, *2*(4), pp. 400–405. [G: Australia]

Kakwani, Nanak. The Relative Deprivation Curve and Its Applications. *J. Bus. Econ. Statist.*, October 1984, *2*(4), pp. 384–94.
[G: Australia]

Kanbur, S. M. Ravi. The Measurement and Decomposition of Inequality and Poverty. In *van der Ploeg, F., ed.*, 1984, pp. 403–32.

Kansal, S. Bangladesh (1973–74) In *van Ginneken, W. and Park, J., eds.*, 1984, pp. 23–31.
[G: Bangladesh]

Kansal, S. Nepal (1976–77) In *van Ginneken, W. and Park, J., eds.*, 1984, pp. 101–06.
[G: Nepal]

Kansal, S. Sierra Leone (1967–69) In *van Ginneken, W. and Park, J., eds.*, 1984, pp. 119–23.
[G: Sierra Leone]

Kansal, S. Sudan (1967–68) In *van Ginneken, W. and Park, J., eds.*, 1984, pp. 131–37.
[G: Sudan]

Kennedy, Thomas E. and Nord, Stephen. The Effect of City Size on the Urban Income Distribution through Time: 1950–70. *Appl. Econ.*, October 1984, *16*(5), pp. 717–28. [G: U.S.]

Kim, Kwan S. and Turrubiate, Gerardo. Structures of Foreign Trade and Income Distribution: The Case of Mexico. *J. Devel. Econ.*, December 1984, *16*(3), pp. 263–78. [G: Mexico]

Kmietowicz, Z. W. The Bivariate Lognormal Model for the Distribution of Household Size and Income. *Manchester Sch. Econ. Soc. Stud.*, June 1984, *52*(2), pp. 196–210.
[G: Iraq; Kenya]

Kocher, James E. Income Distribution and Fertility. In *Schutjer, W. A. and Stokes, C. S., eds.*, 1984, pp. 216–34. [G: LDCs]

Koo, Hagen. The Political Economy of Income Distribution in South Korea: The Impact of the State's Industrialization Policy. *World Devel.*, October 1984, *12*(10), pp. 1029–37.
[G: S. Korea]

Korayem, Karima. Egypt (1974–75) In *van Ginneken, W. and Park, J., eds.*, 1984, pp. 41–48. [G: Egypt]

Kuo, Shirley W. Y. Urbanization and Income Distribution: The Case of Taiwan, 1966–1980. In *[Chenery, H. B.]*, 1984, pp. 217–34.
[G: Taiwan]

Kurz, Rudi. Staatsverschuldung und Einkommensverteilung. Einige kritische Anmerkungen zur These von den unsozialen Verteilungswirkungen. (Public Debt and Income Distribution: Some Critical Notes on Unsocial Distributional Effect. With English summary.) *Konjunkturpolitik*, 1984, *30*(4), pp. 217–32.
[G: W. Germany]

Lam, D. The Variance of Population Characteristics in Stable Populations, with Applications to the Distribution of Income. *Population Stud.*, March 1984, *38*(1), pp. 117–27.
[G: Brazil; U.S.]

Lambert, Peter J. Non-equiproportionate Income Growth, Inequality, and the Income Tax. *Public Finance*, 1984, *39*(1), pp. 104–18.
[G: U.K.]

Lampman, Robert. An Accounting Framework for Transfer Payments and Its Implications for the Size Distribution of Income: Comment. In *Moon, M., ed.*, 1984, pp. 83–86.
[G: U.S.]

Le Grand, Julian. Évaluation de l'impact redistributif des dépenses publiques. Quelques problèmes méthodologiques. (On Measuring the Distributional Impact of Public Expenditures: Some Methodological Problems. With English summary.) *Consommation*, July–September 1984, *31*(3), pp. 3–17. [G: France]

Lee, Byung Sung. Analytical Comparisons of Internal, External and Differential Indices of Income Inequality between Black and White for 1964–1977. *Amer. Econ.*, Fall 1984, *28*(2), pp. 41–47. [G: U.S.]

Lehrer, Evelyn and Nerlove, Marc. A Life-Cycle Analysis of Family Income Distribution. *Econ. Inquiry*, July 1984, *22*(3), pp. 360–74.
[G: U.S.]

Lundborg, Per. The Nexus between Income Distribution, Trade Policy, and Monopoly Power: An Assessment of the Tin Market. *J. Policy Modeling*, February 1984, *6*(1), pp. 69–79.
[G: Malaysia]

Mahmood, Zafar. Income Inequality in Pakistan: An Analysis of Existing Evidence. *Pakistan Devel. Rev.*, Summer–Autumn 1984, *23*(2&3), pp. 365–76. [G: Pakistan]

McDonald, James B. Some Generalized Functions for the Size Distribution of Income. *Econometrica*, May 1984, *52*(3), pp. 647–63.
[G: U.S.]

Mehran, F. Islamic Republic of Iran (1973–74) In *van Ginneken, W. and Park, J., eds.*, 1984, pp. 75–81. [G: Iran]

Mellor, John W. Food Price Policy and Income Distribution in Low-Income Countries. In *Eicher, C. K. and Staatz, J. M., eds.*, 1984, 1978, pp. 147–67. [G: India]

Michel, Richard C., et al. Are We Better Off in 1984? *Challenge*, September/October 1984, *27*(4), pp. 10–17. [G: U.S.]

Moon, Marilyn and Sawhill, Isabel V. Family Incomes: Gainers and Losers. In *Palmer, J. L. and Sawhill, I. V., eds.*, 1984, pp. 317–46.
[G: U.S.]

Morrisson, Christian. Income Distribution in East European and Western Countries. *J. Compar. Econ.*, June 1984, *8*(2), pp. 121–38.
[G: Europe; Canada; U.S.]

Mulkey, David and Espinal, Juan Jose. Income Dimensions of Caribbean Development Problems: The Las Cuevas Region of the Dominican Republic. *Rev. Reg. Stud.*, Fall 1984, *14*(3), pp. 3–8. [G: Dominican Republic]

Muller, Edward N. Financial Dependence in the Capitalist World Economy and the Distribution of Income Within Nations. In *Seligson, M. A., ed.*, 1984, pp. 256–82.
[G: Selected Countries]

Musgrove, Philip. Household Income Distribution in the Dominican Republic: A First Look at New Survey Data. In *[Ferber, R.]*, 1984, pp. 95–121. [G: Dominican Republic]

Negri, Nicola and Santagata, Walter. Distribuzione del reddito e ineguaglianze in un'area urbana. Una analisi empirica. (Inequality and Personal Income Distribution in an Urban Area. With English summary.) *Econ. Lavoro,* July-Sept. 1984, *18*(3), pp. 63–76. **[G: Italy]**

Nelson, Joel I. Income Inequality: The American States. *Soc. Sci. Quart.,* September 1984, *65*(3), pp. 854–60. **[G: U.S.]**

Nevile, J. W. and Warren, Neil A. Inflation and Personal Income Distribution in Australia. *Australian Econ. Rev.,* 1st Quarter 1984, (65), pp. 26–33. **[G: Australia]**

Nord, Stephen. An Economic Analysis of Changes in the Relative Shape of the Interstate Size Distribution of Family Income during the 1960's. *Rivista Int. Sci. Econ. Com.,* August 1984, *31*(8), pp. 787–800. **[G: U.S.]**

Nord, Stephen. An Economic Analysis of Changes in the Relative Shape of the Interstate Size Distribution of Family Income during the 1960's. *Amer. Econ.,* Fall 1984, *28*(2), pp. 18–25. **[G: U.S.]**

Park, J.-G. Panama (1976) In *van Ginneken, W. and Park, J.,* eds., 1984, pp. 107–11. **[G: Panama]**

Park, J.-G. Trinidad and Tobago (1975–76) In *van Ginneken, W. and Park, J.,* eds., 1984, pp. 151–55. **[G: Trinidad and Tabago]**

Park, J.-G. Yugoslavia (1978) In *van Ginneken, W. and Park, J.,* eds., 1984, pp. 163–67. **[G: Yugoslavia]**

Pestieau, Pierre. The Effects of Varying Family Size on the Transmission and Distribution of Wealth. *Oxford Econ. Pap.,* November 1984, *36*(3), pp. 400–417.

Práger, László. The Impoverished Rich and the Well-to-Do Poor (Investigations Concerning Personal Income). *Eastern Europ. Econ.,* Winter 1984–85, *23*(2), pp. 3–28. **[G: Hungary]**

Pratschke, John L. Aspects of the Redistribution of Income in Urban and Rural Ireland, 1973–1980. *Irish J. Agr. Econ. Rural Soc.,* 1984, *10*(1), pp. 13–27. **[G: U.K.]**

Ram, Rati. Population Increase, Economic Growth, Educational Inequality, and Income Distribution: Some Recent Evidence. *J. Devel. Econ.,* April 1984, *14*(3), pp. 419–28.

Rao, B. India (1975–76) In *van Ginneken, W. and Park, J.,* eds., 1984, pp. 69–74. **[G: India]**

Rao, B. Philippines (1970–71) In *van Ginneken, W. and Park, J.,* eds., 1984, pp. 113–17. **[G: Philippines]**

Rao, S. J. Some Reflections on Income Distribution and Poverty in Asia with Special Reference to India. In *Ghosh, P. K.,* ed., no. 18, 1984, *1979,* pp. 239–66. **[G: India; Asia]**

Rosen, Sherwin. The Relative Deprivation Curve and Its Applications. *J. Bus. Econ. Statist.,* October 1984, *2*(4), pp. 395–97. **[G: Australia]**

Rubinson, Richard. The World-Economy and the Distribution of Income Within States: A Cross-National Study. In *Seligson, M. A.,* ed., 1984, *1976,* pp. 156–86. **[G: Selected Countries]**

Ryscavage, Paul and Lamas, Enrique. The Relative Deprivation Curve and Its Applications: Comment. *J. Bus. Econ. Statist.,* October 1984, *2*(4), pp. 398–99. **[G: Australia]**

Sandford, Cedric. Distribution of Income and Wealth. In *Sandford, C. and Bradbury, M.,* eds., 1984, pp. 93–116. **[G: U.K.; Selected Countries]**

Sarma, I. R. K. Recent Trends in the Distribution of Personal Income. *Margin,* January 1984, *16*(2), pp. 86–94. **[G: India]**

Seligson, Mitchell A. Inequality in a Global Perspective: Directions for Further Research. In *Seligson, M. A.,* ed., 1984, pp. 397–408. **[G: Global]**

Sen, Amartya. The Welfare Basis of Real Income Comparisons. In *Sen, A.,* 1984, *1979,* pp. 389–451.

Soroka, Lewis A. City Size and Income Distributions: The Canadian Experience. *Urban Stud.,* November 1984, *21*(4), pp. 359–66. **[G: Canada]**

Srinivasan, T. N. Development, Poverty, and Basic Human Needs: Some Issues. In *Ghosh, P. K.,* ed., no. 13, 1984, *1977,* pp. 7–28. **[G: LDCs]**

Stavenuiter, S. Fiji (1977) In *van Ginneken, W. and Park, J.,* eds., 1984, pp. 49–57. **[G: Fiji]**

Summers, Robert; Kravis, Irving B. and Heston, Alan. Changes in the World Income Distribution. *J. Policy Modeling,* May 1984, *6*(2), pp. 237–69. **[G: Global]**

Tahar, Gabriel. La variance des salaires réels, indicateur d'inégalité. (The Variance of Real Wages as a Measure of Inequality. With English summary.) *Consommation,* 1984, *31*(1), pp. 3–26. **[G: France]**

Tahir, Sayyid. Income Inequality in Pakistan: An Analysis of Existing Evidence: Comment. *Pakistan Devel. Rev.,* Summer-Autumn 1984, *23*(2&3), pp. 377–79. **[G: Pakistan]**

Torrey, Barbara Boyle. Income Transfers and the Economic Status of the Elderly: Comment. In *Moon, M.,* ed., 1984, pp. 276–82. **[G: U.S.]**

Vandermoortele, J. Kenya. In *van Ginneken, W. and Park, J.,* eds., 1984, pp. 89–94. **[G: Kenya]**

Vogel, Robert C. The Effect of Subsidized Agricultural Credit on Income Distribution in Costa Rica. In *Adams, D. W.; Graham, D. H. and Von Pischke, J. D.,* eds., 1984, pp. 133–45. **[G: Costa Rica]**

Weede, Erich and Tiefenbach, Horst. Some Recent Explanations of Income Inequality. In *Seligson, M. A.,* ed., 1984, *1981,* pp. 232–55. **[G: Selected Countries]**

van Weeren, Hans and van Praag, Bernard M. S. The Inequality of Actual Incomes and Earning Capacities between Households in Europe. *Europ. Econ. Rev.,* March 1984, *24*(2), pp. 239–56. **[G: Europe]**

Weil, Gordon. Cyclical and Secular Influences on the Size Distribution of Personal Income in the UK: Some Econometric Tests. *Appl. Econ.,* October 1984, *16*(5), pp. 749–55. **[G: U.K.]**

Wiedemann, Paul. Economic Fluctuations and

Income Distribution: A Comparative Study. *ACES Bull.*, Spring 1984, *26*(1), pp. 59–76. [G: U.S.; U.K.; Yugoslavia; Bulgaria]

Winegarden, Calman R. Income Redistribution versus Accelerated Economic Growth: A Comparison of Demographic Effects. *Oxford Bull. Econ. Statist.*, August 1984, *46*(3), pp. 255–71. [G: LDCs]

von Witzke, Harald. A Model of Income Distribution in Agriculture: Theory and Evidence. *Europ. Rev. Agr. Econ.*, 1984, *11*(1), pp. 65–83. [G: W. Germany]

Yang, Donghyu. Notes on the Wealth Distribution of Farm Households in the United States, 1860: A New Look at Two Manuscript Census Samples. *Exploration Econ. Hist.*, January 1984, *21*(1), pp. 88–102. [G: U.S.]

Yoshida, Tateo. The Gini Coefficient and the Generalized Entrophy Measures: Evidence from the World Bank Data of Income Distributions. (In Japanese. With English summary.) *Osaka Econ. Pap.*, December 1984, *34*(2–3), pp. 125–34. [G: Global]

Zenga, Michele. Proposta per un indice di concentrazione basato sui rapporti fra quantili di popolazione e quantili di reddito. (A Proposal for a Concentration Index Based on the Ratios between the Quantiles of Population and the Quantiles of Income. With English summary.) *Giorn. Econ.*, May–June 1984, *43*(5–6), pp. 301–26. [G: U.K.; Sweden; Italy]

Zwicky, Heinrich. Eine Methode zur Schätzung der personellen Einkommensverteilung in den Schweizer Kantonen. (A Method of Estimating the Personal Distribution of Income in the Swiss Cantons. With English summary.) *Schweiz. Z. Volkswirtsch. Statist.*, June 1984, *120*(2), pp. 191–222. [G: Switzerland]

222 Input-Output

2220 Input-Output

Almon, Clopper. An International System of National Input–Output Models. In *Andersson, Å. E.; Isard, W. and Puu, T., eds.*, 1984, pp. 157–85. [G: U.S.]

Archer, Brian. Tourism and the British Economy. *Rivista Int. Sci. Econ. Com.*, July 1984, *31*(7), pp. 596–613. [G: U.K.]

Auray, J. P. and Duru, G. Structural Analysis, Hierarchical Functions and Weak Structures. In *Ancot, J. P., ed.*, 1984, pp. 49–62.

Bánhidi, Ferenc. Price Model—Price Computations. In *Augusztinovics, M., ed.*, 1984, pp. 246–83. [G: Hungary]

Bezdek, Roger H. Tests of Three Hypotheses Relating to the Leontief Input–Output Model. *J. Roy. Statist. Soc.*, 1984, *147*(3), pp. 499–509. [G: U.S.]

Boda, György. Input–Output Analysis. In *Augusztinovics, M., ed.*, 1984, pp. 215–45. [G: Hungary]

Boisvert, Richard N. Decomposing the Induced Income Changes in Inpug–Output Models. *Amer. J. Agr. Econ.*, February 1984, *66*(1), pp. 99–103.

Bon, Ranko. Comparative Stability Analysis of Multiregional Input–Output Models: Column, Row, and Leontief–Strout Gravity Coefficient Models. *Quart. J. Econ.*, November 1984, *99*(4), pp. 791–815.

Bossier, F.; Biolley, T. and Vandamme, L. Cumulated Costs and Import Contents in the Belgium Input–Output Tables of 1965, 1970 and 1975. *Cah. Écon. Bruxelles*, 1st Trimester 1984, (101), pp. 125–67. [G: Belgium]

Braschler, Curtis; Procter, Michael and Kuehn, John A. Comparison of Non-survey Input–Output Estimates Using Alternative Reduction Techniques. *Rev. Reg. Stud.*, Winter 1984, *14*(1), pp. 22–33. [G: U.S.]

Brejon de Lavargnée, Nicolas. Un réexamen de la dominance économique: théorie et application au cas du Maroc. *Revue Écon. Polit.*, January–February 1984, *94*(1), pp. 116–37. [G: Morocco]

Brodzik, M. L. Final Demand Conversion Coefficients for the 1972 United States Input–Output Table and Their Use in Microeconomic Modelling. In *Avula, X. J. R., et al.*, 1984, pp. 807–14. [G: U.S.]

Cella, Guido. The Input–Output Measurement of Interindustry Linkages. *Oxford Bull. Econ. Statist.*, February 1984, *46*(1), pp. 73–84.

Chander, Parkash. On Material Balances When There Are Capacity Limitations. *J. Compar. Econ.*, June 1984, *8*(2), pp. 159–67.

Chowdhury, Anisuzzaman. Integration of Input–Output and Macroeconometric Models—A Review of Alternative Methodologies. *Singapore Econ. Rev.*, April 1984, *29*(1), pp. 97–115.

Costa, Paolo. La valutazione degli effetti economici del turismo in Italia. (Assessing the Economic Effects of Tourism in Italy. With English summary.) *Rivista Int. Sci. Econ. Com.*, July 1984, *31*(7), pp. 614–26. [G: Italy]

Crama, Yves; Defourny, Jacques and Gazon, Jules. Structural Decompostion of Multipliers in Input–Output or Social Accounting Matrix Analysis. *Écon. Appl.*, 1984, *37*(1), pp. 215–22.

Cronin, Francis J. Analytical Assumptions and Causal Ordering in Interindustry Modeling. *Southern Econ. J.*, October 1984, *51*(2), pp. 521–29. [G: U.S.]

Dániel, Zsuzsa. A Model for Analyzing Desired and Realizable Changes in Housing. *Matekon*, Summer 1984, *20*(4), pp. 3–47. [G: Hungary]

Dasgupta, Dipankar. The Hawkins–Simon Theorem: An Input–Output Analytic Approach. *Indian Econ. Rev.*, July–Dec. 1984, *19*(2), pp. 171–83.

Drabek, Zdenek. A Comparison of Technology in Centrally Planned and Market-Type Economies. *Europ. Econ. Rev.*, August 1984, *25*(3), pp. 293–318. [G: Czechoslovakia; Austria]

Ershov, E. B. Aggregation Analysis of Systems of Linear Equations, Input–Output Models, and Econometric Models. *Matekon*, Fall 1984, *21*(1), pp. 28–53. [G: U.S.S.R.]

Haraszti, Katalin. Long-term Models at Work:

Comparison with Other Countries. In *Augusztinovics, M., ed.*, 1984, pp. 319–48.
[G: Hungary; U.S.; W. Europe]

Harrigan, Frank and Buchanan, Iain. A Quadratic Programming Approach to Input–Output Estimation and Simulation. *J. Reg. Sci.*, August 1984, *24*(3), pp. 339–58. [G: U.K.; U.S.]

Harris, Curtis C., Jr.; McConnell, Virginia D. and Cumberland, John H. A Model for Forecasting the Economic and Environmental Impact of Energy Policy. *Energy Econ.*, July 1984, *6*(3), pp. 167–76. [G: U.S.]

Ishihara, T.; Yabuuchi, H. and Sato, M. A Method of Getting Approximate Input–Output Table for Less Developed Countries. In *Avula, X. J. R., et al.*, 1984, pp. 828–32. [G: LDCs]

Jeong, Ki-Jun. The Relation between Two Different Notions of Direct and Indirect Input Requirements. *J. Macroecon.*, Fall 1984, *6*(4), pp. 473–76.

Karunaratne, Neil Dias. Planning for the Australian Information Economy. *Info. Econ. Policy*, 1984, *1*(4), pp. 345–67. [G: Australia]

Kehoe, Timothy J.; Serra-Puche, Jaime and Solís, Leopoldo. A General Equilibrium Model of Domestic Commerce in Mexico. *J. Policy Modeling*, February 1984, *6*(1), pp. 1–28.
[G: Mexico]

Kjeldsen-Kragh, Søren. Valutaindtjening, beskæftigelse og indtjening i landbruget og industrien. (Foreign Exchange Earnings, Employment Effects, and Income Earnings in Different Sectors of the Danish Economy. With English summary.) *Nationaløkon. Tidsskr.*, 1984, *122*(1), pp. 91–114.
[G: Denmark]

Kuboniwa, Masaaki. Stepwise Aggregation for Material Balances. *J. Compar. Econ.*, March 1984, *8*(1), pp. 41–53. [G: U.S.S.R.]

Marzi, Graziella. Aggregazione ed efficienza produttiva: un'analisi delle distorsioni. (Aggregation and Productive Efficiency: An Analysis of Biases. With English summary.) *Rivista Int. Sci. Econ. Com.*, January 1984, *31*(1), pp. 49–68. [G: Italy]

Morishima, Michio and Prosperetti, Luigi. An Input–Output Analysis of the De-Industrialisation of the U.K. Economy, 1963–1973. *Banca Naz. Lavoro Quart. Rev.*, March 1984, (148), pp. 33–54. [G: U.K.]

Ó hUallacháin, Breandán. Input–Output Linkages and Foreign Direct Investment in Ireland. *Int. Reg. Sci. Rev.*, December 1984, *9*(3), pp. 185–200. [G: Ireland]

Palomo, Manuel Figuerola. Valoración del consumo y la producción turística. (Valuation of Tourism Consumption and Production. With English summary.) *Rivista Int. Sci. Econ. Com.*, July 1984, *31*(7), pp. 627–38.
[G: Spain]

Pasurka, Carl A., Jr. The Short-run Impact of Environmental Protection Costs on U.S. Product Prices. *J. Environ. Econ. Manage.*, December 1984, *11*(4), pp. 380–90. [G: U.S.]

Postner, Harry H. New Developments towards Resolving the Company–Establishment Prob-

lem. *Rev. Income Wealth*, December 1984, *30*(4), pp. 429–59.

ten Raa, Thijs; Chakraborty, Debesh and Small, J. Anthony. An Alternative Treatment of Secondary Products in Input–Output Analysis. *Rev. Econ. Statist.*, February 1984, *66*(1), pp. 88–97. [G: U.S.]

Rhee, Jeong J. and Miranowski, John A. Determination of Income, Production, and Employment under Pollution Control: An Input–Output Approach. *Rev. Econ. Statist.*, February 1984, *66*(1), pp. 146–50.

Schumacher, Dieter. North–South Trade and Shifts in Employment: A Comparative Analysis of Six European Community Countries. *Int. Lab. Rev.*, May–June 1984, *123*(3), pp. 333–48. [G: W. Europe; LDCs]

Skolka, Jiri. Input–Output Anatomy of Changes in Employment Structure in Austria between 1964 and 1976. *Empirica*, 1984, *11*(2), pp. 205–33. [G: Austria]

Skolka, Jiri. Use of Input–Output Models in the Preparation of Price Reform in China. *Industry Devel.*, 1984, (10), pp. 61–73. [G: China]

Truchon, Michel. Using Exogenous Elasticities to Induce Factor Substitution in Input–Output Price Models. *Rev. Econ. Statist.*, May 1984, *66*(2), pp. 329–34.

UNIDO Secretariat. An Input–Output Table for China 1975. *Industry Devel.*, 1984, (10), pp. 47–59. [G: China]

Val'tukh, K. K. Input–Output and the Theory of Value. *Matekon*, Fall 1984, *21*(1), pp. 72–86.

Waugh, Frederick V. Inversion of the Leontief Matrix by Power Series. In *Waugh, F. V.*, 1984, *1950*, pp. 281–93.

Weale, Martin R. Linear Economic Models. In *van der Ploeg, F., ed.*, 1984, pp. 37–56.

Wolsky, Alan Martin. Disaggregating Input–Output Models. *Rev. Econ. Statist.*, May 1984, *66*(2), pp. 283–91.

223 Financial Accounts

2230 Financial Accounts; Financial Statistics; Empirical Analyses of Capital Adequacy

Adachi, Hideyuki. Investment, Replacement and Depreciation Funds. *Kobe Univ. Econ.*, 1984, (30), pp. 47–63. [G: Japan]

Asajima, Shoichi. Flow-of-Funds Analysis of the Sumitomo Zaibatsu. In *Nakagawa, K. and Morikawa, H., eds.*, 1984, pp. 72–103.
[G: Japan]

Bierich, Marcus. More Risk Capital for Private Enterprise: Comment. In *Giersch, H., ed.*, 1984, pp. 40–43.

Brown, J. A. C. and Helou, A. The Fiscal Policy of Japan since 1970. *Oxford Bull. Econ. Statist.*, May 1984, *46*(2), pp. 89–124.
[G: Japan]

Buiter, Willem H. A Comprehensive Balance Sheet and Permanent Income Accounting Framework for the Public Sector: Theory and Applications. In *Masera, R. S. and Triffin, R., eds.*, 1984, pp. 153–95. [G: EEC; U.S.]

Christian, James W. and Wilson, Michael L. Capital Requirements for Housing in the 1980s. *Contemp. Policy Issue*, May 1984, (6), pp. 30–44. [G: U.S.]

Cotula, Franco. Financial Innovation and Monetary Control in Italy. *Banca Naz. Lavoro Quart. Rev.*, September 1984, (150), pp. 219–56. [G: Italy]

Eken, Sena. Integration of Domestic and International Financial Markets: The Japanese Experience. *Int. Monet. Fund Staff Pap.*, September 1984, *31*(3), pp. 499–548. [G: Japan]

Ellman, Michael. Did the Agricultural Surplus Provide the Resources for the Increase in Investment in the USSR 1928–32? In *Ellman, M.*, 1984, *1975*, pp. 27–53. [G: U.S.S.R.]

Ellman, Michael. Seven Theses on Kosyginism. In *Ellman, M.*, 1984, *1977*, pp. 75–96. [G: U.S.S.R.]

Fels, Gerhard. More Risk Capital for Private Enterprise. In *Giersch, H., ed.*, 1984, pp. 29–39. [G: W. Germany; OECD]

Goldsmith, Raymond W. National Balance Sheets as Tools of International Economic Comparisons. In *[Reynolds, L. G.]*, 1984, pp. 280–301. [G: Selected Countries]

Goldsmith, Raymond W. The Stability of the Ratio of Nonfinancial Debt to Income. *Banca Naz. Lavoro Quart. Rev.*, September 1984, (150), pp. 285–305.

Graham, John W. and Bradley, Michael G. Consumer Asset Composition in an Inflationary Environment. In *[Ferber, R.]*, 1984, pp. 39–52. [G: U.S.]

Gupta, Kanhaya L. Financial Intermediation, Interest Rate and Structure of Savings: Evidence from Asia. *J. Econ. Devel.*, July 1984, *9*(1), pp. 7–23. [G: Asia]

Janssen, Jürgen. Strukturen der Ersparnisentwicklung im privatwirtschaftlichen Sektor der Bundesrepublik, 1962–1980. (Changes in the Structure of Private Sector Savings in the Federal Republic of Germany, 1962–1980. With English summary.) *Konjunkturpolitik*, 1984, *30*(5), pp. 304–16. [G: W. Germany]

de Leeuw, Frank. Conflicting Measures of Private Saving. *Surv. Curr. Bus.*, November 1984, *64*(11), pp. 17–23. [G: U.S.]

Marreiros, Luis. Contribution to the Comparative Study of Savings Trends in Latin America: 1973–1983. In *Kessler, D. and Ullmo, P.-A., eds.*, 1984, pp. 281–309. [G: Latin America]

Patrick, Hugh. The Japanese Financial System in Transition: Comment. In *Agmon, T.; Hawkins, R. G. and Levich, R. M., eds.*, 1984, pp. 186–93. [G: Japan]

Pearl, Robert B. and Frankel, Matilda. Composition of the Personal Wealth of American Households at the Start of the Eighties. In *[Ferber, R.]*, 1984, pp. 19–37. [G: U.S.]

Philip, George. Public Enterprise in Mexico. In *Ramanadham, V. V., ed.*, 1984, pp. 28–46. [G: Mexico]

Postner, Harry H. New Developments towards Resolving the Company–Establishment Problem. *Rev. Income Wealth*, December 1984, *30*(4), pp. 429–59.

Sakakibara, Eisuke. The Japanese Financial System in Transition. In *Agmon, T.; Hawkins, R. G. and Levich, R. M., eds.*, 1984, pp. 157–85. [G: Japan; U.S.]

Simpson, Thomas D. Annual Revisions to the Money Stock. *Fed. Res. Bull.*, April 1984, *70*(4), pp. 279–85. [G: U.S.]

Van Fenstermaker, J.; Filer, John E. and Herren, Robert Stanley. Money Statistics of New England, 1785–1837. *J. Econ. Hist.*, June 1984, *44*(2), pp. 441–53. [G: U.S.]

Wood, J. Stuart. Capital Formation in the United States and the Question of a Capital Shortage. In *Siegel, B. N., ed.*, 1984, pp. 73–86. [G: U.S.]

224 National Wealth and Balance Sheets

2240 National Wealth and Balance Sheets

Alam, Mahmudul. Level and Composition of Capital in Irrigated Agriculture of Bangladesh: Evidence from Tubewell Irrigated Villages of Comilla and Rajshahi. *Bangladesh Devel. Stud.*, December 1984, *12*(4), pp. 59–106. [G: Bangladesh]

Arnold, Michael R. Clarification of Miller on Capital Aggregation in the Presence of Obsolescence-inducing Technical Change. *Rev. Income Wealth*, December 1984, *30*(4), pp. 487–92.

Avery, Robert B.; Elliehausen, Gregory E. and Canner, Glenn B. Survey of Consumer Finances, 1983. *Fed. Res. Bull.*, September 1984, *70*(9), pp. 679–92. [G: U.S.]

Bayer, Kurt. Profitability in Austrian Industrial Corporations. In *Holland, D. M., ed.*, 1984, pp. 421–64. [G: Austria]

Beach, Charles M.; Boadway, Robin and Gibbons, Jack O. Social Security and Aggregate Capital Accumulation Revisited: Dynamic Simultaneous Estimates in a Wealth-Generation Model. *Econ. Inquiry*, January 1984, *22*(1), pp. 68–79. [G: U.S.]

Brambilla, Francesco. Povertà e ricchezza. (Poverty and Wealth. With English summary.) *Giorn. Econ.*, Nov.-Dec. 1984, *43*(11–12), pp. 801–50. [G: Italy]

David, Martin and Menchik, Paul L. Nonearned Income, Income Instability, and Inequality: A Life-Cycle Interpretation. In *[Ferber, R.]*, 1984, pp. 53–73. [G: U.S.]

Fal'tsman, V. and Ozhegov, A. The Retirement of Fixed Capital: Investment Opportunities and Limitations. *Prob. Econ.*, May 1984, *27*(1), pp. 3–21. [G: U.S.S.R.]

Fellner, William. Monetary and Fiscal Policy in a Disinflationary Process: Justified and Unjustified Misgivings about Budget Deficits. In *Fellner, W., ed.*, 1984, pp. 55–86. [G: U.S.]

Fouquet, Annie and Strauss-Kahn, Dominique. The Size Distribution of Personal Wealth in France (1977): A First Attempt at the Estate Duty Method. *Rev. Income Wealth*, December 1984, *30*(4), pp. 403–18. [G: France]

Galper, Harvey and Toder, Eric. Transfer Elements in the Taxation of Income from Capital. In *Moon, M., ed.,* 1984, pp. 87–136.
[G: U.S.]

Goldsmith, Raymond W. National Balance Sheets as Tools of International Economic Comparisons. In *[Reynolds, L. G.],* 1984, pp. 280–301.
[G: Selected Countries]

Graham, John W. and Bradley, Michael G. Consumer Asset Composition in an Inflationary Environment. In *[Ferber, R.],* 1984, pp. 39–52.
[G: U.S.]

Hahn, Franz and Schmoranz, Ingo. Estimates of Capital Stock by Industries for Austria. *Rev. Income Wealth,* September 1984, *30*(3), pp. 289–307.
[G: Austria]

Holland, Daniel M. and Myers, Stewart C. Trends in Corporate Profitability and Capital Costs in the United States. In *Holland, D. M., ed.,* 1984, pp. 43–115.
[G: U.S.]

Hulten, Charles R. and Peterson, George E. The Public Capital Stock: Needs, Trends, and Performance. *Amer. Econ. Rev.,* May 1984, *74*(2), pp. 166–73.
[G: U.S.]

Kakwani, Nanak. The Relative Deprivation Curve and Its Applications: Reply. *J. Bus. Econ. Statist.,* October 1984, *2*(4), pp. 400–405.
[G: Australia]

Kakwani, Nanak. The Relative Deprivation Curve and Its Applications. *J. Bus. Econ. Statist.,* October 1984, *2*(4), pp. 384–94.
[G: Australia]

Kearl, James R. and Pope, Clayne L. Mobility and Distribution. *Rev. Econ. Statist.,* May 1984, *66*(2), pp. 192–99.
[G: U.S.]

Martin, Frank D.; Landefeld, J. Steven and Peskin, Janice. The Value of Services Provided by the Stock of Government-owned Fixed Capital in the United States, 1948–79. *Rev. Income Wealth,* September 1984, *30*(3), pp. 331–49.
[G: U.S.]

McHugh, Richard and Widdows, Richard. The Age of Capital and State Unemployment Rates. *J. Reg. Sci.,* February 1984, *24*(1), pp. 85–92.
[G: U.S.]

Menchik, Paul L. Is the Family Wealth Squandered? A Test of the Merry-Widow Model. *J. Econ. Hist.,* September 1984, *44*(3), pp. 835–38.
[G: U.S.]

Moffitt, Robert A. Trends in Social Security Wealth by Cohort. In *Moon, M., ed.,* 1984, pp. 327–53.
[G: U.S.]

Musgrave, John C. Fixed Reproducible Tangible Wealth in the United States, 1980–83. *Surv. Curr. Bus.,* August 1984, *64*(8), pp. 54–57.
[G: U.S.]

Nevile, J. W. and Warren, Neil A. How Much Do We Know about Wealth Distribution in Australia? *Australian Econ. Rev.,* 4th Quarter 1984, (68), pp. 23–33.
[G: Australia]

Norsworthy, J. R. Capital Input Measurement: Options and Inaccuracies. In *Intn'l. Productivity Symp.,* 1984, pp. 73–94.
[G: U.S.]

Norsworthy, J. R. Growth Accounting and Productivity Measurement. *Rev. Income Wealth,* September 1984, *30*(3), pp. 309–29.
[G: U.S.]

Okner, Benjamin A. Transfer Elements in the Taxation of Income from Capital: Comment. In *Moon, M., ed.,* 1984, pp. 136–38.
[G: U.S.]

Patrick, Hugh. The Japanese Financial System in Transition: Comment. In *Agmon, T.; Hawkins, R. G. and Levich, R. M., eds.,* 1984, pp. 186–93.
[G: Japan]

Pearl, Robert B. and Frankel, Matilda. Composition of the Personal Wealth of American Households at the Start of the Eighties. In *[Ferber, R.],* 1984, pp. 19–37.
[G: U.S.]

Pestieau, Pierre. The Effects of Varying Family Size on the Transmission and Distribution of Wealth. *Oxford Econ. Pap.,* November 1984, *36*(3), pp. 400–417.

Piggott, John. The Distribution of Wealth in Australia—A Survey. *Econ. Rec.,* September 1984, *60*(170), pp. 252–65.
[G: Australia]

Quinn, Joseph F. Trends in Social Security Wealth by Cohort: Comment. In *Moon, M., ed.,* 1984, pp. 353–58.
[G: U.S.]

Rosen, Sherwin. The Relative Deprivation Curve and Its Applications. *J. Bus. Econ. Statist.,* October 1984, *2*(4), pp. 395–97.
[G: Australia]

Ryscavage, Paul and Lamas, Enrique. The Relative Deprivation Curve and Its Applications: Comment. *J. Bus. Econ. Statist.,* October 1984, *2*(4), pp. 398–99.
[G: Australia]

Sakakibara, Eisuke. The Japanese Financial System in Transition. In *Agmon, T.; Hawkins, R. G. and Levich, R. M., eds.,* 1984, pp. 157–85.
[G: Japan; U.S.]

Sandford, Cedric. Distribution of Income and Wealth. In *Sandford, C. and Bradbury, M., eds.,* 1984, pp. 93–116.
[G: U.K.; Selected Countries]

Shah, Anup R. Intergenerational Distribution of Wealth in the Presence of Credit Rationing. *Metroecon.,* February 1984, *36*(1), pp. 97–109.

Smith, James D. Trends in the Concentration of Personal Wealth in the United States, 1958 to 1976. *Rev. Income Wealth,* December 1984, *30*(4), pp. 419–28.
[G: U.S.]

Soltow, Lee. Wealth Inequality in the United States in 1798 and 1860. *Rev. Econ. Statist.,* August 1984, *66*(3), pp. 444–51.
[G: U.S.]

Warlick, Jennifer L. and Burkhauser, Richard V. Raising the Normal Retirement Age under Social Security: A Life-Cycle Analysis. In *Moon, M., ed.,* 1984, pp. 359–79.
[G: U.S.]

225 Social Indicators: Data and Analysis

2250 Social Indicators: Data and Analysis

Drechsler, Laszlo. Recent Developments in the National Accounting System of Hungary. *Statist. J.,* August 1984, *2*(3), pp. 243–53.
[G: Hungary]

Ellman, Michael. *Odnowa* in Statistics. In *Ellman, M.,* 1984, *1982,* pp. 242–49.
[G: Poland]

Evans, Jeremy. The Growth of Urban Centres

in Java since 1961. *Bull. Indonesian Econ. Stud.*, April 1984, *20*(1), pp. 44–57.
[G: Indonesia]

Fillenbaum, Gerda G. Development of Functional Status Scales for the Longitudinal Retirement History Survey. *Rev. Public Data Use*, October 1984, *12*(3), pp. 197–209. [G: U.S.]

Foster, James E.; Greer, Joel and Thorbecke, Erik. A Class of Decomposable Poverty Measures. *Econometrica*, May 1984, *52*(3), pp. 761–66. [G: Kenya]

Fox, Karl A. Behavior Settings and Eco-behavioral Science: A New Arena for Mathematical Social Science Permitting a Richer and More Coherent View of Human Activities in Social Systems, Part I: Concepts, Measurements, and Linkages to Economic Data Systems, Time-Allocation Matrices, and Social System Accounts. *Math. Soc. Sci.*, April 1984, *7*(2), pp. 117–38. [G: U.S.]

Fox, Karl A. Behavior Settings and Eco-behavioral Science: A New Arena for Mathematical Social Science Permitting a Richer and More Coherent View of Human Activities in Social Systems, Part II: Relationships to Established Disciplines, and Needs for Mathematical Development. *Math. Soc. Sci.*, April 1984, *7*(2), pp. 139–65. [G: U.S.]

Gunatilleke, Godfrey and Kurukulasuria, G. I. O. M. The Global Economic Crisis and the Impact on Children in Sri Lanka. In *Jolly, R. and Cornia, G. A., eds.*, 1984, pp. 139–58.
[G: Sri Lanka]

Horn, R. V. Social Indicators for Development Planning and Analysis. In *Ghosh, P. K., ed., no. 8*, 1984, *1975*, pp. 166–91. [G: LDCs]

Kao, Charles H. C. and Liu, Ben-chieh. Socioeconomic Advance in the Republic of China (Taiwan): An Intertemporal Analysis of Its Quality of Life Indicators. *Amer. J. Econ. Soc.*, October 1984, *43*(4), pp. 399–412. [G: Taiwan]

Küng, Emil. Güterverteilung. (With English SUmmary.) In *Eucken, W. and Böhm, F., eds.*, 1984, pp. 167–77.

Lambert, Denis-Clair. Amérique Latine: un indicateur synthétique de développement. (With English summary.) *Can. J. Devel. Stud.*, 1984, *5*(1), pp. 25–50. [G: Latin America]

Lim, Chong-Yah. Economic Development of Singapore since Self-government in 1959. In *Boulding, K. E., ed.*, 1984, pp. 105–31.
[G: Singapore]

Martinotti, Guido. Crescita economica, benessere, qualità della vita. (Economic Growth, Welfare, Quality of Life. With English summary.) *Giorn. Econ.*, Nov.-Dec. 1984, *43*(11–12), pp. 867–85.

Miyawaki, Nagasada. Direction of the Civilized Societies of Today Viewed on the Basis of Anomie Indexes. In *Miyawaki, N., ed.*, 1984, pp. 14–43. [G: OECD]

Nissel, Muriel. Indicators of Human Betterment. In *Boulding, K. E., ed.*, 1984, pp. 15–35.
[G: U.K.]

Pack, Howard. Total Factor Productivity and Its

Determinants: Some International Comparisons. In *[Reynolds, L. G.]*, 1984, pp. 17–41.
[G: Israel; Philippines; U.S.]

Perry, Charles S. Economic Activity and Social Indicators: A Rural–Urban Discontinuum? *Amer. J. Econ. Soc.*, January 1984, *43*(1), pp. 61–74. [G: U.S.]

Rao, M. V. S. Socio-economic Indicators for Development Planning. In *Ghosh, P. K., ed., no. 8*, 1984, *1976*, pp. 192–220. [G: India]

Richards, Peter J. Target Setting for Basic-Needs Services: Some Possible Approaches. In *Ghosh, P. K., ed., no. 13*, 1984, *1981*, pp. 173–87. [G: Madagascar; India; Sri Lanka]

Rothchild, Donald. Middle Africa: Hegemonial Exchange and Resource Allocation. In *Groth, A. J. and Wade, L. L., eds.*, 1984, pp. 151–80. [G: Africa]

Sinha, Radha. Culture and Economy: Human Betterment in India and Japan. In *Boulding, K. E., ed.*, 1984, pp. 87–104. [G: India; Japan; OECD]

Strümpel, Burkhard. New Bases of Social and Institutional Conflict. In *Miyawaki, N., ed.*, 1984, pp. 80–88.

Stuart, Edward F. The PQLI as a Measure of Comparative Economic Performance. *ACES Bull.*, Winter 1984, *26*(4), pp. 43–53.
[G: Global]

Wiedemann, Paul. Comparing the Process of Socio-economic Development in Market and Non-market Economies: The EEC and CMEA. *Cambridge J. Econ.*, December 1984, *8*(4), pp. 311–30. [G: EEC; CMEA]

Zerby, J. A. and Khan, M. H. A Comparison of Multivariate Methods for Indexing Socioeconomic Development. *Singapore Econ. Rev.*, April 1984, *29*(1), pp. 47–66. [G: LDCs]

226 Productivity and Growth: Theory and Data

2260 Productivity and Growth: Theory and Data

Adelman, Irma and Morris, Cynthia Taft. Patterns of Economic Growth, 1850–1914, or Chenery–Syrquin in Historical Perspective. In *[Chenery, H. B.]*, 1984, pp. 45–74.

Anderson, Charles W. Worrying about Productivity: A Political, Economic, and Humanistic Analysis. In *Sherman, M., ed.*, 1984, pp. 7–20. [G: U.S.]

Baer, Werner and Birch, Melissa H. Expansion of the Economic Frontier: Paraguayan Growth in the 1970s. *World Devel.*, August 1984, *12*(8), pp. 783–98. [G: Paraguay]

Baily, Martin Neil. The Reagan Administration's Regulatory Relief Effort: A Mid-term Assessment: Comments. In *Eads, G. C. and Fix, M., eds.*, 1984, pp. 81–83. [G: U.S.]

Baily, Martin Neil. Will Productivity Growth Recover? Has It Done So Already? *Amer. Econ. Rev.*, May 1984, *74*(2), pp. 231–35.
[G: U.S.]

Baumol, William J. On Productivity Growth in

the Long Run. *Atlantic Econ. J.*, September 1984, *12*(3), pp. 5–10. [G: U.S.]

Baumol, William J. U.S. Competitiveness and the Productivity Gap. *J. Econ. Educ.*, Summer 1984, *15*(3), pp. 217–24. [G: U.S.]

Baumol, William J. and Wolff, Edward N. Feedback Models: R&D, Information, and Productivity Growth. In *Jussawalla, M. and Ebenfield, H., eds.*, 1984, pp. 73–93.

Baumol, William J. and Wolff, Edward N. On Interindustry Differences in Absolute Productivity. *J. Polit. Econ.*, December 1984, *92*(6), pp. 1017–34.

Berndt, Ernst R. The Role of Energy in Productivity Growth: Comment. In *Kendrick, J. W., ed.*, 1984, pp. 325–34. [G: U.S.]

Bernholz, Peter. The Political Economy of Growth [Review Article]. *Kyklos*, 1984, *37*(2), pp. 291–94. [G: Selected OECD]

Birman, A. M. Tons, Pieces, Rubles. *Prob. Econ.*, July 1984, *27*(3), pp. 22–40. [G: U.S.S.R.]

Borges, Antonio M. and Goulder, Lawrence H. Decomposing the Impact of Higher Energy Prices on Long-term Growth. In *Scarf, H. E. and Shoven, J. B., eds.*, 1984, pp. 319–62. [G: U.S.]

Boserup, Ester. Demographic Pressure, Growth and Productivity in an Historical Perspective. In *Amin, S., ed.*, 1984, pp. 20–32. [G: OECD; U.S.S.R.; LDCs]

Boulier, Bryan L. What Lies behind Verdoorn's Law? *Oxford Econ. Pap.*, June 1984, *36*(2), pp. 259–67.

Bourguignon, François and Levy-Leboyer, M. An Econometric Model of France during the 19th Century. *Europ. Econ. Rev.*, June 1984, *25*(1), pp. 107–41. [G: France]

Bowles, Samuel; Gordon, David M. and Weisskopf, Thomas E. A Social Model for U.S. Productivity Growth. *Challenge*, March/April 1984, *27*(1), pp. 41–48. [G: U.S.]

Brief, Arthur P. Productivity Research in the Behavioral and Social Sciences: Introduction. In *Brief, A. P., ed.*, 1984, pp. 1–3.

Brox, James A. A Note on Capacity Utilization, Productivity, and the Canadian Output Gap. *Empirical Econ.*, 1984, *9*(3), pp. 131–38. [G: Canada]

Bruno, Michael. Petrodollars and the Different Growth Performance of Industrial and Middle-Income Countries in the 1970s. In *[Chenery, H. B.]*, 1984, pp. 363–90. [G: OECD; MDCs]

Bruno, Michael. Raw Materials, Profits, and the Productivity Slowdown. *Quart. J. Econ.*, February 1984, *99*(1), pp. 1–29. [G: Japan; U.S.; U.K.; W. Germany]

Burggraf, Shirley P. Women, Youth, and Minorities and the Case of the Missing Productivity. *Amer. Econ. Rev.*, May 1984, *74*(2), pp. 254–59. [G: U.S.]

Christainsen, Gregory B. and Haveman, Robert H. The Reagan Administration's Regulatory Relief Effort: A Mid-term Assessment. In *Eads, G. C. and Fix, M., eds.*, 1984, pp. 49–80. [G: U.S.]

Christensen, Laurits R. The Diffusion of Economic Growth in the World Economy, 1950–80: Comment. In *Kendrick, J. W., ed.*, 1984, pp. 153–56. [G: Global]

Clark, Peter K. Productivity and Profits in the 1980s: Are They Really Improving? *Brookings Pap. Econ. Act.*, 1984, (1), pp. 133–67. [G: U.S.]

Clark, Peter K. Unemployment and Potential Output in the 1980s: Comment. *Brookings Pap. Econ. Act.*, 1984, (2), pp. 565–67. [G: U.S.]

Clauss, Franz Joachim. Über die Konjunkturabhängigkeit der statistischen Produktivität. (On the Cyclical Dependence of Productivity as Measured Statistically. With English summary.) *Ifo-Studien*, 1984, *30*(4), pp. 273–305. [G: U.S.]

Cohen, Michael A. Cities in Developing Countries: 1975–2000. In *Ghosh, P. K., ed., no. 2*, 1984, *1976*, pp. 27–35. [G: LDCs]

Cole, Sam; Gershuny, Jay and Miles, Ian. Scenarios of World Development. In *Ghosh, P. K., ed., no. 8*, 1984, *1978*, pp. 17–39.

Crafts, N. F. R. Economic Growth in France and Britain, 1830–1910: A Review of the Evidence. *J. Econ. Hist.*, March 1984, *44*(1), pp. 49–67. [G: France; U.K.]

Crafts, N. F. R. Patterns of Development in Nineteenth Century Europe. *Oxford Econ. Pap.*, November 1984, *36*(3), pp. 438–58. [G: Europe]

Cripps, Francis and Ward, Terry. Erratum [European Recession and Problems of Recovery]. *Cambridge J. Econ.*, March 1984, *8*(1), pp. 115. [G: W. Europe]

Darby, Michael R. The U.S. Productivity Slowdown: A Case of Statistical Myopia. *Amer. Econ. Rev.*, June 1984, *74*(3), pp. 301–22. [G: U.S.]

Denison, Edward F. Accounting for Slower Economic Growth: An Update. In *Kendrick, J. W., ed.*, 1984, pp. 1–45. [G: U.S.]

Denison, Edward F. Productivity Analysis Through Growth Accounting. In *Brief, A. P., ed.*, 1984, pp. 7–55. [G: U.S.; OECD]

Di Filippo, Armando. Social Use of the Surplus, Accumulation, Distribution, and Employment. *Cepal Rev.*, 1984, (24), pp. 117–34. [G: Latin America]

Dormont, Brigitte. Productivité-croissance quelle relation a moyen-long terme? Un rapprochement des modèles de Brechling et de Kaldor–Verdoorn. (Productivity and Growth: What Is the Long-Run Relationship? Bringing Together Brechling's and Kaldor–Verdoorn's Models. With English summary.) *Revue Écon.*, May 1984, *35*(3), pp. 447–78. [G: France; W. Germany]

Ettlie, John E. Implementation Strategy for Manufacturing Innovations. In *Warner, M., ed.*, 1984, pp. 31–48.

Fabricant, Solomon. Problems of Productivity Measurement. In *Intn'l. Productivity Symp.*, 1984, pp. 21–39.

Fabricant, Solomon. Productivity Measurement

and Analysis: An Overview. **In** *Intn'l. Productivity Symp.*, 1984, pp. 1–19. **[G: MDCs; LDCs]**

Faini, Riccardo; Annez, Patricia and Taylor, Lance. Defense Spending, Economic Structure, and Growth: Evidence among Countries and Over Time. *Econ. Develop. Cult. Change*, April 1984, *32*(3), pp. 487–98. **[G: India; Global]**

Ferris, Tom. Productivity and Living Standards—Some Further Comparisons. *Irish Banking Rev.*, June 1984, pp. 40–45. **[G: Ireland]**

Figueroa, Adolfo. The Distribution Problem in Different Sociopolitical and Economic Contexts: Peru, 1950–1980. **In** *[Ferber, R.]*, 1984, pp. 145–67. **[G: Peru]**

Frenzel, Bill. In Search of an Optimistic Scenario for the 1980s: Comment. **In** *Wachter, M. L. and Wachter, S. M., eds.*, 1984, pp. 427–30. **[G: Global; U.S.]**

Fröbel, Folker. The Current Development of the World-Economy: Reproduction of Labour and Accumulation of Capital on a World Scale. **In** *Addo, H., ed.*, 1984, pp. 51–118. **[G: Global]**

Fulco, Lawrence J. Strong Post-Recession Gain in Productivity Contributes to Slow Growth in Labor Costs. *Mon. Lab. Rev.*, December 1984, *107*(12), pp. 3–10. **[G: U.S.]**

Geary, Frank. The Cause of the Industrial Revolution and 'Single-Factor' Arguments: An Assessment. *J. Europ. Econ. Hist.*, Spring 1984, *13*(1), pp. 167–73.

Gordon, David M.; Weisskopf, Thomas E. and Bowles, Samuel. Long-term Growth and the Cyclical Restoration of Profitability. **In** *Goodwin, R. M.; Krüger, M. and Vercelli, A., eds.*, 1984, pp. 86–102. **[G: U.S.]**

Gordon, Robert J. An Econometric Model of France during the 19th Century: Comments. *Europ. Econ. Rev.*, June 1984, *25*(1), pp. 143–46. **[G: France]**

Gordon, Robert J. Productivity and Profits in the 1980s: Are They Really Improving? Comments. *Brookings Pap. Econ. Act.*, 1984, (1), pp. 168–72. **[G: U.S.]**

Gordon, Robert J. Unemployment and Potential Output in the 1980s. *Brookings Pap. Econ. Act.*, 1984, (2), pp. 537–64. **[G: U.S.]**

Griliches, Zvi and Lichtenberg, Frank R. Interindustry Technology Flows and Productivity Growth: A Re-examination. *Rev. Econ. Statist.*, May 1984, *66*(2), pp. 324–29. **[G: U.S.]**

Griliches, Zvi and Lichtenberg, Frank R. R&D and Productivity Growth at the Industry Level: Is There Still a Relationship? **In** *Griliches, Z., ed.*, 1984, pp. 465–96. **[G: U.S.]**

Grossman, Elliot S. Company Productivity Measurement. *Bus. Econ.*, July 1984, *19*(4), pp. 18–23. **[G: U.S.]**

Hage, Jerald. Organizational Theory and the Concept of Productivity. **In** *Brief, A. P., ed.*, 1984, pp. 91–126.

den Hartog, Hans. Empirical Vintage Models for the Netherlands: A Review in Outline. *De Economist*, 1984, *132*(3), pp. 326–49. **[G: Netherlands]**

Helleiner, Gerald K. The One World of Economics: Towards Global Economic Analysis. **In** *[Reynolds, L. G.]*, 1984, pp. 63–74. **[G: Global]**

Hjerppe, Riitta; Peltonen, Matti and Pihkala, Erkki. Investment in Finland, 1860–1979. *Scand. Econ. Hist. Rev.*, 1984, *32*(1), pp. 42–59. **[G: Finland]**

Hollard, Michel; Ruffieux, Bernard and Servais, Olivier. Automatisation et productivité: rupture ou continuité? (With English summary.) *Rev. Econ. Ind.*, 2nd Trimester 1984, (28), pp. 59–75. **[G: France]**

Hulten, Charles R. Productivity Change in State and Local Governments. *Rev. Econ. Statist.*, May 1984, *66*(2), pp. 256–66. **[G: U.S.]**

Hulten, Charles R. and Schwab, Robert M. Regional Productivity Growth in U.S. Manufacturing: 1951–78. *Amer. Econ. Rev.*, March 1984, *74*(1), pp. 152–62. **[G: U.S.]**

Jasinowski, Jerry J. In Search of an Optimistic Scenario for the 1980s: Comment. **In** *Wachter, M. L. and Wachter, S. M., eds.*, 1984, pp. 419–24. **[G: Global; U.S.]**

Jones, Reginald H. Responses to the Slowdown in Growth. **In** *Wachter, M. L. and Wachter, S. M., eds.*, 1984, pp. 3–9. **[G: U.S.]**

de Jong, Henk Wouter. Sectoral Development and Sectoral Policies in the EC. **In** *Jacquemin, A., ed.*, 1984, pp. 147–71. **[G: OECD]**

Jonscher, Charles. Productivity and Growth of the Information Economy. **In** *Jussawalla, M. and Ebenfield, H., eds.*, 1984, pp. 95–103. **[G: U.S.]**

Jorgenson, Dale W. The Contribution of Education to U.S. Economic Growth, 1948–73. **In** *Dean, E., ed.*, 1984, pp. 95–162. **[G: U.S.]**

Jorgenson, Dale W. The Role of Energy in Productivity Growth. *Energy J.*, July 1984, *5*(3), pp. 11–26.

Jorgenson, Dale W. The Role of Energy in Productivity Growth. **In** *Kendrick, J. W., ed.*, 1984, pp. 279–323. **[G: U.S.]**

Jorgenson, Dale W. The Role of Energy in Productivity Growth. *Amer. Econ. Rev.*, May 1984, *74*(2), pp. 26–30. **[G: U.S.]**

Kemme, David M. and Crane, Keith. The Polish Economic Collapse: Contributing Factors and Economic Costs. *J. Compar. Econ.*, March 1984, *8*(1), pp. 25–40. **[G: Poland]**

Kendrick, John W. International Comparisons of Recent Productivity Trends. **In** *Intn'l. Productivity Symp.*, 1984, *1981*, pp. 95–140. **[G: OECD]**

Kendrick, John W. Long-Term Economic Projection: Stronger U.S. Growth Ahead. *Southern Econ. J.*, April 1984, *50*(4), pp. 945–64. **[G: U.S.]**

Kendrick, John W. The Implications of Growth Accounting Models. **In** *Hulten, C. R. and Sawhill, I. V., eds.*, 1984, pp. 19–43. **[G: U.S.]**

Kendrick, John W. U.S. Economic Policy and Productivity Growth. *Cato J.*, Fall 1984, *4*(2), pp. 387–400. **[G: U.S.]**

Kjeldsen-Kragh, Søren. Valutaindtjening, beskæftigelse og indtjening i landbruget og indus-

trien. (Foreign Exchange Earnings, Employment Effects, and Income Earnings in Different Sectors of the Danish Economy. With English summary.) *Nationaløkon. Tidsskr.*, 1984, *122*(1), pp. 91–114.
[G: Denmark]

Klein, Lawrence R. In Search of an Optimistic Scenario for the 1980s. In *Wachter, M. L. and Wachter, S. M., eds.*, 1984, pp. 390–412.
[G: Global]

Kravis, Irving B. and Lipsey, Robert E. The Diffusion of Economic Growth in the World Economy, 1950–80. In *Kendrick, J. W., ed.*, 1984, pp. 109–51.
[G: Global]

Krugman, Paul R. The Effects of International Competition on U.S. Economic Growth. In *Hulten, C. R. and Sawhill, I. V., eds.*, 1984, pp. 127–50. [G: U.S.; Japan; W. Germany]

Kurosawa, Kazukiyo. International Comparison of Productivity. In *Intn'l. Productivity Symp.*, 1984, pp. 141–217. [G: OECD; Selected LDCs]

Leichter, Howard M. National Productivity: A Comparative Perspective. In *Holzer, M. and Nagel, S. S., eds.*, 1984, pp. 45–68.
[G: OECD]

Leslie, Derek. The Productivity of Hours in U.S. Manufacturing Industries. *Rev. Econ. Statist.*, August 1984, *66*(3), pp. 486–90. [G: U.S.]

Maddison, Angus. Comparative Analysis of the Productivity Situation in the Advanced Capitalist Countries. In *Kendrick, J. W., ed.*, 1984, pp. 59–92. [G: OECD]

Mahoney, Thomas A. Growth Accounting and Productivity: Comments. In *Brief, A. P., ed.*, 1984, pp. 56–67. [G: U.S.; OECD]

Mann, Arthur J. and Sánchez, Carlos E. Monetarism, Economic Reform and Socio-Economic Consequences: Argentina, 1976–1982. *Int. J. Soc. Econ.*, 1984, *11*(3/4), pp. 12–28.
[G: Argentina]

Manne, Alan S. Decomposing the Impact of Higher Energy Prices on Long-term Growth: Comments. In *Scarf, H. E. and Shoven, J. B., eds.*, 1984, pp. 362–65. [G: U.S.]

Marsden, Keith. Global Development Strategies and the Poor: Alternative Scenarios. In *Ghosh, P. K., ed., no. 8*, 1984, *1978*, pp. 58–83.
[G: Global]

Marshall, Ray. Labor Productivity and Demographics: Comment. In *Wachter, M. L. and Wachter, S. M., eds.*, 1984, pp. 105–08.
[G: Japan; U.S.]

Martinotti, Guido. Crescita economica, benessere, qualità della vita. (Economic Growth, Welfare, Quality of Life. With English summary.) *Giorn. Econ.*, Nov.-Dec. 1984, *43*(11–12), pp. 867–85.

McCombie, J. S. L. and de Ridder, J. R. "The Verdoorn Law Controversy": Some New Empirical Evidence Using U.S. State Data. *Oxford Econ. Pap.*, June 1984, *36*(2), pp. 268–84. [G: U.S.]

McMahon, Walter W. Comparative Analysis of the Productivity Situation in the Advanced Capitalist Countries: Comment. In *Kendrick, J. W., ed.*, 1984, pp. 93–108. [G: OECD]

McMahon, Walter W. The Relation of Education and R&D to Productivity Growth. *Econ. Educ. Rev.*, 1984, *3*(4), pp. 299–313. [G: U.S.]

McNees, Stephen K. Economic Growth: How Much Is Too Much? *New Eng. Econ. Rev.*, January–February 1984, pp. 15–22. [G: U.S.]

Medow, P. I. A New Stage in the Global Biosphere Project: The Simulation of Spatial Processes and of Structural Change. *Écon. Appl.*, 1984, *37*(2), pp. 307–14.

Mitchell, Daniel J. B. The Private Sector Workplace. In *Holzer, M. and Nagel, S. S., eds.*, 1984, pp. 87–112. [G: U.S.; OECD]

de Montbrial, Thierry. An Econometric Model of France during the 19th Century: Comments. *Europ. Econ. Rev.*, June 1984, *25*(1), pp. 147–48. [G: France]

Moore, Geoffrey H. and Cullity, John P. Trends and Cycles in Productivity, Unit Costs, and Prices: An International Perspective. In *Kendrick, J. W., ed.*, 1984, pp. 157–90.
[G: OECD]

Motley, Brian. How Soon Will the U.S. Reach Full Employment? An Assessment Based on Okun's Law. *Fed. Res. Bank San Francisco Econ. Rev.*, Summer 1984, (3), pp. 26–39.
[G: U.S.]

Nelson, Richard R. Where Are We in the Discussion? Retrospect and Prospect. In *Kendrick, J. W., ed.*, 1984, pp. 397–409.

Nichols, Donald A. Federal Spending Priorities and Long-term Economic Growth. In *Hulten, C. R. and Sawhill, I. V., eds.*, 1984, pp. 151–73. [G: U.S.]

Niosi, Jorge. Le déclin de l'industrie américaine. (With English summary.) *Rev. Econ. Ind.*, 4th Trimester 1984, (30), pp. 9–25. [G: U.S.]

Nishimizu, Mieko and Robinson, Sherman. Trade Policies and Productivity Change in Semi-industrialized Countries. *J. Devel. Econ.*, September–October 1984, *16*(1–2), pp. 177–206.
[G: S. Korea; Turkey; Yugoslavia; Japan]

Norsworthy, J. R. Capital Input Measurement: Options and Inaccuracies. In *Intn'l. Productivity Symp.*, 1984, pp. 73–94. [G: U.S.]

Norsworthy, J. R. Growth Accounting and Productivity Measurement. *Rev. Income Wealth*, September 1984, *30*(3), pp. 309–29.
[G: U.S.]

Olson, Mancur. Ideology and Economic Growth. In *Hulten, C. R. and Sawhill, I. V., eds.*, 1984, pp. 229–51. [G: OECD]

Onitsuka, Yusuke. Economic Growth and Social Welfare Policy in the 1980s. In *Miyawaki, N., ed.*, 1984, pp. 220–27.

Oshima, Harry T. The Growth of U.S. Factor Productivity: The Significance of New Technologies in the Early Decades of the Twentieth Century. *J. Econ. Hist.*, March 1984, *44*(1), pp. 161–70. [G: U.S.]

Paauw, Douglas S. Economic Growth, Employment, and Productivity: Prospects for Indonesia. *Singapore Econ. Rev.*, October 1984, *29*(2), pp. 111–25. [G: Indonesia]

Patalinghug, Epictetus. Labor Quality and Growth Accounting: The Philippines. *Philippine Rev. Econ. Bus.*, Sept./Dec. 1984, *21* (3/4), pp. 201–17. [G: Philippines]

Pennings, Johannes M. Productivity: Some Old and New Issues. In *Brief, A. P., ed.*, 1984, pp. 127–40.

Pirages, Dennis. Paths to International Political Economy: An Ecological Approach. In *Strange, S., ed.*, 1984, pp. 53–69. [G: Global]

Plant, Mark W. and Welch, Finis. Measuring the Impact of Education on Productivity. In *Dean, E., ed.*, 1984, pp. 163–93. [G: U.S.]

Pryor, Frederic L. Rent-Seeking and the Growth and Fluctuations of Nations: Empirical Tests of Some Recent Hypotheses. In *Colander, D. C., ed.*, 1984, pp. 155–75. [G: Selected Countries]

Psacharopoulos, George. The Contribution of Education to Economic Growth: International Comparisons. In *Kendrick, J. W., ed.*, 1984, pp. 335–55. [G: Selected Countries]

Rabushka, Alvin. Restoring U.S. Competitiveness [U.S. Economic Policy and Productivity Growth]. *Cato J.*, Fall 1984, *4*(2), pp. 401–06. [G: U.S.]

Ram, Rati. Causal Ordering across Inflation and Productivity Growth in the Post-war United States. *Rev. Econ. Statist.*, August 1984, *66*(3), pp. 472–77. [G: U.S.]

Ricottilli, Massimo. The Investment Performance in Three Industrialized Economies: The U.S.A., West Germany and France. *Econ. Notes*, 1984, (2), pp. 90–120. [G: U.S.; W. Germany; France]

Roberts, Paul Craig. Supply-Side Economics, Growth, and Liberty. In *Moore, J. H., ed.*, 1984, pp. 73–89. [G: U.S.]

Rosen, Ellen Doree. Productivity: Concepts and Measurement. In *Holzer, M. and Nagel, S. S., eds.*, 1984, pp. 19–43.

Rosenberg, Nathan. The Slowdown of Productivity Growth in the American Economy: A Discussion of the Causes. In *Sherman, M., ed.*, 1984, pp. 69–83. [G: U.S.]

Sangha, Kehar S. A Paradox of Productivity [Some Methodological and Political Issues Surrounding Productivity]. *J. Econ. Issues*, December 1984, *18*(4), pp. 1198–1200.

Sawhill, Isabel V. The Reagan Administration's Regulatory Relief Effort: A Mid-term Assessment: Comment. In *Eads, G. C. and Fix, M., eds.*, 1984, pp. 84–86. [G: U.S.]

Scherer, Frederic M. Interindustry Technology Flows and Productivity Growth. In *Scherer, F. M.*, 1984, pp. 270–85. [G: U.S.]

Scherer, Frederic M. Technological Maturity and Waning Economic Growth. In *Scherer, F. M.*, 1984, pp. 261–69. [G: U.S.]

Scherer, Frederic M. The Problem of Declining Productivity Growth. In *Scherer, F. M.*, 1984, pp. 257–59.

Schultz, Theodore W. A Comment on Education and Economic Growth. In *Kendrick, J. W., ed.*, 1984, pp. 357–60. [G: Selected Countries]

Schultze, Charles L. Productivity and Profits in the 1980s: Are They Really Improving? Comments. *Brookings Pap. Econ. Act.*, 1984, (1), pp. 172–79. [G: U.S.]

Schwartz, Sandra L. Up the Down Staircase: The Productivity Decline and Strategies for Recovery. In *Bamberg, G. and Spremann, K., eds.*, 1984, pp. 285–306. [G: OECD]

Seligson, Mitchell A. Inequality in a Global Perspective: Directions for Further Research. In *Seligson, M. A., ed.*, 1984, pp. 397–408. [G: Global]

Simon, Julian L. Research on Population and Productivity Growth. In *Steinmann, G., ed.*, 1984, pp. 50–57.

Simon, Julian L. and Kahn, Herman. The Resourceful Earth: A Response to Global 2000: Introduction. In *Simon, J. L. and Kahn, H., eds.*, 1984, pp. 1–49. [G: Global]

Singer, Hans W. Success Stories of the 1970s: Some Correlations. *World Devel.*, September 1984, *12*(9), pp. 951–52.

Steindl, Josef. Stagnation Theory and Stagnation Policy. In *Foster, J. B. and Szlajfer, H., eds.*, 1984, *1979*, pp. 179–97. [G: U.S.]

Supple, Barry. Revisiting Rostow. *Econ. Hist. Rev., 2nd Ser.*, February 1984, 37(1), pp. 107–14.

Sylos-Labini, Paolo. Factors Affecting Changes in Productivity. In *Sylos-Labini, P.*, 1984, *1983*, pp. 101–19. [G: Italy; U.S.]

Syrquin, Moshe. Resource Reallocation and Productivity Growth. In *[Chenery, H. B.]*, 1984, pp. 75–101. [G: OECD; LDCs; Hungary]

Taira, Koji. Output, Productivity, and Employment: U.S.–Japan Comparison. In *Sherman, M., ed.*, 1984, pp. 87–102. [G: Japan; U.S.]

Terleckyj, Nestor E. R&D and Productivity Growth at the Industry Level: Is There Still a Relationship? Comment. In *Griliches, Z., ed.*, 1984, pp. 496–501. [G: U.S.]

Thomas, Annie and Brief, Arthur P. Unexplored Issues in Productivity Research. In *Brief, A. P., ed.*, 1984, pp. 285–301.

Thor, Carl G.; Sadler, George E. and Grossman, Elliot S. Comparison of Total Factor Productivity in Japan and the Unitied States. In *Intn'l. Productivity Symp.*, 1984, pp. 57–72. [G: Japan; U.S.]

Treat, John. The Effects of Economic Growth on the Oil and Energy Demand. In *Ayoub, A., ed.*, 1984, pp. 111–22. [G: U.S.]

Tung, S. L. An Econometric Analysis of the Effects of Population Change on Economic Growth: A Study of Taiwan. *Appl. Econ.*, August 1984, *16*(4), pp. 523–38. [G: Taiwan]

Vechkanov, V. The Relationship between the Capital–Labor Ratio and Labor Productivity. *Prob. Econ.*, May 1984, 27(1), pp. 22–32. [G: U.S.S.R.]

Vikent'ev, A. On Rates of Economic Growth in the Present Stage. *Prob. Econ.*, September 1984, 27(5), pp. 23–43. [G: CMEA]

Wachter, Michael L. and Wachter, Susan M. The Setting for a Pro-Growth Strategy: An Introduction. In *Wachter, M. L. and Wachter, S. M., eds.*, 1984, pp. xvii–xlii. **[G: U.S.; OECD]**

Waldorf, William H. Trends and Cycles in Productivity, Unit Costs, and Prices: An International Perspective: Comment. In *Kendrick, J. W., ed.*, 1984, pp. 191–95. **[G: OECD]**

Weiss, John. Manufacturing as an Engine of Growth—Revisited. *Industry Devel.*, 1984, (13), pp. 39–62. **[G: Global]**

Williamson, Jeffrey G. Why Was British Growth So Slow during the Industrial Revolution? *J. Econ. Hist.*, September 1984, *44*(3), pp. 687–712. **[G: U.K.]**

Wolff, Edward N. Accounting for Slower Economic Growth: An Update: Comment. In *Kendrick, J. W., ed.*, 1984, pp. 47–58. **[G: U.S.]**

Wolter, Frank. From Economic Miracle to Stagnation: On the German Disease. In *Harberger, A. C., ed.*, 1984, pp. 95–121. **[G: W. Germany]**

Woodham, Douglas M. Potential Output Growth and the Long-Term Inflation Outlook. *Fed. Res. Bank New York Quart. Rev.*, Summer 1984, *9*(2), pp. 16–23. **[G: U.S.]**

Yamaguchi, Mitoshi and Kennedy, George. A Graphic Model of the Effects of Sectoral Technical Change: The Case of Japan, 1880–1970. *Can. J. Agr. Econ.*, March 1984, *32*(1), pp. 71–92. **[G: Japan]**

Zimmermann, Klaus F. Der Beitrag des öffentlichen Sektors zur Entwicklung der Produktivität. (The Contribution of the Public Sector to the Growth of Productivity. With English summary.) *Konjunkturpolitik*, 1984, *30*(2/3), pp. 93–118. **[G: W. Germany]**

227 Prices

2270 Prices

Afriat, S. N. The True Index. In *[Pearce, I. F.]*, 1984, pp. 37–56.

Agarwala, Ramgopal. Price Distortions and Growth. *Finance Develop.*, March 1984, *21*(1), pp. 33–37. **[G: LDCs]**

Arrow, Kenneth J. The Measurement of Price Changes. In *Arrow, K. J., vol. 3*, 1984, *1958*, pp. 85–99.

Aschheim, Joseph and Tavlas, George S. The Simultaneity Problem in Forecasting Inflation. *Atlantic Econ. J.*, September 1984, *12*(3), pp. 20–29. **[G: U.S.]**

Bajt, Aleksander. Changes in Relative Producer Prices in Yugoslavia 1971–80. In *Csikós-Nagy, B.; Hague, D. and Hall, G., eds.*, 1984, pp. 152–78. **[G: Yugoslavia]**

Barnett, Harold J., et al. Global Trends in Nonfuel Minerals. In *Simon, J. L. and Kahn, H., eds.*, 1984, pp. 316–38. **[G: Global]**

Barro, Robert J. Some Evidence on the Real Price of Gold, Its Costs of Production, and Commodity Prices: Comment. In *Bordo, M. D. and Schwartz, A. J., eds.*, 1984, pp. 644–46. **[G: U.S.; U.S.S.R.; S. Africa; Australia]**

Benjamin, Daniel K. and Kochin, Lewis A. War, Prices, and Interest Rates: A Martial Solution to Gibson's Paradox. In *Bordo, M. D. and Schwartz, A. J., eds.*, 1984, pp. 587–604. **[G: U.K.]**

Bessler, David A. Relative Prices and Money: A Vector Autoregression on Brazilian Data. *Amer. J. Agr. Econ.*, February 1984, *66*(1), pp. 25–30. **[G: Brazil]**

Bhagwati, Jagdish N. Why Are Services Cheaper in the Poor Countries? *Econ. J.*, June 1984, *94*(374), pp. 279–86.

Boehm, Ernst A. Money Wages, Consumer Prices, and Causality in Australia. *Econ. Rec.*, September 1984, *60*(170), pp. 236–51. **[G: Australia]**

Brown, Stephen P. A. and Phillips, Keith R. The Effects of Oil Prices and Exchange Rates on World Oil Consumption. *Fed. Res. Bank Dallas Econ. Rev.*, July 1984, pp. 13–21. **[G: OECD]**

Cagan, Phillip. The Consumer Price Index as an Escalator of Social-Security Benefits and Other Payments. In *Campbell, C. D., ed.*, 1984, pp. 207–32. **[G: U.S.]**

Cagan, Phillip. War, Prices, and Interest Rates: A Martial Solution to Gibson's Paradox: Comment. In *Bordo, M. D. and Schwartz, A. J., eds.*, 1984, pp. 604–10. **[G: U.K.]**

Cartaxo, Rui. Equaçoes input–output para os preços da procura final. (With English summary.) *Economia (Portugal)*, May 1984, *8*(2), pp. 381–94. **[G: Portugal]**

Cholewicka-Gozdźik, Krystyna. The Reform of the Price System in Poland. Its Assumptions and First Results. In *Bohnet, A., ed.*, 1984, pp. 97–117.

Chu, Ke-young and Morrison, Thomas K. The 1981–82 Recession and Non-Oil Primary Commodity Prices. *Int. Monet. Fund Staff Pap.*, March 1984, *31*(1), pp. 93–140.

Csikós-Nagy, Béla. Further Development of the Hungarian Price System. *Acta Oecon.*, 1984, *32*(1–2), pp. 21–37. **[G: Hungary]**

Cukierman, Alex and Leiderman, Leonardo. Price Controls and the Variability of Relative Prices. *J. Money, Credit, Banking*, August 1984, *16*(3), pp. 271–84. **[G: Israel]**

Currie, David and Levine, Paul. Exchange Rate and Price Level Volatility under Partial Information. *Greek Econ. Rev.*, August 1984, *6*(2), pp. 149–70.

Dagum, Estela Bee and Morry, Marietta. Basic Issues on the Seasonal Adjustment of the Canadian Consumer Price Index. *J. Bus. Econ. Statist.*, July 1984, *2*(3), pp. 250–59. **[G: Canada]**

Daniels, Edward J. The Cost of Synthetic Fuels in Relation to Oil Prices—Revisited. *Energy J.*, July 1984, *5*(3), pp. 147–57.

De Rosa, Dean A. The International Natural Rubber Agreement and Exchange Rate Changes. *Singapore Econ. Rev.*, April 1984, *29*(1), pp. 30–46. **[G: Global]**

Dwyer, Gerald P., Jr. The Gibson Paradox: A

Cross-Country Analysis. *Economica*, May 1984, *51*(202), pp. 109–27. [G: U.S.; U.K.; France; Belgium]

Eads, George C. R&D and Innovation: Some Empirical Findings: Comment. In *Griliches, Z., ed.*, 1984, pp. 150–53. [G: U.S.]

Early, John F.; Schmidt, Mary Lynn and Mosimann, Thomas J. Inflation and the Business Cycle during the Postwar Period. *Mon. Lab. Rev.*, November 1984, *107*(11), pp. 3–7. [G: U.S.]

Eckstein, Otto. Foundations of Aggregate Supply Price. *Amer. Econ. Rev.*, May 1984, *74*(2), pp. 216–20. [G: U.S.]

Eichhorn, Wolfgang and Pfingsten, Andreas. Sequences of Mechanistic Price Indices. In *[Beckmann, M. J.]*, 1984, pp. 57–64.

Ellman, Michael. The Control of Inflation? Errors in the Interpretation of CPE Data. In *Ellman, M.*, 1984, *1981*, pp. 130–34. [G: E. Europe]

Entov, R. M. Cyclical Factors behind the Movement of Prices. In *Nikitin, S. M., ed.*, 1984, pp. 126–78. [G: U.S.]

Evans, George and Gulamani, Riyaz. Tests for Rationality of the Carlson–Parkin Inflation Expectations Data. *Oxford Bull. Econ. Statist.*, February 1984, *46*(1), pp. 1–19. [G: U.K.]

Fama, Eugene F. and Gibbons, Michael R. A Comparison of Inflation Forecasts. *J. Monet. Econ.*, May 1984, *13*(3), pp. 327–48. [G: U.S.]

Farber, Stephen C. Cyclical Price Flexibility: A Test of Administered Pricing. *J. Ind. Econ.*, June 1984, *32*(4), pp. 465–76. [G: U.S.]

Fieleke, Norman S. Price Behavior during Balance of Payments Adjustment. *New Eng. Econ. Rev.*, November–December 1984, pp. 34–43. [G: Global]

Fishe, Raymond P. H. On Testing Hypotheses Using the Livingston Price Expectations Data: A Note. *J. Money, Credit, Banking*, Part 1 November 1984, *16*(4), pp. 520–27. [G: U.S.]

Fleming, Michael and Nellis, Joseph G. Housing Prices in the United Kingdom: The Problems of Measurement. *Nat. Westminster Bank Quart. Rev.*, November 1984, pp. 43–52. [G: U.K.]

Fortin, Michael and McBean, Edward A. Forecasting Relative Price Movements for Project Evaluation. *Water Resources Res.*, October 1984, *20*(10), pp. 1327–30. [G: Canada]

Franz, A. and Schwarzl, R. ICP 1980—A Brief Account from Austria. *Rev. Income Wealth*, June 1984, *30*(2), pp. 167–84. [G: Austria]

Freebairn, John W. Farm and Retail Food Prices. *Rev. Marketing Agr. Econ.*, August 1984, *52*(2), pp. 71–90. [G: Australia]

Friedman, Milton. The Success of Purchasing Power Parity: Historical Evidence and Its Implications for Macroeconomics: Comment. In *Bordo, M. D. and Schwartz, A. J., eds.*, 1984, pp. 157–62. [G: U.S.; U.K.; Canada]

Fuchs-Seliger, Susanne. A Logical Foundation of the Cost of Living Index. In *[Beckmann, M. J.]*, 1984, pp. 65–74.

Glezakos, Constantine and Nugent, Jeffrey B. Price Instability and Inflation: The Latin American Case. *World Devel.*, July 1984, *12*(7), pp. 755–58. [G: Latin America]

Granziol, M. J. General Price Level Instability and the Variability of Relative Prices in Switzerland. *Empirical Econ.*, 1984, *9*(1), pp. 1–13. [G: Switzerland]

Griliches, Zvi. R&D and Innovation: Some Empirical Findings: Comment. In *Griliches, Z., ed.*, 1984, pp. 148–49. [G: U.S.]

Grilli, Enzo R. and Yang, Maw-Cheng. Real and Monetary Determinants of Non-Oil Primary Commodity Price Movements. In *Storey, G. G.; Schmitz, A. and Sarris, A. H., eds.*, 1984, pp. 3–44. [G: Global]

Hafer, R. W. Examining the Recent Behavior of Inflation. *Fed. Res. Bank St. Louis Rev.*, August/September 1984, *66*(7), pp. 29–37. [G: U.S.]

Hansen, Bent and Lucas, Edward F. On the Accuracy of Index Numbers. *Rev. Income Wealth*, March 1984, *30*(1), pp. 25–38. [G: Egypt]

Heimler, Alberto. Price Behaviour in the Italian Manufacturing Industry. *Europ. Econ. Rev.*, December 1984, *26*(3), pp. 339–51. [G: Italy]

Hickman, Bert G. and Klein, Lawrence R. Wage–Price Behavior in the National Models of Project LINK. *Amer. Econ. Rev.*, May 1984, *74*(2), pp. 150–54. [G: OECD]

Hill, T. P. Introduction: The Special Conference on Purchasing Power Parities. *Rev. Income Wealth*, June 1984, *30*(2), pp. 125–33.

Hooper, Peter. Exchange Rates and the Prices of Nonfood, Nonfuel Products: Comment. *Brookings Pap. Econ. Act.*, 1984, (2), pp. 531–35. [G: U.S.]

Houthakker, Hendrik S. Relative Prices and Floating Exchange Rates—An Empirical Exploration. In *Csikós-Nagy, B.; Hague, D. and Hall, G., eds.*, 1984, pp. 336–46. [G: OECD]

Howell, Craig; Clem, Andrew and Burns, Roger. Inflation Remained Low in 1983 in Face of Strong Recovery. *Mon. Lab. Rev.*, May 1984, *107*(5), pp. 3–9. [G: U.S.]

Howell, Craig; Clem, Andrew and Burns, Roger. Producer Price Trends Continue Moderate in the Third Quarter. *Mon. Lab. Rev.*, January 1984, *107*(1), pp. 76–79. [G: U.S.]

Huntington, Hillard G. Real Oil Prices from 1980 to 1982. *Energy J.*, July 1984, *5*(3), pp. 119–31. [G: OECD]

Johnson, D. Gale. World Food and Agriculture. In *Simon, J. L. and Kahn, H., eds.*, 1984, pp. 67–112. [G: Global]

Johnson, Mark J. Robust Growth and the Strong Dollar Set Pattern for 1983 Import and Export Prices. *Mon. Lab. Rev.*, April 1984, *107*(4), pp. 3–14. [G: U.S.]

Johnson, Mark J. and Szarek, Patricia. Effects of Strong Dollar, Economic Recovery Apparent in First-Half Import and Export Prices. *Mon. Lab. Rev.*, October 1984, *107*(10), pp. 3–17. [G: U.S.]

Kawai, Masahiro. Exchange Rate—Price Causality in the Recent Floating Period. In *Bigman, D. and Taya, T., eds.*, 1984, pp. 189–211.
[G: OECD]

Kawasaki, S.; Gahlen, D. and Buck, Andrew J. The Variability of Relative Price Expectations, the Rate of Inflation and the Phillips Curve. In *Oppenländer, K. H. and Poser, G., eds.*, 1984, pp. 499–539.
[G: W. Germany]

Kay, John A. and Morris, C. Nick. The Gross Earnings Deflator. *Econ. J.*, June 1984, 94(374), pp. 357–69.
[G: U.K.]

Khamis, Salem H. On Aggregation Methods for International Comparisons. *Rev. Income Wealth*, June 1984, 30(2), pp. 185–205.

Kirchgässner, Gebhard. Die Abhängigkeit der Mineralölpreise in der Schweiz von der Entwicklung der Preise auf dem Rotterdamer Spotmarkt und vom Wechselkurs. (The Dependance of Swiss Oil Prices on the Price at Rotterdam and on the Exchange Rate. With English summary.) *Schweiz. Z. Volkswirtsch. Statist.*, September 1984, 120(3), pp. 293–313.
[G: Switzerland]

Kott, Phillip S. A Superpopulation Theory Approach to the Design of Price Index Estimators with Small Sampling Biases. *J. Bus. Econ. Statist.*, January 1984, 2(1), pp. 83–90.
[G: U.S.]

Kravis, Irving B. Comparative Studies of National Incomes and Prices. *J. Econ. Lit.*, March 1984, 22(1), pp. 1–39.
[G: Selected Countries]

Kravis, Irving B. and Lipsey, Robert E. Prices and Terms of Trade for Developed Country Exports of Manufactured Goods. In *Csikós-Nagy, B.; Hague, D. and Hall, G., eds.*, 1984, pp. 415–45.
[G: OECD]

Kumar, Pradeep. The Current Industrial Relations Scene in Canada, 1984: Technical Notes. In *Wood, W. D. and Kumar, P., eds.*, 1984, pp. 483–97.
[G: Canada]

de Leeuw, Frank and McKelvey, Michael J. Price Expectations of Business Firms: Bias in the Short and Long Run. *Amer. Econ. Rev.*, March 1984, 74(1), pp. 99–110.
[G: U.S.]

Lipsey, Robert E. The Success of Purchasing Power Prity: Historical Evidence and Its Implications for Macroeconomics: Comment. In *Bordo, M. D. and Schwartz, A. J., eds.*, 1984, pp. 151–56.
[G: U.S.; U.K.; Canada]

Locker, Hugo Krijnse. On the Estimation of Purchasing Power Parities on the Basic Heading Level. *Rev. Income Wealth*, June 1984, 30(2), pp. 135–52.
[G: Europe]

Locker, Hugo Krijnse and Faerber, H. D. Space and Time Comparisons of Purchasing Power Parities and Real Values. *Rev. Income Wealth*, March 1984, 30(1), pp. 53–83.
[G: EEC]

Mansfield, Edwin. R&D and Innovation: Some Empirical Findings. In *Griliches, Z., ed.*, 1984, pp. 127–48.
[G: U.S.]

Marris, Robin. Comparing the Incomes of Nations: A Critique of the International Comparison Project. *J. Econ. Lit.*, March 1984, 22(1), pp. 40–57.

McCloskey, Donald N. and Zecher, J. Richard.

The Success of Purchasing Power Parity: Historical Evidence and Its Implications for Macroeconomics. In *Bordo, M. D. and Schwartz, A. J., eds.*, 1984, pp. 121–50.
[G: U.S.; U.K.; Canada]

McDonald, Richard J. The "Underground Economy" and BLS Statistical Data. *Mon. Lab. Rev.*, January 1984, 107(1), pp. 4–18.
[G: U.S.]

Milne, William J. and Torous, Walter N. Long-Term Interest Rates and the Price Level: The Canadian Evidence on the Gibson Paradox. *Can. J. Econ.*, May 1984, 17(2), pp. 327–39.
[G: Canada]

Moore, Geoffrey H. and Cullity, John P. Trends and Cycles in Productivity, Unit Costs, and Prices: An International Perspective. In *Kendrick, J. W., ed.*, 1984, pp. 157–90.
[G: OECD]

Murty, G. V. S. N. Inflation and Relative Prices in India. *Indian Econ. J.*, July–Sept. 1984, 32(1), pp. 72–80.
[G: India]

Nagy, Tamás. Das System "weltmarktorientierter" Preise in Ungarn. (With English summary.) In *Bohnet, A., ed.*, 1984, pp. 69–95.
[G: Hungary]

Nikitin, S. M. Trends in Relative World Market Prices. In *Csikós-Nagy, B.; Hague, D. and Hall, G., eds.*, 1984, pp. 285–96.

Pasurka, Carl A., Jr. The Short-run Impact of Environmental Protection Costs on U.S. Product Prices. *J. Environ. Econ. Manage.*, December 1984, 11(4), pp. 380–90.
[G: U.S.]

Peel, David A. and Walters, K. Some Empirical Results on "the Rationality" of Expectations Derived from Survey Data. *Empirical Econ.*, 1984, 9(3), pp. 151–63.

Peña, Daniel and Sánchez-Albornoz, Nicolás. Wheat Prices in Spain, 1857–1890: An Application of the Box–Jenkins Methodology. *J. Europ. Econ. Hist.*, Fall 1984, 13(2), pp. 353–73.
[G: Spain]

Pryor, Frederic L. A Quantitative Study of the Structure and Behavior of Consumption and Prices in Different Economic Systems. In *Bohnet, A., ed.*, 1984, pp. 213–46.
[G: Selected Countries]

Rabil, Floyd A. Average Retail Food Prices: A Brief History of Methods. *Mon. Lab. Rev.*, November 1984, 107(11), pp. 52–53.
[G: U.S.]

Raveh, Adi. Comments on Some Properties of X-11. *Rev. Econ. Statist.*, May 1984, 66(2), pp. 343–48.
[G: U.S.]

Ray, George F. Relative Prices—Methods and Constraints in Forecasting: Some Empirical Considerations. In *Csikós-Nagy, B.; Hague, D. and Hall, G., eds.*, 1984, pp. 89–111.
[G: OECD]

Reekie, W. Duncan. Drug Prices in the UK, USA, Europe and Australia. *Australian Econ. Pap.*, June 1984, 23(42), pp. 71–78.
[G: U.K.; U.S.; Europe; Australia]

Rockoff, Hugh. Some Evidence on the Real Price of Gold, Its Costs of Production, and Commodity Prices. In *Bordo, M. D. and Schwartz, A. J., eds.*, 1984, pp. 613–44. **[G: U.S.; S. Africa; Australia; U.S.S.R.]**

Rockoff, Hugh. Some Evidence on the Real Price of Gold, Its Costs of Production, and Commodity Prices: Reply. In *Bordo, M. D. and Schwartz, A. J., eds.*, 1984, pp. 646–48. **[G: U.S.; U.S.S.R.; S. Africa; Australia]**

Roll, Richard. Orange Juice and Weather. *Amer. Econ. Rev.*, December 1984, *74*(5), pp. 861–80. **[G: U.S.]**

Rosenthal, Leslie. Quarterly Owner-occupied House Price Indices for the U.K., 1975–81. *Manchester Sch. Econ. Soc. Stud.*, September 1984, *52*(3), pp. 272–83. **[G: U.K.]**

Sargan, J. Denis. Wages and Prices in the United Kindgom: A Study in Econometric Methodology. In *Hendry, D. F. and Wallis, K. F., eds.*, 1984, pp. 275–314. **[G: U.K.]**

Sayad, João. Rural Credit and Positive Real Rates of Interest: Brazil's Experience with Rapid Inflation. In *Adams, D. W.; Graham, D. H. and Von Pischke, J. D., eds.*, 1984, pp. 146–60. **[G: Brazil]**

Schultze, Charles L. Cross-Country and Cross-Temporal Differences in Inflation Responsiveness. *Amer. Econ. Rev.*, May 1984, *74*(2), pp. 160–65. **[G: OECD]**

Schumann, Richard. Workers' Purchasing Power Rises Despite Slowdown in Wage and Salary Gains. *Mon. Lab. Rev.*, May 1984, *107*(5), pp. 10–14. **[G: U.S.]**

Sellekaerts, Willy and Sellekaerts, Brigitte H. Both Anticipated and Unanticipated Inflation Determine Relative Price Variability. *J. Post Keynesian Econ.*, Summer 1984, *6*(4), pp. 500–508.

Siddique, Abul K. M. Commodity Price Indices: A Historical and Methodological Review. *Statist. J.*, August 1984, *2*(3), pp. 255–83.

Stockton, David. Perspectives on the Recent Behavior of Inflation. *Fed. Res. Bull.*, June 1984, *70*(6), pp. 483–91. **[G: U.S.]**

Summers, Robert and Heston, Alan. Improved International Comparisons of Real Product and Its Composition: 1950–1980. *Rev. Income Wealth*, June 1984, *30*(2), pp. 207–62. **[G: Global]**

Sylos-Labini, Paolo. Prices and Income Distribution in the Manufacturing Industry. In *Sylos-Labini, P.*, 1984, 1979, pp. 185–209. **[G: Italy; U.S.; U.K.; W. Germany; Argentina]**

Szilágyi, György. Procedures for Updating the Results of International Comparisons. *Rev. Income Wealth*, June 1984, *30*(2), pp. 153–65. **[G: Europe; U.S.]**

Tiraspolsky, Anita. L'effet "taux de change" sur le niveau des prix intra-C.A.E.M. (The Exchange Rate Effect on the Intra-CMEA Price Level. With English summary.) *Écon. Soc.*, February 1984, *18*(2), pp. 139–59. **[G: CMEA]**

Unnevehr, Laurian J. Transport Costs, Tariffs and the Influence of World Markets on Indonesian

Domestic Cassava Prices. *Bull. Indonesian Econ. Stud.*, April 1984, *20*(1), pp. 30–43. **[G: Indonesia]**

Vartia, Pentti L. I. and Mankinen, Reijo. Perceived and Expected Price Changes in Finland. *Weltwirtsch. Arch.*, 1984, *120*(1), pp. 121–32. **[G: Finland]**

Vomfelde, Werner. Die Determinanten der Preisentwicklung in der Bundesrepublik Deutschland. (The Determinants of Price-Developments in the Federal Republic of Germany. With English summary.) *Jahr. Nationalökon. Statist.*, January 1984, *199*(1), pp. 32–48. **[G: W. Germany]**

Waldorf, William H. Trends and Cycles in Productivity, Unit Costs, and Prices: An International Perspective: Comment. In *Kendrick, J. W., ed.*, 1984, pp. 191–95. **[G: OECD]**

Warr, Peter G. Exchange Rate Protection in Indonesia. *Bull. Indonesian Econ. Stud.*, August 1984, *20*(2), pp. 53–89. **[G: Indonesia]**

Warren, Neil A. Some Limitations of the Australian Consumer Price Index. *Australian Bull. Lab.*, September 1984, *10*(4), pp. 211–22. **[G: Australia]**

Waugh, Frederick V. The Marginal Utility of Money in the United States from 1917 to 1921 and from 1922 to 1932. In *Waugh, F. V.*, 1984, 1935, pp. 3–26. **[G: U.S.]**

Weicher, John C. Disinflation in the Housing Market. In *Fellner, W., ed.*, 1984, pp. 155–204. **[G: U.S.]**

Wellington, Donald C. and Gallo, Joseph C. Investment in a Small Antique. *J. Cult. Econ.*, December 1984, *8*(2), pp. 93–98. **[G: U.S.]**

Wiles, Peter. Price Indices under Suppressed Inflation; and an Alternative Approach to Economic Measurement. In *Bohnet, A., ed.*, 1984, pp. 203–11.

Wolters, Jürgen. Preiserwartungen des Ifo-Konjunkturtestes und die tatsächliche Preisentwicklung. (Price Expectations in the IFO-Business Test and the Development of Prices—An Empirical Study. With English summary.) *Ifo-Studien*, 1984, *30*(1), pp. 29–61. **[G: W. Germany]**

Woo, Wing T. Exchange Rates and the Prices of Nonfood, Nonfuel Products. *Brookings Pap. Econ. Act.*, 1984, (2), pp. 511–30.

Wren-Lewis, Simon. Omitted Variables in Equations Relating Prices to Money. *Appl. Econ.*, August 1984, *16*(4), pp. 483–96. **[G: U.K.]**

Zuo, Mu. Price Ratios among Agricultural Products Must Be Well Adjusted. *Chinese Econ. Stud.*, Fall 1984, *18*(1), pp. 34–43. **[G: China]**

228 Regional Statistics

2280 Regional Statistics

Bradbury, Katharine L. Urban Decline and Distress: An Update. *New Eng. Econ. Rev.*, July–August 1984, pp. 39–55. **[G: U.S.]**

Bretzfelder, Robert and Friedenberg, Howard. Regional Nonfarm Wages and Salaries Thus Far in the Recovery. *Surv. Curr. Bus.*, April 1984, *64*(4), pp. 25–26. [G: U.S.]

Browne, Lynn E. How Different Are Regional Wages? A Second Look. *New Eng. Econ. Rev.*, March–April 1984, pp. 40–47. [G: U.S.]

Courbis, Raymond. Multiregional Modeling and Statistical Information. In *Nijkamp, P. and Rietveld, P., eds.*, 1984, pp. 193–201.

Cuthbert, J. R. Proportion Analysis on Cell Data: Distortions Due to Variations in Cell Sizes. *Urban Stud.*, February 1984, *21*(1), pp. 83–88. [G: U.K.]

Friedenberg, Howard and Bretzfelder, Robert. Regional Shifts in Personal Income by Industrial Component, 1959–83. *Surv. Curr. Bus.*, November 1984, *64*(11), pp. 28–36.
[G: U.S.]

Nijkamp, Peter; Rietveld, Piet and Rima, Annemarie. Information Content of Data from Different Spatial Aggregation Levels. In *Nijkamp, P. and Rietveld, P., eds.*, 1984, pp. 215–28.
[G: Netherlands]

O'Farrell, P. N. Components of Manufacturing Employment Change in Ireland, 1973–1981. *Urban Stud.*, May 1984, *21*(2), pp. 155–76.
[G: Ireland]

Pautrat, Charles; Guérard, Agnès and Lafarge, Guy. La dimension régionale dans l'évolution des biens et services. Une nouvelle méthode d'analyse. (With English summary.) *Revue Écon. Polit.*, January–February 1984, *94*(1), pp. 60–91. [G: France]

Peters, Aribert B. Technical Aspects of Computerized Spatial Information Systems. In *Nijkamp, P. and Rietveld, P., eds.*, 1984, pp. 263–69.

Ponsard, Claude and Tranqui, Phuoc. La régionalisation floue de l'économie européenne. (With English summary.) *Revue Écon. Polit.*, January–February 1984, *94*(1), pp. 1–25.
[G: EEC]

Ringleb, Al. Sectoral Shifts and U.S. Regional Economic Growth, 1953–73. *Reg. Sci. Persp.*, 1984, *14*(2), pp. 60–80. [G: U.S.]

Ro, Young Key and Forster, D. Lynn. Regional Input–Output Analysis of an Environmental Regulation. *J. Econ. Devel.*, July 1984, *9*(1), pp. 167–88. [G: U.S.]

Rosen, Richard J. Regional Variations in Employment and Unemployment during 1970–82. *Mon. Lab. Rev.*, February 1984, *107*(2), pp. 38–45. [G: U.S.]

Smith, Stanley K. and Mandell, Marylou. A Comparison of Population Estimation Methods: Housing Unit versus Component II, Ratio Correlation, and Administrative Records. *J. Amer. Statist. Assoc.*, June 1984, *79*(386), pp. 282–89. [G: U.S.]

Stamas, George D. State and Regional Employment and Unemployment in 1983. *Mon. Lab. Rev.*, September 1984, *107*(9), pp. 9–15.
[G: U.S.]

Stevens, Richard L. Measuring Minority Business Formation and Failure. *Rev. Black Polit. Econ.*, Spring 1984, *12*(4), pp. 71–84.
[G: U.S.]

Wigan, M. R. Information Technology and Integrated Regional Development. In *Nijkamp, P. and Rietveld, P., eds.*, 1984, pp. 271–83.

229 Microdata and Database Analysis

2290 Microdata and Database Analysis

Duncan, Greg J.; Juster, F. Thomas and Morgan, James N. The Role of Panel Studies in a World of Scarce Research Resources. In *[Ferber, R.]*, 1984, pp. 301–28. [G: U.S.]

300 Domestic Monetary and Fiscal Theory and Institutions

310 DOMESTIC MONETARY AND FINANCIAL THEORY AND INSTITUTIONS

3100 General

Asztalos, László Gy.; Bokros, Lajos and Surányi, György. Reform and Financial Institutional System in Hungary. *Acta Oecon.*, 1984, *32*(3–4), pp. 251–68. [G: Hungary]

Aziz, Zeti Akhtar. Financial Institutions and Markets in Malaysia. In *Skully, M. T., ed.*, 1984, pp. 110–66. [G: Malaysia]

Clower, Robert W. Monetary History and Positive Economics. In *Clower, R. W.*, 1984, *1964*, pp. 59–77.

Collyns, Charles and Horiguchi, Yusuke. Financial Supermarkets in the United States. *Finance Develop.*, March 1984, *21*(1), pp. 18–22. [G: U.S.]

Eken, Sena. Integration of Domestic and International Financial Markets: The Japanese Experience. *Int. Monet. Fund Staff Pap.*, September 1984, *31*(3), pp. 499–548. [G: Japan]

Evans, Gary R. The Evolution of Financial Institutions and the Ineffectiveness of Modern Monetary Policy. *J. Econ. Issues*, June 1984, *18*(2), pp. 439–48. [G: U.S.]

Gelman, Jorge Daniel. Natural Economies or Money Economies? Silver Production and Monetary Circulation in Spanish America (Late XVI–Early XVII Centuries). *J. Europ. Econ. Hist.*, Spring 1984, *13*(1), pp. 99–115.
[G: Bolivia; Argentina; Paraguay]

Giacometti, Jacques. Langage et monnaie chez Locke et Turgot. (Language and Money: Locke and Turgot. With English summary.) *Écon. Soc.*, March 1984, *18*(3), pp. 119–37.

Gupta, Kanhaya L. Financial Liberalization and Economic Growth: Some Simulation Results. *J. Econ. Devel.*, December 1984, *9*(2), pp. 25–43. [G: Latin America; S.E. Asia]

Kagin, Donald H. Monetary Aspects of the Treasury Notes of the War of 1812. *J. Econ. Hist.*, March 1984, *44*(1), pp. 69–88. [G: U.S.]

Kindleberger, Charles P. Financial Institutions and Economic Development: A Comparison of Great Britain and France in the Eighteenth and Nineteenth Centuries. *Exploration Econ. Hist.*, April 1984, *21*(2), pp. 103–24.
[G: U.K.; France]

Lee, Sheng-Yi. Financial Institutions and Markets in Singapore. In *Skully, M. T., ed.*, 1984, pp. 226–95. [G: Singapore]

Lim, G. C. The Martin Report. *Australian Econ. Rev.*, 2nd Quarter 1984, (66), pp. 26–34. [G: Australia]

McLeod, Ross. Financial Institutions and Markets in Indonesia. In *Skully, M. T., ed.*, 1984, pp. 49–109. [G: Indonesia]

O'Brien, D. P. Monetary Economics. In *Creedy, J. and O'Brien, D. P., eds.*, 1984, pp. 3–45.

Pascual, Alfredo E. Financial Institutions and Markets in the Philippines. In *Skully, M. T., ed.*, 1984, pp. 167–225. [G: Philippines]

Patrick, Hugh. Japanese Financial Development in Historical Perspective, 1868–1980. In *[Reynolds, L. G.]*, 1984, pp. 302–27. [G: Japan]

Redish, Angela. Why Was Specie Scarce in Colonial Economies? An Analysis of the Canadian Currency, 1796–1830. *J. Econ. Hist.*, September 1984, *44*(3), pp. 713–28. [G: Canada]

Rybczynski, Tad M. Industrial Finance System in Europe, U.S. and Japan. *J. Econ. Behav. Organ.*, September–December 1984, *5*(3–4), pp. 275–86. [G: Europe; U.S.; Japan]

Skully, Michael T. Financial Institutions and Markets in Brunei. In *Skully, M. T., ed.*, 1984, pp. 1–48. [G: Brunei]

Skully, Michael T. Financial Institutions and Markets in Thailand. In *Skully, M. T., ed.*, 1984, pp. 296–378. [G: Thailand]

Walker, Donald A. Money and Markets: Introduction. In *Clower, R. W.*, 1984, pp. 1–18.

311 Domestic Monetary and Financial Theory and Policy

3110 Domestic Monetary Theory and Policy

Arnon, Arie. Marx's Theory of Money: The Formative Years. *Hist. Polit. Econ.*, Winter 1984, *16*(4), pp. 555–75.

Ascah, Louis. Sommes-nous tous des néo-keynésiens à la Friedman–Phelps–Lucas maintenant? (Are We All Neo-Keynesians a là Friedman–Phelps–Lucas Now? With English summary.) *L'Actual. Econ.*, March 1984, *60*(1), pp. 132–35.

Barnett, William A.; Offenbacher, Edward K. and Spindt, Paul A. The New Divisia Monetary Aggregates. *J. Polit. Econ.*, December 1984, *92*(6), pp. 1049–85. [G: U.S.]

Blanchard, Olivier J. The Lucas Critique and the Volcker Deflation. *Amer. Econ. Rev.*, May 1984, *74*(2), pp. 211–15. [G: U.S.]

Blanchard, Olivier J. and Summers, Lawrence H. Perspectives on High World Real Interest Rates. *Brookings Pap. Econ. Act.*, 1984, (2), pp. 273–324. [G: U.S.; W. Europe; Japan]

Blinder, Alan S. Perspectives on High World Real Interest Rates: Comment. *Brookings Pap. Econ. Act.*, 1984, (2), pp. 325–33. [G: U.S.; W. Europe; Japan]

Blundell-Wignall, Adrian and Chouraqui, Jean-Claude. The Role of Exchange Market Intervention. *Nat. Westminster Bank Quart. Rev.*, November 1984, pp. 53–68. [G: U.K.]

Boughton, James M. and Wicker, Elmus R. A Reply [The Behavior of the Currency–Deposit Ratio during the Great Depression]. *J. Money, Credit, Banking*, August 1984, *16*(3), pp. 366–67. [G: U.S.]

Brock, Philip L. Inflationary Finance in an Open Economy. *J. Monet. Econ.*, July 1984, *14*(1), pp. 37–53. [G: OECD; LDCs]

Bruni, Franco. Controllo monetario, fabbisogno del settore pubblico e "moneta del Tesoro": Qualche ulteriore riflessione. (Monetary Control, the Public-Sector Requirement and "Treasury Money": Some Further Reflections. With English summary.) *Bancaria*, August 1984, *40*(8), pp. 779–81.

Bruni, Franco. Controllo monetario, fabbisogno del settore pubblico e "moneta del Tesoro." (Monetary Control, the Public-Sector Requirement and "Treasury Money." With English summary.) *Bancaria*, February 1984, *40*(2), pp. 146–58.

Brunner, Karl. Monetary Policy and Monetary Order. *Aussenwirtschaft*, September 1984, *39*(3), pp. 187–206.

Buiter, Willem H. Granger-Causality and Policy Effectiveness. *Economica*, May 1984, *51*(202), pp. 151–62.

Calderón-Rossell, Jorge R. Optimal Financial Structure of Finance Companies in a Regulated Environment of a Developing Country. *J. Banking Finance*, September 1984, *8*(3), pp. 443–57. [G: LDCs]

Camilleri, Arthur P.; Nguyen, Duc-Tho and Campbell, Robert B. Policy Changes and External Disturbances in a Small Open Economy: Stability and Dynamic Responses. *Int. Econ. Rev.*, February 1984, *25*(1), pp. 123–58.

Clark, Truman A. Violations of the Gold Points, 1890–1908. *J. Polit. Econ.*, October 1984, *92*(5), pp. 791–823. [G: U.S.; U.K.]

Clower, Robert W. A Reconsideration of the Microfoundations of Monetary Theory. In *Clower, R. W.*, 1984, *1967*, pp. 81–89.

Clower, Robert W. Classical Monetary Theory Revisited. In *Clower, R. W.*, 1984, *1963*, pp. 27–33.

Clower, Robert W. Is There an Optimal Money Supply? In *Clower, R. W.*, 1984, *1970*, pp. 128–37.

Clower, Robert W. Money and Markets. In *Clower, R. W.*, 1984, pp. 259–72.

Clower, Robert W. Theoretical Foundations of Monetary Policy. In *Clower, R. W.*, 1984, *1971*, pp. 107–19.

Clower, Robert W. What Traditional Monetary Theory Really Wasn't. In *Clower, R. W.*, 1984, *1969*, pp. 123–27.

Connolly, Michael B. and Taylor, Dean. The Exact Timing of the Collapse of an Exchange Rate Regime and Its Impact on the Relative Price of Traded Goods. *J. Money, Credit, Banking*, May 1984, *16*(2), pp. 194–207.

Conti, Giuliano. Indicatori della politica monetaria: il tasso di cambio. (Monetary Policy Indicators: The Exchange Rate. With English summary.) *Giorn. Econ.*, May–June 1984, *43*(5–6), pp. 327–43.

Cross, Rod. Monetarism and Duhem's Thesis: Reply to Comments. In *Wiles, P. and Routh, G., eds.*, 1984, pp. 111–20.

Cross, Rod. Monetarism and Duhem's Thesis. In *Wiles, P. and Routh, G., eds.*, 1984, pp. 78–99.

Cumby, Robert E. and Obstfeld, Maurice. International Interest Rate and Price Level Linkages under Flexible Exchange Rates: A Review of Recent Evidence. In *Bilson, J. F. O. and Marston, R. C., eds.*, 1984, pp. 121–51. [G: Selected OECD]

Dornbusch, Rudiger and Frenkel, Jacob A. The Gold Standard Crisis of 1847. *J. Int. Econ.*, February 1984, *16*(1/2), pp. 1–27. [G: U.K.]

Dow, Sheila C. and Earl, Peter E. Methodology and Orthodox Monetary Policy. *Écon. Appl.*, 1984, *37*(1), pp. 143–63. [G: U.K.]

Engel, Günther. Verstetigung des Geldmengenwachstums und politische Unabhängigkeit der Zentralbank. (Steady Monetary Growth and Political Independence of the Central Bank. With English summary.) *Kredit Kapital*, 1984, *17*(4), pp. 540–55. [G: Germany]

Evans, Paul. The Effects on Output of Money Growth and Interest Rate Volatility in the United States. *J. Polit. Econ.*, April 1984, *92*(2), pp. 204–22. [G: U.S.]

Fazzari, Steve M. and Minsky, Hyman P. Domestic Monetary Policy: If Not Monetarism, What? *J. Econ. Issues*, March 1984, *18*(1), pp. 101–16.

Friedman, Milton. Lessons from the 1979–82 Monetary Policy Experiment. *Amer. Econ. Rev.*, May 1984, *74*(2), pp. 397–400. [G: U.S.]

Friedman, Milton. Monetary Policy for the 1980s. In *Moore, J. H., ed.*, 1984, pp. 23–60. [G: U.S.]

Gilbert, R. Alton. Calculating the Adjusted Monetary Base under Contemporaneous Reserve Requirements. *Fed. Res. Bank St. Louis Rev.*, February 1984, *66*(2), pp. 27–32. [G: U.S.]

Goedhuys, D. W. The Business Cycle and Public Policy. *S. Afr. J. Econ.*, June 1984, *52*(2), pp. 133–45. [G: S. Africa]

Goldstein, Henry N. and Haynes, Stephen E. A Critical Appraisal of McKinnon's World Money Supply Hypothesis [Currency Substitution and Instability in the World Dollar Standard]. *Amer. Econ. Rev.*, March 1984, *74*(1), pp. 217–24. [G: U.S.]

Gonzalez-Vega, Claudio. Credit-Rationing Behavior of Agricultural Lenders: The Iron Law of Interest-Rate Restrictions. In *Adams, D. W.; Graham, D. H. and Von Pischke, J. D., eds.*, 1984, pp. 78–95.

Gramley, Lyle E. Statement to the U.S. House Subcommittee on Domestic Monetary Policy of the Committee on Banking, Finance and Urban Affairs, June 8, 1984. *Fed. Res. Bull.*, June 1984, *70*(6), pp. 499–501. [G: U.S.]

Greenspan, Alan. Removing Structural Barriers

to Growth. In *Wachter, M. L. and Wachter, S. M., eds.*, 1984, pp. 10–14. [G: U.S.]

Gupta, Sanjeev. Causal Relationship between Domestic Credit and International Reserves: The Experience of Developing Countries. *Kredit Kapital*, 1984, *17*(2), pp. 261–70. [G: India; Malaysia; Mexico; Taiwan]

Guttmann, Robert. Stagflation and Credit–Money in the U.S.A. *Brit. Rev. Econ. Issues*, Autumn 1984, *6*(15), pp. 79–119. [G: U.S.]

Hafer, R. W. Comparing Time-Series and Survey Forecasts of Weekly Changes in Money: A Methodological Note. *J. Finance*, September 1984, *39*(4), pp. 1207–13. [G: U.S.]

Hahn, Frank H. Professor Friedman's Views on Money. In *Hahn, F.*, 1984, *1971*, pp. 259–82.

Hartropp, Andrew and Heathfield, David. Monetarism and Duhem's Thesis: Comment. In *Wiles, P. and Routh, G., eds.*, 1984, pp. 105–10.

von Hayek, Friedrich A. The Exchange Value of Money: A Review. In *von Hayek, F. A. (II)*, 1984, pp. 190–94.

Horn, Karen N. Statement to the U.S. House Subcommittee on Domestic Monetary Policy of the Committee on Banking, Finance and Urban Affairs, June 8, 1984. *Fed. Res. Bull.*, June 1984, *70*(6), pp. 502–06. [G: U.S.]

Horsman, Andrew. Money, Banking and Inflation. In *Sandford, C. and Bradbury, M., eds.*, 1984, pp. 164–87. [G: Germany; U.S.]

Humphrey, Thomas M. and Keleher, Robert E. The Lender of Last Resort: A Historical Perspective [International Debt, Bank Failures, and the Money Supply: The Thirties and the Eighties]. *Cato J.*, Spring/Summer 1984, *4*(1), pp. 275–318. [G: U.K.]

Hutchinson, Michael M. and Pigott, Charles. Budget Deficits, Exchange Rates and the Current Account: Theory and U.S. Evidence. *Fed. Res. Bank San Francisco Econ. Rev.*, Fall 1984, (4), pp. 5–25. [G: U.S.]

Klein, Lawrence R. Money in the Wharton Quarterly Model: A Reply. *J. Money, Credit, Banking*, February 1984, *16*(1), pp. 76–79. [G: U.S.]

Kopecky, Kenneth J. Monetary Control under Reverse Lag and Contemporaneous Reserve Accounting: A Comparison [Reserve Requirements: Are They Lagged in the Wrong Direction?]. *J. Money, Credit, Banking*, February 1984, *16*(1), pp. 81–88. [G: U.S.]

Laidler, David. Misconceptions about the Real-Bills Doctrine: A Comment [The Real-Bills Doctrine versus the Quantity Theory: A Reconsideration]. *J. Polit. Econ.*, February 1984, *92*(1), pp. 149–55.

Lane, Timothy D. Money Supply Control and Lagged Reserve Accounting: A Comment. *J. Money, Credit, Banking*, Part 1 November 1984, *16*(4), pp. 536–46. [G: U.S.]

Laney, Leroy O.; Radcliffe, Christopher D. and Willett, Thomas D. Currency Substitution: Comment. *Southern Econ. J.*, April 1984, *50*(4), pp. 1196–1200. [G: U.S.; W. Germany]

Laurent, Robert D. A Reply [Reserve Requirements: Are They Lagged in the Wrong Direction?]. *J. Money, Credit, Banking*, February 1984, *16*(1), pp. 89–92. **[G: U.S.]**

Lecaldano Sasso La Terza, Edoardo. Il prodotto interno lordo a prezzi correnti come obiettivo di politica economica. (Gross Domestic Product at Current Prices as an Economic Policy Objective. With English summary.) *Bancaria*, February 1984, *40*(2), pp. 159–65. **[G: Italy]**

Lee, Joong-Koon and Wellington, Donald C. Angell and the Stable Money Rule. *J. Polit. Econ.*, October 1984, *92*(5), pp. 972–78. **[G: U.S.]**

Mankiw, N. Gregory and Summers, Lawrence H. Do Long-Term Interest Rates Overreact to Short-Term Interest Rates? *Brookings Pap. Econ. Act.*, 1984, (1), pp. 223–42. **[G: U.S.]**

McCormick, Brian J. Monetarism and Duhem's Thesis: Comment. In *Wiles, P. and Routh, G.*, eds., 1984, pp. 100–104.

McKinnon, Ronald I., et al. International Influences on the U.S. Economy: Summary of an Exchange. *Amer. Econ. Rev.*, December 1984, *74*(5), pp. 1132–34. **[G: U.S.]**

Meiselman, David I. The Lender of Last Resort and a Money Supply Rule [International Debt, Bank Failures, and the Money Supply: The Thirties and the Eighties]. *Cato J.*, Spring/Summer 1984, *4*(1), pp. 319–21. **[G: U.K.]**

Meltzer, Allan H. The Cure for Monetary Madness. *Policy Rev.*, Winter 1984, (27), pp. 72–74. **[G: U.S.; OECD]**

Miles, Marc A. Currency Substitution: Reply. *Southern Econ. J.*, April 1984, *50*(4), pp. 1201–03. **[G: U.S.; W. Germany]**

Moore, Basil J. Contemporaneous Reserve Accounting: Can Reserves Be Quantity-constrained? *J. Post Keynesian Econ.*, Fall 1984, *7*(1), pp. 103–13. **[G: U.S.]**

Palash, Carl J. and Radecki, Lawrence J. Did Financial Markets in 1983 Point to Recession? *Fed. Res. Bank New York Quart. Rev.*, Summer 1984, *9*(2), pp. 32–37. **[G: U.S.]**

Pascallon, Pierre. La crise et les reformes monetaires. (The Crisis and Monetary Reforms. With English summary.) *Rivista Int. Sci. Econ. Com.*, October–November 1984, *31*(10–11), pp. 944–75.

Pierce, David A.; Grupe, Michael R. and Cleveland, William P. Seasonal Adjustment of the Weekly Monetary Aggregates: A Model-based Approach. *J. Bus. Econ. Statist.*, July 1984, *2*(3), pp. 260–70. **[G: U.S.]**

Presley, J. R. D. H. Robertson: Some Restoration. *J. Post Keynesian Econ.*, Winter 1983-84, *6*(2), pp. 230–40.

Radcliffe, Christopher D.; Warga, Arthur D. and Willett, Thomas D. Currency Substitution and Instability in the World Dollar Standard: Comment. *Amer. Econ. Rev.*, December 1984, *74*(5), pp. 1129–31. **[G: U.S.]**

Ranuzzi, Paolo. Controllo monetario, fabbisogno del settore pubblico e "moneta del Tesoro": Un commento. (Monetary Control, the Public-Sector Requirement and "Treasury Money":

A Commentary. With English summary.) *Bancaria*, August 1984, *40*(8), pp. 776–78.

Schadler, Susan M. Interest Rates and Exchange Rates. *Finance Develop.*, June 1984, *21*(2), pp. 7–11. **[G: U.S.; Japan]**

Silvia, John E. Monetary Indicators of Economic Activity. *Eastern Econ. J.*, January-March 1984, *10*(1), pp. 15–22. **[G: U.S.]**

Streit, Joachim. Die Relevanz monetärer Innovationen in den USA für die Geldpolitik. (The Importance of U.S. Monetary Innovations for the Monetary Policy. With English summary.) *Kredit Kapital*, 1984, *17*(4), pp. 559–79. **[G: U.S.]**

Trescott, Paul B. The Behavior of the Currency–Deposit Ratio during the Great Depression: A Comment. *J. Money, Credit, Banking*, August 1984, *16*(3), pp. 362–65. **[G: U.S.]**

Urich, Thomas J. and Wachtel, Paul. The Effects of Inflation and Money Supply Announcements on Interest Rates. *J. Finance*, September 1984, *39*(4), pp. 1177–88. **[G: U.S.]**

Vaubel, Roland. The Government's Money Monopoly: Externalities or Natural Monopoly? *Kyklos*, 1984, *37*(1), pp. 27–58. **[G: Selected OECD]**

Vernon, Jack. Interest on Checking Deposits and the Inflation Tax. *Atlantic Econ. J.*, July 1984, *12*(2), pp. 72–73. **[G: U.S.]**

Weintraub, Robert E. Money in the Wharton Quarterly Model: A Rejoinder. *J. Money, Credit, Banking*, February 1984, *16*(1), pp. 79–80. **[G: U.S.]**

Weintraub, Robert E. Money in the Wharton Quarterly Model: A Comment. *J. Money, Credit, Banking*, February 1984, *16*(1), pp. 69–75. **[G: U.S.]**

Weiss, Laurence. Do Long-Term Interest Rates Overreact to Short-Term Interest Rates? Comments. *Brookings Pap. Econ. Act.*, 1984, (1), pp. 243–45. **[G: U.S.]**

White, Lawrence H. Competitive Payments Systems and the Unit of Account. *Amer. Econ. Rev.*, September 1984, *74*(4), pp. 699–712.

3112 Monetary Theory; Empirical Studies Illustrating Theory

Adams, Dale W.; Graham, Douglas H. and Von Pischke, J. D. Overview of the Importance of Interest-Rate Policies. In *Adams, D. W.; Graham, D. H. and Von Pischke, J. D.*, eds., 1984, pp. 61–64.

Ahking, Francis W. A Time Series Analysis of the Relationship between Income Velocity of Money and the Quantity of Money. *Quart. J. Bus. Econ.*, Autumn 1984, *23*(4), pp. 3–12. **[G: U.S.]**

Ahking, Francis W. International Currency Substitution: A Reexamination of Britain's Econometric Evidence: A Comment. *J. Money, Credit, Banking*, Part 1 November 1984, *16*(4), pp. 546–56. **[G: U.S.; W. Germany; U.K.]**

Ahking, Francis W. The Predictive Performance of the Time-Series Model and the Regression Model of the Income Velocity of Money: Evidence from Five EEC Countries. *J. Banking Finance*, September 1984, *8*(3), pp. 389–415. **[G: Italy; U.K.; France; W. Germany; Netherlands]**

Ahmed, Ehsan and Johannes, James M. St. Louis Equation Restrictions and Criticisms Revisited: A Note. *J. Money, Credit, Banking*, Part 1 November 1984, *16*(4), pp. 514–20. **[G: U.S.]**

Ahtiala, Pekka. A Synthesis of the Macroeconomic Approaches to Exchange Rate Determination. *Europ. Econ. Rev.*, March 1984, *24*(2), pp. 117–36.

Åkerholm, Johnny. Penningpolitikens effekter vid duala finansieringsmarknader. (Monetary Policy Effects in Dual Credit Markets. With English summary.) *Ekon. Samfundets Tidskr.*, 1984, *37*(3), pp. 213–22. **[G: Finland]**

Aliber, Robert Z. Structural Change, Monetary Policy and the Foreign Exchange Value of Sterling. In *Griffiths, B. and Wood, G. E., eds.*, 1984, pp. 213–30. **[G: U.K.]**

Amsler, Christine. A "Pure" Long-Term Interest Rate and the Demand for Money. *J. Econ. Bus.*, August 1984, *36*(3), pp. 359–70. **[G: U.S.]**

Andersen, Torben M. Interest-Rate Policy and Rational Expectations. *J. Macroecon.*, Summer 1984, *6*(3), pp. 311–22.

Anderson, Robert; Ando, Albert and Enzler, Jared. Interaction between Fiscal and Monetary Policy and the Real Rate of Interest. *Amer. Econ. Rev.*, May 1984, *74*(2), pp. 55–60. **[G: U.S.]**

Antipova, O. N. and Golosov, V. V. Ideas of Profit and Interest. In *Smirnov, A. D.; Golosov, V. V. and Maximova, V. F., eds.*, 1984, pp. 88–109.

Apostolakis, Bobby E. The Plethora of Antitheses in Empirical Interpretations of Money Demand Functions. *Rivista Int. Sci. Econ. Com.*, October–November 1984, *31*(10–11), pp. 976–91. **[G: Greece]**

Arena, Richard. Monnaie, production et actifs financiers dans une perspective keynésienne: quelques éléments d'interprétation. (Money Production and Financial Assets within a Keynesian Framework: Some Results for an Interpretation. With English summary.) *Écon. Soc.*, April 1984, *18*(4), pp. 259–82.

Arestis, Philip and Driver, Ciaran. A Comparison of the Monetary–Financial Blocks of Two Post-Keynesian Short-Period Models. *Brit. Rev. Econ. Issues*, Autumn 1984, *6*(15), pp. 53–78. **[G: U.K.]**

Arnon, Arie. The Transformation in Thomas Tooke's Monetary Theory Reconsidered. *Hist. Polit. Econ.*, Summer 1984, *16*(2), pp. 311–26.

Artis, M. J. and Lewis, M. K. How Unstable Is the Demand for Money in the United Kingdom? *Economica*, November 1984, *51*(204), pp. 473–76. **[G: U.K.]**

Artus, Jacques R. Effects of United States Monetary Restraint on the DM/$ Exchange Rate and

the German Economy. In *Bilson, J. F. O. and Marston, R. C., eds.*, 1984, pp. 469–94. **[G: U.S.; W. Germany]**

Artus, Patrick. Le fonctionnement du marché du crédit: Diverses analyses dans un cadre de déséquilibre. (The Functioning of the Credit Market: Several Analyses in a Disequilibrium Context. With English summary.) *Revue Écon.*, July 1984, *35*(4), pp. 591–621. **[G: France]**

Aschheim, Joseph and Tavlas, George S. The Monetary Thought–Ideology Nexus: Simons versus Keynes. *Banca Naz. Lavoro Quart. Rev.*, June 1984, (149), pp. 177–96.

Atkinson, Paul, et al. The Efficacy of Monetary Targeting: The Stability of Demand for Money in Major OECD Countries. *OECD Econ. Stud.*, Autumn 1984, (3), pp. 145–76. **[G: OECD]**

Bade, Robin and Parkin, Michael. Is Sterling M_3 the Right Aggregate? In *Griffiths, B. and Wood, G. E., eds.*, 1984, pp. 241–86. **[G: U.K.]**

Batten, Dallas S. and Hafer, R. W. Currency Substitution: A Test of Its Importance. *Fed. Res. Bank St. Louis Rev.*, August/September 1984, *66*(7), pp. 5–11. **[G: Canada; Germany; France; Netherlands; U.K.]**

Batten, Dallas S. and Thornton, Daniel L. Discount Rate Changes and the Foreign Exchange Market. *J. Int. Money Finance*, December 1984, *3*(303), pp. 279–92. **[G: U.S.]**

Batten, Dallas S. and Thornton, Daniel L. How Robust Are the Policy Conclusions of the St. Louis Equation?: Some Further Evidence. *Fed. Res. Bank St. Louis Rev.*, June/July 1984, *66*(6), pp. 26–32. **[G: U.S.]**

Batts, John and Dowling, J. M. The Stability of the Demand-for-Money Function in the United Kingdom: 1880–1975. *Quart. Rev. Econ. Bus.*, Autumn 1984, *24*(3), pp. 37–48. **[G: U.K.]**

Bean, Charles R. A Little Bit More Evidence on the Natural Rate Hypothesis from the U.K. *Europ. Econ. Rev.*, August 1984, *25*(3), pp. 279–92. **[G: U.K.]**

Beenstock, Michael. Structural Change, Monetary Policy and the Foreign Exchange Value of Sterling: Comment. In *Griffiths, B. and Wood, G. E., eds.*, 1984, pp. 231–32. **[G: U.K.]**

Begg, David K. H. Rational Expectations and Bond Pricing: Modelling the Term Structure with and without Certainty Equivalence. *Econ. J.*, 1984 Supplement, *94*, pp. 45–58.

Begg, David K. H. and Haque, Md Badrul. A Nominal Interest Rate Rule and Price Level Indeterminacy Reconsidered. *Greek Econ. Rev.*, April 1984, *6*(1), pp. 31–46.

Belongia, Michael T. Money Growth Variability and GNP. *Fed. Res. Bank St. Louis Rev.*, April 1984, *66*(4), pp. 23–31. **[G: U.S.]**

Ben-Zion, Uri. Recent Literature on the Impact of Taxation and Inflation on Interest Rates. In *Tanzi, V., ed.*, 1984, pp. 69–98. **[G: U.S.; OECD]**

Benavie, Arthur and Froyen, Richard T. Optimal Combination Monetary Policies: A Two-Stage Process. *J. Money, Credit, Banking*, Part 1 November 1984, *16*(4), pp. 497–505.

Benjamin, Daniel K. and Kochin, Levis A. War, Prices, and Interest Rates: A Martial Solution to Gibson's Paradox. In *Bordo, M. D. and Schwartz, A. J., eds.*, 1984, pp. 587–604.
[G: U.K.]

Benninga, Simon and Protopapadakis, Aris. The Neutrality of the Real Equilibrium under Alternative Financing of Government Expenditures. *J. Monet. Econ.*, September 1984, *14*(2), pp. 183–208.

Benoit, J. Pierre V. Artificially Low Interest Rates versus Realistic or Market Interest Rates. In *Kessler, D. and Ullmo, P.-A., eds.*, 1984, pp. 35–78.
[G: LDCs; MDCs]

Berckmans, Annie, et al. Debt Management in a Small Open Economy: A Theoretical and an Empirical Study for Belgium. *J. Policy Modeling*, February 1984, *6*(1), pp. 45–67.
[G: Belgium]

Bergstrand, Jeffrey H. Short-run Domestic Monetary Control in an International Money Market. *New Eng. Econ. Rev.*, July–August 1984, pp. 29–38.

Bessler, David A. Additional Evidence on Money and Prices: U.S. Data, 1870–1913. *Exploration Econ. Hist.*, April 1984, *21*(2), pp. 125–32.
[G: U.S.]

Black, Stanley W. Monetary Targeting: Issues and Alternatives. In *Hewlett, S. A.; Kaufman, H. and Kenen, P. B., eds.*, 1984, pp. 105–21.
[G: U.S.; W. Germany; Japan]

Black, Stanley W. The Relationship between Exchange Rate Policy and Monetary Policy in Ten Industrial Countries. In *Bilson, J. F. O. and Marston, R. C., eds.*, 1984, pp. 499–511.
[G: Selected OECD]

Blake, David. Complete Systems Methods of Estimating Models with Rational and Adaptive Expectations: A Case Study. *Europ. Econ. Rev.*, March 1984, *24*(2), pp. 137–50.
[G: U.S.]

Blanchard, Olivier J. Current and Anticipated Deficits, Interest Rates and Economic Activity. *Europ. Econ. Rev.*, June 1984, *25*(1), pp. 7–27.
[G: EEC; U.S.]

Blinder, Alan S. and Mankiw, N. Gregory. Aggregation and Stabilization Policy in a Multi-Contract Economy. *J. Monet. Econ.*, January 1984, *13*(1), pp. 67–86.

Blomgren-Hansen, Niels and Petersen, Jørgen. Samspillet mellem finans-, penge- og valutakurspolitik. (The Interdependence of Fiscal, Monetary, and Exchange Rate Policies. With English summary.) *Nationaløkon. Tidsskr.*, 1984, *122*(1), pp. 73–90.
[G: Denmark]

Bockelmann, Horst. Orientierungspunkte der Geldpolitik. (Orientation Points for Monetary Policy. With English summary.) *Kredit Kapital*, 1984, *17*(1), pp. 64–83.
[G: W. Germany]

Bonello, Frank J. and Reichenstein, William R. Almon Lags and the St. Louis Equation: An

Addendum. *Rev. Bus. Econ. Res.*, Spring 1984, *19*(2), pp. 102–05.
[G: U.S.]

Bordo, Michael D. The Gold Standard: Myths and Realities. In *Siegel, B. N., ed.*, 1984, pp. 197–237.
[G: U.K.; U.S.]

Bradley, Michael D. Federal Deficits and the Conduct of Monetary Policy. *J. Macroecon.*, Fall 1984, *6*(4), pp. 411–31.
[G: U.S.]

Branson, William H . Effects of United States Monetary Restraint on the DM/$ Exchange Rate and the German Economy: Comment. In *Bilson, J. F. O. and Marston, R. C., eds.*, 1984, pp. 494–97.
[G: U.S.; W. Germany]

Brookins, Oscar T. Monetary Studies of Less-developed Economies: A Review and Survey. *Rivista Int. Sci. Econ. Com.*, October–November 1984, *31*(10–11), pp. 1121–33.
[G: LDCs]

Brunner, Karl. Deficits, Interest Rates and Monetary Policy. In *Shadow Open Market Committee*, 1984, pp. 13–28.
[G: U.S.]

Brunner, Karl. Hat der Monetarismus versagt? (Has Monetarism Failed? With English summary.) *Kredit Kapital*, 1984, *17*(1), pp. 18–63.

Bryant, John and Wallace, Neil. A Price Discrimination Analysis of Monetary Policy. *Rev. Econ. Stud.*, April 1984, *51*(2), pp. 279–88.

Budd, Alan P., et al. Does Monetarism fit the UK Facts? In *Griffiths, B. and Wood, G. E., eds.*, 1984, pp. 75–119.
[G: U.K.]

Buffie, Edward F. Financial Repression, the New Structuralists, and Stabilization Policy in Semi-Industrialized Economies. *J. Devel. Econ.*, April 1984, *14*(3), pp. 305–22.
[G: LDCs]

Buiter, Willem H. Comment: Some Unpleasant Monetarist Arithmetic. In *Griffiths, B. and Wood, G. E., eds.*, 1984, pp. 42–60.
[G: U.K.]

Buscher, Herbert S. The Stability of the West German Demand for Money, 1965–1982. *Weltwirtsch. Arch.*, 1984, *120*(2), pp. 256–78.
[G: W. Germany]

Buscher, Herbert S. Zur Stabilität der Geldnachfrage. Eine empirische Betrachtung. (To the Stability of the Demand for Money: An Empirical Consideration. With English summary.) *Kredit Kapital*, 1984, *17*(4), pp. 507–39.
[G: W. Germany]

Butlin, M. W. Managed Exchange Rates and Exchange Control: A Theoretical Analysis. *Australian Econ. Pap.*, December 1984, *23*(43), pp. 167–78.

Cagan, Phillip. War, Prices, and Interest Rates: A Martial Solution to Gibson's Paradox: Comment. In *Bordo, M. D. and Schwartz, A. J., eds.*, 1984, pp. 604–10.
[G: U.K.]

Calliari, Sergio; Spinelli, Franco and Verga, Giovanni. Money Demand in Italy: A Few More Results. *Manchester Sch. Econ. Soc. Stud.*, June 1984, *52*(2), pp. 141–59.
[G: Italy]

Campbell, John Y. and Shiller, Robert J. A Simple Account of the Behavior of Long-Term Interest Rates. *Amer. Econ. Rev.*, May 1984, *74*(2), pp. 44–48.

Canto, Victor A.; Joines, Douglas H. and Webb, Robert I. Taxation, Rational Expectations, and the Neutrality of Money. *J. Macroecon.*, Winter 1984, *6*(1), pp. 69–78.

Cantoria, Filomena M. The Role of Expectations in Interest-Rate Determination. *Philippine Rev. Econ. Bus.*, Mar./June 1984, *21*(1/2), pp. 77–99. **[G: Philippines]**

Caprara, Ugo. Opinioni e teorie di John Maynard Keynes nella interpretazione di un economista aziendale. (Opinions and Theories of John Maynard Keynes: An Interpretation by a Business Economist. With English summary.) *Bancaria*, March 1984, *40*(3), pp. 256–65.

Cargill, Thomas F. and Meyer, Robert A. Municipal Interest Rates and the Term Structure of Inflationary Expectations. *Financial Rev.*, May 1984, *19*(2), pp. 135–52. **[G: U.S.]**

Carlson, Keith M. Money Growth and the Size of the Federal Debt. *Fed. Res. Bank St. Louis Rev.*, November 1984, *66*(9), pp. 5–16. **[G: U.S.]**

Chambers, Robert G. Agricultural and Financial Market Interdependence in the Short Run. *Amer. J. Agr. Econ.*, February 1984, *66*(1), pp. 12–24. **[G: U.S.]**

Chamley, Christophe and Polemarchakis, Herakles M. Assets, General Equilibrium and the Neutrality of Money. *Rev. Econ. Stud.*, January 1984, *51*(1), pp. 129–38.

Chamouton, Thierry and Piatecki, Cyrille. Anticipations rationnelles et théorie économique. (With English summary.) *Revue Écon. Polit.*, November–December 1984, *94*(6), pp. 754–72.

Chang, Winston W.; Hamberg, Daniel and Hirata, Junichi. On Liquidity Preference—Again: Reply [Liquidity Preference as Behavior toward Risk Is a Demand for Short-term Securities—Not Money]. *Amer. Econ. Rev.*, September 1984, *74*(4), pp. 812–13.

Chiang, Raymond, et al. Adverse Selection as an Explanation of Credit Rationing and Different Lender Types. *J. Macroecon.*, Spring 1984, *6*(2), pp. 159–80.

Chiang, Thomas C. On the Relationship between the Exchange Rate and the Interest Rate Differential in Monetary Models. *Quart. Rev. Econ. Bus.*, Autumn 1984, *24*(3), pp. 49–57. **[G: U.S.]**

Chiappori, Pierre-André and Mongin, Philippe. Un modèle de politique monétaire avec aléas stratégiques. (A Model of Monetary Policy with Strategic Uncertainty. With English summary.) *Revue Écon.*, September 1984, *35*(5), pp. 831–69.

Chick, Victoria. Monetary Increases and Their Consequences: Streams, Backwaters and Floods. In *[Pearce, I. F.]*, 1984, pp. 237–50.

Chung, In-Uk and Jung, W. S. The Currency Ratio with Inflation and Economic Growth. *J. Econ. Devel.*, July 1984, *9*(1), pp. 77–90.

Clarida, Richard H. and Friedman, Benjamin M. The Behavior of U.S. Short-Term Interest Rates since October 1979. *J. Finance*, July 1984, *39*(3), pp. 671–82. **[G: U.S.]**

Clower, Robert W. A Reconsideration of the The-

ory of Inflation. In *Clower, R. W.*, 1984, *1976*, pp. 218–30.

Clower, Robert W. Comment: The Optimal Growth Rate of Money. In *Clower, R. W.*, 1984, *1968*, pp. 90–94.

Clower, Robert W. Monetary Theory: Selected Readings. In *Clower, R. W.*, 1984, *1969*, pp. 95–106.

Clower, Robert W. On the Invariance of Demand for Cash and Other Assets. In *Clower, R. W.*, 1984, *1960*, pp. 138–44.

Clower, Robert W. The Anatomy of Monetary Theory. In *Clower, R. W.*, 1984, *1977*, pp. 231–41.

Clower, Robert W. The Transactions Theory of the Demand for Money: A Reconsideration. In *Clower, R. W.*, 1984, *1978*, pp. 166–84.

Cobham, David. Convergence, Divergence and Realignment in British Macroeconomics. *Banca Naz. Lavoro Quart. Rev.*, June 1984, (149), pp. 159–76. **[G: U.K.]**

Cohen, Jacob. The Money Supply Process: How Much Progress since C. A. Phillips' Bank Credit? *Kredit Kapital*, 1984, *17*(3), pp. 333–51.

Congdon, Tim G. A Comment: The problem of Debt Interest Seen in Historical Perspective [Some Unpleasant Monetarist Arithmetic]. In *Griffiths, B. and Wood, G. E., eds.*, 1984, pp. 67–71.

Costabile, Lilia. Preferenze intertemporali, risparmi e investimenti. Note su due approcci alternativi. (With English summary.) *Econ. Polít.*, December 1984, *1*(3), pp. 335–59.

Courakis, Anthony S. Constraints on Bank Choices and Financial Repression in Less Developed Countries. *Oxford Bull. Econ. Statist.*, November 1984, *46*(4), pp. 341–70. **[G: LDCs]**

Courakis, Anthony S. The Demand for Money in South Africa: Towards a More Accurate Perspective. *S. Afr. J. Econ.*, March 1984, *52*(1), pp. 1–41. **[G: S. Africa]**

Cover, James Peery. What Is Money? *Atlantic Econ. J.*, December 1984, *12*(4), pp. 9–17.

Cox, W. Michael. What Is the Rule for Financing Public Debt? *Fed. Res. Bank Dallas Econ. Rev.*, September 1984, pp. 25–31. **[G: U.S.]**

Craine, Roger. The Behavior of U.S. Short-Term Interest Rates since October 1979: Discussion. *J. Finance*, July 1984, *39*(3), pp. 682–83.

Craine, Roger and Havenner, Arthur. Choosing a Monetary Instrument: The Case of Supply-Side Shocks: Reply. *J. Econ. Dynam. Control*, September 1984, *7*(3), pp. 381–82. **[G: U.S.]**

Cumby, Robert E. Monetary Policy under Dual Exchange Rates. *J. Int. Money Finance*, August 1984, *3*(2), pp. 195–208.

Curran, Ward S. Inflation and Real Interest Rates on Assets with Different Risk Characteristics: Discussion. *J. Finance*, July 1984, *39*(3), pp. 712–14.

Currie, David. Monetary Overshooting and the Exchange Rate. *Manchester Sch. Econ. Soc. Stud.*, March 1984, *52*(1), pp. 28–48.

Cuthbertson, Keith. Techniques of Monetary

Control in the United Kingdom. *J. Econ. Stud.*, 1984, *11*(4), pp. 46–68.   [G: U.K.]

D'Adda, Carlo. Recenti sviluppi nella teoria monetaria. (With English summary.) *Econ. Polít.*, December 1984, *1*(3), pp. 429–56.

Dacy, Douglas C. The Effects of Confidence on Income Velocity in a Politically Unstable Environment: Wartime South Vietnam. *Kyklos*, 1984, *37*(3), pp. 414–23.   [G: Vietnam]

Darby, Jane. Fiscal Policy and Interest Rates. *Nat. Inst. Econ. Rev.*, August 1984, (109), pp. 38–44.   [G: U.K.]

Darby, Michael R. Some Pleasant Monetarist Arithmetic. *Fed. Res. Bank Minn. Rev.*, Spring 1984, *8*(2), pp. 15–20.   [G: U.S.]

Darrat, Ali F. The Dominant Influence of Fiscal Actions in Developing Countries. *Eastern Econ. J.*, July–September 1984, *10*(3), pp. 271–84.   [G: Brazil; Chile; Mexico; Peru; Venezuela]

Darrat, Ali F. The Money Demand Relationship in Saudi Arabia: An Empirical Investigation. *J. Econ. Stud.*, 1984, *11*(3), pp. 43–50.   [G: Saudi Arabia]

De Felice, Gregorio and Porta, Angelo. Credit and Macroeconomic Equilibrium: A Re-examination of Total Domestic Credit Theoretical Framework. (In Italian. With English summary.) *Giorn. Econ.*, September–October 1984, *43*(9–10), pp. 619–50.

De Vany, Arthur S. Modeling the Banking Firm: A Survey: Comment. *J. Money, Credit, Banking*, Part 2 November 1984, *16*(4), pp. 603–09.

De Vroey, Michel. Inflation: A Non-monetarist Monetary Interpretation. *Cambridge J. Econ.*, December 1984, *8*(4), pp. 381–99.

Demery, David. Aggregate Demand, Rational Expectations and Real Output: Some New Evidence for the U.K., 1963.2–1982.2. *Econ. J.*, December 1984, *94*(376), pp. 847–62.   [G: U.K.]

Demery, David and Duck, Nigel W. Inventories and Monetary Growth in the Business Cycle: Some Theoretical Considerations and Empirical Results for the U.K. *Manchester Sch. Econ. Soc. Stud.*, December 1984, *52*(4), pp. 363–79.   [G: U.K.]

Demery, David; Duck, Nigel W. and Musgrave, Simon W. Unanticipated Money Growth, Output and Unemployment in West Germany, 1964–1981. *Weltwirtsch. Arch.*, 1984, *120*(2), pp. 244–55.   [G: Germany]

Di Matteo, M. Alternative Monetary Policies in a Classical Growth Cycle. In *Goodwin, R. M.; Krüger, M. and Vercelli, A., eds.*, 1984, pp. 14–24.

Diamond, Douglas W. Financial Intermediation and Delegated Monitoring. *Rev. Econ. Stud.*, July 1984, *51*(3), pp. 393–414.

Diamond, Peter A. Money in Search Equilibrium. *Econometrica*, January 1984, *52*(1), pp. 1–20.

Dillard, Dudley. Keynes and Marx: A Centennial Appraisal. *J. Post Keynesian Econ.*, Spring 1984, *6*(3), pp. 421–32.

Dornbusch, Rudiger. Exchange Market Intervention Operations: Their Role in Financial Policy and Their Effects: Comment. In *Bilson, J. F. O. and Marston, R. C., eds.*, 1984, pp. 398–402.

Dornbusch, Rudiger. Monetary Policy under Exchange Rate Flexibility. In *Bigman, D. and Taya, T., eds.*, 1984, pp. 3–31.

Dotsey, Michael. An Investigation of Cash Mangement Practices and Their Effects on the Demand for Money. *Fed. Res. Bank Richmond Econ. Rev.*, Sept./Oct. 1984, *70*(5), pp. 3–12.   [G: U.S.]

Dow, Sheila C. Methodology and the Analysis of a Monetary Economy. *Écon. Soc.*, April 1984, *18*(4), pp. 7–35.

Drabicki, John Z. and Takayama, Akira. Money, National Debt, and Economic Growth. *J. Econ. Theory*, August 1984, *33*(2), pp. 356–67.

Drabicki, John Z. and Takayama, Akira. The Stability of a Neoclassical Monetary Growth Model. *Econ. Stud. Quart.*, December 1984, *35*(3), pp. 262–68.

Driskill, Robert A. and McCafferty, Stephen. The Workings of a Commodity Money System in an Incomplete Information Macro Model. *J. Macroecon.*, Spring 1984, *6*(2), pp. 139–57.

Dudler, Hermann-Josef. Domestic Monetary Control in EC Countries under Different Exchange Rate Regimes: National Concerns and Community Options. In *Masera, R. S. and Triffin, R., eds.*, 1984, pp. 227–61.   [G: EEC]

Dwyer, Gerald P., Jr. Inflation and Government Deficits: A Reply. *Econ. Inquiry*, October 1984, *22*(4), pp. 597–601.   [G: U.S.]

Dwyer, Gerald P., Jr. The Gibson Paradox: A Cross-Country Analysis. *Economica*, May 1984, *51*(202), pp. 109–27.   [G: U.S.; U.K.; France; Belgium]

Eaton, Jonathan and Turnovsky, Stephen J. The Forward Exchange Market, Speculation, and Exchange Market Intervention. *Quart. J. Econ.*, February 1984, *99*(1), pp. 45–69.

Eckalbar, John C. Money, Barter, and Convergence to the Competitive Allocation: Menger's Problem. *J. Econ. Theory*, April 1984, *32*(2), pp. 201–11.

Ehrlicher, Werner. Monetarismus und Keynesianismus in der "Neuen Geldpolitik." (Monetarism and Keynesianism in the "New Monetary Policy." With English summary.) *Kredit Kapital*, 1984, *17*(1), pp. 1–17.   [G: W. Germany]

Elyasiani, Elyas. The Multiproduct Deopository Firm, Interest-bearing Transaction Balances, Interest-bearing Reserves, and Uncertainty. *Bull. Econ. Res.*, November 1984, *36*(2), pp. 173–93.   [G: U.S.]

Enders, Walter and Falk, Barry. A Microeconomic Test of Money Neutrality. *Rev. Econ. Statist.*, November 1984, *66*(4), pp. 666–69.   [G: U.S.]

Engel, Charles M. and Frankel, Jeffrey A. Why Interest Rates React to Money Announcements: An Explanation from the Foreign Exchange Market. *J. Monet. Econ.*, January 1984, *13*(1), pp. 31–39. **[G: U.S.]**

Entov, R. M. The "Rule" and Fall of the Phillips Curve. *Prob. Econ.*, February 1984, *26*(10), pp. 3–36.

Ewis, Nabil A. and Fisher, Douglas. The Translog Utility Function and the Demand for Money in the United States. *J. Money, Credit, Banking*, February 1984, *16*(1), pp. 34–52.

Fama, Eugene F. The Information in the Term Structure. *J. Finan. Econ.*, December 1984, *13*(4), pp. 509–28.

Fama, Eugene F. and Gibbons, Michael R. A Comparison of Inflation Forecasts. *J. Monet. Econ.*, May 1984, *13*(3), pp. 327–48.
[G: U.S.]

Farmer, Roger E. A. Bursting Bubbles: On the Rationality of Hyperinflations in Optimizing Models. *J. Monet. Econ.*, July 1984, *14*(1), pp. 29–35.

Fase, Martin M. G. The Monetary Sector of the Netherlands in 50 Equations. A Quarterly Model for the Netherlands (1970–1979). In *Ancot, J. P., ed.*, 1984, pp. 195–228.
[G: Netherlands]

Fender, John. Sectoral and Macroeconomic Effects in a Two Good Open Economy with an Intermediate Input. *Bull. Econ. Res.*, May 1984, *36*(1), pp. 9–32.

Ferro, Angelo. Strumentazione fiscale e monetaria nella politica dell 'offerta. (The Use of Fiscal and Monetary Tools in Supply-Side Policy. With English summary.) *Bancaria*, October 1984, *40*(10), pp. 957–64.

Fethke, Gary C. and Jackman, Richard. Optimal Monetary Policy, Endogenous Supply and Rational Expectations. *J. Monet. Econ.*, March 1984, *13*(2), pp. 211–24.

Field, Alexander James. A New Interpretation of the Onset of the Great Depression. *J. Econ. Hist.*, June 1984, *44*(2), pp. 489–98.
[G: U.S.]

Field, Alexander James. Asset Exchanges and the Transactions Demand for Money, 1919–29. *Amer. Econ. Rev.*, March 1984, *74*(1), pp. 43–59.
[G: U.S.]

Fischer, Edwin O. and Zechner, Josef. Diffusion Process Specifications for Interest Rates. In *Bamberg, G. and Spremann, K., eds.*, 1984, pp. 64–73.
[G: W. Germany]

Flaschel, Peter. The Inflation-based 'Natural' Rate of Unemployment and the Conflict Over Income Distribution. In *Goodwin, R. M.; Krüger, M. and Vercelli, A., eds.*, 1984, pp. 103–26.

Flavin, Marjorie. Time Series Evidence on the Expectations Hypothesis of the Term Structure. *Carnegie-Rochester Conf. Ser. Public Policy*, Spring 1984, *20*, pp. 211–37.
[G: U.S.]

Flavin, Marjorie. Time Series Evidence on the Expectations Hypothesis of the Term Structure: Reply. *Carnegie-Rochester Conf. Ser. Public Policy*, Spring 1984, *20*, pp. 243–45.
[G: U.S.]

Flood, Robert P. and Garber, Peter M. Gold Monetization and Gold Discipline. *J. Polit. Econ.*, February 1984, *92*(1), pp. 90–107.

Flood, Robert P.; Garber, Peter M. and Scott, Louis O. Multi-country Tests for Price Level Bubbles. *J. Econ. Dynam. Control*, December 1984, *8*(3), pp. 329–40. **[G: Germany; Hungary; Poland]**

Forman, Leonard; Groves, Miles and Eichner, Alfred S. The Monetary–Financial Block of a Post-Keynesian Short-Period Model. *Brit. Rev. Econ. Issues*, Autumn 1984, *6*(15), pp. 23–52. **[G: U.S.]**

Frazer, William J., Jr. "The Economics of Supply and Demand" and Friedman. *Econ. Notes*, 1984, (3), pp. 47–73.

Friedman, Benjamin M. Lessons from the 1979–82 Monetary Policy Experiment. *Amer. Econ. Rev.*, May 1984, *74*(2), pp. 382–87.
[G: U.S.]

Fukao, Mitsuhiro and Okubo, Takashi. International Linkage of Interest Rates: The Case of Japan and the United States. *Int. Econ. Rev.*, February 1984, *25*(1), pp. 193–207.
[G: Japan; U.S.]

Garrison, Roger W. Deficits and Inflation: A Comment. *Econ. Inquiry*, October 1984, *22*(4), pp. 593–96. **[G: U.S.]**

Garrison, Roger W. Time and Money: The Universals of Macroeconomic Theorizing. *J. Macroecon.*, Spring 1984, *6*(2), pp. 197–213.

Genberg, Hans. Properties of Innovations in Spot and Forward Exchange Rates and the Role of Money Supply Processes. In *Bilson, J. F. O. and Marston, R. C., eds.*, 1984, pp. 153–74.
[G: Selected OECD]

Gift, Richard E. Regulating the Supply of Money with Enclave Trade and No Foreign Competition for the Home Exportable. *Rivista Int. Sci. Econ. Com.*, October–November 1984, *31*(10–11), pp. 1991–99.

Giovannetti, Giorgia. The Role of the Rate of Interest: From Wicksell to Keynes' Treatise on Money. *Econ. Notes*, 1984, (1), pp. 66–86.

Goldfeld, Stephen M. Modeling the Banking Firm: A Survey: Comment. *J. Money, Credit, Banking*, Part 2 November 1984, *16*(4), pp. 609–16.

Goldsmith, Raymond W. The Stability of the Ratio of Nonfinancial Debt to Income. *Banca Naz. Lavoro Quart. Rev.*, September 1984, (150), pp. 285–305.

Goodhart, Charles A. E. Structural Changes in the Banking System and the Determination of the Stock of Money. In *Masera, R. S. and Triffin, R., eds.*, 1984, pp. 111–49. **[G: OECD]**

Goodman, Laurie S. Eurodollars and the U.S. Monetary Aggregates. *Bus. Econ.*, January 1984, *19*(1), pp. 40–46. **[G: U.S.]**

Gordon, Robert J. Supply Shocks and Monetary Policy Revisited. *Amer. Econ. Rev.*, May 1984, *74*(2), pp. 38–43.

Gordon, Robert J. The Short-run Demand for Money: A Reconsideration. *J. Money, Credit, Banking*, Part 1 November 1984, *16*(4), pp. 403–34. **[G: U.S.]**

de Grauwe, Paul. The Relationship between Exchange Rate Policy and Monetary Policy in Ten Industrial Countries: Comment. In *Bilson, J. F. O. and Marston, R. C., eds.*, 1984, pp. 511–14. **[G: Selected OECD]**

Gray, Jo Anna. Dynamic Instability in Rational Expectations Models: An Attempt to Clarify. *Int. Econ. Rev.*, February 1984, 25(1), pp. 93–122.

Graziani, Augusto. The Debate on Keynes' Finance Motive. *Econ. Notes*, 1984, (1), pp. 5–34.

Gregory, Allan W. A Systems Approach to Simultaneity and the Demand for Money in Canada. *Southern Econ. J.*, October 1984, 51(2), pp. 401–18. **[G: Canada]**

Grice, Joe and Bennett, Adam. Wealth and the Demand for 2M3 in the United Kingdom, 1963–1978. *Manchester Sch. Econ. Soc. Stud.*, September 1984, 52(3), pp. 239–71. **[G: U.K.]**

Griffiths, Brian and Wood, Geoffrey E. Monetarism in the United Kingdom. In *Griffiths, B. and Wood, G. E., eds.*, 1984, pp. 3–12. **[G: U.K.]**

Guttentag, Jack M. and Herring, Richard J. Credit Rationing and Financial Disorder. *J. Finance*, December 1984, 39(5), pp. 1359–82. **[G: U.S.]**

Hafer, R. W. Examining the Recent Behavior of Inflation. *Fed. Res. Bank St. Louis Rev.*, August/September 1984, 66(7), pp. 29–37. **[G: U.S.]**

Hafer, R. W. The Monetary Base or M1? Results from a Small Macromodel. *J. Econ. Bus.*, February 1984, 36(1), pp. 85–93. **[G: U.S.]**

Hafer, R. W. The Money-GNP Link: Assessing Alternative Transaction Measures. *Fed. Res. Bank St. Louis Rev.*, March 1984, 66(3), pp. 19–27. **[G: U.S.]**

Hafer, R. W. and Hein, Scott E. Financial Innovations and the Interest Elasticity of Money Demand: Some Historical Evidence: A Note. *J. Money, Credit, Banking*, May 1984, 16(2), pp. 247–52. **[G: U.S.]**

Hafer, R. W. and Hein, Scott E. Predicting the Money Multiplier: Forecasts from Component and Aggregate Models. *J. Monet. Econ.*, November 1984, 14(3), pp. 375–84. **[G: U.S.]**

von Hagen, Jürgen. The Causal Role of Money in West Germany—Some Contradicting Comments and Evidence. *Weltwirtsch. Arch.*, 1984, 120(3), pp. 558–71. **[G: Germany]**

Hahn, Frank H. Monetarism and Economic Theory. In *Hahn, F.*, 1984, 1980, pp. 283–306.

Hahn, Frank H. On the Foundations of Monetary Theory. In *Hahn, F.*, 1984, 1973, pp. 158–74.

Hahn, Frank H. On Money and Growth. In *Hahn, F.*, 1984, 1969, pp. 195–213.

Hahn, Frank H. On Some Problems of Proving the Existence of Equilibrium in a Monetary Economy. In *Hahn, F.*, 1984, pp. 147–57.

Hahn, Frank H. Professor Friedman's Views on Money. In *Hahn, F.*, 1984, 1971, pp. 259–82.

Hahn, Frank H. Why I Am Not a Monetarist. In *Hahn, F.*, 1984, pp. 307–26.

Hall, Robert E. A Free-Market Policy to Stabilize

the Purchasing Power of the Dollar. In *Siegel, B. N., ed.*, 1984, pp. 303–21. **[G: U.S.]**

Hardouvelis, Gikas A. Market Perceptions of Federal Reserve Policy and the Weekly Monetary Announcements. *J. Monet. Econ.*, September 1984, 14(2), pp. 225–40. **[G: U.S.]**

Hayakawa, Hiroaki. A Dynamic Generalization of the Tobin Model. *J. Econ. Dynam. Control*, September 1984, 7(3), pp. 209–31.

Hayashi, Toshihiko. Note: Deregulated Deposit Rates, Government Financial Intermediation, and Monetary Policy. (In Japanese. With English summary.) *Osaka Econ. Pap.*, December 1984, 34(2–3), pp. 155–59.

von Hayek, Friedrich A. Intertemporal Price Equilibrium and Movements in the Value of Money. In *von Hayek, F. A. (II)*, 1984, 1928, pp. 71–117.

von Hayek, Friedrich A. On 'Neutral Money.' In *von Hayek, F. A. (II)*, 1984, 1933, pp. 159–62.

von Hayek, Friedrich A. On the Problem of the Theory of Interest. In *von Hayek, F. A. (II)*, 1984, 1927, pp. 55–70.

von Hayek, Friedrich A. The Future Monetary Unit of Value. In *Siegel, B. N., ed.*, 1984, pp. 323–35.

Hegji, Charles E. Implicit Information Assumptions and Real Interest Rate Measurements. *Southern Econ. J.*, October 1984, 51(2), pp. 574–81.

Heinsohn, Gunnar and Steiger, Otto. "Marx and Keynes—Private Property and Money." *Écon. Soc.*, April 1984, 18(4), pp. 37–71.

Helpman, Elhanan and Razin, Assaf. The Role of Saving and Investment in Exchange Rate Determination under Alternative Monetary Mechanisms. *J. Monet. Econ.*, May 1984, 13(3), pp. 307–25.

Hendershott, Patric H. Expectations, Surprises and Treasury Bill Rates: 1960–82. *J. Finance*, July 1984, 39(3), pp. 685–96. **[G: U.S.]**

Henderson, Dale W. Exchange Market Intervention Operations: Their Role in Financial Policy and Their Effects. In *Bilson, J. F. O. and Marston, R. C., eds.*, 1984, pp. 359–98.

Hénin, Pierre-Yves and Zylberberg, André. Sur la compatibilité à long terme d'un adjustement partiel des prix avec l'hypothèse de prévisions rationnelles. *Revue Écon. Polit.*, November–December 1984, 94(6), pp. 792–807.

Herman, James. Monetarism: A Paradoxical Counter-revolution. *Hist. Polit. Econ.*, Winter 1984, 16(4), pp. 583–90.

Hetzel, Robert L. A Monetarist Money Demand Function. *Fed. Res. Bank Richmond Econ. Rev.*, Nov./Dec. 1984, 70(6), pp. 15–19.

Hetzel, Robert L. Estimating Money Demand Functions. *J. Money, Credit, Banking*, May 1984, 16(2), pp. 185–93. **[G: U.S.]**

Hetzel, Robert L. The Behavior of the M1 Demand Function in the Early 1980s. *Fed. Res. Bank Richmond Econ. Rev.*, Nov./Dec. 1984, 70(6), pp. 20–29. **[G: U.S.]**

Hicks, John R. A Suggestion for Simplifying the

Theory of Money. In *Hicks, J.*, 1984, *1935*, pp. 168–85.

Hicks, John R. The Credit Economy. In *Hicks, J.*, 1984, pp. 230–39.

Hirschhorn, Eric. Rational Expectations and the Effects of Government Debt. *J. Monet. Econ.*, July 1984, *14*(1), pp. 55–70. [G: U.S.]

Hoffman, Dennis L.; Low, Stuart A. and Schlagenhauf, Don E. Tests of Rationality, Neutrality and Market Efficiency: A Monte Carlo Analysis of Alternative Test Statistics. *J. Monet. Econ.*, November 1984, *14*(3), pp. 339–63.

Holland, A. Steven. Real Interest Rates: What Accounts for Their Recent Rise? *Fed. Res. Bank St. Louis Rev.*, December 1984, *66*(10), pp. 18–29. [G: U.S.]

Holtham, Gerald. Multinational Modelling of Financial Linkages and Exchange Rates. *OECD Econ. Stud.*, Spring 1984, (2), pp. 51–92. [G: OECD]

Honohan, Patrick. Monetary Restraint and the Exchange Rate. *Economica*, May 1984, *51*(202), pp. 163–76.

Honohan, Patrick. The Break-up of a Currency Union Increases the Demand for Money. *Europ. Econ. Rev.*, July 1984, *25*(2), pp. 235–38. [G: Ireland; U.K.]

Hoover, Kevin D. Two Types of Monetarism. *J. Econ. Lit.*, March 1984, *22*(1), pp. 58–76.

Horne, Jocelyn and McDonald, Ian M. Rational Expectations, Gradual Price Adjustment and Monetary Policy in Australia. *Australian Econ. Pap.*, June 1984, *23*(42), pp. 79–90. [G: Australia]

Hosek, William R. and Zahn, Frank. A Comparison of Aggregate Measures of the Real Rate of Interest and the Real Rate of Return on Capital. *Quart. Rev. Econ. Bus.*, Autumn 1984, *24*(3), pp. 58–71. [G: U.S.]

Huang, Roger D. Tests of Variance Bounds Implied by Cagan's Hyperinflation Model. *Int. Econ. Rev.*, October 1984, *25*(3), pp. 545–61. [G: Germany]

Huang, Roger D. and Kracaw, William A. Stock Market Returns and Real Activity: A Note. *J. Finance*, March 1984, *39*(1), pp. 267–73.

Huizinga, John and Mishkin, Frederic S. Inflation and Real Interest Rates on Assets with Different Risk Characteristics. *J. Finance*, July 1984, *39*(3), pp. 699–712. [G: U.S.]

Humphrey, Thomas M. Algebraic Quantity Equations before Fisher and Pigou. *Fed. Res. Bank Richmond Econ. Rev.*, Sept./Oct. 1984, *70*(5), pp. 13–22.

Humphrey, Thomas M. On Nonneutral Relative Price Effects in Monetarist Thought: Some Austrian Misconceptions. *Fed. Res. Bank Richmond Econ. Rev.*, May/June 1984, *70*(3), pp. 13–19.

Husted, Steven L. and Rush, Mark. On Measuring the Nearness of Near Moneys: Revisited. *J. Monet. Econ.*, September 1984, *14*(2), pp. 171–81. [G: U.S.]

Hutchinson, Michael M. and Pyle, David H. The Real Interest Rate/Budget Deficit Link: International Evidence, 1973–82. *Fed. Res. Bank*

San Francisco Econ. Rev., Fall 1984, (4), pp. 26–35. [G: OECD]

IMF Fiscal Affairs Department. Interest Rates and Tax Treatment of Interest Income and Expense. In *Tanzi, V., ed.*, 1984, pp. 3–66. [G: OECD]

Jansen, Dennis W. Choosing a Monetary Instrument: The Case of Supply-Side Shocks: Comment. *J. Econ. Dynam. Control*, September 1984, *7*(3), pp. 377–79. [G: U.S.]

Jao, Y. C. A Libertarian Approach to Monetary Theory and Policy. *Hong Kong Econ. Pap.*, 1984, (15), pp. 1–24.

Jehle, Geoffrey A. Individual Welfare and the Demand for Financial Instruments. *Southern Econ. J.*, July 1984, *51*(1), pp. 116–34. [G: U.S.]

Johansson, Peter. Näkökohtia korkopolitiikasta. (On Interest Rate Policies. With English summary.) *Kansant. Aikak.*, 1984, *80*(2), pp. 163–70.

Johansson, Peter and Rajakangas, Timo. Pääomanliikkeet, sterilointi ja rahapolitiikan itsenäisyys. (Capital Flows, Sterilization and the Independence of Monetary Policy. With English summary.) *Kansant. Aikak.*, 1984, *80*(3), pp. 291–301. [G: Finland]

Jones, Robert A. and Ostroy, Joseph M. Flexibility and Uncertainty. *Rev. Econ. Stud.*, January 1984, *51*(1), pp. 13–32.

Jordan, James V. Tax Effects in Term Structure Estimation. *J. Finance*, June 1984, *39*(2), pp. 393–406. [G: U.S.]

Judd, John P. Money Supply Announcements, Forward Interest Rates and Budget Deficits. *Fed. Res. Bank San Francisco Econ. Rev.*, Fall 1984, (4), pp. 36–46. [G: U.S.]

Judd, John P. and Motley, Brian. The "Great Velocity Decline" of 1982–83: A Comparative Analysis of M1 and M2. *Fed. Res. Bank San Francisco Econ. Rev.*, Summer 1984, (3), pp. 56–74. [G: U.S.]

Kanniainen, Vesa. On Offsetting Capital Flows and Monetary Autonomy of a Small Open Economy. *Economica*, May 1984, *51*(202), pp. 177–86.

Kanniainen, Vesa and Tarkka, Juha. The Role of Capital Flows in the Adjustment of Money Demand: The Case of Finland. *Empirical Econ.*, 1984, *9*(2), pp. 75–85. [G: Finland]

Karacaoglu, Girol. Absence of Gross Substitution in Portfolios and Demand for Finance: Some Macroeconomic Implications. *J. Post Keynesian Econ.*, Summer 1984, *6*(4), pp. 576–89.

Karakitsos, E. and Rustem, Berc. Optimally Derived Fixed Rules and Indicators. *J. Econ. Dynam. Control*, October 1984, *8*(1), pp. 33–64. [G: U.K.]

Katz, Menachem. Inflation, Taxation, and the Rate of Interest in Eight Industrial Countries, 1961–82. In *Tanzi, V., ed.*, 1984, pp. 172–203. [G: OECD]

Kelly, William A., Jr. and Miles, James A. Darby and Fisher: Resolution of a Paradox. *Financial Rev.*, March 1984, *19*(1), pp. 103–10.

Keran, Michael W. Velocity and Inflation Expectations: 1922–1983. *Fed. Res. Bank San Francisco Econ. Rev.*, Summer 1984, (3), pp. 40–55. **[G: U.S.]**

Khan, Shahrukh Rafi. An Economic Analysis of a PLS Model for the Financial Sector. *Pakistan J. Appl. Econ.*, Winter 1984, 3(2), pp. 89–105.

Kimbrough, Kent P. Aggregate Information and the Role of Monetary Policy in an Open Economy. *J. Polit. Econ.*, April 1984, 92(2), pp. 268–85.

Kimbrough, Kent P. and Koray, Faik. Money, Output, and the Trade Balance: Theory and Evidence. *Can. J. Econ.*, August 1984, 17(3), pp. 508–22. **[G: Canada; U.S.]**

King, Robert G. and Plosser, Charles I. Money, Credit, and Prices in a Real Business Cycle. *Amer. Econ. Rev.*, June 1984, 74(3), pp. 363–80. **[G: U.S.]**

King, Robert G. and Trehan, Bharat. Money: Endogeneity and Neutrality. *J. Monet. Econ.*, November 1984, 14(3), pp. 385–93.

Kingston, Geoffrey H. Microeconomic Justification of the Hoarding Function. *Int. Econ. Rev.*, June 1984, 25(2), pp. 385–89.

Klein, Philip A. Economic Policy and the Obligations of the Economist. *J. Econ. Issues*, June 1984, 18(2), pp. 537–46.

Klovland, Jan Tore. Tax Evasion and the Demand for Currency in Norway and Sweden. Is There a Hidden Relationship? *Scand. J. Econ.*, 1984, 86(4), pp. 423–39. **[G: Norway; Sweden]**

Knoester, Anthonie. Theoretical Principles of the Buffer Mechanism, Monetary Quasi-Equilibrium and Its Spillover Effects. *Kredit Kapital*, 1984, 17(2), pp. 243–60.

Kochman, Ladd and Hood, Jerry. The Systematic Understanding of Interest Rates. *Atlantic Econ. J.*, July 1984, 12(2), pp. 69.

Koda, Keiichi. A Note on the Existence of Monetary Equilibria in Overlapping Generations Models with Storage. *J. Econ. Theory*, December 1984, 34(2), pp. 388–95.

Koh, Ai-Tee. Money Shocks and Deviations from Purchasing Power Parity. *J. Monet. Econ.*, July 1984, 14(1), pp. 105–22.

Kohli, Ulrich R. Permanent Prices, Expected Price Changes, and the Demand for Money. *Empirical Econ.*, 1984, 9(4), pp. 233–46. **[G: Canada]**

Komura, Chikara. Money, Income and Causality in Japan—Supplementary Evidence: Reply. *Southern Econ. J.*, April 1984, 50(4), pp. 1219–23. **[G: Japan]**

Kormendi, Roger C. and Meguire, Philip G. Cross-Regime Evidence of Macroeconomic Rationality. *J. Polit. Econ.*, October 1984, 92(5), pp. 875–908. **[G: Selected Countries]**

Koskela, Erkki and Virén, Matti. Credit Rationing and Consumer Intertemporal Choice. *Oxford Econ. Pap.*, June 1984, 36(2), pp. 241–47.

Kouri, Pentti J. K. Monetary Policy, the Balance of Payments, and the Exchange Rate. In *Bigman, D. and Taya, T.*, eds., 1984, pp. 127–59.

Kregel, Jan A. Monetary Production Economics

and Monetary Policy. *Écon. Soc.*, April 1984, 18(4), pp. 221–32.

Krugman, Paul R. The International Role of the Dollar: Theory and Prospect. In *Bilson, J. F. O. and Marston, R. C.*, eds., 1984, pp. 261–78. **[G: OECD; U.S.]**

Kutasovic, Paul; Lackman, Conway L. and Tepperberg, Alfred. A Non-monetarist Test of the Credit Availability Theory. *Rivista Int. Sci. Econ. Com.*, October–November 1984, 31(10–11), pp. 1033–51. **[G: U.S.]**

Ladenson, Mark L. Money Stock Control: The Effects of a Reduction in the Number of Depository Institutions. *J. Bank Res.*, Autumn 1984, 15(3), pp. 160–66. **[G: U.S.]**

Lagos, Luis Felipe. Demanda por dinero y Expectativas Racionales: Una Estimación para Chile. (With English summary.) *Cuadernos Econ.*, August 1984, 21(63), pp. 227–32. **[G: Chile]**

Lahiri, A. K. Non-luxurious Money, Secular Behaviour of Velocity and Implications for Development Planning. *Indian Econ. J.*, July–Sept. 1984, 32(1), pp. 94–99.

Lahiri, Kajal and Zaporowski, Mark. A Note on the Variability of Real Interest Rates, Business Cycles, and the Livingston Data. *J. Banking Finance*, September 1984, 8(3), pp. 483–90. **[G: U.S.]**

Laidler, David. The 'Buffer Stock' Notion in Monetary Economics. *Econ. J.*, 1984 Supplement, 94, pp. 17–34.

Lane, Timothy D. Instrument Instability and Short-Term Monetary Control. *J. Monet. Econ.*, September 1984, 14(2), pp. 209–24.

Lavoie, Marc. The Endogenous Flow of Credit and the Post Keynesian Theory of Money. *J. Econ. Issues*, September 1984, 18(3), pp. 771–97.

Lavoie, Marc. Un modèle post-keynésian d'économie monétaire fondé sur la théorie du circuit. (A Post-Keynesian Model of a Money Economy, Based upon the Theory of the Circuit. With English summary.) *Écon. Soc.*, April 1984, 18(4), pp. 233–58.

Leiderman, Leonardo. On the Monetary-Macro Dynamics of Colombia and Mexico. *J. Devel. Econ.*, January–February 1984, 14(1–2), pp. 183–201. **[G: Colombia; Mexico]**

Leijonhufvud, Axel. Hicks on Time and Money. *Oxford Econ. Pap.*, Supplement November 1984, 36, pp. 26–46.

Leijonhufvud, Axel. Hicks on Time and Money. In *Collard, D. A., et al.*, eds., 1984, pp. 26–46.

Leijonhufvud, Axel. Inflation and Economic Performance. In *Siegel, B. N.*, ed., 1984, pp. 19–36.

Léonard, Jacques. Monnaie, production, circuit. Propositions pour une interprétation théorique. (Money, Production, and Circuit. With English summary.) *Écon. Soc.*, April 1984, 18(4), pp. 73–81.

LeRoy, Stephen F. Nominal Prices and Interest Rates in General Equilibrium: Money Shocks. *J. Bus.*, April 1984, 57(2), pp. 177–95.

LeRoy, Stephen F. Nominal Prices and Interest

Rates in General Equilibrium: Endowment Shocks. *J. Bus.*, April 1984, *57*(2), pp. 197–213.

Levich, Richard M. Comment [Properties of Innovations in Spot and Forward Exchange Rates and the Role of Money Supply Processes] [Exchange Rate Dynamics]. In *Bilson, J. F. O. and Marston, R. C., eds.*, 1984, pp. 189–94. [G: Selected OECD]

Levin, Jay H. On the International Transmission of Monetary Policy under Floating Exchange Rates. *Quart. Rev. Econ. Bus.*, Spring 1984, *24*(1), pp. 78–86.

Liang, Ming-Yih. Keynes's Errors in the Liquidity Preference versus Loanable Funds Controversy. *J. Macroecon.*, Spring 1984, *6*(2), pp. 215–27.

Liang, Ming-Yih. Real *versus* Nominal Specification of the Demand for Money Function. *Econ. Inquiry*, July 1984, *22*(3), pp. 404–13. [G: U.S.]

Lin, Kuan-Pin and Oh, John S. Stability of the U.S. Short-run Money Demand Function, 1959–81. *J. Finance*, December 1984, *39*(5), pp. 1383–96. [G: U.S.]

Lisitsian, N. Commodity and Money Circulation and Bank Credit (Problems of Theory and Management). *Prob. Econ.*, December 1984, *27*(8), pp. 40–54. [G: U.S.S.R.]

Liu, Pak-Wai. A Note on Two Summary Measures of Tax Progressivity. *Public Finance*, 1984, *39*(3), pp. 412–19. [G: Hong Kong]

Liviatan, Nissan. Tight Money and Inflation. *J. Monet. Econ.*, January 1984, *13*(1), pp. 5–15.

Lomax, Rachel. Bade and Parkin: Is £M₃ the Right Aggregate? In *Griffiths, B. and Wood, G. E., eds.*, 1984, pp. 294–300. [G: U.K.]

Lombra, Raymond E. Financial Innovation, Deregulation, and the Effectiveness of Monetary Policy: A Graphical Approach. *Quart. Rev. Econ. Bus.*, Spring 1984, *24*(1), pp. 87–93. [G: U.S.]

Lombra, Raymond E. and Kaufman, Herbert M. The Money Supply Process: Identification, Stability, and Estimation. *Southern Econ. J.*, April 1984, *50*(4), pp. 1147–59. [G: U.S.]

Lopez, Franklin. The Effect of Various Credit Controls on the Level of International Reserves. *Kredit Kapital*, 1984, *17*(3), pp. 404–15. [G: LDCs]

Loranger, Jean-Guy. La théorie qualitative de la monnaie: quelques résultats économétriques pour l'ensemble de l'économie canadienne. (The Qualitative Theory of Money: Some Econometrical Results for the Whole Canadian Economy. With English summary.) *Écon. Soc.*, April 1984, *18*(4), pp. 283–310. [G: Canada]

Lucas, Robert E., Jr. Money in a Theory of Finance. *Carnegie-Rochester Conf. Ser. Public Policy*, Autumn 1984, *21*, pp. 9–45.

MacKinnon, James G. and Milbourne, Ross D. Monetary Anticipations and the Demand for Money. *J. Monet. Econ.*, March 1984, *13*(2), pp. 263–74. [G: U.S.]

Makin, John H. and Tanzi, Vito. Level and Volatility of U.S. Interest Rates: Roles of Expected Inflation, Real Rates, and Taxes. In *Tanzi, V., ed.*, 1984, pp. 110–42. [G: U.S.]

Malinvaud, E. Current and Anticipated Deficits, Interest Rates and Economic Activity: Comments. *Europ. Econ. Rev.*, June 1984, *25*(1), pp. 29–32. [G: EEC; U.S.]

Mankiw, N. Gregory; Runkle, David E. and Shapiro, Matthew D. Are Preliminary Announcements of the Money Stock Rational Forecasts? *J. Monet. Econ.*, July 1984, *14*(1), pp. 15–27. [G: U.S.]

Markose, Sheri M. Non-separability of Consumption and Portfolio Choice with a Precautionary Demand for Money. *Greek Econ. Rev.*, August 1984, *6*(2), pp. 171–202.

Marquez, Jaime. Sustitución de monedas, dualidad e indeterminación del tipo de cambio: análisis empírico de la experiencia venezolana. (With English summary.) *Cuadernos Econ.*, December 1984, *21*(64), pp. 299–313. [G: Venezuela]

Marrelli, Massimo. On Indirect Tax Evasion. *J. Public Econ.*, November 1984, *25*(1/2), pp. 181–96.

Marris, Stephen N. Current and Anticipated Deficits, Interest Rates and Economic Activity: Comments. *Europ. Econ. Rev.*, June 1984, *25*(1), pp. 33–36. [G: U.S.; Japan; Germany; U.K.]

Masera, Rainer S. Monetary Policy and Budget Policy: Blend or Dichotomy? In *Masera, R. S. and Triffin, R., eds.*, 1984, pp. 196–223. [G: Italy; OECD]

Mattesini, Fabrizio. The Wicksell Connection: A Variation on the Theme. *Econ. Notes*, 1984, (2), pp. 121–38.

Mattoscio, Niccola. Intertemporal Coordination and Interest Rates in Neoclassic and Keynesian Models: Problems and Perspectives. (In Italian. With English summary.) *Giorn. Econ.*, September–October 1984, *43*(9–10), pp. 651–69.

Mayer, Thomas. The Government Budget Constraint and Standard Macrotheory. *J. Monet. Econ.*, May 1984, *13*(3), pp. 371–79.

Mayor, Thomas H. and Pearl, Lawrence R. Life-Cycle Effects, Structural Change and Long-Run Movements in the Velocity of Money. *J. Money, Credit, Banking*, May 1984, *16*(2), pp. 175–84. [G: U.S.]

McCallum, Bennett T. A Linearized Version of Lucas's Neutrality Model. *Can. J. Econ.*, February 1984, *17*(1), pp. 138–45.

McCallum, Bennett T. Are Bond-Financed Deficits Inflationary? A Ricardian Analysis. *J. Polit. Econ.*, February 1984, *92*(1), pp. 123–35.

McCallum, Bennett T. Monetarist Rules in the Light of Recent Experience. *Amer. Econ. Rev.*, May 1984, *74*(2), pp. 388–91.

McCallum, Bennett T. On Low-Frequency Estimates of Long-Run Relationships in Macroeconomics. *J. Monet. Econ.*, July 1984, *14*(1), pp. 3–14.

McKenna, Edward J. and Zannoni, Diane C. Comment on Stein and Weintraub: "The Ac-

celeration of Inflation." *J. Post Keynesian Econ.*, Spring 1984, *6*(3), pp. 470–78.
[G: U.S.]

McMahon, Michael R. An Appraisal of the New Classical Macroeconomics. *J. Macroecon.*, Summer 1984, *6*(3), pp. 335–46.

Mehra, Yash P. The Tax Effect, and the Recent Behaviour of the After-Tax Real Rate: Is It Too High? *Fed. Res. Bank Richmond Econ. Rev.*, July/Aug. 1984, *70*(4), pp. 8–20. [G: U.S.]

Melnick, Rafi and Sokoler, Meir. The Government's Revenue from Money Creation and the Inflationary Effects of a Decline in the Rate of Growth of G.N.P. *J. Monet. Econ.*, March 1984, *13*(2), pp. 225–36.
[G: Selected OECD; Israel; Argentina]

Meltzer, Allan H. The Fight Against Inflation: A Comment [Some Unpleasant Monetarist Arithmetic]. In *Griffiths, B. and Wood, G. E., eds.*, 1984, pp. 61–66.

Merrick, John J., Jr. The Anticipated Real Interest Rate, Capital Utilization and the Cyclical Pattern of Real Wages. *J. Monet. Econ.*, January 1984, *13*(1), pp. 17–30. [G: U.S.]

Miller, Edward M. Bank Deposits in the Monetary Theory of Keynes: A Note. *J. Money, Credit, Banking*, May 1984, *16*(2), pp. 242–46.

Miller, Edward M. Extension of the Economics of Keynes to the United States. *Southern Econ. J.*, January 1984, *50*(3), pp. 781–801.

Miller, Preston J. and Sargent, Thomas J. Some Pleasant Monetarist Arithmetic: A Reply. *Fed. Res. Bank Minn. Rev.*, Spring 1984, *8*(2), pp. 21–26. [G: U.S.]

Milne, William J. and Torous, Walter N. Long-Term Interest Rates and the Price Level: The Canadian Evidence on the Gibson Paradox. *Can. J. Econ.*, May 1984, *17*(2), pp. 327–39.
[G: Canada]

Minsky, Hyman P. Frank Hahn's *Money and Inflation:* A Review Article. *J. Post Keynesian Econ.*, Spring 1984, *6*(3), pp. 449–57.

Mishkin, Frederic S. Are Real Interest Rates Equal across Countries? An Empirical Investigation of International Parity Conditions. *J. Finance*, December 1984, *39*(5), pp. 1345–57.
[G: OECD]

Mishkin, Frederic S. The Real Interest Rate: A Multi-Country Empirical Study. *Can. J. Econ.*, May 1984, *17*(2), pp. 283–311.
[G: OECD]

Mistri, Maurizio. Su di un caso di variabilità del saggio di interesse reale in condizioni di inflazione con ipotesi di aspettative razionali. (On a Case of Variability of the Real Interest Rate in Conditions of Inflation under Hypothesis of Rational Expectations. With English summary.) *Giorn. Econ.*, March–April 1984, *43*(3–4), pp. 261–70.

Mitchell, Douglas W. Macro Effects of Interest-sensitive Aggregate Supply. *J. Macroecon.*, Winter 1984, *6*(1), pp. 43–56.

Molho, Lazaros E. Loan Rates as a Selective Credit Control. *J. Banking Finance*, March 1984, *8*(1), pp. 79–98. [G: Greece]

Montiel, Peter. Credit and Fiscal Policies in a "Global Monetarist" Model of the Balance of Payments. *Int. Monet. Fund Staff Pap.*, December 1984, *31*(4), pp. 685–708.

Mookerjee, Rajen. The Demand for Money in Colonial India: A Secular Perspective. *Indian Econ. J.*, July–Sept. 1984, *32*(1), pp. 49–60.
[G: India]

Moore, Basil J. Keynes and the Endogeneity of the Money Stock. *Stud. Econ.*, 1984, *39*(22), pp. 23–69.

Moore, Basil J. and Stuttman, Stephen L. A Causality Analysis of the Determinants of Money Growth. *Brit. Rev. Econ. Issues*, Spring 1984, *6*(14), pp. 1–25. [G: U.S.]

Moosa, Suleman A. Banking Innovations and the Behavior of Measured M1 Velocity. *Rev. Bus. Econ. Res.*, Spring 1984, *19*(2), pp. 13–23.
[G: U.S.]

Motley, Brian. Dynamic Adjustment in Money Demand. *Fed. Res. Bank San Francisco Econ. Rev.*, Winter 1984, (1), pp. 22–26. [G: U.S.]

Mullineaux, Donald J. Expectations, Surprises and Treasury Bill Rates: 1960–82. *J. Finance*, July 1984, *39*(3), pp. 696–98.

von Natzmer, Wulfheinrich and Reim, O. Wirtschaftspolitik und Konjunktur in einem modifizierten ISLM-Modell. (Economic Policy and the Business Cycle in a Modified ISLM Model. With English summary.) *Kredit Kapital*, 1984, *17*(3), pp. 371–95.

Neck, Reinhard. Keynesian and Monetarist Models of Unemployment and Inflation: A Simulation Study for Austria. *Empirica*, 1984, *11*(1), pp. 23–45. [G: Austria]

Niehans, Jürg. National Monetary Policy in an International Capital Market. *Kobe Econ. Bus. Rev.*, 1984, *30*, pp. 1–10.

Nielsen, Peter Erling. Nyere pengeteori—en oversigt. (Recent Trends in Monetary Theory—A Survey Article. With English summary.) *Nationaløkon. Tidsskr.*, 1984, *122*(1), pp. 1–29.

O'Driscoll, Gerald P., Jr. Expectations and Monetary Regimes. *Fed. Res. Bank Dallas Econ. Rev.*, September 1984, pp. 1–11.

Obstfeld, Maurice. Multiple Stable Equilibria in an Optimizing Perfect-Foresight Model. *Econometrica*, January 1984, *52*(1), pp. 223–28.

Olson, Mancur. Beyond Keynesianism and Monetarism. *Econ. Inquiry*, July 1984, *22*(3), pp. 297–322.

Ormerod, Paul. Does Monetarism Fit the UK Facts? A Comment. In *Griffiths, B. and Wood, G. E., eds.*, 1984, pp. 120–28. [G: U.K.]

Osborn, Denise R. Causality Testing and Its Implications for Dynamic Econometric Models. *Econ. J.*, 1984 Supplement, *94*, pp. 82–96.
[G: Canada]

Osborne, Dale K. Ten Approaches to the Definition of Money. *Fed. Res. Bank Dallas Econ. Rev.*, March 1984, pp. 1–23.

Paleologos, John M. The Dynamic Impacts of Fiscal and Monetary Policy on an Aggregate Macroeconomic Model of the Greek Economy—Some Policy Experiments. *Public Finance*, 1984, *39*(2), pp. 261–80. [G: Greece]

Panayotopoulos, Dimitris. Inflationary Expectations and the Demand for Money: The Greek Experience: "A Comment and Some Different Results"—A Rejoinder. *Kredit Kapital*, 1984, 17(2), pp. 272–80. **[G: Greece]**

Papadia, Francesco. Estimates of Ex Ante Real Rates of Interest in the EEC Countries and in the United States, 1973–82: A Note. *J. Money, Credit, Banking*, August 1984, 16(3), pp. 335–44. **[G: EEC; U.S.]**

Parguez, Alain. La Dynamique de la Monnaie. (The Dynamic Theory of Money. With English summary.) *Écon. Soc.*, April 1984, 18(4), pp. 83–118.

Parikh, Ashok. Causality between Money and Prices in Indonesia. *Empirical Econ.*, 1984, 9(4), pp. 217–32. **[G: Indonesia]**

Patterson, K. D. and Ryding, J. Dynamic Time Series Models with Growth Effects Constrained to Zero. *Econ. J.*, March 1984, 94(373), pp. 137–43.

Patterson, K. D. and Ryding, J. The Modified Fisher Hypothesis and the Steady State Demand for Money. *Manchester Sch. Econ. Soc. Stud.*, September 1984, 52(3), pp. 300–313. **[G: U.K.]**

Peek, Joe and Wilcox, James A. The Degree of Fiscal Illusion in Interest Rates: Some Direct Estimates. *Amer. Econ. Rev.*, December 1984, 74(5), pp. 1061–66. **[G: U.S.]**

Peel, David A. and Walters, K. Some Empirical Results on "the Rationality" of Expectations Derived from Survey Data. *Empirical Econ.*, 1984, 9(3), pp. 151–63.

Pellanda, Anna. Keynes' Theory of the Rate of Interest and Its Links with the Mercantilist Theory of Money and Fisher's Theory of Income. *Rivista Int. Sci. Econ. Com.*, March 1984, 31(3), pp. 220–40.

Penm, Jack H. W. and Terrell, Richard D. Multivariate Subset Autoregressive Modelling with Zero Constraints for Detecting 'Overall Causality.' *J. Econometrics*, March 1984, 24(3), pp. 311–30. **[G: Canada]**

Persson, Torsten and Svensson, Lars E. O. Time-Consistent Fiscal Policy and Government Cash-Flow. *J. Monet. Econ.*, November 1984, 14(3), pp. 365–74.

Pesaran, M. H. The New Classical Macroeconomics: A Critical Exposition. In *van der Ploeg, F.*, ed., 1984, pp. 195–215.

Phylaktis, Kate. Structural Change, Monetary Policy and the Foreign Exchange Value of the Pound: Comments. In *Griffiths, B. and Wood, G. E.*, eds., 1984, pp. 233–37. **[G: U.K.]**

Phylaktis, Kate and Wood, Geoffrey E. An Analytical and Taxonomic Framework for the Study of Exchange Controls. In *Black, J. and Dorrance, G. S.*, eds., 1984, pp. 149–66.

Pierce, James L. Did Financial Innovation Hurt the Great Monetarist Experiment? *Amer. Econ. Rev.*, May 1984, 74(2), pp. 392–96. **[G: U.S.]**

Pigott, Charles. Indicators of Long-Term Real Interest Rates. *Fed. Res. Bank San Francisco Econ. Rev.*, Winter 1984, (1), pp. 45–63. **[G: U.S.]**

Plosser, Charles I. Money in a Theory of Finance: Some Observations. *Carnegie-Rochester Conf. Ser. Public Policy*, Autumn 1984, 21, pp. 47–55.

Poloz, Stephen S. The Transactions Demand for Money in a Two-Currency Economy. *J. Monet. Econ.*, September 1984, 14(2), pp. 241–50.

Porta, Angelo. L'"imposta implicita" sulla riserva obbligatoria e il suo gettito per lo Stato: alcune riflessioni sul caso italiano. (The "Hidden Tax" on the Reserve Requirement and Its Yield for Government: A Commentary on the Italian Case. With English summary.) *Bancaria*, July 1984, 40(7), pp. 652–60. **[G: Italy]**

Prodromidis, Kyprianos P. Determinants of Money Demand in Greece, 1966 I–1977 IV. *Kredit Kapital*, 1984, 17(3), pp. 352–70. **[G: Greece]**

Racette, Daniel and Bergeron, Pierre. La Grande dépression américaine et la neutralité de la monnaie: un test économétrique. (U.S. Great Depression and the Neutrality Hypothesis: An Econometric Test. With English summary.) *L'Actual. Econ.*, September 1984, 60(3), pp. 280–307. **[G: U.S.]**

Radecki, Lawrence J. Targeting in a Dynamic Model. *Fed. Res. Bank New York Quart. Rev.*, Summer 1984, 9(2), pp. 9–15. **[G: U.S.]**

Ram, Rati. Money, Income and Causality in Japan—Supplementary Evidence: Comment. *Southern Econ. J.*, April 1984, 50(4), pp. 1214–18. **[G: Japan]**

Ramakrishnan, Ram T. S. and Thakor, Anjan V. Information Reliability and a Theory of Financial Intermediation. *Rev. Econ. Stud.*, July 1984, 51(3), pp. 415–32.

Ramb, Bernd-Thomas. Ineffektivität der Wirtschaftspolitik bei "rationalen Erwartungen"? Eine unkerrekte, aber auch modellspezifische Behauptung. (Ineffectiveness of Economic Policy under "Rational Expectations"? An Incorrect but Also Model-Specific Assertion. With English summary.) *Kredit Kapital*, 1984, 17(2), pp. 165–79.

Rao, V. Lakshmana. Which Money Stock Measure Is to Be Preferred. *Indian Econ. J.*, July–Sept. 1984, 32(1), pp. 100–106. **[G: India]**

Renas, Stephen M. Monetary Policy: Is the Fed's Response to Inflation Accommodative? *Econ. Int.*, August–November 1984, 37(3–4), pp. 364–74. **[G: U.S.]**

Res, Zannis. Comment on Bade and Parkin's Paper on Issues Concerning Monetary Policy in the UK [Is Sterling M_3 the Right Aggregate?]. In *Griffiths, B. and Wood, G. E.*, eds., 1984, pp. 287–93. **[G: U.K.]**

Richard, Alban. La demande de monnaie. Une synthèse fondée sur l'irréversibilité et le risque. (With English summary.) *Revue Écon. Polit.*, March–April 1984, 94(2), pp. 205–25.

Richard, Scott F. Time Series Evidence on the Expectations Hypothesis of the Term Structure: A Comment. *Carnegie-Rochester Conf. Ser. Public Policy*, Spring 1984, *20*, pp. 239–41. **[G: U.S.]**

Rieber, William J. The Expenditure Effects of Supply Side Tax Cuts: The Role of the Interest Elasticity of Money Demand. *Quart. J. Bus. Econ.*, Summer 1984, *23*(3), pp. 29–35.

Robinson, William D. Government Bonds and Unstable Growth Paths. *Quart. J. Bus. Econ.*, Summer 1984, *23*(3), pp. 36–58. **[G: U.S.]**

Rodríguez, Carlos Alfredo. La Estrategia de Estabilización con Tipo de Cambio Flexible y Politica Monetaria Activa. (With English summary.) *Cuadernos Econ.*, August 1984, *21*(63), pp. 103–21.

Rogers, C. and Morgenrood, P. The St Louis Equation and the South African Economy: Some Preliminary Results. *S. Afr. J. Econ.*, June 1984, *52*(2), pp. 172–87. **[G: S. Africa]**

Rogoff, Kenneth. On the Effects of Sterilized Intervention: An Analysis of Weekly Data. *J. Monet. Econ.*, September 1984, *14*(2), pp. 133–50. **[G: U.S.; Canada]**

Roley, V. Vance and Walsh, Carl E. Unanticipated Money and Interest Rates. *Amer. Econ. Rev.*, May 1984, *74*(2), pp. 49–54. **[G: U.S.]**

Rosende, Francisco and Toso, Roberto. Una explicación para la tasa de interés real en Chile en el período, 1975–1983. (With English summary.) *Cuadernos Econ.*, April 1984, *21*(62), pp. 25–36. **[G: Chile]**

Rossiter, Rosemary and Lee, Tong Hun. Statistical Tests of Relative Substitutabilities of Near-Monies over Time. *J. Macroecon.*, Summer 1984, *6*(3), pp. 249–64. **[G: U.S.]**

Rotemberg, Julio J. A Monetary Equilibrium Model with Transactions Costs. *J. Polit. Econ.*, February 1984, *92*(1), pp. 40–58.

Rouzaud, Catherine. Les modèles à générations successives et la monnaie: une présentation introductive. (Overlapping Generations Models and Money: An Introduction. With English summary.) *Écon. Appl.*, 1984, *37*(3–4), pp. 565–91.

Rovelli, Riccardo. Expected Inflation and the Real Interest Rate: A Survey of Current Issues. *Giorn. Econ.*, September–October 1984, *43*(9–10), pp. 671–97.

Royama, Shoichi. An Anatomy of Financial Liberalization. (In Japanese. With English summary.) *Osaka Econ. Pap.*, December 1984, *34*(2–3), pp. 147–54. **[G: Japan]**

Rush, Mark. A Classical Model of a Small Fixed Exchange Rate Economy. *J. Int. Money Finance*, April 1984, *3*(1), pp. 31–49.

Saini, Krishan G. Can Monetary Growth Explain Inflation in India? *Indian Econ. J.*, July–Sept. 1984, *32*(1), pp. 61–71. **[G: India]**

Saint-Étienne, Christian. De l'importance réelle de l'hypothèse de la rationalitè des anticipations. (With English summary.) *Revue Écon. Polit.*, November–December 1984, *94*(6), pp. 773–91.

Salama, Elías. El multiplicador de la base monetaria y los modelos macroeconómicos usuales.

(The Monetary Base Multiplier and the Usual General Equilibrium Macroeconomic Models. With English summary.) *Económica*, January–April 1984, *30*(1), pp. 71–84.

Samuelson, Paul A. and Sato, Ryuzo. Unattainability of Integrability and Definiteness Conditions in the General Case of Demand for Money and Goods. *Amer. Econ. Rev.*, September 1984, *74*(4), pp. 588–604.

Santomero, Anthony M. Modeling the Banking Firm: A Survey. *J. Money, Credit, Banking*, Part 2 November 1984, *16*(4), pp. 576–602.

Saracoglu, Rüşdü. Expectations of Inflation and Interest Rate Determination. *Int. Monet. Fund Staff Pap.*, March 1984, *31*(1), pp. 141–78. **[G: U.S.; France; U.K.; Germany; Japan]**

Sargent, Thomas J. and Wallace, Neil. Some Unpleasant Monetarist Arithmetic. In *Griffiths, B. and Wood, G. E., eds.*, 1984, pp. 15–41.

Sassanpour, Cyrus and Sheen, Jeffrey. An Empirical Analysis of the Effects of Monetary Disequilibria in Open Economies. *J. Monet. Econ.*, January 1984, *13*(1), pp. 127–63. **[G: France; W. Germany]**

Saunders, Anthony and Tress, Richard B. On the Constancy of the International Real Rate of Interest. *J. Monet. Econ.*, January 1984, *13*(1), pp. 113–26. **[G: U.S.; W. Germany; Italy]**

Sayad, João. Rural Credit and Positive Real Rates of Interest: Brazil's Experience with Rapid Inflation. In *Adams, D. W.; Graham, D. H. and Von Pischke, J. D., eds.*, 1984, pp. 146–60. **[G: Brazil]**

Scanagatta, Giovanni. Tasso di interesse e aspettative di inflazione: aspetti teorici ed empirici. (Interest Rates and Inflationary Expectations: Theoretical and Empirical Aspects. With English summary.) *Bancaria*, January 1984, *40*(1), pp. 19–28. **[G: U.S.]**

Scheele, Erwin. Perioden-Gleichgewicht und zeitliche Entwicklung in einem *IS/LM*-Modell mit Finanzierungsrestriktion der Investitionen und Bilanzrestriktion der Unternehmen. (Temporary Equilibrium and Intrinsic Dynamics of an *IS/LM* Model with a Financial Constraint for Investment and a Balance Sheet Restraint for Firms. With English summary.) *Z. Wirtschaft. Sozialwissen.*, 1984, *104*(4), pp. 339–68.

Schmid, A. Allan. Broadening Capital Ownership: The Credit System as a Locus of Power. In *Alperovitz, G. and Skurski, R., eds.*, 1984, pp. 117–37.

Schwartz, Anna J. Does Monetarism Fit the UK Facts? Comments. In *Griffiths, B. and Wood, G. E., eds.*, 1984, pp. 129–36. **[G: U.K.]**

Scott, Robert Haney and Johnson, Dudley W. Rent-Seeking in U.S. Banking and the Optimal Quantity of Money. *Hong Kong Econ. Pap.*, 1984, (15), pp. 67–78. **[G: U.S.]**

Seaks, Terry G. Selden's Model of Inflation: A Reexamination [Monetary Growth and the Long-run Rate of Inflation]. *J. Macroecon.*, Winter 1984, *6*(1), pp. 103–07. **[G: U.S.; Canada; Belgium; Netherlands]**

Seccareccia, Mario S. The Fundamental Macroeconomic Link between Investment Activity, the Structure of Employment and Price Changes: A Theoretical and Empirical Analysis. *Écon. Soc.*, April 1984, *18*(4), pp. 165–219. [G: Canada]

Selden, Richard T. The Lag from Money to Prices [Monetary Growth and the Long-run Rate of Inflation]. *J. Macroecon.*, Winter 1984, *6*(1), pp. 109–11. [G: U.S.; Canada]

Shah, Anup R. Crowding Out, Capital Accumulation, the Stock Market, and Money-financed Fiscal Policy. *J. Money, Credit, Banking*, Part 1 November 1984, *16*(4), pp. 461–73.

Sharma, Ramlal. Causality between Money and Price Level in India. *Indian Econ. Rev.*, July-Dec. 1984, *19*(2), pp. 213–21. [G: India]

Sharpe, Ian G. Covered Interest Rate Parity: The Australian Case. *Appl. Econ.*, October 1984, *16*(5), pp. 655–65. [G: U.S.; Australia]

Sheehey, Edmund J. Money and Output in Latin America: Some Tests of a Rational Expectations Approach. *J. Devel. Econ.*, January–February 1984, *14*(1–2), pp. 203–18. [G: Latin America]

Sheehey, Edmund J. The Neutrality of Money in the Short Run: Some Tests: A Note. *J. Money, Credit, Banking*, May 1984, *16*(2), pp. 237–41. [G: U.S.]

Sheikh, Munir A. An analysis of Some Possible Causes for the Absence or Presence of the Neutrality and Homogeneity Properties in Large Macroeconomic Models. *Empirical Econ.*, 1984, *9*(2), pp. 113–30. [G: Canada]

Shieh, Yeung-Nan. On Monetary Expansion, Terms of Trade and Economic Growth. *Econ. Rec.*, June 1984, *60*(169), pp. 128–32.

Shinkai, Yoichi. Japanese Demand-for-Money Functions. (In Japanese. With English summary.) *Osaka Econ. Pap.*, December 1984, *34*(2–3), pp. 36–44. [G: Japan]

Silvia, John E. Interest Rates, Uncertainty, and Monetary Volatility. *Atlantic Econ. J.*, July 1984, *12*(2), pp. 70. [G: U.S.]

Simkin, Colin. Does Money Matter in Singapore? *Singapore Econ. Rev.*, April 1984, *29*(1), pp. 1–15. [G: Singapore]

Sinn, Hans-Werner. Rationale Erwartungen, Rationierung und Rezession—Braucht keynesianische Politik dumme Bürger? (Rational Expectations, Rationing, and Recession—Does Keynesian Policy Need Dull Citizens? With English summary.) *Jahr. Nationalökon. Statist.*, March 1984, *199*(2), pp. 158–78. [G: W. Germany]

Smith, Bruce D. Money, Nonconvex Preferences, and the Existence of Equilibrium: A Note. *J. Econ. Theory*, April 1984, *32*(2), pp. 359–66.

Smith, Bruce D. Private Information, Deposit Interest Rates, and the 'Stability' of the Banking System. *J. Monet. Econ.*, November 1984, *14*(3), pp. 293–317.

Snower, Dennis J. Rational Expectations, Nonlinearities, and the Effectiveness of Monetary Policy. *Oxford Econ. Pap.*, June 1984, *36*(2), pp. 177–99.

Sørensen, Peter Birch. Er statens budgetunderskud rentedrivende? (The Effects of Government Budget Deficits on Interest Rates. With English summary.) *Nationaløkon. Tidsskr.*, 1984, *122*(1), pp. 41–55.

Sørensen, Peter Birch. Countercyclical versus Passive Monetary Policy in a Medium-run Macro Model. *Scand. J. Econ.*, 1984, *86*(4), pp. 452–67.

Spahn, H.-Peter. Marx–Schumpeter–Keynes: Drei Fragmente über Geld, Zins und Profit. (Marx–Schumpeter–Keynes: Three Approaches to Money, Interest, and Profit. With English summary.) *Jahr. Nationalökon. Statist.*, May 1984, *199*(3), pp. 237–55.

Spanos, Aris. Liquidity as a Latent Variable—An Application of the MIMIC Model. *Oxford Bull. Econ. Statist.*, May 1984, *46*(2), pp. 125–43. [G: U.K.]

Spindt, Paul A. Modelling the Monetary Multiplier and the Controllability of the Divisia Monetary Quantity Aggregates. *Rev. Econ. Statist.*, May 1984, *66*(2), pp. 314–19. [G: U.S.]

Sprenkle, Case M. On Liquidity Preference—Again: Comment [Liquidity Preference as Behavior toward Risk Is a Demand for Short-term Securities—Not Money]. *Amer. Econ. Rev.*, September 1984, *74*(4), pp. 809–11.

Startz, Richard. Can Money Matter? *J. Monet. Econ.*, May 1984, *13*(3), pp. 381–85. [G: U.S.]

Stein, Jerome L. Reply to McKenna and Zannoni: "The Acceleration of Inflation." *J. Post Keynesian Econ.*, Spring 1984, *6*(3), pp. 779–80. [G: U.S.]

Stemp, Peter J. and Turnovsky, Stephen J. Equilibrium, Stability, and Deficit Financing in a Simple Nonlinear Monetary Model under Perfect Foresight. *J. Macroecon.*, Fall 1984, *6*(4), pp. 377–97.

Stern, Gary H.; Supel, Thomas M. and Quah, Danny. Money Market Mutual Funds Are Hardly Money. *Fed. Res. Bank Minn. Rev.*, Summer 1984, *8*(3), pp. 3–8. [G: U.S.]

Struthers, John J. Rational Expectations: A Promising Research Program or a Case of Monetarist Fundamentalism? *J. Econ. Issues*, December 1984, *18*(4), pp. 1133–54.

Strydom, P. D. F. The New Keynesian Approach to Economic Policy. *S. Afr. J. Econ.*, September 1984, *52*(3), pp. 282–95.

Sundaresan, Mahadevan. Consumption and Equilibrium Interest Rates in Stochastic Production Economies. *J. Finance*, March 1984, *39*(1), pp. 77–92.

Swanson, Peggy E. Integer Constraints on the Inventory Theory of Money Demand. *Quart. J. Bus. Econ.*, Winter 1984, *23*(1), pp. 32–37.

Sweeney, Richard James. Anticipate Countercyclical Monetary Policy. *Econ. Inquiry*, January 1984, *22*(1), pp. 28–36.

Sweeney, Richard James. The Transactions Velocity of Money and Its Efficiency. *J. Finan. Quant. Anal.*, September 1984, *19*(3), pp. 339–50. [G: U.S.]

Tanzi, Vito. Inflation and the Incidence of Income Taxes on Interest Income in the United States, 1972–81. In *Tanzi, V., ed.*, 1984, pp. 143–58. [G: U.S.]

Tanzi, Vito. Inflationary Expectations, Taxes, and the Demand for Money in the United States. In *Tanzi, V., ed.*, 1984, pp. 159–71. [G: U.S.]

Taslim, Mohammad Ali. On Rate of Interest and Demand for Money in LDCs: The Case of Bangladesh. *Bangladesh Devel. Stud.*, September 1984, *12*(3), pp. 19–36. [G: Bangladesh]

Tatom, John A. Interest Rate Variability: Its Link to the Variability of Monetary Growth and Economic Performance. *Fed. Res. Bank St. Louis Rev.*, November 1984, *66*(9), pp. 31–47. [G: U.S.]

Taylor, John B. Recent Changes in Macro Policy and Its Effects: Some Time-Series Evidence. *Amer. Econ. Rev.*, May 1984, *74*(2), pp. 206–10. [G: U.S.]

Thomas, Lloyd B., Jr. Short-Term Interest Rates, Inflation, Uncertainty and Monetary Policy: Some Empirical Findings. *Bus. Econ.*, October 1984, *19*(5), pp. 34–39. [G: U.S.]

Thore, Sten. Spatial Models of the Eurodollar Market. *J. Banking Finance*, March 1984, *8*(1), pp. 51–65.

Thornton, Daniel L. Monetizing the Debt. *Fed. Res. Bank St. Louis Rev.*, December 1984, *66*(10), pp. 30–43. [G: U.S.]

Thornton, Daniel L. The Government Budget Constraint with Endogenous Money. *J. Macroecon.*, Winter 1984, *6*(1), pp. 57–67.

Thygesen, Niels. Exchange-rate Policies and Monetary Targets in the EMS Countries. In *Masera, R. S. and Triffin, R., eds.*, 1984, pp. 262–86. [G: EEC]

Tichy, Gunther. Schumpeter's Monetary Theory—An Unjustly Neglected Part of His Work. In *Seidl, C., ed.*, 1984, pp. 125–38.

Turnovsky, Stephen J. Exchange Market Intervention under Alternative Forms of Exogenous Disturbances. *J. Int. Econ.*, November 1984, *17*(3/4), pp. 279–97.

Turnovsky, Stephen J. and Miller, Marcus H. The Effects of Government Expenditure on the Term Structure of Interest Rates. *J. Money, Credit, Banking*, February 1984, *16*(1), pp. 16–33.

Turnovsky, Stephen J. and Wohar, Mark E. Monetarism and the Aggregate Economy: Some Longer-Run Evidence. *Rev. Econ. Statist.*, November 1984, *66*(4), pp. 619–29. [G: U.S.]

Tybout, James R. Interest Control and Credit Allocation in Developing Countries. *J. Money, Credit, Banking*, Part 1 November 1984, *16*(4), pp. 474–87. [G: LDCs; Colombia]

Ueda, Kazuo. Financial Structure and Monetary Policy. (In Japanese. With English summary.) *Osaka Econ. Pap.*, December 1984, *34*(2–3), pp. 160–79. [G: Japan]

Ueda, Kazuo. Supply Shocks and the Interdependence of Macroeconomic Stability under Flexible Exchange Rates. *Europ. Econ. Rev.*, July 1984, *25*(2), pp. 253–77. [G: Japan; Germany]

Urich, Thomas J. and Wachtel, Paul. The Structure of Expectations of the Weekly Money Supply Announcement. *J. Monet. Econ.*, March 1984, *13*(2), pp. 183–94. [G: U.S.]

VanderHoff, James. Evidence on the Varying Effect of Expected Inflation on Interest Rates. *Rev. Econ. Statist.*, August 1984, *66*(3), pp. 477–81. [G: U.S.]

Virén, Matti. Expected Inflation and Interest Rates: Some Cross-Country Evidence. *Liiketaloudellinen Aikak.*, 1984, *33*(4), pp. 433–45. [G: OECD]

Wainhouse, Charles E. Empirical Evidence for Hayek's Theory of Economic Fluctuations. In *Siegel, B. N., ed.*, 1984, pp. 37–71. [G: U.S.]

Wallace, Neil. Some of the Choices for Monetary Policy. *Fed. Res. Bank Minn. Rev.*, Winter 1984, *8*(1), pp. 15–24.

Walsh, Carl E. Interest Rate Volatility and Monetary Policy. *J. Money, Credit, Banking*, May 1984, *16*(2), pp. 133–50.

Watson, Harry S. Credit Markets and Borrower Effort. *Southern Econ. J.*, January 1984, *50*(3), pp. 802–13.

Wenninger, John. Financial Innovation—A Complex Problem Even in a Simple Framework. *Fed. Res. Bank New York Quart. Rev.*, Summer 1984, *9*(2), pp. 1–8. [G: U.S.]

Wenninger, John. The M1-GNP Relationship: A Component Approach. *Fed. Res. Bank New York Quart. Rev.*, Autumn 1984, *9*(3), pp. 6–15. [G: U.S.]

White, Lawrence H. Free Banking as an Alternative Monetary System. In *Siegel, B. N., ed.*, 1984, pp. 269–302.

Whiteman, Charles H. Lucas on the Quantity Theory: Hypothesis Testing without Theory. *Amer. Econ. Rev.*, September 1984, *74*(4), pp. 742–49.

Wildasin, David E. The Welfare Effects of Intergovernmental Grants in an Economy with Distortionary Local Taxes: A Simple General Equilibrium Analysis. *J. Public Econ.*, November 1984, *25*(1/2), pp. 103–25.

Witte, Willard E. Macroeconomic Stability and the Short Run Federal Reserve Reaction Function, 1969–1979. *Econ. Inquiry*, October 1984, *22*(4), pp. 571–78. [G: U.S.]

Wood, John H. The Search for a Monetary Policy Rule in an Uncertain World. *Fed. Res. Bank Dallas Econ. Rev.*, September 1984, pp. 13–23. [G: U.S.; U.K.]

Wren-Lewis, Simon. A Note on Nominal Government Expenditure Targets. *J. Macroecon.*, Winter 1984, *6*(1), pp. 89–95.

Wren-Lewis, Simon. Omitted Variables in Equations Relating Prices to Money. *Appl. Econ.*, August 1984, *16*(4), pp. 483–96. [G: U.K.]

Yun, Young-Sup. The Effects of Inflation and Income Taxes on Interest Rates: Some New Evidence. *J. Finan. Quant. Anal.*, December 1984, *19*(4), pp. 425–48. [G: U.S.]

3116 Monetary Policy, Including All Central Banking Topics

Anderson, Martin. An Economic Bill of Rights. In *Moore, J. H., ed.*, 1984, pp. 1–22.
[G: U.S.]

Arndt, Heinz W. and Sundrum, R. M. Devaluation and Inflation: The 1978 Experience. *Bull. Indonesian Econ. Stud.*, April 1984, *20*(1), pp. 83–97. [G: Indonesia]

Bade, Robin and Parkin, Michael. Is Sterling M₃ the Right Aggregate? In *Griffiths, B. and Wood, G. E., eds.*, 1984, pp. 241–86.
[G: U.K.]

Balles, John J. The Federal Reserve: The Role of Reserve Banks. *J. Money, Credit, Banking*, February 1984, *16*(1), pp. 110–17. [G: U.S.]

Barnard, Doug, Jr. The Future of Payments System Legislation. In *Fed. Res. Bank Atlanta*, 1984, pp. 171–76. [G: U.S.]

Batten, Dallas S. and Ott, Mack. What Can Central Banks Do About the Value of the Dollar? *Fed. Res. Bank St. Louis Rev.*, May 1984, *66*(5), pp. 16–26. [G: U.S.]

Benston, George J. The Effects of Regulation. In *Fed. Res. Bank Atlanta*, 1984, pp. 125–37.
[G: U.S.]

Bernstein, Edward M. A Program for International Monetary Stability: Comment. In *Agmon, T.; Hawkins, R. G. and Levich, R. M., eds.*, 1984, pp. 78–84. [G: OECD]

Bessler, David A. Relative Prices and Money: A Vector Autoregression on Brazilian Data. *Amer. J. Agr. Econ.*, February 1984, *66*(1), pp. 25–30. [G: Brazil]

Biacabe, Pierre. La politique monétaire en France. (With English summary.) *Revue Écon. Polit.*, September–October 1984, *94*(5), pp. 639–48. [G: France]

Black, Robert P. The Fed's Mandate: Help or Hindrance? *Fed. Res. Bank Richmond Econ. Rev.*, July/Aug. 1984, *70*(4), pp. 3–7.
[G: U.S.]

Black, Stanley W. Monetary Targeting: Issues and Alternatives. In *Hewlett, S. A.; Kaufman, H. and Kenen, P. B., eds.*, 1984, pp. 105–21.
[G: U.S.; W. Germany; Japan]

Blinder, Alan S. Changes in the Financial System: Implications for Monetary Policy: Comments. *Brookings Pap. Econ. Act.*, 1984, (1), pp. 266–70. [G: U.S.]

Booth, James R. and Smith, Richard L., II. The Impact of the Community Reinvestment Act on Branching Activity of Financial Institutions. *J. Bank Res.*, Summer 1984, *15*(2), pp. 123–28. [G: U.S.]

Bordo, Michael D. On the Report of the Gold Commission (1982) and Convertible Monetary Systems: A Comment. *Carnegie-Rochester Conf. Ser. Public Policy*, Spring 1984, *20*, pp. 269–73.

Bordo, Michael D. The Gold Standard: Myths and Realities. In *Siegel, B. N., ed.*, 1984, pp. 197–237. [G: U.K.; U.S.]

Boyd, John H. The Use of Inputs by the Federal Reserve System: Comment. *Amer. Econ. Rev.*, December 1984, *74*(5), pp. 1114–17.

Boyes, William J. and Furnish, Dale Beck. A Note on the Use of Incorporation as an Escape from Usury Ceilings. *J. Ind. Econ.*, March 1984, *32*(3), pp. 367–72. [G: U.S.]

Broaddus, Alfred and Goodfriend, Marvin. Base Drift and the Longer Run Growth of M1: Experience from a Decade of Monetary Targeting. *Fed. Res. Bank Richmond Econ. Rev.*, Nov./Dec. 1984, *70*(6), pp. 3–14. [G: U.S.]

Budd, Alan P., et al. Does Monetarism fit the UK Facts? In *Griffiths, B. and Wood, G. E., eds.*, 1984, pp. 75–119. [G: U.K.]

Cagan, Phillip. Monetary Policy and Subduing Inflation. In *Fellner, W., ed.*, 1984, pp. 21–53. [G: U.S.]

Cagan, Phillip. The Report of the Gold Commission (1982). *Carnegie-Rochester Conf. Ser. Public Policy*, Spring 1984, *20*, pp. 247–67.

Campbell, Tim S. and Glenn, David. Deposit Insurance in a Deregulated Environment. *J. Finance*, July 1984, *39*(3), pp. 775–85.
[G: U.S.]

Carli, Guido. Money Markets—Trends and Challenges. *Rev. Econ. Cond. Italy*, Sept.–Dec. 1984, (3), pp. 305–16. [G: U.S.]

Carron, Andrew S. The Australian Financial System. In *Caves, R. E. and Krause, L. B., eds.*, 1984, pp. 195–229. [G: Australia]

Cassese, Sabino. The Long Life of the Financial Institutions Set Up in the Thirties. *J. Europ. Econ. Hist.*, Special Issue 1984, *13*(2), pp. 273–94. [G: OECD]

de Cecco, Marcello and Miller, Marcus H. Monetary Targeting in Europe. In *Hewlett, S. A.; Kaufman, H. and Kenen, P. B., eds.*, 1984, pp. 123–50. [G: OECD]

Chouraqui, Jean-Claude and Price, Robert W. R. Medium-term Financial Strategy: The Coordination of Fiscal and Monetary Policies. *OECD Econ. Stud.*, Spring 1984, (2), pp. 7–49. [G: OECD]

Chrystal, K. Alec. Dutch Disease or Monetarist Medicine? The British Economy under Mrs. Thatcher. *Fed. Res. Bank St. Louis Rev.*, May 1984, *66*(5), pp. 27–37. [G: U.K.]

Ciampi, Carlo Azeglio. Politica di bilancio, politica dei redditi e stabilità monetaria, presupposti di una crescita stabile. (Budget Policy, Incomes Policy and Monetary Stability as Prerequisites for Stable Growth. With English summary.) *Bancaria*, March 1984, *40*(3), pp. 241–55. [G: Italy]

Ciocca, Pierluigi. Economic Analysis and Banking Supervision. In *Banca d'Italia*, 1984, pp. 263–76.

Clair, Robert T. Deposit Insurance, Moral Hazard, and Credit Unions. *Fed. Res. Bank Dallas Econ. Rev.*, July 1984, pp. 1–12.

Cook, Timothy Q. The 1983 M1 Seasonal Factor Revisions: An Illustration of Problems That May Arise in Using Seasonally Adjusted Data for Policy Purposes. *Fed. Res. Bank Richmond Econ. Rev.*, Mar./Apr. 1984, *70*(2), pp. 22–33.
[G: U.S.]

Corrigan, E. Gerald. Statement to the U.S. Senate Committee on Banking, Housing, and Urban Affairs, April 11, 1984. *Fed. Res. Bull.*, May 1984, 70(5), pp. 413–19. **[G: U.S.]**

Cotula, Franco. Financial Innovation and Monetary Control in Italy. *Banca Naz. Lavoro Quart. Rev.*, September 1984, (150), pp. 219–56. **[G: Italy]**

Cross, Sam Y. Treasury and Federal Reserve Foreign Exchange Operations. *Fed. Res. Bank New York Quart. Rev.*, Spring 1984, 9(1), pp. 57–70. **[G: U.S.]**

Cross, Sam Y. Treasury and Federal Reserve Foreign Exchange Operations. *Fed. Res. Bull.*, September 1984, 70(9), pp. 693–704. **[G: U.S.]**

Cross, Sam Y. Treasury and Federal Reserve Foreign Exchange Operations: Interim Report. *Fed. Res. Bull.*, June 1984, 70(6), pp. 492–94. **[G: U.S.]**

Cross, Sam Y. Treasury and Federal Reserve Foreign Exchange Operations. *Fed. Res. Bull.*, March 1984, 70(3), pp. 191–203. **[G: U.S.]**

Cuthbertson, Keith. Techniques of Monetary Control in the United Kingdom. *J. Econ. Stud.*, 1984, 11(4), pp. 46–68. **[G: U.K.]**

Dahl, Frederick R. Statement to the U.S. House Subcommittee on International Economic Policy and Trade of the Committee on Foreign Affairs, June 20, 1984. *Fed. Res. Bull.*, July 1984, 70(7), pp. 575–77. **[G: U.S.]**

Dale, Charles; Wilson, Stephen D. and Capps, Cavan. Forecasting Army Enlistment Rates with Financial Market Indicators. *Atlantic Econ. J.*, March 1984, 12(1), pp. 119 **[G: U.S.]**

Davis, Kevin. Financial Regulation in Australia. *Australian Econ. Rev.*, 3rd Quarter 1984, (67), pp. 135–46. **[G: Australia]**

Diltz, J. David. Commercial Bank Profitability and the New Federal Reserve Operating Procedures: An Empirical Study. *Bus. Econ.*, July 1984, 19(4), pp. 57–62. **[G: U.S.]**

Dorn, James A. A Property Rights View of the Debt Crisis. *Cato J.*, Spring/Summer 1984, 4(1), pp. 1–8. **[G: Global]**

Dornbusch, Rudiger and Frenkel, Jacob A. The Gold Standard and the Bank of England in the Crisis of 1847. In *Bordo, M. D. and Schwartz, A. J.*, eds., 1984, pp. 233–64. **[G: U.K.]**

Dutton, John C., Jr. The Bank of England and the Rules of the Game under the International Gold Standard: New Evidence. In *Bordo, M. D. and Schwartz, A. J.*, eds., 1984, pp. 173–95. **[G: U.K.]**

Dutton, John C., Jr. The Bank of England and the Rules of the Game under the International Gold Standard: New Evidence: Reply. In *Bordo, M. D. and Schwartz, A. J.*, eds., 1984, pp. 199–202. **[G: U.K.]**

Eichengreen, Barry. Central Bank Cooperation under the Interwar Gold Standard. *Exploration Econ. Hist.*, January 1984, 21(1), pp. 64–87. **[G: France; U.K.]**

Eisenbeis, Robert A. Impulsi di innovazione nei servizi finanziari. (Forces for Change in the Financial Service Industry. With English sum-mary.) *Bancaria*, March 1984, 40(3), pp. 266–71. **[G: U.S.]**

Epstein, Gerald and Ferguson, Thomas. Monetary Policy, Loan Liquidation, and Industrial Conflict: The Federal Reserve and the Open Market Operations of 1932. *J. Econ. Hist.*, December 1984, 44(4), pp. 957–83. **[G: U.S.]**

Evans, Gary R. The Evolution of Financial Institutions and the Ineffectiveness of Modern Monetary Policy. *J. Econ. Issues*, June 1984, 18(2), pp. 439–48. **[G: U.S.]**

Felmingham, B. S. The Recovery of World Labor Markets and the U.S. Monetary Stance: Rationale and Evidence. *Kyklôs*, 1984, 37(3), pp. 424–43. **[G: OECD]**

Fleisig, Heywood. Operations of the German Central Bank and the Rules of the Game, 1879–1913: Comment. In *Bordo, M. D. and Schwartz, A. J.*, eds., 1984, pp. 349–58. **[G: Germany]**

Fratianni, Michele and Spinelli, Franco. Italy in the Gold Standard Period, 1861–1914. In *Bordo, M. D. and Schwartz, A. J.*, eds., 1984, pp. 405–41. **[G: Italy]**

Freedman, Charles. Canada and the Interwar Gold Standard, 1920–35: Monetary Policy without a Central Bank: Comment. In *Bordo, M. D. and Schwartz, A. J.*, eds., 1984, pp. 303–08. **[G: U.S.; Canada]**

Frenkel, Jacob A. A Program for International Monetary Stability: Comment. In *Agmon, T.; Hawkins, R. G. and Levich, R. M.*, eds., 1984, pp. 85–89. **[G: OECD]**

Gidlow, R. M. Forward Exchange Arrangements and Exchange Control Policy in South Africa. *S. Afr. J. Econ.*, September 1984, 52(3), pp. 247–55. **[G: S. Africa]**

Gilbert, R. Alton and Holland, A. Steven. Has the Deregulation of Deposit Interest Rates Raised Mortgage Rates? *Fed. Res. Bank St. Louis Rev.*, May 1984, 66(5), pp. 5–15. **[G: U.S.]**

Gleske, Leonhard. Erfahrungen mit flexiblen Wechselkursen. (Experience with Flexible Exchange Rates. With English summary.) *Kredit Kapital*, 1984, 17(4), pp. 455–73. **[G: W. Germany]**

Goodfriend, Marvin. The Promises and Pitfalls of Contemporaneous Reserve Requirements for the Implementation of Monetary Policy. *Fed. Res. Bank Richmond Econ. Rev.*, May/June 1984, 70(3), pp. 3–12. **[G: U.S.]**

Goodhart, Charles A. E. Bank of England Operations, 1893–1913: Comment. In *Bordo, M. D. and Schwartz, A. J.*, eds., 1984, pp. 222–27. **[G: U.K.]**

Goria, Giovanni. Gestione creditizia e politica della finanza pubblica nel quadro della lotta all'inflazione. (Credit Management and Public-Finance Policy in the Struggle against Inflation. With English summary.) *Bancaria*, April 1984, 40(4), pp. 365–70. **[G: Italy]**

Greenwood, John G. Underlying Ingredients of the Recent Hong Kong Dollar Crisis. *Hong Kong Econ. Pap.*, 1984, (15), pp. 119–24. **[G: Hong Kong]**

Hafer, R. W. Money, Debt and Economic Activity. *Fed. Res. Bank St. Louis Rev.*, June/July 1984, *66*(6), pp. 18–25.   [G: U.S.]

Hall, Robert E. A Free-Market Policy to Stabilize the Purchasing Power of the Dollar. In *Siegel, B. N., ed.*, 1984, pp. 303–21.   [G: U.S.]

Hall, Robert E. Bank Regulation and the Effectiveness of Open Market Operations: Comment. *Brookings Pap. Econ. Act.*, 1984, (2), pp. 445–47.   [G: U.S.]

Hall, Robert E. Monetary Policy for Noninflationary Growth. In *Moore, J. H., ed.*, 1984, pp. 61–71.   [G: U.S.]

Hamdani, Kauser. CRR and Excess Reserves: An Early Appraisal. *Fed. Res. Bank New York Quart. Rev.*, Autumn 1984, *9*(3), pp. 16–23.   [G: U.S.]

Hardouvelis, Gikas A. Market Perceptions of Federal Reserve Policy and the Weekly Monetary Announcements. *J. Monet. Econ.*, September 1984, *14*(2), pp. 225–40.   [G: U.S.]

Harper, Ian R. Financial Regulation in Australia: Comment. *Australian Econ. Rev.*, 3rd Quarter 1984, (67), pp. 151–52.   [G: Australia]

Heffernan, Shelagh A. Reflections on the Case for an International Central Bank. *Greek Econ. Rev.*, April 1984, *6*(1), pp. 99–120.   [G: Global]

Heller, H. Robert. Regulatory Aspects of the World Debt Problem: A Comment. *Cato J.*, Spring/Summer 1984, *4*(1), pp. 125–29.   [G: U.S.]

Hicks, John R. Lineamenti storici dei metodi di controllo della moneta. (Methods of Monetary Control. With English summary.) *Bancaria*, November 1984, *40*(11), pp. 1069–75.   [G: U.K.]

Horvitz, Paul M. Deposit Insurance in a Deregulated Environment: Discussion. *J. Finance*, July 1984, *39*(3), pp. 785–87.   [G: U.S.]

Horvitz, Paul M. Payments and Deregulation. In *Fed. Res. Bank Atlanta*, 1984, pp. 163–68.   [G: U.S.]

Hosek, William R. Monetary Aggregate and Interest Rate Volatility. *Bus. Econ.*, April 1984, *19*(3), pp. 35–39.   [G: U.S.]

Hubbard, Carl M.; Davis, Joe C. and Shatto, Gloria M. Uniform Reserves and the Prospects for Monetary Control. *Bus. Econ.*, July 1984, *19*(4), pp. 51–56.   [G: U.S.]

Hughes, Jonathan R. T. Stagnation without 'Flation: The 1930s Again. In *Siegel, B. N., ed.*, 1984, pp. 137–56.   [G: U.S.]

Hughes, Jonathan R. T. The Gold Standard and the Bank of England in the Crisis of 1847: Comment. In *Bordo, M. D. and Schwartz, A. J., eds.*, 1984, pp. 264–71.   [G: U.K.]

Humphrey, David B. Future Networks and the Fed's Role. In *Fed. Res. Bank Atlanta*, 1984, pp. 67–79.   [G: U.S.]

Humphrey, Joseph F. Changing Asset/Liability Structure of Savings Institutions in a Deregulated Environment. *Contemp. Policy Issue*, May 1984, (6), pp. 45–55.   [G: U.S.]

Hutchinson, Michael M. Intervention, Deficit Finance and Real Exchange Rates: The Case of Japan. *Fed. Res. Bank San Francisco Econ. Rev.*, Winter 1984, (1), pp. 27–44.   [G: Japan]

Johannes, James M. and Rasche, Robert H. Recent Behavior of the M1—Adjusted Monetary Base Multiplier and Forecasts for Early 1984. In *Shadow Open Market Committee*, 1984, pp. 51–55.   [G: U.S.]

Jonung, Lars. Swedish Experience under the Classical Gold Standard, 1873–1914. In *Bordo, M. D. and Schwartz, A. J., eds.*, 1984, pp. 361–99.   [G: Sweden]

Jordan, Jerry L. Monetary Policy Options and the Outlook—1984. In *Shadow Open Market Committee*, 1984, pp. 39–43.   [G: U.S.]

Kareken, John H. Bank Regulation and the Effectiveness of Open Market Operations. *Brookings Pap. Econ. Act.*, 1984, (2), pp. 405–44.   [G: U.S.]

Kopcke, Richard W. Inflation and the Choice of "Monetary" Guidelines. *New Eng. Econ. Rev.*, January–February 1984, pp. 5–14.   [G: U.S.]

Korkman, Sixten and Pekkarinen, Jukka. Onko valuuttasäännöstely aikansa elänyt? (Should Exchange Control Be Abandoned? With English summary.) *Kansant. Aikak.*, 1984, *80*(1), pp. 76–85.   [G: Finland]

Krümmel, Hans J. Schutzzweck und Aufsichtseingriffe. Über den Run auf die Bankschalter und seine Verhinderung. (Protective Purpose and Intervention by Supervisory Agencies—On the Run on Bank Counters and Its Prevention. With English summary.) *Kredit Kapital*, 1984, *17*(4), pp. 474–89.   [G: W. Germany]

Latter, A. R. Some Issues Associated with the New Exchange Rate Regime. *Hong Kong Econ. Pap.*, 1984, (15), pp. 125–28.   [G: Hong Kong]

Leaf, Ronald. Competitive Implicit Interest Payments in Commercial Banking. *Amer. Econ.*, Spring 1984, *28*(1), pp. 49–56.   [G: U.S.]

Leijonhufvud, Axel. Constitutional Constraints on the Monetary Powers of Government. In *McKenzie, R. B., ed. (I)*, 1984, pp. 95–107.

Lim, G. C. The Martin Report. *Australian Econ. Rev.*, 2nd Quarter 1984, (66), pp. 26–34.   [G: Australia]

Lim, G. C. The Money Supply in Australia: Prospects for 1984–85. *Australian Econ. Rev.*, 4th Quarter 1984, (68), pp. 18–22.   [G: Australia]

Lindert, Peter H. Swedish Experience under the Classical Gold Standard, 1873–1914: Comment. In *Bordo, M. D. and Schwartz, A. J., eds.*, 1984, pp. 399–404.   [G: Sweden]

Lindsey, David E., et al. Short-Run Monetary Control: Evidence under a Non-Borrowed Reserve Operating Procedure. *J. Monet. Econ.*, January 1984, *13*(1), pp. 87–111.   [G: U.S.]

Litterman, Robert B. Forecasting and Policy Analysis with Bayesian Vector Autoregression Models. *Fed. Res. Bank Minn. Rev.*, Fall 1984, *8*(4), pp. 30–41.   [G: U.S.]

Lomax, Rachel. Bade and Parkin: Is £M$_3$ the Right Aggregate? In *Griffiths, B. and Wood, G. E., eds.*, 1984, pp. 294–300.   [G: U.K.]

Loopesko, Bonnie E. Relationships among Exchange Rates, Intervention, and Interest Rates: An Empirical Investigation. *J. Int. Money Finance*, December 1984, *3*(3), pp. 257–77. **[G: OECD]**

Marreiros, Luis. Contribution to the Comparative Study of Savings Trends in Latin America: 1973–1983. In *Kessler, D. and Ullmo, P.-A., eds.*, 1984, pp. 281–309. **[G: Latin America]**

Marris, Stephen N. Why the Dollar Won't Come Down. *Challenge*, November/December 1984, *27*(5), pp. 19–25. **[G: U.S.]**

Martino, Antonio. Toward Monetary Stability? *Econ. Int.*, February–May 1984, *37*(1–2), pp. 108–22. **[G: Italy]**

Masera, Rainer S. Documentazione statistica e informazione economica. L'esperienza del Servizio Studi della Banca d'Italia. (Statistical Documentation and Economic Information: Experience of the Bank of Italy Research Department. With English summary.) *Bancaria*, October 1984, *40*(10), pp. 979–89. **[G: Italy]**

McCarthy, F. Ward, Jr. The Evolution of the Bank Regulatory Structure: A Reappraisal. *Fed. Res. Bank Richmond Econ. Rev.*, Mar./Apr. 1984, *70*(2), pp. 3–21. **[G: U.S.]**

McGouldrick, Paul. Operations of the German Central Bank and the Rules of the Game, 1879–1913. In *Bordo, M. D. and Schwartz, A. J., eds.*, 1984, pp. 311–49. **[G: Germany]**

McKinnon, Ronald I. A Program for International Monetary Stability. In *Agmon, T.; Hawkins, R. G. and Levich, R. M., eds.*, 1984, pp. 55–77. **[G: OECD]**

McMillin, W. Douglas and Fackler, James S. Monetary vs. Credit Aggregates: An Evaluation of Monetary Policy Targets. *Southern Econ. J.*, January 1984, *50*(3), pp. 711–23.

Meigs, A. James. Regulatory Aspects of the World Debt Problem. *Cato J.*, Spring/Summer 1984, *4*(1), pp. 105–24. **[G: U.S.]**

Meltzer, Allan H. Base Velocity—The Trend Continues. In *Shadow Open Market Committee*, 1984, pp. 29–30. **[G: U.S.]**

Menezes, Victor. Beyond the Peg. *Hong Kong Econ. Pap.*, 1984, (15), pp. 129–31. **[G: Hong Kong]**

Merusi, Fabio. Sulla riforma delle casse di risparmio e dei monti di credito su pegno. (Reform of Savings Banks. With English summary.) *Bancaria*, July 1984, *40*(7), pp. 633–51. **[G: Italy]**

Micossi, S. and Rebecchini, S. A Case Study on the Effectiveness of Foreign Exchange Market Intervention: The Italian Lira (September 1975–March 1977). *J. Banking Finance*, December 1984, *8*(4), pp. 535–55. **[G: Italy]**

Micossi, Stefano. La politica monetaria nella CEE. (Monetary Policy in the EEC. With English summary.) *Bancaria*, August 1984, *40*(8), pp. 759–69. **[G: EEC]**

Moggridge, Donald E. The Bank of England and the Rules of the Game under the International Gold Standard: New Evidence: Comment. In *Bordo, M. D. and Schwartz, A. J., eds.*, 1984, pp. 195–99. **[G: U.K.]**

Neumann, Manfred J. M. Intervention in the Mark/Dollar Market: The Authorities' Reaction Function. *J. Int. Money Finance*, August 1984, *3*(2), pp. 223–39. **[G: U.S.; Germany]**

Nikitin, S. M. and Usoskin, V. M. Bourgeois Political Economy and New Trends in Anti-inflationary Policy. In *Nikitin, S. M., ed.*, 1984, pp. 209–24.

O'Brien, James M. The Information Value of the FOMC Policy Directive under the New Operating Procedures. *J. Money, Credit, Banking*, May 1984, *16*(2), pp. 151–64. **[G: U.S.]**

O'Driscoll, Gerald P., Jr. and Short, Eugenie D. Safety-Net Mechanisms: The Case of International Lending. *Cato J.*, Spring/Summer 1984, *4*(1), pp. 185–204. **[G: U.S.]**

Ohashi, Kenichi. GMDH Forecasting of U.S. Interest Rates. In *Farlow, S. J., ed.*, 1984, pp. 199–214. **[G: U.S.]**

Ormerod, Paul. Does Monetarism Fit the UK Facts? A Comment. In *Griffiths, B. and Wood, G. E., eds.*, 1984, pp. 120–28. **[G: U.K.]**

Parkin, Michael. The United Kingdom: Political Economy and Macroeconomics: A Comment. *Carnegie-Rochester Conf. Ser. Public Policy*, Autumn 1984, *21*, pp. 281–93. **[G: U.K.]**

Perquel, Jean-Jacques. Le marché financier en 1983. (With English summary.) *Revue Écon. Polit.*, September–October 1984, *94*(5), pp. 649–61. **[G: France]**

Péteri, György. The Inflation-Proof Gold Standard: The Foreign Policy of *Riksbankschefen*. Victor Moll and the Origin of the Swedish Ban on Gold Imports in 1924. *J. Europ. Econ. Hist.*, September–December 1984, *13*(3), pp. 635–63. **[G: Sweden]**

Phylaktis, Kate and Wood, Geoffrey E. An Analytical and Taxonomic Framework for the Study of Exchange Controls. In *Black, J. and Dorrance, G. S., eds.*, 1984, pp. 149–66.

Pippenger, John. Bank of England Operations, 1893–1913. In *Bordo, M. D. and Schwartz, A. J., eds.*, 1984, pp. 203–22. **[G: U.K.]**

Porta, Angelo. L'"imposta implicita" sulla riserva obbligatoria e il suo gettito per lo Stato: alcune riflessioni sul caso italiano. (The "Hidden Tax" on the Reserve Requirement and Its Yield for Government: A Commentary on the Italian Case. With English summary.) *Bancaria*, July 1984, *40*(7), pp. 652–60. **[G: Italy]**

Puckett, Richard H. Federal Open Market Committee Structure and Decisions. *J. Monet. Econ.*, July 1984, *14*(1), pp. 97–104. **[G: U.S.]**

Renas, Stephen M. Monetary Policy: Is the Fed's Response to Inflation Accommodative? *Econ. Int.*, August–November 1984, *37*(3–4), pp. 364–74. **[G: U.S.]**

Res, Zannis. Comment on Bade and Parkin's Paper on Issues Concerning Monetary Policy in the UK [Is Sterling M_3 the Right Aggregate?]. In *Griffiths, B. and Wood, G. E., eds.*, 1984, pp. 287–93. **[G: U.K.]**

Reynolds, Alan. Gold and Economic Boom: Five

Case Studies, 1792–1926. In *Siegel, B. N., ed.*, 1984, pp. 249–68. **[G: France; U.K.; U.S.]**

Rich, Georg. Canada without a Central Bank: Operation of the Price-Specie-Flow Mechanism, 1872–1913. In *Bordo, M. D. and Schwartz, A. J., eds.*, 1984, pp. 547–75. **[G: Canada]**

Rogowski, Robert J. Pricing the Money Market Deposit and Super-NOW Accounts in 1983. *J. Bank Res.*, Summer 1984, *15*(2), pp. 72–81. **[G: U.S.]**

Rothbard, Murray N. The Federal Reserve as a Cartelization Device: The Early Years, 1913–1930. In *Siegel, B. N., ed.*, 1984, pp. 89–136. **[G: U.S.]**

Ryan, John E. Statement to the U.S. House Subcommittee on General Oversight and Renegotiation of the Committee on Banking, Finance and Urban Affairs, June 20, 1984. *Fed. Res. Bull.*, July 1984, *70*(7), pp. 573–75. **[G: U.S.]**

Saini, Krishan G. Economic Policy Management in Italy. *Rev. Econ. Cond. Italy*, Sept.–Dec. 1984, (3), pp. 345–63. **[G: Italy]**

Santoni, G. J. A Private Central Bank: Some Olde English Lessons. *Fed. Res. Bank St. Louis Rev.*, April 1984, *66*(4), pp. 12–22. **[G: U.K.]**

Saulnier, Raymond J. The President's Economic Report: A Critique. *J. Portfol. Manage.*, Summer 1984, *10*(4), pp. 81–83. **[G: U.S.]**

Schwartz, Anna J. Does Monetarism Fit the UK Facts? Comments. In *Griffiths, B. and Wood, G. E., eds.*, 1984, pp. 129–36. **[G: U.K.]**

Schwartz, Anna J. International Lending and the Economic Environment [Safety-Net Mechanisms: The Case of International Lending]. *Cato J.*, Spring/Summer 1984, *4*(1), pp. 205–09. **[G: U.S.]**

Shadow Open Market Committee. Policy Statement. In *Shadow Open Market Committee*, 1984, pp. 5–11. **[G: U.S.]**

Sharpley, Jennifer. The Potential of Domestic Stabilisation Measures in Developing Countries. In *Killick, Tony, ed. (II)*, 1984, pp. 55–85. **[G: LDCs]**

Shearer, Ronald A. and Clark, Carolyn. Canada and the Interwar Gold Standard, 1920–35: Monetary Policy without a Central Bank. In *Bordo, M. D. and Schwartz, A. J., eds.*, 1984, pp. 277–302. **[G: U.S.; Canada]**

Shughart, William F., II and Tollison, Robert D. The Use of Inputs by the Federal Reserve System: Reply. *Amer. Econ. Rev.*, December 1984, *74*(5), pp. 1121–23.

Siegel, Barry N. Money in Crisis: Introduction. In *Siegel, B. N., ed.*, 1984, pp. 1–16. **[G: U.S.]**

Simpson, Thomas D. Annual Revisions to the Money Stock. *Fed. Res. Bull.*, April 1984, *70*(4), pp. 279–85. **[G: U.S.]**

Simpson, Thomas D. Changes in the Financial System: Implications for Monetary Policy. *Brookings Pap. Econ. Act.*, 1984, (1), pp. 249–65. **[G: U.S.]**

Skaggs, Neil T. A Theory of the Bureaucratic

Value of Federal Reserve Operating Procedures. *Public Choice*, 1984, *43*(1), pp. 65–76. **[G: U.S.]**

Smith, Bruce D. Money and Inflation in Colonial Massachusetts. *Fed. Res. Bank Minn. Rev.*, Winter 1984, *8*(1), pp. 1–14. **[G: U.S.]**

Smyslov, D. V. The Crisis in the Modern Monetary System of Capitalism and Inflation. In *Nikitin, S. M., ed.*, 1984, pp. 108–25. **[G: OECD]**

Solomon, Anthony M. Some Problems and Prospects for Monetary Policy in 1985. *Fed. Res. Bank New York Quart. Rev.*, Winter 1984–85, *9*(4), pp. 1–6. **[G: U.S.]**

Solomon, Anthony M. Statement to the U.S. Senate Subcommittee on International Finance and Monetary Policy of the Committee on Banking, Housing, and Urban Affairs, May 3, 1984. *Fed. Res. Bull.*, May 1984, *70*(5), pp. 419–23. **[G: U.S.; Argentina]**

Solomon, Anthony M. Unresolved Issues in Monetary Policy. *Fed. Res. Bank New York Quart. Rev.*, Spring 1984, *9*(1), pp. 1–6. **[G: U.S.]**

Spindt, Paul A. and Tarhan, Vefa. Bank Reserve Adjustment Process and the Use of Reserve Carryover as a Reserve Management Tool: A Microeconometric Approach. *J. Banking Finance*, March 1984, *8*(1), pp. 5–20. **[G: U.S.]**

Sternlight, Peter D.; Meulendyke, Ann-Marie and Guentner, Kenneth J. Monetary Policy and Open Market Operations in 1983. *Fed. Res. Bank New York Quart. Rev.*, Spring 1984, *9*(1), pp. 39–56. **[G: U.S.]**

Stone, James M. Monetary Policy: A Reconsideration. In *Alperovitz, G. and Skurski, R., eds.*, 1984, pp. 111–16.

Strong, John S. The Use of Inputs by the Federal Reserve System: Comment. *Amer. Econ. Rev.*, December 1984, *74*(5), pp. 1118–20.

Supel, Thomas M. and Todd, Richard M. Should Currency Be Priced Like Cars? *Fed. Res. Bank Minn. Rev.*, Spring 1984, *8*(2), pp. 3–14. **[G: U.S.]**

Sylla, Richard E. Italy in the Gold Standard Period, 1861–1914: Comment. In *Bordo, M. D. and Schwartz, A. J., eds.*, 1984, pp. 442–46. **[G: Italy]**

Temin, Peter. Canada without a Central Bank: Operation of the Price-Specie-Flow Mechanism, 1872–1913: Comment. In *Bordo, M. D. and Schwartz, A. J., eds.*, 1984, pp. 576–81. **[G: Canada]**

Thornton, Daniel L. An Early Look at the Volatility of Money and Interest Rates under CRR. *Fed. Res. Bank St. Louis Rev.*, October 1984, *66*(8), pp. 26–32.

Thornton, Daniel L. Monetizing the Debt. *Fed. Res. Bank St. Louis Rev.*, December 1984, *66*(10), pp. 30–43. **[G: U.S.]**

Timberlake, Richard H., Jr. Federal Reserve Policy since 1945: The Results of Authority in the Absence of Rules. In *Siegel, B. N., ed.*, 1984, pp. 177–93. **[G: U.S.]**

Tobin, James. Bank Regulation and the Effectiveness of Open Market Operations: Comment.

Brookings Pap. Econ. Act., 1984, (2), pp. 447–53. **[G: U.S.]**

Todd, Richard M. Improving Economic Forecasting with Bayesian Vector Autoregression. *Fed. Res. Bank Minn. Rev.*, Fall 1984, *8*(4), pp. 18–29. **[G: U.S.]**

Usoskin, V. M. Monetary and Budgetary Factors behind Inflation. In *Nikitin, S. M., ed.*, 1984, pp. 25–48. **[G: OECD]**

Valentine, T. J. Financial Regulation in Australia: Comment. *Australian Econ. Rev.*, 3rd Quarter 1984, (67), pp. 147–50. **[G: Australia]**

Vaubel, Roland. International Debt, Bank Failures, and the Money Supply: The Thirties and the Eighties. *Cato J.*, Spring/Summer 1984, *4*(1), pp. 249–67. **[G: U.S.]**

Vogt, Michael G. and Hanna, R. S. Variations of the Federal Funds Rate and Bank Reserve Management. *J. Bank Res.*, Autumn 1984, *15*(3), pp. 188–92. **[G: U.S.]**

Volcker, Paul A. Facing Up to the Twin Deficits. *Challenge*, March/April 1984, *27*(1), pp. 4–9. **[G: U.S.]**

Volcker, Paul A. Statement to the Joint Economic Committee, February 9, 1984. *Fed. Res. Bull.*, February 1984, *70*(2), pp. 105–07. **[G: U.S.]**

Volcker, Paul A. Statement to the U.S. Congress Joint Economic Committee, July 30, 1984. *Fed. Res. Bull.*, August 1984, *70*(8), pp. 632–36. **[G: U.S.]**

Volcker, Paul A. Statement to the U.S. House Committee on Banking, Finance, and Urban Affairs, February 7, 1984. *Fed. Res. Bull.*, February 1984, *70*(2), pp. 96–102. **[G: U.S.]**

Volcker, Paul A. Statement to the U.S. House Committee on Banking, Finance and Urban Affairs, June 12, 1984. *Fed. Res. Bull.*, July 1984, *70*(7), pp. 560–68. **[G: U.S.]**

Volcker, Paul A. Statement to the U.S. Senate Committee on Banking, Housing, and Urban Affairs, Salt Lake City, Utah, January 16, 1984. *Fed. Res. Bull.*, February 1984, *70*(2), pp. 90–95. **[G: U.S.]**

Volcker, Paul A. Statement to the U.S. Senate Committee on Banking, Housing, and Urban Affairs, July 25, 1984. *Fed. Res. Bull.*, August 1984, *70*(8), pp. 626–32. **[G: U.S.]**

Volcker, Paul A. The Federal Reserve Position on Restructuring of Financial Regulation Responsibilities. *Fed. Res. Bull.*, July 1984, *70*(7), pp. 547–57. **[G: OECD]**

Wallace, Myles S. and Warner, John T. Fed Policy and Presidential Elections. *J. Macroecon.*, Winter 1984, *6*(1), pp. 79–88. **[G: U.S.]**

Wallich, Henry C. Floating as Seen from the Central Bank. In *Bigman, D. and Taya, T., eds.*, 1984, pp. 33–42.

Walters, Alan A. The United Kingdom: Political Economy and Macroeconomics. *Carnegie-Rochester Conf. Ser. Public Policy*, Autumn 1984, *21*, pp. 259–79. **[G: U.K.]**

Weintraub, Robert E. The New Role for Gold in U.S. Monetary Policy. In *Siegel, B. N., ed.*, 1984, pp. 239–47. **[G: U.S.]**

Wendt, Peter. Statsfinanser og pengepolitik. (Monetary Policy and Government Deficit Fi-

nancing. With English summary.) *Nationaløkon. Tidsskr.*, 1984, *122*(1), pp. 31–40.
[G: Denmark]

White, Lawrence H. Bank Failures and Monetary Policy [International Debt, Bank Failures, and the Money Supply: The Thirties and the Eighties]. *Cato J.*, Spring/Summer 1984, *4*(1), pp. 269–74. **[G: U.S.]**

Witte, Willard E. Cyclical Variation in the Short-run Federal Reserve Reaction Function, 1969–1978. *J. Macroecon.*, Fall 1984, *6*(4), pp. 457–64. **[G: U.S.]**

Witte, Willard E. Macroeconomic Stability and the Short Run Federal Reserve Reaction Function, 1969–1979. *Econ. Inquiry*, October 1984, *22*(4), pp. 571–78. **[G: U.S.]**

Woerheide, Walt; Hartzog, Jerry and Losey, Robert. The Effect of the "Wild Card" Experiment on Savings Flows at Savings and Loans. *Bus. Econ.*, April 1984, *19*(3), pp. 48–51.
[G: U.S.]

Yeager, Leland B. Constitutional Constraints on the Monetary Powers of Government: Comment. In *McKenzie, R. B., ed. (I)*, 1984, pp. 109–13.

312 Commercial Banking

3120 Commercial Banking

Åkerholm, Johnny. Marginalintäkter och -kostnader i den enskilda bankens långivning. (Marginal Revenue and Cost in Lending of the Individual Bank. With English summary.) *Ekon. Samfundets Tidskr.*, 1984, *37*(2), pp. 103–16.
[G: Finland]

Aliber, Robert Z. Il futuro dell'attività bancaria internazionale. (The Future of International Commercial Banking. With English summary.) *Bancaria*, December 1984, *40*(12), pp. 1201–10. **[G: U.S.]**

Aliber, Robert Z. International Banking: A Survey. *J. Money, Credit, Banking*, Part 2 November 1984, *16*(4), pp. 661–78. **[G: OECD]**

Aziz, Zeti Akhtar. Financial Institutions and Markets in Malaysia. In *Skully, M. T., ed.*, 1984, pp. 110–66. **[G: Malaysia]**

Bähre, Inge Lore. Economic Development and Banking Supervision from 1934 to Today. In *Engels, W. and Pohl, H., eds.*, 1984, pp. 95–106. **[G: W. Germany]**

Bain, Andrew D. and Reid, Richard G. The Finance Sector. In *Hood, N. and Young, S., eds.*, 1984, pp. 365–89. **[G: U.K.]**

Bajetti, Luisa. Note per un'analisi delle implicazioni del rapporto banca-territorio. (Considerations for an Analysis of the Implications of Banks' Support for Geographic Economic Development. With English summary.) *Bancaria*, March 1984, *40*(3), pp. 295–301. **[G: Italy]**

Balossino, Antonio. Pianificazione e controlli direzionali: le implicazioni organizzative in banca. (Planning and Management-Controls in Banking: Organizational Implications. With English summary.) *Bancaria*, September 1984, *40*(9), pp. 862–71. **[G: Italy]**

Bank of Italy. The Branch Distribution Plan 1982. In *Banca d'Italia*, 1984, pp. 229–47.
[G: Italy]

Barth, Herbert. Financial Futures: Neue Risiken für die Kreditinstitute? (Financial Futures: New Risks for the Banks? With English summary.) *Kredit Kapital*, 1984, *17*(1), pp. 120–45. [G: U.S.; W. Germany]

Bashir, B. A. Successful Development of Islamic Banks. *J. Res. Islamic Econ.*, Winter 1984, *1*(2), pp. 63–71. [G: Sudan]

Belongia, Michael T. and Santoni, G. J. Hedging Interest Rate Risk with Financial Futures: Some Basic Principles. *Fed. Res. Bank St. Louis Rev.*, October 1984, *66*(8), pp. 15–25.
[G: U.S.]

Bennett, Barbara A. Bank Regulation and Deposit Insurance: Controlling the FDIC's Losses. *Fed. Res. Bank San Francisco Econ. Rev.*, Spring 1984, (2), pp. 16–30. [G: U.S.]

Bennett, Paul. Applying Portfolio Theory to Global Bank Lending. *J. Banking Finance*, June 1984, *8*(2), pp. 153–69.

Benston, George J. The Effects of Regulation. In *Fed. Res. Bank Atlanta*, 1984, pp. 125–37.
[G: U.S.]

Bertoni, Alberto. The Trend of Banking Profitability in Italy: Determinants and Prospects for 1984. *Rev. Econ. Cond. Italy*, June 1984, (2), pp. 169–225. [G: Italy]

Bierwag, G. O.; Kaufman, George G. and Leonard, Paul A. Interest Rate Effects of Commercial Bank Underwriting of Municipal Revenue Bonds: Additional Evidence. *J. Banking Finance*, March 1984, *8*(1), pp. 35–50.
[G: U.S.]

Billingsley, Randall S. and Fraser, Donald R. Determinants of Bank Holding Company Debt Ratings. *Financial Rev.*, March 1984, *19*(1), pp. 55–66.

Billingsley, Randall S. and Lamy, Robert E. Market Reaction to the Formation of One-Bank Holding Companies and the 1970 Bank Holding Company Act Amendment. *J. Banking Finance*, March 1984, *8*(1), pp. 21–33.
[G: U.S.]

Biscaini, Anna M.; Carosio, Giovanni and Padoa Schioppa, Tommaso. Borrowing and Lending Rates in an Oligopolistic Banking System. In *Banca d'Italia*, 1984, pp. 63–81. [G: Italy]

Bitros, George C. The Fungibility Factor in Credit: Reply [The Fungibility Factor in Credit and the Question of the Efficacy of Selective Controls]. *Oxford Econ. Pap.*, November 1984, *36*(3), pp. 494–98. [G: Greece]

Bogdanowicz-Bindert, Christine A. and Sacks, Paul M. The Role of Information: Closing the Barn Door? In *Feinberg, R. E. and Kallab, V., eds., no. 2*, 1984, pp. 69–78. [G: U.S.]

Booth, James R.; Smith, Richard L., II and Stolz, Richard W. Use of Interest Rate Futures by Financial Institutions. *J. Bank Res.*, Spring 1984, *15*(1), pp. 15–20. [G: U.S.]

Booth, James R. and Smith, Richard L., II. The Impact of the Community Reinvestment Act on Branching Activity of Financial Institutions.

J. Bank Res., Summer 1984, *15*(2), pp. 123–28. [G: U.S.]

Borio, C. E. V. A Test of the Mean-Variance Model of Bank Behaviour on Italian Data. *Greek Econ. Rev.*, April 1984, *6*(1), pp. 77–98. [G: Italy]

Boughton, James M. and Wicker, Elmus R. A Reply [The Behavior of the Currency–Deposit Ratio during the Great Depression]. *J. Money, Credit, Banking*, August 1984, *16*(3), pp. 366–67. [G: U.S.]

Bouvier, Jean. The French Banks, Inflation and the Economic Crisis, 1919–1939. *J. Europ. Econ. Hist.*, Special Issue 1984, *13*(2), pp. 29–80. [G: France]

Boyes, William J. and Furnish, Dale Beck. A Note on the Use of Incorporation as an Escape from Usury Ceilings. *J. Ind. Econ.*, March 1984, *32*(3), pp. 367–72. [G: U.S.]

Brainard, Lawrence J. More Lending to the Third World? A Banker's View. In *Feinberg, R. E. and Kallab, V., eds., no. 2*, 1984, pp. 31–44. [G: LDCs; U.S.]

Brauer, Greggory A. The Value Impacts of Capital Adequacy Regulation and Stochastic Deposits. *J. Finan. Res.*, Summer 1984, *7*(2), pp. 95–103.

Brodt, Abraham I. International Bank Asset and Liability Management. *J. Bank Res.*, Summer 1984, *15*(2), pp. 82–94. [G: U.S.]

Brovedani, Bruno. Cooperazione tra Fondo Monetario e banche internazionali. Strategia di ripiego o collaborazione permanente? (Cooperation between the IMF and International Banks: An Expedient or a Permanent Collaboration Strategy? With English summary.) *Bancaria*, December 1984, *40*(12), pp. 1228–32.

Brown, Stephen J. Benefits of Bank Diversification: The Evidence from Shareholder Returns: Discussion. *J. Finance*, July 1984, *39*(3), pp. 893–94. [G: U.S.]

Bruno, Pietro. Versamenti e compensazione nel conto corrente. Effetto solutorio delle rimesse e revocatoria fallimentare. (Payments into and Withdrawals from Currency Accounts: Release Effect and Revocation of Bankruptcy Proceedings. With English summary.) *Bancaria*, May–June 1984, *40*(5–6), pp. 530–38. [G: Italy]

Burke, Jim. Antitrust Laws, Justice Department Guidelines, and the Limits of Concentration in Local Banking Markets. *Fed. Res. Bull.*, June 1984, *70*(6), pp. 495–96. [G: U.S.]

Burke, Jim and Rhoades, Stephen A. Bank Holding Company Affiliation and Contracyclical Lending by Mortgage Bankers. *J. Econ. Bus.*, May 1984, *36*(2), pp. 275–81. [G: U.S.]

Calderón-Rossell, Jorge R. Optimal Financial Structure of Finance Companies in a Regulated Environment of a Developing Country. *J. Banking Finance*, September 1984, *8*(3), pp. 443–57. [G: LDCs]

Campbell, Tim S. and Glenn, David. Deposit Insurance in a Deregulated Environment. *J. Finance*, July 1984, *39*(3), pp. 775–85.
[G: U.S.]

Campbell, Tim S. and Horvitz, Paul M. Reform

of the Deposit Insurance System: An Appraisal of the FHLBB and FDIC Studies. *Contemp. Policy Issue*, May 1984, (6), pp. 56–68.
[G: U.S.]

Carli, Guido and Savona, Paolo. Il commercio mondiale e la finanza internazionale. Annotazioni per la pianificazione strategica delle banche di credito internazionale. (World Trade and International Finance: Considerations for Strategic Planning by International Banks. With English summary.) *Bancaria*, December 1984, *40*(12), pp. 1233–40. [G: Global]

Carosio, Giovanni. Customer Discrimination and Selective Controls in the Bank Loan Market. In *Banca d'Italia*, 1984, pp. 165–89.
[G: Italy]

Carron, Andrew S. The Australian Financial System. In *Caves, R. E. and Krause, L. B., eds.*, 1984, pp. 195–229. [G: Australia]

Cassese, Sabino. The Long Life of the Financial Institutions Set Up in the Thirties. *J. Europ. Econ. Hist.*, Special Issue 1984, *13*(2), pp. 273–94. [G: OECD]

Cesarini, Francesco. What Scope for Banking Services. *Rev. Econ. Cond. Italy*, June 1984, (2), pp. 227–39. [G: Italy]

Child, John, et al. Microelectronics and the Quality of Employment in Services. In *Marstrand, P., ed.*, 1984, pp. 163–90. [G: U.K.]

Chitariance, Sedrak and Reisman, Arnold. A Strategic Planning Model for Bank Retail Outlet Development. In *Naylor, T. H. and Thomas, C., eds.*, 1984, pp. 91–110.

Choi, Sang-Rim and Tschoegl, Adrian E. Bank Employment in the World's Largest Banks: An Update: A Note. *J. Money, Credit, Banking*, August 1984, *16*(3), pp. 359–62.

Chrystal, K. Alec. International Banking Facilities. *Fed. Res. Bank St. Louis Rev.*, April 1984, *66*(4), pp. 5–11. [G: U.S.]

Ciampi, Carlo Azeglio. Concentrazione bancaria, informazione bancaria e garanzia dei depositi. (Concentration of Banking, Information, and Deposits Guarantee. With English summary.) *Bancaria*, April 1984, *40*(4), pp. 361–64.
[G: Italy]

Cingano, Francesco. Lineamenti per un profilo del nostro sistema bancario. (An Outline of the Italian Banking-System. With English summary.) *Bancaria*, September 1984, *40*(9), pp. 845–55. [G: Italy]

Ciocca, Pierluigi. Economic Analysis and Banking Supervision. In *Banca d'Italia*, 1984, pp. 263–76.

Ciocca, Pierluigi; Giannoni, Anna M. and Nanni, Carla. An Analysis of Customer "Mobility" in the Bank Credit Market (1979–1980). In *Banca d'Italia*, 1984, pp. 191–210. [G: Italy]

Ciocca, Pierluigi; Giussani, Cesare and Lanciotti, Giulio. The Determinants of Banking Costs. In *Banca d'Italia*, 1984, pp. 3–18. [G: Italy]

Ciocca, Pierluigi and Toniolo, Gianni. Industry and Finance in Italy, 1918–1940. *J. Europ. Econ. Hist.*, Special Issue 1984, *13*(2), pp. 113–36. [G: Italy]

Clark, George J. Foreign Banks in the Domestic Markets of Developing Countries. In *Feinberg, R. E. and Kallab, V., eds., no. 2*, 1984, pp. 79–86. [G: LDCs; U.S.]

Clark, Jeffrey A. Estimation of Economies of Scale in Banking Using a Generalized Functional Form. *J. Money, Credit, Banking*, February 1984, *16*(1), pp. 53–68. [G: U.S.]

Clarotti, Paolo. Progress and Future Development of Establishment and Services in the EC in Relation to Banking. *J. Common Market Stud.*, March 1984, *22*(3), pp. 199–226.
[G: EEC]

Coco, Giovanni Silvio. La riforma del diritto penale bancario. (The Reform of Banking Criminal Law. With English summary.) *Bancaria*, January 1984, *40*(1), pp. 38–49. [G: Italy]

Cohen, Kalman J. and Hammer, Frederick S. Linear Programming Models for Optimal Bank Dynamic Balance Sheet Management. In *Naylor, T. H. and Thomas, C., eds.*, 1984, pp. 25–44.

Conigliani, Claudio. Economies of Scale and Efficiency in the Italian Banking System. In *Banca d'Italia*, 1984, pp. 19–40. [G: Italy]

Conigliani, Claudio and Lanciotti, Giulio. Concentration, Competition and Entry Controls: An Analysis of Banking Markets. In *Banca d'Italia*, 1984, pp. 149–64. [G: Italy]

Conigliani, Claudio and Lanciotti, Giulio. Supply Structure and Rates of Interest in the Italian Banking Markets. In *Banca d'Italia*, 1984, pp. 83–108. [G: Italy]

Cooke, Peter. The Basle "Concordat" on the Supervision of Banks' Foreign Establishments. *Aussenwirtschaft*, May 1984, *39*(1/2), pp. 151–65. [G: OECD]

Courakis, Anthony S. Constraints on Bank Choices and Financial Repression in Less Developed Countries. *Oxford Bull. Econ. Statist.*, November 1984, *46*(4), pp. 341–70.
[G: LDCs]

Craven, B. M. and Thompson, R. S. Monopoly Welfare Losses in U.S. Banking: Comment. *J. Monet. Econ.*, July 1984, *14*(1), pp. 123–26. [G: U.S.]

Cullen, L. M. Landlords, Bankers and Merchants: The Early Irish Banking World, 1700–1820. In *Murphy, A. E., ed.*, 1984, pp. 25–44.
[G: Ireland]

Curry, Timothy J. and Rose, John T. Bank Holding Company Presence and Banking Market Performance. *J. Bank Res.*, Winter 1984, *14*(4), pp. 259–65. [G: U.S.]

Curry, Timothy J. and Rose, John T. Bank Structure and Mortgage Rates: A Comment. *J. Econ. Bus.*, May 1984, *36*(2), pp. 283–87.
[G: U.S.]

Curry, Timothy J. and Rose, John T. Diversification and Barriers to Entry: Some Evidence from Banking. *Antitrust Bull.*, Winter 1984, *29*(4), pp. 759–73. [G: U.S.]

Cuthbertson, Keith. Techniques of Monetary Control in the United Kingdom. *J. Econ. Stud.*, 1984, *11*(4), pp. 46–68. [G: U.K.]

Dahl, Frederick R. Statement to the U.S. House Subcommittee on International Economic Policy and Trade of the Committee on Foreign Affairs, June 20, 1984. *Fed. Res. Bull.*, July 1984, 70(7), pp. 575–77. [G: U.S.]

Danker, Deborah J. and McLaughlin, Mary M. Profitability of Insured Commercial Banks in 1983. *Fed. Res. Bull.*, November 1984, 70(11), pp. 802–18. [G: U.S.]

Davis, Kevin. Financial Regulation in Australia. *Australian Econ. Rev.*, 3rd Quarter 1984, (67), pp. 135–46. [G: Australia]

De Vany, Arthur S. Modeling the Banking Firm: A Survey: Comment. *J. Money, Credit, Banking*, Part 2 November 1984, 16(4), pp. 603–09.

Delatour, Leslie. LDC's Debt and the Private Banks. In *Salazar-Carillo, J. and Tirado de Alonso, I., eds., no. 1*, 1984, pp. 1–43. [G: LDCs]

Desenzani, Leonardo and Di Vito, Claus. Riflessioni di marketing per lo sportello bancario. (Over the Counter Marketing Services in Banks. With English summary.) *L'Impresa*, 1984, 26(1), pp. 47–53.

Dewald, William G. Eighth Annual Economic Policy Conference: Introduction. *J. Money, Credit, Banking*, Part 2 November 1984, 16(4), pp. 571–75.

Di Stefano, Guido. Il capitale umano nelle banche: una risorsa sottoutilizzata. (Human Capital in Banks: An Underutilised Resource. With English summary.) *L'Impresa*, 1984, 26(4), pp. 31–40. [G: Italy]

Diamond, Douglas W. Financial Intermediation and Delegated Monitoring. *Rev. Econ. Stud.*, July 1984, 51(3), pp. 393–414.

Diltz, J. David. Commercial Bank Profitability and the New Federal Reserve Operating Procedures: An Empirical Study. *Bus. Econ.*, July 1984, 19(4), pp. 57–62. [G: U.S.]

Dini, Lamberto. Capitale di rischio per le imprese: il ruolo del "merchant banking." (Risk Capital for Businesses: The Role of Merchant Banking. With English summary.) *Bancaria*, May–June 1984, 40(5–6), pp. 487–91. [G: Italy]

Dominguez, Luis V. and Page, Albert L. Formulating a Strategic Portfolio of Profitable Retail Market Segments for Commercial Banks. *J. Econ. Bus.*, May 1984, 36(2), pp. 189–206. [G: U.S.]

Dorrance, G. Morris, Jr. Savings and Investment: Comment. In *Wachter, M. L. and Wachter, S. M., eds.*, 1984, pp. 251–54. [G: U.S.]

Dufey, Gunter and Giddy, Ian H. Eurocurrency Deposit Risk. *J. Banking Finance*, December 1984, 8(4), pp. 567–89. [G: OECD]

Dunham, Constance and Syron, Richard F. Interstate Banking: The Drive to Consolidate. *New Eng. Econ. Rev.*, May–June 1984, pp. 11–28. [G: U.S.]

Dunkelberg, William C.; Scott, Jonathan A. and Cox, Edwin L. Small Business and the Value of Bank–Customer Relationships. *J. Bank Res.*, Winter 1984, 14(4), pp. 248–58. [G: U.S.]

Dutkowsky, Donald H. The Demand for Borrowed Reserves: A Switching Regression Model. *J. Finance*, June 1984, 39(2), pp. 407–24. [G: U.S.]

Eisemann, Peter C. and Timme, Stephen G. Intraweek Seasonality in the Federal Funds Market. *J. Finan. Res.*, Spring 1984, 7(1), pp. 47–56. [G: U.S.]

Eisenbeis, Robert A. Consequences of Deregulation for Commercial Banking: Discussion. *J. Finance*, July 1984, 39(3), pp. 803–05.

Eisenbeis, Robert A. Impulsi di innovazione nei servizi finanziari. (Forces for Change in the Financial Service Industry. With English summary.) *Bancaria*, March 1984, 40(3), pp. 266–71. [G: U.S.]

Eisenbeis, Robert A.; Harris, Robert S. and Lakonishok, Josef. Benefits of Bank Diversification: The Evidence from Shareholder Returns. *J. Finance*, July 1984, 39(3), pp. 881–92. [G: U.S.]

Elyasiani, Elyas. The Multiproduct Deopository Firm, Interest-bearing Transaction Balances, Interest-bearing Reserves, and Uncertainty. *Bull. Econ. Res.*, November 1984, 36(2), pp. 173–93. [G: U.S.]

Epstein, Edythe. Negotiating over Technological Change in Banking and Insurance. *Int. Lab. Rev.*, July–August 1984, 123(4), pp. 405–22.

Feinberg, Richard E. Restoring Confidence in International Credit Markets. In *Feinberg, R. E. and Kallab, V., eds., no. 2*, 1984, pp. 3–20. [G: LDCs; U.S.]

Felgran, Steven D. Bank Entry into Securities Brokerage: Competitive and Legal Aspects. *New Eng. Econ. Rev.*, November–December 1984, pp. 12–33. [G: U.S.]

Felgran, Steven D. Shared ATM Networks: Market Structure and Public Policy. *New Eng. Econ. Rev.*, January–February 1984, pp. 23–38. [G: U.S.]

Flannery, Mark J. The Social Costs of Unit Banking Restrictions. *J. Monet. Econ.*, March 1984, 13(2), pp. 237–49. [G: U.S.]

Flannery, Mark J. and James, Christopher M. Market Evidence on the Effective Maturity of Bank Assets and Liabilities. *J. Money, Credit, Banking*, Part 1 November 1984, 16(4), pp. 435–45. [G: U.S.]

Flannery, Mark J. and James, Christopher M. The Effect of Interest Rate Changes on the Common Stock Returns of Financial Institutions. *J. Finance*, September 1984, 39(4), pp. 1141–53.

Flenda, Carlo. The Internationalization of Banking and Its Economic Advantages. *Rev. Econ. Cond. Italy*, Sept.–Dec. 1984, (3), pp. 365–87. [G: Italy]

Fontana, Francesco. Il capitale proprio e le particolarità di gestione delle banche di deposito con alcune osservazioni sui coefficienti di solvibilità. (Share Capital and Peculiarities of Management of a Deposit-Bank [With Some Observations on Solvency Ratios.] With English summary.) *Bancaria*, April 1984, 40(4), pp. 386–401. [G: Italy]

Forbes, Ronald W. and Leonard, Paul A. The

Effects of Statutory Portfolio Constraints on Tax-Exempt Interest Rates: A Note. *J. Money, Credit, Banking*, February 1984, *16*(1), pp. 92–99. **[G: U.S.]**

Fujita, Masahiro; Mizushima, Kazuya and Mikitani, Ryoichi. Internationalization of Japanese Commercial Banking—The Recent Experience of City Banks. *Kobe Econ. Bus. Rev.*, 1984, *30*, pp. 23–53. **[G: Japan]**

Furlong, Frederick T. A View on Deposit Insurance Coverage. *Fed. Res. Bank San Francisco Econ. Rev.*, Spring 1984, (2), pp. 31–38. **[G: U.S.]**

von Furstenberg, George M. Economic and Financial Stability: Comment. In *Wachter, M. L. and Wachter, S. M., eds.*, 1984, pp. 416–19. **[G: Global; U.S.]**

Gardner, Mona J. Minority Owned Banks: A Managerial and Performance Analysis. *J. Bank Res.*, Spring 1984, *15*(1), pp. 26–34. **[G: U.S.]**

Gilbert, R. Alton. Bank Market Structure and Competition: A Survey. *J. Money, Credit, Banking*, Part 2 November 1984, *16*(4), pp. 617–44. **[G: U.S.]**

Gilbert, R. Alton and Holland, A. Steven. Has the Deregulation of Deposit Interest Rates Raised Mortgage Rates? *Fed. Res. Bank St. Louis Rev.*, May 1984, *66*(5), pp. 5–15. **[G: U.S.]**

Gilligan, Thomas W. and Smirlock, Michael L. An Empirical Study of Joint Production and Scale Economies in Commercial Banking. *J. Banking Finance*, March 1984, *8*(1), pp. 67–77. **[G: U.S.]**

Gilligan, Thomas W.; Smirlock, Michael L. and Marshall, William J. Scale and Scope Economies in the Multi-Product Banking Firm. *J. Monet. Econ.*, May 1984, *13*(3), pp. 393–405. **[G: U.S.]**

Giroux, Gary A. and Rose, Peter S. An Update of Bank Planning Systems: Results of a Nationwide Survey of Large U.S. Banks. *J. Bank Res.*, Autumn 1984, *15*(3), pp. 136–47. **[G: U.S.]**

Goldberg, Michael A. The Sensivity of the Prime Rate to Money Market Conditions. *J. Finan. Res.*, Winter 1984, *7*(4), pp. 269–80. **[G: U.S.]**

Goldfeld, Stephen M. Modeling the Banking Firm: A Survey: Comment. *J. Money, Credit, Banking*, Part 2 November 1984, *16*(4), pp. 609–16. **[G: U.S.]**

Goodhart, Charles A. E. Structural Changes in the Banking System and the Determination of the Stock of Money. In *Masera, R. S. and Triffin, R., eds.*, 1984, pp. 111–49. **[G: OECD]**

Goodman, Laurie S. International Banking: A Survey: Comment. *J. Money, Credit, Banking*, Part 2 November 1984, *16*(4), pp. 678–84. **[G: U.S.]**

Goodman, Laurie S. and Shaffer, Sherrill. The Economics of Deposit Insurance: A Critical Evaluation of Proposed Reforms. *Yale J. Regul.*, 1984, *2*(1), pp. 145–62. **[G: U.S.]**

Graddy, Duane B.; Homaifar, Ghassem and Karna, Adi S. Double Leverage as a Source of Systematic Risk in Bank Holding Company Stocks. *J. Bank Res.*, Summer 1984, *15*(2), pp. 115–22. **[G: U.S.]**

Graddy, Duane B. and Karna, Adi S. Net Interest Margin Sensitivity among Banks of Different Sizes. *J. Bank Res.*, Winter 1984, *14*(4), pp. 283–90. **[G: U.S.]**

Gramley, Lyle E. Statement to the U.S. House Subcommittee on Commerce, Consumer, and Monetary Affairs of the Government Operations Committee, March 14, 1984. *Fed. Res. Bull.*, April 1984, *70*(4), pp. 291–94. **[G: U.S.]**

Guglielmi, Giuseppe. Banca: servizio pubblico o impresa? (Banking: A Public or Business Service? [With a Note by the Editor.] With English summary.) *Bancaria*, April 1984, *40*(4), pp. 377–85. **[G: Italy]**

Gurel, Eitan and Pyle, David H. Bank Income Taxes and Interest Rate Risk Management: A Note. *J. Finance*, September 1984, *39*(4), pp. 1199–206.

Gurwitz, Aaron S. and Rappaport, Julie N. Structural Change and Slower Employment Growth in the Financial Services Sector. *Fed. Res. Bank New York Quart. Rev.*, Winter 1984–85, *9*(4), pp. 39–45. **[G: U.S.]**

Guttentag, Jack M. and Herring, Richard J. Credit Rationing and Financial Disorder. *J. Finance*, December 1984, *39*(5), pp. 1359–82. **[G: U.S.]**

Guttentag, Jack M. and Herring, Richard J. La pianificazione strategica delle banche internazionali contro l'incertezza. (Strategic Planning by International Banks to Cope with Incertitude. With English summary.) *Bancaria*, December 1984, *40*(12), pp. 1183–96.

Guttentag, Jack M. and Herring, Richard J. International Banking: Vulnerability and Crisis. In *Wachter, M. L. and Wachter, S. M., eds.*, 1984, pp. 355–89. **[G: Global; U.S.]**

Hall, Robert E. Bank Regulation and the Effectiveness of Open Market Operations: Comment. *Brookings Pap. Econ. Act.*, 1984, (2), pp. 445–47. **[G: U.S.]**

Hall, Robert E. International Banking: Vulnerability and Crisis: Comment. In *Wachter, M. L. and Wachter, S. M., eds.*, 1984, pp. 424–27. **[G: Global; U.S.]**

Hamdani, Kauser. CRR and Excess Reserves: An Early Appraisal. *Fed. Res. Bank New York Quart. Rev.*, Autumn 1984, *9*(3), pp. 16–23. **[G: U.S.]**

Hannan, Timothy H. Competition between Commercial Banks and Thrift Institutions: An Empirical Examination. *J. Bank Res.*, Spring 1984, *15*(1), pp. 8–14. **[G: U.S.]**

Hannan, Timothy H. and McDowell, John M. Market Concentration and the Diffusion of New Technology in the Banking Industry. *Rev. Econ. Statist.*, November 1984, *66*(4), pp. 686–91. **[G: U.S.]**

Hannan, Timothy H. and McDowell, John M. The Determinants of Technology Adoption: The Case of the Banking Firm. *Rand J. Econ.*, Autumn 1984, *15*(3), pp. 328–35. **[G: U.S.]**

Hanweck, Gerald A. and Kilcollin, Thomas Eric.

Bank Profitability and Interest Rate Risk. *J. Econ. Bus.*, February 1984, *36*(1), pp. 77–84. **[G: U.S.]**

Hanweck, Gerald A. and Rhoades, Stephen A. Dominant Firms, "Deep Pockets," and Local Market Competition in Banking. *J. Econ. Bus.*, December 1984, *36*(4), pp. 391–402. **[G: U.S.]**

Hardach, Gerd. Banking and Industry in Germany in the Interwar Period, 1919–1939. *J. Europ. Econ. Hist.*, Special Issue 1984, *13*(2), pp. 203–34. **[G: Germany]**

Harper, Ian R. Financial Regulation in Australia: Comment. *Australian Econ. Rev.*, 3rd Quarter 1984, (67), pp. 151–52. **[G: Australia]**

Heggestad, Arnold A. Bank Market Structure and Competition: A Survey: Comment. *J. Money, Credit, Banking*, Part 2 November 1984, *16*(4), pp. 645–50.

Heller, H. Robert. Regulatory Aspects of the World Debt Problem: A Comment. *Cato J.*, Spring/Summer 1984, *4*(1), pp. 125–29. **[G: U.S.]**

Hiroyama, Kensuke. Human Factors and the Acquisition of Capital in a National Bank—A Case of the 13th National Bank in Osaka: 1888–1897. (In Japanese. With English summary.) *Osaka Econ. Pap.*, December 1984, *34*(2–3), pp. 362–93. **[G: Japan]**

Hogan, Warren P. and Sharpe, Ian G. Regulation, Risk and the Pricing of Australian Bank Shares, 1957–1976. *Econ. Rec.*, March 1984, *60*(168), pp. 34–44. **[G: Australia]**

Honda, Yuzo. The Japanese Banking Firms. *Econ. Stud. Quart.*, August 1984, *35*(2), pp. 159–80. **[G: Japan]**

Horvitz, Paul M. Deposit Insurance after Deregulation: A Residual Role for Regulation. In *Fed. Home Loan Bank San Francisco*, 1984, pp. 67–94. **[G: U.S.]**

Horvitz, Paul M. Deposit Insurance in a Deregulated Environment: Discussion. *J. Finance*, July 1984, *39*(3), pp. 785–87. **[G: U.S.]**

Horvitz, Paul M. Payments and Deregulation. In *Fed. Res. Bank Atlanta*, 1984, pp. 163–68. **[G: U.S.]**

Houghton, Keith A. Accounting Data and the Prediction of Business Failure: The Setting of Priors and the Age of Data. *J. Acc. Res.*, Spring 1984, *22*(1), pp. 361–68. **[G: Australia]**

Houghton, Keith A. and Sengupta, Ratna. The Effect of Prior Probability Disclosure and Information Set Construction on Bankers' Ability to Predict Failure. *J. Acc. Res.*, Autumn 1984, *22*(2), pp. 768–75. **[G: U.S.]**

Houthakker, Hendrik S. International Banking: A Survey: Comment. *J. Money, Credit, Banking*, Part 2 November 1984, *16*(4), pp. 684–90. **[G: OECD]**

Huertas, Thomas F. An Economic Brief against Glass–Steagall. *J. Bank Res.*, Autumn 1984, *15*(3), pp. 148–59. **[G: U.S.]**

Humphrey, David B. Future Networks and the Fed's Role. In *Fed. Res. Bank Atlanta*, 1984, pp. 67–79. **[G: U.S.]**

Hunter, William C. Insurance, Incentives, and Efficiency in Small Business Lending. *Southern Econ. J.*, April 1984, *50*(4), pp. 1171–84. **[G: U.S.]**

Isaac, William M. The Role of Deposit Insurance in the Emerging Financial Services Industry. *Yale J. Regul.*, 1984, *1*(2), pp. 195–215. **[G: U.S.]**

Jacobs, Rodney L. The Rate Maturity of Prime and Other Indexed Assets or Liabilities. *J. Bank Res.*, Summer 1984, *15*(2), pp. 108–14. **[G: U.S.]**

Jahera, John S., Jr. and Sinkey, Joseph F., Jr. A Note on the Intracyclical Balance-Sheet Behavior of Large Commercial Banks, 1972–1978. *J. Banking Finance*, March 1984, *8*(1), pp. 109–17. **[G: U.S.]**

James, Christopher M. An Analysis of the Effect of State Acquisition Laws on Managerial Efficiency: The Case of the Bank Holding Company Acquisitions. *J. Law Econ.*, April 1984, *27*(1), pp. 211–26. **[G: U.S.]**

James, Harold. The Causes of the German Banking Crisis of 1931. *Econ. Hist. Rev., 2nd Ser.*, February 1984, *37*(1), pp. 68–87. **[G: Germany]**

Jehle, Geoffrey A. Individual Welfare and the Demand for Financial Instruments. *Southern Econ. J.*, July 1984, *51*(1), pp. 116–34. **[G: U.S.]**

Johnson, Douglas A. and Pany, Kurt. Forecasts, Auditor Review, and Bank Loan Decisions. *J. Acc. Res.*, Autumn 1984, *22*(2), pp. 731–43. **[G: U.S.]**

Kareken, John H. Bank Regulation and the Effectiveness of Open Market Operations. *Brookings Pap. Econ. Act.*, 1984, (2), pp. 405–44. **[G: U.S.]**

Karna, Adi S. and Graddy, Duane B. Double Leverage and the Cost of Bank Holding Company Capital. *Quart. J. Bus. Econ.*, Spring 1984, *23*(2), pp. 72–84. **[G: U.S.]**

Kaufman, George G. The Academic Preparation of Economists Employed by Commercial and Investment Banks: A Note. *J. Money, Credit, Banking*, August 1984, *16*(3), pp. 351–59.

Kaufman, George G.; Mote, Larry R. and Rosenblum, Harvey. Consequences of Deregulation for Commercial Banking. *J. Finance*, July 1984, *39*(3), pp. 789–803. **[G: U.S.]**

Kaufman, Henry. Financial Institutions and the Fragile, Volatile Financial Markets. In *Sametz, A. W., ed.*, 1984, pp. 21–27.

Key, Sydney J. International Banking Facilities as a Free Economic Zone. *Aussenwirtschaft*, May 1984, *39*(1/2), pp. 57–74. **[G: U.S.]**

Khan, M. Fahim. Profitability of Islamic Banks Competing with Interest Banks: Comment. *J. Res. Islamic Econ.*, Winter 1984, *1*(2), pp. 73–78.

Khan, Shahrukh Rafi. An Economic Analysis of a PLS Model for the Financial Sector. *Pakistan J. Appl. Econ.*, Winter 1984, *3*(2), pp. 89–105.

Kindleberger, Charles P. Banking and Industry between the Two Wars: An International Comparison. *J. Europ. Econ. Hist.*, Special Issue 1984, *13*(2), pp. 7–28. **[G: U.S.; Europe]**

Kindleberger, Charles P. International Banks and International Business in Historical Perspective. In *Kindleberger, C. P.*, 1984, *1983*, pp. 155–70. **[G: U.S.; Latin America]**

King, Thomas. Thrift Institution Deposits: The Influence of MMCs and MMMFs: A Note. *J. Money, Credit, Banking*, August 1984, *16*(3), pp. 328–34. **[G: U.S.]**

Kolb, Robert W.; Timme, Stephen G. and Gay, Gerald D. Macro versus Micro Futures Hedges at Commercial Banks. *J. Futures Markets*, Spring 1984, *4*(1), pp. 47–54. **[G: U.S.]**

Kopecky, Kenneth J. Monetary Control under Reverse Lag and Contemporaneous Reserve Accounting: A Comparison [Reserve Requirements: Are They Lagged in the Wrong Direction?]. *J. Money, Credit, Banking*, February 1984, *16*(1), pp. 81–88. **[G: U.S.]**

Koppenhaver, G. D. Selectivity Hedging of Bank Assets with Treasury Bill Futures Contracts. *J. Finan. Res.*, Summer 1984, *7*(2), pp. 105–19. **[G: U.S.]**

Krümmel, Hans J. Schutzzweck und Aufsichtseingriffe. Über den Run auf die Bankschalter und seine Verhinderung. (Protective Purpose and Intervention by Supervisory Agencies—On the Run on Bank Counters and Its Prevention. With English summary.) *Kredit Kapital*, 1984, *17*(4), pp. 474–89. **[G: W. Germany]**

Kutasovic, Paul; Lackman, Conway L. and Tepperberg, Alfred. A Non-monetarist Test of the Credit Availability Theory. *Rivista Int. Sci. Econ. Com.*, October–November 1984, *31*(10–11), pp. 1033–51. **[G: U.S.]**

Ladenson, Mark L. and Bombara, Kenneth J. Entry in Commercial Banking: 1962–78. *J. Money, Credit, Banking*, May 1984, *16*(2), pp. 165–74. **[G: U.S.]**

Lamberte, Mario B. Production Technology of Philippine Commercial Banks. *Philippine Rev. Econ. Bus.*, Sept./Dec. 1984, *21*(3/4), pp. 123–43. **[G: Philippines]**

Lanciotti, Giulio. Objectives and Instruments of Structural Supervision: Guidelines and Optimum Rules for Authorising Branch Openings. In *Banca d'Italia*, 1984, pp. 249–61. **[G: Italy]**

Laurent, Robert D. A Reply [Reserve Requirements: Are They Lagged in the Wrong Direction?]. *J. Money, Credit, Banking*, February 1984, *16*(1), pp. 89–92. **[G: U.S.]**

Leaf, Ronald. Competitive Implicit Interest Payments in Commercial Banking. *Amer. Econ.*, Spring 1984, *28*(1), pp. 49–56. **[G: U.S.]**

Lee, Sheng-Yi. Financial Institutions and Markets in Singapore. In *Skully, M. T., ed.*, 1984, pp. 226–95. **[G: Singapore]**

Lee, Sheng-Yi. Issues in Banking and Finance in Singapore. In *Thambipillai, P., ed.*, 1984, pp. 294–307. **[G: Singapore]**

Leite, Sergio Pereira and Vaez-Zadeh, Reza. The Fungibility Factor in Credit: A Comment [The Fungibility Factor in Credit and the Question of the Efficacy of Selective Controls]. *Oxford Econ. Pap.*, November 1984, *36*(3), pp. 490–93. **[G: Greece]**

Leveson, Irving. Restructuring Financial Institutions in the New Financial Environment: Discussion. In *Sametz, A. W., ed.*, 1984, pp. 33–37. **[G: U.S.]**

Lindley, James T.; Selby, Edward B., Jr. and Jackson, John D. Racial Discrimination in the Provision of Financial Services. *Amer. Econ. Rev.*, September 1984, *74*(4), pp. 735–41. **[G: U.S.]**

Lipstein, Benjamin. Marketing Financial Services. In *Sametz, A. W., ed.*, 1984, pp. 49–54. **[G: U.S.]**

Lissakers, Karin. Bank Regulation and International Debt. In *Feinberg, R. E. and Kallab, V., eds., no. 2*, 1984, pp. 45–68. **[G: LDCs; U.S.; W. Europe]**

Llewellyn, David T. Modelling International Banking Flows: An Analytical Framework. In *Black, J. and Dorrance, G. S., eds.*, 1984, pp. 35–76. **[G: OECD]**

Lobue, Marie. Categorical Bank Acquisitions. *J. Bank Res.*, Winter 1984, *14*(4), pp. 274–82. **[G: U.S.]**

Lovett, William A. The Revolution in U.S. Banking. *Challenge*, November/December 1984, *27*(5), pp. 41–46. **[G: U.S.]**

Maccarone, Salvatore. I transferimenti elettronici di fondi nel diritto italiano. (Electronic Transfers of Funds in the Italian Law. With English summary.) *Bancaria*, November 1984, *40*(11), pp. 1090–101. **[G: Italy]**

Mahajan, Arvind and Mehta, Dileep. Strong Form Efficiency of the Foreign Exchange Market and Bank Positions. *J. Finan. Res.*, Fall 1984, *7*(3), pp. 197–207. **[G: U.S.]**

Marais, M. Laurentius; Patell, James M. and Wolfson, Mark A. The Experimental Design of Classification Models: An Application of Recursive Partitioning and Bootstrapping to Commercial Bank Loan Classifications. *J. Acc. Res.*, Supplement 1984, *22*, pp. 87–114. **[G: U.S.]**

Marcus, Alan J. Deregulation and Bank Financial Policy. *J. Banking Finance*, December 1984, *8*(4), pp. 557–65.

Marcus, Alan J. and Shaked, Israel. The Relationship between Accounting Measures and Prospective Probabilities of Insolvency: An Application to the Banking Industry. *Financial Rev.*, March 1984, *19*(1), pp. 67–83. **[G: U.S.]**

Marcus, Alan J. and Shaked, Israel. The Valuation of FDIC Deposit Insurance Using Option-pricing Estimates. *J. Money, Credit, Banking*, Part 1 November 1984, *16*(4), pp. 446–60. **[G: U.S.]**

Marlow, Michael L. Bank Structure and Mortgage Rates: Reply. *J. Econ. Bus.*, May 1984, *36*(2), pp. 289–90.

Marreiros, Luis. Contribution to the Comparative Study of Savings Trends in Latin America: 1973–1983. In *Kessler, D. and Ullmo, P.-A., eds.*, 1984, pp. 281–309. **[G: Latin America]**

Martan, Said S., et al. Islamic vis-à-vis Traditional Banking: A "Fuzzy-Set" Approach. *J. Res. Islamic Econ.*, Summer 1984, *2*(1), pp. 31–48.

Martin, Preston. Statement to the U.S. House Subcommittee on Financial Institutions Supervision, Regulation and Insurance of the Committee on Banking, Finance and Urban Affairs, April 4, 1984. *Fed. Res. Bull.*, April 1984, 70(4), pp. 319–24.   [G: U.S.]

Marzano, A. Conditions in the Italian Economy and Banking Margins. *Rev. Econ. Cond. Italy*, June 1984, (2), pp. 149–67.   [G: Italy]

Maynard, Geoffrey W. The Role of Financial Institutions. In *Black, J. and Dorrance, G. S., eds.*, 1984, pp. 21–34.   [G: LDCs; MDCs]

McCarthy, F. Ward, Jr. A Review of Bank Performance in the Fifth District, 1983. *Fed. Res. Bank Richmond Econ. Rev.*, July/Aug. 1984, 70(4), pp. 21–29.   [G: U.S.]

McCarthy, F. Ward, Jr. The Evolution of the Bank Regulatory Structure: A Reappraisal. *Fed. Res. Bank Richmond Econ. Rev.*, Mar./Apr. 1984, 70(2), pp. 3–21.   [G: U.S.]

McLeod, Ross. Financial Institutions and Markets in Indonesia. In *Skully, M. T., ed.*, 1984, pp. 49–109.   [G: Indonesia]

Meckler, John M. Bank Cash Management Services. In *Fed. Res. Bank Atlanta*, 1984, pp. 27–33.   [G: U.S.]

Meigs, A. James. Regulatory Aspects of the World Debt Problem. *Cato J.*, Spring/Summer 1984, 4(1), pp. 105–24.   [G: U.S.]

Merrill, Peter. Winners and Losers in the Network Race. In *Fed. Res. Bank Atlanta*, 1984, pp. 93–99.   [G: U.S.]

Minsky, Hyman P. Banking and Industry between the Two Wars: The United States. *J. Europ. Econ. Hist.*, Special Issue 1984, 13(2), pp. 235–72.   [G: U.S.]

Morgan, George Emir, III. On the Adequacy of Bank Capital Regulation. *J. Finan. Quant. Anal.*, June 1984, 19(2), pp. 141–62.

Murphy, Antoin E. Richard Cantillon—an Irish Banker in Paris. In *Murphy, A. E., ed.*, 1984, pp. 45–74.   [G: France]

Murphy, Neil B. and Rogers, Ronald C. The Line of Commerce in Retail Financial Institution Mergers: Some Evidence from Consumer Data in New England. *J. Bank Res.*, Spring 1984, 15(1), pp. 21–25.   [G: U.S.]

Murray, John D. International Banking: A Survey: Comment. *J. Money, Credit, Banking*, Part 2 November 1984, 16(4), pp. 690–95.

Nesi, Nerio. Competitività, innovazione ed efficienza nel sistema finanziario italiano. (Competitiveness, Innovation and Efficiency in the Italian Financial System. With English summary.) *L'Impresa*, 1984, 26(2), pp. 13–18.   [G: Italy]

Neubig, Thomas S. The Taxation of Financial Institutions after Deregulation. *Nat. Tax J.*, September 1984, 37(3), pp. 351–59.   [G: U.S.]

Nötel, Rudolf. Money, Banking and Industry in Interwar Austria and Hungary. *J. Europ. Econ. Hist.*, Special Issue 1984, 13(2), pp. 137–202.   [G: Austria; Hungary]

Nothaft, Frank E. ARM Debt Outstanding by Lender Type and Firm Size. *Housing Finance Rev.*, October 1984, 3(4), pp. 447–55.
                                      [G: U.S.]

O'Driscoll, Gerald P., Jr. and Short, Eugenie

D. Safety-Net Mechanisms: The Case of International Lending. *Cato J.*, Spring/Summer 1984, 4(1), pp. 185–204.   [G: U.S.]

Olsen, Chris. The Experimental Design of Classification Models: An Application of Recursive Partitioning and Bootstrapping to Commercial Bank Loan Classifications: Discussion. *J. Acc. Res.*, Supplement 1984, 22, pp. 115–18.
                                      [G: U.S.]

Oteri, Carmelo. The Reform of Bank Shareholdings: Assumptions, Objectives, Implementation and Future Prospects. In *Banca d'Italia*, 1984, pp. 213–27.   [G: Italy]

Parravicini, Giannino. Considerazioni conclusive. (Strategic Planning in International Banking: Concluding Remarks. With English summary.) *Bancaria*, December 1984, 40(12), pp. 1245–47.

Parravicini, Giannino. La banca fra efficienza e innovazione. (Banks between Efficiency and Innovation. With English summary.) *Bancaria*, April 1984, 40(4), pp. 353–60.   [G: Italy]

Parravicini, Giannino. Pianificazione strategica dell'attività di credito internazionale. (Strategic Planning in International Banking. With English summary.) *Bancaria*, December 1984, 40(12), pp. 1179–82.   [G: OECD]

Parravicini, Giannino. Risparmiare per investire. (Savings for Investment. With English summary.) *Bancaria*, May–June 1984, 40(5–6), pp. 469–72.   [G: Italy]

Partee, J. Charles. Statement to the Commerce, Consumer, and Monetary Affairs Subcommittee of the U.S. House Committee on Government Operations, May 3, 1984. *Fed. Res. Bull.*, May 1984, 70(5), pp. 423–26.   [G: U.S.]

Pascual, Alfredo E. Financial Institutions and Markets in the Philippines. In *Skully, M. T., ed.*, 1984, pp. 167–225.   [G: Philippines]

Passacantando, Franco. Costs and Margins in the Italian Banking System: A Comparative Analysis. In *Banca d'Italia*, 1984, pp. 41–59.
                                    [G: OECD]

Peltzman, Sam. Bank Market Structure and Competition: A Survey: Comment. *J. Money, Credit, Banking*, Part 2 November 1984, 16(4), pp. 650–56.   [G: U.S.]

Pepe, Federico. Il sistema contabile delle aziende di credito: analisi e prospettive. (Commercial Banks' Accounting Systems: Analysis and Perspectives. With English summary.) *Bancaria*, November 1984, 40(11), pp. 1082–89.
                                      [G: Italy]

Perkins, Edwin J. Langdon Cheves and the Panic of 1819: A Reassessment. *J. Econ. Hist.*, June 1984, 44(2), pp. 455–61.   [G: U.S.]

Placone, Dennis. The Measurement of Commercial Bank Structure. *Atlantic Econ. J.*, September 1984, 12(3), pp. 81.   [G: U.S.]

Pyle, David H. Deregulation and Deposit Insurance Reform. *Fed. Res. Bank San Francisco Econ. Rev.*, Spring 1984, (2), pp. 5–15.
                                      [G: U.S.]

Pyle, David H. Errata [Deregulation and Deposit

Insurance Reform]. *Fed. Res. Bank San Francisco Econ. Rev.*, Summer 1984, (3), pp. 75. [G: U.S.]

Raganelli, Tullio. Banking Groups in the Italian Banking System: A Discriminant Analysis. In *Banca d'Italia*, 1984, pp. 129–46. [G: Italy]

Randle, William M. Banks. In *Fed. Res. Bank Atlanta*, 1984, pp. 61–66. [G: U.S.]

Reedtz, Paolo Marullo. Market Share of the Banks: Some Explanatory Hypotheses. In *Banca d'Italia*, 1984, pp. 109–28. [G: Italy]

Reese, Richard M. and Stanton, Wilbur W. Further Segmenting a Minority Bank's Customer Set. *J. Bank Res.*, Winter 1984, *14*(4), pp. 297–301. [G: U.S.]

Reichert, Alan K., et al. The Impact of Economic Conditions and Electronic Payments Technology on Federal Reserve Check Volume. *J. Bank Res.*, Winter 1984, *14*(4), pp. 291–96. [G: U.S.]

Rhoades, Stephen A. and White, Alice P. Output in Relation to Labor Input in the Banking and Savings and Loan Industries, 1927–1979. *J. Banking Finance*, March 1984, *8*(1), pp. 119–30. [G: U.S.]

Rogowski, Robert J. Pricing the Money Market Deposit and Super-NOW Accounts in 1983. *J. Bank Res.*, Summer 1984, *15*(2), pp. 72–81. [G: U.S.]

Rolnick, Arthur J. and Weber, Warren E. The Causes of Free Bank Failures: A Detailed Examination. *J. Monet. Econ.*, November 1984, *14*(3), pp. 267–91. [G: U.S.]

del Rosario, Ramon R., Jr. Crisis Management in Financial Institutions. *Philippine Econ. J.*, Winter 1984, *23*(1), pp. 72–78. [G: Philippines]

Rose, John T. and Savage, Donald T. De Novo Entry and Performance: Bank Holding Companies versus Independent Banks. *J. Bank Res.*, Summer 1984, *15*(2), pp. 95–107. [G: U.S.]

Rose, John T. and Talley, Samuel H. Financial Transactions within Bank Holding Companies. *J. Finan. Res.*, Fall 1984, *7*(3), pp. 209–17. [G: U.S.]

Rose, Peter S. and Scott, William L. Heterogeneity in Performance within the Bank Holding Company Sector: Evidence and Implications. *J. Econ. Bus.*, February 1984, *36*(1), pp. 1–14. [G: U.S.]

Rossetti, Alberto. Disintermediazione bancaria e mercato monetario: i certificati di deposito nell'esperienza statunitense. (Banking Disintermediation and the Money Market: Certificates of Deposit in the United States Experience. With English summary.) *Bancaria*, November 1984, *40*(11), pp. 1102–17. [G: Italy; U.S.]

Royama, Shoichi. An Anatomy of Financial Liberalization. (In Japanese. With English summary.) *Osaka Econ. Pap.*, December 1984, *34*(2–3), pp. 147–54. [G: Japan]

Ryan, John E. Statement to the U.S. House Subcommittee on General Oversight and Renegotiation of the Committee on Banking, Finance

and Urban Affairs, June 20, 1984. *Fed. Res. Bull.*, July 1984, *70*(7), pp. 573–75. [G: U.S.]

Rybczynski, Tad M. The U.K. Financial System in Transition. *Nat. Westminster Bank Quart. Rev.*, November 1984, pp. 26–42. [G: U.K.]

Saitoa, Massimo. La banca nell'impresa: il corporate banking. (Corporate Banking. With English summary.) *L'Impresa*, 1984, *26*(5), pp. 57–61.

Saldaña, Cesar G. The Philippine Commercial Banking System: Structure, Performance and the Impact of the Capital Buildup Program of 1972. *Philippine Rev. Econ. Bus.*, Sept./Dec. 1984, *21*(3/4), pp. 145–64. [G: Philippines]

Sandhu, H. S. Impact of Bank Nationalisation on Commercial Bank Deposits in India—A Quantitative Analysis. *Margin*, July 1984, *16*(4), pp. 84–102. [G: India]

Santarelli, Enrico. L'influsso dell'analisi schumpeteriana della funzione imprenditoriale e del credito nel pensiero economico italiano tra le due guerre. (The Influence of Schumepeterian Analysis of the Entrepreneurial Function and of the Banking Function on Italian Economic Thought in the Period between the Two Wars. With English summary.) *Giorn. Econ.*, July–August 1984, *43*(7–8), pp. 507–29. [G: Italy]

Santomero, Anthony M. Modeling the Banking Firm: A Survey. *J. Money, Credit, Banking*, Part 2 November 1984, *16*(4), pp. 576–602.

Santoni, G. J. Interest Rate Risk and the Stock Prices of Financial Institutions. *Fed. Res. Bank St. Louis Rev.*, August/September 1984, *66*(7), pp. 12–20. [G: U.S.]

Savona, Paolo. Banca e borsa. Aspetti internazionali. (Banks and Stock Market: International Impact. With English summary.) *Bancaria*, November 1984, *40*(11), pp. 1076–81. [G: U.S.; Italy]

Schmidt, Peter J. Bank Market Structure and Competition: A Survey: Comment. *J. Money, Credit, Banking*, Part 2 November 1984, *16*(4), pp. 656–60.

Schreiner, Jean-Paul. Le capital financier et le réseau des liaisons personnelles entre les principales sociétés en Suisse. (With English summary.) *Rev. Econ. Ind.*, 3rd Trimester 1984, (29), pp. 78–95.

Schuster, Leo. Profitability and Market Share of Banks. *J. Bank Res.*, Spring 1984, *15*(1), pp. 56–61. [G: U.S.; U.K.; Germany; Switzerland]

Schwartz, Anna J. International Lending and the Economic Environment [Safety-Net Mechanisms: The Case of International Lending]. *Cato J.*, Spring/Summer 1984, *4*(1), pp. 205–09. [G: U.S.]

Scott, Jonathan A. and Dunkelberg, William C. Rural versus Urban Bank Performance: An Analysis of Market Competition for Small Business Loans. *J. Bank Res.*, Autumn 1984, *15*(3), pp. 167–78. [G: U.S.]

Scott, Kenneth E. The Future of Bank Regulation. In *Moore, J. H., ed.*, 1984, pp. 259–73. [G: U.S.]

Scott, Robert Haney and Johnson, Dudley W. Rent-Seeking in U.S. Banking and the Optimal Quantity of Money. *Hong Kong Econ. Pap.*, 1984, (15), pp. 67–78. [G: U.S.]

Scott, Walter Giorgio. L'evoluzione delle aziende di credito: un'analisi bibliografica. (The Development of Credit Organisations: A Bibliographic Analysis. With English summary.) *L'Impresa*, 1984, *26*(2), pp. 19–30. [G: Italy]

Shaffer, Sherrill. Cross-Subsidization in Checking Accounts: A Note. *J. Money, Credit, Banking*, February 1984, *16*(1), pp. 100–109. [G: U.S.]

Shaffer, Sherrill. Scale Economies in Multiproduct Firms. *Bull. Econ. Res.*, May 1984, *36*(1), pp. 51–58. [G: U.S.]

Sherman, H. David. Improving the Productivity of Service Businesses. *Sloan Manage. Rev.*, Spring 1984, *25*(3), pp. 11–23.

Skully, Michael T. Financial Institutions and Markets in Thailand. In *Skully, M. T., ed.*, 1984, pp. 296–378. [G: Thailand]

Skully, Michael T. Financial Institutions and Markets in Brunei. In *Skully, M. T., ed.*, 1984, pp. 1–48. [G: Brunei]

Slovin, Myron B. and Sushka, Marie Elizabeth. A Note on the Evidence on Alternative Models of the Banking Firm: A Cross Section Study of Commercial Loan Rates. *J. Banking Finance*, March 1984, *8*(1), pp. 99–108. [G: U.S.]

Smirlock, Michael L. An Analysis of Bank Risk and Deposit Rate Ceiling: Evidence from the Capital Markets. *J. Monet. Econ.*, March 1984, *13*(2), pp. 195–210. [G: U.S.]

Smith, Bruce D. Private Information, Deposit Interest Rates, and the 'Stability' of the Banking System. *J. Monet. Econ.*, November 1984, *14*(3), pp. 293–317.

Solomon, Anthony M. Banking Deregulation—Where Do We Go from Here? *Fed. Res. Bank New York Quart. Rev.*, Autumn 1984, *9*(3), pp. 1–5. [G: U.S.]

Spedale, Domenico. Misure di redditività delle filiali bancarie. (Measurement of the Profitability of Bank Branches. With English summary.) *Bancaria*, November 1984, *40*(11), pp. 1118–23. [G: Italy]

Spencer, Peter D. Precautionary and Speculative Aspects of the Behaviour of Banks in the United Kingdom under Competition and Credit Control, 1972–1980. *Econ. J.*, September 1984, *94*(375), pp. 554–68. [G: U.K.]

Spiller, Pablo T. and Favaro, Edgardo. The Effects of Entry Regulation on Oligopolistic Interaction: The Uruguayan Banking Sector. *Rand J. Econ.*, Summer 1984, *15*(2), pp. 244–54. [G: Uruguay]

Spindt, Paul A. and Tarhan, Vefa. Bank Reserve Adjustment Process and the Use of Reserve Carryover as a Reserve Management Tool: A Microeconometric Approach. *J. Banking Finance*, March 1984, *8*(1), pp. 5–20. [G: U.S.]

Stutzer, Michael J. Probable Future Competition in Banking Antitrust Determination: Research

Findings. *Fed. Res. Bank Minn. Rev.*, Summer 1984, *8*(3), pp. 9–20. [G: U.S.]

Sullivan, A. Charlene. Competition in the Market for Consumer Loans. *J. Econ. Bus.*, February 1984, *36*(1), pp. 141–49. [G: U.S.]

Sun, I-Shuan. Prospects of the Taipei Offshore Banking Center. *Bull. Int. Fiscal Doc.*, 1984, *38*(6), pp. 259–60. [G: Taiwan]

Sushka, Marie Elizabeth and Barrett, W. Brian. Banking Structure and the National Capital Market, 1869–1914. *J. Econ. Hist.*, June 1984, *44*(2), pp. 463–77. [G: U.S.]

Sweeney, Dennis J. A Practical Evaluation of the Potential of Mixed Integer Programming as a Strategic Planning Tool. In *Naylor, T. H. and Thomas, C., eds.*, 1984, pp. 111–20.

Syron, Richard F. The "New England Experiment" in Interstate Banking. *New Eng. Econ. Rev.*, March–April 1984, pp. 5–17. [G: U.S.]

Taffler, Richard J. and Abassi, B. Country Risk: A Model for Predicting Debt Servicing Problems in Developing Countries. *J. Roy. Statist. Soc.*, 1984, *147*(4), pp. 541–61. [G: LDCs]

Taylor, David Van L., Jr. Debit Cards. In *Fed. Res. Bank Atlanta*, 1984, pp. 11–16. [G: U.S.]

Teeters, Nancy H. Statement to the U.S. House Subcommittee on Consumer Affairs and Coinage of the Committee on Banking, Finance and Urban Affairs, March 27, 1984. *Fed. Res. Bull.*, April 1984, *70*(4), pp. 309–12. [G: U.S.]

Terrell, Henry S. Bank Lending to Developing Countries: Recent Developments and Some Considerations for the Future. *Fed. Res. Bull.*, October 1984, *70*(10), pp. 755–63. [G: U.S.; LDCs]

Terrell, Henry S. Considerazioni sul futuro del credito internazionale. (Some Considerations about the Future of International Lending. With English summary.) *Bancaria*, December 1984, *40*(12), pp. 1211–17. [G: U.S.; LDCs]

Thornton, Daniel L. An Early Look at the Volatility of Money and Interest Rates under CRR. *Fed. Res. Bank St. Louis Rev.*, October 1984, *66*(8), pp. 26–32.

Timberlake, Richard H., Jr. The Central Banking Role of Clearinghouse Associations. *J. Money, Credit, Banking*, February 1984, *16*(1), pp. 1–15. [G: U.S.]

Tobin, James. Bank Regulation and the Effectiveness of Open Market Operations: Comment. *Brookings Pap. Econ. Act.*, 1984, (2), pp. 447–53. [G: U.S.]

Tortella, Gabriel and Palafox, Jordi. Banking and Industry in Spain, 1918–1936. *J. Europ. Econ. Hist.*, Special Issue 1984, *13*(2), pp. 81–111. [G: Spain]

Trescott, Paul B. The Behavior of the Currency–Deposit Ratio during the Great Depression: A Comment. *J. Money, Credit, Banking*, August 1984, *16*(3), pp. 362–65. [G: U.S.]

Tybout, James R. Interest Control and Credit Allocation in Developing Countries. *J. Money, Credit, Banking*, Part 1 November 1984, *16*(4), pp. 474–87. [G: LDCs; Colombia]

Valentine, T. J. Financial Regulation in Australia:

Comment. *Australian Econ. Rev.*, 3rd Quarter 1984, (67), pp. 147–50.　　　**[G: Australia]**

Van Fenstermaker, J.; Filer, John E. and Herren, Robert Stanley. Money Statistics of New England, 1785–1837. *J. Econ. Hist.*, June 1984, *44*(2), pp. 441–53.　　　**[G: U.S.]**

Vaubel, Roland. International Debt, Bank Failures, and the Money Supply: The Thirties and the Eighties. *Cato J.*, Spring/Summer 1984, *4*(1), pp. 249–67.　　　**[G: U.S.]**

Vittas, Dimitri. International Payments Systems. In *Fed. Res. Bank Atlanta*, 1984, pp. 141–48.　　　**[G: Global]**

Vogt, Michael G. and Hanna, R. S. Variations of the Federal Funds Rate and Bank Reserve Management. *J. Bank Res.*, Autumn 1984, *15*(3), pp. 188–92.　　　**[G: U.S.]**

Volcker, Paul A. Statement to the U.S. House Subcommittee on Telecommunications, Consumer Protection, and Finance of the Committee on Energy and Commerce, April 4, 1984. *Fed. Res. Bull.*, April 1984, *70*(4), pp. 312–19.　　　**[G: U.S.]**

Volcker, Paul A. Statement to the U.S. House Committee on Banking, Finance and Urban Affairs, June 12, 1984. *Fed. Res. Bull.*, July 1984, *70*(7), pp. 560–68.　　　**[G: U.S.]**

Volcker, Paul A. Statement to the U.S. Senate Committee on Banking, Housing, and Urban Affairs, March 27, 1984. *Fed. Res. Bull.*, April 1984, *70*(4), pp. 298–308.　　　**[G: U.S.]**

Volcker, Paul A. Statement to the U.S. Senate Committee on Banking, Housing, and Urban Affairs, Salt Lake City, Utah, January 16, 1984. *Fed. Res. Bull.*, February 1984, *70*(2), pp. 90–95.　　　**[G: U.S.]**

Volcker, Paul A. The Federal Reserve Position on Restructuring of Financial Regulation Responsibilities. *Fed. Res. Bull.*, July 1984, *70*(7), pp. 547–57.　　　**[G: OECD]**

Wallison, Peter J. The Emerging Regulatory Structure for Banks: Implications for the Insurance Industry. In *Sametz, A. W., ed.*, 1984, pp. 73–78.　　　**[G: U.S.]**

Warfel, George, Jr. Consumer Acceptance of Technology. In *Fed. Res. Bank Atlanta*, 1984, pp. 103–12.　　　**[G: U.S.]**

Webb, David C. Imperfect Information and Credit Market Equilibrium. *Europ. Econ. Rev.*, October–November 1984, *26*(1–2), pp. 247–58.

Weintraub, Robert E. International Debt: Crisis and Challenge. *Cato J.*, Spring/Summer 1984, *4*(1), pp. 21–61.　　　**[G: LDCs; U.S.]**

Wells, Donald R. and Scruggs, L. S. Free Banking: The Ultimate Deregulation of the Financial System. *Atlantic Econ. J.*, September 1984, *12*(3), pp. 80.　　　**[G: U.S.]**

White, Alice P. "Firm" or "Market" Data: The Proper Test of the Structure–Performance Relationship. *J. Econ. Bus.*, February 1984, *36*(1), pp. 151–60.　　　**[G: U.S.]**

White, Eugene Nelson. A Reinterpretation of the Banking Crisis of 1930. *J. Econ. Hist.*, March 1984, *44*(1), pp. 119–38.　　　**[G: U.S.]**

White, George C. Payments Standards. In *Fed. Res. Bank Atlanta*, 1984, pp. 113–21.

White, Lawrence H. Bank Failures and Monetary Policy [International Debt, Bank Failures, and the Money Supply: The Thirties and the Eighties]. *Cato J.*, Spring/Summer 1984, *4*(1), pp. 269–74.　　　**[G: U.S.]**

White, Lawrence H. Free Banking as an Alternative Monetary System. In *Siegel, B. N., ed.*, 1984, pp. 269–302.

Willman, Paul and Cowan, Rowena. New Technology in Banking: The Impact of Autotellers on Staff Numbers. In *Warner, M., ed.*, 1984, pp. 224–39.　　　**[G: U.K.]**

Woerheide, Walt; Hartzog, Jerry and Losey, Robert. The Effect of the "Wild Card" Experiment on Savings Flows at Savings and Loans. *Bus. Econ.*, April 1984, *19*(3), pp. 48–51.　　　**[G: U.S.]**

Woodard, George D. and Goldsberry, James E. Economic Research as an Aid to Regional Bank Holding Company Expansion. *J. Bank Res.*, Winter 1984, *14*(4), pp. 302–04.　　　**[G: U.S.]**

Wu, Hsiu-Kwang and Cheng, David C. The Effects of Loan and Bank Characteristics on Bank Loan Criticisms Accuracy: A Multivariate Logit Analysis. *Quart. J. Bus. Econ.*, Summer 1984, *23*(3), pp. 3–17.　　　**[G: U.S.]**

Zimmer, Linda Fenner. ATMs. In *Fed. Res. Bank Atlanta*, 1984, pp. 3–9.

313 Capital Markets

3130 General

Arrow, Kenneth J. Risk Perception in Psychology and Economics. In *Arrow, K. J., vol. 3, 1984, 1982*, pp. 261–70.

Ball, Clifford A. and Torous, Walter N. The Maximum Likelihood Estimation of Security Price Volatility: Theory, Evidence, and Application to Option Pricing. *J. Bus.*, Part 1, January 1984, *57*(1), pp. 97–112.　　　**[G: U.S.]**

Carlton, Dennis W. Futures Markets: Their Purpose, Their History, Their Growth, Their Successes and Failures. *J. Futures Markets*, Fall 1984, *4*(3), pp. 237–71.　　　**[G: U.S.]**

Casabona, Patrick A.; Fabozzi, Frank J. and Francis, Jack C. How to Apply Duration to Equity Analysis. *J. Portfol. Manage.*, Winter 1984, *10*(2), pp. 52–58.

Collins, Daniel W. and Dent, Warren T. A Comparison of Alternative Testing Methodologies Used in Capital Market Research. *J. Acc. Res.*, Spring 1984, *22*(1), pp. 48–84.　　　**[G: U.S.]**

De Benedetti, Carlo. Quali strumenti finanziari per lo sviluppo del sistema economico italiano? (Financial Tools for Development of the Italian Economy. With English summary.) *Bancaria*, May–June 1984, *40*(5–6), pp. 479–82.　　　**[G: Italy]**

Farrelly, Gail E. and Reichenstein, William R. Risk Perceptions of Institutional Investors. *J. Portfol. Manage.*, Summer 1984, *10*(4), pp. 5–12.　　　**[G: U.S.]**

Fischer, Stanley. Stock Prices and Social Dynamics: Comment. *Brookings Pap. Econ. Act.*, 1984, (2), pp. 499–504. **[G: U.S.]**

Friedman, Benjamin M. Stock Prices and Social Dynamics: Comment. *Brookings Pap. Econ. Act.*, 1984, (2), pp. 504–08. **[G: U.S.]**

Friedman, Milton. Financial Futures Markets and Tabular Standards. *J. Polit. Econ.*, February 1984, *92*(1), pp. 165–67.

Frinquelli, A. Michael. Implications for Insurance Products and Services: Discussion. In *Sametz, A. W., ed.*, 1984, pp. 67–68. **[G: U.S.]**

Fritz, Richard G. Time Series Evidence of the Causal Relationship between Financial Deepening and Economic Development. *J. Econ. Devel.*, July 1984, *9*(1), pp. 91–111.
[G: Philippines]

Galper, Harvey and Toder, Eric. Transfer Elements in the Taxation of Income from Capital. In *Moon, M., ed.*, 1984, pp. 87–136.
[G: U.S.]

Gourvez, Jean-Yves. Intermediation and Traditional Circuits. Conditions for Mobilizing Financial Savings. In *Kessler, D. and Ullmo, P.-A., eds.*, 1984, pp. 107–20.

Hamon, Jacques and Galesne, Alain. Recherche financière et bases de données bibliographiques: DAUFIN, un nouvel outil pour la recherche financière. (Financial Research and Bibliographic Data Bases: DAUFIN as a New Tool for Financial Research. With English summary.) *Écon. Soc.*, November–December 1984, *18*(11–12), pp. 159–228. **[G: France]**

Jacoby, Jacob. Implications for Insurance Products and Services: Discussion. In *Sametz, A. W., ed.*, 1984, pp. 69–72. **[G: U.S.]**

King, Mervyn A. The Ownership and Financing of Corporations. In *Aoki, M., ed.*, 1984, pp. 311–17. **[G: Japan]**

Kirby, Robert G. The Coffee Can Portfolio. *J. Portfol. Manage.*, Fall 1984, *11*(1), pp. 76–80.

Kolb, Robert W.; Timme, Stephen G. and Gay, Gerald D. Macro versus Micro Futures Hedges at Commercial Banks. *J. Futures Markets*, Spring 1984, *4*(1), pp. 47–54. **[G: U.S.]**

Macsherry, Cathy Daicoff. Infrastructure and an S&P Credit Rating: Questions, Trends, and Considerations. *Public Budg. Finance*, Autumn 1984, *4*(3), pp. 41–45. **[G: U.S.]**

McKinnon, Ronald I. The J-Curve, Stabilizing Speculation, and Capital Constraints on Foreign Exchange Dealers. In *Bigman, D. and Taya, T., eds.*, 1984, pp. 101–25.

Ogawa, Kazuo. On the Substitutability of Public Stocks for Private Stocks under Rational Expectations. *Kobe Univ. Econ.*, 1984, (30), pp. 79–96.

Ohlin, Goran. A New Case for Personal Savings in Development Policy? In *Kessler, D. and Ullmo, P.-A., eds.*, 1984, pp. 79–83.

Okner, Benjamin A. Transfer Elements in the Taxation of Income from Capital: Comment. In *Moon, M., ed.*, 1984, pp. 136–38.
[G: U.S.]

Orlando, Luigi. Mercati e intermediari finanziari: esigenze delle imprese. (Financial Markets and Intermediation: Business Requirements. With English summary.) *Bancaria*, May–June 1984, *40*(5–6), pp. 473–78. **[G: Italy]**

Patrick, Hugh. The Japanese Financial System in Transition: Comment. In *Agmon, T.; Hawkins, R. G. and Levich, R. M., eds.*, 1984, pp. 186–93. **[G: Japan]**

Romiti, Cesare. Una riallocazione efficiente della risorse. (A Reallocation of Resources. With English summary.) *Bancaria*, May–June 1984, *40*(5–6), pp. 483–86. **[G: Italy]**

Rossetti, Alberto. Disintermediazione bancaria e mercato monetario: i certificati di deposito nell'esperienza statunitense. (Banking Disintermediation and the Money Market: Certificates of Deposit in the United States Experience. With English summary.) *Bancaria*, November 1984, *40*(11), pp. 1102–17.
[G: Italy; U.S.]

Sakakibara, Eisuke. The Japanese Financial System in Transition. In *Agmon, T.; Hawkins, R. G. and Levich, R. M., eds.*, 1984, pp. 157–85. **[G: Japan; U.S.]**

Sametz, Arnold W. The New Financial Environment. In *Sametz, A. W., ed.*, 1984, pp. 3–19.
[G: U.S.]

Shea, Gary S. Pitfalls in Smoothing Interest Rate Term Structure Data: Equilibrium Models and Spline Approximations. *J. Finan. Quant. Anal.*, September 1984, *19*(3), pp. 253–69.

Shiller, Robert J. Stock Prices and Social Dynamics. *Brookings Pap. Econ. Act.*, 1984, (2), pp. 457–98. **[G: U.S.]**

Tomek, William G. and Querin, Scott F. Random Processes in Prices and Technical Analysis. *J. Futures Markets*, Spring 1984, *4*(1), pp. 15–23.

Trent, Robert H. and Kemp, Robert S. The Writings of Henry A. Latané: A Compilation and Analysis. *J. Finan. Res.*, Summer 1984, *7*(2), pp. 161–74.

Wachtel, Paul. Observations on Saving by Individuals in Developing Countries. In *Kessler, D. and Ullmo, P.-A., eds.*, 1984, pp. 17–26.

3131 Capital Markets: Theory, Including Portfolio Selection, and Empirical Studies Illustrating Theory

Albouy, Michel. Plan d'épargne logement et théorie des options. (Housing Saving Plan and Option Theory. With English summary.) *Écon. Soc.*, November–December 1984, *18*(11–12), pp. 81–98. **[G: France]**

Allen, Franklin and Postlewaite, Andrew. Rational Expectations and the Measurement of a Stock's Elasticity of Demand. *J. Finance*, September 1984, *39*(4), pp. 1119–25.

Andersen, Torben M. Some Implications of the Efficient Capital Market Hypothesis. *J. Post Keynesian Econ.*, Winter 1983-84, *6*(2), pp. 281–94.

Anderson, Ronald W. and Sundaresan, Mahadevan. Futures Markets and Monopoly. In *Anderson, R. W., ed.*, 1984, pp. 75–105.

Antia, Murad J. and Meyer, Richard L. The Growth Optimal Capital Structure: Manager versus Shareholder Objectives. *J. Finan. Res.*, Fall 1984, 7(3), pp. 259–67.

Aoki, Masahiko. Shareholders' Non-unanimity on Investment Financing: Banks vs. Individual Investors. In *Aoki, M., ed.*, 1984, pp. 193–224. [G: Japan]

Ashton, D. J. and Atkins, D. R. A Partial Theory of Takeover Bids. *J. Finance*, March 1984, 39(1), pp. 167–83.

Babcock, Guilford C. Duration as a Link between Yield and Value. *J. Portfol. Manage.*, Summer 1984, 10(4), pp. 58–65.

Babcock, Guilford C. Duration as a Link between Yield and Value: A Summary. *J. Portfol. Manage.*, Fall 1984, 11(1), pp. 97–98.

Ball, Ray. The Natural Taxation of Capital Gains and Losses When Income Is Taxed. *J. Banking Finance*, September 1984, 8(3), pp. 471–81.

Bamberg, Günter. The Impacts of Variance Reducing Strategies in Dyopolistic Capital Markets. In *Bamberg, G. and Spremann, K., eds.*, 1984, pp. 15–32.

Barry, Christopher B. and Brown, Stephen J. Differential Information and the Small Firm Effect. *J. Finan. Econ.*, June 1984, 13(2), pp. 283–94.

Begg, David K. H. Rational Expectations and Bond Pricing: Modelling the Term Structure with and without Certainty Equivalence. *Econ. J.*, 1984 Supplement, 94, pp. 45–58.

Benesh, Gary A. and Colec, Stephen E. A Simplified Approach for Calculating Bond Duration. *Financial Rev.*, November 1984, 19(4), pp. 394–96.

Bennett, Paul. Applying Portfolio Theory to Global Bank Lending. *J. Banking Finance*, June 1984, 8(2), pp. 153–69.

Benninga, Simon. Futures Markets when Agents Are Myopic. In *Anderson, R. W., ed.*, 1984, pp. 113–33.

Benninga, Simon; Eldor, Rafael and Zilcha, Itzhak. The Optimal Hedge Ratio in Unbiased Futures Markets. *J. Futures Markets*, Summer 1984, 4(2), pp. 155–59.

Bernard, Victor L. The Use of Market Data and Accounting Data in Hedging against Consumer Price Inflation. *J. Acc. Res.*, Autumn 1984, 22(2), pp. 445–66. [G: U.S.]

Bernstein, Peter L. Surprising the Smoothies. *J. Portfol. Manage.*, Fall 1984, 11(1), pp. 7–11.

Bernstein, Peter L. The Surprises of Risk. *J. Portfol. Manage.*, Summer 1984, 10(4), pp. 4.

Bey, Roger P.; Burgess, Richard C. and Kearns, Richard B. Moving Stochastic Dominance: An Alternative Method for Testing Market Efficiency. *J. Finan. Res.*, Fall 1984, 7(3), pp. 185–96. [G: U.S.]

Bhattacharya, Sudipto. Notes on Multiperiod Valuation and the Pricing of Options: A Reply. *J. Finance*, March 1984, 39(1), pp. 309–12.

Bicksler, James L. International Corporate Diversification, Market Valuation, and Size-Adjusted Evidence: Discussion. *J. Finance*, July 1984, 39(3), pp. 743–45.

Blume, Marshall E. The Use of "Alphas" to Improve Performance. *J. Portfol. Manage.*, Fall 1984, 11(1), pp. 86–92.

Bond, Gary E. The Effects of Supply and Interest Rate Shocks in Commodity Futures Markets. *Amer. J. Agr. Econ.*, August 1984, 66(3), pp. 294–301.

Bookstaber, Richard and Clarke, Roger. Option Portfolio Strategies: Measurement and Evaluation. *J. Bus.*, October 1984, 57(4), pp. 469–92. [G: U.S.]

Booth, Laurence D. Bid–Ask Spreads in the Market for Forward Exchange. *J. Int. Money Finance*, August 1984, 3(2), pp. 209–22.

Booth, Laurence D. On the Relationship between Time–State Preference and Capital Asset Pricing Models. *Financial Rev.*, May 1984, 19(2), pp. 251–65.

Borch, Karl. A Note on Option Prices. *Financial Rev.*, March 1984, 19(1), pp. 124–27.

Bos, T. and Newbold, Paul. An Empirical Investigation of the Possibility of Stochastic Systematic Risk in the Market Model. *J. Bus.*, Part 1, January 1984, 57(1), pp. 35–41. [G: U.S.]

Bosshardt, Donald I. Equity Clienteles, Short-Sale Restrictions, and the Miller Equilibrium. *Financial Rev.*, May 1984, 19(2), pp. 240–50.

Bower, Dorothy H.; Bower, Richard S. and Logue, Dennis E. Arbitrage Pricing Theory and Utility Stock Returns. *J. Finance*, September 1984, 39(4), pp. 1041–54. [G: U.S.]

Brauer, Greggory A. 'Open-ending' Closed-End Funds. *J. Finan. Econ.*, December 1984, 13(4), pp. 491–507.

Breeden, Douglas T. Futures Markets and Commodity Options: Hedging and Optimality in Incomplete Markets. *J. Econ. Theory*, April 1984, 32(2), pp. 275–300.

Brennan, Michael J. and Kraus, Allan. Notes on Costless Financial Signalling. In *Bamberg, G. and Spremann, K., eds.*, 1984, pp. 33–51.

Britto, Ronald. The Simultaneous Determination of Spot and Futures Prices in a Simple Model with Production Risk. *Quart. J. Econ.*, May 1984, 99(2), pp. 351–65.

Brown, Robert L. and Achour, Dominique. The Pricing of Land Options. *Urban Stud.*, August 1984, 21(3), pp. 317–23.

Brown, Stephen J. and Barry, Christopher B. Anomalies in Security Returns and the Specification of the Market Model. *J. Finance*, July 1984, 39(3), pp. 807–15. [G: U.S.]

Chambers, Anne E. and Penman, Stephen H. Timeliness of Reporting and the Stock Price Reaction to Earnings Announcements. *J. Acc. Res.*, Spring 1984, 22(1), pp. 21–47. [G: U.S.]

Chambers, Donald R. An Immunization Strategy for Futures Contracts on Government Securities. *J. Futures Markets*, Summer 1984, 4(2), pp. 173–87. [G: U.S.]

Chance, Don M. and Bolster, Paul J. Indexed Bonds: A Comparative Analysis. *J. Econ. Bus.*, May 1984, 36(2), pp. 207–16.

Chen, K. C. and Sears, R. Stephen. How Many Small Firms Are Enough? *J. Finan. Res.*, Winter 1984, 7(4), pp. 341–49. [G: U.S.]

Chen, Son-Nan and Lee, C. F. On the Measurement Errors and Ranking of Three Alternative Composite Performance Measures. *Quart. Rev. Econ. Bus.*, Autumn 1984, 24(3), pp. 6–17.

Chen, Son-Nan and Moore, William T. Multi-Period Asset Pricing: The Effects of Uncertain Inflation. *Financial Rev.*, May 1984, 19(2), pp. 208–21.

Cheng, Pao L. Unbiased Estimators of Long-run Expected Returns Revisited. *J. Finan. Quant. Anal.*, December 1984, 19(4), pp. 375–93.

Chichilnisky, Graciela. Manipulation and Repeated Games in Futures Markets. In *Anderson, R. W., ed.*, 1984, pp. 193–214.

Cho, David Chinhyung. On Testing the Arbitrage Pricing Theory: Inter-battery Factor Analysis. *J. Finance*, December 1984, 39(5), pp. 1485–1502.　　　　　　　　　　　　[G: U.S.]

Cho, David Chinhyung; Elton, Edwin J. and Gruber, Martin J. On the Robustness of the Roll and Ross Arbitrage Pricing Theory. *J. Finan. Quant. Anal.*, March 1984, 19(1), pp. 1–10.
　　　　　　　　　　　　　　　　[G: U.S.]

Choi, Jongmoo Jay. Consumption Basket, Exchange Risk, and Asset Demand. *J. Finan. Quant. Anal.*, September 1984, 19(3), pp. 287–98.

Choksi, Shernaz. Spot and Futures Prices in Copper: The Speculative Link. *J. Post Keynesian Econ.*, Spring 1984, 6(3), pp. 433–48.
　　　　　　　　　　　　　　　　[G: U.K.]

Cole, John A. Are Dividend Surprises Independently Important? *J. Portfol. Manage.*, Summer 1984, 10(4), pp. 45–50.　　[G: U.S.]

Conine, Thomas E., Jr. and Tamarkin, Maurry. A Pedagogic Note on the Derivation of the Comparative Statics of the Option Pricing Model. *Financial Rev.*, November 1984, 19(4), pp. 397–400.

Connor, Gregory. A Unified Beta Pricing Theory. *J. Econ. Theory*, October 1984, 34(1), pp. 13–31.

Constantinides, George M. Optimal Stock Trading with Personal Taxes: Implications for Prices and the Abnormal January Returns. *J. Finan. Econ.*, March 1984, 13(1), pp. 65–89.
　　　　　　　　　　　　　　　　[G: U.S.]

Constantinides, George M. Warrant Exercise and Bond Conversion in Competitive Markets. *J. Finan. Econ.*, September 1984, 13(3), pp. 371–97.

Constantinides, George M. and Ingersoll, Jonathan E., Jr. Optimal Bond Trading with Personal Taxes. *J. Finan. Econ.*, September 1984, 13(3), pp. 299–335.

Constantinides, George M. and Rosenthal, Robert W. Strategic Analysis of the Competitive Exercise of Certain Financial Options. *J. Econ. Theory*, February 1984, 32(1), pp. 128–38.

Danthine, Jean-Pierre. Futures Markets when Agents Are Myopic: Comment. In *Anderson, R. W., ed.*, 1984, pp. 135–37.

Davidson, Paul and Davidson, Greg S. Financial Markets and Williamson's Theory of Governance: Efficiency versus Concentration versus

Power. *Quart. Rev. Econ. Bus.*, Winter 1984, 24(4), pp. 50–63.

Day, Theodore E. Real Stock Returns and Inflation. *J. Finance*, June 1984, 39(2), pp. 493–502.

Dennis, Debra K. and French, Dan W. The CEPS Model for Common Stock Valuation: Comment [CEPS: The Illusion of Corporate Growth] [Integrating Financial Performance and Stock Valuation]. *J. Portfol. Manage.*, Summer 1984, 10(4), pp. 83–85.

Dhrymes, Phoebus J. The Empirical Relevance of Arbitrage Pricing Models. *J. Portfol. Manage.*, Summer 1984, 10(4), pp. 35–44.
　　　　　　　　　　　　　　　　[G: U.S.]

Dhrymes, Phoebus J.; Friend, Irwin and Gultekin, N. Bulent. A Critical Reexamination of the Empirical Evidence on the Arbitrage Pricing Theory. *J. Finance*, June 1984, 39(2), pp. 323–46.

Dodd, Peter, et al. Qualified Audit Opinions and Stock Prices: Information Content, Announcement Dates, and Concurrent Disclosures. *J. Acc. Econ.*, April 1984, 6(1), pp. 3–38.
　　　　　　　　　　　　　　　　[G: U.S.]

Donaldson, John B. and Mehra, Rajnish. Comparative Dynamics of an Equilibrium Intertemporal Asset Pricing Model. *Rev. Econ. Stud.*, July 1984, 51(3), pp. 491–508.

Dotan, Amihud and Ofer, Aharon. Variable versus Stationary Beta in the Market Model: A Comparative Analysis. *J. Banking Finance*, December 1984, 8(4), pp. 525–34.　[G: U.S.]

Dumas, Bernard. International Portfolio Diversification: Short-term Financial Assets and Gold: Comment. In *Bilson, J. F. O. and Marston, R. C., eds.*, 1984, pp. 232–36.
　　　　　　　　　　　[G: Selected OECD]

Dunn, Kenneth B. and Spatt, Chester S. A Strategic Analysis of Sinking Fund Bonds. *J. Finan. Econ.*, September 1984, 13(3), pp. 399–423.

Dybvig, Philip H. Short Sales Restrictions and Kinks on the Mean Variance Frontier. *J. Finance*, March 1984, 39(1), pp. 239–44.

Dye, Ronald A. Inside Trading and Incentives. *J. Bus.*, July 1984, 57(3), pp. 295–313.

Eades, Kenneth M.; Hess, Patrick J. and Kim, E. Han. On Interpreting Security Returns during the Ex-Dividend Period. *J. Finan. Econ.*, March 1984, 13(1), pp. 3–34.　　[G: U.S.]

Elton, Edwin J. and Gruber, Martin J. Non-Standard C.A.P.M.'s and the Market Portfolio. *J. Finance*, July 1984, 39(3), pp. 911–24.

Errunza, Vihang R. and Senbet, Lemma W. International Corporate Diversification, Market Valuation, and Size-Adjusted Evidence. *J. Finance*, July 1984, 39(3), pp. 727–43.
　　　　　　　　　　　　　　　　[G: U.S.]

Evnine, Jeremy and Rudd, Andrew. Option Portfolio Risk Analysis. *J. Portfol. Manage.*, Winter 1984, 10(2), pp. 23–27.

Feldstein, Martin; Slemrod, Joel and Yitzhaki, Shlomo. The Effects of Taxation on the Selling of Corporate Stock and the Realization of Capital Gains: Reply. *Quart. J. Econ.*, February 1984, 99(1), pp. 111–20.　　　　[G: U.S.]

Feuerstein, Jay R. Trading Bond Spreads in the Delivery Month. *J. Futures Markets*, Winter 1984, *4*(4), pp. 579–83.

Figlewski, Stephen. Hedging Performance and Basis Risk in Stock Index Futures. *J. Finance*, July 1984, *39*(3), pp. 657–69. [G: U.S.]

Figlewski, Stephen. Information Diversity and Market Behavior: A Reply. *J. Finance*, March 1984, *39*(1), pp. 299–302.

Firchau, Volker. Variable Information and Capital Market Equilibria. In *Bamberg, G. and Spremann, K., eds.*, 1984, pp. 52–63.

Firth, M. The Extent of Voluntary Disclosure in Corporate Annual Reports and Its Association with Security Risk Measures. *Appl. Econ.*, April 1984, *16*(2), pp. 269–77. [G: U.K.]

Fischer, Stanley and Merton, Robert C. Macroeconomics and Finance: The Role of the Stock Market. *Carnegie-Rochester Conf. Ser. Public Policy*, Autumn 1984, *21*, pp. 57–108.

Fishelson, Gideon. Constraints on Transactions in the Futures Markets for Output and Inputs. *J. Econ. Bus.*, December 1984, *36*(4), pp. 415–20.

Fitzpatrick, Dennis B. A Review of the Theoretical and Empirical Evidence Regarding Equity-Debt Risk Premia for Electric Utilities. In *Foster, J. R., et al., eds.*, 1984, pp. 202–28. [G: U.S.]

Fogler, H. Russell. Bond Portfolio Immunization, Inflation, and the Fisher Equation. *J. Risk Ins.*, June 1984, *51*(2), pp. 244–64.

Fong, H. Gifford and Vasicek, Oldrich A. A Risk Minimizing Strategy for Portfolio Immunization. *J. Finance*, December 1984, *39*(5), pp. 1541–46.

Forsythe, Robert; Palfrey, Thomas R. and Plott, Charles R. Futures Markets and Informational Efficiency: A Laboratory Examination. *J. Finance*, September 1984, *39*(4), pp. 955–81.

Franke, Günter. Conditions for Myopic Valuation and Serial Independence of the Market Excess Return in Discrete Time Models. *J. Finance*, June 1984, *39*(2), pp. 425–42.

Frankel, Jeffrey A. International Portfolio Diversification: Short-term Financial Assets and Gold: Comment. In *Bilson, J. F. O. and Marston, R. C., eds.*, 1984, pp. 236–37. [G: Selected OECD]

French, Kenneth R. Anomalies in Security Returns and the Specification of the Market Model: Discussion. *J. Finance*, July 1984, *39*(3), pp. 815–17. [G: U.S.]

Fuller, Russell J. and Settle, John W. Determinants of Duration and Bond Volatility. *J. Portfol. Manage.*, Summer 1984, *10*(4), pp. 66–72.

Futia, Carl A. Futures Markets when Agents Are Myopic: Comment. In *Anderson, R. W., ed.*, 1984, pp. 139.

Galai, Dan and Geske, Robert. Option Performance Measurement. *J. Portfol. Manage.*, Spring 1984, *10*(3), pp. 42–46.

Gau, George W. Weak Form Tests of the Efficiency of Real Estate Investment Markets. *Financial Rev.*, November 1984, *19*(4), pp. 301–20. [G: Canada]

Gay, Gerald D. and Kolb, Robert W. Removing

Bias in Duration Based Hedging Models: A Note. *J. Futures Markets*, Summer 1984, *4*(2), pp. 225–28.

Gehm, Fred. Techniques for Making Decisions under Uncertainty. *J. Futures Markets*, Spring 1984, *4*(1), pp. 65–73.

Geske, Robert and Johnson, Herb E. The American Put Option Valued Analytically. *J. Finance*, December 1984, *39*(5), pp. 1511–24.

Geske, Robert and Roll, Richard. On Valuing American Call Options with the Black–Scholes European Formula. *J. Finance*, June 1984, *39*(2), pp. 443–55. [G: U.S.]

Giaccotto, Carmelo. A Note on Tests of the Capital Asset Pricing Model. *Financial Rev.*, March 1984, *19*(1), pp. 97–102.

Gilster, John E., Jr. and Lee, William. The Effects of Transaction Costs and Different Borrowing and Lending Rates on the Option Pricing Model: A Note. *J. Finance*, September 1984, *39*(4), pp. 1215–21.

Glick, Reuven. The Geometry of Asset Adjustment with Adjustment Costs. *J. Finan. Res.*, Winter 1984, *7*(4), pp. 303–14.

Gordon, Roger H. Inflation, Taxation, and Corporate Behavior. *Quart. J. Econ.*, May 1984, *99*(2), pp. 312–27.

Grinblatt, Mark S.; Masulis, Ronald W. and Titman, Sheridan. The Valuation Effects of Stock Splits and Stock Dividends. *J. Finan. Econ.*, December 1984, *13*(4), pp. 461–90.

Grinols, Earl L. Production and Risk Leveling in the Intertemporal Capital Asset Pricing Model. *J. Finance*, December 1984, *39*(5), pp. 1571–95.

Grinols, Earl L. Spot Market-Risk Market Interaction and the Protective Effects of a Tariff under Uncertainty. *Econ. J.*, March 1984, *94*(373), pp. 95–103.

Gultekin, N. Bulent and Rogalski, Richard J. Alternative Duration Specifications and the Measurement of Basis Risk: Empirical Tests. *J. Bus.*, April 1984, *57*(2), pp. 241–64. [G: U.S.]

Handjinicolaou, George and Kalay, Avner. Wealth Redistributions or Changes in Firm Value: An Analysis of Returns to Bondholders and Stockholders around Dividend Announcements. *J. Finan. Econ.*, March 1984, *13*(1), pp. 35–63. [G: U.S.]

Harrison, J. Michael; Pitbladdo, Richard and Schaefer, Stephen M. Continuous Price Processes in Frictionless Markets Have Infinite Variation. *J. Bus.*, July 1984, *57*(3), pp. 353–65.

Hart, Oliver. Further Reflections on the Invisible-Hand Theorem: Comment. In *Wiles, P. and Routh, G., eds.*, 1984, pp. 184–89. [G: U.S.]

Hayakawa, Hiroaki. Balance Sheet Identity and Walras' Law. *J. Econ. Theory*, October 1984, *34*(1), pp. 187–202.

Hayes, James. Futures Markets and Monopoly: Comment. In *Anderson, R. W., ed.*, 1984, pp. 109–12.

Hazuka, Thomas B. Consumption Betas and

Backwardation in Commodity Markets. *J. Finance*, July 1984, 39(3), pp. 647–55.

Heaney, W. John and Cheng, Pao L. Continuous Maturity Diversification of Default-Free Bond Portfolios and a Generalization of Efficient Diversification. *J. Finance*, September 1984, 39(4), pp. 1101–17.

Hilliard, Jimmy E. Hedging Interest Rate Risk with Futures Portfolios under Term Structure Effects. *J. Finance*, December 1984, 39(5), pp. 1547–70.   [G: U.S.]

Ho, Thomas S. Y. Intertemporal Commodity Futures Hedging and the Production Decision. *J. Finance*, June 1984, 39(2), pp. 351–76.

Ho, Thomas S. Y. and Macris, Richard G. Dealer Bid–Ask Quotes and Transaction Prices: An Empirical Study of Some AMEX Options. *J. Finance*, March 1984, 39(1), pp. 23–45.
                                              [G: U.S.]

Ho, Thomas S. Y. and Singer, Ronald F. The Value of Corporate Debt with a Sinking-Fund Provision. *J. Bus.*, July 1984, 57(3), pp. 315–36.

Hodrick, Robert J. and Srivastava, Sanjay. An Investigation of Risk and Return in Forward Foreign Exchange. *J. Int. Money Finance*, April 1984, 3(1), pp. 5–29.

Holcombe, Randall G. and Saba, Richard P. The Effects of Heterogeneous Expectations on the Capital Structure of the Firm. *Southern Econ. J.*, October 1984, 51(2), pp. 356–68.

Howard, Charles T. and D'Antonio, Louis J. A Risk-Return Measure of Hedging Effectiveness. *J. Finan. Quant. Anal.*, March 1984, 19(1), pp. 101–12.

Huang, Roger D. and Kracaw, William A. Stock Market Returns and Real Activity: A Note. *J. Finance*, March 1984, 39(1), pp. 267–73.

Huberman, Gur. Capital Asset Pricing in an Overlapping Generations Model. *J. Econ. Theory*, August 1984, 33(2), pp. 232–48.

Husted, Steven L. and Rush, Mark. On Measuring the Nearness of Near Moneys: Revisited. *J. Monet. Econ.*, September 1984, 14(2), pp. 171–81.   [G: U.S.]

Ingersoll, Jonathan E., Jr. Some Results in the Theory of Arbitrage Pricing. *J. Finance*, September 1984, 39(4), pp. 1021–39.

Jagannathan, Ravi. Call Options and the Risk of Underlying Securities. *J. Finan. Econ.*, September 1984, 13(3), pp. 425–34.

Jarrow, Robert A. The Error Learning Hypothesis: The Evidence Reexamined. *J. Econ. Bus.*, May 1984, 36(2), pp. 177–88.   [G: U.S.]

Jarrow, Robert A. and Rosenfeld, Eric R. Jump Risks and the Intertemporal Capital Asset Pricing Model. *J. Bus.*, July 1984, 57(3), pp. 337–51.   [G: U.S.]

Jean, William H. The Harmonic Mean and Other Necessary Conditions for Stochastic Dominance. *J. Finance*, June 1984, 39(2), pp. 527–34.

Jeffrey, Robert H. A New Paradigm for Portfolio Risk. *J. Portfol. Manage.*, Fall 1984, 11(1), pp. 33–40.   [G: U.S.]

Jennings, Robert H. and Barry, Christopher B.

On Information Dissemination and Equilibrium Asset Prices: A Note. *J. Finan. Quant. Anal.*, December 1984, 19(4), pp. 395–402.

Jobson, J. D. and Korkie, Bob. On the Jensen Measure and Marginal Improvements in Portfolio Performance: A Note. *J. Finance*, March 1984, 39(1), pp. 245–51.

John, Kose. Market Resolution and Valuation in Incomplete Markets. *J. Finan. Quant. Anal.*, March 1984, 19(1), pp. 29–44.

Jones, E. Philip. Option Arbitrage and Strategy with Large Price Changes. *J. Finan. Econ.*, March 1984, 13(1), pp. 91–113.

Jüttner, D. Johannes. Information and Futures Trading—Some Missing Facts and Consequences [Informationsaktivitäten und Preisbildungsprozesse auf Terminkontraktmärkten]. *Jahr. Nationalökon. Statist.*, September 1984, 199(5), pp. 460–63.

Kallberg, Jerry G. and Ziemba, William T. Misspecifications in Portfolio Selection Problems. In *Bamberg, G. and Spremann, K., eds.*, 1984, pp. 74–87.

Kandel, Shmuel. On the Exclusion of Assets from Tests of the Mean Variance Efficiency of the Market Portfolio. *J. Finance*, March 1984, 39(1), pp. 63–75.

Kandel, Shmuel. The Likelihood Ratio Test Statistic of Mean-Variance Efficiency without a Riskless Asset. *J. Finan. Econ.*, December 1984, 13(4), pp. 575–92.

Kanniainen, Vesa. Corporation Wealth Tax—A Note. *Liiketaloudellinen Aikak.*, 1984, 33(2), pp. 149–54.   [G: Finland]

Kihlstrom, Richard E. Manipulation and Repeated Games in Futures Markets: Comment. In *Anderson, R. W., ed.*, 1984, pp. 215–24.

Kilcollin, Thomas Eric. A Theory of Futures Market Manipulations: Comment. In *Anderson, R. W., ed.*, 1984, pp. 189–91.

Koskela, Erkki and Kanniainen, Vesa. Changing the Tax Base and Risk-Taking. *Oxford Econ. Pap.*, March 1984, 36(1), pp. 162–74.

Kosmicke, Ralph. The Contradiction between Keynes and the EMH. *J. Portfol. Manage.*, Fall 1984, 11(1), pp. 41–43.

Kroll, Yoram. The Analysis of Risky Investment: A State-Contingent Approach. *J. Banking Finance*, December 1984, 8(4), pp. 509–24.

Kroll, Yoram; Levy, Haim and Markowitz, Harry M. Mean-Variance versus Direct Utility Maximization. *J. Finance*, March 1984, 39(1), pp. 47–61.   [G: U.S.]

Kryzanowski, Lawrence and To, Minh Chau. The Telescopic Effect of Past Return Realizations on Ex-Post Beta Estimates. *Financial Rev.*, March 1984, 19(1), pp. 1–25.

Kwan, Clarence C. Y. Portfolio Analysis Using Single Index, Multi-index, and Constant Correlation Models: A Unified Treatment. *J. Finance*, December 1984, 39(5), pp. 1469–83.

Kyle, Albert S. A Theory of Futures Market Manipulations. In *Anderson, R. W., ed.*, 1984, pp. 141–73.

Kyle, Albert S. Market Structure, Information, Futures Markets, and Price Formation. In *Sto-*

rey, G. G.; Schmitz, A. and Sarris, A. H., eds., 1984, pp. 45–64.

Lackman, Conway L. Dependent Incremental Modeling of Security Prices. *Rivista Int. Sci. Econ. Com.*, February 1984, *31*(2), pp. 156–71. [G: U.S.]

Lai, Tsong-Yue and Boness, A. James. Investment in the Long Run. *Financial Rev.*, November 1984, *19*(4), pp. 285–300.

Landskroner, Yoram and Paroush, Jacob. Human Capital and Financial Equilibrium. *J. Econ. Bus.*, December 1984, *36*(4), pp. 443–52. [G: U.S.]

Leibowitz, Martin L., et al. Horizon Matching: A New Approach to Dedicated Portfolios. *J. Portfol. Manage.*, Fall 1984, *11*(1), pp. 93–96.

LeRoy, Stephen F. Efficiency and the Variability of Asset Prices. *Amer. Econ. Rev.*, May 1984, *74*(2), pp. 183–87.

LeRoy, Stephen F. Nominal Prices and Interest Rates in General Equilibrium: Endowment Shocks. *J. Bus.*, April 1984, *57*(2), pp. 197–213.

Levi, Maurice D. Spot versus Forward Speculation and Hedging: A Diagrammatic Exposition. *J. Int. Money Finance*, April 1984, *3*(1), pp. 105–09.

Levy, Haim. Another Look at the Capital Asset Pricing Model. *Quart. Rev. Econ. Bus.*, Summer 1984, *24*(2), pp. 5–32.

Levy, Haim and Levy, Azriel. Ordering Uncertain Options under Inflation: A Note. *J. Finance*, September 1984, *39*(4), pp. 1223–29.

Li, Raymond K. C. On Grossman's Model of Efficient Stock Markets Where Traders Have Diverse Information. *Hong Kong Econ. Pap.*, 1984, (15), pp. 105–18.

Little, Patricia Knain. Negative Cash Flows, Duration, and Immunization: A Note. *J. Finance*, March 1984, *39*(1), pp. 283–88.

Livingston, Miles. The Cheapest Deliverable Fund for the CBT Treasury Bond Futures Contract. *J. Futures Markets*, Summer 1984, *4*(2), pp. 161–72. [G: U.S.]

Lucas, Robert E., Jr. Money in a Theory of Finance. *Carnegie-Rochester Conf. Ser. Public Policy*, Autumn 1984, *21*, pp. 9–45.

Lys, Thomas. Mandated Accounting Changes and Debt Covenants: The Case of Oil and Gas Accounting. *J. Acc. Econ.*, April 1984, *6*(1), pp. 39–65. [G: U.S.]

de Macedo, Jorge Braga; Goldstein, Jeffrey A. and Meerschwam, David M. International Portfolio Diversification: Short-term Financial Assets and Gold. In *Bilson, J. F. O. and Marston, R. C.*, eds., 1984, pp. 199–232. [G: Selected OECD]

MacMinn, Richard D. A General Diversification Theorem: A Note. *J. Finance*, June 1984, *39*(2), pp. 541–50.

MacMinn, Richard D.; Morgan, George Emir, III and Smith, Stephen D. Forward Market Equilibrium. *Southern Econ. J.*, July 1984, *51*(1), pp. 41–58.

Magill, Michael J. P. Understanding Futures Markets. *Empirica*, 1984, *11*(2), pp. 125–45.

Mandelker, Gershon N. and Rhee, S. Ghon. The Impact of the Degrees of Operating and Financial Leverage on Systematic Risk of Common Stock. *J. Finan. Quant. Anal.*, March 1984, *19*(1), pp. 45–57. [G: U.S.]

Marcus, Alan J. Efficient Asset Portfolios and the Theory of Normal Backwardation: A Comment. *J. Polit. Econ.*, February 1984, *92*(1), pp. 162–64. [G: U.S.]

Markose, Sheri M. Non-separability of Consumption and Portfolio Choice with a Precautionary Demand for Money. *Greek Econ. Rev.*, August 1984, *6*(2), pp. 171–202.

Markowitz, Harry M. The "Two Beta" Trap. *J. Portfol. Manage.*, Fall 1984, *11*(1), pp. 12–20.

McCallum, Bennett T. Macroeconomics and Finance: The Role of the Stock Market: A Comment. *Carnegie-Rochester Conf. Ser. Public Policy*, Autumn 1984, *21*, pp. 109–15.

McDonald, Robert L. and Siegel, Daniel. Option Pricing When the Underlying Asset Earns a Below-Equilibrium Rate of Return: A Note. *J. Finance*, March 1984, *39*(1), pp. 261–65.

McInish, Thomas H. and Srivastava, Rajendra K. Ex-Ante Expectations and Portfolio Selection. *Financial Rev.*, March 1984, *19*(1), pp. 84–96. [G: U.S.]

Metwally, Mokhtar M. The Role of the Stock Exchange in an Islamic Economy. *J. Res. Islamic Econ.*, Summer 1984, *2*(1), pp. 21–30.

Michaud, Richard O. Should Dividend Discount Models Be Yield-Titled? Comment. *J. Portfol. Manage.*, Summer 1984, *10*(4), pp. 85–86. [G: U.S.]

Minarik, Joseph J. The Effects of Taxation on the Selling of Corporate Stock and the Realization of Capital Gains: Comment. *Quart. J. Econ.*, February 1984, *99*(1), pp. 93–110. [G: U.S.]

Minassian, Donald P. Information Diversity and Market Behavior: A Comment. *J. Finance*, March 1984, *39*(1), pp. 295–97.

Mirman, Leonard J. and Reisman, Haim. Price Taking Behavior and Trading in Options. *J. Econ. Theory*, April 1984, *32*(2), pp. 377–83.

Mirus, Rolf. Foreign Currency Options in Exchange Risk Management. *Aussenwirtschaft*, December 1984, *39*(4), pp. 323–34. [G: U.S.]

Möller, Hans-Peter. Stock Market Research in Germany: Some Empirical Results and Critical Remarks. In *Bamberg, G. and Spremann, K.*, eds., 1984, pp. 224–42. [G: W. Germany]

Morse, Joel N. A Multiobjective Expert System for Suppliers of Out-of-the-Money Options. In *Grauer, M. and Wierzbicki, A. P.*, eds., 1984, pp. 186–92.

Mosler, Karl Clemens. Increasing Multivariate Risk: Some Definitions. In *Bamberg, G. and Spremann, K.*, eds., 1984, pp. 88–102.

Mueller, Dennis C. Further Reflections on the Invisible-Hand Theorem. In *Wiles, P. and Routh, G.*, eds., 1984, pp. 159–83. [G: U.S.]

Nawrocki, David. Adaptive Trading Rules and Dynamic Market Disequilibrium. *Appl. Econ.*, February 1984, *16*(1), pp. 1–14. [G: U.S.]

Nawrocki, David. Entropy, Bifurcation and Dynamic Market Disequilibrium. *Financial Rev.*, May 1984, *19*(2), pp. 266–84.

Newbery, David M. G. The Manipulation of Futures Markets by a Dominant Producer. In *Anderson, R. W., ed.*, 1984, pp. 35–62.

O'Hara, Maureen. Commodity Bonds and Consumption Risks. *J. Finance*, March 1984, *39*(1), pp. 193–206.

Ohlson, James A. The Structure of Asset Prices and Socially Useless/Useful Information. *J. Finance*, December 1984, *39*(5), pp. 1417–35.

Oldfield, George S. and Rovira, Carlos E. Futures Contract Options. *J. Futures Markets*, Winter 1984, *4*(4), pp. 479–90.

Pari, Robert A. and Chen, Son-Nan. An Empirical Test of the Arbitrage Pricing Theory. *J. Finan. Res.*, Summer 1984, *7*(2), pp. 121–30. [G: U.S.]

Penman, Stephen H. Abnormal Returns to Investment Strategies Based on the Timing of Earnings Reports. *J. Acc. Econ.*, December 1984, *6*(3), pp. 165–83. [G: U.S.]

Perrakis, Stylianos and Ryan, Peter J. Option Pricing Bounds in Discrete Time. *J. Finance*, June 1984, *39*(2), pp. 519–25.

Peterson, David R. and Waldman, Donald M. A Model of Heterogeneous Expectations as a Determinant of Short Sales. *J. Finan. Res.*, Spring 1984, *7*(1), pp. 1–16. [G: U.S.]

Phlips, Louis. The Manipulation of Futures Markets by a Dominant Producer: Comment. In *Anderson, R. W., ed.*, 1984, pp. 63–65.

Pindyck, Robert S. Risk, Inflation, and the Stock Market. *Amer. Econ. Rev.*, June 1984, *74*(3), pp. 335–51. [G: U.S.]

Plosser, Charles I. Money in a Theory of Finance: Some Observations. *Carnegie-Rochester Conf. Ser. Public Policy*, Autumn 1984, *21*, pp. 47–55.

Polemarchakis, Herakles M. and Rose, D. Another Proposition on the Recoverability of Cardinal Utility. *J. Econ. Theory*, October 1984, *34*(1), pp. 164–68.

Radner, Roy and Stiglitz, Joseph E. A Nonconcavity in the Value of Information. In *Boyer, M. and Kihlstrom, R. E., eds.*, 1984, pp. 33–52.

Ramakrishnan, Ram T. S. and Thakor, Anjan V. The Valuation of Assets under Moral Hazard. *J. Finance*, March 1984, *39*(1), pp. 229–38.

Reinganum, Marc R. Valuation Anomalies—Empirical: Discussion: What the Anomalies Mean. *J. Finance*, July 1984, *39*(3), pp. 837–40.

Robbins, Edward Henry. Pricing Municipal Debt. *J. Finan. Quant. Anal.*, December 1984, *19*(4), pp. 467–83.

Roll, Richard. A Simple Implicit Measure of the Effective Bid–Ask Spread in an Efficient Market. *J. Finance*, September 1984, *39*(4), pp. 1127–39.

Roll, Richard and Ross, Stephen A. A Critical Reexamination of the Empirical Evidence on the Arbitrage Pricing Theory: A Reply. *J. Finance*, June 1984, *39*(2), pp. 347–50.

Rosenthal, Robert W. Futures Markets and Mo-

nopoly: Comment. In *Anderson, R. W., ed.*, 1984, pp. 107–08.

Ross, Stephen A. Reply to Dhrymes: APT *Is* Empirically Relevant. *J. Portfol. Manage.*, Fall 1984, *11*(1), pp. 54–56. [G: U.S.]

Rubinstein, Mark. A Simple Formula for the Expected Rate of Return of an Option over a Finite Holding Period. *J. Finance*, December 1984, *39*(5), pp. 1503–09.

Salant, Stephen F. A Theory of Futures Market Manipulations: Comment. In *Anderson, R. W., ed.*, 1984, pp. 175–88.

Saloner, Garth. Self-regulating Commodity Futures Exchanges. In *Anderson, R. W., ed.*, 1984, pp. 261–73.

Santoni, G. J. Interest Rate Risk and the Stock Prices of Financial Institutions. *Fed. Res. Bank St. Louis Rev.*, August/September 1984, *66*(7), pp. 12–20. [G: U.S.]

Sarris, Alexander H. Speculative Storage, Futures Markets, and the Stability of Commodity Prices. *Econ. Inquiry*, January 1984, *22*(1), pp. 80–97.

Sarris, Alexander H. Speculative Storage, Futures Markets, and the Stability of Agricultural Prices. In *Storey, G. G.; Schmitz, A. and Sarris, A. H., eds.*, 1984, pp. 65–97.

Schaefer, Stephen M. and Schwartz, Eduardo S. A Two-Factor Model of the Term Structure: An Approximate Analytical Solution. *J. Finan. Quant. Anal.*, December 1984, *19*(4), pp. 413–24. [G: U.S.]

Schnabel, Jacques A. On Mean-Variance Portfolio Selection. *Managerial Dec. Econ.*, March 1984, *5*(1), pp. 3–6.

Senbet, Lemma W. and Taggart, Robert A., Jr. Capital Structure Equilibrium under Market Imperfections and Incompleteness. *J. Finance*, March 1984, *39*(1), pp. 93–103.

Shalit, Haim and Yitzhaki, Shlomo. Mean-Gini, Portfolio Theory, and the Pricing of Risky Assets. *J. Finance*, December 1984, *39*(5), pp. 1449–68.

Sharpe, William F. Factor Models, CAPMs, and the ABT. *J. Portfol. Manage.*, Fall 1984, *11*(1), pp. 21–25.

Shefrin, Hersh M. and Statman, Meir. Explaining Investor Preference for Cash Dividends. *J. Finan. Econ.*, June 1984, *13*(2), pp. 253–82. [G: U.S.]

Shiller, Robert J. Theories of Aggregate Stock Price Movements. *J. Portfol. Manage.*, Winter 1984, *10*(2), pp. 28–37. [G: U.S.]

Silber, William L. Marketmaker Behavior in an Auction Market: An Analysis of Scalpers in Futures Markets. *J. Finance*, September 1984, *39*(4), pp. 937–53. [G: U.S.]

Speakes, Jeffrey K. Fixed-Income Risk Measurement and Risk Management. *J. Portfol. Manage.*, Winter 1984, *10*(2), pp. 66–70.

Spence, James G. CML to SML: A Graphical Approach. *Financial Rev.*, November 1984, *19*(4), pp. 388–93.

Stapleton, Richard C. and Subrahmanyam, Marti G. Notes on Multiperiod Valuation and the Pricing of Options: A Comment. *J. Finance*, March 1984, *39*(1), pp. 303–08.

Stapleton, Richard C. and Subrahmanyam, Marti G. The Valuation of Multivariate Contingent Claims in Discrete Time Models. *J. Finance*, March 1984, *39*(1), pp. 207–28.

Stapleton, Richard C. and Subrahmanyam, Marti G. The Valuation of Options When Asset Returns Are Generated by a Binomial Process. *J. Finance*, December 1984, *39*(5), pp. 1525–39.

Streit, Manfred E. Information Processing in Futures Market—An Essay on Adequate Abstraction. *Jahr. Nationalökon. Statist.*, September 1984, *199*(5), pp. 385–400.

Sundaresan, Mahadevan. Consumption and Equilibrium Interest Rates in Stochastic Production Economies. *J. Finance*, March 1984, *39*(1), pp. 77–92.

Taylor, Richard W. Portfolio Management with a Hand-Held Calculator. *J. Portfol. Manage.*, Summer 1984, *10*(4), pp. 27–31.

Telser, Lester G. Theories of Contract Design and Market Organization: Conceptual Bases for Understanding Futures Markets: Comment. In *Anderson, R. W., ed.*, 1984, pp. 307–10.

Tobin, James. A Mean-Variance Approach to Fundamental Valuation. *J. Portfol. Manage.*, Fall 1984, *11*(1), pp. 26–32.

Townsend, Robert M. Theories of Contract Design and Market Organization: Conceptual Bases for Understanding Futures Markets. In *Anderson, R. W., ed.*, 1984, pp. 275–306.

Vermaelen, Theo. Repurchase Tender Offers, Signaling, and Managerial Incentives. *J. Finan. Quant. Anal.*, June 1984, *19*(2), pp. 163–81. [G: U.S.]

Vickers, Douglas. The Uncertainty about Uncertainty: A Paradigmatic Comment on *Professor Weiss' Theory of the Firm:* Capital Markets, Output, and the Demand for Inputs under Uncertainty. *Eastern Econ. J.*, January-March 1984, *10*(1), pp. 71–77.

Vickrey, Don W. An Alternative Interpretation of Unexpected Returns from Accounting Income Numbers. *Quart. Rev. Econ. Bus.*, Spring 1984, *24*(1), pp. 6–21.

Weiss, Nitzan. Capital Markets, Output, and the Demand for Inputs under Uncertainty. *Eastern Econ. J.*, January-March 1984, *10*(1), pp. 51–69.

Weiss, Nitzan. Reply to a Paradigmatic Comment: Capital Markets, Output, and the Demand for Inputs under Uncertainty. *Eastern Econ. J.*, January-March 1984, *10*(1), pp. 79–85.

White, Lawrence J. The Manipulation of Futures Markets by a Dominant Producer: Comment. In *Anderson, R. W., ed.*, 1984, pp. 67–73.

Wilhelm, Jochen E. M. A Consistent Model for the Pricing of Derivative Assets in a Discrete Time Framework. In *Bamberg, G. and Spremann, K., eds.*, 1984, pp. 122–37.

Wolf, Avner. Options of Futures: Pricing and the Effect of an Anticipated Price Change. *J. Futures Markets*, Winter 1984, *4*(4), pp. 491–512.

3132 Capital Markets: Empirical Studies, Including Regulation

Abdel-khalik, A. Rashad. A Note on the Validity of the *WSJ* as a Source of "Event" Dates. *J. Acc. Res.*, Autumn 1984, *22*(2), pp. 758–59. [G: U.S.]

Achour, Dominique and Brown, Robert L. Un marche d'options sur indice de prix fonciers: nouvel instrument d'une politique de l'habitition. (With English summary.) *Can. Public Policy*, September 1984, *10*(3), pp. 287–95. [G: Canada]

Achour, Dominique; Brown, Robert L. and Roy, Yvon. Investment Performance of Canadian Real Estate Stocks Using Sharpe's Performance Index. *Managerial Dec. Econ.*, September 1984, *5*(3), pp. 183–86. [G: Canada]

Ajinkya, Bipin B. and Gift, Michael J. Corporate Managers' Earnings Forecasts and Symmetrical Adjustments of Market Expectations. *J. Acc. Res.*, Autumn 1984, *22*(2), pp. 425–44. [G: U.S.]

Alexander, Gordon J.; Benson, P. George and Kampmeyer, Joan M. Investigating the Valuation Effects of Announcements of Voluntary Corporate Selloffs. *J. Finance*, June 1984, *39*(2), pp. 503–17. [G: U.S.]

Anderson, Ronald W. The Industrial Organization of Futures Markets: A Survey. In *Anderson, R. W., ed.*, 1984, pp. 1–33.

Anderson, Ronald W. The Regulation of Futures Contract Innovations in the United States. *J. Futures Markets*, Fall 1984, *4*(3), pp. 297–332. [G: U.S.]

Ang, James S. and Peterson, David R. An Empirical Study of the Diffusion Process of Securities and Portfolios. *J. Finan. Res.*, Fall 1984, *7*(3), pp. 219–29. [G: U.S.]

Ang, James S. and Peterson, David R. Empirical Properties of the Elasticity Coefficient in the Constant Elasticity of Variance Model. *Financial Rev.*, November 1984, *19*(4), pp. 372–80. [G: U.S.]

Arak, Marcelle and Silver, Andrew. The Value of the Tax Treatment of Original-Issue Deep-Discount Bonds: A Note. *J. Finance*, March 1984, *39*(1), pp. 253–59.

Atoncic, Madelyn and Bennett, Paul. Financial Consequences of Mergers. *Fed. Res. Bank New York Quart. Rev.*, Spring 1984, *9*(1), pp. 26–30. [G: U.S.]

Avery, Robert B.; Elliehausen, Gregory E. and Canner, Glenn B. Survey of Consumer Finances, 1983. *Fed. Res. Bull.*, September 1984, *70*(9), pp. 679–92. [G: U.S.]

Aziz, Zeti Akhtar. Financial Institutions and Markets in Malaysia. In *Skully, M. T., ed.*, 1984, pp. 110–66. [G: Malaysia]

Bailey, DeeVon; Brorsen, B. Wade and Richardson, James W. Dynamic Stochastic Simulation of Daily Cash and Futures Cotton Prices. *Southern J. Agr. Econ.*, December 1984, *16*(2), pp. 109–16. [G: U.S.]

Baldwin, Bruce A. Segment Earnings Disclosure and the Ability of Security Analysts to Forecast

Earnings Per Share. *Accounting Rev.*, July 1984, *59*(3), pp. 376–89. **[G: U.S.]**

Baldwin, Carliss Y.; Tribendis, Joseph J. and Clark, Joel P. The Evolution of Market Risk in the U.S. Steel Industry and Implications for Required Rates of Return. *J. Ind. Econ.*, September 1984, *33*(1), pp. 73–98. **[G: U.S.]**

Barnes, Tom; Johnson, Keith and Shannon, Don. A Test of Fixed-Income Strategies. *J. Portfol. Manage.*, Winter 1984, *10*(2), pp. 60–65. **[G: U.S.]**

Barry, Christopher B. and Starks, Laura T. Investment Management and Risk Sharing with Multiple Managers. *J. Finance*, June 1984, *39*(2), pp. 477–91.

Barth, Herbert. Financial Futures: Neue Risiken für die Kreditinstitute? (Financial Futures: New Risks for the Banks? With English summary.) *Kredit Kapital*, 1984, *17*(1), pp. 120–45. **[G: U.S.; W. Germany]**

Bathke, Allen W., Jr. and Lorek, Kenneth S. The Relationship between Time-Series Models and the Security Market's Expectation of Quarterly Earnings. *Accounting Rev.*, April 1984, *59*(2), pp. 163–76. **[G: U.S.]**

Beckers, Stan. On the Efficiency of the Gold Options Market. *J. Banking Finance*, September 1984, *8*(3), pp. 459–70. **[G: OECD]**

Beedles, William L. The Anomalous and Asymmetric Nature of Equity Returns: An Empirical Synthesis. *J. Finan. Res.*, Summer 1984, *7*(2), pp. 151–60. **[G: U.S.]**

Behr, Robert M. and Ward, Ronald W. A Simultaneous Equation Model of Futures Trading. *Can. J. Agr. Econ.*, July 1984, *32*(2), pp. 377–98.

Belongia, Michael T. and Gregory, Thomas H. Are Options on Treasury Bond Futures Priced Efficiently? *Fed. Res. Bank St. Louis Rev.*, January 1984, *66*(1), pp. 5–13. **[G: U.S.]**

Belongia, Michael T. and Santoni, G. J. Hedging Interest Rate Risk with Financial Futures: Some Basic Principles. *Fed. Res. Bank St. Louis Rev.*, October 1984, *66*(8), pp. 15–25. **[G: U.S.]**

Benesh, Gary A.; Keown, Arthur J. and Pinkerton, John M. An Examination of Market Reaction to Substantial Shifts in Dividend Policy. *J. Finan. Res.*, Summer 1984, *7*(2), pp. 131–42. **[G: U.S.]**

Berges, Angel; McConnell, John J. and Schlarbaum, Gary G. The Turn-of-the-Year in China. *J. Finance*, March 1984, *39*(1), pp. 185–92. **[G: Canada]**

Bertmar, Lars. Measures of Business Performance—The Swedish Case. In *Holland, D. M.*, ed., 1984, pp. 117–53. **[G: Sweden]**

Bey, Roger P. and Howe, Keith M. Gini's Mean Difference and Portfolio Selection: An Empirical Evaluation. *J. Finan. Quant. Anal.*, September 1984, *19*(3), pp. 329–38. **[G: U.S.]**

Bierwag, G. O.; Kaufman, George G. and Leonard, Paul A. Interest Rate Effects of Commercial Bank Underwriting of Municipal Revenue

Bonds: Additional Evidence. *J. Banking Finance*, March 1984, *8*(1), pp. 35–50. **[G: U.S.]**

Billingsley, Randall S. and Fraser, Donald R. Determinants of Bank Holding Company Debt Ratings. *Financial Rev.*, March 1984, *19*(1), pp. 55–66.

Billingsley, Randall S. and Lamy, Robert E. Market Reaction to the Formation of One-Bank Holding Companies and the 1970 Bank Holding Company Act Amendment. *J. Banking Finance*, March 1984, *8*(1), pp. 21–33. **[G: U.S.]**

Bilson, John F. O. Purchasing Power Parity as a Trading Strategy. *J. Finance*, July 1984, *39*(3), pp. 715–24. **[G: U.S.]**

Bird, Peter J. W. N. Commodities as a Hedge against Inflation. *Appl. Econ.*, December 1984, *16*(6), pp. 855–67. **[G: U.K.]**

Blanchard, Olivier J. and Summers, Lawrence H. Perspectives on High World Real Interest Rates. *Brookings Pap. Econ. Act.*, 1984, (2), pp. 273–324. **[G: U.S.; W. Europe; Japan]**

Blanchard, Olivier J. and Watson, Mark W. Bulles, anticipations rationnelles et marchés financiers. (Bubbles, Rational Expectations, and Financial Markets. With English summary.) *Ann. INSEE*, April–June 1984, (54), pp. 79–100. **[G: U.S.]**

Bland, Robert L. The Interest Savings from Optimizing Issue Size and Frequency of Participation in the Municipal Bond Market. *Public Budg. Finance*, Winter 1984, *4*(4), pp. 53–59. **[G: U.S.]**

Blank, Steven C. Cross-hedging Australian Cattle. *Australian J. Agr. Econ.*, August/December 1984, *28*(2–3), pp. 153–62. **[G: Australia]**

Blinder, Alan S. Perspectives on High World Real Interest Rates: Comment. *Brookings Pap. Econ. Act.*, 1984, (2), pp. 325–33. **[G: U.S.; W. Europe; Japan]**

van den Boogaerde, Pierre. The Private SDR: An Assessment of Its Risk and Return. *Int. Monet. Fund Staff Pap.*, March 1984, *31*(1), pp. 25–61.

Booth, Laurence D. and Johnston, David J. The Ex-Dividend Day Behavior of Canadian Stock Prices: Tax Changes and Clientele Effects. *J. Finance*, June 1984, *39*(2), pp. 457–76. **[G: Canada]**

Borio, C. E. V. A Test of the Mean-Variance Model of Bank Behaviour on Italian Data. *Greek Econ. Rev.*, April 1984, *6*(1), pp. 77–98. **[G: Italy]**

Bortz, Gary A. Does the Treasury Bond Futures Market Destabilize the Treasury Bond Cash Market? *J. Futures Markets*, Spring 1984, *4*(1), pp. 25–38. **[G: U.S.]**

Branch, Ben. Special Offerings and Market Efficiency. *Financial Rev.*, March 1984, *19*(1), pp. 26–35. **[G: U.S.]**

Branch, Ben; Gleit, Alan and Schneeweis, Thomas. The Determinants of Risk and Return for Electric Utility Equity Issues. *Quart. J. Bus. Econ.*, Winter 1984, *23*(1), pp. 16–31. **[G: U.S.]**

Branch, Ben, et al. Contract Proliferation: A Study of the Silver Futures Market. *Rivista Int. Sci. Econ. Com.*, October–November 1984, *31*(10–11), pp. 1058–64. [G: U.S.]

Brannen, Pamela P. and Ulveling, Edwin F. Considering an Informational Role for a Futures Market. *Rev. Econ. Stud.*, January 1984, *51*(1), pp. 33–52. [G: U.S.]

Brenner, Menachem and Galai, Dan. On Measuring the Risk of Common Stocks Implied by Options Prices: A Note. *J. Finan. Quant. Anal.*, December 1984, *19*(4), pp. 403–12. [G: U.S.]

Brodsky, David A. Fixed versus Flexible Exchange Rates and the Measurement of Exchange Rate Instability. *J. Int. Econ.*, May 1984, *16*(3/4), pp. 295–306. [G: Global]

Brooks, LeRoy D.; Edwards, Charles E. and Ferreira, Eurico J. Risk-Return Characteristics of Convertible Preferred Stock: Comment [The Risk Return Performance of Convertible Securities]. *J. Portfol. Manage.*, Winter 1984, *10*(2), pp. 76–78. [G: U.S.]

Brown, Stephen J. Benefits of Bank Diversification: The Evidence from Shareholder Returns: Discussion. *J. Finance*, July 1984, *39*(3), pp. 893–94. [G: U.S.]

Brueggeman, W. B.; Chen, Andrew H. and Thibodeau, T. G. Real Estate Investment Funds: Performance and Portfolio Consideration. *Amer. Real Estate Urban Econ. Assoc. J.*, Fall 1984, *12*(3), pp. 333–54. [G: U.S.]

de la Bruslerie, Hubert. Prévision des taux d'intérêt et des taux de change: une étude empirique à partir de données euro-obligataires. (Rates of Exchange and Interest Forecasting. An Empirical Survey Based on Euro-Bond Data. With English summary.) *Écon. Soc.*, January 1984, *18*(1), pp. 53–89.

Bubnys, Edward L.; Primeaux, Walter J., Jr. and Zumwalt, J. Kenton. Risk and Return under Changing Regulation: An Empirical Analysis. *Managerial Dec. Econ.*, December 1984, *5*(4), pp. 234–41. [G: U.S.]

Bühner, Rolf. Shareholder Wealth, Synergy, and the VEBA/Gelsenberg Merger. *Z. ges. Staatswiss.*, June 1984, *140*(2), pp. 259–75. [G: U.S.; U.K.]

Burgstahler, David. An Application of the Bootstrap Method to the Analysis of Squared, Standardized Market Model Prediction Errors: Discussion. *J. Acc. Res.*, Supplement 1984, *22*, pp. 55–58. [G: U.S.]

Buser, Stephen A. and Hendershott, Patric H. Pricing Default-Free Fixed-Rate Mortgages. *Housing Finance Rev.*, October 1984, *3*(4), pp. 405–29.

Cabanilla, Nathaniel B. Directly-Placed Bonds: A Test of Market Efficiency. *J. Portfol. Manage.*, Winter 1984, *10*(2), pp. 72–74. [G: U.S.]

Cantoni, Renato. Le Borse estere nel 1983. (Foreign Stock Markets in 1983. With English summary.) *Bancaria*, February 1984, *40*(2), pp. 166–77. [G: Selected OECD; Belgium; Italy]

Cantoni, Renato. Le Borse italiane nel 1983. (The Italian Stock Exchange in 1983. With English summary.) *Bancaria*, January 1984, *40*(1), pp. 50–60. [G: Italy]

Cargill, Thomas F. and Meyer, Robert A. Municipal Interest Rates and the Term Structure of Inflationary Expectations. *Financial Rev.*, May 1984, *19*(2), pp. 135–52. [G: U.S.]

Carvell, Steven and Strebel, Paul. A New Beta Incorporating Analysis Forecasts. *J. Portfol. Manage.*, Fall 1984, *11*(1), pp. 81–85. [G: U.S.]

Castelino, Mark G. and Vora, Ashok. Spread Volatility in Commodity Futures: The Length Effect. *J. Futures Markets*, Spring 1984, *4*(1), pp. 39–46. [G: U.S.]

Cesarini, Francesco. Le azioni di risparmio: la prassi. (Savings Shares: Practices and Performance. With English summary.) *Bancaria*, October 1984, *40*(10), pp. 965–78. [G: Italy]

Chambers, Donald R.; Carleton, Willard T. and Waldman, Donald M. A New Approach to Estimation of the Term Structure of Interest Rates. *J. Finan. Quant. Anal.*, September 1984, *19*(3), pp. 233–52. [G: U.S.]

Chang, Eric C. and Lewellen, Wilbur G. Market Timing and Mutual Fund Investment Performance. *J. Bus.*, Part 1, January 1984, *57*(1), pp. 57–72. [G: U.S.]

Chen, Carl R. The Structural Stability of the Market Model after the Three Mile Island Accident. *J. Econ. Bus.*, February 1984, *36*(1), pp. 133–40. [G: U.S.]

Cluff, George S. and Farnham, Paul G. Standard & Poor's vs. Moody's: Which City Characteristics Influence Municipal Bond Ratings? *Quart. Rev. Econ. Bus.*, Autumn 1984, *24*(3), pp. 72–94.

Collins, William A.; Hopwood, William S. and McKeown, James C. The Predictability of Interim Earnings over Alternative Quarters. *J. Acc. Res.*, Autumn 1984, *22*(2), pp. 467–79. [G: U.S.]

Conforti, Antonio. I "financial futures." (Financial Futures. With English summary.) *Bancaria*, May–June 1984, *40*(5–6), pp. 539–47. [G: Italy]

Cook, Thomas J. and Rozeff, Michael S. Coskewness, Dividend Yield, and Capital Asset Pricing. *J. Finan. Res.*, Fall 1984, *7*(3), pp. 231–41. [G: U.S.]

Cook, Thomas J. and Rozeff, Michael S. Size and Earnings/Price Ratio Anomalies: One Effect or Two? *J. Finan. Quant. Anal.*, December 1984, *19*(4), pp. 449–66. [G: U.S.]

Copeland, Basil L., Jr. Inflation, Monetary Policy, and the Equity Risk Premium. In *Foster, J. R., et al., eds.*, 1984, pp. 183–201. [G: U.S.]

Corgel, John B. and Gay, Gerald D. The Impact of GNMA Futures Trading on Cash Market Volatility. *Amer. Real Estate Urban Econ. Assoc. J.*, Summer 1984, *12*(2), pp. 176–90. [G: U.S.]

Cornell, Bradford. Purchasing Power Parity as a Trading Strategy: Discussion. *J. Finance*, July 1984, *39*(3), pp. 724–25.

Cornew, Ronald W.; Town, Donald E. and **Crowson, Lawrence D.** Stable Distributions, Futures Prices, and the Measurement of Trading Performance. *J. Futures Markets,* Winter 1984, *4*(4), pp. 531–57. [G: U.S.]

Cummins, J. David and **Outreville, Jean-François.** The Portfolio Behaviour of Pension Funds in the U.S.: An Econometric Analysis of Changes since the New Regulation of 1974. *Appl. Econ.,* October 1984, *16*(5), pp. 687–701. [G: U.S.]

Curran, Ward S. Inflation and Real Interest Rates on Assets with Different Risk Characteristics: Discussion. *J. Finance,* July 1984, *39*(3), pp. 712–14.

Daley, Lane Alan. The Valuation of Reported Pension Measures for Firms Sponsoring Defined Benefit Plans. *Accounting Rev.,* April 1984, *59*(2), pp. 177–98. [G: U.S.]

Danos, Paul; Holt, Doris L. and **Imhoff, Eugene A., Jr.** Bond Raters' Use of Management Financial Forecasts: Experiment in Expert Judgment. *Accounting Rev.,* October 1984, *59*(4), pp. 547–73. [G: U.S.]

Darr, John K. Interest Rate Swaps. In *Fed. Home Loan Bank San Francisco,* 1984, pp. 231–38. [G: U.S.]

Davidson, Wallace N., III. The Effect of Rate Cases on Public Utility Stock Returns. *J. Finan. Res.,* Spring 1984, *7*(1), pp. 81–93. [G: U.S.]

Davidson, Wallace N., III; Chandy, P. R. and **Walker, Mike.** The Stock Market Effects of Airline Deregulation. *Quart. J. Bus. Econ.,* Autumn 1984, *23*(4), pp. 31–45. [G: U.S.]

Devarajan, Shantayanan and **Hubbard, R. Glenn.** Drawing Down the Strategic Petroleum Reserve: The Case for Selling Futures Contracts. In *Alm, A. L. and Weimer, R. J., eds.,* 1984, pp. 187–96. [G: U.S.]

Dhrymes, Phoebus J. The Empirical Relevance of Arbitrage Pricing Models. *J. Portfol. Manage.,* Summer 1984, *10*(4), pp. 35–44. [G: U.S.]

Dielman, Terry E. and **Oppenheimer, Henry R.** An Examination of Investor Behavior during Periods of Large Dividend Changes. *J. Finan. Quant. Anal.,* June 1984, *19*(2), pp. 197–216. [G: U.S.]

Dietrich, J. Richard. Effects of Early Bond Refunding: An Empirical Investigation of Security Returns. *J. Acc. Econ.,* April 1984, *6*(1), pp. 67–96. [G: U.S.]

Diller, Stanley. Options. In *Fed. Home Loan Bank San Francisco,* 1984, pp. 225–29. [G: U.S.]

Dimson, Elroy and **Marsh, Paul R.** An Analysis of Brokers' and Analysts' Unpublished Forecasts of UK Stock Returns. *J. Finance,* December 1984, *39*(5), pp. 1257–92. [G: U.K.]

Dotan, Amihud and **Ofer, Aharon.** Variable versus Stationary Beta in the Market Model: A Comparative Analysis. *J. Banking Finance,* December 1984, *8*(4), pp. 525–34. [G: U.S.]

Draper, Dennis W. The Behavior of Event-related Contracts. *J. Futures Markets,* Summer 1984, *4*(2), pp. 125–32. [G: U.S.]

Dubofsky, David A. and **Groth, John C.** Exchange Listing and Stock Liquidity. *J. Finan. Res.,* Winter 1984, *7*(4), pp. 291–302. [G: U.S.]

Duvall, Richard M. and **Cheney, John M.** Bond Beta and Default Risk. *J. Finan. Res.,* Fall 1984, *7*(3), pp. 243–54. [G: U.S.]

Dyckman, Thomas R.; Philbrick, Donna and **Stephan, Jens.** A Comparison of Event Study Methodologies Using Daily Stock Returns: A Simulation Approach. *J. Acc. Res.,* Supplement 1984, *22*, pp. 1–30. [G: U.S.]

Eckardt, Walter L., Jr. Equivalent Delivery Procedures for GNMA Futures Contracts and Options. *J. Futures Markets,* Spring 1984, *4*(1), pp. 75–85. [G: U.S.]

Edgar, S. Michael and **Swanson, Peggy E.** The Relationship between Selected Domestic and External Dollar Denominated Asset Yields. *Weltwirtsch. Arch.,* 1984, *120*(3), pp. 454–59. [G: U.S.]

Edwards, Franklin R. The Clearing Association in Futures Markets: Guarantor and Regulator. In *Anderson, R. W., ed.,* 1984, pp. 225–54. [G: U.S.]

Edwards, Linda N. and **Edwards, Franklin R.** A Legal and Economic Analysis of Manipulation in Futures Markets. *J. Futures Markets,* Fall 1984, *4*(3), pp. 333–66. [G: U.S.]

Eisenbeis, Robert A.; Harris, Robert S. and **Lakonishok, Josef.** Benefits of Bank Diversification: The Evidence from Shareholder Returns. *J. Finance,* July 1984, *39*(3), pp. 881–92. [G: U.S.]

Elliott, John; Morse, Dale and **Richardson, Gordon.** The Association between Insider Trading and Information Announcements. *Rand J. Econ.,* Winter 1984, *15*(4), pp. 521–36. [G: U.S.]

Elton, Edwin J.; Gruber, Martin J. and **Gultekin, Mustafa N.** Professional Expectations: Accuracy and Diagnosis of Errors. *J. Finan. Quant. Anal.,* December 1984, *19*(4), pp. 351–63. [G: U.S.]

Elton, Edwin J.; Gruber, Martin J. and **Rentzler, Joel.** Intra-Day Tests of the Efficiency of the Treasury Bill Futures Market. *Rev. Econ. Statist.,* February 1984, *66*(1), pp. 129–37. [G: U.S.]

Elton, Edwin J.; Gruber, Martin J. and **Rentzler, Joel.** The Ex-Dividend Day Behavior of Stock Prices; a Re-Examination of the Clientele Effect: A Comment. *J. Finance,* June 1984, *39*(2), pp. 551–56. [G: U.S.]

Engel, Charles M. Testing for the Absence of Expected Real Profits from Forward Market Speculation. *J. Int. Econ.,* November 1984, *17*(3/4), pp. 299–308. [G: OECD]

Eun, Cheol S. and **Resnick, Bruce G.** Estimating the Correlation Structure of International Share Prices. *J. Finance,* December 1984, *39*(5), pp. 1311–24. [G: OECD]

Fama, Eugene F. Forward and Spot Exchange

Rates. *J. Monet. Econ.*, November 1984, *14*(3), pp. 319–38. **[G: OECD]**

Fama, Eugene F. Term Premiums in Bond Returns. *J. Finan. Econ.*, December 1984, *13*(4), pp. 529–46.

Fama, Eugene F. The Information in the Term Structure. *J. Finan. Econ.*, December 1984, *13*(4), pp. 509–28.

Fatemi, Ali M. Shareholder Benefits from Corporate International Diversification. *J. Finance*, December 1984, *39*(5), pp. 1325–44. **[G: U.S.]**

Fellingham, John C. and Wolfson, Mark A. Progressive Income Taxes and the Demand for Risky Assets. *Nat. Tax J.*, March 1984, *37*(1), pp. 127–29. **[G: U.S.]**

Ferri, Michael G.; Goldstein, Steven J. and Oberhelman, H. Dennis. A Second Look at Day-of-the-Week Effects in Treasury Bill Returns. *Quart. J. Bus. Econ.*, Autumn 1984, *23*(4), pp. 46–56. **[G: U.S.]**

Ferri, Michael G.; Oberhelman, H. Dennis and Roenfeldt, Rodney L. Market Timing and Mutual Fund Portfolio Composition. *J. Finan. Res.*, Summer 1984, *7*(2), pp. 143–50. **[G: U.S.]**

Field, Alexander James. Asset Exchanges and the Transactions Demand for Money, 1919–29. *Amer. Econ. Rev.*, March 1984, *74*(1), pp. 43–59. **[G: U.S.]**

Figlewski, Stephen. Margins and Market Integrity: Margin Setting for Stock Index Futures and Options. *J. Futures Markets*, Fall 1984, *4*(3), pp. 385–416. **[G: U.S.]**

Fischel, Daniel R. and Grossman, Sanford J. Customer Protection in Futures and Securities Markets. *J. Futures Markets*, Fall 1984, *4*(3), pp. 273–95. **[G: U.S.]**

Flannery, Mark J. and James, Christopher M. Market Evidence on the Effective Maturity of Bank Assets and Liabilities. *J. Money, Credit, Banking*, Part 1 November 1984, *16*(4), pp. 435–45. **[G: U.S.]**

Flannery, Mark J. and James, Christopher M. The Effect of Interest Rate Changes on the Common Stock Returns of Financial Institutions. *J. Finance*, September 1984, *39*(4), pp. 1141–53.

Fogler, H. Russell. 20% in Real Estate: Can Theory Justify It? *J. Portfol. Manage.*, Winter 1984, *10*(2), pp. 6–13. **[G: U.S.]**

Forbes, Ronald W. and Leonard, Paul A. The Effects of Statutory Portfolio Constraints on Tax-Exempt Interest Rates: A Note. *J. Money, Credit, Banking*, February 1984, *16*(1), pp. 92–99. **[G: U.S.]**

Foster, Chester and Van Order, Robert. An Option-based Model of Mortgage Default. *Housing Finance Rev.*, October 1984, *3*(4), pp. 351–72. **[G: U.S.]**

Foster, George; Olsen, Chris and Shevlin, Terry. Earnings Releases, Anomalies, and the Behavior of Security Returns. *Accounting Rev.*, October 1984, *59*(4), pp. 574–603. **[G: U.S.]**

Frankel, Jeffrey A. and Engel, Charles M. Do Asset-Demand Functions Optimize over the Mean and Variance of Real Returns? A Six-Currency Test. *J. Int. Econ.*, November 1984, *17*(3/4), pp. 309–23. **[G: OECD]**

Fraser, Donald R. and Richards, R. Malcolm. Prices of Deep Discount Bonds and the Revenue Act of 1978: An Evaluation of Market Response. *J. Econ. Bus.*, August 1984, *36*(3), pp. 323–33. **[G: U.S.]**

French, Dan W. The Weekend Effect on the Distribution of Stock Prices: Implications for Option Pricing. *J. Finan. Econ.*, December 1984, *13*(4), pp. 547–59.

Friedman, Daniel; Harrison, Glenn W. and Salmon, Jon W. The Informational Efficiency of Experimental Asset Markets. *J. Polit. Econ.*, June 1984, *92*(3), pp. 349–408. **[G: U.S.]**

Gay, Gerald D. and Manaster, Steven. The Quality Option Implicit in Futures Contracts. *J. Finan. Econ.*, September 1984, *13*(3), pp. 353–70. **[G: U.S.]**

Gebski, Val and McNeil, Don. A Refined Method of Robust Smoothing. *J. Amer. Statist. Assoc.*, September 1984, *79*(387), pp. 616–23. **[G: Australia]**

Geroski, Paul A. On the Relationship between Aggregate Merger Activity and the Stock Market. *Europ. Econ. Rev.*, July 1984, *25*(2), pp. 223–33. **[G: U.S.]**

Geweke, John F. Measures of Conditional Linear Dependence and Feedback between Time Series. *J. Amer. Statist. Assoc.*, December 1984, *79*(388), pp. 907–15. **[G: U.S.]**

Goh, Leng Y. and Allen, David. A Note on Put-Call Parity and the Market Efficiency of the London Traded Options Market. *Managerial Dec. Econ.*, June 1984, *5*(2), pp. 85–90. **[G: U.K.]**

Goldie, Raymond. Are Some Insiders More "Inside" Than Others? Comment. *J. Portfol. Manage.*, Winter 1984, *10*(2), pp. 75. **[G: U.S.]**

Gordon, Douglas. Performance of Thin Futures Markets: Rice and Sunflower Seed Futures. *Agr. Econ. Res.*, Fall 1984, *36*(4), pp. 1–16. **[G: U.S.]**

Gordon, Kathryn M. and Rausser, Gordon C. Country Hedging for Real Income Stabilization: A Case Study of South Korea and Egypt. *J. Futures Markets*, Winter 1984, *4*(4), pp. 449–64. **[G: S. Korea]**

Graddy, Duane B.; Homaifar, Ghassem and Karna, Adi S. Double Leverage as a Source of Systematic Risk in Bank Holding Company Stocks. *J. Bank Res.*, Summer 1984, *15*(2), pp. 115–22. **[G: U.S.]**

Gray, William S. The Stock Market and the Economy in 1988. *J. Portfol. Manage.*, Summer 1984, *10*(4), pp. 73–80. **[G: U.S.]**

Greenberg, Ralph. Adaptive Estimation: An Alternative to the Traditional Stationarity Assumption. *J. Acc. Res.*, Autumn 1984, *22*(2), pp. 719–30. **[G: U.S.]**

Gressis, N.; Vlahos, G. and Philippatos, George C. A CAPM-Based Analysis of Stock Index Futures. *J. Portfol. Manage.*, Spring 1984, *10*(3), pp. 47–52.

Hagerman, Robert L.; Zmijewski, Mark E. and

Shah, Pravin. The Association between the Magnitude of Quarterly Earnings Forecast Errors and Risk-adjusted Stock Returns. *J. Acc. Res.*, Autumn 1984, *22*(2), pp. 526–40. [G: U.S.]

Hakansson, Nils H.; Kunkel, J. Gregory and Ohlson, James A. A Comment on Verrecchia's No Trading "Theorem." *J. Acc. Res.*, Autumn 1984, *22*(2), pp. 765–67.

Hamaui, Rony. Lo sviluppo dei mercati finanziari in ECU: una prima valutazione su rischi e rendimenti. (The Development of Financial Markets in ECU: An Initial Evaluation Regarding Risks and Yields. With English summary.) *Bancaria*, May–June 1984, *40*(5–6), pp. 513–29. [G: EEC]

Hartman, David G. The International Financial Market and U.S. Interest Rates. *J. Int. Money Finance*, April 1984, *3*(1), pp. 91–103. [G: U.S.; Europe]

Hasbrouck, Joel. Stock Returns, Inflation, and Economic Activity: The Survey Evidence. *J. Finance*, December 1984, *39*(5), pp. 1293–1310. [G: U.S.]

Hayenga, Marvin L., et al. Profitable Hedging Opportunities and Risk Premiums for Producers in Live Cattle and Live Hog Futures Markets. *J. Futures Markets*, Summer 1984, *4*(2), pp. 141–54. [G: U.S.]

Hays, Patrick A.; Kidwell, David S. and Marr, M. Wayne. The Effect of Market Uncertainty on Negotiated and Competitively Underwritten Public Utility Bonds. *Financial Rev.*, November 1984, *19*(4), pp. 339–50. [G: U.S.]

Helms, Billy P.; Kaen, Fred R. and Rosenman, Robert E. Memory in Commodity Futures Contracts. *J. Futures Markets*, Winter 1984, *4*(4), pp. 559–67. [G: U.S.]

Hendershott, Patric H. Expectations, Surprises and Treasury Bill Rates: 1960–82. *J. Finance*, July 1984, *39*(3), pp. 685–96. [G: U.S.]

Hendershott, Patric H. and Ling, David C. Trading and the Tax Shelter Value of Depreciable Real Estate. *Nat. Tax J.*, June 1984, *37*(2), pp. 213–23. [G: U.S.]

Henriksson, Roy D. Market Timing and Mutual Fund Performance: An Empirical Investigation. *J. Bus.*, Part 1, January 1984, *57*(1), pp. 73–96. [G: U.S.]

Herbst, Anthony F. and Ordway, Nicholas O. Stock Index Futures Contracts and Separability of Returns. *J. Futures Markets*, Spring 1984, *4*(1), pp. 87–102. [G: U.S.]

Herring, Richard J. Term Premia on Euro Rates: Discussion. *J. Finance*, July 1984, *39*(3), pp. 755–57. [G: EEC]

Hills, John. Deep Discount Bonds—Or How to Get an Interest-free Loan. *Fisc. Stud.*, August 1984, *5*(3), pp. 62–67. [G: U.K.]

Hite, Gailen L.; Owers, James E. and Rogers, Ronald C. The Separation of Real Estate Operations by Spin-off. *Amer. Real Estate Urban Econ. Assoc. J.*, Fall 1984, *12*(3), pp. 318–32. [G: U.S.]

Howe, John S. and Beedles, William L. Defensive Investing Using Fundamental Data. *J.*

Portfol. Manage., Winter 1984, *10*(2), pp. 14–17. [G: U.S.]

Hsu, D. A. The Behavior of Stock Returns: Is It Stationary or Evolutionary? *J. Finan. Quant. Anal.*, March 1984, *19*(1), pp. 11–28. [G: U.S.]

Hughes Hallett, A. J. Optimal Stockpiling in a High-Risk Commodity Market: The Case of Copper. *J. Econ. Dynam. Control*, November 1984, *8*(2), pp. 211–38. [G: Global]

Hughes, John S. and Ricks, William E. Accounting for Retail Land Sales: Analysis of a Mandated Change. *J. Acc. Econ.*, August 1984, *6*(2), pp. 101–32. [G: U.S.]

Huizinga, John and Mishkin, Frederic S. Inflation and Real Interest Rates on Assets with Different Risk Characteristics. *J. Finance*, July 1984, *39*(3), pp. 699–712. [G: U.S.]

Ibbotson, Roger G. and Siegel, Laurence B. Real Estate Returns: A Comparison with Other Investments. *Amer. Real Estate Urban Econ. Assoc. J.*, Fall 1984, *12*(3), pp. 219–42. [G: U.S.]

Imhoff, Eugene A., Jr. and Lobo, Gerald J. Information Content of Analysts' Composite Forecast Revisions. *J. Acc. Res.*, Autumn 1984, *22*(2), pp. 541–54. [G: U.S.]

Jaffee, Dwight M. The Impact of Financial Futures and Options on Capital Formation. *J. Futures Markets*, Fall 1984, *4*(3), pp. 417–47. [G: U.S.]

Jahera, John S., Jr. and Sinkey, Joseph F., Jr. A Note on the Intracyclical Balance-Sheet Behavior of Large Commercial Banks, 1972–1978. *J. Banking Finance*, March 1984, *8*(1), pp. 109–17. [G: U.S.]

Jarrell, Gregg A. Change at the Exchange: The Causes and Effects of Deregulation. *J. Law Econ.*, October 1984, *27*(2), pp. 273–312. [G: U.S.]

Johnson, James M. When Are Zero Coupon Bonds the Better Buy? *J. Portfol. Manage.*, Spring 1984, *10*(3), pp. 36–41.

Johnson, Lewis D. Sources of Risk and Value in Common Stocks: Comment. *J. Portfol. Manage.*, Spring 1984, *10*(3), pp. 84–85. [G: U.S.]

Jones, Charles P.; Rendleman, Richard J., Jr. and Latané, Henry A. Stock Returns and SUEs during the 1970's. *J. Portfol. Manage.*, Winter 1984, *10*(2), pp. 18–22. [G: U.S.]

Jones, L. R. The WPPSS Default: Trouble in the Municipal Bond Market. *Public Budg. Finance*, Winter 1984, *4*(4), pp. 60–77. [G: U.S.]

Jordan, James V. Tax Effects in Term Structure Estimation. *J. Finance*, June 1984, *39*(2), pp. 393–406. [G: U.S.]

Kaen, Fred R.; Simos, Evangelos O. and Hachey, George A. The Response of Forward Exchange Rates to Interest Rate Forecasting Errors. *J. Finan. Res.*, Winter 1984, *7*(4), pp. 281–90. [G: U.S.]

Kalay, Avner. The Ex-Dividend Day Behavior of Stock Prices; a Re-Examination of the Clientele Effect: A Reply. *J. Finance*, June 1984, 39(2), pp. 556–61. [G: U.S.]

Kalay, Avner and Subrahmanyam, Marti G. The Ex-Dividend Day Behavior of Option Prices. *J. Bus.*, Part 1, January 1984, 57(1), pp. 113–28. [G: U.S.]

Kalt, Joseph P. The Congressional–Bureaucratic System: A Principal–Agent Perspective (with Applications to the SEC): A Comment. *Public Choice*, 1984, 44(1), pp. 193–95. [G: U.S.]

Kane, Alex. Coins: Anatomy of a Fad Asset. *J. Portfol. Manage.*, Winter 1984, 10(2), pp. 44–51. [G: U.S.]

Kane, Alex; Lee, Young Ki and Marcus, Alan J. Earnings and Dividend Announcements: Is There a Corroboration Effect? *J. Finance*, September 1984, 39(4), pp. 1091–99. [G: U.S.]

Kane, Alex and Marcus, Alan J. Conversion Factor Risk and Hedging in the Treasury-Bond Futures Market. *J. Futures Markets*, Spring 1984, 4(1), pp. 55–64. [G: U.S.]

Kane, Edward J. Regulatory Structure in Futures Markets: Jurisdictional Competition between the SEC, the CFTC, and Other Agencies. *J. Futures Markets*, Fall 1984, 4(3), pp. 367–84. [G: U.S.]

Karathanassis, G. The Unlisted Securities Market (USM). An Evaluation of the Aims for Its Formation. *Rivista Int. Sci. Econ. Com.*, October–November 1984, 31(10–11), pp. 1065–72. [G: U.K.]

Kawaller, Ira G. and Koch, Timothy W. Cash-and-Carry Trading and the Pricing of Treasury Bill Futures. *J. Futures Markets*, Summer 1984, 4(2), pp. 115–23. [G: U.S.]

Keim, Donald B. and Stambaugh, Robert F. A Further Investigation of the Weekend Effect in Stock Returns. *J. Finance*, July 1984, 39(3), pp. 819–35. [G: U.S.]

Kellogg, Robert L. Accounting Activities, Security Prices, and Class Action Lawsuits. *J. Acc. Econ.*, December 1984, 6(3), pp. 185–204. [G: U.S.]

Kerrigan, Thomas J. When Forecasting Earnings, It Pays to Watch Forecasts. *J. Portfol. Manage.*, Summer 1984, 10(4), pp. 19–26. [G: U.S.]

Khoury, Sarkis J. Dow Theory Is Alive and Well!: Comment. *J. Portfol. Manage.*, Spring 1984, 10(3), pp. 81–83. [G: U.S.]

Kidwell, David S.; Marr, M. Wayne and Thompson, G. Rodney. SEC Rule 415: The Ultimate Competitive Bid. *J. Finan. Quant. Anal.*, June 1984, 19(2), pp. 183–95. [G: U.S.]

King, Raymond D. The Effect of Convertible Bond Equity Values on Dilution and Leverage. *Accounting Rev.*, July 1984, 59(3), pp. 419–31. [G: U.S.]

Klemkosky, Robert C. and Miller, William P. When Forecasting Earnings, It Pays to Be Right! *J. Portfol. Manage.*, Summer 1984, 10(4), pp. 13–18. [G: U.S.]

Koch, Donald L.; Doyle, Joseph T. and Whitt, Joseph A., Jr. Using Dealer Financing Costs to Forecast Turning Points in the Treasury Bill

Market. *Bus. Econ.*, January 1984, 19(1), pp. 30–39. [G: U.S.]

Kon, Stanley J. Models of Stock Returns—A Comparison. *J. Finance*, March 1984, 39(1), pp. 147–65.

Kopcke, Richard W. and Aldrich, Peter C. A Real Estate Crisis: Averted or Just Postponed? *J. Portfol. Manage.*, Spring 1984, 10(3), pp. 21–29.

Kross, William and Schroeder, Douglas A. An Empirical Investigation of the Effect of Quarterly Earnings Announcement Timing on Stock Returns. *J. Acc. Res.*, Spring 1984, 22(1), pp. 153–76. [G: U.S.]

Lakonishok, Josef and Smidt, Seymour. Volume and Turn-of-the-Year Behavior. *J. Finan. Econ.*, September 1984, 13(3), pp. 435–55.

Lease, Ronald C.; McConnell, John J. and Mikkelson, Wayne H. The Market Value of Differential Voting Rights in Closely Held Corporations. *J. Bus.*, October 1984, 57(4), pp. 443–67. [G: U.S.]

Lee, Chi-Wen Jevons. The Speed of Adjustment of Financial Ratios: An Error-in-Variable Problem. *J. Acc. Res.*, Autumn 1984, 22(2), pp. 776–81. [G: U.S.]

Lee, Sheng-Yi. Financial Institutions and Markets in Singapore. In *Skully, M. T., ed.*, 1984, pp. 226–95. [G: Singapore]

Lee, Sheng-Yi. Issues in Banking and Finance in Singapore. In *Thambipillai, P., ed.*, 1984, pp. 294–307. [G: Singapore]

Levy, Haim. Another Look at the Capital Asset Pricing Model. *Quart. Rev. Econ. Bus.*, Summer 1984, 24(2), pp. 5–32.

Litzenberger, Robert H. and Rolfo, Jacques. An International Study of Tax Effects on Government Bonds. *J. Finance*, March 1984, 39(1), pp. 1–22. [G: W. Germany; Japan; U.K.; U.S.]

Litzenberger, Robert H. and Rolfo, Jacques. Arbitrage Pricing, Transaction Costs and Taxation of Capital Gains: A Study of Government Bonds with the Same Maturity Date. *J. Finan. Econ.*, September 1984, 13(3), pp. 337–51. [G: U.S.]

Liu, Pu and Thakor, Anjan V. Interest Yields, Credit Ratings, and Economic Characteristics of State Bonds: An Empirical Analysis: A Note. *J. Money, Credit, Banking*, August 1984, 16(3), pp. 344–51. [G: U.S.]

Lobo, Gerald J. and Nair, R. D. Predictions of Annual Earnings Using Quarterly Earnings, Annual Earnings, and Dividend Payout Ratios. *Managerial Dec. Econ.*, December 1984, 5(4), pp. 228–33. [G: U.S.]

Lobue, Marie. Categorical Bank Acquisitions. *J. Bank Res.*, Winter 1984, 14(4), pp. 274–82. [G: U.S.]

Lofthouse, Stephen. Assessing UK Government Index-Linked Stock. *Irish Banking Rev.*, September 1984, pp. 57–68. [G: U.K.]

Logue, Dennis E. and Sweeney, Richard James. Term Premia on Euro Rates. *J. Finance*, July 1984, 39(3), pp. 747–55. [G: EEC]

Lorek, Kenneth S. and Bathke, Allen W., Jr. A

Time-Series Analysis of Nonseasonal Quarterly Earnings Data. *J. Acc. Res.*, Spring 1984, 22(1), pp. 369–79. **[G: U.S.]**

Lyon, Andrew B. Money Market Funds and Shareholder Dilution. *J. Finance*, September 1984, 39(4), pp. 1011–20. **[G: U.S.]**

Mankiw, N. Gregory and Summers, Lawrence H. Do Long-Term Interest Rates Overreact to Short-Term Interest Rates? *Brookings Pap. Econ. Act.*, 1984, (1), pp. 223–42. **[G: U.S.]**

Mantell, Edmund H. How to Measure Expected Returns on Foreign Investments. *J. Portfol. Manage.*, Winter 1984, 10(2), pp. 38–43. **[G: U.S.]**

Marais, M. Laurentius. An Application of the Bootstrap Method to the Analysis of Squared, Standardized Market Model Prediction Errors. *J. Acc. Res.*, Supplement 1984, 22, pp. 34–54. **[G: U.S.]**

Marr, M. Wayne and Thompson, G. Rodney. The Influence of Offering Yield on Underwriting Spread. *J. Finan. Res.*, Winter 1984, 7(4), pp. 323–28. **[G: U.S.]**

Martin, Larry J. and Hope, David. Risk and Returns from Alternative Marketing Strategies for Corn Producers. *J. Futures Markets*, Winter 1984, 4(4), pp. 513–30. **[G: Canada]**

McCraw, Thomas K. The Public and Private Spheres in Historical Perspective. In *Brooks, H.; Liebman, L. and Schelling, C. S.*, eds., 1984, pp. 31–60. **[G: U.S.]**

McDonald, Bill and Morris, Michael H. The Relevance of SFAS 33 Inflation Accounting Disclosures in the Adjustment of Stock Prices to Inflation. *Accounting Rev.*, July 1984, 59(3), pp. 432–46. **[G: U.S.]**

McDonald, Bill and Nichols, William D. Nonstationarity of Beta and Tests of Market Efficiency. *J. Finan. Res.*, Winter 1984, 7(4), pp. 315–22. **[G: U.S.]**

McInish, Thomas H. and Wood, Robert A. Intertemporal Differences in Movements of Minute-to-Minute Stock Returns. *Financial Rev.*, November 1984, 19(4), pp. 359–71. **[G: U.S.]**

McKenzie, Joseph A. Who Holds Alternative Market-Yield Accounts? *J. Finan. Res.*, Summer 1984, 7(2), pp. 175–83. **[G: U.S.]**

McLeod, Ross. Financial Institutions and Markets in Indonesia. In *Skully, M. T.*, ed., 1984, pp. 49–109. **[G: Indonesia]**

McWilliams, James D. "Watchman, Tell Us of the Night!" *J. Portfol. Manage.*, Spring 1984, 10(3), pp. 75–80.

Meisner, James F. and Labuszewski, John W. Treasury Bond Futures Delivery Bias. *J. Futures Markets*, Winter 1984, 4(4), pp. 569–77. **[G: U.S.]**

Michas, Nicholas A. Pension Funds: More Diversification. *Can. Public Policy*, March 1984, 10(1), pp. 47–53. **[G: Canada]**

Miles, Mike and McCue, Tom. Commercial Real Estate Returns. *Amer. Real Estate Urban Econ. Assoc. J.*, Fall 1984, 12(3), pp. 355–77. **[G: U.S.]**

Miles, Mike and McCue, Tom. Diversification

in the Real Estate Portfolio. *J. Finan. Res.*, Spring 1984, 7(1), pp. 57–68. **[G: U.S.]**

Modest, David M. On the Pricing of Stock Index Futures. *J. Portfol. Manage.*, Summer 1984, 10(4), pp. 51–57. **[G: U.S.]**

Moran, Michael J. Recent Financing Activity of Nonfinancial Corporations. *Fed. Res. Bull.*, May 1984, 70(5), pp. 401–10. **[G: U.S.]**

Morse, Dale. An Econometric Analysis of the Choice of Daily versus Monthly Returns in Tests of Information Content. *J. Acc. Res.*, Autumn 1984, 22(2), pp. 605–23. **[G: U.S.]**

Morucci, Bernard. Le cheminement vers la richesse: les placements financiers et leurs usages tels que les utilisateurs les perçoivent. (The Road to Riches: Investments, Their Uses and Purposes According to Users. With English summary.) *Écon. Soc.*, November–December 1984, 18(11–12), pp. 265–90. **[G: France]**

Muller, Frederick L.; Fielitz, Bruce D. and Greene, Myron T. Portfolio Performance in Relation to Quality, Earnings, Dividends, Firm Size, Leverage, and Return on Equity. *J. Finan. Res.*, Spring 1984, 7(1), pp. 17–26. **[G: U.S.]**

Mullineaux, Donald J. Expectations, Surprises and Treasury Bill Rates: 1960–82. *J. Finance*, July 1984, 39(3), pp. 696–98.

Murfin, Andy and Ormerod, Paul. The Forward Rate for the U.S. Dollar and the Efficient Markets Hypothesis, 1978–1983. *Manchester Sch. Econ. Soc. Stud.*, September 1984, 52(3), pp. 292–99. **[G: U.S.]**

Neftçi, Salih N. and Policano, Andrew J. Can Chartists Outperform the Market? Market Efficiency Tests for "Technical Analysis." *J. Futures Markets*, Winter 1984, 4(4), pp. 465–78. **[G: U.S.]**

Nordhauser, Fred. Using Stock Index Futures to Reduce Market Risk. *J. Portfol. Manage.*, Spring 1984, 10(3), pp. 56–62.

Osteryoung, Jerome S.; McCarty, Daniel E. and Roberts, Gordon S. Riding a Hedged Yield Curve with Treasury Bill Futures. *J. Bank Res.*, Winter 1984, 14(4), pp. 266–73. **[G: U.S.]**

Page, Daniel E. and Sirmans, C. F. Yield Differences on Fixed and Adjustable Rate Mortgages. *Quart. Rev. Econ. Bus.*, Autumn 1984, 24(3), pp. 18–28. **[G: U.S.]**

Pascual, Alfredo E. Financial Institutions and Markets in the Philippines. In *Skully, M. T.*, ed., 1984, pp. 167–225. **[G: Philippines]**

Patell, James M. and Wolfson, Mark A. The Intraday Speed of Adjustment of Stock Prices to Earnings and Dividend Announcements. *J. Finan. Econ.*, June 1984, 13(2), pp. 223–52. **[G: U.S.]**

Pearce, Douglas K. An Empirical Analysis of Expected Stock Price Movements. *J. Money, Credit, Banking*, August 1984, 16(3), pp. 317–27. **[G: U.S.]**

Peavy, John W., III. Forecasting Industrial Bond Rating Changes: A Multivariate Model. *Rev.*

Bus. Econ. Res., Spring 1984, *19*(2), pp. 46–56. [G: U.S.]

Perquel, Jean-Jacques. Le marché financier en 1983. (With English summary.) *Revue Écon. Polit.*, September–October 1984, *94*(5), pp. 649–61. [G: France]

Perry, Larry G.; Henderson, Glenn V., Jr. and Cronan, Timothy P. Multivariate Analysis of Corporate Bond Ratings and Industry Classifications. *J. Finan. Res.*, Spring 1984, *7*(1), pp. 27–36. [G: U.S.]

Pitts, Mark and Kopprasch, Robert W. Reducing Inter-temporal Risk in Financial Futures Hedging. *J. Futures Markets*, Spring 1984, *4*(1), pp. 1–13. [G: U.S.]

Poterba, James M. and Summers, Lawrence H. New Evidence that Taxes Affect the Valuation of Dividends. *J. Finance*, December 1984, *39*(5), pp. 1397–1415. [G: U.K.]

Rana, Pradumna B. Fixed versus Flexible Exchange Rates and the Measurement of Exchange Rate Instability: Comment. *J. Int. Econ.*, May 1984, *16*(3/4), pp. 307–10. [G: Asia]

Raynauld, Jacques and Tessier, Jacques. Risk Premiums in Futures Markets: An Empirical Investigation. *J. Futures Markets*, Summer 1984, *4*(2), pp. 189–211. [G: U.S.]

Reinganum, Marc R. Valuation Anomalies—Empirical: Discussion: What the Anomalies Mean. *J. Finance*, July 1984, *39*(3), pp. 837–40.

Ricks, William E. A Comparison of Event Study Methodologies Using Daily Stock Returns: A Simulation Approach: Discussion. *J. Acc. Res.*, Supplement 1984, *22*, pp. 31–33. [G: U.S.]

Ritter, Jay R. The "Hot Issue" Market of 1980. *J. Bus.*, April 1984, *57*(2), pp. 215–40. [G: U.S.]

Roberts, Gordon S. and Viscione, Jerry A. Note on Who Pays the Agency Costs of Debt. *Financial Rev.*, May 1984, *19*(2), pp. 232–39.

Roberts, Gordon S. and Viscione, Jerry A. The Impact of Seniority and Security Covenants on Bond Yields: A Note. *J. Finance*, December 1984, *39*(5), pp. 1597–1602. [G: U.S.]

Rogalski, Richard J. A Further Investigation of the Weekend Effect in Stock Returns. *J. Finance*, July 1984, *39*(3), pp. 835–37. [G: U.S.]

Rogalski, Richard J. New Findings Regarding Day-of-the-Week Returns over Trading and Non-trading Periods: A Note. *J. Finance*, December 1984, *39*(5), pp. 1603–14. [G: U.S.]

Rogers, Ronald C. and Owers, James E. The Impact of Value Line Special Situation Recommendations on Stock Prices. *Financial Rev.*, May 1984, *19*(2), pp. 195–207.

Roll, Richard. Orange Juice and Weather. *Amer. Econ. Rev.*, December 1984, *74*(5), pp. 861–80. [G: U.S.]

Rosania, Luca. Regime di capitalizzazione nei calcoli finanziari e corso ex estrazione dei titoli a reddito fisso. (Capitalization Method for Calculation of Ex-Redemption Quotations of Fixed-Interest Securities Drawn for Redemption.

With English summary.) *Bancaria*, January 1984, *40*(1), pp. 61–73. [G: Italy]

Rosenberg, Barr. Prediction of Common Stock Investment Risk. *J. Portfol. Manage.*, Fall 1984, *11*(1), pp. 44–53. [G: U.S.]

Rosenfeld, James D. Additional Evidence on the Relation between Divestiture Announcements and Shareholder Wealth. *J. Finance*, December 1984, *39*(5), pp. 1437–48. [G: U.S.]

Rosenfeld, James D. Returns on High-Quality and Low-Quality Preferred Stocks in Periods of Common-Stock Dividend Reductions. *J. Finan. Res.*, Fall 1984, *7*(3), pp. 255–58. [G: U.S.]

Ross, Stephen A. Reply to Dhrymes: APT *Is* Empirically Relevant. *J. Portfol. Manage.*, Fall 1984, *11*(1), pp. 54–56. [G: U.S.]

Rozeff, Michael S. Dividend Yields Are Equity Risk Premiums. *J. Portfol. Manage.*, Fall 1984, *11*(1), pp. 68–75. [G: U.S.]

Ruback, Richard S. and Zimmerman, Martin B. Unionization and Profitability: Evidence from the Capital Market. *J. Polit. Econ.*, December 1984, *92*(6), pp. 1134–57. [G: U.S.]

Rutterford, Janette. The UK Corporate Bond Market: Prospects for Revival. *Nat. Westminster Bank Quart. Rev.*, May 1984, pp. 17–32. [G: U.K.]

Sanderson, Paul. Rational Expectations and Forward Exchange Market Efficiency. *Appl. Econ.*, February 1984, *16*(1), pp. 99–109. [G: Canada; U.K.; W. Germany]

Savona, Paolo. Banca e borsa. Aspetti internazionali. (Banks and Stock Market: International Impact. With English summary.) *Bancaria*, November 1984, *40*(11), pp. 1076–81. [G: U.S.; Italy]

Schmidt, Hartmut. Disclosure, Insider Information and Capital Market Functions. In *Hopt, K. J. and Teubner, G., eds.*, 1984, pp. 338–53.

Schmidt, Hartmut. Venture-Capital-Märkte in Europa. (Venture Capital Markets in Europe. With English summary.) *Kredit Kapital*, 1984, *17*(2), pp. 281–96. [G: Europe]

Schreuder, Hein and Klaassen, Jan. Confidential Revenue and Profit Forecasts by Management and Financial Analysts: Evidence from The Netherlands. *Accounting Rev.*, January 1984, *59*(1), pp. 64–77. [G: Netherlands]

Scott, Louis O. The Stationarity of the Conditional Mean of Real Rates of Return on Common Stocks: An Empirical Investigation. *J. Finan. Quant. Anal.*, June 1984, *19*(2), pp. 217–30. [G: U.S.]

Settle, John W.; Petry, Glenn H. and Hsia, Chi-Cheng. Synergy, Diversification, and Incentive Effects of Corporate Merger on Bondholder Wealth: Some Evidence. *J. Finan. Res.*, Winter 1984, *7*(4), pp. 329–39. [G: U.S.]

Shefrin, Hersh M. Inferior Forecasters, Cycles, and the Efficient-Markets Hypothesis: A Comment [Market 'Efficiency' in a Market with Heterogeneous Information]. *J. Polit. Econ.*, February 1984, *92*(1), pp. 156–61.

Simon, Yves. Les marchés à terme de produits

pétroliers. (Futures Markets of Oil Products. With English summary.) *L'Actual. Econ.*, September 1984, *60*(3), pp. 375–406.   [G: U.S.; U.K.]

Singleton, J. Clay and Grieves, Robin. Synthetic Puts and Portfolio Insurance Strategies. *J. Portfol. Manage.*, Spring 1984, *10*(3), pp. 63–69.

Skully, Michael T. Financial Institutions and Markets in Thailand. In *Skully, M. T., ed.*, 1984, pp. 296–378.   [G: Thailand]

Smith, Donald J. Individual Retirement Accounts and Intermediate Term Holding Periods. *Financial Rev.*, November 1984, *19*(4), pp. 381–87.

Soldofsky, Robert M. Reply [The Risk Return Performance of Convertible Securities]. *J. Portfol. Manage.*, Winter 1984, *10*(2), pp. 79–80.   [G: U.S.]

Soldofsky, Robert M. Risk and Return for Long-term Securities: 1971–1982. *J. Portfol. Manage.*, Fall 1984, *11*(1), pp. 57–64.   [G: U.S.]

Srivastava, Rajendra K.; McInish, Thomas H. and Price, Linda L. Information Costs and Portfolio Selection. *J. Banking Finance*, September 1984, *8*(3), pp. 417–29.   [G: U.S.]

Statman, Meir. Growth Opportunities vs. Growth Stocks. *J. Portfol. Manage.*, Spring 1984, *10*(3), pp. 70–74.

Stock, Duane R. and Schrems, Edward L. Municipal Bond Demand Premiums and Bond Price Volatility: A Note. *J. Finance*, June 1984, *39*(2), pp. 535–39.   [G: U.S.]

Stock, Duane R. and Schrems, Edward L. Return and Price Volatility of Bonds with Different Credit Risk. *J. Econ. Bus.*, August 1984, *36*(3), pp. 291–306.   [G: U.S.]

Stoll, Hans R. The Clearing Association in Futures Markets: Guarantor and Regulator: Comment. In *Anderson, R. W., ed.*, 1984, pp. 257–59.   [G: U.S.]

Stone, James M. The Clearing Association in Futures Markets: Guarantor and Regulator: Comment. In *Anderson, R. W., ed.*, 1984, pp. 255–56.   [G: U.S.]

Sturgess, Brian T. and Wheale, Peter. Merger Performance Evaluation: An Empirical Analysis of a Sample of UK Firms. *J. Econ. Stud.*, 1984, *11*(4), pp. 33–45.   [G: U.K.]

Tehranian, Hassan and Bruning, Edward R. Deregulation and Investor Perception of Motor Carrier Securities. *Logist. Transp. Rev.*, June 1984, *20*(2), pp. 165–86.   [G: U.S.]

Terrebonne, R. Peter. Modeling the Primary Aluminum Spot Market. *Bus. Econ.*, January 1984, *19*(1), pp. 53–60.   [G: OECD]

Theobald, Michael F. and Price, Vera. Seasonality Estimation in Thin Markets. *J. Finance*, June 1984, *39*(2), pp. 377–92.   [G: U.S.]

Tinic, Seha M. and West, Richard R. Risk and Return: January vs. the Rest of the Year. *J. Finan. Econ.*, December 1984, *13*(4), pp. 561–74.

Trainer, Francis H., Jr.; Levine, David A. and Reiss, Jonathan A. A Systematic Approach to

Bond Management in Pension Funds. *J. Portfol. Manage.*, Spring 1984, *10*(3), pp. 30–35.

Tukey, Paul A. and Wachter, Kenneth W. A Demographic Analogy for Shareowner Accounts. *J. Amer. Statist. Assoc.*, September 1984, *79*(387), pp. 525–30.   [G: U.S.]

Urich, Thomas J. and Wachtel, Paul. The Effects of Inflation and Money Supply Announcements on Interest Rates. *J. Finance*, September 1984, *39*(4), pp. 1177–88.   [G: U.S.]

Veit, E. Theodore and Cheney, John M. Managing Investment Portfolios: A Survey of Mutual Funds. *Financial Rev.*, November 1984, *19*(4), pp. 321–38.   [G: U.S.]

Vignola, Anthony J. Financial Futures. In *Fed. Home Loan Bank San Francisco*, 1984, pp. 217–22.   [G: U.S.]

Vock, Thomas and Zimmermann, Heinz. Risiken und Renditen schweizerischer Aktien. (Risk and Return on Swiss Stocks. With English summary.) *Schweiz. Z. Volkswirtsch. Statist.*, December 1984, *120*(4), pp. 547–76.
    [G: Switzerland]

Waymire, Gregory. Additional Evidence on the Information Content of Management Earnings Forecasts. *J. Acc. Res.*, Autumn 1984, *22*(2), pp. 703–18.   [G: U.S.]

Weingast, Barry R. The Congressional–Bureaucratic System: A Principal–Agent Perspective (with Application to the SEC). *Public Choice*, 1984, *44*(1), pp. 147–91.   [G: U.S.]

Weiss, Laurence. Do Long-Term Interest Rates Overreact to Short-Term Interest Rates? Comments. *Brookings Pap. Econ. Act.*, 1984, (1), pp. 243–45.   [G: U.S.]

Welch, Paul R. A Generalized Distributed Lag Model for Predicting Quarterly Earnings. *J. Acc. Res.*, Autumn 1984, *22*(2), pp. 744–57.
    [G: U.S.]

Wellington, Donald C. and Gallo, Joseph C. Investment in a Small Antique. *J. Cult. Econ.*, December 1984, *8*(2), pp. 93–98.   [G: U.S.]

Wescott, Shari H. Accounting Numbers and Socioeconomic Variables as Predictors of Municipal General Obligation Bond Ratings. *J. Acc. Res.*, Spring 1984, *22*(1), pp. 412–23.

Wilson, Earl R. and Howard, Thomas P. The Association between Municipal Market Measures and Selected Financial Reporting Practices: Additional Evidence. *J. Acc. Res.*, Spring 1984, *22*(1), pp. 207–24.   [G: U.S.]

Wong, K. A. and Kwong, K. S. The Behaviour of Hong Kong Stock Prices. *Appl. Econ.*, December 1984, *16*(6), pp. 905–17.
    [G: Hong Kong]

Yun, Young-Sup. The Effects of Inflation and Income Taxes on Interest Rates: Some New Evidence. *J. Finan. Quant. Anal.*, December 1984, *19*(4), pp. 425–48.   [G: U.S.]

Zeghal, Daniel. Firm Size and the Informational Content of Financial Statements. *J. Finan. Quant. Anal.*, September 1984, *19*(3), pp. 299–310.   [G: U.S.]

Zerbst, Robert H. and Cambon, Barbara R. Real Estate: Historical Returns and Risks. *J. Portfol. Manage.*, Spring 1984, *10*(3), pp. 5–20.

314 Financial Intermediaries

3140 Financial Intermediaries

Adam, M. C.; Thys-Clement, F. and Van Regemorter, D. La modélisation des intermédiaires fianciers non monétaires en Belgique: méthodologie et premiers résultats. (With English summary.) *Cah. Écon. Bruxelles*, 2nd Trimester 1984, (102), pp. 202–42. [G: Belgium]

Aziz, Zeti Akhtar. Financial Institutions and Markets in Malaysia. In *Skully, M. T., ed.*, 1984, pp. 110–66. [G: Malaysia]

Bain, Andrew D. and Reid, Richard G. The Finance Sector. In *Hood, N. and Young, S., eds.*, 1984, pp. 365–89. [G: U.K.]

Belongia, Michael T. and Santoni, G. J. Hedging Interest Rate Risk with Financial Futures: Some Basic Principles. *Fed. Res. Bank St. Louis Rev.*, October 1984, 66(8), pp. 15–25. [G: U.S.]

Benston, George J. The Effects of Regulation. In *Fed. Res. Bank Atlanta*, 1984, pp. 125–37. [G: U.S.]

Blackwell, John. Housing Finance in Ireland in the 1980s. *Irish Banking Rev.*, December 1984, pp. 69–84. [G: Ireland]

Bodkin, Ronald G. Comments [Indexed Bonds as an Instrument of Pension Reform] [Registered Pension Accounts (RPAs) as an Instrument of Pension Reform]. In *Conklin, D. W.; Bennett, J. H. and Courchene, T. J., eds.*, 1984, pp. 401–05. [G: Canada]

Booth, James R.; Smith, Richard L., II and Stolz, Richard W. Use of Interest Rate Futures by Financial Institutions. *J. Bank Res.*, Spring 1984, 15(1), pp. 15–20. [G: U.S.]

Booth, James R. and Smith, Richard L., II. The Impact of the Community Reinvestment Act on Branching Activity of Financial Institutions. *J. Bank Res.*, Summer 1984, 15(2), pp. 123–28. [G: U.S.]

Brauer, Greggory A. 'Open-ending' Closed-End Funds. *J. Finan. Econ.*, December 1984, 13(4), pp. 491–507.

Calderón-Rossell, Jorge R. Optimal Financial Structure of Finance Companies in a Regulated Environment of a Developing Country. *J. Banking Finance*, September 1984, 8(3), pp. 443–57. [G: LDCs]

Campbell, Tim S. The Case for Mergers of Depository Institutions and Insurance Companies. In *Fed. Home Loan Bank San Francisco*, 1984, pp. 175–94. [G: U.S.]

Campbell, Tim S. and Glenn, David. Deposit Insurance in a Deregulated Environment. *J. Finance*, July 1984, 39(3), pp. 775–85. [G: U.S.]

Campbell, Tim S. and Horvitz, Paul M. Reform of the Deposit Insurance System: An Appraisal of the FHLBB and FDIC Studies. *Contemp. Policy Issue*, May 1984, (6), pp. 56–68. [G: U.S.]

Carron, Andrew S. The Australian Financial System. In *Caves, R. E. and Krause, L. B., eds.*, 1984, pp. 195–229. [G: Australia]

Causse, Jean. Necessity of and Constraints on the Use of Savings in the Community in Which They Are Collected. In *Kessler, D. and Ullmo, P.-A., eds.*, 1984, pp. 153–81.

Cingano, Francesco. Lineamenti per un profilo del nostro sistema bancario. (An Outline of the Italian Banking-System. With English summary.) *Bancaria*, September 1984, 40(9), pp. 845–55. [G: Italy]

Ciocca, Pierluigi and Toniolo, Gianni. Industry and Finance in Italy, 1918–1940. *J. Europ. Econ. Hist.*, Special Issue 1984, 13(2), pp. 113–36. [G: Italy]

Claggett, E. Tylor and Stansell, Stanley R. Economies of Scale in a Cooperative Financial System: A Study of Production Credit Associations. *Quart. J. Bus. Econ.*, Spring 1984, 23(2), pp. 20–46. [G: U.S.]

Clair, Robert T. Deposit Insurance, Moral Hazard, and Credit Unions. *Fed. Res. Bank Dallas Econ. Rev.*, July 1984, pp. 1–12.

Colton, Kent W. and Cunningham, Donald F. The Role of the Secondary Mortgage Markets in Managing Risk. In *Fed. Home Loan Bank San Francisco*, 1984, pp. 125–55. [G: U.S.]

Cook, Thomas J. and D'Antonio, Louis J. Credit Union Taxation: Competitive Effects. *J. Econ. Bus.*, May 1984, 36(2), pp. 251–62. [G: U.S.]

Cortes, Diane L. Are Lenders Inviting Reregulation by Inadequate Disclosure Practices? *Housing Finance Rev.*, April 1984, 3(2), pp. 201–08. [G: U.S.]

Cox, Edwin B. Integrated Financial Services. In *Fed. Res. Bank Atlanta*, 1984, pp. 17–23. [G: U.S.]

Cummins, J. David and Outreville, Jean-François. The Portfolio Behaviour of Pension Funds in the U.S.: An Econometric Analysis of Changes since the New Regulation of 1974. *Appl. Econ.*, October 1984, 16(5), pp. 687–701. [G: U.S.]

Darr, John K. Interest Rate Swaps. In *Fed. Home Loan Bank San Francisco*, 1984, pp. 231–38. [G: U.S.]

Daubrey, Auguste. Mobilization of Savings for Rural Development in Africa. In *Kessler, D. and Ullmo, P.-A., eds.*, 1984, pp. 231–37.

Davis, Kevin. Financial Regulation in Australia. *Australian Econ. Rev.*, 3rd Quarter 1984, (67), pp. 135–46. [G: Australia]

De Vany, Arthur S. Modeling the Banking Firm: A Survey: Comment. *J. Money, Credit, Banking*, Part 2 November 1984, 16(4), pp. 603–09.

Deguefe, Taffara. Financial Institutions and Rural Development in Africa. In *Kessler, D. and Ullmo, P.-A., eds.*, 1984, pp. 205–16.

Diamond, Douglas W. Financial Intermediation and Delegated Monitoring. *Rev. Econ. Stud.*, July 1984, 51(3), pp. 393–414.

Diller, Stanley. Options. In *Fed. Home Loan Bank San Francisco*, 1984, pp. 225–29. [G: U.S.]

Disharoon, Leslie B. Implications for Strategic

Planning: Discussion. In *Sametz, A. W., ed.*, 1984, pp. 129–30. [G: U.S.]

Eisenbeis, Robert A. Impulsi di innovazione nei servizi finanziari. (Forces for Change in the Financial Service Industry. With English summary.) *Bancaria*, March 1984, *40*(3), pp. 266–71. [G: U.S.]

Elliott, John C. Nonbanks. In *Fed. Res. Bank Atlanta*, 1984, pp. 81–90. [G: U.S.]

Elyasiani, Elyas. The Multiproduct Deopository Firm, Interest-bearing Transaction Balances, Interest-bearing Reserves, and Uncertainty. *Bull. Econ. Res.*, November 1984, *36*(2), pp. 173–93. [G: U.S.]

Felgran, Steven D. Bank Entry into Securities Brokerage: Competitive and Legal Aspects. *New Eng. Econ. Rev.*, November–December 1984, pp. 12–33. [G: U.S.]

Felgran, Steven D. Shared ATM Networks: Market Structure and Public Policy. *New Eng. Econ. Rev.*, January–February 1984, pp. 23–38. [G: U.S.]

Finn, Frank J. and Ziegler, Peter. The Investment Obligations of a Superannuation Fund Trustee and the Commissioner's Discretions. *Australian Tax Forum*, December 1984, *1*(4), pp. 401–11. [G: Australia]

Ford, William F. Product Diversification. In *Fed. Home Loan Bank San Francisco*, 1984, pp. 55–60. [G: U.S.]

Gilbert, R. Alton and Holland, A. Steven. Has the Deregulation of Deposit Interest Rates Raised Mortgage Rates? *Fed. Res. Bank St. Louis Rev.*, May 1984, *66*(5), pp. 5–15. [G: U.S.]

Goldfeld, Stephen M. Modeling the Banking Firm: A Survey: Comment. *J. Money, Credit, Banking*, Part 2 November 1984, *16*(4), pp. 609–16.

Gramley, Lyle E. Statement to the U.S. House Subcommitte on Commerce, Consumer, and Monetary Affairs of the Government Operations Committee, March 14, 1984. *Fed. Res. Bull.*, April 1984, *70*(4), pp. 291–94. [G: U.S.]

Gray, Edwin J. Federal Home Loan Bank of San Francisco: Proceedings of the Ninth Annual Conference: Remarks. In *Fed. Home Loan Bank San Francisco*, 1984, pp. 63–65. [G: U.S.]

Gregg, William P. The Impact of Diversification of the Financial Services Industry on Strategic Planning. In *Sametz, A. W., ed.*, 1984, pp. 123–26.

Gurwitz, Aaron S. and Rappaport, Julie N. Structural Change and Slower Employment Growth in the Financial Services Sector. *Fed. Res. Bank New York Quart. Rev.*, Winter 1984–85, *9*(4), pp. 39–45. [G: U.S.]

Hadaway, Beverly L. and Hadaway, Samuel C. Implications of Savings and Loan Conversions in a Deregulated World. *J. Bank Res.*, Spring 1984, *15*(1), pp. 44–55. [G: U.S.]

Hannan, Timothy H. Competition between Commercial Banks and Thrift Institutions: An Empirical Examination. *J. Bank Res.*, Spring 1984, *15*(1), pp. 8–14. [G: U.S.]

Harper, Ian R. Financial Regulation in Australia: Comment. *Australian Econ. Rev.*, 3rd Quarter 1984, (67), pp. 151–52. [G: Australia]

Hartzog, Jerry. Market Value Decisionmaking. In *Fed. Home Loan Bank San Francisco*, 1984, pp. 197–209. [G: U.S.]

Henderson, John P. Ricardo and the Provident Institutions. In *Samuels, W. J., ed.*, 1984, pp. 65–76. [G: U.K.]

Holst, Juergen U. The Role of Informal Financial Institutions in the Mobilization of Savings. In *Kessler, D. and Ullmo, P.-A., eds.*, 1984, pp. 121–52. [G: LDCs]

Horvitz, Paul M. Deposit Insurance after Deregulation: A Residual Role for Regulation. In *Fed. Home Loan Bank San Francisco*, 1984, pp. 67–94. [G: U.S.]

Horvitz, Paul M. Deposit Insurance in a Deregulated Environment: Discussion. *J. Finance*, July 1984, *39*(3), pp. 785–87. [G: U.S.]

Horvitz, Paul M. Payments and Deregulation. In *Fed. Res. Bank Atlanta*, 1984, pp. 163–68. [G: U.S.]

Huertas, Thomas F. An Economic Brief against Glass–Steagall. *J. Bank Res.*, Autumn 1984, *15*(3), pp. 148–59. [G: U.S.]

Humphrey, David B. Future Networks and the Fed's Role. In *Fed. Res. Bank Atlanta*, 1984, pp. 67–79. [G: U.S.]

Humphrey, Joseph F. Changing Asset/Liability Structure of Savings Institutions in a Deregulated Environment. *Contemp. Policy Issue*, May 1984, (6), pp. 45–55. [G: U.S.]

Jacoby, Jacob. Implications for Insurance Products and Services: Discussion. In *Sametz, A. W., ed.*, 1984, pp. 69–72. [G: U.S.]

Jones, Colin. The Future of Building Societies. *Nat. Westminster Bank Quart. Rev.*, May 1984, pp. 33–46. [G: U.K.]

Julien, Pierre-André; Thibodeau, Jean-Claude and Mathews, Georges. Les nouvelles technologies et l'emploi au Québec. (New Technologies and Employement: Textile, Pulp and Paper, and Savings and Credit Institutions Industries. With English summary.) *L'Actual. Econ.*, September 1984, *60*(3), pp. 326–40.

Jump, G. V. Financing Public Pensions: Some Capital Market Implications. In *Conklin, D. W.; Bennett, J. H. and Courchene, T. J., eds.*, 1984, pp. 295–326. [G: Canada]

Kane, Edward J. Technological and Regulatory Forces in the Developing Fusion of Financial-Services Competition. *J. Finance*, July 1984, *39*(3), pp. 759–72. [G: U.S.]

Kaufman, Henry. Financial Institutions and the Fragile, Volatile Financial Markets. In *Sametz, A. W., ed.*, 1984, pp. 21–27.

Kidwell, David S. Technological and Regulatory Forces in the Developing Fusion of Financial-Services Competition: Discussion. *J. Finance*, July 1984, *39*(3), pp. 772–73.

King, Thomas. Thrift Institution Deposits: The Influence of MMCs and MMMFs: A Note. *J.*

Money, Credit, Banking, August 1984, *16*(3), pp. 328–34. [G: U.S.]

Lee, Sheng-Yi. Financial Institutions and Markets in Singapore. In *Skully, M. T., ed.,* 1984, pp. 226–95. [G: Singapore]

Lee, Sheng-Yi. Issues in Banking and Finance in Singapore. In *Thambipillai, P., ed.,* 1984, pp. 294–307. [G: Singapore]

Leveson, Irving. Restructuring Financial Institutions in the New Financial Environment: Discussion. In *Sametz, A. W., ed.,* 1984, pp. 33–37. [G: U.S.]

Levy, Gerald J. The Secondary Mortgage Market: Amelioration of Risk. In *Fed. Home Loan Bank San Francisco,* 1984, pp. 49–53. [G: U.S.]

Lindley, James T.; Selby, Edward B., Jr. and Jackson, John D. Racial Discrimination in the Provision of Financial Services. *Amer. Econ. Rev.,* September 1984, *74*(4), pp. 735–41. [G: U.S.]

Lipstein, Benjamin. Marketing Financial Services. In *Sametz, A. W., ed.,* 1984, pp. 49–54. [G: U.S.]

Litvak, Larry. Pension Funds and Economic Development. In *Bingham, R. D. and Blair, J. P., eds.,* 1984, pp. 191–98.

Lovett, William A. The Revolution in U.S. Banking. *Challenge,* November/December 1984, *27*(5), pp. 41–46. [G: U.S.]

Lyon, Andrew B. Money Market Funds and Shareholder Dilution. *J. Finance,* September 1984, *39*(4), pp. 1011–20. [G: U.S.]

Marlow, Michael L.; Link, John P. and Trost, Robert P. Market Structure and Rivalry: New Evidence with a Non-linear Model. *Rev. Econ. Statist.,* November 1984, *66*(4), pp. 678–82. [G: U.S.]

Marr, M. Wayne and Thompson, G. Rodney. The Influence of Offering Yield on Underwriting Spread. *J. Finan. Res.,* Winter 1984, 7(4), pp. 323–28. [G: U.S.]

Marreiros, Luis. Contribution to the Comparative Study of Savings Trends in Latin America: 1973–1983. In *Kessler, D. and Ullmo, P.-A., eds.,* 1984, pp. 281–309. [G: Latin America]

Martin, Preston. Statement to the U.S. House Subcommittee on Financial Institutions Supervision, Regulation and Insurance of the Committee on Banking, Finance and Urban Affairs, April 4, 1984. *Fed. Res. Bull.,* April 1984, *70*(4), pp. 319–24. [G: U.S.]

Massey, Pat. The Role of Building Societies in Irish Financial Markets. *Irish Banking Rev.,* March 1984, pp. 6–17. [G: Ireland]

McLeod, Ross. Financial Institutions and Markets in Indonesia. In *Skully, M. T., ed.,* 1984, pp. 49–109. [G: Indonesia]

Meckler, John M. Bank Cash Management Services. In *Fed. Res. Bank Atlanta,* 1984, pp. 27–33. [G: U.S.]

Melnikoff, Meyer. A Note on the Dawn of Property Investment by American Pension Funds. *Amer. Real Estate Urban Econ. Assoc. J.,* Fall 1984, *12*(3), pp. 401–07. [G: U.S.]

Merrill, Peter. Winners and Losers in the Network Race. In *Fed. Res. Bank Atlanta,* 1984, pp. 93–99. [G: U.S.]

Merusi, Fabio. Sulla riforma delle casse di risparmio e dei monti di credito su pegno. (Reform of Savings Banks. With English summary.) *Bancaria,* July 1984, *40*(7), pp. 633–51. [G: Italy]

Michas, Nicholas A. Pension Funds: More Diversification. *Can. Public Policy,* March 1984, *10*(1), pp. 47–53. [G: Canada]

Miles, Mike and McCue, Tom. Commercial Real Estate Returns. *Amer. Real Estate Urban Econ. Assoc. J.,* Fall 1984, *12*(3), pp. 355–77. [G: U.S.]

Mintz, Jack. The Effect of Pension Funding on Investment, Savings, and Financial Intermediation. In *Conklin, D. W.; Bennett, J. H. and Courchene, T. J., eds.,* 1984, pp. 392–400. [G: Canada]

Murphy, Neil B. and Rogers, Ronald C. The Line of Commerce in Retail Financial Institution Mergers: Some Evidence from Consumer Data in New England. *J. Bank Res.,* Spring 1984, *15*(1), pp. 21–25. [G: U.S.]

Nadler, Paul S. The Future of Savings Institutions in an Environment of Risk. In *Fed. Home Loan Bank San Francisco,* 1984, pp. 15–21. [G: U.S.]

Nesi, Nerio. Competitività, innovazione ed efficienza nel sistema finanziario italiano. (Competitiveness, Innovation and Efficiency in the Italian Financial System. With English summary.) *L'Impresa,* 1984, *26*(2), pp. 13–18. [G: Italy]

Neubig, Thomas S. The Taxation of Financial Institutions after Deregulation. *Nat. Tax J.,* September 1984, *37*(3), pp. 351–59. [G: U.S.]

Nothaft, Frank E. ARM Debt Outstanding by Lender Type and Firm Size. *Housing Finance Rev.,* October 1984, *3*(4), pp. 447–55. [G: U.S.]

Orlando, Luigi. Mercati e intermediari finanziari: esigenze delle imprese. (Financial Markets and Intermediation: Business Requirements. With English summary.) *Bancaria,* May–June 1984, *40*(5–6), pp. 473–78. [G: Italy]

Oteri, Carmelo. The Reform of Bank Shareholdings: Assumptions, Objectives, Implementation and Future Prospects. In *Banca d'Italia,* 1984, pp. 213–27. [G: Italy]

Ozanne, Larry. The Financial Stakes in Due-on-Sale: The Case of California's State-chartered Savings and Loans. *Amer. Real Estate Urban Econ. Assoc. J.,* Winter 1984, *12*(4), pp. 473–94. [G: U.S.]

Pascual, Alfredo E. Financial Institutions and Markets in the Philippines. In *Skully, M. T., ed.,* 1984, pp. 167–225. [G: Philippines]

Passacantando, Franco. Costs and Margins in the Italian Banking System: A Comparative Analysis. In *Banca d'Italia,* 1984, pp. 41–59. [G: OECD]

Peters, Helen Frame. Asset/Liability Analysis. In

Fed. Home Loan Bank San Francisco, 1984, pp. 211–15.   [G: U.S.]

Ramakrishnan, Ram T. S. and Thakor, Anjan V. Information Reliability and a Theory of Financial Intermediation. *Rev. Econ. Stud.*, July 1984, *51*(3), pp. 415–32.

Ranieri, Lewis S. Financial Markets and Risk Management. In *Fed. Home Loan Bank San Francisco*, 1984, pp. 5–13.   [G: U.S.]

Reed, David S. Implications for Strategic Planning: Discussion. In *Sametz, A. W., ed.*, 1984, pp. 127–28.

Rhoades, Stephen A. and White, Alice P. Output in Relation to Labor Input in the Banking and Savings and Loan Industries, 1927–1979. *J. Banking Finance*, March 1984, *8*(1), pp. 119–30.   [G: U.S.]

Roessner, Gilbert G. New Views on an Old Problem: Interest Rate Risk and Related Issues. In *Fed. Home Loan Bank San Francisco*, 1984, pp. 31–47.   [G: U.S.]

del Rosario, Ramon R., Jr. Crisis Management in Financial Institutions. *Philippine Econ. J.*, Winter 1984, *23*(1), pp. 72–78.

[G: Philippines]

Royama, Shoichi. An Anatomy of Financial Liberalization. (In Japanese. With English summary.) *Osaka Econ. Pap.*, December 1984, *34*(2–3), pp. 147–54.   [G: Japan]

Rybczynski, Tad M. The U.K. Financial System in Transition. *Nat. Westminster Bank Quart. Rev.*, November 1984, pp. 26–42.

[G: U.K.]

Sametz, Arnold W. The New Financial Environment. In *Sametz, A. W., ed.*, 1984, pp. 3–19.

[G: U.S.]

Sandler, Herbert M. Restructuring and the Role of the Mortgage Instrument. In *Fed. Home Loan Bank San Francisco*, 1984, pp. 25–29.

[G: U.S.]

Santomero, Anthony M. Modeling the Banking Firm: A Survey. *J. Money, Credit, Banking*, Part 2 November 1984, *16*(4), pp. 576–602.

Santoni, G. J. Interest Rate Risk and the Stock Prices of Financial Institutions. *Fed. Res. Bank St. Louis Rev.*, August/September 1984, *66*(7), pp. 12–20.   [G: U.S.]

Schreiner, Jean-Paul. Le capital financier et le réseau des liaisons personnelles entre les principales sociétés en Suisse. (With English summary.) *Rev. Econ. Ind.*, 3rd Trimester 1984, (29), pp. 78–95.

Silverberg, Stanley C. Restricting Brokered Deposits. *Housing Finance Rev.*, January 1984, *3*(1), pp. 99–102.   [G: U.S.]

Skully, Michael T. Financial Institutions and Markets in Thailand. In *Skully, M. T., ed.*, 1984, pp. 296–378.   [G: Thailand]

Skully, Michael T. Financial Institutions and Markets in Brunei. In *Skully, M. T., ed.*, 1984, pp. 1–48.   [G: Brunei]

Smith, Donald J. A Theoretic Framework for the Analysis of Credit Union Decision Making. *J. Finance*, September 1984, *39*(4), pp. 1155–68.

Smith, Louis P. F. British Policy on Building Societies. *Irish Banking Rev.*, December 1984, pp. 52–68.   [G: U.K.; Ireland]

Solomon, Anthony M. Banking Deregulation—Where Do We Go from Here? *Fed. Res. Bank New York Quart. Rev.*, Autumn 1984, *9*(3), pp. 1–5.   [G: U.S.]

Steffins, John L. The Demand for Financial Products. In *Sametz, A. W., ed.*, 1984, pp. 55–60.

[G: U.S.]

Taylor, David Van L., Jr. Debit Cards. In *Fed. Res. Bank Atlanta*, 1984, pp. 11–16.

[G: U.S.]

Teeters, Nancy H. Statement to the U.S. House Subcommittee on Consumer Affairs and Coinage of the Committee on Banking, Finance and Urban Affairs, March 27, 1984. *Fed. Res. Bull.*, April 1984, *70*(4), pp. 309–12.   [G: U.S.]

Timberg, Thomas A. and Aiyar, C. V. Informal Credit Markets in India. *Econ. Develop. Cult. Change*, October 1984, *33*(1), pp. 43–59.

[G: India]

Toevs, Alden L. and Wernick, Jeffrey H. Hedging Interest Rate Risk Inclusive of Prepayment and Credit Risks. In *Fed. Home Loan Bank San Francisco*, 1984, pp. 97–122.   [G: U.S.]

Valentine, T. J. Financial Regulation in Australia: Comment. *Australian Econ. Rev.*, 3rd Quarter 1984, (67), pp. 147–50.   [G: Australia]

Vignola, Anthony J. Financial Futures. In *Fed. Home Loan Bank San Francisco*, 1984, pp. 217–22.   [G: U.S.]

Vittas, Dimitri. International Payments Systems. In *Fed. Res. Bank Atlanta*, 1984, pp. 141–48.

[G: Global]

Volcker, Paul A. Statement to the U.S. House Committee on Banking, Finance and Urban Affairs, June 12, 1984. *Fed. Res. Bull.*, July 1984, *70*(7), pp. 560–68.   [G: U.S.]

Volcker, Paul A. Statement to the U.S. Senate Committee on Banking, Housing, and Urban Affairs, March 27, 1984. *Fed. Res. Bull.*, April 1984, *70*(4), pp. 298–308.   [G: U.S.]

Wachter, Susan M. Indexing Risk: The Special Role of Pension Funds. In *Fed. Home Loan Bank San Francisco*, 1984, pp. 157–73.

[G: U.S.]

Webb, James R. Real Estate Investment Acquisition Rules for Life Insurance Companies and Pension Funds: A Survey. *Amer. Real Estate Urban Econ. Assoc. J.*, Winter 1984, *12*(4), pp. 495–520.   [G: U.S.]

White, George C. Payments Standards. In *Fed. Res. Bank Atlanta*, 1984, pp. 113–21.

Williams, Jeffrey C. Fractional Reserve Banking in Grain. *J. Money, Credit, Banking*, Part 1 November 1984, *16*(4), pp. 488–96.

[G: U.S.]

Woerheide, Walt; Hartzog, Jerry and Losey, Robert. The Effect of the "Wild Card" Experiment on Savings Flows at Savings and Loans. *Bus. Econ.*, April 1984, *19*(3), pp. 48–51.

[G: U.S.]

Zimmer, Linda Fenner. ATMs. In *Fed. Res. Bank Atlanta*, 1984, pp. 3–9.

315 Credit to Business, Consumer, etc. (including mortgages)

3150 General

Allen, Larry and Price, Don. Variations in the Flow of Credit from Regional Financial Institutions as a Source of Cyclical Instability in the Regional Economy: An Application of Causal Analysis. *Reg. Sci. Persp.*, 1984, *14*(2), pp. 3–14. **[G: U.S.]**

Causse, Jean. Necessity of and Constraints on the Use of Savings in the Community in Which They Are Collected. In *Kessler, D. and Ullmo, P.-A., eds.*, 1984, pp. 153–81.

Chiang, Raymond, et al. Adverse Selection as an Explanation of Credit Rationing and Different Lender Types. *J. Macroecon.*, Spring 1984, *6*(2), pp. 159–80.

Ciocca, Pierluigi; Giannoni, Anna M. and Nanni, Carla. An Analysis of Customer "Mobility" in the Bank Credit Market (1979–1980). In *Banca d'Italia*, 1984, pp. 191–210. **[G: Italy]**

Emery, Gary W. A Pure Financial Explanation for Trade Credit. *J. Finan. Quant. Anal.*, September 1984, *19*(3), pp. 271–85.

Goodhart, Charles A. E. Structural Changes in the Banking System and the Determination of the Stock of Money. In *Masera, R. S. and Triffin, R., eds.*, 1984, pp. 111–49. **[G: OECD]**

Guglielmi, Giuseppe. Banca: servizio pubblico o impresa? (Banking: A Public or Business Service? [With a Note by the Editor.] With English summary.) *Bancaria*, April 1984, *40*(4), pp. 377–85. **[G: Italy]**

Hess, James D. Imperfect Information and Credit Rationing: Comment. *Quart. J. Econ.*, November 1984, *99*(4), pp. 865–68.

Jaffee, Dwight M. and Russell, Thomas. Imperfect Information, Uncertainty, and Credit Rationing: A Reply. *Quart. J. Econ.*, November 1984, *99*(4), pp. 869–72.

Lindley, James T.; Selby, Edward B., Jr. and Jackson, John D. Racial Discrimination in the Provision of Financial Services. *Amer. Econ. Rev.*, September 1984, *74*(4), pp. 735–41. **[G: U.S.]**

Macrì, Diego. Per un controllo efficace del credito. (Credit Control. With English summary.) *L'Impresa*, 1984, *26*(1), pp. 55–64. **[G: Italy]**

Molho, Lazaros E. Loan Rates as a Selective Credit Control. *J. Banking Finance*, March 1984, *8*(1), pp. 79–98. **[G: Greece]**

Schmid, A. Allan. Broadening Capital Ownership: The Credit System as a Locus of Power. In *Alperovitz, G. and Skurski, R., eds.*, 1984, pp. 117–37.

Scott, Walter Giorgio. L'evoluzione delle aziende di credito: un'analisi bibliografica. (The Development of Credit Organisations: A Bibliographic Analysis. With English summary.) *L'Impresa*, 1984, *26*(2), pp. 19–30. **[G: Italy]**

Timberg, Thomas A. and Aiyar, C. V. Informal Credit Markets in India. *Econ. Develop. Cult. Change*, October 1984, *33*(1), pp. 43–59. **[G: India]**

Tsutsui, Yoshiro. Credit Rationing and Competitive Loan Markets: A Comment on the Jaffee–Russell Model. *Econ. Stud. Quart.*, December 1984, *35*(3), pp. 269–76.

Vandell, Kerry D. Imperfect Information, Uncertainty, and Credit Rationing: Comment and Extension. *Quart. J. Econ.*, November 1984, *99*(4), pp. 841–63.

Watson, Harry S. Credit Markets and Borrower Effort. *Southern Econ. J.*, January 1984, *50*(3), pp. 802–13.

Webb, David C. Imperfect Information and Credit Market Equilibrium. *Europ. Econ. Rev.*, October–November 1984, *26*(1–2), pp. 247–58.

3151 Consumer Finance

Avery, Robert B., et al. Survey of Consumer Finances, 1983: A Second Report. *Fed. Res. Bull.*, December 1984, *70*(12), pp. 857–68. **[G: U.S.]**

Gregor, William T. Strategic Planning of Consumer Financial Services. In *Sametz, A. W., ed.*, 1984, pp. 117–21.

Koskela, Erkki and Virén, Matti. Hushållens sparande och penningmarknaderna i norden. (Household Saving and Credit Markets in the Nordic Countries. With English summary.) *Ekon. Samfundets Tidskr.*, 1984, *37*(4), pp. 245–65. **[G: Finland; Norway; Sweden]**

Peterson, Richard L. and Black, Dan A. Consumer Credit Search: A Note. *J. Money, Credit, Banking*, Part 1 November 1984, *16*(4), pp. 527–35. **[G: U.S.]**

Rea, Samuel A., Jr. Arm-breaking, Consumer Credit and Personal Bankruptcy. *Econ. Inquiry*, April 1984, *22*(2), pp. 188–208.

Sullivan, A. Charlene. Competition in the Market for Consumer Loans. *J. Econ. Bus.*, February 1984, *36*(1), pp. 141–49. **[G: U.S.]**

Taylor, David Van L., Jr. Debit Cards. In *Fed. Res. Bank Atlanta*, 1984, pp. 11–16. **[G: U.S.]**

Teeters, Nancy H. Statement to the U.S. Senate Subcommittee on Consumer Affairs, Committee on Banking, Housing, and Urban Affairs, February 7, 1984. *Fed. Res. Bull.*, February 1984, *70*(2), pp. 102–05. **[G: U.S.]**

Weber, Edward A. Installment Credit for Autos: A Literature Survey of Sources, Terms and Demand Effects. *J. Bank Res.*, Spring 1984, *15*(1), pp. 35–43. **[G: U.S.]**

3152 Mortgage Market

Agarwal, Vinod B. and Phillips, Richard A. Mortgage Rate Buydowns: Further Evidence. *Housing Finance Rev.*, April 1984, *3*(2), pp. 191–97. **[G: U.S.]**

Agarwal, Vinod B. and Phillips, Richard A. Mortgage Rate Buydowns: Implications for Housing Price Indexes. *Soc. Sci. Quart.*, September 1984, *65*(3), pp. 868–75. **[G: U.S.]**

Albouy, Michel. Plan d'épargne logement et théorie des options. (Housing Saving Plan and Option Theory. With English summary.) *Écon.*

Soc., November–December 1984, *18*(11–12), pp. 81–98. **[G: France]**

Alm, James and Follain, James R., Jr. Alternative Mortgage Instruments, the Tilt Problem, and Consumer Welfare. *J. Finan. Quant. Anal.*, March 1984, *19*(1), pp. 113–26.

Anderson, Gordon J. and Hendry, David F. An Econometric Model of United Kingdom Building Societies. *Oxford Bull. Econ. Statist.*, August 1984, *46*(3), pp. 185–210. **[G: U.K.]**

Blackwell, John. Housing Finance in Ireland in the 1980s. *Irish Banking Rev.*, December 1984, pp. 69–84. **[G: Ireland]**

Boleat, Mark. Alternative Housing Finance Systems. *Nat. Westminster Bank Quart. Rev.*, August 1984, pp. 2–12. **[G: U.S.; U.K.; Germany]**

Boleat, Mark. Housing Finance in Developing Countries. In *Kessler, D. and Ullmo, P.-A.*, eds., 1984, pp. 183–203. **[G: LDCs; MDCs]**

Brueckner, Jan K. Creative Financing and House Prices: A Theoretical Inquiry into the Capitalization Issue. *Amer. Real Estate Urban Econ. Assoc. J.*, Winter 1984, *12*(4), pp. 417–26.

Brueckner, Jan K. The Flexible Mortgage: Optimal Financing of a Consumer Durable. *Amer. Real Estate Urban Econ. Assoc. J.*, Summer 1984, *12*(2), pp. 136–52.

Burke, Jim and Rhoades, Stephen A. Bank Holding Company Affiliation and Contracyclical Lending by Mortgage Bankers. *J. Econ. Bus.*, May 1984, *36*(2), pp. 275–81. **[G: U.S.]**

Buser, Stephen A. and Hendershott, Patric H. Pricing Default-Free Fixed-Rate Mortgages. *Housing Finance Rev.*, October 1984, *3*(4), pp. 405–29.

Capozza, Dennis R. and Gau, George W. Mortgage Rate Insurance and the Canadian Mortgage Market. *Can. Public Policy*, September 1984, *10*(3), pp. 296–304.

Capozza, Dennis R. and Gau, George W. The Pricing and Implementation of Mortgage Rate Insurance. *Housing Finance Rev.*, October 1984, *3*(4), pp. 393–404. **[G: Canada]**

Carr, Jack L. and Smith, Lawrence B. Housing Finance Contracts and the Nonneutrality of Inflation. *Housing Finance Rev.*, January 1984, *3*(1), pp. 39–49. **[G: U.S.]**

Carron, Andrew S. The Australian Financial System. In *Caves, R. E. and Krause, L. B.*, eds., 1984, pp. 195–229. **[G: Australia]**

Christian, James W. and Wilson, Michael L. Capital Requirements for Housing in the 1980s. *Contemp. Policy Issue*, May 1984, (6), pp. 30–44. **[G: U.S.]**

Colton, Kent W. and Cunningham, Donald F. The Role of the Secondary Mortgage Markets in Managing Risk. In *Fed. Home Loan Bank San Francisco*, 1984, pp. 125–55. **[G: U.S.]**

Corgel, John B. and Gay, Gerald D. The Impact of GNMA Futures Trading on Cash Market Volatility. *Amer. Real Estate Urban Econ. Assoc. J.*, Summer 1984, *12*(2), pp. 176–90. **[G: U.S.]**

Cortes, Diane L. Are Lenders Inviting Reregulation by Inadequate Disclosure Practices? *Hous-*

ing Finance Rev., April 1984, *3*(2), pp. 201–08. **[G: U.S.]**

Cunningham, Donald F. and Hendershott, Patric H. Pricing FHA Mortgage Default Insurance. *Housing Finance Rev.*, October 1984, *3*(4), pp. 373–92. **[G: U.S.]**

Curry, Timothy J. and Rose, John T. Bank Structure and Mortgage Rates: A Comment. *J. Econ. Bus.*, May 1984, *36*(2), pp. 283–87. **[G: U.S.]**

Edgren, John A. and Hayworth, Steven C. The Implications of Land Contracts for Property Tax Assessment Practices. *Housing Finance Rev.*, April 1984, *3*(2), pp. 177–89. **[G: U.S.]**

Eichengreen, Barry. Mortgage Interest Rates in the Populist Era. *Amer. Econ. Rev.*, December 1984, *74*(5), pp. 995–1015. **[G: U.S.]**

Esaki, Howard and Wachtenheim, Judy A. Explaining the Recent Level of Single-Family Housing Starts. *Fed. Res. Bank New York Quart. Rev.*, Winter 1984–85, *9*(4), pp. 31–38. **[G: U.S.]**

Ferreira, Eurico J. and Sirmans, G. Stacy. Assumable Loan Value in Creative Financing. *Housing Finance Rev.*, April 1984, *3*(2), pp. 139–47.

Ford, William F. Product Diversification. In *Fed. Home Loan Bank San Francisco*, 1984, pp. 55–60. **[G: U.S.]**

Foster, Chester and Van Order, Robert. An Option-based Model of Mortgage Default. *Housing Finance Rev.*, October 1984, *3*(4), pp. 351–72. **[G: U.S.]**

French, Dan W. and Haney, Richard L., Jr. Pricing the Shared-Appreciation Mortgage in a Stochastic Environment. *Housing Finance Rev.*, October 1984, *3*(4), pp. 431–43.

Gainer, William J. Mortgage Revenue Bonds: Their Costs Outweigh Their Benefits to Homebuyers. *Housing Finance Rev.*, October 1984, *3*(4), pp. 457–65. **[G: U.S.]**

Garnett, Robert and Guttentag, Jack M. The Reverse-Shared-Appreciation Mortgage. *Housing Finance Rev.*, January 1984, *3*(1), pp. 63–84. **[G: U.S.]**

Gilbert, R. Alton and Holland, A. Steven. Has the Deregulation of Deposit Interest Rates Raised Mortgage Rates? *Fed. Res. Bank St. Louis Rev.*, May 1984, *66*(5), pp. 5–15. **[G: U.S.]**

Gray, Edwin J. Federal Home Loan Bank of San Francisco: Proceedings of the Ninth Annual Conference: Remarks. In *Fed. Home Loan Bank San Francisco*, 1984, pp. 63–65. **[G: U.S.]**

Guttentag, Jack M. Recent Changes in the Primary Home Mortgage Market. *Housing Finance Rev.*, July 1984, *3*(3), pp. 221–54. **[G: U.S.]**

Jaffee, Dwight M. Creative Finance: Measures, Sources, and Tests. *Housing Finance Rev.*, January 1984, *3*(1), pp. 1–18. **[G: U.S.]**

Jaffee, Dwight M. House-Price Capitalization of Creative Finance: An Introduction. *Housing Finance Rev.*, April 1984, *3*(2), pp. 107–17.

Kane, Edward J. Change and Progress in Contemporary Mortgage Markets. *Housing Finance Rev.*, July 1984, *3*(3), pp. 257–82. [G: U.S.]

Kaufman, George G. The Role of Traditional Mortgage Lenders in Future Mortgage Lending: Problems and Prospects. *Housing Finance Rev.*, July 1984, *3*(3), pp. 285–315. [G: U.S.]

Leban, Abbott A. The American Homestead Program. *Housing Finance Rev.*, January 1984, *3*(1), pp. 87–90. [G: U.S.]

Levy, Gerald J. The Secondary Mortgage Market: Amelioration of Risk. In *Fed. Home Loan Bank San Francisco*, 1984, pp. 49–53. [G: U.S.]

Marlow, Michael L. Bank Structure and Mortgage Rates: Reply. *J. Econ. Bus.*, May 1984, *36*(2), pp. 289–90.

Martin, Preston. Statement to the U.S. House Subcommittee on Telecommunications, Consumer Protection, and Finance of the Committee on Energy and Commerce, March 14, 1984. *Fed. Res. Bull.*, April 1984, *70*(4), pp. 288–91. [G: U.S.]

Massey, Pat. The Role of Building Societies in Irish Financial Markets. *Irish Banking Rev.*, March 1984, pp. 6–17. [G: Ireland]

Meador, Mark. Assumable vs. Due-on-Sale Mortgages: The Effect on Mortgage Repayment Rates. *Bus. Econ.*, January 1984, *19*(1), pp. 47–52. [G: U.S.]

Modigliani, Franco. I problemi di indicizzazione nel finanziamento dell'edilizia abitativa. Il progetto MIT di mutuo ipotecario per i giovani. (The Inflation Proof Mortgage [IPM]. The Mortgage for the Young. With English summary.) *Bancaria*, July 1984, *40*(7), pp. 607–17. [G: Italy]

Nothaft, Frank E. ARM Debt Outstanding by Lender Type and Firm Size. *Housing Finance Rev.*, October 1984, *3*(4), pp. 447–55. [G: U.S.]

Occhiuto, Antonino. I problemi dell'edilizia abitativa in Italia. (Residential-building Problems in Italy. With English summary.) *Bancaria*, July 1984, *40*(7), pp. 603–06. [G: Italy]

Page, Daniel E. and Sirmans, C. F. Yield Differences on Fixed and Adjustable Rate Mortgages. *Quart. Rev. Econ. Bus.*, Autumn 1984, *24*(3), pp. 18–28. [G: U.S.]

Plaut, Steven E. Endogenous Mortgage Interest and the Consumption of Housing. *J. Urban Econ.*, July 1984, *16*(1), pp. 31–45.

Pollack, Mark B. and Steinbach, Gordon H. Mortgage Guaranty Insurance Risk Management in the 1980s. *Housing Finance Rev.*, April 1984, *3*(2), pp. 209–15. [G: U.S.]

Pozdena, Randall J. and Iben, Ben. Pricing Mortgages: An Options Approach. *Fed. Res. Bank San Francisco Econ. Rev.*, Spring 1984, (2), pp. 39–55.

Ranieri, Lewis S. Financial Markets and Risk Management. In *Fed. Home Loan Bank San Francisco*, 1984, pp. 5–13. [G: U.S.]

Rosen, Kenneth T. Creative Financing and House Prices: A Study of Capitalization Effects. *Housing Finance Rev.*, April 1984, *3*(2), pp. 119–27. [G: U.S.]

Sandler, Herbert M. Restructuring and the Role of the Mortgage Instrument. In *Fed. Home Loan Bank San Francisco*, 1984, pp. 25–29. [G: U.S.]

Schwartz, Arthur L., Jr. and Kapplin, Steven D. Economic Implications of Alternative Home Financing. *Housing Finance Rev.*, April 1984, *3*(2), pp. 165–75. [G: U.S.]

Seiders, David F. The Future of Secondary Mortgage Markets: Economic Forces and Federal Policies. *Housing Finance Rev.*, July 1984, *3*(3), pp. 319–47. [G: U.S.]

Siegel, Jeremy J. The Mortgage Refinancing Decision. *Housing Finance Rev.*, January 1984, *3*(1), pp. 91–97.

Skjoldager, Arne. Housing Finance in Denmark. *Irish Banking Rev.*, June 1984, pp. 24–32. [G: Denmark]

Smith, Stanley D. and Sirmans, G. Stacy. The Shifting of FHA Discount Points: Actual vs. Expectations. *Amer. Real Estate Urban Econ. Assoc. J.*, Summer 1984, *12*(2), pp. 153–61. [G: U.S.]

Smith, Stanley D.; Sirmans, G. Stacy and Sirmans, C. F. The Valuation of Creative Financing in Housing. *Housing Finance Rev.*, April 1984, *3*(2), pp. 129–38. [G: U.S.]

Strathman, James G.; DeLacy, P. Barton and Dueker, Kenneth J. Creative Financing "Concessions" in Residential Sales: Effects and Implications. *Housing Finance Rev.*, April 1984, *3*(2), pp. 149–63. [G: U.S.]

Taylor, William M.; Wichern, Dean W. and Stanley, Craig E. An Intertemporal Analysis of the Shifting of FHA Discount Points to Buyers. *Managerial Dec. Econ.*, December 1984, *5*(4), pp. 242–50. [G: U.S.]

Thom, D. Rodney. Housing Starts and Mortgage Availability: Evidence from the UK Time Series. *Appl. Econ.*, December 1984, *16*(6), pp. 881–93. [G: U.K.]

Toevs, Alden L. and Wernick, Jeffrey H. Hedging Interest Rate Risk Inclusive of Prepayment and Credit Risks. In *Fed. Home Loan Bank San Francisco*, 1984, pp. 97–122. [G: U.S.]

Tuccillo, John A. Disinflation and Housing Investment: A Revisionist Analysis. *Contemp. Policy Issue*, May 1984, (6), pp. 17–29. [G: U.S.]

Vandell, Kerry D. On the Assessment of Default Risk in Commercial Mortgage Lending. *Amer. Real Estate Urban Econ. Assoc. J.*, Fall 1984, *12*(3), pp. 270–96.

Wachter, Susan M. Indexing Risk: The Special Role of Pension Funds. In *Fed. Home Loan Bank San Francisco*, 1984, pp. 157–73. [G: U.S.]

Weicher, John C. Disinflation in the Housing Market. In *Fellner, W., ed.*, 1984, pp. 155–204. [G: U.S.]

Weicher, John C. Housing and Housing Finance in an Era of Inflation and Disinflation: Introduction. *Contemp. Policy Issue*, May 1984, (6), pp. 1–4. [G: U.S.]

Wofford, Larry E. and Burgess, Richard C. Structuring and Pricing Adjustable-Rate Mortgage Products: An Analysis of Critical Parameters. *Housing Finance Rev.*, January 1984, *3*(1), pp. 51–61. **[G: U.S.]**

3153 Business Credit

Akerlof, George A. The Market for "Lemons": Quality Uncertainty and the Market Mechanism. In *Akerlof, G. A.*, 1984, *1970*, pp. 7–22. **[G: India]**

Artus, Patrick. Le fonctionnement du marché du crédit: Diverses analyses dans un cadre de déséquilibre. (The Functioning of the Credit Market: Several Analyses in a Disequilibrium Context. With English summary.) *Revue Écon.*, July 1984, *35*(4), pp. 591–621.
[G: France]

Bitros, George C. The Fungibility Factor in Credit: Reply [The Fungibility Factor in Credit and the Question of the Efficacy of Selective Controls]. *Oxford Econ. Pap.*, November 1984, *36*(3), pp. 494–98. **[G: Greece]**

Carosio, Giovanni. Customer Discrimination and Selective Controls in the Bank Loan Market. In *Banca d'Italia*, 1984, pp. 165–89.
[G: Italy]

De Benedetti, Carlo. Quali strumenti finanziari per lo sviluppo del sistema economico italiano? (Financial Tools for Development of the Italian Economy. With English summary.) *Bancaria*, May–June 1984, *40*(5–6), pp. 479–82.
[G: Italy]

Dini, Lamberto. Capitale di rischio per le imprese: il ruolo del "merchant banking." (Risk Capital for Businesses: The Role of Merchant Banking. With English summary.) *Bancaria*, May–June 1984, *40*(5–6), pp. 487–91.
[G: Italy]

Drukarczyk, Jochen. Credit Contracts, Collateral-Based Security Agreements, and Bankruptcy. In *Bamberg, G. and Spremann, K.*, eds., 1984, pp. 139–59.

Foss, Murray F. Corporate Liquidity under Stagflation and Disinflation. In *Fellner, W., ed.*, 1984, pp. 205–45. **[G: U.S.]**

Giroux, Gary A. and Wiggins, Casper E. An Events Approach to Corporate Bankruptcy. *J. Bank Res.*, Autumn 1984, *15*(3), pp. 179–87.
[G: U.S.]

Goldberg, Michael A. The Sensitivity of the Prime Rate to Money Market Conditions. *J. Finan. Res.*, Winter 1984, *7*(4), pp. 269–80.
[G: U.S.]

Guttentag, Jack M. and Herring, Richard J. Credit Rationing and Financial Disorder. *J. Finance*, December 1984, *39*(5), pp. 1359–82.
[G: U.S.]

Hunter, William C. Insurance, Incentives, and Efficiency in Small Business Lending. *Southern Econ. J.*, April 1984, *50*(4), pp. 1171–84.
[G: U.S.]

Kilby, Peter; Liedholm, Carl E. and Meyer, Richard L. Working Capital and Nonfarm Rural Enterprises. In *Adams, D. W.; Graham, D. H. and Von Pischke, J. D.*, eds., 1984, pp. 266–83.

Leite, Sergio Pereira and Vaez-Zadeh, Reza. The Fungibility Factor in Credit: A Comment [The Fungibility Factor in Credit and the Question

of the Efficacy of Selective Controls]. *Oxford Econ. Pap.*, November 1984, *36*(3), pp. 490–93. **[G: Greece]**

Lombra, Raymond E. and Wasylenko, Michael. The Subsidization of Small Business through Federal Credit Programs: Analytical Foundations. *J. Econ. Bus.*, May 1984, *36*(2), pp. 263–74.

Orlando, Luigi. Mercati e intermediari finanziari: esigenze delle imprese. (Financial Markets and Intermediation: Business Requirements. With English summary.) *Bancaria*, May–June 1984, *40*(5–6), pp. 473–78. **[G: Italy]**

Parravicini, Giannino. Risparmiare per investire. (Savings for Investment. With English summary.) *Bancaria*, May–June 1984, *40*(5–6), pp. 469–72. **[G: Italy]**

Romiti, Cesare. Una riallocazione efficiente della risorse. (A Reallocation of Resources. With English summary.) *Bancaria*, May–June 1984, *40*(5–6), pp. 483–86. **[G: Italy]**

Samuels, J. M. Company Finance in Europe—The Impact on Small Firms. In *Levicki, C.*, ed., 1984, pp. 65–77. **[G: France; U.K.; W. Germany]**

von Stein, Johann Heinrich and Zeigler, Werner. The Prognosis and Surveillance of Risks from Commercial Credit Borrowers. *J. Banking Finance*, June 1984, *8*(2), pp. 249–68.
[G: W. Germany]

Tamari, Meir. The Use of a Bankruptcy Forecasting Model to Analyze Corporate Behavior in Israel. *J. Banking Finance*, June 1984, *8*(2), pp. 293–302. **[G: Israel]**

Tybout, James R. Interest Control and Credit Allocation in Developing Countries. *J. Money, Credit, Banking*, Part 1 November 1984, *16*(4), pp. 474–87. **[G: LDCs; Colombia]**

Walter, Ingo. Project Finance—The Lender's Perspective. In *Pearce, D. W.; Siebert, H. and Walter, I.*, eds., 1984, pp. 249–70.
[G: Selected Countries]

320 Fiscal Theory and Policy; Public Finance

3200 General

Aaron, Henry J. The Social Policy of the Reagan Administration: Comments. In *Bawden, D. L.*, ed., 1984, pp. 241–44. **[G: U.S.]**

Anton, Thomas J. Intergovernmental Change in the United States: An Assessment of the Literature. In *Miller, T. C.*, ed., 1984, pp. 15–64.
[G: U.S.]

Aronson, J. Richard and Schwartz, Eli. Public Sector Performance: A Public Finance Perspective. In *Miller, T. C.*, ed., 1984, pp. 193–223. **[G: U.S.]**

Baruch, Jordan J. Structuring Markets for Public Goods and Services. In *Brooks, H.; Liebman, L. and Schelling, C. S.*, eds., 1984, pp. 111–30. **[G: U.S.]**

Berry, William D. and Lowery, David. The Growing Cost of Government: A Test of Two Explanations. *Soc. Sci. Quart.*, September 1984, *65*(3), pp. 735–49. **[G: U.S.]**

Bosanquet, Nick. Is Privatisation Inevitable? In *Le Grand, J. and Robinson, R., eds.*, 1984, pp. 58–69.

Brooks, Harvey. Seeking Equity and Efficiency: Public and Private Roles. In *Brooks, H.; Liebman, L. and Schelling, C. S., eds.*, 1984, pp. 3–29.   [G: U.S.]

Buchanan, James M. Constitutional Restrictions on the Power of Government. In *Buchanan, J. M. and Tollison, R. D., eds.*, 1984, pp. 439–52.

Creedy, John. Public Finance. In *Creedy, J. and O'Brien, D. P., eds.*, 1984, pp. 84–116.

Culyer, Anthony J. The Quest for Efficiency in the Public Sector: Economists versus Dr. Pangloss (or Why Conservative Economists Are Not Nearly Conservative Enough). In *Hanusch, H., ed.*, 1984, pp. 39–48.

Delorme, Robert. A New View on the Economic Theory of the State: A Case Study of France. *J. Econ. Issues*, September 1984, *18*(3), pp. 715–44.   [G: France]

Elzinga, W. and Klaassen, L. H. Some Thoughts about the Limits to Government Power. In *Cohen, S. I., et al., eds.*, 1984, pp. 199–209.

Emminger, Otmar. Financial Policy at the Crossroads. *Lloyds Bank Rev.*, January 1984, (151), pp. 1–11.   [G: OECD]

Glazer, Nathan. The Social Policy of the Reagan Administration. In *Bawden, D. L., ed.*, 1984, pp. 221–40.   [G: U.S.]

Guibert, G. and Lanvin, B. Decentralization in Government: The United States and France Compared. *J. Policy Anal. Manage.*, Winter 1984, *3*(2), pp. 289–93.   [G: France; U.S.]

Hanusch, Horst. Public Finance and the Quest for Efficiency. In *Hanusch, H., ed.*, 1984, pp. 1–9.

Hills, John. What Is the Public Sector Worth? *Fisc. Stud.*, February 1984, *5*(1), pp. 18–31.   [G: U.K.]

Kirlin, John J. Public Sector Performance: A Political Perspective. In *Miller, T. C., ed.*, 1984, pp. 161–92.   [G: U.S.]

Kirsch, Guy. Social Structure of Developed Societies—Review of the Government's Role. In *Miyawaki, N., ed.*, 1984, pp. 169–78.

Klein, Philip A. Institutionalist Reflections on the Role of the Public Sector. *J. Econ. Issues*, March 1984, *18*(1), pp. 45–68.   [G: U.S.]

Klein, Rudolf. Privatization and the Welfare State. *Lloyds Bank Rev.*, January 1984, (151), pp. 12–29.   [G: U.K.]

Kolderie, Ted. Business Opportunities in the Changing Conceptions of the Public Sector Role. In *Brooks, H.; Liebman, L. and Schelling, C. S., eds.*, 1984, pp. 89–110. [G: U.S.]

Larkey, Patrick D.; Stolp, Chandler and Winer, Mark D. Why Does Government Grow? In *Miller, T. C., ed.*, 1984, pp. 65–101.
[G: OECD]

Liebman, Lance. Political and Economic Markets: The Public, Private and Not-for-Profit Sectors. In *Brooks, H.; Liebman, L. and Schelling, C. S., eds.*, 1984, pp. 341–58.   [G: U.S.]

Masamura, Kimihiro. The Social Structure of Advanced Societies and the Role of the Govern-

ment—Experiences and Problems of Japan. In *Miyawaki, N., ed.*, 1984, pp. 179–83.
[G: Japan]

Miller, Trudi C. Public Sector Performance: Conclusion: A Design Science Perspective. In *Miller, T. C., ed.*, 1984, pp. 251–68.
[G: U.S.]

Peacock, Alan. The Political Economy of Strukturpolitik: A Tribute to the German Council of Economic Experts. *Z. ges. Staatswiss.*, June 1984, *140*(2), pp. 364–70.   [G: Germany]

Raynauld, André. The Canadian Federation. *Can. J. Econ.*, November 1984, *17*(4), pp. 635–53.   [G: Canada]

Rose, Richard and Karran, Terence. Inertia or Incrementalism? A Long-term View of the Growth of Government. In *Groth, A. J. and Wade, L. L., eds.*, 1984, pp. 43–71.
[G: OECD]

Singh, A. K. Planning in a Mixed Economy: The Indian Experience. In *Singh, A. K.; Papola, T. S. and Mathur, R. S., eds.*, 1984, pp. 148–64.   [G: India]

Sundquist, James L. Privatization: No Panacea for What Ails Government. In *Brooks, H.; Liebman, L. and Schelling, C. S., eds.*, 1984, pp. 303–18.   [G: U.S.]

Tian, Yun; Jin, Renxiong and Yuan, Zhenyu. Further Reform and Improve the Financial System. *Chinese Econ. Stud.*, Spring 1984, *17*(3), pp. 53–60.   [G: China]

Tierney, John T. Government Corporations and Managing the Public's Business. *Polit. Sci. Quart.*, Spring 1984, *99*(1), pp. 73–92.
[G: U.S.]

Wolf, Charles, Jr. Government Shortcomings and the Conditions of Demand. In *Hanusch, H., ed.*, 1984, pp. 167–73.

321 Fiscal Theory and Policy

3210 Fiscal Theory and Policy

Barrett, Sean D. Recent Developments in Evaluating Public Expenditure. *Irish Banking Rev.*, June 1984, pp. 33–39.   [G: Ireland]

Bigman, David and Weksler, Itzhak. Emergency Stocks: A Theoretical Analysis and an Illustration for Israel. *J. Policy Modeling*, February 1984, *6*(1), pp. 81–94.   [G: Israel]

Björk, Bo-Christer. Kansantaloudellisen laskentakorkokannan empiirinen määrittäminen. (Measurement of the Social Discount Rate. With English summary.) *Liiketaloudellinen Aikak.*, 1984, *33*(4), pp. 446–74.   [G: OECD]

Blanchard, Olivier J. and Dornbusch, Rudiger. U.S. Deficits, the Dollar and Europe. *Banca Naz. Lavoro Quart. Rev.*, March 1984, (148), pp. 89–113.   [G: U.S.; OECD]

Boskin, Michael J., et al. Budget Policy and Processes: Where Do We Go from Here? *Contemp. Policy Issue*, Fall 1984-85, *3*(1), pp. 53–78.   [G: U.S.]

Bridges, Benjamin, Jr. Post-Fisc Distributions of Income: Further Comment. *Public Finance Quart.*, April 1984, *12*(2), pp. 245–47.
[G: U.S.]

Bridges, Benjamin, Jr. Post-Fisc Distributions of Income: Comment. *Public Finance Quart.*, April 1984, *12*(2), pp. 231–40. **[G: U.S.]**

Bruni, Franco. Controllo monetario, fabbisogno del settore pubblico e "moneta del Tesoro": Qualche ulteriore riflessione. (Monetary Control, the Public-Sector Requirement and "Treasury Money": Some Further Reflections. With English summary.) *Bancaria*, August 1984, *40*(8), pp. 779–81.

Bruni, Franco. Controllo monetario, fabbisogno del settore pubblico e "moneta del Tesoro." (Monetary Control, the Public-Sector Requirement and "Treasury Money." With English summary.) *Bancaria*, February 1984, *40*(2), pp. 146–58.

Buiter, Willem H. Granger-Causality and Policy Effectiveness. *Economica*, May 1984, *51*(202), pp. 151–62.

Camilleri, Arthur P.; Nguyen, Duc-Tho and Campbell, Robert B. Policy Changes and External Disturbances in a Small Open Economy: Stability and Dynamic Responses. *Int. Econ. Rev.*, February 1984, *25*(1), pp. 123–58.

Cox, W. Michael. What Is the Rule for Financing Public Debt? *Fed. Res. Bank Dallas Econ. Rev.*, September 1984, pp. 25–31. **[G: U.S.]**

Dominique, C. René. Choosing the Appropriate Project Appraisal Method for a Labour Surplus Economy. *Industry Devel.*, 1984, (10), pp. 1–37.

Eisner, Robert and Pieper, Paul J. A New View of the Federal Debt and Budget Deficits. *Amer. Econ. Rev.*, March 1984, *74*(1), pp. 11–29. **[G: U.S.]**

Farzin, Y. Hossein. The Effect of the Discount Rate on Depletion of Exhaustible Resources. *J. Polit. Econ.*, October 1984, *92*(5), pp. 841–51.

Fullerton, Don. Which Effective Tax Rate? *Nat. Tax J.*, March 1984, *37*(1), pp. 23–41. **[G: U.S.]**

Goldsmith, K. Energy Planning in Developing Countries: Project Appraisal. In *Baum, V., et al.*, 1984, pp. 100–07. **[G: LDCs]**

Goudard, Daniel. Nouvelles avancées dans le calcul économique public. (Improvements in Public Choice Analysis. With English summary.) *Revue Écon.*, November 1984, *35*(6), pp. 1173–1212. **[G: France]**

Gronchi, Sandro. On Karmel's Criterion for Optimal Truncation. *Econ. Notes*, 1984, (3), pp. 21–30.

Henry, Claude. La microéconomie comme langage et enjeu de négociations. (Economic Appraisal Methodology as Output of Negotiations. With English summary.) *Revue Écon.*, January 1984, *35*(1), pp. 177–97.

Kienzle, Edward C. Post-Fisc Distributions of Income: Reply. *Public Finance Quart.*, April 1984, *12*(2), pp. 241–44. **[G: U.S.]**

Le Grand, Julian. Évaluation de l'impact redistributif des dépenses publiques. Quelques problèmes méthodologiques. (On Measuring the Distributional Impact of Public Expenditures: Some Methodological Problems. With English summary.) *Consommation*, July–September 1984, *31*(3), pp. 3–17. **[G: France]**

Leff, Nathaniel H. Externalities, Information Costs, and Social Benefit–Cost Analysis for Economic Development: An Example from Telecommunications. *Econ. Develop. Cult. Change*, January 1984, *32*(2), pp. 255–76. **[G: LDCs]**

Lewis, David L. and Bodde, David L. Understanding Political Risk in Investment Planning. *J. Policy Anal. Manage.*, Summer 1984, *3*(4), pp. 544–60. **[G: U.S.]**

Lucas, Robert E. B. On the Theory of DRC Criteria. *J. Devel. Econ.*, April 1984, *14*(3), pp. 407–17.

Lybeck, Johan A., et al. A Comparison of the Dynamic Properties of Five Nordic Macro-econometric Models. *Scand. J. Econ.*, 1984, *86*(1), pp. 35–51. **[G: Sweden; Finland; Norway]**

Malliaris, A. G. Economic Stabilization, Social Issues and the Role of Government. *Rev. Soc. Econ.*, October 1984, *42*(2), pp. 117–29. **[G: U.S.]**

Marchand, Maurice; Mintz, J. and Pestieau, Pierre. Shadow Pricing of Labour and Capital in an Economy with Unemployed Labour. *Europ. Econ. Rev.*, July 1984, *25*(2), pp. 239–52.

Marchand, Maurice and Pestieau, Pierre. Discount Rates and Shadow Prices for Public Investment. *J. Public Econ.*, July 1984, *24*(2), pp. 153–69.

Mehdi, Istaqbal. Performance Evaluation of Public Enterprise in Pakistan: Experiment in Social Accounting System. *Pakistan Devel. Rev.*, Summer-Autumn 1984, *23*(2&3), pp. 179–200. **[G: Pakistan]**

Middleton, Roger. The Measurement of Fiscal Influence in Britain in the 1930s [The Constant Employment Budget Balance and British Budgetary Policy, 1929–39]. *Econ. Hist. Rev.*, 2nd Ser., February 1984, *37*(1), pp. 103–06. **[G: U.K.]**

Miller, Edward M. Can the Public's Desire for Future Benefits Be Deduced from Their Private Decisions? Returns from Human Capital and from Public Goods Investments Are Directly Analogous. *Amer. J. Econ. Soc.*, October 1984, *43*(4), pp. 443–49.

Nas, Tevfik. The World Price Methodology for Shadow Pricing: Theory and Practice. *METU*, 1984, *11*(3–4), pp. 295–306.

Palermio, Giovanni. Alcune considerazioni su disavanzo pubblico, inflazione e tasso di sviluppo dell'economia. (Reflections on the Public Sector Deficit, Inflation and Economic Growth Rate. With English summary.) *Bancaria*, March 1984, *40*(3), pp. 272–78.

Pestieau, Pierre. Public Enterprises under Conditions of Unemployment: A Survey of the Issues. *Ann. Pub. Co-op. Econ.*, Oct.–Dec. 1984, *55*(4), pp. 365–82. **[G: Belgium]**

Qureshi, Sarfraz K. The Project Monitoring System in Pakistan: An Evaluation: Comment. *Pa-*

kistan Devel. Rev., Summer-Autumn 1984, 23(2&3), pp. 175–78.

Ranuzzi, Paolo. Controllo monetario, fabbisogno del settore pubblico e "moneta del Tesoro": Un commento. (Monetary Control, the Public-Sector Requirement and "Treasury Money": A Commentary. With English summary.) *Bancaria*, August 1984, 40(8), pp. 776–78.

Rasul, Ghulam. Performance Evaluation of Public Enterprise in Pakistan: Experiment in Social Accounting System: Comment. *Pakistan Devel. Rev.*, Summer-Autumn 1984, 23(2&3), pp. 201–03. **[G: Pakistan]**

Recktenwald, Horst Claus. The Public Waste Syndrome: A Comprehensive Theory of Government Failures. In *Hanusch, H., ed.*, 1984, pp. 11–26.

Reichelstein, Stefan and Osband, Kent. Incentives in Government Contracts. *J. Public Econ.*, July 1984, 24(2), pp. 257–69.

Roberts, Paul Craig. Supply-Side Economics, Growth, and Liberty. In *Moore, J. H., ed.*, 1984, pp. 73–89. **[G: U.S.]**

Sahibzada, Shamim A. and Mahmood, Mir Annice. The Project Monitoring System in Pakistan: An Evaluation. *Pakistan Devel. Rev.*, Summer-Autumn 1984, 23(2&3), pp. 165–74. **[G: Pakistan]**

Sen, Amartya. Approaches to the Choice of Discount Rates for Social Benefit–Cost Analysis. In *Sen, A.*, 1984, 1982, pp. 172–203.

Sen, Amartya. Control Areas and Accounting Prices: An Approach to Economic Evaluation. In *Sen, A.*, 1984, 1972, pp. 224–41.

Sen, Amartya. Isolation, Assurance and the Social Rate of Discount. In *Sen, A.*, 1984, 1967, pp. 135–46.

Stahl, Dale O., II. Monotonic Variations of Consumer Surplus and Comparative Performance Results. *Southern Econ. J.*, October 1984, 51(2), pp. 503–20.

Szychowski, Mario L. and Perazzo, Alfredo C. Protección efectiva y costo doméstico de la divisa: Comparación de su eficiencia en el cumplimiento de objectivos alternativos. (Effective Protection and Domestic Resource Cost: comparison about Their Efficiency in the Achievement of Alternatives Objectives. With English summary.) *Económica*, May-December 1984, 30(2–3), pp. 217–44. **[G: Argentina]**

Tatom, John A. A Perspective on the Federal Deficit Problem. *Fed. Res. Bank St. Louis Rev.*, June/July 1984, 66(6), pp. 5–17. **[G: U.S.]**

Thédié, J. Optimisation des programmes et taux d'actualisation de l'Etat. (Optimization of Programs and Social Discounting Rate. With English summary.) *Écon. Appl.*, 1984, 37(3–4), pp. 593–643.

Tinbergen, Jan. On Collective and Part-Collective Goods. *De Economist*, 1984, 132(2), pp. 171–82.

Whalley, John. Basis Linkage in International Tax Treatment of Goods and Capital Income. *Nat. Tax J.*, June 1984, 37(2), pp. 195–200.

3212 Fiscal Theory; Empirical Studies Illustrating Fiscal Theory

Adachi, Hideyuki. On the Economic Implications of the Growth of the Non-market Sector. *Oxford Econ. Pap.*, November 1984, 36(3), pp. 418–37. **[G: LDCs]**

Ahmad, Ehtisham and Stern, Nicholas H. The Theory of Reform and Indian Indirect Taxes. *J. Public Econ.*, December 1984, 25(3), pp. 259–98. **[G: India]**

Akerlof, George A. The Economics of "Tagging" as Applied to the Optimal Income Tax, Welfare Programs, and Manpower Planning. In *Akerlof, G. A.*, 1984, 1978, pp. 45–68.

Anderson, Robert; Ando, Albert and Enzler, Jared. Interaction between Fiscal and Monetary Policy and the Real Rate of Interest. *Amer. Econ. Rev.*, May 1984, 74(2), pp. 55–60. **[G: U.S.]**

Arnold, Volker. Umweltschutz als international öffentliches Gut: Komparative Kostenvorteile und Verhandlungsgewinne. (Environmental Protection as an International Public Good: Comparative Advantage, and Gains from Bargaining. With English summary.) *Z. Wirtschaft. Sozialwissen.*, 1984, 104(2), pp. 111–29.

Baldassarri, Mario. Optimal "Mix" of Government Expenditure and Optimal Growth Path for an Open Economy within a Three Targets–Three Guns Framework. *Econ. Notes*, 1984, (2), pp. 5–24.

Baldry, J. C. The Enforcement of Income Tax Laws: Efficiency Implications. *Econ. Rec.*, June 1984, 60(169), pp. 156–59.

Ball, Ray. The Natural Taxation of Capital Gains and Losses When Income Is Taxed. *J. Banking Finance*, September 1984, 8(3), pp. 471–81.

Baltensperger, Ernst. Inflation und Staatliche Budgetpolitik. (Inflation and Government Debt Financing. With English summary.) *Z. Wirtschaft. Sozialwissen.*, 1984, 104(6), pp. 675–93.

Bamberg, Günter and Richter, Wolfram F. The Effects of Progressive Taxation on Risk-taking. *Z. Nationalökon.*, 1984, 44(2), pp. 93–102.

Barkume, Anthony J. Some Macroeconomic Consequences of Resource Immobility with Public Production. *Public Finance Quart.*, July 1984, 12(3), pp. 373–84. **[G: U.S.]**

Barth, James R.; Iden, George and Russek, Frank S. Do Federal Deficits Really Matter? *Contemp. Policy Issue*, Fall 1984-85, 3(1), pp. 79–95.

Baumol, William J. Toward a Theory of Public Enterprise. *Atlantic Econ. J.*, March 1984, 12(1), pp. 12–19.

Behuria, Sutanu. Taxation and Employment in General Equilibrium: A Two-Sector Analysis. *J. Devel. Econ.*, January–February 1984, 14(1–2), pp. 219–39.

Benninga, Simon and Protopapadakis, Aris. The Neutrality of the Real Equilibrium under Alternative Financing of Government Expenditures. *J. Monet. Econ.*, September 1984, 14(2), pp. 183–208.

Benson, Bruce L. Spatial Price Theory and an Efficient Congestion Toll Established by the Free Market. *Econ. Inquiry*, April 1984, *22*(2), pp. 244–52.

Berckmans, Annie, et al. Debt Management in a Small Open Economy: A Theoretical and an Empirical Study for Belgium. *J. Policy Modeling*, February 1984, *6*(1), pp. 45–67.
[G: Belgium]

Berglas, Eitan and Pines, David. Resource Constraint, Replicability and Mixed Clubs: A Reply [Clubs, Local Public Goods and Transportation Models: A Synthesis]. *J. Public Econ.*, April 1984, *23*(3), pp. 391–97.

Berglas, Eitan. Quantities, Qualities, and Multiple Public Services in the Tiebout Model. *J. Public Econ.*, December 1984, *25*(3), pp. 299–321.

Biørn, Erik. Inflation, Depreciation, and the Neutrality of the Corporate Income Tax. *Scand. J. Econ.*, 1984, *86*(2), pp. 214–28.
[G: Norway]

Blackorby, Charles and Donaldson, David. Ethical Social Index Numbers and the Measurement of Effective Tax/Benefit Progressivity. *Can. J. Econ.*, November 1984, *17*(4), pp. 683–94.

Blanchard, Olivier J. A Reexamination of the Theory of Automatic Stabilizers: Income Stability and Economic Efficiency under Alternative Tax Schemes: Comments. *Carnegie-Rochester Conf. Ser. Public Policy*, Spring 1984, *20*, pp. 207–08.

Blanchard, Olivier J. Current and Anticipated Deficits, Interest Rates and Economic Activity. *Europ. Econ. Rev.*, June 1984, *25*(1), pp. 7–27.
[G: EEC; U.S.]

Bliss, Christopher and Nalebuff, Barry. Dragonslaying and Ballroom Dancing: The Private Supply of a Public Good. *J. Public Econ.*, November 1984, *25*(1/2), pp. 1–12.

Blomgren-Hansen, Niels and Petersen, Jørgen. Samspillet mellem finans-, penge- og valutakurspolitik. (The Interdependence of Fiscal, Monetary, and Exchange Rate Policies. With English summary.) *Nationaløkon. Tidsskr.*, 1984, *122*(1), pp. 73–90.
[G: Denmark]

Blomquist, N. Sören. The Wage Rate Tax—An Alternative to the Income Tax? *Scand. J. Econ.*, 1984, *86*(2), pp. 269–85.

Blomqvist, Åke and Horn, Henrik. Public Health Insurance and Optimal Income Taxation. *J. Public Econ.*, August 1984, *24*(3), pp. 353–71.

Blume, Lawrence E.; Rubinfeld, Daniel L. and Shapiro, Perry. The Taking of Land: When Should Compensation Be Paid? *Quart. J. Econ.*, February 1984, *99*(1), pp. 71–92.

Boadway, Robin and Bruce, Neil. A General Proposition on the Design of a Neutral Business Tax. *J. Public Econ.*, July 1984, *24*(2), pp. 231–39.

Boadway, Robin; Bruce, Neil and Mintz, Jack. The Role and Design of the Corporate Income Tax. *Scand. J. Econ.*, 1984, *86*(2), pp. 286–99.

Bohanon, Cecil E. and Van Cott, T. Norman. Specific Taxes, Product Quality, and Rate-Revenue Analysis. *Public Finance Quart.*, October 1984, *12*(4), pp. 500–511.

Bohm, Peter. Are There Practicable Demand-Revealing Mechanisms? In *Hanusch, H., ed.*, 1984, pp. 127–39.
[G: Sweden]

Bohm, Peter. Revealing Demand for an Actual Public Good. *J. Public Econ.*, July 1984, *24*(2), pp. 135–51.
[G: Sweden]

Bös, Dieter. Income Taxation, Public Sector Pricing and Redistribution. *Scand. J. Econ.*, 1984, *86*(2), pp. 166–83.

Bowles, David C. and Wang, Leonard F. S. The Efficacy of Bond-financed Fiscal Policy Revisited. *Rivista Int. Sci. Econ. Com.*, October–November 1984, *31*(10–11), pp. 1006–16.

Bradley, Michael D. Federal Deficits and the Conduct of Monetary Policy. *J. Macroecon.*, Fall 1984, *6*(4), pp. 411–31.
[G: U.S.]

Brennan, Geoffrey. Elements of a Fiscal Politics: Public Choice and Public Finance. *Australian Econ. Rev.*, 3rd Quarter 1984, (67), pp. 62–72.

Brennan, Geoffrey; Bohanon, Cecil E. and Carter, Richard. Public Finance and Public Prices: Towards a Reconstruction of Tax Theory. *Public Finance*, 1984, *39*(2), pp. 157–81.

Brennan, Geoffrey and Buchanan, James M. Towards a Tax Constitution for Leviathan. In *Buchanan, J. M. and Tollison, R. D., eds.*, 1984, 1977, pp. 71–89.

Brent, Robert J. Use of Distributional Weights in Cost–Benefit Analysis: A Survey of Schools. *Public Finance Quart.*, April 1984, *12*(2), pp. 213–30.

Browning, Edgar K. and Johnson, William R. The Trade-Off between Equality and Efficiency. *J. Polit. Econ.*, April 1984, *92*(2), pp. 175–203.
[G: U.S.]

Brubaker, Earl R. Demand Disclosures and Conditions on Exclusion: An Experiment. *Econ. J.*, September 1984, *94*(375), pp. 536–53.
[G: U.S.]

Brunner, Karl. Deficits, Interest Rates and Monetary Policy. In *Shadow Open Market Committee*, 1984, pp. 13–28.
[G: U.S.]

Bryant, John. How Fiscal Policy Matters. *Fed. Res. Bank Dallas Econ. Rev.*, January 1984, pp. 15–20.
[G: U.S.]

Buchanan, Cathy and Prior, Elizabeth W. Bureaucrats and Babies: Government Regulation of the Supply of Genetic Material. *Econ. Rec.*, September 1984, *60*(170), pp. 222–30.

Buchanan, James M. The Ethical Limits of Taxation. *Scand. J. Econ.*, 1984, *86*(2), pp. 102–14.

Buchanan, James M. and Lee, Dwight R. Some Simple Analytics of the Laffer Curve. In *Hanusch, H., ed.*, 1984, pp. 281–95.

Buchanan, James M. and Lee, Dwight R. Tax Rates and Tax Revenues in Political Equilibrium: Some Simple Analytics. In *Buchanan, J. M. and Tollison, R. D., eds.*, 1984, 1982, pp. 194–205.

Bucovetsky, Sam. On the Use of Distributional

Waits. *Can. J. Econ.*, November 1984, *17*(4), pp. 699–717.

Buiter, Willem H. and Carmichael, Jeffrey. Government Debt: Comment [Government Debt in an Overlapping-Generations Model with Bequests and Gifts]. *Amer. Econ. Rev.*, September 1984, *74*(4), pp. 762–65. **[G: U.S.]**

Burbidge, John B. Government Debt: Reply [Government Debt in an Overlapping-Generations Model with Bequests and Gifts]. *Amer. Econ. Rev.*, September 1984, *74*(4), pp. 766–67. **[G: U.S.]**

Büttler, Hans-Jürg. Ist eine negative Einkommensteuer auf städtischer Ebene möglich? (Is a Negative Local Income Tax Possible? With English summary.) *Z. Wirtschaft. Sozialwissen.*, 1984, *104*(5), pp. 477–88.

Caniglia, Alan S. Intertemporal Effects, Intertemporal Suitability, and the Analysis of In-Kind Subsidy Programs. *Public Finance Quart.*, October 1984, *12*(4), pp. 395–406.

Carlberg, Michael. Kreditfinanzierung versus Steuerfinanzierung der Staatsausgaben—ein langfristiger Vergleich. (Credit Financing versus Tax Financing of Government Expenditures—A Long-Term Comparison. With English summary.) *Kredit Kapital*, 1984, *17*(1), pp. 84–101.

Chamley, Christophe and Polemarchakis, Herakles M. Assets, General Equilibrium and the Neutrality of Money. *Rev. Econ. Stud.*, January 1984, *51*(1), pp. 129–38.

Chiang, Alpha C. and Fei, John C. H. Growth Epochs and Compensatory Fiscal Policy. *Singapore Econ. Rev.*, October 1984, *29*(2), pp. 38–62. **[G: U.S.]**

Christiano, Lawrence J. A Reexamination of the Theory of Automatic Stabilizers: Reply. *Carnegie-Rochester Conf. Ser. Public Policy*, Spring 1984, *20*, pp. 209–10.

Christiano, Lawrence J. A Reexamination of the Theory of Automatic Stabilizers. *Carnegie-Rochester Conf. Ser. Public Policy*, Spring 1984, *20*, pp. 147–206.

Christiansen, Vidar. Which Commodity Taxes Should Supplement the Income Tax? *J. Public Econ.*, July 1984, *24*(2), pp. 195–220.

Cleeton, David L. Wage and Price Measures of the Excess Burdens from Taxation. *Public Finance*, 1984, *39*(1), pp. 11–24.

Collins, D. J. Elements of a Fiscal Politics: Public Choice and Public Finance: Comment. *Australian Econ. Rev.*, 3rd Quarter 1984, (67), pp. 77–78.

Congleton, Roger D. Committees and Rent-seeking Effort. *J. Public Econ.*, November 1984, *25*(1/2), pp. 197–209.

Cook, Thomas J. and D'Antonio, Louis J. Credit Union Taxation: Competitive Effects. *J. Econ. Bus.*, May 1984, *36*(2), pp. 251–62.
[G: U.S.]

Cornes, Richard and Sandler, Todd. Easy Riders, Joint Production, and Public Goods. *Econ. J.*, September 1984, *94*(375), pp. 580–98.

Cornes, Richard and Sandler, Todd. The Theory of Public Goods: Non-Nash Behaviour. *J. Public Econ.*, April 1984, *23*(3), pp. 367–79.

Coursey, Don and Smith, Vernon L. Experimental Tests of an Allocation Mechanism for Private, Public or Externality Goods. *Scand. J. Econ.*, 1984, *86*(4), pp. 468–84.

Cullis, John G. and Jones, Philip R. The Economic Theory of Bureaucracy, X-Inefficiency and Wagner's Law: A Note. *Public Finance*, 1984, *39*(2), pp. 191–201.

Dahl, Carol A. Vertical Equity Effects and Total Consumer Losses for Emergency Allocation Schemes for the Gasoline Market. *Appl. Econ.*, February 1984, *16*(1), pp. 25–32. **[G: U.S.]**

Darby, Jane. Fiscal Policy and Interest Rates. *Nat. Inst. Econ. Rev.*, August 1984, (109), pp. 38–44. **[G: U.K.]**

Darrat, Ali F. The Dominant Influence of Fiscal Actions in Developing Countries. *Eastern Econ. J.*, July–September 1984, *10*(3), pp. 271–84. **[G: Brazil; Chile; Mexico; Peru; Venezuela]**

De Bondt, Raymond R. and Goovaerts, Marc J. The Effectiveness of Temporary Marginal Cost Subsidies. *Int. J. Ind. Organ.*, September 1984, *2*(3), pp. 235–49.

Deloche, Régis. Aménagement infrastructurel du territoire et politique de concurrence. (With English summary.) *Revue Écon. Polit.*, January–February 1984, *94*(1), pp. 92–115.
[G: France]

Díaz, Francisco Gil. The Incidence of Taxes in Mexico: A Before and After Comparison. In *Aspe, P. and Sigmund, P. E., eds.*, 1984, pp. 59–97. **[G: Mexico]**

Dorfman, Robert. On Optimal Congestion. *J. Environ. Econ. Manage.*, June 1984, *11*(2), pp. 91–106.

Dutt, Amitava Krishna. Stagnation, Income Distribution and Monopoly Power. *Cambridge J. Econ.*, March 1984, *8*(1), pp. 25–40.
[G: India]

Dwyer, Gerald P., Jr. Inflation and Government Deficits: A Reply. *Econ. Inquiry*, October 1984, *22*(4), pp. 597–601. **[G: U.S.]**

Edwards, J. S. S. and Keen, Michael J. Wealth Maximization and the Cost of Capital: A Comment. *Quart. J. Econ.*, February 1984, *99*(1), pp. 211–14.

Eichhorn, Wolfgang and Funke, Helmut. A Characterization of the Proportional Income Tax. In *Hammer, G. and Pallaschke, D., eds.*, 1984, pp. 188–204.

Eichhorn, Wolfgang; Funke, Helmut and Richter, Wolfram F. Tax Progression and Inequality of Income Distribution. *J. Math. Econ.*, October 1984, *13*(2), pp. 127–31.

Eisner, Robert. Which Budget Deficit? Some Issues of Measurement and Their Implications. *Amer. Econ. Rev.*, May 1984, *74*(2), pp. 138–43.

Emerson, Craig and Garnaut, Ross. Mineral Leasing Policy: Competitive Bidding and the Resource Rent Tax Given Various Responses to Risk. *Econ. Rec.*, June 1984, *60*(169), pp. 133–42.

Epple, Dennis; Filimon, Radu and Romer, Thomas. Equilibrium among Local Jurisdictions: Toward an Integrated Treatment of Voting and Residential Choice. *J. Public Econ.*, August 1984, *24*(3), pp. 281–308.

Fane, George. The Incidence of a Tax on Pure Rent: The Old Reason for the Old Answer. *J. Polit. Econ.*, April 1984, *92*(2), pp. 329–33.

Faridi, F. R. Theory of Fiscal Policy in an Islamic State: Rejoinder. *J. Res. Islamic Econ.*, Winter 1984, *1*(2), pp. 81–82.

Ferrari, Francesco. Stabilità macroeconomica e vincolo di bilancio pubblico. (Macroeconomic Stability and Government's Budget Restraint. With English summary.) *Econ. Int.*, August–November 1984, *37*(3–4), pp. 288–307.

Ferro, Angelo. Strumentazione fiscale e monetaria nella politica dell'offerta. (The Use of Fiscal and Monetary Tools in Supply-Side Policy. With English summary.) *Bancaria*, October 1984, *40*(10), pp. 957–64.

Fishburn, Peter C. and Willig, Robert D. Transfer Principles in Income Redistribution. *J. Public Econ.*, December 1984, *25*(3), pp. 323–28.

Flowers, Marilyn R. and Danzon, Patricia M. Separation of the Redistributive and Allocative Functions of Government: A Public Choice Perspective. *J. Public Econ.*, August 1984, *24*(3), pp. 373–80.

Fraser, Clive D. Optimal Compensation for Potential Fatality. *J. Public Econ.*, April 1984, *23*(3), pp. 307–32.

Fung, William K. H. and Theobald, Michael F. Dividends and Debt under Alternative Tax Systems. *J. Finan. Quant. Anal.*, March 1984, *19*(1), pp. 59–72. [G: U.S.; U.K.; France; Germany]

Gahvari, Firouz. Incidence and Efficiency Aspects of Differential Taxation of Residential and Industrial Capital in a Growing Economy. *J. Public Econ.*, November 1984, *25*(1/2), pp. 211–33.

Gahvari, Firouz. The Optimal Taxation of Housing. *Public Finance*, 1984, *39*(2), pp. 213–25.

Garrison, Roger W. Deficits and Inflation: A Comment. *Econ. Inquiry*, October 1984, *22*(4), pp. 593–96. [G: U.S.]

Gilbert, Guy. La Relation entre Recettes Fiscales et Taux d'Imposition dans le Temps: Quelques Résultats Analytiques Simples. (Tax Financing and the Shadow Economy. With English summary.) In *Hanusch, H., ed.*, 1984, pp. 297–312.

Gilbert, Guy and Pommerehne, Werner W. Préférences fiscales et politiques d'imposition. (Fiscal Preferences and Tax Policy. With English summary.) *Public Finance*, 1984, *39*(1), pp. 25–69. [G: Australia]

Goacher, D. J. National Savings, Fiscal Policy and Macroeconomic Stability. *Oxford Econ. Pap.*, March 1984, *36*(1), pp. 16–26.

Goodfriend, Marvin. Income Stability and Economic Efficiency under Alternative Tax Schemes: A Comment. *Carnegie-Rochester Conf. Ser. Public Policy*, Spring 1984, *20*, pp. 143–46. [G: U.S.]

Greenberg, Joseph. Avoiding Tax Avoidance: A (Repeated) Game-Theoretic Approach. *J. Econ. Theory*, February 1984, *32*(1), pp. 1–13.

Grimes, Arthur. The Impact of Taxes on Wages: A Comment. *Econ. Notes*, 1984, (3), pp. 163–66. [G: U.S.]

Groenewold, Nicolaas. Short-Run Tax Incidence. *Oxford Econ. Pap.*, March 1984, *36*(1), pp. 146–61.

Groenewold, Nicolaas. The Effects of Fiscal Policy in a Two-Period Model. *J. Macroecon.*, Winter 1984, *6*(1), pp. 23–41.

Groenewold, Nicolaas. The Short-Run Effects of Fiscal Policy with Useful Government Expenditure. *Bull. Econ. Res.*, May 1984, *36*(1), pp. 85–95.

Guesnerie, Roger and Roberts, Kevin. Effective Policy Tools and Quantity Controls. *Econometrica*, January 1984, *52*(1), pp. 59–86.

Hansson, Ingemar. Marginal Cost of Public Funds for Different Tax Instruments and Government Expenditures. *Scand. J. Econ.*, 1984, *86*(2), pp. 115–30. [G: Sweden]

Harper, Ian R. Taxation and Life Insurance: A Theoretical Analysis. *Econ. Rec.*, June 1984, *60*(169), pp. 165–75.

Hartford, Jon D. Relatively Efficient Pollution Standards under Perfect Competition. *Public Finance Quart.*, April 1984, *12*(2), pp. 183–95.

Haurin, Donald R. The Effects of Output and Factor Subsidies or Taxes on an Urban Area. *Reg. Sci. Urban Econ.*, November 1984, *14*(4), pp. 533–46.

Herber, Bernard P. The Demand for Public Goods and Services: Problems of Identification and Measurement in Western Countries. In *Hanusch, H., ed.*, 1984, pp. 141–53. [G: U.S.]

Hersoug, Tor. Can Tax Cuts Beat the Phillips-Curve? *Europ. Econ. Rev.*, April 1984, *24*(3), pp. 369–81.

Hersoug, Tor. Union Wage Responses to Tax Changes. *Oxford Econ. Pap.*, March 1984, *36*(1), pp. 37–51.

Hill, Martyn B. Friedman's Framework for Economic Stability and the Government Budget Constraint: A Comment. *Manchester Sch. Econ. Soc. Stud.*, March 1984, *52*(1), pp. 75–78.

Hillier, Brian and Malcomson, James M. Dynamic Inconsistency, Rational Expectations, and Optimal Government Policy. *Econometrica*, November 1984, *52*(6), pp. 1437–51.

Hirschhorn, Eric. Rational Expectations and the Effects of Government Debt. *J. Monet. Econ.*, July 1984, *14*(1), pp. 55–70. [G: U.S.]

Hoffman, Ronald F. and Levy, Mickey D. Economic and Budget Issues for Deficit Policy. *Contemp. Policy Issue*, Fall 1984-85, *3*(1), pp. 96–114. [G: U.S.]

Holcombe, Randall G. Is Legislation a Public Good? *Rivista Int. Sci. Econ. Com.*, June 1984, *31*(6), pp. 524–36. [G: U.S.]

Holzmann, Robert. Budgetsanierung und pensionsreform. (With English summary.) *Empirica*, 1984, *11*(2), pp. 235–59.   [G: Austria]

Horner, Melchior. Angebot und Nachfrage von Postdepositen. (Supply and Demand of Post Office Demand Deposits. With English summary.) *Schweiz. Z. Volkswirtsch. Statist.*, March 1984, *120*(1), pp. 65–88.

[G: Switzerland]

Hubbard, R. Glenn. Temporary Tax Reductions as Responses to Oil Shocks. In *Alm, A. L. and Weimer, R. J., eds.*, 1984, pp. 121–28.

[G: U.S.]

Huber, Gérard. Inflation and Nominal Tax System in an Open Economy. *Europ. Econ. Rev.*, February 1984, *24*(1), pp. 23–37.

Ihori, Toshihiro. Partial Welfare Improvements and Capital Income Taxation. *J. Public Econ.*, June 1984, *24*(1), pp. 101–09.

Ihori, Toshihiro. Welfare Implications of Indexing Capital Income Taxation. *Econ. Stud. Quart.*, April 1984, *35*(1), pp. 21–30.

Ikeda, Hisashi. The Analysis of Tax Incidence with Initial Distorting Taxes under Uncertainty. (In Japanese. With English summary.) *Osaka Econ. Pap.*, December 1984, *34*(2–3), pp. 93–101.

Iritani, Jun. Optimal Income Taxation: Approximation and Algorism. (In Japanese. With English summary.) *Econ. Stud. Quart.*, December 1984, *35*(3), pp. 230–44.   [G: Japan]

Iritani, Jun. Optimal Taxation: A Generalized Proposition for Approximation. (In Japanese. With English summary.) *Osaka Econ. Pap.*, December 1984, *34*(2–3), pp. 102–09.

Isaac, R. Mark; Walker, James M. and Thomas, Susan H. Divergent Evidence on Free Riding: An Experimental Examination of Possible Explanations. *Public Choice*, 1984, *43*(2), pp. 113–49.

Kemp, Murray C. On the Applicability and Implementability of the (Finite) Compensation Principle. *Kobe Econ. Bus. Rev.*, 1984, *30*, pp. 17–22.

Kiefer, Donald W. Distributional Tax Progressivity Indexes. *Nat. Tax J.*, December 1984, *37*(4), pp. 497–513.   [G: U.S.]

Koch, Walter A. S. Negative Einkommensteuern und Konjunkturpolitik. (Negative Income Taxes and Stabilization Policy. With English summary.) *Konjunkturpolitik*, 1984, *30*(6), pp. 348–73.   [G: U.S.]

Koenig, Evan F. Uncertainty and Pollution: The Role of Indirect Taxation. *J. Public Econ.*, June 1984, *24*(1), pp. 111–22.

Kofuji, Yasuo. On the Efficacy of Fiscal Policy and Price Level Changes. *Public Finance Quart.*, April 1984, *12*(2), pp. 167–81.

Kolbe, A. Lawrence; Tye, William B. and Baker, Miriam Alexander. Conditions for Investor and Customer Indifference to Transitions among Regulatory Treatments of Deferred Income Taxes. *Rand J. Econ.*, Autumn 1984, *15*(3), pp. 434–46.   [G: U.S.]

Koskela, Erkki and Kanniainen, Vesa. Changing the Tax Base and Risk-Taking. *Oxford Econ. Pap.*, March 1984, *36*(1), pp. 162–74.

Kotlikoff, Laurence J. Economic Impact of Deficit Financing. *Int. Monet. Fund Staff Pap.*, September 1984, *31*(3), pp. 549–82.   [G: U.S.]

Kotlikoff, Laurence J. Taxation and Savings: A Neoclassical Perspective. *J. Econ. Lit.*, December 1984, *22*(4), pp. 1576–1629.

[G: U.S.]

Krashinsky, Michael. Some Limitations on the Usefulness of Revenue Dependency: Why Governments Often Produce What They Subsidize. *Can. Public Policy*, March 1984, *10*(1), pp. 35–46.

Kudrle, Robert Thomas. Excise Tax Incidence in Limit Price Oligopoly. *Public Finance*, 1984, *39*(3), pp. 321–46.

Kurz, Rudi. Staatsverschuldung und Einkommensverteilung. Einige kritische Anmerkungen zur These von den unsozialen Verteilungswirkungen. (Public Debt and Income Distribution: Some Critical Notes on Unsocial Distributional Effect. With English summary.) *Konjunkturpolitik*, 1984, *30*(4), pp. 217–32.

[G: W. Germany]

Lachmann, Werner. Kann die staatliche Kreditaufnahme im Ausland ein "Crowding-out" verhindern? (Does Public Borrowing Abroad Prevent Crowding-out Effects? With English summary.) *Jahr. Nationalökon. Statist.*, November 1984, *199*(6), pp. 522–36.

Lambert, Peter J. Non-equiproportionate Income Growth, Inequality, and the Income Tax. *Public Finance*, 1984, *39*(1), pp. 104–18.

[G: U.K.]

Laumas, G. S. and McMillin, W. D. Anticipated Fiscal Policy and Real Output. *Rev. Econ. Statist.*, August 1984, *66*(3), pp. 468–71.

[G: U.S.]

Le Grand, Julian. Optimal Taxation, the Compensation Principle and the Measurement of Changes in Economic Welfare. *J. Public Econ.*, July 1984, *24*(2), pp. 241–47.

Lee, Dwight R. On the Pricing of Public Goods: Reply. *Southern Econ. J.*, October 1984, *51*(2), pp. 601–02.

León, Carlos Amat Y. Fiscal Deficits and Balance of Payments Disequilibrium in IMF Adjustment Programs: Comment. In *Muns, J., ed.*, 1984, pp. 137–40.   [G: LDCs; Peru]

Lombra, Raymond E. and Wasylenko, Michael. The Subsidization of Small Business through Federal Credit Programs: Analytical Foundations. *J. Econ. Bus.*, May 1984, *36*(2), pp. 263–74.

Long, Ngo Van and Sinn, Hans-Werner. Optimal Taxation and Economic Depreciation: A General Equilibrium Model with Capital and an Exhaustible Resource. In *Kemp, M. C. and Long, N. V., eds.*, 1984, pp. 227–46.

Malinvaud, E. Current and Anticipated Deficits, Interest Rates and Economic Activity: Comments. *Europ. Econ. Rev.*, June 1984, *25*(1), pp. 29–32.   [G: EEC; U.S.]

Marchand, Maurice; Pestieau, Pierre and Weymark, John A. Discount Rates for Public Enterprises in the Presence of Alternative Financial Constraints: A Correction. *Z. Nationalökon.*, 1984, *44*(3), pp. 289–91.

Marion, Nancy Peregrim and Svensson, Lars E. O. World Equilibrium with Oil Price Increases: An Intertemporal Analysis. *Oxford Econ. Pap.*, March 1984, *36*(1), pp. 86–102.

Markusen, James R. The Welfare and Allocative Effects of Export Taxes versus Marketing Boards. *J. Devel. Econ.*, January–February 1984, *14*(1–2), pp. 19–36.

Marris, Stephen N. Current and Anticipated Deficits, Interest Rates and Economic Activity: Comments. *Europ. Econ. Rev.*, June 1984, *25*(1), pp. 33–36. [**G: U.S.; Japan; Germany; U.K.**]

Martin, Lawrence W. The Optimal Magnitude and Enforcement of Evadable Pigovian Charges. *Public Finance*, 1984, *39*(3), pp. 347–58.

Masera, Rainer S. Monetary Policy and Budget Policy: Blend or Dichotomy? In *Masera, R. S. and Triffin, R.*, eds., 1984, pp. 196–223. [**G: Italy; OECD**]

Masson, Paul; Blundell-Wignall, Adrian and Richardson, Peter. Domestic and International Effects of Government Spending under Rational Expectations. *OECD Econ. Stud.*, Autumn 1984, (3), pp. 177–90. [**G: U.S.**]

Mathews, Russell. The Case for Indirect Taxation. *Australian Tax Forum*, March 1984, *1*(1), pp. 54–82. [**G: OECD; Australia**]

Mayer, Thomas. The Government Budget Constraint and Standard Macrotheory. *J. Monet. Econ.*, May 1984, *13*(3), pp. 371–79.

McCallum, Bennett T. Are Bond-Financed Deficits Inflationary? A Ricardian Analysis. *J. Polit. Econ.*, February 1984, *92*(1), pp. 123–35.

McDonald, Ian M. Anti-stagflationary Tax Cuts and the Problem of Investment. *Econ. Rec.*, September 1984, *60*(170), pp. 284–93.

McKinney, Scott. Public Good Producers and Spillovers: An Analysis of Duopoly Behavior. *Public Finance Quart.*, January 1984, *12*(1), pp. 97–116.

Melvin, James R. Taxes, Relative Prices and Trade. In *Csikós-Nagy, B.; Hague, D. and Hall, G.*, eds., 1984, pp. 183–200.

Mestelman, Stuart. The Social Choice of Alternative Corrective Devices. *Public Choice*, 1984, *42*(1), pp. 55–71.

Michel, Philippe; Pestieau, Pierre and Thisse, Jacques-François. A Propos de la répartition interrégionale des investissements. (With English summary.) *Revue Écon. Polit.*, January–February 1984, *94*(1), pp. 49–59.

Miller, Preston J. Income Stability and Economic Efficiency under Alternative Tax Schemes. *Carnegie-Rochester Conf. Ser. Public Policy*, Spring 1984, *20*, pp. 121–41. [**G: U.S.**]

Montiel, Peter. Credit and Fiscal Policies in a "Global Monetarist" Model of the Balance of Payments. *Int. Monet. Fund Staff Pap.*, December 1984, *31*(4), pp. 685–708.

Moreland, Kemper. Public Goods and Optimal Income Taxation. *Public Finance Quart.*, April 1984, *12*(2), pp. 197–212. [**G: U.S.**]

Nerlove, Marc; Razin, Assaf and Sadka, Efraim. Income Distribution Policies with Endogenous Fertility. *J. Public Econ.*, July 1984, *24*(2), pp. 221–30.

Nerlove, Marc; Razin, Assaf and Sadka, Efraim. Investment in Human and Nonhuman Capital, Transfers among Siblings, and the Role of Government. *Econometrica*, September 1984, *52*(5), pp. 1191–98.

O'Hagan, Ciaran. Pigovian Taxes, Polluter Subsidies, Regulation, and the Size of a Polluting Industry: A Note. *Can. J. Econ.*, August 1984, *17*(3), pp. 588–92.

Oates, Wallace E. and Strassmann, Diana L. Effluent Fees and Market Structure. *J. Public Econ.*, June 1984, *24*(1), pp. 29–46.

Oehsen, Johann Hermann. Ein erweitertes umweltökonomisches Standardmodell. (An Extended Standard Model of Environmental Economics. With English summary.) *Jahr. Nationalökon. Statist.*, January 1984, *199*(1), pp. 49–64.

Okuguchi, Koji. Utility Function, Group Size, and the Aggregate Provision of a Pure Public Good. *Public Choice*, 1984, *42*(3), pp. 247–55.

Osborne, Martin J. Why Do Some Goods Bear Higher Taxes than Others? *J. Econ. Theory*, April 1984, *32*(2), pp. 301–16.

Oswald, Andrew J. Three Theorems on Inflation Taxes and Marginal Employment Subsidies. *Econ. J.*, September 1984, *94*(375), pp. 599–611.

Padoa Schioppa, Fiorella. Public Expenditure in a Flexi-price Model. *Public Finance*, 1984, *39*(1), pp. 133–48.

Paleologos, John M. The Dynamic Impacts of Fiscal and Monetary Policy on an Aggregate Macroeconomic Model of the Greek Economy—Some Policy Experiments. *Public Finance*, 1984, *39*(2), pp. 261–80. [**G: Greece**]

Palfrey, Thomas R. and Rosenthal, Howard. Participation and the Provision of Discrete Public Goods: A Strategic Analysis. *J. Public Econ.*, July 1984, *24*(2), pp. 171–93.

Pemberton, James. The Long Run Phillips Curve and the Government Budget Constraint. *Scot. J. Polit. Econ.*, November 1984, *31*(3), pp. 255–64.

Persson, Mats and Wissén, Pehr. Redistributional Aspects of Tax Evasion. *Scand. J. Econ.*, 1984, *86*(2), pp. 131–49.

Persson, Torsten and Svensson, Lars E. O. Time-Consistent Fiscal Policy and Government Cash-Flow. *J. Monet. Econ.*, November 1984, *14*(3), pp. 365–74.

Pfähler, Wilhelm. 'Linear' Income Tax Cuts: Distributional Effects, Social Preferences and Revenue Elasticities. *J. Public Econ.*, August 1984, *24*(3), pp. 381–88.

Pitkänen, Eero. Julkisten liikelaitosten toiminnan tuloksellisuus. (The Efficiency and Effectiveness of Public Enterprises. With English summary.) *Liiketaloudellinen Aikak.*, 1984, *33*(1), pp. 81–106. [**G: Finland; Sweden**]

Porcano, Thomas M. Distributive Justice and Tax

Policy. *Accounting Rev.*, October 1984, *59*(4), pp. 619–36.

Ramb, Bernd-Thomas. Ineffektivität der Wirtschaftspolitik bei "rationalen Erwartungen"? Eine unkerrekte, aber auch modellspezifische Behauptung. (Ineffectiveness of Economic Policy under "Rational Expectations"? An Incorrect but Also Model-Specific Assertion. With English summary.) *Kredit Kapital*, 1984, *17*(2), pp. 165–79.

Raymon, Neil and Stuart, Charles E. Short-Run Politicians and Long-Run Tax Revenue: An Empirical Assessment. *Scand. J. Econ.*, 1984, *86*(3), pp. 314–25. [G: U.S.]

Rieber, William J. The Expenditure Effects of Supply Side Tax Cuts: The Role of the Interest Elasticity of Money Demand. *Quart. J. Bus. Econ.*, Summer 1984, *23*(3), pp. 29–35.

Risager, Ole. Budgetbalanceunderskud, handelsbalanceunderskud og den montetære devalueringsanalyse. (Government Budget Deficits, the Balance of Payments and the Monetary Devaluation Analysis. With English summary.) *Nationaløkon. Tidsskr.*, 1984, *122*(1), pp. 56–72.

Roberts, Kevin. The Theoretical Limits of Redistribution. *Rev. Econ. Stud.*, April 1984, *51*(2), pp. 177–95.

Roberts, Russell D. A Positive Model of Private Charity and Public Transfers. *J. Polit. Econ.*, February 1984, *92*(1), pp. 136–48. [G: U.S.]

Robinson, William D. Government Bonds and Unstable Growth Paths. *Quart. J. Bus. Econ.*, Summer 1984, *23*(3), pp. 36–58. [G: U.S.]

Rødseth, Asbjørn. Progressive Taxes and Automatic Stabilization in an Open Economy. *J. Macroecon.*, Summer 1984, *6*(3), pp. 265–82.

Roy, Subroto. Considerations on Utility, Benevolence, and Taxation. *Hist. Polit. Econ.*, Fall 1984, *16*(3), pp. 349–62.

Rush, Mark. A Classical Model of a Small Fixed Exchange Rate Economy. *J. Int. Money Finance*, April 1984, *3*(1), pp. 31–49.

Sachs, Jeffrey D. and Wyplosz, Charles. La politique budgétaire et le taux de change réel. (Fiscal Policy and the Real Exchange Rate. With English summary.) *Ann. INSEE*, January–March 1984, (53), pp. 63–92.

Sah, Raaj Kumar and Stiglitz, Joseph E. The Economics of Price Scissors. *Amer. Econ. Rev.*, March 1984, *74*(1), pp. 125–38.

Sahni, Balbir S. and Singh, Balvir. On the Causal Directions between National Income and Government Expenditure in Canada. *Public Finance*, 1984, *39*(3), pp. 359–93. [G: Canada]

Sampson, Anthony A. An Optional Tax System. *J. Public Econ.*, August 1984, *24*(3), pp. 389–95.

Sandler, Todd and Tschirhart, John T. Mixed Clubs: Further Observations [Clubs, Local Public Goods and Transportation Models: A Synthesis]. *J. Public Econ.*, April 1984, *23*(3), pp. 381–89.

Sandmo, Agnar. Some Insights from the "New" Theory of Public Finance. *Empirica*, 1984, *11*(2), pp. 111–24.

Sanson, Joao Rogério. An Alternative Model for Studying the Incidence of Indirect Taxes. *J. Public Econ.*, November 1984, *25*(1/2), pp. 245–54. [G: Brazil]

Scarth, William M. Friedman's Framework for Economic Stability: A Reply. *Manchester Sch. Econ. Soc. Stud.*, March 1984, *52*(1), pp. 79–83.

Schwartz, Peter M. On the Pricing of Public Goods: Comment. *Southern Econ. J.*, October 1984, *51*(2), pp. 598–600.

Schweizer, Urs. Welfare Analysis of Excise Tax Evasion. *Z. ges. Staatswiss.*, June 1984, *140*(2), pp. 247–58.

Seidl, Christian. The Tax State in Crisis: Can Schumpeterian Public Finance Claim Modern Relevance? In *Seidl, C., ed.*, 1984, pp. 89–109.

Seidman, Laurence S. Conversion to a Consumption Tax: The Transition in a Life-Cycle Growth Model. *J. Polit. Econ.*, April 1984, *92*(2), pp. 247–67.

Seidman, Laurence S. The Welfare Economics of Taxes: A Three-Class Disposable Income Growth Model. *Public Finance Quart.*, January 1984, *12*(1), pp. 3–26.

Sgontz, L. G. Efficiency and the Tax Treatment of Secondary Workers. *Nat. Tax J.*, June 1984, *37*(2), pp. 249–52.

Shah, Anup R. Crowding Out, Capital Accumulation, the Stock Market, and Money-financed Fiscal Policy. *J. Money, Credit, Banking*, Part 1 November 1984, *16*(4), pp. 461–73.

el Shaikh, Riad. Theory of Fiscal Policy in an Islamic State: Comment. *J. Res. Islamic Econ.*, Winter 1984, *1*(2), pp. 79–80.

Shoven, John B. and Whalley, John. Applied General-Equilibrium Models of Taxation and International Trade: An Introduction and Survey. *J. Econ. Lit.*, September 1984, *22*(3), pp. 1007–51.

Silvestre, Joaquim. Voluntariness and Efficiency in the Provision of Public Goods. *J. Public Econ.*, July 1984, *24*(2), pp. 249–56.

Singh, Balvir and Sahni, Balbir S. Causality between Public Expenditure and National Income. *Rev. Econ. Statist.*, November 1984, *66*(4), pp. 630–44. [G: India]

Smith, Janet Kiholm and Smith, Richard L., II. State and Local Fiscal Policy: Implications for Property Values and Economic Growth. *Public Finance Quart.*, January 1984, *12*(1), pp. 51–76. [G: U.S.]

Søndergaard, Jørgen. Incitamenter, information og offentlige beslutninger. (Incentive, Information, and Public Decision. With English summary.) *Nationaløkon. Tidsskr.*, 1984, *122*(2), pp. 201–12.

Startz, Richard. Prelude to Macroeconomics. *Amer. Econ. Rev.*, December 1984, *74*(5), pp. 881–92.

Steindl, Josef. On Maturity in Capitalist Economies. In *Foster, J. B. and Szlajfer, H., eds.*, 1984, *1966*, pp. 167–78.

Stemp, Peter J. and Turnovsky, Stephen J. Equilibrium, Stability, and Deficit Financing in a Simple Nonlinear Monetary Model under Perfect Foresight. *J. Macroecon.*, Fall 1984, *6*(4), pp. 377–97.

Stern, Nicholas H. Optimum Taxation and Tax Policy. *Int. Monet. Fund Staff Pap.*, June 1984, *31*(2), pp. 339–78.   **[G: India]**

Stournaras, Yannis A. Optimal Taxes and Subsidies in Fix-Price, Open Economies. *Oxford Econ. Pap.*, November 1984, *36*(3), pp. 459–77.

Strydom, P. D. F. The New Keynesian Approach to Economic Policy. *S. Afr. J. Econ.*, September 1984, *52*(3), pp. 282–95.

Stuart, Charles E. Welfare Costs per Dollar of Additional Tax Revenue in the United States. *Amer. Econ. Rev.*, June 1984, *74*(3), pp. 352–62.   **[G: U.S.]**

Stutzer, Michael J. Variable Rate Subsidies: The Inefficiency of In-Kind Transfers Revisited. *Public Finance Quart.*, January 1984, *12*(1), pp. 77–95.   **[G: U.S.]**

Sugden, Robert. Reciprocity: The Supply of Public Goods through Voluntary Contributions. *Econ. J.*, December 1984, *94*(376), pp. 772–87.

Sullivan, Arthur M. The General Equilibrium Effects of the Industrial Property Tax: Incidence and Excess Burden. *Reg. Sci. Urban Econ.*, November 1984, *14*(4), pp. 547–63.

Sumner, Michael T. and Ward, Robert. The Impact of Taxes on Wages: A Further Analysis. *Econ. Notes*, 1984, (3), pp. 155–62.
                    [G: U.S.]

Tanzi, Vito and Blejer, Mario I. Fiscal Deficits and Balance of Payments Disequilibrium in IMF Adjustment Programs. In *Muns, J., ed.*, 1984, pp. 117–36.   **[G: LDCs]**

Thornton, Daniel L. The Government Budget Constraint with Endogenous Money. *J. Macroecon.*, Winter 1984, *6*(1), pp. 57–67.

Throsby, C. D. The Measurement of Willingness-to-Pay for Mixed Goods. *Oxford Bull. Econ. Statist.*, November 1984, *46*(4), pp. 279–89.
                    [G: Australia]

Tideman, T. Nicolaus and Tullock, Gordon. A New and Superior Process for Making Social Choices. In *Buchanan, J. M. and Tollison, R. D., eds.*, 1984, *1976*, pp. 121–33.

Toma, Eugenia Froedge and Toma, Mark. Constitutional Tax Constraints within a Classical Model of Leviathan. *Hist. Polit. Econ.*, Spring 1984, *16*(1), pp. 89–105.

Topham, Neville. A Reappriasal and Recalculation of the Marginal Cost of Public Funds. *Public Finance*, 1984, *39*(3), pp. 394–405.

Truchon, Michel. Nonmyopic Strategic Behavior in the MDP Planning Procedure. *Econometrica*, September 1984, *52*(5), pp. 1179–89.

Tuckman, Howard P. Social Efficiency and the Provision of Collective Services. *Amer. J. Econ. Soc.*, July 1984, *43*(3), pp. 257–68.

Tuomala, Matti. On the Optimal Income Taxation: Some Further Numerical Results. *J. Public Econ.*, April 1984, *23*(3), pp. 351–66.

Tuomala, Matti. Optimal Degree of Progressivity under Income Uncertainty. *Scand. J. Econ.*, 1984, *86*(2), pp. 184–93.

Turnovsky, Stephen J. and Miller, Marcus H. The Effects of Government Expenditure on the Term Structure of Interest Rates. *J. Money, Credit, Banking*, February 1984, *16*(1), pp. 16–33.

Usher, Dan. An Instructive Derivation of the Expression for the Marginal Cost of Public Funds. *Public Finance*, 1984, *39*(3), pp. 406–11.

Vohra, Rajiv. Local Public Goods and Average Cost Pricing. *J. Math. Econ.*, April 1984, *13*(1), pp. 51–67.

Walsh, Cliff. Elements of a Fiscal Politics: Public Choice and Public Finance: Comment. *Australian Econ. Rev.*, 3rd Quarter 1984, (67), pp. 73–76.

Waugh, Frederick V. Excise Taxes and Economic Stability. In *Waugh, F. V.*, 1984, *1948*, pp. 40–51.

Weymark, John A. Majority-Rule Directions of Income Tax Reform and Second-Best Optimality. *Scand. J. Econ.*, 1984, *86*(2), pp. 194–213.

van Wijnbergen, Sweder. The 'Dutch Disease': A Disease after All? *Econ. J.*, March 1984, *94*(373), pp. 41–55.

Wildasin, David E. On Public Good Provision with Distortionary Taxation. *Econ. Inquiry*, April 1984, *22*(2), pp. 227–43.

Wilson, John D. The Excise Tax Effects of the Property Tax. *J. Public Econ.*, August 1984, *24*(3), pp. 309–29.

Wisley, Thomas O. The Effectiveness of Fiscal Policy under a Consumption Tax. *Quart. Rev. Econ. Bus.*, Spring 1984, *24*(1), pp. 33–41.

Wolken, John D. and Navratil, Frank J. The Valuation of Subsidies in Kind and Their Effects on Costs. *J. Econ. Bus.*, May 1984, *36*(2), pp. 217–32.   **[G: U.S.]**

Wyckoff, James H. The Nonexcludable Publicness of Primary and Secondary Public Education. *J. Public Econ.*, August 1984, *24*(3), pp. 331–51.   **[G: U.S.]**

Yandle, Bruce. Groundwater and the Land Value Tax: Some Dimensions of the Problems Facing Fiscal Specialists in Applying Rent Taxation to Underground Resources. *Amer. J. Econ. Soc.*, July 1984, *43*(3), pp. 323–32.

Zee, Howell H. On the Decomposition of the Harberger Tax Incidence Equation. *Atlantic Econ. J.*, December 1984, *12*(4), pp. 41–45.

Zimmermann, Klaus F. Die Inzidenz der Umweltpolitik in theoretischer und empirischer Sicht. (The Incidence of Environmental Policy: Theoretical Aspects and Empirical Evidence. With English summary.) *Jahr. Nationalökon. Statist.*, November 1984, *199*(6), pp. 502–21.
                    [G: U.S.; Sweden]

3216 Fiscal Policy

Aaron, Henry J. and Galper, Harvey. A Tax on Consumption, Gifts, and Bequests and Other Strategies for Reform. In *Pechman, J. A., ed.*, 1984, pp. 106–34.   **[G: U.S.]**

Anderson, Annelise Graebner. The Federal Budget: Problems and Prospects. In *Moore, J. H., ed.*, 1984, pp. 183–98.   **[G: U.S.]**

Anderson, Martin. An Economic Bill of Rights. In *Moore, J. H., ed.*, 1984, pp. 1–22.
[G: U.S.]

Arestis, Philip and Karakitsos, E. The Impact of Fiscal Policy in the UK: Evidence from Two Macroeconomic Models. *Appl. Econ.*, October 1984, *16*(5), pp. 729–47. [G: U.K.]

Auld, D. A. L. Public Revenues and Public Policy: The Impact on the Canadian Economy. In *Block, W. and Walker, M., eds.*, 1984, pp. 66–103. [G: Canada]

Bailey, John J. Public Budgeting in Mexico, 1970–1982. *Public Budg. Finance*, Spring 1984, *4*(1), pp. 76–90. [G: Mexico]

Bird, Richard M. Tax Harmonization and Federal Finance: A Perspective on Recent Canadian Discussion. *Can. Public Policy*, September 1984, *10*(3), pp. 253–66. [G: Canada]

Blinder, Alan S. and Holtz-Eakin, Douglas. Public Opinion and the Balanced Budget. *Amer. Econ. Rev.*, May 1984, *74*(2), pp. 144–49.
[G: U.S.]

Bohm, Peter. Are There Practicable Demand-Revealing Mechanisms? In *Hanusch, H., ed.*, 1984, pp. 127–39. [G: Sweden]

Brennan, Geoffrey. Constitutional Constraints on the Fiscal Powers of Government. In *McKenzie, R. B., ed. (I)*, 1984, pp. 115–31.

Broadberry, S. N. Fiscal Policy in Britain during the 1930s [The Constant Employment Budget Balance and British Budgetary Policy, 1929–39]. *Econ. Hist. Rev., 2nd Ser.*, February 1984, *37*(1), pp. 95–102. [G: U.K.]

Brown, J. A. C. and Helou, A. The Fiscal Policy of Japan since 1970. *Oxford Bull. Econ. Statist.*, May 1984, *46*(2), pp. 89–124.
[G: Japan]

Buchanan, James M. The Limits of Taxation. In *Block, W. and Walker, M., eds.*, 1984, pp. 41–55.

de Buitléir, Donal. The Third Report of the Commission on Taxation. *Irish Banking Rev.*, September 1984, pp. 46–56. [G: Ireland]

de Buitléir, Donal. Whither Tax Policy. *Irish Banking Rev.*, June 1984, pp. 12–23.

Chand, Sheetal K. A Keynesian Fiscal Policy and the New Classical Macroeconomics. *J. Post Keynesian Econ.*, Summer 1984, *6*(4), pp. 509–22.

Chand, Sheetal K. The Stabilizing Role of Fiscal Policy. *Finance Develop.*, March 1984, *21*(1), pp. 38–41. [G: LDCs; U.S.]

Chiang, Alpha C. and Fei, John C. H. Growth Epochs and Compensatory Fiscal Policy. *Singapore Econ. Rev.*, October 1984, *29*(2), pp. 38–62. [G: U.S.]

Chouraqui, Jean-Claude and Price, Robert W. R. Medium-term Financial Strategy: The Coordination of Fiscal and Monetary Policies. *OECD Econ. Stud.*, Spring 1984, (2), pp. 7–49. [G: OECD]

Clotfelter, Charles T. Tax Cut Meets Bracket Creep: The Rise and Fall of Marginal Tax Rates, 1964–1984. *Public Finance Quart.*, April 1984, *12*(2), pp. 131–52. [G: U.S.]

Coen, Robert M. and Hickman, Bert G. Tax Policy, Federal Deficits, and U.S. Growth in the 1980s. *Nat. Tax J.*, March 1984, *37*(1), pp. 89–104. [G: U.S.]

Congdon, Tim G. The Analytical Foundations of the Medium-term Financial Strategy. *Fisc. Stud.*, May 1984, *5*(2), pp. 17–29. [G: U.K.]

Costa, José. Government Budget Deficits, Money Supply, and Inflation in Portugal. *Economia (Portugal)*, January 1984, *8*(1), pp. 97–116.
[G: Portugal]

Coulombe, Serge. Une analyse de la politique fiscale du gouvernement fédéral par l'examen des soldes budgétaires. (An Analysis of the Federal Fiscal Policy. With English summary.) *L'Actual. Econ.*, June 1984, *60*(2), pp. 240–53. [G: Canada]

Davidson, Paul. The Conventional Wisdom on Deficits Is Wrong. *Challenge*, November/December 1984, *27*(5), pp. 54–56. [G: U.S.]

Emminger, Otmar. Financial Policy at the Crossroads. *Lloyds Bank Rev.*, January 1984, (151), pp. 1–11. [G: OECD]

Friedman, Benjamin M. Managing the U.S. Government Deficit in the 1980s. In *Wachter, M. L. and Wachter, S. M., eds.*, 1984, pp. 265–301. [G: U.S.]

Goedhuys, D. W. The Business Cycle and Public Policy. *S. Afr. J. Econ.*, June 1984, *52*(2), pp. 133–45. [G: S. Africa]

Gorton, Slade. Tax Reform and the Tax Legislative Process. In *Pechman, J. A., ed.*, 1984, pp. 33–38. [G: U.S.]

Graetz, Michael J. Can the Income Tax Continue to Be the Major Revenue Source? In *Pechman, J. A., ed.*, 1984, pp. 39–65. [G: U.S.]

Grinspun, Bernardo. Las Perspectivas de las Políticas Económica y Fiscal de la Argentina. (Prospects of the Economic and Fiscal Policies of Argentina. With English summary.) *Bull. Int. Fiscal Doc.*, 1984, *38*(8–9), pp. 352–58.
[G: Argentina]

Halberstadt, Victor; Goudsvaard, Kees and LeBlanc, Bart. Current Control Problems with Public Expenditure in Five European Countries. In *Emerson, M., ed.*, 1984, pp. 122–49.
[G: Belgium; Denmark; Ireland; Italy; Netherlands]

Halperin, Daniel. A Tax on Consumption, Gifts, and Bequests and Other Strategies for Reform: Comment. In *Pechman, J. A., ed.*, 1984, pp. 141–46. [G: U.S.]

Herschtel, Marie-Luise. Les finances publiques françaises 1983–1985: réalisations et perspectives. (With English summary.) *Revue Écon. Polit.*, September–October 1984, *94*(5), pp. 629–38. [G: France]

Hoffman, Ronald F. and Levy, Mickey D. Economic and Budget Issues for Deficit Policy. *Contemp. Policy Issue*, Fall 1984-85, *3*(1), pp. 96–114. [G: U.S.]

Husain, Ishrat. Raising Resources for Development: The Challenge for the Eighties. In *Burki, S. J. and LaPorte, R., Jr., eds.*, 1984, pp. 103–36. [G: Pakistan]

Hutchinson, Michael M. Intervention, Deficit Finance and Real Exchange Rates: The Case of

Japan. *Fed. Res. Bank San Francisco Econ. Rev.*, Winter 1984, (1), pp. 27–44.
[G: Japan]

Jeanrenaud, Claude. Public Procurement and Economic Policy. *Ann. Pub. Co-op. Econ.*, April–June 1984, 55(2), pp. 151–58.
[G: W. Europe; U.S.]

Keller, Robert R. A Macroeconomic History of Supply-Side Fiscal Policies in the 1920s. *Rev. Soc. Econ.*, October 1984, 42(2), pp. 130–42.
[G: U.S.]

Kelly, William A., Jr. and Chambers, Donald R. Inflation, Taxes, and Savings "Incentives." *Financial Rev.*, May 1984, 19(2), pp. 222–31.
[G: U.S.]

Kesselman, Jonathan R. Public Revenues and Public Policy: The Impact on the Canadian Economy: Comment. In *Block, W. and Walker, M., eds.*, 1984, pp. 103–10.
[G: Canada]

Kopits, George and Mutén, Leif. The Relevance of the Unitary Approach for Developing Countries. In *McLure, C. E., Jr., ed.*, 1984, pp. 269–80.

Korff, Hans Clausen. Planning and Budgeting in the Federal Republic of Germany. In *Premchand, A. and Burkhead, J., eds.*, 1984, pp. 39–52.
[G: W. Germany]

Lehment, Harmen. The Macroeconomic Implications of Public-sector Deficits. In *Emerson, M., ed.*, 1984, pp. 150–73.
[G: W. Europe]

Levy, Mickey D. Budget Deficits and the Disarray of Fiscal Policy. In *Shadow Open Market Committee*, 1984, pp. 57–66.
[G: U.S.]

Luger, Michael I. Investment Incentives and the Demand for Labor in U.S. Regions. *Reg. Sci. Urban Econ.*, November 1984, 14(4), pp. 481–503.
[G: U.S.]

McLure, Charles E., Jr. A Tax on Consumption, Gifts, and Bequests and Other Strategies for Reform: Comment. In *Pechman, J. A., ed.*, 1984, pp. 134–41.
[G: U.S.]

Mills, Gregory B. and Palmer, John L. The Federal Budget in Flux. In *Mills, G. B. and Palmer, J. L., eds.*, 1984, pp. 9–41.
[G: U.S.]

Mowery, David C. and Kamlet, Mark S. Games Presidents Do and Do Not Play: Presidential Circumvention of the Executive Branch Budget Process. *Policy Sci.*, March 1984, 16(4), pp. 303–27.
[G: U.S.]

Musgrave, Peggy B. The Relevance of the Unitary Approach for Developing Countries: Comments. In *McLure, C. E., Jr., ed.*, 1984, pp. 281–85.

Musgrave, Richard A. Constitutional Constraints on the Fiscal Powers of Government: Comment. In *McKenzie, R. B., ed. (I)*, 1984, pp. 133–39.

Nolan, John S. Can the Income Tax Continue to Be the Major Revenue Source? Comment. In *Pechman, J. A., ed.*, 1984, pp. 65–69.
[G: U.S.]

Oldman, Oliver. The Relevance of the Unitary Approach for Developing Countries: Com-

ments. In *McLure, C. E., Jr., ed.*, 1984, pp. 286–87.

Ott, Mack. Depreciation, Inflation, and Investment Incentives: The Effects of the Tax Acts of 1981 and 1982. *Fed. Res. Bank St. Louis Rev.*, November 1984, 66(9), pp. 17–30.
[G: U.S.]

Parkin, Michael. The United Kingdom: Political Economy and Macroeconomics: A Comment. *Carnegie-Rochester Conf. Ser. Public Policy*, Autumn 1984, 21, pp. 281–93.
[G: U.K.]

Pedone, Antonio. The 1973–74 Tax Reform in Italy: A Partial Success with Many Shortcomings. *Banca Naz. Lavoro Quart. Rev.*, December 1984, (151), pp. 327–49.
[G: Italy]

Phillips, Ian R. Using the Tax System to Influence Private and Corporate Investment. *Australian Tax Forum*, September 1984, 1(3), pp. 313–22.
[G: U.S.]

Price, Robert W. R. and Muller, Patrice. Structural Budget Indicators and the Interpretation of Fiscal Policy Stance in OECD Economies. *OECD Econ. Stud.*, Autumn 1984, (3), pp. 27–72.
[G: OECD]

Rabushka, Alvin. Controlling the Federal Budget. In *Moore, J. H., ed.*, 1984, pp. 199–215.
[G: U.S.]

Rivlin, Alice M. Reform of the Budget Process. *Amer. Econ. Rev.*, May 1984, 74(2), pp. 133–37.

Saulnier, Raymond J. The President's Economic Report: A Critique. *J. Portfol. Manage.*, Summer 1984, 10(4), pp. 81–83.
[G: U.S.]

Seldon, Arthur. Enhancement of Public Sector Efficiency by Micro-economic Control of Public Supply. In *Hanusch, H., ed.*, 1984, pp. 155–65.

Seth, K. G. Equity in Taxation—A New Interpretation. In *Singh, A. K.; Papola, T. S. and Mathur, R. S., eds.*, 1984, pp. 428–41.
[G: India]

Shadow Open Market Committee. Policy Statement. In *Shadow Open Market Committee*, 1984, pp. 5–11.
[G: U.S.]

Spaventa, Luigi. The Growth of Public Debt in Italy: Past Experience, Perspectives and Policy Problems. *Banca Naz. Lavoro Quart. Rev.*, June 1984, (149), pp. 119–49.
[G: Italy]

Sterks, Cees G. M. The Structural Budget Deficit as an Instrument of Fiscal Policy. *De Economist*, 1984, 132(2), pp. 183–203.
[G: U.S.; Netherlands; W. Germany]

Sufrin, Sidney C. and Liro, Joseph. The Many Faces of Budget Policy. *Rivista Int. Sci. Econ. Com.*, February 1984, 31(2), pp. 147–55.
[G: U.S.]

Sunley, Emil M. Can the Income Tax Continue to Be the Major Revenue Source? Comment. In *Pechman, J. A., ed.*, 1984, pp. 69–73.
[G: U.S.]

Tagao, Francisco G. Philippine Investment Policy Act of 1983 (Batas Pambansa Blg. 391). *Bull. Int. Fiscal Doc.*, March 1984, 38(3), pp. 135–38.
[G: Philippines]

Tatom, John A. The 1981 Personal Income Tax Cuts: A Retrospective Look at Their Effects on the Federal Tax Burden. *Fed. Res. Bank*

St. Louis Rev., December 1984, *66*(10), pp. 5–17. **[G: U.S.]**

Wakefield, Joseph C. Federal Budget Developments. *Surv. Curr. Bus.*, August 1984, *64*(8), pp. 11–17. **[G: U.S.]**

Walters, Alan A. The United Kingdom: Political Economy and Macroeconomics. *Carnegie-Rochester Conf. Ser. Public Policy*, Autumn 1984, *21*, pp. 259–79. **[G: U.K.]**

Weiss, John. Alliance for Production: Mexico's Incentives for Private Sector Industrial Development. *World Devel.*, July 1984, *12*(7), pp. 723–42. **[G: Mexico]**

Wendt, Peter. Statsfinanser og pengepolitik. (Monetary Policy and Government Deficit Financing. With English summary.) *Nationaløkon. Tidsskr.*, 1984, *122*(1), pp. 31–40. **[G: Denmark]**

Wolfson, Dirk J. The Fiscal Policy Aspect of Development Strategy. In *Ghosh, P. K., ed., no. 7*, 1984, *1973*, pp. 302–13.

322 National Government Expenditures and Budgeting

3220 General

Bieri, Stephan. Grundfragen der Submissionspolitik des schweizerischen Bundes. (Basic Problems Relating to the Contracting Policy of the Swiss Federal Authorities. With English summary.) *Ann. Pub. Co-op. Econ.*, April–June 1984, *55*(2), pp. 183–89. **[G: Switzerland]**

Blanchard, Olivier J. Current and Anticipated Deficits, Interest Rates and Economic Activity. *Europ. Econ. Rev.*, June 1984, *25*(1), pp. 7–27. **[G: EEC; U.S.]**

Boskin, Michael J., et al. Budget Policy and Processes: Where Do We Go from Here? *Contemp. Policy Issue*, Fall 1984-85, *3*(1), pp. 53–78. **[G: U.S.]**

Coulombe, Serge. Une analyse de la politique fiscale du gouvernement fédéral par l'examen des soldes budgétaires. (An Analysis of the Federal Fiscal Policy. With English summary.) *L'Actual. Econ.*, June 1984, *60*(2), pp. 240–53. **[G: Canada]**

Emerson, Michael. The European Stagflation Disease in International Perspective and Some Possible Therapy. In *Emerson, M., ed.*, 1984, pp. 195–228. **[G: N. Europe; OECD]**

Hartley, Keith. Policy towards Contracting-Out: The Lessons of Experience. *Fisc. Stud.*, February 1984, *5*(1), pp. 98–105. **[G: U.K.]**

Laxan, Max. Congrès 1984 Buenos-Aires. (Congress Buenos Aires, 1984. With English summary.) *Bull. Int. Fiscal Doc.*, 1984, *38*(8–9), pp. 348–51.

Maddison, Angus. Origins and Impact of the Welfare State, 1883–1983. *Banca Naz. Lavoro Quart. Rev.*, March 1984, (148), pp. 55–87. **[G: Selected OECD]**

Malinvaud, E. Current and Anticipated Deficits, Interest Rates and Economic Activity: Comments. *Europ. Econ. Rev.*, June 1984, *25*(1), pp. 29–32. **[G: EEC; U.S.]**

Marris, Stephen N. Current and Anticipated Def-

icits, Interest Rates and Economic Activity: Comments. *Europ. Econ. Rev.*, June 1984, *25*(1), pp. 33–36. **[G: U.S.; Japan; Germany; U.K.]**

McCraw, Thomas K. The Public and Private Spheres in Historical Perspective. In *Brooks, H.; Liebman, L. and Schelling, C. S., eds.*, 1984, pp. 31–60. **[G: U.S.]**

Meltzer, Eric. Pandora's Convention? *Policy Rev.*, Winter 1984, (27), pp. 53–54. **[G: U.S.]**

Roberti, Paolo. Macroeconomic and Public Finance "Costs" of High Unemployment. *Econ. Lavoro*, Jan.-Mar. 1984, *18*(1), pp. 3–15. **[G: OECD]**

Singh, Balvir and Sahni, Balbir S. Causality between Public Expenditure and National Income. *Rev. Econ. Statist.*, November 1984, *66*(4), pp. 630–44. **[G: India]**

Zimmermann, Klaus F. Der Beitrag des öffentlichen Sektors zur Entwicklung der Produktivität. (The Contribution of the Public Sector to the Growth of Productivity. With English summary.) *Konjunkturpolitik*, 1984, *30*(2/3), pp. 93–118. **[G: W. Germany]**

3221 National Government Expenditures

Aaron, Henry J. Health Care Financing and Pension Programs: Comment. In *Mills, G. B. and Palmer, J. L., eds.*, 1984, pp. 157–61. **[G: U.S.]**

Abedian, I. and Standish, B. An Analysis of the Sources of Growth in State Expenditure in South Africa, 1920–1982. *S. Afr. J. Econ.*, December 1984, *52*(4), pp. 391–408. **[G: S. Africa]**

Alexis, Marcus. Politics and Economics. *Rev. Black Polit. Econ.*, Summer–Fall 1984, *13*(1–2), pp. 9–24. **[G: U.S.]**

Alexis, Marcus. Politics and Economics: Rejoinder. *Rev. Black Polit. Econ.*, Summer–Fall 1984, *13*(1–2), pp. 27–29. **[G: U.S.]**

Ansari, M. M. A Critique of the Developments in Indian Fiscal Federalism. *Margin*, October 1984, *17*(1), pp. 31–47. **[G: India]**

Bailey, John J. Public Budgeting in Mexico, 1970–1982. In *Premchand, A. and Burkhead, J., eds.*, 1984, pp. 199–213. **[G: Mexico]**

Barrett, Sean D. Recent Developments in Evaluating Public Expenditure. *Irish Banking Rev.*, June 1984, pp. 33–39. **[G: Ireland]**

Barth, Michael C. Budget Cuts on the Reagan Administration: A Question of Fairness: Comments. In *Bawden, D. L., ed.*, 1984, pp. 65–67. **[G: U.S.]**

Bertaina, Norberto A. Perspectivas para una Reforma Fiscal en Argentina. (General Outlook for a Tax Reform in Argentina. With English summary.) *Bull. Int. Fiscal Doc.*, 1984, *38*(8–9), pp. 359–66. **[G: Argentina]**

Black, Harold. Politics and Economics: Comments. *Rev. Black Polit. Econ.*, Summer–Fall 1984, *13*(1–2), pp. 25–27. **[G: U.S.]**

Blaug, Mark. Education Vouchers—It All Depends on What You Mean. In *Le Grand,*

J. and Robinson, R., eds., 1984, pp. 160–76.

Brouthers, Lance. Comment on Russett [Defense Expenditures and National Well-Being]. *Amer. Polit. Sci. Rev.,* March 1984, 78(1), pp. 202–04.

Buglione, Enrico and France, George. Skewed Fiscal Federalism in Italy: Implications for Public Expenditure Control. In *Premchand, A. and Burkhead, J., eds.,* 1984, pp. 69–89.
[G: Italy]

Burns, Leland S. and Grebler, Leo. Is Public Construction Countercyclical? *Land Econ.,* November 1984, 60(4), pp. 367–77.
[G: U.S.]

Cockle, Paul. Public Expenditure Policy, 1984–85: Overview. In *Cockle, P., ed.,* 1984, pp. 1–19.
[G: U.K.]

Cockle, Paul. The Public Expenditure Control System. In *Cockle, P., ed.,* 1984, pp. 20–39.
[G: U.K.]

Collings, John. Public Expenditure Policy, 1984–85: Transport. In *Cockle, P., ed.,* 1984, pp. 214–27.
[G: U.K.]

Courchene, Thomas J. An Australian Perspective on Taxation: Comment. In *Block, W. and Walker, M., eds.,* 1984, pp. 426–32.
[G: Australia]

Cutt, James. The Evolution of Expenditure Budgeting in Australia. In *Premchand, A. and Burkhead, J., eds.,* 1984, pp. 1–20.
[G: Australia]

Disney, Richard. Public Expenditure Policy, 1984–85: Social Security. In *Cockle, P., ed.,* 1984, pp. 149–71.
[G: U.K.]

Doern, G. Bruce. Canada's Budgetary Dilemmas: Tax and Expenditure Reform. In *Premchand, A. and Burkhead, J., eds.,* 1984, pp. 21–38.
[G: Canada]

Doh, Joon-Chien. Budgeting as an Instrument of Development: The Malaysian Experience. In *Premchand, A. and Burkhead, J., eds.,* 1984, pp. 187–98.
[G: Malaysia]

Doyle, Denis P. and Hartle, Terry W. Ideology, Pragmatic Politics, and the Education Budget. In *Weicher, J. C., ed.,* 1984, pp. 119–53.
[G: U.S.]

Doyle, Maurice F. Management of the Public Finances in Ireland since 1961. In *Premchand, A. and Burkhead, J., eds.,* 1984, pp. 53–67.
[G: Ireland; Europe]

Dudley, Leonard and Montmarquette, Claude. The Effects of Non-clearing Labor Markets on the Demand for Public Spending. *Econ. Inquiry,* April 1984, 22(2), pp. 151–70.
[G: Selected Countries]

Duffy, Sarah W. and Kraut, Alan G. Understanding and Influencing the Federal Budget for Psychological Research. In *Dusek, E. R., et al., eds.,* 1984, pp. 19–27.
[G: U.S.]

Dunne, John Paul; Pashardes, Panos and Smith, Ronald P. Needs, Costs and Bureaucracy: The Allocation of Public Consumption in the UK. *Econ. J.,* March 1984, 94(373), pp. 1–15.
[G: U.K.]

Eichenberg, Richard C. The Expenditure and Revenue Effects of Defense Spending in the Federal Republic of Germany. *Policy Sci.,* March 1984, 16(4), pp. 391–411.
[G: W. Germany]

Eriksson, Björn. Sweden's Budget System in a Changing World. In *Premchand, A. and Burkhead, J., eds.,* 1984, pp. 91–107.
[G: Sweden]

Fisher, Malcolm R. An Australian Perspective on Taxation. In *Block, W. and Walker, M., eds.,* 1984, pp. 385–426.
[G: Australia]

Foot, David K. The Demographic Future of Fiscal Federalism in Canada. *Can. Public Policy,* December 1984, 10(4), pp. 406–14.
[G: Canada]

Foxley, Alejandro and Raczynski, Dagmar. Vulnerable Groups in Recessionary Situations: The Case of Children and the Young in Chile. In *Jolly, R. and Cornia, G. A., eds.,* 1984, pp. 53–76.
[G: Chile]

Freeman, Katherine B. The Significance of Motivational Variables in International Public Welfare Expenditures. *Econ. Develop. Cult. Change,* July 1984, 32(4), pp. 725–48.
[G: OECD]

Greenwood, David. Public Expenditure Policy, 1984–85: Defence. In *Cockle, P., ed.,* 1984, pp. 172–92.
[G: U.K.]

Halberstadt, Victor; Goudswaard, Kees and LeBlanc, Bart. Current Control Problems with Public Expenditure in Five European Countries. In *Emerson, M., ed.,* 1984, pp. 122–49.
[G: Belgium; Denmark; Ireland; Italy; Netherlands]

Hale, Robert F. The Defense Budget: Comment. In *Mills, G. B. and Palmer, J. L., eds.,* 1984, pp. 116–19.
[G: U.S.; U.S.S.R.]

Heller, Peter S. and Cheasty, Adrienne. Sectoral Adjustment in Government Expenditure in the 1970s: The Educational Sector in Latin America. *World Devel.,* October 1984, 12(10), pp. 1039–49.
[G: Latin America]

Hicks, Norman L. and Kubisch, Anne. Cutting Government Expenditures in LDCs. *Finance Develop.,* September 1984, 21(3), pp. 37–39.
[G: LDCs]

Hoagland, G. William. Perception and Reality in Nutrition Programs. In *Weicher, J. C., ed.,* 1984, pp. 43–71.
[G: U.S.]

Hulten, Charles R. and Peterson, George E. The Public Capital Stock: Needs, Trends, and Performance. *Amer. Econ. Rev.,* May 1984, 74(2), pp. 166–73.
[G: U.S.]

Husain, Ishrat. Raising Resources for Development: The Challenge for the Eighties. In *Burki, S. J. and LaPorte, R., Jr., eds.,* 1984, pp. 103–36.
[G: Pakistan]

Ippolito, Dennis S. Reform, Congress, and the President. In *Wander, W. T.; Hebert, F. T. and Copeland, G. W., eds.,* 1984, pp. 133–50.
[G: U.S.]

Jeanrenaud, Claude. Public Procurement and Economic Policy. *Ann. Pub. Co-op. Econ.,* April–June 1984, 55(2), pp. 151–58.
[G: W. Europe; U.S.]

Kim, Dong-Kun and Kang, In-Jae. The Budget

System and Structure in Korea. In *Premchand, A. and Burkhead, J., eds.*, 1984, pp. 175–86. [G: S. Korea]

Kim, Wan-Soon and Abbott, Graham. Budget Procedures and Policies in the ASEAN Countries. In *Premchand, A. and Burkhead, J., eds.*, 1984, pp. 145–58. [G: ASEAN]

Kraan, D. J. Towards More Flexibility of Government Expenditure: Some Recent Developments in the Netherlands. *Policy Sci.*, March 1984, *16*(4), pp. 413–27. [G: Netherlands]

Le Grand, Julian. Évaluation de l'impact redistributif des dépenses publiques. Quelques problèmes méthodologiques. (On Measuring the Distributional Impact of Public Expenditures: Some Methodological Problems. With English summary.) *Consommation*, July–September 1984, *31*(3), pp. 3–17. [G: France]

Le Grand, Julian and Robinson, Ray. Privatisation and the Welfare State: An Introduction. In *Le Grand, J. and Robinson, R., eds.*, 1984, pp. 1–14. [G: U.K.]

Lee, Fook Hong. A Summary of Singapore's 1984 Budget. *Bull. Int. Fiscal Doc.*, 1984, *38*(5), pp. 202–10. [G: Singapore]

Levitt, M. S. The Growth of Government Expenditure. *Nat. Inst. Econ. Rev.*, May 1984, (108), pp. 34–41. [G: OECD; U.K.]

Mace, John. Public Expenditure Policy, 1984–85: Education and Science. In *Cockle, P., ed.*, 1984, pp. 109–27. [G: U.K.]

Maldague, Robert. La politique des commandes publiques: instrument de politique economique? Le cas de la Belgique. (The Potential of Public Ordering Policy as an Instrument of Economic Policy. With English summary.) *Ann. Pub. Co-op. Econ.*, April–June 1984, *55*(2), pp. 173–82. [G: Belgium]

Marshall, Adriana. El "salario social" en la Argentina. (With English summary.) *Desarrollo Econ.*, April–June 1984, *24*(93), pp. 41–70. [G: Argentina]

Mathiasen, David G. Recent Developments in the Composition and the Formulation of the United States Federal Budget. In *Premchand, A. and Burkhead, J., eds.*, 1984, pp. 131–43. [G: U.S.]

Maynard, Alan. Public Expenditure Policy, 1984–85: Health and Personal Social Services. In *Cockle, P., ed.*, 1984, pp. 128–48. [G: U.K.]

Meyer, Jack A. Budget Cuts in the Reagan Administration: A Question of Fairness. In *Bawden, D. L., ed.*, 1984, pp. 33–64. [G: U.S.]

Meyer, Jack A. Health Care Financing and Pension Programs: Comment. In *Mills, G. B. and Palmer, J. L., eds.*, 1984, pp. 162–64. [G: U.S.]

Mills, Gregory B. The Budget: A Failure of Discipline. In *Palmer, J. L. and Sawhill, I. V., eds.*, 1984, pp. 107–39. [G: U.S.]

Moore, Mary T. Cost Cutting without Goal Setting: A Recipe for Failure. *J. Policy Anal. Manage.*, Winter 1984, *3*(2), pp. 255–63. [G: U.S.]

Mountfield, Peter. Recent Developments in the Control of Public Expenditure in the United

Kingdom. In *Premchand, A. and Burkhead, J., eds.*, 1984, pp. 109–30. [G: U.K.]

Navarro, Vicente. The Crisis of the International Capitalist Order and Its Implications on the Welfare State. In *McKinlay, J. B., ed.*, 1984, pp. 107–40. [G: U.S.]

Neale, A. J. and Wilson, R. A. Public Expenditure Policy, 1984–85: Employment. In *Cockle, P., ed.*, 1984, pp. 193–213. [G: U.K.]

Nichols, Donald A. Federal Spending Priorities and Long-term Economic Growth. In *Hulten, C. R. and Sawhill, I. V., eds.*, 1984, pp. 151–73. [G: U.S.]

Nuñez Miñana, Horacio and Porto, Alberto. Redistribución territorial a través de las finanzas públicas: El caso de los partidos del Gran Buenos Aires. (Territorial Redistribution through Public Finance: The Case of Greater Buenos Aires Districts. With English summary.) *Económica*, January-April 1984, *30*(1), pp. 35–69. [G: Argentina]

Olson, Mancur. Ideology and Economic Growth. In *Hulten, C. R. and Sawhill, I. V., eds.*, 1984, pp. 229–51. [G: OECD]

Palmer, John L. and Torrey, Barbara Boyle. Health Care Financing and Pension Programs. In *Mills, G. B. and Palmer, J. L., eds.*, 1984, pp. 121–56. [G: U.S.]

Pearson, Robert W. The Changing Fortunes of the U.S. Statistical System, 1980–1985. *Rev. Public Data Use*, December 1984, *12*(4), pp. 245–69. [G: U.S.]

Pirie, Robert B. The Defense Budget: Comment. In *Mills, G. B. and Palmer, J. L., eds.*, 1984, pp. 111–15. [G: U.S.; U.S.S.R.]

Prina, L. Edgar. Why Defense Costs So Much: The Rationale for a $300 Billion Budget. *Policy Rev.*, Spring 1984, (28), pp. 80–84. [G: U.S.]

Pryor, Frederic L. Interpretations of Public Expenditure Trends in East and West. In *[Reynolds, L. G.]*, 1984, pp. 362–88. [G: CMEA; OECD]

Redburn, F. Stevens, et al. Federal Economic Development Investments. In *Holzer, M. and Nagel, S. S., eds.*, 1984, pp. 115–43. [G: U.S.]

Rose, Richard and Karran, Terence. Inertia or Incrementalism? A Long-term View of the Growth of Government. In *Groth, A. J. and Wade, L. L., eds.*, 1984, pp. 43–71. [G: OECD]

Rothchild, Donald. Middle Africa: Hegemonial Exchange and Resource Allocation. In *Groth, A. J. and Wade, L. L., eds.*, 1984, pp. 151–80. [G: Africa]

Round, David K. The Impact of Government Purchases on Market Performance in Australia. *Rev. Ind. Organ.*, Summer 1984, *1*(2), pp. 94–113. [G: Australia]

Rubin, Irene S. Marasmus or Recovery? The Effects of Cutbacks in Federal Agencies. *Soc. Sci. Quart.*, March 1984, *65*(1), pp. 74–88. [G: U.S.]

Ruggeri, Giovanni. The Difficult Financing of the Treasury. *Rev. Econ. Cond. Italy*, February 1984, (1), pp. 9–30. [G: Italy]

Sahni, Balbir S. and Singh, Balvir. On the Causal Directions between National Income and Government Expenditure in Canada. *Public Finance*, 1984, *39*(3), pp. 359–93. **[G: Canada]**

Schultze, Charles L. Alternative Measures of Federal Investment Outlays. In *Hulten, C. R. and Sawhill, I. V., eds.*, 1984, pp. 175–78. **[G: U.S.]**

Sharkansky, Ira. Resource Allocation: Environments that Constrain and Governments that Cope. In *Groth, A. J. and Wade, L. L., eds.*, 1984, pp. 73–98. **[G: OECD; Israel; Greece]**

Stubbing, Richard A. The Defense Budget. In *Mills, G. B. and Palmer, J. L., eds.*, 1984, pp. 81–110. **[G: U.S.; U.S.S.R.]**

Suh, Sang Mok. Effects of the Current World Recession on the Welfare of Children: The Case of Korea. In *Jolly, R. and Cornia, G. A., eds.*, 1984, pp. 159–68. **[G: S. Korea]**

Vaubel, Roland. Die Deutschen Staatsausgaben: Wende oder Anstieg ohne Ende? (With English Summary.) In *Eucken, W. and Böhm, F., eds.*, 1984, pp. 3–19. **[G: W. Germany; OECD]**

Wallis, John Joseph. The Birth of the Old Federalism: Financing the New Deal, 1932–1940. *J. Econ. Hist.*, March 1984, *44*(1), pp. 139–59. **[G: U.S.]**

Weicher, John C. The Safety Net after Three Years. In *Weicher, J. C., ed.*, 1984, pp. 1–19. **[G: U.S.]**

Yoingco, Angel Q. and Guevara, Milweda M. Budgetary Practices and Developments in the Philippines. In *Premchand, A. and Burkhead, J., eds.*, 1984, pp. 215–31. **[G: Philippines]**

3226 National Government Budgeting and Deficits

Aaron, Henry J. Health Care Financing and Pension Programs: Comment. In *Mills, G. B. and Palmer, J. L., eds.*, 1984, pp. 157–61. **[G: U.S.]**

Alexander, James R. Curriculum Reform in Budgeting and Financial Management: Preliminary Thoughts on the Dimensions of the Field. *Public Budg. Finance*, Autumn 1984, *4*(3), pp. 91–96. **[G: U.S.]**

Alperovitz, Gar. Government Deficit and Business Cycle: Comment. In *Wachter, M. L. and Wachter, S. M., eds.*, 1984, pp. 337–41. **[G: U.S.]**

Anderson, Annelise Graebner. The Federal Budget: Problems and Prospects. In *Moore, J. H., ed.*, 1984, pp. 183–98. **[G: U.S.]**

Armstrong, William L. Therapy for the Budget. *Policy Rev.*, Winter 1984, (27), pp. 59–61. **[G: U.S.]**

Bailey, John J. Public Budgeting in Mexico, 1970–1982. *Public Budg. Finance*, Spring 1984, *4*(1), pp. 76–90. **[G: Mexico]**

Barth, James R.; Iden, George and Russek, Frank S. Do Federal Deficits Really Matter? *Contemp. Policy Issue*, Fall 1984-85, *3*(1), pp. 79–95.

Beeman, William J. How Bad Are the Large Deficits? Comment. In *Mills, G. B. and Palmer, J. L., eds.*, 1984, pp. 74–78. **[G: U.S.]**

Behn, Robert D. Executive Agency Retrenchment: Comment. In *Mills, G. B. and Palmer, J. L., eds.*, 1984, pp. 337–41. **[G: U.S.]**

Bennet, Douglas J. The Congressional Budget Process: Comment. In *Mills, G. B. and Palmer, J. L., eds.*, 1984, pp. 419–21. **[G: U.S.]**

Bent, Rodney G. Controlling Federal Credit Activity. *Public Budg. Finance*, Autumn 1984, *4*(3), pp. 100–103. **[G: U.S.]**

Bertaina, Norberto A. Perspectivas para una Reforma Fiscal en Argentina. (General Outlook for a Tax Reform in Argentina. With English summary.) *Bull. Int. Fiscal Doc.*, 1984, *38*(8–9), pp. 359–66. **[G: Argentina]**

Blanchard, Olivier J. and Summers, Lawrence H. Perspectives on High World Real Interest Rates. *Brookings Pap. Econ. Act.*, 1984, (2), pp. 273–324. **[G: U.S.; W. Europe; Japan]**

Blinder, Alan S. Perspectives on High World Real Interest Rates: Comment. *Brookings Pap. Econ. Act.*, 1984, (2), pp. 325–33. **[G: U.S.; W. Europe; Japan]**

Blinder, Alan S. Reaganomics and Growth: The Message in the Models. In *Hulten, C. R. and Sawhill, I. V., eds.*, 1984, pp. 199–227. **[G: U.S.]**

Blinder, Alan S. and Holtz-Eakin, Douglas. Public Opinion and the Balanced Budget. *Amer. Econ. Rev.*, May 1984, *74*(2), pp. 144–49. **[G: U.S.]**

Boskin, Michael J. Issues in Budget Accounting: Comment. In *Mills, G. B. and Palmer, J. L., eds.*, 1984, pp. 457–60. **[G: U.S.]**

Bozeman, J. Lisle. The Capital Budget: History and Future Directions. *Public Budg. Finance*, Autumn 1984, *4*(3), pp. 18–30. **[G: U.S.]**

Britton, Andrew J. C. Uncertainty, Forecasting and Budget Changes. *Nat. Inst. Econ. Rev.*, February 1984, (107), pp. 60–62. **[G: U.K.]**

Britton, Andrew J. C. The Budget and the Economic Strategy. *Fisc. Stud.*, May 1984, *5*(2), pp. 1–7. **[G: U.K.]**

Brown, J. A. C. and Helou, A. The Fiscal Policy of Japan since 1970. *Oxford Bull. Econ. Statist.*, May 1984, *46*(2), pp. 89–124. **[G: Japan]**

Buchele, Robert. Reaganomics and the Fairness Issue. *Challenge*, September/October 1984, *27*(4), pp. 25–31. **[G: U.S.]**

Budd, Alan P. Macroeconomic Aspects of the 1984 Budget. *Fisc. Stud.*, May 1984, *5*(2), pp. 8–16. **[G: U.K.]**

Buiter, Willem H. A Comprehensive Balance Sheet and Permanent Income Accounting Framework for the Public Sector: Theory and Applications. In *Masera, R. S. and Triffin, R., eds.*, 1984, pp. 153–95. **[G: EEC; U.S.]**

Buiter, Willem H. Comment: Some Unpleasant Monetarist Arithmetic. In *Griffiths, B. and Wood, G. E., eds.*, 1984, pp. 42–60. **[G: U.K.]**

Burress, Richard T. Congress and the President. In *Moore, J. H., ed.*, 1984, pp. 217–37. **[G: U.S.]**

Carlson, Keith M. Money Growth and the Size of the Federal Debt. *Fed. Res. Bank St. Louis Rev.*, November 1984, *66*(9), pp. 5–16. [G: U.S.]

Champion, Hale. Executive Budget Making: Comment. In *Mills, G. B. and Palmer, J. L., eds.*, 1984, pp. 292–94. [G: U.S.]

Chinwanno, Chulacheeb. Thailand in 1983: The Parliamentary System Survives. In *Thambipillai, P., ed.*, 1984, pp. 311–25. [G: Thailand]

Cockle, Paul. Public Expenditure Policy, 1984–85: The Economic Context. In *Cockle, P., ed.*, 1984, pp. 40–62. [G: U.K.]

Congdon, Tim G. A Comment: The problem of Debt Interest Seen in Historical Perspective [Some Unpleasant Monetarist Arithmetic]. In *Griffiths, B. and Wood, G. E., eds.*, 1984, pp. 67–71.

Copeland, Gary W. Changes in the House of Representatives after the Passage of the Budget Act of 1974. In *Wander, W. T.; Hebert, F. T. and Copeland, G. W., eds.*, 1984, pp. 51–77. [G: U.S.]

Cossiga, Giovanni. The Budget in the Italian Economic Crisis. *Rev. Econ. Cond. Italy*, February 1984, (1), pp. 91–106. [G: Italy]

Costa, José. Government Budget Deficits, Money Supply, and Inflation in Portugal. *Economia (Portugal)*, January 1984, *8*(1), pp. 97–116. [G: Portugal]

Davey, Bernadette P. 1984 Budget Speech. *Bull. Int. Fiscal Doc.*, April 1984, *38*(4), pp. 167–70. [G: Zambia]

Davey, Bernadette P. 1984 Budget Speech. *Bull. Int. Fiscal Doc.*, 1984, *38*(6), pp. 270–71. [G: Botswana]

Davidson, Roger H. The Congressional Budget: How Much Change? How Much Reform? In *Wander, W. T.; Hebert, F. T. and Copeland, G. W., eds.*, 1984, pp. 153–69. [G: U.S.]

Dawkins, Peter and Sloan, Judith. The Australian Labour Market, June 1984. *Australian Bull. Lab.*, June 1984, *10*(3), pp. 113–33. [G: Australia]

Devereux, Michael P. and Morris, C. Nick. The Chancellor's Arithmetic. *Fisc. Stud.*, May 1984, *5*(2), pp. 63–72. [G: U.K.]

Doern, G. Bruce. Canada's Budgetary Dilemmas: Tax and Expenditure Reform. In *Premchand, A. and Burkhead, J., eds.*, 1984, pp. 21–38. [G: Canada]

Doh, Joon-Chien. Budgeting as an Instrument of Development: The Malaysian Experience. *Public Budg. Finance*, Spring 1984, *4*(1), pp. 64–75. [G: Malaysia]

Downs, George W. Budgetary Research in Transition. *Policy Sci.*, March 1984, *16*(4), pp. 297–302. [G: U.S.]

Doyle, Maurice F. Management of the Public Finances in Ireland since 1961. In *Premchand, A. and Burkhead, J., eds.*, 1984, pp. 53–67. [G: Ireland; Europe]

Edgar, Robert. Government Deficit and Business Cycle: Comment. In *Wachter, M. L. and Wachter, S. M., eds.*, 1984, pp. 350–51. [G: U.S.]

Eichner, Alfred S. Budgeting for Peace and Growth. *Challenge*, January/February 1984, *26*(6), pp. 9–20. [G: U.S.]

Eisner, Robert. Which Budget Deficit? Some Issues of Measurement and Their Implications. *Amer. Econ. Rev.*, May 1984, *74*(2), pp. 138–43.

Eisner, Robert and Pieper, Paul J. A New View of the Federal Debt and Budget Deficits. *Amer. Econ. Rev.*, March 1984, *74*(1), pp. 11–29. [G: U.S.]

Ellwood, John W. Budget Reforms and Interchamber Relations. In *Wander, W. T.; Hebert, F. T. and Copeland, G. W., eds.*, 1984, pp. 100–132. [G: U.S.]

Ellwood, John W. Legislative Politics and Budget Outcomes: Comment. In *Mills, G. B. and Palmer, J. L., eds.*, 1984, pp. 368–78. [G: U.S.]

Eriksson, Björn. Sweden's Budget System in a Changing World. In *Premchand, A. and Burkhead, J., eds.*, 1984, pp. 91–107. [G: Sweden]

Fieleke, Norman S. The Budget Deficit: Are the International Consequences Unfavorable? *New Eng. Econ. Rev.*, May–June 1984, pp. 5–10. [G: OECD]

Fischer, Gregory W. and Kamlet, Mark S. Explaining Presidential Priorities: The Competing Aspiration Levels Model of Macrobudgetary Decision Making. *Amer. Polit. Sci. Rev.*, June 1984, *78*(2), pp. 356–71. [G: U.S.]

Fisher, Louis. The Budget Act of 1974: A Further Loss of Spending Control. In *Wander, W. T.; Hebert, F. T. and Copeland, G. W., eds.*, 1984, pp. 170–89. [G: U.S.]

Fisher, Louis. The Congressional Budget Process: Comment. In *Mills, G. B. and Palmer, J. L., eds.*, 1984, pp. 414–18. [G: U.S.]

Friedman, Benjamin M. Managing the U.S. Government Deficit in the 1980s. In *Wachter, M. L. and Wachter, S. M., eds.*, 1984, pp. 265–301. [G: U.S.]

Gammie, Malcolm. Has Nigel Lawson Really Reformed Business Taxation? *Fisc. Stud.*, May 1984, *5*(2), pp. 82–92. [G: U.K.]

Gofran, K. A. Some Highlights of the 1984–85 Budget. *Bull. Int. Fiscal Doc.*, November 1984, *38*(11), pp. 504–06. [G: Bangladesh]

Gramlich, Edward M. How Bad Are the Large Deficits? In *Mills, G. B. and Palmer, J. L., eds.*, 1984, pp. 43–68. [G: U.S.]

Hagelmayer, István. Concept of the State Budget for the New Phase in Hungary. *Acta Oecon.*, 1984, *33*(1–2), pp. 17–30. [G: Hungary]

Halberstadt, Victor; Goudswaard, Kees and LeBlanc, Bart. Current Control Problems with Public Expenditure in Five European Countries. In *Emerson, M., ed.*, 1984, pp. 122–49. [G: Belgium; Denmark; Ireland; Italy; Netherlands]

Hamm, William G. Federal Aid to State and Local Governments: Comment. In *Mills, G. B. and Palmer, J. L., eds.*, 1984, pp. 203–08. [G: U.S.]

Hartman, Robert W. Does Anybody Know the

Way to San Jose? *Nat. Tax J.*, September 1984, 37(3), pp. 389–91. [G: U.S.]

Hartman, Robert W. Issues in Budget Accounting. In *Mills, G. B. and Palmer, J. L., eds.*, 1984, pp. 423–47. [G: U.S.]

Hassan, Mostafa F. Trade Prospects for the Oil Exporters: The Case of Venezuela. In *Jorge, A.; Salazar-Carrillo, J. and Sanchez, E. P.*, 1984, pp. 71–81. [G: Latin America; Venezuela]

Haveman, Robert H. How Bad Are the Large Deficits? Comment. In *Mills, G. B. and Palmer, J. L., eds.*, 1984, pp. 69–73. [G: U.S.]

Haveman, Robert H. How Much Have the Reagan Administration's Tax and Spending Policies Increased Work Effort? In *Hulten, C. R. and Sawhill, I. V., eds.*, 1984, pp. 91–125. [G: U.S.]

Hebert, F. Ted. Congressional Budgeting, 1977–1983: Continuity and Change. In *Wander, W. T.; Hebert, F. T. and Copeland, G. W., eds.*, 1984, pp. 31–48. [G: U.S.]

Heclo, Hugh. Executive Budget Making. In *Mills, G. B. and Palmer, J. L., eds.*, 1984, pp. 255–91. [G: U.S.]

Herschtel, Marie-Luise. Les finances publiques françaises 1983–1985: réalisations et perspectives. (With English summary.) *Revue Écon. Polit.*, September–October 1984, 94(5), pp. 629–38. [G: France]

Hoffman, Ronald F. and Levy, Mickey D. Economic and Budget Issues for Deficit Policy. *Contemp. Policy Issue*, Fall 1984-85, 3(1), pp. 96–114. [G: U.S.]

Holloway, Thomas M. The Economy and the Federal Budget: Guides to the Automatic Effects. *Surv. Curr. Bus.*, July 1984, 64(7), pp. 102–05. [G: U.S.]

Holzmann, Robert. Budgetsanierung und pensionsreform. (With English summary.) *Empirica*, 1984, 11(2), pp. 235–59. [G: Austria]

Horwood, Owen. Budget 1984–85: A Harsh Budget. *Bull. Int. Fiscal Doc.*, 1984, 38(6), pp. 265–69. [G: S. Africa]

Hunt, Lacy H. Using Monetary Control to Dampen the Business Cycle: A New Set of First Principles: Comment. In *Wachter, M. L. and Wachter, S. M., eds.*, 1984, pp. 341–44. [G: U.S.]

Hutchinson, Michael M. and Pigott, Charles. Budget Deficits, Exchange Rates and the Current Account: Theory and U.S. Evidence. *Fed. Res. Bank San Francisco Econ. Rev.*, Fall 1984, (4), pp. 5–25. [G: U.S.]

Hutchinson, Michael M. and Pyle, David H. The Real Interest Rate/Budget Deficit Link: International Evidence, 1973–82. *Fed. Res. Bank San Francisco Econ. Rev.*, Fall 1984, (4), pp. 26–35. [G: OECD]

Johnson, Darwin G. Issues in Budget Accounting: Comment. In *Mills, G. B. and Palmer, J. L., eds.*, 1984, pp. 448–56. [G: U.S.]

Karunaratne, Neil Dias. Short-term Stabilization

and Long-term Development of Fiji in 1983. In *Utrecht, E., ed.*, 1984, pp. 309–15. [G: Fiji]

Kenyon, Daphne A. and Benker, Karen M. Fiscal Discipline: Lessons form the State Experience. *Nat. Tax J.*, September 1984, 37(3), pp. 433–46. [G: U.S.]

Kim, Dong-Kun and Kang, In-Jae. The Budget System and Structure in Korea. In *Premchand, A. and Burkhead, J., eds.*, 1984, pp. 175–86. [G: S. Korea]

King, Ronald F. Tax Expenditures and Systematic Public Policy: An Essay on the Political Economy of the Federal Revenue Code. *Public Budg. Finance*, Spring 1984, 4(1), pp. 14–31. [G: U.S.]

Kirby, Stephen and Cox, Andrew. Defence Budgeting and Accountability in Britain and America: Executive Innovation and Legislative Response in the 1970s. In *Shaw, M., ed.*, 1984, pp. 217–57. [G: U.K.; U.S.]

Korff, Hans Clausen. Planning and Budgeting in the Federal Republic of Germany. In *Premchand, A. and Burkhead, J., eds.*, 1984, pp. 39–52. [G: W. Germany]

Kraan, D. J. Towards More Flexibility of Government Expenditure: Some Recent Developments in the Netherlands. *Policy Sci.*, March 1984, 16(4), pp. 413–27. [G: Netherlands]

Kurz, Rudi. Staatsverschuldung und Einkommensverteilung. Einige kritische Anmerkungen zur These von den unsozialen Verteilungswirkungen. (Public Debt and Income Distribution: Some Critical Notes on Unsocial Distributional Effect. With English summary.) *Konjunkturpolitik*, 1984, 30(4), pp. 217–32. [G: W. Germany]

Ladd, Helen F. Federal Aid to State and Local Governments. In *Mills, G. B. and Palmer, J. L., eds.*, 1984, pp. 165–202. [G: U.S.]

Laney, Leroy O. The Strong Dollar, the Current Account, and Federal Deficits: Cause and Effect. *Fed. Res. Bank Dallas Econ. Rev.*, January 1984, pp. 1–14. [G: U.S.]

de Larosière, Jacques. L'aumento del debito pubblico nel mondo e l'esigenza di maggior rigore nelle politche di bilancio. (The Growth of Public Debt and the Need for Fiscal Discipline. With English summary.) *Bancaria*, September 1984, 40(9), pp. 833–44. [G: OECD]

Lee, Fook Hong. A Summary of Singapore's 1984 Budget. *Bull. Int. Fiscal Doc.*, 1984, 38(5), pp. 202–10. [G: Singapore]

Lehment, Harmen. The Macroeconomic Implications of Public-sector Deficits. In *Emerson, M., ed.*, 1984, pp. 150–73. [G: W. Europe]

LeLoup, Lance T. Appropriations Politics in Congress: The House Appropriations Committee and the Executive Agencies. *Public Budg. Finance*, Winter 1984, 4(4), pp. 78–98. [G: U.S.]

LeLoup, Lance T. The Impact of Budget Reform on the Senate. In *Wander, W. T.; Hebert, F. T. and Copeland, G. W., eds.*, 1984, pp. 78–99. [G: U.S.]

Levy, Mickey D. Budget Deficits and the Disarray

of Fiscal Policy. In *Shadow Open Market Committee*, 1984, pp. 57–66.　　　　[G: U.S.]

Lynn, Laurence E., Jr. Executive Agency Retrenchment: Comment. In *Mills, G. B. and Palmer, J. L., eds.*, 1984, pp. 333–36.
　　　　[G: U.S.]

Masera, Rainer S. Monetary Policy and Budget Policy: Blend or Dichotomy? In *Masera, R. S. and Triffin, R., eds.*, 1984, pp. 196–223.
　　　　[G: Italy; OECD]

Mathiasen, David G. Recent Developments in the Composition and the Formulation of the United States Federal Budget. In *Premchand, A. and Burkhead, J., eds.*, 1984, pp. 131–43.
　　　　[G: U.S.]

McEntee, Gerald W. Government Deficit and Business Cycle: Comment. In *Wachter, M. L. and Wachter, S. M., eds.*, 1984, pp. 344–46.
　　　　[G: U.S.]

Medgyessy, Péter. Debt Policy of the Socialist State. *Acta Oecon.*, 1984, 33(1–2), pp. 31–41.
　　　　[G: Hungary]

Meltzer, Allan H. The Fight Against Inflation: A Comment [Some Unpleasant Monetarist Arithmetic]. In *Griffiths, B. and Wood, G. E., eds.*, 1984, pp. 61–66.

Meyer, Annette. Towards an Alternative Federal Budget. *Atlantic Econ. J.*, December 1984, 12(4), pp. 67.　　　　[G: U.S.]

Meyer, Jack A. Health Care Financing and Pension Programs: Comment. In *Mills, G. B. and Palmer, J. L., eds.*, 1984, pp. 162–64.
　　　　[G: U.S.]

Mills, Gregory B. Prospects for the Restraint of Federal Expenditures. *Nat. Tax J.*, September 1984, 37(3), pp. 361–75.　　　　[G: U.S.]

Mills, Gregory B. The Budget: A Failure of Discipline. In *Palmer, J. L. and Sawhill, I. V., eds.*, 1984, pp. 107–39.　　　　[G: U.S.]

Mills, Gregory B. and Palmer, John L. The Federal Budget in Flux. In *Mills, G. B. and Palmer, J. L., eds.*, 1984, pp. 9–41. [G: U.S.]

Minarik, Joseph J. Tax Policy. In *Mills, G. B. and Palmer, J. L., eds.*, 1984, pp. 209–42.
　　　　[G: U.S.]

Mmusi, P. S. 1984 Budget Speech. *Bull. Int. Fiscal Doc.*, 1984, 38(6), pp. 271–72.
　　　　[G: Botswana]

Moran, Donald W. Perspectives on Proposals for Budget Process Reform. *Nat. Tax J.*, September 1984, 37(3), pp. 377–84.　　[G: U.S.]

Mowery, David C. and Kamlet, Mark S. Games Presidents Do and Do Not Play: Presidential Circumvention of the Executive Branch Budget Process. *Policy Sci.*, March 1984, 16(4), pp. 303–27.　　　　[G: U.S.]

Murphy, D. G. The Zimbabwe 1983 Budget. *Bull. Int. Fiscal Doc.*, 1984, 38(7), pp. 305–10.
　　　　[G: Zimbabwe]

Musgrave, Richard A. Tax Policy: Comment. In *Mills, G. B. and Palmer, J. L., eds.*, 1984, pp. 248–51.　　　　[G: U.S.]

Nagy, Tibor. The 1984 Budget Act and the Tax System. *Bull. Int. Fiscal Doc.*, 1984, 38(7), pp. 311–15.　　　　[G: U.S.S.R.]

Nathan, Richard P. and Doolittle, Fred C. The

Budget Cuts: The Day After. *Challenge*, January/February 1984, 26(6), pp. 29–36.
　　　　[G: U.S.]

Olifin, S. O. Nigeria's Revised Budget for 1984. *Bull. Int. Fiscal Doc.*, December 1984, 38(12), pp. 548–51.　　　　[G: Nigeria]

Pagano, Michael A. Notes on Capital Budgeting. *Public Budg. Finance*, Autumn 1984, 4(3), pp. 31–40.　　　　[G: U.S.]

Palmer, John L. and Torrey, Barbara Boyle. Health Care Financing and Pension Programs. In *Mills, G. B. and Palmer, J. L., eds.*, 1984, pp. 121–56.　　　　[G: U.S.]

Pekkala, Ahti. Vuoden 1985 tulo- ja menoarvioesitys. (The Budget for 1985. With English summary.) *Kansant. Aikak.*, 1984, 80(4), pp. 349–55.　　　　[G: Finland; OECD]

Pepper, H. W. T. Tax Reform in Jamaica: The 1984–85 Budget. *Bull. Int. Fiscal Doc.*, November 1984, 38(11), pp. 507. [G: Jamaica]

Peterson, Peter G. The Government Debt-Imposed Ceiling on Economic Growth. In *Wachter, M. L. and Wachter, S. M., eds.*, 1984, pp. 20–27.　　　　[G: U.S.]

Phaup, Marvin. New Approaches to the Budgetary Treatment of Federal Credit Assistance. *Public Budg. Finance*, Autumn 1984, 4(3), pp. 97–100.　　　　[G: U.S.]

Pick, J. F. No Major Changes in Taxation in the Budget, 1984–85. *Bull. Int. Fiscal Doc.*, October 1984, 38(10), pp. 453–55.　　[G: Israel]

Plassard, Jacques. Le rééquilibrage de l'économie française a commencé au deuxième trimestre 1983. (With English summary.) *Revue Écon. Polit.*, September–October 1984, 94(5), pp. 620–28.　　　　[G: France]

Poole, William. Government Deficit and Business Cycle: Comment. In *Wachter, M. L. and Wachter, S. M., eds.*, 1984, pp. 346–49.
　　　　[G: U.S.]

Price, Robert W. R. and Muller, Patrice. Structural Budget Indicators and the Interpretation of Fiscal Policy Stance in OECD Economies. *OECD Econ. Stud.*, Autumn 1984, (3), pp. 27–72.　　　　[G: OECD]

Rabushka, Alvin. Controlling the Federal Budget. In *Moore, J. H., ed.*, 1984, pp. 199–215.
　　　　[G: U.S.]

Reischauer, Robert D. The Congressional Budget Process. In *Mills, G. B. and Palmer, J. L., eds.*, 1984, pp. 385–413.　　　　[G: U.S.]

Rivlin, Alice M. Congress Can't Face It Alone: Interview. *Challenge*, January/February 1984, 26(6), pp. 21–28.　　　　[G: U.S.]

Rivlin, Alice M. Federal Budget Policy in the 1980s: Introduction. In *Mills, G. B. and Palmer, J. L., eds.*, 1984, pp. 3–8. [G: U.S.]

Rivlin, Alice M. Reform of the Budget Process. *Amer. Econ. Rev.*, May 1984, 74(2), pp. 133–37.

Sargent, Thomas J. and Wallace, Neil. Some Unpleasant Monetarist Arithmetic. In *Griffiths, B. and Wood, G. E., eds.*, 1984, pp. 15–41.

Schiff, Frank W. Comments on "Prospects for

the Restraint of Federal Expenditures." *Nat. Tax J.*, September 1984, *37*(3), pp. 385–88. [G: U.S.]

Schultze, Charles L. Legislative Politics and Budget Outcomes: Comment. In *Mills, G. B. and Palmer, J. L., eds.*, 1984, pp. 379–84. [G: U.S.]

Seaga, Edward. Budget 1984–85. *Bull. Int. Fiscal Doc.*, November 1984, *38*(11), pp. 508–09. [G: Jamaica]

Sharpley, Jennifer. The Potential of Domestic Stabilisation Measures in Developing Countries. In *Killick, Tony, ed. (II)*, 1984, pp. 55–85. [G: LDCs]

Shepsle, Kenneth A. The Congressional Budget Process: Diagnosis, Prescription, Prognosis. In *Wander, W. T.; Hebert, F. T. and Copeland, G. W., eds.*, 1984, pp. 190–217. [G: U.S.]

Shepsle, Kenneth A. and Weingast, Barry R. Legislative Politics and Budget Outcomes. In *Mills, G. B. and Palmer, J. L., eds.*, 1984, pp. 343–67. [G: U.S.]

Sørensen, Peter Birch. Er statens budgetunderskud rentedrivende? (The Effects of Government Budget Deficits on Interest Rates. With English summary.) *Nationaløkon. Tidsskr.*, 1984, *122*(1), pp. 41–55.

Sufrin, Sidney C. and Liro, Joseph. The Many Faces of Budget Policy. *Rivista Int. Sci. Econ. Com.*, February 1984, *31*(2), pp. 147–55. [G: U.S.]

Summers, Lawrence H. The Long-term Effects of Current Macroeconomic Policies. In *Hulten, C. R. and Sawhill, I. V., eds.*, 1984, pp. 179–98. [G: U.S.]

Sunley, Emil M. Big Revenue Options—An Overview. *Nat. Tax J.*, September 1984, *37*(3), pp. 261–63. [G: U.S.]

Tatom, John A. A Perspective on the Federal Deficit Problem. *Fed. Res. Bank St. Louis Rev.*, June/July 1984, *66*(6), pp. 5–17. [G: U.S.]

Thimmaiah, G. Budget Innovations in India: An Evaluation. In *Premchand, A. and Burkhead, J., eds.*, 1984, pp. 159–73. [G: India]

Thimmaiah, G. Budget Innovations in India: An Evaluation. *Public Budg. Finance*, Spring 1984, *4*(1), pp. 40–54. [G: India]

Usoskin, V. M. Monetary and Budgetary Factors behind Inflation. In *Nikitin, S. M., ed.*, 1984, pp. 25–48. [G: OECD]

Verdier, James M. Tax Policy: Comment. In *Mills, G. B. and Palmer, J. L., eds.*, 1984, pp. 243–47. [G: U.S.]

Wakefield, Joseph C. Anatomy of a Federal Government Deficit, Fiscal Year 1983. *Surv. Curr. Bus.*, March 1984, *64*(3), pp. 19–22, 25. [G: U.S.]

Wakefield, Joseph C. Federal Budget Developments. *Surv. Curr. Bus.*, April 1984, *64*(4), pp. 22–24. [G: LDCs]

Wakefield, Joseph C. Federal Budget Developments. *Surv. Curr. Bus.*, August 1984, *64*(8), pp. 11–17. [G: U.S.]

Wakefield, Joseph C. and Ziemer, Richard C.

Federal Fiscal Programs. *Surv. Curr. Bus.*, February 1984, *64*(2), pp. 9–21. [G: U.S.]

Wander, W. Thomas. The Politics of Congressional Budget Reform. In *Wander, W. T.; Hebert, F. T. and Copeland, G. W., eds.*, 1984, pp. 3–30. [G: U.S.]

Wendt, Peter. Statsfinanser og pengepolitik. (Monetary Policy and Government Deficit Financing. With English summary.) *Nationaløkon. Tidsskr.*, 1984, *122*(1), pp. 31–40. [G: Denmark]

Wholey, Joseph S. Executive Agency Retrenchment. In *Mills, G. B. and Palmer, J. L., eds.*, 1984, pp. 295–332. [G: U.S.]

Winer, Mark D. A Description and Analysis of the 1985 Federal Budget. *Public Budg. Finance*, Summer 1984, *4*(2), pp. 73–86. [G: U.S.]

Yoingco, Angel Q. and Guevara, Milweda M. Budgetary Practices and Developments in the Philippines. *Public Budg. Finance*, Summer 1984, *4*(2), pp. 99–115. [G: Philippines]

Yoingco, Angel Q. and Guevara, Milweda M. Budgetary Practices and Developments in the Philippines. In *Premchand, A. and Burkhead, J., eds.*, 1984, pp. 215–31. [G: Philippines]

3228 National Government Debt Management

Baltensperger, Ernst. Inflation und Staatliche Budgetpolitik. (Inflation and Government Debt Financing. With English summary.) *Z. Wirtschaft. Sozialwissen.*, 1984, *104*(6), pp. 675–93.

Barth, James R.; Iden, George and Russek, Frank S. Do Federal Deficits Really Matter? *Contemp. Policy Issue*, Fall 1984-85, *3*(1), pp. 79–95.

Bennett, James T. and DiLorenzo, Thomas J. Political Entrepreneurship and Reform of the Rent-Seeking Society. In *Colander, D. C., ed.*, 1984, pp. 217–27. [G: U.S.]

Berckmans, Annie, et al. Debt Management in a Small Open Economy: A Theoretical and an Empirical Study for Belgium. *J. Policy Modeling*, February 1984, *6*(1), pp. 45–67. [G: Belgium]

Buiter, Willem H. A Comprehensive Balance Sheet and Permanent Income Accounting Framework for the Public Sector: Theory and Applications. In *Masera, R. S. and Triffin, R., eds.*, 1984, pp. 153–95. [G: EEC; U.S.]

Chouraqui, Jean-Claude and Price, Robert W. R. Medium-term Financial Strategy: The Co-ordination of Fiscal and Monetary Policies. *OECD Econ. Stud.*, Spring 1984, (2), pp. 7–49. [G: OECD]

Congdon, Tim G. The Analytical Foundations of the Medium-term Financial Strategy. *Fisc. Stud.*, May 1984, *5*(2), pp. 17–29. [G: U.K.]

Cox, W. Michael. What Is the Rule for Financing Public Debt? *Fed. Res. Bank Dallas Econ. Rev.*, September 1984, pp. 25–31. [G: U.S.]

Eisner, Robert and Pieper, Paul J. A New View of the Federal Debt and Budget Deficits. *Amer. Econ. Rev.*, March 1984, *74*(1), pp. 11–29. [G: U.S.]

Franco, Giampiero and Mengarelli, Gianluigi. Il debito estero dell'Italia. (Italy's Foreign Debt. With English summary.) *Bancaria*, February 1984, *40*(2), pp. 140–45. [G: Italy]

Friedman, Benjamin M. Managing the U.S. Government Deficit in the 1980s. In *Wachter, M. L. and Wachter, S. M., eds.*, 1984, pp. 265–301. [G: U.S.]

Giavazzi, Francesco. A Note on the Italian Public Debt. *Banca Naz. Lavoro Quart. Rev.*, June 1984, (149), pp. 151–58. [G: Italy]

Guess, George and Koford, Kenneth J. Inflation, Recession, and the Federal Budget Deficit (or, Blaming Economic Problems on a Statistical Mirage). *Policy Sci.*, December 1984, *17*(4), pp. 385–402. [G: OECD]

Hafer, R. W. Money, Debt and Economic Activity. *Fed. Res. Bank St. Louis Rev.*, June/July 1984, *66*(6), pp. 18–25. [G: U.S.]

James, John A. Public Debt Management Policy and Nineteenth-Century American Economic Growth. *Exploration Econ. Hist.*, April 1984, *21*(2), pp. 192–217. [G: U.S.]

Kotlikoff, Laurence J. Economic Impact of Deficit Financing. *Int. Monet. Fund Staff Pap.*, September 1984, *31*(3), pp. 549–82. [G: U.S.]

de Larosière, Jacques. L'aumento del debito pubblico nel mondo e l'esigenza di maggior rigore nelle politche di bilancio. (The Growth of Public Debt and the Need for Fiscal Discipline. With English summary.) *Bancaria*, September 1984, *40*(9), pp. 833–44. [G: OECD]

Medgyessy, Péter. Debt Policy of the Socialist State. *Acta Oecon.*, 1984, *33*(1–2), pp. 31–41. [G: Hungary]

Meltzer, Allan H. The Cure for Monetary Madness. *Policy Rev.*, Winter 1984, (27), pp. 72–74. [G: U.S.; OECD]

Mills, Gregory B. The Budget: A Failure of Discipline. In *Palmer, J. L. and Sawhill, I. V., eds.*, 1984, pp. 107–39. [G: U.S.]

Olifin, S. O. Nigeria's Revised Budget for 1984. *Bull. Int. Fiscal Doc.*, December 1984, *38*(12), pp. 548–51. [G: Nigeria]

Ruggeri, Giovanni. The Difficult Financing of the Treasury. *Rev. Econ. Cond. Italy*, February 1984, (1), pp. 9–30. [G: Italy]

Spaventa, Luigi. The Growth of Public Debt in Italy: Past Experience, Perspectives and Policy Problems. *Banca Naz. Lavoro Quart. Rev.*, June 1984, (149), pp. 119–49. [G: Italy]

323 National Taxation, Revenue, and Subsidies

3230 National Taxation, Revenue, and Subsidies

Aaron, Henry J. and Galper, Harvey. A Tax on Consumption, Gifts, and Bequests and Other Strategies for Reform. In *Pechman, J. A., ed.*, 1984, pp. 106–34. [G: U.S.]

Abbin, Byrle M. Alternatives to the Income Tax: Comment. In *Pechman, J. A., ed.*, 1984, pp. 98–105. [G: U.S.]

Abrams, Burton A. and Schmitz, Mark D. The Crowding-Out Effect of Governmental Transfers on Private Charitable Contributions: Cross-Section Evidence. *Nat. Tax J.*, December 1984, *37*(4), pp. 563–68. [G: U.S.]

Ahmad, Ehtisham and Stern, Nicholas H. The Theory of Reform and Indian Indirect Taxes. *J. Public Econ.*, December 1984, *25*(3), pp. 259–98. [G: India]

Albi, Emilio. Fiscal Obstacles to the International Flow of Capital between a Parent and Its Subsidiary: Spain. In *Intn'l. Fisc. Assoc., vol. 69a*, 1984, pp. 311–24. [G: Spain]

Albon, Robert. The Appropriate Tax Treatment of Owner-Occupiers. *Australian Tax Forum*, December 1984, *1*(4), pp. 391–400. [G: Australia]

Albon, Robert; Findlay, Christopher and Piggott, John. The Welfare Costs of Owner–Occupier Housing Subsidies: Inflation, Tax Treatment, and Interest Rate Regulation. *Australian Econ. Pap.*, December 1984, *23*(43), pp. 206–18. [G: Australia]

Alchin, Terry M. A New Measure of Tax Progressivity. *Public Finance*, 1984, *39*(1), pp. 1–10. [G: Australia]

Anderson, William D. Purchase and Sale of Shares. In *Purden, C., ed.*, 1984, pp. 203–44. [G: Canada]

Andic, Fuat M. Tax Harmonization and Economic Integration. In *Núñez del Arco, J.; Margain, E. and Cherol, R., eds.*, 1984, pp. 205–28. [G: Latin America]

Ansari, M. M. A Critique of the Developments in Indian Fiscal Federalism. *Margin*, October 1984, *17*(1), pp. 31–47. [G: India]

Apps, Patricia. Tax Reform and the Tax Unit. *Australian Tax Forum*, December 1984, *1*(4), pp. 467–81. [G: Australia]

Arak, Marcelle and Silver, Andrew. The Value of the Tax Treatment of Original-Issue Deep-Discount Bonds: A Note. *J. Finance*, March 1984, *39*(1), pp. 253–59.

Asher, Martin A. On the Estimation of Payroll Tax Incidence: Comment. *Southern Econ. J.*, April 1984, *50*(4), pp. 1224–30. [G: U.S.]

Auerbach, Alan J. Investment, Taxation, and Growth. In *Wachter, M. L. and Wachter, S. M., eds.*, 1984, pp. 224–50. [G: U.S.]

Auld, D. A. L. Public Revenues and Public Policy: The Impact on the Canadian Economy. In *Block, W. and Walker, M., eds.*, 1984, pp. 66–103. [G: Canada]

Austen-Smith, David. Subsidies to the Arts with Multiple Public Donors. *Econ. Rec.*, December 1984, *60*(171), pp. 381–89.

Baldry, J. C. The Enforcement of Income Tax Laws: Efficiency Implications. *Econ. Rec.*, June 1984, *60*(169), pp. 156–59.

Ball, Ray. The Natural Taxation of Capital Gains and Losses When Income Is Taxed. *J. Banking Finance*, September 1984, *8*(3), pp. 471–81.

Bärlocher, Urs. Steuerliche Behinderungen des internationalen Kapitalflusses zwischen einer Muttergesellschaft und ihrer Tochtergesellschaft: Schweiz. (Fiscal Obstacles to the International Flow of Capital between a Parent and Its Subsidiary: Switzerland. With English summary.) In *Intn'l. Fisc. Assoc.*, *vol. 69a*, 1984, pp. 487–99. **[G: Switzerland]**

Barth, Michael C. and Berk, Edwin. Oil Supply Shocks and Macroeconomic Policy: Economic Response: Administrative Options and Analytical Framework. In *Alm, A. L. and Weimer, R. J., eds.*, 1984, pp. 129–43. **[G: U.S.]**

Baxt, Robert. The Corporate Veil in Tax Law— The Legal Perception of Companies as Separate Entities. *Australian Tax Forum*, September 1984, *1*(3), pp. 239–52. **[G: Australia]**

Beach, Charles M. Who Will Pay for Proposed Public Pension Reforms? In *Conklin, D. W.; Bennett, J. H. and Courchene, T. J., eds.*, 1984, pp. 210–40. **[G: Canada]**

Beardsley, George L., Jr. Examining Flat Tax Rate Proposals: The Equity Issues. *Atlantic Econ. J.*, March 1984, *12*(1), pp. 120. **[G: U.S.]**

Beattie, John R. and Rothschild, Leonard W., Jr. U.S.A.: Foreign Sales Corporation—The Successor to DISC. *Bull. Int. Fiscal Doc.*, December 1984, *38*(12), pp. 552–56. **[G: U.S.]**

Bellon, Bertrand. Conditions de la politique industrielle aux États-Unis. (With English summary.) *Rev. Econ. Ind.*, 4th Trimester 1984, (30), pp. 26–41. **[G: U.S.]**

Ben-Zion, Uri. Recent Literature on the Impact of Taxation and Inflation on the International Financial Market. In *Tanzi, V., ed.*, 1984, pp. 99–109.

Ben-Zion, Uri. Recent Literature on the Impact of Taxation and Inflation on Interest Rates. In *Tanzi, V., ed.*, 1984, pp. 69–98. **[G: U.S.; OECD]**

Ben-Zion, Uri and Weinblatt, J. Purchasing Power, Interest Rate Parities and the Modified Fisher Effect in Presence of Tax Agreements. *J. Int. Money Finance*, April 1984, *3*(1), pp. 67–73.

Bender, Bruce. An Analysis of the Laffer Curve. *Econ. Inquiry*, July 1984, *22*(3), pp. 414–20. **[G: U.S.]**

Bendick, Marc, Jr. Privatization of Public Services: Recent Experience. In *Brooks, H.; Liebman, L. and Schelling, C. S., eds.*, 1984, pp. 153–71. **[G: U.S.]**

Benoit, J. Pierre V. Artificially Low Interest Rates versus Realistic or Market Interest Rates. In *Kessler, D. and Ullmo, P.-A., eds.*, 1984, pp. 35–78. **[G: LDCs; MDCs]**

Benoit, J. Pierre V. International Interest Rates, External Indebtedness of Developing Countries and Foreign Aid. In *Kessler, D. and Ullmo, P.-A., eds.*, 1984, pp. 241–67. **[G: LDCs; MDCs]**

Bergström, Villy and Södersten, Jan. Do Tax Allowances Stimulate Investment? *Scand. J. Econ.*, 1984, *86*(2), pp. 244–68. **[G: Sweden]**

Bertaina, Norberto A. Perspectivas para una Reforma Fiscal en Argentina. (General Outlook for a Tax Reform in Argentina. With English summary.) *Bull. Int. Fiscal Doc.*, 1984, *38*(8–9), pp. 359–66. **[G: Argentina]**

Betson, David and Haveman, Robert H. The Role of Income Transfers in Reducing Inequal-

ity between and within Regions. In *Moon, M., ed.*, 1984, pp. 283–322. **[G: U.S.]**

Bhatia, D. P. Impact of Taxes, Budgetary Deficit & Money Supply on Prices. *Margin*, January 1984, *16*(2), pp. 95–102. **[G: India]**

Biørn, Erik. Inflation, Depreciation, and the Neutrality of the Corporate Income Tax. *Scand. J. Econ.*, 1984, *86*(2), pp. 214–28. **[G: Norway]**

Bird, Richard M. Tax Harmonization and Federal Finance: A Perspective on Recent Canadian Discussion. *Can. Public Policy*, September 1984, *10*(3), pp. 253–66. **[G: Canada]**

Blackorby, Charles and Donaldson, David. Ethical Social Index Numbers and the Measurement of Effective Tax/Benefit Progressivity. *Can. J. Econ.*, November 1984, *17*(4), pp. 683–94.

Blair, Harry W. Agricultural Credit, Political Economy, and Patronage. In *Adams, D. W.; Graham, D. H. and Von Pischke, J. D., eds.*, 1984, pp. 183–93.

Blanchard, Olivier J. A Reexamination of the Theory of Automatic Stabilizers: Income Stability and Economic Efficiency under Alternative Tax Schemes: Comments. *Carnegie-Rochester Conf. Ser. Public Policy*, Spring 1984, *20*, pp. 207–08.

Blejer, Mario I. Financial Market Taxation and International Capital Flows. In *Tanzi, V., ed.*, 1984, pp. 204–19.

Block, Walter and Walker, Michael. Taxation: International Evidence. In *Block, W. and Walker, M., eds.*, 1984, pp. 3–19. **[G: OECD]**

Blomquist, N. Sören. The Wage Rate Tax—An Alternative to the Income Tax? *Scand. J. Econ.*, 1984, *86*(2), pp. 269–85.

Blomqvist, Åke and Horn, Henrik. Public Health Insurance and Optimal Income Taxation. *J. Public Econ.*, August 1984, *24*(3), pp. 353–71.

Blundell, Richard W., et al. On the Reform of the Taxation of Husband and Wife: Are Incentives Important? *Fisc. Stud.*, November 1984, *5*(4), pp. 1–22. **[G: U.K.]**

Boadway, Robin and Bruce, Neil. A General Proposition on the Design of a Neutral Business Tax. *J. Public Econ.*, July 1984, *24*(2), pp. 231–39.

Boadway, Robin; Bruce, Neil and Mintz, Jack. Taxation, Inflation, and the Effective Marginal Tax Rate on Capital in Canada. *Can. J. Econ.*, February 1984, *17*(1), pp. 62–79. **[G: Canada]**

Boadway, Robin; Bruce, Neil and Mintz, Jack. The Role and Design of the Corporate Income Tax. *Scand. J. Econ.*, 1984, *86*(2), pp. 286–99.

Bohanon, Cecil E. and Van Cott, T. Norman. Shapiro on Marginal Tax Rates and Aggregate Labor Supply: A Comment. *Quart. J. Bus. Econ.*, Spring 1984, *23*(2), pp. 15–19.

Bohanon, Cecil E. and Van Cott, T. Norman. Specific Taxes, Product Quality, and Rate-Revenue Analysis. *Public Finance Quart.*, October 1984, *12*(4), pp. 500–511.

Boidman, Nathan. Transfer Pricing Issues: A Critical Discussion of the Revenue Draft Information Circular. *Bull. Int. Fiscal Doc.*, 1984, *38*(8–9), pp. 399–420, 426. **[G: Canada; OECD]**

Bomchil, Maximo, Jr. Argentina's Double Taxation Agreements. *Bull. Int. Fiscal Doc.*, 1984, *38*(8–9), pp. 389–92. **[G: Argentina]**

Booth, Laurence D. and Johnston, David J. The Ex-Dividend Day Behavior of Canadian Stock Prices: Tax Changes and Clientele Effects. *J. Finance*, June 1984, *39*(2), pp. 457–76. **[G: Canada]**

Bortz, Gary A. and Rust, John P. Why Do Companies Pay Dividends? Comment. *Amer. Econ. Rev.*, December 1984, *74*(5), pp. 1135–36.

Bös, Dieter. Income Taxation, Public Sector Pricing and Redistribution. *Scand. J. Econ.*, 1984, *86*(2), pp. 166–83.

Boyd, D. A. C. Pay-as-You-Earn Taxation. *Bull. Int. Fiscal Doc.*, December 1984, *38*(12), pp. 557–65. **[G: Barbados; Jamaica]**

Boyd, Roy. Government Support of Nonindustrial Production: The Case of Private Forests. *Southern Econ. J.*, July 1984, *51*(1), pp. 89–107. **[G: U.S.]**

Brannon, Gerard M. The Value Added Tax Is a Good Utility Infielder. *Nat. Tax J.*, September 1984, *37*(3), pp. 303–12. **[G: U.S.]**

Break, George F. Avenues to Tax Reform: Perils and Possibilities. *Nat. Tax J.*, March 1984, *37*(1), pp. 1–8. **[G: U.S.]**

Break, George F. State Taxation Under the Commerce Clause: The History Revisited: Comments. In *McLure, C. E., Jr., ed.*, 1984, pp. 82–84. **[G: U.S.]**

Brean, Donald J. S. International Portfolio Capital: The Wedge of the Withholding Tax. *Nat. Tax J.*, June 1984, *37*(2), pp. 239–47. **[G: Canada]**

Brennan, Geoffrey. Tax Reform and Tax Limits: Political Process in Public Finance. *Australian Tax Forum*, March 1984, *1*(1), pp. 83–95.

Brennan, Geoffrey; Bohanon, Cecil E. and Carter, Richard. Public Finance and Public Prices: Towards a Reconstruction of Tax Theory. *Public Finance*, 1984, *39*(2), pp. 157–81.

Brennan, Geoffrey and Buchanan, James M. Towards a Tax Constitution for Leviathan. In *Buchanan, J. M. and Tollison, R. D., eds.*, 1984, 1977, pp. 71–89.

Brick, Ivan E. and Fung, William K. H. Taxes and the Theory of Trade Debt. *J. Finance*, September 1984, *39*(4), pp. 1169–76.

Bridges, Benjamin, Jr. Post-Fisc Distributions of Income: Comment. *Public Finance Quart.*, April 1984, *12*(2), pp. 231–40. **[G: U.S.]**

Bridges, Benjamin, Jr. Post-Fisc Distributions of Income: Further Comment. *Public Finance Quart.*, April 1984, *12*(2), pp. 245–47. **[G: U.S.]**

Brown, C. V., et al. Tax Evasion and Avoidance on Earned Income: Some Survey Evidence. *Fisc. Stud.*, August 1984, *5*(3), pp. 1–22. **[G: U.K.]**

Browning, Edgar K. and Johnson, William R.

Taxes in the United States. In *Block, W. and Walker, M., eds.*, 1984, pp. 117–38. **[G: U.S.]**

Browning, Edgar K. and Johnson, William R. Taxes in the United States: Reply. In *Block, W. and Walker, M., eds.*, 1984, pp. 146–52. **[G: U.S.]**

Browning, Edgar K. and Johnson, William R. The Trade-Off between Equality and Efficiency. *J. Polit. Econ.*, April 1984, *92*(2), pp. 175–203. **[G: U.S.]**

van Brunschot, Frank. Fiscal Obstacles to the International Flow of Capital between a Parent and Its Subsidiary: Netherlands. In *Intn'l. Fisc. Assoc.*, vol. 69a, 1984, pp. 417–27. **[G: Netherlands]**

Buchanan, James M. The Ethical Limits of Taxation. *Scand. J. Econ.*, 1984, *86*(2), pp. 102–14.

Buchanan, James M. The Limits of Taxation. In *Block, W. and Walker, M., eds.*, 1984, pp. 41–55.

Buchanan, James M. and Lee, Dwight R. Some Simple Analytics of the Laffer Curve. In *Hanusch, H., ed.*, 1984, pp. 281–95.

Buchanan, James M. and Lee, Dwight R. Tax Rates and Tax Revenues in Political Equilibrium: Some Simple Analytics. In *Buchanan, J. M. and Tollison, R. D., eds.*, 1984, 1982, pp. 194–205.

Buchele, Robert. Reaganomics and the Fairness Issue. *Challenge*, September/October 1984, *27*(4), pp. 25–31. **[G: U.S.]**

Budd, Edward C.; Radner, Daniel B. and Whiteman, T. Cameron. An Accounting Framework for Transfer Payments and Its Implications for the Size Distribution of Income. In *Moon, M., ed.*, 1984, pp. 37–83. **[G: U.S.]**

Buglione, Enrico and France, George. Skewed Fiscal Federalism in Italy: Implications for Public Expenditure Control. In *Premchand, A. and Burkhead, J., eds.*, 1984, pp. 69–89. **[G: Italy]**

de Buitléir, Donal. The Third Report of the Commission on Taxation. *Irish Banking Rev.*, September 1984, pp. 46–56. **[G: Ireland]**

de Buitléir, Donal. Whither Tax Policy. *Irish Banking Rev.*, June 1984, pp. 12–23.

Bulow, Jeremy I. and Summers, Lawrence H. The Taxation of Risky Assets. *J. Polit. Econ.*, February 1984, *92*(1), pp. 20–39. **[G: U.S.]**

Burbidge, John B. Who Will Pay for Proposed Public Pension Reforms? Comments. In *Conklin, D. W.; Bennett, J. H. and Courchene, T. J., eds.*, 1984, pp. 264–65. **[G: Canada]**

Burge, Marianne. Share Purchases Treated as Asset Acquisitions in the U.S.A.—New Section 338. *Bull. Int. Fiscal Doc.*, January 1984, *38*(1), pp. 11–13. **[G: U.S.]**

Burkett, John P. Capitalistic and Market Socialistic Distribution of Lifetime Capital Property: Comment. *Atlantic Econ. J.*, December 1984, *12*(4), pp. 73.

Button, K. J. Subsidies and the Provision of Urban

Public Transport. *Int. J. Transport Econ.*, Aug.-Dec. 1984, *11*(2–3), pp. 177–88. **[G: U.K.]**

Caniglia, Alan S. Intertemporal Effects, Intertemporal Suitability, and the Analysis of In-Kind Subsidy Programs. *Public Finance Quart.*, October 1984, *12*(4), pp. 395–406.

Carlson, George N. and Galper, Harvey. Water's Edge versus Worldwide Unitary Combination. In *McLure, C. E., Jr., ed.*, 1984, pp. 1–40. **[G: U.S.]**

Carlsson, Bo. Industrial Subsidies in the Nordic Countries. In *Mikkelsen, A., et al.*, 1984, pp. 222–29. **[G: Scandinavia]**

Carpenter, Edwin H. and Chester, S. Theodore, Jr. Are Federal Energy Tax Credits Effective? A Western United States Survey. *Energy J.*, April 1984, *5*(2), pp. 139–49. **[G: U.S.]**

Chandrasekhar, S. Tax Policy in India. In *Singh, A. K.; Papola, T. S. and Mathur, R. S., eds.*, 1984, pp. 403–27. **[G: India]**

Chang, Semoon. Do Disaster Areas Benefit from Disasters? *Growth Change*, October 1984, *15*(4), pp. 24–31. **[G: U.S.]**

Chown, John F. The 1984 Budget, the Finance Bill and Corporate Finance. *Fisc. Stud.*, May 1984, *5*(2), pp. 73–81. **[G: U.K.]**

Christian, Ernest S., Jr. Getting Down to Basics: Tax Policy and Tax Politics for the Basic Industries of Today and Tomorrow. *Nat. Tax J.*, September 1984, *37*(3), pp. 347–50. **[G: U.S.]**

Christiano, Lawrence J. A Reexamination of the Theory of Automatic Stabilizers: Reply. *Carnegie-Rochester Conf. Ser. Public Policy*, Spring 1984, *20*, pp. 209–10.

Christiano, Lawrence J. A Reexamination of the Theory of Automatic Stabilizers. *Carnegie-Rochester Conf. Ser. Public Policy*, Spring 1984, *20*, pp. 147–206.

Christiansen, Vidar. Which Commodity Taxes Should Supplement the Income Tax? *J. Public Econ.*, July 1984, *24*(2), pp. 195–220.

Cleeton, David L. Wage and Price Measures of the Excess Burdens from Taxation. *Public Finance*, 1984, *39*(1), pp. 1–24.

Clemmer, Richard B. Measuring Welfare Effects of In-Kind Transfers. *J. Urban Econ.*, January 1984, *15*(1), pp. 46–65. **[G: U.S.]**

Clotfelter, Charles T. Tax Cut Meets Bracket Creep: The Rise and Fall of Marginal Tax Rates, 1964–1984. *Public Finance Quart.*, April 1984, *12*(2), pp. 131–52. **[G: U.S.]**

Cnossen, Sijbren. Alternative Forms of Corporation Tax. *Australian Tax Forum*, September 1984, *1*(3), pp. 253–79. **[G: OECD]**

Cnossen, Sijbren. Corporation Taxes in OECD Member Countries. *Bull. Int. Fiscal Doc.*, November 1984, *38*(11), pp. 483–96. **[G: OECD]**

Cochrane, E. Cal. Use of Vehicles Other Than Corporations in Purchase and Sale Transactions. In *Purden, C., ed.*, 1984, pp. 138–55. **[G: Canada]**

Cockle, Paul. Public Expenditure Policy, 1984–85: Oil. In *Cockle, P., ed.*, 1984, pp. 77–87. **[G: U.K.]**

Coen, Robert M. and Hickman, Bert G. Tax Policy, Federal Deficits, and U.S. Growth in the 1980s. *Nat. Tax J.*, March 1984, *37*(1), pp. 89–104. **[G: U.S.]**

Cohen, Jacques. La T.V.A., un impôt inégalitaire mal connu. (V.A.T.: An Ill-Known Non-Egalitarian Tax. With English summary.) *Consommation*, 1984, *31*(1), pp. 27–58. **[G: France]**

Conrad, Robert F. and Hool, R. Bryce. Intertemporal Extraction of Mineral Resources under Variable Rate Taxes. *Land Econ.*, November 1984, *60*(4), pp. 319–27.

Constantinides, George M. Optimal Stock Trading with Personal Taxes: Implications for Prices and the Abnormal January Returns. *J. Finan. Econ.*, March 1984, *13*(1), pp. 65–89. **[G: U.S.]**

Constantinides, George M. and Ingersoll, Jonathan E., Jr. Optimal Bond Trading with Personal Taxes. *J. Finan. Econ.*, September 1984, *13*(3), pp. 299–335.

Cook, Philip J. The Economics of Alcohol Consumption and Abuse. In *West, L. J., ed.*, 1984, pp. 56–77. **[G: U.S.]**

Cook, Thomas J. and D'Antonio, Louis J. Credit Union Taxation: Competitive Effects. *J. Econ. Bus.*, May 1984, *36*(2), pp. 251–62. **[G: U.S.]**

Cosciani, Cesare. Le distorsioni fiscali nel settore edilizio. (Fiscal Distortions in the Residential-Property Sector. With English summary.) *Bancaria*, July 1984, *40*(7), pp. 623–32. **[G: Italy]**

Courchene, Thomas J. An Australian Perspective on Taxation: Comment. In *Block, W. and Walker, M., eds.*, 1984, pp. 426–32. **[G: Australia]**

Cox, Dennis. Raising Revenue in the Underground Economy. *Nat. Tax J.*, September 1984, *37*(3), pp. 283–88. **[G: U.S.]**

Crampton, Graham. Subsidies to Urban Public Transport and Privatisation. In *Le Grand, J. and Robinson, R., eds.*, 1984, pp. 201–11. **[G: U.K.]**

Creedy, John and Gemmell, Norman. Income Redistribution through Taxes and Transfers in Britain. *Scot. J. Polit. Econ.*, February 1984, *31*(1), pp. 44–59. **[G: U.K.]**

Curry, Robert L., Jr. Problems in Acquiring Mineral Revenues for Financing Economic Development: A Case Study of Zambia during 1970–78. *Amer. J. Econ. Soc.*, January 1984, *43*(1), pp. 37–52. **[G: Zambia]**

Dahl, Carol A. Vertical Equity Effects and Total Consumer Losses for Emergency Allocation Schemes for the Gasoline Market. *Appl. Econ.*, February 1984, *16*(1), pp. 25–32. **[G: U.S.]**

Dal Co, Mario; Longobardi, Ernesto and Vitaletti, Giuseppe. Le liquidazioni e la loro tassazione: un problema di politica economica. (The Taxation of Allowances for Termination of Employment: An Economic-Policy Matter. With English summary.) *Bancaria*, August 1984, *40*(8), pp. 721–40. **[G: Italy]**

Daly, Donald. Recent Developments in the Japa-

nese Tax System: Comment. In *Block, W. and Walker, M., eds.*, 1984, pp. 371–79.
[G: Japan]

Daly, Michael J. and Naqib, Fadle. The Treatment of Registered Retirement Savings Plans at Maturity. *J. Econ. Dynam. Control*, September 1984, 7(3), pp. 233–40.

Danziger, Sheldon, et al. Implications of the Relative Economic Status of the Elderly for Transfer Policy. In *Aaron, H. J. and Burtless, G., eds.*, 1984, pp. 175–93. [G: U.S.]

Danziger, Sheldon, et al. Income Transfers and the Economic Status of the Elderly. In *Moon, M., ed.*, 1984, pp. 239–76. [G: U.S.]

Davey, Bernadette P. 1984 Budget Speech. *Bull. Int. Fiscal Doc.*, April 1984, 38(4), pp. 167–70. [G: Zambia]

Davey, Bernadette P. 1984 Budget Speech. *Bull. Int. Fiscal Doc.*, 1984, 38(6), pp. 270–71.
[G: Botswana]

David, Christina C. Credit and Price Policies in Philippine Agriculture. In *Adams, D. W.; Graham, D. H. and Von Pischke, J. D., eds.*, 1984, pp. 210–25. [G: Philippines]

Davies, James B.; St-Hilaire, France and Whalley, John. Some Calculations of Lifetime Tax Incidence. *Amer. Econ. Rev.*, September 1984, 74(4), pp. 633–49. [G: Canada]

Delwaide, Henry and Malherbe, Jacques. Obstacles fiscaux aux mouvements de capitaux entre une société-mère et ses filiales étrangères: Belgique. (Fiscal Obstacles to the International Flow of Capital between a Parent and Its Subsidiary: Belgium. With English summary.) In *Intn'l. Fisc. Assoc., vol. 69a*, 1984, pp. 255–73. [G: Belgium]

Devereux, Michael P. and Morris, C. Nick. The Chancellor's Arithmetic. *Fisc. Stud.*, May 1984, 5(2), pp. 63–72. [G: U.K.]

Díaz, Francisco Gil. The Incidence of Taxes in Mexico: A Before and After Comparison. In *Aspe, P. and Sigmund, P. E., eds.*, 1984, pp. 59–97. [G: Mexico]

Dilnot, Andrew W. The Impact of the 1984 Budget on the Household Sector. *Fisc. Stud.*, May 1984, 5(2), pp. 57–62. [G: U.K.]

Dilnot, Andrew W.; Kay, John A. and Morris, C. Nick. The UK Tax System, Structure and Progressivity, 1948–1982. *Scand. J. Econ.*, 1984, 86(2), pp. 150–65. [G: U.K.]

Dilnot, Andrew W. and Morris, C. Nick. Progressivity and Graduation in Income Tax. *Fisc. Stud.*, November 1984, 5(4), pp. 23–29.
[G: U.K.]

Dixon, Daryl. Capital Gains and Income Tax Design Alternatives. *Australian Tax Forum*, June 1984, 1(2), pp. 185–95. [G: Australia]

Doern, G. Bruce. Canada's Budgetary Dilemmas: Tax and Expenditure Reform. In *Premchand, A. and Burkhead, J., eds.*, 1984, pp. 21–38.
[G: Canada]

Doh, Joon-Chien. Budgeting as an Instrument of Development: The Malaysian Experience. In *Premchand, A. and Burkhead, J., eds.*, 1984, pp. 187–98. [G: Malaysia]

Doh, Joon-Chien. Budgeting as an Instrument of Development: The Malaysian Experience. *Public Budg. Finance*, Spring 1984, 4(1), pp. 64–75. [G: Malaysia]

Dowell, Richard. Resources Rent Tax and Alternative Forms of Mineral Royalties. *Australian Tax Forum*, December 1984, 1(4), pp. 437–50. [G: Australia]

Doyle, Maurice F. Management of the Public Finances in Ireland since 1961. In *Premchand, A. and Burkhead, J., eds.*, 1984, pp. 53–67.
[G: Ireland; Europe]

Duch, Raymond M. Investment Subsidy Programs in Comparative Perspective. In *Holzer, M. and Nagel, S. S., eds.*, 1984, pp. 145–70.
[G: France; U.K.; Japan]

Due, John F. Accepted v Controversial Sales Tax Structures—Switzerland, Australia, New Zealand, Canada. *Australian Tax Forum*, December 1984, 1(4), pp. 363–77. [G: Switzerland; Australia; New Zealand; Canada]

Due, John F. The Exclusion of Small Firms from Sales and Related Taxes. *Public Finance*, 1984, 39(2), pp. 202–12. [G: Global]

Eades, Kenneth M.; Hess, Patrick J. and Kim, E. Han. On Interpreting Security Returns during the Ex-Dividend Period. *J. Finan. Econ.*, March 1984, 13(1), pp. 3–34. [G: U.S.]

Eckaus, Richard S. and Mohie-Eldin, Amr. Consequences of Changes in Subsidy Policy: The Egyptian Case. In *[Chenery, H. B.]*, 1984, pp. 477–92. [G: Egypt]

Edwards, Jeremy. Does Dividend Policy Matter? *Fisc. Stud.*, February 1984, 5(1), pp. 1–17.
[G: U.S.; U.K.]

Edwards, Jeremy. The 1984 Corporation Tax Reform. *Fisc. Stud.*, May 1984, 5(2), pp. 30–44.
[G: U.K.]

Eichenberg, Richard C. The Expenditure and Revenue Effects of Defense Spending in the Federal Republic of Germany. *Policy Sci.*, March 1984, 16(4), pp. 391–411.
[G: W. Germany]

Eichhorn, Wolfgang and Funke, Helmut. A Characterization of the Proportional Income Tax. In *Hammer, G. and Pallaschke, D., eds.*, 1984, pp. 188–204.

Eichhorn, Wolfgang; Funke, Helmut and Richter, Wolfram F. Tax Progression and Inequality of Income Distribution. *J. Math. Econ.*, October 1984, 13(2), pp. 127–31.

Eisner, Robert. Transfers in a Total Incomes System of Accounts. In *Moon, M., ed.*, 1984, pp. 9–35. [G: U.S.]

Eisner, Robert; Albert, Steven H. and Sullivan, Martin A. Tax Incentives and R&D Expenditures. In *Oppenländer, K. H. and Poser, G., eds.*, 1984, pp. 385–419. [G: U.S.]

Eisner, Robert; Albert, Steven H. and Sullivan, Martin A. The New Incremental Tax Credit for R&D: Incentive or Disincentive? *Nat. Tax J.*, June 1984, 37(2), pp. 171–83. [G: U.S.]

Emerson, Craig; Garnaut, Ross and Ross, Anthony Clunies. Mining Taxation in Indonesia. *Bull. Indonesian Econ. Stud.*, August 1984, 20(2), pp. 107–21. [G: Indonesia]

Emmeluth, Christian. Fiscal Obstacles to the International Flow of Capital between a Parent and Its Subsidiary: Denmark. In *Intn'l. Fisc. Assoc.*, *vol. 69a*, 1984, pp. 307–09.

[G: Denmark]

Emory, Douglas R. and Lewellen, Wilbur G. Refunding Noncallable Debt. *J. Finan. Quant. Anal.*, March 1984, *19*(1), pp. 73–82.

Eshiwani, Arthur A. The 1984–85 Budgetary Measures. *Bull. Int. Fiscal Doc.*, December 1984, *38*(12), pp. 543–45. [G: Kenya]

Estes, Carl, II; Sunley, Emil M. and Zimmerman, Neal W. Fiscal Obstacles to the International Flow of Capital between a Parent and Its Subsidiary: United States. In *Intn'l. Fisc. Assoc.*, *vol. 69a*, 1984, pp. 325–32. [G: U.S.]

Fane, George. The Incidence of a Tax on Pure Rent: The Old Reason for the Old Answer. *J. Polit. Econ.*, April 1984, *92*(2), pp. 329–33.

Feige, Edgar L. Comment: Incidence of Taxation in the U.S. In *Block, W. and Walker, M., eds.*, 1984, pp. 138–46. [G: U.S.]

Feigenbaum, Susan and Jenkinson, Thomas. Government Incentives for Historic Preservation. *Nat. Tax J.*, March 1984, *37*(1), pp. 113–19. [G: U.S.]

Feldstein, Martin; Slemrod, Joel and Yitzhaki, Shlomo. The Effects of Taxation on the Selling of Corporate Stock and the Realization of Capital Gains: Reply. *Quart. J. Econ.*, February 1984, *99*(1), pp. 111–20. [G: U.S.]

Fellingham, John C. and Wolfson, Mark A. Progressive Income Taxes and the Demand for Risky Assets. *Nat. Tax J.*, March 1984, *37*(1), pp. 127–29. [G: U.S.]

Ferro, Angelo. Strumentazione fiscale e monetaria nella politica dell'offerta. (The Use of Fiscal and Monetary Tools in Supply-Side Policy. With English summary.) *Bancaria*, October 1984, *40*(10), pp. 957–64.

Figueroa, Antonio Hugo. Fiscal Obstacles to the International Flow of Capital between a Parent and Its Subsidiary: Argentina. In *Intn'l. Fisc. Assoc.*, *vol. 69a*, 1984, pp. 193–212.

[G: Argentina]

Finch, Johnny C. The Apportionment of Multistate and Multinational Corporate Income for Tax Purposes. *Bull. Int. Fiscal Doc.*, February 1984, *38*(2), pp. 51–59. [G: U.S.]

Finn, Frank J. and Ziegler, Peter. The Investment Obligations of a Superannuation Fund Trustee and the Commissioner's Discretions. *Australian Tax Forum*, December 1984, *1*(4), pp. 401–11. [G: Australia]

Fisher, Jeffrey D.; Lentz, George H. and Stern, Jerrold J. Tax Incentives for Investment in Nonresidential Real Estate. *Nat. Tax J.*, March 1984, *37*(1), pp. 69–87. [G: U.S.]

Fisher, Malcolm R. An Australian Perspective on Taxation. In *Block, W. and Walker, M., eds.*, 1984, pp. 385–426. [G: Australia]

Flath, David. Debt and Taxes: Japan Compared with the U.S. *Int. J. Ind. Organ.*, December 1984, *2*(4), pp. 311–26. [G: Japan; U.S.]

Fleischer, Arthur, Jr. and Raymond, Elizabeth A. Critical Developments in Acquisitions. In *Purden, C., ed.*, 1984, pp. 331–43. [G: U.S.]

Formby, John P.; Seaks, Terry G. and Smith, W. James. Difficulties in the Measurement and Comparison of Tax Progressivity: The Case of North America. *Public Finance*, 1984, *39*(3), pp. 297–313. [G: U.S.; Canada; Mexico]

Fortune, Peter. Tax Exemption and Resource Allocation: Implications for Price, Production, and Factor Choice. *Public Finance Quart.*, July 1984, *12*(3), pp. 347–64. [G: U.S.]

Friedman, Charles S. International Comparison of Tax Rates and Their Effects on National Incomes: Comment. In *Kendrick, J. W., ed.*, 1984, pp. 227–33. [G: OECD]

Fujita, Sei. On the Tax Treatment of Pension Plans. (In Japanese. With English summary.) *Osaka Econ. Pap.*, December 1984, *34*(2–3), pp. 52–62. [G: Japan]

Fullerton, Don. Which Effective Tax Rate? *Nat. Tax J.*, March 1984, *37*(1), pp. 23–41.

[G: U.S.]

Fullerton, Don and Henderson, Yolanda Kodrzycki. Incentive Effects of Taxes on Income from Capital: Alternative Policies in the 1980s. In *Hulten, C. R. and Sawhill, I. V., eds.*, 1984, pp. 45–89. [G: U.S.]

Fullerton, Don; Henderson, Yolanda Kodrzycki and Shoven, John B. A Comparison of Methodologies in Empirical General Equilibrium Models of Taxation. In *Scarf, H. E. and Shoven, J. B., eds.*, 1984, pp. 367–410.

[G: OECD; Mexico]

Fullerton, Don; Lyon, Andrew B. and Rosen, Richard J. Uncertainty, Welfare Cost and the "Adaptability" of U.S. Corporate Taxes. *Scand. J. Econ.*, 1984, *86*(2), pp. 229–43. [G: U.S.]

Fung, William K. H. and Theobald, Michael F. Dividends and Debt under Alternative Tax Systems. *J. Finan. Quant. Anal.*, March 1984, *19*(1), pp. 59–72. [G: U.S.; U.K.; France; Germany]

Gahvari, Firouz. Incidence and Efficiency Aspects of Differential Taxation of Residential and Industrial Capital in a Growing Economy. *J. Public Econ.*, November 1984, *25*(1/2), pp. 211–33.

Galper, Harvey and Toder, Eric. Transfer Elements in the Taxation of Income from Capital. In *Moon, M., ed.*, 1984, pp. 87–136.

[G: U.S.]

Gammie, Malcolm. After Dawson. *Fisc. Stud.*, August 1984, *5*(3), pp. 23–43. [G: U.K.]

Gammie, Malcolm. Has Nigel Lawson Really Reformed Business Taxation? *Fisc. Stud.*, May 1984, *5*(2), pp. 82–92. [G: U.K.]

Gammie, Malcolm. Tax Legislation: Consultation, Enactment and Revenue Practice. *Bull. Int. Fiscal Doc.*, 1984, *38*(5), pp. 195–201.

[G: U.K.]

Gammie, Malcolm. Tax Planning after Dawson. *Bull. Int. Fiscal Doc.*, April 1984, *38*(4), pp. 147–52. [G: U.K.]

Gangemi, Bruno. Fiscal Obstacles to the International Flow of Capital between a Parent and Its Subsidiary: Italy. In *Intn'l. Fisc. Assoc.*, *vol. 69a*, 1984, pp. 375–90. [G: Italy]

García Caballero, M. A. An Overview of the 1983

Tax Reform. *Bull. Int. Fiscal Doc.*, March 1984, *38*(3), pp. 124–29. **[G: Guatemala]**

Gardner, Roy J. Power and Taxes in a One-Party State: The USSR, 1925–1929. *Int. Econ. Rev.*, October 1984, *25*(3), pp. 743–55.
[G: U.S.S.R.]

Garnaut, Ross and Clunies Ross, A. Uncertainty, Risk Aversion and the Taxing of Natural Resource Projects. In *Lloyd, P. J., ed.*, 1984, *1975*, pp. 98–115. **[G: LDCs]**

Gaudet, Gérard and Lasserre, Pierre. L'impôt sur le revenu des sociétés et le coût du capital pour l'entreprise minière. (The Corporate Income Tax and the Cost of Capital for the Mining Firm. With English summary.) *Can. J. Econ.*, November 1984, *17*(4), pp. 778–87.

Gauthier, Anne. Les femmes et l'impôt sur le revenu. (Women and Income Tax. With English summary.) *L'Actual. Econ.*, March 1984, *60*(1), pp. 122–31. **[G: Canada]**

Gephardt, Richard A. The Bradley-Gephardt Fair Tax. In *Pechman, J. A., ed.*, 1984, pp. 74–77.
[G: U.S.]

Gerardi, Geraldine and Toder, Eric. Energy Tax Alernatives. *Nat. Tax J.*, September 1984, *37*(3), pp. 289–301. **[G: U.S.]**

Giertz, J. Fred and Chicoine, David L. Tax Valuation of Farm Land: Non-Neutrality with Respect to Inflation. *Nat. Tax J.*, June 1984, *37*(2), pp. 253–58. **[G: U.S.]**

Gifford, Adam, Jr. and Kenney, Roy W. Socialism and the Revenue Maximizing Leviathan. *Public Choice*, 1984, *42*(1), pp. 101–06.

Gilbert, Guy. La Relation entre Recettes Fiscales et Taux d'Imposition dans le Temps: Quelques Résultats Analytiques Simples. (Tax Financing and the Shadow Economy. With English summary.) In *Hanusch, H., ed.*, 1984, pp. 297–312.

Gilbert, Guy and Pommerehne, Werner W. Préférences fiscales et politiques d'imposition. (Fiscal Preferences and Tax Policy. With English summary.) *Public Finance*, 1984, *39*(1), pp. 25–69. **[G: Australia]**

Glaister, Stephen. The Allocation of Urban Public Transport Subsidy. In *Le Grand, J. and Robinson, R., eds.*, 1984, pp. 177–200. **[G: U.K.]**

Gnazzo Lima, Edison and Valdés Costa, Ramón. Taxation in Latin America. *Bull. Int. Fiscal Doc.*, 1984, *38*(8–9), pp. 367–85, 393.
[G: Latin America]

Goddeeris, John H. Comment on "Self-Employment and the Incidence of the Payroll Tax." *Nat. Tax J.*, December 1984, *37*(4), pp. 575–76. **[G: U.S.]**

Gofran, K. A. The New Draft Income Tax Ordinance: Some Observations. *Bull. Int. Fiscal Doc.*, October 1984, *38*(10), pp. 457–58.
[G: Bangladesh]

Gonzalez-Vega, Claudio. Cheap Agricultural Credit: Redistribution in Reverse. In *Adams, D. W.; Graham, D. H. and Von Pischke, J. D., eds.*, 1984, pp. 120–32.

Goode, Richard. Lessons from Seven Decades of Income Taxation. In *Pechman, J. A., ed.*, 1984, pp. 13–32. **[G: U.S]**

Goodfriend, Marvin. Income Stability and Economic Efficiency under Alternative Tax Schemes: A Comment. *Carnegie-Rochester Conf. Ser. Public Policy*, Spring 1984, *20*, pp. 143–46. **[G: U.S.]**

Gordon, Myron J. Leverage and the Value of a Firm under a Progressive Personal Income Tax: Reply. *J. Banking Finance*, September 1984, *8*(3), pp. 495–97.

Gordon, Roger H. Inflation, Taxation, and Corporate Behavior. *Quart. J. Econ.*, May 1984, *99*(2), pp. 312–27.

Gorton, Slade. Tax Reform and the Tax Legislative Process. In *Pechman, J. A., ed.*, 1984, pp. 33–38. **[G: U.S.]**

Gottschalk, Peter. The Role of Income Transfers in Reducing Inequality between and within Regions: Comment. In *Moon, M., ed.*, 1984, pp. 322–26. **[G: U.S.]**

Goudie, Andrew W. Tax Exhaustion: Estimates from a Disaggregate Model of Corporate Tax Liabilities. *Appl. Econ.*, April 1984, *16*(2), pp. 205–24. **[G: U.K.]**

Goudie, Andrew W. The Dividend Decision in the Presence of Tax Exhaustion. *Scot. J. Polit. Econ.*, November 1984, *31*(3), pp. 265–73.

Govind, Har. Taxation of Foreign Companies. *Bull. Int. Fiscal Doc.*, December 1984, *38*(12), pp. 536–42. **[G: India]**

Graetz, Michael J. Can the Income Tax Continue to Be the Major Revenue Source? In *Pechman, J. A., ed.*, 1984, pp. 39–65. **[G: U.S.]**

Gravelle, Jane G. and Zimmerman, Dennis. Tax Progressivity and the Design of Tax Incentives for Investment. *Public Finance Quart.*, July 1984, *12*(3), pp. 251–89. **[G: U.S.]**

Grbich, Yuri and Grbich, Judith. Tax Expenditures as a Regulatory Tool: Targeting Superannuation Dollars. *Australian Tax Forum*, March 1984, *1*(1), pp. 96–120. **[G: Australia]**

Greenaway, David. A Statistical Analysis of Fiscal Dependence on Trade Taxes and Economic Development. *Public Finance*, 1984, *39*(1), pp. 70–89. **[G: Global]**

Greenberg, Joseph. Avoiding Tax Avoidance: A (Repeated) Game-Theoretic Approach. *J. Econ. Theory*, February 1984, *32*(1), pp. 1–13.

Greenley, Douglas A.; Walsh, Richard G. and Young, Robert A. Option Value: Empirical Evidence from a Case Study of Recreation and Water Quality. In *Ahmad, Y. J.; Dasgupta, P. and Mäler, K.-G., eds.*, 1984, pp. 302–21.
[G: U.S.]

Grimes, Arthur. The Impact of Taxes on Wages: A Comment. *Econ. Notes*, 1984, (3), pp. 163–66. **[G: U.S.]**

Groenewegen, Peter D. Rationalizing Australian Taxation Revisited. *Econ. Rec.*, June 1984, *60*(169), pp. 113–27. **[G: Australia]**

Groenewold, Nicolaas. Short-Run Tax Incidence. *Oxford Econ. Pap.*, March 1984, *36*(1), pp. 146–61.

Grubel, Herbert G. Free Enterprise Zones in Economic Development. In *Giersch, H., ed.*, 1984, pp. 222–35.

Grubel, Herbert G. The Impact of the Tax System—Federal Republic of Germany: Comment. In *Block, W. and Walker, M., eds.,* 1984, pp. 320–23. **[G: W. Germany]**

Guesnerie, Roger and Roberts, Kevin. Effective Policy Tools and Quantity Controls. *Econometrica,* January 1984, 52(1), pp. 59–86.

Guillaume, Y., et al. Etude des incitants financiers aux économies d'énergie dans le secteur domestique. Le cas de la Belgique. (Energy Saving Is One of the Major Economic Problems of This Period. Governments Try to Encourage It by Various Measures. With English summary.) *Cah. Écon. Bruxelles,* 1st Trimester 1984, (101), pp. 57–73. **[G: Belgium]**

Guillaume, Y., et al. Impact of Subsidies and of Tax Deductions on Consumer's Energy Savings—The Belgian Case. In *Avula, X. J. R., et al.,* 1984, pp. 815–21. **[G: Belgium]**

Gurel, Eitan and Pyle, David H. Bank Income Taxes and Interest Rate Risk Management: A Note. *J. Finance,* September 1984, 39(4), pp. 1199–206.

Guttentag, Joseph H. Tax Treaty Shopping. *Bull. Int. Fiscal Doc.,* January 1984, 38(1), pp. 3–10. **[G: U.S.]**

Gwartney, James and Stroup, Richard L. Labor Supply and Tax Rates: Reply. *Amer. Econ. Rev.,* December 1984, 74(5), pp. 1108–09.

Hagelmayer, István. Concept of the State Budget for the New Phase in Hungary. *Acta Oecon.,* 1984, 33(1–2), pp. 17–30. **[G: Hungary]**

Halberstadt, Victor, et al. Inefficiencies in Public Transfer Policies in Western Industrialized Democracies. In *Hanusch, H., ed.,* 1984, pp. 189–208. **[G: OECD]**

Hall, Chris. Fiscal Obstacles to the International Flow of Capital between a Parent and Its Subsidiary: Hong Kong. In *Intn'l. Fisc. Assoc., vol. 69a,* 1984, pp. 359–73. **[G: Hong Kong]**

Hallerbach, Günther. Steuerliche Behinderungen des internationalen Kapitalflusses zwischen einer Muttergesellschaft und ihrer Tochtergesellschaft: Deutschland. (Fiscal Obstacles to the International Flow of Capital between a Parent and Its Subsidiary: Germany. With English summary.) In *Intn'l. Fisc. Assoc., vol. 69a,* 1984, pp. 177–91. **[G: W. Germany]**

Halperin, Daniel. A Tax on Consumption, Gifts, and Bequests and Other Strategies for Reform: Comment. In *Pechman, J. A., ed.,* 1984, pp. 141–46. **[G: U.S.]**

Halperin, Daniel. Broadening the Base—The Case of Fringe Benefits. *Nat. Tax J.,* September 1984, 37(3), pp. 271–81. **[G: U.S.]**

Hamberg, Sten. Fiscal Obstacles to the International Flow of Capital between a Parent and Its Subsidiary: Sweden. In *Intn'l. Fisc. Assoc., vol. 69a,* 1984, pp. 461–85. **[G: Sweden]**

Hamermesh, Daniel S. On the Estimation of Payroll Tax Incidence: Reply. *Southern Econ. J.,* April 1984, 50(4), pp. 1231. **[G: U.S.]**

Hamilton, Roger. Fiscal Obstacles to the International Flow of Capital between a Parent and Its Subsidiary: Australia. In *Intn'l. Fisc. Assoc., vol. 69a,* 1984, pp. 213–26. **[G: Australia]**

Hamm, William G. Federal Aid to State and Local Governments: Comment. In *Mills, G. B. and Palmer, J. L., eds.,* 1984, pp. 203–08. **[G: U.S.]**

Hammer, Richard M. Canadian Acquisition of a U.S. Business: A U.S. Perspective. In *Purden, C., ed.,* 1984, pp. 274–304. **[G: Canada; U.S.]**

Hansen, W. Lee. Economic Growth and Equal Opportunity: Conflicting or Complementary Goals in Higher Education? In *Dean, E., ed.,* 1984, pp. 57–93. **[G: U.S.]**

Hansson, Ingemar. Marginal Cost of Public Funds for Different Tax Instruments and Government Expenditures. *Scand. J. Econ.,* 1984, 86(2), pp. 115–30. **[G: Sweden]**

Harper, Ian R. Taxation and Life Insurance: A Theoretical Analysis. *Econ. Rec.,* June 1984, 60(169), pp. 165–75.

Harriss, C. Lowell. Important Issues and Serious Problems in Flat-Rate Income Taxation. *Amer. J. Econ. Soc.,* April 1984, 43(2), pp. 159–62. **[G: U.S.]**

Harriss, C. Lowell. Proposals to Tax Life Insurance Savings as Personal Income: As Economic, Fiscal and Social Policy Such Expedients Appear Ill-advised. *Amer. J. Econ. Soc.,* October 1984, 43(4), pp. 427–34. **[G: U.S.]**

Hartford, Jon D. Relatively Efficient Pollution Standards under Perfect Competition. *Public Finance Quart.,* April 1984, 12(2), pp. 183–95.

Hartman, David G. Tax Policy and Foreign Direct Investment in the United States. *Nat. Tax J.,* December 1984, 37(4), pp. 475–87. **[G: U.S.]**

Hartog, Joop. On the Private Benefits of Subsidies to Education. *Econ. Educ. Rev.,* 1984, 3(1), pp. 23–35. **[G: Netherlands]**

Hasbrouck, Joel and Friend, Irwin. Why Do Companies Pay Dividends? Comment. *Amer. Econ. Rev.,* December 1984, 74(5), pp. 1137–41.

Hausman, Jerry A. Tax Policy and Unemployment Insurance Effects on Labor Policy. In *Wachter, M. L. and Wachter, S. M., eds.,* 1984, pp. 70–96. **[G: U.S.]**

Hausman, Jerry A. and Ruud, Paul A. Family Labor Supply with Taxes. *Amer. Econ. Rev.,* May 1984, 74(2), pp. 242–48.

Haveman, Robert H. How Much Have the Reagan Administration's Tax and Spending Policies Increased Work Effort? In *Hulten, C. R. and Sawhill, I. V., eds.,* 1984, pp. 91–125. **[G: U.S.]**

Hawkins, Benjamin M. The Impact of the Enterprise Zone on Urban Areas. *Growth Change,* January 1984, 15(1), pp. 35–40. **[G: U.S.]**

Head, John G. Alternative Tax Instruments and Tax Reform Strategies. *Australian Tax Forum,* March 1984, 1(1), pp. 15–38. **[G: Australia]**

Head, John G. Capital Gains Taxation—An Economist's Perspective. *Australian Tax Forum,* June 1984, 1(2), pp. 148–63. **[G: U.S.; U.K.; Canada; Australia]**

Hederman O'Brien, Miriam. Tax Reform in Ireland. *Fisc. Stud.*, November 1984, 5(4), pp. 30–43. **[G: Ireland]**

Heinhold, Michael. The German Nonlinear Income Tax Scale in Linear Programming Models—Linear Approximations and Error Analysis. In *[Beckmann, M. J.]*, 1984, pp. 327–35. **[G: W. Germany]**

Hellerstein, Jerome R. State Taxation Under the Commerce Clause: The History Revisited. In *McLure, C. E., Jr., ed.*, 1984, 1982, pp. 53–81. **[G: U.S.]**

Hendershott, Patric H. and Ling, David C. Prospective Changes in Tax Law and the Value of Depreciable Real Estate. *Amer. Real Estate Urban Econ. Assoc. J.*, Fall 1984, 12(3), pp. 297–317. **[G: U.S.]**

Hendershott, Patric H. and Ling, David C. Trading and the Tax Shelter Value of Depreciable Real Estate. *Nat. Tax J.*, June 1984, 37(2), pp. 213–23. **[G: U.S.]**

Henderson, Gordon D. Alternatives to the Income Tax. In *Pechman, J. A., ed.*, 1984, pp. 78–98. **[G: U.S.]**

Hersoug, Tor. Union Wage Responses to Tax Changes. *Oxford Econ. Pap.*, March 1984, 36(1), pp. 37–51.

Hettich, Walter and Winer, Stanley. A Positive Model of Tax Structure. *J. Public Econ.*, June 1984, 24(1), pp. 67–87. **[G: U.S.]**

Hill, Raymond D. State Enterprise and Income Distribution in Mexico. In *Aspe, P. and Sigmund, P. E., eds.*, 1984, pp. 357–96. **[G: Mexico]**

Hillman, Arye L. and Katz, Eliakim. Excise Taxes, Import Restrictions, and the Allocation of Time to Illegal Income-earning Activity. *Int. Rev. Law Econ.*, December 1984, 4(2), pp. 213–22.

Hills, John. Deep Discount Bonds—Or How to Get an Interest-free Loan. *Fisc. Stud.*, August 1984, 5(3), pp. 62–67. **[G: U.K.]**

Hills, John. Savings Taxation: The Chancellor's "Middle Way." *Fisc. Stud.*, May 1984, 5(2), pp. 45–56. **[G: U.K.]**

Hiltz, Michael A. Section 55: An Update. In *Purden, C., ed.*, 1984, pp. 40–46. **[G: Canada]**

Ho, H. C. Y. Inflation, Depreciation Rules and Profits Tax in Hong Kong. *Hong Kong Econ. Pap.*, 1984, (15), pp. 25–34. **[G: Hong Kong]**

Hofflander, Alfred E. and Nye, Blaine F. Self-Insurance, Captives, and Income Taxation. *J. Risk Ins.*, December 1984, 51(4), pp. 702–09.

Hoffmann, Lutz. Free Enterprise Zones in Economic Development: Comment. In *Giersch, H., ed.*, 1984, pp. 242–48.

Holland, Daniel M. Measuring and Combatting Income Tax Evasion. In *Hanusch, H., ed.*, 1984, pp. 329–48. **[G: U.S.]**

Holland, Daniel M. Measuring Profitability and Capital Costs: Introduction and Summary. In *Holland, D. M., ed.*, 1984, pp. 1–42. **[G: OECD; Finland]**

Homma, Masaaki and Atoda, Naosumi. On the So-called Kuroyon Problem. (In Japanese.

With English summary.) *Osaka Econ. Pap.*, December 1984, 34(2–3), pp. 63–74. **[G: Japan]**

Hongskrailers, M. and Jap, Kim Siong. Taxation of Royalties, License Fees, etc., Paid to Nonresident Licensors. *Bull. Int. Fiscal Doc.*, November 1984, 38(11), pp. 501–03. **[G: Thailand]**

Hongskrailers, M. and Jap, Kim Siong. Thailand: Loss Companies. *Bull. Int. Fiscal Doc.*, 1984, 38(6), pp. 249–50. **[G: Thailand]**

Honkapohja, Seppo and Kanniainen, Vesa. Inventory Valuation Allowance: A Solution to the Problem of the Corporation Tax? *Liiketaloudellinen Aikak.*, 1984, 33(1), pp. 49–59. **[G: Finland; Sweden]**

Hoogendoorn, J. The Netherlands: Current Tax Law Problems for Corporations. *Bull. Int. Fiscal Doc.*, January 1984, 38(1), pp. 15–17. **[G: Netherlands]**

Horwood, Owen. Budget 1984–85: A Harsh Budget. *Bull. Int. Fiscal Doc.*, 1984, 38(6), pp. 265–69. **[G: S. Africa]**

Houck, Oliver A. With Charity for All. *Yale Law J.*, July 1984, 93(8), pp. 1415–563. **[G: U.S.]**

Howard, John. Taxation Reform. *Australian Tax Forum*, March 1984, 1(1), pp. 8–14. **[G: Australia]**

Howick, Wallace M. Purchase and Sale of Assets. In *Purden, C., ed.*, 1984, pp. 156–202. **[G: Canada]**

Hubbard, R. Glenn. Do IRAs and Keoghs Increase Saving? *Nat. Tax J.*, March 1984, 37(1), pp. 43–54. **[G: U.S.]**

Hubbard, R. Glenn. Temporary Tax Reductions as Responses to Oil Shocks. In *Alm, A. L. and Weimer, R. J., eds.*, 1984, pp. 121–28. **[G: U.S.]**

Hughes, Barry. Taxation and Overtime Hours: An Australian Study. *Manchester Sch. Econ. Soc. Stud.*, June 1984, 52(2), pp. 171–95. **[G: Australia]**

Hulten, Charles R. Tax Policy and the Investment Decision. *Amer. Econ. Rev.*, May 1984, 74(2), pp. 236–41. **[G: U.S.]**

Hulten, Charles R. and Robertson, James W. The Taxation of High Technology Industries. *Nat. Tax J.*, September 1984, 37(3), pp. 327–45. **[G: U.S.]**

Husain, Ishrat. Raising Resources for Development: The Challenge for the Eighties. In *Burki, S. J. and LaPorte, R., Jr., eds.*, 1984, pp. 103–36. **[G: Pakistan]**

Hutchens, Robert. The Effect of Different Measures of Benefit on Estimates of the Distributive Consequences of Government Programs: Comment. In *Moon, M., ed.*, 1984, pp. 195–98. **[G: U.S.]**

Ihori, Toshihiro. Partial Welfare Improvements and Capital Income Taxation. *J. Public Econ.*, June 1984, 24(1), pp. 101–09.

Ihori, Toshihiro. Welfare Implications of Indexing Capital Income Taxation. *Econ. Stud. Quart.*, April 1984, 35(1), pp. 21–30.

Ikeda, Hisashi. The Analysis of Tax Incidence with Initial Distorting Taxes under Uncertainty. (In

Japanese. With English summary.) *Osaka Econ. Pap.*, December 1984, *34*(2–3), pp. 93–101.

IMF Fiscal Affairs Department. Interest Rates and Tax Treatment of Interest Income and Expense. In *Tanzi, V., ed.*, 1984, pp. 3–66.
[G: OECD]

Iritani, Jun. Optimal Income Taxation: Approximation and Algorism. (In Japanese. With English summary.) *Econ. Stud. Quart.*, December 1984, *35*(3), pp. 230–44. [G: Japan]

Iritani, Jun. Optimal Taxation: A Generalized Proposition for Approximation. (In Japanese. With English summary.) *Osaka Econ. Pap.*, December 1984, *34*(2–3), pp. 102–09.

Ishi, Hiromitsu. International Tax Evasion and Avoidance in Japan. *Hitotsubashi J. Econ.*, June 1984, *25*(1), pp. 21–29. [G: Japan]

Islam, Iyanatul. Socio-economic Progress in Indonesia under the New Order. In *Thambipillai, P., ed.*, 1984, pp. 137–50. [G: Indonesia]

Jacob, Friedhelm. Unitary Approaches in International Taxation. *Bull. Int. Fiscal Doc.*, March 1984, *38*(3), pp. 99–120. [G: U.S.; Germany; LDCs]

Jaffe, Jeffrey F. and Westerfield, Randolph. Leverage and the Value of a Firm under a Progressive Income Tax: A Correction and Extension. *J. Banking Finance*, September 1984, *8*(3), pp. 491–94.

Jao, Y. C. Hong Kong's New Revenue Proposals and Their Implications. *Bull. Int. Fiscal Doc.*, 1984, *38*(7), pp. 298–302. [G: Hong Kong]

Jap, Kim Siong. Managers' Fees Not Taxable under Malaysia–United Kingdom Treaty. *Bull. Int. Fiscal Doc.*, February 1984, *38*(2), pp. 79–81. [G: U.K.; Malaysia]

Jap, Kim Siong. The Three Tax Reform Laws: Overhaul of an Inherited Tax System. *Bull. Int. Fiscal Doc.*, March 1984, *38*(3), pp. 130–34. [G: Indonesia]

Jarach, Dino. El Impuesto en el Derecho Europeo y Americano. (Taxation in European and American Law. With English summary.) *Bull. Int. Fiscal Doc.*, 1984, *38*(8–9), pp. 387–88.

Jehle, Eugen. The Tax System of Tuvalu: A Brief Survey. *Bull. Int. Fiscal Doc.*, 1984, *38*(5), pp. 211–13. [G: Tuvalu]

Johnson, James A. Federal Sales Tax Reform in Canada: Some Parallels with Australia. *Australian Tax Forum*, December 1984, *1*(4), pp. 379–90. [G: Canada; Australia]

Jordan, James V. Tax Effects in Term Structure Estimation. *J. Finance*, June 1984, *39*(2), pp. 393–406. [G: U.S.]

Juhász, Margit. Enterprise Incomes in Hungary, Their Generation, Distribution and Differentiation. *Acta Oecon.*, 1984, *33*(1–2), pp. 166–80. [G: Hungary]

Juocys, Aleksas. The Supplementary Income Tax on the Remittance of Dividends Abroad Amended. *Bull. Int. Fiscal Doc.*, 1984, *38*(8–9), pp. 392–93. [G: Brazil]

Kaizuka, Keimei. Recent Developments in the Japanese Tax System. In *Block, W. and Walker, M., eds.*, 1984, pp. 357–70.
[G: Japan]

Kanniainen, Vesa. Corporation Wealth Tax—A Note. *Liiketaloudellinen Aikak.*, 1984, *33*(2), pp. 149–54. [G: Finland]

Katz, Menachem. Impact of Taxation on International Capital Flows: Some Empirical Results. In *Tanzi, V., ed.*, 1984, pp. 220–34.
[G: OECD]

Katz, Menachem. Inflation, Taxation, and the Rate of Interest in Eight Industrial Countries, 1961–82. In *Tanzi, V., ed.*, 1984, pp. 172–203.
[G: OECD]

Katz, Stanley N. Influences on Public Policies in the United States. In *Lowry, W. M., ed.*, 1984, pp. 23–37. [G: U.S.]

Kay, John A. The Effect of Increasing Tax Thresholds on the Poverty and Unemployment Traps. *Fisc. Stud.*, February 1984, *5*(1), pp. 32–34.
[G: U.K.]

Kay, John A. and Morris, C. Nick. The Gross Earnings Deflator. *Econ. J.*, June 1984, *94*(374), pp. 357–69. [G: U.K.]

Kazi, Shahnaz. Intersectoral Tax Burdens in Pakistan: A Critical Review of Existing Evidence and Some New Estimates. *Pakistan Devel. Rev.*, Winter 1984, *23*(4), pp. 553–72.
[G: Pakistan]

Keating, Paul J. The Government's Taxation Objectives. *Australian Tax Forum*, March 1984, *1*(1), pp. 2–7. [G: Australia]

Keen, Michael J. The 1984 Budget, the Finance Bill, and Corporate Finance: A Correction. *Fisc. Stud.*, November 1984, *5*(4), pp. 64.
[G: U.K.]

Kelley, Patrick L. Transfer Price Adjustments and Double Taxation: A Sword of Damocles for Multinationals. *Bull. Int. Fiscal Doc.*, October 1984, *38*(10), pp. 448–50. [G: U.S.; EEC]

Kellough, Howard J. Splitting Up the Business of a Private Corporation. In *Purden, C., ed.*, 1984, pp. 12–39. [G: Canada]

Kelly, William A., Jr. and Chambers, Donald R. Inflation, Taxes, and Savings "Incentives." *Financial Rev.*, May 1984, *19*(2), pp. 222–31.
[G: U.S.]

Kelman, Steven. Revenue Recycling Using Check Writing. In *Alm, A. L. and Weimer, R. J., eds.*, 1984, pp. 145–64. [G: U.S.]

Kemp, Alexander G. and Rose, David. Investment in Oil Exploration and Production: The Comparative Influence of Taxation. In *Pearce, D. W.; Siebert, H. and Walter, I., eds.*, 1984, pp. 169–95. [G: Selected Countries]

Kesselman, Jonathan R. Public Revenues and Public Policy: The Impact on the Canadian Economy: Comment. In *Block, W. and Walker, M., eds.*, 1984, pp. 103–10.
[G: Canada]

Key, Sydney J. International Banking Facilities as a Free Economic Zone. *Aussenwirtschaft*, May 1984, *39*(1/2), pp. 57–74. [G: U.S.]

Kiefer, Donald W. Distributional Tax Progressivity Indexes. *Nat. Tax J.*, December 1984, *37*(4), pp. 497–513. [G: U.S.]

Kienzle, Edward C. Post-Fisc Distributions of Income: Reply. *Public Finance Quart.*, April 1984, *12*(2), pp. 241–44.   [G: U.S.]

Kim, Dong-Kun and Kang, In-Jae. The Budget System and Structure in Korea. In *Premchand, A. and Burkhead, J., eds.*, 1984, pp. 175–86.   [G: S. Korea]

Kim, Wan-Soon and Abbott, Graham. Budget Procedures and Policies in the ASEAN Countries. In *Premchand, A. and Burkhead, J., eds.*, 1984, pp. 145–58.   [G: ASEAN]

Kimbell, Larry J. and Harrison, Glenn W. General Equilibrium Analysis of Regional Fiscal Incidence. In *Scarf, H. E. and Shoven, J. B., eds.*, 1984, pp. 275–313.   [G: U.S.]

Kimbrough, Kent P. The Corporation Income Tax in the Open Economy. *Int. Econ. Rev.*, June 1984, *25*(2), pp. 391–407.

King, Ronald F. Tax Expenditures and Systematic Public Policy: An Essay on the Political Economy of the Federal Revenue Code. *Public Budg. Finance*, Spring 1984, *4*(1), pp. 14–31.   [G: U.S.]

Kingston, Geoffrey H. Efficient Timing of Income Taxes. *J. Public Econ.*, July 1984, *24*(2), pp. 271–80.   [G: U.S.]

Kleine, Robert. National Consumption Taxes: The View from the States. *Nat. Tax J.*, September 1984, *37*(3), pp. 313–21.   [G: U.S.]

Klovland, Jan Tore. Tax Evasion and the Demand for Currency in Norway and Sweden. Is There a Hidden Relationship? *Scand. J. Econ.*, 1984, *86*(4), pp. 423–39.   [G: Norway; Sweden]

Koch, Walter A. S. Negative Einkommensteuern und Konjunkturpolitik. (Negative Income Taxes and Stabilization Policy. With English summary.) *Konjunkturpolitik*, 1984, *30*(6), pp. 348–73.   [G: U.S.]

Kock, Heinz. Kumulative Wirkungen des Abgaben- und Transfersystems. (Cumulative Effects of the Levies and Transfer System. With English summary.) *Kredit Kapital*, 1984, *17*(2), pp. 297–318.   [G: Germany]

Koenig, Evan F. Controlling Stock Externalities in a Common Property Fishery Subject to Uncertainty. *J. Environ. Econ. Manage.*, June 1984, *11*(2), pp. 124–38.

Koenig, Evan F. Uncertainty and Pollution: The Role of Indirect Taxation. *J. Public Econ.*, June 1984, *24*(1), pp. 111–22.

Kolbe, A. Lawrence; Tye, William B. and Baker, Miriam Alexander. Conditions for Investor and Customer Indifference to Transitions among Regulatory Treatments of Deferred Income Taxes. *Rand J. Econ.*, Autumn 1984, *15*(3), pp. 434–46.   [G: U.S.]

Koning, H. E. Unitary Taxation—A Foreign Government's View. *Bull. Int. Fiscal Doc.*, 1984, *38*(7), pp. 295–97.   [G: Netherlands; U.S.]

Kopits, George and Mutén, Leif. The Relevance of the Unitary Approach for Developing Countries. In *McLure, C. E., Jr., ed.*, 1984, pp. 269–80.

Koskela, Erkki and Kanniainen, Vesa. Changing the Tax Base and Risk-Taking. *Oxford Econ. Pap.*, March 1984, *36*(1), pp. 162–74.

Kotlikoff, Laurence J. Taxation and Savings: A Neoclassical Perspective. *J. Econ. Lit.*, December 1984, *22*(4), pp. 1576–1629.   [G: U.S.]

Kozub, Robert M. and Trebby, James P. Special Valuation of Farmland and Closely Held Business Realty for Estate Tax Purposes. *Growth Change*, July 1984, *15*(3), pp. 25–29.   [G: U.S.]

Krever, Richard. Apportioning Interest Expenses. *Australian Tax Forum*, December 1984, *1*(4), pp. 413–36.   [G: Australia]

Krever, Richard. Structural Issues in the Taxation of Capital Gains. *Australian Tax Forum*, June 1984, *1*(2), pp. 164–84.   [G: U.S.; Canada; Australia]

Kudrle, Robert Thomas. Excise Tax Incidence in Limit Price Oligopoly. *Public Finance*, 1984, *39*(3), pp. 321–46.

Ladd, Helen F. Federal Aid to State and Local Governments. In *Mills, G. B. and Palmer, J. L., eds.*, 1984, pp. 165–202.   [G: U.S.]

Lambert, Peter J. Non-equiproportionate Income Growth, Inequality, and the Income Tax. *Public Finance*, 1984, *39*(1), pp. 104–18.   [G: U.K.]

Lampman, Robert. An Accounting Framework for Transfer Payments and Its Implications for the Size Distribution of Income: Comment. In *Moon, M., ed.*, 1984, pp. 83–86.   [G: U.S.]

Latcham, Franklin C. Water's Edge versus Worldwide Unitary Combination: Comments. In *McLure, C. E., Jr., ed.*, 1984, pp. 41–44.   [G: U.S.]

Latorraca, Nilton. Fiscal Obstacles to the International Flow of Capital between a Parent and Its Subsidiary: Brazil. In *Intn'l. Fisc. Assoc.*, vol. 69a, 1984, pp. 275–91.   [G: Brazil]

Lau, Lawrence J. Numerical Specification of Applied General Equilibrium Models: Estimation, Calibration, and Data: Comments. In *Scarf, H. E. and Shoven, J. B., eds.*, 1984, pp. 127–37.   [G: U.S.; U.K.]

Lawrence, David B. and Saghafi, Massoud M. The Flat-Rate Income Tax, Tax Burden, and Charitable Contributions. *Nat. Tax J.*, December 1984, *37*(4), pp. 569–74.   [G: U.S.]

Le Grand, Julian. Optimal Taxation, the Compensation Principle and the Measurement of Changes in Economic Welfare. *J. Public Econ.*, July 1984, *24*(2), pp. 241–47.

Ledolter, Johannes and Power, Mark L. A Study of ERISA's Impact on Private Retirement Plan Growth. *J. Risk Ins.*, June 1984, *51*(2), pp. 225–43.   [G: U.S.]

Lee, Dwight R. The Economics of Enforcing Pollution Taxation. *J. Environ. Econ. Manage.*, June 1984, *11*(2), pp. 147–60.

Lee, Fook Hong. A Summary of Singapore's 1984 Budget. *Bull. Int. Fiscal Doc.*, 1984, *38*(5), pp. 202–10.   [G: Singapore]

Lee, Moon H. and Zechner, Josef. Debt, Taxes, and International Equilibrium. *J. Int. Money Finance*, December 1984, *3*(3), pp. 343–55.

Lee, Robert H. Subsidizing the Affluent: The

Case of Medical Education. *J. Policy Anal. Manage.*, Winter 1984, *3*(2), pp. 276–84. [G: U.S.]

Lehmann, Geoffrey. A Lawyer's View of Tax Reform—Building from Discrepancies. *Australian Tax Forum*, December 1984, *1*(4), pp. 451–66. [G: Australia]

Leibler, Mark. Taxation and Deductions for Losses from Highly Geared Rental Investments: Issues of Law and Policy. *Australian Tax Forum*, March 1984, *1*(1), pp. 39–53. [G: Australia]

Leuthold, Jane H. Income Splitting and Women's Labor-Force Participation. *Ind. Lab. Relat. Rev.*, October 1984, *38*(1), pp. 98–105. [G: U.S.]

Levy, Frank. Implications of the Relative Economic Status of the Elderly for Transfer Policy: Comment. In *Aaron, H. J. and Burtless, G., eds.*, 1984, pp. 193–96. [G: U.S.]

Lewis, Gordon H. The Taichman–Young Knot Unravelled [The Day Care Tangle]. *J. Policy Anal. Manage.*, Fall 1984, *4*(1), pp. 119–20. [G: U.S.]

Liebschutz, Saran F. and Lurie, Irene. Evolution in Federalism: The Reagan Program and Legislative Appropriation of Federal Grants in New York. *Public Budg. Finance*, Summer 1984, *4*(2), pp. 24–41. [G: U.S.]

Lindbeck, Assar. The Swedish Tax System—What Can We Learn from It? Comment. In *Block, W. and Walker, M., eds.*, 1984, pp. 251–74. [G: Sweden]

Lindholm, Richard W. The Constitutionality of a Federal Net Wealth Tax: A Socioeconomic Analysis of a Strategy Aimed at Ending Under-Taxation of Land. *Amer. J. Econ. Soc.*, October 1984, *43*(4), pp. 451–54. [G: U.S.]

Lindsay, Robert F. Purchase and Sale of a Canadian Business by a Nonresident of Canada. In *Purden, C., ed.*, 1984, pp. 305–30. [G: Canada; U.S.]

Litzenberger, Robert H. and Rolfo, Jacques. An International Study of Tax Effects on Government Bonds. *J. Finance*, March 1984, *39*(1), pp. 1–22. [G: W. Germany; Japan; U.K.; U.S.]

Litzenberger, Robert H. and Rolfo, Jacques. Arbitrage Pricing, Transaction Costs and Taxation of Capital Gains: A Study of Government Bonds with the Same Maturity Date. *J. Finan. Econ.*, September 1984, *13*(3), pp. 337–51. [G: U.S.]

Liu, Pak-Wai. A Note on Two Summary Measures of Tax Progressivity. *Public Finance*, 1984, *39*(3), pp. 412–19. [G: Hong Kong]

Lloyd, P. J. Individual Mines or Oilfields: Introduction. In *Lloyd, P. J., ed.*, 1984, pp. 35–52. [G: Australia]

Lloyd, P. J. Resource Rent Taxes. *Australian Econ. Rev.*, 2nd Quarter 1984, (66), pp. 37–46. [G: Australia]

Long, James E. Tax Rates and Tax Losses: A Preliminary Analysis Using Aggregate Data. *Public Finance Quart.*, October 1984, *12*(4), pp. 457–72. [G: U.S.]

Long, James E. and Scott, Frank A., Jr. The Impact of the 1981 Tax Act on Fringe Benefits and Federal Tax Revenues. *Nat. Tax J.*, June 1984, *37*(2), pp. 185–94. [G: U.S.]

Lowry, W. McNeil. The Arts & Public Policy in the United States: Introduction. In *Lowry, W. M., ed.*, 1984, pp. 1–22. [G: U.S.]

Luger, Michael I. Federal Tax Incentives as Industrial and Urban Policy. In *Sawers, L. and Tabb, W. K., eds.*, 1984, pp. 201–34. [G: U.S.]

Lustig, Nora. Distribution of Income, Food Consumption, and Fiscal Cost of Alternative Policy Options. In *Aspe, P. and Sigmund, P. E., eds.*, 1984, pp. 439–79. [G: Mexico]

Macón, Jorge and Reig, Enrique J. Social Security Contributions as a Fiscal Burden on Enterprises Engaged in International Activities: General Report. In *Intn'l. Fisc. Assoc., vol. 69b*, 1984, pp. 97–134. [G: Selected Countries]

Makin, John H. and Tanzi, Vito. Level and Volatility of U.S. Interest Rates: Roles of Expected Inflation, Real Rates, and Taxes. In *Tanzi, V., ed.*, 1984, pp. 110–42. [G: U.S.]

Manning, Ian G. Income Tests in the Australian Social Security System. *Australian Econ. Rev.*, 1st Quarter 1984, (65), pp. 34–46. [G: Australia]

Mansfield, Edwin. How Effective Is the R&D Tax Credit? *Challenge*, November/December 1984, *27*(5), pp. 57–61. [G: U.S.]

Mansur, Ahsan Habib and Whalley, John. Numerical Specification of Applied General Equilibrium Models: Estimation, Calibration, and Data. In *Scarf, H. E. and Shoven, J. B., eds.*, 1984, pp. 69–127. [G: U.S.; U.K.]

Marrelli, Massimo. On Indirect Tax Evasion. *J. Public Econ.*, November 1984, *25*(1/2), pp. 181–96.

Marshall, Adriana. El "salario social" en la Argentina. (With English summary.) *Desarrollo Econ.*, April–June 1984, *24*(93), pp. 41–70. [G: Argentina]

Mason, Robert and Calvin, Lyle D. Public Confidence and Admitted Tax Evasion. *Nat. Tax J.*, December 1984, *37*(4), pp. 489–96. [G: U.S.]

Massone, Pedro. The Chilean Income Tax Reform. *Bull. Int. Fiscal Doc.*, October 1984, *38*(10), pp. 433–47. [G: Chile]

Mathews, Russell. The Case for Indirect Taxation. *Australian Tax Forum*, March 1984, *1*(1), pp. 54–82. [G: OECD; Australia]

Matolcsy, Z. P. The Micro Effects of Inflation on Corporate Taxation and Profitability: Some Empirical Evidence for Seventeen Industry Groups. *Econ. Rec.*, December 1984, *60*(171), pp. 356–65. [G: Australia]

McAlpin, Michelle Burge. Economic Policy and the True Believer: The Use of Ricardian Rent Theory in the Bombay Survey and Settlement System. *J. Econ. Hist.*, June 1984, *44*(2), pp. 421–27. [G: India]

McDermott, John. Rational Host Country Use

of a Severance Tax. *J. Environ. Econ. Manage.*, December 1984, *11*(4), pp. 391–402.

McLure, Charles E., Jr. A Tax on Consumption, Gifts, and Bequests and Other Strategies for Reform: Comment. In *Pechman, J. A., ed.*, 1984, pp. 134–41. [G: U.S.]

McLure, Charles E., Jr. Corporate Income Tax: Restoration, Integration, or Elimination? In *Moore, J. H., ed.*, 1984, pp. 303–18.
[G: U.S.]

McLure, Charles E., Jr. General Equilibrium Analysis of Regional Fiscal Incidence: Comments. In *Scarf, H. E. and Shoven, J. B., eds.*, 1984, pp. 313–17. [G: U.S.]

Mehra, Yash P. The Tax Effect, and the Recent Behaviour of the After-Tax Real Rate: Is It Too High? *Fed. Res. Bank Richmond Econ. Rev.*, July/Aug. 1984, *70*(4), pp. 8–20. [G: U.S.]

Melvin, James R. Taxes, Relative Prices and Trade. In *Csikós-Nagy, B.; Hague, D. and Hall, G., eds.*, 1984, pp. 183–200.

Meyer, John R. and Oster, Clinton V., Jr. Small Community Service and the Role of Federal Subsidy. In *Meyer, J. R. and Oster, C. V., Jr., eds.*, 1984, pp. 185–99. [G: U.S.]

Michaud, Richard O. Should Dividend Discount Models Be Yield-Titled? Comment. *J. Portfol. Manage.*, Summer 1984, *10*(4), pp. 85–86.
[G: U.S.]

Michel, Richard C., et al. Are We Better Off in 1984? *Challenge*, September/October 1984, *27*(4), pp. 10–17. [G: U.S.]

Mieszkowski, Peter. A Comparison of Methodologies in Empirical General Equilibrium Models of Taxation: Comments. In *Scarf, H. E. and Shoven, J. B., eds.*, 1984, pp. 410–14.

Miller, Preston J. Income Stability and Economic Efficiency under Alternative Tax Schemes. *Carnegie-Rochester Conf. Ser. Public Policy*, Spring 1984, *20*, pp. 121–41. [G: U.S.]

Mills, Gregory B. The Budget: A Failure of Discipline. In *Palmer, J. L. and Sawhill, I. V., eds.*, 1984, pp. 107–39. [G: U.S.]

Minarik, Joseph J. Tax Policy. In *Mills, G. B. and Palmer, J. L., eds.*, 1984, pp. 209–42.
[G: U.S.]

Minarik, Joseph J. The Effects of Taxation on the Selling of Corporate Stock and the Realization of Capital Gains: Comment. *Quart. J. Econ.*, February 1984, *99*(1), pp. 93–110. [G: U.S.]

Miura, Makoto. The 1984 Tax Amendments. *Bull. Int. Fiscal Doc.*, 1984, *38*(6), pp. 251–54.
[G: Japan]

Mmusi, P. S. 1984 Budget Speech. *Bull. Int. Fiscal Doc.*, 1984, *38*(6), pp. 271–72.
[G: Botswana]

Moffitt, Robert A. Trends in Social Security Wealth by Cohort. In *Moon, M., ed.*, 1984, pp. 327–53. [G: U.S.]

Montgomery, Fred H. Water's Edge verus Worldwide Unitary Combination: Comments. In *McLure, C. E., Jr., ed.*, 1984, pp. 45–52.
[G: U.S.]

Montias, John Michael. Public Support for the Performing Arts in Western Europe and the United States: History and Analysis. In *[Reynolds, L. G.]*, 1984, pp. 409–44. [G: U.S.; W. Europe]

Moore, Robert L. Reply to Goddeeris [Self-Employment and the Incidence of the Payroll Tax]. *Nat. Tax J.*, December 1984, *37*(4), pp. 577–80. [G: U.S.]

Moreland, Kemper. Public Goods and Optimal Income Taxation. *Public Finance Quart.*, April 1984, *12*(2), pp. 197–212. [G: U.S.]

Munnell, Alicia H. Employee Benefits and the Tax Base. *New Eng. Econ. Rev.*, January–February 1984, pp. 39–55. [G: U.S.]

Munnell, Alicia H. ERISA—The First Decade: Was the Legislation Consistent with Other National Goals? *New Eng. Econ. Rev.*, November–December 1984, pp. 44–63. [G: U.S.]

Munnell, Alicia H. and Blais, Lynn E. Do We Want Large Social Security Surpluses? *New Eng. Econ. Rev.*, September–October 1984, pp. 5–21. [G: U.S.]

Murphy, D. G. The Zimbabwe 1983 Budget. *Bull. Int. Fiscal Doc.*, 1984, *38*(7), pp. 305–10.
[G: Zimbabwe]

Murthy, N. R. Vasudeva. Revenue Performance in the Indian Economy. *Atlantic Econ. J.*, December 1984, *12*(4), pp. 66. [G: India]

Musgrave, Peggy B. The Relevance of the Unitary Approach for Developing Countries: Comments. In *McLure, C. E., Jr., ed.*, 1984, pp. 281–85.

Musgrave, Richard A. Tax Policy: Comment. In *Mills, G. B. and Palmer, J. L., eds.*, 1984, pp. 248–51. [G: U.S.]

Mutti, John. Subsidized Production, World Steel Trade and Countervailing Duties. *Southern Econ. J.*, January 1984, *50*(3), pp. 871–80.
[G: Selected Countries]

Nagy, Tibor. The 1984 Budget Act and the Tax System. *Bull. Int. Fiscal Doc.*, 1984, *38*(7), pp. 311–15. [G: U.S.S.R.]

Nerlove, Marc; Razin, Assaf and Sadka, Efraim. Investment in Human and Nonhuman Capital, Transfers among Siblings, and the Role of Government. *Econometrica*, September 1984, *52*(5), pp. 1191–98.

Neubig, Thomas S. The Taxation of Financial Institutions after Deregulation. *Nat. Tax J.*, September 1984, *37*(3), pp. 351–59. [G: U.S.]

Newton, John R. and Sepulveda, Victor. The Puerto Rico Revenue Projection Model: An Econometric Approach. *Rev. Reg. Stud.*, Fall 1984, *14*(3), pp. 17–24. [G: Puerto Rico]

Nishina, Kazuhiko. Recent Trend in Corporate Profitability in Japan. (In Japanese. With English summary.) *Osaka Econ. Pap.*, December 1984, *34*(2–3), pp. 203–17. [G: Japan]

Nolan, John S. Can the Income Tax Continue to Be the Major Revenue Source? Comment. In *Pechman, J. A., ed.*, 1984, pp. 65–69.
[G: U.S.]

Norquist, Grover. Tax-slashing, 1981: The Kindest Cuts of All. *Policy Rev.*, Fall 1984, (30), pp. 59–60. [G: U.S.]

Noto, Nonna A. and Zimmerman, Dennis. Limiting State–Local Tax Deductibility: Effects among the States. *Nat. Tax J.*, December 1984, 37(4), pp. 539–49. [G: U.S.]

Officer, Robert. Capital Gains and Company Taxation. *Australian Tax Forum*, September 1984, 1(3), pp. 281–91. [G: Australia]

Okner, Benjamin A. Transfer Elements in the Taxation of Income from Capital: Comment. In *Moon, M., ed.*, 1984, pp. 136–38. [G: U.S.]

Oldman, Oliver. The Relevance of the Unitary Approach for Developing Countries: Comments. In *McLure, C. E., Jr., ed.*, 1984, pp. 286–87.

Olsen, Edgar O. and York, Kathy A. The Effect of Different Measures of Benefit on Estimates of the Distributive Consequences of Government Programs. In *Moon, M., ed.*, 1984, pp. 177–95. [G: U.S.]

Opaluch, James J. Dynamic Aspects of Effluent Taxation under Uncertainty. *J. Environ. Econ. Manage.*, March 1984, 11(1), pp. 1–13.

Orrock, D. C. Australian Resources Rent Tax. *Bull. Int. Fiscal Doc.*, 1984, 38(6), pp. 261, 291. [G: Australia]

Oswald, Rudolph A. Savings and Investment Comment. In *Wachter, M. L. and Wachter, S. M., eds.*, 1984, pp. 254–57. [G: U.S.]

Ott, Mack. Depreciation, Inflation, and Investment Incentives: The Effects of the Tax Acts of 1981 and 1982. *Fed. Res. Bank St. Louis Rev.*, November 1984, 66(9), pp. 17–30. [G: U.S.]

Parikh, Parimal M. and Peer, Devendra T. Non-Resident Indians—Investment and Taxation. *Bull. Int. Fiscal Doc.*, 1984, 38(6), pp. 243–48. [G: India]

Park, Thae S. Federal Personal Income Taxes: Liabilities and Payments, 1980–82. *Surv. Curr. Bus.*, April 1984, 64(4), pp. 56–57. [G: U.S.]

Parker, Robert P. Improved Adjustments for Misreporting of Tax Return Information Used to Estimate the National Income and Product Accounts, 1977. *Surv. Curr. Bus.*, June 1984, 64(6), pp. 17–25. [G: U.S.]

Parkin, Michael. The United Kingdom: Political Economy and Macroeconomics: A Comment. *Carnegie-Rochester Conf. Ser. Public Policy*, Autumn 1984, 21, pp. 281–93. [G: U.K.]

Parsons, Ross W. Capital Gains Taxation—A Lawyer's Perspective. *Australian Tax Forum*, June 1984, 1(2), pp. 122–47. [G: U.S.; U.K.; Australia; Canada]

Pasurka, Carl A., Jr. Corporate Income Taxes and U.S. Effective Rates of Protection. *Nat. Tax J.*, December 1984, 37(4), pp. 529–37. [G: U.S.]

Patsouratis, Vassilis A. Developmental Aspects of Corporate Taxation: The Case of Greece. *Public Finance*, 1984, 39(1), pp. 119–32. [G: Greece]

Pechman, Joseph A. Options for Tax Reform: Introduction. In *Pechman, J. A., ed.*, 1984, pp. 1–12. [G: U.S.]

Pedone, Antonio. The 1973–74 Tax Reform in Italy: A Partial Success with Many Shortcomings.

Banca Naz. Lavoro Quart. Rev., December 1984, (151), pp. 327–49. [G: Italy]

Peeters, Chris. Scheepsbouw in België: Ontwikkeling van een berekeningsmethode ter bepaling van de financiële implicaties van een indirecte subsidie. (The Belgian Shipbuilding Industry: Development of a Calculation Method to Determine the Financial Implications of an Indirect Subsidy. With English summary.) *Cah. Écon. Bruxelles*, 1st Trimester 1984, (101), pp. 40–56. [G: Belgium]

Peffekoven, Rolf. Anrechnung versus Freistellung—Zur ökonomischen Analyse internationaler Besteuerungsprinzipien. (Foreign Tax Credits versus Tax Exemptions—An Economic Analysis of International Principles of Taxation. With English summary.) *Aussenwirtschaft*, May 1984, 39(1/2), pp. 137–50. [G: Global]

Pepper, H. W. T. Stamp Duties: A Case for Their Abolition. *Bull. Int. Fiscal Doc.*, 1984, 38(7), pp. 303–04.

Pepper, H. W. T. Tax Changes in a Low Tax Country—The 1984–85 Budget in Bermuda. *Bull. Int. Fiscal Doc.*, October 1984, 38(10), pp. 451. [G: Bermuda]

Perkins, John A. Fiscal Policy and Economic Development in XIXth Century Germany. *J. Europ. Econ. Hist.*, Fall 1984, 13(2), pp. 311–44. [G: Germany]

Persson, Mats and Wissén, Pehr. Redistributional Aspects of Tax Evasion. *Scand. J. Econ.*, 1984, 86(2), pp. 131–49.

Peskin, Janice. Approaches to Measuring and Valuing In-Kind Subsidies and the Distribution of Their Benefits: Comment. In *Moon, M., ed.*, 1984, pp. 171–76. [G: U.S.]

Petersen, Hans-Georg. The Impact of the Tax System—Federal Republic of Germany. In *Block, W. and Walker, M., eds.*, 1984, pp. 283–319. [G: W. Germany]

Pfähler, Wilhelm. 'Linear' Income Tax Cuts: Distributional Effects, Social Preferences and Revenue Elasticities. *J. Public Econ.*, August 1984, 24(3), pp. 381–88.

Phaup, Marvin. New Approaches to the Budgetary Treatment of Federal Credit Assistance. *Public Budg. Finance*, Autumn 1984, 4(3), pp. 97–100. [G: U.S.]

Phillips, Ian R. Using the Tax System to Influence Private and Corporate Investment. *Australian Tax Forum*, September 1984, 1(3), pp. 313–22. [G: U.S.]

Pick, J. F. No Major Changes in Taxation in the Budget, 1984–85. *Bull. Int. Fiscal Doc.*, October 1984, 38(10), pp. 453–55. [G: Israel]

Pindyck, Robert S. and Rotemberg, Julio J. Energy Shocks and the Macroeconomy. In *Alm, A. L. and Weimer, R. J., eds.*, 1984, pp. 97–120. [G: U.S.]

Pires, Manuel. Fiscal Obstacles to the International Flow of Capital between a Parent and Its Subsidiary: Portugal. In *Intn'l. Fisc. Assoc.*, vol. 69a, 1984, pp. 429–41. [G: Portugal]

Plant, Mark W. An Empirical Analysis of Welfare Dependence. *Amer. Econ. Rev.*, September 1984, 74(4), pp. 673–84. [G: U.S.]

Plotnick, Robert. The Redistributive Impact of Cash Transfers. *Public Finance Quart.*, January 1984, *12*(1), pp. 27–50. **[G: U.S.]**

Porcano, Thomas M. Distributive Justice and Tax Policy. *Accounting Rev.*, October 1984, *59*(4), pp. 619–36.

Porter, Michael G. Taxation of the Australian Resource Sector. In *Siebert, H., ed.*, 1984, pp. 95–116. **[G: Australia]**

Poterba, James M. Tax Subsidies to Owner-occupied Housing: An Asset-Market Approach. *Quart. J. Econ.*, November 1984, *99*(4), pp. 729–52. **[G: U.S.]**

Poterba, James M. and Summers, Lawrence H. New Evidence that Taxes Affect the Valuation of Dividends. *J. Finance*, December 1984, *39*(5), pp. 1397–1415. **[G: U.K.]**

Pratschke, John L. Aspects of the Redistribution of Income in Urban and Rural Ireland, 1973–1980. *Irish J. Agr. Econ. Rural Soc.*, 1984, *10*(1), pp. 13–27. **[G: U.K.]**

Procter, Robert J. and Tyner, Wallace E. Assessing the Impact of Peak-Load Electricity Pricing and the Solar Tax Credits on the Adoption of Solar Energy. *Land Econ.*, February 1984, *60*(1), pp. 49–55. **[G: U.S.]**

Quick, Perry D. Businesses: Reagan's Industrial Policy. In *Palmer, J. L. and Sawhill, I. V., eds.*, 1984, pp. 287–316. **[G: U.S.]**

Quinn, Joseph F. Trends in Social Security Wealth by Cohort: Comment. In *Moon, M., ed.*, 1984, pp. 353–58. **[G: U.S.]**

Rasmussen, David W.; Bendick, Marc, Jr. and Ledebur, Larry C. A Methodology for Selecting Economic Development Incentives. *Growth Change*, January 1984, *15*(1), pp. 18–25. **[G: U.S.]**

Rathbone, Perry T. Influences of Private Patrons: The Art Museum as an Example. In *Lowry, W. M., ed.*, 1984, pp. 38–56. **[G: U.S.]**

Raymon, Neil and Stuart, Charles E. Short-Run Politicians and Long-Run Tax Revenue: An Empirical Assessment. *Scand. J. Econ.*, 1984, *86*(3), pp. 314–25. **[G: U.S.]**

Redburn, F. Stevens, et al. Federal Economic Development Investments. In *Holzer, M. and Nagel, S. S., eds.*, 1984, pp. 115–43. **[G: U.S.]**

Regan, Donald T. Agendas for Dealing with Deficits: Remarks. *Nat. Tax J.*, September 1984, *37*(3), pp. 323–26. **[G: U.S.]**

Reid, Robert J. Tax Implications of a Change in Control. In *Purden, C., ed.*, 1984, pp. 84–113. **[G: Canada]**

Renaghan, Thomas M. Distributional Effects of Federal Tax Policy 1929–1939. *Exploration Econ. Hist.*, January 1984, *21*(1), pp. 40–63. **[G: U.S.]**

Richardson, James W. and Nixon, Clair J. The Effects of the 1980, 1981, and 1982 Tax Laws on Texas Rice Farmers. *Southern J. Agr. Econ.*, July 1984, *16*(1), pp. 137–44. **[G: U.S.]**

Richupan, Somchai. Measuring Tax Evasion. *Finance Develop.*, December 1984, *21*(4), pp. 38–40.

Ricketts, Martin. On the Simple Macroeconomics of Tax Evasion: An Elaboration of the Peacock-Shaw Approach. *Public Finance*, 1984, *39*(3), pp. 420–24.

Rico B., Guillermo and Arango, Fernando. Fiscal Obstacles to the International Flow of Capital between a Parent and Its Subsidiary: Colombia. In *Intn'l. Fisc. Assoc., vol. 69a*, 1984, pp. 293–306. **[G: Colombia]**

Ricossa, Sergio. A General Description of the Italian Tax System. In *Block, W. and Walker, M., eds.*, 1984, pp. 331–44. **[G: Italy]**

Roberts, Kevin. The Theoretical Limits of Redistribution. *Rev. Econ. Stud.*, April 1984, *51*(2), pp. 177–95.

Roberts, Paul Craig. Supply-Side Economics, Growth, and Liberty. In *Moore, J. H., ed.*, 1984, pp. 73–89. **[G: U.S.]**

Robins, Philip K. The Labor Supply Response of Twenty-Year Families in the Denver Income Maintenance Experiment. *Rev. Econ. Statist.*, August 1984, *66*(3), pp. 491–95. **[G: U.S.]**

Rock, Steven M. The Impact of Deductibility on the Incidence of a General Sales Tax. *Nat. Tax J.*, March 1984, *37*(1), pp. 105–12. **[G: U.S.]**

Rodriguez, Justine Farr. Savings and Investment: Comment. In *Wachter, M. L. and Wachter, S. M., eds.*, 1984, pp. 257–60. **[G: U.S.]**

Rosen, Harvey S.; Rosen, Kenneth T. and Holtz-Eakin, Douglas. Housing Tenure, Uncertainty, and Taxation. *Rev. Econ. Statist.*, August 1984, *66*(3), pp. 405–16. **[G: U.S.]**

Rothschild, Leonard W., Jr. World-Wide Combined Reporting: Recent Developments. *Bull. Int. Fiscal Doc.*, April 1984, *38*(4), pp. 153–56. **[G: U.S.]**

Ryser, Walter. Exterritorialité et Droit Fiscal. (Extra-Territoriality and Fiscal Law. With English summary.) *Aussenwirtschaft*, May 1984, *39*(1/2), pp. 119–36. **[G: OECD]**

Sa-Aadu, Jarjisu. Alternative Estimates of Direct Tenant Benefit and Consumption Inefficiencies from the Section 8 New Construction Program. *Land Econ.*, May 1984, *60*(2), pp. 189–201. **[G: U.S.]**

Sa-Aadu, Jarjisu. Another Look at the Economics of Demand-Side versus Supply-Side Strategies in Low-Income Housing. *Amer. Real Estate Urban Econ. Assoc. J.*, Winter 1984, *12*(4), pp. 427–60. **[G: U.S.]**

Sahling, Leonard and Akhtar, M. A. What Is Behind the Capital Spending Boom? *Fed. Res. Bank New York Quart. Rev.*, Winter 1984–85, *9*(4), pp. 19–30.

Saito, Shin. Structure of Income Tax and Allowances. (In Japanese. With English summary.) *Osaka Econ. Pap.*, December 1984, *34*(2–3), pp. 75–92. **[G: Japan]**

Salamon, Lester M. Nonprofit Organizations: The Lost Opportunity. In *Palmer, J. L. and Sawhill, I. V., eds.*, 1984, pp. 261–85. **[G: U.S.]**

Sampson, Anthony A. An Optional Tax System. *J. Public Econ.*, August 1984, *24*(3), pp. 389–95.

Sander, Jens-Jacob and Truyen, Pieter. Fiscal Obstacles to the International Flow of Capital between a Parent and Its Subsidiary: Norway. In *Intn'l. Fisc. Assoc., vol. 69a*, 1984, pp. 403–15. [G: Norway]

Sandmo, Agnar. Some Insights from the "New" Theory of Public Finance. *Empirica*, 1984, 11(2), pp. 111–24.

Sanson, Joao Rogério. An Alternative Model for Studying the Incidence of Indirect Taxes. *J. Public Econ.*, November 1984, 25(1/2), pp. 245–54. [G: Brazil]

Sarig, Oded H. Why Do Companies Pay Dividends? Comment. *Amer. Econ. Rev.*, December 1984, 74(5), pp. 1142.

Saulter, Kenneth J. Home Energy Costs and the Housing of the Poor and the Elderly: Comment. In *Downs, A. and Bradbury, K. L., eds.*, 1984, pp. 78–84. [G: U.S.]

Savas, E. S. More Insights on Rental Vouchers and Housing Subsidies. *J. Policy Anal. Manage.*, Spring 1984, 3(3), pp. 449–50. [G: U.S.]

Sayeed, Adil. Tax-Transfer Benefits for the Elderly. In *Conklin, D. W.; Bennett, J. H. and Courchene, T. J., eds.*, 1984, pp. 241–63. [G: Canada]

Schall, Lawrence D. Taxes, Inflation and Corporate Financial Policy. *J. Finance*, March 1984, 39(1), pp. 105–26.

Scheuren, Fritz; Schwartz, Otto and Kilss, Beth. Erratum [Statistics from Individual Income Tax Returns: Quality Issues and Budget Cut Impact]. *Rev. Public Data Use*, June 1984, 12(2), pp. 157. [G: U.S.]

Scheuren, Fritz; Schwartz, Otto and Kilss, Beth. Statistics from Individual Income Tax Returns: Quality Issues and Budget Cut Impact. *Rev. Public Data Use*, March 1984, 12(1), pp. 55–67. [G: U.S.]

Schoettle, Ferdinand P. State Taxation Under the Commerce Clause: The History Revisited: Comments. In *McLure, C. E., Jr., ed.*, 1984, pp. 85–88. [G: U.S.]

Schulthess, Walter E. Incidencia de los tributos nacionales por jurisdicciones políticas en la República Argentina. (The Incidences of National Taxes by Political Jurisdictions in the Argentine Republic. With English summary.) *Económica*, January-April 1984, 30(1), pp. 85–117. [G: Argentina]

Schweizer, Urs. Welfare Analysis of Excise Tax Evasion. *Z. ges. Staatswiss.*, June 1984, 140(2), pp. 247–58.

Schwerin, Don S. Historic Compromise and Pluralist Decline? Profits and Capital in the Nordic Countries. In *Goldthorpe, J. H., ed.*, 1984, pp. 231–56. [G: OECD]

Seidl, Christian. The Tax State in Crisis: Can Schumpeterian Public Finance Claim Modern Relevance? In *Seidl, C., ed.*, 1984, pp. 89–109.

Seidman, Laurence S. Conversion to a Consumption Tax: The Transition in a Life-Cycle Growth Model. *J. Polit. Econ.*, April 1984, 92(2), pp. 247–67.

Seidman, Laurence S. The Welfare Economics of Taxes: A Three-Class Disposable Income

Growth Model. *Public Finance Quart.*, January 1984, 12(1), pp. 3–26.

Seldon, Arthur. Taxation in the United Kingdom: Reply. In *Block, W. and Walker, M., eds.*, 1984, pp. 217–21. [G: U.K.]

Seldon, Arthur. Taxation in the United Kingdom. In *Block, W. and Walker, M., eds.*, 1984, pp. 157–213. [G: U.K.; OECD]

Serra, Juan Francisca. Fiscal Obstacles to the International Flow of Capital between a Parent and Its Subsidiary: Uruguay. In *Intn'l. Fisc. Assoc., vol. 69a*, 1984, pp. 501–15. [G: Uruguay]

Seth, K. G. Equity in Taxation—A New Interpretation. In *Singh, A. K.; Papola, T. S. and Mathur, R. S., eds.*, 1984, pp. 428–41. [G: India]

de Seve, Charles W. and Vasquez, Thomas E. The Impact of Changes in the Federal Tax Code on State Tax Revenues. *Nat. Tax J.*, September 1984, 37(3), pp. 393–409. [G: U.S.]

Seyoum, Belayneh. Export Subsidies under the MTN: An Analysis with Particular Emphasis on Developing Countries. *J. World Trade Law*, November:December 1984, 18(6), pp. 512–41. [G: LDCs]

Shafer, Joel. Divestiture and the Courts. In *Purden, C., ed.*, 1984, pp. 47–83. [G: Canada; U.K.]

Shoup, Carl S. Taxation of Capital Gains Abroad. *Australian Tax Forum*, June 1984, 1(2), pp. 196–212. [G: Selected Countries]

Shoven, John B. Saving in the U.S. Economy. In *Wachter, M. L. and Wachter, S. M., eds.*, 1984, pp. 187–223. [G: U.S.]

Shoven, John B. and Whalley, John. Applied General-Equilibrium Models of Taxation and International Trade: An Introduction and Survey. *J. Econ. Lit.*, September 1984, 22(3), pp. 1007–51.

Simon, Julian L. Immigrants, Taxes, and Welfare in the United States. *Population Devel. Rev.*, March 1984, 10(1), pp. 55–69. [G: U.S.]

Sinn, Hans-Werner. Die Bedeutung des Accelerated Cost Recovery System für den internationalen Kapitalverkehr. (The Significance of the Accelerated Cost Recovery System for International Capital Movements. With English summary.) *Kyklos*, 1984, 37(4), pp. 542–76. [G: U.S.]

Sinn, Hans-Werner. Optimal Resource Taxation. In *Pearce, D. W.; Siebert, H. and Walter, I., eds.*, 1984, pp. 197–204.

Slade, Margaret E. Tax Policy and the Supply of Exhaustible Resources: Theory and Practice. *Land Econ.*, May 1984, 60(2), pp. 133–47. [G: U.S.]

Slemrod, Joel and Sorum, Nikki. The Compliance Cost of the U.S. Individual Income Tax System. *Nat. Tax J.*, December 1984, 37(4), pp. 461–74. [G: U.S.]

Smeeding, Timothy M. Approaches to Measuring and Valuing In-Kind Subsidies and the Distribution of Their Benefits. In *Moon, M., ed.*, 1984, pp. 139–71. [G: U.S.]

Smith, Donald J. Individual Retirement Accounts

and Intermediate Term Holding Periods. *Financial Rev.*, November 1984, *19*(4), pp. 381–87.

Spinanger, Dean. Free Enterprise Zones in Economic Development: Comment. In *Giersch, H., ed.*, 1984, pp. 236–41. **[G: LDCs]**

Spindler, Zane A. A General Description of the Italian Tax System: Comment. In *Block, W. and Walker, M., eds.*, 1984, pp. 345–49. **[G: Italy]**

Spiro, Erwin. The 1984 Income Tax Changes in the Republic of South Africa. *Bull. Int. Fiscal Doc.*, 1984, *38*(6), pp. 263–64. **[G: S. Africa]**

Spry, Ian C. F. Some Sceptical Thoughts on Capital Gains Taxes. *Australian Tax Forum*, June 1984, *1*(2), pp. 213–22. **[G: Australia]**

Steinnes, Donald N. Business Climate, Tax Incentives, and Regional Economic Development. *Growth Change*, April 1984, *15*(2), pp. 38–47. **[G: U.S.]**

Stern, Nicholas H. Optimum Taxation and Tax Policy. *Int. Monet. Fund Staff Pap.*, June 1984, *31*(2), pp. 339–78. **[G: India]**

Steuerle, Eugene. Realized Income and Wealth for Owners of Closely Held Farms and Businesses: A Comparison. *Public Finance Quart.*, October 1984, *12*(4), pp. 407–24. **[G: U.S.]**

Stewardt, J. Financial Aids to Small Business. *Irish Banking Rev.*, March 1984, pp. 18–31. **[G: U.K.]**

Struyk, Raymond J. Home Energy Costs and the Housing of the Poor and the Elderly. In *Downs, A. and Bradbury, K. L., eds.*, 1984, pp. 35–78. **[G: U.S.]**

Stuart, Charles E. The Swedish Tax System—What Can We Learn from It? In *Block, W. and Walker, M., eds.*, 1984, pp. 225–50. **[G: Sweden]**

Stuart, Charles E. Welfare Costs per Dollar of Additional Tax Revenue in the United States. *Amer. Econ. Rev.*, June 1984, *74*(3), pp. 352–62. **[G: U.S.]**

Stutzer, Michael J. Variable Rate Subsidies: The Inefficiency of In-Kind Transfers Revisited. *Public Finance Quart.*, January 1984, *12*(1), pp. 77–95. **[G: U.S.]**

Summers, Lawrence H. The After-Tax Rate of Return Affects Private Savings. *Amer. Econ. Rev.*, May 1984, *74*(2), pp. 249–53. **[G: U.S.]**

Sumner, Michael T. The Impact of Stock Relief. *Oxford Bull. Econ. Statist.*, May 1984, *46*(2), pp. 169–79.

Sumner, Michael T. and Ward, Robert. The Impact of Taxes on Wages: A Further Analysis. *Econ. Notes*, 1984, (3), pp. 155–62. **[G: U.S.]**

Sunley, Emil M. Big Revenue Options—An Overview. *Nat. Tax J.*, September 1984, *37*(3), pp. 261–63. **[G: U.S.]**

Sunley, Emil M. Can the Income Tax Continue to Be the Major Revenue Source? Comment. In *Pechman, J. A., ed.*, 1984, pp. 69–73. **[G: U.S.]**

Sutherland, Alister. Capital Transfer Tax: Adieu. *Fisc. Stud.*, August 1984, *5*(3), pp. 68–83. **[G: U.K.]**

Swaine, G. D. Fiscal Obstacles to the International Flow of Capital between a Parent and Its Subsidiary: United Kingdom. In *Intn'l. Fisc. Assoc.*, vol. 69a, 1984, pp. 443–60. **[G: U.K.]**

Swan, Peter L. Capital Gains, Cash Flow Taxes, and Corporate Tax Reform. *Australian Tax Forum*, September 1984, *1*(3), pp. 292–311. **[G: Australia]**

Tagao, Francisco G. Philippine Investment Policy Act of 1983 (Batas Pambansa Blg. 391). *Bull. Int. Fiscal Doc.*, March 1984, *38*(3), pp. 135–38. **[G: Philippines]**

Taichman, Ettie and Young, Dennis R. A Knot in the Day Care Tangle. *J. Policy Anal. Manage.*, Fall 1984, *4*(1), pp. 117–19. **[G: U.S.]**

Tannenwald, Robert. Should We Adopt an Expenditure Tax? *New Eng. Econ. Rev.*, March–April 1984, pp. 29–39. **[G: U.S.]**

Tanzi, Vito. Fiscal Harmonization. *Economia (Portugal)*, January 1984, *8*(1), pp. 43–65. **[G: EEC]**

Tanzi, Vito. Inflation and the Incidence of Income Taxes on Interest Income in the United States, 1972–81. In *Tanzi, V., ed.*, 1984, pp. 143–58. **[G: U.S.]**

Tanzi, Vito. Inflationary Expectations, Taxes, and the Demand for Money in the United States. In *Tanzi, V., ed.*, 1984, pp. 159–71. **[G: U.S.]**

Tatom, John A. The 1981 Personal Income Tax Cuts: A Retrospective Look at Their Effects on the Federal Tax Burden. *Fed. Res. Bank St. Louis Rev.*, December 1984, *66*(10), pp. 5–17. **[G: U.S.]**

Temko, Richard J. Aspetti fiscali, contabili e giuridici del leasing mobiliare in Europa. (An Overview of Tax, Accounting, and Legal Considerations Involved in Structuring Equipment Leases in Europe. With English summary.) *Bancaria*, October 1984, *40*(10), pp. 1004–14. **[G: EEC]**

Temko, Richard J. Aspetti fiscali, contabili e giuridici del leasing mobiliare in Europa. (An Overview of Tax, Accounting, and Legal Considerations Involved in Structuring Equipment Leases in Europe—II. With English summary.) *Bancaria*, November 1984, *40*(11), pp. 1124–31. **[G: EEC]**

Teodori, Giulio. Investimenti in titoli esenti da imposte e imposta di conguaglio. (Investments in Tax-Exempt Securities and the Equalization Tax. With English summary.) *Bancaria*, April 1984, *40*(4), pp. 415–19. **[G: Italy]**

Terkla, David. The Efficiency Value of Effluent Tax Revenues. *J. Environ. Econ. Manage.*, June 1984, *11*(2), pp. 107–23. **[G: U.S.]**

Thac, Cao Duc and Lim, David. Papua New Guinea's Tax Performance, 1965–77. *World Devel.*, April 1984, *12*(4), pp. 451–59. **[G: Papua New Guinea]**

van Thiel, Servaas. Canada–Ivory Coast: Tax

Treaty Concluded. *Bull. Int. Fiscal Doc.*, February 1984, *38*(2), pp. 83–85. **[G: Canada; Ivory Coast]**

van Thiel, Servaas. Tax Incentives for Foreign Investment. *Bull. Int. Fiscal Doc.*, November 1984, *38*(11), pp. 497–500. **[G: Morocco]**

Thomas, W. Scott. New Definition of United States Tax Residency. *Bull. Int. Fiscal Doc.*, October 1984, *38*(10), pp. 459. **[G: U.S.]**

Tichy, Geiserich E. Steuerliche Behinderungen des internationalen Kapitalflusses zwischen einer Muttergesellschaft und ihrer Tochtergesellschaft: Österreich. (Fiscal Obstacles to the International Flow of Capital between a Parent and Its Subsidiary: Austria. With English Summary.) In *Intn'l. Fisc. Assoc.*, *vol. 69a*, 1984, pp. 227–53. **[G: Austria]**

Tikka, Kari S. Fiscal Obstacles to the International Flow of Capital between a Parent and Its Subsidiary: Finland. In *Intn'l. Fisc. Assoc.*, *vol. 69a*, 1984, pp. 333–38. **[G: Finland]**

Tipke, Klaus. On Justice in Taxation. *Bull. Int. Fiscal Doc.*, December 1984, *38*(12), pp. 531–35.

Tirard, Jean-Marc. Tunisia: An Overview of Its Tax System. *Bull. Int. Fiscal Doc.*, January 1984, *38*(1), pp. 27–33. **[G: Tunisia]**

Tolley, George S. and Shear, William B. International Comparison of Tax Rates and Their Effects on National Incomes. In *Kendrick, J. W., ed.*, 1984, pp. 197–225. **[G: OECD]**

Torrey, Barbara Boyle. Income Transfers and the Economic Status of the Elderly: Comment. In *Moon, M., ed.*, 1984, pp. 276–82. **[G: U.S.]**

Tuomala, Matti. On the Optimal Income Taxation: Some Further Numerical Results. *J. Public Econ.*, April 1984, *23*(3), pp. 351–66.

Tuomala, Matti. Optimal Degree of Progressivity under Income Uncertainty. *Scand. J. Econ.*, 1984, *86*(2), pp. 184–93.

Ulmer, John M. Canadian Acquisition of a Foreign Business: A Canadian Perspective. In *Purden, C., ed.*, 1984, pp. 245–73. **[G: Canada]**

Van de Water, Paul N. Social-Security Financing: An Overview of the Issues and Options. In *Campbell, C. D., ed.*, 1984, pp. 59–79. **[G: U.S.]**

Venti, Steven F. The Effects of Income Maintenance on Work, Schooling, and Non-Market Activities of Youth. *Rev. Econ. Statist.*, February 1984, *66*(1), pp. 16–25.

Venti, Steven F. and Wise, David A. Moving and Housing Expenditure: Transaction Costs and Disequilibrium. *J. Public Econ.*, February/March 1984, *23*(1/2), pp. 207–43. **[G: U.S.]**

Verdier, James M. Tax Policy: Comment. In *Mills, G. B. and Palmer, J. L., eds.*, 1984, pp. 243–47. **[G: U.S.]**

Vogel, Klaus. Fiscal Obstacles to the International Flow of Capital between a Parent and Its Subsidiary: General Report. In *Intn'l. Fisc. Assoc.*, *vol. 69a*, 1984, pp. 97–132.

Vogel, Robert C. The Effect of Subsidized Agricultural Credit on Income Distribution in Costa Rica. In *Adams, D. W.; Graham,*

D. H. and Von Pischke, J. D., eds., 1984, pp. 133–45. **[G: Costa Rica]**

Vroman, Susan and Anderson, Gerard. The Effect of Income Taxation on the Demand for Employer–Provided Health Insurance. *Appl. Econ.*, February 1984, *16*(1), pp. 33–43. **[G: U.S.]**

Waincymer, Jeffrey M. Highly Geared Property Investments—A Case-Study in the Operation of Section 51. *Australian Tax Forum*, September 1984, *1*(3), pp. 335–62. **[G: Australia]**

Wakefield, Joseph C. and Ziemer, Richard C. Federal Fiscal Programs. *Surv. Curr. Bus.*, February 1984, *64*(2), pp. 9–21. **[G: U.S.]**

Walsh, Cliff. Political Economy of Capital Gains Tax. *Australian Tax Forum*, June 1984, *1*(2), pp. 223–38. **[G: Australia]**

Walsh, Matthew. Integrating Capital Gains and Income Taxes. *Australian Tax Forum*, September 1984, *1*(3), pp. 323–33. **[G: Australia]**

Walters, Alan A. The United Kingdom: Political Economy and Macroeconomics. *Carnegie-Rochester Conf. Ser. Public Policy*, Autumn 1984, *21*, pp. 259–79. **[G: U.K.]**

Walters, Sir Alan. Taxation in the United Kingdom: Comment. In *Block, W. and Walker, M., eds.*, 1984, pp. 214–17. **[G: U.K.]**

Wang, Bingquian. On Several Problems Involving Financial Work. *Chinese Econ. Stud.*, Summer 1984, *17*(4), pp. 81–98. **[G: China]**

Wanless, P. T. Sales Taxes and Price Subsidies in Poland, 1970–1982. *ACES Bull.*, Summer–Fall 1984, *26*(2–3), pp. 39–61. **[G: Poland]**

Watson, Harry S. A Note on the Effects of Taxation on Charitable Giving over the Life Cycle and Beyond. *Quart. J. Econ.*, August 1984, *99*(3), pp. 639–47.

Watson, William D. and Ridker, Ronald G. Losses from Effluent Taxes and Quotas under Uncertainty. *J. Environ. Econ. Manage.*, December 1984, *11*(4), pp. 310–26. **[G: U.S.]**

Waugh, Frederick V. Excise Taxes and Economic Stability. In *Waugh, F. V.*, 1984, *1948*, pp. 40–51.

Weck, Hannelore and Frey, Bruno S. Tax Financing and the Shadow Economy. In *Hanusch, H., ed.*, 1984, pp. 313–27. **[G: OECD]**

Wellington, Donald C. The English Poor Law: A Negative Income Tax. *Atlantic Econ. J.*, December 1984, *12*(4), pp. 46–50. **[G: U.K.]**

Wetzler, James W. Tax Reform à la the Bradley–Gephardt Bill. *Nat. Tax J.*, September 1984, *37*(3), pp. 265–70. **[G: U.S.]**

Weymark, John A. Majority-Rule Directions of Income Tax Reform and Second-Best Optimality. *Scand. J. Econ.*, 1984, *86*(2), pp. 194–213.

Whalley, John. Basis Linkage in International Tax Treatment of Goods and Capital Income. *Nat. Tax J.*, June 1984, *37*(2), pp. 195–200.

Whalley, John. Regression or Progression: The Taxing Question of Incidence Analysis. *Can. J. Econ.*, November 1984, *17*(4), pp. 654–82. **[G: Canada]**

Whinihan, Michael J. Condominium Conversion and the Tax Reform Acts of 1969 and 1976.

Amer. Real Estate Urban Econ. Assoc. J., Winter 1984, *12*(4), pp. 461–72.   **[G: U.S.]**

Wildasin, David E. On Public Good Provision with Distortionary Taxation. *Econ. Inquiry*, April 1984, *22*(2), pp. 227–43.

Wilde, James A. Labor Supply and Tax Rates: Comment. *Amer. Econ. Rev.*, December 1984, *74*(5), pp. 1103–07.

Williamson, W. G. Purchase and Sale of a Business Within a Family. In *Purden, C., ed.*, 1984, pp. 114–37.   **[G: Canada]**

Wilson, Oliver H. and Smith, William J. Access to Tax Records for Statistical Purposes. *Rev. Public Data Use*, December 1984, *12*(4), pp. 295–305.   **[G: U.S.]**

Wisley, Thomas O. The Effectiveness of Fiscal Policy under a Consumption Tax. *Quart. Rev. Econ. Bus.*, Spring 1984, *24*(1), pp. 33–41.

Wolf, Douglas A. Changes in Household Size and Composition Due to Financial Incentives. *J. Human Res.*, Winter 1984, *19*(1), pp. 87–103.   **[G: U.S.]**

Wolfe, Barbara L., et al. Income Transfers and Work Effort: The Netherlands and the United States in the 1970s. *Kyklos*, 1984, *37*(4), pp. 609–37.   **[G: Netherlands; U.S.]**

Wolfson, Dirk J. The Fiscal Policy Aspect of Development Strategy. In *Ghosh, P. K., ed., no. 7*, 1984, *1973*, pp. 302–13.

Yandle, Bruce. Groundwater and the Land Value Tax: Some Dimensions of the Problems Facing Fiscal Specialists in Applying Rent Taxation to Underground Resources. *Amer. J. Econ. Soc.*, July 1984, *43*(3), pp. 323–32.

Ylä-Liedenpohja, Jouko. On Investment Incentives and Allocational Implications of Corporate Income Taxation. *Liiketaloudellinen Aikak.*, 1984, *33*(3), pp. 264–302.   **[G: Finland]**

Zee, Howell H. On the Decomposition of the Harberger Tax Incidence Equation. *Atlantic Econ. J.*, December 1984, *12*(4), pp. 41–45.

Zimmerman, Dennis. Federal Tax Policy, IDBs and the Market for State and Local Bonds. *Nat. Tax J.*, September 1984, *37*(3), pp. 411–20.   **[G: U.S.]**

Zuberi, A. A. Pakistan: Constraints on the Arbitrary Exercise of Authority and the Income Tax Law. *Bull. Int. Fiscal Doc.*, January 1984, *38*(1), pp. 19–26.   **[G: Pakistan]**

324 State and Local Government Finance

3240 General

Abrams, Jay H. Local Government Finance: Realities and Directions. In *Carr, J. H., ed.*, 1984, *1982*, pp. 384–91.   **[G: U.S.]**

Ansari, M. M. A Critique of the Developments in Indian Fiscal Federalism. *Margin*, October 1984, *17*(1), pp. 31–47.   **[G: India]**

Anton, Thomas J. Intergovernmental Change in the United States: An Assessment of the Literature. In *Miller, T. C., ed.*, 1984, pp. 15–64.   **[G: U.S.]**

Armstrong, John M. The Future of Urban Public

Works: New Ways of Doing Business: Discussion. In *Hanson, R., ed.*, 1984, pp. 204–05.   **[G: U.S.]**

Aronson, J. Richard. Municipal Fiscal Indicators. In *Carr, J. H., ed.*, 1984, *1980*, pp. 3–41.   **[G: U.S.]**

Bahl, Roy. The Fiscal Health of State and Local Governments: 1982 and Beyond. In *Carr, J. H., ed.*, 1984, *1982*, pp. 361–83.   **[G: U.S.]**

Bendick, Marc, Jr. Privatization of Public Services: Recent Experience. In *Brooks, H.; Liebman, L. and Schelling, C. S., eds.*, 1984, pp. 153–71.   **[G: U.S.]**

Bennett, James T. Privatizing Municipal Services. In *Giersch, H., ed.*, 1984, pp. 44–57.

Bennett, R. J. A Bureaucratic Model of Local Government Tax and Expenditure Decisions. *Appl. Econ.*, April 1984, *16*(2), pp. 257–68.   **[G: U.K.]**

Benton, J. Edwin and Gamble, Darwin. City/County Consolidation and Economies of Scale: Evidence from a Time-Series Analysis in Jacksonville, Florida. *Soc. Sci. Quart.*, March 1984, *65*(1), pp. 190–98.   **[G: U.S.]**

Berglas, Eitan and Pines, David. Resource Constraint, Replicability and Mixed Clubs: A Reply [Clubs, Local Public Goods and Transportation Models: A Synthesis]. *J. Public Econ.*, April 1984, *23*(3), pp. 391–97.

Berglas, Eitan. Quantities, Qualities, and Multiple Public Services in the Tiebout Model. *J. Public Econ.*, December 1984, *25*(3), pp. 299–321.

Bradbury, Katharine L. and Yinger, John. Making Ends Meet: Boston's Budget in the 1980s. *New Eng. Econ. Rev.*, March–April 1984, pp. 18–28.   **[G: U.S.]**

Brandl, John. What States and Cities Can Do about Undependable Federal Policy. *Nat. Tax J.*, September 1984, *37*(3), pp. 447–49.   **[G: U.S.]**

Brecher, Charles and Horton, Raymond D. Setting Municipal Priorities: Introduction. In *Brecher, C. and Horton, R. D., eds.*, 1984, pp. 1–12.   **[G: U.S.]**

Burnell, Barbara S. Metropolitan Fiscal Disparities and the Geographic Distribution of Income. *Urban Stud.*, August 1984, *21*(3), pp. 285–93.   **[G: U.S.]**

Carr, James H. Crisis and Constraint in Municipal Finance: Introduction. In *Carr, J. H., ed.*, 1984, pp. ix–xxv.   **[G: U.S.]**

Cohn, Elchanan. Equity Effects of the Educational Finance Act in South Carolina. *Econ. Educ. Rev.*, 1984, *3*(4), pp. 333–39.   **[G: U.S.]**

Courchene, Thomas J. An Australian Perspective on Taxation: Comment. In *Block, W. and Walker, M., eds.*, 1984, pp. 426–32.   **[G: Australia]**

Cushing, Brian J. Capitalization of Interjurisdictional Fiscal Differentials: An Alternative Approach. *J. Urban Econ.*, May 1984, *15*(3), pp. 317–26.   **[G: U.S.]**

Dearborne, Philip. Politics and Urban Public Facilities: Discussion. In *Hanson, R., ed.*, 1984, pp. 169–71. [G: U.S.]

Dhesi, Autar S. and Ghuman, B. S. Aspects of Financing State Plans (With Special Reference to Punjab). *Margin*, April 1984, *16*(3), pp. 31–43. [G: India]

Doolittle, Fred C. State Legislatures and Federal Grants: An Overview. *Public Budg. Finance*, Summer 1984, *4*(2), pp. 7–23. [G: U.S.]

Epple, Dennis; Filimon, Radu and Romer, Thomas. Equilibrium among Local Jurisdictions: Toward an Integrated Treatment of Voting and Residential Choice. *J. Public Econ.*, August 1984, *24*(3), pp. 281–308.

Feeser, Larry J. The Future of Urban Public Works: New Ways of Doing Business: Discussion. In *Hanson, R., ed.*, 1984, pp. 205–07. [G: U.S.]

Feldstein, Martin. Public Education: Reply [Wealth Neutrality and Local Choice in Public Education]. *Amer. Econ. Rev.*, September 1984, *74*(4), pp. 820–21. [G: U.S.]

Fisher, Malcolm R. An Australian Perspective on Taxation. In *Block, W. and Walker, M., eds.*, 1984, pp. 385–426. [G: Australia]

Fisher, Susan M. and Williams, Thomas L. The Economics of Incorporation: An Empirical Study of Lakeland, TN. *Amer. Econ.*, Fall 1984, *28*(2), pp. 64–68. [G: U.S.]

Fisk, Donald M. Measuring Productivity in State and Local Government. *Mon. Lab. Rev.*, June 1984, *107*(6), pp. 47–48. [G: U.S.]

Fortune, Peter. Tax Exemption and Resource Allocation: Implications for Price, Production, and Factor Choice. *Public Finance Quart.*, July 1984, *12*(3), pp. 347–64. [G: U.S.]

Fox, William F. and Quindry, Kenneth E. State and Local Government Fiscal Constraints: Public Sector and Private Sector Effects. *Public Finance Quart.*, October 1984, *12*(4), pp. 425–56. [G: U.S.]

Friedland, Roger; Piven, Frances Fox and Alford, Robert R. Political Conflict, Urban Structure, and the Fiscal Crisis. In *Tabb, W. K. and Sawers, L., eds.*, 1984, *1978*, pp. 273–97. [G: U.S.]

Gardner, Henry. Politics and Urban Public Facilities: Discussion. In *Hanson, R., ed.*, 1984, pp. 173–75. [G: U.S.]

Gramlich, Edward M. "A Fair Go": Fiscal Federalism Arrangements. In *Caves, R. E. and Krause, L. B., eds.*, 1984, pp. 231–74. [G: Australia]

Greene, Kenneth V. Sequential Referenda and Bureaucratic Man. *Public Choice*, 1984, *43*(1), pp. 77–82. [G: U.S.]

Grossman, David A. Setting Municipal Priorities: Financial Resources: State Aid. In *Brecher, C. and Horton, R. D., eds.*, 1984, pp. 115–37. [G: U.S.]

Groves, Sanford M.; Godsey, W. Maureen and Shulman, Martha A. Financial Indicators for Local Government. In *Carr, J. H., ed.*, 1984, *1981*, pp. 42–60. [G: U.S.]

Guibert, G. and Lanvin, B. Decentralization in Government: The United States and France

Compared. *J. Policy Anal. Manage.*, Winter 1984, *3*(2), pp. 289–93. [G: France; U.S.]

Hamer, Eberhard. Creating New Entrepreneurship by Privatizing Municipal Services. In *Giersch, H., ed.*, 1984, pp. 58–69.

Haurin, Donald R. and Gill, H. Leroy. The Spatial Distribution of Public Services: A Structural Model of Voting, Educational Production, and the Government's Allocation of Educational Inputs. *Public Choice*, 1984, *44*(3), pp. 481–500. [G: U.S.]

Hayes, Kathy and Grosskopf, Shawna. The Role of Functional Form in Estimating the Demand for Local Public Goods. *Rev. Econ. Statist.*, February 1984, *66*(1), pp. 169–73. [G: U.S.]

Henton, Douglas C. and Waldhorn, Steven A. The Future of Urban Public Works: New Ways of Doing Business. In *Hanson, R., ed.*, 1984, pp. 178–204. [G: U.S.]

Hill, Richard Child. Fiscal Crisis, Austerity Politics, and Alternative Urban Policies. In *Tabb, W. K. and Sawers, L., eds.*, 1984, pp. 298–322. [G: U.S.]

Hulten, Charles R. Productivity Change in State and Local Governments. *Rev. Econ. Statist.*, May 1984, *66*(2), pp. 256–66. [G: U.S.]

Husain, Ishrat. Raising Resources for Development: The Challenge for the Eighties. In *Burki, S. J. and LaPorte, R., Jr., eds.*, 1984, pp. 103–36. [G: Pakistan]

Ingram, Robert W. Economic Incentives and the Choice of State Government Accounting Practices. *J. Acc. Res.*, Spring 1984, *22*(1), pp. 126–44. [G: U.S.]

Johnson, Scott. Politics and Urban Public Facilities: Discussion. In *Hanson, R., ed.*, 1984, pp. 171–72. [G: U.S.]

Jud, G. Donald. Public Schools in In-Migration in North Carolina Counties, 1975–80. *Amer. J. Econ. Soc.*, July 1984, *43*(3), pp. 313–22. [G: U.S.]

Katz, Judy. Business as Unusual in the Bay State: The Legacy of Proposition 2 1/2. *Policy Rev.*, Spring 1984, (28), pp. 40–41. [G: U.S.]

Kenyon, Daphne A. Preference Revelation and Supply Response in the Arena of Local Government. *Public Choice*, 1984, *42*(2), pp. 147–60. [G: U.S.]

Kolderie, Ted. Business Opportunities in the Changing Conceptions of the Public Sector Role. In *Brooks, H.; Liebman, L. and Schelling, C. S., eds.*, 1984, pp. 89–110. [G: U.S.]

Lerman, Donald L. The Economics of Public School Closings. *J. Urban Econ.*, November 1984, *16*(3), pp. 241–58. [G: U.S.]

Levin, David J. State and Local Government Fiscal Position in 1983. *Surv. Curr. Bus.*, January 1984, *64*(1), pp. 30–34. [G: U.S.]

Litvak, Larry. Pension Funds and Economic Development. In *Bingham, R. D. and Blair, J. P., eds.*, 1984, pp. 191–98.

Masser, Ian and Wilson, Tom. Approaches to Information Management in County Planning Authorities in England and Wales. *Urban Stud.*, November 1984, *21*(4), pp. 415–25. [G: U.K.]

McDonald, Terrence J. San Francisco: Socioeconomic Change, Political Culture, and Fiscal Politics, 1870–1906. In *McDonald, T. J. and Ward, S. K., eds.*, 1984, pp. 39–67.
[G: U.S.]

McDonald, Terrence J. and Ward, Sally K. The Politics of Urban Fiscal Policy: Introduction. In *McDonald, T. J. and Ward, S. K., eds.*, 1984, pp. 13–37.

McGuire, Robert A. Public versus Private Economic Activity: A New Look at School Bus Transportation. *Public Choice*, 1984, *43*(1), pp. 25–43. [G: U.S.]

Mehay, Stephen L. The Effect of Governmental Structure on Special District Expenditures. *Public Choice*, 1984, *44*(2), pp. 339–48.
[G: U.S.]

Mercer, John and Goldberg, Michael A. The Fiscal Condition of American and Canadian Cities. *Urban Stud.*, August 1984, *21*(3), pp. 233–43.
[G: U.S.; Canada]

Meyer, Marshall W. and Solomon, Kenneth A. Risk Management in Local Communities. *Policy Sci.*, February 1984, *16*(3), pp. 245–65.

Muller, Thomas. Public Sector Performance: A Demographic Perspective. In *Miller, T. C., ed.*, 1984, pp. 131–60. [G: U.S.]

Nathan, Richard P. Setting Municipal Priorities: Financial Resources: Federal Aid. In *Brecher, C. and Horton, R. D., eds.*, 1984, pp. 138–68. [G: U.S.]

Neenan, William B. and Ethridge, Marcus E. Competition and Cooperation among Localities. In *Bingham, R. D. and Blair, J. P., eds.*, 1984, pp. 175–90.

Perkins, George M. Public Education: Comment [Wealth Neutrality and Local Choice in Public Education]. *Amer. Econ. Rev.*, September 1984, *74*(4), pp. 814–19. [G: U.S.]

Peterson, George E. Federalism and the States: An Experiment in Decentralization. In *Palmer, J. L. and Sawhill, I. V., eds.*, 1984, pp. 217–59. [G: U.S.]

van der Ploeg, Frederick. The Principle of Political-Economic Assignment. *J. Macroecon.*, Summer 1984, *6*(3), pp. 283–94.

Pommerehne, Werner W. Comment [Privatizing Municipal Services] [Creating New Entrepreneurship by Privatizing Municipal Services]. In *Giersch, H., ed.*, 1984, pp. 70–81.

Proctor, Allen J. Tax Cuts and the Fiscal Management of New York State. *Fed. Res. Bank New York Quart. Rev.*, Winter 1984–85, *9*(4), pp. 7–18. [G: U.S.]

Rubin, Laura S. Recent Developments in the State and Local Government Sector. *Fed. Res. Bull.*, November 1984, *70*(11), pp. 791–801.
[G: U.S.]

Sanders, Heywood T. Politics and Urban Public Facilities. In *Hanson, R., ed.*, 1984, pp. 143–69. [G: U.S.]

Sandler, Todd and Tschirhart, John T. Mixed Clubs: Further Observations [Clubs, Local Public Goods and Transportation Models: A Synthesis]. *J. Public Econ.*, April 1984, *23*(3), pp. 381–89.

Schweizer, Urs. Fiscal Decentralization under Free Mobility. *Reg. Sci. Urban Econ.*, August 1984, *14*(3), pp. 317–29.

Smith, Janet Kiholm and Smith, Richard L., II. State and Local Fiscal Policy: Implications for Property Values and Economic Growth. *Public Finance Quart.*, January 1984, *12*(1), pp. 51–76. [G: U.S.]

Tabb, William K. The New York City Fiscal Crisis. In *Tabb, W. K. and Sawers, L., eds.*, 1984, pp. 323–45. [G: U.S.]

Vaubel, Roland. Comment [Privatizing Municipal Services] [Creating New Entrepreneurship by Privatizing Municipal Services]. In *Giersch, H., ed.*, 1984, pp. 82–86.

Vohra, Rajiv. Local Public Goods and Average Cost Pricing. *J. Math. Econ.*, April 1984, *13*(1), pp. 51–67.

Warren, Ronald S., Jr. Maximizing Models of Legislative Choice. *Public Choice*, 1984, *42*(3), pp. 287–94.

Wildasin, David E. The Welfare Effects of Intergovernmental Grants in an Economy with Distortionary Local Taxes: A Simple General Equilibrium Analysis. *J. Public Econ.*, November 1984, *25*(1/2), pp. 103–25.

3241 State and Local Government Expenditures and Budgeting

Alam, M. Shahid. An Assessment of the Priorities and Efficiency of Pakistan's Public Sector Educational Expenditure: Comment. *Pakistan Devel. Rev.*, Summer-Autumn 1984, *23*(2&3), pp. 425–27. [G: Pakistan]

Augenblick, John. Elementary and Secondary Education: Issues in Budgeting and Financial Management. *Public Budg. Finance*, Winter 1984, *4*(4), pp. 4–6.

Bahl, Roy and Schroeder, Larry. The Role of Multi-year Forecasting in the Annual Budgeting Process for Local Governments. *Public Budg. Finance*, Spring 1984, *4*(1), pp. 3–13.
[G: U.S.]

Beck, John H. Nonmonotonic Demand for Municipal Services: Variation among Communities. *Nat. Tax J.*, March 1984, *37*(1), pp. 55–67.
[G: U.S.]

Benson, Charles S. State Government Contributions to the Public Schools. *Public Budg. Finance*, Winter 1984, *4*(4), pp. 17–29.
[G: U.S.]

Bohm, Peter. Are There Practicable Demand-Revealing Mechanisms? In *Hanusch, H., ed.*, 1984, pp. 127–39. [G: Sweden]

Bozeman, J. Lisle. The Capital Budget: History and Future Directions. *Public Budg. Finance*, Autumn 1984, *4*(3), pp. 18–30. [G: U.S.]

Brecher, Charles and Hartman, James M. Setting Municipal Priorities: Budgeting and Management: Financial Planning. In *Brecher, C. and Horton, R. D., eds.*, 1984, pp. 198–240.
[G: U.S.]

Brecher, Charles and Horton, Raymond D. Setting Municipal Priorities: Budgeting and Man-

agement: Expenditures. In *Brecher, C. and Horton, R. D., eds.*, 1984, pp. 241–69.
[G: U.S.]

Brecher, Charles and Roswick, Diana. Setting Municipal Priorities: Service Delivery: The City's Role in Health Care. In *Brecher, C. and Horton, R. D., eds.*, 1984, pp. 482–518.
[G: U.S.]

Brina, W. T., Jr. and Rowen, John. Capital Planning in the Empire State. *Public Budg. Finance*, Spring 1984, *4*(1), pp. 91–95.
[G: U.S.]

Brown, M. Craig and Halaby, Charles N. Bosses, Reform, and the Socioeconomic Bases of Urban Expenditure, 1890–1940. In *McDonald, T. J. and Ward, S. K., eds.*, 1984, pp. 69–99.
[G: U.S.]

Buglione, Enrico and France, George. Skewed Fiscal Federalism in Italy: Implications for Public Expenditure Control. In *Premchand, A. and Burkhead, J., eds.*, 1984, pp. 69–89.
[G: Italy]

Burkett, Paul. A Note on State and Local Government Expenditures in the United States, 1968–1981. *Econ. Forum*, Summer 1984, *15*(1), pp. 125–37.
[G: U.S.]

Burns, Leland S. and Grebler, Leo. Is Public Construction Countercyclical? *Land Econ.*, November 1984, *60*(4), pp. 367–77.
[G: U.S.]

Caiden, Naomi. An Interview with A. Alan Post, Legislative Analyst for the State of California, 1950–1977. *Public Budg. Finance*, Autumn 1984, *4*(3), pp. 75–90.
[G: U.S.]

Caiden, Naomi. Public Budgeting amidst Uncertainty and Instability. In *Carr, J. H., ed.*, 1984, *1981*, pp. 115–31.
[G: U.S.]

Cockle, Paul. The Public Expenditure Control System. In *Cockle, P., ed.*, 1984, pp. 20–39.
[G: U.K.]

Cole, Richard L. and Caputo, David A. The Public Hearing as an Effective Citizen Participation Mechanism: A Case Study of the General Revenue Sharing Program. *Amer. Polit. Sci. Rev.*, June 1984, *78*(2), pp. 404–16.
[G: U.S.]

Cutt, James. The Evolution of Expenditure Budgeting in Australia. In *Premchand, A. and Burkhead, J., eds.*, 1984, pp. 1–20.
[G: Australia]

Denzau, Arthur and Grier, Kevin. Determinants of Local School Spending: Some Consistent Estimates. *Public Choice*, 1984, *44*(2), pp. 375–83.
[G: U.S.]

Doolittle, Fred C. State Legislatures and Federal Grants: Developments in the Reagan Years. *Public Budg. Finance*, Summer 1984, *4*(2), pp. 3–6.
[G: U.S.]

Downs, George W. and Rocke, David M. Theories of Budgetary Decisionmaking and Revenue Decline. *Policy Sci.*, March 1984, *16*(4), pp. 329–47.
[G: U.S.]

Duncombe, Sydney and Kinney, Richard. Cutbacks—Idaho Style. *Public Budg. Finance*, Summer 1984, *4*(2), pp. 87–98.
[G: U.S.]

Epple, Dennis and Zelenitz, Allan. Profit-Maximizing Communities and the Theory of Local

Public Expenditures: Comment. *J. Urban Econ.*, September 1984, *16*(2), pp. 149–57.

Florestano, Patricia S. and Gordon, Stephen B. A Survey of City and County Use of Private Contracting. In *Carr, J. H., ed.*, 1984, *1981*, pp. 252–63.
[G: U.S.]

Foot, David K. The Demographic Future of Fiscal Federalism in Canada. *Can. Public Policy*, December 1984, *10*(4), pp. 406–14.
[G: Canada]

Gold, Steven D. Contingency Measures and Fiscal Limitations: The Real World Significance of Some Recent State Budget Innovations. *Nat. Tax J.*, September 1984, *37*(3), pp. 421–32.
[G: U.S.]

Gold, Steven D. State Aid for Local Schools: Trends and Prospects. *Public Budg. Finance*, Winter 1984, *4*(4), pp. 30–40. [G: U.S.]

Grosskopf, Shawna and Hayes, Kathy. Measuring the Excess Burden of State Pension Mandates. *Public Finance*, 1984, *39*(1), pp. 90–103.
[G: U.S.]

Grossman, David A. Setting Municipal Priorities: Budgeting and Management: Debt and Capital Management. In *Brecher, C. and Horton, R. D., eds.*, 1984, pp. 270–301. [G: U.S.]

Hartman, James M. Setting Municipal Priorities: Service Delivery: Sanitation. In *Brecher, C. and Horton, R. D., eds.*, 1984, pp. 415–45.
[G: U.S.]

Heller, Peter S. and Cheasty, Adrienne. Sectoral Adjustment in Government Expenditure in the 1970s: The Educational Sector in Latin America. *World Devel.*, October 1984, *12*(10), pp. 1039–49. [G: Latin America]

Horton, Raymond D. and Smith, John Palmer. Setting Municipal Priorities: Service Delivery: Expenditures and Services. In *Brecher, C. and Horton, R. D., eds.*, 1984, pp. 337–79.
[G: U.S.]

Hulten, Charles R. and Peterson, George E. The Public Capital Stock: Needs, Trends, and Performance. *Amer. Econ. Rev.*, May 1984, *74*(2), pp. 166–73. [G: U.S.]

Jackman, Richard. Public Expenditure Policy, 1984–85: Local Authority Finance. In *Cockle, P., ed.*, 1984, pp. 88–108. [G: U.K.]

Jensen, Cristy A. Legislative Response to Federal Cutbacks in California. *Public Budg. Finance*, Summer 1984, *4*(2), pp. 58–72. [G: U.S.]

Kamensky, John M. Budgeting for State and Local Infrastructure: Developing a Strategy. *Public Budg. Finance*, Autumn 1984, *4*(3), pp. 3–17.
[G: U.S.]

Kenyon, Daphne A. and Benker, Karen M. Fiscal Discipline: Lessons form the State Experience. *Nat. Tax J.*, September 1984, *37*(3), pp. 433–46. [G: U.S.]

Khan, Shahrukh Rafi; Mahmood, Naushin and Siddiqui, Rehana. An Assessment of the Priorities and Efficiency of Pakistan's Public Sector Educational Expenditure. *Pakistan Devel. Rev.*, Summer-Autumn 1984, *23*(2&3), pp. 413–23. [G: Pakistan]

Kiefer, David and Miller, Jan. Public Budgets

and Public Capital in Boom Towns. *Policy Sci.*, March 1984, *16*(4), pp. 349–69.   [G: U.S.]

Levin, David J. Receipts and Expenditures of State Governments and of Local Governments, 1980–83. *Surv. Curr. Bus.*, September 1984, *64*(9), pp. 19–23.   [G: U.S.]

Levin, David J. The State and Local Government Fiscal Position: An Alternative Measure. *Surv. Curr. Bus.*, March 1984, *64*(3), pp. 23–25.   [G: U.S.]

Lewis, Carol W. and Logalbo, Anthony T. Cutback Principles and Practices. In *Carr, J. H., ed.*, 1984, pp. 83–92.   [G: U.S.]

Lindsay, Cotton M. and Zycher, Benjamin. Substitution in Public Spending: Who Pays for Canadian National Health Insurance? *Econ. Inquiry*, July 1984, *22*(3), pp. 337–59.   [G: Canada]

MacManus, Susan A. Coping with Retrenchment: Why Local Governments Need to Restructure Their Budget Document Formats. *Public Budg. Finance*, Autumn 1984, *4*(3), pp. 58–66.   [G: U.S.]

Mazy, Jean-Louis, et al. Les budgets régionaux. Compétences et modes de financement. (With English summary.) *Cah. Écon. Bruxelles*, Fourth Trimester 1984, (104), pp. 517–46.   [G: Belgium]

McDowall, David and Loftin, Colin. Conflict, Crime, and Budgetary Constraint: Police Strength in Detroit, 1927–1976. In *McDonald, T. J. and Ward, S. K., eds.*, 1984, pp. 101–24.   [G: U.S.]

McLain, Lewis F., Jr. How Strategic Planning Can Help Put Budgeting in Perspective. In *Carr, J. H., ed.*, 1984, *1981*, pp. 132–45.   [G: U.S.]

Megdal, Sharon Bernstein. A Model of Local Demand for Education. *J. Urban Econ.*, July 1984, *16*(1), pp. 13–30.   [G: U.S.]

Moffitt, Robert A. The Effects of Grants-in-Aid on State and Local Expenditures: The Case of AFDC. *J. Public Econ.*, April 1984, *23*(3), pp. 279–305.   [G: U.S.]

Morehouse, Thomas A. Resource Development and Alaska Wealth Management. In *Morehouse, T. A., ed.*, 1984, pp. 169–97.   [G: U.S.]

Munley, Vincent G. Has the Median Voter Found a Ballot Box That He Can Control? *Econ. Inquiry*, July 1984, *22*(3), pp. 323–36.   [G: U.S.]

Pagano, Michael A. Notes on Capital Budgeting. *Public Budg. Finance*, Autumn 1984, *4*(3), pp. 31–40.   [G: U.S.]

Peterson, George E. Financing the Nation's Infrastructure Requirements. In *Hanson, R., ed.*, 1984, pp. 110–30.   [G: U.S.]

Pommerehne, Werner W. and Schneider, Friedrich. Identification of Individual Preferences for Government Activity from Voting Behavior. In *Hanusch, H., ed.*, 1984, pp. 109–26.   [G: Switzerland]

Raimondo, Henry J. and Stuart, Robert C. Fi-

nancing Soviet Cities. In *Morton, H. W. and Stuart, R. C., eds.*, 1984, pp. 45–64.   [G: U.S.S.R.]

Raines, Franklin D. Financing the Nation's Infrastructure Requirements: Discussion. In *Hanson, R., ed.*, 1984, pp. 131–35. [G: U.S.]

Ravallion, Martin. The Social Appraisal of Local Public Spending Using Revealed Fiscal Preferences. *J. Urban Econ.*, July 1984, *16*(1), pp. 46–64.   [G: Australia]

Rickards, Robert C. How the Spending Patterns of Cities Change: Budgetary Incrementalism Reexamined. *J. Policy Anal. Manage.*, Fall 1984, *4*(1), pp. 56–74.   [G: W. Germany]

Rittenoure, R. Lynn; Warner, Larkin and Steib, Steve B. Oklahoma's Legislative Process in a Period of Fiscal Change. *Public Budg. Finance*, Summer 1984, *4*(2), pp. 42–57.   [G: U.S.]

Romer, Thomas; Rosenthal, Howard and Ladha, Krishna. If at First You Don't Succeed: Budgeting by a Sequence of Referenda. In *Hanusch, H., ed.*, 1984, pp. 87–108.   [G: U.S.]

Round, David K. The Impact of Government Purchases on Market Performance in Australia. *Rev. Ind. Organ.*, Summer 1984, *1*(2), pp. 94–113.   [G: Australia]

Savas, E. S. Alternative Institutional Models for the Delivery of Public Services. In *Carr, J. H., ed.*, 1984, *1981*, pp. 233–42. [G: U.S.]

Schroeder, Larry. Local Government Multi-year Budgetary Forecasting: Some Administrative and Political Issues. In *Carr, J. H., ed.*, 1984, *1982*, pp. 146–58.   [G: U.S.]

Sharkansky, Ira. Resource Allocation: Environments that Constrain and Governments that Cope. In *Groth, A. J. and Wade, L. L., eds.*, 1984, pp. 73–98. [G: OECD; Israel; Greece]

Short, John. Public Finance and Devolution: Money Flows between Government and Regions in the United Kingdom. *Scot. J. Polit. Econ.*, June 1984, *31*(2), pp. 114–30.   [G: U.K.]

Starkie, David. The Specific Effect of Specific Road Grants in South Australia. *Australian Econ. Pap.*, June 1984, *23*(42), pp. 27–37.   [G: Australia]

Wallis, John Joseph. The Birth of the Old Federalism: Financing the New Deal, 1932–1940. *J. Econ. Hist.*, March 1984, *44*(1), pp. 139–59.   [G: U.S.]

Weinberg, Mark. Budget Retrenchment in Small Cities: A Comparative Analysis of Wooster and Athens, Ohio. *Public Budg. Finance*, Autumn 1984, *4*(3), pp. 46–57.   [G: U.S.]

Witsman, Forest. Financing the Nation's Infrastructure Requirements: Discussion. In *Hanson, R., ed.*, 1984, pp. 135–37. [G: U.S.]

Wyckoff, James H. The Nonexcludable Publicness of Primary and Secondary Public Education. *J. Public Econ.*, August 1984, *24*(3), pp. 331–51.   [G: U.S.]

Young, Stephen and Hood, Neil. Industrial Policy and the Scottish Economy. In *Hood, N. and Young, S., eds.*, 1984, pp. 28–56.   [G: U.K.]

3242 State and Local Government Taxation, Subsidies, and Revenue

Anderson, John E. The Choice between Income Tax and Land Tax in Danish Municipalities: A Comment. *Public Finance*, 1984, *39*(2), pp. 292–95.   [G: Denmark]

Aronson, J. Richard and Schwartz, Eli. Public Sector Performance: A Public Finance Perspective. In *Miller, T. C.*, ed., 1984, pp. 193–223.   [G: U.S.]

Auld, D. A. L. Public Revenues and Public Policy: The Impact on the Canadian Economy. In *Block, W. and Walker, M.*, eds., 1984, pp. 66–103.   [G: Canada]

Austen-Smith, David. Subsidies to the Arts with Multiple Public Donors. *Econ. Rec.*, December 1984, *60*(171), pp. 381–89.

Bahl, Roy and Schroeder, Larry. The Role of Multi-year Forecasting in the Annual Budgeting Process for Local Governments. *Public Budg. Finance*, Spring 1984, *4*(1), pp. 3–13.   [G: U.S.]

Ballentine, J. Gregory. Dividing the State Corporate Income Tax Base: Developments in the Supreme Court and Congress: Panel Discussion. In *McLure, C. E., Jr.*, ed., 1984, pp. 330–32.   [G: U.S.]

Barrese, James T. and Nelson, Michael. State Taxation of Multijurisdictional Corporations. *Atlantic Econ. J.*, December 1984, *12*(4), pp. 69.   [G: U.S.]

Barthold, Thomas and Plotnick, Robert. Estate Taxation and Other Determinants of Charitable Bequests. *Nat. Tax J.*, June 1984, *37*(2), pp. 225–37.   [G: U.S.]

Bennett, James T. and DiLorenzo, Thomas J. Off-Budget Activities of Local Government: Reply. *Public Choice*, 1984, *42*(2), pp. 213–15.   [G: U.S.]

Birdseye, Penny and Webb, Tony. Why the Rate Burden on Business Is a Cause for Concern. *Nat. Westminster Bank Quart. Rev.*, February 1984, pp. 2–15.   [G: U.K.]

Bland, Robert L. The Interest Savings from Optimizing Issue Size and Frequency of Participation in the Municipal Bond Market. *Public Budg. Finance*, Winter 1984, *4*(4), pp. 53–59.   [G: U.S.]

Blewett, Robert A. Off-Budget Activities of Local Government: Comment. *Public Choice*, 1984, *42*(2), pp. 205–11.   [G: U.S.]

Bradbury, Katharine L., et al. State Aid to Offset Fiscal Disparities across Communities. *Nat. Tax J.*, June 1984, *37*(2), pp. 151–70.   [G: U.S.]

Break, George F. State Taxation Under the Commerce Clause: The History Revisited: Comments. In *McLure, C. E., Jr.*, ed., 1984, pp. 82–84.   [G: U.S.]

Carlson, George N. and Galper, Harvey. Water's Edge versus Worldwide Unitary Combination. In *McLure, C. E., Jr.*, ed., 1984, pp. 1–40.   [G: U.S.]

Carman, Hoy F. An Analysis of Proposition 13 Impacts on California Land Conservation Act Participation. *Land Econ.*, November 1984, *60*(4), pp. 360–66.   [G: U.S.]

Conn, Robert L.; Williams, Paul F. and Young, William E. Sales Tax Audit Performance among the States. *Public Finance Quart.*, October 1984, *12*(4), pp. 487–99.

Crampton, Graham. Subsidies to Urban Public Transport and Privatisation. In *Le Grand, J. and Robinson, R.*, eds., 1984, pp. 201–11.   [G: U.K.]

Desin, Allan N. Alternative Divisions of the Tax Base: How Much Is at Stake? Comments. In *McLure, C. E., Jr.*, ed., 1984, pp. 214–16.   [G: U.S.]

Dexter, William D. Dividing the State Corporate Income Tax Base: Developments in the Supreme Court and Congress: Panel Discussion. In *McLure, C. E., Jr.*, ed., 1984, pp. 341–48.   [G: U.S.]

Dhesi, Autar S. and Ghuman, B. S. The Responsiveness of State Taxes—A Comparative Study of Punjab and Haryana. *Indian Econ. Rev.*, July-Dec. 1984, *19*(2), pp. 223–34. [G: India]

Downing, Paul B. User Charges and Service Fees. In *Carr, J. H.*, ed., 1984, *1981*, pp. 160–99.   [G: U.S.]

Drennan, Matthew. Setting Municipal Priorities: The Setting: The Local Economy and Local Revenues. In *Brecher, C. and Horton, R. D.*, eds., 1984, pp. 43–68.   [G: U.S.]

Due, John F. Accepted v Controversial Sales Tax Structures—Switzerland, Australia, New Zealand, Canada. *Australian Tax Forum*, December 1984, *1*(4), pp. 363–77.   [G: Switzerland; Australia; New Zealand; Canada]

Duncombe, Sydney and Kinney, Richard. Cutbacks—Idaho Style. *Public Budg. Finance*, Summer 1984, *4*(2), pp. 87–98.   [G: U.S.]

Eatmon, Nile and Kiefer, David. Distributive Consequences of a Property Tax Revolt. *Econ. Inquiry*, October 1984, *22*(4), pp. 508–28.   [G: U.S.]

Edgren, John A. and Hayworth, Steven C. The Implications of Land Contracts for Property Tax Assessment Practices. *Housing Finance Rev.*, April 1984, *3*(2), pp. 177–89. [G: U.S.]

Edwards, Mary E. Site Value Taxation in Australia: Where Land Is Taxed More and Improvements Less, Average Housing Values and Stocks Are Higher. *Amer. J. Econ. Soc.*, October 1984, *43*(4), pp. 481–95.   [G: Australia]

Fisher, Ronald C. and Rasche, Robert H. The Incidence and Incentive Effects of Property Tax Credits: Evidence from Michigan. *Public Finance Quart.*, July 1984, *12*(3), pp. 291–319.   [G: U.S.]

Formby, John P. and Sykes, David. State Income Tax Progressivity. *Public Finance Quart.*, April 1984, *12*(2), pp. 153–65.   [G: U.S.]

Fox, William F. and Campbell, Charles. Stability of the State Sales Tax Income Elasticity. *Nat. Tax J.*, June 1984, *37*(2), pp. 201–12.   [G: U.S.]

Gahvari, Firouz. The Optimal Taxation of Housing. *Public Finance*, 1984, *39*(2), pp. 213–25.

Gainer, William J. Mortgage Revenue Bonds: Their Costs Outweigh Their Benefits to Homebuyers. *Housing Finance Rev.*, October 1984, *3*(4), pp. 457–65. [G: U.S.]

Garnett, Robert and Guttentag, Jack M. The Reverse-Shared-Appreciation Mortgage. *Housing Finance Rev.*, January 1984, *3*(1), pp. 63–84. [G: U.S.]

Glaister, Stephen. The Allocation of Urban Public Transport Subsidy. In *Le Grand, J. and Robinson, R., eds.*, 1984, pp. 177–200. [G: U.K.]

Gold, Steven D. Contingency Measures and Fiscal Limitations: The Real World Significance of Some Recent State Budget Innovations. *Nat. Tax J.*, September 1984, *37*(3), pp. 421–32. [G: U.S.]

Gold, Steven D. State Tax Increases of 1983: Prelude to Another Tax Revolt? *Nat. Tax J.*, March 1984, *37*(1), pp. 9–22. [G: U.S.]

Gramlich, Edward M. and Laren, Deborah S. Migration and Income Redistribution Responsibilities. *J. Human Res.*, Fall 1984, *19*(4), pp. 489–511. [G: U.S.]

Greene, Kenneth V. and Munley, Vincent G. Perceptions of the Ability to Export Nonresidential Property Tax Burdens. *Public Finance Quart.*, January 1984, *12*(1), pp. 117–27. [G: U.S.]

Groenewegen, Peter D. Rationalizing Australian Taxation Revisited. *Econ. Rec.*, June 1984, *60*(169), pp. 113–27. [G: Australia]

Hamm, William G. Federal Aid to State and Local Governments: Comment. In *Mills, G. B. and Palmer, J. L., eds.*, 1984, pp. 203–08. [G: U.S.]

Hellerstein, Jerome R. Defining a Unitary Business: An Economist's View: Comments. In *McLure, C. E., Jr., ed.*, 1984, pp. 127–31. [G: U.S.]

Hellerstein, Jerome R. State Taxation Under the Commerce Clause: The History Revisited. In *McLure, C. E., Jr., ed.*, 1984, *1982*, pp. 53–81. [G: U.S.]

Hellerstein, Walter. Dividing the State Corporate Income Tax Base: Developments in the Supreme Court and Congress. In *McLure, C. E., Jr., ed.*, 1984, pp. 288–329. [G: U.S.]

Hettich, Walter and Winer, Stanley. A Positive Model of Tax Structure. *J. Public Econ.*, June 1984, *24*(1), pp. 67–87. [G: U.S.]

Hirsch, Werner Z. Efficiency Implications of Revenue Limitation Measures. In *Hanusch, H., ed.*, 1984, pp. 349–62. [G: U.S.]

Huddleston, Jack R. Tax Increment Financing as a State Development Policy. *Growth Change*, April 1984, *15*(2), pp. 11–17. [G: U.S.]

Ihlanfeldt, Keith R. Property Taxation and the Demand for Housing: An Econometric Analysis. *J. Urban Econ.*, September 1984, *16*(2), pp. 208–24. [G: U.S.]

Johnson, Michael S. The Impact of Property Tax Revaluation of Wealth-based State Aid to Schools—A Case Study of Tompkins County, New York. *Econ. Educ. Rev.*, 1984, *3*(1), pp. 45–54. [G: U.S.]

Jones, Bryan D. and Bachelor, Lynn W. Local

Policy Discretion and the Corporate Surplus. In *Bingham, R. D. and Blair, J. P., eds.*, 1984, pp. 245–67. [G: U.S.]

Jones, Donald W. and Morrow-Jones, Charles R. Local Taxation and the Consequences of Revenue Distribution Patterns. *Reg. Sci. Urban Econ.*, February 1984, *14*(1), pp. 63–76. [G: U.S.]

Karpoff, Jonathan M. Low-Interest Loans and the Markets for Limited Entry Permits in the Alaska Salmon Fisheries. *Land Econ.*, February 1984, *60*(1), pp. 69–80. [G: U.S.]

Kennedy, Peter. On an Unfair Appraisal of Vertical Equity in Real Estate Assessment. *Econ. Inquiry*, April 1984, *22*(2), pp. 287–90. [G: U.S.]

Kesselman, Jonathan R. Public Revenues and Public Policy: The Impact on the Canadian Economy: Comment. In *Block, W. and Walker, M., eds.*, 1984, pp. 103–10. [G: Canada]

Kidwell, David S.; Koch, Timothy W. and Stock, Duane R. The Impact of State Income Taxes on Municipal Borrowing Costs. *Nat. Tax J.*, December 1984, *37*(4), pp. 551–61. [G: U.S.]

Kimbell, Larry J. and Harrison, Glenn W. General Equilibrium Analysis of Regional Fiscal Incidence. In *Scarf, H. E. and Shoven, J. B., eds.*, 1984, pp. 275–313. [G: U.S.]

Kochin, Levis A. and Parks, Richard W. Vertical Equity in Real Estate Assessment: Reply. *Econ. Inquiry*, April 1984, *22*(2), pp. 291–96. [G: U.S.]

Kozub, Robert M. and Trebby, James P. Special Valuation of Farmland and Closely Held Business Realty for Estate Tax Purposes. *Growth Change*, July 1984, *15*(3), pp. 25–29. [G: U.S.]

Laboe, Norman J. Worldwide Unitary Combination: The California Practice: Comments. In *McLure, C. E., Jr., ed.*, 1984, pp. 173–81. [G: U.S.]

Ladd, Helen F. Federal Aid to State and Local Governments. In *Mills, G. B. and Palmer, J. L., eds.*, 1984, pp. 165–202. [G: U.S.]

Latcham, Franklin C. Water's Edge versus Worldwide Unitary Combination: Comments. In *McLure, C. E., Jr., ed.*, 1984, pp. 41–44. [G: U.S.]

Lee, Robert H. Subsidizing the Affluent: The Case of Medical Education. *J. Policy Anal. Manage.*, Winter 1984, *3*(2), pp. 276–84. [G: U.S.]

LePan, Nicholas D. Principles for Dividing the State Corporate Tax Base: Comments. In *McLure, C. E., Jr., ed.*, 1984, pp. 247–49. [G: Canada]

Levin, David J. Receipts and Expenditures of State Governments and of Local Governments, 1980–83. *Surv. Curr. Bus.*, September 1984, *64*(9), pp. 19–23. [G: U.S.]

Lissner, Will. A. R. Prest's Investigation of the Case for Site Value Taxation. *Amer. J. Econ. Soc.*, April 1984, *43*(2), pp. 163–66.

[G: U.K.; U.S.]

Lissner, Will. Stump Creek, Pa.: Object Lesson in Tax Policy. *Amer. J. Econ. Soc.*, January 1984, *43*(1), pp. 101–02. [G: U.S.]

Mason, Robert and Calvin, Lyle D. Public Confidence and Admitted Tax Evasion. *Nat. Tax J.*, December 1984, *37*(4), pp. 489–96. [G: U.S.]

McLure, Charles E., Jr. Defining a Unitary Business: An Economist's View. In *McLure, C. E., Jr., ed.*, 1984, pp. 89–124. [G: U.S.]

McLure, Charles E., Jr. Dividing the State Corporate Income Tax Base: Developments in the Supreme Court and Congress: Panel Discussion. In *McLure, C. E., Jr., ed.*, 1984, pp. 333–35. [G: U.S.]

McLure, Charles E., Jr. General Equilibrium Analysis of Regional Fiscal Incidence: Comments. In *Scarf, H. E. and Shoven, J. B., eds.*, 1984, pp. 313–17. [G: U.S.]

McLure, Charles E., Jr. Principles for Dividing the State Corporate Tax Base: Comments. In *McLure, C. E., Jr., ed.*, 1984, pp. 250–52. [G: U.S.]

McLure, Charles E., Jr. The State Corporation Income Tax: Introduction. In *McLure, C. E., Jr., ed.*, 1984, pp. xvii–xxvi. [G: U.S.]

Mieszkowski, Peter and Morgan, John. The National Effects of Differential State Corporate Income Taxes on Multistate Corporations. In *McLure, C. E., Jr., ed.*, 1984, pp. 253–63. [G: U.S.]

Mikesell, John L. The Cyclical Sensitivity of State and Local Taxes. *Public Budg. Finance*, Spring 1984, *4*(1), pp. 32–39. [G: U.S.]

Miller, Benjamin F. Worldwide Unitary Combination: The California Practice. In *McLure, C. E., Jr., ed.*, 1984, pp. 132–66. [G: U.S.]

Milton, David R. Worldwide Unitary Combination: The California Practice: Comments. In *McLure, C. E., Jr., ed.*, 1984, pp. 182–91. [G: U.S.]

Montgomery, Fred H. Water's Edge verus Worldwide Unitary Combination: Comments. In *McLure, C. E., Jr., ed.*, 1984, pp. 45–52. [G: U.S.]

Morehouse, Thomas A. Resource Development and Alaska Wealth Management. In *Morehouse, T. A., ed.*, 1984, pp. 169–97. [G: U.S.]

Musgrave, Peggy B. Principles for Dividing the State Corporate Tax Base. In *McLure, C. E., Jr., ed.*, 1984, pp. 228–46. [G: U.S.]

Musgrave, Richard A. The National Effects of Differential State Corporate Income Taxes on Multistate Corporations: Comments. In *McLure, C. E., Jr., ed.*, 1984, pp. 264–66.

Nelson, F. Howard. A Note on the Effects of Commercial and Industrial Property in School Spending Decisions. *Nat. Tax J.*, March 1984, *37*(1), pp. 121–25. [G: U.S.]

Netzer, Dick. On Modernizing Local Public Finance: Why Aren't Property Taxes in Urban Areas Being Reformed into Land Value Taxes? *Amer. J. Econ. Soc.*, October 1984, *43*(4), pp. 497–501. [G: U.S.]

Netzer, Dick. Setting Municipal Priorities: Finan-

cial Resources: Taxes. In *Brecher, C. and Horton, R. D., eds.*, 1984, pp. 76–114. [G: U.S.]

Noto, Nonna A. and Zimmerman, Dennis. Limiting State–Local Tax Deductibility: Effects among the States. *Nat. Tax J.*, December 1984, *37*(4), pp. 539–49. [G: U.S.]

Nunns, James R. Alternative Divisions of the Tax Base: How Much Is at Stake? Comments. In *McLure, C. E., Jr., ed.*, 1984, pp. 220–27. [G: U.S.]

Olson, Dennis O. The Interregional Incidence of Energy-Production Taxes. *Int. Reg. Sci. Rev.*, November 1984, *9*(2), pp. 109–24. [G: U.S.]

Paster, Janice D. School Trust Land and Federal Condemnation for Defense Purposes: Federal Laws in Conflict. *Natural Res. J.*, April 1984, *24*(2), pp. 451–70. [G: U.S.]

Peters, James H. Alternative Divisions of the Tax Base: How Much Is at Stake? Comments. In *McLure, C. E., Jr., ed.*, 1984, pp. 217–19. [G: U.S.]

Peters, James H. Dividing the State Corporate Income Tax Base: Developments in the Supreme Court and Congress: Panel Discussion. In *McLure, C. E., Jr., ed.*, 1984, pp. 336–40. [G: U.S.]

Petersen, Robert A. Worldwide Unitary Combination: The California Practice: Comments. In *McLure, C. E., Jr., ed.*, 1984, pp. 167–72. [G: U.S.]

Phillips, Almarin. Defining a Unitary Business: An Economist's View: Comments. In *McLure, C. E., Jr., ed.*, 1984, pp. 125–26. [G: U.S.]

Piggott, John. The Value of Tenant Benefits from UK Council Housing Subsidies. *Econ. J.*, June 1984, *94*(374), pp. 384–89. [G: U.K.]

Raimondo, Henry J. and Stuart, Robert C. Financing Soviet Cities. In *Morton, H. W. and Stuart, R. C., eds.*, 1984, pp. 45–64. [G: U.S.S.R.]

Rasmussen, David W.; Bendick, Marc, Jr. and Ledebur, Larry C. A Methodology for Selecting Economic Development Incentives. *Growth Change*, January 1984, *15*(1), pp. 18–25. [G: U.S.]

Ring, Raymond J., Jr. A State Corporation Income Tax: Tax Exporting and the Apportionment Formula. *Growth Change*, July 1984, *15*(3), pp. 30–38. [G: U.S.]

Roistacher, Elizabeth and Tobier, Emanuel. Setting Municipal Priorities: Service Delivery: Housing Policy. In *Brecher, C. and Horton, R. D., eds.*, 1984, pp. 446–81. [G: U.S.]

Schoettle, Ferdinand P. State Taxation Under the Commerce Clause: The History Revisited: Comments. In *McLure, C. E., Jr., ed.*, 1984, pp. 85–88. [G: U.S.]

Schulthess, Walter E. Incidencia de los tributos nacionales por jurisdicciones políticas en la República Argentina. (The Incidences of National Taxes by Political Jurisdictions in the Argentine Republic. With English summary.) *Económica*, January-April 1984, *30*(1), pp. 85–117. [G: Argentina]

Seldon, Arthur. Taxation in the United Kingdom:

Reply. In *Block, W. and Walker, M., eds.*, 1984, pp. 217–21.   [G: U.K.]

Seldon, Arthur. Taxation in the United Kingdom. In *Block, W. and Walker, M., eds.*, 1984, pp. 157–213.

                                              [G: U.K.; OECD]

de Seve, Charles W. and Vasquez, Thomas E. The Impact of Changes in the Federal Tax Code on State Tax Revenues. *Nat. Tax J.*, September 1984, *37*(3), pp. 393–409.   [G: U.S.]

Sheffrin, Steven M. and Fulcher, Jack. Alternative Divisions of the Tax Base: How Much Is at Stake? In *McLure, C. E., Jr., ed.*, 1984, pp. 192–213.   [G: U.S.]

Shoven, John B. The National Effects of Differential State Corporate Income Taxes on Multistate Corporations: Comments. In *McLure, C. E., Jr., ed.*, 1984, pp. 267–68.

Stokes, Charles J. Is the New England Urban Tax Rate Too High? *Amer. J. Econ. Soc.*, January 1984, *43*(1), pp. 75–90.   [G: U.S.]

Sullivan, Arthur M. The General Equilibrium Effects of the Industrial Property Tax: Incidence and Excess Burden. *Reg. Sci. Urban Econ.*, November 1984, *14*(4), pp. 547–63.

Tannenwald, Robert. The Pros and Cons of Worldwide Unitary Taxation. *New Eng. Econ. Rev.*, July–August 1984, pp. 17–28.

                                                     [G: U.S.]

Taylor, Carol A. and Charney, Alberta H. The Effects of State Taxation on United States Copper Supply: Comment. *Land Econ.*, May 1984, *60*(2), pp. 211–14.   [G: U.S.]

Thompson, Frederick. How to Stay within the Budget Using Per-Unit Subsidies. *J. Policy Anal. Manage.*, Winter 1984, *3*(2), pp. 285–88.   [G: U.S.]

Walters, Sir Alan. Taxation in the United Kingdom: Comment. In *Block, W. and Walker, M., eds.*, 1984, pp. 214–17.   [G: U.K.]

Wentzler, Nancy A. Net Regional Impact of State Education Aid. *Growth Change*, July 1984, *15*(3), pp. 3–9.   [G: U.S.]

Wheaton, William C. The Incidence of Inter-jurisdictional Differences in Commercial Property Taxes. *Nat. Tax J.*, December 1984, *37*(4), pp. 515–27.   [G: U.S.]

Wilson, John D. The Excise Tax Effects of the Property Tax. *J. Public Econ.*, August 1984, *24*(3), pp. 309–29.

Winkler, Donald R. The Fiscal Consequences of Foreign Students in Public Higher Education: A Case Study of California. *Econ. Educ. Rev.*, 1984, *3*(2), pp. 141–54.   [G: U.S.]

Zodrow, George. The Incidence of Metropolitan Property Tax Base Sharing and Rate Equalization. *J. Urban Econ.*, March 1984, *15*(2), pp. 210–29.   [G: U.S.]

3243 State and Local Government Borrowing

Bennett, James T. and DiLorenzo, Thomas J. Political Entrepreneurship and Reform of the Rent-Seeking Society. In *Colander, D. C., ed.*, 1984, pp. 217–27.   [G: U.S.]

Bierwag, G. O.; Kaufman, George G. and Leonard, Paul A. Interest Rate Effects of Commercial Bank Underwriting of Municipal Revenue Bonds: Additional Evidence. *J. Banking Finance*, March 1984, *8*(1), pp. 35–50.

                                                     [G: U.S.]

Cluff, George S. and Farnham, Paul G. Standard & Poor's vs. Moody's: Which City Characteristics Influence Municipal Bond Ratings? *Quart. Rev. Econ. Bus.*, Autumn 1984, *24*(3), pp. 72–94.

Friedgut, Jac. Setting Municipal Priorities: Financial Resources: Financing. In *Brecher, C. and Horton, R. D., eds.*, 1984, pp. 169–89.

                                                     [G: U.S.]

Gainer, William J. Mortgage Revenue Bonds: Their Costs Outweigh Their Benefits to Homebuyers. *Housing Finance Rev.*, October 1984, *3*(4), pp. 457–65.   [G: U.S.]

Grossman, David A. Setting Municipal Priorities: Budgeting and Management: Debt and Capital Management. In *Brecher, C. and Horton, R. D., eds.*, 1984, pp. 270–301.   [G: U.S.]

Hamilton, Randy. The World Turned Upside Down: The Contemporary Revolution in State and Local Government Capital Financing. In *Carr, J. H., ed.*, 1984, *1983*, pp. 200–20.

                                                     [G: U.S.]

Kidwell, David S.; Koch, Timothy W. and Stock, Duane R. The Impact of State Income Taxes on Municipal Borrowing Costs. *Nat. Tax J.*, December 1984, *37*(4), pp. 551–61.

                                                     [G: U.S.]

Liu, Pu and Thakor, Anjan V. Interest Yields, Credit Ratings, and Economic Characteristics of State Bonds: An Empirical Analysis: A Note. *J. Money, Credit, Banking*, August 1984, *16*(3), pp. 344–51.   [G: U.S.]

Macsherry, Cathy Daicoff. Infrastructure and an S&P Credit Rating: Questions, Trends, and Considerations. *Public Budg. Finance*, Autumn 1984, *4*(3), pp. 41–45.   [G: U.S.]

Monkkonen, Eric H. The Politics of Municipal Indebtedness and Default, 1850–1936. In *McDonald, T. J. and Ward, S. K., eds.*, 1984, pp. 125–59.   [G: U.S.]

Robbins, Edward Henry. Pricing Municipal Debt. *J. Finan. Quant. Anal.*, December 1984, *19*(4), pp. 467–83.

Stock, Duane R. and Schrems, Edward L. Municipal Bond Demand Premiums and Bond Price Volatility: A Note. *J. Finance*, June 1984, *39*(2), pp. 535–39.   [G: U.S.]

Vogt, Michael G. Municipal Bond Banks and Their Effects on the Finances of Local Governments. *Quart. J. Bus. Econ.*, Winter 1984, *23*(1), pp. 38–50.   [G: U.S.]

Wescott, Shari H. Accounting Numbers and Socioeconomic Variables as Predictors of Municipal General Obligation Bond Ratings. *J. Acc. Res.*, Spring 1984, *22*(1), pp. 412–23.

Zimmerman, Dennis. Federal Tax Policy, IDBs and the Market for State and Local Bonds. *Nat. Tax J.*, September 1984, *37*(3), pp. 411–20.

                                                     [G: U.S.]

325 Intergovernmental Financial Relationships

3250 Intergovernmental Financial Relationships

Alperovich, Gershon. The Economics of Choice in the Allocation of Intergovernmental Grants to Local Authorities. *Public Choice*, 1984, 44(2), pp. 285–96. [G: Israel]

Ansari, M. M. A Critique of the Developments in Indian Fiscal Federalism. *Margin*, October 1984, 17(1), pp. 31–47. [G: India]

Anton, Thomas J. Intergovernmental Change in the United States: An Assessment of the Literature. In *Miller, T. C., ed.*, 1984, pp. 15–64. [G: U.S.]

Aronson, J. Richard and Schwartz, Eli. Public Sector Performance: A Public Finance Perspective. In *Miller, T. C., ed.*, 1984, pp. 193–223. [G: U.S.]

Bird, Richard M. Tax Harmonization and Federal Finance: A Perspective on Recent Canadian Discussion. *Can. Public Policy*, September 1984, 10(3), pp. 253–66. [G: Canada]

Bradbury, Katharine L., et al. State Aid to Offset Fiscal Disparities across Communities. *Nat. Tax J.*, June 1984, 37(2), pp. 151–70. [G: U.S.]

Brandl, John. What States and Cities Can Do about Undependable Federal Policy. *Nat. Tax J.*, September 1984, 37(3), pp. 447–49. [G: U.S.]

Buglione, Enrico and France, George. Skewed Fiscal Federalism in Italy: Implications for Public Expenditure Control. In *Premchand, A. and Burkhead, J., eds.*, 1984, pp. 69–89. [G: Italy]

Cole, Richard L. and Caputo, David A. The Public Hearing as an Effective Citizen Participation Mechanism: A Case Study of the General Revenue Sharing Program. *Amer. Polit. Sci. Rev.*, June 1984, 78(2), pp. 404–16. [G: U.S.]

Conlan, Timothy J. The Politics of Federal Block Grants: From Nixon to Reagan. *Polit. Sci. Quart.*, Summer 1984, 99(2), pp. 247–70. [G: U.S.]

DeGrove, John M. State–Local Relations: The Challenge of New Federalism. In *Carr, J. H., ed.*, 1984, 1981, pp. 350–58. [G: U.S.]

Denzau, Arthur and Grier, Kevin. Determinants of Local School Spending: Some Consistent Estimates. *Public Choice*, 1984, 44(2), pp. 375–83. [G: U.S.]

Dhesi, Autar S. and Ghuman, B. S. Aspects of Financing State Plans (With Special Reference to Punjab). *Margin*, April 1984, 16(3), pp. 31–43. [G: India]

Dommel, Paul R. Local Discretion: The CDBG Approach. In *Bingham, R. D. and Blair, J. P., eds.*, 1984, pp. 101–13. [G: U.S.]

Doolittle, Fred C. State Legislatures and Federal Grants: An Overview. *Public Budg. Finance*, Summer 1984, 4(2), pp. 7–23. [G: U.S.]

Doolittle, Fred C. State Legislatures and Federal Grants: Developments in the Reagan Years.

Public Budg. Finance, Summer 1984, 4(2), pp. 3–6. [G: U.S.]

Feldstein, Martin. Public Education: Reply [Wealth Neutrality and Local Choice in Public Education]. *Amer. Econ. Rev.*, September 1984, 74(4), pp. 820–21. [G: U.S.]

Firestine, Robert E.; Weinstein, Bernard L. and Hayden, Shelley M. Intergovernmental Fiscal Cooperation in Growing Metropolitan Economies. In *Carr, J. H., ed.*, 1984, 1978, pp. 221–29. [G: U.S.]

Gatons, Paul K. and Brintnall, Michael. Competitive Grants: The UDAG Approach. In *Bingham, R. D. and Blair, J. P., eds.*, 1984, pp. 115–40. [G: U.S.]

Gist, John R. and Hill, R. Carter. Political and Economic Influences on the Bureaucratic Allocation of Federal Funds: The Case of Urban Development Action Grants. *J. Urban Econ.*, September 1984, 16(2), pp. 158–72. [G: U.S.]

Gold, Steven D. State Aid for Local Schools: Trends and Prospects. *Public Budg. Finance*, Winter 1984, 4(4), pp. 30–40. [G: U.S.]

Gramlich, Edward M. "A Fair Go": Fiscal Federalism Arrangements. In *Caves, R. E. and Krause, L. B., eds.*, 1984, pp. 231–74. [G: Australia]

Grossman, David A. Setting Municipal Priorities: Financial Resources: State Aid. In *Brecher, C. and Horton, R. D., eds.*, 1984, pp. 115–37. [G: U.S.]

Grubb, W. Norton. The Price of Local Discretion: Inequalities in Welfare Spending within Texas. *J. Policy Anal. Manage.*, Spring 1984, 3(3), pp. 359–72. [G: U.S.]

Guibert, G. and Lanvin, B. Decentralization in Government: The United States and France Compared. *J. Policy Anal. Manage.*, Winter 1984, 3(2), pp. 289–93. [G: France; U.S.]

Haar, Charles M. The Joint Venture Approach to Urban Renewal: From Model Cities to Enterprise Zones. In *Brooks, H.; Liebman, L. and Schelling, C. S., eds.*, 1984, pp. 63–87. [G: U.S.]

Hamm, William G. Federal Aid to State and Local Governments: Comment. In *Mills, G. B. and Palmer, J. L., eds.*, 1984, pp. 203–08. [G: U.S.]

Jackman, Richard. Public Expenditure Policy, 1984–85: Local Authority Finance. In *Cockle, P., ed.*, 1984, pp. 88–108. [G: U.K.]

Jensen, Cristy A. Legislative Response to Federal Cutbacks in California. *Public Budg. Finance*, Summer 1984, 4(2), pp. 58–72. [G: U.S.]

Jondrow, James M. and Levy, Robert A. The Displacement of Local Spending for Pollution Control by Federal Construction Grants. *Amer. Econ. Rev.*, May 1984, 74(2), pp. 174–78. [G: U.S.]

Kiefer, David and Miller, Jan. Public Budgets and Public Capital in Boom Towns. *Policy Sci.*, March 1984, 16(4), pp. 349–69. [G: U.S.]

King, John Leslie and Kraemer, Kenneth L. Information Systems and Intergovernmental Relations. In *Miller, T. C., ed.*, 1984, pp. 102–30. [G: U.S.]

Kirlin, John J. Public Sector Performance: A Political Perspective. In *Miller, T. C., ed.*, 1984, pp. 161–92. [G: U.S.]

Ladd, Helen F. Federal Aid to State and Local Governments. In *Mills, G. B. and Palmer, J. L., eds.*, 1984, pp. 165–202. [G: U.S.]

Lakdawala, D. T. Plan Finances in a Federal Economy. In *Singh, A. K.; Papola, T. S. and Mathur, R. S., eds.*, 1984, pp. 363–402. [G: India]

Lindsay, Cotton M. and Zycher, Benjamin. Substitution in Public Spending: Who Pays for Canadian National Health Insurance? *Econ. Inquiry*, July 1984, *22*(3), pp. 337–59. [G: Canada]

Lloyd, P. J. Mineral Economics in Australia: Economy-Wide Effects: Introduction. In *Lloyd, P. J., ed.*, 1984, pp. 275–84. [G: Australia]

Luce, Thomas and Pack, Janet Rothenberg. State Support under the New Federalism. *J. Policy Anal. Manage.*, Spring 1984, *3*(3), pp. 339–58. [G: U.S.]

Mazy, Jean-Louis, et al. Les budgets régionaux. Compétences et modes de financement. (With English summary.) *Cah. Écon. Bruxelles*, Fourth Trimester 1984, (104), pp. 517–46. [G: Belgium]

Megdal, Sharon Bernstein. A Model of Local Demand for Education. *J. Urban Econ.*, July 1984, *16*(1), pp. 13–30. [G: U.S.]

Moffitt, Robert A. The Effects of Grants-in-Aid on State and Local Expenditures: The Case of AFDC. *J. Public Econ.*, April 1984, *23*(3), pp. 279–305. [G: U.S.]

Muller, Thomas. Urban and Regional Change: The Federal Role and National Policy. In *Carr, J. H., ed.*, 1984, *1982*, pp. 342–49. [G: U.S.]

Nathan, Richard P. Setting Municipal Priorities: Financial Resources: Federal Aid. In *Brecher, C. and Horton, R. D., eds.*, 1984, pp. 138–68. [G: U.S.]

Nathan, Richard P. and Doolittle, Fred C. The Budget Cuts: The Day After. *Challenge*, January/February 1984, *26*(6), pp. 29–36. [G: U.S.]

Nuñez Miñana, Horacio and Porto, Alberto. Redistribución territorial a través de las finanzas públicas: El caso de los partidos del Gran Buenos Aires. (Territorial Redistribution through Public Finance: The Case of Greater Buenos Aires Districts. With English summary.) *Económica*, January-April 1984, *30*(1), pp. 35–69. [G: Argentina]

Perkins, George M. Public Education: Comment [Wealth Neutrality and Local Choice in Public Education]. *Amer. Econ. Rev.*, September 1984, *74*(4), pp. 814–19. [G: U.S.]

Peterson, George E. Federalism and the States: An Experiment in Decentralization. In *Palmer, J. L. and Sawhill, I. V., eds.*, 1984, pp. 217–59. [G: U.S.]

Peterson, George E. Financing the Nation's In-

frastructure Requirements. In *Hanson, R., ed.*, 1984, pp. 110–30. [G: U.S.]

Raines, Franklin D. Financing the Nation's Infrastructure Requirements: Discussion. In *Hanson, R., ed.*, 1984, pp. 131–35. [G: U.S.]

Ranjana. Allocative Effects of Inter-Governmental Flows in India: A New Perspective—1952–77. *Margin*, April 1984, *16*(3), pp. 44–55. [G: India]

Raynauld, André. The Canadian Federation. *Can. J. Econ.*, November 1984, *17*(4), pp. 635–53. [G: Canada]

Redburn, F. Stevens, et al. Federal Economic Development Investments. In *Holzer, M. and Nagel, S. S., eds.*, 1984, pp. 115–43. [G: U.S.]

Rittenoure, R. Lynn; Warner, Larkin and Steib, Steve B. Oklahoma's Legislative Process in a Period of Fiscal Change. *Public Budg. Finance*, Summer 1984, *4*(2), pp. 42–57. [G: U.S.]

Rothenberg, Irene Fraser. Regional Coordination of Federal Programs: Has the Difficult Grown Impossible? *J. Policy Anal. Manage.*, Fall 1984, *4*(1), pp. 1–16. [G: U.S.]

Shannon, John. New Federalism in the 1980s. In *Carr, J. H., ed.*, 1984, *1982*, pp. 327–41. [G: U.S.]

Short, John. Public Finance and Devolution: Money Flows between Government and Regions in the United Kingdom. *Scot. J. Polit. Econ.*, June 1984, *31*(2), pp. 114–30. [G: U.K.]

Simon, Richard M. and Conn, W. David. Federal Assistance to Energy-producing Regions: An Evaluation of the 601 Program. *J. Energy Devel.*, Spring 1984, *9*(2), pp. 243–61. [G: U.S.]

Sloan, Frank A. State Discretion in Federal Categorical Assistance Programs: The Case of Medicaid. *Public Finance Quart.*, July 1984, *12*(3), pp. 321–46. [G: U.S.]

Starkie, David. The Specific Effect of Specific Road Grants in South Australia. *Australian Econ. Pap.*, June 1984, *23*(42), pp. 27–37. [G: Australia]

Wallis, John Joseph. The Birth of the Old Federalism: Financing the New Deal, 1932–1940. *J. Econ. Hist.*, March 1984, *44*(1), pp. 139–59. [G: U.S.]

Wildasin, David E. The Welfare Effects of Intergovernmental Grants in an Economy with Distortionary Local Taxes: A Simple General Equilibrium Analysis. *J. Public Econ.*, November 1984, *25*(1/2), pp. 103–25.

Witsman, Forest. Financing the Nation's Infrastructure Requirements: Discussion. In *Hanson, R., ed.*, 1984, pp. 135–37. [G: U.S.]

400 International Economics

4000 General

Addo, Herb. Approaching the New International Economic Order Dialectically and Transformationally. In *Addo, H., ed.*, 1984, pp. 245–98.

Addo, Herb. Pertinent Questions about the NIEO. In *Addo, H., ed.*, 1984, pp. 1–17.

Amacher, Ryan C. International Markets versus the New International Economic Order: Challenges to the Independence of Nation States. In *Jackson, M. R. and Woodson, J. D., Jr., eds.*, 1984, pp. 223–43.

Amin, Samir. After the New International Economic Order: The Future of International Economic Relations. In *Ghosh, P. K., ed., no. 9*, 1984, *1982*, pp. 297–312.

Amin, Samir. Self-Reliance and the New International Economic Order. In *Addo, H., ed.*, 1984, pp. 204–19.

Anell, Lars. An Equitable World Order. In *Ghosh, P. K., ed., no. 9*, 1984, *1980*, pp. 100–16.

Aseniero, George. Technology and Development: NIEO's Quest for Technology Transfer. In *Addo, H., ed.*, 1984, pp. 220–41.

Aziz, Sartaj. The New International Order: Search for Common Ground. In *Ghosh, P. K., ed., no. 9*, 1984, *1978*, pp. 48–58.

Bhagwati, Jagdish N. Annex: A Statement on North–South Economic Strategy. In *Bhagwati, J. N. and Ruggie, J. G., eds.*, 1984, pp. 323–330.

Bhagwati, Jagdish N. North–South Economic Relations: Then and Now. In *Frenkel, J. A. and Mussa, M. L., eds.*, 1984, pp. 49–61.
[G: OECD; LDCs]

Borner, Silvio. Drei Grundperspektiven zur Interpretation des weltwirtschaftlichen Strukturwandels. (Three Perspectives for the Interpretation of Structural Change in the World Economy. With English summary.) *Aussenwirtschaft*, September 1984, *39*(3), pp. 219–40. **[G: Global]**

Boulding, Elise. Retrospective: The Symposium as Mid-Point in a Two-Hundred-Year Present. In *Trent, J. and Lamy, P., eds.*, 1984, pp. 241–51.

Bressand, Albert. Power Passions and Purpose: Prospects for North–South Negotiations: The Time for Painful Rethinking. In *Bhagwati, J. N. and Ruggie, J. G., eds.*, 1984, pp. 49–63.

Bressand, Albert. The Reconstruction of the World Economic Order. In *Miyawaki, N., ed.*, 1984, pp. 101–14.

Brinkman, Richard L. The New International Economic Order and Value Theory. *J. Econ. Issues*, June 1984, *18*(2), pp. 493–506.

Chakravarty, Sukhamoy. New International Economic Order and the Brandt Report. In *Ngo, M., ed., vol. 1*, 1984, pp. 96–103.
[G: Global]

Cole, Sam. Disarmament in the Context of a New International Economic Order. In *Ghosh, P. K., ed., no. 17*, 1984, *1979*, pp. 206–14.

Cooper, Richard N. The United States and the World Economy. In *Frenkel, J. A. and Mussa, M. L., eds.*, 1984, pp. 1–21. **[G: U.S.; Global]**

Cordovez, Diego. Institutional Elements of a New Diplomacy for Development (Notes for a Book

of Memoirs). *Cepal Rev.*, 1984, (23), pp. 29–43. **[G: Global]**

Coussy, J. Intégration ou déconnexion du nord et du sud sous l'impact de la crise: introduction. (North and South under the Impact of the Crisis: Linking or Delinking? Introduction. With English summary.) *Écon. Soc.*, June 1984, *18*(6), pp. 3–17.

Dore, Ronald P. The Future of the International Economy. In *Miyawaki, N., ed.*, 1984, pp. 132–38.

Dostovalov, Y. L. and Allpatov, S. B. The Interpretation of Neocolonialism and the Economies of Developing Countries. In *Smirnov, A. D.; Golosov, V. V. and Maximova, V. F., eds.*, 1984, pp. 190–214.

Dubey, Muchkund. Problems of Establishing a New International Economic Order. In *Ghosh, P. K., ed., no. 9*, 1984, *1980*, pp. 276–96.

Evans, Donald D. Appropriate Technology and Its Role in Development. In *Ghosh, P. K., ed., no. 14*, 1984, *1979*, pp. 7–72.
[G: LDCs]

Faire, Alexandre. Economic Redeployment and Contradictions in the West. In *Ngo, M., ed., vol. 1*, 1984, pp. 5–32. **[G: OECD]**

Frank, Andre Gunder. Global Crisis and Transformation. In *Frank, A. G.*, 1984, *1983*, pp. 208–29.

Frank, Andre Gunder. Policy Ad Hockery: Unemployment and World Crisis of Economic Policy Formation. In *Frank, A. G.*, 1984, *1983*, pp. 230–42.

Frank, Andre Gunder. Rhetoric and Reality of the New International Economic Order. In *Addo, H., ed.*, 1984, pp. 165–203.

Galtung, Johan. Grand Designs on a Collison Course. In *Ghosh, P. K., ed., no. 9*, 1984, *1978*, pp. 59–65.

Galtung, Johan. Grand Designs on a Collision Course. In *Ghosh, P. K., ed., no. 13*, 1984, *1978*, pp. 108–14.

Gaudard, Gaston; Caille, Pierre and Donzé, Laurent. La transformation de l'inégalité économique internationale. (The Change of International Economic Equality. With English summary.) *Schweiz. Z. Volkswirtsch. Statist.*, June 1984, *120*(2), pp. 141–67. **[G: Global]**

Goldstein, Walter. Despair and the UN Development Decade. In *Ghosh, P. K., ed., no. 9*, 1984, *1981*, pp. 335–46.

Hann, Daniel P. Perspectives on the Future of the World Economy: The Energy Situation and the New International Economic Order. In *Ghosh, P. K., ed., no. 4*, 1984, *1981*, pp. 71–77. **[G: Global]**

Harberger, Arnold C. and Wall, David. Harry G. Johnson as a Development Economist. *J. Polit. Econ.*, August 1984, *92*(4), pp. 616–41.

Helleiner, Gerald K. The One World of Economics: Towards Global Economic Analysis. In *[Reynolds, L. G.]*, 1984, pp. 63–74.
[G: Global]

Hesse, Helmut. Discussion of the New Economic World Order. In *Ghosh, P. K., ed., no. 9*, 1984, *1976*, pp. 117–27.

Hewitt, Adrian. The Lomé Conventions: Entering a Second Decade. *J. Common Market Stud.*, December 1984, *23*(2), pp. 95–115.
[G: Global]

Huhle, Fritz. Internationale Institutionen— Hemmschuh oder Förderer weltwirtschaftlicher Integration? (International Institutions— Impeding or Promoting International Economic Integration? With English summary.) *Ifo-Studien*, 1984, *30*(1), pp. 63–78.
[G: Global]

Jungnickel, Rolf and Koopmann, Georg. The Role of Multinationals in the NIEO. In *Ghosh, P. K., ed., no. 11*, 1984, *1976*, pp. 294–301.

Karunaratne, Neil Dias. Foreign Aid, New Economic Order and Basic Human Needs. In *Ghosh, P. K., ed., no. 10*, 1984, *1979*, pp. 205–14.

Koenig, Linda M. Recent Developments in the World Economy and in Non-Oil Developing Countries of the Western Hemisphere. In *Muns, J., ed.*, 1984, pp. 16–29. [G: OECD; LDCs; Latin America]

Kosaka, Masataka. International Political Order. In *Miyawaki, N., ed.*, 1984, pp. 115–20.

Kothari, Rajni. Towards a Just World. In *Ghosh, P. K., ed., no. 9*, 1984, pp. 7–47.

Kreye, Otto. Western Europe's Economic and Social Development and the Rationality and Reality of a New International Economic Order. In *Addo, H., ed.*, 1984, pp. 119–37.
[G: W. Europe]

Lipietz, Alain. Le fordisme périphérique étranglé par le monétarisme central. (Peripheral Fordism Choked by Central Monetarism. With English summary.) *L'Actual. Econ.*, March 1984, *60*(1), pp. 72–94. [G: Global]

Madeuf, B. and Ominami, C. Nouvelle D.I.T. et Keynésianisme planétaire: la fin des illusions. (New International Division of Labour and Worldwide Keynesianism: The End of the Illusions. With English summary.) *Écon. Soc.*, June 1984, *18*(6), pp. 81–98. [G: Global]

Malan, Pedro S. Latin American Countries and the New International Economic Order. In *Ghosh, P. K., ed., no. 19*, 1984, *1980*, pp. 150–70. [G: Latin America]

Malan, Pedro S. The Latin American Countries and the New International Economic Order. In *Ghosh, P. K., ed., no. 9*, 1984, *1980*, pp. 347–67. [G: Latin America]

McFarlane, Bruce. Western Strategies in the Asia–Pacific Region. In *Ngo, M., ed., vol. 1*, 1984, pp. 259–72. [G: Asia; OECD]

Michalski, Wolfgang. The Long-term Prospects for World Development: The Main Results of the Interfutures Project. In *Ghosh, P. K., ed., no. 8*, 1984, *1979*, pp. 277–90.

Mitra, Pijush K. A Note on the New International Economic Order. *Econ. Notes*, 1984, (3), pp. 86–103. [G: Global]

Morrison, Denton E. Energy, Appropriate Technology, and International Interdependence. In *Ghosh, P. K., ed., no. 14*, 1984, pp. 205–37.

Oberg, Jan. The New International Economic and Military Orders as Problems to Peace Research. In *Ghosh, P. K., ed., no. 17*, 1984, *1977*, pp. 269–81.

Ostry, Sylvia. The World Economy in 1983: Marking Time. *Foreign Aff.*, 1984, *62*(3), pp. 533–60. [G: Global]

Preiswerk, Roy. Hidden Dimensions of the So-Called New International Economic Order. In *Addo, H., ed.*, 1984, pp. 33–48.

Putník, Jiří. The Position of Developing Countries in Present-Day International Economic Relations. *Czech. Econ. Digest.*, June 1984, (4), pp. 48–67. [G: LDCs]

Raj, K. N. The Causes and Consequences of World Recession. *World Devel.*, March 1984, *12*(3), pp. 177–85. [G: Global]

Rist, Gilbert. The Not-So-New International Order. In *Ghosh, P. K., ed., no. 9*, 1984, *1978*, pp. 128–34.

Rittberger, Volker. The Role of Science and Technology in the New International Order. In *Ghosh, P. K., ed., no. 9*, 1984, *1978*, pp. 183–97.

Ruggie, John Gerard. Another Round, Another Requiem? Prospects for the Global Negotiations. In *Bhagwati, J. N. and Ruggie, J. G., eds.*, 1984, pp. 33–47.

Saigal, Jagdish C. The Present World Economic Crisis and the International Economic Policy. In *Singh, A. K.; Papola, T. S. and Mathur, R. S., eds.*, 1984, pp. 341–62. [G: Global]

Sakamoto, Masahiro. Scenarios for the 21st Century and Reconstruction of the International Order—The Economic Aspect. In *Miyawaki, N., ed.*, 1984, pp. 139–47.
[G: Selected Countries]

Schiller, Herbert I. Whose New International Economic and Information Order? In *Ngo, M., ed., vol. 1*, 1984, pp. 79–95. [G: Global]

Sewell, John W. and Zartman, I. William. Global Negotiations: Path to the Future or Dead-End Street? In *Bhagwati, J. N. and Ruggie, J. G., eds.*, 1984, pp. 87–124.

Shaw, Timothy M. The Non-Aligned Movement and the New International Economic Order. In *Addo, H., ed.*, 1984, pp. 138–62.

Soedjatmoko. The Social Sciences and Global Transformation. In *Trent, J. and Lamy, P., eds.*, 1984, pp. 17–32.

Strange, Susan. Paths to International Political Economy: What about International Relations? In *Strange, S., ed.*, 1984, pp. 183–97.

Sunkel, Osvaldo. Past, Present and Future of the International Economic Crisis. *Cepal Rev.*, April 1984, (22), pp. 81–105.
[G: Latin America; OECD]

Tooze, Roger. Paths to International Political Economy: Perspectives and Theory: a Consumers' Guide. In *Strange, S., ed.*, 1984, pp. 1–22.

Tumlir, Jan. Economic Policy for a Stable World Order. *Cato J.*, Spring/Summer 1984, *4*(1), pp. 355–64. [G: Global]

Urquidi, Victor L. Population and a New International Economic Order: A Missing Link. In *Ghosh, P. K., ed., no. 9*, 1984, *1979*, pp. 152–63.

Urquidi, Victor L. Population and a New International Order: A Missing Link? In *Ghosh, P. K., ed., no. 5, 1984, 1979*, pp. 294–305.

Wallerstein, Immanuel. An Historical Perspective on the Emergence of the New International Order: Economic, Political, Cultural Aspects. In *Addo, H., ed.*, 1984, pp. 21–32.

Wassermann, Ursula. Gamani Corea, Secretary-General of UNCTAD. *J. World Trade Law*, September–October 1984, *18*(5), pp. 377–80. [G: Global]

Wightman, David. Paths to International Political Economy: Why Economic History? In *Strange, S., ed.*, 1984, pp. 23–32.

Yoshitomi, Masaru. New Challenges to Advanced Economies. In *Miyawaki, N., ed.*, 1984, pp. 148–56.

Zecher, J. Richard. The Interventionist Disease and the IMF's Agency Cost Role [The Impoverishing Effects of Foreign Aid]. *Cato J.*, Spring/Summer 1984, *4*(1), pp. 339–42.

410 INTERNATIONAL TRADE THEORY

411 International Trade Theory

4110 General

Bhagwati, Jagdish N.; Brecher, Richard A. and Srinivasan, T. N. DUP Activities and Economic Theory. *Europ. Econ. Rev.*, April 1984, *24*(3), pp. 291–307.

Borner, Silvio. Internationale Wettbewerbsfähigkeit—Fragmente zu einer Theorie internationaler Unternehmenstätigkeit. (International Competitiveness—Fragments of a Theory on International Entrepreneurial Activity. With English summary.) *Weltwirtsch. Arch.*, 1984, *120*(3), pp. 481–98.

Corden, W. M. Harry Johnson's Contributions to International Trade Theory. *J. Polit. Econ.*, August 1984, *92*(4), pp. 567–91.

Feldman, David H. and Tower, Edward. Welfare Gain from a Stable Exchange Rate: Comment. *Atlantic Econ. J.*, July 1984, *12*(2), pp. 65.

Frey, Bruno S. and Schneider, Friedrich. International Political Economy: A Rising Field. *Econ. Int.*, August–November 1984, *37*(3–4), pp. 308–47. [G: Global]

Scitovsky, Tibor. Lerner's Contribution to Economics. *J. Econ. Lit.*, December 1984, *22*(4), pp. 1547–71.

Shoven, John B. and Whalley, John. Applied General-Equilibrium Models of Taxation and International Trade: An Introduction and Survey. *J. Econ. Lit.*, September 1984, *22*(3), pp. 1007–51.

4112 Theory of International Trade

Arnold, Volker. Umweltschutz als international öffentliches Gut: Komparative Kostenvorteile und Verhandlungsgewinne. (Environmental Protection as an International Public Good: Comparative Advantage, and Gains from Bargaining. With English summary.) *Z. Wirtschaft. Sozialwissen.*, 1984, *104*(2), pp. 111–29.

Baldwin, Robert E. and Hilton, R. Spence. A Technique for Indicating Comparative Costs and Predicting Changes in Trade Ratios. *Rev. Econ. Statist.*, February 1984, *66*(1), pp. 105–10. [G: Selected Countries]

Benson, Bruce L. and Hartigan, James C. An Explanation of Intra-industry Trade in Identical Commodities. *Int. J. Ind. Organ.*, June 1984, *2*(2), pp. 85–97.

Bernhardt, Dan. Dumping, Adjustment Costs, and Uncertainty. *J. Econ. Dynam. Control*, December 1984, *8*(3), pp. 349–70.

Berthelémy, Jean-Claude. La division internationale des processus productifs: une note ricardienne. (With English summary.) *Revue Écon. Polit.*, May–June 1984, *94*(3), pp. 347–57.

Betancourt, Roger; Clague, Christopher K. and Panagariya, Arvind. Trade and Factor Prices in a Model of Capital Utilization. *Southern Econ. J.*, January 1984, *50*(3), pp. 734–42.

Bhagwati, Jagdish N.; Brecher, Richard A. and Hatta, Tatsuo. The Paradoxes of Immiserizing Growth and Donor-enriching "Recipient-immiserizing" Transfers: A Tale of Two Literatures. *Weltwirtsch. Arch.*, 1984, *120*(2), pp. 228–43.

Blair, Roger D. and Cheng, Leonard. On Dumping. *Southern Econ. J.*, January 1984, *50*(3), pp. 857–65.

Bloomfield, Arthur I. Effect of Growth on the Terms of Trade: Some Earlier Views. *Economica*, May 1984, *51*(202), pp. 187–93.

Bond, Eric W. International Trade with Uncertain Product Quality. *Southern Econ. J.*, July 1984, *51*(1), pp. 196–207.

Brecher, Richard A. and Choudhri, Ehsan U. New Products and the Factor Content of International Trade. *J. Polit. Econ.*, October 1984, *92*(5), pp. 965–71. [G: U.S.]

Carlberg, Michael. International Factor Movements, Allocation and Prices. *Schweiz. Z. Volkswirtsch. Statist.*, March 1984, *120*(1), pp. 31–42.

Casas, F. R. Imperfect Factor Mobility: A Generalization and Synthesis of Two-Sector Models of International Trade. *Can. J. Econ.*, November 1984, *17*(4), pp. 747–61.

Casas, F. R. and Choi, E. Kwan. Trade Imbalance and the Leontief Paradox. *Manchester Sch. Econ. Soc. Stud.*, December 1984, *52*(4), pp. 391–401. [G: U.S.]

Cassing, James. Transfers and Presumption with Many Commodities. *Atlantic Econ. J.*, July 1984, *12*(2), pp. 74.

Chaudhuri, T. Datta and Khan, M. Ali. Sector-Specific Capital, Interconnectedness in Production, and Welfare. *Can. J. Econ.*, August 1984, *17*(3), pp. 489–507.

Cheng, Leonard. International Competition in R&D and Technological Leadership: An Examination of the Posner–Hufbauer Hypothesis. *J. Int. Econ.*, August 1984, *17*(1/2), pp. 15–40.

Chichilnisky, Graciela. The Transfer Problem in Stable Markets: A Rejoinder to Rejoinders [Basic Goods, Commodity Transfers, and the International Economic Order]. *J. Devel. Econ.*, December 1984, *16*(3), pp. 319–20.

Clifton, David S., Jr. and Marxsen, William B. An Empirical Investigation of the Heckscher–Ohlin Theorem. *Can. J. Econ.*, February 1984, *17*(1), pp. 32–38. [G: Selected Countries]

Constantopoulos, Maria and Drakos, George E. Measuring Changes in the Gains from Trade—A Contribution to Applied Welfare Economics. In *Csikós-Nagy, B.; Hague, D. and Hall, G., eds.*, 1984, pp. 454–83. [G: Greece]

Corden, W. M. Booming Sector and Dutch Disease Economics: Survey and Consolidation. *Oxford Econ. Pap.*, November 1984, *36*(3), pp. 359–80.

Corden, W. M. The Normative Theory of International Trade. In *Jones, R. W. and Kenen, P., eds.*, 1984, pp. 63–130.

Dalal, Ardeshir J. A Simple Proof of the Concavity of the Transformation Curve. *Atlantic Econ. J.*, July 1984, *12*(2), pp. 67.

Das, Satya P. and Mohanty, Adwait K. Dumping in International Markets and Welfare: A General Equilibrium Analysis. *J. Int. Econ.*, August 1984, *17*(1/2), pp. 149–57.

Deardorff, Alan V. An Exposition and Exploration of Krueger's Trade Model. *Can. J. Econ.*, November 1984, *17*(4), pp. 731–46.

Deardorff, Alan V. Testing Trade Theories and Predicting Trade Flows. In *Jones, R. W. and Kenen, P., eds.*, 1984, pp. 467–517.

Djajic, Slobodan. Exhaustible Resources and the Dynamics of Comparative Advantage. *J. Int. Econ.*, August 1984, *17*(1/2), pp. 55–71.

Dohner, Robert S. Export Pricing, Flexible Exchange Rates, and Divergence in the Prices of Traded Goods. *J. Int. Econ.*, February 1984, *16*(1/2), pp. 79–101.

Dompierre, Michael B. The United Auto Workers vs. the Japanese: Distributional Effects of Alternative United States Trade Policies. *Aussenwirtschaft*, September 1984, *39*(3), pp. 207–18. [G: U.S.; Japan]

Eaton, Jonathan and Kierzkowski, Henryk. Oligopolistic Competition, Product Variety, and International Trade. In *Kierzkowski, H., ed.*, 1984, pp. 69–83.

Economides, Nicholas S. Do Increases in Preference Similarity (Across Countries) Induce Increases in Trade? *J. Int. Econ.*, November 1984, *17*(3/4), pp. 537–81.

Elbers, Chris and Withagen, Cees. Trading in Exhaustible Resources in the Presence of Conversion Costs: A General Equilibrium Approach. *J. Econ. Dynam. Control*, November 1984, *8*(2), pp. 197–209.

Ethier, Wilfred J. Higher Dimensional Issues in Trade Theory. In *Jones, R. W. and Kenen, P., eds.*, 1984, pp. 131–84.

Fisher, Franklin M. and Hillman, Arye L. The Commodity Pattern of Trade and the Heckscher–Ohlin Theorem in the Presence of Aggregate and Commodity-Specific Factor-Intensity Reversals. *J. Int. Econ.*, August 1984, *17*(1/2), pp. 159–72.

Forstner, Helmut. The Changing Pattern of International Trade in Manufactures: A Logit Analysis. *Weltwirtsch. Arch.*, 1984, *120*(1), pp. 1–17. [G: Global]

Frankel, Jeffrey A. The Theory of Trade in Middle Products: An Extension. *Amer. Econ. Rev.*, June 1984, *74*(3), pp. 485–87.

Fried, Joel. Intertemporal Choice and International Trade. *Can. J. Econ.*, May 1984, *17*(2), pp. 217–31.

Gift, Richard E. and Marxsen, William B. Aggregation and the Factoral Content of Trade: Comment. *J. Polit. Econ.*, October 1984, *92*(5), pp. 979–84. [G: U.S.]

Ginsburgh, Victor and Waelbroeck, Jean. Free Trade and Tariff-ridden International Equilibria: Formulation and Computation. In *Andersson, Å. E.; Isard, W. and Puu, T., eds.*, 1984, pp. 133–56.

Gorham, Abby H. Imperfect Price Adjustment, Controlled Price and Multimarket Rationing Models: Their Potential Application to the Modelling of Trade in King and Tanner Crab Products. In *Avula, X. J. R., et al.*, 1984, pp. 837–43.

Gray, H. Peter. Employment Arguments for Protection and the Vita Theory. *Eastern Econ. J.*, January-March 1984, *10*(1), pp. 1–13.

Greenaway, David. The Measurement of Produce Differentiation in Empirical Studies of Trade Flows. In *Kierzkowski, H., ed.*, 1984, pp. 230–49.

Grossman, Gene M. International Competition and the Unionized Sector. *Can. J. Econ.*, August 1984, *17*(3), pp. 541–56.

Grossman, Gene M. The Gains from International Factor Movements. *J. Int. Econ.*, August 1984, *17*(1/2), pp. 73–83.

Hamada, Koichi and Iwata, Kazumasa. National Income, Terms of Trade and Economic Welfare. *Econ. J.*, December 1984, *94*(376), pp. 752–71. [G: Japan]

Hamadani, S. M. Mazahir Hasnain. Factors' Employment Absorption, Growth, and Income Distribution through Foreign Trade: Pakistan's Case. *Pakistan Devel. Rev.*, Summer-Autumn 1984, *23*(2&3), pp. 331–40. [G: Pakistan]

Hamilton, Carl and Svensson, Lars E. O. Do Countries' Factor Endowments Correspond to the Factor Contents in Their Bilateral Trade Flows? *Scand. J. Econ.*, 1984, *86*(1), pp. 84–97. [G: OECD; LDCs]

Harris, Richard G. Applied General Equilibrium Analysis of Small Open Economies with Scale Economies and Imperfect Competition. *Amer. Econ. Rev.*, December 1984, *74*(5), pp. 1016–32. [G: Canada]

Hatta, Tatsuo. Immiserizing Growth in a Many-Commodity Setting. *J. Int. Econ.*, November 1984, *17*(3/4), pp. 335–45.

Haynes, Stephen E. and Stone, Joe A. Cross-Price Effects in Demand between Exports and Imports. *J. Macroecon.*, Spring 1984, *6*(2), pp. 181–95. [G: U.S.]

Helpman, Elhanan. A Simple Theory of International Trade with Multinational Corporations. *J. Polit. Econ.*, June 1984, *92*(3), pp. 451–71.

Helpman, Elhanan. Increasing Returns, Imperfect Markets, and Trade Theory. In *Jones, R. W. and Kenen, P., eds.*, 1984, pp. 325–65.

Helpman, Elhanan. The Factor Content of Foreign Trade. *Econ. J.*, March 1984, *94*(373), pp. 84–94.

Helpman, Elhanan and Razin, Assaf. Increasing Returns, Monopolistic Competition, and Factor Movements: A Welfare Analysis. In *Kierzkowski, H., ed.*, 1984, *1983*, pp. 124–36.

Henner, Henri-F. Un modèle analytique des transferts de technologie. (An Analytical Model of Technology Transfers. With English summary.) *L'Actual. Econ.*, September 1984, *60*(3), pp. 355–74.

Herberg, Horst and Enders, Klaus. More on the Consequences of a Resource Boom and the Cures of the Dutch Disease. In *Siebert, H., ed.*, 1984, pp. 47–94.

Hill, John K. Comparative Statics in General Equilibrium Models with a Unionized Sector. *J. Int. Econ.*, May 1984, *16*(3/4), pp. 345–56.

Hilton, R. Spence. Commodity Trade and Relative Returns to Factors of Production. *J. Int. Econ.*, May 1984, *16*(3/4), pp. 259–70.

Hindley, Brian and Smith, Alasdair. Comparative Advantage and Trade in Services. *World Econ.*, December 1984, *7*(4), pp. 369–89.

Hoftyzer, John. A Further Analysis of the Linder Trade Thesis. *Quart. Rev. Econ. Bus.*, Summer 1984, *24*(2), pp. 57–70.   **[G: OECD]**

Horn, Henrik. Product Diversity, Trade and Welfare. In *Kierzkowski, H., ed.*, 1984, pp. 51–68.

Hwang, Hong. Intra-Industry Trade and Oligopoly: A Conjectural Variations Approach. *Can. J. Econ.*, February 1984, *17*(1), pp. 126–37.

Inoue, Tadashi. The Samuelson Reciprocity Relation in the Joint Production Case. *Econ. Stud. Quart.*, April 1984, *35*(1), pp. 31–38.

Iqbal, Munawar. Factors' Employment Absorption, Growth, and Income Distribution through Foreign Trade: Pakistan's Case. *Pakistan Devel. Rev.*, Summer-Autumn 1984, *23*(2&3), pp. 341–43.   **[G: Pakistan]**

Jones, Ronald W. The Transfer Problem in a Three-Agent Setting. *Can. J. Econ.*, February 1984, *17*(1), pp. 1–14.

Jones, Ronald W. and Neary, J. Peter. The Positive Theory of International Trade. In *Jones, R. W. and Kenen, P., eds.*, 1984, pp. 1–62.

Jussawalla, Meheroo and Cheah, Chee-Wah. International Trade and Information: Some Welfare Implications. In *Jussawalla, M. and Ebenfield, H., eds.*, 1984, pp. 51–71.

Kellman, Mitchell and Landau, Daniel. The Nature of Japan's Comparative Advantage, 1965–80. *World Devel.*, April 1984, *12*(4), pp. 433–38.   **[G: Japan]**

Kemp, Murray C. On the Applicability and Implementability of the (Finite) Compensation Principle. *Kobe Econ. Bus. Rev.*, 1984, *30*, pp. 17–22.

Kemp, Murray C. and Long, Ngo Van. The Optimal Restriction of Resource Imports and the Optimal Investment in Capacity for Substitute Production. In *Kemp, M. C. and Long, N. V., eds.*, 1984, pp. 145–60.

Kemp, Murray C. and Long, Ngo Van. The Role of Natural Resources in Trade Models. In *Jones, R. W. and Kenen, P., eds.*, 1984, pp. 367–417.

Khan, M. Ali. International Trade and Foreign Investment: A Model with Asymmetric Production. *Pakistan Devel. Rev.*, Winter 1984, *23*(4), pp. 509–30.

Kierzkowski, Henryk. Monopolistic Competition and International Trade: Introduction. In *Kierzkowski, H., ed.*, 1984, pp. 1–9.

Kohlmey, Gunther. International Values and the International Division of Labour. In *Csikós-Nagy, B.; Hague, D. and Hall, G., eds.*, 1984, pp. 300–07.

Kojima, Kiyoshi and Ozawa, Terutomo. Micro- and Macro-Economic Models of Direct Foreign Investment: Toward a Synthesis. *Hitotsubashi J. Econ.*, June 1984, *25*(1), pp. 1–20.

Krelle, Wilhelm. De Minimis Non Curate Praetor or: There Might Be Small Disadvantages in Foreign Trade. Don't Mind Them!! In *[Beckmann, M. J.]*, 1984, pp. 23–34.

Kumar, Rishi and Wang, Leonard F. S. Production Externality and the Transfer Problem. *Indian Econ. J.*, January–March 1984, *31*(3), pp. 73–78.

Lassiter, Gregory C. and Sisler, Daniel G. The Factor Proportions Theory of International Trade: Empirical Results from the United States and the Philippines. *Philippine Rev. Econ. Bus.*, Mar./June 1984, *21*(1/2), pp. 59–76.   **[G: U.S.; Philippines]**

Long, Ngo Van. On the Short-run and Long-run Effects of a Resource Boom. In *Siebert, H., ed.*, 1984, pp. 17–45.

Lyons, Bruce R. The Pattern of International Trade in Differentiated Products: An Incentive for the Existence of Multinational Firms. In *Kierzkowski, H., ed.*, 1984, pp. 157–79.

Mantel, Rolf R. Substitutability and the Welfare Effects of Endowment Increases. *J. Int. Econ.*, November 1984, *17*(3/4), pp. 325–34.

Marion, Nancy Peregrim and Svensson, Lars E. O. Adjustment to Expected and Unexpected Oil Price Changes. *Can. J. Econ.*, February 1984, *17*(1), pp. 15–31.

Marion, Nancy Peregrim and Svensson, Lars E. O. World Equilibrium with Oil Price Increases: An Intertemporal Analysis. *Oxford Econ. Pap.*, March 1984, *36*(1), pp. 86–102.

Markusen, James R. Multinationals, Multi-plant Economies, and the Gains from Trade. *J. Int. Econ.*, May 1984, *16*(3/4), pp. 205–26.

Markusen, James R. and Melvin, James R. The Gains-from-Trade Theorem with Increasing Returns to Scale. In *Kierzkowski, H., ed.*, 1984, pp. 10–33.

Martin, Lawrence W. and Panagariya, Arvind. Smuggling, Trade, and Price Disparity: A Crime-Theoretic Approach. *J. Int. Econ.*, November 1984, *17*(3/4), pp. 201–17.

Mejstřík, Michal. Economic Effects of Export and Their Dependence on the Quality of Products. *Czech. Econ. Pap.*, 1984, (22), pp. 57–82. **[G: Czechoslovakia]**

Melvin, James R. Taxes, Relative Prices and Trade. In *Csikós-Nagy, B.; Hague, D. and Hall, G., eds.*, 1984, pp. 183–200.

Momigliano, Franco and Siniscalco, Domenico. Technology and International Specialization. *Banca Naz. Lavoro Quart. Rev.*, September 1984, (150), pp. 257–84. **[G: Italy]**

Moura Roque, Fátima. Factor Endowments, Technology, and Foreign Trade. *S. Afr. J. Econ.*, December 1984, 52(4), pp. 377–90. **[G: S. Africa]**

Neary, J. Peter. The Heckscher–Ohlin Model as an Aggregate. In *[Pearce, I. F.]*, 1984, pp. 57–76.

Newbery, David M. G. and Stiglitz, Joseph E. Pareto Inferior Trade. *Rev. Econ. Stud.*, January 1984, 51(1), pp. 1–12.

Pomery, John. Uncertainty in Trade Models. In *Jones, R. W. and Kenen, P., eds.*, 1984, pp. 419–65.

Postlewaite, Andrew and Webb, Michael. The Possibility of Recipient-harming, Donor-benefiting Transfers with More than Two Countries. *J. Int. Econ.*, May 1984, 16(3/4), pp. 357–64.

Ranney, Susan I. International Capital Transfers and the Choice of Production Technique: A Simple Two-Country Model. *J. Int. Econ.*, August 1984, 17(1/2), pp. 85–99.

Ray, Alok and Ethier, Wilfred J. Presumption, Size of Country, and Gains from Trade. *Indian Econ. J.*, January–March 1984, 31(3), pp. 70–72.

Ray, Debraj. Survival, Growth and Technical Progress in a Small Resource-Importing Economy. *Int. Econ. Rev.*, June 1984, 25(2), pp. 275–95.

Rivera-Batiz, Francisco L. International Migration, Non-traded Goods, and Economic Welfare in a Two-Class Economy: A Reply. *J. Devel. Econ.*, December 1984, 16(3), pp. 325–30.

Ruffin, Roy J. International Factor Movements. In *Jones, R. W. and Kenen, P., eds.*, 1984, pp. 237–88.

Sarkar, Abhirup. A Dynamic Assignment Problem. *Int. Econ. Rev.*, October 1984, 25(3), pp. 663–70.

Schweinberger, A. G. The Austrian Concept of Capital and the Pure Theory of International Trade. In *[Pearce, I. F.]*, 1984, pp. 77–91.

Schydlowsky, Daniel M. A Policymaker's Guide to Comparative Advantage. *World Devel.*, April 1984, 12(4), pp. 439–49.

Shaked, Avner and Sutton, John. Natural Oligopolies and International Trade. In *Kierzkowski, H., ed.*, 1984, pp. 34–50.

Sharma, B. L. Preference Similarity Hypothesis: Survey and Further Empirical Evidence. *Indian Econ. J.*, January–March 1984, 31(3), pp. 79–96. **[G: OECD]**

Siebert, Horst. Allocation Policy in a Resource-Exporting Country. In *Siebert, H., ed.*, 1984, pp. 1–16.

Smith, Alasdair. Capital Theory and Trade Theory. In *Jones, R. W. and Kenen, P., eds.*, 1984, pp. 289–324.

Stewart, Frances. Recent Theories of International Trade: Some Implications for the South. In *Kierzkowski, H., ed.*, 1984, pp. 84–108. **[G: Brazil]**

Svensson, Lars E. O. Factor Trade and Goods Trade. *J. Int. Econ.*, May 1984, 16(3/4), pp. 365–78.

Svensson, Lars E. O. Oil Prices, Welfare, and the Trade Balance. *Quart. J. Econ.*, November 1984, 99(4), pp. 649–72.

Tawada, Makoto. International Trade with a Replenishable Resource: The Steady State Analysis. *Econ. Stud. Quart.*, April 1984, 35(1), pp. 39–45.

Tawada, Makoto and Abe, Kenzo. Production Possibilities and International Trade with a Public Intermediate Good. *Can. J. Econ.*, May 1984, 17(2), pp. 232–48.

Thompson, Henry. International Migration, Non-traded Goods, and Economic Welfare in the Source Country: A Comment. *J. Devel. Econ.*, December 1984, 16(3), pp. 321–24.

Uekawa, Yasuo. Some Theorems of Trade with Joint Production. *J. Int. Econ.*, May 1984, 16(3/4), pp. 319–33.

Vartikar, V. S. International Wage Differentials. *Rivista Int. Sci. Econ. Com.*, January 1984, 31(1), pp. 69–76.

Venables, Anthony J. Multiple Equilibria in the Theory of International Trade with Monopolistically Competitive Commodities. *J. Int. Econ.*, February 1984, 16(1/2), pp. 103–21.

Weale, Martin R. Quantity and Price Effects in an Analysis of World Trade Based on an Accounting Matrix. *Rev. Income Wealth*, March 1984, 30(1), pp. 85–117. **[G: Global]**

Whalley, John and Yeung, Bernard. External Sector 'Closing' Rules in Applied General Equilibrium Models. *J. Int. Econ.*, February 1984, 16(1/2), pp. 123–38.

Winters, L. Alan. Separability and the Specification of Foreign Trade Functions. *J. Int. Econ.*, November 1984, 17(3/4), pp. 239–63. **[G: U.K.]**

Young, Leslie. Uncertainty and the Theory of International Trade in Long-Run Equilibrium. *J. Econ. Theory*, February 1984, 32(1), pp. 67–92.

Zakharov, A. N. and Shagalov, G. L. Methods for Determining the Efficiency of Foreign Economic Relations. *Soviet E. Europ. Foreign Trade*, Spring 1984, 20(1), pp. 76–96.

4113 Theory of Protection

Baldwin, Robert E. Trade Policies in Developed Countries. In *Jones, R. W. and Kenen, P., eds.*, 1984, pp. 571–619.

Bardhan, Pranab K. and Kletzer, Kenneth M. Dynamic Effects of Protection on Productivity. *J. Int. Econ.*, February 1984, 16(1/2), pp. 45–57.

Batra, Raveendra N. Non-traded Goods and the Metzler-Paradox: A Comment. *Int. Econ. Rev.*, October 1984, 25(3), pp. 763–67.

Benassy, Jean-Pascal. Tariffs and Pareto Optimality in International Trade: The Case of Unemployment. *Europ. Econ. Rev.*, December 1984, *26*(3), pp. 261–76.

Benson, Bruce L. and Hartigan, James C. Tariffs and Quotas in a Spatial Duopoly. *Southern Econ. J.*, April 1984, *50*(4), pp. 965–78.

Berlage, L. Commodity Price Stabilization by Buffer Stocks and by Export Quotas. *Tijdschrift Econ. Manage.*, 1984, *29*(3), pp. 437–48. [G: LDCs]

Bhagwati, Jagdish N.; Brecher, Richard A. and Srinivasan, T. N. DUP Activities and Economic Theory. In *Colander, D. C., ed.*, 1984, pp. 17–32.

Bird, Peter J. W. N. The Costs and Benefits of Protection: A Comment. *Kyklos*, 1984, *37*(1), pp. 102–03. [G: U.S.]

Brander, James A. and Spencer, Barbara J. Tariff Protection and Imperfect Competition. In *Kierzkowski, H., ed.*, 1984, pp. 194–206.

Brander, James A. and Spencer, Barbara J. Trade Warfare: Tariffs and Cartels. *J. Int. Econ.*, May 1984, *16*(3/4), pp. 227–42.

Choi, Jai-Young and Yu, Eden S.-H. Customs Unions under Increasing Returns to Scale. *Economica*, May 1984, *51*(202), pp. 195–203.

Choi, Jai-Young and Yu, Eden S.-H. Gains from Trade under Variable Returns to Scale. *Southern Econ. J.*, April 1984, *50*(4), pp. 979–92.

Collinge, Robert A. Generating Optimal Tariffs in the Marketplace. *Econ. J.*, December 1984, *94*(376), pp. 914–23.

Colombatto, Enrico. Riflessioni teoriche su protezionismo, neo-protezionismo e intervento pubblico. (On the Theory of Protectionism, New Protectionism and Public Policy. With English summary.) *Econ. Int.*, August–November 1984, *37*(3–4), pp. 236–54.

Corden, W. M. The Normative Theory of International Trade. In *Jones, R. W. and Kenen, P., eds.*, 1984, pp. 63–130.

Crawford, Vincent P.; Sobel, Joel and Takahashi, Ichiro. Bargaining, Strategic Reserves, and International Trade in Exhaustible Resources. *Amer. J. Agr. Econ.*, November 1984, *66*(4), pp. 472–80.

Curzon, Gerard and Price, Victoria. Is Protection Inevitable? In *Eucken, W. and Böhm, F., eds.*, 1984, pp. 121–36.

Davidson, Carl. Cartel Stability and Tariff Policy. *J. Int. Econ.*, November 1984, *17*(3/4), pp. 219–37.

Deardorff, Alan V. An Exposition and Exploration of Krueger's Trade Model. *Can. J. Econ.*, November 1984, *17*(4), pp. 731–46.

Decaluwe, Bernard and Lee, Y. D. Procédures pour l'estimation des taux de protection effectifs dans les matrices entrées-sorties. (A Procedure to Estimate Effective Rate of Protection Coefficient. With English summary.) *L'Actual. Econ.*, June 1984, *60*(2), pp. 254–62.

Dickinson, D. G.; Driscoll, M. J. and Ford, J. L. Revenue Raising Trade-restricting Policies under Uncertainty: The Sub-optimality of the Expected Welfare Criterion and Some Safety-First Results. *Z. Nationalökon.*, 1984, *44*(4), pp. 387–403.

Diewert, W. Erwin. The Measurement of Deadweight Loss in an Open Economy. *Economica*, February 1984, *51*(201), pp. 23–42.

Dinopoulos, Elias. The Optimal Tariff with Revenue-Seeking: A Contribution to the Theory of DUP Activities. In *Colander, D. C., ed.*, 1984, pp. 129–38.

Dixit, Avinash. International Trade Policy for Oligopolistic Industries. *Econ. J.*, 1984 Supplement, *94*, pp. 1–16.

Eldor, Rafael. On the Risk-Adjusted Effective Protection Rate. *Rev. Econ. Statist.*, May 1984, *66*(2), pp. 235–41. [G: U.S.]

Ethier, Wilfred J. Protection and Real Incomes Once Again. *Quart. J. Econ.*, February 1984, *99*(1), pp. 193–200.

Frey, Bruno S. Die Politische Ökonomie des Protektionismus. Nationalstaatliche Determinanten der Regulierung der internationalen Wirtschafsbeziehungen. (The Political Economics of Protectionism. With English summary.) *Aussenwirtschaft*, May 1984, *39*(1/2), pp. 17–42. [G: U.S.]

Ghosh, Dilip K. Aid or Trade? A Welfare-Theoretic Analysis. In *Ghosh, P. K., ed., no. 16*, 1984, pp. 111–23.

Gibbs, I. and Konovalov, V. Volume Quotas with Heterogeneous Product Categories. *Econ. Rec.*, September 1984, *60*(170), pp. 294–303.

Gray, H. Peter. Employment Arguments for Protection and the Vita Theory. *Eastern Econ. J.*, January–March 1984, *10*(1), pp. 1–13.

Gregory, R. G. Some Implications of the Growth of the Mineral Sector. In *Lloyd, P. J., ed.*, 1984, *1976*, pp. 285–310. [G: Australia]

Grinols, Earl L. Spot Market-Risk Market Interaction and the Protective Effects of a Tariff under Uncertainty. *Econ. J.*, March 1984, *94*(373), pp. 95–103.

Grubel, Herbert G. Free Enterprise Zones in Economic Development. In *Giersch, H., ed.*, 1984, pp. 222–35.

Hager, Wolfgang. North–South Trade and Socioeconomic Autonomy: A Peace Formula. In *Ghosh, P. K., ed., no. 16*, 1984, *1982*, pp. 81–91. [G: EEC]

Harris, Richard G. Applied General Equilibrium Analysis of Small Open Economies with Scale Economies and Imperfect Competition. *Amer. Econ. Rev.*, December 1984, *74*(5), pp. 1016–32. [G: Canada]

Hill, John K. Union Wage Distortions and the Size and Efficiency of the Optimal Tariff. *Can. J. Econ.*, February 1984, *17*(1), pp. 146–55. [G: U.S.]

Hillman, Arye L. and Katz, Eliakim. Excise Taxes, Import Restrictions, and the Allocation of Time to Illegal Income-earning Activity. *Int. Rev. Law Econ.*, December 1984, *4*(2), pp. 213–22.

Hoffmann, Lutz. Free Enterprise Zones in Economic Development: Comment. In *Giersch, H., ed.*, 1984, pp. 242–48.

Itoh, Motoshige and Ono, Yoshiyasu. Tariffs vs. Quotas under Duopoly of Heterogeneous Goods. *J. Int. Econ.*, November 1984, *17*(3/4), pp. 359–73.

Jones, Kent. The Political Economy of Voluntary Export Restraint Agreements. *Kyklos*, 1984, *37*(1), pp. 82–101.

Karp, Larry. Optimality and Consistency in a Differential Game with Non-renewable Resources. *J. Econ. Dynam. Control*, October 1984, *8*(1), pp. 73–97.

Kemp, Murray C. and Long, Ngo Van. The Optimal Restriction of Resource Imports and the Optimal Investment in Capacity for Substitute Production. In *Kemp, M. C. and Long, N. V., eds.*, 1984, pp. 145–60.

Khan, M. Ali. International Trade and Foreign Investment: A Model with Asymmetric Production. *Pakistan Devel. Rev.*, Winter 1984, *23*(4), pp. 509–30.

Kimbrough, Kent P. Commercial Policy and Aggregate Employment under Rational Expectations. *Quart. J. Econ.*, August 1984, *99*(3), pp. 567–85.

Kohli, Ulrich R. Terms of Trade and Welfare: Estimates. *Kyklos*, 1984, *37*(4), pp. 577–97. [G: U.S.; Canada; Australia; Switzerland]

Kostecki, Michel M. Can Tariff Be Effective under Central Planning? *Econ. Int.*, February–May 1984, *37*(1–2), pp. 94–107.

Krueger, Anne O. Problems of Liberalization. In *Harberger, A. C., ed.*, 1984, pp. 403–23.

Krueger, Anne O. Trade Policies in Developing Countries. In *Jones, R. W. and Kenen, P., eds.*, 1984, pp. 519–69. [G: Selected LDCs]

Krugman, Paul R. Import Protection as Export Promotion: International Competition in the Presence of Oligopoly and Economics of Scale. In *Kierzkowski, H., ed.*, 1984, pp. 180–93.

Lancaster, Kelvin. Protection and Product Differentiation. In *Kierzkowski, H., ed.*, 1984, pp. 137–56.

Larcarte, Julio A. Aspects of International Trade and Assistance Relating to the Expansion of Employment in the Developing Countries. In *Ghosh, P. K., ed., no. 16*, 1984, *1972*, pp. 124–51.

Lizondo, Jose Saul. A Note on the Nonequivalence of Import Barriers and Voluntary Export Restraints. *J. Int. Econ.*, February 1984, *16*(1/2), pp. 183–87.

Lucas, Robert E. B. On the Theory of DRC Criteria. *J. Devel. Econ.*, April 1984, *14*(3), pp. 407–17.

Magee, Stephen P. Endogenous Tariff Theory: A Survey. In *Colander, D. C., ed.*, 1984, pp. 41–51.

Maizels, Alfred. International Commodity Agreements. In *Csikós-Nagy, B.; Hague, D. and Hall, G., eds.*, 1984, pp. 491–520.

Markusen, James R. The Welfare and Allocative Effects of Export Taxes versus Marketing Boards. *J. Devel. Econ.*, January–February 1984, *14*(1–2), pp. 19–36.

Martin, Lawrence W. and Panagariya, Arvind. Smuggling, Trade, and Price Disparity: A Crime-Theoretic Approach. *J. Int. Econ.*, November 1984, *17*(3/4), pp. 201–17.

Mayer, Wolfgang. Endogenous Tariff Formation. *Amer. Econ. Rev.*, December 1984, *74*(5), pp. 970–85.

Mayer, Wolfgang. The Infant-Export Industry Argument. *Can. J. Econ.*, May 1984, *17*(2), pp. 249–69.

Ono, Yoshiyasu. Profitability of Export Restraint. *J. Int. Econ.*, May 1984, *16*(3/4), pp. 335–43. [G: OPEC]

Piron, Robert. On Believing the Impossible in Economics. *Challenge*, September/October 1984, *27*(4), pp. 49–51.

Porter, Robert H. Tariff Policies in a Small Open Spatial Economy. *Can. J. Econ.*, May 1984, *17*(2), pp. 270–82.

Rossini, Gianpaolo. Intraindustry Trade and Tariffs: New Wave or Old Fashion? *Econ. Int.*, February–May 1984, *37*(1–2), pp. 130–48. [G: W. Europe]

Rousslang, Donald J. and Young, Philip M. Calculating the Short-Run Welfare Effects of a Tariff Reduction When Wages Are Rigid. *Can. J. Econ.*, February 1984, *17*(1), pp. 39–47.

Ryszkiewicz, Alicja. Norms of Distribution and Protection and Restrictions on Exports and Imports in the Central Plan. *Soviet E. Europ. Foreign Trade*, Spring 1984, *20*(1), pp. 36–56.

Snape, R. H. Effects of Mineral Development on the Economy. In *Lloyd, P. J., ed.*, 1984, 1977, pp. 311–22. [G: Australia]

Spinanger, Dean. Free Enterprise Zones in Economic Development: Comment. In *Giersch, H., ed.*, 1984, pp. 236–41. [G: LDCs]

Stegemann, Klaus. The Social Costs of Monopoly in an Open Economy. *Can. J. Econ.*, November 1984, *17*(4), pp. 718–30.

Stegemann, Klaus. Trade Policy to Promote Entry with Scale Economies: Orthodoxy Restored. *Can. J. Econ.*, November 1984, *17*(4), pp. 774–77.

Thompson, Velma Montoya. The Benefits of Domestic Investment Subsidies and Taxes to Exports in Common Market Countries. *De Economist*, 1984, *132*(1), pp. 61–74. [G: EEC; Netherlands]

Tower, Edward. On a Quick and Dirty Approach to Estimating Second Best Optimum Tariffs. *Rivista Int. Sci. Econ. Com.*, March 1984, *31*(3), pp. 212–19.

Tower, Edward. On the Functional Relationship between Distortions and Welfare. *Atlantic Econ. J.*, March 1984, *12*(1), pp. 65–66.

Wagstaff, Peter. The Cost of Maximum Revenue Trade Taxes. *Economica*, February 1984, *51*(201), pp. 43–52. [G: LDCs]

Webb, Michael. A Theoretical Note on Quota-Reduction Negotiations. *Oxford Econ. Pap.*, June 1984, *36*(2), pp. 288–90.

van Wijnbergen, Sweder. Oil Price Shocks and the Current Account: An Analysis of Short Run Adjustment Measures. *Weltwirtsch. Arch.*, 1984, *120*(3), pp. 460–80. [G: OPEC; LDCs]

Yeh, Yeong-Her. Tariffs vs. Consumption Taxes. *Atlantic Econ. J.*, July 1984, *12*(2), pp. 76.

Zablotsky, Edgardo Enrique. Shocks versus gradualismo: la trayectoria optima de reducción arancelaria. (With English summary.) *Cuadernos Econ.*, December 1984, *21*(64), pp. 263–77.

Zalai, Ernö. Economic Reform, Allocative Efficiency, and Terms of Trade. *Acta Oecon.*, 1984, *33*(3–4), pp. 255–71.

Zylbersztajn, Decio. Price Distortions in Brazilian Agriculture: An Application of Duality Theory and Flexible Functional Forms. *Amer. Econ.*, Fall 1984, *28*(2), pp. 48–59. **[G: Brazil]**

4114 Theory of International Trade and Economic Development

Adelman, Irma. Beyond Export-led Growth. *World Devel.*, September 1984, *12*(9), pp. 937–49. **[G: S. Korea]**

Alam, M. Shahid. Import Substitution Growth: A Simple Intersectoral Analysis. *Philippine Econ. J.*, Winter 1984, *23*(1), pp. 157–60.

Alam, M. Shahid. Import Substitution Growth: A Simple Intersection Analysis. *Pakistan J. Appl. Econ.*, Winter 1984, *3*(2), pp. 157–60.

Bacha, Edmar L. Growth with Limited Supplies of Foreign Exchange: A Reappraisal of the Two-Gap Model. In *[Chenery, H. B.]*, 1984, pp. 263–80.

Bienefeld, Manfred. International Constraints and Opportunities. In *Fransman, M. and King, K., eds.*, 1984, pp. 161–73. **[G: Global]**

Buffie, Edward F. The Macroeconomics of Trade Liberalization. *J. Int. Econ.*, August 1984, *17*(1/2), pp. 121–37. **[G: LDCs]**

Burgstaller, A. and Saavedra-Rivano, Neantro. Capital Mobility and Growth in a North–South Model. *J. Devel. Econ.*, May–June–August 1984, *15*(1,2,3), pp. 213–37.

Chichilnisky, Graciela. North–South Trade and Export-led Policies [Terms of Trade and Domestic Distribution: Export-led Growth with Abundant Labour]. *J. Devel. Econ.*, May–June–August 1984, *15*(1,2,3), pp. 131–60. **[G: U.K.; Sri Lanka]**

Chichilnisky, Graciela. Terms of Trade, Domestic Distribution and Export-led Growth: A Rejoinder to Rejoinders. *J. Devel. Econ.*, May–June–August 1984, *15*(1,2,3), pp. 177–84.

Dixit, Avinash. Growth and Terms of Trade under Imperfect Competition. In *Kierzkowski, H., ed.*, 1984, pp. 109–23.

Dos Santos, Theotonio. The Structure of Dependence. In *Seligson, M. A., ed.*, 1984, *1970*, pp. 95–104.

Evans, David. A Critical Assessment of Some Neo-Marxian Trade Theories. *J. Devel. Stud.*, January 1984, *20*(2), pp. 202–26.

Evans, David and Alizadeh, Parvin. Trade, Industrialisation, and the Visible Hand. *J. Devel. Stud.*, October 1984, *21*(1), pp. 22–46. **[G: S. Korea; Taiwan]**

Evans, David and Alizadeh, Parvin. Trade, Industrialisation, and the Visible Hand. In *Kaplinsky, R., ed.*, 1984, pp. 22–46. **[G: Selected LDCs]**

Ewing, A. F. The Assault on Development Economics: Consequences for Intergovernmental Co-operation. *J. World Trade Law*, May–June 1984, *18*(3), pp. 187–205.

Faini, Riccardo. Increasing Returns, Non-Traded Inputs and Regional Development. *Econ. J.*, June 1984, *94*(374), pp. 308–23.

Findlay, Ronald. A Comment on 'North–South Trade and Export-led Policies' [Terms of Trade and Domestic Distribution: Export-led Growth with Abundant Labour]. *J. Devel. Econ.*, May–June–August 1984, *15*(1,2,3), pp. 161–67.

Findlay, Ronald. Growth and Development in Trade Models. In *Jones, R. W. and Kenen, P., eds.*, 1984, pp. 185–236.

Fishlow, Albert. Summary Comment on Adelman, Balassa and Streeten [Beyond Export-Led Growth] [Adjustment Policies in Developing Countries: A Reassessment] [Basic Needs: Some Unsettled Questions]. *World Devel.*, September 1984, *12*(9), pp. 979–82.

Ghosh, Dilip K. Aid or Trade? A Welfare-Theoretic Analysis. In *Ghosh, P. K., ed., no. 16*, 1984, pp. 111–23.

Glezakos, Constantine. Export Instability and Economic Growth: Reply. *Econ. Develop. Cult. Change*, April 1984, *32*(3), pp. 615–23. **[G: LDCs; MDCs]**

Gregory, R. G. Some Implications of the Growth of the Mineral Sector. In *Lloyd, P. J., ed.*, 1984, *1976*, pp. 285–310. **[G: Australia]**

Grossman, Gene M. International Trade, Foreign Investment, and the Formation of the Entrepreneurial Class. *Amer. Econ. Rev.*, September 1984, *74*(4), pp. 605–14.

Gunning, Jan Willem. Comparative Statics, Stability and Optimal Trade Policy [Terms of Trade and Domestic Distribution: Export-led Growth with Abundant Labour]. *J. Devel. Econ.*, May–June–August 1984, *15*(1,2,3), pp. 169–72.

Gunning, Jan Willem. Export-led Growth with Abundant Labour: A Defense of Orthodoxy. *J. Devel. Econ.*, May–June–August 1984, *15*(1,2,3), pp. 97–103.

Heal, Geoffrey and McLeod, Darryl. Gains from Trade, Stability and Profits: A Comment on Chichilnisky's 'Terms of Trade and Domestic Distribution: Export-led Growth with Abundant Labour.' *J. Devel. Econ.*, May–June–August 1984, *15*(1,2,3), pp. 117–30.

Hicks, Norman L. A Model of Trade and Growth for the Developing World. In *Ghosh, P. K., ed., no. 16*, 1984, *1976*, pp. 92–110. **[G: LDCs]**

Hughes, Helen. Industrializing Small Countries. *Industry Devel.*, 1984, (12), pp. 89–99.

Kaplinsky, Raphael. The International Context for Industrialisation in the Coming Decade. In *Kaplinsky, R., ed.*, 1984, pp. 75–96.

Kavoussi, Rostam M. Export Expansion and Economic Growth: Further Empirical Evidence. *J. Devel. Econ.*, January–February 1984, *14*(1–2), pp. 241–50. **[G: LDCs]**

Kessler, Denis. Foreign Indebtedness, Savings and Growth in Developing Countries. In *Kess-*

ler, D. and Ullmo, P.-A., *eds.*, 1984, pp. 351–63.

Kierzkowski, Henryk. Monopolistic Competition and International Trade: Introduction. In *Kierzkowski, H.*, *ed.*, 1984, pp. 1–9.

Kindleberger, Charles P. Multinationals and the Small Open Economy. In *Kindleberger, C. P.*, 1984, *1980*, pp. 102–17.

Krueger, Anne O. Comparative Advantage and Development Policy 20 Years Later. In *[Chenery, H. B.]*, 1984, pp. 135–56. **[G: LDCs; MDCs]**

Krueger, Anne O. Trade Strategies and Employment in Developing Countries. *Finance Develop.*, June 1984, *21*(2), pp. 23–26. **[G: Selected LDCs]**

Krueger, Anne O. and Tuncer, Baran. An Empirical Test of the Infant Industry Argument: Reply. *Amer. Econ. Rev.*, December 1984, *74*(5), pp. 1112–13. **[G: Turkey]**

Larcarte, Julio A. Aspects of International Trade and Assistance Relating to the Expansion of Employment in the Developing Countries. In *Ghosh, P. K.*, *ed.*, *no. 16*, 1984, *1972*, pp. 124–51.

Leo, Hooi-Eng. Effects of Trade Policies on the Structure and Growth of Manufacturing Industries in Peninsular Malaysia: 1960–1980. *Philippine Rev. Econ. Bus.*, Sept./Dec. 1984, *21*(3/4), pp. 219–38. **[G: Malaysia]**

Loser, Claudio M. The Role of Economy-Wide Prices in the Adjustment Process. In *Muns, J.*, *ed.*, 1984, pp. 84–109. **[G: LDCs]**

Lucas, Robert E. B. An Empirical Test of the Infant Industry Argument: Comment. *Amer. Econ. Rev.*, December 1984, *74*(5), pp. 1110–11. **[G: Turkey]**

Myint, Hla. Exports and Economic Development of Less Developed Countries. In *Eicher, C. K. and Staatz, J. M.*, *eds.*, 1984, *1971*, pp. 222–40.

Myint, Hla. Inward and Outward-Looking Countries Revisited: The Case of Indonesia. *Bull. Indonesian Econ. Stud.*, August 1984, *20*(2), pp. 39–52. **[G: Indonesia]**

Ranney, Susan I. International Capital Transfers and the Choice of Production Technique: A Simple Two-Country Model. *J. Int. Econ.*, August 1984, *17*(1/2), pp. 85–99.

Ranney, Susan I. Terms of Trade and Domestic Distribution: A Comment. *J. Devel. Econ.*, May–June–August 1984, *15*(1,2,3), pp. 89–96.

Riedel, James. Trade as the Engine of Growth in Developing Countries, Revisited. *Econ. J.*, March 1984, *94*(373), pp. 56–73.

Saavedra-Rivano, Neantro. Terms of Trade and Domestic Distribution: A Comment. *J. Devel. Econ.*, May–June–August 1984, *15*(1,2,3), pp. 105–10.

Samli, A. Coskun. Role of Marketing in Economic Development: What Should International Marketers Know? In *Kaynak, E.*, *ed.*, 1984, pp. 34–50.

Savvides, Andreas. Export Instability and Economic Growth: Some New Evidence. *Econ. Develop. Cult. Change*, April 1984, *32*(3), pp. 607–14. **[G: LDCs; MDCs]**

Schmitz, Hubert. Industrialisation Strategies in Less Developed Countries: Some Lessons of Historical Experience. In *Kaplinsky, R.*, *ed.*, 1984, pp. 1–21.

Scitovsky, Tibor. Beyond Export-Led Growth: Comment. *World Devel.*, September 1984, *12*(9), pp. 953–54.

Singer, Hans W. Industrialization: Where Do We Stand? Where Are We Going? *Industry Devel.*, 1984, (12), pp. 79–87.

Snape, R. H. Effects of Mineral Development on the Economy. In *Lloyd, P. J.*, *ed.*, 1984, *1977*, pp. 311–22. **[G: Australia]**

Spechler, Martin and Tovias, Alfred. When Should Developing Countries Use Bilateral State Trading? *World Devel.*, November–December 1984, *12*(11–12), pp. 1077–86. **[G: LDCs]**

Spinanger, Dean. Objectives and Impact of Economic Activity Zones—Some Evidence from Asia. *Weltwirtsch. Arch.*, 1984, *120*(1), pp. 64–89. **[G: Asia]**

Spraos, John. On the Commodity Power of Less Developed Countries. *J. Post Keynesian Econ.*, Summer 1984, *6*(4), pp. 605–13. **[G: LDCs]**

Srinivasan, T. N. and Bhagwati, Jagdish N. A Rejoinder [Terms of Trade and Domestic Distribution: Export-led Growth with Abundant Labour]. *J. Devel. Econ.*, May–June–August 1984, *15*(1,2,3), pp. 173–75.

Srinivasan, T. N. and Bhagwati, Jagdish N. On Transfer Paradoxes and Immiserizing Growth: Part II [Terms of Trade and Domestic Distribution: Export-led Growth with Abundant Labour]. *J. Devel. Econ.*, May–June–August 1984, *15*(1,2,3), pp. 111–15.

Stewart, Frances. Recent Theories of International Trade: Some Implications for the South. In *Kierzkowski, H.*, *ed.*, 1984, pp. 84–108. **[G: Brazil]**

Szychowski, Mario L. and Perazzo, Alfredo C. Protección efectiva y costo doméstico de la divisa: Comparación de su eficiencia en el cumplimiento de objetivos alternativos. (Effective Protection and Domestic Resource Cost: comparison about Their Efficiency in the Achievement of Alternatives Objectives. With English summary.) *Económica*, May-December 1984, *30*(2–3), pp. 217–44. **[G: Argentina]**

Tisdell, Clem A. and Fairbairn, T'eo Ian. Subsistence Economies and Unsustainable Development and Trade: Some Simple Theory. *J. Devel. Stud.*, January 1984, *20*(2), pp. 227–41. **[G: S. Pacific]**

Waelbroeck, Jean. Capital, Foreign Exchange, and Growth: The Two-Gap and Labor-Income-Floor Views. In *[Chenery, H. B.]*, 1984, pp. 281–94.

Wagstaff, Peter. The Cost of Maximum Revenue Trade Taxes. *Economica*, February 1984, *51*(201), pp. 43–52. **[G: LDCs]**

Watanabe, Taro. Industrial Policy and Trade Theory (Part I). *Osaka Econ. Pap.*, March 1984, *33*(3–4), pp. 1–11.

Wellisz, Stanislaw and Findlay, Ronald. Protection and Rent-Seeking in Developing Countries. In *Colander, D. C., ed.*, 1984, pp. 141–53. [G: LDCs]

420 TRADE RELATIONS; COMMERCIAL POLICY; INTERNATIONAL ECONOMIC INTEGRATION

4200 General

Adams, John. Foreign Economic Policy: Challenges of the 1980s. *J. Econ. Issues*, March 1984, *18*(1), pp. 275–94. [G: U.S.]

Bhagwati, Jagdish N. Power Passions and Purpose: Prospects for North–South Negotiations: Introduction. In *Bhagwati, J. N. and Ruggie, J. G., eds.*, 1984, pp. 1–18.

Bhagwati, Jagdish N. Rethinking Global Negotiations. In *Bhagwati, J. N. and Ruggie, J. G., eds.*, 1984, pp. 21–31.

Boyd, Gavin. Foreign Economic and Security Policies. In *Boyd, G., ed.*, 1984, pp. 1–23.

Boyd, Gavin. Political Designing for Pacific Cooperation. In *Downen, R. L. and Dickson, B. J., eds.*, 1984, pp. 57–65.
[G: Pacific Basin]

Capria, Nicola. The Italian Experience. In *Achilli, M. and Khaldi, M., eds.*, 1984, pp. 294–99. [G: Italy]

Chichilnisky, Graciela. Basic Needs, Exhaustible Resources and Growth in a North–South Context. In *Ghosh, P. K., ed., no. 13*, 1984, *1982*, pp. 158–72.

Delson, Roberta M. Sugar Production for the Nineteenth Century British Market: Rethinking the Roles of Brazil and the British West Indies. In *Albert, B. and Graves, A., eds.*, 1984, pp. 59–80. [G: Brazil; Caribbean; U.K.]

Díaz-Alejandro, Carlos F. Some Financial Issues in the North, in the South, and in Between. In *Agmon, T.; Hawkins, R. G. and Levich, R. M., eds.*, 1984, pp. 119–45.

Dubey, Muchkund. A Third-World Perspective. In *Bhagwati, J. N. and Ruggie, J. G., eds.*, 1984, pp. 65–86.

Fikentscher, Wolfgang. Third World Trade Partnership: Supranational Authority vs. National Extraterritorial Antitrust—A Plea for "Harmonized" Regionalism. *Mich. Law Rev.*, April–May 1984, *82*(5 & 6), pp. 1489–1509.

Frey, Bruno S. and Schneider, Friedrich. International Political Economy: A Rising Field. *Econ. Int.*, August–November 1984, *37*(3–4), pp. 308–47. [G: Global]

Gbetibouo, Mathurin and Delgado, Christopher L. Lessons and Constraints of Export Crop-Led Growth: Cocoa in Ivory Coast. In *Zartman, I. W. and Delgado, C. L., eds.*, 1984, pp. 115–47. [G: Ivory Coast]

Groenewegen, John and van Paridon, Kees. *John Groenewegen and Kees van Paridon:* Conference of the Dutch Study Circle on Post-Keynesian Economics on "International Keynesianism," September 1983. *J. Econ. Issues*, March 1984, *18*(1), pp. 315–23. [G: Global]

Hamilton, Bob and Whalley, John. Efficiency and

Distributional Implications of Global Restrictions on Labour Mobility: Calculations and Policy Implications. *J. Devel. Econ.*, January–February 1984, *14*(1–2), pp. 61–75.
[G: Global]

Hoyos, Georges. A New Approach to North–South Co-operation. In *Achilli, M. and Khaldi, M., eds.*, 1984, pp. 145–54.

Khader, Bichara. The Afro–Arab Alliance: an Economic Strategy for the 1980s. In *Achilli, M. and Khaldi, M., eds.*, 1984, pp. 155–93.
[G: OECD; Arab Countries; LDCs]

Krueger, Anne O. The Developing Countries' Role in the World Economy. In *Frenkel, J. A. and Mussa, M. L., eds.*, 1984, pp. 63–83.
[G: LDCs]

Lévai, Imre. Capitalist International Trade: The Contradiction of Equality and Reciprocity. In *Ngo, M., ed., vol. 1*, 1984, pp. 68–78.
[G: LDCs; MDCs]

Lindbeck, Assar. The International Economic Environment and Industrialization Possibilities in Developing Countries. *Industry Devel.*, 1984, (12), pp. 9–42.

Lozoya, Jorge. The Pacific Basin: The Future of a Concept. In *Downen, R. L. and Dickson, B. J., eds.*, 1984, pp. 45–55.
[G: Pacific Basin]

Ohlin, Goran. The Second Chapter in North–South Relations. *Industry Devel.*, 1984, (12), pp. 69–77.

Owen, Henry. The World Economy: The Dollar and the Summit. *Foreign Aff.*, Winter 1984/85, *63*(2), pp. 344–59. [G: OECD]

Paliwoda, Stanley J. East–West Trade Relations and International Marketing Strategy Formulation. In *Kaynak, E., ed.*, 1984, pp. 286–304.

Palmer, Ransford W. Restructuring the Economic Institutions of the Eastern Caribbean. In *Palmer, R. W.*, 1984, pp. 59–65.
[G: E. Caribbean]

Prebisch, Raúl. The Global Crisis of Capitalism and Its Theoretical Background. *Cepal Rev.*, April 1984, (22), pp. 159–78. [G: Global]

de Vries, Barend A. Exports in the New World Environment: The Case of Latin America. In *Ghosh, P. K., ed., no. 16*, 1984, *1977*, pp. 333–76. [G: Latin America]

Wiarda, Howard J. Cancún and After: The United States and the Developing World. In *Wiarda, H. J.*, 1984, *1982*, pp. 1–11.

Wickes, R. J. The New International Economic Order: Progress and Prospects. In *Ghosh, P. K., ed., no. 9*, 1984, *1980*, pp. 66–99.
[G: OECD; Taiwan; Mexico; Brazil; India]

421 Trade Relations

4210 Trade Relations

Abel, Martin E. and Waugh, Frederick V. Measuring Changes in International Trade. In *Waugh, F. V.*, 1984, *1966*, pp. 353–67.
[G: Global]

Acciaris, Ricardo. Cuba's Economic Relations with Latin America and the Caribbean. *Soviet*

E. Europ. Foreign Trade, Fall 1984, *20*(3), pp. 6–77. **[G: Cuba; Latin America]**

Adams, Nassau A. Towards a Global System of Trade Preferences Among Developing Countries. In *Ghosh, P. K., ed., no. 16*, 1984, *1982*, pp. 57–80. **[G: LDCs]**

Adler, Svjetlana and Matejka, Harriet. Soviet Coal Exports. In *Kostecki, M. M., ed.*, 1984, pp. 100–15. **[G: U.S.S.R.; Global]**

Aggarwal, Mangat Ram. Devaluation, Determinants of International Trade Flows and Payments Imbalances. *Indian Econ. J.*, January–March 1984, *31*(3), pp. 24–33. **[G: LDCs]**

Akhtar, M. A. and Hilton, R. Spence. Effects of Exchange Rate Uncertainy on German and U.S. Trade. *Fed. Res. Bank New York Quart. Rev.*, Spring 1984, *9*(1), pp. 7–16. **[G: U.S.; Germany]**

Ali, Ifzal. Estimating the Determinants of Export Supply in India. *Indian Econ. J.*, January–March 1984, *31*(3), pp. 1–12. **[G: India]**

Amsden, Alice H. Exports of Technology by Newly Industrializing Countries: Taiwan. *World Devel.*, May/June 1984, *12*(5/6), pp. 491–503. **[G: Taiwan]**

Anderson, Kym and Ahn, In-Chan. Protection Policy and Changing Comparative Advantage in Korean Agriculture. *Food Res. Inst. Stud.*, 1984, *19*(2), pp. 139–51. **[G: S. Korea]**

Anderson, Kym and Tyers, Rodney. European Community Grain and Meat Policies: Effects on International Prices, Trade and Welfare. *Europ. Rev. Agr. Econ.*, 1984, *11*(4), pp. 367–94. **[G: EEC]**

Andersson, Jan Otto. Intraindustriell handel och produktcykler i Finlands utrikeshandel 1965–80. (Intra-industry Trade and Product Cycles in the Finnish Foreign Trade in 1965–80. With English summary.) *Ekon. Samfundets Tidskr.*, 1984, *37*(3), pp. 153–62. **[G: Finland; OECD]**

Angelis, Ivan. A Forecast of the External Conditions for the Development of the Czechoslovak National Economy (The Outlook until the Year 2000). *Czech. Econ. Pap.*, 1984, (22), pp. 43–56. **[G: Czechoslovakia]**

Anton, Ion. Promotion of Romanian Machine-Tools to the United States: A Marketing Mix Approach. In *Jackson, M. R. and Woodson, J. D., Jr., eds.*, 1984, pp. 187–95. **[G: U.S.; Romania]**

Apostolakis, Bobby E. Substitution between Imports and Primary Inputs in the Netherlands, 1953–1977. *Eastern Econ. J.*, January-March 1984, *10*(1), pp. 43–50. **[G: Netherlands]**

Arce, Horacio. The Trade Liberalization Policy of Argentina: Its Impact on Latin American Integration. In *Núñez del Arco, J.; Margain, E. and Cherol, R., eds.*, 1984, pp. 280–314. **[G: Argentina]**

Archer, Brian. Tourism and the British Economy. *Rivista Int. Sci. Econ. Com.*, July 1984, *31*(7), pp. 596–613. **[G: U.K.]**

Ardeni, Pier Giorgio and Paris, Quirino. Un modello di importazione e di esportazione dei prodotti farinacei. (A Model for Import–Export of

Wheat Products. With English summary.) *Statistica*, April–June 1984, *44*(2), pp. 301–27. **[G: Italy]**

Ariah, T. and Daanoune, A. Development of and Prospects for Trade and Economic Co-operation between Morocco and the Socialist Countries of Eastern Europe. In *U.N.C.T.D.*, 1984, pp. 33–43. **[G: Morocco; CMEA]**

Arndt, Heinz W. Measuring Trade in Financial Services. *Banca Naz. Lavoro Quart. Rev.*, June 1984, (149), pp. 197–213.

Artus, Patrick. Analyse du marché des biens dans les secteurs industriels. (An Analysis of the Disequilibrium on the Markets for Manufactured Goods. With English summary.) *Ann. INSEE*, July–December 1984, (55/56), pp. 77–107. **[G: France]**

Atsain, Achi. Regional Economic Integration and Foreign Policy. In *Zartman, I. W. and Delgado, C. L., eds.*, 1984, pp. 175–218. **[G: Ivory Coast; W. Africa]**

Azhar, Rauf A. and Mahmud, Fakhre. Social Profitability of Alternative Rice Varieties in Pakistan: Basmati vs. IRRI. *Philippine Econ. J.*, Winter 1984, *23*(1), pp. 139–56. **[G: Pakistan]**

Azhar, Rauf A. and Mahmud, Fakhre. Social Profitability of Alternative Rice Varieties in Pakistan: Basmati vs. IRRI. *Pakistan J. Appl. Econ.*, Winter 1984, *3*(2), pp. 139–56. **[G: Pakistan]**

Bach, Christopher L. U.S. International Transactions, Fourth Quarter and Year 1983. *Surv. Curr. Bus.*, March 1984, *64*(3), pp. 38–66. **[G: U.S.]**

Baer, Werner and Birch, Melissa H. Expansion of the Economic Frontier: Paraguayan Growth in the 1970s. *World Devel.*, August 1984, *12*(8), pp. 783–98. **[G: Paraguay]**

Balassa, Bela. Adjustment Policies in Developing Countries: A Reassessment. *World Devel.*, September 1984, *12*(9), pp. 955–72. **[G: LDCs]**

Balassa, Bela. The Policy Experience of Twelve Less Developed Countries, 1973–1979. In *[Reynolds, L. G.]*, 1984, pp. 96–123. **[G: Selected LDCs]**

Balassa, Bela. Trade between Developed and Developing Countries: The Decade Ahead. *OECD Econ. Stud.*, Autumn 1984, (3), pp. 7–25. **[G: LDCs; OECD]**

Balassa, Bela and Balassa, Carol. Industrial Protection in the Developed Countries. *World Econ.*, June 1984, *7*(2), pp. 179–96. **[G: U.S.; Japan; EEC]**

Baldwin, Robert E. and Hilton, R. Spence. A Technique for Indicating Comparative Costs and Predicting Changes in Trade Ratios. *Rev. Econ. Statist.*, February 1984, *66*(1), pp. 105–10. **[G: Selected Countries]**

Ban, Kanemi and Nakamura, Jirou. A Simplified Japan–U.S. Energy Linkage Model. *Osaka Econ. Pap.*, March 1984, *33*(3–4), pp. 81–94. **[G: Japan; U.S.]**

Baretje, René. La contribution nette du tourisme international à la balance des paiements. (The

Net Contribution of International Tourism to the Balance of Payments. With English summary.) *Rivista Int. Sci. Econ. Com.*, July 1984, *31*(7), pp. 649–74. [G: OECD]

Barnouin, Jack P. Trade and Economic Cooperation Among Developing Countries. In *Ghosh, P. K., ed., no. 16*, 1984, *1982*, pp. 37–43. [G: LDCs]

Barnouin, Jack P. Trade and Economic Cooperation Among Developing Countries. In *Ghosh, P. K., ed., no. 15*, 1984, *1982*, pp. 239–47. [G: LDCs]

Barriga, Enrique G. Relative Oil Prices and Oil Pricing Policy in Mexico. In *Csikós-Nagy, B.; Hague, D. and Hall, G., eds.*, 1984, pp. 219–37. [G: Mexico]

Barták, Vlastislav. Treatment of the Economic Maladies of Capitalism. *Czech. Econ. Digest.*, June 1984, (4), pp. 90–101. [G: U.S.; EEC; Japan]

Batten, Dallas S. and Belongia, Michael T. The Recent Decline in Agricultural Exports: Is the Exchange Rate the Culprit? *Fed. Res. Bank St. Louis Rev.*, October 1984, *66*(8), pp. 5–14. [G: U.S.]

Bautista, Romeo M. The Pacific Community Environment and Economic Policy in the Philippines. In *Benjamin, R. and Kudrle, R. T.*, 1984, pp. 105–25. [G: Philippines; Selected Countries]

Baysan, Tercan. Resource Shifts under Tariff Liberalization and Turkey's Comparative Advantage in Agriculture. *Europ. Rev. Agr. Econ.*, 1984, *11*(3), pp. 303–22. [G: Turkey]

Baysan, Tercan. Some Economic Aspects of Turkey's Accession to the EC: Resource Shifts, Comparative Advantage, and Static Gains. *J. Common Market Stud.*, September 1984, *23*(1), pp. 15–34. [G: Turkey; EEC]

Behrman, Jere R. The Importance of Supply and Demand Variations in Earnings Instability: Comment. *Econ. Develop. Cult. Change*, October 1984, *33*(1), pp. 167–70.

Bej, Emil. The CMEA in the 1970's: Commercial Activities and the Patterns of Trade. *Rivista Int. Sci. Econ. Com.*, May 1984, *31*(5), pp. 452–75. [G: EEC]

Bélisle, François J. Food Production and Tourism in Jamaica: Obstacles to Increasing Local Food Supplies to Hotels. *J. Devel. Areas*, October 1984, *19*(1), pp. 1–20. [G: Jamaica]

Bélisle, François J. Tourism and Food Imports: The Case of Jamaica. *Econ. Develop. Cult. Change*, July 1984, *32*(4), pp. 819–42. [G: Jamaica]

Benedict, Philip. Rouen's Foreign Trade during the Era of the Religious Wars (1560–1600). *J. Europ. Econ. Hist.*, Spring 1984, *13*(1), pp. 29–74. [G: France]

Bhagavan, M. R. Angola. In *O'Keefe, P. and Munslow, B., eds., Part I*, 1984, pp. 5–63. [G: Angola]

Bitros, George C. Trade Credit and the Transmission of International Disturbances in a Small Open Economy Context. *Greek Econ. Rev.*, April 1984, *6*(1), pp. 5–30. [G: Greece]

Blanchard, Olivier J. Macroeconomic Policy Coordination among the Industrial Economies: Comments. *Brookings Pap. Econ. Act.*, 1984, (1), pp. 65–68. [G: U.S.; W. Germany; Japan]

Blitzer, Charles R. Energy Demand in Jordan: A Case Study of Energy–Economy Linkages. *Energy J.*, October 1984, *5*(4), pp. 1–19. [G: Jordan]

Bloomfield, Arthur I. Effect of Growth on the Terms of Trade: Some Earlier Views. *Economica*, May 1984, *51*(202), pp. 187–93.

Bolyard, Joan E. International Travel and Passenger Fares, 1983. *Surv. Curr. Bus.*, May 1984, *64*(5), pp. 11–15. [G: U.S.]

Bomhoff, Eduard J. North Sea Oil and Manufacturing Output: Comment. In *Griffiths, B. and Wood, G. E., eds.*, 1984, pp. 200–04. [G: U.K.; Selected Countries]

Bourne, Compton and Joefield-Napier, Wallace. Export Performance and Prospects for the Commonwealth Caribbean. In *Salazar-Carrillo, J. and Tirado de Alonso, I., eds., no. 2*, 1984, pp. 1–26. [G: Caribbean]

Bourne, Compton and Joefield-Napier, Wallace. Export Performance and Prospects for the Commonwealth Caribbean. In *Jorge, A.; Salazar-Carrillo, J. and Sanchez, E. P.*, 1984, pp. 47–59. [G: Caribbean]

Bowen, Harry P. and Pelzman, Joseph. U.S. Export Competitiveness: 1962–77. *Appl. Econ.*, June 1984, *16*(3), pp. 461–73. [G: U.S.; Global]

Bradford, Colin I., Jr. World Economic Outlook and the Prospects for U.S. Exports to Latin America. In *Jorge, A.; Salazar-Carrillo, J. and Sanchez, E. P.*, 1984, pp. 121–25. [G: Global]

Brakman, S.; Jepma, C. J. and Kuipers, S. K. On Export Performance and Export Elasticities: A Reply. *De Economist*, 1984, *132*(2), pp. 232–33. [G: Netherlands]

Branson, William H. The Myth of Deindustrialization. In *McKenzie, R. B., ed. (II)*, 1984, *1983*, pp. 177–90. [G: U.S.]

Brecher, Richard A. and Choudhri, Ehsan U. New Products and the Factor Content of International Trade. *J. Polit. Econ.*, October 1984, *92*(5), pp. 965–71. [G: U.S.]

Brock, William E. The Role of Increased International Trade in Long-term Economic Growth. In *Wachter, M. L. and Wachter, S. M., eds.*, 1984, pp. 439–46. [G: U.S.]

Brock, William E. Trade and Debt: The Vital Linkage. *Foreign Aff.*, Summer 1984, *62*(5), pp. 1037–57. [G: Global]

Bröcker, Johannes. How Do International Trade Barriers Affect Interregional Trade? In *Andersson, Å. E.; Isard, W. and Puu, T., eds.*, 1984, pp. 219–39. [G: EEC]

Brorsen, B. Wade; Chavas, Jean-Paul and Grant, Warren R. Dynamic Relationships of Rice Import Prices in Europe. *Europ. Rev. Agr. Econ.*, 1984, *11*(1), pp. 29–42. [G: U.S.; Thailand; Argentina; Europe]

Burns, Arthur F. The American Trade Deficit

in Perspective. *Foreign Aff.*, Summer 1984, 62(5), pp. 1058–69. **[G: U.S.]**

Burns, E. Bradford. The Modernization of Underdevelopment: El Salvador, 1858–1931. *J. Devel. Areas*, April 1984, 18(3), pp. 293–316. **[G: El Salvador]**

Burton, Daniel F., Jr. The Trade Implications of U.S. Monetary and Fiscal Policy. In *Hewlett, S. A.; Kaufman, H. and Kenen, P. B., eds.*, 1984, pp. 151–65. **[G: U.S.; Brazil; Mexico]**

Byatt, I. C. R. Byatt Report on Subsidies to British Export Credits. *World Econ.*, June 1984, 7(2), pp. 163–78. **[G: U.K.]**

Cadilhe, Miguel. The Portuguese External Deficit and the "Strategy of Humps." *Economia (Portugal)*, May 1984, 8(2), pp. 425–36. **[G: Portugal]**

de Carvalho, Frederico A. As *Trading Companies* no comércio exterior do Brasil: Desempenho recente e perspectivas. (With English summary.) *Economia (Portugal)*, October 1984, 8(3), pp. 509–25. **[G: Brazil]**

Casas, F. R. and Choi, E. Kwan. Trade Imbalance and the Leontief Paradox. *Manchester Sch. Econ. Soc. Stud.*, December 1984, 52(4), pp. 391–401. **[G: U.S.]**

Catinat, Michel. Fondement microéconomique par le déséquilibre des équations d'importation et d'exportation. (Microeconomic Foundation via Disequilibrium: Import and Export Equations. With English summary.) *Ann. INSEE*, July–December 1984, (55/56), pp. 153–81. **[G: France]**

Chabar, Hamid. Arab and Third-World Relations: Genesis of South–South Co-operation and Solidarity. In *Achilli, M. and Khaldi, M., eds.*, 1984, pp. 92–116. **[G: Arab Countries; LDCs]**

Chen, Edward K. Y. Exports of Technology by Newly Industrializing Countries: Hong Kong. *World Devel.*, May/June 1984, 12(5/6), pp. 481–90. **[G: Hong Kong]**

Chichilnisky, Graciela. Necesidades básicas, recursos no renovables y crecimiento en el contexto de las relaciones Norte–Sur. (With English summary.) *Desarrollo Econ.*, July–September 1984, 24(94), pp. 171–85.

Chichilnisky, Graciela. North–South Trade and Export-led Policies [Terms of Trade and Domestic Distribution: Export-led Growth with Abundant Labour]. *J. Devel. Econ.*, May–June–August 1984, 15(1,2,3), pp. 131–60. **[G: U.K.; Sri Lanka]**

Chichilnisky, Graciela. Terms of Trade, Domestic Distribution and Export-led Growth: A Rejoinder to Rejoinders. *J. Devel. Econ.*, May–June–August 1984, 15(1,2,3), pp. 177–84.

Chiesa, Carlo and Castaldo, Pasquale. Il turismo con l'estero dell'Italia. (Foreign Tourism Flows in Italy: Theoretical Model and Empirical Verification. With English summary.) *Rivista Int. Sci. Econ. Com.*, July 1984, 31(7), pp. 639–48. **[G: Italy]**

Chishti, Sumitra. Experience of India in Trade and Economic Relations with the Socialist Countries of Eastern Europe and Its Relevance to Developing Countries. In *U.N.C.T.D.*, 1984, pp. 19–31. **[G: India; CMEA]**

Chu, Ke-young and Morrison, Thomas K. The 1981–82 Recession and Non-Oil Primary Commodity Prices. *Int. Monet. Fund Staff Pap.*, March 1984, 31(1), pp. 93–140.

Clair, Claude; Gaussens, Olivier and Phan, Duc-Loi. Le commerce international intra-branche et ses déterminants d'après le schéma de concurrence monopolistique: une vérification empirique. (Intra-Industry Trade under Perfect Monopolistic Competition Framework: An Empirical Investigation. With English summary.) *Revue Écon.*, March 1984, 35(2), pp. 347–78. **[G: OECD]**

Clifton, David S., Jr. and Marxsen, William B. An Empirical Investigation of the Heckscher–Ohlin Theorem. *Can. J. Econ.*, February 1984, 17(1), pp. 32–38. **[G: Selected Countries]**

Collins, James B. The Role of Atlantic France in the Baltic Trade: Dutch Traders and Polish Grain at Nantes, 1625–1675. *J. Europ. Econ. Hist.*, Fall 1984, 13(2), pp. 239–89. **[G: France]**

Conesa, Eduardo R. The Openness of the Latin American Southern Cone Economies. In *Núñez del Arco, J.; Margain, E. and Cherol, R., eds.*, 1984, pp. 253–79. **[G: Argentina; Chile; Uruguay]**

Constantopoulos, Maria and Drakos, George E. Measuring Changes in the Gains from Trade—A Contribution to Applied Welfare Economics. In *Csikós-Nagy, B.; Hague, D. and Hall, G., eds.*, 1984, pp. 454–83. **[G: Greece]**

Cooper, J. H. Southern Africa and the Threat of Economic Sanctions. *S. Afr. J. Econ.*, September 1984, 52(3), pp. 266–81. **[G: Africa]**

Costa, Paolo. La valutazione degli effetti economici del turismo in Italia. (Assessing the Economic Effects of Tourism in Italy. With English summary.) *Rivista Int. Sci. Econ. Com.*, July 1984, 31(7), pp. 614–26. **[G: Italy]**

Courakis, Anthony S. and Moura Roque, Fátima. An Enquiry into the Determinants of the Net Exports Pattern of Portugal's Trade in Manufactures. *Economia (Portugal)*, May 1984, 8(2), pp. 299–331. **[G: Portugal]**

Crowe, Marshall A. An Assessment of the Recent Record in Canada. In *Fried, E. R. and Trezise, P. H., eds.*, 1984, pp. 114–21. **[G: U.S.; Canada]**

Cruz, Robert David. The Impact of Foreign Trade on the Economy of South Florida: An Econometric Model Forecast. In *Jorge, A.; Salazar-Carrillo, J. and Sanchez, E. P.*, 1984, pp. 143–54. **[G: U.S.; Latin America]**

Cruz, Robert David. The Impact of Foreign Trade on the Economy of South Florida: An Econometric Model Forecast. In *Salazar-Carrillo, J. and Tirado de Alonso, I., eds., no. 2*, 1984, pp. 1–13. **[G: U.S.; Latin America]**

Culem, Claudy. Comparative Advantage and Industrial Restructuring: The Belgian Case, 1970–1980. *Cah. Écon. Bruxelles*, 3rd Trimester 1984, (103), pp. 457–84. **[G: Belgium]**

Curran, Robert F. The Effect of Changes in the

Exchange Rate on Commodity Diversification in Less Developed Countries. *Eastern Econ. J.*, October-December 1984, *10*(4), pp. 409–20. **[G: LDCs]**

Dahlman, Carl J. and Cortes, Mariluz. Exports of Technology by Newly Industrializing Countries: Mexico. *World Devel.*, May/June 1984, *12*(5/6), pp. 601–24. **[G: Mexico]**

Dahlman, Carl J. and Sercovich, Francisco Colman. Exports of Technology from Semi-industrial Economies and Local Technological Development. *J. Devel. Econ.*, September–October 1984, *16*(1–2), pp. 63–99.
[G: Argentina; Brazil; India; Korea; Mexico]

Daniel, Terrence E.; Goldberg, Henry M. and Weyant, John P. Canadian Natural Gas Exports to the United States: A Monopolistic Intertemporal Analysis. *Energy J.*, October 1984, *5*(4), pp. 21–34. **[G: Canada; U.S.]**

Darling, John R. and Piha, Kalevi. Strategic Marketing of Finnish Products in the U.S. *Liiketaloudellinen Aikak.*, 1984, *33*(2), pp. 131–48.
[G: Finland; U.S.]

De Bandt, J. La dynamique des échanges de produits industriels: interdépendance, maîtrise ou dépendance? (The Dynamics of Trade in Manufactured Goods: Interdependence, Control or Dependence? With English summary.) *Écon. Soc.*, June 1984, *18*(6), pp. 101–23.
[G: Global]

Deardorff, Alan V. Testing Trade Theories and Predicting Trade Flows. In *Jones, R. W. and Kenen, P.*, eds., 1984, pp. 467–517.

Deese, David. The Vulnerability of Modern Economies. In *McCormick, G. H. and Bissell, R. E.*, eds., 1984, pp. 148–80. **[G: OECD; CMEA]**

Desai, Padma. The Soviet Union and the Third World: A Faltering Partnership? In *Bhagwati, J. N. and Ruggie, J. G.*, eds., 1984, pp. 261–85. **[G: U.S.S.R.; LDCs]**

Díaz-Alejandro, Carlos F. The U.S. Response to Foreign Industrial Targeting: Comments. *Brookings Pap. Econ. Act.*, 1984, (1), pp. 122–25. **[G: U.S.]**

Dick, Hermann, et al. Stabilisation Strategies in Primary Commodity Exporting Countries: A Case Study of Chile. *J. Devel. Econ.*, May–June–August 1984, *15*(1,2,3), pp. 47–75.
[G: Chile]

DiLullo, Anthony J. U.S. International Transactions, Third Quarter, 1984. *Surv. Curr. Bus.*, December 1984, *64*(12), pp. 41–64.
[G: U.S.]

Dixon, Peter B.; Parmenter, B. R. and Powell, Alan A. Trade Liberalization and Labor Market Disruption. *J. Policy Modeling*, November 1984, *6*(4), pp. 431–54. **[G: Australia]**

Dixon, William J. Trade Concentration, Economic Growth, and the Provision of Basic Human Needs. *Soc. Sci. Quart.*, September 1984, *65*(3), pp. 761–74. **[G: LDCs]**

Donaldson, Graham. Food Security and the Role of the Grain Trade. *Amer. J. Agr. Econ.*, May 1984, *66*(2), pp. 188–93.

Dornbusch, Rudiger. On the Consequences of Muddling through the Debt Crisis. *World Econ.*, June 1984, *7*(2), pp. 145–61.
[G: Latin America; U.S.]

Dornbusch, Rudiger. The Overvalued Dollar. *Lloyds Bank Rev.*, April 1984, (152), pp. 1–12. **[G: U.S.; Japan; W. Germany]**

Drabek, Zdenek. Exports of Primary Commodities and the Soviet Terms of Trade. In *Kostecki, M. M.*, ed., 1984, pp. 26–67. **[G: U.S.S.R.; CMEA; Global]**

Dyer, Mark. Export Production in Western Libya, 1750–1793. *African Econ. Hist.*, 1984, (13), pp. 117–36. **[G: Libya]**

Echavarria S., Juan José. Trade Prospects for Latin America: The Case of Colombia. In *Salazar-Carrillo, J. and Tirado de Alonso, I.*, eds., no. 2, 1984, pp. 1–12. **[G: LDCs; Latin America; Colombia]**

Echavarria S., Juan José. Trade Prospects for Latin America: The Case of Colombia. In *Jorge, A.; Salazar-Carrillo, J. and Sanchez, E. P.*, 1984, pp. 83–92. **[G: Latin America; Colombia; LDCs]**

Edwards, Geoff W. and Freebairn, John W. The Gains from Research into Tradable Commodities. *Amer. J. Agr. Econ.*, February 1984, *66*(1), pp. 41–49. **[G: Australia]**

Ellman, Michael. Odnowa in Statistics. In *Ellman, M.*, 1984, *1982*, pp. 242–49.
[G: Poland]

Ellman, Michael. Soviet Grain Imports and the Weather. In *Ellman, M.*, 1984, pp. 97–107.
[G: U.S.S.R.]

Ernst, Dieter. Recent Developments in the Semiconductor Industry: Implications for International Restructuring and Global Patterns of Technological Dominance and Dependence. *Industry Devel.*, 1984, (11), pp. 1–42.
[G: Global]

Etgar, Michael. Marketing of Export Commodities: The Case of Ivory Coast. In *Kaynak, E. and Savitt, R.*, eds., 1984, pp. 71–89.
[G: Ivory Coast]

Faber, Gerrit. The Economics of Stabex. *J. World Trade Law*, January:February 1984, *18*(1), pp. 52–62. **[G: EEC; Selected LDCs]**

Feldman, Robert A. The Impact of the Recent Strength of the Dollar on the U.S. Merchandise Trade Balance: Some "First-Round" Effects and Feedbacks from Exchange Rate Induced Changes in U.S.-Relative Inflation. *J. Policy Modeling*, February 1984, *6*(1), pp. 29–44. **[G: U.S.]**

Feldstein, Martin. From Crisis to Renewed Growth. *Challenge*, July/August 1984, *27*(3), pp. 27–30. **[G: Latin America]**

Fendt, Roberto, Jr. Trade Prospects for Brazil after the Devaluation. In *Jorge, A.; Salazar-Carrillo, J. and Sanchez, E. P.*, 1984, pp. 93–96. **[G: Brazil]**

Fichet, Gerard and Gonzalez, Norberto. The Production Structure and the Dynamics of Development. In *Ghosh, P. K.*, ed., no. 7, 1984, *1976*, pp. 362–407. **[G: Latin America; OECD]**

Fieleke, Norman S. Price Behavior during Balance of Payments Adjustment. *New Eng. Econ. Rev.*, November–December 1984, pp. 34–43. **[G: Global]**

Filippucci, Carlo and Paris, Quirino. Importazione di grano: un caso di mercati "controllati." (Wheat Prices and Administered Prices. With English summary.) *Statistica*, April–June 1984, *44*(2), pp. 271–300. **[G: Italy; EEC]**

Findlay, Ronald. A Comment on 'North–South Trade and Export-led Policies' [Terms of Trade and Domestic Distribution: Export-led Growth with Abundant Labour]. *J. Devel. Econ.*, May–June–August 1984, *15*(1,2,3), pp. 161–67.

Finlayson, Jock A. and Haglund, David G. Oil Politics and Canada–United States Relations. *Polit. Sci. Quart.*, Summer 1984, *99*(2), pp. 271–88. **[G: Canada; U.S.]**

Fischer, Lewis A. The USSR as a Major Factor in International Cotton Markets. In *Kostecki, M. M., ed.*, 1984, pp. 218–36. **[G: U.S.S.R.; Global]**

Fishlow, Albert. Reciprocal Trade Growth: The Latin American Integration Experience. In *[Chenery, H. B.]*, 1984, pp. 235–60. **[G: Latin America]**

Fishlow, Albert. The Debt Crisis: Solution by Economic Integration? In *Núñez del Arco, J.; Margain, E. and Cherol, R., eds.*, 1984, pp. 64–91. **[G: Latin America]**

Fitzpatrick, Jim. The Geographical Pattern of Irish Foreign Trade: Test of a Gravity Model. *Econ. Soc. Rev.*, October 1984, *16*(1), pp. 19–30. **[G: Ireland]**

Forstner, Helmut. The Changing Pattern of International Trade in Manufactures: A Logit Analysis. *Weltwirtsch. Arch.*, 1984, *120*(1), pp. 1–17. **[G: Global]**

Frank, Andre Gunder. Economic Crisis, Export Promotion and Political Repression in the Third World. In *Ngo, M., ed., vol. 1*, 1984, pp. 54–67. **[G: LDCs; S. Korea]**

Frank, Andre Gunder. On Commercial Imbalances in the Third World. In *Frank, A. G.*, 1984, *1976*, pp. 77–81.

Fraser, Malcolm. Pacific Community: Further Steps. In *Downen, R. L. and Dickson, B. J., eds.*, 1984, pp. 3–11. **[G: Pacific Basin]**

Freeman, John R. and Duvall, Raymond D. International Economic Relations and the Entrepreneurial State. *Econ. Develop. Cult. Change*, January 1984, *32*(2), pp. 373–400. **[G: Ireland]**

Fröbel, Folker. The Current Development of the World-Economy: Reproduction of Labour and Accumulation of Capital on a World Scale. In *Addo, H., ed.*, 1984, pp. 51–118. **[G: Global]**

Fuller, Stephen; Makus, Larry and Gallimore, William. Effects of Increasing Panama Canal Toll Rates on U.S. Grain Exports. *Southern J. Agr. Econ.*, December 1984, *16*(2), pp. 9–19. **[G: U.S.; Panama]**

Gafar, John. Devaluation and Its Impact on the Demand for Imports in an Open Economy: The Case of Jamaica. *Indian Econ. J.*, January–March 1984, *31*(3), pp. 34–44. **[G: Jamaica]**

Gerken, Egbert. Diversification and Stabilization

in a Resource-Exporting Country. In *Siebert, H., ed.*, 1984, pp. 117–55. **[G: Chile]**

Ghibutiu, Aurel. Effects of Most Favored Nation and Generalized System of Preferences Treatment on Romania's Exports to the United States. In *Jackson, M. R. and Woodson, J. D., Jr., eds.*, 1984, pp. 103–15. **[G: Romania; U.S.]**

Giannaros, Demetrios S. Estimation of Structural Changes in the Trade Sector Resulting from the Integration with the E.E.C.: The Case of Greece. *J. Econ. Devel.*, December 1984, *9*(2), pp. 145–70. **[G: Greece; EEC]**

Gift, Richard E. and Marxsen, William B. Aggregation and the Factoral Content of Trade: Comment. *J. Polit. Econ.*, October 1984, *92*(5), pp. 979–84. **[G: U.S.]**

Goldina, I. Soviet Export Potential and Several Aspects of Soviet Foreign Trade. *Prob. Econ.*, March 1984, *26*(11), pp. 3–14. **[G: U.S.S.R.]**

Gomane, Jean-Pierre. The Future for France in the Pacific. In *Downen, R. L. and Dickson, B. J., eds.*, 1984, pp. 91–99. **[G: France; Pacific Basin]**

Gordon, Kathryn M.; Lagrange, Sylvie and Riboud, Christophe. Measuring Country Exposure to Commodity Price Uncertainty. *Europ. Rev. Agr. Econ.*, 1984, *11*(3), pp. 285–301. **[G: Selected Countries]**

Gordon, Kathryn M. and Rausser, Gordon C. Country Hedging for Real Income Stabilization: A Case Study of South Korea and Egypt. *J. Futures Markets*, Winter 1984, *4*(4), pp. 449–64. **[G: S. Korea]**

Gordon, Wendell C. The Implementation of Economic Development. *J. Econ. Issues*, March 1984, *18*(1), pp. 295–313. **[G: Global]**

Greenaway, David. The Measurement of Produce Differentiation in Empirical Studies of Trade Flows. In *Kierzkowski, H., ed.*, 1984, pp. 230–49.

Greenaway, David and Milner, Chris. A Cross Section Analysis of Intra-industry Trade in the U.K. *Europ. Econ. Rev.*, August 1984, *25*(3), pp. 319–44. **[G: U.K.]**

Gregory, R. G. Some Implications of the Growth of the Mineral Sector. In *Lloyd, P. J., ed.*, 1984, *1976*, pp. 285–310. **[G: Australia]**

Grinols, Earl L. A Thorn in the Lion's Paw: Has Britain Paid Too Much for Common Market Membership? *J. Int. Econ.*, May 1984, *16*(3/4), pp. 271–93. **[G: U.K.; EEC]**

Guarini, Renato and Cantoloni, Alessandro. La domanda di turismo in Italia. Un'analisi interpretativa. (Tourism Demand in Italy. An Interpretive Analysis. With English summary.) *Rivista Int. Sci. Econ. Com.*, July 1984, *31*(7), pp. 675–95. **[G: Italy]**

Gunning, Jan Willem. Comparative Statics, Stability and Optimal Trade Policy [Terms of Trade and Domestic Distribution: Export-led Growth with Abundant Labour]. *J. Devel. Econ.*, May–June–August 1984, *15*(1,2,3), pp. 169–72.

Gunning, Jan Willem. Export-led Growth with Abundant Labour: A Defense of Orthodoxy.

J. Devel. Econ., May–June–August 1984, 15(1,2,3), pp. 97–103.

Gupta, Sanjeev. Unrecorded Trade at Black Exchange Rate: Analysis, Implications and Estimates. *Aussenwirtschaft*, May 1984, 39(1/2), pp. 75–90. **[G: India; Pakistan; Turkey]**

Gupta, Sanjeev and Togan, Sübidey. Who Benefits from the Adjustment Process in Developing Countries? A Test on India, Kenya, and Turkey. *J. Policy Modeling*, February 1984, 6(1), pp. 95–109. **[G: India; Kenya; Turkey]**

Hamada, Koichi and Iwata, Kazumasa. National Income, Terms of Trade and Economic Welfare. *Econ. J.*, December 1984, 94(376), pp. 752–71. **[G: Japan]**

Hamadani, S. M. Mazahir Hasnain. Factors' Employment Absorption, Growth, and Income Distribution through Foreign Trade: Pakistan's Case. *Pakistan Devel. Rev.*, Summer-Autumn 1984, 23(2&3), pp. 331–40. **[G: Pakistan]**

Hamilton, Bob; Mohammad, Sharif and Whalley, John. Rent Seeking and the North–South Terms of Trade. *J. Policy Modeling*, November 1984, 6(4), pp. 485–511. **[G: Global]**

Hamilton, Carl and Lars, E. O. Svensson. Potential and Realized Trade Patterns: The Case of Sweden. *Scand. J. Econ.*, 1984, 86(3), pp. 371–78. **[G: Sweden; OECD]**

Hamilton, Carl and Svensson, Lars E. O. Do Countries' Factor Endowments Correspond to the Factor Contents in Their Bilateral Trade Flows? *Scand. J. Econ.*, 1984, 86(1), pp. 84–97. **[G: OECD; LDCs]**

Hanel, Petr. The Soviet Impact on International Trade in Asbestos. In *Kostecki, M. M., ed.*, 1984, pp. 173–93. **[G: U.S.S.R.; Global]**

Hannigan, J. B. and McMillan, C. H. The Soviet Union and World Trade in Oil and Gas. In *Kostecki, M. M., ed.*, 1984, pp. 68–99. **[G: U.S.S.R.; Global]**

Hasan, Parvez. Adjustment to External Shocks. *Finance Develop.*, December 1984, 21(4), pp. 14–17. **[G: E. Asia]**

Hausman, William J. Market Power in the London Coal Trade: The Limitation of the Vend, 1770–1845. *Exploration Econ. Hist.*, October 1984, 21(4), pp. 383–405. **[G: U.K.]**

Havrylyshyn, Oli and Wolf, Martin. Promoting Trade Among Developing Countries: An Assessment. In *Ghosh, P. K., ed., no. 16*, 1984, 1982, pp. 44–56. **[G: LDCs]**

Haynes, Stephen E. and Stone, Joe A. Cross-Price Effects in Demand between Exports and Imports. *J. Macroecon.*, Spring 1984, 6(2), pp. 181–95. **[G: U.S.]**

Hazilla, Michael and Kopp, Raymond J. Assessing U.S. Vulnerability to Raw Material Supply Disruptions: An Application to Nonfuel Minerals. *Southern Econ. J.*, October 1984, 51(2), pp. 341–55. **[G: U.S.]**

Heal, Geoffrey and McLeod, Darryl. Gains from Trade, Stability and Profits: A Comment on Chichilnisky's 'Terms of Trade and Domestic Distribution: Export-led Growth with Abundant Labour.' *J. Devel. Econ.*, May–June–August 1984, 15(1,2,3), pp. 117–30.

Helliwell, John F.; MacGregor, Mary E. and Plourde, Andre. Changes in Canadian Energy Demand, Supply, and Policies, 1974–1986. *Natural Res. J.*, April 1984, 24(2), pp. 297–324. **[G: Canada]**

Helpman, Elhanan. The Factor Content of Foreign Trade. *Econ. J.*, March 1984, 94(373), pp. 84–94.

Hester, Susan B. and Hinkle, Dennis E. Balancing U.S. Trade Interests: The Impact of Chinese Textile Imports on the Market Shares of American Manufacturers. *Bus. Econ.*, April 1984, 19(3), pp. 27–34. **[G: U.S.]**

Hewitt, Adrian. The Lomé Conventions: Entering a Second Decade. *J. Common Market Stud.*, December 1984, 23(2), pp. 95–115. **[G: Global]**

Hilton, R. Spence. Commodity Trade and Relative Returns to Factors of Production. *J. Int. Econ.*, May 1984, 16(3/4), pp. 259–70.

Hitiris, T. and Petoussis, E. Price and Tariff Effects in a Dynamic Specification of the Demand for Imports. *Appl. Econ.*, February 1984, 16(1), pp. 15–24. **[G: Greece; EEC]**

Hoftyzer, John. A Further Analysis of the Linder Trade Thesis. *Quart. Rev. Econ. Bus.*, Summer 1984, 24(2), pp. 57–70. **[G: OECD]**

Högberg, Bengt and Wahlbin, Clas. East–West Industrial Cooperation: The Swedish Case. *J. Int. Bus. Stud.*, Spring/Summer 1984, 15(1), pp. 63–79. **[G: Sweden]**

Holstius, Karin. Does It Pay to Invest in Export Marketing during Recession? *Liiketaloudellinen Aikak.*, 1984, 33(3), pp. 303–09. **[G: Finland]**

Hopkins, Raymond F. and Puchala, Donald J. Perspectives on the International Relations of Food. In *Ghosh, P. K., ed., no. 6*, 1984, 1978, pp. 87–124. **[G: Global]**

Horlick, Gary. Development of Trade and Trade Conflicts in the Pacific Basin. In *Downen, R. L. and Dickson, B. J., eds.*, 1984, pp. 113–17. **[G: Pacific Basin]**

Horwitz, Eva Christina. Export Performance of the Nordic Countries 1965–82. In *Mikkelsen, A., et al.*, 1984, pp. 260–84. **[G: Scandinavia]**

Horwitz, Eva Christina. Intra Nordic Trade. In *Mikkelsen, A., et al.*, 1984, pp. 286–99. **[G: Scandinavia]**

Houck, James P. Food Security and the Role of the Grain Trade: Discussion. *Amer. J. Agr. Econ.*, May 1984, 66(2), pp. 194–95.

Hugon, Ph. Crise économique et vulnérabilité externe en Afrique sub-saharienne. (Economic Crisis and External Vulnerability in Sub-Saharian Africa. With English summary.) *Écon. Soc.*, June 1984, 18(6), pp. 159–94. **[G: Sub-Saharan Africa]**

Huguel, Catherine. La balance des paiements française: une contrainte extérieure qui demeure. (With English summary.) *Revue Écon. Polit.*, September–October 1984, 94(5), pp. 662–75. **[G: France]**

Hussain, M. Nureldin and Thirlwall, A. P. The IMF Supply-Side Approach to Devaluation: An

Assessment with Reference to the Sudan. *Oxford Bull. Econ. Statist.*, May 1984, *46*(2), pp. 145–67. [G: Sudan]

Husted, Steven L. and Kollintzas, Tryphon E. Import Demand with Rational Expectations: Estimates for Bauxite, Cocoa, Coffee, and Petroleum. *Rev. Econ. Statist.*, November 1984, *66*(4), pp. 608–18. [G: U.S.]

Iqbal, Munawar. Factors' Employment Absorption, Growth, and Income Distribution through Foreign Trade: Pakistan's Case. *Pakistan Devel. Rev.*, Summer-Autumn 1984, *23*(2&3), pp. 341–43. [G: Pakistan]

Isard, Peter. U.S. International Transactions in 1983. *Fed. Res. Bull.*, April 1984, *70*(4), pp. 269–78. [G: U.S.]

Jackson, Marvin R. and Woodson, James D., Jr. New Horizons in East–West Relations: Introduction. In *Jackson, M. R. and Woodson, J. D., Jr., eds.*, 1984, pp. 1–10. [G: Romania; U.S.]

Jager, Henk and de Jong, Eelke. On Export Performance and Export Elasticities: A Macroeconomic Approach. *De Economist*, 1984, *132*(2), pp. 224–31. [G: Netherlands]

Johnson, Mark J. Robust Growth and the Strong Dollar Set Pattern for 1983 Import and Export Prices. *Mon. Lab. Rev.*, April 1984, *107*(4), pp. 3–14. [G: U.S.]

Johnson, Mark J. and Szarek, Patricia. Effects of Strong Dollar, Economic Recovery Apparent in First-Half Import and Export Prices. *Mon. Lab. Rev.*, October 1984, *107*(10), pp. 3–17. [G: U.S.]

Jolly, Richard. Restructuring Out of Recession. In *Ghosh, P. K., ed., no. 16*, 1984, *1980*, pp. 29–36. [G: Global]

Jorge, Antonio. Trade, Debt and Growth in Latin America: By Way of a Brief Overview. In *Jorge, A.; Salazar-Carrillo, J. and Sanchez, E. P.*, 1984, pp. 1–6.

Jussawalla, Meheroo and Cheah, Chee-Wah. International Trade and Information: Some Welfare Implications. In *Jussawalla, M. and Ebenfield, H., eds.*, 1984, pp. 51–71.

Kádár, Béla. The External Economic Framework and the Conditions of Accelerating Hungarian Growth. *Acta Oecon.*, 1984, *33*(1–2), pp. 89–104. [G: Hungary]

Kaser, Michael C. The Soviet Impact on World Trade in Gold and Platinum. In *Kostecki, M. M., ed.*, 1984, pp. 156–72. [G: U.S.S.R.; Global]

Katz, Jorge M. Domestic Technological Innovations and Dynamic Comparative Advantage: Further Reflections on a Comparative Case-Study Program. *J. Devel. Econ.*, September–October 1984, *16*(1–2), pp. 13–37. [G: Latin America]

Kavoussi, Rostam M. Export Expansion and Economic Growth: Further Empirical Evidence. *J. Devel. Econ.*, January–February 1984, *14*(1–2), pp. 241–50. [G: LDCs]

Kay, John A. North Sea Oil and Manufacturing Output. In *Griffiths, B. and Wood, G. E., eds.*, 1984, pp. 185–99. [G: U.K.; Selected Countries]

Kellman, Mitchell and Landau, Daniel. The Nature of Japan's Comparative Advantage, 1965–80. *World Devel.*, April 1984, *12*(4), pp. 433–38. [G: Japan]

Khanna, Ashok. Market Distortions and Export Performance: India's Exports of Manufactures in the 1970s. *Weltwirtsch. Arch.*, 1984, *120*(2), pp. 348–60. [G: India]

Kibola, Hamisi S. Stabex and Lomé III. *J. World Trade Law*, January:February 1984, *18*(1), pp. 32–51. [G: EEC; Selected LDCs]

Kim, Chongyoul. Structural Shifts in Foreign Trade and Economic Growth: A Bayesian Test of Paremeter Shifts with an Application to Korea. *J. Econ. Devel.*, December 1984, *9*(2), pp. 109–20. [G: Korea]

Kim, Kwan S. and Turrubiate, Gerardo. Structures of Foreign Trade and Income Distribution: The Case of Mexico. *J. Devel. Econ.*, December 1984, *16*(3), pp. 263–78. [G: Mexico]

Kincaid, G. Russell. A Test of the Efficacy of Exchange Rate Adjustments in Indonesia. *Int. Monet. Fund Staff Pap.*, March 1984, *31*(1), pp. 62–92. [G: Indonesia]

Kirmani, Naheed; Molajoni, Pierluigi and Mayer, Thomas. Effects of Increased Market Access on Exports of Developing Countries. *Int. Monet. Fund Staff Pap.*, December 1984, *31*(4), pp. 661–84. [G: LDCs; OECD]

Kleiman, Ephraim and Kop, Yaakov. Who Trades with Whom—The Income Pattern of International Trade. *Weltwirtsch. Arch.*, 1984, *120*(3), pp. 499–521. [G: Global]

Kleinschmidt, Elko J. and Cooper, Robert G. A Typology of Export Strategies Applied to the Export Performance of Industrial Firms. In *Kaynak, E., ed.*, 1984, pp. 217–31. [G: Canada]

Klíma, Arnŏst. Glassmaking Industry and Trade in Bohemia in the XVIIth and XVIIIth Centuries. *J. Europ. Econ. Hist.*, September–December 1984, *13*(3), pp. 499–520. [G: Czechoslovakia]

Knudsen, Odin K. and Harbert, Lloyd S. The Causes of Export Instability: Comparing the Experiences of Two Decades. In *Bigman, D. and Taya, T., eds.*, 1984, pp. 241–58. [G: LDCs]

Koekkoek, K. Ad and Mennes, Loet B. M. Revealed Comparative Advantage in Manufacturing Industry: The Case of the Netherlands. *De Economist*, 1984, *132*(1), pp. 30–48. [G: W. Germany; Belgium; Netherlands]

Koenig, Linda M. Recent Developments in the World Economy and in Non-Oil Developing Countries of the Western Hemisphere. In *Muns, J., ed.*, 1984, pp. 16–29. [G: OECD; LDCs; Latin America]

Koester, Ulrich and Valdés, Alberto. The EC's Potential Role in Food Security for LDC's: Adjustments in Its STABEX and Stock Policies. *Europ. Rev. Agr. Econ.*, 1984, *11*(4), pp. 415–37. [G: EEC]

Kohli, Ulrich R. Terms of Trade and Welfare: Estimates. *Kyklos*, 1984, *37*(4), pp. 577–97. **[G: U.S.; Canada; Australia; Switzerland]**

Kollintzas, Tryphon E. and Husted, Steven L. Distributed Lags and Intermediate Good Imports. *J. Econ. Dynam. Control*, December 1984, *8*(3), pp. 303–27.

Kolstad, Charles D. and Abbey, David S. Erratum [The Effect of Market Conduct on International Steam Coal Trade]. *Europ. Econ. Rev.*, December 1984, *26*(3), pp. 379. **[G: Selected Countries]**

Kolstad, Charles D. and Abbey, David S. The Effect of Market Conduct on International Steam Coal Trade. *Europ. Econ. Rev.*, February 1984, *24*(1), pp. 39–59. **[G: Selected Countries]**

Kondonassis, A. J. Some Major Trade and Development Programs of the European Economic Community with the LDCs: Toward a Common Development Policy? *J. Econ. Issues*, June 1984, *18*(2), pp. 651–62. **[G: EEC; LDCs]**

Koo, Anthony Y. C. and Martin, Stephen. Market Structure and U.S. Trade Flows. *Int. J. Ind. Organ.*, September 1984, *2*(3), pp. 173–97. **[G: U.S.]**

Kostecki, Michel M. The Soviet Union in International Grain Markets. In *Kostecki, M. M., ed.*, 1984, pp. 194–217. **[G: U.S.S.R.; Global]**

Kovács, András. The Relationship between Producers and Foreign Trade Enterprises: Observations on Cooperation between an Impex and Its Producers. *Soviet E. Europ. Foreign Trade*, Summer 1984, *20*(2), pp. 69–87. **[G: Hungary]**

Köves, András. On New Trends in International Industrial Development and the Division of Labour. *Acta Oecon.*, 1984, *33*(1–2), pp. 147–53. **[G: Hungary]**

Krause, Lawrence B. Australia's Comparative Advantage in International Trade. In *Caves, R. E. and Krause, L. B., eds.*, 1984, pp. 275–311. **[G: Australia]**

Kravis, Irving B. and Lipsey, Robert E. Prices and Terms of Trade for Developed Country Exports of Manufactured Goods. In *Csikós-Nagy, B.; Hague, D. and Hall, G., eds.*, 1984, pp. 415–45. **[G: OECD]**

Kreinin, Mordechai E. Wage Competitiveness in the U.S. Auto and Steel Industries. *Contemp. Policy Issue*, January 1984, (4), pp. 39–50. **[G: U.S.]**

Kronish, Rich. Latin America and the World Motor Vehicle Industry: The Turn to Exports. In *Kronish, R. and Mericle, K. S., eds.*, 1984, pp. 75–93. **[G: Latin America; Global]**

Krueger, Russell C. U.S. International Transactions, Second Quarter 1984. *Surv. Curr. Bus.*, September 1984, *64*(9), pp. 34–57. **[G: U.S.]**

Krueger, Russell C. U.S. International Transactions, First Quarter 1984. *Surv. Curr. Bus.*, June 1984, *64*(6), pp. 35–73. **[G: U.S.]**

Krugman, Paul R. The Effects of International Competition on U.S. Economic Growth. In

Hulten, C. R. and Sawhill, I. V., eds., 1984, pp. 127–50. **[G: U.S.; Japan; W. Germany]**

Krugman, Paul R. The U.S. Response to Foreign Industrial Targeting. *Brookings Pap. Econ. Act.*, 1984, (1), pp. 77–121. **[G: U.S.]**

Kubarych, Roger M. Financing the U.S. Current Account Deficit. *Fed. Res. Bank New York Quart. Rev.*, Summer 1984, *9*(2), pp. 24–31. **[G: U.S.]**

Kueh, Yak-Yeow. China's Foodgrain Production, Consumption, and Trade: Recent Trends and Prospects. *Rivista Int. Sci. Econ. Com.*, September 1984, *31*(9), pp. 910–26. **[G: China]**

Kuznets, Paul W. Economic Development, Export Structure, and Shifting Comparative Advantage in the Pacific Basin Region. In *Benjamin, R. and Kudrle, R. T.*, 1984, pp. 35–58. **[G: Selected Countries]**

Labys, Walter. The Role of the Soviet Union in Metals Markets: A Case Study of Copper, Manganese and Chromite. In *Kostecki, M. M., ed.*, 1984, pp. 135–55. **[G: U.S.S.R.; Global]**

Laird, Samuel. Intra-industry Trade and the Expansion, Diversification and Integration of the Trade of the Developing Countries. In *Ghosh, P. K., ed., no. 16*, 1984, *1981*, pp. 163–89. **[G: MDCs; LDCs]**

Lall, Sanjaya. Exports of Technology by Newly Industrializing Countries: An Overview. *World Devel.*, May/June 1984, *12*(5/6), pp. 471–80. **[G: LDCs]**

Lall, Sanjaya. Exports of Technology by Newly Industrializing Countries: India. *World Devel.*, May/June 1984, *12*(5/6), pp. 535–65. **[G: India]**

Lall, Sanjaya. South–South Economic Cooperation and Global Negotiations. In *Bhagwati, J. N. and Ruggie, J. G., eds.*, 1984, pp. 287–322. **[G: India; LDCs]**

Langhammer, Rolf J. Regional Integration and Cooperation in Africa: A History of Disappointments? In *Ghosh, P. K., ed., no. 12*, 1984, *1977*, pp. 203–15. **[G: Africa]**

Lányi, Kamilla. Constraints on Profitable Growth and Exports in Hungarian Agriculture. *Acta Oecon.*, 1984, *33*(3–4), pp. 293–304. **[G: Hungary]**

Larcarte, Julio A. Aspects of International Trade and Assistance Relating to the Expansion of Employment in the Developing Countries. In *Ghosh, P. K., ed., no. 16*, 1984, *1972*, pp. 124–51.

Larkin, John A. The International Face of the Philippine Sugar Industry, 1836–1920. *Philippine Rev. Econ. Bus.*, Mar./June 1984, *21*(1/2), pp. 39–58. **[G: Philippines]**

Lassudrie-Duchêne, Bernard. Les incidences régionales des échanges internationaux. (With English summary.) *Revue Écon. Polit.*, January–February 1984, *94*(1), pp. 26–48. **[G: France]**

Lawrence, Robert Z. The U.S. Response to Foreign Industrial Targeting: Comments. *Brookings Pap. Econ. Act.*, 1984, (1), pp. 125–29. **[G: U.S.]**

Lazer, William. Comparative Insights into Japanese Marketing: Myths and Realities. In *Kaynak, E. and Savitt, R., eds.*, 1984, pp. 233–46. **[G: Japan]**

Le Van, Cuong. Specification of the Import Function and the Determination of Short and Long Term Equilibria in a Macroeconometric Model. In *Ancot, J. P., ed.*, 1984, pp. 229–45.

Ledić, Michèle and Silberston, Aubrey. The Technological Balance of Payments in Perspective. *Greek Econ. Rev.*, December 1984, *6*(3), pp. 356–86. **[G: OECD]**

Lehmann, Jean-Pierre. Agenda for Action on Issues in Euro-Japanese Relations. *World Econ.*, September 1984, *7*(3), pp. 257–76. **[G: EEC; Japan]**

Lemperière, J. La restructuration des échanges internationaux. (The Restructuring of Trade. With English summary.) *Écon. Soc.*, June 1984, *18*(6), pp. 21–58. **[G: Global]**

van Lennep, Jonkheer Emile. Strengthening the International Trade and Financial Systems. *World Econ.*, March 1984, *7*(1), pp. 23–32. **[G: OECD]**

Leskelä, Jukka. A Note on Export Specialization in the Nordic Countries. In *Mikkelsen, A., et al.*, 1984, pp. 302–08. **[G: Scandinavia]**

Levine, Leonard B. Changes in Policies Affecting U.S. Natural Gas Trade. *J. Energy Devel.*, Autumn 1984, *10*(1), pp. 117–20. **[G: U.S.]**

Levy, Mickey D. The Impact of Foreign Trade on the Economy of South Florida: An Econometric Model Forecast. In *Jorge, A.; Salazar-Carrillo, J. and Sanchez, E. P.*, 1984, pp. 155–56. **[G: U.S.; Latin America]**

Liang, Kuo-shu and Liang, Ching-ing Hou. Trade, Technology Transfers, and Risks of Protectionism: The Experience of the Republic of China. In *Downen, R. L. and Dickson, B. J., eds.*, 1984, pp. 145–59. **[G: Taiwan]**

Liebman, Howard M. GATT and Countertrade Requirements: Comment [The International Treatment of State Trading]. *J. World Trade Law*, May–June 1984, *18*(3), pp. 252–61.

Lipner, J. Kenneth and Dutt, Amitava Krishna. South Florida as a Gateway to U.S. Trade with Latin America. In *Jorge, A.; Salazar-Carrillo, J. and Sanchez, E. P.*, 1984, pp. 131–40. **[G: Latin America; U.S.]**

Lipner, J. Kenneth and Dutt, Amitava Krishna. South Florida as a Gateway to U.S. Trade with Latin America. In *Salazar-Carrillo, J. and Tirado de Alonso, I., eds., no. 2*, 1984, pp. 1–12. **[G: U.S.; Latin America]**

Lipsey, Robert E. Recent Trends in U.S. Trade and Investment. In *Miyawaki, N., ed.*, 1984, pp. 58–79. **[G: U.S.; OECD]**

Lipsey, Robert E. and Weiss, Merle Yahr. Foreign Production and Exports of Individual Firms. *Rev. Econ. Statist.*, May 1984, *66*(2), pp. 304–08. **[G: U.S.]**

Longworth, David. A Comment on 'The Small Country Assumption: A Note on Canadian Exports.' *Appl. Econ.*, December 1984, *16*(6), pp. 933–34. **[G: Canada]**

Love, James. External Market Conditions, Competitiveness, Diversification, and LDCs' Exports. *J. Devel. Econ.*, December 1984, *16*(3), pp. 279–91. **[G: LDCs]**

Lovejoy, Paul E. Commercial Sectors in the Economy of the Nineteenth-Century Central Sudan: The Trans-Saharan Trade and the Desert-Side Salt Trade. *African Econ. Hist.*, 1984, (13), pp. 85–116. **[G: Sudan]**

Lundahl, Mats. Economic Effects of a Trade and Investment Boycott against South Africa. *Scand. J. Econ.*, 1984, *86*(1), pp. 68–83. **[G: S. Africa]**

Lunn, John. Trade-adjusted Concentration Ratios. *Antitrust Bull.*, Fall 1984, *29*(3), pp. 523–34. **[G: U.S.]**

Mac Bean, A. I. Export Instability and Economic Growth. *METU*, 1984, *11*(1–2), pp. 195–205. **[G: LDCs]**

Maddock, Rodney and McLean, Ian. Supply-Side Shocks: The Case of Australian Gold. *J. Econ. Hist.*, December 1984, *44*(4), pp. 1047–67. **[G: Australia]**

Maizels, Alfred. A Conceptual Framework for Analysis of Primary Commodity Markets. *World Devel.*, January 1984, *12*(1), pp. 25–41. **[G: Global]**

Malý, Bohuslav. Conditions for the Specialization of the Czechoslovak National Economic Complex. *Czech. Econ. Pap.*, 1984, (22), pp. 25–41. **[G: Czechoslovakia; CMEA]**

Manne, Alan S. and Preckel, Paul V. North–South Trade, Capital Flows, and Economic Growth: An Almost Neoclassical Model. In *[Chenery, H. B.]*, 1984, pp. 409–27.

Marks, Stephen V. Wage Competitiveness in the U.S. Auto and Steel Industries: Comment. *Contemp. Policy Issue*, January 1984, (4), pp. 51–53. **[G: U.S.]**

Marquez, Jaime and Pauly, Peter. OPEC's Pricing Policy and the International Transmission of Oil Price Effects. *Energy Econ.*, October 1984, *6*(4), pp. 267–75. **[G: MDCs; OPEC; Non-OPEC LDCs]**

Marris, Stephen N. Macroeconomic Policy Coordination among the Industrial Economies: Comments. *Brookings Pap. Econ. Act.*, 1984, (1), pp. 68–71. **[G: U.S.; W. Germany; Japan]**

Marsh, John S. The Reform of the CAP: National Interests and Financial Implications. *Europ. Rev. Agr. Econ.*, 1984, *11*(2), pp. 141–50. **[G: EEC]**

Marsh, Peter. The European Community and East–West Economic Relations. *J. Common Market Stud.*, September 1984, *23*(1), pp. 1–13. **[G: EEC; CMEA]**

Martellaro, Joseph A. China's Two Economies and the USA Factor. *Rivista Int. Sci. Econ. Com.*, September 1984, *31*(9), pp. 875–97. **[G: China; Taiwan]**

Massad, Carlos and Zahler, Roberto. The Adjustment Process in the 1980s: The Need for a Global Approach. *Cepal Rev.*, 1984, (23), pp. 83–105. **[G: Latin America]**

McCutchen, William W., Jr. The Use of Box Jenkins Techniques for Forecasting U.S. Merchandise Exports: An Update and Extension. *Quart. J. Bus. Econ.*, Autumn 1984, *23*(4), pp. 64–75. [G: U.S.]

Melo, Oscar and Vogt, Michael G. Determinants of the Demand for Imports of Venezuela. *J. Devel. Econ.*, April 1984, *14*(3), pp. 351–58. [G: Venezuela]

Melvin, Michael and Bernstein, David. Trade Concentration, Openness, and Deviations from Purchasing Power Parity. *J. Int. Money Finance*, December 1984, *3*(3), pp. 369–76. [G: Global]

Mercenier, Jean and Waelbroeck, Jean. The Sensitivity of Developing Countries to External Shocks in an Interdependent World. *J. Policy Modeling*, May 1984, *6*(2), pp. 209–35. [G: OECD; LDCs]

Michel, Gilles and Noel, Michel. The Ivorian Economy and Alternative Trade Regimes. In *Zartman, I. W. and Delgado, C. L., eds.*, 1984, pp. 77–114. [G: Ivory Coast]

Minford, Patrick. North Sea Oil and Manufacturing Output: Comment. In *Griffiths, B. and Wood, G. E., eds.*, 1984, pp. 205–10. [G: U.K.; Selected Countries]

Mohabbat, Khan A.; Dalal, Ardeshir J. and Williams, Martin. Import Demand for India: A Translog Cost Function Approach. *Econ. Develop. Cult. Change*, April 1984, *32*(3), pp. 593–605. [G: India]

Möller, Kristian. Role of Promotional Management in Exporting to the Soviet Union and OECD Countries. In *Kaynak, E., ed.*, 1984, pp. 318–34. [G: U.S.S.R.; OECD]

Momigliano, Franco and Siniscalco, Domenico. Technology and International Specialization. *Banca Naz. Lavoro Quart. Rev.*, September 1984, (150), pp. 257–84. [G: Italy]

Monke, Eric and Petzel, Todd. Market Integration: An Application to International Trade in Cotton. *Amer. J. Agr. Econ.*, November 1984, *66*(4), pp. 481–87. [G: Selected Countries]

Morgan, Ann D. Protectionism and European Trade in Manufactures. *Nat. Inst. Econ. Rev.*, August 1984, (109), pp. 45–57. [G: EEC; EFTA]

Motono, Moriyuki. World Trade Issues Require More than a Piecemeal Approach. *World Econ.*, September 1984, *7*(3), pp. 229–39. [G: Global]

Moura Roque, Fátima. Factor Endowments, Technology, and Foreign Trade. *S. Afr. J. Econ.*, December 1984, *52*(4), pp. 377–90. [G: S. Africa]

Mucchielli, Jean-Louis. Investissements internationaux et dynamique des avantages comparatifs des nouveaux pays industrialisés. (International Investments and the Changing Pattern of Comparative Advantages—An Application to the New Industrializing Countries. With English summary.) *Revue Écon.*, May 1984, *35*(3), pp. 537–70. [G: Global]

Munteanu, Catalin and Pop, Napoleon. Romanian–United States Trade: Achievements and Prospects. In *Jackson, M. R. and Woodson, J. D., Jr., eds.*, 1984, pp. 13–21. [G: Romania; U.S.]

Munting, Roger. The Russian Beet Sugar Industry in the XIXth Century. *J. Europ. Econ. Hist.*, Fall 1984, *13*(2), pp. 291–309. [G: U.S.S.R.]

Murray, David. The Importance of Supply and Demand Variations in Earnings Instability: Reply. *Econ. Develop. Cult. Change*, October 1984, *33*(1), pp. 171–72.

Mytelka, Lynn Krieger. Competition, Conflict and Decline in the Union Douanière et Economique de l'Afrique Centrale (UDEAC). In *Mazzeo, D., ed.*, 1984, pp. 131–49. [G: Central Africa]

Nagy, András. Structural and Intensity Changes in International Trade. In *Andersson, Å. E.; Isard, W. and Puu, T., eds.*, 1984, pp. 187–218.

Nappi, Carmine. The USSR and The International Aluminium Market. In *Kostecki, M. M., ed.*, 1984, pp. 116–34. [G: U.S.S.R.; Global]

Naqvi, Syed Nawab Haider; Ahmed, Ather Maqsood and Khan, Ashfaque H. Possibilities of Regional Trade Expansion: A Link Model for Pakistan, India, Bangladesh, and Sri Lanka. *Pakistan Devel. Rev.*, Spring 1984, *23*(1), pp. 9–35. [G: Pakistan; India; Bangladesh; Sri Lanka]

Narongchai, Akransanee. Industrialization of ASEAN and Structural Adjustment in the Pacific. In *Benjamin, R. and Kudrle, R. T.*, 1984, pp. 59–78. [G: ASEAN]

Neuberger, Egon and Ben-Ner, Avner. Romania's Reactions to International Commodity Inflation. In *Jackson, M. R. and Woodson, J. D., Jr., eds.*, 1984, pp. 55–99. [G: Romania; CMEA]

Nicholas, Stephen J. The Overseas Marketing Performance of British Industry, 1870–1914. *Econ. Hist. Rev.*, 2nd Ser., November 1984, *37*(4), pp. 489–506. [G: U.K.]

Nicholson, Norman K. and Esseks, John D. The Politics of Food Scarcities in Developing Countries. In *Ghosh, P. K., ed., no. 6*, 1984, *1978*, pp. 153–98. [G: LDCs]

Nikitin, S. M. Trends in Relative World Market Prices. In *Csikós-Nagy, B.; Hague, D. and Hall, G., eds.*, 1984, pp. 285–96.

Nikitin, S. M. and Tulin, I. V. Prices on the World Capitalist Market and Inflation. In *Nikitin, S. M., ed.*, 1984, pp. 93–107. [G: Global]

Nobel, Peter. Internationalisierung der Tatbestände und nationalstaatliches Recht. (International Facts and National Law. With English summary.) *Aussenwirtschaft*, May 1984, *39*(1/2), pp. 91–118. [G: Global]

Norman, George and Dunning, John H. Intra-industry Foreign Direct Investment: Its Rationale and Trade Effects. *Weltwirtsch. Arch.*, 1984, *120*(3), pp. 522–40. [G: U.S.; U.K.; Germany; France; Japan]

North, Michael. A Small Baltic Port in the Early Modern Period: The Port of Elbing in the Six-

teenth and Seventeenth Century. *J. Europ. Econ. Hist.*, Spring 1984, *13*(1), pp. 117–27.
[G: Poland]

Nyers, Rezso. Tendencies of Tradition and Reform in CMEA Cooperation. *Soviet E. Europ. Foreign Trade*, Summer 1984, *20*(2), pp. 6–36. [G: CMEA]

O'Hagan, John W. and Harrison, M. J. Market Shares of U.S. Tourist Expenditure in Europe: An Econometric Analysis. *Appl. Econ.*, December 1984, *16*(6), pp. 919–31. [G: U.S.; Europe]

O'Hagan, John W. and Harrison, M. J. U.K. and U.S. Visitor Expenditure in Ireland: Some Econometric Findings. *Econ. Soc. Rev.*, April 1984, *15*(3), pp. 195–207. [G: Ireland; OECD]

O'Neill, Helen. HICs, MICs, NICs and LICs: Some Elements in the Political Economy of Graduation and Differentiation. *World Devel.*, July 1984, *12*(7), pp. 693–712. [G: LDCs; MDCs]

Offutt, Susan Elizabeth and Blandford, David. The Impact of the Soviet Union upon the U.S Feed/Livestock Sector—An Assessment. *J. Policy Modeling*, August 1984, *6*(3), pp. 311–40. [G: U.S.; U.S.S.R.]

Okólski, Marek and Winiecki, Jan. Structural Change and Adaptation: On Reintegrating Planned Economies into the World Economy. *Konjunkturpolitik*, 1984, *30*(2/3), pp. 148–69. [G: Europe]

Olmer, Lionel H. Trade, Debt and Growth in Latin America: Closing Statement. In *Jorge, A.; Salazar-Carrillo, J. and Sanchez, E. P.*, 1984, pp. 157–65. [G: U.S.; Latin America]

Olson, Mancur. Australia in Perspective of the Rise and Decline of Nations. *Australian Econ. Rev.*, 3rd Quarter 1984, (67), pp. 7–17. [G: Global]

Orlandi, Alberto. Latin American Commodity Exports: The Case of Cotton Fibre. *Cepal Rev.*, April 1984, (22), pp. 137–58. [G: Latin America]

Oudiz, Gilles and Sachs, Jeffrey D. Macroeconomic Policy Coordination among the Industrial Economies. *Brookings Pap. Econ. Act.*, 1984, (1), pp. 1–64. [G: U.S.; W. Germany; Japan]

Palomo, Manuel Figuerola. Valoración del consumo y la producción turística. (Valuation of Tourism Consumption and Production. With English summary.) *Rivista Int. Sci. Econ. Com.*, July 1984, *31*(7), pp. 627–38. [G: Spain]

Pamuk, Şevket. The Ottoman Empire in the "Great Depression" of 1873–1896. *J. Econ. Hist.*, March 1984, *44*(1), pp. 107–18. [G: Middle East; S. Europe; Turkey]

Park, Eul Y. Patterns of Foreign Direct Investment, Foreign Ownership, and Industrial Performance: The Case of the Korean Manufacturing Industry. In *Benjamin, R. and Kudrle, R. T.*, 1984, pp. 127–60. [G: S. Korea]

Peeters, Th. Structural Adjustment and Trade Specialisation: U.S., Japan, and the EC. *Tijd-*

schrift Econ. Manage., 1984, *29*(3), pp. 449–58. [G: U.S.; EEC; Japan]

Pickering, J. F. and Sheldon, I. M. International Trade Performance and Concentration in British Industry. *Appl. Econ.*, June 1984, *16*(3), pp. 421–42. [G: U.K.]

Pletcher, David M. 1861–1898: Economic Growth and Diplomatic Adjustment. In *Becker, W. H. and Wells, S. F., Jr., eds.*, 1984, pp. 119–71. [G: U.S.]

Ponte Ferreira, Margarida and Rayment, Paul. Exports of Manufactures from South European Countries: Demand and Competitiveness Factors. *J. World Trade Law*, May–June 1984, *18*(3), pp. 235–51. [G: Selected Countries]

Radetzki, Marian and Van Duyne, Carl. The Response of Mining Investment to a Decline in Economic Growth: The Case of Copper in the 1970s. *J. Devel. Econ.*, May–June–August 1984, *15*(1,2,3), pp. 19–45. [G: LDCs]

Rahman, Sultan H. Analysis of a Flexible Market Stabilization Policy in the Jute Sector and Its Sensitivity to a Parametric Change in Demand. *Bangladesh Devel. Stud.*, September 1984, *12*(3), pp. 64–73. [G: Bangladesh]

Rallo, Joseph. The European Communities' Industrial Policy Revisited: The Case of Aerospace. *J. Common Market Stud.*, March 1984, *22*(3), pp. 245–67. [G: OECD; EEC]

Ramadhyani, M. Export Promotion in an Import Substitution Framework: An Analysis of the 100% Export Oriented Units Scheme. *Margin*, April 1984, *16*(3), pp. 56–69.

Ramhorst, Guntholf. Eine konzeptionelle Alternative zur Messung des interindustriellen Handels. Replik auf K. Nobel: "Intra- vs. Interindustry Trade: The Case of Many Countries and Industries." (An Alternative Concept of Measuring Inter-industry Trade. Reply to K. Nobel: The Case of Many Countries and Industries. With English summary.) *Z. Wirtschaft. Sozialwissen.*, 1984, *104*(5), pp. 457–75. [G: OECD]

Rangarajan, L. The Politics of International Trade. In *Strange, S., ed.*, 1984, pp. 126–63. [G: Global]

Ranney, Susan I. Terms of Trade and Domestic Distribution: A Comment. *J. Devel. Econ.*, May–June–August 1984, *15*(1,2,3), pp. 89–96.

Ray, George F. European Energy Alternatives and Future Developments. *Natural Res. J.*, April 1984, *24*(2), pp. 325–49. [G: Europe]

Redish, Angela. Why Was Specie Scarce in Colonial Economies? An Analysis of the Canadian Currency, 1796–1830. *J. Econ. Hist.*, September 1984, *44*(3), pp. 713–28. [G: Canada]

Reynolds, Bruce. China in the International Economy. In *Harding, H., ed.*, 1984, pp. 71–106. [G: China]

Reynolds, Clark; Ramos, Raul and McCleery, Robert. The Impact of Foreign Trade and Export Strategies on Distribution of Income for Low-Income Households in Mexico. In *Aspe, P. and Sigmund, P. E., eds.*, 1984, pp. 203–46. [G: Mexico]

Rhoades, Stephen A. Wages, Concentration, and

Import Penetration: An Analysis of the Interrelationships. *Atlantic Econ. J.*, July 1984, *12*(2), pp. 23–31. [G: U.S.]

Richonnier, Michel. Europe's Decline Is Not Irreversible. *J. Common Market Stud.*, March 1984, *22*(3), pp. 227–43. [G: U.S.; Japan; EEC]

Riedel, James. Trade as the Engine of Growth in Developing Countries, Revisited. *Econ. J.*, March 1984, *94*(373), pp. 56–73.

Riedel, James; Hall, Chris and Grawe, Roger. Determinants of Indian Export Performance in the 1970s. *Weltwirtsch. Arch.*, 1984, *120*(1), pp. 40–63. [G: India]

Ross, Gary N. U.S. Oil and Gas Imports. In *Ayoub, A.*, ed., 1984, pp. 249–61. [G: U.S.]

Rossini, Gianpaolo. Intraindustry Trade and Tariffs: New Wave or Old Fashion? *Econ. Int.*, February–May 1984, *37*(1–2), pp. 130–48. [G: W. Europe]

Rous, Jan and Hejl, Lubomir. Contributions to the Evaluation and Stimulation of Effectiveness in External Economic Relations. *Soviet E. Europ. Foreign Trade*, Winter 1984-85, *20*(4), pp. 77–105. [G: Czechoslovakia]

Rousslang, Donald J. and Parker, Stephen. Cross-Price Elasticities of U.S. Import Demand. *Rev. Econ. Statist.*, August 1984, *66*(3), pp. 518–23. [G: U.S.]

Ruta, Gianni. L'Europa comunitaria e la cooperazione allo sviluppo. (The European Community and the Cooperation to Development. With English summary.) *Mondo Aperto*, November–December 1984, *38*(6), pp. 337–42. [G: EEC; Africa; Caribbean; Pacific Countries]

Saavedra-Rivano, Neantro. Terms of Trade and Domestic Distribution: A Comment. *J. Devel. Econ.*, May–June–August 1984, *15*(1,2,3), pp. 105–10.

Sagafi-Nejad, Tagi. Exports of Technology by Newly Industrializing Countries: Egypt. *World Devel.*, May/June 1984, *12*(5/6), pp. 567–73. [G: Egypt]

Sakisaka, Masao. Japan's Energy Supply/Demand Structure and Its Trade Relationship with the United States and the Middle East. *J. Energy Devel.*, Autumn 1984, *10*(1), pp. 1–11. [G: Japan]

Salazar-Carrillo, Jorge. Trade and Debt in Central America in the 1970s. In *Salazar-Carrillo, J. and Tirado de Alonso, I.*, eds., no. 2, 1984, pp. 1–7. [G: Central America]

Salazar-Carrillo, Jorge. Trade and Debt in Central America in the 1970s. In *Jorge, A.; Salazar-Carrillo, J. and Sanchez, E. P.*, 1984, pp. 37–40. [G: Central America]

Salazar-Carrillo, Jorge and Tirado de Alonso, Irma. Trade, Debt, and Development in the Caribbean Basin. In *Salazar-Carrillo, J. and Tirado de Alonso, I.*, eds., no. 2, 1984, pp. 1–9. [G: Caribbean Basin]

Samson, I. La coopération économique entre la R.D.A. et ses partenaires du C.A.E.M.: une forme exemplaire d'insertion dans la D.I.S.T.? (Economic Cooperation between the G.D.R.

and Its CMEA Partners: A Model Form of Insertion within the International Social Division of Labour. With English summary.) *Écon. Soc.*, February 1984, *18*(2), pp. 79–114. [G: E. Germany; CMEA]

Sanchez, Enrique P. Latin American Outlook Under IMF Conditionality. In *Jorge, A.; Salazar-Carrillo, J. and Sanchez, E. P.*, 1984, pp. 11–19. [G: Latin America]

Sarris, Alexander H. Agricultural Problems in EC Enlargement: The Case of Greece. *Europ. Rev. Agr. Econ.*, 1984, *11*(2), pp. 195–205. [G: EEC; Greece]

Savvides, Andreas. Export Instability and Economic Growth: Some New Evidence. *Econ. Develop. Cult. Change*, April 1984, *32*(3), pp. 607–14. [G: LDCs; MDCs]

Sawyer, W. Charles. The Effects of the Second Enlargement of the EC on U.S. Exports to Europe. *Weltwirtsch. Arch.*, 1984, *120*(3), pp. 572–79. [G: EEC; U.S.]

Schiller, László. The Socialist Foreign Trade Contacts of Budaflax. *Soviet E. Europ. Foreign Trade*, Summer 1984, *20*(2), pp. 88–99. [G: CMEA]

Schneider, Hans K. and Schulz, Walter. The Importing Country's Perspective: A Case Study of LNG. In *Pearce, D. W.; Siebert, H. and Walter, I.*, eds., 1984, pp. 295–310. [G: Global]

Schumacher, Dieter. North–South Trade and Shifts in Employment: A Comparative Analysis of Six European Community Countries. *Int. Lab. Rev.*, May–June 1984, *123*(3), pp. 333–48. [G: W. Europe; LDCs]

Sell, Axel. Staatliche Regulierung und Arbeitslosigkeit im internationalen Sektor. (Regulation and Unemployment in the International Sector. With English summary.) *Konjunkturpolitik*, 1984, *30*(4), pp. 189–216. [G: W. Germany]

Sercovich, Francisco Colman. Exports of Technology by Newly Industrializing Countries: Brazil. *World Devel.*, May/June 1984, *12*(5/6), pp. 575–99. [G: Brazil]

Shaaf, Mohammad. Strong Dollar, Low Inflation, and OPEC's Terms of Trade. *J. Energy Devel.*, Autumn 1984, *10*(1), pp. 121–29. [G: OPEC]

Shahi, M. A.; Khawja, N. and Contogiannis, E. A Model of the Nigerian Foreign Trade Sector. *J. Stud. Econ. Econometrics*, January 1984, (18), pp. 48–65. [G: Nigeria]

Shepherd, Geoffrey. Industrial Change in European Countries: The Experience of Six Sectors. In *Jacquemin, A.*, ed., 1984, pp. 191–214. [G: OECD]

Shishido, Shuntaro. A Multisector Approach to Global Econometric Modeling, with Special Reference to Heavy Industries. In *[Chenery, H. B.]*, 1984, pp. 391–405. [G: OECD; LDCs]

Siamwalla, Ammar and Valdés, Alberto. Food Security in Developing Countries: International Issues. In *Eicher, C. K. and Staatz, J. M.*, eds., 1984, *1980*, pp. 189–206. [G: LDCs]

Sinan, I. M. UNCTAD and Flags of Convenience. *J. World Trade Law*, March–April 1984, *18*(2), pp. 95–109.

Smart, Ian. The Importing Country's Perspective: A Case Study of LNG: Comment. In *Pearce, D. W.; Siebert, H. and Walter, I., eds.*, 1984, pp. 311–18. [G: Global]

Smith, Edward K. South Florida as a Gateway to U.S. Trade with Latin America. In *Jorge, A.; Salazar-Carrillo, J. and Sanchez, E. P.*, 1984, pp. 141. [G: U.S.; Latin America]

Smith, John T. Sugar Dependency in Cuba: Capitalism versus Socialism. In *Seligson, M. A., ed.*, 1984, pp. 366–78. [G: Cuba]

Snape, R. H. Effects of Mineral Development on the Economy. In *Lloyd, P. J., ed.*, 1984, *1977*, pp. 311–22. [G: Australia]

Sobhan, Rehman. Regional Economic Cooperation in South Asia: Legacy and Prospects. In *Ghosh, P. K., ed., no. 18*, 1984, *1979*, pp. 267–93. [G: S. Asia]

Soifer, Ricardo J. Exports of Technology by Newly Industrializing Countries: Argentina. *World Devel.*, May/June 1984, *12*(5/6), pp. 625–44. [G: Argentina]

Sorsa, Kalevi. Det internationella handels-, finans- och valutasystemet. Utvecklingstrender och reformsynpunkter. (The International Trade, Finance and Currency System: Trends and Views on Reforms. With English summary.) *Ekon. Samfundets Tidskr.*, 1984, *37*(2), pp. 65–73. [G: Global]

Spencer, Grant H. The World Trade Model: Revised Estimates. *Int. Monet. Fund Staff Pap.*, September 1984, *31*(3), pp. 469–98. [G: W. Europe; U.S.; Canada; Japan]

Spinanger, Dean. Objectives and Impact of Economic Activity Zones—Some Evidence from Asia. *Weltwirtsch. Arch.*, 1984, *120*(1), pp. 64–89. [G: Asia]

Srinivasan, T. N. and Bhagwati, Jagdish N. A Rejoinder [Terms of Trade and Domestic Distribution: Export-led Growth with Abundant Labour]. *J. Devel. Econ.*, May–June–August 1984, *15*(1,2,3), pp. 173–75.

Srinivasan, T. N. and Bhagwati, Jagdish N. On Transfer Paradoxes and Immiserizing Growth: Part II [Terms of Trade and Domestic Distribution: Export-led Growth with Abundant Labour]. *J. Devel. Econ.*, May–June–August 1984, *15*(1,2,3), pp. 111–15.

Sveikauskas, Leo. Science and Technology in Many Different Industries: Data for the Analysis of International Trade. *Rev. Public Data Use*, June 1984, *12*(2), pp. 133–56. [G: U.S.]

Tanskanen, Antti. Kilpailukyky ja työllisyys Suomessa. (Competitiveness and Employment in Finland. With English summary.) *Kansant. Aikak.*, 1984, *80*(4), pp. 383–93. [G: Finland]

Tapia, Humberto S. The Experience of Latin America in Marketing Exports to the United States: Some Lessons for Romania. In *Jackson, M. R. and Woodson, J. D., Jr., eds.*, 1984, pp. 245–77. [G: U.S.; Latin America; Romania]

Teitel, Simón and Sercovich, Francisco Colman. Exports of Technology by Newly Industrializing Countries: Latin America. *World Devel.*, May/June 1984, *12*(5/6), pp. 645–60. [G: Latin America]

Teubal, Morris. The Role of Technological Learning in the Exports of Manufactured Goods: The Case of Selected Capital Goods in Brazil. *World Devel.*, August 1984, *12*(8), pp. 849–65. [G: Brazil]

Tharakan, P. K. M. Intra-industry Trade between the Industrial Countries and the Developing World. *Europ. Econ. Rev.*, October–November 1984, *26*(1–2), pp. 213–27. [G: OECD; LDCs]

Thursby, Jerry G. and Thursby, Marie C. How Reliable Are Simple, Single Equation Specifications of Import Demand? *Rev. Econ. Statist.*, February 1984, *66*(1), pp. 120–28. [G: Canada; Germany; U.K.; Japan; U.S.]

Tirado de Alonso, Irma. Economic Growth and International Trade in the Caribbean Basin. In *Salazar-Carrillo, J. and Tirado de Alonso, I., eds., no. 2*, 1984, pp. 1–7. [G: Caribbean Basin]

Tirado de Alonso, Irma. Economic Growth and International Trade in the Caribbean Basin. In *Jorge, A.; Salazar-Carrillo, J. and Sanchez, E. P.*, 1984, pp. 25–35. [G: Latin America; Caribbean Basin]

Tiraspolsky, Anita. An Evaluation of Gains and Losses in Intra-CMEA Trade: Terms of Trade from 1970 to 1982. *Soviet E. Europ. Foreign Trade*, Winter 1984-85, *20*(4), pp. 32–62. [G: CMEA]

Török, Ádám. Sectoral and Enterprise Structure of Net Exports Settled in Convertible Currency of the Hungarian Industry. *Acta Oecon.*, 1984, *33*(1–2), pp. 127–45. [G: Hungary]

Toye, John. The Recession, the Third World and the Base Metals Industries. *World Devel.*, September 1984, *12*(9), pp. 923–34.

Triffin, Robert. The Relationship between the International Monetary System and Regional Monetary Systems. In *[Reynolds, L. G.]*, 1984, pp. 75–95. [G: Global]

Truett, Dale B. and Truett, Lila J. The Maquiladoras: Prospects for Mexico. *J. Econ. Devel.*, December 1984, *9*(2), pp. 45–66. [G: Mexico]

Tubiana, L. Le commerce mondial des produits agricoles: de la régulation globale au fractionnement des marchés. (World Food Trade: From Global Regulation to Markets Fragmentation. With English summary.) *Écon. Soc.*, June 1984, *18*(6), pp. 125–56. [G: Global]

Turner, Philip and Tuveri, Jean-Pierre. Some Effects of Export Restraints on Japanese Trading Behaviour. *OECD Econ. Stud.*, Spring 1984, (2), pp. 93–107. [G: Japan]

Ueda, Kazuo. Supply Shocks and the Interdependence of Macroeconomic Stability under Flexible Exchange Rates. *Europ. Econ. Rev.*, July 1984, *25*(2), pp. 253–77. [G: Japan; Germany]

Ullmann, John E. Can Business Become a Participant? In *Gordon, S. and McFadden, D., eds.*, 1984, pp. 164–74. [G: U.S.]

UNCTAD Secretariat. Bulgaria—Policies, Developments and Institutional Framework. In *U.N.C.T.D.*, 1984, pp. 57–78. [G: Bulgaria]

UNCTAD Secretariat. Czechoslovakia—Policies, Developments and Institutional Framework. In *U.N.C.T.D.*, 1984, pp. 79–96. [G: Czechoslovakia]

UNCTAD Secretariat. German Democratic Republic—Policies, Developments and Institutional Framework. In *U.N.C.T.D.*, 1984, pp. 97–110. [G: E. Germany]

UNCTAD Secretariat. Hungary—Policies, Developments and Institutional Framework. In *U.N.C.T.D.*, 1984, pp. 111–28. [G: Hungary]

UNCTAD Secretariat. Prospects for Trade and Economic Co-operation between Nigeria and the Socialist Countries of Eastern Europe. In *U.N.C.T.D.*, 1984, pp. 45–55. [G: Nigeria; CMEA]

UNCTAD Secretariat. Trends, Policies and Prospects in Trade and Economic Co-operation Between Argentina and the Socialist Countries of Eastern Europe. In *U.N.C.T.D.*, 1984, pp. 5–18. [G: Argentina; CMEA]

UNCTAD Secretariat. Union of Soviet Socialist Republics—Policies, Developments and Institutional Framework. In *U.N.C.T.D.*, 1984, pp. 129–45. [G: U.S.S.R.]

UNIDO Secretariat. Patterns and Prospects for East–South Trade in the 1980s. *Industry Devel.*, 1984, (11), pp. 67–98. [G: CMEA]

Unnevehr, Laurian J. Transport Costs, Tariffs and the Influence of World Markets on Indonesian Domestic Cassava Prices. *Bull. Indonesian Econ. Stud.*, April 1984, 20(1), pp. 30–43. [G: Indonesia]

Valdés, Alberto. Comercio de Productos Agrícolas entre Países en Desarrollo: América Latina durante, 1962–1979. (With English summary.) *Cuadernos Econ.*, August 1984, 21(63), pp. 169–206. [G: Latin America]

Velev, Todor. The Influence of Bulgaria's Economic Ties with CMEA Members on Some Proportions in Its Economy. *Soviet E. Europ. Foreign Trade*, Summer 1984, 20(2), pp. 56–68. [G: Bulgaria; CMEA]

Viviani, Alessandro. Importazione di alcuni prodotti tropicali: un caso di mercati aperti. (Import of Tropical Products: A Case of Open Markets. With English summary.) *Statistica*, April–June 1984, 44(2), pp. 329–39. [G: Italy]

Vogel, Ezra F. Japanese and American Societies in the 1980s. In *Miyawaki, N., ed.*, 1984, pp. 49–57. [G: U.S.; Japan]

Volcker, Paul A. Statement to the U.S. House Subcommittee on Trade of the Committee on Ways and Means, April 10, 1984. *Fed. Res. Bull.*, April 1984, 70(4), pp. 324–28. [G: U.S.]

Volcker, Paul A. Statement to the U.S. Senate Subcommittee on International Economic Policy of the Committee on Foreign Relations, June 15, 1984. *Fed. Res. Bull.*, July 1984, 70(7), pp. 568–73. [G: U.S.]

de Vos, Gerrit Th. B and Zurawicki, Leon. International Trading Companies for Developing Countries—Latin America. *METU*, 1984, 11(3–4), pp. 307–24. [G: Brazil; E. Asia; Latin America]

Wallich, Henry C. Statement to the U.S. House Subcommittee on Commerce, Transportation, and Tourism of the Committee on Energy and Commerce, March 6, 1984. *Fed. Res. Bull.*, March 1984, 70(3), pp. 210–12. [G: U.S.]

Wassermann, Ursula. The Economic Situation in Africa. *J. World Trade Law*, November:December 1984, 18(6), pp. 555–62. [G: Africa]

Weale, Martin R. Quantity and Price Effects in an Analysis of World Trade Based on an Accounting Matrix. *Rev. Income Wealth*, March 1984, 30(1), pp. 85–117. [G: Global]

Weiss, Charles and Lepkowski, Wil. Cotton Development International. In *Weiss, C. and Jéquier, N., eds.*, 1984, pp. 295–311. [G: LDCs]

Weiss, Frank D. Aspects of Real Exchange Rates—East and West. In *Csikós-Nagy, B.; Hague, D. and Hall, G., eds.*, 1984, pp. 317–32. [G: CMEA; OECD]

Westphal, Larry E., et al. Exports of Technology by Newly Industrializing Countries: Republic of Korea. *World Devel.*, May/June 1984, 12(5/6), pp. 505–33. [G: Korea]

Whalley, John. Trade, Industrial Policy, and Canadian Manufacturing by Richard G. Harris (with the Assistance of David Cox): A Review Article. *Can. J. Econ.*, May 1984, 17(2), pp. 386–98. [G: Canada]

Whalley, John. The North–South Debate and the Terms of Trade: An Applied General Equilibrium Approach. *Rev. Econ. Statist.*, May 1984, 66(2), pp. 224–34. [G: Global]

Wheeler, David. Sources of Stagnation in Sub-Saharan Africa. *World Devel.*, January 1984, 12(1), pp. 1–23. [G: Sub-Saharan Africa]

Whichard, Obie G. U.S. International Trade and Investment in Services: Data Needs and Availability. *Surv. Curr. Bus.*, September 1984, 64(9), pp. 18. [G: U.S.]

Widyono, Benny. Transnational Corporations and Export-Oriented Primary Commodities: A Conceptual Framework for Research. In *Ngo, M., ed., vol. 1*, 1984, pp. 107–23. [G: LDCs]

Wignjowijoto, Hartojo. Regional Trade and Investment: Conflict and Cooperation Ahead. In *Downen, R. L. and Dickson, B. J., eds.*, 1984, pp. 119–20.

Wilkinson, Bruce W. Canada–U.S. Trade Policy Relations. *Can. Public Policy*, March 1984, 10(1), pp. 96–103. [G: U.S.; Canada]

Williams, Gary W. and Thompson, Robert L. Brazilian Soybean Policy: The International Effects of Intervention. *Amer. J. Agr. Econ.*, November 1984, 66(4), pp. 488–98. [G: Brazil; U.S.]

Winters, L. Alan. British Imports of Manufactures

and the Common Market. *Oxford Econ. Pap.*, March 1984, *36*(1), pp. 103–18. [G: U.K.; EEC]

Winters, L. Alan. Separability and the Specification of Foreign Trade Functions. *J. Int. Econ.*, November 1984, *17*(3/4), pp. 239–63. [G: U.K.]

Woo, Wing T. Macroeconomic Policy Coordination among the Industrial Economies: Comments. *Brookings Pap. Econ. Act.*, 1984, (1), pp. 71–74. [G: U.S.]

Yannopoulos, George N. Prospects for the Manufacturing Exports of the Non-candidate Mediterranean Countries in a Community of Twelve. *World Devel.*, November–December 1984, *12*(11–12), pp. 1087–94. [G: EEC]

Yeats, Alexander J. On the Analysis of Tariff Escalation: Is There a Methodological Bias against the Interest of Developing Countries? *J. Devel. Econ.*, May–June–August 1984, *15*(1,2,3), pp. 77–88. [G: LDCs]

Zakharov, A. N. and Shagalov, G. L. Methods for Determining the Efficiency of Foreign Economic Relations. *Soviet E. Europ. Foreign Trade*, Spring 1984, *20*(1), pp. 76–96.

Zalai, Ernö. Economic Reform, Allocative Efficiency, and Terms of Trade. *Acta Oecon.*, 1984, *33*(3–4), pp. 255–71.

van Zyl, J. C. South Africa in World Trade. *S. Afr. J. Econ.*, March 1984, *52*(1), pp. 42–62. [G: S. Africa]

422 Commercial Policy

4220 Commercial Policy

Adams, F. Gerard and Marquez, Jaime. Petroleum Price Elasticity, Income Effects, and OPEC's Pricing Policy. *Energy J.*, January 1984, *5*(1), pp. 115–28. [G: OECD]

Adams, Nassau A. Towards a Global System of Trade Preferences Among Developing Countries. In *Ghosh, P. K., ed., no. 16*, 1984, *1982*, pp. 57–80. [G: LDCs]

Adams, Walter. "Laissez-Faire," Import Restraints, and Industry Performance: A Case Study of Automobiles. In *[Reynolds, L. G.]*, 1984, pp. 389–408. [G: U.S.]

Adelman, Irma. Development Strategies and the Size Distribution of World Income. *METU*, 1984, *11*(1–2), pp. 177–93. [G: LDCs]

Adelman, M. A. International Oil Agreements. *Energy J.*, July 1984, *5*(3), pp. 1–9.

Al-Husseini, Farouk. An Experiment in the Pricing Stratagy of OPEC Countries. *J. Energy Devel.*, Spring 1984, *9*(2), pp. 337–43. [G: OPEC]

Al-Sowayegh, Abdulaziz and Sharif, Walid. The Security of Oil Supplies: Prevalent Views among Oil Consumers and Producers. *J. Energy Devel.*, Autumn 1984, *10*(1), pp. 29–38. [G: Global]

Ali, M. Shaukat. Employment Expansion—Import Substitution or Export Promotion? A General Equilibrium Study of Pakistan. *Indian Econ. J.*, January–March 1984, *31*(3), pp. 53–61. [G: Pakistan]

Anderson, Kym and Ahn, In-Chan. Protection Policy and Changing Comparative Advantage in Korean Agriculture. *Food Res. Inst. Stud.*, 1984, *19*(2), pp. 139–51. [G: S. Korea]

Andic, Fuat M. Tax Harmonization and Economic Integration. In *Núñez del Arco, J.; Margain, E. and Cherol, R., eds.*, 1984, pp. 205–28. [G: Latin America]

Arce, Horacio. The Trade Liberalization Policy of Argentina: Its Impact on Latin American Integration. In *Núñez del Arco, J.; Margain, E. and Cherol, R., eds.*, 1984, pp. 280–314. [G: Argentina]

Ariah, T. and Daanoune, A. Development of and Prospects for Trade and Economic Co-operation between Morocco and the Socialist Countries of Eastern Europe. In *U.N.C.T.D.*, 1984, pp. 33–43. [G: Morocco; CMEA]

Arndt, Sven W. Exchange Rates and Trade Policy: Comment. *Contemp. Policy Issue*, January 1984, (4), pp. 19–22.

Atsain, Achi. Regional Economic Integration and Foreign Policy. In *Zartman, I. W. and Delgado, C. L., eds.*, 1984, pp. 175–218. [G: Ivory Coast; W. Africa]

Baer, Werner. Industrialization in Latin America: Successes and Failures. *J. Econ. Educ.*, Spring 1984, *15*(2), pp. 124–35. [G: Latin America]

Baer, Werner. Semi-industrialization and Semi-development: The Legacy of Import-Substitution on Development Problems and on Development Economics. *METU*, 1984, *11*(1–2), pp. 151–62. [G: LDCs]

Balassa, Bela. External Shocks and Policy Responses in Sub-Saharan Africa, 1973–78. *Finance Develop.*, March 1984, *21*(1), pp. 10–12. [G: Sub-Saharan Africa]

Balassa, Bela. Prices, Incentives, and Economic Growth. *Weltwirtsch. Arch.*, 1984, *120*(4), pp. 611–30. [G: Global]

Balassa, Bela. The Policy Experience of Twelve Less Developed Countries, 1973–1979. In *[Reynolds, L. G.]*, 1984, pp. 96–123. [G: Selected LDCs]

Balassa, Bela. Trade between Developed and Developing Countries: The Decade Ahead. *OECD Econ. Stud.*, Autumn 1984, (3), pp. 7–25. [G: LDCs; OECD]

Balassa, Bela and Balassa, Carol. Industrial Protection in the Developed Countries. *World Econ.*, June 1984, *7*(2), pp. 179–96. [G: U.S.; Japan; EEC]

Baldwin, Robert E. Rent-seeking and Trade Policy: An Industry Approach. *Weltwirtsch. Arch.*, 1984, *120*(4), pp. 662–77. [G: U.S.]

Baldwin, Robert E. Trade Policies in Developed Countries. In *Jones, R. W. and Kenen, P., eds.*, 1984, pp. 571–619.

Baldwin, Robert E. and Thompson, T. Scott. Responding to Trade-Distorting Policies of Other Countries. *Amer. Econ. Rev.*, May 1984, *74*(2), pp. 271–76.

Ball, George W. Overview of Canadian–U.S. Relations. In *Fried, E. R. and Trezise, P. H., eds.*, 1984, pp. 21–27. [G: U.S.; Canada]

Ballance, Robert and Sinclair, Stuart. Re-industrialising America: Policy Makers and Interest Groups. *World Econ.*, June 1984, 7(2), pp. 197–214. **[G: U.S.]**

Bardhan, Pranab K. and Kletzer, Kenneth M. Dynamic Effects of Protection on Productivity. *J. Int. Econ.*, February 1984, 16(1/2), pp. 45–57.

Barnouin, Jack P. Trade and Economic Cooperation Among Developing Countries. In *Ghosh, P. K., ed., no. 16*, 1984, *1982*, pp. 37–43. **[G: LDCs]**

Barnouin, Jack P. Trade and Economic Cooperation Among Developing Countries. In *Ghosh, P. K., ed., no. 15*, 1984, *1982*, pp. 239–47. **[G: LDCs]**

Baysan, Tercan. Resource Shifts under Tariff Liberalization and Turkey's Comparative Advantage in Agriculture. *Europ. Rev. Agr. Econ.*, 1984, 11(3), pp. 303–22. **[G: Turkey]**

Beattie, John R. and Rothschild, Leonard W., Jr. U.S.A.: Foreign Sales Corporation—The Successor to DISC. *Bull. Int. Fiscal Doc.*, December 1984, 38(12), pp. 552–56. **[G: U.S.]**

Behrman, Jere R. Rethinking Global Negotiations: Trade. In *Bhagwati, J. N. and Ruggie, J. G., eds.*, 1984, pp. 232–58.

Beladi, Hamid. Welfare Effects of Trade Restrictions: The Case of the U.S. Dairy Industry. *Atlantic Econ. J.*, December 1984, 12(4), pp. 70. **[G: U.S.]**

Bell, Martin; Ross-Larson, Bruce and Westphal, Larry E. Assessing the Performance of Infant Industries. *J. Devel. Econ.*, September–October 1984, 16(1–2), pp. 101–28. **[G: LDCs]**

Bennett, James T. and DiLorenzo, Thomas J. Unions, Politics, and Protectionism. *J. Lab. Res.*, Summer 1984, 5(3), pp. 287–307. **[G: U.S.]**

Berlage, L. Commodity Price Stabilization by Buffer Stocks and by Export Quotas. *Tijdschrift Econ. Manage.*, 1984, 29(3), pp. 437–48. **[G: LDCs]**

Bernhardt, Dan. Dumping, Adjustment Costs, and Uncertainty. *J. Econ. Dynam. Control*, December 1984, 8(3), pp. 349–70.

Beshai, Adel A. The Economics of a Primary Commodity: Gum Arabic. *Oxford Bull. Econ. Statist.*, November 1984, 46(4), pp. 371–81. **[G: Sudan; Nigeria; Tanzania; W. Africa]**

Bhagwati, Jagdish N. Industrial Expansion in Developing Countries and Implications for Trade Policies. In *Ghosh, P. K., ed., no. 16*, 1984, *1979*, pp. 152–62.

Bhagwati, Jagdish N. Splintering and Disembodiment of Services and Developing Nations. *World Econ.*, June 1984, 7(2), pp. 133–43. **[G: LDCs; U.K.; U.S.]**

Bhagwati, Jagdish N.; Schatz, Klaus-Werner and Wong, Kar-yiu. The West German *Gastarbeiter* System of Immigration. *Europ. Econ. Rev.*, December 1984, 26(3), pp. 277–94. **[G: W. Germany]**

Bils, Mark. Tariff Protection and Production in the Early U.S. Cotton Textile Industry. *J. Econ. Hist.*, December 1984, 44(4), pp. 1033–45. **[G: U.S.]**

Bird, Peter J. W. N. The Costs and Benefits of Protection: A Comment. *Kyklos*, 1984, 37(1), pp. 102–03. **[G: U.S.]**

Biswas, Basudeb and Shahrokni, Ahmad. A Static Analysis of Domestic Production Loss in the Presence of Negative Value-Added: The Case of Iranian Automobile Industry. *J. Econ. Devel.*, July 1984, 9(1), pp. 113–24. **[G: Iran]**

Black, C. J. and Bowers, J. K. The Level of Protection of UK Agriculture. *Oxford Bull. Econ. Statist.*, November 1984, 46(4), pp. 291–310. **[G: U.K.]**

Blyth, Nicola. The EEC Sheepmeat Market and Voluntary Export Restraint Agreements. *Australian J. Agr. Econ.*, April 1984, 28(1), pp. 33–43. **[G: EEC; Australia; New Zealand]**

Bonker, Don. Reconciling Export Opportunities and National Security Policy: Renewal of the Export Administration Act. In *Czinkota, M. R., ed.*, 1984, pp. 153–60. **[G: U.S.]**

Bradford, Colin I., Jr. The NICs: Confronting U.S. "Autonomy." In *Feinberg, R. E. and Kallab, V., eds., no. 1*, 1984, pp. 119–38. **[G: LDCs]**

Brander, James A. and Spencer, Barbara J. Trade Warfare: Tariffs and Cartels. *J. Int. Econ.*, May 1984, 16(3/4), pp. 227–42.

Bright, Samuel L. and McKinney, Joseph A. The Economics of the Steel Trigger Price Mechanism. *Bus. Econ.*, July 1984, 19(4), pp. 40–46. **[G: U.S.]**

Brock, William E. Canadian–U.S. Trade Negotiations: A Status Report. In *Fried, E. R. and Trezise, P. H., eds.*, 1984, pp. 65–67. **[G: Canada; U.S.]**

Brock, William E. Developing Multilateral Trade Controls. In *Czinkota, M. R., ed.*, 1984, pp. 45–49. **[G: CMEA; OECD]**

Brock, William E. The Role of Increased International Trade in Long-term Economic Growth. In *Wachter, M. L. and Wachter, S. M., eds.*, 1984, pp. 439–46. **[G: U.S.]**

Buffie, Edward F. The Macroeconomics of Trade Liberalization. *J. Int. Econ.*, August 1984, 17(1/2), pp. 121–37. **[G: LDCs]**

Burbidge, John B. and Harrison, Alan. Testing for the Effects of Oil-Price Rises Using Vector Autoregressions. *Int. Econ. Rev.*, June 1984, 25(2), pp. 459–84. **[G: U.S.; Japan; W. Germany; U.K.; Canada]**

Burián, Gustav. Czechoslovak Economic Law and External Economic Relations. *Czech. Econ. Digest.*, May 1984, (3), pp. 63–88. **[G: Czechoslovakia]**

Buswell, David H. Fiatallis North America, Inc., and the Pipeline Sanctions. In *Czinkota, M. R., ed.*, 1984, pp. 103–10. **[G: U.S.; U.S.S.R.]**

Byatt, I. C. R. Byatt Report on Subsidies to British Export Credits. *World Econ.*, June 1984, 7(2), pp. 163–78. **[G: U.K.]**

Byatt, I. C. R. Reflections on the Byatt Report: Rejoinder [Byatt Report on Subsidies to British Export Credits]. *World Econ.*, September 1984, 7(3), pp. 345–46. **[G: U.K.]**

Cairns, Robert D. Changing Structure in the World Nickel Industry. *Antitrust Bull.*, Fall 1984, *29*(3), pp. 561–75. **[G: U.S.]**

Canto, Victor A. The Effect of Voluntary Restraint Agreements: A Case Study of the Steel Industry. *Appl. Econ.*, April 1984, *16*(2), pp. 175–86. **[G: U.S.]**

Capriglioni, Francesco. Azione promozionale dello Stato negli scambi commerciali con l'estero. (Government Promotion in the Area of Foreign Trade. With English summary.) *Bancaria*, May–June 1984, *40*(5–6), pp. 492–512. **[G: Italy]**

de Carvalho, Frederico A. As *Trading Companies* no comércio exterior do Brasil: Desempenho recente e perspectivas. (With English summary.) *Economia (Portugal)*, October 1984, *8*(3), pp. 509–25. **[G: Brazil]**

Chalmin, Ph. G. The Important Trends in Sugar Diplomacy before 1914. In *Albert, B. and Graves, A.*, eds., 1984, pp. 9–19.
[G: Global]

Charnovitz, Steve. Caribbean Basin Initiative: Setting Labor Standards. *Mon. Lab. Rev.*, November 1984, *107*(11), pp. 54–56.
[G: Caribbean]

Chishti, Sumitra. Experience of India in Trade and Economic Relations with the Socialist Countries of Eastern Europe and Its Relevance to Developing Countries. In *U.N.C.T.D.*, 1984, pp. 19–31. **[G: India; CMEA]**

Clark, Paul G. Step-by-Step Liberalization of a Controlled Economy: Experience in Egypt. In *[Chenery, H. B.]*, 1984, pp. 179–203.
[G: Egypt]

Co, Nemesio. Crisis Management Directions for the Export Sector. *Philippine Econ. J.*, Winter 1984, *23*(1), pp. 66–71. **[G: Philippines]**

Cohen, Jon S.; Rubin, Jeffrey and Saunders, Ronald S. Chasing the Bandwagon: Government Policy for the Electronics Industry. *Can. Public Policy*, March 1984, *10*(1), pp. 25–34.
[G: OECD]

Conesa, Eduardo R. Latin American Integration in the Eighties. In *Salazar-Carrillo, J. and Tirado de Alonso, I.*, eds., no. 2, 1984, pp. 1–14. **[G: Latin America]**

Conesa, Eduardo R. Latin American Integration in the Eighties. In *Jorge, A.; Salazar-Carrillo, J. and Sanchez, E. P.*, 1984, pp. 97–101.
[G: Latin America]

Conesa, Eduardo R. The Openness of the Latin American Southern Cone Economies. In *Núñez del Arco, J.; Margain, E. and Cherol, R.*, eds., 1984, pp. 253–79. **[G: Argentina; Chile; Uruguay]**

Conybeare, John. Politicians and Protection: Tariffs and Elections in Australia. *Public Choice*, 1984, *43*(2), pp. 203–09. **[G: Australia]**

Cordovez, Diego. Institutional Elements of a New Diplomacy for Development (Notes for a Book of Memoirs). *Cepal Rev.*, 1984, (23), pp. 29–43. **[G: Global]**

Cornell, Robert A. The New Nexus among Trade, Industrial and Exchange-Rate Policies: Com-

ment. In *Agmon, T.; Hawkins, R. G. and Levich, R. M.*, eds., 1984, pp. 280–83.

Costa, Antonio Maria. The Pressure towards Protectionism: Is It Systemic? A Legacy of the Regression? The Result of Policy to Promote Recovery? *World Devel.*, October 1984, *12*(10), pp. 1051–61. **[G: Global]**

Costick, Miles M. The Dangers of Dependence. In *Czinkota, M. R.*, ed., 1984, pp. 70–75.
[G: CMEA; OECD]

Cronin, M. R. Protection and Employment in the Motor Car Sector. *Australian Econ. Pap.*, June 1984, *23*(42), pp. 38–51.

Csaba, Laszlo. The Role of CMEA in the World Economy in the 1980s. *ACES Bull.*, Summer–Fall 1984, *26*(2–3), pp. 1–28. **[G: CMEA]**

Curlee, T. Randall. Monitoring the Potential for Future Oil Supply Crises: The Lack of Information. *J. Energy Devel.*, Spring 1984, *9*(2), pp. 289–97. **[G: OPEC]**

Czinkota, Michael R. International Economic Sanctions and Trade Controls: A Taxonomic Analysis. In *Czinkota, M. R.*, ed., 1984, pp. 3–17. **[G: Global]**

Das, Bhagirath L. The Gatt Ministerial Meeting, 1982: An Interpretative Note. *J. World Trade Law*, January:February 1984, *18*(1), pp. 3–15.

Das, Dilip K. GATT: Complaints between the United States and the European Community. *J. World Trade Law*, September–October 1984, *18*(5), pp. 456–59. **[G: U.S.; EEC]**

Das, Satya P. and Mohanty, Adwait K. Dumping in International Markets and Welfare: A General Equilibrium Analysis. *J. Int. Econ.*, August 1984, *17*(1/2), pp. 149–57.

Davidson, Carl. Cartel Stability and Tariff Policy. *J. Int. Econ.*, November 1984, *17*(3/4), pp. 219–37.

De Rosa, Dean A. The International Natural Rubber Agreement and Exchange Rate Changes. *Singapore Econ. Rev.*, April 1984, *29*(1), pp. 30–46. **[G: Global]**

Dealy, John F. Realism in Trade with Adversaries. In *Czinkota, M. R.*, ed., 1984, pp. 76–81. **[G: U.S.]**

Decaluwe, Bernard and Lee, Y. D. Procédures pour l'estimation des taux de protection effectifs dans les matrices entrées-sorties. (A Procedure to Estimate Effective Rate of Protection Coefficient. With English summary.) *L'Actual. Econ.*, June 1984, *60*(2), pp. 254–62.

Deese, David. The Vulnerability of Modern Economies. In *McCormick, G. H. and Bissell, R. E.*, eds., 1984, pp. 148–80. **[G: OECD; CMEA]**

Díaz-Alejandro, Carlos F. The U.S. Response to Foreign Industrial Targeting: Comments. *Brookings Pap. Econ. Act.*, 1984, (1), pp. 122–25. **[G: U.S.]**

Dick, Hermann, et al. Stabilisation Strategies in Primary Commodity Exporting Countries: A Case Study of Chile. *J. Devel. Econ.*, May–June–August 1984, *15*(1,2,3), pp. 47–75.
[G: Chile]

Dixon, Peter B.; Parmenter, B. R. and Powell, Alan A. Trade Liberalization and Labor Market

Disruption. *J. Policy Modeling,* November 1984, *6*(4), pp. 431–54. **[G: Australia]**

Dompierre, Michael B. The United Auto Workers vs. the Japanese: Distributional Effects of Alternative United States Trade Policies. *Aussenwirtschaft,* September 1984, *39*(3), pp. 207–18. **[G: U.S.; Japan]**

Donaghue, Hugh P. Establishing Principles for Trade in Computer Services. In *Fried, E. R. and Trezise, P. H., eds.,* 1984, pp. 87–95.

Dornbusch, Rudiger. On the Consequences of Muddling through the Debt Crisis. *World Econ.,* June 1984, *7*(2), pp. 145–61.
[G: Latin America; U.S.]

Drabek, Zdenek. Exports of Primary Commodities and the Soviet Terms of Trade. In *Kostecki, M. M., ed.,* 1984, pp. 26–67. **[G: U.S.S.R.; CMEA; Global]**

Drabek, Zdenek and Greenaway, David. Economic Integration and Intra-industry Trade: The EEC and CMEA Compared. *Kyklos,* 1984, *37*(3), pp. 444–69. **[G: EEC; CMEA]**

Driscoll, Robert E. and Behrman, Jack N. National Industrial Policies: Introduction. In *Driscoll, R. E. and Behrman, J. N., eds.,* 1984, pp. 1–24. **[G: LDCs; MDCs]**

Dror, David M. Aspects of Labour Law and Relations in Selected Export Processing Zones. *Int. Lab. Rev.,* November–December 1984, *123*(6), pp. 705–22. **[G: Mauritius; Sri Lanka; Pakistan; Philippines]**

Dunkel, Arthur. Lessons from Textile Experience for General Trade Policy. *World Econ.,* December 1984, *7*(4), pp. 361–68.

Eckaus, Richard S. and Mohie-Eldin, Amr. Consequences of Changes in Subsidy Policy: The Egyptian Case. In *[Chenery, H. B.],* 1984, pp. 477–92. **[G: Egypt]**

Eichengreen, Barry. Keynes and Protection. *J. Econ. Hist.,* June 1984, *44*(2), pp. 363–73.
[G: U.K.]

Eldor, Rafael. On the Risk-Adjusted Effective Protection Rate. *Rev. Econ. Statist.,* May 1984, *66*(2), pp. 235–41. **[G: U.S.]**

Estanislao, Jesus P. Philippine Industrialization Policy. In *Driscoll, R. E. and Behrman, J. N., eds.,* 1984, pp. 121–36. **[G: Philippines]**

Ewing, A. F. Non-Tariff Barriers and Non-Adjustment *or* International Trade: Review Article. *J. World Trade Law,* January:February 1984, *18*(1), pp. 63–80. **[G: Global]**

Faber, Gerrit. The Economics of Stabex. *J. World Trade Law,* January:February 1984, *18*(1), pp. 52–62. **[G: EEC; Selected LDCs]**

Falkenheim, Victor C. Chinese Trade Policy Reforms: Domestic Determinants and International Implications. In *Downen, R. L. and Dickson, B. J., eds.,* 1984, pp. 131–44.
[G: China]

Feketekuty, Geza and Aronson, Jonathan D. Meeting the Challenges of the World Information Economy. *World Econ.,* March 1984, *7*(1), pp. 63–86. **[G: Global]**

Fiallo, Fabio R. The Negotiations Strategy of Developing Countries in the Field of Trade Liber-

alization. In *Ghosh, P. K., ed., no. 16,* 1984, *1977,* pp. 240–49.

Filippucci, Carlo and Paris, Quirino. Importazione di grano: un caso di mercati "controllati." (Wheat Prices and Administered Prices. With English summary.) *Statistica,* April–June 1984, *44*(2), pp. 271–300. **[G: Italy; EEC]**

Flacco, Paul R., et al. Exchange Rates and Trade Policy. *Contemp. Policy Issue,* January 1984, (4), pp. 6–18. **[G: U.S.]**

Folkerts-Landau, Elena. The Social Cost of Imported Oil. *Energy J.,* July 1984, *5*(3), pp. 41–58.

Frank, Andre Gunder. Economic Crisis, Export Promotion and Political Repression in the Third World. In *Ngo, M., ed., vol. 1,* 1984, pp. 54–67. **[G: LDCs; S. Korea]**

Fraser, Malcolm. Pacific Community: Further Steps. In *Downen, R. L. and Dickson, B. J., eds.,* 1984, pp. 3–11. **[G: Pacific Basin]**

Frazee, Rowland C. Traded Computer Services: A Bilateral Beginning. In *Fried, E. R. and Trezise, P. H., eds.,* 1984, pp. 77–86.
[G: U.S.; Canada]

Freedenberg, Paul. High Technology and the Export Administration Act. In *Czinkota, M. R., ed.,* 1984, pp. 169–76. **[G: U.S.]**

Frenzel, Bill. In Search of an Optimistic Scenario for the 1980s: Comment. In *Wachter, M. L. and Wachter, S. M., eds.,* 1984, pp. 427–30.
[G: Global; U.S.]

Frey, Bruno S. Die Politische Ökonomie des Protektionismus. Nationalstaatliche Determinanten der Regulierung der internationalen Wirtschafsbeziehungen. (The Political Economics of Protectionism. With English summary.) *Aussenwirtschaft,* May 1984, *39*(1/2), pp. 17–42. **[G: U.S.]**

Fried, Edward R. and Trezise, Philip H. U.S.–Canadian Economic Relations *Next Steps?* An Introductory Perspective. In *Fried, E. R. and Trezise, P. H., eds.,* 1984, pp. 1–7.
[G: Canada; U.S.]

Fukushima, Kiyohiko. Public Use of Private Interests: Japan's Industrial Policy. In *Driscoll, R. E. and Behrman, J. N., eds.,* 1984, pp. 73–84. **[G: Japan]**

Gang, Ira N. The Private Cost of Labor Adjustment: Comment. *Contemp. Policy Issue,* January 1984, (4), pp. 37–38. **[G: Canada]**

Garavoglia, Guido. From Rambouillet to Williamsburg: A Historical Assessment. In *Merlini, C., ed.,* 1984, pp. 1–42. **[G: OECD]**

Gately, Dermot. A Ten-Year Retrospective: OPEC and the World Oil Market. *J. Econ. Lit.,* September 1984, *22*(3), pp. 1100–114.
[G: OPEC]

Gerken, Egbert. Diversification and Stabilization in a Resource-Exporting Country. In *Siebert, H., ed.,* 1984, pp. 117–55. **[G: Chile]**

Ghibutiu, Aurel. Effects of Most Favored Nation and Generalized System of Preferences Treatment on Romania's Exports to the United States. In *Jackson, M. R. and Woodson, J. D., Jr., eds.,* 1984, pp. 103–15. **[G: Romania; U.S.]**

Ghosh, S.; Gilbert, C. L. and Hughes Hallett, Andrew J. Commodity Market Stabilization: A Comparison of Simple and Optimal Intervention Strategies in the World Copper Market. *J. Policy Modeling*, November 1984, *6*(4), pp. 555–72. [G: Global]

Ghosh, S.; Gilbert, C. L. and Hughes Hallett, Andrew J. Simple and Optimal Control Rules for Stabilising Commodity Markets. In *Hughes Hallet, A.J., ed.*, 1984, pp. 209–48.

Gibbs, I. and Konovalov, V. Volume Quotas with Heterogeneous Product Categories. *Econ. Rec.*, September 1984, *60*(170), pp. 294–303.

Gilpin, Robert. Structural Constraints on Economic Leverage: Market-Type Systems. In *McCormick, G. H. and Bissell, R. E., eds.*, 1984, pp. 105–28.

Giordano, Yvonne. Analyse de la politique française du commerce extérieur depuis le VIe Plan. (With English summary.) *Rev. Econ. Ind.*, 3rd Trimester 1984, (29), pp. 46–61. [G: France]

Glenday, Graham and Jenkins, Glenn P. Industrial Dislocation and the Private Cost of Labor Adjustment. *Contemp. Policy Issue*, January 1984, (4), pp. 23–36. [G: Canada]

Goldina, I. Soviet Export Potential and Several Aspects of Soviet Foreign Trade. *Prob. Econ.*, March 1984, *26*(11), pp. 3–14. [G: U.S.S.R.]

Goldstein, Judith L. and Krasner, Stephen D. Unfair Trade Practices: The Case for a Differential Response. *Amer. Econ. Rev.*, May 1984, *74*(2), pp. 282–87. [G: U.S.; Japan]

Gómez-Ibáñez, José A. and Morgan, Ivor P. Deregulating International Markets: The Examples of Aviation and Ocean Shipping. *Yale J. Regul.*, 1984, *2*(1), pp. 107–44. [G: U.S.]

Gordon, Kathryn M. and Rausser, Gordon C. Country Hedging for Real Income Stabilization: A Case Study of South Korea and Egypt. *J. Futures Markets*, Winter 1984, *4*(4), pp. 449–64. [G: S. Korea]

Gotlieb, Allan E. Managing Canadian–U.S. Interdependence. In *Fried, E. R. and Trezise, P. H., eds.*, 1984, pp. 127–34. [G: U.S.; Canada]

Greenaway, David. A Statistical Analysis of Fiscal Dependence on Trade Taxes and Economic Development. *Public Finance*, 1984, *39*(1), pp. 70–89. [G: Global]

Greenaway, David. Multilateral Trade Policy in the 1980s. *Lloyds Bank Rev.*, January 1984, (151), pp. 30–44. [G: LDCs; MDCs]

Grubel, Herbert G. Free Economic Zones: Good or Bad? *Aussenwirtschaft*, May 1984, *39*(1/2), pp. 43–56. [G: U.S.; U.K.]

Guy, Donna J. Sugar Industries at the Periphery of the World Market: Argentina, 1860–1914. In *Albert, B. and Graves, A., eds.*, 1984, pp. 147–62. [G: Argentina]

Gwin, Catherine. Strengthening the Framework of the Global Economic Organizations. In *Bhagwati, J. N. and Ruggie, J. G., eds.*, 1984, pp. 125–77.

Hager, Wolfgang. North–South Trade and Socioeconomic Autonomy: A Peace Formula. In

Ghosh, P. K., ed., no. 16, 1984, *1982*, pp. 81–91. [G: EEC]

Haggart, Veronica A. Economic and Financial Stability: Comment. In *Wachter, M. L. and Wachter, S. M., eds.*, 1984, pp. 413–15. [G: U.S.]

Hansson, Göte and Lundahl, Mats. A Social Clause against Discrimination in the Labor Market. *J. Devel. Econ.*, April 1984, *14*(3), pp. 395–405.

Harper, Edwin L. Do We Need an Industrial Policy? In *Wachter, M. L. and Wachter, S. M., eds.*, 1984, pp. 457–69. [G: U.S.]

Harris, Richard G. Applied General Equilibrium Analysis of Small Open Economies with Scale Economies and Imperfect Competition. *Amer. Econ. Rev.*, December 1984, *74*(5), pp. 1016–32. [G: Canada]

Heinz, John. The Export Administration Act: The Senate View. In *Czinkota, M. R., ed.*, 1984, pp. 161–68. [G: U.S.]

Helleiner, Gerald K. The New Industrial Protectionism and the Developing Countries. In *Ghosh, P. K., ed., no. 16*, 1984, *1979*, pp. 190–218. [G: OECD]

Herander, Mark G. and Schwartz, J. Brad. An Empirical Test of the Impact of the Threat of U.S. Trade Policy: The Case of Antidumping Duties. *Southern Econ. J.*, July 1984, *51*(1), pp. 59–79. [G: U.S.]

Hervitz, Hugo M. Some Thoughts about Latin American Integration in the Eighties. In *Jorge, A.; Salazar-Carrillo, J. and Sanchez, E. P.*, 1984, pp. 103–04. [G: Latin America]

Hickson, Allister B. Estimation of Producer Losses Arising from the Partial Embargo of Grain Exports to the Soviet Union: A Comment. *Can. J. Agr. Econ.*, March 1984, *32*(1), pp. 235–36. [G: Canada; U.S.]

Higgs, Peter J.; Parmenter, B. R. and Powell, Alan A. The Scope for Tariff Reform Created by a Resources Boom: Simulations with the ORANI Model. *Australian Econ. Pap.*, June 1984, *23*(42), pp. 1–26. [G: Australia]

Hill, John K. and Méndez, José A. The Effect of Commercial Policy on International Migration Flows: The Case of the United States and Mexico. *J. Int. Econ.*, August 1984, *17*(1/2), pp. 41–53. [G: U.S.; Mexico]

Hillman, Arye L. Declining Industries and Political-Support Protectionist Motives: Errata. *Amer. Econ. Rev.*, March 1984, *74*(1), pp. 260.

Hitiris, T. and Petoussis, E. Price and Tariff Effects in a Dynamic Specification of the Demand for Imports. *Appl. Econ.*, February 1984, *16*(1), pp. 15–24. [G: Greece; EEC]

Hollerman, Leon. Japan's Direct Investment in California and the New Protectionism. *J. World Trade Law*, July–August 1984, *18*(4), pp. 309–19. [G: Japan; U.S.]

Hufbauer, Gary Clyde and Schott, Jeffrey J. Economic Sanctions: An Often Used and Occasionally Effective Tool of Foreign Policy. In *Czinkota, M. R., ed.*, 1984, pp. 18–33. [G: Global]

Huguel, Catherine. La balance des paiements

française: une contrainte extérieure qui demeure. (With English summary.) *Revue Écon. Polit.*, September–October 1984, *94*(5), pp. 662–75.   [G: France]

Isarescu, Mugur and Timofei, Emil. Ensuring a Stable Legal Framework for the Development of Economic Relations between the United States and Romania. In *Jackson, M. R. and Woodson, J. D., Jr., eds.*, 1984, pp. 145–49.
[G: U.S.; Romania]

Itoh, Motoshige and Ono, Yoshiyasu. Tariffs vs. Quotas under Duopoly of Heterogeneous Goods. *J. Int. Econ.*, November 1984, *17*(3/4), pp. 359–73.

Jackson, John H. Perspectives on the Jurisprudence of International Trade. *Amer. Econ. Rev.*, May 1984, *74*(2), pp. 277–81.

Jackson, John H. Perspectives on the Jurisprudence of International Trade: Costs and Benefits of Legal Procedures in the United States. *Mich. Law Rev.*, April–May 1984, *82*(5 & 6), pp. 1570–87.   [G: U.S.]

Jackson, Marvin R. and Woodson, James D., Jr. New Horizons in East–West Relations: Introduction. In *Jackson, M. R. and Woodson, J. D., Jr., eds.*, 1984, pp. 1–10.
[G: Romania; U.S.]

Jenkins, Kempton B. The Business Perspective of Trade with Adversaries. In *Czinkota, M. R., ed.*, 1984, pp. 55–62.   [G: U.S.; CMEA]

Jones, Kent. The Political Economy of Voluntary Export Restraint Agreements. *Kyklos*, 1984, *37*(1), pp. 82–101.

Kanbur, S. M. Ravi. How to Analyse Commodity Price Stabilization? A Review Article. *Oxford Econ. Pap.*, November 1984, *36*(3), pp. 336–58.   [G: LDCs]

Kaplinsky, Raphael. The International Context for Industrialisation in the Coming Decade. *J. Devel. Stud.*, October 1984, *21*(1), pp. 75–96.

Kaplinsky, Raphael. The International Context for Industrialisation in the Coming Decade. In *Kaplinsky, R., ed.*, 1984, pp. 75–96.

Kaufman, Richard F. The Strategic Dimensions of Trade: A Framework for Discussion. In *Czinkota, M. R., ed.*, 1984, pp. 34–39.   [G: U.S.; U.S.S.R.]

Khanna, Ashok. Market Distortions and Export Performance: India's Exports of Manufactures in the 1970s. *Weltwirtsch. Arch.*, 1984, *120*(2), pp. 348–60.   [G: India]

Kibola, Hamisi S. Stabex and Lomé III. *J. World Trade Law*, January:February 1984, *18*(1), pp. 32–51.   [G: EEC; Selected LDCs]

Kimbrough, Kent P. Commercial Policy and Aggregate Employment under Rational Expectations. *Quart. J. Econ.*, August 1984, *99*(3), pp. 567–85.

Kindleberger, Charles P. A GATT for International Direct Investment: Further Reflections. In *Kindleberger, C. P.*, 1984, *1980*, pp. 247–65.

Kindleberger, Charles P. and Goldberg, Paul M. Toward a GATT for Investment: A Proposal

for Supervision of the International Corporation. In *Kindleberger, C. P.*, 1984, *1970*, pp. 202–31.

Kirmani, Naheed; Molajoni, Pierluigi and Mayer, Thomas. Effects of Increased Market Access on Exports of Developing Countries. *Int. Monet. Fund Staff Pap.*, December 1984, *31*(4), pp. 661–84.   [G: LDCs; OECD]

Kissinger, Henry A. Foreign Policy and Economics. In *Wachter, M. L. and Wachter, S. M., eds.*, 1984, pp. 447–56.   [G: U.S.]

Knorr, Klaus. Economic Relations as an Instrument of National Power. In *McCormick, G. H. and Bissell, R. E., eds.*, 1984, pp. 183–207.

Kohli, Ulrich R. Terms of Trade and Welfare: Estimates. *Kyklos*, 1984, *37*(4), pp. 577–97.
[G: U.S.; Canada; Australia; Switzerland]

Kostecki, Michel M. Can Tariff Be Effective under Central Planning? *Econ. Int.*, February–May 1984, *37*(1–2), pp. 94–107.

Krause, Lawrence B. Australia's Comparative Advantage in International Trade. In *Caves, R. E. and Krause, L. B., eds.*, 1984, pp. 275–311.   [G: Australia]

Kreinin, Mordechai E. and Finger, J. M. A Critical Survey of the New International Economic Order. In *Ghosh, P. K., ed., no. 9*, 1984, *1976*, pp. 313–34.

Krueger, Anne O. Trade Policies in Developing Countries. In *Jones, R. W. and Kenen, P., eds.*, 1984, pp. 519–69.   [G: Selected LDCs]

Krugman, Paul R. Import Protection as Export Promotion: International Competition in the Presence of Oligopoly and Economics of Scale. In *Kierzkowski, H., ed.*, 1984, pp. 180–93.

Krugman, Paul R. The U.S. Response to Foreign Industrial Targeting. *Brookings Pap. Econ. Act.*, 1984, (1), pp. 77–121.   [G: U.S.]

Lall, Sanjaya. India's Technological Capacity: Effects of Trade, Industrial, Science and Technology Policies. In *Fransman, M. and King, K., eds.*, 1984, pp. 225–43.   [G: India]

Lall, Sanjaya. South–South Economic Cooperation and Global Negotiations. In *Bhagwati, J. N. and Ruggie, J. G., eds.*, 1984, pp. 287–322.
[G: India; LDCs]

Lavigne, Marie. Long-term Commodity Agreements and the USSR. In *Kostecki, M. M., ed.*, 1984, pp. 15–25.   [G: U.S.S.R.; CMEA; Global]

Lawrence, Robert Z. The U.S. Response to Foreign Industrial Targeting: Comments. *Brookings Pap. Econ. Act.*, 1984, (1), pp. 125–29.
[G: U.S.]

Lehmann, Jean-Pierre. Agenda for Action on Issues in Euro-Japanese Relations. *World Econ.*, September 1984, *7*(3), pp. 257–76. [G: EEC; Japan]

van Lennep, Jonkheer Emile. Strengthening the International Trade and Financial Systems. *World Econ.*, March 1984, *7*(1), pp. 23–32.
[G: OECD]

Leo, Hooi-Eng. Effects of Trade Policies on the Structure and Growth of Manufacturing Industries in Peninsular Malaysia: 1960–1980. *Philip-*

pine Rev. Econ. Bus., Sept./Dec. 1984, *21*(3/4), pp. 219–38. **[G: Malaysia]**

Levine, Herbert S. Structural Constraints on Economic Leverage: Command-Type Systems. In *McCormick, G. H. and Bissell, R. E., eds.*, 1984, pp. 129–47.

Li, Kuo-Lee. The Law of GATT: Study and Research. *J. World Trade Law*, July–August 1984, *18*(4), pp. 357–65. **[G: Global]**

Liang, Kuo-shu and Liang, Ching-ing Hou. Trade, Technology Transfers, and Risks of Protectionism: The Experience of the Republic of China. In *Downen, R. L. and Dickson, B. J., eds.*, 1984, pp. 145–59. **[G: Taiwan]**

Liebman, Howard M. GATT and Countertrade Requirements: Comment [The International Treatment of State Trading]. *J. World Trade Law*, May–June 1984, *18*(3), pp. 252–61.

Lim, Hua Sing. Japanese Perspectives on Malaysia's "Look East" Policy. In *Thambipillai, P., ed.*, 1984, pp. 231–45. **[G: Malaysia; Japan]**

Little, I. M. D. Import Controls and Exports in Developing Countries. In *Ghosh, P. K., ed., no. 16*, 1984, *1982*, pp. 268–77.

Livingstone, Neil C. The Politics of Trade with Adversaries. In *Czinkota, M. R., ed.*, 1984, pp. 63–69. **[G: U.S.; Selected countries]**

Longworth, David. A Comment on 'The Small Country Assumption: A Note on Canadian Exports.' *Appl. Econ.*, December 1984, *16*(6), pp. 933–34. **[G: Canada]**

Lundahl, Mats. Economic Effects of a Trade and Investment Boycott against South Africa. *Scand. J. Econ.*, 1984, *86*(1), pp. 68–83. **[G: S. Africa]**

Lundborg, Per. The Nexus between Income Distribution, Trade Policy, and Monopoly Power: An Assessment of the Tin Market. *J. Policy Modeling*, February 1984, *6*(1), pp. 69–79. **[G: Malaysia]**

Marer, Paul. United States Market Disruption Procedures Involving Romanian and Other CPE Products, with Policy Recommendations. In *Jackson, M. R. and Woodson, J. D., Jr., eds.*, 1984, pp. 117–44. **[G: U.S.; Romania]**

Markusen, James R. The Welfare and Allocative Effects of Export Taxes versus Marketing Boards. *J. Devel. Econ.*, January–February 1984, *14*(1–2), pp. 19–36.

Marsh, Peter. The European Community and East–West Economic Relations. *J. Common Market Stud.*, September 1984, *23*(1), pp. 1–13. **[G: EEC; CMEA]**

Mattera, A. Protectionism inside the European Community: Decisions of the European Court. *J. World Trade Law*, July–August 1984, *18*(4), pp. 283–308. **[G: EEC]**

McFarland, Henry. Transport Costs and Processing. *J. Transp. Econ. Policy*, September 1984, *18*(3), pp. 311–15. **[G: U.S.]**

Michel, Gilles and Noel, Michel. The Ivorian Economy and Alternative Trade Regimes. In *Zartman, I. W. and Delgado, C. L., eds.*, 1984, pp. 77–114. **[G: Ivory Coast]**

Milward, Alan S. Restriction of Supply as a Strate-gic Choice. In *McCormick, G. H. and Bissell, R. E., eds.*, 1984, pp. 44–58. **[G: Japan; Germany; U.K.]**

Mohammad, Sharif and Whalley, John. Rent Seeking in India: Its Costs and Policy Significance. *Kyklos*, 1984, *37*(3), pp. 387–413. **[G: India]**

Mohammad, Yousuf Hasan. Recent Developments within OPEC: An Economic Perspective. *J. Energy Devel.*, Spring 1984, *9*(2), pp. 223–41. **[G: OPEC]**

Morales, Juan Antonio. Problems Surrounding the Common External Tariff: The Andean Group Case. In *Núñez del Arco, J.; Margain, E. and Cherol, R., eds.*, 1984, pp. 185–204. **[G: Latin America]**

Morgan, Ann D. Protectionism and European Trade in Manufactures. *Nat. Inst. Econ. Rev.*, August 1984, (109), pp. 45–57. **[G: EEC; EFTA]**

Morris, D. J. Reflections on the Byatt Report [Byatt Report on Subsidies to British Export Credits]. *World Econ.*, September 1984, *7*(3), pp. 341–44. **[G: U.K.]**

Motono, Moriyuki. World Trade Issues Require More than a Piecemeal Approach. *World Econ.*, September 1984, *7*(3), pp. 229–39. **[G: Global]**

Munger, Michael C. The Costs of Protectionism. *Challenge*, January/February 1984, *26*(6), pp. 54–58. **[G: U.S.]**

Mutti, John. Subsidized Production, World Steel Trade and Countervailing Duties. *Southern Econ. J.*, January 1984, *50*(3), pp. 871–80. **[G: Selected Countries]**

Newbery, David M. G. Commodity Price Stabilization in Imperfect or Cartelized Markets. *Econometrica*, May 1984, *52*(3), pp. 563–78.

Nishimizu, Mieko and Robinson, Sherman. Trade Policies and Productivity Change in Semi-industrialized Countries. *J. Devel. Econ.*, September–October 1984, *16*(1–2), pp. 177–206. **[G: S. Korea; Turkey; Yugoslavia; Japan]**

Nobel, Peter. Internationalisierung der Tatbestände und nationalstaatliches Recht. (International Facts and National Law. With English summary.) *Aussenwirtschaft*, May 1984, *39*(1/2), pp. 91–118. **[G: Global]**

Nogués, Julio J. Políticas agrícolas y los países en desarrollo en el GATT: una propuesta para aumentar la capacidad exportadora. (With English summary.) *Cuadernos Econ.*, December 1984, *21*(64), pp. 279–97. **[G: Global]**

Nollen, Stanley D. The Case of John Brown Engineering and the Soviet Gas Pipeline. In *Czinkota, M. R., ed.*, 1984, pp. 111–42. **[G: U.K.; U.S.; U.S.S.R.; W. Europe]**

Nusbaumer, Jacques. The GATT Standards Code in Operation. *J. World Trade Law*, November:December 1984, *18*(6), pp. 542–52. **[G: Selected Countries]**

O'Neill, Helen. HICs, MICs, NICs and LICs: Some Elements in the Political Economy of Graduation and Differentiation. *World Devel.*, July 1984, *12*(7), pp. 693–712. **[G: LDCs; MDCs]**

Okita, Saburo. Role of the Trade Ombudsman in Liberalising Japan's Market. *World Econ.*, September 1984, 7(3), pp. 241–56.
[G: Japan]

Olmer, Lionel H. Objectives and Goals of U.S. Export Control Policy. In *Czinkota, M. R., ed.*, 1984, pp. 40–44. [G: U.S.]

Olson, Mancur. Australia in Perspective of the Rise and Decline of Nations. *Australian Econ. Rev.*, 3rd Quarter 1984, (67), pp. 7–17.
[G: Global]

Ono, Yoshiyasu. Profitability of Export Restraint. *J. Int. Econ.*, May 1984, 16(3/4), pp. 335–43.
[G: OPEC]

Oweiss, Ibrahim M. Petrodollar Surpluses: Trends and Economic Impact. *J. Energy Devel.*, Spring 1984, 9(2), pp. 177–202.
[G: OPEC]

Paarlberg, Philip L. When Are Export Subsidies Rational? *Agr. Econ. Res.*, January 1984, 36(1), pp. 1–7. [G: U.S.]

Paarlberg, Philip L. and Abbott, Philip C. Towards a Countervailing Power Theory of World Wheat Trade. In *Storey, G. G.; Schmitz, A. and Sarris, A. H., eds.*, 1984, pp. 185–210.
[G: Canada; Japan; U.S.]

Paddock, Brian. Estimation of Producer Losses Arising from the Partial Embargo of Grain Exports to the Soviet Union: Reply. *Can. J. Agr. Econ.*, March 1984, 32(1), pp. 237–38.
[G: U.S.; Canada]

Palmer, Ransford W. U.S. Economic Policy toward the Caribbean. In *Palmer, R. W.*, 1984, pp. 67–87.

Palmeter, N. David. The U.S. International Trade Commission at Common Law: Unfair Competition, Trademark, and Section 337 of the Tariff Act. *J. World Trade Law*, November:December 1984, 18(6), pp. 497–511.
[G: U.S.]

Pantelides, Pantelis I. Testing the USA Generalized Systems of Preferences. *J. Econ. Devel.*, December 1984, 9(2), pp. 87–107. [G: U.S.; LDCs]

Pasurka, Carl A., Jr. Corporate Income Taxes and U.S. Effective Rates of Protection. *Nat. Tax J.*, December 1984, 37(4), pp. 529–37.
[G: U.S.]

Patterson, Eliza. Features of the Omnibus Trade Act in the United States. *World Econ.*, December 1984, 7(4), pp. 407–20. [G: U.S.]

Pattison, Joseph E. Extraterritorial Enforcement of the Export Administration Act. In *Czinkota, M. R., ed.*, 1984, pp. 87–102. [G: U.S.; Selected countries]

Peffekoven, Rolf. Anrechnung versus Freistellung—Zur ökonomischen Analyse internationaler Besteuerungsprinzipien. (Foreign Tax Credits versus Tax Exemptions—An Economic Analysis of International Principles of Taxation. With English summary.) *Aussenwirtschaft*, May 1984, 39(1/2), pp. 137–50. [G: Global]

Pelkmans, Jacques. Collective Management and Economic Cooperation. In *Merlini, C., ed.*, 1984, pp. 89–136. [G: OECD]

Perez, Lorenzo L. Export Subsidies in Developing Countries and the GATT. In *Ghosh, P. K., ed., no. 16*, 1984, 1976, pp. 250–67.

Perkins, John A. Fiscal Policy and Economic Development in XIXth Century Germany. *J. Europ. Econ. Hist.*, Fall 1984, 13(2), pp. 311–44. [G: Germany]

Pinar, Musa; Stennis, Earl A. and Turay, Abdul M. Transportation Cost Subsidies: A Criterion for Policy to Promote International Trade. *J. World Trade Law*, May–June 1984, 18(3), pp. 224–34. [G: Selected Countries]

Piron, Robert. On Believing the Impossible in Economics. *Challenge*, September/October 1984, 27(4), pp. 49–51.

Pitt, Mark M. Smuggling and the Black Market for Foreign Exchange. *J. Int. Econ.*, May 1984, 16(3/4), pp. 243–57.

Pomfret, Richard. The Quiet Shift in U.S. Trade Policy. *Challenge*, November/December 1984, 27(5), pp. 61–64. [G: U.S.]

Prybyla, Jan S. China's Special Economic Zones. *ACES Bull.*, Winter 1984, 26(4), pp. 1–23.
[G: China]

Putnam, Robert. The Western Economic Summits: A Political Interpretation. In *Merlini, C., ed.*, 1984, pp. 43–88. [G: OECD]

Quick, Perry D. Businesses: Reagan's Industrial Policy. In *Palmer, J. L. and Sawhill, I. V., eds.*, 1984, pp. 287–316. [G: U.S.]

Ramadhyani, M. Export Promotion in an Import Substitution Framework: An Analysis of the 100% Export Oriented Units Scheme. *Margin*, April 1984, 16(3), pp. 56–69.

Rangarajan, L. The Politics of International Trade. In *Strange, S., ed.*, 1984, pp. 126–63.
[G: Global]

Rashish, Myer. Reducing Nontariff Barriers. In *Fried, E. R. and Trezise, P. H., eds.*, 1984, pp. 52–56. [G: U.S.; Canada]

Ray, Edward John and Marvel, Howard P. The Pattern of Protection in the Industrialized World. *Rev. Econ. Statist.*, August 1984, 66(3), pp. 452–58. [G: U.S.; Japan; EEC; Canada]

Razavi, Hossein. An Economic Model of OPEC Coalition. *Southern Econ. J.*, October 1984, 51(2), pp. 419–28. [G: OPEC]

Reisman, Simon S. The Issue of Free Trade. In *Fried, E. R. and Trezise, P. H., eds.*, 1984, pp. 35–51. [G: Canada; U.S.]

Reynolds, Bruce. China in the International Economy. In *Harding, H., ed.*, 1984, pp. 71–106. [G: China]

Reynolds, Clark; Ramos, Raul and McCleery, Robert. The Impact of Foreign Trade and Export Strategies on Distribution of Income for Low-Income Households in Mexico. In *Aspe, P. and Sigmund, P. E., eds.*, 1984, pp. 203–46. [G: Mexico]

Reza, Ali M. The Price of Oil and Conflict in OPEC. *Energy J.*, April 1984, 5(2), pp. 29–33. [G: OPEC]

Richardson, J. David. The New Nexus among Trade, Industrial and Exchange-Rate Policies. In *Agmon, T.; Hawkins, R. G. and Levich, R. M., eds.*, 1984, pp. 253–79.

Rom, Michael. Export Controls in GATT. *J.*

World Trade Law, March–April 1984, *18*(2), pp. 125–54.

Rooth, T. J. T. Limits of Leverage: The Anglo–Danish Trade Agreements of 1933. *Econ. Hist. Rev.*, 2nd Ser., May 1984, *37*(2), pp. 211–28. **[G: U.K.; Denmark]**

Rossini, Gianpaolo. Intraindustry Trade and Tariffs: New Wave or Old Fashion? *Econ. Int.*, February–May 1984, *37*(1–2), pp. 130–48. **[G: W. Europe]**

Rossmiller, George E. The U.S. Agricultural Trade Issue Decision Process: An Illustrated Partial Anatomy. In *Storey, G. G.; Schmitz, A. and Sarris, A. H., eds.*, 1984, pp. 165–83. **[G: U.S.]**

Rousslang, Donald J. and Lindsey, John. The Benefits to Caribbean Basin Countries from the U.S. CBI Tariff Eliminations. *J. Policy Modeling*, November 1984, *6*(4), pp. 513–30. **[G: U.S.; Caribbean]**

Rousslang, Donald J. and Parker, Stephen. Cross-Price Elasticities of U.S. Import Demand. *Rev. Econ. Statist.*, August 1984, *66*(3), pp. 518–23. **[G: U.S.]**

Rudanko, Kalervo. Handelshinder vid Importen. En kommentar. (Import Trade Barriers: A Comment. With English summary.) [Protektionismen i världshandeln. (Protectionism in World Trade.)]. *Ekon. Samfundets Tidskr.*, 1984, *37*(2), pp. 123–24. **[G: Finland]**

Ryser, Walter. Exterritorialité et Droit Fiscal. (Extra-Territoriality and Fiscal Law. With English summary.) *Aussenwirtschaft*, May 1984, *39*(1/2), pp. 119–36. **[G: OECD]**

Santos, Leonard. The Implementation of Trade Sanctions. In *Czinkota, M. R., ed.*, 1984, pp. 143–48. **[G: U.S.; Selected Countries]**

Sawyer, W. Charles. The Effects of the Second Enlargement of the EC on U.S. Exports to Europe. *Weltwirtsch. Arch.*, 1984, *120*(3), pp. 572–79. **[G: EEC; U.S.]**

Sawyer, W. Charles and Sprinkle, Richard L. Caribbean Basin Economic Recovery Act: Export Expansion Effects. *J. World Trade Law*, September–October 1984, *18*(5), pp. 429–36. **[G: U.S.; Caribbean]**

Schlesinger, James R. Hard-Earned Lessons about U.S.–Canadian Energy Relations. In *Fried, E. R. and Trezise, P. H., eds.*, 1984, pp. 107–13. **[G: U.S.; Canada]**

Schmitz, Peter Michael and Koester, Ulrich. The Sugar Market Policy of the European Community and the Stability of World Market Prices for Sugar. In *Storey, G. G.; Schmitz, A. and Sarris, A. H., eds.*, 1984, pp. 235–59. **[G: EEC; Global]**

Schoenbaum, Thomas J. Trade Friction with Japan and the American Policy Response. *Mich. Law Rev.*, April–May 1984, *82*(5 & 6), pp. 1647–61. **[G: U.S.; Japan]**

Schultz, Siegfried and Schumacher, Dieter. The Re-Liberalization of World Trade: Some Ideas for Reducing Trade Barriers against Industrial Products from Developing Countries. *J. World Trade Law*, May–June 1984, *18*(3), pp. 206–23. **[G: OECD]**

Seyoum, Belayneh. Export Subsidies under the MTN: An Analysis with Particular Emphasis on Developing Countries. *J. World Trade Law*, November:December 1984, *18*(6), pp. 512–41. **[G: LDCs]**

Shaaf, Mohammad. Strong Dollar, Low Inflation, and OPEC's Terms of Trade. *J. Energy Devel.*, Autumn 1984, *10*(1), pp. 121–29. **[G: OPEC]**

Sharp, Mitchell. Canada's Independence and U.S. Domination. In *Fried, E. R. and Trezise, P. H., eds.*, 1984, pp. 11–20. **[G: Canada; U.S.]**

Singer, Hans W. Industrialisation: Where Do We Stand? Where Are We Going? *METU*, 1984, *11*(1–2), pp. 163–75. **[G: LDCs]**

Snape, R. H. Australia's Relations with GATT. *Econ. Rec.*, March 1984, *60*(168), pp. 16–27. **[G: Australia]**

Sobhan, Rehman. Regional Economic Cooperation in South Asia: Legacy and Prospects. In *Ghosh, P. K., ed., no. 18*, 1984, *1979*, pp. 267–93. **[G: S. Asia]**

Sorsa, Kalevi. Det internationella handels-, finans- och valutasystemet. Utvecklingstrender och reformsynpunkter. (The International Trade, Finance and Currency System: Trends and Views on Reforms. With English summary.) *Ekon. Samfundets Tidskr.*, 1984, *37*(2), pp. 65–73. **[G: Global]**

Spechler, Martin and Tovias, Alfred. When Should Developing Countries Use Bilateral State Trading? *World Devel.*, November–December 1984, *12*(11–12), pp. 1077–86. **[G: LDCs]**

Spinanger, Dean. Objectives and Impact of Economic Activity Zones—Some Evidence from Asia. *Weltwirtsch. Arch.*, 1984, *120*(1), pp. 64–89. **[G: Asia]**

Spraos, John. On the Commodity Power of Less Developed Countries. *J. Post Keynesian Econ.*, Summer 1984, *6*(4), pp. 605–13. **[G: LDCs]**

Stanton, J. Protection, Market Structure, and Firm Behaviour: Inefficiency in the Early Australian Tyre Industry. *Australian Econ. Hist. Rev.*, September 1984, *24*(2), pp. 91–114. **[G: Australia]**

Stubbs, Richard. The International Natural Rubber Agreement: Its Negotiation and Operation. *J. World Trade Law*, January:February 1984, *18*(1), pp. 16–31.

Szychowski, Mario L. and Perazzo, Alfredo C. Protección efectiva y costo doméstico de la divisa: Comparación de su eficiencia en el cumplimiento de objectivos alternativos. (Effective Protection and Domestic Resource Cost: comparison about Their Efficiency in the Achievement of Alternatives Objectives. With English summary.) *Económica*, May-December 1984, *30*(2–3), pp. 217–44. **[G: Argentina]**

Teitel, Simón. Technology Creation in Semi-industrial Economies. *J. Devel. Econ.*, September–October 1984, *16*(1–2), pp. 39–61. **[G: Latin America]**

Tharakan, P. K. M. Political Economy of Protection: An Analysis of the Belgian Case. *Cah.*

Écon. Bruxelles, 1st Trimester 1984, (101), pp. 3–39. **[G: Belgium]**

Thomas, Mark. Discussion [Keynes and Protection] [Macroeconomic Instability and the "Natural" Processes in Early Neoclassical Economics]. *J. Econ. Hist.*, June 1984, *44*(2), pp. 375–79. **[G: U.K.]**

Tumlir, Jan. Trade Restrictions Imposed in 1983. In *Shadow Open Market Committee*, 1984, pp. 31–37. **[G: U.S.; Selected Countries]**

Turner, Philip and Tuveri, Jean-Pierre. Some Effects of Export Restraints on Japanese Trading Behaviour. *OECD Econ. Stud.*, Spring 1984, (2), pp. 93–107. **[G: Japan]**

UNCTAD Secretariat. Bulgaria—Policies, Developments and Institutional Framework. In *U.N.C.T.D.*, 1984, pp. 57–78. **[G: Bulgaria]**

UNCTAD Secretariat. Czechoslovakia—Policies, Developments and Institutional Framework. In *U.N.C.T.D.*, 1984, pp. 79–96. **[G: Czechoslovakia]**

UNCTAD Secretariat. German Democratic Republic—Policies, Developments and Institutional Framework. In *U.N.C.T.D.*, 1984, pp. 97–110. **[G: E. Germany]**

UNCTAD Secretariat. Hungary—Policies, Developments and Institutional Framework. In *U.N.C.T.D.*, 1984, pp. 111–28. **[G: Hungary]**

UNCTAD Secretariat. Prospects for Trade and Economic Co-operation between Nigeria and the Socialist Countries of Eastern Europe. In *U.N.C.T.D.*, 1984, pp. 45–55. **[G: Nigeria; CMEA]**

UNCTAD Secretariat. Trends, Policies and Prospects in Trade and Economic Co-operation Between Argentina and the Socialist Countries of Eastern Europe. In *U.N.C.T.D.*, 1984, pp. 5–18. **[G: Argentina; CMEA]**

UNCTAD Secretariat. Union of Soviet Socialist Republics—Policies, Developments and Institutional Framework. In *U.N.C.T.D.*, 1984, pp. 129–45. **[G: U.S.S.R.]**

Vernon, Raymond. Soviet Commodity Power in International Economic Relations. In *Kostecki, M. M., ed.*, 1984, pp. 6–14. **[G: U.S.S.R.]**

Viita, Pentti. Näivettääkö valtio Suomen teollisuutta. (The State Withering Industry in Finland? With English summary.) *Kansant. Aikak.*, 1984, *80*(3), pp. 261–70. **[G: Finland]**

Waelbroeck, Jean. The Logic of EC Commercial and Industrial Policy Making. In *Jacquemin, A., ed.*, 1984, pp. 99–144. **[G: EEC]**

Waldmann, Raymond J. Improving Foreign Policy Trade Controls. In *Czinkota, M. R., ed.*, 1984, pp. 177–91. **[G: U.S.]**

Wallén, Axel. Export Credit Subsidization and the Consensus Arrangement. *Aussenwirtschaft*, September 1984, *39*(3), pp. 261–69. **[G: OECD]**

Walters, S. George. Management Issues in United States–Romanian Trade and Cooperation. In *Jackson, M. R. and Woodson, J. D., Jr., eds.*, 1984, pp. 197–219. **[G: Romania; U.S.]**

Wang, N. T. Reforms in Foreign Trade and Investment in China. *Hong Kong Econ. Pap.*, 1984, (15), pp. 87–97. **[G: China]**

Wannacott, Ronald J. The Canadian Content Proposals of the Task Force on the Automobile Industry. *Can. Public Policy*, March 1984, *10*(1), pp. 1–9. **[G: U.S.; Canada; Japan]**

Warr, Peter G. Exchange Rate Protection in Indonesia. *Bull. Indonesian Econ. Stud.*, August 1984, *20*(2), pp. 53–89. **[G: Indonesia]**

Wassermann, Ursula. Gamani Corea, Secretary-General of UNCTAD. *J. World Trade Law*, September–October 1984, *18*(5), pp. 377–80. **[G: Global]**

Wassermann, Ursula. UNCTAD: International Agreement on Jute and Jute Products, 1982. *J. World Trade Law*, March–April 1984, *18*(2), pp. 173–74.

Wassermann, Ursula. UNCTAD: International Tropical Timber Agreement. *J. World Trade Law*, January:February 1984, *18*(1), pp. 89–91.

Webb, Michael. A Theoretical Note on Quota-Reduction Negotiations. *Oxford Econ. Pap.*, June 1984, *36*(2), pp. 288–90.

Weinrod, W. Bruce. National Security Dimensions of International Trade. In *Czinkota, M. R., ed.*, 1984, pp. 192–203. **[G: U.S.]**

Weiss, Frank D. Industrial Policy and International Competitiveness in West Germany. In *Driscoll, R. E. and Behrman, J. N., eds.*, 1984, pp. 229–44. **[G: W. Germany]**

Whalley, John. The North–South Debate and the Terms of Trade: An Applied General Equilibrium Approach. *Rev. Econ. Statist.*, May 1984, *66*(2), pp. 224–34. **[G: Global]**

Wihlborg, Clas G. The New Nexus among Trade, Industrial and Exchange-Rate Policies: Comment. In *Agmon, T.; Hawkins, R. G. and Levich, R. M., eds.*, 1984, pp. 284–90.

Wilkinson, Bruce W. Canada–U.S. Trade Policy Relations. *Can. Public Policy*, March 1984, *10*(1), pp. 96–103. **[G: U.S.; Canada]**

Wilkinson, Christopher. Trends in Industrial Policy in the EC: Theory and Practice. In *Jacquemin, A., ed.*, 1984, pp. 39–83. **[G: EEC]**

Willett, Thomas D.; Tower, Edward and Christenson, D. B. The Relevance of Modern Economic Research. *Contemp. Policy Issue*, January 1984, (4), pp. 1–5. **[G: U.S.]**

Williams, Phil; Wallace, William and Woolcock, Stephen. Atlantic Relations. In *Boyd, G., ed.*, 1984, pp. 25–52. **[G: U.S.; W. Europe]**

Willoughby, John. Economic Nationalism, the Left and the World Economy. *Rev. Radical Polit. Econ.*, Winter 1984, *16*(4), pp. 1–13.

de Wilmars, J. Mertens and Steenbergen, J. The Court of Justice of the European Communities and Governance in an Economic Crisis. *Mich. Law Rev.*, April–May 1984, *82*(5 & 6), pp. 1377–98. **[G: EEC]**

Winham, Gilbert R. The Canadian Automobile Industry and Trade-related Performance Requirements. *J. World Trade Law*, November: December 1984, *18*(6), pp. 471–96. **[G: Canada; U.S.]**

Wogart, Jan Peter and Marques, Jose Siverio.

Trade Liberalization, Tariff Redundancy and Inflation: A Methodological Exploration Applied to Argentina. *Weltwirtsch. Arch.*, 1984, *120*(1), pp. 18–39. **[G: Argentina]**

Wolf, Martin. Two-Edged Sword: Demands of Developing Countries and the Trading System. In *Bhagwati, J. N. and Ruggie, J. G., eds.*, 1984, pp. 201–29.

Wonnacott, Paul. Industrial Allocation in the Andean Pact. In *Núñez del Arco, J.; Margain, E. and Cherol, R., eds.*, 1984, pp. 103–14. **[G: Latin America]**

Wonnacott, Paul and Wonnacott, Ronald. How General Is the Case for Unilateral Tariff Reduction? *Amer. Econ. Rev.*, June 1984, *74*(3), pp. 491.

Yeats, Alexander J. On the Analysis of Tariff Escalation: Is There a Methodological Bias against the Interest of Developing Countries? *J. Devel. Econ.*, May–June–August 1984, *15*(1,2,3), pp. 77–88. **[G: LDCs]**

Wolf, Martin. Two-Edged Sword: Demands of Developing Countries and the Trading System. In *Bhagwati, J. N. and Ruggie, J. G., eds.*, 1984, pp. 201–29.

Wonnacott, Paul. Industrial Allocation in the Andean Pact. In *Núñez del Arco, J.; Margain, E. and Cherol, R., eds.*, 1984, pp. 103–14. **[G: Latin America]**

Wonnacott, Paul and Wonnacott, Ronald. How General Is the Case for Unilateral Tariff Reduction? *Amer. Econ. Rev.*, June 1984, *74*(3), pp. 491.

Yeats, Alexander J. On the Analysis of Tariff Escalation: Is There a Methodological Bias against the Interest of Developing Countries? *J. Devel. Econ.*, May–June–August 1984, *15*(1,2,3), pp. 77–88. **[G: LDCs]**

Young, Stephen and Hood, Neil. Industrial Policy in The United Kingdom. In *Driscoll, R. E. and Behrman, J. N., eds.*, 1984, pp. 197–214. **[G: U.K.]**

van Zyl, J. C. South Africa in World Trade. *S. Afr. J. Econ.*, March 1984, *52*(1), pp. 42–62. **[G: S. Africa]**

423 Economic Integration

4230 General

Balassa, Bela and Stoutjesdijk, Ardy. Economic Integration Among Developing Countries. In *Ghosh, P. K., ed., no. 12*, 1984, *1978*, pp. 33–50. **[G: LDCs]**

Elkan, Peter G. Measuring the Impact of Economic Integration Among Developing Countries. In *Ghosh, P. K., ed., no. 12*, 1984, *1975*, pp. 190–202. **[G: Central America; E. Africa]**

Fishlow, Albert. Reciprocal Trade Growth: The Latin American Integration Experience. In *[Chenery, H. B.]*, 1984, pp. 235–60. **[G: Latin America]**

Ghosh, Pradip K. Economic Integration and Third World Development: Introduction. In *Ghosh, P. K., ed., no. 12*, 1984, pp. 3–6.

Gilbert, Gary G. Investment Planning for Latin American Economic Integration. In *Ghosh, P. K., ed., no. 12*, 1984, *1973*, pp. 177–89. **[G: Latin America]**

Langhammer, Rolf J. Regional Integration and Cooperation in Africa: A History of Disappointments? In *Ghosh, P. K., ed., no. 15*, 1984, *1977*, pp. 263–74. **[G: Africa]**

Miller, J. D. B. Raw Materials and Their Role in Regional Economic Cooperation. In *Downen, R. L. and Dickson, B. J., eds.*, 1984, pp. 121–28. **[G: Pacific Basin]**

Ondráček, Mojmír. Views of Economists from the Socialist Countries on Handling Currency Matters in the CMEA—The Role of Exchange Rates (Coefficients) in Planned Economic Management. *Soviet E. Europ. Foreign Trade*, Summer 1984, *20*(2), pp. 37–55. **[G: CMEA]**

Strauss, Robert S. Pacific Trade: The Perils of Economic Nationalism. In *Downen, R. L. and Dickson, B. J., eds.*, 1984, pp. 175–78.

Thompson, Velma Montoya. The Benefits of Domestic Investment Subsidies and Taxes to Exports in Common Market Countries. *De Economist*, 1984, *132*(1), pp. 61–74. **[G: EEC; Netherlands]**

Wignjowijoto, Hartojo. Regional Trade and Investment: Conflict and Cooperation Ahead. In *Downen, R. L. and Dickson, B. J., eds.*, 1984, pp. 119–20.

4232 Theory of Economic Integration

Atkinson, Glen W. Legal Foundations of European Economic Integration. *J. Econ. Issues*, June 1984, *18*(2), pp. 507–15.

Axline, W. Andrew. Underdevelopment, Dependence, and Integration: The Politics of Regionalism in the Third World. In *Ghosh, P. K., ed., no. 12*, 1984, *1977*, pp. 7–32.

Bittante, Elena. Price, Discrimination and Economic Integration: Some Theoretical Considerations. (In Italian. With English summary.) *Giorn. Econ.*, September–October 1984, *43*(9–10), pp. 699–712.

Choi, Jai-Young and Yu, Eden S.-H. Customs Unions under Increasing Returns to Scale. *Economica*, May 1984, *51*(202), pp. 195–203.

Ethier, Wilfred J. and Horn, Henrik. A New Look at Economic Integration. In *Kierzkowski, H., ed.*, 1984, pp. 207–29.

Falvey, Rodney E. and Fried, Harold O. Sectoral Trading Arrangements. *Int. Econ. Rev.*, October 1984, *25*(3), pp. 671–85.

Fries, Timothy L. Uncertainty as a Possible Rationale for Customs Unions. *J. Int. Econ.*, November 1984, *17*(3/4), pp. 347–57.

Ghai, Dharam P. Alternative Concepts of Economic Integration. In *Ghosh, P. K., ed., no. 12*, 1984, *1973*, pp. 67–73. **[G: LDCs]**

Orantes, Isaac Cohen. The Concept of Integration. In *Ghosh, P. K., ed., no. 12*, 1984, *1981*, pp. 51–66.

Wonnacott, Paul and Wonnacott, Ronald. How General Is the Case for Unilateral Tariff Reduction? *Amer. Econ. Rev.*, June 1984, *74*(3), pp. 491.

4233 Economic Integration: Policy and Empirical Studies

Agmon, Tamir. OPEC and International Financial Markets: Redistribution and Recycling: Comment. In *Agmon, T.; Hawkins, R. G. and Levich, R. M., eds.*, 1984, pp. 246–51.
[G: OPEC]

Anderson, Kym and Tyers, Rodney. European Community Grain and Meat Policies: Effects on International Prices, Trade and Welfare. *Europ. Rev. Agr. Econ.*, 1984, *11*(4), pp. 367–94.
[G: EEC]

Andic, Fuat M. Tax Harmonization and Economic Integration. In *Núñez del Arco, J.; Margain, E. and Cherol, R., eds.*, 1984, pp. 205–28.
[G: Latin America]

Armstrong, H. W. Competition Policy in the Common Market: A Comment. *Reg. Stud.*, February 1984, *18*(1), pp. 69–71. [G: EEC]

Asante, S. K. B. ECOWAS, the EEC and the Lomé Convention. In *Mazzeo, D., ed.*, 1984, pp. 171–95. [G: EEC; W. Africa]

Atsain, Achi. Regional Economic Integration and Foreign Policy. In *Zartman, I. W. and Delgado, C. L., eds.*, 1984, pp. 175–218.
[G: Ivory Coast; W. Africa]

Barbero, Giuseppe and Croci-Angelini, Elisabetta. Towards a Better Structural Policy. *Europ. Rev. Agr. Econ.*, 1984, *11*(2), pp. 245–54. [G: EEC]

Barbero, Giuseppe, et al. The Siena Memorandum on 'The Reform of the Common Agricultural Policy.' *Europ. Rev. Agr. Econ.*, 1984, *11*(2), pp. 255–59. [G: EEC]

Barnouin, Jack P. Trade and Economic Cooperation Among Developing Countries. In *Ghosh, P. K., ed., no. 15*, 1984, *1982*, pp. 239–47.
[G: LDCs]

Barnouin, Jack P. Trade and Economic Cooperation Among Developing Countries. In *Ghosh, P. K., ed., no. 16*, 1984, *1982*, pp. 37–43.
[G: LDCs]

Baysan, Tercan. Some Economic Aspects of Turkey's Accession to the EC: Resource Shifts, Comparative Advantage, and Static Gains. *J. Common Market Stud.*, September 1984, *23*(1), pp. 15–34. [G: Turkey; EEC]

Bergmann, Denis. North-South Balances and Conflicts within the Community. *Europ. Rev. Agr. Econ.*, 1984, *11*(2), pp. 151–57.
[G: W. Europe]

Blyth, Nicola. The EEC Sheepmeat Market and Voluntary Export Restraint Agreements. *Australian J. Agr. Econ.*, April 1984, *28*(1), pp. 33–43. [G: EEC; Australia; New Zealand]

Boyd, Gavin. Pacific Community Building. In *Boyd, G., ed.*, 1984, pp. 83–117.
[G: ASEAN]

Boyd, Gavin. Regional Designing. In *Boyd, G., ed.*, 1984, pp. 175–91. [G: LDCs]

Boyd, Gavin and Ferguson, Yale. Latin American Regionalism. In *Boyd, G., ed.*, 1984, pp. 119–45. [G: Latin America]

Bublot, Georges. Gradual Re-nationalization of the CAP? *Europ. Rev. Agr. Econ.*, 1984, *11*(2), pp. 187–93. [G: EEC]

Castro, Amado A. The Outlook for Cooperation: An ASEAN View. In *Downen, R. L. and Dickson, B. J., eds.*, 1984, pp. 161–65.
[G: ASEAN]

Cho, Lee-Jay. The Industrial Future of the Pacific Basin: Conclusion. In *Benjamin, R. and Kudrle, R. T.*, 1984, pp. 237–47.

Clarotti, Paolo. Progress and Future Development of Establishment and Services in the EC in Relation to Banking. *J. Common Market Stud.*, March 1984, *22*(3), pp. 199–226.
[G: EEC]

Conesa, Eduardo R. Latin American Integration in the Eighties. In *Salazar-Carrillo, J. and Tirado de Alonso, I., eds., no. 2*, 1984, pp. 1–14. [G: Latin America]

Conesa, Eduardo R. Latin American Integration in the Eighties. In *Jorge, A.; Salazar-Carrillo, J. and Sanchez, E. P.*, 1984, pp. 97–101.
[G: Latin America]

Csaba, Laszlo. COMECON Perspectives for the 1980's. *Écon. Soc.*, February 1984, *18*(2), pp. 5–44. [G: CMEA]

Csaba, Laszlo. The Role of CMEA in the World Economy in the 1980s. *ACES Bull.*, Summer–Fall 1984, *26*(2–3), pp. 1–28. [G: CMEA]

Csikós-Nagy, Béla. The Role of the Law of Values in Socialist Economy. *Eastern Europ. Econ.*, Spring–Summer 1984, *22*(3–4), pp. 102–21.
[G: Hungary; CMEA]

Davies, Robert and Jones, Philip R. International Trade. In *Sandford, C. and Bradbury, M., eds.*, 1984, pp. 188–218. [G: EEC]

Deese, David. The Vulnerability of Modern Economies. In *McCormick, G. H. and Bissell, R. E., eds.*, 1984, pp. 148–80. [G: OECD; CMEA]

Denton, Geoffrey. Re-structuring the EC Budget: Implications of the Fontainebleau Agreement. *J. Common Market Stud.*, December 1984, *23*(2), pp. 117–40. [G: EEC]

Dini, Lamberto. Un nuovo codice per la cooperazione internazionale. (A New Code for International Cooperation. With English summary.) *Bancaria*, October 1984, *40*(10), pp. 949–56.
[G: EEC]

Donges, Juergen B. Is European Integration Now Due to Inertia or Conviction? *World Econ.*, March 1984, *7*(1), pp. 33–46. [G: EEC]

Drabek, Zdenek and Greenaway, David. Economic Integration and Intra-industry Trade: The EEC and CMEA Compared. *Kyklos*, 1984, *37*(3), pp. 444–69. [G: EEC; CMEA]

Dudler, Hermann-Josef. Domestic Monetary Control in EC Countries under Different Exchange Rate Regimes: National Concerns and Community Options. In *Masera, R. S. and Triffin, R., eds.*, 1984, pp. 227–61. [G: EEC]

El-Agraa, Ali M. Has Membership of the European Communities Been a Disaster for Britain? *Appl. Econ.*, April 1984, *16*(2), pp. 299–315.
[G: U.K.]

El-Agraa, Ali M. and Hu, Yao-Su. National versus Supranational Interests and the Problem of Establishing an Effective EC Energy Policy. *J. Common Market Stud.*, June 1984, *22*(4), pp. 333–49. **[G: EEC]**

Ferrere, Daniel. The Uruguayan–Argentinian Trade Co-operation Agreement. *J. World Trade Law*, July–August 1984, *18*(4), pp. 320–34. **[G: Uruguay; Argentina]**

Fichet, Gerard and Gonzalez, Norberto. The Production Structure and the Dynamics of Development. In *Ghosh, P. K., ed., no. 7, 1984, 1976*, pp. 362–407. **[G: Latin America; OECD]**

Fingerland, Jaroslav. CMEA Looks ahead Realistically and with Optimism. *Czech. Econ. Digest.*, May 1984, (3), pp. 55–62. **[G: CMEA]**

Fishlow, Albert. The Debt Crisis: Solution by Economic Integration? In *Núñez del Arco, J.; Margain, E. and Cherol, R., eds.*, 1984, pp. 64–91. **[G: Latin America]**

Fraser, Malcolm. Pacific Community: Further Steps. In *Downen, R. L. and Dickson, B. J., eds.*, 1984, pp. 3–11. **[G: Pacific Basin]**

Fredland, R. A. OCAM: One Scene in the Drama of West African Development. In *Mazzeo, D., ed.*, 1984, pp. 103–30. **[G: W. Africa]**

Friedeberg, Alfred S. Milk Surpluses till the Cows Come Home? *World Econ.*, December 1984, *7*(4), pp. 421–33. **[G: EEC]**

Frost, Hans. Fisheries Management and Uncertainty within the EEC. *Marine Resource Econ.*, 1984, *1*(1), pp. 97–103. **[G: EEC]**

Gaillard, William. The Rationalization of the Trade of Agricultural Products and the National Objectives of Self-Sufficiency in Common Markets. In *Núñez del Arco, J.; Margain, E. and Cherol, R., eds.*, 1984, pp. 147–53. **[G: EEC]**

Giannaros, Demetrios S. Estimation of Structural Changes in the Trade Sector Resulting from the Integration with the E.E.C.: The Case of Greece. *J. Econ. Devel.*, December 1984, *9*(2), pp. 145–70. **[G: Greece; EEC]**

Gilbert, J.-P. Un cas de coopération économique Pologne-R.D.A.: la filature de coton polonoallemande de Zawiercie "Przyjazn-Freundschaft" (Amitié). (An Example of Economic Cooperation between Poland and the G.D.R. With English summary.) *Écon. Soc.*, February 1984, *18*(2), pp. 115–37. **[G: Poland; E. Germany]**

Grinols, Earl L. A Thorn in the Lion's Paw: Has Britain Paid Too Much for Common Market Membership? *J. Int. Econ.*, May 1984, *16*(3/4), pp. 271–93. **[G: U.K.; EEC]**

Gruhn, Isebill V. The Economic Commission for Africa. In *Mazzeo, D., ed.*, 1984, pp. 27–48. **[G: Africa]**

Grunwald, Joseph. Some Reflections on Latin American Industrial Integration. In *Núñez del Arco, J.; Margain, E. and Cherol, R., eds.*, 1984, pp. 115–25. **[G: Latin America]**

Haferkamp, Wilhelm. EC and EFTA Liberalize Industrial Trade. *Bull. Int. Fiscal Doc.*, February 1984, *38*(2), pp. 86–87.

ul Haq, Obaid. The Pacific Basin Community:

Problems and Prospects. In *Downen, R. L. and Dickson, B. J., eds.*, 1984, pp. 35–43. **[G: Pacific Basin]**

Herrmann, Roland and Schmitz, Peter Michael. Stabilizing Producers' Revenue by Fixing Agricultural Prices within the EC? *Europ. Rev. Agr. Econ.*, 1984, *11*(4), pp. 395–414. **[G: EEC]**

Hervitz, Hugo M. Some Thoughts about Latin American Integration in the Eighties. In *Jorge, A.; Salazar-Carrillo, J. and Sanchez, E. P.*, 1984, pp. 103–04. **[G: Latin America]**

Horlick, Gary. Development of Trade and Trade Conflicts in the Pacific Basin. In *Downen, R. L. and Dickson, B. J., eds.*, 1984, pp. 113–17. **[G: Pacific Basin]**

Hradecký, Stanislav. Structural Changes and International Socialist Economic Integration. *Czech. Econ. Digest.*, February 1984, (1), pp. 70–83. **[G: CMEA]**

Inter-Amer. Devel. Bank, Integration Sub-Dept. Integration in Latin America and Its Outlook for the Future. In *Núñez del Arco, J.; Margain, E. and Cherol, R., eds.*, 1984, pp. 53–63. **[G: Latin America]**

Ionescu, Nicolae. Coordination of Economic Development Plans among the CMEA Member Countries. *Soviet E. Europ. Foreign Trade*, Spring 1984, *20*(1), pp. 27–35. **[G: CMEA]**

Jacobs, Francis G. Civil Enforcement of EEC Antitrust Law. *Mich. Law Rev.*, April–May 1984, *82*(5 & 6), pp. 1364–76. **[G: EEC]**

Jirges, Miloslav. Irreplaceability of Czechoslovak–Soviet Cooperation in Intensification of Economic Processes. *Czech. Econ. Digest.*, February 1984, (1), pp. 84–98. **[G: U.S.S.R.; Czechoslovakia]**

de Jong, Henk Wouter. Sectoral Development and Sectoral Policies in the EC. In *Jacquemin, A., ed.*, 1984, pp. 147–71. **[G: OECD]**

Kanapathy, V. ASEAN and the Pacific Community: Problems and Prospects. In *Downen, R. L. and Dickson, B. J., eds.*, 1984, pp. 71–79. **[G: Pacific Basin]**

Kanchuger, Robert. The Caribbean Group: Its Evolution and Role. *Finance Develop.*, September 1984, *21*(3), pp. 44–46. **[G: Caribbean]**

Kervyn de Lettenhove, Albert. Steel: A Case Study in Industrial Policy. In *Jacquemin, A., ed.*, 1984, pp. 215–26. **[G: EEC]**

Khaldi, Mohamed. Arab Aid in the World Economy. In *Achilli, M. and Khaldi, M., eds.*, 1984, pp. 7–39. **[G: Arab Countries; LDCs]**

Koester, Ulrich. The Role of the CAP in the Process of European Integration. *Europ. Rev. Agr. Econ.*, 1984, *11*(2), pp. 129–40. **[G: EEC]**

Koester, Ulrich and Valdés, Alberto. The EC's Potential Role in Food Security for LDC's: Adjustments in Its STABEX and Stock Policies. *Europ. Rev. Agr. Econ.*, 1984, *11*(4), pp. 415–37. **[G: EEC]**

Konstantinov, Iu. A. The Interaction of National Currencies with International Socialist Currency. *Soviet E. Europ. Foreign Trade*, Spring 1984, *20*(1), pp. 57–75. **[G: CMEA]**

Langhammer, Rolf J. Regional Integration and Cooperation in Africa: A History of Disappointments? In *Ghosh, P. K., ed., no. 12, 1984, 1977*, pp. 203–15. [G: Africa]

Larsen, Arne. Major Factors behind the Problems of the Common Agricultural Policy. *Europ. Rev. Agr. Econ.*, 1984, *11*(2), pp. 121–27. [G: EEC]

Lee, Joseph. Perspectives on Ireland in the EEC—A Review Essay. *Econ. Soc. Rev.*, October 1984, *16*(1), pp. 51–58. [G: Ireland; EEC]

Lewis, Vaughan A. Regional Integration and Theories of Regionalism in the Commonwealth Caribbean. In *Núñez del Arco, J.; Margain, E. and Cherol, R., eds.*, 1984, pp. 27–42. [G: Caribbean]

Lozoya, Jorge. The Pacific Basin: The Future of a Concept. In *Downen, R. L. and Dickson, B. J., eds.*, 1984, pp. 45–55. [G: Pacific Basin]

Mahé, Louis P. A Lower but More Balanced Protection for European Agriculture. *Europ. Rev. Agr. Econ.*, 1984, *11*(2), pp. 217–34. [G: EEC]

Malý, Bohuslav. Conditions for the Specialization of the Czechoslovak National Economic Complex. *Czech. Econ. Pap.*, 1984, (22), pp. 25–41. [G: Czechoslovakia; CMEA]

Marsh, John S. The Reform of the CAP: National Interests and Financial Implications. *Europ. Rev. Agr. Econ.*, 1984, *11*(2), pp. 141–50. [G: EEC]

Marsh, Peter. The European Community and East–West Economic Relations. *J. Common Market Stud.*, September 1984, *23*(1), pp. 1–13. [G: EEC; CMEA]

Mattera, A. Protectionism inside the European Community: Decisions of the European Court. *J. World Trade Law*, July–August 1984, *18*(4), pp. 283–308. [G: EEC]

Matthews, Jacqueline. Economic Integration in Southern Africa: Progress or Decline? *S. Afr. J. Econ.*, September 1984, *52*(3), pp. 256–65. [G: S. Africa]

Mazzeo, Domenico. Conclusion: Problems and Prospects of Intra-African Cooperation. In *Mazzeo, D., ed.*, 1984, pp. 225–42. [G: Africa]

Mazzeo, Domenico. Introduction: The Regional Trend. In *Mazzeo, D., ed.*, 1984, pp. 1–12. [G: Africa]

Mazzeo, Domenico. The Experience of the East African Community: Implications for the Theory and Practice of Regional Cooperation in Africa. In *Mazzeo, D., ed.*, 1984, pp. 150–70. [G: E. Africa]

McAleese, Dermot. Regional Disequilibria. *Economia (Portugal)*, January 1984, *8*(1), pp. 19–41. [G: EEC]

Mestmäcker, Ernst-Joachim. The Applicability of the ECSC-Cartel Prohibition (Article 65) during a "Manifest Crisis." *Mich. Law Rev.*, April–May 1984, *82*(5 & 6), pp. 1399–1414. [G: EEC]

Meyns, Peter. The Southern African Development Coordination Conference (SADCC) and Regional Cooperation in Southern Africa. In *Mazzeo, D., ed.*, 1984, pp. 196–224. [G: Southern Africa]

Morales, Juan Antonio. Problems Surrounding the Common External Tariff: The Andean Group Case. In *Núñez del Arco, J.; Margain, E. and Cherol, R., eds.*, 1984, pp. 185–204. [G: Latin America]

Mytelka, Lynn Krieger. Competition, Conflict and Decline in the Union Douanière et Economique de l'Afrique Centrale (UDEAC). In *Mazzeo, D., ed.*, 1984, pp. 131–49. [G: Central Africa]

Neuberger, Egon and Ben-Ner, Avner. Romania's Reactions to International Commodity Inflation. In *Jackson, M. R. and Woodson, J. D., Jr., eds.*, 1984, pp. 55–99. [G: Romania; CMEA]

Nicoll, W. The Luxembourg Compromise. *J. Common Market Stud.*, September 1984, *23*(1), pp. 35–43. [G: EEC]

Nsouli, Saleh M. Monetary Integration in Developing Countries. In *Ghosh, P. K., ed., no. 12, 1984, 1981*, pp. 153–58.

Nyers, Rezso. Tendencies of Tradition and Reform in CMEA Cooperation. *Soviet E. Europ. Foreign Trade*, Summer 1984, *20*(2), pp. 6–36. [G: CMEA]

Palmer, Ransford W. Restructuring the Economic Institutions of the Eastern Caribbean. In *Palmer, R. W.*, 1984, pp. 59–65. [G: E. Caribbean]

Pérez, Carlos Andrés. The Geopolitics of Integration in Latin America. In *Núñez del Arco, J.; Margain, E. and Cherol, R., eds.*, 1984, pp. 17–26. [G: Latin America]

Petersen, Volker and Schmitt, Günther. Ordnungs- und finanzpolitische Irrwege der europäischen Agrarpolitik. (With English Summary.) In *Eucken, W. and Böhm, F., eds.*, 1984, pp. 71–108. [G: EEC]

Petit, Bernard. Euro–Arab Co-financing. In *Achilli, M. and Khaldi, M., eds.*, 1984, pp. 244–51. [G: EEC]

Pitta e Cunha, Paulo and de Macedo, Jorge Braga. Economic Policy in an Enlarged European Community. *Economia (Portugal)*, January 1984, *8*(1), pp. 3–6. [G: EEC]

Poller, Roland and Tesner, István. Socialist Economic Integration and the Investment Cooperation of the CMEA Countries. *Soviet E. Europ. Foreign Trade*, Spring 1984, *20*(1), pp. 6–26. [G: CMEA]

Ponsard, Claude and Tranqui, Phuoc. La régionalisation floue de l'économie européenne. (With English summary.) *Revue Écon. Polit.*, January–February 1984, *94*(1), pp. 1–25. [G: EEC]

Porto, Manuel Carlos Lopes. Os países da Península Ibérica e a problemática regional no seio da CEE. (With English summary.) *Economia (Portugal)*, October 1984, *8*(3), pp. 471–507. [G: Spain; Portugal; EEC]

Průcha, Václav. 35th Anniversary of the Council

for Mutual Economic Assistance. *Czech. Econ. Digest.*, May 1984, (3), pp. 47–54.
[G: CMEA]

Rashish, Myer. Reducing Nontariff Barriers. **In** *Fried, E. R. and Trezise, P. H., eds.,* 1984, pp. 52–56. [G: U.S.; Canada]

Richonnier, Michel. Europe's Decline Is Not Irreversible. *J. Common Market Stud.*, March 1984, *22*(3), pp. 227–43. [G: U.S.; Japan; EEC]

Ritson, Christopher and Fearne, Andrew. Long-term Goals for the CAP. *Europ. Rev. Agr. Econ.*, 1984, *11*(2), pp. 207–16. [G: EEC]

Ronkainen, Ilkka A. Project Exports and the CMEA. **In** *Kaynak, E., ed.,* 1984, pp. 305–17. [G: CMEA]

Rusmich, Ladislav. Value Aspects in Developing the Process of International Socialist Integration. *Soviet E. Europ. Foreign Trade*, Winter 1984-85, *20*(4), pp. 7–31. [G: CMEA]

Ruta, Gianni. L'Europa comunitaria e la cooperazione allo sviluppo. (The European Community and the Cooperation to Development. With English summary.) *Mondo Aperto*, November–December 1984, *38*(6), pp. 337–42.
[G: EEC; Africa; Caribbean; Pacific Countries]

Salgado Penaherrera, Germanico. Economic Integration of Developing Countries and the Role of Joint Industrial Planning. **In** *Ghosh, P. K., ed., no. 12,* 1984, *1975*, pp. 120–52.
[G: Latin America]

Salgado Penaherrera, Germanico. Viable Integration and the Economic Co-operation Problems of the Developing World. **In** *Ghosh, P. K., ed., no. 12,* 1984, *1978*, pp. 74–119.
[G: Global]

Samson, I. La coopération économique entre la R.D.A. et ses partenaires du C.A.E.M.: une forme exemplaire d'insertion dans la D.I.S.T.? (Economic Cooperation between the G.D.R. and Its CMEA Partners: A Model Form of Insertion within the International Social Division of Labour. With English summary.) *Écon. Soc.*, February 1984, *18*(2), pp. 79–114.
[G: E. Germany; CMEA]

Schwartz, Hugh. Industrial Project Identification in an Economic Integration Context. **In** *Núñez del Arco, J.; Margain, E. and Cherol, R., eds.,* 1984, pp. 126–41. [G: Latin America]

Sereghyová, Jana. The Role of Advertising in Developing Economic Cooperation among Members of the CMEA. *Soviet E. Europ. Foreign Trade*, Winter 1984-85, *20*(4), pp. 63–76.
[G: CMEA]

Sheeny, Seamus. The Agri-monetary System—A Reinterpretation. *Europ. Rev. Agr. Econ.*, 1984, *11*(2), pp. 177–86. [G: EEC]

Sobhan, Rehman. Regional Economic Cooperation in South Asia: Legacy and Prospects. **In** *Ghosh, P. K., ed., no. 18,* 1984, *1979*, pp. 267–93. [G: S. Asia]

Solomon, Robert. The European Monetary System: Tombstone or Cornerstone?: Discussion. **In** *Fed. Res. Bank Boston,* 1984, pp. 174–77. [G: OECD]

Sonntag, Niels and Featherstone, Kevin. Looking towards the 1984 European Elections: Problems of Political Integration. *J. Common Market Stud.*, March 1984, *22*(3), pp. 269–82.
[G: U.K.; France; Italy; W. Germany]

Sternlight, David. OPEC and International Financial Markets: Redistribution and Recycling. **In** *Agmon, T.; Hawkins, R. G. and Levich, R. M., eds.,* 1984, pp. 231–45. [G: OPEC]

Straubhaar, Thomas. Die Süderweiterung der EG unter arbeitsmarkpolitischen Gesichtspunkten—Das Migrationspotential der neuen Mitglieder auf dem Gemeinsamen Arbeitsmarkt. (The Southern Expansion of the EC from the Political Point of View of the Labour Market—The Migration Potential of the New Members of the Common Labour Market. With English summary.) *Schweiz. Z. Volkswirtsch. Statist.*, December 1984, *120*(4), pp. 577–88. [G: EEC]

Tangermann, Stefan. Guarantee Thresholds: A Device for Solving the CAP Surplus Problem? *Europ. Rev. Agr. Econ.*, 1984, *11*(2), pp. 157–68. [G: EEC]

Tanzi, Vito. Fiscal Harmonization. *Economia (Portugal)*, January 1984, *8*(1), pp. 43–65.
[G: EEC]

Tarditi, Secondo. Direct Financial Support to Agriculture. *Europ. Rev. Agr. Econ.*, 1984, *11*(2), pp. 235–43. [G: EEC]

Tetreault, Mary Ann. Middle East Community Building. **In** *Boyd, G., ed.,* 1984, pp. 147–73.
[G: OPEC; OAPEC]

Ting, Chung-Chiang and Lee, Thomas B. Taiwan's Role in the Pacific Community in Relationship to the Soviet Threat. **In** *Downen, R. L. and Dickson, B. J., eds.,* 1984, pp. 221–25. [G: Taiwan; Pacific Basin]

Tiraspolsky, Anita. An Evaluation of Gains and Losses in Intra-CMEA Trade: Terms of Trade from 1970 to 1982. *Soviet E. Europ. Foreign Trade*, Winter 1984-85, *20*(4), pp. 32–62.
[G: CMEA]

Triffin, Robert. The European Monetary System: Tombstone or Cornerstone? **In** *Fed. Res. Bank Boston,* 1984, pp. 127–73. [G: EEC]

Tsardanidis, Charalambos. The EC–Cyprus Association Agreement: Ten Years of a Troubled Relationship, 1973–1983. *J. Common Market Stud.*, June 1984, *22*(4), pp. 351–76.
[G: EEC; Cyprus]

Tvrdík, Zdeněk. The Coordinated Scientific–Technological Policy of the CMEA Member States. *Czech. Econ. Digest.*, September 1984, (6), pp. 56–79. [G: CMEA]

Uhalley, Stephen, Jr. The Membership Dilemma and What to Do About It: The Non-Market Economy Nations and the Pacific Community. **In** *Downen, R. L. and Dickson, B. J., eds.,* 1984, pp. 81–90. [G: Pacific Basin]

UNIDO Secretariat. Patterns and Prospects for East–South Trade in the 1980s. *Industry Devel.*, 1984, (11), pp. 67–98. [G: CMEA]

Ushakova, N. Industrial Co-operation between the Council for Mutual Economic Assistance and Developing Countries. *Industry Devel.*, 1984, (11), pp. 59–66. **[G: CMEA]**

Van den Bempt, Paul. Autonomy in Economic Policy: The Case of a Small Open Economy. *Economia (Portugal)*, January 1984, 8(1), pp. 89–95. **[G: Portugal; EEC]**

Van Houtte, H. The EEC Draft Regulation on Selective Distribution of Automobiles. *J. World Trade Law*, July–August 1984, 18(4), pp. 349–57. **[G: EEC]**

Vandamme, François. The Revised European Social Fund and Action to Combat Unemployment in the European Community. *Int. Lab. Rev.*, March-April 1984, 123(2), pp. 167–81. **[G: EEC]**

Vandamme, Jacques. The Conflict about the Budget. *Economia (Portugal)*, January 1984, 8(1), pp. 81–88. **[G: EEC]**

Velev, Todor. The Influence of Bulgaria's Economic Ties with CMEA Members on Some Proportions in Its Economy. *Soviet E. Europ. Foreign Trade*, Summer 1984, 20(2), pp. 56–68. **[G: Bulgaria; CMEA]**

Waelbroeck, Michel. Competition, Integration, and Economic Efficiency in the EEC from the Point of View of the Private Firm. *Mich. Law Rev.*, April–May 1984, 82(5 & 6), pp. 1439–46. **[G: EEC]**

Warner, Harriet. EC Social Policy in Practice: Community Action on Behalf of Women and Its Impact in the Member States. *J. Common Market Stud.*, December 1984, 23(2), pp. 141–67. **[G: EEC]**

Wassermann, Ursula. EEC: Air Pollution Directive. *J. World Trade Law*, September–October 1984, 18(5), pp. 459–61. **[G: EEC]**

Weiss, Frank D. Aspects of Real Exchange Rates—East and West. In *Csikós-Nagy, B.; Hague, D. and Hall, G., eds.*, 1984, pp. 317–32. **[G: CMEA; OECD]**

White, Geoff. Intra-Industry Trade Adjustment and European Industrial Policies. In *Jacquemin, A., ed.*, 1984, pp. 172–90. **[G: EEC]**

de Wilmars, J. Mertens and Steenbergen, J. The Court of Justice of the European Communities and Governance in an Economic Crisis. *Mich. Law Rev.*, April–May 1984, 82(5 & 6), pp. 1377–98. **[G: EEC]**

Winters, L. Alan. British Imports of Manufactures and the Common Market. *Oxford Econ. Pap.*, March 1984, 36(1), pp. 103–18. **[G: U.K.; EEC]**

Wonnacott, Paul. Industrial Allocation in the Andean Pact. In *Núñez del Arco, J.; Margain, E. and Cherol, R., eds.*, 1984, pp. 103–14. **[G: Latin America]**

Woolcock, Stephen. Information Technology: The Challenge to Europe. *J. Common Market Stud.*, June 1984, 22(4), pp. 315–31. **[G: Europe]**

Yannopoulos, George N. Prospects for the Manufacturing Exports of the Non-candidate Mediterranean Countries in a Community of Twelve. *World Devel.*, November–December 1984, 12(11–12), pp. 1087–94. **[G: EEC]**

430 Open Economy Macroeconomics; Exchange Rates; International Finance

4300 General

Adams, John. Foreign Economic Policy: Challenges of the 1980s. *J. Econ. Issues*, March 1984, 18(1), pp. 275–94. **[G: U.S.]**

Diaz-Alejandro, Carlos F. Latin American Debt: I Don't Think We Are in Kansas Anymore. *Brookings Pap. Econ. Act.*, 1984, (2), pp. 335–89. **[G: Latin America]**

Hewlett, Sylvia Ann. Overview and Policy Options. In *Hewlett, S. A.; Kaufman, H. and Kenen, P. B., eds.*, 1984, pp. 199–221.

Iglesias, Enrique V. Latin America: Crisis and Development Options. *Cepal Rev.*, 1984, (23), pp. 7–28. **[G: Latin America]**

Krugman, Paul R. Latin American Debt: I Don't Think We Are in Kansas Anymore: Comment. *Brookings Pap. Econ. Act.*, 1984, (2), pp. 390–93. **[G: Latin America]**

Owen, Henry. The World Economy: The Dollar and the Summit. *Foreign Aff.*, Winter 1984/85, 63(2), pp. 344–59. **[G: OECD]**

Prebisch, Raúl. The Global Crisis of Capitalism and Its Theoretical Background. *Cepal Rev.*, April 1984, (22), pp. 159–78. **[G: Global]**

Sachs, Jeffrey D. Latin American Debt: I Don't Think We Are in Kansas Anymore: Comment. *Brookings Pap. Econ. Act.*, 1984, (2), pp. 393–401. **[G: Latin America]**

431 Open Economy Macroeconomics; Exchange Rates

4310 General

Ahking, Francis W. International Currency Substitution: A Reexamination of Britain's Econometric Evidence: A Comment. *J. Money, Credit, Banking*, Part 1 November 1984, 16(4), pp. 546–56. **[G: U.S.; W. Germany; U.K.]**

Aliber, Robert Z. Capital Flows, External Debt and the International Adjustment Process. In *Black, J. and Dorrance, G. S., eds.*, 1984, pp. 1–20. **[G: LDCs]**

Baqai, Moinuddin. A New Framework for International Financial Co-operation for Development. In *Ghosh, P. K., ed., no. 15*, 1984, 1979, pp. 222–38.

Baretje, René. La contribution nette du tourisme international à la balance des paiements. (The Net Contribution of International Tourism to the Balance of Payments. With English summary.) *Rivista Int. Sci. Econ. Com.*, July 1984, 31(7), pp. 649–74. **[G: OECD]**

Bigman, David and Taya, Teizo. Floating Exchange Rates and the State of World Trade and Payments: Introduction. In *Bigman, D. and Taya, T., eds.*, 1984, pp. xvii–xxvi.

Buffie, Edward F. Financial Repression, the New Structuralists, and Stabilization Policy in Semi-Industrialized Economies. *J. Devel. Econ.*, April 1984, 14(3), pp. 305–22. **[G: LDCs]**

Calleo, David P. and Strange, Susan. Paths to International Political Economy: Money and World Politics. In *Strange, S., ed.*, 1984, pp. 91–125. [G: U.S.; Global]

Chipman, J. S. Balance of Payments Theory. In *Creedy, J. and O'Brien, D. P., eds.*, 1984, pp. 186–217.

Dornbusch, Rudiger and Frenkel, Jacob A. The Gold Standard Crisis of 1847. *J. Int. Econ.*, February 1984, *16*(1/2), pp. 1–27. [G: U.K.]

Guglielmi, Jean-Louis. Mutations techniques. Formation du capital et monnaie. Essai sur une nouvelle révolution industrielle: 1952–1983. (With English summary.) *Revue Écon. Polit.*, March–April 1984, *94*(2), pp. 181–201. [G: OECD]

Laney, Leroy O.; Radcliffe, Christopher D. and Willett, Thomas D. Currency Substitution: Comment. *Southern Econ. J.*, April 1984, *50*(4), pp. 1196–1200. [G: U.S.; W. Germany]

Miles, Marc A. Currency Substitution: Reply. *Southern Econ. J.*, April 1984, *50*(4), pp. 1201–03. [G: U.S.; W. Germany]

Scitovsky, Tibor. Lerner's Contribution to Economics. *J. Econ. Lit.*, December 1984, *22*(4), pp. 1547–71.

Shoven, John B. and Whalley, John. Applied General-Equilibrium Models of Taxation and International Trade: An Introduction and Survey. *J. Econ. Lit.*, September 1984, *22*(3), pp. 1007–51.

Williamson, John. Is There an External Constraint? *Nat. Inst. Econ. Rev.*, August 1984, (109), pp. 73–77. [G: U.K.]

4312 Open Economy Macroeconomic Theory: Balance of Payments and Adjustment Mechanisms

Ahtiala, Pekka. A Synthesis of the Macroeconomic Approaches to Exchange Rate Determination. *Europ. Econ. Rev.*, March 1984, *24*(2), pp. 117–36.

Aizenman, Joshua. Optimal Wage Re-Negotiation in a Closed and Open Economy. *J. Monet. Econ.*, March 1984, *13*(2), pp. 251–62.

Arndt, Sven W. The External Effects of U.S. Disinflation. In *Fellner, W., ed.*, 1984, pp. 131–53. [G: OECD; U.S.]

Aurikko, Esko. Exchange Rate Policies Simulated by Means of a Disequilibrium Model of the Finnish Economy. *J. Policy Modeling*, November 1984, *6*(4), pp. 531–54. [G: Finland]

Ben-Zion, Uri. Recent Literature on the Impact of Taxation and Inflation on the International Financial Market. In *Tanzi, V., ed.*, 1984, pp. 99–109.

Benavie, Arthur. Imported Inflation and Monetary-Fiscal Policy under a Flexible Exchange Rate. *Atlantic Econ. J.*, March 1984, *12*(1), pp. 41–49.

Bhandari, Jagdeep S. A Computational Stochastic Equilibrium Model of Oil-importing Economies. *Weltwirtsch. Arch.*, 1984, *120*(2), pp. 301–28.

Bhandari, Jagdeep S. Wage Contracting and Aggregate Adjustment in an Open Economy. *Aussenwirtschaft*, December 1984, *39*(4), pp. 335–56.

Bhandari, Jagdeep S. Wage Contracting and Exchange Rate Intervention in a Model with Intermediate Imports. *Z. ges. Staatswiss.*, December 1984, *140*(4), pp. 685–711.

Bhandari, Jagdeep S. and Turnovsky, Stephen J. Materials Price Increases and Aggregate Adjustment in an Open Economy: A Stochastic Approach. *Europ. Econ. Rev.*, July 1984, *25*(2), pp. 151–82.

Bigman, David. Semi-Rational Expectations and Exchange-Rate Dynamics. *J. Int. Money Finance*, April 1984, *3*(1), pp. 51–66.

Bilson, John F. O. The Process of Balance of Payments Adjustment. In *Muns, J., ed.*, 1984, pp. 34–57.

Bird, Graham. Balance of Payments Policy in Developing Countries. In *Killick, Tony, ed. (II)*, 1984, pp. 86–127.

Black, Stanley W. The Relationship between Exchange Rate Policy and Monetary Policy in Ten Industrial Countries. In *Bilson, J. F. O. and Marston, R. C., eds.*, 1984, pp. 499–511. [G: Selected OECD]

Blanchard, Olivier J. Macroeconomic Policy Coordination among the Industrial Economies: Comments. *Brookings Pap. Econ. Act.*, 1984, (1), pp. 65–68. [G: U.S.; W. Germany; Japan]

Blejer, Mario I. Financial Market Taxation and International Capital Flows. In *Tanzi, V., ed.*, 1984, pp. 204–19.

Boughton, James M. Some Aspects of the Adjustment Problem in an Interdependent World: Comment. In *Agmon, T.; Hawkins, R. G. and Levich, R. M., eds.*, 1984, pp. 221–27.

Branson, William H. Exchange Rate Policy after a Decade of "Floating." In *Bilson, J. F. O. and Marston, R. C., eds.*, 1984, pp. 79–108. [G: Japan; U.K.; U.S.; W. Germany]

Breuss, Fritz. Robinson and Marshall–Lerner Conditions with Positive Import Content of Exports. *Europ. Econ. Rev.*, July 1984, *25*(2), pp. 183–85.

Brock, Philip L. Inflationary Finance in an Open Economy. *J. Monet. Econ.*, July 1984, *14*(1), pp. 37–53. [G: OECD; LDCs]

Browne, F. X. The International Transmission of Inflation to a Small Open Economy under Fixed Exchange Rates and Highly Interest-sensitive Capital Flows: An Empirical Analysis. *Europ. Econ. Rev.*, July 1984, *25*(2), pp. 187–212.

Buiter, Willem H. A Comprehensive Balance Sheet and Permanent Income Accounting Framework for the Public Sector: Theory and Applications. In *Masera, R. S. and Triffin, R., eds.*, 1984, pp. 153–95. [G: EEC; U.S.]

Buiter, Willem H. Exchange Rate Policy after a Decade of "Floating": Comment. In *Bilson,*

J. F. O. and Marston, R. C., eds., 1984, pp. 108–12. **[G: Japan; U.K.; U.S.; W. Germany]**

Buiter, Willem H. Real Exchange Rates in the 1970s: Comment. In *Bilson, J. F. O. and Marston, R. C., eds.*, 1984, pp. 321–30. **[G: Selected OECD]**

Buiter, Willem H. Saddlepoint Problems in Continuous Time Rational Expectations Models: A General Method and Some Macroeconomic Examples. *Econometrica*, May 1984, 52(3), pp. 665–80.

Burns, Arthur F. The American Trade Deficit in Perspective. *Foreign Aff.*, Summer 1984, 62(5), pp. 1058–69. **[G: U.S.]**

Butlin, M. W. Managed Exchange Rates and Exchange Control: A Theoretical Analysis. *Australian Econ. Pap.*, December 1984, 23(43), pp. 167–78.

Cadilhe, Miguel. The Portuguese External Deficit and the "Strategy of Humps." *Economia (Portugal)*, May 1984, 8(2), pp. 425–36. **[G: Portugal]**

Canzoneri, Matthew and Gray, Jo Anna. Some Aspects of the Adjustment Problem in an Interdependent World. In *Agmon, T.; Hawkins, R. G. and Levich, R. M., eds.*, 1984, pp. 195–220.

Chrystal, K. Alec. On the Theory of International Money. In *Black, J. and Dorrance, G. S., eds.*, 1984, pp. 77–92.

Corden, W. M. Booming Sector and Dutch Disease Economics: Survey and Consolidation. *Oxford Econ. Pap.*, November 1984, 36(3), pp. 359–80.

Corden, W. M. International Liquidity: Are the Supply and Composition Appropriate? Discussion. In *Fed. Res. Bank Boston*, 1984, pp. 78–82.

Corden, W. M. Macroeconomic Targets and Instruments for a Small Open Economy. *Singapore Econ. Rev.*, October 1984, 29(2), pp. 27–37.

Cornell, Robert A. The New Nexus among Trade, Industrial and Exchange-Rate Policies: Comment. In *Agmon, T.; Hawkins, R. G. and Levich, R. M., eds.*, 1984, pp. 280–83.

Currie, David and Levine, Paul. Stochastic Macroeconomic Policy Simulations for a Small Open Economy. In *van der Ploeg, F., ed.*, 1984, pp. 217–48.

Debonneuil, Michèle and Sterdyniak, Henri. La boucle prix-salaires dans l'inflation. (Inflation and Wage–Price Feed-Back. With English summary.) *Revue Écon.*, March 1984, 35(2), pp. 267–311.

Djajić, Slobodan. Currency Management and Economic Stability. *Econ. J.*, June 1984, 94(374), pp. 324–39.

Dornbusch, Rudiger. Exchange Market Intervention Operations: Their Role in Financial Policy and Their Effects: Comment. In *Bilson, J. F. O. and Marston, R. C., eds.*, 1984, pp. 398–402.

Dornbusch, Rudiger. Monetary Policy under Exchange Rate Flexibility. In *Bigman, D. and Taya, T., eds.*, 1984, pp. 3–31.

Dornbusch, Rudiger. The Theory of Exchange Rate Determination: Comment. In *Bilson, J. F. O. and Marston, R. C., eds.*, 1984, pp. 63–66.

Duck, Nigel W. Prices, Output and the Balance of Payments in an Open Economy with Rational Expectations. *J. Int. Econ.*, February 1984, 16(1/2), pp. 59–77.

Eaton, Jonathan and Turnovsky, Stephen J. The Forward Exchange Market, Speculation, and Exchange Market Intervention. *Quart. J. Econ.*, February 1984, 99(1), pp. 45–69.

Eichhorn, Wolfgang and Buhl, Hans Ulrich. Optimal Growth Policies for Resource-Dependent Open Economies. In *Hammer, G. and Pallaschke, D., eds.*, 1984, pp. 175–87.

Enders, Klaus. The Dutch Disease or Problems of a Sectoral Boom. *Z. Wirtschaft. Sozialwissen.*, 1984, 104(1), pp. 1–20.

Engel, Charles M. and Frankel, Jeffrey A. The Secular Inflation Term in Open-Economy Phillips Curves. *Europ. Econ. Rev.*, March 1984, 24(2), pp. 161–64.

Fender, John. Sectoral and Macroeconomic Effects in a Two Good Open Economy with an Intermediate Input. *Bull. Econ. Res.*, May 1984, 36(1), pp. 9–32.

Flood, Robert P. and Hodrick, Robert J. Exchange Rate and Price Dynamics with Asymmetric Information. *Int. Econ. Rev.*, October 1984, 25(3), pp. 513–26.

Fourgeaud, Claude; Lenclud, Bernard and Picard, Pierre. Calcul économique prix fictifs et contrainte extérieure. (Cost–Benefit Analysis, Shadow Prices and Foreign Trade Constraint. With English summary.) *Revue Écon.*, May 1984, 35(3), pp. 425–45.

Frankel, Jeffrey A. Tests of Monetary and Portfolio Balance Models of Exchange Rate Determination. In *Bilson, J. F. O. and Marston, R. C., eds.*, 1984, pp. 239–60. **[G: Selected OECD]**

Frenkel, Jacob A. Does Devaluation Improve the Current Account? Comments. *Europ. Econ. Rev.*, June 1984, 25(1), pp. 65–68. **[G: Global]**

Frenkel, Jacob A. The Theory of Exchange Rate Determination: Comment. In *Bilson, J. F. O. and Marston, R. C., eds.*, 1984, pp. 58–62.

Giavazzi, Francesco and Vyplosz, Charles. The Real Exchange Rate, the Current Account, and the Speed of Adjustment. In *Bilson, J. F. O. and Marston, R. C., eds.*, 1984, pp. 335–53.

Goldstein, Henry N. and Haynes, Stephen E. A Critical Appraisal of McKinnon's World Money Supply Hypothesis [Currency Substitution and Instability in the World Dollar Standard]. *Amer. Econ. Rev.*, March 1984, 74(1), pp. 217–24. **[G: U.S.]**

de Grauwe, Paul. The Relationship between Exchange Rate Policy and Monetary Policy in Ten Industrial Countries: Comment. In *Bilson, J. F. O. and Marston, R. C., eds.*, 1984, pp. 511–14. **[G: Selected OECD]**

Greenwood, Jeremy. Non-traded Goods, the Trade Balance, and the Balance of Payments. *Can. J. Econ.*, November 1984, *17*(4), pp. 806–23.

Gupta, Sanjeev. Causal Relationship between Domestic Credit and International Reserves: The Experience of Developing Countries. *Kredit Kapital*, 1984, *17*(2), pp. 261–71. **[G: India; Malaysia; Mexico; Taiwan]**

Gylfason, Thorvaldur and Risager, Ole. Does Devaluation Improve the Current Account? *Europ. Econ. Rev.*, June 1984, *25*(1), pp. 37–64. **[G: Global]**

Hahn, Frank H. The Balance of Payments in a Monetary Economy. In *Hahn, F.*, 1984, *1959*, pp. 217–36.

Hahn, Frank H. The Monetary Approach to the Balance of Payments. In *Hahn, F.*, 1984, *1977*, pp. 237–58.

Harkness, Jon. Optimal Oil Pricing in a Small Open Economy: A Macro-economic Perspective. *Can. J. Econ.*, November 1984, *17*(4), pp. 762–73.

Haynes, Stephen E. and Stone, Joe A. Cross-Price Effects in Demand between Exports and Imports. *J. Macroecon.*, Spring 1984, *6*(2), pp. 181–95. **[G: U.S.]**

Henderson, Dale W. Exchange Market Intervention Operations: Their Role in Financial Policy and Their Effects. In *Bilson, J. F. O. and Marston, R. C., eds.*, 1984, pp. 359–98.

Herberg, Horst and Enders, Klaus. More on the Consequences of a Resource Boom and the Cures of the Dutch Disease. In *Siebert, H., ed.*, 1984, pp. 47–94.

Holly, Sean and Corker, R. Optimal Feedback and Feedforward Stabilisation of Exchange Rates, Money, Prices and Output under Rational Expectations. In *Hughes Hallet, A.J., ed.*, 1984, pp. 33–60. **[G: U.K.]**

Hsu, John C. Adjustment to Oil Shocks in a Small Open Less Developed Country: Problems and Policy Alternatives. *Singapore Econ. Rev.*, April 1984, *29*(1), pp. 16–29. **[G: Taiwan]**

Huber, Gérard. Inflation and Nominal Tax System in an Open Economy. *Europ. Econ. Rev.*, February 1984, *24*(1), pp. 23–37.

Islam, Shafiqul. Devaluation, Stabilization Policies and the Developing Countries: A Macroeconomic Analysis. *J. Devel. Econ.*, January–February 1984, *14*(1–2), pp. 37–60.

Johnson, R. Stafford and Zuber, Richard A. The Economic Cost of Correcting External Imbalances. *Rivista Int. Sci. Econ. Com.*, March 1984, *31*(3), pp. 193–211.

Jones, Michael. Optimal Foreign Exchange Market Intervention: Evidence from the Bretton Woods Era. *Rev. Econ. Statist.*, May 1984, *66*(2), pp. 242–55. **[G: OECD]**

Kanniainen, Vesa. On Offsetting Capital Flows and Monetary Autonomy of a Small Open Economy. *Economica*, May 1984, *51*(202), pp. 177–86.

Kemp, Murray C. and Long, Ngo Van. The Problem of Survival: An Open Economy. In *Kemp, M. C. and Long, N. V., eds.*, 1984, pp. 27–35.

Kenen, Peter B. Exchange Rate Policy after a Decade of "Floating": Comment. In *Bilson, J. F. O. and Marston, R. C., eds.*, 1984, pp. 112–16. **[G: Japan; U.K.; U.S.; W. Germany]**

Kenen, Peter B. Exchange Rate Unions as an Alternative to Flexible Rates: The Effects of Real and Monetary Disturbances: Comment. In *Bilson, J. F. O. and Marston, R. C., eds.*, 1984, pp. 437–41.

Kimbrough, Kent P. Aggregate Information and the Role of Monetary Policy in an Open Economy. *J. Polit. Econ.*, April 1984, *92*(2), pp. 268–85.

Kimbrough, Kent P. The Corporation Income Tax in the Open Economy. *Int. Econ. Rev.*, June 1984, *25*(2), pp. 391–407.

Kimbrough, Kent P. The Forward Rate as a Predictor of the Future Spot Rate, the Role of Policy, and Exchange Rate Regime Choice. *Int. Econ. Rev.*, October 1984, *25*(3), pp. 527–43.

Kimbrough, Kent P. and Koray, Faik. Money, Output, and the Trade Balance: Theory and Evidence. *Can. J. Econ.*, August 1984, *17*(3), pp. 508–22. **[G: Canada; U.S.]**

Kingston, Geoffrey H. Microeconomic Justification of the Hoarding Function. *Int. Econ. Rev.*, June 1984, *25*(2), pp. 385–89.

Korkman, Sixten and Pekkarinen, Jukka. Onko valuuttasäännöstely aikansa elänyt? (Should Exchange Control Be Abandoned? With English summary.) *Kansant. Aikak.*, 1984, *80*(1), pp. 76–85. **[G: Finland]**

Kouri, Pentti, J. K. The Theory of Exchange Rate Determination: Comment. In *Bilson, J. F. O. and Marston, R. C., eds.*, 1984, pp. 67–72.

Krugman, Paul R. The International Role of the Dollar: Theory and Prospect. In *Bilson, J. F. O. and Marston, R. C., eds.*, 1984, pp. 261–78. **[G: OECD; U.S.]**

Krugman, Paul R. The Real Exchange Rate, the Current Account, and the Speed of Adjustment: Comment. In *Bilson, J. F. O. and Marston, R. C., eds.*, 1984, pp. 353–55.

Lai, Ching-chong. Exchange Rate Expectations, Monetary Effect of Devaluation, and Macroeconomic Policies. *Atlantic Econ. J.*, December 1984, *12*(4), pp. 55–58.

Lai, Ching-chong and Chen, Chau-nan. Flexible Exchange Rates, Tight Money Effects, and Macroeconomic Policy. *J. Post Keynesian Econ.*, Fall 1984, *7*(1), pp. 128–33.

Lawrence, Colin. The Role of Information and the International Business Cycle. *J. Int. Econ.*, August 1984, *17*(1/2), pp. 101–20.

Le Van, Cuong. Specification of the Import Function and the Determination of Short and Long Term Equilibria in a Macroeconometric Model. In *Ancot, J. P., ed.*, 1984, pp. 229–45.

Lee, Moon H. and Zechner, Josef. Debt, Taxes, and International Equilibrium. *J. Int. Money Finance*, December 1984, *3*(3), pp. 343–55.

León, Carlos Amat Y. Fiscal Deficits and Balance

of Payments Disequilibrium in IMF Adjustment Programs: Comment. In *Muns, J., ed.*, 1984, pp. 137–40. **[G: LDCs; Peru]**

Levin, Jay H. Non-sterilization, Pegged Exchange Rates, and Stabilization Policy. *Metroecon.*, February 1984, *36*(1), pp. 77–96.

Levin, Jay H. On the International Transmission of Monetary Policy under Floating Exchange Rates. *Quart. Rev. Econ. Bus.*, Spring 1984, *24*(1), pp. 78–86.

Liviatan, Oded. A Macro-Absorption Approach for Estimating the Foreign Debt Burden. *Econ. Develop. Cult. Change*, July 1984, *32*(4), pp. 803–18. **[G: LDCs]**

Lopez, Franklin. The Effect of Various Credit Controls on the Level of International Reserves. *Kredit Kapital*, 1984, *17*(3), pp. 404–15. **[G: LDCs]**

MacDonald, Ronald. The Monetary Approach to the Exchange Rate and the 1920s' Experience with Floating Exchange Rates. *J. Econ. Stud.*, 1984, *11*(3), pp. 14–25. **[G: U.S.; U.K.; France]**

Malan, Pedro S. and Wells, John R. 'Structural' Models of Inflation and Balance of Payments Disequilibria in Semi-industrialised Economies—Some Implications for Stabilisation and Growth Policies. In *Csikós-Nagy, B.; Hague, D. and Hall, G., eds.*, 1984, pp. 391–408.

Marion, Nancy Peregrim. Nontraded Goods, Oil Price Increases and the Current Account. *J. Int. Econ.*, February 1984, *16*(1/2), pp. 29–44.

Marion, Nancy Peregrim and Svensson, Lars E. O. World Equilibrium with Oil Price Increases: An Intertemporal Analysis. *Oxford Econ. Pap.*, March 1984, *36*(1), pp. 86–102.

Marris, Stephen N. Macroeconomic Policy Coordination among the Industrial Economies: Comments. *Brookings Pap. Econ. Act.*, 1984, (1), pp. 68–71. **[G: U.S.; W. Germany; Japan]**

Marston, Richard C. Exchange Rate Unions as an Alternative to Flexible Rates: The Effects of Real and Monetary Disturbances. In *Bilson, J. F. O. and Marston, R. C., eds.*, 1984, pp. 407–37.

Marston, Richard C. Real Wages and the Terms of Trade: Alternative Indexation Rules for an Open Economy. *J. Money, Credit, Banking*, August 1984, *16*(3), pp. 285–301.

McKinnon, Ronald I., et al. International Influences on the U.S. Economy: Summary of an Exchange. *Amer. Econ. Rev.*, December 1984, *74*(5), pp. 1132–34. **[G: U.S.]**

Meade, J. E. Structural Changes in the Rate of Interest and the Rate of Foreign Exchange to Preserve Equilibrium in the Balance of Payments and the Budget Balance. *Oxford Econ. Pap.*, March 1984, *36*(1), pp. 52–66.

Michener, Ron. A Neoclassical Model of the Balance of Payments. *Rev. Econ. Stud.*, October 1984, *51*(4), pp. 651–64.

de Montbrial, Thierry. Does Devaluation Improve the Current Account? Comments. *Eu-rop. Econ. Rev.*, June 1984, *25*(1), pp. 69–70. **[G: Global]**

Montiel, Peter. Credit and Fiscal Policies in a "Global Monetarist" Model of the Balance of Payments. *Int. Monet. Fund Staff Pap.*, December 1984, *31*(4), pp. 685–708.

Moses, Eleanor R. The Policy Implications of Internationally Mobile Capital under Fixed Exchange Rates. *Economica*, August 1984, *51*(203), pp. 341–49.

Mussa, Michael. The Theory of Exchange Rate Determination. In *Bilson, J. F. O. and Marston, R. C., eds.*, 1984, pp. 13–58.

Nowak, Michael. Quantitative Controls and Unofficial Markets in Foreign Exchange: A Theoretical Framework. *Int. Monet. Fund Staff Pap.*, June 1984, *31*(2), pp. 404–31.

O'Connell, Joan. Stock Adjustment and the Balance of Payments. *Econ. Notes*, 1984, (1), pp. 136–45.

Obstfeld, Maurice. Balance-of-Payments Crises and Devaluation. *J. Money, Credit, Banking*, May 1984, *16*(2), pp. 208–17.

Oudiz, Gilles and Sachs, Jeffrey D. Macroeconomic Policy Coordination among the Industrial Economies. *Brookings Pap. Econ. Act.*, 1984, (1), pp. 1–64. **[G: U.S.; W. Germany; Japan]**

Padoa Schioppa, Tommaso and Papadia, Francesco. Competing Currencies and Monetary Stability. In *Masera, R. S. and Triffin, R., eds.*, 1984, pp. 79–110.

Papadia, Francesco. Multilateral Exchange Rate Determination: A Model for the Analysis of the European Monetary System: Comment. In *Bilson, J. F. O. and Marston, R. C., eds.*, 1984, pp. 461–64. **[G: Selected OECD]**

Papell, David H. Activist Monetary Policy and Exchange-Rate Overshooting: The Deutsche Mark/Dollar Rate. *J. Int. Money Finance*, December 1984, *3*(3), pp. 293–310. **[G: U.S.; W. Germany]**

Persson, Torsten. Real Transfers in Fixed Exchange Rate Systems and the International Adjustment Mechanism. *J. Monet. Econ.*, May 1984, *13*(3), pp. 349–69.

Persson, Torsten and Svensson, Lars E. O. Misperceptions, Rigidity and Welfare. *Europ. Econ. Rev.*, August 1984, *25*(3), pp. 387–99.

Pesaran, M. H. Macroeconomic Policy in an Oil-exporting Economy with Foreign Exchange Controls. *Economica*, August 1984, *51*(203), pp. 253–70.

Pikoulakis, Emmanuel. Fiscal and Monetary Policies in a Flexible Exchange Rate Model with Full Employment and Static Expectations. In *Black, J. and Dorrance, G. S., eds.*, 1984, pp. 167–86.

Radcliffe, Christopher D.; Warga, Arthur D. and Willett, Thomas D. Currency Substitution and Instability in the World Dollar Standard: Comment. *Amer. Econ. Rev.*, December 1984, *74*(5), pp. 1129–31. **[G: U.S.]**

Razin, Assaf. Capital Movements, Intersectoral Resource Shifts and the Trade Balance. *Europ.*

Econ. Rev., October–November 1984, *26*(1–2), pp. 135–52.

Ribas, Armando P. The Process of Balance of Payments Adjustment: Comment. In *Muns, J., ed.*, 1984, pp. 58–66.

Richardson, J. David. The New Nexus among Trade, Industrial and Exchange-Rate Policies. In *Agmon, T.; Hawkins, R. G. and Levich, R. M., eds.*, 1984, pp. 253–79.

Risager, Ole. Budgetbalanceunderskud, handelsbalanceunderskud og den montetære devalueringsanalyse. (Government Budget Deficits, the Balance of Payments and the Monetary Devaluation Analysis. With English summary.) *Nationaløkon. Tidsskr.*, 1984, *122*(1), pp. 56–72.

Rosner, Peter, et al. Lohnbestimmung, aussenwirtschaftliche Stabilität und internationale Stagnation. (Wage Determination, External Economic Stability and International Stagnation. With English summary.) *Jahr. Nationalökon. Statist.*, May 1984, *199*(3), pp. 193–212. **[G: Global]**

Rothengatter, Werner. The Dynamics of Financial Adjustments in an Open Economy and the Effects of Stabilization Policy. *Z. ges. Staatswiss.*, June 1984, *140*(2), pp. 308–29.

Rous, Jan and Hejl, Lubomir. Contributions to the Evaluation and Stimulation of Effectiveness in External Economic Relations. *Soviet E. Europ. Foreign Trade*, Winter 1984-85, *20*(4), pp. 77–105. **[G: Czechoslovakia]**

Rush, Mark. A Classical Model of a Small Fixed Exchange Rate Economy. *J. Int. Money Finance*, April 1984, *3*(1), pp. 31–49.

Sampson, Anthony A. Real Balances, Relative Prices and the Marshall–Lerner Conditions in an Open Model Temporary Equilibrium with Rationing. *Bull. Econ. Res.*, May 1984, *36*(1), pp. 33–49.

Sarantis, Nicholas C. Foreign Influences, Exchange Rates, Expectations and Price Inflation in a Developing Economy: The Case of Greece. *J. Devel. Econ.*, January–February 1984, *14*(1–2), pp. 1–18. **[G: Greece]**

Shafer, Jeffrey R. Stabilization Policies in Open Economies. *Amer. Econ. Rev.*, May 1984, *74*(2), pp. 305–10.

Shieh, Yeung-Nan. On Monetary Expansion, Terms of Trade and Economic Growth. *Econ. Rec.*, June 1984, *60*(169), pp. 128–32.

Siebert, Horst. Allocation Policy in a Resource-Exporting Country. In *Siebert, H., ed.*, 1984, pp. 1–16.

Spanos, Aris and Taylor, Mark P. The Monetary Approach to the Balance of Payments: A Critical Appraisal of Some Empirical Evidence. *Oxford Bull. Econ. Statist.*, November 1984, *46*(4), pp. 329–40. **[G: U.K.]**

Stournaras, Yannis A. Optimal Taxes and Subsidies in Fix-Price, Open Economies. *Oxford Econ. Pap.*, November 1984, *36*(3), pp. 459–77.

Svensson, Lars E. O. Oil Prices, Welfare, and the Trade Balance. *Quart. J. Econ.*, November 1984, *99*(4), pp. 649–72.

Tanzi, Vito and Blejer, Mario I. Fiscal Deficits and Balance of Payments Disequilibrium in IMF Adjustment Programs. In *Muns, J., ed.*, 1984, pp. 117–36. **[G: LDCs]**

Turnovsky, Stephen J. Exchange Market Intervention under Alternative Forms of Exogenous Disturbances. *J. Int. Econ.*, November 1984, *17*(3/4), pp. 279–97.

Ueda, Kazuo. Supply Shocks and the Interdependence of Macroeconomic Stability under Flexible Exchange Rates. *Europ. Econ. Rev.*, July 1984, *25*(2), pp. 253–77. **[G: Japan; Germany]**

Ursprung, Heinrich W. Structural Balance of Trade Deficits in a Small Open Economy with Exogenous Capital Flows: A Monetary Approach. *Econ. Rec.*, December 1984, *60*(171), pp. 326–39. **[G: New Zealand]**

Wihlborg, Clas G. The New Nexus among Trade, Industrial and Exchange-Rate Policies: Comment. In *Agmon, T.; Hawkins, R. G. and Levich, R. M., eds.*, 1984, pp. 284–90.

van Wijnbergen, Sweder. Inflation, Employment, and the Dutch Disease in Oil-Exporting Countries: A Short-Run Disequilibrium Analysis. *Quart. J. Econ.*, May 1984, *99*(2), pp. 233–50.

van Wijnbergen, Sweder. Oil Price Shocks and the Current Account: An Analysis of Short Run Adjustment Measures. *Weltwirtsch. Arch.*, 1984, *120*(3), pp. 460–80. **[G: OPEC; LDCs]**

van Wijnbergen, Sweder. The 'Dutch Disease': A Disease after All? *Econ. J.*, March 1984, *94*(373), pp. 41–55.

van Wijnbergen, Sweder. The Optimal Investment and Current Account Response to Oil Price Shocks under Putty–Clay Technology. *J. Int. Econ.*, August 1984, *17*(1/2), pp. 139–47.

Willett, Thomas D. Macroeconomic Policy Coordination Issues under Flexible Exchange Rates. In *Eucken, W. and Böhm, F., eds.*, 1984, pp. 137–49. **[G: U.S.]**

Williamson, John. International Liquidity: Are the Supply and Composition Appropriate? In *Fed. Res. Bank Boston*, 1984, pp. 59–77.

Woo, Wing T. Macroeconomic Policy Coordination among the Industrial Economies: Comments. *Brookings Pap. Econ. Act.*, 1984, (1), pp. 71–74. **[G: U.S.]**

de Zeeuw, Aart J. Policy Evaluation with Conflicting Goals for a Linked Two Country Model. In *Despontin, M.; Nijkamp, P. and Spronk, J., eds.*, 1984, pp. 99–124. **[G: W. Germany; Netherlands]**

4313 Open Economy Macroeconomic Studies: Balance of Payments and Adjustment Mechanisms

Abella, Manolo I. Labour Migration from South and South–East Asia: Some Policy Issues. *Int. Lab. Rev.*, July–August 1984, *123*(4), pp. 491–506. **[G: Asia]**

Aggarwal, Mangat Ram. Devaluation, Determinants of International Trade Flows and Payments Imbalances. *Indian Econ. J.*, January–March 1984, *31*(3), pp. 24–33. **[G: LDCs]**

Agmon, Tamir. OPEC and International Financial Markets: Redistribution and Recycling: Comment. In *Agmon, T.; Hawkins, R. G. and Levich, R. M., eds.*, 1984, pp. 246–51.
[G: OPEC]

Ahmad, Jaleel. Inflationary Expectations and Transmission of Inflation under Floating Exchange Rates. *Weltwirtsch. Arch.*, 1984, *120*(3), pp. 424–35.

Albach, Horst. Structural Change in the Economy—A Challenge to Enterprise. In *Engels, W. and Pohl, H., eds.*, 1984, pp. 107–17.
[G: W. Germany]

Aliber, Robert Z. Capital Movements—the Tail That Wags the Dog: Discussion. In *Fed. Res. Bank Boston*, 1984, pp. 188–94.

Arndt, Sven W. The External Effects of U.S. Disinflation. In *Fellner, W., ed.*, 1984, pp. 131–53.
[G: OECD; U.S.]

Bach, Christopher L. U.S. International Transactions, Fourth Quarter and Year 1983. *Surv. Curr. Bus.*, March 1984, *64*(3), pp. 38–66.
[G: U.S.]

Bahmani-Oskooee, Mohsen. Gold Price as Another Determinant of Demand for International Reserves. *J. Econ. Stud.*, 1984, *11*(4), pp. 23–32.
[G: OECD]

Balassa, Bela. Adjustment to External Shocks in Developing Countries. In *Csikós-Nagy, B.; Hague, D. and Hall, G., eds.*, 1984, pp. 352–84.
[G: LDCs]

Balassa, Bela. Adjustment Policies and Development Strategies in Sub-Saharan Africa, 1973–1978. In *[Chenery, H. B.]*, 1984, pp. 317–40.
[G: Africa]

Balassa, Bela. External Shocks and Policy Responses in Sub-Saharan Africa, 1973–78. *Finance Develop.*, March 1984, *21*(1), pp. 10–12.
[G: Sub-Saharan Africa]

Balassa, Bela. The Policy Experience of Twelve Less Developed Countries, 1973–1979. In *[Reynolds, L. G.]*, 1984, pp. 96–123.
[G: Selected LDCs]

Bensión, Alberto. The Role of Commercial Banks in the Adjustment Process: Comment. In *Muns, J., ed.*, 1984, pp. 211–14. [G: LDCs]

Bhandari, Jagdeep S. Speculation and the Crawling Peg: Some Further Issues. *Z. ges. Staatswiss.*, September 1984, *140*(3), pp. 528–36.

Bitros, George C. Trade Credit and the Transmission of International Disturbances in a Small Open Economy Context. *Greek Econ. Rev.*, April 1984, *6*(1), pp. 5–30. [G: Greece]

Borchardt, Knut. Could and Should Germany Have Followed Great Britain in Leaving the Gold Standard? *J. Europ. Econ. Hist.*, September–December 1984, *13*(3), pp. 471–97.
[G: Germany]

Bourne, Compton and Joefield-Napier, Wallace. Export Performance and Prospects for the Commonwealth Caribbean. In *Jorge, A.; Salazar-Carrillo, J. and Sanchez, E. P.*, 1984, pp. 47–59. [G: Caribbean]

Bourne, Compton and Joefield-Napier, Wallace. Export Performance and Prospects for the Commonwealth Caribbean. In *Salazar-Car-*

rillo, J. and Tirado de Alonso, I., eds., no. 2, 1984, pp. 1–26. [G: Caribbean]

Brada, Josef C.; Jackson, Marvin R. and King, Arthur E. The Romanian Balance of Payments Crisis: An Econometric Study of its Causes and Cures. In *Jackson, M. R. and Woodson, J. D., Jr., eds.*, 1984, pp. 23–53. [G: Romania]

Bradford, Colin I., Jr. The NICs: Confronting U.S. "Autonomy." In *Feinberg, R. E. and Kallab, V., eds., no. 1*, 1984, pp. 119–38.
[G: LDCs]

Brissimis, Sophocles N. and Leventakis, John A. An Empirical Inquiry into the Short-Run Dynamics of Output, Prices and Exchange Market Pressure. *J. Int. Money Finance*, April 1984, *3*(1), pp. 75–89. [G: Greece]

Burton, Daniel F., Jr. The Trade Implications of U.S. Monetary and Fiscal Policy. In *Hewlett, S. A.; Kaufman, H. and Kenen, P. B., eds.*, 1984, pp. 151–65. [G: U.S.; Brazil; Mexico]

Carli, Guido. Money Markets—Trends and Challenges. *Rev. Econ. Cond. Italy*, Sept.–Dec. 1984, (3), pp. 305–16. [G: U.S.]

Choi, Jongmoo Jay. Consumption Basket, Exchange Risk, and Asset Demand. *J. Finan. Quant. Anal.*, September 1984, *19*(3), pp. 287–98.

Cohen, Jacob. International Implications of U.S. Macroeconomic Policy. *Singapore Econ. Rev.*, October 1984, *29*(2), pp. 11–26. [G: OECD]

Constantopoulos, Maria and Drakos, George E. Measuring Changes in the Gains from Trade—A Contribution to Applied Welfare Economics. In *Csikós-Nagy, B.; Hague, D. and Hall, G., eds.*, 1984, pp. 454–83. [G: Greece]

Cooper, Richard N. Linkage Effects. In *Hewlett, S. A.; Kaufman, H. and Kenen, P. B., eds.*, 1984, pp. 27–35. [G: U.S.]

Courtney, M. M. South African Exchange-Rate Policy under Managed Floating. *Finance Trade Rev.*, 1983/84, *15*(3), pp. 112–44.
[G: S. Africa]

Díaz-Alejandro, Carlos F. Some Economic Lessons of the Early 1980s. In *Bhagwati, J. N. and Ruggie, J. G., eds.*, 1984, pp. 181–200.
[G: LDCs]

Díaz-Alejandro, Carlos F. The 1940s in Latin America. In *[Chenery, H. B.]*, 1984, pp. 341–62. [G: Latin America]

Dornbusch, Rudiger. Adjustments in World Payments: An Evaluation: Discussion. In *Fed. Res. Bank Boston*, 1984, pp. 208–12.
[G: Selected Countries]

Dornbusch, Rudiger. U.S. Monetary and Fiscal Policy, the Dollar and the International Financial System. In *Frenkel, J. A. and Mussa, M. L., eds.*, 1984, pp. 23–48. [G: U.S.; OECD; Latin America]

Dumas, Bernard. International Portfolio Diversification: Short-term Financial Assets and Gold: Comment. In *Bilson, J. F. O. and Marston, R. C., eds.*, 1984, pp. 232–36.
[G: Selected OECD]

Edwards, Sebastian. Coffee, Money, and Inflation

in Colombia. *World Devel.*, November–December 1984, *12*(11–12), pp. 1107–17.
[G: Colombia]

Edwards, Sebastian. The Demand for International Reserves and Monetary Equilibrium: Some Evidence from Developing Countries. *Rev. Econ. Statist.*, August 1984, *66*(3), pp. 495–500. [G: LDCs; Greece]

Edwards, Sebastian. The Role of International Reserves and Foreign Debt in the External Adjustment Process. In *Muns, J., ed.*, 1984, pp. 143–73. [G: LDCs; Latin America]

Eichengreen, Barry. Keynes and Protection. *J. Econ. Hist.*, June 1984, *44*(2), pp. 363–73.
[G: U.K.]

Eken, Sena. Integration of Domestic and International Financial Markets: The Japanese Experience. *Int. Monet. Fund Staff Pap.*, September 1984, *31*(3), pp. 499–548. [G: Japan]

Emminger, Otmar. Adjustments in World Payments: An Evaluation. In *Fed. Res. Bank Boston*, 1984, pp. 196–207.

Espinosa, Juan Guillermo. The Role of International Reserves and Foreign Debt in the External Adjustment Process: Comment. In *Muns, J., ed.*, 1984, pp. 174–79. [G: LDCs; Latin America]

Feinberg, Richard E. The Adjustment Imperative and U.S. Policy. In *Feinberg, R. E. and Kallab, V., eds., no. 1*, 1984, pp. 3–18. [G: LDCs; U.S.]

Fieleke, Norman S. Price Behavior during Balance of Payments Adjustment. *New Eng. Econ. Rev.*, November–December 1984, pp. 34–43.
[G: Global]

Fieleke, Norman S. The Budget Deficit: Are the International Consequences Unfavorable? *New Eng. Econ. Rev.*, May–June 1984, pp. 5–10.
[G: OECD]

Franco, Giampiero and Mengarelli, Gianluigi. Il debito estero dell'Italia. (Italy's Foreign Debt. With English summary.) *Bancaria*, February 1984, *40*(2), pp. 140–45. [G: Italy]

Frankel, Jeffrey A. International Portfolio Diversification: Short-term Financial Assets and Gold: Comment. In *Bilson, J. F. O. and Marston, R. C., eds.*, 1984, pp. 236–37.
[G: Selected OECD]

Frenkel, Jacob A. Does Devaluation Improve the Current Account? Comments. *Europ. Econ. Rev.*, June 1984, *25*(1), pp. 65–68.
[G: Global]

Frenkel, Jacob A. The Demand for International Reserves under Pegged and Flexible Exchange Rate Regimes and Aspects of the Economics of Managed Float. In *Bigman, D. and Taya, T., eds.*, 1984, pp. 161–87. [G: MDCs; MDCs]

Goldfarb, Robert S.; Havrylyshyn, Oli and Mangum, Stephen L. Can Remittances Compensate for Manpower Outflows: The Case of Philippine Physicians. *J. Devel. Econ.*, May–June–August 1984, *15*(1,2,3), pp. 1–17.
[G: Philippines]

Guenther, Jack D. The Role of Commercial Banks

in the Adjustment Process. In *Muns, J., ed.*, 1984, pp. 184–205. [G: LDCs]

Gylfason, Thorvaldur and Risager, Ole. Does Devaluation Improve the Current Account? *Europ. Econ. Rev.*, June 1984, *25*(1), pp. 37–64. [G: Global]

Haberler, Gottfried. The International Monetary System in the World Recession. In *Fellner, W., ed.*, 1984, pp. 87–129. [G: OECD]

Hartman, David G. The International Financial Market and U.S. Interest Rates. *J. Int. Money Finance*, April 1984, *3*(1), pp. 91–103.
[G: U.S.; Europe]

Holtham, Gerald. Multinational Modelling of Financial Linkages and Exchange Rates. *OECD Econ. Stud.*, Spring 1984, (2), pp. 51–92.
[G: OECD]

Isard, Peter. U.S. International Transactions in 1983. *Fed. Res. Bull.*, April 1984, *70*(4), pp. 269–78. [G: U.S.]

Kaufman, Henry. Complexities of U.S. Stabilization Policies in an International Context. In *Hewlett, S. A.; Kaufman, H. and Kenen, P. B., eds.*, 1984, pp. 1–12. [G: U.S.]

Kenen, Peter B. Beyond Recovery: Challenges to U.S. Economic Policy in the 1980s. In *Hewlett, S. A.; Kaufman, H. and Kenen, P. B., eds.*, 1984, pp. 13–25. [G: U.S.]

Killick, Tony. IMF Stabilisation Programmes. In *Killick, Tony, ed. (II)*, 1984, pp. 183–226.

Killick, Tony. The Impact of Fund Stabilisation Programmes. In *Killick, Tony, ed. (II)*, 1984, pp. 227–69. [G: LDCs]

Killick, Tony and Sharpley, Jennifer. Extent, Causes and Consequences of Disequilibria in Developing Countries. In *Killick, Tony, ed. (II)*, 1984, pp. 15–54. [G: LDCs; MDCs]

Killick, Tony, et al. Towards a Real Economy Approach. In *Killick, Tony, ed. (II)*, 1984, pp. 270–320. [G: LDCs]

Koenig, Linda M. Recent Developments in the World Economy and in Non-Oil Developing Countries of the Western Hemisphere. In *Muns, J., ed.*, 1984, pp. 16–29. [G: OECD; LDCs; Latin America]

Koskela, Erkki and Virén, Matti. Bytesbalansen i OECD-länderna. (Current Balances of OECD Countries. With English summary.) *Ekon. Samfundets Tidskr.*, 1984, 37(2), pp. 75–87. [G: OECD]

Krueger, Russell C. U.S. International Transactions, Second Quarter 1984. *Surv. Curr. Bus.*, September 1984, *64*(9), pp. 34–57. [G: U.S.]

Krueger, Russell C. U.S. International Transactions, First Quarter 1984. *Surv. Curr. Bus.*, June 1984, *64*(6), pp. 35–73. [G: U.S.]

Kubarych, Roger M. Financing the U.S. Current Account Deficit. *Fed. Res. Bank New York Quart. Rev.*, Summer 1984, 9(2), pp. 24–31.
[G: U.S.]

Lächler, Ulrich. Stabilization Policy in an Open-Economy Equilibrium Model. *Weltwirtsch. Arch.*, 1984, *120*(3), pp. 403–23.

Laney, Leroy O. The Strong Dollar, the Current Account, and Federal Deficits: Cause and Effect. *Fed. Res. Bank Dallas Econ. Rev.*, January 1984, pp. 1–14. **[G: U.S.]**

Laursen, Karsten. Dansk økonomi på længere sigt. (Long Term Perspectives in the Danish Economy. With English summary.) *Nationaløkon. Tidsskr.*, 1984, *122*(1), pp. 115–23.
[G: Denmark]

Ledić Michèle. Debt Analysis and Debt-Related Issues: The Case of Yugoslavia. *Econ. Anal. Worker's Manage.*, 1984, *18*(1), pp. 35–64.
[G: Yugoslavia]

Lehment, Harmen. The Macroeconomic Implications of Public-sector Deficits. In *Emerson, M., ed.*, 1984, pp. 150–73. **[G: W. Europe]**

Lelart, M. Le nord et le sud face à la crise financière internationale. (The North and South in the International Financial Crisis. With English summary.) *Écon. Soc.*, June 1984, *18*(6), pp. 59–79. **[G: Global]**

Lipschitz, Leslie. Domestic Credit and Exchange Rates in Developing Countries: Some Policy Experiments with Korean Data. *Int. Monet. Fund Staff Pap.*, December 1984, *31*(4), pp. 595–635. **[G: Korea]**

Llewellyn, David T. Modelling International Banking Flows: An Analytical Framework. In *Black, J. and Dorrance, G. S., eds.*, 1984, pp. 35–76. **[G: OECD]**

Looney, Robert E. Inflation and Oil Based Development: Failure of the Monetarist Model in Saudi Arabia. *Rivista Int. Sci. Econ. Com.*, October–November 1984, *31*(10–11), pp. 1100–20. **[G: Saudi Arabia]**

de Macedo, Jorge Braga; Goldstein, Jeffrey A. and Meerschwam, David M. International Portfolio Diversification: Short-term Financial Assets and Gold. In *Bilson, J. F. O. and Marston, R. C., eds.*, 1984, pp. 199–232.
[G: Selected OECD]

Málaga, Sergio. The Role of International Reserves and Foreign Debt in the External Adjustment Process: Comment. In *Muns, J., ed.*, 1984, pp. 180–83. **[G: LDCs; Latin America]**

Mammen, Thumpy. A Trade Gap Model and IMF Loan to India. *Indian Econ. J.*, January–March 1984, *31*(3), pp. 45–52. **[G: India]**

Maramba, Felix K., Jr. The State of Domestic Essential Industries Today. *Philippine Econ. J.*, Winter 1984, *23*(1), pp. 60–65.
[G: Philippines]

Massad, Carlos. The Role of Commercial Banks in the Adjustment Process: Comment. In *Muns, J., ed.*, 1984, pp. 206–10. **[G: LDCs]**

Massad, Carlos and Zahler, Roberto. The Adjustment Process in the 1980s: The Need for a Global Approach. *Cepal Rev.*, 1984, (23), pp. 83–105. **[G: Latin America]**

de Montbrial, Thierry. Does Devaluation Improve the Current Account? Comments. *Europ. Econ. Rev.*, June 1984, *25*(1), pp. 69–70.
[G: Global]

Mutoh, Takahiko and Hamada, Koichi. International Short Term Capital Flow and the Foreign Exchange Rate: Japan, 1973–1980. *Econ. Stud. Quart.*, August 1984, *35*(2), pp. 97–115.
[G: Japan]

Naya, Seiji. Effects of External Shocks on the Balance of Payments, Policy Responses and Debt Problems of Asian Developing Countries. *Philippine Econ. J.*, Winter 1984, *23*(1), pp. 23–49. **[G: Asia]**

Nötel, Rudolf. Money, Banking and Industry in Interwar Austria and Hungary. *J. Europ. Econ. Hist.*, Special Issue 1984, *13*(2), pp. 137–202.
[G: Austria; Hungary]

O'Leary, J. Some Implications of the Revisions to the Balance of Payments and the National Accounts. *Irish Banking Rev.*, September 1984, pp. 13–34. **[G: Ireland]**

Okita, Saburo. Role of the Trade Ombudsman in Liberalising Japan's Market. *World Econ.*, September 1984, *7*(3), pp. 241–56.
[G: Japan]

Olgun, Hasan. An Analysis of the Black Market Exchange Rate in a Developing Economy— The Case of Turkey. *Weltwirtsch. Arch.*, 1984, *120*(2), pp. 329–47. **[G: Turkey]**

Otani, Ichiro. Exchange Rate Instability and Capital Controls: The Japanese Experience, 1978–1981. In *Bigman, D. and Taya, T., eds.*, 1984, pp. 213–39. **[G: Japan]**

Oweiss, Ibrahim M. Petrodollar Surpluses: Trends and Economic Impact. *J. Energy Devel.*, Spring 1984, *9*(2), pp. 177–202.
[G: OPEC]

Papell, David H. Anticipated and Unanticipated Disturbances: The Dynamics of the Exchange Rate and the Current Account. *J. Int. Money Finance*, August 1984, *3*(2), pp. 179–93.
[G: U.S.; U.K.; Germany; Japan]

Patel, Meena. Private Foreign Investment and Balance of Payments Effects in India during 1960–1970. *Indian Econ. J.*, January–March 1984, *31*(3), pp. 62–69. **[G: India]**

Plassard, Jacques. Le rééquilibrage de l'économie française a commencé au deuxième trimestre 1983. (With English summary.) *Revue Écon. Polit.*, September–October 1984, *94*(5), pp. 620–28. **[G: France]**

Quinn, William T. The Current Account and Macroeconomic Adjustment: The Italian Experience. *Rev. Econ. Cond. Italy*, Sept.–Dec. 1984, (3), pp. 317–44. **[G: Italy]**

Ragazzi, Giorgio. LDCs Debt and Net Financial Transfers: The Search for Equilibrium between Stocks and Flows. *Giorn. Econ.*, May–June 1984, *43*(5–6), pp. 359–67. **[G: LDCs]**

Rich, Georg. Canada without a Central Bank: Operation of the Price-Specie-Flow Mechanism, 1872–1913. In *Bordo, M. D. and Schwartz, A. J., eds.*, 1984, pp. 547–75. **[G: Canada]**

Rogoff, Kenneth. On the Effects of Sterilized Intervention: An Analysis of Weekly Data. *J. Monet. Econ.*, September 1984, *14*(2), pp. 133–50. **[G: U.S.; Canada]**

Rose, Andrew K. and Selody, Jack G. Exchange Market Efficiency: A Semi-strong Test Using Multiple Markets and Daily Data. *Rev. Econ. Statist.*, November 1984, *66*(4), pp. 669–72.
[G: Canada; U.S.]

Rous, Jan and Hejl, Lubomir. Contributions to the Evaluation and Stimulation of Effectiveness in External Economic Relations. *Soviet E. Europ. Foreign Trade*, Winter 1984-85, *20*(4), pp. 77–105. **[G: Czechoslovakia]**

Salvatore, Dominick. Petroleum Prices, Exchange Rates, and Domestic Inflation in Developing Nations. *Weltwirtsch. Arch.*, 1984, *120*(3), pp. 580–89. **[G: LDCs]**

Sassanpour, Cyrus and Sheen, Jeffrey. An Empirical Analysis of the Effects of Monetary Disequilibria in Open Economies. *J. Monet. Econ.*, January 1984, *13*(1), pp. 127–63. **[G: France; W. Germany]**

Scholl, Russell B. The International Investment Position of the United States in 1983. *Surv. Curr. Bus.*, June 1984, *64*(6), pp. 74–78. **[G: U.S.]**

Smeets, Heinz-Dieter. Wechselkurssystem und Phillips-Kurve. (Exchange Rate System and Phillips Curve. With English summary.) *Kredit Kapital*, 1984, *17*(3), pp. 396–403. **[G: W. Germany]**

Spanos, Aris and Taylor, Mark P. The Monetary Approach to the Balance of Payments: A Critical Appraisal of Some Empirical Evidence. *Oxford Bull. Econ. Statist.*, November 1984, *46*(4), pp. 329–40. **[G: U.K.]**

Spencer, Grant H. The World Trade Model: Revised Estimates. *Int. Monet. Fund Staff Pap.*, September 1984, *31*(3), pp. 469–98. **[G: W. Europe; U.S.; Canada; Japan]**

Sternlight, David. OPEC and International Financial Markets: Redistribution and Recycling. In *Agmon, T.; Hawkins, R. G. and Levich, R. M., eds.*, 1984, pp. 231–45. **[G: OPEC]**

Swanson, Peggy E. External Currency Market Data: An Application from BIS Series. *J. Int. Money Finance*, April 1984, *3*(1), pp. 111–17.

Talele, Chaitram J. The 1966 Devaluation of Rupee: Empirical Analysis from the Point of View of the Monetary Theory of the Balance of Payments. *Indian Econ. J.*, January–March 1984, *31*(3), pp. 13–23. **[G: India]**

Temin, Peter. Canada without a Central Bank: Operation of the Price-Specie-Flow Mechanism, 1872–1913: Comment. In *Bordo, M. D. and Schwartz, A. J., eds.*, 1984, pp. 576–81. **[G: Canada]**

Tomašić, Vjekoslav. Effects of Foreign Direct Investments on the Balance of Payments in Industrial Ventures in SR Croatia. *Econ. Anal. Worker's Manage.*, 1984, *18*(4), pp. 333–41. **[G: Yugoslavia]**

Török, Ádám. Sectoral and Enterprise Structure of Net Exports Settled in Convertible Currency of the Hungarian Industry. *Acta Oecon.*, 1984, *33*(1–2), pp. 127–45. **[G: Hungary]**

Triffin, Robert. How to End the World 'Infession': Crisis Management or Fundamental Reforms? In *Masera, R. S. and Triffin, R., eds.*, 1984, pp. 13–76. **[G: U.S.; Global]**

Turner, Brian and Williams, Lynn R. Economic Policy in a Global Economy: The Future of American Industry. In *Hewlett, S. A.; Kaufman, H. and Kenen, P. B., eds.*, 1984, pp. 181–98. **[G: U.S.]**

Ursprung, Heinrich W. Structural Balance of

Trade Deficits in a Small Open Economy with Exogenous Capital Flows: A Monetary Approach. *Econ. Rec.*, December 1984, *60*(171), pp. 326–39. **[G: New Zealand]**

Volcker, Paul A. Statement to the U.S. House Subcommittee on Trade of the Committee on Ways and Means, April 10, 1984. *Fed. Res. Bull.*, April 1984, *70*(4), pp. 324–28. **[G: U.S.]**

Wallich, Henry C. Capital Movements—the Tail That Wags the Dog. In *Fed. Res. Bank Boston*, 1984, pp. 179–87.

Wallich, Henry C. Institutional Cooperation in the World Economy. In *Frenkel, J. A. and Mussa, M. L., eds.*, 1984, pp. 85–99. **[G: OECD]**

Wallich, Henry C. Statement to the U.S. Senate Committee on Finance, March 23, 1984. *Fed. Res. Bull.*, April 1984, *70*(4), pp. 294–98. **[G: U.S.]**

Worrell, DeLisle. Central America and the Caribbean: Adjustment in Small, Open Economies. In *Feinberg, R. E. and Kallab, V., eds., no. 1*, 1984, pp. 159–81. **[G: Barbados; Costa Rica; Jamaica; Nicaragua]**

Zis, George. Flexible Exchange Rates: Lessons from the Last Decade. *Greek Econ. Rev.*, April 1984, *6*(1), pp. 47–76. **[G: OECD]**

Zulu, Justin B. and Nsouli, Saleh M. Adjustment Programs in Africa. *Finance Develop.*, March 1984, *21*(1), pp. 5–7, 9. **[G: Africa]**

4314 Exchange Rates and Markets: Theory and Studies

Ahtiala, Pekka. A Synthesis of the Macroeconomic Approaches to Exchange Rate Determination. *Europ. Econ. Rev.*, March 1984, *24*(2), pp. 117–36.

Aizenman, Joshua. Modeling Deviations from Purchasing Power Parity (PPP). *Int. Econ. Rev.*, February 1984, *25*(1), pp. 175–91.

Akhtar, M. A. and Hilton, R. Spence. Effects of Exchange Rate Uncertainty on German and U.S. Trade. *Fed. Res. Bank New York Quart. Rev.*, Spring 1984, *9*(1), pp. 7–16. **[G: U.S.; Germany]**

Aliber, Robert Z. Structural Change, Monetary Policy and the Foreign Exchange Value of Sterling. In *Griffiths, B. and Wood, G. E., eds.*, 1984, pp. 213–30. **[G: U.K.]**

Anderson, Robert O. Exchange Rate Regimes: How the Dollar Stole Christmas. In *Hewlett, S. A.; Kaufman, H. and Kenen, P. B., eds.*, 1984, pp. 97–103.

Andrews, Michael D. Recent Trends in the U.S. Foreign Exchange Market. *Fed. Res. Bank New York Quart. Rev.*, Summer 1984, *9*(2), pp. 38–47. **[G: U.S.]**

Arce, Horacio. The Trade Liberalization Policy of Argentina: Its Impact on Latin American Integration. In *Núñez del Arco, J.; Margain, E. and Cherol, R., eds.*, 1984, pp. 280–314. **[G: Argentina]**

Arndt, Heinz W. and Sundrum, R. M. Devaluation and Inflation: The 1978 Experience. *Bull.*

Indonesian Econ. Stud., April 1984, *20*(1), pp. 83–97. [G: Indonesia]

Arndt, Sven W. Exchange Rates and Trade Policy: Comment. *Contemp. Policy Issue*, January 1984, (4), pp. 19–22.

Arndt, Sven W. The External Effects of U.S. Disinflation. In *Fellner, W., ed.*, 1984, pp. 131–53. [G: OECD; U.S.]

Artus, Jacques R. Effects of United States Monetary Restraint on the DM/$ Exchange Rate and the German Economy. In *Bilson, J. F. O. and Marston, R. C., eds.*, 1984, pp. 469–94. [G: U.S.; W. Germany]

Asheim, Geir B. Properties of a System of Currency Baskets. *J. Int. Econ.*, May 1984, *16*(3/4), pp. 311–17.

Aurikko, Esko. Exchange Rate Policies Simulated by Means of a Disequilibrium Model of the Finnish Economy. *J. Policy Modeling*, November 1984, *6*(4), pp. 531–54. [G: Finland]

Backus, David. Empirical Models of the Exchange Rate: Separating the Wheat from the Chaff. *Can. J. Econ.*, November 1984, *17*(4), pp. 824–46. [G: Canada; U.S.]

Bade, Robin and Parkin, Michael. Is Sterling M_3 the Right Aggregate? In *Griffiths, B. and Wood, G. E., eds.*, 1984, pp. 241–86. [G: U.K.]

Bailey, Ralph W.; Baillie, Richard T. and McMahon, Patrick C. Interpreting Econometric Evidence on Efficiency in the Foreign Exchange Market. *Oxford Econ. Pap.*, March 1984, *36*(1), pp. 67–85. [G: U.K.; W. Germany; France; Italy]

Baillie, Richard T. and Bailey, Ralph W. International Currency Speculation, Market Stability and Efficiency in the 1920s: A Time Series Approach. *J. Macroecon.*, Spring 1984, *6*(2), pp. 127–37. [G: Belgium; France; Netherlands; U.S.; Germany]

Barro, Robert J. Some Evidence on the Real Price of Gold, Its Costs of Production, and Commodity Prices: Comment. In *Bordo, M. D. and Schwartz, A. J., eds.*, 1984, pp. 644–46. [G: U.S.; U.S.S.R.; S. Africa; Australia]

Bartoli, Gloria. An Assessment of the Scandinavian Model of Inflation. *Econ. Int.*, August–November 1984, *37*(3–4), pp. 215–35. [G: Sweden]

Basevi, Giorgio and Calzolari, Michele. Multilateral Exchange Rate Determination: A Model for the Analysis of the European Monetary System. In *Bilson, J. F. O. and Marston, R. C., eds.*, 1984, pp. 443–61. [G: Selected OECD]

Batten, Dallas S. and Belongia, Michael T. The Recent Decline in Agricultural Exports: Is the Exchange Rate the Culprit? *Fed. Res. Bank St. Louis Rev.*, October 1984, *66*(8), pp. 5–14. [G: U.S.]

Batten, Dallas S. and Hafer, R. W. Currency Substitution: A Test of Its Importance. *Fed. Res. Bank St. Louis Rev.*, August/September 1984, *66*(7), pp. 5–11. [G: Canada; Germany; France; Netherlands; U.K.]

Batten, Dallas S. and Ott, Mack. What Can Cen-

tral Banks Do About the Value of the Dollar? *Fed. Res. Bank St. Louis Rev.*, May 1984, *66*(5), pp. 16–26. [G: U.S.]

Batten, Dallas S. and Thornton, Daniel L. Discount Rate Changes and the Foreign Exchange Market. *J. Int. Money Finance*, December 1984, *3*(303), pp. 279–92. [G: U.S.]

Beenstock, Michael. Structural Change, Monetary Policy and the Foreign Exchange Value of Sterling: Comment. In *Griffiths, B. and Wood, G. E., eds.*, 1984, pp. 231–32. [G: U.K.]

Ben-Zion, Uri and Weinblatt, J. Purchasing Power, Interest Rate Parities and the Modified Fisher Effect in Presence of Tax Agreements. *J. Int. Money Finance*, April 1984, *3*(1), pp. 67–73.

Bernstein, Edward M. A Program for International Monetary Stability: Comment. In *Agmon, T.; Hawkins, R. G. and Levich, R. M., eds.*, 1984, pp. 78–84. [G: OECD]

Bhandari, Jagdeep S. Exchange Rate Overshooting: Reply and Further Clarifications. *Manchester Sch. Econ. Soc. Stud.*, December 1984, *52*(4), pp. 425–30.

Bhandari, Jagdeep S. Wage Contracting and Exchange Rate Intervention in a Model with Intermediate Imports. *Z. ges. Staatswiss.*, December 1984, *140*(4), pp. 685–711.

Bhandari, Jagdeep S.; Driskill, Robert A. and Frenkel, Jacob A. Capital Mobility and Exchange Rate Overshooting. *Europ. Econ. Rev.*, April 1984, *24*(3), pp. 309–20.

Bigman, David. Exchange Rate Determination: Some Old Myths and New Paradigms. In *Bigman, D. and Taya, T., eds.*, 1984, pp. 71–100.

Bigman, David. Semi-Rational Expectations and Exchange-Rate Dynamics. *J. Int. Money Finance*, April 1984, *3*(1), pp. 51–66.

Bilson, John F. O. Exchange Rate Dynamics. In *Bilson, J. F. O. and Marston, R. C., eds.*, 1984, pp. 175–89. [G: U.K.; U.S.; W. Germany]

Bilson, John F. O. Purchasing Power Parity as a Trading Strategy. *J. Finance*, July 1984, *39*(3), pp. 715–24. [G: U.S.]

Bilson, John F. O. The Process of Balance of Payments Adjustment. In *Muns, J., ed.*, 1984, pp. 34–57.

Bird, Graham. Balance of Payments Policy in Developing Countries. In *Killick, Tony, ed. (II)*, 1984, pp. 86–127.

Bird, Roger. International Financial Disorder. In *Jorge, A.; Salazar-Carrillo, J. and Sanchez, E. P.*, 1984, pp. 105–20. [G: Global]

Black, Stanley W. Monetary Targeting: Issues and Alternatives. In *Hewlett, S. A.; Kaufman, H. and Kenen, P. B., eds.*, 1984, pp. 105–21. [G: U.S.; W. Germany; Japan]

Black, Stanley W. The Relationship between Exchange Rate Policy and Monetary Policy in Ten Industrial Countries. In *Bilson, J. F. O. and Marston, R. C., eds.*, 1984, pp. 499–511. [G: Selected OECD]

Blanchard, Olivier J. and Dornbusch, Rudiger. U.S. Deficits, the Dollar and Europe. *Banca*

Naz. Lavoro Quart. Rev., March 1984, (148), pp. 89–113. **[G: U.S.; OECD]**

Blejer, Mario I. Financial Market Taxation and International Capital Flows. In *Tanzi, V., ed.*, 1984, pp. 204–19.

Blomgren-Hansen, Niels and Petersen, Jørgen. Samspillet mellem finans-, penge- og valutakurspolitik. (The Interdependence of Fiscal, Monetary, and Exchange Rate Policies. With English summary.) *Nationaløkon. Tidsskr.*, 1984, *122*(1), pp. 73–90. **[G: Denmark]**

Blundell-Wignall, Adrian. Exchange Rate Modelling and the Role of Asset Supplies: The Case of the Deutschemark Effective Rate, 1973 to 1983. *Manchester Sch. Econ. Soc. Stud.*, March 1984, 52(1), pp. 14–27.
[G: W. Germany]

Blundell-Wignall, Adrian and Chouraqui, Jean-Claude. The Role of Exchange Market Intervention. *Nat. Westminster Bank Quart. Rev.*, November 1984, pp. 53–68. **[G: U.K.]**

Boloña, Carlos. The Role of Economy-Wide Prices in the Adjustment Process: Comment. In *Muns, J., ed.*, 1984, pp. 110–12.
[G: LDCs]

van den Boogaerde, Pierre. The Private SDR: An Assessment of Its Risk and Return. *Int. Monet. Fund Staff Pap.*, March 1984, 31(1), pp. 25–61.

Booth, G. Geoffrey and Seifert, Bruce. "News" and Exchange Rates: Some Empirical Tests. *Rivista Int. Sci. Econ. Com.*, October–November 1984, 31(10–11), pp. 1017–32.
[G: Selected OECD]

Booth, Laurence D. Bid–Ask Spreads in the Market for Forward Exchange. *J. Int. Money Finance*, August 1984, 3(2), pp. 209–22.

Bordo, Michael D. The Gold Standard: Myths and Realities. In *Siegel, B. N., ed.*, 1984, pp. 197–237. **[G: U.K.; U.S.]**

Bordo, Michael D. The Gold Standard: The Traditional Approach. In *Bordo, M. D. and Schwartz, A. J., eds.*, 1984, pp. 23–113.

Boughton, James M. Exchange Rate Movements and Adjustment in Financial Markets: Quarterly Estimates for Major Currencies. *Int. Monet. Fund Staff Pap.*, September 1984, 31(3), pp. 445–68. **[G: U.S.; U.K.; Japan; Germany; France]**

Branson, William H. Effects of United States Monetary Restraint on the DM/$ Exchange Rate and the German Economy: Comment. In *Bilson, J. F. O. and Marston, R. C., eds.*, 1984, pp. 494–97. **[G: U.S.; W. Germany]**

Branson, William H. Exchange Rate Policy after a Decade of "Floating." In *Bilson, J. F. O. and Marston, R. C., eds.*, 1984, pp. 79–108.
[G: Japan; U.K.; U.S.; W. Germany]

Brissimis, Sophocles N. and Leventakis, John A. An Empirical Inquiry into the Short-Run Dynamics of Output, Prices and Exchange Market Pressure. *J. Int. Money Finance*, April 1984, 3(1), pp. 75–89. **[G: Greece]**

Brodsky, David A. Fixed versus Flexible Exchange Rates and the Measurement of Exchange Rate Instability. *J. Int. Econ.*, May 1984, 16(3/4), pp. 295–306. **[G: Global]**

Brodsky, David A. and Sampson, Gary P. The Sources of Exchange Rate Instability in Developing Countries: Dollar, French Franc and SDR Pegging Countries. *Weltwirtsch. Arch.*, 1984, *120*(1), pp. 133–54. **[G: LDCs; U.S.; France]**

Brown, Stephen P. A. and Phillips, Keith R. The Effects of Oil Prices and Exchange Rates on World Oil Consumption. *Fed. Res. Bank Dallas Econ. Rev.*, July 1984, pp. 13–21.
[G: OECD]

de la Bruslerie, Hubert. Prévision des taux d'intérêt et des taux de change: une étude empirique à partir de données euro-obligataires. (Rates of Exchange and Interest Forecasting. An Empirical Survey Based on Euro-Bond Data. With English summary.) *Écon. Soc.*, January 1984, *18*(1), pp. 53–89.

Bruton, Henry J. Economic Development with Unlimited Supplies of Foreign Exchange. In *[Reynolds, L. G.]*, 1984, pp. 124–44.
[G: LDCs]

Buiter, Willem H. Exchange Rate Policy after a Decade of "Floating": Comment. In *Bilson, J. F. O. and Marston, R. C., eds.*, 1984, pp. 108–12. **[G: Japan; U.K.; U.S.; W. Germany]**

Buiter, Willem H. Real Exchange Rates in the 1970s: Comment. In *Bilson, J. F. O. and Marston, R. C., eds.*, 1984, pp. 321–30.
[G: Selected OECD]

Burns, Arthur F. The American Trade Deficit in Perspective. *Foreign Aff.*, Summer 1984, 62(5), pp. 1058–69. **[G: U.S.]**

Butlin, M. W. Managed Exchange Rates and Exchange Control: A Theoretical Analysis. *Australian Econ. Pap.*, December 1984, 23(43), pp. 167–78.

Camilleri, Arthur P.; Nguyen, Duc-Tho and Campbell, Robert B. Policy Changes and External Disturbances in a Small Open Economy: Stability and Dynamic Responses. *Int. Econ. Rev.*, February 1984, 25(1), pp. 123–58.

Carli, Guido. Contributo all'aggiornamento della disciplina valutaria nella prospettiva della unificazione dei mercati finanziari europei. (A Contribution of Amendment of Foreign-Exchange Regulations in the Prospect of Unification of European Financial Markets. With English summary.) *Bancaria*, January 1984, *40*(1), pp. 29–37. **[G: Italy]**

Carli, Guido. Floating Exchange Rates: A Practical Lesson on the Automaticity of Adjustment Mechanisms. In *Bigman, D. and Taya, T., eds.*, 1984, pp. 291–99.

de Cecco, Marcello and Miller, Marcus H. Monetary Targeting in Europe. In *Hewlett, S. A.; Kaufman, H. and Kenen, P. B., eds.*, 1984, pp. 123–50. **[G: OECD]**

Chan-Lee, James H. and Kato, Hiromi. A Comparison of Simulation Properties of National Econometric Models. *OECD Econ. Stud.*, Spring 1984, (2), pp. 109–50. **[G: OECD]**

Chiang, Thomas C. On the Relationship between the Exchange Rate and the Interest Rate Differential in Monetary Models. *Quart. Rev. Econ. Bus.*, Autumn 1984, *24*(3), pp. 49–57. [G: U.S.]

Chrystal, K. Alec. A Guide to Foreign Exchange Markets. *Fed. Res. Bank St. Louis Rev.*, March 1984, *66*(3), pp. 5–18.

Clark, Truman A. Violations of the Gold Points, 1890–1908. *J. Polit. Econ.*, October 1984, *92*(5), pp. 791–823. [G: U.S.; U.K.]

Conci, Paolo and Ferrarese, Giulio. Coordinamento internazionale delle politiche economiche. Indispensabile o superfluo? (With English summary.) *Econ. Int.*, August–November 1984, *37*(3–4), pp. 255–67. [G: U.S.; W. Germany; Japan]

Conesa, Eduardo R. The Openness of the Latin American Southern Cone Economies. In *Núñez del Arco, J.; Margain, E. and Cherol, R., eds.*, 1984, pp. 253–79. [G: Argentina; Chile; Uruguay]

Connolly, Michael B. The Gold Standard and the Transmission of Business Cycles, 1833–1932: Comment. In *Bordo, M. D. and Schwartz, A. J., eds.*, 1984, pp. 507–11. [G: U.S.; U.K.]

Connolly, Michael B. and Taylor, Dean. The Exact Timing of the Collapse of an Exchange Rate Regime and Its Impact on the Relative Price of Traded Goods. *J. Money, Credit, Banking*, May 1984, *16*(2), pp. 194–207.

Conti, Giuliano. Indicatori della politica monetaria: il tasso di cambio. (Monetary Policy Indicators: The Exchange Rate. With English summary.) *Giorn. Econ.*, May–June 1984, *43*(5–6), pp. 327–43.

Cooper, Richard N. Recent History of World Monetary Problems. In *Agmon, T.; Hawkins, R. G. and Levich, R. M., eds.*, 1984, pp. 11–22.

Cornell, Bradford. Purchasing Power Parity as a Trading Strategy: Discussion. *J. Finance*, July 1984, *39*(3), pp. 724–25.

Cosset, Jean-Claude. On the Presence of Risk Premiums in Foreign Exchange Markets. *J. Int. Econ.*, February 1984, *16*(1/2), pp. 139–54. [G: Selected OECD]

Courtney, M. M. South African Exchange-Rate Policy under Managed Floating. *Finance Trade Rev.*, 1983/84, *15*(3), pp. 112–44. [G: S. Africa]

Cross, Sam Y. Treasury and Federal Reserve Foreign Exchange Operations. *Fed. Res. Bank New York Quart. Rev.*, Spring 1984, *9*(1), pp. 57–70. [G: U.S.]

Cross, Sam Y. Treasury and Federal Reserve Foreign Exchange Operations. *Fed. Res. Bull.*, March 1984, *70*(3), pp. 191–203. [G: U.S.]

Cross, Sam Y. Treasury and Federal Reserve Foreign Exchange Operations. *Fed. Res. Bull.*, September 1984, *70*(9), pp. 693–704. [G: U.S.]

Cross, Sam Y. Treasury and Federal Reserve Foreign Exchange Operations: Interim Report. *Fed. Res. Bull.*, June 1984, *70*(6), pp. 492–94. [G: U.S.]

Culbertson, William Patterson, Jr. and Amacher, Ryan C. Inflation in the Planned Economies: Reply [Inflation in the Planned Economies: Some Estimates for Eastern Europe]. *Southern Econ. J.*, October 1984, *51*(2), pp. 613–14. [G: E. Europe]

Cumby, Robert E. Monetary Policy under Dual Exchange Rates. *J. Int. Money Finance*, August 1984, *3*(2), pp. 195–208.

Cumby, Robert E. and Obstfeld, Maurice. International Interest Rate and Price Level Linkages under Flexible Exchange Rates: A Review of Recent Evidence. In *Bilson, J. F. O. and Marston, R. C., eds.*, 1984, pp. 121–51. [G: Selected OECD]

Curran, Robert F. The Effect of Changes in the Exchange Rate on Commodity Diversification in Less Developed Countries. *Eastern Econ. J.*, October-December 1984, *10*(4), pp. 409–20. [G: LDCs]

Currie, David. Monetary Overshooting and the Exchange Rate. *Manchester Sch. Econ. Soc. Stud.*, March 1984, *52*(1), pp. 28–48.

Currie, David and Levine, Paul. Exchange Rate and Price Level Volatility under Partial Information. *Greek Econ. Rev.*, August 1984, *6*(2), pp. 149–70.

Davies, Robert and Jones, Philip R. International Trade. In *Sandford, C. and Bradbury, M., eds.*, 1984, pp. 188–218. [G: EEC]

Davila, Alberto E.; Schmidt, Ronald H. and Ziegler, Gary M. Industrial Diversification, Exchange Rate Shocks, and the Texas–Mexico Border. *Fed. Res. Bank Dallas Econ. Rev.*, May 1984, pp. 1–9. [G: U.S.; Mexico]

De Rosa, Dean A. The International Natural Rubber Agreement and Exchange Rate Changes. *Singapore Econ. Rev.*, April 1984, *29*(1), pp. 30–46. [G: Global]

Demery, David. Exchange Rate Dynamics: The Swiss/U.S. Case. *Europ. Econ. Rev.*, March 1984, *24*(2), pp. 151–59. [G: Switzerland; U.S.]

DiLullo, Anthony J. U.S. International Transactions, Third Quarter, 1984. *Surv. Curr. Bus.*, December 1984, *64*(12), pp. 41–64. [G: U.S.]

Dini, Lamberto. The Changing International Monetary System. *Banca Naz. Lavoro Quart. Rev.*, December 1984, (151), pp. 423–31.

Djajić, Slobodan. Currency Management and Economic Stability. *Econ. J.*, June 1984, *94*(374), pp. 324–39.

Dohner, Robert S. Export Pricing, Flexible Exchange Rates, and Divergence in the Prices of Traded Goods. *J. Int. Econ.*, February 1984, *16*(1/2), pp. 79–101.

Dooley, Michael P. and Shafer, Jeffrey R. Analysis of Short-run Exchange Rate Behavior: March 1973 to November 1981. In *Bigman, D. and Taya, T., eds.*, 1984, pp. 43–69. [G: OECD]

Dornbusch, Rudiger. Adjustments in World Pay-

ments: An Evaluation: Discussion. In *Fed. Res. Bank Boston*, 1984, pp. 208–12.
[G: Selected Countries]

Dornbusch, Rudiger. Monetary Policy under Exchange Rate Flexibility. In *Bigman, D. and Taya, T., eds.*, 1984, pp. 3–31.

Dornbusch, Rudiger. The Overvalued Dollar. *Lloyds Bank Rev.*, April 1984, (152), pp. 1–12. [G: U.S.; Japan; W. Germany]

Dornbusch, Rudiger. The Theory of Exchange Rate Determination: Comment. In *Bilson, J. F. O. and Marston, R. C., eds.*, 1984, pp. 63–66.

Dornbusch, Rudiger. U.S. Monetary and Fiscal Policy, the Dollar and the International Financial System. In *Frenkel, J. A. and Mussa, M. L., eds.*, 1984, pp. 23–48. [G: U.S.; OECD; Latin America]

Dornbusch, Rudiger and Frenkel, Jacob A. The Gold Standard and the Bank of England in the Crisis of 1847. In *Bordo, M. D. and Schwartz, A. J., eds.*, 1984, pp. 233–64. [G: U.K.]

Drechsler, Laszlo. International Comparisons of Real Product and of Purchasing Power Parities. A Review of the Development of the Methodology. *Econ. Int.*, August–November 1984, 37(3–4), pp. 280–87. [G: Global]

Duck, Nigel W. Prices, Output and the Balance of Payments in an Open Economy with Rational Expectations. *J. Int. Econ.*, February 1984, 16(1/2), pp. 59–77.

Dudler, Hermann-Josef. Domestic Monetary Control in EC Countries under Different Exchange Rate Regimes: National Concerns and Community Options. In *Masera, R. S. and Triffin, R., eds.*, 1984, pp. 227–61. [G: EEC]

Dutton, John C., Jr. The Bank of England and the Rules of the Game under the International Gold Standard: New Evidence. In *Bordo, M. D. and Schwartz, A. J., eds.*, 1984, pp. 173–95. [G: U.K.]

Dutton, John C., Jr. The Bank of England and the Rules of the Game under the International Gold Standard: New Evidence: Reply. In *Bordo, M. D. and Schwartz, A. J., eds.*, 1984, pp. 199–202. [G: U.K.]

Easton, Stephen T. Real Output and the Gold Standard Years, 1830–1913. In *Bordo, M. D. and Schwartz, A. J., eds.*, 1984, pp. 513–38. [G: OECD]

Edwards, Sebastian. Exchange Rates and 'News': Reply. *J. Int. Money Finance*, April 1984, 3(1), pp. 123–26.

Eken, Sena. Integration of Domestic and International Financial Markets: The Japanese Experience. *Int. Monet. Fund Staff Pap.*, September 1984, 31(3), pp. 499–548. [G: Japan]

Eldridge, Robert M. Intertemporal Price Volatility of Foreign Currency Futures Contracts. *J. Futures Markets*, Summer 1984, 4(2), pp. 133–40. [G: W. Germany; Canada; Japan; U.S.]

Emminger, Otmar. Adjustments in World Payments: An Evaluation. In *Fed. Res. Bank Boston*, 1984, pp. 196–207.

Emminger, Otmar. The Exchange Rate as an In-strument of Policy. In *Bigman, D. and Taya, T., eds.*, 1984, pp. 267–83.

Engel, Charles M. Testing for the Absence of Expected Real Profits from Forward Market Speculation. *J. Int. Econ.*, November 1984, 17(3/4), pp. 299–308. [G: OECD]

Engel, Charles M. and Frankel, Jeffrey A. Why Interest Rates React to Money Announcements: An Explanation from the Foreign Exchange Market. *J. Monet. Econ.*, January 1984, 13(1), pp. 31–39. [G: U.S.]

Fama, Eugene F. Forward and Spot Exchange Rates. *J. Monet. Econ.*, November 1984, 14(3), pp. 319–38. [G: OECD]

Farrell, John P. Inflation in the Planned Economies: Comment [Inflation in the Planned Economies: Some Estimates for Eastern Europe]. *Southern Econ. J.*, October 1984, 51(2), pp. 603–12. [G: Europe]

Feldman, David H. and Tower, Edward. Welfare Gain from a Stable Exchange Rate: Comment. *Atlantic Econ. J.*, July 1984, 12(2), pp. 65.

Feldman, Robert A. The Impact of the Recent Strength of the Dollar on the U.S. Merchandise Trade Balance: Some "First-Round" Effects and Feedbacks from Exchange Rate Induced Changes in U.S.-Relative Inflation. *J. Policy Modeling*, February 1984, 6(1), pp. 29–44. [G: U.S.]

Feldstein, Martin. Why the Dollar Is Strong. *Challenge*, January/February 1984, 26(6), pp. 37–41. [G: U.S.]

Fendt, Roberto, Jr. Trade Prospects for Brazil after the Devaluation. In *Jorge, A.; Salazar-Carrillo, J. and Sanchez, E. P.*, 1984, pp. 93–96. [G: Brazil]

Fieleke, Norman S. Price Behavior during Balance of Payments Adjustment. *New Eng. Econ. Rev.*, November–December 1984, pp. 34–43. [G: Global]

Finnerty, Joseph E. The Mexican Peso and the Chicago International Money Market: A Case Study in Foreign Currency Futures. *J. Futures Markets*, Summer 1984, 4(2), pp. 213–24. [G: U.S.; Mexico]

Flacco, Paul R., et al. Exchange Rates and Trade Policy. *Contemp. Policy Issue*, January 1984, (4), pp. 6–18. [G: U.S.]

Fleisig, Heywood. Operations of the German Central Bank and the Rules of the Game, 1879–1913: Comment. In *Bordo, M. D. and Schwartz, A. J., eds.*, 1984, pp. 349–58. [G: Germany]

Flood, Robert P. and Garber, Peter M. Collapsing Exchange-Rate Regimes: Some Linear Examples. *J. Int. Econ.*, August 1984, 17(1/2), pp. 1–13.

Flood, Robert P. and Hodrick, Robert J. Exchange Rate and Price Dynamics with Asymmetric Information. *Int. Econ. Rev.*, October 1984, 25(3), pp. 513–26.

Fouquin, Michel. Qu'est-ce qui arrêtera le Japon? (With English summary.) *Revue Écon. Polit.*, September–October 1984, 94(5), pp. 555–61. [G: Japan]

Frankel, Jeffrey A. Tests of Monetary and Portfo-

lio Balance Models of Exchange Rate Determination. In *Bilson, J. F. O. and Marston, R. C., eds.*, 1984, pp. 239–60.
[G: Selected OECD]

Frankel, Jeffrey A. and Engel, Charles M. Do Asset-Demand Functions Optimize over the Mean and Variance of Real Returns? A Six-Currency Test. *J. Int. Econ.*, November 1984, 17(3/4), pp. 309–23. **[G: OECD]**

Fratianni, Michele and Spinelli, Franco. Italy in the Gold Standard Period, 1861–1914. In *Bordo, M. D. and Schwartz, A. J., eds.*, 1984, pp. 405–41. **[G: Italy]**

Freedman, Charles. Canada and the Interwar Gold Standard, 1920–35: Monetary Policy without a Central Bank: Comment. In *Bordo, M. D. and Schwartz, A. J., eds.*, 1984, pp. 303–08. **[G: U.S.; Canada]**

Frenkel, Jacob A. A Program for International Monetary Stability: Comment. In *Agmon, T.; Hawkins, R. G. and Levich, R. M., eds.*, 1984, pp. 85–89. **[G: OECD]**

Frenkel, Jacob A. Exchange Rate Arrangements in the Eighties: Discussion. In *Fed. Res. Bank Boston*, 1984, pp. 119–25.

Frenkel, Jacob A. The Demand for International Reserves under Pegged and Flexible Exchange Rate Regimes and Aspects of the Economics of Managed Float. In *Bigman, D. and Taya, T., eds.*, 1984, pp. 161–87. **[G: LDCs; MDCs]**

Frenkel, Jacob A. The Theory of Exchange Rate Determination: Comment. In *Bilson, J. F. O. and Marston, R. C., eds.*, 1984, pp. 58–62.

Friedman, Milton. The Success of Purchasing Power Parity: Historical Evidence and Its Implications for Macroeconomics: Comment. In *Bordo, M. D. and Schwartz, A. J., eds.*, 1984, pp. 157–62. **[G: U.S.; U.K.; Canada]**

Fukao, Mitsuhiro and Okubo, Takashi. International Linkage of Interest Rates: The Case of Japan and the United States. *Int. Econ. Rev.*, February 1984, 25(1), pp. 193–207.
[G: Japan; U.S.]

Gazioglou, Shaziye. Exchange Rate Overshooting: Clarification and Extensions. *Manchester Sch. Econ. Soc. Stud.*, September 1984, 52(3), pp. 314–21.

Genberg, Hans. On Choosing the Right Rules for Exchange-Rate Management. *World Econ.*, December 1984, 7(4), pp. 391–406.

Genberg, Hans. Properties of Innovations in Spot and Forward Exchange Rates and the Role of Money Supply Processes. In *Bilson, J. F. O. and Marston, R. C., eds.*, 1984, pp. 153–74.
[G: Selected OECD]

Gerken, Egbert. Diversification and Stabilization in a Resource-Exporting Country. In *Siebert, H., ed.*, 1984, pp. 117–55. **[G: Chile]**

Gidlow, R. M. Forward Exchange Arrangements and Exchange Control Policy in South Africa. *S. Afr. J. Econ.*, September 1984, 52(3), pp. 247–55. **[G: S. Africa]**

Gift, Richard E. Regulating the Supply of Money with Enclave Trade and No Foreign Competition for the Home Exportable. *Rivista Int. Sci.*

Econ. Com., October–November 1984, 31(10–11), pp. 1991–99.

Gleske, Leonhard. Erfahrungen mit flexiblen Wechselkursen. (Experience with Flexible Exchange Rates. With English summary.) *Kredit Kapital*, 1984, 17(4), pp. 455–73.
[G: W. Germany]

Gold, Joseph [Sir]. Effects of Variable Exchange Rates on Treaties. In *Gold, J.*, 1984, 1982, pp. 580–623.

Gold, Joseph [Sir]. Legal Models for the International Regulation of Exchange Rates. *Mich. Law Rev.*, April–May 1984, 82(5 & 6), pp. 1533–54.

Gold, Joseph [Sir]. Legal Models for the International Regulation of Exchange Rates. In *Gold, J.*, 1984, pp. 624–55.

Gold, Joseph [Sir]. Strengthening the Soft International Law of Exchange Arrangements. In *Gold, J.*, 1984, 1983, pp. 515–79.

Goldstein, Morris. Whither the Exchange Rate System? *Finance Develop.*, June 1984, 21(2), pp. 2–6.

Goodhart, Charles A. E. Bank of England Operations, 1893–1913: Comment. In *Bordo, M. D. and Schwartz, A. J., eds.*, 1984, pp. 222–27.
[G: U.K.]

de Grauwe, Paul. The Relationship between Exchange Rate Policy and Monetary Policy in Ten Industrial Countries: Comment. In *Bilson, J. F. O. and Marston, R. C., eds.*, 1984, pp. 511–14. **[G: Selected OECD]**

Greenwood, John G. Underlying Ingredients of the Recent Hong Kong Dollar Crisis. *Hong Kong Econ. Pap.*, 1984, (15), pp. 119–24.
[G: Hong Kong]

Gregory, Allan W. and McCurdy, Thomas H. Testing the Unbiasedness Hypothesis in the Forward Foreign Exchange Market: A Specification Analysis. *J. Int. Money Finance*, December 1984, 3(3), pp. 357–68. **[G: Canada; U.S.]**

Gudac, Toma. Pricing and Exchange Rates in Planned Economies. *Finance Develop.*, September 1984, 21(3), pp. 40–43.

Guillaumont, Sylviane. La situation monétaire et finacière des États africains de la zone franc. (With English summary.) *Revue Écon. Polit.*, September–October 1984, 94(5), pp. 592–601.
[G: Africa]

Gupta, Sanjeev. Unrecorded Trade at Black Exchange Rate: Analysis, Implications and Estimates. *Aussenwirtschaft*, May 1984, 39(1/2), pp. 75–90. **[G: India; Pakistan; Turkey]**

Haberler, Gottfried. The International Monetary System in the World Recession. In *Fellner, W., ed.*, 1984, pp. 87–129. **[G: OECD]**

Hakkio, Craig S. A Re-examination of Purchasing Power Parity: A Multi-country and Multi-period Study. *J. Int. Econ.*, November 1984, 17(3/4), pp. 265–77. **[G: U.K.; Canada; France; Japan]**

Hamaui, Rony. Lo sviluppo dei mercati finanziari in ECU: una prima valutazione su rischi e rendimenti. (The Development of Financial Markets in ECU: An Initial Evaluation Regarding

Risks and Yields. With English summary.) *Bancaria*, May–June 1984, *40*(5–6), pp. 513–29. **[G: EEC]**

Harberger, Arnold C. La Crisis Cambiaria Chilena de 1982. (With English summary.) *Cuadernos Econ.*, August 1984, *21*(63), pp. 123–36. **[G: Chile]**

Hardouvelis, Gikas A. Market Perceptions of Federal Reserve Policy and the Weekly Monetary Announcements. *J. Monet. Econ.*, September 1984, *14*(2), pp. 225–40. **[G: U.S.]**

Harley, C. Knick. The Gold Standard: The Traditional Approach: Comment. In *Bordo, M. D. and Schwartz, A. J.*, eds., 1984, pp. 113–17.

von Hayek, Friedrich A. The Fate of the Gold Standard. In *von Hayek, F. A. (II)*, 1984, *1932*, pp. 118–35. **[G: U.K.; U.S.]**

Helpman, Elhanan and Razin, Assaf. The Role of Saving and Investment in Exchange Rate Determination under Alternative Monetary Mechanisms. *J. Monet. Econ.*, May 1984, *13*(3), pp. 307–25.

Heri, Erwin W. Wechselkursbewegungen—Einige Ergebnisse einer Analyse der kurzen Frist. (Exchange Rate Movements—Some Results of an Analysis of the Short-Run. With English summary.) *Kredit Kapital*, 1984, *17*(2), pp. 223–42. **[G: U.S.; Germany; U.K.; France; Italy]**

Heri, Erwin W. Zur Prognostizierbarkeit von Wechselkursänderungen. Ein empirischer Vergleich verschiedener Prognosefunktionen. (Forecasting Exchange Rate Changes: An Empirical Comparison of Different Models. With English summary.) *Z. Wirtschaft. Sozialwissen.*, 1984, *104*(4), pp. 369–88. **[G: U.S.; U.K.; Germany; Switzerland]**

Herring, Richard J. Term Premia on Euro Rates: Discussion. *J. Finance*, July 1984, *39*(3), pp. 755–57. **[G: EEC]**

Hill, T. P. Introduction: The Special Conference on Purchasing Power Parities. *Rev. Income Wealth*, June 1984, *30*(2), pp. 125–33.

Hodrick, Robert J. and Srivastava, Sanjay. An Investigation of Risk and Return in Forward Foreign Exchange. *J. Int. Money Finance*, April 1984, *3*(1), pp. 5–29.

Holtham, Gerald. Multinational Modelling of Financial Linkages and Exchange Rates. *OECD Econ. Stud.*, Spring 1984, (2), pp. 51–92. **[G: OECD]**

Honohan, Patrick. Expectation Errors and Exchange-Rate Volatility. *J. Macroecon.*, Summer 1984, *6*(3), pp. 323–34.

Honohan, Patrick. Monetary Restraint and the Exchange Rate. *Economica*, May 1984, *51*(202), pp. 163–76.

Honohan, Patrick. The Break-up of a Currency Union Increases the Demand for Money. *Europ. Econ. Rev.*, July 1984, *25*(2), pp. 235–38. **[G: Ireland; U.K.]**

Hooper, Peter. Exchange Rates and the Prices of Nonfood, Nonfuel Products: Comment. *Brookings Pap. Econ. Act.*, 1984, (2), pp. 531–35. **[G: U.S.]**

Houthakker, Hendrik S. Relative Prices and

Floating Exchange Rates—An Empirical Exploration. In *Csikós-Nagy, B.; Hague, D. and Hall, G.*, eds., 1984, pp. 336–46. **[G: OECD]**

Hsieh, David A. International Risk Sharing and the Choice of Exchange-Rate Regime. *J. Int. Money Finance*, August 1984, *3*(2), pp. 141–51.

Hsieh, David A. Tests of Rational Expectations and No Risk Premium in Forward Exchange Markets. *J. Int. Econ.*, August 1984, *17*(1/2), pp. 173–84. **[G: W. Europe; Japan; Canada]**

Huang, Roger D. Exchange Rate and Relative Monetary Expansions: The Case of Simultaneous Hyperinflation and Rational Expectations. *Europ. Econ. Rev.*, March 1984, *24*(2), pp. 189–95. **[G: Poland; Germany]**

Huang, Roger D. Some Alternative Tests of Forward Exchange Rates as Predictors of Future Spot Rates. *J. Int. Money Finance*, August 1984, *3*(2), pp. 153–67. **[G: Selected OECD]**

Huang, Roger D. Tests of Variance Bounds Implied by Cagan's Hyperinflation Model. *Int. Econ. Rev.*, October 1984, *25*(3), pp. 545–61. **[G: Germany]**

Huffman, Wallace E. and Lothian, James R. The Gold Standard and the Transmission of Business Cycles, 1833–1932. In *Bordo, M. D. and Schwartz, A. J.*, eds., 1984, pp. 455–507. **[G: U.S.; U.K.]**

Hughes, Jonathan R. T. The Gold Standard and the Bank of England in the Crisis of 1847: Comment. In *Bordo, M. D. and Schwartz, A. J.*, eds., 1984, pp. 264–71. **[G: U.K.]**

Huguel, Catherine. La balance des paiements française: une contrainte extérieure qui demeure. (With English summary.) *Revue Écon. Polit.*, September–October 1984, *94*(5), pp. 662–75. **[G: France]**

Hussain, M. Nureldin and Thirlwall, A. P. The IMF Supply-Side Approach to Devaluation: An Assessment with Reference to the Sudan. *Oxford Bull. Econ. Statist.*, May 1984, *46*(2), pp. 145–67. **[G: Sudan]**

Hutchinson, Michael M. Intervention, Deficit Finance and Real Exchange Rates: The Case of Japan. *Fed. Res. Bank San Francisco Econ. Rev.*, Winter 1984, (1), pp. 27–44. **[G: Japan]**

Hutchinson, Michael M. and Pigott, Charles. Budget Deficits, Exchange Rates and the Current Account: Theory and U.S. Evidence. *Fed. Res. Bank San Francisco Econ. Rev.*, Fall 1984, (4), pp. 5–25. **[G: U.S.]**

Jarchow, Hans-Joachim. Devisenmarktinterventionen und Liquiditätswirkungen. (Exchange Market Interventions and Liquidity Effects. With English summary.) *Aussenwirtschaft*, December 1984, *39*(4), pp. 299–321. **[G: U.S.; W. Europe]**

Johansson, Peter and Rajakangas, Timo. Pääomanliikkeet, sterilointi ja rahapolitiikan itsenäisyys. (Capital Flows, Sterilization and the Independence of Monetary Policy. With English summary.) *Kansant. Aikak.*, 1984, *80*(3), pp. 291–301. **[G: Finland]**

Johnson, Mark J. and Szarek, Patricia. Effects of Strong Dollar, Economic Recovery Apparent in First-Half Import and Export Prices. *Mon. Lab. Rev.*, October 1984, *107*(10), pp. 3–17. [G: U.S.]

Johnson, R. Stafford and Zuber, Richard A. The Construction of International Currency Cocktails—An Argument for the Use of the Markowitz Portfolio Model. *Amer. Econ.*, Spring 1984, *28*(1), pp. 69–73.

Jones, Michael. Optimal Foreign Exchange Market Intervention: Evidence from the Bretton Woods Era. *Rev. Econ. Statist.*, May 1984, *66*(2), pp. 242–55. [G: OECD]

Jonung, Lars. Swedish Experience under the Classical Gold Standard, 1873–1914. In *Bordo, M. D. and Schwartz, A. J., eds.*, 1984, pp. 361–99. [G: Sweden]

Junge, Georg. Purchasing Power Parity in the 1920s and the 1970s: A Note. *Europ. Econ. Rev.*, October–November 1984, *26*(1–2), pp. 73–82. [G: Switzerland]

Kaen, Fred R.; Simos, Evangelos O. and Hachey, George A. The Response of Forward Exchange Rates to Interest Rate Forecasting Errors. *J. Finan. Res.*, Winter 1984, *7*(4), pp. 281–90. [G: U.S.]

Kanniainen, Vesa. On Offsetting Capital Flows and Monetary Autonomy of a Small Open Economy. *Economica*, May 1984, *51*(202), pp. 177–86.

Karamouzis, Nicholas V. The Use of the Interest Rate Differential in Empirical Studies. *Atlantic Econ. J.*, July 1984, *12*(2), pp. 77. [G: U.S.; W. Germany]

Katseli, Louka T. Real Exchange Rates in the 1970s. In *Bilson, J. F. O. and Marston, R. C., eds.*, 1984, pp. 281–321. [G: Selected OECD]

Kawai, Masahiro. Exchange Rate—Price Causality in the Recent Floating Period. In *Bigman, D. and Taya, T., eds.*, 1984, pp. 189–211. [G: OECD]

Kawai, Masahiro. The Effect of Forward Exchange on Spot-Rate Volatility under Risk and Rational Expectations. *J. Int. Econ.*, February 1984, *16*(1/2), pp. 155–72.

Kenen, Peter B. Exchange Rate Policy after a Decade of "Floating": Comment. In *Bilson, J. F. O. and Marston, R. C., eds.*, 1984, pp. 112–16. [G: Japan; U.K.; U.S.; W. Germany]

Khan, Waseem and Willett, Thomas D. The Monetary Approach to Exchange Rates: A Review of Recent Empirical Studies. *Kredit Kapital*, 1984, *17*(2), pp. 199–222. [G: U.S.; Germany]

Kimbrough, Kent P. The Forward Rate as a Predictor of the Future Spot Rate, the Role of Policy, and Exchange Rate Regime Choice. *Int. Econ. Rev.*, October 1984, *25*(3), pp. 527–43.

Kimbrough, Kent P. and Koray, Faik. Money, Output, and the Trade Balance: Theory and Evidence. *Can. J. Econ.*, August 1984, *17*(3), pp. 508–22. [G: Canada; U.S.]

Kincaid, G. Russell. A Test of the Efficacy of Exchange Rate Adjustments in Indonesia. *Int. Monet. Fund Staff Pap.*, March 1984, *31*(1), pp. 62–92. [G: Indonesia]

Kirchgässner, Gebhard. Die Abhängigkeit der Mineralölpreise in der Schweiz von der Entwicklung der Preise auf dem Rotterdamer Spotmarkt und vom Wechselkurs. (The Dependance of Swiss Oil Prices on the Price at Rotterdam and on the Exchange Rate. With English summary.) *Schweiz. Z. Volkswirtsch. Statist.*, September 1984, *120*(3), pp. 293–313. [G: Switzerland]

Kjeldsen-Kragh, Søren. Valutaindtjening, beskæftigelse og indtjening i landbruget og industrien. (Foreign Exchange Earnings, Employment Effects, and Income Earnings in Different Sectors of the Danish Economy. With English summary.) *Nationaløkon. Tidsskr.*, 1984, *122*(1), pp. 91–114. [G: Denmark]

Klein, Lawrence R.; Fardoust, S. and Filatov, V. Endogenous Exchange Rate in the Medium Term: A Weak Law of Purchasing Power Parity for the LINK System. In *[Pearce, I. F.]*, 1984, pp. 171–90. [G: OECD]

Koh, Ai-Tee. Money Shocks and Deviations from Purchasing Power Parity. *J. Monet. Econ.*, July 1984, *14*(1), pp. 105–22.

Komura, Chikara. Money, Income and Causality in Japan—Supplementary Evidence: Reply. *Southern Econ. J.*, April 1984, *50*(4), pp. 1219–23. [G: Japan]

Konstantinov, Iu. A. The Interaction of National Currencies with International Socialist Currency. *Soviet E. Europ. Foreign Trade*, Spring 1984, *20*(1), pp. 57–75. [G: CMEA]

Koromzay, Val; Llewellyn, John and Potter, Stephen. Exchange Rates and Policy Choices: Some Lessons from Interdependence in a Multilateral Perspective. *Amer. Econ. Rev.*, May 1984, *74*(2), pp. 311–15.

Kouri, Pentti J. K. Monetary Policy, the Balance of Payments, and the Exchange Rate. In *Bigman, D. and Taya, T., eds.*, 1984, pp. 127–59.

Kouri, Pentti, J. K. The Theory of Exchange Rate Determination: Comment. In *Bilson, J. F. O. and Marston, R. C., eds.*, 1984, pp. 67–72.

Lai, Ching-chong. Exchange Rate Expectations, Monetary Effect of Devaluation, and Macroeconomic Policies. *Atlantic Econ. J.*, December 1984, *12*(4), pp. 55–58.

Lai, Ching-chong and Chen, Chau-nan. Flexible Exchange Rates, Tight Money Effects, and Macroeconomic Policy. *J. Post Keynesian Econ.*, Fall 1984, *7*(1), pp. 128–33.

Laney, Leroy O. The Strong Dollar, the Current Account, and Federal Deficits: Cause and Effect. *Fed. Res. Bank Dallas Econ. Rev.*, January 1984, pp. 1–14. [G: U.S.]

de Larosière, Jacques. Exchange Rates and the Adjustment Process. In *Bigman, D. and Taya, T., eds.*, 1984, pp. 259–65.

Latter, A. R. Some Issues Associated with the

New Exchange Rate Regime. *Hong Kong Econ. Pap.*, 1984, (15), pp. 125–28. **[G: Hong Kong]**

Le Fort Varela, Guillermo. El tipo de cambio real y la experienca de los países del Cono Sur, 1974–1982. (With English summary.) *Cuadernos Econ.*, April 1984, 21(62), pp. 37–61. **[G: Argentina; Chile; Uruguay]**

Le Fort Varela, Guillermo. Fe de erratas [El tipo de cambio real y la experiencia de los países del Cono Sur, 1974–1982]. *Cuadernos Econ.*, August 1984, 21(63), pp. 239. **[G: Argentina; Chile; Uruguay]**

Levi, Maurice D. Spot versus Forward Speculation and Hedging: A Diagrammatic Exposition. *J. Int. Money Finance*, April 1984, 3(1), pp. 105–09.

Levich, Richard M. Comment [Properties of Innovations in Spot and Forward Exchange Rates and the Role of Money Supply Processes] [Exchange Rate Dynamics]. In *Bilson, J. F. O. and Marston, R. C., eds.*, 1984, pp. 189–94. **[G: Selected OECD]**

Levin, Jay H. Non-sterilization, Pegged Exchange Rates, and Stabilization Policy. *Metroecon.*, February 1984, 36(1), pp. 77–96.

Levin, Jay H. On the International Transmission of Monetary Policy under Floating Exchange Rates. *Quart. Rev. Econ. Bus.*, Spring 1984, 24(1), pp. 78–86.

Lindert, Peter H. Swedish Experience under the Classical Gold Standard, 1873–1914: Comment. In *Bordo, M. D. and Schwartz, A. J., eds.*, 1984, pp. 399–404. **[G: Sweden]**

Lipsey, Robert E. The Success of Purchasing Power Prity: Historical Evidence and Its Implications for Macroeconomics: Comment. In *Bordo, M. D. and Schwartz, A. J., eds.*, 1984, pp. 151–56. **[G: U.S.; U.K.; Canada]**

Locker, Hugo Krijnse and Faerber, H. D. Space and Time Comparisons of Purchasing Power Parities and Real Values. *Rev. Income Wealth*, March 1984, 30(1), pp. 53–83. **[G: EEC]**

Logue, Dennis E. and Sweeney, Richard James. Term Premia on Euro Rates. *J. Finance*, July 1984, 39(3), pp. 747–55. **[G: EEC]**

Lomax, David F. The European Monetary System, Real Exchange Rates and the European Currency Unit. *Irish Banking Rev.*, December 1984, pp. 37–51. **[G: W. Europe]**

Lomax, Rachel. Bade and Parkin: Is £M₃ the Right Aggregate? In *Griffiths, B. and Wood, G. E., eds.*, 1984, pp. 294–300. **[G: U.K.]**

Longworth, David. Exchange Rates and 'News': A Comment. *J. Int. Money Finance*, April 1984, 3(1), pp. 119–21.

Loopesko, Bonnie E. Relationships among Exchange Rates, Intervention, and Interest Rates: An Empirical Investigation. *J. Int. Money Finance*, December 1984, 3(3), pp. 257–77. **[G: OECD]**

Lybeck, Johan A., et al. A Comparison of the Dynamic Properties of Five Nordic Macroeconometric Models. *Scand. J. Econ.*, 1984, 86(1), pp. 35–51. **[G: Sweden; Finland; Norway]**

MacDonald, Ronald. The Monetary Approach to the Exchange Rate Revisited. *Appl. Econ.*, October 1984, 16(5), pp. 771–82. **[G: U.S.; U.K.; Japan; Germany]**

MacDonald, Ronald. The Monetary Approach to the Exchange Rate and the 1920s' Experience with Floating Exchange Rates. *J. Econ. Stud.*, 1984, 11(3), pp. 14–25. **[G: U.S.; U.K.; France]**

Madura, Jeff. Construction of Currency Cocktails for Export Pricing. *Bus. Econ.*, April 1984, 19(3), pp. 40–47.

Mahajan, Arvind and Mehta, Dileep. Strong Form Efficiency of the Foreign Exchange Market and Bank Positions. *J. Finan. Res.*, Fall 1984, 7(3), pp. 197–207. **[G: U.S.]**

Mansur, Ahsan Habib. Determining the Appropriate Exchange Rate in LDCs. *Finance Develop.*, December 1984, 21(4), pp. 18–21. **[G: LDCs]**

Mantell, Edmund H. How to Measure Expected Returns on Foreign Investments. *J. Portfol. Manage.*, Winter 1984, 10(2), pp. 38–43. **[G: U.S.]**

Marion, Nancy Peregrim. Exchange Rate Regimes: The Problem of Rate Swings. In *Hewlett, S. A.; Kaufman, H. and Kenen, P. B., eds.*, 1984, pp. 77–95.

Marquez, Jaime. Sustitución de monedas, dualidad e indeterminación del tipo de cambio: análisis empírico de la experiencia venezolana. (With English summary.) *Cuadernos Econ.*, December 1984, 21(64), pp. 299–313. **[G: Venezuela]**

Marris, Stephen N. Why the Dollar Won't Come Down. *Challenge*, November/December 1984, 27(5), pp. 19–25. **[G: U.S.]**

Marston, Richard C. Exchange Rate Unions as an Alternative to Flexible Rates: The Effects of Real and Monetary Disturbances. In *Bilson, J. F. O. and Marston, R. C., eds.*, 1984, pp. 407–37.

Marwah, Kanta and Bodkin, Ronald G. A Model of the Canadian Global Exchange Rate: A Test of the 1970s. *J. Policy Modeling*, November 1984, 6(4), pp. 455–83. **[G: Canada]**

McCloskey, Donald N. and Zecher, J. Richard. The Success of Purchasing Power Parity: Historical Evidence and Its Implications for Macroeconomics. In *Bordo, M. D. and Schwartz, A. J., eds.*, 1984, pp. 121–50. **[G: U.S.; U.K.; Canada]**

McGouldrick, Paul. Operations of the German Central Bank and the Rules of the Game, 1879–1913. In *Bordo, M. D. and Schwartz, A. J., eds.*, 1984, pp. 311–49. **[G: Germany]**

McKinnon, Ronald I. A Program for International Monetary Stability. In *Agmon, T.; Hawkins, R. G. and Levich, R. M., eds.*, 1984, pp. 55–77. **[G: OECD]**

McKinnon, Ronald I. The J-Curve, Stabilizing Speculation, and Capital Constraints on Foreign Exchange Dealers. In *Bigman, D. and Taya, T., eds.*, 1984, pp. 101–25.

Meese, Richard A. Is the Sticky Price Assumption Reasonable for Exchange Rate Models? *J. Int.*

Money Finance, August 1984, *3*(2), pp. 131–39. **[G: U.S.; U.K.; Germany; Japan]**

Mehra, Yash P. and Chiang, Thomas C. Tests of Exogeneity and Causality Specification in Monetary Models of Exchange Rate Determination. *Atlantic Econ. J.,* July 1984, *12*(2), pp. 54–60. **[G: U.K.; Canada; W. Germany]**

Melvin, Michael and Bernstein, David. Trade Concentration, Openness, and Deviations from Purchasing Power Parity. *J. Int. Money Finance,* December 1984, *3*(3), pp. 369–76. **[G: Global]**

Menezes, Victor. Beyond the Peg. *Hong Kong Econ. Pap.,* 1984, (15), pp. 129–31. **[G: Hong Kong]**

Michel, Gilles and Noel, Michel. The Ivorian Economy and Alternative Trade Regimes. In *Zartman, I. W. and Delgado, C. L., eds.,* 1984, pp. 77–114. **[G: Ivory Coast]**

Micossi, Stefano. La politica monetaria nella CEE. (Monetary Policy in the EEC. With English summary.) *Bancaria,* August 1984, *40*(8), pp. 759–69. **[G: EEC]**

Micossi, Stefano and Rebecchini, S. A Case Study on the Effectiveness of Foreign Exchange Market Intervention: The Italian Lira (September 1975–March 1977). *J. Banking Finance,* December 1984, *8*(4), pp. 535–55. **[G: Italy]**

Miller, Stephen. Purchasing Power Parity and Relative Price Variability: Evidence from the 1970s. *Europ. Econ. Rev.,* December 1984, *26*(3), pp. 353–67. **[G: U.S.; U.K.; France; W. Germany]**

Mirus, Rolf. Foreign Currency Options in Exchange Risk Management. *Aussenwirtschaft,* December 1984, *39*(4), pp. 323–34. **[G: U.S.]**

Mishkin, Frederic S. Are Real Interest Rates Equal across Countries? An Empirical Investigation of International Parity Conditions. *J. Finance,* December 1984, *39*(5), pp. 1345–57. **[G: OECD]**

Modigliani, Franco. Opportunities and Implications of a Return to Fixed Exchange Rates—Is Gold an Answer for International Adjustment? Comment. In *Agmon, T.; Hawkins, R. G. and Levich, R. M., eds.,* 1984, pp. 46–53.

Moggridge, Donald E. The Bank of England and the Rules of the Game under the International Gold Standard: New Evidence: Comment. In *Bordo, M. D. and Schwartz, A. J., eds.,* 1984, pp. 195–99. **[G: U.K.]**

Murfin, Andy and Ormerod, Paul. The Forward Rate for the U.S. Dollar and the Efficient Markets Hypothesis, 1978–1983. *Manchester Sch. Econ. Soc. Stud.,* September 1984, *52*(3), pp. 292–99. **[G: U.S.]**

Mussa, Michael. The Theory of Exchange Rate Determination. In *Bilson, J. F. O. and Marston, R. C., eds.,* 1984, pp. 13–58.

Mutoh, Takahiko and Hamada, Koichi. International Short Term Capital Flow and the Foreign Exchange Rate: Japan, 1973–1980. *Econ. Stud. Quart.,* August 1984, *35*(2), pp. 97–115. **[G: Japan]**

Neumann, Manfred J. M. Intervention in the Mark/Dollar Market: The Authorities' Reaction Function. *J. Int. Money Finance,* August 1984, *3*(2), pp. 223–39. **[G: U.S.; Germany]**

Newton, C. C. S. The Sterling Crisis of 1947 and the British Response to the Marshall Plan. *Econ. Hist. Rev., 2nd Ser.,* August 1984, *37*(3), pp. 391–408. **[G: U.K.; U.S.]**

Nickelsburg, Gerald. Dynamic Exchange Rate Equilibria with Uncertain Government Policy. *Rev. Econ. Stud.,* July 1984, *51*(3), pp. 509–19.

Niehans, Jürg. National Monetary Policy in an International Capital Market. *Kobe Econ. Bus. Rev.,* 1984, *30,* pp. 1–10.

Nowak, Michael. Quantitative Controls and Unofficial Markets in Foreign Exchange: A Theoretical Framework. *Int. Monet. Fund Staff Pap.,* June 1984, *31*(2), pp. 404–31.

Obstfeld, Maurice and Rogoff, Kenneth. Exchange Rate Dynamics with Sluggish Prices under Alternative Price-Adjustment Rules. *Int. Econ. Rev.,* February 1984, *25*(1), pp. 159–74.

Ondráček, Mojmír. Views of Economists from the Socialist Countries on Handling Currency Matters in the CMEA—The Role of Exchange Rates (Coefficients) in Planned Economic Management. *Soviet E. Europ. Foreign Trade,* Summer 1984, *20*(2), pp. 37–55. **[G: CMEA]**

Otani, Ichiro. Exchange Rate Instability and Capital Controls: The Japanese Experience, 1978–1981. In *Bigman, D. and Taya, T., eds.,* 1984, pp. 213–39. **[G: Japan]**

Padoa Schioppa, Tommaso and Papadia, Francesco. Competing Currencies and Monetary Stability. In *Masera, R. S. and Triffin, R., eds.,* 1984, pp. 79–110.

Papell, David H. Activist Monetary Policy and Exchange-Rate Overshooting: The Deutsche Mark/Dollar Rate. *J. Int. Money Finance,* December 1984, *3*(3), pp. 293–310. **[G: U.S.; W. Germany]**

Papell, David H. Anticipated and Unanticipated Disturbances: The Dynamics of the Exchange Rate and the Current Account. *J. Int. Money Finance,* August 1984, *3*(2), pp. 179–93. **[G: U.S.; U.K.; Germany; Japan]**

Park, Keehwan. Tests of the Hypothesis of the Existence of Risk Premium in the Foreign Exchange Market. *J. Int. Money Finance,* August 1984, *3*(2), pp. 169–78. **[G: U.S.; Germany]**

Penati, Alessandro and Dooley, Michael P. Current Account Imbalances and Capital Formation in Industrial Countries, 1949–81. *Int. Monet. Fund Staff Pap.,* March 1984, *31*(1), pp. 1–24. **[G: OECD]**

Pesaran, M. H. Macroeconomic Policy in an Oil-exporting Economy with Foreign Exchange Controls. *Economica,* August 1984, *51*(203), pp. 253–70.

Phylaktis, Kate. Structural Change, Monetary Policy and the Foreign Exchange Value of the Pound: Comments. In *Griffiths, B. and Wood, G. E., eds.,* 1984, pp. 233–37. **[G: U.K.]**

Phylaktis, Kate and Wood, Geoffrey E. An Analytical and Taxonomic Framework for the Study of Exchange Controls. In *Black, J. and Dorrance, G. S., eds.*, 1984, pp. 149–66.

Pigott, Charles. Indicators of Long-Term Real Interest Rates. *Fed. Res. Bank San Francisco Econ. Rev.*, Winter 1984, (1), pp. 45–63.
[G: U.S.]

Pinho, Manuel A. Approches monétaires des taux de change: 1e FF/DM pendant les annés soixante-dix. (With English summary.) *Economia (Portugal)*, May 1984, 8(2), pp. 233–56.
[G: France; Germany]

Pippenger, John. Bank of England Operations, 1893–1913. In *Bordo, M. D. and Schwartz, A. J., eds.*, 1984, pp. 203–22. [G: U.K.]

Pitt, Mark M. Smuggling and the Black Market for Foreign Exchange. *J. Int. Econ.*, May 1984, 16(3/4), pp. 243–57.

Postiaux, Jean-Marie. La maîtrise de l'inflation aux Etats-Unis, une condition nécessaire pour un scénario de redressement économique— L'exemple de l'Allemagne, de la France et de la Belgique—1984–1986. (With English summary.) *Cah. Écon. Bruxelles*, 3rd Trimester 1984, (103), pp. 419–39. [G: Germany; France; Belgium]

Potter, Stephen and Feiner, Michael. Macroeconomic Policies and Exchange Rates. *OECD Econ. Stud.*, Autumn 1984, (3), pp. 119–44.
[G: OECD]

Ram, Rati. Money, Income and Causality in Japan—Supplementary Evidence: Comment. *Southern Econ. J.*, April 1984, 50(4), pp. 1214–18. [G: Japan]

Rana, Pradumna B. Fixed versus Flexible Exchange Rates and the Measurement of Exchange Rate Instability: Comment. *J. Int. Econ.*, May 1984, 16(3/4), pp. 307–10.
[G: Asia]

Redish, Angela. Why Was Specie Scarce in Colonial Economies? An Analysis of the Canadian Currency, 1796–1830. *J. Econ. Hist.*, September 1984, 44(3), pp. 713–28. [G: Canada]

Redmond, John. The Sterling Overvaluation in 1925: A Multilateral Approach. *Econ. Hist. Rev., 2nd Ser.*, November 1984, 37(4), pp. 520–32. [G: U.K.]

Res, Zannis. Comment on Bade and Parkin's Paper on Issues Concerning Monetary Policy in the UK [Is Sterling M₃ the Right Aggregate?]. In *Griffiths, B. and Wood, G. E., eds.*, 1984, pp. 287–93. [G: U.K.]

Ribas, Armando P. The Process of Balance of Payments Adjustment: Comment. In *Muns, J., ed.*, 1984, pp. 58–66.

Rich, Georg. Canada without a Central Bank: Operation of the Price-Specie-Flow Mechanism, 1872–1913. In *Bordo, M. D. and Schwartz, A. J., eds.*, 1984, pp. 547–75. [G: Canada]

Rockoff, Hugh. Some Evidence on the Real Price of Gold, Its Costs of Production, and Commodity Prices: Reply. In *Bordo, M. D. and Schwartz, A. J., eds.*, 1984, pp. 646–48.
[G: U.S.; U.S.S.R.; S. Africa; Australia]

Rockoff, Hugh. Some Evidence on the Real Price of Gold, Its Costs of Production, and Commod-

ity Prices. In *Bordo, M. D. and Schwartz, A. J., eds.*, 1984, pp. 613–44. [G: U.S.; S. Africa; Australia; U.S.S.R.]

Rodríguez, Carlos Alfredo. Inflación, salario real y tipo real de cambio. (With English summary.) *Cuadernos Econ.*, December 1984, 21(64), pp. 247–61. [G: Argentina]

Rodríguez, Carlos Alfredo. La Estrategia de Estabilización con Tipo de Cambio Flexible y Politica Monetaria Activa. (With English summary.) *Cuadernos Econ.*, August 1984, 21(63), pp. 103–21.

Rodríguez, Carlos Alfredo. The Role of Economy-Wide Prices in the Adjustment Process: Comment. In *Muns, J., ed.*, 1984, pp. 113–16.
[G: LDCs]

Roosa, Robert V. Exchange Rate Arrangements in the Eighties. In *Fed. Res. Bank Boston*, 1984, pp. 104–18.

Rothengatter, Werner. The Dynamics of Financial Adjustments in an Open Economy and the Effects of Stabilization Policy. *Z. ges. Staatswiss.*, June 1984, 140(2), pp. 308–29.

Rusmich, Ladislav. Value Aspects in Developing the Process of International Socialist Integration. *Soviet E. Europ. Foreign Trade*, Winter 1984-85, 20(4), pp. 7–31. [G: CMEA]

Sachs, Jeffrey D. and Wyplosz, Charles. La politique budgétaire et le taux de change réel. (Fiscal Policy and the Real Exchange Rate. With English summary.) *Ann. INSEE*, January–March 1984, (53), pp. 63–92.

Sanderson, Paul. Rational Expectations and Forward Exchange Market Efficiency. *Appl. Econ.*, February 1984, 16(1), pp. 99–109.
[G: Canada; U.K.; W. Germany]

Schadler, Susan M. Interest Rates and Exchange Rates. *Finance Develop.*, June 1984, 21(2), pp. 7–11. [G: U.S.; Japan]

von der Schulenberg, J.-Matthias Graf. Who Wants to Go Shopping with a Currency Basket? A Risk Theoretical Study. *Jahr. Nationalökon. Statist.*, January 1984, 199(1), pp. 65–75.

Schwartz, Anna J. A Retrospective on the Classical Gold Standard, 1821–1931: Introduction. In *Bordo, M. D. and Schwartz, A. J., eds.*, 1984, pp. 1–20. [G: U.K.]

Schwartz, Anna J. Opportunities and Implications of a Return to Fixed Exchange Rates—Is Gold an Answer for International Adjustment? Comment. In *Agmon, T.; Hawkins, R. G. and Levich, R. M., eds.*, 1984, pp. 42–45.

Shaaf, Mohammad. Strong Dollar, Low Inflation, and OPEC's Terms of Trade. *J. Energy Devel.*, Autumn 1984, 10(1), pp. 121–29. [G: OPEC]

Shapiro, Alan C. Currency Risk and Relative Price Risk. *J. Finan. Quant. Anal.*, December 1984, 19(4), pp. 365–73.

Sharpe, Ian G. Covered Interest Rate Parity: The Australian Case. *Appl. Econ.*, October 1984, 16(5), pp. 655–65. [G: U.S.; Australia]

Shearer, Ronald A. and Clark, Carolyn. Canada and the Interwar Gold Standard, 1920–35: Monetary Policy without a Central Bank. In *Bordo, M. D. and Schwartz, A. J., eds.*, 1984, pp. 277–302. [G: U.S.; Canada]

Sheffrin, Steven M. and Russell, Thomas. Sterling and Oil Discoveries: The Mystery of Nonappreciation. *J. Int. Money Finance,* December 1984, *3*(3), pp. 311–26. **[G: U.K.]**

Simkin, Colin. Does Money Matter in Singapore? *Singapore Econ. Rev.,* April 1984, *29*(1), pp. 1–15. **[G: Singapore]**

Smeets, Heinz-Dieter. Wechselkurssystem und Phillips-Kurve. (Exchange Rate System and Phillips Curve. With English summary.) *Kredit Kapital,* 1984, *17*(3), pp. 396–403. **[G: W. Germany]**

Smyslov, D. V. The Crisis in the Modern Monetary System of Capitalism and Inflation. In *Nikitin, S. M., ed.,* 1984, pp. 108–25. **[G: OECD]**

Somanath, V. S. Exchange Rate Expectations and the Current Exchange Rate: A Test of the Monetarist Approach. *J. Int. Bus. Stud.,* Spring/Summer 1984, *15*(1), pp. 131–40. **[G: U.S.]**

Spencer, Peter D. The Effect of Oil Discoveries on the British Economy—Theoretical Ambiguities and the Consistent Expectations Simulation Approach. *Econ. J.,* September 1984, *94*(375), pp. 633–44. **[G: U.K.]**

Spiro, Peter S. Exchange Rate Risk and the Cost of Foreign Capital. *Can. Public Policy,* March 1984, *10*(1), pp. 54–63. **[G: U.K.; N. America; Japan; W. Germany; Switzerland]**

Stulz, René M. Currency Preferences, Purchasing Power Risks, and the Determination of Exchange Rates in an Optimizing Model. *J. Money, Credit, Banking,* August 1984, *16*(3), pp. 302–16.

Stulz, René M. Optimal Hedging Policies. *J. Finan. Quant. Anal.,* June 1984, *19*(2), pp. 127–40.

Summers, Robert and Heston, Alan. Improved International Comparisons of Real Product and Its Composition: 1950–1980. *Rev. Income Wealth,* June 1984, *30*(2), pp. 207–62. **[G: Global]**

Suni, Paavo. A Comparison of the External Values of Nordic Currencies 1970–83. In *Mikkelsen, A., et al.,* 1984, pp. 242–58. **[G: Scandinavia]**

Suzuki, Hideo. On the Efficacy of the Generalized Floating System. In *Bigman, D. and Taya, T., eds.,* 1984, pp. 285–89.

Sylla, Richard E. Italy in the Gold Standard Period, 1861–1914: Comment. In *Bordo, M. D. and Schwartz, A. J., eds.,* 1984, pp. 442–46. **[G: Italy]**

Szilágyi, György. Procedures for Updating the Results of International Comparisons. *Rev. Income Wealth,* June 1984, *30*(2), pp. 153–65. **[G: Europe; U.S.]**

Temin, Peter. Canada without a Central Bank: Operation of the Price-Specie-Flow Mechanism, 1872–1913: Comment. In *Bordo, M. D. and Schwartz, A. J., eds.,* 1984, pp. 576–81. **[G: Canada]**

Thygesen, Niels. Exchange-rate Policies and Monetary Targets in the EMS Countries. In *Masera, R. S. and Triffin, R., eds.,* 1984, pp. 262–86. **[G: EEC]**

Tiraspolsky, Anita. L'effet "taux de change" sur le niveau des prix intra-C.A.E.M. (The Exchange Rate Effect on the Intra-CMEA Price Level. With English summary.) *Écon. Soc.,* February 1984, *18*(2), pp. 139–59. **[G: CMEA]**

Turnovsky, Stephen J. Exchange Market Intervention under Alternative Forms of Exogenous Disturbances. *J. Int. Econ.,* November 1984, *17*(3/4), pp. 279–97.

Vartia, Yrjö O. and Vartia, Pentti L. I. Descriptive Index Number Theory and the Bank of Finland Currency Index. *Scand. J. Econ.,* 1984, *86*(3), pp. 352–64. **[G: Finland]**

Wallich, Henry C. Floating as Seen from the Central Bank. In *Bigman, D. and Taya, T., eds.,* 1984, pp. 33–42.

Wallich, Henry C. Institutional Cooperation in the World Economy. In *Frenkel, J. A. and Mussa, M. L., eds.,* 1984, pp. 85–99. **[G: OECD]**

Warr, Peter G. Exchange Rate Protection in Indonesia. *Bull. Indonesian Econ. Stud.,* August 1984, *20*(2), pp. 53–89. **[G: Indonesia]**

Weiss, Frank D. Aspects of Real Exchange Rates—East and West. In *Csikós-Nagy, B.; Hague, D. and Hall, G., eds.,* 1984, pp. 317–32. **[G: CMEA; OECD]**

Whitman, Marina v.N. Assessing Greater Variability of Exchange Rates: A Private Sector Perspective. *Amer. Econ. Rev.,* May 1984, *74*(2), pp. 298–304.

van Wijnbergen, Sweder. Oil Price Shocks and the Current Account: An Analysis of Short Run Adjustment Measures. *Weltwirtsch. Arch.,* 1984, *120*(3), pp. 460–80. **[G: OPEC; LDCs]**

Willett, Thomas D. Macroeconomic Policy Coordination Issues under Flexible Exchange Rates. In *Eucken, W. and Böhm, F., eds.,* 1984, pp. 137–49. **[G: U.S.]**

Witzel, Ruprecht. Overshooting des Wechselkurses, Substituierbarkeit der Finanzaktiva und J-Kurve. (Overshooting of the Exchange Rate, Substitutability of Financial Assets and J-Curve. With English summary.) *Weltwirtsch. Arch.,* 1984, *120*(3), pp. 436–53.

Wogart, Jan Peter and Marques, Jose Siverio. Trade Liberalization, Tariff Redundancy and Inflation: A Methodological Exploration Applied to Argentina. *Weltwirtsch. Arch.,* 1984, *120*(1), pp. 18–39. **[G: Argentina]**

Woo, Wing T. Exchange Rates and the Prices of Nonfood, Nonfuel Products. *Brookings Pap. Econ. Act.,* 1984, (2), pp. 511–30.

Wood, Geoffrey E. Real Output and the Gold Standard Years, 1830–1913: Comment. In *Bordo, M. D. and Schwartz, A. J., eds.,* 1984, pp. 538–44. **[G: OECD]**

Yeager, Leland B. Opportunities and Implications of a Return to Fixed Exchange Rates—Is Gold an Answer for International Adjustment? In *Agmon, T.; Hawkins, R. G. and Levich, R. M., eds.,* 1984, pp. 25–41.

Yeager, Leland B. The Image of the Gold Standard. In *Bordo, M. D. and Schwartz, A. J.,* eds., 1984, pp. 651–69.

Zis, George. Flexible Exchange Rates: Lessons from the Last Decade. *Greek Econ. Rev.,* April 1984, 6(1), pp. 47–76.   **[G: OECD]**

Zis, George. The European Monetary System, 1979–84: An Assessment. *J. Common Market Stud.,* September 1984, 23(1), pp. 45–72.
                                        [G: EEC]

Zylbersztajn, Decio. Price Distortions in Brazilian Agriculture: An Application of Duality Theory and Flexible Functional Forms. *Amer. Econ.,* Fall 1984, 28(2), pp. 48–59.   **[G: Brazil]**

432 International Monetary Arrangements

4320 International Monetary Arrangements

Agmon, Tamir; Hawkins, Robert G. and Levich, Richard M. The Future of the International Monetary System: Introduction. In *Agmon, T.; Hawkins, R. G. and Levich, R. M.,* eds., 1984, pp. 1–9.

Aliber, Robert Z. The Potential for Financial Crises: Comment. In *Agmon, T.; Hawkins, R. G. and Levich, R. M.,* eds., 1984, pp. 110–15.

Asheim, Geir B. Properties of a System of Currency Baskets. *J. Int. Econ.,* May 1984, 16(3/4), pp. 311–17.

Bacha, Edmar L. Brazil and the IMF: Prologue to the Third Letter of Intent. *Industry Devel.,* 1984, (12), pp. 101–13.   **[G: Brazil]**

Bahmani-Oskooee, Mohsen. Gold Price as Another Determinant of Demand for International Reserves. *J. Econ. Stud.,* 1984, 11(4), pp. 23–32.   **[G: OECD]**

Baqai, Moinuddin. A New Framework for International Financial Co-operation for Development. In *Ghosh, P. K., ed., no. 15,* 1984, 1979, pp. 222–38.

Bergsten, C. Fred. The Role of the Fund: Discussion. In *Fed. Res. Bank Boston,* 1984, pp. 267–71.

Bergstrand, Jeffrey H. Bretton Woods Revisited. *New Eng. Econ. Rev.,* September–October 1984, pp. 23–33.

Bergstrand, Jeffrey H. The International Monetary System: Forty Years after Bretton Woods: Summary. In *Fed. Res. Bank Boston,* 1984, pp. 1–14.

Bernstein, Edward M. A Program for International Monetary Stability: Comment. In *Agmon, T.; Hawkins, R. G. and Levich, R. M.,* eds., 1984, pp. 78–84.   **[G: OECD]**

Bernstein, Edward M. Do We Need a New Bretton Woods? *Finance Devel.,* September 1984, 21(3), pp. 5–7.   **[G: Global]**

Bernstein, Edward M. Reflections on Bretton Woods. In *Fed. Res. Bank Boston,* 1984, pp. 15–20.

Bird, Graham. Relationships, Resource Uses and the Conditionality Debate. In *Killick, Tony, ed. (II),* 1984, pp. 145–82.   **[G: LDCs]**

Bird, Roger. International Financial Disorder. In *Jorge, A.; Salazar-Carrillo, J. and Sanchez, E. P.,* 1984, pp. 105–20.   **[G: Global]**

Blanchard, Olivier J. Macroeconomic Policy Coordination among the Industrial Economies: Comments. *Brookings Pap. Econ. Act.,* 1984, (1), pp. 65–68.   **[G: U.S.; W. Germany; Japan]**

Boeck, Klaus. The Supply of International Liquidity to Developing Countries. In *Ghosh, P. K., ed., no. 7,* 1984, 1977, pp. 195–203.

van den Boogaerde, Pierre. The Private SDR: An Assessment of Its Risk and Return. *Int. Monet. Fund Staff Pap.,* March 1984, 31(1), pp. 25–61.

Borchardt, Knut. Could and Should Germany Have Followed Great Britain in Leaving the Gold Standard? *J. Europ. Econ. Hist.,* September–December 1984, 13(3), pp. 471–97.
                                        [G: Germany]

Bordo, Michael D. On the Report of the Gold Commission (1982) and Convertible Monetary Systems: A Comment. *Carnegie-Rochester Conf. Ser. Public Policy,* Spring 1984, 20, pp. 269–73.

Bradford, Colin I., Jr. World Economic Outlook and the Prospects for U.S. Exports to Latin America. In *Jorge, A.; Salazar-Carrillo, J. and Sanchez, E. P.,* 1984, pp. 121–25.
                                        [G: Global]

Brodsky, David A. and Sampson, Gary P. The Sources of Exchange Rate Instability in Developing Countries: Dollar, French Franc and SDR Pegging Countries. *Weltwirtsch. Arch.,* 1984, 120(1), pp. 133–54.   **[G: LDCs; U.S.; France]**

Brunner, Karl. Monetary Policy and Monetary Order. *Aussenwirtschaft,* September 1984, 39(3), pp. 187–206.

Buira, Ariel. Is There a Need for Reform? Discussion. In *Fed. Res. Bank Boston,* 1984, pp. 44–51.

Cagan, Phillip. The Report of the Gold Commission (1982). *Carnegie-Rochester Conf. Ser. Public Policy,* Spring 1984, 20, pp. 247–67.

Calika, Nur. Somalia's Adjustment Experience, 1981–83. *Finance Devel.,* March 1984, 21(1), pp. 8.   **[G: Somalia]**

Calleo, David P. and Strange, Susan. Paths to International Political Economy: Money and World Politics. In *Strange, S., ed.,* 1984, pp. 91–125.   **[G: U.S.; Global]**

Carli, Guido. Contributo all'aggiornamento della disciplina valutaria nella prospettiva della unificazione dei mercati finanziari europei. (A Contribution of Amendment of Foreign-Exchange Regulations in the Prospect of Unification of European Financial Markets. With English summary.) *Bancaria,* January 1984, 40(1), pp. 29–37.   **[G: Italy]**

de Cecco, Marcello and Miller, Marcus H. Monetary Targeting in Europe. In *Hewlett, S. A.; Kaufman, H. and Kenen, P. B., eds.,* 1984, pp. 123–50.   **[G: OECD]**

Chaufournier, Roger. The Coming of Age. *Finance Devel.,* June 1984, 21(2), pp. 32–35.

Clark, Truman A. Violations of the Gold Points, 1890–1908. *J. Polit. Econ.,* October 1984, 92(5), pp. 791–823.   **[G: U.S.; U.K.]**

Clarotti, Paolo. Progress and Future Development of Establishment and Services in the EC in Relation to Banking. *J. Common Market Stud.*, March 1984, *22*(3), pp. 199–226. [G: EEC]

Cooke, Peter. The Basle "Concordat" on the Supervision of Banks' Foreign Establishments. *Aussenwirtschaft*, May 1984, *39*(1/2), pp. 151–65. [G: OECD]

Cooper, Richard N. A Monetary System for the Future. *Foreign Aff.*, Fall 1984, *63*(1), pp. 166–84. [G: Global]

Cooper, Richard N. Is There a Need for Reform? In *Fed. Res. Bank Boston*, 1984, pp. 21–39.

Cooper, Richard N. Recent History of World Monetary Problems. In *Agmon, T.; Hawkins, R. G. and Levich, R. M., eds.*, 1984, pp. 11–22.

Corden, W. M. International Liquidity: Are the Supply and Composition Appropriate? Discussion. In *Fed. Res. Bank Boston*, 1984, pp. 78–82.

Dale, William B. The IMF's Role in a Changing World. *Finance Develop.*, March 1984, *21*(1), pp. 2–4.

Davies, Robert and Jones, Philip R. International Trade. In *Sandford, C. and Bradbury, M., eds.*, 1984, pp. 188–218. [G: EEC]

Dhesi, Autar S. Recent Books on the International Monetary System. *Indian Econ. J.*, January–March 1984, *31*(3), pp. 97–102.

Dini, Lamberto. The Changing International Monetary System. *Banca Naz. Lavoro Quart. Rev.*, December 1984, (151), pp. 423–31.

Dini, Lamberto. Un nuovo codice per la cooperazione internazionale. (A New Code for International Cooperation. With English summary.) *Bancaria*, October 1984, *40*(10), pp. 949–56. [G: EEC]

Diz, Adolfo C. The Conditions Attached to Adjustment Financing; Evolution of the IMF Practice. In *Fed. Res. Bank Boston*, 1984, pp. 214–35.

Dufey, Gunter and Giddy, Ian H. Eurocurrency Deposit Risk. *J. Banking Finance*, December 1984, *8*(4), pp. 567–89. [G: OECD]

Eichengreen, Barry. Central Bank Cooperation under the Interwar Gold Standard. *Exploration Econ. Hist.*, January 1984, *21*(1), pp. 64–87. [G: France; U.K.]

Endres, Werner. Euro-Märkte: Entstehung—Funktion—Bedeutung. (Euro-markets: Genesis—Function—Significance. With English summary.) *Konjunkturpolitik*, 1984, *30*(2/3), pp. 119–47. [G: EEC]

Epstein, José D. Some Financial Issues in the North, in the South, and in Between: Comment. In *Agmon, T.; Hawkins, R. G. and Levich, R. M., eds.*, 1984, pp. 146–50.

Fabbri, Miguel A. The IMF's Conditionality Re-Examined: Comment. In *Muns, J., ed.*, 1984, pp. 80–83. [G: LDCs]

Fischer, Bernhard. South Bank and Third World Money. A Critical Assessment. *Konjunkturpolitik*, 1984, *30*(5), pp. 317–25. [G: LDCs]

Flood, Robert P. and Garber, Peter M. Collaps-ing Exchange-Rate Regimes: Some Linear Examples. *J. Int. Econ.*, August 1984, *17*(1/2), pp. 1–13.

Frenkel, Jacob A. A Program for International Monetary Stability: Comment. In *Agmon, T.; Hawkins, R. G. and Levich, R. M., eds.*, 1984, pp. 85–89. [G: OECD]

Frenkel, Jacob A. Exchange Rate Arrangements in the Eighties: Discussion. In *Fed. Res. Bank Boston*, 1984, pp. 119–25.

von Furstenberg, George M. Economic and Financial Stability: Comment. In *Wachter, M. L. and Wachter, S. M., eds.*, 1984, pp. 416–19. [G: Global; U.S.]

Garavoglia, Guido. From Rambouillet to Williamsburg: A Historical Assessment. In *Merlini, C., ed.*, 1984, pp. 1–42. [G: OECD]

Gleske, Leonhard. Erfahrungen mit flexiblen Wechselkursen. (Experience with Flexible Exchange Rates. With English summary.) *Kredit Kapital*, 1984, *17*(4), pp. 455–73. [G: W. Germany]

Gold, Joseph [Sir]. A New Universal and A New Regional Monetary Asset: SDR and ECU. In *Gold, J.*, 1984, *1983*, pp. 659–722.

Gold, Joseph [Sir]. Continuity and Change in the International Monetary Fund. In *Gold, J.*, 1984, pp. 381–452.

Gold, Joseph [Sir]. Convertible Currency Clauses Under Present International Monetary Arrangements. In *Gold, J.*, 1984, *1979*, pp. 803–38.

Gold, Joseph [Sir]. Developments in the International Monetary System, the International Monetary Fund, and International Monetary Law Since 1971. In *Gold, J.*, 1984, *1982*, pp. 17–254.

Gold, Joseph [Sir]. Effects of Variable Exchange Rates on Treaties. In *Gold, J.*, 1984, *1982*, pp. 580–623.

Gold, Joseph [Sir]. Gold in International Monetary Law: Change, Uncertainty, and Ambiguity. In *Gold, J.*, 1984, *1981*, pp. 723–77.

Gold, Joseph [Sir]. Keynes on Legal Problems of International Organization. In *Gold, J.*, 1984, *1981*, pp. 841–61.

Gold, Joseph [Sir]. Legal and Institutional Aspects of the International Monetary System: Selected Essays: Introduction. In *Gold, J.*, 1984, pp. 1–14.

Gold, Joseph [Sir]. Legal Models for the International Regulation of Exchange Rates. In *Gold, J.*, 1984, pp. 624–55.

Gold, Joseph [Sir]. Legal Models for the International Regulation of Exchange Rates. *Mich. Law Rev.*, April–May 1984, *82*(5 & 6), pp. 1533–54.

Gold, Joseph [Sir]. Relations Between Banks' Loan Agreements and Fund Stand-By Arrangements. In *Gold, J.*, 1984, *1983*, pp. 781–802.

Gold, Joseph [Sir]. Some Impressions of the Early Fund. *Finance Develop.*, March 1984, *21*(1), pp. 23–25.

Gold, Joseph [Sir]. Strengthening the Soft International Law of Exchange Arrangements. In *Gold, J.*, 1984, *1983*, pp. 515–79.

Gold, Joseph [Sir]. Substitution in the International Monetary System. In *Gold, J.*, 1984, *1980*, pp. 308–78.

Gold, Joseph [Sir]. Symmetry as a Legal Objective of the International Monetary System. In *Gold, J.*, 1984, *1980*, pp. 255–307.

Gold, Joseph [Sir]. The Distinction Between "Intergovernmental" and "Interstate" Treaties and Organizations: The International Monetary Fund Agreement—A Note on Mr. Obeyesekere's Note. In *Gold, J.*, 1984, pp. 876–89.

Gold, Joseph [Sir]. The Fund Agreement in the Courts—XX. *Int. Monet. Fund Staff Pap.*, December 1984, *31*(4), pp. 709–41.

Gold, Joseph [Sir]. The Fund Agreement in the Courts—XIX. *Int. Monet. Fund Staff Pap.*, March 1984, *31*(1), pp. 179–234.

Gold, Joseph [Sir]. The General Arrangements to Borrow of the International Monetary Fund. In *Gold, J.*, 1984, pp. 478–511.

Gold, Joseph [Sir]. The Relationship Between the International Monetary Fund and the World Bank. In *Gold, J.*, 1984, *1981*, pp. 453–77.

Gold, Joseph [Sir]. Trust Funds in International Law: The Contribution of the International Monetary Fund to a Code of Principles. In *Gold, J.*, 1984, *1978*, pp. 862–75.

Goldman, Morris B. The United States Treasury Review of the Multilateral Development Banks: An Economic Critique. *J. Monet. Econ.*, March 1984, *13*(2), pp. 275–93. [G: U.S.]

Goldstein, Morris. Whither the Exchange Rate System? *Finance Develop.*, June 1984, *21*(2), pp. 2–6.

Gollas, Manuel. Mexico's Perspectives under a Three-Year Agreement with the IMF: Remarks. In *Jorge, A.; Salazar-Carrillo, J. and Sanchez, E. P.*, 1984, pp. 69–70. [G: Mexico]

Goodman, Laurie S. Eurodollars and the U.S. Monetary Aggregates. *Bus. Econ.*, January 1984, *19*(1), pp. 40–46. [G: U.S.]

Guillaumont, Sylviane. La situation monétaire et finacière des États africains de la zone franc. (With English summary.) *Revue Écon. Polit.*, September–October 1984, *94*(5), pp. 592–601. [G: Africa]

Guttentag, Jack M. and Herring, Richard J. International Banking: Vulnerability and Crisis. In *Wachter, M. L. and Wachter, S. M., eds.*, 1984, pp. 355–89. [G: Global; U.S.]

Gwin, Catherine. Strengthening the Framework of the Global Economic Organizations. In *Bhagwati, J. N. and Ruggie, J. G., eds.*, 1984, pp. 125–77.

Gwin, Catherine. The IMF and the World Bank: Measures to Improve the System. In *Feinberg, R. E. and Kallab, V., eds., no. 2*, 1984, pp. 87–106. [G: LDCs; OECD]

Haberler, Gottfried. The International Monetary System in the World Recession. In *Fellner, W., ed.*, 1984, pp. 87–129. [G: OECD]

Hall, Robert E. International Banking: Vulnerability and Crisis: Comment. In *Wachter,*

M. L. and Wachter, S. M., eds., 1984, pp. 424–27. [G: Global; U.S.]

Hamaui, Rony. Lo sviluppo dei mercati finanziari in ECU: una prima valutazione su rischi e rendimenti. (The Development of Financial Markets in ECU: An Initial Evaluation Regarding Risks and Yields. With English summary.) *Bancaria*, May–June 1984, *40*(5–6), pp. 513–29. [G: EEC]

Hasche-Preusse, Christine. ECU—Von der Insider- zur Parallelwährung? Entwicklung, Be standsaufnahme und Perspektiven. *Kredit Kapital*, 1984, *17*(3), pp. 416–40. [G: EEC]

von Hayek, Friedrich A. The Fate of the Gold Standard. In *von Hayek, F. A. (II)*, 1984, *1932*, pp. 118–35. [G: U.K.; U.S.]

Heffernan, Shelagh A. Reflections on the Case for an International Central Bank. *Greek Econ. Rev.*, April 1984, *6*(1), pp. 99–120. [G: Global]

Hicks, John R. Lineamenti storici dei metodi di controllo della moneta. (Methods of Monetary Control. With English summary.) *Bancaria*, November 1984, *40*(11), pp. 1069–75. [G: U.K.]

Hood, William C. Outlook for the World Financial System: The IMF Perspective. *Contemp. Policy Issue*, January 1984, (4), pp. 76–82. [G: Global]

Hoopengardner, Thomas and Garcia-Thoumi, Ines. The World Bank in a Changing Financial Environment. *Finance Develop.*, June 1984, *21*(2), pp. 12–14.

Humphrey, Thomas M. and Keleher, Robert E. The Lender of Last Resort: A Historical Perspective [International Debt, Bank Failures, and the Money Supply: The Thirties and the Eighties]. *Cato J.*, Spring/Summer 1984, *4*(1), pp. 275–318. [G: U.K.]

Hürni, Bettina. Der Beitritt der Schweiz zu den Institutionen von Bretton Woods: Wirtschaftliche Aspekte. (The Swiss Accession to the Bretton Woods: Economic Aspects. With English summary.) *Schweiz. Z. Volkswirtsch. Statist.*, June 1984, *120*(2), pp. 123–39.

Islam, Nurul. New Mechanisms for the Transfer of Resources to Developing Countries. In *Ghosh, P. K., ed., no. 10*, 1984, *1976*, pp. 145–89.

Jarchow, Hans-Joachim. Devisenmarktinterventionen und Liquiditätswirkungen. (Exchange Market Interventions and Liquidity Effects. With English summary.) *Aussenwirtschaft*, December 1984, *39*(4), pp. 299–321. [G: U.S.; W. Europe]

Kamarck, Andrew M. The World Bank and Development: A Personal Perspective. *Finance Develop.*, December 1984, *21*(4), pp. 26–28. [G: Global]

Karunaratne, Neil Dias. Foreign Aid, New Economic Order and Basic Human Needs. In *Ghosh, P. K., ed., no. 9*, 1984, *1979*, pp. 135–44.

Killick, Tony. An Introduction to the International Monetary Fund. In *Killick, Tony, ed. (II)*, 1984, pp. 128–44. [G: Global]

Killick, Tony. IMF Stabilisation Programmes. In *Killick, Tony, ed. (II),* 1984, pp. 183–226.

Killick, Tony. The Impact of Fund Stabilisation Programmes. In *Killick, Tony, ed. (II),* 1984, pp. 227–69. **[G: LDCs]**

Killick, Tony. The IMF and Stabilisation: Kenya, 1975–81. In *Killick, Tony, ed. (I),* 1984, pp. 164–216. **[G: Kenya]**

Killick, Tony, et al. The IMF: Case for a Change in Emphasis. In *Feinberg, R. E. and Kallab, V., eds., no. 1,* 1984, pp. 59–81. **[G: LDCs; OECD]**

Killick, Tony, et al. Towards a Real Economy Approach. In *Killick, Tony, ed. (II),* 1984, pp. 270–320. **[G: LDCs]**

Konstantinov, Iu. A. The Interaction of National Currencies with International Socialist Currency. *Soviet E. Europ. Foreign Trade,* Spring 1984, *20*(1), pp. 57–75. **[G: CMEA]**

Krugman, Paul R. The International Role of the Dollar: Theory and Prospect. In *Bilson, J. F. O. and Marston, R. C., eds.,* 1984, pp. 261–78. **[G: OECD; U.S.]**

Kuhn, W. E. Settling for Less: European Monetary System vs. European Monetary Union. *J. Econ. Issues,* June 1984, *18*(2), pp. 517–26.

Laney, Leroy O.; Radcliffe, Christopher D. and Willett, Thomas D. Currency Substitution: Comment. *Southern Econ. J.,* April 1984, *50*(4), pp. 1196–1200. **[G: U.S.; W. Germany]**

Lara, Juan. Mexico's Perspectives under a Three-Year Agreement with the IMF. In *Jorge, A.; Salazar-Carrillo, J. and Sanchez, E. P.,* 1984, pp. 61–68. **[G: Mexico]**

Lessard, Donald R. Some Financial Issues in the North, in the South, and in Between: Comment. In *Agmon, T.; Hawkins, R. G. and Levich, R. M., eds.,* 1984, pp. 151–56.

Lomax, David F. The European Monetary System, Real Exchange Rates and the European Currency Unit. *Irish Banking Rev.,* December 1984, pp. 37–51. **[G: W. Europe]**

Marris, Stephen N. Macroeconomic Policy Coordination among the Industrial Economies: Comments. *Brookings Pap. Econ. Act.,* 1984, (1), pp. 68–71. **[G: U.S.; W. Germany; Japan]**

Masera, Rainer S. and Triffin, Robert. Europe's Money: Introduction. In *Masera, R. S. and Triffin, R., eds.,* 1984, pp. 1–10.

Maynard, Geoffrey W. The Role of Financial Institutions. In *Black, J. and Dorrance, G. S., eds.,* 1984, pp. 21–34. **[G: LDCs; MDCs]**

McKinnon, Ronald I. A Program for International Monetary Stability. In *Agmon, T.; Hawkins, R. G. and Levich, R. M., eds.,* 1984, pp. 55–77. **[G: OECD]**

Meiselman, David I. The Lender of Last Resort and a Money Supply Rule [International Debt, Bank Failures, and the Money Supply: The Thirties and the Eighties]. *Cato J.,* Spring/Summer 1984, *4*(1), pp. 319–21. **[G: U.K.]**

Metghalchi, Massoud. The European Monetary System: Has It Worked? *Atlantic Econ. J.,* July 1984, *12*(2), pp. 78. **[G: EEC]**

Micossi, Stefano. La politica monetaria nella CEE. (Monetary Policy in the EEC. With English summary.) *Bancaria,* August 1984, *40*(8), pp. 759–69. **[G: EEC]**

Miles, Marc A. Currency Substitution: Reply. *Southern Econ. J.,* April 1984, *50*(4), pp. 1201–03. **[G: U.S.; W. Germany]**

Minsky, Hyman P. The Potential for Financial Crises. In *Agmon, T.; Hawkins, R. G. and Levich, R. M., eds.,* 1984, pp. 91–109.

Moncarz, Raul. The Economic Outlook for Latin America and the IMF. In *Jorge, A.; Salazar-Carrillo, J. and Sanchez, E. P.,* 1984, pp. 21–23. **[G: Latin America]**

Nesi, Nerio. Il sistema monetario internazionale e la crisi dell'indebitamento: necessità di soluzioni strutturali. (The International Monetary System and the Debt Crisis: Need for a Structural Solution. With English summary.) *Bancaria,* April 1984, *40*(4), pp. 371–76.

Niehans, Jürg. National Monetary Policy in an International Capital Market. *Kobe Econ. Bus. Rev.,* 1984, *30*, pp. 1–10.

Nsouli, Saleh M. Monetary Integration in Developing Countries. In *Ghosh, P. K., ed., no. 12, 1984, 1981,* pp. 153–58.

Olmer, Lionel H. Trade, Debt and Growth in Latin America: Closing Statement. In *Jorge, A.; Salazar-Carrillo, J. and Sanchez, E. P.,* 1984, pp. 157–65. **[G: U.S.; Latin America]**

Oudiz, Gilles and Sachs, Jeffrey D. Macroeconomic Policy Coordination among the Industrial Economies. *Brookings Pap. Econ. Act.,* 1984, (1), pp. 1–64. **[G: U.S.; W. Germany; Japan]**

Oweiss, Ibrahim M. Petrodollar Surpluses: Trends and Economic Impact. *J. Energy Devel.,* Spring 1984, *9*(2), pp. 177–202. **[G: OPEC]**

Pelkmans, Jacques. Collective Management and Economic Cooperation. In *Merlini, C., ed.,* 1984, pp. 89–136. **[G: OECD]**

Péteri, György. The Inflation-Proof Gold Standard: The Foreign Policy of *Riksbankschefen.* Victor Moll and the Origin of the Swedish Ban on Gold Imports in 1924. *J. Europ. Econ. Hist.,* September–December 1984, *13*(3), pp. 635–63. **[G: Sweden]**

Polak, Jacques J. The Role of the Fund. In *Fed. Res. Bank Boston,* 1984, pp. 245–66. **[G: OECD]**

Pozo, Susan. Composition and Variability of the SDR. *Rev. Econ. Statist.,* May 1984, *66*(2), pp. 308–14.

Prussia, Leland S. Outlook for the World Financial System: A Banker's Perspective. *Contemp. Policy Issue,* January 1984, (4), pp. 64–70. **[G: Global]**

Putnam, Robert. The Western Economic Summits: A Political Interpretation. In *Merlini, C., ed.,* 1984, pp. 43–88. **[G: OECD]**

Ray, Edward John and Marvel, Howard P. The Pattern of Protection in the Industrialized World. *Rev. Econ. Statist.,* August 1984, *66*(3), pp. 452–58. **[G: U.S.; Japan; EEC; Canada]**

Riolo, Franco. Il mercato privato dell'ECU Profili

giuridici. (The ECU Private Market: Some Juridical Aspects. With English summary.) *Bancaria*, August 1984, *40*(8), pp. 741–58. [G: EEC]

Robichek, E. Walter. The IMF's Conditionality Re-Examined. In *Muns, J., ed.*, 1984, pp. 67–75. [G: LDCs]

Rodriguez-Pastor, Carlos. Outlook for the World Financial System: A Borrower's Perspective. *Contemp. Policy Issue*, January 1984, (4), pp. 71–75. [G: Global; Peru]

Roll, Eric [Lord]. Is There a Need for Reform? Discussion. In *Fed. Res. Bank Boston*, 1984, pp. 40–43.

Roosa, Robert V. Exchange Rate Arrangements in the Eighties. In *Fed. Res. Bank Boston*, 1984, pp. 104–18.

von Rosen, Rüdiger. Zuversicht bei der IWF-Währungskonferenz. (A Mood of Confidence at the IMF Meeting. With English summary.) *Kredit Kapital*, 1984, *17*(4), pp. 580–93. [G: Global]

Salda, Anne C. M. The International Monetary Fund, 1983: A Selected Bibliography. *Int. Monet. Fund Staff Pap.*, Supplement, December 1984, *31*, pp. 763–809.

Salerno, Joseph. The International Gold Standard: A New Perspective. *Eastern Econ. J.*, October-December 1984, *10*(4), pp. 488–98.

Sanchez, Enrique P. Latin American Outlook Under IMF Conditionality. In *Jorge, A.; Salazar-Carrillo, J. and Sanchez, E. P.*, 1984, pp. 11–19. [G: Latin America]

von der Schulenberg, J.-Matthias Graf. Who Wants to Go Shopping with a Currency Basket? A Risk Theoretical Study. *Jahr. Nationalökon. Statist.*, January 1984, *199*(1), pp. 65–75.

Schwartz, Anna J. A Retrospective on the Classical Gold Standard, 1821–1931: Introduction. In *Bordo, M. D. and Schwartz, A. J., eds.*, 1984, pp. 1–20. [G: U.K.]

Sharpley, Jennifer. The IMF and Stabilisation: Jamaica, 1972–80. In *Killick, Tony, ed. (I)*, 1984, pp. 115–63. [G: Jamaica]

Smith, Fred L., Jr. The Politics of IMF Lending. *Cato J.*, Spring/Summer 1984, *4*(1), pp. 211–41.

Sobhan, Rehman. OPEC as a Source of Capital for the Third World: The Current Perspective. *Bangladesh Devel. Stud.*, December 1984, *12*(4), pp. 1–28. [G: OPEC; LDCs]

Solomon, Anthony M. Is There a Need for Reform? Discussion. In *Fed. Res. Bank Boston*, 1984, pp. 52–57.

Solomon, Anthony M. Statement to the U.S. Senate Subcommittee on International Finance and Monetary Policy of the Committee on Banking, Housing, and Urban Affairs, May 3, 1984. *Fed. Res. Bull.*, May 1984, *70*(5), pp. 419–23. [G: U.S.; Argentina]

Solomon, Robert. The European Monetary System: Tombstone or Cornerstone?: Discussion. In *Fed. Res. Bank Boston*, 1984, pp. 174–77. [G: OECD]

Solomon, Robert. The Politics of IMF Lending:

A Comment. *Cato J.*, Spring/Summer 1984, *4*(1), pp. 243–47. [G: U.S.]

Sommers, Davidson. An Institution Emerges. *Finance Develop.*, June 1984, *21*(2), pp. 30–32.

Sorsa, Kalevi. Det internationella handels-, finans- och valutasystemet. Utvecklingstrender och reformsynpunkter. (The International Trade, Finance and Currency System: Trends and Views on Reforms. With English summary.) *Ekon. Samfundets Tidskr.*, 1984, *37*(2), pp. 65–73. [G: Global]

Sutton, Mary. Structuralism: The Latin American Record and the New Critique. In *Killick, Tony, ed. (I)*, 1984, pp. 19–67. [G: Chile; Peru]

Sutton, Mary. The IMF and Stabilisation: Indonesia, 1966–70. In *Killick, Tony, ed. (I)*, 1984, pp. 68–114. [G: Indonesia]

Swanson, Peggy E. External Currency Market Data: An Application from BIS Series. *J. Int. Money Finance*, April 1984, *3*(1), pp. 111–17.

Swoboda, Alexander K. Sui compiti futuri delle istituzioni finanziarie internazionali. (Some Reflections on the Future Role of Intergovernmental Financial Institutions. With English summary.) *Bancaria*, December 1984, *40*(12), pp. 1218–27. [G: Global]

Sylos-Labini, Paolo. Rigid Prices, Flexible Prices, and Inflation. In *Sylos-Labini, P.*, 1984, *1982*, pp. 147–82.

di Tella, Guido. The IMF's Conditionality Re-Examined: Comment. In *Muns, J., ed.*, 1984, pp. 76–79. [G: LDCs]

Thore, Sten. Spatial Models of the Eurodollar Market. *J. Banking Finance*, March 1984, *8*(1), pp. 51–65.

Thygesen, Niels. Exchange-rate Policies and Monetary Targets in the EMS Countries. In *Masera, R. S. and Triffin, R., eds.*, 1984, pp. 262–86. [G: EEC]

Triffin, Robert. How to End the World 'Infession': Crisis Management or Fundamental Reforms? In *Masera, R. S. and Triffin, R., eds.*, 1984, pp. 13–76. [G: U.S.; Global]

Triffin, Robert. The European Monetary System: Tombstone or Cornerstone? In *Fed. Res. Bank Boston*, 1984, pp. 127–73. [G: EEC]

Triffin, Robert. The Relationship between the International Monetary System and Regional Monetary Systems. In *[Reynolds, L. G.]*, 1984, pp. 75–95. [G: Global]

Tumlir, Jan. Economic Policy for a Stable World Order. *Cato J.*, Spring/Summer 1984, *4*(1), pp. 355–64. [G: Global]

Valencia, Mario R. Gómez. The Implications of Financial and Monetary Integration in Latin America. In *Núñez del Arco, J.; Margain, E. and Cherol, R., eds.*, 1984, pp. 229–41. [G: Latin America]

Wallich, Christine I. The World Bank's Currency Swaps. *Finance Develop.*, June 1984, *21*(2), pp. 15–19.

Wallich, Henry C. Institutional Cooperation in the World Economy. In *Frenkel, J. A. and Mussa, M. L., eds.*, 1984, pp. 85–99. [G: OECD]

Wallich, Henry C. Outlook for the World Financial System: A Central Banker's Perspective. *Contemp. Policy Issue*, January 1984, (4), pp. 54–63. [G: Global]

Wiesner, Eduardo. The Conditions Attached to Adjustment Financing; Evolution of the IMF Practice: Discussion. In *Fed. Res. Bank Boston*, 1984, pp. 236–43.

Williams, Phil; Wallace, William and Woolcock, Stephen. Atlantic Relations. In *Boyd, G., ed.*, 1984, pp. 25–52. [G: U.S.; W. Europe]

Williamson, John. International Liquidity: Are the Supply and Composition Appropriate? In *Fed. Res. Bank Boston*, 1984, pp. 59–77.

Witteveen, H. Johannes. Verso un nuovo sistema monetario internazionale: prospettiva di lungo periodo. (Developing a New Monetary System: A Long Term View. With English summary.) *Bancaria*, February 1984, *40*(2), pp. 129–39. [G: Global]

Woo, Wing T. Macroeconomic Policy Coordination among the Industrial Economies: Comments. *Brookings Pap. Econ. Act.*, 1984, (1), pp. 71–74. [G: U.S.]

Zis, George. Flexible Exchange Rates: Lessons from the Last Decade. *Greek Econ. Rev.*, April 1984, *6*(1), pp. 47–76. [G: OECD]

Zis, George. The European Monetary System, 1979–84: An Assessment. *J. Common Market Stud.*, September 1984, *23*(1), pp. 45–72. [G: EEC]

433 Private International Lending

4330 Private International Lending

Ahn, Kookshin. Optimal Foreign Borrowing and Altruism in an Overlapping Generations Model. *J. Econ. Devel.*, December 1984, *9*(2), pp. 171–90.

Aliber, Robert Z. Capital Flows, External Debt and the International Adjustment Process. In *Black, J. and Dorrance, G. S., eds.*, 1984, pp. 1–20. [G: LDCs]

Aliber, Robert Z. Il futuro dell'attività bancaria internazionale. (The Future of International Commercial Banking. With English summary.) *Bancaria*, December 1984, *40*(12), pp. 1201–10. [G: U.S.]

Aliber, Robert Z. International Banking: A Survey. *J. Money, Credit, Banking*, Part 2 November 1984, *16*(4), pp. 661–78. [G: OECD]

Altman, Edward I. Company and Country Risk Models: Introduction. *J. Banking Finance*, June 1984, *8*(2), pp. 151.

Arndt, Sven W. Liberalization Policies and the Implementation Question [The Impoverishing Effects of Foreign Aid]. *Cato J.*, Spring/Summer 1984, *4*(1), pp. 335–37.

Ayau, Manuel F. The Impoverishing Effects of Foreign Aid. *Cato J.*, Spring/Summer 1984, *4*(1), pp. 323–34.

Bensión, Alberto. The Role of Commercial Banks in the Adjustment Process: Comment. In *Muns, J., ed.*, 1984, pp. 211–14. [G: LDCs]

Bernal, Richard L. Economic Growth and External Debt of Jamaica. In *Salazar-Carillo, J. and*

Tirado de Alonso, I., eds., no. 1, 1984, pp. 1–27. [G: Jamaica]

Bernholz, Peter. Inflation, Over-indebtedness, Crisis and Consolidation: Argentina and the Baring Crisis (1884–1900). *Z. ges. Staatswiss.*, December 1984, *140*(4), pp. 669–84. [G: Argentina]

Biagioli, Antonello. Principali aspetti evolutivi del debito estero dell'Italia. (Principal Aspects of the Development of Italy's Foreign Debt. With English summary.) *Bancaria*, February 1984, *40*(2), pp. 178–82. [G: Italy]

Boffito, Carlo. Il finanziamento bancario internazionale dei paesi in via di sviluppo e dei paesi europei del Comecon negli anni '70 e '80. (International Financing for Developing Countries and for the European Comecon Countries in the 1970s and 1980s. With English summary.) *Bancaria*, March 1984, *40*(3), pp. 279–94. [G: LDCs; CMEA]

Bogdanowicz-Bindert, Christine A. and Sacks, Paul M. The Role of Information: Closing the Barn Door? In *Feinberg, R. E. and Kallab, V., eds., no. 2*, 1984, pp. 69–78. [G: U.S.]

van den Boogaerde, Pierre. The Private SDR. *Finance Develop.*, June 1984, *21*(2), pp. 20–22.

Brainard, Lawrence J. More Lending to the Third World? A Banker's View. In *Feinberg, R. E. and Kallab, V., eds., no. 2*, 1984, pp. 31–44. [G: LDCs; U.S.]

Brock, William E. Trade and Debt: The Vital Linkage. *Foreign Aff.*, Summer 1984, *62*(5), pp. 1037–57. [G: Global]

Brovedani, Bruno. Cooperazione tra Fondo Monetario e banche internazionali. Strategia di ripiego o collaborazione permanente? (Cooperation between the IMF and International Banks: An Expedient or a Permanent Collaboration Strategy? With English summary.) *Bancaria*, December 1984, *40*(12), pp. 1228–32.

Brunner, Karl. Resolving the Debt Problem: Some Policy Considerations [U.S. Macroeconomic Policy and Third World Debt]. *Cato J.*, Spring/Summer 1984, *4*(1), pp. 97–103. [G: U.S.; LDCs]

Burnham, James B. World Debt and Monetary Order: Learning from the Past. *Cato J.*, Spring/Summer 1984, *4*(1), pp. 71–80. [G: Global]

Carli, Guido and Savona, Paolo. Il commercio mondiale e la finanza internazionale. Annotazioni per la pianificazione strategica delle banche di credito internazionale. (World Trade and International Finance: Considerations for Strategic Planning by International Banks. With English summary.) *Bancaria*, December 1984, *40*(12), pp. 1233–40. [G: Global]

Chapman, Sheila A. The Foreign Debt of CMEA Nations: A Move towards Adjustment? *Econ. Notes*, 1984, (2), pp. 51–75. [G: CMEA]

Clark, George J. Foreign Banks in the Domestic Markets of Developing Countries. In *Feinberg, R. E. and Kallab, V., eds., no. 2*, 1984, pp. 79–86. [G: LDCs; U.S.]

Cline, William R. Restoring Credibility to International Lending: A Comment. *Cato J.*, Spring/

Summer 1984, *4*(1), pp. 141–46. **[G: Global]**

Cline, William R. The Issue Is Illiquidity, Not Insolvency. *Challenge*, July/August 1984, *27*(3), pp. 12–20. **[G: Latin America]**

Cline, William R.; Vidal, D. and Seaberry, J. Banca e Finanza nell' America Latina. (Debt Recovery: A Qualified Hope for Latin America. With English summary.) *Mondo Aperto*, March-April 1984, *38*(2), pp. 77–94. **[G: Latin America]**

Cockaerts, M. The Debt Problem: A Challenge for the Banks. *Tijdschrift Econ. Manage.*, 1984, *29*(4), pp. 539–52. **[G: LDCs]**

Cohen, Benjamin J. High Finance, High Politics. In *Feinberg, R. E. and Kallab, V., eds., no. 2*, 1984, pp. 107–24. **[G: LDCs; U.S.]**

Cucinotta, Giovanni. L'analisi delle condizioni dei prestiti internazionali con particolare riferimento alle determinanti degli "spread." (An Analysis of the Terms and Conditions of International Loans, with Particular Reference to the Spread Determinants. With English summary.) *Bancaria*, April 1984, *40*(4), pp. 402–14. **[G: Global]**

Delatour, Leslie. LDC's Debt and the Private Banks. In *Salazar-Carillo, J. and Tirado de Alonso, I., eds., no. 1*, 1984, pp. 1–43. **[G: LDCs]**

Devlin, Robert. The Burden of Debt and the Crisis: Is It Time for a Unilateral Solution? *Cepal Rev.*, April 1984, (22), pp. 107–20. **[G: Latin America]**

Díaz-Alejandro, Carlos F. Some Financial Issues in the North, in the South, and in Between. In *Agmon, T.; Hawkins, R. G. and Levich, R. M., eds.*, 1984, pp. 119–45.

Donovan, Donal J. Nature and Origins of Debt-servicing Difficulties: Some Empirical Evidence. *Finance Develop.*, December 1984, *21*(4), pp. 22–25. **[G: LDCs]**

Dorn, James A. A Property Rights View of the Debt Crisis. *Cato J.*, Spring/Summer 1984, *4*(1), pp. 1–8. **[G: Global]**

Dornbusch, Rudiger. On the Consequences of Muddling through the Debt Crisis. *World Econ.*, June 1984, *7*(2), pp. 145–61. **[G: Latin America; U.S.]**

Dornbusch, Rudiger. The Latin American Dimension. *Challenge*, July/August 1984, *27*(3), pp. 4–11. **[G: U.S.; Latin America]**

Edwards, Sebastian. LDC Foreign Borrowing and Default Risk: An Empirical Investigation, 1976–80. *Amer. Econ. Rev.*, September 1984, *74*(4), pp. 726–34. **[G: LDCs]**

Epstein, José D. Some Financial Issues in the North, in the South, and in Between: Comment. In *Agmon, T.; Hawkins, R. G. and Levich, R. M., eds.*, 1984, pp. 146–50.

Feder, Gershon and Just, Richard E. Debt Crisis in an Increasingly Pessimistic International Market: The Case of Egyptian Credit, 1862–1876. *Econ. J.*, June 1984, *94*(374), pp. 340–56. **[G: Egypt]**

Feinberg, Richard E. Restoring Confidence in International Credit Markets. In *Feinberg,*

R. E. and Kallab, V., eds., no. 2, 1984, pp. 3–20. **[G: LDCs; U.S.]**

Feldstein, Martin. From Crisis to Renewed Growth. *Challenge*, July/August 1984, *27*(3), pp. 27–30. **[G: Latin America]**

Fishlow, Albert. The Debt Crisis: Round Two Ahead? In *Feinberg, R. E. and Kallab, V., eds., no. 1*, 1984, pp. 31–58. **[G: LDCs; OECD]**

Flenda, Carlo. The Internationalization of Banking and Its Economic Advantages. *Rev. Econ. Cond. Italy*, Sept.–Dec. 1984, (3), pp. 365–87. **[G: Italy]**

Franco, Giampiero and Mengarelli, Gianluigi. Il debito estero dell'Italia. (Italy's Foreign Debt. With English summary.) *Bancaria*, February 1984, *40*(2), pp. 140–45. **[G: Italy]**

von Furstenberg, George M. Economic and Financial Stability: Comment. In *Wachter, M. L. and Wachter, S. M., eds.*, 1984, pp. 416–19. **[G: Global; U.S.]**

Gold, Joseph [Sir]. Relations Between Banks' Loan Agreements and Fund Stand-By Arrangements. In *Gold, J.*, 1984, *1983*, pp. 781–802.

Gonçalves, Reinaldo. Brazil and Mexico: The IMF Stabilization Programmes and Banks' Rescheduling. *Econ. Int.*, February–May 1984, *37*(1–2), pp. 76–93. **[G: Brazil; Mexico]**

Goodman, Laurie S. International Banking: A Survey: Comment. *J. Money, Credit, Banking*, Part 2 November 1984, *16*(4), pp. 678–84.

de Grauwe, Paul and Fratianni, Michele. The Political Economy of International Lending. *Cato J.*, Spring/Summer 1984, *4*(1), pp. 147–70. **[G: Global]**

Griffith-Jones, Stephany and Rodriguez, Ennio. Private International Finance and Industrialisation of LDCs. In *Kaplinsky, R., ed.*, 1984, pp. 47–74. **[G: LDCs]**

Griffith-Jones, Stephany and Rodriguez, Ennio. Private International Finance and Industrialisation of LDCs. *J. Devel. Stud.*, October 1984, *21*(1), pp. 47–74. **[G: Brazil; Chile]**

Guenther, Jack D. The Role of Commercial Banks in the Adjustment Process. In *Muns, J., ed.*, 1984, pp. 184–205. **[G: LDCs]**

Guerguil, Martine. The International Financial Crisis: Diagnoses and Prescriptions. *Cepal Rev.*, 1984, (24), pp. 147–69.

Guttentag, Jack M. and Herring, Richard. La pianificazione strategica delle banche internazionali contro l'incertezza. (Strategic Planning by International Banks to Cope with Incertitude. With English summary.) *Bancaria*, December 1984, *40*(12), pp. 1183–96.

Guttentag, Jack M. and Herring, Richard J. International Banking: Vulnerability and Crisis. In *Wachter, M. L. and Wachter, S. M., eds.*, 1984, pp. 355–89. **[G: Global; U.S.]**

Gwin, Catherine. The IMF and the World Bank: Measures to Improve the System. In *Feinberg, R. E. and Kallab, V., eds., no. 2*, 1984, pp. 87–106. **[G: LDCs; OECD]**

Hall, Robert E. International Banking: Vulnerability and Crisis: Comment. In *Wachter,*

M. L. and Wachter, S. M., eds., 1984, pp. 424–27. [G: Global; U.S.]

Hassan, Abdul Razek. The Arab Assistance organs and their Role in Economic Development. In *Achilli, M. and Khaldi, M.*, eds., 1984, pp. 201–19. [G: Arab Countries]

Heller, H. Robert. Regulatory Aspects of the World Debt Problem: A Comment. *Cato J.*, Spring/Summer 1984, *4*(1), pp. 125–29. [G: U.S.]

Hood, William C. Outlook for the World Financial System: The IMF Perspective. *Contemp. Policy Issue*, January 1984, (4), pp. 76–82. [G: Global]

Hope, Nicholas C. and McMurray, David W. Loan Capital in Development Finance, the Role of Banks, and Some Implications for Managing Debt. In *Black, J. and Dorrance, G. S.*, eds., 1984, pp. 93–139. [G: LDCs]

Houthakker, Hendrik S. International Banking: A Survey: Comment. *J. Money, Credit, Banking*, Part 2 November 1984, *16*(4), pp. 684–90. [G: OECD]

Hugon, Ph. Crise économique et vulnérabilité externe en Afrique sub-saharienne. (Economic Crisis and External Vulnerability in Sub-Saharian Africa. With English summary.) *Écon. Soc.*, June 1984, *18*(6), pp. 159–94. [G: Sub-Saharan Africa]

Jordan, Jerry L. Restoring Credibility to International Lending. *Cato J.*, Spring/Summer 1984, *4*(1), pp. 131–39. [G: Global]

Kharas, Homi. The Long-Run Creditworthiness of Developing Countries: Theory and Practice. *Quart. J. Econ.*, August 1984, *99*(3), pp. 415–39. [G: LDCs]

Kindleberger, Charles P. International Banks and International Business in Historical Perspective. In *Kindleberger, C. P.*, 1984, *1983*, pp. 155–70. [G: U.S.; Latin America]

Kindleberger, Charles P. International Emergency Lending Facilities—Are They Adequate? Discussion. In *Fed. Res. Bank Boston*, 1984, pp. 99–101. [G: Latin America]

Kletzer, Kenneth M. Asymmetries of Information and LDC Borrowing with Sovereign Risk. *Econ. J.*, June 1984, *94*(374), pp. 287–307.

Kuczynski, Pedro-Pablo. International Emergency Lending Facilities—Are They Adequate? In *Fed. Res. Bank Boston*, 1984, pp. 84–98. [G: LDCs; Latin America]

Kugler, Peter. Economic Indicators and Debt Reschedulings, 1977–1981: Empirical Results from a Logit Model. *Rivista Int. Sci. Econ. Com.*, October–November 1984, *31*(10–11), pp. 992–1005. [G: LDCs]

Lachmann, Werner. Kann die staatliche Kreditaufnahme im Ausland ein "Crowding-out" verhindern? (Does Public Borrowing Abroad Prevent Crowding-out Effects? With English summary.) *Jahr. Nationalökon. Statist.*, November 1984, *199*(6), pp. 522–36.

Langoni, Carlos Geraldo. Country Debt Problems: The Brazilian Case. *Cato J.*, Spring/Summer 1984, *4*(1), pp. 343–53. [G: Brazil]

Latortue, Paul R. The External Debt Situation of Haiti. In *Salazar-Carillo, J. and Tirado de Alonso, I.*, eds., no. 1, 1984, pp. 1–11. [G: Latin America; Haiti]

Ledić Michèle. Debt Analysis and Debt-Related Issues: The Case of Yugoslavia. *Econ. Anal. Worker's Manage.*, 1984, *18*(1), pp. 35–64. [G: Yugoslavia]

Leeds, Roger S. External Financing of Development: Challenges and Concerns. In *Ghosh, P. K.*, ed., no. 10, 1984, *1980*, pp. 7–30. [G: LDCs]

Lelart, M. Le nord et le sud face à la crise financière internationale. (The North and South in the International Financial Crisis. With English summary.) *Écon. Soc.*, June 1984, *18*(6), pp. 59–79. [G: Global]

van Lennep, Jonkheer Emile. Strengthening the International Trade and Financial Systems. *World Econ.*, March 1984, *7*(1), pp. 23–32. [G: OECD]

Lessard, Donald R. Some Financial Issues in the North, in the South, and in Between: Comment. In *Agmon, T.; Hawkins, R. G. and Levich, R. M.*, eds., 1984, pp. 151–56.

Lipietz, Alain. Le fordisme périphérique étranglé par le monétarisme central. (Peripheral Fords7ism Choked by Central Monetarism. With English summary.) *L'Actual. Econ.*, March 1984, *60*(1), pp. 72–94. [G: Global]

Lissakers, Karin. Bank Regulation and International Debt. In *Feinberg, R. E. and Kallab, V.*, eds., no. 2, 1984, pp. 45–68. [G: LDCs; U.S.; W. Europe]

Llewellyn, David T. Modelling International Banking Flows: An Analytical Framework. In *Black, J. and Dorrance, G. S.*, eds., 1984, pp. 35–76. [G: OECD]

Madeuf, B. and Ominami, C. Nouvelle D.I.T. et Keynésianisme planétaire: la fin des illusions. (New International Division of Labour and Worldwide Keynesianism: The End of the Illusions. With English summary.) *Écon. Soc.*, June 1984, *18*(6), pp. 81–98. [G: Global]

Martin, Ricardo and Selowsky, Marcelo. Energy Prices, Substitution, and Optimal Borrowing in the Short Run: An Analysis of Adjustment in Oil Importing Developing Countries. *J. Devel. Econ.*, April 1984, *14*(3), pp. 331–50. [G: LDCs]

Masera, Rainer S. Rischi macro e microeconomici del sistema bancario internazionale: un approccio alternativo. (Macroeconomic and Microeconomic Risks of the International Banking System: An Alternative Approach. With English summary.) *Bancaria*, December 1984, *40*(12), pp. 1197–1200. [G: LDCs]

Massad, Carlos. The Role of Commercial Banks in the Adjustment Process: Comment. In *Muns, J.*, ed., 1984, pp. 206–10. [G: LDCs]

Massad, Carlos and Zahler, Roberto. The Adjustment Process in the 1980s: The Need for a Global Approach. *Cepal Rev.*, 1984, (23), pp. 83–105. [G: Latin America]

Maynard, Geoffrey W. The Role of Financial Institutions. In *Black, J. and Dorrance, G. S.*, eds., 1984, pp. 21–34. [G: LDCs; MDCs]

Meigs, A. James. Regulatory Aspects of the World Debt Problem. *Cato J.*, Spring/Summer 1984, *4*(1), pp. 105–24. **[G: U.S.]**

Meltzer, Allan H. The International Debt Problem. *Cato J.*, Spring/Summer 1984, *4*(1), pp. 63–69. **[G: LDCs]**

Murray, John D. International Banking: A Survey: Comment. *J. Money, Credit, Banking*, Part 2 November 1984, *16*(4), pp. 690–95.

Mussa, Michael. U.S. Macroeconomic Policy and Third World Debt. *Cato J.*, Spring/Summer 1984, *4*(1), pp. 81–95. **[G: U.S.; LDCs]**

Nardolilli, Rocco. Trasferimento internazionale di risorse per lo sviluppo: il ruolo delle istituzioni multilaterali. (International Transfer of Development Resources: The Role of the Multilateral Institutions. With English summary.) *Bancaria*, October 1984, *40*(10), pp. 990–1003. **[G: Global]**

Naya, Seiji. Effects of External Shocks on the Balance of Payments, Policy Responses and Debt Problems of Asian Developing Countries. *Philippine Econ. J.*, Winter 1984, *23*(1), pp. 23–49. **[G: Asia]**

Nesi, Nerio. Il sistema monetario internazionale e la crisi dell'indebitamento: necessità di soluzioni strutturali. (The International Monetary System and the Debt Crisis: Need for a Structural Solution. With English summary.) *Bancaria*, April 1984, *40*(4), pp. 371–76.

Niehans, Jürg. La pianificazione strategica con riferimento ai crediti non esigibili. (Strategic Planning with Unenforceable Claims. With English summary.) *Bancaria*, December 1984, *40*(12), pp. 1241–44.

O'Driscoll, Gerald P., Jr. and Short, Eugenie D. Safety-Net Mechanisms: The Case of International Lending. *Cato J.*, Spring/Summer 1984, *4*(1), pp. 185–204. **[G: U.S.]**

Palmer, Ransford W. The Financial Implications of Caribbean Industrialization. In *Palmer, R. W.*, 1984, pp. 17–22. **[G: Caribbean]**

Parravicini, Giannino. Considerazioni conclusive. (Strategic Planning in International Banking: Concluding Remarks. With English summary.) *Bancaria*, December 1984, *40*(12), pp. 1245–47.

Parravicini, Giannino. Pianificazione strategica dell'attività di credito internazionale. (Strategic Planning in International Banking. With English summary.) *Bancaria*, December 1984, *40*(12), pp. 1179–82. **[G: OECD]**

Prussia, Leland S. Outlook for the World Financial System: A Banker's Perspective. *Contemp. Policy Issue*, January 1984, (4), pp. 64–70. **[G: Global]**

Qureshi, Moeen A. Mobilizing Finance for Development. *Finance Develop.*, September 1984, *21*(3), pp. 2–4. **[G: Global]**

Ragazzi, Giorgio. LDCs Debt and Net Financial Transfers: The Search for Equilibrium between Stocks and Flows. *Giorn. Econ.*, May–June 1984, *43*(5–6), pp. 359–67. **[G: LDCs]**

Ranis, Gustav. Needed: Commitment to Structural Adjustment. *Challenge*, July/August 1984, *27*(3), pp. 21–26. **[G: LDCs]**

Rodriguez-Pastor, Carlos. Outlook for the World Financial System: A Borrower's Perspective. *Contemp. Policy Issue*, January 1984, (4), pp. 71–75. **[G: Global; Peru]**

Roett, Riordan. Democracy and Debt in South America: A Continent's Dilemma. *Foreign Aff.*, 1984, *62*(3), pp. 695–720. **[G: Latin America]**

Rothgeb, John M., Jr. Investment Penetration in Manufacturing and Extraction and External Public Debt in Third World States. *World Devel.*, November–December 1984, *12*(11–12), pp. 1063–75. **[G: LDCs]**

Sachs, I. Internationalisation de l'économie ou développement endogène? les enjeux de la crise au Brésil. (Internationalization of the Economy or Endogenous Development? The Challengers of the Brazilian Crisis. With English summary.) *Écon. Soc.*, June 1984, *18*(6), pp. 195–220. **[G: Brazil]**

Saini, Krishan G. and Bates, Philip S. A Survey of the Quantitative Approaches to Country Risk Analysis. *J. Banking Finance*, June 1984, *8*(2), pp. 341–56. **[G: LDCs]**

Schmidt, Reinhart. Early Warning of Debt Rescheduling. *J. Banking Finance*, June 1984, *8*(2), pp. 357–70. **[G: LDCs]**

Schwartz, Anna J. International Lending and the Economic Environment [Safety-Net Mechanisms: The Case of International Lending]. *Cato J.*, Spring/Summer 1984, *4*(1), pp. 205–09. **[G: U.S.]**

Shapiro, Alan C. The Impact of Taxation on the Currency-of-Denomination Decision for Long-Term Foreign Borrowing and Lending. *J. Int. Bus. Stud.*, Spring/Summer 1984, *15*(1), pp. 15–25.

Sjaastad, Larry A. Reflections on the International Debt Crisis [The Political Economy of International Lending]. *Cato J.*, Spring/Summer 1984, *4*(1), pp. 171–75. **[G: Global]**

Sullivan, Barry. In difesa del libero scambio. (Down with Protectionism. With English summary.) *Mondo Aperto*, March-April 1984, *38*(2), pp. 69–75. **[G: Global]**

Sun, I-Shuan. Prospects of the Taipei Offshore Banking Center. *Bull. Int. Fiscal Doc.*, 1984, *38*(6), pp. 259–60. **[G: Taiwan]**

Swoboda, Alexander K. Sui compiti futuri delle istituzioni finanziarie internazionali. (Some Reflections on the Future Role of Intergovernmental Financial Institutions. With English summary.) *Bancaria*, December 1984, *40*(12), pp. 1218–27. **[G: Global]**

Taffler, Richard J. and Abassi, B. Country Risk: A Model for Predicting Debt Servicing Problems in Developing Countries. *J. Roy. Statist. Soc.*, 1984, *147*(4), pp. 541–61. **[G: LDCs]**

Terrell, Henry S. Bank Lending to Developing Countries: Recent Developments and Some Considerations for the Future. *Fed. Res. Bull.*, October 1984, *70*(10), pp. 755–63. **[G: U.S.; LDCs]**

Terrell, Henry S. Considerazioni sul futuro del credito internazionale. (Some Considerations about the Future of International Lending. With English summary.) *Bancaria*, December 1984, *40*(12), pp. 1211–17. **[G: U.S.; LDCs]**

Thore, Sten. Spatial Models of the Eurodollar Market. *J. Banking Finance*, March 1984, *8*(1), pp. 51–65.

Tomassini, Luciano. The International Scene and Latin America's External Debt. *Cepal Rev.*, 1984, (24), pp. 135–46. **[G: Latin America]**

Vaubel, Roland. International Debt, Bank Failures, and the Money Supply: The Thirties and the Eighties. *Cato J.*, Spring/Summer 1984, *4*(1), pp. 249–67. **[G: U.S.]**

Villasuso E., Juan Manuel. Foreign Debt and Economic Development: The Case of Costa Rica. In *Salazar-Carillo, J. and Tirado de Alonso, I., eds., no. 1*, 1984, pp. 1–6. **[G: Costa Rica]**

Volcker, Paul A. Statement to the U.S. House Committee on Foreign Affairs, August 8, 1984. *Fed. Res. Bull.*, August 1984, *70*(8), pp. 636–42.

de Vries, Rimmer. Key Issues in the World Debt Problem [The Political Economy of International Lending]. *Cato J.*, Spring/Summer 1984, *4*(1), pp. 177–84. **[G: Global]**

Wallich, Henry C. Outlook for the World Financial System: A Central Banker's Perspective. *Contemp. Policy Issue*, January 1984, (4), pp. 54–63. **[G: Global]**

Walter, Ingo. Project Finance—The Lender's Perspective. In *Pearce, D. W.; Siebert, H. and Walter, I., eds.*, 1984, pp. 249–70. **[G: Selected Countries]**

Wassermann, Ursula. Latin America's Debt Crisis. *J. World Trade Law*, July–August 1984, *18*(4), pp. 342–48. **[G: Latin America]**

Weinert, Richard S. International Indebtedness: Coping with LDC Debt. In *Hewlett, S. A.; Kaufman, H. and Kenen, P. B., eds.*, 1984, pp. 37–51.

Weintraub, Robert E. International Debt: Crisis and Challenge. *Cato J.*, Spring/Summer 1984, *4*(1), pp. 21–61. **[G: LDCs; U.S.]**

White, Lawrence H. Bank Failures and Monetary Policy [International Debt, Bank Failures, and the Money Supply: The Thirties and the Eighties]. *Cato J.*, Spring/Summer 1984, *4*(1), pp. 269–74. **[G: U.S.]**

Wilmots-Vandendaele, André. Les perspectives économiques des pays en voie de développement non exportateurs de pétrole. L'amélioration des perspectives dans le domaine de l'énergie. (With English summary.) *Revue Écon. Polit.*, September–October 1984, *94*(5), pp. 602–14. **[G: LDCs]**

Yener, Demir and Mambrito, Fulvia. An Early Warning Model for International Debt Servicing Problems. *METU*, 1984, *11*(3–4), pp. 263–84. **[G: LDCs]**

Zecher, J. Richard. The Interventionist Disease and the IMF's Agency Cost Role [The Impoverishing Effects of Foreign Aid]. *Cato J.*, Spring/Summer 1984, *4*(1), pp. 339–42.

440 INTERNATIONAL INVESTMENT AND FOREIGN AID

441 International Investment and Long-term Capital Movements

4410 General

Aliber, Robert Z. The Potential for Financial Crises: Comment. In *Agmon, T.; Hawkins, R. G. and Levich, R. M., eds.*, 1984, pp. 110–15.

Dompierre, Michael B. The United Auto Workers vs. the Japanese: Distributional Effects of Alternative United States Trade Policies. *Aussenwirtschaft*, September 1984, *39*(3), pp. 207–18. **[G: U.S.; Japan]**

Hara, Masayuki. An Economic Analysis of National Ownership in Australia. *Osaka Econ. Pap.*, December 1984, *34*(2–3), pp. 218–27. **[G: Australia]**

Kindleberger, Charles P. A GATT for International Direct Investment: Further Reflections. In *Kindleberger, C. P., 1984, 1980*, pp. 247–65.

Kindleberger, Charles P. Restrictions on Direct Investment in Host Countries. In *Kindleberger, C. P., 1984, 1972*, pp. 51–59.

Minsky, Hyman P. The Potential for Financial Crises. In *Agmon, T.; Hawkins, R. G. and Levich, R. M., eds.*, 1984, pp. 91–109.

Ruffin, Roy J. International Factor Movements. In *Jones, R. W. and Kenen, P., eds.*, 1984, pp. 237–88.

4411 International Investment and Long-term Capital Movements: Theory

Burgstaller, A. and Saavedra-Rivano, Neantro. Capital Mobility and Growth in a North–South Model. *J. Devel. Econ.*, May–June–August 1984, *15*(1,2,3), pp. 213–37.

Eaton, Jonathan and Gersovitz, Mark. A Theory of Expropriation and Deviations from Perfect Capital Mobility. *Econ. J.*, March 1984, *94*(373), pp. 16–40.

Frank, Andre Gunder. On Some Questionable Questions about Marxist Theory and International Capital Flows [Marxist Theory and International Capital Flows]. In *Frank, A. G., 1984, 1976*, pp. 82–86.

Grossman, Gene M. and Razin, Assaf. International Capital Movements under Uncertainty. *J. Polit. Econ.*, April 1984, *92*(2), pp. 286–306.

Helpman, Elhanan and Razin, Assaf. Increasing Returns, Monopolistic Competition, and Factor Movements: A Welfare Analysis. In *Kierzkowski, H., ed., 1984, 1983*, pp. 124–36.

Katz, Menachem. Impact of Taxation on International Capital Flows: Some Empirical Results. In *Tanzi, V., ed.*, 1984, pp. 220–34. **[G: OECD]**

Khan, M. Ali. International Trade and Foreign Investment: A Model with Asymmetric Production. *Pakistan Devel. Rev.*, Winter 1984, *23*(4), pp. 509–30.

Kindleberger, Charles P. Direct Investment in Less Developed Countries: Historical Wrongs and Present Values. In *Kindleberger, C. P.*, 1984, *1972*, pp. 60–76.

Kojima, Kiyoshi and Ozawa, Terutomo. Micro- and Macro-Economic Models of Direct Foreign Investment: Toward a Synthesis. *Hitotsubashi J. Econ.*, June 1984, *25*(1), pp. 1–20.

Lee, Chung H. On Japanese Macroeconomic Theories of Direct Foreign Investment. *Econ. Develop. Cult. Change*, July 1984, *32*(4), pp. 713–23. **[G: Japan]**

Méndez, José A. The Effects of Foreign Investment in the Presence of a Factor Market Monopsony. *J. Int. Econ.*, February 1984, *16*(1/2), pp. 173–82.

Ranney, Susan I. International Capital Transfers and the Choice of Production Technique: A Simple Two-Country Model. *J. Int. Econ.*, August 1984, *17*(1/2), pp. 85–99.

Sinn, Hans-Werner. Die Bedeutung des Accerated Cost Recovery System für den internationalen Kapitalverkehr. (The Significance of the Accelerated Cost Recovery System for International Capital Movements. With English summary.) *Kyklos*, 1984, *37*(4), pp. 542–76. **[G: U.S.]**

Whynes, David K. International Political Economy. In *Whynes, D. K., ed.*, 1984, pp. 162–86.

4412 International Investment and Long-term Capital Movements: Studies

Albi, Emilio. Fiscal Obstacles to the International Flow of Capital between a Parent and Its Subsidiary: Spain. In *Intn'l. Fisc. Assoc., vol. 69a*, 1984, pp. 311–24. **[G: Spain]**

Aliber, Robert Z. Capital Movements—the Tail That Wags the Dog: Discussion. In *Fed. Res. Bank Boston*, 1984, pp. 188–94.

Amsden, Alice H. Exports of Technology by Newly Industrializing Countries: Taiwan. *World Devel.*, May/June 1984, *12*(5/6), pp. 491–503. **[G: Taiwan]**

Balasubramanyam, Venkataraman N. Incentives and Disincentives for Foreign Direct Investment in Less Developed Countries. *Weltwirtsch. Arch.*, 1984, *120*(4), pp. 720–35. **[G: LDCs]**

Belli, R. David. Foreign Direct Investment in the United States in 1983. *Surv. Curr. Bus.*, October 1984, *64*(10), pp. 26–48. **[G: U.S.; Global]**

Belli, R. David. U.S. Business Enterprises Acquired or Established by Foreign Direct Investors in 1983. *Surv. Curr. Bus.*, May 1984, *64*(5), pp. 16–20. **[G: U.S.]**

Berberoglu, Berch. The Nature and Contradictions of U.S. Transnational Expansion Abroad since World War II. In *Zarembka, P., ed.*, 1984, pp. 1–35. **[G: U.S.; Selected Countries]**

Caceres, Luis René. Savings in a Global Context. In *Kessler, D. and Ullmo, P.-A., eds.*, 1984, pp. 323–49. **[G: Latin America]**

Caron, François. Foreign Investments and Technology Transfers: The Case of the French Chemical Industry in the 1950s and 1960s as Viewed by the *Direction des Industries Chimiques*. In *Okochi, A. and Inoue, T., eds.*, 1984, pp. 261–80. **[G: France]**

Chen, Edward K. Y. Exports of Technology by Newly Industrializing Countries: Hong Kong. *World Devel.*, May/June 1984, *12*(5/6), pp. 481–90. **[G: Hong Kong]**

Dahlman, Carl J. and Cortes, Mariluz. Exports of Technology by Newly Industrializing Countries: Mexico. *World Devel.*, May/June 1984, *12*(5/6), pp. 601–24. **[G: Mexico]**

El Shibly, Mekki. Foreign Capital Inflow, Domestic Savings and Economic Growth: The Experience of the Sudan (1960/61–1974/75). *J. Econ. Devel.*, July 1984, *9*(1), pp. 125–45. **[G: Sudan]**

Emmeluth, Christian. Fiscal Obstacles to the International Flow of Capital between a Parent and Its Subsidiary: Denmark. In *Intn'l. Fisc. Assoc., vol. 69a*, 1984, pp. 307–09. **[G: Denmark]**

Faire, Alexandre. Economic Redeployment and Contradictions in the West. In *Ngo, M., ed., vol. 1*, 1984, pp. 5–32. **[G: OECD]**

Flamm, Kenneth. The Volatility of Offshore Investment. *J. Devel. Econ.*, December 1984, *16*(3), pp. 231–48. **[G: U.S.; LDCs]**

Globerman, Steven R. The Consistency of Canada's Foreign Investment Review Process—A Temporal Analysis. *J. Int. Bus. Stud.*, Spring/Summer 1984, *15*(1), pp. 119–29. **[G: Canada]**

Graziani, Giovanni. Les mouvements de capital au sein du Comecon. (Capital Movements within the CMEA. With English summary.) *Écon. Soc.*, February 1984, *18*(2), pp. 45–77. **[G: CMEA]**

Griffith-Jones, Stephany and Rodriguez, Ennio. Private International Finance and Industrialisation of LDCs. In *Kaplinsky, R., ed.*, 1984, pp. 47–74. **[G: LDCs]**

Hartman, David G. Tax Policy and Foreign Direct Investment in the United States. *Nat. Tax J.*, December 1984, *37*(4), pp. 475–87. **[G: U.S.]**

Hollerman, Leon. Japan's Direct Investment in California and the New Protectionism. *J. World Trade Law*, July–August 1984, *18*(4), pp. 309–19. **[G: Japan; U.S.]**

Howenstine, Ned G. U.S. Affiliates of Foreign Companies: Operations in 1982. *Surv. Curr. Bus.*, December 1984, *64*(12), pp. 26–40. **[G: U.S.]**

Howenstine, Ned G. U.S. Direct Investment Abroad in 1983. *Surv. Curr. Bus.*, August 1984, *64*(8), pp. 18–40. **[G: U.S.]**

Jackman, Robert W. Dependence on Foreign Investment and Economic Growth in the Third World. In *Seligson, M. A., ed.*, 1984, *1982*, pp. 211–31. **[G: LDCs]**

Johansson, Peter and Rajakangas, Timo. Pääomanliikkeet, sterilointi ja rahapolitiikan itsenäisyys. (Capital Flows, Sterilization and the Independence of Monetary Policy. With English summary.) *Kansant. Aikak.*, 1984, *80*(3), pp. 291–301. [G: Finland]

Kindleberger, Charles P. Origins of U.S. Direct Investment in France. In *Kindleberger, C. P.*, 1984, *1974*, pp. 118–54. [G: France; U.S.]

Kinugasa, Yosuke. Japanese Firms' Foreign Direct Investment in the U.S. In *Okochi, A. and Inoue, T., eds.*, 1984, pp. 21–60. [G: Japan]

Kozlow, Ralph. Capital Expenditures by Majority-owned Foreign Affiliates of U.S. Companies, 1984 and 1985. *Surv. Curr. Bus.*, September 1984, *64*(9), pp. 28–33. [G: U.S.]

Kozlow, Ralph. Capital Expenditures by Majority-Owned Foreign Affiliates of U.S. Companies, 1984. *Surv. Curr. Bus.*, March 1984, *64*(3), pp. 32–37. [G: U.S.]

Krause, Lawrence B. Australia's Comparative Advantage in International Trade. In *Caves, R. E. and Krause, L. B., eds.*, 1984, pp. 275–311. [G: Australia]

Kudrle, Robert Thomas. The Correlates of Direct Foreign Investment in Developing Countries: A Look at Recent Experience. In *Benjamin, R. and Kudrle, R. T.*, 1984, pp. 211–34. [G: LDCs; OECD]

Lall, Sanjaya. Exports of Technology by Newly Industrializing Countries: India. *World Devel.*, May/June 1984, *12*(5/6), pp. 535–65. [G: India]

Lall, Sanjaya. Exports of Technology by Newly Industrializing Countries: An Overview. *World Devel.*, May/June 1984, *12*(5/6), pp. 471–80. [G: LDCs]

Lall, Sanjaya. Transnationals and the Third World: Changing Perceptions. *Nat. Westminster Bank Quart. Rev.*, May 1984, pp. 2–16. [G: OECD]

Lanteri, Marc. La multinationalisation des firmes européennes aux États-Unis: une approche dynamique. (The Spreading of European Multinational Firms in the U.S.A.: A Dynamic Approach. With English summary.) *Revue Écon.*, July 1984, *35*(4), pp. 733–49. [G: U.S.]

LaPalombara, Joseph and Blank, Stephen. Multinational Corporations and Developing Countries. In *Ghosh, P. K., ed., no. 11*, 1984, *1980*, pp. 7–29. [G: OECD; LDCs]

Lee, Chung H. Direct Foreign Investment and Industrial Development in the Pacific Basin. In *Benjamin, R. and Kudrle, R. T.*, 1984, pp. 191–209. [G: S.E. Asia; U.S.]

Lee, Chung H. Transfer of Technology from Japan and the United States to Korean Manufacturing Industries: A Comparative Study. *Hitotsubashi J. Econ.*, December 1984, *25*(2), pp. 125–36. [G: U.S.; Japan; Korea]

Little, Jane Sneddon. The Industrial Composition of Foreign Direct Investment in the United States and Abroad: A Preliminary Look. *New Eng. Econ. Rev.*, May–June 1984, pp. 38–48. [G: OECD]

Lundahl, Mats. Economic Effects of a Trade and Investment Boycott against South Africa. *Scand. J. Econ.*, 1984, *86*(1), pp. 68–83. [G: S. Africa]

McColl, G. D. Foreign Investment in Australian Mining. In *Lloyd, P. J., ed.*, 1984, pp. 176–207. [G: Australia]

Mucchielli, Jean-Louis. Investissements internationaux et dynamique des avantages comparatifs des nouveaux pays industrialisés. (International Investments and the Changing Pattern of Comparative Advantages—An Application to the New Industrializing Countries. With English summary.) *Revue Écon.*, May 1984, *35*(3), pp. 537–70. [G: Global]

Murphy, Robert G. Capital Mobility and the Relationship between Saving and Investment Rates in OECD Countries. *J. Int. Money Finance*, December 1984, *3*(3), pp. 327–42. [G: OECD]

Mytelka, Lynn Krieger. Foreign Business and Economic Development. In *Zartman, I. W. and Delgado, C. L., eds.*, 1984, pp. 149–73. [G: Ivory Coast]

Nakagawa, Keiichiro. A Comparison of the Emergence of Multinational Manufacturing by U.S., European, and Japanese Firms: Japanese Firms' Foreign Direct Investment in the U.S.: Comments. In *Okochi, A. and Inoue, T., eds.*, 1984, pp. 61–63. [G: Europe; Japan; U.S.]

Nardolilli, Rocco. Trasferimento internazionale di risorse per lo sviluppo: il ruolo delle istituzioni multilaterali. (International Transfer of Development Resources: The Role of the Multilateral Institutions. With English summary.) *Bancaria*, October 1984, *40*(10), pp. 990–1003. [G: Global]

Norman, George and Dunning, John H. Intra-industry Foreign Direct Investment: Its Rationale and Trade Effects. *Weltwirtsch. Arch.*, 1984, *120*(3), pp. 522–40. [G: U.S.; U.K.; Germany; France; Japan]

Ó hUallacháin, Breandán. Input–Output Linkages and Foreign Direct Investment in Ireland. *Int. Reg. Sci. Rev.*, December 1984, *9*(3), pp. 185–200. [G: Ireland]

Ó hUallacháin, Breandán. Linkages and Foreign Direct Investment in the United States. *Econ. Geogr.*, July 1984, *60*(3), pp. 238–53. [G: U.S.]

Olle, Werner. Auslandsinvestitionen deutscher Unternehmen in Entwicklungsländern—empirische Trends zu Beginn der 80er Jahre. (Foreign Investments of German Enterprises in Developing Countries—Empirical Trends at the Beginning of the 1980s. With English summary.) *Aussenwirtschaft*, September 1984, *39*(3), pp. 241–60. [G: W. Germany; LDCs]

Palmer, Ransford W. Technology and Caribbean Development. In *Palmer, R. W.*, 1984, pp. 39–47. [G: Selected Countries]

Palmer, Ransford W. The Financial Implications of Caribbean Industrialization. In *Palmer, R. W.*, 1984, pp. 17–22. [G: Caribbean]

Pamuk, Şevket. The Ottoman Empire in the "Great Depression" of 1873–1896. *J. Econ. Hist.*, March 1984, *44*(1), pp. 107–18. [G: Middle East; S. Europe; Turkey]

Park, Eul Y. Patterns of Foreign Direct Investment, Foreign Ownership, and Industrial Performance: The Case of the Korean Manufacturing Industry. In *Benjamin, R. and Kudrle, R. T.*, 1984, pp. 127–60. [G: S. Korea]

Patel, Meena. Private Foreign Investment and Balance of Payments Effects in India during 1960–1970. *Indian Econ. J.*, January–March 1984, *31*(3), pp. 62–69. [G: India]

Penati, Alessandro and Dooley, Michael P. Current Account Imbalances and Capital Formation in Industrial Countries, 1949–81. *Int. Monet. Fund Staff Pap.*, March 1984, *31*(1), pp. 1–24. [G: OECD]

Petrochilos, G. The Determinants of Foreign Direct Investment in the Greek Economy. *Brit. Rev. Econ. Issues*, Spring 1984, *6*(14), pp. 27–54. [G: Greece]

Poller, Roland and Tesner, István. Socialist Economic Integration and the Investment Cooperation of the CMEA Countries. *Soviet E. Europ. Foreign Trade*, Spring 1984, *20*(1), pp. 6–26. [G: CMEA]

Prybyla, Jan S. China's Special Economic Zones. *ACES Bull.*, Winter 1984, *26*(4), pp. 1–23. [G: China]

Riedel, Jürgen. Attitudes in the Federal Republic of Germany to the Policies of Developing Countries Regarding Foreign Investors. *Industry Devel.*, 1984, (13), pp. 1–38. [G: W. Germany; LDCs]

Rothgeb, John M., Jr. Investment Penetration in Manufacturing and Extraction and External Public Debt in Third World States. *World Devel.*, November–December 1984, *12*(11–12), pp. 1063–75. [G: LDCs]

Scholl, Russell B. The International Investment Position of the United States in 1983. *Surv. Curr. Bus.*, June 1984, *64*(6), pp. 74–78. [G: U.S.]

Sercovich, Francisco Colman. Exports of Technology by Newly Industrializing Countries: Brazil. *World Devel.*, May/June 1984, *12*(5/6), pp. 575–99. [G: Brazil]

Shihata, Ibrahim F. I. Increasing Private Capital Flows to LDCs. *Finance Develop.*, December 1984, *21*(4), pp. 6–9. [G: OECD; LDCs]

Sigmund, Paul E. The Regulation of Foreign Investment in Mexico and Its Impact on Income Distribution. In *Aspe, P. and Sigmund, P. E., eds.*, 1984, pp. 247–64. [G: Mexico]

Soifer, Ricardo J. Exports of Technology by Newly Industrializing Countries: Argentina. *World Devel.*, May/June 1984, *12*(5/6), pp. 625–44. [G: Argentina]

Thee, Kian Wie. Japanese Direct Investment in Indonesian Manufacturing. *Bull. Indonesian Econ. Stud.*, August 1984, *20*(2), pp. 90–106. [G: Indonesia]

van Thiel, Servaas. Tax Incentives for Foreign Investment. *Bull. Int. Fiscal Doc.*, November 1984, *38*(11), pp. 497–500. [G: Morocco]

Thrall, Grant Ian. Geoinvestment: The Interdependence among Space, Market Size, and Political Turmoil in Attracting Foreign Direct Investment. *Conflict Manage. Peace Sci.*, Fall 1984, *8*(1), pp. 17–47. [G: U.S.]

Tichy, Geiserich E. Steuerliche Behinderungen

des internationalen Kapitalflusses zwischen einer Muttergesellschaft und ihrer Tochtergesellschaft: Österreich. (Fiscal Obstacles to the International Flow of Capital between a Parent and Its Subsidiary: Austria. With English Summary.) In *Intn'l. Fisc. Assoc.*, vol. 69a, 1984, pp. 227–53. [G: Austria]

Tomašić, Vjekoslav. Effects of Foreign Direct Investments on the Balance of Payments in Industrial Ventures in SR Croatia. *Econ. Anal. Worker's Manage.*, 1984, *18*(4), pp. 333–41. [G: Yugoslavia]

Turner, Philip and Tuveri, Jean-Pierre. Some Effects of Export Restraints on Japanese Trading Behaviour. *OECD Econ. Stud.*, Spring 1984, (2), pp. 93–107. [G: Japan]

Vaitsos, Constantine V. Strategic Choices in the Commercialization of Technology: The Point of View of Developing Countries. In *Ghosh, P. K., ed., no. 3*, 1984, *1973*, pp. 273–91. [G: LDCs]

Vogel, Klaus. Fiscal Obstacles to the International Flow of Capital between a Parent and Its Subsidiary: General Report. In *Intn'l. Fisc. Assoc.*, vol. 69a, 1984, pp. 97–132.

Wallich, Henry C. Capital Movements—the Tail That Wags the Dog. In *Fed. Res. Bank Boston*, 1984, pp. 179–87.

Wang, N. T. Reforms in Foreign Trade and Investment in China. *Hong Kong Econ. Pap.*, 1984, (15), pp. 87–97. [G: China]

Westphal, Larry E., et al. Exports of Technology by Newly Industrializing Countries: Republic of Korea. *World Devel.*, May/June 1984, *12*(5/6), pp. 505–33. [G: Korea]

Wheelwright, E. The Political Economy of Foreign Domination. In *Lloyd, P. J., ed.*, 1984, *1982*, pp. 208–25. [G: Australia]

Winham, Gilbert R. The Canadian Automobile Industry and Trade-related Performance Requirements. *J. World Trade Law*, November:December 1984, *18*(6), pp. 471–96. [G: Canada; U.S.]

Wu, Friedrich. Realities Confronting China's Foreign Investment Policy. *World Econ.*, September 1984, *7*(3), pp. 295–311. [G: China]

Yang, Tien-yi. Foreign Business Activities and the Chinese Response, 1842–1937. In *Okochi, A. and Inoue, T., eds.*, 1984, pp. 215–57. [G: China]

442 International Business and Multinational Enterprises

4420 International Business and Multinational Enterprises

Achumba, Iheanyi C.; Harvey, Michael G. and Rothe, James T. Marketing of Nonconsumer Goods in Foreign Markets: The Case of High-Technology Products. In *Kaynak, E., ed.*, 1984, pp. 121–35.

Albi, Emilio. Fiscal Obstacles to the International Flow of Capital between a Parent and Its Subsidiary: Spain. In *Intn'l. Fisc. Assoc.*, vol. 69a, 1984, pp. 311–24. [G: Spain]

Antonelli, Cristiano. Multinational Firms, International Trade, and International Telecommunications. *Info. Econ. Policy,* 1984, *1*(4), pp. 333–43.   [G: Selected Countries]

Armstrong, Christopher and Nelles, H. V. A Curious Capital Flow: Canadian Investment in Mexico, 1902–1910. *Bus. Hist. Rev.,* Summer 1984, *58*(2), pp. 178–203.   [G: Canada; Mexico]

Artisien, Patrick F. R. and Buckley, Peter J. Joint Ventures in Yugoslavia: Comment [An Economic Analysis of Yugoslav Joint Ventures]. *J. World Trade Law,* March–April 1984, *18*(2), pp. 163–70.   [G: Yugoslavia]

Balasubramanyam, Venkataraman N. Factor Proportions and Productive Efficiency of Foreign Owned Firms in the Indonesian Manufacturing Sector. *Bull. Indonesian Econ. Stud.,* December 1984, *20*(3), pp. 70–94.
                                                            [G: Indonesia]

Balasubramanyam, Venkataraman N. Incentives and Disincentives for Foreign Direct Investment in Less Developed Countries. *Weltwirtsch. Arch.,* 1984, *120*(4), pp. 720–35.
                                                                   [G: LDCs]

Barksdale, Hiram C. and Anderson, L. McTier. Toward a Conceptual Framework for Comparative Marketing. In *Kaynak, E. and Savitt, R.,* eds., 1984, pp. 17–33.

Bärlocher, Urs. Steuerliche Behinderungen des internationalen Kapitalflusses zwischen einer Muttergesellschaft und ihrer Tochtergesellschaft: Schweiz. (Fiscal Obstacles to the International Flow of Capital between a Parent and Its Subsidiary: Switzerland. With English summary.) In *Intn'l. Fisc. Assoc.,* vol. 69a, 1984, pp. 487–99.   [G: Switzerland]

Bartels, Robert. National Culture-International Business Relations: Two Dominant Markets Contrasted. In *Kaynak, E.,* ed., 1984, pp. 261–70.   [G: U.S.; Japan]

Belli, R. David. U.S. Business Enterprises Acquired or Established by Foreign Direct Investors in 1983. *Surv. Curr. Bus.,* May 1984, *64*(5), pp. 16–20.   [G: U.S.]

Bennett, Douglas and Sharpe, Kenneth. Agenda Setting and Bargaining Power: The Mexican State versus Transnational Automobile Corporations. In *Kronish, R. and Mericle, K. S.,* eds., 1984, *1979,* pp. 195–229.   [G: Mexico]

Berberoglu, Berch. The Nature and Contradictions of U.S. Transnational Expansion Abroad since World War II. In *Zarembka, P.,* ed., 1984, pp. 1–35.   [G: U.S.; Selected Countries]

Berrefjord, Ole and Heum, Per. Nordic Engineering Industries and the Norwegian Offshore Market. In *Mikkelsen, A., et al.,* 1984, pp. 204–19.   [G: Scandinavia]

Bhagwati, Jagdish N. Incentives and Disincentives: International Migration. *Weltwirtsch. Arch.,* 1984, *120*(4), pp. 678–701.   [G: U.S.; Global]

Bicksler, James L. International Corporate Diversification, Market Valuation, and Size-Adjusted Evidence: Discussion. *J. Finance,* July 1984, *39*(3), pp. 743–45.

Blainey, Geoffrey. The History of Multinational Factories in Australia. In *Okochi, A. and Inoue, T.,* eds., 1984, pp. 183–210.
                                                                [G: Australia]

Blanchflower, David. Comparative Pay Levels in Domestically-owned and Foreign-owned Manufacturing Plants: A Comment. *Brit. J. Ind. Relat.,* July 1984, *22*(2), pp. 265–67.
                                                                   [G: U.K.]

Blitzer, Charles R.; Lessard, Donald R. and Paddock, James L. Risk-Bearing and the Choice of Contract Forms for Oil Exploration and Development. *Energy J.,* January 1984, *5*(1), pp. 1–28.   [G: Ecuador]

Bodenheimer, Thomas S. The Transnational Pharmaceutical Industry and the Health of the World's People. In *McKinlay, J. B.,* ed., 1984, pp. 187–216.

Bodó-Vértes, Ágnes. Results of Co-operation Strategy in the 70's—Exemplified by the Production Co-operation between Machine Tool Manufacturers in the FRG and in Hungary. In *Rába, A. and Schenk, K.-E.,* eds., 1984, pp. 189–214.   [G: Hungary; W. Germany]

Boidman, Nathan. Transfer Pricing Issues: A Critical Discussion of the Revenue Draft Information Circular. *Bull. Int. Fiscal Doc.,* 1984, *38*(8–9), pp. 399–420, 426.   [G: Canada; OECD]

Borner, Silvio. Drei Grundperspektiven zur Interpretation des weltwirtschaftlichen Strukturwandels. (Three Perspectives for the Interpretation of Structural Change in the World Economy. With English summary.) *Aussenwirtschaft,* September 1984, *39*(3), pp. 219–40.   [G: Global]

Borner, Silvio. Internationale Wettbewerbsfähigkeit—Fragmente zu einer Theorie internationaler Unternehmenstätigkeit. (International Competitiveness—Fragments of a Theory on International Entrepreneurial Activity. With English summary.) *Weltwirtsch. Arch.,* 1984, *120*(3), pp. 481–98.

Bornschier, Volker. Multinational Corporations, Economic Policy and National Development in the World System. In *Ghosh, P. K.,* ed., no. 11, 1984, *1980,* pp. 30–46.

Borrow, Davis B. and Kudrle, Robert Thomas. MNE Disclosure Alternatives and Their Consequences. *J. World Trade Law,* September–October 1984, *18*(5), pp. 437–54.
                                                                   [G: OECD]

Break, George F. State Taxation Under the Commerce Clause: The History Revisited: Comments. In *McLure, C. E., Jr.,* ed., 1984, pp. 82–84.   [G: U.S.]

Brown, Wilson B. Firm-like Behavior in Markets: The Administered Channel. *Int. J. Ind. Organ.,* September 1984, *2*(3), pp. 263–76.

van Brunschot, Frank. Fiscal Obstacles to the International Flow of Capital between a Parent and Its Subsidiary: Netherlands. In *Intn'l. Fisc. Assoc.,* vol. 69a, 1984, pp. 417–27.
                                                            [G: Netherlands]

Buckley, Peter J. Managing Multinational Organisations. In *Pickering, J. F. and Cockerill, T. A. J., eds.*, 1984, pp. 324–43.

Burton, F. N. and Inoue, Hisashi. Expropriations of Foreign-owned Firms in Developing Countries: A Cross-National Analysis. *J. World Trade Law*, September–October 1984, *18*(5), pp. 396–414.   [G: LDCs]

Buswell, David H. Fiatallis North America, Inc., and the Pipeline Sanctions. In *Czinkota, M. R., ed.*, 1984, pp. 103–10.   [G: U.S.; U.S.S.R.]

Cairns, Robert D. Changing Structure in the World Nickel Industry. *Antitrust Bull.*, Fall 1984, *29*(3), pp. 561–75.   [G: U.S.]

Carlson, George N. and Galper, Harvey. Water's Edge versus Worldwide Unitary Combination. In *McLure, C. E., Jr., ed.*, 1984, pp. 1–40.   [G: U.S.]

Caron, François. Foreign Investments and Technology Transfers: The Case of the French Chemical Industry in the 1950s and 1960s as Viewed by the *Direction des Industries Chimiques.* In *Okochi, A. and Inoue, T., eds.*, 1984, pp. 261–80.   [G: France]

Cavusgil, S. Tamer. Changing Nature of Firms' International Market Research Activities During the Internationalization Process. In *Kaynak, E., ed.*, 1984, pp. 207–16.   [G: U.S.]

Chung, Byung Soo and Lee, Chung H. The Choice of Production Techniques by Foreign and Local Firms in Korea: Reply. *Econ. Develop. Cult. Change*, April 1984, *32*(3), pp. 629–31.   [G: S. Korea]

Cieslik, Jerzy. Restrictive Clauses in Licensing Agreements: The Pharmaceutical Industry in Developing Countries. *J. World Trade Law*, September–October 1984, *18*(5), pp. 415–28.   [G: LDCs]

Clairmonte, Frederick F. and Cavanagh, John H. Transnational Corporations and Global Markets: Changing Power Relations. In *Ghosh, P. K., ed., no. 11*, 1984, *1982*, pp. 47–91.   [G: LDCs; OECD]

Clark, George J. Foreign Banks in the Domestic Markets of Developing Countries. In *Feinberg, R. E. and Kallab, V., eds., no. 2*, 1984, pp. 79–86.   [G: LDCs; U.S.]

Coughlin, Cletus C. Reply [An Economic Analysis of Yugoslav Joint Ventures]. *J. World Trade Law*, March–April 1984, *18*(2), pp. 170–72.   [G: Yugoslavia]

Daser, Sayeste. International Marketing Information Systems: A Neglected Prerequisite for Foreign Marketing Planning. In *Kaynak, E., ed.*, 1984, pp. 139–54.

Davidson, W. H. and McFetridge, Donald G. International Technology Transactions and the Theory of the Firm. *J. Ind. Econ.*, March 1984, *32*(3), pp. 253–64.   [G: U.S.]

Delapierre, Michel and Zimmermann, Jean-Benoît. Les multinationales de l'électronique: des stratégies différenciées. (With English summary.) *Rev. Econ. Ind.*, 2nd Trimester 1984, (28), pp. 9–35.   [G: OECD]

Delwaide, Henry and Malherbe, Jacques. Obsta-

cles fiscaux aux mouvements de capitaux entre une société-mère et ses filiales étrangères: Belgique. (Fiscal Obstacles to the International Flow of Capital between a Parent and Its Subsidiary: Belgium. With English summary.) In *Intn'l. Fisc. Assoc., vol. 69a*, 1984, pp. 255–73.   [G: Belgium]

Desin, Allan N. Alternative Divisions of the Tax Base: How Much Is at Stake? Comments. In *McLure, C. E., Jr., ed.*, 1984, pp. 214–16.   [G: U.S.]

Dow, Alexander. Finance and Foreign Control in Canadian Base Metal Mining, 1918–55 *Econ. Hist. Rev., 2nd Ser.*, February 1984, *37*(1), pp. 54–67.   [G: Canada]

Droucopoulos, Vassilis. The Changing Remittance Behaviour of U.S. Manufacturing Firms in Latin America: A Comment and an Update. *World Devel.*, January 1984, *12*(1), pp. 97–100.   [G: Latin America; U.S.]

Eads, George C. R&D and Innovation: Some Empirical Findings: Comment. In *Griliches, Z., ed.*, 1984, pp. 150–53.   [G: U.S.]

Eaton, Jonathan and Gersovitz, Mark. A Theory of Expropriation and Deviations from Perfect Capital Mobility. *Econ. J.*, March 1984, *94*(373), pp. 16–40.

El-Ansary, Adel I. and Liebrenz, Marilyn L. Comparative Marketing Systems Analysis: Revisited. In *Kaynak, E. and Savitt, R., eds.*, 1984, pp. 34–50.

Emmanuel, Arghiri. The Multinational Corporations and Inequality of Development. In *Ghosh, P. K., ed., no. 11*, 1984, *1976*, pp. 92–113.

Errunza, Vihang R. and Senbet, Lemma W. International Corporate Diversification, Market Valuation, and Size-Adjusted Evidence. *J. Finance*, July 1984, *39*(3), pp. 727–43.   [G: U.S.]

Eshiwani, Arthur A. The 1984–85 Budgetary Measures. *Bull. Int. Fiscal Doc.*, December 1984, *38*(12), pp. 543–45.   [G: Kenya]

Estes, Carl, II; Sunley, Emil M. and Zimmerman, Neal W. Fiscal Obstacles to the International Flow of Capital between a Parent and Its Subsidiary: United States. In *Intn'l. Fisc. Assoc., vol. 69a*, 1984, pp. 325–32. [G: U.S.]

Etemad, Hamid. A Generalized Model of Comparative Marketing: Formal Development, Methodological Implications and Examples. In *Kindra, G. S., ed.*, 1984, pp. 188–215.

Fatemi, Ali M. Shareholder Benefits from Corporate International Diversification. *J. Finance*, December 1984, *39*(5), pp. 1325–44.   [G: U.S.]

Figueroa, Antonio Hugo. Fiscal Obstacles to the International Flow of Capital between a Parent and Its Subsidiary: Argentina. In *Intn'l. Fisc. Assoc., vol. 69a*, 1984, pp. 193–212.   [G: Argentina]

Figura, Ivan. Crisis of the Concepts of the Defence of Neo-Colonialism. *Czech. Econ. Digest.*, June 1984, (4), pp. 68–89. [G: Global]

Finch, Johnny C. The Apportionment of Multistate and Multinational Corporate Income for

Tax Purposes. *Bull. Int. Fiscal Doc.*, February 1984, *38*(2), pp. 51–59. **[G: U.S.]**

Finlayson, Jock A. and Haglund, David G. Oil Politics and Canada–United States Relations. *Polit. Sci. Quart.*, Summer 1984, *99*(2), pp. 271–88. **[G: Canada; U.S.]**

Firn, John R. and Roberts, David. High-technology Industries. In *Hood, N. and Young, S., eds.*, 1984, pp. 288–325. **[G: U.K.]**

Flamm, Kenneth. The Volatility of Offshore Investment. *J. Devel. Econ.*, December 1984, *16*(3), pp. 231–48. **[G: U.S.; LDCs]**

Fleet, Michael. Bargaining Relations in the Colombian Motor Vehicle Industry. In *Kronish, R. and Mericle, K. S., eds.*, 1984, pp. 231–60. **[G: Colombia]**

Fontagné, Lionel. La notion de produit-système et la décomposition internationale des processus productifs dans l'industrie automobile. (With English summary.) *Revue Écon. Polit.*, May–June 1984, *94*(3), pp. 358–74.

Fujita, Masahiro; Mizushima, Kazuya and Mikitani, Ryoichi. Internationalization of Japanese Commercial Banking—The Recent Experience of City Banks. *Kobe Econ. Bus. Rev.*, 1984, *30*, pp. 23–53. **[G: Japan]**

Gabor, André. On the Theory and Practice of Transfer Pricing. In *[Pearce, I. F.]*, 1984, pp. 149–70.

Gangemi, Bruno. Fiscal Obstacles to the International Flow of Capital between a Parent and Its Subsidiary: Italy. In *Intn'l. Fisc. Assoc.*, vol. 69a, 1984, pp. 375–90. **[G: Italy]**

García Caballero, M. A. An Overview of the 1983 Tax Reform. *Bull. Int. Fiscal Doc.*, March 1984, *38*(3), pp. 124–29. **[G: Guatemala]**

Germidis, Dimitrios. Technology Transfer, Regional Co-operation and Multinational Firms. In *Ghosh, P. K., ed., no. 11*, 1984, 1977, pp. 246–58.

Geyikdagi, Yasar M. On International Diversification and the Interrelationship of Major Economies. *Rivista Int. Sci. Econ. Com.*, August 1984, *31*(8), pp. 801–07. **[G: U.S.]**

Globerman, Steven R. The Consistency of Canada's Foreign Investment Review Process—A Temporal Analysis. *J. Int. Bus. Stud.*, Spring/Summer 1984, *15*(1), pp. 119–29.
[G: Canada]

Glover, David J. Contract Farming and Smallholder Outgrower Schemes in Less-developed Countries. *World Devel.*, November–December 1984, *12*(11–12), pp. 1143–57.
[G: LDCs]

Gomane, Jean-Pierre. The Future for France in the Pacific. In *Downen, R. L. and Dickson, B. J., eds.*, 1984, pp. 91–99. **[G: France; Pacific Basin]**

Gouedard-Comte, Olivier. Formes et degrés d'insertion régionale des groupes: une comparaison entre groupes français et groupes étrangers. (Regional Insertions of Groups: A Comparison between French and Foreign Groups. With English summary.) *Revue Écon.*, March 1984, *35*(2), pp. 313–46. **[G: France]**

Govind, Har. Taxation of Foreign Companies. *Bull. Int. Fiscal Doc.*, December 1984, *38*(12), pp. 536–42. **[G: India]**

Gray, S. J. and Radebaugh, Lee H. International Segment Disclosures by U.S. and U.K. Multinational Enterprises: A Descriptive Study. *J. Acc. Res.*, Spring 1984, *22*(1), pp. 351–60.
[G: U.S.; U.K.]

Graziani, Giovanni. Des multinationales à l'Est? (With English summary.) *Rev. Econ. Ind.*, 2nd Trimester 1984, (28), pp. 36–58. **[G: CMEA]**

Griliches, Zvi. R&D and Innovation: Some Empirical Findings: Comment. In *Griliches, Z., ed.*, 1984, pp. 148–49. **[G: U.S.]**

Gürol, Metin N.; Kaynak, Erdener and Yucel, Ahmet A. Computer Systems Marketing in the Emerging Economies of the Middle East: Managerial and Public Policy Implications. In *Kaynak, E., ed.*, 1984, pp. 271–85. **[G: U.S.; Turkey; Saudi Arabia]**

Guy, Donna J. Dependency, the Credit Market, and Argentine Industrialization, 1860–1940. *Bus. Hist. Rev.*, Winter 1984, *58*(4), pp. 532–61. **[G: Argentina]**

Hall, Chris. Fiscal Obstacles to the International Flow of Capital between a Parent and Its Subsidiary: Hong Kong. In *Intn'l. Fisc. Assoc.*, vol. 69a, 1984, pp. 359–73. **[G: Hong Kong]**

Hallerbach, Günther. Steuerliche Behinderungen des internationalen Kapitalflusses zwischen einer Muttergesellschaft und ihrer Tochtergesellschaft: Deutschland. (Fiscal Obstacles to the International Flow of Capital between a Parent and Its Subsidiary: Germany. With English summary.) In *Intn'l. Fisc. Assoc., vol. 69a*, 1984, pp. 177–91. **[G: W. Germany]**

Hamberg, Sten. Fiscal Obstacles to the International Flow of Capital between a Parent and Its Subsidiary: Sweden. In *Intn'l. Fisc. Assoc.*, vol. 69a, 1984, pp. 461–85. **[G: Sweden]**

Hamilton, Roger. Fiscal Obstacles to the International Flow of Capital between a Parent and Its Subsidiary: Australia. In *Intn'l. Fisc. Assoc.*, vol. 69a, 1984, pp. 213–26. **[G: Australia]**

Hammer, Richard M. Canadian Acquisition of a U.S. Business: A U.S. Perspective. In *Purden, C., ed.*, 1984, pp. 274–304. **[G: Canada; U.S.]**

Harris, Stuart. Dimensions of Resource Dependence in Exporting Countries. In *Pearce, D. W.; Siebert, H. and Walter, I., eds.*, 1984, pp. 113–33. **[G: Papua New Guinea; LDCs]**

Hellerstein, Jerome R. State Taxation Under the Commerce Clause: The History Revisited. In *McLure, C. E., Jr., ed.*, 1984, 1982, pp. 53–81. **[G: U.S.]**

Helpman, Elhanan. A Simple Theory of International Trade with Multinational Corporations. *J. Polit. Econ.*, June 1984, *92*(3), pp. 451–71.

Heyzer, Noeleen. The Merging of State with Foreign Investment: Building a Technocratic Elite in Singapore. In *Ngo, M., ed., vol. 1*, 1984, pp. 404–26. **[G: Singapore]**

Higgins, Benjamin. Jan Boeke and the Doctrine of 'The Little Push.' *Bull. Indonesian Econ. Stud.*, December 1984, *20*(3), pp. 55–69.
[G: Indonesia]

Hollander, Abraham. Foreign Location Decisions by U.S. Transnational Firms: An Empirical Study. *Managerial Dec. Econ.*, March 1984, 5(1), pp. 7–18. [G: U.S.]

Howard, Michael C. and Chand, Anand. Australian Based Companies in Fiji. In *Utrecht, E., ed.*, 1984, pp. 285–305. [G: Fiji]

Howenstine, Ned G. U.S. Direct Investment Abroad in 1983. *Surv. Curr. Bus.*, August 1984, 64(8), pp. 18–40. [G: U.S.]

Hung, C. L. Economic and Market Environment: The Case of Hong Kong. In *Kindra, G. S., ed.*, 1984, pp. 95–114. [G: Hong Kong]

Inoue, Tadakatsu. A Comparison of the Emergence of Multinational Manufacturing by U.S., European, and Japanese Firms. In *Okochi, A. and Inoue, T., eds.*, 1984, pp. 3–20. [G: Europe; Japan; U.S.]

Ishi, Hiromitsu. International Tax Evasion and Avoidance in Japan. *Hitotsubashi J. Econ.*, June 1984, 25(1), pp. 21–29. [G: Japan]

Jain, S. C. and Puri, Y. Role of Multinational Corporations in Developing Countries: Policy Makers' Views. In *Ghosh, P. K., ed., no. 11*, 1984, *1981*, pp. 114–30.

Jansson, Hans. Industrial Marketing Strategies of Transnational Corporations in Third World Markets. In *Kaynak, E., ed.*, 1984, pp. 75–90.

Jap, Kim Siong. Managers' Fees Not Taxable under Malaysia–United Kingdom Treaty. *Bull. Int. Fiscal Doc.*, February 1984, 38(2), pp. 79–81. [G: U.K.; Malaysia]

Jenkins, Kempton B. The Business Perspective of Trade with Adversaries. In *Czinkota, M. R., ed.*, 1984, pp. 55–62. [G: U.S.; CMEA]

Jenkins, Rhys. The Rise and Fall of the Argentine Motor Vehicle Industry. In *Kronish, R. and Mericle, K. S., eds.*, 1984, pp. 41–73. [G: Argentina]

Ji, Chongwei. China's Utilization of Foreign Funds and Relevant Policies. *Chinese Econ. Stud.*, Winter 1983–84, 17(2), pp. 37–49. [G: China]

Jones, Charles A. Competition and Structural Change in the Buenos Aires Fire Insurance Market: The Local Board of Agents, 1875–1921. In *Westall, O. M., ed.*, 1984, pp. 114–29. [G: Argentina; U.K.]

Jones, Geoffrey. The Expansion of British Multinational Manufacturing, 1890–1939. In *Okochi, A. and Inoue, T., eds.*, 1984, pp. 125–53. [G: U.K.]

Jones, Geoffrey. The Growth and Performance of British Multinational Firms before 1939: The Case of Dunlop. *Econ. Hist. Rev., 2nd Ser.*, February 1984, 37(1), pp. 35–53. [G: U.K.]

Jones, Randall J., Jr. Empirical Models of Political Risks in U.S. Oil Production Operations in Venezuela. *J. Int. Bus. Stud.*, Spring/Summer 1984, 15(1), pp. 81–95. [G: U.S.]

Jungnickel, Rolf and Koopmann, Georg. The Role of Multinationals in the NIEO. In *Ghosh, P. K., ed., no. 9*, 1984, *1976*, pp. 198–205.

Jungnickel, Rolf and Koopmann, Georg. The Role of Multinationals in the NIEO. In *Ghosh, P. K., ed., no. 11*, 1984, *1976*, pp. 294–301.

Kaplinsky, Raphael. Computer-Aided-Design: An Assessment of the Current International Economic Setting and Policy Implications. *Industry Devel.*, 1984, (11), pp. 43–57. [G: LDCs]

Katrak, Homi. Pricing Policies of Multinational Enterprises: Host Country Regulation and Welfare. *Int. J. Ind. Organ.*, December 1984, 2(4), pp. 327–40.

Kaynak, Erdener. Future Directions of Research in International Marketing. In *Kaynak, E., ed.*, 1984, pp. 337–44.

Kaynak, Erdener. The Use of Marketing Research to Facilitate International Marketing Within Developing Countries. In *Kaynak, E., ed.*, 1984, pp. 155–71.

Kaynak, Erdener and Savitt, Ronald. Comparative Marketing: Integrative Statement. In *Kaynak, E. and Savitt, R., eds.*, 1984, pp. 3–13.

Kelley, Patrick L. Transfer Price Adjustments and Double Taxation: A Sword of Damocles for Multinationals. *Bull. Int. Fiscal Doc.*, October 1984, 38(10), pp. 448–50. [G: U.S.; EEC]

Kindleberger, Charles P. Book Review: Magdoff, The Age of Imperialism. In *Kindleberger, C. P.*, 1984, *1971*, pp. 177–79.

Kindleberger, Charles P. A GATT for International Direct Investment: Further Reflections. In *Kindleberger, C. P.*, 1984, *1980*, pp. 247–65.

Kindleberger, Charles P. Direct Investment in Less Developed Countries: Historical Wrongs and Present Values. In *Kindleberger, C. P.*, 1984, *1972*, pp. 60–76.

Kindleberger, Charles P. Multinational Companies in World Affairs. In *Kindleberger, C. P.*, 1984, pp. 1–13.

Kindleberger, Charles P. Multinationals and the Small Open Economy. In *Kindleberger, C. P.*, 1984, *1980*, pp. 102–17.

Kindleberger, Charles P. Ownership and Contract in International Business. In *Kindleberger, C. P.*, 1984, pp. 89–101.

Kindleberger, Charles P. Plus ça change—A Look at the New Literature. In *Kindleberger, C. P.*, 1984, pp. 180–88.

Kindleberger, Charles P. Restrictions on Direct Investment in Host Countries. In *Kindleberger, C. P.*, 1984, *1972*, pp. 51–59.

Kindleberger, Charles P. Size of Firm and Size of Nation. In *Kindleberger, C. P.*, 1984, *1974*, pp. 14–34.

Kindleberger, Charles P. Statement before the International Finance Subcommittee of the Senate Banking, Housing, and Urban Affairs Committee. In *Kindleberger, C. P.*, 1984, *1974*, pp. 189–93.

Kindleberger, Charles P. Statement Submitted to the Sixth Meeting of Members of Congress and of the European Parliament. In *Kindleberger, C. P.*, 1984, *1975*, pp. 238–41.

Kindleberger, Charles P. Testimony before Hearings of the Subcommittee on Foreign Economic Policy of the Joint Economic Committee, Congress of the United States, 91st Congress, 2d Session, July 27, 1970, on the Multinational Corporation and International Investment. In *Kindleberger, C. P.*, 1984, 1970, pp. 242–46.

Kindleberger, Charles P. The Clash of Economics and Sociology and Politics in the Internationalization of Business. In *Kindleberger, C. P.*, 1984, 1973, pp. 35–50.

Kindleberger, Charles P. The International Corporation in the Atlantic Community: An Economist's View. In *Kindleberger, C. P.*, 1984, 1971, pp. 232–37.

Kindleberger, Charles P. The International Corporation in the Late Sixties and Early Seventies. In *Kindleberger, C. P.*, 1984, pp. 194–201.

Kindleberger, Charles P. The Multinational Corporation in a World of Militant Developing Countries. In *Kindleberger, C. P.*, 1984, 1975, pp. 77–88.

Kindleberger, Charles P. and Goldberg, Paul M. Toward a GATT for Investment: A Proposal for Supervision of the International Corporation. In *Kindleberger, C. P.*, 1984, 1970, pp. 202–31.

Kinugasa, Yosuke. Japanese Firms' Foreign Direct Investment in the U.S. In *Okochi, A. and Inoue, T.*, eds., 1984, pp. 21–60. [G: Japan]

Klein, Ronald D. Adding International Business to the Core Program via the Simulation Game. *J. Int. Bus. Stud.*, Spring/Summer 1984, 15(1), pp. 151–59.

Kleinschmidt, Elko J. and Cooper, Robert G. A Typology of Export Strategies Applied to the Export Performance of Industrial Firms. In *Kaynak, E.*, ed., 1984, pp. 217–31.
[G: Canada]

Kobrin, Stephen J. Multinational Corporations, Sociocultural Dependence, and Industrialization: Need Satisfaction or Want Creation? In *Ghosh, P. K.*, ed., no. 11, 1984, 1979, pp. 195–218. [G: LDCs; U.S.]

Kobrin, Stephen J. The Nationalisation of Oil Production, 1918–80. In *Pearce, D. W.; Siebert, H. and Walter, I.*, eds., 1984, pp. 137–64.
[G: LDCs]

Kojima, Kiyoshi and Ozawa, Terutomo. Micro- and Macro-Economic Models of Direct Foreign Investment: Toward a Synthesis. *Hitotsubashi J. Econ.*, June 1984, 25(1), pp. 1–20.

Kopits, George and Mutén, Leif. The Relevance of the Unitary Approach for Developing Countries. In *McLure, C. E., Jr.*, ed., 1984, pp. 269–80.

Kronish, Rich. Latin America and the World Motor Vehicle Industry: The Turn to Exports. In *Kronish, R. and Mericle, K. S.*, eds., 1984, pp. 75–93. [G: Latin America; Global]

Kronish, Rich and Mericle, Kenneth S. The Development of the Latin American Motor Vehicle Industry, 1900-1980: A Class Analysis. In *Kronish, R. and Mericle, K. S.*, eds., 1984, pp. 261–306. [G: Latin America]

Kumar, Krishna and Kim, Kee Young. The Korean Manufacturing Multinationals. *J. Int. Bus.*

Stud., Spring/Summer 1984, 15(1), pp. 45–61.
[G: Korea]

Kumar, Manmohan Singh. Comparative Analysis of UK Domestic and International Firms. *J. Econ. Stud.*, 1984, 11(3), pp. 26–42.
[G: U.K.]

Kumar, Nagesh. Social Cost–Benefit Analysis of an Export-Oriented Project with Foreign Collaboration in India. *Industry Devel.*, 1984, (10), pp. 39–46. [G: India]

Laband, David N. Restriction of Farm Ownership as Rent-Seeking Behavior: Family Farmers Have It Their Way. *Amer. J. Econ. Soc.*, April 1984, 43(2), pp. 179–89. [G: U.S.]

Laboe, Norman J. Worldwide Unitary Combination: The California Practice: Comments. In *McLure, C. E., Jr.*, ed., 1984, pp. 173–81.
[G: U.S.]

Lall, Sanjaya. Transnationals and the Third World: Changing Perceptions. *Nat. Westminster Bank Quart. Rev.*, May 1984, pp. 2–16.
[G: OECD]

Lanteri, Marc. La multinationalisation des firmes européennes aux États-Unis: une approche dynamique. (The Spreading of European Multinational Firms in the U.S.A.: A Dynamic Approach. With English summary.) *Revue Écon.*, July 1984, 35(4), pp. 733–49. [G: U.S.]

LaPalombara, Joseph and Blank, Stephen. Multinational Corporations and Developing Countries. In *Ghosh, P. K.*, ed., no. 11, 1984, 1980, pp. 7–29. [G: OECD; LDCs]

Latcham, Franklin C. Water's Edge versus Worldwide Unitary Combination: Comments. In *McLure, C. E., Jr.*, ed., 1984, pp. 41–44.
[G: U.S.]

Latorraca, Nilton. Fiscal Obstacles to the International Flow of Capital between a Parent and Its Subsidiary: Brazil. In *Intn'l. Fisc. Assoc.*, vol. 69a, 1984, pp. 275–91. [G: Brazil]

Lauter, G. Peter. East–West Trade: Organizational Structures and Problems of U.S. Multinational Corporations. In *Jackson, M. R. and Woodson, J. D., Jr.*, eds., 1984, pp. 153–85.

Lecraw, Donald J. Bargaining Power, Ownership, and Profitability of Transnational Corporations in Developing Countries. *J. Int. Bus. Stud.*, Spring/Summer 1984, 15(1), pp. 27–43.

Lesourne, Jacques. The Changing Context of Industrial Policy: External and Internal Developments. In *Jacquemin, A.*, ed., 1984, pp. 13–38. [G: OECD]

Lim, Hua Sing. Japanese Perspectives on Malaysia's "Look East" Policy. In *Thambipillai, P.*, ed., 1984, pp. 231–45. [G: Malaysia; Japan]

Lindsay, Robert F. Purchase and Sale of a Canadian Business by a Nonresident of Canada. In *Purden, C.*, ed., 1984, pp. 305–30.
[G: Canada; U.S.]

Lipsey, Robert E. and Weiss, Merle Yahr. Foreign Production and Exports of Individual Firms. *Rev. Econ. Statist.*, May 1984, 66(2), pp. 304–08. [G: U.S.]

Litvak, Isaiah A. and Maule, Christopher J. Assessing Industry Concentration: The Case of

Aluminum. *J. Int. Bus. Stud.*, Spring/Summer 1984, *15*(1), pp. 97–104.

Lloyd, P. J. Mineral Economics in Australia: Linkages With Other Sectors of the Economy: Introduction. In *Lloyd, P. J., ed.*, 1984, pp. 158–69. **[G: Australia]**

Long, Franklin A. Potential Contributions of Western Business to the Service Sector of LDCs. In *Brooks, H.; Liebman, L. and Schelling, C. S., eds.*, 1984, pp. 319–37. **[G: LDCs]**

Lyons, Bruce R. The Pattern of International Trade in Differentiated Products: An Incentive for the Existence of Multinational Firms. In *Kierzkowski, H., ed.*, 1984, pp. 157–79.

Madura, Jeff. Construction of Currency Cocktails for Export Pricing. *Bus. Econ.*, April 1984, *19*(3), pp. 40–47.

Magallona, Merlin M. The Export of Free-Enterprise Capitalism: The Politics of TNCs. In *Ngo, M., ed., vol. 1*, 1984, pp. 124–42. **[G: LDCs]**

Magee, Stephen P. Multinational Corporations, the Industry Technology Cycle and Development. In *Ghosh, P. K., ed., no. 11*, 1984, *1977*, pp. 219–45. **[G: LDCs]**

Maizels, Alfred. A Conceptual Framework for Analysis of Primary Commodity Markets. *World Devel.*, January 1984, *12*(1), pp. 25–41. **[G: Global]**

Mansfield, Edwin. R&D and Innovation: Some Empirical Findings. In *Griliches, Z., ed.*, 1984, pp. 127–48. **[G: U.S.]**

Mansfield, Edwin. R&D and Innovation: Some Empirical Findings: Reply. In *Griliches, Z., ed.*, 1984, pp. 154. **[G: U.S.]**

Markusen, James R. Multinationals, Multi-plant Economies, and the Gains from Trade. *J. Int. Econ.*, May 1984, *16*(3/4), pp. 205–26.

McColl, G. D. Foreign Investment in Australian Mining. In *Lloyd, P. J., ed.*, 1984, pp. 176–207. **[G: Australia]**

McDermott, John. Rational Host Country Use of a Severance Tax. *J. Environ. Econ. Manage.*, December 1984, *11*(4), pp. 391–402.

Mercusa, Antonio. Existing Opportunities and Prospects for Investment in Southern Italy. *Rev. Econ. Cond. Italy*, Sept.–Dec. 1984, (3), pp. 389–97. **[G: Italy]**

Meredith, Lindsay Norman. U.S. Multinational Investment in Canadian Manufacturing Industries. *Rev. Econ. Statist.*, February 1984, *66*(1), pp. 111–19. **[G: U.S.; Canada]**

Miller, Benjamin F. Worldwide Unitary Combination: The California Practice. In *McLure, C. E., Jr., ed.*, 1984, pp. 132–66. **[G: U.S.]**

Milton, David R. Worldwide Unitary Combination: The California Practice: Comments. In *McLure, C. E., Jr., ed.*, 1984, pp. 182–91. **[G: U.S.]**

Miyamoto, Matao. Multinational Growth of Japanese Manufacturing Enterprises in the Postwar Period: Comments. In *Okochi, A. and Inoue, T., eds.*, 1984, pp. 121–23. **[G: Japan; U.S.; W. Europe]**

Möller, Kristian. Role of Promotional Management in Exporting to the Soviet Union and

OECD Countries. In *Kaynak, E., ed.*, 1984, pp. 318–34. **[G: U.S.S.R.; OECD]**

Montgomery, Fred H. Water's Edge verus Worldwide Unitary Combination: Comments. In *McLure, C. E., Jr., ed.*, 1984, pp. 45–52. **[G: U.S.]**

Mucchielli, Jean-Louis. Investissements internationaux et dynamique des avantages comparatifs des nouveaux pays industrialisés. (International Investments and the Changing Pattern of Comparative Advantages—An Application to the New Industrializing Countries. With English summary.) *Revue Écon.*, May 1984, *35*(3), pp. 537–70. **[G: Global]**

Muller, Edward N. Financial Dependence in the Capitalist World Economy and the Distribution of Income Within Nations. In *Seligson, M. A., ed.*, 1984, pp. 256–82. **[G: Selected Countries]**

Musgrave, Peggy B. The Relevance of the Unitary Approach for Developing Countries: Comments. In *McLure, C. E., Jr., ed.*, 1984, pp. 281–85.

Mytelka, Lynn Krieger. Foreign Business and Economic Development. In *Zartman, I. W. and Delgado, C. L., eds.*, 1984, pp. 149–73. **[G: Ivory Coast]**

Nakagawa, Keiichiro. A Comparison of the Emergence of Multinational Manufacturing by U.S., European, and Japanese Firms: Japanese Firms' Foreign Direct Investment in the U.S.: Comments. In *Okochi, A. and Inoue, T., eds.*, 1984, pp. 61–63. **[G: Europe; Japan; U.S.]**

Niosi, Jorge. La multinationalisation des pétrolières canadiennes. (Multinationalization of Canadian Oil and Gas Industries. With English summary.) *L'Actual. Econ.*, March 1984, *60*(1), pp. 106–21. **[G: Canada]**

Nollen, Stanley D. The Case of John Brown Engineering and the Soviet Gas Pipeline. In *Czinkota, M. R., ed.*, 1984, pp. 111–42. **[G: U.K.; U.S.; U.S.S.R.; W. Europe]**

Nunez del Prado, Arturo. The Transnational Corporations in a New Planning Process. In *Ghosh, P. K., ed., no. 11*, 1984, *1981*, pp. 273–93. **[G: Latin America]**

Nunns, James R. Alternative Divisions of the Tax Base: How Much Is at Stake? Comments. In *McLure, C. E., Jr., ed.*, 1984, pp. 220–27. **[G: U.S.]**

Ó hUallacháin, Breandán. Input–Output Linkages and Foreign Direct Investment in Ireland. *Int. Reg. Sci. Rev.*, December 1984, *9*(3), pp. 185–200. **[G: Ireland]**

Odell, Peter R. Dimensions of Resource Dependence in Exporting Countries: Comment. In *Pearce, D. W.; Siebert, H. and Walter, I., eds.*, 1984, pp. 134–36. **[G: Papua New Guinea; LDCs]**

Oldman, Oliver. The Relevance of the Unitary Approach for Developing Countries: Comments. In *McLure, C. E., Jr., ed.*, 1984, pp. 286–87.

Pack, Howard. The Choice of Production Techniques by Foreign and Local Firms in Korea:

Comment. *Econ. Develop. Cult. Change,* April 1984, *32*(3), pp. 625–28. **[G: S. Korea]**

Paliwoda, Stanley J. East–West Trade Relations and International Marketing Strategy Formulation. In *Kaynak, E., ed.,* 1984, pp. 286–304.

Park, Eul Y. Patterns of Foreign Direct Investment, Foreign Ownership, and Industrial Performance: The Case of the Korean Manufacturing Industry. In *Benjamin, R. and Kudrle, R. T.,* 1984, pp. 127–60. **[G: S. Korea]**

Peet, Richard. Class Struggle, the Relocation of Employment, and Economic Crisis. *Sci. Soc.,* Spring 1984, *48*(1), pp. 38–51. **[G: U.S.]**

Penrose, Edith. The Management of Conflict in Natural-Resource Projects. In *Pearce, D. W.; Siebert, H. and Walter, I., eds.,* 1984, pp. 37–56.

Peters, James H. Alternative Divisions of the Tax Base: How Much Is at Stake? Comments. In *McLure, C. E., Jr., ed.,* 1984, pp. 217–19. **[G: U.S.]**

Petersen, Robert A. Worldwide Unitary Combination: The California Practice: Comments. In *McLure, C. E., Jr., ed.,* 1984, pp. 167–72. **[G: U.S.]**

Picciotto, Sol. Political Economy and International Law. In *Strange, S., ed.,* 1984, pp. 164–82. **[G: Global]**

Pires, Manuel. Fiscal Obstacles to the International Flow of Capital between a Parent and Its Subsidiary: Portugal. In *Intn'l. Fisc. Assoc., vol. 69a,* 1984, pp. 429–41. **[G: Portugal]**

Prud'homme, Rémy. Les investissements des multinationales de l'automobile dans le Tiers-Monde. (With English summary.) *Rev. Econ. Ind.,* 3rd Trimester 1984, (29), pp. 62–77. **[G: LDCs]**

Prybyla, Jan S. China's Special Economic Zones. *ACES Bull.,* Winter 1984, *26*(4), pp. 1–23. **[G: China]**

Reid, Robert J. Tax Implications of a Change in Control. In *Purden, C., ed.,* 1984, pp. 84–113. **[G: Canada]**

Reid, Stan D. Market Expansion and Firm Internationalization. In *Kaynak, E., ed.,* 1984, pp. 197–206.

Reutlinger, Shlomo. Project Food Aid and Equitable Growth: Income–Transfer Efficiency First! *World Devel.,* September 1984, *12*(9), pp. 901–11. **[G: Egypt; India; Pakistan]**

Rhodes, Harold L. British Public Enterprises and Project Initiation in the Developing World. In *Ramanadham, V. V., ed.,* 1984, pp. 87–108. **[G: U.K.]**

Rice, Gillian. An Empirical Study of the Effect of Political Uncertainty on International Marketing Strategy. In *Kaynak, E., ed.,* 1984, pp. 51–69. **[G: U.S.]**

Rico B., Guillermo and Arango, Fernando. Fiscal Obstacles to the International Flow of Capital between a Parent and Its Subsidiary: Colombia. In *Intn'l. Fisc. Assoc., vol. 69a,* 1984, pp. 293–306. **[G: Colombia]**

Riedel, Jürgen. Attitudes in the Federal Republic of Germany to the Policies of Developing Countries Regarding Foreign Investors. *Industry Devel.,* 1984, (13), pp. 1–38. **[G: W. Germany; LDCs]**

Rosson, Philip J. Success Factors in Manufacturer–Overseas Distributor Relationships in International Marketing. In *Kaynak, E., ed.,* 1984, pp. 91–107.

Rothschild, Leonard W., Jr. World-Wide Combined Reporting: Recent Developments. *Bull. Int. Fiscal Doc.,* April 1984, *38*(4), pp. 153–56. **[G: U.S.]**

Sales, Hubert. La recherche-développement dans la stratégie des grandes entreprises chimiques de l'entre-deux-guerres: Du Pont de Nemours, Imperial chemical industries, I. G. Farben. (With English summary.) *Revue Écon. Polit.,* July–August 1984, *94*(4), pp. 446–64. **[G: Germany]**

Samiee, Saeed. Transnational Data Flow Constraints: A New Challenge for Multinational Corporations. *J. Int. Bus. Stud.,* Spring/Summer 1984, *15*(1), pp. 141–50.

Sander, Jens-Jacob and Truyen, Pieter. Fiscal Obstacles to the International Flow of Capital between a Parent and Its Subsidiary: Norway. In *Intn'l. Fisc. Assoc., vol. 69a,* 1984, pp. 403–15. **[G: Norway]**

Savary, Julien. L'impact de l'investissement étranger en France sur l'emploi industriel (1974–1983). (With English summary.) *Revue Écon. Polit.,* September–October 1984, *94*(5), pp. 688–97. **[G: France]**

Schneider, Hans K. and Schulz, Walter. The Importing Country's Perspective: A Case Study of LNG. In *Pearce, D. W.; Siebert, H. and Walter, I., eds.,* 1984, pp. 295–310. **[G: Global]**

Schoettle, Ferdinand P. State Taxation Under the Commerce Clause: The History Revisited: Comments. In *McLure, C. E., Jr., ed.,* 1984, pp. 85–88. **[G: U.S.]**

Schwab, Bernhard. Financial Risk and Capital Structure: Theory and Practice in an International Context. In *Bamberg, G. and Spremann, K., eds.,* 1984, pp. 271–84. **[G: OECD]**

Serra, Juan Francisca. Fiscal Obstacles to the International Flow of Capital between a Parent and Its Subsidiary: Uruguay. In *Intn'l. Fisc. Assoc., vol. 69a,* 1984, pp. 501–15. **[G: Uruguay]**

Shapiro, Alan C. Currency Risk and Relative Price Risk. *J. Finan. Quant. Anal.,* December 1984, *19*(4), pp. 365–73.

Sharma, D. Deo. Management Contract and International Marketing of Industrial Goods. In *Kaynak, E., ed.,* 1984, pp. 108–20. **[G: Sweden]**

Sharp, Mitchell. Canada's Independence and U.S. Domination. In *Fried, E. R. and Trezise, P. H., eds.,* 1984, pp. 11–20. **[G: Canada; U.S.]**

Sheffrin, Steven M. and Fulcher, Jack. Alternative Divisions of the Tax Base: How Much Is at Stake? In *McLure, C. E., Jr., ed.,* 1984, pp. 192–213. **[G: U.S.]**

Shihata, Ibrahim F. I. Increasing Private Capital

Flows to LDCs. *Finance Develop.*, December 1984, *21*(4), pp. 6–9. **[G: OECD; LDCs]**

Sigmund, Paul E. The Regulation of Foreign Investment in Mexico and Its Impact on Income Distribution. In *Aspe, P. and Sigmund, P. E., eds.*, 1984, pp. 247–64. **[G: Mexico]**

Smart, Ian. The Importing Country's Perspective: A Case Study of LNG: Comment. In *Pearce, D. W.; Siebert, H. and Walter, I., eds.*, 1984, pp. 311–18. **[G: Global]**

Spence, A. Michael. Industrial Organization and Competitive Advantage in Multinational Industries. *Amer. Econ. Rev.*, May 1984, *74*(2), pp. 356–60.

Stanley, Marjorie T. and Block, Stanley B. A Survey of Multinational Capital Budgeting. *Financial Rev.*, March 1984, *19*(1), pp. 36–54. **[G: U.S.]**

Stock, John R. and Lambert, Douglas M. International Distribution Systems: A Comparative Approach. In *Kaynak, E. and Savitt, R., eds.*, 1984, pp. 183–99. **[G: U.S.; U.K.; Japan; Australia]**

Stopford, John. Joint Ventures between Multinational Corporations and Local State Enterprises. In *Ramanadham, V. V., ed.*, 1984, pp. 71–86. **[G: Selected LDCs]**

Sudit, Ephraim F. The Role of Comparative Productivity Accounting in Export Decisions. *J. Int. Bus. Stud.*, Spring/Summer 1984, *15*(1), pp. 105–18. **[G: U.S.; Japan]**

Sunoo, Harold Hakwon. The Transnational Development of South Korea. In *Ngo, M., ed., vol. 1,* 1984, pp. 427–50. **[G: S. Korea]**

Svejnar, Jan and Smith, Stephen C. The Economics of Joint Ventures in Less Developed Countries. *Quart. J. Econ.*, February 1984, *99*(1), pp. 149–67.

Swaine, G. D. Fiscal Obstacles to the International Flow of Capital between a Parent and Its Subsidiary: United Kingdom. In *Intn'l. Fisc. Assoc., vol. 69a,* 1984, pp. 443–60. **[G: U.K.]**

Tannenwald, Robert. The Pros and Cons of Worldwide Unitary Taxation. *New Eng. Econ. Rev.*, July–August 1984, pp. 17–28. **[G: U.S.]**

Tapia, Humberto S. The Experience of Latin America in Marketing Exports to the United States: Some Lessons for Romania. In *Jackson, M. R. and Woodson, J. D., Jr., eds.*, 1984, pp. 245–77. **[G: U.S.; Latin America; Romania]**

Tichy, Geiserich E. Steuerliche Behinderungen des internationalen Kapitalflusses zwischen einer Muttergesellschaft und ihrer Tochtergesellschaft: Österreich. (Fiscal Obstacles to the International Flow of Capital between a Parent and Its Subsidiary: Austria. With English Summary.) In *Intn'l. Fisc. Assoc., vol. 69a,* 1984, pp. 227–53. **[G: Austria]**

Tikka, Kari S. Fiscal Obstacles to the International Flow of Capital between a Parent and Its Subsidiary: Finland. In *Intn'l. Fisc. Assoc., vol. 69a,* 1984, pp. 333–38. **[G: Finland]**

Tsokhas, K. 'A Touch of Midas': The Rise of West-ern Mining Corporation, 1945–1975. *Australian Econ. Hist. Rev.*, September 1984, *24*(2), pp. 132–49. **[G: Australia]**

Udagawa, Masaru. The Contribution of Sogo Shosha to the Multinationalization of Japanese Industrial Enterprises in Historical Perspective: Comments. In *Okochi, A. and Inoue, T., eds.*, 1984, pp. 93–94. **[G: Japan]**

Ulmer, John M. Canadian Acquisition of a Foreign Business: A Canadian Perspective. In *Purden, C., ed.*, 1984, pp. 245–73. **[G: Canada]**

Usui, Mikoto. Transnational Enterprises and International Development: A New Focus in the Perspective of Industrial and Technological Cooperation. In *Ghosh, P. K., ed., no. 11,* 1984, pp. 259–72.

Utrecht, Ernst. Structural Distortions in Indonesia's Economic Development. In *Ngo, M., ed., vol. 1,* 1984, pp. 378–403. **[G: Indonesia]**

Vaitsos, Constantine V. Strategic Choices in the Commercialization of Technology: The Point of View of Developing Countries. In *Ghosh, P. K., ed., no. 3,* 1984, *1973*, pp. 273–91. **[G: LDCs]**

Varvello, Pietro. Esportare o internazionalizzarsi? (Export or Go International? With English summary.) *L'Impresa*, 1984, *26*(5), pp. 33–43.

Vogel, Klaus. Fiscal Obstacles to the International Flow of Capital between a Parent and Its Subsidiary: General Report. In *Intn'l. Fisc. Assoc., vol. 69a,* 1984, pp. 97–132.

de Vos, Gerrit Th. B and Zurawicki, Leon. International Trading Companies for Developing Countries—Latin America. *METU*, 1984, *11*(3–4), pp. 307–24. **[G: Brazil; E. Asia; Latin America]**

Walter, Ingo. Project Finance—The Lender's Perspective. In *Pearce, D. W.; Siebert, H. and Walter, I., eds.*, 1984, pp. 249–70. **[G: Selected Countries]**

Watanabe, Susumu. Multinational Enterprises, Employment and Technology Adaptations. In *Ghosh, P. K., ed., no. 11,* 1984, *1981*, pp. 175–94. **[G: LDCs]**

Westphal, Larry E.; Rhee, Yung W. and Pursell, Garry. Sources of Technological Capability in South Korea. In *Fransman, M. and King, K., eds.*, 1984, pp. 279–300. **[G: S. Korea]**

Wheelwright, E. The Political Economy of Foreign Domination. In *Lloyd, P. J., ed.*, 1984, *1982*, pp. 208–25. **[G: Australia]**

Whitley, Glenn R. Project Financing: The Borrower's View. In *Pearce, D. W.; Siebert, H. and Walter, I., eds.*, 1984, pp. 271–91. **[G: Selected Countries]**

Whynes, David K. International Political Economy. In *Whynes, D. K., ed.*, 1984, pp. 162–86.

Widyono, Benny. Transnational Corporations and Export-Oriented Primary Commodities: A Conceptual Framework for Research. In *Ngo, M., ed., vol. 1,* 1984, pp. 107–23. **[G: LDCs]**

Williams, Roger. The International Political Economy of Technology. In *Strange, S., ed.*, 1984, pp. 70–90. **[G: Global]**

Wilpert, Bernhard. Participation in Organizations: Evidence from International Comparative Research. *Int. Soc. Sci. J.*, 1984, *36*(2), pp. 355–66. [G: W. Europe]

Winham, Gilbert R. The Canadian Automobile Industry and Trade-related Performance Requirements. *J. World Trade Law*, November: December 1984, *18*(6), pp. 471–96. [G: Canada; U.S.]

Wu, Friedrich. Realities Confronting China's Foreign Investment Policy. *World Econ.*, September 1984, *7*(3), pp. 295–311. [G: China]

Yang, Tien-yi. Foreign Business Activities and the Chinese Response, 1842–1937. In *Okochi, A. and Inoue, T., eds.*, 1984, pp. 215–57. [G: China]

Yaprak, Attila and Parameswaran, Ravi. Reliability Measurement in Cross-National Survey Research: An Empirical Evaluation. In *Kaynak, E., ed.*, 1984, pp. 172–93. [G: Turkey; U.S.; W. Germany; Japan; Italy]

Yaprak, Attila; Sorek, Christopher and Parameswaran, Ravi. Competitive Strategy in Multinational Oligopolies: The Role of Promotion in the Computer Industry. In *Kaynak, E., ed.*, 1984, pp. 232–55. [G: U.K.; U.S.]

Yasumuro, Ken'ichi. The Contribution of Sogo Shosha to the Multinationalization of Japanese Industrial Enterprises in Historical Perspective. In *Okochi, A. and Inoue, T., eds.*, 1984, pp. 65–92. [G: Japan]

Yoshihara, Hideki. Multinational Growth of Japanese Manufacturing Enterprises in the Postwar Period. In *Okochi, A. and Inoue, T., eds.*, 1984, pp. 95–120. [G: Japan; U.S.; W. Europe]

Yoshino, M. Yotaro. The Evolution of United States Multinational Enterprises. In *Okochi, A. and Inoue, T., eds.*, 1984, pp. 157–81. [G: U.S.]

Young, Stephen. The Foreign-Owned Manufacturing Sector. In *Hood, N. and Young, S., eds.*, 1984, pp. 93–127. [G: U.K.]

Yuzawa, Takeshi. The History of Multinational Factories in Australia: Comments. In *Okochi, A. and Inoue, T., eds.*, 1984, pp. 211–13. [G: Australia]

443 International Lending and Aid (public)

4430 International Lending and Aid (public)

Abdelmula, Yousef. Lafico and the Libyan Contribution to Development Assistance. In *Achilli, M. and Khaldi, M., eds.*, 1984, pp. 194–200. [G: Libya]

Acciaris, Ricardo. Cuba's Economic Relations with Latin America and the Caribbean. *Soviet E. Europ. Foreign Trade*, Fall 1984, *20*(3), pp. 6–77. [G: Cuba; Latin America]

Achilli, Michele. The Role of the Arab Development Funds in the World Economy: Introduction. In *Achilli, M. and Khaldi, M., eds.*, 1984, pp. 1–6.

Adam, Abdallah. The Arab Fund for Technical Assistance to African and Arab Countries. In *Achilli, M. and Khaldi, M., eds.*, 1984, pp. 220–30. [G: Africa; Arab Countries]

Ahmed, Abel Kader Sid. Arab Development Agencies and South–South Co-operation. In *Achilli, M. and Khaldi, M., eds.*, 1984, pp. 117–44. [G: Arab Countries; LDCs]

Ahn, Kookshin. Optimal Foreign Borrowing and Altruism in an Overlapping Generations Model. *J. Econ. Devel.*, December 1984, *9*(2), pp. 171–90.

Al-Ani, Awri. OPEC Aid to Developing Countries. In *Achilli, M. and Khaldi, M., eds.*, 1984, pp. 40–45. [G: OPEC]

Al-Humaidi, Bader. The Kuwait Fund for Arab Economic Development: The Loan Grant Policy and Procedure in Favour of Developing Countries. In *Achilli, M. and Khaldi, M., eds.*, 1984, pp. 59–66. [G: Kuwait]

Al-Salem, Suleiman. The Co-financing Operations of the Islamic Development Bank. In *Achilli, M. and Khaldi, M., eds.*, 1984, pp. 73–82. [G: Arab Countries; LDCs]

Aliber, Robert Z. Capital Flows, External Debt and the International Adjustment Process. In *Black, J. and Dorrance, G. S., eds.*, 1984, pp. 1–20. [G: LDCs]

Aliber, Robert Z. The Potential for Financial Crises: Comment. In *Agmon, T.; Hawkins, R. G. and Levich, R. M., eds.*, 1984, pp. 110–15.

Aloisi, Francesco. Perspectives of Bi-and Multilateral Co-financing within the Italian Policy of Co-operation for Development. In *Achilli, M. and Khaldi, M., eds.*, 1984, pp. 288–93. [G: Italy]

Amaral, Samuel. El empréstito de Londres de 1824. (With English summary.) *Desarrollo Econ.*, January-March 1984, *23*(92), pp. 559–88. [G: Argentina]

Ariah, T. and Daanoune, A. Development of and Prospects for Trade and Economic Co-operation between Morocco and the Socialist Countries of Eastern Europe. In *U.N.C.T.D.*, 1984, pp. 33–43. [G: Morocco; CMEA]

Arndt, Sven W. Liberalization Policies and the Implementation Question [The Impoverishing Effects of Foreign Aid]. *Cato J.*, Spring/Summer 1984, *4*(1), pp. 335–37.

Ayau, Manuel F. The Impoverishing Effects of Foreign Aid. *Cato J.*, Spring/Summer 1984, *4*(1), pp. 323–34.

Baer, Donald E. Issues in Country Risk Assessment. In *Jorge, A.; Salazar-Carrillo, J. and Sanchez, E. P.*, 1984, pp. 129–30.

Baqai, Moinuddin. A New Framework for International Financial Co-operation for Development. In *Ghosh, P. K., ed., no. 15*, 1984, *1979*, pp. 222–38.

Baron, Christopher. Appropriate Technology Comes of Age: A Review of Some Recent Literature and Aid Policy Statements. In *Ghosh, P. K., ed., no. 14*, 1984, *1978*, pp. 117–27. [G: LDCs]

Bartsch, J. M. and Stock, Ruth. Co-operation between the OECD, DAC Member Countries and the ARAB Development Funds. In *Achilli, M. and Khaldi, M., eds.*, 1984, pp. 256–61.

Bassetti, Piero. International Economic Co-operation and Arab Development Funds. In *Achilli, M. and Khaldi, M., eds.*, 1984, pp. 300–02.

Bauer, P. T. Multinational Aid: An Improvement? In *Bauer, P. T.*, 1984, pp. 63–72.

Bauer, P. T. and Yamey, B. S. Foreign Aid: Issues and Implications. In *Bauer, P. T.*, 1984, pp. 38–62.

Behrman, Jere R. and Sah, Raaj Kumar. What Role Does Equity Play in the International Distribution of Development Aid? In *[Chenery, H. B.]*, 1984, pp. 295–315. **[G: LDCs]**

Beim, David O. International Indebtedness: A New Perspective on LDC Debt. In *Hewlett, S. A.; Kaufman, H. and Kenen, P. B., eds.*, 1984, pp. 53–60. **[G: LDCs]**

Benoit, J. Pierre V. International Interest Rates, External Indebtedness of Developing Countries and Foreign Aid. In *Kessler, D. and Ullmo, P.-A., eds.*, 1984, pp. 241–67.
[G: LDCs; MDCs]

Bensión, Alberto. The Role of Commercial Banks in the Adjustment Process: Comment. In *Muns, J., ed.*, 1984, pp. 211–14. **[G: LDCs]**

Bernal, Richard L. Economic Growth and External Debt of Jamaica. In *Salazar-Carillo, J. and Tirado de Alonso, I., eds., no. 1*, 1984, pp. 1–27. **[G: Jamaica]**

Betz, Joachim. The Internationalization of Development Policy. In *Ghosh, P. K., ed., no. 8*, 1984, 1979, pp. 240–52. **[G: LDCs]**

Bhagwati, Jagdish N.; Brecher, Richard A. and Hatta, Tatsuo. The Paradoxes of Immiserizing Growth and Donor-enriching "Recipient-immiserizing" Transfers: A Tale of Two Literatures. *Weltwirtsch. Arch.*, 1984, 120(2), pp. 228–43.

Bharier, Julian. Water Supply and Waste Disposal. In *Weiss, C. and Jéquier, N., eds.*, 1984, pp. 107–24.

Biagioli, Antonello. Principali aspetti evolutivi del debito estero dell'Italia. (Principal Aspects of the Development of Italy's Foreign Debt. With English summary.) *Bancaria*, February 1984, 40(2), pp. 178–82. **[G: Italy]**

Bigman, David and Taya, Teizo. Floating Exchange Rates and the State of World Trade and Payments: Introduction. In *Bigman, D. and Taya, T., eds.*, 1984, pp. xvii–xxvi.

Blackwell, Michael. Aid Flows: The Role of the DAC. *Finance Develop.*, March 1984, 21(1), pp. 42–43. **[G: LDCs; OECD]**

Boeck, Klaus. The Supply of International Liquidity to Developing Countries. In *Ghosh, P. K., ed., no. 7*, 1984, 1977, pp. 195–203.

Boffito, Carlo. Il finanziamento bancario internazionale dei paesi in via di sviluppo e dei paesi europei del Comecon negli anni '70 e '80. (International Financing for Developing Countries and for the European Comecon Countries in the 1970s and 1980s. With English summary.) *Bancaria*, March 1984, 40(3), pp. 279–94. **[G: LDCs; CMEA]**

Boleat, Mark. Housing Finance in Developing Countries. In *Kessler, D. and Ullmo, P.-A., eds.*, 1984, pp. 183–203. **[G: LDCs; MDCs]**

Boloña, Carlos. The Role of Economy-Wide

Prices in the Adjustment Process: Comment. In *Muns, J., ed.*, 1984, pp. 110–12.
[G: LDCs]

Bourne, Compton. External Debt and Economic Growth in the Commonwealth Caribbean. In *Salazar-Carillo, J. and Tirado de Alonso, I., eds., no. 1*, 1984, pp. 1–5. **[G: Caribbean]**

Bradford, Colin I., Jr. The NICs: Confronting U.S. "Autonomy." In *Feinberg, R. E. and Kallab, V., eds., no. 1*, 1984, pp. 119–38.
[G: LDCs]

Brady, Philip F. The Rubik's Cube of Canadian International Development Co-operation in the 1980s. *Can. J. Devel. Stud.*, 1984, 5(1), pp. 129–39. **[G: Canada]**

Brock, William E. Trade and Debt: The Vital Linkage. *Foreign Aff.*, Summer 1984, 62(5), pp. 1037–57. **[G: Global]**

Brovedani, Bruno. Cooperazione tra Fondo Monetario e banche internazionali. Strategia di ripiego o collaborazione permanente? (Cooperation between the IMF and International Banks: An Expedient or a Permanent Collaboration Strategy? With English summary.) *Bancaria*, December 1984, 40(12), pp. 1228–32.

Burnham, James B. World Debt and Monetary Order: Learning from the Past. *Cato J.*, Spring/Summer 1984, 4(1), pp. 71–80. **[G: Global]**

Calika, Nur. Somalia's Adjustment Experience, 1981–83. *Finance Develop.*, March 1984, 21(1), pp. 8. **[G: Somalia]**

Canela-Bueno, Luis A. The Dominican Republic External Debt: An Assessment of Its Evolution Over the Last Six Years. In *Salazar-Carillo, J. and Tirado de Alonso, I., eds., no. 1*, 1984, pp. 1–5. **[G: Dominican Republic]**

Carli, Guido and Savona, Paolo. Il commercio mondiale e la finanza internazionale. Annotazioni per la pianificazione strategica delle banche di credito internazionale. (World Trade and International Finance: Considerations for Strategic Planning by International Banks. With English summary.) *Bancaria*, December 1984, 40(12), pp. 1233–40. **[G: Global]**

Chabar, Hamid. Arab and Third-World Relations: Genesis of South–South Co-operation and Solidarity. In *Achilli, M. and Khaldi, M., eds.*, 1984, pp. 92–116. **[G: Arab Countries; LDCs]**

Chalumeau, Jean-Luc. La situation économique du Brésil. (With English summary.) *Revue Écon. Polit.*, September–October 1984, 94(5), pp. 615–19. **[G: Brazil]**

Chapman, Sheila A. The Foreign Debt of CMEA Nations: A Move towards Adjustment? *Econ. Notes*, 1984, (2), pp. 51–75. **[G: CMEA]**

Chichilnisky, Graciela. The Transfer Problem in Stable Markets: A Rejoinder to Rejoinders [Basic Goods, Commodity Transfers, and the International Economic Order]. *J. Devel. Econ.*, December 1984, 16(3), pp. 319–20.

Chishti, Sumitra. Experience of India in Trade and Economic Relations with the Socialist Countries of Eastern Europe and Its Relevance to Developing Countries. In *U.N.C.T.D.*, 1984, pp. 19–31. **[G: India; CMEA]**

Clark, George J. International Indebtedness: Economic Development. In *Hewlett, S. A.; Kaufman, H. and Kenen, P. B.*, eds., 1984, pp. 61–76. [G: LDCs]

Clausen, A. W. Toward Sustained Development: A Joint Program of Action for Sub-Saharan Africa. *Finance Develop.*, December 1984, *21*(4), pp. 29–30. [G: Sub-Saharan Africa]

Cline, William R. Restoring Credibility to International Lending: A Comment. *Cato J.*, Spring/Summer 1984, *4*(1), pp. 141–46. [G: Global]

Cline, William R. The Issue Is Illiquidity, Not Insolvency. *Challenge*, July/August 1984, *27*(3), pp. 12–20. [G: Latin America]

Cline, William R.; Vidal, D. and Seaberry, J. Banca e Finanza nell' America Latina. (Debt Recovery: A Qualified Hope for Latin America. With English summary.) *Mondo Aperto*, March-April 1984, *38*(2), pp. 77–94. [G: Latin America]

Cockaerts, M. The Debt Problem: A Challenge for the Banks. *Tijdschrift Econ. Manage.*, 1984, *29*(4), pp. 539–52. [G: LDCs]

Cohen, Benjamin J. High Finance, High Politics. In *Feinberg, R. E. and Kallab, V.*, eds., no. 2, 1984, pp. 107–24. [G: LDCs; U.S.]

Corea, Gamani. The Debt Problem of Developing Countries. In *Ghosh, P. K.*, ed., no. 7, 1984, *1976*, pp. 216–43.

Costales, Rene. Inter-American Development Bank: Electricity Tariffs, Policies and Practices. In *Munasinghe, M. and Rungta, S.*, eds., 1984, pp. 537–42. [G: Latin America]

Coukis, Basil P. and Jéquier, Nicolas. Civil Works Construction. In *Weiss, C. and Jéquier, N.*, eds., 1984, pp. 55–67.

Dawson, A. Suggestions for an Approach to Rural Development by Foreign Aid Programmes. In *Ghosh, P. K.*, ed., no. 10, 1984, *1978*, pp. 190–204.

Dell, Sidney. A Note on Stabilization and the World Bank. *World Devel.*, February 1984, *12*(2), pp. 165–67.

Desai, Padma. The Soviet Union and the Third World: A Faltering Partnership? In *Bhagwati, J. N. and Ruggie, J. G.*, eds., 1984, pp. 261–85. [G: U.S.S.R.; LDCs]

Diaz-Alejandro, Carlos F. Latin American Debt: I Don't Think We Are in Kansas Anymore. *Brookings Pap. Econ. Act.*, 1984, (2), pp. 335–89. [G: Latin America]

Díaz-Alejandro, Carlos F. Some Economic Lessons of the Early 1980s. In *Bhagwati, J. N. and Ruggie, J. G.*, eds., 1984, pp. 181–200. [G: LDCs]

Díaz-Alejandro, Carlos F. Some Financial Issues in the North, in the South, and in Between. In *Agmon, T.; Hawkins, R. G. and Levich, R. M.*, eds., 1984, pp. 119–45.

Donaldson, Graham. Technology in Agricultural Development. In *Weiss, C. and Jéquier, N.*, eds., 1984, pp. 19–34. [G: Global]

Donovan, Donal J. Nature and Origins of Debt-servicing Difficulties: Some Empirical Evidence. *Finance Develop.*, December 1984, *21*(4), pp. 22–25. [G: LDCs]

Dorn, James A. A Property Rights View of the Debt Crisis. *Cato J.*, Spring/Summer 1984, *4*(1), pp. 1–8. [G: Global]

Dornbusch, Rudiger. Adjustments in World Payments: An Evaluation: Discussion. In *Fed. Res. Bank Boston*, 1984, pp. 208–12. [G: Selected Countries]

Dornbusch, Rudiger. On the Consequences of Muddling through the Debt Crisis. *World Econ.*, June 1984, *7*(2), pp. 145–61. [G: Latin America; U.S.]

Dornbusch, Rudiger. The Latin American Dimension. *Challenge*, July/August 1984, *27*(3), pp. 4–11. [G: U.S.; Latin America]

Dornbusch, Rudiger. U.S. Monetary and Fiscal Policy, the Dollar and the International Financial System. In *Frenkel, J. A. and Mussa, M. L.*, eds., 1984, pp. 23–48. [G: U.S.; OECD; Latin America]

Dos Santos, Theotonio. The Structure of Dependence. In *Seligson, M. A.*, ed., 1984, *1970*, pp. 95–104.

Drewes, Wolfram U. and Sirkin, Abraham M. The Uses of Satellite Remote Sensing. In *Weiss, C. and Jéquier, N.*, eds., 1984, pp. 85–102.

Edwards, Sebastian. LDC Foreign Borrowing and Default Risk: An Empirical Investigation, 1976–80. *Amer. Econ. Rev.*, September 1984, *74*(4), pp. 726–34. [G: LDCs]

Edwards, Sebastian. Deuda externa y riesgo de pais. (With English summary.) *Cuadernos Econ.*, April 1984, *21*(62), pp. 3–23. [G: LDCs]

Edwards, Sebastian. Domestic Policies and Foreign Resource Requirements: Comment. *Quart. J. Econ.*, February 1984, *99*(1), pp. 201–06.

Edwards, Sebastian. The Role of International Reserves and Foreign Debt in the External Adjustment Process. In *Muns, J.*, ed., 1984, pp. 143–73. [G: LDCs; Latin America]

El-Helw, Mahmoud. Co-operation among Arab Development Financing Agencies. In *Achilli, M. and Khaldi, M.*, eds., 1984, pp. 83–91. [G: Arab Countries]

El-Helw, Mahmoud. The Role of the Arab Fund for Economic and Social Development. In *Achilli, M. and Khaldi, M.*, eds., 1984, pp. 46–58. [G: Arab Countries]

El Shibly, Mekki. Foreign Capital Inflow, Domestic Savings and Economic Growth: The Experience of the Sudan (1960/61–1974/75). *J. Econ. Devel.*, July 1984, *9*(1), pp. 125–45. [G: Sudan]

Emminger, Otmar. Adjustments in World Payments: An Evaluation. In *Fed. Res. Bank Boston*, 1984, pp. 196–207.

Epstein, José D. Some Financial Issues in the North, in the South, and in Between: Comment. In *Agmon, T.; Hawkins, R. G. and Levich, R. M.*, eds., 1984, pp. 146–50.

Espinosa, Juan Guillermo. The Role of International Reserves and Foreign Debt in the Exter-

nal Adjustment Process: Comment. **In** *Muns,
J., ed.*, 1984, pp. 174–79.   **[G: LDCs;
Latin America]**

Fabbri, Miguel A. The IMF's Conditionality Re-
Examined: Comment. **In** *Muns, J., ed.*, 1984,
pp. 80–83.   **[G: LDCs]**

Faber, Gerrit. The Economics of Stabex. *J. World
Trade Law*, January:February 1984, *18*(1), pp.
52–62.   **[G: EEC; Selected LDCs]**

Falcon, Walter P. The Role of the United States
in Alleviating World Hunger. **In** *Eicher,
C. K. and Staatz, J. M., eds.*, 1984, pp. 176–88.
                          [G: U.S.]

Feinberg, Richard E. The Adjustment Imperative
and U.S. Policy. **In** *Feinberg, R. E. and Kallab,
V., eds., no. 1*, 1984, pp. 3–18. **[G: LDCs;
U.S.]**

Feldstein, Martin. From Crisis to Renewed
Growth. *Challenge*, July/August 1984, *27*(3),
pp. 27–30.   **[G: Latin America]**

Fischer, Bernhard. South Bank and Third World
Money. A Critical Assessment. *Konjunkturpolitik*, 1984, *30*(5), pp. 317–25.   **[G: LDCs]**

Fishlow, Albert. The Debt Crisis: Round Two
Ahead? **In** *Feinberg, R. E. and Kallab, V.,
eds., no. 1*, 1984, pp. 31–58.   **[G: LDCs;
OECD]**

Fishlow, Albert. The Debt Crisis: Solution by
Economic Integration? **In** *Núñez del Arco, J.;
Margain, E. and Cherol, R., eds.*, 1984, pp.
64–91.   **[G: Latin America]**

Franco, Giampiero and Mengarelli, Gianluigi.
Il debito estero dell'Italia. (Italy's Foreign
Debt. With English summary.) *Bancaria*, Feb-
ruary 1984, *40*(2), pp. 140–45.   **[G: Italy]**

Frey, Bruno S. The Function of Governments
and Intergovernmental Organizations in the
International Resource Transfer—The Case of
the World Bank. *Weltwirtsch. Arch.*, 1984,
120(4), pp. 702–19.   **[G: Global]**

Friedman, Kenneth S. and Garcha, Balwant S.
Sustaining Recovery, Reviving Development.
Finance Develop., December 1984, *21*(4), pp.
31–33.   **[G: Global]**

Gold, Joseph [Sir]. The General Arrangements
to Borrow of the International Monetary Fund.
In *Gold, J.*, 1984, pp. 478–511.

Gold, Joseph [Sir]. The Relationship Between the
International Monetary Fund and the World
Bank. **In** *Gold, J.*, 1984, *1981*, pp. 453–77.

Goldman, Morris B. The United States Treasury
Review of the Multilateral Development
Banks: An Economic Critique. *J. Monet.
Econ.*, March 1984, *13*(2), pp. 275–93.
                          [G: U.S.]

Goldwater, Carmel. Humanitarian Situation in
Kampuchea. **In** *Thambipillai, P., ed.*, 1984,
pp. 162–76.   **[G: Cambodia]**

Gollas, Manuel. Mexico's Perspectives under a
Three-Year Agreement with the IMF: Re-
marks. **In** *Jorge, A.; Salazar-Carrillo, J. and
Sanchez, E. P.*, 1984, pp. 69–70.
                          [G: Mexico]

Gonçalves, Reinaldo. Brazil and Mexico: The
IMF Stabilization Programmes and Banks' Re-

scheduling. *Econ. Int.*, February–May 1984,
37(1–2), pp. 76–93.   **[G: Brazil; Mexico]**

Gordon, Wendell C. The Implementation of Economic Development. *J. Econ. Issues*, March
1984, *18*(1), pp. 295–313.   **[G: Global]**

de Grauwe, Paul and Fratianni, Michele. The
Political Economy of International Lending.
Cato J., Spring/Summer 1984, *4*(1), pp. 147–
70.   **[G: Global]**

Graziani, Giovanni. Les mouvements de capital
au sein du Comecon. (Capital Movements
within the CMEA. With English summary.)
Écon. Soc., February 1984, *18*(2), pp. 45–77.
                          [G: CMEA]

Griffith-Jones, Stephany and Rodriguez, Ennio.
Private International Finance and Industrialisation of LDCs. *J. Devel. Stud.*, October 1984,
21(1), pp. 47–74.   **[G: Brazil; Chile]**

Ground, Richard Lynn. Orthodox Adjustment
Programmes in Latin America: A Critical Look
at the Policies of the International Monetary
Fund. *Cepal Rev.*, 1984, (23), pp. 45–82.
                          [G: Latin America]

Guenther, Jack D. The Role of Commercial Banks
in the Adjustment Process. **In** *Muns, J., ed.*,
1984, pp. 184–205.   **[G: LDCs]**

Guerguil, Martine. The International Financial
Crisis: Diagnoses and Prescriptions. *Cepal
Rev.*, 1984, (24), pp. 147–69.

Guillaumont, Sylviane. La situation monétaire et
finacière des États africains de la zone franc.
(With English summary.) *Revue Écon. Polit.*,
September–October 1984, *94*(5), pp. 592–601.
                          [G: Africa]

Gwin, Catherine. Strengthening the Framework
of the Global Economic Organizations. **In**
Bhagwati, J. N. and Ruggie, J. G., eds., 1984,
pp. 125–77.

Gwin, Catherine. The IMF and the World Bank:
Measures to Improve the System. **In** *Feinberg,
R. E. and Kallab, V., eds., no. 2*, 1984, pp.
87–106.   **[G: LDCs; OECD]**

Hassan, Abdul Razek. The Arab Assistance organs
and their Role in Economic Development. **In**
Achilli, M. and Khaldi, M., eds., 1984, pp.
201–19.   **[G: Arab Countries]**

Hassan, Mostafa F. Trade Prospects for the Oil
Exporters: The Case of Venezuela. **In** *Jorge,
A.; Salazar-Carrillo, J. and Sanchez, E. P.*,
1984, pp. 71–81.   **[G: Latin America;
Venezuela]**

Hewitt, Adrian. The Lomé Conventions: Entering a Second Decade. *J. Common Market
Stud.*, December 1984, *23*(2), pp. 95–115.
                          [G: Global]

Hilton, H. Geoffrey. The International Finance
Corporation. **In** *Weiss, C. and Jéquier, N.,
eds.*, 1984, pp. 227–45.

Hood, William C. Outlook for the World Financial
System: The IMF Perspective. *Contemp. Policy Issue*, January 1984, (4), pp. 76–82.
                          [G: Global]

**Hoopengardner, Thomas and Garcia-Thoumi,
Ines.** The World Bank in a Changing Financial
Environment. *Finance Develop.*, June 1984,
21(2), pp. 12–14.

Hope, Nicholas C. and McMurray, David W. Loan Capital in Development Finance, the Role of Banks, and Some Implications for Managing Debt. In *Black, J. and Dorrance, G. S., eds.*, 1984, pp. 93–139. **[G: LDCs]**

Hormats, Robert D. New Factors in the World Economy in the Wake of the Debt Crisis. In *Hewlett, S. A.; Kaufman, H. and Kenen, P. B., eds.*, 1984, pp. 167–79.

Humaidan, Saleh H. The Activities of the Saudi Fund for Development. In *Achilli, M. and Khaldi, M., eds.*, 1984, pp. 67–72.
[G: Saudi Arabia]

Hürni, Bettina. Der Beitritt der Schweiz zu den Institutionen von Bretton Woods: Wirtschaftliche Aspekte. (The Swiss Accession to the Bretton Woods: Economic Aspects. With English summary.) *Schweiz. Z. Volkswirtsch. Statist.*, June 1984, *120*(2), pp. 123–39.

Hussain, M. Nureldin and Thirlwall, A. P. The IMF Supply-Side Approach to Devaluation: An Assessment with Reference to the Sudan. *Oxford Bull. Econ. Statist.*, May 1984, *46*(2), pp. 145–67. **[G: Sudan]**

Ishimine, Tomotaka. Food, Energy and Debt Servicing as Reserve and Development Constraints of Less Developed Countries. *Rivista Int. Sci. Econ. Com.*, April 1984, *31*(4), pp. 371–79. **[G: LDCs]**

Islam, Nurul. New Mechanisms for the Transfer of Resources to Developing Countries. In *Ghosh, P. K., ed., no. 10*, 1984, *1976*, pp. 145–89.

Jéquier, Nicolas and Weiss, Charles. Introduction: The World Bank as a Technological Institution. In *Weiss, C. and Jéquier, N., eds.*, 1984, pp. 1–13.

Jéquier, Nicolas and Weiss, Charles. Technology, Finance, and Development: General Conclusions. In *Weiss, C. and Jéquier, N., eds.*, 1984, pp. 313–28.

Ji, Chongwei. China's Utilization of Foreign Funds and Relevant Policies. *Chinese Econ. Stud.*, Winter 1983–84, *17*(2), pp. 37–49.
[G: China]

Jordan, Jerry L. Restoring Credibility to International Lending. *Cato J.*, Spring/Summer 1984, *4*(1), pp. 131–39. **[G: Global]**

Kaplinsky, Raphael. The International Context for Industrialisation in the Coming Decade. *J. Devel. Stud.*, October 1984, *21*(1), pp. 75–96.

Karunaratne, Neil Dias. Foreign Aid, New Economic Order and Basic Human Needs. In *Ghosh, P. K., ed., no. 10*, 1984, *1979*, pp. 205–14.

Karunaratne, Neil Dias. Foreign Aid, New Economic Order and Basic Human Needs. In *Ghosh, P. K., ed., no. 9*, 1984, *1979*, pp. 135–44.

Kaufman, Henry. Complexities of U.S. Stabilization Policies in an International Context. In *Hewlett, S. A.; Kaufman, H. and Kenen, P. B., eds.*, 1984, pp. 1–12. **[G: U.S.]**

Khader, Bichara. The Afro–Arab Alliance: an

Economic Strategy for the 1980s. In *Achilli, M. and Khaldi, M., eds.*, 1984, pp. 155–93.
[G: OECD; Arab Countries; LDCs]

Khaldi, Mohamed. Arab Aid in the World Economy. In *Achilli, M. and Khaldi, M., eds.*, 1984, pp. 7–39. **[G: Arab Countries; LDCs]**

Kharas, Homi. The Long-Run Creditworthiness of Developing Countries: Theory and Practice. *Quart. J. Econ.*, August 1984, *99*(3), pp. 415–39. **[G: LDCs]**

Kibola, Hamisi S. Stabex and Lomé III. *J. World Trade Law*, January:February 1984, *18*(1), pp. 32–51. **[G: EEC; Selected LDCs]**

Killick, Tony, et al. The IMF: Case for a Change in Emphasis. In *Feinberg, R. E. and Kallab, V., eds., no. 1*, 1984, pp. 59–81. **[G: LDCs; OECD]**

Kindleberger, Charles P. International Emergency Lending Facilities—Are They Adequate? Discussion. In *Fed. Res. Bank Boston*, 1984, pp. 99–101. **[G: Latin America]**

Kinley, David; Collins, Joseph and Lappé, Moore. United States Aid to Asia: A Critique. In *Ngo, M., ed., vol. 1*, 1984, pp. 165–87.
[G: Asian LDCs; U.S.]

Kirpich, Phillip Z. Water Resources Development. In *Weiss, C. and Jéquier, N., eds.*, 1984, pp. 179–95. **[G: Selected Countries]**

Kleemeier, L. Domestic Policies versus Poverty-Oriented Foreign Assistance in Tanzania. *J. Devel. Stud.*, January 1984, *20*(2), pp. 171–201. **[G: Tanzania]**

Knorr, Klaus. Economic Relations as an Instrument of National Power. In *McCormick, G. H. and Bissell, R. E., eds.*, 1984, pp. 183–207.

Kondonassis, A. J. Some Major Trade and Development Programs of the European Economic Community with the LDCs: Toward a Common Development Policy? *J. Econ. Issues*, June 1984, *18*(2), pp. 651–62. **[G: EEC; LDCs]**

Krueger, Anne O. Debt Problems of Developing Countries. *METU*, 1984, *11*(3–4), pp. 249–61.
[G: LDCs]

Krueger, Anne O. The Developing Countries' Role in the World Economy. In *Frenkel, J. A. and Mussa, M. L., eds.*, 1984, pp. 63–83.
[G: LDCs]

Krugman, Paul R. Latin American Debt: I Don't Think We Are in Kansas Anymore: Comment. *Brookings Pap. Econ. Act.*, 1984, (2), pp. 390–93. **[G: Latin America]**

Kuczynski, Pedro-Pablo. International Emergency Lending Facilities—Are They Adequate? In *Fed. Res. Bank Boston*, 1984, pp. 84–98. **[G: LDCs; Latin America]**

Kugler, Peter. Economic Indicators and Debt Reschedulings, 1977–1981: Empirical Results from a Logit Model. *Rivista Int. Sci. Econ. Com.*, October–November 1984, *31*(10–11), pp. 992–1005.

Laird, Robbin F. Soviet Arms Trade with the Noncommunist Third World. In *Hoffmann, E. P., ed.*, 1984, pp. 196–213. **[G: U.S.S.R.; LDCs]**

Langoni, Carlos Geraldo. Country Debt Problems: The Brazilian Case. *Cato J.*, Spring/Summer 1984, *4*(1), pp. 343–53. **[G: Brazil]**

Lara, Juan. Mexico's Perspectives under a Three-Year Agreement with the IMF. **In** *Jorge, A.; Salazar-Carrillo, J. and Sanchez, E. P.*, 1984, pp. 61–68. **[G: Mexico]**

Larcarte, Julio A. Aspects of International Trade and Assistance Relating to the Expansion of Employment in the Developing Countries. **In** *Ghosh, P. K., ed., no. 16*, 1984, *1972*, pp. 124–51.

Latortue, Paul R. The External Debt Situation of Haiti. **In** *Salazar-Carillo, J. and Tirado de Alonso, I., eds., no. 1*, 1984, pp. 1–11.
[G: Latin America; Haiti]

Ledić Michèle. Debt Analysis and Debt-Related Issues: The Case of Yugoslavia. *Econ. Anal. Worker's Manage.*, 1984, *18*(1), pp. 35–64.
[G: Yugoslavia]

Leeds, Roger S. External Financing of Development: Challenges and Concerns. **In** *Ghosh, P. K., ed., no. 10*, 1984, *1980*, pp. 7–30.
[G: LDCs]

Leipziger, Danny M. The Concessionality of Foreign Assistance. *Finance Develop.*, March 1984, *21*(1), pp. 44–46. **[G: LDCs; MDCs]**

Lelart, M. Le nord et le sud face à la crise financière internationale. (The North and South in the International Financial Crisis. With English summary.) *Écon. Soc.*, June 1984, *18*(6), pp. 59–79. **[G: Global]**

Lele, Uma. Rural Africa: Modernization, Equity, and Long-term Development. **In** *Eicher, C. K. and Staatz, J. M., eds.*, 1984, *1981*, pp. 436–52. **[G: Africa]**

Lembke, Hans H. Entwicklungshilfepolitik im internationalen Vergleich—die nicht-projektgebundene Finanzierung. (Development Co-operation Policy in a Cross-Country Perspective—Rationale and Practice of Non-Project Aid. With English summary.) *Konjunkturpolitik*, 1984, *30*(2/3), pp. 170–87.
[G: OECD]

van Lennep, Jonkheer Emile. Strengthening the International Trade and Financial Systems. *World Econ.*, March 1984, *7*(1), pp. 23–32.
[G: OECD]

León, Carlos Amat Y. Fiscal Deficits and Balance of Payments Disequilibrium in IMF Adjustment Programs: Comment. **In** *Muns, J., ed.*, 1984, pp. 137–40. **[G: LDCs; Peru]**

Lessard, Donald R. Some Financial Issues in the North, in the South, and in Between: Comment. **In** *Agmon, T.; Hawkins, R. G. and Levich, R. M., eds.*, 1984, pp. 151–56.

Lethbridge, Christopher. European Community Financial Co-operation in the Arab Countries: The Role of the European Investment Bank. **In** *Achilli, M. and Khaldi, M., eds.*, 1984, pp. 269–75.

Lethem, Francis J. Basic Education. **In** *Weiss, C. and Jéquier, N., eds.*, 1984, pp. 157–74.

Levy, Victor. The Savings Gap and the Productivity of Foreign Aid to a Developing Economy: Egypt. *J. Devel. Areas*, October 1984, *19*(1), pp. 21–34. **[G: Egypt]**

Lim, Hua Sing. Japanese Perspectives on Malaysia's "Look East" Policy. **In** *Thambipillai, P., ed.*, 1984, pp. 231–45. **[G: Malaysia; Japan]**

Liviatan, Oded. A Macro-Absorption Approach for Estimating the Foreign Debt Burden. *Econ. Develop. Cult. Change*, July 1984, *32*(4), pp. 803–18. **[G: LDCs]**

Loser, Claudio M. The Role of Economy-Wide Prices in the Adjustment Process. **In** *Muns, J., ed.*, 1984, pp. 84–109. **[G: LDCs]**

Lubell, Harold. Third World Urbanization and International Assistance. *Urban Stud.*, February 1984, *21*(1), pp. 1–13. **[G: LDCs]**

Lucas, Adetokunbo O. The Tropical Diseases Research Program. **In** *Weiss, C. and Jéquier, N., eds.*, 1984, pp. 283–94.

Maizels, Alfred and Nissanke, Machiko K. Motivations for Aid to Developing Countries. *World Devel.*, September 1984, *12*(9), pp. 879–900.
[G: LDCs]

Málaga, Sergio. The Role of International Reserves and Foreign Debt in the External Adjustment Process: Comment. **In** *Muns, J., ed.*, 1984, pp. 180–83. **[G: LDCs; Latin America]**

Mammen, Thumpy. A Trade Gap Model and IMF Loan to India. *Indian Econ. J.*, January–March 1984, *31*(3), pp. 45–52. **[G: India]**

Marsden, Keith. Global Development Strategies and the Poor: Alternative Scenarios. **In** *Ghosh, P. K., ed., no. 8*, 1984, *1978*, pp. 58–83.
[G: Global]

Marsden, Keith and Roe, Alan. The Political Economy of Foreign Aid: A World Bank Perspective. **In** *Ghosh, P. K., ed., no. 10*, 1984, *1983*, pp. 133–44.

Masera, Rainer S. Rischi macro e microeconomici del sistema bancario internazionale: un approccio alternativo. (Macroeconomic and Microeconomic Risks of the International Banking System: An Alternative Approach. With English summary.) *Bancaria*, December 1984, *40*(12), pp. 1197–1200. **[G: LDCs]**

Massad, Carlos. The Role of Commercial Banks in the Adjustment Process: Comment. **In** *Muns, J., ed.*, 1984, pp. 206–10. **[G: LDCs]**

Meehan, Sheila. On the Spot. *Finance Develop.*, September 1984, *21*(3), pp. 47–48.

Meltzer, Allan H. The International Debt Problem. *Cato J.*, Spring/Summer 1984, *4*(1), pp. 63–69. **[G: LDCs]**

Minsky, Hyman P. The Potential for Financial Crises. **In** *Agmon, T.; Hawkins, R. G. and Levich, R. M., eds.*, 1984, pp. 91–109.

Moore, Mick. Institutional Development, the World Bank, and India's New Agricultural Extension Programme. *J. Devel. Stud.*, July 1984, *20*(4), pp. 303–17. **[G: India]**

Morss, Elliott R. Institutional Destruction Resulting from Donor and Project Proliferation in Sub-Saharan African Countries. *World Devel.*, April 1984, *12*(4), pp. 465–70. **[G: Africa]**

Most, Benjamin A. Latin America: The Case of Argentina. **In** *Groth, A. J. and Wade, L. L., eds.*, 1984, pp. 181–211. **[G: Argentina]**

Mould, Maurice C. World Bank: Financial Covenants and Their Use in the Development of

Pricing Policies. In *Munasinghe, M. and Rungta, S., eds.*, 1984, pp. 543–67.
[G: LDCs]

Muller, Edward N. Financial Dependence in the Capitalist World Economy and the Distribution of Income Within Nations. In *Seligson, M. A., ed.*, 1984, pp. 256–82.
[G: Selected Countries]

Mytelka, Lynn Krieger. Competition, Conflict and Decline in the Union Douanière et Economique de l'Afrique Centrale (UDEAC). In *Mazzeo, D., ed.*, 1984, pp. 131–49.
[G: Central Africa]

Nardolilli, Rocco. Trasferimento internazionale di risorse per lo sviluppo: il ruolo delle istituzioni multilaterali. (International Transfer of Development Resources: The Role of the Multilateral Institutions. With English summary.) *Bancaria*, October 1984, *40*(10), pp. 990–1003.
[G: Global]

Naru, Saleem M. Khan. Pakistan–U.S. Relations: Strategies of Growthmanship. In *Ngo, M., ed., vol. 1*, 1984, pp. 188–204. [G: Pakistan; U.S.]

Nelson, Joan M. The Political Economy of Stabilization: Commitment, Capacity, and Public Response. *World Devel.*, October 1984, *12*(10), pp. 983–1006. [G: Ghana; Zambia; Kenya; Sri Lanka; Jamaica]

Nelson, Joan M. The Politics of Stabilization. In *Feinberg, R. E. and Kallab, V., eds., no. 1*, 1984, pp. 99–118. [G: LDCs]

Nesi, Nerio. Il sistema monetario internazionale e la crisi dell'indebitamento: necessità di soluzioni strutturali. (The International Monetary System and the Debt Crisis: Need for a Structural Solution. With English summary.) *Bancaria*, April 1984, *40*(4), pp. 371–76.

Newton, C. C. S. The Sterling Crisis of 1947 and the British Response to the Marshall Plan. *Econ. Hist. Rev., 2nd Ser.*, August 1984, *37*(3), pp. 391–408. [G: U.K.; U.S.]

Nowzad, Bahram. The Debt Burden Problem. In *Black, J. and Dorrance, G. S., eds.*, 1984, pp. 140–48.

Odeh, A. F. The Canadian International Development Agency and the Arab World. In *Achilli, M. and Khaldi, M., eds.*, 1984, pp. 276–87.
[G: Canada; Selected LDCs]

Olmer, Lionel H. Trade, Debt and Growth in Latin America: Closing Statement. In *Jorge, A.; Salazar-Carrillo, J. and Sanchez, E. P.*, 1984, pp. 157–65. [G: U.S.; Latin America]

Osman, Hussein Elsayed. The Role of the Arab Bank for Economic Development in Africa in Arab–African Co-operation. In *Achilli, M. and Khaldi, M., eds.*, 1984, pp. 231–43.
[G: Africa; Arab Countries]

Painter, David S. Oil and the Marshall Plan. *Bus. Hist. Rev.*, Autumn 1984, *58*(3), pp. 359–83.
[G: U.S.; W. Europe]

Palma, Pedro A. Venezuela's Foreign Public Debt. In *Salazar-Carillo, J. and Tirado de Alonso, I., eds., no. 1*, 1984, pp. 1–5.
[G: Venezuela]

Palmer, Ransford W. The Financial Implications of Caribbean Industrialization. In *Palmer, R. W.*, 1984, pp. 17–22. [G: Caribbean]

Please, Stanley. The World Bank: Lending for Structural Adjustment. In *Feinberg, R. E. and Kallab, V., eds., no. 1*, 1984, pp. 83–98.
[G: LDCs]

Pratt, Christopher J. Fertilizer Production. In *Weiss, C. and Jéquier, N., eds.*, 1984, pp. 209–26. [G: LDCs]

Prussia, Leland S. Outlook for the World Financial System: A Banker's Perspective. *Contemp. Policy Issue*, January 1984, (4), pp. 64–70.
[G: Global]

Quibria, M. G. Domestic Policies and Foreign Resource Requirements: A Reply. *Quart. J. Econ.*, February 1984, *99*(1), pp. 207–09.

Qureshi, Moeen A. Mobilizing Finance for Development. *Finance Develop.*, September 1984, *21*(3), pp. 2–4. [G: Global]

Ragazzi, Giorgio. LDCs Debt and Net Financial Transfers: The Search for Equilibrium between Stocks and Flows. *Giorn. Econ.*, May–June 1984, *43*(5–6), pp. 359–67. [G: LDCs]

Ranis, Gustav. Needed: Commitment to Structural Adjustment. *Challenge*, July/August 1984, *27*(3), pp. 21–26. [G: LDCs]

Rao, K. Nagaraja and Weiss, Charles. Government Promotion of Industrial Innovation. In *Weiss, C. and Jéquier, N., eds.*, 1984, pp. 35–54. [G: Spain; Israel; S. Korea]

Robichek, E. Walter. The IMF's Conditionality Re-Examined. In *Muns, J., ed.*, 1984, pp. 67–75. [G: LDCs]

Rodríguez, Carlos Alfredo. The Role of Economy-Wide Prices in the Adjustment Process: Comment. In *Muns, J., ed.*, 1984, pp. 113–16.
[G: LDCs]

Rodriguez-Pastor, Carlos. Outlook for the World Financial System: A Borrower's Perspective. *Contemp. Policy Issue*, January 1984, (4), pp. 71–75. [G: Global; Peru]

Roett, Riordan. Brazil's Debt Crisis and U.S. Policy. In *Feinberg, R. E. and Kallab, V., eds., no. 1*, 1984, pp. 139–46. [G: Brazil; U.S.]

Roett, Riordan. Democracy and Debt in South America: A Continent's Dilemma. *Foreign Aff.*, 1984, *62*(3), pp. 695–720.
[G: Latin America]

von Rosen, Rüdiger. Zuversicht bei der IWF-Währungskonferenz. (A Mood of Confidence at the IMF Meeting. With English summary.) *Kredit Kapital*, 1984, *17*(4), pp. 580–93.
[G: Global]

Ruta, Gianni. L'Europa comunitaria e la cooperazione allo sviluppo. (The European Community and the Cooperation to Development. With English summary.) *Mondo Aperto*, November–December 1984, *38*(6), pp. 337–42.
[G: EEC; Africa; Caribbean; Pacific Countries]

Sachs, I. Internationalisation de l'économie ou développement endogène? les enjeux de la crise au Brésil. (Internationalization of the Economy or Endogenous Development? The Challengers of the Brazilian Crisis. With English summary.) *Écon. Soc.*, June 1984, *18*(6), pp. 195–220. **[G: Brazil]**

Sachs, Jeffrey D. Latin American Debt: I Don't Think We Are in Kansas Anymore: Comment. *Brookings Pap. Econ. Act.*, 1984, (2), pp. 393–401. **[G: Latin America]**

Salazar-Carrillo, Jorge. Trade and Debt in Central America in the 1970s. In *Salazar-Carrillo, J. and Tirado de Alonso, I., eds., no. 2*, 1984, pp. 1–7. **[G: Central America]**

Salazar-Carrillo, Jorge. Trade and Debt in Central America in the 1970s. In *Jorge, A.; Salazar-Carrillo, J. and Sanchez, E. P.*, 1984, pp. 37–40. **[G: Central America]**

Salazar-Carrillo, Jorge and Tirado de Alonso, Irma. Latin American External Debt and Economic Growth: Introduction. In *Salazar-Carrillo, J. and Tirado de Alonso, I., eds., no. 1*, 1984, pp. 1–9.

Salazar-Carrillo, Jorge and Tirado de Alonso, Irma. Trade, Debt, and Development in the Caribbean Basin. In *Salazar-Carrillo, J. and Tirado de Alonso, I., eds., no. 2*, 1984, pp. 1–9. **[G: Caribbean Basin]**

Sarkesian, Sam C. African Community Building. In *Boyd, G., ed.*, 1984, pp. 53–82. **[G: Africa]**

Sheehan, Richard H. and Ramachandran, S. Power Generation and Distribution. In *Weiss, C. and Jéquier, N., eds.*, 1984, pp. 197–207.

Shubik, Martin and Bracken, Paul. Strategic Purpose and the International Economy. In *McCormick, G. H. and Bissell, R. E., eds.*, 1984, pp. 208–28. **[G: Selected LDCs]**

Siamwalla, Ammar and Valdés, Alberto. Food Security in Developing Countries: International Issues. In *Eicher, C. K. and Staatz, J. M., eds.*, 1984, *1980*, pp. 189–206. **[G: LDCs]**

Sjaastad, Larry A. Reflections on the International Debt Crisis [The Political Economy of International Lending]. *Cato J.*, Spring/Summer 1984, *4*(1), pp. 171–75. **[G: Global]**

Smith, Fred L., Jr. The Politics of IMF Lending. *Cato J.*, Spring/Summer 1984, *4*(1), pp. 211–41.

Sobhan, Rehman. OPEC as a Source of Capital for the Third World: The Current Perspective. *Bangladesh Devel. Stud.*, December 1984, *12*(4), pp. 1–28. **[G: OPEC; LDCs]**

Solomon, Robert. The Politics of IMF Lending: A Comment. *Cato J.*, Spring/Summer 1984, *4*(1), pp. 243–47. **[G: U.S.]**

Spiro, Peter S. Exchange Rate Risk and the Cost of Foreign Capital. *Can. Public Policy*, March 1984, *10*(1), pp. 54–63. **[G: U.K.; N. America; Japan; W. Germany; Switzerland]**

Spraos, John. IMF Conditionality—A Better Way. *Banca Naz. Lavoro Quart. Rev.*, December 1984, (151), pp. 411–21.

Steckhan, Rainer B. International Co-financing and International Co-operation. In *Achilli, M. and Khaldi, M., eds.*, 1984, pp. 262–68.

Street, James H. Values in Conflict: Developing

Countries as Social Laboratories. *J. Econ. Issues*, June 1984, *18*(2), pp. 633–41. **[G: Mexico; Argentina; Chile; Uruguay; Brazil]**

Sullivan, Barry. In difesa del libero scambio. (Down with Protectionism. With English summary.) *Mondo Aperto*, March-April 1984, *38*(2), pp. 69–75. **[G: Global]**

Swoboda, Alexander K. Sui compiti futuri delle istituzioni finanziarie internazionali. (Some Reflections on the Future Role of Intergovernmental Financial Institutions. With English summary.) *Bancaria*, December 1984, *40*(12), pp. 1218–27. **[G: Global]**

Tanzi, Vito and Blejer, Mario I. Fiscal Deficits and Balance of Payments Disequilibrium in IMF Adjustment Programs. In *Muns, J., ed.*, 1984, pp. 117–36. **[G: LDCs]**

Taylor, Lance. IMF Conditionality: Incomplete Theory, Policy Malpractice. *METU*, 1984, *11*(1–2), pp. 233–47. **[G: LDCs]**

Taylor, Lance. Mexico's Adjustment in the 1980s: Look Back Before Leaping Ahead. In *Feinberg, R. E. and Kallab, V., eds., no. 1*, 1984, pp. 147–58. **[G: Mexico]**

Tayyarah, S. UNICEF and the Arab Funds: Perspectives for the Future. In *Achilli, M. and Khaldi, M., eds.*, 1984, pp. 252–55.

di Tella, Guido. The IMF's Conditionality Re-Examined: Comment. In *Muns, J., ed.*, 1984, pp. 76–79. **[G: LDCs]**

Tetreault, Mary Ann. Middle East Community Building. In *Boyd, G., ed.*, 1984, pp. 147–73. **[G: OPEC; OAPEC]**

Tseng, Wanda. The Effects of Adjustment. *Finance Develop.*, December 1984, *21*(4), pp. 2–5. **[G: LDCs]**

Ullmo, Pierre-Antoine. Financial Crisis and Development Strategy. In *Kessler, D. and Ullmo, P.-A., eds.*, 1984, pp. 269–80. **[G: LDCs]**

UNCTAD Secretariat. Hungary—Policies, Developments and Institutional Framework. In *U.N.C.T.D.*, 1984, pp. 111–28. **[G: Hungary]**

UNCTAD Secretariat. Trends, Policies and Prospects in Trade and Economic Co-operation Between Argentina and the Socialist Countries of Eastern Europe. In *U.N.C.T.D.*, 1984, pp. 5–18. **[G: Argentina; CMEA]**

UNCTAD Secretariat. Union of Soviet Socialist Republics—Policies, Developments and Institutional Framework. In *U.N.C.T.D.*, 1984, pp. 129–45. **[G: U.S.S.R.]**

Ushakova, N. Industrial Co-operation between the Council for Mutual Economic Assistance and Developing Countries. *Industry Devel.*, 1984, (11), pp. 59–66. **[G: CMEA]**

Villamil, J. Antonio. Assessing Country Risk: Lessons from the Recent Experience with Latin America. In *Jorge, A.; Salazar-Carrillo, J. and Sanchez, E. P.*, 1984, pp. 127–28.

Villasuso E., Juan Manuel. Foreign Debt and Economic Development: The Case of Costa Rica. In *Salazar-Carillo, J. and Tirado de Alonso, I., eds., no. 1*, 1984, pp. 1–6. **[G: Costa Rica]**

Volcker, Paul A. Statement to the U.S. House Committee on Foreign Affairs, August 8, 1984. *Fed. Res. Bull.*, August 1984, *70*(8), pp. 636–42.

de Vries, Barend A. Exports in the New World Environment: The Case of Latin America. In *Ghosh, P. K., ed., no. 16, 1984, 1977*, pp. 333–76. **[G: Latin America]**

de Vries, Rimmer. Key Issues in the World Debt Problem [The Political Economy of International Lending]. *Cato J.*, Spring/Summer 1984, *4*(1), pp. 177–84. **[G: Global]**

Waelbroeck, Jean. Capital, Foreign Exchange, and Growth: The Two-Gap and Labor-Income-Floor Views. In *[Chenery, H. B.]*, 1984, pp. 281–94.

Wallich, Christine I. The World Bank's Currency Swaps. *Finance Develop.*, June 1984, *21*(2), pp. 15–19.

Wallich, Henry C. Outlook for the World Financial System: A Central Banker's Perspective. *Contemp. Policy Issue*, January 1984, (4), pp. 54–63. **[G: Global]**

Walton, Christopher. Lessons from East African Agriculture. *Finance Develop.*, March 1984, *21*(1), pp. 13–16. **[G: East Africa]**

Wassermann, Ursula. Latin America's Debt Crisis. *J. World Trade Law*, July–August 1984, *18*(4), pp. 342–48. **[G: Latin America]**

Wassermann, Ursula. The Economic Situation in Africa. *J. World Trade Law*, November:December 1984, *18*(6), pp. 555–62. **[G: Africa]**

Weinert, Richard S. International Indebtedness: Coping with LDC Debt. In *Hewlett, S. A.; Kaufman, H. and Kenen, P. B., eds.*, 1984, pp. 37–51.

Weintraub, Robert E. International Debt: Crisis and Challenge. *Cato J.*, Spring/Summer 1984, *4*(1), pp. 21–61. **[G: LDCs; U.S.]**

Werlin, Herbert H. Urban Shelter and Community Development. In *Weiss, C. and Jéquier, N., eds.*, 1984, pp. 141–55.
[G: Selected Countries]

Wharton, Clifton R., Jr. Thirty Years of American Commitment to Development: Where Do We Stand Today? *Singapore Econ. Rev.*, October 1984, *29*(2), pp. 126–31. **[G: U.S.]**

Wickes, R. J. The New International Economic Order: Progress and Prospects. In *Ghosh, P. K., ed., no. 9, 1984, 1980*, pp. 66–99.
[G: OECD; Taiwan; Mexico; Brazil; India]

Wodie, Francis. The African Development Bank and the African Development Fund. In *Mazzeo, D., ed.*, 1984, pp. 85–102. **[G: Africa]**

Worrell, DeLisle. Central America and the Caribbean: Adjustment in Small, Open Economies. In *Feinberg, R. E. and Kallab, V., eds., no. 1*, 1984, pp. 159–81. **[G: Barbados; Costa Rica; Jamaica; Nicaragua]**

Yener, Demir and Mambrito, Fulvia. An Early Warning Model for International Debt Servicing Problems. *METU*, 1984, *11*(3–4), pp. 263–84. **[G: LDCs]**

Yudelman, Montague. Agricultural Lending by the Bank, 1974–84: A Retrospective Analysis.

Finance Develop., December 1984, *21*(4), pp. 45–47. **[G: Global]**

Zecher, J. Richard. The Interventionist Disease and the IMF's Agency Cost Role [The Impoverishing Effects of Foreign Aid]. *Cato J.*, Spring/Summer 1984, *4*(1), pp. 339–42.

Zimonyi, I. L. Asian Development Bank: The Objectives of Financial Covenants in the Context of Efficient Electricity Tariffs. In *Munasinghe, M. and Rungta, S., eds.*, 1984, pp. 531–35.
[G: Asia]

Zulu, Justin B. and Nsouli, Saleh M. Adjustment Programs in Africa. *Finance Develop.*, March 1984, *21*(1), pp. 5–7, 9. **[G: Africa]**

500 Administration; Business Finance; Marketing; Accounting

5000 General

Watanabe, Hisashi. A History of the Process Leading to the Formation of Fuji Electric. In *Nakagawa, K. and Morikawa, H., eds.*, 1984, pp. 47–71. **[G: Japan]**

510 Administration

511 Organization and Decision Theory

5110 Organization and Decision Theory

Aigrain, Pierre and Blockmar, Gunnar. Overview of Policy Issues: Panel Report on University Participation in Strategic Business Planning. In *Fusfeld, H. I. and Haklisch, C. S., eds.*, 1984, pp. 125–27.

Arrow, Kenneth J. Decision Theory and the Choice of a Level of Significance for the *t*-Test. In *Arrow, K. J., vol. 4, 1984, 1960*, pp. 66–76.

Arrow, Kenneth J. Decision Theory and Operations Research. In *Arrow, K. J., vol. 4, 1984, 1957*, pp. 55–65.

Arrow, Kenneth J. On the Agenda of Organizations. In *Arrow, K. J., vol. 4, 1984, 1974*, pp. 167–84.

Arrow, Kenneth J. Risk Perception in Psychology and Economics. In *Arrow, K. J., vol. 3, 1984, 1982*, pp. 261–70.

Ashton, Alison Hubbard. A Field Test of Implications of Laboratory Studies of Decision Making. *Accounting Rev.*, July 1984, *59*(3), pp. 361–75. **[G: U.S.]**

Badea-Dincă, N., et al. Problems Deriving from the Directives of the XIIIth Congress of the Romanian Communist Party Concerning the Problems of Economic Efficiency in Introducing Information Systems for Processes Management. *Econ. Computat. Cybern. Stud. Res.*, 1984, *19*(4), pp. 13–20. **[G: Romania]**

Barach, Jeffrey A. Is There a Cure for the Paralyzed Family Board? *Sloan Manage. Rev.*, Fall 1984, *26*(1), pp. 3–12.

Barry, Christopher B. and Starks, Laura T. Investment Management and Risk Sharing with Multiple Managers. *J. Finance*, June 1984, *39*(2), pp. 477–91.

Bartmann, Dieter. Reduction of State Space in Dynamic Programming with Integrated Forecasting. In *[Beckmann, M. J.]*, 1984, pp. 183–93.

Beckmann, Martin J. Hierarchy vs. Partnership. *J. Econ. Behav. Organ.*, June 1984, *5*(2), pp. 237–45.

Beckmann, Martin J. Zur Bewertung von Karrieren. (On the Utility of a Career. With English summary.) *Jahr. Nationalökon. Statist.*, July 1984, *199*(4), pp. 289–307.   [G: U.S.]

Bhagat, Sanjai and Brickley, James A. Cumulative Voting: The Value of Minority Shareholder Voting Rights. *J. Law Econ.*, October 1984, *27*(2), pp. 339–65.   [G: U.S.]

Bischoff, Eberhard E. A Posteriori Trade-Off Analysis in Reference Point Approaches. In *Grauer, M. and Wierzbicki, A. P., eds.*, 1984, pp. 139–45.

Bossard, M. I sistemi informativi nelle piccole imprese. (The Information System within Low-sized Firms. With English summary.) *Mondo Aperto*, September–October 1984, *38*(5), pp. 245–50.

Boudreau, John W. Decision Theory Contributions to HRM Research and Practice. *Ind. Relat.*, Spring 1984, *23*(2), pp. 198–217.
    [G: U.S.]

Briefs, Henry W. Solidarity within the Firm: Principles, Concepts and Reflections. *Rev. Soc. Econ.*, December 1984, *42*(3), pp. 295–317.

Brockett, Patrick L., et al. A Chance-constrained Programming Approach to Cost–Volume–Profit Analysis. *Accounting Rev.*, July 1984, *59*(3), pp. 474–87.

Buccola, Steven T. and Subaei, Abdelbagi. Mean-Gini Analysis, Stochastic Efficiency and Weak Risk Aversion. *Australian J. Agr. Econ.*, August/December 1984, *28*(2–3), pp. 77–86.

Bullinger, H. J. and Warschat, J. Production–Inventory Systems with State Constraints—Control Policies and Objective Functions. In *Avula, X. J. R., et al.*, 1984, pp. 202–07.

Bunich, P. G. Economic Stimulation of High Final Results. *Prob. Econ.*, November 1984, *27*(7), pp. 3–25.   [G: U.S.S.R.]

Burgelman, Robert A. Managing the Internal Corporate Venturing Process. *Sloan Manage. Rev.*, Winter 1984, *25*(2), pp. 33–48.

Burton, Richard M.; Damon, William W. and Obel, Børge. Operations Planning and Investment Strategy in the Owner Financed Firm. In *Naylor, T. H. and Thomas, C., eds.*, 1984, pp. 53–65.

Butler, F. P. and Mihăiţă, N. V. Management System: Analytical Paradigm and Holistic Paradigm Synthesis. A Theoretical Framework and Application. *Econ. Computat. Cybern. Stud. Res.*, 1984, *19*(3), pp. 55–68.

Carlsson, Christer. Handling Conflicts in Fuzzy Multiple-Criteria Optimization. In *Grauer, M. and Wierzbicki, A. P., eds.*, 1984, pp. 31–40.

Caswell, Julie A. An Institutional Perspective on Corporate Control and the Network of Inter-

locking Directorates. *J. Econ. Issues*, June 1984, *18*(2), pp. 619–26.

Chambers, David J. Corporate Plans as Commitments. In *Ramanadham, V. V., ed.*, 1984, pp. 119–37.

Chuang, David T. Further Theory of Stable Decisions. In *Kadane, J. B., ed.*, 1984, pp. 166–228.

Ciobanu, G. and Ciubotaru, I. Cybernetic Modelling of the Manufacturing Processes with the Help of the Co-ordinating Graphs. *Econ. Computat. Cybern. Stud. Res.*, 1984, *19*(3), pp. 9–20.   [G: Romania]

Clayson, James. Micro-Operational Research: A Simple Modeling Tool for Managers. In *Richardson, J., ed.*, 1984, pp. 247–63.

Coate, Malcolm B. Optimization for Business Portfolio Planning. In *Naylor, T. H. and Thomas, C., eds.*, 1984, pp. 13–23.

Cockerill, T. A. J. and Pickering, J. F. Introduction: The Firm in Economics. In *Pickering, J. F. and Cockerill, T. A. J., eds.*, 1984, pp. 1–22.

Cohen, Michael D. Conflict and Complexity: Goal Diversity and Organizational Search Effectiveness. *Amer. Polit. Sci. Rev.*, June 1984, *78*(2), pp. 435–51.

DeAngelo, Harry; DeAngelo, Linda and Rice, Edward M. Going Private: Minority Freezeouts and Stockholder Wealth. *J. Law Econ.*, October 1984, *27*(2), pp. 367–401.   [G: U.S.]

Dembo, Ron S. The Correct Degree of Resolution and Aggregation in Strategic Planning Models. In *Naylor, T. H. and Thomas, C., eds.*, 1984, pp. 157–67.

Dill, William R. University Participation in Strategic Business Planning. In *Fusfeld, H. I. and Haklisch, C. S., eds.*, 1984, pp. 119–24.

Dutton, John M.; Thomas, Annie and Butler, John E. The History of Progress Functions as a Managerial Technology. *Bus. Hist. Rev.*, Summer 1984, *58*(2), pp. 204–33.   [G: U.S.]

Dyer, Lee. Studying Human Resource Strategy: An Approach and an Agenda. *Ind. Relat.*, Spring 1984, *23*(2), pp. 156–69.

Fatehi-Sedeh, K. Conversion to a Just-in-Time Production System: Structural Considerations. *J. Behav. Econ.*, Winter 1984, *13*(2), pp. 111–32.

Ferrand, Dominique-J. and Martel, Jean-Marc. Le choix d'un processus de rationalisation dans l'organisation. (Choice of a Rationalization Method in the Organization. With English summary.) *Écon. Soc.*, November–December 1984, *18*(11–12), pp. 5–27.

Ferschl, Franz. An Optimization Problem in Assemblage Systems. In *[Beckmann, M. J.]*, 1984, pp. 215–30.

Fettig, Lester A. Power Mapping and the Practice of Innovation in Management. In *[Kozmetsky, G.]*, 1984, pp. 207–11.

Fiore, Claude. L'impact de la logistique sur l'industrie: la production flexible. (With English summary.) *Rev. Econ. Ind.*, 3rd Trimester 1984, (29), pp. 18–25.

FitzRoy, Felix R. and Mueller, Dennis C. Cooperation and Conflict in Contractual Organizations. *Quart. Rev. Econ. Bus.*, Winter 1984, *24*(4), pp. 24–49.

Forgó, Ferenc. A Game–Theoretic Approach for Multicriteria Decision Making. In *Grauer, M. and Wierzbicki, A. P., eds.*, 1984, pp. 41–46.

Gaede, Karl-Walter. Optimal Replacement under Differing Amounts of Information. In *[Beckmann, M. J.]*, 1984, pp. 231–42.

Gaibisso, Anna Maria. Quando sistemi direzionali e obiettivi non coincidono. (Management Systems and Business Objectives. With English summary.) *L'Impresa*, 1984, *26*(4), pp. 41–47. [G: Italy]

Galbraith, J. N. Organizzare per l'innovazione. (Designing the Innovating Organization. With English summary.) *Mondo Aperto*, November–December 1984, *38*(6), pp. 317–36.

Gimpel, Franco. Pianificazione operativa e strategia. (Operational Planning and Strategy. With English summary.) *L'Impresa*, 1984, *26*(5), pp. 27–31.

Giordano, Yvonne. La gestion des organisations obéit-elle à des normes? (Does Organization Management Obey to Norms? With English summary.) *Écon. Soc.*, November–December 1984, *18*(11–12), pp. 325–48.

Giroux, Gary A. and Rose, Peter S. An Update of Bank Planning Systems: Results of a Nationwide Survey of Large U.S. Banks. *J. Bank Res.*, Autumn 1984, *15*(3), pp. 136–47. [G: U.S.]

Grauer, Manfred; Lewandowski, A. and Wierzbicki, A. DIDASS—Theory, Implementation and Experiences. In *Grauer, M. and Wierzbicki, A. P., eds.*, 1984, pp. 22–30. [G: Austria]

Green, Edward J. On the Difficulty of Eliciting Summary Information. *J. Econ. Theory*, April 1984, *32*(2), pp. 228–45.

Gvishiani, D. and Mil'ner, B. Organizational Reserves of Management. *Prob. Econ.*, August 1984, *27*(4), pp. 29–45. [G: U.S.S.R.]

Hage, Jerald. Organizational Theory and the Concept of Productivity. In *Brief, A. P., ed.*, 1984, pp. 91–126.

Hague, Douglas [Sir]. Managing in the Macroeconomic Environment. In *Pickering, J. F. and Cockerill, T. A. J., eds.*, 1984, pp. 252–76.

Hartulari, Carmen. The Systemic Approach on the Problem of Production Operative Programming and Scheduling. *Econ. Computat. Cybern. Stud. Res.*, 1984, *19*(2), pp. 63–68.

Hatchuel, Armand and Moisdon, Jean-Claude. Théorie de la décision et pratiques organisationnelles: Le cas des investissements pétroliers. (Decision Theory and Organizational Practices: The Case Study of Oil Investments. With English summary.) *Écon. Soc.*, January 1984, *18*(1), pp. 249–89.

Hauptmann, Harry. Evolution of Organizations. In *[Beckmann, M. J.]*, 1984, pp. 257–66.

Hazelton, Jared. Bureaucracy, Creativity, and the Need for New Organizational Forms and Relations. In *[Kozmetsky, G.]*, 1984, pp. 239–45.

Hey, John D. Decision Under Uncertainty. In *van der Ploeg, F., ed.*, 1984, pp. 433–55.

Hill, C. W. L. Organisational Structure, the Development of the Firm and Business Behaviour. In *Pickering, J. F. and Cockerill, T. A. J., eds.*, 1984, pp. 52–71.

Hill, Lewis E. A Comment on Solidarity within the Firm [Solidarity within the Firm: Principles, Concepts and Reflections] [Industrial Justice in a Practical Sense]. *Rev. Soc. Econ.*, December 1984, *42*(3), pp. 328–29.

Hirshfeld, David S. An Overview of Mathematical Programming for Strategic Planning. In *Naylor, T. H. and Thomas, C., eds.*, 1984, pp. 121–37.

Holler, M. J. A Collective Choice Approach to Individual Decision Making. In *Holler, M. J., ed.*, 1984, pp. 338–44.

Holtzman, Wayne H. Psychology and Managerial Creativity. In *[Kozmetsky, G.]*, 1984, pp. 187–205.

Honko, Jaakko. Challenges of Future Changes for Management and Management Development. *Liiketaloudellinen Aikak.*, 1984, *33*(3), pp. 239–52.

Horowitz, Ira and Dennis, Samuel. Decision-making in the Two-Act Antitrust Decision Problem. *Managerial Dec. Econ.*, December 1984, *5*(4), pp. 194–203. [G: U.S.]

Hughes Hallett, A. J. Optimal Stockpiling in a High-Risk Commodity Market: The Case of Copper. *J. Econ. Dynam. Control*, November 1984, *8*(2), pp. 211–38. [G: Global]

Imai, Ken-ichi and Itami, Hiroyuki. Interpenetration of Organization and Market: Japan's Firm and Market in Comparison with the U.S. *Int. J. Ind. Organ.*, December 1984, *2*(4), pp. 285–310. [G: Japan; U.S.]

Jelinek, Mariann and Goldhar, Joel D. The Strategic Implications of the Factory of the Future. *Sloan Manage. Rev.*, Summer 1984, *25*(4), pp. 29–37.

Jones, Kirk M. Implementing Optimization in a Decision Support System. In *Naylor, T. H. and Thomas, C., eds.*, 1984, pp. 169–73.

Kadane, Joseph B. and Chuang, David T. Stable Decision Problems. In *Kadane, J. B., ed.*, 1984, pp. 146–63.

Kanter, Rosabeth Moss. Innovation—The Only Hope for Times Ahead? *Sloan Manage. Rev.*, Summer 1984, *25*(4), pp. 51–55.

Kaplan, Robert S. The Evolution of Management Accounting. *Accounting Rev.*, July 1984, *59*(3), pp. 390–418. [G: U.S.]

Karagedov, R. G. On the Organizational Structure of Industrial Management. *Prob. Econ.*, April 1984, *26*(12), pp. 3–24. [G: U.S.S.R.]

Knoke, David and Prensky, David. What Relevance Do Organization Theories Have for Voluntary Associations? *Soc. Sci. Quart.*, March 1984, *65*(1), pp. 3–20.

Korhonen, Pekka and Laakso, Jukka. A Visual Interactive Method for Solving the Multiple-Criteria Problem. In *Grauer, M. and Wierzbicki, A. P., eds.*, 1984, pp. 146–53.

Kurashvili, B. P. The Fate of Branch Management. *Prob. Econ.*, August 1984, *27*(4), pp. 3–28. [G: U.S.S.R.]

Langlois, Richard N. Internal Organization in a Dynamic Context: Some Theoretical Considerations. In *Jussawalla, M. and Ebenfield, H.*, eds., 1984, pp. 23–49.

Leibenstein, Harvey. The Japanese Management System: An X-Efficiency-Game Theory Analysis. In *Aoki, M., ed.*, 1984, pp. 331–57. **[G: Japan]**

Loasby, Brian J. Organisational Control and Performance. In *Pickering, J. F. and Cockerill, T. A. J.*, eds., 1984, pp. 72–100.

MacCrimmon, Kenneth R. and Wehrung, Donald A. The Risk In-Basket. *J. Bus.*, July 1984, 57(3), pp. 367–87. **[G: U.S.]**

Mahé, Henry. Un outil de diagnostic stratégique la grille dépendance/technologie/avantage. (A Tool of Strategic Diagnosis: The [Dependence/Technology/Advantage] Grid. With English summary.) *Écon. Soc.*, January 1984, 18(1), pp. 5–32.

Manca, Gavino. I "fattori critici di successo." ("Critical Success Factors." With English summary.) *L'Impresa*, 1984, 26(5), pp. 23–26.

Marc, F. La difficoltá ad ainnovare nelle piccole e medie imprese. (Obstacles to the Innovating Process within Low and Medium Sized Firms. With English summary.) *Mondo Aperto*, January-February 1984, 38(1), pp. 13–25. **[G: U.S.]**

Masten, Scott E. The Organization of Production: Evidence from the Aerospace Industry. *J. Law Econ.*, October 1984, 27(2), pp. 403–17. **[G: U.S.]**

McGinnis, Michael A. The Key to Strategic Planning: Integrating Analysis and Intuition. *Sloan Manage. Rev.*, Fall 1984, 26(1), pp. 45–52.

McMeekin, Gordon C. Delegation and Symmetry Approaches to Committee Decision Problems. *Atlantic Econ. J.*, December 1984, 12(4), pp. 64–65.

McNulty, Paul J. On the Nature and Theory of Economic Organization: The Role of the Firm Reconsidered. *Hist. Polit. Econ.*, Summer 1984, 16(2), pp. 233–53.

Miliukov, A. New Aspects of the Cost-accounting Independence and Responsibility of Enterprises. *Prob. Econ.*, October 1984, 27(6), pp. 39–53. **[G: U.S.S.R.]**

Milkovich, George. Personnel Strategy and Evaluation. *Ind. Relat.*, Spring 1984, 23(2), pp. 151–55.

Murphy, John W. Organizational Issues in Worker Ownership: Problems of Organizational Order in Worker Control of Production in Plants Dropped as Obsolete. *Amer. J. Econ. Soc.*, July 1984, 43(3), pp. 287–99.

Navarre, Christian. Propositions pour une méthodologie du diagnostic. (Proposals for a Diagnosis Method. With English summary.) *Écon. Soc.*, January 1984, 18(1), pp. 33–50.

Naylor, Thomas H. A Matrix Management Approach to Strategic Planning. In *Naylor, T. H. and Thomas, C.*, eds., 1984, pp. 175–84.

Naylor, Thomas H. and Thomas, Celia. Optimization Models in Strategic Planning. In *Naylor, T. H. and Thomas, C.*, eds., 1984, pp. 1–11.

Nickerson, David and Sandler, Todd. Intertemporal Incentive Allocation in Simple Hierarchies. *Math. Soc. Sci.*, February 1984, 7(1), pp. 33–57.

Olian, Judy D. and Rynes, Sara L. Organizational Staffing: Integrating Practice with Strategy. *Ind. Relat.*, Spring 1984, 23(2), pp. 170–83.

Ouchi, William. M-Form: Making Decisions and Building Concensus. *Challenge*, July/August 1984, 27(3), pp. 31–37. **[G: U.S.]**

Papanek, Gábor. "Medium-term" Planning in the Hungarian Industrial Enterprises (A Research Report.) *Acta Oecon.*, 1984, 33(3–4), pp. 361–75. **[G: Hungary]**

Penno, Mark. Asymmetry of Pre-Decision Information and Managerial Accounting. *J. Acc. Res.*, Spring 1984, 22(1), pp. 177–91.

Révész, Gábor. Enterprise Business Partnerships (VGMK) in Hungary—A Case Study. *Acta Oecon.*, 1984, 33(3–4), pp. 337–59. **[G: Hungary]**

Saaty, Thomas L. Multicriterion Decisions in Systems with Feedback. In *Avula, X. J. R., et al.*, 1984, pp. 26–36.

Smith, J. M. Punti di forza e di debolezza del management giapponese. (Demystifying Japanese Management. With English summary.) *Mondo Aperto*, September–October 1984, 38(5), pp. 237–44. **[G: Japan]**

Sousa, António. A Dynamic Model for Organizational Action. *Economia (Portugal)*, May 1984, 8(2), pp. 257–97.

Sugihara, Nobuo and Ichikawa, Mitsugu. The Systems Approach and Contingency View in Managerial Behavior and Management Organization. In *Grauer, M. and Wierzbicki, A. P.*, eds., 1984, pp. 47–53.

Sweeney, Dennis J. A Practical Evaluation of the Potential of Mixed Integer Programming as a Strategic Planning Tool. In *Naylor, T. H. and Thomas, C.*, eds., 1984, pp. 111–20.

Tichy, Noel M. and Ulrich, David O. The Leadership Challenge—A Call for the Transformational Leader. *Sloan Manage. Rev.*, Fall 1984, 26(1), pp. 59–68. **[G: U.S.]**

Tisdell, Clem A. Slack and Strain in Efficient Budgeting and Resource Allocation by Organizations. *Managerial Dec. Econ.*, March 1984, 5(1), pp. 54–57.

Tomasini, Luigi M. A Game Theoretic Approach to the Marschak Optimal Incentives Problem. *Econ. Notes*, 1984, (3), pp. 104–14.

Waldron, Jerome M. Methodological Problems with Portfolio Planning. In *Naylor, T. H. and Thomas, C.*, eds., 1984, pp. 139–55.

Wierzbicki, A. Interactive Decision Analysis and Interpretative Computer Intelligence. In *Grauer, M. and Wierzbicki, A. P.*, eds., 1984, pp. 2–19.

Williams, Edward E. and Findlay, M. Chapman, III. Corporate Governance: A Problem of Hierarchies and Self Interest. *Amer. J. Econ. Soc.*, January 1984, 43(1), pp. 19–36.

Williamson, Oliver E. Corporate Governance. *Yale Law J.*, June 1984, 93(7), pp. 1197–1230.

Williamson, Oliver E. The Incentive Limits of

Firms: A Comparative Institutional Assessment of Bureaucracy. *Weltwirtsch. Arch.*, 1984, *120*(4), pp. 736–63. **[G: U.S.]**

Woodward, S. N. Corporate Planning, Commitment and Public Enterprises. In *Ramanadham, V. V., ed.*, 1984, pp. 138–58.

Yoshino, M. Yotaro. The Evolution of United States Multinational Enterprises. In *Okochi, A. and Inoue, T., eds.*, 1984, pp. 157–81. **[G: U.S.]**

Zionts, Stanley and Wallenius, Jyrki. Recent Developments in Our Approach to Multiple-Criteria Decision Making. In *Grauer, M. and Wierzbicki, A. P., eds.*, 1984, pp. 54–62.

512 Managerial Economics

5120 Managerial Economics

Aho, Teemu and Virtanen, Ilkka. Inflaation vaikutuksesta koneen edullisimpaan pitoaikaan. (The Impact of Inflation on the Optimal Service Life of a Machine. With English summary.) *Liiketaloudellinen Aikak.*, 1984, *33*(1), pp. 60–80.

Aiginger, K. Economic Rational Expectations and their Influence on Production and Inventory Decisions. In *Oppenländer, K. H. and Poser, G., eds.*, 1984, pp. 541–97. **[G: Japan; Austria]**

Albach, Horst. Investment in Inventory. In *[Beckmann, M. J.]*, 1984, pp. 3–13. **[G: W. Germany]**

Alchian, Armen A. Specificity, Specialization, and Coalitions. *Z. ges. Staatswiss.*, March 1984, *140*(1), pp. 34–49.

Altman, Edward I. The Success of Business Failure Prediction Models: An International Survey. *J. Banking Finance*, June 1984, *8*(2), pp. 171–98. **[G: OECD; Brazil]**

Anderson, Evan E. The Growth and Performance of Franchise Systems: Company versus Franchisee Ownership. *J. Econ. Bus.*, December 1984, *36*(4), pp. 421–31. **[G: U.S.]**

Aoki, Masahiko. Aspects of the Japanese Firm. In *Aoki, M., ed.*, 1984, pp. 3–43. **[G: Japan]**

Appetiti, Sandro. Identifying Unsound Firms in Italy: An Attempt to Use Trend Variables. *J. Banking Finance*, June 1984, *8*(2), pp. 269–79. **[G: Italy]**

Arrow, Kenneth J. Decision Theory and Operations Research. In *Arrow, K. J., vol. 4*, 1984, *1957*, pp. 55–65.

Artto, Eero. Kansainvälinen kilpailukyky yritys-ja toimialatasolla -IV. (International Competitiveness at Enterprise and Industry Level IV. With English summary.) *Liiketaloudellinen Aikak.*, 1984, *33*(3), pp. 321–75. **[G: Finland; Sweden; Canada; W. Germany; U.S.]**

Ashton, Alison Hubbard. A Field Test of Implications of Laboratory Studies of Decision Making. *Accounting Rev.*, July 1984, *59*(3), pp. 361–75. **[G: U.S.]**

Ashton, D. J. and Atkins, D. R. A Partial Theory of Takeover Bids. *J. Finance*, March 1984, *39*(1), pp. 167–83.

Auerbach, Alan J. Taxes, Firm Financial Policy

and the Cost of Capital: An Empirical Analysis. *J. Public Econ.*, February/March 1984, *23*(1/2), pp. 27–57. **[G: U.S.]**

Barach, Jeffrey A. Is There a Cure for the Paralyzed Family Board? *Sloan Manage. Rev.*, Fall 1984, *26*(1), pp. 3–12.

Barry, Christopher B. and Starks, Laura T. Investment Management and Risk Sharing with Multiple Managers. *J. Finance*, June 1984, *39*(2), pp. 477–91.

Barry, Christopher B.; Velez-Arocho, Jorge I. and Welch, Paul R. A Bayesian Approach to CVP Analysis under Parameter Uncertainty. *Quart. Rev. Econ. Bus.*, Summer 1984, *24*(2), pp. 71–90.

Beged-Dov, Aharon G. Application of Operations Research in Paper Procurement. In *Avula, X. J. R., et al.*, 1984, pp. 271–77. **[G: U.S.]**

Bennett, R. C. and Cooper, G. Il cattivo uso del marketing. (The Misuse of Marketing. With English summary.) *Mondo Aperto*, June–August 1984, *38*(3–4), pp. 163–78.

Bianchi, Marcello and Donna, Giorgio. Errori strategici di gestione finanziaria. (Strategic Errors in Financial Management. With English summary.) *L'Impresa*, 1984, *26*(4), pp. 21–29.

Bresnahan, Timothy F. Comment on "Conjoint Analysis of Price Premiums for Hotel Amenities." *J. Bus.*, Part 2, January 1984, *57*(1), pp. S133–38.

Brown, Wilson B. Firm-like Behavior in Markets: The Administered Channel. *Int. J. Ind. Organ.*, September 1984, *2*(3), pp. 263–76.

Bullinger, H. J. and Warschat, J. Production–Inventory Systems with State Constraints—Control Policies and Objective Functions. In *Avula, X. J. R., et al.*, 1984, pp. 202–07.

Burton, Richard M.; Damon, William W. and Obel, Børge. Operations Planning and Investment Strategy in the Owner Financed Firm. In *Naylor, T. H. and Thomas, C., eds.*, 1984, pp. 53–65.

Carlsson, Christer. Handling Conflicts in Fuzzy Multiple-Criteria Optimization. In *Grauer, M. and Wierzbicki, A. P., eds.*, 1984, pp. 31–40.

Carson, R. The Optimal Size of the Competitive Firm. *J. Econ. Bus.*, February 1984, *36*(1), pp. 15–28.

Caves, Richard E. Economic Analysis and the Quest for Competitive Advantage. *Amer. Econ. Rev.*, May 1984, *74*(2), pp. 127–32.

Chiappori, Pierre-André. Sélection naturelle et rationalité absolue des entreprises. (Natural Selection and Substantive Rationality of Business Firms. With English summary.) *Revue Écon.*, January 1984, *35*(1), pp. 87–107.

Chisholm, Rupert F. A Systems Approach to Organizational Productivity. In *Holzer, M. and Nagel, S. S., eds.*, 1984, pp. 261–85. **[G: U.S.]**

Ciobanu, G. and Ciubotaru, I. Cybernetic Modelling of the Manufacturing Processes with the Help of the Co-ordinating Graphs. *Econ. Computat. Cybern. Stud. Res.*, 1984, *19*(3), pp. 9–20. **[G: Romania]**

Ciscel, David H. and Evans, Richard D. Returns

to Corporate Diversification in the 1970s. *Managerial Dec. Econ.*, June 1984, *5*(2), pp. 67–71. **[G: U.S.]**

Clarke, Darral G. and Dolan, Robert J. A Simulation Analysis of Alternative Pricing Strategies for Dynamic Environments. *J. Bus.*, Part 2, January 1984, *57*(1), pp. S179–200.

Clayson, James. Micro-Operational Research: A Simple Modeling Tool for Managers. In *Richardson, J., ed.*, 1984, pp. 247–63.

Coate, Malcolm B. Optimization for Business Portfolio Planning. In *Naylor, T. H. and Thomas, C., eds.*, 1984, pp. 13–23.

Cochran, Philip L.; Wartick, Steven L. and Wood, Robert A. The Average Age of Boards and Financial Performance, Revisited. *Quart. J. Bus. Econ.*, Autumn 1984, *23*(4), pp. 57–63. **[G: U.S.]**

Cockerill, T. A. J. and Kinloch, H. Managing Risk and Uncertainty. In *Pickering, J. F. and Cockerill, T. A. J., eds.*, 1984, pp. 221–51. **[G: U.K.]**

Costello, Dennis and Posner, David. The Application of Venture Analysis to Public Policy Decisions: A Case Study of Photovoltaics. *Policy Sci.*, February 1984, *16*(3), pp. 267–80.

Crain, W. Mark; Shughart, William F., II and Tollison, Robert D. The Convergence of Satisficing to Marginalism: An Empirical Test. *J. Econ. Behav. Organ.*, September–December 1984, *5*(3–4), pp. 375–85. **[G: U.S.]**

Cremer, Jacques. On the Economics of Repeat Buying. *Rand J. Econ.*, Autumn 1984, *15*(3), pp. 396–403.

Danielsson, Christer. Företagsutveckling. Utkast och bakgrund till en modell. (Development of the Firm. Draft and Background of a Model. With English summary.) *Ekon. Samfundets Tidskr.*, 1984, *37*(4), pp. 267–83. **[G: Sweden]**

Davidson, W. H. and McFetridge, Donald G. International Technology Transactions and the Theory of the Firm. *J. Ind. Econ.*, March 1984, *32*(3), pp. 253–64. **[G: U.S.]**

Doi, M. and Ōsawa, H. A Storage Process with Non-constant Inflow and Outflow. In *Avula, X. J. R., et al.*, 1984, pp. 305–310.

Drexel, Gerhard. Ein Frühwarnsystem für die Praxis—dargestellt am Beispiel eines Einzelhandelsunternehmens. (With English summary.) *Z. Betriebswirtshaft*, January 1984, *54*(1), pp. 89–105.

Dreyfus, Stuart E. Mathematical Modeling and Long Range Planning. In *Avula, X. J. R., et al.*, 1984, pp. 37–43.

Eppen, Gary D. and Liebermann, Yehoshua. Why Do Retailers Deal? An Inventory Explanation. *J. Bus.*, October 1984, *57*(4), pp. 519–30. **[G: U.S.]**

Faith, Roger L.; Higgins, Richard S. and Tollison, Robert D. Managerial Rents and Outside Recruitment in the Coasian Firm. *Amer. Econ. Rev.*, September 1984, *74*(4), pp. 660–72. **[G: U.S.]**

Ferschl, Franz. An Optimization Problem in Assemblage Systems. In *[Beckmann, M. J.]*, 1984, pp. 215–30.

Forgionne, Guisseppi A. Economic Tools Used by Management in large American Operated Corporations. *Bus. Econ.*, April 1984, *19*(3), pp. 5–17. **[G: U.S.]**

French, Kenneth R. and McCormick, Robert E. Sealed Bids, Sunk Costs, and the Process of Competition. *J. Bus.*, October 1984, *57*(4), pp. 417–41.

Friedman, James W. Comments on "A Simulation Analysis of Alternative Pricing Strategies for Dynamic Environments." *J. Bus.*, Part 2, January 1984, *57*(1), pp. S201–04.

Gaede, Karl-Walter. Optimal Replacement under Differing Amounts of Information. In *[Beckmann, M. J.]*, 1984, pp. 231–42.

Garvin, David A. What Does "Product Quality" Really Mean? *Sloan Manage. Rev.*, Fall 1984, *26*(1), pp. 25–43.

Godfrey, James; Roshwalb, Alan and Wright, Roger L. Model-based Stratification in Inventory Cost Estimation. *J. Bus. Econ. Statist.*, January 1984, *2*(1), pp. 1–9. **[G: U.S.]**

Goldberg, Stephen M.; Green, Paul E. and Wind, Yoram. Conjoint Analysis of Price Premiums for Hotel Amenities. *J. Bus.*, Part 2, January 1984, *57*(1), pp. S111–32.

Górecki, H., et al. A Multiobjective Procedure for Project Formulation—Design of a Chemical Installation. In *Grauer, M. and Wierzbicki, A. P., eds.*, 1984, pp. 248–59.

Gould, John P. Comments on "Firm-Specific Differentiation and Competition among Multiproduct Firms." *J. Bus.*, Part 2, January 1984, *57*(1), pp. S173–77.

Greenhut, M. L.; Hwang, M. and Shwiff, S. Differences in Spatial Pricing in the United States: A Statistical Analysis and Case Studies. *Ann. Reg. Sci.*, November 1984, *18*(3), pp. 49–66. **[G: U.S.]**

Grossman, Elliot S. Company Productivity Measurement. *Bus. Econ.*, July 1984, *19*(4), pp. 18–23. **[G: U.S.]**

Hague, Douglas [Sir]. Managing in the Macroeconomic Environment. In *Pickering, J. F. and Cockerill, T. A. J., eds.*, 1984, pp. 252–76.

Harris, Milton. Comment on "Pricing a Product Line." *J. Bus.*, Part 2, January 1984, *57*(1), pp. S109–10.

Harris, Robert G. The Values of Economic Theory in Management Education. *Amer. Econ. Rev.*, May 1984, *74*(2), pp. 122–26.

Hartulari, Carmen. The Systemic Approach on the Problem of Production Operative Programming and Scheduling. *Econ. Computat. Cybern. Stud. Res.*, 1984, *19*(2), pp. 63–68.

Hauser, John R. Pricing Theory and the Role of Marketing Science [Pricing Research in Marketing: The State of the Art]. *J. Bus.*, Part 2, January 1984, *57*(1), pp. S65–71.

Hirschey, Mark and Wichern, Dean W. Accounting and Market-Value Measures of Profitability: Consistency, Determinants, and Uses. *J. Bus. Econ. Statist.*, October 1984, *2*(4), pp. 375–83. **[G: U.S.]**

Hirshfeld, David S. An Overview of Mathematical Programming for Strategic Planning. **In** *Naylor, T. H. and Thomas, C., eds.*, 1984, pp. 121–37.

Horsky, Dan. Comments on "Conjoint Analysis of Price Premiums for Hotel Amenities." *J. Bus.*, Part 2, January 1984, 57(1), pp. S139–47.

Howell, Robert A. Strategic Planning in a Volatile Economy. **In** *Sametz, A. W., ed.*, 1984, pp. 113–16.

Imai, Ken-ichi and Itami, Hiroyuki. Interpenetration of Organization and Market: Japan's Firm and Market in Comparison with the U.S. *Int. J. Ind. Organ.*, December 1984, 2(4), pp. 285–310. **[G: Japan; U.S.]**

Intrator, Jacob and Weiss, Joseph. About Some Special Cases of Transportation Problems. *Econ. Computat. Cybern. Stud. Res.*, 1984, 19(1), pp. 83–91.

Irvine, F. Owen, Jr. Intrafirm Inventory Policy: Theory and Tests. *Can. J. Econ.*, February 1984, 17(1), pp. 156–74. **[G: U.S.]**

Iwai, Katsuhito. Schumpeterian Dynamics, Part II: Technological Progress, Firm Growth and 'Economic Selection.' *J. Econ. Behav. Organ.*, September–December 1984, 5(3–4), pp. 321–51.

Izan, H. Y. Corporate Distress in Australia. *J. Banking Finance*, June 1984, 8(2), pp. 303–20. **[G: Australia]**

Jelinek, Mariann and Goldhar, Joel D. The Strategic Implications of the Factory of the Future. *Sloan Manage. Rev.*, Summer 1984, 25(4), pp. 29–37.

Kalish, Shlomo. Comments on "A Simulation Analysis of Alternative Pricing Strategies in a Dynamic Environment." *J. Bus.*, Part 2, January 1984, 57(1), pp. S205–09.

Katz, Michael L. Firm-Specific Differentiation and Competition among Multiproduct Firms. *J. Bus.*, Part 2, January 1984, 57(1), pp. S149–66.

Khalil, Z. S. and Leonard, K. J. A Markov Process Model for Cash Management. **In** *Avula, X. J. R., et al.*, 1984, pp. 215–19.

Klingman, Darwin D.; Ross, G. Terry and Schneider, Robert F. Optimization-Based Facility Location Planning: An Application and Some Insights. **In** *Naylor, T. H. and Thomas, C., eds.*, 1984, pp. 79–90. **[G: U.S.]**

Knudsen, Torben Finn. Interne afregningspriser i decentraliserede virksomheder. (Transfer Prices in Decentralized Firms. With English summary.) *Nationaløkon. Tidsskr.*, 1984, 122(2), pp. 240–52.

König, H. and Nerlove, Marc. Response of Prices and Production to Unanticipated Demand Shocks: Some Micro-economic Evidence. **In** *Oppenländer, K. H. and Poser, G., eds.*, 1984, pp. 349–84. **[G: W. Germany; France]**

Kumar, Manmohan Singh. Comparative Analysis of UK Domestic and International Firms. *J. Econ. Stud.*, 1984, 11(3), pp. 26–42.
[G: U.K.]

Kumar, Nagesh. Public Policy, Marris Model and Corporate Growth in India. *Indian Econ. J.*, Oct.–Dec. 1984, 32(2), pp. 74–83. **[G: India]**

Lahti, Arto. Yrityksen strategia ja menestyksellisyys. (Strategy and Performance of a Firm. With English summary.) *Liiketaloudellinen Aikak.*, 1984, 33(2), pp. 228–33.
[G: Finland]

Laitinen, Erkki K. Empirical Evidence on the Measurement of the Firm. *Liiketaloudellinen Aikak.*, 1984, 33(4), pp. 405–32.
[G: Finland]

Laki, Mihály. The Enterprise Crisis. *Acta Oecon.*, 1984, 32(1–2), pp. 113–24. **[G: Hungary]**

Lambert, Richard A. Income Smoothing as Rational Equilibrium Behavior. *Accounting Rev.*, October 1984, 59(4), pp. 604–18.

Lawriwsky, Michael L. A Critical View of Studies Examining the Performance Effects of the Separation of Ownership from Control. *Rivista Int. Sci. Econ. Com.*, April 1984, 31(4), pp. 312–28. **[G: Australia]**

Leahey, Cary. Linking Business Decisions to Macroeconomic Models. *Bus. Econ.*, October 1984, 19(5), pp. 49–56. **[G: U.S.]**

Lease, Ronald C.; McConnell, John J. and Mikkelson, Wayne H. The Market Value of Differential Voting Rights in Closely Held Corporations. *J. Bus.*, October 1984, 57(4), pp. 443–67. **[G: U.S.]**

LeBlanc, Larry J. Optimization Models for Distribution Planning. **In** *Bamberg, G. and Spremann, K., eds.*, 1984, pp. 203–23.

Leibenstein, Harvey. The Japanese Management System: An X-Efficiency-Game Theory Analysis. **In** *Aoki, M., ed.*, 1984, pp. 331–57.
[G: Japan]

Liberman, E. G. and Khaikin, V. P. A Simpler, More Accurate Method of Calculating Profitability. *Prob. Econ.*, March 1984, 26(11), pp. 40–52. **[G: U.S.S.R.]**

Lincoln, Mervyn. An Empirical Study of the Usefulness of Accounting Ratios to Describe Levels of Insolvency Risk. *J. Banking Finance*, June 1984, 8(2), pp. 321–40.

Loescher, Samuel M. Bureaucratic Measurement, Shuttling Stock Shares, and Shortened Time Horizons: Implications for Economic Growth. *Quart. Rev. Econ. Bus.*, Winter 1984, 24(4), pp. 8–23.

Lombardi, Maria Ludovica and Vardelli, Riccardo. Il tempo manageriale come fattore strategico. (Managerial Time as a Strategic Factor. With English summary.) *L'Impresa*, 1984, 26(1), pp. 39–46. **[G: Sweden; Korea; Italy]**

Long, Robert A., Jr. A Theory of Hypothetical Contract. *Yale Law J.*, December 1984, 94(2), pp. 415–34.

Lyons, J. L. An Evaluation Procedure for Electronics Equipment Life Cycle Costs. **In** *Avula, X. J. R., et al.*, 1984, pp. 133–38.

MacCrimmon, Kenneth R. and Wehrung, Donald A. The Risk In-Basket. *J. Bus.*, July 1984, 57(3), pp. 367–87. **[G: U.S.]**

Mahé, Henry. Un outil de diagnostic stratégique la grille dépendance/technologie/avantage. (A Tool of Strategic Diagnosis: The [Dependence/

Technology/Advantage] Grid. With English summary.) *Écon. Soc.*, January 1984, *18*(1), pp. 5–32.

Manes, Rene P.; Shoumaker, Francoise and Silhan, Peter A. Demand Relationships and Pricing Decisions for Related Products. *Managerial Dec. Econ.*, June 1984, *5*(2), pp. 120–22.

Mangoni, Gustavo and Taverna, Piero. La strumentazione, aspetto trascurato dei grandi progetti. (Instrumentation and Control for Large Projects. With English summary.) *L'Impresa*, 1984, *26*(4), pp. 55–61.

Marcinko, David and Petri, Enrico. Use of the Production Function in Calculation of Standard Cost Variances—An Extension. *Accounting Rev.*, July 1984, *59*(3), pp. 488–95.

Marvel, Howard P. and McCafferty, Stephen. Resale Price Maintenance and Quality Certification. *Rand J. Econ.*, Autumn 1984, *15*(3), pp. 346–59. **[G: U.S.]**

Masten, Scott E. The Organization of Production: Evidence from the Aerospace Industry. *J. Law Econ.*, October 1984, *27*(2), pp. 403–17. **[G: U.S.]**

McGinnis, Michael A. The Key to Strategic Planning: Integrating Analysis and Intuition. *Sloan Manage. Rev.*, Fall 1984, *26*(1), pp. 45–52.

Mehrez, Abraham; Regev, U. and Spivak, A. An Analysis of Risky Financial Decisions. *Managerial Dec. Econ.*, March 1984, *5*(1), pp. 19–24.

Meško, Ivan. Optimizing Multiphase Business Processes. *Econ. Anal. Worker's Manage.*, 1984, *18*(3), pp. 269–75.

Micha, Bernard. Analysis of Business Failures in France. *J. Banking Finance*, June 1984, *8*(2), pp. 281–91. **[G: France]**

Moorthy, K. Sridhar. Comments on "Firm-Specific Differentiation and Competition among Multiproduct Firms." *J. Bus.*, Part 2, January 1984, *57*(1), pp. S167–71.

Nagel, Stuart S. Productivity Improvement, Management Science, and Policy Evaluation. In *Holzer, M. and Nagel, S. S., eds.*, 1984, pp. 235–59.

Naggl, W. and Nerb, G. Zur Aussagefähigkeit von Beschäftigungsplänen der Unternehmen in der Europäischen Gemeinschaft. (The Information Content of the Employment Plans in European Business Surveys. With English summary.) *Ifo-Studien*, 1984, *30*(1), pp. 1–28. **[G: U.S.; W. Europe]**

Nagle, Thomas. Economic Foundations for Pricing. *J. Bus.*, Part 2, January 1984, *57*(1), pp. S3–26.

Narasimhan, Chakravarthi. Comments on "Economic Foundations for Pricing." *J. Bus.*, Part 2, January 1984, *57*(1), pp. S27–34.

Naylor, Thomas H. A Matrix Management Approach to Strategic Planning. In *Naylor, T. H. and Thomas, C., eds.*, 1984, pp. 175–84.

Naylor, Thomas H. and Thomas, Celia. Optimization Models in Strategic Planning. In *Naylor, T. H. and Thomas, C., eds.*, 1984, pp. 1–11.

Nickerson, David and Sandler, Todd. Intertemporal Incentive Allocation in Simple Hierarchies. *Math. Soc. Sci.*, February 1984, *7*(1), pp. 33–57.

Oehler, Wolfgang. Corporation Law and the New Institutional Economics: Comment. *Z. ges. Staatswiss.*, March 1984, *140*(1), pp. 153–55.

Oren, Shmuel S. Comments on "Pricing Research in Marketing: The State of the Art." *J. Bus.*, Part 2, January 1984, *57*(1), pp. S61–64.

Oren, Shmuel S.; Smith, Stephen and Wilson, Robert B. Pricing a Product Line. *J. Bus.*, Part 2, January 1984, *57*(1), pp. S73–99.

Ottenwaelter, B. and Vuong, Quang H. An Empirical Analysis of Backlog, Inventory, Production, and Price Adjustments: An Application of Recursive Systems of Log-Linear Models. *J. Bus. Econ. Statist.*, July 1984, *2*(3), pp. 224–34. **[G: France]**

Papanek, Gábor. "Medium-term" Planning in the Hungarian Industrial Enterprises (A Research Report.) *Acta Oecon.*, 1984, *33*(3–4), pp. 361–75. **[G: Hungary]**

Petrescu, G. Note on the Utilization of Dynamic Series in the Study of a Stock and Waiting System. *Econ. Computat. Cybern. Stud. Res.*, 1984, *19*(4), pp. 47–54.

Picot, Arnold. Specificity, Specialization, and Coalitions: Comment. *Z. ges. Staatswiss.*, March 1984, *140*(1), pp. 50–53.

Pike, R. H. Sophisticated Capital Budgeting Systems and Their Association with Corporate Performance. *Managerial Dec. Econ.*, June 1984, *5*(2), pp. 91–97. **[G: U.K.]**

Putterman, Louis. On Some Recent Explanations of Why Capital Hires Labor. *Econ. Inquiry*, April 1984, *22*(2), pp. 171–87.

Ramakrishnan, Ram T. S. and Thakor, Anjan V. The Valuation of Assets under Moral Hazard. *J. Finance*, March 1984, *39*(1), pp. 229–38.

Rao, Vithala R. Pricing Research in Marketing: The State of the Art. *J. Bus.*, Part 2, January 1984, *57*(1), pp. S39–60.

Raviv, Artur. Comments on "Economic Foundations for Pricing." *J. Bus.*, Part 2, January 1984, *57*(1), pp. S35–38.

Rogerson, William P. Efficient Reliance and Damage Measures for Breach of Contract. *Rand J. Econ.*, Spring 1984, *15*(1), pp. 39–53.

Rushinek, Avi and Rushinek, Sara F. Mini/Micro Computer Evaluation of System Features: An Empirical Discriminant Model of Software and Hardware Expandability, Compatibility, Cost-Efficiency, Installation, and Delivery. *Managerial Dec. Econ.*, September 1984, *5*(3), pp. 150–59. **[G: U.S.]**

Salmi, Timo, et al. Extracting and Analyzing the Time Series for Profitability Measurement from Published Financial Statements: With Results on Publicly Traded Finnish Metal Industry Firms: Part III. *Liiketaloudellinen Aikak.*, 1984, *33*(1), pp. 23–48. **[G: Finland]**

Schwartz, Steven. An Empirical Test of a Managerial, Life-Cycle, and Cost of Capital Model of Merger Activity. *J. Ind. Econ.*, March 1984, *32*(3), pp. 265–76. **[G: U.S.]**

Scott, John T. and Pascoe, George. Capital Costs

and Profitability. *Int. J. Ind. Organ.*, September 1984, 2(3), pp. 217–33. **[G: U.S.]**

Scott, Kenneth E. Corporate Governance and the New Institutional Economics. *Z. ges. Staatswiss.*, March 1984, 140(1), pp. 136–52.

Shapiro, Jeremy F. Practical Experience with Optimization Models. In *Naylor, T. H. and Thomas, C., eds.*, 1984, pp. 67–77.

Shugan, Steven M. Comments on "Pricing a Product Line." *J. Bus.*, Part 2, January 1984, 57(1), pp. S101–07.

von Stein, Johann Heinrich and Zeigler, Werner. The Prognosis and Surveillance of Risks from Commercial Credit Borrowers. *J. Banking Finance*, June 1984, 8(2), pp. 249–68.
[G: W. Germany]

Steuer, Ralph E. Operating Considerations Pertaining to the Interactive Weighted Tchebycheff Procedure. In *Grauer, M. and Wierzbicki, A. P., eds.*, 1984, pp. 132–38.

Steuerle, Eugene. Realized Income and Wealth for Owners of Closely Held Farms and Businesses: A Comparison. *Public Finance Quart.*, October 1984, 12(4), pp. 407–24. **[G: U.S.]**

Stowe, John D. and Ingene, Charles A. Microeconomic Influences on Operating Leverage. *J. Econ. Bus.*, May 1984, 36(2), pp. 233–41.

Sturgess, Brian T. and Wilson, Nicholas. Advertising Expenditure and Aggregate Consumption in Britain and West Germany: An Analysis of Causality. *Managerial Dec. Econ.*, December 1984, 5(4), pp. 219–27. **[G: U.K.; W. Germany]**

Sudit, Ephraim F. The Role of Comparative Productivity Accounting in Export Decisions. *J. Int. Bus. Stud.*, Spring/Summer 1984, 15(1), pp. 105–18. **[G: U.S.; Japan]**

Sutalaksana, Iftikar Z. and Van Wassenhove, Luk N. Integrating Human Factor Aspects in Cost Function Development: A Quality Inspection Case. In *Avula, X. J. R., et al.*, 1984, pp. 920–24.

Taffler, Richard J. Empirical Models for the Monitoring of UK Corporations. *J. Banking Finance*, June 1984, 8(2), pp. 199–227.
[G: U.K.]

Takahashi, Kichinosuke; Kurokawa, Yukiharu and Watase, Kazunori. Corporate Bankruptcy Prediction in Japan. *J. Banking Finance*, June 1984, 8(2), pp. 229–47. **[G: Japan]**

Tamari, Meir. The Use of a Bankruptcy Forecasting Model to Analyze Corporate Behavior in Israel. *J. Banking Finance*, June 1984, 8(2), pp. 293–302. **[G: Israel]**

Tamminen, Rauno. Tilastollisesti estimoidun kannattavuuden tulkinnasta. (Interpretations for Statistically Estimated Profitability. With English summary.) *Liiketaloudellinen Aikak.*, 1984, 33(1), pp. 107–13. **[G: Finland]**

Teece, David J. and Winter, Sidney G. The Limits of Neoclassical Theory in Management Education. *Amer. Econ. Rev.*, May 1984, 74(2), pp. 116–21.

Teller, Robert. Évolution et insuffisance des analyses "profit–coût–volume" pour le contrôle de gestion. (Evolution and Insufficiency of the Analyses "Profit–Cost–Volume" for the Budgetary Control. With English summary.) *Écon. Soc.*, November–December 1984, 18(11–12), pp. 293–321.

Thompson, Gerald L. and Teng, Jinn-Tsair. Optimal Pricing and Advertising Policies for New Product Oligopoly Models. *Marketing Sci.*, Spring 1984, 3(2), pp. 148–68.

Thompson, Howard E. Estimating Individual Company Costs of Capital from Cross-sectional Data: A Random Coefficients Approach. *Managerial Dec. Econ.*, September 1984, 5(3), pp. 130–40. **[G: U.S.]**

Tisdell, Clem A. Slack and Strain in Efficient Budgeting and Resource Allocation by Organizations. *Managerial Dec. Econ.*, March 1984, 5(1), pp. 54–57.

Todd, Douglas. Productive Performance in the Firm: The Economic Approach. In *Pickering, J. F. and Cockerill, T. A. J., eds.*, 1984, pp. 101–31. **[G: Ireland]**

Todd, Jerry D. A Retirement Plan Decision Model for Small Business. *J. Risk Ins.*, June 1984, 51(2), pp. 265–85. **[G: U.S.]**

Waldron, Jerome M. Methodological Problems with Portfolio Planning. In *Naylor, T. H. and Thomas, C., eds.*, 1984, pp. 139–55.

Walkling, Ralph A. and Long, Michael S. Agency Theory, Managerial Welfare, and Takeover Bid Resistance. *Rand J. Econ.*, Spring 1984, 15(1), pp. 54–68. **[G: U.S.]**

Williams, Arlington W. and Smith, Vernon L. Cyclical Double-Auction Markets with and without Speculators. *J. Bus.*, Part 1, January 1984, 57(1), pp. 1–33.

Williamson, Oliver E. Perspectives on the Modern Corporation. *Quart. Rev. Econ. Bus.*, Winter 1984, 24(4), pp. 64–71.

Wu, Lung Chiang and Wilson, Richard C. Modelling Manpower Allocation of Mixed Multiproduct Assembly Line. In *Avula, X. J. R., et al.*, 1984, pp. 220–23.

Yakushiji, Taizo. Reshuffling Firms for Technology? An Aggregate Time-Series Analysis of B. Klein's "Dynamic Efficiency." In *Aoki, M., ed.*, 1984, pp. 359–85. **[G: Japan]**

Yoshihara, Kunio. Indigenous Entrepreneurs in the ASEAN Countries. *Singapore Econ. Rev.*, October 1984, 29(2), pp. 132–47.
[G: ASEAN]

513 Business and Public Administration

5130 General

Bhatt, V. V. Institutional Framework and Public Enterprise Performance. *World Devel.*, July 1984, 12(7), pp. 713–21.

Butler, F. P. and Mihăiţă, N. V. Management System: Analytical Paradigm and Holistic Paradigm Synthesis. A Theoretical Framework and Application. *Econ. Computat. Cybern. Stud. Res.*, 1984, 19(3), pp. 55–68.

Davis, Otto A. Similarities and Differences in Innovation for Governmental and Private Enterprise Management. In *[Kozmetsky, G.]*, 1984, pp. 61–68.

Drexel, Gerhard. Ein Frühwarnsystem für die Praxis—dargestellt am Beispiel eines Einzelhandelsunternehmens. (With English summary.) *Z. Betriebswirtshaft*, January 1984, *54*(1), pp. 89–105.

Fettig, Lester A. Power Mapping and the Practice of Innovation in Management. In *[Kozmetsky, G.]*, 1984, pp. 207–11.

Hazelton, Jared. Bureaucracy, Creativity, and the Need for New Organizational Forms and Relations. In *[Kozmetsky, G.]*, 1984, pp. 239–45.

Holtzman, Wayne H. Psychology and Managerial Creativity. In *[Kozmetsky, G.]*, 1984, pp. 187–205.

Kozmetsky, George. Creative and Innovative Management: A New Academic Frontier. In *[Kozmetsky, G.]*, 1984, pp. 3–25.

Kubicek, Herbert. Führungsgrundsätze als Organisationsmythen und die Notwendigkeit von Entmythologisierungsversuchen. (With English summary.) *Z. Betriebswirtshaft*, January 1984, *54*(1), pp. 4–29.

Kuhn, Robert Lawrence. Creative and Innovative Management—A Challenge to Academia. In *[Kozmetsky, G.]*, 1984, pp. 27–37.

Milkovich, George. Personnel Strategy and Evaluation. *Ind. Relat.*, Spring 1984, *23*(2), pp. 151–55.

Newell, Allen. On Computers, Creativity, and Management. In *[Kozmetsky, G.]*, 1984, pp. 213–37.

Ouchi, William. M-Form: Making Decisions and Building Concensus. *Challenge*, July/August 1984, *27*(3), pp. 31–37. [G: U.S.]

Schneider, Benjamin. Industrial and Organizational Psychology Perspective. In *Brief, A. P., ed.*, 1984, pp. 174–206.

Smith, J. M. Punti di forza e di debolezza del management giapponese. (Demystifying Japanese Management. With English summary.) *Mondo Aperto*, September–October 1984, *38*(5), pp. 237–44. [G: Japan]

Weinert, Ansfried B. Menschenbilder in Organisations- und Führungstheorien: Erste Ergebnisse einer empirischen Überprüfung. (With English summary.) *Z. Betriebswirtshaft*, January 1984, *54*(1), pp. 30–62. [G: W. Germany]

5131 Business Administration

Aigrain, Pierre and Blockmar, Gunnar. Overview of Policy Issues: Panel Report on University Participation in Strategic Business Planning. In *Fusfeld, H. I. and Haklisch, C. S., eds.*, 1984, pp. 125–27.

Belli, Claudio and Ratti, Franco. Per una gestione più efficace delle risorse umane. (Towards an Integrated Management of Human Resources. With English summary.) *L'Impresa*, 1984, *26*(4), pp. 49–53.

Benjamin, Robert I., et al. Information Technology: A Strategic Opportunity. *Sloan Manage. Rev.*, Spring 1984, *25*(3), pp. 3–10.

Bernardi, Bruno. Il "tessuto causale" delle imprese di ingegneria. ("Casual Fabric" in Engineering Companies. With English summary.) *L'Impresa*, 1984, *26*(1), pp. 17–26. [G: LDCs]

Blair, David C. The Management of Information: Basic Distinctions. *Sloan Manage. Rev.*, Fall 1984, *26*(1), pp. 13–23.

Blumenthal, Tuvia. Some Reflections on the Japanese Motivation System. In *Aoki, M., ed.*, 1984, pp. 413–16. [G: Japan]

Bossard, M. I sistemi informativi nelle piccole imprese. (The Information System within Low-sized Firms. With English summary.) *Mondo Aperto*, September–October 1984, *38*(5), pp. 245–50.

Boudreau, John W. Decision Theory Contributions to HRM Research and Practice. *Ind. Relat.*, Spring 1984, *23*(2), pp. 198–217. [G: U.S.]

Burgelman, Robert A. Managing the Internal Corporate Venturing Process. *Sloan Manage. Rev.*, Winter 1984, *25*(2), pp. 33–48.

Crockett, Geoffrey and Elias, Peter. British Managers: A Study of their Education, Training, Mobility and Earnings. *Brit. J. Ind. Relat.*, March 1984, *22*(1), pp. 34–46. [G: U.K.]

Di Stefano, Guido. Il capitale umano nelle banche: una risorsa sottoutilizzata. (Human Capital in Banks: An Underutilised Resource. With English summary.) *L'Impresa*, 1984, *26*(4), pp. 31–40. [G: Italy]

Dill, William R. University Participation in Strategic Business Planning. In *Fusfeld, H. I. and Haklisch, C. S., eds.*, 1984, pp. 119–24.

Dye, Ronald A. The Trouble with Tournaments. *Econ. Inquiry*, January 1984, *22*(1), pp. 147–49.

Dyer, Lee. Studying Human Resource Strategy: An Approach and an Agenda. *Ind. Relat.*, Spring 1984, *23*(2), pp. 156–69.

Faith, Roger L.; Higgins, Richard S. and Tollison, Robert D. Managerial Rents and Outside Recruitment in the Coasian Firm. *Amer. Econ. Rev.*, September 1984, *74*(4), pp. 660–72. [G: U.S.]

Fatehi-Sedeh, K. Conversion to a Just-in-Time Production System: Structural Considerations. *J. Behav. Econ.*, Winter 1984, *13*(2), pp. 111–32.

Flora, Elio and Nunziata, Eugenio. Controllo di gestione e processi produttivi. (Management Control and Production Processes. With English summary.) *L'Impresa*, 1984, *26*(1), pp. 65–73.

Foote, Susan Bartlett. Changing Regulatory Strategies—What Managers Should Know about Federal Preemption. *Sloan Manage. Rev.*, Fall 1984, *26*(1), pp. 69–73.

Glick, Henry A. and Feuer, Michael J. Employer-sponsored Training and the Governance of Specific Human Capital Investments. *Quart. Rev. Econ. Bus.*, Summer 1984, *24*(2), pp. 91–103.

Hessen, Robert. The Agenda for Corporate Reform. In *Moore, J. H., ed.*, 1984, pp. 287–302. [G: U.S.]

House, Robert J. Commentary on Management

Research. In *Brief, A. P., ed.*, 1984, pp. 268–82.

Kanter, Rosabeth Moss. Variations in Managerial Career Structures in High-Technology Firms: The Impact of Organizational Characteristics on Internal Labor Market Patterns. In *Osterman, P., ed.*, 1984, *1983*, pp. 109–31.

Kaplan, Robert S. The Evolution of Management Accounting. *Accounting Rev.*, July 1984, *59*(3), pp. 390–418. **[G: U.S.]**

Kerr, Steven. Leadership and Participation. In *Brief, A. P., ed.*, 1984, pp. 229–51.

Koike, Kazuo. Skill Formation Systems in the U.S. and Japan: A Comparative Study. In *Aoki, M., ed.*, 1984, pp. 47–75. **[G: U.S.; Japan]**

Lambert, Richard A. Income Smoothing as Rational Equilibrium Behavior. *Accounting Rev.*, October 1984, *59*(4), pp. 604–18.

Lauter, G. Peter. East–West Trade: Organizational Structures and Problems of U.S. Multinational Corporations. In *Jackson, M. R. and Woodson, J. D., Jr., eds.*, 1984, pp. 153–85.

Leibenstein, Harvey. The Japanese Management System: An X-Efficiency-Game Theory Analysis. In *Aoki, M., ed.*, 1984, pp. 331–57.
[G: Japan]

Lombardi, Maria Ludovica and Vardelli, Riccardo. Il tempo manageriale come fattore strategico. (Managerial Time as a Strategic Factor. With English summary.) *L'Impresa*, 1984, *26*(1), pp. 39–46. **[G: Sweden; Korea; Italy]**

Maidique, Modesto A. and Hayes, Robert H. The Art of High-Technology Management. *Sloan Manage. Rev.*, Winter 1984, *25*(2), pp. 17–31.

Mangoni, Gustavo and Taverna, Piero. La strumentazione, aspetto trascurato dei grandi progetti. (Instrumentation and Control for Large Projects. With English summary.) *L'Impresa*, 1984, *26*(4), pp. 55–61.

Okuno, Masahiro. Corporate Loyalty and Bonus Payments: An Analysis of Work Incentives in Japan. In *Aoki, M., ed.*, 1984, pp. 387–411.
[G: Japan]

Olian, Judy D. and Rynes, Sara L. Organizational Staffing: Integrating Practice with Strategy. *Ind. Relat.*, Spring 1984, *23*(2), pp. 170–83.

Rapping, Leonard A. Bureaucracy, the Corporation, and Economic Policy. *J. Post Keynesian Econ.*, Spring 1984, *6*(3), pp. 337–53.
[G: U.S.]

Sherman, H. David. Improving the Productivity of Service Businesses. *Sloan Manage. Rev.*, Spring 1984, *25*(3), pp. 11–23.

Tsui, Anne S. Personnel Department Effectiveness: A Tripartite Approach. *Ind. Relat.*, Spring 1984, *23*(2), pp. 184–97.

Walkling, Ralph A. and Long, Michael S. Agency Theory, Managerial Welfare, and Takeover Bid Resistance. *Rand J. Econ.*, Spring 1984, *15*(1), pp. 54–68. **[G: U.S.]**

Williamson, Oliver E. The Incentive Limits of Firms: A Comparative Institutional Assessment of Bureaucracy. *Weltwirtsch. Arch.*, 1984, *120*(4), pp. 736–63. **[G: U.S.]**

Yui, Tsunehiko. The Development of the Organizational Structure of Top Management in Meiji Japan. In *Nakagawa, K. and Morikawa, H., eds.*, 1984, pp. 1–23. **[G: Japan]**

5132 Public Administration

Alexander, James R. Curriculum Reform in Budgeting and Financial Management: Preliminary Thoughts on the Dimensions of the Field. *Public Budg. Finance*, Autumn 1984, *4*(3), pp. 91–96. **[G: U.S.]**

Borsting, Jack R. Perspectives from the U.S. Department of Defense on Requirements and Opportunities for Innovation in Government. In *[Kozmetsky, G.]*, 1984, pp. 69–76. **[G: U.S.]**

Caiden, Naomi. An Interview with A. Alan Post, Legislative Analyst for the State of California, 1950–1977. *Public Budg. Finance*, Autumn 1984, *4*(3), pp. 75–90. **[G: U.S.]**

Cocks, Paul. Rethinking the Organizational Weapon: The Soviet System in a Systems Age. In *Hoffmann, E. P. and Laird, R. F., eds.*, 1984, *1980*, pp. 331–58. **[G: U.S.S.R.]**

Coe, Charles K. and Borthick, A. Faye. Computer Auditing in the Federal Government. *Public Budg. Finance*, Autumn 1984, *4*(3), 67–74. **[G: U.S.]**

Feller, Irwin and Johnston, Irene. The Innovation–Productivity Connection. In *Holzer, M. and Nagel, S. S., eds.*, 1984, pp. 171–89.
[G: U.S.]

Greenhalgh, Leonard and McKersie, Robert B. Cost-effectiveness of Alternative Strategies for Cutback Management. In *Carr, J. H., ed.*, 1984, *1980*, pp. 93–112. **[G: U.S.]**

Holzer, Marc. Public Administration under Pressure. In *Holzer, M. and Nagel, S. S., eds.*, 1984, pp. 71–86.

Johnson, Ronald W. and Lewin, Arie Y. Management and Accountability Models of Public Sector Performance. In *Miller, T. C., ed.*, 1984, pp. 224–50. **[G: U.S.]**

Jonsson, Ernst. Recurrent Cost and Performance Comparisons within Public Administration: A Method of Generating Efficiency-Promoting Competition. *Public Choice*, 1984, *42*(2), pp. 185–92. **[G: Sweden]**

Kelman, Steven. Using Implementation Research to Solve Implementation Problems: The Case of Energy Emergency Assistance. *J. Policy Anal. Manage.*, Fall 1984, *4*(1), pp. 75–91.
[G: U.S.]

Kirby, Michael J. L. Innovation in Government: Problems and Possibilities. In *[Kozmetsky, G.]*, 1984, pp. 41–59.

Kirlin, John J. Public Sector Performance: A Political Perspective. In *Miller, T. C., ed.*, 1984, pp. 161–92. **[G: U.S.]**

LaPorte, Robert, Jr. Administering Development. In *Burki, S. J. and LaPorte, R., Jr., eds.*, 1984, pp. 239–70. **[G: Pakistan]**

Levine, Charles H. Organizational Decline and Cutback Management. In *Carr, J. H., ed.*, 1984, *1978*, pp. 63–82. **[G: U.S.]**

Lewis, Carol W. and Logalbo, Anthony T. Cutback Principles and Practices. In *Carr, J. H., ed.*, 1984, pp. 83–92. **[G: U.S.]**

Makolo, Philomène. Reflections on Development Administration with Special Reference to Africa. *Can. J. Devel. Stud.*, 1984, *5*(1), pp. 79–112. **[G: Africa]**

Masser, Ian and Wilson, Tom. Approaches to Information Management in County Planning Authorities in England and Wales. *Urban Stud.*, November 1984, *21*(4), pp. 415–25. **[G: U.K.]**

Rivlin, Alice M. Out of the Trenches: A Public Policy Paradox. *J. Policy Anal. Manage.*, Fall 1984, *4*(1), pp. 17–22. **[G: U.S.]**

Staats, Elmer B. Changing Approaches to Accountability in an Increasingly Complex Society. In *[Kozmetsky, G.]*, 1984, pp. 77–92.

Vernon, Raymond. Linking Managers with Ministers: Dilemmas of the State-owned Enterprise. *J. Policy Anal. Manage.*, Fall 1984, *4*(1), pp. 39–55.

Withane, Sirinimal. Changing Patterns of Local Administration in Sri Lanka: Loose-Coupling between Planning and Implementation. *Can. J. Devel. Stud.*, 1984, *5*(2), pp. 243–55. **[G: Sri Lanka]**

514 Goals and Objectives of Firms

5140 Goals and Objectives of Firms

Akers, John F. A Responsible Future—An Address to the Computer Industry. *Sloan Manage. Rev.*, Fall 1984, *26*(1), pp. 53–57. **[G: U.S.]**

Albach, Horst. Structural Change in the Economy—A Challenge to Enterprise. In *Engels, W. and Pohl, H.*, eds., 1984, pp. 107–17. **[G: W. Germany]**

Baruch, Jordan J. Structuring Markets for Public Goods and Services. In *Brooks, H.; Liebman, L. and Schelling, C. S.*, eds., 1984, pp. 111–30. **[G: U.S.]**

Baumol, William J. Matching Private Incentives to Public Goals. In *Brooks, H.; Liebman, L. and Schelling, C. S.*, eds., 1984, pp. 175–94.

Bennett, John. A Model of Income Distribution in a Revenue-sharing Firm. *J. Compar. Econ.*, September 1984, *8*(3), pp. 237–46.

Boyle, Anthony J. The Private Law Enforcement of Directors' Duties. In *Hopt, K. J. and Teubner, G.*, eds., 1984, pp. 261–82.

Braun, Jerome S. Industrial Justice in a Practical Sense. *Rev. Soc. Econ.*, December 1984, *42*(3), pp. 318–27.

Brooks, Harvey. Seeking Equity and Efficiency: Public and Private Roles. In *Brooks, H.; Liebman, L. and Schelling, C. S.*, eds., 1984, pp. 3–29. **[G: U.S.]**

Chrisman, James J. and Carroll, Archie B. Corporate Responsibility—Reconciling Economic and Social Goals. *Sloan Manage. Rev.*, Winter 1984, *25*(2), pp. 59–65.

Clark, Robert C. What Is the Proper Role of the Corporation? In *Brooks, H.; Liebman, L. and Schelling, C. S.*, eds., 1984, pp. 195–220.

Coleman, James S. Responsibility in Corporate Action: A Sociologist's View. In *Hopt, K. J. and Teubner, G.*, eds., 1984, pp. 69–91.

Crain, W. Mark; Shughart, William F., II and Tollison, Robert D. The Convergence of Satisficing to Marginalism: An Empirical Test. *J. Econ. Behav. Organ.*, September–December 1984, *5*(3–4), pp. 375–85. **[G: U.S.]**

Davidson, Paul and Davidson, Greg S. Financial Markets and Williamson's Theory of Governance: Efficiency versus Concentration versus Power. *Quart. Rev. Econ. Bus.*, Winter 1984, *24*(4), pp. 50–63.

Dierkes, Meinolf. Corporate Social Reporting and Auditing: Theory and Practice. In *Hopt, K. J. and Teubner, G.*, eds., 1984, pp. 354–79.

Drucker, Peter F. Doing Good to Do Well: The New Opportunities for Business Enterprise. In *Brooks, H.; Liebman, L. and Schelling, C. S.*, eds., 1984, pp. 285–302. **[G: U.S.]**

Duus, Peter. The Reaction of Japanese Big Business to a State-controlled Economy in the 1930s. *Rivista Int. Sci. Econ. Com.*, September 1984, *31*(9), pp. 819–32. **[G: Japan]**

Fanara, Philip, Jr. and Sweet, David M. What Do Regulated Firms Maximize? Some Empirical Evidence from the Natural Gas Pipeline Industry. *Amer. Econ.*, Spring 1984, *28*(1), pp. 44–48. **[G: U.S.]**

FitzRoy, Felix R. and Mueller, Dennis C. Cooperation and Conflict in Contractual Organizations. *Quart. Rev. Econ. Bus.*, Winter 1984, *24*(4), pp. 24–49.

Gaibisso, Anna Maria. Quando sistemi direzionali e obiettivi non coincidono. (Management Systems and Business Objectives. With English summary.) *L'Impresa*, 1984, *26*(4), pp. 41–47. **[G: Italy]**

Gitelman, H. M. Management's Crisis of Confidence and the Origin of the National Industrial Conference Board, 1914–1916. *Bus. Hist. Rev.*, Summer 1984, *58*(2), pp. 153–77. **[G: U.S.]**

Gomard, Bernhard. Board Members' Liability for Damages. In *Hopt, K. J. and Teubner, G.*, eds., 1984, pp. 208–60.

Gruenberg, Gladys W. Prospects: Solidarity within the Firm. *Rev. Soc. Econ.*, December 1984, *42*(3), pp. 424–26.

Hattwick, Richard E.; Shin, Bong-Gon P. and Wall, Larry C. Business Ethics—Findings of a Survey of America's Business Leaders. *J. Behav. Econ.*, Winter 1984, *13*(2), pp. 157–85. **[G: U.S.]**

Hopt, Klaus J. Self-dealing and Use of Corporate Opportunity and Information: Regulating Directors' Conflicts of Interest. In *Hopt, K. J. and Teubner, G.*, eds., 1984, pp. 285–326.

Keim, Gerald D.; Zeithaml, Carl P. and Baysinger, Barry D. New Directions for Corporate Political Strategy. *Sloan Manage. Rev.*, Spring 1984, *25*(3), pp. 53–62. **[G: U.S.]**

Kolderie, Ted. Business Opportunities in the Changing Conceptions of the Public Sector Role. In *Brooks, H.; Liebman, L. and Schelling, C. S.*, eds., 1984, pp. 89–110. **[G: U.S.]**

Kraakman, Reinier H. The Economic Functions of Corporate Liability. In *Hopt, K. J. and Teubner, G.*, eds., 1984, pp. 178–207.

Krause, Detlef. Corporate Social Responsibility: Interests and Goals. In *Hopt, K. J. and Teubner, G., eds.,* 1984, pp. 95–121.

Kübler, Friedrich. Dual Loyalty of Labor Representatives. In *Hopt, K. J. and Teubner, G., eds.,* 1984, pp. 429–44. **[G: W. Germany]**

Lawriwsky, Michael L. A Critical View of Studies Examining the Performance Effects of the Separation of Ownership from Control. *Rivista Int. Sci. Econ. Com.,* April 1984, *31*(4), pp. 312–28. **[G: Australia]**

Liebman, Lance. Political and Economic Markets: The Public, Private and Not-for-Profit Sectors. In *Brooks, H.; Liebman, L. and Schelling, C. S., eds.,* 1984, pp. 341–58. **[G: U.S.]**

Linowes, David F. Socioeconomic Reporting and Expanded Accountability for Management Actions. In *[Kozmetsky, G.],* 1984, pp. 111–19.

Loasby, Brian J. Entrepreneurs and Organisation. *J. Econ. Stud.,* 1984, *11*(2), pp. 75–88.

Loescher, Samuel M. Bureaucratic Measurement, Shuttling Stock Shares, and Shortened Time Horizons: Implications for Economic Growth. *Quart. Rev. Econ. Bus.,* Winter 1984, *24*(4), pp. 8–23.

Martin, James R. Market Structure and Corporate Accounting Strategy. *Amer. Econ.,* Spring 1984, *28*(1), pp. 34–43. **[G: U.S.]**

Mashaw, Jerry L. The Economic Context of Corporate Social Responsibility. In *Hopt, K. J. and Teubner, G., eds.,* 1984, pp. 55–68.

McKenzie, Richard B. The Case for Plant Closures. In *McKenzie, R. B., ed. (II),* 1984, *1981,* pp. 205–19. **[G: U.S.]**

Norris, William C. A New Role for Corporations. In *Brooks, H.; Liebman, L. and Schelling, C. S., eds.,* 1984, pp. 243–62. **[G: U.S.]**

Pickering, J. F. and Jones, Trefor T. The Firm and its Social Environment. In *Pickering, J. F. and Cockerill, T. A. J., eds.,* 1984, pp. 277–323.

Rapping, Leonard A. Bureaucracy, the Corporation, and Economic Policy. *J. Post Keynesian Econ.,* Spring 1984, *6*(3), pp. 337–53. **[G: U.S.]**

Schelling, Thomas C. Command and Control. In *Schelling, T. C.,* 1984, pp. 27–56.

Scherillo, Maria Teresa. Controllo totale per la qualità. (Total Quality Control. With English summary.) *L'Impresa,* 1984, *26*(5), pp. 51–56.

Steinmann, Horst. The Enterprise as a Political System. In *Hopt, K. J. and Teubner, G., eds.,* 1984, pp. 401–28.

Stewart, John F.; Harris, Robert S. and Carleton, Willard T. The Role of Market Structure in Merger Behavior. *J. Ind. Econ.,* March 1984, *32*(3), pp. 293–312. **[G: U.S.]**

Stollenwerk, James H. *Rexworks:* A Case Study of Applied Social Economic Justice. *Rev. Soc. Econ.,* December 1984, *42*(3), pp. 253–56. **[G: U.S.]**

Stone, Cristopher D. Public Interest Representation: Economic and Social Policy Inside the Enterprise. In *Hopt, K. J. and Teubner, G., eds.,* 1984, pp. 122–46.

Teubner, Gunther. Corporate Fiduciary Duties and Their Beneficiaries: A Functional Approach to the Legal Institutionalization of Corporate Responsibility. In *Hopt, K. J. and Teubner, G., eds.,* 1984, pp. 149–77.

Tichy, Noel M. and Ulrich, David O. The Leadership Challenge—A Call for the Transformational Leader. *Sloan Manage. Rev.,* Fall 1984, *26*(1), pp. 59–68. **[G: U.S.]**

Wedderburn, K. W. [Lord]. The Legal Development of Corporate Responsibility: For Who Will Corporate Managers Be Trustees? In *Hopt, K. J. and Teubner, G., eds.,* 1984, pp. 3–54. **[G: U.K.]**

Williams, Edward E. and Findlay, M. Chapman, III. Corporate Governance: A Problem of Hierarchies and Self Interest. *Amer. J. Econ. Soc.,* January 1984, *43*(1), pp. 19–36.

Williamson, Oliver E. Perspectives on the Modern Corporation. *Quart. Rev. Econ. Bus.,* Winter 1984, *24*(4), pp. 64–71.

Worthy, James C. Managing the "Social Markets" Business. In *Brooks, H.; Liebman, L. and Schelling, C. S., eds.,* 1984, pp. 221–40.

Yoshihara, Kunio. Indigenous Entrepreneurs in the ASEAN Countries. *Singapore Econ. Rev.,* October 1984, *29*(2), pp. 132–47.
[G: ASEAN]

520 BUSINESS FINANCE AND INVESTMENT

5200 Business Finance and Investment

Aoki, Masahiko. Aspects of the Japanese Firm. In *Aoki, M., ed.,* 1984, pp. 3–43. **[G: Japan]**

Bierich, Marcus. More Risk Capital for Private Enterprise: Comment. In *Giersch, H., ed.,* 1984, pp. 40–43.

van Breda, Michael F. Integrating Capital and Operating Budgets. *Sloan Manage. Rev.,* Winter 1984, *25*(2), pp. 49–58.

Chappell, Henry W., Jr. and Cheng, David C. Firms' Acquisition Decisions and Tobin's *q* Ratio. *J. Econ. Bus.,* February 1984, *36*(1), pp. 29–42. **[G: U.S.]**

Chen, Gavin M. Business Formation and Investment in the Minority Community. In *Bingham, R. D. and Blair, J. P., eds.,* 1984, pp. 79–98. **[G: U.S.]**

Chen, Son-Nan. Capital Budgeting and Uncertain Inflation. *J. Econ. Bus.,* August 1984, *36*(3), pp. 335–44.

Coate, Malcolm B. Optimization for Business Portfolio Planning. In *Naylor, T. H. and Thomas, C., eds.,* 1984, pp. 13–23.

Feldenkirchen, Wilfried. Capital Raised and its Use by German Mechanical Engineering Firms in the 19th and Early 20th Centuries. In *Engels, W. and Pohl, H., eds.,* 1984, pp. 19–55. **[G: W. Germany]**

Fels, Gerhard. More Risk Capital for Private Enterprise. In *Giersch, H., ed.,* 1984, pp. 29–39. **[G: W. Germany; OECD]**

Howe, Keith M. A Search Model of Capital Budgeting Behavior. *Quart. J. Bus. Econ.*, Winter 1984, *23*(1), pp. 65–76.

Jaffee, Dwight M. The Impact of Financial Futures and Options on Capital Formation. *J. Futures Markets*, Fall 1984, *4*(3), pp. 417–47.
[G: U.S.]

Jones, Trefor T. and Cockerill, T. A. J. Public Enterprise Management. In *Pickering, J. F. and Cockerill, T. A. J., eds.*, 1984, pp. 344–87. [G: U.K.]

King, Mervyn A. The Ownership and Financing of Corporations. In *Aoki, M., ed.*, 1984, pp. 311–17. [G: Japan]

Laitinen, Erkki K. Empirical Evidence on the Measurement of the Firm. *Liiketaloudellinen Aikak.*, 1984, *33*(4), pp. 405–32.
[G: Finland]

Littler, D. A.; Pickering, J. F. and Cockerill, T. A. J. The Management of the Small Firm. In *Pickering, J. F. and Cockerill, T. A. J., eds.*, 1984, pp. 388–415. [G: U.K.; OECD]

Makhija, Anil K. and Thompson, Howard E. Comparison of Alternative Models for Estimating the Cost of Equity Capital for Electric Utilities. *J. Econ. Bus.*, February 1984, *36*(1), pp. 107–31. [G: U.S.]

Mehrez, Abraham and Stulman, Alan. A Note on Capital Budgeting in the Purchase of Information. *Managerial Dec. Econ.*, December 1984, *5*(4), pp. 251–54. [G: U.S.]

Miyamoto, Masaaki. Budgetary Control and ROI. (In Japanese. With English summary.) *Osaka Econ. Pap.*, December 1984, *34*(2–3), pp. 290–98.

Miyamoto, Matao and Hiroyama, Kensuke. The Retreat from Diversification and the Desire for Specialization in Kōnoike: Late Meiji to Early Shōwa. In *Nakagawa, K. and Morikawa, H., eds.*, 1984, pp. 104–30. [G: Japan]

Okimoto, Daniel I. Competitive Edge: Conclusions. In *Okimoto, D. I.; Sugano, T. and Weinstein, F. B., eds.*, 1984, pp. 177–235.
[G: Japan; U.S.]

Pike, R. H. Sophisticated Capital Budgeting Systems and Their Association with Corporate Performance. *Managerial Dec. Econ.*, June 1984, *5*(2), pp. 91–97. [G: U.K.]

Schmidt, Hartmut. Venture-Capital-Märkte in Europa. (Venture Capital Markets in Europe. With English summary.) *Kredit Kapital*, 1984, *17*(2), pp. 281–96. [G: Europe]

Scott, David F., Jr. and Petty, J. William, II. Capital Budgeting Practices in Large American Firms: A Retrospective Analysis and Synthesis. *Financial Rev.*, March 1984, *19*(1), pp. 111–23. [G: U.S.]

Stanley, Marjorie T. and Block, Stanley B. A Survey of Multinational Capital Budgeting. *Financial Rev.*, March 1984, *19*(1), pp. 36–54.
[G: U.S.]

Stapleton, Richard C. Financial Management. In *Pickering, J. F. and Cockerill, T. A. J., eds.*, 1984, pp. 153–78.

Sugiyama, Kazuo. Business Finance in Japanese

Business History. In *Nakagawa, K. and Morikawa, H., eds.*, 1984, pp. 24–46. [G: U.K.; U.S.; W. Germany; Japan]

521 Business Finance

5210 Business Finance

Abel, Andrew B. R&D and the Market Value of the Firm: A Note. In *Griliches, Z., ed.*, 1984, pp. 261–69.

Albach, Horst. The Rate of Return in German Manufacturing Industry: Measurement and Policy Implications. In *Holland, D. M., ed.*, 1984, pp. 273–311. [G: W. Germany]

Altman, Edward I. A Further Empirical Investigation of the Bankruptcy Cost Question. *J. Finance*, September 1984, *39*(4), pp. 1067–89.
[G: U.S.]

Altman, Edward I. Company and Country Risk Models: Introduction. *J. Banking Finance*, June 1984, *8*(2), pp. 151.

Altman, Edward I. The Success of Business Failure Prediction Models: An International Survey. *J. Banking Finance*, June 1984, *8*(2), pp. 171–98. [G: OECD; Brazil]

Anderson, William D. Purchase and Sale of Shares. In *Purden, C., ed.*, 1984, pp. 203–44.
[G: Canada]

Ang, James S. and Peterson, Pamela P. The Leasing Puzzle. *J. Finance*, September 1984, *39*(4), pp. 1055–65. [G: U.S.]

Antia, Murad J. and Meyer, Richard L. The Growth Optimal Capital Structure: Manager versus Shareholder Objectives. *J. Finan. Res.*, Fall 1984, *7*(3), pp. 259–67.

Aoki, Masahiko. Shareholders' Non-unanimity on Investment Financing: Banks vs. Individual Investors. In *Aoki, M., ed.*, 1984, pp. 193–224.
[G: Japan]

Appetiti, Sandro. Identifying Unsound Firms in Italy: An Attempt to Use Trend Variables. *J. Banking Finance*, June 1984, *8*(2), pp. 269–79. [G: Italy]

Artus, Patrick. Le fonctionnement du marché du crédit: Diverses analyses dans un cadre de déséquilibre. (The Functioning of the Credit Market: Several Analyses in a Disequilibrium Context. With English summary.) *Revue Écon.*, July 1984, *35*(4), pp. 591–621.
[G: France]

Asajima, Shoichi. Flow-of-Funds Analysis of the Sumitomo Zaibatsu. In *Nakagawa, K. and Morikawa, H., eds.*, 1984, pp. 72–90.
[G: Japan]

Auerbach, Alan J. Taxes, Firm Financial Policy and the Cost of Capital: An Empirical Analysis. *J. Public Econ.*, February/March 1984, *23*(1/2), pp. 27–57. [G: U.S.]

Bathke, Allen W., Jr. and Lorek, Kenneth S. The Relationship between Time-Series Models and the Security Market's Expectation of Quarterly Earnings. *Accounting Rev.*, April 1984, *59*(2), pp. 163–76. [G: U.S.]

Bayer, Kurt. Profitability in Austrian Industrial

Corporations. In *Holland, D. M., ed.,* 1984, pp. 421–64. **[G: Austria]**

Ben-Zion, Uri. The R&D and Investment Decision and Its Relationship to the Firm's Market Value: Some Preliminary Results. In *Griliches, Z., ed.,* 1984, pp. 299–312. **[G: U.S.]**

Benesh, Gary A.; Keown, Arthur J. and Pinkerton, John M. An Examination of Market Reaction to Substantial Shifts in Dividend Policy. *J. Finan. Res.,* Summer 1984, 7(2), pp. 131–42. **[G: U.S.]**

Bertmar, Lars. Measures of Business Performance—The Swedish Case. In *Holland, D. M., ed.,* 1984, pp. 117–53. **[G: Sweden]**

Bezza, El Mostafa. Le concept d'intérêts cumulés: un algorithme pour dépasser le problème de multiplicité des T.I.R. (The Cumulative Interest Concept: An Algorithm to Overstep the IRR's Multiplicity. With English summary.) *Écon. Soc.,* November–December 1984, 18(11–12), pp. 99–132.

Bianchi, Marcello and Donna, Giorgio. Errori strategici di gestione finanziaria. (Strategic Errors in Financial Management. With English summary.) *L'Impresa,* 1984, 26(4), pp. 21–29.

Bicksler, James L. International Corporate Diversification, Market Valuation, and Size-Adjusted Evidence: Discussion. *J. Finance,* July 1984, 39(3), pp. 743–45.

Bodenheimer, Thomas S. The Transnational Pharmaceutical Industry and the Health of the World's People. In *McKinlay, J. B., ed.,* 1984, pp. 187–216.

le Bon, Claude. Old and "New" Concepts of Competition and Concentration. In *[Kozmetsky, G.],* 1984, pp. 151–53.

Bortz, Gary A. and Rust, John P. Why Do Companies Pay Dividends? Comment. *Amer. Econ. Rev.,* December 1984, 74(5), pp. 1135–36.

Bosshardt, Donald I. Equity Clienteles, Short-Sale Restrictions, and the Miller Equilibrium. *Financial Rev.,* May 1984, 19(2), pp. 240–50.

Boultbee, Jack A. Public Company Split-ups. In *Purden, C., ed.,* 1984, pp. 1–11.
[G: Canada]

Bowman, Edward H. Risk-Return Tradeoffs for Strategic Management: A Response. *Sloan Manage. Rev.,* Spring 1984, 25(3), pp. 50–51.
[G: U.S.]

Boyes, William J. and Furnish, Dale Beck. A Note on the Use of Incorporation as an Escape from Usury Ceilings. *J. Ind. Econ.,* March 1984, 32(3), pp. 367–72. **[G: U.S.]**

Bradley, Michael; Jarrell, Gregg A. and Kim, E. Han. On the Existence of an Optimal Capital Structure: Theory and Evidence. *J. Finance,* July 1984, 39(3), pp. 857–78.
[G: U.S.]

Brean, Donald J. S. International Portfolio Capital: The Wedge of the Withholding Tax. *Nat. Tax J.,* June 1984, 37(2), pp. 239–47.
[G: Canada]

Brennan, Michael J. and Kraus, Allan. Notes on Costless Financial Signalling. In *Bamberg, G. and Spremann, K., eds.,* 1984, pp. 33–51.

Brennan, Michael J. and Schwartz, Eduardo S.

Optimal Financial Policy and Firm Valuation. *J. Finance,* July 1984, 39(3), pp. 593–607.

Brick, Ivan E. and Fung, William K. H. Taxes and the Theory of Trade Debt. *J. Finance,* September 1984, 39(4), pp. 1169–76.

Brockett, Patrick L.; Cox, Samuel H., Jr. and Witt, Robert C. Self-Insurance and the Probability of Financial Regret. *J. Risk Ins.,* December 1984, 51(4), pp. 720–29. **[G: U.S.]**

Brockett, Patrick L., et al. A Chance-constrained Programming Approach to Cost–Volume–Profit Analysis. *Accounting Rev.,* July 1984, 59(3), pp. 474–87.

Brodt, Abraham I. International Bank Asset and Liability Management. *J. Bank Res.,* Summer 1984, 15(2), pp. 82–94. **[G: U.S.]**

Chang, Eric C. and Lewellen, Wilbur G. Market Timing and Mutual Fund Investment Performance. *J. Bus.,* Part 1, January 1984, 57(1), pp. 57–72. **[G: U.S.]**

Chen, Andrew H. External Financing and Liquidity: Discussion. *J. Finance,* July 1984, 39(3), pp. 908–10.

Choi, Dosoung and Philippatos, George C. Post-Merger Performance among Homogeneous Firm Samples. *Financial Rev.,* May 1984, 19(2), pp. 173–94. **[G: U.S.]**

Chown, John F. The 1984 Budget, the Finance Bill and Corporate Finance. *Fisc. Stud.,* May 1984, 5(2), pp. 73–81. **[G: U.K.]**

Churchill, Neil C. Improved Accountability and Comprehensive Audit as Portents for the Future. In *[Kozmetsky, G.],* 1984, pp. 93–109.
[G: U.S.]

Clippinger, Marni. Financial Strategies for the New Entrepreneurs. In *Meyer, J. R. and Oster, C. V., Jr., eds.,* 1984, pp. 105–22.
[G: U.S.]

Cochrane, E. Cal. Use of Vehicles Other Than Corporations in Purchase and Sale Transactions. In *Purden, C., ed.,* 1984, pp. 138–55.
[G: Canada]

Cockerill, T. A. J. and Kinloch, H. Managing Risk and Uncertainty. In *Pickering, J. F. and Cockerill, T. A. J., eds.,* 1984, pp. 221–51.
[G: U.K.]

Cohen, Kalman J. and Hammer, Frederick S. Linear Programming Models for Optimal Bank Dynamic Balance Sheet Management. In *Naylor, T. H. and Thomas, C., eds.,* 1984, pp. 25–44.

Collomb, B. and Ponssard, J. P. Creative Management in Mature Capital Intensive Industries: The Case of Cement. In *[Kozmetsky, G.],* 1984, pp. 123–43. **[G: OECD; Selected LDCs]**

Colton, Kent W. and Cunningham, Donald F. The Role of the Secondary Mortgage Markets in Managing Risk. In *Fed. Home Loan Bank San Francisco,* 1984, pp. 125–55. **[G: U.S.]**

Constantinides, George M. Warrant Exercise and Bond Conversion in Competitive Markets. *J. Finan. Econ.,* September 1984, 13(3), pp. 371–97.

Constantinides, George M. and Rosenthal, Robert W. Strategic Analysis of the Competitive

Exercise of Certain Financial Options. *J. Econ. Theory*, February 1984, *32*(1), pp. 128–38.

Dann, Larry Y. and Mikkelson, Wayne H. Convertible Debt Issuance, Capital Structure Change and Financing-Related Information: Some New Evidence. *J. Finan. Econ.*, June 1984, *13*(2), pp. 157–86. [G: U.S.]

Danos, Paul; Holt, Doris L. and Imhoff, Eugene A., Jr. Bond Raters' Use of Management Financial Forecasts: Experiment in Expert Judgment. *Accounting Rev.*, October 1984, *59*(4), pp. 547–73. [G: U.S.]

Davis, Harry Z.; Kahn, Nathan and Rozen, Etzmun. LIFO Inventory Liquidations: An Empirical Study. *J. Acc. Res.*, Autumn 1984, *22*(2), pp. 480–96. [G: U.S.]

Denneberg, Dieter. Elements of Finance under Risk, an Average Deviation Approach to Risk. *Écon. Appl.*, 1984, *37*(1), pp. 165–99.

Desin, Allan N. Alternative Divisions of the Tax Base: How Much Is at Stake? Comments. In *McLure, C. E., Jr., ed.*, 1984, pp. 214–16. [G: U.S.]

Dietrich, J. Richard. Methodological Issues Related to the Estimation of Financial Distress Prediction Models: Discussion. *J. Acc. Res.*, Supplement 1984, *22*, pp. 83–86. [G: U.S.]

Drukarczyk, Jochen. Credit Contracts, Collateral-Based Security Agreements, and Bankruptcy. In *Bamberg, G. and Spremann, K., eds.*, 1984, pp. 139–59.

Dunn, Kenneth B. and Spatt, Chester S. A Strategic Analysis of Sinking Fund Bonds. *J. Finan. Econ.*, September 1984, *13*(3), pp. 399–423.

Dye, Ronald A. Inside Trading and Incentives. *J. Bus.*, July 1984, *57*(3), pp. 295–313.

Easterbrook, Frank H. Two Agency-Cost Explanations of Dividends. *Amer. Econ. Rev.*, September 1984, *74*(4), pp. 650–59.

Edwards, J. S. S. and Keen, Michael J. Wealth Maximization and the Cost of Capital: A Comment. *Quart. J. Econ.*, February 1984, *99*(1), pp. 211–14.

Edwards, Jeremy. Does Dividend Policy Matter? *Fisc. Stud.*, February 1984, *5*(1), pp. 1–17. [G: U.S.; U.K.]

Edwards, Jeremy. The 1984 Corporation Tax Reform. *Fisc. Stud.*, May 1984, *5*(2), pp. 30–44. [G: U.K.]

Elton, Edwin J.; Gruber, Martin J. and Rentzler, Joel. The Ex-Dividend Day Behavior of Stock Prices; a Re-Examination of the Clientele Effect: A Comment. *J. Finance*, June 1984, *39*(2), pp. 551–56. [G: U.S.]

Emanuel, David. Optimal Financial Policy and Firm Valuation: Discussion. *J. Finance*, July 1984, *39*(3), pp. 607–09.

Emery, Gary W. A Pure Financial Explanation for Trade Credit. *J. Finan. Quant. Anal.*, September 1984, *19*(3), pp. 271–85.

Emory, Douglas R. and Lewellen, Wilbur G. Refunding Noncallable Debt. *J. Finan. Quant. Anal.*, March 1984, *19*(1), pp. 73–82.

Engels, Wolfram. Die Eignung von Massgütern für den intertemporalen Vermögensvergleich. (The Suitability of Yardstick Goods for Intertemporal Wealth Comparisons. With English summary.) *Kredit Kapital*, 1984, *17*(4), pp. 490–506.

Errunza, Vihang R. and Senbet, Lemma W. International Corporate Diversification, Market Valuation, and Size-Adjusted Evidence. *J. Finance*, July 1984, *39*(3), pp. 727–43. [G: U.S.]

Estrella, Arturo. Corporate Use of Pension Overfunding. *Fed. Res. Bank New York Quart. Rev.*, Spring 1984, *9*(1), pp. 17–25. [G: U.S.]

Evenson, Robert E. The R&D and Investment Decision and Its Relationship to the Firm's Market Value: Some Preliminary Results: Comment. In *Griliches, Z., ed.*, 1984, pp. 312–14. [G: U.S.]

Farmer, Roger E. A. Unemployment, Bankruptcy and Asymmetric Information. *Manchester Sch. Econ. Soc. Stud.*, September 1984, *52*(3), pp. 284–91.

Feldstein, Martin; Slemrod, Joel and Yitzhaki, Shlomo. The Effects of Taxation on the Selling of Corporate Stock and the Realization of Capital Gains: Reply. *Quart. J. Econ.*, February 1984, *99*(1), pp. 111–20. [G: U.S.]

Finsinger, Jörg and Pauly, Mark V. Reserve Levels and Reserve Requirements for Profit-maximizing Insurance Firms. In *Bamberg, G. and Spremann, K., eds.*, 1984, pp. 160–80.

Fisher, Lawrence. Contingent Claims Analysis of Corporate Capital Structures: An Empirical Investigation. *J. Finance*, July 1984, *39*(3), pp. 625–27.

Flaherty, M. Therese and Itami, Hiroyuki. Competitive Edge: Finance. In *Okimoto, D. I.; Sugano, T. and Weinstein, F. B., eds.*, 1984, pp. 134–76. [G: Japan; U.S.]

Flath, David. Debt and Taxes: Japan Compared with the U.S. *Int. J. Ind. Organ.*, December 1984, *2*(4), pp. 311–26. [G: Japan; U.S.]

Fleischer, Arthur, Jr. and Raymond, Elizabeth A. Critical Developments in Acquisitions. In *Purden, C., ed.*, 1984, pp. 331–43. [G: U.S.]

Foss, Murray F. Corporate Liquidity under Stagflation and Disinflation. In *Fellner, W., ed.*, 1984, pp. 205–45.

Foster, George; Olsen, Chris and Shevlin, Terry. Earnings Releases, Anomalies, and the Behavior of Security Returns. *Accounting Rev.*, October 1984, *59*(4), pp. 574–603. [G: U.S.]

Fung, William K. H. and Theobald, Michael F. Dividends and Debt under Alternative Tax Systems. *J. Finan. Quant. Anal.*, March 1984, *19*(1), pp. 59–72. [G: U.S.; U.K.; France; Germany]

Gabor, André. On the Theory and Practice of Transfer Pricing. In *[Pearce, I. F.]*, 1984, pp. 149–70.

Gaul, Wolfgang. Financial Planning via Stochastic Programming: A Stochastic Flows-With-Gains Approach. In *Bamberg, G. and Spremann, K., eds.*, 1984, pp. 181–97.

Gehr, Adam K., Jr. Financial Structure and Financial Strategy. *J. Finan. Res.*, Spring 1984, *7*(1), pp. 69–80.

Geske, Robert and Johnson, Herb E. The Valuation of Corporate Liabilities as Compound Options: A Correction. *J. Finan. Quant. Anal.*, June 1984, *19*(2), pp. 231–32.

Giroux, Gary A. and Wiggins, Casper E. An Events Approach to Corporate Bankruptcy. *J. Bank Res.*, Autumn 1984, *15*(3), pp. 179–87. [G: U.S.]

Gordon, Myron J. Leverage and the Value of a Firm under a Progressive Personal Income Tax: Reply. *J. Banking Finance*, September 1984, *8*(3), pp. 495–97.

Gordon, Roger H. Inflation, Taxation, and Corporate Behavior. *Quart. J. Econ.*, May 1984, *99*(2), pp. 312–27.

Goudie, Andrew W. The Dividend Decision in the Presence of Tax Exhaustion. *Scot. J. Polit. Econ.*, November 1984, *31*(3), pp. 265–73.

Green, Richard C. Investment Incentives, Debt, and Warrants. *J. Finan. Econ.*, March 1984, *13*(1), pp. 115–36.

Greenwald, Bruce C.; Stiglitz, Joseph E. and Weiss, Andrew. Informational Imperfections in the Capital Market and Macroeconomic Fluctuations. *Amer. Econ. Rev.*, May 1984, *74*(2), pp. 194–99.

Griliches, Zvi. Market Value, R&D, and Patents. In *Griliches, Z., ed.*, 1984, pp. 249–52. [G: U.S.]

Grinblatt, Mark S.; Masulis, Ronald W. and Titman, Sheridan. The Valuation Effects of Stock Splits and Stock Dividends. *J. Finan. Econ.*, December 1984, *13*(4), pp. 461–90.

Grinols, Earl L. Competition and Optimal Departures from Stock Market Value Maximization by Firms. *J. Econ. Dynam. Control*, December 1984, *8*(3), pp. 277–89.

Gröner, Helmut. Marktsystem, Unternehmenskontrollen und Insolvenzen: Volkswirtschaftliche Überlegungen zur Reform des Insolvenzrechts. (With English Summary.) In *Eucken, W. and Böhm, F., eds.*, 1984, pp. 247–67. [G: W. Germany]

Hadley, Eleanor. Counterpoint on Business Groupings and Government–Industry Relations in Automobiles. In *Aoki, M., ed.*, 1984, pp. 319–27. [G: Japan]

Hammond, Peter J. What to Do about Business Cycles? In *Seidl, C., ed.*, 1984, pp. 59–75.

Hamon, Jacques and Galesne, Alain. Recherche financière et bases de données bibliographiques: DAUFIN, un nouvel outil pour la recherche financière. (Financial Research and Bibliographic Data Bases: DAUFIN as a New Tool for Financial Research. With English summary.) *Écon. Soc.*, November–December 1984, *18*(11–12), pp. 159–228. [G: France]

Hansen, Robert S. and Pinkerton, John M. Direct Equity Financing; A Resolution of a Paradox: A Reply. *J. Finance*, December 1984, *39*(5), pp. 1619–24. [G: U.S.]

Harris, Frederick H. deB. Growth Expectations, Excess Value, and the Risk-Adjusted Return to Market Power. *Southern Econ. J.*, July 1984, *51*(1), pp. 166–79. [G: U.S.]

Harrison, Bennett and Bluestone, Barry. The Incidence and Regulation of Plant Closings. In

Sawers, L. and Tabb, W. K., eds., 1984, *1982*, pp. 368–402. [G: U.S.]

Hartzog, Jerry. Market Value Decisionmaking. In *Fed. Home Loan Bank San Francisco*, 1984, pp. 197–209. [G: U.S.]

Hasbrouck, Joel and Friend, Irwin. Why Do Companies Pay Dividends? Comment. *Amer. Econ. Rev.*, December 1984, *74*(5), pp. 1137–41.

Henriksson, Roy D. Market Timing and Mutual Fund Performance: An Empirical Investigation. *J. Bus.*, Part 1, January 1984, *57*(1), pp. 73–96. [G: U.S.]

Hills, John. Deep Discount Bonds—Or How to Get an Interest-free Loan. *Fisc. Stud.*, August 1984, *5*(3), pp. 62–67. [G: U.K.]

Hiltz, Michael A. Section 55: An Update. In *Purden, C., ed.*, 1984, pp. 40–46. [G: Canada]

Hirschey, Mark and Wichern, Dean W. Accounting and Market-Value Measures of Profitability: Consistency, Determinants, and Uses. *J. Bus. Econ. Statist.*, October 1984, *2*(4), pp. 375–83. [G: U.S.]

Ho, Thomas S. Y. and Singer, Ronald F. The Value of Corporate Debt with a Sinking-Fund Provision. *J. Bus.*, July 1984, *57*(3), pp. 315–36.

Holcombe, Randall G. and Saba, Richard P. The Effects of Heterogeneous Expectations on the Capital Structure of the Firm. *Southern Econ. J.*, October 1984, *51*(2), pp. 356–68.

Holland, Daniel M. and Myers, Stewart C. Trends in Corporate Profitability and Capital Costs in the United States. In *Holland, D. M., ed.*, 1984, pp. 43–115. [G: U.S.]

Honkapohja, Seppo and Kanniainen, Vesa. Inventory Valuation Allowance: A Solution to the Problem of the Corporation Tax? *Liiketaloudellinen Aikak.*, 1984, *33*(1), pp. 49–59. [G: Finland; Sweden]

Houghton, Keith A. Accounting Data and the Prediction of Business Failure: The Setting of Priors and the Age of Data. *J. Acc. Res.*, Spring 1984, *22*(1), pp. 361–68. [G: Australia]

Houghton, Keith A. and Sengupta, Ratna. The Effect of Prior Probability Disclosure and Information Set Construction on Bankers' Ability to Predict Failure. *J. Acc. Res.*, Autumn 1984, *22*(2), pp. 768–75. [G: U.S.]

Howick, Wallace M. Purchase and Sale of Assets. In *Purden, C., ed.*, 1984, pp. 156–202. [G: Canada]

Huberman, Gur. External Financing and Liquidity. *J. Finance*, July 1984, *39*(3), pp. 895–908.

Ijiri, Yuji and Noel, James. A Reliability Comparison of the Measurement of Wealth, Income, and Force. *Accounting Rev.*, January 1984, *59*(1), pp. 52–63.

Isermann, Heinz. Investment and Financial Planning in a General Partnership. In *Grauer, M. and Wierzbicki, A. P., eds.*, 1984, pp. 175–85.

Izan, H. Y. Corporate Distress in Australia. *J. Banking Finance*, June 1984, *8*(2), pp. 303–20. [G: Australia]

Jaffe, Jeffrey F. and Westerfield, Randolph.

Leverage and the Value of a Firm under a Progressive Income Tax: A Correction and Extension. *J. Banking Finance*, September 1984, 8(3), pp. 491–94.

Jalilvand, Abolhassan and Harris, Robert S. Corporate Behavior in Adjusting to Capital Structure and Dividend Targets: An Econometric Study. *J. Finance*, March 1984, 39(1), pp. 127–45.　　　　　　　　　　　　**[G: U.S.]**

Jones, E. Philip; Mason, Scott P. and Rosenfeld, Eric R. Contingent Claims Analysis of Corporate Capital Structures: An Empirical Investigation. *J. Finance*, July 1984, 39(3), pp. 611–25.

Juhász, Margit. Enterprise Incomes in Hungary, Their Generation, Distribution and Differentiation. *Acta Oecon.*, 1984, 33(1–2), pp. 166–80.　　　　　　　　　　　**[G: Hungary]**

Kalaba, Robert E., et al. Estimation of Implicit Bankruptcy Costs. *J. Finance*, July 1984, 39(3), pp. 629–42.

Kalay, Avner. The Ex-Dividend Day Behavior of Stock Prices; a Re-Examination of the Clientele Effect: A Reply. *J. Finance*, June 1984, 39(2), pp. 556–61.　　　　　**[G: U.S.]**

Kane, Alex; Lee, Young Ki and Marcus, Alan J. Earnings and Dividend Announcements: Is There a Corroboration Effect? *J. Finance*, September 1984, 39(4), pp. 1091–99.　　**[G: U.S.]**

Kane, Alex; Marcus, Alan J. and McDonald, Robert L. How Big Is the Tax Advantage to Debt? *J. Finance*, July 1984, 39(3), pp. 841–53.

Kaplan, Robert S. The Evolution of Management Accounting. *Accounting Rev.*, July 1984, 59(3), pp. 390–418.　　　　　　　　　　　**[G: U.S.]**

Keen, Michael J. The 1984 Budget, the Finance Bill, and Corporate Finance: A Correction. *Fisc. Stud.*, November 1984, 5(4), pp. 64.　　　　　　　　　　　　　　　**[G: U.K.]**

Kellough, Howard J. Splitting Up the Business of a Private Corporation. In *Purden, C., ed.*, 1984, pp. 12–39.　　　　　　　　**[G: Canada]**

Khalil, Z. S. and Leonard, K. J. A Markov Process Model for Cash Management. In *Avula, X. J. R., et al.*, 1984, pp. 215–19.

Kidwell, David S.; Marr, M. Wayne and Thompson, G. Rodney. SEC Rule 415: The Ultimate Competitive Bid. *J. Finan. Quant. Anal.*, June 1984, 19(2), pp. 183–95.　　　　　**[G: U.S.]**

Koskenkylä, Heikki. Rates of Return, Cost of Capital, and Valuation Rates in Finnish Manufacturing 1960–1980. In *Holland, D. M., ed.*, 1984, pp. 387–419.　　　　　　**[G: Finland]**

Krever, Richard. Apportioning Interest Expenses. *Australian Tax Forum*, December 1984, 1(4), pp. 413–36.　　　　**[G: Australia]**

Kumar, S. and Khurana, P. K. Determinants of Corporate Dividend in India. *Indian Econ. J.*, Oct.–Dec. 1984, 32(2), pp. 98–103.
　　　　　　　　　　　　　　　　　[G: India]

Laumas, Prem S. and Williams, Martin. The Demand for Working Capital. *Appl. Econ.*, December 1984, 16(6), pp. 791–98.　　**[G: India]**

Lawrence, Kenneth D. and Guerard, John B., Jr. Strategic Planning and the Problem of Capital Budgeting in a Steel Firm: A Multi-Criteria

Approach. In *Naylor, T. H. and Thomas, C., eds.*, 1984, pp. 45–52.

Lee, Chi-Wen Jevons. The Speed of Adjustment of Financial Ratios: An Error-in-Variable Problem. *J. Acc. Res.*, Autumn 1984, 22(2), pp. 776–81.　　　　　　　　　　　**[G: U.S.]**

Lee, Moon H. and Zechner, Josef. Debt, Taxes, and International Equilibrium. *J. Int. Money Finance*, December 1984, 3(3), pp. 343–55.

Leibowitz, Martin L., et al. Horizon Matching: A New Approach to Dedicated Portfolios. *J. Portfol. Manage.*, Fall 1984, 11(1), pp. 93–96.

Likierman, Andrew. The Use of Profitability in Assessing the Performance of Public Enterprises. In *Ramanadham, V. V., ed.*, 1984, pp. 159–70.　　　　　　　　　　　**[G: U.K.]**

Lincoln, Mervyn. An Empirical Study of the Usefulness of Accounting Ratios to Describe Levels of Insolvency Risk. *J. Banking Finance*, June 1984, 8(2), pp. 321–40.

Linke, Charles M. Equity-Debt Risk Premia Issues in Utility Rate Regulation. In *Foster, J. R., et al., eds.*, 1984, pp. 229–36.

Loasby, Brian J. Organisational Control and Performance. In *Pickering, J. F. and Cockerill, T. A. J., eds.*, 1984, pp. 72–100.

Lobo, Gerald J. and Nair, R. D. Predictions of Annual Earnings Using Quarterly Earnings, Annual Earnings, and Dividend Payout Ratios. *Managerial Dec. Econ.*, December 1984, 5(4), pp. 228–33.　　　　　　　　　　　**[G: U.S.]**

Loss, Louis. Disclosure as Preventive Enforcement. In *Hopt, K. J. and Teubner, G., eds.*, 1984, pp. 327–37.　　　　　　　**[G: U.S.]**

Lusht, Kenneth M. and Fisher, Jeffrey D. Anticipated Growth and the Specification of Debt in Real Estate Value Models. *Amer. Real Estate Urban Econ. Assoc. J.*, Spring 1984, 12(1), pp. 1–11.　　　　　　　　　　　**[G: U.S.]**

Madura, Jeff. Construction of Currency Cocktails for Export Pricing. *Bus. Econ.*, April 1984, 19(3), pp. 40–47.

Makhija, Anil K. and Thompson, Howard E. Capitalized Interest and the Cost of Money to Electric Utilities. *Land Econ.*, August 1984, 60(3), pp. 278–91.　　　　　　　　　　　**[G: U.S.]**

Malécot, Jean-François. Risque de faillite, coûts de faillite et structure du capital: réexamen et nouvelles propositions. (Capital Structure and Risk with Cost of Bankruptcy: Critical Examination and New Propositions. With English summary.) *Écon. Soc.*, November–December 1984, 18(11–12), pp. 229–64.

Mandelker, Gershon N. and Rhee, S. Ghon. The Impact of the Degrees of Operating and Financial Leverage on Systematic Risk of Common Stock. *J. Finan. Quant. Anal.*, March 1984, 19(1), pp. 45–57.　　　　　　**[G: U.S.]**

Marsh, Terry A. and Swanson, Douglas S. Risk-Return Tradeoffs for Strategic Management. *Sloan Manage. Rev.*, Spring 1984, 25(3), pp. 35–49.　　　　　　　　　　　**[G: U.S.]**

Marshall, William J.; Yawitz, Jess B. and Greenberg, Edward. Incentives for Diversification and the Structure of the Conglomerate Firm.

Southern Econ. J., July 1984, *51*(1), pp. 1–23. [G: U.S.]

Martin, Linda J. and Henderson, Glenn V., Jr. Industry Influence on Financial Structure: A Matter of Interpretation. *Rev. Bus. Econ. Res.*, Spring 1984, *19*(2), pp. 57–67. [G: U.S.]

Masulis, Ronald W. How Big Is the Tax Advantage to Debt? Discussion. *J. Finance*, July 1984, *39*(3), pp. 853–55.

Mehdi, Istaqbal. Performance Evaluation of Public Enterprise in Pakistan: Experiment in Social Accounting System. *Pakistan Devel. Rev.*, Summer-Autumn 1984, *23*(2&3), pp. 179–200. [G: Pakistan]

Mehrez, Abraham; Regev, U. and Spivak, A. An Analysis of Risky Financial Decisions. *Managerial Dec. Econ.*, March 1984, *5*(1), pp. 19–24.

Mensah, Yaw M. An Examination of the Stationarity of Multivariate Bankruptcy Prediction Models: A Methodological Study. *J. Acc. Res.*, Spring 1984, *22*(1), pp. 380–95.

Meric, Gulser and Meric, Ilhan. Size, Operating Leverage, and Financial Structure. *Rivista Int. Sci. Econ. Com.*, October–November 1984, *31*(10–11), pp. 1052–57. [G: Turkey]

Micha, Bernard. Analysis of Business Failures in France. *J. Banking Finance*, June 1984, *8*(2), pp. 281–91. [G: France]

Mikkelson, Wayne H. On the Existence of an Optimal Capital Structure: Theory and Evidence: Discussion. *J. Finance*, July 1984, *39*(3), pp. 878–80. [G: U.S.]

Milne, Frank and Shefrin, Hersh M. Clarifying Some Misconceptions about Stock Market Economies. *Quart. J. Econ.*, August 1984, *99*(3), pp. 615–27.

Minard, Frank P. L. Implications for Investment or Portfolio Management: Discussion. In *Sametz, A. W., ed.*, 1984, pp. 105–07.

Minarik, Joseph J. The Effects of Taxation on the Selling of Corporate Stock and the Realization of Capital Gains: Comment. *Quart. J. Econ.*, February 1984, *99*(1), pp. 93–110. [G: U.S.]

Mirus, Rolf. Foreign Currency Options in Exchange Risk Management. *Aussenwirtschaft*, December 1984, *39*(4), pp. 323–34. [G: U.S.]

Moore, William T. and Chen, Son-Nan. Implementing the IRR Criterion When Cash Flow Parameters Are Unknown. *Financial Rev.*, November 1984, *19*(4), pp. 351–58.

Moran, Michael J. Recent Financing Activity of Nonfinancial Corporations. *Fed. Res. Bull.*, May 1984, *70*(5), pp. 401–10. [G: U.S.]

Myers, Stewart C. The Capital Structure Puzzle. *J. Finance*, July 1984, *39*(3), pp. 575–92.

Myers, Stewart C. and Majluf, Nicholas S. Corporate Financing and Investment Decisions When Firms Have Information That Investors Do Not Have. *J. Finan. Econ.*, June 1984, *13*(2), pp. 187–221.

Nakatani, Iwao. The Economic Role of Financial Corporate Grouping. In *Aoki, M., ed.*, 1984, pp. 227–58. [G: Japan]

Nishina, Kazuhiko. Recent Trend in Corporate Profitability in Japan. (In Japanese. With En-

glish summary.) *Osaka Econ. Pap.*, December 1984, *34*(2–3), pp. 203–17. [G: Japan]

Nunns, James R. Alternative Divisions of the Tax Base: How Much Is at Stake? Comments. In *McLure, C. E., Jr., ed.*, 1984, pp. 220–27. [G: U.S.]

Onofri, Paolo and Stagni, Anna. Rate of Profit and Return on Financial Assets in Italian Industry 1951–1981. In *Holland, D. M., ed.*, 1984, pp. 465–80. [G: Italy]

Ooghe, Humbert and Verbaere, Eric. Investeringsgedrag en financiële structuur. (With English summary.) *Cah. Écon. Bruxelles*, 3rd Trimester 1984, (103), pp. 440–56. [G: Belgium]

Osborne, M. F. M. and Murphy, Joseph E., Jr. Financial Analogs of Physical Brownian Motion, as Illustrated by Earnings. *Financial Rev.*, May 1984, *19*(2), pp. 153–72. [G: U.S.]

Patsouratis, Vassilis A. Developmental Aspects of Corporate Taxation: The Case of Greece. *Public Finance*, 1984, *39*(1), pp. 119–32. [G: Greece]

Patterson, Cleveland S. The Effects of Leverage on k. In *Foster, J. R., et al., eds.*, 1984, pp. 237–60. [G: U.S.]

Peters, Helen Frame. Asset/Liability Analysis. In *Fed. Home Loan Bank San Francisco*, 1984, pp. 211–15. [G: U.S.]

Peters, James H. Alternative Divisions of the Tax Base: How Much Is at Stake? Comments. In *McLure, C. E., Jr., ed.*, 1984, pp. 217–19. [G: U.S.]

Price, Robert W. Small Businesses. In *Fed. Res. Bank Atlanta*, 1984, pp. 35–40. [G: U.S.]

Rao, T. V. S. Ramamohan and Sharma, Rita. Primacy of Corporate Dividend Decisions. *Indian Econ. J.*, Oct.–Dec. 1984, *32*(2), pp. 56–73. [G: India]

Ravenscraft, David J. Collusion vs. Superiority: A Monte Carlo Analysis. *Int. J. Ind. Organ.*, December 1984, *2*(4), pp. 385–402.

Reid, Robert J. Tax Implications of a Change in Control. In *Purden, C., ed.*, 1984, pp. 84–113. [G: Canada]

Ritter, Jay R. Signaling and the Valuation of Unseasoned New Issues: A Comment. *J. Finance*, September 1984, *39*(4), pp. 1231–37. [G: U.S.]

Roberts, Gordon S. and Viscione, Jerry A. Note on Who Pays the Agency Costs of Debt. *Financial Rev.*, May 1984, *19*(2), pp. 232–39.

Roessner, Gilbert G. New Views on an Old Problem: Interest Rate Risk and Related Issues. In *Fed. Home Loan Bank San Francisco*, 1984, pp. 31–47. [G: U.S.]

Rose, John T. and Talley, Samuel H. Financial Transactions within Bank Holding Companies. *J. Finan. Res.*, Fall 1984, *7*(3), pp. 209–17. [G: U.S.]

Rose, Peter S. and Giroux, Gary A. Predicting Corporate Bankruptcy: An Analytical and Empirical Evaluation. *Rev. Bus. Econ. Res.*, Spring 1984, *19*(2), pp. 1–12. [G: U.S.]

Ruback, Richard S. Estimation of Implicit Bankruptcy Costs: Discussion. *J. Finance*, July 1984, *39*(3), pp. 643–45.

Rutterford, Janette. The UK Corporate Bond Market: Prospects for Revival. *Nat. Westminster Bank Quart. Rev.*, May 1984, pp. 17–32. **[G: U.K.]**

Rybczynski, Tad M. Industrial Finance System in Europe, U.S. and Japan. *J. Econ. Behav. Organ.*, September–December 1984, *5*(3–4), pp. 275–86. **[G: Europe; U.S.; Japan]**

Saias, Maurice. Creative and Noncreative Uses of Portfolio Planning Tools and Strategies. In *[Kozmetsky, G.]*, 1984, pp. 145–49.

Samuels, J. M. Company Finance in Europe—The Impact on Small Firms. In *Levicki, C.*, *ed.*, 1984, pp. 65–77. **[G: France; U.K.; W. Germany]**

Sarig, Oded H. Why Do Companies Pay Dividends? Comment. *Amer. Econ. Rev.*, December 1984, *74*(5), pp. 1142.

Saunders, Anthony. The Effect of Changing Regulation on Investment Policy of Life Insurance Companies. In *Sametz, A. W.*, *ed.*, 1984, pp. 85–94. **[G: U.S.]**

Savona, Paolo. Banca e borsa. Aspetti internazionali. (Banks and Stock Market: International Impact. With English summary.) *Bancaria*, November 1984, *40*(11), pp. 1076–81. **[G: U.S.; Italy]**

Schaefer, T. F. The Information Content of Current Cost Income Relative to Dividends and Historical Cost Income. *J. Acc. Res.*, Autumn 1984, *22*(2), pp. 647–56. **[G: U.S.]**

Schall, Lawrence D. Taxes, Inflation and Corporate Financial Policy. *J. Finance*, March 1984, *39*(1), pp. 105–26.

Scheid, Jean-Claude. Nouveaux résultats et maintien du capital des entreprises. (New Results and Maintenance of the Capital of the Company. With English summary.) *Écon. Soc.*, January 1984, *18*(1), pp. 91–119.

Schmidt, Hartmut. Disclosure, Insider Information and Capital Market Functions. In *Hopt, K. J. and Teubner, G.*, *eds.*, 1984, pp. 338–53.

Schnabel, Jacques A. Bankruptcy, Interest Tax Shields and 'Optimal' Capital Structure: A Cash Flow Formulation. *Managerial Dec. Econ.*, June 1984, *5*(2), pp. 116–19.

Schnabel, Jacques A. and Frank, Jonathan. Bankruptcy Risk and Impaired Investment Decisions. *Managerial Dec. Econ.*, September 1984, *5*(3), pp. 187–90.

Schreuder, Hein and Klaassen, Jan. Confidential Revenue and Profit Forecasts by Management and Financial Analysts: Evidence from The Netherlands. *Accounting Rev.*, January 1984, *59*(1), pp. 64–77. **[G: Netherlands]**

Schwab, Bernhard. Financial Risk and Capital Structure: Theory and Practice in an International Context. In *Bamberg, G. and Spremann, K.*, *eds.*, 1984, pp. 271–84. **[G: OECD]**

Schwartz, Steven. An Empirical Test of a Managerial, Life-Cycle, and Cost of Capital Model of Merger Activity. *J. Ind. Econ.*, March 1984, *32*(3), pp. 265–76. **[G: U.S.]**

Scott, John T. and Pascoe, George. Capital Costs and Profitability. *Int. J. Ind. Organ.*, September 1984, *2*(3), pp. 217–33. **[G: U.S.]**

Seelbach, Horst. Ersatztheorie. (With English summary.) *Z. Betriebswirtshaft*, January 1984, *54*(1), pp. 106–27.

Senbet, Lemma W. and Taggart, Robert A., Jr. Capital Structure Equilibrium under Market Imperfections and Incompleteness. *J. Finance*, March 1984, *39*(1), pp. 93–103.

Shafer, Joel. Divestiture and the Courts. In *Purden, C.*, *ed.*, 1984, pp. 47–83. **[G: Canada; U.K.]**

Shapiro, Alan C. Currency Risk and Relative Price Risk. *J. Finan. Quant. Anal.*, December 1984, *19*(4), pp. 365–73.

Shapiro, Alan C. The Impact of Taxation on the Currency-of-Denomination Decision for Long-Term Foreign Borrowing and Lending. *J. Int. Bus. Stud.*, Spring/Summer 1984, *15*(1), pp. 15–25.

Sheffrin, Steven M. and Fulcher, Jack. Alternative Divisions of the Tax Base: How Much Is at Stake? In *McLure, C. E., Jr.*, *ed.*, 1984, pp. 192–213. **[G: U.S.]**

Shefrin, Hersh M. Inferior Forecasters, Cycles, and the Efficient-Markets Hypothesis: A Comment [Market 'Efficiency' in a Market with Heterogeneous Information]. *J. Polit. Econ.*, February 1984, *92*(1), pp. 156–61.

Shefrin, Hersh M. and Statman, Meir. Explaining Investor Preference for Cash Dividends. *J. Finan. Econ.*, June 1984, *13*(2), pp. 253–82. **[G: U.S.]**

Smith, Richard L., II and Dhatt, Manjeet. Direct Equity Financing; A Resolution of a Paradox: A Comment. *J. Finance*, December 1984, *39*(5), pp. 1615–18. **[G: U.S.]**

Steele, Anthony. Difference Equation Solutions to the Valuation of Lease Contracts. *J. Finan. Quant. Anal.*, September 1984, *19*(3), pp. 311–28.

von Stein, Johann Heinrich. Rescue Operations in Business Crises: Management's Role in an Economic Perspective. In *Hopt, K. J. and Teubner, G.*, *eds.*, 1984, pp. 380–98. **[G: W. Germany]**

von Stein, Johann Heinrich and Zeigler, Werner. The Prognosis and Surveillance of Risks from Commercial Credit Borrowers. *J. Banking Finance*, June 1984, *8*(2), pp. 249–68. **[G: W. Germany]**

Stone, Bernell K. Corporate Perspectives on Cash Management. In *Fed. Res. Bank Atlanta*, 1984, pp. 41–58.

Stowe, John D. and Ingene, Charles A. Microeconomic Influences on Operating Leverage. *J. Econ. Bus.*, May 1984, *36*(2), pp. 233–41.

Stulz, René M. Optimal Hedging Policies. *J. Finan. Quant. Anal.*, June 1984, *19*(2), pp. 127–40.

Sturgess, Brian T. and Wheale, Peter. Merger Performance Evaluation: An Empirical Analysis of a Sample of UK Firms. *J. Econ. Stud.*, 1984, *11*(4), pp. 33–45. **[G: U.K.]**

Suret, Jean-Marc. Facteurs explicatifs des structures financières des P.M.E. québécoises. (Financial Structure of Small and Medium Size Firms in the Province of Quebec. With English summary.) *L'Actual. Econ.*, March 1984, *60*(1), pp. 58–71.   [G: Canada]

Suzuki, Toshiro A. Distribution of Value Added in Enterprises in Japan. In *Intn'l. Productivity Symp.*, 1984, pp. 267–81.   [G: Japan; U.S.; W. Germany]

Taffler, Richard J. Empirical Models for the Monitoring of UK Corporations. *J. Banking Finance*, June 1984, *8*(2), pp. 199–227.
    [G: U.K.]

Takahashi, Kichinosuke; Kurokawa, Yukiharu and Watase, Kazunori. Corporate Bankruptcy Prediction in Japan. *J. Banking Finance*, June 1984, *8*(2), pp. 229–47.   [G: Japan]

Talmor, Eli. The Determination of Corporate Optimal Capital Structure under Value Maximization and Informational Asymmetry. *J. Econ. Bus.*, February 1984, *36*(1), pp. 65–75.

Tamari, Meir. The Use of a Bankruptcy Forecasting Model to Analyze Corporate Behavior in Israel. *J. Banking Finance*, June 1984, *8*(2), pp. 293–302.   [G: Israel]

Tamminen, Rauno. The Estimation of Causal Revenue Contributions. *Liiketaloudellinen Aikak.*, 1984, *33*(2), pp. 155–62.
    [G: Finland]

Tarasofsky, Abraham. Aggregate Rates of Return in Canada. In *Holland, D. M., ed.*, 1984, pp. 313–44.   [G: Canada]

Temko, Richard J. Aspetti fiscali, contabili e giuridici del leasing mobiliare in Europa. (An Overview of Tax, Accounting, and Legal Considerations Involved in Structuring Equipment Leases in Europe—II. With English summary.) *Bancaria*, November 1984, *40*(11), pp. 1124–31.   [G: EEC]

Temko, Richard J. Aspetti fiscali, contabili e giuridici del leasing mobiliare in Europa. (An Overview of Tax, Accounting, and Legal Considerations Involved in Structuring Equipment Leases in Europe. With English summary.) *Bancaria*, October 1984, *40*(10), pp. 1004–14.
    [G: EEC]

Teodori, Giulio. Investimenti in titoli esenti da imposte e imposta di conguaglio. (Investments in Tax-Exempt Securities and the Equalization Tax. With English summary.) *Bancaria*, April 1984, *40*(4), pp. 415–19.   [G: Italy]

Thompson, Alexander M., III. The Allocation of Surplus to Non-Productive, Oligopolistic Rivalry: A Contradiction for Accumulation in Advanced Capitalist Economies. In *Zarembka, P., ed.*, 1984, pp. 37–80.   [G: U.S.]

Thompson, Howard E. Estimating Individual Company Costs of Capital from Cross-sectional Data: A Random Coefficients Approach. *Managerial Dec. Econ.*, September 1984, *5*(3), pp. 130–40.   [G: U.S.]

Titman, Sheridan. The Effect of Capital Structure on a Firm's Liquidation Decision. *J. Finan. Econ.*, March 1984, *13*(1), pp. 137–51.

Tobin, James. A Mean-Variance Approach to

Fundamental Valuation. *J. Portfol. Manage.*, Fall 1984, *11*(1), pp. 26–32.

Valcarcel, Lina J. On the Ability of Accounting Ratios to Predict Failure of Philippine Business Firms. *Philippine Rev. Econ. Bus.*, Sept./Dec. 1984, *21*(3/4), pp. 165–99.   [G: Philippines]

Vermaelen, Theo. Repurchase Tender Offers, Signaling, and Managerial Incentives. *J. Finan. Quant. Anal.*, June 1984, *19*(2), pp. 163–81.
    [G: U.S.]

Verni, Ralph F. Implications for Investment or Portfolio Management: Discussion. In *Sametz, A. W., ed.*, 1984, pp. 109–10.

Vickers, Douglas. The Uncertainty about Uncertainty: A Paradigmatic Comment on *Professor Weiss' Theory of the Firm:* Capital Markets, Output, and the Demand for Inputs under Uncertainty. *Eastern Econ. J.*, January-March 1984, *10*(1), pp. 71–77.

Vickrey, Don W. An Alternative Interpretation of Unexpected Returns from Accounting Income Numbers. *Quart. Rev. Econ. Bus.*, Spring 1984, *24*(1), pp. 6–21.

Wacht, Richard F. A Financial Management Theory of the Nonprofit Organization. *J. Finan. Res.*, Spring 1984, *7*(1), pp. 37–45.

Wakasugi, Takaaki, et al. Measuring the Profitability of the Nonfinancial Corporate Sector in Japan. In *Holland, D. M., ed.*, 1984, pp. 345–86.   [G: Japan]

Waldron, Jerome M. Methodological Problems with Portfolio Planning. In *Naylor, T. H. and Thomas, C., eds.*, 1984, pp. 139–55.

Wallace, Wanda A. The Effects of Delays by Accounting Policy-Setters in Reconciling the Accounting Treatment of Stock Options and Stock Appreciation Rights. *Accounting Rev.*, April 1984, *59*(2), pp. 325–41.   [G: U.S.]

Weinberger, Alfred. New Solutions to Investment Management Problems. In *Sametz, A. W., ed.*, 1984, pp. 99–103.

Weiss, Nitzan. Capital Markets, Output, and the Demand for Inputs under Uncertainty. *Eastern Econ. J.*, January-March 1984, *10*(1), pp. 51–69.

Weiss, Nitzan. Reply to a Paradigmatic Comment: Capital Markets, Output, and the Demand for Inputs under Uncertainty. *Eastern Econ. J.*, January-March 1984, *10*(1), pp. 79–85.

White, Bob. International Differences in Gearing: How Important Are They? *Nat. Westminster Bank Quart. Rev.*, November 1984, pp. 14–25. [G: U.S.; U.K.; Japan; France; Germany]

Whitley, Glenn R. Project Financing: The Borrower's View. In *Pearce, D. W.; Siebert, H. and Walter, I., eds.*, 1984, pp. 271–91.
    [G: Selected Countries]

Whittred, Greg and Zimmer, Ian. Timeliness of Financial Reporting and Financial Distress. *Accounting Rev.*, April 1984, *59*(2), pp. 287–95.   [G: Australia]

Williams, Norman P. The Profitability of United Kingdom Industrial and Commercial Companies 1963–1981. In *Holland, D. M., ed.*, 1984, pp. 155–75.   [G: U.K.]

Williams, Norman P. United Kingdom Industrial

Sectors' Rates of Return. In *Holland, D. M., ed.*, 1984, pp. 177–219. **[G: U.K.]**

Williamson, Robert W. Evidence on the Selective Reporting of Financial Ratios. *Accounting Rev.*, April 1984, *59*(2), pp. 296–99.
[G: U.S.]

Williamson, W. G. Purchase and Sale of a Business Within a Family. In *Purden, C., ed.*, 1984, pp. 114–37. **[G: Canada]**

Wood, J. Stuart. Some Refinements in Austrian Trade-Cycle Theory. *Managerial Dec. Econ.*, September 1984, *5*(3), pp. 141–49.

Yaprak, Attila; Sorek, Christopher and Parameswaran, Ravi. Competitive Strategy in Multinational Oligopolies: The Role of Promotion in the Computer Industry. In *Kaynak, E., ed.*, 1984, pp. 232–55. **[G: U.K.; U.S.]**

Zinbarg, Edward D. Asset Management: The Parts versus the Whole. In *Sametz, A. W., ed.*, 1984, pp. 95–97. **[G: U.S.]**

Zmijewski, Mark E. Methodological Issues Related to the Estimation of Financial Distress Prediction Models. *J. Acc. Res.*, Supplement 1984, *22*, pp. 59–82. **[G: U.S.]**

522 Business Investment

5220 Business Investment

Aaron, Henry J. and Galper, Harvey. A Tax on Consumption, Gifts, and Bequests and Other Strategies for Reform. In *Pechman, J. A., ed.*, 1984, pp. 106–34. **[G: U.S.]**

Abel, Andrew B. The Effects of Uncertainty on Investment and the Expected Long-Run Capital Stock. *J. Econ. Dynam. Control*, February 1984, *7*(1), pp. 39–53.

Aho, Teemu and Virtanen, Ilkka. Inflaation vaikutuksesta koneen edullisimpaan pitoaikaan. (The Impact of Inflation on the Optimal Service Life of a Machine. With English summary.) *Liiketaloudellinen Aikak.*, 1984, *33*(1), pp. 60–80.

Aiginger, K. Economic Rational Expectations and their Influence on Production and Inventory Decisions. In *Oppenländer, K. H. and Poser, G., eds.*, 1984, pp. 541–97. **[G: Japan; Austria]**

Albach, Horst. Investment in Inventory. In *[Beckmann, M. J.]*, 1984, pp. 3–13.
[G: W. Germany]

Albach, Horst. The Rate of Return in German Manufacturing Industry: Measurement and Policy Implications. In *Holland, D. M., ed.*, 1984, pp. 273–311. **[G: W. Germany]**

Aoki, Masahiko. Shareholders' Non-unanimity on Investment Financing: Banks vs. Individual Investors. In *Aoki, M., ed.*, 1984, pp. 193–224.
[G: Japan]

Appelbaum, Elie and Ullah, Aman. An Empirical Test of the Risk Aversion Hypothesis. *Pakistan J. Appl. Econ.*, Summer 1984, *3*(1), pp. 57–64. **[G: U.S.]**

Arnold, Michael R. Clarification of Miller on Capital Aggregation in the Presence of Obsolescence-inducing Technical Change. *Rev. Income Wealth*, December 1984, *30*(4), pp. 487–92.

Arzac, Enrique R. and Marcus, Matityahu. Erratum: Flotation Cost Adjustment in Rate of Return Regulation: A Reply. *J. Finance*, June 1984, *39*(2), pp. 563.

Arzac, Enrique R. and Marcus, Matityahu. Flotation Cost Allowance for the Regulated Firm: A Reply. *J. Finance*, March 1984, *39*(1), pp. 293–94.

Auerbach, Alan J. Investment, Taxation, and Growth. In *Wachter, M. L. and Wachter, S. M., eds.*, 1984, pp. 224–50. **[G: U.S.]**

Baldwin, Carliss Y.; Tribendis, Joseph J. and Clark, Joel P. The Evolution of Market Risk in the U.S. Steel Industry and Implications for Required Rates of Return. *J. Ind. Econ.*, September 1984, *33*(1), pp. 73–98. **[G: U.S.]**

Bayer, Kurt. Profitability in Austrian Industrial Corporations. In *Holland, D. M., ed.*, 1984, pp. 421–64. **[G: Austria]**

Beggs, John J. An Extended Accelerator Model of R&D and Physical Investment: Comment. In *Griliches, Z., ed.*, 1984, pp. 295–97.
[G: U.S.]

Bélyácz, Iván. Investment Policy and Structural Transformation in Hungary. *Acta Oecon.*, 1984, *33*(3–4), pp. 273–91. **[G: Hungary]**

Ben-Zion, Uri. The R&D and Investment Decision and Its Relationship to the Firm's Market Value: Some Preliminary Results. In *Griliches, Z., ed.*, 1984, pp. 299–312. **[G: U.S.]**

Bergström, Villy and Södersten, Jan. Do Tax Allowances Stimulate Investment? *Scand. J. Econ.*, 1984, *86*(2), pp. 244–68. **[G: Sweden]**

Bernhard, Richard H. Risk-Adjusted Values, Timing of Uncertainty Resolution, and the Measurement of Project Worth. *J. Finan. Quant. Anal.*, March 1984, *19*(1), pp. 83–99.

Bertmar, Lars. Measures of Business Performance—The Swedish Case. In *Holland, D. M., ed.*, 1984, pp. 117–53. **[G: Sweden]**

Bezza, El Mostafa. Le concept d'intérêts cumulés: un algorithme pour dépasser le problème de multiplicité des T.I.R. (The Cumulative Interest Concept: An Algorithm to Overstep the IRR's Multiplicity. With English summary.) *Écon. Soc.*, November–December 1984, *18*(11–12), pp. 99–132.

Biørn, Erik. Inflation, Depreciation, and the Neutrality of the Corporate Income Tax. *Scand. J. Econ.*, 1984, *86*(2), pp. 214–28.
[G: Norway]

Bitros, George C. The Fungibility Factor in Credit: Reply [The Fungibility Factor in Credit and the Question of the Efficacy of Selective Controls]. *Oxford Econ. Pap.*, November 1984, *36*(3), pp. 494–98. **[G: Greece]**

Blejer, Mario I. and Khan, Mohsin S. Government Policy and Private Investment in Developing Countries. *Int. Monet. Fund Staff Pap.*, June 1984, *31*(2), pp. 379–403. **[G: LDCs]**

Blejer, Mario I. and Khan, Mohsin S. Private Investment in Developing Countries. *Finance Develop.*, June 1984, *21*(2), pp. 26–29.
[G: Selected LDCs]

Boadway, Robin; Bruce, Neil and Mintz, Jack. Taxation, Inflation, and the Effective Marginal

Tax Rate on Capital in Canada. *Can. J. Econ.*, February 1984, *17*(1), pp. 62–79.

[G: Canada]

Brada, Josef C. The Political Business Cycle and Investment Fluctuations in France. *Rivista Int. Sci. Econ. Com.*, April 1984, *31*(4), pp. 305–11.

[G: France]

van Breda, Michael F. The Misuse of Accounting Rates of Return: Comment. *Amer. Econ. Rev.*, June 1984, *74*(3), pp. 507–08.

Bulow, Jeremy I. and Summers, Lawrence H. The Taxation of Risky Assets. *J. Polit. Econ.*, February 1984, *92*(1), pp. 20–39. [G: U.S.]

Burton, Richard M.; Damon, William W. and Obel, Børge. Operations Planning and Investment Strategy in the Owner Financed Firm. In *Naylor, T. H. and Thomas, C., eds.*, 1984, pp. 53–65.

Christy, George A. Original Cost and Fair Value: Pseudo-Science Versus Judgement. In *Foster, J. R., et al., eds.*, 1984, pp. 154–72.

[G: U.S.]

Conine, Thomas E., Jr. and Tamarkin, Maurry. On the Theory of Inflation and Optimal Investment Policy: Equilibrium Considerations. *Southern Econ. J.*, January 1984, *50*(3), pp. 755–60.

Dorrance, G. Morris, Jr. Savings and Investment: Comment. In *Wachter, M. L. and Wachter, S. M., eds.*, 1984, pp. 251–54.

[G: U.S.]

Dumler, Georg. Ertragslage und Rentabilität des Unternehmenssektors 1966–1981. (The Profit Situation and the Profitability of the Business Sector in West Germany, 1966–1981. With English summary.) *Konjunkturpolitik*, 1984, *30*(1), pp. 23–44. [G: W. Germany]

Edwards, Jeremy. The 1984 Corporation Tax Reform. *Fisc. Stud.*, May 1984, *5*(2), pp. 30–44.

[G: U.K.]

Emerson, Craig. Economic Evaluation of Mineral-Processing Projects. In *Lloyd, P. J., ed.*, 1984, pp. 253–72. [G: Australia]

Erdös, Tibor. The Development of Investment Purchasing Power: Theoretical Questions. *Acta Oecon.*, 1984, *33*(1–2), pp. 105–26.

[G: Hungary]

Evenson, Robert E. The R&D and Investment Decision and Its Relationship to the Firm's Market Value: Some Preliminary Results: Comment. In *Griliches, Z., ed.*, 1984, pp. 312–14. [G: U.S.]

Farber, Kit D.; Dreiling, Frederick J. and Rutledge, Gary L. Pollution Abatement and Control Expenditures, 1972–82. *Surv. Curr. Bus.*, February 1984, *64*(2), pp. 22–30. [G: U.S.]

Fiorito, Riccardo. Multisectoral Inventory Cycles under Different Expectations and Technologies. *Econ. Notes*, 1984, (1), pp. 109–20.

[G: Italy]

Fisher, Franklin M. The Misuse of Accounting Rates of Return: Reply. *Amer. Econ. Rev.*, June 1984, *74*(3), pp. 509–17.

Flaherty, M. Therese and Itami, Hiroyuki. Competitive Edge: Finance. In *Okimoto, D. I.; Su-*

gano, T. and Weinstein, F. B., eds., 1984, pp. 134–76. [G: Japan; U.S.]

Fortune, J. Neill. Inventory Accumulation and Expectations of Real Income, Inflation and Interest Rates. *Appl. Econ.*, June 1984, *16*(3), pp. 411–19. [G: U.S.]

Fullerton, Don and Henderson, Yolanda Kodrzycki. Incentive Effects of Taxes on Income from Capital: Alternative Policies in the 1980s. In *Hulten, C. R. and Sawhill, I. V., eds.*, 1984, pp. 45–89. [G: U.S.]

Fullerton, Don; Lyon, Andrew B. and Rosen, Richard J. Uncertainty, Welfare Cost and the "Adaptability" of U.S. Corporate Taxes. *Scand. J. Econ.*, 1984, *86*(2), pp. 229–43. [G: U.S.]

Galeotti, Marzio. Recent Developments in Investment Theory. *Giorn. Econ.*, May–June 1984, *43*(5–6), pp. 393–415.

Gibbons, Joel C. The Optimal Durability of Fixed Capital When Demand Is Uncertain. *J. Bus.*, July 1984, *57*(3), pp. 389–403. [G: U.S.]

Gordon, Roger H. Inflation, Taxation, and Corporate Behavior. *Quart. J. Econ.*, May 1984, *99*(2), pp. 312–27.

Goudie, Andrew W. Tax Exhaustion: Estimates from a Disaggregate Model of Corporate Tax Liabilities. *Appl. Econ.*, April 1984, *16*(2), pp. 205–24. [G: U.K.]

Gravelle, Jane G. and Zimmerman, Dennis. Tax Progressivity and the Design of Tax Incentives for Investment. *Public Finance Quart.*, July 1984, *12*(3), pp. 251–89. [G: U.S.]

Green, Richard C. Investment Incentives, Debt, and Warrants. *J. Finan. Econ.*, March 1984, *13*(1), pp. 115–36.

Greenwald, Bruce C.; Stiglitz, Joseph E. and Weiss, Andrew. Informational Imperfections in the Capital Market and Macroeconomic Fluctuations. *Amer. Econ. Rev.*, May 1984, *74*(2), pp. 194–99.

Gronchi, Sandro. On Karmel's Criterion for Optimal Truncation. *Econ. Notes*, 1984, (3), pp. 21–30.

Grosen, Anders and Møller, Peder Fredslund. Immunisering af porteføljer. (Immunization of Future Obligations. With English summary.) *Nationaløkon. Tidsskr.*, 1984, *122*(2), pp. 253–65.

Halperin, Daniel. A Tax on Consumption, Gifts, and Bequests and Other Strategies for Reform: Comment. In *Pechman, J. A., ed.*, 1984, pp. 141–46. [G: U.S.]

Hambrick, Donald C. and MacMillan, Ian C. Asset Parsimony—Managing Assets to Manage Profits. *Sloan Manage. Rev.*, Winter 1984, *25*(2), pp. 67–74.

Hansson, Ingemar. Determinants of Investment Volatility. *Z. Nationalökon.*, 1984, *44*(1), pp. 11–26.

Hellwig, Klaus. Corporate Planning and Capital Maintenance. In *Bamberg, G. and Spremann, K., eds.*, 1984, pp. 198–202.

Ho, H. C. Y. Inflation, Depreciation Rules and Profits Tax in Hong Kong. *Hong Kong Econ. Pap.*, 1984, (15), pp. 25–34. [G: Hong Kong]

Holland, Daniel M. Measuring Profitability and

Capital Costs: Introduction and Summary. In *Holland, D. M., ed.*, 1984, pp. 1–42.
[G: OECD; Finland]
Holland, Daniel M. and Myers, Stewart C. Trends in Corporate Profitability and Capital Costs in the United States. In *Holland, D. M., ed.*, 1984, pp. 43–115. **[G: U.S.]**
Honkapohja, Seppo and Kanniainen, Vesa. Inventory Valuation Allowance: A Solution to the Problem of the Corporation Tax? *Liiketaloudellinen Aikak.*, 1984, 33(1), pp. 49–59.
[G: Finland; Sweden]
Horowitz, Ira. The Misuse of Accounting Rates of Return: Comment. *Amer. Econ. Rev.*, June 1984, 74(3), pp. 492–93.
Howe, Keith M. Flotation Cost Allowance for the Regulated Firm: A Comment. *J. Finance*, March 1984, 39(1), pp. 289–91.
Howrey, E. Philip. Data Revision, Reconstruction, and Prediction: An Application to Inventory Investment. *Rev. Econ. Statist.*, August 1984, 66(3), pp. 386–93. **[G: U.S.]**
Hulten, Charles R. Tax Policy and the Investment Decision. *Amer. Econ. Rev.*, May 1984, 74(2), pp. 236–41. **[G: U.S.]**
Irvine, F. Owen, Jr. Intrafirm Inventory Policy: Theory and Tests. *Can. J. Econ.*, February 1984, 17(1), pp. 156–74. **[G: U.S.]**
Isermann, Heinz. Investment and Financial Planning in a General Partnership. In *Grauer, M. and Wierzbicki, A. P., eds.*, 1984, pp. 175–85.
Kemp, Alexander G. and Rose, David. Investment in Oil Exploration and Production: The Comparative Influence of Taxation. In *Pearce, D. W.; Siebert, H. and Walter, I., eds.*, 1984, pp. 169–95. **[G: Selected Countries]**
King, Mervyn A. and Mairesse, Jacques. Profitability in Britain and France 1956–1975: A Comparative Study. In *Holland, D. M., ed.*, 1984, pp. 221–71. **[G: U.K.; France]**
Koskenkylä, Heikki. Rates of Return, Cost of Capital, and Valuation Rates in Finnish Manufacturing 1960–1980. In *Holland, D. M., ed.*, 1984, pp. 387–419. **[G: Finland]**
Kozlow, Ralph. Capital Expenditures by Majority-Owned Foreign Affiliates of U.S. Companies, 1984. *Surv. Curr. Bus.*, March 1984, 64(3), pp. 32–37. **[G: U.S.]**
Kračun, Davorin. Aktivizacijska doba investicij v Jugoslaviji—Metodologija in izračun. (Maturation Period of Investment in Yugoslavia—Methodology and Computation. With English summary.) *Econ. Anal. Worker's Manage.*, 1984, 18(3), pp. 201–16. **[G: Yugoslavia]**
Lackó, Mária. Behavioral Rules in the Distribution of Sectoral Investments in Hungary, 1951–1980. *J. Compar. Econ.*, September 1984, 8(3), pp. 290–300. **[G: Hungary]**
Landefeld, J. Steven and Seskin, Eugene P. Plant and Equipment Expenditures, First and Second Quarters and Second Half of 1984. *Surv. Curr. Bus.*, March 1984, 64(3), pp. 26–31.
[G: U.S.]
Lawrence, Kenneth D. and Guerard, John B., Jr. Strategic Planning and the Problem of Capi-

tal Budgeting in a Steel Firm: A Multi-Criteria Approach. In *Naylor, T. H. and Thomas, C., eds.*, 1984, pp. 45–52.
Leite, Sergio Pereira and Vaez-Zadeh, Reza. The Fungibility Factor in Credit: A Comment [The Fungibility Factor in Credit and the Question of the Efficacy of Selective Controls]. *Oxford Econ. Pap.*, November 1984, 36(3), pp. 490–93. **[G: Greece]**
Long, William F. and Ravenscraft, David J. The Misuse of Accounting Rates of Return: Comment. *Amer. Econ. Rev.*, June 1984, 74(3), pp. 494–500.
Luger, Michael I. Federal Tax Incentives as Industrial and Urban Policy. In *Sawers, L. and Tabb, W. K., eds.*, 1984, pp. 201–34.
[G: U.S.]
Luger, Michael I. Investment Incentives and the Demand for Labor in U.S. Regions. *Reg. Sci. Urban Econ.*, November 1984, 14(4), pp. 481–503. **[G: U.S.]**
Lusht, Kenneth M. and Fisher, Jeffrey D. Anticipated Growth and the Specification of Debt in Real Estate Value Models. *Amer. Real Estate Urban Econ. Assoc. J.*, Spring 1984, 12(1), pp. 1–11. **[G: U.S.]**
Maccini, Louis J. and Rossana, Robert J. Joint Production, Quasi-Fixed Factors of Production, and Investement in Finished Goods Inventories. *J. Money, Credit, Banking*, May 1984, 16(2), pp. 218–36. **[G: U.S.]**
Mairesse, Jacques and Siu, Alan K. An Extended Accelerator Model of R&D and Physical Investment. In *Griliches, Z., ed.*, 1984, pp. 271–95. **[G: U.S.]**
Martin, Stephen. The Misuse of Accounting Rates of Return: Comment. *Amer. Econ. Rev.*, June 1984, 74(3), pp. 501–06.
McLure, Charles E., Jr. A Tax on Consumption, Gifts, and Bequests and Other Strategies for Reform: Comment. In *Pechman, J. A., ed.*, 1984, pp. 134–41. **[G: U.S.]**
Mercusa, Antonio. Existing Opportunities and Prospects for Investment in Southern Italy. *Rev. Econ. Cond. Italy*, Sept.–Dec. 1984, (3), pp. 389–97. **[G: Italy]**
Miller, Edward M. Extent of Economies of Scale: An Update. *Southern Econ. J.*, October 1984, 51(2), pp. 582–87.
Milne, Frank and Shefrin, Hersh M. Clarifying Some Misconceptions about Stock Market Economies. *Quart. J. Econ.*, August 1984, 99(3), pp. 615–27.
Miyamoto, Masaaki, et al. Theoretical and Empirical Studies of New ROI. *Osaka Econ. Pap.*, March 1984, 33(3–4), pp. 12–63. **[G: Japan]**
Moore, William T. and Chen, Son-Nan. Implementing the IRR Criterion When Cash Flow Parameters Are Unknown. *Financial Rev.*, November 1984, 19(4), pp. 351–58.
Myers, Stewart C. and Majluf, Nicholas S. Corporate Financing and Investment Decisions When Firms Have Information That Investors Do Not Have. *J. Finan. Econ.*, June 1984, 13(2), pp. 187–221.
Nadji, Mehrzad and Harris, Curtis C., Jr. A Note

on Regional Investment Functions. *J. Reg. Sci.*, May 1984, *24*(2), pp. 271–75.

Naylor, Thomas H. and Thomas, Celia. Optimization Models in Strategic Planning. In *Naylor, T. H. and Thomas, C., eds.*, 1984, pp. 1–11.

Novikov, O. Stimulating the Growth of the Effectiveness of Capital Investments. *Prob. Econ.*, February 1984, *26*(10), pp. 37–49. [G: U.S.S.R.]

Onofri, Paolo and Stagni, Anna. Rate of Profit and Return on Financial Assets in Italian Industry 1951–1981. In *Holland, D. M., ed.*, 1984, pp. 465–80. [G: Italy]

Ooghe, Humbert and Verbaere, Eric. Investeringsgedrag en financiële structuur. (With English summary.) *Cah. Écon. Bruxelles*, 3rd Trimester 1984, (103), pp. 440–56.
[G: Belgium]

Oswald, Rudolph A. Savings and Investment: Comment. In *Wachter, M. L. and Wachter, S. M., eds.*, 1984, pp. 254–57. [G: U.S.]

Ott, Mack. Depreciation, Inflation, and Investment Incentives: The Effects of the Tax Acts of 1981 and 1982. *Fed. Res. Bank St. Louis Rev.*, November 1984, *66*(9), pp. 17–30.
[G: U.S.]

Pakes, Ariel and Griliches, Zvi. Estimating Distributed Lags in Short Panels with an Application to the Specification of Depreciation Patterns and Capital Stock Constructs. *Rev. Econ. Stud.*, April 1984, *51*(2), pp. 243–62.
[G: U.S.]

Pakes, Ariel and Schankerman, Mark. The Rate of Obsolescence of Patents, Research Gestation Lags, and the Private Rate of Return to Research Resources. In *Griliches, Z., ed.*, 1984, pp. 73–88.

Peiser, Richard B. Risk Analysis in Land Development. *Amer. Real Estate Urban Econ. Assoc. J.*, Spring 1984, *12*(1), pp. 12–29.

Persson, Håkan. A Way of Modelling Investment in a Multisectoral Model. *Reg. Sci. Urban Econ.*, August 1984, *14*(3), pp. 331–43.

Phillips, Ian R. Using the Tax System to Influence Private and Corporate Investment. *Australian Tax Forum*, September 1984, *1*(3), pp. 313–22. [G: U.S.]

Polasek, Wolfgang. Multivariate Regression Systems. In *Kadane, J. B., ed.*, 1984, pp. 231–309. [G: U.S.]

Pyyhtiä, I. The Realization of Investment Plans of Finnish Manufacturing Firms. In *Oppenländer, K. H. and Poser, G., eds.*, 1984, pp. 421–58. [G: Finland]

Ricottilli, Massimo. The Investment Performance in Three Industrialized Economies: The U.S.A., West Germany and France. *Econ. Notes*, 1984, (2), pp. 90–120. [G: U.S.; W. Germany; France]

Rodriguez, Justine Farr. Savings and Investment: Comment. In *Wachter, M. L. and Wachter, S. M., eds.*, 1984, pp. 257–60. [G: U.S.]

Russo, William J., Jr. and Rutledge, Gary L. Plant and Equipment Expenditures by Business for Pollution Abatement, 1983 and

Planned 1984. *Surv. Curr. Bus.*, June 1984, *64*(6), pp. 31–34. [G: U.S.]

Sahling, Leonard and Akhtar, M. A. What Is Behind the Capital Spending Boom? *Fed. Res. Bank New York Quart. Rev.*, Winter 1984–85, *9*(4), pp. 19–30. [G: U.S.]

Schankerman, Mark and Nadiri, M. Ishaq. Investment in R&D, Costs of Adjustment, and Expectations. In *Griliches, Z., ed.*, 1984, pp. 315–38. [G: U.S.]

Scherer, Frederic M. Market Structure and the Employment of Scientists and Engineers. In *Scherer, F. M.*, 1984, pp. 239–48. [G: U.S.]

Scherer, Frederic M. The Investment Decision Phases in Modern Invention and Innovation. In *Scherer, F. M.*, 1984, pp. 3–7. [G: U.S.]

Schnabel, Jacques A. and Frank, Jonathan. Bankruptcy Risk and Impaired Investment Decisions. *Managerial Dec. Econ.*, September 1984, *5*(3), pp. 187–90.

Schwartz, Steven. An Empirical Test of a Managerial, Life-Cycle, and Cost of Capital Model of Merger Activity. *J. Ind. Econ.*, March 1984, *32*(3), pp. 265–76. [G: U.S.]

Seskin, Eugene P. Plant and Equipment Expenditures, the Four Quarters of 1984. *Surv. Curr. Bus.*, September 1984, *64*(9), pp. 24–27.
[G: U.S.]

Seskin, Eugene P. and Landefeld, J. Steven. Plant and Equipment Expenditures, 1984. *Surv. Curr. Bus.*, January 1984, *64*(1), pp. 26–29. [G: U.S.]

Seskin, Eugene P. and Landefeld, J. Steven. Plant and Equipment Expenditures, the Four Quarters of 1984. *Surv. Curr. Bus.*, June 1984, *64*(6), pp. 26–30. [G: U.S.]

Sheffrin, Steven M. The Dispersion Hypothesis in Macroeconomics. *Rev. Econ. Statist.*, August 1984, *66*(3), pp. 482–85. [G: U.S.]

Siebert, Horst. The Economics of Natural Resources Ventures. In *Pearce, D. W.; Siebert, H. and Walter, I., eds.*, 1984, pp. 11–35.
[G: Selected Countries]

Smith, Richard L., II. On Strategic Behavior as a Basis for Antitrust Action. *Antitrust Bull.*, Fall 1984, *29*(3), pp. 501–22.

Spremann, Klaus. A Firm in Statu Nascendi—Initial and Final Shareholders. In *Bamberg, G. and Spremann, K., eds.*, 1984, pp. 103–21.

Sumner, Michael T. The Impact of Stock Relief. *Oxford Bull. Econ. Statist.*, May 1984, *46*(2), pp. 169–79.

Tamminen, Rauno. The Estimation of Causal Revenue Contributions. *Liiketaloudellinen Aikak.*, 1984, *33*(2), pp. 155–62. [G: Finland]

Tarasofsky, Abraham. Aggregate Rates of Return in Canada. In *Holland, D. M., ed.*, 1984, pp. 313–44. [G: Canada]

Turunen, I.; Järveläinen, M. and Dohnal, M. Fuzzy Models in Capital Cost Estimation of Chemical Plants. In *Avula, X. J. R., et al.*, 1984, pp. 500–06.

Wakasugi, Takaaki, et al. Measuring the Profitability of the Nonfinancial Corporate Sector in

Japan. In *Holland, D. M., ed.*, 1984, pp. 345–86. [G: Japan]

Watkins, G. Campbell; Kirkby, R. G. and Lawrey, Roger N. Risk and the Rate of Return on Arctic Natural Gas: An Illustrative Analysis. In *Pearce, D. W.; Siebert, H. and Walter, I., eds.*, 1984, pp. 87–109. [G: U.S.; Canada]

Wildasin, David E. The *q* Theory of Investment with Many Capital Goods. *Amer. Econ. Rev.*, March 1984, 74(1), pp. 203–10.

Williams, Norman P. The Profitability of United Kingdom Industrial and Commercial Companies 1963–1981. In *Holland, D. M., ed.*, 1984, pp. 155–75. [G: U.K.]

Williams, Norman P. United Kingdom Industrial Sectors' Rates of Return. In *Holland, D. M., ed.*, 1984, pp. 177–219. [G: U.K.]

Wong, Robert E. and Fan, Yiu-Kwan. Capital Accumulation and Financing Programs in a Neoclassical Investment Model. *Atlantic Econ. J.*, July 1984, 12(2), pp. 3–11.

Wood, J. Stuart. Some Refinements in Austrian Trade-Cycle Theory. *Managerial Dec. Econ.*, September 1984, 5(3), pp. 141–49.

Yandle, Bruce. "Polluters' Profits": An Empirical Note. *J. Ind. Econ.*, March 1984, 32(3), pp. 359–66. [G: U.S.]

Ylä-Liedenpohja, Jouko. On Investment Incentives and Allocational Implications of Corporate Income Taxation. *Liiketaloudellinen Aikak.*, 1984, 33(3), pp. 264–302. [G: Finland]

Zotov, M. Intensification of the Investment Process. *Prob. Econ.*, October 1984, 27(6), pp. 24–38. [G: U.S.S.R.]

530 MARKETING AND ADVERTISING

531 Marketing and Advertising

5310 Marketing and Advertising

Achumba, Iheanyi C.; Harvey, Michael G. and Rothe, James T. Marketing of Nonconsumer Goods in Foreign Markets: The Case of High-Technology Products. In *Kaynak, E., ed.*, 1984, pp. 121–35.

Albaum, Gerald and Peterson, Robert A. Empirical Research in International Marketing: 1976–1982. *J. Int. Bus. Stud.*, Spring/Summer 1984, 15(1), pp. 161–73.

Anderson, Erin and Schmittlein, David C. Integration of the Sales Force: An Empirical Examination. *Rand J. Econ.*, Autumn 1984, 15(3), pp. 385–95. [G: U.S.]

Andreasen, Alan R. Life Status Changes and Changes in Consumer Preferences and Satisfaction. *J. Cons. Res.*, December 1984, 11(3), pp. 784–94. [G: U.S.]

Anton, Ion. Promotion of Romanian Machine-Tools to the United States: A Marketing Mix Approach. In *Jackson, M. R. and Woodson, J. D., Jr., eds.*, 1984, pp. 187–95. [G: U.S.; Romania]

Anttila, Mai and Möller, Kristian. Conjoint Analysis Models in Explaining Consumer Price Utility Structures. *Liiketaloudellinen Aikak.*, 1984, 33(4), pp. 379–404. [G: Finland]

Baldani, Jeffrey and Masson, Robert T. Economies of Scale, Strategic Advertising and Fully Credible Entry Deterrence. *Rev. Ind. Organ.*, Fall 1984, 1(3), pp. 190–205.

Barksdale, Hiram C. and Anderson, L. McTier. Toward a Conceptual Framework for Comparative Marketing. In *Kaynak, E. and Savitt, R., eds.*, 1984, pp. 17–33.

Bass, Frank M., et al. An Investigation into the Order of the Brand Choice Process. *Marketing Sci.*, Fall 1984, 3(4), pp. 267–87. [G: U.S.]

Belk, Russell; Mayer, Robert and Driscoll, Amy. Children's Recognition of Consumption Symbolism in Children's Products. *J. Cons. Res.*, March 1984, 10(4), pp. 386–97. [G: U.S.]

Bennett, R. C. and Cooper, G. Il cattivo uso del marketing. (The Misuse of Marketing. With English summary.) *Mondo Aperto*, June–August 1984, 38(3–4), pp. 163–78.

Berkowitz, Michael K. and Haines, George H., Jr. The Relationship between Relative Attributes, Relative Preferences, and Market Share: The Case of Solar Energy in Canada. *J. Cons. Res.*, December 1984, 11(3), pp. 754–62. [G: Canada]

Bernardo, John J. A Heuristic Model to Predict Brand Switching in Consumer Choice. *J. Behav. Econ.*, Winter 1984, 13(2), pp. 25–51.

Blackburn, Joseph and Clancy, Kevin. An Empirical Comparison of Awareness Forecasting Models of New Product Introduction: Comment. *Marketing Sci.*, Summer 1984, 3(3), pp. 198–201. [G: U.S.]

Bond, Eric W. Test of the Lemons Model: Reply [A Direct Test of the 'Lemons' Model: The Market for Used Pickup Trucks]. *Amer. Econ. Rev.*, September 1984, 74(4), pp. 801–04. [G: U.S.]

Boyer, Marcel; Kihlstrom, Richard E. and Laffont, Jean-Jacques. Market Determinants of Misleading Advertising. In *Boyer, M. and Kihlstrom, R. E., eds.*, 1984, pp. 241–70.

Bresnahan, Timothy F. Comment on "Conjoint Analysis of Price Premiums for Hotel Amenities." *J. Bus.*, Part 2, January 1984, 57(1), pp. S133–38.

Brown, Wilson B. Firm-like Behavior in Markets: The Administered Channel. *Int. J. Ind. Organ.*, September 1984, 2(3), pp. 263–76.

Buxton, A. J.; Davies, Stephen W. and Lyons, Bruce R. Concentration and Advertising in Consumer and Producer Markets. *J. Ind. Econ.*, June 1984, 32(4), pp. 451–64. [G: U.K.]

Capon, Noel and Davis, Roger. Basic Cognitive Ability Measures as Predictors of Consumer Information Processing Strategies. *J. Cons. Res.*, June 1984, 11(1), pp. 551–63. [G: U.S.]

Cartwright, Phillip A. A Note on Using State-Dependent Models with a Time-Dependent Variance. *J. Bus. Econ. Statist.*, October 1984, 2(4), pp. 410–13. [G: U.S.]

Cattin, Philippe and Punj, Girish N. Factors Influencing the Selection of Preference Model Form for Continuous Utility Functions in Conjoint Analysis. *Marketing Sci.*, Winter 1984, 3(1), pp. 73–82.

Cavusgil, S. Tamer. Changing Nature of Firms' International Market Research Activities During the Internationalization Process. In *Kaynak, E., ed.*, 1984, pp. 207–16. **[G: U.S.]**

Cavusgil, S. Tamer and Kaynak, Erdener. Critical Issues in the Cross-Cultural Measurement of Consumer Dissatisfaction: Developed versus LDC Practices. In *Kaynak, E. and Savitt, R., eds.*, 1984, pp. 114–30.

Charnes, A., et al. An MDI Model and an Algorithm for Composite Hypotheses Testing and Estimation in Marketing. *Marketing Sci.*, Winter 1984, 3(1), pp. 55–72.

Chitariance, Sedrak and Reisman, Arnold. A Strategic Planning Model for Bank Retail Outlet Development. In *Naylor, T. H. and Thomas, C., eds.*, 1984, pp. 91–110.

Ciobanu, G. and Ciubotaru, I. Cybernetic Modelling of the Manufacturing Processes with the Help of the Co-ordinating Graphs. *Econ. Computat. Cybern. Stud. Res.*, 1984, 19(3), pp. 9–20. **[G: Romania]**

Clarke, Darral G. and Dolan, Robert J. A Simulation Analysis of Alternative Pricing Strategies for Dynamic Environments. *J. Bus.*, Part 2, January 1984, 57(1), pp. S179–200.

Claycamp, H. J.; Dodson, Joe A., Jr. and Doughty, N. An Empirical Comparison of Awareness Forecasting Models of New Product Introduction: Comment. *Marketing Sci.*, Summer 1984, 3(3), pp. 201–02. **[G: U.S.]**

Collins, William H. and Collins, Carol B. Advertising and Monopoly Power: The Case of the Electric Utility Industry. *Atlantic Econ. J.*, September 1984, 12(3), pp. 45–53.

Dalal, S. R.; Lee, J. C. and Sabavala, D. J. Prediction of Individual Buying Behavior: A Poisson–Bernoulli Model with Arbitrary Heterogeneity. *Marketing Sci.*, Fall 1984, 3(4), pp. 352–67. **[G: U.S.]**

Darling, John R. and Piha, Kalevi. Strategic Marketing of Finnish Products in the U.S. *Liiketaloudellinen Aikak.*, 1984, 33(2), pp. 131–48. **[G: Finland; U.S.]**

Daser, Sayeste. International Marketing Information Systems: A Neglected Prerequisite for Foreign Marketing Planning. In *Kaynak, E., ed.*, 1984, pp. 139–54.

Deighton, John. The Interaction of Advertising and Evidence. *J. Cons. Res.*, December 1984, 11(3), pp. 763–70. **[G: U.S.]**

Desenzani, Leonardo and Di Vito, Claus. Riflessioni di marketing per lo sportello bancario. (Over the Counter Marketing Services in Banks. With English summary.) *L'Impresa*, 1984, 26(1), pp. 47–53.

Dholakia, Nikhilesh. Marketing in Less Developed Countries: Its Nature and Prospects. In *Kindra, G. S., ed.*, 1984, pp. 10–28. **[G: LDCs]**

Dholakia, Nikhilesh and Dholakia, Ruby Roy. Missing Links: Marketing and the Newer Theories of Development. In *Kindra, G. S., ed.*, 1984, pp. 57–75. **[G: LDCs]**

Dodson, Joe A., Jr. An Empirical Comparison of Awareness Forecasting Models of New Product Introduction: Comment. *Marketing Sci.*, Summer 1984, 3(3), pp. 202. **[G: U.S.]**

Douglas, Susan P. and Craig, C. Samuel. Establishing Equivalence in Comparative Consumer Research. In *Kaynak, E. and Savitt, R., eds.*, 1984, pp. 93–113.

Doyle, Peter. Marketing Management. In *Pickering, J. F. and Cockerill, T. A. J., eds.*, 1984, pp. 132–52.

El-Ansary, Adel I. and Liebrenz, Marilyn L. Comparative Marketing Systems Analysis: Revisited. In *Kaynak, E. and Savitt, R., eds.*, 1984, pp. 34–50.

Eppen, Gary D. and Liebermann, Yehoshua. Why Do Retailers Deal? An Inventory Explanation. *J. Bus.*, October 1984, 57(4), pp. 519–30. **[G: U.S.]**

Etemad, Hamid. A Generalized Model of Comparative Marketing: Formal Development, Methodological Implications and Examples. In *Kindra, G. S., ed.*, 1984, pp. 188–215.

Etemad, Hamid. Is Marketing the Catalyst in the Economic Development Process? In *Kindra, G. S., ed.*, 1984, pp. 29–56. **[G: LDCs]**

Etgar, Michael. Marketing of Export Commodities: The Case of Ivory Coast. In *Kaynak, E. and Savitt, R., eds.*, 1984, pp. 71–89. **[G: Ivory Coast]**

Fershtman, Chaim. Goodwill and Market Shares in Oligopoly. *Economica*, August 1984, 51(203), pp. 271–81.

Folkes, Valerie S. Consumer Reactions to Product Failure: An Attributional Approach. *J. Cons. Res.*, March 1984, 10(4), pp. 398–409. **[G: U.S.]**

Fraser, Cynthia and Bradford, John W. Competitive Market Structure Analysis: A Reply [Competitive Market Structure Analysis: Principal Partitioning of Revealed Substitutabilities]. *J. Cons. Res.*, December 1984, 11(3), pp. 842–47. **[G: U.S.]**

Fudenberg, Drew and Tirole, Jean. The Fat-Cat Effect, the Puppy-Dog Ploy, and the Lean and Hungry Look. *Amer. Econ. Rev.*, May 1984, 74(2), pp. 361–66.

Furse, David H.; Punj, Girish N. and Stewart, David W. A Typology of Individual Search Strategies among Purchasers of New Automobiles. *J. Cons. Res.*, March 1984, 10(4), pp. 417–31. **[G: U.S.]**

Gabor, André. On the Theory and Practice of Transfer Pricing. In *[Pearce, I. F.]*, 1984, pp. 149–70.

Gatignon, Hubert. Toward a Methodology for Measuring Advertising Copy Effects. *Marketing Sci.*, Fall 1984, 3(4), pp. 308–26.

Gensch, Dennis H. Targeting the Switchable Industrial Customer. *Marketing Sci.*, Winter 1984, 3(1), pp. 41–54. **[G: U.S.]**

Givon, Moshe. Variety Seeking through Brand Switching. *Marketing Sci.*, Winter 1984, 3(1), pp. 1–22. **[G: U.S.]**

Glazer, Rashi. Multiattribute Perceptual Bias as

Revealing of Preference Structure. *J. Cons. Res.*, June 1984, *11*(1), pp. 510–21. [G: U.S.]

Gochet, W. and Vandenbosch, P. Location of Depots at the Maes Brewery. *Tijdschrift Econ. Manage.*, 1984, *29*(1), pp. 33–43[G: Belgium]

Golanty, John L. Clarification of the Tracker Methodology and Limitations [An Empirical Comparison of Awareness Forecasting Models of New Product Introduction]. *Marketing Sci.*, Summer 1984, *3*(3), pp. 203. [G: U.S.]

Goldberg, Stephen M.; Green, Paul E. and Wind, Yoram. Conjoint Analysis of Price Premiums for Hotel Amenities. *J. Bus.*, Part 2, January 1984, *57*(1), pp. S111–32.

Goldman, Arieh. The Development and Implementation of a Marketing-Based Economic Development Project in the Agricultural Sector—An Israeli Case. **In** *Kaynak, E. and Savitt, R., eds.*, 1984, pp. 53–70. [G: Israel]

Goodhardt, G. J.; Ehrenberg, A. S. C. and Chatfield, C. The Dirichlet: A Comprehensive Model of Buying Behaviour. *J. Roy. Statist. Soc.*, 1984, *147*(5), pp. 621–43. [G: U.K.]

Gould, John P. Comments on "Firm-Specific Differentiation and Competition among Multiproduct Firms." *J. Bus.*, Part 2, January 1984, *57*(1), pp. S173–77.

Greenwald, Anthony G. and Leavitt, Clark. Audience Involvement in Advertising: Four Levels. *J. Cons. Res.*, June 1984, *11*(1), pp. 581–92. [G: U.S.]

Grossman, Gene M. and Shapiro, Carl. Informative Advertising with Differentiated Products. *Rev. Econ. Stud.*, January 1984, *51*(1), pp. 63–81.

Gürol, Metin N.; Kaynak, Erdener and Yucel, Ahmet A. Computer Systems Marketing in the Emerging Economies of the Middle East: Managerial and Public Policy Implications. **In** *Kaynak, E., ed.*, 1984, pp. 271–85. [G: U.S.; Turkey; Saudi Arabia]

Hagerty, Michael R. and Aaker, David A. A Normative Model of Consumer Information Processing. *Marketing Sci.*, Summer 1984, *3*(3), pp. 227–46.

Hannah, Darlene B. and Sternthal, Brian. Detecting and Explaining the Sleeper Effect. *J. Cons. Res.*, September 1984, *11*(2), pp. 632–42.

Harris, Milton. Comment on "Pricing a Product Line." *J. Bus.*, Part 2, January 1984, *57*(1), pp. S109–10.

Hauser, John R. Pricing Theory and the Role of Marketing Science [Pricing Research in Marketing: The State of the Art]. *J. Bus.*, Part 2, January 1984, *57*(1), pp. S65–71.

Hauser, John R. and Gaskin, Steven P. Application of the "Defender" Consumer Model. *Marketing Sci.*, Fall 1984, *3*(4), pp. 327–51. [G: U.S.]

Heede, Søren. International Marketing: A Comparative System Perspective. **In** *Kaynak, E., ed.*, 1984, pp. 25–33.

Hensher, David A. Achieving Representativeness of the Observable Component of the Indirect Utility Function in Logit Choice Models: An Empirical Revelation. *J. Bus.*, April 1984, *57*(2), pp. 265–80. [G: U.S.]

Hilke, John C. and Nelson, Philip B. Noisy Advertising and the Predation Rule in Antitrust Analysis. *Amer. Econ. Rev.*, May 1984, *74*(2), pp. 367–71. [G: U.S.]

Holstius, Karin. Does It Pay to Invest in Export Marketing during Recession? *Liiketaloudellinen Aikak.*, 1984, *33*(3), pp. 303–09. [G: Finland]

Horsky, Dan. Comments on "Conjoint Analysis of Price Premiums for Hotel Amenities." *J. Bus.*, Part 2, January 1984, *57*(1), pp. S139–47.

Hoyer, Wayne D. An Examination of Consumer Decision Making for a Common Repeat Purchase Product. *J. Cons. Res.*, December 1984, *11*(3), pp. 822–29. [G: U.S.]

Hung, C. L. Economic and Market Environment: The Case of Hong Kong. **In** *Kindra, G. S., ed.*, 1984, pp. 95–114. [G: Hong Kong]

Jacoby, Jacob. Perspectives on Information Overload. *J. Cons. Res.*, March 1984, *10*(4), pp. 432–35.

Jansson, Hans. Industrial Marketing Strategies of Transnational Corporations in Third World Markets. **In** *Kaynak, E., ed.*, 1984, pp. 75–90.

Joachimsthaler, Erich A. and Lastovicka, John L. Optimal Stimulation Level—Exploratory Behavior Models. *J. Cons. Res.*, December 1984, *11*(3), pp. 830–35. [G: U.S.]

Johnson, Eric J. and Meyer, Robert J. Compensatory Choice Models of Noncompensatory Processes: The Effect of Varying Context. *J. Cons. Res.*, June 1984, *11*(1), pp. 528–41. [G: U.S.]

Johnson, Eric J. and Russo, J. Edward. Product Familiarity and Learning New Information. *J. Cons. Res.*, June 1984, *11*(1), pp. 542–50. [G: U.S.]

Johnson, Michael D. Consumer Choice Strategies for Comparing Noncomparable Alternatives. *J. Cons. Res.*, December 1984, *11*(3), pp. 741–53.

Kardasz, Stanley W. and Stollery, Kenneth R. Simultaneous Equation Models of Profitability, Advertising and Concentration for Canadian Manufacturing Industries. *Quart. J. Bus. Econ.*, Winter 1984, *23*(1), pp. 51–64. [G: Canada]

Katz, Michael L. Firm-Specific Differentiation and Competition among Multiproduct Firms. *J. Bus.*, Part 2, January 1984, *57*(1), pp. S149–66.

Kaynak, Erdener. Comparative Marketing Systems: Past, Present, and Future. **In** *Kaynak, E. and Savitt, R., eds.*, 1984, pp. 263–77.

Kaynak, Erdener. Current Status of International Marketing Management. **In** *Kaynak, E., ed.*, 1984, pp. 3–21.

Kaynak, Erdener. Future Directions of Research in International Marketing. **In** *Kaynak, E., ed.*, 1984, pp. 337–44.

Kaynak, Erdener. Marketing-Research Techniques and Approaches for LDCs. In *Kindra, G. S., ed.*, 1984, pp. 238–52. **[G: LDCs]**

Kaynak, Erdener. The Use of Marketing Research to Facilitate International Marketing Within Developing Countries. In *Kaynak, E., ed.*, 1984, pp. 155–71.

Kaynak, Erdener and Savitt, Ronald. Comparative Marketing: Integrative Statement. In *Kaynak, E. and Savitt, R., eds.*, 1984, pp. 3–13.

Kaynak, Erdener and Savitt, Ronald. The Future Directions of Comparative Marketing: An Agenda for Research Priorities. In *Kaynak, E. and Savitt, R., eds.*, 1984, pp. 278–85.

Kehret-Ward, Trudy and Yalch, Richard F. To Take or Not to Take the Only One: Effects of Changing the Meaning of a Product Attribute on Choice Behavior. *J. Cons. Res.*, March 1984, 10(4), pp. 410–16. **[G: U.S.]**

Kihlstrom, Richard E. and Riordan, Michael H. Advertising as a Signal. *J. Polit. Econ.*, June 1984, 92(3), pp. 427–50.

Kindra, G. S.; Dholakia, Ruby Roy and Pangotra, Prem. The Public Sector and the Marketing of Birth Control in LDCs. In *Kindra, G. S., ed.*, 1984, pp. 138–55. **[G: India; LDCs]**

Kleinschmidt, Elko J. and Cooper, Robert G. A Typology of Export Strategies Applied to the Export Performance of Industrial Firms. In *Kaynak, E., ed.*, 1984, pp. 217–31.
[G: Canada]

Koford, Kenneth J. Was "Free" TV a Price Control that Increased Consumers' Welfare? *Quart. Rev. Econ. Bus.*, Spring 1984, 24(1), pp. 67–77.

Kwoka, John E., Jr. Advertising and the Price and Quality of Optometric Services. *Amer. Econ. Rev.*, March 1984, 74(1), pp. 211–16.
[G: U.S.]

Lazer, William. Comparative Insights into Japanese Marketing: Myths and Realities. In *Kaynak, E. and Savitt, R., eds.*, 1984, pp. 233–46. **[G: Japan]**

Lee, Li Way. Franchising and Interbrand Competition. *Southern Econ. J.*, July 1984, 51(1), pp. 219–34. **[G: U.S.]**

Lehtonen, Pekka and Lehtinen, Uolevi. Mainonnan merkityksestä. (On the Importance of Advertising. With English summary.) *Liiketaloudellinen Aikak.*, 1984, 33(3), pp. 310–20.
[G: W. Europe]

Leroux, François and Zaccour, Georges. Structures de marché et intensité de la publicité. (Market Structures and Intensity of Publicity. With English summary.) *L'Actual. Econ.*, September 1984, 60(3), pp. 341–54. **[G: Canada]**

Lerviks, Alf-Erik. The Predictive Accuracy of a Combined Segmentation-Diffusion Model for New Consumer Durables. *Liiketaloudellinen Aikak.*, 1984, 33(1), pp. 3–22. **[G: Finland]**

Lipstein, Benjamin. Marketing Financial Services. In *Sametz, A. W., ed.*, 1984, pp. 49–54. **[G: U.S.]**

Mahajan, Vijay; Muller, Eitan and Sharma, Subhash. An Empirical Comparison of Awareness Forecasting Models of New Product Introduc-

tion. *Marketing Sci.*, Summer 1984, 3(3), pp. 179–97. **[G: U.S.]**

Mahajan, Vijay; Muller, Eitan and Sharma, Subhash. Reflections on Awareness Forecasting Models of New Product Introduction: Rejoinder. *Marketing Sci.*, Summer 1984, 3(3), pp. 205–06. **[G: U.S.]**

Maheswaran, Durairaj. State Enterprises: A Marketing Perspective. In *Kindra, G. S., ed.*, 1984, pp. 216–37. **[G: LDCs]**

Mahmoud, Essam and Rice, Gillian. Marketing Problems in LDCs: The Case of Egypt. In *Kindra, G. S., ed.*, 1984, pp. 76–94. **[G: Egypt]**

Malhotra, Naresh K. Reflections on the Information Overload Paradigm in Consumer Decision Making [Perspectives on Information Overload]. *J. Cons. Res.*, March 1984, 10(4), pp. 436–40.

Marvel, Howard P. and McCafferty, Stephen. Resale Price Maintenance and Quality Certification. *Rand J. Econ.*, Autumn 1984, 15(3), pp. 346–59. **[G: U.S.]**

Maynes, E. Scott, et al. Informationally Imperfect Markets: Implications for Consumers. In *[Ferber, R.]*, 1984, pp. 185–97. **[G: U.S.]**

McSweeney, Frances K. and Bierley, Calvin. Recent Developments in Classical Conditioning. *J. Cons. Res.*, September 1984, 11(2), pp. 619–31.

Meredith, Lindsay Norman. U.S. Multinational Investment in Canadian Manufacturing Industries. *Rev. Econ. Statist.*, February 1984, 66(1), pp. 111–19. **[G: U.S.; Canada]**

Micallef, André. Positivisme et relativisme en théorie commerciale. Analyse d'une évolution et nouvelle formulation. (Positivism and Relativism in Marketing Theory. Analysis of an Evolution and of a New Formulation. With English summary.) *Écon. Soc.*, November–December 1984, 18(11–12), pp. 31–61.

Midgley, David F. Parsimony or Explanation: On the Estimation of Systems Defined by Nonlinear Differential Equations [A Simple Mathematical Theory of Innovative Behavior]. *J. Cons. Res.*, March 1984, 10(4), pp. 445–48.

Möller, Kristian. Role of Promotional Management in Exporting to the Soviet Union and OECD Countries. In *Kaynak, E., ed.*, 1984, pp. 318–34. **[G: U.S.S.R.; OECD]**

Monahan, George E. A Pure Birth Model of Optimal Advertising with Word-of-Mouth. *Marketing Sci.*, Spring 1984, 3(2), pp. 169–78.

Moorthy, K. Sridhar. Comments on "Firm-Specific Differentiation and Competition among Multiproduct Firms." *J. Bus.*, Part 2, January 1984, 57(1), pp. S167–71.

Moorthy, K. Sridhar. Market Segmentation, Self-Selection, and Product Line Design. *Marketing Sci.*, Fall 1984, 3(4), pp. 288–307.

Mueller, Willard F. and Rogers, Richard T. Changes in Market Concentration of Manufacturing Industries 1947–1977. *Rev. Ind. Organ.*, Spring 1984, 1(1), pp. 1–14. **[G: U.S.]**

Mun, Kin-chok. Marketing in the PRC. In *Kaynak, E. and Savitt, R., eds.*, 1984, pp. 247–60. **[G: China]**

Murfin, Andy. Market Shares in the UK Passenger Car Market: Marketing, Expenditure and Price Effects, 1975–80. *Appl. Econ.*, August 1984, *16*(4), pp. 611–32. **[G: U.K.]**

Nagle, Thomas. Economic Foundations for Pricing. *J. Bus.*, Part 2, January 1984, *57*(1), pp. S3–26.

Narasimhan, Chakravarthi. A Price Discrimination Theory of Coupons. *Marketing Sci.*, Spring 1984, *3*(2), pp. 128–47. **[G: U.S.]**

Narasimhan, Chakravarthi. Comments on "Economic Foundations for Pricing." *J. Bus.*, Part 2, January 1984, *57*(1), pp. S27–34.

Nerlove, Marc and Waugh, Frederick V. Advertising without Supply Control: Some Implications of a Study of the Advertising of Oranges. In *Waugh, F. V.*, 1984, *1961*, pp. 63–87. **[G: U.S.]**

Nomura, Junji. A Method for Predicting Sales Amount by the Use of IWSM and GMDH. In *Farlow, S. J.*, ed., 1984, pp. 215–24. **[G: Japan]**

Oren, Shmuel S. Comments on "Pricing Research in Marketing: The State of the Art." *J. Bus.*, Part 2, January 1984, *57*(1), pp. S61–64.

Oren, Shmuel S. and Rothkopf, Michael H. A Market Dynamics Model for New Industrial Products and Its Application. *Marketing Sci.*, Summer 1984, *3*(3), pp. 247–65.

Oren, Shmuel S.; Smith, Stephen and Wilson, Robert B. Pricing a Product Line. *J. Bus.*, Part 2, January 1984, *57*(1), pp. S73–99.

Paliwoda, Stanley J. East–West Trade Relations and International Marketing Strategy Formulation. In *Kaynak, E.*, ed., 1984, pp. 286–304.

Peters, Michael. Restrictions on Price Advertising. *J. Polit. Econ.*, June 1984, *92*(3), pp. 472–85.

Pratt, Michael D. and Hoffer, George E. Test of the Lemons Model: Comment [A Direct Test of the 'Lemons' Model: The Market for Used Pickup Trucks]. *Amer. Econ. Rev.*, September 1984, *74*(4), pp. 798–800. **[G: U.S.]**

Pringle, Lewis G. An Audience Flow Model of Television Viewing Choice: A Comment. *Marketing Sci.*, Spring 1984, *3*(2), pp. 125–26. **[G: U.S.]**

Pringle, Lewis G.; Wilson, R. Dale and Brody, Edward I. Issues in Comparing the Awareness Component of New Product Models. *Marketing Sci.*, Summer 1984, *3*(3), pp. 203–05. **[G: U.S.]**

Rao, Vithala R. Pricing Research in Marketing: The State of the Art. *J. Bus.*, Part 2, January 1984, *57*(1), pp. S39–60.

Raviv, Artur. Comments on "Economic Foundations for Pricing." *J. Bus.*, Part 2, January 1984, *57*(1), pp. S35–38.

Reid, Stan D. Market Expansion and Firm Internationalization. In *Kaynak, E.*, ed., 1984, pp. 197–206.

Reingen, Peter H., et al. Brand Congruence in Interpersonal Relations: A Social Network Analysis. *J. Cons. Res.*, December 1984, *11*(3), pp. 771–83. **[G: U.S.]**

Rice, Gillian. An Empirical Study of the Effect of Political Uncertainty on International Marketing Strategy. In *Kaynak, E.*, ed., 1984, pp. 51–69. **[G: U.S.]**

Rogers, Gordon A. Microcomputer Support for Market Penetration via Regional Transfer Yards. *Logist. Transp. Rev.*, December 1984, *20*(4), pp. 367–72. **[G: U.S.; Canada]**

Ross, Christopher A. and McTavish, Ronald. The Marketing-Education Task in Third World Countries. In *Kindra, G. S.*, ed., 1984, pp. 156–71. **[G: LDCs]**

Rosson, Philip J. Success Factors in Manufacturer–Overseas Distributor Relationships in International Marketing. In *Kaynak, E.*, ed., 1984, pp. 91–107.

Rust, Roland T. and Alpert, Mark I. An Audience Flow Model of Television Viewing Choice. *Marketing Sci.*, Spring 1984, *3*(2), pp. 113–24. **[G: U.S.]**

Rust, Roland T. and Alpert, Mark I. On Establishing a Dialogue in Television Viewing Research. *Marketing Sci.*, Spring 1984, *3*(2), pp. 126–27. **[G: U.S.]**

Samli, A. Coskun. Comparative Marketing Systems in Eastern Europe: An Illustration of Marketing Evolution. In *Kaynak, E. and Savitt, R.*, eds., 1984, pp. 217–32. **[G: E. Europe]**

Samli, A. Coskun. Role of Marketing in Economic Development: What Should International Marketers Know? In *Kaynak, E.*, ed., 1984, pp. 34–50.

Samuels, Warren J. Samaritan Advertising. *J. Econ. Issues*, September 1984, *18*(3), pp. 893–94. **[G: U.S.]**

Schmittlein, David C. Assessing Validity and Test-Retest Reliability for "Pick K of N" Data. *Marketing Sci.*, Winter 1984, *3*(1), pp. 23–40. **[G: U.S.]**

Scott, Walter Giorgio. Una funzione da riscoprire: il marketing. (A Neglected Area: Marketing. With English summary.) *L'Impresa*, 1984, *26*(4), pp. 11–20. **[G: Italy]**

Sereghyová, Jana. The Role of Advertising in Developing Economic Cooperation among Members of the CMEA. *Soviet E. Europ. Foreign Trade*, Winter 1984-85, *20*(4), pp. 63–76. **[G: CMEA]**

Seymour, Daniel and Lessne, Greg. Spousal Conflict Arousal: Scale Development. *J. Cons. Res.*, December 1984, *11*(3), pp. 810–21. **[G: U.S.]**

Shapiro, Jeremy F. Practical Experience with Optimization Models. In *Naylor, T. H. and Thomas, C.*, eds., 1984, pp. 67–77.

Sharma, D. Deo. Management Contract and International Marketing of Industrial Goods. In *Kaynak, E.*, ed., 1984, pp. 108–20. **[G: Sweden]**

Shimp, Terence A. and Kavas, Alican. The Theory of Reasoned Action Applied to Coupon Usage. *J. Cons. Res.*, December 1984, *11*(3), pp. 795–809. **[G: U.S.]**

Shocker, Allan D.; Zahorik, Anthony J. and Stewart, David W. Competitive Market Structure Analysis: A Comment on Problems. [Competitive Market Structure Analysis: Principal Partitioning of Revealed Substitutabilities]. *J. Cons. Res.*, December 1984, *11*(3), pp. 836–41. [G: U.S.]

Shugan, Steven M. Comments on "Pricing a Product Line." *J. Bus.*, Part 2, January 1984, *57*(1), pp. S101–07.

Silver, Steven D. A Simple Mathematical Theory of Innovative Behavior: Comment. *J. Cons. Res.*, March 1984, *10*(4), pp. 441–44.

Simon-Miller, Françoise. African Marketing: The Next Frontier. In *Kindra, G. S., ed.*, 1984, pp. 115–29. [G: Sub-Saharan Africa]

Spulber, Daniel F. Nonlinear Pricing, Advertising and Welfare. *Southern Econ. J.*, April 1984, *50*(4), pp. 1025–35.

Stock, John R. and Lambert, Douglas M. International Distribution Systems: A Comparative Approach. In *Kaynak, E. and Savitt, R., eds.*, 1984, pp. 183–99. [G: U.S.; U.K.; Japan; Australia]

Sturgess, Brian T. and Wilson, Nicholas. Advertising Expenditure and Aggregate Consumption in Britain and West Germany: An Analysis of Causality. *Managerial Dec. Econ.*, December 1984, *5*(4), pp. 219–27. [G: U.K.; W. Germany]

Szabo, Laszlo. Marketing and Marketing Research in the Socialist Countries. In *Kaynak, E. and Savitt, R., eds.*, 1984, pp. 131–43. [G: Hungary]

Thompson, Gerald L. and Teng, Jinn-Tsair. Optimal Pricing and Advertising Policies for New Product Oligopoly Models. *Marketing Sci.*, Spring 1984, *3*(2), pp. 148–68.

Thompson, R. S. Structure and Conduct in Local Advertising Markets: The Case of Irish Provincial Newspapers. *J. Ind. Econ.*, December 1984, *33*(2), pp. 241–49. [G: U.K.]

Thorelli, Hans B. Informatics: Impact on Marketing. In *[Ferber, R.]*, 1984, pp. 171–84.

Urban, Glen L.; Johnson, Philip L. and Hauser, John R. Testing Competitive Market Structures. *Marketing Sci.*, Spring 1984, *3*(2), pp. 83–112. [G: U.S.]

Urrila, Matti. Palvelu tulevaisuuden markkinoinnissa. (The Potentials of Service in Marketing. With English summary.) *Liiketaloudellinen Aikak.*, 1984, *33*(4), pp. 475–83.

Vedrine, Jean-Pierre. Vers un marketing adapté aux pays en développement. (Towards a Marketing Adapted to Developing Countries. With English summary.) *Écon. Soc.*, November–December 1984, *18*(11–12), pp. 63–78. [G: LDC]

Yalch, Richard F. and Elmore-Yalch, Rebecca. The Effect of Numbers on the Route to Persuasion. *J. Cons. Res.*, June 1984, *11*(1), pp. 522–27. [G: U.S.]

Yaprak, Attila and Parameswaran, Ravi. Reliability Measurement in Cross-National Survey Research: An Empirical Evaluation. In *Kaynak, E., ed.*, 1984, pp. 172–93. [G: Turkey; U.S.; W. Germany; Japan; Italy]

Yaprak, Attila; Sorek, Christopher and Parameswaran, Ravi. Competitive Strategy in Multinational Oligopolies: The Role of Promotion in the Computer Industry. In *Kaynak, E., ed.*, 1984, pp. 232–55. [G: U.K.; U.S.]

Yucelt, Ugur and Kaynak, Erdener. A Study of Measuring Influence of Advertising and Forecasting Cigarette Sales. *Managerial Dec. Econ.*, December 1984, *5*(4), pp. 213–18. [G: U.S.]

540 ACCOUNTING

541 Accounting

5410 Accounting

Adams, Steven J.; Lightner, Sharon M. and Ricketts, Donald E. Implications of Reported Accounting Information on Corporate Expenditures for Research and Development. *Rev. Bus. Econ. Res.*, Spring 1984, *19*(2), pp. 35–45. [G: U.S.]

Adelberg, Arthur H. and Razek, Joseph R. The Cloze Procedure: A Methodology for Determining the Understandability of Accounting Textbooks. *Accounting Rev.*, January 1984, *59*(1), pp. 109–22. [G: U.S.]

Amernic, Joel H. and Beechy, Thomas H. Accounting Students' Performance and Cognitive Complexity: Some Empirical Evidence. *Accounting Rev.*, April 1984, *59*(2), pp. 300–313.

Antle, Rick. Auditor Independence. *J. Acc. Res.*, Spring 1984, *22*(1), pp. 1–20.

Aranya, Nissim and Ferris, Kenneth R. A Reexamination of Accountants' Organizational–Professional Conflict. *Accounting Rev.*, January 1984, *59*(1), pp. 1–15. [G: U.S.]

Arens, Alvin A. and Ward, D. Dewey. The Use of a Systems Understanding Aid in the Accounting Curriculum. *Accounting Rev.*, January 1984, *59*(1), pp. 98–108. [G: U.S.]

Arnold, Donald F. and Geiselhart, Thomas J. Practitioners' Views on Five-Year Educational Requirements for CPAs. *Accounting Rev.*, April 1984, *59*(2), pp. 314–24. [G: U.S.]

Artto, Eero. Kansainvälinen kilpailukyky yritys- ja toimialatasolla -IV. (International Competitiveness at Enterprise and Industry Level IV. With English summary.) *Liiketaloudellinen Aikak.*, 1984, *33*(3), pp. 321–75. [G: Finland; Sweden; Canada; W. Germany; U.S.]

Ashton, Alison Hubbard. A Field Test of Implications of Laboratory Studies of Decision Making. *Accounting Rev.*, July 1984, *59*(3), pp. 361–75. [G: U.S.]

Ashton, Robert H. Integrating Research and Teaching in Auditing: Fifteen Cases on Judgment and Decision Making. *Accounting Rev.*, January 1984, *59*(1), pp. 78–97.

Baldwin, Bruce A. Segment Earnings Disclosure and the Ability of Security Analysts to Forecast Earnings Per Share. *Accounting Rev.*, July 1984, *59*(3), pp. 376–89. [G: U.S.]

Barry, Christopher B.; Velez-Arocho, Jorge I. and Welch, Paul R. A Bayesian Approach to CVP Analysis under Parameter Uncertainty. *Quart. Rev. Econ. Bus.*, Summer 1984, *24*(2), pp. 71–90.

Bathke, Allen W., Jr. and Lorek, Kenneth S. The Relationship between Time-Series Models and the Security Market's Expectation of Quarterly Earnings. *Accounting Rev.*, April 1984, 59(2), pp. 163–76. **[G: U.S.]**

Beaver, William H.; Griffin, Paul A. and Landsman, Wayne R. Testing for Incremental Information Content in the Presence of Collinearity: A Comment. *J. Acc. Econ.*, December 1984, 6(3), pp. 219–23.

Boskin, Michael J. Issues in Budget Accounting: Comment. In *Mills, G. B. and Palmer, J. L., eds.*, 1984, pp. 457–60. **[G: U.S.]**

Boussard, Daniel. La comptabilité comme image de l'entreprise: un modèle "faible." (Accounting as an Image of the Firm: A "Weak" Model. With English summary.) *Écon. Soc.*, November–December 1984, 18(11–12), pp. 133–57. **[G: France]**

van Breda, Michael F. The Misuse of Accounting Rates of Return: Comment. *Amer. Econ. Rev.*, June 1984, 74(3), pp. 507–08.

Brockett, Patrick L., et al. A Chance-constrained Programming Approach to Cost–Volume–Profit Analysis. *Accounting Rev.*, July 1984, 59(3), pp. 474–87.

Bruno, Pietro. Versamenti e compensazione nel conto corrente. Effetto solutorio delle rimesse e revocatoria fallimentare. (Payments into and Withdrawals from Currency Accounts: Release Effect and Revocation of Bankruptcy Proceedings. With English summary.) *Bancaria*, May–June 1984, 40(5–6), pp. 530–38. **[G: Italy]**

Chambers, Anne E. and Penman, Stephen H. Timeliness of Reporting and the Stock Price Reaction to Earnings Announcements. *J. Acc. Res.*, Spring 1984, 22(1), pp. 21–47. **[G: U.S.]**

Chasteen, Lanny. A Taxonomy of Price Change Models. *Accounting Rev.*, July 1984, 59(3), pp. 515–23.

Christie, Andrew A., et al. Testing for Incremental Information Content in the Presence of Collinearity. *J. Acc. Econ.*, December 1984, 6(3), pp. 205–17.

Churchill, Neil C. Improved Accountability and Comprehensive Audit as Portents for the Future. In *[Kozmetsky, G.]*, 1984, pp. 93–109. **[G: U.S.]**

Coe, Charles K. and Borthick, A. Faye. Computer Auditing in the Federal Government. *Public Budg. Finance*, Autumn 1984, 4(3), pp. 67–74. **[G: U.S.]**

Collins, Daniel W. and Dent, Warren T. A Comparison of Alternative Testing Methodologies Used in Capital Market Research. *J. Acc. Res.*, Spring 1984, 22(1), pp. 48–84. **[G: U.S.]**

Daley, Lane Alan. The Valuation of Reported Pension Measures for Firms Sponsoring Defined Benefit Plans. *Accounting Rev.*, April 1984, 59(2), pp. 177–98. **[G: U.S.]**

Danos, Paul; Holt, Doris L. and Imhoff, Eugene A., Jr. Bond Raters' Use of Management Financial Forecasts: Experiment in Expert Judgment. *Accounting Rev.*, October 1984, 59(4), pp. 547–73. **[G: U.S.]**

Davis, Harry Z.; Kahn, Nathan and Rozen, Etzmun. LIFO Inventory Liquidations: An Empirical Study. *J. Acc. Res.*, Autumn 1984, 22(2), pp. 480–96. **[G: U.S.]**

Demski, Joel S.; Patell, James M. and Wolfson, Mark A. Decentralized Choice of Monitoring Systems. *Accounting Rev.*, January 1984, 59(1), pp. 16–34.

Dharan, Bala G. Expectation Models and Potential Information Content of Oil and Gas Reserve Value Disclosures. *Accounting Rev.*, April 1984, 59(2), pp. 199–217. **[G: U.S.]**

Dierkes, Meinolf. Corporate Social Reporting and Auditing: Theory and Practice. In *Hopt, K. J. and Teubner, G., eds.*, 1984, pp. 354–79.

Dietrich, J. Richard. Methodological Issues Related to the Estimation of Financial Distress Prediction Models: Discussion. *J. Acc. Res.*, Supplement 1984, 22, pp. 83–86. **[G: U.S.]**

Dockweiler, Raymond C. and Willis, Carl G. On the Use of Entry Requirements for Undergraduate Accounting Programs. *Accounting Rev.*, July 1984, 59(3), pp. 496–504. **[G: U.S.]**

Dodd, Peter, et al. Qualified Audit Opinions and Stock Prices: Information Content, Announcement Dates, and Concurrent Disclosures. *J. Acc. Econ.*, April 1984, 6(1), pp. 3–38. **[G: U.S.]**

Dunn, W. Marcus and Hall, Thomas W. An Empirical Analysis of the Relationships between CPA Examination Candidate Attributes and Candidate Performance. *Accounting Rev.*, October 1984, 59(4), pp. 674–89. **[G: U.S.]**

Dworin, Lowell and Grimlund, Richard A. Dollar Unit Sampling for Accounts Receivable and Inventory. *Accounting Rev.*, April 1984, 59(2), pp. 218–41.

Dyckman, Thomas R.; Philbrick, Donna and Stephan, Jens. A Comparison of Event Study Methodologies Using Daily Stock Returns: A Simulation Approach. *J. Acc. Res.*, Supplement 1984, 22, pp. 1–30. **[G: U.S.]**

Dyckman, Thomas R. and Zeff, Stephen A. Two Decades of the *Journal of Accounting Research*. *J. Acc. Res.*, Spring 1984, 22(1), pp. 225–97.

Edmonds, Thomas P. On the Benefits of Cumulative Exams: An Experimental Study. *Accounting Rev.*, October 1984, 59(4), pp. 660–68. **[G: U.S.]**

Elliott, John, et al. The Impact of SFAS No. 2 on Firm Expenditures on Research and Development: Replications and Extensions. *J. Acc. Res.*, Spring 1984, 22(1), pp. 85–102. **[G: U.S.]**

Filios, Vassilios P. The Methodology of Accounting Research and the Underlying Philosophy. *Rivista Int. Sci. Econ. Com.*, August 1984, 31(8), pp. 762–86.

Firth, M. The Extent of Voluntary Disclosure in Corporate Annual Reports and Its Association with Security Risk Measures. *Appl. Econ.*, April 1984, 16(2), pp. 269–77. **[G: U.K.]**

Fisher, Franklin M. The Misuse of Accounting Rates of Return: Reply. *Amer. Econ. Rev.*, June 1984, 74(3), pp. 509–17.

Fonfeder, Robert and Fabozzi, Frank J. Interim Review and the Quality of Interim Report Numbers. *Rev. Bus. Econ. Res.*, Spring 1984, *19*(2), pp. 24–34. [G: U.S.]

Foster, George; Olsen, Chris and Shevlin, Terry. Earnings Releases, Anomalies, and the Behavior of Security Returns. *Accounting Rev.*, October 1984, *59*(4), pp. 574–603. [G: U.S.]

Francis, Jere R. The Effect of Audit Firm Size on Audit Prices: A Study of the Australian Market. *J. Acc. Econ.*, August 1984, *6*(2), pp. 133–51. [G: Australia]

Fullerton, Don and Henderson, Yolanda Kodrzycki. Incentive Effects of Taxes on Income from Capital: Alternative Policies in the 1980s. In *Hulten, C. R. and Sawhill, I. V., eds.*, 1984, pp. 45–89. [G: U.S.]

Godfrey, James and Neter, John. Bayesian Bounds for Monetary Unit Sampling in Accounting and Auditing. *J. Acc. Res.*, Autumn 1984, *22*(2), pp. 497–525.

Godfrey, James; Roshwalb, Alan and Wright, Roger L. Model-based Stratification in Inventory Cost Estimation. *J. Bus. Econ. Statist.*, January 1984, *2*(1), pp. 1–9. [G: U.S.]

Gray, Dahli. Corporate Preferences for Foreign Currency Accounting Standards. *J. Acc. Res.*, Autumn 1984, *22*(2), pp. 760–64. [G: U.S.]

Gray, S. J. and Radebaugh, Lee H. International Segment Disclosures by U.S. and U.K. Multinational Enterprises: A Descriptive Study. *J. Acc. Res.*, Spring 1984, *22*(1), pp. 351–60. [G: U.S.; U.K.]

Hartman, Robert W. Issues in Budget Accounting. In *Mills, G. B. and Palmer, J. L., eds.*, 1984, pp. 423–47. [G: U.S.]

Hellerstein, Jerome R. Defining a Unitary Business: An Economist's View: Comments. In *McLure, C. E., Jr., ed.*, 1984, pp. 127–31. [G: U.S.]

Hirschey, Mark and Wichern, Dean W. Accounting and Market-Value Measures of Profitability: Consistency, Determinants, and Uses. *J. Bus. Econ. Statist.*, October 1984, *2*(4), pp. 375–83. [G: U.S.]

Hopt, Klaus J. Self-dealing and Use of Corporate Opportunity and Information: Regulating Directors' Conflicts of Interest. In *Hopt, K. J. and Teubner, G., eds.*, 1984, pp. 285–326.

Horowitz, Ira. The Misuse of Accounting Rates of Return: Comment. *Amer. Econ. Rev.*, June 1984, *74*(3), pp. 492–93.

Houghton, Keith A. Accounting Data and the Prediction of Business Failure: The Setting of Priors and the Age of Data. *J. Acc. Res.*, Spring 1984, *22*(1), pp. 361–68. [G: Australia]

Hughes, John S. and Ricks, William E. Accounting for Retail Land Sales: Analysis of a Mandated Change. *J. Acc. Econ.*, August 1984, *6*(2), pp. 101–32. [G: U.S.]

Ijiri, Yuji and Noel, James. A Reliability Comparison of the Measurement of Wealth, Income, and Force. *Accounting Rev.*, January 1984, *59*(1), pp. 52–63.

Ingram, Robert W. Economic Incentives and the Choice of State Government Accounting Prac-

tices. *J. Acc. Res.*, Spring 1984, *22*(1), pp. 126–44. [G: U.S.]

Iyoda, Takatoshi. A Consideration of the Concept of a "True and Fair View." *Osaka Econ. Pap.*, March 1984, *33*(3–4), pp. 135–43. [G: U.K.]

Izan, H. Y. Corporate Distress in Australia. *J. Banking Finance*, June 1984, *8*(2), pp. 303–20. [G: Australia]

Johnson, Darwin G. Issues in Budget Accounting: Comment. In *Mills, G. B. and Palmer, J. L., eds.*, 1984, pp. 448–56. [G: U.S.]

Johnson, Douglas A. and Pany, Kurt. Forecasts, Auditor Review, and Bank Loan Decisions. *J. Acc. Res.*, Autumn 1984, *22*(2), pp. 731–43. [G: U.S.]

Johnson, Ronald W. and Lewin, Arie Y. Management and Accountability Models of Public Sector Performance. In *Miller, T. C., ed.*, 1984, pp. 224–50. [G: U.S.]

Johnson, Steven B. Demand-Revealing Processes and Accounting Standard-Setting. *Public Choice*, 1984, *42*(1), pp. 3–24. [G: U.S.]

Kaplan, Robert S. The Evolution of Management Accounting. *Accounting Rev.*, July 1984, *59*(3), pp. 390–418. [G: U.S.]

Kellogg, Robert L. Accounting Activities, Security Prices, and Class Action Lawsuits. *J. Acc. Econ.*, December 1984, *6*(3), pp. 185–204. [G: U.S.]

King, John Leslie and Kraemer, Kenneth L. Information Systems and Intergovernmental Relations. In *Miller, T. C., ed.*, 1984, pp. 102–30. [G: U.S.]

King, Raymond D. The Effect of Convertible Bond Equity Values on Dilution and Leverage. *Accounting Rev.*, July 1984, *59*(3), pp. 419–31. [G: U.S.]

Knudsen, Torben Finn. Interne afregningspriser i decentraliserede virksomheder. (Transfer Prices in Decentralized Firms. With English summary.) *Nationaløkon. Tidsskr.*, 1984, *122*(2), pp. 240–52.

Lambert, Richard A. Income Smoothing as Rational Equilibrium Behavior. *Accounting Rev.*, October 1984, *59*(4), pp. 604–18.

Likierman, Andrew. The Use of Profitability in Assessing the Performance of Public Enterprises. In *Ramanadham, V. V., ed.*, 1984, pp. 159–70. [G: U.K.]

Lincoln, Mervyn. An Empirical Study of the Usefulness of Accounting Ratios to Describe Levels of Insolvency Risk. *J. Banking Finance*, June 1984, *8*(2), pp. 321–40.

Linowes, David F. Socioeconomic Reporting and Expanded Accountability for Management Actions. In *[Kozmetsky, G.]*, 1984, pp. 111–19.

Lobo, Gerald J. and Nair, R. D. Predictions of Annual Earnings Using Quarterly Earnings, Annual Earnings, and Dividend Payout Ratios. *Managerial Dec. Econ.*, December 1984, *5*(4), pp. 228–33. [G: U.S.]

Long, William F. and Ravenscraft, David J. The Misuse of Accounting Rates of Return: Comment. *Amer. Econ. Rev.*, June 1984, *74*(3), pp. 494–500.

Loss, Louis. Disclosure as Preventive Enforcement. **In** *Hopt, K. J. and Teubner, G., eds.,* 1984, pp. 327–37. **[G: U.S.]**

Lotti, Eraldo. Il budget monetario. (Monetary Budget. With English summary.) *L'Impresa,* 1984, *26*(1), pp. 75–79.

Lys, Thomas. Mandated Accounting Changes and Debt Covenants: The Case of Oil and Gas Accounting. *J. Acc. Econ.,* April 1984, *6*(1), pp. 39–65. **[G: U.S.]**

Mann, Harvey. A Worksheet for Demonstrating the Articulation of Financial Statements. *Accounting Rev.,* October 1984, *59*(4), pp. 669–73.

Marais, M. Laurentius; Patell, James M. and Wolfson, Mark A. The Experimental Design of Classification Models: An Application of Recursive Partitioning and Bootstrapping to Commercial Bank Loan Classifications. *J. Acc. Res.,* Supplement 1984, *22,* pp. 87–114. **[G: U.S.]**

Marcinko, David and Petri, Enrico. Use of the Production Function in Calculation of Standard Cost Variances—An Extension. *Accounting Rev.,* July 1984, *59*(3), pp. 488–95.

Martin, James R. Market Structure and Corporate Accounting Strategy. *Amer. Econ.,* Spring 1984, *28*(1), pp. 34–43. **[G: U.S.]**

Martin, Stephen. The Misuse of Accounting Rates of Return: Comment. *Amer. Econ. Rev.,* June 1984, *74*(3), pp. 501–06.

Matolcsy, Z. P. Evidence on the Joint and Marginal Information Content of Inflation-adjusted Accounting Income Numbers. *J. Acc. Res.,* Autumn 1984, *22*(2), pp. 555–69. **[G: U.S.]**

McCray, John H. A Quasi-Bayesian Audit Risk Model for Dollar Unit Sampling: A Reply. *Accounting Rev.,* July 1984, *59*(3), pp. 526–27.

McCray, John H. A Quasi-Bayesian Audit Risk Model for Dollar Unit Sampling. *Accounting Rev.,* January 1984, *59*(1), pp. 35–51.

McDonald, Bill and Morris, Michael H. The Relevance of SFAS 33 Inflation Accounting Disclosures in the Adjustment of Stock Prices to Inflation. *Accounting Rev.,* July 1984, *59*(3), pp. 432–46. **[G: U.S.]**

McKee, A. James, Jr.; Bell, Timothy B. and Boatsman, James R. Management Preferences over Accounting Standards: A Replication and Additional Tests. *Accounting Rev.,* October 1984, *59*(4), pp. 647–59.

McLure, Charles E., Jr. Defining a Unitary Business: An Economist's View. **In** *McLure, C. E., Jr., ed.,* 1984, pp. 89–124. **[G: U.S.]**

Menzefricke, Ulrich. Using Decision Theory for Planning Audit Sample Size with Dollar Unit Sampling. *J. Acc. Res.,* Autumn 1984, *22*(2), pp. 570–87.

Menzefricke, Ulrich and Smieliauskas, Wally. A Simulation Study of the Performance of Parametric Dollar Unit Sampling Statistical Procedures. *J. Acc. Res.,* Autumn 1984, *22*(2), pp. 588–604.

Miyamoto, Masaaki, et al. Theoretical and Empirical Studies of New ROI. *Osaka Econ. Pap.,* March 1984, *33*(3–4), pp. 12–63. **[G: Japan]**

Mohr, Rosanne M. and Dilley, Steven C. Current Cost and ACRS Depreciation Expense: A Com-

parison. *Accounting Rev.,* October 1984, *59*(4), pp. 690–701.

Moore, Peter G. Present Position and Potential Developments: Some Personal Views: Statistics in Business and Commerce. *J. Roy. Statist. Soc.,* 1984, *147*(2), pp. 268–77.

Morris, Michael H. and Ricketts, Donald E. The Relevance of Inflation-Adjusted Accounting Data in the Assessment of Systematic Risk. *Rev. Bus. Econ. Res.,* Spring 1984, *19*(2), pp. 90–101. **[G: U.S.]**

Most, Kenneth S. Depreciation Expense and the Effect of Inflation [Fixed Asset Lives and Replacement Accounting]. *J. Acc. Res.,* Autumn 1984, *22*(2), pp. 782–88. **[G: U.K.]**

Nagahama, Bokuryo. The Basic Problems of the Management Accounting. (In Japanese. With English summary.) *Osaka Econ. Pap.,* December 1984, *34*(2–3), pp. 299–305.

Nakamura, Nobuichiro. The Conceptual Foundations of Accounting Theory. (In Japanese. With English summary.) *Osaka Econ. Pap.,* December 1984, *34*(2–3), pp. 306–14.

Nakamura, Nobuichiro; Takao, Hiroji and Iyoda, Takatoshi. A Note of Study on the Accounting Institutions in France (1)—Concerning "Plan Comptable Général 1982". (In Japanese. With English summary.) *Osaka Econ. Pap.,* June 1984, *34*(1), pp. 20–103. **[G: France]**

Olsen, Chris. The Experimental Design of Classification Models: An Application of Recursive Partitioning and Bootstrapping to Commercial Bank Loan Classifications: Discussion. *J. Acc. Res.,* Supplement 1984, *22,* pp. 115–18. **[G: U.S.]**

Penno, Mark. Asymmetry of Pre-Decision Information and Managerial Accounting. *J. Acc. Res.,* Spring 1984, *22*(1), pp. 177–91.

Pepe, Federico. Il sistema contabile delle aziende di credito: analisi e prospettive. (Commercial Banks' Accounting Systems: Analysis and Perspectives. With English summary.) *Bancaria,* November 1984, *40*(11), pp. 1082–89. **[G: Italy]**

Peterson, Timothy M. Loss Reserving—Property/Casualty Insurance: A Summary of the Book. *J. Risk Ins.,* March 1984, *51*(1), pp. 115–21.

Phillips, Almarin. Defining a Unitary Business: An Economist's View: Comments. **In** *McLure, C. E., Jr., ed.,* 1984, pp. 125–26. **[G: U.S.]**

Postner, Harry H. New Developments towards Resolving the Company–Establishment Problem. *Rev. Income Wealth,* December 1984, *30*(4), pp. 429–59.

Puro, Marsha. Audit Firm Lobbying before the Financial Accounting Standards Board: An Empirical Study. *J. Acc. Res.,* Autumn 1984, *22*(2), pp. 624–46. **[G: U.S.]**

Radaeva, K. M. Non-Marxian Conceptions of Management Accounting. **In** *Smirnov, A. D.; Golosov, V. V. and Maximova, V. F., eds.,* 1984, pp. 272–81.

Revsine, Lawrence. The Rationale Underlying the Functional Currency Choice. *Accounting Rev.,* July 1984, *59*(3), pp. 505–14. **[G: U.S.]**

Ricks, William E. A Comparison of Event Study

Methodologies Using Daily Stock Returns: A Simulation Approach: Discussion. *J. Acc. Res.*, Supplement 1984, 22, pp. 31–33. [G: U.S.]

Salmi, Timo, et al. Extracting and Analyzing the Time Series for Profitability Measurement from Published Financial Statements: With Results on Publicly Traded Finnish Metal Industry Firms: Part III. *Liiketaloudellinen Aikak.*, 1984, 33(1), pp. 23–48. [G: Finland]

Schaefer, T. F. The Information Content of Current Cost Income Relative to Dividends and Historical Cost Income. *J. Acc. Res.*, Autumn 1984, 22(2), pp. 647–56. [G: U.S.]

Scheid, Jean-Claude. Nouveaux résultats et maintien du capital des entreprises. (New Results and Maintenance of the Capital of the Company. With English summary.) *Écon. Soc.*, January 1984, 18(1), pp. 91–119.

Scheiner, James H. An Empirical Assessment of the Impact of SEC Nonaudit Service Disclosure Requirements on Independent Auditors and Their Clients. *J. Acc. Res.*, Autumn 1984, 22(2), pp. 789–97. [G: U.S.]

Schmidt, Hartmut. Disclosure, Insider Information and Capital Market Functions. In *Hopt, K. J. and Teubner, G., eds.*, 1984, pp. 338–53.

Schneider, Arnold. Modeling External Auditors' Evaluations of Internal Auditing. *J. Acc. Res.*, Autumn 1984, 22(2), pp. 657–78. [G: U.S.]

Schreuder, Hein and Klaassen, Jan. Confidential Revenue and Profit Forecasts by Management and Financial Analysts: Evidence from The Netherlands. *Accounting Rev.*, January 1984, 59(1), pp. 64–77. [G: Netherlands]

Simunic, Dan A. Auditing, Consulting, and Auditor Independence. *J. Acc. Res.*, Autumn 1984, 22(2), pp. 679–702. [G: U.S.]

Smith, David B.; Stettler, Howard and Beedles, William L. An Investigation of the Information Content of Foreign Sensitive Payment Disclosures. *J. Acc. Econ.*, August 1984, 6(2), pp. 153–62. [G: U.S.]

Smith, Millard E. A Quasi-Bayesian Audit Risk Model for Dollar Unit Sampling: A Comment. *Accounting Rev.*, July 1984, 59(3), pp. 524–25.

Staats, Elmer B. Changing Approaches to Accountability in an Increasingly Complex Society. In *[Kozmetsky, G.]*, 1984, pp. 77–92.

von Stein, Johann Heinrich and Zeigler, Werner. The Prognosis and Surveillance of Risks from Commercial Credit Borrowers. *J. Banking Finance*, June 1984, 8(2), pp. 249–68.
[G: W. Germany]

Stock, Duane R. and Watson, Collin J. Human Judgment Accuracy, Multidimensional Graphics, and Human versus Models. *J. Acc. Res.*, Spring 1984, 22(1), pp. 192–206. [G: U.S.]

Stone, Mary and Bublitz, Bruce. An Analysis of the Reliability of the FASB Data Bank of Changing Price and Pension Information. *Accounting Rev.*, July 1984, 59(3), pp. 469–73.
[G: U.S.]

Sunder, Shyam and Waymire, Gregory. Accuracy of Exchange Valuation Rules: Additivity

and Unbiased Estimation. *J. Acc. Res.*, Spring 1984, 22(1), pp. 396–405.

Swieringa, Robert J. When Current Is Noncurrent and Vice Versa! *Accounting Rev.*, January 1984, 59(1), pp. 123–30. [G: U.S.]

Tamminen, Rauno. The Estimation of Causal Revenue Contributions. *Liiketaloudellinen Aikak.*, 1984, 33(2), pp. 155–62.
[G: Finland]

Tamminen, Rauno. Tilastollisesti estimoidun kannattavuuden tulkinnasta. (Interpretations for Statistically Estimated Profitability. With English summary.) *Liiketaloudellinen Aikak.*, 1984, 33(1), pp. 107–13.
[G: Finland]

Temko, Richard J. Aspetti fiscali, contabili e giuridici del leasing mobiliare in Europa. (An Overview of Tax, Accounting, and Legal Considerations Involved in Structuring Equipment Leases in Europe. With English summary.) *Bancaria*, October 1984, 40(10), pp. 1004–14.
[G: EEC]

Temko, Richard J. Aspetti fiscali, contabili e giuridici del leasing mobiliare in Europa. (An Overview of Tax, Accounting, and Legal Considerations Involved in Structuring Equipment Leases in Europe—II. With English summary.) *Bancaria*, November 1984, 40(11), pp. 1124–31. [G: EEC]

Valcarcel, Lina J. On the Ability of Accounting Ratios to Predict Failure of Philippine Business Firms. *Philippine Rev. Econ. Bus.*, Sept./Dec. 1984, 21(3/4), pp. 165–99. [G: Philippines]

Vickrey, Don W. An Alternative Interpretation of Unexpected Returns from Accounting Income Numbers. *Quart. Rev. Econ. Bus.*, Spring 1984, 24(1), pp. 6–21.

Walker, Martin. Risk Attitudes, Value-restricted Preferences, and Public Choice over Lotteries and Information Systems. *Accounting Rev.*, April 1984, 59(2), pp. 278–86.

Wallace, Wanda A. The Effects of Delays by Accounting Policy-Setters in Reconciling the Accounting Treatment of Stock Options and Stock Appreciation Rights. *Accounting Rev.*, April 1984, 59(2), pp. 325–41. [G: U.S.]

Waller, William S. and Felix, William L., Jr. The Effects of Incomplete Outcome Feedback on Auditors' Self-perceptions of Judgment Ability. *Accounting Rev.*, October 1984, 59(4), pp. 637–46.

Wescott, Shari H. Accounting Numbers and Socioeconomic Variables as Predictors of Municipal General Obligation Bond Ratings. *J. Acc. Res.*, Spring 1984, 22(1), pp. 412–23.

Whittred, Greg and Zimmer, Ian. Timeliness of Financial Reporting and Financial Distress. *Accounting Rev.*, April 1984, 59(2), pp. 287–95. [G: Australia]

Williamson, Robert W. Evidence on the Selective Reporting of Financial Ratios. *Accounting Rev.*, April 1984, 59(2), pp. 296–99.
[G: U.S.]

Wilson, Earl R. and Howard, Thomas P. The Association between Municipal Market Measures and Selected Financial Reporting Practices: Additional Evidence. *J. Acc. Res.*, Spring 1984, *22*(1), pp. 207–24. [G: U.S.]

Zeff, Stephen A. Some Junctures in the Evolution of the Process of Establishing Accounting Principles in the U.S.A.: 1917–1972. *Accounting Rev.*, July 1984, *59*(3), pp. 447–68. [G: U.S.]

Zeff, Stephen A. and Johansson, Sven-Erik. The Curious Accounting Treatment of the Swedish Government Loan to Uddeholm. *Accounting Rev.*, April 1984, *59*(2), pp. 342–50.
[G: Sweden]

Zeghal, Daniel. Firm Size and the Informational Content of Financial Statements. *J. Finan. Quant. Anal.*, September 1984, *19*(3), pp. 299–310. [G: U.S.]

Zmijewski, Mark E. Methodological Issues Related to the Estimation of Financial Distress Prediction Models. *J. Acc. Res.*, Supplement 1984, *22*, pp. 59–82. [G: U.S.]

600 Industrial Organization; Technological Change; Industry Studies

610 INDUSTRIAL ORGANIZATION AND PUBLIC POLICY

611 Market Structure: Industrial Organization and Corporate Strategy

6110 Market Structure: Industrial Organization and Corporate Strategy

Adams, John. Foreign Economic Policy: Challenges of the 1980s. *J. Econ. Issues*, March 1984, *18*(1), pp. 275–94. [G: U.S.]

Adams, Walter and Brock, James W. Countervailing or Coalescing Power? The Problem of Labor/Management Coalitions. *J. Post Keynesian Econ.*, Winter 1983-84, *6*(2), pp. 180–97.
[G: U.S.]

Albach, Horst. Structural Change in the Economy—A Challenge to Enterprise. In *Engels, W. and Pohl, H., eds.*, 1984, pp. 107–17.
[G: W. Germany]

Alberts, William W. Do Oligopolists Earn "Noncompetitive" Rates of Return? *Amer. Econ. Rev.*, September 1984, *74*(4), pp. 624–32.

Alchian, Armen A. Specificity, Specialization, and Coalitions. *Z. ges. Staatswiss.*, March 1984, *140*(1), pp. 34–49.

Alexander, Gordon J.; Benson, P. George and Kampmeyer, Joan M. Investigating the Valuation Effects of Announcements of Voluntary Corporate Selloffs. *J. Finance*, June 1984, *39*(2), pp. 503–17. [G: U.S.]

Allen, Bruce T. Merger Statistics and Merger Policy. *Rev. Ind. Organ.*, Summer 1984, *1*(2), pp. 78–92. [G: U.S.]

Allen, Robert F. Efficiency, Market Power and Profitability in American Manufacturing: Reply. *Southern Econ. J.*, July 1984, *51*(1), pp. 278–81. [G: U.S.]

Andersen, Arthur T.; Moody, Carlisle E., Jr. and Rasmussen, Jon A. Strategy, Structure and

Performance of Major U.S. Oil Companies: Evidence from Line of Business Data. *Rev. Ind. Organ.*, Winter 1984, *1*(4), pp. 290–306.
[G: U.S.]

Anderson, Erin and Schmittlein, David C. Integration of the Sales Force: An Empirical Examination. *Rand J. Econ.*, Autumn 1984, *15*(3), pp. 385–95. [G: U.S.]

Anderson, Evan E. The Growth and Performance of Franchise Systems: Company versus Franchisee Ownership. *J. Econ. Bus.*, December 1984, *36*(4), pp. 421–31. [G: U.S.]

Anderson, James E. Indentification of Interactive Behavior in Air Service Markets: 1973–76. *J. Ind. Econ.*, June 1984, *32*(4), pp. 489–507.
[G: U.S.]

Aoki, Masahiko. Aspects of the Japanese Firm. In *Aoki, M., ed.*, 1984, pp. 3–43. [G: Japan]

Aoki, Masahiko. Innovative Adaptation through the Quasi-tree Structure: An Emerging Aspect of Japanese Entrepreneurship. *Z. Nationalökon.*, Supplement 1984, pp. 177–98.
[G: Japan]

Aoki, Masahiko. Risk-sharing in the Corporate Group. In *Aoki, M., ed.*, 1984, pp. 259–64.

Arrow, Kenneth J. Vertical Integration and Communication. In *Arrow, K. J., vol. 4*, 1984, *1975*, pp. 185–96.

Artto, Eero. Kansainvälinen kilpailukyky yritys- ja toimialatasolla -III. (International Competitiveness at Enterprise and Industry Level-III. With English summary.) *Liiketaloudellinen Aikak.*, 1984, *33*(2), pp. 181–217. [G: U.S.; Finland; Sweden; Canada; Germany]

Ashton, D. J. and Atkins, D. R. A Partial Theory of Takeover Bids. *J. Finance*, March 1984, *39*(1), pp. 167–83.

Atoncic, Madelyn and Bennett, Paul. Financial Consequences of Mergers. *Fed. Res. Bank New York Quart. Rev.*, Spring 1984, *9*(1), pp. 26–30. [G: U.S.]

Badelt, Christoph. Freiwilligengruppen als Problem der ökonomischen Klubtheorie. (A Club Theoretical View of Volunteer Groups. With English summary.) *Kyklos*, 1984, *37*(1), pp. 59–81.

Bailey, Elizabeth E. and Baumol, William J. Deregulation and the Theory of Contestable Markets. *Yale J. Regul.*, 1984, *1*(2), pp. 111–37.
[G: U.S.]

Baldani, Jeffrey and Masson, Robert T. Economies of Scale, Strategic Advertising and Fully Credible Entry Deterrence. *Rev. Ind. Organ.*, Fall 1984, *1*(3), pp. 190–205.

Baldwin, E. Dean; Thraen, Cameron S. and Larson, Donald W. A Discriminant Analysis of Grain Market Structure in Selected States of the South and Cornbelt. *Southern J. Agr. Econ.*, December 1984, *16*(2), pp. 117–25.
[G: U.S.]

Bank of Italy. The Branch Distribution Plan 1982. In *Banca d'Italia*, 1984, pp. 229–47.
[G: Italy]

Barton, David M. and Sherman, Roger. The Price and Profit Effects of Horizontal Merger:

A Case Study. *J. Ind. Econ.*, December 1984, 33(2), pp. 165–77. [G: U.S.]

Beckmann, Martin J. Hierarchy vs. Partnership. *J. Econ. Behav. Organ.*, June 1984, 5(2), pp. 237–45.

Beesley, Michael E. Government, Nationalised Industries and Creating Enterprise. In *Ramanadham, V. V.*, ed., 1984, pp. 192–208. [G: U.K.]

Beesley, Michael E. and Hamilton, R. T. Small Firms' Seedbed Role and the Concept of Turbulence. *J. Ind. Econ.*, December 1984, 33(2), pp. 217–31. [G: U.K.]

van den Berg, Kent T. Approval of Take-Out Mergers by Minority Shareholders: From Substantive to Procedural Fairness. *Yale Law J.*, May 1984, 93(6), pp. 1113–26.

Bernheim, B. Douglas. Strategic Deterrence of Sequential Entry into an Industry. *Rand J. Econ.*, Spring 1984, 15(1), pp. 1–11.

Biscaini, Anna M.; Carosio, Giovanni and Padoa Schioppa, Tommaso. Borrowing and Lending Rates in an Oligopolistic Banking System. In *Banca d'Italia*, 1984, pp. 63–81. [G: Italy]

le Bon, Claude. Old and "New" Concepts of Competition and Concentration. In *[Kozmetsky, G.]*, 1984, pp. 151–53.

Bond, Eric W. and Samuelson, Larry. Durable Good Monopolies with Rational Expectations and Replacement Sales. *Rand J. Econ.*, Autumn 1984, 15(3), pp. 336–45.

Bossányi, Katalin. The Newly Independent Enterprises in Hungary. *Acta Oecon.*, 1984, 32(3–4), pp. 269–86. [G: Hungary]

Bothwell, James L.; Cooley, Thomas F. and Hall, Thomas E. A New View of the Market Structure–Performance Debate. *J. Ind. Econ.*, June 1984, 32(4), pp. 397–417. [G: U.S.]

Bowen, Harry P. and Pelzman, Joseph. U.S. Export Competitiveness: 1962–77. *Appl. Econ.*, June 1984, 16(3), pp. 461–73. [G: U.S.; Global]

Bowman, Edward H. Risk-Return Tradeoffs for Strategic Management: A Response. *Sloan Manage. Rev.*, Spring 1984, 25(3), pp. 50–51. [G: U.S.]

Boyer, Kenneth D. Is There a Principle for Defining Industries? *Southern Econ. J.*, January 1984, 50(3), pp. 761–70.

Boyes, William J. and Furnish, Dale Beck. A Note on the Use of Incorporation as an Escape from Usury Ceilings. *J. Ind. Econ.*, March 1984, 32(3), pp. 367–72. [G: U.S.]

Boyle, Stanley E. and Piette, Michael J. Neglected Elements in Vertical Integration Analysis: The Case of Retail Price Preticketing. *Rev. Ind. Organ.*, Spring 1984, 1(1), pp. 69–77. [G: U.S.]

Braeutigam, Ronald R. Socially Optimal Pricing with Rivalry and Economies of Scale. *Rand J. Econ.*, Spring 1984, 15(1), pp. 127–34.

Brander, James A. and Eaton, Jonathan. Product Line Rivalry. *Amer. Econ. Rev.*, June 1984, 74(3), pp. 323–34.

Brannman, Lance; Klein, J. Douglass and Weiss, Leonard W. Concentration and Winning Bids

in Auctions. *Antitrust Bull.*, Spring 1984, 29(1), pp. 27–31.

van Breda, Michael F. The Misuse of Accounting Rates of Return: Comment. *Amer. Econ. Rev.*, June 1984, 74(3), pp. 507–08.

Briefs, Henry W. Solidarity within the Firm: Principles, Concepts and Reflections. *Rev. Soc. Econ.*, December 1984, 42(3), pp. 295–317.

Brock, Gerald. Vertical Restraints in Industrial Gases. In *Lafferty, R. N.; Lande, R. H. and Kirkwood, J. B.*, eds., 1984, pp. 386–427. [G: U.S.]

Brock, James W. Industry Structure and Market Power: The Relevance of the "Relevant Market." *Antitrust Bull.*, Fall 1984, 29(3), pp. 535–60. [G: U.S.]

Bronsteen, Peter. A Review of the Revised Merger Guidelines. *Antitrust Bull.*, Winter 1984, 29(4), pp. 613–52. [G: U.S.]

Brown, William, et al. Product and Labour Markets in Wage Determination: Some Australian Evidence. *Brit. J. Ind. Relat.*, July 1984, 22(2), pp. 169–76. [G: Australia]

Brush, Brian C. and Crane, Steven E. Wage Share, Market Power and Unionism: Some Contrary U.S. Evidence. *Manchester Sch. Econ. Soc. Stud.*, December 1984, 52(4), pp. 417–24. [G: U.S.]

Bryant, John. Sunk Cost, "Contestable" Markets, and Long-Term Contracts. *Public Finance Quart.*, July 1984, 12(3), pp. 385–87.

Buckley, Peter J.; Dunning, John H. and Pearce, Robert D. An Analysis of the Growth and Profitability of the World's Largest Firms, 1972 to 1977. *Kyklos*, 1984, 37(1), pp. 3–26. [G: Global]

Bueno, Eduardo and Lamothe, Prosper. Dimension et rentabilité de la grande entreprise espagnole. (With English summary.) *Rev. Econ. Ind.*, 2nd Trimester 1984, (28), pp. 1–8.

Bühner, Rolf. Shareholder Wealth, Synergy, and the VEBA/Gelsenberg Merger. *Z. ges. Staatswiss.*, June 1984, 140(2), pp. 259–75. [G: U.S.; U.K.]

Burstein, M. L. Diffusion of Knowledge-based Products: Applications to Developing Economies. *Econ. Inquiry*, October 1984, 22(4), pp. 612–33. [G: LDCs]

Buxton, A. J.; Davies, Stephen W. and Lyons, Bruce R. Concentration and Advertising in Consumer and Producer Markets. *J. Ind. Econ.*, June 1984, 32(4), pp. 451–64. [G: U.K.]

Calem, Paul S. and Spulber, Daniel F. Multiproduct Two Part Tariffs. *Int. J. Ind. Organ.*, June 1984, 2(2), pp. 105–15.

Campbell, Tim S. The Case for Mergers of Depository Institutions and Insurance Companies. In *Fed. Home Loan Bank San Francisco*, 1984, pp. 175–94. [G: U.S.]

Carter, John R. Concentration Change and the Structure–Performance Debate: An Interpretive Essay. *Managerial Dec. Econ.*, December 1984, 5(4), pp. 204–12.

Casson, Mark. The Theory of Vertical Integration:

A Survey and Synthesis. *J. Econ. Stud.*, 1984, *11*(2), pp. 3–43.

Caswell, Julie A. An Institutional Perspective on Corporate Control and the Network of Interlocking Directorates. *J. Econ. Issues*, June 1984, *18*(2), pp. 619–26.

Caves, Richard E. Economic Analysis and the Quest for Competitive Advantage. *Amer. Econ. Rev.*, May 1984, *74*(2), pp. 127–32.

Caves, Richard E. Scale, Openness, and Productivity in Manufacturing Industries. In *Caves, R. E. and Krause, L. B., eds.*, 1984, pp. 313–47. **[G: Australia; U.S.]**

Caves, Richard E. Vertical Restraints as Integration by Contract: Evidence and Policy Implications. In *Lafferty, R. N.; Lande, R. H. and Kirkwood, J. B., eds.*, 1984, pp. 430–77. **[G: U.S.]**

Caves, Richard E.; Fortunato, Michael and Ghemawat, Pankaj. The Decline of Dominant Firms, 1905–1929. *Quart. J. Econ.*, August 1984, *99*(3), pp. 523–46. **[G: U.S.]**

Centner, Terence J. and Wetzstein, Michael E. Cooperative Antitrust Monopolization and the Theory of Contestable Markets. *Southern J. Agr. Econ.*, July 1984, *16*(1), pp. 129–35.

Chambers, David J. Corporate Plans as Commitments. In *Ramanadham, V. V., ed.*, 1984, pp. 119–37.

Chandler, Alfred D., Jr. The Emergence of Managerial Capitalism. *Bus. Hist. Rev.*, Winter 1984, *58*(4), pp. 473–503. **[G: U.S.; U.K.; Germany; Japan]**

Chappell, Henry W., Jr. and Cheng, David C. Firms' Acquisition Decisions and Tobin's q Ratio. *J. Econ. Bus.*, February 1984, *36*(1), pp. 29–42. **[G: U.S.]**

Chen, Fu-Sen. An Optimal Timing of Withdrawal. *Hong Kong Econ. Pap.*, 1984, (15), pp. 98–104.

Choi, Dosoung and Philippatos, George C. Post-Merger Performance among Homogeneous Firm Samples. *Financial Rev.*, May 1984, *19*(2), pp. 173–94. **[G: U.S.]**

Chung, Kwang S. Forward Integration by a Monopolist: Some Extensions. *Southern Econ. J.*, January 1984, *50*(3), pp. 690–710.

Ciscel, David H. and Evans, Richard D. Returns to Corporate Diversification in the 1970s. *Managerial Dec. Econ.*, June 1984, *5*(2), pp. 67–71. **[G: U.S.]**

Clairmonte, Frederick F. and Cavanagh, John H. Transnational Corporations and Global Markets: Changing Power Relations. In *Ghosh, P. K., ed., no. 11*, 1984, *1982*, pp. 47–91. **[G: LDCs; OECD]**

Clarke, R. Profit Margins and Market Concentration in UK Manufacturing Industry: 1970–6. *Appl. Econ.*, February 1984, *16*(1), pp. 57–71. **[G: U.K.]**

Clarke, Richard N. Scale Economies, Entry, and Welfare. *J. Econ. Bus.*, May 1984, *36*(2), pp. 161–76.

Clarke, Roger; Davies, Stephen W. and Waterson, Michael. The Profitability–Concentration Relation: Market Power or Efficiency? *J. Ind. Econ.*, June 1984, *32*(4), pp. 435–50. **[G: U.K.]**

Coate, Malcolm B. Efficiency, Market Power and Profitability in American Manufacturing: Comment. *Southern Econ. J.*, July 1984, *51*(1), pp. 274–77. **[G: U.S.]**

Cockerill, T. A. J. and Pickering, J. F. Introduction: The Firm in Economics. In *Pickering, J. F. and Cockerill, T. A. J., eds.*, 1984, pp. 1–22.

Collins, William H. and Collins, Carol B. Advertising and Monopoly Power: The Case of the Electric Utility Industry. *Atlantic Econ. J.*, September 1984, *12*(3), pp. 45–53.

Collomb, B. and Ponssard, J. P. Creative Management in Mature Capital Intensive Industries: The Case of Cement. In *[Kozmetsky, G.]*, 1984, pp. 123–43. **[G: OECD; Selected LDCs]**

Conigliani, Claudio and Lanciotti, Giulio. Concentration, Competition and Entry Controls: An Analysis of Banking Markets. In *Banca d'Italia*, 1984, pp. 149–64. **[G: Italy]**

Conigliani, Claudio and Lanciotti, Giulio. Supply Structure and Rates of Interest in the Italian Banking Markets. In *Banca d'Italia*, 1984, pp. 83–108. **[G: Italy]**

Connolly, Robert A. and Hirschey, Mark. R&D, Market Structure, and Profits: A Value-based Approach. *Rev. Econ. Statist.*, November 1984, *66*(4), pp. 682–86. **[G: U.S.]**

Contini, Bruno. Firm Size and the Division of Labor. *Banca Naz. Lavoro Quart. Rev.*, December 1984, (151), pp. 367–80. **[G: Italy]**

Coursey, Don; Isaac, R. Mark and Smith, Vernon L. Natural Monopoly and Contested Markets: Some Experimental Results. *J. Law Econ.*, April 1984, *27*(1), pp. 91–113.

Coursey, Don, et al. Market Contestability in the Presence of Sunk (Entry) Costs. *Rand J. Econ.*, Spring 1984, *15*(1), pp. 69–84.

Curry, Timothy J. and Rose, John T. Diversification and Barriers to Entry: Some Evidence from Banking. *Antitrust Bull.*, Winter 1984, *29*(4), pp. 759–73. **[G: U.S.]**

Dahmén, Erik. Industriens villkor nu och på 1930-talet. (With English summary.) *Nationaløkon. Tidsskr.*, 1984, *122*(3), pp. 333–46. **[G: Nordic Countries]**

Daniel, Coldwell, III. Competition, Imperfect Competition, and Dynamic Market Processes. *Amer. J. Econ. Soc.*, July 1984, *43*(3), pp. 301–12.

Dao, Thi D. Drug Innovation and Price Competition. In *Lindgren, B., ed.*, 1984, pp. 207–16. **[G: U.S.]**

Dao, Thi D. Drug Innovation and Price Competition. *Managerial Dec. Econ.*, June 1984, *5*(2), pp. 80–84. **[G: U.S.]**

Daughety, Andrew F. Regulation and Industrial Organization. *J. Polit. Econ.*, October 1984, *92*(5), pp. 932–53.

Davidson, Carl and Deneckere, Raymond. Horizontal Mergers and Collusive Behavior. *Int. J. Ind. Organ.*, June 1984, *2*(2), pp. 117–32.

Davidson, Paul and Davidson, Greg S. Financial Markets and Williamson's Theory of Governance: Efficiency versus Concentration versus Power. *Quart. Rev. Econ. Bus.*, Winter 1984, 24(4), pp. 50–63.

Davidson, W. H. and McFetridge, Donald G. International Technology Transactions and the Theory of the Firm. *J. Ind. Econ.*, March 1984, 32(3), pp. 253–64. [G: U.S.]

DeAngelo, Harry; DeAngelo, Linda and Rice, Edward M. Going Private: Minority Freezeouts and Stockholder Wealth. *J. Law Econ.*, October 1984, 27(2), pp. 367–401. [G: U.S.]

DiLorenzo, Thomas J. Corporate Management, Property Rights and the X-istence of X-inefficiency: Reply. *Southern Econ. J.*, April 1984, 50(4), pp. 1209–13.

Doi, Noriyuki. Industrial Concentration and Employee Compensation: Some Evidence from Japan. *Rivista Int. Sci. Econ. Com.*, September 1984, 31(9), pp. 844–57. [G: Japan]

Dolan, Robert C. Price Behavior in Tight Oligopoly. *Rev. Ind. Organ.*, Fall 1984, 1(3), pp. 160–88. [G: U.S.]

Dollery, B. E. A South African Test of the Blair Target Return Model. *J. Stud. Econ. Econometrics*, July 1984, (20), pp. 28–39. [G: S. Africa]

Dollery, B. E. Market Structure and Inflation in South Africa: A Test of the Administered Price Hypothesis. *S. Afr. J. Econ.*, December 1984, 52(4), pp. 345–58. [G: S. Africa]

Donsimoni, Marie-Paule; Geroski, Paul A. and Jacquemin, Alexis. Concentration Indices and Market Power: Two Views. *J. Ind. Econ.*, June 1984, 32(4), pp. 419–34.

Dowell, Richard. Asset Salvageability and the Potential for Trade Restraint through Merger. *Rand J. Econ.*, Winter 1984, 15(4), pp. 537–45.

Dudley, David M. Industrial Concentration and Price Stability: An Empirical Analysis. *Amer. Econ.*, Fall 1984, 28(2), pp. 26–35. [G: U.S.]

Duetsch, Larry L. An Examination of Industry Exit Patterns. *Rev. Ind. Organ.*, Spring 1984, 1(1), pp. 60–68. [G: U.S.]

Duetsch, Larry L. Entry and the Extent of Multiplant Operations. *J. Ind. Econ.*, June 1984, 32(4), pp. 477–87. [G: U.S.]

Eads, George C. Discussion of "New Developments on the Cartel Front." *Antitrust Bull.*, Spring 1984, 29(1), pp. 77–83. [G: U.S.]

Eads, George C. R&D and Innovation: Some Empirical Findings: Comment. In *Griliches, Z., ed.*, 1984, pp. 150–53. [G: U.S.]

Eckel, Catherine C. and Goldberg, Michael A. Regulation and Deregulation of the Brewing Industry: The British Columbia Example. *Can. Public Policy*, September 1984, 10(3), pp. 316–27. [G: Canada]

Eliasson, Gunnar. The Micro-Foundations of Industrial Policies. In *Jacquemin, A., ed.*, 1984, pp. 295–326.

Ellman, Michael. Economic Reform in Chinese Industry. In *Ellman, M.*, 1984, 1981, pp. 215–41. [G: China]

Elzinga, Kenneth G. New Developments on the Cartel Front. *Antitrust Bull.*, Spring 1984, 29(1), pp. 3–26. [G: U.S.]

Entov, R. M. Cyclical Factors behind the Movement of Prices. In *Nikitin, S. M., ed.*, 1984, pp. 126–78. [G: U.S.]

Ergas, Henry. Corporate Strategies in Transition. In *Jacquemin, A., ed.*, 1984, pp. 327–42.

Eriksson, Göran. Growth, Entry and Exit of Firms. *Scand. J. Econ.*, 1984, 86(1), pp. 52–67.

Eswaran, Mukesh and Lewis, Tracy R. Ultimate Recovery of an Exhaustible Resource under Different Market Structures. *J. Environ. Econ. Manage.*, March 1984, 11(1), pp. 55–69.

Evans, Robert, Jr. Pay Differentials: The Case of Japan. *Mon. Lab. Rev.*, October 1984, 107(10), pp. 24–29. [G: Japan; U.S.]

Farber, Stephen C. Cyclical Price Flexibility: A Test of Administered Pricing. *J. Ind. Econ.*, June 1984, 32(4), pp. 465–76. [G: U.S.]

Feinberg, Robert M. Conglomerate Mergers and Subsequent Industry Effects. *Rev. Ind. Organ.*, Summer 1984, 1(2), pp. 128–37. [G: U.S.]

Felgran, Steven D. Shared ATM Networks: Market Structure and Public Policy. *New Eng. Econ. Rev.*, January–February 1984, pp. 23–38. [G: U.S.]

Fershtman, Chaim. Goodwill and Market Shares in Oligopoly. *Economica*, August 1984, 51(203), pp. 271–81.

Field, Alexander James. Microeconomics, Norms, and Rationality. *Econ. Develop. Cult. Change*, July 1984, 32(4), pp. 683–711.

Filer, John E., et al. Impact of Regulation on Vertical Integration in the Electric Industry. *Rev. Ind. Organ.*, Fall 1984, 1(3), pp. 216–31. [G: U.S.]

Finsinger, Jörg. Zur Stabilität von Submissionskartellen. (Collusive Bidding for Contracts. With English summary.) *Jahr. Nationalökon. Statist.*, November 1984, 199(6), pp. 575–85. [G: W. Germany]

Fisher, Franklin M. The Misuse of Accounting Rates of Return: Reply. *Amer. Econ. Rev.*, June 1984, 74(3), pp. 509–17.

FitzRoy, Felix R. and Mueller, Dennis C. Cooperation and Conflict in Contractual Organizations. *Quart. Rev. Econ. Bus.*, Winter 1984, 24(4), pp. 24–49.

Fleischer, Arthur, Jr. and Raymond, Elizabeth A. Critical Developments in Acquisitions. In *Purden, C., ed.*, 1984, pp. 331–43. [G: U.S.]

Formby, John P. and Smith, W. James. Collusion, Entry, and Market Shares. *Rev. Ind. Organ.*, Spring 1984, 1(1), pp. 15–25.

Fourie, F. C. v. N. Industriële Konsentrasie en Inflasie in Suid-Afrika 1972–1979. *S. Afr. J. Econ.*, December 1984, 52(4), pp. 359–76. [G: S. Africa]

Frantz, Roger S. Corporate Management, Property Rights and the X-istence of X-inefficiency: Comment. *Southern Econ. J.*, April 1984, 50(4), pp. 1204–08.

Furubotn, Eirik G. and Richter, Rudolf. The

New Institutional Economics: Symposium June 6–10, 1983, Mettlach/Saar. *Z. ges. Staatswiss.*, March 1984, *140*(1), pp. 1–6.

Gable, Wayne E. Horizontal Restraints of Competition. *Eastern Econ. J.*, October-December 1984, *10*(4), pp. 421–31.

Gal-Or, Esther. Price Dispersion with Uncertain Demand. *Int. Econ. Rev.*, June 1984, *25*(2), pp. 441–57.

Galbraith, James K. Galbraith and the Theory of the Corporation. *J. Post Keynesian Econ.*, Fall 1984, *7*(1), pp. 43–60.

Gallini, Nancy T. Deterrence by Market Sharing: A Strategic Incentive for Licensing. *Amer. Econ. Rev.*, December 1984, *74*(5), pp. 931–41.

Gegax, Douglas and Tschirhart, John T. An Analysis of Interfirm Cooperation: Theory and Evidence from Electric Power Pools. *Southern Econ. J.*, April 1984, *50*(4), pp. 1077–97.
[G: U.S.]

Geroski, Paul A. On the Relationship between Aggregate Merger Activity and the Stock Market. *Europ. Econ. Rev.*, July 1984, *25*(2), pp. 223–33.
[G: U.S.]

Geroski, Paul A. The Incidence of Entry in Three Oligopoly Models. *Economica*, August 1984, *51*(203), pp. 283–93.

Geroski, Paul A. and Jacquemin, Alexis. Dominant Firms and Their Alleged Decline. *Int. J. Ind. Organ.*, March 1984, *2*(1), pp. 1–27.

Geroski, Paul A. and Jacquemin, Alexis. Large Firms in the European Corporate Economy and Industrial Policy in the 1980s. In *Jacquemin, A., ed.*, 1984, pp. 343–67.
[G: EEC]

Ghemawat, Pankaj. Capacity Expansion in the Titanium Dioxide Industry. *J. Ind. Econ.*, December 1984, *33*(2), pp. 145–63.
[G: U.S.]

Giannini, Mirella. Strategie aziendali e comportamento dei lavoratori nelle organizzazioni industriali: il caso Italsider–Taranto. (Managerial Strategies and Workers' Behaviour in Industrial Organization: The Case of Italsider–Taranto. With English summary.) *Econ. Lavoro*, Oct.-Dec. 1984, *18*(4), pp. 47–68.
[G: Italy]

Gibbons, Joel C. The Optimal Durability of Fixed Capital When Demand Is Uncertain. *J. Bus.*, July 1984, *57*(3), pp. 389–403.
[G: U.S.]

Gilbert, Richard J. and Newbery, David M. G. Preemptive Patenting and the Persistence of Monopoly: Reply. *Amer. Econ. Rev.*, March 1984, *74*(1), pp. 251–53.

Gilbert, Richard J. and Newbery, David M. G. Uncertain Innovation and the Persistence of Monopoly: Comment. *Amer. Econ. Rev.*, March 1984, *74*(1), pp. 238–42.

Giroux, Gary A. and Wiggins, Casper E. An Events Approach to Corporate Bankruptcy. *J. Bank Res.*, Autumn 1984, *15*(3), pp. 179–87.
[G: U.S.]

Gisser, Micha. Price Leadership and Dynamic Aspects of Oligopoly in U.S. Manufacturing. *J. Polit. Econ.*, December 1984, *92*(6), pp. 1035–48.
[G: U.S.]

Görgens, Egon. Nachfragemacht im Lebensmittelhandel als Instrument der Strukturanpas-

sung. (With English Summary.) In *Eucken, W. and Böhm, F., eds.*, 1984, pp. 231–45.
[G: W. Germany]

Gort, Michael and Wall, Richard A. The Effect of Technical Change on Market Structure. *Econ. Inquiry*, October 1984, *22*(4), pp. 668–75.
[G: U.S.]

Green, Edward J. and Porter, Robert H. Noncooperative Collusion under Imperfect Price Information. *Econometrica*, January 1984, *52*(1), pp. 87–100.

Green, Milford B. and Cromley, Robert G. Merger and Acquisition Fields for Large United States Cities, 1955–1970. *Reg. Stud.*, August 1984, *18*(4), pp. 291–301.
[G: U.S.]

Greening, Timothy. Analysis of the Impact of the Florsheim Shoe Case. In *Lafferty, R. N.; Lande, R. H. and Kirkwood, J. B., eds.*, 1984, pp. 92–199.
[G: U.S.]

Greer, Douglas F. Size, Efficiency, and *Fortune* Magazine. *Rev. Ind. Organ.*, Spring 1984, *1*(1), pp. 53–59.

Grether, David M. and Plott, Charles R. The Effects of Market Practices in Oligopolistic Markets: An Experimental Examination of the Ethyl Case. *Econ. Inquiry*, October 1984, *22*(4), pp. 479–507.
[G: U.S.]

Griliches, Zvi. R&D and Innovation: Some Empirical Findings: Comment. In *Griliches, Z., ed.*, 1984, pp. 148–49.
[G: U.S.]

Grimm, Curtis M. An Evaluation of Economic Issues in the UP–MP–WP Railroad Merger. *Logist. Transp. Rev.*, September 1984, *20*(3), pp. 239–59.
[G: U.S.]

Gröner, Helmut. Marktsystem, Unternehmenskontrollen und Insolvenzen: Volkswirtschaftliche Überlegungen zur Reform des Insolvenzrechts. (With English Summary.) In *Eucken, W. and Böhm, F., eds.*, 1984, pp. 247–67.
[G: W. Germany]

Grubel, Herbert G. Free Economic Zones: Good or Bad? *Aussenwirtschaft*, May 1984, *39*(1/2), pp. 43–56.
[G: U.S.; U.K.]

Guth, William D. Productivity and Corporate Strategy. In *Brief, A. P., ed.*, 1984, pp. 252–67.

Hadley, Eleanor. Counterpoint on Business Groupings and Government–Industry Relations in Automobiles. In *Aoki, M., ed.*, 1984, pp. 319–27.
[G: Japan]

Hahn, Robert W. Market Power and Transferable Property Rights. *Quart. J. Econ.*, November 1984, *99*(4), pp. 753–65.

Haining, Robert P. Testing a Spatial Interacting-Markets Hypothesis. *Rev. Econ. Statist.*, November 1984, *66*(4), pp. 576–83.
[G: U.K.]

Hall, William P. The Learning Curve, Demand Growth, and Market Concentration. *Int. J. Ind. Organ.*, June 1984, *2*(2), pp. 147–57.

Hammer, Richard M. Canadian Acquisition of a U.S. Business: A U.S. Perspective. In *Purden, C., ed.*, 1984, pp. 274–304.
[G: Canada; U.S.]

Hammond, Peter J. Must Monopoly Power Accompany Innovation? In *Seidl, C., ed.*, 1984, pp. 45–56.

Handy, John and Swinton, David H. The Determinants of the Rate of Growth of Black-Owned Businesses: A Preliminary Analysis. *Rev. Black Polit. Econ.*, Spring 1984, *12*(4), pp. 85–110.
[G: U.S.]

Hannah, Leslie. Entrepreneurs and the Social Sciences. *Economica*, August 1984, *51*(203), pp. 219–34.
[G: U.K.]

Hannan, Timothy H. and McDowell, John M. Market Concentration and the Diffusion of New Technology in the Banking Industry. *Rev. Econ. Statist.*, November 1984, *66*(4), pp. 686–91.
[G: U.S.]

Hanweck, Gerald A. and Rhoades, Stephen A. Dominant Firms, "Deep Pockets," and Local Market Competition in Banking. *J. Econ. Bus.*, December 1984, *36*(4), pp. 391–402.
[G: U.S.]

Harris, Frederick H. deB. Growth Expectations, Excess Value, and the Risk-Adjusted Return to Market Power. *Southern Econ. J.*, July 1984, *51*(1), pp. 166–79.
[G: U.S.]

Hartley, Keith. Policy towards Contracting-Out: The Lessons of Experience. *Fisc. Stud.*, February 1984, *5*(1), pp. 98–105.
[G: U.K.]

Harvel, Howard P. Vertical Restraints in the Hearing Aids Industry. In *Lafferty, R. N.; Lande, R. H. and Kirkwood, J. B., eds.*, 1984, pp. 272–384.
[G: U.S.]

Hause, John C. and Du Rietz, Gunnar. Entry, Industry Growth, and the Microdynamics of Industry Supply. *J. Polit. Econ.*, August 1984, *92*(4), pp. 733–57.
[G: Sweden]

Hax, Herbert. The Economics of Governance: Framework and Implications: Comment. *Z. ges. Staatswiss.*, March 1984, *140*(1), pp. 227–28.

Hazledine, Tim. The Possibility of Price Umbrellas in Canadian Manufacturing Industries. *Int. J. Ind. Organ.*, September 1984, *2*(3), pp. 251–62.
[G: Canada]

van Heemst, Jan J. P. Sub-Contracting between Small-Scale Enterprises in Developing Countries: A Note. *J. Ind. Econ.*, March 1984, *32*(3), pp. 373–76.
[G: LDCs]

Hellerstein, Jerome R. Defining a Unitary Business: An Economist's View: Comments. In *McLure, C. E., Jr., ed.*, 1984, pp. 127–31.
[G: U.S.]

Helpman, Elhanan. Increasing Returns, Imperfect Markets, and Trade Theory. In *Jones, R. W. and Kenen, P., eds.*, 1984, pp. 325–65.

Hergert, Michael. Market Share and Profitability: Is Bigger Really Better? *Bus. Econ.*, October 1984, *19*(5), pp. 45–48.

Hilke, John C. Excess Capacity and Entry: Some Empirical Evidence. *J. Ind. Econ.*, December 1984, *33*(2), pp. 233–40.
[G: U.S.]

Hill, C. W. L. Organisational Structure, the Development of the Firm and Business Behaviour. In *Pickering, J. F. and Cockerill, T. A. J., eds.*, 1984, pp. 52–71.

Hill, Lewis E. A Comment on Solidarity within the Firm [Solidarity within the Firm: Principles, Concepts and Reflections] [Industrial Justice in a Practical Sense]. *Rev. Soc. Econ.*, December 1984, *42*(3), pp. 328–29.

Hindley, Brian. Economics and Small Enterprises. In *Levicki, C., ed.*, 1984, pp. 42–54.
[G: OECD]

Hinterhuber, Giovanni. L'analisi dei raggruppamenti strategici di imprese. (Analysis of Strategic Company Groupings. With English summary.) *L'Impresa*, 1984, *26*(5), pp. 13–21.

Hollander, Abraham. Market Structure and Performance in Intellectual Property: The Case of Copyright Collectives. *Int. J. Ind. Organ.*, September 1984, *2*(3), pp. 199–216.

Horowitz, Ira. Market Growth, Demand Uncertainty, and Potential Entry. *Quart. Rev. Econ. Bus.*, Summer 1984, *24*(2), pp. 33–40.

Horowitz, Ira. On the Use and Nonuse of Entry Deterrents. *J. Econ. Bus.*, December 1984, *36*(4), pp. 371–89.

Horowitz, Ira. The Misuse of Accounting Rates of Return: Comment. *Amer. Econ. Rev.*, June 1984, *74*(3), pp. 492–93.

Hughes, Alan and Kumar, Manmohan Singh. Recent Trends in Aggregate Concentration in the United Kingdom Economy: Revised Estimates. *Cambridge J. Econ.*, December 1984, *8*(4), pp. 401–02.

Hughes, Alan and Kumar, Manmohan Singh. Recent Trends in Aggregate Concentration in the United Kingdom Economy. *Cambridge J. Econ.*, September 1984, *8*(3), pp. 235–50.
[G: U.K.]

Imai, Ken-ichi and Itami, Hiroyuki. Interpenetration of Organization and Market: Japan's Firm and Market in Comparison with the U.S. *Int. J. Ind. Organ.*, December 1984, *2*(4), pp. 285–310.
[G: Japan; U.S.]

Isaac, R. Mark; Ramey, Valerie and Williams, Arlington W. The Effects of Market Organization on Conspiracies in Restraint of Trade. *J. Econ. Behav. Organ.*, June 1984, *5*(2), pp. 191–222.

Iwai, Katsuhito. Schumpeterian Dynamics, Part II: Technological Progress, Firm Growth and 'Economic Selection.' *J. Econ. Behav. Organ.*, September–December 1984, *5*(3–4), pp. 321–51.

Jehle, Geoffrey A. Individual Welfare and the Demand for Financial Instruments. *Southern Econ. J.*, July 1984, *51*(1), pp. 116–34.
[G: U.S.]

Jorgensen, Jan J.; Hafsi, Taieb and Kiggundu, Moses N. Market Imperfections and Organizational Structure: The LDC Perspective. In *Kindra, G. S., ed.*, 1984, pp. 172–87.
[G: LDCs]

Juhász, Margit. Enterprise Incomes in Hungary, Their Generation, Distribution and Differentiation. *Acta Oecon.*, 1984, *33*(1–2), pp. 166–80.
[G: Hungary]

Kardasz, Stanley W. and Stollery, Kenneth R. Simultaneous Equation Models of Profitability, Advertising and Concentration for Canadian Manufacturing Industries. *Quart. J. Bus. Econ.*, Winter 1984, *23*(1), pp. 51–64.
[G: Canada]

Katrak, Homi. Pricing Policies of Multinational Enterprises: Host Country Regulation and Welfare. *Int. J. Ind. Organ.*, December 1984, *2*(4), pp. 327–40.

Kaufer, Erich. On the Economics of Conventions and Institutions: An Exploratory Essay: Comment. *Z. ges. Staatswiss.*, March 1984, *140*(1), pp. 87–89.

Kay, Neil M. Innovation, Markets and Hierarchies. *J. Econ. Stud.*, 1984, *11*(2), pp. 44–60.

Keeley, Michael C. The Economics of Firm Size: Implications from Labor-Market Studies. *Fed. Res. Bank San Francisco Econ. Rev.*, Winter 1984, (1), pp. 5–21. **[G: U.S.]**

Keim, Gerald D.; Zeithaml, Carl P. and Baysinger, Barry D. New Directions for Corporate Political Strategy. *Sloan Manage. Rev.*, Spring 1984, *25*(3), pp. 53–62. **[G: U.S.]**

Ketcham, Jon; Smith, Vernon L. and Williams, Arlington W. A Comparison of Posted-Offer and Double-Auction Pricing Institutions. *Rev. Econ. Stud.*, October 1984, *51*(4), pp. 595–614.

Keyes, Lucile S. Revised Guidelines—1984. *Rev. Ind. Organ.*, Summer 1984, *1*(2), pp. 154–58. **[G: U.S.]**

Keyes, Lucile S. The New Merger Guidelines of the Department of Justice. *Rev. Ind. Organ.*, Spring 1984, *1*(1), pp. 26–52. **[G: U.S.]**

Kim, Jae Won. CES Production Functions in Manufacturing and Problems of Industrialization in LDCs: Evidence from Korea. *Econ. Develop. Cult. Change*, October 1984, *33*(1), pp. 143–65.

Klausinger, Hansjörg. Fristigkeitsaspekte in der Theorie der Stabilisierungspolitik. (Maturity Aspects in the Theory of Stabilization Policy. With English summary.) *Kredit Kapital*, 1984, *17*(2), pp. 180–98.

Kochan, Thomas A.; McKersie, Robert B. and Cappelli, Peter. Strategic Choice and Industrial Relations Theory. *Ind. Relat.*, Winter 1984, *23*(1), pp. 16–39. **[G: U.S.]**

Koo, Anthony Y. C. and Martin, Stephen. Market Structure and U.S. Trade Flows. *Int. J. Ind. Organ.*, September 1984, *2*(3), pp. 173–97. **[G: U.S.]**

Kooiman, P. Smoothing the Aggregate Fix-Price Model and the Use of Business Survey Data. *Econ. J.*, December 1984, *94*(376), pp. 899–913. **[G: Netherlands]**

Koutsoyiannis, Anna. Goals of Oligopolistic Firms: An Empirical Test of Competing Hypotheses. *Southern Econ. J.*, October 1984, *51*(2), pp. 540–67. **[G: U.S.]**

Krouse, Clement G. Brand Name as a Barrier to Entry: The ReaLemon Case. *Southern Econ. J.*, October 1984, *51*(2), pp. 495–502. **[G: U.S.]**

Kudrle, Robert Thomas. Excise Tax Incidence in Limit Price Oligopoly. *Public Finance*, 1984, *39*(3), pp. 321–46.

Kumar, Nagesh. Public Policy, Marris Model and Corporate Growth in India. *Indian Econ. J.*, Oct.–Dec. 1984, *32*(2), pp. 74–83. **[G: India]**

Kwoka, John E., Jr. Market Power and Market

Change in the U.S. Automobile Industry. *J. Ind. Econ.*, June 1984, *32*(4), pp. 509–22. **[G: U.S.]**

Kwoka, John E., Jr. The Effect of Market Share Distribution on Industry Performance: Reply. *Rev. Econ. Statist.*, May 1984, *66*(2), pp. 358–61. **[G: U.S.]**

LaFrance, Jeffrey T.; Schmitz, Andrew and Zilberman, David. Small Leading Firms. *Econ. Rec.*, June 1984, *60*(169), pp. 160–64.

Lafferty, Ronald N.; Lande, Robert H. and Kirkwood, John B. Impact Evaluations of Federal Trade Commission Vertical Restraints Cases: Introduction and Overview. In *Lafferty, R. N.; Lande, R. H. and Kirkwood, J. B.*, eds., 1984, pp. 1–45. **[G: U.S.]**

Lahti, Arto. Yrityksen strategia ja menestyksellisyys. (Strategy and Performance of a Firm. With English summary.) *Liiketaloudellinen Aikak.*, 1984, *33*(2), pp. 228–33. **[G: Finland]**

Laky, Teréz. Small Enterprises in Hungary—Myth and Reality. *Acta Oecon.*, 1984, *32*(1–2), pp. 39–63. **[G: Hungary]**

Lam, Chun H. and Boudreaux, Kenneth J. Conglomerate Merger, Wealth Redistribution and Debt: A Note. *J. Finance*, March 1984, *39*(1), pp. 275–81.

Landes, William M. Harm to Competition: Cartels, Mergers, and Joint Ventures. In *Fox, E. M. and Halverson, J. T.*, eds., 1984, pp. 73–82. **[G: U.S.]**

Lapsley, Irvine. Reconstructing British Rail: In Search of a Profitable Railway. *Managerial Dec. Econ.*, March 1984, *5*(1), pp. 32–48. **[G: U.K.]**

Laumas, Prem S. and Williams, Martin. The Demand for Working Capital. *Appl. Econ.*, December 1984, *16*(6), pp. 791–98. **[G: India]**

Lawriwsky, Michael L. A Critical View of Studies Examining the Performance Effects of the Separation of Ownership from Control. *Rivista Int. Sci. Econ. Com.*, April 1984, *31*(4), pp. 312–28. **[G: Australia]**

Lawriwsky, Michael L. Some Tests of the Influence of Control Type on the Market for Corporate Control in Australia. *J. Ind. Econ.*, March 1984, *32*(3), pp. 277–91. **[G: Australia]**

Lease, Ronald C.; McConnell, John J. and Mikkelson, Wayne H. The Market Value of Differential Voting Rights in Closely Held Corporations. *J. Bus.*, October 1984, *57*(4), pp. 443–67. **[G: U.S.]**

Lecraw, Donald J. Diversification Strategy and Performance. *J. Ind. Econ.*, December 1984, *33*(2), pp. 179–98. **[G: Canada]**

Lederer, Emil. Social Control vs. Economic Law: An Old Dogma and a New Situation. *Soc. Res.*, Spring & Summer 1984, *51*(1&2), pp. 91–110.

Lee, Li Way. Franchising and Interbrand Competition. *Southern Econ. J.*, July 1984, *51*(1), pp. 219–34. **[G: U.S.]**

Lee, Lung-Fei and Porter, Robert H. Switching Regression Models with Imperfect Sample Separation Information—With an Application on Cartel Stability. *Econometrica*, March 1984, 52(2), pp. 391–418. [G: U.S.]

Leibenstein, Harvey. On the Economics of Conventions and Institutions: An Exploratory Essay *Z. ges. Staatswiss.*, March 1984, 140(1), pp. 74–86.

Leroux, François and Zaccour, Georges. Structures de marché et intensité de la publicité. (Market Structures and Intensity of Publicity. With English summary.) *L'Actual. Econ.*, September 1984, 60(3), pp. 341–54. [G: Canada]

Lesourne, Jacques. The Changing Context of Industrial Policy: External and Internal Developments. In *Jacquemin, A., ed.*, 1984, pp. 13–38. [G: OECD]

Levin, Richard C. and Reiss, Peter C. Tests of a Schumpeterian Model of R&D and Market Structure. In *Griliches, Z., ed.*, 1984, pp. 175–204. [G: U.S.]

Levin, Sharon G. Mergers and Corporate Control. *Rivista Int. Sci. Econ. Com.*, October–November 1984, 31(10–11), pp. 1073–90. [G: U.S.]

Levy, David T. Testing Stigler's Interpretation of "The Division of Labor Is Limited by the Extent of the Market." *J. Ind. Econ.*, March 1984, 32(3), pp. 377–89. [G: U.S.]

Levy, David T. Variation in the Concentration–Profit Relationship across Industries. *Southern Econ. J.*, July 1984, 51(1), pp. 267–73. [G: U.S.]

Libecap, Gary D. and Wiggins, Steven N. Contractual Responses to the Common Pool: Prorationing of Crude Oil Production. *Amer. Econ. Rev.*, March 1984, 74(1), pp. 87–98. [G: U.S.]

Lieberman, Marvin B. The Learning Curve and Pricing in the Chemical Processing Industries. *Rand J. Econ.*, Summer 1984, 15(2), pp. 213–28. [G: U.S.]

Lindsay, Robert F. Purchase and Sale of a Canadian Business by a Nonresident of Canada. In *Purden, C., ed.*, 1984, pp. 305–30. [G: Canada; U.S.]

Link, Albert N. Firm versus Industry Variability in R&D Intensity: Comment. In *Griliches, Z., ed.*, 1984, pp. 245–48. [G: U.S.]

Link, Albert N. and Lunn, John. Concentration and the Returns to R&D. *Rev. Ind. Organ.*, Fall 1984, 1(3), pp. 232–39. [G: U.S.]

Lipiński, Jan and Mujżel, Jan. Price Formation, Market Structure, Economic System of Enterprises. In *Bohnet, A., ed.*, 1984, pp. 153–81. [G: Poland]

Littlechild, Stephen C. German "Ordnungspolitik" as Institutional Choice. *Z. ges. Staatswiss.*, March 1984, 140(1), pp. 71–73. [G: Germany; U.S.; U.K.]

Litvak, Isaiah A. and Maule, Christopher J. Assessing Industry Concentration: The Case of Aluminum. *J. Int. Bus. Stud.*, Spring/Summer 1984, 15(1), pp. 97–104.

Loescher, Samuel M. Bureaucratic Measurement, Shuttling Stock Shares, and Shortened Time Horizons: Implications for Economic Growth. *Quart. Rev. Econ. Bus.*, Winter 1984, 24(4), pp. 8–23.

Lofthouse, Stephen. Issues Raised by the Acquisition of F. W. Woolworth by a Consortium of Financial Institutions. *Rivista Int. Sci. Econ. Com.*, June 1984, 31(6), pp. 545–57. [G: U.K.]

Long, William F. and Ravenscraft, David J. The Misuse of Accounting Rates of Return: Comment. *Amer. Econ. Rev.*, June 1984, 74(3), pp. 494–500.

Lundborg, Per. The Nexus between Income Distribution, Trade Policy, and Monopoly Power: An Assessment of the Tin Market. *J. Policy Modeling*, February 1984, 6(1), pp. 69–79. [G: Malaysia]

Lunn, John. Trade-adjusted Concentration Ratios. *Antitrust Bull.*, Fall 1984, 29(3), pp. 523–34. [G: U.S.]

Lynk, William J. Interpreting Rising Concentration: The Case of Beer. *J. Bus.*, Part 1, January 1984, 57(1), pp. 43–55. [G: U.S.]

MacDonald, James M. Diversification, Market Growth, and Concentration in U.S. Manufacturing. *Southern Econ. J.*, April 1984, 50(4), pp. 1098–111. [G: U.S.]

Mahajan, Arvind. Profitability Measures as Indicators of Post-Merger Efficiency Revisited. *J. Ind. Econ.*, September 1984, 33(1), pp. 135–38.

Malécot, Jean-François. Risque de faillite, coûts de faillite et structure du capital: réexamen et nouvelles propositions. (Capital Structure and Risk with Cost of Bankruptcy: Critical Examination and New Propositions. With English summary.) *Écon. Soc.*, November–December 1984, 18(11–12), pp. 229–64.

Mangum, Stephen L. Response to Schiller on Small Business Training [Small Business Training: A Negative-Sum Game]. *Challenge*, January/February 1984, 26(6), pp. 64. [G: U.S.]

Mann, H. Michael. Discussion of "Credible Commitments." *Antitrust Bull.*, Spring 1984, 29(1), pp. 85–88. [G: U.S.]

Mansfield, Edwin. R&D and Innovation: Some Empirical Findings. In *Griliches, Z., ed.*, 1984, pp. 127–48. [G: U.S.]

Marcus, Alan J. and Shaked, Israel. The Relationship between Accounting Measures and Prospective Probabilities of Insolvency: An Application to the Banking Industry. *Financial Rev.*, March 1984, 19(1), pp. 67–83. [G: U.S.]

Mardones, José Luis; Silva, Enrique and Martínez, Cristián. Las industrias del cobre y del aluminio: una revisión de cambios estructurales. (With English summary.) *Cuadernos Econ.*, December 1984, 21(64), pp. 329–45. [G: Global]

Marlow, Michael L.; Link, John P. and Trost, Robert P. Market Structure and Rivalry: New Evidence with a Non-linear Model. *Rev. Econ. Statist.*, November 1984, 66(4), pp. 678–82. [G: U.S.]

Marris, Robin. A New Model of the Process of Business Concentration. In *Levicki, C., ed.*, 1984, pp. 55–64.

Marsh, Terry A. and Swanson, Douglas S. Risk-Return Tradeoffs for Strategic Management. *Sloan Manage. Rev.*, Spring 1984, *25*(3), pp. 35–49. [G: U.S.]

Marshall, William J.; Yawitz, Jess B. and Greenberg, Edward. Incentives for Diversification and the Structure of the Conglomerate Firm. *Southern Econ. J.*, July 1984, *51*(1), pp. 1–23. [G: U.S.]

Martin, James R. Market Structure and Corporate Accounting Strategy. *Amer. Econ.*, Spring 1984, *28*(1), pp. 34–43. [G: U.S.]

Martin, Linda J. and Henderson, Glenn V., Jr. Industry Influence on Financial Structure: A Matter of Interpretation. *Rev. Bus. Econ. Res.*, Spring 1984, *19*(2), pp. 57–67. [G: U.S.]

Martin, Stephen. A Bainsian Interpretation of Von Weisäcker's Model of Scale Economies [A Welfare Analysis of Barriers to Entry]. *Southern Econ. J.*, April 1984, *50*(4), pp. 1192–95.

Martin, Stephen. Comment on the Specification of Structure–Performance Relationships. *Europ. Econ. Rev.*, March 1984, *24*(2), pp. 197–201.

Martin, Stephen. Structure and Performance of U.S. Wholesale Trade. *Managerial Dec. Econ.*, September 1984, *5*(3), pp. 160–67. [G: U.S.]

Martin, Stephen. Testing the Interaction between Concentration and Barriers to Entry. *Rev. Ind. Organ.*, Summer 1984, *1*(2), pp. 114–26. [G: U.S.]

Martin, Stephen. The Misuse of Accounting Rates of Return: Comment. *Amer. Econ. Rev.*, June 1984, *74*(3), pp. 501–06.

Marvel, Howard P. The Locus of Collusion in U.S. Manufacturing. *Quart. Rev. Econ. Bus.*, Winter 1984, *24*(4), pp. 82–99. [G: U.S.]

Marvel, Howard P. and McCafferty, Stephen. Resale Price Maintenance and Quality Certification. *Rand J. Econ.*, Autumn 1984, *15*(3), pp. 346–59. [G: U.S.]

Masson, Robert T. and Shaanan, Joseph. Social Costs of Oligopoly and the Value of Competition. *Econ. J.*, September 1984, *94*(375), pp. 520–35.

Mathewson, G. F. and Winter, R. A. An Economic Theory of Vertical Restraints. *Rand J. Econ.*, Spring 1984, *15*(1), pp. 27–38.

Mayo, John W. The Technological Determinants of the U.S. Energy Industry Structure. *Rev. Econ. Statist.*, February 1984, *66*(1), pp. 51–58. [G: U.S.]

McEachern, William A. and Romeo, Anthony A. Vertical Restraints in the Audio Components Industry: An Economic Analysis of FTC Intervention. **In** *Lafferty, R. N.; Lande, R. H. and Kirkwood, J. B., eds.*, 1984, pp. 202–57. [G: U.S.]

McEachern, William A. and Romeo, Anthony A. Vertical Restraints in the Audio Component Industry: Possibilities for Future Empirical Work. **In** *Lafferty, R. N.; Lande, R. H. and Kirkwood, J. B., eds.*, 1984, pp. 258–69. [G: U.S.]

McLure, Charles E., Jr. Defining a Unitary Business: An Economist's View. **In** *McLure, C. E., Jr., ed.*, 1984, pp. 89–124. [G: U.S.]

McNulty, Paul J. On the Nature and Theory of Economic Organization: The Role of the Firm Reconsidered. *Hist. Polit. Econ.*, Summer 1984, *16*(2), pp. 233–53.

Mead, Donald C. Of Contracts and Subcontracts: Small Firms in Vertically Dis-integrated Production/Distribution Systems in LDCs. *World Devel.*, November–December 1984, *12*(11–12), pp. 1095–1106. [G: LDCs]

Mead, Walter J.; Moseidjord, Asbjorn and Sorensen, Philip E. Competitive Bidding under Asymmetrical Information: Behavior and Performance in Gulf of Mexico Drainage Lease Sales, 1959–1969. *Rev. Econ. Statist.*, August 1984, *66*(3), pp. 505–08. [G: U.S.]

Meeks, G. and Meeks, J. G. Profitability Measures as Indicators of Post-Merger Efficiency: Reply. *J. Ind. Econ.*, September 1984, *33*(1), pp. 139–42.

Mensah, Yaw M. An Examination of the Stationarity of Multivariate Bankruptcy Prediction Models: A Methodological Study. *J. Acc. Res.*, Spring 1984, *22*(1), pp. 380–95.

Meric, Gulser and Meric, Ilhan. Size, Operating Leverage, and Financial Structure. *Rivista Int. Sci. Econ. Com.*, October–November 1984, *31*(10–11), pp. 1052–57. [G: Turkey]

Metzer, Jacob. Railroads and the Efficiency of Internal Markets: Some Conceptual and Practical Considerations. *Econ. Develop. Cult. Change*, October 1984, *33*(1), pp. 61–70. [G: U.S.S.R.]

Miller, Edward M. Extent of Economies of Scale: An Update. *Southern Econ. J.*, October 1984, *51*(2), pp. 582–87.

Miller, Jeffrey B. The Big Nail and Other Stories: Product Quality Control in the Soviet Union. *ACES Bull.*, Spring 1984, *26*(1), pp. 43–57. [G: U.S.S.R.]

Miller, Richard A. Notes on the 1984 Merger Guidelines: Clarification of the Policy or Repeal of the Celler–Kefauver Act? *Antitrust Bull.*, Winter 1984, *29*(4), pp. 653–62. [G: U.S.]

Millward, Robert. The Early Stages of European Industrialization: Economic Organization under Serfdom. *Exploration Econ. Hist.*, October 1984, *21*(4), pp. 406–28. [G: U.S.S.R.; E. Europe]

Mirucki, Jean. Vérification des conditions d'efficacité dans les décisions de production à partir de l'hypothèse Averch-Johnson: étude de cas. (With English summary.) *Rev. Econ. Ind.*, 4th Trimester 1984, (30), pp. 60–76. [G: Canada]

Modani, Naval K.; Lloyd, William P. and Hand, John H. Behavior of Risk Proxies and Merger Activity. *Rev. Bus. Econ. Res.*, Spring 1984, *19*(2), pp. 81–89. [G: U.S.]

Mongar, Tom. Monopoly Pricing and Stagnation. *Econ. Forum*, Summer 1984, *15*(1), pp. 63–87. [G: U.S.]

Monke, Eric and Petzel, Todd. Market Integration: An Application to International Trade in

Cotton. *Amer. J. Agr. Econ.*, November 1984, *66*(4), pp. 481–87.   **[G: Selected Countries]**

Moorthy, K. Sridhar. Market Segmentation, Self-Selection, and Product Line Design. *Marketing Sci.*, Fall 1984, *3*(4), pp. 288–307.

Mowery, David C. Firm Structure, Government Policy, and the Organization of Industrial Research: Great Britain and the United States, 1900–1950. *Bus. Hist. Rev.*, Winter 1984, *58*(4), pp. 504–31.   **[G: U.S.; U.K.]**

Mueller, Willard F. and Greer, Douglas F. The Effect of Market Share Distribution on Industry Performance Re-examined. *Rev. Econ. Statist.*, May 1984, *66*(2), pp. 353–58.   **[G: U.S.]**

Mueller, Willard F. and Rogers, Richard T. Changes in Market Concentration of Manufacturing Industries 1947–1977. *Rev. Ind. Organ.*, Spring 1984, *1*(1), pp. 1–14.   **[G: U.S.]**

Murfin, Andy. Market Shares in the UK Passenger Car Market: Marketing, Expenditure and Price Effects, 1975–80. *Appl. Econ.*, August 1984, *16*(4), pp. 611–32.   **[G: U.K.]**

Murphy, Neil B. and Rogers, Ronald C. The Line of Commerce in Retail Financial Institution Mergers: Some Evidence from Consumer Data in New England. *J. Bank Res.*, Spring 1984, *15*(1), pp. 21–25.   **[G: U.S.]**

Nakatani, Iwao. The Economic Role of Financial Corporate Grouping. In *Aoki, M., ed.*, 1984, pp. 227–58.   **[G: Japan]**

Newbery, David M. G. Commodity Price Stabilization in Imperfect or Cartelized Markets. *Econometrica*, May 1984, *52*(3), pp. 563–78.

Nikitin, S. M., et al. Big Companies and Inflation. In *Nikitin, S. M., ed.*, 1984, pp. 49–73.   **[G: U.S.]**

Noam, Eli M. Market Power and Regulation: A Simultaneous Approach. *J. Ind. Econ.*, March 1984, *32*(3), pp. 335–47.   **[G: U.S.]**

Noam, Eli M. Private Sector Monopolies: The Case of Cable Television Franchises. In *Holzer, M. and Nagel, S. S., eds.*, 1984, pp. 193–217.   **[G: U.S.]**

Nomura, Hidekazu. Capital Accumulation by Large Enterprises in Japan. *Kyoto Univ. Econ. Rev.*, April 1984, *54*(1), pp. 11–39.
   [G: Japan]

North, Douglass C. Government and the Cost of Exchange in History. *J. Econ. Hist.*, June 1984, *44*(2), pp. 255–64.

Nuti, Fabio. Gli effetti dell'innovazione microelettronica sull'organizzazione della produzione industriale. (Effects of the Micro-electronic Innovation on the Organization of Industrial Production. With English summary.) *Econ. Lavoro*, Oct.-Dec. 1984, *18*(4), pp. 35–46.

Oehler, Wolfgang. Corporation Law and the New Institutional Economics: Comment. *Z. ges. Staatswiss.*, March 1984, *140*(1), pp. 153–55.

Olson, Dennis O. and Bumpass, Donald L. An Intertemporal Analysis of the Welfare Cost of Monopoly Power: U.S. Manufacturing 1967–1981. *Rev. Ind. Organ.*, Winter 1984, *1*(4), pp. 308–22.   **[G: U.S.]**

Olson, Dennis O. and Bumpass, Donald L. Welfare Cost of Monopoly Power. *Atlantic Econ. J.*, December 1984, *12*(4), pp. 63.   **[G: U.S.]**

Ordover, Janusz A. and Willig, Robert D. The 1982 Department of Justice Merger Guidelines: An Economic Assessment. In *Fox, E. M. and Halverson, J. T., eds.*, 1984, pp. 267–304.   **[G: U.S.]**

Oster, Sharon. The FTC v. Levi Strauss: An Analysis of the Economic Issues. In *Lafferty, R. N.; Lande, R. H. and Kirkwood, J. B., eds.*, 1984, pp. 48–90.   **[G: U.S.]**

Ottenwaelter, B. and Vuong, Quang H. An Empirical Analysis of Backlog, Inventory, Production, and Price Adjustments: An Application of Recursive Systems of Log-Linear Models. *J. Bus. Econ. Statist.*, July 1984, *2*(3), pp. 224–34.   **[G: France]**

Ouchi, William. M-Form: Making Decisions and Building Concensus. *Challenge*, July/August 1984, *27*(3), pp. 31–37.   **[G: U.S.]**

Page, John M., Jr. Firm Size and Technical Efficiency: Applications of Production Frontiers to Indian Survey Data. *J. Devel. Econ.*, September–October 1984, *16*(1–2), pp. 129–52.
   [G: India]

Parker, William N. M. Schuman and His Plan. In *Parker, W. N.*, 1984, *1952*, pp. 125–38.
   [G: W. Europe]

Parker, William N. The Organization of Rapid Expansion. In *Parker, W. N.*, 1984, pp. 76–91.   **[G: W. Europe]**

Parkman, Allen. Crossownership and Media Concentration. *Rev. Ind. Organ.*, Summer 1984, *1*(2), pp. 138–47.   **[G: U.S.]**

Perry, Martin K. Scale Economies, Imperfect Competition, and Public Policy. *J. Ind. Econ.*, March 1984, *32*(3), pp. 313–33.

Perry, Martin K. Vertical Equilibrium in a Competitive Input Market. *Int. J. Ind. Organ.*, June 1984, *2*(2), pp. 159–70.

Perry, Motty. Sustainable Positive Profit Multiple-Price Strategies in Contestable Markets. *J. Econ. Theory*, April 1984, *32*(2), pp. 246–65.

Pfouts, Ralph W. Modelling Non-price Competition and Market Share. In *Avula, X. J. R., et al.*, 1984, pp. 795–98.

Phillips, Almarin. Defining a Unitary Business: An Economist's View: Comments. In *McLure, C. E., Jr., ed.*, 1984, pp. 125–26.   **[G: U.S.]**

Phillips, David A. Choice of Technology and Industrial Transformation: The Case of the United Republic of Tanzania. In *Ghosh, P. K., ed., no. 3*, 1984, *1980*, pp. 325–51.
   [G: Tanzania]

Pickering, J. F. The Development of the Firm. In *Pickering, J. F. and Cockerill, T. A. J., eds.*, 1984, pp. 23–51.

Pickering, J. F. and Sheldon, I. M. International Trade Performance and Concentration in British Industry. *Appl. Econ.*, June 1984, *16*(3), pp. 421–42.   **[G: U.K.]**

Picot, Arnold. Specificity, Specialization, and Coalitions: Comment. *Z. ges. Staatswiss.*, March 1984, *140*(1), pp. 50–53.

Pittman, Russell W. Predatory Investment: U.S.

vs. IBM. *Int. J. Ind. Organ.*, December 1984, 2(4), pp. 341–65.   **[G: U.S.]**

ten Raa, Thijs. Fixed Points of Compositions. *Europ. Econ. Rev.*, October–November 1984, 26(1–2), pp. 209–12.

ten Raa, Thijs. Resolution of Conjectures on the Sustainability of Natural Monopoly. *Rand J. Econ.*, Spring 1984, 15(1), pp. 135–41.

Raab, Raymond L. A Note on Dominant Firm Market Share and Economic Performance. *Rev. Ind. Organ.*, Summer 1984, 1(2), pp. 148–53.

Raganelli, Tullio. Banking Groups in the Italian Banking System: A Discriminant Analysis. In *Banca d'Italia*, 1984, pp. 129–46.   **[G: Italy]**

Ravenscraft, David J. Collusion vs. Superiority: A Monte Carlo Analysis. *Int. J. Ind. Organ.*, December 1984, 2(4), pp. 385–402.

Razavi, Hossein. An Economic Model of OPEC Coalition. *Southern Econ. J.*, October 1984, 51(2), pp. 419–28.   **[G: OPEC]**

Reedtz, Paolo Marullo. Market Share of the Banks: Some Explanatory Hypotheses. In *Banca d'Italia*, 1984, pp. 109–28.   **[G: Italy]**

Reekie, W. Duncan. Minimum Efficient Scale in South African Industry: An Application of the Survivor Technique. *S. Afr. J. Econ.*, September 1984, 52(3), pp. 223–32.   **[G: S. Africa]**

Reekie, W. Duncan. The Structure-Conduct-Performance Paradigm in a South African Setting. *S. Afr. J. Econ.*, June 1984, 52(2), pp. 146–55.   **[G: S. Africa]**

Reinganum, Jennifer F. Uncertain Innovation and the Persistence of Monopoly: Reply. *Amer. Econ. Rev.*, March 1984, 74(1), pp. 243–46.

Révész, Gábor. Enterprise Business Partnerships (VGMK) in Hungary—A Case Study. *Acta Oecon.*, 1984, 33(3–4), pp. 337–59.
                                [G: Hungary]

Reynolds, Peter John. An Empirical Analysis of the Degree of Monopoly Theory of Distribution. *Bull. Econ. Res.*, May 1984, 36(1), pp. 59–84.   **[G: U.K.]**

Rhoades, Stephen A. Wages, Concentration, and Import Penetration: An Analysis of the Interrelationships. *Atlantic Econ. J.*, July 1984, 12(2), pp. 23–31.   **[G: U.S.]**

Roberts, Mark J. Testing Oligopolistic Behavior. *Int. J. Ind. Organ.*, December 1984, 2(4), pp. 367–83.   **[G: U.S.]**

Rose, Peter S. and Giroux, Gary A. Predicting Corporate Bankruptcy: An Analytical and Empirical Evaluation. *Rev. Bus. Econ. Res.*, Spring 1984, 19(2), pp. 1–12.   **[G: U.S.]**

Round, David K. The Impact of Government Purchases on Market Performance in Australia. *Rev. Ind. Organ.*, Summer 1984, 1(2), pp. 94–113.   **[G: Australia]**

Rozek, Richard P. The Role of Market Power Measures in the Search for an Antitrust Case. *Amer. Econ.*, Fall 1984, 28(2), pp. 36–40.

Rumor, Raimondo. Una storia di diversificazioni. (History of Diversification. With English summary.) *L'Impresa*, 1984, 26(3), pp. 59–66.
                                [G: Italy]

Saias, Maurice. Creative and Noncreative Uses

of Portfolio Planning Tools and Strategies. In *[Kozmetsky, G.]*, 1984, pp. 145–49.

Salant, Stephen W. Preemptive Patenting and the Persistence of Monopoly: Comment. *Amer. Econ. Rev.*, March 1984, 74(1), pp. 247–50.

Salinger, Michael A. Tobin's q, Unionization, and the Concentration–Profits Relationship. *Rand J. Econ.*, Summer 1984, 15(2), pp. 159–70.
                                [G: U.S.]

Salop, Steven C. and Simons, Joseph J. A Practical Guide to Merger Analysis. *Antitrust Bull.*, Winter 1984, 29(4), pp. 663–703.   **[G: U.S.]**

Samuels, J. M. and Morrish, P. A. An Analysis of Concentration. In *Levicki, C., ed.*, 1984, pp. 19–41.   **[G: U.K.; W. Europe]**

Santos, Anibal and da Silva, J. M. Amado. Rivalidade e barreiras à entrada no sector público empresarial (Um ensaio de análise económica). (With English summary.) *Economia (Portugal)*, May 1984, 8(2), pp. 361–79.

Sato, Ryuzo and Tsutsui, Shunichi. Technical Progress, the Schumpeterian Hypothesis, and Market Structure. *Z. Nationalökon.*, Supplement 1984, pp. 1–37.

Scharfstein, David. A Policy to Prevent Rational Test-Market Predation. *Rand J. Econ.*, Summer 1984, 15(2), pp. 229–43.

Schenk, Karl-Ernst and Wass von Czege, Andreas. Industrial Organization and Interfirm Co-operation in a Regime of Central Regulation—The Hungarian Case. In *Rába, A. and Schenk, K.-E., eds.*, 1984, pp. 1–32.
                                [G: Hungary]

Scherer, Frederic M. Concentration, R&D, and Productivity Change. In *Scherer, F. M.*, 1984, 1983, pp. 249–55.   **[G: U.S.]**

Scherer, Frederic M. Corporate Size, Diversification, and Innovative Activity. In *Scherer, F. M.*, 1984, pp. 222–38.   **[G: U.S.; U.K.; W. Germany; France; Japan]**

Scherer, Frederic M. Firm Size, Market Structure, Opportunity, and the Output of Patented Inventions. In *Scherer, F. M.*, 1984, pp. 175–206.   **[G: U.S.]**

Scherer, Frederic M. Market Structure and the Employment of Scientists and Engineers. In *Scherer, F. M.*, 1984, pp. 239–48.   **[G: U.S.]**

Scherer, Frederic M. Market Structure and Innovation: Statistical Studies. In *Scherer, F. M.*, 1984, pp. 169–73.

Scherer, Frederic M. Measuring Surplus Attributable to Differentiated Products: Reply. *J. Ind. Econ.*, September 1984, 33(1), pp. 133.

Scherer, Frederic M. The Economics of Vertical Restraints. In *Fox, E. M. and Halverson, J. T., eds.*, 1984, pp. 429–48.   **[G: U.S.]**

Scherer, Frederic M. The Theory of Market Structure and Innovation. In *Scherer, F. M.*, 1984, pp. 59–65.

Scherer, Frederic M. The Welfare Economics of Product Variety: An Application to the Ready-to-Eat Cereals Industry. In *Scherer, F. M.*, 1984, 1979, pp. 142–67.   **[G: U.S.]**

Scherer, Frederic M. and Ravenscraft, David J. Growth by Diversification: Entrepreneurial Behavior in Large-Scale United States Enterprises. *Z. Nationalökon.*, Supplement 1984, pp. 199–218. [G: U.S.]

Schmalensee, Richard and Golub, Bennett W. Estimating Effective Concentration in Deregulated Wholesale Electricity Markets. *Rand J. Econ.*, Spring 1984, *15*(1), pp. 12–26. [G: U.S.]

Schmidtchen, Dieter. German *"Ordnungspolitik"* as Institutional Choice. *Z. ges. Staatswiss.*, March 1984, *140*(1), pp. 54–70. [G: Germany]

Schreiner, Jean-Paul. Le capital financier et le réseau des liaisons personnelles entre les principales sociétés en Suisse. (With English summary.) *Rev. Econ. Ind.*, 3rd Trimester 1984, (29), pp. 78–95.

Schuster, Leo. Profitability and Market Share of Banks. *J. Bank Res.*, Spring 1984, *15*(1), pp. 56–61. [G: U.S.; U.K.; Germany; Switzerland]

Schwartz, Steven. An Empirical Test of a Managerial, Life-Cycle, and Cost of Capital Model of Merger Activity. *J. Ind. Econ.*, March 1984, *32*(3), pp. 265–76. [G: U.S.]

Schweitzer, Iván. Size and Market Behaviour of the Hungarian Engineering Enterprises. In *Rába, A. and Schenk, K.-E., eds.*, 1984, pp. 73–98. [G: Hungary; Europe]

Scott, A. J. Industrial Organization and the Logic of Intra-Metropolitan Location, III: A Case Study of the Women's Dress Industry in the Greater Los Angeles Region. *Econ. Geogr.*, January 1984, *60*(1), pp. 3–27. [G: U.S.]

Scott, John T. Firm versus Industry Variability in R&D Intensity. In *Griliches, Z., ed.*, 1984, pp. 233–45. [G: U.S.]

Scott, John T. and Pascoe, George. Capital Costs and Profitability. *Int. J. Ind. Organ.*, September 1984, *2*(3), pp. 217–33. [G: U.S.]

Scott, Kenneth E. Corporate Governance and the New Institutional Economics. *Z. ges. Staatswiss.*, March 1984, *140*(1), pp. 136–52.

Settle, John W.; Petry, Glenn H. and Hsia, Chi-Cheng. Synergy, Diversification, and Incentive Effects of Corporate Merger on Bondholder Wealth: Some Evidence. *J. Finan. Res.*, Winter 1984, *7*(4), pp. 329–39. [G: U.S.]

Sharma, S. C. New Trends of Concentration of Economic Power. In *Ngo, M., ed., vol. 1*, 1984, pp. 324–40. [G: India]

Shaw, Richard W. and Shaw, Susan A. Late Entry, Market Shares and Competitive Survival: The Case of Synthetic Fibers. *Managerial Dec. Econ.*, June 1984, *5*(2), pp. 72–79. [G: W. Europe]

Shepherd, William G. "Contestability" vs. Competition. *Amer. Econ. Rev.*, September 1984, *74*(4), pp. 572–87.

Shepherd, William G. Discussion of "Concentration and Winning Bids in Auctions." *Antitrust Bull.*, Spring 1984, *29*(1), pp. 89–100.

Shimotani, Masahiro. Formation of "New Zaibatsu" in Prewar Japan: Case Study on Nisso Konzern. *Kyoto Univ. Econ. Rev.*, April 1984, *54*(1), pp. 40–59. [G: Japan]

Shughart, William F., II and Tollison, Robert D. The Random Character of Merger Activity. *Rand J. Econ.*, Winter 1984, *15*(4), pp. 500–509. [G: U.S.]

Smirlock, Michael L.; Gilligan, Thomas W. and Marshall, William J. Tobin's *q* and the Structure–Performance Relationship. *Amer. Econ. Rev.*, December 1984, *74*(5), pp. 1051–60. [G: U.S.]

Smith, Richard L., II. On Strategic Behavior as a Basis for Antitrust Action. *Antitrust Bull.*, Fall 1984, *29*(3), pp. 501–22.

Spence, A. Michael. Cost Reduction, Competition, and Industry Performance. *Econometrica*, January 1984, *52*(1), pp. 101–21.

Spence, A. Michael. Industrial Organization and Competitive Advantage in Multinational Industries. *Amer. Econ. Rev.*, May 1984, *74*(2), pp. 356–60.

Spiller, Pablo T. and Favaro, Edgardo. The Effects of Entry Regulation on Oligopolistic Interaction: The Uruguayan Banking Sector. *Rand J. Econ.*, Summer 1984, *15*(2), pp. 244–54. [G: Uruguay]

Sternthal, János. Co-operation and Size-Structure in the Hungarian Engineering Industry. In *Rába, A. and Schenk, K.-E., eds.*, 1984, pp. 127–64. [G: Hungary]

Stewart, John F.; Harris, Robert S. and Carleton, Willard T. The Role of Market Structure in Merger Behavior. *J. Ind. Econ.*, March 1984, *32*(3), pp. 293–312. [G: U.S.]

Stiglitz, Joseph E. Price Rigidities and Market Structure. *Amer. Econ. Rev.*, May 1984, *74*(2), pp. 350–55.

Sturgess, Brian T. and Wheale, Peter. Merger Performance Evaluation: An Empirical Analysis of a Sample of UK Firms. *J. Econ. Stud.*, 1984, *11*(4), pp. 33–45. [G: U.K.]

Suret, Jean-Marc. Facteurs explicatifs des structures financières des P.M.E. québécoises. (Financial Structure of Small and Medium Size Firms in the Province of Quebec. With English summary.) *L'Actual. Econ.*, March 1984, *60*(1), pp. 58–71. [G: Canada]

Suzuki, Toshiro A. Distribution of Value Added in Enterprises in Japan. In *Intn'l. Productivity Symp.*, 1984, pp. 267–81. [G: Japan; U.S.; W. Germany]

Tandon, Pankaj. Innovation, Market Structure, and Welfare. *Amer. Econ. Rev.*, June 1984, *74*(3), pp. 394–403.

Tandon, Pankaj. Tests of a Schumpeterian Model of R&D and Market Structure: Comment. In *Griliches, Z., ed.*, 1984, pp. 205–08. [G: U.S.]

Taxell, Christoffer. Tankar om den economiska lagstiftningen. (Views on Economic Legislation. With English summary.) *Ekon. Samfundets Tidskr.*, 1984, *37*(4), pp. 237–44. [G: Finland]

Telser, Lester G. Innovation: Its Public and Private Aspects and Some of Their Empirical Implications for Mergers. *Econ. Inquiry*, October 1984, *22*(4), pp. 334–59. [G: U.S.]

Telser, Lester G. Theories of Contract Design and Market Organization: Conceptual Bases for

Understanding Futures Markets: Comment. In *Anderson, R. W., ed.,* 1984 , pp. 307–10.

Thompson, Alexander M., III. The Allocation of Surplus to Non-Productive, Oligopolistic Rivalry: A Contradiction for Accumulation in Advanced Capitalist Economies. In *Zarembka, P., ed.,* 1984, pp. 37–80. [G: U.S.]

Thompson, R. S. Diversification Strategy and Systematic Risk: An Empirical Inquiry. *Managerial Dec. Econ.,* June 1984, 5(2), pp. 98–103. [G: U.K.]

Todd, D. Strategies of Growth, Diversification and Rationalization in the Evolution of Concentration in British Shipbuilding. *Reg. Stud.,* February 1984, 18(1), pp. 55–67. [G: U.K.]

Ulen, Thomas S. The Efficiency of Specific Performance: Toward a Unified Theory of Contract Remedies. *Mich. Law Rev.,* November 1984, 83(2), pp. 341–403. [G: U.S.]

Ulmer, John M. Canadian Acquisition of a Foreign Business: A Canadian Perspective. In *Purden, C., ed.,* 1984, pp. 245–73. [G: Canada]

Urban, Glen L.; Johnson, Philip L. and Hauser, John R. Testing Competitive Market Structures. *Marketing Sci.,* Spring 1984, 3(2), pp. 83–112. [G: U.S.]

Utton, M. A. Concentration, Competition and the Small Firm. In *Levicki, C., ed.,* 1984, pp. 5–18. [G: U.K.]

Valcarcel, Lina J. On the Ability of Accounting Ratios to Predict Failure of Philippine Business Firms. *Philippine Rev. Econ. Bus.,* Sept./Dec. 1984, 21(3/4), pp. 165–99. [G: Philippines]

Van Herck, Gustaaf. Entry, Exit and Profitability. *Managerial Dec. Econ.,* March 1984, 5(1), pp. 25–31. [G: Belgium]

Vince, Péter. Enterprise Size—As Reflected in Market Position and International Comparison. In *Rába, A. and Schenk, K.-E., eds.,* 1984, pp. 165–88. [G: Hungary]

Wahlroos, Björn. Monopoly Welfare Losses under Uncertainty. *Southern Econ. J.,* October 1984, 51(2), pp. 429–42. [G: Finland; U.S.]

Wahlroos, Björn; Berglund, Tom and Cabell, Nina. The Social Cost of Imperfections in Domestic Trade: The Case of Finland. *Appl. Econ.,* February 1984, 16(1), pp. 119–29. [G: Finland]

Walkling, Ralph A. and Long, Michael S. Agency Theory, Managerial Welfare, and Takeover Bid Resistance. *Rand J. Econ.,* Spring 1984, 15(1), pp. 54–68. [G: U.S.]

Walter, C. K. and Rives, Janet M. A Discriminant Analysis of Industry Classification by Input Mix. *Rivista Int. Sci. Econ. Com.,* May 1984, 31(5), pp. 417–31. [G: U.S.]

Ware, Roger. Lumpy Investment in a Growing Differentiated Market. *Economica,* November 1984, 51(204), pp. 377–91.

Ware, Roger. Sunk Costs and Strategic Commitment: A Proposed Three-Stage Equilibrium. *Econ. J.,* June 1984, 94(374), pp. 370–78.

Wass von Czege, Andreas. New Possibilities of Institutional Choice in the Hungarian Industry—Legal Aspects, First Experiences and

Problems. In *Rába, A. and Schenk, K.-E., eds.,* 1984, pp. 33–71. [G: Hungary]

Wedderburn, K. W. [Lord]. The Legal Development of Corporate Responsibility: For Who Will Corporate Managers Be Trustees? In *Hopt, K. J. and Teubner, G., eds.,* 1984, pp. 3–54. [G: U.K.]

Weinstein, Bernard L. and Gross, Harold T. Grassroots Industrial Policy. *Challenge,* July/August 1984, 27(3), pp. 52–55. [G: U.S.]

Weinstock, David S. Some Little-known Properties of the Herfindahl–Hirschman Index: Problems of Translation and Specification. *Antitrust Bull.,* Winter 1984, 29(4), pp. 705–17. [G: U.S.]

von Weizsäcker, Carl Christian. The Costs of Substitution. *Econometrica,* September 1984, 52(5), pp. 1085–1116.

Wernerfelt, Birger. Consumers with Differing Reaction Speeds, Scale Advantages and Industry Structure. *Europ. Econ. Rev.,* March 1984, 24(2), pp. 257–70.

Wernerfelt, Birger. Stagflation, New Products, and Speculation. *J. Macroecon.,* Summer 1984, 6(3), pp. 295–309.

Wessel, Horst A. The German Feeble Current Cable Association (DSV)—Background, Foundation and Early Years (1876–1917.) In *Engels, W. and Pohl, H., eds.,* 1984, pp. 57–75. [G: W. Germany]

West, Douglas S. and Von Hohenbalken, Balder. Spatial Predation in a Canadian Retail Oligopoly. *J. Reg. Sci.,* August 1984, 24(3), pp. 415–29. [G: Canada]

Wiggins, Steven N. Organizational Structures and Economic Efficiency: Comment. *Z. ges. Staatswiss.,* March 1984, 140(1), pp. 224–26.

Wilder, Ronald P. and Tucker, Irvin B. Trends in Vertical Integration: Reply. *J. Ind. Econ.,* March 1984, 32(3), pp. 391–92. [G: U.S.]

Wildman, Steven S. A Note on Measuring Surplus Attributable to Differentiated Products. *J. Ind. Econ.,* September 1984, 33(1), pp. 123–32.

Williamson, Oliver E. Corporate Governance. *Yale Law J.,* June 1984, 93(7), pp. 1197–1230.

Williamson, Oliver E. Credible Commitments: Further Remarks. *Amer. Econ. Rev.,* June 1984, 74(3), pp. 488–90.

Williamson, Oliver E. Perspectives on the Modern Corporation. *Quart. Rev. Econ. Bus.,* Winter 1984, 24(4), pp. 64–71.

Williamson, Oliver E. The Economics of Governance: Framework and Implications. *Z. ges. Staatswiss.,* March 1984, 140(1), pp. 195–223.

Williamson, Oliver E. The Incentive Limits of Firms: A Comparative Institutional Assessment of Bureaucracy. *Weltwirtsch. Arch.,* 1984, 120(4), pp. 736–63. [G: U.S.]

Winter, Sidney G. Schumpeterian Competition in Alternative Technological Regimes. *J. Econ. Behav. Organ.,* September–December 1984, 5(3–4), pp. 287–320.

Woodward, S. N. Corporate Planning, Commitment and Public Enterprises. In *Ramanadham, V. V., ed.,* 1984, pp. 138–58.

Yamawaki, Hideki. Market Structure, Capacity

Expansion, and Pricing: A Model Applied to the Japanese Iron and Steel Industry. *Int. J. Ind. Organ.*, March 1984, *2*(1), pp. 29–62.
[G: Japan]

Yoshihara, Hideki. Diversification of Large Japanese Manufacturing Firms. *Kobe Econ. Bus. Rev.*, 1984, *30*, pp. 61–71. [G: Japan; U.S.]

Young, Leslie and Schmitz, Andrew. Storage under a Cartel. In *Storey, G. G.; Schmitz, A. and Sarris, A. H., eds.*, 1984, pp. 285–303.

Yu, Ben T. A Contractual Remedy to Premature Innovation: The Vertical Integration of Brand-Name Specific Research. *Econ. Inquiry*, October 1984, *22*(4), pp. 660–67.

Yu, Shirley S. Some Determinants of Entry into Therapeutic Drug Markets. *Rev. Ind. Organ.*, Winter 1984, *1*(4), pp. 260–75. [G: U.S.]

Zardkoohi, Asghar and Sheer, Alain. Public versus Private Liquor Retailing: An Investigation into the Behavior of the State Governments. *Southern Econ. J.*, April 1984, *50*(4), pp. 1058–76. [G: U.S.]

612 Public Policy toward Monopoly and Competition

6120 Public Policy toward Monopoly and Competition

Adams, Walter and Brock, James W. Countervailing or Coalescing Power? The Problem of Labor/Management Coalitions. *J. Post Keynesian Econ.*, Winter 1983-84, *6*(2), pp. 180–97.
[G: U.S.]

Alberts, William W. Do Oligopolists Earn "Noncompetitive" Rates of Return? *Amer. Econ. Rev.*, September 1984, *74*(4), pp. 624–32.

Allen, Bruce T. Merger Statistics and Merger Policy. *Rev. Ind. Organ.*, Summer 1984, *1*(2), pp. 78–92. [G: U.S.]

Alpert, Geraldine and McCarthy, Thomas R. Beyond *Goldfarb:* Applying Traditional Antitrust Analysis to Changing Health Markets. *Antitrust Bull.*, Summer 1984, *29*(2), pp. 165–204.

Andic, Suphan and Cao-García, Ramón J. Regulation in a Democracy: Inefficiency or Efficiency? In *Hanusch, H., ed.*, 1984, pp. 209–22.

Areeda, Phillip E. Introduction to Antitrust Economics. In *Fox, E. M. and Halverson, J. T., eds.*, 1984, pp. 45–59. [G: U.S.]

Bailey, Elizabeth E. A Comment on the Papers by Theodore Keeler and Barry Weingast [Theories of Regulation and the Deregulation Movement] [The Congressional–Bureaucratic System: A Principal–Agent Perspective (with Application to the SEC)]. *Public Choice*, 1984, *44*(1), pp. 197–200. [G: U.S.]

Bailey, Elizabeth E. and Baumol, William J. Deregulation and the Theory of Contestable Markets. *Yale J. Regul.*, 1984, *1*(2), pp. 111–37.
[G: U.S.]

Ballentine, J. Gregory. Dividing the State Corporate Income Tax Base: Developments in the Supreme Court and Congress: Panel Discussion. In *McLure, C. E., Jr., ed.*, 1984, pp. 330–32. [G: U.S.]

Barron, John M. and Umbeck, John R. The Effects of Different Contractual Arrangements: The Case of Retail Gasoline Markets. *J. Law Econ.*, October 1984, *27*(2), pp. 313–28.
[G: U.S.]

Barton, David M. and Sherman, Roger. The Price and Profit Effects of Horizontal Merger: A Case Study. *J. Ind. Econ.*, December 1984, *33*(2), pp. 165–77. [G: U.S.]

Baxter, William F. Comments [The Role of Economic Analysis in the Antitrust Division before and after the Establishment of the Economic Policy Office: A Lawyer's View] [Pigeonholes in antitrust]. *Antitrust Bull.*, Spring 1984, *29*(1), pp. 147–50.

Baxter, William F. Responding to the Reaction: The Draftsman's View. In *Fox, E. M. and Halverson, J. T., eds.*, 1984, pp. 305–18.
[G: U.S.]

Baxter, William F. Vertical Restraints—Half Slave, Half Free. In *Fox, E. M. and Halverson, J. T., eds.*, 1984, pp. 477–88. [G: U.S.]

Beesley, Michael E. and Littlechild, Stephen C. Privatization: Principles, Problems and Priorities: Reply. *Lloyds Bank Rev.*, January 1984, (151), pp. 47–48. [G: U.K.]

Beggs, John J. Long-run Trends in Patenting. In *Griliches, Z., ed.*, 1984, pp. 155–69.
[G: U.S.]

Blackstone, Erwin A. and Fuhr, Joseph P., Jr. Antitrust and Exclusive Agreements: The Case of Hospital-based Physicians. *Antitrust Bull.*, Winter 1984, *29*(4), pp. 739–58. [G: U.S.]

Bolze, Ray S. and Pennak, Mark W. Reconciliation of the Sherman Act with Federal Health-planning Legislation: Implied Antitrust Immunity in the Health Care Field. *Antitrust Bull.*, Summer 1984, *29*(2), pp. 225–52. [G: U.S.]

Bound, John, et al. Who Does R&D and Who Patents? In *Griliches, Z., ed.*, 1984, pp. 21–54. [G: U.S.]

Break, George F. State Taxation Under the Commerce Clause: The History Revisited: Comments. In *McLure, C. E., Jr., ed.*, 1984, pp. 82–84. [G: U.S.]

Brock, Gerald. Vertical Restraints in Industrial Gases. In *Lafferty, R. N.; Lande, R. H. and Kirkwood, J. B., eds.*, 1984, pp. 386–427.
[G: U.S.]

Brock, James W. Industry Structure and Market Power: The Relevance of the "Relevant Market." *Antitrust Bull.*, Fall 1984, *29*(3), pp. 535–60. [G: U.S.]

Brodley, Joseph F. Potential Competition under the Merger Guidelines. In *Fox, E. M. and Halverson, J. T., eds.*, 1984, pp. 199–223.
[G: U.S.]

Bronsteen, Peter. A Review of the Revised Merger Guidelines. *Antitrust Bull.*, Winter 1984, *29*(4), pp. 613–52. [G: U.S.]

Brown, Charles L. Disconnecting Bell: The Impact of the AT&T Divestiture: A Personal Introduction. In *Shooshan, H. M., III, ed.*, 1984, pp. 1–7. [G: U.S.]

Burke, Jim. Antitrust Laws, Justice Department Guidelines, and the Limits of Concentration in Local Banking Markets. *Fed. Res. Bull.*, June 1984, *70*(6), pp. 495–96. **[G: U.S.]**

Campbell, Thomas J. and Ware, Charles J. *Russell Stover* and the Vertical Agreement Puzzle. In *Fox, E. M. and Halverson, J. T.*, eds., 1984, pp. 371–81. **[G: U.S.]**

Caves, Richard E. Vertical Restraints as Integration by Contract: Evidence and Policy Implications. In *Lafferty, R. N.; Lande, R. H. and Kirkwood, J. B.*, eds., 1984, pp. 430–77. **[G: U.S.]**

Centner, Terence J. and Wetzstein, Michael E. Cooperative Antitrust Monopolization and the Theory of Contestable Markets. *Southern J. Agr. Econ.*, July 1984, *16*(1), pp. 129–35.

Comanor, William S. and Frech, H. E., III. Strategic Behavior and Antitrust Analysis. *Amer. Econ. Rev.*, May 1984, *74*(2), pp. 372–76.

Conard, Alfred F. The Supervision of Corporate Management: A Comparison of Developments in European Community and United States Law. *Mich. Law Rev.*, April–May 1984, *82*(5 & 6), pp. 1459–88. **[G: U.S.; EEC]**

Costilo, L. Barry and Kazon, Peter M. Preferred Provider Plans: Avoiding Problems of Horizontal Price-fixing. *Antitrust Bull.*, Summer 1984, *29*(2), pp. 403–22. **[G: U.S.]**

Coustel, Jean-Pierre. La déréglementation des Télécommunications. Le poids du démembrement d'ATT dans la dynamique de diffusion du mouvement. (With English summary.) *Rev. Econ. Ind.*, 4th Trimester 1984, (30), pp. 42–59. **[G: U.S.]**

Crandall, Robert W. The Emerging Competition in the U.S. Telecommunications Market. In *Giersch, H.*, ed., 1984, pp. 87–106. **[G: U.S.]**

Crandall, Robert W. and Owen, Bruce M. Disconnecting Bell: The Marketplace: Economic Implications of Divestiture. In *Shooshan, H. M., III*, ed., 1984, pp. 47–70. **[G: U.S.]**

Dansby, Robert E. and Conrad, Cecilia A. Commodity Bundling. *Amer. Econ. Rev.*, May 1984, *74*(2), pp. 377–81.

DeCanio, Stephen J. Delivered Pricing and Multiple Basing Point Equilibria: A Reevaluation. *Quart. J. Econ.*, May 1984, *99*(2), pp. 329–49.

Dexter, William D. Dividing the State Corporate Income Tax Base: Developments in the Supreme Court and Congress: Panel Discussion. In *McLure, C. E., Jr.*, ed., 1984, pp. 341–48. **[G: U.S.]**

Donnenfeld, Shabtai. Domestic Price Regulation and the Exporting Monopolist. *Oxford Econ. Pap.*, June 1984, *36*(2), pp. 285–87.

Eads, George C. Discussion of "New Developments on the Cartel Front." *Antitrust Bull.*, Spring 1984, *29*(1), pp. 77–83. **[G: U.S.]**

Elzinga, Kenneth G. New Developments on the Cartel Front. *Antitrust Bull.*, Spring 1984, *29*(1), pp. 3–26. **[G: U.S.]**

Feinberg, Robert M. Strategic and Deterrent Pricing Responses to Antitrust Investigations.

Int. J. Ind. Organ., March 1984, *2*(1), pp. 75–84. **[G: U.S.]**

Feinberg, Robert M. The Timing of Antitrust Effects on Pricing. *Appl. Econ.*, June 1984, *16*(3), pp. 397–409. **[G: U.S.]**

Fikentscher, Wolfgang. Third World Trade Partnership: Supranational Authority vs. National Extraterritorial Antitrust—A Plea for "Harmonized" Regionalism. *Mich. Law Rev.*, April–May 1984, *82*(5 & 6), pp. 1489–1509.

Filer, Randall K. A Theoretical Analysis of the Economic Impact of Artists' Resale Royalties Legislation. *J. Cult. Econ.*, June 1984, *8*(1), pp. 1–28.

Forsyth, Peter. Airlines and Airports: Privatisation, Competition, and Regulation. *Fisc. Stud.*, February 1984, *5*(1), pp. 61–75. **[G: U.K.]**

Gallini, Nancy T. Deterrence by Market Sharing: A Strategic Incentive for Licensing. *Amer. Econ. Rev.*, December 1984, *74*(5), pp. 931–41.

Geller, Henry. Disconnecting Bell: Regulation and Public Policy after Divestiture: The FCC and Congress. In *Shooshan, H. M., III*, ed., 1984, pp. 83–99. **[G: U.S.]**

Gilbert, Richard J. and Newbery, David M. G. Preemptive Patenting and the Persistence of Monopoly: Reply. *Amer. Econ. Rev.*, March 1984, *74*(1), pp. 251–53.

Görgens, Egon. Nachfragemacht im Lebensmittelhandel als Instrument der Strukturanpassung. (With English Summary.) In *Eucken, W. and Böhm, F.*, eds., 1984, pp. 231–45. **[G: W. Germany]**

Greening, Timothy. Analysis of the Impact of the Florsheim Shoe Case. In *Lafferty, R. N.; Lande, R. H. and Kirkwood, J. B.*, eds., 1984, pp. 92–199. **[G: U.S.]**

Grether, David M. and Plott, Charles R. The Effects of Market Practices in Oligopolistic Markets: An Experimental Examination of the Ethyl Case. *Econ. Inquiry*, October 1984, *22*(4), pp. 479–507. **[G: U.S.]**

Griliches, Zvi. Market Value, R&D, and Patents. In *Griliches, Z.*, ed., 1984, pp. 249–52. **[G: U.S.]**

Guesnerie, Roger and Laffont, Jean-Jacques. Indirect Public Control of Self-Managed Monopolies. *J. Compar. Econ.*, June 1984, *8*(2), pp. 139–58.

Guesnerie, Roger and Laffont, Jean-Jacques. The Government Control of Public Firms and the Economics of Incomplete Information: An Introduction. In *Marchand, M.; Pestieau, P. and Tulkens, H.*, eds., 1984, pp. 159–78.

Harris, Robert G. and Jorde, Thomas M. Market Definition in the Merger Guidelines: Implications for Antitrust Enforcement. In *Fox, E. M. and Halverson, J. T.*, eds., 1984, pp. 225–51. **[G: U.S.]**

Hartley, Keith. Policy towards Contracting-Out: The Lessons of Experience. *Fisc. Stud.*, February 1984, *5*(1), pp. 98–105. **[G: U.K.]**

Harvel, Howard P. Vertical Restraints in the Hearing Aids Industry. In *Lafferty, R. N.;*

Lande, R. H. and Kirkwood, J. B., eds., 1984, pp. 272–384.   [G: U.S.]

Haverson, James T. An Overview of the Legal and Economic Issues Regarding Vertical Arrangements. In *Fox, E. M. and Halverson, J. T., eds.*, 1984, pp. 343–70.   [G: U.S.]

Hay, George A. Pigeonholes in Antitrust. *Antitrust Bull.*, Spring 1984, 29(1), pp. 133–45.

Hellerstein, Jerome R. Defining a Unitary Business: An Economist's View: Comments. In *McLure, C. E., Jr., ed.*, 1984, pp. 127–31.
                                                  [G: U.S.]

Hellerstein, Jerome R. State Taxation Under the Commerce Clause: The History Revisited. In *McLure, C. E., Jr., ed.*, 1984, 1982, pp. 53–81.   [G: U.S.]

Hellerstein, Walter. Dividing the State Corporate Income Tax Base: Developments in the Supreme Court and Congress. In *McLure, C. E., Jr., ed.*, 1984, pp. 288–329. [G: U.S.]

Hilke, John C. and Nelson, Philip B. Noisy Advertising and the Predation Rule in Antitrust Analysis. *Amer. Econ. Rev.*, May 1984, 74(2), pp. 367–71.   [G: U.S.]

Hollander, Abraham. Market Structure and Performance in Intellectual Property: The Case of Copyright Collectives. *Int. J. Ind. Organ.*, September 1984, 2(3), pp. 199–216.

Horowitz, Ira and Dennis, Samuel. Decision-making in the Two-Act Antitrust Decision Problem. *Managerial Dec. Econ.*, December 1984, 5(4), pp. 194–203.   [G: U.S.]

Isaac, R. Mark; Ramey, Valerie and Williams, Arlington W. The Effects of Market Organization on Conspiracies in Restraint of Trade. *J. Econ. Behav. Organ.*, June 1984, 5(2), pp. 191–222.

Jacobs, Francis G. Civil Enforcement of EEC Antitrust Law. *Mich. Law Rev.*, April–May 1984, 82(5 & 6), pp. 1364–76.   [G: EEC]

Kamien, Morton I. and Tauman, Yair. The Private Value of a Patent: A Game Theoretic Analysis. *Z. Nationalökon.*, Supplement 1984, pp. 93–118.

Katz, Eliakim and Paroush, Jacob. Royalty vs. Partnership Agreement in the Creative Arts. *Atlantic Econ. J.*, July 1984, 12(2), pp. 41–46.

Kauper, Thomas E. The Role of Economic Analysis in the Antitrust Division before and after the Establishment of the Economic Policy Office: A Lawyer's View. *Antitrust Bull.*, Spring 1984, 29(1), pp. 111–32.

Kauper, Thomas E. The 1982 Horizontal Merger Guidelines: Of Collusion, Efficiency, and Failure. In *Fox, E. M. and Halverson, J. T., eds.*, 1984, pp. 171–98.   [G: U.S.]

Keeler, Theodore E. Theories of Regulation and the Deregulation Movement. *Public Choice*, 1984, 44(1), pp. 103–45.   [G: U.S.]

Keenan, Donald C. and Paul, Chris. An Economic Explanation for Political Action and Inaction. *Atlantic Econ. J.*, July 1984, 12(2), pp. 12–22.

Keyes, Lucile S. Armentano's *Antitrust and Mo-*

nopoly: A Review Article. *J. Post Keynesian Econ.*, Spring 1984, 6(3), pp. 354–59.
                                                  [G: U.S.]

Keyes, Lucile S. Revised Guidelines—1984. *Rev. Ind. Organ.*, Summer 1984, 1(2), pp. 154–58.
                                                  [G: U.S.]

Keyes, Lucile S. The New Merger Guidelines of the Department of Justice. *Rev. Ind. Organ.*, Spring 1984, 1(1), pp. 26–52.   [G: U.S.]

Kuhlman, John M. and Johnson, S. R. Estimating Damages on Highway Construction Contracts. *Antitrust Bull.*, Winter 1984, 29(4), pp. 719–38.   [G: U.S.]

Kunnas, Heikki J. Hinta- ja kilpailuvalvonta inflaation torjunnan osana. (Price and Competition Controls for Anti-Inflationary Policy. With English summary.) *Kansant. Aikak.*, 1984, 80(1), pp. 17–27.   [G: Finland]

Laboe, Norman J. Worldwide Unitary Combination: The California Practice: Comments. In *McLure, C. E., Jr., ed.*, 1984, pp. 173–81.
                                                  [G: U.S.]

Lafferty, Ronald N.; Lande, Robert H. and Kirkwood, John B. Impact Evaluations of Federal Trade Commission Vertical Restraints Cases: Introduction and Overview. In *Lafferty, R. N.; Lande, R. H. and Kirkwood, J. B., eds.*, 1984, pp. 1–45.   [G: U.S.]

Lanciotti, Giulio. Objectives and Instruments of Structural Supervision: Guidelines and Optimum Rules for Authorising Branch Openings. In *Banca d'Italia*, 1984, pp. 249–61.
                                                  [G: Italy]

Landes, William M. Harm to Competition: Cartels, Mergers, and Joint Ventures. In *Fox, E. M. and Halverson, J. T., eds.*, 1984, pp. 73–82.   [G: U.S.]

Lerner, Arthur N. Federal Trade Commission Antitrust Activities in the Health Care Services Field. *Antitrust Bull.*, Summer 1984, 29(2), pp. 205–24.   [G: U.S.]

Lynk, William J. Interpreting Rising Concentration: The Case of Beer. *J. Bus.*, Part 1, January 1984, 57(1), pp. 43–55.   [G: U.S.]

Mahoney, Paul G. A Market Power Test for Noncommercial Boycotts. *Yale Law J.*, January 1984, 93(3), pp. 523–40.   [G: U.S.]

Manne, Henry G. Antitrust and Economic Analysis of Law: Comments. *Z. ges. Staatswiss.*, March 1984, 140(1), pp. 172–75.   [G: U.S.]

Mansfield, Edwin. Using Linked Patent and R&D Data to Measure Interindustry Technology Flows: Comment. In *Griliches, Z., ed.*, 1984, pp. 461–64.   [G: U.S.]

Martin, James R. Market Structure and Corporate Accounting Strategy. *Amer. Econ.*, Spring 1984, 28(1), pp. 34–43.   [G: U.S.]

Martin, John W., Jr. Use of Section 2 to Control Conduct in Vertical Relationships—An Opportunity or an Abuse? In *Fox, E. M. and Halverson, J. T., eds.*, 1984, pp. 397–420.
                                                  [G: U.S.]

Marvel, Howard P. The Locus of Collusion in U.S. Manufacturing. *Quart. Rev. Econ. Bus.*, Winter 1984, 24(4), pp. 82–99.   [G: U.S.]

Maynard, Alan and Hartley, Keith. The Regulation of the Pharmaceutical Industry. In *Lindgren, B., ed.*, 1984, pp. 123–37. **[G: U.K.]**

McEachern, William A. and Romeo, Anthony A. Vertical Restraints in the Audio Component Industry: Possibilities for Future Empirical Work. In *Lafferty, R. N.; Lande, R. H. and Kirkwood, J. B., eds.*, 1984, pp. 258–69. **[G: U.S.]**

McEachern, William A. and Romeo, Anthony A. Vertical Restraints in the Audio Components Industry: An Economic Analysis of FTC Intervention. In *Lafferty, R. N.; Lande, R. H. and Kirkwood, J. B., eds.*, 1984, pp. 202–57. **[G: U.S.]**

McLure, Charles E., Jr. Defining a Unitary Business: An Economist's View. In *McLure, C. E., Jr., ed.*, 1984, pp. 89–124. **[G: U.S.]**

McLure, Charles E., Jr. Dividing the State Corporate Income Tax Base: Developments in the Supreme Court and Congress: Panel Discussion. In *McLure, C. E., Jr., ed.*, 1984, pp. 333–35. **[G: U.S.]**

McRae, James J. and Tapon, Francis. Compulsory Licensing as a Policy Instrument. *Can. Public Policy*, March 1984, *10*(1), pp. 74–77. **[G: Canada]**

Mestmäcker, Ernst-Joachim. The Applicability of the ECSC-Cartel Prohibition (Article 65) during a "Manifest Crisis." *Mich. Law Rev.*, April–May 1984, *82*(5 & 6), pp. 1399–1414. **[G: EEC]**

Miles, John J. Hospital Mergers and the Antitrust Laws: An Overview. *Antitrust Bull.*, Summer 1984, *29*(2), pp. 253–99. **[G: U.S.]**

Miller, Benjamin F. Worldwide Unitary Combination: The California Practice. In *McLure, C. E., Jr., ed.*, 1984, pp. 132–66. **[G: U.S.]**

Miller, Richard A. Notes on the 1984 Merger Guidelines: Clarification of the Policy or Repeal of the Celler–Kefauver Act? *Antitrust Bull.*, Winter 1984, *29*(4), pp. 653–62. **[G: U.S.]**

Millstein, Ira M. Economics: Use and Misuse— A Response to Professor Areeda. In *Fox, E. M. and Halverson, J. T., eds.*, 1984, pp. 61–72. **[G: U.S.]**

Milton, David R. Worldwide Unitary Combination: The California Practice: Comments. In *McLure, C. E., Jr., ed.*, 1984, pp. 182–91. **[G: U.S.]**

Möschel, Wernhard. Antitrust and Economic Analysis of Law. *Z. ges. Staatswiss.*, March 1984, *140*(1), pp. 156–71.

Novos, Ian E. and Waldman, Michael. The Effects of Increased Copyright Protection: An Analytic Approach. *J. Polit. Econ.*, April 1984, *92*(2), pp. 236–46.

Ordover, Janusz A. and Willig, Robert D. The 1982 Department of Justice Merger Guidelines: An Economic Assessment. In *Fox, E. M. and Halverson, J. T., eds.*, 1984, pp. 267–304. **[G: U.S.]**

Oster, Sharon. The FTC v. Levi Strauss: An Analysis of the Economic Issues. In *Lafferty, R. N.; Lande, R. H. and Kirkwood, J. B., eds.*, 1984, pp. 48–90. **[G: U.S.]**

Owen, Bruce M. Comments [The Role of Economic Analysis in the Antitrust Division before and after the Establishment of the Economic Policy Office: A Lawyer's View] [Pigeonholes in Antitrust]. *Antitrust Bull.*, Spring 1984, *29*(1), pp. 151–52.

Pakes, Ariel and Griliches, Zvi. Patents and R&D at the Firm Level: A First Look. In *Griliches, Z., ed.*, 1984, pp. 55–72. **[G: U.S.]**

Pakes, Ariel and Schankerman, Mark. The Rate of Obsolescence of Patents, Research Gestation Lags, and the Private Rate of Return to Research Resources. In *Griliches, Z., ed.*, 1984, pp. 73–88.

Palmer, John P. Patents, Licensing and Restrictions on Competition. *Econ. Inquiry*, October 1984, *22*(4), pp. 676–83.

Palmeter, N. David. The U.S. International Trade Commission at Common Law: Unfair Competition, Trademark, and Section 337 of the Tariff Act. *J. World Trade Law*, November:December 1984, *18*(6), pp. 497–511. **[G: U.S.]**

Paul, Ellen Frankel. Taking by Regulation: Resolving the Constitutional Muddle. In *McKenzie, R. B., ed. (I)*, 1984, pp. 161–82. **[G: U.S.]**

Perri, Timothy J. The Social Loss from Private Monopoly and Optimal Antitrust Enforcement. *Rev. Ind. Organ.*, Winter 1984, *1*(4), pp. 276–88.

Perry, Martin K. Scale Economies, Imperfect Competition, and Public Policy. *J. Ind. Econ.*, March 1984, *32*(3), pp. 313–33.

Perry, Motty. Sustainable Positive Profit Multiple-Price Strategies in Contestable Markets. *J. Econ. Theory*, April 1984, *32*(2), pp. 246–65.

Peters, James H. Dividing the State Corporate Income Tax Base: Developments in the Supreme Court and Congress: Panel Discussion. In *McLure, C. E., Jr., ed.*, 1984, pp. 336–40. **[G: U.S.]**

Petersen, Robert A. Worldwide Unitary Combination: The California Practice: Comments. In *McLure, C. E., Jr., ed.*, 1984, pp. 167–72. **[G: U.S.]**

Phillips, Almarin. Defining a Unitary Business: An Economist's View: Comments. In *McLure, C. E., Jr., ed.*, 1984, pp. 125–26. **[G: U.S.]**

Pittman, Russell W. Predatory Investment: U.S. vs. IBM. *Int. J. Ind. Organ.*, December 1984, *2*(4), pp. 341–65. **[G: U.S.]**

Popofsky, M. Laurence. The Economics of Vertical Restraints: A Lawyer's Response. In *Fox, E. M. and Halverson, J. T., eds.*, 1984, pp. 449–59. **[G: U.S.]**

Prudhon, Bernard. Intermédiation financière française et intermédiation financiére ouest-allemande: perspectives pour une réforme. (With English summary.) *Rev. Econ. Ind.*, 4th Trimester 1984, (30), pp. 77–88. **[G: France; W. Germany]**

Reekie, W. Duncan. The Structure-Conduct-Performance Paradigm in a South African Setting. *S. Afr. J. Econ.*, June 1984, *52*(2), pp. 146–55. **[G: S. Africa]**

Richman, Daniel C. Antitrust Standing, Antitrust Injury, and the Per Se Standard. *Yale Law J.*, June 1984, 93(7), pp. 1309–329. [G: U.S.]

Rill, James F. Non-price Vertical Restraints since Sylvania: Market Conditions and Dual Distribution. In *Fox, E. M. and Halverson, J. T., eds.*, 1984, pp. 383–96. [G: U.S.]

Ross, Thomas W. Winners and Losers under the Robinson–Patman Act. *J. Law Econ.*, October 1984, 27(2), pp. 243–71. [G: U.S.]

Rozek, Richard P. The Role of Market Power Measures in the Search for an Antitrust Case. *Amer. Econ.*, Fall 1984, 28(2), pp. 36–40.

Salant, Stephen W. Preemptive Patenting and the Persistence of Monopoly: Comment. *Amer. Econ. Rev.*, March 1984, 74(1), pp. 247–50.

Salop, Steven C. and Simons, Joseph J. A Practical Guide to Merger Analysis. *Antitrust Bull.*, Winter 1984, 29(4), pp. 663–703. [G: U.S.]

Sárközy, Tamás. The Problems of Contracts Containing Co-operation among Enterprises in Hungary. In *Rába, A. and Schenk, K.-E., eds.*, 1984, pp. 99–126. [G: Hungary]

Scharfstein, David. A Policy to Prevent Rational Test-Market Predation. *Rand J. Econ.*, Summer 1984, 15(2), pp. 229–43.

Scherer, Frederic M. Nordhaus's Theory of Optimal Patent Life: A Geometric Reinterpretation. In *Scherer, F. M.*, 1984, pp. 130–41.

Scherer, Frederic M. Statistical Evidence on Antitrust Decree Effects. In *Scherer, F. M.*, 1984, pp. 207–21. [G: U.S.]

Scherer, Frederic M. The Economics of Vertical Restraints. In *Fox, E. M. and Halverson, J. T., eds.*, 1984, pp. 429–48. [G: U.S.]

Scherer, Frederic M. Using Linked Patent and R&D Data to Measure Interindustry Technology Flows. In *Griliches, Z., ed.*, 1984, pp. 417–61. [G: U.S.]

Schoettle, Ferdinand P. State Taxation Under the Commerce Clause: The History Revisited: Comments. In *McLure, C. E., Jr., ed.*, 1984, pp. 85–88. [G: U.S.]

Seldon, Zena A. and Seldon, James R. Natural Monopolies versus Desirable Monopolies and Regulation in the Public Interest: Two Quibbles and a Policy Note. *Quart. J. Bus. Econ.*, Spring 1984, 23(2), pp. 58–71.

Selten, Reinhard. Are Cartel Laws Bad for Business? In *[Beckmann, M. J.]*, 1984, pp. 85–117.

Sharpe, Tom. Privatisation, Regulation and Competition. *Fisc. Stud.*, February 1984, 5(1), pp. 47–60. [G: U.K.; U.S.]

Shooshan, Harry M., III. The Bell Breakup: Putting it in Perspective. In *Shooshan, H. M., III, ed.*, 1984, pp. 8–22. [G: U.S.]

Silcox, Clark R. Unfair Methods of Competition: The Courts Revive Proof of Injury to Competition in Antitrust Cases under Section 5 of the FTC Act. *Antitrust Bull.*, Fall 1984, 29(3), pp. 423–74. [G: U.S.]

Smith, Richard L., II. On Strategic Behavior as a Basis for Antitrust Action. *Antitrust Bull.*, Fall 1984, 29(3), pp. 501–22.

de Sola Pool, Ithiel. Disconnecting Bell: Competition and Universal Service: Can We Get There

from Here? In *Shooshan, H. M., III, ed.*, 1984, pp. 112–31. [G: U.S.]

Spivack, Gordon B. The Chicago School Approach to Single Firm Exercises of Monopoly Power: A Response. In *Fox, E. M. and Halverson, J. T., eds.*, 1984, pp. 83–106. [G: U.S.]

Stanbury, W. T. How Wide the Ocean? The Regulated Conduct Exemption in Canada. *Antitrust Bull.*, Fall 1984, 29(3), pp. 577–604. [G: Canada]

Stoller, Michael A. On the Economics of Antitrust and Competition in a Collectibles Market: The Strange Case of the Baseball Card Industry. *Bus. Econ.*, April 1984, 19(3), pp. 18–26. [G: U.S.]

Sullivan, Lawrence A. The New Merger Guidelines: An Afterword. In *Fox, E. M. and Halverson, J. T., eds.*, 1984, pp. 319–35. [G: U.S.]

Trebilcock, Michael. Restrictive Covenants in the Sale of a Business: An Economic Perspective. *Int. Rev. Law Econ.*, December 1984, 4(2), pp. 137–61. [G: U.K.; U.S.; Canada]

Trebing, Harry M. Public Control of Enterprise: Neoclassical Assault and Neoinstitutional Reform: Remarks upon Receipt of the Veblens–Commons Award. *J. Econ. Issues*, June 1984, 18(2), pp. 353–68.

Tullock, Gordon. Taking by Regulation: Resolving the Constitutional Muddle: Comment. In *McKenzie, R. B., ed. (I)*, 1984, pp. 183–86.

von Ungern-Sternberg, Thomas. Innovator Protection and the Rate of Technical Progress. *J. Econ. Behav. Organ.*, March 1984, 5(1), pp. 115–29.

Van Houtte, H. The EEC Draft Regulation on Selective Distribution of Automobiles. *J. World Trade Law*, July–August 1984, 18(4), pp. 349–57. [G: EEC]

Waelbroeck, Michel. Competition, Integration, and Economic Efficiency in the EEC from the Point of View of the Private Firm. *Mich. Law Rev.*, April–May 1984, 82(5 & 6), pp. 1439–46. [G: EEC]

Weinstock, David S. Some Little-known Properties of the Herfindahl–Hirschman Index: Problems of Translation and Specification. *Antitrust Bull.*, Winter 1984, 29(4), pp. 705–17. [G: U.S.]

White, Lawrence H. Comments [The Role of Economic Analysis in the Antitrust Division before and after the Establishment of the Economic Policy Office: A Lawyer's View] [Pigeonholes in Antitrust]. *Antitrust Bull.*, Spring 1984, 29(1), pp. 153–57.

Wiley, Richard E. Disconnecting Bell: The End of Monopoly: Regulatory Change and the Promotion of Competition. In *Shooshan, H. M., III, ed.*, 1984, pp. 23–46. [G: U.S.]

Williamson, John. Privatization: Principles, Problems and Priorities: Comment. *Lloyds Bank Rev.*, January 1984, (151), pp. 45–46. [G: U.K.]

Williamson, Oliver E. Pretrial Uses of Economists: On the Use of "Incentive Logic" to Screen Predation. *Antitrust Bull.*, Fall 1984, 29(3), pp. 475–500. [G: U.S.]

Williamson, Oliver E. Vertical Merger Guidelines: Interpreting the 1982 Reforms. In *Fox, E. M. and Halverson, J. T., eds.*, 1984, pp. 253–66. [G: U.S.]

Youle, Robert E. and Daw, Paul C. Preferred Provider Organizations: An Antitrust Perspective. *Antitrust Bull.*, Summer 1984, 29(2), pp. 301–401. [G: U.S.]

Zielinski, Charles A. Disconnecting Bell: Regulation and Public Policy after Divestiture: The FCC and Congress. In *Shooshan, H. M., III, ed.*, 1984, pp. 100–11. [G: U.S.]

Zwicker, Dieter G. Trade Associations in Germany and the United States of America—Antitrust Restrictions on the Ability of Trade Associations to Regulate Themselves. *Antitrust Bull.*, Winter 1984, 29(4), pp. 775–831. [G: U.S.; W. Germany]

613 Regulation of Public Utilities

6130 Regulation of Public Utilities

Abidin, Ahmad Abid. Malaysia: National Electricity Board Tariffs. In *Munasinghe, M. and Rungta, S., eds.*, 1984, pp. 479–97. [G: Malaysia]

Aigner, Dennis J. The Welfare Econometrics of Peak-Load Pricing for Electricity: Editor's Introduction. *J. Econometrics*, September/October 1984, 26(1/2), pp. 1–15. [G: U.S.]

Aigner, Dennis J. and Leamer, Edward E. Estimation of Time-of-Use Pricing Response in the Absence of Experimental Data: An Application of the Methodology of Data Transferability. *J. Econometrics*, September/October 1984, 26(1/2), pp. 205–27. [G: U.S.]

Aigner, Dennis J. and Lillard, Lee A. Measuring Peak Load Pricing Response from Experimental Data: An Exploratory Analysis. *J. Bus. Econ. Statist.*, January 1984, 2(1), pp. 21–39. [G: U.S.]

Ammons, Jane Chumley. An Analytic Study of Critical Terminal Conditions in Long Range Generation Expansion Planning For Electric Utilities. In *Lev, B., et al., eds.*, 1984, pp. 83–93.

Andersson, Roland. Electricity Tariffs in Sweden. *Energy Econ.*, April 1984, 6(2), pp. 122–30. [G: Sweden]

Andic, Suphan and Cao-García, Ramón J. Regulation in a Democracy: Inefficiency or Efficiency? In *Hanusch, H., ed.*, 1984, pp. 209–22.

Arzac, Enrique R. and Marcus, Matityahu. Erratum: Flotation Cost Adjustment in Rate of Return Regulation: A Reply. *J. Finance*, June 1984, 39(2), pp. 563.

Arzac, Enrique R. and Marcus, Matityahu. Flotation Cost Allowance for the Regulated Firm: A Reply. *J. Finance*, March 1984, 39(1), pp. 293–94.

Asplund, Rita. Kotitaloussähkön kysynnästä Suomessa. (Household Electricity Demand in Finland. With English summary.) *Kansant. Aikak.*, 1984, 80(1), pp. 66–75. [G: Finland]

Atkinson, Scott E. and Halvorsen, Robert. Parametric Efficiency Tests, Economies of Scale, and Input Demand in U.S. Electric Power Generation. *Int. Econ. Rev.*, October 1984, 25(3), pp. 647–62. [G: U.S.]

Balkin, Steven and McDonald, John F. A Market Analysis for Handguns and Gun Control Issues. In *Kates, D. B., Jr., ed.*, 1984, pp. 259–93. [G: U.S.]

Barcella, Mary L. In Defense of Price Controls for "Old" Natural Gas. *Bus. Econ.*, July 1984, 19(4), pp. 24–33. [G: U.S.]

Baron, David P. Regulatory Strategies under Asymmetric Information. In *Boyer, M. and Kihlstrom, R. E., eds.*, 1984, pp. 155–80.

Barrett, Edward M. Proposed Regulatory Treatment of Costs of Extraordinary Large Additions to Plant in Service. In *Foster, J. R., et al., eds.*, 1984, pp. 117–35. [G: U.S.]

Bauer, Kurt W. Assessing Infrastructure Needs: The State of the Art: Discussion. In *Hanson, R., ed.*, 1984, pp. 104–06. [G: U.S.]

Beebe, Raymond. Government Participation in Resource Markets: Comment. In *Pearce, D. W.; Siebert, H. and Walter, I., eds.*, 1984, pp. 242–46. [G: Australia; LDCs]

Bohn, Roger E.; Caramanis, Michael C. and Schweppe, Fred C. Optimal Pricing in Electrical Networks over Space and Time. *Rand J. Econ.*, Autumn 1984, 15(3), pp. 360–76. [G: U.S.]

Bohn, Roger E., et al. Deregulating the Generation of Electricity through the Creation of Spot Markets for Bulk Power. *Energy J.*, April 1984, 5(2), pp. 71–91. [G: U.S.]

Bös, Dieter and Tillmann, Georg. Cost-Axiomatic versus Welfare-Maximizing Marginal Cost Pricing. In *Marchand, M.; Pestieau, P. and Tulkens, H., eds.*, 1984, pp. 101–17.

Bower, Dorothy H.; Bower, Richard S. and Logue, Dennis E. Arbitrage Pricing Theory and Utility Stock Returns. *J. Finance*, September 1984, 39(4), pp. 1041–54. [G: U.S.]

Branch, Ben; Gleit, Alan and Schneeweis, Thomas. The Determinants of Risk and Return for Electric Utility Equity Issues. *Quart. J. Bus. Econ.*, Winter 1984, 23(1), pp. 16–31. [G: U.S.]

Breslaw, J. and Smith, J. Barry. The Restrictiveness of Flexible Functional Forms and the Measurement of Regulatory Constraint: Reply. *Land Econ.*, May 1984, 60(2), pp. 222–27.

Brown, Gardner M., Jr. and McGuire, C. B. A Socially Optimum Pricing Policy for a Public Water Agency. In *Ahmad, Y. J.; Dasgupta, P. and Mäler, K.-G., eds.*, 1984, pp. 176–97. [G: U.S.]

Bubnys, Edward L.; Primeaux, Walter J., Jr. and Zumwalt, J. Kenton. Risk and Return under Changing Regulation: An Empirical Analysis. *Managerial Dec. Econ.*, December 1984, 5(4), pp. 234–41. [G: U.S.]

Buckland, Roger and Davis, Edward W. Privatisation Techniques and the PSBR. *Fisc. Stud.*, August 1984, 5(3), pp. 44–53. [G: U.K.]

Canes, Michael E. and Norman, Donald A. Long-term Contracts and Market Forces in the Natural Gas Market. *J. Energy Devel.*, Autumn 1984, *10*(1), pp. 73–96. [G: U.S.]

Carter, Richard. Le Canada est-il entraîné dans la déréglementation: le cas des communications. (With English summary.) *Can. Public Policy*, March 1984, *10*(1), pp. 10–24. [G: U.S.; Canada]

Carver, John A., Jr. Reciprocal Performance Obligation of Utilities and Government. In *Foster, J. R., et al., eds.*, 1984, pp. 69–76.

Caves, Douglas W.; Christensen, Laurits R. and Herriges, Joseph A. Consistency of Residential Customer Response in Time-of-Use Electricity Pricing Experiments. *J. Econometrics*, September/October 1984, *26*(1/2), pp. 179–203. [G: U.S.]

Caves, Douglas W.; Christensen, Laurits R. and Herriges, Joseph A. Modelling Alternative Residential Peak-Load Electricity Rate Structures. *J. Econometrics*, March 1984, *24*(3), pp. 249–68. [G: U.S.]

Caves, Douglas W., et al. A Comparison of Different Methodologies in a Case Study of Residential Time-of-Use Electricity Pricing: Cost–Benefit Analysis. *J. Econometrics*, September/October 1984, *26*(1/2), pp. 17–34. [G: U.S.]

Christensen, Jens. DANSK OLIE OG NATURGAS A/S—en statsejet erhvervsvirksomhed? (DONG A/S—How Ought It Be Organized? With English summary.) *Nationaløkon. Tidsskr.*, 1984, *122*(1), pp. 124–32. [G: Denmark]

Christy, George A. Original Cost and Fair Value: Pseudo-Science Versus Judgement. In *Foster, J. R., et al., eds.*, 1984, pp. 154–72. [G: U.S.]

Ciliano, Robert and Hery, William. An Overview of the Tenrac Oil and Gas Supply Model. In *Lev, B., et al., eds.*, 1984, pp. 317–35.

Costales, Rene. Inter-American Development Bank: Electricity Tariffs, Policies and Practices. In *Munasinghe, M. and Rungta, S., eds.*, 1984, pp. 537–42. [G: Latin America]

Costello, Kenneth W. Electing Regulators: The Case of Public Utility Commissioners. *Yale J. Regul.*, 1984, *2*(1), pp. 83–105. [G: U.S.]

Coustel, Jean-Pierre. La déréglementation des Télécommunications. Le poids du démembrement d'ATT dans la dynamique de diffusion du mouvement. (With English summary.) *Rev. Econ. Ind.*, 4th Trimester 1984, (30), pp. 42–59. [G: U.S.]

Cowan, William J. Use of Rule-Making in Lieu of Ad Hoc Case-by-Case Adjudication. In *Foster, J. R., et al., eds.*, 1984, pp. 63–68.

Crain, W. Mark and McCormick, Robert E. Regulators as an Interest Group. In *Buchanan, J. M. and Tollison, R. D., eds.*, 1984, pp. 287–304. [G: U.S.]

Crandall, Robert W. The Emerging Competition in the U.S. Telecommunications Market. In *Giersch, H., ed.*, 1984, pp. 87–106. [G: U.S.]

Danielsen, Albert L. and Kamerschen, David R. Economic Regulation: Old Wine in New Bottles. In *Foster, J. R., et al., eds.*, 1984, pp. 45–57.

Davidson, Wallace N., III and Glascock, John L. Rate-of-Return Attrition and Inflation-induced Penalties in Public Utility Common Stocks. *Energy J.*, October 1984, *5*(4), pp. 65–72. [G: U.S.]

Dechert, W. Davis. Has the Averch–Johnson Effect Been Theoretically Justified? *J. Econ. Dynam. Control*, October 1984, *8*(1), pp. 1–17.

Dingell, John D.; Nulty, Timothy E. and McCarthy, Mark. Telephone Deregulation: . . . Or a Free Ride for AT&T? *Challenge*, March/April 1984, *27*(1), pp. 30–33. [G: U.S.]

Evans, Nigel. Sizewell Decision: A Sensitivity Analysis. *Energy Econ.*, January 1984, *6*(1), pp. 14–20. [G: U.K.]

Fanara, Philip, Jr. and Sweet, David M. What Do Regulated Firms Maximize? Some Empirical Evidence from the Natural Gas Pipeline Industry. *Amer. Econ.*, Spring 1984, *28*(1), pp. 44–48. [G: U.S.]

Färe, Rolf and Logan, James. The Restrictiveness of Flexible Functional Forms and the Measurement of Regulatory Constraint: Comment. *Land Econ.*, May 1984, *60*(2), pp. 219–21.

Filer, John E., et al. Impact of Regulation on Vertical Integration in the Electric Industry. *Rev. Ind. Organ.*, Fall 1984, *1*(3), pp. 216–31. [G: U.S.]

Foster, J. Rhoads. Commentary on the State of the Regulatory Art: Emerging Concepts and Procedures. In *Foster, J. R., et al., eds.*, 1984, pp. 4–42. [G: U.S.]

Gallant, A. Ronald and Koenker, Roger W. Costs and Benefits of Peak-Load Pricing of Electricity: A Continuous-Time Econometric Approach. *J. Econometrics*, September/October 1984, *26*(1/2), pp. 83–113. [G: U.S.]

Gallavan, William M. Rate and Service Options: Achieving a Balance between the Utility Ability to Provide Service and Customer Demand for Service. In *Foster, J. R., et al., eds.*, 1984, pp. 77–85. [G: U.S.]

Gardner, Richard L. and Young, Robert A. The Effects of Electricity Rates and Rate Structures on Pump Irrigation: An Eastern Colorado Case Study. *Land Econ.*, November 1984, *60*(4), pp. 352–59. [G: U.S.]

Geller, Henry. Disconnecting Bell: Regulation and Public Policy after Divestiture: The FCC and Congress. In *Shooshan, H. M., III, ed.*, 1984, pp. 83–99. [G: U.S.]

Glismann, Hans H. Comment [The Emerging Competition in the U.S. Telecommunications Market] [Free Entry into Telecommunications?]. In *Giersch, H., ed.*, 1984, pp. 132–35.

Godden, Edward and Crouch, Tom. Papua New Guinea: Electricity Pricing Policy and Practice. In *Munasinghe, M. and Rungta, S., eds.*, 1984, pp. 370–404. [G: Papua New Guinea]

Goudard, Daniel. Tarifs et équilibre financier des entreprises publiques. (Tariffs and Financial Balance of Public Firms. With English summary.) *Revue Écon.*, November 1984, 35(6), pp. 1213–38.   [G: France]

Green, David Jay. A Small Scale, Partial Equilibrium Model of Natural Gas Markets: Responses to Alternative Deregulation Scenarios and Oil Price Changes. *Southern Econ. J.*, April 1984, 50(4), pp. 1112–30.   [G: U.S.]

Greene, William H. and Smiley, Robert H. The Effectiveness of Utility Regulation in a Period of Changing Economic Conditions. In *Marchand, M.; Pestieau, P. and Tulkens, H., eds.*, 1984, pp. 269–87.   [G: U.S.]

Greenwald, Bruce C. Rate Base Selection and the Structure of Regulation. *Rand J. Econ.*, Spring 1984, 15(1), pp. 85–95.

Gurwitz, Aaron S. and Chall, Daniel E. Nuclear Power Plant Construction: Paying the Bill. *Fed. Res. Bank New York Quart. Rev.*, Summer 1984, 9(2), pp. 48–57.   [G: U.S.]

Hall, George R. Comments on Revenue Requirements Papers. In *Foster, J. R., et al., eds.*, 1984, pp. 58–62.

Harrison, J. Michael. Selection of the Appropriate Test Year. In *Foster, J. R., et al., eds.*, 1984, pp. 89–95.   [G: U.S.]

Hartley, Peter and Trengove, Chris. The Marginal Costs of Electricity Supply in Victoria. *Econ. Rec.*, December 1984, 60(171), pp. 340–55.   [G: Australia]

Hatry, Harry. Assessing Infrastructure Needs: The State of the Art: Discussion. In *Hanson, R., ed.*, 1984, pp. 102–04.   [G: U.S.]

Hausman, Jerry A. and Trimble, John. Appliance Purchase and Usage Adaptation to a Permanent Time-of-Day Electricity Rate Schedule. *J. Econometrics*, September/October 1984, 26(1/2), pp. 115–39.   [G: U.S.]

Hausman, William J. and Neufeld, John L. Time-of-Day Pricing in the U.S. Electric Power Industry at the Turn of the Century. *Rand J. Econ.*, Spring 1984, 15(1), pp. 116–26.   [G: U.S.]

Helman, Leonard A. Rulemaking in Lieu of Ad Hoc Case-by-Case Adjudication: Automatic Adjustment Clauses, the New Mexico Experiment. In *Foster, J. R., et al., eds.*, 1984, pp. 148–53.   [G: U.S.]

Hillman, Arye L. Producer and Consumer Interests, the State-Owned Pipeline, and Public Authority Pricing of Natural Gas. *Econ. Rec.*, March 1984, 60(168), pp. 28–33.

Hölker, Franz-Josef. Die ordnung der energiewirtschaft der Bundesrepublik Deutschland. Leitbild—Reale Probleme. (The Organisation of the Energy Sector in the Federal Republic of Germany. With English summary.) *Ann. Pub. Co-op. Econ.*, Oct.–Dec. 1984, 55(4), pp. 413–31.   [G: W. Germany]

Hoover, Donald R. The Test Year Nemesis. In *Foster, J. R., et al., eds.*, 1984, pp. 96–102.   [G: U.S.]

Howe, Keith M. Flotation Cost Allowance for the Regulated Firm: A Comment. *J. Finance*, March 1984, 39(1), pp. 289–91.

Howrey, E. Philip and Varian, Hal R. Estimating the Distributional Impact of Time-of-Day Pric-

ing of Electricity. *J. Econometrics*, September/October 1984, 26(1/2), pp. 65–82.   [G: U.S.]

Itchon, Gabriel Y. Philippines: National Power Corporation Power Tariff Policy. In *Munasinghe, M. and Rungta, S., eds.*, 1984, pp. 363–69.   [G: Philippines]

Jahangir, Mohammad. Pakistan: Electricity Tariff Policy. In *Munasinghe, M. and Rungta, S., eds.*, 1984, pp. 498–509.   [G: Pakistan]

Kahn, Alfred E. Telephone Deregulation: A Needed Dose of Competition . . . *Challenge*, March/April 1984, 27(1), pp. 24–29.
                    [G: U.S.]

Kahn, Alfred E. The Road to More Intelligent Telephone Pricing. *Yale J. Regul.*, 1984, 1(2), pp. 139–57.   [G: U.S.]

Kaserman, David L.; Kavanaugh, L. Roy and Tepel, Richard C. To Which Fiddle Does the Regulator Dance? Some Empirical Evidence. *Rev. Ind. Organ.*, Winter 1984, 1(4), pp. 246–58.   [G: U.S.]

Keane, John K., Jr. CWIP: An Empty Fishbowl? In *Foster, J. R., et al., eds.*, 1984, pp. 103–09.   [G: U.S.]

Kohler, Daniel F. and Mitchell, Bridger M. Response to Residential Time-of-Use Electricity Rates: How Transferable Are the Findings? *J. Econometrics*, September/October 1984, 26(1/2), pp. 141–77.   [G: U.S.]

Lawrey, Roger N.; Kirkby, R. G. and Watkins, G. Campbell. Regulated Pipeline Tariffs in Canada—A Sensitivity Analysis. *Logist. Transp. Rev.*, September 1984, 20(3), pp. 195–203.   [G: Canada]

Levine, Leonard B. Changes in Policies Affecting U.S. Natural Gas Trade. *J. Energy Devel.*, Autumn 1984, 10(1), pp. 117–20.   [G: U.S.]

Lillard, Lee A. and Aigner, Dennis J. Time-of-Day Electricity Consumption Response to Temperature and the Ownership of Air Conditioning Appliances. *J. Bus. Econ. Statist.*, January 1984, 2(1), pp. 40–53.   [G: U.S.]

Linke, Charles M. Equity-Debt Risk Premia Issues in Utility Rate Regulation. In *Foster, J. R., et al., eds.*, 1984, pp. 229–36.

Lloyd, P. J. Protection and Structural Change from a Contestable Market Perspective: Comment. *Australian Econ. Rev.*, 3rd Quarter 1984, (67), pp. 90–91.

Makhija, Anil K. and Thompson, Howard E. Capitalized Interest and the Cost of Money to Electric Utilities. *Land Econ.*, August 1984, 60(3), pp. 278–91.   [G: U.S.]

Maloney, Michael T.; McCormick, Robert E. and Tollison, Robert D. Economic Regulation, Competitive Governments, and Specialized Resources. *J. Law Econ.*, October 1984, 27(2), pp. 329–38.   [G: U.S.]

Mayo, John W. Multiproduct Monopoly, Regulation, and Firm Costs. *Southern Econ. J.*, July 1984, 51(1), pp. 208–18.   [G: U.S.]

Mestmäcker, Ernst-Joachim. Comment [The Emerging Competition in the U.S. Telecommunications Market] [Free Entry into Telecommunications?]. In *Giersch, H., ed.*, 1984, pp. 129–32.

Mirucki, Jean. A Study of the Averch–Johnson Hypothesis in the Telecommunications Industry. *Atlantic Econ. J.*, March 1984, *12*(1), pp. 121. **[G: Canada]**

Mitra, A. K. India: Power Tariffs and Policy in Calcutta. In *Munasinghe, M. and Rungta, S., eds.*, 1984, pp. 405–19. **[G: India]**

Mould, Maurice C. World Bank: Financial Covenants and Their Use in the Development of Pricing Policies. In *Munasinghe, M. and Rungta, S., eds.*, 1984, pp. 543–67. **[G: LDCs]**

Munasinghe, Mohan. Comment [Sri Lanka: Costs of Supplying Electricity and Tariff Policy] [Indonesia: Development of Electricity Tariffs] [Malaysia: National Electricity Board Tariffs] [Pakistan: Electricity Tariff Policy]. In *Munasinghe, M. and Rungta, S., eds.*, 1984, pp. 510–15. **[G: Sri Lanka; Malaysia; Indonesia; Pakistan]**

Munasinghe, Mohan. Implementing Long-run Marginal Cost-based Tariff Structures. In *Munasinghe, M. and Rungta, S., eds.*, 1984, pp. 193–211.

Munasinghe, Mohan and Rungta, Shyam. Power Tariffs: An Overview. In *Munasinghe, M. and Rungta, S., eds.*, 1984, pp. 1–51. **[G: LDCs; MDCs]**

Nelson, Randy A. Regulation, Capital Vintage, and Technical Change in the Electric Utility Industry. *Rev. Econ. Statist.*, February 1984, *66*(1), pp. 59–69. **[G: U.S.]**

Nelson, Randy A. and Primeaux, Walter J., Jr. Rate Base Valuation Procedures and the Behavior of Regulated Firms. *Quart. Rev. Econ. Bus.*, Winter 1984, *24*(4), pp. 72–81. **[G: U.S.]**

O'Day, D. Kelly and Neumann, Lance A. Assessing Infrastructure Needs: The State of the Art. In *Hanson, R., ed.*, 1984, pp. 67–101. **[G: U.S.]**

Palmer, H. C. Accounting Costs as a Basis for Time-of-Use Tariffs. In *Munasinghe, M. and Rungta, S., eds.*, 1984, pp. 119–35. **[G: Canada]**

Park, Rolla Edward and Acton, Jan Paul. Large Business Customer Response to Time-of-Day Electricity Rates. *J. Econometrics*, September/October 1984, *26*(1/2), pp. 229–52. **[G: U.S.]**

Parks, Richard W. and Weitzel, David. Measuring the Consumer Welfare Effects of Time-differentiated Electricity Prices. *J. Econometrics*, September/October 1984, *26*(1/2), pp. 35–64. **[G: U.S.]**

Patterson, Cleveland S. The Effects of Leverage on k. In *Foster, J. R., et al., eds.*, 1984, pp. 237–60. **[G: U.S.]**

Pincus, Jonathan J. Protection and Structural Change from a Contestable Market Perspective. *Australian Econ. Rev.*, 3rd Quarter 1984, (67), pp. 79–89.

Porter, Michael G. Private Resource Development and Public Utilities: Some Hazards of Sleeping with Elephants. In *Pearce, D. W.; Siebert, H. and Walter, I., eds.*, 1984, pp. 225–41. **[G: Australia]**

Primeaux, Walter J., Jr., et al. Determinants of Regulatory Policies toward Competition in the Electric Utility Industry. *Public Choice*, 1984, *43*(2), pp. 173–86. **[G: U.S.]**

Primeaux, Walter J., Jr.; Bubnys, Edward L. and Rasche, Robert H. Fair Value versus Original Cost Rate Base Valuation during Inflation. *Energy J.*, April 1984, *5*(2), pp. 93–108. **[G: U.S.]**

Procter, Robert J. and Tyner, Wallace E. Assessing the Impact of Peak-Load Electricity Pricing and the Solar Tax Credits on the Adoption of Solar Energy. *Land Econ.*, February 1984, *60*(1), pp. 49–55. **[G: U.S.]**

Rahman, A. K. M. Anisur. Bangladesh: Electricity Tariff Policy and Methodology. In *Munasinghe, M. and Rungta, S., eds.*, 1984, pp. 336–46. **[G: Bangladesh]**

Rajagopalan, R. Implementing Long-run Marginal Cost-based Tariff Structures: Comment. In *Munasinghe, M. and Rungta, S., eds.*, 1984, pp. 214–17. **[G: India]**

Rhys, J. M. W. The Implications of Nuclear Energy for Electricity Tariffs. In *Brookes, L. G. and Motamen, H., eds.*, 1984, pp. 316–31.

Riordan, Michael H. On Delegating Price Authority to a Regulated Firm. *Rand J. Econ.*, Spring 1984, *15*(1), pp. 108–15.

Robinson, Frank S. Regulatory Treatment of Cancelled Construction Project Costs. In *Foster, J. R., et al., eds.*, 1984, pp. 110–16. **[G: U.S.]**

Roux, J. Pl. Marginal Cost Pricing: Updating the French Electricity Tariffs. In *Munasinghe, M. and Rungta, S., eds.*, 1984, pp. 231–65. **[G: France]**

Schmalensee, Richard and Golub, Bennett W. Estimating Effective Concentration in Deregulated Wholesale Electricity Markets. *Rand J. Econ.*, Spring 1984, *15*(1), pp. 12–26. **[G: U.S.]**

Schmidt, Michael. Rulemaking in Lieu of Case-by-Case Adjudication: An Overview of Automatic Adjustment. In *Foster, J. R., et al., eds.*, 1984, pp. 136–47. **[G: U.S.]**

Schwartz, Eli. "Excess Capacity" in Utility Industries: An Inventory Theoretic Approach. *Land Econ.*, February 1984, *60*(1), pp. 40–48. **[G: U.S.]**

Schwarz, Peter M. The Estimated Effects on Industry of Time-of-Day Demand and Energy Electricity Prices. *J. Ind. Econ.*, June 1984, *32*(4), pp. 523–39. **[G: U.S.]**

Scott, Frank A., Jr. Uncertain Input Prices, Profit Risk, and the Rate-of-Return Regulated Firm: Reply. *Land Econ.*, November 1984, *60*(4), pp. 411–13.

Sedlik, Barry. A New Method for Assessing Cogeneration Potential: Northeast Utilities' Case Study. In *Lev, B., et al., eds.*, 1984, pp. 213–29. **[G: U.S.]**

Senadhipathy, D. G. Sri Lanka: Costs of Supplying Electricity and Tariff Policy. In *Munasinghe, M. and Rungta, S., eds.*, 1984, pp. 438–65. **[G: Sri Lanka]**

Shapleigh, John C. Rate of Change Regulation:

Incentive Restoration Clause. In *Foster, J. R., et al., eds.*, 1984, pp. 173–80.

Soejitno, Soejanto. Indonesia: Development of Electricity Tariffs. In *Munasinghe, M. and Rungta, S., eds.*, 1984, pp. 468–79.
[G: Indonesia]

Stark, A. W. Uncertain Input Prices, Profit Risk, and the Rate-of-Return Regulated Firm: Comment. *Land Econ.*, November 1984, *60*(4), pp. 404–07.

Trebing, Harry M. Public Utility Regulation: A Case Study in the Debate over Effectiveness of Economic Regulation. *J. Econ. Issues*, March 1984, *18*(1), pp. 223–50. **[G: U.S.]**

Tun, U Tin. Burma: Electricity Tariff Study. In *Munasinghe, M. and Rungta, S., eds.*, 1984, pp. 308–35. **[G: Burma]**

Turnbull, Geoffrey K. Uncertain Input Prices, Profit Risk, and the Rate-of-Return Regulated Firm: Comment. *Land Econ.*, November 1984, *60*(4), pp. 408–10.

Turvey, Ralph. Accounting Costs as a Basis for Time-of-Use Tariffs: Comment. In *Munasinghe, M. and Rungta, S., eds.*, 1984, pp. 138–43. **[G: Canada]**

Turvey, Ralph. Estimating and Using Marginal Cost Pricing Concepts. In *Munasinghe, M. and Rungta, S., eds.*, 1984, pp. 153–70.
[G: France; U.K.]

Turvey, Ralph. Marginal Cost Pricing: Updating the French Electricity Tariffs: Comment. In *Munasinghe, M. and Rungta, S., eds.*, 1984, pp. 266–71. **[G: France]**

Turvey, Ralph. Philippines: National Power Corporation Power Tariff Policy: Comment. In *Munasinghe, M. and Rungta, S., eds.*, 1984, pp. 425–28. **[G: Philippines]**

Vennard, Edwin. Accounting Costs as a Basis for Time-of-Use Tariffs: Comment. In *Munasinghe, M. and Rungta, S., eds.*, 1984, pp. 136–38. **[G: Canada]**

Vennard, Edwin. Review of Electricity Industry Trends and Rate Making. In *Munasinghe, M. and Rungta, S., eds.*, 1984, pp. 70–98.
[G: U.S.]

Wallis, J. L. Piecemeal Optimization and Public Utility Pricing. *S. Afr. J. Econ.*, September 1984, *52*(3), pp. 233–46. **[G: S. Africa]**

Warford, Jeremy. Comments [Philippines: National Power Corporation Power Tariff Policy] [Papua New Guinea: Electricity Pricing Policy and Practice] [India: Power Tariffs and Policy in Calcutta]. In *Munasinghe, M. and Rungta, S., eds.*, 1984, pp. 420–25. **[G: Philippines; Papua New Guinea; India]**

Warford, Jeremy. The Objectives of Electricity Tariff Policy. In *Munasinghe, M. and Rungta, S., eds.*, 1984, pp. 61–69. **[G: LDCs]**

von Weizsäcker, Carl Christian. Free Entry into Telecommunications? *Info. Econ. Policy*, 1984, *1*(3), pp. 197–216.

von Weizsäcker, Carl Christian. Free Entry into Telecommunications? In *Giersch, H., ed.*, 1984, pp. 107–28.

Wenders, John T. Two-Part Tariffs and the "Spiral of Impossibility" in the Market for Electricity

[Disequilibrium Processes in the Market for Electricity: The Case of Municipal Ownership]. *Energy J.*, January 1984, *5*(1), pp. 177–79. **[G: U.S.]**

Wiley, Richard E. Disconnecting Bell: The End of Monopoly: Regulatory Change and the Promotion of Competition. In *Shooshan, H. M., III, ed.*, 1984, pp. 23–46. **[G: U.S.]**

Woo, Chi-Keung. A Note on Measuring Household Welfare Effects of Time-of-Use (TOU) Pricing. *Energy J.*, July 1984, *5*(3), pp. 170–81. **[G: U.S.]**

Yoon, Hi Woo. Korea: Peak-load Pricing Based on LRMC. In *Munasinghe, M. and Rungta, S., eds.*, 1984, pp. 295–308. **[G: S. Korea]**

Zielinski, Charles A. Disconnecting Bell: Regulation and Public Policy after Divestiture: The FCC and Congress. In *Shooshan, H. M., III, ed.*, 1984, pp. 100–11. **[G: U.S.]**

Zimonyi, I. L. Asian Development Bank: The Objectives of Financial Covenants in the Context of Efficient Electricity Tariffs. In *Munasinghe, M. and Rungta, S., eds.*, 1984, pp. 531–35.
[G: Asia]

614 Public Enterprises

6140 Public Enterprises

Allali, Badre-Eddine and Mdaghri, Driss Alaoui. Economic Performance of Public Enterprises. In *U.N. Dept. Tech. Coop. Devel.*, 1984, pp. 221–27.

Asher, Martin A. and Popkin, Joel. Industrial and Labor Relations Review: Comment. *Ind. Lab. Relat. Rev.*, October 1984, *38*(1), pp. 36. **[G: U.S.]**

Asher, Martin A. and Popkin, Joel. The Effect of Gender and Race Differentials on Public–Private Wage Comparisons: A Study of Postal Workers. *Ind. Lab. Relat. Rev.*, October 1984, *38*(1), pp. 16–25. **[G: U.S.]**

Baer, Werner and Villela, Annibal V. Evaluating Public Enterprises: Some Dilemmas in Formulating Guidelines. In *[Ferber, R.]*, 1984, pp. 289–98.

Baklanoff, Eric N. Changing Systems: The Portuguese Revolution and the Public Enterprise Sector. *ACES Bull.*, Summer–Fall 1984, *26*(2–3), pp. 63–76. **[G: Portugal]**

Barenstein, Jorge. Evaluation and Control of Public Enterprises in Mexico: Some Organisational and Normative Issues. In *U.N. Dept. Tech. Coop. Devel.*, 1984, pp. 206–20. **[G: Mexico]**

Basu, P. K. Evaluation of Economic Performance of Public Enterprises in India. In *U.N. Dept. Tech. Coop. Devel.*, 1984, pp. 120–205. **[G: India]**

Baumol, William J. Toward a Theory of Public Enterprise. *Atlantic Econ. J.*, March 1984, *12*(1), pp. 12–19.

Beato, Paulina and Mas-Colell, Andreu. The Marginal Cost Pricing Rule as a Regulation Mechanism in Mixed Markets. In *Marchand, M.; Pestieau, P. and Tulkens, H., eds.*, 1984, pp. 81–100.

Beebe, Raymond. Government Participation in Resource Markets: Comment. In *Pearce, D. W.; Siebert, H. and Walter, I., eds.*, 1984, pp. 242–46. **[G: Australia; LDCs]**

Beesley, Michael E. Government, Nationalised Industries and Creating Enterprise. In *Ramanadham, V. V., ed.*, 1984, pp. 192–208. **[G: U.K.]**

Beesley, Michael E. and Littlechild, Stephen C. Privatization: Principles, Problems and Priorities: Reply. *Lloyds Bank Rev.*, January 1984, (151), pp. 47–48. **[G: U.K.]**

Bennett, James T. Privatizing Municipal Services. In *Giersch, H., ed.*, 1984, pp. 44–57.

Bhatt, V. V. Institutional Framework and Public Enterprise Performance. *World Devel.*, July 1984, 12(7), pp. 713–21.

Boneo, Horacio. Evaluation of Economic Performance in Public Enterprises. In *U.N. Dept. Tech. Coop. Devel.*, 1984, pp. 43–71. **[G: Argentina]**

Bös, Dieter; Tillmann, Georg and Zimmermann, Hans-Georg. Bureaucratic Public Enterprises. *Z. Nationalökon.*, Supplement 1984, pp. 127–76. **[G: U.K.]**

Buckland, Roger and Davis, Edward W. Privatisation Techniques and the PSBR. *Fisc. Stud.*, August 1984, 5(3), pp. 44–53. **[G: U.K.]**

Calogero, Giuseppe. La diffusion de l'innovation et le rôle des participations de l'etat en Italie. (The Propagation of Innovations. The Role of State Share Holdings in Italy. With English summary.) *Ann. Pub. Co-op. Econ.*, Oct.–Dec. 1984, 55(4), pp. 395–411. **[G: Italy]**

Chambers, David J. Corporate Plans as Commitments. In *Ramanadham, V. V., ed.*, 1984, pp. 119–37.

Cvetanović, Milivoje. Performance Evaluation of Yugoslav Enterprises. In *U.N. Dept. Tech. Coop. Devel.*, 1984, pp. 275–95. **[G: Yugoslavia]**

Davis, Evan. Express Coaching since 1980: Liberalisation in Practice. *Fisc. Stud.*, February 1984, 5(1), pp. 76–86. **[G: U.K.]**

Deprins, Dominique; Simar, Léopold and Tulkens, Henry. Measuring Labor-Efficiency in Post Offices. In *Marchand, M.; Pestieau, P. and Tulkens, H., eds.*, 1984, pp. 243–67. **[G: Belgium]**

Diwan, Rauf and Hamid, Javed. The Potential for Industrial Development. In *Burki, S. J. and LaPorte, R., Jr., eds.*, 1984, pp. 84–102. **[G: Pakistan]**

Drèze, Jacques H. Second-best Analysis with Markets in Disequilibrium: Public Sector Pricing in a Keynesian Regime. In *Marchand, M.; Pestieau, P. and Tulkens, H., eds.*, 1984, pp. 45–79.

Emmerich, Volker. Anmerkungen zu den Postfinanzen. (With English Summary.) In *Eucken, W. and Böhm, F., eds.*, 1984, pp. 43–69. **[G: W. Germany]**

Fadahunsi, Olu. Institutional Arrangements for Monitoring the Performance of Nigerian Public Enterprises. In *U.N. Dept. Tech. Coop. Devel.*, 1984, pp. 228–33. **[G: Nigeria]**

Finsinger, Jörg. The Performance of Public Enterprises in Insurance Markets. In *Marchand, M.; Pestieau, P. and Tulkens, H., eds.*, 1984, pp. 223–41. **[G: W. Germany]**

Forsyth, Peter. Airlines and Airports: Privatisation, Competition, and Regulation. *Fisc. Stud.*, February 1984, 5(1), pp. 61–75. **[G: U.K.]**

Freeman, John R. and Duvall, Raymond D. International Economic Relations and the Entrepreneurial State. *Econ. Develop. Cult. Change*, January 1984, 32(2), pp. 373–400. **[G: Ireland]**

Garner, Maurice R. Public Enterprise in Thailand. In *Ramanadham, V. V., ed.*, 1984, pp. 14–27. **[G: Thailand]**

Ghai, Yash. Law and Public Enterprise in Developing Countries. In *Ramanadham, V. V., ed.*, 1984, pp. 59–70.

Goudard, Daniel. Tarifs et équilibre financier des entreprises publiques. (Tariffs and Financial Balance of Public Firms. With English summary.) *Revue Écon.*, November 1984, 35(6), pp. 1213–38. **[G: France]**

Gravelle, Hugh S. E. Bargaining and Efficiency in Public and Private Sector Firms. In *Marchand, M.; Pestieau, P. and Tulkens, H., eds.*, 1984, pp. 193–220.

Guesnerie, Roger and Laffont, Jean-Jacques. The Government Control of Public Firms and the Economics of Incomplete Information: An Introduction. In *Marchand, M.; Pestieau, P. and Tulkens, H., eds.*, 1984, pp. 159–78.

Hamer, Eberhard. Creating New Entrepreneurship by Privatizing Municipal Services. In *Giersch, H., ed.*, 1984, pp. 58–69.

Hassan, Mostafa F. Trade Prospects for the Oil Exporters: The Case of Venezuela. In *Jorge, A.; Salazar-Carrillo, J. and Sanchez, E. P.*, 1984, pp. 71–81. **[G: Latin America; Venezuela]**

Heald, David. Privatisation: Analysing Its Appeal and Limitations. *Fisc. Stud.*, February 1984, 5(1), pp. 36–46. **[G: U.K.]**

Heath, John B. Public Enterprises in the UK: Relevant Experiences for the Developing Countries. In *Ramanadham, V. V., ed.*, 1984, pp. 109–18. **[G: U.K.]**

Hill, Raymond D. State Enterprise and Income Distribution in Mexico. In *Aspe, P. and Sigmund, P. E., eds.*, 1984, pp. 357–96. **[G: Mexico]**

Hillman, Arye L. Producer and Consumer Interests, the State-Owned Pipeline, and Public Authority Pricing of Natural Gas. *Econ. Rec.*, March 1984, 60(168), pp. 28–33.

Horner, Melchior. Angebot und Nachfrage von Postdepositen. (Supply and Demand of Post Office Demand Deposits. With English summary.) *Schweiz. Z. Volkswirtsch. Statist.*, March 1984, 120(1), pp. 65–88. **[G: Switzerland]**

Jeanrenaud, Claude and Meyer, Daniel. L'incidence a moyen et long terme des commandes de materiel de telecommunication: deux etudes de cas. (The Medium- and Long-term Incidence of Orders of Telecommunication Material: Two Case Studies. With English summary.) *Ann. Pub. Co-op. Econ.*, April–June 1984, 55(2), pp. 191–203. **[G: Switzerland]**

Jones, Trefor T. and Cockerill, T. A. J. Public Enterprise Management. In *Pickering, J. F. and Cockerill, T. A. J.*, eds., 1984, pp. 344–87. **[G: U.K.]**

Kornai, János and Matits, Ágnes. Softness of the Budget Constraint—An Analysis Relying on Data of Firms. *Acta Oecon.*, 1984, 32(3–4), pp. 223–49. **[G: Hungary]**

Lewis, David L. and Bodde, David L. Understanding Political Risk in Investment Planning. *J. Policy Anal. Manage.*, Summer 1984, 3(4), pp. 544–60. **[G: U.S.]**

Likierman, Andrew. The Use of Profitability in Assessing the Performance of Public Enterprises. In *Ramanadham, V. V.*, ed., 1984, pp. 159–70. **[G: U.K.]**

Lloyd, P. J. Protection and Structural Change from a Contestable Market Perspective: Comment. *Australian Econ. Rev.*, 3rd Quarter 1984, (67), pp. 90–91.

Maheswaran, Durairaj. State Enterprises: A Marketing Perspective. In *Kindra, G. S.*, ed., 1984, pp. 216–37. **[G: LDCs]**

Marchand, Maurice; Pestieau, Pierre and Tulkens, Henry. The Performance of Public Enterprises: Normative, Positive and Empirical Issues. In *Marchand, M.; Pestieau, P. and Tulkens, H.*, eds., 1984, pp. 3–42.

Marchand, Maurice; Pestieau, Pierre and Weymark, John A. Discount Rates for Public Enterprises in the Presence of Alternative Financial Constraints: A Correction. *Z. Nationalökon.*, 1984, 44(3), pp. 289–91.

McCraw, Thomas K. The Public and Private Spheres in Historical Perspective. In *Brooks, H.; Liebman, L. and Schelling, C. S.*, eds., 1984, pp. 31–60. **[G: U.S.]**

Mehdi, Istaqbal. Performance Evaluation of Public Enterprise in Pakistan: Experiment in Social Accounting System. *Pakistan Devel. Rev.*, Summer-Autumn 1984, 23(2&3), pp. 179–200. **[G: Pakistan]**

Monsen, R. Joseph. French Socialists March to the Right. *Challenge*, September/October 1984, 27(4), pp. 37–42. **[G: France]**

Müller, Jens. Facilitating an Indigenous Social Organisation of Production in Tanzania. In *Fransman, M. and King, K.*, eds., 1984, pp. 375–90. **[G: Tanzania]**

Perloff, Jeffrey M. and Wachter, Michael L. Postal Service Wage Comparability: Comment. *Ind. Lab. Relat. Rev.*, October 1984, 38(1), pp. 37. **[G: U.S.]**

Perloff, Jeffrey M. and Wachter, Michael L. Wage Comparability in the U.S. Postal Service. *Ind. Lab. Relat. Rev.*, October 1984, 38(1), pp. 26–35. **[G: U.S.]**

Pestieau, Pierre. Public Enterprises under Conditions of Unemployment: A Survey of the Issues. *Ann. Pub. Co-op. Econ.*, Oct.–Dec. 1984, 55(4), pp. 365–82. **[G: Belgium]**

Philip, George. Public Enterprise in Mexico. In *Ramanadham, V. V.*, ed., 1984, pp. 28–46. **[G: Mexico]**

Pincus, Jonathan J. Protection and Structural Change from a Contestable Market Perspective. *Australian Econ. Rev.*, 3rd Quarter 1984, (67), pp. 79–89.

Pitkänen, Eero. Julkisten liikelaitosten toiminnan tuloksellisuus. (The Efficiency and Effectiveness of Public Enterprises. With English summary.) *Liiketaloudellinen Aikak.*, 1984, 33(1), pp. 81–106. **[G: Finland; Sweden]**

Pommerehne, Werner W. Comment [Privatizing Municipal Services] [Creating New Entrepreneurship by Privatizing Municipal Services]. In *Giersch, H.*, ed., 1984, pp. 70–81.

Porter, Michael G. Private Resource Development and Public Utilities: Some Hazards of Sleeping with Elephants. In *Pearce, D. W.; Siebert, H. and Walter, I.*, eds., 1984, pp. 225–41. **[G: Australia]**

Pryke, Richard. The Monitoring and Control of Nationalised Industries in Great Britain. In *U.N. Dept. Tech. Coop. Devel.*, 1984, pp. 234–74. **[G: U.K.]**

Qadir, Asghar. The Profitability of Public Enterprises in Pakistan: Comment. *Pakistan Devel. Rev.*, Summer-Autumn 1984, 23(2&3), pp. 161–63. **[G: Pakistan]**

Ramanadham, V. V. Public Enterprise and the Developing World: A Concluding Review. In *Ramanadham, V. V.*, ed., 1984, pp. 209–29.

Ramanadham, V. V. Public Enterprise in Developing Countries: The Development Context. In *Ramanadham, V. V.*, ed., 1984, pp. 1–13. **[G: Selected LDCs]**

Rasul, Ghulam. Performance Evaluation of Public Enterprise in Pakistan: Experiment in Social Accounting System: Comment. *Pakistan Devel. Rev.*, Summer-Autumn 1984, 23(2&3), pp. 201–03. **[G: Pakistan]**

Rees, Ray. A Positive Theory of the Public Enterprise. In *Marchand, M.; Pestieau, P. and Tulkens, H.*, eds., 1984, pp. 179–91.

Rees, Ray. The Public Enterprise Game. *Econ. J.*, 1984 Supplement, 94, pp. 109–23.

Rhodes, Harold L. British Public Enterprises and Project Initiation in the Developing World. In *Ramanadham, V. V.*, ed., 1984, pp. 87–108. **[G: U.K.]**

Rizzo, Socrates C. Generation and Allocation of Oil Economic Surpluses. In *Aspe, P. and Sigmund, P. E.*, eds., 1984, pp. 99–127. **[G: Mexico]**

Ronson, George. Financial Accountability of Public Enterprises in Bangladesh. In *Ramanadham, V. V.*, ed., 1984, pp. 47–58. **[G: Bangladesh]**

Ruiz Dueñas, Jorge. Public Enterprise and Planning in Mexico. *Ann. Pub. Co-op. Econ.*, January–March 1984, 55(1), pp. 91–107. **[G: Mexico]**

Santos, Anibal and da Silva, J. M. Amado. Rivalidade e barreiras à entrada no sector público empresarial (Um ensaio de análise económica).

(With English summary.) *Economia (Portugal)*, May 1984, *8*(2), pp. 361–79.

Sarmad, Khwaja. The Profitability of Public Enterprises in Pakistan. *Pakistan Devel. Rev.*, Summer-Autumn 1984, *23*(2&3), pp. 147–60. [G: Pakistan]

Shackleton, J. R. Privatization: The Case Examined. *Nat. Westminster Bank Quart. Rev.*, May 1984, pp. 59–73. [G: U.K.]

Sharpe, Tom. Privatisation, Regulation and Competition. *Fisc. Stud.*, February 1984, *5*(1), pp. 47–60. [G: U.K.; U.S.]

Steel, David. Government and the New Hybrids: A Trail of Unanswered Questions. *Fisc. Stud.*, February 1984, *5*(1), pp. 87–97. [G: U.K.]

Stopford, John. Joint Ventures between Multinational Corporations and Local State Enterprises. In *Ramanadham, V. V., ed.*, 1984, pp. 71–86. [G: Selected LDCs]

Straussman, Jeffrey D. and Rosenberg, Alexander. Public Sector Monopolies. In *Holzer, M. and Nagel, S. S., eds.*, 1984, pp. 219–34.

Subrahmanyam, Marti G. and Swirski, Moises. The Public Investment Decision under Uncertainty: A Mean-Variance Synthesis. In *Marchand, M.; Pestieau, P. and Tulkens, H., eds.*, 1984, pp. 119–55.

Tanner, Lucretia Dewey. Modernizing the Federal Government: Effect on Its Employees. In *Collins, E. L. and Tanner, L. D., eds.*, 1984, pp. 97–114. [G: U.S.]

Thompson, Mark and Ponak, Allen. Industrial Relations in Canadian Public Enterprises. *Int. Lab. Rev.*, September–October 1984, *123*(5), pp. 647–63. [G: Canada]

Tian, Jiyun. Problems in the "Substitution of Taxes for Profits" in State-Run Enterprises. *Chinese Econ. Stud.*, Winter 1983–84, *17*(2), pp. 68–77. [G: China]

Tierney, John T. Government Corporations and Managing the Public's Business. *Polit. Sci. Quart.*, Spring 1984, *99*(1), pp. 73–92. [G: U.S.]

Vaubel, Roland. Comment [Privatizing Municipal Services] [Creating New Entrepreneurship by Privatizing Municipal Services]. In *Giersch, H., ed.*, 1984, pp. 82–86.

Vernon, Raymond. Linking Managers with Ministers: Dilemmas of the State-owned Enterprise. *J. Policy Anal. Manage.*, Fall 1984, *4*(1), pp. 39–55.

Vernon, Raymond. Uncertainty in the Resource Industries: The Special Role of State-owned Enterprises. In *Pearce, D. W.; Siebert, H. and Walter, I., eds.*, 1984, pp. 207–23. [G: LDCs]

Walsh, Vivien. The Post Office, the Unions and the New Technology. In *Warner, M., ed.*, 1984, pp. 210–23. [G: U.K.]

von Weizsäcker, Carl Christian. Free Entry into Telecommunications? *Info. Econ. Policy*, 1984, *1*(3), pp. 197–216.

Williamson, John. Privatization: Principles, Problems and Priorities: Comment. *Lloyds Bank Rev.*, January 1984, (151), pp. 45–46. [G: U.K.]

Woodward, S. N. Corporate Planning, Commitment and Public Enterprises. In *Ramanadham, V. V., ed.*, 1984, pp. 138–58.

Zardkoohi, Asghar and Sheer, Alain. Public versus Private Liquor Retailing: An Investigation into the Behavior of the State Governments. *Southern Econ. J.*, April 1984, *50*(4), pp. 1058–76. [G: U.S.]

615 Economics of Transportation

6150 Economics of Transportation

Aberle, Gerd. Deregulating Ground Transportation: Comment. In *Giersch, H., ed.*, 1984, pp. 174–82. [G: W. Germany]

Adams, Walter and Brock, James W. Countervailing or Coalescing Power? The Problem of Labor/Management Coalitions. *J. Post Keynesian Econ.*, Winter 1983-84, *6*(2), pp. 180–97. [G: U.S.]

Anderson, James E. Indentification of Interactive Behavior in Air Service Markets: 1973–76. *J. Ind. Econ.*, June 1984, *32*(4), pp. 489–507. [G: U.S.]

Anderson, S. and Glazer, A. Public Opinion and Regulatory Behavior. *Public Choice*, 1984, *43*(2), pp. 187–94. [G: U.S.]

Babcock, Michael W. and German, H. Wade. The Impact of Deregulation on Rail TOFC Carloadings. *Logist. Transp. Rev.*, September 1984, *20*(3), pp. 205–12. [G: U.S.]

Bailey, Elizabeth E. A Comment on the Papers by Theodore Keeler and Barry Weingast [Theories of Regulation and the Deregulation Movement] [The Congressional–Bureaucratic System: A Principal–Agent Perspective (with Application to the SEC)]. *Public Choice*, 1984, *44*(1), pp. 197–200. [G: U.S.]

Bailey, Elizabeth E. and Baumol, William J. Deregulation and the Theory of Contestable Markets. *Yale J. Regul.*, 1984, *1*(2), pp. 111–37. [G: U.S.]

Bajic, Vladimir. Choice of Travel Mode for Work Trips: Some Findings for Metropolitan Toronto. *Int. J. Transport Econ.*, April 1984, *11*(1), pp. 79–96. [G: Canada]

Bauer, Kurt W. Assessing Infrastructure Needs: The State of the Art: Discussion. In *Hanson, R., ed.*, 1984, pp. 104–06. [G: U.S.]

Baum, Herbert. Deregulation of Rates for International Road Haulage within the European Community. *J. Transp. Econ. Policy*, January 1984, *18*(1), pp. 23–50. [G: EEC]

Baumol, William J. Some Subtle Pricing Issue in Railroad Regulation: Reply. *Int. J. Transport Econ.*, Aug.-Dec. 1984, *11*(2–3), pp. 217–18. [G: U.S.]

Bee, C. K. and Sargious, M. A. Modeling Community Reactions to Transportation Impacts. In *Avula, X. J. R., et al.*, 1984, pp. 847–52. [G: Canada]

Beggs, John J. The Value of Travel to Recreational Facilities: The Uncertainty Issue. *Int. J. Transport Econ.*, April 1984, *11*(1), pp. 53–59. [G: Australia]

Beilock, Richard and Freeman, James. Florida Motor Carrier Deregulation: Perspectives of Urban and Rural Shipper/Receivers. *Amer. J. Agr. Econ.*, February 1984, *66*(1), pp. 91–98. [G: U.S.]

Benabi, B. Elasticity Parameters of Disaggregate Models of Freight Modal Choice. In *Pitfield, D. E., ed.*, 1984, pp. 122–40. [G: U.K.]

Benson, Bruce L. Spatial Price Theory and an Efficient Congestion Toll Established by the Free Market. *Econ. Inquiry*, April 1984, *22*(2), pp. 244–52.

Berglas, Eitan; Fresko, David and Pines, David. Right of Way and Congestion Toll. *J. Transp. Econ. Policy*, May 1984, *18*(2), pp. 165–87. [G: U.S.]

Black, William R. An Evaluation of Nine Methods of Projecting Rail Branch Line Traffic. *Logist. Transp. Rev.*, March 1984, *20*(1), pp. 67–76. [G: U.S.]

Blair, Roger D.; Kaserman, David L. and Tepel, Richard C. The Impact of Improved Mileage on Gasoline Consumption. *Econ. Inquiry*, April 1984, *22*(2), pp. 209–17. [G: U.S.]

Blankart, Charles B. Deregulating Surface Transportation in Germany: New Opportunities for Entrepreneurship and New Opportunities for Political Entrepreneurship? In *Giersch, H., ed.*, 1984, pp. 158–73. [G: W. Germany]

Bohlander, George W. and Farris, Martin T. Collective Bargaining in Trucking—The Effects of Deregulation. *Logist. Transp. Rev.*, September 1984, *20*(3), pp. 223–38. [G: U.S.]

Bongaerts, J. C. and van Schaik, A. S. The Demand for Regulation. The Case of Dutch Inland Shipping. *Int. Rev. Law Econ.*, December 1984, *4*(2), pp. 199–212. [G: Netherlands]

Borins, Sandford F. The Economic Effects of Non-Optimal Pricing and Investment Policies for Substitutable Transport Facilities. *Can. J. Econ.*, February 1984, *17*(1), pp. 80–98. [G: Canada]

Boyer, Marcel and Dionne, Georges. Sécurité routière: efficacité, subvention et réglementation. (Road Security: Efficiency, Subsidies, Regulation. With English summary.) *L'Actual. Econ.*, June 1984, *60*(2), pp. 200–222.

Braeutigam, Ronald R.; Daughety, Andrew F. and Turnquist, Mark A. A Firm Specific Analysis of Economies of Density in the U.S. Railroad Industry. *J. Ind. Econ.*, September 1984, *33*(1), pp. 3–20. [G: U.S.]

Braeutigam, Ronald R. and Noll, Roger G. The Regulation of Surface Freight Transportation: The Welfare Effects Revisited. *Rev. Econ. Statist.*, February 1984, *66*(1), pp. 80–87. [G: U.S.]

Brent, Robert J. A Three-Objective Social Welfare Function for Cost–Benefit Analysis. *Appl. Econ.*, June 1984, *16*(3), pp. 369–78. [G: U.K.]

Bryan, Ingrid A. Conference Freight Rates and Eastern Canadian Ports. *Can. Public Policy*, June 1984, *10*(2), pp. 193–200. [G: Canada]

Button, K. J. Subsidies and the Provision of Urban

Public Transport. *Int. J. Transport Econ.*, Aug.-Dec. 1984, *11*(2–3), pp. 177–88. [G: U.K.]

Carlos, Ann M. Steel Rails versus Iron Rails: Evidence from Canada. *Exploration Econ. Hist.*, April 1984, *21*(2), pp. 169–75. [G: Canada]

Caves, Douglas W.; Christensen, Laurits R. and Tretheway, Michael W. Economies of Density versus Economies of Scale: Why Trunk and Local Service Airline Costs Differ. *Rand J. Econ.*, Winter 1984, *15*(4), pp. 471–89. [G: U.S.]

Cha, Dong-deuck and Saklas, James G. Integration of Choice Set Reduction in Behavioral Choice Travel Demand Models. In *Avula, X. J. R., et al.*, 1984, pp. 853–59.

Chebat, Jean-Charles. Le temps comme intrant des attitudes à l'égard de la sécurité routière: le cas québécois. (Time as an Input Variable of Attitudes toward Road Security: The Case of Québec. With English summary.) *L'Actual. Econ.*, December 1984, *60*(4), pp. 495–513. [G: Canada]

Chen, M.-L.; Francis, R. L. and Lowe, T. J. P-Centers on Bitrees. *J. Reg. Sci.*, May 1984, *24*(2), pp. 203–17.

Chow, Garland and Poist, Richard F. The Measurement of Quality of Service and the Transportation Purchase Decision. *Logist. Transp. Rev.*, March 1984, *20*(1), pp. 25–43.

Clippinger, Marni. Financial Strategies for the New Entrepreneurs. In *Meyer, J. R. and Oster, C. V., Jr., eds.*, 1984, pp. 105–22. [G: U.S.]

Coffin, H. Garth. Western Grain Transportation Initiatives and Agriculture in Eastern Canada. *Can. J. Agr. Econ.*, July 1984, *32*(2), pp. 269–81. [G: Canada]

Collings, John. Public Expenditure Policy, 1984–85: Transport. In *Cockle, P., ed.*, 1984, pp. 214–27. [G: U.K.]

Collins, James B. The Role of Atlantic France in the Baltic Trade: Dutch Traders and Polish Grain at Nantes, 1625–1675. *J. Europ. Econ. Hist.*, Fall 1984, *13*(2), pp. 239–89. [G: France]

Corsi, Thomas M.; Fanara, Philip, Jr. and Roberts, Merrill J. Linkages between Motor Carrier Accidents and Safety Regulation. *Logist. Transp. Rev.*, June 1984, *20*(2), pp. 149–64. [G: U.S.]

Crampton, Graham. Subsidies to Urban Public Transport and Privatisation. In *Le Grand, J. and Robinson, R., eds.*, 1984, pp. 201–11. [G: U.K.]

Current, John; ReVelle, Charles and Cohon, Jared. The Shortest Covering Path Problem: An Application of Locational Constraints to Network Design. *J. Reg. Sci.*, May 1984, *24*(2), pp. 161–83.

Daly, A. Cost Saving Methods in Travel Demand Forecasting. In *Pitfield, D. E., ed.*, 1984, pp. 102–13.

Damus, Sylvester. Ramsey Pricing by U.S. Railroads: Can It Exist? *J. Transp. Econ. Policy*, January 1984, *18*(1), pp. 51–62. [G: U.S.]

Davidson, Wallace N., III; Chandy, P. R. and Walker, Mike. The Stock Market Effects of Airline Deregulation. *Quart. J. Bus. Econ.*, Autumn 1984, *23*(4), pp. 31–45. [G: U.S.]

Davies, J. E. Freight Rate Stability in Liner Shipping: Implicit Peak Load Pricing? *Int. J. Transport Econ.*, Aug.-Dec. 1984, *11*(2–3), pp. 163–76. [G: Canada; U.K.]

Davis, Evan. Express Coaching since 1980: Liberalisation in Practice. *Fisc. Stud.*, February 1984, *5*(1), pp. 76–86. [G: U.K.]

Dawson, D. A. and Parent, L. P. Second Thoughts on Tariff Bureaus—A Note. *Can. Public Policy*, March 1984, *10*(1), pp. 92–93. [G: Canada]

De Borger, Bruno L. Cost and Productivity in Regional Bus Transportation: The Belgian Case. *J. Ind. Econ.*, September 1984, *33*(1), pp. 37–54. [G: Belgium]

Dewatripont, Mathias. Analyse et prévision du choix modal de transport terrestre de marchandises en Belgique. (With English summary.) *Cah. Écon. Bruxelles*, 2nd Trimester 1984, (102), pp. 179–201. [G: Belgium]

Dewatripont, Mathias. Evaluation et prévision du volume total de transport terrestre de marchandises en Belgique. (With English summary.) *Cah. Écon. Bruxelles*, 1st Trimester 1984, (101), pp. 74–104. [G: Belgium]

Dodgson, J. S. Railway Costs and Closures. *J. Transp. Econ. Policy*, September 1984, *18*(3), pp. 219–36. [G: U.K.]

Dorfman, Robert. On Optimal Congestion. *J. Environ. Econ. Manage.*, June 1984, *11*(2), pp. 91–106.

Dougan, William R. Railway Abandonments, Cross-Subsidies, and the Theory of Regulation. *Public Choice*, 1984, *44*(2), pp. 297–305. [G: U.S.]

Dunne, John Paul. Elasticity Measures and Disaggregate Choice Models. *J. Transp. Econ. Policy*, May 1984, *18*(2), pp. 189–97. [G: U.K.]

Ellison, Anthony P. Regulatory Reform in Canada: A Different Ball Game. In *Thompson, F., ed.*, 1984, pp. 103–32. [G: Canada]

Ferris, Richard J. Playing the Game after the Rules Change. *Logist. Transp. Rev.*, March 1984, *20*(1), pp. 77–81.

Forester, Thomas H.; McNown, Robert F. and Singell, Larry D. A Cost–Benefit Analysis of the 55 MPH Speed Limit. *Southern Econ. J.*, January 1984, *50*(3), pp. 631–41. [G: U.S.]

Forsyth, Peter. Transport Infrastructure and Mining Industry Development. In *Lloyd, P. J., ed.*, 1984, pp. 226–52. [G: Australia]

Forsyth, Peter. Airlines and Airports: Privatisation, Competition, and Regulation. *Fisc. Stud.*, February 1984, *5*(1), pp. 61–75. [G: U.K.]

Friedman, Samuel R. The Work Process and Worker Mobilization among Teamster Drivers. In *Zarembka, P., ed.*, 1984, pp. 161–83.

Fuller, Stephen; Makus, Larry and Gallimore, William. Effects of Increasing Panama Canal Toll Rates on U.S. Grain Exports. *Southern J. Agr. Econ.*, December 1984, *16*(2), pp. 9–19. [G: U.S.; Panama]

Garrod, Peter V. and Miklius, Walter. Owner-Operators, Demand Fluctuations and the Choice of Technology. *J. Transp. Econ. Policy*, September 1984, *18*(3), pp. 293–302. [G: U.S.]

Gaul, Wolfgang. Optimal Routes in Compound Transportation Systems. In *[Beckmann, M. J.]*, 1984, pp. 309–19.

Georgescu Pipera, Constantino and Georgescu Pipera, Paul. Fluvial Interconnection: A Basic Element of Latin American Integration. In *Núñez del Arco, J.; Margain, E. and Cherol, R., eds.*, 1984, pp. 161–79. [G: Latin America]

Ghonima, Hazem. Microcomputers in Economic Planning of the St. Lawrence Seaway System. *Logist. Transp. Rev.*, December 1984, *20*(4), pp. 449–61. [G: Canada; U.S.]

Giannopoulos, George A. Modelling of International Freight Transport for Greece. *Int. J. Transport Econ.*, April 1984, *11*(1), pp. 61–78. [G: Greece]

Gilbert, Geoffrey. Maritime Enterprise in the New Republic: Investment in Baltimore Shipping, 1789–1793. *Bus. Hist. Rev.*, Spring 1984, *58*(1), pp. 14–29. [G: U.S.]

Gillen, David W. and Oum, Tae Hoon. A Study of the Cost Structures of the Canadian Intercity Motor Coach Industry. *Can. J. Econ.*, May 1984, *17*(2), pp. 369–85. [G: Canada]

Glaister, Stephen. The Allocation of Urban Public Transport Subsidy. In *Le Grand, J. and Robinson, R., eds.*, 1984, pp. 177–200. [G: U.K.]

Glickman, Theodore S. and Heimann, David I. Risk Analysis of Railroad Freight Transportation Disasters. In *Avula, X. J. R., et al.*, 1984, pp. 844–46.

Goldstein, Gerald S. and Pittman, Robert H. Transportation and the Commodity Composition of Interstate Trade. *Growth Change*, July 1984, *15*(3), pp. 15–24. [G: U.S.]

Gómez-Ibáñez, José A. and Morgan, Ivor P. Deregulating International Markets: The Examples of Aviation and Ocean Shipping. *Yale J. Regul.*, 1984, *2*(1), pp. 107–44. [G: U.S.]

Goodman, Allen C. Port Planning and Financing for Bulk Cargo Ships: Theory and a North American Example. *J. Transp. Econ. Policy*, September 1984, *18*(3), pp. 237–52. [G: U.S.]

Graham, John D. Technology, Behavior, and Safety: An Empirical Study of Automobile Occupant-Protection Regulation. *Policy Sci.*, October 1984, *17*(2), pp. 141–51. [G: U.S.]

Graham, John D. and Garber, Steven. Evaluating the Effects of Automobile Safety Regulation. *J. Policy Anal. Manage.*, Winter 1984, *3*(2), pp. 206–24. [G: U.S.]

Graves, Stephen C.; Horwitch, Mel and Bowman, Edward H. Deep-Draft Dredging of U.S. Coal Ports: A Cost–Benefit Analysis. *Policy Sci.*, October 1984, *17*(2), pp. 153–78. [G: U.S.]

Grimm, Curtis M. An Evaluation of Economic Issues in the UP–MP–WP Railroad Merger.

Logist. Transp. Rev., September 1984, *20*(3), pp. 239–59. **[G: U.S.]**

Guinet, A. and Dussauchoy, A. A Tour Management System for the Industrial Carrier Problems. In *Avula, X. J. R., et al.*, 1984, pp. 860–65.

Guo, Hongtao. Current Status of China's Transport and Prospects in the Near Future. *Chinese Econ. Stud.*, Summer 1984, *17*(4), pp. 63–71. **[G: China]**

Harmatuck, Donald J. A Methodology for Decomposing Motor Carrier Profits. *Logist. Transp. Rev.*, June 1984, *20*(2), pp. 99–109.

Hatry, Harry. Assessing Infrastructure Needs: The State of the Art: Discussion. In *Hanson, R., ed.*, 1984, pp. 102–04. **[G: U.S.]**

Hausman, William J. Profitability of English Colliers in the Eighteenth Century: Reply to a Reappraisal. *Bus. Hist. Rev.*, Spring 1984, *58*(1), pp. 121–25. **[G: U.K.]**

Hazard, John L. Comparative Transportation Systems. In *Kaynak, E. and Savitt, R., eds.*, 1984, pp. 200–13. **[G: U.K.; U.S.; W. Germany; France]**

Hensher, David A. A Rejoinder [The Value of Commuter Travel Time Savings: Empirical Estimation Using an Alternative Valuation Model]. *J. Transp. Econ. Policy*, May 1984, *18*(2), pp. 201–03.

Hensher, David A. Accounting for Curvilinearity in Explanatory Variables: A Simplified Alternative. *Int. J. Transport Econ.*, April 1984, *11*(1), pp. 43–51. **[G: Australia]**

Horn, Kevin. Shipper Support and Entry into Regulated Interstate Trucking. *Logist. Transp. Rev.*, June 1984, *20*(2), pp. 111–26. **[G: U.S.]**

Hu, Michael and Bruning, Edward R. Prior Experience and Misperceptions of Airline Service. *Logist. Transp. Rev.*, September 1984, *20*(3), pp. 213–22. **[G: U.S.]**

Intrator, Jacob and Weiss, Joseph. About Some Special Cases of Transportation Problems. *Econ. Computat. Cybern. Stud. Res.*, 1984, *19*(1), pp. 83–91.

Jordan, Jeffrey L. and Thompson, Stanley R. Forecasting Rail Freight Traffic from a Statewide Economic Model. *Southern J. Agr. Econ.*, December 1984, *16*(2), pp. 83–90. **[G: U.S.]**

Kanemoto, Yoshitsugu. Pricing and Investment Policies in a System of Competitive Commuter Railways. *Rev. Econ. Stud.*, October 1984, *51*(4), pp. 665–81.

Kania, John J. Economics of Coal Transport by Slurry Pipeline versus Unit Train: A Case Study. *Energy Econ.*, April 1984, *6*(2), pp. 131–38. **[G: U.S.]**

Karasek, Mirek. Modelling the Future Air Traffic Demands in Saudi Arabia. In *Avula, X. J. R., et al.*, 1984, pp. 866–71. **[G: Saudi Arabia]**

Karatzas, George. Greek Earnings from Ocean Transportation in 1960–77: An Analysis. *Rivista Int. Sci. Econ. Com.*, February 1984, *31*(2), pp. 172–86. **[G: Greece]**

Keeler, Theodore E. Theories of Regulation and the Deregulation Movement. *Public Choice*, 1984, *44*(1), pp. 103–45. **[G: U.S.]**

Kim, Moshe. The Beneficiaries of Trucking Regulation, Revisited. *J. Law Econ.*, April 1984, *27*(1), pp. 227–41. **[G: Canada]**

Koo, Won W. and Uhm, Ihn H. United States and Canadian Rail Freight-Rate Structures: A Comparative Analysis. *Can. J. Agr. Econ.*, July 1984, *32*(2), pp. 301–26. **[G: Canada; U.S.]**

Kuhlman, John M. and Johnson, S. R. Estimating Damages on Highway Construction Contracts. *Antitrust Bull.*, Winter 1984, *29*(4), pp. 719–38. **[G: U.S.]**

La Croix, Sumner J. Airline Coupons and Pricing Adjustments. *J. Transp. Econ. Policy*, September 1984, *18*(3), pp. 253–62. **[G: U.S.]**

Lang, Otto. Western Grain Transportation Initiatives and Agriculture in Eastern Canada: Discussion. *Can. J. Agr. Econ.*, July 1984, *32*(2), pp. 287–90. **[G: Canada]**

Lapsley, Irvine. Reconstructing British Rail: In Search of a Profitable Railway. *Managerial Dec. Econ.*, March 1984, *5*(1), pp. 32–48. **[G: U.K.]**

Layton, Allan P. The Impact of Increased Penalties on Australian Drink/Driving Behavior—A Procedural Note. *Logist. Transp. Rev.*, June 1984, *20*(2), pp. 187–89. **[G: Australia]**

Layton, Allan P. The Value of Commuter Travel Time Savings: Some Clarifications. *J. Transp. Econ. Policy*, May 1984, *18*(2), pp. 199–201.

LeBlanc, Larry J. Optimization Models for Distribution Planning. In *Bamberg, G. and Spremann, K., eds.*, 1984, pp. 203–23.

Lee, David D. Herbert Hoover and the Development of Commercial Aviation, 1921–1926. *Bus. Hist. Rev.*, Spring 1984, *58*(1), pp. 78–102. **[G: U.S.]**

Lee, Li Way. An Economic Theory of the Distribution of Traffic Speeds. *J. Urban Econ.*, May 1984, *15*(3), pp. 302–09.

Lee, Li Way. The Economics of Carpools. *Econ. Inquiry*, January 1984, *22*(1), pp. 128–35.

Lee, Lung-Fei and Porter, Robert H. Switching Regression Models with Imperfect Sample Separation Information—With an Application on Cartel Stability. *Econometrica*, March 1984, *52*(2), pp. 391–418. **[G: U.S.]**

Lewis, David L. and Bodde, David L. Understanding Political Risk in Investment Planning. *J. Policy Anal. Manage.*, Summer 1984, *3*(4), pp. 544–60. **[G: U.S.]**

Lewis, Frank D. and Robinson, David R. The Timing of Railway Construction on the Canadian Prairies. *Can. J. Econ.*, May 1984, *17*(2), pp. 340–52. **[G: Canada]**

Liew, Chong K. and Liew, Chung J. Measuring the Development Impact of a Proposed Transportation System. *Reg. Sci. Urban Econ.*, May 1984, *14*(2), pp. 175–98. **[G: U.S.]**

Liew, Chong K. and Liew, Chung J. Multi-Modal, Multi-Output, Multiregional Variable Input–Output Model. *Reg. Sci. Urban Econ.*, May 1984, *14*(2), pp. 265–81.

Littlefield, Douglas R. The Potomac Company: A Misadventure in Financing an Early Ameri-

can Internal Improvement Project. *Bus. Hist. Rev.*, Winter 1984, *58*(4), pp. 562–85.
[G: U.S.]

Loeb, Peter D. and Gilad, Benjamin. The Efficacy and Cost-Effectiveness of Vehicle Inspection: A State Specific Analysis Using Time Series Data. *J. Transp. Econ. Policy*, May 1984, *18*(2), pp. 145–64. [G: U.S.]

Marcus, Henry S.; Martland, Carl D. and Raymond, George B., Jr. Microcomputer Preparation of Volume-Variable Budgets: Terminals on the Boston & Maine Railroad. *Logist. Transp. Rev.*, December 1984, *20*(4), pp. 373–86.
[G: U.S.]

Martin, Albro. Introductory Essay: Transportation and the Evolution of the American Economic Republic. *Bus. Hist. Rev.*, Spring 1984, *58*(1), pp. 1–13. [G: U.S.]

Mażbic-Kulma, Barbara. Methods of Determining Systems of Time-Table Arranging with Predetermined Area. In *Hammer, G. and Pallaschke, D., eds.*, 1984, pp. 457–64.

McCarthy, Patrick S. The Shared Vehicle Fleet: A Study of Its Impact upon Accessibility and Vehicle Ownership. *J. Transp. Econ. Policy*, January 1984, *18*(1), pp. 75–94. [G: U.S.]

McFarland, Henry. Transport Costs and Processing. *J. Transp. Econ. Policy*, September 1984, *18*(3), pp. 311–15. [G: U.S.]

McGeehan, H. Forecasting the Demand for Inter-Urban Railway Travel in the Republic of Ireland. *J. Transp. Econ. Policy*, September 1984, *18*(3), pp. 275–92. [G: Ireland]

McGuire, Robert A. Public versus Private Economic Activity: A New Look at School Bus Transportation. *Public Choice*, 1984, *43*(1), pp. 25–43. [G: U.S.]

McLeod, A. D. Western Grain Transportation Initiatives and Agriculture in Eastern Canada: Discussion. *Can. J. Agr. Econ.*, July 1984, *32*(2), pp. 283–86. [G: Canada]

Merkel, Philip L. The Origins of an Expanded Federal Court Jurisdiction: Railroad Development and the Ascendancy of the Federal Judiciary. *Bus. Hist. Rev.*, Autumn 1984, *58*(3), pp. 336–58. [G: U.S.]

Metzer, Jacob. Railroads and the Efficiency of Internal Markets: Some Conceptual and Practical Considerations. *Econ. Develop. Cult. Change*, October 1984, *33*(1), pp. 61–70.
[G: U.S.S.R.]

Meyer, John R. and Oster, Clinton V., Jr. Airline Industry Structure and Public Policy. In *Meyer, J. R. and Oster, C. V., Jr., eds.*, 1984, pp. 201–23. [G: U.S.]

Meyer, John R. and Oster, Clinton V., Jr. Competitive Strategies of New Entrant Jets. In *Meyer, J. R. and Oster, C. V., Jr., eds.*, 1984, pp. 123–37. [G: U.S.]

Meyer, John R. and Oster, Clinton V., Jr. Opportunities in a Deregulated Industry. In *Meyer, J. R. and Oster, C. V., Jr., eds.*, 1984, pp. 1–10. [G: U.S.]

Meyer, John R. and Oster, Clinton V., Jr. Progenitors: Entrepreneurial Opportunities before

Deregulation. In *Meyer, J. R. and Oster, C. V., Jr., eds.*, 1984, pp. 11–25. [G: U.S.]

Meyer, John R. and Oster, Clinton V., Jr. Small Community Service and the Role of Federal Subsidy. In *Meyer, J. R. and Oster, C. V., Jr., eds.*, 1984, pp. 185–99. [G: U.S.]

Moore, Thomas Gale. Deregulating Ground Transportation. In *Giersch, H., ed.*, 1984, pp. 136–57. [G: U.S.]

Morrison, Steven A. An Economic Analysis of Aircraft Design. *J. Transp. Econ. Policy*, May 1984, *18*(2), pp. 123–43.

Mosler, Karl Clemens. Location Theory of the Firm Facing Uncertain Prices and Transport Rates. In *[Beckmann, M. J.]*, 1984, pp. 163–74.

Murayama, Yuzo. Contractors, Collusion, and Competition: Japanese Immigrant Railroad Laborers in the Pacific Northwest, 1898–1911. *Exploration Econ. Hist.*, July 1984, *21*(3), pp. 290–305. [G: Japan; U.S.]

North, Michael. A Small Baltic Port in the Early Modern Period: The Port of Elbing in the Sixteenth and Seventeenth Century. *J. Europ. Econ. Hist.*, Spring 1984, *13*(1), pp. 117–27.
[G: Poland]

O'Day, D. Kelly and Neumann, Lance A. Assessing Infrastructure Needs: The State of the Art. In *Hanson, R., ed.*, 1984, pp. 67–101.
[G: U.S.]

Oster, Clinton V., Jr. and McKey, Andrew. The Cost Structure of Short-Haul Air Service. In *Meyer, J. R. and Oster, C. V., Jr., eds.*, 1984, pp. 51–86. [G: U.S.]

Oster, Clinton V., Jr. and Strong, John S. Competitive Strategies of Commuters. In *Meyer, J. R. and Oster, C. V., Jr., eds.*, 1984, pp. 139–64. [G: U.S.]

Oster, Clinton V., Jr. and Zorn, C. Kurt. Commuter Airline Safety. In *Meyer, J. R. and Oster, C. V., Jr., eds.*, 1984, pp. 87–101. [G: U.S.]

Oum, Tae Hoon and Tretheway, Michael W. Reforming Canadian Airline Regulation. *Logist. Transp. Rev.*, September 1984, *20*(3), pp. 261–84. [G: Canada; U.S.]

Owen, Wilfred. Transportation and World Development. *Int. J. Transport Econ.*, Aug.-Dec. 1984, *11*(2–3), pp. 123–33.

Pearman, A. D. and Button, K. J. The Value of Time in Road Investment Appraisal in Less Developed Countries. *Int. J. Transport Econ.*, Aug.-Dec. 1984, *11*(2–3), pp. 135–48.
[G: LDCs]

Peccei, Riccardo and Guest, David. Evaluating the Introduction of New Technology: The Case of Word-Processors in British Rail. In *Warner, M., ed.*, 1984, pp. 84–109.

Peiser, Richard B. Land Use versus Road Network Design in Community Transport Cost Evaluation. *Land Econ.*, February 1984, *60*(1), pp. 95–109.

Phillips, Karen Borlaug and Phillips, Laurence T. Research, Politics, and the Dynamics of Policy Development: A Case Study of Motor Carrier Regulatory Reform. *Policy Sci.*, December 1984, *17*(4), pp. 367–84.   [G: U.S.]

Pickrell, Don H. Airport Congestion and New Entrant Access. In *Meyer, J. R. and Oster, C. V., Jr., eds.*, 1984, pp. 167–84. [G: U.S.]

Pickrell, Don H. The Demand for Short-Haul Air Service. In *Meyer, J. R. and Oster, C. V., Jr., eds.*, 1984, pp. 29–49.   [G: U.S.]

Pitkänen, Eero. Julkisten liikelaitosten toiminnan tuloksellisuus. (The Efficiency and Effectiveness of Public Enterprises. With English summary.) *Liiketaloudellinen Aikak.*, 1984, *33*(1), pp. 81–106.   [G: Finland; Sweden]

Primožić, Miroslav. Udio tehnološkog progresa u razvoju saobraćaja u periodu, 1959–1978. (Contribution of Technological Progress to the Traffic Development in the Period 1959–1978. With English summary.) *Econ. Anal. Worker's Manage.*, 1984, *18*(2), pp. 127–39.
                                        [G: Yugoslavia]

Quinet, Emile and Hamel, Zohra. Les modèles de flux de transport et al théorie économique du consommateur. (With English summary.) *Revue Écon. Polit.*, May–June 1984, *94*(3), pp. 329–46.

Radharamanan, R.; Sortica, G. B. and Camargo, M. E. A Branch and Bound Model for the Transportation Routing Problem. In *Avula, X. J. R., et al.*, 1984, pp. 877–82. [G: Brazil]

Rhodes, Harold L. British Public Enterprises and Project Initiation in the Developing World. In *Ramanadham, V. V., ed.*, 1984, pp. 87–108.
                                              [G: U.K.]

Rogers, Gordon A. Microcomputer Support for Market Penetration via Regional Transfer Yards. *Logist. Transp. Rev.*, December 1984, *20*(4), pp. 367–72.   [G: U.S.; Canada]

Ropertz, Henry. Western Grain Transportation Initiatives and Agriculture in Eastern Canada: Discussion. *Can. J. Agr. Econ.*, July 1984, *32*(2), pp. 291–95.   [G: Canada]

Samples, Karl C. and Prescott, James H. The Use of Sail-Assisted Commercial Fishing Vessels in the Pacific: An Economic Appraisal. In *Gopalakrishnan, C., ed.*, 1984, pp. 87–106.

Savage, Ian P. "Unnecessary and Wasteful" Competition in Bus Transport. *J. Transp. Econ. Policy*, September 1984, *18*(3), pp. 303–09.

Schmidt, Peter J. and Sickles, Robin C. Production Frontiers and Panel Data. *J. Bus. Econ. Statist.*, October 1984, *2*(4), pp. 367–74.
                                              [G: U.S.]

Schrier, Elliot; Nadel, Ernest and Rifas, Bertram E. Forces Shaping International Maritime Transport. *World Econ.*, March 1984, *7*(1), pp. 87–102.   [G: Global]

Seely, Bruce E. Engineers and Government–Business Cooperation: Highway Standards and the Bureau of Public Roads, 1900–1940. *Bus. Hist. Rev.*, Spring 1984, *58*(1), pp. 51–77.
                                              [G: U.S.]

Sinan, I. M. UNCTAD and Flags of Convenience. *J. World Trade Law*, March–April 1984, *18*(2), pp. 95–109.

St. Seidenfus, Hellmuth. Deregulating Ground Transportation: Comment. In *Giersch, H., ed.*, 1984, pp. 183–89.   [G: W. Europe]

Stanbury, W. T. Airline Regulation Contretemps. In *Thompson, F., ed.*, 1984, pp. 137–38.
                                        [G: Canada; U.S.]

Stanbury, W. T. Slouching toward Airline Deregulation: Canada's Reluctant Journey. In *Thompson, F., ed.*, 1984, pp. 57–79.
                                              [G: Canada]

Stanbury, W. T. Trucking Wars. In *Thompson, F., ed.*, 1984, pp. 133–35. [G: Canada; U.S.]

Starkie, David. Price Competition and Fair Competition in the U.K. Freight Market. *Int. J. Transport Econ.*, Aug.-Dec. 1984, *11*(2–3), pp. 149–62.   [G: U.K.]

Starkie, David. The Specific Effect of Specific Road Grants in South Australia. *Australian Econ. Pap.*, June 1984, *23*(42), pp. 27–37.
                                        [G: Australia]

Starkie, David and Starrs, Margaret. Contestability and Sustainability in Regional Airline Markets. *Econ. Rec.*, September 1984, *60*(170), pp. 274–83.   [G: Australia]

Stephanedes, Y. J. and Kumar, V. Comparative Evaluation of Intercity Demand Models. In *Pitfield, D. E., ed.*, 1984, pp. 114–21.
                                              [G: U.S.]

Tehranian, Hassan and Bruning, Edward R. Deregulation and Investor Perception of Motor Carrier Securities. *Logist. Transp. Rev.*, June 1984, *20*(2), pp. 165–86.   [G: U.S.]

Thobani, Mateen. Passenger Transport in Karachi. In *van Ginneken, W. and Baron, C., eds.*, 1984, pp. 211–37.   [G: Pakistan]

Tobin, Roger L. A Network Programming System for Studying Coal Transportation. In *Lev, B., et al., eds.*, 1984, pp. 21–32.   [G: U.S.]

Tolliver, Denver D. Economies in Density in Railroad Cost Finding: Applications to Rail Form A. *Logist. Transp. Rev.*, March 1984, *20*(1), pp. 3–24.   [G: U.S.]

Totten, George O., III. The Reconstruction of the Japanese Shipbuilding Industry. In *Friedheim, R. L., et al.*, 1984, pp. 130–72.
                                              [G: Japan]

Trent, Darrell M. Transportation: Policy, Goals, Accomplishments. In *Moore, J. H., ed.*, 1984, pp. 275–86.   [G: U.S.]

Tye, William B. Some Subtle Pricing Issues in Railroad Regulation: Rejoinder. *Int. J. Transport Econ.*, Aug.-Dec. 1984, *11*(2), pp. 219–20.   [G: U.S.]

Tye, William B. Some Subtle Pricing Issues in Railroad Regulation: Comment. *Int. J. Transport Econ.*, Aug.-Dec. 1984, *11*(2–3), pp. 207–16.   [G: U.S.]

Tyrchniewicz, E. W. Western Grain Transportation Initiatives: Where Do We Go from Here? *Can. J. Agr. Econ.*, July 1984, *32*(2), pp. 253–68.   [G: Canada]

Ulusoy, G. Routing in Strategic Airlift: a Study in Bottleneck Routing. In *Avula, X. J. R., et al.*, 1984, pp. 872–76.

Usselman, Steven W. Air Brakes for Freight Trains: Technological Innovation in the American Railroad Industry, 1869–1900. *Bus. Hist. Rev.*, Spring 1984, *58*(1), pp. 30–50. [G: U.S.]

Vickerman, R. W. and Barmby, T. A. The Structure of Shopping Travel: Some Developments of the Trip Generation Model. *J. Transp. Econ. Policy*, May 1984, *18*(2), pp. 109–21. [G: U.S.]

Ville, Simon. Note: Size and Profitability of English Colliers in the Eighteenth Century—A Reappraisal. *Bus. Hist. Rev.*, Spring 1984, *58*(1), pp. 103–20. [G: U.K.]

Wang Chiang, S. Judy and Friedlaender, Ann F. Output Aggregation, Network Effects, and the Measurement of Trucking Technology. *Rev. Econ. Statist.*, May 1984, *66*(2), pp. 267–76. [G: U.S.]

Ward, Frank A. Specification Considerations for the Price Variable in Travel Cost Demand Models. *Land Econ.*, August 1984, *60*(3), pp. 301–05.

Warley, T. K. Western Grain Transportation Initiatives and Agriculture in Eastern Canada: Discussion. *Can. J. Agr. Econ.*, July 1984, *32*(2), pp. 297–300. [G: Canada]

Werlin, Herbert H. Urban Traffic Management. In *Weiss, C. and Jéquier, N., eds.*, 1984, pp. 69–84. [G: Selected Countries]

Wilcox, James A. Automobile Fuel Efficiency: Measurement and Explanation. *Econ. Inquiry*, July 1984, *22*(3), pp. 375–85. [G: U.S.]

Wilkins, Bill. Airline Deregulation: Neoclassical Theory as Public Policy. *J. Econ. Issues*, June 1984, *18*(2), pp. 419–27. [G: U.S.]

Zlatoper, Thomas J. Regression Analysis of Time Series Data on Motor Vehicle Deaths in the United States. *J. Transp. Econ. Policy*, September 1984, *18*(3), pp. 263–74. [G: U.S.]

616 Industrial Policy

6160 Industrial Policy

Ahmad, Q. K. Policies and Institutions Concerning Promotion of Rural Industries in Bangladesh. *Bangladesh Devel. Stud.*, March-June 1984, *12*(1–2), pp. 163–95. [G: Bangladesh]

Ahmed, Meekal Aziz. Issues in the Economics of Industrialization in Developing Countries: A Case Study from Pakistan's Light Engineering Sector: Comment. *Pakistan Devel. Rev.*, Summer-Autumn 1984, *23*(2&3), pp. 327–29. [G: Pakistan]

Albertine, John M. Breaking the Barriers to U.S. Economic Growth. *Cato J.*, Fall 1984, *4*(2), pp. 609–17. [G: U.S.]

Anderson, Charles W. Worrying about Productivity: A Political, Economic, and Humanistic Analysis. In *Sherman, M., ed.*, 1984, pp. 7–20. [G: U.S.]

Aubrey, Agnès. La conjoncture de l'économie allemande des années 80. (With English summary.) *Revue Écon. Polit.*, September–October 1984, *94*(5), pp. 571–80. [G: Germany]

Baer, Werner. Industrialization in Latin America: Successes and Failures. *J. Econ. Educ.*, Spring 1984, *15*(2), pp. 124–35. [G: Latin America]

Ballance, Robert and Sinclair, Stuart. Re-industrialising America: Policy Makers and Interest Groups. *World Econ.*, June 1984, *7*(2), pp. 197–214. [G: U.S.]

Bartlett, Bruce. Is Industrial Innovation Destroying Jobs? *Cato J.*, Fall 1984, *4*(2), pp. 625–43. [G: U.S.]

Bautista, Romeo M. The Pacific Community Environment and Economic Policy in the Philippines. In *Benjamin, R. and Kudrle, R. T.*, 1984, pp. 105–25. [G: Philippines; Selected Countries]

Beesley, Michael E. and Wilson, P. E. B. Public Policy and Small Firms in Britain. In *Levicki, C., ed.*, 1984, pp. 111–26. [G: U.K.]

Behrman, Jack N. Industrial Strategies in the United States. In *Driscoll, R. E. and Behrman, J. N., eds.*, 1984, pp. 215–28. [G: U.S.]

Behrman, Jack N. Japanese Industrial Policy: A View from Outside. In *Driscoll, R. E. and Behrman, J. N., eds.*, 1984, pp. 85–91. [G: Japan]

Belfrage, Bengt and Molleryd, Bengt. Swedish Industrial Policy. In *Driscoll, R. E. and Behrman, J. N., eds.*, 1984, pp. 177–85. [G: Sweden]

Bellon, Bertrand. Conditions de la politique industrielle aux États-Unis. (With English summary.) *Rev. Econ. Ind.*, 4th Trimester 1984, (30), pp. 26–41. [G: U.S.]

Bennett, Douglas and Sharpe, Kenneth. Agenda Setting and Bargaining Power: The Mexican State versus Transnational Automobile Corporations. In *Kronish, R. and Mericle, K. S., eds.*, 1984, *1979*, pp. 195–229. [G: Mexico]

Bhalla, A. S. Technological Transformation in China. *Econ. Int.*, February–May 1984, *37*(1–2), pp. 4–19. [G: China]

Bierbaum, C. B. Structural Change: The South Australian Experience. *Australian Econ. Pap.*, December 1984, *23*(43), pp. 281–90. [G: Australia]

Brabec, František. Propects Justified by Experience. *Czech. Econ. Digest.*, June 1984, (4), pp. 14–24. [G: Czechoslovakia]

Brada, Josef C. Industrial Policy in Hungary: Lessons for America. *Cato J.*, Fall 1984, *4*(2), pp. 485–505. [G: Hungary]

Brada, Josef C. and Montias, John Michael. Industrial Policy in Eastern Europe: A Three-Country Comparison. *J. Compar. Econ.*, December 1984, *8*(4), pp. 377–419. [G: Czechoslovakia; Poland; Hungary]

Branson, William H. The Myth of Deindustrialization. In *McKenzie, R. B., ed. (II)*, 1984, *1983*, pp. 177–90. [G: U.S.]

Butler, Stuart M. Free Zones in the Inner City. In *Bingham, R. D. and Blair, J. P., eds.*, 1984, pp. 141–53. [G: U.K.; U.S.]

Byatt, I. C. R. Reflections on the Byatt Report: Rejoinder [Byatt Report on Subsidies to British Export Credits]. *World Econ.*, September 1984, *7*(3), pp. 345–46. [G: U.K.]

Calogero, Giuseppe. La diffusion de l'innovation et le rôle des participations de l'état en Italie. (The Propagation of Innovations. The Role of

State Share Holdings in Italy. With English summary.) *Ann. Pub. Co-op. Econ.*, Oct.–Dec. 1984, *55*(4), pp. 395–411. **[G: Italy]**

Campbell, Donald E. Enforcement of Resource Allocation Mechanisms and Second Best Industrial Policy. *J. Econ. Theory*, December 1984, *34*(2), pp. 319–41.

Carlsson, Bo. Industrial Subsidies in the Nordic Countries. In *Mikkelsen, A., et al.*, 1984, pp. 222–29. **[G: Scandinavia]**

Carnoy, Martin and Shearer, Derek. Towards a Democratic Alternative: Neo-liberals vs. Economic Democrats. In *Alperovitz, G. and Skurski, R., eds.*, 1984, pp. 167–89. **[G: U.S.]**

Chakrabarti, Alok K. Reindustrialization of the United States: Three Perspectives on Organizational Adaptation: Review Article. *Quart. Rev. Econ. Bus.*, Summer 1984, *24*(2), pp. 51–56. **[G: U.S.]**

Conrad, Cecilia A. Industrial Policy: Minority Economic Interests and American Political Response: Comments. *Rev. Black Polit. Econ.*, Summer–Fall 1984, *13*(1–2), pp. 99–102.

Corrêa do Lago, Luiz A. Brazilian Industrial Policy and International Restructuring of Industry. In *Driscoll, R. E. and Behrman, J. N., eds.*, 1984, pp. 25–38. **[G: Brazil]**

Crawford, Allan R. Putting Realism into Hi-Tech Policy. *Can. Public Policy*, June 1984, *10*(2), pp. 230–34. **[G: Canada]**

De Benedetti, Carlo. Strategie per uno sviluppo industriale. (Strategies for Industrial Development. With English summary.) *L'Impresa*, 1984, *26*(3), pp. 15–21. **[G: Italy; U.S.]**

De Bondt, Raymond R. and Goovaerts, Marc J. The Effectiveness of Temporary Marginal Cost Subsidies. *Int. J. Ind. Organ.*, September 1984, *2*(3), pp. 235–49.

Defraigne, Pierre. Towards Concerted Industrial Policies in the EC. In *Jacquemin, A., ed.*, 1984, pp. 368–77. **[G: EEC]**

Dervis, Kemal and Page, John M., Jr. Industrial Policy in Developing Countries. *J. Compar. Econ.*, December 1984, *8*(4), pp. 436–51. **[G: LDCs]**

Díaz-Alejandro, Carlos F. The U.S. Response to Foreign Industrial Targeting: Comments. *Brookings Pap. Econ. Act.*, 1984, (1), pp. 122–25. **[G: U.S.]**

DiLorenzo, Thomas J. The Political Economy of National Industrial Policy. *Cato J.*, Fall 1984, *4*(2), pp. 587–607. **[G: U.S.]**

Diwan, Rauf and Hamid, Javed. The Potential for Industrial Development. In *Burki, S. J. and LaPorte, R., Jr., eds.*, 1984, pp. 84–102. **[G: Pakistan]**

Dobson, Wendy A. Industrial Policy in Canada: An Overview. In *Driscoll, R. E. and Behrman, J. N., eds.*, 1984, pp. 39–56. **[G: Canada]**

Dorn, James A. Planning America: Government or the Market? Introduction. *Cato J.*, Fall 1984, *4*(2), pp. 365–80. **[G: U.S.]**

Driscoll, Robert E. and Behrman, Jack N. National Industrial Policies: Introduction. In *Driscoll, R. E. and Behrman, J. N., eds.*, 1984, pp. 1–24. **[G: LDCs; MDCs]**

Duch, Raymond M. Investment Subsidy Programs in Comparative Perspective. In *Holzer, M. and Nagel, S. S., eds.*, 1984, pp. 145–70. **[G: France; U.K.; Japan]**

Dumas, Lloyd J. Making Peace Possible: The Legislative Approach to Economic Conversion. In *Gordon, S. and McFadden, D., eds.*, 1984, pp. 67–85. **[G: U.S.]**

Eizenstat, Stuart E. Reindustrialization through Coordination or Chaos? *Yale J. Regul.*, 1984, *2*(1), pp. 39–51. **[G: U.S.]**

Elbaum, Bernard and Lazonick, William. The Decline of the British Economy: An Institutional Perspective. *J. Econ. Hist.*, June 1984, *44*(2), pp. 567–83. **[G: U.K.]**

Eliasson, Gunnar. The Micro-Foundations of Industrial Policies. In *Jacquemin, A., ed.*, 1984, pp. 295–326.

Ellman, Michael. Investment Planning in the State Socialist Countries and its Relevance for Reindustrialisation. In *Ellman, M., 1984, 1980*, pp. 174–97. **[G: E. Europe]**

Ellman, Michael. Natural Gas, Restructuring and Re-industrialisation: The Dutch Experience of Industrial Policy. In *Ellman, M., 1984, 1981*, pp. 253–72. **[G: Netherlands]**

Estanislao, Jesus P. Philippine Industrialization Policy. In *Driscoll, R. E. and Behrman, J. N., eds.*, 1984, pp. 121–36. **[G: Philippines]**

Faire, Alexandre. Economic Redeployment and Contradictions in the West. In *Ngo, M., ed., vol. 1*, 1984, pp. 5–32. **[G: OECD]**

Fleet, Michael. Bargaining Relations in the Colombian Motor Vehicle Industry. In *Kronish, R. and Mericle, K. S., eds.*, 1984, pp. 231–60. **[G: Colombia]**

Flynn, Patricia M. Lowell: A High Technology Success Story. *New Eng. Econ. Rev.*, September–October 1984, pp. 39–49. **[G: U.S.]**

Fong, Pang Eng. Industrial Policy and Economic Restructuring in Singapore. In *Driscoll, R. E. and Behrman, J. N., eds.*, 1984, pp. 151–66. **[G: Singapore]**

Ford, William D. Statements in Support of the National Employment Priorities Act. In *McKenzie, R. B., ed. (II)*, 1984, pp. 315–27. **[G: U.S.]**

Frank, C. E. J.; Miall, R. H. C. and Rees, R. D. Issues in Small Firms Research of Relevance to Policy Making. *Reg. Stud.*, June 1984, *18*(3), pp. 257–66. **[G: U.K.]**

Franko, Lawrence G. and Behrman, Jack N. Industrial Policy in France. In *Driscoll, R. E. and Behrman, J. N., eds.*, 1984, pp. 57–71. **[G: France]**

Frenkel, Orit. Flying High: A Case Study of Japanese Industrial Policy. *J. Policy Anal. Manage.*, Spring 1984, *3*(3), pp. 406–20. **[G: Japan]**

Fukushima, Kiyohiko. Public Use of Private Interests: Japan's Industrial Policy. In *Driscoll, R. E. and Behrman, J. N., eds.*, 1984, pp. 73–84. **[G: Japan]**

Galbraith, James K. The Debate about Industrial Policy. In *Alperovitz, G. and Skurski, R., eds.*, 1984, pp. 89–108. **[G: U.S.]**

Geiser, Kenneth. Converting Economic Conversion: An Argument for Building Broader Coalitions. In *Gordon, S. and McFadden, D., eds.,* 1984, pp. 175–90.   [G: U.S.]

Geroski, Paul A. and Jacquemin, Alexis. Large Firms in the European Corporate Economy and Industrial Policy in the 1980s. In *Jacquemin, A., ed.,* 1984, pp. 343–67.   [G: EEC]

Giordano, Yvonne. Analyse de la politique française du commerce extérieur depuis le VIe Plan. (With English summary.) *Rev. Econ. Ind.,* 3rd Trimester 1984, (29), pp. 46–61.
[G: France]

Gold, David. Conversion and Industrial Policy. In *Gordon, S. and McFadden, D., eds.,* 1984, pp. 191–203.   [G: U.S.]

Goldsmith, William W. Bringing the Third World Home: Enterprise Zones for America? In *Sawers, L. and Tabb, W. K., eds.,* 1984, *1982,* pp. 339–50.   [G: U.S.]

Gordon, Suzanne. Economic Conversion Activity in Western Europe. In *Gordon, S. and McFadden, D., eds.,* 1984, pp. 108–29.
[G: W. Europe]

Gordon, Suzanne and McFadden, Dave. Economic Conversion: Revitalizing America's Economy: Introduction. In *Gordon, S. and McFadden, D., eds.,* 1984, pp. xiii–xxi.

Green, Diana. Cable TV in France: A Non-market Approach to Industrial Development. *Nat. Westminster Bank Quart. Rev.,* August 1984, pp. 13–24.   [G: France; U.K.]

Grubel, Herbert G. Free Economic Zones: Good or Bad? *Aussenwirtschaft,* May 1984, 39(1/2), pp. 43–56.   [G: U.S.; U.K.]

Grubel, Herbert G. Free Enterprise Zones in Economic Development. In *Giersch, H., ed.,* 1984, pp. 222–35.

Gruchy, Allan G. Uncertainty, Indicative Planning, and Industrial Policy. *J. Econ. Issues,* March 1984, 18(1), pp. 159–80.   [G: U.S.]

Haar, Charles M. The Joint Venture Approach to Urban Renewal: From Model Cities to Enterprise Zones. In *Brooks, H.; Liebman, L. and Schelling, C. S., eds.,* 1984, pp. 63–87.
[G: U.S.]

Hadley, Eleanor. Counterpoint on Business Groupings and Government–Industry Relations in Automobiles. In *Aoki, M., ed.,* 1984, pp. 319–27.   [G: Japan]

Harper, Edwin L. Do We Need an Industrial Policy? In *Wachter, M. L. and Wachter, S. M., eds.,* 1984, pp. 457–69.   [G: U.S.]

Haug, Peter. Regional Policy Incentives in the Scottish Electronics Industry: Survey Evidence. *Scot. J. Polit. Econ.,* November 1984, 31(3), pp. 274–83.   [G: U.K.]

Hawkins, Benjamin M. The Impact of the Enterprise Zone on Urban Areas. *Growth Change,* January 1984, 15(1), pp. 35–40.   [G: U.S.]

Heald, David. Privatisation: Analysing Its Appeal and Limitations. *Fisc. Stud.,* February 1984, 5(1), pp. 36–46.   [G: U.K.]

Heim, Carol E. Limits to Intervention: The Bank of England and Industrial Diversification in the Depressed Areas. *Econ. Hist. Rev., 2nd Ser.,* November 1984, 37(4), pp. 533–50.
[G: U.K.]

Hekman, John S. and Strong, John S. Is There a Case for Plant-Closing Laws? In *McKenzie, R. B., ed. (II),* 1984, *1980,* pp. 49–77.
[G: U.S.]

Herzberg, Ernesto. Mexico's Industrialization. In *Driscoll, R. E. and Behrman, J. N., eds.,* 1984, pp. 111–19.   [G: Mexico]

Hieronymi, Otto; Gabus, André and Afheldt, Heik. National Industrial Strategies and International Industrial Mobility: The Case of Switzerland. In *Driscoll, R. E. and Behrman, J. N., eds.,* 1984, pp. 187–95 [G: Switzerland]

Hindley, Brian. Empty Economics in the Case for Industrial Policy. *World Econ.,* September 1984, 7(3), pp. 277–94.   [G: Japan; U.S.; Europe]

Hoffmann, Lutz. Free Enterprise Zones in Economic Development: Comment. In *Giersch, H., ed.,* 1984, pp. 242–48.

Horvath, Janos. Economic Review in Hungary: Role of Plan and Market [Industrial Policy in Hungary: Lessons for America]. *Cato J.,* Fall 1984, 4(2), pp. 511–20.   [G: Hungary]

Hurwicz, Leonid. Economic Planning and the Knowledge Problem: A Comment. *Cato J.,* Fall 1984, 4(2), pp. 419–25.

Int'l Assoc. of Machinists and Aerospace Workers. Coping with Technology. In *Gordon, S. and McFadden, D., eds.,* 1984, pp. 61–66.
[G: U.S.]

Jacquemin, Alexis. Introduction: Which Policy for Industry? In *Jacquemin, A., ed.,* 1984, pp. 1–10.

Jacquemin, Alexis and Rainelli, Michel. Filières de la nation et filières de l'entreprise. (State and Firm "Filieres." With English summary.) *Revue Écon.,* March 1984, 35(2), pp. 379–92.
[G: France]

James, Franklin J. Urban Economic Development: A Zero-Sum Game? In *Bingham, R. D. and Blair, J. P., eds.,* 1984, pp. 157–74.
[G: U.S.]

Jeanrenaud, Claude and Meyer, Daniel. L'incidence a moyen et long terme des commandes de materiel de telecommunication: deux etudes de cas. (The Medium- and Long-term Incidence of Orders of Telecommunication Material: Two Case Studies. With English summary.) *Ann. Pub. Co-op. Econ.,* April–June 1984, 55(2), pp. 191–203. [G: Switzerland]

Jenkins, Rhys. The Rise and Fall of the Argentine Motor Vehicle Industry. In *Kronish, R. and Mericle, K. S., eds.,* 1984, pp. 41–73.
[G: Argentina]

Johnson, Peter S. and Thomas, R. Barry. Government Policies towards Business Formation: An Economic Appraisal of a Training Scheme. *Scot. J. Polit. Econ.,* June 1984, 31(2), pp. 131–46.   [G: U.K.]

Jones, Bryan D. and Bachelor, Lynn W. Local Policy Discretion and the Corporate Surplus. In *Bingham, R. D. and Blair, J. P., eds.,* 1984, pp. 245–67.   [G: U.S.]

de Jong, Henk Wouter. Sectoral Development and Sectoral Policies in the EC. In *Jacquemin, A., ed.*, 1984, pp. 147–71. [G: OECD]

Kale, Steven R. U.S. Industrial Development Incentives and Manufacturing Growth during the 1970s. *Growth Change*, January 1984, *15*(1), pp. 26–34. [G: U.S.]

Kanapathy, V. Why Malaysia Needs an Industrial Policy. In *Driscoll, R. E. and Behrman, J. N., eds.*, 1984, pp. 93–110. [G: Malaysia]

Kapstein, Ethan B. The Marshall Plan and Industrial Policy. *Challenge*, May/June 1984, *27*(2), pp. 54–59. [G: EEC]

Kendrick, John W. U.S. Economic Policy and Productivity Growth. *Cato J.*, Fall 1984, *4*(2), pp. 387–400. [G: U.S.]

Key, Sydney J. International Banking Facilities as a Free Economic Zone. *Aussenwirtschaft*, May 1984, *39*(1/2), pp. 57–74. [G: U.S.]

Kirzner, Israel M. Economic Planning and the Knowledge Problem. *Cato J.*, Fall 1984, *4*(2), pp. 407–18.

Kronish, Rich and Mericle, Kenneth S. The Development of the Latin American Motor Vehicle Industry, 1900-1980: A Class Analysis. In *Kronish, R. and Mericle, K. S., eds.*, 1984, pp. 261–306. [G: Latin America]

Krugman, Paul R. The U.S. Response to Foreign Industrial Targeting. *Brookings Pap. Econ. Act.*, 1984, (1), pp. 77–121. [G: U.S.]

Kumar, Nagesh. Public Policy, Marris Model and Corporate Growth in India. *Indian Econ. J.*, Oct.–Dec. 1984, *32*(2), pp. 74–83. [G: India]

Lall, Sanjaya. India's Technological Capacity: Effects of Trade, Industrial, Science and Technology Policies. In *Fransman, M. and King, K., eds.*, 1984, pp. 225–43. [G: India]

Lassila, Jaakko. Industripolitik—reglering versus marknadskrafter. (With English summary.) *Nationaløkon. Tidsskr.*, 1984, *122*(3), pp. 347–56. [G: Nordic Countries]

Lavoie, Don. Two Varieties of Industrial Policy: A Critique. *Cato J.*, Fall 1984, *4*(2), pp. 457–84. [G: U.S.; Japan]

Lawrence, Robert Z. The U.S. Response to Foreign Industrial Targeting: Comments. *Brookings Pap. Econ. Act.*, 1984, (1), pp. 125–29. [G: U.S.]

Lesourne, Jacques. The Changing Context of Industrial Policy: External and Internal Developments. In *Jacquemin, A., ed.*, 1984, pp. 13–38. [G: OECD]

Levačić, Rosalind. Do Mercantilist Industrial Policies Work? A Comparison of British and French TV Manufacturing. *Nat. Westminster Bank Quart. Rev.*, May 1984, pp. 47–58. [G: U.K.; France]

van Liemt, G. Adjusting To Change. *Int. Lab. Rev.*, November–December 1984, *123*(6), pp. 693–703. [G: OECD]

Littman, Daniel A. and Lee, Myung-Hoon. Plant Closings and Worker Dislocation. In *McKenzie, R. B., ed. (II)*, 1984, *1983*, pp. 127–54. [G: U.S.]

Litvak, Larry. Pension Funds and Economic De-

velopment. In *Bingham, R. D. and Blair, J. P., eds.*, 1984, pp. 191–98.

Liu, Tai-Ying and Chan, Yie-Lang. Industrial Policy and Strategies In the Republic of China. In *Driscoll, R. E. and Behrman, J. N., eds.*, 1984, pp. 137–49. [G: Republic of China]

Livingstone, Ian. Resource-Based Industrial Development: Past Experience and Future Prospects in Malawi. *Industry Devel.*, 1984, (10), pp. 75–135. [G: Malawi]

Looney, Robert E. Mexican Optimism and Economic Reality: An Analysis of the Mexican Industrial Development Plan. *Rivista Int. Sci. Econ. Com.*, May 1984, *31*(5), pp. 432–51. [G: Mexico]

Mackay, Tony. The Oil and Oil-Related Sector. In *Hood, N. and Young, S., eds.*, 1984, pp. 326–64. [G: U.K.]

Maldague, Robert. La politique des commandes publiques: instrument de politique economique? Le cas de la Belgique. (The Potential of Public Ordering Policy as an Instrument of Economic Policy. With English summary.) *Ann. Pub. Co-op. Econ.*, April–June 1984, *55*(2), pp. 173–82. [G: Belgium]

Malkin, Daniel. Mutations industrielles et IXe Plan. (Industrial Mutations and the IXth Plan. With English summary.) *Revue Écon.*, November 1984, *35*(6), pp. 1091–145. [G: France]

Marlin, Matthew R. Industrial Development Bonds: Reviewing the Evidence in the Norfolk–Virginia Beach SMSA. *Rev. Reg. Stud.*, Winter 1984, *14*(1), pp. 45–53. [G: U.S.]

Marsden, Keith. Services for Small Firms: The Roles of Government Programmes and Market Networks in Thailand. *Int. Lab. Rev.*, March-April 1984, *123*(2), pp. 235–49. [G: Thailand]

McCracken, Paul W. Is Industrial Policy for the U.S.? *Bus. Econ.*, January 1984, *19*(1), pp. 24–29. [G: U.S.]

McDonell, Michael. Recent Developments in Medium-term Planning and Policy Implementation in Ireland. *Econ. Lavoro*, Oct.-Dec. 1984, *18*(4), pp. 85–90. [G: Ireland]

McGahey, Richard. Industrial Policy: Minority Economic Interests and American Political Response. *Rev. Black Polit. Econ.*, Summer–Fall 1984, *13*(1–2), pp. 81–98. [G: U.S.]

McHone, W. Warren. State Industrial Development Incentives and Employment Growth in Multistate SMSAs. *Growth Change*, October 1984, *15*(4), pp. 8–15. [G: U.S.]

McKenzie, Richard B. A Pro-market National Industrial Policy [Breaking the Barriers to U.S. Economic Growth]. *Cato J.*, Fall 1984, *4*(2), pp. 619–24. [G: U.S.]

McKenzie, Richard B. Business Mobility: Economic Myths and Realities. In *McKenzie, R. B., ed. (II)*, 1984, pp. 11–27. [G: U.S.]

McKenzie, Richard B. Summary Remarks. In *McKenzie, R. B., ed. (II)*, 1984, pp. 309–13. [G: U.S.]

McKenzie, Richard B. The Case for Plant Closures. In *McKenzie, R. B., ed. (II)*, 1984, *1981*, pp. 205–19. [G: U.S.]

McKenzie, Richard B. The Right to Close Up Shop. In *McKenzie, R. B., ed. (II)*, 1984, pp. 3–8. **[G: U.S.]**

Metcalf, David. Employment and Industrial Assistance. In *Jacquemin, A., ed.*, 1984, pp. 84–98. **[G: U.K.; Belgium; France; Norway; Netherlands]**

Mier, Robert. Job Generation as a Road to Recovery. In *Porter, P. R. and Sweet, D. C., eds.*, 1984, pp. 160–72. **[G: U.S.]**

Miller, James C., III. Reindustrialization Policy: Atari Mercantilism. In *McKenzie, R. B., ed. (II)*, 1984, pp. 221–29. **[G: U.S.]**

Miller, James C., III. The Case against "Industrial Policy." *Cato J.*, Fall 1984, *4*(2), pp. 651–60. **[G: U.S.]**

Miller, James C., III, et al. Industrial Policy: Reindustrialization through Competition or Coordinated Action? *Yale J. Regul.*, 1984, *2*(1), pp. 1–37. **[G: U.S.; Japan; W. Europe]**

Møller, J. Ørstøm. Industripolitik i Danmark. (Danish Industrial Policy. With English summary.) *Nationaløkon. Tidsskr.*, 1984, *122*(2), pp. 228–39. **[G: Denmark]**

Morishima, Michio and Prosperetti, Luigi. An Input–Output Analysis of the De-Industrialisation of the U.K. Economy, 1963–1973. *Banca Naz. Lavoro Quart. Rev.*, March 1984, (148), pp. 33–54. **[G: U.K.]**

Morris, D. J. Reflections on the Byatt Report [Byatt Report on Subsidies to British Export Credits]. *World Econ.*, September 1984, *7*(3), pp. 341–44. **[G: U.K.]**

Most, Benjamin A. Latin America: The Case of Argentina. In *Groth, A. J. and Wade, L. L., eds.*, 1984, pp. 181–211. **[G: Argentina]**

Nabi, Ijaz. Issues in the Economics of Industrialization in Developing Countries: A Case Study from Pakistan's Light Engineering Sector. *Pakistan Devel. Rev.*, Summer-Autumn 1984, *23*(2&3), pp. 311–25. **[G: Pakistan]**

Niosi, Jorge. Le déclin de l'industrie américaine. (With English summary.) *Rev. Econ. Ind.*, 4th Trimester 1984, (30), pp. 9–25. **[G: U.S.]**

Niskanen, William A. A "Supply-Side" Industrial Policy. *Cato J.*, Fall 1984, *4*(2), pp. 381–86. **[G: U.S.]**

Okimoto, Daniel I. Competitive Edge: Conclusions. In *Okimoto, D. I.; Sugano, T. and Weinstein, F. B., eds.*, 1984, pp. 177–235. **[G: Japan; U.S.]**

Okimoto, Daniel I. Competitive Edge: Political Context. In *Okimoto, D. I.; Sugano, T. and Weinstein, F. B., eds.*, 1984, pp. 78–133. **[G: Japan; U.S.]**

Pugel, Thomas A. Japan's Industrial Policy: Instruments, Trends, and Effects. *J. Compar. Econ.*, December 1984, *8*(4), pp. 420–35. **[G: Japan]**

Quick, Perry D. Businesses: Reagan's Industrial Policy. In *Palmer, J. L. and Sawhill, I. V., eds.*, 1984, pp. 287–316. **[G: U.S.]**

Rabushka, Alvin. Restoring U.S. Competitiveness [U.S. Economic Policy and Productivity Growth]. *Cato J.*, Fall 1984, *4*(2), pp. 401–06. **[G: U.S.]**

Rallo, Joseph. The European Communities' Industrial Policy Revisited: The Case of Aerospace. *J. Common Market Stud.*, March 1984, *22*(3), pp. 245–67. **[G: OECD; EEC]**

Rapping, Leonard A. Bureaucracy, the Corporation, and Economic Policy. *J. Post Keynesian Econ.*, Spring 1984, *6*(3), pp. 337–53. **[G: U.S.]**

Rapping, Leonard A. Economic Change, Bureaucracy, and the Innovative Process. In *Alperovitz, G. and Skurski, R., eds.*, 1984, pp. 56–75. **[G: U.S.]**

Rasmussen, David W.; Bendick, Marc, Jr. and Ledebur, Larry C. A Methodology for Selecting Economic Development Incentives. *Growth Change*, January 1984, *15*(1), pp. 18–25. **[G: U.S.]**

Redburn, F. Stevens, et al. Federal Economic Development Investments. In *Holzer, M. and Nagel, S. S., eds.*, 1984, pp. 115–43. **[G: U.S.]**

Reich, Robert B. Matching Public Policies and Business Strategies: The New Context. In *Brooks, H.; Liebman, L. and Schelling, C. S., eds.*, 1984, pp. 263–84. **[G: U.S.]**

Richonnier, Michel. Europe's Decline Is Not Irreversible. *J. Common Market Stud.*, March 1984, *22*(3), pp. 227–43. **[G: U.S.; Japan; EEC]**

Roberts, Markley. A Labor Perspective on Technological Change. In *Collins, E. L. and Tanner, L. D., eds.*, 1984, pp. 183–205. **[G: U.S.]**

Roberts, Paul Craig. Industrial Policy in Hungary: A Comment. *Cato J.*, Fall 1984, *4*(2), pp. 507–09. **[G: Hungary]**

Rothwell, Roy. Creating a Regional Innovation-oriented Infrastructure: The Role of Public Procurement. *Ann. Pub. Co-op. Econ.*, April–June 1984, *55*(2), pp. 159–72. **[G: U.K.]**

Rothwell, Roy. Reindustrialisation, Innovation and Public Policy. *Greek Econ. Rev.*, December 1984, *6*(3), pp. 317–35. **[G: OECD]**

Ruane, Frances P. The White Paper on Industrial Policy. *Irish Banking Rev.*, September 1984, pp. 35–45. **[G: Ireland]**

Sakoh, Katsuro. Japanese Economic Success: Industrial Policy or Free Market? *Cato J.*, Fall 1984, *4*(2), pp. 521–43. **[G: Japan]**

Salgado Penaherrera, Germanico. Economic Integration of Developing Countries and the Role of Joint Industrial Planning. In *Ghosh, P. K., ed., no. 12*, 1984, *1975*, pp. 120–52. **[G: Latin America]**

Sauer, Willibrord. Small Firms and the German Economic Miracle. In *Levicki, C., ed.*, 1984, pp. 78–88. **[G: W. Germany]**

Schmitz, Hubert. Industrialisation Strategies in Less Developed Countries: Some Lessons of Historical Experience. *J. Devel. Stud.*, October 1984, *21*(1), pp. 1–21. **[G: LDCs]**

Schultze, Charles L. Industrial Policy: A Dissent. *Australian Bull. Lab.*, June 1984, *10*(3), pp. 134–43. **[G: Japan; U.S.]**

Schultze, Charles L. Industrial Policy: A Dissent.

In *McKenzie, R. B., ed. (II)*, 1984, *1983*, pp. 155–75. [G: U.S.; Japan]

Schwartz, Gail Garfield. The Hard Realities of Industrial Policy. In *Alperovitz, G. and Skurski, R., eds.*, 1984, pp. 79–88. [G: U.S.]

Sekiguchi, Sueo and Horiuchi, Toshihiro. Foreign Trade and Industrial Policies: A Review of Japanese Experience. In *Benjamin, R. and Kudrle, R. T.*, 1984, pp. 81–103. [G: Japan]

Shackleton, J. R. Privatization: The Case Examined. *Nat. Westminster Bank Quart. Rev.*, May 1984, pp. 59–73. [G: U.K.]

Sharpe, Tom. Privatisation, Regulation and Competition. *Fisc. Stud.*, February 1984, 5(1), pp. 47–60. [G: U.K.; U.S.]

Skurski, Roger. The Need for New Directions and a Progressive Response. In *Alperovitz, G. and Skurski, R., eds.*, 1984, pp. 1–14.

Soifer, Ricardo J. Exports of Technology by Newly Industrializing Countries: Argentina. *World Devel.*, May/June 1984, 12(5/6), pp. 625–44. [G: Argentina]

Solo, Robert A. American Economic Policy: Lessons from Elsewhere. In *Alperovitz, G. and Skurski, R., eds.*, 1984, pp. 43–55. [G: Japan]

Solo, Robert A. Industrial Policy. *J. Econ. Issues*, September 1984, 18(3), pp. 697–714. [G: U.S.]

Spence, A. Michael. Industrial Organization and Competitive Advantage in Multinational Industries. *Amer. Econ. Rev.*, May 1984, 74(2), pp. 356–60.

Spinanger, Dean. Free Enterprise Zones in Economic Development: Comment. In *Giersch, H., ed.*, 1984, pp. 236–41. [G: LDCs]

Steel, David. Government and the New Hybrids: A Trail of Unanswered Questions. *Fisc. Stud.*, February 1984, 5(1), pp. 87–97. [G: U.K.]

Stewardt, J. Financial Aids to Small Business. *Irish Banking Rev.*, March 1984, pp. 18–31. [G: U.K.]

Stoffaës, Christian. French Industrial Strategy in Sunrise Sectors. In *Jacquemin, A., ed.*, 1984, pp. 274–92. [G: France]

Stutchbury, Michael. The Playford Legend and the Industrialization of South Australia. *Australian Econ. Hist. Rev.*, March 1984, 24(1), pp. 1–19. [G: Australia]

Sun, Yefang. To Raise Production Four-Fold in Two Decades Is Not Only Politically Probable but Technologically Feasible. *Chinese Econ. Stud.*, Winter 1983–84, 17(2), pp. 50–67. [G: China]

Teitel, Simón and Sercovich, Francisco Colman. Exports of Technology by Newly Industrializing Countries: Latin America. *World Devel.*, May/June 1984, 12(5/6), pp. 645–60. [G: Latin America]

Thurow, Lester C. The Need for Industrial Policies: The Case of the U.S.A. *Ann. Pub. Coop. Econ.*, January–March 1984, 55(1), pp. 3–31. [G: U.S.]

Tiffany, Paul A. The Roots of Decline: Business–Government Relations in the American Steel Industry, 1945–1960. *J. Econ. Hist.*, June 1984, 44(2), pp. 407–19. [G: U.S.]

Tokman, Víctor E. Global Monetarism and Destruction of Industry. *Cepal Rev.*, 1984, (23), pp. 107–21. [G: Argentina; Chile]

Trezise, Philip H. Japanese Economic Success: A Comment. *Cato J.*, Fall 1984, 4(2), pp. 545–86. [G: Japan]

Truett, Dale B. and Truett, Lila J. The Maquiladoras: Prospects for Mexico. *J. Econ. Devel.*, December 1984, 9(2), pp. 45–66. [G: Mexico]

Ullmann, John E. Can Business Become a Participant? In *Gordon, S. and McFadden, D., eds.*, 1984, pp. 164–74. [G: U.S.]

Varga, György. The Long-run Development of Hungarian Industry (Outlines of an Approach to Industrial Policy). *Acta Oecon.*, 1984, 32(1–2), pp. 91–112. [G: Hungary]

Vieira, Edwin, Jr. The Constitutional Chaos of Industrial Policy. *Cato J.*, Fall 1984, 4(2), pp. 549–86. [G: U.S.]

Viita, Pentti. Näivettääkö valtio Suomen teollisuutta. (The State Withering Industry in Finland? With English summary.) *Kansant. Aikak.*, 1984, 80(3), pp. 261–70. [G: Finland]

de Vries, Barend A. Industrial Policy in Small Developing Countries. *Finance Develop.*, June 1984, 21(2), pp. 39–41. [G: Selected LDCs]

Waelbroeck, Jean. The Logic of EC Commercial and Industrial Policy Making. In *Jacquemin, A., ed.*, 1984, pp. 99–144. [G: EEC]

Watanabe, Taro. Industrial Policy and Trade Theory (Part I). *Osaka Econ. Pap.*, March 1984, 33(3–4), pp. 1–11.

Watson, William G. It's Still Not Time for an Industrial Strategy. *Can. Public Policy*, June 1984, 10(2), pp. 201–10. [G: Canada]

Weinstein, Bernard L. and Gross, Harold T. Grassroots Industrial Policy. *Challenge*, July/August 1984, 27(3), pp. 52–55. [G: U.S.]

Weiss, Frank D. Industrial Policy and International Competitiveness in West Germany. In *Driscoll, R. E. and Behrman, J. N., eds.*, 1984, pp. 229–44. [G: W. Germany]

Weiss, John. Alliance for Production: Mexico's Incentives for Private Sector Industrial Development. *World Devel.*, July 1984, 12(7), pp. 723–42. [G: Mexico]

Whalley, John. *Trade, Industrial Policy, and Canadian Manufacturing* by Richard G. Harris (with the Assistance of David Cox): A Review Article. *Can. J. Econ.*, May 1984, 17(2), pp. 386–98. [G: Canada]

White, Geoff. Intra-Industry Trade Adjustment and European Industrial Policies. In *Jacquemin, A., ed.*, 1984, pp. 172–90. [G: EEC]

Wilkinson, Christopher. Trends in Industrial Policy in the EC: Theory and Practice. In *Jacquemin, A., ed.*, 1984, pp. 39–83. [G: EEC]

Wilmoth, David. Regional Economic Policy and the New Corporatism. In *Sawers, L. and Tabb, W. K., eds.*, 1984, pp. 235–58. [G: U.S.]

Wilson, P. E. B. The Role of the Public Sector

in the Development of Small Enterprise. In *Ramanadham, V. V., ed.*, 1984, pp. 171–91.
[G: LDCs; MDCs]

Winpisinger, William W. Why Labor Unions Do Not Accept the New Economic Policy. In *Wachter, M. L. and Wachter, S. M., eds.*, 1984, pp. 28–33. [G: U.S.]

Wolff, Goetz. Reindustrialization: A Debate among Capitalists. In *Sawers, L. and Tabb, W. K., eds.*, 1984, pp. 259–68.

Yakushiji, Taizo. The Government in a Spiral Dilemma: Dynamic Policy Interventions vis-à-vis Auto Firms. C.1900–C.1960. In *Aoki, M., ed.*, 1984, pp. 265–310. [G: Japan]

Yeager, Leland B. Is Industrial Innovation Destroying Jobs? A Comment. *Cato J.*, Fall 1984, *4*(2), pp. 645–50. [G: U.S.]

Yokoyama, Taizo. The Japanese Industrial Policy. *Rivista Int. Sci. Econ. Com.*, September 1984, *31*(9), pp. 812–18. [G: Japan]

Yoo, Young. Industrial Policy of South Korea: Past and Future. In *Driscoll, R. E. and Behrman, J. N., eds.*, 1984, pp. 167–76. [G: S. Korea]

Young, Stephen and Hood, Neil. Industrial Policy and the Scottish Economy. In *Hood, N. and Young, S., eds.*, 1984, pp. 28–56. [G: U.K.]

Young, Stephen and Hood, Neil. Industrial Policy in The United Kingdom. In *Driscoll, R. E. and Behrman, J. N., eds.*, 1984, pp. 197–214.
[G: U.K.]

Zacchia, Carlo. Rural Industrialization in Italy. *J. World Trade Law*, March–April 1984, *18*(2), pp. 110–24. [G: Italy]

van Zyl, J. C. South Africa in World Trade. *S. Afr. J. Econ.*, March 1984, *52*(1), pp. 42–62.
[G: S. Africa]

619 Economics of Regulation

6190 Economics of Regulation

Anderson, Lee G. Uncertainty in the Fisheries Management Process. *Marine Resource Econ.*, 1984, *1*(1), pp. 77–87. [G: U.S.]

Anderson, Ronald W. The Regulation of Futures Contract Innovations in the United States. *J. Futures Markets*, Fall 1984, *4*(3), pp. 297–332.
[G: U.S.]

Aranson, Peter H. Constitutionalizing the Regulatory Process. In *McKenzie, R. B., ed. (I)*, 1984, pp. 187–206. [G: U.S.]

Bailey, Elizabeth E. A Comment on the Papers by Theodore Keeler and Barry Weingast [Theories of Regulation and the Deregulation Movement] [The Congressional–Bureaucratic System: A Principal–Agent Perspective (with Application to the SEC)]. *Public Choice*, 1984, *44*(1), pp. 197–200. [G: U.S.]

Baily, Martin Neil. The Reagan Administration's Regulatory Relief Effort: Comments. In *Eads, G. C. and Fix, M., eds.*, 1984, pp. 81–83. [G: U.S.]

Balassa, Bela. Prices, Incentives, and Economic Growth. *Weltwirtsch. Arch.*, 1984, *120*(4), pp. 611–30. [G: Global]

Baron, David P. Regulatory Strategies under As-

ymmetric Information. In *Boyer, M. and Kihlstrom, R. E., eds.*, 1984, pp. 155–80.

Baron, David P. and Besanko, David. Regulation and Information in a Continuing Relationship. *Info. Econ. Policy*, 1984, *1*(3), pp. 267–302.

Baron, David P. and Besanko, David. Regulation, Asymmetric Information, and Auditing. *Rand J. Econ.*, Winter 1984, *15*(4), pp. 447–70.

Bennett, John. Alternative Price and Quantity Controls for Regulation under Uncertainty. *Z. Nationalökon.*, 1984, *44*(2), pp. 103–15.

Bird, Richard M. Put Up or Shut Up: Self-Assessment and Asymmetric Information. *J. Policy Anal. Manage.*, Summer 1984, *3*(4), pp. 618–20.

Bohlander, George W. and Farris, Martin T. Collective Bargaining in Trucking—The Effects of Deregulation. *Logist. Transp. Rev.*, September 1984, *20*(3), pp. 223–38. [G: U.S.]

Braeutigam, Ronald R. Socially Optimal Pricing with Rivalry and Economies of Scale. *Rand J. Econ.*, Spring 1984, *15*(1), pp. 127–34.

Braeutigam, Ronald R. and Quirk, James P. Demand Uncertainty and the Regulated Firm. *Int. Econ. Rev.*, February 1984, *25*(1), pp. 45–60.

Breit, William. Constitutionalizing the Regulatory Process: Comment. In *McKenzie, R. B., ed. (I)*, 1984, pp. 207–11. [G: U.S.]

Buxbaum, Richard M. Federalism and Company Law. *Mich. Law Rev.*, April–May 1984, *82*(5 & 6), pp. 1163–81. [G: U.S.]

Christainsen, Gregory B. and Haveman, Robert H. The Reagan Administration's Regulatory Relief Effort: A Mid-term Assessment. In *Eads, G. C. and Fix, M., eds.*, 1984, pp. 49–80.
[G: U.S.]

Crain, W. Mark and McCormick, Robert E. Regulators as an Interest Group. In *Buchanan, J. M. and Tollison, R. D., eds.*, 1984, pp. 287–304. [G: U.S.]

Crandall, Robert W. Regulatory Reform under the Reagan Administration: Comments. In *Eads, G. C. and Fix, M., eds.*, 1984, pp. 42–44. [G: U.S.]

Daughety, Andrew F. Regulation and Industrial Organization. *J. Polit. Econ.*, October 1984, *92*(5), pp. 932–53.

Dechert, W. Davis. Has the Averch–Johnson Effect Been Theoretically Justified? *J. Econ. Dynam. Control*, October 1984, *8*(1), pp. 1–17.

Dougan, William R. Railway Abandonments, Cross-Subsidies, and the Theory of Regulation. *Public Choice*, 1984, *44*(2), pp. 297–305.
[G: U.S.]

Dudenhöffer, Ferdi. The Regulation of Intensities and Productivities: Concepts in Environmental Policy. *Z. ges. Staatswiss.*, June 1984, *140*(2), pp. 276–87.

Eads, George C. and Fix, Michael. The Reagan Regulatory Strategy: Introduction. In *Eads, G. C. and Fix, M., eds.*, 1984, pp. 1–13.
[G: U.S.]

Eckard, E. Woodrow. Regulatory Relief and the

Automobile Industry: Comments. In *Eads, G. C. and Fix, M.*, eds., 1984, pp. 106–09. [G: U.S.]

Eckel, Catherine C. and Goldberg, Michael A. Regulation and Deregulation of the Brewing Industry: The British Columbia Example. *Can. Public Policy*, September 1984, *10*(3), pp. 316–27. [G: Canada]

Ellison, Anthony P. Regulatory Reform in Canada: A Different Ball Game. In *Thompson, F.*, ed., 1984, pp. 103–32. [G: Canada]

Fix, Michael. Transferring Regulatory Authority to the States. In *Eads, G. C. and Fix, M.*, eds., 1984, pp. 153–79. [G: U.S.]

Foreman, Christopher H., Jr. Congress and Social Regulation in the Reagan Era. In *Eads, G. C. and Fix, M.*, eds., 1984, pp. 187–214. [G: U.S.]

Goldman, M. Barry; Leland, Hayne E. and Sibley, David S. Optimal Nonuniform Prices. *Rev. Econ. Stud.*, April 1984, *51*(2), pp. 305–19.

Hambright, James K. Transferring Regulatory Authority to the States: Comments. In *Eads, G. C. and Fix, M.*, eds., 1984, pp. 180–83. [G: U.S.]

Harrison, David, Jr. Federalism and Regulation: Comments. In *Eads, G. C. and Fix, M.*, eds., 1984, pp. 146–52. [G: U.S.]

Jasinowski, Jerry J. Regulatory Reform under the Reagan Administration: Comments. In *Eads, G. C. and Fix, M.*, eds., 1984, pp. 45–47. [G: U.S.]

Jones, L. R. and Thompson, Frederick. Incremental vs. Comprehensive Reform of Economic Regulation: Predictable Outcomes and Unintended Consequences. *Amer. J. Econ. Soc.*, January 1984, *43*(1), pp. 1–17. [G: U.S.]

Kalt, Joseph P. The Congressional–Bureaucratic System: A Principal–Agent Perspective (with Applications to the SEC): A Comment. *Public Choice*, 1984, *44*(1), pp. 193–95. [G: U.S.]

Keeler, Theodore E. Theories of Regulation and the Deregulation Movement. *Public Choice*, 1984, *44*(1), pp. 103–45. [G: U.S.]

Keenan, Donald C. and Keenan, Taewon K. First and Second-Best Pricing with Uncertain Demand. *Southern Econ. J.*, July 1984, *51*(1), pp. 80–88.

Keenan, Donald C. and Paul, Chris. An Economic Explanation for Political Action and Inaction. *Atlantic Econ. J.*, July 1984, *12*(2), pp. 12–22.

Koenig, Evan F. Fisheries Regulation under Uncertainty: A Dynamic Analysis. *Marine Resource Econ.*, 1984, *1*(2), pp. 193–208.

Lanciotti, Giulio. Objectives and Instruments of Structural Supervision: Guidelines and Optimum Rules for Authorising Branch Openings. In *Banca d'Italia*, 1984, pp. 249–61. [G: Italy]

Lave, Lester B. Controlling Contradictions among Regulations. *Amer. Econ. Rev.*, June 1984, *74*(3), pp. 471–75. [G: U.S.]

Lecraw, Donald J. Some Economic Effects of

Standards. *Appl. Econ.*, August 1984, *16*(4), pp. 507–22. [G: Canada]

Leone, Robert A. Regulatory Relief and the Automobile Industry. In *Eads, G. C. and Fix, M.*, eds., 1984, pp. 87–105. [G: U.S.]

Lewis, Albert E. Restructuring Financial Institutions in the New Financial Environment: Discussion. In *Sametz, A. W.*, ed., 1984, pp. 43–46. [G: U.S.]

Libecap, Gary D. and Wiggins, Steven N. Contractual Responses to the Common Pool: Prorationing of Crude Oil Production. *Amer. Econ. Rev.*, March 1984, *74*(1), pp. 87–98. [G: U.S.]

Linder, Stephen H. and McBride, Mark E. Enforcement Costs and Regulatory Reform: The Agency and Firm Response. *J. Environ. Econ. Manage.*, December 1984, *11*(4), pp. 327–46.

Lipsey, Robert E. and Weiss, Merle Yahr. Foreign Production and Exports of Individual Firms. *Rev. Econ. Statist.*, May 1984, *66*(2), pp. 304–08. [G: U.S.]

Maloney, Michael T.; McCormick, Robert E. and Tollison, Robert D. Economic Regulation, Competitive Governments, and Specialized Resources. *J. Law Econ.*, October 1984, *27*(2), pp. 329–38. [G: U.S.]

Maloney, Michael T. and Yandle, Bruce. Estimation of the Cost of Air Pollution Control Regulation. *J. Environ. Econ. Manage.*, September 1984, *11*(3), pp. 244–63. [G: U.S.]

Mashaw, Jerry L. and Rose-Ackerman, Susan. Federalism and Regulation. In *Eads, G. C. and Fix, M.*, eds., 1984, pp. 111–45. [G: U.S.]

Maynard, Alan and Hartley, Keith. The Regulation of the Pharmaceutical Industry. In *Lindgren, B.*, ed., 1984, pp. 123–37. [G: U.K.]

McCormick, Robert E.; Shughart, William F., II and Tollison, Robert D. The Disinterest in Deregulation. *Amer. Econ. Rev.*, December 1984, *74*(5), pp. 1075–79.

McLain, Patrick. Congress and Social Regulation in the Reagan Era: Comments. In *Eads, G. C. and Fix, M.*, eds., 1984, pp. 215–17. [G: U.S.]

Moore, Thomas Gale. Reagan's Regulatory Record. In *Moore, J. H.*, ed., 1984, pp. 239–58. [G: U.S.]

Noam, Eli M. Market Power and Regulation: A Simultaneous Approach. *J. Ind. Econ.*, March 1984, *32*(3), pp. 335–47. [G: U.S.]

Parker, John. Regulatory Stringency and the International Diffusion of Drugs. In *Lindgren, B.*, ed., 1984, pp. 139–58. [G: Selected Countries; U.K.]

Pashigian, B. Peter. The Effect of Environmental Regulation on Optimal Plant Size and Factor Shares. *J. Law Econ.*, April 1984, *27*(1), pp. 1–28. [G: U.S.]

Paul, Ellen Frankel. Taking by Regulation: Resolving the Constitutional Muddle. In *McKenzie, R. B.*, ed. (1), 1984, pp. 161–82. [G: U.S.]

Peeters, Chris. Scheepsbouw in België: Ontwikkeling van een berekeningsmethode ter bepaling van de financiële implicaties van een indirecte subsidie. (The Belgian Shipbuilding Industry: Development of a Calculation Method to Determine the Financial Implications of an Indirect Subsidy. With English summary.) *Cah. Écon. Bruxelles*, 1st Trimester 1984, (101), pp. 40–56. **[G: Belgium]**

Perry, Martin K. Scale Economies, Imperfect Competition, and Public Policy. *J. Ind. Econ.*, March 1984, *32*(3), pp. 313–33.

Prywes, Menahem. The Cost in Lost Productivity of New Regulation in the U.S. Chemical Industry. *J. Policy Modeling*, August 1984, *6*(3), pp. 411–19. **[G: U.S.]**

Quick, Perry D. Businesses: Reagan's Industrial Policy. In *Palmer, J. L. and Sawhill, I. V., eds.*, 1984, pp. 287–316. **[G: U.S.]**

Quirk, Paul J. Congress and Social Regulation in the Reagan Era: Comments. In *Eads, G. C. and Fix, M., eds.*, 1984, pp. 218–22. **[G: U.S.]**

Reynolds, R. Larry. The Regulatory Matrix and Rigidity in the Economic System. *J. Econ. Issues*, June 1984, *18*(2), pp. 627–31.

Ross, Thomas W. Uncovering Regulators' Social Welfare Weights. *Rand J. Econ.*, Spring 1984, *15*(1), pp. 152–55.

Ruane, Frances P. and John, A. Andrew. Government Intervention and the Cost of Capital to Irish Manufacturing Industry. *Econ. Soc. Rev.*, October 1984, *16*(1), pp. 31–50. **[G: Ireland]**

Samuelson, Douglas A. Identifying Changes in Patterns of Production to Support Petroleum Price Control Litigation. In *Lev, B., et al., eds.*, 1984, pp. 47–49.

Saunders, Anthony. The Effect of Changing Regulation on Investment Policy of Life Insurance Companies. In *Sametz, A. W., ed.*, 1984, pp. 85–94. **[G: U.S.]**

Sawhill, Isabel V. The Reagan Administration's Regulatory Relief Effort: A Mid-term Assessment: Comment. In *Eads, G. C. and Fix, M., eds.*, 1984, pp. 84–86. **[G: U.S.]**

Scott, Kenneth E. The Future of Bank Regulation. In *Moore, J. H., ed.*, 1984, pp. 259–73. **[G: U.S.]**

Sell, Axel. Staatliche Regulierung und Arbeitslosigkeit im internationalen Sektor. (Regulation and Unemployment in the International Sector. With English summary.) *Konjunkturpolitik*, 1984, *30*(4), pp. 189–216. **[G: W. Germany]**

Shaffer, Sherrill. Regulation and Risk Preferences. *J. Ind. Econ.*, March 1984, *32*(3), pp. 349–57.

Sharpe, Tom. Privatisation, Regulation and Competition. *Fisc. Stud.*, February 1984, *5*(1), pp. 47–60. **[G: U.K.; U.S.]**

Shavell, Steven. A Model of the Optimal Use of Liability and Safety Regulation. *Rand J. Econ.*, Summer 1984, *15*(2), pp. 271–80.

Siegan, Bernard H. The Economic Constitution in Historical Perspective. In *McKenzie, R. B., ed. (I)*, 1984, pp. 39–53. **[G: U.S.]**

Stigler, George J. Gioie e dolori del capitalismo moderno. (The Pleasures and Pains of Modern Capitalism. With English summary.) *Mondo Aperto*, January-February 1984, *38*(1), pp. 1–11. **[G: U.S.]**

Thompson, Frederick and Stanbury, W. T. The Comparative Politics of Regulation: A Contingency Theory of the Function of Interest Groups in the Legislative Process. In *Thompson, F., ed.*, 1984, pp. 81–102. **[G: Canada; U.S.]**

Tollison, Robert D. The Economic Constitution in Historical Perspective: Comment. In *McKenzie, R. B., ed. (I)*, 1984, pp. 55–60. **[G: U.S.]**

Trebing, Harry M. Public Control of Enterprise: Neoclassical Assault and Neoinstitutional Reform: Remarks upon Receipt of the Veblens–Commons Award. *J. Econ. Issues*, June 1984, *18*(2), pp. 353–68.

Trent, Darrell M. Transportation: Policy, Goals, Accomplishments. In *Moore, J. H., ed.*, 1984, pp. 275–86. **[G: U.S.]**

Tullock, Gordon. Taking by Regulation: Resolving the Constitutional Muddle: Comment. In *McKenzie, R. B., ed. (I)*, 1984, pp. 183–86.

Viscusi, W. Kip. Regulating Uncertain Health Hazards When There Is Changing Risk Information. *J. Health Econ.*, December 1984, *3*(3), pp. 259–73.

Wallison, Peter J. The Emerging Regulatory Structure for Banks: Implications for the Insurance Industry. In *Sametz, A. W., ed.*, 1984, pp. 73–78. **[G: U.S.]**

Wardell, William M. and Sheck, Lorraine E. Is Pharmaceutical Innovation Declining? Interpreting Measures of Pharmaceutical Innovation and Regulatory Impact in the USA, 1950–1980. In *Lindgren, B., ed.*, 1984, pp. 177–89. **[G: U.S.]**

Watson, William D. and Bernknopf, Richard. Maximum Economic Recovery of Federal Coal. *Energy J.*, July 1984, *5*(3), pp. 59–80. **[G: U.S.]**

Weidenbaum, Murray L. Regulatory Reform Under the Reagan Administration. In *Eads, G. C. and Fix, M., eds.*, 1984, pp. 15–41. **[G: U.S.]**

Weingast, Barry R. The Congressional–Bureaucratic System: A Principal–Agent Perspective (with Application to the SEC). *Public Choice*, 1984, *44*(1), pp. 147–91. **[G: U.S.]**

de Wilmars, J. Mertens and Steenbergen, J. The Court of Justice of the European Communities and Governance in an Economic Crisis. *Mich. Law Rev.*, April–May 1984, *82*(5 & 6), pp. 1377–98. **[G: EEC]**

Yohe, Gary W. Regulation under Uncertainty: An Intuitive Survey and Application to Fisheries. *Marine Resource Econ.*, 1984, *1*(2), pp. 171–92.

Zardkoohi, Asghar and Sheer, Alain. Public versus Private Liquor Retailing: An Investigation into the Behavior of the State Governments.

Southern Econ. J., April 1984, *50*(4), pp. 1058–76. **[G: U.S.]**

620 ECONOMICS OF TECHNOLOGICAL CHANGE

621 Technological Change; Innovation; Research and Development

6210 General

Adam, Abdallah. The Arab Fund for Technical Assistance to African and Arab Countries. In *Achilli, M. and Khaldi, M., eds.*, 1984, pp. 220–30. **[G: Africa; Arab Countries]**

Alam, M. Shahid. Hirschman's Taxonomy of Industries: Some Hypotheses and Evidence. *Econ. Develop. Cult. Change*, January 1984, *32*(2), pp. 367–72. **[G: Pakistan]**

Amendola, Mario. Productive Transformations and Economic Theory. *Banca Naz. Lavoro Quart. Rev.*, December 1984, (151), pp. 351–66.

Amendola, Mario. Towards a Dynamic Analysis of the "Traverse." *Eastern Econ. J.*, April-June 1984, *10*(2), pp. 203–10.

Badea-Dincă, N., et al. Problems Deriving from the Directives of the XIIIth Congress of the Romanian Communist Party Concerning the Problems of Economic Efficiency in Introducing Information Systems for Processes Management. *Econ. Computat. Cybern. Stud. Res.*, 1984, *19*(4), pp. 13–20. **[G: Romania]**

Bandyopadhyay, T. and Ghatak, S. Errata [Some Remarks on Agricultural Backwardness under Semi-feudalism]. *Indian Econ. Rev.*, January–June 1984, *19*(1), pp. 157. **[G: India]**

Bartlett, Bruce. Is Industrial Innovation Destroying Jobs? *Cato J.*, Fall 1984, *4*(2), pp. 625–43. **[G: U.S.]**

Beckers, H. L. The Role of Industry. In *Fusfeld, H. I. and Haklisch, C. S., eds.*, 1984, pp. 143–49.

Bell, Martin. 'Learning' and the Accumulation of Industrial Technological Capacity in Developing Countries. In *Fransman, M. and King, K., eds.*, 1984, pp. 187–209. **[G: LDCs]**

Bosworth, Derek and Westaway, Tony. The Influence of Demand and Supply Side Pressures on the Quantity and Quality of Inventive Activity. *Appl. Econ.*, February 1984, *16*(1), pp. 131–46. **[G: U.K.]**

Bugliarello, George. Technology and Economic Development. *Metroecon.*, February 1984, *36*(1), pp. 111–19. **[G: Global]**

Bugliarello, George. The Generation of Knowledge in Advanced Countries. In *Fusfeld, H. I. and Haklisch, C. S., eds.*, 1984, pp. 15–23.

Caillods, Françoise. Education, Organisation of Work and Indigenous Technological Capacity. In *Fransman, M. and King, K., eds.*, 1984, pp. 211–22. **[G: LDCs]**

Carlsson, Ingvar. University–Industry Research Interactions: Summing Up. In *Fusfeld, H. I. and Haklisch, C. S., eds.*, 1984, pp. 139–43.

Chabbal, Robert. Overview of Policy Issues: Panel Report on the Role of the Universities in Economic Development. In *Fusfeld, H. I. and Haklisch, C. S., eds.*, 1984, pp. 113–17.

Chen, Edward K. Y. Exports of Technology by Newly Industrializing Countries: Hong Kong. *World Devel.*, May/June 1984, *12*(5/6), pp. 481–90. **[G: Hong Kong]**

Chung, Byung Soo and Lee, Chung H. The Choice of Production Techniques by Foreign and Local Firms in Korea: Reply. *Econ. Develop. Cult. Change*, April 1984, *32*(3), pp. 629–31. **[G: S. Korea]**

CIMMYT Economics Staff. The Farming Systems Perspective and Farmer Participation in the Development of Appropriate Technology. In *Eicher, C. K. and Staatz, J. M., eds.*, 1984, pp. 362–77.

Crawford, Allan R. Putting Realism into Hi-Tech Policy. *Can. Public Policy*, June 1984, *10*(2), pp. 230–34. **[G: Canada]**

Dahlman, Carl J. and Sercovich, Francisco Colman. Exports of Technology from Semi-industrial Economies and Local Technological Development. *J. Devel. Econ.*, September–October 1984, *16*(1–2), pp. 63–99. **[G: Argentina; Brazil; India; Korea; Mexico]**

Dao, Thi D. Drug Innovation and Price Competition. *Managerial Dec. Econ.*, June 1984, *5*(2), pp. 80–84. **[G: U.S.]**

Davies, Duncan. Actions to Strengthen University–Industry Cooperation. In *Fusfeld, H. I. and Haklisch, C. S., eds.*, 1984, pp. 161–67.

Denielou, Guy. The Role of The University. In *Fusfeld, H. I. and Haklisch, C. S., eds.*, 1984, pp. 151–54.

Desai, Ashok V. Achievements and Limitations of India's Technological Capability. In *Fransman, M. and King, K., eds.*, 1984, pp. 245–61. **[G: India]**

DiLorenzo, Thomas J. The Domain of Rent-seeking Behavior: Private or Public Choice? *Int. Rev. Law Econ.*, December 1984, *4*(2), pp. 185–97.

Dore, Ronald P. Technological Self-reliance: Sturdy Ideal or Self-serving Rhetoric. In *Fransman, M. and King, K., eds.*, 1984, pp. 65–80. **[G: India]**

Drewes, Wolfram U. and Sirkin, Abraham M. The Uses of Satellite Remote Sensing. In *Weiss, C. and Jéquier, N., eds.*, 1984, pp. 85–102.

Eisemon, Thomas Owen. Insular and Open Strategies for Enhancing Scientific and Technological Capacities: Indian Educational Expansion and its Implications for African Countries. In *Fransman, M. and King, K., eds.*, 1984, pp. 263–77. **[G: India]**

Eliasson, Gunnar. Micro Heterogeneity of Firms and the Stability of Industrial Growth. *J. Econ. Behav. Organ.*, September–December 1984, *5*(3–4), pp. 249–74. **[G: Sweden]**

Fel'zenbaum, V. The Management of Scientific–Technical Progress. *Prob. Econ.*, September 1984, *27*(5), pp. 44–65. **[G: U.S.S.R.]**

Frank, Andre Gunder. Science and Underdevelopment in the Third World. In *Frank, A. G., 1984, 1968,* pp. 6–19.

Freeman, John R. and Duvall, Raymond D. International Economic Relations and the Entrepreneurial State. *Econ. Develop. Cult. Change,* January 1984, *32*(2), pp. 373–400. [G: Ireland]

Gallini, Nancy T. Deterrence by Market Sharing: A Strategic Incentive for Licensing. *Amer. Econ. Rev.,* December 1984, *74*(5), pp. 931–41.

Gilbert, Richard J. and Newbery, David M. G. Preemptive Patenting and the Persistence of Monopoly: Reply. *Amer. Econ. Rev.,* March 1984, *74*(1), pp. 251–53.

Gilbert, Richard J. and Newbery, David M. G. Uncertain Innovation and the Persistence of Monopoly: Comment. *Amer. Econ. Rev.,* March 1984, *74*(1), pp. 238–42.

Gowdy, John M. Marx and Resource Scarcity: An Institutionalist Approach. *J. Econ. Issues,* June 1984, *18*(2), pp. 393–400.

Hall, P. H. The Theory and Practice of Innovation Policy: An Overview. *Greek Econ. Rev.,* December 1984, *6*(3), pp. 253–86.

Hauschildt, Jürgen. Opportunities for New Entrepreneurship in Old Firms. In *Giersch, H., ed.,* 1984, pp. 249–56.

Hollick, Ann L. Planning Science and Technology Policy. *J. Policy Anal. Manage.,* Summer 1984, *3*(4), pp. 516–31. [G: U.S.]

Jéquier, Nicolas and Weiss, Charles. Introduction: The World Bank as a Technological Institution. In *Weiss, C. and Jéquier, N., eds.,* 1984, pp. 1–13.

Jéquier, Nicolas and Weiss, Charles. Technology, Finance, and Development: General Conclusions. In *Weiss, C. and Jéquier, N., eds.,* 1984, pp. 313–28.

Julien, Pierre-André; Thibodeau, Jean-Claude and Mathews, Georges. Les nouvelles technologies et l'emploi au Québec. (New Technologies and Employement: Textile, Pulp and Paper, and Savings and Credit Institutions Industries. With English summary.) *L'Actual. Econ.,* September 1984, *60*(3), pp. 326–40.

Kamien, Morton I. and Tauman, Yair. The Private Value of a Patent: A Game Theoretic Analysis. *Z. Nationalökon.,* Supplement 1984, pp. 93–118.

Kaplinsky, Raphael. Trade in Technology—Who, What, Where and When? In *Fransman, M. and King, K., eds.,* 1984, pp. 139–60. [G: LDCs]

Katz, Jorge M. Domestic Technological Innovations and Dynamic Comparative Advantage: Further Reflections on a Comparative Case-Study Program. *J. Devel. Econ.,* September–October 1984, *16*(1–2), pp. 13–37. [G: Latin America]

Kheinman, S. The Production and Scientific Potential of the USSR. *Prob. Econ.,* February 1984, *26*(10), pp. 50–67. [G: U.S.S.R.]

Kienbaum, Gerhard. Opportunities for New Entrepreneurship in Old Firms: Comment. In *Giersch, H., ed.,* 1984, pp. 257–60.

Kiuranov, Chartar. The Information Revolution: Substantive Issues and Methodological Challenges: Comment. In *Trent, J. and Lamy, P., eds.,* 1984, pp. 235–37.

Lall, Sanjaya. India's Technological Capacity: Effects of Trade, Industrial, Science and Technology Policies. In *Fransman, M. and King, K., eds.,* 1984, pp. 225–43. [G: India]

Lamberton, D. M.; Macdonald, Stuart and Mandeville, Thomas D. Information and Technological Change—A Research Program in Retrospect. *Greek Econ. Rev.,* December 1984, *6*(3), pp. 483–95. [G: U.K.]

Ledić, Michèle and Silberston, Aubrey. The Technological Balance of Payments in Perspective. *Greek Econ. Rev.,* December 1984, *6*(3), pp. 356–86. [G: OECD]

Makarov, V. L. The Introduction of Nontechnical Innovations. *Prob. Econ.,* August 1984, *27*(4), pp. 64–77. [G: U.S.S.R.]

von Massow, Valentin. The Role of Universities in Economic Development: National, Regional, and International. In *Fusfeld, H. I. and Haklisch, C. S., eds.,* 1984, pp. 105–11.

Novek, Joel. The Mechanization of Work: Paradise or Purgatory? *Challenge,* September/October 1984, *27*(4), pp. 43–48. [G: U.S.; Global]

Okimoto, Daniel I. Competitive Edge: Conclusions. In *Okimoto, D. I.; Sugano, T. and Weinstein, F. B., eds.,* 1984, pp. 177–235. [G: Japan; U.S.]

Ordover, Janusz A. and Shapiro, Carl. Advances in Supervision Technology and Economic Welfare: A General Equilibrium Analysis. *J. Public Econ.,* December 1984, *25*(3), pp. 371–89.

Pack, Howard. The Choice of Production Techniques by Foreign and Local Firms in Korea: Comment. *Econ. Develop. Cult. Change,* April 1984, *32*(3), pp. 625–28. [G: S. Korea]

Premus, Robert. Urban Growth and Technological Innovation. In *Bingham, R. D. and Blair, J. P., eds.,* 1984, pp. 47–61. [G: U.S.]

Pulley, Lawrence B. and Braunstein, Yale M. Scope and Scale Augmenting Technological Change: An Application in the Information Sector. In *Jussawalla, M. and Ebenfield, H., eds.,* 1984, pp. 105–18. [G: U.S.]

Ranis, Gustav. Determinants and Consequences of Indigenous Technological Activity. In *Fransman, M. and King, K., eds.,* 1984, pp. 95–112. [G: LDCs]

Reinganum, Jennifer F. Uncertain Innovation and the Persistence of Monopoly: Reply. *Amer. Econ. Rev.,* March 1984, *74*(1), pp. 243–46.

Rush, H. J. Source of Technology in Development. In *Ghosh, P. K., ed., no. 14,* 1984, *1981,* pp. 102–16.

Ruttan, Vernon W. Induced Innovation and Agricultural Development. In *Douglass, G. K., ed.,* 1984, pp. 107–34. [G: LDCs; MDCs]

Ryan, James G. Efficiency and Equity Considerations in the Design of Agricultural Technology in Developing Countries. *Australian J. Agr.*

Econ., August/December 1984, *28*(2–3), pp. 109–35. **[G: LDCs]**

Rybczynski, Tad M. Industrial Finance System in Europe, U.S. and Japan. *J. Econ. Behav. Organ.*, September–December 1984, *5*(3–4), pp. 275–86. **[G: Europe; U.S.; Japan]**

Šafář, Jiří. Scientific and Technical Progress in Intensive Development. *Czech. Econ. Digest.*, February 1984, (1), pp. 51–69.
[G: Czechoslovakia]

Salant, Stephen W. Preemptive Patenting and the Persistence of Monopoly: Comment. *Amer. Econ. Rev.*, March 1984, *74*(1), pp. 247–50.

Scherer, Frederic M. Concentration, R&D, and Productivity Change. In *Scherer, F. M.*, 1984, *1983*, pp. 249–55. **[G: U.S.]**

Scherer, Frederic M. Interindustry Technology Flows and Productivity Growth. In *Scherer, F. M.*, 1984, pp. 270–85. **[G: U.S.]**

Scherer, Frederic M. Market Structure and the Employment of Scientists and Engineers. In *Scherer, F. M.*, 1984, pp. 239–48. **[G: U.S.]**

Scherer, Frederic M. Market Structure and Innovation: Statistical Studies. In *Scherer, F. M.*, 1984, pp. 169–73.

Scherer, Frederic M. Nordhaus's Theory of Optimal Patent Life: A Geometric Reinterpretation. In *Scherer, F. M.*, 1984, pp. 130–41.

Scherer, Frederic M. The Microeconomics of Decision Making for Innovation. In *Scherer, F. M.*, 1984, pp. 120–29.

Schwartz, Alan G.; Garb, Gerald and Schwartz, Eli. Predatory Pricing, the Courts, and Public Policy. *Eastern Econ. J.*, July-September 1984, *10*(3), pp. 259–69. **[G: U.S.]**

Senanayake, Ranil. The Ecological, Energetic, and Agronomic Systems of Ancient and Modern Sri Lanka. In *Douglass, G. K., ed.*, 1984, pp. 227–37. **[G: Sri Lanka]**

Seregard, Ingvar. The Role of Scientists and Engineers. In *Fusfeld, H. I. and Haklisch, C. S., eds.*, 1984, pp. 155–59.

Simpson, David. Technology, Communications, Economics and Progress. In *Boulding, K. E., ed.*, 1984, pp. 58–70.

Singer, Hans W. Appropriate Technology for a Basic Human Needs Strategy. In *Ghosh, P. K., ed., no. 13*, 1984, *1977*, pp. 226–31.

Skolnikoff, E. B. The Information Revolution: Substantive Issues and Methodological Challenges: Comment. In *Trent, J. and Lamy, P., eds.*, 1984, pp. 227–33.

Sonis, M. Dynamic Choice of Alternatives, Innovation Diffusion, and Ecological Dynamics of the Volterra-Lotka Model. In *Pitfield, D. E., ed.*, 1984, pp. 29–43.

Starnick, Jürgen and Allesch, Jürgen. Compatibility of University Integrity with Industrial Cooperation. In *Fusfeld, H. I. and Haklisch, C. S., eds.*, 1984, pp. 129–33.

Šteffl, Zdeněk. Scientific and Technical Development in Agriculture. *Czech. Econ. Digest.*, November 1984, (7), pp. 3–28.
[G: Czechoslovakia]

Stewart, Frances. Facilitating Indigenous Technical Change in Third World Countries. In

Fransman, M. and King, K., eds., 1984, pp. 81–94. **[G: LDCs]**

Streeten, Paul. Technology Gaps between Rich and Poor Countries. In *Ghosh, P. K., ed., no. 3*, 1984, *1972*, pp. 7–26. **[G: MDCs]**

Sveikauskas, Leo. Science and Technology in Many Different Industries: Data for the Analysis of International Trade. *Rev. Public Data Use*, June 1984, *12*(2), pp. 133–56. **[G: U.S.]**

Tandon, Pankaj. Innovation, Market Structure, and Welfare. *Amer. Econ. Rev.*, June 1984, *74*(3), pp. 394–403.

Teitel, Simón. Technology Creation in Semi-industrial Economies. *J. Devel. Econ.*, September–October 1984, *16*(1–2), pp. 39–61.
[G: Latin America]

Thiemann, Hugo. Overview of Policy Issues: Panel Report on Compatibility of University Integrity with Industrial Cooperation. In *Fusfeld, H. I. and Haklisch, C. S., eds.*, 1984, pp. 135–38.

Tvrdík, Zdeněk. The Coordinated Scientific–Technological Policy of the CMEA Member States. *Czech. Econ. Digest.*, September 1984, (6), pp. 56–79. **[G: CMEA]**

Vaitsos, Constantine V. Strategic Choices in the Commercialization of Technology: The Point of View of Developing Countries. In *Ghosh, P. K., ed., no. 3*, 1984, *1973*, pp. 273–91.
[G: LDCs]

Valaskakis, Kimon. The Information Revolution: Substantive Issues and Methodological Challenges. In *Trent, J. and Lamy, P., eds.*, 1984, pp. 211–26.

Warner, Malcolm. Microprocessors, Manpower and Society: Epilogue. In *Warner, M., ed.*, 1984, pp. 361–63.

von Weizsäcker, Carl Christian. Rights and Relations in Modern Economic Theory. *J. Econ. Behav. Organ.*, June 1984, *5*(2), pp. 133–57.

Wiggins, Steven N. The Effect of U.S. Pharmaceutical Regulation on New Introductions. In *Lindgren, B., ed.*, 1984, pp. 191–205.
[G: U.S.]

Yeager, Leland B. Is Industrial Innovation Destroying Jobs? A Comment. *Cato J.*, Fall 1984, *4*(2), pp. 645–50. **[G: U.S.]**

6211 Technological Change and Innovation

Ahammed, C. S. and Herdt, Robert W. Measuring the Impact of Consumption Linkages on the Employment Effects of Mechanisation in Philippine Rice Production. *J. Devel. Stud.*, January 1984, *20*(2), pp. 242–55.
[G: Philippines]

Albin, Peter S. Job Design within Changing Patterns of Technical Development. In *Collins, E. L. and Tanner, L. D., eds.*, 1984, pp. 125–61. **[G: U.S.]**

Alderman, Harold. Attributing Technological Bias to Public Goods. *J. Devel. Econ.*, April 1984, *14*(3), pp. 375–93. **[G: Japan]**

Amsden, Alice H. Exports of Technology by Newly Industrializing Countries: Taiwan. *World Devel.*, May/June 1984, *12*(5/6), pp. 491–503. **[G: Taiwan]**

Antonelli, Cristiano. Multinational Firms, International Trade, and International Telecommunications. *Info. Econ. Policy,* 1984, *1*(4), pp. 333–43. **[G: Selected Countries]**

Apostolakis, Bobby E. A Translogarithmic Cost Function Approach: Greece, 1953–1977. *Empirical Econ.,* 1984, *9*(4), pp. 247–62. **[G: Greece]**

Appelbaum, Eileen. High Tech and the Structural Employment Problems of the 1980s. In *Collins, E. L. and Tanner, L. D., eds.,* 1984, pp. 23–48. **[G: U.S.]**

Armstrong, P. J. Work, Rest or Play? Changes in Time Spent at Work. In *Marstrand, P., ed.,* 1984, pp. 26–44. **[G: U.K.]**

Arnold, Michael R. Clarification of Miller on Capital Aggregation in the Presence of Obsolescence-inducing Technical Change. *Rev. Income Wealth,* December 1984, *30*(4), pp. 487–92.

Artisien, Patrick F. R. and Buckley, Peter J. Joint Ventures in Yugoslavia: Comment [An Economic Analysis of Yugoslav Joint Ventures]. *J. World Trade Law,* March–April 1984, *18*(2), pp. 163–70. **[G: Yugoslavia]**

Aryee, George A. Income Distribution, Technology and Employment in the Footwear Industry in Ghana. In *van Ginneken, W. and Baron, C., eds.,* 1984, pp. 120–47. **[G: Ghana]**

Aseniero, George. Technology and Development: NIEO's Quest for Technology Transfer. In *Addo, H., ed.,* 1984, pp. 220–41.

Bajracharya, Deepak. Organizing for Energy Need Assessment and Innovation: Action Research in Nepal. In *Islam, M. N.; Morse, R. and Soesastro, M. H., eds.,* 1984, pp. 279–336. **[G: Nepal]**

Balcer, Yves and Lippman, Steven A. Technological Expectations and Adoption of Improved Technology. *J. Econ. Theory,* December 1984, *34*(2), pp. 292–318.

Bardhan, Pranab K. and Kletzer, Kenneth M. Quality Variations and the Choice between Foreign and Indigenous Goods or Technology. *J. Devel. Econ.,* April 1984, *14*(3), pp. 323–30. **[G: LDCs]**

Barnes, Trevor and Sheppard, Eric. Technical Choice and Reswitching in Space Economies. *Reg. Sci. Urban Econ.,* August 1984, *14*(3), pp. 345–62.

Baron, Christopher. Appropriate Technology Comes of Age: A Review of Some Recent Literature and Aid Policy Statements. In *Ghosh, P. K., ed., no. 14,* 1984, *1978,* pp. 117–27. **[G: LDCs]**

Barras, R. and Swann, J. Information Technology and the Service Sector: Quality of Services and Quantity of Jobs. In *Marstrand, P., ed.,* 1984, pp. 214–33. **[G: U.K.]**

Barzel, Yoram. Discussion of Innovation Papers. *Econ. Inquiry,* October 1984, *22*(4), pp. 684–85.

Baumgartner, Thomas and Burns, Tom R. Transitions to Alternative Energy Systems: Analysis, Theory, and Normative Conclusions: Selec-

tive Observations. In *Baumgartner, T. and Burns, T. R., eds.,* 1984, pp. 241–54.

Bayliss-Smith, Tim P. Energy Flows and Agrarian Change in Karnataka: the Green Revolution at Micro-Scale. In *[Farmer, B. H.],* 1984, pp. 153–72. **[G: India]**

Beckford, George L. Induced Innovation Model of Agricultural Development: Comment. In *Eicher, C. K. and Staatz, J. M., eds.,* 1984, *1972,* pp. 75–81.

Benjamin, Robert I., et al. Information Technology: A Strategic Opportunity. *Sloan Manage. Rev.,* Spring 1984, *25*(3), pp. 3–10.

Bertram, Christoph. Arms Control and Technological Change. In *Ghosh, P. K., ed., no. 17,* 1984, *1981,* pp. 120–34.

Bhagavan, M. R. A Critique of "Appropriate" Technology for Underdeveloped Countries. In *Ngo, M., ed., vol. 1,* 1984, pp. 143–61. **[G: LDCs]**

Bhalla, A. S. and James, J. New Technology Revolution: Myth or Reality for Developing Countries? *Greek Econ. Rev.,* December 1984, *6*(3), pp. 387–423. **[G: LDCs]**

Bhattacharya, Gautam. Optimal Resource Extraction and Uncertainty about New Technology. *J. Environ. Econ. Manage.,* March 1984, *11*(1), pp. 39–54.

Bienefeld, Manfred. International Constraints and Opportunities. In *Fransman, M. and King, K., eds.,* 1984, pp. 161–73. **[G: Global]**

Bixler, Gordon and Shemilt, L. W. Chemistry and World Food Supplies. In *Bixler, G. and Shemilt, L. W., eds.,* 1984, pp. 5–23.

Blair, Larry M. Worker Adjustment to Changing Technology: Techniques, Processes, and Policy Considerations. In *Collins, E. L. and Tanner, L. D., eds.,* 1984, pp. 207–52. **[G: U.S.]**

Blanchard, Francis. Technology, Work and Society: Some Pointers from ILO Research. *Int. Lab. Rev.,* May–June 1984, *123*(3), pp. 267–76. **[G: Global]**

Bloch, Erich. Development of Competence in a World of Rapid Technical Change. In *Fusfeld, H. I. and Haklisch, C. S., eds.,* 1984, pp. 73–82. **[G: U.S.]**

Block, Fred. Technological Change and Employment: New Perspectives on an Old Controversy. *Econ. Lavoro,* July-Sept. 1984, *18*(3), pp. 3–21. **[G: France; U.S.]**

Bonfiglioli, Alberto. Universal Science, Appropriate Technology and Underdevelopment—A Reprise of the Latin American Case. In *Ghosh, P. K., ed., no. 14,* 1984, *1981,* pp. 248–65. **[G: Latin America]**

Borrow, Davis B. and Kudrle, Robert Thomas. MNE Disclosure Alternatives and Their Consequences. *J. World Trade Law,* September–October 1984, *18*(5), pp. 437–54. **[G: OECD]**

Bowles, Samuel; Gordon, David M. and Weisskopf, Thomas E. A Social Model for U.S. Productivity Growth. *Challenge,* March/April 1984, *27*(1), pp. 41–48. **[G: U.S.]**

Brabec, František. Propects Justified by Experience. *Czech. Econ. Digest.*, June 1984, (4), pp. 14–24. **[G: Czechoslovakia]**

Browne, Lynn E. Conflicting Views of Technological Progress and the Labor Market. *New Eng. Econ. Rev.*, July–August 1984, pp. 5–16. **[G: U.S.]**

Burns, Tom R. and Baumgartner, Thomas. Technology, Society, and Social Change. In *Baumgartner, T. and Burns, T. R., eds.*, 1984, pp. 11–24.

Burns, Tom R. and Baumgartner, Thomas. Transitions to Alternative Energy Systems: Toward a Theory of New Technological Developments. In *Baumgartner, T. and Burns, T. R., eds.*, 1984, pp. 255–78.

Burstein, M. L. Diffusion of Knowledge-based Products: Applications to Developing Economies. *Econ. Inquiry*, October 1984, *22*(4), pp. 612–33. **[G: LDCs]**

Calogero, Giuseppe. La diffusion de l'innovation et le rôle des participations de l'etat en Italie. (The Propagation of Innovations. The Role of State Share Holdings in Italy. With English summary.) *Ann. Pub. Co-op. Econ.*, Oct.–Dec. 1984, *55*(4), pp. 395–411. **[G: Italy]**

Carlsson, Bo. The Development and Use of Machine Tools in Historical Perspective. *J. Econ. Behav. Organ.*, March 1984, *5*(1), pp. 91–114.

Carnall, Colin A. and Medland, Anthony J. Computer-Aided Design: Social and Technical Choices for Development. In *Warner, M., ed.*, 1984, pp. 49–65.

Caron, François. Foreign Investments and Technology Transfers: The Case of the French Chemical Industry in the 1950s and 1960s as Viewed by the *Direction des Industries Chimiques.* In *Okochi, A. and Inoue, T., eds.*, 1984, pp. 261–80. **[G: France]**

Carter, Mary E. Implications of Emerging Biotechnologies. *Southern J. Agr. Econ.*, July 1984, *16*(1), pp. 7–9.

Chattopadhyay, Manabendu. Transformation of Labour Use in Indian Agriculture. *Cambridge J. Econ.*, September 1984, *8*(3), pp. 289–96. **[G: India]**

Checchi, Daniele. Some Notes Regarding Goodwin's Model "A Growth Cycle." *Econ. Notes*, 1984, (1), pp. 121–35.

Child, John, et al. Microelectronics and the Quality of Employment in Services. In *Marstrand, P., ed.*, 1984, pp. 163–90. **[G: U.K.]**

Choi, E. Kwan and Hicks, W. Whitney. Agricultural Mechanization Policy and Human Fertility. In *Schutjer, W. A. and Stokes, C. S., eds.*, 1984, pp. 252–68. **[G: LDCs]**

Choucri, Nazli. Population, Resources, Technology, and Environment: Trends and Implications. In *Trent, J. and Lamy, P., eds.*, 1984, pp. 187–203.

Chowdhury, Tawfiq E. Technological Diffusion in Agriculture: Theories and Evidence. *Bangladesh Devel. Stud.*, September 1984, *12*(3), pp. 75–85.

Chudnovsky, Daniel. Regulating Technology Imports in Some Developing Countries. In

Ghosh, P. K., ed., no. 16, 1984, *1981*, pp. 219–39. **[G: LDCs]**

Cieslik, Jerzy. Restrictive Clauses in Licensing Agreements: The Pharmaceutical Industry in Developing Countries. *J. World Trade Law*, September–October 1984, *18*(5), pp. 415–28. **[G: LDCs]**

Clapp, John M. and Richardson, Harry W. Technological Change in Information-processing Industries and Regional Income Differentials in Developing Countries. *Int. Reg. Sci. Rev.*, December 1984, *9*(3), pp. 241–56. **[G: LDCs]**

Clarke, Robin. The Pressing Need for Alternative Technology. In *Ghosh, P. K., ed., no. 14*, 1984, *1973*, pp. 128–41.

Clarke, Robin. The Pressing Need for Alternative Technology. In *Ghosh, P. K., ed., no. 3*, 1984, *1973*, pp. 202–17.

Cohen, Avi J. Technological Change as Historical Process: The Case of the U.S. Pulp and Paper Industry, 1915–1940. *J. Econ. Hist.*, September 1984, *44*(3), pp. 775–99. **[G: U.S.]**

Cooke, Philip; Morgan, Kevin and Jackson, David. New Technology and Regional Development in Austerity Britain: The Case of the Semiconductor Industry. *Reg. Stud.*, August 1984, *18*(4), pp. 277–89. **[G: U.K.]**

Coombs, R. W. Long-term Trends in Automation. In *Marstrand, P., ed.*, 1984, pp. 146–62. **[G: U.K.; MDCs]**

Coughlin, Cletus C. Reply [An Economic Analysis of Yugoslav Joint Ventures]. *J. World Trade Law*, March–April 1984, *18*(2), pp. 170–72. **[G: Yugoslavia]**

Craig, Paul P. Fuel Efficiency Incentives for Cars Oil Import Vulnerability Reduction. *Energy J.*, January 1984, *5*(1), pp. 141–48. **[G: U.S.]**

Dahlman, Carl J. Foreign Technology and Indigenous Technological Capability in Brazil. In *Fransman, M. and King, K., eds.*, 1984, pp. 317–34. **[G: Brazil]**

Dahlman, Carl J. and Cortes, Mariluz. Exports of Technology by Newly Industrializing Countries: Mexico. *World Devel.*, May/June 1984, *12*(5/6), pp. 601–24. **[G: Mexico]**

Danzin, Andre. Are Science and Technology Leading to a New Pattern of Development? In *Ghosh, P. K., ed., no. 3*, 1984, *1979*, pp. 182–94.

Dao, Thi D. Drug Innovation and Price Competition. In *Lindgren, B., ed.*, 1984, pp. 207–16. **[G: U.S.]**

Das, Ram. Appropriate Technology: Concept, Scope and Rationale. In *Singh, A. K.; Papola, T. S. and Mathur, R. S., eds.*, 1984, pp. 33–52. **[G: India; LDCs]**

Date, Anil. Understanding Appropriate Technology. In *Ghosh, P. K., ed., no. 14*, 1984, *1981*, pp. 163–83.

Date-Bah, Eugenia. Rural Women, Their Activities and Technology in Ghana: An Overview. In *Intn'l. Lab. Office*, 1984, pp. 89–98. **[G: Ghana]**

Davidson, W. H. and McFetridge, Donald G. International Technology Transactions and the

Theory of the Firm. *J. Ind. Econ.*, March 1984, 32(3), pp. 253–64. [G: U.S.]

Davies, Annette. Management-Union Participation during Microtechnological Change. In *Warner, M., ed.*, 1984, pp. 149–70.

[G: U.K.]

Delfino, José A. Análisis económico de la tecnología del sector manufacturero Argentino. (Economic Analysis of Argentina's Manufacturing Technology. With English summary.) *Económica*, May–December 1984, 30(2–3), pp. 149–202. [G: Argentina]

Donaghue, Hugh P. Establishing Principles for Trade in Computer Services. In *Fried, E. R. and Trezise, P. H., eds.*, 1984, pp. 87–95.

Drabek, Zdenek. A Comparison of Technology in Centrally Planned and Market-Type Economies. *Europ. Econ. Rev.*, August 1984, 25(3), pp. 293–318. [G: Czechoslovakia; Austria]

Duchin, Faye. Automation and Its Effect on Employment and Income. In *Collins, E. L. and Tanner, L. D., eds.*, 1984, pp. 49–75.

[G: U.S.]

Dugger, William M. The Nature of Capital Accumulation and Technological Progress in the Modern Economy. *J. Econ. Issues*, September 1984, 18(3), pp. 799–823. [G: U.S.]

Eilers, William L. Dong More with Less: The Future of Technology in the Third World. In *Ghosh, P. K., ed., no. 3, 1984, 1980*, pp. 175–81.

Enos, J. L. Public Policy in an Economy with Different Types of Agents. *Greek Econ. Rev.*, December 1984, 6(3), pp. 424–52.

Epstein, Edythe. Negotiating over Technological Change in Banking and Insurance. *Int. Lab. Rev.*, July–August 1984, 123(4), pp. 405–22.

Epstein, Eugene. Innovation and Growth. *Challenge*, July/August 1984, 27(3), pp. 49–52.

[G: U.S.]

Ettlie, John E. Implementation Strategy for Manufacturing Innovations. In *Warner, M., ed.*, 1984, pp. 31–48.

Evans, Donald D. Appropriate Technology and Its Role in Development. In *Ghosh, P. K., ed., no. 14, 1984, 1979*, pp. 7–72.

[G: LDCs]

Fadem, Joel A. Automation and Work Design in the U.S.: Case Studies of Quality of Working Life Impacts. In *Warner, M., ed.*, 1984, pp. 294–310. [G: U.S.]

Fal'tsman, V. and Ozhegov, A. The Retirement of Fixed Capital: Investment Opportunities and Limitations. *Prob. Econ.*, May 1984, 27(1), pp. 3–21. [G: U.S.S.R.]

Falkinger, Josef. Grenzen der innovatorischen Anpassung: Ein skeptisches Wachstumsmodell. (Limits of Innovational Capacity: A Sceptical Growth Model. With English summary.) *Jahr. Nationalökon. Statist.*, July 1984, 199(4), pp. 321–33.

Färe, Rolf; Grabowski, Richard and Yoon, Bong Joon. An Alternative View of Production and Technical Change in Agriculture: Weak Disposability of Inputs. *J. Devel. Areas*, January 1984, 18(2), pp. 219–26. [G: Korea]

Farstad, Halfdan. Solar Branch Development in Israel. In *Baumgartner, T. and Burns, T. R., eds.*, 1984, pp. 27–52. [G: Israel]

Feder, Gershon and Slade, Roger. The Acquisition of Information and the Adoption of New Technology. *Amer. J. Agr. Econ.*, August 1984, 66(3), pp. 312–20. [G: India]

Fei, John C. H. and Ranis, Gustav. Task Orientation and Technology Change: A Suggested Approach. In *[Reynolds, L. G.]*, 1984, pp. 1–16.

[G: Taiwan]

Fischoff, Baruch; Watson, Stephen R. and Hope, Chris. Defining Risk. *Policy Sci.*, October 1984, 17(2), pp. 123–39.

Flaherty, M. Therese. Field Research on the Link between Technological Innovation and Growth: Evidence from the International Semiconductor Industry. *Amer. Econ. Rev.*, May 1984, 74(2), pp. 67–72.

Florescu, M. Present Trends of Industrial Cybernetics. *Econ. Computat. Cybern. Stud. Res.*, 1984, 19(1), pp. 13–23. [G: Romania]

Fong, Chan Onn. Basic Needs and Appropriate Technology in the Malaysian Bicycle Industry. In *van Ginneken, W. and Baron, C., eds.*, 1984, pp. 54–83. [G: Malaysia]

Foray, Dominique. Changements techniques et structure du capital en fonderie: pour une explicitation des choix d'accumulation du capital et de gestion du changement technologique. (With English summary.) *Rev. Econ. Ind.*, 3rd Trimester 1984, (29), pp. 26–45. [G: OECD]

Ford, Bill. Technology, Women and Employment: The Australian Experience. In *Warner, M., ed.*, 1984, pp. 339–48. [G: Australia]

Fransman, Martin. Some Hypotheses Regarding Indigenous Technological Capability and the Case of Machine Production in Hong Kong. In *Fransman, M. and King, K., eds.*, 1984, pp. 301–16. [G: Hong Kong]

Fransman, Martin. Technological Capability in the Third World: An Overview and Introduction to Some of the Issues Raised in This Book. In *Fransman, M. and King, K., eds.*, 1984, pp. 3–30. [G: LDCs]

Freedenberg, Paul. High Technology and the Export Administration Act. In *Czinkota, M. R., ed.*, 1984, pp. 169–76. [G: U.S.]

Freeman, Christopher. Keynes or Kondratiev? How Can We Get Back to Full Employment? In *Marstrand, P., ed.*, 1984, pp. 103–23.

[G: U.K.]

Frosch, Robert A. Improving American Innovation: The Role of Industry in Innovation. In *Coles, J. S., ed.*, 1984, pp. 56–81. [G: U.S.]

Fudenberg, Drew and Tirole, Jean. The Fat-Cat Effect, the Puppy-Dog Ploy, and the Lean and Hungry Look. *Amer. Econ. Rev.*, May 1984, 74(2), pp. 361–66.

Fusfeld, Herbert I. The Slow Rate of Technical Change. In *Miyawaki, N., ed.*, 1984, pp. 238–53.

Garrod, Peter V. and Miklius, Walter. Owner-Operators, Demand Fluctuations and the

Choice of Technology. *J. Transp. Econ. Policy*, September 1984, *18*(3), pp. 293–302.
[**G: U.S.**]

Georgescu-Roegen, Nicholas. Feasible Recipes versus Viable Technologies. *Atlantic Econ. J.*, March 1984, *12*(1), pp. 20–31.

Germidis, Dimitrios. Technology Transfer, Regional Co-operation and Multinational Firms. In *Ghosh, P. K., ed., no. 11, 1984, 1977*, pp. 246–58.

Gerwin, Donald. Innovation, Microelectronics and Manufacturing Technology. In *Warner, M., ed.*, 1984, pp. 66–83.

Gligo, Nicolo. Energy and the Prevailing Model of Agricultural Technology in Latin America. *Cepal Rev.*, April 1984, (22), pp. 121–36.
[**G: Global**]

Goddard, J. B. and Thwaites, A. T. Unemployment in the North: Jobs in the South. In *Marstrand, P., ed.*, 1984, pp. 45–72. [**G: U.K.**]

Goddeeris, John H. Insurance and Incentives for Innovation in Medical Care. *Southern Econ. J.*, October 1984, *51*(2), pp. 530–39.

Goddeeris, John H. Medical Insurance, Technological Change, and Welfare. *Econ. Inquiry*, January 1984, *22*(1), pp. 56–67.

Goodell, Grace E. Bugs, Bunds, Banks, and Bottlenecks: Organizational Contradictions in the New Rice Technology. *Econ. Develop. Cult. Change*, October 1984, *33*(1), pp. 23–41.
[**G: S.E. Asia**]

Gort, Michael and Wall, Richard A. The Effect of Technical Change on Market Structure. *Econ. Inquiry*, October 1984, *22*(4), pp. 668–75. [**G: U.S.**]

Goulet, Denis. Can Values Shape Third World Technology Policy? In *Ghosh, P. K., ed., no. 3, 1984, 1979*, pp. 50–74.

Grabowski, Henry and Vernon, John. A Computer Simulation Model of Pharmaceutical Innovation. In *Lindgren, B., ed.*, 1984, pp. 159–75. [**G: U.S.**]

Green, Diana. Cable TV in France: A Non-market Approach to Industrial Development. *Nat. Westminster Bank Quart. Rev.*, August 1984, pp. 13–24. [**G: France; U.K.**]

Griffin, Tony. Technological Change and Craft Control in the Newspaper Industry: An International Comparison. *Cambridge J. Econ.*, March 1984, *8*(1), pp. 41–61. [**G: U.S.; U.K.; Australia**]

Griliches, Zvi. R&D, Patents, and Productivity: Introduction. In *Griliches, Z., ed.*, 1984, pp. 1–19.

Gruchy, Allan G. Uncertainty, Indicative Planning, and Industrial Policy. *J. Econ. Issues*, March 1984, *18*(1), pp. 159–80. [**G: U.S.**]

Gupta, Manash Ranjan. The Productivity of Workers' Consumption and the Choice of Techniques: A Comment. *Indian Econ. Rev.*, July-Dec. 1984, *19*(2), pp. 241–42.

Gupta, Suraj B. The Productivity of Workers' Consumption and the Choice of Techniques: A Reply. *Indian Econ. Rev.*, July-Dec. 1984, *19*(2), pp. 243–45.

Hafter, Daryl M. The Business of Invention in the Paris Industrial Exposition of 1806. *Bus. Hist. Rev.*, Autumn 1984, *58*(3), pp. 317–35.
[**G: France**]

Haltmaier, Jane. Measuring Technical Change. *Econ. J.*, December 1984, *94*(376), pp. 924–30. [**G: U.S.**]

Hammond, Peter J. Must Monopoly Power Accompany Innovation? In *Seidl, C., ed.*, 1984, pp. 45–56.

Hannan, Timothy H. and McDowell, John M. Market Concentration and the Diffusion of New Technology in the Banking Industry. *Rev. Econ. Statist.*, November 1984, *66*(4), pp. 686–91. [**G: U.S.**]

Hannan, Timothy H. and McDowell, John M. The Determinants of Technology Adoption: The Case of the Banking Firm. *Rand J. Econ.*, Autumn 1984, *15*(3), pp. 328–35. [**G: U.S.**]

Hardaker, J. Brian; Anderson, Jock R. and Dillon, John L. Perspectives on Assessing the Impacts of Improved Agricultural Technologies in Developing Countries. *Australian J. Agr. Econ.*, August/December 1984, *28*(2–3), pp. 87–108. [**G: LDCs**]

Hartmann, Gert, et al. Consequences of CNC Technology: A Study of British and West German Manufacturing Firms. In *Warner, M., ed.*, 1984, pp. 311–24. [**G: W. Germany; U.K.**]

Hayami, Yujiro. Assessment of the Green Revolution. In *Eicher, C. K. and Staatz, J. M., eds.*, 1984, 1981, pp. 389–96. [**G: Asia**]

von Hayek, Friedrich A. Technical Progress and Excess Capacity. In *von Hayek, F. A. (II)*, 1984, 1936, pp. 163–80.

Hazell, Peter B. R. and Anderson, Jock R. Public Policy toward Technical Change in Agriculture. *Greek Econ. Rev.*, December 1984, *6*(3), pp. 453–82. [**G: Global**]

Hederman, William F., Jr. and Gordon, Laura Cohen. Investment in Geothermal Direct Heat Applications. *Energy J.*, January 1984, *5*(1), pp. 85–97. [**G: U.S.**]

Henner, Henri-F. Un modèle analytique des transferts de technologie. (An Analytical Model of Technology Transfers. With English summary.) *L'Actual. Econ.*, September 1984, *60*(3), pp. 355–74.

Hingel, Anders J. A Promethean Change of Industrial Relations: A Comparative Study of Western European Unions and Technological Developments. In *Warner, M., ed.*, 1984, pp. 255–72. [**G: W. Europe**]

Hollard, Michel; Ruffieux, Bernard and Servais, Olivier. Automatisation et productivité: rupture ou continuité? (With English summary.) *Rev. Econ. Ind.*, 2nd Trimester 1984, (28), pp. 59–75. [**G: France**]

Hornig, Donald F. The Role of Government in Scientific Innovation. In *Coles, J. S., ed.*, 1984, pp. 30–55. [**G: U.S.**]

House, William J. Product Choice and Employment in Furniture-making in Kenya. In *van Ginneken, W. and Baron, C., eds.*, 1984, pp. 148–67. [**G: Kenya**]

Huang, Cliff J. Estimation of Stochastic Frontier

Production Function and Technical Inefficiency via the EM Algorithm. *Southern Econ. J.*, January 1984, *50*(3), pp. 847–56.
[G: India]

Int'l Assoc. of Machinists and Aerospace Workers. Coping with Technology. In *Gordon, S. and McFadden, D., eds.*, 1984, pp. 61–66.
[G: U.S.]

Ishikawa, Akihiro. Microelectronics and Japanese Industrial Relations. In *Warner, M., ed.*, 1984, pp. 349–60.
[G: Japan]

Islam, M. Nurul. Field-Based Assessment and Development of Improved Stoves. In *Islam, M. N.; Morse, R. and Soesastro, M. H., eds.*, 1984, pp. 337–79.
[G: Asian LDCs]

Iwai, Katsuhito. Schumpeterian Dynamics, Part II: Technological Progress, Firm Growth and 'Economic Selection.' *J. Econ. Behav. Organ.*, September–December 1984, *5*(3–4), pp. 321–51.

Iwai, Katsuhito. Schumpeterian Dynamics: An Evolutionary Model of Innovation and Imitation. *J. Econ. Behav. Organ.*, June 1984, *5*(2), pp. 159–90.
[G: U.S.]

Jackson, Charles L. Disconnecting Bell: Technology: The Anchor of the Bell System. In *Shooshan, H. M., III, ed.*, 1984, pp. 71–82.
[G: U.S.]

Jackson, Sarah. Economically Appropriate Technologies for Developing Countries: A Survey. In *Ghosh, P. K., ed., no. 14*, 1984, pp. 73–101.

James, Jeffrey. Appropriate Technologies and Inappropriate Policy Instruments. In *Ghosh, P. K., ed., no. 14*, 1984, *1980*, pp. 238–47.

James, Jeffrey. Technology, Products and Income Distribution: The Soap Market in Barbados. In *van Ginneken, W. and Baron, C., eds.*, 1984, pp. 168–94.
[G: Barbados]

Jelinek, Mariann and Goldhar, Joel D. The Strategic Implications of the Factory of the Future. *Sloan Manage. Rev.*, Summer 1984, *25*(4), pp. 29–37.

Jorgenson, Dale W. The Role of Energy in Productivity Growth. *Amer. Econ. Rev.*, May 1984, *74*(2), pp. 26–30.
[G: U.S.]

Kahn, Lawrence M. The Effect of Collective Bargaining on Production Technique: A Theoretical Analysis. *J. Lab. Res.*, Winter 1984, *5*(1), pp. 1–12.

Kalawar, Jayant. Institutionalizing the Appropriate Technology Process in India. In *Ghosh, P. K., ed., no. 14*, 1984, *1981*, pp. 266–76.
[G: India]

Kalirajan, K. P. Farm-specific Technical Efficiencies and Development Policies. *J. Econ. Stud.*, 1984, *11*(3), pp. 3–13.
[G: Philippines]

Kamenetzky, Mario. The Socio-economic Iceberg and the Design of Policies for Scientific and Technological Development. In *Ghosh, P. K., ed., no. 3*, 1984, pp. 239–54.

Kanter, Rosabeth Moss. Innovation—The Only Hope for Times Ahead? *Sloan Manage. Rev.*, Summer 1984, *25*(4), pp. 51–55.

Kaplinsky, Raphael. Computer-Aided-Design: An Assessment of the Current International

Economic Setting and Policy Implications. *Industry Devel.*, 1984, (11), pp. 43–57.
[G: LDCs]

Kaplinsky, Raphael. Indigenous Technical Change: What We Can Learn from Sugar Processing. *World Devel.*, April 1984, *12*(4), pp. 419–32.
[G: India; Kenya]

Katsoulacos, Y. Product Innovation and Employment. *Europ. Econ. Rev.*, October–November 1984, *26*(1–2), pp. 83–108.

Katz, Jorge M. Technological Innovation, Industrial Organisation and Comparative Advantages of Latin American Metalworking Industries. In *Fransman, M. and King, K., eds.*, 1984, pp. 113–36.
[G: Latin America]

Kay, Neil M. Innovation, Markets and Hierarchies. *J. Econ. Stud.*, 1984, *11*(2), pp. 44–60.

Kim, Jae Won. CES Production Functions in Manufacturing and Problems of Industrialization in LDCs: Evidence from Korea. *Econ. Develop. Cult. Change*, October 1984, *33*(1), pp. 143–65.

King, Kenneth. Science, Technology and Education in the Development of Indigenous Technological Capability. In *Fransman, M. and King, K., eds.*, 1984, pp. 31–63. [G: LDCs]

Kiyokawa, Yukihiko. The Diffusion of New Technologies in the Japanese Sericulture Industry: The Case of the Hybrid Silkworm. *Hitotsubashi J. Econ.*, June 1984, *25*(1), pp. 31–59.
[G: Japan]

Kleinknecht, Alfred. Prosperity, Crisis and Innovation Patterns. *Cambridge J. Econ.*, September 1984, *8*(3), pp. 251–70. [G: N. America; U.K.; W. Germany; Japan; France]

Kohlmey, Gunther. International Values and the International Division of Labour. In *Csikós-Nagy, B.; Hague, D. and Hall, G., eds.*, 1984, pp. 300–07.

Kul'bovskaia, N. The Social and Economic Effect of New Technology. *Prob. Econ.*, February 1984, *26*(10), pp. 68–83.

Kul'bovskaia, N. The Socioeconomic Effectiveness of Technical Retooling. *Prob. Econ.*, November 1984, *27*(7), pp. 76–89.
[G: U.S.S.R.]

Kuroda, Masahiro; Yoshioka, Kanji and Jorgenson, Dale W. Relative Price Changes and Biases of Technical Change in Japan. *Econ. Stud. Quart.*, August 1984, *35*(2), pp. 116–38.
[G: Japan; U.S.]

Kurz, Heinz D. Ricardo and Lowe on Machinery. *Eastern Econ. J.*, April-June 1984, *10*(2), pp. 211–29.

Laitner, John P. Resource Extraction Costs and Competitive Steady-State Growth. *Int. Econ. Rev.*, June 1984, *25*(2), pp. 297–314.

Lall, Sanjaya. Exports of Technology by Newly Industrializing Countries: An Overview. *World Devel.*, May/June 1984, *12*(5/6), pp. 471–80.
[G: LDCs]

Lall, Sanjaya. Exports of Technology by Newly Industrializing Countries: India. *World Devel.*, May/June 1984, *12*(5/6), pp. 535–65.
[G: India]

Langdon, Steven. Indigenous Technological Capability in Africa: The Case of Textiles and Wood Products in Kenya. In *Fransman, M. and King, K., eds.*, 1984, pp. 355–74.

[G: Kenya]

Langmantel, Erich. Die Beschäftigungswirkungen sättigungsbedingten Strukturwandels— Eine Analyse anhand von Pasinettis "Structural Change and Economic Growth." (Employment Effects of Structural Change Induced by Saturation of Markets—An Analysis on the Basis of Pasinetti's "Structural Change and Economic Growth." With English summary.) *Ifo-Studien*, 1984, *30*(3), pp. 231–41.

Lazonick, William. Rings and Mules in Britain: Reply [Factor Costs and the Diffusion of Ring Spinning in Britain Prior to World War I]. *Quart. J. Econ.*, May 1984, *99*(2), pp. 393–98.

[G: U.K.]

Leach, Bernard and Shutt, John. Chips and Crisps: The Impact of New Technology on Food Processing Jobs in Greater Manchester. In *Marstrand, P., ed.*, 1984, pp. 73–92.

[G: U.K.]

Lee, Chung H. The Diffusion of Technology and Growth of Factor Productivity in Korean Manufacturing Industries. *J. Econ. Devel.*, July 1984, *9*(1), pp. 25–44. [G: S. Korea]

Lee, Chung H. Transfer of Technology from Japan and the United States to Korean Manufacturing Industries: A Comparative Study. *Hitotsubashi J. Econ.*, December 1984, *25*(2), pp. 125–36.

[G: U.S.; Japan; Korea]

Lemperière, J. La restructuration des échanges internationaux. (The Restructuring of Trade. With English summary.) *Écon. Soc.*, June 1984, *18*(6), pp. 21–58. [G: Global]

Levy, Robert A.; Bowes, Marianne and Jondrow, James M. Technical Advance and Other Sources of Employment Change in Basic Industry. In *Collins, E. L. and Tanner, L. D., eds.*, 1984, pp. 77–95. [G: U.S.]

Leys, Colin. Relations of Production and Technology. In *Fransman, M. and King, K., eds.*, 1984, pp. 175–84. [G: LDCs]

Lindsay, Franklin A.; Rubin, Jerome S. and Cohen, Richard L. The Need for New Private and Public Policies. In *Wachter, M. L. and Wachter, S. M., eds.*, 1984, pp. 115–43.

[G: U.S.]

Loasby, Brian J. Entrepreneurs and Organisation. *J. Econ. Stud.*, 1984, *11*(2), pp. 75–88.

Löbl, Karel. Condition for Initiative. *Czech. Econ. Digest.*, June 1984, (4), pp. 34–47.

[G: Czechoslovakia]

Lock, Peter and Wulf, Herbert. Consequences of the Transfer of Military-Oriented Technology on the Development Process. In *Ghosh, P. K., ed., no. 17*, 1984, *1977*, pp. 104–19.

[G: LDCs]

Long, Richard J. Microelectronics and Quality of Working Life in the Office: A Canadian Perspective. In *Warner, M., ed.*, 1984, pp. 273–93. [G: Canada]

Lopez, Louis. NASA–DOD Technology. In *Fed. Res. Bank Atlanta*, 1984, pp. 153–59.

Lundine, Stan. Motivation and New Technolo-

gies: Comment. In *Wachter, M. L. and Wachter, S. M., eds.*, 1984, pp. 179–82.

[G: U.S.]

Magee, Stephen P. Multinational Corporations, the Industry Technology Cycle and Development. In *Ghosh, P. K., ed., no. 11*, 1984, *1977*, pp. 219–45. [G: LDCs]

Marc, F. La difficoltá ad ainnovare nelle piccole e medie imprese. (Obstacles to the Innovating Process within Low and Medium Sized Firms. With English summary.) *Mondo Aperto*, January-February 1984, *38*(1), pp. 13–25[G: U.S.]

Marcy, Willard. Enhancements and Impediments in the Innovation Process. In *Coles, J. S., ed.*, 1984, pp. 82–108. [G: U.S.]

Margolick, Michael; Hansson, Ardo H. and Helliwell, John F. Competing Energy Uses for Wood Wastes in British Columbia. *Energy J.*, January 1984, *5*(1), pp. 65–84. [G: Canada]

Marsden, Keith. Progressive Technologies for Developing Countries. In *Ghosh, P. K., ed., no. 3*, 1984, *1970*, pp. 292–324. [G: Japan; Middle East]

Marsh, James B. The Potential Economic Impact of Technological Progress on the Development of Manganese Nodule Mining. In *Gopalakrishnan, C., ed.*, 1984, pp. 49–59.

Martin, Roderick. New Technology and Industrial Relations in Fleet Street: 'New Technology Will Make it Possible for Managers to Manage.' In *Warner, M., ed.*, 1984, pp. 240–52.

[G: U.K.]

Metcalfe, J. S. Technological Innovation and the Competitive Process. *Greek Econ. Rev.*, December 1984, *6*(3), pp. 287–316.

Milenkovitch, Deborah Duff. The Incentive to Innovate under Alternative Property Rights: A Comment. *Cato J.*, Fall 1984, *4*(2), pp. 447–55. [G: Japan; U.S.S.R.; U.S.]

Mitchell, Thomas M. A Functional Equation Approach to the Theory of Production, Technical Change, and Invariance. *Z. Nationalökon.*, 1984, *44*(2), pp. 177–87.

Møller, J. Ørstøm. Industripolitik i Danmark. (Danish Industrial Policy. With English summary.) *Nationaløkon. Tidsskr.*, 1984, *122*(2), pp. 228–39. [G: Denmark]

Momigliano, Franco and Siniscalco, Domenico. Technology and International Specialization. *Banca Naz. Lavoro Quart. Rev.*, September 1984, (150), pp. 257–84. [G: Italy]

Morrison, Denton E. Energy, Appropriate Technology and International Interdependence. In *Ghosh, P. K., ed., no. 4*, 1984, pp. 102–37.

Morrison, Denton E. Energy, Appropriate Technology, and International Interdependence. In *Ghosh, P. K., ed., no. 14*, 1984, pp. 205–37.

Moss, Scott J. Imbalance Theory and the Analysis of Investment and Technical Change by Firms. *J. Econ. Stud.*, 1984, *11*(2), pp. 61–74.

Mubin, A. K. A. and Forsyth, David J. C. Technology, Employment and Income Distribution: The Soap Industry in Bangladesh. In *van Ginneken, W. and Baron, C., eds.*, 1984, pp. 14–53. [G: Bangladesh]

Müller, Jens. Facilitating an Indigenous Social

Organisation of Production in Tanzania. In *Fransman, M. and King, K., eds.*, 1984, pp. 375–90. [G: Tanzania]

Muller, Steven. Research Universities and Industrial Innovation in America. In *Coles, J. S., ed.*, 1984, pp. 8–29. [G: U.S.]

Murrin, Thomas J. Motivation and New Technologies: Comment. In *Wachter, M. L. and Wachter, S. M., eds.*, 1984, pp. 175–78. [G: U.S.]

Nakatani, Takeshi. Technical Change and the Rate of Profit: Considering Fixed Capital. *Kobe Univ. Econ.*, 1984, (30), pp. 65–78.

Neale, Walter C. Technology as Social Process: A Commentary on Knowledge and Human Capital. *J. Econ. Issues*, June 1984, 18(2), pp. 573–80.

Nelson, Randy A. Regulation, Capital Vintage, and Technical Change in the Electric Utility Industry. *Rev. Econ. Statist.*, February 1984, 66(1), pp. 59–69. [G: U.S.]

Newell, Allen. On Computers, Creativity, and Management. In *[Kozmetsky, G.]*, 1984, pp. 213–37.

Nicholson, Norman K. Landholding, Agricultural Modernization, and Local Institutions in India. *Econ. Develop. Cult. Change*, April 1984, 32(3), pp. 569–92. [G: India]

Nuti, Fabio. Gli effetti dell'innovazione microelettronica sull'organizzazione della produzione industriale. (Effects of the Micro-electronic Innovation on the Organization of Industrial Production. With English summary.) *Econ. Lavoro*, Oct.-Dec. 1984, 18(4), pp. 35–46.

Ó Gráda, Cormac. Technical Change in the Mid-Nineteenth Century British Cotton Industry: A Note. *J. Europ. Econ. Hist.*, Fall 1984, 13(2), pp. 345–52. [G: U.K.]

Oakey, Raymond P. Innovation and Regional Growth in Small High Technology Firms: Evidence from Britain and the USA. *Reg. Stud.*, June 1984, 18(3), pp. 237–51. [G: U.S.; U.K.]

Odhiambo, Thomas R. Biological Constraints on Food Production and on the Level and Efficient Use of Chemical Inputs. In *Bixler, G. and Shemilt, L. W., eds.*, 1984, pp. 65–88. [G: Global]

Oshima, Harry T. The Growth of U.S. Factor Productivity: The Significance of New Technologies in the Early Decades of the Twentieth Century. *J. Econ. Hist.*, March 1984, 44(1), pp. 161–70. [G: U.S.]

Özol, Cengiz. Parable and Realism in Production Theory: The Surrogate Wage Function. *Can. J. Econ.*, May 1984, 17(2), pp. 353–68.

Pack, Howard. Productivity and Technical Choice: Applications to the Textile Industry. *J. Devel. Econ.*, September–October 1984, 16(1–2), pp. 153–76. [G: Philippines]

Palmer, Ransford W. Technology and Caribbean Development. In *Palmer, R. W.*, 1984, pp. 39–47. [G: Selected Countries]

Patel, Surendra J. Technological Transformation of the Third World. In *Singh, A. K.; Papola,*

T. S. and Mathur, R. S., eds., 1984, pp. 3–16. [G: LDCs]

Peccei, Riccardo and Guest, David. Evaluating the Introduction of New Technology: The Case of Word-Processors in British Rail. In *Warner, M., ed.*, 1984, pp. 84–109.

Pejovich, Steve. The Incentive to Innovate under Alternative Property Rights. *Cato J.*, Fall 1984, 4(2), pp. 427–46. [G: Yugoslavia]

Phillips, David A. Choice of Technology and Industrial Transformation: The Case of the United Republic of Tanzania. In *Ghosh, P. K., ed., no. 3*, 1984, *1980*, pp. 325–51. [G: Tanzania]

Phillips, David A. Technological Innovation and Social Cost Benefit Analysis in Developing Countries. *Industry Devel.*, 1984, (13), pp. 63–75.

Pirie, N. W. Technological Approaches to Plant Productivity. *Écon. Appl.*, 1984, 37(2), pp. 363–76. [G: LDCs]

Polèse, Mario. Population, Resources, Technology, and Environment: Trends and Implications: Comment. In *Trent, J. and Lamy, P., eds.*, 1984, pp. 205–10.

Primožič, Miroslav. Udio tehnološkog progresa u razvoju saobraćaja u periodu, 1959–1978. (Contribution of Technological Progress to the Traffic Development in the Period 1959–1978. With English summary.) *Econ. Anal. Worker's Manage.*, 1984, 18(2), pp. 127–39. [G: Yugoslavia]

Rao, P. S. and Preston, R. S. Inter-factor Substitution, Economies of Scale and Technical Change: Evidence from Canadian Industries. *Empirical Econ.*, 1984, 9(2), pp. 87–111. [G: Canada]

Ray, Debraj. Survival, Growth and Technical Progress in a Small Resource-Importing Economy. *Int. Econ. Rev.*, June 1984, 25(2), pp. 275–95.

Rees, John; Briggs, Ronald and Oakey, Raymond P. The Adoption of New Technology in the American Machinery Industry. *Reg. Stud.*, December 1984, 18(6), pp. 489–504. [G: U.S.]

Reimers, Niels. The Government-Industry-University Interface: Improving the Innovative Process. In *Coles, J. S., ed.*, 1984, pp. 109–48. [G: U.S.]

Roberts, Markley. A Labor Perspective on Technological Change. In *Collins, E. L. and Tanner, L. D., eds.*, 1984, pp. 183–205. [G: U.S.]

Roffe, Pedro. UNCTAD: Transfer of Technology Code: Fifth Session of the UN Conference. *J. World Trade Law*, March–April 1984, 18(2), pp. 176–82.

Romeo, Anthony A.; Wagner, Judith L. and Lee, Robert H. Prospective Reimbursement and the Diffusion of New Technologies in Hospitals. *J. Health Econ.*, April 1984, 3(1), pp. 1–24. [G: U.S.]

Rosenberg, Nathan and Frischtak, Claudio R. Technological Innovation and Long Waves.

Cambridge J. Econ., March 1984, *8*(1), pp. 7–24.

Rosenbrock, H. H. Designing Automated Systems—Need Skill Be Lost? In *Marstrand, P., ed.*, 1984, pp. 124–32.

Rothwell, Roy. Reindustrialisation, Innovation and Public Policy. *Greek Econ. Rev.*, December 1984, *6*(3), pp. 317–35. **[G: OECD]**

Rothwell, Sheila G. Company Employment Policies and New Technology in Manufacturing and Service Sectors. In *Warner, M., ed.*, 1984, pp. 111–33. **[G: U.K.]**

Rozenova, L. The Price and Effectiveness of Machine-building Output. *Prob. Econ.*, November 1984, *27*(7), pp. 44–60. **[G: U.S.S.R.]**

Rush, H. J. Sources of Technology in Development. In *Ghosh, P. K., ed.*, no. 3, 1984, *1981*, pp. 35–49.

Ruttan, Vernon W. and Hayami, Yujiro. Induced Innovation Model of Agricultural Development. In *Eicher, C. K. and Staatz, J. M., eds.*, 1984, *1972*, pp. 59–74.

Ruttan, Vernon W. and Hayami, Yujiro. Toward a Theory of Induced Institutional Innovation. *J. Devel. Stud.*, July 1984, *20*(4), pp. 203–23. **[G: Philippines]**

Sagafi-Nejad, Tagi. Exports of Technology by Newly Industrializing Countries: Egypt. *World Devel.*, May/June 1984, *12*(5/6), pp. 567–73. **[G: Egypt]**

Sanchez, Pedro A.; Nicholaides, John J., III and Couto, Walter. Physical and Chemical Constraints to Food Production in the Tropics. In *Bixler, G. and Shemilt, L. W., eds.*, 1984, pp. 89–105. **[G: Asia; Latin America; Africa]**

Sandberg, Lars G. The Remembrance of Things Past: Rings and Mules Revisited [Factor Costs and the Diffusion of Ring Spinning in Britain Prior to World War I]. *Quart. J. Econ.*, May 1984, *99*(2), pp. 387–92. **[G: U.K.]**

Sato, Ryuzo. Technological Advances and Economic Progress: Short-run and Long-run Adjustments. In *Miyawaki, N., ed.*, 1984, pp. 254–65.

Savane, Landing. Problems of Scientific and Technological Development in Black Africa. In *Ghosh, P. K., ed.*, no. 3, 1984, *1973*, pp. 371–79. **[G: Africa]**

Scherer, Frederic M. Firm Size, Market Structure, Opportunity, and the Output of Patented Inventions. In *Scherer, F. M.*, 1984, pp. 175–206. **[G: U.S.]**

Scherer, Frederic M. Interindustry Technology Flows in the United States. In *Scherer, F. M.*, 1984, pp. 32–58. **[G: U.S.]**

Scherer, Frederic M. Invention and Innovation in the Watt–Boulton Steam Engine Venture. In *Scherer, F. M.*, 1984, pp. 8–31. **[G: Europe]**

Schlesinger, Robert J. Industrial Robots, Work and Industry: Past, Present and Future. In *Warner, M., ed.*, 1984, pp. 11–30. **[G: U.S.; U.K.; Japan]**

Selby, Cecily Cannan. Current Trends in Mathematics, Science, and Technology Education:

Implications for Technological Innovation. In *Coles, J. S., ed.*, 1984, pp. 149–82. **[G: U.S.]**

Sellekaerts, Willy and Sellekaerts, Brigitte H. Technical Change, Capital Formation, and Capacity Unemployment in the United States. *Eastern Econ. J.*, July-September 1984, *10*(3), pp. 231–41. **[G: U.S.]**

Semmler, Willi. Marx and Schumpeter on Competition, Transient Surplus Profit and Technical Change. *Écon. Appl.*, 1984, *37*(3–4), pp. 419–55.

Sen, Amartya. Employment, Institutions and Technology: Some Policy Issues. In *Sen, A.*, 1984, *1975*, pp. 242–73. **[G: LDCs]**

Senker, Peter. Engineering Skills in the Robot Age. In *Marstrand, P., ed.*, 1984, pp. 133–45. **[G: U.K.]**

Senker, Peter. Training for Automation. In *Warner, M., ed.*, 1984, pp. 134–46.

Sercovich, Francisco Colman. Exports of Technology by Newly Industrializing Countries: Brazil. *World Devel.*, May/June 1984, *12*(5/6), pp. 575–99. **[G: Brazil]**

Shaffer, Sherrill. Selective Cost-reducing Innovation. *Rev. Ind. Organ.*, Fall 1984, *1*(3), pp. 240–45.

Siggel, Eckhard. On the Nature of Technology Shelves Facing Less Developed Countries: Some Hypotheses and Case Studies. *J. Devel. Areas*, January 1984, *18*(2), pp. 227–45. **[G: Zaire; U.K.; Canada]**

Silverberg, Gerald. Embodied Technical Progress in a Dynamic Economic Model: The Self-Organization Paradigm. In *Goodwin, R. M.; Krüger, M. and Vercelli, A., eds.*, 1984, pp. 192–208.

Soete, Luc and Turner, Roy. Technology Diffusion and the Rate of Technical Change. *Econ. J.*, September 1984, *94*(375), pp. 612–23.

Soifer, Ricardo J. Exports of Technology by Newly Industrializing Countries: Argentina. *World Devel.*, May/June 1984, *12*(5/6), pp. 625–44. **[G: Argentina]**

Sporleder, Thomas L. Policy Considerations of Emerging Information Technologies. *Southern J. Agr. Econ.*, July 1984, *16*(1), pp. 15–21.

Standing, Guy. The Notion of Technological Unemployment. *Int. Lab. Rev.*, March-April 1984, *123*(2), pp. 127–47.

Steinmann, Gunter. A Model of the History of Demographic-Economic Growth. In *Steinmann, G., ed.*, 1984, pp. 29–49.

Stevens, Yvette. Technologies for Rural Women's Activities: Problems and Prospects in Sierra Leone. In *Intn'l. Lab. Office*, 1984, pp. 79–88. **[G: Sierra Leone]**

Subrahmanian, K. K. Some Observations on Technology Planning. In *Singh, A. K.; Papola, T. S. and Mathur, R. S., eds.*, 1984, pp. 17–32. **[G: LDCs]**

Sullivan, Richard J. Measurement of English Farming Technological Change, 1523–1900. *Exploration Econ. Hist.*, July 1984, *21*(3), pp. 270–89. **[G: U.K.]**

Sumner, Daniel A. Labor Supply Uncertainty and

Technology Adoption: Discussion. In *Emerson, R. D., ed.*, 1984, pp. 224–29.

Swords-Isherwood, N.; Zmroczek, C. and Henwood, F. Technical Change and its Effect on Employment Opportunities for Women. In *Marstrand, P., ed.*, 1984, pp. 191–213. [G: U.K.]

Sylos-Labini, Paolo. Technological Change under Contemporary Conditions: An Economist's View. In *Sylos-Labini, P.*, 1984, *1981*, pp. 81–99.

Tanner, Lucretia Dewey. Modernizing the Federal Government: Effect on Its Employees. In *Collins, E. L. and Tanner, L. D., eds.*, 1984, pp. 97–114. [G: U.S.]

Tarpley, Fred A., Jr. Technological Diffusion. In *Fed. Res. Bank Atlanta*, 1984, pp. 149–52.

Teitel, Simón and Sercovich, Francisco Colman. Exports of Technology by Newly Industrializing Countries: Latin America. *World Devel.*, May/June 1984, *12*(5/6), pp. 645–60. [G: Latin America]

Teitel, Simón and Westphal, Larry E. Symposium on Technological Change and Industrial Development: Editors' Introduction. *J. Devel. Econ.*, September–October 1984, *16*(1–2), pp. 1–11.

Telser, Lester G. Innovation: Its Public and Private Aspects and Some of Their Empirical Implications for Mergers. *Econ. Inquiry*, October 1984, *22*(4), pp. 334–59. [G: U.S.]

Thakur, C. P. Computers, Manpower and the Indian Labour Market: Some Experiences in a Labour-Surplus Economy. In *Warner, M., ed.*, 1984, pp. 325–38. [G: India]

Treu, Tiziano. Nuove tecnologie e (vecchie) relazioni industriali. (New Technologies and [Old] Industrial Relations. With English summary.) *L'Impresa*, 1984, *26*(2), pp. 83–86. [G: Italy]

von Ungern-Sternberg, Thomas. Innovator Protection and the Rate of Technical Progress. *J. Econ. Behav. Organ.*, March 1984, *5*(1), pp. 115–29.

Uri, Noel D. The Impact of Technical Change on the Aggregate Production Function. *Appl. Econ.*, August 1984, *16*(4), pp. 555–67. [G: U.S.]

Ursprung, Heinrich W. Schumpeterian Entrepreneurs and Catastrophe Theory or a New Chapter to the Foundations of Economic Analysis. *Z. Nationalökon.*, Supplement 1984, pp. 39–69.

Useem, Elizabeth L. Education and High-Technology Industry: The Case of Silicon Valley. *Econ. Educ. Rev.*, 1984, *3*(3), pp. 215–21. [G: U.S.]

Usselman, Steven W. Air Brakes for Freight Trains: Technological Innovation in the American Railroad Industry, 1869–1900. *Bus. Hist. Rev.*, Spring 1984, *58*(1), pp. 30–50. [G: U.S.]

Usui, Mikoto. Transnational Enterprises and International Development: A New Focus in the Perspective of Industrial and Technological Cooperation. In *Ghosh, P. K., ed., no. 11*, 1984, pp. 259–72.

Vrooman, John. Effect of Technology on the Distribution of Labor Income. In *Collins, E. L. and Tanner, L. D., eds.*, 1984, pp. 115–23. [G: U.S.]

Wallace, Phyllis A. Motivation and New Technologies: Comment. In *Wachter, M. L. and Wachter, S. M., eds.*, 1984, pp. 171–75. [G: U.S.]

Ward, James. Solar Water Heating in California: Policy Evolution and Industry Development. In *Baumgartner, T. and Burns, T. R., eds.*, 1984, pp. 53–90. [G: U.S.]

Wardell, William M. and Sheck, Lorraine E. Is Pharmaceutical Innovation Declining? Interpreting Measures of Pharmaceutical Innovation and Regulatory Impact in the USA, 1950–1980. In *Lindgren, B., ed.*, 1984, pp. 177–89. [G: U.S.]

Warfel, George, Jr. Consumer Acceptance of Technology. In *Fed. Res. Bank Atlanta*, 1984, pp. 103–12. [G: U.S.]

Warner, Malcolm. Microprocessors, Manpower and Society: Introduction. In *Warner, M., ed.*, 1984, pp. 1–7.

Watanabe, Susumu. Institutional Factors, Government Policies and Appropriate Technologies. In *Ghosh, P. K., ed., no. 14*, 1984, *1980*, pp. 142–62.

Watanabe, Susumu. Multinational Enterprises, Employment and Technology Adaptations. In *Ghosh, P. K., ed., no. 11*, 1984, *1981*, pp. 175–94. [G: LDCs]

Watts, Geof and Quiggin, John. A Note on the Use of a Logarithmic Time Trend. *Rev. Marketing Agr. Econ.*, August 1984, *52*(2), pp. 91–99. [G: Australia]

Weinstein, Franklin B.; Uenohara, Michiyuki and Linvill, John G. Competitive Edge: Technological Resources. In *Okimoto, D. I.; Sugano, T. and Weinstein, F. B., eds.*, 1984, pp. 35–77. [G: Japan; U.S.]

Weiss, Charles, Jr.; Kamenetzky, Mario and Maybury, Robert H. Guiding Technological Change. In *Ghosh, P. K., ed., no. 3*, 1984, pp. 229–38.

Wernerfelt, Birger. Stagflation, New Products, and Speculation. *J. Macroecon.*, Summer 1984, *6*(3), pp. 295–309.

Westoby, Richard. Models of Interfuel Substitution in the UK. *J. Econ. Stud.*, 1984, *11*(1), pp. 27–39. [G: U.K.]

Westphal, Larry E. Research on Appropriate Technology. In *Ghosh, P. K., ed., no. 14*, 1984, *1978*, pp. 184–204.

Westphal, Larry E.; Rhee, Yung W. and Pursell, Garry. Sources of Technological Capability in South Korea. In *Fransman, M. and King, K., eds.*, 1984, pp. 279–300. [G: S. Korea]

Westphal, Larry E., et al. Exports of Technology by Newly Industrializing Countries: Republic of Korea. *World Devel.*, May/June 1984, *12*(5/6), pp. 505–33. [G: Korea]

van Wijnbergen, Sweder. The 'Dutch Disease': A Disease after All? *Econ. J.*, March 1984, *94*(373), pp. 41–55.

Wilcox, James A. Automobile Fuel Efficiency:

Measurement and Explanation. *Econ. Inquiry,* July 1984, *22*(3), pp. 375–85. [G: U.S.]

Williams, Bruce. Technical Change and Employment. *Greek Econ. Rev.,* December 1984, *6*(3), pp. 336–55. [G: U.K.]

Williams, Roger. The International Political Economy of Technology. In *Strange, S., ed.,* 1984, pp. 70–90. [G: Global]

Willman, Paul and Cowan, Rowena. New Technology in Banking: The Impact of Autotellers on Staff Numbers. In *Warner, M., ed.,* 1984, pp. 224–39. [G: U.K.]

Winch, Graham, et al. Industrial Relations, New Technology and the BL Metro. In *Warner, M., ed.,* 1984, pp. 189–209. [G: U.K.]

Wionczek, Miguel S. Technology Transfer: What Do the Developing Countries Want? In *Ghosh, P. K., ed., no. 3,* 1984, *1976,* pp. 195–201.

Woolcock, Stephen. Information Technology: The Challenge to Europe. *J. Common Market Stud.,* June 1984, *22*(4), pp. 315–31. [G: Europe]

Woolf, Arthur G. Electricity, Productivity, and Labor Saving: American Manufacturing, 1900–1929. *Exploration Econ. Hist.,* April 1984, *21*(2), pp. 176–91. [G: U.S.]

Wozniak, Gregory D. The Adoption of Interrelated Innovations: A Human Capital Approach. *Rev. Econ. Statist.,* February 1984, *66*(1), pp. 70–79. [G: U.S.]

Wu, S. Y. Social and Private Rates of Returns Derived from Pharmaceutical Innovations: Some Empirical Findings. In *Lindgren, B., ed.,* 1984, pp. 217–54. [G: U.S.]

Wyatt, Joe B. Science, Technology, and Employment: The Reindustrialization of America. In *Ullrich, R. A., ed.,* 1984, pp. 59–80. [G: U.S.]

Yakushiji, Taizo. Reshuffling Firms for Technology? An Aggregate Time-Series Analysis of B. Klein's "Dynamic Efficiency." In *Aoki, M., ed.,* 1984, pp. 359–85. [G: Japan]

Yamaguchi, Mitoshi and Kennedy, George. A Graphic Model of the Effects of Sectoral Technical Change: The Case of Japan, 1880–1970. *Can. J. Agr. Econ.,* March 1984, *32*(1), pp. 71–92. [G: Japan]

Yu, Ben T. A Contractual Remedy to Premature Innovation: The Vertical Integration of Brand-Name Specific Research. *Econ. Inquiry,* October 1984, *22*(4), pp. 660–67.

Zilberman, David and Just, Richard E. Labor Supply Uncertainty and Technology Adoption. In *Emerson, R. D., ed.,* 1984, pp. 200–24.

Zweifel, Peter. Technological Change in Health Care: Why Are Opinions So Divided? *Managerial Dec. Econ.,* September 1984, *5*(3), pp. 177–82. [G: U.S.]

6212 Research and Development

Abel, Andrew B. R&D and the Market Value of the Firm: A Note. In *Griliches, Z., ed.,* 1984, pp. 261–69.

Adams, Steven J.; Lightner, Sharon M. and Ricketts, Donald E. Implications of Reported Accounting Information on Corporate Expenditures for Research and Development. *Rev. Bus. Econ. Res.,* Spring 1984, *19*(2), pp. 35–45. [G: U.S.]

Antle, John M. and Goodger, William J. Measuring Stochastic Technology: The Case of Tulare Milk Production. *Amer. J. Agr. Econ.,* August 1984, *66*(3), pp. 342–50. [G: U.S.]

Aoki, Masahiko. Innovative Adaptation through the Quasi-tree Structure: An Emerging Aspect of Japanese Entrepreneurship. *Z. Nationalökon.,* Supplement 1984, pp. 177–98. [G: Japan]

Aylen, Jonathan. Prospects for Steel. *Lloyds Bank Rev.,* April 1984, (152), pp. 13–30. [G: U.K.]

Baldini, Vittorio. Parchi Scientifici per l'innovazione. (Scientific Brains Trusts for Innovation. With English summary.) *L'Impresa,* 1984, *26*(1), pp. 29–38. [G: U.S.; Germany; U.K.; Sweden]

Baumol, William J. and Wolff, Edward N. Feedback Models: R&D, Information, and Productivity Growth. In *Jussawalla, M. and Ebenfield, H., eds.,* 1984, pp. 73–93.

Beggs, John J. An Extended Accelerator Model of R&D and Physical Investment: Comment. In *Griliches, Z., ed.,* 1984, pp. 295–97. [G: U.S.]

Beggs, John J. Long-run Trends in Patenting. In *Griliches, Z., ed.,* 1984, pp. 155–69. [G: U.S.]

Ben-Zion, Uri. The R&D and Investment Decision and Its Relationship to the Firm's Market Value: Some Preliminary Results. In *Griliches, Z., ed.,* 1984, pp. 299–312. [G: U.S.]

Berkowitz, Michael K. and Haines, George H., Jr. The Relationship between Relative Attributes, Relative Preferences, and Market Share: The Case of Solar Energy in Canada. *J. Cons. Res.,* December 1984, *11*(3), pp. 754–62. [G: Canada]

Bernardi, Bruno. Il "tessuto causale" delle imprese di ingegneria. ("Casual Fabric" in Engineering Companies. With English summary.) *L'Impresa,* 1984, *26*(1), pp. 17–26. [G: LDCs]

Bhalla, A. S. Technological Transformation in China. *Econ. Int.,* February–May 1984, *37*(1–2), pp. 4–19. [G: China]

Bhattacharya, Gautam. Learning and the Behavior of Potential Entrants. *Rand J. Econ.,* Summer 1984, *15*(2), pp. 281–89.

Bound, John, et al. Who Does R&D and Who Patents? In *Griliches, Z., ed.,* 1984, pp. 21–54. [G: U.S.]

Brooks, H. G. and Furtan, W. H. An Analysis of Public Agricultural Research in the Canadian Prairie Provinces. *Can. J. Agr. Econ.,* July 1984, *32*(2), pp. 355–75. [G: Canada]

Burke, Marti E. Approaching Foundations and Other Private Organizations for Research Support. In *Dusek, E. R., et al., eds.,* 1984, pp. 305–19. [G: U.S.]

Calvin, Melvin. Basic Chemical Research and Future Food Supplies. In *Bixler, G. and Shemilt, L. W., eds.,* 1984, pp. 107–24.

Cardani, Angelo M. and Mohnen, Pierre A. Labor Productivity in a Dynamic Model with Energy, Capital and R&D for Italian and French Manufacturing. *Giorn. Econ.*, July–August 1984, *43*(7–8), pp. 471–90. [G: Italy; France]

Cheng, Leonard. International Competition in R&D and Technological Leadership: An Examination of the Posner–Hufbauer Hypothesis. *J. Int. Econ.*, August 1984, *17*(1/2), pp. 15–40.

Clark, Kim B. and Griliches, Zvi. Productivity Growth and R&D at the Business Level: Results from the PIMS Data Base. In *Griliches, Z., ed.*, 1984, pp. 393–416. [G: U.S.]

Cohen, Jon S.; Rubin, Jeffrey and Saunders, Ronald S. Chasing the Bandwagon: Government Policy for the Electronics Industry. *Can. Public Policy*, March 1984, *10*(1), pp. 25–34. [G: OECD]

Connolly, Robert A. and Hirschey, Mark. R&D, Market Structure, and Profits: A Value-based Approach. *Rev. Econ. Statist.*, November 1984, *66*(4), pp. 682–86. [G: U.S.]

Coulter, John K. The Consultative Group on International Agricultural Research. In *Weiss, C. and Jéquier, N., eds.*, 1984, pp. 265–81. [G: LDCs]

Cuneo, Philippe and Mairesse, Jacques. Productivity and R&D at the Firm Level in French Manufacturing. In *Griliches, Z., ed.*, 1984, pp. 375–92. [G: France]

Dow, Gregory K. Pools and Streams: A Stochastic Process Model of Applied Research. *J. Econ. Dynam. Control*, October 1984, *8*(1), pp. 117–33.

Duffy, Sarah W. and Kraut, Alan G. Understanding and Influencing the Federal Budget for Psychological Research. In *Dusek, E. R., et al., eds.*, 1984, pp. 19–27. [G: U.S.]

Eads, George C. R&D and Innovation: Some Empirical Findings: Comment. In *Griliches, Z., ed.*, 1984, pp. 150–53. [G: U.S.]

Edwards, Geoff W. and Freebairn, John W. The Gains from Research into Tradable Commodities. *Amer. J. Agr. Econ.*, February 1984, *66*(1), pp. 41–49. [G: Australia]

Eisner, Robert; Albert, Steven H. and Sullivan, Martin A. Tax Incentives and R&D Expenditures. In *Oppenländer, K. H. and Poser, G., eds.*, 1984, pp. 385–419. [G: U.S.]

Eisner, Robert; Albert, Steven H. and Sullivan, Martin A. The New Incremental Tax Credit for R&D: Incentive or Disincentive? *Nat. Tax J.*, June 1984, *37*(2), pp. 171–83. [G: U.S.]

Elliott, John, et al. The Impact of SFAS No. 2 on Firm Expenditures on Research and Development: Replications and Extensions. *J. Acc. Res.*, Spring 1984, *22*(1), pp. 85–102. [G: U.S.]

Evenson, Robert E. Benefits and Obstacles in Developing Appropriate Agricultural Technology. In *Eicher, C. K. and Staatz, J. M., eds.*, 1984, *1981*, pp. 348–61.

Evenson, Robert E. International Invention: Implications for Technology Market Analysis. In *Griliches, Z., ed.*, 1984, pp. 89–123. [G: Global]

Evenson, Robert E. The R&D and Investment Decision and Its Relationship to the Firm's Market Value: Some Preliminary Results: Comment. In *Griliches, Z., ed.*, 1984, pp. 312–14. [G: U.S.]

Fakstorp, Jørgen. University–Industry Research Interactions: Overview of Policy Issues: Panel Report on Mechanical Engineering. In *Fusfeld, H. I. and Haklisch, C. S., eds.*, 1984, pp. 67–72.

Falkinger, Josef. Grenzen der innovatorischen Anpassung: Ein skeptisches Wachstumsmodell. (Limits of Innovational Capacity: A Sceptical Growth Model. With English summary.) *Jahr. Nationalökon. Statist.*, July 1984, *199*(4), pp. 321–33.

Frosch, Robert A. Improving American Innovation: The Role of Industry in Innovation. In *Coles, J. S., ed.*, 1984, pp. 56–81. [G: U.S.]

Fusfeld, Herbert I. and Haklisch, Carmela S. University–Industry Research Interactions: A Guide to the Proceedings. In *Fusfeld, H. I. and Haklisch, C. S., eds.*, 1984, pp. 1–7. [G: U.S.]

Gannicott, K. The Determinants of Industrial R&D in Australia. *Econ. Rec.*, September 1984, *60*(170), pp. 231–35. [G: Australia]

Garnier, Francis. University–Industry Research Interactions: Petroleum. In *Fusfeld, H. I. and Haklisch, C. S., eds.*, 1984, pp. 43–45. [G: France]

Gates, John M.; Grigalunas, Thomas A. and Vieira, Luis F. Cost Effectiveness of Publicly Funded Research: A Case Study of the United States Academic Research Fleet. *Appl. Econ.*, June 1984, *16*(3), pp. 355–67. [G: U.S.]

Grabowski, Henry and Vernon, John. A Computer Simulation Model of Pharmaceutical Innovation. In *Lindgren, B., ed.*, 1984, pp. 159–75. [G: U.S.]

Graham, Loren R. Science and Computers in Soviet Society. In *Hoffmann, E. P., ed.*, 1984, pp. 124–34. [G: U.S.S.R.]

Griliches, Zvi. Market Value, R&D, and Patents. In *Griliches, Z., ed.*, 1984, pp. 249–52. [G: U.S.]

Griliches, Zvi. R&D and Innovation: Some Empirical Findings: Comment. In *Griliches, Z., ed.*, 1984, pp. 148–49. [G: U.S.]

Griliches, Zvi. R&D, Patents, and Productivity: Introduction. In *Griliches, Z., ed.*, 1984, pp. 1–19.

Griliches, Zvi and Lichtenberg, Frank R. Interindustry Technology Flows and Productivity Growth: A Re-examination. *Rev. Econ. Statist.*, May 1984, *66*(2), pp. 324–29. [G: U.S.]

Griliches, Zvi and Lichtenberg, Frank R. R&D and Productivity Growth at the Industry Level: Is There Still a Relationship? In *Griliches, Z., ed.*, 1984, pp. 465–96. [G: U.S.]

Griliches, Zvi and Mairesse, Jacques. Productivity and R&D at the Firm Level. In *Griliches, Z., ed.*, 1984, pp. 339–74. [G: U.S.]

Hausman, Jerry A.; Hall, Bronwyn H. and Griliches, Zvi. Econometric Models for Count Data with an Application to the Patents–R&D Relationship. *Econometrica*, July 1984, *52*(4), pp. 909–38. [G: U.S.]

Hillman, Arye L. and Katz, Eliakim. Oil Price Instability and Domestic Energy Substitution for Imported Oil. *Econ. Rec.*, March 1984, *60*(168), pp. 85–89.

Holt, Virginia E. Federal Funding Trends for Research in Psychology. In *Dusek, E. R., et al., eds.*, 1984, pp. 29–39. [G: U.S.]

Hornig, Donald F. The Role of Government in Scientific Innovation. In *Coles, J. S., ed.*, 1984, pp. 30–55. [G: U.S.]

Howells, J. R. L. The Location of Research and Development: Some Observations and Evidence from Britain. *Reg. Stud.*, February 1984, *18*(1), pp. 13–29. [G: U.K.]

Ishii, Takemochi. Future Trend of Technological Research and Development and its Potential Impact on Society. In *Miyawaki, N., ed.*, 1984, pp. 266–70.

Johnson, Steven B. Comparing R&D Strategies of Japanese and U.S. Firms. *Sloan Manage. Rev.*, Spring 1984, *25*(3), pp. 25–34. [G: U.S.; Japan]

Koekkoek, K. Ad and Mennes, Loet B. M. Revealed Comparative Advantage in Manufacturing Industry: The Case of the Netherlands. *De Economist*, 1984, *132*(1), pp. 30–48. [G: W. Germany; Belgium; Netherlands]

Koga, Mamoru and Nakahara, Hiroyuki. Japanese Ocean Science and Technology Policy and the National Budget. In *Friedheim, R. L., et al.*, 1984, pp. 108–29. [G: Japan]

Krupp, Helmar. Overview of Policy Issues: Panel Report on the Functions of Non-University Research Institutes in National R&D and Innovation Systems and the Contributions of Universities. In *Fusfeld, H. I. and Haklisch, C. S., eds.*, 1984, pp. 95–100. [G: W. Germany]

Krupp, Helmar and Englund, Bjorn. Overview of Policy Issues: Panel Report on the Role of Middle-Level Research in the R&D Systems. In *Fusfeld, H. I. and Haklisch, C. S., eds.*, 1984, pp. 101–03.

Lakhtin, G. and Pavlenko, Iu. The Science-Intensiveness Indicator of an Economic Branch. *Prob. Econ.*, November 1984, *27*(7), pp. 61–75. [G: U.S.S.R.; U.S.]

Landefeld, J. Steven. Measuring the Returns to Biomedical Research: Issues and Problems. In *Lindgren, B., ed.*, 1984, pp. 255–86. [G: U.S.]

Lavoie, Don. Two Varieties of Industrial Policy: A Critique. *Cato J.*, Fall 1984, *4*(2), pp. 457–84. [G: U.S.; Japan]

Lecraw, Donald J. Some Economic Effects of Standards. *Appl. Econ.*, August 1984, *16*(4), pp. 507–22. [G: Canada]

Levin, Richard C. and Reiss, Peter C. Tests of a Schumpeterian Model of R&D and Market Structure. In *Griliches, Z., ed.*, 1984, pp. 175–204. [G: U.S.]

Lichtenberg, Frank R. The Relationship between Federal Contract R&D and Company R&D. *Amer. Econ. Rev.*, May 1984, *74*(2), pp. 73–78. [G: U.S.]

Lieberman, Marvin B. The Learning Curve and Pricing in the Chemical Processing Industries. *Rand J. Econ.*, Summer 1984, *15*(2), pp. 213–28. [G: U.S.]

Link, Albert N. Firm versus Industry Variability in R&D Intensity: Comment. In *Griliches, Z., ed.*, 1984, pp. 245–48. [G: U.S.]

Link, Albert N. and Lunn, John. Concentration and the Returns to R&D. *Rev. Ind. Organ.*, Fall 1984, *1*(3), pp. 232–39. [G: U.S.]

Long, Franklin A. Potential Contributions of Western Business to the Service Sector of LDCs. In *Brooks, H.; Liebman, L. and Schelling, C. S., eds.*, 1984, pp. 319–37. [G: LDCs]

Lovett, J. Robert. University–Industry Research Interactions: Chemicals. In *Fusfeld, H. I. and Haklisch, C. S., eds.*, 1984, pp. 51–57.

Lowman, Robert P. and Dusek, E. Ralph. Federal Research Support: A Primer for Proposal Writers. In *Dusek, E. R., et al., eds.*, 1984, pp. 41–53. [G: U.S.]

Lubin, Moshe and Een, Gillis. University–Industry Research Interactions: Overview of Policy Issues: Panel Report on Petroleum. In *Fusfeld, H. I. and Haklisch, C. S., eds.*, 1984, pp. 47–50.

Lyu, Syu-Jyun Larry; White, Fred C. and Lu, Yao-Chi. Estimating Effects of Agricultural Research and Extension Expenditures on Productivity: A Translog Production Function Approach. *Southern J. Agr. Econ.*, December 1984, *16*(2), pp. 1–8. [G: U.S.]

Mairesse, Jacques and Siu, Alan K. An Extended Accelerator Model of R&D and Physical Investment. In *Griliches, Z., ed.*, 1984, pp. 271–95. [G: U.S.]

Mansfield, Edwin. How Effective Is the R&D Tax Credit? *Challenge*, November/December 1984, *27*(5), pp. 57–61. [G: U.S.]

Mansfield, Edwin. R&D and Innovation: Some Empirical Findings. In *Griliches, Z., ed.*, 1984, pp. 127–48. [G: U.S.]

Mansfield, Edwin. R&D and Innovation: Some Empirical Findings: Reply. In *Griliches, Z., ed.*, 1984, pp. 154. [G: U.S.]

Mansfield, Edwin. Using Linked Patent and R&D Data to Measure Interindustry Technology Flows: Comment. In *Griliches, Z., ed.*, 1984, pp. 461–64. [G: U.S.]

Marc, F. La difficoltá ad ainnovare nelle piccole e medie imprese. (Obstacles to the Innovating Process within Low and Medium Sized Firms. With English summary.) *Mondo Aperto*, January-February 1984, *38*(1), pp. 13–25. [G: U.S.]

McMahon, Walter W. The Relation of Education and R&D to Productivity Growth. *Econ. Educ. Rev.*, 1984, *3*(4), pp. 299–313. [G: U.S.]

Mendelsohn, Robert. Endogenous Technical Change and Environmental Regulation. *J. Environ. Econ. Manage.*, September 1984, *11*(3), pp. 202–07.

Moe, Johannes. Functions of Research Institutes. In *Fusfeld, H. I. and Haklisch, C. S., eds.*, 1984, pp. 85–93. **[G: Norway]**

Mowery, David C. Firm Structure, Government Policy, and the Organization of Industrial Research: Great Britain and the United States, 1900–1950. *Bus. Hist. Rev.*, Winter 1984, 58(4), pp. 504–31. **[G: U.S.; U.K.]**

Muller, Steven. Research Universities and Industrial Innovation in America. In *Coles, J. S., ed.*, 1984, pp. 8–29. **[G: U.S.]**

Murnane, Richard J. and Nelson, Richard R. Production and Innovation When Techniques Are Tacit: The Case of Education. *J. Econ. Behav. Organ.*, September–December 1984, 5(3–4), pp. 353–73. **[G: U.S.]**

Nelson, Richard R. Incentives for Entrepreneurship and Supporting Institutions. *Weltwirtsch. Arch.*, 1984, 120(4), pp. 646–61. **[G: U.S.]**

Nichols, Donald A. Federal Spending Priorities and Long-term Economic Growth. In *Hulten, C. R. and Sawhill, I. V., eds.*, 1984, pp. 151–73. **[G: U.S.]**

Okimoto, Daniel I. Competitive Edge: Political Context. In *Okimoto, D. I.; Sugano, T. and Weinstein, F. B., eds.*, 1984, pp. 78–133. **[G: Japan; U.S.]**

Pakes, Ariel. Patents, R&D, and the Stock Market Rate of Return: A Summary of Some Empirical Results. In *Griliches, Z., ed.*, 1984, pp. 253–59.

Pakes, Ariel and Griliches, Zvi. Patents and R&D at the Firm Level: A First Look. In *Griliches, Z., ed.*, 1984, pp. 55–72. **[G: U.S.]**

Pakes, Ariel and Schankerman, Mark. An Exploration into the Determinants of Research Intensity. In *Griliches, Z., ed.*, 1984, pp. 209–32. **[G: U.S.]**

Pakes, Ariel and Schankerman, Mark. The Rate of Obsolescence of Patents, Research Gestation Lags, and the Private Rate of Return to Research Resources. In *Griliches, Z., ed.*, 1984, pp. 73–88.

Palmer, John P. Patents, Licensing and Restrictions on Competition. *Econ. Inquiry*, October 1984, 22(4), pp. 676–83.

Peters, Lois S. University–Industry Research Interactions: Pharmaceuticals. In *Fusfeld, H. I. and Haklisch, C. S., eds.*, 1984, pp. 35–40.

Piekarz, Rolf; Thomas, Eleanor and Jennings, Donna. International Comparisons of Research and Development Expenditures. In *Kendrick, J. W., ed.*, 1984, pp. 235–73. **[G: OECD]**

Rao, K. Nagaraja and Weiss, Charles. Government Promotion of Industrial Innovation. In *Weiss, C. and Jéquier, N., eds.*, 1984, pp. 35–54. **[G: Spain; Israel; S. Korea]**

Reimers, Niels. The Government-Industry-University Interface: Improving the Innovative Process. In *Coles, J. S., ed.*, 1984, pp. 109–48. **[G: U.S.]**

Reinganum, Jennifer F. Practical Implications of Game Theoretic Models of R&D. *Amer. Econ. Rev.*, May 1984, 74(2), pp. 61–66.

Rittberger, Volker. The Role of Science and Technology in the New International Order. In *Ghosh, P. K., ed., no. 9, 1984, 1978*, pp. 183–97.

Rothwell, Roy. Creating a Regional Innovation-oriented Infrastructure: The Role of Public Procurement. *Ann. Pub. Co-op. Econ.*, April–June 1984, 55(2), pp. 159–72. **[G: U.K.]**

Sales, Hubert. La recherche-développement dans la stratégie des grandes entreprises chimiques de l'entre-deux-guerres: Du Pont de Nemours, Imperial chemical industries, I. G. Farben. (With English summary.) *Revue Écon. Polit.*, July–August 1984, 94(4), pp. 446–64. **[G: Germany]**

Sato, Ryuzo and Tsutsui, Shunichi. Technical Progress, the Schumpeterian Hypothesis, and Market Structure. *Z. Nationalökon.*, Supplement 1984, pp. 1–37.

Schankerman, Mark. Long-run Trends in Patenting: Comment. In *Griliches, Z., ed.*, 1984, pp. 169–73. **[G: U.S.]**

Schankerman, Mark and Nadiri, M. Ishaq. Investment in R&D, Costs of Adjustment, and Expectations. In *Griliches, Z., ed.*, 1984, pp. 315–38. **[G: U.S.]**

Scherer, Frederic M. Corporate Size, Diversification, and Innovative Activity. In *Scherer, F. M.*, 1984, pp. 222–38. **[G: U.S.; U.K.; W. Germany; France; Japan]**

Scherer, Frederic M. International Invention: Implications for Technology Market Analysis: Comment. In *Griliches, Z., ed.*, 1984, pp. 123–26. **[G: Global]**

Scherer, Frederic M. R&D and Declining Productivity Growth. In *Scherer, F. M.*, 1984, 1983, pp. 286–92. **[G: U.S.]**

Scherer, Frederic M. Research and Development Resource Allocation under Rivalry. In *Scherer, F. M.*, 1984, pp. 83–119.

Scherer, Frederic M. Statistical Evidence on Antitrust Decree Effects. In *Scherer, F. M.*, 1984, pp. 207–21. **[G: U.S.]**

Scherer, Frederic M. The Investment Decision Phases in Modern Invention and Innovation. In *Scherer, F. M.*, 1984, pp. 3–7. **[G: U.S.]**

Scherer, Frederic M. The Theory of Market Structure and Innovation. In *Scherer, F. M.*, 1984, pp. 59–65.

Scherer, Frederic M. Time–Cost Trade-offs in Uncertain Empirical Research Projects. In *Scherer, F. M.*, 1984, pp. 67–82.

Scherer, Frederic M. Using Linked Patent and R&D Data to Measure Interindustry Technology Flows. In *Griliches, Z., ed.*, 1984, pp. 417–61.

Scherer, Frederic M. and Ravenscraft, David J. Growth by Diversification: Entrepreneurial Behavior in Large-Scale United States Enterprises. *Z. Nationalökon.*, Supplement 1984, pp. 199–218. **[G: U.S.]**

Schultz, Theodore W. The Economics of Agricultural Research. In *Eicher, C. K. and Staatz, J. M., eds.*, 1984, 1979, pp. 335–47.

Schultze, Charles L. Alternative Measures of Federal Investment Outlays. In *Hulten, C. R. and Sawhill, I. V., eds.*, 1984, pp. 175–78. **[G: U.S.]**

Scobie, Grant M. and Posada T., Rafael. The Impact of Technical Change on Income Distribution: The Case of Rice in Colombia. In *Eicher, C. K. and Staatz, J. M., eds.*, 1984, 1978, pp. 378–88. [G: Colombia]

Scott, John T. Firm versus Industry Variability in R&D Intensity. In *Griliches, Z., ed.*, 1984, pp. 233–45. [G: U.S.]

Smith, J. M. Punti di forza e di debolezza del management giapponese. (Demystifying Japanese Management. With English summary.) *Mondo Aperto*, September–October 1984, 38(5), pp. 237–44. [G: Japan]

Solo, Robert A. Industrial Policy. *J. Econ. Issues*, September 1984, 18(3), pp. 697–714. [G: U.S.]

Sosin, Kim H. and Fairchild, Loretta G. Nonhomotheticity and Technological Bias in Production. *Rev. Econ. Statist.*, February 1984, 66(1), pp. 44–50. [G: Latin America]

Spence, A. Michael. Cost Reduction, Competition, and Industry Performance. *Econometrica*, January 1984, 52(1), pp. 101–21.

Spence, A. Michael. Industrial Organization and Competitive Advantage in Multinational Industries. *Amer. Econ. Rev.*, May 1984, 74(2), pp. 356–60.

Stolte-Heiskanen, Veronica. Societal Use of Scientific and Technical Research: Existing and Alternative Models. In *Richardson, J., ed.*, 1984, pp. 185–207.

Svedberg, Bjorn. University–Industry Research Interactions: Electronics. In *Fusfeld, H. I. and Haklisch, C. S., eds.*, 1984, pp. 25–29.

Swanson, S. A. V. University–Industry Research Interactions: Mechanical Engineering. In *Fusfeld, H. I. and Haklisch, C. S., eds.*, 1984, pp. 61–65. [G: U.K.]

Switzer, Lorne. The Determinants of Industrial R&D: A Funds Flow Simultaneous Equation Approach. *Rev. Econ. Statist.*, February 1984, 66(1), pp. 163–68. [G: U.S.]

Tandon, Pankaj. Tests of a Schumpeterian Model of R&D and Market Structure: Comment. In *Griliches, Z., ed.*, 1984, pp. 205–08. [G: U.S.]

Terleckyj, Nestor E. A Growth Model of the U.S. Communication Industry, 1948–80. In *Jussawalla, M. and Ebenfield, H., eds.*, 1984, pp. 119–45. [G: U.S.]

Terleckyj, Nestor E. R&D and Productivity Growth at the Industry Level: Is There Still a Relationship? Comment. In *Griliches, Z., ed.*, 1984, pp. 496–501. [G: U.S.]

Teubal, Morris. The Role of Technological Learning in the Exports of Manufactured Goods: The Case of Selected Capital Goods in Brazil. *World Devel.*, August 1984, 12(8), pp. 849–65. [G: Brazil]

Teubal, Morris and Steinmueller, Edward. The Introduction of a Major New Technology—Externalities and Government Policy. In *Csikós-Nagy, B.; Hague, D. and Hall, G., eds.*, 1984, pp. 117–39.

Thompson, John K. L. International Comparisons of Research and Development Expenditures:

Comment. In *Kendrick, J. W., ed.*, 1984, pp. 275–78. [G: OECD]

Thurow, Lester C. The Need for Industrial Policies: The Case of the U.S.A. *Ann. Pub. Co-op. Econ.*, January–March 1984, 55(1), pp. 3–31. [G: U.S.]

Uenohara, Michiyuki, et al. Competitive Edge: Background. In *Okimoto, D. I.; Sugano, T. and Weinstein, F. B., eds.*, 1984, pp. 9–34. [G: Japan; U.S.]

von Ungern-Sternberg, Thomas. Innovator Protection and the Rate of Technical Progress. *J. Econ. Behav. Organ.*, March 1984, 5(1), pp. 115–29.

White, Geoff. Intra-Industry Trade Adjustment and European Industrial Policies. In *Jacquemin, A., ed.*, 1984, pp. 172–90. [G: EEC]

Winter, Sidney G. Schumpeterian Competition in Alternative Technological Regimes. *J. Econ. Behav. Organ.*, September–December 1984, 5(3–4), pp. 287–320.

Wu, S. Y. Social and Private Rates of Returns Derived from Pharmaceutical Innovations: Some Empirical Findings. In *Lindgren, B., ed.*, 1984, pp. 217–54. [G: U.S.]

Yu, Shirley S. Some Determinants of Entry into Therapeutic Drug Markets. *Rev. Ind. Organ.*, Winter 1984, 1(4), pp. 260–75. [G: U.S.]

Zentner, R. P. and Peterson, W. L. An Economic Evaluation of Public Wheat Research and Extension Expenditures in Canada. *Can. J. Agr. Econ.*, July 1984, 32(2), pp. 327–53. [G: Canada]

630 INDUSTRY STUDIES

6300 General

Alexis, Marcus. Politics and Economics. *Rev. Black Polit. Econ.*, Summer–Fall 1984, 13(1–2), pp. 9–24. [G: U.S.]

Alexis, Marcus. Politics and Economics: Rejoinder. *Rev. Black Polit. Econ.*, Summer–Fall 1984, 13(1–2), pp. 27–29. [G: U.S.]

Alvarez, Donato and Cooper, Brian. Productivity Trends in Manufacturing in the U.S. and 11 Other Countries. *Mon. Lab. Rev.*, January 1984, 107(1), pp. 52–58. [G: OECD]

Apostolakis, Bobby E. A Translogarithmic Cost Function Approach: Greece, 1953–1977. *Empirical Econ.*, 1984, 9(4), pp. 247–62. [G: Greece]

Apostolakis, Bobby E. Substitution between Imports and Primary Inputs in the Netherlands, 1953–1977. *Eastern Econ. J.*, January-March 1984, 10(1), pp. 43–50. [G: Netherlands]

Appelbaum, Eileen. High Tech and the Structural Employment Problems of the 1980s. In *Collins, E. L. and Tanner, L. D., eds.*, 1984, pp. 23–48. [G: U.S.]

Armstrong, E. G. A. Employers Associations in Great Britain. In *Windmuller, J. P. and Gladstone, A., eds.*, 1984, pp. 44–78. [G: U.K.]

Asajima, Shoichi. Flow-of-Funds Analysis of the Sumitomo Zaibatsu. In *Nakagawa, K. and Morikawa, H., eds.*, 1984, pp. 72–103. [G: Japan]

Auster, Ellen and Aldrich, Howard. Small Business Vulnerability, Ethnic Enclaves and Ethnic Enterprise. In *Ward, R. and Jenkins, R., eds.*, 1984, pp. 39–54. **[G: U.S.]**

Babic, Stojan. The Problem of Choosing Indicators of Efficiency in the Yugoslav Economic System, 1976–1980. *Eastern Europ. Econ.*, Winter 1984–85, 23(2), pp. 43–70.
[G: Yugoslavia]

Baer, Werner. Semi-industrialization and Semi-development: The Legacy of Import-Substitution on Development Problems and on Development Economics. *METU*, 1984, 11(1–2), pp. 151–62. **[G: LDCs]**

Bamford, Julia. Small Business in Italy—The Submerged Economy. In *Levicki, C., ed.*, 1984, pp. 97–110. **[G: Italy]**

Barreyre, Pierre-Yves. The Small Firm in the French Economy. In *Levicki, C., ed.*, 1984, pp. 89–96. **[G: France]**

Baysan, Tercan. Some Economic Aspects of Turkey's Accession to the EC: Resource Shifts, Comparative Advantage, and Static Gains. *J. Common Market Stud.*, September 1984, 23(1), pp. 15–34. **[G: Turkey; EEC]**

Becker, Eugene H. and Bowers, Norman. Employment and Unemployment Improvements Widespread in 1983. *Mon. Lab. Rev.*, February 1984, 107(2), pp. 3–14. **[G: U.S.]**

Beesley, Michael E. and Wilson, P. E. B. Public Policy and Small Firms in Britain. In *Levicki, C., ed.*, 1984, pp. 111–26. **[G: U.K.]**

Bell, David. Trends in Scottish Industry. In *Hood, N. and Young, S., eds.*, 1984, pp. 1–27.
[G: U.K.]

Berndt, Ernst R. The Role of Energy in Productivity Growth: Comment. In *Kendrick, J. W., ed.*, 1984, pp. 325–34. **[G: U.S.]**

Bertmar, Lars. Measures of Business Performance—The Swedish Case. In *Holland, D. M., ed.*, 1984, pp. 117–53. **[G: Sweden]**

Bessler, David A. Relative Prices and Money: A Vector Autoregression on Brazilian Data. *Amer. J. Agr. Econ.*, February 1984, 66(1), pp. 25–30. **[G: Brazil]**

Birch, David. The Contribution of Small Enterprise to Growth and Employment. In *Giersch, H., ed.*, 1984, pp. 1–17. **[G: U.S.]**

Birdseye, Penny and Webb, Tony. Why the Rate Burden on Business Is a Cause for Concern. *Nat. Westminster Bank Quart. Rev.*, February 1984, pp. 2–15. **[G: U.K.]**

Black, Harold. Politics and Economics: Comments. *Rev. Black Polit. Econ.*, Summer–Fall 1984, 13(1–2), pp. 25–27. **[G: U.S.]**

Boissevain, Jeremy. Small Entrepreneurs in Contemporary Europe. In *Ward, R. and Jenkins, R., eds.*, 1984, pp. 20–38. **[G: EEC]**

Bossányi, Katalin. The Newly Independent Enterprises in Hungary. *Acta Oecon.*, 1984, 32(3–4), pp. 269–86. **[G: Hungary]**

Bossier, F.; Biolley, T. and Vandamme, L. Cumulated Costs and Import Contents in the Belgium Input–Output Tables of 1965, 1970 and 1975. *Cah. Écon. Bruxelles*, 1st Trimester 1984, (101), pp. 125–67. **[G: Belgium]**

Bouissou, Michel-Benoît; Laffont, Jean-Jacques and Vuong, Quang H. Économétrie du déséquilibre sur données microéconomiques. (Econometrics of Disequilibrium with Microeconomic Data. With English summary.) *Ann. INSEE*, July–December 1984, (55/56), pp. 109–51. **[G: France]**

Boyer, Kenneth D. Is There a Principle for Defining Industries? *Southern Econ. J.*, January 1984, 50(3), pp. 761–70.

Brown, William, et al. Product and Labour Markets in Wage Determination: Some Australian Evidence. *Brit. J. Ind. Relat.*, July 1984, 22(2), pp. 169–76. **[G: Australia]**

Browne, Lynn E. Conflicting Views of Technological Progress and the Labor Market. *New Eng. Econ. Rev.*, July–August 1984, pp. 5–16.
[G: U.S.]

Bruch, Mathias. The Contribution of Small Enterprise to Growth and Employment: Comment. In *Giersch, H., ed.*, 1984, pp. 18–22.
[G: U.S.]

Bunel, Jean and Saglio, Jean. Employers Associations in France. In *Windmuller, J. P. and Gladstone, A., eds.*, 1984, pp. 232–63.
[G: France]

Bunn, Ronald F. Employers Association in the Federal Republic of Germany. In *Windmuller, J. P. and Gladstone, A., eds.*, 1984, pp. 169–201. **[G: W. Germany]**

Buxton, A. J.; Davies, Stephen W. and Lyons, Bruce R. Concentration and Advertising in Consumer and Producer Markets. *J. Ind. Econ.*, June 1984, 32(4), pp. 451–64.
[G: U.K.]

Carlsson, Bo. Industrial Subsidies in the Nordic Countries. In *Mikkelsen, A., et al.*, 1984, pp. 222–29. **[G: Scandinavia]**

Carter, Jane. Energy Conservation in the United Kingdom: A Major Industrial Opportunity. *Energy J.*, January 1984, 5(1), pp. 149–58.
[G: U.K.]

Cronin, Francis J. Analytical Assumptions and Causal Ordering in Interindustry Modeling. *Southern Econ. J.*, October 1984, 51(2), pp. 521–29. **[G: U.S.]**

Curran, James and Stanworth, John. Small Business Research in Britain. In *Levicki, C., ed.*, 1984, pp. 127–52. **[G: U.K.]**

Dahlman, Carl J. and Cortes, Mariluz. Exports of Technology by Newly Industrializing Countries: Mexico. *World Devel.*, May/June 1984, 12(5/6), pp. 601–24. **[G: Mexico]**

Dahlman, Carl J. and Sercovich, Francisco Colman. Exports of Technology from Semi-industrial Economies and Local Technological Development. *J. Devel. Econ.*, September–October 1984, 16(1–2), pp. 63–99.
[G: Argentina; Brazil; India; Korea; Mexico]

Davies, Duncan. Actions to Strengthen University–Industry Cooperation. In *Fusfeld, H. I. and Haklisch, C. S., eds.*, 1984, pp. 161–67.

Davila, Alberto E.; Schmidt, Ronald H. and Ziegler, Gary M. Industrial Diversification, Exchange Rate Shocks, and the Texas–Mexico

Border. *Fed. Res. Bank Dallas Econ. Rev.*, May 1984, pp. 1–9. **[G: U.S.; Mexico]**

Decaluwe, Bernard. Le modèle scandinave et l'économie canadienne. (The Scandinavian Model and the Canadian Economy. With English summary.) *L'Actual. Econ.*, June 1984, *60*(2), pp. 164–85. **[G: Canada]**

Derber, Milton. Employers Associations in the United States. In *Windmuller, J. P. and Gladstone, A., eds.*, 1984, pp. 79–114. **[G: U.S.]**

Devens, Richard M., Jr. Employment in the First Half: Robust Recovery Continues. *Mon. Lab. Rev.*, August 1984, *107*(8), pp. 3–7. **[G: U.S.]**

Dewatripont, Mathias. Analyse et prévision du choix modal de transport terrestre de marchandises en Belgique. (With English summary.) *Cah. Écon. Bruxelles*, 2nd Trimester 1984, (102), pp. 179–201. **[G: Belgium]**

Dixon, Peter B.; Parmenter, B. R. and Powell, Alan A. Trade Liberalization and Labor Market Disruption. *J. Policy Modeling*, November 1984, *6*(4), pp. 431–54. **[G: Australia]**

Dollery, B. E. Market Structure and Inflation in South Africa: A Test of the Administered Price Hypothesis. *S. Afr. J. Econ.*, December 1984, *52*(4), pp. 345–58. **[G: S. Africa]**

Dorfman, Adolfo. The Structural Crisis in Argentine Industry. *Cepal Rev.*, 1984, (23), pp. 123–34. **[G: Argentina]**

Dormayer, H.-J. and Lindlbauer, J. D. Sectoral Indicators by Use of Survey Data. In *Oppenländer, K. H. and Poser, G., eds.*, 1984, pp. 467–98. **[G: W. Germany]**

Duetsch, Larry L. An Examination of Industry Exit Patterns. *Rev. Ind. Organ.*, Spring 1984, *1*(1), pp. 60–68. **[G: U.S.]**

Dufty, Norman F. Employers Associations in Australia. In *Windmuller, J. P. and Gladstone, A., eds.*, 1984, pp. 115–48. **[G: Australia]**

Dumler, Georg. Ertragslage und Rentabilität des Unternehmenssektors 1966–1981. (The Profit Situation and the Profitability of the Business Sector in West Germany, 1966–1981. With English summary.) *Konjunkturpolitik*, 1984, *30*(1), pp. 23–44. **[G: W. Germany]**

Evans, Robert, Jr. Pay Differentials: The Case of Japan. *Mon. Lab. Rev.*, October 1984, *107*(10), pp. 24–29. **[G: Japan; U.S.]**

Fal'tsman, V. and Ozhegov, A. The Retirement of Fixed Capital: Investment Opportunities and Limitations. *Prob. Econ.*, May 1984, *27*(1), pp. 3–21. **[G: U.S.S.R.]**

Fatemi, Ali M. Shareholder Benefits from Corporate International Diversification. *J. Finance*, December 1984, *39*(5), pp. 1325–44. **[G: U.S.]**

Florescu, M. Present Trends of Industrial Cybernetics. *Econ. Computat. Cybern. Stud. Res.*, 1984, *19*(1), pp. 13–23. **[G: Romania]**

Fourie, F. C. v. N. Industriële Konsentrasie en Inflasie in Suid-Afrika 1972–1979. *S. Afr. J. Econ.*, December 1984, *52*(4), pp. 359–76. **[G: S. Africa]**

Friedenberg, Howard and Bretzfelder, Robert. Regional Shifts in Personal Income by Indus-

trial Component, 1959–83. *Surv. Curr. Bus.*, November 1984, *64*(11), pp. 28–36. **[G: U.S.]**

Gardini, Attilio. Indici settoriali per l'analisi territoriale delle tecniche e della produttivita'. Un'applicazione al confronto fra l'economia italiana e quella emiliano-romagnola. (Multisectoral Indices for the Spatial Analysis of the Techniques and of Productivity. An Application for the Comparison between the Economic Structure of Italy and of Emilia Romagna. With English summary.) *Statistica*, July–September 1984, *44*(3), pp. 443–62. **[G: Italy]**

Geroski, Paul A. and Jacquemin, Alexis. Large Firms in the European Corporate Economy and Industrial Policy in the 1980s. In *Jacquemin, A., ed.*, 1984, pp. 343–67. **[G: EEC]**

Gibbons, Joel C. Capital–Energy Substitution in the Long Run. *Energy J.*, April 1984, *5*(2), pp. 109–18. **[G: W. Europe; Canada; U.S.]**

Gibbons, Joel C. Energy Prices and Capital Obsolescence: Evidence from the Oil Embargo Period. *Energy J.*, January 1984, *5*(1), pp. 29–43. **[G: U.S.]**

Giordano, Yvonne. Analyse de la politique française du commerce extérieur depuis le VIe Plan. (With English summary.) *Rev. Econ. Ind.*, 3rd Trimester 1984, (29), pp. 46–61. **[G: France]**

Gouedard-Comte, Olivier. Formes et degrés d'insertion régionale des groupes: une comparaison entre groupes français et groupes étrangers. (Regional Insertions of Groups: A Comparison between French and Foreign Groups. With English summary.) *Revue Écon.*, March 1984, *35*(2), pp. 313–46. **[G: France]**

Greenaway, David and Milner, Chris. A Cross Section Analysis of Intra-industry Trade in the U.K. *Europ. Econ. Rev.*, August 1984, *25*(3), pp. 319–44. **[G: U.K.]**

Greer, Douglas F. Size, Efficiency, and *Fortune* Magazine. *Rev. Ind. Organ.*, Spring 1984, *1*(1), pp. 53–59.

Hahn, Franz and Schmoranz, Ingo. Estimates of Capital Stock by Industries for Austria. *Rev. Income Wealth*, September 1984, *30*(3), pp. 289–307. **[G: Austria]**

Hekman, John S. and Strong, John S. Is There a Case for Plant-Closing Laws? In *McKenzie, R. B., ed. (II)*, 1984, *1980*, pp. 49–77. **[G: U.S.]**

Herman, Arthur S. Productivity Declined in 1982 in a Majority of Industries Measured. *Mon. Lab. Rev.*, January 1984, *107*(1), pp. 80–83. **[G: U.S.]**

Higgs, Peter J.; Parmenter, B. R. and Powell, Alan A. The Scope for Tariff Reform Created by a Resources Boom: Simulations with the ORANI Model. *Australian Econ. Pap.*, June 1984, *23*(42), pp. 1–26. **[G: Australia]**

Hillman, Arye L. Declining Industries and Political-Support Protectionist Motives: Errata. *Amer. Econ. Rev.*, March 1984, *74*(1), pp. 260.

Holland, Daniel M. and Myers, Stewart C. Trends in Corporate Profitability and Capital

Costs in the United States. In *Holland, D. M.*, *ed.*, 1984, pp. 43–115. [G: U.S.]

Hollard, Michel; Ruffieux, Bernard and Servais, Olivier. Automatisation et productivité: rupture ou continuité? (With English summary.) *Rev. Econ. Ind.*, 2nd Trimester 1984, (28), pp. 59–75. [G: France]

Hood, Neil and Young, Stephen. Conclusions: The Way Ahead. In *Hood, N. and Young, S.*, *eds.*, 1984, pp. 390–412. [G: U.K.]

Hossain, Mahabub. Productivity and Profitability in Bangladesh Rural Industries. *Bangladesh Devel. Stud.*, March-June 1984, *12*(1–2), pp. 127–61. [G: Bangladesh]

Hughes, Alan and Kumar, Manmohan Singh. Recent Trends in Aggregate Concentration in the United Kingdom Economy: Revised Estimates. *Cambridge J. Econ.*, December 1984, *8*(4), pp. 401–02.

Hughes, Alan and Kumar, Manmohan Singh. Recent Trends in Aggregate Concentration in the United Kingdom Economy. *Cambridge J. Econ.*, September 1984, *8*(3), pp. 235–50. [G: U.K.]

Hui, Lim Mah. Industrial Development in Malaysia and the Dependency Debate. In *Ngo, M.*, *ed.*, *vol. 1*, 1984, pp. 357–77. [G: Malaysia]

Hunt, Lester Charles. Energy and Capital: Substitutes or Complements? Some Results for the UK Industrial Sector. *Appl. Econ.*, October 1984, *16*(5), pp. 783–89. [G: U.K.]

Jabine, Thomas B. Industry Classification and Coding in a Decentralized Statistical System. In *[Ferber, R.]*, 1984, pp. 355–92. [G: U.S.]

Jackson, Randall W. An Evaluation of Alternative Measures of Regional Industrial Diversification. *Reg. Stud.*, April 1984, *18*(2), pp. 103–12. [G: U.S.]

Jones, Gavin W. Links between Urbanization and Sectoral Shifts in Employment in Java. *Bull. Indonesian Econ. Stud.*, December 1984, *20*(3), pp. 120–57. [G: Indonesia]

Jorgenson, Dale W. Econometric Methods for Applied General Equilibrium Analysis. In *Scarf, H. E. and Shoven, J. B.*, *eds.*, 1984, pp. 139–203. [G: U.S.]

Jorgenson, Dale W. The Role of Energy in Productivity Growth. In *Kendrick, J. W.*, *ed.*, 1984, pp. 279–323.

Jusenius, Carol L. and Ledebur, Larry C. Where Have All the Firms Gone? An Analysis of the New England Economy. In *McKenzie, R. B.*, *ed. (II)*, 1984, 1977, pp. 79–117. [G: U.S.]

Kain, Peter G. and Dawkins, Peter. The Australian Labour Market, December 1984. *Australian Bull. Lab.*, December 1984, *11*(1), pp. 3–29. [G: Australia; OECD]

Kaufman, Roger T. On Wage Stickiness in Britain's Competitive Sector. *Brit. J. Ind. Relat.*, March 1984, *22*(1), pp. 101–12. [G: U.K.]

Keeley, Michael C. The Economics of Firm Size: Implications from Labor-Market Studies. *Fed. Res. Bank San Francisco Econ. Rev.*, Winter 1984, (1), pp. 5–21. [G: U.S.]

Kemme, David M. Discriminating among Alter-

native Production Functions in Polish Industry. *Empirical Econ.*, 1984, *9*(1), pp. 59–66. [G: Poland]

Ketkar, Kusum W. Environmental Protection Policies and the Structure of the U.S. Economy. *Appl. Econ.*, April 1984, *16*(2), pp. 237–56. [G: U.S.]

Kjeldsen-Kragh, Søren. Valutaindtjening, beskæftigelse og indtjening i landbruget og industrien. (Foreign Exchange Earnings, Employment Effects, and Income Earnings in Different Sectors of the Danish Economy. With English summary.) *Nationaløkon. Tidsskr.*, 1984, *122*(1), pp. 91–[G: Denmark]

Kmietowicz, Z. W. and Silver, Mick S. Some Problems in the Construction of Indexes of Industrial Production for Developing Countries: The Case of Tanzania, 1965–1972. *J. Devel. Areas*, July 1984, *18*(4), pp. 481–99. [G: Tanzania]

Koike, Kazuo. Skill Formation Systems in the U.S. and Japan: A Comparative Study. In *Aoki, M.*, *ed.*, 1984, pp. 47–75. [G: U.S.; Japan]

Kozlow, Ralph. Capital Expenditures by Majority-Owned Foreign Affiliates of U.S. Companies, 1984. *Surv. Curr. Bus.*, March 1984, *64*(3), pp. 32–37. [G: U.S.]

Kumar, Manmohan Singh. Comparative Analysis of UK Domestic and International Firms. *J. Econ. Stud.*, 1984, *11*(3), pp. 26–42. [G: U.K.]

Kunze, Kent. A New BLS Survey Measures the Ratio of Hours Worked to Hours Paid. *Mon. Lab. Rev.*, June 1984, *107*(6), pp. 3–7. [G: U.S.]

Kuroda, Masahiro; Yoshioka, Kanji and Jorgenson, Dale W. Relative Price Changes and Biases of Technical Change in Japan. *Econ. Stud. Quart.*, August 1984, *35*(2), pp. 116–38. [G: Japan; U.S.]

Kwoka, John E., Jr. The Effect of Market Share Distribution on Industry Performance: Reply. *Rev. Econ. Statist.*, May 1984, *66*(2), pp. 358–61. [G: U.S.]

Lackó, Mária. Behavioral Rules in the Distribution of Sectoral Investments in Hungary, 1951–1980. *J. Compar. Econ.*, September 1984, *8*(3), pp. 290–300. [G: Hungary]

Ladbury, Sarah. Choice, Chance or No Alternative? Turkish Cypriots in Business in London. In *Ward, R. and Jenkins, R.*, *eds.*, 1984, pp. 105–24. [G: U.K.]

Laitinen, Erkki K. Empirical Evidence on the Measurement of the Firm. *Liiketaloudellinen Aikak.*, 1984, *33*(4), pp. 405–32. [G: Finland]

Lall, Sanjaya. Exports of Technology by Newly Industrializing Countries: India. *World Devel.*, May/June 1984, *12*(5/6), pp. 535–65. [G: India]

Landefeld, J. Steven and Seskin, Eugene P. Plant and Equipment Expenditures, First and Second Quarters and Second Half of 1984. *Surv. Curr. Bus.*, March 1984, *64*(3), pp. 26–31. [G: U.S.]

Lecraw, Donald J. Diversification Strategy and Performance. *J. Ind. Econ.*, December 1984, *33*(2), pp. 179–98. **[G: Canada]**

de Leeuw, Frank and McKelvey, Michael J. Price Expectations of Business Firms: Bias in the Short and Long Run. *Amer. Econ. Rev.*, March 1984, *74*(1), pp. 99–110. **[G: U.S.]**

Levine, Solomon B. Employers Associations in Japan. In *Windmuller, J. P. and Gladstone, A., eds.*, 1984, pp. 318–56. **[G: Japan]**

Levy, Robert A.; Bowes, Marianne and Jondrow, James M. Technical Advance and Other Sources of Employment Change in Basic Industry. In *Collins, E. L. and Tanner, L. D., eds.*, 1984, pp. 77–95. **[G: U.S.]**

Little, Jane Sneddon. The Industrial Composition of Foreign Direct Investment in the United States and Abroad: A Preliminary Look. *New Eng. Econ. Rev.*, May–June 1984, pp. 38–48. **[G: OECD]**

Littler, D. A.; Pickering, J. F. and Cockerill, T. A. J. The Management of the Small Firm. In *Pickering, J. F. and Cockerill, T. A. J., eds.*, 1984, pp. 388–415. **[G: U.K.; OECD]**

Lubrano, Michel and Sneessens, Henri R. Un modèle de production CES–Léontief pour l'industrie française. (A Léontief–CES Production Model for the French Industry. With English summary.) *Ann. INSEE*, April–June 1984, (54), pp. 3–30. **[G: France]**

MacKinnon, James G. Econometric Methods for Applied General Equilibrium Analysis: Comments. In *Scarf, H. E. and Shoven, J. B., eds.*, 1984, pp. 203–07. **[G: U.S.]**

Maramba, Felix K., Jr. The State of Domestic Essential Industries Today. *Philippine Econ. J.*, Winter 1984, *23*(1), pp. 60–65. **[G: Philippines]**

Marco, Luc. Les défaillances d'entreprises et la crise en France (1974–1983). (With English summary.) *Revue Écon. Polit.*, September–October 1984, *94*(5), pp. 676–87. **[G: France]**

Mars, Gerald and Ward, Robin. Ethnic Business Development in Britain: Opportunities and Resources. In *Ward, R. and Jenkins, R., eds.*, 1984, pp. 1–19. **[G: U.K.]**

Martin, Linda J. and Henderson, Glenn V., Jr. Industry Influence on Financial Structure: A Matter of Interpretation. *Rev. Bus. Econ. Res.*, Spring 1984, *19*(2), pp. 57–67. **[G: U.S.]**

Martinelli, Alberto and Treu, Tiziano. Employers Associations in Italy. In *Windmuller, J. P. and Gladstone, A., eds.*, 1984, pp. 264–93. **[G: Italy]**

Matthews, Nancy Torrance. Shutdown: Twenty-Two Industrial Plant Closings in the U.S., 1977–1982. *Rev. Reg. Stud.*, Winter 1984, *14*(1), pp. 34–44. **[G: U.S.]**

McLennan, Kenneth. Industry Perspectives on Adjustment to Economic Change. In *Collins, E. L. and Tanner, L. D., eds.*, 1984, pp. 163–82. **[G: U.S.]**

Mead, Donald C. Of Contracts and Subcontracts: Small Firms in Vertically Dis-integrated Production/Distribution Systems in LDCs. *World Devel.*, November–December 1984, *12*(11–12), pp. 1095–1106. **[G: LDCs]**

Mohabbat, Khan A.; Dalal, Ardeshir J. and Williams, Martin. Import Demand for India: A Translog Cost Function Approach. *Econ. Develop. Cult. Change*, April 1984, *32*(3), pp. 593–605. **[G: India]**

Morishima, Michio and Prosperetti, Luigi. An Input–Output Analysis of the De-Industrialisation of the U.K. Economy, 1963–1973. *Banca Naz. Lavoro Quart. Rev.*, March 1984, (148), pp. 33–54. **[G: U.K.]**

Mueller, Willard F. and Greer, Douglas F. The Effect of Market Share Distribution on Industry Performance Re-examined. *Rev. Econ. Statist.*, May 1984, *66*(2), pp. 353–58. **[G: U.S.]**

Musgrave, John C. Fixed Reproducible Tangible Wealth in the United States, 1980–83. *Surv. Curr. Bus.*, August 1984, *64*(8), pp. 54–57. **[G: U.S.]**

Mytelka, Lynn Krieger. Foreign Business and Economic Development. In *Zartman, I. W. and Delgado, C. L., eds.*, 1984, pp. 149–73. **[G: Ivory Coast]**

Nakatani, Iwao. The Economic Role of Financial Corporate Grouping. In *Aoki, M., ed.*, 1984, pp. 227–58. **[G: Japan]**

Nomura, Hidekazu. Capital Accumulation by Large Enterprises in Japan. *Kyoto Univ. Econ. Rev.*, April 1984, *54*(1), pp. 11–39. **[G: Japan]**

Oksanen, E. H. and Williams, J. R. Industrial Location and Inter-industry Linkages. *Empirical Econ.*, 1984, *9*(3), pp. 139–50. **[G: Canada]**

Olson, Mancur. Australia in Perspective of the Rise and Decline of Nations. *Australian Econ. Rev.*, 3rd Quarter 1984, (67), pp. 7–17. **[G: Global]**

Palloix, Christian. Crisis and Third World Industrialization. In *Ngo, M., ed., vol. 1*, 1984, pp. 33–53. **[G: LDCs; MDCs]**

Park, Rolla Edward and Acton, Jan Paul. Large Business Customer Response to Time-of-Day Electricity Rates. *J. Econometrics*, September/October 1984, *26*(1/2), pp. 229–52. **[G: U.S.]**

Pashigian, B. Peter. The Effect of Environmental Regulation on Optimal Plant Size and Factor Shares. *J. Law Econ.*, April 1984, *27*(1), pp. 1–28. **[G: U.S.]**

Pasurka, Carl A., Jr. The Short-run Impact of Environmental Protection Costs on U.S. Product Prices. *J. Environ. Econ. Manage.*, December 1984, *11*(4), pp. 380–90. **[G: U.S.]**

Peng, Tian. A Rational Economic Structure Is the Precondition for Healthy Development of the National Economy. *Chinese Econ. Stud.*, Summer 1984, *17*(4), pp. 10–15. **[G: China]**

Pollins, Harold. The Development of Jewish Business in the United Kingdom. In *Ward, R. and Jenkins, R., eds.*, 1984, pp. 73–88. **[G: U.K.]**

Popkin, Joel. The Business Cycle at Various Stages of Process. *J. Bus. Econ. Statist.*, July 1984, *2*(3), pp. 215–23. **[G: U.S.]**

Prosperetti, Luigi. Procedure ottimali di destagionalizzazione e di stima del trend. Alcuni esperimenti con gli indice della produzione industriale. (Optimal Seasonal Adjustment and Trend Estimation: Some Experiments with Industrial Production Indexes. With English summary.) *Statistica*, April–June 1984, *44*(2), pp. 219–33. **[G: Italy]**

Rao, P. S. and Preston, R. S. Inter-factor Substitution, Economies of Scale and Technical Change: Evidence from Canadian Industries. *Empirical Econ.*, 1984, *9*(2), pp. 87–111. **[G: Canada]**

Ray, George F. Changes in Industrial Structure. *Nat. Inst. Econ. Rev.*, February 1984, (107), pp. 50–53. **[G: U.K.]**

Reati, Angelo. Taux de profit et composition organique du capital dans le cycle long de l'après-guerre: le cas de l'industrie du Royaume-Uni de 1959 à 1981. (With English summary.) *Cah. Écon. Bruxelles*, Fourth Trimester 1984, (104), pp. 547–609. **[G: U.K.]**

Reekie, W. Duncan. The Structure-Conduct-Performance Paradigm in a South African Setting. *S. Afr. J. Econ.*, June 1984, *52*(2), pp. 146–55. **[G: S. Africa]**

Reich, Michael. Segmented Labour: Time Series Hypothesis and Evidence. *Cambridge J. Econ.*, March 1984, *8*(1), pp. 63–81. **[G: U.S.]**

Reich, Robert B. Matching Public Policies and Business Strategies: The New Context. **In** *Brooks, H.; Liebman, L. and Schelling, C. S., eds.*, 1984, pp. 263–84. **[G: U.S.]**

Riedel, James; Hall, Chris and Grawe, Roger. Determinants of Indian Export Performance in the 1970s. *Weltwirtsch. Arch.*, 1984, *120*(1), pp. 40–63. **[G: India]**

Rothwell, Sheila G. Company Employment Policies and New Technology in Manufacturing and Service Sectors. **In** *Warner, M., ed.*, 1984, pp. 111–33. **[G: U.K.]**

Rousslang, Donald J. and Parker, Stephen. Cross-Price Elasticities of U.S. Import Demand. *Rev. Econ. Statist.*, August 1984, *66*(3), pp. 518–23. **[G: U.S.]**

Ruben, George. Economy Improves; Bargaining Problems Persist in 1983. *Mon. Lab. Rev.*, January 1984, *107*(1), pp. 33–43. **[G: U.S.]**

Sagafi-Nejad, Tagi. Exports of Technology by Newly Industrializing Countries: Egypt. *World Devel.*, May/June 1984, *12*(5/6), pp. 567–73. **[G: Egypt]**

Samuels, J. M. Company Finance in Europe—The Impact on Small Firms. **In** *Levicki, C., ed.*, 1984, pp. 65–77. **[G: France; U.K.; W. Germany]**

Samuels, J. M. and Morrish, P. A. An Analysis of Concentration. **In** *Levicki, C., ed.*, 1984, pp. 19–41. **[G: U.K.; W. Europe]**

Sauer, Willibrord. Small Firms and the German Economic Miracle. **In** *Levicki, C., ed.*, 1984, pp. 78–88. **[G: W. Germany]**

Scherer, Frederic M. Interindustry Technology Flows in the United States. **In** *Scherer, F. M.*, 1984, pp. 32–58. **[G: U.S.]**

Schreiner, Jean-Paul. Le capital financier et le réseau des liaisons personnelles entre les prin-

cipales sociétés en Suisse. (With English summary.) *Rev. Econ. Ind.*, 3rd Trimester 1984, (29), pp. 78–95.

Schwartz, Sandra L. Up the Down Staircase: The Productivity Decline and Strategies for Recovery. **In** *Bamberg, G. and Spremann, K., eds.*, 1984, pp. 285–306. **[G: OECD]**

Schwarz, Peter M. The Estimated Effects on Industry of Time-of-Day Demand and Energy Electricity Prices. *J. Ind. Econ.*, June 1984, *32*(4), pp. 523–39. **[G: U.S.]**

Sekiguchi, Sueo and Horiuchi, Toshihiro. Foreign Trade and Industrial Policies: A Review of Japanese Experience. **In** *Benjamin, R. and Kudrle, R. T.*, 1984, pp. 81–103. **[G: Japan]**

Sell, Axel. Staatliche Regulierung und Arbeitslosigkeit im internationalen Sektor. (Regulation and Unemployment in the International Sector. With English summary.) *Konjunkturpolitik*, 1984, *30*(4), pp. 189–216. **[G: W. Germany]**

Seskin, Eugene P. Plant and Equipment Expenditures: Quarters of 1984, First and Second Quarters of 1985, Year 1985. *Surv. Curr. Bus.*, December 1984, *64*(12), pp. 23–25. **[G: U.S.]**

Seskin, Eugene P. and Landefeld, J. Steven. Plant and Equipment Expenditures, 1984. *Surv. Curr. Bus.*, January 1984, *64*(1), pp. 26–29. **[G: U.S.]**

Shirom, Arie. Employers Associations in Israel. **In** *Windmuller, J. P. and Gladstone, A., eds.*, 1984, pp. 294–317. **[G: Israel]**

Singer, Hans W. Industrialisation: Where Do We Stand? Where Are We Going? *METU*, 1984, *11*(1–2), pp. 163–75. **[G: LDCs]**

Skogh, Göran. Employers Associations in Sweden. **In** *Windmuller, J. P. and Gladstone, A., eds.*, 1984, pp. 149–68. **[G: Sweden]**

Starnick, Jürgen and Allesch, Jürgen. Compatibility of University Integrity with Industrial Cooperation. **In** *Fusfeld, H. I. and Haklisch, C. S., eds.*, 1984, pp. 129–33.

Stevens, Richard L. Measuring Minority Business Formation and Failure. *Rev. Black Polit. Econ.*, Spring 1984, *12*(4), pp. 71–84. **[G: U.S.]**

Sun, Te-Hsiung. Urban-Industrial Development as a Force in Rural Fertility Change: The Case of Taiwan, Republic of China. **In** *Schutjer, W. A. and Stokes, C. S., eds.*, 1984, pp. 49–76. **[G: Taiwan]**

Sveikauskas, Leo. Science and Technology in Many Different Industries: Data for the Analysis of International Trade. *Rev. Public Data Use*, June 1984, *12*(2), pp. 133–56. **[G: U.S.]**

Tahar, Gabriel. La variance des salaires réels, indicateur d'inégalité. (The Variance of Real Wages as a Measure of Inequality. With English summary.) *Consommation*, 1984, *31*(1), pp. 3–26. **[G: France]**

Tâm, Lê Hông. Vietnam: Building Industrial–Agricultural Complexes. **In** *Ngo, M., ed., vol. 1*, 1984, pp. 523–35. **[G: Vietnam]**

Tannenwald, Robert. The Pros and Cons of

Worldwide Unitary Taxation. *New Eng. Econ. Rev.*, July–August 1984, pp. 17–28.
[G: U.S.]

Tarasofsky, Abraham. Aggregate Rates of Return in Canada. In *Holland, D. M., ed.*, 1984, pp. 313–44. [G: Canada]

Thiemann, Hugo. Overview of Policy Issues: Panel Report on Compatibility of University Integrity with Industrial Cooperation. In *Fusfeld, H. I. and Haklisch, C. S., eds.*, 1984, pp. 135–38.

Tschetter, John H. An Evaluation of BLS' Projections of 1980 Industry Employment. *Mon. Lab. Rev.*, August 1984, *107*(8), pp. 12–22.
[G: U.S.]

Udagawa, Masaru. The Contribution of Sogo Shosha to the Multinationalization of Japanese Industrial Enterprises in Historical Perspective: Comments. In *Okochi, A. and Inoue, T., eds.*, 1984, pp. 93–94. [G: Japan]

Udovenko, V. Location of the Productive Forces and the Effectiveness of Social Production. *Prob. Econ.*, June 1984, *27*(2), pp. 57–74.
[G: U.S.S.R.]

Urquhart, Michael. The Employment Shift to Services: Where Did It Come From? *Mon. Lab. Rev.*, April 1984, *107*(4), pp. 15–22.
[G: U.S.]

Utton, M. A. Concentration, Competition and the Small Firm. In *Levicki, C., ed.*, 1984, pp. 5–18. [G: U.K.]

Van Herck, Gustaaf. Entry, Exit and Profitability. *Managerial Dec. Econ.*, March 1984, *5*(1), pp. 25–31. [G: Belgium]

van Voorden, William. Employers Associations in the Netherlands. In *Windmuller, J. P. and Gladstone, A., eds.*, 1984, pp. 202–31.
[G: Netherlands]

Wakasugi, Takaaki, et al. Measuring the Profitability of the Nonfinancial Corporate Sector in Japan. In *Holland, D. M., ed.*, 1984, pp. 345–86. [G: Japan]

Walter, C. K. and Rives, Janet M. A Discriminant Analysis of Industry Classification by Input Mix. *Rivista Int. Sci. Econ. Com.*, May 1984, *31*(5), pp. 417–31. [G: U.S.]

Wass von Czege, Andreas. New Possibilities of Institutional Choice in the Hungarian Industry—Legal Aspects, First Experiences and Problems. In *Rába, A. and Schenk, K.-E., eds.*, 1984, pp. 33–71. [G: Hungary]

Weiss, Frank D. The Contribution of Small Enterprise to Growth and Employment: Comment. In *Giersch, H., ed.*, 1984, pp. 23–28.
[G: U.S.]

Wessel, Horst A. A Review of the New Literature on Business History and Biography. In *Engels, W. and Pohl, H., eds.*, 1984, pp. 119–53.
[G: W. Germany]

Westphal, Larry E., et al. Exports of Technology by Newly Industrializing Countries: Republic of Korea. *World Devel.*, May/June 1984, *12*(5/6), pp. 505–33. [G: Korea]

Wibe, Sören A. Engineering Production Functions: A Survey. *Economica*, November 1984, *51*(204), pp. 401–11.

Williams, Norman P. The Profitability of United Kingdom Industrial and Commercial Companies 1963–1981. In *Holland, D. M., ed.*, 1984, pp. 155–75. [G: U.K.]

Williams, Norman P. United Kingdom Industrial Sectors' Rates of Return. In *Holland, D. M., ed.*, 1984, pp. 177–219. [G: U.K.]

Wilson, P. E. B. The Role of the Public Sector in the Development of Small Enterprise. In *Ramanadham, V. V., ed.*, 1984, pp. 171–91.
[G: LDCs; MDCs]

Winters, L. Alan. Separability and the Specification of Foreign Trade Functions. *J. Int. Econ.*, November 1984, *17*(3/4), pp. 239–63.
[G: U.K.]

Wright, M.; Coyne, J. and Lockley, H. Regional Aspects of Management Buyouts: Some Evidence. *Reg. Stud.*, October 1984, *18*(5), pp. 428–31. [G: U.K.]

Wyatt, Geoffrey J. Trends in Total Factor Productivity in Finnish and Swedish Industries. In *Mikkelsen, A., et al.*, 1984, pp. 232–40.
[G: Finland; Sweden]

Yasumuro, Ken'ichi. The Contribution of Sogo Shosha to the Multinationalization of Japanese Industrial Enterprises in Historical Perspective. In *Okochi, A. and Inoue, T., eds.*, 1984, pp. 65–92. [G: Japan]

631 Industry Studies: Manufacturing

6310 General

Åberg, Rune. Market-Independent Income Distribution: Efficiency and Legitimacy. In *Goldthorpe, J. H., ed.*, 1984, pp. 209–30.
[G: U.S.; Sweden]

Alam, M. Shahid. Hirschman's Taxonomy of Industries: Some Hypotheses and Evidence. *Econ. Develop. Cult. Change*, January 1984, *32*(2), pp. 367–72. [G: Pakistan]

Alameda, José I. and Mann, Arthur J. Technology Dependency and Energy Substitutability in a Small, Open, and Petroleum-importing Developing Economy: The Case of Puerto Rico. *J. Econ. Devel.*, July 1984, *9*(1), pp. 147–66. [G: Puerto Rico]

Albach, Horst. The Rate of Return in German Manufacturing Industry: Measurement and Policy Implications. In *Holland, D. M., ed.*, 1984, pp. 273–311. [G: W. Germany]

Allen, Robert F. Efficiency, Market Power and Profitability in American Manufacturing: Reply. *Southern Econ. J.*, July 1984, *51*(1), pp. 278–81. [G: U.S.]

Amsden, Alice H. Exports of Technology by Newly Industrializing Countries: Taiwan. *World Devel.*, May/June 1984, *12*(5/6), pp. 491–503. [G: Taiwan]

Artus, Jacques R. Are Real Wages Too High in Europe? *Finance Develop.*, December 1984, *21*(4), pp. 10–13. [G: W. Europe; U.S.; Canada; Japan]

Artus, Jacques R. The Disequilibrium Real Wage Rate Hypothesis: An Empirical Evaluation. *Int. Monet. Fund Staff Pap.*, June 1984, *31*(2), pp. 249–302. [G: OECD]

Artus, Patrick. Analyse du marché des biens dans les secteurs industriels. (An Analysis of the Disequilibrium on the Markets for Manufactured Goods. With English summary.) *Ann. INSEE,* July–December 1984, (55/56), pp. 77–107. **[G: France]**

Balasubramanyam, Venkataraman N. Factor Proportions and Productive Efficiency of Foreign Owned Firms in the Indonesian Manufacturing Sector. *Bull. Indonesian Econ. Stud.,* December 1984, 20(3), pp. 70–94. **[G: Indonesia]**

Ballance, Robert and Sinclair, Stuart. Re-industrialising America: Policy Makers and Interest Groups. *World Econ.,* June 1984, 7(2), pp. 197–214. **[G: U.S.]**

Balydon, R.; Woods, Adrian and Zafiris, N. Inner City versus New Town: A Comparison of Manufacturing Performance. *Oxford Bull. Econ. Statist.,* February 1984, 46(1), pp. 21–29. **[G: U.K.]**

Ban, Kanemi. Energy Prices and Interrelated Factor Demands: A Multivariate Time Series Analysis for the Japanese Manufacturing. (In Japanese. With English summary.) *Osaka Econ. Pap.,* December 1984, 34(2–3), pp. 180–88. **[G: Japan]**

Bayer, Kurt. Profitability in Austrian Industrial Corporations. In *Holland, D. M., ed.,* 1984, pp. 421–64. **[G: Austria]**

Beckers, H. L. The Role of Industry. In *Fusfeld, H. I. and Haklisch, C. S., eds.,* 1984, pp. 143–49.

Beesley, Michael E. and Hamilton, R. T. Small Firms' Seedbed Role and the Concept of Turbulence. *J. Ind. Econ.,* December 1984, 33(2), pp. 217–31. **[G: U.K.]**

Bell, Martin; Ross-Larson, Bruce and Westphal, Larry E. Assessing the Performance of Infant Industries. *J. Devel. Econ.,* September–October 1984, 16(1–2), pp. 101–28. **[G: LDCs]**

Bennett, Adam. Output Expectations of Manufacturing Industry. *Appl. Econ.,* December 1984, 16(6), pp. 869–79. **[G: U.K.]**

ter Berg, Peter and Harkema, Rins. Bayesian Limited-Information Analysis of Nonlinear Simultaneous Equations Systems. *J. Econometrics,* March 1984, 24(3), pp. 379–95. **[G: Netherlands]**

Berg, Sigbjørn Atle. Estimation of Production Capacities in a Putty-Clay Production Model: Norwegian Manufacturing Industries, 1962–81. *Scand. J. Econ.,* 1984, 86(3), pp. 379–84. **[G: Norway]**

Berger, Mark C. Increases in Energy Prices, Costs of Production, and Plant Size. *J. Econ. Bus.,* August 1984, 36(3), pp. 345–57. **[G: U.S.]**

Bhagavan, M. R. A Critique of "Appropriate" Technology for Underdeveloped Countries. In *Ngo, M., ed., vol. 1,* 1984, pp. 143–61. **[G: LDCs]**

Bhagwati, Jagdish N.; Schatz, Klaus-Werner and Wong, Kar-yiu. The West German *Gastar-*

beiter System of Immigration. *Europ. Econ. Rev.,* December 1984, 26(3), pp. 277–94. **[G: W. Germany]**

Bhalla, A. S. and James, J. New Technology Revolution: Myth or Reality for Developing Countries? *Greek Econ. Rev.,* December 1984, 6(3), pp. 387–423. **[G: LDCs]**

Bierbaum, C. B. Structural Change: The South Australian Experience. *Australian Econ. Pap.,* December 1984, 23(43), pp. 281–90. **[G: Australia]**

Blackley, Paul R. A Hedonic Approach to the Decentralization of Manufacturing Activity. *J. Reg. Sci.,* November 1984, 24(4), pp. 541–57. **[G: U.S.]**

Blackley, Paul R.; Follain, James R., Jr. and Ondrich, Jan. Box–Cox Estimation of Hedonic Models: How Serious Is the Iterative OLS Variance Bias? *Rev. Econ. Statist.,* May 1984, 66(2), pp. 348–53. **[G: U.S.]**

Blanchflower, David. Comparative Pay Levels in Domestically-owned and Foreign-owned Manufacturing Plants: A Comment. *Brit. J. Ind. Relat.,* July 1984, 22(2), pp. 265–67. **[G: U.K.]**

Bomhoff, Eduard J. North Sea Oil and Manufacturing Output: Comment. In *Griffiths, B. and Wood, G. E., eds.,* 1984, pp. 200–04. **[G: U.K.; Selected Countries]**

Bos, Henk C. The Role of Industry and Industrial Policies in the Third Development Decade. In *Ghosh, P. K., ed., no. 1,* 1984, *1978,* pp. 30–49. **[G: LDCs]**

Bosi, Paolo and Stagni, Anna. Domanda di fattori e sostituibilità nell'industria italiana: una verifica dell'ipotesi "putty–clay." (With English summary.) *Econ. Polít.,* August 1984, 1(2), pp. 197–241. **[G: Italy]**

Bosworth, Derek and Westaway, Tony. The Influence of Demand and Supply Side Pressures on the Quantity and Quality of Inventive Activity. *Appl. Econ.,* February 1984, 16(1), pp. 131–46. **[G: U.K.]**

Bothwell, James L.; Cooley, Thomas F. and Hall, Thomas E. A New View of the Market Structure–Performance Debate. *J. Ind. Econ.,* June 1984, 32(4), pp. 397–417. **[G: U.S.]**

Bound, John, et al. Who Does R&D and Who Patents? In *Griliches, Z., ed.,* 1984, pp. 21–54. **[G: U.S.]**

Bowman, Edward H. Risk-Return Tradeoffs for Strategic Management: A Response. *Sloan Manage. Rev.,* Spring 1984, 25(3), pp. 50–51. **[G: U.S.]**

Brabec, František. Propects Justified by Experience. *Czech. Econ. Digest.,* June 1984, (4), pp. 14–24. **[G: Czechoslovakia]**

Brada, Josef C. Industrial Policy in Hungary: Lessons for America. *Cato J.,* Fall 1984, 4(2), pp. 485–505. **[G: Hungary]**

Bradley, Michael; Jarrell, Gregg A. and Kim, E. Han. On the Existence of an Optimal Capital Structure: Theory and Evidence. *J. Finance,* July 1984, 39(3), pp. 857–78. **[G: U.S.]**

Bruno, Michael. Raw Materials, Profits, and the

Productivity Slowdown. *Quart. J. Econ.*, February 1984, *99*(1), pp. 1–29. [**G: Japan; U.S.; U.K.; W. Germany**]

Cardani, Angelo M. and Mohnen, Pierre A. Labor Productivity in a Dynamic Model with Energy, Capital and R&D for Italian and French Manufacturing. *Giorn. Econ.*, July–August 1984, *43*(7–8), pp. 471–90. [**G: Italy; France**]

Carlsson, Bo. The Development and Use of Machine Tools in Historical Perspective. *J. Econ. Behav. Organ.*, March 1984, *5*(1), pp. 91–114.

Carlton, Dennis W. Energy and the Location of Industry: Comment. In *Downs, A. and Bradbury, K. L.*, eds., 1984, pp. 219–25. [**G: U.S.**]

Casella, Allesandra. L'elasticità di sostituzione tra lavoro, capitale ed energia nell'industria manifatturiera italiana (1960–78). (The Elasticity of Substitution between Labour, Capital, and Energy in Italian Manufacturing Industry [1960–1978]. With English summary.) *Giorn. Econ.*, July–August 1984, *43*(7–8), pp. 491–505. [**G: Italy**]

Casetti, Emilio. Manufacturing Productivity and Snowbelt–Sunbelt Shifts. *Econ. Geogr.*, October 1984, *60*(4), pp. 313–24. [**G: U.S.**]

Caves, Richard E. Scale, Openness, and Productivity in Manufacturing Industries. In *Caves, R. E. and Krause, L. B.*, eds., 1984, pp. 313–47. [**G: Australia; U.S.**]

Caves, Richard E.; Fortunato, Michael and Ghemawat, Pankaj. The Decline of Dominant Firms, 1905–1929. *Quart. J. Econ.*, August 1984, *99*(3), pp. 523–46. [**G: U.S.**]

Chen, Edward K. Y. Exports of Technology by Newly Industrializing Countries: Hong Kong. *World Devel.*, May/June 1984, *12*(5/6), pp. 481–90. [**G: Hong Kong**]

Cho, David Chinhyung. On Testing the Arbitrage Pricing Theory: Inter-battery Factor Analysis. *J. Finance*, December 1984, *39*(5), pp. 1485–1502. [**G: U.S.**]

Chung, Byung Soo and Lee, Chung H. The Choice of Production Techniques by Foreign and Local Firms in Korea: Reply. *Econ. Develop. Cult. Change*, April 1984, *32*(3), pp. 629–31. [**G: S. Korea**]

Clair, Claude; Gaussens, Olivier and Phan, Duc-Loi. Le commerce international intra-branche et ses déterminants d'après le schéma de concurrence monopolistique: une vérification empirique. (Intra-Industry Trade under Perfect Monopolistic Competition Framework: An Empirical Investigation. With English summary.) *Revue Écon.*, March 1984, *35*(2), pp. 347–78. [**G: OECD**]

Clark, Kim B. Unionization and Firm Performance: The Impact on Profits, Growth, and Productivity. *Amer. Econ. Rev.*, December 1984, *74*(5), pp. 893–919. [**G: U.S.**]

Clark, Kim B. and Griliches, Zvi. Productivity Growth and R&D at the Business Level: Results from the PIMS Data Base. In *Griliches, Z.*, ed., 1984, pp. 393–416. [**G: U.S.**]

Clarke, R. Profit Margins and Market Concentration in UK Manufacturing Industry: 1970–6. *Appl. Econ.*, February 1984, *16*(1), pp. 57–71. [**G: U.K.**]

Clarke, Roger; Davies, Stephen W. and Waterson, Michael. The Profitability–Concentration Relation: Market Power or Efficiency? *J. Ind. Econ.*, June 1984, *32*(4), pp. 435–50. [**G: U.K.**]

Cluver, F. H. and Contogiannis, E. Energy Substitution Responses of South African Manufacturing: An Application of the Translog Production Function. *J. Stud. Econ. Econometrics*, January 1984, (18), pp. 15–35. [**G: S. Africa**]

Coate, Malcolm B. Efficiency, Market Power and Profitability in American Manufacturing: Comment. *Southern Econ. J.*, July 1984, *51*(1), pp. 274–77. [**G: U.S.**]

Contini, Bruno. Firm Size and the Division of Labor. *Banca Naz. Lavoro Quart. Rev.*, December 1984, (151), pp. 367–80. [**G: Italy**]

Culem, Claudy. Comparative Advantage and Industrial Restructuring: The Belgian Case, 1970–1980. *Cah. Écon. Bruxelles*, 3rd Trimester 1984, (103), pp. 457–84. [**G: Belgium**]

Cuneo, Philippe and Mairesse, Jacques. Productivity and R&D at the Firm Level in French Manufacturing. In *Griliches, Z.*, ed., 1984, pp. 375–92. [**G: France**]

Delfino, José A. Análisis económico de la tecnología del sector manufacturero Argentino. (Economic Analysis of Argentina's Manufacturing Technology. With English summary.) *Económica*, May-December 1984, *30*(2–3), pp. 149–202. [**G: Argentina**]

Dimsdale, N. H. Employment and Real Wages in the Inter-war Period. *Nat. Inst. Econ. Rev.*, November 1984, (110), pp. 94–103. [**G: U.K.**]

Diwan, Rauf and Hamid, Javed. The Potential for Industrial Development. In *Burki, S. J. and LaPorte, R., Jr.*, eds., 1984, pp. 84–102. [**G: Pakistan**]

Dolan, Robert C. Price Behavior in Tight Oligopoly. *Rev. Ind. Organ.*, Fall 1984, *1*(3), pp. 160–88. [**G: U.S.**]

Dollery, B. E. A South African Test of the Blair Target Return Model. *J. Stud. Econ. Econometrics*, July 1984, (20), pp. 28–39. [**G: S. Africa**]

Dormont, Brigitte. Productivité-croissance quelle relation a moyen-long terme? Un rapprochement des modèles de Brechling et de Kaldor–Verdoorn. (Productivity and Growth: What Is the Long-Run Relationship? Bringing Together Brechling's and Kaldor–Verdoorn's Models. With English summary.) *Revue Écon.*, May 1984, *35*(3), pp. 447–78. [**G: France; W. Germany**]

Dornbusch, Rudiger. The Overvalued Dollar. *Lloyds Bank Rev.*, April 1984, (152), pp. 1–12. [**G: U.S.; Japan; W. Germany**]

Ducos, Gilbert and Laffont, Jean-Jacques. Stock et déséquilibre: une analyse comparative et internationale. (Inventories and Disequilibrium: A Comparative International Analysis. With

English summary.) *Ann. INSEE*, July–December 1984, (55/56), pp. 183–202. [G: U.S.; France; Canada; Japan]

Dudley, David M. Industrial Concentration and Price Stability: An Empirical Analysis. *Amer. Econ.*, Fall 1984, 28(2), pp. 26–35. [G: U.S.]

Duetsch, Larry L. Entry and the Extent of Multiplant Operations. *J. Ind. Econ.*, June 1984, 32(4), pp. 477–87. [G: U.S.]

Edelstein, Michael. Discussion [The Decline of the British Economy: An Institutional Perspective] [Structural Transformation and the Demand for New Labor in Advanced Economies: Interwar Britain]. *J. Econ. Hist.*, June 1984, 44(2), pp. 599–602. [G: U.K.]

Elbaum, Bernard and Lazonick, William. The Decline of the British Economy: An Institutional Perspective. *J. Econ. Hist.*, June 1984, 44(2), pp. 567–83. [G: U.K.]

Ellman, Michael. Seven Theses on Kosyginism. In *Ellman, M.*, 1984, 1977, pp. 75–96. [G: U.S.S.R.]

Enders, Klaus. Strukturelle Konsequenzen eines Rohstoffbooms in einem Industrieland: De-Industrialisierungstheorie und norwegische Erfahrungen. (Structural Consequences of a Resource Boom in an Industrialized Economy: De-industrialization Theory and Norwegian Experience. With English summary.) *Konjunkturpolitik*, 1984, 30(6), pp. 328–47. [G: Norway]

Ersenkal, Caryl R. and Dillman, B. L. The Product Cycle and Shifts in the Location of Manufacturing. *Reg. Sci. Persp.*, 1984, 14(1), pp. 30–39. [G: U.S.]

Ershov, E. B. Aggregation Analysis of Systems of Linear Equations, Input–Output Models, and Econometric Models. *Matekon*, Fall 1984, 21(1), pp. 28–53. [G: U.S.S.R.]

Ettlie, John E. Implementation Strategy for Manufacturing Innovations. In *Warner, M.*, ed., 1984, pp. 31–48.

Evenson, Robert E. International Invention: Implications for Technology Market Analysis. In *Griliches, Z.*, ed., 1984, pp. 89–123. [G: Global]

Farber, Stephen C. Cyclical Price Flexibility: A Test of Administered Pricing. *J. Ind. Econ.*, June 1984, 32(4), pp. 465–76. [G: U.S.]

Feinberg, Robert M. Strategic and Deterrent Pricing Responses to Antitrust Investigations. *Int. J. Ind. Organ.*, March 1984, 2(1), pp. 75–84. [G: U.S.]

Fichet, Gerard and Gonzalez, Norberto. The Production Structure and the Dynamics of Development. In *Ghosh, P. K.*, ed., no. 7, 1984, 1976, pp. 362–407. [G: Latin America; OECD]

FitzRoy, Felix R. and Kraft, Kornelius. Mitarbeiterbeteiligung bei deutschen Industrieakitiengesellschaften—Ein Kommetar. (With English summary.) *Z. Betriebswirtshaft*, January 1984, 54(1), pp. 79–83. [G: W. Germany]

Fothergill, Stephen, et al. Differences in the Profitability of the U.K. Manufacturing Sector between Conurbations and Other Areas. *Scot. J. Polit. Econ.*, February 1984, 31(1), pp. 72–91. [G: U.K.]

Franz, Wolfgang. Inflation und interindustrielle Lohnstruktur. (Inflation and the Interindustrial Wage Structure. With English summary.) *Ifo-Studien*, 1984, 30(2), pp. 81–106. [G: Germany]

Gallant, A. Ronald and Golub, Gene H. Imposing Curvature Restrictions on Flexible Functional Forms. *J. Econometrics*, December 1984, 26(3), pp. 295–321. [G: U.S.]

Garofalo, Gasper A. and Malhotra, Devinder M. Input Substitution in the Manufacturing Sector during the 1970's: A Regional Analysis. *J. Reg. Sci.*, February 1984, 24(1), pp. 51–63. [G: U.S.]

Gay, Robert S. Union Settlements and Aggregate Wage Behavior in the 1980s. *Fed. Res. Bull.*, December 1984, 70(12), pp. 843–56. [G: U.S.]

Gertler, Meric S. The Dynamics of Regional Capital Accumulation. *Econ. Geogr.*, April 1984, 60(2), pp. 150–74. [G: U.S.]

Geyikdagi, Yasar M. On International Diversification and the Interrelationship of Major Economies. *Rivista Int. Sci. Econ. Com.*, August 1984, 31(8), pp. 801–07. [G: U.S.]

Gibbons, Joel C. The Optimal Durability of Fixed Capital When Demand Is Uncertain. *J. Bus.*, July 1984, 57(3), pp. 389–403. [G: U.S.]

Gisser, Micha. Price Leadership and Dynamic Aspects of Oligopoly in U.S. Manufacturing. *J. Polit. Econ.*, December 1984, 92(6), pp. 1035–48. [G: U.S.]

Goudie, Andrew W. and Meeks, G. Individual Economic Agents in a Macroeconomic Model: UK Companies in Cambridge MDM. *J. Policy Modeling*, August 1984, 6(3), pp. 289–309. [G: U.K.]

Gould, Andrew and Keeble, David. New Firms and Rural Industrialization in East Anglia. *Reg. Stud.*, June 1984, 18(3), pp. 189–201. [G: U.K.]

Griliches, Zvi and Lichtenberg, Frank R. Interindustry Technology Flows and Productivity Growth: A Re-examination. *Rev. Econ. Statist.*, May 1984, 66(2), pp. 324–29. [G: U.S.]

Griliches, Zvi and Lichtenberg, Frank R. R&D and Productivity Growth at the Industry Level: Is There Still a Relationship? In *Griliches, Z.*, ed., 1984, pp. 465–96. [G: U.S.]

Grimes, Arthur. The Impact of Taxes on Wages: A Comment. *Econ. Notes*, 1984, (3), pp. 163–66. [G: U.S.]

Grunwald, Joseph. Some Reflections on Latin American Industrial Integration. In *Núñez del Arco, J.; Margain, E. and Cherol, R.*, eds., 1984, pp. 115–25. [G: Latin America]

Gudgin, G. and Fothergill, Stephen. Geographical Variation in the Rate of Formation of New Manufacturing Firms. *Reg. Stud.*, June 1984, 18(3), pp. 203–06. [G: U.K.]

Hall, V. B. and Saunders, Peter. Further Evidence from Survey Data on Australian Manufacturing Price Changes. *Econ. Rec.*, March 1984, *60*(168), pp. 68–84. **[G: Australia]**

Haltmaier, Jane. Measuring Technical Change. *Econ. J.*, December 1984, *94*(376), pp. 924–30. **[G: U.S.]**

Hamada, Koichi and Kurosaka, Yoshio. The Relationship between Production and Unemployment in Japan: Okun's Law in Comparative Perspective. *Europ. Econ. Rev.*, June 1984, *25*(1), pp. 71–94. **[G: U.S.; Japan]**

Haraf, William S. The Relationship between Production and Unemployment in Japan: Okun's Law in Comparative Perspective: Comments. *Europ. Econ. Rev.*, June 1984, *25*(1), pp. 95–98. **[G: U.S.; Japan]**

Harris, Richard G. Applied General Equilibrium Analysis of Small Open Economies with Scale Economies and Imperfect Competition. *Amer. Econ. Rev.*, December 1984, *74*(5), pp. 1016–32. **[G: Canada]**

Hartmann, Gert, et al. Consequences of CNC Technology: A Study of British and West German Manufacturing Firms. In *Warner, M.*, ed., 1984, pp. 311–24. **[G: W. Germany; U.K.]**

den Hartog, Hans. Empirical Vintage Models for the Netherlands: A Review in Outline. *De Economist*, 1984, *132*(3), pp. 326–49. **[G: Netherlands]**

Hause, John C. and Du Rietz, Gunnar. Entry, Industry Growth, and the Microdynamics of Industry Supply. *J. Polit. Econ.*, August 1984, *92*(4), pp. 733–57. **[G: Sweden]**

Hazilla, Michael and Kopp, Raymond J. Assessing U.S. Vulnerability to Raw Material Supply Disruptions: An Application to Nonfuel Minerals. *Southern Econ. J.*, October 1984, *51*(2), pp. 341–55. **[G: U.S.]**

Hazledine, Tim. The Possibility of Price Umbrellas in Canadian Manufacturing Industries. *Int. J. Ind. Organ.*, September 1984, *2*(3), pp. 251–62. **[G: Canada]**

Healey, Michael and Clark, David. Industrial Decline and Government Response in the West Midlands: The Case of Coventry. *Reg. Stud.*, August 1984, *18*(4), pp. 303–18. **[G: U.K.]**

Heim, Carol E. Structural Transformation and the Demand for New Labor in Advanced Economies: Interwar Britain. *J. Econ. Hist.*, June 1984, *44*(2), pp. 585–95. **[G: U.K.]**

Heimler, Alberto. Price Behaviour in the Italian Manufacturing Industry. *Europ. Econ. Rev.*, December 1984, *26*(3), pp. 339–51. **[G: Italy]**

Held, Thomas. Mitarbeiterbeteiligung bei deutschen Industrieaktiengesellschaften: Eine Entgegnung. (With English summary.) *Z. Betriebswirtshaft*, January 1984, *54*(1), pp. 84–88. **[G: W. Germany]**

Henderson, Robert A. The Employment Performance of Established Manufacturing Industry in the Scottish New Towns. *Urban Stud.*, August 1984, *21*(3), pp. 295–315. **[G: U.K.]**

Hiemenz, Ulrich. Structural Change in Manufacturing: Issues and Perspectives for Developing Asian Countries. In *Benjamin, R. and Kudrle, R. T.*, 1984, pp. 13–34. **[G: S.E. Asia; U.S.]**

Hilton, H. Geoffrey. The International Finance Corporation. In *Weiss, C. and Jéquier, N.*, eds., 1984, pp. 227–45.

Hindley, Brian. Economics and Small Enterprises. In *Levicki, C., ed.*, 1984, pp. 42–54. **[G: OECD]**

Hirsch, Barry T. and Berger, Mark C. Union Membership Determination and Industry Characteristics. *Southern Econ. J.*, January 1984, *50*(3), pp. 665–79. **[G: U.S.]**

Hirsch, Barry T. and Link, Albert N. Unions, Productivity, and Productivity Growth. *J. Lab. Res.*, Winter 1984, *5*(1), pp. 29–37. **[G: U.S.]**

Hirschey, Mark and Wichern, Dean W. Accounting and Market-Value Measures of Profitability: Consistency, Determinants, and Uses. *J. Bus. Econ. Statist.*, October 1984, *2*(4), pp. 375–83. **[G: U.S.]**

Holland, Daniel M. Measuring Profitability and Capital Costs: Introduction and Summary. In *Holland, D. M., ed.*, 1984, pp. 1–42. **[G: OECD; Finland]**

Hood, Neil. The Small-Firm Sector. In *Hood, N. and Young, S., eds.*, 1984, pp. 57–92. **[G: U.K.; OECD]**

Howland, Marie. Age of Capital and Regional Business Cycles. *Growth Change*, April 1984, *15*(2), pp. 29–37. **[G: U.S.]**

Hulten, Charles R. and Schwab, Robert M. Regional Productivity Growth in U.S. Manufacturing: 1951–78. *Amer. Econ. Rev.*, March 1984, *74*(1), pp. 152–62. **[G: U.S.]**

Humphrey, John. The Growth of Female Employment in Brazilian Manufacturing Industry in the 1970s. *J. Devel. Stud.*, July 1984, *20*(4), pp. 224–47. **[G: Brazil]**

Inoue, Tadakatsu. A Comparison of the Emergence of Multinational Manufacturing by U.S., European, and Japanese Firms. In *Okochi, A. and Inoue, T., eds.*, 1984, pp. 3–20. **[G: Europe; Japan; U.S.]**

Jacoby, Sanford M. The Development of Internal Labor Markets in American Manufacturing Firms. In *Osterman, P., ed.*, 1984, pp. 23–69. **[G: U.S.]**

Jacquemin, Alexis and Rainelli, Michel. Filières de la nation et filières de l'entreprise. (State and Firm "Filieres." With English summary.) *Revue Écon.*, March 1984, *35*(2), pp. 379–92. **[G: France]**

Johansson, Börje and Marksjö, Bertil. Interactive Systems for Regional Analysis of Industrial Sectors. In *Nijkamp, P. and Rietveld, P., eds.*, 1984, pp. 231–49. **[G: Sweden]**

Jones, Geoffrey. The Expansion of British Multinational Manufacturing, 1890–1939. In *Okochi, A. and Inoue, T., eds.*, 1984, pp. 125–53. **[G: U.K.]**

Jones, J. C. H. and Walsh, W. D. Inter-Industry Strike Frequencies: Some Pooled Cross-Sectional Evidence from Canadian Secondary Manufacturing. *J. Lab. Res.*, Fall 1984, *5*(4), pp. 419–25. **[G: Canada]**

Jorgenson, Dale W. The Role of Energy in Productivity Growth. *Amer. Econ. Rev.*, May 1984, *74*(2), pp. 26–30. [G: U.S.]

Jorgenson, Dale W. The Role of Energy in Productivity Growth. *Energy J.*, July 1984, *5*(3), pp. 11–26.

Kale, Steven R. U.S. Industrial Development Incentives and Manufacturing Growth during the 1970s. *Growth Change*, January 1984, *15*(1), pp. 26–34. [G: U.S.]

Kardasz, Stanley W. and Stollery, Kenneth R. Simultaneous Equation Models of Profitability, Advertising and Concentration for Canadian Manufacturing Industries. *Quart. J. Bus. Econ.*, Winter 1984, *23*(1), pp. 51–64. [G: Canada]

Kawasaki, S.; Gahlen, D. and Buck, Andrew J. The Variability of Relative Price Expectations, the Rate of Inflation and the Phillips Curve. In *Oppenländer, K. H. and Poser, G., eds.*, 1984, pp. 499–539. [G: W. Germany]

Kay, John A. North Sea Oil and Manufacturing Output. In *Griffiths, B. and Wood, G. E., eds.*, 1984, pp. 185–99. [G: U.K.; Selected Countries]

Kendrick, John W. U.S. Economic Policy and Productivity Growth. *Cato J.*, Fall 1984, *4*(2), pp. 387–400. [G: U.S.]

Khanna, Ashok. Market Distortions and Export Performance: India's Exports of Manufactures in the 1970s. *Weltwirtsch. Arch.*, 1984, *120*(2), pp. 348–60. [G: India]

Kim, Jae Won. CES Production Functions in Manufacturing and Problems of Industrialization in LDCs: Evidence from Korea. *Econ. Develop. Cult. Change*, October 1984, *33*(1), pp. 143–65.

King, Mervyn A. and Mairesse, Jacques. Profitability in Britain and France 1956–1975: A Comparative Study. In *Holland, D. M., ed.*, 1984, pp. 221–71. [G: U.K.; France]

Kinugasa, Yosuke. Japanese Firms' Foreign Direct Investment in the U.S. In *Okochi, A. and Inoue, T., eds.*, 1984, pp. 21–60. [G: Japan]

Kipnis, Baruch A. Plant Size and Urban Growth. *Urban Stud.*, February 1984, *21*(1), pp. 53–61. [G: Brazil]

Kleinknecht, Alfred. Prosperity, Crisis and Innovation Patterns. *Cambridge J. Econ.*, September 1984, *8*(3), pp. 251–70. [G: N. America; U.K.; W. Germany; Japan; France]

Koekkoek, K. Ad and Mennes, Loet B. M. Revealed Comparative Advantage in Manufacturing Industry: The Case of the Netherlands. *De Economist*, 1984, *132*(1), pp. 30–48. [G: W. Germany; Belgium; Netherlands]

Kohn, Robert E. Input–Output Analysis and Air Pollution Control. In *Ahmad, Y. J.; Dasgupta, P. and Mäler, K.-G., eds.*, 1984, pp. 322–58. [G: U.S.]

Kokkelenberg, Edward C. The Specification and Estimation of Interrelated Factor Demands under Uncertainty. *J. Econ. Dynam. Control*, September 1984, *7*(3), pp. 181–207. [G: U.S.]

Koo, Anthony Y. C. and Martin, Stephen. Market

Structure and U.S. Trade Flows. *Int. J. Ind. Organ.*, September 1984, *2*(3), pp. 173–97. [G: U.S.]

Koskenkylä, Heikki. Rates of Return, Cost of Capital, and Valuation Rates in Finnish Manufacturing 1960–1980. In *Holland, D. M., ed.*, 1984, pp. 387–419. [G: Finland]

Koutsoyiannis, Anna. Goals of Oligopolistic Firms: An Empirical Test of Competing Hypotheses. *Southern Econ. J.*, October 1984, *51*(2), pp. 540–67. [G: U.S.]

Kračun, Davorin. Aktivizacijska doba investicij v Jugoslaviji—Metodologija in izračun. (Maturation Period of Investment in Yugoslavia—Methodology and Computation. With English summary.) *Econ. Anal. Worker's Manage.*, 1984, *18*(3), pp. 201–16. [G: Yugoslavia]

Kumar, Krishna and Kim, Kee Young. The Korean Manufacturing Multinationals. *J. Int. Bus. Stud.*, Spring/Summer 1984, *15*(1), pp. 45–61. [G: Korea]

Lakhtin, G. and Pavlenko, Iu. The Science-Intensiveness Indicator of an Economic Branch. *Prob. Econ.*, November 1984, *27*(7), pp. 61–75. [G: U.S.S.R.; U.S.]

Lakhshmanan, T. R.; Anderson, W. and Jourabchi, M. Regional Dimensions of Factor and Fuel Substitution in U.S. Manufacturing. *Reg. Sci. Urban Econ.*, August 1984, *14*(3), pp. 381–98. [G: U.S.]

Lanteri, Marc. La multinationalisation des firmes européennes aux États-Unis: une approche dynamique. (The Spreading of European Multinational Firms in the U.S.A.: A Dynamic Approach. With English summary.) *Revue Écon.*, July 1984, *35*(4), pp. 733–49. [G: U.S.]

Laumas, Prem S. and Williams, Martin. The Demand for Working Capital. *Appl. Econ.*, December 1984, *16*(6), pp. 791–98. [G: India]

Lawrence, R. J. The Lognormal Distribution of the Duration of Strikes. *J. Roy. Statist. Soc.*, 1984, *147*(3), pp. 464–83. [G: U.K.]

Lee, Chung H. The Diffusion of Technology and Growth of Factor Productivity in Korean Manufacturing Industries. *J. Econ. Devel.*, July 1984, *9*(1), pp. 25–44. [G: S. Korea]

Lee, Chung H. Transfer of Technology from Japan and the United States to Korean Manufacturing Industries: A Comparative Study. *Hitotsubashi J. Econ.*, December 1984, *25*(2), pp. 125–36. [G: U.S.; Japan; Korea]

Leo, Hooi-Eng. Effects of Trade Policies on the Structure and Growth of Manufacturing Industries in Peninsular Malaysia: 1960–1980. *Philippine Rev. Econ. Bus.*, Sept./Dec. 1984, *21*(3/4), pp. 219–38. [G: Malaysia]

Leroux, François and Zaccour, Georges. Structures de marché et intensité de la publicité. (Market Structures and Intensity of Publicity. With English summary.) *L'Actual. Écon.*, September 1984, *60*(3), pp. 341–54. [G: Canada]

Leslie, Derek. The Productivity of Hours in U.S. Manufacturing Industries. *Rev. Econ. Statist.*, August 1984, *66*(3), pp. 486–90. [G: U.S.]

Levy, David T. Testing Stigler's Interpretation of "The Division of Labor Is Limited by the

Extent of the Market." *J. Ind. Econ.*, March 1984, *32*(3), pp. 377–89.   [G: U.S.]

Liew, Chong K. and Liew, Chung J. Measuring the Development Impact of a Proposed Transportation System. *Reg. Sci. Urban Econ.*, May 1984, *14*(2), pp. 175–98.   [G: U.S.]

Lipschitz, Leslie and Schadler, Susan M. Relative Prices, Real Wages, and Macroeconomic Policies: Some Evidence from Manufacturing in Japan and the United Kingdom. *Int. Monet. Fund Staff Pap.*, June 1984, *31*(2), pp. 303–38.   [G: Japan; U.K.]

Littman, Daniel A. and Lee, Myung-Hoon. Plant Closings and Worker Dislocation. In *McKenzie, R. B., ed. (II)*, 1984, *1983*, pp. 127–54.   [G: U.S.]

Livingstone, Ian. Resource-Based Industrial Development: Past Experience and Future Prospects in Malawi. *Industry Devel.*, 1984, (10), pp. 75–135.   [G: Malawi]

Lloyd, P. E. and Mason, C. M. Spatial Variations in New Firm Formation in the United Kingdom: Comparative Evidence from Merseyside, Greater Manchester and South Hampshire. *Reg. Stud.*, June 1984, *18*(3), pp. 207–20.   [G: U.K.]

Maccini, Louis J. and Rossana, Robert J. Joint Production, Quasi-Fixed Factors of Production, and Investement in Finished Goods Inventories. *J. Money, Credit, Banking*, May 1984, *16*(2), pp. 218–36.   [G: U.S.]

MacDonald, James M. Diversification, Market Growth, and Concentration in U.S. Manufacturing. *Southern Econ. J.*, April 1984, *50*(4), pp. 1098–111.   [G: U.S.]

Mairesse, Jacques. The Relationship between Production and Unemployment in Japan: Okun's Law in Comparative Perspective: Comments. *Europ. Econ. Rev.*, June 1984, *25*(1), pp. 99–105.   [G: U.S.; Japan; EEC]

Mangan, John and Stokes, Leigh. The Determinants of Labour Demand in Australian Manufacturing. *S. Afr. J. Econ.*, September 1984, *52*(3), pp. 296–308.   [G: Australia]

Mangan, John and Stokes, Leigh. The Determinants of Labour Demand in Australian Manufacturing. *Appl. Econ.*, June 1984, *16*(3), pp. 449–59.   [G: Australia]

Mansfield, Edwin. Using Linked Patent and R&D Data to Measure Interindustry Technology Flows: Comment. In *Griliches, Z., ed.*, 1984, pp. 461–64.   [G: U.S.]

Marsden, Keith. Services for Small Firms: The Roles of Government Programmes and Market Networks in Thailand. *Int. Lab. Rev.*, March-April 1984, *123*(2), pp. 235–49.
                                    [G: Thailand]

Marsh, Terry A. and Swanson, Douglas S. Risk-Return Tradeoffs for Strategic Management. *Sloan Manage. Rev.*, Spring 1984, *25*(3), pp. 35–49.   [G: U.S.]

Marshall, William J.; Yawitz, Jess B. and Greenberg, Edward. Incentives for Diversification and the Structure of the Conglomerate Firm. *Southern Econ. J.*, July 1984, *51*(1), pp. 1–23.   [G: U.S.]

Martin, Robert E. Stochastic Input Supply: Theory and Evidence. *Appl. Econ.*, June 1984, *16*(3), pp. 343–54.   [G: U.S.]

Maruo, Naomi. Productivity Improvement in Japan: An Econometric Analysis. In *Intn'l. Productivity Symp.*, 1984, pp. 219–65.
                                    [G: Japan]

Marvel, Howard P. The Locus of Collusion in U.S. Manufacturing. *Quart. Rev. Econ. Bus.*, Winter 1984, *24*(4), pp. 82–99.   [G: U.S.]

Masson, Robert T. and Shaanan, Joseph. Social Costs of Oligopoly and the Value of Competition. *Econ. J.*, September 1984, *94*(375), pp. 520–35.   [G: U.S.]

Matolcsy, Z. P. The Micro Effects of Inflation on Corporate Taxation and Profitability: Some Empirical Evidence for Seventeen Industry Groups. *Econ. Rec.*, December 1984, *60*(171), pp. 356–65.   [G: Australia]

McCawley, Peter. A Slowdown in Industrial Growth? *Bull. Indonesian Econ. Stud.*, December 1984, *20*(3), pp. 158–74.
                                    [G: Indonesia]

McCombie, J. S. L. and de Ridder, J. R. "The Verdoorn Law Controversy": Some New Empirical Evidence Using U.S. State Data. *Oxford Econ. Pap.*, June 1984, *36*(2), pp. 268–84.   [G: U.S.]

McHugh, Richard and Widdows, Richard. The Age of Capital and State Unemployment Rates. *J. Reg. Sci.*, February 1984, *24*(1), pp. 85–92.
                                    [G: U.S.]

Meredith, Lindsay Norman. U.S. Multinational Investment in Canadian Manufacturing Industries. *Rev. Econ. Statist.*, February 1984, *66*(1), pp. 111–19.   [G: U.S.; Canada]

Mikkelson, Wayne H. On the Existence of an Optimal Capital Structure: Theory and Evidence: Discussion. *J. Finance*, July 1984, *39*(3), pp. 878–80.   [G: U.S.]

Miller, James P. Manufacturing Relocations in the United States, 1969–1975. In *McKenzie, R. B., ed. (II)*, 1984, pp. 29–47.   [G: U.S.]

Minford, Patrick. North Sea Oil and Manufacturing Output: Comment. In *Griffiths, B. and Wood, G. E., eds.*, 1984, pp. 205–10.
                        [G: U.K.; Selected Countries]

Miyamoto, Matao. Multinational Growth of Japanese Manufacturing Enterprises in the Postwar Period: Comments. In *Okochi, A. and Inoue, T., eds.*, 1984, pp. 121–23. [G: Japan; U.S.; W. Europe]

Momigliano, Franco and Siniscalco, Domenico. Technology and International Specialization. *Banca Naz. Lavoro Quart. Rev.*, September 1984, (150), pp. 257–84.   [G: Italy]

Morgan, Ann D. Protectionism and European Trade in Manufactures. *Nat. Inst. Econ. Rev.*, August 1984, (109), pp. 45–57.   [G: EEC; EFTA]

Mueller, Willard F. and Rogers, Richard T. Changes in Market Concentration of Manufacturing Industries 1947–1977. *Rev. Ind. Organ.*, Spring 1984, *1*(1), pp. 1–14. [G: U.S.]

Muramatsu, Kuramitsu. The Effect of Trade Unions on Productivity in Japanese Manufacturing Industries. In *Aoki, M., ed.*, 1984, pp. 103–23. **[G: Japan]**

Narongchai, Akransanee. Industrialization of ASEAN and Structural Adjustment in the Pacific. In *Benjamin, R. and Kudrle, R. T.*, 1984, pp. 59–78. **[G: ASEAN]**

Nemoto, Jiro. On Substitution Possibilities between Energy and Non-energy Inputs—A Nested CES Production Function Analysis. (In Japanese. With English summary.) *Econ. Stud. Quart.*, August 1984, *35*(2), pp. 139–58. **[G: Japan]**

Neumann, George R. and Reder, Melvin W. Output and Strike Activity in U.S. Manufacturing: How Large Are the Losses? *Ind. Lab. Relat. Rev.*, January 1984, *37*(2), pp. 197–211. **[G: U.S.]**

Nickell, Stephen J. An Investigation of the Determinants of Manufacturing Employment in the United Kingdom. *Rev. Econ. Stud.*, October 1984, *51*(4), pp. 529–57. **[G: U.K.]**

Nilsen, Diane M. Employment in Durable Goods Anything But Durable in 1979–82. *Mon. Lab. Rev.*, February 1984, *107*(2), pp. 15–24. **[G: U.S.]**

Nishimizu, Mieko and Robinson, Sherman. Trade Policies and Productivity Change in Semi-industrialized Countries. *J. Devel. Econ.*, September–October 1984, *16*(1–2), pp. 177–206. **[G: S. Korea; Turkey; Yugoslavia; Japan]**

Nishina, Kazuhiko. Recent Trend in Corporate Profitability in Japan. (In Japanese. With English summary.) *Osaka Econ. Pap.*, December 1984, *34*(2–3), pp. 203–17. **[G: Japan]**

Norman, George and Dunning, John H. Intra-industry Foreign Direct Investment: Its Rationale and Trade Effects. *Weltwirtsch. Arch.*, 1984, *120*(3), pp. 522–40. **[G: U.S.; U.K.; Germany; France; Japan]**

Nove, Alec. The Soviet Economy: Problems and Prospects. In *Hoffmann, E. P. and Laird, R. F., eds.*, 1984, *1980*, pp. 447–65. **[G: U.S.S.R.]**

O'Farrell, P. N. Components of Manufacturing Employment Change in Ireland, 1973–1981. *Urban Stud.*, May 1984, *21*(2), pp. 155–76. **[G: Ireland]**

O'Farrell, P. N. and Crouchley, Robert. An Industrial and Spatial Analysis of New Firm Formation in Ireland. *Reg. Stud.*, June 1984, *18*(3), pp. 221–36. **[G: Ireland]**

Odaka, Konosuke. Skill Formation in Development: Case Studies of Philippine Manufacturing (II). *Hitotsubashi J. Econ.*, December 1984, *25*(2), pp. 105–23. **[G: Philippines]**

Olson, Dennis O. and Bumpass, Donald L. An Intertemporal Analysis of the Welfare Cost of Monopoly Power: U.S. Manufacturing 1967–1981. *Rev. Ind. Organ.*, Winter 1984, *1*(4), pp. 308–22. **[G: U.S.]**

Olson, Dennis O. and Bumpass, Donald L. Welfare Cost of Monopoly Power. *Atlantic Econ. J.*, December 1984, *12*(4), pp. 63. **[G: U.S.]**

Onofri, Paolo and Stagni, Anna. Rate of Profit and Return on Financial Assets in Italian Indus-

try 1951–1981. In *Holland, D. M., ed.*, 1984, pp. 465–80. **[G: Italy]**

Oxelheim, Lars. The Largest Nordic Manufacturing Companies. In *Mikkelsen, A., et al.*, 1984, pp. 184–201. **[G: Scandinavia]**

Pack, Howard. The Choice of Production Techniques by Foreign and Local Firms in Korea: Comment. *Econ. Develop. Cult. Change*, April 1984, *32*(3), pp. 625–28. **[G: S. Korea]**

Pack, Howard. Total Factor Productivity and Its Determinants: Some International Comparisons. In *[Reynolds, L. G.]*, 1984, pp. 17–41. **[G: Israel; Philippines; U.S.]**

Page, John M., Jr. Firm Size and Technical Efficiency: Applications of Production Frontiers to Indian Survey Data. *J. Devel. Econ.*, September–October 1984, *16*(1–2), pp. 129–52. **[G: India]**

Pakes, Ariel and Schankerman, Mark. An Exploration into the Determinants of Research Intensity. In *Griliches, Z., ed.*, 1984, pp. 209–32. **[G: U.S.]**

Park, Eul Y. Patterns of Foreign Direct Investment, Foreign Ownership, and Industrial Performance: The Case of the Korean Manufacturing Industry. In *Benjamin, R. and Kudrle, R. T.*, 1984, pp. 127–60. **[G: S. Korea]**

Pasha, Hafiz A. and Qureshi, Tahira. Capacity Utilisation in Selected Industries of Pakistan. *Pakistan J. Appl. Econ.*, Summer 1984, *3*(1), pp. 29–56. **[G: Pakistan]**

Peck, Francis and Townsend, Alan. Contrasting Experience of Recession and Spatial Restructuring: British Shipbuilders, Plessey and Metal Box. *Reg. Stud.*, August 1984, *18*(4), pp. 319–38. **[G: U.K.]**

Peet, Richard. Class Struggle, the Relocation of Employment, and Economic Crisis. *Sci. Soc.*, Spring 1984, *48*(1), pp. 38–51. **[G: U.S.]**

Phillips, David A. Choice of Technology and Industrial Transformation: The Case of the United Republic of Tanzania. In *Ghosh, P. K., ed., no. 3*, 1984, *1980*, pp. 325–51. **[G: Tanzania]**

Pickering, J. F. and Sheldon, I. M. International Trade Performance and Concentration in British Industry. *Appl. Econ.*, June 1984, *16*(3), pp. 421–42. **[G: U.K.]**

Pindyck, Robert S. and Rotemberg, Julio J. Energy Price Shocks and Macroeconomic Adjustments. *Natural Res. J.*, April 1984, *24*(2), pp. 277–96.

Plaut, Thomas R. A Supply-Side Model of Texas Manufacturing Growth. *J. Reg. Sci.*, August 1984, *24*(3), pp. 373–89. **[G: U.S.]**

Pollak, Robert A.; Sickles, Robin C. and Wales, Terence J. The CES-Translog: Specification and Estimation of a New Cost Function. *Rev. Econ. Statist.*, November 1984, *66*(4), pp. 602–07. **[G: U.S.]**

Porter, Richard C. Apartheid, the Job Ladder, and the Evolutionary Hypothesis: Empirical Evidence from South African Manufacturing, 1960–1977. *Econ. Develop. Cult. Change*, October 1984, *33*(1), pp. 117–41. **[G: S. Africa]**

Pyror, Frederic L. Incentives in Manufacturing:

The Carrot and the Stick. *Mon. Lab. Rev.*, July 1984, *107*(7), pp. 40–43. [G: U.S.]

Pyyhtiä, I. The Realization of Investment Plans of Finnish Manufacturing Firms. In *Oppenländer, K. H. and Poser, G., eds.*, 1984, pp. 421–58. [G: Finland]

Ray, George F. Industrial Labour Costs, 1971–1983. *Nat. Inst. Econ. Rev.*, November 1984, (110), pp. 62–67. [G: OECD]

Reekie, W. Duncan. Minimum Efficient Scale in South African Industry: An Application of the Survivor Technique. *S. Afr. J. Econ.*, September 1984, *52*(3), pp. 223–32. [G: S. Africa]

Riefler, Roger F. and Lamphear, F. Charles. Climate and Manufacturing Location. *Reg. Sci. Persp.*, 1984, *14*(2), pp. 46–59. [G: U.S.]

Rizzi, Alfredo. Some Mathematical Properties of Cluster Methods. *Econ. Notes*, 1984, (2), pp. 139–55. [G: Italy]

Roberts, Paul Craig. Industrial Policy in Hungary: A Comment. *Cato J.*, Fall 1984, *4*(2), pp. 507–09. [G: Hungary]

Roomkin, Myron J. and Harris, Dawn A. Interindustry Patterns in Unfair Labor Practice Cases. *J. Lab. Res.*, Spring 1984, *5*(2), pp. 113–26. [G: U.S.]

Ross, Marc. Industrial Energy Conservation. *Natural Res. J.*, April 1984, *24*(2), pp. 369–404. [G: U.S.]

Rozenova, L. The Price and Effectiveness of Machine-building Output. *Prob. Econ.*, November 1984, *27*(7), pp. 44–60. [G: U.S.S.R.]

Ruane, Frances P. and John, A. Andrew. Government Intervention and the Cost of Capital to Irish Manufacturing Industry. *Econ. Soc. Rev.*, October 1984, *16*(1), pp. 31–50. [G: Ireland]

Ruback, Richard S. and Zimmerman, Martin B. Unionization and Profitability: Evidence from the Capital Market. *J. Polit. Econ.*, December 1984, *92*(6), pp. 1134–57. [G: U.S.]

Rubin, Jeffrey. Economic Incentives and Safety Regulation: An Analytical Framework: Comments. *Amer. Econ.*, Spring 1984, *28*(1), pp. 25–26.

Rushdi, Ali Ahmed. Industrial Demand for Electricity in South Australia. *Australian Econ. Pap.*, December 1984, *23*(43), pp. 259–80. [G: Australia]

Ryan, Paul. Job Training, Employment Practices, and the Large Enterprise: The Case of Costly Transferable Skills. In *Osterman, P., ed.*, 1984, pp. 191–229. [G: U.S.]

Sakoh, Katsuro. Japanese Economic Success: Industrial Policy or Free Market? *Cato J.*, Fall 1984, *4*(2), pp. 521–43. [G: Japan]

Salgado Penaherrera, Germanico. Economic Integration of Developing Countries and the Role of Joint Industrial Planning. In *Ghosh, P. K., ed., no. 12*, 1984, *1975*, pp. 120–52. [G: Latin America]

Sawyer, W. Charles. The Effects of the Second Enlargement of the EC on U.S. Exports to Europe. *Weltwirtsch. Arch.*, 1984, *120*(3), pp. 572–79. [G: EEC; U.S.]

Scherer, Frederic M. Interindustry Technology Flows and Productivity Growth. In *Scherer, F. M.*, 1984, pp. 270–85. [G: U.S.]

Scherer, Frederic M. International Invention: Implications for Technology Market Analysis: Comment. In *Griliches, Z., ed.*, 1984, pp. 123–26. [G: Global]

Scherer, Frederic M. Using Linked Patent and R&D Data to Measure Interindustry Technology Flows. In *Griliches, Z., ed.*, 1984, pp. 417–61. [G: U.S.]

Scherer, Frederic M. and Ravenscraft, David J. Growth by Diversification: Entrepreneurial Behavior in Large-Scale United States Enterprises. *Z. Nationalökon.*, Supplement 1984, pp. 199–218. [G: U.S.]

Schmenner, Roger W. Energy and the Location of Industry. In *Downs, A. and Bradbury, K. L., eds.*, 1984, pp. 188–219. [G: U.S.]

Sellekaerts, Willy and Sellekaerts, Brigitte H. Technical Change, Capital Formation, and Capacity Unemployment in the United States. *Eastern Econ. J.*, July-September 1984, *10*(3), pp. 231–41. [G: U.S.]

Senker, Peter. Engineering Skills in the Robot Age. In *Marstrand, P., ed.*, 1984, pp. 133–45. [G: U.K.]

Shen, T. Y. The Estimation of X-Inefficiency in Eighteen Countries. *Rev. Econ. Statist.*, February 1984, *66*(1), pp. 98–104. [G: Selected Countries]

Shepherd, Geoffrey. Industrial Change in European Countries: The Experience of Six Sectors. In *Jacquemin, A., ed.*, 1984, pp. 191–214. [G: OECD]

Shishido, Shuntaro. A Multisector Approach to Global Econometric Modeling, with Special Reference to Heavy Industries. In *[Chenery, H. B.]*, 1984, pp. 391–405. [G: OECD; LDCs]

Sider, Hal. Economic Incentives and Safety Regulation: An Analytical Framework. *Amer. Econ.*, Spring 1984, *28*(1), pp. 18–24. [G: U.S.]

Siggel, Eckhard. On the Nature of Technology Shelves Facing Less Developed Countries: Some Hypotheses and Case Studies. *J. Devel. Areas*, January 1984, *18*(2), pp. 227–45. [G: Zaire; U.K.; Canada]

Sláma, Jiří. Empirische Prüfung der Wirkung der Reformen in den planwirtschaftlichen Ländern. (An Empirical Analysis of the Effects of Economic Reforms in Countries with Planned Economy. With English summary.) *Jahr. Nationalökon. Statist.*, November 1984, *199*(6), pp. 537–56. [G: Yugoslavia; Czechoslovakia]

Smyth, David J. Short-Run Employment Functions When the Speed of Adjustment Depends on the Unemployment Rate. *Rev. Econ. Statist.*, February 1984, *66*(1), pp. 138–42. [G: OECD]

Sokoloff, Kenneth L. Investment in Fixed and Working Capital during Early Industrialization: Evidence from U.S. Manufacturing Firms. *J. Econ. Hist.*, June 1984, *44*(2), pp. 545–56. [G: U.S.]

Sokoloff, Kenneth L. Was the Transition from the Artisanal Shop to the Nonmechanized Factory

Associated with Gains in Efficiency? Evidence from the U.S. Manufacturing Censuses of 1820 and 1850. *Exploration Econ. Hist.*, October 1984, *21*(4), pp. 351–82. **[G: U.S.]**

Sosin, Kim H. and Fairchild, Loretta G. Nonhomotheticity and Technological Bias in Production. *Rev. Econ. Statist.*, February 1984, *66*(1), pp. 44–50. **[G: Latin America]**

Soza, Hector. The Industrialization Debate in Latin America. In *Ghosh, P. K., ed., no. 1*, 1984, *1981*, pp. 309–29. **[G: Latin America]**

Stallaerts, Robert. The Interindustry Wage Structure of a Labour-Managed Economy: The Yugoslav Case, 1976–1981. *Econ. Anal. Worker's Manage.*, 1984, *18*(2), pp. 109–25. **[G: Yugoslavia]**

Stutchbury, Michael. The Playford Legend and the Industrialization of South Australia. *Australian Econ. Hist. Rev.*, March 1984, *24*(1), pp. 1–19. **[G: Australia]**

Sumner, Michael T. and Ward, Robert. The Impact of Taxes on Wages: A Further Analysis. *Econ. Notes*, 1984, (3), pp. 155–62. **[G: U.S.]**

Suzuki, Toshiro A. Distribution of Value Added in Enterprises in Japan. In *Intn'l. Productivity Symp.*, 1984, pp. 267–81. **[G: Japan; U.S.; W. Germany]**

Svejnar, Jan. The Determinants of Industrial-Sector Earnings in Senegal. *J. Devel. Econ.*, May–June–August 1984, *15*(1,2,3), pp. 289–311. **[G: Senegal]**

Swamy, T. L. N. Factor Substitution in Indian Industries: Some Cross-Section Evidence. *Margin*, January 1984, *16*(2), pp. 31–38. **[G: India]**

Sylos-Labini, Paolo. Factors Affecting Changes in Productivity. *J. Post Keynesian Econ.*, Winter 1983-84, *6*(2), pp. 161–79. **[G: Italy; U.S.]**

Sylos-Labini, Paolo. Prices and Income Distribution in the Manufacturing Industry. In *Sylos-Labini, P.*, 1984, *1979*, pp. 185–209. **[G: Italy; U.S.; U.K.; W. Germany; Argentina]**

Symons, J. and Layard, R. Neoclassical Demand for Labour Functions for Six Major Economies. *Econ. J.*, December 1984, *94*(376), pp. 788–99. **[G: N. America; U.K.; Germany; Japan; France]**

Telser, Lester G. Innovation: Its Public and Private Aspects and Some of Their Empirical Implications for Mergers. *Econ. Inquiry*, October 1984, *22*(4), pp. 334–59. **[G: U.S.]**

Terleckyj, Nestor E. R&D and Productivity Growth at the Industry Level: Is There Still a Relationship? Comment. In *Griliches, Z., ed.*, 1984, pp. 496–501. **[G: U.S.]**

Teubal, Morris. The Role of Technological Learning in the Exports of Manufactured Goods: The Case of Selected Capital Goods in Brazil. *World Devel.*, August 1984, *12*(8), pp. 849–65. **[G: Brazil]**

Tharakan, P. K. M. Intra-industry Trade between the Industrial Countries and the Developing

World. *Europ. Econ. Rev.*, October–November 1984, *26*(1–2), pp. 213–27. **[G: OECD; LDCs]**

Thee, Kian Wie. Japanese Direct Investment in Indonesian Manufacturing. *Bull. Indonesian Econ. Stud.*, August 1984, *20*(2), pp. 90–106. **[G: Indonesia]**

Tokman, Víctor E. Global Monetarism and Destruction of Industry. *Cepal Rev.*, 1984, (23), pp. 107–21. **[G: Argentina; Chile]**

Török, Ádám. Sectoral and Enterprise Structure of Net Exports Settled in Convertible Currency of the Hungarian Industry. *Acta Oecon.*, 1984, *33*(1–2), pp. 127–45. **[G: Hungary]**

Trezise, Philip H. Japanese Economic Success: A Comment. *Cato J.*, Fall 1984, *4*(2), pp. 545–86. **[G: Japan]**

Ullmann, John E. Can Business Become a Participant? In *Gordon, S. and McFadden, D., eds.*, 1984, pp. 164–74. **[G: U.S.]**

UNIDO Secretariat. Patterns and Prospects for East–South Trade in the 1980s. *Industry Devel.*, 1984, (11), pp. 67–98. **[G: CMEA]**

Utrecht, Ernst. Manufacturing and the Corporate Sector. In *Utrecht, E., ed.*, 1984, pp. 235–66. **[G: Fiji]**

Valppu, Pirkko. Kapasiteetin Käyttöaste 1960–1982: menetelmä ja tulokset. (Capacity Utilization in Finland in 1960–1982: Method and Results. With English summary.) *Kansant. Aikak.*, 1984, *80*(3), pp. 302–12. **[G: Finland]**

Varga, György. The Long-run Development of Hungarian Industry (Outlines of an Approach to Industrial Policy). *Acta Oecon.*, 1984, *32*(1–2), pp. 91–112. **[G: Hungary]**

Vashist, D. C. Substitution Possibilities and Price Sensitivity of Energy Demand in Indian Manufacturing. *Indian Econ. J.*, Oct.–Dec. 1984, *32*(2), pp. 84–97. **[G: India]**

Viita, Pentti. Näivettääkö valtio Suomen teollisuutta. (The State Withering Industry in Finland? With English summary.) *Kansant. Aikak.*, 1984, *80*(3), pp. 261–70. **[G: Finland]**

Vroman, Wayne. Wage Contract Settlements in U.S. Manufacturing. *Rev. Econ. Statist.*, November 1984, *66*(4), pp. 661–65. **[G: U.S.]**

Waskett, George. The Role of Information Activities in Total Canadian Manufacturing: Separability and Substitutability. *Appl. Econ.*, October 1984, *16*(5), pp. 763–70. **[G: Canada]**

Weiss, Frank D. Industrial Policy and International Competitiveness in West Germany. In *Driscoll, R. E. and Behrman, J. N., eds.*, 1984, pp. 229–44. **[G: W. Germany]**

Weiss, John. Alliance for Production: Mexico's Incentives for Private Sector Industrial Development. *World Devel.*, July 1984, *12*(7), pp. 723–42. **[G: Mexico]**

Weiss, John. Manufacturing as an Engine of Growth—Revisited. *Industry Devel.*, 1984, (13), pp. 39–62. **[G: Global]**

Wilder, Ronald P. and Tucker, Irvin B. Trends in Vertical Integration: Reply. *J. Ind. Econ.*, March 1984, *32*(3), pp. 391–92. **[G: U.S.]**

Williams, Martin and Laumas, Prem S. Economies of Scale for Various Types of Manufacturing Production Technologies in an Underdeveloped Economy. *Econ. Develop. Cult. Change*, January 1984, *32*(2), pp. 401–12. **[G: India]**

Wogart, Jan Peter and Marques, Jose Siverio. Trade Liberalization, Tariff Redundancy and Inflation: A Methodological Exploration Applied to Argentina. *Weltwirtsch. Arch.*, 1984, *120*(1), pp. 18–39. **[G: Argentina]**

Wonnacott, Paul. Industrial Allocation in the Andean Pact. In *Núñez del Arco, J.; Margain, E. and Cherol, R., eds.*, 1984, pp. 103–14. **[G: Latin America]**

Woolf, Arthur G. Electricity, Productivity, and Labor Saving: American Manufacturing, 1900–1929. *Exploration Econ. Hist.*, April 1984, *21*(2), pp. 176–91. **[G: U.S.]**

Wren-Lewis, Simon. The Roles of Output Expectations and Liquidity in Explaining Recent Productivity Movements. *Nat. Inst. Econ. Rev.*, May 1984, (108), pp. 42–53. **[G: U.K.]**

Wright, Gavin. Rethinking the Postbellum Southern Political Economy: A Review Essay. *Bus. Hist. Rev.*, Autumn 1984, *58*(3), pp. 409–16. **[G: U.S.]**

Yakushiji, Taizo. Reshuffling Firms for Technology? An Aggregate Time-Series Analysis of B. Klein's "Dynamic Efficiency." In *Aoki, M., ed.*, 1984, pp. 359–85. **[G: Japan]**

Yandle, Bruce. "Polluters' Profits": An Empirical Note. *J. Ind. Econ.*, March 1984, *32*(3), pp. 359–66. **[G: U.S.]**

Yandle, Bruce. Environmental Control and Regional Growth. *Growth Change*, July 1984, *15*(3), pp. 39–42. **[G: U.S.]**

Yoshihara, Hideki. Diversification of Large Japanese Manufacturing Firms. *Kobe Econ. Bus. Rev.*, 1984, *30*, pp. 61–71. **[G: Japan; U.S.]**

Yoshihara, Hideki. Multinational Growth of Japanese Manufacturing Enterprises in the Postwar Period. In *Okochi, A. and Inoue, T., eds.*, 1984, pp. 95–120. **[G: Japan; U.S.; W. Europe]**

Yoshikawa, Hiroshi. Demand–Supply Constraints and Inventory Stock in Macroeconomic Analysis. *Econ. Stud. Quart.*, December 1984, *35*(3), pp. 193–205. **[G: Japan]**

Young, Stephen. The Foreign-Owned Manufacturing Sector. In *Hood, N. and Young, S., eds.*, 1984, pp. 93–127. **[G: U.K.]**

6312 Metals (iron, steel, and other)

Adams, Walter and Brock, James W. Countervailing or Coalescing Power? The Problem of Labor/Management Coalitions. *J. Post Keynesian Econ.*, Winter 1983-84, *6*(2), pp. 180–97. **[G: U.S.]**

Albin, Peter S. Job Design within Changing Patterns of Technical Development. In *Collins, E. L. and Tanner, L. D., eds.*, 1984, pp. 125–61. **[G: U.S.]**

Aylen, Jonathan. Prospects for Steel. *Lloyds Bank Rev.*, April 1984, (152), pp. 13–30. **[G: U.K.]**

Baldwin, Carliss Y.; Tribendis, Joseph J. and Clark, Joel P. The Evolution of Market Risk in the U.S. Steel Industry and Implications

for Required Rates of Return. *J. Ind. Econ.*, September 1984, *33*(1), pp. 73–98. **[G: U.S.]**

Bright, Samuel L. and McKinney, Joseph A. The Economics of the Steel Trigger Price Mechanism. *Bus. Econ.*, July 1984, *19*(4), pp. 40–46. **[G: U.S.]**

Canto, Victor A. The Effect of Voluntary Restraint Agreements: A Case Study of the Steel Industry. *Appl. Econ.*, April 1984, *16*(2), pp. 175–86. **[G: U.S.]**

Carlson, Norma W. Pay Gains Tempered in Basic Steel Mills. *Mon. Lab. Rev.*, August 1984, *107*(8), pp. 28–30. **[G: U.S.]**

Chakravarty, S. P. and Wibe, Sören A. Energy Conservation: An Elasticity of Substitution Approach. *Energy Econ.*, October 1984, *6*(4), pp. 255–58. **[G: Sweden]**

Dahlman, Carl J. Foreign Technology and Indigenous Technological Capability in Brazil. In *Fransman, M. and King, K., eds.*, 1984, pp. 317–34. **[G: Brazil]**

Duffus, LuAnn McClernan and Chern, Wen S. An Energy Demand and Generalized Fuel Choice Model for the Primary Metals Industry. *Energy J.*, April 1984, *5*(2), pp. 35–52. **[G: U.S.]**

Elbaum, Bernard. The Making and Shaping of Job and Pay Structures in the Iron and Steel Industry. In *Osterman, P., ed.*, 1984, pp. 71–107. **[G: OECD]**

Emerson, Craig. Economic Evaluation of Mineral-Processing Projects. In *Lloyd, P. J., ed.*, 1984, pp. 253–72. **[G: Australia]**

Foray, Dominique. Changements techniques et structure du capital en fonderie: pour une explicitation des choix d'accumulation du capital et de gestion du changement technologique. (With English summary.) *Rev. Econ. Ind.*, 3rd Trimester 1984, (29), pp. 26–45. **[G: OECD]**

Hazilla, Michael and Kopp, Raymond J. A Factor Demand Model for Strategic Nonfuel Minerals in the Primary Metals Sector. *Land Econ.*, November 1984, *60*(4), pp. 328–39. **[G: U.S.]**

Katz, Jorge M. Technological Innovation, Industrial Organisation and Comparative Advantages of Latin American Metalworking Industries. In *Fransman, M. and King, K., eds.*, 1984, pp. 113–36. **[G: Latin America]**

Kelly, James. Management Strategy and the Reform of Collective Bargaining: Cases from the British Steel Corporation. *Brit. J. Ind. Relat.*, July 1984, *22*(2), pp. 135–53. **[G: U.K.]**

Kervyn de Lettenhove, Albert. Steel: A Case Study in Industrial Policy. In *Jacquemin, A., ed.*, 1984, pp. 215–26. **[G: EEC]**

Kreinin, Mordechai E. Wage Competitiveness in the U.S. Auto and Steel Industries. *Contemp. Policy Issue*, January 1984, (4), pp. 39–50. **[G: U.S.]**

Labys, Walter. The Role of the Soviet Union in Metals Markets: A Case Study of Copper, Manganese and Chromite. In *Kostecki, M. M., ed.*, 1984, pp. 135–55. **[G: U.S.S.R.; Global]**

Litvak, Isaiah A. and Maule, Christopher J. Assessing Industry Concentration: The Case of

Aluminum. *J. Int. Bus. Stud.*, Spring/Summer 1984, *15*(1), pp. 97–104.

Lynch, Frances M. B. Resolving the Paradox of the Monnet Plan: National and International Planning in French Reconstruction. *Econ. Hist. Rev.*, 2nd Ser., May 1984, *37*(2), pp. 229–43. **[G: France]**

Marks, Stephen V. Wage Competitiveness in the U.S. Auto and Steel Industries: Comment. *Contemp. Policy Issue*, January 1984, (4), pp. 51–53. **[G: U.S.]**

Mestmäcker, Ernst-Joachim. The Applicability of the ECSC-Cartel Prohibition (Article 65) during a "Manifest Crisis." *Mich. Law Rev.*, April–May 1984, *82*(5 & 6), pp. 1399–1414.
[G: EEC]

Monash University, Centre of Pol. Stud. The Environment: The Aluminium Industry in Australia in the 1980s. In *Lloyd, P. J., ed.*, 1984, *1981*, pp. 116–25. **[G: Australia]**

Mutti, John. Subsidized Production, World Steel Trade and Countervailing Duties. *Southern Econ. J.*, January 1984, *50*(3), pp. 871–80.
[G: Selected Countries]

Nappi, Carmine. The USSR and The International Aluminium Market. In *Kostecki, M. M., ed.*, 1984, pp. 116–34. **[G: U.S.S.R.; Global]**

Papola, T. S. and Sinha, R. C. Metal Household Utensils and Basic Needs in India. In *van Ginneken, W. and Baron, C., eds.*, 1984, pp. 84–119. **[G: India]**

Parker, William N. The Interruption of Expansion. In *Parker, W. N.*, 1984, *1957*, pp. 57–75. **[G: Europe]**

Parker, William N. The Organization of Rapid Expansion. In *Parker, W. N.*, 1984, pp. 76–91. **[G: W. Europe]**

Pierenkemper, Toni. Pre-1900 Industrial White Collar Employees at the Krupp Steel Casting Works: A New Occupational Category in Germany. *Bus. Hist. Rev.*, Autumn 1984, *58*(3), pp. 384–408. **[G: Germany]**

Porter, Michael G. Private Resource Development and Public Utilities: Some Hazards of Sleeping with Elephants. In *Pearce, D. W.; Siebert, H. and Walter, I., eds.*, 1984, pp. 225–41. **[G: Australia]**

Roderick, David M. U.S. Steelmakers Fight Back. *Challenge*, January/February 1984, *26*(6), pp. 51–53. **[G: U.S.]**

Salmi, Timo, et al. Extracting and Analyzing the Time Series for Profitability Measurement from Published Financial Statements: With Results on Publicly Traded Finnish Metal Industry Firms: Part III. *Liiketaloudellinen Aikak.*, 1984, *33*(1), pp. 23–48. **[G: Finland]**

Schorsch, Louis. The Abdication of Big Steel. *Challenge*, March/April 1984, *27*(1), pp. 34–40. **[G: U.S.]**

Tarr, David G. The Minimum Efficient Size Steel Plant. *Atlantic Econ. J.*, March 1984, *12*(1), pp. 122.

Terrebonne, R. Peter. Modeling the Primary Aluminum Spot Market. *Bus. Econ.*, January 1984, *19*(1), pp. 53–60. **[G: OECD]**

Tiffany, Paul A. The Roots of Decline: Business–Government Relations in the American Steel Industry, 1945–1960. *J. Econ. Hist.*, June 1984, *44*(2), pp. 407–19. **[G: U.S.]**

Tsokhas, K. 'A Touch of Midas': The Rise of Western Mining Corporation, 1945–1975. *Australian Econ. Hist. Rev.*, September 1984, *24*(2), pp. 132–49. **[G: Australia]**

Turnovsky, Michelle H. L. and Donnelly, William A. Energy Substitution, Separability, and Technical Progress in the Australian Iron and Steel Industry. *J. Bus. Econ. Statist.*, January 1984, *2*(1), pp. 54–63. **[G: Australia]**

Wigren, Rune. Measuring Regional Efficiency: A Method Tested on the Fabricated Metal Products Industry in Sweden, 1973–75. *Reg. Sci. Urban Econ.*, August 1984, *14*(3), pp. 363–79. **[G: Sweden]**

Yamawaki, Hideki. Market Structure, Capacity Expansion, and Pricing: A Model Applied to the Japanese Iron and Steel Industry. *Int. J. Ind. Organ.*, March 1984, *2*(1), pp. 29–62. **[G: Japan]**

Young, Stephen and Reeves, Alan. The Engineering and Metals Sector. In *Hood, N. and Young, S., eds.*, 1984, pp. 128–73. **[G: U.K.]**

6313 Machinery (tools, electrical equipment, computers, communication equipment, and appliances)

Ahmed, Meekal Aziz. Issues in the Economics of Industrialization in Developing Countries: A Case Study from Pakistan's Light Engineering Sector: Comment. *Pakistan Devel. Rev.*, Summer-Autumn 1984, *23*(2&3), pp. 327–29. **[G: Pakistan]**

Akers, John F. A Responsible Future—An Address to the Computer Industry. *Sloan Manage. Rev.*, Fall 1984, *26*(1), pp. 53–57. **[G: U.S.]**

Albach, Horst. Investment in Inventory. In *[Beckmann, M. J.]*, 1984, pp. 3–13. **[G: W. Germany]**

Anderson, Erin and Schmittlein, David C. Integration of the Sales Force: An Empirical Examination. *Rand J. Econ.*, Autumn 1984, *15*(3), pp. 385–95. **[G: U.S.]**

Anton, Ion. Promotion of Romanian Machine-Tools to the United States: A Marketing Mix Approach. In *Jackson, M. R. and Woodson, J. D., Jr., eds.*, 1984, pp. 187–95. **[G: U.S.; Romania]**

Aoki, Masahiko. Innovative Adaptation through the Quasi-tree Structure: An Emerging Aspect of Japanese Entrepreneurship. *Z. Nationalökon.*, Supplement 1984, pp. 177–98.
[G: Japan]

Berrefjord, Ole and Heum, Per. Nordic Engineering Industries and the Norwegian Offshore Market. In *Mikkelsen, A., et al.*, 1984, pp. 204–19. **[G: Scandinavia]**

Bloch, Erich. Development of Competence in a World of Rapid Technical Change. In *Fusfeld, H. I. and Haklisch, C. S., eds.*, 1984, pp. 73–82. **[G: U.S.]**

Bodó-Vértes, Ágnes. Results of Co-operation

Strategy in the 70's—Exemplified by the Production Co-operation between Machine Tool Manufacturers in the FRG and in Hungary. In *Rába, A. and Schenk, K.-E., eds.*, 1984, pp. 189–214. **[G: Hungary; W. Germany]**

Brand, Horst and Huffstutler, Clyde. Productivity in Making Air Conditioners, Refrigeration Equipment, and Furnaces. *Mon. Lab. Rev.*, December 1984, *107*(12), pp. 11–17.
[G: U.S.]

Carnall, Colin A. and Medland, Anthony J. Computer-Aided Design: Social and Technical Choices for Development. In *Warner, M., ed.*, 1984, pp. 49–65.

Chang, Chien-Min and Chen, Kar-Nin Peter. Factors Affecting Industrial Relations in the Electronics Industry of Hong Kong—An Empirical Research Analysis. *Managerial Dec. Econ.*, June 1984, *5*(2), pp. 104–15.
[G: Hong Kong]

Cohen, Jon S.; Rubin, Jeffrey and Saunders, Ronald S. Chasing the Bandwagon: Government Policy for the Electronics Industry. *Can. Public Policy*, March 1984, *10*(1), pp. 25–34.
[G: OECD]

Cooke, Philip; Morgan, Kevin and Jackson, David. New Technology and Regional Development in Austerity Britain: The Case of the Semiconductor Industry. *Reg. Stud.*, August 1984, *18*(4), pp. 277–89. **[G: U.K.]**

Delapierre, Michel and Zimmermann, Jean-Benoît. Les multinationales de l'électronique: des stratégies différenciées. (With English summary.) *Rev. Econ. Ind.*, 2nd Trimester 1984, (28), pp. 9–35. **[G: OECD]**

English, Maurice. The European Information Technology Industry. In *Jacquemin, A., ed.*, 1984, pp. 227–73. **[G: OECD]**

Ernst, Dieter. Recent Developments in the Semiconductor Industry: Implications for International Restructuring and Global Patterns of Technological Dominance and Dependence. *Industry Devel.*, 1984, (11), pp. 1–42.
[G: Global]

Feldenkirchen, Wilfried. Capital Raised and its Use by German Mechanical Engineering Firms in the 19th and Early 20th Centuries. In *Engels, W. and Pohl, H., eds.*, 1984, pp. 19–55. **[G: W. Germany]**

Firn, John R. and Roberts, David. High-technology Industries. In *Hood, N. and Young, S., eds.*, 1984, pp. 288–325. **[G: U.K.]**

Flaherty, M. Therese. Field Research on the Link between Technological Innovation and Growth: Evidence from the International Semiconductor Industry. *Amer. Econ. Rev.*, May 1984, *74*(2), pp. 67–72.

Flaherty, M. Therese and Itami, Hiroyuki. Competitive Edge: Finance. In *Okimoto, D. I.; Sugano, T. and Weinstein, F. B., eds.*, 1984, pp. 134–76. **[G: Japan; U.S.]**

Fransman, Martin. Some Hypotheses Regarding Indigenous Technological Capability and the Case of Machine Production in Hong Kong. In *Fransman, M. and King, K., eds.*, 1984, pp. 301–16. **[G: Hong Kong]**

Gerwin, Donald. Innovation, Microelectronics and Manufacturing Technology. In *Warner, M., ed.*, 1984, pp. 66–83.

Gilder, George. Triumph of the American Mind. *Policy Rev.*, Winter 1984, (27), pp. 20–26.
[G: U.S.]

Graham, Loren R. Science and Computers in Soviet Society. In *Hoffmann, E. P., ed.*, 1984, pp. 124–34. **[G: U.S.S.R.]**

Gürol, Metin N.; Kaynak, Erdener and Yucel, Ahmet A. Computer Systems Marketing in the Emerging Economies of the Middle East: Managerial and Public Policy Implications. In *Kaynak, E., ed.*, 1984, pp. 271–85. **[G: U.S.; Turkey; Saudi Arabia]**

Haug, Peter. Regional Policy Incentives in the Scottish Electronics Industry: Survey Evidence. *Scot. J. Polit. Econ.*, November 1984, *31*(3), pp. 274–83. **[G: U.K.]**

Herman, Arthur S. and Otto, Phyllis F. Productivity Growth in the Switchgear Industry Slows after 1973. *Mon. Lab. Rev.*, March 1984, *107*(3), pp. 33–36. **[G: U.S.]**

Herranen, Timo and Myllyntaus, Timo. Effects of the First World War on the Engineering Industries of Estonia and Finland. *Scand. Econ. Hist. Rev.*, 1984, *32*(3), pp. 121–42.
[G: U.S.S.R.; Finland]

Jackson, Charles L. Disconnecting Bell: Technology: The Anchor of the Bell System. In *Shooshan, H. M., III, ed.*, 1984, pp. 71–82.
[G: U.S.]

Kanter, Rosabeth Moss. Variations in Managerial Career Structures in High-Technology Firms: The Impact of Organizational Characteristics on Internal Labor Market Patterns. In *Osterman, P., ed.*, 1984, *1983*, pp. 109–31.

Kleinschmidt, Elko J. and Cooper, Robert G. A Typology of Export Strategies Applied to the Export Performance of Industrial Firms. In *Kaynak, E., ed.*, 1984, pp. 217–31.
[G: Canada]

Levačić, Rosalind. Do Mercantilist Industrial Policies Work? A Comparison of British and French TV Manufacturing. *Nat. Westminster Bank Quart. Rev.*, May 1984, pp. 47–58.
[G: U.K.; France]

Mathews, R. G. Initial Growth Pains in the Development of the Indian Machine Tool Industry. *Indian Econ. J.*, Oct.–Dec. 1984, *32*(2), pp. 41–55. **[G: India]**

McEachern, William A. and Romeo, Anthony A. Vertical Restraints in the Audio Component Industry: Possibilities for Future Empirical Work. In *Lafferty, R. N.; Lande, R. H. and Kirkwood, J. B., eds.*, 1984, pp. 258–69.
[G: U.S.]

McEachern, William A. and Romeo, Anthony A. Vertical Restraints in the Audio Components Industry: An Economic Analysis of FTC Intervention. In *Lafferty, R. N.; Lande, R. H. and Kirkwood, J. B., eds.*, 1984, pp. 202–57.
[G: U.S.]

Moore, Frederick T. The Engineering Industries. In *Weiss, C. and Jéquier, N., eds.*, 1984, pp. 247–60. **[G: S. Korea; Thailand]**

Nabi, Ijaz. Issues in the Economics of Industrialization in Developing Countries: A Case Study from Pakistan's Light Engineering Sector. *Pakistan Devel. Rev.*, Summer-Autumn 1984, 23(2&3), pp. 311–25. [G: Pakistan]

Okimoto, Daniel I. Competitive Edge: Conclusions. In *Okimoto, D. I.; Sugano, T. and Weinstein, F. B., eds.*, 1984, pp. 177–235. [G: Japan; U.S.]

Okimoto, Daniel I. Competitive Edge: Political Context. In *Okimoto, D. I.; Sugano, T. and Weinstein, F. B., eds.*, 1984, pp. 78–133. [G: Japan; U.S.]

Pittman, Russell W. Predatory Investment: U.S. vs. IBM. *Int. J. Ind. Organ.*, December 1984, 2(4), pp. 341–65. [G: U.S.]

Rees, John; Briggs, Ronald and Oakey, Raymond P. The Adoption of New Technology in the American Machinery Industry. *Reg. Stud.*, December 1984, 18(6), pp. 489–504. [G: U.S.]

Richonnier, Michel. Europe's Decline Is Not Irreversible. *J. Common Market Stud.*, March 1984, 22(3), pp. 227–43. [G: U.S.; Japan; EEC]

Rill, James F. Non-price Vertical Restraints since Sylvania: Market Conditions and Dual Distribution. In *Fox, E. M. and Halverson, J. T., eds.*, 1984, pp. 383–96. [G: U.S.]

Rush, Howard and Williams, Robin. Consultation and Change: New Technology and Manpower in the Electronics Industry. In *Warner, M., ed.*, 1984, pp. 171–88. [G: U.K.]

Rushinek, Avi and Rushinek, Sara F. Mini/Micro Computer Evaluation of System Features: An Empirical Discriminant Model of Software and Hardware Expandability, Compatibility, Cost-Efficiency, Installation, and Delivery. *Managerial Dec. Econ.*, September 1984, 5(3), pp. 150–59. [G: U.S.]

Saxenian, AnnaLee. The Urban Contradictions of Silicon Valley: Regional Growth and the Restructuring of the Semiconductor Industry. In *Sawers, L. and Tabb, W. K., eds.*, 1984, pp. 163–97. [G: U.S.]

Schlesinger, Robert J. Industrial Robots, Work and Industry: Past, Present and Future. In *Warner, M., ed.*, 1984, pp. 11–30. [G: U.S.; U.K.; Japan]

Schweitzer, Iván. Size and Market Behaviour of the Hungarian Engineering Enterprises. In *Rába, A. and Schenk, K.-E., eds.*, 1984, pp. 73–98. [G: Hungary; Europe]

Snooks, G. D. Growth and Productivity Change in the Australian Mechanical Engineering Industry, 1910–1940. *Australian Econ. Hist. Rev.*, March 1984, 24(1), pp. 53–70. [G: Australia]

St. Louis, Robert D. Short-Time Compensation: At Home and Abroad: Arizona, Motorola, and STC. In *MaCoy, R. and Morand, M. J., eds.*, 1984, pp. 82–94. [G: U.S.]

Sternthal, János. Co-operation and Size-Structure in the Hungarian Engineering Industry. In *Rába, A. and Schenk, K.-E., eds.*, 1984, pp. 127–64. [G: Hungary]

Stoffaës, Christian. French Industrial Strategy in Sunrise Sectors. In *Jacquemin, A., ed.*, 1984, pp. 274–92. [G: France]

Svedberg, Bjorn. University–Industry Research Interactions: Electronics. In *Fusfeld, H. I. and Haklisch, C. S., eds.*, 1984, pp. 25–29.

Taira, Koji. The Management of Employment Adjustment in Electric and Electronics Firms in the 1970s. *Rivista Int. Sci. Econ. Com.*, September 1984, 31(9), pp. 833–43. [G: Japan]

Uenohara, Michiyuki and Starfelt, Nils. University–Industry Research Interactions: Overview of Policy Issues: Panel Report on Electronics. In *Fusfeld, H. I. and Haklisch, C. S., eds.*, 1984, pp. 31–33.

Uenohara, Michiyuki, et al. Competitive Edge: Background. In *Okimoto, D. I.; Sugano, T. and Weinstein, F. B., eds.*, 1984, pp. 9–34. [G: Japan; U.S.]

Useem, Elizabeth L. Education and High-Technology Industry: The Case of Silicon Valley. *Econ. Educ. Rev.*, 1984, 3(3), pp. 215–21. [G: U.S.]

Warner, Malcolm. Microprocessors, Manpower and Society: Introduction. In *Warner, M., ed.*, 1984, pp. 1–7.

Warner, P. C. Manufacturing Industry and Nuclear Power. In *Brookes, L. G. and Motamen, H., eds.*, 1984, pp. 88–113. [G: U.K.]

Weinstein, Franklin B.; Uenohara, Michiyuki and Linvill, John G. Competitive Edge: Technological Resources. In *Okimoto, D. I.; Sugano, T. and Weinstein, F. B., eds.*, 1984, pp. 35–77. [G: Japan; U.S.]

Wessel, Horst A. The German Feeble Current Cable Association (DSV)—Background, Foundation and Early Years (1876–1917.) In *Engels, W. and Pohl, H., eds.*, 1984, pp. 57–75. [G: W. Germany]

Woolcock, Stephen. Information Technology: The Challenge to Europe. *J. Common Market Stud.*, June 1984, 22(4), pp. 315–31. [G: Europe]

Yaprak, Attila; Sorek, Christopher and Parameswaran, Ravi. Competitive Strategy in Multinational Oligopolies: The Role of Promotion in the Computer Industry. In *Kaynak, E., ed.*, 1984, pp. 232–55. [G: U.K.; U.S.]

Young, Stephen and Reeves, Alan. The Engineering and Metals Sector. In *Hood, N. and Young, S., eds.*, 1984, pp. 128–73. [G: U.K.]

6314 Transportation Equipment

Adams, Walter. "Laissez-Faire," Import Restraints, and Industry Performance: A Case Study of Automobiles. In *[Reynolds, L. G.]*, 1984, pp. 389–408. [G: U.S.]

Adams, Walter and Brock, James W. Countervailing or Coalescing Power? The Problem of Labor/Management Coalitions. *J. Post Keynesian Econ.*, Winter 1983-84, 6(2), pp. 180–97. [G: U.S.]

Atkinson, Scott E. and Halvorsen, Robert. A New Hedonic Technique for Estimating Attribute Demand: An Application to the Demand for

Automobile Fuel Efficiency. *Rev. Econ. Statist.*, August 1984, *66*(3), pp. 417–26.
[G: U.S.]

Bennett, Douglas and Sharpe, Kenneth. Agenda Setting and Bargaining Power: The Mexican State versus Transnational Automobile Corporations. In *Kronish, R. and Mericle, K. S., eds.,* 1984, *1979*, pp. 195–229. [G: Mexico]

Biswas, Basudeb and Shahrokni, Ahmad. A Static Analysis of Domestic Production Loss in the Presence of Negative Value-Added: The Case of Iranian Automobile Industry. *J. Econ. Devel.*, July 1984, *9*(1), pp. 113–24.
[G: Iran]

Blair, Roger D.; Kaserman, David L. and Tepel, Richard C. The Impact of Improved Mileage on Gasoline Consumption. *Econ. Inquiry,* April 1984, *22*(2), pp. 209–17. [G: U.S.]

Bond, Eric W. Test of the Lemons Model: Reply [A Direct Test of the 'Lemons' Model: The Market for Used Pickup Trucks]. *Amer. Econ. Rev.,* September 1984, *74*(4), pp. 801–04.
[G: U.S.]

Bowles, Roger. Theory of the Firm. In *Sandford, C. and Bradbury, M., eds.,* 1984, pp. 66–92.
[G: Belgium; U.K.]

Boyle, Stanley E. and Piette, Michael J. Neglected Elements in Vertical Integration Analysis: The Case of Retail Price Preticketing. *Rev. Ind. Organ.,* Spring 1984, *1*(1), pp. 69–77.
[G: U.S.]

Brodley, Joseph F. Potential Competition under the Merger Guidelines. In *Fox, E. M. and Halverson, J. T., eds.,* 1984, pp. 199–223.
[G: U.S.]

Cappelli, Peter. Auto Industry Experiments with the Guaranteed Income Stream. *Mon. Lab. Rev.,* July 1984, *107*(7), pp. 37–39. [G: U.S.]

Carlos, Ann M. Steel Rails versus Iron Rails: Evidence from Canada. *Exploration Econ. Hist.,* April 1984, *21*(2), pp. 169–75. [G: Canada]

Cockerill, T. A. J. and Kinloch, H. Managing Risk and Uncertainty. In *Pickering, J. F. and Cockerill, T. A. J., eds.,* 1984, pp. 221–51.
[G: U.K.]

Craig, Paul P. Fuel Efficiency Incentives for Cars Oil Import Vulnerability Reduction. *Energy J.,* January 1984, *5*(1), pp. 141–48. [G: U.S.]

Cronin, M. R. Protection and Employment in the Motor Car Sector. *Australian Econ. Pap.,* June 1984, *23*(42), pp. 38–51.

Dahlman, Carl J. Foreign Technology and Indigenous Technological Capability in Brazil. In *Fransman, M. and King, K., eds.,* 1984, pp. 317–34. [G: Brazil]

Deighton, John. The Interaction of Advertising and Evidence. *J. Cons. Res.,* December 1984, *11*(3), pp. 763–70. [G: U.S.]

Eckard, E. Woodrow. Alternative Vertical Structures: The Case of the Japanese Auto Industry. *Bus. Econ.,* October 1984, *19*(5), pp. 57–61.
[G: Japan]

Eckard, E. Woodrow. Regulatory Relief and the Automobile Industry: Comments. In *Eads, G. C. and Fix, M., eds.,* 1984, pp. 106–09.
[G: U.S.]

Evans, Judith; Hoeffel, Paul Heath and James, Daniel. Reflections on Argentine Auto Workers and Their Unions. In *Kronish, R. and Mericle, K. S., eds.,* 1984, pp. 133–59.
[G: Argentina]

Fleet, Michael. Bargaining Relations in the Colombian Motor Vehicle Industry. In *Kronish, R. and Mericle, K. S., eds.,* 1984, pp. 231–60. [G: Colombia]

Fong, Chan Onn. Basic Needs and Appropriate Technology in the Malaysian Bicycle Industry. In *van Ginneken, W. and Baron, C., eds.,* 1984, pp. 54–83. [G: Malaysia]

Fontagné, Lionel. La notion de produit-système et la décomposition internationale des processus productifs dans l'industrie automobile. (With English summary.) *Revue Écon. Polit.,* May–June 1984, *94*(3), pp. 358–74.

Fox, Douglas R. Motor Vehicles, Model Year 1984. *Surv. Curr. Bus.,* October 1984, *64*(10), pp. 20–23. [G: U.S.]

Frenkel, Orit. Flying High: A Case Study of Japanese Industrial Policy. *J. Policy Anal. Manage.,* Spring 1984, *3*(3), pp. 406–20. [G: Japan]

Gallasch, H. Frederick, Jr. Price Elasticities of Demand at Retail and Wholesale Levels: An Automotive Example. *Bus. Econ.,* January 1984, *19*(1), pp. 61–62.

Hadley, Eleanor. Counterpoint on Business Groupings and Government–Industry Relations in Automobiles. In *Aoki, M., ed.,* 1984, pp. 319–27. [G: Japan]

Hoffer, George E. and Reilly, Robert J. Automobile Styling as a Shift Variable: An Investigation by Firm and by Industry. *Appl. Econ.,* April 1984, *16*(2), pp. 291–97. [G: U.S.]

Humphrey, John. Labor in the Brazilian Motor Vehicle Industry. In *Kronish, R. and Mericle, K. S., eds.,* 1984, pp. 95–131. [G: Brazil]

Jenkins, Rhys. The Rise and Fall of the Argentine Motor Vehicle Industry. In *Kronish, R. and Mericle, K. S., eds.,* 1984, pp. 41–73.
[G: Argentina]

Katz, Harry C. The U.S. Automobile Collective Bargaining System in Transition. *Brit. J. Ind. Relat.,* July 1984, *22*(2), pp. 205–17.
[G: U.S.]

Keen, Howard, Jr. Composite Models Reduce Forecast Errors: The Case of New Automobile Sales, 1979–1983. *Bus. Econ.,* July 1984, *19*(4), pp. 47–50. [G: U.S.]

Kim, Kyoo H. Price Elasticity of Demand at Retail and Wholesale: A Comment. *Bus. Econ.,* October 1984, *19*(5), pp. 62.

Koshiro, Kazutoshi. Robots Are a Big Success at Auto Plant in Japan. *Mon. Lab. Rev.,* August 1984, *107*(8), pp. 35–36. [G: Japan]

Kreinin, Mordechai E. Wage Competitiveness in the U.S. Auto and Steel Industries. *Contemp. Policy Issue,* January 1984, (4), pp. 39–50.
[G: U.S.]

Kronish, Rich. Latin America and the World Motor Vehicle Industry: The Turn to Exports. In *Kronish, R. and Mericle, K. S., eds.,* 1984, pp. 75–93. [G: Latin America; Global]

Kronish, Rich and Mericle, Kenneth S. The Development of the Latin American Motor Vehicle Industry, 1900-1980: A Class Analysis. In *Kronish, R. and Mericle, K. S., eds.*, 1984, pp. 261–306. [G: Latin America]

Kwoka, John E., Jr. Market Power and Market Change in the U.S. Automobile Industry. *J. Ind. Econ.*, June 1984, *32*(4), pp. 509–22. [G: U.S.]

Larsen, Hans Kryger and Nilsson, Carl-Axel. Consumption and Production of Bicycles in Denmark, 1890–1980. *Scand. Econ. Hist. Rev.*, 1984, *32*(3), pp. 143–58. [G: Denmark]

Lave, Lester B. Controlling Contradictions among Regulations. *Amer. Econ. Rev.*, June 1984, *74*(3), pp. 471–75. [G: U.S.]

Leone, Robert A. Regulatory Relief and the Automobile Industry. In *Eads, G. C. and Fix, M.*, eds., 1984, pp. 87–105. [G: U.S.]

Lorenz, Edward H. Two Patterns of Development: The Labour Process in the British and French Shipbuilding Industries 1880 to 1930. *J. Europ. Econ. Hist.*, September–December 1984, *13*(3), pp. 599–634. [G: U.K.; France]

Marks, Stephen V. Wage Competitiveness in the U.S. Auto and Steel Industries: Comment. *Contemp. Policy Issue*, January 1984, (4), pp. 51–53. [G: U.S.]

Masten, Scott E. The Organization of Production: Evidence from the Aerospace Industry. *J. Law Econ.*, October 1984, *27*(2), pp. 403–17. [G: U.S.]

Mericle, Kenneth S. The Political Economy of the Brazilian Motor Vehicle Industry. In *Kronish, R. and Mericle, K. S.*, eds., 1984, pp. 1–40. [G: Brazil]

Morrison, Steven A. An Economic Analysis of Aircraft Design. *J. Transp. Econ. Policy*, May 1984, *18*(2), pp. 123–43.

Murfin, Andy. Market Shares in the UK Passenger Car Market: Marketing, Expenditure and Price Effects, 1975–80. *Appl. Econ.*, August 1984, *16*(4), pp. 611–32. [G: U.K.]

Peeters, Chris. Scheepsbouw in België: Ontwikkeling van een berekeningsmethode ter bepaling van de financiële implicaties van een indirecte subsidie. (The Belgian Shipbuilding Industry: Development of a Calculation Method to Determine the Financial Implications of an Indirect Subsidy. With English summary.) *Cah. Écon. Bruxelles*, 1st Trimester 1984, (101), pp. 40–56. [G: Belgium]

Pratt, Michael D. and Hoffer, George E. Test of the Lemons Model: Comment [A Direct Test of the 'Lemons' Model: The Market for Used Pickup Trucks]. *Amer. Econ. Rev.*, September 1984, *74*(4), pp. 798–800. [G: U.S.]

Prud'homme, Rémy. Les investissements des multinationales de l'automobile dans le Tiers-Monde. (With English summary.) *Rev. Econ. Ind.*, 3rd Trimester 1984, (29), pp. 62–77. [G: LDCs]

Rallo, Joseph. The European Communities' Industrial Policy Revisited: The Case of Aerospace. *J. Common Market Stud.*, March 1984, *22*(3), pp. 245–67. [G: OECD; EEC]

Rhys, Garel. Heavy Commercial Vehicles: A Decade of Change. *Nat. Westminster Bank Quart. Rev.*, August 1984, pp. 25–35. [G: U.K.]

Rossano, Geoffrey. Suburbia Armed: Nassau County Development and the Rise of the Aerospace Industry, 1909–60. In *Lotchin, R. W.*, ed., 1984, pp. 61–87. [G: U.S.]

Roxborough, Ian. Labor in the Mexican Motor Vehicle Industry. In *Kronish, R. and Mericle, K. S.*, eds., 1984, pp. 161–94. [G: Mexico]

Schiesl, Martin J. Airplanes to Aerospace: Defense Spending and Economic Growth in the Los Angeles Region, 1945–60. In *Lotchin, R. W.*, ed., 1984, pp. 135–49. [G: U.S.]

Stoffaës, Christian. French Industrial Strategy in Sunrise Sectors. In *Jacquemin, A.*, ed., 1984, pp. 274–92. [G: France]

Todd, D. Strategies of Growth, Diversification and Rationalization in the Evolution of Concentration in British Shipbuilding. *Reg. Stud.*, February 1984, *18*(1), pp. 55–67. [G: U.K.]

Totten, George O., III. The Reconstruction of the Japanese Shipbuilding Industry. In *Friedheim, R. L., et al.*, 1984, pp. 130–72. [G: Japan]

Urban, Glen L.; Johnson, Philip L. and Hauser, John R. Testing Competitive Market Structures. *Marketing Sci.*, Spring 1984, *3*(2), pp. 83–112. [G: U.S.]

Van Houtte, H. The EEC Draft Regulation on Selective Distribution of Automobiles. *J. World Trade Law*, July–August 1984, *18*(4), pp. 349–57. [G: EEC]

Wannacott, Ronald J. The Canadian Content Proposals of the Task Force on the Automobile Industry. *Can. Public Policy*, March 1984, *10*(1), pp. 1–9. [G: U.S.; Canada; Japan]

Wilcox, James A. Automobile Fuel Efficiency: Measurement and Explanation. *Econ. Inquiry*, July 1984, *22*(3), pp. 375–85. [G: U.S.]

Winch, Graham, et al. Industrial Relations, New Technology and the BL Metro. In *Warner, M.*, ed., 1984, pp. 189–209. [G: U.K.]

Winham, Gilbert R. The Canadian Automobile Industry and Trade-related Performance Requirements. *J. World Trade Law*, November: December 1984, *18*(6), pp. 471–96. [G: Canada; U.S.]

Yakushiji, Taizo. The Government in a Spiral Dilemma: Dynamic Policy Interventions vis-à-vis Auto Firms. C.1900–C.1960. In *Aoki, M.*, ed., 1984, pp. 265–310. [G: Japan]

Young, Stephen and Reeves, Alan. The Engineering and Metals Sector. In *Hood, N. and Young, S.*, eds., 1984, pp. 128–73. [G: U.K.]

Yudken, Joel S. Conversion in the Aerospace Industry: The McDonnell Douglas Project. In *Gordon, S. and McFadden, D.*, eds., 1984, pp. 130–43. [G: U.S.]

6315 Chemicals, Drugs, Plastics, Ceramics, Glass, Cement, and Rubber

Albach, Horst. Investment in Inventory. In *[Beckmann, M. J.]*, 1984, pp. 3–13. [G: W. Germany]

Auty, R. M. The Product Life-Cycle and the Location of the Global Petrochemical Industry after the Second Oil Shock. *Econ. Geogr.*, October 1984, *60*(4), pp. 325–38. **[G: OECD]**

Avery, William H. OTEC Methanol: A New Approach. In *Gopalakrishnan, C., ed.*, 1984, pp. 17–30.

Barton, David M. and Sherman, Roger. The Price and Profit Effects of Horizontal Merger: A Case Study. *J. Ind. Econ.*, December 1984, *33*(2), pp. 165–77. **[G: U.S.]**

Bodenheimer, Thomas S. The Transnational Pharmaceutical Industry and the Health of the World's People. In *McKinlay, J. B., ed.*, 1984, pp. 187–216.

le Bon, Claude. Old and "New" Concepts of Competition and Concentration. In *[Kozmetsky, G.]*, 1984, pp. 151–53.

Brock, James W. Industry Structure and Market Power: The Relevance of the "Relevant Market." *Antitrust Bull.*, Fall 1984, *29*(3), pp. 535–60. **[G: U.S.]**

Butterfield, David W.; Kubursi, Atif A. and Welland, J. Douglas. A Model of the Petrochemical Industry. *J. Energy Devel.*, Spring 1984, *9*(2), pp. 299–335. **[G: Global]**

Caron, François. Foreign Investments and Technology Transfers: The Case of the French Chemical Industry in the 1950s and 1960s as Viewed by the *Direction des Industries Chimiques*. In *Okochi, A. and Inoue, T., eds.*, 1984, pp. 261–80. **[G: France]**

Cieslik, Jerzy. Restrictive Clauses in Licensing Agreements: The Pharmaceutical Industry in Developing Countries. *J. World Trade Law*, September–October 1984, *18*(5), pp. 415–28. **[G: LDCs]**

Collomb, B. and Ponssard, J. P. Creative Management in Mature Capital Intensive Industries: The Case of Cement. In *[Kozmetsky, G.]*, 1984, pp. 123–43. **[G: OECD; Selected LDCs]**

Dao, Thi D. Drug Innovation and Price Competition. *Managerial Dec. Econ.*, June 1984, *5*(2), pp. 80–84. **[G: U.S.]**

Dao, Thi D. Drug Innovation and Price Competition. In *Lindgren, B., ed.*, 1984, pp. 207–16. **[G: U.S.]**

Eichenbaum, Martin S. Rational Expectations and the Smoothing Properties of Inventories of Finished Goods. *J. Monet. Econ.*, July 1984, *14*(1), pp. 71–96. **[G: U.S.]**

Fernández, Manuel A. British Nitrate Companies and the Emergence of Chile's Proletariat, 1880–1914. In *Munslow, B. and Finch, H., eds.*, 1984, pp. 42–76. **[G: Chile]**

Fowler, David J. and Gordon, Myron J. The Effect of Public Policy Initiatives on Drug Prices in Canada. *Can. Public Policy*, March 1984, *10*(1), pp. 64–73. **[G: Canada; U.S.]**

Funke, Ursula H. The Locational Behaviour of the Chemical Industry in the United States after World War II. In *[Beckmann, M. J.]*, 1984, pp. 151–61. **[G: U.S.]**

Ghemawat, Pankaj. Capacity Expansion in the Titanium Dioxide Industry. *J. Ind. Econ.*, December 1984, *33*(2), pp. 145–63. **[G: U.S.]**

Grabowski, Henry and Vernon, John. A Computer Simulation Model of Pharmaceutical Innovation. In *Lindgren, B., ed.*, 1984, pp. 159–75. **[G: U.S.]**

Hay, Joel W. Variation in U.S. Per Capita Pharmaceutical Expenditures: Are Drugs Health Care Complements or Substitutes? In *Lindgren, B., ed.*, 1984, pp. 21–35. **[G: U.S.]**

James, Jeffrey. Technology, Products and Income Distribution: The Soap Market in Barbados. In *van Ginneken, W. and Baron, C., eds.*, 1984, pp. 168–94. **[G: Barbados]**

Jones, Geoffrey. The Growth and Performance of British Multinational Firms before 1939: The Case of Dunlop. *Econ. Hist. Rev., 2nd Ser.*, February 1984, *37*(1), pp. 35–53. **[G: U.K.]**

Klíma, Arnŏst. Glassmaking Industry and Trade in Bohemia in the XVIIth and XVIIIth Centuries. *J. Europ. Econ. Hist.*, September–December 1984, *13*(3), pp. 499–520. **[G: Czechoslovakia]**

Kumar, Nagesh. Social Cost–Benefit Analysis of an Export-Oriented Project with Foreign Collaboration in India. *Industry Devel.*, 1984, (10), pp. 39–46. **[G: India]**

Lieberman, Marvin B. The Learning Curve and Pricing in the Chemical Processing Industries. *Rand J. Econ.*, Summer 1984, *15*(2), pp. 213–28. **[G: U.S.]**

Lovett, J. Robert. University–Industry Research Interactions: Chemicals. In *Fusfeld, H. I. and Haklisch, C. S., eds.*, 1984, pp. 51–57.

Maynard, Alan and Hartley, Keith. The Regulation of the Pharmaceutical Industry. In *Lindgren, B., ed.*, 1984, pp. 123–37. **[G: U.K.]**

McRae, James J. and Tapon, Francis. Compulsory Licensing as a Policy Instrument. *Can. Public Policy*, March 1984, *10*(1), pp. 74–77. **[G: Canada]**

Mounier, Alain and Byé, Pascal. Les futurs alimentaires et énergétiques des biotechnologies. (With English summary.) *Écon. Soc.*, September 1984, *18*(9), pp. 7–340. **[G: Global]**

Mubin, A. K. A. and Forsyth, David J. C. Technology, Employment and Income Distribution: The Soap Industry in Bangladesh. In *van Ginneken, W. and Baron, C., eds.*, 1984, pp. 14–53. **[G: Bangladesh]**

Narayana, P. L. Indian Pharmaceutical Industry: Problems & Prospects. *Margin*, January 1984, *16*(2), pp. 39–52. **[G: India]**

Parker, John. Regulatory Stringency and the International Diffusion of Drugs. In *Lindgren, B., ed.*, 1984, pp. 139–58. **[G: Selected Countries; U.K.]**

Pedroni, Gabriella. Drugs and Adverse Reactions: An Economic View of a Medical Problem. In *Lindgren, B., ed.*, 1984, pp. 67–95. **[G: Selected Countries]**

Peters, Lois S. University–Industry Research Interactions: Pharmaceuticals. In *Fusfeld, H. I. and Haklisch, C. S., eds.*, 1984, pp. 35–40.

von Planta, Louis. The Future Role of Chemistry in Removing Constraints on Food Production and Utilization. In *Bixler, G. and Shemilt, L. W., eds.*, 1984, pp. 55–63.

Pratt, Christopher J. Fertilizer Production. In *Weiss, C. and Jéquier, N., eds.*, 1984, pp. 209–26. [G: LDCs]

Prywes, Menahem. The Cost in Lost Productivity of New Regulation in the U.S. Chemical Industry. *J. Policy Modeling*, August 1984, 6(3), pp. 411–19. [G: U.S.]

Reekie, W. Duncan. Drug Prices in the UK, USA, Europe and Australia. *Australian Econ. Pap.*, June 1984, 23(42), pp. 71–78. [G: U.K.; U.S.; Europe; Australia]

Saias, Maurice. Creative and Noncreative Uses of Portfolio Planning Tools and Strategies. In *[Kozmetsky, G.]*, 1984, pp. 145–49.

Sales, Hubert. La recherche-développement dans la stratégie des grandes entreprises chimiques de l'entre-deux-guerres: Du Pont de Nemours, Imperial chemical industries, I. G. Farben. (With English summary.) *Revue Écon. Polit.*, July–August 1984, 94(4), pp. 446–64. [G: Germany]

Shimotani, Masahiro. Formation of "New Zaibatsu" in Prewar Japan: Case Study on Nisso Konzern. *Kyoto Univ. Econ. Rev.*, April 1984, 54(1), pp. 40–59. [G: Japan]

Stanton, J. Protection, Market Structure, and Firm Behaviour: Inefficiency in the Early Australian Tyre Industry. *Australian Econ. Hist. Rev.*, September 1984, 24(2), pp. 91–114. [G: Australia]

Viscusi, W. Kip and O'Connor, Charles J. Adaptive Responses to Chemical Labeling: Are Workers Bayesian Decision Makers? *Amer. Econ. Rev.*, December 1984, 74(5), pp. 942–56. [G: U.S.]

Wardell, William M. and Sheck, Lorraine E. Is Pharmaceutical Innovation Declining? Interpreting Measures of Pharmaceutical Innovation and Regulatory Impact in the USA, 1950–1980. In *Lindgren, B., ed.*, 1984, pp. 177–89. [G: U.S.]

Wiggins, Steven N. The Effect of U.S. Pharmaceutical Regulation on New Introductions. In *Lindgren, B., ed.*, 1984, pp. 191–205. [G: U.S.]

Wu, S. Y. Social and Private Rates of Returns Derived from Pharmaceutical Innovations: Some Empirical Findings. In *Lindgren, B., ed.*, 1984, pp. 217–54. [G: U.S.]

Yu, Shirley S. Some Determinants of Entry into Therapeutic Drug Markets. *Rev. Ind. Organ.*, Winter 1984, 1(4), pp. 260–75. [G: U.S.]

Ziegler, Joseph A. and Bell, Stephen E. Estimating Demand for Intake Water by Self-Supplied Firms. *Water Resources Res.*, January 1984, 20(1), pp. 4–8. [G: U.S.]

6316 Textiles, Leather, and Clothing

Albach, Horst. Investment in Inventory. In *[Beckmann, M. J.]*, 1984, pp. 3–13. [G: W. Germany]

Appelbaum, Elie and Ullah, Aman. An Empirical Test of the Risk Aversion Hypothesis. *Pakistan J. Appl. Econ.*, Summer 1984, 3(1), pp. 57–64. [G: U.S.]

Aryee, George A. Income Distribution, Technology and Employment in the Footwear Industry in Ghana. In *van Ginneken, W. and Baron, C., eds.*, 1984, pp. 120–47. [G: Ghana]

Beatty, Bess. Textile Labor in the North Carolina Piedmont: Mill Owner Images and Mill Worker Response, 1830–1900. *Labor Hist.*, Fall 1984, 25(4), pp. 485–503. [G: U.S.]

Bils, Mark. Tariff Protection and Production in the Early U.S. Cotton Textile Industry. *J. Econ. Hist.*, December 1984, 44(4), pp. 1033–45. [G: U.S.]

Crichton, David. The Textile and Clothing Sectors. In *Hood, N. and Young, S., eds.*, 1984, pp. 213–48. [G: U.K.]

Dublin, Thomas. The Merrimack Valley Textile Museum—An Appreciation. *Labor Hist.*, Spring 1984, 25(2), pp. 240–42. [G: U.S.]

Dunkel, Arthur. Lessons from Textile Experience for General Trade Policy. *World Econ.*, December 1984, 7(4), pp. 361–68.

Gilbert, J.-P. Un cas de coopération économique Pologne-R.D.A.: la filature de coton polono-allemande de Zawiercie "Przyjazn-Freundschaft" (Amitié). (An Example of Economic Cooperation between Poland and the G.D.R. With English summary.) *Écon. Soc.*, February 1984, 18(2), pp. 115–37. [G: Poland; E. Germany]

Gupta, Kanhaya L. and Taher, M. A. Technological Progress and Factor Substitution in the U.S. Textile Industry, 1949–1974. *Empirical Econ.*, 1984, 9(2), pp. 67–74. [G: U.S.]

Hester, Susan B. and Hinkle, Dennis E. Balancing U.S. Trade Interests: The Impact of Chinese Textile Imports on the Market Shares of American Manufacturers. *Bus. Econ.*, April 1984, 19(3), pp. 27–34. [G: U.S.]

Julien, Pierre-André; Thibodeau, Jean-Claude and Mathews, Georges. Les nouvelles technologies et l'emploi au Québec. (New Technologies and Employement: Textile, Pulp and Paper, and Savings and Credit Institutions Industries. With English summary.) *L'Actual. Econ.*, September 1984, 60(3), pp. 326–40.

Kelton, Christina M. L. Nonstationary Markov Modeling: An Application to Wage-influenced Industrial Relocation. *Int. Reg. Sci. Rev.*, September 1984, 9(1), pp. 75–90. [G: U.S.]

Kibria, M. G. and Tisdell, Clem A. Comparative Aspects of Capacity Utilization: Evidence from Bangladesh Jute Weaving Industry. *J. Econ. Devel.*, July 1984, 9(1), pp. 45–66. [G: Bangladesh]

Langdon, Steven. Indigenous Technological Capability in Africa: The Case of Textiles and Wood Products in Kenya. In *Fransman, M. and King, K., eds.*, 1984, pp. 355–74. [G: Kenya]

Lazonick, William. Rings and Mules in Britain: Reply [Factor Costs and the Diffusion of Ring Spinning in Britain Prior to World War I]. *Quart. J. Econ.*, May 1984, 99(2), pp. 393–98. [G: U.K.]

McHugh, Cathy L. Earning in the Post-Bellum

Southern Cotton Textile Industry: A Case Study. *Exploration Econ. Hist.*, January 1984, *21*(1), pp. 28–39. [G: U.S.]

Mondal, Abdul Hye and Ahmad, Salahuddin. Factor Proportions and Factor Productivity Changes in Jute and Cotton Textile Manufacturing Industries in Bangladesh (1962/63–1977/78). *Bangladesh Devel. Stud.*, September 1984, *12*(3), pp. 37–63. [G: Bangladesh]

Ó Gráda, Cormac. Technical Change in the Mid-Nineteenth Century British Cotton Industry: A Note. *J. Europ. Econ. Hist.*, Fall 1984, *13*(2), pp. 345–52. [G: U.K.]

Orlandi, Alberto. Latin American Commodity Exports: The Case of Cotton Fibre. *Cepal Rev.*, April 1984, (22), pp. 137–58.
[G: Latin America]

Pack, Howard. Productivity and Technical Choice: Applications to the Textile Industry. *J. Devel. Econ.*, September–October 1984, *16*(1–2), pp. 153–76. [G: Philippines]

Sandberg, Lars G. The Remembrance of Things Past: Rings and Mules Revisited [Factor Costs and the Diffusion of Ring Spinning in Britain Prior to World War I]. *Quart. J. Econ.*, May 1984, *99*(2), pp. 387–92. [G: U.K.]

Saxonhouse, Gary R. and Wright, Gavin. New Evidence on the Stubborn English Mule and the Cotton Industry, 1878–1920. *Econ. Hist. Rev., 2nd Ser.*, November 1984, *37*(4), pp. 507–19. [G: U.K.]

Schiller, László. The Socialist Foreign Trade Contacts of Budaflax. *Soviet E. Europ. Foreign Trade*, Summer 1984, *20*(2), pp. 88–99.
[G: CMEA]

Schwartz, Hugh. Industrial Project Identification in an Economic Integration Context. In *Núñez del Arco, J.; Margain, E. and Cherol, R., eds.*, 1984, pp. 126–41. [G: Latin America]

Scott, A. J. Industrial Organization and the Logic of Intra-Metropolitan Location, III: A Case Study of the Women's Dress Industry in the Greater Los Angeles Region. *Econ. Geogr.*, January 1984, *60*(1), pp. 3–27. [G: U.S.]

Seiler, Eric. Piece Rate vs. Time Rate: The Effect of Incentives on Earnings. *Rev. Econ. Statist.*, August 1984, *66*(3), pp. 363–76. [G: U.S.]

Shaw, Richard W. and Shaw, Susan A. Late Entry, Market Shares and Competitive Survival: The Case of Synthetic Fibers. *Managerial Dec. Econ.*, June 1984, *5*(2), pp. 72–79.
[G: W. Europe]

Weiss, Charles and Lepkowski, Wil. Cotton Development International. In *Weiss, C. and Jéquier, N., eds.*, 1984, pp. 295–311.
[G: LDCs]

Werbner, Pnina. Business on Trust: Pakistani Entrepreneurship in the Manchester Garment Trade. In *Ward, R. and Jenkins, R., eds.*, 1984, pp. 166–88. [G: U.K.]

Williams, Martin. The Structure of Production in the United States Textile Industry: The Postwar Period. *Weltwirtsch. Arch.*, 1984, *120*(1), pp. 155–64. [G: U.S.]

6317 Forest Products, Lumber, Paper, and Printing and Publishing

Artto, Eero. Kansainvälinen kilpailukyky yritys-ja toimialatasolla -IV. (International Competitiveness at Enterprise and Industry Level IV. With English summary.) *Liiketaloudellinen Aikak.*, 1984, *33*(3), pp. 321–75. [G: Finland; Sweden; Canada; W. Germany; U.S.]

Artto, Eero. Kansainvälinen kilpailukyky yritys-ja toimialatasolla -III. (International Competitiveness at Enterprise and Industry Level-III. With English summary.) *Liiketaloudellinen Aikak.*, 1984, *33*(2), pp. 181–217. [G: U.S.; Finland; Sweden; Canada; Germany]

Beged-Dov, Aharon G. Application of Operations Research in Paper Procurement. In *Avula, X. J. R., et al.*, 1984, pp. 271–77. [G: U.S.]

Chakrabarty, Gurupada. Minor Forest Products and Amelioration of Rural Unemployment. *Margin*, January 1984, *16*(2), pp. 53–76.
[G: India]

Cohen, Avi J. Technological Change as Historical Process: The Case of the U.S. Pulp and Paper Industry, 1915–1940. *J. Econ. Hist.*, September 1984, *44*(3), pp. 775–99. [G: U.S.]

Durutalo, Simione. "Factory Forestry": Fiji's Throwaway Forests. In *Utrecht, E., ed.*, 1984, pp. 181–231. [G: Fiji]

Greenberg, Edward S. Producer Cooperatives and Democratic Theory: The Case of the Plywood Firms. In *Jackall, R. and Levin, H. M., eds.*, 1984, pp. 171–214. [G: U.S.]

Gunn, Christopher. Hoedads Co-op: Democracy and Cooperation at Work. In *Jackall, R. and Levin, H. M., eds.*, 1984, pp. 141–70.
[G: U.S.]

Henderson, David M. The Natural Resource-Based Sector. In *Hood, N. and Young, S., eds.*, 1984, pp. 249–87. [G: U.K.]

House, William J. Product Choice and Employment in Furniture-making in Kenya. In *van Ginneken, W. and Baron, C., eds.*, 1984, pp. 148–67. [G: Kenya]

Hunter, Lachlan. Tropical Forest Plantations and Natural Stand Management: A National Lesson from East Kalimantan? *Bull. Indonesian Econ. Stud.*, April 1984, *20*(1), pp. 98–116.
[G: Indonesia]

Julien, Pierre-André; Thibodeau, Jean-Claude and Mathews, Georges. Les nouvelles technologies et l'emploi au Québec. (New Technologies and Employement: Textile, Pulp and Paper, and Savings and Credit Institutions Industries. With English summary.) *L'Actual. Econ.*, September 1984, *60*(3), pp. 326–40.

Kalleberg, Arne L.; Wallace, Michael and Raffalovich, Lawrence E. Accounting for Labor's Share: Class and Income Distribution in the Printing Industry. *Ind. Lab. Relat. Rev.*, April 1984, *37*(3), pp. 386–402. [G: U.S.]

Kinkley, Chu-Chu and Lahiri, Kajal. Testing the Rational Expectations Hypothesis in a Second-

ary Materials Market. *J. Environ. Econ. Manage.*, September 1984, *11*(3), pp. 282–91.
[G: U.S.]

Langdon, Steven. Indigenous Technological Capability in Africa: The Case of Textiles and Wood Products in Kenya. In *Fransman, M. and King, K., eds.*, 1984, pp. 355–74.
[G: Kenya]

Larson, David. Wages in the Paper Industries among Highest in Manufacturing. *Mon. Lab. Rev.*, March 1984, *107*(3), pp. 52–54.
[G: U.S.]

Margolick, Michael; Hansson, Ardo H. and Helliwell, John F. Competing Energy Uses for Wood Wastes in British Columbia. *Energy J.*, January 1984, *5*(1), pp. 65–84. [G: Canada]

Merrifield, David E. and Haynes, Richard W. The Adjustment of Product and Factor Markets: An Application to the Pacific Northwest Forest Products Industry. *Amer. J. Agr. Econ.*, February 1984, *66*(1), pp. 79–87. [G: U.S.]

Mickwitz, Gösta. Skogarnas öde. (The Fate of the Forests. With English summary.) *Ekon. Samfundets Tidskr.*, 1984, *37*(2), pp. 63–64.
[G: Europe]

Pencavel, John H. The Empirical Performance of a Model of Trade Union Behavior. In *Rosa, J.-J., ed.*, 1984, pp. 221–76. [G: U.S.]

Tamminen, Rauno; Laitinen, Erkki K. and Rajahonka, Raimo J. Forecasting the Sales Volume of a Novel and Optimizing the Size of Edition. *Liiketaloudellinen Aikak.*, 1984, *33*(3), pp. 253–63. [G: Finland]

Ziegler, Joseph A. and Bell, Stephen E. Estimating Demand for Intake Water by Self-Supplied Firms. *Water Resources Res.*, January 1984, *20*(1), pp. 4–8. [G: U.S.]

6318 Food Processing, Tobacco, and Beverages

Adekanye, Tomilayo O. A Study of Bread Baking Costs in Nigeria: Some Considerations for Development. *Reg. Stud.*, October 1984, *18*(5), pp. 381–84. [G: Nigeria]

Burke, R. H. and Naughtin, J. C. Productivity in the Meat Processing Industry in Queensland. *Rev. Marketing Agr. Econ.*, April 1984, *52*(1), pp. 49–60. [G: Australia]

Campbell, Thomas J. and Ware, Charles J. *Russell Stover* and the Vertical Agreement Puzzle. In *Fox, E. M. and Halverson, J. T., eds.*, 1984, pp. 371–81. [G: U.S.]

Carnes, Richard B. Meatpacking and Prepared Meats Industry: Above-Average Productivity Gains. *Mon. Lab. Rev.*, April 1984, *107*(4), pp. 37–42. [G: U.S.]

Clarence-Smith, W. G. The Sugar and Rum Industries in the Portuguese Empire, 1850–1914. In *Albert, B. and Graves, A., eds.*, 1984, 227–35. [G: Africa]

Cordonnier, J. L.; Lesourd, J. B. and Ruiz, J. M. Substitutions in the French Food Industry from a Translog Cost Function Model. In *Avula, X. J. R., et al.*, 1984, pp. 833–36.
[G: France]

Delson, Roberta M. Sugar Production for the

Nineteenth Century British Market: Rethinking the Roles of Brazil and the British West Indies. In *Albert, B. and Graves, A., eds.*, 1984, pp. 59–80. [G: Brazil; Caribbean; U.K.]

Eckel, Catherine C. and Goldberg, Michael A. Regulation and Deregulation of the Brewing Industry: The British Columbia Example. *Can. Public Policy*, September 1984, *10*(3), pp. 316–27. [G: Canada]

Gochet, W. and Vandenbosch, P. Location of Depots at the Maes Brewery. *Tijdschrift Econ. Manage.*, 1984, *29*(1), pp. 33–43.
[G: Belgium]

Guy, Donna J. Sugar Industries at the Periphery of the World Market: Argentina, 1860–1914. In *Albert, B. and Graves, A., eds.*, 1984, pp. 147–62. [G: Argentina]

Haraksingh, Kusha. Labour, Technology and the Sugar Estates in Trinidad, 1870–1914. In *Albert, B. and Graves, A., eds.*, 1984, pp. 133–45. [G: Trinidad]

Ingram, A. H. and Sloane, P. J. The Growth of Shiftwork in the British Food, Drink, and Tobacco Industries. *Managerial Dec. Econ.*, September 1984, *5*(3), pp. 168–76. [G: U.K.]

Kaplinsky, Raphael. Indigenous Technical Change: What We Can Learn from Sugar Processing. *World Devel.*, April 1984, *12*(4), pp. 419–32. [G: India; Kenya]

Krouse, Clement G. Brand Name as a Barrier to Entry: The ReaLemon Case. *Southern Econ. J.*, October 1984, *51*(2), pp. 495–502.
[G: U.S.]

Landgren-Gudina, Marie-Ann. Weaning Food and Low-income Consumers in Ethiopia. In *van Ginneken, W. and Baron, C., eds.*, 1984, pp. 195–210. [G: Ethiopia]

Larkin, John A. The International Face of the Philippine Sugar Industry, 1836–1920. *Philippine Rev. Econ. Bus.*, Mar./June 1984, *21*(1/2), pp. 39–58. [G: Philippines]

Leach, Bernard and Shutt, John. Chips and Crisps: The Impact of New Technology on Food Processing Jobs in Greater Manchester. In *Marstrand, P., ed.*, 1984, pp. 73–92.
[G: U.K.]

Lutton, Thomas J. and LeBlanc, Michael R. A Comparison of Multivariate Logit and Translog Models for Energy and Nonenergy Input Cost Share Analysis. *Energy J.*, October 1984, *5*(4), pp. 35–44. [G: U.S.]

Lynk, William J. Interpreting Rising Concentration: The Case of Beer. *J. Bus.*, Part 1, January 1984, *57*(1), pp. 43–55. [G: U.S.]

Marion, Donald R. and Grinnell, Gerald. Estimates of Consumer Loss Due to Monopoly in the U.S. Food Manufacturing Industries: Comment. *Amer. J. Agr. Econ.*, November 1984, *66*(4), pp. 520–23. [G: U.S.]

Mattei, Andres A. Ramos. The Growth of the Puerto Rican Sugar Industry under North American Domination: 1899–1910. In *Albert, B. and Graves, A., eds.*, 1984, pp. 121–31.
[G: Puerto Rico]

Mounier, Alain and Byé, Pascal. Les futurs alimentaires et énergétiques des biotechnologies. (With English summary.) *Écon. Soc.*, September 1984, *18*(9), pp. 7–340. [G: Global]

Mujica Ateaga, Rodrigo and Oncken Bonta, Hermann. Análisis econométrico de la industria vitivinícola en Chile. (With English summary.) *Cuadernos Econ.*, December 1984, *21*(64), pp. 315–27. [G: Chile]

Munting, Roger. The Russian Beet Sugar Industry in the XIXth Century. *J. Europ. Econ. Hist.*, Fall 1984, *13*(2), pp. 291–309. [G: U.S.S.R.]

Munting, Roger. The State and the Beet Sugar Industry in Russia before 1914. In *Albert, B. and Graves, A., eds.*, 1984, pp. 21–28. [G: U.S.S.R.]

O'Neil, Brian F. Direct Store Delivery Distribution—An Evaluation. *Logist. Transp. Rev.*, March 1984, *20*(1), pp. 83–89. [G: U.S.]

Owen, Roger. The Egyptian Sugar Industry, 1870–1914: From State to Private Ownership and from Export Orientation to Production for the Local Market. In *Albert, B. and Graves, A., eds.*, 1984, pp. 217–25. [G: Egypt]

Palairet, Michael. Beet Sugar and Peasant Economy in the Balkans before 1914. In *Albert, B. and Graves, A., eds.*, 1984, pp. 47–57. [G: Bulgaria; Yugoslavia]

Parker, Russell C. and Connor, John M. Estimates of Consumer Loss Due to Monopoly in the U.S. Food Manufacturing Industries: Second Reply. *Amer. J. Agr. Econ.*, November 1984, *66*(4), pp. 524–28. [G: U.S.]

Perkins, John A. The Political Economy of Sugar Beet in Imperial Germany. In *Albert, B. and Graves, A., eds.*, 1984, pp. 31–45. [G: Germany]

Prochaska, Fred J. Principal Types of Uncertainty in Seafood Processing and Marketing. *Marine Resource Econ.*, 1984, *1*(1), pp. 51–66. [G: U.S.]

Remy, Dorothy and Sawers, Larry. Urban Industrial Decline and the Dynamics of Sexual and Racial Oppression. In *Sawers, L. and Tabb, W. K., eds.*, 1984, pp. 128–51.

Richardson, Peter. The Natal Sugar Industry in the Nineteenth Century. In *Albert, B. and Graves, A., eds.*, 1984, pp. 237–58. [G: S. Africa]

Roberts, Mark J. Testing Oligopolistic Behavior. *Int. J. Ind. Organ.*, December 1984, *2*(4), pp. 367–83. [G: U.S.]

Scherer, Frederic M. The Welfare Economics of Product Variety: An Application to the Ready-to-Eat Cereals Industry. In *Scherer, F. M.*, 1984, *1979*, pp. 142–67. [G: U.S.]

Schnakenbourg, Christian. From Sugar Estate to Central Factory: The Industrial Revolution in the Caribbean (1840–1905). In *Albert, B. and Graves, A., eds.*, 1984, pp. 83–93. [G: Caribbean]

Silkman, Richard. The Commons Problems Revisited: Shellfishing on Long Island. *J. Policy Anal. Manage.*, Spring 1984, *3*(3), pp. 451–53. [G: U.S.]

Small, Drummond B. and Smith, Lawrence D.

The Food, Drink, and Tobacco Sectors. In *Hood, N. and Young, S., eds.*, 1984, pp. 174–212. [G: U.K.]

Timmer, C. Peter. Choice of Technique in Rice Milling on Java: A Reply. In *Eicher, C. K. and Staatz, J. M., eds.*, 1984, pp. 292–95. [G: Indonesia]

Timmer, C. Peter. Choice of Technique in Rice Milling on Java. In *Eicher, C. K. and Staatz, J. M., eds.*, 1984, *1973*, pp. 278–88. [G: Indonesia]

Warman, Arturo. The Cauldron of the Revolution: Agrarian Capitalism and Sugar Industry in Morelos, Mexico, 1880–1910. In *Albert, B. and Graves, A., eds.*, 1984, pp. 165–79. [G: Mexico]

6319 Other Industries

Bradbury, Malcolm. Variation of Cost with Output. In *Sandford, C. and Bradbury, M., eds.*, 1984, pp. 42–65. [G: U.K.]

Stoller, Michael A. On the Economics of Antitrust and Competition in a Collectibles Market: The Strange Case of the Baseball Card Industry. *Bus. Econ.*, April 1984, *19*(3), pp. 18–26. [G: U.S.]

Ward, James. Solar Water Heating in California: Policy Evolution and Industry Development. In *Baumgartner, T. and Burns, T. R., eds.*, 1984, pp. 53–90. [G: U.S.]

632 Industry Studies: Extractive Industries

6320 General

Beebe, Raymond. Government Participation in Resource Markets: Comment. In *Pearce, D. W.; Siebert, H. and Walter, I., eds.*, 1984, pp. 242–46. [G: Australia; LDCs]

Lloyd, P. J. Mineral Economics in Australia: Linkages With Other Sectors of the Economy: Introduction. In *Lloyd, P. J., ed.*, 1984, pp. 158–69. [G: Australia]

McColl, G. D. Foreign Investment in Australian Mining. In *Lloyd, P. J., ed.*, 1984, pp. 176–207. [G: Australia]

Noam, Eli M. Market Power and Regulation: A Simultaneous Approach. *J. Ind. Econ.*, March 1984, *32*(3), pp. 335–47. [G: U.S.]

Shah, Farhed A. A Note on "The Optimal Depletion of Exhaustible Resources." *Rev. Econ. Stud.*, April 1984, *51*(2), pp. 351.

Siebert, Horst. The Economics of Natural Resources Ventures. In *Pearce, D. W.; Siebert, H. and Walter, I., eds.*, 1984, pp. 11–35. [G: Selected Countries]

Szidarovszky, Ferenc. A Multiobjective Observation Network Design Procedure and Its Application in Hydrology and Mining. In *Grauer, M. and Wierzbicki, A. P., eds.*, 1984, pp. 210–17.

Vernon, Raymond. Uncertainty in the Resource Industries: The Special Role of State-owned Enterprises. In *Pearce, D. W.; Siebert, H. and Walter, I., eds.*, 1984, pp. 207–23. [G: LDCs]

Walter, Ingo. Project Finance—The Lender's Perspective. In *Pearce, D. W.; Siebert, H. and Walter, I., eds.*, 1984, pp. 249–70. [G: Selected Countries]

Wheelwright, E. The Political Economy of Foreign Domination. In *Lloyd, P. J., ed.*, 1984, 1982, pp. 208–25. [G: Australia]

Whitley, Glenn R. Project Financing: The Borrower's View. In *Pearce, D. W.; Siebert, H. and Walter, I., eds.*, 1984, pp. 271–91. [G: Selected Countries]

6322 Mining (metal, coal, and other nonmetallic minerals)

Adler, Svjetlana and Matejka, Harriet. Soviet Coal Exports. In *Kostecki, M. M., ed.*, 1984, pp. 100–15. [G: U.S.S.R.; Global]

Appleton, William C. and Baker, Joe G. The Effect of Unionization on Safety in Bituminous Deep Mines. *J. Lab. Res.*, Spring 1984, 5(2), pp. 139–47. [G: U.S.]

Barro, Robert J. Some Evidence on the Real Price of Gold, Its Costs of Production, and Commodity Prices: Comment. In *Bordo, M. D. and Schwartz, A. J., eds.*, 1984, pp. 644–46. [G: U.S.; U.S.S.R.; S. Africa; Australia]

Beckmann, Petr. The Resourceful Earth: A Response to Global 2000: Coal. In *Simon, J. L. and Kahn, H., eds.*, 1984, pp. 428–38. [G: Global]

Brockhoff, Klaus. The Production Ceiling According to the United Nations Convention on the Law of the Sea. *Weltwirtsch. Arch.*, 1984, 120(3), pp. 541–57. [G: Global]

Cairns, Robert D. Changing Structure in the World Nickel Industry. *Antitrust Bull.*, Fall 1984, 29(3), pp. 561–75. [G: U.S.]

Carlson, Norma W. Pay in Mountain Region Coal Mines Outstrips National Average. *Mon. Lab. Rev.*, March 1984, 107(3), pp. 49–52. [G: U.S.]

Carr, David W. Difficulty of Restoring Economic Viability with Lopsided Development: The Mauritanian Case. *J. Devel. Areas*, April 1984, 18(3), pp. 373–86. [G: Mauritania]

Choksi, Shernaz. Spot and Futures Prices in Copper: The Speculative Link. *J. Post Keynesian Econ.*, Spring 1984, 6(3), pp. 433–48. [G: U.K.]

Conrad, Robert F. and Hool, R. Bryce. Intertemporal Extraction of Mineral Resources under Variable Rate Taxes. *Land Econ.*, November 1984, 60(4), pp. 319–27.

Crisp, Jeff. The Labour Question in the Gold Coast, 1870–1906. In *Munslow, B. and Finch, H., eds.*, 1984, pp. 18–41. [G: Ghana]

Curry, Robert L., Jr. Problems in Acquiring Mineral Revenues for Financing Economic Development: A Case Study of Zambia during 1970–78. *Amer. J. Econ. Soc.*, January 1984, 43(1), pp. 37–52. [G: Zambia]

Dale, Larry L. The Pace of Mineral Depletion in the United States. *Land Econ.*, August 1984, 60(3), pp. 255–67. [G: U.S.]

Dow, Alexander. Finance and Foreign Control in Canadian Base Metal Mining, 1918–55 *Econ. Hist. Rev.*, 2nd Ser., February 1984, 37(1), pp. 54–67. [G: Canada]

Dowell, Richard. Resources Rent Tax and Alternative Forms of Mineral Royalties. *Australian Tax Forum*, December 1984, 1(4), pp. 437–50. [G: Australia]

Eisenhauer, J. L. Comparative Analysis of Coal-based Electric Energy Delivery Systems. In *Lev, B., et al., eds.*, 1984, pp. 33–45. [G: U.S.]

Emerson, Craig. Economic Evaluation of Mineral-Processing Projects. In *Lloyd, P. J., ed.*, 1984, pp. 253–72. [G: Australia]

Emerson, Craig and Garnaut, Ross. Mineral Leasing Policy: Competitive Bidding and the Resource Rent Tax Given Various Responses to Risk. *Econ. Rec.*, June 1984, 60(169), pp. 133–42.

Emerson, Craig; Garnaut, Ross and Ross, Anthony Clunies. Mining Taxation in Indonesia. *Bull. Indonesian Econ. Stud.*, August 1984, 20(2), pp. 107–21. [G: Indonesia]

Fishback, Price. Segregation in Job Hierarchies: West Virginia Coal Mining, 1906–1932. *J. Econ. Hist.*, September 1984, 44(3), pp. 755–74. [G: U.S.]

Forsyth, Peter. Transport Infrastructure and Mining Industry Development. In *Lloyd, P. J., ed.*, 1984, pp. 226–52. [G: Australia]

Foster, James C. Western Miners and Silicosis: "The Scourge of the Underground Toiler," 1890–1943. *Ind. Lab. Relat. Rev.*, April 1984, 37(3), pp. 371–85. [G: U.S.]

Franssen, Herman T. OECD Coal Demand in the 1980s. In *Hawdon, D., ed.*, 1984, pp. 104–31. [G: OECD]

Garcia, Timothy L. United States Supreme Court Upholds Indiana Mineral Lapse Statute. *Natural Res. J.*, January 1984, 24(1), pp. 203–12. [G: U.S.]

Ghosh, S.; Gilbert, C. L. and Hughes Hallett, Andrew J. Commodity Market Stabilization: A Comparison of Simple and Optimal Intervention Strategies in the World Copper Market. *J. Policy Modeling*, November 1984, 6(4), pp. 555–72. [G: Global]

Ghosh, S.; Gilbert, C. L. and Hughes Hallett, Andrew J. Simple and Optimal Control Rules for Stabilising Commodity Markets. In *Hughes Hallet, A. J., ed.*, 1984, pp. 209–48.

Gordon, Richard L. Resource Procurement: A Case Study of U.S. Electric Utilities. In *Pearce, D. W.; Siebert, H. and Walter, I., eds.*, 1984, pp. 319–37. [G: U.S.]

Graves, Stephen C.; Horwitch, Mel and Bowman, Edward H. Deep-Draft Dredging of U.S. Coal Ports: A Cost–Benefit Analysis. *Policy Sci.*, October 1984, 17(2), pp. 153–78. [G: U.S.]

Gregory, R. G. Some Implications of the Growth of the Mineral Sector. In *Lloyd, P. J., ed.*, 1984, 1976, pp. 285–310. [G: Australia]

Halvorsen, Robert and Smith, Tim R. On Mea-

suring Natural Resource Scarcity. *J. Polit. Econ.*, October 1984, *92*(5), pp. 954–64.
[G: Canada]

Hanel, Petr. The Soviet Impact on International Trade in Asbestos. In *Kostecki, M. M., ed.*, 1984, pp. 173–93. [G: U.S.S.R.; Global]

Harries, Heinrich. Adaptation of Long-term Contracts. In *Pearce, D. W.; Siebert, H. and Walter, I., eds.*, 1984, pp. 165–68.

Harris, Stuart. Dimensions of Resource Dependence in Exporting Countries. In *Pearce, D. W.; Siebert, H. and Walter, I., eds.*, 1984, pp. 113–33. [G: Papua New Guinea; LDCs]

Hausman, William J. Market Power in the London Coal Trade: The Limitation of the Vend, 1770–1845. *Exploration Econ. Hist.*, October 1984, *21*(4), pp. 383–405. [G: U.K.]

Hazilla, Michael and Kopp, Raymond J. A Factor Demand Model for Strategic Nonfuel Minerals in the Primary Metals Sector. *Land Econ.*, November 1984, *60*(4), pp. 328–39.

Heery, Edmund. Group Incentives and the Mining Supervisor: The Effects of a Payment System on First-Line Management. *Brit. J. Ind. Relat.*, November 1984, *22*(3), pp. 333–45.
[G: U.K.]

Helliwell, John F. Natural Resources and the Australian Economy. In *Caves, R. E. and Krause, L. B., eds.*, 1984, pp. 81–126. [G: Australia]

Henderson, David M. The Natural Resource-Based Sector. In *Hood, N. and Young, S., eds.*, 1984, pp. 249–87. [G: U.K.]

Hughes Hallett, A. J. Optimal Stockpiling in a High-Risk Commodity Market: The Case of Copper. *J. Econ. Dynam. Control*, November 1984, *8*(2), pp. 211–38. [G: Global]

Hyett, A. J. The Structure and Economics of the Nuclear Fuel Cycle Service Industry. In *Brookes, L. G. and Motamen, H., eds.*, 1984, pp. 162–89. [G: Selected Countries]

Kania, John J. Economics of Coal Transport by Slurry Pipeline versus Unit Train: A Case Study. *Energy Econ.*, April 1984, *6*(2), pp. 131–38. [G: U.S.]

Kaser, Michael C. The Soviet Impact on World Trade in Gold and Platinum. In *Kostecki, M. M., ed.*, 1984, pp. 156–72. [G: U.S.S.R.; Global]

Kolstad, Charles D. and Abbey, David S. Erratum [The Effect of Market Conduct on International Steam Coal Trade]. *Europ. Econ. Rev.*, December 1984, *26*(3), pp. 379.
[G: Selected Countries]

Kolstad, Charles D. and Abbey, David S. The Effect of Market Conduct on International Steam Coal Trade. *Europ. Econ. Rev.*, February 1984, *24*(1), pp. 39–59.
[G: Selected Countries]

Kononov, Iu. D. The Fuel-Energy Complex in the System of National Economic Relations. *Prob. Econ.*, May 1984, *27*(1), pp. 33–46.
[G: U.S.S.R.]

Labys, Walter. The Role of the Soviet Union in Metals Markets: A Case Study of Copper, Manganese and Chromite. In *Kostecki, M. M., ed.*, 1984, pp. 135–55. [G: U.S.S.R.; Global]

Lloyd, P. J. Individual Mines or Oilfields: Introduction. In *Lloyd, P. J., ed.*, 1984, pp. 35–52. [G: Australia]

Lloyd, P. J. Major Issues of the Current Resources Boom. In *Lloyd, P. J., ed.*, 1984, pp. 3–9.
[G: Australia]

Lloyd, P. J. Mineral Economics in Australia: Economy-Wide Effects: Introduction. In *Lloyd, P. J., ed.*, 1984, pp. 275–84.
[G: Australia]

Lloyd, P. J. Mineral Economics in Australia: Conclusion. In *Lloyd, P. J., ed.*, 1984, pp. 323–25. [G: Australia]

Lloyd, P. J. Mining Rights as a Component of Aboriginal Land Rights: An Economic Assessment. In *Lloyd, P. J., ed.*, 1984, pp. 138–56.
[G: Australia]

Lloyd, P. J. Resource Rent Taxes. *Australian Econ. Rev.*, 2nd Quarter 1984, (66), pp. 37–46. [G: Australia]

Lundborg, Per. The Nexus between Income Distribution, Trade Policy, and Monopoly Power: An Assessment of the Tin Market. *J. Policy Modeling*, February 1984, *6*(1), pp. 69–79.
[G: Malaysia]

Mardones, José Luis; Silva, Enrique and Martínez, Cristián. Las industrias del cobre y del aluminio: una revisión de cambios estructurales. (With English summary.) *Cuadernos Econ.*, December 1984, *21*(64), pp. 329–45.
[G: Global]

Marsh, James B. The Potential Economic Impact of Technological Progress on the Development of Manganese Nodule Mining. In *Gopalakrishnan, C., ed.*, 1984, pp. 49–59.

Mirlin, G. Mineral Resources and the Economy. *Prob. Econ.*, March 1984, *26*(11), pp. 53–72.
[G: U.S.S.R.; Global]

Naganna, N. Structural Composition of Costs in Coal Industry: New Perspectives. *Indian Econ. J.*, Oct.–Dec. 1984, *32*(2), pp. 104–32.
[G: India]

Nappi, Carmine. The USSR and The International Aluminium Market. In *Kostecki, M. M., ed.*, 1984, pp. 116–34. [G: U.S.S.R.; Global]

Odell, Peter R. Dimensions of Resource Dependence in Exporting Countries: Comment. In *Pearce, D. W.; Siebert, H. and Walter, I., eds.*, 1984, pp. 134–36. [G: Papua New Guinea; LDCs]

Parker, William N. Kartelle und Konzerne: The German Coal Syndicate under the Steel Mills' Domination. In *Parker, W. N.*, 1984, *1954*, pp. 103–24. [G: Germany]

Parker, William N. Law and Enterprise: Ore-Mining on Two Sides of the Franco–German Border [National States and National Development: French and German Ore-Mining in the Late Nineteenth Century]. In *Parker, W. N.*, 1984, *1959*, pp. 91–102. [G: France; Germany]

Parker, William N. M. Schuman and His Plan. In *Parker, W. N.*, 1984, *1952*, pp. 125–38.
[G: W. Europe]

Parker, William N. The Interruption of Expansion. In *Parker, W. N.*, 1984, *1957*, pp. 57–75. [G: Europe]

Porter, Michael G. Taxation of the Australian Resource Sector. In *Siebert, H.*, ed., 1984, pp. 95–116. [G: Australia]

Price, Jeffrey P. Coal Supply Models: The State of the Art. In *Lev, B., et al.*, eds., 1984, pp. 3–20. [G: U.S.]

Price, T. Uranium Production and Distribution: The Balance of Supply and Demand. In *Brookes, L. G. and Motamen, H.*, eds., 1984, pp. 145–60. [G: Selected Countries]

Radetzki, Marian and Van Duyne, Carl. The Response of Mining Investment to a Decline in Economic Growth: The Case of Copper in the 1970s. *J. Devel. Econ.*, May–June–August 1984, *15*(1,2,3), pp. 19–45. [G: LDCs]

Reed, J. David and Hoag, John H. Regional Coal-mining Employment in the United States from 1985 to 2000. *Growth Change*, July 1984, *15*(3), pp. 43–50. [G: U.S.]

Rhodes, Harold L. British Public Enterprises and Project Initiation in the Developing World. In *Ramanadham, V. V.*, ed., 1984, pp. 87–108. [G: U.K.]

Richardson, Peter and Van Helten, Jean-Jacques. The Development of the South African Gold-Mining Industry, 1895–1918. *Econ. Hist. Rev.*, 2nd Ser., August 1984, *37*(3), pp. 319–40. [G: S. Africa]

Ritchie, Carol J. Wide Pattern *Pedis Possessio*: The Expansion of Prediscovery Mineral Claim Protection in New Mexico. *Natural Res. J.*, April 1984, *24*(2), pp. 437–49. [G: U.S.]

Ro, Young Key and Forster, D. Lynn. Regional Input–Output Analysis of an Environmental Regulation. *J. Econ. Devel.*, July 1984, *9*(1), pp. 167–88. [G: U.S.]

Robotham, F. P. The Case Against Uranium Mining. In *Lloyd, P. J.*, ed., 1984, *1980*, pp. 131–35. [G: Australia; Selected Countries]

Rockoff, Hugh. Some Evidence on the Real Price of Gold, Its Costs of Production, and Commodity Prices. In *Bordo, M. D. and Schwartz, A. J.*, eds., 1984, pp. 613–44. [G: U.S.; S. Africa; Australia; U.S.S.R.]

Rockoff, Hugh. Some Evidence on the Real Price of Gold, Its Costs of Production, and Commodity Prices: Reply. In *Bordo, M. D. and Schwartz, A. J.*, eds., 1984, pp. 646–48. [G: U.S.; U.S.S.R.; S. Africa; Australia]

Simon, Richard M. and Conn, W. David. Federal Assistance to Energy-producing Regions: An Evaluation of the 601 Program. *J. Energy Devel.*, Spring 1984, *9*(2), pp. 243–61. [G: U.S.]

Slade, Margaret E. Tax Policy and the Supply of Exhaustible Resources: Theory and Practice. *Land Econ.*, May 1984, *60*(2), pp. 133–47. [G: U.S.]

Taylor, Carol A. and Charney, Alberta H. The Effects of State Taxation on United States Copper Supply: Comment. *Land Econ.*, May 1984, *60*(2), pp. 211–14. [G: U.S.]

Titterton, E. [Sir]. Uranium and the Energy Fu-

ture. In *Lloyd, P. J.*, ed., 1984, *1980*, pp. 126–30. [G: Australia]

Tobin, Roger L. A Network Programming System for Studying Coal Transportation. In *Lev, B., et al.*, eds., 1984, pp. 21–32. [G: U.S.]

Toye, John. The Recession, the Third World and the Base Metals Industries. *World Devel.*, September 1984, *12*(9), pp. 923–34.

Tsokhas, K. 'A Touch of Midas': The Rise of Western Mining Corporation, 1945–1975. *Australian Econ. Hist. Rev.*, September 1984, *24*(2), pp. 132–49. [G: Australia]

Tuck, Bradford H. Alaskan Resources Development: Nonfuel Minerals and Coal. In *Morehouse, T. A.*, ed., 1984, pp. 79–104. [G: U.S.]

Ueta, Kuzuhiro and Sueishi, Tomitaro. The Control of the Use Pattern and the Life of Metals for Environmental Risk Management; The Case of Lead. *Kyoto Univ. Econ. Rev.*, October 1984, *54*(2), pp. 13–30. [G: Japan]

Watson, William D. and Bernknopf, Richard. Maximum Economic Recovery of Federal Coal. *Energy J.*, July 1984, *5*(3), pp. 59–80. [G: U.S.]

Williams, Richard M. Uranium Production and Distribution: Prospects and Concepts. In *Brookes, L. G. and Motamen, H.*, eds., 1984, pp. 116–44. [G: Global]

Wright, Sanford. Struggling against Apartheid: The Use of Economic Sanctions on South Africa. *Rev. Black Polit. Econ.*, Winter 1984–85, *13*(3), pp. 37–47. [G: S. Africa]

6323 Oil, Gas, and Other Fuels

Adams, F. Gerard and Marquez, Jaime. Petroleum Price Elasticity, Income Effects, and OPEC's Pricing Policy. *Energy J.*, January 1984, *5*(1), pp. 115–28. [G: OECD]

Agmon, Tamir; Lessard, Donald R. and Paddock, James L. Appropriate Financing for Petroleum Development in Developing Countries. *Energy J.*, July 1984, *5*(3), pp. 27–40.

Al-Sowayegh, Abdulaziz and Sharif, Walid. The Security of Oil Supplies: Prevalent Views among Oil Consumers and Producers. *J. Energy Devel.*, Autumn 1984, *10*(1), pp. 29–38. [G: Global]

Andersen, Arthur T.; Moody, Carlisle E., Jr. and Rasmussen, Jon A. Strategy, Structure and Performance of Major U.S. Oil Companies: Evidence from Line of Business Data. *Rev. Ind. Organ.*, Winter 1984, *1*(4), pp. 290–306. [G: U.S.]

Attanasi, E. D. A Note on Petroleum Industry Exploration Efficiency. *Energy J.*, July 1984, *5*(3), pp. 133–45. [G: U.S.]

Barriga, Enrique G. Relative Oil Prices and Oil Pricing Policy in Mexico. In *Csikós-Nagy, B.; Hague, D. and Hall, G.*, eds., 1984, pp. 219–37. [G: Mexico]

Basile, Paul S. and de La Grandville, Baudoin. The Evolution and Role of Non-OPEC Production in the International Oil Market. In *Ayoub, A.*, ed., 1984, pp. 123–51. [G: Global]

Baum, Herbert and Kneip, Markus. Einflussgrössen des Heizöpreises—Ergebnisse einer Regressionsrechnung. (Determinants of the Prices for Fuel Oil—Results of a Regression-Analysis. With English summary.) *Jahr. Nationalökon. Statist.*, July 1984, *199*(4), pp. 334–50. [G: W. Germany]

Baxendell, Peter [Sir]. Oil Companies and the Changing Energy Market. In *Hawdon, D., ed.*, 1984, pp. 48–56.

Berrefjord, Ole and Heum, Per. Nordic Engineering Industries and the Norwegian Offshore Market. In *Mikkelsen, A., et al.*, 1984, pp. 204–19. [G: Scandinavia]

Best, E. W. The Conditions & Limits of Oil Substitution in Canada. In *Ayoub, A., ed.*, 1984, pp. 262–83. [G: Canada]

Blanco, Herminio and Walter, John P. An Analysis of the U.S. Oil and Gas Drilling Cycle, 1940–1983. *J. Energy Devel.*, Autumn 1984, *10*(1), pp. 39–43. [G: U.S.]

Blitzer, Charles R.; Lessard, Donald R. and Paddock, James L. Risk-Bearing and the Choice of Contract Forms for Oil Exploration and Development. *Energy J.*, January 1984, *5*(1), pp. 1–28. [G: Ecuador]

Bopp, Anthony E. Tests for Structural Change in U.S. Oil Consumption, 1967–1982. *Energy Econ.*, October 1984, *6*(4), pp. 223–30. [G: U.S.]

Brock, Gerald. Vertical Restraints in Industrial Gases. In *Lafferty, R. N.; Lande, R. H. and Kirkwood, J. B., eds.*, 1984, pp. 386–427. [G: U.S.]

Canes, Michael E. and Norman, Donald A. Long-term Contracts and Market Forces in the Natural Gas Market. *J. Energy Devel.*, Autumn 1984, *10*(1), pp. 73–96. [G: U.S.]

Ciliano, Robert and Hery, William. An Overview of the Tenrac Oil and Gas Supply Model. In *Lev, B., et al., eds.*, 1984, pp. 317–35.

Cockle, Paul. Public Expenditure Policy, 1984–85: Oil. In *Cockle, P., ed.*, 1984, pp. 77–87. [G: U.K.]

Considine, Timothy J. Interfuel Substitution and Cyclical Volatility in U.S. Natural Gas Markets. *J. Energy Devel.*, Autumn 1984, *10*(1), pp. 97–109. [G: U.S.]

Dahl, Carol A. and Laumas, G. S. Stability of Canadian Refinery Response to Petroleum Product Prices. *Appl. Econ.*, October 1984, *16*(5), pp. 667–75. [G: Canada; U.S.]

Dale, Larry L. The Pace of Mineral Depletion in the United States. *Land Econ.*, August 1984, *60*(3), pp. 255–67. [G: U.S.]

Daniel, Terrence E.; Goldberg, Henry M. and Weyant, John P. Canadian Natural Gas Exports to the United States: A Monopolistic Intertemporal Analysis. *Energy J.*, October 1984, *5*(4), pp. 21–34. [G: Canada; U.S.]

Desvousges, William H. and Piette, Michael J. Problems and Prospects: U.S. Outer Continental Shelf Petroleum Resources. *Growth Change*, April 1984, *15*(2), pp. 3–10. [G: U.S.]

Dharan, Bala G. Expectation Models and Poten-

tial Information Content of Oil and Gas Reserve Value Disclosures. *Accounting Rev.*, April 1984, *59*(2), pp. 199–217. [G: U.S.]

Donnelly, William A. The Australian Demand for Petrol. *Int. J. Transport Econ.*, Aug.-Dec. 1984, *11*(2–3), pp. 189–205. [G: Australia]

Dowell, Richard. Resources Rent Tax and Alternative Forms of Mineral Royalties. *Australian Tax Forum*, December 1984, *1*(4), pp. 437–50. [G: Australia]

Drouet, Pierre. The Restructuring of the Petroleum Refining Sector and Its Social Consequences. *Int. Lab. Rev.*, July–August 1984, *123*(4), pp. 423–40. [G: Global]

Enders, Klaus. Strukturelle Konsequenzen eines Rohstoffbooms in einem Industrieland: De-Industrialisierungstheorie und norwegische Erfahrungen. (Structural Consequences of a Resource Boom in an Industrialized Economy: De-industrialization Theory and Norwegian Experience. With English summary.) *Konjunkturpolitik*, 1984, *30*(6), pp. 328–47. [G: Norway]

Finlayson, Jock A. and Haglund, David G. Oil Politics and Canada–United States Relations. *Polit. Sci. Quart.*, Summer 1984, *99*(2), pp. 271–88. [G: Canada; U.S.]

Fišer, Miroslav. The Development of the Fuel and Energy Balance during the Period of the 7th Five-Year Plan. *Czech. Econ. Digest.*, September 1984, (6), pp. 80–98. [G: Czechoslovakia]

Franssen, Herman T. International Energy Agency Strategies to Cope with Energy Uncertainties. *J. Energy Devel.*, Autumn 1984, *10*(1), pp. 13–28. [G: Global]

Garnier, Francis. University–Industry Research Interactions: Petroleum. In *Fusfeld, H. I. and Haklisch, C. S., eds.*, 1984, pp. 43–45. [G: France]

Gately, Dermot. A Ten-Year Retrospective: OPEC and the World Oil Market. *J. Econ. Lit.*, September 1984, *22*(3), pp. 1100–114. [G: OPEC]

Hannigan, J. B. and McMillan, C. H. The Soviet Union and World Trade in Oil and Gas. In *Kostecki, M. M., ed.*, 1984, pp. 68–99. [G: U.S.S.R.; Global]

Harkness, Jon. Optimal Oil Pricing in a Small Open Economy: A Macro-economic Perspective. *Can. J. Econ.*, November 1984, *17*(4), pp. 762–73.

Hatchuel, Armand and Moisdon, Jean-Claude. Théorie de la décision et pratiques organisationnelles: Le cas des investissements pétroliers. (Decision Theory and Organizational Practices: The Case Study of Oil Investments. With English summary.) *Écon. Soc.*, January 1984, *18*(1), pp. 249–89.

Helliwell, John F.; MacGregor, Mary E. and Plourde, Andre. Changes in Canadian Energy Demand, Supply, and Policies, 1974–1986. *Natural Res. J.*, April 1984, *24*(2), pp. 297–324. [G: Canada]

Helliwell, John F.; MacGregor, Mary E. and Plourde, Andre. Energy Policy and Industrial

Activity: A Reply [The National Energy Program Meets Falling World Energy Prices]. *Can. Public Policy*, December 1984, *10*(4), pp. 476–80. **[G: Canada]**

Iwayemi, Akin. Nigeria's Internal Petroleum Problems: Perspectives and Choices. *Energy J.*, October 1984, *5*(4), pp. 45–54.
[G: Nigeria]

Jarrin, Manuel Lauro Tobar. The Petroleum Industry in Ecuador. In *Baum, V., et al.*, 1984, pp. 185–95. **[G: Ecuador]**

Jones, Randall J., Jr. Empirical Models of Political Risks in U.S. Oil Production Operations in Venezuela. *J. Int. Bus. Stud.*, Spring/Summer 1984, *15*(1), pp. 81–95. **[G: U.S.]**

Kassler, Peter. Risk and Oil Exploration. In *Pearce, D. W.; Siebert, H. and Walter, I., eds.*, 1984, pp. 75–86.

Kemp, Alexander G. and Rose, David. Investment in Oil Exploration and Production: The Comparative Influence of Taxation. In *Pearce, D. W.; Siebert, H. and Walter, I., eds.*, 1984, pp. 169–95. **[G: Selected Countries]**

Kobrin, Stephen J. The Nationalisation of Oil Production, 1918–80. In *Pearce, D. W.; Siebert, H. and Walter, I., eds.*, 1984, pp. 137–64.
[G: LDCs]

Kononov, Iu. D. The Fuel-Energy Complex in the System of National Economic Relations. *Prob. Econ.*, May 1984, *27*(1), pp. 33–46.
[G: U.S.S.R.]

Krapels, Edward N., et al. The Domestic Refining Industry: Economics and Regulation. In *Alm, A. L. and Weimer, R. J., eds.*, 1984, pp. 55–76. **[G: U.S.]**

Langston, Vicky C. An Investment Model for the U.S. Gulf Coast Refining/Petrochemical Complex for Policy Analysis. In *Lev, B., et al., eds.*, 1984, pp. 355–71. **[G: U.S.]**

Lawrey, Roger N.; Kirkby, R. G. and Watkins, G. Campbell. Regulated Pipeline Tariffs in Canada—A Sensitivity Analysis. *Logist. Transp. Rev.*, September 1984, *20*(3), pp. 195–203. **[G: Canada]**

Libecap, Gary D. and Wiggins, Steven N. Contractual Responses to the Common Pool: Prorationing of Crude Oil Production. *Amer. Econ. Rev.*, March 1984, *74*(1), pp. 87–98.
[G: U.S.]

Lowinger, Thomas C. and Ram, Rati. Product Value as a Determinant of OPEC's Official Crude Oil Prices: Additional Evidence [The Determinants of Official OPEC Crude Prices]. *Rev. Econ. Statist.*, November 1984, *66*(4), pp. 691–95. **[G: OPEC]**

Lubin, Moshe and Een, Gillis. University–Industry Research Interactions: Overview of Policy Issues: Panel Report on Petroleum. In *Fusfeld, H. I. and Haklisch, C. S., eds.*, 1984, pp. 47–50.

Lys, Thomas. Mandated Accounting Changes and Debt Covenants: The Case of Oil and Gas Accounting. *J. Acc. Econ.*, April 1984, *6*(1), pp. 39–65. **[G: U.S.]**

Mackay, Tony. The Oil and Oil-Related Sector.

In *Hood, N. and Young, S., eds.*, 1984, pp. 326–64. **[G: U.K.]**

Manuel, David P. Unemployment and Drilling Activity in Major Energy-producing States. *J. Energy Devel.*, Autumn 1984, *10*(1), pp. 44–62. **[G: U.S.]**

Mayo, John W. The Technological Determinants of the U.S. Energy Industry Structure. *Rev. Econ. Statist.*, February 1984, *66*(1), pp. 51–58. **[G: U.S.]**

Mead, Walter J.; Moseidjord, Asbjorn and Sorensen, Philip E. Competitive Bidding under Asymmetrical Information: Behavior and Performance in Gulf of Mexico Drainage Lease Sales, 1959–1969. *Rev. Econ. Statist.*, August 1984, *66*(3), pp. 505–08. **[G: U.S.]**

Mounier, Alain and Byé, Pascal. Les futurs alimentaires et énergétiques des biotechnologies. (With English summary.) *Écon. Soc.*, September 1984, *18*(9), pp. 7–340. **[G: Global]**

Nikitin, S. M. and Tulin, I. V. Prices on the World Capitalist Market and Inflation. In *Nikitin, S. M., ed.*, 1984, pp. 93–107. **[G: Global]**

Niosi, Jorge. La multinationalisation des pétrolières canadiennes. (Multinationalization of Canadian Oil and Gas Industries. With English summary.) *L'Actual. Econ.*, March 1984, *60*(1), pp. 106–21. **[G: Canada]**

Painter, David S. Oil and the Marshall Plan. *Bus. Hist. Rev.*, Autumn 1984, *58*(3), pp. 359–83.
[G: U.S.; W. Europe]

Pakravan, Karim. Estimation of User's Cost for a Depletable Resource Such as Oil. *Energy Econ.*, January 1984, *6*(1), pp. 35–40.
[G: Middle East]

Porter, Richard C. The Optimal Timing of an Exhaustible, Reversible Wilderness Development Project. *Land Econ.*, August 1984, *60*(3), pp. 247–54. **[G: U.S.]**

Rasmussen, Jon A. and Piette, Michael J. A Comparison of the Costs and the Results in the Onshore and Offshore Search for Oil and Gas. *Energy J.*, January 1984, *5*(1), pp. 159–64.
[G: U.S.]

Rizzo, Socrates C. Generation and Allocation of Oil Economic Surpluses. In *Aspe, P. and Sigmund, P. E., eds.*, 1984, pp. 99–127.
[G: Mexico]

Robinson, Colin. The Changing Energy Market: What Can We Learn from the Last Ten Years? In *Hawdon, D., ed.*, 1984, pp. 7–36.
[G: Global]

Ross, Gary N. U.S. Oil and Gas Imports. In *Ayoub, A., ed.*, 1984, pp. 249–61. **[G: U.S.]**

Scarfe, Brian L. The New Oil Price Scenario and the Chrétien–Zaozirny Agreement: A Comment [Symposium on the New Oil Price Scenario]. *Can. Public Policy*, September 1984, *10*(3), pp. 340–46. **[G: Canada]**

Schmidt, Ronald H. The Effect of Price Expectations on Drilling Activity. *Fed. Res. Bank Dallas Econ. Rev.*, November 1984, pp. 1–12.
[G: U.S.]

Schneider, Hans K. and Schulz, Walter. The Importing Country's Perspective: A Case Study

of LNG. In *Pearce, D. W.; Siebert, H. and Walter, I.*, eds., 1984, pp. 295–310.
[G: Global]

Schramm, Gunter. The Changing World of Natural Gas Utilization. *Natural Res. J.*, April 1984, 24(2), pp. 405–36. [G: Global]

Sinn, Hans-Werner. Common Property Resources, Storage Facilities and Ownership Structures: A Cournot Model of the Oil Market. *Economica*, August 1984, 51(203), pp. 235–52.

Smart, Ian. The Importing Country's Perspective: A Case Study of LNG: Comment. In *Pearce, D. W.; Siebert, H. and Walter, I.*, eds., 1984, pp. 311–18. [G: Global]

Smith, James L. Further Results on Equilibrium Patterns of Competition in OCS Lease Sales. *Econ. Inquiry*, January 1984, 22(1), pp. 142–46. [G: U.S.]

Smith, James L. and Paddock, James L. Regional Modelling of Oil Discovery and Production. *Energy Econ.*, January 1984, 6(1), pp. 5–13. [G: Selected Countries]

Sproule-Jones, Mark and Richards, Patricia L. Toward a Theory of the Regulated Environment. *Can. Public Policy*, September 1984, 10(3), pp. 305–15. [G: Canada]

Takeyama, Masayuki. Japan's Foreign Negotiations Over Offshore Petroleum Development. In *Friedheim, R. L., et al.*, 1984, pp. 276–313. [G: Japan]

Tussing, Arlon R. Alaska's Petroleum-Based Economy. In *Morehouse, T. A.*, ed., 1984, pp. 51–78. [G: U.S.]

Visintini, Alfredo Aldo. Un ensayo sobre la determinación del precio de los combustibles. (An Essay on the Determination of Fuel Prices. With English summary.) *Económica*, May-December 1984, 30(2–3), pp. 245–84. [G: Argentina]

Watkins, G. Campbell; Kirkby, R. G. and Lawrey, Roger N. Risk and the Rate of Return on Arctic Natural Gas: An Illustrative Analysis. In *Pearce, D. W.; Siebert, H. and Walter, I.*, eds., 1984, pp. 87–109. [G: U.S.; Canada]

Yang, Bong-Min and Hu, Teh-wei. Gasoline Demand and Supply under a Disequilibrium Market. *Energy Econ.*, October 1984, 6(4), pp. 276–82. [G: U.S.]

633 Industry Studies: Distributive Trades

6330 General

Gallasch, H. Frederick, Jr. Price Elasticities of Demand at Retail and Wholesale Levels: An Automotive Example. *Bus. Econ.*, January 1984, 19(1), pp. 61–62.

Kim, Kyoo H. Price Elasticity of Demand at Retail and Wholesale: A Comment. *Bus. Econ.*, October 1984, 19(5), pp. 62.

Ross, Thomas W. Winners and Losers under the Robinson–Patman Act. *J. Law Econ.*, October 1984, 27(2), pp. 243–71. [G: U.S.]

Wahlroos, Björn; Berglund, Tom and Cabell,

Nina. The Social Cost of Imperfections in Domestic Trade: The Case of Finland. *Appl. Econ.*, February 1984, 16(1), pp. 119–29. [G: Finland]

6332 Wholesale Trade

Martin, Stephen. Structure and Performance of U.S. Wholesale Trade. *Managerial Dec. Econ.*, September 1984, 5(3), pp. 160–67. [G: U.S.]

O'Neil, Brian F. Direct Store Delivery Distribution—An Evaluation. *Logist. Transp. Rev.*, March 1984, 20(1), pp. 83–89. [G: U.S.]

6333 Retail Trade

Aldrich, Howard; Jones, Trevor P. and McEvoy, David. Ethnic Advantage and Minority Business Development. In *Ward, R. and Jenkins, R.*, eds., 1984, pp. 189–210. [G: U.K.]

Babb, Florence E. Women in the Marketplace: Petty Commerce in Peru. *Rev. Radical Polit. Econ.*, Spring 1984, 16(1), pp. 45–59. [G: Peru]

Bain, John S. Transfer Payment Impacts on Rural Retail Markets: A Regression Analysis. *Reg. Sci. Persp.*, 1984, 14(1), pp. 3–17. [G: U.S.]

Barron, John M. and Umbeck, John R. The Effects of Different Contractual Arrangements: The Case of Retail Gasoline Markets. *J. Law Econ.*, October 1984, 27(2), pp. 313–28. [G: U.S.]

Brambilla, Francesco. Inchiesta sul mercato dell'antiquariato in Italia. Un modello interpretativo. (An Inquiry into the Antiques Market in Italy. An Interpretive Model. With English summary.) *Giorn. Econ.*, January–February 1984, 43(1–2), pp. 3–35. [G: Italy]

Caves, Richard E. Vertical Restraints as Integration by Contract: Evidence and Policy Implications. In *Lafferty, R. N.; Lande, R. H. and Kirkwood, J. B.*, eds., 1984, pp. 430–77. [G: U.S.]

Child, John, et al. Microelectronics and the Quality of Employment in Services. In *Marstrand, P.*, ed., 1984, pp. 163–90. [G: U.K.]

Crouchley, Robert. Some Corrections to Coelho and Wilson, 1976: The Optimum Location and Size of Shopping Centres. *Reg. Stud.*, October 1984, 18(5), pp. 393–96. [G: U.S.]

Darden, William R. and Lumpkin, James R. Psychographic and Demographic Profile of Convenience Food Store Users: Why People Convenience Shop. *Rev. Bus. Econ. Res.*, Spring 1984, 19(2), pp. 68–80. [G: U.S.]

Dawson, John A. Structural-Spatial Relationships in the Spread of Hypermarket Retailing. In *Kaynak, E. and Savitt, R.*, eds., 1984, pp. 156–82. [G: Selected Countries]

Eppen, Gary D. and Liebermann, Yehoshua. Why Do Retailers Deal? An Inventory Explanation. *J. Bus.*, October 1984, 57(4), pp. 519–30. [G: U.S.]

Friedman, Brian. Apparel Stores Display Above-

Average Productivity. *Mon. Lab. Rev.*, October 1984, *107*(10), pp. 37–42. [G: U.S.]

Glazer, Nona Y. Servants to Capital: Unpaid Domestic Labor and Paid Work. *Rev. Radical Polit. Econ.*, Spring 1984, *16*(1), pp. 61–87. [G: U.S.]

Görgens, Egon. Nachfragemacht im Lebensmittelhandel als Instrument der Strukturanpassung. (With English Summary.) In *Eucken, W. and Böhm, F., eds.*, 1984, pp. 231–45. [G: W. Germany]

Greening, Timothy. Analysis of the Impact of the Florsheim Shoe Case. In *Lafferty, R. N.; Lande, R. H. and Kirkwood, J. B., eds.*, 1984, pp. 92–199. [G: U.S.]

Grigg, Trevor. Parameters of the Retail Trade Model: A Utility Based Interpretation. *Urban Stud.*, February 1984, *21*(1), pp. 73–79. [G: U.S.]

Haining, Robert P. Testing a Spatial Interacting-Markets Hypothesis. *Rev. Econ. Statist.*, November 1984, *66*(4), pp. 576–83. [G: U.K.]

Harvel, Howard P. Vertical Restraints in the Hearing Aids Industry. In *Lafferty, R. N.; Lande, R. H. and Kirkwood, J. B., eds.*, 1984, pp. 272–384. [G: U.S.]

Irvine, F. Owen, Jr. Intrafirm Inventory Policy: Theory and Tests. *Can. J. Econ.*, February 1984, *17*(1), pp. 156–74. [G: U.S.]

Jackall, Robert. Paradoxes of Collective Work: A Study of the Cheeseboard, Berkeley, California. In *Jackall, R. and Levin, H. M., eds.*, 1984, pp. 109–35. [G: U.S.]

Kehoe, Timothy J.; Serra-Puche, Jaime and Solís, Leopoldo. A General Equilibrium Model of Domestic Commerce in Mexico. *J. Policy Modeling*, February 1984, *6*(1), pp. 1–28. [G: Mexico]

Ketcham, Jon; Smith, Vernon L. and Williams, Arlington W. A Comparison of Posted-Offer and Double-Auction Pricing Institutions. *Rev. Econ. Stud.*, October 1984, *51*(4), pp. 595–614.

Lawler, John J. The Influence of Management Consultants on the Outcome of Union Certification Elections. *Ind. Lab. Relat. Rev.*, October 1984, *38*(1), pp. 38–51. [G: U.S.]

Lerman, S. R. and Liu, T.-K. Microlevel Econometric Analysis of Retail CLosure. In *Pitfield, D. E., ed.*, 1984, pp. 181–201. [G: U.S.]

Marvel, Howard P. and McCafferty, Stephen. Resale Price Maintenance and Quality Certification. *Rand J. Econ.*, Autumn 1984, *15*(3), pp. 346–59. [G: U.S.]

McEachern, William A. and Romeo, Anthony A. Vertical Restraints in the Audio Components Industry: An Economic Analysis of FTC Intervention. In *Lafferty, R. N.; Lande, R. H. and Kirkwood, J. B., eds.*, 1984, pp. 202–57. [G: U.S.]

McEachern, William A. and Romeo, Anthony A. Vertical Restraints in the Audio Component Industry: Possibilities for Future Empirical Work. In *Lafferty, R. N.; Lande, R. H. and Kirkwood, J. B., eds.*, 1984, pp. 258–69. [G: U.S.]

de Meza, David. The Fourth Commandment: Is it Pareto Efficient? *Econ. J.*, June 1984, *94*(374), pp. 379–83.

Moorhouse, John C. Is Tullock Correct about Sunday Closing Laws? *Public Choice*, 1984, *42*(2), pp. 197–203. [G: U.S.]

Oster, Sharon. The FTC v. Levi Strauss: An Analysis of the Economic Issues. In *Lafferty, R. N.; Lande, R. H. and Kirkwood, J. B., eds.*, 1984, pp. 48–90. [G: U.S.]

Raab, Raymond L. Statistical Determinants of Several Retail Activities for Various Homogeneous Regions in the State of Minnesota. *Reg. Sci. Persp.*, 1984, *14*(1), pp. 40–51. [G: U.S.]

Ring, Raymond J., Jr. The Effect of Permanent Income on Retail Sales by Sales Category. *Quart. J. Bus. Econ.*, Autumn 1984, *23*(4), pp. 13–30. [G: U.S.]

Roy, John R. and Johansson, Börje. On Planning and Forecasting the Location of Retail and Service Activity. *Reg. Sci. Urban Econ.*, August 1984, *14*(3), pp. 433–52.

Savitt, Ronald. An Historical Approach to Comparative Retailing. In *Kaynak, E. and Savitt, R., eds.*, 1984, pp. 147–55.

Schroeder, Gertrude E. Retail Trade and Personal Services in Soviet Cities. In *Morton, H. W. and Stuart, R. C., eds.*, 1984, pp. 203–20. [G: U.S.S.R.]

Solís, Leopoldo. Food Marketing and Income Distribution. In *Aspe, P. and Sigmund, P. E., eds.*, 1984, pp. 481–522. [G: Mexico]

Taylor, David Van L., Jr. Debit Cards. In *Fed. Res. Bank Atlanta*, 1984, pp. 11–16. [G: U.S.]

Thurik, A. R. and Vollebregt, J. A. C. A Generalized Labour Cost Relation for French Retailing. *Ann. INSEE*, January–March 1984, (53), pp. 93–106. [G: France]

Timmermans, H. J. P. Discrete Choice Models versus Decompositional Multiattribute Preference Models: A Comparative Analysis of Model Performance in the Context of Spatial Shopping-Behaviour. In *Pitfield, D. E., ed.*, 1984, pp. 88–101. [G: Netherlands]

Urban Land Institute. Revitalizing Downtown Retailing: Trends and Opportunities. In *Carr, J. H., ed.*, 1984, *1983*, pp. 289–323. [G: U.S.]

Von Hohenbalken, Balder and West, Douglas S. Predation among Supermarkets: An Algorithmic Locational Analysis. *J. Urban Econ.*, March 1984, *15*(2), pp. 244–57. [G: Canada]

West, Douglas S. and Von Hohenbalken, Balder. Spatial Predation in a Canadian Retail Oligopoly. *J. Reg. Sci.*, August 1984, *24*(3), pp. 415–29. [G: Canada]

Zardkoohi, Asghar and Sheer, Alain. Public versus Private Liquor Retailing: An Investigation into the Behavior of the State Governments. *Southern Econ. J.*, April 1984, *50*(4), pp. 1058–76. [G: U.S.]

634 Industry Studies: Construction

6340 Construction

Allen, Steven G. Unionized Construction Workers Are More Productive. *Quart. J. Econ.*, May 1984, 99(2), pp. 251–74. **[G: U.S.]**

Coukis, Basil P. and Jéquier, Nicolas. Civil Works Construction. In *Weiss, C. and Jéquier, N., eds.*, 1984, pp. 55–67.

Diamond, Douglas B., Jr. The Impact of Inflation on New House Prices. *Contemp. Policy Issue*, May 1984, (6), pp. 5–16. **[G: U.S.]**

Doucet, Michael and Weaver, John. The North American Shelter Business, 1860–1920: A Study of a Canadian Real Estate and Property Management Agency. *Bus. Hist. Rev.*, Summer 1984, 58(2), pp. 234–62. **[G: Canada]**

Fraundorf, Martha Norby; Farrell, John P. and Mason, Robert. The Effect of the Davis–Bacon Act on Construction Costs in Rural Areas. *Rev. Econ. Statist.*, February 1984, 66(1), pp. 142–46. **[G: U.S.]**

Goldfarb, Robert S. A Davis–Bacon Musicale: Symphony Orchestras as Migrant Labor. *J. Lab. Res.*, Fall 1984, 5(4), pp. 427–33. **[G: U.S.]**

Hinterhuber, Giovanni. L'analisi dei raggruppamenti strategici di imprese. (Analysis of Strategic Company Groupings. With English summary.) *L'Impresa*, 1984, 26(5), pp. 13–21.

Jaffee, Dwight M. New Residential Construction and Energy Costs. In *Downs, A. and Bradbury, K. L., eds.*, 1984, pp. 143–84. **[G: U.S.]**

Kilbridge, Maurice D. Problems Often Encountered in Implementing Industrial Projects in Developing Countries. In *Ghosh, P. K., ed., no. 1*, 1984, 1970, pp. 270–89. **[G: India]**

Kuhlman, John M. and Johnson, S. R. Estimating Damages on Highway Construction Contracts. *Antitrust Bull.*, Winter 1984, 29(4), pp. 719–38. **[G: U.S.]**

Lohman, Jeff and Mayer, Henry C. Top Notch Is More than a Slogan. *Rev. Soc. Econ.*, December 1984, 42(3), pp. 330–38. **[G: U.S.]**

Novikov, O. Stimulating the Growth of the Effectiveness of Capital Investments. *Prob. Econ.*, February 1984, 26(10), pp. 37–49. **[G: U.S.S.R.]**

Sheehan, Robert J. New Residential Construction and Energy Costs: Comment. In *Downs, A. and Bradbury, K. L., eds.*, 1984, pp. 184–87. **[G: U.S.]**

Shulenburger, David; McLean, Robert A. and Rasch, Sara B. CISC Controls and the Union/Non-union Wage Ratio. *J. Behav. Econ.*, Summer 1984, 13(1), pp. 57–66. **[G: U.S.]**

Thom, D. Rodney. Housing Starts and Mortgage Availability: Evidence from the UK Time Series. *Appl. Econ.*, December 1984, 16(6), pp. 881–93. **[G: U.K.]**

Weistroffer, H. Roland. Modelling the Demand for Construction. *J. Stud. Econ. Econometrics*, January 1984, (18), pp. 36–47. **[G: S. Africa]**

Williams, Ross A. An Australian Housing Model. *Econ. Rec.*, June 1984, 60(169), pp. 143–55. **[G: Australia]**

635 Industry Studies: Services and Related Industries

6350 General

Anderson, Evan E. The Growth and Performance of Franchise Systems: Company versus Franchisee Ownership. *J. Econ. Bus.*, December 1984, 36(4), pp. 421–31. **[G: U.S.]**

Barras, R. and Swann, J. Information Technology and the Service Sector: Quality of Services and Quantity of Jobs. In *Marstrand, P., ed.*, 1984, pp. 214–33. **[G: U.K.]**

Bennell, Paul. The Utilisation of Professional Engineering Skills in Kenya. In *Fransman, M. and King, K., eds.*, 1984, pp. 335–53. **[G: Kenya]**

Bhagwati, Jagdish N. Why Are Services Cheaper in the Poor Countries? *Econ. J.*, June 1984, 94(374), pp. 279–86.

Crew, Michael A. Royalty Contracts: An Efficient Form of Contracting? *Southern Econ. J.*, January 1984, 50(3), pp. 724–33.

Gershuny, Jonathan I. The Future of Service Employment. In *Marstrand, P., ed.*, 1984, pp. 234–55. **[G: U.K.]**

Ginzberg, Eli. The Service Economy and the Changing Job Structures. In *Ullrich, R. A., ed.*, 1984, pp. 81–94. **[G: U.S.]**

Kojima, Ichiro. The Interrelation between Extensions of Service Industry Sector and Information Industry Sector. (In Japanese. With English summary.) *Osaka Econ. Pap.*, December 1984, 34(2–3), pp. 228–38. **[G: Japan]**

Roy, John R. and Johansson, Börje. On Planning and Forecasting the Location of Retail and Service Activity. *Reg. Sci. Urban Econ.*, August 1984, 14(3), pp. 433–52.

Sbytova, L. Employment and Raising the Effectiveness of Labor in the Service Sector. *Prob. Econ.*, January 1984, 26(9), pp. 64–80. **[G: U.S.S.R.]**

Sherman, H. David. Improving the Productivity of Service Businesses. *Sloan Manage. Rev.*, Spring 1984, 25(3), pp. 11–23.

6352 Electrical, Gas, Communication, and Information Services

Abidin, Ahmad Abid. Malaysia: National Electricity Board Tariffs. In *Munasinghe, M. and Rungta, S., eds.*, 1984, pp. 479–97. **[G: Malaysia]**

Aigner, Dennis J. The Welfare Econometrics of Peak-Load Pricing for Electricity: Editor's Introduction. *J. Econometrics*, September/October 1984, 26(1/2), pp. 1–15. **[G: U.S.]**

Aigner, Dennis J. and Lillard, Lee A. Measuring Peak Load Pricing Response from Experimental Data: An Exploratory Analysis. *J. Bus. Econ. Statist.*, January 1984, 2(1), pp. 21–39. **[G: U.S.]**

Aigner, Dennis J.; Sorooshian, Cyrus and Kerwin, Pamela. Conditional Demand Analysis for Estimating Residential End-Use Load Profiles. *Energy J.*, July 1984, *5*(3), pp. 81–97.
[G: U.S.]

Ammons, Jane Chumley. An Analytic Study of Critical Terminal Conditions in Long Range Generation Expansion Planning For Electric Utilities. In *Lev, B., et al., eds.*, 1984, pp. 83–93.

Antonelli, Cristiano. Multinational Firms, International Trade, and International Telecommunications. *Info. Econ. Policy*, 1984, *1*(4), pp. 333–43.
[G: Selected Countries]

Armstrong, Christopher and Nelles, H. V. A Curious Capital Flow: Canadian Investment in Mexico, 1902–1910. *Bus. Hist. Rev.*, Summer 1984, *58*(2), pp. 178–203.
[G: Canada; Mexico]

Asplund, Rita. Hushållens efterfrågan på eluppvärmning: En empirisk undersökning för åren 1975–82. (Residential Demand of Electric Space Heating: An Empirical Investigation for 1975–82. With English summary.) *Ekon. Samfundets Tidskr.*, 1984, *37*(3), pp. 163–79.
[G: Finland]

Asplund, Rita. Kotitaloussähkön kysynnästä Suomessa. (Household Electricity Demand in Finland. With English summary.) *Kansant. Aikak.*, 1984, *80*(1), pp. 66–75.
[G: Finland]

Bailey, Elizabeth E. A Comment on the Papers by Theodore Keeler and Barry Weingast [Theories of Regulation and the Deregulation Movement] [The Congressional–Bureaucratic System: A Principal–Agent Perspective (with Application to the SEC)]. *Public Choice*, 1984, *44*(1), pp. 197–200.
[G: U.S.]

Banks, Ferdinand E. A Note on Optimal System Planning. *Energy J.*, October 1984, *5*(4), pp. 79–80.

Barrett, Edward M. Proposed Regulatory Treatment of Costs of Extraordinary Large Additions to Plant in Service. In *Foster, J. R., et al., eds.*, 1984, pp. 117–35.
[G: U.S.]

Baumier, J. and Duchatelle, L. The Case for Developing the Liquid Metal Fast Breeder Reactor in France. In *Brookes, L. G. and Motamen, H., eds.*, 1984, pp. 234–54.
[G: France]

Bernard, Jean-Thomas; Bridges, Glenn E. and Scott, Anthony D. Une évaluation de la rente potentielle des sites hydro-électriques au Canada. (With English summary.) *Rev. Econ. Ind.*, 3rd Trimester 1984, (29), pp. 1–17.
[G: Canada]

Bernard, Jean-Thomas and Chatel, Josée. The Role of Energy Limited Hydro Equipment in an Optimal Plant Mix. *Energy Econ.*, April 1984, *6*(2), pp. 139–44.
[G: Canada]

Berrie, T. W. Nuclear and Non-nuclear Electricity: Decision-making for Optimal Economic Performance. In *Brookes, L. G. and Motamen, H., eds.*, 1984, pp. 67–86.

Bjerkholt, Olav and Olsen, Øystein. Uncertainty in Hydroelectric Power Supply. *Energy Econ.*, July 1984, *6*(3), pp. 159–66.

Bloch, Harry and Wirth, Michael. The Demand for Pay Services on Cable Television. *Info. Econ. Policy*, 1984, *1*(4), pp. 311–32.
[G: U.S.]

Boardman, Anthony E. and Vining, Aidan R. Canadian and British TV Markets: Why the CBC Should Not Be Like the BBC [Market Structure and Television Programming Performance in Canada and the U.K.]. *Can. Public Policy*, September 1984, *10*(3), pp. 347–52.
[G: U.K.; Canada]

Bohn, Roger E.; Caramanis, Michael C. and Schweppe, Fred C. Optimal Pricing in Electrical Networks over Space and Time. *Rand J. Econ.*, Autumn 1984, *15*(3), pp. 360–76.
[G: U.S.]

Bohn, Roger E., et al. Deregulating the Generation of Electricity through the Creation of Spot Markets for Bulk Power. *Energy J.*, April 1984, *5*(2), pp. 71–91.
[G: U.S.]

Branch, Ben; Gleit, Alan and Schneeweis, Thomas. The Determinants of Risk and Return for Electric Utility Equity Issues. *Quart. J. Bus. Econ.*, Winter 1984, *23*(1), pp. 16–31.
[G: U.S.]

Brookes, L. G. and Motamen, H. The Economics of Nuclear Energy: Introduction. In *Brookes, L. G. and Motamen, H., eds.*, 1984, pp. 1–28.
[G: Selected Countries]

Brookes, L. G. and Motamen, H. The Economics of Nuclear Energy: Conclusions. In *Brookes, L. G. and Motamen, H., eds.*, 1984, pp. 404–08.

Brooks, Robert E. The Tenrac Gas Pipeline Competition Model. In *Lev, B., et al., eds.*, 1984, pp. 337–54.

Brown, Charles L. Disconnecting Bell: The Impact of the AT&T Divestiture: A Personal Introduction. In *Shooshan, H. M., III, ed.*, 1984, pp. 1–7.
[G: U.S.]

Canes, Michael E. and Norman, Donald A. Long-term Contracts and Market Forces in the Natural Gas Market. *J. Energy Devel.*, Autumn 1984, *10*(1), pp. 73–96.
[G: U.S.]

Carter, Richard. Le Canada est-il entraîné dans la déréglementation: le cas des communications. (With English summary.) *Can. Public Policy*, March 1984, *10*(1), pp. 10–24.
[G: U.S.; Canada]

Caves, Douglas W., et al. A Comparison of Different Methodologies in a Case Study of Residential Time-of-Use Electricity Pricing: Cost–Benefit Analysis. *J. Econometrics*, September/October 1984, *26*(1/2), pp. 17–34. [G: U.S.]

Chen, Carl R. The Structural Stability of the Market Model after the Three Mile Island Accident. *J. Econ. Bus.*, February 1984, *36*(1), pp. 133–40.
[G: U.S.]

Collins, William H. and Collins, Carol B. Advertising and Monopoly Power: The Case of the Electric Utility Industry. *Atlantic Econ. J.*, September 1984, *12*(3), pp. 45–53.

Considine, Timothy J. Interfuel Substitution and Cyclical Volatility in U.S. Natural Gas Markets. *J. Energy Devel.*, Autumn 1984, *10*(1), pp. 97–109.
[G: U.S.]

Corduas, Marcella. Distanza tra modelli: problemi metodologici ed indici statistici. (On Distance between Models: Methodological Problems and Statistical Indices. With English summary.) *Statistica,* July–September 1984, *44*(3), pp. 513–24.

Corey, G. R. The Comparative Costs of Nuclear and Fossil Fuelled Power Plants in an American Electricity Utility. In *Brookes, L. G. and Motamen, H., eds.,* 1984, pp. 274–87. [G: U.S.]

Costales, Rene. Inter-American Development Bank: Electricity Tariffs, Policies and Practices. In *Munasinghe, M. and Rungta, S., eds.,* 1984, pp. 537–42. [G: Latin America]

Coustel, Jean-Pierre. La déréglementation des Télécommunications. Le poids du démembrement d'ATT dans la dynamique de diffusion du mouvement. (With English summary.) *Rev. Econ. Ind.,* 4th Trimester 1984, (30), pp. 42–59. [G: U.S.]

Crandall, Robert W. The Emerging Competition in the U.S. Telecommunications Market. In *Giersch, H., ed.,* 1984, pp. 87–106. [G: U.S.]

Crandall, Robert W. and Owen, Bruce M. Disconnecting Bell: The Marketplace: Economic Implications of Divestiture. In *Shooshan, H. M., III, ed.,* 1984, pp. 47–70. [G: U.S.]

Dingell, John D.; Nulty, Timothy E. and McCarthy, Mark. Telephone Deregulation: . . . Or a Free Ride for AT&T? *Challenge,* March/April 1984, *27*(1), pp. 30–33. [G: U.S.]

Dunbar, Lyle E. OTEC Market Potential in Small Pacific Islands. In *Gopalakrishnan, C., ed.,* 1984, pp. 31–47. [G: Pacific Islands]

Eisenhauer, J. L. Comparative Analysis of Coal-based Electric Energy Delivery Systems. In *Lev, B., et al., eds.,* 1984, pp. 33–45. [G: U.S.]

Emmerich, Volker. Anmerkungen zu den Postfinanzen. (With English Summary.) In *Eucken, W. and Böhm, F., eds.,* 1984, pp. 43–69. [G: W. Germany]

Evans, David S. and Heckman, James J. A Test for Subadditivity of the Cost Function with an Application to the Bell System. *Amer. Econ. Rev.,* September 1984, *74*(4), pp. 615–23.

Farmer, A. A. Assessing the Economics of the Liquid Metal Fast Breeder Reactor. In *Brookes, L. G. and Motamen, H., eds.,* 1984, pp. 192–233.

Farstad, Halfdan. Solar Branch Development in Israel. In *Baumgartner, T. and Burns, T. R., eds.,* 1984, pp. 27–52. [G: Israel]

Farstad, Halfdan and Ward, James. Wind Energy in Denmark. In *Baumgartner, T. and Burns, T. R., eds.,* 1984, pp. 91–125. [G: Denmark]

Feketekuty, Geza and Aronson, Jonathan D. Meeting the Challenges of the World Information Economy. *World Econ.,* March 1984, *7*(1), pp. 63–86. [G: Global]

Filer, John E., et al. Impact of Regulation on Vertical Integration in the Electric Industry. *Rev. Ind. Organ.,* Fall 1984, *1*(3), pp. 216–31. [G: U.S.]

Flavin, Christopher. The Demise of Nuclear Power: What Comes Next? *Challenge,* July/August 1984, *27*(3), pp. 38–45. [G: Global]

Foster, J. Rhoads. Commentary on the State of the Regulatory Art: Emerging Concepts and Procedures. In *Foster, J. R., et al., eds.,* 1984, pp. 4–42. [G: U.S.]

Frazee, Rowland C. Traded Computer Services: A Bilateral Beginning. In *Fried, E. R. and Trezise, P. H., eds.,* 1984, pp. 77–86. [G: U.S.; Canada]

Gallant, A. Ronald and Koenker, Roger W. Costs and Benefits of Peak-Load Pricing of Electricity: A Continuous-Time Econometric Approach. *J. Econometrics,* September/October 1984, *26*(1/2), pp. 83–113. [G: U.S.]

Gallavan, William M. Rate and Service Options: Achieving a Balance between the Utility Ability to Provide Service and Customer Demand for Service. In *Foster, J. R., et al., eds.,* 1984, pp. 77–85. [G: U.S.]

Gegax, Douglas and Tschirhart, John T. An Analysis of Interfirm Cooperation: Theory and Evidence from Electric Power Pools. *Southern Econ. J.,* April 1984, *50*(4), pp. 1077–97. [G: U.S.]

Geller, Henry. Disconnecting Bell: Regulation and Public Policy after Divestiture: The FCC and Congress. In *Shooshan, H. M., III, ed.,* 1984, pp. 83–99. [G: U.S.]

Glismann, Hans H. Comment [The Emerging Competition in the U.S. Telecommunications Market] [Free Entry into Telecommunications?]. In *Giersch, H., ed.,* 1984, pp. 132–35.

Godden, Edward and Crouch, Tom. Papua New Guinea: Electricity Pricing Policy and Practice. In *Munasinghe, M. and Rungta, S., eds.,* 1984, pp. 370–404. [G: Papua New Guinea]

Goldstein, Jonah. Broadcasting Vouchers: A Reply [Communication, Property Rights, and Broadcasting Vouchers]. *Can. Public Policy,* December 1984, *10*(4), pp. 474–75. [G: Canada]

Gordon, Richard L. Resource Procurement: A Case Study of U.S. Electric Utilities. In *Pearce, D. W.; Siebert, H. and Walter, I., eds.,* 1984, pp. 319–37. [G: U.S.]

Gouni, L. Economic Principles of Optimizing Mixed Nuclear and Non-nuclear Electricity Systems. In *Brookes, L. G. and Motamen, H., eds.,* 1984, pp. 46–66. [G: France; W. Europe]

Grant, Linda. Disconnecting Bell: Through a Glass Brightly: Consumers and the New Tomorrow. In *Shooshan, H. M., III, ed.,* 1984, pp. 132–47. [G: U.S.]

Gray, Clive S. The Jakarta Telephone Connection Charge and Financing Indonesian Telecommunications Development. *Bull. Indonesian Econ. Stud.,* August 1984, *20*(2), pp. 139–50. [G: Indonesia]

Green, David Jay. A Small Scale, Partial Equilibrium Model of Natural Gas Markets: Responses to Alternative Deregulation Scenarios and Oil

Price Changes. *Southern Econ. J.*, April 1984, *50*(4), pp. 1112–30. [G: U.S.]

Green, Diana. Cable TV in France: A Non-market Approach to Industrial Development. *Nat. Westminster Bank Quart. Rev.*, August 1984, pp. 13–24. [G: France; U.K.]

Greene, William H. and Smiley, Robert H. The Effectiveness of Utility Regulation in a Period of Changing Economic Conditions. In *Marchand, M.; Pestieau, P. and Tulkens, H., eds.*, 1984, pp. 269–87. [G: U.S.]

Griffin, Tony. Technological Change and Craft Control in the Newspaper Industry: An International Comparison. *Cambridge J. Econ.*, March 1984, *8*(1), pp. 41–61. [G: U.S.; U.K.; Australia]

Guldmann, Jean-Michel. A Further Note on the Structure of Gas Distribution Costs in Urban Areas. *Reg. Sci. Urban Econ.*, November 1984, *14*(4), pp. 583–88.

Gurwitz, Aaron S. and Chall, Daniel E. Nuclear Power Plant Construction: Paying the Bill. *Fed. Res. Bank New York Quart. Rev.*, Summer 1984, *9*(2), pp. 48–57. [G: U.S.]

Habibollahzadeh, H., et al. Optimization of Hydroelectric Power System Operation. In *Lev, B., et al., eds.*, 1984, pp. 109–19.

Häfele, Wolf. The Future of Nuclear Energy. In *Hawdon, D., ed.*, 1984, pp. 79–103.

Harrison, J. Michael. Selection of the Appropriate Test Year. In *Foster, J. R., et al., eds.*, 1984, pp. 89–95. [G: U.S.]

Hartley, Peter and Trengove, Chris. The Marginal Costs of Electricity Supply in Victoria. *Econ. Rec.*, December 1984, *60*(171), pp. 340–55. [G: Australia]

Hartman, Raymond S. The Importance of Technology and Fuel Choice in the Analysis of Utility-sponsored Conservation Strategies for Residential Water Heating. *Energy J.*, July 1984, *5*(3), pp. 99–118. [G: U.S.]

Hausman, William J. and Neufeld, John L. Time-of-Day Pricing in the U.S. Electric Power Industry at the Turn of the Century. *Rand J. Econ.*, Spring 1984, *15*(1), pp. 116–26. [G: U.S.]

Henderson, David M. The Natural Resource-Based Sector. In *Hood, N. and Young, S., eds.*, 1984, pp. 249–87. [G: U.K.]

Highton, Nicolas H. and Webb, Michael G. The Effects on Electricity Prices in England and Wales of Notional Sulphur Dioxide Emission Standards for Power Stations. *J. Environ. Econ. Manage.*, March 1984, *11*(1), pp. 70–83. [G: U.K.]

Hirst, Eric and Goeltz, Richard. The Economics of Utility Residential Energy Conservation Programs: A Pacific Northwest Example. *Energy J.*, July 1984, *5*(3), pp. 159–69. [G: U.S.]

Hobbs, Benjamin F. Regional Energy Facility Location Models for Power System Planning and Policy Analysis. In *Lev, B., et al., eds.*, 1984, pp. 53–66.

Hölker, Franz-Josef. Die ordnung der energiewirtschaft der Bundesrepublik Deutschland.

Leitbild—Reale Probleme. (The Organisation of the Energy Sector in the Federal Republic of Germany. With English summary.) *Ann. Pub. Co-op. Econ.*, Oct.–Dec. 1984, *55*(4), pp. 413–31. [G: W. Germany]

Hoskins, Colin and McFadyen, Stuart. The Role of the CBC in the Canadian Broadcasting System: Revisited [Canadian and British TV Markets: Why the CBC Should Not Be Like the BBC]. *Can. Public Policy*, September 1984, *10*(3), pp. 352–58. [G: U.K.; Canada]

Inose, Hiroshi. Challenges for Policy of Network Oriented Society: A Japanese View. *Info. Econ. Policy*, 1984, *1*(4), pp. 369–79. [G: Japan]

Itchon, Gabriel Y. Philippines: National Power Corporation Power Tariff Policy. In *Munasinghe, M. and Rungta, S., eds.*, 1984, pp. 363–69. [G: Philippines]

Jackson, Charles L. Disconnecting Bell: Technology: The Anchor of the Bell System. In *Shooshan, H. M., III, ed.*, 1984, pp. 71–82. [G: U.S.]

Jahangir, Mohammad. Pakistan: Electricity Tariff Policy. In *Munasinghe, M. and Rungta, S., eds.*, 1984, pp. 498–509. [G: Pakistan]

Jeanrenaud, Claude and Meyer, Daniel. L'incidence a moyen et long terme des commandes de materiel de telecommunication: deux etudes de cas. (The Medium- and Long-term Incidence of Orders of Telecommunication Material: Two Case Studies. With English summary.) *Ann. Pub. Co-op. Econ.*, April–June 1984, *55*(2), pp. 191–203. [G: Switzerland]

Kahn, Alfred E. Telephone Deregulation: A Needed Dose of Competition . . . *Challenge*, March/April 1984, *27*(1), pp. 24–29. [G: U.S.]

Kahn, Alfred E. The Road to More Intelligent Telephone Pricing. *Yale J. Regul.*, 1984, *1*(2), pp. 139–57. [G: U.S.]

Karunaratne, Neil Dias. Planning for the Australian Information Economy. *Info. Econ. Policy*, 1984, *1*(4), pp. 345–67. [G: Australia]

Keeler, Theodore E. Theories of Regulation and the Deregulation Movement. *Public Choice*, 1984, *44*(1), pp. 103–45. [G: U.S.]

Kemeny, L. The Practical Problems and Issues Pertaining to Nuclear Energy in Less-developed Countries. In *Brookes, L. G. and Motamen, H., eds.*, 1984, pp. 334–59. [G: LDCs; CMEA; Australia]

King, J. C. Assessment of Electric Power Conservation and Supply Resources in the Pacific Northwest: An Overview. In *Lev, B., et al., eds.*, 1984, pp. 95–108. [G: U.S.]

King, Michael J. and Scott, Michael J. Forecasting Electricity Demand with an End-Use/Econometric Model. In *Lev, B., et al., eds.*, 1984, pp. 151–64. [G: U.S.]

Koford, Kenneth J. Was "Free" TV a Price Control that Increased Consumers' Welfare? *Quart. Rev. Econ. Bus.*, Spring 1984, *24*(1), pp. 67–77.

Kononov, Iu. D. The Fuel-Energy Complex in

the System of National Economic Relations. *Prob. Econ.*, May 1984, *27*(1), pp. 33–46. [G: U.S.S.R.]

Leff, Nathaniel H. Externalities, Information Costs, and Social Benefit–Cost Analysis for Economic Development: An Example from Telecommunications. *Econ. Develop. Cult. Change*, January 1984, *32*(2), pp. 255–76. [G: LDCs]

Leff, Nathaniel H. Social Benefit–Cost Analysis and Telecommunications Investment in Developing Countries. *Info. Econ. Policy*, 1984, *1*(3), pp. 217–27. [G: LDCs]

Lillard, Lee A. and Aigner, Dennis J. Time-of-Day Electricity Consumption Response to Temperature and the Ownership of Air Conditioning Appliances. *J. Bus. Econ. Statist.*, January 1984, *2*(1), pp. 40–53. [G: U.S.]

Lunning, W. H. The Economics of Final Decommissioning and Disposal of Nuclear Power Plant. In *Brookes, L. G. and Motamen, H., eds.*, 1984, pp. 303–13. [G: U.K.]

Makhija, Anil K. and Thompson, Howard E. Capitalized Interest and the Cost of Money to Electric Utilities. *Land Econ.*, August 1984, *60*(3), pp. 278–91. [G: U.S.]

Makhija, Anil K. and Thompson, Howard E. Comparison of Alternative Models for Estimating the Cost of Equity Capital for Electric Utilities. *J. Econ. Bus.*, February 1984, *36*(1), pp. 107–31. [G: U.S.]

Martin, Roderick. New Technology and Industrial Relations in Fleet Street: 'New Technology Will Make it Possible for Managers to Manage.' In *Warner, M., ed.*, 1984, pp. 240–52. [G: U.K.]

Mayo, John W. Multiproduct Monopoly, Regulation, and Firm Costs. *Southern Econ. J.*, July 1984, *51*(1), pp. 208–18. [G: U.S.]

McConnell, L. G. and Woodhead, L. W. The Economics of the Candu Reactor. In *Brookes, L. G. and Motamen, H., eds.*, 1984, pp. 255–72. [G: Canada]

Mirucki, Jean. Vérification des conditions d'efficacité dans les décisions de production à partir de l'hypothèse Averch-Johnson: étude de cas. (With English summary.) *Rev. Econ. Ind.*, 4th Trimester 1984, (30), pp. 60–76. [G: Canada]

Mitra, A. K. India: Power Tariffs and Policy in Calcutta. In *Munasinghe, M. and Rungta, S., eds.*, 1984, pp. 405–19. [G: India]

Mould, Maurice C. World Bank: Financial Covenants and Their Use in the Development of Pricing Policies. In *Munasinghe, M. and Rungta, S., eds.*, 1984, pp. 543–67. [G: LDCs]

Munasinghe, Mohan. Comment [Sri Lanka: Costs of Supplying Electricity and Tariff Policy] [Indonesia: Development of Electricity Tariffs] [Malaysia: National Electricity Board Tariffs] [Pakistan: Electricity Tariff Policy]. In *Munasinghe, M. and Rungta, S., eds.*, 1984, pp. 510–15. [G: Sri Lanka; Malaysia; Indonesia; Pakistan]

Munasinghe, Mohan. Implementing Long-run

Marginal Cost-based Tariff Structures. In *Munasinghe, M. and Rungta, S., eds.*, 1984, pp. 193–211.

Munasinghe, Mohan and Rungta, Shyam. Power Tariffs: An Overview. In *Munasinghe, M. and Rungta, S., eds.*, 1984, pp. 1–51. [G: LDCs; MDCs]

Nawaz, Shuja. Mass Media and Development. In *Burki, S. J. and LaPorte, R., Jr., eds.*, 1984, pp. 310–50. [G: Pakistan]

Nelson, Randy A. Regulation, Capital Vintage, and Technical Change in the Electric Utility Industry. *Rev. Econ. Statist.*, February 1984, *66*(1), pp. 59–69. [G: U.S.]

Noam, Eli M. Private Sector Monopolies: The Case of Cable Television Franchises. In *Holzer, M. and Nagel, S. S., eds.*, 1984, pp. 193–217. [G: U.S.]

O'Neill, Richard P., et al. The Gas Analysis Modeling System. In *Lev, B., et al., eds.*, 1984, pp. 265–83.

Palmer, H. C. Accounting Costs as a Basis for Time-of-Use Tariffs. In *Munasinghe, M. and Rungta, S., eds.*, 1984, pp. 119–35. [G: Canada]

Park, Rolla Edward and Acton, Jan Paul. Large Business Customer Response to Time-of-Day Electricity Rates. *J. Econometrics*, September/October 1984, *26*(1/2), pp. 229–52. [G: U.S.]

Parker, William N. Communication Techniques and Social Organization in the World Economy. In *Parker, W. N.*, 1984, *1982*, pp. 150–63.

Parkman, Allen. Crossownership and Media Concentration. *Rev. Ind. Organ.*, Summer 1984, *1*(2), pp. 138–47. [G: U.S.]

Pencavel, John H. The Tradeoff between Wages and Employment in Trade Union Objectives. *Quart. J. Econ.*, May 1984, *99*(2), pp. 215–31. [G: U.S.]

Podmore, Chris. Broadcasting Vouchers Rejected [Communication, Property Rights, and Broadcasting Vouchers]. *Can. Public Policy*, December 1984, *10*(4), pp. 472–73. [G: Canada]

Polasek, Wolfgang. Extreme Bound Analysis for Residential Load Curve Models: Empirical Evidence for a 16-Household Example. *Empirical Econ.*, 1984, *9*(3), pp. 165–81. [G: U.S.]

Primeaux, Walter J., Jr.; Bubnys, Edward L. and Rasche, Robert H. Fair Value versus Original Cost Rate Base Valuation during Inflation. *Energy J.*, April 1984, *5*(2), pp. 93–108. [G: U.S.]

Pringle, Lewis G. An Audience Flow Model of Television Viewing Choice: A Comment. *Marketing Sci.*, Spring 1984, *3*(2), pp. 125–26. [G: U.S.]

Pulley, Lawrence B. and Braunstein, Yale M. Scope and Scale Augmenting Technological Change: An Application in the Information Sector. In *Jussawalla, M. and Ebenfield, H., eds.*, 1984, pp. 105–18. [G: U.S.]

Quester, George H. Coping with Transborder Penetration: The Politics of Television. *J. Policy Anal. Manage.*, Summer 1984, *3*(4), pp. 532–43.

Radharamanan, R.; Sortica, G. B. and Camargo, M. E. A Branch and Bound Model for the Transportation Routing Problem. In *Avula, X. J. R., et al.*, 1984, pp. 877–82. [G: Brazil]

Rahman, A. K. M. Anisur. Bangladesh: Electricity Tariff Policy and Methodology. In *Munasinghe, M. and Rungta, S., eds.*, 1984, pp. 336–46. [G: Bangladesh]

Rajagopalan, R. Implementing Long-run Marginal Cost-based Tariff Structures: Comment. In *Munasinghe, M. and Rungta, S., eds.*, 1984, pp. 214–17. [G: India]

Rhys, J. M. W. The Implications of Nuclear Energy for Electricity Tariffs. In *Brookes, L. G. and Motamen, H., eds.*, 1984, pp. 316–31.

Roux, J. Pl. Marginal Cost Pricing: Updating the French Electricity Tariffs. In *Munasinghe, M. and Rungta, S., eds.*, 1984, pp. 231–65.
[G: France]

Rushdi, Ali Ahmed. Industrial Demand for Electricity in South Australia. *Australian Econ. Pap.*, December 1984, 23(43), pp. 259–80.
[G: Australia]

Rust, Roland T. and Alpert, Mark I. An Audience Flow Model of Television Viewing Choice. *Marketing Sci.*, Spring 1984, 3(2), pp. 113–24. [G: U.S.]

Rust, Roland T. and Alpert, Mark I. On Establishing a Dialogue in Television Viewing Research. *Marketing Sci.*, Spring 1984, 3(2), pp. 126–27. [G: U.S.]

Schmitt, Dieter and Junk, H. The Comparative Costs of Nuclear and Coal-Fired Power Stations in West Germany. In *Brookes, L. G. and Motamen, H., eds.*, 1984, pp. 288–302.
[G: W. Germany]

Schwartz, Eli. "Excess Capacity" in Utility Industries: An Inventory Theoretic Approach. *Land Econ.*, February 1984, 60(1), pp. 40–48.
[G: U.S.]

Senadhipathy, D. G. Sri Lanka: Costs of Supplying Electricity and Tariff Policy. In *Munasinghe, M. and Rungta, S., eds.*, 1984, pp. 438–65. [G: Sri Lanka]

Sheehan, Richard H. and Ramachandran, S. Power Generation and Distribution. In *Weiss, C. and Jéquier, N., eds.*, 1984, pp. 197–207.

Shiller, Robert J. Smoothness Priors and Nonlinear Regression. *J. Amer. Statist. Assoc.*, September 1984, 79(387), pp. 609–15. [G: U.S.]

Shooshan, Harry M., III. The Bell Breakup: Putting it in Perspective. In *Shooshan, H. M., III, ed.*, 1984, pp. 8–22. [G: U.S.]

Shore, Haim. Summer Time and Electricity Conservation: The Israeli Case. *Energy J.*, April 1984, 5(2), pp. 53–70. [G: Israel]

Soejitno, Soejanto. Indonesia: Development of Electricity Tariffs. In *Munasinghe, M. and Rungta, S., eds.*, 1984, pp. 468–79.
[G: Indonesia]

de Sola Pool, Ithiel. Disconnecting Bell: Competition and Universal Service: Can We Get There from Here? In *Shooshan, H. M., III, ed.*, 1984, pp. 112–31. [G: U.S.]

Starr, C. and Yu, O. The Role of Centralized Energy In National Energy Systems. In

Brookes, L. G. and Motamen, H., eds., 1984, pp. 30–45. [G: Selected Countries]

Terleckyj, Nestor E. A Growth Model of the U.S. Communication Industry, 1948–80. In *Jussawalla, M. and Ebenfield, H., eds.*, 1984, pp. 119–45. [G: U.S.]

Thompson, Howard E. Estimating Individual Company Costs of Capital from Cross-sectional Data: A Random Coefficients Approach. *Managerial Dec. Econ.*, September 1984, 5(3), pp. 130–40. [G: U.S.]

Thompson, R. S. Structure and Conduct in Local Advertising Markets: The Case of Irish Provincial Newspapers. *J. Ind. Econ.*, December 1984, 33(2), pp. 241–49. [G: U.K.]

Tun, U Tin. Burma: Electricity Tariff Study. In *Munasinghe, M. and Rungta, S., eds.*, 1984, pp. 308–35. [G: Burma]

Turvey, Ralph. Accounting Costs as a Basis for Time-of-Use Tariffs: Comment. In *Munasinghe, M. and Rungta, S., eds.*, 1984, pp. 138–43. [G: Canada]

Turvey, Ralph. Estimating and Using Marginal Cost Pricing Concepts. In *Munasinghe, M. and Rungta, S., eds.*, 1984, pp. 153–70.
[G: France; U.K.]

Turvey, Ralph. Marginal Cost Pricing: Updating the French Electricity Tariffs: Comment. In *Munasinghe, M. and Rungta, S., eds.*, 1984, pp. 266–71. [G: France]

Turvey, Ralph. Philippines: National Power Corporation Power Tariff Policy: Comment. In *Munasinghe, M. and Rungta, S., eds.*, 1984, pp. 425–28. [G: Philippines]

Uri, Noel D. The Pricing and Allocation of Electrical Energy. *Energy Econ.*, April 1984, 6(2), pp. 94–101. [G: U.S.]

Vennard, Edwin. Accounting Costs as a Basis for Time-of-Use Tariffs: Comment. In *Munasinghe, M. and Rungta, S., eds.*, 1984, pp. 136–38. [G: Canada]

Vennard, Edwin. Review of Electricity Industry Trends and Rate Making. In *Munasinghe, M. and Rungta, S., eds.*, 1984, pp. 70–98.
[G: U.S.]

Walsh, Vivien. The Post Office, the Unions and the New Technology. In *Warner, M., ed.*, 1984, pp. 210–23. [G: U.K.]

Warford, Jeremy. Comments [Philippines: National Power Corporation Power Tariff Policy] [Papua New Guinea: Electricity Pricing Policy and Practice] [India: Power Tariffs and Policy in Calcutta]. In *Munasinghe, M. and Rungta, S., eds.*, 1984, pp. 420–25. [G: Philippines; Papua New Guinea; India]

Warford, Jeremy. The Objectives of Electricity Tariff Policy. In *Munasinghe, M. and Rungta, S., eds.*, 1984, pp. 61–69. [G: LDCs]

Warner, P. C. Manufacturing Industry and Nuclear Power. In *Brookes, L. G. and Motamen, H., eds.*, 1984, pp. 88–113. [G: U.K.]

Watanabe, Hisashi. A History of the Process Leading to the Formation of Fuji Electric. In *Nakagawa, K. and Morikawa, H., eds.*, 1984, pp. 47–71. [G: Japan]

Webb, Michael G. and Pinto, N. M. Power System Economics: The Value of Natural Gas in Electricity Generation. *Energy Econ.*, October 1984, *6*(4), pp. 245–54.

von Weizsäcker, Carl Christian. Free Entry into Telecommunications? *Info. Econ. Policy*, 1984, *1*(3), pp. 197–216.

von Weizsäcker, Carl Christian. Free Entry into Telecommunications? In *Giersch, H., ed.*, 1984, pp. 107–28.

Wellenius, Bjorn. Telecommunications in Developing Countries. *Finance Develop.*, September 1984, *21*(3), pp. 33–36. **[G: LDCs]**

Westley, Glenn D. Electricity Demand in a Developing Country. *Rev. Econ. Statist.*, August 1984, *66*(3), pp. 459–67. **[G: Paraguay]**

Westoby, Richard and McGuire, Alistair. Factor Substitution and Complementarity in Energy: A Case Study of the UK Electricity Industry. *Appl. Econ.*, February 1984, *16*(1), pp. 111–18. **[G: U.K.]**

Wiley, Richard E. Disconnecting Bell: The End of Monopoly: Regulatory Change and the Promotion of Competition. In *Shooshan, H. M., III, ed.*, 1984, pp. 23–46. **[G: U.S.]**

Woolcock, Stephen. Information Technology: The Challenge to Europe. *J. Common Market Stud.*, June 1984, *22*(4), pp. 315–31. **[G: Europe]**

Woolf, Arthur G. Electricity, Productivity, and Labor Saving: American Manufacturing, 1900–1929. *Exploration Econ. Hist.*, April 1984, *21*(2), pp. 176–91. **[G: U.S.]**

Yoon, Hi Woo. Korea: Peak-load Pricing Based on LRMC. In *Munasinghe, M. and Rungta, S., eds.*, 1984, pp. 295–308. **[G: S. Korea]**

Zielinski, Charles A. Disconnecting Bell: Regulation and Public Policy after Divestiture: The FCC and Congress. In *Shooshan, H. M., III, ed.*, 1984, pp. 100–11. **[G: U.S.]**

Zimonyi, I. L. Asian Development Bank: The Objectives of Financial Covenants in the Context of Efficient Electricity Tariffs. In *Munasinghe, M. and Rungta, S., eds.*, 1984, pp. 531–35. **[G: Asia]**

6353 Personal Services

Kwoka, John E., Jr. Advertising and the Price and Quality of Optometric Services. *Amer. Econ. Rev.*, March 1984, *74*(1), pp. 211–16. **[G: U.S.]**

Schroeder, Gertrude E. Retail Trade and Personal Services in Soviet Cities. In *Morton, H. W. and Stuart, R. C., eds.*, 1984, pp. 203–20. **[G: U.S.S.R.]**

Shataev, I. The Economics and Organization of Personal Services. *Prob. Econ.*, December 1984, *27*(8), pp. 55–70. **[G: U.S.S.R.]**

Warfel, George, Jr. Consumer Acceptance of Technology. In *Fed. Res. Bank Atlanta*, 1984, pp. 103–12. **[G: U.S.]**

6354 Business and Legal Services

Cox, Edwin B. Integrated Financial Services. In *Fed. Res. Bank Atlanta*, 1984, pp. 17–23. **[G: U.S.]**

Feinberg, Robert M. Paralegals and Substitution among Labor Inputs in the Law Firm. *J. Ind. Econ.*, September 1984, *33*(1), pp. 99–104. **[G: U.S.]**

Francis, Jere R. The Effect of Audit Firm Size on Audit Prices: A Study of the Australian Market. *J. Acc. Econ.*, August 1984, *6*(2), pp. 133–51. **[G: Australia]**

Lipstein, Benjamin. Marketing Financial Services. In *Sametz, A. W., ed.*, 1984, pp. 49–54. **[G: U.S.]**

Meckler, John M. Bank Cash Management Services. In *Fed. Res. Bank Atlanta*, 1984, pp. 27–33. **[G: U.S.]**

Merrill, Peter. Winners and Losers in the Network Race. In *Fed. Res. Bank Atlanta*, 1984, pp. 93–99. **[G: U.S.]**

Polèse, Mario and Stafford, Robert. Le rôle de Montréal comme centre de services: une analyse pour certains services aux entreprises. (Montreal as a Regional Business Service Center: An Analysis. With English summary.) *L'Actual. Econ.*, March 1984, *60*(1), pp. 39–57. **[G: Canada]**

Price, Robert W. Small Businesses. In *Fed. Res. Bank Atlanta*, 1984, pp. 35–40. **[G: U.S.]**

Thompson, R. S. Structure and Conduct in Local Advertising Markets: The Case of Irish Provincial Newspapers. *J. Ind. Econ.*, December 1984, *33*(2), pp. 241–49. **[G: U.K.]**

Vittas, Dimitri. International Payments Systems. In *Fed. Res. Bank Atlanta*, 1984, pp. 141–48. **[G: Global]**

White, George C. Payments Standards. In *Fed. Res. Bank Atlanta*, 1984, pp. 113–21.

6356 Insurance

Arrow, Kenneth J. Insurance, Risk, and Resource Allocation. In *Arrow, K. J., vol. 4*, 1984, *1965*, pp. 77–86.

Arrow, Kenneth J. Optimal Insurance and Generalized Deductibles. In *Arrow, K. J., vol. 3*, 1984, *1974*, pp. 212–60.

Bardsley, Peter; Abey, Arun and Davenport, Scott. The Economics of Insuring Crops against Drought. *Australian J. Agr. Econ.*, April 1984, *28*(1), pp. 1–14. **[G: Australia]**

Beliveau, Barbara C. Theoretical and Empirical Aspects of Implicit Information in the Market for Life Insurance. *J. Risk Ins.*, June 1984, *51*(2), pp. 286–307. **[G: U.S.]**

Bladen, Ashby. Evolving Investment Policy. In *Sametz, A. W., ed.*, 1984, pp. 81–83.

Borch, Karl. Equilibrium Premiums in an Insurance Market. *J. Risk Ins.*, September 1984, *51*(3), pp. 468–76.

Borch, Karl. Premiums in a Competitive Insurance Market. *J. Banking Finance*, September 1984, *8*(3), pp. 431–41.

Brady, Dennis P.; Brookshire, Michael L. and Cobb, William E. The Development and Solution of a Tax-Adjusted Model for Personal Injury Awards. *J. Risk Ins.*, March 1984, *51*(1), pp. 138–42. **[G: U.S.]**

Breyer, Friedrich. Moral Hazard und der optimale Krankenversicherungsvertrag. Eine Übersicht. (Moral Hazard and the Optimal Health Insurance Contract: A Survey. With English summary.) *Z. ges. Staatswiss.*, June 1984, *140*(2), pp. 288–307.

Brockett, Patrick L.; Cox, Samuel H., Jr. and Witt, Robert C. Self-Insurance and the Probability of Financial Regret. *J. Risk Ins.*, December 1984, *51*(4), pp. 720–29.   [G: U.S.]

Brunt, Maureen. The Economics of Law: Economic Imperialism in Negligence Law, No-Fault Insurance, Occupational Licensing and Criminology: Comment. *Australian Econ. Rev.*, 3rd Quarter 1984, (67), pp. 113–19.
  [G: Australia; New Zealand]

Burnett, John T. and Palmer, Bruce A. Examining Life Insurance Ownership through Demographic and Psychographic Characteristics. *J. Risk Ins.*, September 1984, *51*(3), pp. 453–67.   [G: U.S.]

Butt, John. Life Assurance in War and Depression: The Standard Life Assurance Company and Its Environment, 1914–39. In *Westall, O. M., ed.*, 1984, pp. 155–72.   [G: U.K.]

Campbell, Tim S. The Case for Mergers of Depository Institutions and Insurance Companies. In *Fed. Home Loan Bank San Francisco*, 1984, pp. 175–94.   [G: U.S.]

Capozza, Dennis R. and Gau, George W. The Pricing and Implementation of Mortgage Rate Insurance. *Housing Finance Rev.*, October 1984, *3*(4), pp. 393–404.   [G: Canada]

Carlson, Robert. The Evolving Life Insurance Industry. In *Sametz, A. W., ed.*, 1984, pp. 29–32.   [G: U.S.]

Chapman, S. D. Hogg Robinson: The Rise of a Lloyd's Broker. In *Westall, O. M., ed.*, 1984, pp. 173–89.   [G: U.K.]

Cho, Dongsae. Rehabilitation for Workers' Compensation Loss Exposures. *J. Risk Ins.*, March 1984, *51*(1), pp. 80–98.   [G: U.S.]

Collesano, Stephen; Greenwald, Mathew and Katosh, John P. Consumer Information Seeking in Purchasing Life Insurance. In *[Ferber, R.]*, 1984, pp. 199–216.   [G: U.S.]

Crawford, Peter. Restructuring Financial Institutions in the New Financial Environment: Discussion. In *Sametz, A. W., ed.*, 1984, pp. 39–42.   [G: U.S.]

Cunningham, Donald F. and Hendershott, Patric H. Pricing FHA Mortgage Default Insurance. *Housing Finance Rev.*, October 1984, *3*(4), pp. 373–92.   [G: U.S.]

Dionne, Georges. Search and Insurance. *Int. Econ. Rev.*, June 1984, *25*(2), pp. 357–67.

Disharoon, Leslie B. Implications for Strategic Planning: Discussion. In *Sametz, A. W., ed.*, 1984, pp. 129–30.   [G: U.S.]

Doherty, Neil A. Portfolio Efficient Insurance Buying Strategies. *J. Risk Ins.*, June 1984, *51*(2), pp. 205–24.

Epstein, Edythe. Negotiating over Technological Change in Banking and Insurance. *Int. Lab. Rev.*, July–August 1984, *123*(4), pp. 405–22.

Finsinger, Jörg. The Performance of Public Enterprises in Insurance Markets. In *Marchand,*

M.; Pestieau, P. and Tulkens, H., eds., 1984, pp. 223–41.   [G: W. Germany]

Finsinger, Jörg and Kraft, Kornelius. Marktordnung und Kostenstruktur in der Privaten Krankenversicherung. (The Private Health Insurance Market and the Cost Structure of the Insurance Firms. With English summary.) *Z. Wirtschaft. Sozialwissen.*, 1984, *104*(4), pp. 389–415.   [G: Germany]

Finsinger, Jörg and Kraft, Kornelius. Markup Pricing and Firm Decisions. *Z. ges. Staatswiss.*, September 1984, *140*(3), pp. 500–509.
  [G: Germany]

Finsinger, Jörg and Pauly, Mark V. Reserve Levels and Reserve Requirements for Profit-maximizing Insurance Firms. In *Bamberg, G. and Spremann, K., eds.*, 1984, pp. 160–80.

Friedman, Bernard; Ross, Caroline and Misek, Glen. On the Surprisingly Low Cost of State Catastrophic Health Insurance Programs. *J. Risk Ins.*, March 1984, *51*(1), pp. 31–48.
  [G: U.S.]

Halperin, Sanford B. and Mabry, Rodney H. Property and Casualty Insurance Lines Comparison: A Shift-Share Analysis. *J. Risk Ins.*, September 1984, *51*(3), pp. 524–35.
  [G: U.S.]

Hamwi, Iskandar S. and Nissan, Edward. Determination of Net Rate in Property and Liability Insurance: An Alternative Approach. *J. Risk Ins.*, September 1984, *51*(3), pp. 536–48.
  [G: U.S.]

Harper, Ian R. Taxation and Life Insurance: A Theoretical Analysis. *Econ. Rec.*, June 1984, *60*(169), pp. 165–75.

Harrington, Scott. The Impact of Rate Regulation on Prices and Underwriting Results in the Property-Liability Insurance Industry: A Survey. *J. Risk Ins.*, December 1984, *51*(4), pp. 577–623.   [G: U.S.]

Harris, William G. Problems in the Use of Historical Data in Estimating Economic Loss in Wrongful Death and Injury Cases: Comment. *J. Risk Ins.*, March 1984, *51*(1), pp. 122–26.
  [G: U.S.]

Harriss, C. Lowell. Proposals to Tax Life Insurance Savings as Personal Income: As Economic, Fiscal and Social Policy Such Expedients Appear Ill-advised. *Amer. J. Econ. Soc.*, October 1984, *43*(4), pp. 427–34.   [G: U.S.]

Heyne, Paul. The Economics of Law: Economic Imperialism in Negligence Law, No-Fault Insurance, Occupational Licensing and Criminology: Comment. *Australian Econ. Rev.*, 3rd Quarter 1984, (67), pp. 109–12.
  [G: Australia; New Zealand]

Hofflander, Alfred E. and Nye, Blaine F. Self-Insurance, Captives, and Income Taxation. *J. Risk Ins.*, December 1984, *51*(4), pp. 702–09.

Hogan, Andrew J. and Audrey, Robert T. Compulsory Insurance and Allocative Efficiency in Agriculture. *J. Risk Ins.*, June 1984, *51*(2), pp. 342–48.

Holmer, Martin. Tax Policy and the Demand for Health Insurance. *J. Health Econ.*, December 1984, *3*(3), pp. 203–21.   [G: U.S.]

Horvitz, Paul M. Deposit Insurance after Deregulation: A Residual Role for Regulation. In *Fed. Home Loan Bank San Francisco*, 1984, pp. 67–94. [G: U.S.]

Hosek, William R. Problems in the Use of Historical Data in Estimating Economic Loss in Wrongful Death and Injury Cases: Reply. *J. Risk Ins.*, March 1984, *51*(1), pp. 127–30. [G: U.S.]

Hoy, Michael. The Impact of Imperfectly Categorizing Risks on Income Inequality and Social Welfare. *Can. J. Econ.*, August 1984, *17*(3), pp. 557–68.

Jenkins, D. T. The Practice of Insurance Against Fire, 1750–1840, and Historical Research. In *Westall, O. M., ed.*, 1984, pp. 9–38. [G: U.K.]

Jones, Charles A. Competition and Structural Change in the Buenos Aires Fire Insurance Market: The Local Board of Agents, 1875–1921. In *Westall, O. M., ed.*, 1984, pp. 114–29. [G: Argentina; U.K.]

Kahane, Yehuda and Porat, M. Moshe. Financial Analysis of Underwriting Results—A Corrected Approach to Loss Ratio Analysis, with a Special Reference to Inflation. *J. Risk Ins.*, December 1984, *51*(4), pp. 710–19.

Keeton, William R. and Kwerel, Evan. Externalities in Automobile Insurance and the Underinsured Driver Problem. *J. Law Econ.*, April 1984, *27*(1), pp. 149–79. [G: U.S.]

Klingman, Darwin D.; Ross, G. Terry and Schneider, Robert F. Optimization-Based Facility Location Planning: An Application and Some Insights. In *Naylor, T. H. and Thomas, C., eds.*, 1984, pp. 79–90. [G: U.S.]

Klugman, Stuart A. and Murray, Michael L. Bodily Injury Claim Payments as a Function of Automobile Liability Insurance Limits. *J. Risk Ins.*, September 1984, *51*(3), pp. 412–32. [G: U.S.]

Lau, Hon-Shiang. An Effective Approach for Estimating the Aggregate Loss of an Insurance Portfolio. *J. Risk Ins.*, March 1984, *51*(1), pp. 20–30.

Leveson, Irving. Restructuring Financial Institutions in the New Financial Environment: Discussion. In *Sametz, A. W., ed.*, 1984, pp. 33–37. [G: U.S.]

Lewis, Albert E. Restructuring Financial Institutions in the New Financial Environment: Discussion. In *Sametz, A. W., ed.*, 1984, pp. 43–46. [G: U.S.]

Lusk, William B. Evolving Insurance Products and Services: The Supply Side. In *Sametz, A. W., ed.*, 1984, pp. 61–65.

Marlin, Paul. Fitting the Log-Normal Distribution to Loss Data Subject to Multiple Deductions. *J. Risk Ins.*, December 1984, *51*(4), pp. 687–701.

McLeod, Ross. Financial Institutions and Markets in Indonesia. In *Skully, M. T., ed.*, 1984, pp. 49–109. [G: Indonesia]

Minard, Frank P. L. Implications for Investment or Portfolio Management: Discussion. In *Sametz, A. W., ed.*, 1984, pp. 105–07.

Nielson, Norma. Capacity of the Property-Casualty Insurance Industry. *J. Risk Ins.*, September 1984, *51*(3), pp. 393–411. [G: U.S.]

Outreville, Jean-François. The Impact of the Government No-Fault Plan for Automobile Insurance in the Province of Quebec. *J. Risk Ins.*, June 1984, *51*(2), pp. 320–35. [G: Canada]

Palmer, Sarah. The Indemnity in the London Marine Insurance Market, 1824–50. In *Westall, O. M., ed.*, 1984, pp. 74–94. [G: U.K.]

Peterson, Timothy M. Loss Reserving—Property/Casualty Insurance: A Summary of the Book. *J. Risk Ins.*, March 1984, *51*(1), pp. 115–21.

Ryan, Roger. The Norwich Union and the British Fire Insurance Market in the Early Nineteenth Century. In *Westall, O. M., ed.*, 1984, pp. 39–73. [G: U.K.]

Sahin, Izzet. Bruce's Spider and the Employee's Risk under a Pension System. *J. Risk Ins.*, March 1984, *51*(1), pp. 143–49.

Saunders, Anthony. The Effect of Changing Regulation on Investment Policy of Life Insurance Companies. In *Sametz, A. W., ed.*, 1984, pp. 85–94. [G: U.S.]

Schlesinger, Harris. Optimal Insurance for Irreplaceable Commodities. *J. Risk Ins.*, March 1984, *51*(1), pp. 131–37.

Scholz, John T. In Search of Regulatory Alternatives. *J. Policy Anal. Manage.*, Fall 1984, *4*(1), pp. 113–16. [G: U.S.]

Sherden, William A. An Analysis of the Determinants of the Demand for Automobile Insurance. *J. Risk Ins.*, March 1984, *51*(1), pp. 49–62. [G: U.S.]

Skinner, Steven J. and Dubinsky, Alan J. Purchasing Insurance: Predictors of Family Decision-making Responsibility. *J. Risk Ins.*, September 1984, *51*(3), pp. 513–23. [G: U.S.]

Skully, Michael T. Financial Institutions and Markets in Brunei. In *Skully, M. T., ed.*, 1984, pp. 1–48. [G: Brunei]

Skully, Michael T. Financial Institutions and Markets in Thailand. In *Skully, M. T., ed.*, 1984, pp. 296–378. [G: Thailand]

Supple, Barry. Insurance in British History. In *Westall, O. M., ed.*, 1984, pp. 1–8. [G: U.K.]

Swan, Peter L. The Economics of Law: Economic Imperialism in Negligence Law, No-Fault Insurance, Occupational Licensing and Criminology? *Australian Econ. Rev.*, 3rd Quarter 1984, (67), pp. 92–108. [G: Australia; New Zealand]

Tapiero, Charles S. A Mutual Insurance Diffusion Stochastic Control Problem. *J. Econ. Dynam. Control*, September 1984, *7*(3), pp. 241–60.

Treble, J. H. The Record of the Standard Life Assurance Company in the Life Insurance Market of the United Kingdom, 1850–64. In *Westall, O. M., ed.*, 1984, pp. 95–113. [G: U.K.]

Venezia, Itzhak. Aspects of Optimal Automobile Insurance. *J. Risk Ins.*, March 1984, *51*(1), pp. 63–79.

Venezian, Emilio C. Are Insurers Under-Earning? *J. Risk Ins.*, March 1984, *51*(1), pp. 150–56. [G: U.S.]

Venezian, Emilio C. Cost-based Pricing and Price-based Costing in Private Passenger Automobile Insurance. *J. Risk Ins.*, September 1984, *51*(3), pp. 433–52. [G: U.S.]

Venezian, Emilio C. Efficiency and Equity in Insurance. *J. Risk Ins.*, June 1984, *51*(2), pp. 190–204.

Verni, Ralph F. Implications for Investment or Portfolio Management: Discussion. In *Sametz, A. W., ed.*, 1984, pp. 109–10.

Vroman, Susan and Anderson, Gerard. The Effect of Income Taxation on the Demand for Employer–Provided Health Insurance. *Appl. Econ.*, February 1984, *16*(1), pp. 33–43. [G: U.S.]

Wallison, Peter J. The Emerging Regulatory Structure for Banks: Implications for the Insurance Industry. In *Sametz, A. W., ed.*, 1984, pp. 73–78. [G: U.S.]

Watson, Harry S. The Effects of Compensation for Uninsured but Insurable Losses. *J. Risk Ins.*, September 1984, *51*(3), pp. 498–512.

Weinberger, Alfred. New Solutions to Investment Management Problems. In *Sametz, A. W., ed.*, 1984, pp. 99–103.

Weisberg, Herbert I.; Tomberlin, Thomas J. and Chatterjee, Sangit. Predicting Insurance Losses under Cross-Classification: A Comparison of Alternative Approaches. *J. Bus. Econ. Statist.*, April 1984, *2*(2), pp. 170–78. [G: U.S.]

Weissbrod, Doran. Index-Linked Life Insurance in Israel and the Sharir Committee. *J. Risk Ins.*, June 1984, *51*(2), pp. 336–41. [G: Israel]

West, Peter A. Private Health Insurance. In *Le Grand, J. and Robinson, R., eds.*, 1984, pp. 111–15. [G: U.K.]

Westall, Oliver M. David and Goliath: The Fire Offices Committee and Non-tariff Competition, 1898–1907. In *Westall, O. M., ed.*, 1984, pp. 130–54. [G: U.K.]

White, Lawrence H. The Title Insurance Industry, Reverse Competition, and Controlled Business—A Different View [The High Price of 'Reform': Title Insurance Rates and the Benefits of Rating Bureaus]. *J. Risk Ins.*, June 1984, *51*(2), pp. 308–19. [G: U.S.]

Zinbarg, Edward D. Asset Management: The Parts versus the Whole. In *Sametz, A. W., ed.*, 1984, pp. 95–97. [G: U.S.]

Zweifel, Peter. Drugs as an Ambulatory Care Technology: Costs and Benefits to the Insurer. In *Lindgren, B., ed.*, 1984, pp. 37–65. [G: Switzerland]

6357 Real Estate

Achour, Dominique and Brown, Robert L. Un marche d'options sur indice de prix fonciers: nouvel instrument d'une politique de l'habitition. (With English summary.) *Can. Public Policy*, September 1984, *10*(3), pp. 287–95. [G: Canada]

Brennan, Thomas P.; Cannaday, Roger E. and

Colwell, Peter F. Office Rent in the Chicago CBD. *Amer. Real Estate Urban Econ. Assoc. J.*, Fall 1984, *12*(3), pp. 243–60. [G: U.S.]

Brown, Robert L. and Achour, Dominique. The Pricing of Land Options. *Urban Stud.*, August 1984, *21*(3), pp. 317–23.

Brueggeman, W. B.; Chen, Andrew H. and Thibodeau, T. G. Real Estate Investment Funds: Performance and Portfolio Consideration. *Amer. Real Estate Urban Econ. Assoc. J.*, Fall 1984, *12*(3), pp. 333–54. [G: U.S.]

Cater, John. Acquiring Premises: A Case Study of Asians in Bradford. In *Ward, R. and Jenkins, R., eds.*, 1984, pp. 211–28. [G: U.K.]

Drennan, Matthew. Setting Municipal Priorities: The Setting: The Local Economy and Local Revenues. In *Brecher, C. and Horton, R. D., eds.*, 1984, pp. 43–68. [G: U.S.]

Fogler, H. Russell. 20% in Real Estate: Can Theory Justify It? *J. Portfol. Manage.*, Winter 1984, *10*(2), pp. 6–13. [G: U.S.]

Hendershott, Patric H. and Ling, David C. Prospective Changes in Tax Law and the Value of Depreciable Real Estate. *Amer. Real Estate Urban Econ. Assoc. J.*, Fall 1984, *12*(3), pp. 297–317. [G: U.S.]

Hite, Gailen L.; Owers, James E. and Rogers, Ronald C. The Separation of Real Estate Operations by Spin-off. *Amer. Real Estate Urban Econ. Assoc. J.*, Fall 1984, *12*(3), pp. 318–32. [G: U.S.]

Ibbotson, Roger G. and Siegel, Laurence B. Real Estate Returns: A Comparison with Other Investments. *Amer. Real Estate Urban Econ. Assoc. J.*, Fall 1984, *12*(3), pp. 219–42. [G: U.S.]

Jaffe, Austin J. and Sirmans, C. F. The Theory and Evidence on Real Estate Financial Decisions: A Review of the Issues. *Amer. Real Estate Urban Econ. Assoc. J.*, Fall 1984, *12*(3), pp. 378–400.

Kau, James B. and Sirmans, C. F. Changes in Urban Land Values: 1836–1970. *J. Urban Econ.*, January 1984, *15*(1), pp. 18–25. [G: U.S.]

Kennedy, Peter. On an Unfair Appraisal of Vertical Equity in Real Estate Assessment. *Econ. Inquiry*, April 1984, *22*(2), pp. 287–90. [G: U.S.]

Kochin, Levis A. and Parks, Richard W. Vertical Equity in Real Estate Assessment: Reply. *Econ. Inquiry*, April 1984, *22*(2), pp. 291–96. [G: U.S.]

Kopcke, Richard W. and Aldrich, Peter C. A Real Estate Crisis: Averted or Just Postponed? *J. Portfol. Manage.*, Spring 1984, *10*(3), pp. 21–29.

Kozub, Robert M. and Trebby, James P. Special Valuation of Farmland and Closely Held Business Realty for Estate Tax Purposes. *Growth Change*, July 1984, *15*(3), pp. 25–29. [G: U.S.]

Leibler, Mark. Taxation and Deductions for Losses from Highly Geared Rental Investments: Issues of Law and Policy. *Australian Tax Forum*, March 1984, *1*(1), pp. 39–53. [G: Australia]

Lusht, Kenneth M. and Fisher, Jeffrey D. Anticipated Growth and the Specification of Debt in Real Estate Value Models. *Amer. Real Estate Urban Econ. Assoc. J.*, Spring 1984, *12*(1), pp. 1–11. **[G: U.S.]**

Miles, Mike. Institutional Real Estate Investment. *Amer. Real Estate Urban Econ. Assoc. J.*, Fall 1984, *12*(3), pp. 215–18. **[G: U.S.]**

Miles, Mike and McCue, Tom. Commercial Real Estate Returns. *Amer. Real Estate Urban Econ. Assoc. J.*, Fall 1984, *12*(3), pp. 355–77. **[G: U.S.]**

Peiser, Richard B. Risk Analysis in Land Development. *Amer. Real Estate Urban Econ. Assoc. J.*, Spring 1984, *12*(1), pp. 12–29.

Rabiega, William A.; Lin, Ta-Win and Robinson, Linda M. The Property Value Impacts of Public Housing Projects in Low and Moderate Density Residential Neighborhoods. *Land Econ.*, May 1984, *60*(2), pp. 174–79. **[G: U.S.]**

Rosen, Kenneth T. Toward a Model of the Office Building Sector. *Amer. Real Estate Urban Econ. Assoc. J.*, Fall 1984, *12*(3), pp. 261–69. **[G: U.S.]**

Schloss, Nathan. Use of Employment Data to Estimate Office Space Demand. *Mon. Lab. Rev.*, December 1984, *107*(12), pp. 40–44. **[G: U.S.]**

Srivastava, Rajendra K., et al. Analysis of the Characteristics of Individual Investors in Real Estate Securities and Income-producing Property. *Amer. Real Estate Urban Econ. Assoc. J.*, Winter 1984, *12*(4), pp. 521–41. **[G: U.S.]**

Webb, James R. Real Estate Investment Acquisition Rules for Life Insurance Companies and Pension Funds: A Survey. *Amer. Real Estate Urban Econ. Assoc. J.*, Winter 1984, *12*(4), pp. 495–520. **[G: U.S.]**

Zerbst, Robert H. and Cambon, Barbara R. Real Estate: Historical Returns and Risks. *J. Portfol. Manage.*, Spring 1984, *10*(3), pp. 5–20.

6358 Entertainment, Recreation, Tourism

Archer, Brian. Tourism and the British Economy. *Rivista Int. Sci. Econ. Com.*, July 1984, *31*(7), pp. 596–613. **[G: U.K.]**

Asch, Peter; Malkiel, Burton G. and Quandt, Richard E. Market Efficiency in Racetrack Betting. *J. Bus.*, April 1984, *57*(2), pp. 165–75. **[G: U.S.]**

Austen-Smith, David. Subsidies to the Arts with Multiple Public Donors. *Econ. Rec.*, December 1984, *60*(171), pp. 381–89.

Baretje, René. La contribution nette du tourisme international à la balance des paiements. (The Net Contribution of International Tourism to the Balance of Payments. With English summary.) *Rivista Int. Sci. Econ. Com.*, July 1984, *31*(7), pp. 649–74. **[G: OECD]**

Bélisle, François J. Food Production and Tourism in Jamaica: Obstacles to Increasing Local Food Supplies to Hotels. *J. Devel. Areas*, October 1984, *19*(1), pp. 1–20. **[G: Jamaica]**

Bélisle, François J. Tourism and Food Imports: The Case of Jamaica. *Econ. Develop. Cult. Change*, July 1984, *32*(4), pp. 819–42. **[G: Jamaica]**

Bradbury, Malcolm. Supply and Demand. In *Sandford, C. and Bradbury, M., eds.*, 1984, pp. 1–26. **[G: U.K.]**

Brambilla, Francesco. Inchiesta sul mercato dell'antiquariato in Italia. Un modello interpretativo. (An Inquiry into the Antiques Market in Italy. An Interpretive Model. With English summary.) *Giorn. Econ.*, January–February 1984, *43*(1–2), pp. 3–35. **[G: Italy]**

Bresnahan, Timothy F. Comment on "Conjoint Analysis of Price Premiums for Hotel Amenities." *J. Bus.*, Part 2, January 1984, *57*(1), pp. S133–38.

Campbell, Colin S. and Ponting, J. Rick. The Evolution of Casino Gambling in Alberta. *Can. Public Policy*, June 1984, *10*(2), pp. 142–55. **[G: Canada]**

Chiesa, Carlo and Castaldo, Pasquale. Il turismo con l'estero dell'Italia. (Foreign Tourism Flows in Italy: Theoretical Model and Empirical Verification. With English summary.) *Rivista Int. Sci. Econ. Com.*, July 1984, *31*(7), pp. 639–48. **[G: Italy]**

Costa, Paolo. La valutazione degli effetti economici del turismo in Italia. (Assessing the Economic Effects of Tourism in Italy. With English summary.) *Rivista Int. Sci. Econ. Com.*, July 1984, *31*(7), pp. 614–26. **[G: Italy]**

Daly, A. Cost Saving Methods in Travel Demand Forecasting. In *Pitfield, D. E., ed.*, 1984, pp. 102–13.

DiMaggio, Paul J. The Nonprofit Instrument and the Influence of the Marketplace on Policies in the Arts. In *Lowry, W. M., ed.*, 1984, pp. 57–99. **[G: U.S.]**

Filer, Randall K. A Theoretical Analysis of the Economic Impact of Artists' Resale Royalties Legislation. *J. Cult. Econ.*, June 1984, *8*(1), pp. 1–28.

Gambling, Trevor and Andrews, Gordon. Does Baumol's Disease Exist? Some Findings from the Royal Shakespeare Company. *J. Cult. Econ.*, December 1984, *8*(2), pp. 73–92. **[G: U.K.]**

Gapinski, James H. The Economics of Performing Shakespeare. *Amer. Econ. Rev.*, June 1984, *74*(3), pp. 458–66.

Goldberg, Stephen M.; Green, Paul E. and Wind, Yoram. Conjoint Analysis of Price Premiums for Hotel Amenities. *J. Bus.*, Part 2, January 1984, *57*(1), pp. S111–32.

Green, J. Ronald. Film and Video: An Institutional Paradigm and Some Issues of National Policy. *J. Cult. Econ.*, June 1984, *8*(1), pp. 61–79. **[G: U.S.]**

Guarini, Renato and Cantoloni, Alessandro. La domanda di turismo in Italia. Un'analisi interpretativa. (Tourism Demand in Italy. An Interpretive Analysis. With English summary.) *Rivista Int. Sci. Econ. Com.*, July 1984, *31*(7), pp. 675–95. **[G: Italy]**

Heilbrun, James. Keynes and the Economics of

the Arts. *J. Cult. Econ.*, December 1984, *8*(2), pp. 37–49.

Hensher, David A. and Louviere, J. J. Towards an Approach to Forecasting Attendance at Unique Events Using a Discrete Choice Model and Experimental Design Data. In *Pitfield, D. E., ed.*, 1984, pp. 67–87. **[G: Australia]**

Hill, James Richard and Spellman, William. Pay Discrimination in Baseball: Data from the Seventies. *Ind. Relat.*, Winter 1984, *23*(1), pp. 103–12. **[G: U.S.]**

Horsky, Dan. Comments on "Conjoint Analysis of Price Premiums for Hotel Amenities." *J. Bus.*, Part 2, January 1984, *57*(1), pp. S139–47.

Jennett, Nicholas I. Attendances, Uncertainty of Outcome and Policy in Scottish League Football. *Scot. J. Polit. Econ.*, June 1984, *31*(2), pp. 176–98. **[G: U.K.]**

Jones, J. C. H. Winners, Losers and Hosers: Demand and Survival in the National Hockey League. *Atlantic Econ. J.*, September 1984, *12*(3), pp. 54–63. **[G: Canada]**

Jones, Trefor T. Restrictive Practices in the Supply of Inclusive Tours. *Nat. Westminster Bank Quart. Rev.*, February 1984, pp. 31–40. **[G: U.K.]**

Katz, Stanley N. Influences on Public Policies in the United States. In *Lowry, W. M., ed.*, 1984, pp. 23–37. **[G: U.S.]**

Lange, Mark D. and Luksetich, William A. Demand Elasticities for Symphony Orchestras. *J. Cult. Econ.*, June 1984, *8*(1), pp. 29–47. **[G: U.S.]**

Lehn, Kenneth. Information Asymmetries in Baseball's Free Agent Market. *Econ. Inquiry*, January 1984, *22*(1), pp. 37–44. **[G: U.S.]**

Leonard, John E. and Prinzinger, Joseph M. An Investigation into the Monopsonistic Market Structure of Division One NCAA Football and Its Effect on College Football Players. *Eastern Econ. J.*, October-December 1984, *10*(4), pp. 455–67. **[G: U.S.]**

Lin, Tzong-biau. A Comparative Econometric Study of Tourist Expenditure Behavior in Asia. *Hong Kong Econ. Pap.*, 1984, (15), pp. 35–66. **[G: Hong Kong; Nepal; Sri Lanka]**

Lowry, W. McNeil. The Arts & Public Policy in the United States: Introduction. In *Lowry, W. M., ed.*, 1984, pp. 1–22. **[G: U.S.]**

McCormack, Thelma. Culture and the State. *Can. Public Policy*, September 1984, *10*(3), pp. 267–77.

Mogull, Robert G. Racial Discrimination in Professional Basketball: A Retort. *Amer. Econ.*, Fall 1984, *28*(2), pp. 69–70. **[G: U.S.]**

Montias, John Michael. Public Support for the Performing Arts in Western Europe and the United States: History and Analysis. In *[Reynolds,L.G.]*,1984,pp.409–44. **[G: U.S.; W. Europe]**

Morash, Tal. The Economic Impact of Marine Recreation. In *Gopalakrishnan, C., ed.*, 1984, pp. 179–86.

Morey, Edward R. The Choice of Ski Areas: Estimation of a Generalized CES Preference Or-

dering with Characteristics. *Rev. Econ. Statist.*, November 1984, *66*(4), pp. 584–90. **[G: U.S.]**

Murph, A. Franklin. The Classical Record Industry in the United States. *J. Cult. Econ.*, June 1984, *8*(1), pp. 81–89. **[G: U.S.]**

O'Hagan, John W. and Harrison, M. J. Market Shares of U.S. Tourist Expenditure in Europe: An Econometric Analysis. *Appl. Econ.*, December 1984, *16*(6), pp. 919–31. **[G: U.S.; Europe]**

O'Hagan, John W. and Harrison, M. J. U.K. and U.S. Visitor Expenditure in Ireland: Some Econometric Findings. *Econ. Soc. Rev.*, April 1984, *15*(3), pp. 195–207. **[G: Ireland; OECD]**

Palomo, Manuel Figuerola. Valoración del consumo y la producción turística. (Valuation of Tourism Consumption and Production. With English summary.) *Rivista Int. Sci. Econ. Com.*, July 1984, *31*(7), pp. 627–38. **[G: Spain]**

Rathbone, Perry T. Influences of Private Patrons: The Art Museum as an Example. In *Lowry, W. M., ed.*, 1984, pp. 38–56. **[G: U.S.]**

Sahota, Gian S. and Sahota, Chander K. A Theory of Human Investment in Physical Skills and Its Application to Achievement in Tennis. *Southern Econ. J.*, January 1984, *50*(3), pp. 642–64. **[G: U.S.]**

Shoesmith, Eddie. Long-term Trends in Performing Arts Expenditures. *J. Cult. Econ.*, December 1984, *8*(2), pp. 51–72. **[G: U.S.; U.K.]**

Stephens, R. J. Forestry or a National Park: A New Zealand Case Study. *Int. J. Soc. Econ.*, 1984, *11*(3/4), pp. 29–44. **[G: New Zealand]**

Stoller, Michael A. The Economics of Collectible Goods. *J. Cult. Econ.*, June 1984, *8*(1), pp. 91–104. **[G: Israel]**

Vaughan, D. R. The Cultural Heritage: An Approach to Analyzing Income and Employment Effects. *J. Cult. Econ.*, December 1984, *8*(2), pp. 1–36. **[G: U.K.]**

636 Nonprofit Industries: Theory and Studies

6360 Nonprofit Industries: Theory and Studies

Badelt, Christoph. New Concepts for the Supply of Government Services. In *Hanusch, H., ed.*, 1984, pp. 267–78.

Bertsch, Dale F. Non-profit Institutions and Urban Revitalization. In *Porter, P. R. and Sweet, D. C., eds.*, 1984, pp. 52–64. **[G: U.S.]**

Busche, Kelly and Kennedy, Peter. On Economists' Belief in the Law of Small Numbers. *Econ. Inquiry*, October 1984, *22*(4), pp. 602–03. **[G: U.S.]**

Coughlin, Cletus C. and Erekson, O. Homer. An Examination of Contributions to Support Intercollegiate Athletics. *Southern Econ. J.*, July 1984, *51*(1), pp. 180–95. **[G: U.S.]**

Cullis, John G.; Jones, Philip R. and Thanassoulas, Constantine. Are Charities Efficient 'Firms'? A Preliminary Test of the UK Charitable Sector. *Public Choice*, 1984, *44*(2), pp. 367–73. **[G: U.K.]**

DiMaggio, Paul J. The Nonprofit Instrument and the Influence of the Marketplace on Policies in the Arts. In *Lowry, W. M., ed.*, 1984, pp. 57–99. [G: U.S.]

Hamermesh, Daniel S. The Role of Time in the Measurement of Transfers and Well-Being: Comment. In *Moon, M., ed.*, 1984, pp. 234–38. [G: U.S.]

Houck, Oliver A. With Charity for All. *Yale Law J.*, July 1984, 93(8), pp. 1415–563. [G: U.S.]

Jacobs, Philip and Wilder, Ronald P. Pricing Behavior of Non-profit Agencies: The Case of Blood Products. *J. Health Econ.*, April 1984, 3(1), pp. 49–61. [G: U.S.]

Kass, David I. and Pautler, Paul A. On Economists' Belief in the Law of Small Numbers: A Reply [The Administration Costs of Non-profit Health Insurers]. *Econ. Inquiry*, October 1984, 22(4), pp. 604–06. [G: U.S.]

Kolderie, Ted. Business Opportunities in the Changing Conceptions of the Public Sector Role. In *Brooks, H.; Liebman, L. and Schelling, C. S., eds.*, 1984, pp. 89–110. [G: U.S.]

Liebman, Lance. Political and Economic Markets: The Public, Private and Not-for-Profit Sectors. In *Brooks, H.; Liebman, L. and Schelling, C. S., eds.*, 1984, pp. 341–58. [G: U.S.]

Lowry, W. McNeil. The Arts & Public Policy in the United States: Introduction. In *Lowry, W. M., ed.*, 1984, pp. 1–22. [G: U.S.]

Morgan, James N. The Role of Time in the Measurement of Transfers and Well-Being. In *Moon, M., ed.*, 1984, pp. 199–234. [G: U.S.]

Pitts, Robert E. and Skelly, Gerald U. Economic Self-Interest and Other Motivational Factors Underlying Charitable Giving. *J. Behav. Econ.*, Winter 1984, 13(2), pp. 93–109. [G: U.S.]

Rathbone, Perry T. Influences of Private Patrons: The Art Museum as an Example. In *Lowry, W. M., ed.*, 1984, pp. 38–56. [G: U.S.]

Rudney, Gabriel and Weitzman, Murray. Trends in Employment and Earnings in the Philanthropic Sector. *Mon. Lab. Rev.*, September 1984, 107(9), pp. 16–20. [G: U.S.]

Salamon, Lester M. Nonprofit Organizations: The Lost Opportunity. In *Palmer, J. L. and Sawhill, I. V., eds.*, 1984, pp. 261–85. [G: U.S.]

Schill, Michael H. The Participation of Charities in Limited Partnerships. *Yale Law J.*, June 1984, 93(7), pp. 1355–374. [G: U.S.]

Sugden, Robert. Voluntary Organisations and the Welfare State. In *Le Grand, J. and Robinson, R., eds.*, 1984, pp. 70–89.

Swint, John Michael. Collective Bargaining in Not-For-Profit Hospitals: A Model amd Its Implications for the Likelihood of Strikes. *Southern Econ. J.*, July 1984, 51(1), pp. 24–40.

Wacht, Richard F. A Financial Management Theory of the Nonprofit Organization. *J. Finan. Res.*, Spring 1984, 7(1), pp. 37–45.

Wolpert, Julian and Reiner, Thomas A. Service Provision by the Not-for-Profit Sector: A Comparative Study. *Econ. Geogr.*, January 1984, 60(1), pp. 28–37. [G: U.S.]

Wolpert, Julian and Reiner, Thomas A. The Philanthropy Marketplace. *Econ. Geogr.*, July 1984, 60(3), pp. 197–209. [G: U.S.]

640 ECONOMIC CAPACITY

641 Economic Capacity

6410 Economic Capacity

Banks, Ferdinand E. A Note on Optimal System Planning. *Energy J.*, October 1984, 5(4), pp. 79–80.

Berg, Sigbjørn Atle. Estimation of Production Capacities in a Putty-Clay Production Model: Norwegian Manufacturing Industries, 1962–81. *Scand. J. Econ.*, 1984, 86(3), pp. 379–84. [G: Norway]

Braeutigam, Ronald R. and Quirk, James P. Demand Uncertainty and the Regulated Firm. *Int. Econ. Rev.*, February 1984, 25(1), pp. 45–60.

Calvo, Guillermo A. and Thoumi, Francisco E. Demand Fluctuations, Inventories and Capacity Utilization. *Southern Econ. J.*, January 1984, 50(3), pp. 743–54.

Färe, Rolf. The Existence of Plant Capacity. *Int. Econ. Rev.*, February 1984, 25(1), pp. 209–13.

Foster, John Bellamy. The Limits of U.S. Capitalism: Surplus Capacity and Capacity Surplus. In *Foster, J. B. and Szlajfer, H., eds.*, 1984, pp. 198–213. [G: U.S.]

von Hayek, Friedrich A. Technical Progress and Excess Capacity. In *von Hayek, F. A. (II)*, 1984, 1936, pp. 163–80.

Hulten, Charles R. and Peterson, George E. The Public Capital Stock: Needs, Trends, and Performance. *Amer. Econ. Rev.*, May 1984, 74(2), pp. 166–73. [G: U.S.]

Jaffee, Dwight M. The Impact of Financial Futures and Options on Capital Formation. *J. Futures Markets*, Fall 1984, 4(3), pp. 417–47. [G: U.S.]

Kibria, M. G. and Tisdell, Clem A. Comparative Aspects of Capacity Utilization: Evidence from Bangladesh Jute Weaving Industry. *J. Econ. Devel.*, July 1984, 9(1), pp. 45–66. [G: Bangladesh]

Pasha, Hafiz A. and Qureshi, Tahira. Capacity Utilisation in Selected Industries of Pakistan. *Pakistan J. Appl. Econ.*, Summer 1984, 3(1), pp. 29–56. [G: Pakistan]

Schwartz, Eli. "Excess Capacity" in Utility Industries: An Inventory Theoretic Approach. *Land Econ.*, February 1984, 60(1), pp. 40–48. [G: U.S.]

Szarvas, Péter. Capital Formation in Hungary in International Comparison. *Acta Oecon.*, 1984, 32(3–4), pp. 303–16. [G: Selected Countries]

Valppu, Pirkko. Kapasiteetin Käyttöaste 1960–1982: menetelmä ja tulokset. (Capacity Utilization in Finland in 1960–1982: Method and Results. With English summary.) *Kansant. Aikak.*, 1984, 80(3), pp. 302–12. [G: Finland]

Yamawaki, Hideki. Market Structure, Capacity Expansion, and Pricing: A Model Applied to

the Japanese Iron and Steel Industry. *Int. J. Ind. Organ.*, March 1984, 2(1), pp. 29–62.
[G: Japan]

700 Agriculture; Natural Resources

710 AGRICULTURE

7100 Agriculture

Baker, Christopher J. Frogs and Farmers: The Green Revolution in India, and its Murky Past. In *[Farmer, B. H.]*, 1984, pp. 37–52.
[G: India]

Balakrishnan, Pulapre. On the Significance of Interlinked Factor Markets in Agrarian Economies. *Indian Econ. J.*, April–June 1984, 31(4), pp. 62–72.

Beckford, George L. Induced Innovation Model of Agricultural Development: Comment. In *Eicher, C. K. and Staatz, J. M., eds.*, 1984, 1972, pp. 75–81.

Berry, Wendell. The Agricultural Crisis as a Crisis of Culture. In *Douglass, G. K., ed.*, 1984, pp. 219–25.

Bessler, David A. Relative Prices and Money: A Vector Autoregression on Brazilian Data. *Amer. J. Agr. Econ.*, February 1984, 66(1), pp. 25–30.
[G: Brazil]

Blandford, David. Changes in Food Consumption Patterns in the OECD Area. *Europ. Rev. Agr. Econ.*, 1984, 11(1), pp. 43–64.
[G: OECD]

Bradnock, Robert W. Agricultural Development in Tamil Nadu: Two Decades of Land Use Change at Village Level. In *[Farmer, B. H.]*, 1984, pp. 136–52.
[G: India]

Chacon, Ramón D. Labor Unrest and Industrialized Agriculture in California: The Case of the 1933 San Joaquin Valley Cotton Strike. *Soc. Sci. Quart.*, June 1984, 65(2), pp. 336–53.
[G: U.S.]

Chambers, Robert. Beyond the Green Revolution: A Selective Essay. In *[Farmer, B. H.]*, 1984, pp. 362–79.

Chambers, Robert G. Agricultural and Financial Market Interdependence in the Short Run. *Amer. J. Agr. Econ.*, February 1984, 66(1), pp. 12–24.
[G: U.S.]

Choate, Stephen. Agricultural Development and Government Policy in Settler Economies: A Comment. *Econ. Hist. Rev., 2nd Ser.*, August 1984, 37(3), pp. 409–13.
[G: Rhodesia]

Cobb, John B. Theology, Perception, and Agriculture. In *Douglass, G. K., ed.*, 1984, pp. 205–17.

Csizmadia, Ernö. Lasting Elements and Changing Circumstances in the Hungarian Agrarian Development. *Acta Oecon.*, 1984, 32(3–4), pp. 343–61.
[G: Hungary]

Donghi, Tulio Halperin. Canción de otoño en primavera: previsiones sobre la crisis de la agricultura cerealera argentina (1894–1930). (With English summary.) *Desarrollo Econ.*, October–December 1984, 24(95), pp. 367–86.
[G: Argentina]

Drewes, Wolfram U. and Sirkin, Abraham M. The Uses of Satellite Remote Sensing. In *Weiss, C. and Jéquier, N., eds.*, 1984, pp. 85–102.

Eicher, Carl K. and Staatz, John M. Agricultural Growth and the Transformation of Rural Institutions: Introduction. In *Eicher, C. K. and Staatz, J. M., eds.*, 1984, pp. 255–62.

Eicher, Carl K. and Staatz, John M. Models of Agricultural Development: Introduction. In *Eicher, C. K. and Staatz, J. M., eds.*, 1984, pp. 33–37.

Ellis, Frank. Relative Agricultural Prices and the Urban Bias Model: A Comparative Analysis of Tanzania and Fiji. *J. Devel. Stud.*, April 1984, 20(3), pp. 28–51.
[G: Tanzania; Fiji]

Fishlow, Albert. Summary Comment on Adelman, Balassa and Streeten [Beyond Export-Led Growth] [Adjustment Policies in Developing Countries: A Reassessment] [Basic Needs: Some Unsettled Questions]. *World Devel.*, September 1984, 12(9), pp. 979–82.

Frank, Andre Gunder. Reflections on Green, Red and White Revolutions in India. In *Frank, A. G.*, 1984, 1973, pp. 62–73.
[G: India]

Gbetibouo, Mathurin and Delgado, Christopher L. Lessons and Constraints of Export Crop-Led Growth: Cocoa in Ivory Coast. In *Zartman, I. W. and Delgado, C. L., eds.*, 1984, pp. 115–47.
[G: Ivory Coast]

Goodman, David; Sorj, Bernardo and Wilkinson, John. Agro-Industry, State Policy and Rural Social Structures: Recent Analyses of Proletarianisation in Brazilian Agriculture. In *Munslow, B. and Finch, H., eds.*, 1984, pp. 189–215.
[G: Brazil]

Grigg, David B. The Agricultural Revolution in Western Europe. In *[Farmer, B. H.]*, 1984, pp. 1–17.
[G: W. Europe]

Hardaker, J. Brian; Anderson, Jock R. and Dillon, John L. Perspectives on Assessing the Impacts of Improved Agricultural Technologies in Developing Countries. *Australian J. Agr. Econ.*, August/December 1984, 28(2–3), pp. 87–108.
[G: LDCs]

Harriss, Barbara and Harriss, John C. 'Generative' or 'Parasitic' Urbanism? Some Observations from the Recent History of a South Indian Market Town. *J. Devel. Stud.*, April 1984, 20(3), pp. 82–101.
[G: India]

Harriss, Barbara and Harriss, John C. 'Generative' or 'Parasitic' Urbanism? Some Observations from the Recent History of a South Indian Market Town. In *Harriss, J. and Moore, M., eds.*, 1984, pp. 82–101.
[G: India]

Hayami, Yujiro. Assessment of the Green Revolution. In *Eicher, C. K. and Staatz, J. M., eds.*, 1984, 1981, pp. 389–96.
[G: Asia]

Hayami, Yujiro and Ruttan, Vernon W. The Green Revolution: Inducement and Distribution. *Pakistan Devel. Rev.*, Spring 1984, 23(1), pp. 37–63.
[G: Asia]

Holdcroft, Lane E. The Rise and Fall of Community Development, 1950–65: A Critical Assessment. In *Eicher, C. K. and Staatz, J. M., eds.*, 1984, 1978, pp. 46–58.

Ishimine, Tomotaka. Food, Energy and Debt Servicing as Reserve and Development Constraints of Less Developed Countries. *Rivista Int. Sci. Econ. Com.*, April 1984, *31*(4), pp. 371–79. [G: LDCs]

Kozyr, M. I. New Features of Labour Relations in Soviet Agriculture. *Int. Soc. Sci. J.*, 1984, *36*(2), pp. 285–97. [G: U.S.S.R.]

Lardy, Nicholas R. Prices, Markets, and the Chinese Peasant. In *Eicher, C. K. and Staatz, J. M., eds.*, 1984, pp. 420–35. [G: China]

Leisinger, Klaus M. "Grüne Revolution": Eine revidierte Beurteilung im Lichte neuer empirischer Erfahrungen. (The Green Revolution: A Review on the Basis of New Empirical Evidence. With English summary.) *Aussenwirtschaft*, December 1984, *39*(4), pp. 357–81. [G: LDCs]

Lele, Uma. Rural Africa: Modernization, Equity, and Long-term Development. In *Eicher, C. K. and Staatz, J. M., eds.*, 1984, *1981*, pp. 436–52. [G: Africa]

Léons, Madeline Barbara. Political Pentration and Conflict Resolution in the Bolivian Yungas. *J. Devel. Areas*, July 1984, *18*(4), pp. 465–80. [G: Bolivia]

Lim, Manuel. Directions for Management: Agriculture. *Philippine Econ. J.*, Winter 1984, *23*(1), pp. 53–59. [G: Philippines]

Ludden, David. Productive Power in Agriculture: A Survey of Work on the Local History of British India. In *Desai, M.; Rudolph, S. H. and Rudra, A., eds.*, 1984, pp. 51–99. [G: India]

Mănescu, B.; Davidovici, I. and Stroe, R. Agricultural Production—A Dynamic Complex System (II). *Econ. Computat. Cybern. Stud. Res.*, 1984, *19*(2), pp. 49–56. [G: Romania]

Mate, Mavis. Agrarian Economy after the Black Death: The Manors of Canterbury Cathedral Priory, 1348–91. *Econ. Hist. Rev., 2nd Ser.*, August 1984, *37*(3), pp. 341–54. [G: U.K.]

McCalla, Alex F. Macro Prices and Structural Change: Discussion. *Amer. J. Agr. Econ.*, May 1984, *66*(2), pp. 202–03.

Mellor, John W. Agricultural Development and the Intersectoral Transfer of Resources. In *Eicher, C. K. and Staatz, J. M., eds.*, 1984, *1973*, pp. 136–46. [G: Taiwan]

Mellor, John W. and Johnston, Bruce F. The World Food Equation: Interrelations among Development, Employment, and Food Consumption. *J. Econ. Lit.*, June 1984, *22*(2), pp. 53–74. [G: Global]

Mishra, S. N. Agricultural Development in India: A Communitarian Strategy. In *Ngo, M., ed., vol. 2*, 1984, pp. 785–96. [G: India]

Mohammad, Faiz. The Performance of Pakistan's Agricultural Markets in the Green Revolution Perspective. *Pakistan Devel. Rev.*, Summer-Autumn 1984, *23*(2&3), pp. 287–303. [G: Pakistan]

Moore, Mick. Institutional Development, the World Bank, and India's New Agricultural Extension Programme. *J. Devel. Stud.*, July 1984, *20*(4), pp. 303–17. [G: India]

Mosley, Paul. Agricultural Development and

Government Policy: A Reply. *Econ. Hist. Rev., 2nd Ser.*, August 1984, *37*(3), pp. 414–16. [G: Rhodesia]

Mounier, Alain and Byé, Pascal. Les futurs alimentaires et énergétiques des biotechnologies. (With English summary.) *Écon. Soc.*, September 1984, *18*(9), pp. 7–340. [G: Global]

Myint, Hla. Exports and Economic Development of Less Developed Countries. In *Eicher, C. K. and Staatz, J. M., eds.*, 1984, *1971*, pp. 222–40.

Nicholson, Norman K. Landholding, Agricultural Modernization, and Local Institutions in India. *Econ. Develop. Cult. Change*, April 1984, *32*(3), pp. 569–92. [G: India]

Norgaard, Richard B. Coevolutionary Agricultural Development. *Econ. Develop. Cult. Change*, April 1984, *32*(3), pp. 525–46.

Norton, George W.; Coffey, Joseph D. and Frye, E. Berrier. Estimating Returns to Agricultural Research, Extension, and Teaching at the State Level. *Southern J. Agr. Econ.*, July 1984, *16*(1), pp. 121–28. [G: U.S.]

Pirie, N. W. Technological Approaches to Plant Productivity. *Écon. Appl.*, 1984, *37*(2), pp. 363–76. [G: LDCs]

Pitra, František. Present Tasks and Long-term Development of Agriculture and Other Branches Ensuring Food Supplies. *Czech. Econ. Digest.*, December 1984, (8), pp. 3–62. [G: Czechoslovakia]

von Planta, Louis. The Future Role of Chemistry in Removing Constraints on Food Production and Utilization. In *Bixler, G. and Shemilt, L. W., eds.*, 1984, pp. 55–63.

Pray, Carl E. The Impact of Agricultural Research in British India. *J. Econ. Hist.*, June 1984, *44*(2), pp. 429–40. [G: India]

Robinson, Warren and Schutjer, Wayne A. Agricultural Development and Demographic Change: A Generalization of the Boserup Model. *Econ. Develop. Cult. Change*, January 1984, *32*(2), pp. 355–66. [G: LDCs]

Ruttan, Vernon W. Models of Agricultural Development. In *Eicher, C. K. and Staatz, J. M., eds.*, 1984, *1980*, pp. 38–45.

Ruttan, Vernon W. and Hayami, Yujiro. Induced Innovation Model of Agricultural Development. In *Eicher, C. K. and Staatz, J. M., eds.*, 1984, *1972*, pp. 59–74.

Ruttan, Vernon W. and Hayami, Yujiro. Toward a Theory of Induced Institutional Innovation. *J. Devel. Stud.*, July 1984, *20*(4), pp. 203–23. [G: Philippines]

Ryan, James G. Efficiency and Equity Considerations in the Design of Agricultural Technology in Developing Countries. *Australian J. Agr. Econ.*, August/December 1984, *28*(2–3), pp. 109–35. [G: LDCs]

Sah, Raaj Kumar and Stiglitz, Joseph E. The Economics of Price Scissors. *Amer. Econ. Rev.*, March 1984, *74*(1), pp. 125–38.

Salam, Abdul. The Performance of Pakistan's Agricultural Markets in the Green Revolution

Perspective. *Pakistan Devel. Rev.*, Summer-Autumn 1984, *23*(2&3), pp. 305–08.
[G: Pakistan]

Schuh, G. Edward. The Political Economy of Rural Development in Latin America: Comment. In *Eicher, C. K. and Staatz, J. M., eds.*, 1984, pp. 96–109. [G: Latin America]

Shari, Ishak and Sundaram, Jomo Kwame. Capital Accumulation, Technological Change and the Social Relations of Rice-Farming: The Political Economy of Malaysia's "Green Revolution" In *Ngo, M., ed., vol. 2*, 1984, pp. 691–723. [G: Malaysia]

Smith, Clifford T. Land Reform as a Pre-condition for Green Revolution in Latin America. In *[Farmer, B. H.]*, 1984, pp. 18–36.
[G: Latin America]

Staatz, John M. and Eicher, Carl K. Agricultural Development Ideas in Historical Perspective. In *Eicher, C. K. and Staatz, J. M., eds.*, 1984, pp. 3–30.

Šteffl, Zdeněk. Scientific and Technical Development in Agriculture. *Czech. Econ. Digest.*, November 1984, (7), pp. 3–28.
[G: Czechoslovakia]

Than, Mya. Burma's Agricultural Development Since 1962—From Stagnancy to Breakthrough. In *Ngo, M., ed., vol. 2*, 1984, pp. 741–61.
[G: Burma]

Timmer, C. Peter. Developing a Food Strategy. In *Eicher, C. K. and Staatz, J. M., eds.*, 1984, *1981*, pp. 119–35.

Timmer, C. Peter. Macro Prices and Structural Change. *Amer. J. Agr. Econ.*, May 1984, *66*(2), pp. 196–201. [G: Selected Countries]

Utrecht, Ernst. Land and Agriculture, Fishing and Mining. In *Utrecht, E., ed.*, 1984, pp. 121–77. [G: Fiji]

Varga, Július. Progress of Socialist Agriculture. *Czech. Econ. Digest.*, August 1984, (5), pp. 67–76. [G: Czechoslovakia]

Von Witzke, Harald. Poverty, Agriculture, and Economic Development: A Survey. *Europ. Rev. Agr. Econ.*, 1984, *11*(4), pp. 439–53.

Walker, Paul C. The Value of the Canadian Census of Agriculture. *Can. J. Agr. Econ.*, March 1984, *32*(1), pp. 163–74. [G: Canada]

Warman, Arturo. The Cauldron of the Revolution: Agrarian Capitalism and Sugar Industry in Morelos, Mexico, 1880–1910. In *Albert, B. and Graves, A., eds.*, 1984, pp. 165–79.
[G: Mexico]

West, Robert L. Energy and Agricultural Development in the Third World. In *[Reynolds, L. G.]*, 1984, pp. 445–77. [G: LDCs]

Wright, Gavin. Rethinking the Postbellum Southern Political Economy: A Review Essay. *Bus. Hist. Rev.*, Autumn 1984, *58*(3), pp. 409–16.
[G: U.S.]

Yamaguchi, Mitoshi and Kennedy, George. A Graphic Model of the Effects of Sectoral Technical Change: The Case of Japan, 1880–1970. *Can. J. Agr. Econ.*, March 1984, *32*(1), pp. 71–92. [G: Japan]

Yusuf, Shahid. Institutional Change and Agricultural Development in Pakistan: The Possibility

of Labour-Intensive Farming. In *Burki, S. J. and LaPorte, R., Jr., eds.*, 1984, pp. 271–309.
[G: Pakistan]

711 Agricultural Supply and Demand Analysis

7110 Agricultural Supply and Demand Analysis

Abel, Martin E. and Waugh, Frederick V. Measuring Changes in International Trade. In *Waugh, F. V.*, 1984, *1966*, pp. 353–67.
[G: Global]

Adamowicz, W. L.; Baah, S. O. and Hawkins, M. H. Pricing Efficiency in Hog Markets. *Can. J. Agr. Econ.*, November 1984, *32*(3), pp. 462–77. [G: Canada; U.S.]

Adams, Richard M.; Crocker, Thomas D. and Katz, Richard W. Assessing the Adequacy of Natural Science Information: A Bayesian Approach. *Rev. Econ. Statist.*, November 1984, *66*(4), pp. 568–75. [G: U.S.]

Agarwal, Bina. Tractors, Tubewells and Cropping Intensity in the Indian Punjab. *J. Devel. Stud.*, July 1984, *20*(4), pp. 290–302. [G: India]

Ahammed, C. S. and Herdt, Robert W. Measuring the Impact of Consumption Linkages on the Employment Effects of Mechanisation in Philippine Rice Production. *J. Devel. Stud.*, January 1984, *20*(2), pp. 242–55.
[G: Philippines]

Alderman, Harold. Attributing Technological Bias to Public Goods. *J. Devel. Econ.*, April 1984, *14*(3), pp. 375–93. [G: Japan]

Allen, Franklin. Mixed Wage and Rent Contracts as Reinterpretations of Share Contracts. *J. Devel. Econ.*, December 1984, *16*(3), pp. 313–17.

Altieri, Miguel A.; Letourneau, Deborah K. and Davis, James R. The Requirements of Sustainable Agroecosystems. In *Douglass, G. K., ed.*, 1984, pp. 175–89.

Anderson, Kym and Ahn, In-Chan. Protection Policy and Changing Comparative Advantage in Korean Agriculture. *Food Res. Inst. Stud.*, 1984, *19*(2), pp. 139–51. [G: S. Korea]

Antle, John M. Human Capital, Infrastructure, and the Productivity of Indian Rice Farmers. *J. Devel. Econ.*, January–February 1984, *14*(1–2), pp. 163–81. [G: India]

Antle, John M. The Structure of U.S. Agricultural Technology, 1910–78. *Amer. J. Agr. Econ.*, November 1984, *66*(4), pp. 414–21.
[G: U.S.]

Antle, John M. and Goodger, William J. Measuring Stochastic Technology: The Case of Tulare Milk Production. *Amer. J. Agr. Econ.*, August 1984, *66*(3), pp. 342–50. [G: U.S.]

Ardeni, Pier Giorgio and Paris, Quirino. Un modello di importazione e di esportazione dei prodotti farinacei. (A Model for Import–Export of Wheat Products. With English summary.) *Statistica*, April–June 1984, *44*(2), pp. 301–27.
[G: Italy]

Ashton, Basil, et al. Famine in China, 1958–61. *Population Devel. Rev.*, December 1984, *10*(4), pp. 613–45. [G: China]

Attwood, Donald W. Capital and the Transformation of Agrarian Class Systems: Sugar Production in India. In *Desai, M.; Rudolph, S. H. and Rudra, A., eds.*, 1984, pp. 20–50. [G: India]

Azhar, Rauf A. and Mahmud, Fakhre. Social Profitability of Alternative Rice Varieties in Pakistan: Basmati vs. IRRI. *Pakistan J. Appl. Econ.*, Winter 1984, *3*(2), pp. 139–56. [G: Pakistan]

Azhar, Rauf A. and Mahmud, Fakhre. Social Profitability of Alternative Rice Varieties in Pakistan: Basmati vs. IRRI. *Philippine Econ. J.*, Winter 1984, *23*(1), pp. 139–56. [G: Pakistan]

Bandyopadhyay, T. and Ghatak, S. Errata [Some Remarks on Agricultural Backwardness under Semi-feudalism]. *Indian Econ. Rev.*, January–June 1984, *19*(1), pp. 157. [G: India]

Barker, F. S. The Macro-economic Consequences of the Drought. *J. Stud. Econ. Econometrics*, July 1984, (20), pp. 17–27. [G: S. Africa]

Batten, Dallas S. and Belongia, Michael T. The Recent Decline in Agricultural Exports: Is the Exchange Rate the Culprit? *Fed. Res. Bank St. Louis Rev.*, October 1984, *66*(8), pp. 5–14. [G: U.S.]

Bayliss-Smith, Tim P. Energy Flows and Agrarian Change in Karnataka: the Green Revolution at Micro-Scale. In *[Farmer, B. H.]*, 1984, pp. 153–72. [G: India]

Bélisle, François J. Food Production and Tourism in Jamaica: Obstacles to Increasing Local Food Supplies to Hotels. *J. Devel. Areas*, October 1984, *19*(1), pp. 1–20. [G: Jamaica]

Belongia, Michael T. The Dairy Price Support Program: A Study of Misdirected Economic Incentives. *Fed. Res. Bank St. Louis Rev.*, February 1984, *66*(2), pp. 5–14. [G: U.S.]

Bengtsson, Tommy. Harvest Fluctuations and Demographic Response: Southern Sweden 1751–1859. In *Bengtsson, T.; Fridlizius, G. and Ohlsson, R., eds.*, 1984, pp. 329–55. [G: Sweden]

Berck, Peter and Schmitz, Andrew. Price Supports in the Context of International Trade. In *Storey, G. G.; Schmitz, A. and Sarris, A. H., eds.*, 1984, pp. 127–43. [G: U.S.]

Berthélémy, Jean-Claude and Gagey, Frédéric. Élasticité-prix de l'offre agricole dans les pays en développement: une note sur la rationalité des agriculteurs dans un contexte non-Walrasien. (Price Elasticity of Agricultural Production in LDC's: A Note on Behavior of Peasants in a Non-Walrasian Context. With English summary.) *Ann. INSEE*, July–December 1984, (55/56), pp. 203–21. [G: Cameroon]

Beshai, Adel A. The Economics of a Primary Commodity: Gum Arabic. *Oxford Bull. Econ. Statist.*, November 1984, *46*(4), pp. 371–81. [G: Sudan; Nigeria; Tanzania; W. Africa]

Bessler, David A. An Analysis of Dynamic Economic Relationships: An Application to the U.S. Hog Market. *Can. J. Agr. Econ.*, March 1984, *32*(1), pp. 109–24. [G: U.S.]

Binswanger, Hans P.; Quizon, Jaime B. and

Swamy, Gurushri. The Demand for Food and Foodgrain Quality in India. *Indian Econ. J.*, April–June 1984, *31*(4), pp. 73–96. [G: India]

Bixler, Gordon and Shemilt, L. W. Chemistry and World Food Supplies. In *Bixler, G. and Shemilt, L. W., eds.*, 1984, pp. 5–23.

Bockstael, Nancy E. The Welfare Implications of Minimum Quality Standards. *Amer. J. Agr. Econ.*, November 1984, *66*(4), pp. 466–71.

Borlaug, Norman E. Feeding the World during the Next Doubling of the World Population. In *Bixler, G. and Shemilt, L. W., eds.*, 1984, pp. 133–58.

Brennan, John P. Measuring the Contribution of New Varieties to Increasing Wheat Yields. *Rev. Marketing Agr. Econ.*, December 1984, *52*(3), pp. 175–95. [G: Australia]

Bronshtein, M. The Equalization of Cost-Accounting Conditions in Agriculture. *Prob. Econ.*, June 1984, *27*(2), pp. 75–90. [G: U.S.S.R.]

Brorsen, B. Wade; Chavas, Jean-Paul and Grant, Warren R. Dynamic Relationships of Rice Import Prices in Europe. *Europ. Rev. Agr. Econ.*, 1984, *11*(1), pp. 29–42. [G: U.S.; Thailand; Argentina; Europe]

Brorsen, B. Wade; Grant, Warren R. and Rister, M. Edward. A Hedonic Price Model for Rough Rice Bid/Acceptance Markets. *Amer. J. Agr. Econ.*, May 1984, *66*(2), pp. 156–63. [G: U.S.]

Brown, Deborah J. and Smith, Martha. Crop Substitution in the Estimation of Economic Benefits Due to Ozone Reduction. *J. Environ. Econ. Manage.*, December 1984, *11*(4), pp. 347–62. [G: U.S.]

Brown, Lester R. World Population Growth, Soil Erosion, and Food Security. In *Douglass, G. K., ed.*, 1984, pp. 31–48.

Brystrakov, Iu. and Orlovskaia, S. The Development of Grain Farming. *Prob. Econ.*, May 1984, *27*(1), pp. 47–62. [G: U.S.S.R.]

Byerlee, Derek. Autarky in Food: Evidence and Prospects: Comment. *Pakistan Devel. Rev.*, Summer-Autumn 1984, *23*(2&3), pp. 269–71. [G: Pakistan]

Calvin, Melvin. Basic Chemical Research and Future Food Supplies. In *Bixler, G. and Shemilt, L. W., eds.*, 1984, pp. 107–24.

Carter, Colin A. Pooling Sales versus Forward Selling and the Management of Risk: The Case of Wheat. In *Storey, G. G.; Schmitz, A. and Sarris, A. H., eds.*, 1984, pp. 145–63. [G: Australia; Canada]

Carter, Colin A.; Hickson, Allister B. and Kraft, D. F. The Welfare Effects of Export Constraints on the Canadian Feed Grain Market. *Can. J. Agr. Econ.*, March 1984, *32*(1), pp. 25–36. [G: Canada]

Carter, Michael R. Identification of the Inverse Relationship between Farm Size and Productivity: An Empirical Analysis of Peasant Agricultural Production. *Oxford Econ. Pap.*, March 1984, *36*(1), pp. 131–45. [G: India]

Centre for World Food Studies. A Computable General Equilibrium Model for Thailand with

Emphasis on the Agricultural Sector. In *Cohen, S. I., et al., eds.*, 1984, pp. 407–43.
[G: Thailand]

Chakravarty, Sukhamoy. Power Structure and Agricultural Productivity. In *Desai, M.; Rudolph, S. H. and Rudra, A., eds.*, 1984, pp. 345–73.

Chalfant, James A. Comparison of Alternative Functional Forms with Application to Agricultural Input Data. *Amer. J. Agr. Econ.*, May 1984, *66*(2), pp. 216–20.
[G: U.S.]

Chattopadhyay, Manabendu. Transformation of Labour Use in Indian Agriculture. *Cambridge J. Econ.*, September 1984, *8*(3), pp. 289–96.
[G: India]

Chaudhry, M. Ghaffar. Autarky in Food: Evidence and Prospects. *Pakistan Devel. Rev.*, Summer-Autumn 1984, *23*(2&3), pp. 257–67.
[G: Pakistan]

Chaudhuri, B. B. Rural Power Structure and Agricultural Productivity in Eastern India, 1757–1947. In *Desai, M.; Rudolph, S. H. and Rudra, A., eds.*, 1984, pp. 100–70. [G: India]

Clarence-Smith, W. G. The Sugar and Rum Industries in the Portuguese Empire, 1850–1914. In *Albert, B. and Graves, A., eds.*, 1984, pp. 227–35. [G: Africa]

Colburn, Forrest D. Class, State, and Revolution in Rural Nicaragua: The Case of *Los Cafetaleros*. *J. Devel. Areas*, July 1984, *18*(4), pp. 501–18. [G: Nicaragua]

Collier, William L., et al. Choice of Technique in Rice Milling on Java: A Comment. In *Eicher, C. K. and Staatz, J. M., eds.*, 1984, pp. 289–91. [G: Indonesia]

Cook, Michael C. F. The Yield Response of N. Ireland Seed Potatoes to Economic and Technological Factors. *Irish J. Agr. Econ. Rural Soc.*, 1984, *10*(1), pp. 65–83. [G: U.K.]

Cornelisse, Peter A. Wheat-Market Flows in the Punjab. *Pakistan Devel. Rev.*, Spring 1984, *23*(1), pp. 65–79. [G: Pakistan]

Cornia, Giovanni Andrea. The Long-Term Agricultural Production Function: An Analysis on Farm Level Data for Fifteen Developing Countries. *Statistica*, July–September 1984, *44*(3), pp. 525–38. [G: LDCs]

Coulter, John K. The Consultative Group on International Agricultural Research. In *Weiss, C. and Jéquier, N., eds.*, 1984, pp. 265–81.
[G: LDCs]

Cox, Pamela M. J. Implementing Agricultural Development Policy in Kenya. *Food Res. Inst. Stud.*, 1984, *19*(2), pp. 153–76. [G: Kenya]

Crom, Richard. Effects of Simulated Changes in Consumer Preference on the Meat and Poultry Industries. *Agr. Econ. Res.*, Spring 1984, *36*(2), pp. 16–24. [G: U.S.]

Cuddy, Michael P. Supply Response in the Irish Dairy Sector: A Reply [Response of Irish Creamery Milk Supply to Price Changes]. *Europ. Rev. Agr. Econ.*, 1984, *11*(3), pp. 353–57. [G: Ireland]

Delson, Roberta M. Sugar Production for the Nineteenth Century British Market: Rethinking the Roles of Brazil and the British West

Indies. In *Albert, B. and Graves, A., eds.*, 1984, pp. 59–80. [G: Brazil; Caribbean; U.K.]

Disney, Richard and Elbashir, A. A. Mechanisation, Employment, and Productivity in Sudanese Agriculture. *J. Devel. Econ.*, December 1984, *16*(3), pp. 249–62. [G: Sudan]

Dixon, Bruce L.; Batte, Marvin T. and Sonka, Steven T. Random Coefficients Estimation of Average Total Product Costs for Multiproduct Firms. *J. Bus. Econ. Statist.*, October 1984, *2*(4), pp. 360–66. [G: U.S.]

Dixon, Bruce L. and Chen, Wu-Hsiung. Endogenous versus Exogenous Price Targets for Commodity Market Stabilisation. In *Hughes Hallet, A.J., ed.*, 1984, pp. 181–207. [G: Taiwan]

Eckstein, Zvi. A Rational Expectations Model of Agricultural Supply. *J. Polit. Econ.*, February 1984, *92*(1), pp. 1–19. [G: Egypt]

Edwards, Clark. Wheat Prices: Past and Future Levels and Volatility. *Agr. Econ. Res.*, Summer 1984, *36*(3), pp. 28–31. [G: U.S.]

Edwards, Geoff W. and Freebairn, John W. The Gains from Research into Tradable Commodities. *Amer. J. Agr. Econ.*, February 1984, *66*(1), pp. 41–49. [G: Australia]

Ellis, Frank. Relative Agricultural Prices and the Urban Bias Model: A Comparative Analysis of Tanzania and Fiji. In *Harriss, J. and Moore, M., eds.*, 1984, pp. 28–51. [G: Tanzania; Fiji]

Ellman, Michael. Did the Agricultural Surplus Provide the Resources for the Increase in Investment in the USSR 1928–32? In *Ellman, M.*, 1984, 1975, pp. 27–53. [G: U.S.S.R.]

Ellman, Michael. On a Mistake of Preobrazhensky and Stalin. In *Ellman, M.*, 1984, pp. 54–57. [G: U.S.S.R.; China]

Ellman, Michael. Soviet Grain Imports and the Weather. In *Ellman, M.*, 1984, pp. 97–107. [G: U.S.S.R.]

Ellman, Michael. The Control of Inflation? Errors in the Interpretation of CPE Data. In *Ellman, M.*, 1984, 1981, pp. 130–34. [G: E. Europe]

Evenson, Robert E. Benefits and Obstacles in Developing Appropriate Agricultural Technology. In *Eicher, C. K. and Staatz, J. M., eds.*, 1984, 1981, pp. 348–61. [G: LDCs]

Färe, Rolf; Grabowski, Richard and Yoon, Bong Joon. An Alternative View of Production and Technical Change in Agriculture: Weak Disposability of Inputs. *J. Devel. Areas*, January 1984, *18*(2), pp. 219–26. [G: Korea]

Fei, John C. H. and Ranis, Gustav. Task Orientation and Technology Change: A Suggested Approach. In *[Reynolds, L. G.]*, 1984, pp. 1–16. [G: Taiwan]

Filippucci, Carlo and Paris, Quirino. Importazione di grano: un caso di mercati "controllati." (Wheat Prices and Administered Prices. With English summary.) *Statistica*, April–June 1984, *44*(2), pp. 271–300. [G: Italy; EEC]

Fischer, Lewis A. The USSR as a Major Factor in International Cotton Markets. In *Kostecki, M. M., ed.*, 1984, pp. 218–36. [G: U.S.S.R.; Global]

Freebairn, John W. Farm and Retail Food Prices. *Rev. Marketing Agr. Econ.*, August 1984, 52(2), pp. 71–90. **[G: Australia]**

Freebairn, John W.; Rausser, Gordon C. and de Gorter, Harry. Monetary Policy and U.S. Agriculture. In *Storey, G. G.; Schmitz, A. and Sarris, A. H., eds.*, 1984, pp. 99–123. **[G: U.S.]**

Freeman, Orville L. A Global Strategy for Agriculture. In *Douglass, G. K., ed.*, 1984, pp. 135–43.

Gallant, A. Ronald. The Fourier Flexible Form. *Amer. J. Agr. Econ.*, May 1984, 66(2), pp. 204–08.

Gligo, Nicolo. Energy and the Prevailing Model of Agricultural Technology in Latin America. *Cepal Rev.*, April 1984, (22), pp. 121–36. **[G: Global]**

Glover, David J. Contract Farming and Smallholder Outgrower Schemes in Less-developed Countries. *World Devel.*, November–December 1984, 12(11–12), pp. 1143–57. **[G: LDCs]**

Goodell, Grace E. Bugs, Bunds, Banks, and Bottlenecks: Organizational Contradictions in the New Rice Technology. *Econ. Develop. Cult. Change*, October 1984, 33(1), pp. 23–41. **[G: S.E. Asia]**

Govinden, Noel, et al. Intercropping in the Tropics: Advantages and Relevance to the Small Farmer. *Can. J. Devel. Stud.*, 1984, 5(2), pp. 213–32.

Grant, Warren R., et al. Economic Impacts of Increased Price Variability: A Case Study with Rice. *Agr. Econ. Res.*, Fall 1984, 36(4), pp. 17–27. **[G: U.S.]**

Graves, Adrian. Crisis and Change in the Queensland Sugar Industry, 1862–1906. In *Albert, B. and Graves, A., eds.*, 1984, pp. 261–79. **[G: Australia]**

Grigg, David B. The Agricultural Revolution in Western Europe. In *[Farmer, B. H.]*, 1984, pp. 1–17. **[G: W. Europe]**

Grilli, Enzo R. and Yang, Maw-Cheng. Real and Monetary Determinants of Non-Oil Primary Commodity Price Movements. In *Storey, G. G.; Schmitz, A. and Sarris, A., eds.*, 1984, pp. 3–44. **[G: Global]**

Guy, Donna J. Sugar Industries at the Periphery of the World Market: Argentina, 1860–1914. In *Albert, B. and Graves, A., eds.*, 1984, pp. 147–62. **[G: Argentina]**

Haraksingh, Kusha. Labour, Technology and the Sugar Estates in Trinidad, 1870–1914. In *Albert, B. and Graves, A., eds.*, 1984, pp. 133–45. **[G: Trinidad]**

Harvey, D. R. and Hubbard, L. J. A Comparative Static Analysis of Welfare Impacts of Supply-restricting Marketing Boards: A Comment. *Can. J. Agr. Econ.*, November 1984, 32(3), pp. 570–74. **[G: Canada]**

Hayenga, Marvin L., et al. Profitable Hedging Opportunities and Risk Premiums for Producers in Live Cattle and Live Hog Futures Markets. *J. Futures Markets*, Summer 1984, 4(2), pp. 141–54. **[G: U.S.]**

Hazell, Peter B. R. Sources of Increased Instability in Indian and U.S. Cereal Production. *Amer. J. Agr. Econ.*, August 1984, 66(3), pp. 302–11. **[G: U.S.; India]**

Helmberger, Peter G. and Akinyosoye, Vincent O. Competitive Pricing and Storage under Uncertainty with an Application to the U.S. Soybean Market. *Amer. J. Agr. Econ.*, May 1984, 66(2), pp. 119–30. **[G: U.S.]**

Herdt, Robert W. Differing Perspectives on the World Food Problem: Discussion. *Amer. J. Agr. Econ.*, May 1984, 66(2), pp. 186–87.

Ho, Thomas S. Y. Intertemporal Commodity Futures Hedging and the Production Decision. *J. Finance*, June 1984, 39(2), pp. 351–76.

Holland, David M. Energy and Agriculture: Conflicts and Potentials for Structural Reform. In *Geisler, C. C. and Popper, F. J., eds.*, 1984, pp. 88–97. **[G: U.S.]**

Hopkins, Raymond F. and Puchala, Donald J. Perspectives on the International Relations of Food. In *Ghosh, P. K., ed., no. 6, 1984, 1978*, pp. 87–124. **[G: Global]**

Hossain, Mahabub. Agricultural Development in Bangladesh: A Historical Perspective. *Bangladesh Devel. Stud.*, December 1984, 12(4), pp. 29–57. **[G: Bangladesh]**

Husain, Tariq. Potential for Irrigated Agricultural Development in Pakistan. In *Burki, S. J. and LaPorte, R., Jr., eds.*, 1984, pp. 45–83. **[G: Pakistan]**

Jamison, Dean T. and Moock, Peter R. Farmer Education and Farm Efficiency in Nepal: The Role of Schooling, Extension Services, and Cognitive Skills. *World Devel.*, January 1984, 12(1), pp. 67–86. **[G: Nepal]**

Johnson, D. Gale. World Food and Agriculture. In *Simon, J. L. and Kahn, H., eds.*, 1984, pp. 67–112. **[G: Global]**

Jones, Steve. Agrarian Structure and Agricultural Innovation in Bangladesh: Panimara Village, Dhaka District. In *[Farmer, B. H.]*, 1984, pp. 194–211. **[G: Bangladesh]**

Kainth, G. S. and Bawa, R. S. Cropping Intensity in Punjab—Flow, Spatial Disparity, and Determinants. *Margin*, July 1984, 16(4), pp. 64–83. **[G: India]**

Kanbur, S. M. Ravi. How to Analyse Commodity Price Stabilization? A Review Article. *Oxford Econ. Pap.*, November 1984, 36(3), pp. 336–58. **[G: LDCs]**

Kaukiainen, Yrjö. Harvest Fluctuations and Mortality in Agrarian Finland (1810–1870). In *Bengtsson, T.; Fridlizius, G. and Ohlsson, R., eds.*, 1984, pp. 235–54. **[G: Finland]**

Keuning, Steven J. Farm Size, Land Use and Profitability of Food Crops in Indonesia. *Bull. Indonesian Econ. Stud.*, April 1984, 20(1), pp. 58–82. **[G: Indonesia]**

Kilmer, Richard L. and Armbruster, Walter J. Methods for Evaluating Economic Efficiency in Agricultural Marketing. *Southern J. Agr. Econ.*, July 1984, 16(1), pp. 101–09.

Kim, Sung-Hoon and Dixon, John A. Economic Valuation of Environmental Quality Aspects of Upland Agricultural Projects in Korea. In *Ah-*

mad, Y. J.; Dasgupta, P. and Mäler, K.-G., eds., 1984, pp. 21–37. **[G: S. Korea]**

King, Gordon A. Estimating Functional Forms with Special Reference to Agriculture: Discussion. *Amer. J. Agr. Econ.*, May 1984, *66*(2), pp. 221–22.

Koester, Ulrich. The Role of the CAP in the Process of European Integration. *Europ. Rev. Agr. Econ.*, 1984, *11*(2), pp. 129–40. **[G: EEC]**

Kostecki, Michel M. The Soviet Union in International Grain Markets. In *Kostecki, M. M., ed.*, 1984, pp. 194–217. **[G: U.S.S.R.; Global]**

Kostrowicka, Irena. Changes in Agricultural Productivity in the Kingdom of Poland in the XIXth and Early XXth Centuries. *J. Europ. Econ. Hist.*, Spring 1984, *13*(1), pp. 75–97. **[G: Poland]**

Kueh, Yak-Yeow. China's Foodgrain Production, Consumption, and Trade: Recent Trends and Prospects. *Rivista Int. Sci. Econ. Com.*, September 1984, *31*(9), pp. 910–26. **[G: China]**

Lányi, Kamilla. Constraints on Profitable Growth and Exports in Hungarian Agriculture. *Acta Oecon.*, 1984, *33*(3–4), pp. 293–304. **[G: Hungary]**

Lebow, William M., et al. Forecasting Applications of GMDH in Agricultural and Meteorological Time Series. In *Farlow, S. J., ed.*, 1984, pp. 121–47. **[G: Canada]**

Lee, Jonq-Ying. Demand Interrelationships among Fruit Beverages. *Southern J. Agr. Econ.*, December 1984, *16*(2), pp. 135–43. **[G: U.S.]**

Lele, Uma and Candler, Wilfred. Food Security in Developing Countries: National Issues. In *Eicher, C. K. and Staatz, J. M., eds.*, 1984, pp. 207–21. **[G: Tanzania]**

Lockeretz, William. Energy and the Sustainability of the American Agricultural System. In *Douglass, G. K., ed.*, 1984, pp. 77–88.

Lopez, Ramon E. Estimating Substitution and Expansion Effects Using a Profit Function Framework. *Amer. J. Agr. Econ.*, August 1984, *66*(3), pp. 358–67. **[G: Canada]**

Lutton, Thomas J. The Elasticity of Substitution and Land Use in Agricultural Production: A Cause for Optimism? *Agr. Econ. Res.*, Summer 1984, *36*(3), pp. 20–27.

Lyu, Syu-Jyun Larry; White, Fred C. and Lu, Yao-Chi. Estimating Effects of Agricultural Research and Extension Expenditures on Productivity: A Translog Production Function Approach. *Southern J. Agr. Econ.*, December 1984, *16*(2), pp. 1–8. **[G: U.S.]**

Madduma Bandara, C. M. Green Revolution and Water Demand: Irrigation and Ground Water in Sri Lanka and Tamil Nadu. In *[Farmer, B. H.]*, 1984, pp. 296–314. **[G: Sri Lanka]**

Mahé, Louis P. A Lower but More Balanced Protection for European Agriculture. *Europ. Rev. Agr. Econ.*, 1984, *11*(2), pp. 217–34. **[G: EEC]**

Mears, Leon A. Rice and Food Self-Sufficiency in Indonesia. *Bull. Indonesian Econ. Stud.*, August 1984, *20*(2), pp. 122–38. **[G: Indonesia]**

Meerman, Jacob and Cochrane, Susan Hill. Population Growth and Food Supply in Sub-Saharan Africa. In *Ghosh, P. K., ed., no. 6, 1984, 1982*, pp. 340–51. **[G: Sub-Saharan Africa]**

Meerman, Jacob and Cochrane, Susan Hill. Population Growth and Food Supply in Sub-Saharan Africa. In *Ghosh, P. K., ed., no. 5, 1984, 1982*, pp. 331–42. **[G: Sub-Saharan Africa]**

Miller, Stephen E.; Capps, Oral, Jr. and Wells, Gary J. Confidence Intervals for Elasticities and Flexibilities from Linear Equations. *Amer. J. Agr. Econ.*, August 1984, *66*(3), pp. 392–96. **[G: U.S.]**

Moschini, Giancarlo. Quota Values and Price Uncertainty. *Can. J. Agr. Econ.*, March 1984, *32*(1), pp. 231–34. **[G: Canada]**

Mounier, Alain and Byé, Pascal. Les futurs alimentaires et énergétiques des biotechnologies. (With English summary.) *Écon. Soc.*, September 1984, *18*(9), pp. 7–340. **[G: Global]**

Munting, Roger. The State and the Beet Sugar Industry in Russia before 1914. In *Albert, B. and Graves, A., eds.*, 1984, pp. 21–28. **[G: U.S.S.R.]**

Murray, Jane. Retail Demand for Meat in Australia: A Utility Theory Approach. *Econ. Rec.*, March 1984, *60*(168), pp. 45–56. **[G: Australia]**

Musser, Wesley N. and Tew, Bernard V. Use of Biophysical Simulation in Production Economics. *Southern J. Agr. Econ.*, July 1984, *16*(1), pp. 77–86.

Nadkarni, M. V. Growth and Instability in Indian Agriculture—Another Look. In *Singh, A. K.; Papola, T. S. and Mathur, R. S., eds.*, 1984, pp. 233–47. **[G: India]**

Narayana, N. S. S. and Shah, M. M. Farm Supply Response in Kenya: Acreage Allocation Model. *Europ. Rev. Agr. Econ.*, 1984, *11*(1), pp. 85–105. **[G: Kenya]**

Nicholson, Norman K. and Esseks, John D. The Politics of Food Scarcities in Developing Countries. In *Ghosh, P. K., ed., no. 6, 1984, 1978*, pp. 153–98. **[G: LDCs]**

Norrie, Kenneth H. and Percy, Michael B. Sustained Harvest Fluctuations and Economic Change: A General Equilibrium Analysis. In *Bengtsson, T.; Fridlizius, G. and Ohlsson, R., eds.*, 1984, pp. 391–418.

Ó Gráda, Cormac. Irish Agricultural Output before and after the Famine. *J. Europ. Econ. Hist.*, Spring 1984, *13*(1), pp. 149–65. **[G: Ireland]**

Odhiambo, Thomas R. Biological Constraints on Food Production and on the Level and Efficient Use of Chemical Inputs. In *Bixler, G. and Shemilt, L. W., eds.*, 1984, pp. 65–88. **[G: Global]**

Offutt, Susan Elizabeth and Blandford, David. The Impact of the Soviet Union upon the U.S Feed/Livestock Sector—An Assessment. *J. Policy Modeling*, August 1984, *6*(3), pp. 311–40. **[G: U.S.; U.S.S.R.]**

Ominde, S. H. The Former Scheduled Areas. In *Ominde, S. H., ed.*, 1984, pp. 18–22. **[G: Kenya]**

Ominde, S. H. The Pattern of Land Classification. In *Ominde, S. H., ed.*, 1984, pp. 6–17.
[G: Kenya]

Orlandi, Alberto. Latin American Commodity Exports: The Case of Cotton Fibre. *Cepal Rev.*, April 1984, (22), pp. 137–58.
[G: Latin America]

Oros, Iván. Small-Scale Agricultural Production in Hungary. *Acta Oecon.*, 1984, *32*(1–2), pp. 65–90.
[G: Hungary]

Oskam, A. J. Supply Response in the Irish Dairy Sector: A Comment [Response of Irish Creamery Milk Supply to Price Changes]. *Europ. Rev. Agr. Econ.*, 1984, *11*(3), pp. 343–51.
[G: Ireland]

Overton, Mark. Agricultural Productivity in Eighteenth-Century England: Some Further Speculation. *Econ. Hist. Rev., 2nd Ser.*, May 1984, *37*(2), pp. 244–51.
[G: U.K.]

Owen, Roger. The Egyptian Sugar Industry, 1870–1914: From State to Private Ownership and from Export Orientation to Production for the Local Market. In *Albert, B. and Graves, A., eds.*, 1984, pp. 217–25.
[G: Egypt]

Paarlberg, Philip L. and Abbott, Philip C. Towards a Countervailing Power Theory of World Wheat Trade. In *Storey, G. G.; Schmitz, A. and Sarris, A. H., eds.*, 1984, pp. 185–210.
[G: Canada; Japan; U.S.]

Palairet, Michael. Beet Sugar and Peasant Economy in the Balkans before 1914. In *Albert, B. and Graves, A., eds.*, 1984, pp. 47–57.
[G: Bulgaria; Yugoslavia]

Pandey, R. K. and Sarin, B. S. Economic Study of Acreage Response of Rice in Uttar Pradesh. *Margin*, October 1984, *17*(1), pp. 55–60.
[G: India]

Pandey, R. K. and Sarin, B. S. Estimation of Demand for Foodgrains in Uttar Pradesh. *Margin*, April 1984, *16*(3), pp. 70–76. [G: India]

Peña, Daniel and Sánchez-Albornoz, Nicolás. Wheat Prices in Spain, 1857–1890: An Application of the Box–Jenkins Methodology. *J. Europ. Econ. Hist.*, Fall 1984, *13*(2), pp. 353–73.
[G: Spain]

Perkins, John A. The Political Economy of Sugar Beet in Imperial Germany. In *Albert, B. and Graves, A., eds.*, 1984, pp. 31–45.
[G: Germany]

Pitts, Eamonn. Effects of Rainfall on Milk Yields in Areas with Drainage Difficulties. *Irish J. Agr. Econ. Rural Soc.*, 1984, *10*(1), pp. 29–42.
[G: U.K.]

Plato, Gerald and Gordon, Douglas. Stockpiling U.S. Agricultural Commodities with Volatile World Markets: The Case of Soybeans. *Agr. Econ. Res.*, Spring 1984, *36*(2), pp. 1–9.
[G: U.S.]

Pope, Rulon D. Estimating Functional Forms with Special Reference to Agriculture: Discussion. *Amer. J. Agr. Econ.*, May 1984, *66*(2), pp. 223–24.

Porter, George. Food and Energy Interdependent World Needs. In *Bixler, G. and Shemilt, L. W., eds.*, 1984, pp. 125–32.

Prasad, Pradhan H. Changing Class Relations in India's Agriculture: A Statistical Appraisal. In *Ngo, M., ed., vol. 2*, 1984, pp. 567–605.
[G: India]

Pratt, Christopher J. Fertilizer Production. In *Weiss, C. and Jéquier, N., eds.*, 1984, pp. 209–26.
[G: LDCs]

Rahman, Sultan H. Analysis of a Flexible Market Stabilization Policy in the Jute Sector and Its Sensitivity to a Parametric Change in Demand. *Bangladesh Devel. Stud.*, September 1984, *12*(3), pp. 64–73.
[G: Bangladesh]

Richardson, Peter. The Natal Sugar Industry in the Nineteenth Century. In *Albert, B. and Graves, A., eds.*, 1984, pp. 237–58.
[G: S. Africa]

Roberts, Kenneth D. Agricultural Development and Labor Mobility: A Study of Four Mexican Subregions. In *Jones, R. C., ed.*, 1984, pp. 74–92.
[G: Mexico; U.S.]

Rossi, Nicola. The Estimation of Product Supply and Input Demand by the Differential Approach. *Amer. J. Agr. Econ.*, August 1984, *66*(3), pp. 368–75.
[G: Italy]

Rucker, Randal R.; Burt, Oscar R. and LaFrance, Jeffrey T. An Econometric Model of Cattle Inventories. *Amer. J. Agr. Econ.*, May 1984, *66*(2), pp. 131–44.
[G: U.S.]

Rudra, Ashok. Local Power and Farm-Level Decision-Making. In *Desai, M.; Rudolph, S. H. and Rudra, A., eds.*, 1984, pp. 250–80.
[G: India]

Ruttan, Vernon W. Induced Innovation and Agricultural Development. In *Douglass, G. K., ed.*, 1984, pp. 107–34.
[G: LDCs; MDCs]

Sanchez, Pedro A.; Nicholaides, John J., III and Couto, Walter. Physical and Chemical Constraints to Food Production in the Tropics. In *Bixler, G. and Shemilt, L. W., eds.*, 1984, pp. 89–105.
[G: Asia; Latin America; Africa]

Sarris, Alexander H. Agricultural Problems in EC Enlargement: The Case of Greece. *Europ. Rev. Agr. Econ.*, 1984, *11*(2), pp. 195–205.
[G: EEC; Greece]

Sarris, Alexander H. Speculative Storage, Futures Markets, and the Stability of Commodity Prices. *Econ. Inquiry*, January 1984, *22*(1), pp. 80–97.

Sarris, Alexander H. and Freebairn, John W. Domestic Price Policies and International Rice Trade. In *Storey, G. G.; Schmitz, A. and Sarris, A. H., eds.*, 1984, pp. 213–33.
[G: Global]

Schmitz, Peter Michael and Koester, Ulrich. The Sugar Market Policy of the European Community and the Stability of World Market Prices for Sugar. In *Storey, G. G.; Schmitz, A. and Sarris, A. H., eds.*, 1984, pp. 235–59.
[G: EEC; Global]

Schnakenbourg, Christian. From Sugar Estate to Central Factory: The Industrial Revolution in the Caribbean (1840–1905). In *Albert, B. and Graves, A., eds.*, 1984, pp. 83–93.
[G: Caribbean]

Schultz, Theodore W. The Economics of Agricultural Research. In *Eicher, C. K. and Staatz, J. M., eds.*, 1984, *1979*, pp. 335–47.

Sen, Amartya. Ingredients of Famine Analysis: Availability and Entitlements. In *Sen, A., 1984, 1981*, pp. 452–84. [G: India; Bangladesh]

Shaw, Anthony B. Impact of New Technology on the Guyanese Rice Industry: Efficiency and Equity Considerations. *J. Devel. Areas,* January 1984, *18*(2), pp. 191–217. [G: Guyana]

Sheeny, Seamus. The Agri-monetary System—A Reinterpretation. *Europ. Rev. Agr. Econ.,* 1984, *11*(2), pp. 177–86. [G: EEC]

Shonkwiler, J. S. and Taylor, Timothy G. The Implications of Estimating Market Demand Curves by Least Squares Regression. *Europ. Rev. Agr. Econ.,* 1984, *11*(1), pp. 107–18. [G: U.S.]

Siamwalla, Ammar and Valdés, Alberto. Food Security in Developing Countries: International Issues. In *Eicher, C. K. and Staatz, J. M., eds.,* 1984, *1980,* pp. 189–206. [G: LDCs]

Singh, H. K. Manmohan and Singh, Surender. Growth of Agriculture in Punjab and Haryana: A Comparative Study. In *Singh, A. K.; Papola, T. S. and Mathur, R. S., eds.,* 1984, pp. 248–91. [G: India]

Soetrisno, Noer. Supply Response of Sugar Cane in Indonesia. *Philippine Rev. Econ. Bus.,* Sept./Dec. 1984, *21*(3/4), pp. 239–65. [G: Indonesia]

Spreen, Thomas H. and Arnade, Carlos A. Use of Forecasts in Decisionmaking: The Case of Stocker Cattle in Florida. *Southern J. Agr. Econ.,* July 1984, *16*(1), pp. 145–50. [G: U.S.]

Spriggs, John; Van Kooten, G. C. and Hayward, Keith. Canadian Feed Grains Policy: A Comparison of Price Variability between Canada and the United States. *Can. J. Agr. Econ.,* November 1984, *32*(3), pp. 540–47. [G: Canada; U.S.]

Stuart, Robert C. Wheat Yields in Socialist and Capitalist Economic Systems: A Statistical Comparison. *ACES Bull.,* Spring 1984, *26*(1), pp. 77–85.

Surry, Yves and Moschini, Giancarlo. Input Substitutability in the EC Compound Feed Industry. *Europ. Rev. Agr. Econ.,* 1984, *11*(4), pp. 455–64. [G: Belgium; Netherlands]

Swaminathan, M. S. Our Greatest Challenge: Feeding a Hungry World. In *Bixler, G. and Shemilt, L. W., eds.,* 1984, pp. 25–46. [G: LDCs]

Taylor, Timothy G. and Wilkowske, Gary H. Productivity Growth in the Florida Fresh Winter Vegetable Industry. *Southern J. Agr. Econ.,* December 1984, *16*(2), pp. 55–61. [G: U.S.]

Thaman, R. R. Food Dependency and Malnutrition: Deterioration of Traditional Pacific Food Systems. In *Utrecht, E., ed.,* 1984, pp. 69–117. [G: Pacific Islands]

Turner, Michael. Agricultural Productivity in Eighteenth-Century England: Further Strains of Speculation. *Econ. Hist. Rev., 2nd Ser.,* May 1984, *37*(2), pp. 252–57. [G: U.K.]

Valdés, Alberto. Comercio de Productos Agrícolas entre Países en Desarrollo: América Latina durante, 1962–1979. (With English summary.) *Cuadernos Econ.,* August 1984, *21*(63), pp. 169–206. [G: Latin America]

Van Kooten, G. C. and Spriggs, John. A Comparative Static Analysis of the Welfare Impacts of Supply-Restricting Marketing Boards. *Can. J. Agr. Econ.,* March 1984, *32*(1), pp. 221–30. [G: Canada]

Van Kooten, G. C. and Spriggs, John. A Comparative Static Analysis of the Welfare Impacts of Supply-restricting Marketing Boards: Reply. *Can. J. Agr. Econ.,* November 1984, *32*(3), pp. 576–78. [G: Canada]

de Veer, Jan. Cereal Substitutes, Fat Tax and Price Distortion. *Europ. Rev. Agr. Econ.,* 1984, *11*(2), pp. 169–76. [G: EEC]

Watts, Geof and Quiggin, John. A Note on the Use of a Logarithmic Time Trend. *Rev. Marketing Agr. Econ.,* August 1984, *52*(2), pp. 91–99. [G: Australia]

Waugh, Frederick V. Factors Influencing the Price of New Jersey Potatoes on the New York Market. In *Waugh, F. V.,* 1984, *1923,* pp. 385–408. [G: U.S.]

Waugh, Frederick V. Regressions between Sets of Variables. In *Waugh, F. V.,* 1984, *1942,* pp. 251–71. [G: U.S.; Canada]

Waugh, Frederick V. Reserve Stocks of Farm Products. In *Waugh, F. V.,* 1984, *1967,* pp. 198–247. [G: U.S.]

Waugh, Frederick V. and Ogren, Kenneth E. An Interpretation of Changes in Agricultural Marketing Costs. In *Waugh, F. V.,* 1984, *1961,* pp. 183–97. [G: U.S.]

Weaver, Robert D. Caveats on the Application of the Fourier Flexible Form: Discussion. *Amer. J. Agr. Econ.,* May 1984, *66*(2), pp. 209–10.

West, Robert L. Energy and Agricultural Development in the Third World. In *[Reynolds, L. G.],* 1984, pp. 445–77. [G: LDCs]

Wohlgenant, Michael K. Conceptual and Functional Form Issues in Estimating Demand Elasticities for Food. *Amer. J. Agr. Econ.,* May 1984, *66*(2), pp. 211–15. [G: U.S.]

Womack, Abner W., et al. An Evaluation of the 1981 Farm Program for Crops: Implications for the 1985 Farm Bill. *Southern J. Agr. Econ.,* July 1984, *16*(1), pp. 27–37. [G: U.S.]

Yousefi, Mahmood and Abizadeh, Sohrab. An Analysis and Forecast of Demand for Food in Iran. *Econ. Anal. Worker's Manage.,* 1984, *18*(1), pp. 65–76. [G: Iran]

Zagaitov, I. and Polovinkin, P. The Stability of Agricultural Production. *Prob. Econ.,* September 1984, *27*(5), pp. 66–84. [G: U.S.S.R.]

Ziemer, Rod F. and Collins, Glenn S. Granger Causality and U.S. Crop and Livestock Prices. *Southern J. Agr. Econ.,* July 1984, *16*(1), pp. 115–20. [G: U.S.]

Zuo, Mu. Price Ratios among Agricultural Products Must Be Well Adjusted. *Chinese Econ. Stud.,* Fall 1984, *18*(1), pp. 34–43. [G: China]

Zylbersztajn, Decio. Price Distortions in Brazilian Agriculture: An Application of Duality Theory and Flexible Functional Forms. *Amer. Econ.*, Fall 1984, *28*(2), pp. 48–59. **[G: Brazil]**

712 Agricultural Situation and Outlook

7120 Agricultural Situation and Outlook

Abercrombie, Keith and McCormack, Arthur. Population Growth and Food Supplies in Different Time Perspectives. In *Ghosh, P. K., ed., no. 6*, 1984, *1976*, pp. 18–39. **[G: Global]**

Ahmed, Meekal Aziz. Issues in the Economics of Industrialization in Developing Countries: A Case Study from Pakistan's Light Engineering Sector: Comment. *Pakistan Devel. Rev.*, Summer-Autumn 1984, *23*(2&3), pp. 327–29. **[G: Pakistan]**

Alam, Mahmudul. Level and Composition of Capital in Irrigated Agriculture of Bangladesh: Evidence from Tubewell Irrigated Villages of Comilla and Rajshahi. *Bangladesh Devel. Stud.*, December 1984, *12*(4), pp. 59–106. **[G: Bangladesh]**

Baumeister, Eduardo. Estructura y reforma agraria en el proceso sandinista. (With English summary.) *Desarrollo Econ.*, July–September 1984, *24*(94), pp. 187–202. **[G: Nicaragua]**

Bélisle, François J. Food Production and Tourism in Jamaica: Obstacles to Increasing Local Food Supplies to Hotels. *J. Devel. Areas*, October 1984, *19*(1), pp. 1–20. **[G: Jamaica]**

Borlaug, Norman E. Feeding the World during the Next Doubling of the World Population. In *Bixler, G. and Shemilt, L. W., eds.*, 1984, pp. 133–58.

Brown, George E., Jr. Stewardship in Agriculture. In *Douglass, G. K., ed.*, 1984, pp. 147–57.

Buttel, Frederick H. Socioeconomic Equity and Environmental Quality in North American Agriculture: Alternative Trajectories for Future Development. In *Douglass, G. K., ed.*, 1984, pp. 89–106. **[G: U.S.]**

Byerlee, Derek. Autarky in Food: Evidence and Prospects: Comment. *Pakistan Devel. Rev.*, Summer-Autumn 1984, *23*(2&3), pp. 269–71. **[G: Pakistan]**

Calvin, Melvin. Basic Chemical Research and Future Food Supplies. In *Bixler, G. and Shemilt, L. W., eds.*, 1984, pp. 107–24.

Carter, Mary E. Implications of Emerging Biotechnologies. *Southern J. Agr. Econ.*, July 1984, *16*(1), pp. 7–9.

Cavaco, Carminda. A pequena horticultura doméstica de nao agricultores das periferias urbanas: o caso de Lisboa. (With English summary.) *Economia (Portugal)*, May 1984, *8*(2), pp. 395–423. **[G: Portugal]**

Chaudhry, M. Ghaffar. Autarky in Food: Evidence and Prospects. *Pakistan Devel. Rev.*, Summer-Autumn 1984, *23*(2&3), pp. 257–67. **[G: Pakistan]**

Choonhavan, Kraisak. Thailand: Economic Development and Rural Poverty—A Country Report. In *Ngo, M., ed., vol. 1*, 1984, pp. 479–504. **[G: Thailand]**

Coffin, H. Garth. Western Grain Transportation Initiatives and Agriculture in Eastern Canada. *Can. J. Agr. Econ.*, July 1984, *32*(2), pp. 269–81. **[G: Canada]**

Donaldson, Graham. Food Security and the Role of the Grain Trade. *Amer. J. Agr. Econ.*, May 1984, *66*(2), pp. 188–93.

Douglass, Gordon K. Agricultural Sustainability in a Changing World Order: Conclusions: Sustainability for Whom? In *Douglass, G. K., ed.*, 1984, pp. 271–75.

Douglass, Gordon K. The Meanings of Agricultural Sustainability. In *Douglass, G. K., ed.*, 1984, pp. 3–29.

Eicher, Carl K. Facing Up to Africa's Food Crisis. In *Eicher, C. K. and Staatz, J. M., eds.*, 1984, *1982*, pp. 453–79. **[G: Africa]**

Evenson, Robert E. Benefits and Obstacles in Developing Appropriate Agricultural Technology. In *Eicher, C. K. and Staatz, J. M., eds.*, 1984, *1981*, pp. 348–61.

Farrell, Kenneth R. The Sustainability of U.S. Agriculture: Economic Perspectives and Policy Issues. In *Douglass, G. K., ed.*, 1984, pp. 51–59. **[G: U.S.]**

Feuer, Carl Henry. Better Must Come: Sugar and Jamaica in the 20th Century. *Soc. Econ. Stud.*, December 1984, *33*(4), pp. 1–49. **[G: Jamaica]**

Forster, Bruce A. An Economic Assessment of the Significance of Long-range Transported Air Pollutants for Agriculture in Eastern Canada. *Can. J. Agr. Econ.*, November 1984, *32*(3), pp. 498–525. **[G: Canada]**

Frank, Andre Gunder. Reflections on Green, Red and White Revolutions in India. In *Frank, A. G.*, 1984, *1973*, pp. 62–73. **[G: India]**

Freeman, Orville L. A Global Strategy for Agriculture. In *Douglass, G. K., ed.*, 1984, pp. 135–43.

Goldwater, Carmel. Humanitarian Situation in Kampuchea. In *Thambipillai, P., ed.*, 1984, pp. 162–76. **[G: Cambodia]**

Hopper, W. David. Economic and Social Factors Influencing the Use of Chemicals in Agriculture. In *Bixler, G. and Shemilt, L. W., eds.*, 1984, pp. 47–53.

Houck, James P. Food Security and the Role of the Grain Trade: Discussion. *Amer. J. Agr. Econ.*, May 1984, *66*(2), pp. 194–95.

Jensen, Ken. An Economic View of the Debate on Farm Size in Saskatchewan. *Can. J. Agr. Econ.*, March 1984, *32*(1), pp. 187–200. **[G: Canada]**

Johnson, D. Gale. Food for the Future: A Perspective. In *Ghosh, P. K., ed., no. 6*, 1984, *1976*, pp. 40–60.

Johnson, D. Gale. World Food and Agriculture. In *Simon, J. L. and Kahn, H., eds.*, 1984, pp. 67–112. **[G: Global]**

Joshi, P. C. Conflicting Pulls of Productivity and Employment: Contemporary Choices in the

Light of Historical Experience. In *Ngo, M.,* *ed., vol. 2,* 1984, pp. 797–814. **[G: India; Japan; U.K.]**

Lang, Otto. Western Grain Transportation Initiatives and Agriculture in Eastern Canada: Discussion. *Can. J. Agr. Econ.,* July 1984, *32*(2), pp. 287–90. **[G: Canada]**

Lim, Manuel. Directions for Management: Agriculture. *Philippine Econ. J.,* Winter 1984, *23*(1), pp. 53–59. **[G: Philippines]**

McLeod, A. D. Western Grain Transportation Initiatives and Agriculture in Eastern Canada: Discussion. *Can. J. Agr. Econ.,* July 1984, *32*(2), pp. 283–86. **[G: Canada]**

Moles, Jerry A. and Riker, James V. Hope, Ideas, and Our Only Alternative—Ourselves and Our Values: National Heritage and the Future of Sri Lanka Agriculture. In *Douglass, G. K., ed.,* 1984, pp. 239–70. **[G: Sri Lanka]**

Nabi, Ijaz. Issues in the Economics of Industrialization in Developing Countries: A Case Study from Pakistan's Light Engineering Sector. *Pakistan Devel. Rev.,* Summer-Autumn 1984, *23*(2&3), pp. 311–25. **[G: Pakistan]**

Oros, Iván. Small-Scale Agricultural Production in Hungary. *Acta Oecon.,* 1984, *32*(1–2), pp. 65–90. **[G: Hungary]**

Revelle, Roger. The World Supply of Agricultural Land. In *Simon, J. L. and Kahn, H., eds.,* 1984, pp. 184–201. **[G: Global]**

Rister, M. Edward; Skees, Jerry R. and Black, J. Roy. Evaluating Use of Outlook Information in Grain Sorghum Storage Decisions. *Southern J. Agr. Econ.,* July 1984, *16*(1), pp. 151–58. **[G: U.S.]**

Ropertz, Henry. Western Grain Transportation Initiatives and Agriculture in Eastern Canada: Discussion. *Can. J. Agr. Econ.,* July 1984, *32*(2), pp. 291–95. **[G: Canada]**

Rossiter, Bryant W. World Hunger: Problems and Opportunities. In *Bixler, G. and Shemilt, L. W., eds.,* 1984, pp. 159–64.

Shanmugaratnam, N. Emerging Agrarian Trends in Sri Lanka. In *Ngo, M., ed., vol. 2,* 1984, pp. 666–87. **[G: Sri Lanka]**

Shmelev, G. and Steksov, Iu. Personal Household Plots under Conditions of Interfarm and Agroindustrial Integration. *Prob. Econ.,* January 1984, *26*(9), pp. 81–92. **[G: U.S.S.R.]**

Siamwalla, Ammar and Valdés, Alberto. Food Security in Developing Countries: International Issues. In *Eicher, C. K. and Staatz, J. M., eds.,* 1984, *1980,* pp. 189–206. **[G: LDCs]**

Sporleder, Thomas L. Policy Considerations of Emerging Information Technologies. *Southern J. Agr. Econ.,* July 1984, *16*(1), pp. 15–21.

Walton, Christopher. Lessons from East African Agriculture. *Finance Develop.,* March 1984, *21*(1), pp. 13–16. **[G: East Africa]**

Warley, T. K. Western Grain Transportation Initiatives and Agriculture in Eastern Canada: Discussion. *Can. J. Agr. Econ.,* July 1984, *32*(2), pp. 297–300. **[G: Canada]**

713 Agricultural Policy, Domestic and International

7130 Agricultural Policy, Domestic and International

Adams, Dale W. and Graham, Douglas H. A Critique of Traditional Agricultural Credit Projects and Policies. In *Eicher, C. K. and Staatz, J. M., eds.,* 1984, *1981,* pp. 313–28. **[G: LDCs]**

Adelman, Irma. Development Strategies and the Size Distribution of World Income. *METU,* 1984, *11*(1–2), pp. 177–93. **[G: LDCs]**

Ahmad, Q. K. Policies and Institutions Concerning Promotion of Rural Industries in Bangladesh. *Bangladesh Devel. Stud.,* March-June 1984, *12*(1–2), pp. 163–95. **[G: Bangladesh]**

Alagh, Yoginder K.; Kashyap, S. P. and Murty, G. V. S. N. Policy Modelling for Planning in India. In *Cohen, S. I., et al., eds.,* 1984, pp. 59–88. **[G: India]**

Allam, Mohamed N. and Marks, David H. Irrigated Agricultural Expansion Planning in Developing Countries: Investment Scheduling Incorporating Drainage Water Reuse. *Water Resources Res.,* July 1984, *20*(7), pp. 757–66. **[G: Egypt]**

Allam, Mohamed N. and Marks, David H. Irrigated Agricultural Expansion Planning in Developing Countries: Resilient System Design. *Water Resources Res.,* July 1984, *20*(7), pp. 775–84.

Allam, Mohamed N. and Marks, David H. Irrigated Agricultural Expansion Planning in Developing Countries: Income Redistribution Objective. *Water Resources Res.,* July 1984, *20*(7), pp. 767–74.

Alston, Lee J. Farm Foreclosure Moratorium Legislation: A Lesson from the Past. *Amer. Econ. Rev.,* June 1984, *74*(3), pp. 445–57. **[G: U.S.]**

Anderson, Kym and Ahn, In-Chan. Protection Policy and Changing Comparative Advantage in Korean Agriculture. *Food Res. Inst. Stud.,* 1984, *19*(2), pp. 139–51. **[G: S. Korea]**

Anderson, Kym and Tyers, Rodney. European Community Grain and Meat Policies: Effects on International Prices, Trade and Welfare. *Europ. Rev. Agr. Econ.,* 1984, *11*(4), pp. 367–94. **[G: EEC]**

Aziz, Sartaj. Rural Development—Some Essential Prerequisites. *Int. Lab. Rev.,* May–June 1984, *123*(3), pp. 277–85. **[G: LDCs]**

Bagi, Faqir Singh. A Logit Model of an Extension Agent's Choice to Visit Individual Farms. *Can. J. Agr. Econ.,* March 1984, *32*(1), pp. 211–20. **[G: U.S.]**

Barbero, Giuseppe and Croci-Angelini, Elisabetta. Towards a Better Structural Policy. *Europ. Rev. Agr. Econ.,* 1984, *11*(2), pp. 245–54. **[G: EEC]**

Barbero, Giuseppe, et al. The Siena Memorandum on 'The Reform of the Common Agricultural Policy.' *Europ. Rev. Agr. Econ.,* 1984, *11*(2), pp. 255–59. **[G: EEC]**

Barchfield, John W. The Continuity of Injustice: Agrarian and Alimentary Policy under Mexico's New Administration. *J. Econ. Issues*, March 1984, *18*(1), pp. 325–34. **[G: Mexico]**

Barrett, Richard E. Share Tenancy and Fixed Rent in Taiwan. *Econ. Develop. Cult. Change*, January 1984, *32*(2), pp. 413–22. **[G: Taiwan]**

Baumeister, Eduardo. Estructura y reforma agraria en el proceso sandinista. (With English summary.) *Desarrollo Econ.*, July–September 1984, *24*(94), pp. 187–202. **[G: Nicaragua]**

Baysan, Tercan. Resource Shifts under Tariff Liberalization and Turkey's Comparative Advantage in Agriculture. *Europ. Rev. Agr. Econ.*, 1984, *11*(3), pp. 303–22. **[G: Turkey]**

Beladi, Hamid. Welfare Effects of Trade Restrictions: The Case of the U.S. Dairy Industry. *Atlantic Econ. J.*, December 1984, *12*(4), pp. 70. **[G: U.S.]**

Belongia, Michael T. The Dairy Price Support Program: A Study of Misdirected Economic Incentives. *Fed. Res. Bank St. Louis Rev.*, February 1984, *66*(2), pp. 5–14. **[G: U.S.]**

Belshaw, Deryke G. R. Planning and Agrarian Change in East Africa: Appropriate and Inappropriate Models for Land Settlement Schemes. In *[Farmer, B. H.]*, 1984, pp. 270–79. **[G: E. Africa]**

Berck, Peter and Schmitz, Andrew. Price Supports in the Context of International Trade. In *Storey, G. G.; Schmitz, A. and Sarris, A. H.*, eds., 1984, pp. 127–43. **[G: U.S.]**

Bergmann, Denis. North–South Balances and Conflicts within the Community. *Europ. Rev. Agr. Econ.*, 1984, *11*(2), pp. 151–57. **[G: W. Europe]**

Black, C. J. and Bowers, J. K. The Level of Protection of UK Agriculture. *Oxford Bull. Econ. Statist.*, November 1984, *46*(4), pp. 291–310. **[G: U.K.]**

Blair, Harry W. Agricultural Credit, Political Economy, and Patronage. In *Adams, D. W.; Graham, D. H. and Von Pischke, J. D.*, eds., 1984, pp. 183–93.

Blyth, Nicola. The EEC Sheepmeat Market and Voluntary Export Restraint Agreements. *Australian J. Agr. Econ.*, April 1984, *28*(1), pp. 33–43. **[G: EEC; Australia; New Zealand]**

Boyd, Roy. Government Support of Nonindustrial Production: The Case of Private Forests. *Southern Econ. J.*, July 1984, *51*(1), pp. 89–107. **[G: U.S.]**

Brada, Josef C. Industrial Policy in Hungary: Lessons for America. *Cato J.*, Fall 1984, *4*(2), pp. 485–505. **[G: Hungary]**

Brannon, Jeffery T. and Baklanoff, Eric N. The Political Economy of Agrarian Reform in Yucatán, Mexico. *World Devel.*, November–December 1984, *12*(11–12), pp. 1131–41. **[G: Mexico]**

Bronshtein, M. The Equalization of Cost-Accounting Conditions in Agriculture. *Prob. Econ.*, June 1984, *27*(2), pp. 75–90. **[G: U.S.S.R.]**

Brooks, H. G. and Furtan, W. H. An Analysis of Public Agricultural Research in the Canadian Prairie Provinces. *Can. J. Agr. Econ.*, July 1984, *32*(2), pp. 355–75. **[G: Canada]**

Brystrakov, Iu. and Orlovskaia, S. The Development of Grain Farming. *Prob. Econ.*, May 1984, *27*(1), pp. 47–62. **[G: U.S.S.R.]**

Bublot, Georges. Gradual Re-nationalization of the CAP? *Europ. Rev. Agr. Econ.*, 1984, *11*(2), pp. 187–93. **[G: EEC]**

Bullock, J. Bruce. Future Directions for Agricultural Policy. *Amer. J. Agr. Econ.*, May 1984, *66*(2), pp. 234–39. **[G: U.S.]**

Buttel, Frederick H. Agricultural Land Reform in America. In *Geisler, C. C. and Popper, F. J.*, eds., 1984, pp. 55–72. **[G: U.S.]**

Byerlee, Derek. Autarky in Food: Evidence and Prospects: Comment. *Pakistan Devel. Rev.*, Summer-Autumn 1984, *23*(2&3), pp. 269–71. **[G: Pakistan]**

Carmody, M. J., et al. An Economic Evaluation of the Footrot Eradication Program in the New England Region of New South Wales. *Rev. Marketing Agr. Econ.*, April 1984, *52*(1), pp. 9–21. **[G: Australia]**

Carter, Colin A. Pooling Sales versus Forward Selling and the Management of Risk: The Case of Wheat. In *Storey, G. G.; Schmitz, A. and Sarris, A. H.*, eds., 1984, pp. 145–63. **[G: Australia; Canada]**

Carter, Colin A.; Hickson, Allister B. and Kraft, D. F. The Welfare Effects of Export Constraints on the Canadian Feed Grain Market. *Can. J. Agr. Econ.*, March 1984, *32*(1), pp. 25–36. **[G: Canada]**

Cernea, Michael M. Can Local Participation Help Development? *Finance Develop.*, December 1984, *21*(4), pp. 41–44. **[G: Mexico]**

Chaudhry, M. Ghaffar. Autarky in Food: Evidence and Prospects. *Pakistan Devel. Rev.*, Summer-Autumn 1984, *23*(2&3), pp. 257–67. **[G: Pakistan]**

Chavas, Jean-Paul. Future Directions for Domestic Food Policy. *Amer. J. Agr. Econ.*, May 1984, *66*(2), pp. 225–31. **[G: U.S.]**

Choi, E. Kwan and Hicks, W. Whitney. Agricultural Mechanization Policy and Human Fertility. In *Schutjer, W. A. and Stokes, C. S.*, eds., 1984, pp. 252–68. **[G: LDCs]**

Choonhavan, Kraisak. Thailand: Economic Development and Rural Poverty—A Country Report. In *Ngo, M.*, ed., vol. 1, 1984, pp. 479–504. **[G: Thailand]**

Coffin, H. Garth. Western Grain Transportation Initiatives and Agriculture in Eastern Canada. *Can. J. Agr. Econ.*, July 1984, *32*(2), pp. 269–81. **[G: Canada]**

Cohen, John M. Participatory Planning and Kenya's National Food Policy Paper. *Food Res. Inst. Stud.*, 1984, *19*(2), pp. 187–213. **[G: Kenya]**

Colburn, Forrest D. Class, State, and Revolution in Rural Nicaragua: The Case of *Los Cafetaleros*. *J. Devel. Areas*, July 1984, *18*(4), pp. 501–18. **[G: Nicaragua]**

Corbridge, Stuart. Agrarian Policy and Agrarian

Change in Tribal India. In *[Farmer, B. H.]*, 1984, pp. 87–108. [G: India]

Cox, Pamela M. J. Implementing Agricultural Development Policy in Kenya. *Food Res. Inst. Stud.*, 1984, *19*(2), pp. 153–76. [G: Kenya]

Crawford, Vincent P.; Sobel, Joel and Takahashi, Ichiro. Bargaining, Strategic Reserves, and International Trade in Exhaustible Resources. *Amer. J. Agr. Econ.*, November 1984, *66*(4), pp. 472–80.

Csizmadia, Ernö. Lasting Elements and Changing Circumstances in the Hungarian Agrarian Development. *Acta Oecon.*, 1984, *32*(3–4), pp. 343–61. [G: Hungary]

David, Christina C. Credit and Price Policies in Philippine Agriculture. In *Adams, D. W.; Graham, D. H. and Von Pischke, J. D., eds.*, 1984, pp. 210–25. [G: Philippines]

De Rosa, Dean A. The International Natural Rubber Agreement and Exchange Rate Changes. *Singapore Econ. Rev.*, April 1984, *29*(1), pp. 30–46. [G: Global]

Deaton, Brady J. and Johnson, Thomas G. State Legislation for Rural Development: The Role of the University. *Rev. Reg. Stud.*, Spring 1984, *14*(2), pp. 29–37. [G: U.S.]

Dewey, Peter E. British Farming Profits and Government Policy during the First World War. *Econ. Hist. Rev., 2nd Ser.*, August 1984, *37*(3), pp. 373–90. [G: U.K.]

Dixon, Bruce L. and Chen, Wu-Hsiung. Endogenous versus Exogenous Price Targets for Commodity Market Stabilisation. In *Hughes Hallet, A.J., ed.*, 1984, pp. 181–207. [G: Taiwan]

Dobson, W. D. Future Directions for Agricultural Policy: Discussion. *Amer. J. Agr. Econ.*, May 1984, *66*(2), pp. 240–41. [G: U.S.]

Eicher, Carl K. and Staatz, John M. Policy Analysis in a General Equilibrium Framework: Introduction. In *Eicher, C. K. and Staatz, J. M., eds.*, 1984, pp. 113–18.

Ellis, Frank. Relative Agricultural Prices and the Urban Bias Model: A Comparative Analysis of Tanzania and Fiji. *J. Devel. Stud.*, April 1984, *20*(3), pp. 28–51. [G: Tanzania; Fiji]

Erickson, Elizabeth and House, Robert. Multiple Objective Policy Analysis: A Factor Analysis and Tradeoff Approach Applied to the Agricultural Sector of the Dominican Republic. *J. Policy Modeling*, August 1984, *6*(3), pp. 369–87. [G: Dominican Republic]

Falcon, Walter P. Recent Food Policy Lessons from Developing Countries. *Amer. J. Agr. Econ.*, May 1984, *66*(2), pp. 180–85.

Falcon, Walter P. The Role of the United States in Alleviating World Hunger. In *Eicher, C. K. and Staatz, J. M., eds.*, 1984, pp. 176–88. [G: U.S.]

Faminow, M. D. and Benson, Bruce L. Rent Seeking and Supply Management in Canadian Agriculture. *Can. J. Agr. Econ.*, November 1984, *32*(3), pp. 548–58. [G: Canada]

Friedeberg, Alfred S. Milk Surpluses till the Cows Come Home? *World Econ.*, December 1984, *7*(4), pp. 421–33. [G: EEC]

Gaillard, William. The Rationalization of the Trade of Agricultural Products and the National Objectives of Self-Sufficiency in Common Markets. In *Núñez del Arco, J.; Margain, E. and Cherol, R., eds.*, 1984, pp. 147–53. [G: EEC]

Gardner, Bruce. Seasonal Farm Labor and U.S. Farm Policy. In *Emerson, R. D., ed.*, 1984, pp. 450–76. [G: U.S.]

Gbetibouo, Mathurin and Delgado, Christopher L. Lessons and Constraints of Export Crop-Led Growth: Cocoa in Ivory Coast. In *Zartman, I. W. and Delgado, C. L., eds.*, 1984, pp. 115–47. [G: Ivory Coast]

Ghosh, S.; Gilbert, C. L. and Hughes Hallett, Andrew J. Simple and Optimal Control Rules for Stabilising Commodity Markets. In *Hughes Hallet, A.J., ed.*, 1984, pp. 209–48.

Gonzalez-Vega, Claudio. Cheap Agricultural Credit: Redistribution in Reverse. In *Adams, D. W.; Graham, D. H. and Von Pischke, J. D., eds.*, 1984, pp. 120–32.

Goodman, David; Sorj, Bernardo and Wilkinson, John. Agro-Industry, State Policy and Rural Social Structures: Recent Analyses of Proletarianisation in Brazilian Agriculture. In *Munslow, B. and Finch, H., eds.*, 1984, pp. 189–215. [G: Brazil]

Gorecki, Paul K. Regulating Price and Output in Canadian Agriculture. In *Thompson, F., ed.*, 1984, pp. 31–56. [G: Canada]

Grant, Warren R., et al. Economic Impacts of Increased Price Variability: A Case Study with Rice. *Agr. Econ. Res.*, Fall 1984, *36*(4), pp. 17–27. [G: U.S.]

Gustafson, Thane. Lessons of the Brezhnev Policies on Land and Water and the Future of Reform. In *Hoffmann, E. P. and Laird, R. F., eds.*, 1984, *1981*, pp. 511–27. [G: U.S.S.R.]

Hardy, Stuart B. Farm Policy at a Crossroads: Critical Choices Facing U.S. Agriculture. In *Moore, J. H., ed.*, 1984, pp. 169–82. [G: U.S.]

Harriss, Barbara. Agrarian Change and the Merchant State in Tamil Nadu. In *[Farmer, B. H.]*, 1984, pp. 53–83. [G: India]

Hayden, F. Gregory. A Geobased National Agricultural Policy for Rural Community Enhancement, Environmental Vitality, and Income Stabilization. *J. Econ. Issues*, March 1984, *18*(1), pp. 181–221. [G: U.S.]

Hazell, Peter B. R. and Anderson, Jock R. Public Policy toward Technical Change in Agriculture. *Greek Econ. Rev.*, December 1984, *6*(3), pp. 453–82. [G: Global]

Heien, Dale. Future Directions for U.S. Food, Agricultural, and Trade Policy: Discussion. *Amer. J. Agr. Econ.*, May 1984, *66*(2), pp. 232–33. [G: U.S.]

Helmberger, Peter G. and Akinyosoye, Vincent O. Competitive Pricing and Storage under Uncertainty with an Application to the U.S. Soybean Market. *Amer. J. Agr. Econ.*, May 1984, *66*(2), pp. 119–30. [G: U.S.]

Herdt, Robert W. Differing Perspectives on the World Food Problem: Discussion. *Amer. J. Agr. Econ.*, May 1984, *66*(2), pp. 186–87.

Herrmann, Roland and Schmitz, Peter Michael. Stabilizing Producers' Revenue by Fixing Agricultural Prices within the EC? *Europ. Rev. Agr. Econ.*, 1984, *11*(4), pp. 395–414.
[G: EEC]

Hickson, Allister B. Estimation of Producer Losses Arising from the Partial Embargo of Grain Exports to the Soviet Union: A Comment. *Can. J. Agr. Econ.*, March 1984, *32*(1), pp. 235–36. [G: Canada; U.S.]

Horvath, Janos. Economic Review in Hungary: Role of Plan and Market [Industrial Policy in Hungary: Lessons for America]. *Cato J.*, Fall 1984, *4*(2), pp. 511–20. [G: Hungary]

Husain, Tariq. Potential for Irrigated Agricultural Development in Pakistan. In *Burki, S. J. and LaPorte, R., Jr., eds.*, 1984, pp. 45–83.
[G: Pakistan]

Hyman, Eric L. Providing Public Lands for Smallholder Agroforestry in the Province of Ilocos Norte, Philippines. *J. Devel. Areas*, January 1984, *18*(2), pp. 177–90. [G: Philippines]

Jarrett, F. G. and McColl, J. C. Comments on the Balderstone Report: Reply [Agricultural Policy: Issues and Options for the 1980s]. *Australian J. Agr. Econ.*, April 1984, *28*(2–3), pp. 56–65. [G: Australia]

Johnson, D. Gale. Food for the Future: A Perspective. In *Ghosh, P. K., ed., no. 6, 1984, 1976*, pp. 40–60.

Johnston, J. H. The Current State of Developments on Wheat Marketing Arrangements. *Rev. Marketing Agr. Econ.*, August 1984, *52*(2), pp. 129–34. [G: Australia]

Johnston, J. H. Wheat Marketing Symposium 1984: An Introduction. *Rev. Marketing Agr. Econ.*, August 1984, *52*(2), pp. 101–05.
[G: Australia]

Jones, William O. Economic Tasks for Food Marketing Boards in Tropical Africa. *Food Res. Inst. Stud.*, 1984, *19*(2), pp. 113–38.
[G: Sub-Saharan Africa]

Josling, Timothy E. Future Directions for Food and Agricultural Trade Policy: Discussion. *Amer. J. Agr. Econ.*, May 1984, *66*(2), pp. 248–49. [G: U.S.]

Kanbur, S. M. Ravi. How to Analyse Commodity Price Stabilization? A Review Article. *Oxford Econ. Pap.*, November 1984, *36*(3), pp. 336–58. [G: LDCs]

Kane, Edward J. Political Economy of Subsidizing Agricultural Credit in Developing Countries. In *Adams, D. W.; Graham, D. H. and Von Pischke, J. D., eds.*, 1984, pp. 166–82.

Kazi, Shahnaz. Intersectoral Tax Burdens in Pakistan: A Critical Review of Existing Evidence and Some New Estimates. *Pakistan Devel. Rev.*, Winter 1984, *23*(4), pp. 553–72.
[G: Pakistan]

Khan, Mahmood Hasan. Agricultural Policy Issues in Pakistan. *Pakistan Devel. Rev.*, Summer-Autumn 1984, *23*(2&3), pp. 241–51.
[G: Pakistan]

Kleemeier, L. Domestic Policies versus Poverty-Oriented Foreign Assistance in Tanzania. *J.*

Devel. Stud., January 1984, *20*(2), pp. 171–201. [G: Tanzania]

Koester, Ulrich. The Role of the CAP in the Process of European Integration. *Europ. Rev. Agr. Econ.*, 1984, *11*(2), pp. 129–40. [G: EEC]

Koester, Ulrich and Valdés, Alberto. The EC's Potential Role in Food Security for LDC's: Adjustments in Its STABEX and Stock Policies. *Europ. Rev. Agr. Econ.*, 1984, *11*(4), pp. 415–37. [G: EEC]

Kueh, Yak-Yeow. China's Foodgrain Production, Consumption, and Trade: Recent Trends and Prospects. *Rivista Int. Sci. Econ. Com.*, September 1984, *31*(9), pp. 910–26. [G: China]

Kueh, Yak-Yeow. China's New Agricultural-Policy Program: Major Economic Consequences, 1979–1983. *J. Compar. Econ.*, December 1984, *8*(4), pp. 353–75. [G: China]

Lamont, M. P. Characteristics of and Prospects for Agricultural Finance in Australia, the United States and South Africa. *Finance Trade Rev.*, 1983/84, *15*(3), pp. 73–111.
[G: Australia; U.S.; S. Africa]

Lang, Otto. Western Grain Transportation Initiatives and Agriculture in Eastern Canada: Discussion. *Can. J. Agr. Econ.*, July 1984, *32*(2), pp. 287–90. [G: Canada]

Lányi, Kamilla. Constraints on Profitable Growth and Exports in Hungarian Agriculture. *Acta Oecon.*, 1984, *33*(3–4), pp. 293–304.
[G: Hungary]

Lardy, Nicholas R. Prices, Markets, and the Chinese Peasant. In *Eicher, C. K. and Staatz, J. M., eds.*, 1984, pp. 420–35. [G: China]

Larsen, Arne. Major Factors behind the Problems of the Common Agricultural Policy. *Europ. Rev. Agr. Econ.*, 1984, *11*(2), pp. 121–27.
[G: EEC]

Lavigne, Marie. Long-term Commodity Agreements and the USSR. In *Kostecki, M. M., ed.*, 1984, pp. 15–25. [G: U.S.S.R.; CMEA; Global]

Leisinger, Klaus M. "Grüne Revolution": Eine revidierte Beurteilung im Lichte neuer empirischer Erfahrungen. (The Green Revolution: A Review on the Basis of New Empirical Evidence. With English summary.) *Aussenwirtschaft*, December 1984, *39*(4), pp. 357–81.
[G: LDCs]

Lele, Uma and Candler, Wilfred. Food Security in Developing Countries: National Issues. In *Eicher, C. K. and Staatz, J. M., eds.*, 1984, pp. 207–21. [G: Tanzania]

Leonard, David K. Disintegrating Agricultural Development. *Food Res. Inst. Stud.*, 1984, *19*(2), pp. 177–86. [G: Kenya]

Lundahl, Mats. Defense and Distribution: Agricultural Policy in Haiti during the Reign of Jean-Jacques Dessalines, 1804–1806. *Scand. Econ. Hist. Rev.*, 1984, *32*(2), pp. 77–103.
[G: Haiti]

Mahé, Louis P. A Lower but More Balanced Protection for European Agriculture. *Europ. Rev. Agr. Econ.*, 1984, *11*(2), pp. 217–34.
[G: EEC]

Mansell, Robert L.; Wright, Robert W. and

Kerr, William A. An Economic Evaluation of Formula Pricing for Fluid Milk. *Can. J. Agr. Econ.*, March 1984, *32*(1), pp. 3–24. [G: Canada]

Marsh, John S. The Reform of the CAP: National Interests and Financial Implications. *Europ. Rev. Agr. Econ.*, 1984, *11*(2), pp. 141–50. [G: EEC]

Matoušek, Jiří. The Agrarian Policy of the Communist Party of Czechoslovakia and Thirty-Five Years of the Development of Socialism in the Countryside. *Czech. Econ. Digest.*, November 1984, (7), pp. 29–55. [G: Czechoslovakia]

McCalla, Alex F. Macro Prices and Structural Change: Discussion. *Amer. J. Agr. Econ.*, May 1984, *66*(2), pp. 202–03.

McLeod, A. D. Western Grain Transportation Initiatives and Agriculture in Eastern Canada: Discussion. *Can. J. Agr. Econ.*, July 1984, *32*(2), pp. 283–86. [G: Canada]

Mears, Leon A. Rice and Food Self-Sufficiency in Indonesia. *Bull. Indonesian Econ. Stud.*, August 1984, *20*(2), pp. 122–38. [G: Indonesia]

Mellor, John W. Food Price Policy and Income Distribution in Low-Income Countries. In *Eicher, C. K. and Staatz, J. M., eds.*, 1984, 1978, pp. 147–67. [G: India]

Mieli, Stefano. Fabbisogno di capitale in agricoltura e credito agrario. (Capital Requirements in Agriculture and Rural Credit. With English summary.) *Bancaria*, August 1984, *40*(8), pp. 769–75. [G: Italy]

Mishra, S. N. Agricultural Development in India: A Communitarian Strategy. In *Ngo, M., ed., vol. 2*, 1984, pp. 785–96. [G: India]

Moore, Mick. Categorizing Space: Urban–Rural or Core-Periphery in Sri Lanka. *J. Devel. Stud.*, April 1984, *20*(3), pp. 102–22. [G: Sri Lanka]

Moschini, Giancarlo. Quota Values and Price Uncertainty. *Can. J. Agr. Econ.*, March 1984, *32*(1), pp. 231–34. [G: Canada]

Munting, Roger. The State and the Beet Sugar Industry in Russia before 1914. In *Albert, B. and Graves, A., eds.*, 1984, pp. 21–28. [G: U.S.S.R.]

Nabi, Ijaz. Agricultural Policy Issues in Pakistan: Comment. *Pakistan Devel. Rev.*, Summer-Autumn 1984, *23*(2&3), pp. 253–55. [G: Pakistan]

Newbery, David M. G. Commodity Price Stabilization in Imperfect or Cartelized Markets. *Econometrica*, May 1984, *52*(3), pp. 563–78.

Newbery, David M. G. Commodity Price Stabilization in Imperfectly Competitive Markets. In *Storey, G. G.; Schmitz, A. and Sarris, A. H., eds.*, 1984, pp. 261–84.

Nogués, Julio J. Políticas agrícolas y los países en desarrollo en el GATT: una propuesta para aumentar la capacidad exportadora. (With English summary.) *Cuadernos Econ.*, December 1984, *21*(64), pp. 279–97. [G: Global]

Paarlberg, Philip L. When Are Export Subsidies Rational? *Agr. Econ. Res.*, January 1984, *36*(1), pp. 1–7. [G: U.S.]

Paarlberg, Philip L. and Abbott, Philip C. Towards a Countervailing Power Theory of World Wheat Trade. In *Storey, G. G.; Schmitz, A. and Sarris, A. H., eds.*, 1984, pp. 185–210. [G: Canada; Japan; U.S.]

Paddock, Brian. Estimation of Producer Losses Arising from the Partial Embargo of Grain Exports to the Soviet Union: Reply. *Can. J. Agr. Econ.*, March 1984, *32*(1), pp. 237–38. [G: U.S.; Canada]

Paddock, Brian. The Economic Effects of Policy Intervention in Canadian Agriculture: Comment. *Can. J. Agr. Econ.*, July 1984, *32*(2), pp. 437–42.

Perkins, John A. The Political Economy of Sugar Beet in Imperial Germany. In *Albert, B. and Graves, A., eds.*, 1984, pp. 31–45. [G: Germany]

Petersen, Volker and Schmitt, Günther. Ordnungs- und finanzpolitische Irrwege der europäischen Agrarpolitik. (With English summary.) In *Eucken, W. and Böhm, F., eds.*, 1984, pp. 71–108. [G: EEC]

Pinstrup-Andersen, Per and Kumar, Shubh K. Food Policy, Human Nutrition, and Fertility. In *Schutjer, W. A. and Stokes, C. S., eds.*, 1984, pp. 235–51. [G: LDCs]

Plato, Gerald and Gordon, Douglas. Stockpiling U.S. Agricultural Commodities with Volatile World Markets: The Case of Soybeans. *Agr. Econ. Res.*, Spring 1984, *36*(2), pp. 1–9. [G: U.S.]

Portney, Paul R. Natural Resources and the Environment: More Controversy than Change. In *Palmer, J. L. and Sawhill, I. V., eds.*, 1984, pp. 141–75. [G: U.S.]

Rahman, Sultan H. Analysis of a Flexible Market Stabilization Policy in the Jute Sector and Its Sensitivity to a Parametric Change in Demand. *Bangladesh Devel. Stud.*, September 1984, *12*(3), pp. 64–73. [G: Bangladesh]

Ravallion, Martin and Van de Walle, Dominique. Measuring Ex-Ante Information: What the Newspapers Said during the 1974 Famine in Bangladesh. *Rev. Public Data Use*, October 1984, *12*(3), pp. 169–84. [G: Bangladesh]

Redclift, M. R. 'Urban Bias' and Rural Poverty: A Latin American Perspective. *J. Devel. Stud.*, April 1984, *20*(3), pp. 123–38. [G: Mexico; Brazil]

Richardson, James W. and Nixon, Clair J. The Effects of the 1980, 1981, and 1982 Tax Laws on Texas Rice Farmers. *Southern J. Agr. Econ.*, July 1984, *16*(1), pp. 137–44. [G: U.S.]

Ritson, Christopher and Fearne, Andrew. Long-term Goals for the CAP. *Europ. Rev. Agr. Econ.*, 1984, *11*(2), pp. 207–16. [G: EEC]

Roberts, Paul Craig. Industrial Policy in Hungary: A Comment. *Cato J.*, Fall 1984, *4*(2), pp. 507–09. [G: Hungary]

Roberts, Roland K. and Martin, William J. State-Level Analysis of National Beef Policy: The Use of State Econometric Models. *Southern*

J. Agr. Econ., December 1984, *16*(2), pp. 63–72. **[G: U.S.]**

Ropertz, Henry. Western Grain Transportation Initiatives and Agriculture in Eastern Canada: Discussion. *Can. J. Agr. Econ.*, July 1984, *32*(2), pp. 291–95. **[G: Canada]**

Rossmiller, George E. The U.S. Agricultural Trade Issue Decision Process: An Illustrated Partial Anatomy. In *Storey, G. G.; Schmitz, A. and Sarris, A. H.*, eds., 1984, pp. 165–83. **[G: U.S.]**

Ryan, Timothy J. Wheat Marketing. *Rev. Marketing Agr. Econ.*, August 1984, *52*(2), pp. 117–28. **[G: Australia]**

Salathe, Larry; Price, J. Michael and Banker, David E. An Analysis of the Farmer-Owned Reserve Program, 1977–82. *Amer. J. Agr. Econ.*, February 1984, *66*(1), pp. 1–11. **[G: U.S.]**

Sarris, Alexander H. and Freebairn, John W. Domestic Price Policies and International Rice Trade. In *Storey, G. G.; Schmitz, A. and Sarris, A. H.*, eds., 1984, pp. 213–33. **[G: Global]**

Sawyer, W. Charles. The Effects of the Second Enlargement of the EC on U.S. Exports to Europe. *Weltwirtsch. Arch.*, 1984, *120*(3), pp. 572–79. **[G: EEC; U.S.]**

Schmitz, Peter Michael and Koester, Ulrich. The Sugar Market Policy of the European Community and the Stability of World Market Prices for Sugar. In *Storey, G. G.; Schmitz, A. and Sarris, A. H.*, eds., 1984, pp. 235–59. **[G: EEC; Global]**

Schuh, G. Edward. Future Directions for Food and Agricultural Trade Policy. *Amer. J. Agr. Econ.*, May 1984, *66*(2), pp. 242–47. **[G: U.S.]**

Schuh, G. Edward. Seasonal Farm Labor and U.S. Farm Policy: Discussion. In *Emerson, R. D.*, ed., 1984, pp. 476–81. **[G: U.S.]**

Senior Nello, Susan. An Application of Public Choice Theory to the Question of CAP Reform. *Europ. Rev. Agr. Econ.*, 1984, *11*(3), pp. 261–83. **[G: EEC]**

Shabman, Leonard A. Water Resources Management: Policy Economics for an Era of Transitions. *Southern J. Agr. Econ.*, July 1984, *16*(1), pp. 53–65. **[G: U.S.]**

Shalit, Haim. Does It Pay to Stabilise the Price of Vegetables? An Empirical Evaluation of Agricultural Price Policies. *Europ. Rev. Agr. Econ.*, 1984, *11*(1), pp. 1–16. **[G: Israel]**

Shaw, Anthony B. Impact of New Technology on the Guyanese Rice Industry: Efficiency and Equity Considerations. *J. Devel. Areas*, January 1984, *18*(2), pp. 191–217. **[G: Guyana]**

Sheeny, Seamus. The Agri-monetary System—A Reinterpretation. *Europ. Rev. Agr. Econ.*, 1984, *11*(2), pp. 177–86. **[G: EEC]**

Spriggs, John; Van Kooten, G. C. and Hayward, Keith. Canadian Feed Grains Policy: A Comparison of Price Variability between Canada and the United States. *Can. J. Agr. Econ.*, November 1984, *32*(3), pp. 540–47. **[G: Canada; U.S.]**

Stubbs, Richard. The International Natural Rubber Agreement: Its Negotiation and Operation. *J. World Trade Law*, January:February 1984, *18*(1), pp. 16–31.

Tangermann, Stefan. Guarantee Thresholds: A Device for Solving the CAP Surplus Problem? *Europ. Rev. Agr. Econ.*, 1984, *11*(2), pp. 157–68. **[G: EEC]**

Tarditi, Secondo. Direct Financial Support to Agriculture. *Europ. Rev. Agr. Econ.*, 1984, *11*(2), pp. 235–43. **[G: EEC]**

Thompson, Velma Montoya. The Benefits of Domestic Investment Subsidies and Taxes to Exports in Common Market Countries. *De Economist*, 1984, *132*(1), pp. 61–74. **[G: EEC; Netherlands]**

Timmer, C. Peter. Developing a Food Strategy. In *Eicher, C. K. and Staatz, J. M.*, eds., 1984, *1981*, pp. 119–35.

Timmer, C. Peter. Macro Prices and Structural Change. *Amer. J. Agr. Econ.*, May 1984, *66*(2), pp. 196–201. **[G: Selected Countries]**

Tyrchniewicz, E. W. Western Grain Transportation Initiatives: Where Do We Go from Here? *Can. J. Agr. Econ.*, July 1984, *32*(2), pp. 253–68. **[G: Canada]**

Van Kooten, G. C. and Spriggs, John. A Comparative Static Analysis of the Welfare Impacts of Supply-Restricting Marketing Boards. *Can. J. Agr. Econ.*, March 1984, *32*(1), pp. 221–30. **[G: Canada]**

de Veer, Jan. Cereal Substitutes, Fat Tax and Price Distortion. *Europ. Rev. Agr. Econ.*, 1984, *11*(2), pp. 169–76. **[G: EEC]**

Vogel, Robert C. The Effect of Subsidized Agricultural Credit on Income Distribution in Costa Rica. In *Adams, D. W.; Graham, D. H. and Von Pischke, J. D.*, eds., 1984, pp. 133–45. **[G: Costa Rica]**

Vogel, Robert C. and Larson, Donald W. Illusion and Reality in Allocating Agricultural Credit: The Example of Colombia. In *Adams, D. W.; Graham, D. H. and Von Pischke, J. D.*, eds., 1984, pp. 49–58. **[G: Colombia]**

Warley, T. K. Western Grain Transportation Initiatives and Agriculture in Eastern Canada: Discussion. *Can. J. Agr. Econ.*, July 1984, *32*(2), pp. 297–300. **[G: Canada]**

Watson, A. S. Wheat in 1984. *Rev. Marketing Agr. Econ.*, August 1984, *52*(2), pp. 107–16. **[G: Australia]**

Waugh, Frederick V. A Price Policy for Agriculture, Consistent with Economic Progress That Will Promote Adequate and More Stable Income from Farming. In *Waugh, F. V.*, 1984, *1945*, pp. 157–68.

Waugh, Frederick V. Excise Taxes and Economic Stability. In *Waugh, F. V.*, 1984, *1948*, pp. 40–51.

Waugh, Frederick V. Programs for Using Agricultural Surpluses to Reduce Malnutrition and to Benefit Farmers. In *Waugh, F. V.*, 1984, *1940*, pp. 146–56. **[G: U.S.]**

Waugh, Frederick V. Reserve Stocks of Farm Products. In *Waugh, F. V.*, 1984, *1967*, pp. 198–247. **[G: U.S.]**

Waugh, Frederick V. and Cavin, James P. Contributions of Agricultural Policies to General Economic Growth. In *Waugh, F. V.*, 1984, 1955, pp. 169–82.

Wells, Miriam J. and Climo, Jacob. Parallel Process in the World System: Intermediate Agencies and Local Factionalism in the United States and Mexico. *J. Devel. Stud.*, January 1984, 20(2), pp. 151–70. [G: Mexico; U.S.]

White, T. Kelley. World Agricultural Markets: Implications for U.S. Food and Agricultural Policy. *Southern J. Agr. Econ.*, July 1984, 16(1), pp. 91–97.

Williams, Gary W. and Thompson, Robert L. Brazilian Soybean Policy: The International Effects of Intervention. *Amer. J. Agr. Econ.*, November 1984, 66(4), pp. 488–98. [G: Brazil; U.S.]

Womack, Abner W., et al. An Evaluation of the 1981 Farm Program for Crops: Implications for the 1985 Farm Bill. *Southern J. Agr. Econ.*, July 1984, 16(1), pp. 27–37. [G: U.S.]

Wright, Brian D. and Williams, Jeffrey C. Antihoarding Laws: A Stock Condemnation Reconsidered. *Amer. J. Agr. Econ.*, November 1984, 66(4), pp. 447–55.

Zentner, R. P. and Peterson, W. L. An Economic Evaluation of Public Wheat Research and Extension Expenditures in Canada. *Can. J. Agr. Econ.*, July 1984, 32(2), pp. 327–53. [G: Canada]

Zuo, Mu. Price Ratios among Agricultural Products Must Be Well Adjusted. *Chinese Econ. Stud.*, Fall 1984, 18(1), pp. 34–43. [G: China]

714 Agricultural Finance

7140 Agricultural Finance

Adams, Dale W. Are the Arguments for Cheap Agricultural Credit Sound? In *Adams, D. W.; Graham, D. H. and Von Pischke, J. D., eds.*, 1984, pp. 65–77.

Adams, Dale W. Effects of Finance on Rural Development. In *Adams, D. W.; Graham, D. H. and Von Pischke, J. D., eds.*, 1984, pp. 11–21.

Adams, Dale W. and Graham, Douglas H. A Critique of Traditional Agricultural Credit Projects and Policies. In *Eicher, C. K. and Staatz, J. M., eds.*, 1984, 1981, pp. 313–28. [G: LDCs]

Adams, Dale W.; Graham, Douglas H. and Von Pischke, J. D. Overview of the Importance of Interest-Rate Policies. In *Adams, D. W.; Graham, D. H. and Von Pischke, J. D., eds.*, 1984, pp. 61–64.

Adams, Dale W.; Graham, Douglas H. and Von Pischke, J. D. Undermining Rural Development with Cheap Credit. In *Adams, D. W.; Graham, D. H. and Von Pischke, J. D., eds.*, 1984, pp. 1–7.

Ahmad, Mushtaq. Rural Credit and Rural Development: Some Issues: Comment. *Pakistan Devel. Rev.*, Summer-Autumn 1984, 23(2&3), pp. 283–85. [G: Pakistan]

Ahmed, Momtaz Uddin. Financing Rural Industries in Bangladesh. *Bangladesh Devel. Stud.*, March-June 1984, 12(1–2), pp. 59–79. [G: Bangladesh]

Alston, Lee J. Farm Foreclosure Moratorium Legislation: A Lesson from the Past. *Amer. Econ. Rev.*, June 1984, 74(3), pp. 445–57. [G: U.S.]

Argyle, D. Brian. The Impact of Interest Rates on Savings in Rural Financial Markets. In *Kessler, D. and Ullmo, P.-A., eds.*, 1984, pp. 27–33.

Bardsley, Peter; Abey, Arun and Davenport, Scott. The Economics of Insuring Crops against Drought. *Australian J. Agr. Econ.*, April 1984, 28(1), pp. 1–14. [G: Australia]

Basu, Kaushik. Implicit Interest Rates, Usury and Isolation in Backward Agriculture. *Cambridge J. Econ.*, June 1984, 8(2), pp. 145–59. [G: India]

Blair, Harry W. Agricultural Credit, Political Economy, and Patronage. In *Adams, D. W.; Graham, D. H. and Von Pischke, J. D., eds.*, 1984, pp. 183–93.

Bouman, F. J. A. Informal Saving and Credit Arrangements in Developing Countries: Observations from Sri Lanka. In *Adams, D. W.; Graham, D. H. and Von Pischke, J. D., eds.*, 1984, pp. 232–47. [G: Sri Lanka]

Bourne, Compton and Graham, Douglas H. Problems with Specialized Agricultural Lenders. In *Adams, D. W.; Graham, D. H. and Von Pischke, J. D., eds.*, 1984, pp. 36–48.

Brannon, Jeffery T. and Baklanoff, Eric N. The Political Economy of Agrarian Reform in Yucatán, Mexico. *World Devel.*, November–December 1984, 12(11–12), pp. 1131–41. [G: Mexico]

Braverman, Avishay and Guasch, J. Luis. Capital Requirements, Screening and Interlinked Sharecropping and Credit Contracts. *J. Devel. Econ.*, April 1984, 14(3), pp. 359–74.

Claggett, E. Tylor and Stansell, Stanley R. Economies of Scale in a Cooperative Financial System: A Study of Production Credit Associations. *Quart. J. Bus. Econ.*, Spring 1984, 23(2), pp. 20–46. [G: U.S.]

Cuevas, Carlos E. and Graham, Douglas H. Agricultural Lending Costs in Honduras. In *Adams, D. W.; Graham, D. H. and Von Pischke, J. D., eds.*, 1984, pp. 96–103. [G: Honduras]

David, Christina C. Credit and Price Policies in Philippine Agriculture. In *Adams, D. W.; Graham, D. H. and Von Pischke, J. D., eds.*, 1984, pp. 210–25. [G: Philippines]

Deguefe, Taffara. Financial Institutions and Rural Development in Africa. In *Kessler, D. and Ullmo, P.-A., eds.*, 1984, pp. 205–16.

Donaldson, Graham. Technology in Agricultural Development. In *Weiss, C. and Jéquier, N., eds.*, 1984, pp. 19–34. [G: Global]

Eichengreen, Barry. Mortgage Interest Rates in the Populist Era. *Amer. Econ. Rev.*, December 1984, 74(5), pp. 995–1015. [G: U.S.]

Garcia, Philip; Leuthold, Raymond M. and Sarhan, Mohamed E. Basis Risk: Measurement and Analysis of Basis Fluctuations for Selected Livestock Markets. *Amer. J. Agr. Econ.*, November 1984, *66*(4), pp. 499–504. **[G: U.S.]**

Gonzalez-Vega, Claudio. Cheap Agricultural Credit: Redistribution in Reverse. In *Adams, D. W.; Graham, D. H. and Von Pischke, J. D., eds.*, 1984, pp. 120–32.

Gonzalez-Vega, Claudio. Credit-Rationing Behavior of Agricultural Lenders: The Iron Law of Interest-Rate Restrictions. In *Adams, D. W.; Graham, D. H. and Von Pischke, J. D., eds.*, 1984, pp. 78–95.

Gonzalez-Vega, Claudio. Interest Rate Restrictions and Income Distribution. In *Eicher, C. K. and Staatz, J. M., eds.*, 1984, *1977*, pp. 329–34. **[G: LDCs]**

Graham, Douglas H. and Firestine, Robert E. An Agenda for Reform of Rural Financial Markets in Low-Income Countries. In *Adams, D. W.; Graham, D. H. and Von Pischke, J. D., eds.*, 1984, pp. 298–307.

Haruvi, Nava and Kislev, Yoav. Cooperation in the Moshav. *J. Compar. Econ.*, March 1984, *8*(1), pp. 54–73. **[G: Israel]**

Kane, Edward J. Political Economy of Subsidizing Agricultural Credit in Developing Countries. In *Adams, D. W.; Graham, D. H. and Von Pischke, J. D., eds.*, 1984, pp. 166–82.

Ladman, Jerry R. Loan-Transactions Costs, Credit Rationing, and Market Structure: The Case of Bolivia. In *Adams, D. W.; Graham, D. H. and Von Pischke, J. D., eds.*, 1984, pp. 104–19. **[G: Bolivia]**

Lamont, M. P. Characteristics of and Prospects for Agricultural Finance in Australia, the United States and South Africa. *Finance Trade Rev.*, 1983/84, *15*(3), pp. 73–111.

[G: Australia; U.S.; S. Africa]

Ligeti, Sandor. Rural Savings and Agricultural Credits. In *Kessler, D. and Ullmo, P.-A., eds.*, 1984, pp. 87–106.

Melichar, Emanuel. A Financial Perspective on Agriculture. *Fed. Res. Bull.*, January 1984, *70*(1), pp. 1–13. **[G: U.S.]**

Meyer, Richard L. and Alicbusan, Adelaida P. Farm-Household Heterogeneity and Rural Financial Markets: Insights from Thailand. In *Adams, D. W.; Graham, D. H. and Von Pischke, J. D., eds.*, 1984, pp. 22–35. **[G: Thailand]**

Mieli, Stefano. Fabbisogno di capitale in agricoltura e credito agrario. (Capital Requirements in Agriculture and Rural Credit. With English summary.) *Bancaria*, August 1984, *40*(8), pp. 769–75. **[G: Italy]**

Mittendorf, Hans. Savings Mobilization for Agricultural and Rural Development in Africa. In *Kessler, D. and Ullmo, P.-A., eds.*, 1984, pp. 217–29. **[G: Zimbabwe]**

Qureshi, Sarfraz K. Rural Credit and Rural Development: Some Issues. *Pakistan Devel. Rev.*, Summer-Autumn 1984, *23*(2&3), pp. 273–82. **[G: Pakistan]**

Ray, Debraj. Intertemporal Borrowing to Sustain Exogenous Consumption Standards under Uncertainty. *J. Econ. Theory*, June 1984, *33*(1), pp. 72–87.

Ray, Edward John. Economic Distortions and Financial Reforms. In *Adams, D. W.; Graham, D. H. and Von Pischke, J. D., eds.*, 1984, pp. 194–209.

Sayad, João. Rural Credit and Positive Real Rates of Interest: Brazil's Experience with Rapid Inflation. In *Adams, D. W.; Graham, D. H. and Von Pischke, J. D., eds.*, 1984, pp. 146–60. **[G: Brazil]**

Stock, James H. Real Estate Mortgages, Foreclosures, and Midwestern Agrarian Unrest, 1865–1920. *J. Econ. Hist.*, March 1984, *44*(1), pp. 89–105. **[G: U.S.]**

Vogel, Robert C. Savings Mobilization: The Forgotten Half of Rural Finance. In *Adams, D. W.; Graham, D. H. and Von Pischke, J. D., eds.*, 1984, pp. 248–65. **[G: Peru]**

Vogel, Robert C. The Effect of Subsidized Agricultural Credit on Income Distribution in Costa Rica. In *Adams, D. W.; Graham, D. H. and Von Pischke, J. D., eds.*, 1984, pp. 133–45. **[G: Costa Rica]**

Vogel, Robert C. and Larson, Donald W. Illusion and Reality in Allocating Agricultural Credit: The Example of Colombia. In *Adams, D. W.; Graham, D. H. and Von Pischke, J. D., eds.*, 1984, pp. 49–58. **[G: Colombia]**

Von Pischke, J. D. Improving Donor Intervention in Rural Finance. In *Adams, D. W.; Graham, D. H. and Von Pischke, J. D., eds.*, 1984, pp. 284–97.

Williams, Jeffrey C. Fractional Reserve Banking in Grain. *J. Money, Credit, Banking*, Part 1 November 1984, *16*(4), pp. 488–96.

[G: U.S.]

Yudelman, Montague. Agricultural Lending by the Bank, 1974–84: A Retrospective Analysis. *Finance Develop.*, December 1984, *21*(4), pp. 45–47. **[G: Global]**

715 Agricultural Markets and Marketing; Cooperatives

7150 Agricultural Markets and Marketing; Cooperatives

Adamowicz, W. L.; Baah, S. O. and Hawkins, M. H. Pricing Efficiency in Hog Markets. *Can. J. Agr. Econ.*, November 1984, *32*(3), pp. 462–77. **[G: Canada; U.S.]**

Ardeni, Pier Giorgio and Paris, Quirino. Un modello di importazione e di esportazione dei prodotti farinacei. (A Model for Import–Export of Wheat Products. With English summary.) *Statistica*, April–June 1984, *44*(2), pp. 301–27. **[G: Italy]**

Bailey, DeeVon; Brorsen, B. Wade and Richardson, James W. Dynamic Stochastic Simulation of Daily Cash and Futures Cotton Prices. *Southern J. Agr. Econ.*, December 1984, *16*(2), pp. 109–16. **[G: U.S.]**

Bakht, Zaid. Marketing of Rural Industrial Products in Bangladesh. *Bangladesh Devel. Stud.*, March-June 1984, *12*(1–2), pp. 101–26. **[G: Bangladesh]**

Baldwin, E. Dean; Thraen, Cameron S. and Lar-

son, **Donald W.** A Discriminant Analysis of Grain Market Structure in Selected States of the South and Cornbelt. *Southern J. Agr. Econ.*, December 1984, *16*(2), pp. 117–25. [G: U.S.]

Behr, Robert M. and Ward, Ronald W. A Simultaneous Equation Model of Futures Trading. *Can. J. Agr. Econ.*, July 1984, *32*(2), pp. 377–98.

Beilock, Richard and Freeman, James. Florida Motor Carrier Deregulation: Perspectives of Urban and Rural Shipper/Receivers. *Amer. J. Agr. Econ.*, February 1984, *66*(1), pp. 91–98. [G: U.S.]

Blank, Steven C. Cross-hedging Australian Cattle. *Australian J. Agr. Econ.*, August/December 1984, *28*(2–3), pp. 153–62. [G: Australia]

Brorsen, B. Wade; Chavas, Jean-Paul and Grant, Warren R. Dynamic Relationships of Rice Import Prices in Europe. *Europ. Rev. Agr. Econ.*, 1984, *11*(1), pp. 29–42. [G: U.S.; Thailand; Argentina; Europe]

Brorsen, B. Wade; Grant, Warren R. and Rister, M. Edward. A Hedonic Price Model for Rough Rice Bid/Acceptance Markets. *Amer. J. Agr. Econ.*, May 1984, *66*(2), pp. 156–63. [G: U.S.]

Buccola, Steven T. and Subaei, Abdelbagi. Mean-Gini Analysis, Stochastic Efficiency and Weak Risk Aversion. *Australian J. Agr. Econ.*, August/December 1984, *28*(2–3), pp. 77–86.

Carter, Colin A. Pooling Sales versus Forward Selling and the Management of Risk: The Case of Wheat. In *Storey, G. G.; Schmitz, A. and Sarris, A. H.*, eds., 1984, pp. 145–63. [G: Australia; Canada]

Centner, Terence J. and Wetzstein, Michael E. Cooperative Antitrust Monopolization and the Theory of Contestable Markets. *Southern J. Agr. Econ.*, July 1984, *16*(1), pp. 129–35.

Chengappa, P. G., et al. Market Margin Analysis of India Tea. *Margin*, January 1984, *16*(2), pp. 77–85. [G: India]

Cornelisse, Peter A. Wheat-Market Flows in the Punjab. *Pakistan Devel. Rev.*, Spring 1984, *23*(1), pp. 65–79. [G: Pakistan]

Cox, Pamela M. J. Implementing Agricultural Development Policy in Kenya. *Food Res. Inst. Stud.*, 1984, *19*(2), pp. 153–76. [G: Kenya]

Edwards, Clark. Wheat Prices: Past and Future Levels and Volatility. *Agr. Econ. Res.*, Summer 1984, *36*(3), pp. 28–31. [G: U.S.]

Faminow, M. D. and Benson, Bruce L. Rent Seeking and Supply Management in Canadian Agriculture. *Can. J. Agr. Econ.*, November 1984, *32*(3), pp. 548–58. [G: Canada]

Fischer, Lewis A. The USSR as a Major Factor in International Cotton Markets. In *Kostecki, M. M.*, ed., 1984, pp. 218–36. [G: U.S.S.R.; Global]

Fuller, Stephen; Makus, Larry and Gallimore, William. Effects of Increasing Panama Canal Toll Rates on U.S. Grain Exports. *Southern J. Agr. Econ.*, December 1984, *16*(2), pp. 9–19. [G: U.S.; Panama]

Garcia, Philip; Leuthold, Raymond M. and Sar-

han, Mohamed E. Basis Risk: Measurement and Analysis of Basis Fluctuations for Selected Livestock Markets. *Amer. J. Agr. Econ.*, November 1984, *66*(4), pp. 499–504. [G: U.S.]

Gay, Gerald D. and Manaster, Steven. The Quality Option Implicit in Futures Contracts. *J. Finan. Econ.*, September 1984, *13*(3), pp. 353–70. [G: U.S.]

Goldman, Arieh. The Development and Implementation of a Marketing-Based Economic Development Project in the Agricultural Sector—An Israeli Case. In *Kaynak, E. and Savitt, R.*, eds., 1984, pp. 53–70. [G: Israel]

Gordon, Douglas. Performance of Thin Futures Markets: Rice and Sunflower Seed Futures. *Agr. Econ. Res.*, Fall 1984, *36*(4), pp. 1–16. [G: U.S.]

Gordon, Kathryn M.; Lagrange, Sylvie and Riboud, Christophe. Measuring Country Exposure to Commodity Price Uncertainty. *Europ. Rev. Agr. Econ.*, 1984, *11*(3), pp. 285–301. [G: Selected Countries]

Gorecki, Paul K. Regulating Price and Output in Canadian Agriculture. In *Thompson, F.*, ed., 1984, pp. 31–56. [G: Canada]

Harriss, Barbara. Agrarian Change and the Merchant State in Tamil Nadu. In *[Farmer, B. H.]*, 1984, pp. 53–83. [G: India]

Haruvi, Nava and Kislev, Yoav. Cooperation in the Moshav. *J. Compar. Econ.*, March 1984, *8*(1), pp. 54–73. [G: Israel]

Harvey, D. R. and Hubbard, L. J. A Comparative Static Analysis of Welfare Impacts of Supply-restricting Marketing Boards: A Comment. *Can. J. Agr. Econ.*, November 1984, *32*(3), pp. 570–74. [G: Canada]

Hayenga, Marvin L., et al. Profitable Hedging Opportunities and Risk Premiums for Producers in Live Cattle and Live Hog Futures Markets. *J. Futures Markets*, Summer 1984, *4*(2), pp. 141–54. [G: U.S.]

Helmberger, Peter G. and Akinyosoye, Vincent O. Competitive Pricing and Storage under Uncertainty with an Application to the U.S. Soybean Market. *Amer. J. Agr. Econ.*, May 1984, *66*(2), pp. 119–30. [G: U.S.]

Johnston, J. H. The Current State of Developments on Wheat Marketing Arrangements. *Rev. Marketing Agr. Econ.*, August 1984, *52*(2), pp. 129–34. [G: Australia]

Jones, William O. Economic Tasks for Food Marketing Boards in Tropical Africa. *Food Res. Inst. Stud.*, 1984, *19*(2), pp. 113–38. [G: Sub-Saharan Africa]

Kilmer, Richard L. and Armbruster, Walter J. Methods for Evaluating Economic Efficiency in Agricultural Marketing. *Southern J. Agr. Econ.*, July 1984, *16*(1), pp. 101–09.

Kostecki, Michel M. The Soviet Union in International Grain Markets. In *Kostecki, M. M.*, ed., 1984, pp. 194–217. [G: U.S.S.R.; Global]

Lányi, Kamilla. Constraints on Profitable Growth and Exports in Hungarian Agriculture. *Acta Oecon.*, 1984, *33*(3–4), pp. 293–304. [G: Hungary]

Lele, Uma and Candler, Wilfred. Food Security

in Developing Countries: National Issues. In *Eicher, C. K. and Staatz, J. M., eds.*, 1984, pp. 207–21. [G: Tanzania]

Lopez, Rigoberto A. and Spreen, Thomas H. The Impact of Alternative Payment Arrangements on the Performance of Florida Sugarcane Cooperatives. *Southern J. Agr. Econ.*, December 1984, *16*(2), pp. 99–107. [G: U.S.]

Love, Ross O. and Robison, Lindon J. An Empirical Analysis of the Intertemporal Stability of Risk Preference. *Southern J. Agr. Econ.*, July 1984, *16*(1), pp. 159–65. [G: U.S.]

MacMinn, Richard D.; Morgan, George Emir, III and Smith, Stephen D. Forward Market Equilibrium. *Southern Econ. J.*, July 1984, *51*(1), pp. 41–58.

Maizels, Alfred. A Conceptual Framework for Analysis of Primary Commodity Markets. *World Devel.*, January 1984, *12*(1), pp. 25–41. [G: Global]

Mansell, Robert L.; Wright, Robert W. and Kerr, William A. An Economic Evaluation of Formula Pricing for Fluid Milk. *Can. J. Agr. Econ.*, March 1984, *32*(1), pp. 3–24. [G: Canada]

Marion, Donald R. and Grinnell, Gerald. Estimates of Consumer Loss Due to Monopoly in the U.S. Food Manufacturing Industries: Comment. *Amer. J. Agr. Econ.*, November 1984, *66*(4), pp. 520–23. [G: U.S.]

Martin, Larry J. and Hope, David. Risk and Returns from Alternative Marketing Strategies for Corn Producers. *J. Futures Markets*, Winter 1984, *4*(4), pp. 513–30. [G: Canada]

McCloskey, Donald N. and Nash, John. Corn at Interest: The Extent and Cost of Grain Storage in Medieval England. *Amer. Econ. Rev.*, March 1984, *74*(1), pp. 174–87. [G: U.K.]

Mohammad, Faiz. The Performance of Pakistan's Agricultural Markets in the Green Revolution Perspective. *Pakistan Devel. Rev.*, Summer-Autumn 1984, *23*(2&3), pp. 287–303. [G: Pakistan]

Monke, Eric and Petzel, Todd. Market Integration: An Application to International Trade in Cotton. *Amer. J. Agr. Econ.*, November 1984, *66*(4), pp. 481–87. [G: Selected Countries]

Moschini, Giancarlo. Quota Values and Price Uncertainty. *Can. J. Agr. Econ.*, March 1984, *32*(1), pp. 231–34. [G: Canada]

Nerlove, Marc and Waugh, Frederick V. Advertising without Supply Control: Some Implications of a Study of the Advertising of Oranges. In *Waugh, F. V.*, 1984, *1961*, pp. 63–87. [G: U.S.]

Paddock, Brian. The Economic Effects of Policy Intervention in Canadian Agriculture: Comment. *Can. J. Agr. Econ.*, July 1984, *32*(2), pp. 437–42.

Parker, Russell C. and Connor, John M. Estimates of Consumer Loss Due to Monopoly in the U.S. Food Manufacturing Industries: Second Reply. *Amer. J. Agr. Econ.*, November 1984, *66*(4), pp. 524–28. [G: U.S.]

Platteau, Jean-Philippe. Projet cooperatif et realite rurale dans le tiers-monde. Vers une re-

definition des termes du debat. (The Co-operative Design and Rural Realities in the Third World. With English summary.) *Ann. Pub. Co-op. Econ.*, July–September 1984, *55*(3), pp. 283–307. [G: LDCs]

Raynauld, Jacques and Tessier, Jacques. Risk Premiums in Futures Markets: An Empirical Investigation. *J. Futures Markets*, Summer 1984, *4*(2), pp. 189–211. [G: U.S.]

Rister, M. Edward; Skees, Jerry R. and Black, J. Roy. Evaluating Use of Outlook Information in Grain Sorghum Storage Decisions. *Southern J. Agr. Econ.*, July 1984, *16*(1), pp. 151–58. [G: U.S.]

Rucker, Randal R.; Burt, Oscar R. and LaFrance, Jeffrey T. An Econometric Model of Cattle Inventories. *Amer. J. Agr. Econ.*, May 1984, *66*(2), pp. 131–44. [G: U.S.]

Ryan, Timothy J. Wheat Marketing. *Rev. Marketing Agr. Econ.*, August 1984, *52*(2), pp. 117–28. [G: Australia]

Salam, Abdul. The Performance of Pakistan's Agricultural Markets in the Green Revolution Perspective. *Pakistan Devel. Rev.*, Summer-Autumn 1984, *23*(2&3), pp. 305–08. [G: Pakistan]

Salathe, Larry; Price, J. Michael and Banker, David E. An Analysis of the Farmer-Owned Reserve Program, 1977–82. *Amer. J. Agr. Econ.*, February 1984, *66*(1), pp. 1–11. [G: U.S.]

Sarris, Alexander H. Speculative Storage, Futures Markets, and the Stability of Agricultural Prices. In *Storey, G. G.; Schmitz, A. and Sarris, A. H., eds.*, 1984, pp. 65–97.

Sexton, Richard J. Perspectives on the Development of the Economic Theory of Co-operatives. *Can. J. Agr. Econ.*, July 1984, *32*(2), pp. 423–36.

Solís, Leopoldo. Food Marketing and Income Distribution. In *Aspe, P. and Sigmund, P. E., eds.*, 1984, pp. 481–522. [G: Mexico]

Soulas de Russel, D. J. M. Les coopératives des pays les plus pauvres: rôle fixateur de populations rurales et conditions de succès. (Co-operatives in the Poorest Countries: Their Role in the Stabilisation of the Population in Rural Areas; Conditions for Success. With English summary.) *Ann. Pub. Co-op. Econ.*, January–March 1984, *55*(1), pp. 71–90. [G: Ghana]

Spriggs, John; Van Kooten, G. C. and Hayward, Keith. Canadian Feed Grains Policy: A Comparison of Price Variability between Canada and the United States. *Can. J. Agr. Econ.*, November 1984, *32*(3), pp. 540–47. [G: Canada; U.S.]

Subrahmanyam, P. and Taimni, K. K. Growth and Development of Cooperatives in Maharashtra: An Analytical Study. *Ann. Pub. Co-op. Econ.*, July–September 1984, *55*(3), pp. 315–31. [G: India]

Tubiana, L. Le commerce mondial des produits agricoles: de la régulation globale au fractionnement des marchés. (World Food Trade: From Global Regulation to Markets Fragmentation. With English summary.) *Écon. Soc.*, June 1984, *18*(6), pp. 125–56. **[G: Global]**

Tyrchniewicz, E. W. Western Grain Transportation Initiatives: Where Do We Go from Here? *Can. J. Agr. Econ.*, July 1984, *32*(2), pp. 253–68. **[G: Canada]**

Unnevehr, Laurian J. Transport Costs, Tariffs and the Influence of World Markets on Indonesian Domestic Cassava Prices. *Bull. Indonesian Econ. Stud.*, April 1984, *20*(1), pp. 30–43. **[G: Indonesia]**

Valdés, Alberto. Comercio de Productos Agrícolas entre Países en Desarrollo: América Latina durante, 1962–1979. (With English summary.) *Cuadernos Econ.*, August 1984, *21*(63), pp. 169–206. **[G: Latin America]**

Van Kooten, G. C. and Spriggs, John. A Comparative Static Analysis of the Welfare Impacts of Supply-restricting Marketing Boards: Reply. *Can. J. Agr. Econ.*, November 1984, *32*(3), pp. 576–78. **[G: Canada]**

Van Kooten, G. C. and Spriggs, John. A Comparative Static Analysis of the Welfare Impacts of Supply-Restricting Marketing Boards. *Can. J. Agr. Econ.*, March 1984, *32*(1), pp. 221–30. **[G: Canada]**

Watson, A. S. Wheat in 1984. *Rev. Marketing Agr. Econ.*, August 1984, *52*(2), pp. 107–16. **[G: Australia]**

Waugh, Frederick V. Distribution Among Markets. In *Waugh, F. V.*, 1984, pp. 107–26. **[G: U.S.]**

Waugh, Frederick V. Market Prorates and Social Welfare. In *Waugh, F. V.*, 1984, *1938*, pp. 132–45.

Waugh, Frederick V. and Ogren, Kenneth E. An Interpretation of Changes in Agricultural Marketing Costs. In *Waugh, F. V.*, 1984, *1961*, pp. 183–97. **[G: U.S.]**

White, T. Kelley. World Agricultural Markets: Implications for U.S. Food and Agricultural Policy. *Southern J. Agr. Econ.*, July 1984, *16*(1), pp. 91–97.

Woodworth, Warner. Cooperative Movements in the U.S.A.: The Third Stage. *Ann. Pub. Co-op. Econ.*, July–September 1984, *55*(3), pp. 239–51. **[G: U.S.]**

Wright, Brian D. and Williams, Jeffrey C. Anti-hoarding Laws: A Stock Condemnation Reconsidered. *Amer. J. Agr. Econ.*, November 1984, *66*(4), pp. 447–55.

Young, Leslie and Schmitz, Andrew. Storage under a Cartel. In *Storey, G. G.; Schmitz, A. and Sarris, A. H., eds.*, 1984, pp. 285–303.

7151 Corporate Agriculture

Baklanoff, Eric N. and Brannon, Jeffery T. Forward and Backward Linkages in a Plantation Economy: Imigrant Entrepreneurship and Industrial Development in Yucatan, Mexico. *J. Devel. Areas*, October 1984, *19*(1), pp. 83–94. **[G: Mexico]**

Beladi, Hamid. Welfare Effects of Trade Restrictions: The Case of the U.S. Dairy Industry. *Atlantic Econ. J.*, December 1984, *12*(4), pp. 70. **[G: U.S.]**

Cuddy, Michael P. Supply Response in the Irish Dairy Sector: A Reply [Response of Irish Creamery Milk Supply to Price Changes]. *Europ. Rev. Agr. Econ.*, 1984, *11*(3), pp. 353–57. **[G: Ireland]**

Friedeberg, Alfred S. Milk Surpluses till the Cows Come Home? *World Econ.*, December 1984, *7*(4), pp. 421–33. **[G: EEC]**

Glover, David J. Contract Farming and Smallholder Outgrower Schemes in Less-developed Countries. *World Devel.*, November–December 1984, *12*(11–12), pp. 1143–57. **[G: LDCs]**

Kiyokawa, Yukihiko. The Diffusion of New Technologies in the Japanese Sericulture Industry: The Case of the Hybrid Silkworm. *Hitotsubashi J. Econ.*, June 1984, *25*(1), pp. 31–59. **[G: Japan]**

Larkin, John A. The International Face of the Philippine Sugar Industry, 1836–1920. *Philippine Rev. Econ. Bus.*, Mar./June 1984, *21*(1/2), pp. 39–58. **[G: Philippines]**

Offutt, Susan Elizabeth and Blandford, David. The Impact of the Soviet Union upon the U.S Feed/Livestock Sector—An Assessment. *J. Policy Modeling*, August 1984, *6*(3), pp. 311–40. **[G: U.S.; U.S.S.R.]**

Oskam, A. J. Supply Response in the Irish Dairy Sector: A Comment [Response of Irish Creamery Milk Supply to Price Changes]. *Europ. Rev. Agr. Econ.*, 1984, *11*(3), pp. 343–51. **[G: Ireland]**

Pitts, Eamonn. Effects of Rainfall on Milk Yields in Areas with Drainage Difficulties. *Irish J. Agr. Econ. Rural Soc.*, 1984, *10*(1), pp. 29–42. **[G: U.K.]**

Reidy, K. A Survey of Pig Producers' Intentions. *Irish J. Agr. Econ. Rural Soc.*, 1984, *10*(1), pp. 1–12. **[G: U.K.]**

Roll, Richard. Orange Juice and Weather. *Amer. Econ. Rev.*, December 1984, *74*(5), pp. 861–80. **[G: U.S.]**

Shmueli, A. and Tapiero, Charles S. Adaptive Econometric Forecasting by an Approximate Filtering-Smoothing Algorithm: The Case of the Israeli Meat Sector. In *Hughes Hallet, A.J., ed.*, 1984, pp. 63–84. **[G: Israel]**

Sporleder, Thomas L. Policy Considerations of Emerging Information Technologies. *Southern J. Agr. Econ.*, July 1984, *16*(1), pp. 15–21.

Weiss, Charles and Lepkowski, Wil. Cotton Development International. In *Weiss, C. and Jéquier, N., eds.*, 1984, pp. 295–311. **[G: LDCs]**

716 Farm Management

7160 Farm Management

Adeyemo, Remi. Management and Production Problems in Group Farming Cooperatives in the Savannah Zones of South-Western Nigeria. *Econ. Anal. Worker's Manage.*, 1984, *18*(2), pp. 179–86. **[G: Nigeria]**

Adulavidhaya, Kamphol, et al. The Comparative Statics of the Behavior of Agricultural Households in Thailand. *Singapore Econ. Rev.*, April 1984, *29*(1), pp. 67–96.   [**G: Thailand**]

Agarwal, Bina. Tractors, Tubewells and Cropping Intensity in the Indian Punjab. *J. Devel. Stud.*, July 1984, *20*(4), pp. 290–302.   [**G: India**]

Alston, Lee J.; Datta, Samar K. and Nugent, Jeffrey B. Tenancy Choice in a Competitive Framework with Transactions Costs. *J. Polit. Econ.*, December 1984, *92*(6), pp. 1121–33.
[**G: U.S.**]

Antle, John M. Human Capital, Infrastructure, and the Productivity of Indian Rice Farmers. *J. Devel. Econ.*, January–February 1984, *14*(1–2), pp. 163–81.   [**G: India**]

Antle, John M. and Goodger, William J. Measuring Stochastic Technology: The Case of Tulare Milk Production. *Amer. J. Agr. Econ.*, August 1984, *66*(3), pp. 342–50.   [**G: U.S.**]

Apland, Jeffrey; Barnes, Robert N. and Justus, Fred. The Farm Lease: An Analysis of Owner–Tenant and Landlord Preferences under Risk. *Amer. J. Agr. Econ.*, August 1984, *66*(3), pp. 376–84.   [**G: U.S.**]

Babcock, Bruce, et al. Identifying Least-Cost Sources of Required Fertilizer Nutrients. *Amer. J. Agr. Econ.*, August 1984, *66*(3), pp. 385–91.   [**G: U.S.**]

Basu, Arati. Production Systems and Productivity of Labour: An Analysis on the Existence of Surplus Labour. *Indian Econ. Rev.*, July-Dec. 1984, *19*(2), pp. 185–201.

Berck, Peter and Schmitz, Andrew. Price Supports in the Context of International Trade. In *Storey, G. G.; Schmitz, A. and Sarris, A. H., eds.*, 1984, pp. 127–43.   [**G: U.S.**]

Buccola, Steven T. and Subaei, Abdelbagi. Mean-Gini Analysis, Stochastic Efficiency and Weak Risk Aversion. *Australian J. Agr. Econ.*, August/December 1984, *28*(2–3), pp. 77–86.

Carmody, M. J., et al. An Economic Evaluation of the Footrot Eradication Program in the New England Region of New South Wales. *Rev. Marketing Agr. Econ.*, April 1984, *52*(1), pp. 9–21.   [**G: Australia**]

Carter, Michael R. Identification of the Inverse Relationship between Farm Size and Productivity: An Empirical Analysis of Peasant Agricultural Production. *Oxford Econ. Pap.*, March 1984, *36*(1), pp. 131–45.   [**G: India**]

Carter, Michael R. Resource Allocation and Use under Collective Rights and Labour Management in Peruvian Coastal Agriculture. *Econ. J.*, December 1984, *94*(376), pp. 826–46.
[**G: Peru**]

Chapman, Graham P. A Structural Analysis of Two Farms in Bangladesh. In *[Farmer, B. H.]*, 1984, pp. 212–49.   [**G: Bangladesh**]

Chowdhury, Tawfiq E. Technological Diffusion in Agriculture: Theories and Evidence. *Bangladesh Devel. Stud.*, September 1984, *12*(3), pp. 75–85.

CIMMYT Economics Staff. The Farming Systems Perspective and Farmer Participation in the Development of Appropriate Technology. In *Eicher, C. K. and Staatz, J. M., eds.*, 1984, pp. 362–77.

Clary, G. M.; Jordan, J. W. and Thompson, C. E. Economics of Purchasing Genetically Superior Beef Bulls. *Southern J. Agr. Econ.*, December 1984, *16*(2), pp. 31–36.

Cordts, W.; Deerberg, K.-H. and Hanf, C.-H. Analysis of the Intrasectoral Income Differences in West German Agriculture. *Europ. Rev. Agr. Econ.*, 1984, *11*(3), pp. 323–42.
[**G: W. Germany**]

Dawson, P. J. An Economic View of the Debate on Farm Size in Saskatchewan. *Can. J. Agr. Econ.*, November 1984, *32*(3), pp. 480–82.
[**G: Canada**]

Dawson, P. J. Family Labour Supply: Some Empirical Results from Agriculture. *Appl. Econ.*, December 1984, *16*(6), pp. 895–904.
[**G: U.K.**]

Dewey, Peter E. British Farming Profits and Government Policy during the First World War. *Econ. Hist. Rev., 2nd Ser.*, August 1984, *37*(3), pp. 373–90.   [**G: U.K.**]

Disney, Richard and Elbashir, A. A. Mechanisation, Employment, and Productivity in Sudanese Agriculture. *J. Devel. Econ.*, December 1984, *16*(3), pp. 249–62.   [**G: Sudan**]

Dixon, Bruce L.; Batte, Marvin T. and Sonka, Steven T. Random Coefficients Estimation of Average Total Product Costs for Multiproduct Firms. *J. Bus. Econ. Statist.*, October 1984, *2*(4), pp. 360–66.   [**G: U.S.**]

Eckstein, Zvi. A Rational Expectations Model of Agricultural Supply. *J. Polit. Econ.*, February 1984, *92*(1), pp. 1–19.   [**G: Egypt**]

Ellman, Michael. Agricultural Productivity under Socialism. In *Ellman, M.*, 1984, *1981*, pp. 198–214.   [**G: China; U.S.S.R.**]

Ellman, Michael. Fifty Years of Collectivised Soviet Agriculture, 1929–79. In *Ellman, M.*, 1984, pp. 58–71.   [**G: U.S.S.R.**]

Elterich, G. Joachim. Seasonality of Farm Labor Use Patterns in the United States: Discussion. In *Emerson, R. D., ed.*, 1984, pp. 96–103.
[**G: U.S.**]

Faminow, M. D. and Benson, Bruce L. Rent Seeking and Supply Management in Canadian Agriculture. *Can. J. Agr. Econ.*, November 1984, *32*(3), pp. 548–58.   [**G: Canada**]

Farnsworth, Richard L. and Moffitt, L. Joe. Farmers' Perceptions and Information Sources: A Quantitative Analysis. *Agr. Econ. Res.*, January 1984, *36*(1), pp. 8–11.   [**G: U.S.**]

Feder, Gershon and Slade, Roger. The Acquisition of Information and the Adoption of New Technology. *Amer. J. Agr. Econ.*, August 1984, *66*(3), pp. 312–20.   [**G: India**]

Fritsch, Conrad F. Seasonality of Farm Labor Use Patterns in the United States. In *Emerson, R. D., ed.*, 1984, pp. 64–95.   [**G: U.S.**]

Garcia, Philip and Sonka, Steven T. Farm Size, Tenure, and Economic Efficiency in a Sample of Illinois Grain Farms: Reply. *Amer. J. Agr. Econ.*, November 1984, *66*(4), pp. 517–19.
[**G: U.S.**]

Gliessman, Stephen R. Resource Management in Traditional Tropical Agroecosystems in Southeast Mexico. In *Douglass, G. K., ed.*, 1984, pp. 191–201. [G: Mexico]

Glover, Terry. An Intertemporal Approach to Seasonal Agricultural Labor Markets: Discussion. In *Emerson, R. D., ed.*, 1984, pp. 249–53.

Goodell, Grace E. Bugs, Bunds, Banks, and Bottlenecks: Organizational Contradictions in the New Rice Technology. *Econ. Develop. Cult. Change*, October 1984, 33(1), pp. 23–41. [G: S.E. Asia]

Gordon, D. V.; Haufe, W. O. and Klein, K. K. Determination of Economic Thresholds for Horn Fly Control in Western Canada: A Farm Level Simulation Approach. *Can. J. Agr. Econ.*, July 1984, 32(2), pp. 399–421.

Gunter, Lewell and Smathers, Webb M., Jr. Financial Analysis of Solar Energy Applications with Endogenous System Sizing. *Southern J. Agr. Econ.*, December 1984, 16(2), pp. 21–29. [G: U.S.]

Hanson, Gregory D. Opportunities in Farm Management: Discussion/Challenge. *Southern J. Agr. Econ.*, July 1984, 16(1), pp. 71–76. [G: U.S.]

Hanson, Gregory D.; Martin, Neil R., Jr. and Flynn, John B. Production, Price and Risk Factors in Channel Catfish Farming. *Southern J. Agr. Econ.*, July 1984, 16(1), pp. 173–82. [G: U.S.]

Ho, Thomas S. Y. Intertemporal Commodity Futures Hedging and the Production Decision. *J. Finance*, June 1984, 39(2), pp. 351–76.

Hogan, Andrew J. and Audrey, Robert T. Compulsory Insurance and Allocative Efficiency in Agriculture. *J. Risk Ins.*, June 1984, 51(2), pp. 342–48.

Holland, David M. Energy and Agriculture: Conflicts and Potentials for Structural Reform. In *Geisler, C. C. and Popper, F. J., eds.*, 1984, pp. 88–97. [G: U.S.]

Holt, James S. Introduction to the Seasonal Farm Labor Problem. In *Emerson, R. D., ed.*, 1984, pp. 3–32. [G: U.S.]

Huang, Cliff J. Estimation of Stochastic Frontier Production Function and Technical Inefficiency via the EM Algorithm. *Southern Econ. J.*, January 1984, 50(3), pp. 847–56. [G: India]

Huang, Cliff J. and Bagi, Faqir Singh. Technical Efficiency on Individual Farms in Northwest India. *Southern Econ. J.*, July 1984, 51(1), pp. 108–15. [G: India]

Huffman, Wallace E. Some Analytical Approaches for Human Resource Issues of Seasonal Farm Labor. In *Emerson, R. D., ed.*, 1984, pp. 33–63. [G: U.S.]

Hurst, Christopher. A Model of an Indian Village: A Study of Alternative Sources of Energy for Irrigation. *World Devel.*, February 1984, 12(2), pp. 141–56. [G: India]

Jamison, Dean T. and Moock, Peter R. Farmer Education and Farm Efficiency in Nepal: The Role of Schooling, Extension Services, and Cognitive Skills. *World Devel.*, January 1984, 12(1), pp. 67–86. [G: Nepal]

Jensen, Ken. An Economic View of the Debate on Farm Size in Saskatchewan. *Can. J. Agr. Econ.*, March 1984, 32(1), pp. 187–200. [G: Canada]

Johnson, Sam H., III. Temporal Land Resource Concerns and Farming Systems Research: Chiang Mai Valley, Northern Thailand. *Land Econ.*, May 1984, 60(2), pp. 202–10. [G: Thailand]

Kalirajan, K. P. Farm-specific Technical Efficiencies and Development Policies. *J. Econ. Stud.*, 1984, 11(3), pp. 3–13. [G: Philippines]

Kalirajan, K. P. and Shand, R. T. Schooling, Non-formal Education and Productivity. *Indian Econ. J.*, April–June 1984, 31(4), pp. 35–44. [G: India]

Karp, Larry and Pope, C. Arden, III. Range Management under Uncertainty. *Amer. J. Agr. Econ.*, November 1984, 66(4), pp. 437–46. [G: U.S.]

Kertesi, Gábor and Sziráczki, György. The Second Economy and Workers' Behaviour on the Labour Market in Hungary. *Econ. Lavoro*, Jan.-Mar. 1984, 18(1), pp. 119–27. [G: Hungary]

Keuning, Steven J. Farm Size, Land Use and Profitability of Food Crops in Indonesia. *Bull. Indonesian Econ. Stud.*, April 1984, 20(1), pp. 58–82. [G: Indonesia]

Kiker, Clyde and Bauman, Eric. Producer Gas Fueled Irrigation: Evaluating the Potential of Technology. *Southern J. Agr. Econ.*, December 1984, 16(2), pp. 127–34. [G: U.S.]

Kilmer, Richard L. and Armbruster, Walter J. Methods for Evaluating Economic Efficiency in Agricultural Marketing. *Southern J. Agr. Econ.*, July 1984, 16(1), pp. 101–09.

Kiyokawa, Yukihiko. The Diffusion of New Technologies in the Japanese Sericulture Industry: The Case of the Hybrid Silkworm. *Hitotsubashi J. Econ.*, June 1984, 25(1), pp. 31–59. [G: Japan]

Lang, Rikard and Nikić, Gorazd. Dispersion of Industrial Activities into Rural Areas and Employment. In *Amin, S., ed.*, 1984, pp. 265–72. [G: Yugoslavia]

Lazarus, William F. and Dixon, Bruce L. Agricultural Pests as Common Property: Control of the Corn Rootworm. *Amer. J. Agr. Econ.*, November 1984, 66(4), pp. 456–65. [G: U.S.]

Levins, Richard. The Significance of the Variability of Agricultural Parameters. *Écon. Appl.*, 1984, 37(2), pp. 377–92.

Lockeretz, William. Energy and the Sustainability of the American Agricultural System. In *Douglass, G. K., ed.*, 1984, pp. 77–88.

Lopez, Ramon E. Estimating Labor Supply and Production Decisions of Self-Employed Farm Producers. *Europ. Econ. Rev.*, February 1984, 24(1), pp. 61–82. [G: Canada]

Love, Ross O. and Robison, Lindon J. An Empirical Analysis of the Intertemporal Stability of Risk Preference. *Southern J. Agr. Econ.*, July 1984, 16(1), pp. 159–65. [G: U.S.]

Lynne, Gary D.; Boggess, William G. and Portier, Kenneth M. Irrigation Water Supply as a Bioeconomic Process. *Southern J. Agr. Econ.*, December 1984, *16*(2), pp. 73–82. **[G: U.S.]**

Marcus, Alan J. and Modest, David M. Futures Markets and Production Decisions. *J. Polit. Econ.*, June 1984, *92*(3), pp. 409–26. **[G: U.S.]**

McCarl, Bruce A. Model Validation: An Overview with Some Emphasis on Risk Models. *Rev. Marketing Agr. Econ.*, December 1984, *52*(3), pp. 153–73.

McCloskey, Donald N. and Nash, John. Corn at Interest: The Extent and Cost of Grain Storage in Medieval England. *Amer. Econ. Rev.*, March 1984, *74*(1), pp. 174–87. **[G: U.K.]**

Meyer, Richard L. and Alicbusan, Adelaida P. Farm-Household Heterogeneity and Rural Financial Markets: Insights from Thailand. In *Adams, D. W.; Graham, D. H. and Von Pischke, J. D., eds.*, 1984, pp. 22–35. **[G: Thailand]**

Miranowski, John A. Impacts of Productivity Loss on Crop Production and Management in a Dynamic Economic Model. *Amer. J. Agr. Econ.*, February 1984, *66*(1), pp. 61–71. **[G: U.S.]**

Moffitt, L. Joe; Hall, Darwin C. and Osteen, Craig D. Economic Thresholds under Uncertainty with Application to Corn Nematode Management. *Southern J. Agr. Econ.*, December 1984, *16*(2), pp. 151–57.

Narayana, N. S. S. and Shah, M. M. Farm Supply Response in Kenya: Acreage Allocation Model. *Europ. Rev. Agr. Econ.*, 1984, *11*(1), pp. 85–105. **[G: Kenya]**

Pope, C. Arden, III and Shumway, C. Richard. Management of Intensive Forage-Beef Production under Yield Uncertainty. *Southern J. Agr. Econ.*, December 1984, *16*(2), pp. 37–43. **[G: U.S.]**

Pope, Rulon D. and Ziemer, Rod F. Stochastic Efficiency, Normality, and Sampling Errors in Agricultural Risk Analysis. *Amer. J. Agr. Econ.*, February 1984, *66*(1), pp. 31–40.

Quibria, M. G. and Rashid, Salim. The Puzzle of Sharecropping: A Survey of Theories. *World Devel.*, February 1984, *12*(2), pp. 103–14.

Rahm, Michael R. and Huffman, Wallace E. The Adoption of Reduced Tillage: The Role of Human Capital and Other Variables. *Amer. J. Agr. Econ.*, November 1984, *66*(4), pp. 405–13. **[G: U.S.]**

Rister, M. Edward; Skees, Jerry R. and Black, J. Roy. Evaluating Use of Outlook Information in Grain Sorghum Storage Decisions. *Southern J. Agr. Econ.*, July 1984, *16*(1), pp. 151–58. **[G: U.S.]**

Roumasset, James. Explaining Patterns in Landowner Shares: Rice, Corn, Coconut, and Abaca in the Philippines. In *Binswanger, H. P. and Rosenzweig, R., eds.*, 1984, pp. 82–95. **[G: Philippines]**

Rudra, Ashok. Local Power and Farm-Level Decision-Making. In *Desai, M.; Rudolph, S. H. and Rudra, A., eds.*, 1984, pp. 250–80. **[G: India]**

Samarasinghe, Vidyamali and Samarasinghe, S. W. R. de A. Income and Wealth Disparities

in a Land Settlement of the Sri Lanka Dry Zone. In *[Farmer, B. H.]*, 1984, pp. 173–93. **[G: Sri Lanka]**

Senanayake, Ranil. The Ecological, Energetic, and Agronomic Systems of Ancient and Modern Sri Lanka. In *Douglass, G. K., ed.*, 1984, pp. 227–37. **[G: Sri Lanka]**

Shaw, Anthony B. Impact of New Technology on the Guyanese Rice Industry: Efficiency and Equity Considerations. *J. Devel. Areas*, January 1984, *18*(2), pp. 191–217. **[G: Guyana]**

Shmelev, G. and Steksov, Iu. Personal Household Plots under Conditions of Interfarm and Agroindustrial Integration. *Prob. Econ.*, January 1984, *26*(9), pp. 81–92. **[G: U.S.S.R.]**

Shumway, C. Richard; Pope, Rulon D. and Nash, Elizabeth K. Allocatable Fixed Inputs and Jointness in Agricultural Production: Implications for Economic Modeling. *Amer. J. Agr. Econ.*, February 1984, *66*(1), pp. 72–78.

Sporleder, Thomas L. Policy Considerations of Emerging Information Technologies. *Southern J. Agr. Econ.*, July 1984, *16*(1), pp. 15–21.

Spreen, Thomas H. An Intertemporal Approach to Seasonal Agricultural Labor Markets. In *Emerson, R. D., ed.*, 1984, pp. 230–49.

Spreen, Thomas H. and Arnade, Carlos A. Use of Forecasts in Decisionmaking: The Case of Stocker Cattle in Florida. *Southern J. Agr. Econ.*, July 1984, *16*(1), pp. 145–50. **[G: U.S.]**

Steuerle, Eugene. Realized Income and Wealth for Owners of Closely Held Farms and Businesses: A Comparison. *Public Finance Quart.*, October 1984, *12*(4), pp. 407–24. **[G: U.S.]**

Stonehouse, D. Peter and Narayanan, A. V. S. The Contributions of Livestock Manure to Profitability and to Self-Sufficiency in Plant Nutrients on Mixed Farms. *Can. J. Agr. Econ.*, March 1984, *32*(1), pp. 201–10. **[G: Canada]**

Stonehouse, D. Peter, et al. Economics of an Integrated Manurial Biogas and Protein Recovery System for Beef Cattle. *Can. J. Agr. Econ.*, November 1984, *32*(3), pp. 478–97. **[G: Canada]**

Strasser, Rudolf. The Austrian Experience of Social and Economic Cooperation: Comment. In *Cavaco Silva, A. A., ed.*, 1984, pp. 109–12. **[G: Austria]**

Strauss, John. Marketed Surpluses of Agricultural Households in Sierra Leone. *Amer. J. Agr. Econ.*, August 1984, *66*(3), pp. 321–31. **[G: Sierra Leone]**

Sullivan, Richard J. Measurement of English Farming Technological Change, 1523–1900. *Exploration Econ. Hist.*, July 1984, *21*(3), pp. 270–89. **[G: U.K.]**

Sumner, Daniel A. Labor Supply Uncertainty and Technology Adoption: Discussion. In *Emerson, R. D., ed.*, 1984, pp. 224–29.

Surry, Yves and Moschini, Giancarlo. Input Substitutability in the EC Compound Feed Industry. *Europ. Rev. Agr. Econ.*, 1984, *11*(4), pp. 455–64. **[G: Belgium; Netherlands]**

Swanson, Earl R. and Heady, Earl O. Soil Erosion in the United States. In *Simon, J. L. and Kahn, H., eds.*, 1984, pp. 202–23. [G: U.S.]

Taylor, C. Robert and Burt, Oscar R. Near-Optimal Management Strategies for Controlling Wild Oats in Spring Wheat. *Amer. J. Agr. Econ.*, February 1984, *66*(1), pp. 50–60.
[G: U.S.]

Teague, Paul W. Farm Size, Tenure, and Economic Efficiency in a Sample of Illinois Grain Farms: Comment. *Amer. J. Agr. Econ.*, November 1984, *66*(4), pp. 515–16. [G: U.S.]

Tew, Bernard V. and Boggess, William G. Risk–Return Assessment of Irrigation Decisions in Humid Regions: An Extension. *Southern J. Agr. Econ.*, December 1984, *16*(2), pp. 159–60.

Waugh, Frederick V. Cobweb Models. In *Waugh, F. V.*, 1984, *1964*, pp. 88–106.

Waugh, Frederick V. Factor Analysis: Some Basic Principles and an Application. In *Waugh, F. V.*, 1984, *1962*, pp. 349–52. [G: U.S.]

Wozniak, Gregory D. The Adoption of Interrelated Innovations: A Human Capital Approach. *Rev. Econ. Statist.*, February 1984, *66*(1), pp. 70–79. [G: U.S.]

Wright, Brian D. and Williams, Jeffrey C. Antihoarding Laws: A Stock Condemnation Reconsidered. *Amer. J. Agr. Econ.*, November 1984, *66*(4), pp. 447–55.

Wyatts, Myles J.; Held, Larry J. and Helmers, Glenn A. A Comparison of Target MOTAD to MOTAD. *Can. J. Agr. Econ.*, March 1984, *32*(1), pp. 175–86. [G: U.S.]

Young, C. Edwin and Shortle, James S. Investments in Soil Conservation Structures: The Role of Operator and Operation Characteristics. *Agr. Econ. Res.*, Spring 1984, *36*(2), pp. 10–15. [G: U.S.]

Zentner, R. P., et al. An Economic Evaluation of Crop Rotations in Southwestern Saskatchewan. *Can. J. Agr. Econ.*, March 1984, *32*(1), pp. 37–54. [G: Canada]

Zilberman, David and Just, Richard E. Labor Supply Uncertainty and Technology Adoption. In *Emerson, R. D., ed.*, 1984, pp. 200–24.

717 Land Reform and Land Use

7170 General

Alam, Mahmudul. Level and Composition of Capital in Irrigated Agriculture of Bangladesh: Evidence from Tubewell Irrigated Villages of Comilla and Rajshahi. *Bangladesh Devel. Stud.*, December 1984, *12*(4), pp. 59–106.
[G: Bangladesh]

Bjork, Gordon C. Ownership and Outcome: An Economic Analysis of the Privatization of Land Tenure on Forest and Rangeland. In *Brubaker, S., ed.*, 1984, pp. 181–92. [G: U.S.]

Bradnock, Robert W. Agricultural Development in Tamil Nadu: Two Decades of Land Use Change at Village Level. In *[Farmer, B. H.]*, 1984, pp. 136–52. [G: India]

Brown, David L.; Heaton, Tim B. and Huffman, Benjamin L. Sociodemographic Pressures on Farmland Value in Nonmetropolitan America. *Soc. Sci. Quart.*, September 1984, *65*(3), pp. 789–802. [G: U.S.]

Brubaker, Sterling. Issues and Summary of Federal Land Tenure. In *Brubaker, S., ed.*, 1984, pp. 1–31. [G: U.S.]

Cavaco, Carminda. A pequena horticultura doméstica de nao agricultores das periferias urbanas: o caso de Lisboa. (With English summary.) *Economia (Portugal)*, May 1984, *8*(2), pp. 395–423. [G: Portugal]

Cirillo, Renato. Economists and Social Reformers on Land Ownership and Economic Rents. *Rivista Int. Sci. Econ. Com.*, March 1984, *31*(3), pp. 241–56.

Clawson, Marion. Major Alternatives for Future Management of the Federal Lands. In *Brubaker, S., ed.*, 1984, pp. 195–234. [G: U.S.]

Gardner, B. Delworth. The Case for Divestiture. In *Brubaker, S., ed.*, 1984, pp. 156–80.
[G: U.S.]

Hart, John. Land Reform and the Church. In *Geisler, C. C. and Popper, F. J., eds.*, 1984, pp. 73–87. [G: U.S.]

Keuning, Steven J. Farm Size, Land Use and Profitability of Food Crops in Indonesia. *Bull. Indonesian Econ. Stud.*, April 1984, *20*(1), pp. 58–82. [G: Indonesia]

Leshy, John D. Sharing Federal Multiple-Use Lands: Historic Lessons and Speculations for the Future. In *Brubaker, S., ed.*, 1984, pp. 235–73. [G: U.S.]

Menra, Naresh Kumar. Dualism and Surplus Labour: A Case Study of Indian Agriculture. *Margin*, October 1984, *17*(1), pp. 48–54.
[G: India]

Milon, J. Walter; Gressel, Jonathan and Mulkey, David. Hedonic Amenity Valuation and Functional Form Specification. *Land Econ.*, November 1984, *60*(4), pp. 378–87. [G: U.S.]

Nelson, Robert H. Ideology and Public Land Policy: The Current Crisis. In *Brubaker, S., ed.*, 1984, pp. 275–98. [G: U.S.]

Phipps, Tim T. Land Prices and Farm-based Returns. *Amer. J. Agr. Econ.*, November 1984, *66*(4), pp. 422–29. [G: U.S.]

Sax, Joseph L. The Claim for Retention of the Public Lands. In *Brubaker, S., ed.*, 1984, pp. 125–48. [G: U.S.]

Stroup, Richard L. Weaknesses in the Case for Retention. In *Brubaker, S., ed.*, 1984, pp. 149–55. [G: U.S.]

7171 Land Ownership and Tenure; Land Reform

Ahmad, Nigar. Changes in Agrarian Relations in Pakistan: A Study of Five Villages. In *Ngo, M., ed., vol. 2*, 1984, pp. 640–65.
[G: Pakistan]

Ahmed, Feroz. Transformation of Agrarian Structures in Pakistan: The Punjab: A Preliminary Analysis. In *Ngo, M., ed., vol. 2*, 1984, pp. 606–39. [G: Pakistan]

Akerlof, George A. The Economics of Caste and of the Rat Race and Other Woeful Tales. In *Akerlof, G. A.*, 1984, *1976*, pp. 23–44.

Allen, Franklin. Mixed Wage and Rent Contracts as Reinterpretations of Share Contracts. *J. Devel. Econ.*, December 1984, *16*(3), pp. 313–17.

Alston, Lee J.; Datta, Samar K. and Nugent, Jeffrey B. Tenancy Choice in a Competitive Framework with Transactions Costs. *J. Polit. Econ.*, December 1984, *92*(6), pp. 1121–33. **[G: U.S.]**

Apland, Jeffrey; Barnes, Robert N. and Justus, Fred. The Farm Lease: An Analysis of Owner–Tenant and Landlord Preferences under Risk. *Amer. J. Agr. Econ.*, August 1984, *66*(3), pp. 376–84. **[G: U.S.]**

Aziz, Sartaj. Rural Development—Some Essential Prerequisites. *Int. Lab. Rev.*, May–June 1984, *123*(3), pp. 277–85. **[G: LDCs]**

Barrett, Richard E. Share Tenancy and Fixed Rent in Taiwan. *Econ. Develop. Cult. Change*, January 1984, *32*(2), pp. 413–22.
[G: Taiwan]

Basu, Arati. Production Systems and Productivity of Labour: An Analysis on the Existence of Surplus Labour. *Indian Econ. Rev.*, July-Dec. 1984, *19*(2), pp. 185–201.

Baumeister, Eduardo. Estructura y reforma agraria en el proceso sandinista. (With English summary.) *Desarrollo Econ.*, July–September 1984, *24*(94), pp. 187–202. **[G: Nicaragua]**

Beckett, J. V. The Pattern of Landownership in England and Wales, 1660–1880. *Econ. Hist. Rev.*, *2nd Ser.*, February 1984, *37*(1), pp. 1–22. **[G: U.K.]**

Binswanger, Hans P. and Rosenzweig, Mark R. Contractual Arrangements, Employment, and Wages in Rural Labor Markets: A Critical Review. In *Binswanger, H. P. and Rosenzweig, R., eds.*, 1984, pp. 1–40.

Bose, Arun. Agrarian Reform, International Trade and Development. In *Ngo, M., ed., vol. 2*, 1984, pp. 765–84.

Brannon, Jeffery T. and Baklanoff, Eric N. The Political Economy of Agrarian Reform in Yucatán, Mexico. *World Devel.*, November–December 1984, *12*(11–12), pp. 1131–41.
[G: Mexico]

Braverman, Avishay and Guasch, J. Luis. Capital Requirements, Screening and Interlinked Sharecropping and Credit Contracts. *J. Devel. Econ.*, April 1984, *14*(3), pp. 359–74.

Braverman, Avishay and Srinivasan, T. N. Agrarian Reforms in Developing Rural Economies Characterized by Interlinked Credit and Tenancy Markets. In *Binswanger, H. P. and Rosenzweig, R., eds.*, 1984, pp. 63–81.

Bromley, Daniel W. The Role of Land Reform in Economic Development: Comment. In *Eicher, C. K. and Staatz, J. M., eds.*, 1984, *1981*, pp. 275–77.

Brown, Keith C. and Brown, Deborah J. Heterogenous Expectations and Farmland Prices. *Amer. J. Agr. Econ.*, May 1984, *66*(2), pp. 164–69. **[G: U.S.]**

Buttel, Frederick H. Agricultural Land Reform in America. In *Geisler, C. C. and Popper, F. J., eds.*, 1984, pp. 55–72. **[G: U.S.]**

Carter, Michael R. Resource Allocation and Use under Collective Rights and Labour Management in Peruvian Coastal Agriculture. *Econ. J.*, December 1984, *94*(376), pp. 826–46.
[G: Peru]

Chakravarty, Sukhamoy. Power Structure and Agricultural Productivity. In *Desai, M.; Rudolph, S. H. and Rudra, A., eds.*, 1984, pp. 345–73.

Chapman, John. The Chronology of English Enclosure. *Econ. Hist. Rev.*, *2nd Ser.*, November 1984, *37*(4), pp. 557–59. **[G: U.K.]**

Colburn, Forrest D. Class, State, and Revolution in Rural Nicaragua: The Case of *Los Cafetaleros*. *J. Devel. Areas*, July 1984, *18*(4), pp. 501–18. **[G: Nicaragua]**

Cooley, Richard A. Evolution of Alaska Land Policy. In *Morehouse, T. A., ed.*, 1984, pp. 13–49. **[G: U.S.]**

Corbridge, Stuart. Agrarian Policy and Agrarian Change in Tribal India. In *[Farmer, B. H.]*, 1984, pp. 87–108. **[G: India]**

Crist, Raymond E. Development and Agrarian Land Reform in Venezuela's Pioneer Zone: Social Progress along the Llano-Andes Border in a Half Century of Political Advance. *Amer. J. Econ. Soc.*, April 1984, *43*(2), pp. 149–58.
[G: Venezuela]

Davis, John Emmeus. Reallocating Equity: A Land Trust Model of Land Reform. In *Geisler, C. C. and Popper, F. J., eds.*, 1984, pp. 209–32. **[G: U.S.]**

Desai, Meghnad. Power and Agrarian Relations: Some Concepts and Measurements. In *Desai, M.; Rudolph, S. H. and Rudra, A., eds.*, 1984, pp. 171–97.

Fenoaltea, Stefano. Slavery and Supervision in Comparative Perspective: A Model. *J. Econ. Hist.*, September 1984, *44*(3), pp. 635–68.
[G: U.S.; U.K.; Italy; Latin America]

Gaventa, John and Horton, Bill. Land Ownership and Land Reform in Appalachia. In *Geisler, C. C. and Popper, F. J., eds.*, 1984, pp. 233–44. **[G: U.S.]**

Geisler, Charles C. and Popper, Frank J. Land Reform, American Style: Introduction. In *Geisler, C. C. and Popper, F. J., eds.*, 1984, pp. 3–6. **[G: U.S.]**

Ghai, Dharam P. Income Distribution and Labour Utilisation under Different Agrarian Systems. In *Amin, S., ed.*, 1984, pp. 116–43.
[G: Asia; Tanzania]

Giertz, J. Fred and Chicoine, David L. Tax Valuation of Farm Land: Non-Neutrality with Respect to Inflation. *Nat. Tax J.*, June 1984, *37*(2), pp. 253–58. **[G: U.S.]**

Graaff, Jan. Economic Theory and the Economy of Palanpur: A Review Article. *Oxford Econ. Pap.*, November 1984, *36*(3), pp. 327–35.
[G: India]

Hane Ba, Fama, et al. The Impact of Territorial Administration Reform on the Situation of Women in Senegal. In *Intn'l. Lab. Office*, 1984, pp. 107–15. **[G: Senegal]**

Hayami, Yujiro and Ruttan, Vernon W. The Green Revolution: Inducement and Distribution. *Pakistan Devel. Rev.*, Spring 1984, *23*(1), pp. 37–63. [G: Asia]

Ike, Don N. The System of Land Rights in Nigerian Agriculture. *Amer. J. Econ. Soc.*, October 1984, *43*(4), pp. 469–80. [G: Nigeria]

Islam, Iyanatul. Socio-economic Progress in Indonesia under the New Order. In *Thambipillai, P., ed.*, 1984, pp. 137–50. [G: Indonesia]

James, William and Roumasset, James. Migration and the Evolution of Tenure Contracts in Newly Settled Regions. *J. Devel. Econ.*, January–February 1984, *14*(1–2), pp. 147–62. [G: Philippines]

de Janvry, Alain. The Role of Land Reform in Economic Development: Policies and Politics. In *Eicher, C. K. and Staatz, J. M., eds.*, 1984, *1981*, pp. 263–74.

Jaynes, Gerald David. Economic Theory and Land Tenure. In *Binswanger, H. P. and Rosenzweig, R., eds.*, 1984, pp. 43–62.

Jodha, N. S. Agricultural Tenancy in Semiarid Tropical India. In *Binswanger, H. P. and Rosenzweig, R., eds.*, 1984, pp. 96–113. [G: India]

Jonsson, Ulf. Population Growth and Agrarian Economic and Social Structure: Some Swedish Examples. In *Bengtsson, T.; Fridlizius, G. and Ohlsson, R., eds.*, 1984, pp. 223–34. [G: Sweden]

Joshi, P. C. Land Reforms and the Indian Elite: Problems and Dilemmas of Land Reforms in the Second Stage. In *Singh, A. K.; Papola, T. S. and Mathur, R. S., eds.*, 1984, pp. 165–88. [G: India]

Kozub, Robert M. and Trebby, James P. Special Valuation of Farmland and Closely Held Business Realty for Estate Tax Purposes. *Growth Change*, July 1984, *15*(3), pp. 25–29. [G: U.S.]

Laband, David N. Restriction of Farm Ownership as Rent-Seeking Behavior: Family Farmers Have It Their Way. *Amer. J. Econ. Soc.*, April 1984, *43*(2), pp. 179–89. [G: U.S.]

Lapping, Mark B. and Forster, V. Dale. From Insurgency to Policy: Land Reform in Prince Edward Island. In *Geisler, C. C. and Popper, F. J., eds.*, 1984, pp. 245–70. [G: Canada]

Lee, W. Robert. Mortality Levels and Agrarian Reform in Early 19th Century Prussia: Some Regional Evidence. In *Bengtsson, T.; Fridlizius, G. and Ohlsson, R., eds.*, 1984, pp. 161–90. [G: Germany]

Léons, Madeline Barbara. Political Pentration and Conflict Resolution in the Bolivian Yungas. *J. Devel. Areas*, July 1984, *18*(4), pp. 465–80. [G: Bolivia]

Liden, David. Pulling the Pillars: Energy Development and Land Reform in Appalachia. In *Geisler, C. C. and Popper, F. J., eds.*, 1984, pp. 101–16. [G: U.S.]

Lloyd, P. J. Mining Rights as a Component of Aboriginal Land Rights: An Economic Assessment. In *Lloyd, P. J., ed.*, 1984, pp. 138–56. [G: Australia]

Ludden, David. Productive Power in Agriculture: A Survey of Work on the Local History of Brit-

ish India. In *Desai, M.; Rudolph, S. H. and Rudra, A., eds.*, 1984, pp. 51–99. [G: India]

Lux, Guillermo. Ancient Aspirations: A Mexican-American View of Land Reform. In *Geisler, C. C. and Popper, F. J., eds.*, 1984, pp. 188–205. [G: U.S.]

Mantelli, Roberto. The Sale of Crown Lands in Spain in the Early Modern Era: Review Article. *J. Europ. Econ. Hist.*, Spring 1984, *13*(1), pp. 201–05. [G: Spain]

Matoušek, Jiří. The Agrarian Policy of the Communist Party of Czechoslovakia and Thirty-Five Years of the Development of Socialism in the Countryside. *Czech. Econ. Digest.*, November 1984, (7), pp. 29–55. [G: Czechoslovakia]

McDougall, Harold A. Land Reform and the Struggle for Black Liberation: From Reconstruction to Remote Claims. In *Geisler, C. C. and Popper, F. J., eds.*, 1984, pp. 172–87. [G: U.S.]

Mencinger, Jože. The Limit on Landholdings. *Eastern Europ. Econ.*, Winter 1984–85, *23*(2), pp. 29–42. [G: Yugoslavia]

Nicholson, Norman K. Landholding, Agricultural Modernization, and Local Institutions in India. *Econ. Develop. Cult. Change*, April 1984, *32*(3), pp. 569–92. [G: India]

Olwig, Karen Fog. 'Witnesses in Spite of Themselves': Reconstructing Afro-Caribbean Culture in the Danish W. Indian Archives. *Scand. Econ. Hist. Rev.*, 1984, *32*(2), pp. 61–76. [G: Danish W. Indies; Caribbean]

Ortiz, Roxanne Dunbar. Land Reform and Indian Survival in the United States. In *Geisler, C. C. and Popper, F. J., eds.*, 1984, pp. 151–71. [G: U.S.]

Popper, Frank J. The Ambiguous End of the Sagebrush Rebellion. In *Geisler, C. C. and Popper, F. J., eds.*, 1984, pp. 117–28. [G: U.S.]

Quibria, M. G. and Rashid, Salim. The Puzzle of Sharecropping: A Survey of Theories. *World Devel.*, February 1984, *12*(2), pp. 103–14.

Roumasset, James. Explaining Patterns in Landowner Shares: Rice, Corn, Coconut, and Abaca in the Philippines. In *Binswanger, H. P. and Rosenzweig, R., eds.*, 1984, pp. 82–95. [G: Philippines]

Rudolph, Lloyd I. and Rudolph, Susanne Hoeber. Determinants and Varieties of Agrarian Mobilization. In *Desai, M.; Rudolph, S. H. and Rudra, A., eds.*, 1984, pp. 281–344. [G: India]

Shanmugaratnam, N. Emerging Agrarian Trends in Sri Lanka. In *Ngo, M., ed., vol. 2*, 1984, pp. 666–87. [G: Sri Lanka]

Shaw, Anthony B. Impact of New Technology on the Guyanese Rice Industry: Efficiency and Equity Considerations. *J. Devel. Areas*, January 1984, *18*(2), pp. 191–217. [G: Guyana]

Silagi, Michael. Land Reform in Kiaochow, China: From 1898 to 1914 the Menace of Disastrous Land Speculation Was Averted by Taxation. *Amer. J. Econ. Soc.*, April 1984, *43*(2), pp. 167–78. [G: China]

Skold, Melvin D.; Atty El Shinnawi, Shinnawi Abdel and Nasr, M. Lofty. Irrigation Water Distribution along Branch Canals in Egypt: Economic Effects. *Econ. Develop. Cult. Change*, April 1984, *32*(3), pp. 547–67.
[G: Egypt]

Smith, Clifford T. Land Reform as a Pre-condition for Green Revolution in Latin America. In *[Farmer, B. H.]*, 1984, pp. 18–36.
[G: Latin America]

Stokes, C. Shannon and Schutjer, Wayne A. Access to Land and Fertility in Developing Countries. In *Schutjer, W. A. and Stokes, C. S.*, *eds.*, 1984, pp. 195–215. [G: LDCs]

Sturgess, N. H.; Wijaya, Hesti and Dow, N. Usufruct and Usury: An Analysis of Land Leasing in East Java. *Australian J. Agr. Econ.*, April 1984, *28*(1), pp. 15–32. [G: Indonesia]

Taylor, Elizabeth. Peasants or Proletarians? The Transformation of Agrarian Production Relations in Egypt. In *Munslow, B. and Finch, H.*, *eds.*, 1984, pp. 164–88. [G: Egypt]

Toumanoff, Peter G. Some Effects of Land Tenure Reforms on Russian Agricultural Productivity, 1901–1913. *Econ. Develop. Cult. Change*, July 1984, *32*(4), pp. 861–72. [G: U.S.S.R.]

Wiest, Raymond E. External Dependency and the Perpetuation of Temporary Migration to the United States. In *Jones, R. C.*, *ed.*, 1984, pp. 110–35. [G: U.S.; Mexico]

Witney, K. P. The Economic Position of Husbandmen at the time of Domesday Book: A Kentish Perspective. *Econ. Hist. Rev.*, *2nd Ser.*, February 1984, *37*(1), pp. 23–34. [G: U.K.]

Wordie, J. R. The Chronology of English Enclosure: A Reply. *Econ. Hist. Rev.*, *2nd Ser.*, November 1984, *37*(4), pp. 560–62. [G: U.K.]

7172 Land Development; Land Use; Irrigation Policy

Allam, Mohamed N. and Marks, David H. Irrigated Agricultural Expansion Planning in Developing Countries: Income Redistribution Objective. *Water Resources Res.*, July 1984, *20*(7), pp. 767–74.

Allam, Mohamed N. and Marks, David H. Irrigated Agricultural Expansion Planning in Developing Countries: Investment Scheduling Incorporating Drainage Water Reuse. *Water Resources Res.*, July 1984, *20*(7), pp. 757–66.
[G: Egypt]

Allam, Mohamed N. and Marks, David H. Irrigated Agricultural Expansion Planning in Developing Countries: Resilient System Design. *Water Resources Res.*, July 1984, *20*(7), pp. 775–84.

Altieri, Miguel A.; Letourneau, Deborah K. and Davis, James R. The Requirements of Sustainable Agroecosystems. In *Douglass, G. K.*, *ed.*, 1984, pp. 175–89.

Belshaw, Deryke G. R. Planning and Agrarian Change in East Africa: Appropriate and Inappropriate Models for Land Settlement Schemes. In *[Farmer, B. H.]*, 1984, pp. 270–79. [G: E. Africa]

Brown, Gardner M., Jr. and McGuire, C. B. A Socially Optimum Pricing Policy for a Public Water Agency. In *Ahmad, Y. J.; Dasgupta, P. and Mäler, K.-G.*, *eds.*, 1984, pp. 176–97.
[G: U.S.]

Brown, Lester R. World Population Growth, Soil Erosion, and Food Security. In *Douglass, G. K.*, *ed.*, 1984, pp. 31–48.

Carman, Hoy F. An Analysis of Proposition 13 Impacts on California Land Conservation Act Participation. *Land Econ.*, November 1984, *60*(4), pp. 360–66. [G: U.S.]

Chattopadhyay, Manabendu. Transformation of Labour Use in Indian Agriculture. *Cambridge J. Econ.*, September 1984, *8*(3), pp. 289–96.
[G: India]

Davidson, B. R. A Preliminary Benefit Cost Analysis of the Inland Diversion of the Coastal Rivers of New South Wales. *Rev. Marketing Agr. Econ.*, April 1984, *52*(1), pp. 23–47.
[G: Australia]

Dobitz, Clifford P. Energy Substitution in Irrigation. *Reg. Sci. Persp.*, 1984, *14*(1), pp. 25–29.
[G: U.S.]

Dowdle, Barney. Why Have We Retained the Federal Lands? An Alternative Hypothesis. In *Brubaker, S.*, *ed.*, 1984, pp. 61–73.
[G: U.S.]

Duncan, Myrl L. Toward a Theory of Broad-Based Planning for the Preservation of Agricultural Land. *Natural Res. J.*, January 1984, *24*(1), pp. 61–135. [G: U.S.]

Ervin, David E.; Heffernan, William D. and Green, Gary P. Cross-Compliance for Erosion Control: Anticipating Efficiency and Distributive Impacts. *Amer. J. Agr. Econ.*, August 1984, *66*(3), pp. 273–78. [G: U.S.]

Franklin, Douglas R. and Hageman, Ronda K. Cost Sharing with Irrigated Agriculture: Promise versus Performance. *Water Resources Res.*, August 1984, *20*(8), pp. 1047–51. [G: U.S.]

Gardner, Richard L. and Young, Robert A. The Effects of Electricity Rates and Rate Structures on Pump Irrigation: An Eastern Colorado Case Study. *Land Econ.*, November 1984, *60*(4), pp. 352–59. [G: U.S.]

Gates, Paul W. The Federal Lands: Why We Retained Them. In *Brubaker, S.*, *ed.*, 1984, pp. 35–60. [G: U.S.]

Hagenstein, Perry R. The Federal Lands Today: Uses and Limits. In *Brubaker, S.*, *ed.*, 1984, pp. 74–107. [G: U.S.]

Hardie, Ian W. Comparative Rents for Farmland and Timberland in a Subregion of the South. *Southern J. Agr. Econ.*, December 1984, *16*(2), pp. 45–53. [G: U.S.]

Harriss, John C. Social Organisation and Irrigation: Ideology, Planning and Practice in Sri Lanka's Settlement Schemes. In *[Farmer, B. H.]*, 1984, pp. 315–38. [G: Sri Lanka]

Hart, John Fraser. Cropland Change in the United States, 1944–78. In *Simon, J. L. and Kahn, H.*, *eds.*, 1984, pp. 224–49. [G: U.S.]

Harvey, D. Michael. Uses and Limits of the Federal Lands Today: Who Cares and How Should

Current Law Work? In *Brubaker, S., ed.*, 1984, pp. 108–21. **[G: U.S.]**

Hayden, F. Gregory. A Geobased National Agricultural Policy for Rural Community Enhancement, Environmental Vitality, and Income Stabilization. *J. Econ. Issues*, March 1984, *18*(1), pp. 181–221. **[G: U.S.]**

Hossain, Mahabub. Agricultural Development in Bangladesh: A Historical Perspective. *Bangladesh Devel. Stud.*, December 1984, *12*(4), pp. 29–57. **[G: Bangladesh]**

Hurst, Christopher. A Model of an Indian Village: A Study of Alternative Sources of Energy for Irrigation. *World Devel.*, February 1984, *12*(2), pp. 141–56. **[G: India]**

Husain, Tariq. Potential for Irrigated Agricultural Development in Pakistan. In *Burki, S. J. and LaPorte, R., Jr., eds.*, 1984, pp. 45–83. **[G: Pakistan]**

Hyman, Eric L. Land-Use Planning to Help Sustain Tropical Forest Resources. *World Devel.*, August 1984, *12*(8), pp. 837–47. **[G: Global]**

Hyman, Eric L. Providing Public Lands for Smallholder Agroforestry in the Province of Ilocos Norte, Philippines. *J. Devel. Areas*, January 1984, *18*(2), pp. 177–90. **[G: Philippines]**

Ionescu, V. and Berar, U. Simulation and Optimization of Some Hydro-Improvement Processes with the Help of Systems' Medium-State Concept. *Econ. Computat. Cybern. Stud. Res.*, 1984, *19*(2), pp. 85–91.

Jackson, Wes. Toward a Unifying Concept for Agriculture. In *Douglass, G. K., ed.*, 1984, pp. 159–73.

Jayawardena, Kumari. The Plantation Sector in Sri Lanka: Recent Changes in the Welfare of Children and Women. *World Devel.*, March 1984, *12*(3), pp. 317–28. **[G: Sri Lanka]**

Johnson, Sam H., III. Temporal Land Resource Concerns and Farming Systems Research: Chiang Mai Valley, Northern Thailand. *Land Econ.*, May 1984, *60*(2), pp. 202–10. **[G: Thailand]**

Johnson, Sam H., III and Reuss, John O. Economic Results of Simulated Changes in Pakistan's Irrigation System. *Water Resources Res.*, May 1984, *20*(5), pp. 629–32. **[G: Pakistan]**

Kim, Sung-Hoon and Dixon, John A. Economic Valuation of Environmental Quality Aspects of Upland Agricultural Projects in Korea. In *Ahmad, Y. J.; Dasgupta, P. and Mäler, K.-G., eds.*, 1984, pp. 21–37. **[G: S. Korea]**

Knapp, Keith C. Steady-State Solutions to Soil Salinity Optimization Problems. *Amer. J. Agr. Econ.*, August 1984, *66*(3), pp. 279–85. **[G: U.S.]**

Korten, David C. and Carner, George. Reorienting Bureaucracies to Serve People: Two Experiences from the Philippines. *Can. J. Devel. Stud.*, 1984, *5*(1), pp. 7–24.

Larson, W. E. Changes in the Availability of Agricultural Land, the Quality of Soil, and the Sustainability of Agriculture. In *Douglass, G. K., ed.*, 1984, pp. 61–76. **[G: U.S.]**

Lynne, Gary D.; Boggess, William G. and Portier, Kenneth M. Irrigation Water Supply as

a Bioeconomic Process. *Southern J. Agr. Econ.*, December 1984, *16*(2), pp. 73–82. **[G: U.S.]**

Madariaga, Bruce and McConnell, Kenneth E. Value of Irrigation Water in the Middle Atlantic States: An Econometric Approach. *Southern J. Agr. Econ.*, December 1984, *16*(2), pp. 91–98. **[G: U.S.]**

Madduma Bandara, C. M. Green Revolution and Water Demand: Irrigation and Ground Water in Sri Lanka and Tamil Nadu. In *[Farmer, B. H.]*, 1984, pp. 296–314. **[G: Sri Lanka]**

Matoussi, Mohamed Salah. Intégration de l'aléatoire et de l'allocation temporelle dans la planification des ressources hydrauliques "Modèle Anasim." (With English summary.) *Revue Écon. Polit.*, March–April 1984, *94*(2), pp. 226–53. **[G: Tunisia]**

Miranowski, John A. Impacts of Productivity Loss on Crop Production and Management in a Dynamic Economic Model. *Amer. J. Agr. Econ.*, February 1984, *66*(1), pp. 61–71. **[G: U.S.]**

Montgomery, John D. Inferences from Third World Experience: Public Participation and Water Allocation. In *Groth, A. J. and Wade, L. L., eds.*, 1984, pp. 213–36. **[G: LDCs]**

Murshid, Khan Ahmed Sayed. Modernization and Technology in Bangladesh: The Case of Deep Tube-Wells. In *Ngo, M., ed., vol. 2*, 1984, pp. 724–40. **[G: Bangladesh]**

Nosov, S. Improvement in the Utilization of Land. *Prob. Econ.*, October 1984, *27*(6), pp. 87–102. **[G: U.S.S.R.]**

O'Mara, Gerald T. and Duloy, John H. Modeling Efficient Water Allocation in a Conjunctive Use Regime: The Indus Basin of Pakistan. *Water Resources Res.*, November 1984, *20*(11), pp. 1489–98. **[G: Pakistan]**

Revelle, Roger. The World Supply of Agricultural Land. In *Simon, J. L. and Kahn, H., eds.*, 1984, pp. 184–201. **[G: Global]**

Rielley, Kevin J.; Larsen, Wendy U. and Weaver, Clifford L. Partnership in the Pinelands. In *Geisler, C. C. and Popper, F. J., eds.*, 1984, pp. 129–48. **[G: U.S.]**

Rose, Jerome G. Farmland Preservation Policy and Programs. *Natural Res. J.*, July 1984, *24*(3), pp. 591–640. **[G: U.S.]**

Sampath, Rajan K. Income Distribution Impacts of Irrigation Water Distribution Policy. *Water Resources Res.*, June 1984, *20*(6), pp. 647–54.

Sampath, Rajan K. and Nobe, Kenneth. Optimum Investment for Irrigation Development in India. *Margin*, July 1984, *16*(4), pp. 30–47. **[G: India]**

Shabman, Leonard A. Water Resources Management: Policy Economics for an Era of Transitions. *Southern J. Agr. Econ.*, July 1984, *16*(1), pp. 53–65. **[G: U.S.]**

Skold, Melvin D.; Atty El Shinnawi, Shinnawi Abdel and Nasr, M. Lofty. Irrigation Water Distribution along Branch Canals in Egypt: Economic Effects. *Econ. Develop. Cult. Change*, April 1984, *32*(3), pp. 547–67. **[G: Egypt]**

Stoddart, David R. and Pethick, John S. Environmental Hazard and Coastal Reclamation: Problems and Prospects in Bangladesh. In *[Farmer, B. H.]*, 1984, pp. 339–61.   [G: Bangladesh]

Swanson, Earl R. and Heady, Earl O. Soil Erosion in the United States. In *Simon, J. L. and Kahn, H.*, eds., 1984, pp. 202–23. [G: U.S.]

Tew, Bernard V. and Boggess, William G. Risk–Return Assessment of Irrigation Decisions in Humid Regions: An Extension. *Southern J. Agr. Econ.*, December 1984, *16*(2), pp. 159–60.

Wade, Robert. Irrigation Reform in Conditions of Populist Anarchy: An Indian Case. *J. Devel. Econ.*, April 1984, *14*(3), pp. 285–303.
[G: India]

Weimer, A. M. A Note on the Early History of Land Economics. *Amer. Real Estate Urban Econ. Assoc. J.*, Fall 1984, *12*(3), pp. 408–16.
[G: U.S.]

Young, C. Edwin and Shortle, James S. Investments in Soil Conservation Structures: The Role of Operator and Operation Characteristics. *Agr. Econ. Res.*, Spring 1984, *36*(2), pp. 10–15. [G: U.S.]

718 Rural Economics

7180 Rural Economics

Adams, Dale W. Do Rural Financial Savings Matter? In *Kessler, D. and Ullmo, P.-A.*, eds., 1984, pp. 9–15.

Ahmad, Mushtaq. Rural Credit and Rural Development: Some Issues: Comment. *Pakistan Devel. Rev.*, Summer-Autumn 1984, *23*(2&3), pp. 283–85. [G: Pakistan]

Ahmad, Nigar. Changes in Agrarian Relations in Pakistan: A Study of Five Villages. In *Ngo, M.*, ed., vol. 2, 1984, pp. 640–65.
[G: Pakistan]

Ahmad, Q. K. Policies and Institutions Concerning Promotion of Rural Industries in Bangladesh. *Bangladesh Devel. Stud.*, March-June 1984, *12*(1–2), pp. 163–95. [G: Bangladesh]

Ahmad, Zubeida. Rural Women and Their Work: Dependence and Alternatives for Change. *Int. Lab. Rev.*, January-February 1984, *123*(1), pp. 71–86. [G: LDCs]

Ahmed, Momtaz Uddin. Financing Rural Industries in Bangladesh. *Bangladesh Devel. Stud.*, March-June 1984, *12*(1–2), pp. 59–79.
[G: Bangladesh]

Akande, Jadesola O. Participation of Women in Rural Development (Nigeria). In *Intn'l. Lab. Office*, 1984, pp. 129–35. [G: Nigeria]

Alagh, Yoginder K. and Shah, Vinod K. Spatial Spread of Facilities in Rural India. In *Singh, A. K.; Papola, T. S. and Mathur, R. S.*, eds., 1984, pp. 323–38. [G: India]

Allaghi, Farida. Rural Women in a Resettlement Project: The Case of the Libyan Arab Jamahiriya. In *Intn'l. Lab. Office*, 1984, pp. 137–45.
[G: Libya]

Argyle, D. Brian. The Impact of Interest Rates on Savings in Rural Financial Markets. In *Kessler, D. and Ullmo, P.-A.*, eds., 1984, pp. 27–33.

Attwood, Donald W. Capital and the Transformation of Agrarian Class Systems: Sugar Production in India. In *Desai, M.; Rudolph, S. H. and Rudra, A.*, eds., 1984, pp. 20–50.
[G: India]

Aziz, Sartaj. Rural Development—Some Essential Prerequisites. *Int. Lab. Rev.*, May–June 1984, *123*(3), pp. 277–85. [G: LDCs]

Bajracharya, Deepak. Organizing for Energy Need Assessment and Innovation: Action Research in Nepal. In *Islam, M. N.; Morse, R. and Soesastro, M. H.*, eds., 1984, pp. 279–336. [G: Nepal]

Bakht, Zaid. Entrepreneurship in Bangladesh Rural Industries. *Bangladesh Devel. Stud.*, March-June 1984, *12*(1–2), pp. 25–57.
[G: Bangladesh]

Bakht, Zaid. Marketing of Rural Industrial Products in Bangladesh. *Bangladesh Devel. Stud.*, March-June 1984, *12*(1–2), pp. 101–26.
[G: Bangladesh]

Baklanoff, Eric N. and Brannon, Jeffery T. Forward and Backward Linkages in a Plantation Economy: Imigrant Entrepreneurship and Industrial Development in Yucatan, Mexico. *J. Devel. Areas*, October 1984, *19*(1), pp. 83–94.
[G: Mexico]

Balakrishnan, Pulapre. On the Significance of Interlinked Factor Markets in Agrarian Economies. *Indian Econ. J.*, April–June 1984, *31*(4), pp. 62–72.

Banerjee, Biswajit. The Probability, Size, and Uses of Remittances from Urban to Rural Areas in India. *J. Devel. Econ.*, December 1984, *16*(3), pp. 293–311. [G: India]

Bar-El, Raphael. Rural Industrialization Objectives: The Income–Employment Conflict. *World Devel.*, February 1984, *12*(2), pp. 129–40. [G: Brazil]

Barchfield, John W. The Continuity of Injustice: Agrarian and Alimentary Policy under Mexico's New Administration. *J. Econ. Issues*, March 1984, *18*(1), pp. 325–34. [G: Mexico]

Bardhan, Kalpana. Work Patterns and Social Differentiation: Rural Women of West Bengal. In *Binswanger, H. P. and Rosenzweig, R.*, eds., 1984, pp. 184–207. [G: India]

Barnes, Carolyn; Ensminger, Jean and O'Keefe, Philip. Energy Environment and Development in Africa: Introduction. In *Barnes, C.; Ensminger, J. and O'Keefe, P.*, eds., 1984, pp. 1–13. [G: Kenya]

Bausell, Charles W., Jr. and Anders, Gary C. Impacts of Back to the Land Policies. *J. Devel. Econ.*, April 1984, *14*(3), pp. 429–39.
[G: LDCs]

Bayliss-Smith, Tim P. Energy Flows and Agrarian Change in Karnataka: the Green Revolution at Micro-Scale. In *[Farmer, B. H.]*, 1984, pp. 153–72. [G: India]

Berry, Sara S. Oil and the Disappearing Peasantry: Accumulation, Differentiation and Underdevelopment in Western Nigeria. *African Econ. Hist.*, 1984, (13), pp. 1–22.
[G: Nigeria]

Berthelémy, Jean-Claude and Gagey, Frédéric.

Élasticité-prix de l'offre agricole dans les pays en développement: une note sur la rationalité des agriculteurs dans un contexte non-Walrasien. (Price Elasticity of Agricultural Production in LDC's: A Note on Behavior of Peasants in a Non-Walrasian Context. With English summary.) *Ann. INSEE*, July–December 1984, (55/56), pp. 203–21. **[G: Cameroon]**

Binswanger, Hans P. and Rosenzweig, Mark R. Contractual Arrangements, Employment, and Wages in Rural Labor Markets: A Critical Review. In *Binswanger, H. P. and Rosenzweig, R., eds.*, 1984, pp. 1–40.

Binswanger, Hans P., et al. Common Features and Contrasts in Labor Relations in the Semiarid Tropics of India. In *Binswanger, H. P. and Rosenzweig, R., eds.*, 1984, pp. 143–68. **[G: India]**

Boserup, Ester. Technical Change and Human Fertility in Rural Areas of Developing Countries. In *Schutjer, W. A. and Stokes, C. S., eds.*, 1984, pp. 23–33. **[G: LDCs]**

Bouman, F. J. A. Informal Saving and Credit Arrangements in Developing Countries: Observations from Sri Lanka. In *Adams, D. W.; Graham, D. H. and Von Pischke, J. D., eds.*, 1984, pp. 232–47. **[G: Sri Lanka]**

Bradnock, Robert W. Agricultural Development in Tamil Nadu: Two Decades of Land Use Change at Village Level. In *[Farmer, B. H.]*, 1984, pp. 136–52. **[G: India]**

Caballero, José María. Unequal Pricing and Unequal Exchange between the Peasant and Capitalist Economies. *Cambridge J. Econ.*, December 1984, 8(4), pp. 347–59.

Chakrabarty, Gurupada. Minor Forest Products and Amelioration of Rural Unemployment. *Margin*, January 1984, 16(2), pp. 53–76. **[G: India]**

Chirarattananon, Surapong. Analysis of Rural Energy Development in Thailand. In *Islam, M. N.; Morse, R. and Soesastro, M. H., eds.*, 1984, pp. 169–240. **[G: Thailand]**

Chisholm, M. The Development Commission's Factory Programme. *Reg. Stud.*, December 1984, 18(6), pp. 514–17. **[G: U.K.]**

Choonhavan, Kraisak. Thailand: Economic Development and Rural Poverty—A Country Report. In *Ngo, M., ed., vol. 1*, 1984, pp. 479–504. **[G: Thailand]**

Chuta, Enyinna and Liedholm, Carl E. Rural Small-Scale Industry: Empirical Evidence and Policy Issues. In *Eicher, C. K. and Staatz, J. M., eds.*, 1984, pp. 296–312. **[G: LDCs]**

Cohen, Alvin. Review Article: The Macroeconomic versus the Microeconomic Approach to Development: The Futility of Development Efforts as a Function of Institutional Inertia. *Econ. Develop. Cult. Change*, January 1984, 32(2), pp. 423–30. **[G: LDCs]**

Collier, Paul and Lal, Deepak. Why Poor People Get Rich: Kenya, 1960–79. *World Devel.*, October 1984, 12(10), pp. 1007–18. **[G: Kenya]**

Date-Bah, Eugenia. Rural Women, Their Activi-

ties and Technology in Ghana: An Overview. In *Intn'l. Lab. Office*, 1984, pp. 89–98. **[G: Ghana]**

Datta-Chaudhuri, Mrinal. Approach to Rural Development in South Asia. In *Ghosh, P. K., ed., no. 18*, 1984, 1980, pp. 294–309. **[G: S. Asia]**

Datta, Samar K. and Nugent, Jeffrey B. Are Old-Age Security and the Utility of Children in Rural India Really Unimportant? *Population Stud.*, November 1984, 38(3), pp. 507–09. **[G: India]**

Daubrey, Auguste. Mobilization of Savings for Rural Development in Africa. In *Kessler, D. and Ullmo, P.-A., eds.*, 1984, pp. 231–37.

Dawson, A. Suggestions for an Approach to Rural Development by Foreign Aid Programmes. In *Ghosh, P. K., ed., no. 10*, 1984, 1978, pp. 190–204.

Deaton, Brady J. and Johnson, Thomas G. State Legislation for Rural Development: The Role of the University. *Rev. Reg. Stud.*, Spring 1984, 14(2), pp. 29–37. **[G: U.S.]**

Deb, Nibaran C. and Hossain, Mahabub. Demand for Rural Industries Products in Bangladesh. *Bangladesh Devel. Stud.*, March–June 1984, 12(1–2), pp. 81–99. **[G: Bangladesh]**

Deguefe, Taffara. Financial Institutions and Rural Development in Africa. In *Kessler, D. and Ullmo, P.-A., eds.*, 1984, pp. 205–16.

Desai, Meghnad. Power and Agrarian Relations: Some Concepts and Measurements. In *Desai, M.; Rudolph, S. H. and Rudra, A., eds.*, 1984, pp. 171–97.

Dhamija, Jasleen. Income-Generating Activities for Rural Women in Africa: Some Successes and Failures. In *Intn'l. Lab. Office*, 1984, pp. 75–78. **[G: Africa]**

Doeringer, Peter B. Internal Labor Markets and Paternalism in Rural Areas. In *Osterman, P., ed.*, 1984, pp. 271–89. **[G: U.S.]**

Du, Runsheng. New Developments in the Contracting System of United Production and the Cooperative Economy in the Countryside. *Chinese Econ. Stud.*, Summer 1984, 17(4), pp. 16–39. **[G: China]**

Dutt, Amitava Krishna. Rent, Income Distribution and Growth in an Underdeveloped Agrarian Economy. *J. Devel. Econ.*, May–June–August 1984, 15(1,2,3), pp. 185–211. **[G: LDCs]**

Ellis, Frank. Relative Agricultural Prices and the Urban Bias Model: A Comparative Analysis of Tanzania and Fiji. In *Harriss, J. and Moore, M., eds.*, 1984, pp. 28–51. **[G: Tanzania; Fiji]**

Ercelawn, Aly. Income Inequality in Rural Pakistan: A Study of Sample Villages. *Pakistan J. Appl. Econ.*, Summer 1984, 3(1), pp. 1–28. **[G: Pakistan]**

Feng, Jixin. Bring out the Superiority of the System of Contracted Responsibilities on the Household Basis. *Chinese Econ. Stud.*, Spring 1984, 17(3), pp. 18–26. **[G: China]**

Furtan, W. H. and Clark, J. S. An Application of the New Household Economics to Explaining Farm Income Distributions. *Can. J. Agr. Econ.*, March 1984, *32*(1), pp. 151–62. [G: Canada]

Gaude, J.; Phan-Thuy, N. and Van Kempen, C. Evaluation of Special Public Works Programmes: Some Policy Conclusions. *Int. Lab. Rev.*, March-April 1984, *123*(2), pp. 203–19. [G: Selected Countries]

Geertz, Clifford. Capital-Intensive Agriculture in Peasant Society: A Case Study. *Soc. Res.*, Spring & Summer 1984, *51*(1&2), pp. 419–36. [G: Java]

Ghai, Dharam P. Income Distribution and Labour Utilisation under Different Agrarian Systems. In *Amin, S., ed.*, 1984, pp. 116–43. [G: Asia; Tanzania]

Glover, David J. Contract Farming and Smallholder Outgrower Schemes in Less-developed Countries. *World Devel.*, November–December 1984, *12*(11–12), pp. 1143–57. [G: LDCs]

Goldscheider, Calvin. Migration and Rural Fertility in Less Developed Countries. In *Schutjer, W. A. and Stokes, C. S., eds.*, 1984, pp. 34–48. [G: LDCs]

Gonzalez-Vega, Claudio. Interest Rate Restrictions and Income Distribution. In *Eicher, C. K. and Staatz, J. M., eds.*, 1984, *1977*, pp. 329–34. [G: LDCs]

Goodman, David; Sorj, Bernardo and Wilkinson, John. Agro-Industry, State Policy and Rural Social Structures: Recent Analyses of Proletarianisation in Brazilian Agriculture. In *Munslow, B. and Finch, H., eds.*, 1984, pp. 189–215. [G: Brazil]

Goodwin, H. L., Jr.; Doeksen, Gerald A. and Oehrtman, Robert L. Determination of Settlement Patterns in Rapidly Growing Rural Areas. *Ann. Reg. Sci.*, November 1984, *18*(3), pp. 67–80. [G: U.S.]

Gould, Andrew and Keeble, David. New Firms and Rural Industrialization in East Anglia. *Reg. Stud.*, June 1984, *18*(3), pp. 189–201. [G: U.K.]

Graaff, Jan. Economic Theory and the Economy of Palanpur: A Review Article. *Oxford Econ. Pap.*, November 1984, *36*(3), pp. 327–35. [G: India]

Greider, Thomas and Krannich, Richard S. Diffusion and Development in the Rocky Mountain Region, 1970–80. *Growth Change*, January 1984, *15*(1), pp. 41–49. [G: U.S.]

Haq, M. T. Industrialization in Relation to Integrated Rural Development with Reference to Bangladesh. In *Ghosh, P. K., ed., no. 1*, 1984, *1979*, pp. 290–308. [G: Bangladesh]

Harriss, Barbara and Harriss, John C. 'Generative' or 'Parasitic' Urbanism? Some Observations from the Recent History of a South Indian Market Town. *J. Devel. Stud.*, April 1984, *20*(3), pp. 82–101. [G: India]

Harriss, Barbara and Harriss, John C. 'Generative' or 'Parasitic' Urbanism? Some Observations from the Recent History of a South Indian Market Town. In *Harriss, J. and Moore, M., eds.*, 1984, pp. 82–101. [G: India]

Hayden, F. Gregory. A Geobased National Agricultural Policy for Rural Community Enhancement, Environmental Vitality, and Income Stabilization. *J. Econ. Issues*, March 1984, *18*(1), pp. 181–221. [G: U.S.]

Hayes, Michael N. and Olmstead, Alan L. Farm Size and Community Quality: Arvin and Dinuba Revisited. *Amer. J. Agr. Econ.*, November 1984, *66*(4), pp. 430–36. [G: U.S.]

Henry, Mark S. and Martin, Thomas L. Rural Area Consumer Demand and Regional Input–Output Analysis: Reply. *Amer. J. Agr. Econ.*, May 1984, *66*(2), pp. 176–79. [G: U.S.]

Herring, Ronald J. Economic Consequences of Local Power Configurations in Rural South Asia. In *Desai, M.; Rudolph, S. H. and Rudra, A., eds.*, 1984, pp. 198–249. [G: S. Asia]

Hogg, M. V. Industrialization and Rural Development: An Analysis of Basic Issues. In *Ghosh, P. K., ed., no. 1*, 1984, *1978*, pp. 153–83.

Holdcroft, Lane E. The Rise and Fall of Community Development, 1950–65: A Critical Assessment. In *Eicher, C. K. and Staatz, J. M., eds.*, 1984, *1978*, pp. 46–58.

Hosier, Richard. Domestic Energy Consumption in Rural Kenya: Results of a Nationwide Survey. In *Barnes, C.; Ensminger, J. and O'Keefe, P., eds.*, 1984, pp. 14–60. [G: Kenya]

Hossain, Mahabub. Employment and Labour in Bangladesh Rural Industries. *Bangladesh Devel. Stud.*, March-June 1984, *12*(1–2), pp. 1–24. [G: Bangladesh]

Hossain, Mahabub. Productivity and Profitability in Bangladesh Rural Industries. *Bangladesh Devel. Stud.*, March-June 1984, *12*(1–2), pp. 127–61. [G: Bangladesh]

Hyman, Eric L. Providing Public Lands for Smallholder Agroforestry in the Province of Ilocos Norte, Philippines. *J. Devel. Areas*, January 1984, *18*(2), pp. 177–90. [G: Philippines]

Islam, M. Nurul. Energy and Rural Development: Critical Assessment of the Bangladesh Situation. In *Islam, M. N.; Morse, R. and Soesastro, M. H., eds.*, 1984, pp. 43–88. [G: Bangladesh]

Islam, M. Nurul. Field-Based Assessment and Development of Improved Stoves. In *Islam, M. N.; Morse, R. and Soesastro, M. H., eds.*, 1984, pp. 337–79. [G: Asian LDCs]

de Janvry, Alain. The Political Economy of Rural Development in Latin America: An Interpretation. In *Eicher, C. K. and Staatz, J. M., eds.*, 1984, *1975*, pp. 82–95. [G: Latin America]

Johnson, Nan E. Rural Development and the Value of Children: Implications for Human Fertility. In *Schutjer, W. A. and Stokes, C. S., eds.*, 1984, pp. 172–93. [G: LDCs]

Johnson, Thomas G. and Capps, Oral, Jr. Rural Area Consumer Demand and Regional Input–Output Analysis: Comment. *Amer. J. Agr. Econ.*, May 1984, *66*(2), pp. 173–76. [G: U.S.]

Jones, Steve. Agrarian Structure and Agricultural Innovation in Bangladesh: Panimara Village, Dhaka District. In *[Farmer, B. H.]*, 1984, pp. 194–211. [G: Bangladesh]

Jordan, Jeffrey L. and Brooks, Rusty. IO/EAM: An Input–Output Economic Assessment Model. *Southern J. Agr. Econ.*, December 1984, *16*(2), pp. 145–49.

Khan, Qaiser M. The Impact of Household Endowment Constraints on Nutrition and Health: A Simultaneous Equation Test of Human Capital Divestment. *J. Devel. Econ.*, May–June–August 1984, *15*(1,2,3), pp. 313–28. [G: Bangladesh]

Kilby, Peter; Liedholm, Carl E. and Meyer, Richard L. Working Capital and Nonfarm Rural Enterprises. In *Adams, D. W.; Graham, D. H. and Von Pischke, J. D., eds.*, 1984, pp. 266–83.

Kinley, David; Collins, Joseph and Lappé, Moore. United States Aid to Asia: A Critique. In *Ngo, M., ed., vol. 1*, 1984, pp. 165–87. [G: Asian LDCs; U.S.]

Kleemeier, L. Domestic Policies versus Poverty-Oriented Foreign Assistance in Tanzania. *J. Devel. Stud.*, January 1984, *20*(2), pp. 171–201. [G: Tanzania]

Kumar, T. M. Vinod. Integrated Rural Development Planning and Energy Priorities: Participatory Surveys in India Microregions. In *Islam, M. N.; Morse, R. and Soesastro, M. H., eds.*, 1984, pp. 241–78. [G: India]

Lang, Rikard and Nikić, Gorazd. Dispersion of Industrial Activities into Rural Areas and Employment. In *Amin, S., ed.*, 1984, pp. 265–72. [G: Yugoslavia]

Lele, Uma. Rural Africa: Modernization, Equity, and Long-term Development. In *Eicher, C. K. and Staatz, J. M., eds.*, 1984, *1981*, pp. 436–52. [G: Africa]

Li, Zili. Again on "Standard Output": A Further Inquiry into the Distribution Form of United Production with Remuneration Calculated According to the Standard Output. *Chinese Econ. Stud.*, Spring 1984, *17*(3), pp. 3–17. [G: China]

Lieberman, Samuel S. Accommodation and Control of Population Growth. In *Burki, S. J. and LaPorte, R., Jr., eds.*, 1984, pp. 139–200. [G: Pakistan]

Lipton, Michael. Family, Fungibility and Formality: Rural Advantages of Informal Non-farm Enterprise versus the Urban-Formal State. In *Amin, S., ed.*, 1984, pp. 189–242.

Lipton, Michael. Urban Bias Revisited. *J. Devel. Stud.*, April 1984, *20*(3), pp. 139–66. [G: LDCs]

Longhurst, Richard. Rural Development Planning and the Sexual Division of Labour: A Case Study of a Moslem Hausa Village in Northern Nigeria. In *Intn'l. Lab. Office*, 1984, pp. 117–22. [G: Nigeria]

Mandala, Elias. Capitalism, Kinship and Gender in the Lower Tchiri (Shire) Valley of Malawi, 1860–1960: An Alterntive Theoretical Framework. *African Econ. Hist.*, 1984, (13), pp. 137–69.

McGregor, Patrick. The Impact of the Blight upon the Pre-Famine Rural Economy in Ire-

land. *Econ. Soc. Rev.*, July 1984, *15*(4), pp. 289–303. [G: U.K.]

McIntosh, James. An Oligopsonistic Model of Wage Determination in Agrarian Societies. *Econ. J.*, September 1984, *94*(375), pp. 569–79. [G: LDCs]

Menra, Naresh Kumar. Dualism and Surplus Labour: A Case Study of Indian Agriculture. *Margin*, October 1984, *17*(1), pp. 48–54. [G: India]

Mernissi, Fatima. Capitalist Development and Perceptions of Women in Arab-Muslim Society: An Illustration of Peasant Women in Gharb, Morocco. In *Intn'l. Lab. Office*, 1984, pp. 123–28. [G: Morocco]

Mines, Richard. Network Migration and Mexican Rural Development: A Case Study. In *Jones, R. C., ed.*, 1984, pp. 136–55. [G: U.S.; Mexico]

Mishra, G. P. Approaches to Planning for Employment Creation in Rural Areas. In *Singh, A. K.; Papola, T. S. and Mathur, R. S., eds.*, 1984, pp. 53–65. [G: India; LDCs]

Mittendorf, Hans. Savings Mobilization for Agricultural and Rural Development in Africa. In *Kessler, D. and Ullmo, P.-A., eds.*, 1984, pp. 217–29. [G: Zimbabwe]

Moore, Mick. Categorising Space: Urban–Rural or Core–Periphery in Sri Lanka. In *Harriss, J. and Moore, M., eds.*, 1984, pp. 102–22. [G: Sri Lanka]

Moore, Mick. Political Economy and the Rural-Urban Divide, 1767–1981. *J. Devel. Stud.*, April 1984, *20*(3), pp. 5–27. [G: LDCs]

Morrissey, Michael P. A Rural–Urban Stratification of Jamaica for Sampling Procedures. *Soc. Econ. Stud.*, December 1984, *33*(4), pp. 101–23. [G: Jamaica]

Morse, Richard; Soesastro, M. Hadi and Schlegel, Charles. Energy for Rural Development: Principals, Issues, and Methods. In *Islam, M. N.; Morse, R. and Soesastro, M. H., eds.*, 1984, pp. 1–42. [G: Asian LDCs]

Morse, Richard, et al. Converting Rural Energy Needs to Opportunities. In *Islam, M. N.; Morse, R. and Soesastro, M. H., eds.*, 1984, pp. 519–47. [G: Asian LDCs]

Morse, Richard, et al. Organizing Current Information for Rural Energy and Development Planning. In *Islam, M. N.; Morse, R. and Soesastro, M. H., eds.*, 1984, pp. 473–518. [G: Asian LDCs]

Mott, Frank L. and Shapiro, David. Seasonal Variations in Labor-Force Activity and Intra-household Substitution of Labor in Rural Keyna. *J. Devel. Areas*, July 1984, *18*(4), pp. 449–63. [G: Kenya]

Mueller, Eva. Income, Aspirations, and Fertility in Rural Areas of Less Developed Countries. In *Schutjer, W. A. and Stokes, C. S., eds.*, 1984, pp. 121–50. [G: LDCs]

Mueller, Eva. The Value and Allocation of Time in Rural Botswana. *J. Devel. Econ.*, May–June–August 1984, *15*(1,2,3), pp. 329–60. [G: Botswana]

Nabi, Ijaz. Village-End Considerations in Rural-

Urban Migration. *J. Devel. Econ.*, January–February 1984, *14*(1–2), pp. 129–45.
[G: Pakistan]

Nelson, James R. and Doeksen, Gerald A. Agricultural Economists in Rural Development: Responsibilities, Opportunities, Risks, and Payoffs. *Southern J. Agr. Econ.*, July 1984, *16*(1), pp. 41–47. [G: U.S.]

Nevadomsky, Joseph. Economic Organization, Social Mobility and Changing Social Status among the East Indians in Rural Trinidad. *Soc. Econ. Stud.*, September 1984, *33*(3), pp. 31–62. [G: Trinidad and Tobago]

Nolan, Peter and White, Gordon. Urban Bias, Rural Bias or State Bias? Urban–Rural Relations in Post-revolutionary China. In *Harriss, J. and Moore, M., eds.*, 1984, pp. 52–81.
[G: China]

Nolan, Peter and White, Gordon. Urban Bias, Rural Bias or State Bias? Urban–Rural Relations in Post-Revolutionary China. *J. Devel. Stud.*, April 1984, *20*(3), pp. 52–81.
[G: China]

O'Keefe, Philip. Poverty, Proletarianisation and the Production of Uneven Development: A Kenyan Village. In *Munslow, B. and Finch, H., eds.*, 1984, pp. 148–63. [G: Kenya]

Papola, T. S. Industrialisation for Rural Development. In *Singh, A. K.; Papola, T. S. and Mathur, R. S., eds.*, 1984, pp. 309–22.
[G: India]

Perry, Charles S. Economic Activity and Social Indicators: A Rural–Urban Discontinuum? *Amer. J. Econ. Soc.*, January 1984, *43*(1), pp. 61–74. [G: U.S.]

Planning Ser., Ministry of Energy, Philippines. Philippine Rural Energy Resource and Consumption Survey. In *Islam, M. N.; Morse, R. and Soesastro, M. H., eds.*, 1984, pp. 135–68. [G: Philippines]

Platteau, Jean-Philippe. Projet cooperatif et realite rurale dans le tiers-monde. Vers une redefinition des termes du debat. (The Co-operative Design and Rural Realities in the Third World. With English summary.) *Ann. Pub. Co-op. Econ.*, July–September 1984, *55*(3), pp. 283–307. [G: LDCs]

Prasad, Pradhan H. Changing Class Relations in India's Agriculture: A Statistical Appraisal. In *Ngo, M., ed., vol. 2*, 1984, pp. 567–605.
[G: India]

Pratschke, John L. Aspects of the Redistribution of Income in Urban and Rural Ireland, 1973–1980. *Irish J. Agr. Econ. Rural Soc.*, 1984, *10*(1), pp. 13–27. [G: U.K.]

Qureshi, Sarfraz K. Rural Credit and Rural Development: Some Issues. *Pakistan Devel. Rev.*, Summer-Autumn 1984, *23*(2&3), pp. 273–82.
[G: Pakistan]

Rao, V. M. Rural Development Personnel—Location, Status and Development Characteristics. In *Singh, A. K.; Papola, T. S. and Mathur, R. S., eds.*, 1984, pp. 189–206. [G: India]

Ravallion, Martin. How Much Is a Transfer Pay-

ment Worth to a Rural Worker? *Oxford Econ. Pap.*, November 1984, *36*(3), pp. 478–89.
[G: LDCs]

Ray, Edward John. Economic Distortions and Financial Reforms. In *Adams, D. W.; Graham, D. H. and Von Pischke, J. D., eds.*, 1984, pp. 194–209.

Redclift, M. R. 'Urban Bias' and Rural Poverty: A Latin American Perspective. In *Harriss, J. and Moore, M., eds.*, 1984, pp. 123–38.
[G: Latin America]

Reidy, K. A Survey of Pig Producers' Intentions. *Irish J. Agr. Econ. Rural Soc.*, 1984, *10*(1), pp. 1–12. [G: U.K.]

Roberts, Kenneth D. Agricultural Development and Labor Mobility: A Study of Four Mexican Subregions. In *Jones, R. C., ed.*, 1984, pp. 74–92. [G: Mexico; U.S.]

Rosenzweig, Mark R. Determinants of Wage Rates and Labor Supply Behavior in the Rural Sector of a Developing Country. In *Binswanger, H. P. and Rosenzweig, R., eds.*, 1984, pp. 211–41. [G: India]

Rudolph, Lloyd I. and Rudolph, Susanne Hoeber. Determinants and Varieties of Agrarian Mobilization. In *Desai, M.; Rudolph, S. H. and Rudra, A., eds.*, 1984, pp. 281–344.
[G: India]

Rudolph, Susanne Hoeber. Agrarian Power and Agricultural Productivity in Southern Asia: Introduction. In *Desai, M.; Rudolph, S. H. and Rudra, A., eds.*, 1984, pp. 1–19.

Ruttan, Vernon W. Integrated Rural Development Programmes: A Historical Perspective. *World Devel.*, April 1984, *12*(4), pp. 393–401.
[G: LDCs]

Ryan, James G. and Ghodake, R. D. Labor Market Behavior in Rural Villages in South India: Effects of Season, Sex, and Socioeconomic Status. In *Binswanger, H. P. and Rosenzweig, R., eds.*, 1984, pp. 169–83. [G: India]

Salinas de Gortari, Carlos. Production and Participation in Rural Areas: Some Political Considerations. In *Aspe, P. and Sigmund, P. E., eds.*, 1984, pp. 523–542. [G: Mexico]

Sampath, Rajan K. Income Distribution Impacts of Irrigation Water Distribution Policy. *Water Resources Res.*, June 1984, *20*(6), pp. 647–54.

Santerre, Michael T. Financial and Resource Analyses of Anaerobic Digestion (Biogas) Systems. In *Islam, M. N.; Morse, R. and Soesastro, M. H., eds.*, 1984, pp. 415–71.
[G: China; India; Asian LDCs]

Schuh, G. Edward. The Political Economy of Rural Development in Latin America: Comment. In *Eicher, C. K. and Staatz, J. M., eds.*, 1984, pp. 96–109. [G: Latin America]

Schutjer, Wayne A. and Stokes, C. Shannon. Rural Development and Human Fertility in Developing Nations. In *Schutjer, W. A. and Stokes, C. S., eds.*, 1984, pp. 1–22.
[G: LDCs]

Scobie, Grant M. and Posada T., Rafael. The Impact of Technical Change on Income Distribution: The Case of Rice in Colombia. In

Eicher, C. K. and Staatz, J. M., eds., 1984, 1978, pp. 378–88.   [G: Colombia]

Sen, Amartya. Peasants and Dualism with or without Surplus Labour. In Sen, A., 1984, 1966, pp. 37–72.

Simmons, Ozzie G. Rural Development and Human Fertility: Conclusions and Policy Implications. In Schutjer, W. A. and Stokes, C. S., eds., 1984, pp. 291–308.   [G: LDCs]

Sinha, J. N. Development Strategy and Demographic Change. In Singh, A. K.; Papola, T. S. and Mathur, R. S., eds., 1984, pp. 66–88.   [G: India]

Smith, Hilary H. Farmers and Economic Shocks: Ranking Texas Agricultural Production Regions. Fed. Res. Bank Dallas Econ. Rev., July 1984, pp. 23–34.   [G: U.S.]

Smith, Stephen M. Export Orientation of Nonmanufacturing Businesses in Nonmetropolitan Communities. Amer. J. Agr. Econ., May 1984, 66(2), pp. 145–55.   [G: U.S.]

Soesastro, M. Hadi. Policy Analysis of Rural Household Energy Needs in West Java. In Islam, M. N.; Morse, R. and Soesastro, M. H., eds., 1984, pp. 89–134.   [G: Indonesia]

Soulas de Russel, D. J. M. Les coopératives des pays les plus pauvres: rôle fixateur de populations rurales et conditions de succès. (Co-operatives in the Poorest Countries: Their Role in the Stabilisation of the Population in Rural Areas; Conditions for Success. With English summary.) Ann. Pub. Co-op. Econ., January–March 1984, 55(1), pp. 71–90.   [G: Ghana]

Stark, Oded. Rural-to-Urban Migration in LDCs: A Relative Deprivation Approach. Econ. Develop. Cult. Change, April 1984, 32(3), pp. 475–86.   [G: LDCs]

Stark, Oded. Rural-to-Urban Migration in LDCs: A Relative Deprivation Approach. Econ. Develop. Cult. Change, April 1984, 32(3), pp. 475–86.

Stark, Oded. Rural-to-Urban Migration in LDCs: A Relative Deprivation Approach. Econ. Develop. Cult. Change, April 1984, 32(3), pp. 475–86.   [G: LDCs]

Stevens, Yvette. Technologies for Rural Women's Activities: Problems and Prospects in Sierra Leone. In Intn'l. Lab. Office, 1984, pp. 79–88.   [G: Sierra Leone]

Strauss, John. Joint Determination of Food Consumption and Production in Rural Sierra Leone: Estimates of a Household-Firm Model. J. Devel. Econ., January–February 1984, 14(1–2), pp. 77–103.   [G: Sierra Leone]

Strauss, John. Marketed Surpluses of Agricultural Households in Sierra Leone. Amer. J. Agr. Econ., August 1984, 66(3), pp. 321–31.   [G: Sierra Leone]

Tadesse, Zenebeworke. Studies on Rural Women in Africa: An Overview. In Intn'l. Lab. Office, 1984, pp. 65–73.   [G: Africa]

Tâm, Lê Hông. Vietnam: Building Industrial–Agricultural Complexes. In Ngo, M., ed., vol. 1, 1984, pp. 523–35.   [G: Vietnam]

Tilak, Jandhyala B. G. Urban Bias and Rural Neglect in Education: A Study on Rural–Urban

Disparities in Education in Andhra Pradesh. Margin, October 1984, 17(1), pp. 61–86.
                                     [G: India]

Traoré, Aminata. Women's Access to Resources in the Ivory Coast: Women and Land in Adioukrou District. In Intn'l. Lab. Office, 1984, pp. 99–106.   [G: Ivory Coast]

Tricker, M. and Martin, S. The Developing Role of the Commission. Reg. Stud., December 1984, 18(6), pp. 507–14.   [G: U.K.]

Turchi, Boone A. Rural Development Policy and Fertility: A Framework for Analysis at the Household Level. In Schutjer, W. A. and Stokes, C. S., eds., 1984, pp. 97–120.
                                     [G: LDCs]

Van Den Beldt, Rick J. Supplying Firewood for Household Energy. In Islam, M. N.; Morse, R. and Soesastro, M. H., eds., 1984, pp. 381–414.   [G: Asian LDCs]

Vidyarthi, Varun. Energy and the Poor in an Indian Village. World Devel., August 1984, 12(8), pp. 821–36.   [G: India]

Vinovskis, Maris A. Historical Perspectives on Rural Development and Human Fertility in Nineteenth-Century America. In Schutjer, W. A. and Stokes, C. S., eds., 1984, pp. 77–96.   [G: U.S.]

Vlassoff, M. A Rejoinder to S. K. Datta and J. B. Nugent [Old Age Security and the Utility of Children in Rural India]. Population Stud., November 1984, 38(3), pp. 510–12.
                                     [G: India]

Vogel, Robert C. Savings Mobilization: The Forgotten Half of Rural Finance. In Adams, D. W.; Graham, D. H. and Von Pischke, J. D., eds., 1984, pp. 248–65.   [G: Peru]

Von Pischke, J. D. Improving Donor Intervention in Rural Finance. In Adams, D. W.; Graham, D. H. and Von Pischke, J. D., eds., 1984, pp. 284–97.

Wanmali, Sudhir. Rural-based Models for Rural Development: The Indian Experience. In [Farmer, B. H.], 1984, pp. 253–69.
                                     [G: India]

Watanabe, Barbara and Mueller, Eva. A Poverty Profile for Rural Botswana. World Devel., February 1984, 12(2), pp. 115–27. [G: Botswana]

Watts, Susan J. Rural Women as Food Processors and Traders: Eko Making in the Ilorin Area of Nigeria. J. Devel. Areas, October 1984, 19(1), pp. 71–82.   [G: Nigeria]

Weller, Robert H. The Gainful Employment of Females and Fertility—With Special Reference to Rural Areas of Developing Countries. In Schutjer, W. A. and Stokes, C. S., eds., 1984, pp. 151–71.   [G: LDCs]

Wells, Miriam J. and Climo, Jacob. Parallel Process in the World System: Intermediate Agencies and Local Factionalism in the United States and Mexico. J. Devel. Stud., January 1984, 20(2), pp. 151–70.   [G: Mexico; U.S.]

Whittaker, William. Migration and Agrarian Change in Garhwal District, Uttar Pradesh. In [Farmer, B. H.], 1984, pp. 109–35.
                                     [G: India]

Wiest, Raymond E. External Dependency and

the Perpetuation of Temporary Migration to the United States. In *Jones, R. C., ed.*, 1984, pp. 110–35. [G: U.S.; Mexico]

Williams, G. Promoting the Rural Economy: The Role of Development Agencies in Remoter Rural Areas. *Reg. Stud.*, February 1984, *18*(1), pp. 73–77. [G: U.K.]

Witney, K. P. The Economic Position of Husbandmen at the time of Domesday Book: A Kentish Perspective. *Econ. Hist. Rev., 2nd Ser.*, February 1984, *37*(1), pp. 23–34. [G: U.K.]

von Witzke, Harald. A Model of Income Distribution in Agriculture: Theory and Evidence. *Europ. Rev. Agr. Econ.*, 1984, *11*(1), pp. 65–83. [G: W. Germany]

Wu, King. Energy Sources in China—Present and Future. In *Baum, V., et al.*, 1984, pp. 174–84. [G: China]

Yang, Donghyu. Notes on the Wealth Distribution of Farm Households in the United States, 1860: A New Look at Two Manuscript Census Samples. *Exploration Econ. Hist.*, January 1984, *21*(1), pp. 88–102. [G: U.S.]

Zacchia, Carlo. Rural Industrialization in Italy. *J. World Trade Law*, March–April 1984, *18*(2), pp. 110–24. [G: Italy]

Zachariah, Mathew. The Berger Commission Inquiry Report and the Revitalization of Indigenous Cultures. *Can. J. Devel. Stud.*, 1984, *5*(1), pp. 65–77. [G: Canada]

Zhang, Chunsheng and Song, Dahan. Separation of Government Administration from Commune Management Is a Need of Rural Economic Development and of Building Political Power. *Chinese Econ. Stud.*, Spring 1984, *17*(3), pp. 76–83. [G: China]

720 NATURAL RESOURCES

7200 General

Pirages, Dennis. Paths to International Political Economy: An Ecological Approach. In *Strange, S., ed.*, 1984, pp. 53–69. [G: Global]

Simon, Julian L. and Kahn, Herman. The Resourceful Earth: A Response to Global 2000: Introduction. In *Simon, J. L. and Kahn, H., eds.*, 1984, pp. 1–49. [G: Global]

721 Natural Resources

7210 General

Aage, Hans. Economic Arguments on the Sufficiency of Natural Resources. *Cambridge J. Econ.*, March 1984, *8*(1), pp. 105–13.

Akaha, Tsuneo. A Cybernetic Analysis of Japan's Fishery Policy Process. In *Friedheim, R. L., et al.*, 1984, pp. 173–226. [G: Japan]

Allam, Mohamed N. and Marks, David H. Irrigated Agricultural Expansion Planning in Developing Countries: Investment Scheduling Incorporating Drainage Water Reuse. *Water Resources Res.*, July 1984, *20*(7), pp. 757–66. [G: Egypt]

Allen, Richard C. and Gisser, Micha. Competition versus Optimal Control in Groundwater Pumping when Demand Is Nonlinear. *Water Resources Res.*, July 1984, *20*(7), pp. 752–56. [G: U.S.]

Andersen, Peder and Sutinen, Jon G. Stochastic Bioeconomics: A Review of Basic Methods and Results. *Marine Resource Econ.*, 1984, *1*(2), pp. 117–36.

Anderson, Lee G. Uncertainty in the Fisheries Management Process. *Marine Resource Econ.*, 1984, *1*(1), pp. 77–87. [G: U.S.]

As-Sammani, Mohammed Osman. Private Sector and Government Commercial Fishing in the Sudd Area, Southern Sudan. *Econ. Geogr.*, July 1984, *60*(3), pp. 210–16. [G: Sudan]

Avery, William H. OTEC Methanol: A New Approach. In *Gopalakrishnan, C., ed.*, 1984, pp. 17–30.

Ayubi, Nazih N. M. The Arab States and Major Sea Issues. In *Luciani, G., ed.*, 1984, pp. 126–47.

Barnett, Harold J., et al. Global Trends in Nonfuel Minerals. In *Simon, J. L. and Kahn, H., eds.*, 1984, pp. 316–38. [G: Global]

Beckmann, Petr. The Resourceful Earth: A Response to Global 2000: Coal. In *Simon, J. L. and Kahn, H., eds.*, 1984, pp. 428–38. [G: Global]

Beddington, John R. and Clark, Colin W. Allocation Problems between National and Foreign Fisheries with a Fluctuating Fish Resource. *Marine Resource Econ.*, 1984, *1*(2), pp. 137–54.

Berck, Peter and Perloff, Jeffrey M. An Open-Access Fishery with Rational Expectations. *Econometrica*, March 1984, *52*(2), pp. 489–506.

Berman, Matthew D. Alaskan Resources Development: Renewable Resources. In *Morehouse, T. A., ed.*, 1984, pp. 105–33. [G: U.S.]

Bernard, Jean-Thomas; Bridges, Glenn E. and Scott, Anthony D. Une évaluation de la rente potentielle des sites hydro-électriques au Canada. (With English summary.) *Rev. Econ. Ind.*, 3rd Trimester 1984, (29), pp. 1–17. [G: Canada]

Bernard, Jean-Thomas and Chatel, Josée. The Role of Energy Limited Hydro Equipment in an Optimal Plant Mix. *Energy Econ.*, April 1984, *6*(2), pp. 139–44. [G: Canada]

Bharier, Julian. Water Supply and Waste Disposal. In *Weiss, C. and Jéquier, N., eds.*, 1984, pp. 107–24.

Bhattacharya, Gautam. Optimal Resource Extraction and Uncertainty about New Technology. *J. Environ. Econ. Manage.*, March 1984, *11*(1), pp. 39–54.

Bjork, Gordon C. Ownership and Outcome: An Economic Analysis of the Privatization of Land Tenure on Forest and Rangeland. In *Brubaker, S., ed.*, 1984, pp. 181–92. [G: U.S.]

Blake, Gerald H. Mediterranean Non-energy Resources: Scope for Cooperation and Dangers of Conflict. In *Luciani, G., ed.*, 1984, pp. 41–74. [G: Mediterranean]

Boulding, Kenneth E. Sources of Reasonable Hope for the Future. *Amer. Econ. Rev.*, May 1984, *74*(2), pp. 221–25. [G: Global]

Boyd, Roy. Government Support of Nonindustrial Production: The Case of Private Forests. *Southern Econ. J.*, July 1984, *51*(1), pp. 89–107. [G: U.S.]

Brewer, William A. and Corbin, John S. Aquaculture Development for the Pacific Islands. In *Gopalakrishnan, C., ed.*, 1984, pp. 153–75. [G: Pacific Islands]

Brockhoff, Klaus. The Production Ceiling According to the United Nations Convention on the Law of the Sea. *Weltwirtsch. Arch.*, 1984, *120*(3), pp. 541–57. [G: Global]

Brooks, Hugh A. and Probert, Thomas H. Let's Ask GMDH What Effect the Environment Has on Fisheries. In *Farlow, S. J., ed.*, 1984, pp. 169–78. [G: U.S.]

Brown, Gardner M., Jr. and McGuire, C. B. A Socially Optimum Pricing Policy for a Public Water Agency. In *Ahmad, Y. J.; Dasgupta, P. and Mäler, K.-G., eds.*, 1984, pp. 176–97. [G: U.S.]

Brubaker, Sterling. Issues and Summary of Federal Land Tenure. In *Brubaker, S., ed.*, 1984, pp. 1–31. [G: U.S.]

Bulgaru, M. and Bulgaru, Ana. Scenarios of the Water Resources. *Econ. Computat. Cybern. Stud. Res.*, 1984, *19*(1), pp. 31–44.

Burchi, Stefano. Legislation on Domestic and Industrial Uses of Water: A Comparative Review. *Natural Res. J.*, January 1984, *24*(1), pp. 143–59. [G: Selected Countries]

Campbell, David C. The Pick–Sloan Program: A Case of Bureaucratic Economic Power. *J. Econ. Issues*, June 1984, *18*(2), pp. 449–56. [G: U.S.]

Charney, Alberta H. and Woodard, Gary C. A Test of Consumer Demand Response to Water Prices: Comment [Urban Residential Demand for Water in the United States: Further Discussion]. *Land Econ.*, November 1984, *60*(4), pp. 414–16. [G: U.S.]

Chiarella, Carl, et al. On the Economics of International Fisheries. In *Kemp, M. C. and Long, N. V., eds.*, 1984, pp. 189–98.

Chiarella, Carl, et al. On the Economics of International Fisheries. *Int. Econ. Rev.*, February 1984, *25*(1), pp. 85–92.

Chichilnisky, Graciela. Necesidades básicas, recursos no renovables y crecimiento en el contexto de las relaciones Norte–Sur. (With English summary.) *Desarrollo Econ.*, July–September 1984, *24*(94), pp. 171–85.

Chilton, John. The Pricing of Durable Exhaustible Resources: Comment. *Quart. J. Econ.*, August 1984, *99*(3), pp. 629–37.

Choucri, Nazli. Population, Resources, Technology, and Environment: Trends and Implications. In *Trent, J. and Lamy, P., eds.*, 1984, pp. 187–203.

Chyba, Antonín. The Problem of Raw Material and Energy Supplies in Today's World. *Czech. Econ. Digest.*, March 1984, (2), pp. 50–68. [G: Global]

Clawson, Marion. Major Alternatives for Future Management of the Federal Lands. In *Brubaker, S., ed.*, 1984, pp. 195–234. [G: U.S.]

Comolli, Paul M. A Proposition on Imperfect Stumpage Markets. *Land Econ.*, August 1984, *60*(3), pp. 297–300.

Conrad, Robert F. and Hool, R. Bryce. Intertemporal Extraction of Mineral Resources under Variable Rate Taxes. *Land Econ.*, November 1984, *60*(4), pp. 319–27.

Cooley, Richard A. Evolution of Alaska Land Policy. In *Morehouse, T. A., ed.*, 1984, pp. 13–49. [G: U.S.]

Copes, Parzival. The Market as an Open Access Commons: A Neglected Aspect of Excess Capacity. *De Economist*, 1984, *132*(1), pp. 49–60.

Crawford, Vincent P.; Sobel, Joel and Takahashi, Ichiro. Bargaining, Strategic Reserves, and International Trade in Exhaustible Resources. *Amer. J. Agr. Econ.*, November 1984, *66*(4), pp. 472–80.

Dalsted, Norman L. and Green, John W. Water Requirements for Coal-Fired Power Plants. *Natural Res. J.*, January 1984, *24*(1), pp. 137–41. [G: U.S.]

Dandy, G. C.; McBean, Edward A. and Hutchinson, B. G. A Model for Constrained Optimum Water Pricing and Capacity Expansion. *Water Resources Res.*, May 1984, *20*(5), pp. 511–20.

Datta, Bithin and Houck, Mark H. A Stochastic Optimization Model for Real-Time Operation of Reservoirs Using Uncertain Forecasts. *Water Resources Res.*, August 1984, *20*(8), pp. 1039–46.

David, Elizabeth L. and Peskin, Henry M. The USGS National Water Use Data System: An Optimal Data Base? *Rev. Public Data Use*, June 1984, *12*(2), pp. 97–105. [G: U.S.]

Davidson, B. R. A Preliminary Benefit Cost Analysis of the Inland Diversion of the Coastal Rivers of New South Wales. *Rev. Marketing Agr. Econ.*, April 1984, *52*(1), pp. 23–47. [G: Australia]

Deason, J. P. and White, K. P., Jr. Specification of Objectives by Group Processes in Multiobjective Water Resources Planning. *Water Resources Res.*, February 1984, *20*(2), pp. 189–96. [G: U.S.]

Desvousges, William H. and Piette, Michael J. Problems and Prospects: U.S. Outer Continental Shelf Petroleum Resources. *Growth Change*, April 1984, *15*(2), pp. 3–10. [G: U.S.]

Diffenderfer, Mark. Wood for Industrial Energy in Northern New England. In *Baumgartner, T. and Burns, T. R., eds.*, 1984, pp. 187–215. [G: U.S.]

Djajic, Slobodan. Exhaustible Resources and the Dynamics of Comparative Advantage. *J. Int. Econ.*, August 1984, *17*(1/2), pp. 55–71.

Dowdle, Barney. Why Have We Retained the Federal Lands? An Alternative Hypothesis. In *Brubaker, S., ed.*, 1984, pp. 61–73. [G: U.S.]

Duckstein, Lucien; Kempf, Jim and Casti, John.

Design and Management of Regional Systems by Fuzzy Ratings and Polyhedral Dynamics (MCQA). In *Despontin, M.; Nijkamp, P. and Spronk, J., eds.,* 1984, pp. 223–37. [G: U.S.]

DuMars, Charles T., et al. The Impact of Recent Court Decisions Concerning Water and Interstate Commerce on Water Resources of the State of New Mexico. *Natural Res. J.,* July 1984, *24*(3), pp. 689–744. [G: U.S.]

Durutalo, Simione. "Factory Forestry": Fiji's Throwaway Forests. In *Utrecht, E., ed.,* 1984, pp. 181–231. [G: Fiji]

Elbers, Chris and Withagen, Cees. Trading in Exhaustible Resources in the Presence of Conversion Costs: A General Equilibrium Approach. *J. Econ. Dynam. Control,* November 1984, *8*(2), pp. 197–209.

Emerson, Craig and Garnaut, Ross. Mineral Leasing Policy: Competitive Bidding and the Resource Rent Tax Given Various Responses to Risk. *Econ. Rec.,* June 1984, *60*(169), pp. 133–42.

Enders, Klaus. Strukturelle Konsequenzen eines Rohstoffbooms in einem Industrieland: De-Industrialisierungstheorie und norwegische Erfahrungen. (Structural Consequences of a Resource Boom in an Industrialized Economy: De-industrialization Theory and Norwegian Experience. With English summary.) *Konjunkturpolitik,* 1984, *30*(6), pp. 328–47. [G: Norway]

Enders, Klaus. The Dutch Disease or Problems of a Sectoral Boom. *Z. Wirtschaft. Sozialwissen.,* 1984, *104*(1), pp. 1–20.

Eswaran, Mukesh and Lewis, Tracy R. Appropriability and the Extraction of a Common Property Resource. *Economica,* November 1984, *51*(204), pp. 393–400.

Eswaran, Mukesh and Lewis, Tracy R. Ultimate Recovery of an Exhaustible Resource under Different Market Structures. *J. Environ. Econ. Manage.,* March 1984, *11*(1), pp. 55–69.

Fakhraei, S. Hamid; Narayanan, Rangesan and Hughes, Trevor C. Price Rigidity and Quantity Rationing Rules under Stochastic Water Supply. *Water Resources Res.,* June 1984, *20*(6), pp. 664–70.

Farzin, Y. Hossein. The Effect of the Discount Rate on Depletion of Exhaustible Resources. *J. Polit. Econ.,* October 1984, *92*(5), pp. 841–51.

Finney, Ben R. The Ocean and the Quality of Life. In *Gopalakrishnan, C., ed.,* 1984, pp. 187–92. [G: U.S.]

Fortin, Michael and McBean, Edward A. Forecasting Relative Price Movements for Project Evaluation. *Water Resources Res.,* October 1984, *20*(10), pp. 1327–30. [G: Canada]

Frank, Jeff and Babunovic, Mark. An Investment Model of Natural Resource Markets. *Economica,* February 1984, *51*(201), pp. 83–95. [G: U.S.]

Franklin, Douglas R. and Hageman, Ronda K. Cost Sharing with Irrigated Agriculture: Promise versus Performance. *Water Resources Res.,* August 1984, *20*(8), pp. 1047–51. [G: U.S.]

Freeman, A. Myrick, III. The Quasi-Option Value of Irreversible Development. *J. Environ. Econ. Manage.,* September 1984, *11*(3), pp. 292–95.

Freeman, A. Myrick, III. The Sign and Size of Option Value. *Land Econ.,* February 1984, *60*(1), pp. 1–13.

Friedheim, Robert L. Japan's Ocean Policy: An Assessment. In *Friedheim, R. L., et al.,* 1984, pp. 353–73. [G: Japan]

Friedheim, Robert L. and Akaha, Tsuneo. Japan and the Ocean. In *Friedheim, R. L., et al.,* 1984, pp. 1–20. [G: Japan]

Friedman, Robert, et al. The Use of Models for Water Resources Management, Planning, and Policy. *Water Resources Res.,* July 1984, *20*(7), pp. 793–802. [G: U.S.]

Frost, Hans. Fisheries Management and Uncertainty within the EEC. *Marine Resource Econ.,* 1984, *1*(1), pp. 97–103. [G: EEC]

Fukui, Haruhiro. How Japan Handled UNCLOS Issues: Does Japan Have an Ocean Policy? In *Friedheim, R. L., et al.,* 1984, pp. 21–74. [G: Japan]

Garcia, Timothy L. United States Supreme Court Upholds Indiana Mineral Lapse Statute. *Natural Res. J.,* January 1984, *24*(1), pp. 203–12. [G: U.S.]

Gardner, B. Delworth. The Case for Divestiture. In *Brubaker, S., ed.,* 1984, pp. 156–80. [G: U.S.]

Garnaut, Ross and Clunies Ross, A. Uncertainty, Risk Aversion and the Taxing of Natural Resource Projects. In *Lloyd, P. J., ed.,* 1984, *1975,* pp. 98–115. [G: LDCs]

Gates, John M. Principal Types of Uncertainty in Fishing Operations. *Marine Resource Econ.,* 1984, *1*(1), pp. 31–49.

Gates, Paul W. The Federal Lands: Why We Retained Them. In *Brubaker, S., ed.,* 1984, pp. 35–60. [G: U.S.]

Gaudet, Gérard and Lasserre, Pierre. L'impôt sur le revenu des sociétés et le coût du capital pour l'entreprise minière. (The Corporate Income Tax and the Cost of Capital for the Mining Firm. With English summary.) *Can. J. Econ.,* November 1984, *17*(4), pp. 778–87.

Gibson, Bill. Profit and Rent in a Classical Theory of Exhaustible and Renewable Resources. *Z. Nationalökon.,* 1984, *44*(2), pp. 131–49.

Gowdy, John M. Marx and Resource Scarcity: An Institutionalist Approach. *J. Econ. Issues,* June 1984, *18*(2), pp. 393–400.

Grigg, Richard W. Economics and Future Development of the Precious Coral Fishery in the Pacific. In *Gopalakrishnan, C., ed.,* 1984, pp. 77–85. [G: Japan; Taiwan]

Grilli, Enzo R. and Yang, Maw-Cheng. Real and Monetary Determinants of Non-Oil Primary Commodity Price Movements. In *Storey, G. G.; Schmitz, A. and Sarris, A. H., eds.,* 1984, pp. 3–44. [G: Global]

Gross, Sharon P. Commerce Clause Curbs State Control of Interstate Use of Ground Water: *City of El Paso v. Reynolds. Natural Res. J.,* January 1984, *24*(1), pp. 213–20. [G: U.S.]

Guppy, Nicholas. Tropical Deforestation: A Global View. *Foreign Aff.*, Spring 1984, *62*(4), pp. 928–65. [G: Global]

Hagenstein, Perry R. The Federal Lands Today: Uses and Limits. In *Brubaker, S., ed.*, 1984, pp. 74–107. [G: U.S.]

Hall, Darwin C. and Hall, Jane V. Concepts and Measures of Natural Resource Scarcity with a Summary of Recent Trends. *J. Environ. Econ. Manage.*, December 1984, *11*(4), pp. 363–79. [G: U.S.]

Halvorsen, Robert and Smith, Tim R. On Measuring Natural Resource Scarcity. *J. Polit. Econ.*, October 1984, *92*(5), pp. 954–64. [G: Canada]

Hanke, Steve H. On Water: A Critique of *Global 2000*. In *Simon, J. L. and Kahn, H., eds.*, 1984, pp. 267–71. [G: Global]

Hannesson, Rögnvaldur. Fisheries Management and Uncertainty. *Marine Resource Econ.*, 1984, *1*(1), pp. 89–96. [G: Europe]

Hardie, Ian W. Comparative Rents for Farmland and Timberland in a Subregion of the South. *Southern J. Agr. Econ.*, December 1984, *16*(2), pp. 45–53. [G: U.S.]

Harries, Heinrich. Adaptation of Long-term Contracts. In *Pearce, D. W.; Siebert, H. and Walter, I., eds.*, 1984, pp. 165–68.

Harris, Stuart. Dimensions of Resource Dependence in Exporting Countries. In *Pearce, D. W.; Siebert, H. and Walter, I., eds.*, 1984, pp. 113–33. [G: Papua New Guinea; LDCs]

Hartje, Volkmar J. Zur Effizienz von Institutionen der Meeresnutzung. Eine ökonomische Analyse neuerer seerechtlicher Entwicklungen. (Efficient Institutions for Utilization of the Ocean—An Economic Analysis of Recent Developments of the Law of the Sea. With English summary.) *Z. ges. Staatswiss.*, December 1984, *140*(4), pp. 712–36.

Harvey, D. Michael. Uses and Limits of the Federal Lands Today: Who Cares and How Should Current Law Work? In *Brubaker, S., ed.*, 1984, pp. 108–21. [G: U.S.]

Hazilla, Michael and Kopp, Raymond J. A Factor Demand Model for Strategic Nonfuel Minerals in the Primary Metals Sector. *Land Econ.*, November 1984, *60*(4), pp. 328–39.

Hazilla, Michael and Kopp, Raymond J. Assessing U.S. Vulnerability to Raw Material Supply Disruptions: An Application to Nonfuel Minerals. *Southern Econ. J.*, October 1984, *51*(2), pp. 341–55. [G: U.S.]

Heaps, Terry. The Forestry Maximum Principle. *J. Econ. Dynam. Control*, May 1984, *7*(2), pp. 131–51.

Helliwell, John F. Natural Resources and the Australian Economy. In *Caves, R. E. and Krause, L. B., eds.*, 1984, pp. 81–126. [G: Australia]

Henderson, David M. The Natural Resource-Based Sector. In *Hood, N. and Young, S., eds.*, 1984, pp. 249–87. [G: U.K.]

Henderson, J. V. and Tugwell, M. Exploitation of the Lobster Fishery: Some Empirical Re-

sults. In *Ahmad, Y. J.; Dasgupta, P. and Mäler, K.-G., eds.*, 1984, pp. 71–82. [G: Canada]

Herberg, Horst and Enders, Klaus. More on the Consequences of a Resource Boom and the Cures of the Dutch Disease. In *Siebert, H., ed.*, 1984, pp. 47–94.

Hoel, Michael. Extraction of a Resource with a Substitute for Some of Its Uses. *Can. J. Econ.*, August 1984, *17*(3), pp. 593–602.

Hori, Hajime. Competitive Price Paths of an Exhaustible Resource with Increasing Extraction Costs. *J. Econ. Dynam. Control*, October 1984, *8*(1), pp. 19–32.

Hung, Nguyen Manh; Kemp, Murray C. and Long, Ngo Van. On the Transition from an Exhaustible Resource Stock to an Inexhaustible Substitute. In *[Pearce, I. F.]*, 1984, pp. 105–21.

Hung, Nguyen Manh; Kemp, Murray C. and Long, Ngo Van. On the Transition from an Exhaustible Resource-Stock to an Inexhaustible Substitute. In *Kemp, M. C. and Long, N. V., eds.*, 1984, pp. 105–22.

Hunter, Lachlan. Tropical Forest Plantations and Natural Stand Management: A National Lesson from East Kalimantan? *Bull. Indonesian Econ. Stud.*, April 1984, *20*(1), pp. 98–116. [G: Indonesia]

Hyman, Eric L. Land-Use Planning to Help Sustain Tropical Forest Resources. *World Devel.*, August 1984, *12*(8), pp. 837–47. [G: Global]

Hyman, Eric L. Providing Public Lands for Smallholder Agroforestry in the Province of Ilocos Norte, Philippines. *J. Devel. Areas*, January 1984, *18*(2), pp. 177–90. [G: Philippines]

Ikeda, Saburo. Nonlinear Prediction Models for River Flows and Typhoon Precipitation by Self-Organizing Methods. In *Farlow, S. J., ed.*, 1984, pp. 149–67. [G: Japan]

Ingram, Helen M., et al. Guidelines for Improved Institutional Analysis in Water Resources Planning. *Water Resources Res.*, March 1984, *20*(3), pp. 323–34. [G: U.S.]

Jackson, R. G. Resource Development and Our Future. In *Lloyd, P. J., ed.*, 1984, *1982*, pp. 29–32. [G: Australia]

Jones, C. Vaughan and Morris, John R. Instrumental Price Estimates and Residential Water Demand. *Water Resources Res.*, February 1984, *20*(2), pp. 197–202. [G: U.S.]

Kabir, M. and Ridler, N. B. The Demand for Atlantic Salmon in Canada. *Can. J. Agr. Econ.*, November 1984, *32*(3), pp. 560–68. [G: Canada]

Kaden, S. Analysis of Regional Water Policies in Open-Cast Mining Areas—A Multicriteria Approach. In *Grauer, M. and Wierzbicki, A. P., eds.*, 1984, pp. 218–26.

Karp, Larry. Optimality and Consistency in a Differential Game with Non-renewable Resources. *J. Econ. Dynam. Control*, October 1984, *8*(1), pp. 73–97.

Karp, Larry and Pope, C. Arden, III. Range

Management under Uncertainty. *Amer. J. Agr. Econ.*, November 1984, *66*(4), pp. 437–46. **[G: U.S.]**

Karpoff, Jonathan M. Low-Interest Loans and the Markets for Limited Entry Permits in the Alaska Salmon Fisheries. *Land Econ.*, February 1984, *60*(1), pp. 69–80. **[G: U.S.]**

Kasanen, Eero. Turnpikes and Detours in the Renewable Resource Exploitation under Price Shocks. *J. Econ. Dynam. Control*, February 1984, *7*(1), pp. 1–20. **[G: Finland]**

Kassler, Peter. Risk and Oil Exploration. In *Pearce, D. W.; Siebert, H. and Walter, I., eds.*, 1984, pp. 75–86.

Katekaru, Alvin Z. A Cost-Revenue Assessment of the Hawaiian Fish Aggregating System. In *Gopalakrishnan, C., ed.*, 1984, pp. 145–51. **[G: U.S.]**

Keith, Kent M. An Ethic for Ocean Resource Development: Lessons from Hawaii. In *Gopalakrishnan, C., ed.*, 1984, pp. 229–41. **[G: U.S.]**

Kemp, Murray C. and Long, Ngo Van. On the Development of a Substitute for an Exhaustible Natural Resource. In *Kemp, M. C. and Long, N. V., eds.*, 1984, *1982*, pp. 123–43.

Kemp, Murray C. and Long, Ngo Van. On the Economics of Forests. In *Kemp, M. C. and Long, N. V., eds.*, 1984, *1983*, pp. 163–87.

Kemp, Murray C. and Long, Ngo Van. The Efficiency of Competitive Markets in a Context of Exhaustible Resources. In *Kemp, M. C. and Long, N. V., eds.*, 1984, *1982*, pp. 219–25.

Kemp, Murray C. and Long, Ngo Van. The Optimal Restriction of Resource Imports and the Optimal Investment in Capacity for Substitute Production. In *Kemp, M. C. and Long, N. V., eds.*, 1984, pp. 145–60.

Kemp, Murray C. and Long, Ngo Van. The Problem of Survival: An Open Economy. In *Kemp, M. C. and Long, N. V., eds.*, 1984, pp. 27–35.

Kemp, Murray C. and Long, Ngo Van. The Role of Natural Resources in Trade Models. In *Jones, R. W. and Kenen, P., eds.*, 1984, pp. 367–417.

Kemp, Murray C. and Long, Ngo Van. The State of the Art. In *Kemp, M. C. and Long, N. V., eds.*, 1984, pp. 3–10.

Kemp, Murray C. and Long, Ngo Van. Towards a More General Theory of the Order of Exploitation of Non-renewable Resource-Deposits. In *Kemp, M. C. and Long, N. V., eds.*, 1984, pp. 39–74.

Kemp, Murray C.; Long, Ngo Van and Shimomura, Kazuo. The Problem of Survival: A Closed Economy. In *Kemp, M. C. and Long, N. V., eds.*, 1984, pp. 13–26.

Khan, M. Ali. International Trade and Foreign Investment: A Model with Asymmetric Production. *Pakistan Devel. Rev.*, Winter 1984, *23*(4), pp. 509–30.

Kimmel, Sheldon. A Note on Extraction with Nonconvex Costs [On the Nonexistence of Market Equilibria in Exhaustible Resource

Markets with Decreasing Costs]. *J. Polit. Econ.*, December 1984, *92*(6), pp. 1158–67.

Kirke, J. and Arthur, J. Water Supply Issues. In *Richards, P. J. and Thomson, A. M., eds.*, 1984, pp. 123–51. **[G: LDCs]**

Kirpich, Phillip Z. Water Resources Development. In *Weiss, C. and Jéquier, N., eds.*, 1984, pp. 179–95. **[G: Selected Countries]**

Koenig, Evan F. Controlling Stock Externalities in a Common Property Fishery Subject to Uncertainty. *J. Environ. Econ. Manage.*, June 1984, *11*(2), pp. 124–38.

Koenig, Evan F. Fisheries Regulation under Uncertainty: A Dynamic Analysis. *Marine Resource Econ.*, 1984, *1*(2), pp. 193–208.

Koga, Mamoru. Developing a Manganese Nodule Policy for Japan. In *Friedheim, R. L., et al.*, 1984, pp. 227–75. **[G: Japan; Other Countries]**

Koga, Mamoru and Nakahara, Hiroyuki. Japanese Ocean Science and Technology Policy and the National Budget. In *Friedheim, R. L., et al.*, 1984, pp. 108–29. **[G: Japan]**

Krelle, Wilhelm. Economic Growth with Exhaustible Resources and Environmental Protection. *Z. ges. Staatswiss.*, September 1984, *140*(3), pp. 399–429.

Laitner, John P. Resource Extraction Costs and Competitive Steady-State Growth. *Int. Econ. Rev.*, June 1984, *25*(2), pp. 297–314.

Lasserre, Pierre. Reserve and Land Prices with Exploration under Uncertainty. *J. Environ. Econ. Manage.*, September 1984, *11*(3), pp. 191–201.

Lavigne, Marie. Long-term Commodity Agreements and the USSR. In *Kostecki, M. M., ed.*, 1984, pp. 15–25. **[G: U.S.S.R.; CMEA; Global]**

Leitzinger, Jeffrey J. and Stiglitz, Joseph E. Information Externalities in Oil and Gas Leasing. *Contemp. Policy Issue*, March 1984, (5), pp. 44–57. **[G: U.S.]**

Leshy, John D. Sharing Federal Multiple-Use Lands: Historic Lessons and Speculations for the Future. In *Brubaker, S., ed.*, 1984, pp. 235–73. **[G: U.S.]**

Lewis, Stephen R., Jr. Development Problems of the Mineral-Rich Countries. In *[Chenery, H. B.]*, 1984, pp. 157–77.

Liden, David. Pulling the Pillars: Energy Development and Land Reform in Appalachia. In *Geisler, C. C. and Popper, F. J., eds.*, 1984, pp. 101–16. **[G: U.S.]**

Llewellyn, Othman Abd ar-Rahman. Islamic Jurisprudence and Environmental Planning. *J. Res. Islamic Econ.*, Winter 1984, *1*(2), pp. 25–49.

Lloyd, P. J. Individual Mines or Oilfields: Introduction. In *Lloyd, P. J., ed.*, 1984, pp. 35–52. **[G: Australia]**

Lloyd, P. J. Major Issues of the Current Resources Boom. In *Lloyd, P. J., ed.*, 1984, pp. 3–9. **[G: Australia]**

Lloyd, P. J. Mineral Economics in Australia: Conclusion. In *Lloyd, P. J., ed.*, 1984, pp. 323–25. **[G: Australia]**

Lloyd, P. J. Mineral Economics in Australia: Economy-Wide Effects: Introduction. In *Lloyd, P. J., ed.,* 1984, pp. 275–84.
[G: Australia]

Lloyd, P. J. Mining Rights as a Component of Aboriginal Land Rights: An Economic Assessment. In *Lloyd, P. J., ed.,* 1984, pp. 138–56.
[G: Australia]

Löfgren, Karl Gustaf. Endowments and Timber Supply. *Europ. Rev. Agr. Econ.,* 1984, *11*(1), pp. 17–28.

Long, Ngo Van. On the Short-run and Long-run Effects of a Resource Boom. In *Siebert, H., ed.,* 1984, pp. 17–45.

Long, Ngo Van. Risk and Resource Economics: The State of the Art. In *Pearce, D. W.; Siebert, H. and Walter, I., eds.,* 1984, pp. 59–73.

Long, Ngo Van and Sinn, Hans-Werner. Optimal Taxation and Economic Depreciation: A General Equilibrium Model with Capital and an Exhaustible Resource. In *Kemp, M. C. and Long, N. V., eds.,* 1984, pp. 227–46.

Lotov, A. V. and Stolyarova, H. M. Multiobjective Analysis of Forestry Management Models Using the Generalized Reachable Set Method. In *Grauer, M. and Wierzbicki, A. P., eds.,* 1984, pp. 236–47.

Lynne, Gary D.; Boggess, William G. and Portier, Kenneth M. Irrigation Water Supply as a Bioeconomic Process. *Southern J. Agr. Econ.,* December 1984, *16*(2), pp. 73–82.
[G: U.S.]

MacDonald, J. Douglas and Mazany, R. L. Quality Improvement: Panacea for the Atlantic Fishing Industry? *Can. Public Policy,* September 1984, *10*(3), pp. 278–86. [G: Canada]

Madariaga, Bruce and McConnell, Kenneth E. Value of Irrigation Water in the Middle Atlantic States: An Econometric Approach. *Southern J. Agr. Econ.,* December 1984, *16*(2), pp. 91–98. [G: U.S.]

Marion, Nancy Peregrim and Svensson, Lars E. O. Adjustment to Expected and Unexpected Oil Price Changes. *Can. J. Econ.,* February 1984, *17*(1), pp. 15–31.

Marjoram, Tony. The Potential Impacts of the Exploitation of New Ocean Resources on the Pacific. In *Gopalakrishnan, C., ed.,* 1984, pp. 61–73. [G: S. Pacific]

Marsh, James B. The Potential Economic Impact of Technological Progress on the Development of Manganese Nodule Mining. In *Gopalakrishnan, C., ed.,* 1984, pp. 49–59.

Marston, Geoffrey. Extension and Delimitation of National Sea Boundaries in the Mediterranean. In *Luciani, G., ed.,* 1984, pp. 75–125.
[G: Mediterranean]

Masud, Ross. The Asian–African Legal Consultative Committee: A Survey of Activities. *J. World Trade Law,* January:February 1984, *18*(1), pp. 81–88. [G: Asia; Africa]

Matoussi, Mohamed Salah. Intégration de l'aléatoire et de l'allocation temporelle dans la planification des ressources hydrauliques "Modèle Anasim." (With English summary.) *Revue Écon. Polit.,* March–April 1984, *94*(2), pp. 226–53. [G: Tunisia]

McConnell, Kenneth E. and Phipps, Tim T. Optimum Forest Rotation in an Imperfect Stumpage Market: Comment. *Land Econ.,* May 1984, *60*(2), pp. 215–17.

McDermott, John. Rational Host Country Use of a Severance Tax. *J. Environ. Econ. Manage.,* December 1984, *11*(4), pp. 391–402.

McEvoy, Arthur F. and Scheiber, Harry N. Scientists, Entrepreneurs, and the Policy Process: A Study of the Post-1945 California Sardine Depletion. *J. Econ. Hist.,* June 1984, *44*(2), pp. 393–406. [G: U.S.]

McMillan, John and Sinn, Hans-Werner. Oligopolistic Extraction of a Common-Property Resource: Dynamic Equilibria. In *Kemp, M. C. and Long, N. V., eds.,* 1984, pp. 199–214.

Mead, Walter J. and Moseidjord, Asbjorn. A New Market-based Method for Estimating Oil Field Reserves: An Application to the Santa Maria Basin. *J. Energy Devel.,* Spring 1984, *9*(2), pp. 163–76. [G: U.S.]

Mead, Walter J.; Moseidjord, Asbjorn and Muraoka, Dennis D. Alternative Bid Variables as Instruments of OCS Leasing Policy. *Contemp. Policy Issue,* March 1984, (5), pp. 30–43.
[G: U.S.]

Merrifield, David E. and Haynes, Richard W. The Adjustment of Product and Factor Markets: An Application to the Pacific Northwest Forest Products Industry. *Amer. J. Agr. Econ.,* February 1984, *66*(1), pp. 79–87. [G: U.S.]

Miller, J. D. B. Raw Materials and Their Role in Regional Economic Cooperation. In *Downen, R. L. and Dickson, B. J., eds.,* 1984, pp. 121–28. [G: Pacific Basin]

Mirman, Leonard J. and Spulber, Daniel F. Uncertainty and Markets for Renewable Resources. *J. Econ. Dynam. Control,* December 1984, *8*(3), pp. 239–64.

Morehouse, Thomas A. Alaskan Resources Development: Conclusion: The Limits of Policy. In *Morehouse, T. A., ed.,* 1984, pp. 199–206.
[G: U.S.]

Morehouse, Thomas A. Alaskan Resources Development: Introduction. In *Morehouse, T. A., ed.,* 1984, pp. 1–12. [G: U.S.]

Morehouse, Thomas A. Resource Development and Alaska Wealth Management. In *Morehouse, T. A., ed.,* 1984, pp. 169–97.
[G: U.S.]

Morey, Edward R. The Choice of Ski Areas: Estimation of a Generalized CES Preference Ordering with Characteristics. *Rev. Econ. Statist.,* November 1984, *66*(4), pp. 584–90.
[G: U.S.]

Moussavian, Mohammed and Samuelson, Larry. On the Extraction of an Exhaustible Resource by a Monopoly. *J. Environ. Econ. Manage.,* June 1984, *11*(2), pp. 139–46.

Mumy, Gene E. Competitive Equilibria in Exhaustible Resource Markets with Decreasing Costs: A Comment on Eswaran, Lewis, and Heaps's Demonstration of Nonexistence. *J. Po-*

lit. Econ., December 1984, *92*(6), pp. 1168–74.

Murota, Takeshi. Heat Economy of the Water Planet Earth: An Entropic Analysis and the Water–Soil Matrix Theory. *Hitotsubashi J. Econ.*, December 1984, *25*(2), pp. 161–72. **[G: U.K.; Japan]**

Nakahara, Hiroyuki. Consensus Building in the Council for Ocean Development. In *Friedheim, R. L., et al.*, 1984, pp. 75–107. **[G: Japan]**

Nautiyal, J. C. Optimum Forest Rotation in an Imperfect Stumpage Market: Reply. *Land Econ.*, May 1984, *60*(2), pp. 218.

Nautiyal, J. C. and Innes, M. R. Optimal Economic Rotation for a Mixed Species Even-aged Forest. *Can. J. Agr. Econ.*, November 1984, *32*(3), pp. 526–38. **[G: Canada]**

Neary, J. Peter and van Wijnbergen, Sweder. Can an Oil Discovery Lead to a Recession? A Comment. *Econ. J.*, June 1984, *94*(374), pp. 390–95. **[G: U.K.]**

Nelson, Robert H. Ideology and Public Land Policy: The Current Crisis. In *Brubaker, S., ed.*, 1984, pp. 275–98. **[G: U.S.]**

Newbery, David M. G. The Economics of Oil. In *van der Ploeg, F., ed.*, 1984, pp. 519–67.

Ng, Yew-Kwang. Quasi-Pareto Social Improvements. *Amer. Econ. Rev.*, December 1984, *74*(5), pp. 1033–50.

Norgaard, Richard B. Coevolutionary Development Potential. *Land Econ.*, May 1984, *60*(2), pp. 160–73.

O'Mara, Gerald T. and Duloy, John H. Modeling Efficient Water Allocation in a Conjunctive Use Regime: The Indus Basin of Pakistan. *Water Resources Res.*, November 1984, *20*(11), pp. 1489–98. **[G: Pakistan]**

Odell, Peter R. Dimensions of Resource Dependence in Exporting Countries: Comment. In *Pearce, D. W.; Siebert, H. and Walter, I., eds.*, 1984, pp. 134–36. **[G: Papua New Guinea; LDCs]**

Opaluch, James J. A Test of Consumer Demand Response to Water Prices: Reply [Urban Residential Demand for Water in the United States: Further Discussion]. *Land Econ.*, November 1984, *60*(4), pp. 417–21. **[G: U.S.]**

Opaluch, James J. and Bockstael, Nancy E. Behavioral Modeling and Fisheries Management. *Marine Resource Econ.*, 1984, *1*(1), pp. 105–15. **[G: U.S.]**

Ortiz, Roxanne Dunbar. Land Reform and Indian Survival in the United States. In *Geisler, C. C. and Popper, F. J., eds.*, 1984, pp. 151–71. **[G: U.S.]**

Ovsienko, Iu. V. and Sobolev, I. I. Optimizing Forestry Use in a Way Which Takes Account of Its Ecological Impact. *Matekon*, Summer 1984, *20*(4), pp. 64–80. **[G: U.S.S.R.]**

Pakravan, Karim. Estimation of User's Cost for a Depletable Resource Such as Oil. *Energy Econ.*, January 1984, *6*(1), pp. 35–40. **[G: Middle East]**

Palanisami, K. and Easter, K. William. Ex Post

Evaluation of Flood Control Investments: A Case Study in North Dakota. *Water Resources Res.*, December 1984, *20*(12), pp. 1785–90. **[G: U.S.]**

Pardo, Arvid. The Emerging Marine Economy of Micronesia and Polynesia: A Possible Scenario. In *Gopalakrishnan, C., ed.*, 1984, pp. 3–13. **[G: Pacific Basin]**

Penrose, Edith. The Management of Conflict in Natural-Resource Projects. In *Pearce, D. W.; Siebert, H. and Walter, I., eds.*, 1984, pp. 37–56.

Pesaran, M. H. Macroeconomic Policy in an Oil-exporting Economy with Foreign Exchange Controls. *Economica*, August 1984, *51*(203), pp. 253–70.

Pethig, Rüdiger. International Common Property Resources. In *Pearce, D. W.; Siebert, H. and Walter, I., eds.*, 1984, pp. 339–56. **[G: Global]**

Pindyck, Robert S. Uncertainty in the Theory of Renewable Resource Markets. *Rev. Econ. Stud.*, April 1984, *51*(2), pp. 289–303.

Plourde, Charles and Bodell, Richard. Uncertainty in Fisheries Economics: The Role of the Discount Rate. *Marine Resource Econ.*, 1984, *1*(2), pp. 155–70.

Polèse, Mario. Population, Resources, Technology, and Environment: Trends and Implications: Comment. In *Trent, J. and Lamy, P., eds.*, 1984, pp. 205–10.

Poliak, A. The Assessment of Material Resources. *Prob. Econ.*, December 1984, *27*(8), pp. 71–88. **[G: U.S.S.R.]**

Popper, Frank J. The Ambiguous End of the Sagebrush Rebellion. In *Geisler, C. C. and Popper, F. J., eds.*, 1984, pp. 117–28. **[G: U.S.]**

Porter, Richard C. The Optimal Timing of an Exhaustible, Reversible Wilderness Development Project. *Land Econ.*, August 1984, *60*(3), pp. 247–54. **[G: U.S.]**

Portney, Paul R. Natural Resources and the Environment: More Controversy than Change. In *Palmer, J. L. and Sawhill, I. V., eds.*, 1984, pp. 141–75. **[G: U.S.]**

Prager, Michael H. and Saila, Saul B. Predictive GMDH Models of Shrimp Catches: Some Practical Considerations. In *Farlow, S. J., ed.*, 1984, pp. 179–97. **[G: U.S.]**

Prewo, Wilfried E. International Common Property Resources: Comment. In *Pearce, D. W.; Siebert, H. and Walter, I., eds.*, 1984, pp. 357–63. **[G: Global]**

Prochaska, Fred J. Principal Types of Uncertainty in Seafood Processing and Marketing. *Marine Resource Econ.*, 1984, *1*(1), pp. 51–66. **[G: U.S.]**

Radetzki, Marian and Van Duyne, Carl. The Response of Mining Investment to a Decline in Economic Growth: The Case of Copper in the 1970s. *J. Devel. Econ.*, May–June–August 1984, *15*(1,2,3), pp. 19–45. **[G: LDCs]**

Ray, Debraj. Survival, Growth and Technical Progress in a Small Resource-Importing Economy. *Int. Econ. Rev.*, June 1984, *25*(2), pp. 275–95.

Reed, William J. The Effects of the Risk of Fire on the Optimal Rotation of a Forest. *J. Environ. Econ. Manage.*, June 1984, *11*(2), pp. 180–90.

Rielley, Kevin J.; Larsen, Wendy U. and Weaver, Clifford L. Partnership in the Pinelands. In *Geisler, C. C. and Popper, F. J., eds.*, 1984, pp. 129–48.   [G: U.S.]

Robb, Dean H. Foreign Fishing Access Regimes in the Pacific Basin. In *Gopalakrishnan, C., ed.*, 1984, pp. 107–19.   [G: Pacific Basin]

Runge, Carlisle Ford. Energy Exploration on Wilderness: "Privatization" and Public Lands Management. *Land Econ.*, February 1984, *60*(1), pp. 56–68.   [G: U.S.]

Samples, Karl C. and Prescott, James H. The Use of Sail-Assisted Commercial Fishing Vessels in the Pacific: An Economic Appraisal. In *Gopalakrishnan, C., ed.*, 1984, pp. 87–106.

Sax, Joseph L. The Claim for Retention of the Public Lands. In *Brubaker, S., ed.*, 1984, pp. 125–48.   [G: U.S.]

Schoolmaster, F. Andrew. Water Development Referenda and Planning in Texas. *Soc. Sci. Quart.*, December 1984, *65*(4), pp. 1147–56.   [G: U.S.]

Sedjo, Roger A. and Clawson, Marion. Global Forests. In *Simon, J. L. and Kahn, H., eds.*, 1984, pp. 128–70.   [G: Global]

Shabman, Leonard A. Water Resources Management: Policy Economics for an Era of Transitions. *Southern J. Agr. Econ.*, July 1984, *16*(1), pp. 53–65.   [G: U.S.]

Sharefkin, Mark; Shechter, Mordechai and Kneese, Allen V. Impacts, Costs, and Techniques for Mitigation of Contaminated Groundwater: A Review. *Water Resources Res.*, December 1984, *20*(12), pp. 1771–83. [G: U.S.]

Shimomura, Kazuo. The Optimal Order of Exploitation of Deposits of a Renewable Resource. In *Kemp, M. C. and Long, N. V., eds.*, 1984, pp. 75–104.

Siebert, Horst. Allocation Policy in a Resource-Exporting Country. In *Siebert, H., ed.*, 1984, pp. 1–16.

Siebert, Horst. The Economics of Natural Resources Ventures. In *Pearce, D. W.; Siebert, H. and Walter, I., eds.*, 1984, pp. 11–35.   [G: Selected Countries]

Silkman, Richard. The Commons Problems Revisited: Shellfishing on Long Island. *J. Policy Anal. Manage.*, Spring 1984, *3*(3), pp. 451–53.   [G: U.S.]

Simmons, Randy T. and Mitchell, William C. Politics and the New Resource Economics. *Contemp. Policy Issue*, March 1984, (5), pp. 1–13.

Simon, Julian L. and Wildavsky, Aaron. On Species Loss, the Absence of Data, and Risks to Humanity. In *Simon, J. L. and Kahn, H., eds.*, 1984, pp. 171–83.   [G: Global]

Sinn, Hans-Werner. Common Property Resources, Storage Facilities and Ownership Structures: A Cournot Model of the Oil Market. *Economica*, August 1984, *51*(203), pp. 235–52.

Sinn, Hans-Werner. Optimal Resource Taxation. In *Pearce, D. W.; Siebert, H. and Walter, I., eds.*, 1984, pp. 197–204.

Sissenwine, M. P. The Uncertain Environment of Fishery Scientists and Managers. *Marine Resource Econ.*, 1984, *1*(1), pp. 1–30.

Slade, Margaret E. Tax Policy and the Supply of Exhaustible Resources: Theory and Practice. *Land Econ.*, May 1984, *60*(2), pp. 133–47.   [G: U.S.]

Smith, Stanton R. Energy Supply Management. In *Baum, V., et al.*, 1984, pp. 36–52.   [G: LDCs]

Smith, V. Kerry. A Bound for Option Value. *Land Econ.*, August 1984, *60*(3), pp. 292–96.

Smith, V. Kerry and Krutilla, John V. Economic Growth, Resource Availability, and Environmental Quality. *Amer. Econ. Rev.*, May 1984, *74*(2), pp. 226–30.

Smith, Zachary A. Centralized Decisionmaking in the Administration of Groundwater Rights: The Experience of Arizona, California and New Mexico and Suggestions for the Future. *Natural Res. J.*, July 1984, *24*(3), pp. 641–88.   [G: U.S.]

Snape, R. H. Effects of Mineral Development on the Economy. In *Lloyd, P. J., ed.*, 1984, 1977, pp. 311–22.   [G: Australia]

Solow, Robert M. The Economics of Resources or the Resources of Economics. In *Lloyd, P. J., ed.*, 1984, *1974*, pp. 53–70.

Spence, A. Michael. Blue Whales and Applied Control Theory. In *Ahmad, Y. J.; Dasgupta, P. and Mäler, K.-G., eds.*, 1984, pp. 43–68.

Stroup, Richard L. In Defense of Asset Management: The Privatization Component. *Contemp. Policy Issue*, March 1984, (5), pp. 14–21.   [G: U.S.]

Stroup, Richard L. Weaknesses in the Case for Retention. In *Brubaker, S., ed.*, 1984, pp. 149–55.   [G: U.S.]

Sundaresan, Suresh M. Equilibrium Valuation of Natural Resources. *J. Bus.*, October 1984, *57*(4), pp. 493–518.

Swerdloff, Stanley N. Hawaii's Fisheries: An Overview. In *Gopalakrishnan, C., ed.*, 1984, pp. 121–43.   [G: U.S.]

Taylor, Carol A. and Charney, Alberta H. The Effects of State Taxation on United States Copper Supply: Comment. *Land Econ.*, May 1984, *60*(2), pp. 211–14.   [G: U.S.]

Tisdell, Clem A. The Provision of Wilderness by Clubs. *Rivista Int. Sci. Econ. Com.*, August 1984, *31*(8), pp. 758–61.

Tuck, Bradford H. Alaskan Resources Development: Nonfuel Minerals and Coal. In *Morehouse, T. A., ed.*, 1984, pp. 79–104.   [G: U.S.]

Tucker, Richard P. The Historical Context of Social Forestry in the Kumaon Himalayas. *J. Devel. Areas*, April 1984, *18*(3), pp. 341–55.   [G: India]

Tussing, Arlon R. Alaska's Petroleum-Based Economy. In *Morehouse, T. A., ed.*, 1984, pp. 51–78.   [G: U.S.]

Utrecht, Ernst. Land and Agriculture, Fishing

and Mining. In *Utrecht, E., ed.*, 1984, pp. 121–77. **[G: Fiji]**

Van Den Beldt, Rick J. Supplying Firewood for Household Energy. In *Islam, M. N.; Morse, R. and Soesastro, M. H., eds.*, 1984, pp. 381–414. **[G: Asian LDCs]**

Vaux, H. J., Jr. and Howitt, Richard E. Managing Water Scarcity: An Evaluation of Interregional Transfers. *Water Resources Res.*, July 1984, *20*(7), pp. 785–92. **[G: U.S.]**

Walker, John L. Tall Trees, People, and Politics: The Opportunity Costs of the Redwood National Park. *Contemp. Policy Issue*, March 1984, (5), pp. 22–29. **[G: U.S.]**

Walsh, Richard G.; Loomis, John B. and Gillman, Richard A. Valuing Option, Existence, and Bequest Demands for Wilderness. *Land Econ.*, February 1984, *60*(1), pp. 14–29. **[G: U.S.]**

Wandschneider, Philip R. Managing River Systems: Centralization versus Decentralization. *Natural Res. J.*, October 1984, *24*(4), pp. 1043–66. **[G: U.S.]**

Wassermann, Ursula. UNCTAD: International Tropical Timber Agreement. *J. World Trade Law*, January:February 1984, *18*(1), pp. 89–91.

Watkins, G. Campbell; Kirkby, R. G. and Lawrey, Roger N. Risk and the Rate of Return on Arctic Natural Gas: An Illustrative Analysis. In *Pearce, D. W.; Siebert, H. and Walter, I., eds.*, 1984, pp. 87–109. **[G: U.S.; Canada]**

Waugh, Frederick V. and Miller, Morton M. Fish Cycles: A Harmonic Analysis. In *Waugh, F. V.*, 1984, *1970*, pp. 440–48. **[G: U.S.]**

Weimer, A. M. A Note on the Early History of Land Economics. *Amer. Real Estate Urban Econ. Assoc. J.*, Fall 1984, *12*(3), pp. 408–16. **[G: U.S.]**

White, Gilbert F. Water Resource Adequacy: Illusion and Reality. In *Simon, J. L. and Kahn, H., eds.*, 1984, pp. 250–66. **[G: Global]**

Williams, Richard M. Uranium Production and Distribution: Prospects and Concepts. In *Brookes, L. G. and Motamen, H., eds.*, 1984, pp. 116–44. **[G: Global]**

Willis, Robert; Finney, Brad A. and Chu, Wen-Sen. Monte Carlo Optimization for Reservoir Operation. *Water Resources Res.*, September 1984, *20*(9), pp. 1177–82. **[G: U.S.]**

Wise, John P. The Future of Food from the Sea. In *Simon, J. L. and Kahn, H., eds.*, 1984, pp. 113–27. **[G: Global]**

Yandle, Bruce. Groundwater and the Land Value Tax: Some Dimensions of the Problems Facing Fiscal Specialists in Applying Rent Taxation to Underground Resources. *Amer. J. Econ. Soc.*, July 1984, *43*(3), pp. 323–32.

Yohe, Gary W. Regulation under Uncertainty: An Intuitive Survey and Application to Fisheries. *Marine Resource Econ.*, 1984, *1*(2), pp. 171–92.

Zeller, Susan. New Mexico's Water Exportation Statute: Will It Float? *Natural Res. J.*, April 1984, *24*(2), pp. 471–86. **[G: U.S.]**

Ziegler, Joseph A. and Bell, Stephen E. Estimat-

ing Demand for Intake Water by Self-Supplied Firms. *Water Resources Res.*, January 1984, *20*(1), pp. 4–8. **[G: U.S.]**

7211 Recreational Aspects of Natural Resources

Adamowicz, W. L. and Phillips, W. E. A Comparison of Extra Market Benefit Evaluation Techniques: A Reply. *Can. J. Agr. Econ.*, November 1984, *32*(3), pp. 590–92. **[G: Canada]**

Beggs, John J. The Value of Travel to Recreational Facilities: The Uncertainty Issue. *Int. J. Transport Econ.*, April 1984, *11*(1), pp. 53–59. **[G: Australia]**

Bennett, J. W. Using Direct Questioning to Value the Existence Benefits of Preserved Natural Areas. *Australian J. Agr. Econ.*, August/December 1984, *28*(2–3), pp. 135–52.

Brown, Gardner M., Jr. and Mendelsohn, Robert. The Hedonic Travel Cost Method. *Rev. Econ. Statist.*, August 1984, *66*(3), pp. 427–33. **[G: U.S.]**

Clawson, Marion. Major Alternatives for Future Management of the Federal Lands. In *Brubaker, S., ed.*, 1984, pp. 195–234. **[G: U.S.]**

Cooley, Richard A. Evolution of Alaska Land Policy. In *Morehouse, T. A., ed.*, 1984, pp. 13–49. **[G: U.S.]**

Hagenstein, Perry R. The Federal Lands Today: Uses and Limits. In *Brubaker, S., ed.*, 1984, pp. 74–107. **[G: U.S.]**

Hanemann, W. Michael. Welfare Evaluations in Contingent Valuation Experiments with Discrete Responses. *Amer. J. Agr. Econ.*, August 1984, *66*(3), pp. 332–41. **[G: U.S.]**

Hay, Michael J. and McConnell, Kenneth E. Harvesting and Nonconsumptive Wildlife Recreation Decisions. *Land Econ.*, November 1984, *60*(4), pp. 388–96. **[G: U.S.]**

Lieber, Stanley R. and Fesenmaier, Daniel R. Modelling Recreation Choice: A Case Study of Management Alternatives in Chicago. *Reg. Stud.*, February 1984, *18*(1), pp. 31–43. **[G: U.S.]**

Milon, J. Walter; Gressel, Jonathan and Mulkey, David. Hedonic Amenity Valuation and Functional Form Specification. *Land Econ.*, November 1984, *60*(4), pp. 378–87. **[G: U.S.]**

Morash, Tal. The Economic Impact of Marine Recreation. In *Gopalakrishnan, C., ed.*, 1984, pp. 179–86.

Ribaudo, Marc O. and Epp, Donald J. The Importance of Sample Dicrimination in Using the Travel Cost Method to Estimate the Benefits of Improved Water Quality. *Land Econ.*, November 1984, *60*(4), pp. 397–403.

Stephens, R. J. Forestry or a National Park: A New Zealand Case Study. *Int. J. Soc. Econ.*, 1984, *11*(3/4), pp. 29–44. **[G: New Zealand]**

Van Kooten, G. C. A Comparison of Extra Market Benefit Evaluation Techniques: Comment. *Can. J. Agr. Econ.*, November 1984, *32*(3), pp. 584–89.

Ward, Frank A. Specification Considerations for the Price Variable in Travel Cost Demand Models. *Land Econ.*, August 1984, *60*(3), pp. 301–05.

722 Conservation and Pollution

7220 Conservation and Pollution

Adams, Richard M.; Crocker, Thomas D. and Katz., Richard W. Assessing the Adequacy of Natural Science Information: A Bayesian Approach. *Rev. Econ. Statist.*, November 1984, *66*(4), pp. 568–75. [G: U.S.]

Andrews, Richard N. L. Economics and Environmental Decisions, Past and Present. In *Smith, V. K., ed.*, 1984, pp. 43–85. [G: U.S.]

Atkinson, Scott E. and Tietenberg, T. H. Approaches for Reaching Ambient Standards in Non-Attainment Areas: Financial Burden and Efficiency Considerations. *Land Econ.*, May 1984, *60*(2), pp. 148–59. [G: U.S.]

Baumann, Duane D.; Boland, John J. and Sims, John H. Water Conservation: The Struggle Over Definition. *Water Resources Res.*, April 1984, *20*(4), pp. 428–34. [G: U.S.]

Baumol, William J. and Mills, Edwin S. Incentives for Solving Social Problems. *Challenge*, November/December 1984, *27*(5), pp. 47–53.

Baumol, William J. and Oates, Wallace E. Long-run Trends in Environmental Quality. In *Simon, J. L. and Kahn, H., eds.*, 1984, pp. 439–75. [G: U.S.; Selected Countries]

Bennett, J. W. Using Direct Questioning to Value the Existence Benefits of Preserved Natural Areas. *Australian J. Agr. Econ.*, August/December 1984, *28*(2–3), pp. 135–52.

Berman, Matthew D. Alaskan Resources Development: Renewable Resources. In *Morehouse, T. A., ed.*, 1984, pp. 105–33. [G: U.S.]

Bharier, Julian. Water Supply and Waste Disposal. In *Weiss, C. and Jéquier, N., eds.*, 1984, pp. 107–24.

Bird, Richard M. Put Up or Shut Up: Self-Assessment and Asymmetric Information. *J. Policy Anal. Manage.*, Summer 1984, *3*(4), pp. 618–20.

Bjornstad, David J. and Vogt, David P. Some Comments Relating to Model Specification on "Effects of Nuclear Plants on Residential Property Values." *J. Reg. Sci.*, February 1984, *24*(1), pp. 135–36. [G: U.S.]

Blake, Gerald H. Mediterranean Non-energy Resources: Scope for Cooperation and Dangers of Conflict. In *Luciani, G., ed.*, 1984, pp. 41–74. [G: Mediterranean]

Brown, Deborah J. and Smith, Martha. Crop Substitution in the Estimation of Economic Benefits Due to Ozone Reduction. *J. Environ. Econ. Manage.*, December 1984, *11*(4), pp. 347–62. [G: U.S.]

Brown, Gardner M., Jr. and Goldstein, Jon H. A Model for Valuing Endangered Species. *J. Environ. Econ. Manage.*, December 1984, *11*(4), pp. 303–09.

Brown, Gardner M., Jr. and Johnson, Ralph W. Pollution Control by Effluent Charges: It Works in the Federal Republic of Germany, Why Not in the United States? *Natural Res. J.*, October 1984, *24*(4), pp. 929–66. [G: U.S.; W. Germany]

Brown, Keith C. Conservation: Illiberal Motives? *Land Econ.*, August 1984, *60*(3), pp. 310–13.

Buttel, Frederick H. Socioeconomic Equity and Environmental Quality in North American Agriculture: Alternative Trajectories for Future Development. In *Douglass, G. K., ed.*, 1984, pp. 89–106. [G: U.S.]

Campbell, Laurence S. Using Market Incentives to Curb Acid Rain. *Eastern Econ. J.*, October-December 1984, *10*(4), pp. 389–401. [G: U.S.; Canada]

Carlson, J. Lon; Johnson, Gary V. and Ulen, Thomas S. An Economic Analysis of Illinois' New Hazardous Waste Law—P.A. 82–572. *Natural Res. J.*, October 1984, *24*(4), pp. 865–85. [G: U.S.]

Carman, Hoy F. An Analysis of Proposition 13 Impacts on California Land Conservation Act Participation. *Land Econ.*, November 1984, *60*(4), pp. 360–66. [G: U.S.]

Choucri, Nazli. Population, Resources, Technology, and Environment: Trends and Implications. In *Trent, J. and Lamy, P., eds.*, 1984, pp. 187–203.

Clements, Kendrick A. Herbert Hoover and Conservation, 1921–33. *Amer. Hist. Rev.*, February 1984, *89*(1), pp. 67–88. [G: U.S.]

Cochrane, Harold C. and Huszar, Paul C. Economics of Timing Storm Drainage Improvements. *Water Resources Res.*, October 1984, *20*(10), pp. 1331–36.

Cohen, Bernard L. The Hazards of Nuclear Power. In *Simon, J. L. and Kahn, H., eds.*, 1984, pp. 545–65. [G: U.S.]

Crandall, Robert W. The Political Economy of Clean Air: Practical Constraints on White House Review. In *Smith, V. K., ed.*, 1984, pp. 205–25. [G: U.S.]

Crocker, Thomas D., et al. The Sixty-City Limit. In *Ahmad, Y. J.; Dasgupta, P. and Mäler, K.-G., eds.*, 1984, pp. 114–61. [G: U.S.]

Dorman, Peter. Environmental Protection, Employment, and Profit: The Politics of Public Interest in the Tacoma/Asarco Arsenic Dispute. *Rev. Radical Polit. Econ.*, Winter 1984, *16*(4), pp. 151–64. [G: U.S.]

Douglass, Gordon K. The Meanings of Agricultural Sustainability. In *Douglass, G. K., ed.*, 1984, pp. 3–29.

Dudenhöffer, Ferdi. The Regulation of Intensities and Productivities: Concepts in Environmental Policy. *Z. ges. Staatswiss.*, June 1984, *140*(2), pp. 276–87.

Duncan, Myrl L. Toward a Theory of Broad-Based Planning for the Preservation of Agricultural Land. *Natural Res. J.*, January 1984, *24*(1), pp. 61–135. [G: U.S.]

Dunlap, Riley E. and Van Liere, Kent D. Commitment to the Dominant Social Paradigm and Concern for Environmental Quality. *Soc. Sci. Quart.*, December 1984, *65*(4), pp. 1013–28. [G: U.S.]

Epple, Dennis and Visscher, Michael. Environmental Pollution: Modeling Occurrence, Detection, and Deterrence. *J. Law Econ.*, April 1984, *27*(1), pp. 29–60. [G: U.S.]

Ervin, David E.; Heffernan, William D. and Green, Gary P. Cross-Compliance for Erosion Control: Anticipating Efficiency and Distributive Impacts. *Amer. J. Agr. Econ.*, August 1984, *66*(3), pp. 273–78.   [G: U.S.]

Evans, John S. Theoretically Optimal Environmental Metrics and Their Surrogates. *J. Environ. Econ. Manage.*, March 1984, *11*(1), pp. 18–27.

Farber, Kit D.; Dreiling, Frederick J. and Rutledge, Gary L. Pollution Abatement and Control Expenditures, 1972–82. *Surv. Curr. Bus.*, February 1984, *64*(2), pp. 22–30.   [G: U.S.]

Farber, Stephen C. Pareto-Optimal Effluent Taxation and Market Structure in the Presence of Uncertain Demand and Detection. *J. Ind. Econ.*, September 1984, *33*(1), pp. 105–11.

Farzin, Y. Hossein. The Effect of the Discount Rate on Depletion of Exhaustible Resources. *J. Polit. Econ.*, October 1984, *92*(5), pp. 841–51.

Feigenbaum, Susan and Jenkinson, Thomas. Government Incentives for Historic Preservation. *Nat. Tax J.*, March 1984, *37*(1), pp. 113–19.   [G: U.S.]

Finn, Daniel P. Radioactive Waste Disposal in the Pacific Basin and International Cooperation on Nuclear Waste Management. In *Gopalakrishnan, C., ed.*, 1984, pp. 193–206.
        [G: Pacific Basin]

Fisher, Ann. An Overview and Evaluation of EPA's Guidelines for Conducting Regulatory Impact Analyses. In *Smith, V. K., ed.*, 1984, pp. 99–118.   [G: U.S.]

Fornaciari Davoli, Maria Livia. In margine all'economia dell'ambiente: l'esigenza di nuovi sviluppi teorici. (On Environmental Economy: The Need for New Developments. With English summary.) *Giorn. Econ.*, January–February 1984, *43*(1–2), pp. 77–88.

Forster, Bruce A. An Economic Assessment of the Significance of Long-range Transported Air Pollutants for Agriculture in Eastern Canada. *Can. J. Agr. Econ.*, November 1984, *32*(3), pp. 498–525.   **[G: Canada]**

Forster, Bruce A. The Backward Incidence of Pollution Control: A Dual Approach. *J. Environ. Econ. Manage.*, March 1984, *11*(1), pp. 14–17.

Fraas, Arthur G. Benefit–Cost Analysis for Environmental Regulation. In *Smith, V. K., ed.*, 1984, pp. 86–98.   [G: U.S.]

Fraas, Arthur G. and Munley, Vincent G. Municipal Wastewater Treatment Cost. *J. Environ. Econ. Manage.*, March 1984, *11*(1), pp. 28–38.   [G: U.S.]

Frankenhoff, Charles A. and Giulini, Lorenzo T. Environment and Development: The Caribbean Region. In *Ghosh, P. K., ed., no. 5, 1984, 1975*, pp. 363–73.   **[G: Caribbean]**

Freeman, A. Myrick, III. Depletable Externalities and Pigouvian Taxation. *J. Environ. Econ. Manage.*, June 1984, *11*(2), pp. 173–79.

Freeman, A. Myrick, III. On the Tactics of Bene-

fit Estimation under Executive Order 12291. In *Smith, V. K., ed.*, 1984, pp. 167–86.
        [G: U.S.]

Freeman, A. Myrick, III. The Quasi-Option Value of Irreversible Development. *J. Environ. Econ. Manage.*, September 1984, *11*(3), pp. 292–95.

Friedheim, Robert L. Coastal Management and Nuclear Power. In *Friedheim, R. L., et al.*, 1984, pp. 314–52.   **[G: Japan]**

Fujita, Shin-ichi and Koi, Hiroshi. Application of GMDH to Environmental System Modeling and Management. In *Farlow, S. J., ed.*, 1984, pp. 257–75.   **[G: Japan]**

Gamble, Hays B. and Downing, Roger H. Some Comments Relating to Model Specification on "Effects of Nuclear Power Plants on Residential Property Values": Reply. *J. Reg. Sci.*, February 1984, *24*(1), pp. 137–38.   [G: U.S.]

Gaventa, John and Horton, Bill. Land Ownership and Land Reform in Appalachia. In *Geisler, C. C. and Popper, F. J., eds.*, 1984, pp. 233–44.   [G: U.S.]

Geiser, Kenneth. Converting Economic Conversion: An Argument for Building Broader Coalitions. In *Gordon, S. and McFadden, D., eds.*, 1984, pp. 175–90.   [G: U.S.]

Godard, Olivier. Autonomie socio-économique et externalisation de l'environnement: la théorie néo-classique mise en perspective. (Socio-economic Autonomy and the Externalization of the Environment: The Neo-classical Theory in Perspective. With English summary.) *Écon. Appl.*, 1984, *37*(2), pp. 315–45.

Gottinger, Hans W. Lower-Bound Benefits of Air Pollution Reductions in the Munich Metropolitan Area (MMA) In *[Beckmann, M. J.]*, 1984, pp. 243–55.   **[G: W. Germany]**

Greenley, Douglas A.; Walsh, Richard G. and Young, Robert A. Option Value: Empirical Evidence from a Case Study of Recreation and Water Quality. In *Ahmad, Y. J.; Dasgupta, P. and Mäler, K.-G., eds.*, 1984, pp. 302–21.
        [G: U.S.]

Griffin, Ronald C. and Stoll, John R. Evolutionary Processes in Soil Conservation Policy. *Land Econ.*, February 1984, *60*(1), pp. 30–39.
        [G: U.S.]

Grubb, W. Norton; Whittington, Dale and Humphries, Michael. The Ambiguities of Benefit–Cost Analysis: An Evaluation of Regulatory Impact Analyses under Executive Order 12291. In *Smith, V. K., ed.*, 1984, pp. 121–64.
        [G: U.S.]

Gunnerson, Charles G. Sanitation Systems for Developing Countries. In *Weiss, C. and Jéquier, N., eds.*, 1984, pp. 125–39.

Guppy, Nicholas. Tropical Deforestation: A Global View. *Foreign Aff.*, Spring 1984, *62*(4), pp. 928–65.   **[G: Global]**

Hafkamp, Wim and Nijkamp, Peter. A Multiple-Layer Model for Economic-Environmental-Energy Policy Analysis. In *Grauer, M. and Wierzbicki, A. P., eds.*, 1984, pp. 193–201.
        [G: Netherlands]

Hafkamp, Wim and Nijkamp, Peter. An Operational Multi-component Multi-actor Policy Model for Economic-Environmental Scenarios. In *Despontin, M.; Nijkamp, P. and Spronk, J., eds.*, 1984, pp. 157–82. [G: Netherlands]

Hahn, Robert W. Market Power and Transferable Property Rights. *Quart. J. Econ.*, November 1984, 99(4), pp. 753–65.

Harford, Jon D. Averting Behavior and the Benefits of Reduced Soiling. *J. Environ. Econ. Manage.*, September 1984, 11(3), pp. 296–302.

Harris, Curtis C., Jr.; McConnell, Virginia D. and Cumberland, John H. A Model for Forecasting the Economic and Environmental Impact of Energy Policy. *Energy Econ.*, July 1984, 6(3), pp. 167–76. [G: U.S.]

Hartford, Jon D. Relatively Efficient Pollution Standards under Perfect Competition. *Public Finance Quart.*, April 1984, 12(2), pp. 183–95.

Hartje, Volkmar J. Oil Pollution Caused by Tanker Accidents: Liability versus Regulation. *Natural Res. J.*, January 1984, 24(1), pp. 41–60.

Hartman, Raymond S. The Importance of Technology and Fuel Choice in the Analysis of Utility-sponsored Conservation Strategies for Residential Water Heating. *Energy J.*, July 1984, 5(3), pp. 99–118. [G: U.S.]

Hayden, F. Gregory. A Geobased National Agricultural Policy for Rural Community Enhancement, Environmental Vitality, and Income Stabilization. *J. Econ. Issues*, March 1984, 18(1), pp. 181–221. [G: U.S.]

Henry, Claude. La microéconomie comme langage et enjeu de négociations. (Economic Appraisal Methodology as Output of Negotiations. With English summary.) *Revue Écon.*, January 1984, 35(1), pp. 177–97.

Highton, Nicolas H. and Webb, Michael G. The Effects on Electricity Prices in England and Wales of Notional Sulphur Dioxide Emission Standards for Power Stations. *J. Environ. Econ. Manage.*, March 1984, 11(1), pp. 70–83. [G: U.K.]

Hirst, Eric and Goeltz, Richard. The Economics of Utility Residential Energy Conservation Programs: A Pacific Northwest Example. *Energy J.*, July 1984, 5(3), pp. 159–69. [G: U.S.]

Hoy, Don R. and Bélisle, François J. Environmental Protection and Economic Development in Guatemala's Western Highlands. *J. Devel. Areas*, January 1984, 18(2), pp. 161–76. [G: Guatemala]

Hrezo, Margaret S. and Hrezo, William E. Judicial Regulation of the Environment under Posner's Economic Model of the Law. *J. Econ. Issues*, December 1984, 18(4), pp. 1071–91. [G: U.S.]

Hyman, Eric L. Land-Use Planning to Help Sustain Tropical Forest Resources. *World Devel.*, August 1984, 12(8), pp. 837–47. [G: Global]

Ikeda, Saburo. Nonlinear Prediction Models for River Flows and Typhoon Precipitation by Self-Organizing Methods. In *Farlow, S. J., ed.*, 1984, pp. 149–67. [G: Japan]

Ilgen, Thomas L. Between Europe and America: Regulating Toxic Substances in Canada. In *Thompson, F., ed.*, 1984, pp. 1–30. [G: Canada]

Jackson, Wes. Toward a Unifying Concept for Agriculture. In *Douglass, G. K., ed.*, 1984, pp. 159–73.

Johnson, Sam H., III. Temporal Land Resource Concerns and Farming Systems Research: Chiang Mai Valley, Northern Thailand. *Land Econ.*, May 1984, 60(2), pp. 202–10. [G: Thailand]

Jondrow, James M. and Levy, Robert A. The Displacement of Local Spending for Pollution Control by Federal Construction Grants. *Amer. Econ. Rev.*, May 1984, 74(2), pp. 174–78. [G: U.S.]

Joyner, Christopher C. Oceanic Pollution and the Southern Ocean: Rethinking the International Legal Implications for Antarctica. *Natural Res. J.*, January 1984, 24(1), pp. 1–40.

Kaden, S. Analysis of Regional Water Policies in Open-Cast Mining Areas—A Multicriteria Approach. In *Grauer, M. and Wierzbicki, A. P., eds.*, 1984, pp. 218–26.

Kalt, Joseph P. and Zupan, Mark A. Capture and Ideology in the Economic Theory of Politics. *Amer. Econ. Rev.*, June 1984, 74(3), pp. 279–300. [G: U.S.]

Keith, Kent M. An Ethic for Ocean Resource Development: Lessons from Hawaii. In *Gopalakrishnan, C., ed.*, 1984, pp. 229–41. [G: U.S.]

Ketkar, Kusum W. Environmental Protection Policies and the Structure of the U.S. Economy. *Appl. Econ.*, April 1984, 16(2), pp. 237–56. [G: U.S.]

Kim, Sung-Hoon and Dixon, John A. Economic Valuation of Environmental Quality Aspects of Upland Agricultural Projects in Korea. In *Ahmad, Y. J.; Dasgupta, P. and Mäler, K.-G., eds.*, 1984, pp. 21–37. [G: S. Korea]

King, J. C. Assessment of Electric Power Conservation and Supply Resources in the Pacific Northwest: An Overview. In *Lev, B., et al., eds.*, 1984, pp. 95–108. [G: U.S.]

Kinkley, Chu-Chu and Lahiri, Kajal. Testing the Rational Expectations Hypothesis in a Secondary Materials Market. *J. Environ. Econ. Manage.*, September 1984, 11(3), pp. 282–91. [G: U.S.]

Kjeldsen-Kragh, Søren. Mål og midler i miljøpolitikken. (Ends of Means in Environmental Policy. With English summary.) *Nationaløkon. Tidsskr.*, 1984, 122(2), pp. 213–27.

Knapp, Keith C. Steady-State Solutions to Soil Salinity Optimization Problems. *Amer. J. Agr. Econ.*, August 1984, 66(3), pp. 279–85. [G: U.S.]

Kneese, Allen V. and Bower, Blair T. Regional Residuals Management Models and the Lower Delaware Valley Case Study. In *Ahmad, Y. J.; Dasgupta, P. and Mäler, K.-G., eds.*, 1984, pp. 222–301. [G: U.S.]

Koenig, Evan F. Uncertainty and Pollution: The

Role of Indirect Taxation. *J. Public Econ.*, June 1984, *24*(1), pp. 111–22.

Kohn, Robert E. Input–Output Analysis and Air Pollution Control. In *Ahmad, Y. J.; Dasgupta, P. and Mäler, K.-G.*, eds., 1984, pp. 322–58. [G: U.S.]

Kosobud, Richard F. and Daly, Thomas A. Global Conflict or Cooperation over the CO_2 Climate Impact? *Kyklos*, 1984, *37*(4), pp. 638–59. [G: Global]

Kraft, Michael E. and Vig, Norman J. Environmental Policy in the Reagan Presidency. *Polit. Sci. Quart.*, Fall 1984, *99*(3), pp. 415–39. [G: U.S.]

Krutilla, John V. and Fisher, Anthony C. The Trans-Alaska Pipeline: Environmental Consequences and Alternatives. In *Ahmad, Y. J.; Dasgupta, P. and Mäler, K.-G.*, eds., 1984, pp. 83–113. [G: U.S.]

Kucera, V.; Ghullman, J. and Swartlang, P. Atmospheric Corrosion of Materials. In *Ahmad, Y. J.; Dasgupta, P. and Mäler, K.-G.*, eds., 1984, pp. 198–221. [G: OECD]

Labeyrie, Vincent. Contraintes écologiques, équilibres et activités humaines. (Ecological Constraints, Equilibrium, and Human Activities. With English summary.) *Écon. Appl.*, 1984, *37*(2), pp. 243–77.

Landsberg, H. E. Global Climatic Trends. In *Simon, J. L. and Kahn, H.*, eds., 1984, pp. 272–315. [G: Global]

Lee, Dwight R. The Economics of Enforcing Pollution Taxation. *J. Environ. Econ. Manage.*, June 1984, *11*(2), pp. 147–60.

Libecap, Gary D. The Political Allocation of Mineral Rights: A Re-Evaluation of Teapot Dome. *J. Econ. Hist.*, June 1984, *44*(2), pp. 381–91. [G: U.S.]

Liew, Chung J. Pollution-Related Variable Input–Output Model: The Tulsa SMSA as a Case Study. *J. Urban Econ.*, May 1984, *15*(3), pp. 327–49. [G: U.S.]

Linder, Stephen H. and McBride, Mark E. Enforcement Costs and Regulatory Reform: The Agency and Firm Response. *J. Environ. Econ. Manage.*, December 1984, *11*(4), pp. 327–46.

Lipfert, Frederick W. Air Pollution and Mortality: Specification Searches Using SMSA-Based Data. *J. Environ. Econ. Manage.*, September 1984, *11*(3), pp. 208–43. [G: U.S.]

Llewellyn, Othman Abd ar-Rahman. Islamic Jurisprudence and Environmental Planning. *J. Res. Islamic Econ.*, Winter 1984, *1*(2), pp. 25–49.

Lloyd, P. J. Individual Mines or Oilfields: Introduction. In *Lloyd, P. J.*, ed., 1984, pp. 35–52. [G: Australia]

Maloney, Michael T. and Yandle, Bruce. Estimation of the Cost of Air Pollution Control Regulation. *J. Environ. Econ. Manage.*, September 1984, *11*(3), pp. 244–63. [G: U.S.]

Martin, Lawrence W. The Optimal Magnitude and Enforcement of Evadable Pigovian Charges. *Public Finance*, 1984, *39*(3), pp. 347–58.

Masud, Ross. The Asian–African Legal Consulta-

tive Committee: A Survey of Activities. *J. World Trade Law*, January:February 1984, *18*(1), pp. 81–88. [G: Asia; Africa]

McEvoy, Arthur F. and Scheiber, Harry N. Scientists, Entrepreneurs, and the Policy Process: A Study of the Post-1945 California Sardine Depletion. *J. Econ. Hist.*, June 1984, *44*(2), pp. 393–406. [G: U.S.]

Mel'nik, L. Accounting for Ecological Indicators in Solving Economic Problems. *Prob. Econ.*, March 1984, *26*(11), pp. 15–26. [G: U.S.S.R.]

Mendelsohn, Robert. Endogenous Technical Change and Environmental Regulation. *J. Environ. Econ. Manage.*, September 1984, *11*(3), pp. 202–07.

Mickwitz, Gösta. Skogarnas öde. (The Fate of the Forests. With English summary.) *Ekon. Samfundets Tidskr.*, 1984, *37*(2), pp. 63–64. [G: Europe]

Miller, Jon R. and Lad, Frank. Flexibility, Learning, and Irreversibility in Environmental Decisions: A Bayesian Approach. *J. Environ. Econ. Manage.*, June 1984, *11*(2), pp. 161–72.

Mirlin, G. Mineral Resources and the Economy. *Prob. Econ.*, March 1984, *26*(11), pp. 53–72. [G: U.S.S.R.; Global]

Moe, R. J. and Adams, R. C. Residential Energy Use and Improved Building Thermal Efficiency: An Econometric Analysis. In *Lev, B., et al.*, eds., 1984, pp. 135–49. [G: U.S.]

Monash University, Centre of Pol. Stud. The Environment: The Aluminium Industry in Australia in the 1980s. In *Lloyd, P. J.*, ed., 1984, *1981*, pp. 116–25. [G: Australia]

Movassaghi, Kam K. and Thibodeaux, K. G. A Computer Model in Solid Waste Management. In *Avula, X. J. R., et al.*, 1984, pp. 265–70.

Nordhaus, William D. Economic Growth and Climate: The Carbon-Dioxide Problem. In *Ahmad, Y. J.; Dasgupta, P. and Mäler, K.-G.*, eds., 1984, pp. 162–75.

Norgaard, Richard B. Coevolutionary Agricultural Development. *Econ. Develop. Cult. Change*, April 1984, *32*(3), pp. 525–46.

Norgaard, Richard B. Coevolutionary Development Potential. *Land Econ.*, May 1984, *60*(2), pp. 160–73.

O'Hagan, Ciaran. Pigovian Taxes, Polluter Subsidies, Regulation, and the Size of a Polluting Industry: A Note. *Can. J. Econ.*, August 1984, *17*(3), pp. 588–92.

O'Keefe, Philip. Poverty, Proletarianisation and the Production of Uneven Development: A Kenyan Village. In *Munslow, B. and Finch, H.*, eds., 1984, pp. 148–63. [G: Kenya]

Oates, Wallace E. Markets for Pollution Control. *Challenge*, May/June 1984, *27*(2), pp. 11–17. [G: U.S.]

Oates, Wallace E. and Strassmann, Diana L. Effluent Fees and Market Structure. *J. Public Econ.*, June 1984, *24*(1), pp. 29–46.

Oehsen, Johann Hermann. Ein erweitertes umweltökonomisches Standardmodell. (An Extended Standard Model of Environmental Economics. With English summary.) *Jahr.*

Nationalökon. Statist., January 1984, *199*(1), pp. 49–64.

Opaluch, James J. Dynamic Aspects of Effluent Taxation under Uncertainty. *J. Environ. Econ. Manage.*, March 1984, *11*(1), pp. 1–13.

Opaluch, James J. and Grigalunas, Thomas A. Controlling Stochastic Pollution Events through Liability Rules: Some Evidence from OCS Leasing. *Rand J. Econ.*, Spring 1984, *15*(1), pp. 142–51. [G: U.S.]

Ovsienko, Iu. V. and Sobolev, I. I. Optimizing Forestry Use in a Way Which Takes Account of Its Ecological Impact. *Matekon*, Summer 1984, *20*(4), pp. 64–80. [G: U.S.S.R.]

Paez, Ellen. The 1977 Procedural Amendments to the Clean Air Act—Have They Made a Difference? *Natural Res. J.*, July 1984, *24*(3), pp. 745–60. [G: U.S.]

Palanisami, K. and Easter, K. William. Ex Post Evaluation of Flood Control Investments: A Case Study in North Dakota. *Water Resources Res.*, December 1984, *20*(12), pp. 1785–90. [G: U.S.]

Pandit, A. and Anand, S. C. Finite Element Modeling of Contaminant Transport in Saturated Aquifers. In *Avula, X. J. R., et al.*, 1984, pp. 377–82.

Pashigian, B. Peter. The Effect of Environmental Regulation on Optimal Plant Size and Factor Shares. *J. Law Econ.*, April 1984, *27*(1), pp. 1–28. [G: U.S.]

Pasurka, Carl A., Jr. The Short-run Impact of Environmental Protection Costs on U.S. Product Prices. *J. Environ. Econ. Manage.*, December 1984, *11*(4), pp. 380–90. [G: U.S.]

Patti, Salvatore. Environmental Protection in Italy: The Emerging Concept of a Right to a Healthful Environment. *Natural Res. J.*, July 1984, *24*(3), pp. 535–47. [G: Italy]

Pechan, Edward H. and Graves, Kristin. The Emissions Strategy Integration Model: A Proposed Conceptual Approach. In *Lev, B., et al.*, eds., 1984, pp. 121–31. [G: U.S.]

Perlov, Diane Catherine. Exploiting the Forest: Patterns and Perceptions in Highland Samburu. In *Barnes, C.; Ensminger, J. and O'Keefe, P.*, eds., 1984, pp. 141–63. [G: Kenya]

Polèse, Mario. Population, Resources, Technology, and Environment: Trends and Implications: Comment. In *Trent, J. and Lamy, P.*, eds., 1984, pp. 205–10.

Portney, Paul R. Natural Resources and the Environment: More Controversy than Change. In *Palmer, J. L. and Sawhill, I. V.*, eds., 1984, pp. 141–75. [G: U.S.]

Portney, Paul R. The Benefits and Costs of Regulatory Analysis. In *Smith, V. K.*, ed., 1984, pp. 226–40. [G: U.S.]

Preda, G., et al. Instruction and Education in the Field of Energy Conservation in Romania. *Econ. Computat. Cybern. Stud. Res.*, 1984, *19*(1), pp. 67–73. [G: Romania]

Rhee, Jeong J. and Miranowski, John A. Determination of Income, Production, and Employment under Pollution Control: An Input–Output Approach. *Rev. Econ. Statist.*, February 1984, *66*(1), pp. 146–50.

Ro, Young Key and Forster, D. Lynn. Regional Input–Output Analysis of an Environmental Regulation. *J. Econ. Devel.*, July 1984, *9*(1), pp. 167–88. [G: U.S.]

Robotham, F. P. The Case Against Uranium Mining. In *Lloyd, P. J.*, ed., 1984, *1980*, pp. 131–35. [G: Australia; Selected Countries]

Runge, Carlisle Ford. Economic Criteria and "Net Social Risk" in the Analysis of Environmental Regulation. In *Smith, V. K.*, ed., 1984, pp. 187–202. [G: U.S.]

Runge, Carlisle Ford. Energy Exploration on Wilderness: "Privatization" and Public Lands Management. *Land Econ.*, February 1984, *60*(1), pp. 56–68. [G: U.S.]

Russo, William J., Jr. and Rutledge, Gary L. Plant and Equipment Expenditures by Business for Pollution Abatement, 1983 and Planned 1984. *Surv. Curr. Bus.*, June 1984, *64*(6), pp. 31–34. [G: U.S.]

Sedjo, Roger A. and Clawson, Marion. Global Forests. In *Simon, J. L. and Kahn, H.*, eds., 1984, pp. 128–70. [G: Global]

Sharefkin, Mark; Shechter, Mordechai and Kneese, Allen V. Impacts, Costs, and Techniques for Mitigation of Contaminated Groundwater: A Review. *Water Resources Res.*, December 1984, *20*(12), pp. 1771–83. [G: U.S.]

Shibata, Hirofumi. Reconsideration of the Optimal Governmental Policies against Pollution. (In Japanese. With English summary.) *Osaka Econ. Pap.*, December 1984, *34*(2–3), pp. 45–51.

Simon, Julian L. and Wildavsky, Aaron. On Species Loss, the Absence of Data, and Risks to Humanity. In *Simon, J. L. and Kahn, H.*, eds., 1984, pp. 171–83. [G: Global]

Singer, S. Fred. Acid Raid. *Policy Rev.*, Winter 1984, (27), pp. 56–58. [G: U.S.; Canada]

Smith, V. Kerry. Environmental Policy Making under Executive Order 12291: An Introduction. In *Smith, V. K.*, ed., 1984, pp. 3–40. [G: U.S.]

Smith, V. Kerry and Krutilla, John V. Economic Growth, Resource Availability, and Environmental Quality. *Amer. Econ. Rev.*, May 1984, *74*(2), pp. 226–30.

Solow, Robert M. The Economics of Resources or the Resources of Economics. In *Lloyd, P. J.*, ed., 1984, *1974*, pp. 53–70.

Sorenson, Jay B. The Assurance of Reasonable Toxic Risk? *Natural Res. J.*, July 1984, *24*(3), pp. 549–69. [G: U.S.]

Sproule-Jones, Mark and Richards, Patricia L. Toward a Theory of the Regulated Environment. *Can. Public Policy*, September 1984, *10*(3), pp. 305–15. [G: Canada]

Stevens, Joe B. Satisfaction with Environmental Change: An Empirical Analysis of Attitudes toward Air Quality by Recent Interstate Migrants. *J. Environ. Econ. Manage.*, September 1984, *11*(3), pp. 264–81. [G: U.S.]

Stewart, Thomas R.; Dennis, Robin L. and Ely, Daniel W. Citizen Participation and Judgment in Policy Analysis: A Case Study of Urban Air Quality Policy. *Policy Sci.*, May 1984, *17*(1), pp. 67–87. **[G: U.S.]**

Stoddart, David R. and Pethick, John S. Environmental Hazard and Coastal Reclamation: Problems and Prospects in Bangladesh. In *[Farmer, B. H.],* 1984, pp. 339–61. **[G: Bangladesh]**

Sussman, Frances G. A Note on the Willingness to Pay Approach to the Valuation of Longevity. *J. Environ. Econ. Manage.*, March 1984, *11*(1), pp. 84–89.

Swanson, Earl R. and Heady, Earl O. Soil Erosion in the United States. In *Simon, J. L. and Kahn, H., eds.,* 1984, pp. 202–23. **[G: U.S.]**

Swanson, Larry D. Shifting the Burden of Environmental Protection. *J. Econ. Issues*, March 1984, *18*(1), pp. 251–74. **[G: U.S.]**

Tamanoï, Yoshiro; Tsuchida, Atsushi and Murota, Takeshi. Towards an Entropic Theory of Economy and Ecology: Beyond the Mechanistic Equilibrium Approach. *Écon. Appl.*, 1984, *37*(2), pp. 279–94.

Terkla, David. The Efficiency Value of Effluent Tax Revenues. *J. Environ. Econ. Manage.*, June 1984, *11*(2), pp. 107–23. **[G: U.S.]**

TerKonda, Purush K. Energy Conservation and Modeling of Indoor Pollution. In *Avula, X. J. R., et al.,* 1984, pp. 981–84.

U.N. Environment Programme. Air and Water Quality. In *Simon, J. L. and Kahn, H., eds.,* 1984, pp. 476–89. **[G: Global]**

Ueta, Kuzuhiro and Sueishi, Tomitaro. The Control of the Use Pattern and the Life of Metals for Environmental Risk Management; The Case of Lead. *Kyoto Univ. Econ. Rev.*, October 1984, *54*(2), pp. 13–30. **[G: Japan]**

Uri, Noel D. The Pricing and Allocation of Electrical Energy. *Energy Econ.*, April 1984, *6*(2), pp. 94–101. **[G: U.S.]**

Vidal, J. E. Appréciation des conséquences écologiques et économiques de la défoliation chimique au Viêt Nam. (Evaluation of the Economic and Ecological Consequences of Chemical Defoliation in Viet Nam. With English summary.) *Écon. Appl.*, 1984, *37*(2), pp. 393–403. **[G: Vietnam]**

Walsh, Richard G.; Loomis, John B. and Gillman, Richard A. Valuing Option, Existence, and Bequest Demands for Wilderness. *Land Econ.*, February 1984, *60*(1), pp. 14–29. **[G: U.S.]**

Wandschneider, Philip R. Managing River Systems: Centralization versus Decentralization. *Natural Res. J.*, October 1984, *24*(4), pp. 1043–66. **[G: U.S.]**

Wassermann, Ursula. EEC: Air Pollution Directive. *J. World Trade Law*, September–October 1984, *18*(5), pp. 459–61. **[G: EEC]**

Watson, William D. and Ridker, Ronald G. Losses from Effluent Taxes and Quotas under Uncertainty. *J. Environ. Econ. Manage.*, December 1984, *11*(4), pp. 310–26. **[G: U.S.]**

Weeden, Robert B. Alaskan Resources Development: Environmental Issues. In *Morehouse, T. A., ed.,* 1984, pp. 135–68. **[G: U.S.]**

von Weizsäcker, Carl Christian. The Influence of Property Rights on Tastes. *Z. ges. Staatswiss.*, March 1984, *140*(1), pp. 90–95.

Williams, D. G. T. Developments in British Environmental Law. *Natural Res. J.*, July 1984, *24*(3), pp. 511–34. **[G: U.K.]**

Yandle, Bruce. "Polluters' Profits": An Empirical Note. *J. Ind. Econ.*, March 1984, *32*(3), pp. 359–66. **[G: U.S.]**

Yandle, Bruce. Environmental Control and Regional Growth. *Growth Change*, July 1984, *15*(3), pp. 39–42. **[G: U.S.]**

Yandle, Bruce. Sulfur Dioxide: State versus Federal Control. *J. Energy Devel.*, Autumn 1984, *10*(1), pp. 63–72. **[G: U.S.]**

Yohe, Gary W. Comparative Results in Pollution Control. *Amer. Econ.*, Spring 1984, *28*(1), pp. 10–17.

Young, C. Edwin and Shortle, James S. Investments in Soil Conservation Structures: The Role of Operator and Operation Characteristics. *Agr. Econ. Res.*, Spring 1984, *36*(2), pp. 10–15. **[G: U.S.]**

Zimmermann, Klaus F. Die Inzidenz der Umweltpolitik in theoretischer und empirischer Sicht. (The Incidence of Environmental Policy: Theoretical Aspects and Empirical Evidence. With English summary.) *Jahr. Nationalökon. Statist.*, November 1984, *199*(6), pp. 502–21. **[G: U.S.; Sweden]**

723 Energy

7230 Energy

Abdallah, Hussein. The Energy Situation in the Arab Republic of Egypt. In *Baum, V., et al.,* 1984, pp. 196–204. **[G: Egypt]**

Adams, F. Gerard and Marquez, Jaime. Petroleum Price Elasticity, Income Effects, and OPEC's Pricing Policy. *Energy J.*, January 1984, *5*(1), pp. 115–28. **[G: OECD]**

Adelman, M. A. International Oil Agreements. *Energy J.*, July 1984, *5*(3), pp. 1–9.

Adelman, M. A. Oil Supply and Demand. In *Hawdon, D., ed.,* 1984, pp. 57–78.

Adelman, M. A. Sense and Nonsense about World Oil. *Energy J.*, January 1984, *5*(1), pp. 169–71.

Adj, Mamadou. The Energy Situation in Senegal. In *Baum, V., et al.,* 1984, pp. 280–87. **[G: Senegal]**

Adler, Svjetlana and Matejka, Harriet. Soviet Coal Exports. In *Kostecki, M. M., ed.,* 1984, pp. 100–15. **[G: U.S.S.R.; Global]**

Agmon, Tamir. OPEC and International Financial Markets: Redistribution and Recycling: Comment. In *Agmon, T.; Hawkins, R. G. and Levich, R. M., eds.,* 1984, pp. 246–51. **[G: OPEC]**

Agmon, Tamir; Lessard, Donald R. and Paddock, James L. Appropriate Financing for Petroleum Development in Developing Countries. *Energy J.*, July 1984, *5*(3), pp. 27–40.

Aigner, Dennis J. The Welfare Econometrics of Peak-Load Pricing for Electricity: Editor's Introduction. *J. Econometrics*, September/October 1984, *26*(1/2), pp. 1–15. **[G: U.S.]**

Akins, James E. Prospects for the New OPEC. In *Ayoub, A., ed.*, 1984, pp. 152–69. [G: OPEC]

Al-Husseini, Farouk. An Experiment in the Pricing Stratagy of OPEC Countries. *J. Energy Devel.*, Spring 1984, 9(2), pp. 337–43. [G: OPEC]

Al-Khereiji, Ahmed. The Role and Effects of Saudi Arabia's Oil Policy on the International Oil Market: Prospect for the Eighties. In *Ayoub, A., ed.*, 1984, pp. 170–93. [G: Saudi Arabia]

Al-Sowayegh, Abdulaziz and Sharif, Walid. The Security of Oil Supplies: Prevalent Views among Oil Consumers and Producers. *J. Energy Devel.*, Autumn 1984, 10(1), pp. 29–38. [G: Global]

Alameda, José I. and Mann, Arthur J. Technology Dependency and Energy Substitutability in a Small, Open, and Petroleum-importing Developing Economy: The Case of Puerto Rico. *J. Econ. Devel.*, July 1984, 9(1), pp. 147–66. [G: Puerto Rico]

Alm, Alvin L. Managing Oil Shocks. In *Alm, A. L. and Weimer, R. J., eds.*, 1984, pp. 1–29. [G: U.S.]

Ammons, Jane Chumley. An Analytic Study of Critical Terminal Conditions in Long Range Generation Expansion Planning For Electric Utilities. In *Lev, B., et al., eds.*, 1984, pp. 83–93.

Amuzegar, Jahangir. Prospects for a New "Oil Dialogue." *Finance Develop.*, September 1984, 21(3), pp. 28–31. [G: OPEC; OECD]

Attanasi, E. D. A Note on Petroleum Industry Exploration Efficiency. *Energy J.*, July 1984, 5(3), pp. 133–45. [G: U.S.]

Avery, William H. OTEC Methanol: A New Approach. In *Gopalakrishnan, C., ed.*, 1984, pp. 17–30.

Badger, Daniel B., Jr. The Anatomy of a "Minor Disruption": Missed Opportunities. In *Alm, A. L. and Weimer, R. J., eds.*, 1984, pp. 33–53. [G: OPEC]

Bajracharya, Deepak. Organizing for Energy Need Assessment and Innovation: Action Research in Nepal. In *Islam, M. N.; Morse, R. and Soesastro, M. H., eds.*, 1984, pp. 279–336. [G: Nepal]

Baltagi, Badi H. and Griffin, James M. U.S. Gasoline Demand: What Next? *Energy J.*, January 1984, 5(1), pp. 129–40. [G: U.S.]

Ban, Kanemi. Energy Prices and Interrelated Factor Demands: A Multivariate Time Series Analysis for the Japanese Manufacturing. (In Japanese. With English summary.) *Osaka Econ. Pap.*, December 1984, 34(2–3), pp. 180–88. [G: Japan]

Ban, Kanemi and Nakamura, Jirou. A Simplified Japan–U.S. Energy Linkage Model. *Osaka Econ. Pap.*, March 1984, 33(3–4), pp. 81–94. [G: Japan; U.S.]

Barcella, Mary L. In Defense of Price Controls for "Old" Natural Gas. *Bus. Econ.*, July 1984, 19(4), pp. 24–33. [G: U.S.]

Barnes, Carolyn. The Historical Context of the Fuelwood Situation in Kisii District. In *Barnes,*

C.; Ensminger, J. and O'Keefe, P., eds., 1984, pp. 61–78. [G: Kenya]

Barnes, Carolyn; Ensminger, Jean and O'Keefe, Philip. Energy Environment and Development in Africa: Introduction. In *Barnes, C.; Ensminger, J. and O'Keefe, P., eds.*, 1984, pp. 1–13. [G: Kenya]

Baron, Christopher. Energy Policy and Social Progress in Developing Countries. In *Ghosh, P. K., ed., no. 4*, 1984, *1980*, pp. 148–67. [G: LDCs]

Barriga, Enrique G. Relative Oil Prices and Oil Pricing Policy in Mexico. In *Csikós-Nagy, B.; Hague, D. and Hall, G., eds.*, 1984, pp. 219–37. [G: Mexico]

Barth, Michael C. and Berk, Edwin. Oil Supply Shocks and Macroeconomic Policy: Economic Response: Administrative Options and Analytical Framework. In *Alm, A. L. and Weimer, R. J., eds.*, 1984, pp. 129–43. [G: U.S.]

Barzelay, Michael and Iusem, Alfredo. Consumer Behavior and Energy Demand Forecasts for the United States: A Synthesis of Neoclassical and Behavioral Approaches Using the Stanford Pilot CESM. *J. Policy Modeling*, August 1984, 6(3), pp. 389–410. [G: U.S.]

Basile, Paul S. and de La Grandville, Baudoin. The Evolution and Role of Non-OPEC Production in the International Oil Market. In *Ayoub, A., ed.*, 1984, pp. 123–51. [G: Global]

Battista, Giampero and Cataldi, Carlo. Production and Utilization of High-Temperature Geothermal Energy—Statistical Data Processing Methodology. *Statist. J.*, January 1984, 2(1), pp. 63–71. [G: Italy]

Baum, Herbert and Kneip, Markus. Einflussgrössen des Heizöpreises—Ergebnisse einer Regressionsrechnung. (Determinants of the Prices for Fuel Oil—Results of a Regression-Analysis. With English summary.) *Jahr. Nationalökon. Statist.*, July 1984, 199(4), pp. 334–50. [G: W. Germany]

Baumgartner, Thomas and Burns, Tom R. Transitions to Alternative Energy Systems: Analysis, Theory, and Normative Conclusions: Selective Observations. In *Baumgartner, T. and Burns, T. R., eds.*, 1984, pp. 241–54.

Baumier, J. and Duchatelle, L. The Case for Developing the Liquid Metal Fast Breeder Reactor in France. In *Brookes, L. G. and Motamen, H., eds.*, 1984, pp. 234–54. [G: France]

Baxendell, Peter [Sir]. Energy in the 2000's: What Happens to the Have Nots? In *Ghosh, P. K., ed., no. 4*, 1984, *1981*, pp. 78–89. [G: LDCs]

Baxendell, Peter [Sir]. Oil Companies and the Changing Energy Market. In *Hawdon, D., ed.*, 1984, pp. 48–56.

Beckmann, Petr. Solar Energy and Other "Alternative" Energy Sources. In *Simon, J. L. and Kahn, H., eds.*, 1984, pp. 415–27. [G: Global]

Behrens, Alfredo. Energy and Output Implications of Income Redistribution in Brazil. *Energy Econ.*, April 1984, 6(2), pp. 110–16. [G: Brazil]

Berger, Mark C. Increases in Energy Prices, Costs of Production, and Plant Size. *J. Econ. Bus.*, August 1984, *36*(3), pp. 345–57.
[G: U.S.]

Berkowitz, Michael K. and Haines, George H., Jr. The Relationship between Relative Attributes, Relative Preferences, and Market Share: The Case of Solar Energy in Canada. *J. Cons. Res.*, December 1984, *11*(3), pp. 754–62.
[G: Canada]

Bernard, Jean-Thomas; Bridges, Glenn E. and Scott, Anthony D. Une évaluation de la rente potentielle des sites hydro-électriques au Canada. (With English summary.) *Rev. Econ. Ind.*, 3rd Trimester 1984, (29), pp. 1–17.
[G: Canada]

Berndt, Ernst R. The Role of Energy in Productivity Growth: Comment. In *Kendrick, J. W., ed.*, 1984, pp. 325–34. [G: U.S.]

Berndt, Ernst R. and Samaniego, Ricardo. Residential Electricity Demand in Mexico: A Model Distinguishing Access from Consumption. *Land Econ.*, August 1984, *60*(3), pp. 268–77.
[G: Mexico]

Berrie, T. W. Nuclear and Non-nuclear Electricity: Decision-making for Optimal Economic Performance. In *Brookes, L. G. and Motamen, H., eds.*, 1984, pp. 67–86.

Berry, Sara S. Oil and the Disappearing Peasantry: Accumulation, Differentiation and Underdevelopment in Western Nigeria. *African Econ. Hist.*, 1984, (13), pp. 1–22.
[G: Nigeria]

Best, E. W. The Conditions & Limits of Oil Substitution in Canada. In *Ayoub, A., ed.*, 1984, pp. 262–83. [G: Canada]

Bhagavan, M. R. Angola. In *O'Keefe, P. and Munslow, B., eds., Part I*, 1984, pp. 5–63.
[G: Angola]

Bhandari, Jagdeep S. A Computational Stochastic Equilibrium Model of Oil-importing Economies. *Weltwirtsch. Arch.*, 1984, *120*(2), pp. 301–28.

Bharier, Julian. Energy Demand Management. In *Baum, V., et al.*, 1984, pp. 25–35.
[G: LDCs]

Bir, Omer. The General Energy Situation and National Energy Strategy of Turkey. In *Baum, V., et al.*, 1984, pp. 288–92. [G: Turkey]

Bjerkholt, Olav and Olsen, Øystein. Uncertainty in Hydroelectric Power Supply. *Energy Econ.*, July 1984, *6*(3), pp. 159–66.

Blitzer, Charles R. Energy Demand in Jordan: A Case Study of Energy–Economy Linkages. *Energy J.*, October 1984, *5*(4), pp. 1–19.
[G: Jordan]

Bohn, Roger E., et al. Deregulating the Generation of Electricity through the Creation of Spot Markets for Bulk Power. *Energy J.*, April 1984, *5*(2), pp. 71–91. [G: U.S.]

Bomhoff, Eduard J. North Sea Oil and Manufacturing Output: Comment. In *Griffiths, B. and Wood, G. E., eds.*, 1984, pp. 200–04.
[G: U.K.; Selected Countries]

Bopp, Anthony E. Tests for Structural Change

in U.S. Oil Consumption, 1967–1982. *Energy Econ.*, October 1984, *6*(4), pp. 223–30.
[G: U.S.]

Borges, Antonio M. and Goulder, Lawrence H. Decomposing the Impact of Higher Energy Prices on Long-term Growth. In *Scarf, H. E. and Shoven, J. B., eds.*, 1984, pp. 319–62.
[G: U.S.]

Boughton, James M. Some Aspects of the Adjustment Problem in an Interdependent World: Comment. In *Agmon, T.; Hawkins, R. G. and Levich, R. M., eds.*, 1984, pp. 221–27.

Breitenecker, F. and Schmid, A. Decision Support via Simulation for a Multipurpose Hydroenergetic System. In *Grauer, M. and Wierzbicki, A. P., eds.*, 1984, pp. 227–35.

Brookes, L. G. Long-term Equilibrium Effects of Constraints in Energy Supply. In *Brookes, L. G. and Motamen, H., eds.*, 1984, 1982, pp. 381–402. [G: OECD]

Brookes, L. G. and Motamen, H. The Economics of Nuclear Energy: Conclusions. In *Brookes, L. G. and Motamen, H., eds.*, 1984, pp. 404–08.

Brookes, L. G. and Motamen, H. The Economics of Nuclear Energy: Introduction. In *Brookes, L. G. and Motamen, H., eds.*, 1984, pp. 1–28. [G: Selected Countries]

Brooks, Robert E. The Tenrac Gas Pipeline Competition Model. In *Lev, B., et al., eds.*, 1984, pp. 337–54.

Brown, Keith C. Conservation: Illiberal Motives? *Land Econ.*, August 1984, *60*(3), pp. 310–13.

Brown, Stephen P. A. and Phillips, Keith R. The Effects of Oil Prices and Exchange Rates on World Oil Consumption. *Fed. Res. Bank Dallas Econ. Rev.*, July 1984, pp. 13–21.
[G: OECD]

Brown, William M. The Outlook for Future Petroleum Supplies. In *Simon, J. L. and Kahn, H., eds.*, 1984, pp. 361–86. [G: Global]

Burbidge, John B. and Harrison, Alan. Testing for the Effects of Oil-Price Rises Using Vector Autoregressions. *Int. Econ. Rev.*, June 1984, *25*(2), pp. 459–84. [G: U.S.; Japan; W. Germany; U.K.; Canada]

Burgess, David F. Energy Prices, Capital Formation, and Potential GNP. *Energy J.*, April 1984, *5*(2), pp. 1–27. [G: U.S.]

Burns, Tom R. and Baumgartner, Thomas. The Shaping of Alternative Energy Systems: Introduction. In *Baumgartner, T. and Burns, T. R., eds.*, 1984, pp. 3–9.

Burns, Tom R. and Baumgartner, Thomas. Transitions to Alternative Energy Systems: Analysis, Theory, and Normative Conclusions: Policy and Normative Implications. In *Baumgartner, T. and Burns, T. R., eds.*, 1984, pp. 279–92.

Burns, Tom R. and Baumgartner, Thomas. Transitions to Alternative Energy Systems: Toward a Theory of New Technological Developments. In *Baumgartner, T. and Burns, T. R., eds.*, 1984, pp. 255–78.

Byer, Trevor A. Institutional Problems and Requirements for Energy Planning and Plan Implementation. **In** *Baum, V., et al.*, 1984, pp. 146–56. **[G: LDCs]**

Canes, Michael E. and Norman, Donald A. Longterm Contracts and Market Forces in the Natural Gas Market. *J. Energy Devel.*, Autumn 1984, *10*(1), pp. 73–96. **[G: U.S.]**

Canzoneri, Matthew and Gray, Jo Anna. Some Aspects of the Adjustment Problem in an Interdependent World. **In** *Agmon, T.; Hawkins, R. G. and Levich, R. M., eds.*, 1984, pp. 195–220.

Carlevaro, Fabrizio and Spierer, Charles. Nouvelles perspectives d'évolution de la demande d'énergie en Suisse jusqu'à l'an 2000. (New Prospects for Swiss Energy Demand until the Year 2000. With English summary.) *Schweiz. Z. Volkswirtsch. Statist.*, December 1984, *120*(4), pp. 483–520. **[G: Switzerland]**

Carlton, Dennis W. Energy and the Location of Industry: Comment. **In** *Downs, A. and Bradbury, K. L., eds.*, 1984, pp. 219–25. **[G: U.S.]**

Carpenter, Edwin H. and Chester, S. Theodore, Jr. Are Federal Energy Tax Credits Effective? A Western United States Survey. *Energy J.*, April 1984, *5*(2), pp. 139–49. **[G: U.S.]**

Carter, Jane. Energy Conservation in the United Kingdom: A Major Industrial Opportunity. *Energy J.*, January 1984, *5*(1), pp. 149–58. **[G: U.K.]**

Case, Charles W. and Actouka, Marcelino. Five Small-Scale Energy Projects in the United States Pacific Territories. **In** *Gopalakrishnan, C., ed.*, 1984, pp. 207–27. **[G: U.S.]**

Caves, Douglas W., et al. A Comparison of Different Methodologies in a Case Study of Residential Time-of-Use Electricity Pricing: Cost–Benefit Analysis. *J. Econometrics*, September/October 1984, *26*(1/2), pp. 17–34. **[G: U.S.]**

Chakravarty, S. P. and Wibe, Sören A. Energy Conservation: An Elasticity of Substitution Approach. *Energy Econ.*, October 1984, *6*(4), pp. 255–58. **[G: Sweden]**

Chirarattananon, Surapong. Analysis of Rural Energy Development in Thailand. **In** *Islam, M. N.; Morse, R. and Soesastro, M. H., eds.*, 1984, pp. 169–240. **[G: Thailand]**

Choe, B. J. World Bank Energy Model. *Finance Develop.*, September 1984, *21*(3), pp. 32. **[G: OPEC]**

Choucri, Nazli and Lahiri, Supriya. Short-Run Energy–Economy Interactions in Egypt. *World Devel.*, August 1984, *12*(8), pp. 799–820. **[G: Egypt]**

Christensen, Jens. DANSK OLIE OG NATURGAS A/S—en statsejet erhvervsvirksomhed? (DONG A/S—How Ought It Be Organized? With English summary.) *Nationaløkon. Tidsskr.*, 1984, *122*(1), pp. 124–32. **[G: Denmark]**

Chyba, Antonín. The Problem of Raw Material and Energy Supplies in Today's World. *Czech. Econ. Digest.*, March 1984, (2), pp. 50–68. **[G: Global]**

Ciampicali, Pierantonio. The Adjustment to the Oil Shocks in Western European Countries. **In** *Csikós-Nagy, B.; Hague, D. and Hall, G., eds.*, 1984, pp. 259–78. **[G: OECD]**

Ciliano, Robert and Hery, William. An Overview of the Tenrac Oil and Gas Supply Model. **In** *Lev, B., et al., eds.*, 1984, pp. 317–35.

Clô, Alberto. Mutamenti di breve e di lungo periodo nel sistema energetico internazionale e nazionale. (Short- and Long-Run Changes in the National and International Energy System. With English summary.) *Rivista Int. Sci. Econ. Com.*, August 1984, *31*(8), pp. 734–57. **[G: Italy; U.S.; France; Spain]**

Cluver, F. H. and Contogiannis, E. Energy Substitution Responses of South African Manufacturing: An Application of the Translog Production Function. *J. Stud. Econ. Econometrics*, January 1984, (18), pp. 15–35. **[G: S. Africa]**

Cockle, Paul. Public Expenditure Policy, 1984–85: Oil. **In** *Cockle, P., ed.*, 1984, pp. 77–87. **[G: U.K.]**

Cohen, Karl. The Resourceful Earth: A Response to Global 2000: Nuclear Power. **In** *Simon, J. L. and Kahn, H., eds.*, 1984, pp. 387–414. **[G: Global]**

Conant, Melvin A. Energy Policies of the United States: A Different Perspective. **In** *Ayoub, A., ed.*, 1984, pp. 194–204. **[G: U.S.]**

Conant, Melvin A. Sense and Nonsense about World Oil: Reply. *Energy J.*, January 1984, *5*(1), pp. 171–72.

Considine, Timothy J. Interfuel Substitution and Cyclical Volatility in U.S. Natural Gas Markets. *J. Energy Devel.*, Autumn 1984, *10*(1), pp. 97–109. **[G: U.S.]**

Considine, Timothy J. and Mount, Timothy D. The Use of Linear Logit Models for Dynamic Input Demand Systems. *Rev. Econ. Statist.*, August 1984, *66*(3), pp. 434–43. **[G: U.S.]**

Corey, G. R. The Comparative Costs of Nuclear and Fossil Fuelled Power Plants in an American Electricity Utility. **In** *Brookes, L. G. and Motamen, H., eds.*, 1984, pp. 274–87. **[G: U.S.]**

Craig, Paul P. Fuel Efficiency Incentives for Cars Oil Import Vulnerability Reduction. *Energy J.*, January 1984, *5*(1), pp. 141–48. **[G: U.S.]**

Crowe, Marshall A. An Assessment of the Recent Record in Canada. **In** *Fried, E. R. and Trezise, P. H., eds.*, 1984, pp. 114–21. **[G: U.S.; Canada]**

Csikós-Nagy, Béla. The Oil Price Shock in a Planned Economy—The Case of Hungary. **In** *Csikós-Nagy, B.; Hague, D. and Hall, G., eds.*, 1984, pp. 242–53. **[G: Hungary]**

Curlee, T. Randall. Monitoring the Potential for Future Oil Supply Crises: The Lack of Information. *J. Energy Devel.*, Spring 1984, *9*(2), pp. 289–97. **[G: OPEC]**

Dahl, Carol A. Vertical Equity Effects and Total Consumer Losses for Emergency Allocation Schemes for the Gasoline Market. *Appl. Econ.*, February 1984, *16*(1), pp. 25–32. **[G: U.S.]**

Dalsted, Norman L. and Green, John W. Water Requirements for Coal-Fired Power Plants. *Natural Res. J.*, January 1984, *24*(1), pp. 137–41. **[G: U.S.]**

Daniels, Edward J. The Cost of Synthetic Fuels in Relation to Oil Prices—Revisited. *Energy J.*, July 1984, *5*(3), pp. 147–57.

Devarajan, Shantayanan and Hubbard, R. Glenn. Drawing Down the Strategic Petroleum Reserve: The Case for Selling Futures Contracts. In *Alm, A. L. and Weimer, R. J.*, eds., 1984, pp. 187–96. [G: U.S.]

Dick, Hermann, et al. The Effect of Oil Price Increases on Four Oil-Poor Developing Countries: A Comparative Analysis. *Energy Econ.*, January 1984, *6*(1), pp. 59–70. [G: Ivory Coast; Kenya; S. Korea; Turkey]

Diefenbacher, Hans. Heat Pump Use in the Federal Republic of Germany. In *Baumgartner, T. and Burns, T. R.*, eds., 1984, pp. 127–64. [G: W. Germany]

Diffenderfer, Mark. Wood for Industrial Energy in Northern New England. In *Baumgartner, T. and Burns, T. R.*, eds., 1984, pp. 187–215. [G: U.S.]

Dobitz, Clifford P. Energy Substitution in Irrigation. *Reg. Sci. Persp.*, 1984, *14*(1), pp. 25–29. [G: U.S.]

Donnelly, William A. Residential Electricity Demand Modeling in the Australian Capital Territory: Preliminary Results. *Energy J.*, April 1984, *5*(2), pp. 119–31. [G: Australia]

Donnelly, William A. The Australian Demand for Petrol. *Int. J. Transport Econ.*, Aug.-Dec. 1984, *11*(2–3), pp. 189–205. [G: Australia]

Donnelly, William A. and Saddler, H. D. W. The Retail Demand for Electricity in Tasmania. *Australian Econ. Pap.*, June 1984, *23*(42), pp. 52–60. [G: Tasmania]

Downs, Anthony and Bradbury, Katharine L. What Does It All Mean? In *Downs, A. and Bradbury, K. L.*, eds., 1984, pp. 1–34. [G: U.S.]

Draper, Dennis W. The Behavior of Event-related Contracts. *J. Futures Markets*, Summer 1984, *4*(2), pp. 125–32. [G: U.S.]

Drollas, Leonidas P. The Demand for Gasoline: Further Evidence. *Energy Econ.*, January 1984, *6*(1), pp. 71–82. [G: U.S.; W. Europe]

Dubin, Jeffrey A. and McFadden, Daniel L. An Econometric Analysis of Residential Electric Appliance Holdings and Consumption. *Econometrica*, March 1984, *52*(2), pp. 345–62. [G: U.S.]

Duffus, LuAnn McClernan and Chern, Wen S. An Energy Demand and Generalized Fuel Choice Model for the Primary Metals Industry. *Energy J.*, April 1984, *5*(2), pp. 35–52. [G: U.S.]

Dunbar, Lyle E. OTEC Market Potential in Small Pacific Islands. In *Gopalakrishnan, C.*, ed., 1984, pp. 31–47. [G: Pacific Islands]

Eichhorn, Wolfgang and Buhl, Hans Ulrich. Optimal Growth Policies for Resource-Dependent Open Economies. In *Hammer, G. and Pallaschke, D.*, eds., 1984, pp. 175–87.

Einhorn, Michael. FEA Efficiency Standards and Energy Usage: Resolving Khazzoom versus Besen and Johnson [Economic Implications of Mandated Efficiency Standards for Household Appliances]. *Energy J.*, January 1984, *5*(1), pp. 173–76.

Eisenhauer, J. L. Comparative Analysis of Coal-based Electric Energy Delivery Systems. In *Lev, B., et al.*, eds., 1984, pp. 33–45. [G: U.S.]

El-Agraa, Ali M. and Hu, Yao-Su. National versus Supranational Interests and the Problem of Establishing an Effective EC Energy Policy. *J. Common Market Stud.*, June 1984, *22*(4), pp. 333–49. [G: EEC]

El Mallakh, Ragaei. The World Oil Market: Lessons from the Past and Implications for the Future. In *Ayoub, A.*, ed., 1984, pp. 23–32. [G: OPEC]

Ellis, James E., et al. Aspects of Energy Consumption in a Pastoral Ecosystem: Wood Use by the South Turkana. In *Barnes, C.; Ensminger, J. and O'Keefe, P.*, eds., 1984, pp. 164–87. [G: Kenya]

Ellman, Michael. Natural Gas, Restructuring and Re-industrialisation: The Dutch Experience of Industrial Policy. In *Ellman, M.*, 1984, *1981*, pp. 253–72. [G: Netherlands]

Enders, Klaus. The Dutch Disease or Problems of a Sectoral Boom. *Z. Wirtschaft. Sozialwissen.*, 1984, *104*(1), pp. 1–20.

Ensminger, Jean. Monetization of the Galole Orma Economy: Changes in the Use of Fuel and Woodstock. In *Barnes, C.; Ensminger, J. and O'Keefe, P.*, eds., 1984, pp. 124–40. [G: Kenya]

Evans, Nigel. Sizewell Decision: A Sensitivity Analysis. *Energy Econ.*, January 1984, *6*(1), pp. 14–20. [G: U.K.]

Farmer, A. A. Assessing the Economics of the Liquid Metal Fast Breeder Reactor. In *Brookes, L. G. and Motamen, H.*, eds., 1984, pp. 192–233.

Farstad, Halfdan. Solar Branch Development in Israel. In *Baumgartner, T. and Burns, T. R.*, eds., 1984, pp. 27–52. [G: Israel]

Farstad, Halfdan and Ward, James. Wind Energy in Denmark. In *Baumgartner, T. and Burns, T. R.*, eds., 1984, pp. 91–125. [G: Denmark]

Fender, John. Sectoral and Macroeconomic Effects in a Two Good Open Economy with an Intermediate Input. *Bull. Econ. Res.*, May 1984, *36*(1), pp. 9–32.

Fischoff, Baruch; Watson, Stephen R. and Hope, Chris. Defining Risk. *Policy Sci.*, October 1984, *17*(2), pp. 123–39.

Fišer, Miroslav. The Development of the Fuel and Energy Balance during the Period of the 7th Five-Year Plan. *Czech. Econ. Digest.*, September 1984, (6), pp. 80–98. [G: Czechoslovakia]

Flavin, Christopher. The Demise of Nuclear Power: What Comes Next? *Challenge*, July/August 1984, *27*(3), pp. 38–45. [G: Global]

Folkerts-Landau, Elena. The Social Cost of Imported Oil. *Energy J.*, July 1984, *5*(3), pp. 41–58.

Fortin, Pierre. Chocs pétroliers et stagflation dans les pays industriels: une synthèse de la décen-

nie. (with English Summary.) In *Ayoub, A.,
ed.*, 1984, pp. 33–56.   **[G: OECD]**

Franssen, Herman T. International Energy
Agency Strategies to Cope with Energy Uncertainties. *J. Energy Devel.*, Autumn 1984, *10*(1),
pp. 13–28.   **[G: Global]**

Franssen, Herman T. OECD Coal Demand in
the 1980s. In *Hawdon, D., ed.*, 1984, pp. 104–
31.   **[G: OECD]**

Freedman, David A. and Peters, Stephen C.
Bootstrapping a Regression Equation: Some
Empirical Results. *J. Amer. Statist. Assoc.*,
March 1984, *79*(385), pp. 97–106.   **[G: U.S.]**

**Freudenburg, William R. and Baxter, Rodney
K.** Host Community Attitudes toward Nuclear
Power Plants: A Reassessment. *Soc. Sci.
Quart.*, December 1984, *65*(4), pp. 1129–36.
          [G: U.S.]

Friedheim, Robert L. Coastal Management and
Nuclear Power. In *Friedheim, R. L., et al.*,
1984, pp. 314–52.   **[G: Japan]**

Frolich, Alan. Lesotho. In *O'Keefe, P. and Munslow, B., eds., Part I*, 1984, pp. 135–70.
          [G: Lesotho]

Fujii, Edwin T. and Mak, James. A Model of
Household Electricity Conservation Behavior.
Land Econ., November 1984, *60*(4), pp. 340–
51.   **[G: U.S.]**

Gallant, A. Ronald and Koenker, Roger W. Costs
and Benefits of Peak-Load Pricing of Electricity: A Continuous-Time Econometric Approach. *J. Econometrics*, September/October
1984, *26*(1/2), pp. 83–113.   **[G: U.S.]**

Gallavan, William M. Rate and Service Options:
Achieving a Balance between the Utility Ability
to Provide Service and Customer Demand for
Service. In *Foster, J. R., et al., eds.*, 1984,
pp. 77–85.   **[G: U.S.]**

Garbacz, Christopher. A National Micro-Data
Based Model of Residential Electricity Demand: New Evidence on Seasonal Variation.
Southern Econ. J., July 1984, *51*(1), pp. 235–
49.   **[G: U.S.]**

Garbacz, Christopher. Residential Electricity
Demand: A Suggested Appliance Stock Equation. *Energy J.*, April 1984, *5*(2), pp. 151–54.
          [G: U.S.]

Garcia-Nuñez, Luis. Energy Planning in Peru.
In *Baum, V., et al.*, 1984, pp. 267–79.
          [G: Peru]

Gardner, Richard L. and Young, Robert A. The
Effects of Electricity Rates and Rate Structures
on Pump Irrigation: An Eastern Colorado Case
Study. *Land Econ.*, November 1984, *60*(4), pp.
352–59.   **[G: U.S.]**

Garofalo, Gasper A. and Malhotra, Devinder M.
Input Substitution in the Manufacturing Sector
during the 1970's: A Regional Analysis. *J. Reg.
Sci.*, February 1984, *24*(1), pp. 51–63.
          [G: U.S.]

Gately, Dermot. A Ten-Year Retrospective:
OPEC and the World Oil Market. *J. Econ.
Lit.*, September 1984, *22*(3), pp. 1100–114.
          [G: OPEC]

Gerardi, Geraldine and Toder, Eric. Energy Tax

Alernatives. *Nat. Tax J.*, September 1984,
37(3), pp. 289–301.   **[G: U.S.]**

Gerisch, G. On the Conceptual Development of
Energy Statistics in Terms of Useful Energy.
Statist. J., August 1984, *2*(3), pp. 307–24.

Gholamnezhad, H. Energy Conservation: A Policy Model for the United States. In *Avula,
X. J. R., et al.*, 1984, pp. 969–74.   **[G: U.S.]**

Gibbons, Joel C. Capital–Energy Substitution in
the Long Run. *Energy J.*, April 1984, *5*(2),
pp. 109–18.   **[G: W. Europe; Canada; U.S.]**

Gibbons, Joel C. Energy Prices and Capital Obsolescence: Evidence from the Oil Embargo Period. *Energy J.*, January 1984, *5*(1), pp. 29–
43.   **[G: U.S.]**

Gilbert, Richard J. and Mork, Knut Anton. Will
Oil Markets Tighten Again? A Survey of Policies to Manage Possible Oil Supply Disruptions. *J. Policy Modeling*, February 1984, *6*(1),
pp. 111–42.   **[G: U.S.]**

Gillingham, Robert and Hagemann, Robert P.
Household Demand for Fuel Oil. *Appl. Econ.*,
August 1984, *16*(4), pp. 475–82.   **[G: U.S.]**

Gligo, Nicolo. Energy and the Prevailing Model
of Agricultural Technology in Latin America.
Cepal Rev., April 1984, (22), pp. 121–36.
          [G: Global]

Goldsmith, K. Energy Planning in Developing
Countries: Project Appraisal. In *Baum, V., et
al.*, 1984, pp. 100–07.   **[G: LDCs]**

Goldsmith, K. Financial Considerations in Energy
Planning. In *Baum, V., et al.*, 1984, pp. 94–
99.   **[G: LDCs]**

Goodman, Raymond. Managing the Demand for
Energy in the Developing World. In *Ghosh,
P. K., ed., no. 4*, 1984, *1980*, pp. 138–47.
          [G: LDCs]

Gouni, L. Economic Principles of Optimizing
Mixed Nuclear and Non-nuclear Electricity
Systems. In *Brookes, L. G. and Motamen, H.,
eds.*, 1984, pp. 46–66.   **[G: France;
W. Europe]**

Grauer, Manfred; Lewandowski, A. and Wierzbicki, A. DIDASS—Theory, Implementation
and Experiences. In *Grauer, M. and Wierzbicki, A. P., eds.*, 1984, pp. 22–30.
          [G: Austria]

Green, David Jay. A Small Scale, Partial Equilibrium Model of Natural Gas Markets: Responses
to Alternative Deregulation Scenarios and Oil
Price Changes. *Southern Econ. J.*, April 1984,
50(4), pp. 1112–30.   **[G: U.S.]**

Greene, David L. and Roberts, Glenn F. Fuel
Consumption for Road Transport in the USA—
A Comment. *Energy Econ.*, April 1984, *6*(2),
pp. 145–47.   **[G: U.S.]**

Greene, William H. and Smiley, Robert H. The
Effectiveness of Utility Regulation in a Period
of Changing Economic Conditions. In *Marchand, M.; Pestieau, P. and Tulkens, H., eds.*,
1984, pp. 269–87.   **[G: U.S.]**

Gross, Sharon P. Energy Conservation—A New
Factor in Certain Utility Rate Regulation. *Natural Res. J.*, April 1984, *24*(2), pp. 487–96.
          [G: U.S.]

Guadagni, Alieto Aldo. La revolución energética:

el rol de la sustitución del petróleo y la conservación de energía. (With English summary.) *Desarrollo Econ.*, October–December 1984, *24*(95), pp. 339–66. [G: Global]

Guillaume, Y., et al. Etude des incitants financiers aux économies d'énergie dans le secteur domestique. Le cas de la Belgique. (Energy Saving Is One of the Major Economic Problems of This Period. Governments Try to Encourage It by Various Measures. With English summary.) *Cah. Écon. Bruxelles*, 1st Trimester 1984, (101), pp. 57–73. [G: Belgium]

Guillaume, Y., et al. Impact of Subsidies and of Tax Deductions on Consumer's Energy Savings—The Belgian Case. In *Avula, X. J. R., et al.*, 1984, pp. 815–21. [G: Belgium]

Gunter, Lewell and Smathers, Webb M., Jr. Financial Analysis of Solar Energy Applications with Endogenous System Sizing. *Southern J. Agr. Econ.*, December 1984, *16*(2), pp. 21–29. [G: U.S.]

Gurwitz, Aaron S. and Chall, Daniel E. Nuclear Power Plant Construction: Paying the Bill. *Fed. Res. Bank New York Quart. Rev.*, Summer 1984, *9*(2), pp. 48–57. [G: U.S.]

Habibollahzadeh, H., et al. Optimization of Hydroelectric Power System Operation. In *Lev, B., et al., eds.*, 1984, pp. 109–19.

Häfele, Wolf. The Future of Nuclear Energy. In *Hawdon, D., ed.*, 1984, pp. 79–103.

Häfele, Wolf and Rogner, H-H. A Technical Appraisal of the IIASA Energy Scenarios? A Rebuttal. *Policy Sci.*, December 1984, *17*(4), pp. 341–65. [G: U.S.; Selected Countries]

Hafkamp, Wim and Nijkamp, Peter. A Multiple-Layer Model for Economic-Environmental-Energy Policy Analysis. In *Grauer, M. and Wierzbicki, A. P., eds.*, 1984, pp. 193–201. [G: Netherlands]

Hafkamp, Wim and Nijkamp, Peter. An Operational Multi-component Multi-actor Policy Model for Economic-Environmental Scenarios. In *Despontin, M.; Nijkamp, P. and Spronk, J., eds.*, 1984, pp. 157–82. [G: Netherlands]

Hamilton, K. E.; Hoffman, R. B. and Sande, G. T. Energy Modelling in SERF: The Socio-Economic-Resource Framework. In *Lev, B., et al., eds.*, 1984, pp. 233–53. [G: Canada]

Hammond, P. Brett. The Energy Model Muddle. *Policy Sci.*, February 1984, *16*(3), pp. 227–43.

Hammoudeh, Shawkat; Ayyash, Saud and Suri, R. K. Conventional and Solar Cooling Systems for Kuwait: An Economic Analysis. *Energy Econ.*, October 1984, *6*(4), pp. 259–66. [G: Kuwait]

Hann, Daniel P. Perspectives on the Future of the World Economy: The Energy Situation and the New International Economic Order. In *Ghosh, P. K., ed., no. 4*, 1984, *1981*, pp. 71–77. [G: Global]

Hannigan, J. B. and McMillan, C. H. The Soviet Union and World Trade in Oil and Gas. In *Kostecki, M. M., ed.*, 1984, pp. 68–99. [G: U.S.S.R.; Global]

Haque, Abu Mohammad Izharul. Energy Planning in Pakistan—Problems and Prospects. In *Baum, V., et al.*, 1984, pp. 257–66. [G: Pakistan]

Haraf, William S. Japanese Macroeconomic Performance since 1970: Comments. *Carnegie-Rochester Conf. Ser. Public Policy*, Spring 1984, *20*, pp. 115–20. [G: Japan]

Harkness, Jon. Optimal Oil Pricing in a Small Open Economy: A Macro-economic Perspective. *Can. J. Econ.*, November 1984, *17*(4), pp. 762–73.

Harris, Curtis C., Jr.; McConnell, Virginia D. and Cumberland, John H. A Model for Forecasting the Economic and Environmental Impact of Energy Policy. *Energy Econ.*, July 1984, *6*(3), pp. 167–76. [G: U.S.]

Hartley, Peter and Trengove, Chris. The Marginal Costs of Electricity Supply in Victoria. *Econ. Rec.*, December 1984, *60*(171), pp. 340–55. [G: Australia]

Hartshorn, J. E. Recast Roles in the World Oil Performance. In *Ayoub, A., ed.*, 1984, pp. 205–19. [G: Global]

Haugerud, Angelique. Economy, Ecology and the Unequal Impact of Woodfuel Scarcity in Embu, Kenya. In *Barnes, C.; Ensminger, J. and O'Keefe, P., eds.*, 1984, pp. 79–101. [G: Kenya]

Hawdon, David. The Energy Crisis: Introduction and Summary. In *Hawdon, D., ed.*, 1984, pp. iii–vi.

Hayes, Denis. Transitions to Alternative Energy Systems: Toward a Sustainable Future. In *Baumgartner, T. and Burns, T. R., eds.*, 1984, pp. xiii–xvi.

Hederman, William F., Jr. and Gordon, Laura Cohen. Investment in Geothermal Direct Heat Applications. *Energy J.*, January 1984, *5*(1), pp. 85–97. [G: U.S.]

Helliwell, John F.; MacGregor, Mary E. and Plourde, Andre. Changes in Canadian Energy Demand, Supply, and Policies, 1974–1986. *Natural Res. J.*, April 1984, *24*(2), pp. 297–324. [G: Canada]

Helliwell, John F.; MacGregor, Mary E. and Plourde, Andre. Energy Policy and Industrial Activity: A Reply [The National Energy Program Meets Falling World Energy Prices]. *Can. Public Policy*, December 1984, *10*(4), pp. 476–80. [G: Canada]

Henson, Steven E. Electricity Demand Estimates under Increasing-Block Rates. *Southern Econ. J.*, July 1984, *51*(1), pp. 147–56. [G: U.S.]

Hillman, Arye L. Producer and Consumer Interests, the State-Owned Pipeline, and Public Authority Pricing of Natural Gas. *Econ. Rec.*, March 1984, *60*(168), pp. 28–33.

Hillman, Arye L. and Katz, Eliakim. Oil Price Instability and Domestic Energy Substitution for Imported Oil. *Econ. Rec.*, March 1984, *60*(168), pp. 85–89.

Hjort, Lars. The Swedish Experience in Energy Planning. In *Baum, V., et al.*, 1984, pp. 53–62. [G: Sweden]

Hobbs, Benjamin F. Regional Energy Facility Location Models for Power System Planning and

Policy Analysis. In *Lev, B., et al., eds.*, 1984, pp. 53–66.

Hochman, Eithan; LaFrance, Jeffrey T. and Zilberman, David. Solar Energy and Hydroelectric Power Generation in the Dead Sea: A Dynamic Analysis. *Water Resources Res.*, November 1984, *20*(11), pp. 1469–76.
[G: Israel]

Hölker, Franz-Josef. Die ordnung der energiewirtschaft der Bundesrepublik Deutschland. Leitbild—Reale Probleme. (The Organisation of the Energy Sector in the Federal Republic of Germany. With English summary.) *Ann. Pub. Co-op. Econ.*, Oct.–Dec. 1984, *55*(4), pp. 413–31.
[G: W. Germany]

Holland, David M. Energy and Agriculture: Conflicts and Potentials for Structural Reform. In *Geisler, C. C. and Popper, F. J., eds.*, 1984, pp. 88–97.
[G: U.S.]

Hopkins, Frank. Energy and Regional Development: Comment. In *Downs, A. and Bradbury, K. L., eds.*, 1984, pp. 283–86.
[G: U.S.]

Hosier, Richard. Domestic Energy Consumption in Rural Kenya: Results of a Nationwide Survey. In *Barnes, C.; Ensminger, J. and O'Keefe, P., eds.*, 1984, pp. 14–60.
[G: Kenya]

Hosier, Richard. Zimbabwe. In *O'Keefe, P. and Munslow, B., eds., Part II*, 1984, pp. 171–210.
[G: Zimbabwe]

Hourcade, Jean-Charles. Energy, Development Styles and Capital Requirements in Third World Countries. In *Ghosh, P. K., ed., no. 4*, 1984, *1981*, pp. 90–101.
[G: LDCs]

Hsu, John C. Adjustment to Oil Shocks in a Small Open Less Developed Country: Problems and Policy Alternatives. *Singapore Econ. Rev.*, April 1984, *29*(1), pp. 16–29.
[G: Taiwan]

Hubbard, R. Glenn. Temporary Tax Reductions as Responses to Oil Shocks. In *Alm, A. L. and Weimer, R. J., eds.*, 1984, pp. 121–28.
[G: U.S.]

Hubbard, R. Glenn and Weiner, Robert J. Oil Shock: Policy Response and Implementation: Government Stockpiles in a Multicountry World: Coordination versus Competition. In *Alm, A. L. and Weimer, R. J., eds.*, 1984, pp. 197–218.
[G: OECD]

Hung, Nguyen Manh; Kemp, Murray C. and Long, Ngo Van. On the Transition from an Exhaustible Resource-Stock to an Inexhaustible Substitute. In *Kemp, M. C. and Long, N. V., eds.*, 1984, pp. 105–22.

Hunt, Lester Charles. Energy and Capital: Substitutes or Complements? Some Results for the UK Industrial Sector. *Appl. Econ.*, October 1984, *16*(5), pp. 783–89.
[G: U.K.]

Huntington, Hillard G. Real Oil Prices from 1980 to 1982. *Energy J.*, July 1984, *5*(3), pp. 119–31.
[G: OECD]

Hurst, Christopher. A Model of an Indian Village: A Study of Alternative Sources of Energy for Irrigation. *World Devel.*, February 1984, *12*(2), pp. 141–56.
[G: India]

Hutton, Sandra. Domestic Fuel Expenditure: An Analysis of Three National Surveys. *Energy Econ.*, January 1984, *6*(1), pp. 52–58.
[G: U.K.]

Hyett, A. J. The Structure and Economics of the Nuclear Fuel Cycle Service Industry. In *Brookes, L. G. and Motamen, H., eds.*, 1984, pp. 162–89.
[G: Selected Countries]

Iqbal, Mahmood. Residential Energy Demand: A Case Study of Pakistan. *J. Econ. Stud.*, 1984, *11*(1), pp. 40–48.
[G: Pakistan]

Ironmonger, Duncan; Manning, Ian G. and Tran, Van Hoa. Longitudinal Working Models: Estimates of Household Energy Consumption in Australia. *Energy Econ.*, January 1984, *6*(1), pp. 41–46.
[G: Australia]

Ishimine, Tomotaka. Food, Energy and Debt Servicing as Reserve and Development Constraints of Less Developed Countries. *Rivista Int. Sci. Econ. Com.*, April 1984, *31*(4), pp. 371–79.
[G: LDCs]

Islam, M. Nurul. Energy and Rural Development: Critical Assessment of the Bangladesh Situation. In *Islam, M. N.; Morse, R. and Soesastro, M. H., eds.*, 1984, pp. 43–88.
[G: Bangladesh]

Islam, M. Nurul. Field-Based Assessment and Development of Improved Stoves. In *Islam, M. N.; Morse, R. and Soesastro, M. H., eds.*, 1984, pp. 337–79.
[G: Asian LDCs]

Jaffee, Dwight M. New Residential Construction and Energy Costs. In *Downs, A. and Bradbury, K. L., eds.*, 1984, pp. 143–84.
[G: U.S.]

Jarrin, Manuel Lauro Tobar. The Petroleum Industry in Ecuador. In *Baum, V., et al.*, 1984, pp. 185–95.
[G: Ecuador]

Jensen, Cynthia L. Wood Use by the Amboseli Maasai. In *Barnes, C.; Ensminger, J. and O'Keefe, P., eds.*, 1984, pp. 188–204.
[G: Kenya]

Jorgenson, Dale W. The Role of Energy in Productivity Growth. *Amer. Econ. Rev.*, May 1984, *74*(2), pp. 26–30.
[G: U.S.]

Jorgenson, Dale W. The Role of Energy in Productivity Growth. *Energy J.*, July 1984, *5*(3), pp. 11–26.

Jorgenson, Dale W. The Role of Energy in Productivity Growth. In *Kendrick, J. W., ed.*, 1984, pp. 279–323.
[G: U.S.]

Karp, Larry. Demand for Energy and Insulation. *Energy Econ.*, July 1984, *6*(3), pp. 208–10.

Kassum, Al Noor. Energy Planning in Tanzania. In *Baum, V., et al.*, 1984, pp. 1 [G: Tanzania]

Kay, John A. North Sea Oil and Manufacturing Output. In *Griffiths, B. and Wood, G. E., eds.*, 1984, pp. 185–99.
[G: U.K.; Selected Countries]

Keepin, Bill. A Technical Appraisal of the IIASA Energy Scenarios. *Policy Sci.*, November 1984, *17*(3), pp. 199–276.
[G: Global]

Kelman, Steven. Revenue Recycling Using Check Writing. In *Alm, A. L. and Weimer, R. J., eds.*, 1984, pp. 145–64.
[G: U.S.]

Kelman, Steven. Using Implementation Research to Solve Implementation Problems: The Case of Energy Emergency Assistance. *J. Policy Anal. Manage.*, Fall 1984, 4(1), pp. 75–91. [G: U.S.]

Kemeny, L. The Practical Problems and Issues Pertaining to Nuclear Energy in Less-developed Countries. In *Brookes, L. G. and Motamen, H., eds.*, 1984, pp. 334–59. [G: LDCs; CMEA; Australia]

Kieschnick, Robert L., Jr. State Energy Modeling and Planning: The Current Texas Experience. In *Lev, B., et al., eds.*, 1984, pp. 311–16. [G: U.S.]

King, Michael J. and Scott, Michael J. Forecasting Electricity Demand with an End-Use/Econometric Model. In *Lev, B., et al., eds.*, 1984, pp. 151–64. [G: U.S.]

Kirchgässner, Gebhard. Die Abhängigkeit der Mineralölpreise in der Schweiz von der Entwicklung der Preise auf dem Rotterdamer Spotmarkt und vom Wechselkurs. (The Dependance of Swiss Oil Prices on the Price at Rotterdam and on the Exchange Rate. With English summary.) *Schweiz. Z. Volkswirtsch. Statist.*, September 1984, 120(3), pp. 293–313. [G: Switzerland]

Komiya, Ryutaro and Yasui, Kazuo. Japan's Macroeconomic Performance since the First Oil Crisis: Review and Appraisal. *Carnegie-Rochester Conf. Ser. Public Policy*, Spring 1984, 20, pp. 69–114. [G: Japan]

Kononov, Iu. D. The Fuel-Energy Complex in the System of National Economic Relations. *Prob. Econ.*, May 1984, 27(1), pp. 33–46. [G: U.S.S.R.]

Kouris, George. Fuel Consumption for Road Transport in the USA—A Reply. *Energy Econ.*, April 1984, 6(2), pp. 148. [G: U.S.]

Krapels, Edward N., et al. The Domestic Refining Industry: Economics and Regulation. In *Alm, A. L. and Weimer, R. J., eds.*, 1984, pp. 55–76. [G: U.S.]

Krasulja, Petar. Development of Energy Production and Consumption in the Socialist Federal Republic of Yugoslavia. In *Baum, V., et al.*, 1984, pp. 293–98. [G: Yugoslavia]

Krutilla, John V. and Fisher, Anthony C. The Trans-Alaska Pipeline: Environmental Consequences and Alternatives. In *Ahmad, Y. J.; Dasgupta, P. and Mäler, K.-G., eds.*, 1984, pp. 83–113. [G: U.S.]

Kumar, T. M. Vinod. Integrated Rural Development Planning and Energy Priorities: Participatory Surveys in India Microregions. In *Islam, M. N.; Morse, R. and Soesastro, M. H., eds.*, 1984, pp. 241–78. [G: India]

Langston, Vicky C. An Investment Model for the U.S. Gulf Coast Refining/Petrochemical Complex for Policy Analysis. In *Lev, B., et al., eds.*, 1984, pp. 355–71. [G: U.S.]

Lantzke, Ulf. Energy Policies in Industrialized Countries: An Evaluation of the Past Decade. In *Ayoub, A., ed.*, 1984, pp. 15–22.

Lantzke, Ulf. Energy: Still a Problem for the Health of the World Economy. *Schweiz. Z. Volkswirtsch. Statist.*, September 1984, 120(3), pp. 241–47. [G: OECD]

Lantzke, Ulf. The Oil Market: The Role of International Cooperation. In *Alm, A. L. and Weimer, R. J., eds.*, 1984, pp. 77–93. [G: OECD]

Lawson, Nigel. Energy Economics and Policy: Lessons from the Past. In *Hawdon, D., ed.*, 1984, pp. 1–6. [G: U.K.]

Légrády, K., et al. Multicriteria Decision Analysis to Aid Budget Allocation. In *Grauer, M. and Wierzbicki, A. P., eds.*, 1984, pp. 164–74. [G: Netherlands]

Leitzinger, Jeffrey J. and Stiglitz, Joseph E. Information Externalities in Oil and Gas Leasing. *Contemp. Policy Issue*, March 1984, (5), pp. 44–57. [G: U.S.]

Leu, Robert E., et al. Externe Kosten der Energie am Beispiel von Mortalität und Morbidität. (External Costs of Energy: Effects on Mortality and Morbidity. With English summary.) *Schweiz. Z. Volkswirtsch. Statist.*, September 1984, 120(3), pp. 383–408. [G: Switzerland]

Leung, Ping Sun and Hsu, George J. Y. An Integrated Energy Planning Model for Hawaii. *Energy Econ.*, April 1984, 6(2), pp. 117–21. [G: U.S.]

Levin, Nissan; Tishler, Asher and Zahavi, Jacob. A Model for Planning Investments in the Energy Sector in the Medium Range. In *Lev, B., et al., eds.*, 1984, pp. 285–308. [G: Israel]

Levine, Leonard B. Changes in Policies Affecting U.S. Natural Gas Trade. *J. Energy Devel.*, Autumn 1984, 10(1), pp. 117–20. [G: U.S.]

Lin, Ching-yuan. Global Pattern of Energy Consumption before and after the 1974 Oil Crisis. *Econ. Develop. Cult. Change*, July 1984, 32(4), pp. 781–802. [G: Global]

Lind, Jan-Inge. Peat for Energy in Finland: History of a Development Process. In *Baumgartner, T. and Burns, T. R., eds.*, 1984, pp. 217–37. [G: Finland]

Lockeretz, William. Energy and the Sustainability of the American Agricultural System. In *Douglass, G. K., ed.*, 1984, pp. 77–88.

Lowinger, Thomas C. and Ram, Rati. Product Value as a Determinant of OPEC's Official Crude Oil Prices: Additional Evidence [The Determinants of Official OPEC Crude Prices]. *Rev. Econ. Statist.*, November 1984, 66(4), pp. 691–95. [G: OPEC]

Luciani, Giacomo. The Mediterranean and the Energy Picture. In *Luciani, G., ed.*, 1984, pp. 1–40. [G: Mediterranean]

Lunning, W. H. The Economics of Final Decommissioning and Disposal of Nuclear Power Plant. In *Brookes, L. G. and Motamen, H., eds.*, 1984, pp. 303–13. [G: U.K.]

Lutton, Thomas J. and LeBlanc, Michael R. A Comparison of Multivariate Logit and Translog Models for Energy and Nonenergy Input Cost Share Analysis. *Energy J.*, October 1984, 5(4), pp. 35–44. [G: U.S.]

Mabuchi, Noritoshi. Energy Finance and Investment in a Changing Environment. *J. Energy Devel.*, Autumn 1984, 10(1), pp. 111–15. [G: Japan]

Mackay, Tony. The Oil and Oil-Related Sector. In *Hood, N. and Young, S., eds.*, 1984, pp. 326–64. **[G: U.K.]**

Manne, Alan S. Decomposing the Impact of Higher Energy Prices on Long-term Growth: Comments. In *Scarf, H. E. and Shoven, J. B., eds.*, 1984, pp. 362–65. **[G: U.S.]**

Manne, Alan S. and Schrattenholzer, Leo. International Energy Workshop: A Summary of the 1983 Poll Responses. *Energy J.*, January 1984, 5(1), pp. 45–64.

Manuel, David P. Unemployment and Drilling Activity in Major Energy-producing States. *J. Energy Devel.*, Autumn 1984, 10(1), pp. 44–62. **[G: U.S.]**

Margolick, Michael; Hansson, Ardo H. and Helliwell, John F. Competing Energy Uses for Wood Wastes in British Columbia. *Energy J.*, January 1984, 5(1), pp. 65–84. **[G: Canada]**

Marion, Nancy Peregrim. Nontraded Goods, Oil Price Increases and the Current Account. *J. Int. Econ.*, February 1984, 16(1/2), pp. 29–44.

Marion, Nancy Peregrim and Svensson, Lars E. O. Adjustment to Expected and Unexpected Oil Price Changes. *Can. J. Econ.*, February 1984, 17(1), pp. 15–31.

Marion, Nancy Peregrim and Svensson, Lars E. O. World Equilibrium with Oil Price Increases: An Intertemporal Analysis. *Oxford Econ. Pap.*, March 1984, 36(1), pp. 86–102.

Marquez, Jaime and Pauly, Peter. OPEC's Pricing Policy and the International Transmission of Oil Price Effects. *Energy Econ.*, October 1984, 6(4), pp. 267–75. **[G: MDCs; OPEC; Non-OPEC LDCs]**

Martin, Ricardo and Selowsky, Marcelo. Energy Prices, Substitution, and Optimal Borrowing in the Short Run: An Analysis of Adjustment in Oil Importing Developing Countries. *J. Devel. Econ.*, April 1984, 14(3), pp. 331–50. **[G: LDCs]**

Martz, John D. Venezuela: Democratic Politics of Petroleum. In *Wesson, R., ed.*, 1984, pp. 161–87. **[G: Venezuela]**

Mathur, Vijay K. Effectiveness of Building Energy Performance Standards to Curtail Household Energy Demand: A Theoretical Analysis. *Energy J.*, January 1984, 5(1), pp. 99–114.

Mayo, John W. Multiproduct Monopoly, Regulation, and Firm Costs. *Southern Econ. J.*, July 1984, 51(1), pp. 208–18. **[G: U.S.]**

Mayo, John W. The Technological Determinants of the U.S. Energy Industry Structure. *Rev. Econ. Statist.*, February 1984, 66(1), pp. 51–58. **[G: U.S.]**

McConnell, L. G. and Woodhead, L. W. The Economics of the Candu Reactor. In *Brookes, L. G. and Motamen, H., eds.*, 1984, pp. 255–72. **[G: Canada]**

Mead, Walter J. and Moseidjord, Asbjorn. A New Market-based Method for Estimating Oil Field Reserves: An Application to the Santa Maria Basin. *J. Energy Devel.*, Spring 1984, 9(2), pp. 163–76. **[G: U.S.]**

Mead, Walter J.; Moseidjord, Asbjorn and Mu- raoka, Dennis D. Alternative Bid Variables as Instruments of OCS Leasing Policy. *Contemp. Policy Issue*, March 1984, (5), pp. 30–43. **[G: U.S.]**

Miernyk, William H. Energy and Regional Development. In *Downs, A. and Bradbury, K. L., eds.*, 1984, pp. 226–83. **[G: U.S.]**

Minford, Patrick. North Sea Oil and Manufacturing Output: Comment. In *Griffiths, B. and Wood, G. E., eds.*, 1984, pp. 205–10. **[G: U.K.; Selected Countries]**

Moe, R. J. and Adams, R. C. Residential Energy Use and Improved Building Thermal Efficiency: An Econometric Analysis. In *Lev, B., et al., eds.*, 1984, pp. 135–49. **[G: U.S.]**

Mohammad, Yousuf Hasan. Recent Developments within OPEC: An Economic Perspective. *J. Energy Devel.*, Spring 1984, 9(2), pp. 223–41. **[G: OPEC]**

Molnár, Antal. Statistics on the Production and Use of Low-Temperature Thermal Water in Hungary. *Statist. J.*, January 1984, 2(1), pp. 73–83. **[G: Hungary]**

Morehouse, Thomas A. Resource Development and Alaska Wealth Management. In *Morehouse, T. A., ed.*, 1984, pp. 169–97. **[G: U.S.]**

Morgenstern, Richard D. Energy Prices and Urban Decentralization: Comment. In *Downs, A. and Bradbury, K. L., eds.*, 1984, pp. 104–09. **[G: U.S.]**

Morlan, Terry H. Energy and the Existing Stock of Housing: Comment. In *Downs, A. and Bradbury, K. L., eds.*, 1984, pp. 139–42. **[G: U.S.]**

Morrison, Denton E. Energy, Appropriate Technology, and International Interdependence. In *Ghosh, P. K., ed., no. 14*, 1984, pp. 205–37.

Morse, Richard; Soesastro, M. Hadi and Schlegel, Charles. Energy for Rural Development: Principals, Issues, and Methods. In *Islam, M. N.; Morse, R. and Soesastro, M. H., eds.*, 1984, pp. 1–42. **[G: Asian LDCs]**

Morse, Richard, et al. Converting Rural Energy Needs to Opportunities. In *Islam, M. N.; Morse, R. and Soesastro, M. H., eds.*, 1984, pp. 519–47. **[G: Asian LDCs]**

Morse, Richard, et al. Organizing Current Information for Rural Energy and Development Planning. In *Islam, M. N.; Morse, R. and Soesastro, M. H., eds.*, 1984, pp. 473–518. **[G: Asian LDCs]**

Mounier, Alain and Byé, Pascal. Les futurs alimentaires et énergétiques des biotechnologies. (With English summary.) *Écon. Soc.*, September 1984, 18(9), pp. 7–340. **[G: Global]**

Munasinghe, Mohan. Energy Strategies for Oil Importing Developing Countries. *Natural Res. J.*, April 1984, 24(2), pp. 351–68. **[G: LDCs]**

Munasinghe, Mohan. Integrated National Energy Planning in Developing Countries. In *Ghosh, P. K., ed., no. 4*, 1984, 1980, pp. 199–212.

Mung'ala, Patrick Mutula and Openshaw, Keith. Estimation of Present and Future demand for Woodfuel in the Machakos District. In *Barnes,*

C.; Ensminger, J. and O'Keefe, P., eds., 1984, pp. 102–23. **[G: Kenya]**

Munslow, Barry. Mozambique. In O'Keefe, P. and Munslow, B., eds., Part II, 1984, pp. 5–47. **[G: Mozambique]**

Munslow, Barry. Swaziland. In O'Keefe, P. and Munslow, B., eds., Part II, 1984, pp. 49–85. **[G: Swaziland]**

Murphy, Frederic H., et al. An Introduction to the Intermediate Future Forecasting System. In Lev, B., et al., eds., 1984, pp. 255–64.

Muth, Richard F. Energy Prices and Urban Decentralization. In Downs, A. and Bradbury, K. L., eds., 1984, pp. 85–104. **[G: U.S.]**

Nasr, Faisal A. Implications of the Recent OPEC "Crisis." J. Econ. Issues, June 1984, 18(2), pp. 483–91.

Nasseh, Ali Reza and Elyasiani, Elyas. Energy Price Shocks in the 1970s: Impact in Industrialized Economies. Energy Econ., October 1984, 6(4), pp. 231–44. **[G: U.S.; U.K.; Canada; Germany; France]**

Nasseh, Ali Reza and Elyasiani, Elyas. Energy Price Shocks, Aggregate Supply Displacement, and Macroeconomic Activity. Eastern Econ. J., October-December 1984, 10(4), pp. 468–87. **[G: U.S.]**

Neels, Kevin and Murray, Michael P. Energy and the Existing Stock of Housing. In Downs, A. and Bradbury, K. L., eds., 1984, pp. 110–39. **[G: U.S.]**

Nemetz, Peter N., et al. Threat in Opportunity and Opportunity in Threat: Energy Prospects for Australia and New Zealand. J. Energy Devel., Spring 1984, 9(2), pp. 263–88. **[G: Australia; New Zealand]**

Nemoto, Jiro. On Substitution Possibilities between Energy and Non-energy Inputs—A Nested CES Production Function Analysis. (In Japanese. With English summary.) Econ. Stud. Quart., August 1984, 35(2), pp. 139–58. **[G: Japan]**

Newbery, David M. G. The Economics of Oil. In van der Ploeg, F., ed., 1984, pp. 519–67.

Nguyen, The-Hiep. Energy Consumption and Economic Growth. Managerial Dec. Econ., March 1984, 5(1), pp. 49–53. **[G: OECD]**

Nguyen, The-Hiep. On Energy Coefficients and Ratios. Energy Econ., April 1984, 6(2), pp. 102–09. **[G: OECD]**

Niculescu, I. and Boconcios, Rodica. Modelling Problems of the Efficient Utilization of the Existing Energy Resources. Econ. Computat. Cybern. Stud. Res., 1984, 19(2), pp. 57–62.

O'Keefe, Philip; Goodman, Gordon and Kristoferson, Lars. Policy Issues in Ethiopian Development. In Baum, V., et al., 1984, pp. 205–18. **[G: Ethiopia]**

O'Neill, Richard P., et al. The Gas Analysis Modeling System. In Lev, B., et al., eds., 1984, pp. 265–83.

Ojanen, Karla. Preemption—Atomic Energy. Natural Res. J., July 1984, 24(3), pp. 761–82. **[G: U.S.]**

Olsen, Marvin E. and Cluett, Christopher. Public Willingness to Invest in Household Weath-

erization. Energy J., January 1984, 5(1), pp. 165–68.

Olson, Dennis O. The Interregional Incidence of Energy-Production Taxes. Int. Reg. Sci. Rev., November 1984, 9(2), pp. 109–24. **[G: U.S.]**

Openshaw, Keith. Tanzania. In O'Keefe, P. and Munslow, B., eds., Part II, 1984, pp. 87–132. **[G: Tanzania]**

Oweiss, Ibrahim M. Petrodollar Surpluses: Trends and Economic Impact. J. Energy Devel., Spring 1984, 9(2), pp. 177–202. **[G: OPEC]**

Palmedo, Philip F. and Chatterjee, Romir. Information Needs for Energy Planning. In Baum, V., et al., 1984, pp. 108–24. **[G: Argentina]**

Pandjaitan, M. Energy Planning and Energy Policy in Indonesia. In Baum, V., et al., 1984, pp. 230–40. **[G: Indonesia]**

Park, Rolla Edward and Acton, Jan Paul. Large Business Customer Response to Time-of-Day Electricity Rates. J. Econometrics, September/October 1984, 26(1/2), pp. 229–52. **[G: U.S.]**

Parks, Richard W. and Weitzel, David. Measuring the Consumer Welfare Effects of Time-differentiated Electricity Prices. J. Econometrics, September/October 1984, 26(1/2), pp. 35–64. **[G: U.S.]**

Pearce, David W. and Edwards, Ronald. Energy Policy in a Price-Regulated Developing Economy: A Study of Egypt. J. Econ. Stud., 1984, 11(1), pp. 3–26. **[G: Egypt]**

Pelkmans, Jacques. Collective Management and Economic Cooperation. In Merlini, C., ed., 1984, pp. 89–136. **[G: OECD]**

Penrose, Edith. OPEC and the World Oil Market in the 1980s. In Hawdon, D., ed., 1984, pp. 37–47. **[G: OPEC]**

Perlov, Diane Catherine. Exploiting the Forest: Patterns and Perceptions in Highland Samburu. In Barnes, C.; Ensminger, J. and O'Keefe, P., eds., 1984, pp. 141–63. **[G: Kenya]**

Pillet, Gonzague and Odum, Howard T. Energy Externality and the Economy of Switzerland. Schweiz. Z. Volkswirtsch. Statist., September 1984, 120(3), pp. 409–35. **[G: Switzerland]**

Pindyck, Robert S. and Rotemberg, Julio J. Energy Price Shocks and Macroeconomic Adjustments. Natural Res. J., April 1984, 24(2), pp. 277–96.

Pindyck, Robert S. and Rotemberg, Julio J. Energy Shocks and the Macroeconomy. In Alm, A. L. and Weimer, R. J., eds., 1984, pp. 97–120. **[G: U.S.]**

Pines, David and Sadka, Efraim. Gasoline Prices, Welfare and Congestion Tolls. Scand. J. Econ., 1984, 86(4), pp. 440–51.

Planning Ser., Ministry of Energy, Philippines. Philippine Rural Energy Resource and Consumption Survey. In Islam, M. N.; Morse, R. and Soesastro, M. H., eds., 1984, pp. 135–68. **[G: Philippines]**

Plummer, James L. Institutional Alternatives for Financing and Operating the Strategic Petroleum Reserve. In Alm, A. L. and Weimer, R. J., eds., 1984, pp. 167–86. **[G: U.S.]**

Polasek, Wolfgang. Extreme Bound Analysis for Residential Load Curve Models: Empirical Evidence for a 16-Household Example. *Empirical Econ.*, 1984, 9(3), pp. 165–81. [G: U.S.]

Polzin, Paul E. The Specification of Price in Studies of Consumer Demand under Block Price Scheduling: Additional Empirical Evidence. *Land Econ.*, August 1984, 60(3), pp. 306–09. [G: U.S.]

Portney, Paul R. Natural Resources and the Environment: More Controversy than Change. In *Palmer, J. L. and Sawhill, I. V.*, eds., 1984, pp. 141–75. [G: U.S.]

Preda, G., et al. Instruction and Education in the Field of Energy Conservation in Romania. *Econ. Computat. Cybern. Stud. Res.*, 1984, 19(1), pp. 67–73. [G: Romania]

Price, Jeffrey P. Coal Supply Models: The State of the Art. In *Lev, B., et al.*, eds., 1984, pp. 3–20. [G: U.S.]

Procter, Robert J. and Tyner, Wallace E. Assessing the Impact of Peak-Load Electricity Pricing and the Solar Tax Credits on the Adoption of Solar Energy. *Land Econ.*, February 1984, 60(1), pp. 49–55. [G: U.S.]

Promboin, Ronald L. Energy Shocks and the U.S. Economy: How Much Has OPEC Helped Recently? *Bus. Econ.*, July 1984, 19(4), pp. 34–39. [G: U.S.]

Proops, John L. R. Modelling the Energy-Output Ratio. *Energy Econ.*, January 1984, 6(1), pp. 47–51.

Qu, Yu. Cogeneration in the People's Republic of China. *Energy J.*, April 1984, 5(2), pp. 133–37. [G: China]

Quigley, John M. Residential Energy Standards and the Housing Market: A Regional Analysis. *Int. Reg. Sci. Rev.*, December 1984, 9(3), pp. 201–16. [G: U.S.]

Qurashi, M. M. Renewable Sources of Energy in Pakistan. *Pakistan Devel. Rev.*, Summer-Autumn 1984, 23(2&3), pp. 457–72. [G: Pakistan]

Rasmussen, Jon A. and Piette, Michael J. A Comparison of the Costs and the Results in the Onshore and Offshore Search for Oil and Gas. *Energy J.*, January 1984, 5(1), pp. 159–64. [G: U.S.]

Ray, George F. European Energy Alternatives and Future Developments. *Natural Res. J.*, April 1984, 24(2), pp. 325–49. [G: Europe]

Razavi, Hossein. An Economic Model of OPEC Coalition. *Southern Econ. J.*, October 1984, 51(2), pp. 419–28. [G: OPEC]

Redclift, M. R. 'Urban Bias' and Rural Poverty: A Latin American Perspective. *J. Devel. Stud.*, April 1984, 20(3), pp. 123–38. [G: Mexico; Brazil]

Reza, Ali M. The Price of Oil and Conflict in OPEC. *Energy J.*, April 1984, 5(2), pp. 29–33. [G: OPEC]

Rhys, J. M. W. The Implications of Nuclear Energy for Electricity Tariffs. In *Brookes, L. G. and Motamen, H.*, eds., 1984, pp. 316–31.

Riaz, T. Pakistan: Energy Consumption and Eco-

nomic Growth. *Pakistan Devel. Rev.*, Summer-Autumn 1984, 23(2&3), pp. 431–53. [G: Pakistan]

Rizzo, Socrates C. Generation and Allocation of Oil Economic Surpluses. In *Aspe, P. and Sigmund, P. E.*, eds., 1984, pp. 99–127. [G: Mexico]

Robinson, Colin. The Changing Energy Market: What Can We Learn from the Last Ten Years? In *Hawdon, D.*, ed., 1984, pp. 7–36. [G: Global]

Rogers, J. S. Planning Models are for Insight Not Numbers: A Complementary Modelling Approach. In *Lev, B., et al.*, eds., 1984, pp. 67–81. [G: Canada]

Rosner, Peter, et al. Lohnbestimmung, aussenwirtschaftliche Stabilität und internationale Stagnation. (Wage Determination, External Economic Stability and International Stagnation. With English summary.) *Jahr. Nationalökon. Statist.*, May 1984, 199(3), pp. 193–212. [G: Global]

Ross, Gary N. U.S. Oil and Gas Imports. In *Ayoub, A.*, ed., 1984, pp. 249–61. [G: U.S.]

Ross, Marc. Industrial Energy Conservation. *Natural Res. J.*, April 1984, 24(2), pp. 369–404. [G: U.S.]

Rovard, Rafael Alfonzo. Energy Planning in Venezuela. In *Baum, V., et al.*, 1984, pp. 16–21. [G: Venezuela]

Runge, Carlisle Ford. Energy Exploration on Wilderness: "Privatization" and Public Lands Management. *Land Econ.*, February 1984, 60(1), pp. 56–68. [G: U.S.]

Rycroft, Robert W. and Regens, James L. International Cooperation in Energy Policy: The United States and the Third World. *J. Energy Devel.*, Spring 1984, 9(2), pp. 203–22. [G: U.S.; LDCs]

Sabato, Jorge A. Technological Development in Latin America and the Caribbean. In *Ghosh, P. K.*, ed., no. 3, 1984, 1980, pp. 352–70. [G: Latin America; Caribbean]

Saebö, Hans Viggo. Modelling Energy Demand: Considerations of Price Impacts and Statistics. *Statist. J.*, August 1984, 2(3), pp. 285–305. [G: Global]

Saeed, Fawzi S. Recovery of Waste Energy in Iraqi Industry. In *Baum, V., et al.*, 1984, pp. 241–46.

Sakisaka, Masao. Japan's Energy Supply/Demand Structure and Its Trade Relationship with the United States and the Middle East. *J. Energy Devel.*, Autumn 1984, 10(1), pp. 1–11. [G: Japan]

Salant, Stephen W. The Design of a Self-enforcing Multilateral Agreement among Oil-importing Countries. *Contemp. Policy Issue*, March 1984, (5), pp. 58–75. [G: U.S.]

Sambamurti, M. K. The Energy Scene in India. In *Baum, V., et al.*, 1984, pp. 219–29. [G: India]

Samouilidis, J.-E. and Mitropoulos, C. S. Energy and Economic Growth in Industrializing Countries: The Case of Greece. *Energy Econ.*, July 1984, 6(3), pp. 191–201. [G: Greece]

Samuelson, Douglas A. Identifying Changes in Patterns of Production to Support Petroleum Price Control Litigation. In *Lev, B., et al., eds.*, 1984, pp. 47–49.

Sankar, T. L. A Soft Energy Scenario for India. In *Ghosh, P. K., ed., no. 4, 1984, 1981*, pp. 192–98. [G: India]

Sankar, T. L. Institutional Aspects of Energy Planning and Plan Implementation. In *Baum, V., et al.*, 1984, pp. 125–33. [G: LDCs]

Santerre, Michael T. Financial and Resource Analyses of Anaerobic Digestion (Biogas) Systems. In *Islam, M. N.; Morse, R. and Soesastro, M. H., eds.*, 1984, pp. 415–71.
[G: China; India; Asian LDCs]

Saros, Georg. A Model for Planning Energy Requirements for Residential Heating. *Energy Econ.*, July 1984, *6*(3), pp. 202–07.
[G: Sweden]

Saulter, Kenneth J. Home Energy Costs and the Housing of the Poor and the Elderly: Comment. In *Downs, A. and Bradbury, K. L., eds.*, 1984, pp. 78–84. [G: U.S.]

Saunders, Harry D. A Note on Rowen and Weyant, "Reducing the Economic Impacts of Oil Supply Interruptions: An International Perspective." *Energy J.*, October 1984, *5*(4), pp. 55–59.

Saunders, Harry D. Reducing the Economic Impacts of Oil Supply Interruptions: An International Perspective: Rejoinder. *Energy J.*, October 1984, *5*(4), pp. 62–64.

Saunders, Harry D. The Macrodynamics of Energy Shocks, Short- and Long-Run. *Energy Econ.*, January 1984, *6*(1), pp. 21–34.
[G: OECD]

Sav, G. Thomas. Micro Engineering Foundations of Energy–Capital Complementarity: Solar Domestic Water Heaters. *Rev. Econ. Statist.*, May 1984, *66*(2), pp. 334–38. [G: U.S.]

Sav, G. Thomas. The Engineering Approach to Economic Production Functions Revisited: An Application to Solar Processes. *J. Ind. Econ.*, September 1984, *33*(1), pp. 21–35. [G: U.S.]

Scarfe, Brian L. The New Oil Price Scenario and the Chrétien–Zaozirny Agreement: A Comment [Symposium on the New Oil Price Scenario]. *Can. Public Policy*, September 1984, *10*(3), pp. 340–46. [G: Canada]

Schlesinger, James R. Hard-Earned Lessons about U.S.–Canadian Energy Relations. In *Fried, E. R. and Trezise, P. H., eds.*, 1984, pp. 107–13. [G: U.S.; Canada]

Schmenner, Roger W. Energy and the Location of Industry. In *Downs, A. and Bradbury, K. L., eds.*, 1984, pp. 188–219. [G: U.S.]

Schmidt, Ronald H. The Effect of Price Expectations on Drilling Activity. *Fed. Res. Bank Dallas Econ. Rev.*, November 1984, pp. 1–12.
[G: U.S.]

Schmitt, Dieter and Junk, H. The Comparative Costs of Nuclear and Coal-Fired Power Stations in West Germany. In *Brookes, L. G. and Motamen, H., eds.*, 1984, pp. 288–302.
[G: W. Germany]

Schramm, Gunter. The Changing World of Natu-ral Gas Utilization. *Natural Res. J.*, April 1984, *24*(2), pp. 405–36. [G: Global]

Schramm, Gunter and Munasinghe, Mohan. Symposium on Structural Changes in Energy Demand and Supply: Introduction and Overview. *Natural Res. J.*, April 1984, *24*(2), pp. 267–75.

Schurr, S. H. Energy, Economic Growth, and Human Welfare. In *Brookes, L. G. and Motamen, H., eds.*, 1984, *1978*, pp. 362–70.
[G: U.S.]

Schwartz, Eli. "Excess Capacity" in Utility Industries: An Inventory Theoretic Approach. *Land Econ.*, February 1984, *60*(1), pp. 40–48.
[G: U.S.]

Schwarz, Peter M. The Estimated Effects on Industry of Time-of-Day Demand and Energy Electricity Prices. *J. Ind. Econ.*, June 1984, *32*(4), pp. 523–39. [G: U.S.]

Scobey, Richard. Malawi. In *O'Keefe, P. and Munslow, B., eds., Part I*, 1984, pp. 171–86.
[G: Malawi]

Secrest, T. J. Economic and Energy End-Use Assessment. In *Lev, B., et al., eds.*, 1984, pp. 185–200. [G: U.S.]

Sheehan, Robert J. New Residential Construction and Energy Costs: Comment. In *Downs, A. and Bradbury, K. L., eds.*, 1984, pp. 184–87.
[G: U.S.]

Sheffrin, Steven M. and Russell, Thomas. Sterling and Oil Discoveries: The Mystery of Nonappreciation. *J. Int. Money Finance*, December 1984, *3*(3), pp. 311–26. [G: U.K.]

Shore, Haim. Summer Time and Electricity Conservation: The Israeli Case. *Energy J.*, April 1984, *5*(2), pp. 53–70. [G: Israel]

Simon, Richard M. and Conn, W. David. Federal Assistance to Energy-producing Regions: An Evaluation of the 601 Program. *J. Energy Devel.*, Spring 1984, *9*(2), pp. 243–61.
[G: U.S.]

Simon, Yves. Les marchés à terme de produits pétroliers. (Futures Markets of Oil Products. With English summary.) *L'Actual. Econ.*, September 1984, *60*(3), pp. 375–406. [G: U.S.; U.K.]

Singer, S. Fred. World Demand for Oil. In *Simon, J. L. and Kahn, H., eds.*, 1984, pp. 339–60. [G: Global]

Smith, James L. Further Results on Equilibrium Patterns of Competition in OCS Lease Sales. *Econ. Inquiry*, January 1984, *22*(1), pp. 142–46. [G: U.S.]

Smith, James L. and Paddock, James L. Regional Modelling of Oil Discovery and Production. *Energy Econ.*, January 1984, *6*(1), pp. 5–13.
[G: Selected Countries]

Smith, Stanton R. Energy Supply Management. In *Baum, V., et al.*, 1984, pp. 36–52.
[G: LDCs]

Soesastro, M. Hadi. Policy Analysis of Rural Household Energy Needs in West Java. In *Islam, M. N.; Morse, R. and Soesastro, M. H., eds.*, 1984, pp. 89–134. [G: Indonesia]

Spencer, Peter D. The Effect of Oil Discoveries on the British Economy—Theoretical Ambiguities and the Consistent Expectations Simulation Approach. *Econ. J.*, September 1984, *94*(375), pp. 633–44. [G: U.K.]

Starr, C. and Yu, O. The Role of Centralized Energy In National Energy Systems. In *Brookes, L. G. and Motamen, H., eds.*, 1984, pp. 30–45. [G: Selected Countries]

Stern, Nicholas H. Pakistan: Energy Consumption and Economic Growth: Comment. *Pakistan Devel. Rev.*, Summer-Autumn 1984, *23*(2&3), pp. 455–56. [G: Pakistan]

Sternlight, David. OPEC and International Financial Markets: Redistribution and Recycling. In *Agmon, T.; Hawkins, R. G. and Levich, R. M., eds.*, 1984, pp. 231–45. [G: OPEC]

Stocks, K. J. Discount Rate for Technology Assessment: An Application to the Energy Sector. *Energy Econ.*, July 1984, *6*(3), pp. 177–85. [G: Australia]

Stoffaës, Christian. French Industrial Strategy in Sunrise Sectors. In *Jacquemin, A., ed.*, 1984, pp. 274–92. [G: France]

Stonehouse, D. Peter, et al. Economics of an Integrated Manurial Biogas and Protein Recovery System for Beef Cattle. *Can. J. Agr. Econ.*, November 1984, *32*(3), pp. 478–97. [G: Canada]

Strom, David. Opportunities for Cogeneration in Commercial Buildings. In *Lev, B., et al., eds.*, 1984, pp. 201–12. [G: U.S.]

Strong, Maurice F. Energy Planning in Developing Countries: Keynote Address. In *Baum, V., et al.*, 1984, pp. 6–9. [G: LDCs]

Struyk, Raymond J. Home Energy Costs and the Housing of the Poor and the Elderly. In *Downs, A. and Bradbury, K. L., eds.*, 1984, pp. 35–78. [G: U.S.]

Suárez, Carlos E. Energy Planning Methodology and Manpower Requirements. In *Baum, V., et al.*, 1984, pp. 63–73. [G: LDCs]

Susman, Paul. Zambia. In *O'Keefe, P. and Munslow, B., eds., Part II*, 1984, pp. 133–70. [G: Zambia]

Svensson, Lars E. O. Oil Prices, Welfare, and the Trade Balance. *Quart. J. Econ.*, November 1984, *99*(4), pp. 649–72.

Sweeney, James L. The Response of Energy Demand to Higher Prices: What Have We Learned? *Amer. Econ. Rev.*, May 1984, *74*(2), pp. 31–37. [G: U.S.]

Takeyama, Masayuki. Japan's Foreign Negotiations Over Offshore Petroleum Development. In *Friedheim, R. L., et al.*, 1984, pp. 276–313. [G: Japan]

TerKonda, Purush K. Energy Conservation and Modeling of Indoor Pollution. In *Avula, X. J. R., et al.*, 1984, pp. 981–84.

Thiriet, L. Nuclear Energy as an Instrument of Economic Policy. In *Brookes, L. G. and Motamen, H., eds.*, 1984, pp. 371–80. [G: France]

Thompson, Michael. Among the Energy Tribes: A Cultural Framework for the Analysis and Design of Energy Policy. *Policy Sci.*, November 1984, *17*(3), pp. 321–39.

Titterton, E. [Sir]. Uranium and the Energy Future. In *Lloyd, P. J., ed.*, 1984, *1980*, pp. 126–30. [G: Australia]

Tobin, Roger L. A Network Programming System for Studying Coal Transportation. In *Lev, B., et al., eds.*, 1984, pp. 21–32. [G: U.S.]

Treat, John. The Effects of Economic Growth on the Oil and Energy Demand. In *Ayoub, A., ed.*, 1984, pp. 111–22. [G: U.S.]

Turnovsky, Michelle H. L. and Donnelly, William A. Energy Substitution, Separability, and Technical Progress in the Australian Iron and Steel Industry. *J. Bus. Econ. Statist.*, January 1984, *2*(1), pp. 54–63. [G: Australia]

Ulph, A. and Folie, M. An Economic Analysis of Oil Self-sufficiency in Australia. In *Lloyd, P. J., ed.*, 1984, *1981*, pp. 76–97. [G: Australia]

Uri, Noel D. The Pricing and Allocation of Electrical Energy. *Energy Econ.*, April 1984, *6*(2), pp. 94–101. [G: U.S.]

Uslaner, E. M. Energy Policy and the Logic of Collective Inaction. In *Holler, M. J., ed.*, 1984, pp. 320–37. [G: Canada; U.S.]

Ussher, Miguel Santiago. The Current Situation and Future Prospects for Argentina's Energy Resources. In *Baum, V., et al.*, 1984, pp. 159–73. [G: Argentina]

del Valle, Alfredo. Regional Aspects of Energy Planning and Development. In *Baum, V., et al.*, 1984, pp. 84–93. [G: Latin America]

Van Den Beldt, Rick J. Supplying Firewood for Household Energy. In *Islam, M. N.; Morse, R. and Soesastro, M. H., eds.*, 1984, pp. 381–414. [G: Asian LDCs]

Vargas, Adolfo. National Energy Balances. In *Baum, V., et al.*, 1984, pp. 74–83.

Vashist, D. C. Substitution Possibilities and Price Sensitivity of Energy Demand in Indian Manufacturing. *Indian Econ. J.*, Oct.–Dec. 1984, *32*(2), pp. 84–97. [G: India]

Vidyarthi, Varun. Energy and the Poor in an Indian Village. *World Devel.*, August 1984, *12*(8), pp. 821–36. [G: India]

Viñals, Jose M. Energy–Capital Substitutions, Wage Flexibility and Aggregate Output Supply. *Europ. Econ. Rev.*, October–November 1984, *26*(1–2), pp. 229–45. [G: U.S.; Europe]

Visintini, Alfredo Aldo. Un ensayo sobre la determinación del precio de los combustibles. (An Essay on the Determination of Fuel Prices. With English summary.) *Económica*, May-December 1984, *30*(2–3), pp. 245–84. [G: Argentina]

Ward, James. Geothermal Electricity in California. In *Baumgartner, T. and Burns, T. R., eds.*, 1984, pp. 167–86. [G: U.S.]

Ward, James. Solar Water Heating in California: Policy Evolution and Industry Development. In *Baumgartner, T. and Burns, T. R., eds.*, 1984, pp. 53–90. [G: U.S.]

Waverman, Leonard. Energy Conservation Policies: Value or Waste. In *Ayoub, A., ed.*, 1984, pp. 223–39. [G: OECD; Selected Countries]

Webb, Michael G. and Pinto, N. M. Power System Economics: The Value of Natural Gas in

Electricity Generation. *Energy Econ.*, October 1984, *6*(4), pp. 245–54.

West, Robert L. Energy and Agricultural Development in the Third World. In *[Reynolds, L. G.]*, 1984, pp. 445–77. **[G: LDCs]**

Westoby, Richard. Models of Interfuel Substitution in the UK. *J. Econ. Stud.*, 1984, *11*(1), pp. 27–39. **[G: U.K.]**

Westoby, Richard and Pearce, David W. Energy Consumption in Eastern Europe: A Cross-Sectional Analysis. *Energy Econ.*, January 1984, *6*(1), pp. 2–4. **[G: E. Europe]**

Westoby, Richard and Pearce, David W. Single Equation Models for the Projection of Energy Demand in the United Kingdom, 1954–80. *Scot. J. Polit. Econ.*, November 1984, *31*(3), pp. 229–54. **[G: U.K.]**

Weyant, John P. Reducing the Economic Impacts of Oil Supply Interruptions: An International Perspective: Reply. *Energy J.*, October 1984, *5*(4), pp. 59–62.

Weyant, John P. The Continuing Threat of Oil Supply Interruptions. *J. Policy Anal. Manage.*, Spring 1984, *3*(3), pp. 393–405.

van Wijnbergen, Sweder. Inflation, Employment, and the Dutch Disease in Oil-Exporting Countries: A Short-Run Disequilibrium Analysis. *Quart. J. Econ.*, May 1984, *99*(2), pp. 233–50.

van Wijnbergen, Sweder. The 'Dutch Disease': A Disease after All? *Econ. J.*, March 1984, *94*(373), pp. 41–55.

Willars, Jaime Mario. Principal Characteristics of Mexico's Energy Programme. In *Baum, V., et al.*, 1984, pp. 247–56. **[G: Mexico]**

Wilmots-Vandendaele, André. Les perspectives économiques des pays en voie de développement non exportateurs de pétrole. L'amélioration des perspectives dans le domaine de l'énergie. (With English summary.) *Revue Écon. Polit.*, September–October 1984, *94*(5), pp. 602–14. **[G: LDCs]**

Winett, Richard A. and Kagel, John H. Effects of Information Presentation Format on Resource Use in Field Studies. *J. Cons. Res.*, September 1984, *11*(2), pp. 655–67.

Wisner, Ben. Botswana. In *O'Keefe, P. and Munslow, B., eds., Part I*, 1984, pp. 65–133. **[G: Botswana]**

Wu, King. Energy Sources in China—Present and Future. In *Baum, V., et al.*, 1984, pp. 174–84. **[G: China]**

Wynne, Brian. The Institutional Context of Science, Models, and Policy: The IIASA Energy Study. *Policy Sci.*, November 1984, *17*(3), pp. 277–320.

Yamaguchi, S. and Kuczek, E. The Social and Economic Impact of Large-Scale Energy Projects on the Local Community. *Int. Lab. Rev.*, March-April 1984, *123*(2), pp. 149–65. **[G: U.S.]**

Yang, Bong-Min and Hu, Teh-wei. Gasoline Demand and Supply under a Disequilibrium Market. *Energy Econ.*, October 1984, *6*(4), pp. 276–82. **[G: U.S.]**

Yano, Yuko. Energy and Economic Development

in Japan. In *Baum, V., et al.*, 1984, pp. 134–45. **[G: Japan]**

Yohe, Gary W. Interpreting the International Energy Workshop Survey Results—Uncertainty and the Need for Consistent Modeling [International Energy Workshop: A Summary of 1983 Poll Responses]. *Energy J.*, October 1984, *5*(4), pp. 73–77.

Yu, Eden S.-H. and Hwang, Been Kwei. The Relationship between Energy and GNP: Further Results. *Energy Econ.*, July 1984, *6*(3), pp. 186–90. **[G: U.S.]**

Zingel, Wolfgang-Peter. Renewable Sources of Energy in Pakistan: Comment. *Pakistan Devel. Rev.*, Summer-Autumn 1984, *23*(2&3), pp. 473–75. **[G: Pakistan]**

730 ECONOMIC GEOGRAPHY

731 Economic Geography

7310 Economic Geography

Auty, R. M. The Product Life-Cycle and the Location of the Global Petrochemical Industry after the Second Oil Shock. *Econ. Geogr.*, October 1984, *60*(4), pp. 325–38. **[G: OECD]**

Bahrenberg, G. Spatial Analysis: A Retrospective View. In *Bahrenberg, G.; Fischer, M. M., and Nijkamp, P.*, 1984, pp. 35–49.

Brouwer, Floor and Nijkamp, Peter. Linear Logit Models for Categorical Data in Spatial Mobility Analysis. *Econ. Geogr.*, April 1984, *60*(2), pp. 102–10. **[G: Netherlands]**

Church, Richard L. The Planar Maximal Covering Location Problem. *J. Reg. Sci.*, May 1984, *24*(2), pp. 185–201.

Cornia, Giovanni Andrea. The Impact of World Recession on Children: A Survey of Cross-Sectional and Time-Series Literature on Factors Affecting Child Welfare. *World Devel.*, March 1984, *12*(3), pp. 187–202. **[G: Global]**

Crouchley, Robert. Some Corrections to Coelho and Wilson, 1976: The Optimum Location and Size of Shopping Centres. *Reg. Stud.*, October 1984, *18*(5), pp. 393–96. **[G: U.S.]**

Dendrinos, Dimitrios S. Regions, Antiregions, and Their Dynamic Stability: The U.S. Case (1929–1979). *J. Reg. Sci.*, February 1984, *24*(1), pp. 65–83. **[G: U.S.]**

Ettlinger, Nancy. A Note on Rank-Size and Primacy: In Pursuit of a Parsimonious Explanation. *Urban Stud.*, May 1984, *21*(2), pp. 195–97.

Georgescu Pipera, Constantino and Georgescu Pipera, Paul. Fluvial Interconnection: A Basic Element of Latin American Integration. In *Núñez del Arco, J.; Margain, E. and Cherol, R., eds.*, 1984, pp. 161–79. **[G: Latin America]**

Green, Milford B. and Cromley, Robert G. Merger and Acquisition Fields for Large United States Cities, 1955–1970. *Reg. Stud.*, August 1984, *18*(4), pp. 291–301. **[G: U.S.]**

Griffith, D. A. Measuring the Arrangement of Property of a System of Areal Units Generated by Partitioning a Planar Surface. In *Bahren-*

berg, G.; Fischer, M. M., and Nijkamp, P., 1984, pp. 191–99.

Hanjoul, Pierre and Thisse, Jacques-François. The Location of a Firm on a Network. In *Hughes Hallet, A.J., ed.*, 1984, pp. 289–326.

Hauer, J. Towards Multilevel Analysis: General and Theoretical Considerations. In *Bahrenberg, G.; Fischer, M. M., and Nijkamp, P.*, 1984, pp. 117–30.

Johnston, R. J. Quantitative Ecological Analysis in Human Geography: An Evaluation of Four Problem Areas. In *Bahrenberg, G.; Fischer, M. M., and Nijkamp, P.*, 1984, pp. 131–41.

Katzman, Martin T. The Land and People of Northeast Brazil: Is Geography a Useful Guide to Development Policy? Review Article. *Econ. Develop. Cult. Change*, April 1984, *32*(3), pp. 633–38.   **[G: Brazil]**

Kemper, Franz-Josef. Categorical Regression Models for Large Samples. In *Bahrenberg, G.; Fischer, M. M., and Nijkamp, P.*, 1984, pp. 303–16.   **[G: W. Germany]**

Lieber, Stanley R. and Fesenmaier, Daniel R. Modelling Recreation Choice: A Case Study of Management Alternatives in Chicago. *Reg. Stud.*, February 1984, *18*(1), pp. 31–43.
[G: U.S.]

Mai, Chao-cheng. Location and the Theory of the Imperfectly Competitive Firm under Demand Uncertainty. *Southern Econ. J.*, April 1984, *50*(4), pp. 1160–70.

Mai, Chao-cheng and Shieh, Yeung-Nan. Transport Rates Structure, Optimum Location, and Theory of Production: Reexamination. *J. Urban Econ.*, September 1984, *16*(2), pp. 225–31.

Nijkamp, Peter and Voogd, Henk. Multidimensional and Homogeneous Scaling in Spatial Analysis. In *Bahrenberg, G.; Fischer, M. M., and Nijkamp, P.*, 1984, pp. 201–14.

O'Brien, L. G. and Wrigley, N. A Generalised Linear Models Approach to Categorical Data Analysis: Theory and Applications in Geography and Regional Science. In *Bahrenberg, G.; Fischer, M. M., and Nijkamp, P.*, 1984, pp. 231–51.

Ochitwa, Jerome M. Applicability and Efficiency in a Land Use Plan Design Model: An Input–Output Linear Programming Approach. *Urban Stud.*, May 1984, *21*(2), pp. 149–54.

Ominde, S. H. Introduction: A Bird's Eye View of the Republic in the Modern World. In *Ominde, S. H., ed.*, 1984, pp. 1–5.
[G: Kenya]

Ominde, S. H. The Former Scheduled Areas. In *Ominde, S. H., ed.*, 1984, pp. 18–22.
[G: Kenya]

Ominde, S. H. The Pattern of Land Classification. In *Ominde, S. H., ed.*, 1984, pp. 6–17.
[G: Kenya]

Pitts, Eamonn. Effects of Rainfall on Milk Yields in Areas with Drainage Difficulties. *Irish J. Agr. Econ. Rural Soc.*, 1984, *10*(1), pp. 29–42.   **[G: U.K.]**

Plane, David A. A Systemic Demographic Efficiency Analysis of U.S. Interstate Population

Exchange, 1935–1980. *Econ. Geogr.*, October 1984, *60*(4), pp. 294–312.   **[G: U.S.]**

ten Raa, Thijs. The Distribution Approach to Spatial Economics. *J. Reg. Sci.*, February 1984, *24*(1), pp. 105–17.

Riefler, Roger F. and Lamphear, F. Charles. Climate and Manufacturing Location. *Reg. Sci. Persp.*, 1984, *14*(2), pp. 46–59.   **[G: U.S.]**

Rushton, Gerard. Use of Location-Allocation Models for Improving the Geographical Accessibility of Rural Services in Developing Countries. *Int. Reg. Sci. Rev.*, December 1984, *9*(3), pp. 217–40.   **[G: LDCs]**

Scott, A. J. Industrial Organization and the Logic of Intra-Metropolitan Location, III: A Case Study of the Women's Dress Industry in the Greater Los Angeles Region. *Econ. Geogr.*, January 1984, *60*(1), pp. 3–27.   **[G: U.S.]**

Şerban, R. and Albu, C. Model and Algorithms for the Optimal Management of a Thermoelectric Power Station. *Econ. Computat. Cybern. Stud. Res.*, 1984, *19*(2), pp. 69–76.

Strickland, Donald and Aiken, Michael. Corporate Influence and the German Urban System: Headquarters Location of German Industrial Corporations, 1950–1982. *Econ. Geogr.*, January 1984, *60*(1), pp. 38–54.   **[G: Germany]**

Timmermans, H. J. P. Decision Models for Predicting Preferences among Multiattribute Choice Alternatives. In *Bahrenberg, G.; Fischer, M. M., and Nijkamp, P.*, 1984, pp. 337–54.

Von Hohenbalken, Balder and West, Douglas S. Manhattan versus Euclid: Market Areas Computed and Compared. *Reg. Sci. Urban Econ.*, February 1984, *14*(1), pp. 19–35.
[G: Canada]

Wendell, Richard E. and Peterson, Elmor L. A Dual Approach for Obtaining Lower Bounds to the Weber Problem. *J. Reg. Sci.*, May 1984, *24*(2), pp. 219–28.

Wolpert, Julian and Reiner, Thomas A. Service Provision by the Not-for-Profit Sector: A Comparative Study. *Econ. Geogr.*, January 1984, *60*(1), pp. 28–37.   **[G: U.S.]**

800 Manpower; Labor; Population

8000 General

Bennett, John. Bibliography, 1982. *Brit. J. Ind. Relat.*, July 1984, *22*(2), pp. 218–64.

Emmerij, Louis. Basic Needs and Employment-oriented Strategies Reconsidered. In *Amin, S., ed.*, 1984, pp. 147–69.

810 MANPOWER TRAINING AND DEVELOPMENT; LABOR FORCE AND SUPPLY

8100 General

Szentes, Tamas. The Structural Defects of Periphery Economies. In *Amin, S., ed.*, 1984, pp. 33–51.

811 Manpower Training and Development

8110 Manpower Training and Development

Adnett, N. J. On-the-Job Search and the Public Employment Service. *J. Econ. Stud.*, 1984, *11*(3), pp. 51–61. **[G: U.K.]**

Bassi, Laurie J. Estimating the Effect of Training Programs with Non-Random Selection. *Rev. Econ. Statist.*, February 1984, *66*(1), pp. 36–43. **[G: U.S.]**

Baxter, J. L. and McCormick, Brian J. Seventy Per Cent of Our Future: The Education, Training and Employment of Young People. *Nat. Westminster Bank Quart. Rev.*, August 1984, pp. 36–44.

Blakemore, Arthur E. Human Capital Investment and the Reduction in the Unemployment Rate Consistent with Nonaccelerating Inflation. *Quart. J. Bus. Econ.*, Spring 1984, *23*(2), pp. 3–14. **[G: U.S.]**

Bloom, Howard S. Estimating the Effect of Job-training Programs, Using Longitudinal Data: Ashenfelter's Findings Reconsidered. *J. Human Res.*, Fall 1984, *19*(4), pp. 544–56. **[G: U.S.]**

Chambers, David I. Adult Education in Urban-Industrial China: Problems, Policies, and Prospects. In *Hayhoe, R., ed.*, 1984, pp. 178–204. **[G: China]**

Chizhova, L. Balancing Labor Resources with Economic Demands. *Prob. Econ.*, May 1984, *27*(1), pp. 63–78. **[G: U.S.S.R.]**

Dore, Ronald P. and Oxenham, John. Educational Reform and Selection for Employment—An Overview. In *Oxenham, J., ed.*, 1984, pp. 3–40.

Eck, Alan. New Occupational Separation Data Improve Estimates of Job Replacement Needs. *Mon. Lab. Rev.*, March 1984, *107*(3), pp. 3–10. **[G: U.S.]**

Gaude, J.; Phan-Thuy, N. and Van Kempen, C. Evaluation of Special Public Works Programmes: Some Policy Conclusions. *Int. Lab. Rev.*, March-April 1984, *123*(2), pp. 203–19. **[G: Selected Countries]**

Ginzberg, Eli. Expanding the Knowledge Base for Informed Public Policy: The U.S. Department of Labor's Research Program 1963–1978. In *Robson, R. T., ed.*, 1984, pp. 1–41. **[G: U.S.]**

Henze, Jürgen. Higher Education: The Tension between Quality and Equality. In *Hayhoe, R., ed.*, 1984, pp. 93–153. **[G: China]**

Jeffries, John M. and Stanback, Howard. Employment and Training Policy for Black America: Beyond Placebo to Progressive Public Policy. *Rev. Black Polit. Econ.*, Summer–Fall 1984, *13*(1–2), pp. 119–37.

Johnson, George E. Employment and Training Programs in the United States: What Do We Know, and Where Should We Go From Here? In *Ullrich, R. A., ed.*, 1984, pp. 25–39. **[G: U.S.]**

Johnson, Peter S. and Thomas, R. Barry. Government Policies towards Business Formation:

An Economic Appraisal of a Training Scheme. *Scot. J. Polit. Econ.*, June 1984, *31*(2), pp. 131–46. **[G: U.K.]**

Kotliar, A. Full Employment and Proportionality of Factors in Socialist Production. *Prob. Econ.*, June 1984, *27*(2), pp. 38–56. **[G: U.S.S.R.]**

Kuenstler, Peter. Local Employment Initiatives in Western Europe. *Int. Lab. Rev.*, March-April 1984, *123*(2), pp. 221–33. **[G: W. Europe]**

Kutas, János. Innovation, Social Environment, Human Factors. *Acta Oecon.*, 1984, *32*(1–2), pp. 125–36. **[G: Hungary]**

Lee, Gloria and Wrench, John. Routes into Segmented Youth Labour Markets. *Int. J. Soc. Econ.*, 1984, *11*(7), pp. 77–90. **[G: U.K.]**

Löbl, Karel. Condition for Initiative. *Czech. Econ. Digest.*, June 1984, (4), pp. 34–47. **[G: Czechoslovakia]**

MacLennan, Emma and Weitzel, Renate. Labour Market Policy in Four Countries: Are Women Adequately Represented? In *Schmid, G. and Weitzel, R., eds.*, 1984, pp. 202–48. **[G: Sweden; U.K.; U.S.; W. Germany]**

Malmygin, I. The Balance of Workplaces and Manpower. *Prob. Econ.*, July 1984, *27*(3), pp. 80–93. **[G: U.S.S.R.]**

Malveaux, Julianne. Employment and Training Policy for Black America: Beyond Placebo to Progressive Public Policy: Comments. *Rev. Black Polit. Econ.*, Summer–Fall 1984, *13*(1–2), pp. 138–44. **[G: U.S.]**

Mangum, Stephen L. Response to Schiller on Small Business Training [Small Business Training: A Negative-Sum Game]. *Challenge*, January/February 1984, *26*(6), pp. 64. **[G: U.S.]**

Marshall, Ray. Selective Employment Programs and Economic Policy. *J. Econ. Issues*, March 1984, *18*(1), pp. 117–42. **[G: U.S.]**

Mathur, Gautam. Employment and Manpower Generation. In *Amin, S., ed.*, 1984, pp. 67–93.

Merrilees, W. J. Do Wage Subsidies Stimulate Training? An Evaluation of the Craft Rebate Scheme. *Australian Econ. Pap.*, December 1984, *23*(43), pp. 235–48. **[G: Australia]**

Perkins, Frances. Manpower Forecasting and Resource Development—Examples from the Hunter Region of NSW. *Australian Bull. Lab.*, March 1984, *10*(2), pp. 77–104. **[G: Australia]**

Psacharopoulos, George. Assessing Training Priorities in Developing Countries: Current Practice and Possible Alternatives. *Int. Lab. Rev.*, September–October 1984, *123*(5), pp. 569–83. **[G: LDCs]**

Richter, Lothar. Manpower Planning in Developing Countries: Changing Approaches and Emphases. *Int. Lab. Rev.*, November–December 1984, *123*(6), pp. 677–92. **[G: LDCs]**

Rochin, Refugio I. Farm Worker Service and Employment Programs. In *Emerson, R. D., ed.*, 1984, pp. 412–46. **[G: U.S.]**

Rosen, Howard. Employment and Training R&D: An Administrator's Reflections. In *Robson, R. T., ed.*, 1984, pp. 73–104. **[G: U.S.]**

Rumberger, Russell W. The Incidence and Wage Effects of Occupational Training among Young Men. *Soc. Sci. Quart.*, September 1984, *65*(3), pp. 775–88.   [G: U.S.]

Ryan, Paul. Job Training, Employment Practices, and the Large Enterprise: The Case of Costly Transferable Skills. In *Osterman, P., ed.*, 1984, pp. 191–229.   [G: U.S.]

Ryan, Paul. The New Training Initiative after Two Years. *Lloyds Bank Rev.*, April 1984, (152), pp. 31–45.   [G: U.K.]

Saks, Daniel H. A Research Agenda for Employment and Training Policy in the Eighties. In *Robson, R. T., ed.*, 1984, pp. 43–71.
                     [G: U.S.]

Senker, Peter. Training for Automation. In *Warner, M., ed.*, 1984, pp. 134–46.

Shapley, Allen E. Farm Worker Service and Employment Programs: Discussion. In *Emerson, R. D., ed.*, 1984, pp. 446–49.   [G: U.S.]

Simpson, Wayne. An Econometric Analysis of Industrial Training in Canada. *J. Human Res.*, Fall 1984, *19*(4), pp. 435–51.   [G: Canada]

Streker-Seeborg, Irmtraud; Seeborg, Michael C. and Zegeye, Abera. The Impact of Nontraditional Training on the Occupational Attainment of Women. *J. Human Res.*, Fall 1984, *19*(4), pp. 452–71.   [G: U.S.]

Sullivan, Sean. Employment versus Training in Federal Manpower Programs. In *Weicher, J. C., ed.*, 1984, pp. 154–66.   [G: U.S.]

Thakur, C. P. Computers, Manpower and the Indian Labour Market: Some Experiences in a Labour-Surplus Economy. In *Warner, M., ed.*, 1984, pp. 325–38.   [G: India]

Vandamme, François. The Revised European Social Fund and Action to Combat Unemployment in the European Community. *Int. Lab. Rev.*, March-April 1984, *123*(2), pp. 167–81.
                     [G: EEC]

Wachter, Michael L. The Training Component of Growth Policies. In *Wachter, M. L. and Wachter, S. M., eds.*, 1984, pp. 41–69.
                     [G: U.S.]

812 Occupation

8120 Occupation

Altman, Stuart H. The Growing Physician Surplus: Will It Benefit or Bankrupt the U.S. Health System? In *Ginzberg, E. and Ostow, M., eds.*, 1984, pp. 9–36.   [G: U.S.]

Amelang, James S. Barristers and Judges in Early Modern Barcelona: The Rise of a Legal Elite. *Amer. Hist. Rev.*, December 1984, *89*(5), pp. 1264–84.   [G: Spain]

Appelbaum, Eileen. High Tech and the Structural Employment Problems of the 1980s. In *Collins, E. L. and Tanner, L. D., eds.*, 1984, pp. 23–48.

Aranya, Nissim and Ferris, Kenneth R. A Reexamination of Accountants' Organizational–Professional Conflict. *Accounting Rev.*, January 1984, *59*(1), pp. 1–15.   [G: U.S.]

Arnold, Donald F. and Geiselhart, Thomas J.

Practitioners' Views on Five-Year Educational Requirements for CPAs. *Accounting Rev.*, April 1984, *59*(2), pp. 314–24.   [G: U.S.]

Baksh, Ishmael J. Factors Influencing Occupational Expectations of Secondary School Students in Trinidad and Tobago. *Soc. Econ. Stud.*, September 1984, *33*(3), pp. 1–29.
                     [G: Trinidad and Tobago]

Bardhan, Kalpana. Work Patterns and Social Differentiation: Rural Women of West Bengal. In *Binswanger, H. P. and Rosenzweig, R., eds.*, 1984, pp. 184–207.   [G: India]

Blakemore, Arthur E. and Low, Stuart A. Sex Differences in Occupational Selection: The Case of College Majors. *Rev. Econ. Statist.*, February 1984, *66*(1), pp. 157–63. [G: U.S.]

Bonnell, Sheila M.; Chew, T. C. and Dixon, Peter B. Measuring the Impact of Structural Change on Groups in the Australian Labour Market. In *Steinmann, G., ed.*, 1984, pp. 343–59.   [G: Australia]

Bourguignon, François and Morrisson, Christian. La mobilité des salaires sur le cycle de vie: un échantillon de cadres français sur trente ans. (Earning Mobility over the Life-Cycle: A Thirty-Years Panel Sample of French "Cadres." With English summary.) *Revue Écon.*, September 1984, *35*(5), pp. 929–70.

Boyes, William J.; Happel, Stephen K. and Hogan, Timothy D. Publish or Perish: Fact or Fiction? *J. Econ. Educ.*, Spring 1984, *15*(2), pp. 136–41.   [G: U.S.; Canada]

Brimmer, Andrew F. Long-Term Economic Growth and Black Employment Opportunities. *Rev. Black Polit. Econ.*, Summer–Fall 1984, *13*(1–2), pp. 61–73.   [G: U.S.]

Bubnys, Edward L. Ethnicity and Occupational Mobility: Chicago, 1870 and 1900. *Rev. Soc. Econ.*, April 1984, *42*(1), pp. 50–62.
                     [G: U.S.]

Clogg, Clifford C. and Shockey, James W. Mismatch between Occupation and Schooling: A Prevalence Measure, Recent Trends and Demographic Analysis. *Demography*, May 1984, *21*(2), pp. 235–57.   [G: U.S.]

Covey, Charles D. Occupational Structure and the Industrialization of Agriculture: Discussion. In *Emerson, R. D., ed.*, 1984, pp. 323–27.   [G: U.S.]

Coyte, Peter C. Optimal Job Assignment and Investment in Specific Human Capital: An Application to Professional Teachers. *Appl. Econ.*, October 1984, *16*(5), pp. 703–15.
                     [G: Canada]

Crockett, Geoffrey and Elias, Peter. British Managers: A Study of their Education, Training, Mobility and Earnings. *Brit. J. Ind. Relat.*, March 1984, *22*(1), pp. 34–46.   [G: U.K.]

Dauffenbach, Robert C. and Greer, Charles R. A Comparison of Job Analytic and Conventional Economic Variables as Explanations of Occupational Earnings Differentials. *J. Econ. Bus.*, February 1984, *36*(1), pp. 43–64.
                     [G: U.S.]

Davis, Karen. Physician Supply and Health Care

Costs. In *Ginzberg, E. and Ostow, M., eds.,* 1984, pp. 37–48. **[G: U.S.]**

Dederick, Robert G. A Primer on Surviving in Washington. *Bus. Econ.,* October 1984, *19*(5), pp. 5–8.

Delaney, John Thomas; Feuille, Peter and Hendricks, Wallace E. Police Salaries, Interest Arbitration, and the Leveling Effect. *Ind. Relat.,* Fall 1984, *23*(3), pp. 417–23. **[G: U.S.]**

Dixon, Peter B.; Parmenter, B. R. and Powell, Alan A. Trade Liberalization and Labor Market Disruption. *J. Policy Modeling,* November 1984, *6*(4), pp. 431–54. **[G: Australia]**

Dunn, W. Marcus and Hall, Thomas W. An Empirical Analysis of the Relationships between CPA Examination Candidate Attributes and Candidate Performance. *Accounting Rev.,* October 1984, *59*(4), pp. 674–89. **[G: U.S.]**

Eck, Alan. New Occupational Separation Data Improve Estimates of Job Replacement Needs. *Mon. Lab. Rev.,* March 1984, *107*(3), pp. 3–10. **[G: U.S.]**

Fagnani, Jeanne. Marital Status and Occupational Structures in the Ile-de-France Region. *Urban Stud.,* May 1984, *21*(2), pp. 139–48. **[G: France]**

Filer, Randall K. A Theoretical Analysis of the Economic Impact of Artists' Resale Royalties Legislation. *J. Cult. Econ.,* June 1984, *8*(1), pp. 1–28.

Fossett, Mark A. City Differences in Racial Occupational Differentiation: A Note on the Use of Odds Ratios. *Demography,* November 1984, *21*(4), pp. 655–66. **[G: U.S.]**

Fujino, Shozaburo. Why Does the Age Distribution of Economists in Japan Have Two Peaks?—Demand–Supply Adjustment in the Labor Market for Economists. (In Japanese. With English summary.) *Econ. Stud. Quart.,* April 1984, *35*(1), pp. 63–84. **[G: Japan]**

Gilson, Ronald J. Value Creation by Business Lawyers: Legal Skills and Asset Pricing. *Yale Law J.,* December 1984, *94*(2), pp. 239–313.

Ginzberg, Eli. Conference Summary: The Expanding Physician Supply: Policy Options. In *Ginzberg, E. and Ostow, M., eds.,* 1984, pp. 1–8. **[G: U.S.]**

Glazer, Nona Y. Servants to Capital: Unpaid Domestic Labor and Paid Work. *Rev. Radical Polit. Econ.,* Spring 1984, *16*(1), pp. 61–87. **[G: U.S.]**

Goldfarb, Robert S.; Havrylyshyn, Oli and Mangum, Stephen L. Can Remittances Compensate for Manpower Outflows: The Case of Philippine Physicians. *J. Devel. Econ.,* May–June–August 1984, *15*(1,2,3), pp. 1–17. **[G: Philippines]**

Goldfield, Michael. The Causes of U.S. Trade Union Decline and Their Future Prospects. In *Zarembka, P., ed.,* 1984, pp. 81–159. **[G: U.S.]**

Goldin, Claudia. The Historical Evolution of Female Earnings Functions and Occupations. *Exploration Econ. Hist.,* January 1984, *21*(1), pp. 1–27. **[G: U.S.]**

Gottfried, Heidi and Fasenfest, David. Gender

and Class Formation: Female Clerical Workers. *Rev. Radical Polit. Econ.,* Spring 1984, *16*(1), pp. 89–103. **[G: U.S.]**

Granick, David. Central Physical Planning, Incentives and Job Rights. In *Zimbalist, A., ed.,* 1984, pp. 133–57. **[G: U.S.; U.S.S.R.]**

Grossman, Jean Baldwin. The Occupational Attainment of Immigrant Women in Sweden. *Scand. J. Econ.,* 1984, *86*(3), pp. 337–51. **[G: Sweden]**

Hamilton, Earl G. Long-Term Economic Growth and Black Employment Opportunities: Comments. *Rev. Black Polit. Econ.,* Summer–Fall 1984, *13*(1–2), pp. 74–79. **[G: U.S.]**

He, Xiaopei. An Investigation into the Current Compensation System for Mental and Manual Labor. *Chinese Econ. Stud.,* Fall 1984, *18*(1), pp. 77–95. **[G: China]**

Hobsbawm, E. J. Artisan or Labour Aristocrat? *Econ. Hist. Rev., 2nd Ser.,* August 1984, *37*(3), pp. 355–72. **[G: U.K.]**

Horn, Ernst-Jürgen. Reassessing Consumer Safety Regulation: Comment. In *Giersch, H., ed.,* 1984, pp. 216–21.

Jaussaud, Danielle P. Can Job Evaluation Systems Help Determine the Comparable Worth of Male and Female Occupations? *J. Econ. Issues,* June 1984, *18*(2), pp. 473–82. **[G: U.S.]**

Jones, Richard C.; Harris, Richard J. and Valdez, Avelardo. Occupational and Spatial Mobility of Undocumented Migrants from Dolores Hidalgo, Guanajuato. In *Jones, R. C., ed.,* 1984, pp. 159–82. **[G: U.S.; Mexico]**

Jonung, Christina. Patterns of Occupational Segregation by Sex in the Labor Market. In *Schmid, G. and Weitzel, R., eds.,* 1984, pp. 44–68. **[G: Sweden]**

Kaufman, George G. The Academic Preparation of Economists Employed by Commercial and Investment Banks: A Note. *J. Money, Credit, Banking,* August 1984, *16*(3), pp. 351–59.

Kaun, David E. Faculty Advancement in a Nontraditional University Environment. *Ind. Lab. Relat. Rev.,* July 1984, *37*(4), pp. 592–606.

Koike, Kazuo. Skill Formation Systems in the U.S. and Japan: A Comparative Study. In *Aoki, M., ed.,* 1984, pp. 47–75. **[G: U.S.; Japan]**

Lane, David. Social Stratification and Class. In *Hoffmann, E. P. and Laird, R. F., eds.,* 1984, 1982, pp. 563–605. **[G: U.S.S.R.]**

Leonard, Jonathan S. Employment and Occupational Advance under Affirmative Action. *Rev. Econ. Statist.,* August 1984, *66*(3), pp. 377–85. **[G: U.S.]**

Mamer, John W. Occupational Structure and the Industrialization of Agriculture. In *Emerson, R. D., ed.,* 1984, pp. 286–323. **[G: U.S.]**

Martellaro, Joseph A. Business and Economics as Pre-law Majors. *Soc. Econ. Stud.,* December 1984, *33*(4), pp. 125–49. **[G: U.S.]**

Marvel, Mary K. Sunset: An Early Evaluation. *Public Choice,* 1984, *42*(2), pp. 193–96. **[G: U.S.]**

Maurice, Marc; Sellier, François and Silvestre, Jean-Jacques. The Search for a Societal Effect in the Production of Company Hierarchy: A

Comparison of France and Germany. In *Osterman, P., ed.*, 1984, pp. 231–70.
[G: W. Germany; France]

Mellor, Earl F. Investigating the Differences in Weekly Earnings of Women and Men. *Mon. Lab. Rev.*, June 1984, *107*(6), pp. 17–28.
[G: U.S.]

Mitchell, Janet B. Why Do Women Physicians Work Fewer Hours than Men Physicians? *Inquiry*, Winter 1984, *21*(4), pp. 361–68.
[G: U.S.]

Murnane, Richard J. Selection and Survival in the Teacher Labor Market. *Rev. Econ. Statist.*, August 1984, *66*(3), pp. 513–18. [G: U.S.]

Nevadomsky, Joseph. Economic Organization, Social Mobility and Changing Social Status among the East Indians in Rural Trinidad. *Soc. Econ. Stud.*, September 1984, *33*(3), pp. 31–62. [G: Trinidad and Tobago]

Nichol, W. The Medical Profession in New South Wales, 1788–1850. *Australian Econ. Hist. Rev.*, September 1984, *24*(2), pp. 115–31.
[G: Australia]

Nissim, Joseph. An Examination of the Differential Patterns in the Cyclical Behaviour of the Employment, Hours and Wages of Labour of Different Skills: British Mechanical Engineering, 1963–1978. *Economica*, November 1984, *51*(204), pp. 423–36. [G: U.K.]

O'Boyle, Edward J. On the University Researcher as an Entrepreneur. *Int. J. Soc. Econ.*, 1984, *11*(3/4), pp. 114–23. [G: U.S.]

Osterman, Paul. White-Collar Internal Labor Markets. In *Osterman, P., ed.*, 1984, pp. 163–89. [G: U.S.]

Paul, Chris. Physician Licensure Legislation and the Quality of Medical Care. *Atlantic Econ. J.*, December 1984, *12*(4), pp. 18–30.
[G: U.S.]

Perkins, Frances. Manpower Forecasting and Resource Development—Examples from the Hunter Region of NSW. *Australian Bull. Lab.*, March 1984, *10*(2), pp. 77–104.
[G: Australia]

Personick, Martin E. White-Collar Pay Determination under Range-of-Rate Systems. *Mon. Lab. Rev.*, December 1984, *107*(12), pp. 25–30. [G: U.S.]

Pierenkemper, Toni. Pre-1900 Industrial White Collar Employees at the Krupp Steel Casting Works: A New Occupational Category in Germany. *Bus. Hist. Rev.*, Autumn 1984, *58*(3), pp. 384–408. [G: Germany]

Prieser, Carl. Occupational Salary Levels for White-Collar Workers, 1984. *Mon. Lab. Rev.*, October 1984, *107*(10), pp. 43–45. [G: U.S.]

Reeves, Frank and Ward, Robin. West Indian Business in Britain. In *Ward, R. and Jenkins, R., eds.*, 1984, pp. 125–46. [G: U.K.]

Rickman, Bill D. Faculty Salaries at a Small University: Does Sex Matter? *Quart. J. Bus. Econ.*, Spring 1984, *23*(2), pp. 47–57. [G: U.S.]

Ryan, Paul. Job Training, Employment Practices, and the Large Enterprise: The Case of Costly Transferable Skills. In *Osterman, P., ed.*, 1984, pp. 191–229. [G: U.S.]

Rytina, Nancy F. and Bianchi, Suzanne M. Occupational Reclassification and Changes in Distribution by Gender. *Mon. Lab. Rev.*, March 1984, *107*(3), pp. 11–17. [G: U.S.]

Schlottmann, Alan M. and Herzog, Henry W., Jr. Career and Geographic Mobility Interactions: Implications for the Age Selectivity of Migration. *J. Human Res.*, Winter 1984, *19*(1), pp. 72–86. [G: U.S.]

Sehgal, Ellen. Occupational Mobility and Job Tenure in 1983. *Mon. Lab. Rev.*, October 1984, *107*(10), pp. 18–23. [G: U.S.]

Semyonov, Moshe; Hoyt, Danny R. and Scott, Richard Ira. The Place of Odds Ratios in the Study of Place, Race and Differential Occupational Opportunities. *Demography*, November 1984, *21*(4), pp. 667–71.

Shaw, Kathryn L. A Formulation of the Earnings Function Using the Concept of Occupational Investment. *J. Human Res.*, Summer 1984, *19*(3), pp. 319–40. [G: U.S.]

Shulman, Steven. The Measurement and Interpretation of Black Wage and Occupational Gains: A Reevaluation. *Rev. Black Polit. Econ.*, Spring 1984, *12*(4), pp. 59–69. [G: U.S.]

Sieling, Mark S. Staffing Patterns Prominent in Female–Male Earnings Gap. *Mon. Lab. Rev.*, June 1984, *107*(6), pp. 29–33. [G: U.S.]

Siow, Aloysius. Occupational Choice under Uncertainty. *Econometrica*, May 1984, *52*(3), pp. 631–45. [G: U.S.]

Snipp, C. Matthew and Tienda, Marta. Mexican American Occupational Mobility. *Soc. Sci. Quart.*, June 1984, *65*(2), pp. 364–80.
[G: U.S.]

Stanbury, W. T. How Wide the Ocean? The Regulated Conduct Exemption in Canada. *Antitrust Bull.*, Fall 1984, *29*(3), pp. 577–604.
[G: Canada]

Stevens, Rosemary A. Defining and Certifying the Specialists. In *Ginzberg, E. and Ostow, M., eds.*, 1984, pp. 83–98. [G: U.S.]

Stewart, Mark B. and Greenhalgh, Christine A. Work History Patterns and the Occupational Attainment of Women. *Econ. J.*, September 1984, *94*(375), pp. 493–519. [G: U.K.]

Streit, Manfred E. Reassessing Consumer Safety Regulation. In *Giersch, H., ed.*, 1984, pp. 190–215. [G: W. Germany]

Sveikauskas, Leo. Science and Technology in Many Different Industries: Data for the Analysis of International Trade. *Rev. Public Data Use*, June 1984, *12*(2), pp. 133–56. [G: U.S.]

Svejnar, Jan. The Determinants of Industrial-Sector Earnings in Senegal. *J. Devel. Econ.*, May–June–August 1984, *15*(1,2,3), pp. 289–311.
[G: Senegal]

Swords-Isherwood, N.; Zmroczek, C. and Henwood, F. Technical Change and its Effect on Employment Opportunities for Women. In *Marstrand, P., ed.*, 1984, pp. 191–213.
[G: U.K.]

Trager, Lillian. Migration and Remittances: Urban Income and Rural Households in the Philippines. *J. Devel. Areas*, April 1984, *18*(3), pp. 317–40. [G: Philippines]

Tuckman, Barbara H. and Tuckman, Howard P. The Labor Market for Part-Time Faculty at Business Schools. *Quart. Rev. Econ. Bus.,* Autumn 1984, *24*(3), pp. 95–103. [G: U.S.]

Unger, Jonathan. Severing the Links between Education and Careers: The Sobering Experience of China's Urban Schools. In *Oxenham, J., ed.,* 1984, pp. 176–91. [G: China]

Warner, John T. and Goldberg, Matthew S. The Influence of Non-Pecuniary Factors on Labor Supply: The Case of Navy Enlisted Personnel. *Rev. Econ. Statist.,* February 1984, *66*(1), pp. 26–35. [G: U.S.]

Wolfram, Charles W. The Second Set of Players: Lawyers, Fee Shifting, and the Limits of Professional Discipline. *Law Contemp. Probl.,* Winter 1984, *47*(1), pp. 293–320. [G: U.S.]

Zarca, Bernard. Travail familial et travail salarié: un modèle de formation du revenu des artisans. (Family Work and Wage Work: A Model of Artisans Income Formation. With English summary.) *Consommation,* Oct.–Dec. 1984, *31*(4), pp. 3–27. [G: France]

Zubrzycki, Jerzy. Immigration and Population Change in Australia: A Test of the Dual Labour Market Hypothesis. In *Steinmann, G., ed.,* 1984, pp. 360–85. [G: Australia]

813 Labor Force

8130 General

Abella, Manolo I. Labour Migration from South and South–East Asia: Some Policy Issues. *Int. Lab. Rev.,* July–August 1984, *123*(4), pp. 491–506. [G: Asia]

Ashenfelter, Orley C. Macroeconomic Analyses and Microeconomic Analyses of Labor Supply. *Carnegie-Rochester Conf. Ser. Public Policy,* Autumn 1984, *21*, pp. 117–55. [G: U.S.; U.K.; Canada]

Bakht, Zaid. Entrepreneurship in Bangladesh Rural Industries. *Bangladesh Devel. Stud.,* March-June 1984, *12*(1–2), pp. 25–57. [G: Bangladesh]

Bartlett, Bruce. Is Industrial Innovation Destroying Jobs? *Cato J.,* Fall 1984, *4*(2), pp. 625–43. [G: U.S.]

Becker, Eugene H. Self-Employed Workers: An Update to 1983. *Mon. Lab. Rev.,* July 1984, *107*(7), pp. 14–18. [G: U.S.]

Becker, Eugene H. and Bowers, Norman. Employment and Unemployment Improvements Widespread in 1983. *Mon. Lab. Rev.,* February 1984, *107*(2), pp. 3–14. [G: U.S.]

Berger, Mark C. and Fleisher, Belton M. Husband's Health and Wife's Labor Supply. *J. Health Econ.,* April 1984, *3*(1), pp. 63–75. [G: U.S.]

Blandy, Richard. Labour Problems of the Minerals Boom. In *Lloyd, P. J., ed.,* 1984, *1981*, pp. 170–75. [G: Australia]

Boothby, Daniel. The Continuity of Married Women's Labour Force Participation in Canada. *Can. J. Econ.,* August 1984, *17*(3), pp. 471–80. [G: Canada]

Bregger, John E. The Current Population Survey: A Historical Perspective and BLS' Role. *Mon. Lab. Rev.,* June 1984, *107*(6), pp. 8–14. [G: U.S.]

Brown, Lisa Jo. Neoclassical Economics and the Sexual Division of Labor. *Eastern Econ. J.,* October-December 1984, *10*(4), pp. 367–79.

Browne, Lynn E. Conflicting Views of Technological Progress and the Labor Market. *New Eng. Econ. Rev.,* July–August 1984, pp. 5–16. [G: U.S.]

Bryceson, Deborah Fahy and Vuorela, Ulla. Outside the Domestic Labor Debate: Towards a Theory of Modes of Human Reproduction. *Rev. Radical Polit. Econ.,* Summer & Fall 1984, *16*(2&3), pp. 137–66. [G: Global]

Burdett, Kenneth, et al. Earnings, Unemployment, and the Allocation of Time over Time. *Rev. Econ. Stud.,* October 1984, *51*(4), pp. 559–78. [G: U.S.]

Burtless, Gary and Moffitt, Robert A. The Effect of Social Security Benefits on the Labor Supply of the Aged. In *Aaron, H. J. and Burtless, G., eds.,* 1984, pp. 135–71. [G: U.S.]

Cain, Glen. Estimating the Impact of Labor Market Policies on Women: A Discussion of the Four-Country Studies on the Employment of Women. In *Schmid, G. and Weitzel, R., eds.,* 1984, pp. 249–63. [G: Sweden; U.K.; U.S.; W. Germany]

Chamberlain, Gary. Panel Data. In *Griliches, Z. and Intriligator, M. D., eds.,* 1984, pp. 1248–1318. [G: U.S.]

Chirikos, Thomas N. and Nestel, Gilbert. Economic Determinants and Consequences of Self-reported Work Disability. *J. Health Econ.,* August 1984, *3*(2), pp. 117–36. [G: U.S.]

Coates, Mary Lou. Human Resources and Labour Markets: Summary Outline. In *Wood, W. D. and Kumar, P., eds.,* 1984, pp. 41–89. [G: Canada; OECD]

Davis, Kingsley. Wives and Work: The Sex Role Revolution and Its Consequences. *Population Devel. Rev.,* September 1984, *10*(3), pp. 397–417. [G: U.S.; U.K.; Sweden]

DeBoer, Larry and Seeborg, Michael C. The Female–Male Unemployment Differential: Effects of Changes in Industry Employment. *Mon. Lab. Rev.,* November 1984, *107*(11), pp. 8–15. [G: U.S.]

Devens, Richard M., Jr. Employment in the First Half: Robust Recovery Continues. *Mon. Lab. Rev.,* August 1984, *107*(8), pp. 3–7. [G: U.S.]

Dieguez, Héctor L. and Gerchunoff, Pablo. La dinámica del mercado laboral urbano en la Argentina, 1976–1981. (With English summary.) *Desarrollo Econ.,* April–June 1984, *24*(93), pp. 3–40. [G: Argentina]

Doeringer, Peter B. Internal Labor Markets and Paternalism in Rural Areas. In *Osterman, P., ed.,* 1984, pp. 271–89. [G: U.S.]

Dooley, Martin D. and Gottschalk, Peter. Earnings Inequality among Males in the United States: Trends and the Effect of Labor Force

Growth. *J. Polit. Econ.*, February 1984, *92*(1), pp. 59–89. [G: U.S.]

Duggan, James E. The Labor-Force Participation of Older Workers. *Ind. Lab. Relat. Rev.*, April 1984, *37*(3), pp. 416–30. [G: U.S.]

Eck, Alan. New Occupational Separation Data Improve Estimates of Job Replacement Needs. *Mon. Lab. Rev.*, March 1984, *107*(3), pp. 3–10. [G: U.S.]

Eichengreen, Barry. Experience and the Male–Female Earnings Gap in the 1890s. *J. Econ. Hist.*, September 1984, *44*(3), pp. 822–34. [G: U.S.]

Flaim, Paul O. Discouraged Workers: How Strong Are Their Links to the Job Market? *Mon. Lab. Rev.*, August 1984, *107*(8), pp. 8–11. [G: U.S.]

García, Norberto and Tokman, Víctor E. Changes in Employment and the Crisis. *Cepal Rev.*, 1984, (24), pp. 103–15. [G: Latin America]

Grasmick, Harold G.; Finley, Nancy J. and Glaser, Deborah L. Labor Force Participation, Sex-Role Attitudes, and Female Crime. *Soc. Sci. Quart.*, September 1984, *65*(3), pp. 703–18. [G: U.S.]

Gregory, Peter. The Mexican Labor Market, 1940–1980. In *[Reynolds, L. G.]*, 1984, pp. 245–79. [G: Mexico]

Grossman, Jean Baldwin. The Occupational Attainment of Immigrant Women in Sweden. *Scand. J. Econ.*, 1984, *86*(3), pp. 337–51. [G: Sweden]

Ham, John and Hsiao, Cheng. Two-Stage Estimation of Structural Labor Supply Parameters Using Interval Data from the 1971 Canadian Census. *J. Econometrics*, January/February 1984, *24*(1/2), pp. 133–58. [G: Canada]

Hausman, Jerry A. Tax Policy and Unemployment Insurance Effects on Labor Policy. In *Wachter, M. L. and Wachter, S. M., eds.*, 1984, pp. 70–96. [G: U.S.]

Hausman, Jerry A. and Ruud, Paul A. Family Labor Supply with Taxes. *Amer. Econ. Rev.*, May 1984, *74*(2), pp. 242–48.

Haveman, Robert H.; Halberstadt, Victor and Burkhauser, Richard V. Public Policy toward Disabled Workers: The Ameliorative Response: Effects on Program Growth and Labor Supply. In *Haveman, R. H.; Halberstadt, V. and Burkhauser, R. V.*, 1984, pp. 81–116. [G: OECD; Israel]

Haveman, Robert H.; Halberstadt, Victor and Burkhauser, Richard V. The Extent and Character of Measured Disability among the Working-Age Population. In *Haveman, R. H.; Halberstadt, V. and Burkhauser, R. V.*, 1984, pp. 8–27. [G: U.S.; OECD]

Haveman, Robert H. and Wolfe, Barbara L. The Decline in Male Labor Force Participation: Comment. *J. Polit. Econ.*, June 1984, *92*(3), pp. 532–41. [G: U.S.]

Hayghe, Howard. Working Mothers Reach Record Number in 1984. *Mon. Lab. Rev.*, December 1984, *107*(12), pp. 31–34. [G: U.S.]

Heroles, Jesús F. Reyes. The Distribution of La-

bor Income in Mexico. In *Aspe, P. and Sigmund, P. E., eds.*, 1984, pp. 129–86. [G: Mexico]

Hughes, Barry. Taxation and Overtime Hours: An Australian Study. *Manchester Sch. Econ. Soc. Stud.*, June 1984, *52*(2), pp. 171–95. [G: Australia]

Johri, C. K. Labour Supply Factors in Earnings' Differentials. In *Singh, A. K.; Papola, T. S. and Mathur, R. S., eds.*, 1984, pp. 109–37. [G: India]

Jones, Richard C.; Harris, Richard J. and Valdez, Avelardo. Occupational and Spatial Mobility of Undocumented Migrants from Dolores Hidalgo, Guanajuato. In *Jones, R. C., ed.*, 1984, pp. 159–82. [G: U.S.; Mexico]

Jonung, Christina. Patterns of Occupational Segregation by Sex in the Labor Market. In *Schmid, G. and Weitzel, R., eds.*, 1984, pp. 44–68. [G: Sweden]

Kausker, Karl. Encouraging Domesticity: A Closer Look. *J. Policy Anal. Manage.*, Summer 1984, *3*(4), pp. 603–07.

Kaztman, Rubén. Sectoral Transformations in Employment in Latin America. *Cepal Rev.*, 1984, (24), pp. 83–101. [G: Latin America]

Keeley, Michael C. Cyclical Unemployment and Employment: Effects of Labor Force Entry and Exit. *Fed. Res. Bank San Francisco Econ. Rev.*, Summer 1984, (3), pp. 5–25. [G: U.S.]

Kogut, Edy Luiz and Langoni, Carlos Geraldo. Population Growth, Income Distribution and Economic Development. In *Ghosh, P. K., ed.*, no. 5, 1984, *1975*, pp. 147–60. [G: Latin America; U.S.]

Kotliar, A. Full Employment and Proportionality of Factors in Socialist Production. *Prob. Econ.*, June 1984, *27*(2), pp. 38–56. [G: U.S.S.R.]

Kristiansson, Karl-Erik. Gross-Flow Estimates in the Swedish Labour Force Surveys. *Statist. J.*, December 1984, *2*(4), pp. 357–67. [G: Sweden]

Kutas, János. Innovation, Social Environment, Human Factors. *Acta Oecon.*, 1984, *32*(1–2), pp. 125–36. [G: Hungary]

Lamonde, Pierre and Polèse, Mario. L'évolution de la structure économique de Montréal 1971–1981: désindustrialisation ou reconversion? (The Evolution of Montreal's Economic Structure, 1971–1981: Deindustrialization or Reconversion? With English summary.) *L'Actual. Econ.*, December 1984, *60*(4), pp. 471–94. [G: Canada]

Leppel, Karen. Determinants of Expectations of Retirement: Evidence from a Less Developed Country. *Appl. Econ.*, October 1984, *16*(5), pp. 677–86. [G: U.S.; Malaysia]

Leuthold, Jane H. Income Splitting and Women's Labor-Force Participation. *Ind. Lab. Relat. Rev.*, October 1984, *38*(1), pp. 98–105. [G: U.S.]

Mason, Andrew; Koo, Sung-Yeal and Song, Wi-Sup. Labor Force and Industrial Development in the Pacific Basin. In *Benjamin, R. and Kudrle, R. T.*, 1984, pp. 163–89. [G: Selected Countries]

Maurice, Marc; Sellier, François and Silvestre, Jean-Jacques. The Search for a Societal Effect in the Production of Company Hierarchy: A Comparison of France and Germany. In *Osterman, P., ed.*, 1984, pp. 231–70.
[G: W. Germany; France]

Michael, Robert T. and Tuma, Nancy Brandon. Youth Employment: Does Life Begin at 16? *J. Lab. Econ.*, October 1984, *2*(4), pp. 464–76.
[G: U.S.]

Mitchell, Daniel J. B. The Australian Labor Market. In *Caves, R. E. and Krause, L. B., eds.*, 1984, pp. 127–93.
[G: Australia]

Moffitt, Robert. Profiles of Fertility, Labour Supply and Wages of Married Women: A Complete Life-Cycle Model. *Rev. Econ. Stud.*, April 1984, *51*(2), pp. 263–78.
[G: U.S.]

Moffitt, Robert. The Estimation of a Joint Wage–Hours Labor Supply Model. *J. Lab. Econ.*, October 1984, *2*(4), pp. 550–66.
[G: U.S.]

Molho, Ian and Elias, Peter. A Study of Regional Trends in the Labour Force Participation of Married Women in the UK, 1968–1977. *Appl. Econ.*, April 1984, *16*(2), pp. 163–73.
[G: U.K.]

Moskoff, William. The Soviet Urban Labor Supply. In *Morton, H. W. and Stuart, R. C., eds.*, 1984, pp. 65–83.
[G: U.S.S.R.]

Mott, Frank L. and Shapiro, David. Seasonal Variations in Labor-Force Activity and Intrahousehold Substitution of Labor in Rural Keyna. *J. Devel. Areas*, July 1984, *18*(4), pp. 449–63.
[G: Kenya]

Moy, Joyanna. Recent Labor Market Developments in the U.S. and Nine Other Countries. *Mon. Lab. Rev.*, January 1984, *107*(1), pp. 44–51.
[G: OECD]

Müller, A. L. Employment Policies in the Soviet Bloc (Review Note). *S. Afr. J. Econ.*, March 1984, *52*(1), pp. 90–95.
[G: U.S.S.R.; Poland; E. Germany; Czechoslovakia; Hungary]

Newbold, Paul and Thury, Gerhard. Seasonal Adjustment of Austrian Labour Force Series. *Empirica*, 1984, *11*(2), pp. 147–204.
[G: Austria]

Novek, Joel. The Mechanization of Work: Paradise or Purgatory? *Challenge*, September/October 1984, *27*(4), pp. 43–48.
[G: U.S.; Global]

Oberai, A. S. and Singh, H. K. Manmohan. Migration, Employment and the Urban Labour Market: A Study in the Indian Punjab. *Int. Lab. Rev.*, July–August 1984, *123*(4), pp. 507–23.
[G: India]

Oi, Walter Y. A Comment on the Ashenfelter Analysis of Labor Market Fluctuations [Macroeconomic Analyses and Microeconomic Analyses of Labor Supply]. *Carnegie-Rochester Conf. Ser. Public Policy*, Autumn 1984, *21*, pp. 157–72.
[G: U.S.; U.K.; Canada]

Ortiz, Vilma and Cooney, Rosemary Santana. Sex-Role Attitudes and Labor Force Participation among Young Hispanic Females and Non-Hispanic White Females. *Soc. Sci. Quart.*, June 1984, *65*(2), pp. 392–400.
[G: U.S.]

Owen, D. W.; Gillespie, A. E. and Coombes, M. G. 'Job Shortfalls' in British Local Labour Market Areas: A Classification of Labour Supply and Demand Trends, 1971–1981. *Reg. Stud.*, December 1984, *18*(6), pp. 469–88.
[G: U.K.]

Parsons, Donald O. Disability Insurance and Male Labor Force Participation: A Response. *J. Polit. Econ.*, June 1984, *92*(3), pp. 542–49.
[G: U.S.]

Perkins, Frances. Manpower Forecasting and Resource Development—Examples from the Hunter Region of NSW. *Australian Bull. Lab.*, March 1984, *10*(2), pp. 77–104.
[G: Australia]

Petrella, Ricardo. Europe at Work: Challenges and Prospects. In *Marstrand, P., ed.*, 1984, pp. 1–18.
[G: W. Europe]

Plotnick, Robert. The Redistributive Impact of Cash Transfers. *Public Finance Quart.*, January 1984, *12*(1), pp. 27–50.
[G: U.S.]

Portes, Alejandro and Benton, Lauren. Industrial Development and Labor Absorption: A Reinterpretation. *Population Devel. Rev.*, December 1984, *10*(4), pp. 589–611.
[G: Latin America]

Presser, Harriet B. Job Characteristics of Spouses and Their Work Shifts. *Demography*, November 1984, *21*(4), pp. 575–89.
[G: U.S.]

Ramos, Joseph. Urbanization and the Labour Market. *Cepal Rev.*, 1984, (24), pp. 63–81.
[G: Latin America]

Ries, John C. Unemployment in 1982: Beyond the Official Labor Force Statistics. *New Eng. Econ. Rev.*, May–June 1984, pp. 29–37.
[G: U.S.]

Robins, Philip K. The Labor Supply Response of Twenty-Year Families in the Denver Income Maintenance Experiment. *Rev. Econ. Statist.*, August 1984, *66*(3), pp. 491–95.
[G: U.S.]

Rosen, Sherwin. The Effect of Social Security Benefits on the Labor Supply of the Aged: Comment. In *Aaron, H. J. and Burtless, G., eds.*, 1984, pp. 171–74.
[G: U.S.]

Rytina, Nancy F. and Bianchi, Suzanne M. Occupational Reclassification and Changes in Distribution by Gender. *Mon. Lab. Rev.*, March 1984, *107*(3), pp. 11–17.
[G: U.S.]

Saracino, Alberto. L'offerta di lavoro: uno verifica empirica sul "Panel" delle regioni italiane (1967–1979). (Labour Supply: Empirical Results from the Panel of the Italian Regions [1967–1979]. With English summary.) *Econ. Lavoro*, Jan.-Mar. 1984, *18*(1), pp. 43–52.
[G: Italy]

Schmidt, Rainer. Population Change, Labour Market and Unemployment—The Case of the German Domestic Labour Force from 1965–1982. In *Steinmann, G., ed.*, 1984, pp. 278–94.
[G: W. Germany]

Skolka, Jiri. Input–Output Anatomy of Changes in Employment Structure in Austria between 1964 and 1976. *Empirica*, 1984, *11*(2), pp. 205–33.
[G: Austria]

Slade, Frederic P. Older Men: Disability Insurance and the Incentive to Work. *Ind. Relat.*, Spring 1984, *23*(2), pp. 260–69.   [G: U.S.]

Spitze, Glenna. The Effect of Family Migration on Wives' Employment: How Long Does It Last? *Soc. Sci. Quart.*, March 1984, *65*(1), pp. 21–36.   [G: U.S.]

Stewart, Mark B. and Greenhalgh, Christine A. Work History Patterns and the Occupational Attainment of Women. *Econ. J.*, September 1984, *94*(375), pp. 493–519.   [G: U.K.]

Tschetter, John H. An Evaluation of BLS' Projections of 1980 Industry Employment. *Mon. Lab. Rev.*, August 1984, *107*(8), pp. 12–22.   [G: U.S.]

Urquhart, Michael. The Employment Shift to Services: Where Did It Come From? *Mon. Lab. Rev.*, April 1984, *107*(4), pp. 15–22.   [G: U.S.]

van der Veen, Anne and Evers, Gerard H. M. A Labour-Supply Function for Females in the Netherlands. *De Economist*, 1984, *132*(3), pp. 367–76.   [G: Netherlands]

Wachter, Michael L. The Training Component of Growth Policies. In *Wachter, M. L. and Wachter, S. M., eds.*, 1984, pp. 41–69.   [G: U.S.]

Wachter, Michael L. Unemployment in the American Economy: Types, Causes, and Outlooks for the 1980's. In *Ullrich, R. A., ed.*, 1984, pp. 1–24.   [G: U.S.]

Weller, Robert H. The Gainful Employment of Females and Fertility—With Special Reference to Rural Areas of Developing Countries. In *Schutjer, W. A. and Stokes, C. S., eds.*, 1984, pp. 151–71.   [G: LDCs]

Winegarden, Calman R. Women's Fertility, Market Work and Marital Status: A Test of the New Household Economics with International Data. *Economica*, November 1984, *51*(204), pp. 447–56.   [G: W. Europe]

Wolfe, Barbara L. Measuring Disability and Health. *J. Health Econ.*, August 1984, *3*(2), pp. 187–93.   [G: U.S.]

Yeager, Leland B. Is Industrial Innovation Destroying Jobs? A Comment. *Cato J.*, Fall 1984, *4*(2), pp. 645–50.   [G: U.S.]

Young, Anne McDougall. Fewer Students in Work Force as School Age Population Declines. *Mon. Lab. Rev.*, July 1984, *107*(7), pp. 34–37.

Young, Anne McDougall and Hayghe, Howard. More U.S. Workers Are College Graduates. *Mon. Lab. Rev.*, March 1984, *107*(3), pp. 46–49.   [G: U.S.]

Zimmermann, Klaus F. The Dynamics of Women's Labor Force Participation and Fertility: A Simultaneous ARX-Model. In *Steinmann, G., ed.*, 1984, pp. 386–403.
    [G: W. Germany]

8131 Agriculture

Albert, Bill. The Creation of a Proletariat on Peru's Coastal Sugar Plantations: 1880–1920. In *Munslow, B. and Finch, H., eds.*, 1984, pp. 99–120.   [G: Peru]

Albert, Bill. The Labour Force on Peru's Sugar Plantations 1820–1930: A Survey. In *Albert, B. and Graves, A., eds.*, 1984, pp. 199–215.
    [G: Peru]

Armstrong, Thomas F. The Transformation of Work: Turpentine Workers in Coastal Georgia, 1865–1901. *Labor Hist.*, Fall 1984, *25*(4), pp. 518–32.   [G: U.S.]

Bardhan, Pranab K. Determinants of Supply and Demand for Labor in a Poor Agrarian Economy: An Analysis of Household Survey Data from Rural West Bengal. In *Binswanger, H. P. and Rosenzweig, R., eds.*, 1984, pp. 242–62.   [G: India]

Beechert, Ed. Labour Relations in the Hawaiian Sugar Industry, 1850–1937. In *Albert, B. and Graves, A., eds.*, 1984, pp. 281–92.
    [G: U.S.]

Binswanger, Hans P. and Rosenzweig, Mark R. Contractual Arrangements, Employment, and Wages in Rural Labor Markets: A Critical Review. In *Binswanger, H. P. and Rosenzweig, R., eds.*, 1984, pp. 1–40.

Binswanger, Hans P., et al. Common Features and Contrasts in Labor Relations in the Semiarid Tropics of India. In *Binswanger, H. P. and Rosenzweig, R., eds.*, 1984, pp. 143–68.
    [G: India]

von Braun, Joachim. Demographic-Economic Interaction in a Shrinking Agricultural Sector: Population and Labor Market Effects in the Federal Republic of Germany. In *Steinmann, G., ed.*, 1984, pp. 203–16.
    [G: W. Germany]

Breman, Jan C. Seasonal Migration and Cooperative Capitalism: The Crushing of Cane and Labor by the Sugar Factories of Bardoli, South Gujarat. In *Binswanger, H. P. and Rosenzweig, R., eds.*, 1984, pp. 131–42.   [G: India]

Chacon, Ramón D. Labor Unrest and Industrialized Agriculture in California: The Case of the 1933 San Joaquin Valley Cotton Strike. *Soc. Sci. Quart.*, June 1984, *65*(2), pp. 336–53.
    [G: U.S.]

Chattopadhyay, Manabendu. Transformation of Labour Use in Indian Agriculture. *Cambridge J. Econ.*, September 1984, *8*(3), pp. 289–96.
    [G: India]

Coffey, Joseph D. The California Agricultural Labor Relations Act and National Agricultural Labor Relations Legislation: Discussion. In *Emerson, R. D., ed.*, 1984, pp. 370–75. [G: U.S.]

Coltrane, Robert. The Off-Farm Work of Hired Farm Workers: Discussion. In *Emerson, R. D., ed.*, 1984, pp. 164–67.   [G: U.S.]

Covey, Charles D. Occupational Structure and the Industrialization of Agriculture: Discussion. In *Emerson, R. D., ed.*, 1984, pp. 323–27.   [G: U.S.]

Dawson, P. J. Family Labour Supply: Some Empirical Results from Agriculture. *Appl. Econ.*, December 1984, *16*(6), pp. 895–904.
    [G: U.K.]

Disney, Richard and Elbashir, A. A. Mechanisation, Employment, and Productivity in Sudanese Agriculture. *J. Devel. Econ.*, December 1984, *16*(3), pp. 249–62. [G: Sudan]

Domar, Evsey D. and Machina, Mark J. On the Profitability of Russian Serfdom. *J. Econ. Hist.*, December 1984, *44*(4), pp. 919–55. [G: U.S.S.R.]

Elterich, G. Joachim. Seasonality of Farm Labor Use Patterns in the United States: Discussion. In *Emerson, R. D., ed.*, 1984, pp. 96–103. [G: U.S.]

Emerson, Robert D. Migration in Farm Labor Markets. In *Emerson, R. D., ed.*, 1984, pp. 104–35. [G: U.S.]

Emerson, Robert D. Seasonal Agricultural Labor Markets in the United States: Summary. In *Emerson, R. D., ed.*, 1984, pp. 482–523. [G: U.S.]

Erven, Bernard L. Impact of Labor Laws and Regulations on Agricultural Labor Markets. In *Emerson, R. D., ed.*, 1984, pp. 376–405. [G: U.S.]

Friedland, William H. Unstructured Labor Markets and Alternative Labor Market Forms: Discussion. In *Emerson, R. D., ed.*, 1984, pp. 279–85. [G: U.S.]

Fritsch, Conrad F. Seasonality of Farm Labor Use Patterns in the United States. In *Emerson, R. D., ed.*, 1984, pp. 64–95. [G: U.S.]

Gardner, Bruce. Seasonal Farm Labor and U.S. Farm Policy. In *Emerson, R. D., ed.*, 1984, pp. 450–76. [G: U.S.]

Glover, Robert W. Unstructured Labor Markets and Alternative Labor Market Forms. In *Emerson, R. D., ed.*, 1984, pp. 254–79. [G: U.S.]

Glover, Terry. An Intertemporal Approach to Seasonal Agricultural Labor Markets: Discussion. In *Emerson, R. D., ed.*, 1984, pp. 249–53.

Hayes, Sue Eileen. The California Agricultural Labor Relations Act and National Agricultural Labor Relations Legislation. In *Emerson, R. D., ed.*, 1984, pp. 328–70. [G: U.S.]

Holt, James S. Introduction to the Seasonal Farm Labor Problem. In *Emerson, R. D., ed.*, 1984, pp. 3–32. [G: U.S.]

Hossain, Mahabub. Agricultural Development in Bangladesh: A Historical Perspective. *Bangladesh Devel. Stud.*, December 1984, *12*(4), pp. 29–57. [G: Bangladesh]

Huffman, Wallace E. Some Analytical Approaches for Human Resource Issues of Seasonal Farm Labor. In *Emerson, R. D., ed.*, 1984, pp. 33–63. [G: U.S.]

Kikuchi, Masao; Hafid, Anwar and Hayami, Yujiro. Changes in Rice Harvesting Contracts and Wages in Java. In *Binswanger, H. P. and Rosenzweig, R., eds.*, 1984, pp. 117–30. [G: Indonesia]

Mamer, John W. Occupational Structure and the Industrialization of Agriculture. In *Emerson, R. D., ed.*, 1984, pp. 286–323. [G: U.S.]

Marshall, Dawn I. Vincentian Contract Labour Migration to Barbados: The Satisfaction of Mutual Needs? *Soc. Econ. Stud.*, September 1984, *33*(3), pp. 63–92. [G: Barbados; St. Vincent]

Martin, Philip L. and North, David S. Nonimmigrant Aliens in American Agriculture. In *Emerson, R. D., ed.*, 1984, pp. 168–93. [G: U.S.]

Mason, Andrew; Koo, Sung-Yeal and Song, Wi-Sup. Labor Force and Industrial Development in the Pacific Basin. In *Benjamin, R. and Kudrle, R. T.*, 1984, pp. 163–89. [G: Selected Countries]

Matta, Benjamin N., Jr. The Off-Farm Work of Hired Farm Workers. In *Emerson, R. D., ed.*, 1984, pp. 140–64. [G: U.S.]

Menra, Naresh Kumar. Dualism and Surplus Labour: A Case Study of Indian Agriculture. *Margin*, October 1984, *17*(1), pp. 48–54. [G: India]

O'Brien, Jay. The Political Economy of Semi-Proletarianisation under Colonialism: Sudan 1925–50. In *Munslow, B. and Finch, H., eds.*, 1984, pp. 121–47. [G: Sudan]

Parks, Alfred L. Migration in Farm Labor Markets: Discussion. In *Emerson, R. D., ed.*, 1984, pp. 136–39. [G: U.S.]

Polopolus, Leo. Impact of Labor Laws and Regulations on Agricultural Labor Markets: Discussion. In *Emerson, R. D., ed.*, 1984, pp. 406–11. [G: U.S.]

Roberts, Kenneth D. Agricultural Development and Labor Mobility: A Study of Four Mexican Subregions. In *Jones, R. C., ed.*, 1984, pp. 74–92. [G: Mexico; U.S.]

Rochin, Refugio I. Farm Worker Service and Employment Programs. In *Emerson, R. D., ed.*, 1984, pp. 412–46. [G: U.S.]

Rosenzweig, Mark R. Determinants of Wage Rates and Labor Supply Behavior in the Rural Sector of a Developing Country. In *Binswanger, H. P. and Rosenzweig, R., eds.*, 1984, pp. 211–41. [G: India]

Rudra, Ashok. Local Power and Farm-Level Decision-Making. In *Desai, M.; Rudolph, S. H. and Rudra, A., eds.*, 1984, pp. 250–80. [G: India]

Ryan, James G. and Ghodake, R. D. Labor Market Behavior in Rural Villages in South India: Effects of Season, Sex, and Socioeconomic Status. In *Binswanger, H. P. and Rosenzweig, R., eds.*, 1984, pp. 169–83. [G: India]

Schuh, G. Edward. Seasonal Farm Labor and U.S. Farm Policy: Discussion. In *Emerson, R. D., ed.*, 1984, pp. 476–81. [G: U.S.]

Shapley, Allen E. Farm Worker Service and Employment Programs: Discussion. In *Emerson, R. D., ed.*, 1984, pp. 446–49. [G: U.S.]

Spreen, Thomas H. An Intertemporal Approach to Seasonal Agricultural Labor Markets. In *Emerson, R. D., ed.*, 1984, pp. 230–49.

Sumner, Daniel A. Labor Supply Uncertainty and Technology Adoption: Discussion. In *Emerson, R. D., ed.*, 1984, pp. 224–29.

Taylor, Elizabeth. Peasants or Proletarians? The Transformation of Agrarian Production Relations in Egypt. In *Munslow, B. and Finch, H., eds.*, 1984, pp. 164–88. [G: Egypt]

Welch, Finis. Nonimmigrant Aliens in American Agriculture: Discussion. In *Emerson, R. D., ed.*, 1984, pp. 194–99. [G: U.S.]

Whitener, Leslie A. A Statistical Portrait of Hired Farmworkers. *Mon. Lab. Rev.*, June 1984, *107*(6), pp. 49–53. [G: U.S.]

Zilberman, David and Just, Richard E. Labor Supply Uncertainty and Technology Adoption. In *Emerson, R. D., ed.*, 1984, pp. 200–24.

8132 Manufacturing

Elbaum, Bernard. The Making and Shaping of Job and Pay Structures in the Iron and Steel Industry. In *Osterman, P., ed.*, 1984, pp. 71–107. [G: OECD]

Fernández, Manuel A. British Nitrate Companies and the Emergence of Chile's Proletariat, 1880–1914. In *Munslow, B. and Finch, H., eds.*, 1984, pp. 42–76. [G: Chile]

Freudenberger, Herman; Mather, Frances J. and Nardinelli, Clark. A New Look at the Early Factory Labor Force. *J. Econ. Hist.*, December 1984, *44*(4), pp. 1085–90. [G: U.K.]

Hossain, Mahabub. Employment and Labour in Bangladesh Rural Industries. *Bangladesh Devel. Stud.*, March-June 1984, *12*(1–2), pp. 1–24. [G: Bangladesh]

Humphrey, John. The Growth of Female Employment in Brazilian Manufacturing Industry in the 1970s. *J. Devel. Stud.*, July 1984, *20*(4), pp. 224–47. [G: Brazil]

Mangan, John and Stokes, Leigh. The Determinants of Labour Demand in Australian Manufacturing. *S. Afr. J. Econ.*, September 1984, *52*(3), pp. 296–308. [G: Australia]

Nilsen, Diane M. Employment in Durable Goods Anything But Durable in 1979–82. *Mon. Lab. Rev.*, February 1984, *107*(2), pp. 15–24. [G: U.S.]

Peet, Richard. Class Struggle, the Relocation of Employment, and Economic Crisis. *Sci. Soc.*, Spring 1984, *48*(1), pp. 38–51. [G: U.S.]

Pierenkemper, Toni. Pre-1900 Industrial White Collar Employees at the Krupp Steel Casting Works: A New Occupational Category in Germany. *Bus. Hist. Rev.*, Autumn 1984, *58*(3), pp. 384–408. [G: Germany]

Ragan, James F., Jr. Investigating the Decline in Manufacturing Quit Rates. *J. Human Res.*, Winter 1984, *19*(1), pp. 53–71. [G: U.S.]

Timmer, C. Peter. Choice of Technique in Rice Milling on Java. In *Eicher, C. K. and Staatz, J. M., eds.*, 1984, *1973*, pp. 278–88. [G: Indonesia]

Timmer, C. Peter. Choice of Technique in Rice Milling on Java: A Reply. In *Eicher, C. K. and Staatz, J. M., eds.*, 1984, pp. 292–95. [G: Indonesia]

Tokman, Víctor E. Global Monetarism and Destruction of Industry. *Cepal Rev.*, 1984, (23), pp. 107–21. [G: Argentina; Chile]

8133 Service

Barras, R. and Swann, J. Information Technology and the Service Sector: Quality of Services and Quantity of Jobs. In *Marstrand, P., ed.*, 1984, pp. 214–33. [G: U.K.]

Gershuny, Jonathan I. The Future of Service Employment. In *Marstrand, P., ed.*, 1984, pp. 234–55. [G: U.K.]

Ginzberg, Eli. The Service Economy and the Changing Job Structures. In *Ullrich, R. A., ed.*, 1984, pp. 81–94. [G: U.S.]

Lo, Billie L. C. Teacher Education in the Eighties. In *Hayhoe, R., ed.*, 1984, pp. 154–77. [G: China]

Nene, Daphne Sbongile. A Survey of African Women Petty Traders and Self-employed in Town and Country in South Africa. In *Intn'l. Lab. Office*, 1984, pp. 147–54. [G: S. Africa]

Osterman, Paul. White-Collar Internal Labor Markets. In *Osterman, P., ed.*, 1984, pp. 163–89. [G: U.S.]

Sbytova, L. Employment and Raising the Effectiveness of Labor in the Service Sector. *Prob. Econ.*, January 1984, *26*(9), pp. 64–80. [G: U.S.S.R.]

8134 Professional

Agarwal, Vinod B. and Winkler, Donald R. Migration of Professional Manpower to the United States. *Southern Econ. J.*, January 1984, *50*(3), pp. 814–30. [G: U.S.; Selected Countries]

Aranya, Nissim and Ferris, Kenneth R. A Reexamination of Accountants' Organizational–Professional Conflict. *Accounting Rev.*, January 1984, *59*(1), pp. 1–15. [G: U.S.]

Bennell, Paul. The Utilisation of Professional Engineering Skills in Kenya. In *Fransman, M. and King, K., eds.*, 1984, pp. 335–53. [G: Kenya]

Davis, Karen. Physician Supply and Health Care Costs. In *Ginzberg, E. and Ostow, M., eds.*, 1984, pp. 37–48. [G: U.S.]

Derber, Charles. Physicians and Their Sponsors: The New Medical Relations of Production. In *McKinlay, J. B., ed.*, 1984, pp. 217–54.

Fougere, Denis. Insertion professionnelle, mobilité, salaire: le cas des sortants de l'enseignement technique court. (Insertion into the Labour Market, Mobility, Wage: The Case of Young Men with Professional Training Diplomas. With English summary.) *Consommation*, Oct.–Dec. 1984, *31*(4), pp. 29–64. [G: France]

Ginzberg, Eli. Conference Summary: The Expanding Physician Supply: Policy Options. In *Ginzberg, E. and Ostow, M., eds.*, 1984, pp. 1–8. [G: U.S.]

Ginzberg, Eli. The Future Supply of Physicians: Directions for Policy. In *Ginzberg, E. and Ostow, M., eds.*, 1984, pp. 116–25. [G: U.S.]

Gordon, Michael E.; Beauvais, Laura L. and Ladd, Robert T. The Job Satisfaction and Union Commitment of Unionized Engineers. *Ind. Lab. Relat. Rev.*, April 1984, *37*(3), pp. 359–70. [G: U.S.]

Hiestand, Dale L. Medical Residencies in a Period of Expanding Physician Supply. In *Ginzberg, E. and Ostow, M., eds.*, 1984, pp. 69–82. [G: U.S.]

Mitchell, Janet B. Why Do Women Physicians

Work Fewer Hours than Men Physicians? *Inquiry*, Winter 1984, *21*(4), pp. 361–68. [G: U.S.]

Nissim, Joseph. The Price Responsiveness of the Demand for Labour by Skill: British Mechanical Engineering: 1963–1978. *Econ. J.*, December 1984, *94*(376), pp. 812–25. [G: U.K.]

Seregard, Ingvar. The Role of Scientists and Engineers. In *Fusfeld, H. I. and Haklisch, C. S., eds.*, 1984, pp. 155–59.

Sloan, Frank A. Physicians and Hospitals: Implications of an Expanding Physician Supply. In *Ginzberg, E. and Ostow, M., eds.*, 1984, pp. 99–115. [G: U.S.]

Soldofsky, Robert M. Age and Productivity of University Faculties: A Case Study. *Econ. Educ. Rev.*, 1984, *3*(4), pp. 289–98. [G: U.S.]

Swanson, August G. Implications of the Expanding Physician Supply for Medical Schools and Medical Students. In *Ginzberg, E. and Ostow, M., eds.*, 1984, pp. 49–68. [G: U.S.]

Waits, C. Richard and McNertney, Edward M. An Economic Model of Artistic Behavior. *J. Cult. Econ.*, June 1984, *8*(1), pp. 49–60.

Zweifel, Peter. Drugs as an Ambulatory Care Technology: Costs and Benefits to the Insurer. In *Lindgren, B., ed.*, 1984, pp. 37–65. [G: Switzerland]

8135 Government Employees

Borjas, George J. Electoral Cycles and the Earnings of Federal Bureaucrats. *Econ. Inquiry*, October 1984, *22*(4), pp. 447–59. [G: U.S.]

Fisk, Donald M. Public Sector Productivity and Relative Efficiency: The State of Art in the United States. In *Hanusch, H., ed.*, 1984, pp. 241–49. [G: U.S.]

Gomez-Mejia, Luis R. and Balkin, David B. Union Impacts on Secretarial Earnings: A Public Sector Case. *Ind. Relat.*, Winter 1984, *23*(1), pp. 97–102. [G: U.S.]

Greenhalgh, Leonard and McKersie, Robert B. Cost-effectiveness of Alternative Strategies for Cutback Management. In *Carr, J. H., ed.*, 1984, *1980*, pp. 93–112. [G: U.S.]

Horn, Robert N. and McGuire, William J. Determinants of Secondary School Teacher Salaries in a Large Urban School District. *Southern Econ. J.*, October 1984, *51*(2), pp. 481–94. [G: U.S.]

Horton, Raymond D. and Smith, John Palmer. Setting Municipal Priorities: Service Delivery: Expenditures and Services. In *Brecher, C. and Horton, R. D., eds.*, 1984, pp. 337–79. [G: U.S.]

Leon, Carol Boyd. Working for Uncle Sam—A Look at Members of the Armed Forces. *Mon. Lab. Rev.*, July 1984, *107*(7), pp. 3–9. [G: U.S.]

McCormick, Mary. Setting Municipal Priorities: Budgeting and Management: Labor Relations. In *Brecher, C. and Horton, R. D., eds.*, 1984, pp. 302–28. [G: U.S.]

Münch, Klaus-Norbert; Länger, Wolfgang and

Rauscher, Gerhard. Productivity in the Local Government Sector—A Framework for Empirical Research. In *Hanusch, H., ed.*, 1984, pp. 251–65. [G: W. Germany]

Sider, Hal and Cole, Cheryl. The Changing Composition of the Military and the Effect on Labor Force Data. *Mon. Lab. Rev.*, July 1984, *107*(7), pp. 10!nd13. [G: U.S.]

Tanner, Lucretia Dewey. Modernizing the Federal Government: Effect on Its Employees. In *Collins, E. L. and Tanner, L. D., eds.*, 1984, pp. 97–114. [G: U.S.]

Warner, John T. and Goldberg, Matthew S. The Influence of Non-Pecuniary Factors on Labor Supply: The Case of Navy Enlisted Personnel. *Rev. Econ. Statist.*, February 1984, *66*(1), pp. 26–35. [G: U.S.]

820 LABOR MARKETS; PUBLIC POLICY

8200 General

Gilreath, James. Labor History Sources in the Library of Congress Rare Book and Special Collections Division. *Labor Hist.*, Spring 1984, *25*(2), pp. 243–51. [G: U.S.]

Osterman, Paul. Introduction: The Nature and Importance of Internal Labor Markets. In *Osterman, P., ed.*, 1984, pp. 1–22.

Storper, Michael. Who Benefits from Industrial Decentralization? Social Power in the Labour Market, Income Distribution and Spatial Policy in Brazil. *Reg. Stud.*, April 1984, *18*(2), pp. 143–64. [G: Brazil]

Townroe, Peter M. and Hamer, Andrew M. Who Benefits from Industrial Decentralization? Response. *Reg. Stud.*, August 1984, *18*(4), pp. 339–44. [G: Brazil]

821 Labor Economics

8210 Labor Economics: Theory and Empirical Studies Illustrating Theory

Aizenman, Joshua. Optimal Wage Re-Negotiation in a Closed and Open Economy. *J. Monet. Econ.*, March 1984, *13*(2), pp. 251–62.

Akerlof, George A. A Theory of Social Custom, of Which Unemployment May Be One Consequence. In *Akerlof, G. A.*, 1984, *1980*, pp. 69–99.

Akerlof, George A. Gift Exchange and Efficiency-Wage Theory: Four Views. *Amer. Econ. Rev.*, May 1984, *74*(2), pp. 79–83.

Akerlof, George A. Jobs as Dam Sites. In *Akerlof, G. A.*, 1984, *1981*, pp. 101–22.

Akerlof, George A. Labor Contracts as Partial Gift Exchange. In *Akerlof, G. A.*, 1984, *1982*, pp. 145–74. [G: U.S.]

Akerlof, George A. Loyalty Filters. In *Akerlof, G. A.*, 1984, *1983*, pp. 175–91.

Akerlof, George A. The Economics of Caste and of the Rat Race and Other Woeful Tales. In *Akerlof, G. A.*, 1984, *1976*, pp. 23–44.

Akerlof, George A. and Dickens, William T. The Economic Consequences of Cognitive Dissonance. In *Akerlof, G. A.*, 1984, *1982*, pp. 123–44.

Albrecht, James W. and Axell, Bo. An Equilibrium Model of Search Unemployment. *J. Polit. Econ.*, October 1984, *92*(5), pp. 824–40.

Alexis, Marcus and Medoff, Marshall H. Becker's Utility Approach to Discrimination: A Review of the Issues. *Rev. Black Polit. Econ.*, Spring 1984, *12*(4), pp. 41–58.

Allen, Franklin. Mixed Wage and Rent Contracts as Reinterpretations of Share Contracts. *J. Devel. Econ.*, December 1984, *16*(3), pp. 313–17.

Allen, Kathryn E. The Phillips Curve Controversy and Orthodox Visions of the Labor Market. In *Darity, W., Jr.*, ed., 1984, pp. 219–37.

Alston, Lee J.; Datta, Samar K. and Nugent, Jeffrey B. Tenancy Choice in a Competitive Framework with Transactions Costs. *J. Polit. Econ.*, December 1984, *92*(6), pp. 1121–33. [G: U.S.]

Annable, James. The Free Market Needs Help: Incomes Policy. *Challenge*, May/June 1984, *27*(2), pp. 59–61. [G: U.S.]

Arai, Kazuhiro. Expected-Utility-Maximizing Search. *Hitotsubashi J. Econ.*, June 1984, *25*(1), pp. 71–92.

Arrow, Kenneth J. Permanent and Transitory Substitution Effects in Health Insurance Experiments. *J. Lab. Econ.*, April 1984, *2*(2), pp. 259–67.

Ashenfelter, Orley C. Macroeconomic Analyses and Microeconomic Analyses of Labor Supply. *Carnegie-Rochester Conf. Ser. Public Policy*, Autumn 1984, *21*, pp. 117–55. [G: U.S.; U.K.; Canada]

Ashton, D. N. and Maguire, M. J. Dual Labour Market Theory and the Organisation of Local Labour Markets. *Int. J. Soc. Econ.*, 1984, *11*(7), pp. 106–20. [G: U.K.]

Babkina, Z. Employment under Socialism and Its Bourgeois Interpretations. *Prob. Econ.*, April 1984, *26*(12), pp. 54–74. [G: U.S.S.R.]

Bagella, Michele. Note sul concetto di disoccupazione involontaria. (Some Notes on the Concept of Involuntary Unemployment. With English summary.) *Giorn. Econ.*, March–April 1984, *43*(3–4), pp. 213–36.

Baldry, J. C. Wage Indexation in a Two-Sector Economy: A Generalisation. *Australian Econ. Pap.*, December 1984, *23*(43), pp. 219–34.

Baltz, Richard B. An Incentive Early Retirement Model for College and University Faculty. *J. Risk Ins.*, September 1984, *51*(3), pp. 477–97.

Bandyopadhyay, Pradeep. Value and Post-Sraffa Marxian Analysis. *Sci. Soc.*, Winter 1984-1985, *48*(4), pp. 433–48.

Barro, Robert J. and King, Robert G. Time-separable Preferences and Intertemporal-Substitution Models of Business Cycles. *Quart. J. Econ.*, November 1984, *99*(4), pp. 817–39.

Barron, John M.; Loewenstein, Mark A. and Black, Dan A. On Recalls, Layoffs, Variable Hours, and Labor Adjustment Costs. *J. Econ.*

Dynam. Control, December 1984, *8*(3), pp. 265–75.

Barzel, Yoram and Yu, Ben T. The Effect of the Utilization Rate on the Division of Labor. *Econ. Inquiry*, January 1984, *22*(1), pp. 18–27.

Basu, Arati. Production Systems and Productivity of Labour: An Analysis on the Existence of Surplus Labour. *Indian Econ. Rev.*, July-Dec. 1984, *19*(2), pp. 185–201.

Batchelor, Roy A. A Natural Interpretation of the Present Unemployment. In *Griffiths, B. and Wood, G. E.*, eds., 1984, pp. 139–71. [G: U.K.; U.S.; EEC]

van Batenburg, Paul and Tinbergen, Jan. Income Distribution: A Correction and a Generalization. *Weltwirtsch. Arch.*, 1984, *120*(2), pp. 361–65.

Bean, Charles R. Optimal Wage Bargains. *Economica*, May 1984, *51*(202), pp. 141–49.

Beck, Nathaniel. Comment on Hibbs [Political Parties and Macroeconomic Policy]. *Amer. Polit. Sci. Rev.*, June 1984, *78*(2), pp. 499–502. [G: N. America; W. Europe]

Beckmann, Martin J. Zur Bewertung von Karrieren. (On the Utility of a Career. With English summary.) *Jahr. Nationalökon. Statist.*, July 1984, *199*(4), pp. 289–307. [G: U.S.]

Behrend, Hilde. The Effort Bargain. In *Behrend, H.*, 1984, *1957*, pp. 110–31.

Behuria, Sutanu. Taxation and Employment in General Equilibrium: A Two-Sector Analysis. *J. Devel. Econ.*, January–February 1984, *14*(1–2), pp. 219–39.

Berg, Ivar. Current Conceptions of Unemployment: Some Logical and Empirical Difficulties. In *Ullrich, R. A.*, ed., 1984, pp. 95–126. [G: U.S.]

Berg, Ivar. Unemployment, Productivity, and Inflation: Misgivings About the Sapient Orthodoxy. In *Brief, A. P.*, ed., 1984, pp. 71–89.

Berry, Albert and Sabot, R. H. Unemployment and Economic Development. *Econ. Develop. Cult. Change*, October 1984, *33*(1), pp. 99–116. [G: LDCs]

Bhandari, Jagdeep S. Wage Contracting and Aggregate Adjustment in an Open Economy. *Aussenwirtschaft*, December 1984, *39*(4), pp. 335–56.

Bilas, Richard A. Monopsony, Overtime Wages, and Worker's Surplus. *Rivista Int. Sci. Econ. Com.*, August 1984, *31*(8), pp. 725–33.

Binswanger, Hans P. and Rosenzweig, Mark R. Contractual Arrangements, Employment, and Wages in Rural Labor Markets: A Critical Review. In *Binswanger, H. P. and Rosenzweig, R.*, eds., 1984, pp. 1–40.

Birg, Herwig. Demographic Aspects of Labour Market Efficiency. In *Steinmann, G.*, ed., 1984, pp. 303–22. [G: W. Germany]

Black, Philip A. The 'Demonstration Effect' and Labour Unemployment in Developing Countries. *J. Stud. Econ. Econometrics*, March 1984, (19), pp. 31–40. [G: LDCs]

Blair, Douglas H. and Crawford, David L. Labor Union Objectives and Collective Bargaining.

Quart. J. Econ., August 1984, *99*(3), pp. 547–66.

Blakemore, Arthur E. and Hoffman, Dennis L. Hiring Decisions, Labor Flows, and Short-Run Productivity. *Southern Econ. J.*, April 1984, *50*(4), pp. 993–1004. [G: U.S.]

Blau, Francine D. Discrimination Against Women: Theory and Evidence. In *Darity, W., Jr., ed.*, 1984, pp. 53–89. [G: U.S.]

Blumenthal, Tuvia. Some Reflections on the Japanese Motivation System. In *Aoki, M., ed.*, 1984, pp. 413–16. [G: Japan]

Bortis, Heinrich. Employment in a Capitalist Economy. *J. Post Keynesian Econ.*, Summer 1984, *6*(4), pp. 590–604.

Bosworth, Derek and Dawkins, Peter. Modelling Labour Demand: The Role of Economics. *Int. J. Soc. Econ.*, 1984, *11*(7), pp. 91–105.

Bourguignon, François. Rationalité individuelle ou rationalité stratégique: le cas de l'offre familiale de travail. (Individual or Strategic Rationality: The Case of Family Labor Supply. With English summary.) *Revue Écon.*, January 1984, *35*(1), pp. 147–62.

Bowles, Samuel. Class Alliances and Surplus Labor Time. In *[Chenery, H. B.]*, 1984, pp. 103–14.

Brown, Lisa Jo. Neoclassical Economics and the Sexual Division of Labor. *Eastern Econ. J.*, October-December 1984, *10*(4), pp. 367–79.

Brun, J. Ricardo Ramirez and Díaz, Ernesta Guizar. Employment and Development: The Mexican Case. In *Amin, S., ed.*, 1984, pp. 3–19. [G: Mexico]

Brunner, Karl and Meltzer, Allan H. Essays on Macroeconomic Implications of Financial and Labor Markets and Political Processes. *Carnegie-Rochester Conf. Ser. Public Policy*, Autumn 1984, *21*, pp. 1–8.

Bruno, Sergio. Heterogeneous Labour, Employment and Distribution: A Micro–Macro Theoretical Framework for the Analysis of Segmented Labour Markets. *Econ. Lavoro*, Apr.-June 1984, *18*(2), pp. 3–30.

Buchanan, James M. and Lee, Dwight R. Some Simple Analytics of the Laffer Curve. In *Hanusch, H., ed.*, 1984, pp. 281–95.

Bull, Clive and Frydman, Roman. A Reply [The Derivation and Interpretation of the Lucas Supply Function]. *J. Money, Credit, Banking*, August 1984, *16*(3), pp. 377–79.

Burdett, Kenneth, et al. Earnings, Unemployment, and the Allocation of Time over Time. *Rev. Econ. Stud.*, October 1984, *51*(4), pp. 559–78. [G: U.S.]

Burmeister, Edwin. Sraffa, Labor Theories of Value, and the Economics of Real Wage Rate Determination. *J. Polit. Econ.*, June 1984, *92*(3), pp. 508–26.

Burton, John. Strike Cost and Wage Rates: Cross-Industry Differences: Comment. In *Rosa, J.-J., ed.*, 1984, pp. 37–41. [G: U.S.]

Burton, John. The Economic Analysis of the Trade Union as a Political Institution. In *Rosa, J.-J., ed.*, 1984, pp. 123–54.

Butler, Richard J. The Effect of Education on Wages—Hedonic Makes Selectivity Bias (Sort of) Simpler. *Econ. Inquiry*, January 1984, *22*(1), pp. 109–20.

Cagan, Phillip and Fellner, William. The Cost of Disinflation, Credibility, and the Deceleration of Wages 1982–1983. In *Fellner, W., ed.*, 1984, pp. 7–19. [G: U.S.]

Calmfors, Lars. Stabilization Policy and Wage Formation in Economies with Strong Trade Unions. In *Emerson, M., ed.*, 1984, pp. 89–121. [G: Scandinavia; Belgium; Austria; Netherlands]

Carling, Alan. Observations on the Labor Theory of Value. *Sci. Soc.*, Winter 1984-1985, *48*(4), pp. 407–18.

Carmichael, H. Lorne. Reputations in the Labor Market. *Amer. Econ. Rev.*, September 1984, *74*(4), pp. 713–25.

Cassidy, George W. L. R. Dual Market and Human Capital Theories Revisited: The Role of Secondary Labor Market Intermediaries. *Rivista Int. Sci. Econ. Com.*, February 1984, *31*(2), pp. 109–25.

Chalkley, Martin. Adaptive Job Search and Null Offers: A Model of Quantity Constrained Search. *Econ. J.*, 1984 Supplement, *94*, pp. 148–57.

Chapman, Bruce J. Labour Markets from the Microeconomic Perspective: Implicit Contract Theory: Comment. *Australian Econ. Rev.*, 3rd Quarter 1984, (67), pp. 132–34.

Chapman, Paul G. and Fisher, Malcolm R. Union Wage Policies: Comment [Wage Bargaining and Employment]. *Amer. Econ. Rev.*, September 1984, *74*(4), pp. 755–58.

Chaudhuri, T. Datta and Khan, M. Ali. Educated Unemployed, Educational Subsidies, and Growth. *Pakistan Devel. Rev.*, Summer-Autumn 1984, *23*(2&3), pp. 395–409.

Chillemi, Ottorino. Un modello per l'analisi della produzione di capitale umano specifico. (A Model for the Analysis of the Production of Specific Human Capital. With English summary.) *Rivista Int. Sci. Econ. Com.*, December 1984, *31*(12), pp. 1201–20.

Chisari, Omar O. Oferta de trabajo a varios sectores bajo incertidumbre e irreversibilidad. (Multi-sector Labor Supply under Uncertainty and Irreversibility. With English summary.) *Económica*, May-December 1984, *30*(2–3), pp. 133–47.

Clark, Kim B. Unionization and Firm Performance: The Impact on Profits, Growth, and Productivity. *Amer. Econ. Rev.*, December 1984, *74*(5), pp. 893–919. [G: U.S.]

Colander, David C. and Olson, Mancur. Coalitions and Macroeconomics. In *Colander, D. C., ed.*, 1984, pp. 115–28. [G: U.S.]

Collier, Paul and Pemberton, James. Unemployment, Information, and Job Competition. *Greek Econ. Rev.*, April 1984, *6*(1), pp. 121–40.

Cooley, Thomas F.; LeRoy, Stephen F. and Raymon, Neil. Econometric Policy Evaluation: Note. *Amer. Econ. Rev.*, June 1984, *74*(3), pp. 467–70.

Costrell, Robert M. Equilibrium Unemployment and Excess Capacity in Steady-State and Growth Cycles. *Economica*, February 1984, *51*(201), pp. 69–82.

Coyte, Peter C. Optimal Job Assignment and Investment in Specific Human Capital: An Application to Professional Teachers. *Appl. Econ.*, October 1984, *16*(5), pp. 703–15.
[G: Canada]

Coyte, Peter C. Specific Human Capital and Sorting Mechanisms in Labor Markets. *Southern Econ. J.*, October 1984, *51*(2), pp. 469–80.

Cross, Rod. Friedman and Phelps on the Natural Rate of Unemployment. *Atlantic Econ. J.*, July 1984, *12*(2), pp. 47–53.

Danziger, Leif. Stochastic Inflation and Wage Indexation. *Scand. J. Econ.*, 1984, *86*(3), pp. 326–36.

Darity, William A., Jr. Reflections on the State of the Art in Labor Economics. In *Darity, W., Jr., ed.*, 1984, pp. 3–20.

Debonneuil, Michèle and Sterdyniak, Henri. La boucle prix-salaires dans l'inflation. (Inflation and Wage–Price Feed-Back. With English summary.) *Revue Écon.*, March 1984, *35*(2), pp. 267–311.

Del Boca, Daniela. Differenziali salariali e alternative di orario. (Wage Differentials in Alternative Working Schedules. With English summary.) *Econ. Lavoro*, Oct.-Dec. 1984, *18*(4), pp. 3–16. [G: Italy]

Desai, Meghnad. Wages, Prices and Unemployment a Quarter Century after the Phillips Curve. In *Hendry, D. F. and Wallis, K. F., eds.*, 1984, pp. 253–73.

Diamond, Peter A. Money in Search Equilibrium. *Econometrica*, January 1984, *52*(1), pp. 1–20.

Dickens, William T. Occupational Safety and Health Regulation and Economic Theory. In *Darity, W., Jr., ed.*, 1984, pp. 133–73.
[G: U.S.]

Donaldson, David and Eaton, B. Curtis. Person-Specific Costs of Production: Hours of Work, Rates of Pay, Labour Contracts. *Can. J. Econ.*, August 1984, *17*(3), pp. 441–49.

Driehuis, Wim. Macroeconomic Investment and Employment Functions. In *van der Ploeg, F., ed.*, 1984, pp. 131–61.

Dudley, Leonard and Montmarquette, Claude. The Effects of Non-clearing Labor Markets on the Demand for Public Spending. *Econ. Inquiry*, April 1984, *22*(2), pp. 151–70.
[G: Selected Countries]

Duffy, Martyn H. The Relationship between Unemployment and Unfilled Vacancies in Great Britain: An Extended Job-Search, Labour Turnover View. *Bull. Econ. Res.*, November 1984, *36*(2), pp. 143–72. [G: U.K.]

Dye, Ronald A. The Trouble with Tournaments. *Econ. Inquiry*, January 1984, *22*(1), pp. 147–49.

Dye, Ronald A. and Antle, Rick. Self-Selection via Fringe Benefits. *J. Lab. Econ.*, July 1984, *2*(3), pp. 388–411.

Earle, John S. and Kniesner, Thomas J. Did Reaganomics Shift the Phillips Curve? *Indian Econ. Rev.*, July-Dec. 1984, *19*(2), pp. 235–40. [G: U.S.]

Ellman, Michael. Full Employment—Lessons from State Socialism. In *Ellman, M., 1984, 1979*, pp. 149–73. [G: E. Europe; U.S.S.R.; China]

Entov, R. M. The "Rule" and Fall of the Phillips Curve. *Prob. Econ.*, February 1984, *26*(10), pp. 3–36.

Evenson, Robert E. and Binswanger, Hans P. Estimating Labor Demand Functions for Indian Agriculture. In *Binswanger, H. P. and Rosenzweig, R., eds.*, 1984, pp. 263–79.
[G: India]

Farmer, Roger E. A. Unemployment, Bankruptcy and Asymmetric Information. *Manchester Sch. Econ. Soc. Stud.*, September 1984, *52*(3), pp. 284–91.

Fehr, Ernst. Workers' Management and Capitalism in a Nutshell. *Econ. Anal. Worker's Manage.*, 1984, *18*(4), pp. 319–31.

Fethke, Gary C. and Policano, Andrew J. Cyclical Implications of Indexing the Minimum Wage. *J. Macroecon.*, Winter 1984, *6*(1), pp. 1–21.
[G: U.S.]

Fethke, Gary C. and Policano, Andrew J. Wage Contingencies, the Patterns of Negotiation and Aggregate Implications of Alternative Contract Structures. *J. Monet. Econ.*, September 1984, *14*(2), pp. 151–70.

Flanagan, Robert J. Implicit Contracts, Explicit Contracts, and Wages. *Amer. Econ. Rev.*, May 1984, *74*(2), pp. 345–49.

Flaschel, Peter. The Inflation-based 'Natural' Rate of Unemployment and the Conflict Over Income Distribution. In *Goodwin, R. M.; Krüger, M. and Vercelli, A., eds.*, 1984, pp. 103–26.

Foster, James E. and Wan, Henry Y., Jr. Involuntary Unemployment as a Principal–Agent Equilibrium. *Amer. Econ. Rev.*, June 1984, *74*(3), pp. 476–84.

Francesco, Farina. "Inefficient" Equilibrium in V. Lutz's Two-Sector Model: A Critique. *Econ. Notes*, 1984, (2), pp. 25–50.

Frank, Robert H. Are Workers Paid Their Marginal Products? *Amer. Econ. Rev.*, September 1984, *74*(4), pp. 549–71. [G: U.S.]

Frank, Robert H. Interdependent Preferences and the Competitive Wage Structure. *Rand J. Econ.*, Winter 1984, *15*(4), pp. 510–20.

Franz, Wolfgang. Inflation und interindustrielle Lohnstruktur. (Inflation and the Interindustrial Wage Structure. With English summary.) *Ifo-Studien*, 1984, *30*(2), pp. 81–106.
[G: Germany]

Franz, Wolfgang. Wohin treibt die Phillipskurve? Theoretische und empirische Überlegungen zur inflationsstabilen Arbeitslosenquote in der Bundesrepublik Deutschland. (The Shift of the Phillips Curve. Theoretical and Empirical Considerations about the Non-accelerating Inflation Rate of Unemployment for the Federal Republic of Germany. With English summary.)

Z. *Wirtschaft. Sozialwissen.*, 1984, *104*(6), pp. 603–29. **[G: W. Germany]**

Fraser, R. W. Demand Uncertainty and Unemployment. *Oxford Econ. Pap.*, March 1984, *36*(1), pp. 27–36.

Friedman, Samuel R. Structure, Process, and the Labor Market. In *Darity, W., Jr., ed.*, 1984, pp. 175–217.

Furubotn, Eirik G. and Wiggins, Steven N. Plant Closings, Worker Reallocation Costs and Efficiency Gains to Labor Representation on Boards of Directors. *Z. ges. Staatswiss.*, March 1984, *140*(1), pp. 176–92. **[G: U.S.]**

Galeotti, Marzio. On the Micro-foundations of the Lucas Supply Function. *Econ. Notes*, 1984, (3), pp. 115–27.

Garrison, Charles B. Friedman versus Keynes on the Theory of Employment. *J. Post Keynesian Econ.*, Fall 1984, *7*(1), pp. 114–27.

Gershuny, Jonathan I. Growth, Social Innovation and Time Use. In *Boulding, K. E., ed.*, 1984, pp. 36–57. **[G: OECD]**

Gilbert, Guy. La Relation entre Recettes Fiscales et Taux d'Imposition dans le Temps: Quelques Résultats Analytiques Simples. (Tax Financing and the Shadow Economy. With English summary.) In *Hanusch, H., ed.*, 1984, pp. 297–312.

Gill, Flora. The Costs of Adjustment and the Invisible Hand; with Special Reference to the Labour Market. *Écon. Appl.*, 1984, *37*(3–4), pp. 523–41.

Glombowski, Jörg and Krüger, Michael. Unemployment Insurance and Cyclical Growth. In *Goodwin, R. M.; Krüger, M. and Vercelli, A., eds.*, 1984, pp. 25–46.

Glover, Terry. An Intertemporal Approach to Seasonal Agricultural Labor Markets: Discussion. In *Emerson, R. D., ed.*, 1984, pp. 249–53.

Graham, John W. Why Is Consumption Out of Labor Income Greater Than Consumption Out of Nonlabor Income? *Quart. J. Bus. Econ.*, Summer 1984, *23*(3), pp. 59–69.

Graham, John W. and Green, Carole A. Estimating the Parameters of a Household Production Function with Joint Products. *Rev. Econ. Statist.*, May 1984, *66*(2), pp. 277–82. **[G: U.S.]**

Greenwood, Daphne. The Economic Significance of "Woman's Place" in Society: A New-Institutionalist View. *J. Econ. Issues*, September 1984, *18*(3), pp. 663–80. **[G: U.S.]**

Greenwood, Daphne. The Institutional Inadequacy of the Market in Determining Comparable Worth: Implications for Value Theory. *J. Econ. Issues*, June 1984, *18*(2), pp. 457–64. **[G: U.S.]**

Grossbard-Shechtman, Amyra. A Theory of Allocation of Time in Markets for Labour and Marriage. *Econ. J.*, December 1984, *94*(376), pp. 863–82.

Grossman, Gene M. International Competition and the Unionized Sector. *Can. J. Econ.*, August 1984, *17*(3), pp. 541–56.

Grout, Paul A. Investment and Wages in the Absence of Binding Contracts: A Nash Bargaining

Approach. *Econometrica*, March 1984, *52*(2), pp. 449–60.

Gupta, Manash Ranjan. The Productivity of Workers' Consumption and the Choice of Techniques: A Comment. *Indian Econ. Rev.*, July-Dec. 1984, *19*(2), pp. 241–42.

Gupta, Suraj B. The Productivity of Workers' Consumption and the Choice of Techniques: A Reply. *Indian Econ. Rev.*, July-Dec. 1984, *19*(2), pp. 243–45.

Gwartney, James and Stroup, Richard L. Labor Supply and Tax Rates: Reply. *Amer. Econ. Rev.*, December 1984, *74*(5), pp. 1108–09.

Gylfason, Thorvaldur and Lindbeck, Assar. Competing Wage Claims, Cost Inflation, and Capacity Utilization. *Europ. Econ. Rev.*, February 1984, *24*(1), pp. 1–21.

Gylfason, Thorvaldur and Lindbeck, Assar. Union Rivalry and Wages: An Oligopolistic Approach. *Economica*, May 1984, *51*(202), pp. 129–39.

Hahn, Frank H. Wages and Employment. In *Collard, D. A., et al., eds.*, 1984, pp. 47–58.

Hahn, Frank H. Wages and Employment. *Oxford Econ. Pap.*, Supplement November 1984, *36*, pp. 47–58.

Hall, Robert E. and Lazear, Edward P. The Excess Sensitivity of Layoffs and Quits to Demand. *J. Lab. Econ.*, April 1984, *2*(2), pp. 233–57.

Haltiwanger, John C. The Distinguishing Characteristics of Temporary and Permanent Layoffs. *J. Lab. Econ.*, October 1984, *2*(4), pp. 523–38.

Haltiwanger, John C. Asymmetric Information, Multiperiod Labor Contracts, and Inefficient Job Separations. *Southern Econ. J.*, April 1984, *50*(4), pp. 1005–24.

Hamermesh, Daniel S. Life-Cycle Effects on Consumption and Retirement. *J. Lab. Econ.*, July 1984, *2*(3), pp. 353–70. **[G: U.S.]**

Hammond, Peter J. What to Do about Business Cycles? In *Seidl, C., ed.*, 1984, pp. 59–75.

Harris, Milton and Weiss, Yoram. Job Matching with Finite Horizon and Risk Aversion. *J. Polit. Econ.*, August 1984, *92*(4), pp. 758–79.

Hart, Robert A. Worksharing and Factor Prices. *Europ. Econ. Rev.*, March 1984, *24*(2), pp. 165–88. **[G: OECD]**

Hartog, Joop. On the Efficiency of Labor Markets. *De Economist*, 1984, *132*(3), pp. 279–99. **[G: Netherlands]**

Hausman, Jerry A. and Ruud, Paul A. Family Labor Supply with Taxes. *Amer. Econ. Rev.*, May 1984, *74*(2), pp. 242–48.

Haveman, Robert H. How Much Have the Reagan Administration's Tax and Spending Policies Increased Work Effort? In *Hulten, C. R. and Sawhill, I. V., eds.*, 1984, pp. 91–125. **[G: U.S.]**

von Hayek, Friedrich A. Inflation, the Misdirection of Labour, and Unemployment. In *von Hayek, F. A. (I)*, 1984, *1975*, pp. 3–17.

Hayes, Beth. Unions and Strikes with Asymmetric Information. *J. Lab. Econ.*, January 1984, *2*(1), pp. 57–83.

Heckman, James J. Comments on the Ashenfelter and Kydland Papers [Macroeconomic Analyses and Microeconomic Analyses of Labor Supply] [Labor-Force Heterogeneity and the Business Cycle]. *Carnegie-Rochester Conf. Ser. Public Policy*, Autumn 1984, *21*, pp. 209–24.

Heckman, James J. and Singer, Burton. A Method for Minimizing the Impact of Distributional Assumptions in Econometric Models for Duration Data. *Econometrica*, March 1984, *52*(2), pp. 271–320.

Heckman, James J. and Singer, Burton. Econometric Duration Analysis. *J. Econometrics*, January/February 1984, *24*(1/2), pp. 63–132.

Heckman, James J. and Singer, Burton. The Identifiability of the Proportional Hazard Model. *Rev. Econ. Stud.*, April 1984, *51*(2), pp. 231–41.

Hendricks, Wallace E. and Kahn, Lawrence M. The Demand for Labor Market Structure: An Economic Approach. *J. Lab. Econ.*, July 1984, *2*(3), pp. 412–38. [G: U.S.]

Henry, S. G. B. Real Wage Implications of Wage Inflation Models. *Bull. Econ. Res.*, November 1984, *36*(2), pp. 119–42. [G: U.K.]

Hersoug, Tor. Union Wage Responses to Tax Changes. *Oxford Econ. Pap.*, March 1984, *36*(1), pp. 37–51.

High, Jack. Knowledge, Maximizing, and Conjecture: A Critical Analysis of Search Theory. *J. Post Keynesian Econ.*, Winter 1983-84, *6*(2), pp. 252–64.

Hirsch, Barry T. and Link, Albert N. Unions, Productivity, and Productivity Growth. *J. Lab. Res.*, Winter 1984, *5*(1), pp. 29–37. [G: U.S.]

Hoffman, Saul D. Comment [Discrimination Against Women: Theory and Evidence] [The Effect of Racial Differences in Background on Schooling: A Survey]. In *Darity, W., Jr., ed.*, 1984, pp. 241–55. [G: U.S.]

Hojman, David E. Minimum Wages, Union Membership, and Differentials: The Phillips Curve and the Chilean Labour Market Revisited. *J. Econ. Stud.*, 1984, *11*(4), pp. 3–22. [G: Chile]

Holland, A. Steven. The Impact of Inflation Uncertainty on the Labor Market. *Fed. Res. Bank St. Louis Rev.*, August/September 1984, *66*(7), pp. 21–28. [G: U.S.]

Holländer, Heinz. A Further Note on Sraffa's Negative Quantities of Allegedly Embodied Labour. *Econ. J.*, March 1984, *94*(373), pp. 155–57.

Hollander, Samuel. Marx and Malthusianism: Marx's Secular Path of Wages. *Amer. Econ. Rev.*, March 1984, *74*(1), pp. 139–51.

Hollander, Samuel. The Wage Path in Classical Growth Models: Ricardo, Malthus and Mill. *Oxford Econ. Pap.*, June 1984, *36*(2), pp. 200–212.

Holmlund, Bertil. Income Prospects and Job Mobility: The Case of Sweden. *Europ. Econ. Rev.*, April 1984, *24*(3), pp. 383–400. [G: Sweden]

Holt, Charles C. Triplett's Essay on Labor Cost: Comments. *Rev. Public Data Use*, March 1984, *12*(1), pp. 85–87.

Hosios, Arthur J. A Welfare Analysis of Employment Contracts with and without Asymmetric Information. *Rev. Econ. Stud.*, July 1984, *51*(3), pp. 471–89.

Humphries, Jane and Rubery, Jill. The Reconstitution of the Supply Side of the Labour Market: The Relative Autonomy of Social Reproduction. *Cambridge J. Econ.*, December 1984, *8*(4), pp. 331–46.

Ireland, Norman J. Codetermination, Wage Bargaining and the Horizon Problem. *Z. Nationalökon.*, 1984, *44*(1), pp. 1–10.

Jaeger, Franz and Schips, Bernd. Teuerungsausgleich und funktionelle Einkommensverteilung. (Wage Indexation and Income Distribution. With English summary.) *Schweiz. Z. Volkswirtsch. Statist.*, March 1984, *120*(1), pp. 43–63. [G: Switzerland]

Johnson, Terry R. and Pencavel, John H. Dynamic Hours of Work Functions for Husbands, Wives, and Single Females. *Econometrica*, March 1984, *52*(2), pp. 363–89.

Jovanovic, Boyan. Matching, Turnover, and Unemployment. *J. Polit. Econ.*, February 1984, *92*(1), pp. 108–22.

Junankar, P. N. and Price, Simon. The Dynamics of Unemployment: Structural Change and Unemployment Flows. *Econ. J.*, 1984 Supplement, *94*, pp. 158–65. [G: U.K.]

Kahana, Nava and Paroush, Jacob. A Multi-factor Labor-managed Firm under Price Uncertainty. *Eastern Econ. J.*, January-March 1984, *10*(1), pp. 23–29.

Kahn, Lawrence M. The Effect of Collective Bargaining on Production Technique: A Theoretical Analysis. *J. Lab. Res.*, Winter 1984, *5*(1), pp. 1–12.

Kahn, Lawrence M. and Low, Stuart A. An Empirical Model of Employed Search, Unemployed Search, and Nonsearch. *J. Human Res.*, Winter 1984, *19*(1), pp. 104–17. [G: U.S.]

Katsoulacos, Y. Product Innovation and Employment. *Europ. Econ. Rev.*, October–November 1984, *26*(1–2), pp. 83–108.

Kaufman, Roger T. and Woglom, Geoffrey. The Effects of Expectations on Union Wages. *Amer. Econ. Rev.*, June 1984, *74*(3), pp. 418–32. [G: U.S.]

Keeley, Michael C. Cyclical Unemployment and Employment: Effects of Labor Force Entry and Exit. *Fed. Res. Bank San Francisco Econ. Rev.*, Summer 1984, (3), pp. 5–25. [G: U.S.]

Kemp, Murray C. Craft Unions, Wages and Employment. *Kobe Econ. Bus. Rev.*, 1984, *30*, pp. 11–16.

Kenyon, Peter D. Trying to Understand Stagflation: Comment. *Australian Econ. Rev.*, 3rd Quarter 1984, (67), pp. 59–61. [G: Australia]

Kierzkowski, Henryk. Trade Unions, Wage Relativities and Employment. *Australian Econ. Pap.*, June 1984, *23*(42), pp. 91–104.

Kihlstrom, Richard E. A Simple Example of the Radner–Stiglitz Nonconcavity in the Value of

Information. In *Boyer, M. and Kihlstrom, R. E., eds.*, 1984, pp. 53–61.

Kimbrough, Kent P. Commercial Policy and Aggregate Employment under Rational Expectations. *Quart. J. Econ.*, August 1984, *99*(3), pp. 567–85.

Kimbrough, Kent P. The Derivation and Interpretation of the Lucas Supply Function: A Comment. *J. Money, Credit, Banking*, August 1984, *16*(3), pp. 367–77.

Klein, Benjamin. Contract Costs and Administered Prices: An Economic Theory of Rigid Wages. *Amer. Econ. Rev.*, May 1984, *74*(2), pp. 332–38.

Kleinhückelskoten, Hans-Dieter. Die umbiegende Arbeitsangebotskurve—ein altes Problem neu interpretiert. (The Backbending Supply Curve of Labour—An Old Problem Interpreted Once Again. With English summary.) *Jahr. Nationalökon. Statist.*, March 1984, *199*(2), pp. 145–57.

Kleinhückelskoten, Hans-Dieter. Optimale Strategien unternehmerischer Humankapitalinvestitionen und deren Einfluss auf Lohnentwicklung und Lohnstruktur. (Optimal Strategies for the Firm's Investment in Human Capital and Their Influence on Wage Movements and Wage Structure. With English summary.) *Z. ges. Staatswiss.*, September 1984, *140*(3), pp. 510–27.

Koizumi, Susumu. Wage–Employment Contract and Okun's Law. (In Japanese. With English summary.) *Osaka Econ. Pap.*, December 1984, *34*(2–3), pp. 27–35. **[G: Japan; U.S.]**

Kromphardt, Jürgen. Die Phillips-Kurve bei informierter Erwartungsbildung. Eine keynesianische Alternative zur Theorie der natürlichen Arbeitslosenquote. (Informed Expectations and the Phillips Curve. With English summary.) *Z. Wirtschaft. Sozialwissen.*, 1984, *104*(6), pp. 631–44.

Kydland, Finn E. A Clarification: Using the Growth Model to Account for Fluctuations: Reply [Labor-Force Heterogeneity and the Business Cycle]. *Carnegie-Rochester Conf. Ser. Public Policy*, Autumn 1984, *21*, pp. 225–30.

Kydland, Finn E. Labor-Force Heterogeneity and the Business Cycle. *Carnegie-Rochester Conf. Ser. Public Policy*, Autumn 1984, *21*, pp. 173–208.

Laibman, David. Value: A Dialog in One Act. *Sci. Soc.*, Winter 1984-1985, *48*(4), pp. 449–65.

Lang, Kevin. Unions, Firms, and the Return to Seniority. *J. Lab. Res.*, Winter 1984, *5*(1), pp. 81–92.

Lange, Peter. Unions, Workers and Wage Regulation: The Rational Bases of Consent. In *Goldthorpe, J. H., ed.*, 1984, pp. 98–123.

Lazear, Edward P. Incentives and Wage Rigidity. *Amer. Econ. Rev.*, May 1984, *74*(2), pp. 339–44.

Lazear, Edward P. and Moore, Robert L. Incentives, Productivity, and Labor Contracts. *Quart. J. Econ.*, May 1984, *99*(2), pp. 275–96. **[G: U.S.]**

Leigh, Duane E. Why Is There Mandatory Retirement? An Empirical Reexamination. *J. Human Res.*, Fall 1984, *19*(4), pp. 512–31. **[G: U.S.]**

Lévy-Garboua, Louis. Homo Economicus and the Labour Market: Comment. In *Wiles, P. and Routh, G., eds.*, 1984, pp. 154–58.

Lewis, Philip E. T. and Makepeace, Gerald H. The Estimation of a Disequilibrium Real Wage Equation for Britain. *J. Macroecon.*, Fall 1984, *6*(4), pp. 399–410. **[G: U.K.]**

Lopez, Ramon E. Estimating Labor Supply and Production Decisions of Self-Employed Farm Producers. *Europ. Econ. Rev.*, February 1984, *24*(1), pp. 61–82. **[G: Canada]**

Lundahl, Mats. Employer Discrimination with and without Substitution: A Note on the Thurow Model. *Rivista Int. Sci. Econ. Com.*, June 1984, *31*(6), pp. 537–44.

Malcomson, James M. Work Incentives, Hierarchy, and Internal Labor Markets. *J. Polit. Econ.*, June 1984, *92*(3), pp. 486–507.

Malveaux, Julianne. Theoretical Explanations of the Persistence of Racial Unemployment Differentials. In *Darity, W., Jr., ed.*, 1984, pp. 91–118. **[G: U.S.]**

Mangan, John and Stokes, Leigh. The Determinants of Labour Demand in Australian Manufacturing. *Appl. Econ.*, June 1984, *16*(3), pp. 449–59. **[G: Australia]**

Marcus, Alan J. Efficient Risk Sharing, Non-marketable Labor Income and Fixed-Wage Contracts. *Europ. Econ. Rev.*, August 1984, *25*(3), pp. 373–85.

Marsden, David. Homo Economicus and the Labour Market. In *Wiles, P. and Routh, G., eds.*, 1984, pp. 121–53.

Marshall, John M. Gambles and the Shadow Price of Death. *Amer. Econ. Rev.*, March 1984, *74*(1), pp. 73–86.

Marston, Richard C. Real Wages and the Terms of Trade: Alternative Indexation Rules for an Open Economy. *J. Money, Credit, Banking*, August 1984, *16*(3), pp. 285–301.

Martin, Donald L. The Agency Problem in a Nonproprietary Theory of Union Behavior. In *Rosa, J.-J., ed.*, 1984, pp. 191–220.

Maruyama, Shigeru. Wage Stickiness and Unemployment Due to the Part of Firms. *Econ. Stud. Quart.*, December 1984, *35*(3), pp. 206–15.

Maynard, Geoffrey W. A Natural Interpretation of The Present Unemployment: Comment. In *Griffiths, B. and Wood, G. E., eds.*, 1984, pp. 172–75. **[G: U.K.; U.S.; EEC]**

McDonald, Ian M. Trying to Understand Stagflation. *Australian Econ. Rev.*, 3rd Quarter 1984, (67), pp. 32–56. **[G: Australia]**

McDonald, Ian M. and Solow, Robert M. Union Wage Policies: Reply [Wage Bargaining and Employment]. *Amer. Econ. Rev.*, September 1984, *74*(4), pp. 759–61.

McIntosh, James. An Oligopsonistic Model of Wage Determination in Agrarian Societies. *Econ. J.*, September 1984, *94*(375), pp. 569–79. **[G: LDCs]**

Menra, Naresh Kumar. Dualism and Surplus

Labour: A Case Study of Indian Agriculture. *Margin*, October 1984, *17*(1), pp. 48–54.

[G: India]

Merrick, John J., Jr. The Anticipated Real Interest Rate, Capital Utilization and the Cyclical Pattern of Real Wages. *J. Monet. Econ.*, January 1984, *13*(1), pp. 17–30. [G: U.S.]

de Meza, David. Wage Uncertainty, Expected Utility, and Occupation Choice. *Int. Econ. Rev.*, October 1984, *25*(3), pp. 757–62.

Micheli, Giuseppe A. Costruire un sistema informativo del mercato del lavoro "User Oriented": trasparenza dell'informazione, razionalità delle attese. (Building a Labour Market Information System "User Oriented": Information's Transparence, Expectations' Rationality. With English summary.) *Econ. Lavoro*, Apr.-June 1984, *18*(2), pp. 85–104. [G: Italy]

Mikhalkina, T. Y.; Lebedev, V. N. and Maryganova, E. A. Western Views of Wages and Unemployment. In *Smirnov, A. D.; Golosov, V. V. and Maximova, V. F., eds.*, 1984, pp. 71–87.

Miller, Paul W. and Volker, Paul A. The Screening Hypothesis: An Application of the Wiles Test. *Econ. Inquiry*, January 1984, *22*(1), pp. 121–27. [G: Australia]

Miller, Robert A. Job Matching and Occupational Choice. *J. Polit. Econ.*, December 1984, *92*(6), pp. 1086–120. [G: U.S.]

Minford, Patrick. A Review of *Unemployment: Cause and Cure*, by Patrick Minford with David Davies, Michael Peel and Alison Sprague: Response. *Econ. J.*, December 1984, *94*(376), pp. 954–59. [G: U.K.]

Minsky, Hyman P. and Ferri, Piero. Prices, Employment, and Profits. *J. Post Keynesian Econ.*, Summer 1984, *6*(4), pp. 489–99.

Mitchell, Olivia S. and Fields, Gary S. The Economics of Retirement Behavior. *J. Lab. Econ.*, January 1984, *2*(1), pp. 84–105. [G: U.S.]

Miyazaki, Hajime. Internal Bargaining, Labor Contracts, and a Marshallian Theory of the Firm. *Amer. Econ. Rev.*, June 1984, *74*(3), pp. 381–93.

Miyazaki, Hajime. Work Norms and Involuntary Unemployment. *Quart. J. Econ.*, May 1984, *99*(2), pp. 297–311.

Moffitt, Robert. Profiles of Fertility, Labour Supply and Wages of Married Women: A Complete Life-Cycle Model. *Rev. Econ. Stud.*, April 1984, *51*(2), pp. 263–78. [G: U.S.]

Moffitt, Robert. The Estimation of a Joint Wage-Hours Labor Supply Model. *J. Lab. Econ.*, October 1984, *2*(4), pp. 550–66. [G: U.S.]

Mohun, Simon. Abstract Labor and Its Value-Form. *Sci. Soc.*, Winter 1984-1985, *48*(4), pp. 388–406.

Montgomery, Edward. Aggregate Dynamics and Staggered Contracts: A Test of the Importance of Spillover Effects: A Note. *J. Money, Credit, Banking*, Part 1 November 1984, *16*(4), pp. 505–14. [G: U.S.]

Mori, Nobuhiro. The Oil Crises and the Phillips Curve. *Osaka Econ. Pap.*, March 1984, *33*(3–4), pp. 123–34. [G: Japan]

Münker, Horst. Reallohn and Marktmacht. (Real Wages and Market Power. With English summary.) *Jahr. Nationalökon. Statist.*, March 1984, *199*(2), pp. 123–44.

Myers, Samuel L., Jr. Labor Economics, Preferences, and the Rationality Assumption: A Comment on Blau, Dickens, and Malveaux. In *Darity, W., Jr., ed.*, 1984, pp. 257–68. [G: U.S.]

Nakatani, Iwao. Growth and Distribution Policy of the Firm and Workers' Morale. (In Japanese. With English summary.) *Osaka Econ. Pap.*, December 1984, *34*(2–3), pp. 189–202.

Neck, Reinhard. Keynesian and Monetarist Models of Unemployment and Inflation: A Simulation Study for Austria. *Empirica*, 1984, *11*(1), pp. 23–45. [G: Austria]

Neffa, Julio César. Enfoques alternativos para el análisis del empleo en los países en vías de desarrollo. (Alternative Focusing for the Analysis of Employment in Developing Countries. With English summary.) *Económica*, January-April 1984, *30*(1), pp. 3–33.

[G: Latin America]

Neipp, Joachim. Stabilitätspolitische Auswirkungen einer Reduzierung der Lohnfortzahlung bei Arbeitsunfähigkeit. (Reducing Social Benefits in Case of Disability to Work: A Contribution to the Achievement of Stabilization Policy Goals? With English summary.) *Jahr. Nationalökon. Statist.*, September 1984, *199*(5), pp. 401–14. [G: Germany]

Nickell, Stephen J. A Review of *Unemployment: Cause and Cure*, by Patrick Minford with David Davies, Michael Peel and Alison Sprague. *Econ. J.*, December 1984, *94*(376), pp. 946–53. [G: U.K.]

Nickell, Stephen J. Discussants' Comments on: A Natural Interpretation of the Present Unemployment, by Roy A. Batchelor, presented at the City University Conference on Monetarism in the United Kingdom, September 1981. In *Griffiths, B. and Wood, G. E., eds.*, 1984, pp. 176–81. [G: U.K.; U.S.; EEC]

Nickell, Stephen J. The Modelling of Wages and Employment. In *Hendry, D. F. and Wallis, K. F., eds.*, 1984, pp. 13–35.

Norris, Keith. Labour Markets from the Microeconomic Perspective: Implicit Contract Theory: Comment. *Australian Econ. Rev.*, 3rd Quarter 1984, (67), pp. 130–31.

O'Keeffe, Mary; Viscusi, W. Kip and Zeckhauser, Richard J. Economic Contests: Comparative Reward Schemes. *J. Lab. Econ.*, January 1984, *2*(1), pp. 27–56.

Oi, Walter Y. A Comment on the Ashenfelter Analysis of Labor Market Fluctuations [Macroeconomic Analyses and Microeconomic Analyses of Labor Supply]. *Carnegie-Rochester Conf. Ser. Public Policy*, Autumn 1984, *21*, pp. 157–72. [G: U.S.; U.K.; Canada]

Okuno, Masahiro. Corporate Loyalty and Bonus Payments: An Analysis of Work Incentives in Japan. In *Aoki, M., ed.*, 1984, pp. 387–411.

[G: Japan]

Opromolla, Paolo. Indicizzazione saliare a punto unico e a punto variabile: un'analisi teorica.

(Wage Indexation at a Single and Fixed Point, and at a Flexible Point: A Theoretical Analysis. With English summary.) *Giorn. Econ.*, July–August 1984, *43*(7–8), pp. 547–61.

Ordover, Janusz A. and Shapiro, Carl. Advances in Supervision Technology and Economic Welfare: A General Equilibrium Analysis. *J. Public Econ.*, December 1984, *25*(3), pp. 371–89.

Osborne, Martin J. Capitalist–Worker Conflict and Involuntary Unemployment. *Rev. Econ. Stud.*, January 1984, *51*(1), pp. 111–27.

Oswald, Andrew J. Three Theorems on Inflation Taxes and Marginal Employment Subsidies. *Econ. J.*, September 1984, *94*(375), pp. 599–611.

Oswald, Andrew J. Wage and Employment Structure in an Economy with Internal Labor Markets. *Quart. J. Econ.*, November 1984, *99*(4), pp. 693–716.

Paldam, Martin. Ved Phillipskurvens sølvbryllup—Hvad ved vi om løndannelsen? (At the Silver Wedding of the Phillips Curve—What Have We Learned about Wage Formation? With English summary.) *Nationaløkon. Tidsskr.*, 1984, *122*(1), pp. 133–51.
[G: OECD; U.S.]

Pemberton, James. Equilibrium Unemployment and the Long-run Phillips Curve in a Partially Unionized Economy. *Manchester Sch. Econ. Soc. Stud.*, December 1984, *52*(4), pp. 402–16.

Pemberton, James. The Long Run Phillips Curve and the Government Budget Constraint. *Scot. J. Polit. Econ.*, November 1984, *31*(3), pp. 255–64.

Pencavel, John H. The Empirical Performance of a Model of Trade Union Behavior. In *Rosa, J.-J., ed.*, 1984, pp. 221–76. [G: U.S.]

Pencavel, John H. The Tradeoff between Wages and Employment in Trade Union Objectives. *Quart. J. Econ.*, May 1984, *99*(2), pp. 215–31. [G: U.S.]

Pesando, James E. Employee Evaluation of Pension Claims and the Impact of Indexing Initiatives. *Econ. Inquiry*, January 1984, *22*(1), pp. 1–17. [G: U.S.; Canada]

Piacentini, Paolo. The Real Wage/Employment Relationship in the Short-Run in Flex-Price and Fix-Price Markets. *Econ. Notes*, 1984, (1), pp. 87–108.

Pickles, Andrew and Rogerson, Peter A. Wage Distributions and Spatial Preferences in Competitive Job Search and Migration. *Reg. Stud.*, April 1984, *18*(2), pp. 131–42.

Piersanti, Giovanni. Tasso naturale di disoccupazione, aspettative razionali e incertezza sul tasso di inflazione: alcune evidenze empiriche per l'Italia. (Natural Rate of Unemployment, Rational Expectations and Inflation Uncertainty: Some Empirical Evidence for Italy. With English summary.) *Giorn. Econ.*, May–June 1984, *43*(5–6), pp. 369–92. [G: Italy]

Pissarides, Christopher A. Efficient Job Rejection. *Econ. J.*, 1984 Supplement, *94*, pp. 97–108.

Pissarides, Christopher A. Search Intensity, Job

Advertising, and Efficiency. *J. Lab. Econ.*, January 1984, *2*(1), pp. 128–43.

Plant, Mark W. An Empirical Analysis of Welfare Dependence. *Amer. Econ. Rev.*, September 1984, *74*(4), pp. 673–84. [G: U.S.]

Pohjola, Matti. Union Rivalry and Economic Growth: A Differential Game Approach. *Scand. J. Econ.*, 1984, *86*(3), pp. 365–70.

Prescott, Edward C. and Townsend, Robert M. Pareto Optima and Competitive Equilibria with Adverse Selection and Moral Hazard. *Econometrica*, January 1984, *52*(1), pp. 21–45.

Qadir, Asghar. Educated Unemployed, Educational Subsidies, and Growth: Comment. *Pakistan Devel. Rev.*, Summer-Autumn 1984, *23*(2&3), pp. 411–12.

Radner, Roy and Stiglitz, Joseph E. A Nonconcavity in the Value of Information. In *Boyer, M. and Kihlstrom, R. E., eds.*, 1984, pp. 33–52.

Raschke, Freddy. Demographic Influences on the Mobility of German Labor Stock. In *Steinmann, G., ed.*, 1984, pp. 323–42.
[G: W. Germany]

Ravallion, Martin. How Much Is a Transfer Payment Worth to a Rural Worker? *Oxford Econ. Pap.*, November 1984, *36*(3), pp. 478–89.
[G: LDCs]

Reder, Melvin W. Strike Cost and Wage Rates: Cross-Industry Differences. In *Rosa, J.-J., ed.*, 1984, pp. 27–37. [G: U.S.]

Reich, Michael. Segmented Labour: Time Series Hypothesis and Evidence. *Cambridge J. Econ.*, March 1984, *8*(1), pp. 63–81.
[G: U.S.]

Reichlin, Lucrezia. Il sistema di assicurazione alla disoccupazione negli Stati Uniti: descrizione del sistema e rassegna del dibattito teorico. (Unemployment Insurance in the United States: Practical Working of the System and Review of Theoretical Literature. With English summary.) *Econ. Lavoro*, Oct.-Dec. 1984, *18*(4), pp. 17–33. [G: U.S.]

Renaud, Paul S. A. and Siegers, Jacques J. Income and Substitution Effects in Family Labour Supply. *De Economist*, 1984, *132*(3), pp. 350–66. [G: Netherlands; U.S.]

Riebel, Volker. Arbeitszeitverkürzung und Schwarzarbeit. Auswirkungen einer Verkürzung der Wochenarbeitszeit auf das individuelle Arbeitsangebot. (Shorter Work Week and Moonlighting. Effects of a Reduction of Work Week on Individual Labour Supply. With English summary.) *Z. Wirtschaft. Sozialwissen.*, 1984, *104*(5), pp. 515–38.

Rima, Ingrid H. Involuntary Unemployment and the Respecified Labor Supply Curve. *J. Post Keynesian Econ.*, Summer 1984, *6*(4), pp. 540–50.

Rima, Ingrid H. Whatever Happened to the Concept of Involuntary Unemployment? *Int. J. Soc. Econ.*, 1984, *11*(3/4), pp. 62–71.

Roemer, John E. Exploitation, Class, and Property Relations. In *Ball, T. and Farr, J., eds.*, 1984, pp. 184–211.

Romer, David. The Theory of Social Custom: A

Modification and Some Extensions. *Quart. J. Econ.*, November 1984, *99*(4), pp. 717–27.

Rosa, Jean-Jacques. Toward a Theory of the Union Firm. In *Rosa, J.-J., ed.*, 1984, pp. 157–86.

Rosenberg, Jacob. Wage Indexation and Labour Market Indicators: A Proposal. *Econ. Int.*, February–May 1984, *37*(1–2), pp. 123–29.

Rosenzweig, Mark R. Determinants of Wage Rates and Labor Supply Behavior in the Rural Sector of a Developing Country. In *Binswanger, H. P. and Rosenzweig, R., eds.*, 1984, pp. 211–41. **[G: India]**

Rosner, Peter, et al. Lohnbestimmung, aussenwirtschaftliche Stabilität und internationale Stagnation. (Wage Determination, External Economic Stability and International Stagnation. With English summary.) *Jahr. Nationalökon. Statist.*, May 1984, *199*(3), pp. 193–212. **[G: Global]**

Rossana, Robert J. A Model of the Demand for Investment in Inventories of Finished Goods and Employment. *Int. Econ. Rev.*, October 1984, *25*(3), pp. 731–41.

Roth, Alvin E. Stability and Polarization of Interests in Job Matching. *Econometrica*, January 1984, *52*(1), pp. 47–57.

Roth, Alvin E. The Evolution of the Labor Market for Medical Interns and Residents: A Case Study in Game Theory. *J. Polit. Econ.*, December 1984, *92*(6), pp. 991–1016. **[G: U.S.]**

Sampson, Anthony A. Unemployment and the Distribution of Income. *Australian Econ. Pap.*, December 1984, *23*(43), pp. 249–58.

Sattinger, Michael. Factor Pricing in the Assignment Problem. *Scand. J. Econ.*, 1984, *86*(1), pp. 17–34.

Schiller, Bradley R. Job-Search Clubs for Dislocated Workers. *Challenge*, May/June 1984, *27*(2), pp. 51–55. **[G: U.S.]**

Schlicht, Ekkehart. Plant Closings, Worker Reallocation Costs and Efficiency Gains to Labor Representation on Board of Directors: Comment. *Z. ges. Staatswiss.*, March 1984, *140*(1), pp. 193–94.

Schmid, Günther. The Political Economy of Labor Market Discrimination: A Theoretical and Comparative Analysis of Sex Discrimination. In *Schmid, G. and Weitzel, R., eds.*, 1984, pp. 264–308. **[G: Sweden; U.K.; U.S.; W. Germany Managemt,]**

Schmidt, Rainer. Population Change, Labour Market and Unemployment—The Case of the German Domestic Labour Force from 1965–1982. In *Steinmann, G., ed.*, 1984, pp. 278–94. **[G: W. Germany]**

Schott, Kerry. Investment, Order and Conflict in a Simple Dynamic Model of Capitalism. In *Goldthorpe, J. H., ed.*, 1984, pp. 81–97.

Sekine, Thomas T. An Uno School Seminar on the Theory of Value. *Sci. Soc.*, Winter 1984-1985, *48*(4), pp. 419–32.

Sen, Amartya. Control Areas and Accounting Prices: An Approach to Economic Evaluation. In *Sen, A.*, 1984, *1972*, pp. 224–41.

Sen, Amartya. Employment, Institutions and Technology: Some Policy Issues. In *Sen, A.*, 1984, *1975*, pp. 242–73. **[G: LDCs]**

Sen, Amartya. Labour Allocation in a Cooperative Enterprise. In *Sen, A.*, 1984, *1966*, pp. 72–89.

Sgontz, L. G. Efficiency and the Tax Treatment of Secondary Workers. *Nat. Tax J.*, June 1984, *37*(2), pp. 249–52.

Shaked, Avner and Sutton, John. Involuntary Unemployment as a Perfect Equilibrium in a Bargaining Model. *Econometrica*, November 1984, *52*(6), pp. 1351–64.

Shapiro, Carl and Stiglitz, Joseph E. Equilibrium Unemployment as a Worker Discipline Device. *Amer. Econ. Rev.*, June 1984, *74*(3), pp. 433–44.

Shimomura, Kazuo. A Simple General Equilibrium Model Involving a Maximizing Labour Union. *Kobe Econ. Bus. Rev.*, 1984, *30*, pp. 87–96.

Shorey, John. Employment Discrimination and the Employer Tastes Model. *Scot. J. Polit. Econ.*, June 1984, *31*(2), pp. 157–75.

Sloan, Judith and Wooden, Mark. Labour Markets from the Microeconomic Perspective: Implicit Contract Theory. *Australian Econ. Rev.*, 3rd Quarter 1984, (67), pp. 120–29.

Smeets, Heinz-Dieter. Wechselkurssystem und Phillips-Kurve. (Exchange Rate System and Phillips Curve. With English summary.) *Kredit Kapital*, 1984, *17*(3), pp. 396–403. **[G: W. Germany]**

Smith, Stephen C. Does Employment Matter to the Labour-managed Firm? Some Theory and an Empirical Illustration. *Econ. Anal. Worker's Manage.*, 1984, *18*(4), pp. 303–18. **[G: U.S.; Italy]**

Smithin, John Nicholas. Medio and Musu's Keynesian Analysis of Money Wage Changes: A Comment [Changes in Money Wages and Employment in a Keynesian Analysis]. *Econ. Notes*, 1984, (3), pp. 167–71.

Smyth, David J. Short-Run Employment Functions When the Speed of Adjustment Depends on the Unemployment Rate. *Rev. Econ. Statist.*, February 1984, *66*(1), pp. 138–42. **[G: OECD]**

Sorensen, Elaine. Equal Pay for Comparable Worth: A Policy for Eliminating the Undervaluation of Women's Work. *J. Econ. Issues*, June 1984, *18*(2), pp. 465–72. **[G: U.S.]**

Spreen, Thomas H. An Intertemporal Approach to Seasonal Agricultural Labor Markets. In *Emerson, R. D., ed.*, 1984, pp. 230–49.

Standing, Guy. The Notion of Technological Unemployment. *Int. Lab. Rev.*, March-April 1984, *123*(2), pp. 127–47.

Steigum, Erling, Jr. Intersectoral Transfer of Labour in a Small Open Economy. *Europ. Econ. Rev.*, March 1984, *24*(2), pp. 225–37.

Stenius, Marianne and Virén, Matti. Some Further Results on Rosen and Quandt's Labor Market Model. *Europ. Econ. Rev.*, December 1984, *26*(3), pp. 369–77. **[G: U.S.]**

Stewart, Geoff. Labour-managed Firms and Monopsony Power. *Int. J. Ind. Organ.*, March 1984, *2*(1), pp. 63–74.

Stiglitz, Joseph E. Information, Screening, and Welfare. In *Boyer, M. and Kihlstrom, R. E., eds.*, 1984, pp. 209–39.

Storper, Michael and Walker, Richard. The Spatial Division of Labor: Labor and the Location of Industries. In *Sawers, L. and Tabb, W. K., eds.*, 1984, pp. 19–47.

Stournaras, Yannis A. Optimal Taxes and Subsidies in Fix-Price, Open Economies. *Oxford Econ. Pap.*, November 1984, *36*(3), pp. 459–77.

Straszheim, Mahlon R. Urban Agglomeration Effects and Employment and Wage Gradients. *J. Urban Econ.*, September 1984, *16*(2), pp. 187–207.

Takagi, Yasuoki. Urban Unemployment and Rural–Urban Migration in LDC's: A Survey. (In Japanese. With English summary.) *Econ. Stud. Quart.*, December 1984, *35*(3), pp. 216–29. **[G: LDCs]**

Tinbergen, Jan. Allocation of Workers over Jobs. *De Economist*, 1984, *132*(1), pp. 23–29. **[G: U.S.]**

Tirelli, Daniele. Osservazioni sui modelli allocativi del consumo e del tempo di lavoro. (Some Observations on Allocative Models of Consumption and Leisure. With English summary.) *Econ. Lavoro*, Jan.-Mar. 1984, *18*(1), pp. 53–75. **[G: W. Europe; U.S.; Canada; Australia]**

Tisdell, Clem A. and Fairbairn, T'eo Ian. Labor Supply Constraints on Industrialization, and Production Deficiencies in Traditional Sharing Societies. *J. Econ. Devel.*, December 1984, *9*(2), pp. 7–23. **[G: LDCs]**

Toker, Mehmet Ayhan. A Note on the 'Negative' Quantities of Embodied Labour. *Econ. J.*, March 1984, *94*(373), pp. 149–54.

Topel, Robert H. Equilibrium Earnings, Turnover, and Unemployment: New Evidence. *J. Lab. Econ.*, October 1984, *2*(4), pp. 500–522. **[G: U.S.]**

Triplett, Jack E. A Conceptual Model for Labor Market Data. *Rev. Public Data Use*, March 1984, *12*(1), pp. 1–16.

Tullock, Gordon. Toward a Theory of the Union Firm: Comment. In *Rosa, J.-J., ed.*, 1984, pp. 187–89.

Uthoff, Andras and Riveros, Luis. La Curva de Phillips y el sector urbano informal Chile, 1964–1981. (With English summary.) *Cuadernos Econ.*, April 1984, *21*(62), pp. 63–81. **[G: Chile]**

Van Rompuy, G. The Effect of Unemployment Legislation on Labor Supply Decisions. *Tijdschrift Econ. Manage.*, 1984, *29*(2), pp. 217–31. **[G: Belgium]**

Vasche, Jon David. Unemployment Benefits for Work Sharing: A Further Consideration. *Bus. Econ.*, April 1984, *19*(3), pp. 59–61. **[G: U.S.]**

Waits, C. Richard and McNertney, Edward M. An Economic Model of Artistic Behavior. *J. Cult. Econ.*, June 1984, *8*(1), pp. 49–60.

Waldman, Michael. Job Assignments, Signalling, and Efficiency. *Rand J. Econ.*, Summer 1984, *15*(2), pp. 255–67.

Waldman, Michael. Worker Allocation, Hierarchies and the Wage Distribution. *Rev. Econ. Stud.*, January 1984, *51*(1), pp. 95–109.

Warner, John T. and Goldberg, Matthew S. The Influence of Non-Pecuniary Factors on Labor Supply: The Case of Navy Enlisted Personnel. *Rev. Econ. Statist.*, February 1984, *66*(1), pp. 26–35. **[G: U.S.]**

Weiss, Andrew. Determinants of Quit Behavior. *J. Lab. Econ.*, July 1984, *2*(3), pp. 371–87. **[G: U.S.]**

Weiss, Andrew and Landau, Henry J. Wages, Hiring Standards, and Firm Size. *J. Lab. Econ.*, October 1984, *2*(4), pp. 477–99. **[G: U.S.]**

Weiss, Yoram. Wage Contracts When Output Grows Stochastically: The Roles of Mobility Costs and Capital Market Imperfections. *J. Lab. Econ.*, April 1984, *2*(2), pp. 155–73.

Wilde, James A. Labor Supply and Tax Rates: Comment. *Amer. Econ. Rev.*, December 1984, *74*(5), pp. 1103–07.

Williams, Rhonda M. The Methodology and Practice of Modern Labor Economics: A Critique. In *Darity, W., Jr., ed.*, 1984, pp. 23–51.

Wolcowitz, Jeffrey. Dynamic Effects of the Unemployment Insurance Tax on Temporary Layoffs. *J. Public Econ.*, November 1984, *25*(1/2), pp. 35–51.

Wolfstetter, Elmar; Brown, Murray and Meran, Georg. Optimal Employment and Risk Sharing in Illyria: The Labor Managed Firm Reconsidered. *Z. ges. Staatswiss.*, December 1984, *140*(4), pp. 655–68.

Woodbury, Stephen A. Occupational Safety and Health Regulation and Economic Theory: Comment. In *Darity, W., Jr., ed.*, 1984, pp. 269–78.

Yellen, Janet L. Efficiency Wage Models of Unemployment. *Amer. Econ. Rev.*, May 1984, *74*(2), pp. 200–205.

Zamagni, Stefano. Ricardo and Hayek Effects in a Fixwage Model of Traverse. *Oxford Econ. Pap.*, Supplement November 1984, *36*, pp. 135–51.

Zamagni, Stefano. Ricardo and Hayek Effects in a Fixwage Model of Traverse. In *Collard, D. A., et al., eds.*, 1984, pp. 135–51.

Zarca, Bernard. Travail familial et travail salarié: un modèle de formation du revenu des artisans. (Family Work and Wage Work: A Model of Artisans Income Formation. With English summary.) *Consommation*, Oct.–Dec. 1984, *31*(4), pp. 3–27. **[G: France]**

Zarembka, Paul. A Comment on the Market in Labor Power. In *Darity, W., Jr., ed.*, 1984, pp. 279–84.

Zubrzycki, Jerzy. Immigration and Population Change in Australia: A Test of the Dual Labour Market Hypothesis. In *Steinmann, G., ed.*, 1984, pp. 360–85. **[G: Australia]**

Zuckerman, Dror. On Preserving the Reservation Wage Property in a Continuous Job Search

Model. *J. Econ. Theory*, October 1984, *34*(1), pp. 175–79.

822 Public Policy; Role of Government

8220 General

Aaron, Benjamin. Future Trends in Industrial Relations Law. *Ind. Relat.*, Winter 1984, *23*(1), pp. 52–57. **[G: U.S.]**

Balassa, Bela. Prices, Incentives, and Economic Growth. *Weltwirtsch. Arch.*, 1984, *120*(4), pp. 611–30. **[G: Global]**

Balassa, Bela. The Economic Consequences of Social Policies in the Industrial Countries. *Weltwirtsch. Arch.*, 1984, *120*(2), pp. 213–27. **[G: U.S.; EEC]**

Balcer, Yves and Sahin, Izzet. Dynamics of Pension Reform: The Case of Ontario. *J. Risk Ins.*, December 1984, *51*(4), pp. 652–86. **[G: Canada]**

Banting, Keith G. The Decision Rules: Federalism and Pension Reform. In *Conklin, D. W.; Bennett, J. H. and Courchene, T. J., eds.*, 1984, pp. 189–209. **[G: Canada]**

Cain, Glen. Estimating the Impact of Labor Market Policies on Women: A Discussion of the Four-Country Studies on the Employment of Women. In *Schmid, G. and Weitzel, R., eds.*, 1984, pp. 249–63. **[G: Sweden; U.K.; U.S.; W. Germany]**

Coffey, Joseph D. The California Agricultural Labor Relations Act and National Agricultural Labor Relations Legislation: Discussion. In *Emerson, R. D., ed.*, 1984, pp. 370–75. **[G: U.S.]**

Córdova, Efrén. Industrial Relations in Latin America: Tripartite Cooperation. In *Cérdova, E., ed.*, 1984, pp. 147–66. **[G: Latin America]**

Córdova, Efrén. Industrial Relations in Latin America: Departments of Labor. In *Cérdova, E., ed.*, 1984, pp. 69–83. **[G: Latin America]**

Dickens, Linda, et al. The British Experience under a Statute Prohibiting Unfair Dismissal. *Ind. Lab. Relat. Rev.*, July 1984, *37*(4), pp. 497–514. **[G: U.K.]**

Disney, Richard and Szyszczak, E. M. Protective Legislation and Part-Time Employment in Britain. *Brit. J. Ind. Relat.*, March 1984, *22*(1), pp. 78–100. **[G: U.K.]**

Dror, David M. Aspects of Labour Law and Relations in Selected Export Processing Zones. *Int. Lab. Rev.*, November–December 1984, *123*(6), pp. 705–22. **[G: Mauritius; Sri Lanka; Pakistan; Philippines]**

Emerson, Robert D. Seasonal Agricultural Labor Markets in the United States: Summary. In *Emerson, R. D., ed.*, 1984, pp. 482–523. **[G: U.S.]**

Erven, Bernard L. Impact of Labor Laws and Regulations on Agricultural Labor Markets. In *Emerson, R. D., ed.*, 1984, pp. 376–405. **[G: U.S.]**

Folbre, Nancy R.; Leighton, Julia L. and Roder-ick, **Melissa R.** Plant Closings and Their Regulation in Maine, 1971–1982. *Ind. Lab. Relat. Rev.*, January 1984, 37(2), pp. 185–96. **[G: U.S.]**

Ford, William D. Statements in Support of the National Employment Priorities Act. In *McKenzie, R. B., ed. (II)*, 1984, pp. 315–27. **[G: U.S.]**

Gitelman, H. M. Being of Two Minds: American Employers Confront the Labor Problem, 1915–1919. *Labor Hist.*, Spring 1984, *25*(2), pp. 189–216. **[G: U.S.]**

Harrison, Bennett. The International Movement for Prenotification of Plant Closures. *Ind. Relat.*, Fall 1984, *23*(3), pp. 387–409. **[G: U.S.; Europe]**

Hayes, Sue Eileen. The California Agricultural Labor Relations Act and National Agricultural Labor Relations Legislation. In *Emerson, R. D., ed.*, 1984, pp. 328–70. **[G: U.S.]**

Horn, Ernst-Jürgen. Reassessing Consumer Safety Regulation: Comment. In *Giersch, H., ed.*, 1984, pp. 216–21.

Marshall, Ray. Selective Employment Programs and Economic Policy. *J. Econ. Issues*, March 1984, *18*(1), pp. 117–42. **[G: U.S.]**

Mayer, Jean. Regional Employment Development: The Evolution of Theory and Practice. *Int. Lab. Rev.*, January–February 1984, *123*(1), pp. 17–34. **[G: Global]**

McKenzie, Richard B. Summary Remarks. In *McKenzie, R. B., ed. (II)*, 1984, pp. 309–13. **[G: U.S.]**

McKenzie, Richard B. The Case for Plant Closures. In *McKenzie, R. B., ed. (II)*, 1984, *1981*, pp. 205–19. **[G: U.S.]**

McMurray, David. Labour Legislation and Policy: Summary Outline. In *Wood, W. D. and Kumar, P., eds.*, 1984, pp. 93–216. **[G: Canada]**

Munnell, Alicia H. ERISA—The First Decade: Was the Legislation Consistent with Other National Goals? *New Eng. Econ. Rev.*, November–December 1984, pp. 44–63. **[G: U.S.]**

Nelson, Richard R. State Labor Legislation Enacted in 1983. *Mon. Lab. Rev.*, January 1984, *107*(1), pp. 59–75. **[G: U.S.]**

Polopolus, Leo. Impact of Labor Laws and Regulations on Agricultural Labor Markets: Discussion. In *Emerson, R. D., ed.*, 1984, pp. 406–11. **[G: U.S.]**

Sengenberger, Werner. West German Employment Policy: Restoring Worker Competition. *Ind. Relat.*, Fall 1984, *23*(3), pp. 323–43. **[G: W. Germany]**

Shalev, Michael. Labor, State, and Crisis: An Israeli Case Study. *Ind. Relat.*, Fall 1984, *23*(3), pp. 362–86. **[G: Israel]**

Soskice, David. Industrial Relations and the British Economy, 1979–1983. *Ind. Relat.*, Fall 1984, *23*(3), pp. 306–22. **[G: U.K.]**

Streit, Manfred E. Reassessing Consumer Safety Regulation. In *Giersch, H., ed.*, 1984, pp. 190–215. **[G: W. Germany]**

Süssekind, Arnaldo. The Influence of International Labour Standards on Brazilian Legislation. *Int. Lab. Rev.*, July–August 1984, *123*(4), pp. 441–56. **[G: Brazil]**

8221 Wages and Hours

Dieguez, Héctor L. and Gerchunoff, Pablo. La dinámica del mercado laboral urbano en la Argentina, 1976–1981. (With English summary.) *Desarrollo Econ.*, April–June 1984, *24*(93), pp. 3–40. **[G: Argentina]**

Fethke, Gary C. and Policano, Andrew J. Cyclical Implications of Indexing the Minimum Wage. *J. Macroecon.*, Winter 1984, *6*(1), pp. 1–21. **[G: U.S.]**

Fraundorf, Martha Norby; Farrell, John P. and Mason, Robert. The Effect of the Davis–Bacon Act on Construction Costs in Rural Areas. *Rev. Econ. Statist.*, February 1984, *66*(1), pp. 142–46. **[G: U.S.]**

Glucklich, Pauline. The Effects of Statutory Employment Policies on Women in the United Kingdom Labour Market. In *Schmid, G. and Weitzel, R., eds.*, 1984, pp. 107–31. **[G: U.K.]**

Goldfarb, Robert S. A Davis–Bacon Musicale: Symphony Orchestras as Migrant Labor. *J. Lab. Res.*, Fall 1984, *5*(4), pp. 427–33. **[G: U.S.]**

Hojman, David E. Minimum Wages, Union Membership, and Differentials: The Phillips Curve and the Chilean Labour Market Revisited. *J. Econ. Stud.*, 1984, *11*(4), pp. 3–22. **[G: Chile]**

Hunnicutt, Benjamin Kline. The End of Shorter Hours. *Labor Hist.*, Summer 1984, *25*(3), pp. 373–404. **[G: U.S.]**

Hylton, Keith. Illusory Wage Differentials: Comment [The Narrowing of Black–White Wage Differentials Is Illusory]. *Amer. Econ. Rev.*, December 1984, *74*(5), pp. 1124–27. **[G: U.S.]**

Lange, Peter. Unions, Workers and Wage Regulation: The Rational Bases of Consent. In *Goldthorpe, J. H., ed.*, 1984, pp. 98–123.

Lazear, Edward P. Illusory Wage Differentials: Reply. *Amer. Econ. Rev.*, December 1984, *74*(5), pp. 1128.

McKee, Michael and West, Edwin G. Minimum Wage Effects on Part-time Employment. *Econ. Inquiry*, July 1984, *22*(3), pp. 421–28. **[G: U.S.; Canada]**

Meyer-Thomas, Gerold. Vom Sinn und Unsinn der 35-Stunden-Woche. (Sense and Nonsense of the 35-Hour Working Week. With English summary.) *Z. Wirtschaft. Sozialwissen.*, 1984, *104*(5), pp. 489–513. **[G: W. Germany]**

Sellekaerts, Brigitte H. and Welch, Stephen W. An Econometric Analysis of Minimum Wage Noncompliance. *Ind. Relat.*, Spring 1984, *23*(2), pp. 244–59. **[G: U.S.]**

Tomášek, Přemysl. Egalitarianism Is Harmful. *Czech. Econ. Digest.*, June 1984, (4), pp. 3–13. **[G: Czechoslovakia]**

8222 Workmen's Compensation and Vocational Rehabilitation

Angel, Ronald. The Costs of Disability for Hispanic Males. *Soc. Sci. Quart.*, June 1984, *65*(2), pp. 426–43. **[G: U.S.]**

Baglini, Norman A. Towards a Comprehensive Compensation Programme. *Int. J. Soc. Econ.*, 1984, *11*(1/2), pp. 41–48. **[G: U.S.]**

Benjamin, Daniel K. Insurance in the Workplace: Experience Is the Best Guide. In *Moore, J. H., ed.*, 1984, pp. 153–68. **[G: U.S.]**

Bissell, Thomas St.G.; Skadden, Donald H. and White, Frederic E. Social Security Contributions as a Fiscal Burden on Enterprises Engaged in International Activities: United States. In *Intn'l. Fisc. Assoc., vol. 69b*, 1984, pp. 317–37. **[G: U.S.]**

Cho, Dongsae. Rehabilitation for Workers' Compensation Loss Exposures. *J. Risk Ins.*, March 1984, *51*(1), pp. 80–98. **[G: U.S.]**

Emanuel, Han; Halberstadt, Victor and Petersen, Carel. Disability Policy in the Netherlands. In *Haveman, R. H.; Halberstadt, V. and Burkhauser, R. V.*, 1984, pp. 399–443. **[G: Netherlands]**

Englander, Valerie. Treatment and Comparison Groups in an Evaluation of Vocational Rehabilitation: Comparability, Costs and Other Issues [A Cost Effectiveness Evaluation of the Federal/State Vocational Rehabilitation Program—Using a Comparison Group]. *Amer. Econ.*, Fall 1984, *28*(2), pp. 71–73. **[G: U.S.]**

Habib, Jack; Factor, Haim and Mor, Vincent. Disability Policy in Israel. In *Haveman, R. H.; Halberstadt, V. and Burkhauser, R. V.*, 1984, pp. 292–345. **[G: Israel]**

Haveman, Robert H.; Halberstadt, Victor and Burkhauser, Richard V. An Economic View of Disability and Disability Policy. In *Haveman, R. H.; Halberstadt, V. and Burkhauser, R. V.*, 1984, pp. 28–43.

Haveman, Robert H.; Halberstadt, Victor and Burkhauser, Richard V. Approaches to Disability Policy: The United States System in a Comparative Assessment with Other Industrialized Nations. In *Haveman, R. H.; Halberstadt, V. and Burkhauser, R. V.*, 1984, pp. 44–80. **[G: U.S.; Israel; Selected OECD]**

Haveman, Robert H.; Halberstadt, Victor and Burkhauser, Richard V. Fundamental Issues in the Evolution of Disability Policy. In *Haveman, R. H.; Halberstadt, V. and Burkhauser, R. V.*, 1984, pp. 172–87.

Haveman, Robert H.; Halberstadt, Victor and Burkhauser, Richard V. Public Policy toward Disabled Workers: The Ameliorative Response: Effects on Program Growth and Labor Supply. In *Haveman, R. H.; Halberstadt, V. and Burkhauser, R. V.*, 1984, pp. 81–116. **[G: OECD; Israel]**

Haveman, Robert H.; Halberstadt, Victor and Burkhauser, Richard V. Public Policy toward Disabled Workers: Corrective Responses: Approaches and Outcomes. In *Haveman,*

R. H.; Halberstadt, V. and Burkhauser, R. V., 1984, pp. 135–71. [G: OECD]

Haveman, Robert H.; Halberstadt, Victor and Burkhauser, Richard V. Public Policy toward Disabled Workers: Ameliorative Responses: Has Adequacy Been Guaranteed? In Haveman, R. H.; Halberstadt, V. and Burkhauser, R. V., 1984, pp. 117–34. [G: OECD; Israel]

Haveman, Robert H.; Halberstadt, Victor and Burkhauser, Richard V. The Economics of Disability Policy toward Those of Working Age: An Introduction. In Haveman, R. H.; Halberstadt, V. and Burkhauser, R. V., 1984, pp. 3–7.

Haveman, Robert H.; Halberstadt, Victor and Burkhauser, Richard V. The Extent and Character of Measured Disability among the Working-Age Population. In Haveman, R. H.; Halberstadt, V. and Burkhauser, R. V., 1984, pp. 8–27. [G: U.S.; OECD]

Haveman, Robert H. and Wolfe, Barbara L. Disability Transfers and Early Retirement: A Causal Relationship? J. Public Econ., June 1984, 24(1), pp. 47–66. [G: W. Europe; U.S.]

d'Intignano, Beatrice Majnoni and Repellin, Jacqueline. Disability Policy in France. In Haveman, R. H.; Halberstadt, V. and Burkhauser, R. V., 1984, pp. 240–91. [G: France]

Leigh, J. Paul and Folsom, Roger N. Estimates of the Value of Accident Avoidance at the Job Depend on the Concavity of the Equalizing Differences Curve. Quart. Rev. Econ. Bus., Spring 1984, 24(1), pp. 56–66. [G: U.S.]

McCrostie, M. J. and Peacock, Alan. Disability Policy in the United Kingdom. In Haveman, R. H.; Halberstadt, V. and Burkhauser, R. V., 1984, pp. 517–73. [G: U.K.]

Neipp, Joachim. Stabilitätspolitische Auswirkungen einer Reduzierung der Lohnfortzahlung bei Arbeitsunfähigkeit. (Reducing Social Benefits in Case of Disability to Work: A Contribution to the Achievement of Stabilization Policy Goals? With English summary.) Jahr. Nationalökon. Statist., September 1984, 199(5), pp. 401–14. [G: Germany]

Nowak, Laura. Reply to Englander's Comments [A Cost Effectiveness Evaluation of the Federal/State Vocational Rehabilitation Program—Using a Comparison Group]. Amer. Econ., Fall 1984, 28(2), pp. 74–75. [G: U.S.]

Parsons, Donald O. Disability Insurance and Male Labor Force Participation: A Response. J. Polit. Econ., June 1984, 92(3), pp. 542–49. [G: U.S.]

Pfaff, Martin and Huber, Walter. Disability Policy in the Federal Republic of Germany. In Haveman, R. H.; Halberstadt, V. and Burkhauser, R. V., 1984, pp. 193–239. [G: W. Germany]

Slade, Frederic P. Older Men: Disability Insurance and the Incentive to Work. Ind. Relat., Spring 1984, 23(2), pp. 260–69. [G: U.S.]

Tinsley, LaVerne C. Workers' Compensation: Significant Enactments in 1983. Mon. Lab. Rev., February 1984, 107(2), pp. 55–61. [G: U.S.]

Vitali, Lucia. Disability Policy in Italy. In Haveman, R. H.; Halberstadt, V. and Burkhauser, R. V., 1984, pp. 346–98. [G: Italy]

Wadensjö, Eskil. Disability Policy in Sweden. In Haveman, R. H.; Halberstadt, V. and Burkhauser, R. V., 1984, pp. 444–516. [G: Sweden]

8223 Factory Act and Safety Legislation

Anderson, Gary M. and Tollison, Robert D. A Rent-Seeking Explanation of the British Factory Acts. In Colander, D. C., ed., 1984, pp. 187–201. [G: U.K.]

Bequele, Assefa. The Costs and Benefits of Protecting and Saving Lives at Work: Some Issues. Int. Lab. Rev., January-February 1984, 123(1), pp. 1–16.

Dickens, William T. Differences between Risk Premiums in Union and Nonunion Wages and the Case for Occupational Safety Regulation. Amer. Econ. Rev., May 1984, 74(2), pp. 320–23. [G: U.S.]

Dickens, William T. Occupational Safety and Health Regulation and Economic Theory. In Darity, W., Jr., ed., 1984, pp. 133–73. [G: U.S.]

Hrezo, Margaret S. and Hrezo, William E. Judicial Regulation of the Environment under Posner's Economic Model of the Law. J. Econ. Issues, December 1984, 18(4), pp. 1071–91. [G: U.S.]

Macon, Janet. BLS' 1982 Survey of Work-Related Deaths. Mon. Lab. Rev., March 1984, 107(3), pp. 43–45. [G: U.S.]

Miller, James C., III. Is Organized Labor Rational in Supporting OSHA? Southern Econ. J., January 1984, 50(3), pp. 881–85. [G: U.S.]

Myers, Samuel L., Jr. Labor Economics, Preferences, and the Rationality Assumption: A Comment on Blau, Dickens, and Malveaux. In Darity, W., Jr., ed., 1984, pp. 257–68. [G: U.S.]

Peacock, A. E. The Successful Prosecution of the Factory Acts, 1833–55. Econ. Hist. Rev., 2nd Ser., May 1984, 37(2), pp. 197–210. [G: U.K.]

Reber, Robert A.; Wallen, Jerry A. and Chhokar, Jagdeep S. Reducing Industrial Accidents: A Behavioral Experiment. Ind. Relat., Winter 1984, 23(1), pp. 119–25. [G: U.S.]

Rosner, David and Markowitz, Gerald. Safety and Health on the Job as a Class Issue: The Workers' Health Bureau of America in the 1920s. Sci. Soc., Winter 1984-1985, 48(4), pp. 464–82. [G: U.S.]

Rubin, Jeffrey. Economic Incentives and Safety Regulation: An Analytical Framework: Comments. Amer. Econ., Spring 1984, 28(1), pp. 25–26.

Scholz, John T. In Search of Regulatory Alternatives. J. Policy Anal. Manage., Fall 1984, 4(1), pp. 113–16. [G: U.S.]

Sider, Hal. Economic Incentives and Safety Regulation: An Analytical Framework. *Amer. Econ.*, Spring 1984, *28*(1), pp. 18–24. [G: U.S.]

Spyropoulos, Georges. Working Conditions in the Industrial Nations: What Lies Ahead? *Int. Lab. Rev.*, July–August 1984, *123*(4), pp. 391–404. [G: OECD]

Viscusi, W. Kip. Structuring an Effective Occupational Disease Policy: Victim Compensation and Risk Regulation. *Yale J. Regul.*, 1984, *2*(1), pp. 53–81. [G: U.S.]

Woodbury, Stephen A. Occupational Safety and Health Regulation and Economic Theory: Comment. In *Darity, W., Jr., ed.*, 1984, pp. 269–78.

8224 Unemployment Insurance

Aaron, Henry J. Social Welfare in Australia. In *Caves, R. E. and Krause, L. B., eds.*, 1984, pp. 349–90. [G: Australia]

Atkinson, Anthony B., et al. Unemployment Benefit, Duration and Incentives in Britain: How Robust Is the Evidence? *J. Public Econ.*, February/March 1984, *23*(1/2), pp. 3–26. [G: U.K.]

Benjamin, Daniel K. Insurance in the Workplace: Experience Is the Best Guide. In *Moore, J. H., ed.*, 1984, pp. 153–68. [G: U.S.]

Bissell, Thomas St.G.; Skadden, Donald H. and White, Frederic E. Social Security Contributions as a Fiscal Burden on Enterprises Engaged in International Activities: United States. In *Intn'l. Fisc. Assoc., vol. 69b*, 1984, pp. 317–37. [G: U.S.]

Blumrosen, Ruth Gerber. Work Sharing, STC, and Affirmative Action. In *MaCoy, R. and Morand, M. J., eds.*, 1984, pp. 139–57. [G: U.S.]

Burgess, Paul L.; Kingston, Jerry L. and St. Louis, Robert D. Unemployment Insurance: Identifying Payment Errors. *Mon. Lab. Rev.*, December 1984, *107*(12), pp. 34–37. [G: U.S.]

Disney, Richard. The Regional Impact of Unemployment Insurance in the United Kingdom. *Oxford Bull. Econ. Statist.*, August 1984, *46*(3), pp. 241–54. [G: U.K.]

Feldstein, Martin and Poterba, James M. Unemployment Insurance and Reservation Wages. *J. Public Econ.*, February/March 1984, *23*(1/2), pp. 141–67. [G: U.S.]

Glombowski, Jörg and Krüger, Michael. Unemployment Insurance and Cyclical Growth. In *Goodwin, R. M.; Krüger, M. and Vercelli, A., eds.*, 1984, pp. 25–46.

Gustman, Alan L. Modeling Individuals' Behavior: Evaluation of a Policymaker's Tool. *J. Policy Anal. Manage.*, Winter 1984, *3*(2), pp. 191–205. [G: U.S.]

Hausman, Jerry A. Tax Policy and Unemployment Insurance Effects on Labor Policy. In *Wachter, M. L. and Wachter, S. M., eds.*, 1984, pp. 70–96. [G: U.S.]

Holen, Arlene. Federal Supplemental Compensation and Unemployment Insurance Recipients. *Mon. Lab. Rev.*, April 1984, *107*(4), pp. 43–44. [G: U.S.]

Hunter, Donna. Oregon Tries the "Workshare" Idea. In *MaCoy, R. and Morand, M. J., eds.*, 1984, pp. 95–105. [G: U.S.]

Ittner, Linda A. The Federal Response to Short-Time Compensation. In *MaCoy, R. and Morand, M. J., eds.*, 1984, pp. 120–35. [G: U.S.]

Lammers, John and Lockwood, Timothy. Short-Time Compensation: At Home and Abroad: The California Experiment. In *MaCoy, R. and Morand, M. J., eds.*, 1984, pp. 61–81. [G: U.S.]

Lupo, Nancy Altman. Influencing Retirement Behavior: A Further Analysis. *J. Policy Anal. Manage.*, Spring 1984, *3*(3), pp. 439–46. [G: U.S.]

MacLennan, Emma and Weitzel, Renate. Labour Market Policy in Four Countries: Are Women Adequately Represented? In *Schmid, G. and Weitzel, R., eds.*, 1984, pp. 202–48. [G: Sweden; U.K.; U.S.; W. Germany]

MaCoy, Ramelle and Morand, Martin J. Short-Time Compensation: The Implications for Management. In *MaCoy, R. and Morand, M. J., eds.*, 1984, pp. 14–35. [G: U.S.]

MaCoy, Ramelle and Morand, Martin J. Short-Time Compensation: An Alternative to Layoff: A Labor Viewpoint. In *MaCoy, R. and Morand, M. J., eds.*, 1984, pp. 36–50. [G: U.S.]

MaCoy, Ramelle and Morand, Martin J. Short-Time Compensation: A Formula for Work Sharing: Afterword. In *MaCoy, R. and Morand, M. J., eds.*, 1984, pp. 196–99. [G: U.S.]

MaCoy, Ramelle and Morand, Martin J. STC and Labor–Management Cooperation. In *MaCoy, R. and Morand, M. J., eds.*, 1984, pp. 183–95. [G: U.S.]

MaCoy, Ramelle and Morand, Martin J. Work Sharing and Short-time Compensation: An Overview. In *MaCoy, R. and Morand, M. J., eds.*, 1984, pp. 3–13. [G: U.S.]

Maguire, Maria. Components of Growth of Income Maintenance Expenditure in Ireland 1951–1979. *Econ. Soc. Rev.*, January 1984, *15*(2), pp. 75–85. [G: Ireland]

Marks, Denton. Incomplete Experience Rating in State Unemployment Insurance. *Mon. Lab. Rev.*, November 1984, *107*(11), pp. 45–51. [G: U.S.]

Meisel, Harry. The Pioneers: STC in the Federal Republic of Germany. In *MaCoy, R. and Morand, M. J., eds.*, 1984, pp. 53–60. [G: W. Germany]

Mesa, Juan M. Short-Time Working or Lay-Offs? Experience from Canada and California. *Int. Lab. Rev.*, January-February 1984, *123*(1), pp. 99–115. [G: Canada; U.S.]

Nemirow, Martin. Short-Time Compensation: Some Policy Considerations. In *MaCoy, R. and Morand, M. J., eds.*, 1984, pp. 158–82. [G: U.S.; W. Germany]

Ragan, James F., Jr. The Voluntary Leaver Provisions of Unemployment Insurance and Their Effect on Quit and Unemployment Rates. *Southern Econ. J.*, July 1984, *51*(1), pp. 135–46.   [G: U.S.]

Reichlin, Lucrezia. Il sistema di assicurazione alla disoccupazione negli Stati Uniti: descrizione del sistema e rassegna del dibattito teorico. (Unemployment Insurance in the United States: Practical Working of the System and Review of Theoretical Literature. With English summary.) *Econ. Lavoro*, Oct.-Dec. 1984, *18*(4), pp. 17–33.   [G: U.S.]

Reid, Frank and Meltz, Noah M. Canada's STC: A Comparison with the California Version. In *MaCoy, R. and Morand, M. J., eds.*, 1984, pp. 106–19.   [G: Canada; U.S.]

Roberti, Paolo. Macroeconomic and Public Finance "Costs" of High Unemployment. *Econ. Lavoro*, Jan.-Mar. 1984, *18*(1), pp. 3–15.
                    [G: OECD]

Runner, Diana. Changes in Unemployment Insurance Legislation during 1983. *Mon. Lab. Rev.*, February 1984, *107*(2), pp. 46–54.
                    [G: U.S.]

Solon, Gary. The Effects of Unemployment Insurance Eligibility Rules on Job Quitting Behavior. *J. Human Res.*, Winter 1984, *19*(1), pp. 118–26.   [G: U.S.]

St. Louis, Robert D. Short-Time Compensation: At Home and Abroad: Arizona, Motorola, and STC. In *MaCoy, R. and Morand, M. J., eds.*, 1984, pp. 82–94.   [G: U.S.]

Topel, Robert H. Equilibrium Earnings, Turnover, and Unemployment: New Evidence. *J. Lab. Econ.*, October 1984, *2*(4), pp. 500–522.
                    [G: U.S.]

Topel, Robert H. Experience Rating of Unemployment Insurance and the Incidence of Unemployment. *J. Law Econ.*, April 1984, *27*(1), pp. 61–90.   [G: U.S.]

Van Rompuy, G. The Effect of Unemployment Legislation on Labor Supply Decisions. *Tijdschrift Econ. Manage.*, 1984, *29*(2), pp. 217–31.   [G: Belgium]

Vasche, Jon David. Unemployment Benefits for Work Sharing: A Further Consideration. *Bus. Econ.*, April 1984, *19*(3), pp. 59–61.[G: U.S.]

Wachter, Michael L. The Training Component of Growth Policies. In *Wachter, M. L. and Wachter, S. M., eds.*, 1984, pp. 41–69.
                    [G: U.S.]

Wolcowitz, Jeffrey. Dynamic Effects of the Unemployment Insurance Tax on Temporary Layoffs. *J. Public Econ.*, November 1984, *25*(1/2), pp. 35–51.

8225 Government Employment Policies (including employment services)

Abella, Manolo I. Labour Migration from South and South–East Asia: Some Policy Issues. *Int. Lab. Rev.*, July–August 1984, *123*(4), pp. 491–506.   [G: Asia]

Adnett, N. J. On-the-Job Search and the Public Employment Service. *J. Econ. Stud.*, 1984, *11*(3), pp. 51–61.   [G: U.K.]

Anderson, Bernard E. Labor Productivity and Demographics: Comment. In *Wachter, M. L. and Wachter, S. M., eds.*, 1984, pp. 100–03.
                    [G: U.S.]

Bequele, Assefa and Freedman, David H. Employment and Basic Needs: An Overview. In *Ghosh, P. K., ed., no. 13*, 1984, *1979*, pp. 188–204.

Bresnick, David. Policymaking by Partnership: Reshaping Youth Employment Policy. *J. Policy Anal. Manage.*, Fall 1984, *4*(1), pp. 23–38.
                    [G: U.S.; W. Europe; Japan]

Burtless, Gary and Haveman, Robert H. Policy Lessons from Three Labor Market Experiments. In *Robson, R. T., ed.*, 1984, pp. 105–33.   [G: U.S.]

Dumas, Lloyd J. Making Peace Possible: The Legislative Approach to Economic Conversion. In *Gordon, S. and McFadden, D., eds.*, 1984, pp. 67–85.   [G: U.S.]

Farber, Henry S. Right-to-Work Laws and the Extent of Unionization. *J. Lab. Econ.*, July 1984, *2*(3), pp. 319–52.   [G: U.S.]

Fedrau, Ruth H. Easing the Worker's Transition from Job Loss to Employment. *Mon. Lab. Rev.*, May 1984, *107*(5), pp. 38–40.
                    [G: U.S.]

Ford, William D. Statements in Support of the National Employment Priorities Act. In *McKenzie, R. B., ed. (II)*, 1984, pp. 315–27.
                    [G: U.S.]

Gordon, Suzanne. Economic Conversion Activity in Western Europe. In *Gordon, S. and McFadden, D., eds.*, 1984, pp. 108–29.
                    [G: W. Europe]

Int'l Assoc. of Machinists and Aerospace Workers. Coping with Technology. In *Gordon, S. and McFadden, D., eds.*, 1984, pp. 61–66.
                    [G: U.S.]

Islam, Iyanatul. Socio-economic Progress in Indonesia under the New Order. In *Thambipillai, P., ed.*, 1984, pp. 137–50. [G: Indonesia]

Jeffries, John M. and Stanback, Howard. Employment and Training Policy for Black America: Beyond Placebo to Progressive Public Policy. *Rev. Black Polit. Econ.*, Summer–Fall 1984, *13*(1–2), pp. 119–37.

Johnson, George E. Employment and Training Programs in the United States: What Do We Know, and Where Should We Go From Here? In *Ullrich, R. A., ed.*, 1984, pp. 25–39.
                    [G: U.S.]

Johnson, Peter S. and Thomas, R. Barry. Government Policies towards Business Formation: An Economic Appraisal of a Training Scheme. *Scot. J. Polit. Econ.*, June 1984, *31*(2), pp. 131–46.   [G: U.K.]

Kotliar, A. The Job Placement System in the USSR. *Prob. Econ.*, December 1984, *27*(8), pp. 20–39.   [G: U.S.S.R.]

Lacroix, Robert. Québec: les politiques et programmes gouvernementaux et la création d'emplois. (Quebec: Government Policies and Programs and Job Creation. With English summary.) *Can. Public Policy*, December 1984, *10*(4), pp. 429–35.   [G: OECD]

Leonard, Jonathan S. The Impact of Affirmative Action on Employment. *J. Lab. Econ.*, October 1984, *2*(4), pp. 439–63.   [G: U.S.]

van Liemt, G. Adjusting To Change. *Int. Lab. Rev.*, November–December 1984, *123*(6), pp. 693–703.   [G: OECD]

Lovell, Malcolm R. Labor Productivity and Demographics: Comment. In *Wachter, M. L. and Wachter, S. M., eds.*, 1984, pp. 108–10.
                                         [G: U.S.]

MacLennan, Emma and Weitzel, Renate. Labour Market Policy in Four Countries: Are Women Adequately Represented? In *Schmid, G. and Weitzel, R., eds.*, 1984, pp. 202–48.
                  [G: Sweden; U.K.; U.S.; W. Germany]

Malveaux, Julianne. Employment and Training Policy for Black America: Beyond Placebo to Progressive Public Policy: Comments. *Rev. Black Polit. Econ.*, Summer–Fall 1984, *13*(1–2), pp. 138–44.   [G: U.S.]

Merrilees, W. J. Do Wage Subsidies Stimulate Training? An Evaluation of the Craft Rebate Scheme. *Australian Econ. Pap.*, December 1984, *23*(43), pp. 235–48.   [G: Australia]

Metcalf, David. Employment and Industrial Assistance. In *Jacquemin, A., ed.*, 1984, pp. 84–98.   [G: U.K.; Belgium; France; Norway; Netherlands]

Mishra, G. P. Approaches to Planning for Employment Creation in Rural Areas. In *Singh, A. K.; Papola, T. S. and Mathur, R. S., eds.*, 1984, pp. 53–65.   [G: India; LDCs]

Müller, A. L. Employment Policies in the Soviet Bloc (Review Note). *S. Afr. J. Econ.*, March 1984, *52*(1), pp. 90–95.   [G: U.S.S.R.; Poland; E. Germany; Czechoslovakia; Hungary]

Neale, A. J. and Wilson, R. A. Public Expenditure Policy, 1984–85: Employment. In *Cockle, P., ed.*, 1984, pp. 193–213.   [G: U.K.]

Nemirow, Martin. Work-Sharing Approaches: Past and Present. *Mon. Lab. Rev.*, September 1984, *107*(9), pp. 34–39. [G: U.S.; Germany]

Norris, William C. A New Role for Corporations. In *Brooks, H.; Liebman, L. and Schelling, C. S., eds.*, 1984, pp. 243–62.   [G: U.S.]

Pachal, Tapan and Chakrabarty, Gurupada. Placement through Employment Exchange—A Case Study of the Delhi Metropolitan Area. *Margin*, October 1984, *17*(1), pp. 87–93.
                                         [G: India]

Peden, G. C. The "Treasury View" on Public Works and Employment in the Interwar Period. *Econ. Hist. Rev.*, 2nd Ser., May 1984, *37*(2), pp. 167–81.   [G: U.S.]

Rochin, Refugio I. Farm Worker Service and Employment Programs. In *Emerson, R. D., ed.*, 1984, pp. 412–46.   [G: U.S.]

Schuster, Michael and Miller, Christopher S. An Empirical Assessment of the Age Discrimination in Employment Act. *Ind. Lab. Relat. Rev.*, October 1984, *38*(1), pp. 64–74.   [G: U.S.]

Shapley, Allen E. Farm Worker Service and Em-

ployment Programs: Discussion. In *Emerson, R. D., ed.*, 1984, pp. 446–49.   [G: U.S.]

Smith, James P. and Welch, Finis. Affirmative Action and Labor Markets. *J. Lab. Econ.*, April 1984, *2*(2), pp. 269–301.   [G: U.S.]

Tokman, Víctor E. The Employment Crisis in Latin America. *Int. Lab. Rev.*, September–October 1984, *123*(5), pp. 585–97.
                              [G: Latin America]

Wachter, Michael L. The Training Component of Growth Policies. In *Wachter, M. L. and Wachter, S. M., eds.*, 1984, pp. 41–69.
                                         [G: U.S.]

8226 Employment in the Public Sector

Blair, Larry M. Worker Adjustment to Changing Technology: Techniques, Processes, and Policy Considerations. In *Collins, E. L. and Tanner, L. D., eds.*, 1984, pp. 207–52.   [G: U.S.]

Burtless, Gary and Haveman, Robert H. Policy Lessons from Three Labor Market Experiments. In *Robson, R. T., ed.*, 1984, pp. 105–33.   [G: U.S.]

Cousineau, Jean-Michel. La détermination des salaires des policiers municipaux au Québec. (The Determinants of Wages in the Municipal Police Services in Quebec. With English summary.) *L'Actual. Econ.*, June 1984, *60*(2), pp. 186–99.   [G: Canada]

Dalton, Amy H. The Organization of State and Local Government Employees: Reply. *J. Lab. Res.*, Spring 1984, *5*(2), pp. 201–04.
                                         [G: U.S.]

Dometrius, Nelson C. Minorities and Women among State Agency Leaders. *Soc. Sci. Quart.*, March 1984, *65*(1), pp. 127–37.   [G: U.S.]

Enns, John H.; Nelson, Gary R. and Warner, John T. Retention and Retirement: The Case of the U.S. Military. *Policy Sci.*, October 1984, *17*(2), pp. 101–21.   [G: U.S.]

Grosskopf, Shawna and Hayes, Kathy. Measuring the Excess Burden of State Pension Mandates. *Public Finance*, 1984, *39*(1), pp. 90–103.
                                         [G: U.S.]

Lacroix, Robert and Dussault, François. The Spillover Effect of Public-Sector Wage Contracts in Canada. *Rev. Econ. Statist.*, August 1984, *66*(3), pp. 509–12.   [G: Canada]

Leon, Carol Boyd. Working for Uncle Sam—A Look at Members of the Armed Forces. *Mon. Lab. Rev.*, July 1984, *107*(7), pp. 3–9.
                                         [G: U.S.]

Reid, Joseph D., Jr. and Kurth, Michael M. The Organization of State and Local Government Employees: Comment. *J. Lab. Res.*, Spring 1984, *5*(2), pp. 191–99.   [G: U.S.]

Sullivan, Sean. Employment versus Training in Federal Manpower Programs. In *Weicher, J. C., ed.*, 1984, pp. 154–66.   [G: U.S.]

Taylor, Patricia A. and Shields, Susan Walker. Mexican Americans and Employment Inequality in the Federal Civil Service. *Soc. Sci. Quart.*, June 1984, *65*(2), pp. 381–91.
                                         [G: U.S.]

Wietfeldt, Richard A. The Role of the State in

Retirement Income Policy: Some Fundamental Considerations. In *Conklin, D. W.; Bennett, J. H. and Courchene, T. J., eds.*, 1984, pp. 445–53. [G: Canada]

Yandle, Bruce. The Wages of Regulation. *J. Lab. Res.*, Fall 1984, *5*(4), pp. 435–39.

823 Labor Mobility; National and International Migration

8230 Labor Mobility; National and International Migration

Abella, Manolo I. Labour Migration from South and South–East Asia: Some Policy Issues. *Int. Lab. Rev.*, July–August 1984, *123*(4), pp. 491–506. [G: Asia]

Agarwal, Vinod B. and Winkler, Donald R. Migration of Professional Manpower to the United States. *Southern Econ. J.*, January 1984, *50*(3), pp. 814–30. [G: U.S.; Selected Countries]

Armstrong, Thomas F. The Transformation of Work: Turpentine Workers in Coastal Georgia, 1865–1901. *Labor Hist.*, Fall 1984, *25*(4), pp. 518–32. [G: U.S.]

Banerjee, Biswajit. Information Flow, Expectations and Job Search: Rural-to-Urban Migration Process in India. *J. Devel. Econ.*, May–June–August 1984, *15*(1,2,3), pp. 239–57. [G: India]

Banerjee, Biswajit. The Probability, Size, and Uses of Remittances from Urban to Rural Areas in India. *J. Devel. Econ.*, December 1984, *16*(3), pp. 293–311. [G: India]

Bauer, P. T. and Yamey, B. S. The Economics of Post-war Immigration Policy in British West Africa. In *Bauer, P. T.*, 1984, pp. 128–39. [G: Nigeria; Gold Coast]

Bennell, Paul. The Utilisation of Professional Engineering Skills in Kenya. In *Fransman, M. and King, K., eds.*, 1984, pp. 335–53. [G: Kenya]

Bhagwati, Jagdish N. Incentives and Disincentives: International Migration. *Weltwirtsch. Arch.*, 1984, *120*(4), pp. 678–701. [G: U.S.; Global]

Bhagwati, Jagdish N.; Schatz, Klaus-Werner and Wong, Kar-yiu. The West German *Gastarbeiter* System of Immigration. *Europ. Econ. Rev.*, December 1984, *26*(3), pp. 277–94. [G: W. Germany]

Birks, Stace and Sinclair, Clive. Libya: Problems of a Rentier State. In *Lawless, R. and Findlay, A., eds.*, 1984, pp. 241–75. [G: Libya]

Borjas, George J. Race, Turnover, and Male Earnings. *Ind. Relat.*, Winter 1984, *23*(1), pp. 73–89. [G: U.S.]

Bruton, Henry J. Economic Development with Unlimited Supplies of Foreign Exchange. In *[Reynolds, L. G.]*, 1984, pp. 124–44. [G: LDCs]

Bukowczyk, John J. The Transformation of Working-Class Ethnicity: Corporate Control, Americanization, and the Polish Immigrant Middle Class in Bayonne, New Jersey, 1915–1925. *Labor Hist.*, Winter 1984, *25*(1), pp. 53–82. [G: U.S.]

Bustamante, Jorge A. Changing Patterns of Undocumented Migration from Mexican States in Recent Years. In *Jones, R. C., ed.*, 1984, pp. 15–32. [G: U.S.; Mexico]

Cooper, J. H. Southern Africa and the Threat of Economic Sanctions. *S. Afr. J. Econ.*, September 1984, *52*(3), pp. 266–81. [G: Africa]

Cullison, William E. Equalizing Regional Differences in Wages: A Study of Wages and Migration in the South and Other Regions. *Fed. Res. Bank Richmond Econ. Rev.*, May/June 1984, *70*(3), pp. 20–33. [G: U.S.]

Dagodag, W. Tim. Illegal Mexican Aliens in Los Angeles: Locational Characteristics. In *Jones, R. C., ed.*, 1984, pp. 199–217. [G: U.S.]

Dagodag, W. Tim. Illegal Mexican Immigration to California from Western Mexico. In *Jones, R. C., ed.*, 1984, pp. 61–73. [G: U.S.; Mexico]

van Delft, A. and Suyker, W. B. C. Interregional Migration in a Multiregional Labour Market Model for the Netherlands. In *ter Heide, H. and Willekens, F. J., eds.*, 1984, pp. 253–69. [G: Netherlands]

Denslow, David A., Jr. and Eaton, Peter J. Migration and Intervening Opportunities. *Southern Econ. J.*, October 1984, *51*(2), pp. 369–87. [G: Brazil; U.S.; Venezuela; Japan; Mexico]

Dhar, Sanjay. Interstate and Within-State Migration in India. In *Binswanger, H. P. and Rosenzweig, R., eds.*, 1984, pp. 280–304. [G: India]

Emerson, Robert D. Migration in Farm Labor Markets. In *Emerson, R. D., ed.*, 1984, pp. 104–35. [G: U.S.]

Findlay, Allan; Findlay, Anne M. and Paddison, Ronan. Maintaining the Status Quo: An Analysis of Social Space in Post-Colonial Rabat. *Urban Stud.*, February 1984, *21*(1), pp. 41–51. [G: Morocco]

Foot, David K. and Milne, William J. Net Migration Estimation in an Extended, Multiregional Gravity Model. *J. Reg. Sci.*, February 1984, *24*(1), pp. 119–33. [G: Canada]

Freeman, Richard B. The Structure of Labor Markets: A Book Review Three Decades Later. In *[Reynolds, L. G.]*, 1984, pp. 201–26. [G: U.S.]

Galenson, David W. The Rise and Fall of Indentured Servitude in the Americas: An Economic Analysis. *J. Econ. Hist.*, March 1984, *44*(1), pp. 1–26. [G: Caribbean; Latin America; U.S.]

Glover, Terry. An Intertemporal Approach to Seasonal Agricultural Labor Markets: Discussion. In *Emerson, R. D., ed.*, 1984, pp. 249–53.

Goldfarb, Robert S.; Havrylyshyn, Oli and Mangum, Stephen L. Can Remittances Compensate for Manpower Outflows: The Case of Philippine Physicians. *J. Devel. Econ.*, May–June–August 1984, *15*(1,2,3), pp. 1–17. [G: Philippines]

Gordijn, H. E.; Heida, H. R. and ter Heide, Henk. Monitoring Migration and Population Redistribution. In *ter Heide, H. and Willekens, F. J., eds.*, 1984, pp. 95–110.
[G: Netherlands]

Goss, Ernst P. and Schoening, Niles C. Search Time, Unemployment, and the Migration Decision. *J. Human Res.*, Fall 1984, *19*(4), pp. 570–79. [G: U.S.]

Graves, Philip E. and Knapp, Thomas A. A Theory of International Migration Flows: United States Immigration from Mexico. *Rev. Reg. Stud.*, Winter 1984, *14*(1), pp. 1–7.
[G: U.S.; Mexico]

Greenwood, Michael J. and Hunt, Gary L. Migration and Interregional Employment Redistribution in the United States. *Amer. Econ. Rev.*, December 1984, *74*(5), pp. 957–69.
[G: U.S.]

Grossman, Jean Baldwin. Illegal Immigrants and Domestic Employment. *Ind. Lab. Relat. Rev.*, January 1984, *37*(2), pp. 240–51. [G: U.S.]

Grossman, Jean Baldwin. The Occupational Attainment of Immigrant Women in Sweden. *Scand. J. Econ.*, 1984, *86*(3), pp. 337–51.
[G: Sweden]

Guisinger, Stephen E. The Impact of Temporary Worker Migration on Pakistan. In *Burki, S. J. and LaPorte, R., Jr., eds.*, 1984, pp. 201–23.
[G: Pakistan]

Guttierrez, Phillip R. The Channelization of Mexicans Nationals to the San Luis Valley of Colorado. In *Jones, R. C., ed.*, 1984, pp. 183–98.
[G: U.S.; Mexico]

Hamilton, Bob and Whalley, John. Efficiency and Distributional Implications of Global Restrictions on Labour Mobility: Calculations and Policy Implications. *J. Devel. Econ.*, January–February 1984, *14*(1–2), pp. 61–75.
[G: Global]

Harrison, David S. The Impact of Immigration on a Depressed Labour Market: The South Australian Experience. *Econ. Rec.*, March 1984, *60*(168), pp. 57–67. [G: Australia]

Herzog, Henry W., Jr. and Schlottmann, Alan M. Labor Force Mobility in the United States: Migration, Unemployment, and Remigration. *Int. Reg. Sci. Rev.*, September 1984, *9*(1), pp. 43–58. [G: U.S.]

Hill, John K. and Méndez, José A. The Effect of Commercial Policy on International Migration Flows: The Case of the United States and Mexico. *J. Int. Econ.*, August 1984, *17*(1/2), pp. 41–53. [G: U.S.; Mexico]

Hoenack, Stephen A.; Peris, Jose Antonio and Weiler, William C. Can Economic Incentives Explain the Recent Population Movements to Nonmetropolitan Areas? *Ann. Reg. Sci.*, November 1984, *18*(3), pp. 81–93. [G: U.S.]

Holmlund, Bertil. Income Prospects and Job Mobility: The Case of Sweden. *Europ. Econ. Rev.*, April 1984, *24*(3), pp. 383–400. [G: Sweden]

House, William J. Nairobi's Informal Sector: Dynamic Entrepreneurs or Surplus Labor? *Econ. Develop. Cult. Change*, January 1984, *32*(2), pp. 277–302. [G: Kenya]

Inoki, Takenori. Japanese Emigration to Hawaii and North America in 1890s. (In Japanese. With English summary.) *Osaka Econ. Pap.*, December 1984, *34*(2–3), pp. 239–47.
[G: Japan; U.S.]

Izraeli, Oded and Lin, An-Loh. Recent Evidence on the Effect of Real Earnings on Net Migration. *Reg. Stud.*, April 1984, *18*(2), pp. 113–20. [G: U.S.]

Jones, Richard C. Changing Patterns of Undocumented Mexican Migration to South Texas. *Soc. Sci. Quart.*, June 1984, *65*(2), pp. 465–81. [G: U.S.]

Jones, Richard C. Macro-patterns of Undocumented Migration between Mexico and the U.S. In *Jones, R. C., ed.*, 1984, pp. 33–57.
[G: U.S.; Mexico]

Jones, Richard C. Patterns of Undocumented Migration: Introduction. In *Jones, R. C., ed.*, 1984, pp. 1–12. [G: U.S.; Mexico]

Jones, Richard C.; Harris, Richard J. and Valdez, Avelardo. Occupational and Spatial Mobility of Undocumented Migrants from Dolores Hidalgo, Guanajuato. In *Jones, R. C., ed.*, 1984, pp. 159–82. [G: U.S.; Mexico]

Jovanovic, Boyan. Matching, Turnover, and Unemployment. *J. Polit. Econ.*, February 1984, *92*(1), pp. 108–22.

Katz, Eliakim and Stark, Oded. Migration and Asymmetric Information: Comment. *Amer. Econ. Rev.*, June 1984, *74*(3), pp. 533–34.

Kawanabe, Noboru. Urban Traditional Sector and Rural–Urban Migration in LDCs. (In Japanese. With English summary.) *Osaka Econ. Pap.*, December 1984, *34*(2–3), pp. 248–60.
[G: LDCs]

Kelley, Allen C. and Williamson, Jeffrey G. Population Growth, Industrial Revolutions, and the Urban Transition. *Population Devel. Rev.*, September 1984, *10*(3), pp. 419–41.
[G: LDCs]

van der Knaap, G. A. and Sleegers, W. F. Structural Analysis of Interregional and Intraregional Migration Patterns. In *ter Heide, H. and Willekens, F. J., eds.*, 1984, pp. 113–31.
[G: Netherlands]

Kossov, V. V. and Tatevosov, R. V. Geographical Mobility of Manpower in the USSR. *Int. Lab. Rev.*, January-February 1984, *123*(1), pp. 87–97. [G: U.S.S.R.]

Kwok, Peter and Leland, Hayne E. Migration and Asymmetric Information: Reply. *Amer. Econ. Rev.*, June 1984, *74*(3), pp. 535.

Lane, A. T. American Trade Unions, Mass Immigration and the Literacy Test: 1900–1917. *Labor Hist.*, Winter 1984, *25*(1), pp. 5–25.
[G: U.S.]

Latos, Charles J. Non-white Migration Patterns in Northern Metropolitan Areas, 1960–1970: The Interaction between Economic and Affinitive Factors. *Rev. Black Polit. Econ.*, Winter 1984–85, *13*(3), pp. 5–19. [G: U.S.]

Lecaillon, Jacques and Germidis, Dimitrios. Income Differentials and the Dynamics of Development. In *Ghosh, P. K., ed., no. 7*, 1984, 1976, pp. 176–94. [G: Africa]

Lee, Kye S. The Direction of Migration: A Dynamic General Equilibrium Model. *J. Reg. Sci.*, November 1984, *24*(4), pp. 509–17.

Levine, Bruce C. Immigrant Workers, "Equal Rights," and Anti-Slavery: The Germans of Newark, New Jersey. *Labor Hist.*, Winter 1984, *25*(1), pp. 26–52.   [G: U.S.]

Maillat, Denis. Mobility Channels: An Instrument for Analysing and Regulating the Local Labour Market. *Int. Lab. Rev.*, May–June 1984, *123*(3), pp. 349–62.   [G: Switzerand]

Marshall, Dawn I. Vincentian Contract Labour Migration to Barbados: The Satisfaction of Mutual Needs? *Soc. Econ. Stud.*, September 1984, *33*(3), pp. 63–92.   [G: Barbados; St. Vincent]

Martin, Philip L. and North, David S. Nonimmigrant Aliens in American Agriculture. In *Emerson, R. D., ed.*, 1984, pp. 168–93. [G: U.S.]

Massiah, Gustave. Immigrant Workers in Europe. In *Amin, S., ed.*, 1984, pp. 275–302.
[G: W. Europe]

McCormick, Barry and Hughes, Gordon. The Influence of Pensions on Job Mobility. *J. Public Econ.*, February/March 1984, *23*(1/2), pp. 183–206.   [G: U.K.]

McKay, R. Reynolds. The Impact of the Great Depression on Immigrant Mexican Labor: Repatriation of the Bridgeport, Texas, Coal Miners. *Soc. Sci. Quart.*, June 1984, *65*(2), pp. 354–63.   [G: U.S.; Mexico]

Miller, Lawrence W.; Polinard, Jerry L. and Wrinkle, Robert D. Attitudes toward Undocumented Workers: The Mexican American Perspective. *Soc. Sci. Quart.*, June 1984, *65*(2), pp. 482–94.   [G: U.S.; Mexico]

Miller, Michael V. and Valdez, Avelardo. Immigration and Perceptions of Economic Deprivation among Working-Class Mexican American Men. *Soc. Sci. Quart.*, June 1984, *65*(2), pp. 455–64.   [G: U.S.]

Mines, Richard. Network Migration and Mexican Rural Development: A Case Study. In *Jones, R. C., ed.*, 1984, pp. 136–55.   [G: U.S.; Mexico]

Molho, Ian. A Dynamic Model of Interregional Migration Flows in Great Britain. *J. Reg. Sci.*, August 1984, *24*(3), pp. 317–37.   [G: U.K.]

Molho, Ian. Distance Deterrence Relationships in Multi-Stream Migration Models. *Manchester Sch. Econ. Soc. Stud.*, March 1984, *52*(1), pp. 49–69.   [G: U.K.]

Murayama, Yuzo. Contractors, Collusion, and Competition: Japanese Immigrant Railroad Laborers in the Pacific Northwest, 1898–1911. *Exploration Econ. Hist.*, July 1984, *21*(3), pp. 290–305.   [G: Japan; U.S.]

Nabi, Ijaz. Village-End Considerations in Rural–Urban Migration. *J. Devel. Econ.*, January–February 1984, *14*(1–2), pp. 129–45.
[G: Pakistan]

van den Noord, P. J. Relocation of State Services and Regional Unemployment in the Netherlands. *De Economist*, 1984, *132*(4), pp. 451–67.   [G: Netherlands]

O'Brien, Jay. The Political Economy of Semi-Proletarianisation under Colonialism: Sudan 1925–50. In *Munslow, B. and Finch, H., eds.*, 1984, pp. 121–47.   [G: Sudan]

Oberai, A. S. and Singh, H. K. Manmohan. Migration, Employment and the Urban Labour Market: A Study in the Indian Punjab. *Int. Lab. Rev.*, July–August 1984, *123*(4), pp. 507–23.   [G: India]

Op 't Veld, A.; Bijlsma, E. and Starmans, J. Explanatory Analysis of Interregional Migration in the Nineteen-Seventies. In *ter Heide, H. and Willekens, F. J., eds.*, 1984, pp. 171–200.
[G: Netherlands]

Palmer, Ransford W. The Impact of Emigration of Human Capital on the Jamaican Economy: An Empirical Assessment. In *Palmer, R. W.*, 1984, pp. 31–38.   [G: Jamaica]

Palmer, Ransford W. The Phenomenon of Caribbean Emigration to the United States. In *Palmer, R. W.*, 1984, pp. 23–29.
[G: Caribbean]

Parks, Alfred L. Migration in Farm Labor Markets: Discussion. In *Emerson, R. D., ed.*, 1984, pp. 136–39.   [G: U.S.]

Pickles, Andrew and Rogerson, Peter A. Wage Distributions and Spatial Preferences in Competitive Job Search and Migration. *Reg. Stud.*, April 1984, *18*(2), pp. 131–42.

Piore, Michael J. Alien Workers in the American Economy: Economic Consequences and Alternative Policies. In *Ullrich, R. A., ed.*, 1984, pp. 41–58.   [G: U.S.]

Ragan, James F., Jr. Investigating the Decline in Manufacturing Quit Rates. *J. Human Res.*, Winter 1984, *19*(1), pp. 53–71.   [G: U.S.]

Raschke, Freddy. Demographic Influences on the Mobility of German Labor Stock. In *Steinmann, G., ed.*, 1984, pp. 323–42.
[G: W. Germany]

Reichert, Joshua S. and Massey, Douglas S. Patterns of U.S. Migration from a Mexican Town. In *Jones, R. C., ed.*, 1984, pp. 93–109.
[G: Mexico; U.S.]

Renard, Robrecht. Rural-to-Urban Migration and the Shadow Wage in LDCs. *Europ. Econ. Rev.*, April 1984, *24*(3), pp. 401–07.
[G: LDCs]

Reynolds, Clark; Ramos, Raul and McCleery, Robert. The Impact of Foreign Trade and Export Strategies on Distribution of Income for Low-Income Households in Mexico. In *Aspe, P. and Sigmund, P. E., eds.*, 1984, pp. 203–46.   [G: Mexico]

Rivera-Batiz, Francisco L. International Migration, Non-traded Goods, and Economic Welfare in a Two-Class Economy: A Reply. *J. Devel. Econ.*, December 1984, *16*(3), pp. 325–30.

Roberts, Kenneth D. Agricultural Development and Labor Mobility: A Study of Four Mexican Subregions. In *Jones, R. C., ed.*, 1984, pp. 74–92.   [G: Mexico; U.S.]

Salvatore, Dominick. An Econometric Model of Internal Migration and Development: Extensions and Tests. *Reg. Sci. Urban Econ.*, February 1984, *14*(1), pp. 77–87.   [G: Italy]

Schäfer, Hermann. Italian Migrant Workers in Germany, 1890–1914. In *Engels, W. and Pohl, H., eds.*, 1984, pp. 77–94. **[G: W. Germany]**

Scheurwater, Jan. Toward a Spatial Demographic Information System. In *ter Heide, H. and Willekens, F. J., eds.*, 1984, pp. 69–93. **[G: Netherlands]**

Schlottmann, Alan M. and Herzog, Henry W., Jr. Career and Geographic Mobility Interactions: Implications for the Age Selectivity of Migration. *J. Human Res.*, Winter 1984, *19*(1), pp. 72–86. **[G: U.S.]**

Sherbiny, Naiem A. Expatriate Labor in Arab Oil-producing Countries. *Finance Develop.*, December 1984, *21*(4), pp. 34–37. **[G: OAPEC]**

Snipp, C. Matthew and Tienda, Marta. Mexican American Occupational Mobility. *Soc. Sci. Quart.*, June 1984, *65*(2), pp. 364–80. **[G: U.S.]**

Spitze, Glenna. The Effect of Family Migration on Wives' Employment: How Long Does It Last? *Soc. Sci. Quart.*, March 1984, *65*(1), pp. 21–36. **[G: U.S.]**

Spreen, Thomas H. An Intertemporal Approach to Seasonal Agricultural Labor Markets. In *Emerson, R. D., ed.*, 1984, pp. 230–49.

Stark, Oded. A Note on Modelling Labour Migration in LDCs. *J. Devel. Stud.*, July 1984, *20*(4), pp. 318–22.

Stark, Oded. Discontinuity and the Theory of International Migration. *Kyklos*, 1984, *37*(2), pp. 206–22. **[G: Taiwan; U.S.; U.K.]**

Stark, Oded. Rural-to-Urban Migration in LDCs: A Relative Deprivation Approach. *Econ. Develop. Cult. Change*, April 1984, *32*(3), pp. 475–86. **[G: LDCs]**

Stark, Oded. Rural-to-Urban Migration in LDCs: A Relative Deprivation Approach. *Econ. Develop. Cult. Change*, April 1984, *32*(3), pp. 475–86.

Staroverov, O. V. Markov Models of Mobility. *Matekon*, Spring 1984, *20*(3), pp. 3–21.

Stewart, James B. and Hyclak, Thomas. An Analysis of the Earnings Profiles of Immigrants. *Rev. Econ. Statist.*, May 1984, *66*(2), pp. 292–96. **[G: U.S.]**

Straubhaar, Thomas. Die Süderweiterung der EG unter arbeitsmarkpolitischen Gesichtspunkten—Das Migrationspotential der neuen Mitglieder auf dem Gemeinsamen Arbeitsmarkt. (The Southern Expansion of the EC from the Political Point of View of the Labour Market—The Migration Potential of the New Members of the Common Labour Market. With English summary.) *Schweiz. Z. Volkswirtsch. Statist.*, December 1984, *120*(4), pp. 577–88. **[G: EEC]**

Tachibanaki, Toshiaki. Labor Mobility and Job Tenure. In *Aoki, M., ed.*, 1984, pp. 77–102. **[G: Japan; U.S.]**

Takagi, Yasuoki. The Migration Function and the Todaro Parodox. *Reg. Sci. Urban Econ.*, May 1984, *14*(2), pp. 219–30.

Takagi, Yasuoki. Urban Unemployment and Rural–Urban Migration in LDC's: A Survey. (In

Japanese. With English summary.) *Econ. Stud. Quart.*, December 1984, *35*(3), pp. 216–29. **[G: LDCs]**

Thompson, Henry. International Migration, Non-traded Goods, and Economic Welfare in the Source Country: A Comment. *J. Devel. Econ.*, December 1984, *16*(3), pp. 321–24.

Trager, Lillian. Migration and Remittances: Urban Income and Rural Households in the Philippines. *J. Devel. Areas*, April 1984, *18*(3), pp. 317–40. **[G: Philippines]**

Tsakok, Isabelle. The Export of Manpower from Pakistan to the Middle East, 1975–85. In *Burki, S. J. and LaPorte, R., Jr., eds.*, 1984, pp. 224–36. **[G: Pakistan]**

Valdez, Avelardo and Jones, Richard C. Geographical Patterns of Undocumented Mexicans and Chicanos in San Antonio, Texas: 1970 and 1980. In *Jones, R. C., ed.*, 1984, pp. 218–35. **[G: U.S.]**

Verster, A. C. P. A Double Allocation Model for Interregional Residential and Job Mobility. In *ter Heide, H. and Willekens, F. J., eds.*, 1984, pp. 201–31. **[G: Netherlands]**

Vickerman, R. W. Urban and Regional Change, Migration and Commuting—The Dynamics of Workplace, Residence and Transport Choice. *Urban Stud.*, February 1984, *21*(1), pp. 15–29. **[G: U.K.]**

Welch, Finis. Nonimmigrant Aliens in American Agriculture: Discussion. In *Emerson, R. D., ed.*, 1984, pp. 194–99. **[G: U.S.]**

Whittaker, William. Migration and Agrarian Change in Garhwal District, Uttar Pradesh. In *[Farmer, B. H.]*, 1984, pp. 109–35. **[G: India]**

Wiest, Raymond E. External Dependency and the Perpetuation of Temporary Migration to the United States. In *Jones, R. C., ed.*, 1984, pp. 110–35. **[G: U.S.; Mexico]**

Zubrzycki, Jerzy. Immigration and Population Change in Australia: A Test of the Dual Labour Market Hypothesis. In *Steinmann, G., ed.*, 1984, pp. 360–85. **[G: Australia]**

824 Labor Market Studies, Wages, Employment

8240 General

Aaron, Henry J. and Burtless, Gary. Retirement and Economic Behavior: Introduction and Summary. In *Aaron, H. J. and Burtless, G., eds.*, 1984, pp. 1–22. **[G: U.S.]**

Allen, Steven G. Trade Unions, Absenteeism, and Exit-Voice. *Ind. Lab. Relat. Rev.*, April 1984, *37*(3), pp. 331–45. **[G: U.S.]**

Anderson, Joan and Frantz, Roger S. The Response of Labour Effort to Falling Real Wages: The Mexican Peso Devaluation of February 1982. *World Devel.*, July 1984, *12*(7), pp. 759–66. **[G: Mexico]**

Ashenfelter, Orley C. Macroeconomic Analyses and Microeconomic Analyses of Labor Supply.

Carnegie-Rochester Conf. Ser. Public Policy, Autumn 1984, *21*, pp. 117–55. [G: U.S.; U.K.; Canada]

Ashton, D. N. and Maguire, M. J. Dual Labour Market Theory and the Organisation of Local Labour Markets. *Int. J. Soc. Econ.,* 1984, *11*(7), pp. 106–20. [G: U.K.]

Beckmann, Martin J. Zur Bewertung von Karrieren. (On the Utility of a Career. With English summary.) *Jahr. Nationalökon. Statist.,* July 1984, *199*(4), pp. 289–307. [G: U.S.]

Behrman, Jere R. and Wolfe, Barbara L. Labor Force Participation and Earnings Determinants for Women in the Special Conditions of Developing Countries. *J. Devel. Econ.,* May–June–August 1984, *15*(1,2,3), pp. 259–88. [G: Nicaragua]

Bequele, Assefa and Freedman, David H. Employment and Basic Needs: An Overview. In *Ghosh, P. K., ed., no. 13,* 1984, *1979,* pp. 188–204.

Berry, Albert and Sabot, R. H. Unemployment and Economic Development. *Econ. Develop. Cult. Change,* October 1984, *33*(1), pp. 99–116. [G: LDCs]

Binswanger, Hans P., et al. Common Features and Contrasts in Labor Relations in the Semiarid Tropics of India. In *Binswanger, H. P. and Rosenzweig, R., eds.,* 1984, pp. 143–68. [G: India]

Blair, Larry M. Worker Adjustment to Changing Technology: Techniques, Processes, and Policy Considerations. In *Collins, E. L. and Tanner, L. D., eds.,* 1984, pp. 207–52. [G: U.S.]

Blandy, Richard. Labour Problems of the Minerals Boom. In *Lloyd, P. J., ed.,* 1984, *1981,* pp. 170–75. [G: Australia]

Blandy, Richard and Wooden, Mark. The Australian Labour Market, March 1984. *Australian Bull. Lab.,* March 1984, *10*(2), pp. 55–76. [G: Australia]

Botham, R. Employment Subsidies: A New Direction for Local Government Economic Initiatives. *Reg. Stud.,* February 1984, *18*(1), pp. 84–88. [G: U.K.]

Bustamante, Jorge A. Changing Patterns of Undocumented Migration from Mexican States in Recent Years. In *Jones, R. C., ed.,* 1984, pp. 15–32. [G: U.S.; Mexico]

Cameron, David R. Social Democracy, Corporatism, Labour Quiescence and the Representation of Economic Interest in Advanced Capitalist Society. In *Goldthorpe, J. H., ed.,* 1984, pp. 143–78. [G: OECD]

Coates, Mary Lou. Human Resources and Labour Markets: Summary Outline. In *Wood, W. D. and Kumar, P., eds.,* 1984, pp. 41–89. [G: Canada; OECD]

Coffey, Joseph D. The California Agricultural Labor Relations Act and National Agricultural Labor Relations Legislation: Discussion. In *Emerson, R. D., ed.,* 1984, pp. 370–75. [G: U.S.]

Curtis, Fred. "Cheap" African Labor-Power and South African Capitalism: 1948–1978. In *Zarembka, P., ed.,* 1984, pp. 185–235. [G: S. Africa]

Dawkins, Peter and Sloan, Judith. The Australian Labour Market, September 1984. *Australian Bull. Lab.,* September 1984, *10*(4), pp. 179–95. [G: Australia]

Doeringer, Peter B. Internal Labor Markets and Paternalism in Rural Areas. In *Osterman, P., ed.,* 1984, pp. 271–89. [G: U.S.]

Drouet, Pierre. The Restructuring of the Petroleum Refining Sector and Its Social Consequences. *Int. Lab. Rev.,* July–August 1984, *123*(4), pp. 423–40. [G: Global]

Dudley, Leonard and Montmarquette, Claude. The Effects of Non-clearing Labor Markets on the Demand for Public Spending. *Econ. Inquiry,* April 1984, *22*(2), pp. 151–70. [G: Selected Countries]

Fields, Gary S. Employment, Income Distribution and Economic Growth in Seven Small Open Economies. *Econ. J.,* March 1984, *94*(373), pp. 74–83. [G: Selected LDCs]

Fields, Gary S. and Mitchell, Olivia S. Economic Determinants of the Optimal Retirement Age: An Empirical Investigation. *J. Human Res.,* Spring 1984, *19*(2), pp. 245–62. [G: U.S.]

Freeman, Richard B. De-mystifying the Japanese Labor Markets. In *Aoki, M., ed.,* 1984, pp. 125–29. [G: Japan]

Friedland, William H. Unstructured Labor Markets and Alternative Labor Market Forms: Discussion. In *Emerson, R. D., ed.,* 1984, pp. 279–85. [G: U.S.]

Gardner, Bruce. Seasonal Farm Labor and U.S. Farm Policy. In *Emerson, R. D., ed.,* 1984, pp. 450–76. [G: U.S.]

Glover, Robert W. Unstructured Labor Markets and Alternative Labor Market Forms. In *Emerson, R. D., ed.,* 1984, pp. 254–79. [G: U.S.]

Graham, John W. and Green, Carole A. Estimating the Parameters of a Household Production Function with Joint Products. *Rev. Econ. Statist.,* May 1984, *66*(2), pp. 277–82. [G: U.S.]

Hayes, Sue Eileen. The California Agricultural Labor Relations Act and National Agricultural Labor Relations Legislation. In *Emerson, R. D., ed.,* 1984, pp. 328–70. [G: U.S.]

Hojman, David E. Minimum Wages, Union Membership, and Differentials: The Phillips Curve and the Chilean Labour Market Revisited. *J. Econ. Stud.,* 1984, *11*(4), pp. 3–22. [G: Chile]

Hope, Kempe Ronald. Unemployment, Labour Force Participation, and Urbanization in the Caribbean. *Rev. Reg. Stud.,* Fall 1984, *14*(3), pp. 9–16. [G: Caribbean]

House, William J. Labour Market Segmentation: Evidence from Cyprus. *World Devel.,* April 1984, *12*(4), pp. 403–18. [G: Cyprus]

House, William J. Nairobi's Informal Sector: Dynamic Entrepreneurs or Surplus Labor? *Econ. Develop. Cult. Change,* January 1984, *32*(2), pp. 277–302. [G: Kenya]

Humphrey, John. Labor in the Brazilian Motor Vehicle Industry. In *Kronish, R. and Mericle, K. S., eds.,* 1984, pp. 95–131. [G: Brazil]

Keeley, Michael C. The Economics of Firm Size: Implications from Labor-Market Studies. *Fed.*

Res. Bank San Francisco Econ. Rev., Winter 1984, (1), pp. 5–21. **[G: U.S.]**

Kertesi, Gábor and Sziráczki, György. The Second Economy and Workers' Behaviour on the Labour Market in Hungary. *Econ. Lavoro*, Jan.-Mar. 1984, *18*(1), pp. 119–27.
[G: Hungary]

Koizumi, Susumu. Wage–Employment Contract and Okun's Law. (In Japanese. With English summary.) *Osaka Econ. Pap.*, December 1984, *34*(2–3), pp. 27–35. **[G: Japan; U.S.]**

Kuenstler, Peter. Local Employment Initiatives in Western Europe. *Int. Lab. Rev.*, March-April 1984, *123*(2), pp. 221–33.
[G: W. Europe]

Lehn, Kenneth. Information Asymmetries in Baseball's Free Agent Market. *Econ. Inquiry*, January 1984, *22*(1), pp. 37–44. **[G: U.S.]**

Lehrer, Evelyn and Nerlove, Marc. A Life-Cycle Analysis of Family Income Distribution. *Econ. Inquiry*, July 1984, *22*(3), pp. 360–74.
[G: U.S.]

Leigh, J. Paul. Unionization and Absenteeism. *Appl. Econ.*, February 1984, *16*(1), pp. 147–57. **[G: U.S.]**

Liebschutz, Saran F. and Lurie, Irene. Evolution in Federalism: The Reagan Program and Legislative Appropriation of Federal Grants in New York. *Public Budg. Finance*, Summer 1984, *4*(2), pp. 24–41. **[G: U.S.]**

Lloyd, P. J. Mineral Economics in Australia: Linkages With Other Sectors of the Economy: Introduction. In *Lloyd, P. J., ed.*, 1984, pp. 158–69. **[G: Australia]**

Manwaring, Tony. The Extended Internal Labour Market. *Cambridge J. Econ.*, June 1984, *8*(2), pp. 161–87. **[G: U.K.]**

Martin, Philip L. and North, David S. Nonimmigrant Aliens in American Agriculture. In *Emerson, R. D., ed.*, 1984, pp. 168–93. **[G: U.S.]**

Millar, James R. The Household Sector: The View from the Bottom. In *Hoffmann, E. P. and Laird, R. F., eds.*, 1984, *1981*, pp. 529–61. **[G: U.S.S.R.]**

Mines, Richard. Network Migration and Mexican Rural Development: A Case Study. In *Jones, R. C., ed.*, 1984, pp. 136–55. **[G: U.S.; Mexico]**

Mines, Richard and Martin, Philip L. Immigrant Workers and the California Citrus Industry. *Ind. Relat.*, Winter 1984, *23*(1), pp. 139–49.
[G: U.S.]

Moffitt, Robert. Profiles of Fertility, Labour Supply and Wages of Married Women: A Complete Life-Cycle Model. *Rev. Econ. Stud.*, April 1984, *51*(2), pp. 263–78. **[G: U.S.]**

Moskoff, William. The Soviet Urban Labor Supply. In *Morton, H. W. and Stuart, R. C., eds.*, 1984, pp. 65–83. **[G: U.S.S.R.]**

Oi, Walter Y. A Comment on the Ashenfelter Analysis of Labor Market Fluctuations [Macroeconomic Analyses and Microeconomic Analyses of Labor Supply]. *Carnegie-Rochester Conf. Ser. Public Policy*, Autumn 1984, *21*, pp. 157–72. **[G: U.S.; U.K.; Canada]**

Oxenham, John. Employers, Jobs and Qualifications. In *Oxenham, J., ed.*, 1984, pp. 41–86.
[G: Tanzania; Kenya; Zambia; Sri Lanka; Mexico]

Pencavel, John H. The Empirical Performance of a Model of Trade Union Behavior. In *Rosa, J.-J., ed.*, 1984, pp. 221–76. **[G: U.S.]**

Reich, Michael. Segmented Labour: Time Series Hypothesis and Evidence. *Cambridge J. Econ.*, March 1984, *8*(1), pp. 63–81.
[G: U.S.]

Roth, Alvin E. The Evolution of the Labor Market for Medical Interns and Residents: A Case Study in Game Theory. *J. Polit. Econ.*, December 1984, *92*(6), pp. 991–1016. **[G: U.S.]**

Santiago, Carlos E. and Thorbecke, Erik. Regional and Technological Dualism: A Dual–Dual Development Framework Applied to Puerto Rico. *J. Devel. Stud.*, July 1984, *20*(4), pp. 271–89. **[G: Puerto Rico]**

Schuh, G. Edward. Seasonal Farm Labor and U.S. Farm Policy: Discussion. In *Emerson, R. D., ed.*, 1984, pp. 476–81. **[G: U.S.]**

Sengenberger, Werner. West German Employment Policy: Restoring Worker Competition. *Ind. Relat.*, Fall 1984, *23*(3), pp. 323–43.
[G: W. Germany]

Siow, Aloysius. Occupational Choice under Uncertainty. *Econometrica*, May 1984, *52*(3), pp. 631–45. **[G: U.S.]**

Smith, James P. and Welch, Finis. Affirmative Action and Labor Markets. *J. Lab. Econ.*, April 1984, *2*(2), pp. 269–301. **[G: U.S.]**

Tichy, Gunther. Strategy and Implementation of Employment Policy in Austria: Successful Experiments with Unconventional Assignment of Instruments to Goals. *Kyklos*, 1984, *37*(3), pp. 363–86. **[G: Austria]**

Tirelli, Daniele. Osservazioni sui modelli allocativi del consumo e del tempo di lavoro. (Some Observations on Allocative Models of Consumption and Leisure. With English summary.) *Econ. Lavoro*, Jan.-Mar. 1984, *18*(1), pp. 53–75. **[G: W. Europe; U.S.; Canada; Australia]**

Viscusi, W. Kip and O'Connor, Charles J. Adaptive Responses to Chemical Labeling: Are Workers Bayesian Decision Makers? *Amer. Econ. Rev.*, December 1984, *74*(5), pp. 942–56. **[G: U.S.]**

Weinberg, Edgar. BLS and the Economy: A Centennial Timetable. *Mon. Lab. Rev.*, November 1984, *107*(11), pp. 29–37. **[G: U.S.]**

Welch, Finis. Nonimmigrant Aliens in American Agriculture: Discussion. In *Emerson, R. D., ed.*, 1984, pp. 194–99. **[G: U.S.]**

Wolfe, Barbara L., et al. Income Transfers and Work Effort: The Netherlands and the United States in the 1970s. *Kyklos*, 1984, *37*(4), pp. 609–37. **[G: Netherlands; U.S.]**

Wray, Kathleen. Labour Market Operation, Recruitment Strategies, and Workforce Structures. *Int. J. Soc. Econ.*, 1984, *11*(7), pp. 6–31. **[G: U.K.]**

824 Labor Market Studies, Wages, Employment

8241 Geographic Labor Market Studies

Bardhan, Pranab K. Determinants of Supply and Demand for Labor in a Poor Agrarian Economy: An Analysis of Household Survey Data from Rural West Bengal. In *Binswanger, H. P. and Rosenzweig, R., eds.*, 1984, pp. 242–62. **[G: India]**

van Delft, A. and Suyker, W. B. C. Interregional Migration in a Multiregional Labour Market Model for the Netherlands. In *ter Heide, H. and Willekens, F. J., eds.*, 1984, pp. 253–69. **[G: Netherlands]**

Fagnani, Jeanne. Marital Status and Occupational Structures in the Ile-de-France Region. *Urban Stud.*, May 1984, *21*(2), pp. 139–48. **[G: France]**

Flynn, Patricia M. Lowell: A High Technology Success Story. *New Eng. Econ. Rev.*, September–October 1984, pp. 39–49. **[G: U.S.]**

Guttierrez, Phillip R. The Channelization of Mexicans Nationals to the San Luis Valley of Colorado. In *Jones, R. C., ed.*, 1984, pp. 183–98. **[G: U.S.; Mexico]**

Jones, Richard C. Macro-patterns of Undocumented Migration between Mexico and the U.S. In *Jones, R. C., ed.*, 1984, pp. 33–57. **[G: U.S.; Mexico]**

Jusenius, Carol L. and Ledebur, Larry C. Where Have All the Firms Gone? An Analysis of the New England Economy. In *McKenzie, R. B., ed. (II)*, 1984, 1977, pp. 79–117. **[G: U.S.]**

Luger, Michael I. Investment Incentives and the Demand for Labor in U.S. Regions. *Reg. Sci. Urban Econ.*, November 1984, *14*(4), pp. 481–503. **[G: U.S.]**

Luria, Dan and Russell, Jack. Motor City Changeover. In *Sawers, L. and Tabb, W. K., eds.*, 1984, pp. 271–312. **[G: U.S.]**

MacCannell, Dean and White, Jerry. The Social Costs of Large-Scale Agriculture: The Prospects of Land Reform in California. In *Geisler, C. C. and Popper, F. J., eds.*, 1984, pp. 35–54. **[G: U.S.]**

Maillat, Denis. Mobility Channels: An Instrument for Analysing and Regulating the Local Labour Market. *Int. Lab. Rev.*, May–June 1984, *123*(3), pp. 349–62. **[G: Switzerand]**

Manuel, David P. Unemployment and Drilling Activity in Major Energy-producing States. *J. Energy Devel.*, Autumn 1984, *10*(1), pp. 44–62. **[G: U.S.]**

Martin, Ronald L. Redundancies, Labour Turnover and Employment Contraction in the Recession: A Regional Analysis. *Reg. Stud.*, December 1984, *18*(6), pp. 445–58. **[G: U.K.]**

Meager, Nigel. Job Loss and the Regions: How Important Is Redundancy? *Reg. Stud.*, December 1984, *18*(6), pp. 459–67. **[G: U.K.]**

Owen, D. W.; Gillespie, A. E. and Coombes, M. G. 'Job Shortfalls' in British Local Labour Market Areas: A Classification of Labour Supply and Demand Trends, 1971–1981. *Reg. Stud.*, December 1984, *18*(6), pp. 469–88. **[G: U.K.]**

Rietveld, Piet. Information Systems for Regional Labor Markets. In *Nijkamp, P. and Rietveld, P., eds.*, 1984, pp. 163–76.

Rosen, Richard J. Regional Variations in Employment and Unemployment during 1970–82. *Mon. Lab. Rev.*, February 1984, *107*(2), pp. 38–45. **[G: U.S.]**

Ryan, James G. and Ghodake, R. D. Labor Market Behavior in Rural Villages in South India: Effects of Season, Sex, and Socioeconomic Status. In *Binswanger, H. P. and Rosenzweig, R., eds.*, 1984, pp. 169–83. **[G: India]**

Stamas, George D. State and Regional Employment and Unemployment in 1983. *Mon. Lab. Rev.*, September 1984, *107*(9), pp. 9–15. **[G: U.S.]**

8242 Wage and Fringe Benefit Studies

Aaron, Henry J. Social Welfare in Australia. In *Caves, R. E. and Krause, L. B., eds.*, 1984, pp. 349–90. **[G: Australia]**

Åberg, Rune. Market-Independent Income Distribution: Efficiency and Legitimacy. In *Goldthorpe, J. H., ed.*, 1984, pp. 209–30. **[G: U.S.; Sweden]**

Addison, John T. Changes Over Time in the Union–Nonunion Wage Differential in the United States: Comment. In *Rosa, J.-J., ed.*, 1984, pp. 20–25. **[G: U.S.; U.K.]**

Adnett, N. J. On-the-Job Search and the Public Employment Service. *J. Econ. Stud.*, 1984, *11*(3), pp. 51–61. **[G: U.K.]**

Allen, Steven G.; Clark, Robert L. and Sumner, Daniel A. A Comparison of Pension Benefit Increases and Inflation, 1973–79. *Mon. Lab. Rev.*, May 1984, *107*(5), pp. 42–46. **[G: U.S.]**

Angel, Ronald. The Costs of Disability for Hispanic Males. *Soc. Sci. Quart.*, June 1984, *65*(2), pp. 426–43. **[G: U.S.]**

Antonelli, Gilberto. Risorse umane e redditi da lavoro. Domanda di istruzione, offerta di lavoro e comparazioni tra settore privato e settore pubblico. (Human Resources and Labour Incomes. Demand for Education, Labour Supply and Comparison between Private and Public Sector. With English summary.) *Econ. Lavoro*, Jan.-Mar. 1984, *18*(1), pp. 17–41. **[G: Italy]**

Appelbaum, Eileen. High Tech and the Structural Employment Problems of the 1980s. In *Collins, E. L. and Tanner, L. D., eds.*, 1984, pp. 23–48. **[G: U.S.]**

Armstrong, P. J. Work, Rest or Play? Changes in Time Spent at Work. In *Marstrand, P., ed.*, 1984, pp. 26–44. **[G: U.K.]**

Artus, Jacques R. Are Real Wages Too High in Europe? *Finance Develop.*, December 1984, *21*(4), pp. 10–13. **[G: W. Europe; U.S.; Canada; Japan]**

Artus, Jacques R. The Disequilibrium Real Wage Rate Hypothesis: An Empirical Evaluation. *Int. Monet. Fund Staff Pap.*, June 1984, *31*(2), pp. 249–302. **[G: OECD]**

Ascah, Louis. Recent Pension Reports in Canada: A Survey. *Can. Public Policy*, December 1984, *10*(4), pp. 415–28. **[G: Canada]**

Asher, Martin A. On the Estimation of Payroll Tax Incidence: Comment. *Southern Econ. J.*, April 1984, *50*(4), pp. 1224–30.   [**G: U.S.**]

Asher, Martin A. and Popkin, Joel. Industrial and Labor Relations Review: Comment. *Ind. Lab. Relat. Rev.*, October 1984, *38*(1), pp. 36.
[**G: U.S.**]

Asher, Martin A. and Popkin, Joel. The Effect of Gender and Race Differentials on Public–Private Wage Comparisons: A Study of Postal Workers. *Ind. Lab. Relat. Rev.*, October 1984, *38*(1), pp. 16–25.   [**G: U.S.**]

Aspe, Pedro and Beristain, Javier. Toward a First Estimate of the Evolution of Inequality in Mexico. In *Aspe, P. and Sigmund, P. E., eds.*, 1984, pp. 31–57.   [**G: Mexico**]

Balcer, Yves and Sahin, Izzet. Dynamics of Pension Reform: The Case of Ontario. *J. Risk Ins.*, December 1984, *51*(4), pp. 652–86.
[**G: Canada**]

Banaji, Jairus. Accumulation and Exploitability: Wage Determination and Pay Conflict. In *Ngo, M., ed., vol. 1*, 1984, pp. 295–323.
[**G: India**]

Banting, Keith G. The Decision Rules: Federalism and Pension Reform. In *Conklin, D. W.; Bennett, J. H. and Courchene, T. J., eds.*, 1984, pp. 189–209.   [**G: Canada**]

Bartlett, Robin L. and Callahan, Charles, III. Wage Determination and Marital Status: Another Look. *Ind. Relat.*, Winter 1984, *23*(1), pp. 90–96.   [**G: U.S.**]

Bassi, Laurie J. Estimating the Effect of Training Programs with Non-Random Selection. *Rev. Econ. Statist.*, February 1984, *66*(1), pp. 36–43.   [**G: U.S.**]

Beach, Charles M. Who Will Pay for Proposed Public Pension Reforms? In *Conklin, D. W.; Bennett, J. H. and Courchene, T. J., eds.*, 1984, pp. 210–40.   [**G: Canada**]

Behrend, Hilde. Financial Incentives as the Expression of a System of Beliefs. In *Behrend, H.*, 1984, *1959*, pp. 132–44.

Behrend, Hilde. Inflation and Attitudes to Pay Increases: The Major Issues. In *Behrend, H.*, 1984, pp. 206–17.

Behrend, Hilde. Problems of Labour and Inflation: Concluding Comments. In *Behrend, H.*, 1984, pp. 224–43.

Behrend, Hilde. Research into Inflation and Conceptions of Earnings. In *Behrend, H.*, 1984, pp. 178–90.   [**G: U.K.**]

Behrend, Hilde. Some Aspects of Company Wage Policy. In *Behrend, H.*, 1984, pp. 164–77.

Behrend, Hilde. The Effort Bargain. In *Behrend, H.*, 1984, *1957*, pp. 110–31.

Bell, Donald and Graham, Avy. Surviving Spouse's Benefits in Private Pension Plans. *Mon. Lab. Rev.*, April 1984, *107*(4), pp. 23–31.   [**G: U.S.**]

Bell, Donald and Hill, Diane. How Social Security Payments Affect Private Pensions. *Mon. Lab. Rev.*, May 1984, *107*(5), pp. 15–20.
[**G: U.S.**]

Berger, Mark C. Cohort Size and the Earnings

Growth of Young Workers. *Ind. Lab. Relat. Rev.*, July 1984, *37*(4), pp. 582–91. [**G: U.S.**]

Birdsall, Nancy and Behrman, Jere R. Does Geographical Aggregation Cause Overestimates of the Returns to Schooling? *Oxford Bull. Econ. Statist.*, February 1984, *46*(1), pp. 55–72.
[**G: Brazil**]

Bisset, Terry. Pensions and Divorce. In *Conklin, D. W.; Bennett, J. H. and Courchene, T. J., eds.*, 1984, pp. 426–31.   [**G: Canada**]

Blakemore, Arthur E. and Low, Stuart A. The High-School Dropout Decision and Its Wage Consequences. *Econ. Educ. Rev.*, 1984, *3*(2), pp. 111–19.   [**G: U.S.**]

Blanchflower, David. Comparative Pay Levels in Domestically-owned and Foreign-owned Manufacturing Plants: A Comment. *Brit. J. Ind. Relat.*, July 1984, *22*(2), pp. 265–67.
[**G: U.K.**]

Blanchflower, David. Union Relative Wage Effects: A Cross-Section Analysis Using Establishment Data. *Brit. J. Ind. Relat.*, November 1984, *22*(3), pp. 311–32.   [**G: U.K.**]

Blau, David M. Family Earnings and Wage Inequality Early in the Life Cycle. *Rev. Econ. Statist.*, May 1984, *66*(2), pp. 200–207.
[**G: U.S.**]

Bloom, Howard S. Estimating the Effect of Job-training Programs, Using Longitudinal Data: Ashenfelter's Findings Reconsidered. *J. Human Res.*, Fall 1984, *19*(4), pp. 544–56.
[**G: U.S.**]

Blumrosen, Ruth Gerber. Work Sharing, STC, and Affirmative Action. In *MaCoy, R. and Morand, M. J., eds.*, 1984, pp. 139–57.
[**G: U.S.**]

Bodkin, Ronald G. Comments [Indexed Bonds as an Instrument of Pension Reform] [Registered Pension Accounts (RPAs) as an Instrument of Pension Reform]. In *Conklin, D. W.; Bennett, J. H. and Courchene, T. J., eds.*, 1984, pp. 401–05.   [**G: Canada**]

Boehm, Ernst A. Money Wages, Consumer Prices, and Causality in Australia. *Econ. Rec.*, September 1984, *60*(170), pp. 236–51.
[**G: Australia**]

Borjas, George J. Electoral Cycles and the Earnings of Federal Bureaucrats. *Econ. Inquiry*, October 1984, *22*(4), pp. 447–59. [**G: U.S.**]

Borjas, George J. Race, Turnover, and Male Earnings. *Ind. Relat.*, Winter 1984, *23*(1), pp. 73–89.   [**G: U.S.**]

Borus, Michael E. A Description of Employed and Unemployed Youth in 1981. In *Borus, M. E., ed.*, 1984, pp. 13–55.   [**G: U.S.**]

Bossons, John. Indexed Bonds as an Instrument of Pension Reform. In *Conklin, D. W.; Bennett, J. H. and Courchene, T. J., eds.*, 1984, pp. 327–59.   [**G: Canada**]

Boucher, Michel. Les Canadiens français dans la Ligue nationale de hockey: une analyse statistique. (French-Canadians in the National Hockey League: A Statistical Note. With English summary.) *L'Actual. Econ.*, September 1984, *60*(3), pp. 308–25.   [**G: Canada**]

Bourguignon, François and Morrisson, Christian.

La mobilité des salaires sur le cycle de vie: un échantillon de cadres français sur trente ans. (Earning Mobility over the Life-Cycle: A Thirty-Years Panel Sample of French "Cadres." With English summary.) *Revue Écon.*, September 1984, *35*(5), pp. 929–70.

Bretzfelder, Robert and Friedenberg, Howard. Regional Nonfarm Wages and Salaries Thus Far in the Recovery. *Surv. Curr. Bus.*, April 1984, *64*(4), pp. 25–26. **[G: U.S.]**

Briguglio, Pasquale Lino. The Specification and Estimation of a Disequilibrium Labour Market Model. *Appl. Econ.*, August 1984, *16*(4), pp. 539–54. **[G: Malta]**

Brown, Charles. Black–White Earnings Ratios since the Civil Rights Act of 1964: The Importance of Labor Market Dropouts. *Quart. J. Econ.*, February 1984, *99*(1), pp. 31–44. **[G: U.S.]**

Brown, William, et al. Product and Labour Markets in Wage Determination: Some Australian Evidence. *Brit. J. Ind. Relat.*, July 1984, *22*(2), pp. 169–76. **[G: Australia]**

Browne, Lynn E. How Different Are Regional Wages? A Second Look. *New Eng. Econ. Rev.*, March–April 1984, pp. 40–47. **[G: U.S.]**

Burbidge, John B. Who Will Pay for Proposed Public Pension Reforms? Comments. In *Conklin, D. W.; Bennett, J. H. and Courchene, T. J., eds.*, 1984, pp. 264–65. **[G: Canada]**

Burkhauser, Richard V. Pension Plan Equity: Second-Round Consequences. *J. Policy Anal. Manage.*, Summer 1984, *3*(4), pp. 613–18. **[G: U.S.]**

Burton, John. Strike Cost and Wage Rates: Cross-Industry Differences: Comment. In *Rosa, J.-J., ed.*, 1984, pp. 37–41. **[G: U.S.]**

Cagan, Phillip and Fellner, William. The Cost of Disinflation, Credibility, and the Deceleration of Wages 1982–1983. In *Fellner, W., ed.*, 1984, pp. 7–19. **[G: U.S.]**

Cain, Glen. Estimating the Impact of Labor Market Policies on Women: A Discussion of the Four-Country Studies on the Employment of Women. In *Schmid, G. and Weitzel, R., eds.*, 1984, pp. 249–63. **[G: Sweden; U.K.; U.S.; W. Germany]**

Calmfors, Lars. Stabilization Policy and Wage Formation in Economies with Strong Trade Unions. In *Emerson, M., ed.*, 1984, pp. 89–121. **[G: Scandinavia; Belgium; Austria; Netherlands]**

Cappelli, Peter. Auto Industry Experiments with the Guaranteed Income Stream. *Mon. Lab. Rev.*, July 1984, *107*(7), pp. 37–39. **[G: U.S.]**

Carlson, Norma W. Pay in Mountain Region Coal Mines Outstrips National Average. *Mon. Lab. Rev.*, March 1984, *107*(3), pp. 49–52. **[G: U.S.]**

Carlson, Norma W. Pay Gains Tempered in Basic Steel Mills. *Mon. Lab. Rev.*, August 1984, *107*(8), pp. 28–30. **[G: U.S.]**

Chamberlin, John. Pension Plan Equity: The Debate Continued [Equity between the Sexes: The Pension Problem]. *J. Policy Anal. Manage.*, Fall 1984, *4*(1), pp. 121. **[G: U.S.]**

Charpin, Jean-Michel. The Adaptation of Working Time as a Response to the Unemployment Problem. In *Emerson, M., ed.*, 1984, pp. 174–94. **[G: France; Netherlands; U.K.; W. Germany]**

Chomitz, Kenneth M. and Lave, Charles A. Part-Time Labour, Work Rules, and Urban Transit Costs. *J. Transp. Econ. Policy*, January 1984, *18*(1), pp. 63–73. **[G: U.S.]**

Christl, Josef. The Explanatory Power of the Human Capital Earnings Function. *Empirica*, 1984, *11*(1), pp. 47–57. **[G: Austria]**

Clark, Robert L.; Gohmann, Stephan F. and Sumner, Daniel A. Wages and Hours of Work of Elderly Men. *Atlantic Econ. J.*, December 1984, *12*(4), pp. 31–40. **[G: U.S.]**

Clark, Robert M. Comments [Reforming Public Pensions in Canada: Issues and Options] [Tax-Transfer Benefits for the Elderly]. In *Conklin, D. W.; Bennett, J. H. and Courchene, T. J., eds.*, 1984, pp. 266–73. **[G: Canada]**

Coltrane, Robert. The Off-Farm Work of Hired Farm Workers: Discussion. In *Emerson, R. D., ed.*, 1984, pp. 164–67. **[G: U.S.]**

Conway, Delores A. and Roberts, Harry V. Rejoinder to Comments on "Reverse Regression, Fairness, and Employment Discrimination." *J. Bus. Econ. Statist.*, April 1984, *2*(2), pp. 126–39. **[G: U.S.]**

Corbett, Marie. The Impact of Pension Reforms on Women: Employment Pension Plans. In *Conklin, D. W.; Bennett, J. H. and Courchene, T. J., eds.*, 1984, pp. 417–25. **[G: Canada]**

Courant, Paul N. The Private Pension System to the Year 2020: Comment. In *Aaron, H. J. and Burtless, G., eds.*, 1984, pp. 342–44. **[G: U.S.]**

Cousineau, Jean-Michel. La détermination des salaires des policiers municipaux au Québec. (The Determinants of Wages in the Municipal Police Services in Quebec. With English summary.) *L'Actual. Écon.*, June 1984, *60*(2), pp. 186–99. **[G: Canada]**

Cox, Donald. Panel Estimates of the Effects of Career Interruptions on the Earnings of Women. *Econ. Inquiry*, July 1984, *22*(3), pp. 386–403. **[G: U.S.]**

Coxe, Donald. A Look at the Pension Iceberg. In *Conklin, D. W.; Bennett, J. H. and Courchene, T. J., eds.*, 1984, pp. 439–44. **[G: Canada]**

Coyte, Peter C. Optimal Job Assignment and Investment in Specific Human Capital: An Application to Professional Teachers. *Appl. Econ.*, October 1984, *16*(5), pp. 703–15. **[G: Canada]**

Crockett, Geoffrey and Elias, Peter. British Managers: A Study of their Education, Training, Mobility and Earnings. *Brit. J. Ind. Relat.*, March 1984, *22*(1), pp. 34–46. **[G: U.K.]**

Cullison, William E. Equalizing Regional Differences in Wages: A Study of Wages and Migration in the South and Other Regions. *Fed. Res. Bank Richmond Econ. Rev.*, May/June 1984, *70*(3), pp. 20–33. **[G: U.S.]**

D'Amico, Ronald. The Time-Use Behavior of

Young Adults. In *Borus, M. E., ed.*, 1984, pp. 193–238. [G: U.S.]

Dabscheck, Braham and Niland, John. Recent Trends in Collective Bargaining in Australia. *Int. Lab. Rev.*, September–October 1984, *123*(5), pp. 631–46. [G: Australia]

Dal Co, Mario; Longobardi, Ernesto and Vitaletti, Giuseppe. Le liquidazioni e la loro tassazione: un problema di politica economica. (The Taxation of Allowances for Termination of Employment: An Economic-Policy Matter. With English summary.) *Bancaria*, August 1984, *40*(8), pp. 721–40. [G: Italy]

Dauffenbach, Robert C. and Greer, Charles R. A Comparison of Job Analytic and Conventional Economic Variables as Explanations of Occupational Earnings Differentials. *J. Econ. Bus.*, February 1984, *36*(1), pp. 43–64. [G: U.S.]

Davila, Alberto E. Racial Earnings Differentials in Texas. *Fed. Res. Bank Dallas Econ. Rev.*, November 1984, pp. 13–23. [G: U.S.]

Davis, Lance. Discussion [The Decline of the British Economy: An Institutional Perspective] [Structural Transformation and the Demand for New Labor in Advanced Economies: Interwar Britain]. *J. Econ. Hist.*, June 1984, *44*(2), pp. 596–99. [G: U.K.]

Dawkins, Peter and Sloan, Judith. The Australian Labour Market, June 1984. *Australian Bull. Lab.*, June 1984, *10*(3), pp. 113–33. [G: Australia]

Daymont, Thomas N. and Andrisani, Paul J. Job Preferences, College Major, and the Gender Gap in Earnings. *J. Human Res.*, Summer 1984, *19*(3), pp. 408–28. [G: U.S.]

Decaluwe, Bernard. Le modèle scandinave et l'économie canadienne. (The Scandinavian Model and the Canadian Economy. With English summary.) *L'Actual. Econ.*, June 1984, *60*(2), pp. 164–85. [G: Canada]

Del Boca, Daniela. Differenziali salariali e alternative di orario. (Wage Differentials in Alternative Working Schedules. With English summary.) *Econ. Lavoro*, Oct.-Dec. 1984, *18*(4), pp. 3–16. [G: Italy]

Delaney, John Thomas; Feuille, Peter and Hendricks, Wallace E. Police Salaries, Interest Arbitration, and the Leveling Effect. *Ind. Relat.*, Fall 1984, *23*(3), pp. 417–23. [G: U.S.]

Desai, Meghnad. An Econometric Model of the Share of Wages in National Income: UK 1855–1965. In *Goodwin, R. M.; Krüger, M. and Vercelli, A., eds.*, 1984, pp. 253–77. [G: U.K.]

Dickens, William T. Differences between Risk Premiums in Union and Nonunion Wages and the Case for Occupational Safety Regulation. *Amer. Econ. Rev.*, May 1984, *74*(2), pp. 320–23. [G: U.S.]

Dicks-Mireaux, Louis and King, Mervyn A. Pension Wealth and Household Savings: Tests of Robustness. *J. Public Econ.*, February/March 1984, *23*(1/2), pp. 115–39. [G: Canada]

Dieguez, Héctor L. and Gerchunoff, Pablo. La dinámica del mercado laboral urbano en la Argentina, 1976–1981. (With English summary.) *Desarrollo Econ.*, April–June 1984, *24*(93), pp. 3–40. [G: Argentina]

Dimsdale, N. H. Employment and Real Wages in the Inter-war Period. *Nat. Inst. Econ. Rev.*, November 1984, (110), pp. 94–103. [G: U.K.]

Disney, Richard and Szyszczak, E. M. Protective Legislation and Part-Time Employment in Britain. *Brit. J. Ind. Relat.*, March 1984, *22*(1), pp. 78–100. [G: U.K.]

Doeringer, Peter B. Unions: Economic Performance and Labor Market Structure. In *Rosa, J.-J., ed.*, 1984, pp. 315–38. [G: U.S.; OECD]

Doi, Noriyuki. Industrial Concentration and Employee Compensation: Some Evidence from Japan. *Rivista Int. Sci. Econ. Com.*, September 1984, *31*(9), pp. 844–57. [G: Japan]

Dooley, Martin D. and Gottschalk, Peter. Earnings Inequality among Males in the United States: Trends and the Effect of Labor Force Growth. *J. Polit. Econ.*, February 1984, *92*(1), pp. 59–89. [G: U.S.]

Douty, H. M. A Century of Wage Statistics: The BLS Contribution. *Mon. Lab. Rev.*, November 1984, *107*(11), pp. 16–28. [G: U.S.]

Duchin, Faye. Automation and Its Effect on Employment and Income. In *Collins, E. L. and Tanner, L. D., eds.*, 1984, pp. 49–75. [G: U.S.]

Earle, John S. and Kniesner, Thomas J. Inflation, Unemployment and the Reagan Administration. *Bus. Econ.*, October 1984, *19*(5), pp. 26–33. [G: U.S.]

Eckstein, Otto. Foundations of Aggregate Supply Price. *Amer. Econ. Rev.*, May 1984, *74*(2), pp. 216–20. [G: U.S.]

Ehrenberg, Ronald G. and Schumann, Paul L. Compensating Wage Differentials for Mandatory Overtime? *Econ. Inquiry*, October 1984, *22*(4), pp. 460–78. [G: U.S.]

Eichengreen, Barry. Experience and the Male–Female Earnings Gap in the 1890s. *J. Econ. Hist.*, September 1984, *44*(3), pp. 822–34. [G: U.S.]

Elbaum, Bernard. The Making and Shaping of Job and Pay Structures in the Iron and Steel Industry. In *Osterman, P., ed.*, 1984, pp. 71–107. [G: OECD]

Ellman, Michael. Income Distribution in the USSR. In *Ellman, M.*, 1984, pp. 112–29. [G: U.S.S.R.]

Ellman, Michael. The Distribution of Earnings under Brezhnev. In *Ellman, M.*, 1984, *1980*, pp. 108–11. [G: U.S.S.R.]

Emerson, Robert D. Migration in Farm Labor Markets. In *Emerson, R. D., ed.*, 1984, pp. 104–35. [G: U.S.]

Esping-Andersen, Gösta and Korpi, Walter. Social Policy as Class Politics in Post-war Capitalism: Scandinavia, Austria, and Germany. In *Goldthorpe, J. H., ed.*, 1984, pp. 179–208. [G: Scandinavia; Austria; Germany]

Estrella, Arturo. Corporate Use of Pension Overfunding. *Fed. Res. Bank New York Quart. Rev.*, Spring 1984, *9*(1), pp. 17–25. [G: U.S.]

Evans, Robert, Jr. 'Lifetime Earnings' in Japan for the Class of 1955. *Mon. Lab. Rev.*, April 1984, *107*(4), pp. 32–36.　　　　[G: Japan]

Evans, Robert, Jr. Pay Differentials: The Case of Japan. *Mon. Lab. Rev.*, October 1984, *107*(10), pp. 24–29.　　[G: Japan; U.S.]

Falus-Szikra, Katalin. Distribution According to Work and Reform in Hungary. *Acta Oecon.*, 1984, *33*(1–2), pp. 1–16.　　[G: Hungary]

Farber, Henry S. Right-to-Work Laws and the Extent of Unionization. *J. Lab. Econ.*, July 1984, *2*(3), pp. 319–52.　　　　[G: U.S.]

Feldstein, Martin and Poterba, James M. Unemployment Insurance and Reservation Wages. *J. Public Econ.*, February/March 1984, *23*(1/2), pp. 141–67.　　　　[G: U.S.]

Ferber, Marianne A. and Green, Carole A. What Kind of Fairness Is Fair? A Comment [Reverse Regression, Fairness, and Employment Discrimination]. *J. Bus. Econ. Statist.*, April 1984, *2*(2), pp. 111–13.　　　[G: U.S.]

Ferber, Marianne A. and Spaeth, Joe L. Work Characteristics and the Male–Female Earnings Gap. *Amer. Econ. Rev.*, May 1984, *74*(2), pp. 260–64.　　　　[G: U.S.]

Fil'ev, V. The Relationship between the Growth of Labor Productivity and Wages. *Prob. Econ.*, October 1984, *27*(6), pp. 71–86.[G: U.S.S.R.]

Fishback, Price. Segregation in Job Hierarchies: West Virginia Coal Mining, 1906–1932. *J. Econ. Hist.*, September 1984, *44*(3), pp. 755–74.　　　　[G: U.S.]

Flaim, Paul O. Proposed Spendable Earnings Series Retains Basic Faults of Earlier One. *Mon. Lab. Rev.*, November 1984, *107*(11), pp. 43–44.　　　　[G: U.S.]

Flanagan, Robert J. Wage Concessions and Long-Term Union Wage Flexibility. *Brookings Pap. Econ. Act.*, 1984, (1), pp. 183–216. [G: U.S.]

Foster, Nigel; Henry, S. G. B. and Trinder, Chris. Public and Private Sector Pay: A Partly Disaggregated Study. *Nat. Inst. Econ. Rev.*, February 1984, (107), pp. 63–73.　[G: U.K.]

Fosu, Augustin Kwasi. Unions and Fringe Benefits: Additional Evidence. *J. Lab. Res.*, Summer 1984, *5*(3), pp. 247–54.　　[G: U.S.]

Fougere, Denis. Insertion professionnelle, mobilité, salaire: le cas des sortants de l'enseignement technique court. (Insertion into the Labour Market, Mobility, Wage: The Case of Young Men with Professional Training Diplomas. With English summary.) *Consommation*, Oct.–Dec. 1984, *31*(4), pp. 29–64.
　　　　[G: France]

Frank, Robert H. Are Workers Paid Their Marginal Products? *Amer. Econ. Rev.*, September 1984, *74*(4), pp. 549–71.　　[G: U.S.]

Franz, Wolfgang. Inflation und interindustrielle Lohnstruktur. (Inflation and the Interindustrial Wage Structure. With English summary.) *Ifo-Studien*, 1984, *30*(2), pp. 81–106.
　　　　[G: Germany]

Franz, Wolfgang. Is Less More? The Current Discussion about Reduced Working Time in Western Germany: A Survey of the Debate. *Z. ges. Staatswiss.*, December 1984, *140*(4), pp. 626–54.　　　　[G: W. Germany]

Freeman, Richard B. Longitudinal Analyses of the Effects of Trade Unions. *J. Lab. Econ.*, January 1984, *2*(1), pp. 1–26.　　[G: U.S.]

Freeman, Richard B. The Structure of Labor Markets: A Book Review Three Decades Later. In [Reynolds, L. G.], 1984, pp. 201–26.
　　　　[G: U.S.]

Frenkel, Roberto. Salarios industriales e inflación. El período 1976–82. (With English summary.) *Desarrollo Econ.*, October–December 1984, *24*(95), pp. 387–414.　　[G: Argentina]

Fry, Vanessa C. Inequality in Family Earnings. *Fisc. Stud.*, August 1984, *5*(3), pp. 54–61.
　　　　[G: U.K.]

Fujita, Sei. On the Tax Treatment of Pension Plans. (In Japanese. With English summary.) *Osaka Econ. Pap.*, December 1984, *34*(2–3), pp. 52–62.　　　　[G: Japan]

Fulco, Lawrence J. Strong Post-Recession Gain in Productivity Contributes to Slow Growth in Labor Costs. *Mon. Lab. Rev.*, December 1984, *107*(12), pp. 3–10.　　[G: U.S.]

García, Norberto and Tokman, Víctor E. Changes in Employment and the Crisis. *Cepal Rev.*, 1984, (24), pp. 103–15.
　　　　[G: Latin America]

Gardini, Attilio. Indici settoriali per l'analisi territoriale delle tecniche e della produttivita'. Un'applicazione al confronto fra l'economia italiana e quella emiliano-romagnola. (Multisectoral Indices for the Spatial Analysis of the Techniques and of Productivity. An Application for the Comparison between the Economic Structure of Italy and of Emilia Romagna. With English summary.) *Statistica*, July–September 1984, *44*(3), pp. 443–62.　　[G: Italy]

Gay, Robert S. Union Settlements and Aggregate Wage Behavior in the 1980s. *Fed. Res. Bull.*, December 1984, *70*(12), pp. 843–56.
　　　　[G: U.S.]

Giannola, Giuseppina. Il "potere sindacale" ed i modelli di "inflazione salariale": un'analisi statistica dell'esperienza italiana per il periodo 1951–1977. (Trade-union Power and the Models of "Wage Inflation": A Statistical Analysis for Italy, 1951–1977. With English summary.) *Econ. Lavoro*, Apr.-June 1984, *18*(2), pp. 105–18.　　　　[G: Italy]

van Ginneken, Wouter. Employment and the Reduction of the Work Week: A Comparison of Seven European Macro-Economic Models. *Int. Lab. Rev.*, January-February 1984, *123*(1), pp. 35–52.　　　[G: W. Europe]

Glucklich, Pauline. The Effects of Statutory Employment Policies on Women in the United Kingdom Labour Market. In *Schmid, G. and Weitzel, R., eds.*, 1984, pp. 107–31.
　　　　[G: U.K.]

Goldberger, Arthur S. Redirecting Reverse Regression [Reverse Regression, Fairness, and Employment Discrimination]. *J. Bus. Econ. Statist.*, April 1984, *2*(2), pp. 114–16.
　　　　[G: U.S.]

Goldberger, Arthur S. Reverse Regression and

Salary Discrimination. *J. Human Res.*, Summer 1984, *19*(3), pp. 293–318. [G: U.S.]

Goldin, Claudia. The Historical Evolution of Female Earnings Functions and Occupations. *Exploration Econ. Hist.*, January 1984, *21*(1), pp. 1–27. [G: U.S.]

Gomez-Mejia, Luis R. and Balkin, David B. Union Impacts on Secretarial Earnings: A Public Sector Case. *Ind. Relat.*, Winter 1984, *23*(1), pp. 97–102. [G: U.S.]

Gramlich, Edward M. and Laren, Deborah S. How Widespread Are Income Losses in a Recession? In *Bawden, D. L., ed.*, 1984, pp. 157–80. [G: U.S.]

Green, Carole A. and Ferber, Marianne A. Employment Discrimination: An Empirical Test of Forward versus Reverse Regression. *J. Human Res.*, Fall 1984, *19*(4), pp. 557–69. [G: U.S.]

Greene, William H. Reverse Regression: The Algebra of Discrimination [Reverse Regression, Fairness, and Employment Discrimination]. *J. Bus. Econ. Statist.*, April 1984, *2*(2), pp. 117–20. [G: U.S.]

Gregory, Peter. The Mexican Labor Market, 1940–1980. In *[Reynolds, L. G.]*, 1984, pp. 245–79. [G: Mexico]

Grenier, Gilles. The Effects of Language Characteristics on the Wages of Hispanic-American Males. *J. Human Res.*, Winter 1984, *19*(1), pp. 35–52. [G: U.S.]

Grimes, Arthur. The Impact of Taxes on Wages: A Comment. *Econ. Notes*, 1984, (3), pp. 163–66. [G: U.S.]

Grosskopf, Shawna and Hayes, Kathy. Measuring the Excess Burden of State Pension Mandates. *Public Finance*, 1984, *39*(1), pp. 90–103. [G: U.S.]

Grubb, D.; Layard, R. and Symons, J. Wages, Unemployment, and Incomes Policies. In *Emerson, M., ed.*, 1984, pp. 57–88. [G: OECD]

Grubel, Herbert G. and Spindler, Zane A. Bonus Pay Systems for Greater Economic Stability. *Can. Public Policy*, June 1984, *10*(2), pp. 185–92. [G: Canada]

Guisinger, Stephen E.; Henderson, James W. and Scully, Gerald W. Earnings, Rates of Return to Education and the Earnings Distribution in Pakistan. *Econ. Educ. Rev.*, 1984, *3*(4), pp. 257–67. [G: Pakistan]

Halperin, Daniel. Broadening the Base—The Case of Fringe Benefits. *Nat. Tax J.*, September 1984, *37*(3), pp. 271–81. [G: U.S.]

Hamermesh, Daniel S. On the Estimation of Payroll Tax Incidence: Reply. *Southern Econ. J.*, April 1984, *50*(4), pp. 1231. [G: U.S.]

Harris, William G. Problems in the Use of Historical Data in Estimating Economic Loss in Wrongful Death and Injury Cases: Comment. *J. Risk Ins.*, March 1984, *51*(1), pp. 122–26. [G: U.S.]

He, Xiaopei. An Investigation into the Current Compensation System for Mental and Manual Labor. *Chinese Econ. Stud.*, Fall 1984, *18*(1), pp. 77–95. [G: China]

Healy, C. Ross. Pensions and the Capital Markets:

Independence or Intervention? In *Conklin, D. W.; Bennett, J. H. and Courchene, T. J., eds.*, 1984, pp. 283–94. [G: Canada]

Heery, Edmund. Group Incentives and the Mining Supervisor: The Effects of a Payment System on First-Line Management. *Brit. J. Ind. Relat.*, November 1984, *22*(3), pp. 333–45. [G: U.K.]

Hennart, Jean-François. The Determinants of Union Staff Salaries: A New Meaning to Business Unionism: Comment. In *Rosa, J.-J., ed.*, 1984, pp. 306–11. [G: U.S.; France]

Hennart, Jean-François. The Relative Wage Effect of French Unions. In *Rosa, J.-J., ed.*, 1984, pp. 63–81. [G: France]

Heroles, Jesús F. Reyes. The Distribution of Labor Income in Mexico. In *Aspe, P. and Sigmund, P. E., eds.*, 1984, pp. 129–86. [G: Mexico]

Hickman, Bert G. and Klein, Lawrence R. Wage–Price Behavior in the National Models of Project LINK. *Amer. Econ. Rev.*, May 1984, *74*(2), pp. 150–54. [G: OECD]

Hill, James Richard and Spellman, William. Pay Discrimination in Baseball: Data from the Seventies. *Ind. Relat.*, Winter 1984, *23*(1), pp. 103–12. [G: U.S.]

Hill, John K. Union Wage Distortions and the Size and Efficiency of the Optimal Tariff. *Can. J. Econ.*, February 1984, *17*(1), pp. 146–55. [G: U.S.]

Hill, Raymond D. State Enterprise and Income Distribution in Mexico. In *Aspe, P. and Sigmund, P. E., eds.*, 1984, pp. 357–96. [G: Mexico]

Hirsch, Barry T. Physical Capital, Human Capital and the Distribution of Earnings. *Econ. Educ. Rev.*, 1984, *3*(1), pp. 55–64. [G: U.S.]

Hoffman, Saul D. Black–White Differences in Returns to Higher Education: Evidence from the 1970s. *Econ. Educ. Rev.*, 1984, *3*(1), pp. 13–21. [G: U.S.]

Hoffman, Saul D. and Link, Charles R. Selectivity Bias in Male Wage Equations: Black–White Comparisons. *Rev. Econ. Statist.*, May 1984, *66*(2), pp. 320–24. [G: U.S.]

Holland, A. Steven. The Impact of Inflation Uncertainty on the Labor Market. *Fed. Res. Bank St. Louis Rev.*, August/September 1984, *66*(7), pp. 21–28. [G: U.S.]

Holmlund, Bertil. Income Prospects and Job Mobility: The Case of Sweden. *Europ. Econ. Rev.*, April 1984, *24*(3), pp. 383–400. [G: Sweden]

Horn, Robert N. and McGuire, William J. Determinants of Secondary School Teacher Salaries in a Large Urban School District. *Southern Econ. J.*, October 1984, *51*(2), pp. 481–94. [G: U.S.]

Hosek, William R. Problems in the Use of Historical Data in Estimating Economic Loss in Wrongful Death and Injury Cases: Reply. *J. Risk Ins.*, March 1984, *51*(1), pp. 127–30. [G: U.S.]

Hughes, Barry. Taxation and Overtime Hours:

An Australian Study. *Manchester Sch. Econ. Soc. Stud.*, June 1984, *52*(2), pp. 171–95.
[G: Australia]

Hunnicutt, Benjamin Kline. The End of Shorter Hours. *Labor Hist.*, Summer 1984, *25*(3), pp. 373–404. [G: U.S.]

Hunter, Donna. Oregon Tries the "Workshare" Idea. In *MaCoy, R. and Morand, M. J., eds.*, 1984, pp. 95–105. [G: U.S.]

Hylton, Keith. Illusory Wage Differentials: Comment [The Narrowing of Black–White Wage Differentials Is Illusory]. *Amer. Econ. Rev.*, December 1984, *74*(5), pp. 1124–27.
[G: U.S.]

Hyman, Jeffrey and Schuller, Tom. Occupational Pension Schemes and Collective Bargaining. *Brit. J. Ind. Relat.*, November 1984, *22*(3), pp. 289–310. [G: U.K.]

Ingberg, Mikael. Eläkkeet ja tulonjako. (Pensions and Redistribution. With English summary.) *Kansant. Aikak.*, 1984, *80*(2), pp. 141–62.
[G: Finland]

Ishikawa, Tsuneo and Ueda, Kazuo. The Bonus Payment System and Japanese Personal Savings. In *Aoki, M., ed.*, 1984, pp. 133–92.
[G: Japan]

Ittner, Linda A. The Federal Response to Short-Time Compensation. In *MaCoy, R. and Morand, M. J., eds.*, 1984, pp. 120–35.
[G: U.S.]

Jacobson, Louis. A Tale of Employment Decline in Two Cities: How Bad Was the Worst of Times? *Ind. Lab. Relat. Rev.*, July 1984, *37*(4), pp. 557–69. [G: U.S.]

Jaussaud, Danielle P. Can Job Evaluation Systems Help Determine the Comparable Worth of Male and Female Occupations? *J. Econ. Issues*, June 1984, *18*(2), pp. 473–82. [G: U.S.]

Jensen, Gail; Feldman, Roger and Dowd, Bryan. Corporate Benefit Policies and Health Insurance Costs. *J. Health Econ.*, December 1984, *3*(3), pp. 275–96. [G: U.S.]

Johnson, George E. Changes Over Time in the Union–Nonunion Wage Differential in the United States. In *Rosa, J.-J., ed.*, 1984, pp. 3–19. [G: U.S.]

Johnson, Paul. Self-Help versus State Help: Old Age Pensions and Personal Savings in Great Britain, 1906–1937. *Exploration Econ. Hist.*, October 1984, *21*(4), pp. 329–50. [G: U.K.]

Johnson, Terry R. and Pencavel, John H. Dynamic Hours of Work Functions for Husbands, Wives, and Single Females. *Econometrica*, March 1984, *52*(2), pp. 363–89.

Johnson, William G. and Heler, Edward. Compensation for Death from Asbestos. *Ind. Lab. Relat. Rev.*, July 1984, *37*(4), pp. 529–40.

Johri, C. K. Labour Supply Factors in Earnings' Differentials. In *Singh, A. K.; Papola, T. S. and Mathur, R. S., eds.*, 1984, pp. 109–37.
[G: India]

Jump, G. V. Financing Public Pensions: Some Capital Market Implications. In *Conklin, D. W.; Bennett, J. H. and Courchene, T. J., eds.*, 1984, pp. 295–326. [G: Canada]

Kahn, George A. International Differences in

Wage Behavior: Real, Nominal, or Exaggerated? *Amer. Econ. Rev.*, May 1984, *74*(2), pp. 155–59. [G: OECD]

Kalleberg, Arne L.; Wallace, Michael and Raffalovich, Lawrence E. Accounting for Labor's Share: Class and Income Distribution in the Printing Industry. *Ind. Lab. Relat. Rev.*, April 1984, *37*(3), pp. 386–402. [G: U.S.]

Kaufman, Roger T. On Wage Stickiness in Britain's Competitive Sector. *Brit. J. Ind. Relat.*, March 1984, *22*(1), pp. 101–12. [G: U.K.]

Kaufman, Roger T. and Woglom, Geoffrey. The Effects of Expectations on Union Wages. *Amer. Econ. Rev.*, June 1984, *74*(3), pp. 418–32.
[G: U.S.]

Kaun, David E. Faculty Advancement in a Nontraditional University Environment. *Ind. Lab. Relat. Rev.*, July 1984, *37*(4), pp. 592–606.

Keyfitz, Nathan. Pension Plan Equity: The Debate Continued [Equity between the Sexes: The Pension Problem]. *J. Policy Anal. Manage.*, Fall 1984, *4*(1), pp. 120–21. [G: U.S.]

Kiker, B. F. and Roberts, R. Blaine. A Note on the Effect of Schooling, Experience and Aging on Wage Growth. *Econ. Educ. Rev.*, 1984, *3*(2), pp. 155–58. [G: U.S.]

Kiker, B. F. and Roberts, R. Blaine. The Durability of Human Capital: Some New Evidence. *Econ. Inquiry*, April 1984, *22*(2), pp. 269–81.
[G: U.S.]

King, Francis P. An Increasing Annuity Based on Nominal Interest Rates and Debt Instruments. *J. Risk Ins.*, December 1984, *51*(4), pp. 624–39. [G: U.S.]

Kirschen, E. S. La valeur horaire du temps. (With English summary.) *Cah. Écon. Bruxelles*, 2nd Trimester 1984, (102), pp. 243–78.
[G: Belgium]

Kosters, Marvin H. Disinflation in the Labor Market. In *Fellner, W., ed.*, 1984, pp. 247–86.
[G: U.S.]

Kosters, Marvin H. Wage Concessions and Long-Term Union Wage Flexibility: Comments. *Brookings Pap. Econ. Act.*, 1984, (1), pp. 217–20. [G: U.S.]

Kottis, Athena Petraki. Female–Male Earnings Differentials in the Founder Countries of the European Economic Community: An Econometric Investigation. *De Economist*, 1984, *132*(2), pp. 204–23. [G: Selected EEC]

Kovács, Ilona. The Development of Living Standards in Hungary from 1975 to 1983. *Acta Oecon.*, 1984, *33*(1–2), pp. 155–66.
[G: Hungary]

Kreinin, Mordechai E. Wage Competitiveness in the U.S. Auto and Steel Industries. *Contemp. Policy Issue*, January 1984, (4), pp. 39–50.
[G: U.S.]

Krugman, Paul R. The Effects of International Competition on U.S. Economic Growth. In *Hulten, C. R. and Sawhill, I. V., eds.*, 1984, pp. 127–50. [G: U.S.; Japan; W. Germany]

Krumm, Ronald J. Regional Wage Differentials, Labor Supply Responses, and Race. *J. Reg. Sci.*, August 1984, *24*(3), pp. 431–42.
[G: U.S.]

Kumar, Pradeep. Wages, Productivity and Labour Costs: Summary Outline. In *Wood, W. D. and Kumar, P., eds.*, 1984, pp. 429–79. [G: Canada; OECD]

Kunze, Kent. A New BLS Survey Measures the Ratio of Hours Worked to Hours Paid. *Mon. Lab. Rev.*, June 1984, *107*(6), pp. 3–7. [G: U.S.]

Kuzmin, Franc. Razlike v osebnih dohodkih znotraj panog in med njimi ter njihov vpliv na splošno rast osebnih dohodkov. (The Effects of Inter- and Intra-Industry Wage Differentials on Overall Wage Increase. With English summary.) *Econ. Anal. Worker's Manage.*, 1984, *18*(4), pp. 343–63. [G: Yugoslavia]

Laaksonen, Seppo. Palkkojen kehitys ja palkkapoliittinen keskustelu 1900-luvulla. (Development of Wages and Salaries and Wage Policy Discussion in Finland in the 20th Century. With English summary.) *Kansant. Aikak.*, 1984, *80*(1), pp. 34–65. [G: Finland]

Lacroix, Robert and Dussault, François. The Spillover Effect of Public-Sector Wage Contracts in Canada. *Rev. Econ. Statist.*, August 1984, *66*(3), pp. 509–12. [G: Canada]

Lammers, John and Lockwood, Timothy. Short-Time Compensation: At Home and Abroad: The California Experiment. In *MaCoy, R. and Morand, M. J., eds.*, 1984, pp. 61–81. [G: U.S.]

Landau, C. E. Recent Legislation and Case Law in the EEC on Sex Equality in Employment. *Int. Lab. Rev.*, January-February 1984, *123*(1), pp. 53–70. [G: EEC]

Lane, David. Social Stratification and Class. In *Hoffmann, E. P. and Laird, R. F., eds.*, 1984, *1982*, pp. 563–605. [G: U.S.S.R.]

Lang, Kevin. Unions, Firms, and the Return to Seniority. *J. Lab. Res.*, Winter 1984, *5*(1), pp. 81–92.

Lang, Rikard and Nikić, Gorazd. Dispersion of Industrial Activities into Rural Areas and Employment. In *Amin, S., ed.*, 1984, pp. 265–72. [G: Yugoslavia]

Larson, David. Wages in the Paper Industries among Highest in Manufacturing. *Mon. Lab. Rev.*, March 1984, *107*(3), pp. 52–54. [G: U.S.]

Lazear, Edward P. Illusory Wage Differentials: Reply. *Amer. Econ. Rev.*, December 1984, *74*(5), pp. 1128.

Lazear, Edward P. and Moore, Robert L. Incentives, Productivity, and Labor Contracts. *Quart. J. Econ.*, May 1984, *99*(2), pp. 275–96. [G: U.S.]

Lecaillon, Jacques. Disparités de revenus et stratégie politique. (With English summary.) *Revue Écon. Polit.*, July–August 1984, *94*(4), pp. 433–45. [G: France]

Lecaillon, Jacques and Germidis, Dimitrios. Income Differentials and the Dynamics of Development. In *Ghosh, P. K., ed., no. 7*, 1984, *1976*, pp. 176–94. [G: Africa]

Ledolter, Johannes and Power, Mark L. A Study of ERISA's Impact on Private Retirement Plan

Growth. *J. Risk Ins.*, June 1984, *51*(2), pp. 225–43. [G: U.S.]

Lee, Don. Pensions in Other Nations: The Implications for Reform in Canada. In *Conklin, D. W.; Bennett, J. H. and Courchene, T. J., eds.*, 1984, pp. 174–88. [G: Canada; U.S.; Sweden; U.K.]

Leigh, J. Paul. Do Union Members Receive Compensating Wages for Accepting Employment in Strike-Prone or Hazardous Industries? *Soc. Sci. Quart.*, March 1984, *65*(1), pp. 89–99. [G: U.S.]

Leigh, J. Paul and Folsom, Roger N. Estimates of the Value of Accident Avoidance at the Job Depend on the Concavity of the Equalizing Differences Curve. *Quart. Rev. Econ. Bus.*, Spring 1984, *24*(1), pp. 56–66. [G: U.S.]

Lentz, Bernard. The Determinants of Union Staff Salaries: A New Meaning to Business Unionism. In *Rosa, J.-J., ed.*, 1984, pp. 277–305. [G: U.S.]

Levine, Victor and Moock, Peter R. Labor Force Experience and Earnings: Women and Children. *Econ. Educ. Rev.*, 1984, *3*(3), pp. 183–93. [G: U.S.]

Lipschitz, Leslie and Schadler, Susan M. Relative Prices, Real Wages, and Macroeconomic Policies: Some Evidence from Manufacturing in Japan and the United Kingdom. *Int. Monet. Fund Staff Pap.*, June 1984, *31*(2), pp. 303–38. [G: Japan; U.K.]

Long, James E. and Scott, Frank A., Jr. The Impact of the 1981 Tax Act on Fringe Benefits and Federal Tax Revenues. *Nat. Tax J.*, June 1984, *37*(2), pp. 185–94. [G: U.S.]

Lupo, Nancy Altman. Influencing Retirement Behavior: A Further Analysis. *J. Policy Anal. Manage.*, Spring 1984, *3*(3), pp. 439–46. [G: U.S.]

MaCoy, Ramelle and Morand, Martin J. Short-Time Compensation: A Formula for Work Sharing: Afterword. In *MaCoy, R. and Morand, M. J., eds.*, 1984, pp. 196–99. [G: U.S.]

MaCoy, Ramelle and Morand, Martin J. Short-Time Compensation: The Implications for Management. In *MaCoy, R. and Morand, M. J., eds.*, 1984, pp. 14–35. [G: U.S.]

MaCoy, Ramelle and Morand, Martin J. Short-Time Compensation: An Alternative to Layoff: A Labor Viewpoint. In *MaCoy, R. and Morand, M. J., eds.*, 1984, pp. 36–50. [G: U.S.]

MaCoy, Ramelle and Morand, Martin J. STC and Labor–Management Cooperation. In *MaCoy, R. and Morand, M. J., eds.*, 1984, pp. 183–95. [G: U.S.]

MaCoy, Ramelle and Morand, Martin J. Work Sharing and Short-time Compensation: An Overview. In *MaCoy, R. and Morand, M. J., eds.*, 1984, pp. 3–13. [G: U.S.]

Marchant, C. K. Registered Pension Accounts (RPAs) as an Instrument of Pension Reform. In *Conklin, D. W.; Bennett, J. H. and Courchene, T. J., eds.*, 1984, pp. 360–91. [G: Canada]

Markham, Jesse. Inflation and the Wage-Price

Issue: A Reappraisal. In *[Reynolds, L. G.]*, 1984, pp. 227–44. [G: U.S.]

Marks, Stephen V. Wage Competitiveness in the U.S. Auto and Steel Industries: Comment. *Contemp. Policy Issue*, January 1984, (4), pp. 51–53. [G: U.S.]

Marshall, Adriana. El "salario social" en la Argentina. (With English summary.) *Desarrollo Econ.*, April–June 1984, *24*(93), pp. 41–70. [G: Argentina]

Martin, Stephen and Rence, Cynthia. Vertical Spillovers, Market Concentration, Union Coverage, and Wages. *J. Lab. Res.*, Spring 1984, *5*(2), pp. 177–89. [G: U.S.]

Masera, Rainer S. Monetary Policy and Budget Policy: Blend or Dichotomy? In *Masera, R. S. and Triffin, R.*, eds., 1984, pp. 196–223. [G: Italy; OECD]

Matta, Benjamin N., Jr. The Off-Farm Work of Hired Farm Workers. In *Emerson, R. D.*, ed., 1984, pp. 140–64. [G: U.S.]

Maurice, Marc; Sellier, François and Silvestre, Jean-Jacques. Rules, Contexts, and Actors: Observations Based on a Comparison between France and Germany. *Brit. J. Ind. Relat.*, November 1984, *22*(3), pp. 346–63. [G: France; Germany]

McCormick, Barry and Hughes, Gordon. The Influence of Pensions on Job Mobility. *J. Public Econ.*, February/March 1984, *23*(1/2), pp. 183–206. [G: U.K.]

McCormick, Robert E. and Tollison, Robert D. Legislatures as Unions. In *Buchanan, J. M. and Tollison, R. D.*, eds., 1984, *1978*, pp. 323–37. [G: U.S.]

McHone, W. Warren. State Industrial Development Incentives and Employment Growth in Multistate SMSAs. *Growth Change*, October 1984, *15*(4), pp. 8–15. [G: U.S.]

McHugh, Cathy L. Earning in the Post-Bellum Southern Cotton Textile Industry: A Case Study. *Exploration Econ. Hist.*, January 1984, *21*(1), pp. 28–39. [G: U.S.]

McKee, Michael and West, Edwin G. Minimum Wage Effects on Part-time Employment. *Econ. Inquiry*, July 1984, *22*(3), pp. 421–28. [G: U.S.; Canada]

Meisel, Harry. The Pioneers: STC in the Federal Republic of Germany. In *MaCoy, R. and Morand, M. J.*, eds., 1984, pp. 53–60. [G: W. Germany]

Mellor, Earl F. Investigating the Differences in Weekly Earnings of Women and Men. *Mon. Lab. Rev.*, June 1984, *107*(6), pp. 17–28. [G: U.S.]

Mesa, Juan M. Short-Time Working or Lay-Offs? Experience from Canada and California. *Int. Lab. Rev.*, January-February 1984, *123*(1), pp. 99–115. [G: Canada; U.S.]

Michael, Robert T. and Tuma, Nancy Brandon. Youth Employment: Does Life Begin at 16? *J. Lab. Econ.*, October 1984, *2*(4), pp. 464–76. [G: U.S.]

Michelson, Stephan and Blattenberger, Gail. Reverse Regression and Employment Discrimination [Reverse Regression, Fairness, and Employment Discrimination]. *J. Bus. Econ. Statist.*, April 1984, *2*(2), pp. 121–22. [G: U.S.]

Micklewright, John. Male Unemployment and the Family Expenditure Survey 1972–80. *Oxford Bull. Econ. Statist.*, February 1984, *46*(1), pp. 31–53. [G: U.K.]

Miller, Edward M. Extent of Economies of Scale: An Update. *Southern Econ. J.*, October 1984, *51*(2), pp. 582–87.

Miller, John J. Some Observations, a Suggestion, and Some Comments on the Conway–Roberts Article [Reverse Regression, Fairness, and Employment Discrimination]. *J. Bus. Econ. Statist.*, April 1984, *2*(2), pp. 123–25. [G: U.S.]

Miller, Paul W. and Volker, Paul A. The Screening Hypothesis: An Application of the Wiles Test. *Econ. Inquiry*, January 1984, *22*(1), pp. 121–27. [G: Australia]

Minford, Patrick. A Review of *Unemployment: Cause and Cure*, by Patrick Minford with David Davies, Michael Peel and Alison Sprague: Response. *Econ. J.*, December 1984, *94*(376), pp. 954–59. [G: U.K.]

Mintz, Jack. The Effect of Pension Funding on Investment, Savings, and Financial Intermediation. In *Conklin, D. W.; Bennett, J. H. and Courchene, T. J.*, eds., 1984, pp. 392–400. [G: Canada]

Mitchell, Daniel J. B. The Australian Labor Market. In *Caves, R. E. and Krause, L. B.*, eds., 1984, pp. 127–93. [G: Australia]

Mitchell, Daniel J. B. The Private Sector Workplace. In *Holzer, M. and Nagel, S. S.*, eds., 1984, pp. 87–112. [G: U.S.; OECD]

Mitchell, Janet B. Why Do Women Physicians Work Fewer Hours than Men Physicians? *Inquiry*, Winter 1984, *21*(4), pp. 361–68. [G: U.S.]

Moffitt, Robert. The Estimation of a Joint Wage–Hours Labor Supply Model. *J. Lab. Econ.*, October 1984, *2*(4), pp. 550–66. [G: U.S.]

Mori, Nobuhiro. The Oil Crises and the Phillips Curve. *Osaka Econ. Pap.*, March 1984, *33*(3–4), pp. 123–34. [G: Japan]

Moss, Richard Loring and Curtis, Thomas D. Flextime and Sick Leave Use. *Atlantic Econ. J.*, July 1984, *12*(2), pp. 79. [G: U.S.]

Munnell, Alicia H. Employee Benefits and the Tax Base. *New Eng. Econ. Rev.*, January–February 1984, pp. 39–55. [G: U.S.]

Munnell, Alicia H. ERISA—The First Decade: Was the Legislation Consistent with Other National Goals? *New Eng. Econ. Rev.*, November–December 1984, pp. 44–63. [G: U.S.]

Nemirow, Martin. Short-Time Compensation: Some Policy Considerations. In *MaCoy, R. and Morand, M. J.*, eds., 1984, pp. 158–82. [G: U.S.; W. Germany]

Nickell, Stephen J. A Review of *Unemployment: Cause and Cure*, by Patrick Minford with David Davies, Michael Peel and Alison Sprague. *Econ. J.*, December 1984, *94*(376), pp. 946–53. [G: U.K.]

Nickell, Stephen J. An Investigation of the Determinants of Manufacturing Employment in the United Kingdom. *Rev. Econ. Stud.*, October 1984, *51*(4), pp. 529–57. **[G: U.K.]**

Nissim, Joseph. An Examination of the Differential Patterns in the Cyclical Behaviour of the Employment, Hours and Wages of Labour of Different Skills: British Mechanical Engineering, 1963–1978. *Economica*, November 1984, *51*(204), pp. 423–36. **[G: U.K.]**

O'Neill, June A. Earnings Differentials: Empirical Evidence and Causes. In *Schmid, G. and Weitzel, R., eds.*, 1984, pp. 69–91. **[G: OECD]**

Parks, Alfred L. Migration in Farm Labor Markets: Discussion. In *Emerson, R. D., ed.*, 1984, pp. 136–39. **[G: U.S.]**

Pencavel, John H. and Hartsog, Catherine E. A Reconsideration of the Effects of Unionism on Relative Wages and Employment in the United States, 1920–1980. *J. Lab. Econ.*, April 1984, *2*(2), pp. 193–232. **[G: U.S.]**

Penley, Larry E.; Gould, Sam and de la Viña, Lynda Y. The Comparative Salary Position of Mexican American College Graduates in Business. *Soc. Sci. Quart.*, June 1984, *65*(2), pp. 444–54. **[G: U.S.]**

Perloff, Jeffrey M. and Wachter, Michael L. Postal Service Wage Comparability: Comment. *Ind. Lab. Relat. Rev.*, October 1984, *38*(1), pp. 37. **[G: U.S.]**

Perloff, Jeffrey M. and Wachter, Michael L. Wage Comparability in the U.S. Postal Service. *Ind. Lab. Relat. Rev.*, October 1984, *38*(1), pp. 26–35. **[G: U.S.]**

Personick, Martin E. White-Collar Pay Determination under Range-of-Rate Systems. *Mon. Lab. Rev.*, December 1984, *107*(12), pp. 25–30. **[G: U.S.]**

Pesando, James E. An Economic Analysis of the Green Paper Proposals for the Reform of Employer-Sponsored Plans. In *Conklin, D. W.; Bennett, J. H. and Courchene, T. J., eds.*, 1984, pp. 138–73.

Pesando, James E. Employee Evaluation of Pension Claims and the Impact of Indexing Initiatives. *Econ. Inquiry*, January 1984, *22*(1), pp. 1–17. **[G: U.S.; Canada]**

Pesando, James E. Valuing Pensions (Annuities) with Different Types of Inflation Protection in Total Compensation Comparisons. *Can. J. Econ.*, August 1984, *17*(3), pp. 569–87. **[G: Canada]**

Pilkey, Clifford G. Public Versus Private Pensions. In *Conklin, D. W.; Bennett, J. H. and Courchene, T. J., eds.*, 1984, pp. 432–38. **[G: Canada]**

Pitman, David. The Determination of Junior Wages in Australia: Needs, Work Value and Employment. *Australian Bull. Lab.*, June 1984, *10*(3), pp. 144–66. **[G: Australia]**

Plotnick, Robert. The Redistributive Impact of Cash Transfers. *Public Finance Quart.*, January 1984, *12*(1), pp. 27–50. **[G: U.S.]**

Porter, Richard C. Apartheid, the Job Ladder, and the Evolutionary Hypothesis: Empirical Evidence from South African Manufacturing,

1960–1977. *Econ. Develop. Cult. Change*, October 1984, *33*(1), pp. 117–41. **[G: S. Africa]**

Práger, László. The Impoverished Rich and the Well-to-Do Poor (Investigations Concerning Personal Income). *Eastern Europ. Econ.*, Winter 1984–85, *23*(2), pp. 3–28. **[G: Hungary]**

Prieser, Carl. Occupational Salary Levels for White-Collar Workers, 1984. *Mon. Lab. Rev.*, October 1984, *107*(10), pp. 43–45. **[G: U.S.]**

Psacharopoulos, George and Zabalza, Antonio. The Effect of Diversified Schools on Employment Status and Earnings in Colombia. *Econ. Educ. Rev.*, 1984, *3*(4), pp. 315–31. **[G: Colombia]**

Purvis, Douglas D. Indexed Bonds as an Instrument of Pension Reform: Comments. In *Conklin, D. W.; Bennett, J. H. and Courchene, T. J., eds.*, 1984, pp. 406–11. **[G: Canada]**

Pyror, Frederic L. Incentives in Manufacturing: The Carrot and the Stick. *Mon. Lab. Rev.*, July 1984, *107*(7), pp. 40–43. **[G: U.S.]**

Quan, Nguyen T. Unionism and the Size Distribution of Earnings. *Ind. Relat.*, Spring 1984, *23*(2), pp. 270–77. **[G: U.S.]**

Ray, George F. Industrial Labour Costs, 1971–1983. *Nat. Inst. Econ. Rev.*, November 1984, (110), pp. 62–67. **[G: OECD]**

Reder, Melvin W. Strike Cost and Wage Rates: Cross-Industry Differences. In *Rosa, J.-J., ed.*, 1984, pp. 27–37. **[G: U.S.]**

Reid, Frank and Meltz, Noah M. Canada's STC: A Comparison with the California Version. In *MaCoy, R. and Morand, M. J., eds.*, 1984, pp. 106–19. **[G: Canada; U.S.]**

Reimers, Cordelia. The Wage Structure of Hispanic Men: Implications for Policy. *Soc. Sci. Quart.*, June 1984, *65*(2), pp. 401–16. **[G: U.S.]**

Rejda, George E. and Schmidt, James R. The Impact of Social Security and ERISA on Insured Private Pension Contributions. *J. Risk Ins.*, December 1984, *51*(4), pp. 640–51. **[G: U.S.]**

Renaud, Paul S. A. and Siegers, Jacques J. Income and Substitution Effects in Family Labour Supply. *De Economist*, 1984, *132*(3), pp. 350–66. **[G: Netherlands; U.S.]**

Rhoades, Stephen A. Wages, Concentration, and Import Penetration: An Analysis of the Interrelationships. *Atlantic Econ. J.*, July 1984, *12*(2), pp. 23–31. **[G: U.S.]**

Rickman, Bill D. Faculty Salaries at a Small University: Does Sex Matter? *Quart. J. Bus. Econ.*, Spring 1984, *23*(2), pp. 47–57. **[G: U.S.]**

Roberts, Markley. A Labor Perspective on Technological Change. In *Collins, E. L. and Tanner, L. D., eds.*, 1984, pp. 183–205. **[G: U.S.]**

Robins, Philip K. The Labor Supply Response of Twenty-Year Families in the Denver Income Maintenance Experiment. *Rev. Econ. Statist.*, August 1984, *66*(3), pp. 491–95. **[G: U.S.]**

Robinson, Chris and Tomes, Nigel. Union Wage Differentials in the Public and Private Sectors:

A Simultaneous Equations Specification. *J. Lab. Econ.*, January 1984, *2*(1), pp. 106–27. [G: Canada]

Rodríguez, Carlos Alfredo. Inflación, salario real y tipo real de cambio. (With English summary.) *Cuadernos Econ.*, December 1984, *21*(64), pp. 247–61. [G: Argentina]

Rosenzweig, Mark R. Determinants of Wage Rates and Labor Supply Behavior in the Rural Sector of a Developing Country. In *Binswanger, H. P. and Rosenzweig, R.*, eds., 1984, pp. 211–41. [G: India]

Rubin, Jeffrey. Economic Incentives and Safety Regulation: An Analytical Framework: Comments. *Amer. Econ.*, Spring 1984, *28*(1), pp. 25–26.

Rudd, D. S. The Coverage Question in the Pension Debate. In *Conklin, D. W.; Bennett, J. H. and Courchene, T. J.*, eds., 1984, pp. 454–73. [G: Canada]

Rudney, Gabriel and Weitzman, Murray. Trends in Employment and Earnings in the Philanthropic Sector. *Mon. Lab. Rev.*, September 1984, *107*(9), pp. 16–20. [G: U.S.]

Rumberger, Russell W. The Changing Economic Benefits of College Graduates. *Econ. Educ. Rev.*, 1984, *3*(1), pp. 3–11. [G: U.S.]

Rumberger, Russell W. The Incidence and Wage Effects of Occupational Training among Young Men. *Soc. Sci. Quart.*, September 1984, *65*(3), pp. 775–88. [G: U.S.]

Rürup, Bert and Struwe, Jochen. Arbeitszeitflexibilisierung als Instrument der Beschäftigungspolitik. (Flexibilisation of Working Times as an Instrument of Employment Policies. With English summary.) *Konjunkturpolitik*, 1984, *30*(1), pp. 1–22. [G: W. Germany]

Ryan, James G. and Ghodake, R. D. Labor Market Behavior in Rural Villages in South India: Effects of Season, Sex, and Socioeconomic Status. In *Binswanger, H. P. and Rosenzweig, R.*, eds., 1984, pp. 169–83. [G: India]

Sahin, Izzet. Bruce's Spider and the Employee's Risk under a Pension System. *J. Risk Ins.*, March 1984, *51*(1), pp. 143–49.

Samarasinghe, Vidyamali and Samarasinghe, S. W. R. de A. Income and Wealth Disparities in a Land Settlement of the Sri Lanka Dry Zone. In *[Farmer, B. H.]*, 1984, pp. 173–93. [G: Sri Lanka]

Sargan, J. Denis. Wages and Prices in the United Kindgom: A Study in Econometric Methodology. In *Hendry, D. F. and Wallis, K. F.*, eds., 1984, pp. 275–314. [G: U.K.]

Savané, Marie Angelique. The Employment of Women with Social Change and Freedom of Women: The Case of Africa. In *Amin, S.*, ed., 1984, pp. 52–66. [G: Africa]

Sawhill, Isabel V. How Widespread Are Income Losses in a Recession? Comments. In *Bawden, D. L.*, ed., 1984, pp. 181–84. [G: U.S.]

Sayeed, Adil. A Survey of Pension Reform Recommendations. In *Conklin, D. W.; Bennett, J. H. and Courchene, T. J.*, eds., 1984, pp. 17–61. [G: Canada]

Schmitt, Donald G. Postretirement Increases under Private Pension Plans. *Mon. Lab. Rev.*, September 1984, *107*(9), pp. 3–8. [G: U.S.]

Schumann, Richard. Workers' Purchasing Power Rises Despite Slowdown in Wage and Salary Gains. *Mon. Lab. Rev.*, May 1984, *107*(5), pp. 10–14. [G: U.S.]

Schwerin, Don S. Historic Compromise and Pluralist Decline? Profits and Capital in the Nordic Countries. In *Goldthorpe, J. H.*, ed., 1984, pp. 231–56. [G: OECD]

Seiler, Eric. Piece Rate vs. Time Rate: The Effect of Incentives on Earnings. *Rev. Econ. Statist.*, August 1984, *66*(3), pp. 363–76. [G: U.S.]

Sellekaerts, Brigitte H. and Welch, Stephen W. An Econometric Analysis of Minimum Wage Noncompliance. *Ind. Relat.*, Spring 1984, *23*(2), pp. 244–59. [G: U.S.]

Shack-Marquez, Janice. Earnings Differences between Men and Women: An Introductory Note. *Mon. Lab. Rev.*, June 1984, *107*(6), pp. 15–16. [G: U.S.]

Shah, Anup R. Job Attributes and the Size of the Union/Non-union Wage Differential. *Economica*, November 1984, *51*(204), pp. 437–46. [G: U.K.]

Shapiro, David. Wage Differentials among Black, Hispanic, and White Young Men. *Ind. Lab. Relat. Rev.*, July 1984, *37*(4), pp. 570–81. [G: U.S.]

Shore, Harvey. Employee Assistance Programs— Reaping the Benefits. *Sloan Manage. Rev.*, Spring 1984, *25*(3), pp. 69–73. [G: U.S.]

Shulenburger, David; McLean, Robert A. and Rasch, Sara R. CISC Controls and the Union/Non-union Wage Ratio. *J. Behav. Econ.*, Summer 1984, *13*(1), pp. 57–66. [G: U.S.]

Sider, Hal. Economic Incentives and Safety Regulation: An Analytical Framework. *Amer. Econ.*, Spring 1984, *28*(1), pp. 18–24. [G: U.S.]

Sieling, Mark S. Staffing Patterns Prominent in Female–Male Earnings Gap. *Mon. Lab. Rev.*, June 1984, *107*(6), pp. 29–33. [G: U.S.]

Sloan, Frank A. and Adamache, Killard W. The Role of Unions in Hospital Cost Inflation. *Ind. Lab. Relat. Rev.*, January 1984, *37*(2), pp. 252–62. [G: U.S.]

Smith, James P. Race and Human Capital. *Amer. Econ. Rev.*, September 1984, *74*(4), pp. 685–98. [G: U.S.]

St. Louis, Robert D. Short-Time Compensation: At Home and Abroad: Arizona, Motorola, and STC. In *MaCoy, R. and Morand, M. J.*, eds., 1984, pp. 82–94. [G: U.S.]

Stallaerts, Robert. The Interindustry Wage Structure of a Labour-Managed Economy: The Yugoslav Case, 1976–1981. *Econ. Anal. Worker's Manage.*, 1984, *18*(2), pp. 109–25. [G: Yugoslavia]

Stapleton, David C. and Young, Douglas J. The Effects of Demographic Change on the Distribution of Wages, 1967–1990. *J. Human Res.*, Spring 1984, *19*(2), pp. 175–201. [G: U.S.]

Stewart, James B. and Hyclak, Thomas. An Analysis of the Earnings Profiles of Immigrants. *Rev. Econ. Statist.*, May 1984, *66*(2), pp. 292–96. [G: U.S.]

Streker-Seeborg, Irmtraud; Seeborg, Michael C. and Zegeye, Abera. The Impact of Nontraditional Training on the Occupational Attainment of Women. *J. Human Res.*, Fall 1984, *19*(4), pp. 452–71. [G: U.S.]

Sumner, Michael T. and Ward, Robert. The Impact of Taxes on Wages: A Further Analysis. *Econ. Notes*, 1984, (3), pp. 155–62. [G: U.S.]

Svejnar, Jan. The Determinants of Industrial-Sector Earnings in Senegal. *J. Devel. Econ.*, May–June–August 1984, *15*(1,2,3), pp. 289–311. [G: Senegal]

Sylos-Labini, Paolo. Prices and Income Distribution in the Manufacturing Industry. In *Sylos-Labini, P.*, 1984, *1979*, pp. 185–209. [G: Italy; U.S.; U.K.; W. Germany; Argentina]

Syverson, William M. Identification of Regional Wage Leadership within a System of Labor Markets. *Reg. Sci. Persp.*, 1984, *14*(1), pp. 52–64. [G: U.S.]

Szymanski, Al. Productivity Growth and Capitalist Stagnation. *Sci. Soc.*, Fall 1984, *48*(3), pp. 295–322. [G: U.S.; Japan; W. Europe]

Tahar, Gabriel. La variance des salaires réels, indicateur d'inégalité. (The Variance of Real Wages as a Measure of Inequality. With English summary.) *Consommation*, 1984, *31*(1), pp. 3–26. [G: France]

Thurik, A. R. and Vollebregt, J. A. C. A Generalized Labour Cost Relation for French Retailing. *Ann. INSEE*, January–March 1984, (53), pp. 93–106. [G: France]

Tienda, Marta and Neidert, Lisa J. Language, Education, and the Socioeconomic Achievement of Hispanic Origin Men. *Soc. Sci. Quart.*, June 1984, *65*(2), pp. 519–36. [G: U.S.]

Tinbergen, Jan. The Future of Incomes Policies. In *[Chenery, H. B.]*, 1984, pp. 205–15. [G: U.S.; Netherlands]

Tokman, Víctor E. The Employment Crisis in Latin America. *Int. Lab. Rev.*, September–October 1984, *123*(5), pp. 585–97. [G: Latin America]

Tomes, Nigel. The Effects of Religion and Denomination Earnings and the Returns to Human Capital. *J. Human Res.*, Fall 1984, *19*(4), pp. 472–88. [G: Canada]

Townson, Monica. Pension Reform for Women. In *Conklin, D. W.; Bennett, J. H. and Courchene, T. J.*, eds., 1984, pp. 412–16. [G: Canada]

Treble, John G. Does the Union/Non-Union Wage Differential Exist? *Manchester Sch. Econ. Soc. Stud.*, June 1984, *52*(2), pp. 160–70. [G: U.K.]

Trost, Robert P. and Lee, Lung-Fei. Technical Training and Earnings: A Polychotomous Choice Model with Selectivity. *Rev. Econ. Statist.*, February 1984, *66*(1), pp. 151–56. [G: U.S.]

Tzannatos, P. Z. and Zabalza, Antonio. The Anatomy of the Rise of British Female Relative Wages in the 1970s: Evidence from the New

Earnings Survey. *Brit. J. Ind. Relat.*, July 1984, *22*(2), pp. 177–94. [G: U.K.]

Uthoff, Andras and Riveros, Luis. La Curva de Phillips y el sector urbano informal Chile, 1964–1981. (With English summary.) *Cuadernos Econ.*, April 1984, *21*(62), pp. 63–81. [G: Chile]

Vaillancourt, François and Payette, Micheline. Antécédents familiaux et revenu de travail des hommes québécois. (Some Family Characteristics and the Earnings of Quebec Males. With English summary.) *L'Actual. Econ.*, March 1984, *60*(1), pp. 24–38. [G: Canada]

Varadarajan, Poondi and Futrell, Charles. Factors Affecting Perceptions of Smallest Meaningful Pay Increases. *Ind. Relat.*, Spring 1984, *23*(2), pp. 278–86. [G: U.S.]

Verdugo, Naomi Turner and Verdugo, Richard R. Earnings Differentials among Mexican American, Black, and White Male Workers. *Soc. Sci. Quart.*, June 1984, *65*(2), pp. 417–25. [G: U.S.]

Vroman, Wayne. The Wage Deceleration of 1982–83. *Challenge*, May/June 1984, *27*(2), pp. 35–41. [G: U.S.]

Vrooman, John. Effect of Technology on the Distribution of Labor Income. In *Collins, E. L. and Tanner, L. D.*, eds., 1984, pp. 115–23. [G: U.S.]

Wanik, Bernhard. The Development of Wages of German Industrial Corporations. *J. Ind. Econ.*, September 1984, *33*(1), pp. 113–21. [G: Germany]

van Weeren, Hans and van Praag, Bernard M. S. The Inequality of Actual Incomes and Earning Capacities between Households in Europe. *Europ. Econ. Rev.*, March 1984, *24*(2), pp. 239–56. [G: Europe]

Weiler, William C. Time Effects in Earnings of Faculty Members. *Econ. Educ. Rev.*, 1984, *3*(3), pp. 223–30. [G: U.S.]

Weiss, Andrew and Landau, Henry J. Wages, Hiring Standards, and Firm Size. *J. Lab. Econ.*, October 1984, *2*(4), pp. 477–99. [G: U.S.]

Weisskopf, Thomas E. Use of Hourly Earnings Proposed to Revive Spendable Earnings Series. *Mon. Lab. Rev.*, November 1984, *107*(11), pp. 38–43. [G: U.S.]

Weitzman, Martin L. The Case for a Share Economy. *Challenge*, November/December 1984, *27*(5), pp. 34–40. [G: U.S.]

Wietfeldt, Richard A. The Role of the State in Retirement Income Policy: Some Fundamental Considerations. In *Conklin, D. W.; Bennett, J. H. and Courchene, T. J.*, eds., 1984, pp. 445–53. [G: Canada]

Wright, J. F. Real Wage Resistance: Eighty Years of the British Cost of Living. *Oxford Econ. Pap.*, Supplement November 1984, *36*, pp. 152–67. [G: U.K.]

Wright, J. F. Real Wage Resistance: Eighty Years of the British Cost of Living. In *Collard, D. A., et al.*, eds., 1984, pp. 152–67.

Yandle, Bruce. The Wages of Regulation. *J. Lab. Res.*, Fall 1984, *5*(4), pp. 435–39.

Zedlewski, Sheila R. The Private Pension System to the Year 2020. In *Aaron, H. J. and Burtless, G., eds.*, 1984, pp. 315–42. [G: U.S.]

8243 Employment Studies, Unemployment and Vacancies; Retirements and Quits

Åberg, Rune. Market-Independent Income Distribution: Efficiency and Legitimacy. In *Goldthorpe, J. H., ed.*, 1984, pp. 209–30.
[G: U.S.; Sweden]

Abowd, John M. and Killingsworth, Mark R. Do Minority/White Unemployment Differences Really Exist? *J. Bus. Econ. Statist.*, January 1984, 2(1), pp. 64–72. [G: U.S.]

Abraham, Katharine G. and Medoff, James L. Length of Service and Layoffs in Union and Nonunion Work Groups. *Ind. Lab. Relat. Rev.*, October 1984, 38(1), pp. 87–97.
[G: U.S.]

Addison, John T. Trade Unions and Restrictive Practices. In *Rosa, J.-J., ed.*, 1984, pp. 83–114. [G: U.S.]

Ahammed, C. S. and Herdt, Robert W. Measuring the Impact of Consumption Linkages on the Employment Effects of Mechanisation in Philippine Rice Production. *J. Devel. Stud.*, January 1984, 20(2), pp. 242–55.
[G: Philippines]

Ahlburg, Dennis A. and Schapiro, Morton Owen. The Social Cost of Economic Decline: Some Earlier Evidence. *J. Post Keynesian Econ.*, Winter 1983-84, 6(2), pp. 303–04. [G: U.S.]

Alagh, Yoginder K.; Kashyap, S. P. and Murty, G. V. S. N. Policy Modelling for Planning in India. In *Cohen, S. I., et al., eds.*, 1984, pp. 59–88. [G: India]

Alam, M. Shahid. Consumption and Employment Effects of Income Redistribution in Pakistan: Comment. *Pakistan Devel. Rev.*, Summer-Autumn 1984, 23(2&3), pp. 361–63.
[G: Pakistan]

Ali, M. Shaukat. Employment Expansion—Import Substitution or Export Promotion? A General Equilibrium Study of Pakistan. *Indian Econ. J.*, January–March 1984, 31(3), pp. 53–61. [G: Pakistan]

Anderson, Bernard E. Labor Productivity and Demographics: Comment. In *Wachter, M. L. and Wachter, S. M., eds.*, 1984, pp. 100–03.
[G: U.S.]

Antonelli, Gilberto. Risorse umane e redditi da lavoro. Domanda di istruzione, offerta di lavoro e comparazioni tra settore privato e settore pubblico. (Human Resources and Labour Incomes. Demand for Education, Labour Supply and Comparison between Private and Public Sector. With English summary.) *Econ. Lavoro*, Jan.-Mar. 1984, 18(1), pp. 17–41. [G: Italy]

Appelbaum, Eileen. High Tech and the Structural Employment Problems of the 1980s. In *Collins, E. L. and Tanner, L. D., eds.*, 1984, pp. 23–48. [G: U.S.]

Armstrong, P. J. Work, Rest or Play? Changes in Time Spent at Work. In *Marstrand, P., ed.*, 1984, pp. 26–44. [G: U.K.]

Aspe, Pedro and Blanco, Herminio. Macroeconomic Uncertainty and Employment: The Case of Mexico. In *Aspe, P. and Sigmund, P. E., eds.*, 1984, pp. 187–202. [G: Mexico]

Atkinson, Anthony B., et al. Unemployment Benefit, Duration and Incentives in Britain: How Robust Is the Evidence? *J. Public Econ.*, February/March 1984, 23(1/2), pp. 3–26.
[G: U.K.]

Babkina, Z. Employment under Socialism and Its Bourgeois Interpretations. *Prob. Econ.*, April 1984, 26(12), pp. 54–74. [G: U.S.S.R.]

Baily, Martin Neil. The Retirement and Unemployment Behavior of Older Men: Comment. In *Aaron, H. J. and Burtless, G., eds.*, 1984, pp. 132–34. [G: U.S.]

Ball, Joseph. Implementation of the Supported Work Program Model. In *Hollister, R. G., Jr.; Kemper, P. and Maynard, R. A., eds.*, 1984, pp. 50–89. [G: U.S.]

Baltz, Richard B. An Incentive Early Retirement Model for College and University Faculty. *J. Risk Ins.*, September 1984, 51(3), pp. 477–97.

Baranenkova, T. Reducing Labor Turnover under Conditions of Intensification of Production. *Prob. Econ.*, June 1984, 27(2), pp. 20–37.
[G: U.S.S.R.]

Bardhan, Kalpana. Work Patterns and Social Differentiation: Rural Women of West Bengal. In *Binswanger, H. P. and Rosenzweig, R., eds.*, 1984, pp. 184–207. [G: India]

Barras, R. and Swann, J. Information Technology and the Service Sector: Quality of Services and Quantity of Jobs. In *Marstrand, P., ed.*, 1984, pp. 214–33. [G: U.K.]

Barre, Raymond. National versus International Solutions for Unemployment. In *Pierre, A. J., ed.*, 1984, pp. 53–78. [G: U.S.; W. Europe]

Bartlett, Bruce. Is Industrial Innovation Destroying Jobs? *Cato J.*, Fall 1984, 4(2), pp. 625–43. [G: U.S.]

Batchelor, Roy A. A Natural Interpretation of the Present Unemployment. In *Griffiths, B. and Wood, G. E., eds.*, 1984, pp. 139–71.
[G: U.K.; U.S.; EEC]

Baxter, J. L. and McCormick, Brian J. Seventy Per Cent of Our Future: The Education, Training and Employment of Young People. *Nat. Westminster Bank Quart. Rev.*, August 1984, pp. 36–44.

Becker, Eugene H. Self-Employed Workers: An Update to 1983. *Mon. Lab. Rev.*, July 1984, 107(7), pp. 14–18. [G: U.S.]

Becker, Eugene H. and Bowers, Norman. Employment and Unemployment Improvements Widespread in 1983. *Mon. Lab. Rev.*, February 1984, 107(2), pp. 3–14. [G: U.S.]

Bennell, Paul. The Utilisation of Professional Engineering Skills in Kenya. In *Fransman, M. and King, K., eds.*, 1984, pp. 335–53.
[G: Kenya]

Berg, Ivar. Current Conceptions of Unemployment: Some Logical and Empirical Difficulties. In *Ullrich, R. A., ed.*, 1984, pp. 95–126.
[G: U.S.]

Birch, David. The Contribution of Small Enterprise to Growth and Employment. In *Giersch, H., ed.,* 1984, pp. 1–17. [G: U.S.]

Birg, Herwig. Demographic Aspects of Labor Market Efficiency. In *Steinmann, G., ed.,* 1984, pp. 303–22. [G: W. Germany]

Björklund, Anders. A Look at the Male–Female Unemployment Differentials in the Federal Republic of Germany, Sweden, United Kingdom, and the United States of America. In *Schmid, G. and Weitzel, R., eds.,* 1984, pp. 20–43. [G: Sweden; U.K.; U.S.; W. Germany]

Blanchard, Olivier J. The Lucas Critique and the Volcker Deflation. *Amer. Econ. Rev.,* May 1984, 74(2), pp. 211–15. [G: U.S.]

Block, Fred. Technological Change and Employment: New Perspectives on an Old Controversy. *Econ. Lavoro,* July-Sept. 1984, 18(3), pp. 3–21. [G: France; U.S.]

Blumrosen, Ruth Gerber. Work Sharing, STC, and Affirmative Action. In *MaCoy, R. and Morand, M. J., eds.,* 1984, pp. 139–57. [G: U.S.]

Bodo, Giorgio. Demand for Labour in the Italian Industry (1970–80). *Appl. Econ.,* August 1984, 16(4), pp. 583–95. [G: Italy]

Boissevain, Jeremy. Small Entrepreneurs in Contemporary Europe. In *Ward, R. and Jenkins, R., eds.,* 1984, pp. 20–38. [G: EEC]

Bonnell, Sheila M.; Chew, T. C. and Dixon, Peter B. Measuring the Impact of Structural Change on Groups in the Australian Labour Market. In *Steinmann, G., ed.,* 1984, pp. 343–59. [G: Australia]

Boothby, Daniel. The Continuity of Married Women's Labour Force Participation in Canada. *Can. J. Econ.,* August 1984, 17(3), pp. 471–80. [G: Canada]

Borowski, Allan. A Comparison of Youth Unemployment in Australia and the United States. *Mon. Lab. Rev.,* October 1984, 107(10), pp. 30–36. [G: Australia; U.S.]

Borus, Michael E. A Description of Employed and Unemployed Youth in 1981. In *Borus, M. E., ed.,* 1984, pp. 13–55. [G: U.S.]

Bourdon, F.; Bourdon, J. and Hallak, J. The EDFOREM Model: A Case Study of Thailand. In *Cohen, S. I., et al., eds.,* 1984, pp. 139–59. [G: Thailand]

Bowers, Norman and Horvath, Francis W. Keeping Time: An Analysis of Errors in the Measurement of Unemployment Duration. *J. Bus. Econ. Statist.,* April 1984, 2(2), pp. 140–49. [G: U.S.]

Bregger, John E. The Current Population Survey: A Historical Perspective and BLS' Role. *Mon. Lab. Rev.,* June 1984, 107(6), pp. 8–14. [G: U.S.]

Bresnick, David. Policymaking by Partnership: Reshaping Youth Employment Policy. *J. Policy Anal. Manage.,* Fall 1984, 4(1), pp. 23–38. [G: U.S.; W. Europe; Japan]

Briguglio, Pasquale Lino. The Specification and Estimation of a Disequilibrium Labour Market Model. *Appl. Econ.,* August 1984, 16(4), pp. 539–54. [G: Malta]

Brimmer, Andrew F. Long-Term Economic Growth and Black Employment Opportunities. *Rev. Black Polit. Econ.,* Summer–Fall 1984, 13(1–2), pp. 61–73. [G: U.S.]

Browne, Lynn E. Conflicting Views of Technological Progress and the Labor Market. *New Eng. Econ. Rev.,* July–August 1984, pp. 5–16. [G: U.S.]

Bruch, Mathias. The Contribution of Small Enterprise to Growth and Employment: Comment. In *Giersch, H., ed.,* 1984, pp. 18–22. [G: U.S.]

Bruno, Michael. Stagflation in the EC Countries 1973–1981: A Cross-sectional View. In *Emerson, M., ed.,* 1984, pp. 33–56. [G: EEC]

Buchele, Robert. Reaganomics and the Fairness Issue. *Challenge,* September/October 1984, 27(4), pp. 25–31. [G: U.S.]

Burdett, Kenneth, et al. Earnings, Unemployment, and the Allocation of Time over Time. *Rev. Econ. Stud.,* October 1984, 51(4), pp. 559–78. [G: U.S.]

Burtless, Gary and Haveman, Robert H. Policy Lessons from Three Labor Market Experiments. In *Robson, R. T., ed.,* 1984, pp. 105–33. [G: U.S.]

Cebula, Richard J. Unemployment and the 1976 Presidential Election. *Atlantic Econ. J.,* March 1984, 12(1), pp. 123. [G: U.S.]

Charpin, Jean-Michel. The Adaptation of Working Time as a Response to the Unemployment Problem. In *Emerson, M., ed.,* 1984, pp. 174–94. [G: France; Netherlands; U.K.; W. Germany]

Cheema, Aftab Ahmad and Malik, Muhammad Hussain. Consumption and Employment Effects of Income Redistribution in Pakistan. *Pakistan Devel. Rev.,* Summer-Autumn 1984, 23(2&3), pp. 347–59. [G: Pakistan]

Chiswick, Barry R. and Chiswick, Carmel U. Race and Public Policy: The Statistical Connection. *Challenge,* September/October 1984, 27(4), pp. 51–55. [G: U.S.]

Choi, Sang-Rim and Tschoegl, Adrian E. Bank Employment in the World's Largest Banks: An Update: A Note. *J. Money, Credit, Banking,* August 1984, 16(3), pp. 359–62.

Clark, Gordon L. The Changing Composition of Regional Employment. *Econ. Geogr.,* April 1984, 60(2), pp. 175–93. [G: U.S.]

Clark, Peter K. Unemployment and Potential Output in the 1980s: Comment. *Brookings Pap. Econ. Act.,* 1984, (2), pp. 565–67. [G: U.S.]

Cohen, Yinon and Pfeffer, Jeffrey. Employment Practices in the Dual Economy. *Ind. Relat.,* Winter 1984, 23(1), pp. 58–72. [G: U.S.]

Coltrane, Robert. The Off-Farm Work of Hired Farm Workers: Discussion. In *Emerson, R. D., ed.,* 1984, pp. 164–67. [G: U.S.]

Connaughton, John E. and Madsen, Ronald A. Explaining Differentials in State Unemployment Rates during Recessions. *Reg. Sci. Persp.,* 1984, 14(1), pp. 18–24. [G: U.S.]

Corman, Hope and Davidson, Patricia K. Economic Aspects of Post-secondary Schooling Decisions. *Econ. Educ. Rev.*, 1984, 3(2), pp. 131–39. [G: U.S.]

Couriel, Alberto. Poverty and Underemployment in Latin America. *Cepal Rev.*, 1984, (24), pp. 39–62. [G: Latin America]

Cronin, M. R. Protection and Employment in the Motor Car Sector. *Australian Econ. Pap.*, June 1984, 23(42), pp. 38–51.

Crowley, Joan E. Delinquency and Employment: Substitutions or Spurious Associations. In *Borus, M. E., ed.*, 1984, pp. 239–95. [G: U.S.]

Cullis, John G. Opportunity Cost and Choice. In *Sandford, C. and Bradbury, M., eds.*, 1984, pp. 27–41. [G: U.K.]

Dabscheck, Braham and Niland, John. Recent Trends in Collective Bargaining in Australia. *Int. Lab. Rev.*, September–October 1984, 123(5), pp. 631–46. [G: Australia]

Davila, Alberto E.; Schmidt, Ronald H. and Ziegler, Gary M. Industrial Diversification, Exchange Rate Shocks, and the Texas–Mexico Border. *Fed. Res. Bank Dallas Econ. Rev.*, May 1984, pp. 1–9. [G: U.S.; Mexico]

Dawkins, Peter and Sloan, Judith. The Australian Labour Market, June 1984. *Australian Bull. Lab.*, June 1984, 10(3), pp. 113–33. [G: Australia]

DeBoer, Larry and Seeborg, Michael C. The Female–Male Unemployment Differential: Effects of Changes in Industry Employment. *Mon. Lab. Rev.*, November 1984, 107(11), pp. 8–15. [G: U.S.]

DeCanio, Stephen J. Expectations and Business Confidence during the Great Depression. In *Siegel, B. N., ed.*, 1984, pp. 157–75. [G: U.S.]

Del Boca, Daniela. Differenziali salariali e alternative di orario. (Wage Differentials in Alternative Working Schedules. With English summary.) *Econ. Lavoro*, Oct.-Dec. 1984, 18(4), pp. 3–16. [G: Italy]

Demery, David; Duck, Nigel W. and Musgrave, Simon W. Unanticipated Money Growth, Output and Unemployment in West Germany, 1964–1981. *Weltwirtsch. Arch.*, 1984, 120(2), pp. 244–55. [G: Germany]

Devens, Richard M., Jr. Employment in the First Half: Robust Recovery Continues. *Mon. Lab. Rev.*, August 1984, 107(8), pp. 3–7. [G: U.S.]

Diamond, Peter A. and Hausman, Jerry A. Individual Retirement and Savings Behavior. *J. Public Econ.*, February/March 1984, 23(1/2), pp. 81–114. [G: U.S.]

Diamond, Peter A. and Hausman, Jerry A. The Retirement and Unemployment Behavior of Older Men. In *Aaron, H. J. and Burtless, G., eds.*, 1984, pp. 97–132. [G: U.S.]

Dieguez, Héctor L. and Gerchunoff, Pablo. La dinámica del mercado laboral urbano en la Argentina, 1976–1981. (With English summary.) *Desarrollo Econ.*, April–June 1984, 24(93), pp. 3–40. [G: Argentina]

Dimsdale, N. H. Employment and Real Wages

in the Inter-war Period. *Nat. Inst. Econ. Rev.*, November 1984, (110), pp. 94–103. [G: U.K.]

Disney, Richard and Szyszczak, E. M. Protective Legislation and Part-Time Employment in Britain. *Brit. J. Ind. Relat.*, March 1984, 22(1), pp. 78–100. [G: U.K.]

Dixon, Peter B.; Parmenter, B. R. and Powell, Alan A. Trade Liberalization and Labor Market Disruption. *J. Policy Modeling*, November 1984, 6(4), pp. 431–54. [G: Australia]

Dore, Ronald P. and Oxenham, John. Educational Reform and Selection for Employment—An Overview. In *Oxenham, J., ed.*, 1984, pp. 3–40.

Duchin, Faye. Automation and Its Effect on Employment and Income. In *Collins, E. L. and Tanner, L. D., eds.*, 1984, pp. 49–75. [G: U.S.]

Duffy, Martyn H. The Relationship between Unemployment and Unfilled Vacancies in Great Britain: An Extended Job-Search, Labour Turnover View. *Bull. Econ. Res.*, November 1984, 36(2), pp. 143–72. [G: U.K.]

Earle, John S. and Kniesner, Thomas J. Inflation, Unemployment and the Reagan Administration. *Bus. Econ.*, October 1984, 19(5), pp. 26–33. [G: U.S.]

Eck, Alan. New Occupational Separation Data Improve Estimates of Job Replacement Needs. *Mon. Lab. Rev.*, March 1984, 107(3), pp. 3–10. [G: U.S.]

Edelstein, Michael. Discussion [The Decline of the British Economy: An Institutional Perspective] [Structural Transformation and the Demand for New Labor in Advanced Economies: Interwar Britain]. *J. Econ. Hist.*, June 1984, 44(2), pp. 599–602. [G: U.K.]

Ellman, Michael. Full Employment—Lessons from State Socialism. In *Ellman, M.*, 1984, 1979, pp. 149–73. [G: E. Europe; U.S.S.R.; China]

Elterich, G. Joachim. Seasonality of Farm Labor Use Patterns in the United States: Discussion. In *Emerson, R. D., ed.*, 1984, pp. 96–103. [G: U.S.]

Emerson, Michael. The European Stagflation Disease in International Perspective and Some Possible Therapy. In *Emerson, M., ed.*, 1984, pp. 195–228. [G: N. Europe; OECD]

Eriksson, Tor. Den finländska arbetslöshetens struktur. (The Structure of Finnish Unemployment. With English summary.) *Ekon. Samfundets Tidskr.*, 1984, 37(3), pp. 181–90. [G: Finland]

Faxén, Karl O. Risk Management. In *[Kozmetsky, G.]*, 1984, pp. 155–75. [G: U.S.; Sweden]

Fedrau, Ruth H. Easing the Worker's Transition from Job Loss to Employment. *Mon. Lab. Rev.*, May 1984, 107(5), pp. 38–40. [G: U.S.]

Felbinger, Claire L. Economic Development or Economic Disaster? Joliet, Illinois. In *Bingham, R. D. and Blair, J. P., eds.*, 1984, pp. 223–44. [G: U.S.]

Felmingham, B. S. The Recovery of World Labor

Markets and the U.S. Monetary Stance: Rationale and Evidence. *Kyklos*, 1984, 37(3), pp. 424–43. [G: OECD]

Felmlee, Diane H. A Dynamic Analysis of Women's Employment Exits. *Demography*, May 1984, 21(2), pp. 171–83. [G: U.S.]

Fichtenbaum, Rudy. Trends and Cycles in Ohio's Unemployment Rate. *Growth Change*, January 1984, 15(1), pp. 50–55. [G: U.S.]

Fields, Gary S. and Mitchell, Olivia S. The Effects of Social Security Reforms on Retirement Ages and Retirement Incomes. *J. Public Econ.*, November 1984, 25(1/2), pp. 143–59. [G: U.S.]

Firn, John R. and Roberts, David. High-technology Industries. In *Hood, N. and Young, S.*, eds., 1984, pp. 288–325. [G: U.K.]

Flaim, Paul O. Discouraged Workers: How Strong Are Their Links to the Job Market? *Mon. Lab. Rev.*, August 1984, 107(8), pp. 8–11. [G: U.S.]

Flaim, Paul O. Unemployment in 1982: The Cost to Workers and Their Families. *Mon. Lab. Rev.*, February 1984, 107(2), pp. 30–37. [G: U.S.]

Folbre, Nancy R.; Leighton, Julia L. and Roderick, Melissa R. Plant Closings and Their Regulation in Maine, 1971–1982. *Ind. Lab. Relat. Rev.*, January 1984, 37(2), pp. 185–96. [G: U.S.]

Forbes, John F. and McGregor, Alan. Unemployment and Mortality in Post-war Scotland. *J. Health Econ.*, December 1984, 3(3), pp. 239–57. [G: Scotland]

Ford, William D. Statements in Support of the National Employment Priorities Act. In *McKenzie, R. B., ed. (II)*, 1984, pp. 315–27. [G: U.S.]

Fougere, Denis. Insertion professionnelle, mobilité, salaire: le cas des sortants de l'enseignement technique court. (Insertion into the Labour Market, Mobility, Wage: The Case of Young Men with Professional Training Diplomas. With English summary.) *Consommation*, Oct.–Dec. 1984, 31(4), pp. 29–64. [G: France]

Freedman, David. Employment and Unemployment in the 1980s: Economic Dilemmas and Socio-political Challenges. *Int. Lab. Rev.*, September–October 1984, 123(5), pp. 557–68. [G: OECD]

Freeman, Christopher. Keynes or Kondratiev? How Can We Get Back to Full Employment? In *Marstrand, P., ed.*, 1984, pp. 103–23. [G: U.K.]

Fritsch, Conrad F. Seasonality of Farm Labor Use Patterns in the United States. In *Emerson, R. D., ed.*, 1984, pp. 64–95. [G: U.S.]

Fuller, Rex and Seninger, Stephen F. A Discriminant Analysis of Factors Affecting the Employment of Urban Youth. *Appl. Econ.*, October 1984, 16(5), pp. 757–62. [G: U.S.]

Gafni, Amiram and Peled, Dan. The Effect of Labelling on Illness Related Absenteeism: An Economic Explanation for the Case of Hyper-

tension. *J. Health Econ.*, August 1984, 3(2), pp. 173–78. [G: U.S.]

Galbraith, James K. The Case for Rapid Growth. *Challenge*, March/April 1984, 27(1), pp. 10–14. [G: U.S.]

Gang, Ira N. The Private Cost of Labor Adjustment: Comment. *Contemp. Policy Issue*, January 1984, (4), pp. 37–38. [G: Canada]

Gannon, Martin J. Preferences of Temporary Workers: Time, Variety, and Flexibility. *Mon. Lab. Rev.*, August 1984, 107(8), pp. 26–28. [G: U.S.]

García, Norberto and Tokman, Víctor E. Changes in Employment and the Crisis. *Cepal Rev.*, 1984, (24), pp. 103–15. [G: Latin America]

Gastwirth, Joseph L. Statistical Methods for Analyzing Claims of Employment Discrimination. *Ind. Lab. Relat. Rev.*, October 1984, 38(1), pp. 75–86. [G: U.S.]

Geiser, Kenneth. Converting Economic Conversion: An Argument for Building Broader Coalitions. In *Gordon, S. and McFadden, D., eds.*, 1984, pp. 175–90. [G: U.S.]

Gershuny, Jonathan I. The Future of Service Employment. In *Marstrand, P., ed.*, 1984, pp. 234–55. [G: U.K.]

van Ginneken, Wouter. Employment and the Reduction of the Work Week: A Comparison of Seven European Macro-Economic Models. *Int. Lab. Rev.*, January-February 1984, 123(1), pp. 35–52. [G: W. Europe]

Ginzberg, Eli. The Service Economy and the Changing Job Structures. In *Ullrich, R. A., ed.*, 1984, pp. 81–94. [G: U.S.]

Ginzberg, Eli; Nathan, Richard P. and Solow, Robert M. The Lessons of the Supported Work Demonstration. In *Hollister, R. G., Jr.; Kemper, P. and Maynard, R. A., eds.*, 1984, pp. 305–19. [G: U.S.]

Glenday, Graham and Jenkins, Glenn P. Industrial Dislocation and the Private Cost of Labor Adjustment. *Contemp. Policy Issue*, January 1984, (4), pp. 23–36. [G: Canada]

Goddard, J. B. and Thwaites, A. T. Unemployment in the North: Jobs in the South. In *Marstrand, P., ed.*, 1984, pp. 45–72. [G: U.K.]

Gordon, Robert J. Unemployment and Potential Output in the 1980s. *Brookings Pap. Econ. Act.*, 1984, (2), pp. 537–64. [G: U.S.]

Gordon, Suzanne and McFadden, Dave. Economic Conversion: Revitalizing America's Economy: Introduction. In *Gordon, S. and McFadden, D., eds.*, 1984, pp. xiii–xxi.

Gramlich, Edward M. and Laren, Deborah S. How Widespread Are Income Losses in a Recession? In *Bawden, D. L., ed.*, 1984, pp. 157–80. [G: U.S.]

Gravelle, Hugh S. E. Time Series Analysis of Mortality and Unemployment [Unemployment and Mortality in Post-war Scotland]. *J. Health Econ.*, December 1984, 3(3), pp. 297–305.

Greenhalgh, Leonard and McKersie, Robert B. Cost-effectiveness of Alternative Strategies for Cutback Management. In *Carr, J. H., ed.*, 1984, 1980, pp. 93–112. [G: U.S.]

Greenwood, Michael J. and Hunt, Gary L. Migration and Interregional Employment Redistribution in the United States. *Amer. Econ. Rev.*, December 1984, 74(5), pp. 957–69.
[G: U.S.]

Gregory, Peter. The Mexican Labor Market, 1940–1980. In [*Reynolds, L. G.*], 1984, pp. 245–79. [G: Mexico]

Grossman, Jean Baldwin. Illegal Immigrants and Domestic Employment. *Ind. Lab. Relat. Rev.*, January 1984, 37(2), pp. 240–51. [G: U.S.]

Grubb, D.; Layard, R. and Symons, J. Wages, Unemployment, and Incomes Policies. In *Emerson, M., ed.*, 1984, pp. 57–88. [G: OECD]

Gueron, Judith. Lessons from Managing the Supported Work Demonstration. In *Hollister, R. G., Jr.; Kemper, P. and Maynard, R. A., eds.*, 1984, pp. 286–304. [G: U.S.]

Gurwitz, Aaron S. and Rappaport, Julie N. Structural Change and Slower Employment Growth in the Financial Services Sector. *Fed. Res. Bank New York Quart. Rev.*, Winter 1984–85, 9(4), pp. 39–45. [G: U.S.]

Gustafsson, Björn. Macroeconomic Performance, Old Age Security and the Rate of Social Assistance Recipients in Sweden. *Europ. Econ. Rev.*, December 1984, 26(3), pp. 319–38.
[G: Sweden]

Gustafsson, Siv. Equal Opportunity Policies in Sweden. In *Schmid, G. and Weitzel, R., eds.*, 1984, pp. 132–54. [G: Sweden]

Gustman, Alan L. and Steinmeier, Thomas L. Modeling the Retirement Process for Policy Evaluation and Research. *Mon. Lab. Rev.*, July 1984, 107(7), pp. 26–33. [G: U.S.]

Gustman, Alan L. and Steinmeier, Thomas L. Partial Retirement and the Analysis of Retirement Behavior. *Ind. Lab. Relat. Rev.*, April 1984, 37(3), pp. 403–15. [G: U.S.]

Hamada, Koichi and Kurosaka, Yoshio. The Relationship between Production and Unemployment in Japan: Okun's Law in Comparative Perspective. *Europ. Econ. Rev.*, June 1984, 25(1), pp. 71–94. [G: U.S.; Japan]

Hamadani, S. M. Mazahir Hasnain. Factors' Employment Absorption, Growth, and Income Distribution through Foreign Trade: Pakistan's Case. *Pakistan Devel. Rev.*, Summer-Autumn 1984, 23(2&3), pp. 331–40. [G: Pakistan]

Hamermesh, Daniel S. Life-Cycle Effects on Consumption and Retirement. *J. Lab. Econ.*, July 1984, 2(3), pp. 353–70. [G: U.S.]

Hamilton, Earl G. Long-Term Economic Growth and Black Employment Opportunities: Comments. *Rev. Black Polit. Econ.*, Summer–Fall 1984, 13(1–2), pp. 74–79. [G: U.S.]

Haraf, William S. The Relationship between Production and Unemployment in Japan: Okun's Law in Comparative Perspective: Comments. *Europ. Econ. Rev.*, June 1984, 25(1), pp. 95–98. [G: U.S.; Japan]

Harrison, Bennett and Bluestone, Barry. The Incidence and Regulation of Plant Closings. In *Sawers, L. and Tabb, W. K., eds.*, 1984, 1982, pp. 368–402. [G: U.S.]

Harrison, David S. The Impact of Immigration

on a Depressed Labour Market: The South Australian Experience. *Econ. Rec.*, March 1984, 60(168), pp. 57–67. [G: Australia]

Haveman, Robert H. and Wolfe, Barbara L. Disability Transfers and Early Retirement: A Causal Relationship? *J. Public Econ.*, June 1984, 24(1), pp. 47–66. [G: W. Europe; U.S.]

Haveman, Robert H.; Wolfe, Barbara L. and Warlick, Jennifer L. Disability Transfers, Early Retirement, and Retrenchment. In *Aaron, H. J. and Burtless, G., eds.*, 1984, pp. 65–93. [G: U.S.]

Heckman, James J. and Singer, Burton. A Method for Minimizing the Impact of Distributional Assumptions in Econometric Models for Duration Data. *Econometrica*, March 1984, 52(2), pp. 271–320.

Heim, Carol E. Structural Transformation and the Demand for New Labor in Advanced Economies: Interwar Britain. *J. Econ. Hist.*, June 1984, 44(2), pp. 585–95. [G: U.K.]

Hekman, John S. and Strong, John S. Is There a Case for Plant-Closing Laws? In *McKenzie, R. B., ed. (II)*, 1984, 1980, pp. 49–77.
[G: U.S.]

Henderson, Robert A. The Employment Performance of Established Manufacturing Industry in the Scottish New Towns. *Urban Stud.*, August 1984, 21(3), pp. 295–315. [G: U.K.]

Henschel, Rudolf. Ursachen der Beschäftigungskrise im Meinungsspektrum der Gewerkschaften. (The Spectrum of Opinions on the Causes of the Employment Crisis in the German Trade Union Movement. With English summary.) *Konjunkturpolitik*, 1984, 30(2/3), pp. 73–92.
[G: W. Germany]

Higgs, Peter J.; Parmenter, B. R. and Powell, Alan A. The Scope for Tariff Reform Created by a Resources Boom: Simulations with the ORANI Model. *Australian Econ. Pap.*, June 1984, 23(42), pp. 1–26. [G: Australia]

Hollister, Robinson G., Jr. The Design and Implementation of the Supported Work Evaluation. In *Hollister, R. G., Jr.; Kemper, P. and Maynard, R. A., eds.*, 1984, pp. 12–49.
[G: U.S.]

Hollister, Robinson G., Jr. The National Supported Work Demonstration: Introduction. In *Hollister, R. G., Jr.; Kemper, P. and Maynard, R. A., eds.*, 1984, pp. 3–11. [G: U.S.]

Hollister, Robinson G., Jr. and Maynard, Rebecca A. The Impacts of Supported Work on AFDC Recipients. In *Hollister, R. G., Jr.; Kemper, P. and Maynard, R. A., eds.*, 1984, pp. 90–135. [G: U.S.]

Holt, James S. Introduction to the Seasonal Farm Labor Problem. In *Emerson, R. D., ed.*, 1984, pp. 3–32. [G: U.S.]

Hood, Neil. The Small-Firm Sector. In *Hood, N. and Young, S., eds.*, 1984, pp. 57–92.
[G: U.K.; OECD]

Hormats, Robert D. Unemployment and Growth in the Western Economies: Introduction. In *Pierre, A. J., ed.*, 1984, pp. 1–13.

Hossain, Mahabub. Employment and Labour in

Bangladesh Rural Industries. *Bangladesh Devel. Stud.*, March-June 1984, *12*(1–2), pp. 1–24. **[G: Bangladesh]**

Howenstine, Ned G. U.S. Affiliates of Foreign Companies: Operations in 1982. *Surv. Curr. Bus.*, December 1984, *64*(12), pp. 26–40. **[G: U.S.]**

Huffman, Wallace E. Some Analytical Approaches for Human Resource Issues of Seasonal Farm Labor. In *Emerson, R. D., ed.*, 1984, pp. 33–63. **[G: U.S.]**

Hunter, Donna. Oregon Tries the "Workshare" Idea. In *MaCoy, R. and Morand, M. J., eds.*, 1984, pp. 95–105. **[G: U.S.]**

Hurd, Michael D. and Boskin, Michael J. The Effect of Social Security on Retirement in the Early 1970s. *Quart. J. Econ.*, November 1984, *99*(4), pp. 767–90. **[G: U.S.]**

Hutchinson, G.; Barr, N. A. and Drobny, A. The Employment of Young Males in a Segmented Labour Market: The Case of Great Britain. *Appl. Econ.*, April 1984, *16*(2), pp. 187–204. **[G: U.K.]**

Ingram, A. H. and Sloane, P. J. The Growth of Shiftwork in the British Food, Drink, and Tobacco Industries. *Managerial Dec. Econ.*, September 1984, *5*(3), pp. 168–76. **[G: U.K.]**

Iqbal, Munawar. Factors' Employment Absorption, Growth, and Income Distribution through Foreign Trade: Pakistan's Case. *Pakistan Devel. Rev.*, Summer-Autumn 1984, *23*(2&3), pp. 341–43. **[G: Pakistan]**

Ittner, Linda A. The Federal Response to Short-Time Compensation. In *MaCoy, R. and Morand, M. J., eds.*, 1984, pp. 120–35. **[G: U.S.]**

Jackson, Christine. Policies and Implementation of Anti-discrimination Strategies. In *Schmid, G. and Weitzel, R., eds.*, 1984, pp. 191–201. **[G: Sweden; U.K.; U.S.]**

Jacobson, Louis. A Tale of Employment Decline in Two Cities: How Bad Was the Worst of Times? *Ind. Lab. Relat. Rev.*, July 1984, *37*(4), pp. 557–69. **[G: U.S.]**

Jacoby, Sanford M. The Development of Internal Labor Markets in American Manufacturing Firms. In *Osterman, P., ed.*, 1984, pp. 23–69. **[G: U.S.]**

Jahoda, Marie. Unemployment—Curse or Liberation? In *Marstrand, P., ed.*, 1984, pp. 19–25. **[G: U.K.]**

Jenkins, Richard. Acceptability, Suitability, and the Search for the Habituated Worker: How Ethnic Minorities and Women Lose Out. *Int. J. Soc. Econ.*, 1984, *11*(7), pp. 64–76. **[G: U.K.]**

Jones, Gavin W. Links between Urbanization and Sectoral Shifts in Employment in Java. *Bull. Indonesian Econ. Stud.*, December 1984, *20*(3), pp. 120–57. **[G: Indonesia]**

Junankar, P. N. and Price, Simon. The Dynamics of Unemployment: Structural Change and Unemployment Flows. *Econ. J.*, 1984 Supplement, *94*, pp. 158–65. **[G: U.K.]**

Kahn, Lawrence M. and Low, Stuart A. An Empirical Model of Employed Search, Unemployed Search, and Nonsearch. *J. Human Res.*, Winter 1984, *19*(1), pp. 104–17. **[G: U.S.]**

Kain, Peter G. and Dawkins, Peter. The Australian Labour Market, December 1984. *Australian Bull. Lab.*, December 1984, *11*(1), pp. 3–29. **[G: Australia; OECD]**

Kaliski, S. F. Why Must Unemployment Remain so High? *Can. Public Policy*, June 1984, *10*(2), pp. 127–41. **[G: Canada]**

Kay, John A. The Effect of Increasing Tax Thresholds on the Poverty and Unemployment Traps. *Fisc. Stud.*, February 1984, *5*(1), pp. 32–34. **[G: U.K.]**

Kaztman, Rubén. Sectoral Transformations in Employment in Latin America. *Cepal Rev.*, 1984, (24), pp. 83–101. **[G: Latin America]**

Keeley, Michael C. Cyclical Unemployment and Employment: Effects of Labor Force Entry and Exit. *Fed. Res. Bank San Francisco Econ. Rev.*, Summer 1984, (3), pp. 5–25. **[G: U.S.]**

Keil, Teresa, et al. Does Occupational Status Matter? The Case of Recruitment. *Int. J. Soc. Econ.*, 1984, *11*(7), pp. 32–48. **[G: U.K.]**

Kemper, Peter; Long, David A. and Thornton, Craig. A Benefit–Cost Analysis of the Supported Work Experiment. In *Hollister, R. G., Jr.; Kemper, P. and Maynard, R. A., eds.*, 1984, pp. 239–85. **[G: U.S.]**

Kiefer, Nicholas M. A Simple Test for Heterogeneity in Exponential Models of Duration. *J. Lab. Econ.*, October 1984, *2*(4), pp. 539–49. **[G: U.S.]**

Kikuchi, Masao; Hafid, Anwar and Hayami, Yujiro. Changes in Rice Harvesting Contracts and Wages in Java. In *Binswanger, H. P. and Rosenzweig, R., eds.*, 1984, pp. 117–30. **[G: Indonesia]**

Kooiman, P. Smoothing the Aggregate Fix-Price Model and the Use of Business Survey Data. *Econ. J.*, December 1984, *94*(376), pp. 899–913. **[G: Netherlands]**

Koshiro, Kazutoshi. Lifetime Employment in Japan: Three Models of the Concept. *Mon. Lab. Rev.*, August 1984, *107*(8), pp. 34–35. **[G: Japan]**

Kotliar, A. Full Employment and Proportionality of Factors in Socialist Production. *Prob. Econ.*, June 1984, *27*(2), pp. 38–56. **[G: U.S.S.R.]**

Kotliar, A. The Job Placement System in the USSR. *Prob. Econ.*, December 1984, *27*(8), pp. 20–39. **[G: U.S.S.R.]**

Lacroix, Robert. Québec: les politiques et programmes gouvernementaux et la création d'emplois. (Quebec: Government Policies and Programs and Job Creation. With English summary.) *Can. Public Policy*, December 1984, *10*(4), pp. 429–35. **[G: OECD]**

Lagos, Ricardo and Tokman, Víctor E. Monetarism, Employment and Social Stratification. *World Devel.*, January 1984, *12*(1), pp. 43–65. **[G: Argentina; Chile]**

Lambert, Jean-Pierre; Lubrano, Michel and Sneessens, Henri R. Emploi et chômage en France de 1955 à 1982: un modèle macroéconomique annuel avec rationnement. (Employment and Unemployment in France: An Annual Macroeconomic Model with Rationing. With English summary.) *Ann. INSEE*, July–December 1984, (55/56), pp. 39–76. [G: France]

Lammers, John and Lockwood, Timothy. Short-Time Compensation: At Home and Abroad: The California Experiment. In *MaCoy, R. and Morand, M. J., eds.*, 1984, pp. 61–81. [G: U.S.]

Lamonde, Pierre and Polèse, Mario. L'évolution de la structure économique de Montréal 1971–1981: désindustrialisation ou reconversion? (The Evolution of Montreal's Economic Structure, 1971–1981: Deindustrialization or Reconversion? With English summary.) *L'Actual. Econ.*, December 1984, 60(4), pp. 471–94. [G: Canada]

Langmantel, Erich. Die Beschäftigungswirkungen sättigungsbedingten Strukturwandels—Eine Analyse anhand von Pasinettis "Structural Change and Economic Growth." (Employment Effects of Structural Change Induced by Saturation of Markets—An Analysis on the Basis of Pasinetti's "Structural Change and Economic Growth." With English summary.) *Ifo-Studien*, 1984, 30(3), pp. 231–41.

Laursen, Karsten. Dansk økonomi på længere sigt. (Long Term Perspectives in the Danish Economy. With English summary.) *Nationaløkon. Tidsskr.*, 1984, 122(1), pp. 115–23. [G: Denmark]

Leach, Bernard and Shutt, John. Chips and Crisps: The Impact of New Technology on Food Processing Jobs in Greater Manchester. In *Marstrand, P., ed.*, 1984, pp. 73–92. [G: U.K.]

Lee, Gloria and Wrench, John. Routes into Segmented Youth Labour Markets. *Int. J. Soc. Econ.*, 1984, 11(7), pp. 77–90. [G: U.K.]

Leigh, Duane E. Why Is There Mandatory Retirement? An Empirical Reexamination. *J. Human Res.*, Fall 1984, 19(4), pp. 512–31. [G: U.S.]

Leonard, John E. and Prinzinger, Joseph M. An Investigation into the Monopsonistic Market Structure of Division One NCAA Football and Its Effect on College Football Players. *Eastern Econ. J.*, October–December 1984, 10(4), pp. 455–67. [G: U.S.]

Leonard, Jonathan S. Employment and Occupational Advance under Affirmative Action. *Rev. Econ. Statist.*, August 1984, 66(3), pp. 377–85. [G: U.S.]

Leonard, Jonathan S. The Impact of Affirmative Action on Employment. *J. Lab. Econ.*, October 1984, 2(4), pp. 439–63. [G: U.S.]

Leppel, Karen. Determinants of Expectations of Retirement: Evidence from a Less Developed Country. *Appl. Econ.*, October 1984, 16(5), pp. 677–86. [G: U.S.; Malaysia]

Levin, Henry M. Employment and Productivity of Producer Cooperatives. In *Jackall, R. and Levin, H. M., eds.*, 1984, pp. 16–31. [G: Spain]

Levy, Robert A.; Bowes, Marianne and Jondrow, James M. Technical Advance and Other Sources of Employment Change in Basic In-

dustry. In *Collins, E. L. and Tanner, L. D., eds.*, 1984, pp. 77–95. [G: U.S.]

Lipschitz, Leslie and Schadler, Susan M. Relative Prices, Real Wages, and Macroeconomic Policies: Some Evidence from Manufacturing in Japan and the United Kingdom. *Int. Monet. Fund Staff Pap.*, June 1984, 31(2), pp. 303–38. [G: Japan; U.K.]

Littler, D. A.; Pickering, J. F. and Cockerill, T. A. J. The Management of the Small Firm. In *Pickering, J. F. and Cockerill, T. A. J., eds.*, 1984, pp. 388–415. [G: U.K.; OECD]

Littman, Daniel A. and Lee, Myung-Hoon. Plant Closings and Worker Dislocation. In *McKenzie, R. B., ed. (II)*, 1984, 1983, pp. 127–54. [G: U.S.]

Livingstone, Ian. Resource-Based Industrial Development: Past Experience and Future Prospects in Malawi. *Industry Devel.*, 1984, (10), pp. 75–135. [G: Malawi]

Lovell, Malcolm R. Labor Productivity and Demographics: Comment. In *Wachter, M. L. and Wachter, S. M., eds.*, 1984, pp. 108–10. [G: U.S.]

Lupo, Nancy Altman. Influencing Retirement Behavior: A Further Analysis. *J. Policy Anal. Manage.*, Spring 1984, 3(3), pp. 439–46. [G: U.S.]

Lynch, Gerald J. and Hyclak, Thomas. Cyclical and Noncyclical Unemployment Differences among Demographic Groups. *Growth Change*, January 1984, 15(1), pp. 9–17. [G: U.S.]

Mackay, Tony. The Oil and Oil-Related Sector. In *Hood, N. and Young, S., eds.*, 1984, pp. 326–64. [G: U.K.]

MaCoy, Ramelle and Morand, Martin J. Short-Time Compensation: The Implications for Management. In *MaCoy, R. and Morand, M. J., eds.*, 1984, pp. 14–35. [G: U.S.]

MaCoy, Ramelle and Morand, Martin J. Short-Time Compensation: A Formula for Work Sharing: Afterword. In *MaCoy, R. and Morand, M. J., eds.*, 1984, pp. 196–99. [G: U.S.]

MaCoy, Ramelle and Morand, Martin J. Short-Time Compensation: An Alternative to Layoff: A Labor Viewpoint. In *MaCoy, R. and Morand, M. J., eds.*, 1984, pp. 36–50. [G: U.S.]

MaCoy, Ramelle and Morand, Martin J. STC and Labor–Management Cooperation. In *MaCoy, R. and Morand, M. J., eds.*, 1984, pp. 183–95. [G: U.S.]

MaCoy, Ramelle and Morand, Martin J. Work Sharing and Short-time Compensation: An Overview. In *MaCoy, R. and Morand, M. J., eds.*, 1984, pp. 3–13. [G: U.S.]

Mairesse, Jacques. The Relationship between Production and Unemployment in Japan: Okun's Law in Comparative Perspective: Comments. *Europ. Econ. Rev.*, June 1984, 25(1), pp. 99–105. [G: U.S.; Japan; EEC]

Malmygin, I. The Balance of Workplaces and Manpower. *Prob. Econ.*, July 1984, 27(3), pp. 80–93. [G: U.S.S.R.]

Malveaux, Julianne. Theoretical Explanations of the Persistence of Racial Unemployment Differentials. In *Darity, W., Jr., ed.,* 1984, pp. 91–118. [G: U.S.]

Mangan, John and Stokes, Leigh. The Determinants of Labour Demand in Australian Manufacturing. *S. Afr. J. Econ.,* September 1984, *52*(3), pp. 296–308. [G: Australia]

Mangan, John and Stokes, Leigh. The Determinants of Labour Demand in Australian Manufacturing. *Appl. Econ.,* June 1984, *16*(3), pp. 449–59. [G: Australia]

Manwaring, Tony and Wood, Stephen. Recruitment and the Recession. *Int. J. Soc. Econ.,* 1984, *11*(7), pp. 49–63. [G: U.K.]

Martin, Ronald L. Redundancies, Labour Turnover and Employment Contraction in the Recession: A Regional Analysis. *Reg. Stud.,* December 1984, *18*(6), pp. 445–58. [G: U.K.]

Mathur, R. S. Dynamics of Sectoral Shifts in Employment: An Inter-state Analysis. In *Singh, A. K.; Papola, T. S. and Mathur, R. S., eds.,* 1984, pp. 461–67. [G: India]

Matta, Benjamin N., Jr. The Off-Farm Work of Hired Farm Workers. In *Emerson, R. D., ed.,* 1984, pp. 140–64. [G: U.S.]

Mayer, Jean. Regional Employment Development: The Evolution of Theory and Practice. *Int. Lab. Rev.,* January-February 1984, *123*(1), pp. 17–34. [G: Global]

Maynard, Geoffrey W. A Natural Interpretation of The Present Unemployment: Comment. In *Griffiths, B. and Wood, G. E., eds.,* 1984, pp. 172–75. [G: U.K.; U.S.; EEC]

Maynard, Rebecca A. The Impacts of Supported Work on Youth. In *Hollister, R. G., Jr.; Kemper, P. and Maynard, R. A., eds.,* 1984, pp. 205–38. [G: U.S.]

McAvinchey, Ian D. Economic Factors and Mortality—Some Aspects of the Scottish Case, 1950–1978. *Scot. J. Polit. Econ.,* February 1984, *31*(1), pp. 1–27. [G: U.K.]

McDonald, Richard J. The "Underground Economy" and BLS Statistical Data. *Mon. Lab. Rev.,* January 1984, *107*(1), pp. 4–18. [G: U.S.]

McHugh, Richard and Widdows, Richard. The Age of Capital and State Unemployment Rates. *J. Reg. Sci.,* February 1984, *24*(1), pp. 85–92. [G: U.S.]

McKee, Michael and West, Edwin G. Minimum Wage Effects on Part-time Employment. *Econ. Inquiry,* July 1984, *22*(3), pp. 421–28. [G: U.S.; Canada]

McKenzie, Richard B. Business Mobility: Economic Myths and Realities. In *McKenzie, R. B., ed. (II),* 1984, pp. 11–27. [G: U.S.]

McKenzie, Richard B. Summary Remarks. In *McKenzie, R. B., ed. (II),* 1984, pp. 309–13. [G: U.S.]

McKenzie, Richard B. The Case for Plant Closures. In *McKenzie, R. B., ed. (II),* 1984, *1981,* pp. 205–19. [G: U.S.]

McKenzie, Richard B. The Right to Close Up Shop. In *McKenzie, R. B., ed. (II),* 1984, pp. 3–8. [G: U.S.]

McLennan, Kenneth. Industry Perspectives on Adjustment to Economic Change. In *Collins,*

E. L. and Tanner, L. D., eds., 1984, pp. 163–82. [G: U.S.]

Meager, Nigel. Job Loss and the Regions: How Important Is Redundancy? *Reg. Stud.,* December 1984, *18*(6), pp. 459–67. [G: U.K.]

Medoff, Marshall H. Christian Politics and the Economic Status of Women. *J. Behav. Econ.,* Summer 1984, *13*(1), pp. 23–40. [G: U.S.]

Meisel, Harry. The Pioneers: STC in the Federal Republic of Germany. In *MaCoy, R. and Morand, M. J., eds.,* 1984, pp. 53–60. [G: W. Germany]

Mesa, Juan M. Short-Time Working or Lay-Offs? Experience from Canada and California. *Int. Lab. Rev.,* January-February 1984, *123*(1), pp. 99–115. [G: Canada; U.S.]

Metcalf, David. Employment and Industrial Assistance. In *Jacquemin, A., ed.,* 1984, pp. 84–98. [G: U.K.; Belgium; France; Norway; Netherlands]

Metcalf, David. On the Measurement of Employment and Unemployment. *Nat. Inst. Econ. Rev.,* August 1984, (109), pp. 59–67. [G: OECD; U.K.]

Meyer-Thomas, Gerold. Vom Sinn und Unsinn der 35-Stunden-Woche. (Sense and Nonsense of the 35-Hour Working Week. With English summary.) *Z. Wirtschaft. Sozialwissen.,* 1984, *104*(5), pp. 489–513. [G: W. Germany]

Micklewright, John. Male Unemployment and the Family Expenditure Survey 1972–80. *Oxford Bull. Econ. Statist.,* February 1984, *46*(1), pp. 31–53. [G: U.K.]

Miles, Ian. Work, Well-being and Unemployment: A Study of Men in Brighton. In *Marstrand, P., ed.,* 1984, pp. 93–102. [G: U.K.]

Miller, Robert A. Job Matching and Occupational Choice. *J. Polit. Econ.,* December 1984, *92*(6), pp. 1086–120. [G: U.S.]

Minford, Patrick. A Review of *Unemployment: Cause and Cure,* by Patrick Minford with David Davies, Michael Peel and Alison Sprague: Response. *Econ. J.,* December 1984, *94*(376), pp. 954–59. [G: U.K.]

Mitchell, Daniel J. B. The Australian Labor Market. In *Caves, R. E. and Krause, L. B., eds.,* 1984, pp. 127–93. [G: Australia]

Mitchell, Olivia S. and Fields, Gary S. The Economics of Retirement Behavior. *J. Lab. Econ.,* January 1984, *2*(1), pp. 84–105. [G: U.S.]

Moser, James W. A Principal Component Analysis of Labor Market Indicators. *Eastern Econ. J.,* July-September 1984, *10*(3), pp. 243–57. [G: U.S.]

Motley, Brian. How Soon Will the U.S. Reach Full Employment? An Assessment Based on Okun's Law. *Fed. Res. Bank San Francisco Econ. Rev.,* Summer 1984, (3), pp. 26–39. [G: U.S.]

Moy, Joyanna. Recent Labor Market Developments in the U.S. and Nine Other Countries. *Mon. Lab. Rev.,* January 1984, *107*(1), pp. 44–51. [G: OECD]

Müller, A. L. Employment Policies in the Soviet

Bloc (Review Note). *S. Afr. J. Econ.*, March 1984, *52*(1), pp. 90–95. **[G: U.S.S.R.; Poland; E. Germany; Czechoslovakia; Hungary]**

Murphy, Kevin J. and Hofler, Richard A. Determinants of Geographic Unemployment Rates: A Selectively Pooled–Simultaneous Model. *Rev. Econ. Statist.*, May 1984, *66*(2), pp. 216–23. **[G: U.S.]**

Myers, Samuel L., Jr. Labor Economics, Preferences, and the Rationality Assumption: A Comment on Blau, Dickens, and Malveaux. In *Darity, W., Jr., ed.*, 1984, pp. 257–68. **[G: U.S.]**

Naggl, W. and Nerb, G. Zur Aussagefähigkeit von Beschäftigungsplänen der Unternehmen in der Europäischen Gemeinschaft. (The Information Content of the Employment Plans in European Business Surveys. With English summary.) *Ifo-Studien*, 1984, *30*(1), pp. 1–28. **[G: U.S.; W. Europe]**

Naslund, Bertil. Uncertainty and the Need for Innovation in Management Techniques and Methods. In *[Kozmetsky, G.]*, 1984, pp. 177–80. **[G: Sweden]**

Nasseh, Ali Reza and Elyasiani, Elyas. Energy Price Shocks in the 1970s: Impact in Industrialized Economies. *Energy Econ.*, October 1984, *6*(4), pp. 231–44. **[G: U.S.; U.K.; Canada; Germany; France]**

Neftçi, Salih N. Are Economic Time Series Asymmetric over the Business Cycle? *J. Polit. Econ.*, April 1984, *92*(2), pp. 307–28. **[G: U.S.]**

Nemirow, Martin. Short-Time Compensation: Some Policy Considerations. In *MaCoy, R. and Morand, M. J., eds.*, 1984, pp. 158–82. **[G: U.S.; W. Germany]**

Nemirow, Martin. Work-Sharing Approaches: Past and Present. *Mon. Lab. Rev.*, September 1984, *107*(9), pp. 34–39. **[G: U.S.; Germany]**

Newbold, Paul and Thury, Gerhard. Seasonal Adjustment of Austrian Labour Force Series. *Empirica*, 1984, *11*(2), pp. 147–204. **[G: Austria]**

Newhouse, Joseph P. Disability Transfers, Early Retirement, and Retrenchment: Comment. In *Aaron, H. J. and Burtless, G., eds.*, 1984, pp. 93–96. **[G: U.S.]**

Nickell, Stephen J. A Review of *Unemployment: Cause and Cure,* by Patrick Minford with David Davies, Michael Peel and Alison Sprague. *Econ. J.*, December 1984, *94*(376), pp. 946–53. **[G: U.K.]**

Nickell, Stephen J. Discussants' Comments on: A Natural Interpretation of the Present Unemployment, by Roy A. Batchelor, presented at the City University Conference on Monetarism in the United Kingdom, September 1981. In *Griffiths, B. and Wood, G. E., eds.*, 1984, pp. 176–81. **[G: U.K.; U.S.; EEC]**

Nilsen, Diane M. Employment in Durable Goods Anything But Durable in 1979–82. *Mon. Lab. Rev.*, February 1984, *107*(2), pp. 15–24. **[G: U.S.]**

Nilsen, Sigurd R. Recessionary Impacts on the Unemployment of Men and Women. *Mon. Lab. Rev.*, May 1984, *107*(5), pp. 21–25. **[G: U.S.]**

Nissim, Joseph. An Examination of the Differential Patterns in the Cyclical Behaviour of the Employment, Hours and Wages of Labour of Different Skills: British Mechanical Engineering, 1963–1978. *Economica*, November 1984, *51*(204), pp. 423–36. **[G: U.K.]**

Nissim, Joseph. The Price Responsiveness of the Demand for Labour by Skill: British Mechanical Engineering: 1963–1978. *Econ. J.*, December 1984, *94*(376), pp. 812–25. **[G: U.K.]**

van den Noord, P. J. Relocation of State Services and Regional Unemployment in the Netherlands. *De Economist*, 1984, *132*(4), pp. 451–67. **[G: Netherlands]**

Norquist, Grover. Four Million New Jobs: The American Employment Boom That Stunned the World. *Policy Rev.*, Spring 1984, (28), pp. 27–29. **[G: U.S.]**

O'Farrell, P. N. Components of Manufacturing Employment Change in Ireland, 1973–1981. *Urban Stud.*, May 1984, *21*(2), pp. 155–76. **[G: Ireland]**

Oberai, A. S. and Singh, H. K. Manmohan. Migration, Employment and the Urban Labour Market: A Study in the Indian Punjab. *Int. Lab. Rev.*, July–August 1984, *123*(4), pp. 507–23. **[G: India]**

Ogunbameru, Olakunle Abiona. The African Proletariat in Industrial Employment: A Reappraisal. *Int. Soc. Sci. J.*, 1984, *36*(2), pp. 341–54. **[G: Nigeria]**

Oppenländer, Karl Heinrich. Reicht die Arbeit für alle? Zur Entwicklung von Wirtschaft und Arbeitsmarkt in den achtziger Jahren. (Is There Enough Work for Everyone? On the Economy and the Labour Market in the 1980s. With English summary.) *Ifo-Studien*, 1984, *30*(3), pp. 193–207. **[G: W. Germany]**

Paauw, Douglas S. Economic Growth, Employment, and Productivity: Prospects for Indonesia. *Singapore Econ. Rev.*, October 1984, *29*(2), pp. 111–25. **[G: Indonesia]**

Pachal, Tapan and Chakrabarty, Gurupada. Placement through Employment Exchange— A Case Study of the Delhi Metropolitan Area. *Margin*, October 1984, *17*(1), pp. 87–93. **[G: India]**

Palazzi, Paolo. The Segmentation of the Labor Market in the United States. The Role of Young People. *Econ. Lavoro*, July-Sept. 1984, *18*(3), pp. 47–61. **[G: U.S.]**

Palmer, Ransford W. Absorbing the Caribbean Labor Surplus: The Need for an Indigenous Engine of Growth. In *Palmer, R. W.,* 1984, pp. 3–15. **[G: Jamaica]**

Parsons, D. Employment Stimulation and the Local Labour Market: A Case Study of Airport Growth. *Reg. Stud.*, October 1984, *18*(5), pp. 423–28. **[G: U.K.]**

Peck, Francis and Townsend, Alan. Contrasting Experience of Recession and Spatial Restructuring: British Shipbuilders, Plessey and Metal

Box. *Reg. Stud.*, August 1984, *18*(4), pp. 319–38. **[G: U.K.]**

Peet, Richard. Class Struggle, the Relocation of Employment, and Economic Crisis. *Sci. Soc.*, Spring 1984, *48*(1), pp. 38–51. **[G: U.S.]**

Pellechio, Anthony J. Pension Coverage, Pension Vesting, and the Distribution of Job Tenures: Comment. In *Aaron, H. J. and Burtless, G.*, eds., 1984, pp. 61–63. **[G: U.S.]**

Pencavel, John H. Trade Unions and Restrictive Practices: Comment. In *Rosa, J.-J.*, ed., 1984, pp. 115–19. **[G: U.S.]**

Petrella, Ricardo. Europe at Work: Challenges and Prospects. In *Marstrand, P.*, ed., 1984, pp. 1–18. **[G: W. Europe]**

Pfarr, Heide M. and Eitel, Ludwig. Equal Opportunity Policies for Women in the Federal Republic of Germany. In *Schmid, G. and Weitzel, R.*, eds., 1984, pp. 155–90.
[G: W. Germany]

Piliavin, Irving and Gartner, Rosemary. The Impacts of Supported Work on Ex-offenders. In *Hollister, R. G., Jr.; Kemper, P. and Maynard, R. A.*, eds., 1984, pp. 172–204. **[G: U.S.]**

Pittin, Renée. Documentation and Analysis of the Invisible Work of Invisible Women: A Nigerian Case-Study. *Int. Lab. Rev.*, July–August 1984, *123*(4), pp. 473–90. **[G: Nigeria]**

Podgursky, Michael. Sources of Secular Increases in the Unemployment Rate, 1969–82. *Mon. Lab. Rev.*, July 1984, *107*(7), pp. 19–25.
[G: U.S.]

Pollard, Tom K. Changes over the 1970s in the Employment Patterns of Black and White Young Men. In *Borus, M. E.*, ed., 1984, pp. 57–79. **[G: U.S.]**

Porter, Richard C. Apartheid, the Job Ladder, and the Evolutionary Hypothesis: Empirical Evidence from South African Manufacturing, 1960–1977. *Econ. Develop. Cult. Change*, October 1984, *33*(1), pp. 117–41. **[G: S. Africa]**

Poterba, James M. and Summers, Lawrence H. Response Variation in the CPS: Caveats for the Unemployment Analyst. *Mon. Lab. Rev.*, March 1984, *107*(3), pp. 37–43. **[G: U.S.]**

Premus, Robert and Fichtenbaum, Rudy. Labor Turnover and the Sunbelt/Frostbelt Controversy: An Empirical Test. In *McKenzie, R. B.*, ed. (II), 1984, 1977, pp. 119–26. **[G: U.S.]**

Ragan, James F., Jr. Investigating the Decline in Manufacturing Quit Rates. *J. Human Res.*, Winter 1984, *19*(1), pp. 53–71. **[G: U.S.]**

Ragan, James F., Jr. The Voluntary Leaver Provisions of Unemployment Insurance and Their Effect on Quit and Unemployment Rates. *Southern Econ. J.*, July 1984, *51*(1), pp. 135–46. **[G: U.S.]**

Ramos, Joseph. Urbanization and the Labour Market. *Cepal Rev.*, 1984, (24), pp. 63–81.
[G: Latin America]

Raschke, Freddy. Demographic Influences on the Mobility of German Labor Stock. In *Steinmann, G.*, ed., 1984, pp. 323–42.
[G: W. Germany]

Reed, J. David and Hoag, John H. Regional Coalmining Employment in the United States from 1985 to 2000. *Growth Change*, July 1984, *15*(3), pp. 43–50. **[G: U.S.]**

Reeves, Frank and Ward, Robin. West Indian Business in Britain. In *Ward, R. and Jenkins, R.*, eds., 1984, pp. 125–46. **[G: U.K.]**

Reid, Frank and Meltz, Noah M. Canada's STC: A Comparison with the California Version. In *MaCoy, R. and Morand, M. J.*, eds., 1984, pp. 106–19. **[G: Canada; U.S.]**

Reynolds, Clark; Ramos, Raul and McCleery, Robert. The Impact of Foreign Trade and Export Strategies on Distribution of Income for Low-Income Households in Mexico. In *Aspe, P. and Sigmund, P. E.*, eds., 1984, pp. 203–46. **[G: Mexico]**

Ries, John C. Unemployment in 1982: Beyond the Official Labor Force Statistics. *New Eng. Econ. Rev.*, May–June 1984, pp. 29–37.
[G: U.S.]

Roberti, Paolo. Macroeconomic and Public Finance "Costs" of High Unemployment. *Econ. Lavoro*, Jan.-Mar. 1984, *18*(1), pp. 3–15.
[G: OECD]

Rogalski, Michel and Yakubovich, Carlos. Strategies for Reconversion of Armaments Industry. In *Ghosh, P. K.*, ed., no. 17, 1984, 1982, pp. 260–68. **[G: U.S.]**

Rones, Philip L. Recent Recessions Swell Ranks of the Long-Term Unemployment. *Mon. Lab. Rev.*, February 1984, *107*(2), pp. 25–29.
[G: U.S.]

Rudney, Gabriel and Weitzman, Murray. Trends in Employment and Earnings in the Philanthropic Sector. *Mon. Lab. Rev.*, September 1984, *107*(9), pp. 16–20. **[G: U.S.]**

Rürup, Bert and Struwe, Jochen. Arbeitszeitflexibilisierung als Instrument der Beschäftigungspolitik. (Flexibilisation of Working Times as an Instrument of Employment Policies. With English summary.) *Konjunkturpolitik*, 1984, *30*(1), pp. 1–22. **[G: W. Germany]**

Santoni, G. J. Employment Trends in St. Louis: 1954–82. *Fed. Res. Bank St. Louis Rev.*, January 1984, *66*(1), pp. 14–20. **[G: U.S.]**

Savané, Marie Angelique. The Employment of Women with Social Change and Freedom of Women: The Case of Africa. In *Amin, S.*, ed., 1984, pp. 52–66. **[G: Africa]**

Savary, Julien. L'impact de l'investissement étranger en France sur l'emploi industriel (1974–1983). (With English summary.) *Revue Écon. Polit.*, September–October 1984, *94*(5), pp. 688–97. **[G: France]**

Sawhill, Isabel V. How Widespread Are Income Losses in a Recession? Comments. In *Bawden, D. L.*, ed., 1984, pp. 181–84. **[G: U.S.]**

Sawhill, Isabel V. Labor Productivity and Demographics: Comment. In *Wachter, M. L. and Wachter, S. M.*, eds., 1984, pp. 97–100.
[G: U.S.]

Sbytova, L. Employment and Raising the Effectiveness of Labor in the Service Sector. *Prob. Econ.*, January 1984, *26*(9), pp. 64–80.
[G: U.S.S.R.]

Scharpf, Fritz W. Economic and Institutional Constraints of Full-Employment Strategies:

Sweden, Austria, and Western Germany, 1973–1982. In *Goldthorpe, J. H., ed.*, 1984, pp. 257–90. **[G: Sweden; Austria; W. Germany]**

Schellhaass, Horst-Manfred and Weis, Peter. Die beschäftigungspolitischen Auswirkungen einer Vorruhestandsregelung. (The Effects of Early Retirement Schemes upon the Level of Employment. With English summary.) *Z. ges. Staatswiss.*, September 1984, *140*(3), pp. 448–74. **[G: Germany]**

Schmidt, Rainer. Population Change, Labour Market and Unemployment—The Case of the German Domestic Labour Force from 1965–1982. In *Steinmann, G., ed.*, 1984, pp. 278–94. **[G: W. Germany]**

Schroeder, Patricia. Short-Time Compensation: Looking Ahead to Work-sharing. *Challenge*, November/December 1984, *27*(5), pp. 56–57. **[G: Canada; U.S.]**

Schumacher, Dieter. North–South Trade and Shifts in Employment: A Comparative Analysis of Six European Community Countries. *Int. Lab. Rev.*, May–June 1984, *123*(3), pp. 333–48. **[G: W. Europe; LDCs]**

Sehgal, Ellen. Occupational Mobility and Job Tenure in 1983. *Mon. Lab. Rev.*, October 1984, *107*(10), pp. 18–23. **[G: U.S.]**

Sehgal, Ellen. Work Experience in 1983 Reflects the Effects of the Recovery. *Mon. Lab. Rev.*, December 1984, *107*(12), pp. 18–24. **[G: U.S.]**

Sellekaerts, Willy and Sellekaerts, Brigitte H. Technical Change, Capital Formation, and Capacity Unemployment in the United States. *Eastern Econ. J.*, July-September 1984, *10*(3), pp. 231–41. **[G: U.S.]**

Shulman, Steven. Competition and Racial Discrimination: The Employment Effects of Reagan's Labor Market Policies. *Rev. Radical Polit. Econ.*, Winter 1984, *16*(4), pp. 111–28. **[G: U.S.]**

Skolka, Jiri. Input–Output Anatomy of Changes in Employment Structure in Austria between 1964 and 1976. *Empirica*, 1984, *11*(2), pp. 205–33. **[G: Austria]**

Sly, David F. Modern Economic-Sector Development and Population Change. In *Ominde, S. H., ed.*, 1984, pp. 91–100. **[G: Kenya]**

Small, Drummond B. and Smith, Lawrence D. The Food, Drink, and Tobacco Sectors. In *Hood, N. and Young, S., eds.*, 1984, pp. 174–212. **[G: U.K.]**

Smyth, David J. Short-Run Employment Functions When the Speed of Adjustment Depends on the Unemployment Rate. *Rev. Econ. Statist.*, February 1984, *66*(1), pp. 138–42. **[G: OECD]**

Solon, Gary. The Effects of Unemployment Insurance Eligibility Rules on Job Quitting Behavior. *J. Human Res.*, Winter 1984, *19*(1), pp. 118–26. **[G: U.S.]**

Sorrentino, Constance. Japan's Low Unemployment: An In-Depth Analysis. *Mon. Lab. Rev.*, March 1984, *107*(3), pp. 18–27. **[G: Japan]**

Squires, Gregory D. Capital Mobility versus Upward Mobility: The Racially Discriminatory Consequences of Plant Closings and Corporate Relocations. In *Sawers, L. and Tabb, W. K., eds.*, 1984, pp. 152–62.

St. Louis, Robert D. Short-Time Compensation: At Home and Abroad: Arizona, Motorola, and STC. In *MaCoy, R. and Morand, M. J., eds.*, 1984, pp. 82–94. **[G: U.S.]**

Stamas, George D. State and Regional Employment and Unemployment in 1983. *Mon. Lab. Rev.*, September 1984, *107*(9), pp. 9–15. **[G: U.S.]**

Standing, Guy. The Notion of Technological Unemployment. *Int. Lab. Rev.*, March-April 1984, *123*(2), pp. 127–47. **[G: U.S.]**

Stenius, Marianne and Virén, Matti. Some Further Results on Rosen and Quandt's Labor Market Model. *Europ. Econ. Rev.*, December 1984, *26*(3), pp. 369–77. **[G: U.S.]**

Stewart, Mark B. and Greenhalgh, Christine A. Work History Patterns and the Occupational Attainment of Women. *Econ. J.*, September 1984, *94*(375), pp. 493–519. **[G: U.K.]**

Swords-Isherwood, N.; Zmroczek, C. and Henwood, F. Technical Change and its Effect on Employment Opportunities for Women. In *Marstrand, P., ed.*, 1984, pp. 191–213. **[G: U.K.]**

Symons, J. and Layard, R. Neoclassical Demand for Labour Functions for Six Major Economies. *Econ. J.*, December 1984, *94*(376), pp. 788–99. **[G: N. America; U.K.; Germany; Japan; France]**

Tachibanaki, Toshiaki. Labor Mobility and Job Tenure. In *Aoki, M., ed.*, 1984, pp. 77–102. **[G: Japan; U.S.]**

Taira, Koji. Output, Productivity, and Employment: U.S.–Japan Comparison. In *Sherman, M., ed.*, 1984, pp. 87–102. **[G: Japan; U.S.]**

Taira, Koji. The Management of Employment Adjustment in Electric and Electronics Firms in the 1970s. *Rivista Int. Sci. Econ. Com.*, September 1984, *31*(9), pp. 833–43. **[G: Japan]**

Tannenwald, Robert. Why Has the Unemployment Rate Declined so Rapidly? *New Eng. Econ. Rev.*, September–October 1984, pp. 34–38. **[G: U.S.]**

Tanskanen, Antti. Kilpailukyky ja työllisyys Suomessa. (Competitiveness and Employment in Finland. With English summary.) *Kansant. Aikak.*, 1984, *80*(4), pp. 383–93. **[G: Finland]**

Taylor, John B. Recent Changes in Macro Policy and Its Effects: Some Time-Series Evidence. *Amer. Econ. Rev.*, May 1984, *74*(2), pp. 206–10. **[G: U.S.]**

Thore, Sten. Uncertainty and the Opportunities for Innovation and Investment. In *[Kozmetsky, G.]*, 1984, pp. 181–83. **[G: U.S.; Sweden]**

Tiller, Richard B. Labor Market Efficiency and the Dynamic Behavior of Regional Unemployment Differentials. *Ann. Reg. Sci.*, November 1984, *18*(3), pp. 21–32. **[G: U.S.]**

Tinbergen, Jan. Allocation of Workers over Jobs. *De Economist*, 1984, *132*(1), pp. 23–29. **[G: U.S.]**

Tobin, James. Impasse of the 1980s: Locomotives Who Can't or Won't. *World Econ.*, March 1984, 7(1), pp. 5–21. [G: OECD]

Todaro, Michael P. Urbanization in Developing Nations: Trends, Prospects, and Policies. In *Ghosh, P. K., ed., no. 2*, 1984, pp. 7–26. [G: LDCs]

Todd, Jerry D. A Retirement Plan Decision Model for Small Business. *J. Risk Ins.*, June 1984, 51(2), pp. 265–85. [G: U.S.]

Tokman, Víctor E. Global Monetarism and Destruction of Industry. *Cepal Rev.*, 1984, (23), pp. 107–21. [G: Argentina; Chile]

Tokman, Víctor E. The Employment Crisis in Latin America. *Int. Lab. Rev.*, September–October 1984, 123(5), pp. 585–97. [G: Latin America]

Topel, Robert H. Equilibrium Earnings, Turnover, and Unemployment: New Evidence. *J. Lab. Econ.*, October 1984, 2(4), pp. 500–522. [G: U.S.]

Topel, Robert H. Experience Rating of Unemployment Insurance and the Incidence of Unemployment. *J. Law Econ.*, April 1984, 27(1), pp. 61–90. [G: U.S.]

Truett, Dale B. and Truett, Lila J. The Maquiladoras: Prospects for Mexico. *J. Econ. Devel.*, December 1984, 9(2), pp. 45–66. [G: Mexico]

Tschetter, John H. An Evaluation of BLS' Projections of 1980 Industry Employment. *Mon. Lab. Rev.*, August 1984, 107(8), pp. 12–22. [G: U.S.]

Tuckman, Barbara H. and Tuckman, Howard P. The Labor Market for Part-Time Faculty at Business Schools. *Quart. Rev. Econ. Bus.*, Autumn 1984, 24(3), pp. 95–103. [G: U.S.]

Tuomainen, Eero. Työaika ja työllisyys. (Working Time and Employment. With English summary.) *Kansant. Aikak.*, 1984, 80(2), pp. 131–38. [G: Finland]

Ulman, Lloyd and Sorensen, Elaine. Exit, Voice, and Muscle: A Note. *Ind. Relat.*, Fall 1984, 23(3), pp. 424–28. [G: U.S.]

Urquhart, Michael. The Employment Shift to Services: Where Did It Come From? *Mon. Lab. Rev.*, April 1984, 107(4), pp. 15–22. [G: U.S.]

Van Rompuy, G. The Effect of Unemployment Legislation on Labor Supply Decisions. *Tijdschrift Econ. Manage.*, 1984, 29(2), pp. 217–31. [G: Belgium]

Vandamme, François. The Revised European Social Fund and Action to Combat Unemployment in the European Community. *Int. Lab. Rev.*, March-April 1984, 123(2), pp. 167–81. [G: EEC]

Vartiainen, Henri J. Public Finance, Social Policy and the Creation of Employment. *Kansant. Aikak.*, 1984, 80(1), pp. 86–96. [G: Finland]

van der Veen, Anne and Evers, Gerard H. M. A Labour-Supply Function for Females in the Netherlands. *De Economist*, 1984, 132(3), pp. 367–76. [G: Netherlands]

Venti, Steven F. The Effects of Income Maintenance on Work, Schooling, and Non-Market

Activities of Youth. *Rev. Econ. Statist.*, February 1984, 66(1), pp. 16–25.

Vipond, Joan. The Intra-urban Unemployment Gradient: The Influence of Location on Unemployment. *Urban Stud.*, November 1984, 21(4), pp. 377–88. [G: Australia]

Wachter, Michael L. The Training Component of Growth Policies. In *Wachter, M. L. and Wachter, S. M., eds.*, 1984, pp. 41–69. [G: U.S.]

Wachter, Michael L. Unemployment in the American Economy: Types, Causes, and Outlooks for the 1980's. In *Ullrich, R. A., ed.*, 1984, pp. 1–24. [G: U.S.]

Wagner, Adolf. Aspects of Demographic Unemployment. In *Steinmann, G., ed.*, 1984, pp. 295–302. [G: W. Germany]

Walsh, Brendan M. Employment and Competitiveness in the European Community. *World Econ.*, March 1984, 7(1), pp. 47–62. [G: EEC; U.S.]

Weiss, Andrew. Determinants of Quit Behavior. *J. Lab. Econ.*, July 1984, 2(3), pp. 371–87. [G: U.S.]

Weiss, Frank D. The Contribution of Small Enterprise to Growth and Employment: Comment. In *Giersch, H., ed.*, 1984, pp. 23–28. [G: U.S.]

Whitener, Leslie A. A Statistical Portrait of Hired Farmworkers. *Mon. Lab. Rev.*, June 1984, 107(6), pp. 49–53. [G: U.S.]

Whitman, Marina v.N. Persistent Unemployment: Economic Policy Perspectives in United States and Western Europe. In *Pierre, A. J., ed.*, 1984, pp. 14–52. [G: U.S.; W. Europe]

Williams, Bruce. Technical Change and Employment. *Greek Econ. Rev.*, December 1984, 6(3), pp. 336–55. [G: U.K.]

Willman, Paul and Cowan, Rowena. New Technology in Banking: The Impact of Autotellers on Staff Numbers. In *Warner, M., ed.*, 1984, pp. 224–39. [G: U.K.]

Wolf, Douglas A. and Levy, Frank. Pension Coverage, Pension Vesting, and the Distribution of Job Tenures. In *Aaron, H. J. and Burtless, G., eds.*, 1984, pp. 23–61. [G: U.S.]

Wren-Lewis, Simon. The Roles of Output Expectations and Liquidity in Explaining Recent Productivity Movements. *Nat. Inst. Econ. Rev.*, May 1984, (108), pp. 42–53. [G: U.K.]

Wyatt, Joe B. Science, Technology, and Employment: The Reindustrialization of America. In *Ullrich, R. A., ed.*, 1984, pp. 59–80. [G: U.S.]

Yaun, P. J. Econometric and Empirical Evidence on the Relationship between Survey Data and Official Data and its Relevance for Monitoring the Business Cycle. In *Oppenländer, K. H. and Poser, G., eds.*, 1984, pp. 47–66. [G: U.K.]

Yeager, Leland B. Is Industrial Innovation Destroying Jobs? A Comment. *Cato J.*, Fall 1984, 4(2), pp. 645–50. [G: U.S.]

Young, Stephen and Reeves, Alan. The Engineering and Metals Sector. In *Hood, N. and Young, S., eds.*, 1984, pp. 128–73. **[G: U.K.]**

825 Productivity Studies: Labor, Capital, and Total Factor

8250 Productivity Studies: Labor, Capital, and Total Factor

Addison, John T. Trade Unions and Restrictive Practices. In *Rosa, J.-J., ed.*, 1984, pp. 83–114. **[G: U.S.]**

Akerlof, George A. Labor Contracts as Partial Gift Exchange. In *Akerlof, G. A.*, 1984, *1982*, pp. 145–74. **[G: U.S.]**

Alam, M. Shahid. Hirschman's Taxonomy of Industries: Some Hypotheses and Evidence. *Econ. Develop. Cult. Change*, January 1984, *32*(2), pp. 367–72. **[G: Pakistan]**

Allen, Steven G. Unionized Construction Workers Are More Productive. *Quart. J. Econ.*, May 1984, *99*(2), pp. 251–74. **[G: U.S.]**

Alvarez, Donato and Cooper, Brian. Productivity Trends in Manufacturing in the U.S. and 11 Other Countries. *Mon. Lab. Rev.*, January 1984, *107*(1), pp. 52–58. **[G: OECD]**

Anderson, Charles W. Worrying about Productivity: A Political, Economic, and Humanistic Analysis. In *Sherman, M., ed.*, 1984, pp. 7–20. **[G: U.S.]**

Anderson, Joan and Frantz, Roger S. The Response of Labour Effort to Falling Real Wages: The Mexican Peso Devaluation of February 1982. *World Devel.*, July 1984, *12*(7), pp. 759–66. **[G: Mexico]**

Arai, Joji. U.S. and European Approaches to Improving Labor Productivity and the Quality of Work Life: Comments. In *Kendrick, J. W., ed.*, 1984, pp. 393–96. **[G: U.S.; W. Europe]**

Artus, Jacques R. The Disequilibrium Real Wage Rate Hypothesis: An Empirical Evaluation. *Int. Monet. Fund Staff Pap.*, June 1984, *31*(2), pp. 249–302. **[G: OECD]**

Baily, Martin Neil. The Reagan Administration's Regulatory Relief Effort: A Mid-term Assessment: Comments. In *Eads, G. C. and Fix, M., eds.*, 1984, pp. 81–83. **[G: U.S.]**

Bardhan, Pranab K. and Kletzer, Kenneth M. Dynamic Effects of Protection on Productivity. *J. Int. Econ.*, February 1984, *16*(1/2), pp. 45–57.

Basu, Arati. Production Systems and Productivity of Labour: An Analysis on the Existence of Surplus Labour. *Indian Econ. Rev.*, July-Dec. 1984, *19*(2), pp. 185–201.

Baumol, William J. On Productivity Growth in the Long Run. *Atlantic Econ. J.*, September 1984, *12*(3), pp. 5–10. **[G: U.S.]**

Baumol, William J. U.S. Competitiveness and the Productivity Gap. *J. Econ. Educ.*, Summer 1984, *15*(3), pp. 217–24. **[G: U.S.]**

Baumol, William J. and Wolff, Edward N. Feedback Models: R&D, Information, and Productivity Growth. In *Jussawalla, M. and Ebenfield, H., eds.*, 1984, pp. 73–93.

Baumol, William J. and Wolff, Edward N. On

Interindustry Differences in Absolute Productivity. *J. Polit. Econ.*, December 1984, *92*(6), pp. 1017–34.

Behrend, Hilde. Voluntary Absence from Work. In *Behrend, H.*, 1984, *1959*, pp. 58–89. **[G: U.K.]**

Berndt, Ernst R. The Role of Energy in Productivity Growth: Comment. In *Kendrick, J. W., ed.*, 1984, pp. 325–34. **[G: U.S.]**

Binswanger, Hans P. and Rosenzweig, Mark R. Contractual Arrangements, Employment, and Wages in Rural Labor Markets: A Critical Review. In *Binswanger, H. P. and Rosenzweig, R., eds.*, 1984, pp. 1–40.

Blakemore, Arthur E. and Hoffman, Dennis L. Hiring Decisions, Labor Flows, and Short-Run Productivity. *Southern Econ. J.*, April 1984, *50*(4), pp. 993–1004. **[G: U.S.]**

Boulier, Bryan L. What Lies behind Verdoorn's Law? *Oxford Econ. Pap.*, June 1984, *36*(2), pp. 259–67.

Bowles, Samuel; Gordon, David M. and Weisskopf, Thomas E. A Social Model for U.S. Productivity Growth. *Challenge*, March/April 1984, *27*(1), pp. 41–48. **[G: U.S.]**

Brand, Horst and Huffstutler, Clyde. Productivity in Making Air Conditioners, Refrigeration Equipment, and Furnaces. *Mon. Lab. Rev.*, December 1984, *107*(12), pp. 11–17. **[G: U.S.]**

Bruno, Michael. Raw Materials, Profits, and the Productivity Slowdown. *Quart. J. Econ.*, February 1984, *99*(1), pp. 1–29. **[G: Japan; U.S.; U.K.; W. Germany]**

Burggraf, Shirley P. Women, Youth, and Minorities and the Case of the Missing Productivity. *Amer. Econ. Rev.*, May 1984, *74*(2), pp. 254–59. **[G: U.S.]**

Cardani, Angelo M. and Mohnen, Pierre A. Labor Productivity in a Dynamic Model with Energy, Capital and R&D for Italian and French Manufacturing. *Giorn. Econ.*, July-August 1984, *43*(7–8), pp. 471–90. **[G: Italy; France]**

Carnes, Richard B. Meatpacking and Prepared Meats Industry: Above-Average Productivity Gains. *Mon. Lab. Rev.*, April 1984, *107*(4), pp. 37–42. **[G: U.S.]**

Caves, Richard E. Scale, Openness, and Productivity in Manufacturing Industries. In *Caves, R. E. and Krause, L. B., eds.*, 1984, pp. 313–47. **[G: Australia; U.S.]**

Chisholm, Rupert F. A Systems Approach to Organizational Productivity. In *Holzer, M. and Nagel, S. S., eds.*, 1984, pp. 261–85. **[G: U.S.]**

Christainsen, Gregory B. and Haveman, Robert H. The Reagan Administration's Regulatory Relief Effort: A Mid-term Assessment. In *Eads, G. C. and Fix, M., eds.*, 1984, pp. 49–80. **[G: U.S.]**

Clark, Gordon L. The Changing Composition of Regional Employment. *Econ. Geogr.*, April 1984, *60*(2), pp. 175–93. **[G: U.S.]**

Clark, Kim B. Unionization and Firm Performance: The Impact on Profits, Growth, and

Productivity. *Amer. Econ. Rev.*, December 1984, *74*(5), pp. 893–919. [G: U.S.]

Clark, Kim B. and Griliches, Zvi. Productivity Growth and R&D at the Business Level: Results from the PIMS Data Base. In *Griliches, Z., ed.*, 1984, pp. 393–416. [G: U.S.]

Clark, Peter K. Productivity and Profits in the 1980s: Are They Really Improving? *Brookings Pap. Econ. Act.*, 1984, (1), pp. 133–67. [G: U.S.]

Clauss, Franz Joachim. Über die Konjunkturabhängigkeit der statistischen Produktivität. (On the Cyclical Dependence of Productivity as Measured Statistically. With English summary.) *Ifo-Studien*, 1984, *30*(4), pp. 273–305. [G: U.S.]

Crafts, N. F. R. Economic Growth in France and Britain, 1830–1910: A Review of the Evidence. *J. Econ. Hist.*, March 1984, *44*(1), pp. 49–67. [G: France; U.K.]

Cuneo, Philippe and Mairesse, Jacques. Productivity and R&D at the Firm Level in French Manufacturing. In *Griliches, Z., ed.*, 1984, pp. 375–92. [G: France]

Darby, Michael R. The U.S. Productivity Slowdown: A Case of Statistical Myopia. *Amer. Econ. Rev.*, June 1984, *74*(3), pp. 301–22. [G: U.S.]

Denison, Edward F. Accounting for Slower Economic Growth: An Update. In *Kendrick, J. W., ed.*, 1984, pp. 1–45. [G: U.S.]

Deprins, Dominique; Simar, Léopold and Tulkens, Henry. Measuring Labor-Efficiency in Post Offices. In *Marchand, M.; Pestieau, P. and Tulkens, H., eds.*, 1984, pp. 243–67. [G: Belgium]

Eberts, Randall W. Union Effects on Teacher Productivity. *Ind. Lab. Relat. Rev.*, April 1984, *37*(3), pp. 346–58. [G: U.S.]

Edwards, Richard. Productivity as an Organizational Variable. In *Sherman, M., ed.*, 1984, pp. 103–16. [G: U.S.]

Ellman, Michael. Agricultural Productivity under Socialism. In *Ellman, M.*, 1984, *1981*, pp. 198–214. [G: China; U.S.S.R.]

Fabricant, Solomon. Problems of Productivity Measurement. In *Intn'l. Productivity Symp.*, 1984, pp. 21–39.

Fabricant, Solomon. Productivity Measurement and Analysis: An Overview. In *Intn'l. Productivity Symp.*, 1984, pp. 1–19. [G: MDCs; LDCs]

Feller, Irwin and Johnston, Irene. The Innovation–Productivity Connection. In *Holzer, M. and Nagel, S. S., eds.*, 1984, pp. 171–89. [G: U.S.]

Fichtenbaum, Rudy. The False Claim of Declining Productivity and Its Political Use: A Comment. *Sci. Soc.*, Winter 1984-1985, *48*(4), pp. 484–89. [G: U.S.]

Fil'ev, V. The Relationship between the Growth of Labor Productivity and Wages. *Prob. Econ.*, October 1984, *27*(6), pp. 71–86. [G: U.S.S.R.]

Fisk, Donald M. Measuring Productivity in State and Local Government. *Mon. Lab. Rev.*, June 1984, *107*(6), pp. 47–48. [G: U.S.]

Fisk, Donald M. Public Sector Productivity and Relative Efficiency: The State of Art in the United States. In *Hanusch, H., ed.*, 1984, pp. 241–49. [G: U.S.]

Forte, Francesco. Controlling the Productivity of Bureaucratic Behavior. *Atlantic Econ. J.*, March 1984, *12*(1), pp. 32–40.

Frank, Robert H. Are Workers Paid Their Marginal Products? *Amer. Econ. Rev.*, September 1984, *74*(4), pp. 549–71. [G: U.S.]

Friedman, Brian. Apparel Stores Display Above-Average Productivity. *Mon. Lab. Rev.*, October 1984, *107*(10), pp. 37–42. [G: U.S.]

Fulco, Lawrence J. Strong Post-Recession Gain in Productivity Contributes to Slow Growth in Labor Costs. *Mon. Lab. Rev.*, December 1984, *107*(12), pp. 3–10. [G: U.S.]

Gordon, Robert J. Productivity and Profits in the 1980s: Are They Really Improving? Comments. *Brookings Pap. Econ. Act.*, 1984, (1), pp. 168–72. [G: U.S.]

Gregory, Peter. The Mexican Labor Market, 1940–1980. In *[Reynolds, L. G.]*, 1984, pp. 245–79. [G: Mexico]

Griliches, Zvi. R&D, Patents, and Productivity: Introduction. In *Griliches, Z., ed.*, 1984, pp. 1–19.

Griliches, Zvi and Lichtenberg, Frank R. R&D and Productivity Growth at the Industry Level: Is There Still a Relationship? In *Griliches, Z., ed.*, 1984, pp. 465–96. [G: U.S.]

Griliches, Zvi and Mairesse, Jacques. Productivity and R&D at the Firm Level. In *Griliches, Z., ed.*, 1984, pp. 339–74. [G: U.S.]

Grossman, Elliot S. Company Productivity Measurement. *Bus. Econ.*, July 1984, *19*(4), pp. 18–23. [G: U.S.]

Guth, William D. Productivity and Corporate Strategy. In *Brief, A. P., ed.*, 1984, pp. 252–67.

Hamada, Koichi and Kurosaka, Yoshio. The Relationship between Production and Unemployment in Japan: Okun's Law in Comparative Perspective. *Europ. Econ. Rev.*, June 1984, *25*(1), pp. 71–94. [G: U.S.; Japan]

Haraf, William S. The Relationship between Production and Unemployment in Japan: Okun's Law in Comparative Perspective: Comments. *Europ. Econ. Rev.*, June 1984, *25*(1), pp. 95–98. [G: U.S.; Japan]

Helliwell, John F. Stagflation and Productivity Decline in Canada, 1974–82. *Can. J. Econ.*, May 1984, *17*(2), pp. 191–216. [G: Canada]

Herman, Arthur S. Productivity Declined in 1982 in a Majority of Industries Measured. *Mon. Lab. Rev.*, January 1984, *107*(1), pp. 80–83. [G: U.S.]

Herman, Arthur S. and Otto, Phyllis F. Productivity Growth in the Switchgear Industry Slows after 1973. *Mon. Lab. Rev.*, March 1984, *107*(3), pp. 33–36. [G: U.S.]

Hinomoto, Hirohide. Measuring White-Collar

Productivity in a Computer Environment. In *Intn'l. Productivity Symp.*, 1984, pp. 41–56. [G: Japan]

Hirsch, Barry T. and Link, Albert N. Unions, Productivity, and Productivity Growth. *J. Lab. Res.*, Winter 1984, *5*(1), pp. 29–37. [G: U.S.]

Holzer, Marc. Public Administration under Pressure. In *Holzer, M. and Nagel, S. S., eds.*, 1984, pp. 71–86.

Hossain, Mahabub. Productivity and Profitability in Bangladesh Rural Industries. *Bangladesh Devel. Stud.*, March-June 1984, *12*(1–2), pp. 127–61. [G: Bangladesh]

Jonscher, Charles. Productivity and Growth of the Information Economy. In *Jussawalla, M. and Ebenfield, H., eds.*, 1984, pp. 95–103. [G: U.S.]

Jonsson, Ernst. Recurrent Cost and Performance Comparisons within Public Administration: A Method of Generating Efficiency-Promoting Competition. *Public Choice*, 1984, *42*(2), pp. 185–92. [G: Sweden]

Jorgenson, Dale W. The Contribution of Education to U.S. Economic Growth, 1948–73. In *Dean, E., ed.*, 1984, pp. 95–162. [G: U.S.]

Jorgenson, Dale W. The Role of Energy in Productivity Growth. In *Kendrick, J. W., ed.*, 1984, pp. 279–323. [G: U.S.]

Kendrick, John W. International Comparisons of Recent Productivity Trends. In *Intn'l. Productivity Symp.*, 1984, *1981*, pp. 95–140. [G: OECD]

Kumar, Pradeep. Wages, Productivity and Labour Costs: Summary Outline. In *Wood, W. D. and Kumar, P., eds.*, 1984, pp. 429–79. [G: Canada; OECD]

Kunze, Kent. A New BLS Survey Measures the Ratio of Hours Worked to Hours Paid. *Mon. Lab. Rev.*, June 1984, *107*(6), pp. 3–7. [G: U.S.]

Kurosawa, Kazukiyo. International Comparison of Productivity. In *Intn'l. Productivity Symp.*, 1984, pp. 141–217. [G: OECD; Selected LDCs]

Lazear, Edward P. and Moore, Robert L. Incentives, Productivity, and Labor Contracts. *Quart. J. Econ.*, May 1984, *99*(2), pp. 275–96. [G: U.S.]

Lee, Chung H. The Diffusion of Technology and Growth of Factor Productivity in Korean Manufacturing Industries. *J. Econ. Devel.*, July 1984, *9*(1), pp. 25–44. [G: S. Korea]

Leibenstein, Harvey. Motivations and Constraints in the Supply-Cost of Government Services: A Game Theoretic Analysis. In *Hanusch, H., ed.*, 1984, pp. 223–40.

Leichter, Howard M. National Productivity: A Comparative Perspective. In *Holzer, M. and Nagel, S. S., eds.*, 1984, pp. 45–68. [G: OECD]

Leonard, Jonathan S. Antidiscrimination or Reverse Discrimination: The Impact of Changing Demographics, Title VII, and Affirmative Action on Productivity. *J. Human Res.*, Spring 1984, *19*(2), pp. 145–74. [G: U.S.]

Leslie, Derek. The Productivity of Hours in U.S. Manufacturing Industries. *Rev. Econ. Statist.*, August 1984, *66*(3), pp. 486–90. [G: U.S.]

Levin, Henry M. Employment and Productivity of Producer Cooperatives. In *Jackall, R. and Levin, H. M., eds.*, 1984, pp. 16–31. [G: Spain]

Levitan, Sar A. and Werneke, Diane. Worker Participation and Productivity Change. *Mon. Lab. Rev.*, September 1984, *107*(9), pp. 28–33. [G: U.S.]

Liebschutz, Saran F. and Lurie, Irene. Evolution in Federalism: The Reagan Program and Legislative Appropriation of Federal Grants in New York. *Public Budg. Finance*, Summer 1984, *4*(2), pp. 24–41. [G: U.S.]

Lindner, Clausjohann. Demokratisierung von Organisationen und Leistungssteigerung. (Democratisation of Organisations and Performance. With English summary.) *Z. Wirtschaft. Sozialwissen.*, 1984, *104*(1), pp. 45–74.

Little, Angela. Education, Earnings and Productivity—the Eternal Triangle. In *Oxenham, J., ed.*, 1984, pp. 87–110. [G: Selected LDCs]

Lundeen, Robert W. Labor Productivity and Demographics: Comment. In *Wachter, M. L. and Wachter, S. M., eds.*, 1984, pp. 103–05. [G: U.S.]

Maddison, Angus. Comparative Analysis of the Productivity Situation in the Advanced Capitalist Countries. In *Kendrick, J. W., ed.*, 1984, pp. 59–92. [G: OECD]

Mairesse, Jacques. The Relationship between Production and Unemployment in Japan: Okun's Law in Comparative Perspective: Comments. *Europ. Econ. Rev.*, June 1984, *25*(1), pp. 99–105. [G: U.S.; Japan; EEC]

Mandel, Ernest. Gold, Money and the Transformation Problem. In *Mandel, E. and Freeman, A., eds.*, 1984, pp. 141–63.

Maranto, Cheryl L. and Rodgers, Robert C. Does Work Experience Increase Productivity? A Test of the On-the-Job Training Hypothesis. *J. Human Res.*, Summer 1984, *19*(3), pp. 341–57. [G: U.S.]

Marshall, Ray. Labor Productivity and Demographics: Comment. In *Wachter, M. L. and Wachter, S. M., eds.*, 1984, pp. 105–08. [G: Japan; U.S.]

Maruo, Naomi. Productivity Improvement in Japan: An Econometric Analysis. In *Intn'l. Productivity Symp.*, 1984, pp. 219–65. [G: Japan]

McCombie, J. S. L. and de Ridder, J. R. "The Verdoorn Law Controversy": Some New Empirical Evidence Using U.S. State Data. *Oxford Econ. Pap.*, June 1984, *36*(2), pp. 268–84. [G: U.S.]

McDonald, Richard J. The "Underground Economy" and BLS Statistical Data. *Mon. Lab. Rev.*, January 1984, *107*(1), pp. 4–18. [G: U.S.]

McMahon, Walter W. Comparative Analysis of the Productivity Situation in the Advanced

Capitalist Countries: Comment. In *Kendrick, J. W., ed.*, 1984, pp. 93–108. [G: OECD]

Miller, Edward M. Extent of Economies of Scale: An Update. *Southern Econ. J.*, October 1984, *51*(2), pp. 582–87.

Mills, Ted. U.S. and European Approaches to Improving Labor Productivity and the Quality of Work Life. In *Kendrick, J. W., ed.*, 1984, pp. 361–91. [G: U.S.; W. Europe]

Mitchell, Daniel J. B. The Private Sector Workplace. In *Holzer, M. and Nagel, S. S., eds.*, 1984, pp. 87–112. [G: U.S.; OECD]

Mitter, P. and Skolka, Jiri. Labour Productivity in Austria between 1964 and 1980. *Empirical Econ.*, 1984, *9*(1), pp. 27–49. [G: Austria]

Mondal, Abdul Hye and Ahmad, Salahuddin. Factor Proportions and Factor Productivity Changes in Jute and Cotton Textile Manufacturing Industries in Bangladesh (1962/63–1977/78). *Bangladesh Devel. Stud.*, September 1984, *12*(3), pp. 37–63. [G: Bangladesh]

Moore, Geoffrey H. and Cullity, John P. Trends and Cycles in Productivity, Unit Costs, and Prices: An International Perspective. In *Kendrick, J. W., ed.*, 1984, pp. 157–90. [G: OECD]

Münch, Klaus-Norbert; Länger, Wolfgang and Rauscher, Gerhard. Productivity in the Local Government Sector—A Framework for Empirical Research. In *Hanusch, H., ed.*, 1984, pp. 251–65. [G: W. Germany]

Muramatsu, Kuramitsu. The Effect of Trade Unions on Productivity in Japanese Manufacturing Industries. In *Aoki, M., ed.*, 1984, pp. 103–23. [G: Japan]

Nagel, Stuart S. Productivity Improvement, Management Science, and Policy Evaluation. In *Holzer, M. and Nagel, S. S., eds.*, 1984, pp. 235–59.

Nasseh, Ali Reza and Elyasiani, Elyas. Energy Price Shocks in the 1970s: Impact in Industrialized Economies. *Energy Econ.*, October 1984, *6*(4), pp. 231–44. [G: U.S.; U.K.; Canada; Germany; France]

Nelson, Richard R. Where Are We in the Discussion? Retrospect and Prospect. In *Kendrick, J. W., ed.*, 1984, pp. 397–409.

Nishimizu, Mieko and Robinson, Sherman. Trade Policies and Productivity Change in Semi-industrialized Countries. *J. Devel. Econ.*, September–October 1984, *16*(1–2), pp. 177–206. [G: S. Korea; Turkey; Yugoslavia; Japan]

Norsworthy, J. R. Capital Input Measurement: Options and Inaccuracies. In *Intn'l. Productivity Symp.*, 1984, pp. 73–94. [G: U.S.]

Odaka, Konosuke. Skill Formation in Development: Case Studies of Philippine Manufacturing (II). *Hitotsubashi J. Econ.*, December 1984, *25*(2), pp. 105–23. [G: Philippines]

Paauw, Douglas S. Economic Growth, Employment, and Productivity: Prospects for Indonesia. *Singapore Econ. Rev.*, October 1984, *29*(2), pp. 111–25. [G: Indonesia]

Pack, Howard. Productivity and Technical Choice: Applications to the Textile Industry. *J. Devel. Econ.*, September–October 1984, *16*(1–2), pp. 153–76. [G: Philippines]

Pack, Howard. Total Factor Productivity and Its Determinants: Some International Comparisons. In *[Reynolds, L. G.]*, 1984, pp. 17–41. [G: Israel; Philippines; U.S.]

Pencavel, John H. Trade Unions and Restrictive Practices: Comment. In *Rosa, J.-J., ed.*, 1984, pp. 115–19. [G: U.S.]

Plant, Mark W. and Welch, Finis. Measuring the Impact of Education on Productivity. In *Dean, E., ed.*, 1984, pp. 163–93. [G: U.S.]

Prywes, Menahem. The Cost in Lost Productivity of New Regulation in the U.S. Chemical Industry. *J. Policy Modeling*, August 1984, *6*(3), pp. 411–19. [G: U.S.]

Rosen, Ellen Doree. Productivity: Concepts and Measurement. In *Holzer, M. and Nagel, S. S., eds.*, 1984, pp. 19–43.

Rosenberg, Nathan. The Slowdown of Productivity Growth in the American Economy: A Discussion of the Causes. In *Sherman, M., ed.*, 1984, pp. 69–83. [G: U.S.]

Sangha, Kehar S. A Paradox of Productivity [Some Methodological and Political Issues Surrounding Productivity]. *J. Econ. Issues*, December 1984, *18*(4), pp. 1198–1200.

Sawhill, Isabel V. The Reagan Administration's Regulatory Relief Effort: A Mid-term Assessment: Comment. In *Eads, G. C. and Fix, M., eds.*, 1984, pp. 84–86. [G: U.S.]

Scherer, Frederic M. Concentration, R&D, and Productivity Change. In *Scherer, F. M.*, 1984, *1983*, pp. 249–55. [G: U.S.]

Scherer, Frederic M. Interindustry Technology Flows and Productivity Growth. In *Scherer, F. M.*, 1984, pp. 270–85. [G: U.S.]

Scherer, Frederic M. R&D and Declining Productivity Growth. In *Scherer, F. M.*, 1984, *1983*, pp. 286–92. [G: U.S.]

Scherer, Frederic M. Technological Maturity and Waning Economic Growth. In *Scherer, F. M.*, 1984, pp. 261–69. [G: U.S.]

Scherer, Frederic M. The Problem of Declining Productivity Growth. In *Scherer, F. M.*, 1984, pp. 257–59.

Schultze, Charles L. Productivity and Profits in the 1980s: Are They Really Improving? Comments. *Brookings Pap. Econ. Act.*, 1984, (1), pp. 172–79. [G: U.S.]

Schwartz, Sandra L. Up the Down Staircase: The Productivity Decline and Strategies for Recovery. In *Bamberg, G. and Spremann, K., eds.*, 1984, pp. 285–306. [G: OECD]

Shen, T. Y. The Estimation of X-Inefficiency in Eighteen Countries. *Rev. Econ. Statist.*, February 1984, *66*(1), pp. 98–104. [G: Selected Countries]

Sylos-Labini, Paolo. Factors Affecting Changes in Productivity. In *Sylos-Labini, P.*, 1984, *1983*, pp. 101–19. [G: Italy; U.S.]

Sylos-Labini, Paolo. Factors Affecting Changes in Productivity. *J. Post Keynesian Econ.*, Winter 1983-84, *6*(2), pp. 161–79. [G: Italy; U.S.]

Syrquin, Moshe. Resource Reallocation and Productivity Growth. In *[Chenery, H. B.]*, 1984, pp. 75–101.   [G: OECD; LDCs; Hungary]

Szymanski, Al. Productivity Growth and Capitalist Stagnation. *Sci. Soc.*, Fall 1984, *48*(3), pp. 295–322.   [G: U.S.; Japan; W. Europe]

Taira, Koji. Output, Productivity, and Employment: U.S.–Japan Comparison. In *Sherman, M., ed.*, 1984, pp. 87–102.   [G: Japan; U.S.]

Thor, Carl G.; Sadler, George E. and Grossman, Elliot S. Comparison of Total Factor Productivity in Japan and the Unitied States. In *Intn'l. Productivity Symp.*, 1984, pp. 57–72.
[G: Japan; U.S.]

Thurow, Lester C. The Need for Industrial Policies: The Case of the U.S.A. *Ann. Pub. Co-op. Econ.*, January–March 1984, *55*(1), pp. 3–31.   [G: U.S.]

Uri, Noel D. The Impact of Technical Change on the Aggregate Production Function. *Appl. Econ.*, August 1984, *16*(4), pp. 555–67.
[G: U.S.]

Vechkanov, V. The Relationship between the Capital–Labor Ratio and Labor Productivity. *Prob. Econ.*, May 1984, *27*(1), pp. 22–32.
[G: U.S.S.R.]

Waldorf, William H. Trends and Cycles in Productivity, Unit Costs, and Prices: An International Perspective: Comment. In *Kendrick, J. W., ed.*, 1984, pp. 191–95.   [G: OECD]

Wolff, Edward N. Accounting for Slower Economic Growth: An Update: Comment. In *Kendrick, J. W., ed.*, 1984, pp. 47–58. [G: U.S.]

Wren-Lewis, Simon. The Roles of Output Expectations and Liquidity in Explaining Recent Productivity Movements. *Nat. Inst. Econ. Rev.*, May 1984, (108), pp. 42–53. [G: U.K.]

Wyatt, Geoffrey J. Trends in Total Factor Productivity in Finnish and Swedish Industries. In *Mikkelsen, A., et al.*, 1984, pp. 232–40.
[G: Finland; Sweden]

Yakushiji, Taizo. Reshuffling Firms for Technology? An Aggregate Time-Series Analysis of B. Klein's "Dynamic Efficiency." In *Aoki, M., ed.*, 1984, pp. 359–85.   [G: Japan]

Yu, Guangyuan. The Key Lies in Enhancing Economic Efficiency. *Chinese Econ. Stud.*, Summer 1984, *17*(4), pp. 99–109.   [G: China]

826 Labor Markets: Demographic Characteristics

8260 Labor Markets: Demographic Characteristics

Banister, Judith. An Analysis of Recent Data on the Population of China. *Population Devel. Rev.*, June 1984, *10*(2), pp. 241–71.
[G: China]

Bates, Timothy. Black Economic Well-Being Since the 1950s. *Rev. Black Polit. Econ.*, Spring 1984, *12*(4), pp. 5–39.   [G: U.S.]

Behrman, Jere R. and Wolfe, Barbara L. Labor Force Participation and Earnings Determinants for Women in the Special Conditions of

Developing Countries. *J. Devel. Econ.*, May–June–August 1984, *15*(1,2,3), pp. 259–88.
[G: Nicaragua]

Berger, Mark C. and Fleisher, Belton M. Husband's Health and Wife's Labor Supply. *J. Health Econ.*, April 1984, *3*(1), pp. 63–75.
[G: U.S.]

Betson, David and van der Gaag, Jacques. Working Married Women and the Distribution of Income. *J. Human Res.*, Fall 1984, *19*(4), pp. 532–43.   [G: U.S.]

Björklund, Anders. A Look at the Male–Female Unemployment Differentials in the Federal Republic of Germany, Sweden, United Kingdom, and the United States of America. In *Schmid, G. and Weitzel, R., eds.*, 1984, pp. 20–43.   [G: Sweden; U.K.; U.S.; W. Germany]

Bonnell, Sheila M.; Chew, T. C. and Dixon, Peter B. Measuring the Impact of Structural Change on Groups in the Australian Labour Market. In *Steinmann, G., ed.*, 1984, pp. 343–59.   [G: Australia]

Borowski, Allan. A Comparison of Youth Unemployment in Australia and the United States. *Mon. Lab. Rev.*, October 1984, *107*(10), pp. 30–36.   [G: Australia; U.S.]

Borus, Michael E. A Description of Employed and Unemployed Youth in 1981. In *Borus, M. E., ed.*, 1984, pp. 13–55.   [G: U.S.]

Borus, Michael E. Youth and the Labor Market: Introduction and Summary. In *Borus, M. E., ed.*, 1984, pp. 1–12.   [G: U.S.]

Bresnick, David. Policymaking by Partnership: Reshaping Youth Employment Policy. *J. Policy Anal. Manage.*, Fall 1984, *4*(1), pp. 23–38.
[G: U.S.; W. Europe; Japan]

Brimmer, Andrew F. Long-Term Economic Growth and Black Employment Opportunities. *Rev. Black Polit. Econ.*, Summer–Fall 1984, *13*(1–2), pp. 61–73.   [G: U.S.]

Brown, Lisa Jo. Neoclassical Economics and the Sexual Division of Labor. *Eastern Econ. J.*, October-December 1984, *10*(4), pp. 367–79.

Chapman, Bruce J. Affirmative Action for Women: Economic Issues. *Australian Bull. Lab.*, December 1984, *11*(1), pp. 30–42.
[G: Australia]

Chirikos, Thomas N. and Nestel, Gilbert. Economic Determinants and Consequences of Self-reported Work Disability. *J. Health Econ.*, August 1984, *3*(2), pp. 117–36.
[G: U.S.]

Chizhova, L. Balancing Labor Resources with Economic Demands. *Prob. Econ.*, May 1984, *27*(1), pp. 63–78.   [G: U.S.S.R.]

Clark, Robert L.; Gohmann, Stephan F. and Sumner, Daniel A. Wages and Hours of Work of Elderly Men. *Atlantic Econ. J.*, December 1984, *12*(4), pp. 31–40.   [G: U.S.]

Clogg, Clifford C. and Shockey, James W. Mismatch between Occupation and Schooling: A Prevalence Measure, Recent Trends and Demographic Analysis. *Demography*, May 1984, *21*(2), pp. 235–57.   [G: U.S.]

Coates, Mary Lou. Human Resources and Labour

Markets: Summary Outline. In *Wood, W. D. and Kumar, P., eds.*, 1984, pp. 41–89.
[G: Canada; OECD]

Coltrane, Robert. The Off-Farm Work of Hired Farm Workers: Discussion. In *Emerson, R. D., ed.*, 1984, pp. 164–67. [G: U.S.]

Cox, Donald. Panel Estimates of the Effects of Career Interruptions on the Earnings of Women. *Econ. Inquiry*, July 1984, *22*(3), pp. 386–403. [G: U.S.]

Crowley, Joan E. Delinquency and Employment: Substitutions or Spurious Associations. In *Borus, M. E., ed.*, 1984, pp. 239–95. [G: U.S.]

D'Amico, Ronald. The Time-Use Behavior of Young Adults. In *Borus, M. E., ed.*, 1984, pp. 193–238. [G: U.S.]

Dalsimer, Marlyn and Nisonoff, Laurie. The New Economic Readjustment Policies: Implications for Chinese Urban Working Women. *Rev. Radical Polit. Econ.*, Spring 1984, *16*(1), pp. 17–43. [G: China]

DeBoer, Larry and Seeborg, Michael C. The Female–Male Unemployment Differential: Effects of Changes in Industry Employment. *Mon. Lab. Rev.*, November 1984, *107*(11), pp. 8–15. [G: U.S.]

Devens, Richard M., Jr. Employment in the First Half: Robust Recovery Continues. *Mon. Lab. Rev.*, August 1984, *107*(8), pp. 3–7.
[G: U.S.]

Duggan, James E. The Labor-Force Participation of Older Workers. *Ind. Lab. Relat. Rev.*, April 1984, *37*(3), pp. 416–30. [G: U.S.]

Emanuel, Han; Halberstadt, Victor and Petersen, Carel. Disability Policy in the Netherlands. In *Haveman, R. H.; Halberstadt, V. and Burkhauser, R. V.*, 1984, pp. 399–443.
[G: Netherlands]

Fagnani, Jeanne. Marital Status and Occupational Structures in the Ile-de-France Region. *Urban Stud.*, May 1984, *21*(2), pp. 139–48.
[G: France]

Felmlee, Diane H. A Dynamic Analysis of Women's Employment Exits. *Demography*, May 1984, *21*(2), pp. 171–83. [G: U.S.]

Ferber, Marianne A. and Spaeth, Joe L. Work Characteristics and the Male–Female Earnings Gap. *Amer. Econ. Rev.*, May 1984, *74*(2), pp. 260–64. [G: U.S.]

Flaim, Paul O. Unemployment in 1982: The Cost to Workers and Their Families. *Mon. Lab. Rev.*, February 1984, *107*(2), pp. 30–37.
[G: U.S.]

Fossett, Mark A. City Differences in Racial Occupational Differentiation: A Note on the Use of Odds Ratios. *Demography*, November 1984, *21*(4), pp. 655–66. [G: U.S.]

Fuller, Rex and Seninger, Stephen F. A Discriminant Analysis of Factors Affecting the Employment of Urban Youth. *Appl. Econ.*, October 1984, *16*(5), pp. 757–62. [G: U.S.]

Gottfried, Heidi and Fasenfest, David. Gender and Class Formation: Female Clerical Workers. *Rev. Radical Polit. Econ.*, Spring 1984, *16*(1), pp. 89–103. [G: U.S.]

Greenwood, Daphne. The Institutional Inadequacy of the Market in Determining Comparable Worth: Implications for Value Theory. *J. Econ. Issues*, June 1984, *18*(2), pp. 457–64.
[G: U.S.]

Grossman, Jean Baldwin. The Occupational Attainment of Immigrant Women in Sweden. *Scand. J. Econ.*, 1984, *86*(3), pp. 337–51.
[G: Sweden]

Gustman, Alan L. and Steinmeier, Thomas L. Partial Retirement and the Analysis of Retirement Behavior. *Ind. Lab. Relat. Rev.*, April 1984, *37*(3), pp. 403–15. [G: U.S.]

Habib, Jack; Factor, Haim and Mor, Vincent. Disability Policy in Israel. In *Haveman, R. H.; Halberstadt, V. and Burkhauser, R. V.*, 1984, pp. 292–345. [G: Israel]

Hamilton, Earl G. Long-Term Economic Growth and Black Employment Opportunities: Comments. *Rev. Black Polit. Econ.*, Summer–Fall 1984, *13*(1–2), pp. 74–79. [G: U.S.]

Harrison, David S. The Impact of Immigration on a Depressed Labour Market: The South Australian Experience. *Econ. Rec.*, March 1984, *60*(168), pp. 57–67. [G: Australia]

Haveman, Robert H. How Much Have the Reagan Administration's Tax and Spending Policies Increased Work Effort? In *Hulten, C. R. and Sawhill, I. V., eds.*, 1984, pp. 91–125.
[G: U.S.]

Haveman, Robert H. and Wolfe, Barbara L. The Decline in Male Labor Force Participation: Comment. *J. Polit. Econ.*, June 1984, *92*(3), pp. 532–41. [G: U.S.]

Hayghe, Howard. Working Mothers Reach Record Number in 1984. *Mon. Lab. Rev.*, December 1984, *107*(12), pp. 31–34. [G: U.S.]

Hein, Catherine. Jobs for the Girls: Export Manufacturing in Mauritius. *Int. Lab. Rev.*, March–April 1984, *123*(2), pp. 251–65.
[G: Mauritius]

Hill, M. Anne. Female Labor Force Participation in Japan: An Aggregate Model. *J. Human Res.*, Spring 1984, *19*(2), pp. 280–87. [G: Japan]

Humphrey, John. The Growth of Female Employment in Brazilian Manufacturing Industry in the 1970s. *J. Devel. Stud.*, July 1984, *20*(4), pp. 224–47. [G: Brazil]

Hutchinson, G.; Barr, N. A. and Drobny, A. The Employment of Young Males in a Segmented Labour Market: The Case of Great Britain. *Appl. Econ.*, April 1984, *16*(2), pp. 187–204.
[G: U.K.]

Kain, Peter G. and Dawkins, Peter. The Australian Labour Market, December 1984. *Australian Bull. Lab.*, December 1984, *11*(1), pp. 3–29. [G: Australia; OECD]

Kausker, Karl. Encouraging Domesticity: A Closer Look. *J. Policy Anal. Manage.*, Summer 1984, *3*(4), pp. 603–07.

Kogut, Edy Luiz and Langoni, Carlos Geraldo. Population Growth, Income Distribution and Economic Development. In *Ghosh, P. K., ed.*, no. 5, 1984, *1975*, pp. 147–60.
[G: Latin America; U.S.]

Krumm, Ronald J. Regional Wage Differentials,

Labor Supply Responses, and Race. *J. Reg. Sci.*, August 1984, *24*(3), pp. 431–42. [G: U.S.]

Lee, Gloria and Wrench, John. Routes into Segmented Youth Labour Markets. *Int. J. Soc. Econ.*, 1984, *11*(7), pp. 77–90. [G: U.K.]

Leonard, Jonathan S. Antidiscrimination or Reverse Discrimination: The Impact of Changing Demographics, Title VII, and Affirmative Action on Productivity. *J. Human Res.*, Spring 1984, *19*(2), pp. 145–74. [G: U.S.]

Maekawa, Kaichi. A Study on Public Policy for the Aged Workers. *Kyoto Univ. Econ. Rev.*, October 1984, *54*(2), pp. 1–12. [G: Japan]

Mathur, R. S. Dynamics of Sectoral Shifts in Employment: An Inter-state Analysis. In *Singh, A. K.; Papola, T. S. and Mathur, R. S., eds.*, 1984, pp. 461–67. [G: India]

Matta, Benjamin N., Jr. The Off-Farm Work of Hired Farm Workers. In *Emerson, R. D., ed.*, 1984, pp. 140–64. [G: U.S.]

Maynard, Rebecca A. The Impacts of Supported Work on Youth. In *Hollister, R. G., Jr.; Kemper, P. and Maynard, R. A., eds.*, 1984, pp. 205–38. [G: U.S.]

Mellor, Earl F. Investigating the Differences in Weekly Earnings of Women and Men. *Mon. Lab. Rev.*, June 1984, *107*(6), pp. 17–28. [G: U.S.]

Meng, Ronald and Sentance, Jim. Religion and the Determination of Earnings: Further Results. *Can. J. Econ.*, August 1984, *17*(3), pp. 481–88. [G: Canada]

Michael, Robert T. and Tuma, Nancy Brandon. Youth Employment: Does Life Begin at 16? *J. Lab. Econ.*, October 1984, *2*(4), pp. 464–76. [G: U.S.]

Mott, Frank L. and Shapiro, David. Seasonal Variations in Labor-Force Activity and Intrahousehold Substitution of Labor in Rural Keyna. *J. Devel. Areas*, July 1984, *18*(4), pp. 449–63. [G: Kenya]

Moy, Joyanna. Recent Labor Market Developments in the U.S. and Nine Other Countries. *Mon. Lab. Rev.*, January 1984, *107*(1), pp. 44–51. [G: OECD]

Mueller, Eva. The Value and Allocation of Time in Rural Botswana. *J. Devel. Econ.*, May–June–August 1984, *15*(1,2,3), pp. 329–60. [G: Botswana]

Nilsen, Sigurd R. Recessionary Impacts on the Unemployment of Men and Women. *Mon. Lab. Rev.*, May 1984, *107*(5), pp. 21–25. [G: U.S.]

Oberai, A. S. and Singh, H. K. Manmohan. Migration, Employment and the Urban Labour Market: A Study in the Indian Punjab. *Int. Lab. Rev.*, July–August 1984, *123*(4), pp. 507–23. [G: India]

Owen, D. W.; Gillespie, A. E. and Coombes, M. G. 'Job Shortfalls' in British Local Labour Market Areas: A Classification of Labour Supply and Demand Trends, 1971–1981. *Reg. Stud.*, December 1984, *18*(6), pp. 469–88. [G: U.K.]

Palazzi, Paolo. The Segmentation of the Labor Market in the United States. The Role of Young People. *Econ. Lavoro*, July-Sept. 1984, *18*(3), pp. 47–61. [G: U.S.]

Papagni, Erasmo. Stratificazione delle famiglie secondo la forza-lavoro e segmentazione in un mercato locale del lavoro. (The Distribution of Labour Force in the Economic Structure of the Families and Segmentation in a Local Labour Market. With English summary.) *Econ. Lavoro*, Jan.-Mar. 1984, *18*(1), pp. 77–87. [G: Italy]

Parsons, Donald O. Disability Insurance and Male Labor Force Participation: A Response. *J. Polit. Econ.*, June 1984, *92*(3), pp. 542–49. [G: U.S.]

Pfaff, Martin and Huber, Walter. Disability Policy in the Federal Republic of Germany. In *Haveman, R. H.; Halberstadt, V. and Burkhauser, R. V.*, 1984, pp. 193–239. [G: W. Germany]

Phillips, Llad and Votey, Harold L., Jr. Black Women, Economic Disadvantage, and Incentives to Crime. *Amer. Econ. Rev.*, May 1984, *74*(2), pp. 293–97. [G: U.S.]

Podgursky, Michael. Sources of Secular Increases in the Unemployment Rate, 1969–82. *Mon. Lab. Rev.*, July 1984, *107*(7), pp. 19–25. [G: U.S.]

Pollard, Tom K. Changes over the 1970s in the Employment Patterns of Black and White Young Men. In *Borus, M. E., ed.*, 1984, pp. 57–79. [G: U.S.]

Presser, Harriet B. Job Characteristics of Spouses and Their Work Shifts. *Demography*, November 1984, *21*(4), pp. 575–89. [G: U.S.]

Raschke, Freddy. Demographic Influences on the Mobility of German Labor Stock. In *Steinmann, G., ed.*, 1984, pp. 323–42. [G: W. Germany]

Ries, John C. Unemployment in 1982: Beyond the Official Labor Force Statistics. *New Eng. Econ. Rev.*, May–June 1984, pp. 29–37. [G: U.S.]

Rones, Philip L. Recent Recessions Swell Ranks of the Long-Term Unemployment. *Mon. Lab. Rev.*, February 1984, *107*(2), pp. 25–29. [G: U.S.]

Rumberger, Russell W. and Daymont, Thomas N. The Economic Value of Academic and Vocational Training Acquired in High School. In *Borus, M. E., ed.*, 1984, pp. 157–91. [G: U.S.]

Rytina, Nancy F. and Bianchi, Suzanne M. Occupational Reclassification and Changes in Distribution by Gender. *Mon. Lab. Rev.*, March 1984, *107*(3), pp. 11–17. [G: U.S.]

Sehgal, Ellen. Occupational Mobility and Job Tenure in 1983. *Mon. Lab. Rev.*, October 1984, *107*(10), pp. 18–23. [G: U.S.]

Sehgal, Ellen. Work Experience in 1983 Reflects the Effects of the Recovery. *Mon. Lab. Rev.*, December 1984, *107*(12), pp. 18–24. [G: U.S.]

Semyonov, Moshe; Hoyt, Danny R. and Scott, Richard Ira. Place, Race and Differential Occupational Opportunities. *Demography*, May 1984, *21*(2), pp. 259–70. [G: U.S.]

Semyonov, Moshe; Hoyt, Danny R. and Scott, Richard Ira. The Place of Odds Ratios in the Study of Place, Race and Differential Occupational Opportunities. *Demography*, November 1984, *21*(4), pp. 667–71.

Shack-Marquez, Janice. Earnings Differences between Men and Women: An Introductory Note. *Mon. Lab. Rev.*, June 1984, *107*(6), pp. 15–16. [G: U.S.]

Shapiro, David. Wage Differentials among Black, Hispanic, and White Young Men. *Ind. Lab. Relat. Rev.*, July 1984, *37*(4), pp. 570–81. [G: U.S.]

Shulman, Steven. The Measurement and Interpretation of Black Wage and Occupational Gains: A Reevaluation. *Rev. Black Polit. Econ.*, Spring 1984, *12*(4), pp. 59–69. [G: U.S.]

Sieling, Mark S. Staffing Patterns Prominent in Female–Male Earnings Gap. *Mon. Lab. Rev.*, June 1984, *107*(6), pp. 29–33. [G: U.S.]

Stapleton, David C. and Young, Douglas J. The Effects of Demographic Change on the Distribution of Wages, 1967–1990. *J. Human Res.*, Spring 1984, *19*(2), pp. 175–201. [G: U.S.]

Stevans, Lonnie K.; Register, Charles and Grimes, Paul. Civil Rights Legislation and Racial Employment Differentials. *Rev. Black Polit. Econ.*, Winter 1984–85, *13*(3), pp. 49–59. [G: U.S.]

Stewart, Mark B. and Greenhalgh, Christine A. Work History Patterns and the Occupational Attainment of Women. *Econ. J.*, September 1984, *94*(375), pp. 493–519. [G: U.K.]

Stolzenberg, Ross M. and Waite, Linda J. Local Labor Markets, Children and Labor Force Participation of Wives. *Demography*, May 1984, *21*(2), pp. 157–70. [G: U.S.]

Svejnar, Jan. The Determinants of Industrial-Sector Earnings in Senegal. *J. Devel. Econ.*, May–June–August 1984, *15*(1,2,3), pp. 289–311. [G: Senegal]

Tomes, Nigel. The Effects of Religion and Denomination Earnings and the Returns to Human Capital. *J. Human Res.*, Fall 1984, *19*(4), pp. 472–88. [G: Canada]

Turbin, Carole. Reconceptualizing Family, Work, and Labor Organizing: Working Women in Troy, 1860–1890. *Rev. Radical Polit. Econ.*, Spring 1984, *16*(1), pp. 1–16. [G: U.S.]

Wachter, Michael L. Unemployment in the American Economy: Types, Causes, and Outlooks for the 1980's. In *Ullrich, R. A., ed.*, 1984, pp. 1–24. [G: U.S.]

Wadensjö, Eskil. Disability Policy in Sweden. In *Haveman, R. H.; Halberstadt, V. and Burkhauser, R. V.*, 1984, pp. 444–516. [G: Sweden]

Whitener, Leslie A. A Statistical Portrait of Hired Farmworkers. *Mon. Lab. Rev.*, June 1984, *107*(6), pp. 49–53. [G: U.S.]

Winegarden, Calman R. Women's Fertility, Market Work and Marital Status: A Test of the New Household Economics with International

Data. *Economica*, November 1984, *51*(204), pp. 447–56. [G: W. Europe]

Wolfe, Barbara L. Measuring Disability and Health. *J. Health Econ.*, August 1984, *3*(2), pp. 187–93. [G: U.S.]

Wray, Kathleen. Labour Market Operation, Recruitment Strategies, and Workforce Structures. *Int. J. Soc. Econ.*, 1984, *11*(7), pp. 6–31. [G: U.K.]

Young, Anne McDougall. Fewer Students in Work Force as School Age Population Declines. *Mon. Lab. Rev.*, July 1984, *107*(7), pp. 34–37.

Young, Anne McDougall and Hayghe, Howard. More U.S. Workers Are College Graduates. *Mon. Lab. Rev.*, March 1984, *107*(3), pp. 46–49. [G: U.S.]

Zubrzycki, Jerzy. Immigration and Population Change in Australia: A Test of the Dual Labour Market Hypothesis. In *Steinmann, G., ed.*, 1984, pp. 360–85. [G: Australia]

830 Trade Unions; Collective Bargaining; Labor–Management Relations

8300 General

Aaron, Benjamin. Future Trends in Industrial Relations Law. *Ind. Relat.*, Winter 1984, *23*(1), pp. 52–57. [G: U.S.]

Cameron, David R. Social Democracy, Corporatism, Labour Quiescence and the Representation of Economic Interest in Advanced Capitalist Society. In *Goldthorpe, J. H., ed.*, 1984, pp. 143–78. [G: OECD]

Chaloupek, Gunter. The Austrian Experience of Social and Economic Cooperation: Comment. In *Cavaco Silva, A. A., ed.*, 1984, pp. 105–08. [G: Austria]

Compa, Lance. Labor and the Military—A History. In *Gordon, S. and McFadden, D., eds.*, 1984, pp. 33–43. [G: U.S.]

Córdova, Efrén. Industrial Relations in Latin America: Tripartite Cooperation. In *Cérdova, E., ed.*, 1984, pp. 147–66. [G: Latin America]

Drouet, Pierre. The Restructuring of the Petroleum Refining Sector and Its Social Consequences. *Int. Lab. Rev.*, July–August 1984, *123*(4), pp. 423–40. [G: Global]

Elbaum, Bernard. The Making and Shaping of Job and Pay Structures in the Iron and Steel Industry. In *Osterman, P., ed.*, 1984, pp. 71–107. [G: OECD]

Farnleitner, Johannes. The Austrian Experience of Social and Economic Cooperation: Comment. In *Cavaco Silva, A. A., ed.*, 1984, pp. 99–103. [G: Austria]

Freeman, Richard B. De-mystifying the Japanese Labor Markets. In *Aoki, M., ed.*, 1984, pp. 125–29. [G: Japan]

Gaudio, Ricardo and Pilone, Jorge. Estado y relaciones laborales en el período previo al surgimiento del peronismo, 1935–1943. (With English summary.) *Desarrollo Econ.*, July–September 1984, *24*(94), pp. 235–73.

[G: Argentina]

Lorenz, Edward H. Two Patterns of Development: The Labour Process in the British and French Shipbuilding Industries 1880 to 1930. *J. Europ. Econ. Hist.*, September–December 1984, *13*(3), pp. 599–634. [G: U.K.; France]

Miller, Harold. The American Bureau of Industrial Research and the Origins of the "Wisconsin School" of Labor History. *Labor Hist.*, Spring 1984, *25*(2), pp. 165–88.

Murray, Martin J. The Development of Capitalism and the Making of the Working Class in Colonial Indochina, 1870–1940. In *Munslow, B. and Finch, H., eds.*, 1984, pp. 216–33.

[G: Indochina]

Pelinka, Anton. The Austrian Experience of Social and Economic Cooperation. In *Cavaco Silva, A. A., ed.*, 1984, pp. 83–97. [G: Austria]

Roomkin, Myron J. and Harris, Dawn A. Interindustry Patterns in Unfair Labor Practice Cases. *J. Lab. Res.*, Spring 1984, *5*(2), pp. 113–26.

[G: U.S.]

Ruben, George. Economy Improves; Bargaining Problems Persist in 1983. *Mon. Lab. Rev.*, January 1984, *107*(1), pp. 33–43. [G: U.S.]

Schatz, Ronald W. Connecticut's Working Class in the 1950s: A Catholic Perspective. *Labor Hist.*, Winter 1984, *25*(1), pp. 83–101.

[G: U.S.]

Schmitz, Wolfgang. Economic and Social Partnership and Incomes Policy and the Social Doctrine of the Church. In *Cavaco Silva, A. A., ed.*, 1984, pp. 195–217.

Strasser, Rudolf. The Austrian Experience of Social and Economic Cooperation: Comment. In *Cavaco Silva, A. A., ed.*, 1984, pp. 109–12.

[G: Austria]

Strauss, George. Industrial Relations: Time of Change. *Ind. Relat.*, Winter 1984, *23*(1), pp. 1–15. [G: U.S.]

Ulman, Lloyd. Labor Relations and High Unemployment Abroad: Symposium Introduction. *Ind. Relat.*, Fall 1984, *23*(3), pp. 299–305.

[G: OECD]

Weinberg, Edgar. BLS and the Economy: A Centennial Timetable. *Mon. Lab. Rev.*, November 1984, *107*(11), pp. 29–37. [G: U.S.]

831 Trade Unions

8310 Trade Unions

Abraham, Katharine G. and Medoff, James L. Length of Service and Layoffs in Union and Nonunion Work Groups. *Ind. Lab. Relat. Rev.*, October 1984, *38*(1), pp. 87–97.

[G: U.S.]

Adams, Larry T. Labor Organization Mergers, 1979–84: Adapting to Change. *Mon. Lab. Rev.*, September 1984, *107*(9), pp. 21–27.

[G: U.S.]

Addison, John T. Changes Over Time in the Union–Nonunion Wage Differential in the United States: Comment. In *Rosa, J.-J., ed.*, 1984, pp. 20–25. [G: U.S.; U.K.]

Addison, John T. Trade Unions and Restrictive Practices. In *Rosa, J.-J., ed.*, 1984, pp. 83–114. [G: U.S.]

Addison, John T. Trade Unions, Corporatism, and Inflation. *J. Lab. Res.*, Winter 1984, *5*(1), pp. 39–62.

Ahlburg, Dennis A. Majority Voting Rules and the Union Success Rate in National Labor Relations Board Representation Elections. *J. Lab. Res.*, Summer 1984, *5*(3), pp. 229–36.

[G: U.S.]

Ahlburg, Dennis A. and Dworkin, James B. The Influence of Macroeconomic Variables on the Probability of Union Decertification. *J. Lab. Res.*, Winter 1984, *5*(1), pp. 13–28.

[G: U.S.]

Allen, Christopher S. Trade Unions and Paths toward Economic Conversion: European and American Contrasts. In *Gordon, S. and McFadden, D., eds.*, 1984, pp. 204–18.

[G: U.S.; W. Europe]

Allen, Steven G. Trade Unions, Absenteeism, and Exit-Voice. *Ind. Lab. Relat. Rev.*, April 1984, *37*(3), pp. 331–45. [G: U.S.]

Allen, Steven G. Unionized Construction Workers Are More Productive. *Quart. J. Econ.*, May 1984, *99*(2), pp. 251–74. [G: U.S.]

Almaguer, Tomás. Racial Domination and Class Conflict in Capitalist Agriculture: The Oxnard Sugar Beet Workers' Strike of 1903. *Labor Hist.*, Summer 1984, *25*(3), pp. 325–50.

[G: U.S.]

Appleton, William C. and Baker, Joe G. The Effect of Unionization on Safety in Bituminous Deep Mines. *J. Lab. Res.*, Spring 1984, *5*(2), pp. 139–47. [G: U.S.]

Ashenfelter, Orley C. and Bloom, David E. Models of Arbitrator Behavior: Theory and Evidence. *Amer. Econ. Rev.*, March 1984, *74*(1), pp. 111–24. [G: U.S.]

Barker, Allan; Lewis, Paul and McCann, Michael. Trades Unions and the Organisation of the Unemployed. *Brit. J. Ind. Relat.*, November 1984, *22*(3), pp. 391–404. [G: U.K.]

Beaumont, P. B. Trade Union Recognition in Northern Ireland. *Brit. J. Ind. Relat.*, November 1984, *22*(3), pp. 364–71. [G: U.K.]

Benello, C. George. Workplace Democracy in the United States: Present Trends and Counter-Trends. *Econ. Anal. Worker's Manage.*, 1984, *18*(4), pp. 385–97. [G: U.S.]

Bennett, James T. Privatizing Municipal Services. In *Giersch, H., ed.*, 1984, pp. 44–57.

Bennett, James T. Unions and Politics: Introductory Remarks. *J. Lab. Res.*, Summer 1984, *5*(3), pp. 263–64. [G: U.S.]

Bennett, James T. and DiLorenzo, Thomas J. Unions, Politics, and Protectionism. *J. Lab. Res.*, Summer 1984, *5*(3), pp. 287–307.

[G: U.S.]

Biles, Roger. Ed Crump versus the Unions: The Labor Movement in Memphis during the 1930s. *Labor Hist.*, Fall 1984, *25*(4), pp. 533–52. [G: U.S.]

Blair, Douglas H. and Crawford, David L. Labor Union Objectives and Collective Bargaining.

Quart. J. Econ., August 1984, *99*(3), pp. 547–66.

Blanchflower, David. Union Relative Wage Effects: A Cross-Section Analysis Using Establishment Data. *Brit. J. Ind. Relat.*, November 1984, *22*(3), pp. 311–32. **[G: U.K.]**

Booth, Alison L. A Public Choice Model of Trade Union Behaviour and Membership. *Econ. J.*, December 1984, *94*(376), pp. 883–98.

Bornstein, Stephen and Gourevitch, Peter. Unions in a Declining Economy: The Case of the British TUC. In *Gourevitch, P., et al.*, 1984, pp. 15–88. **[G: U.K.]**

Brinker, Paul A. Labor Union Coercion: The Misuse of the Grievance Procedure. *J. Lab. Res.*, Winter 1984, *5*(1), pp. 93–102. **[G: U.S.]**

Brown, William and Sisson, Keith. Current Trends and Future Possibilities. In *Poole, M., et al.*, 1984, pp. 13–38. **[G: U.K.]**

Brush, Brian C. and Crane, Steven E. Wage Share, Market Power and Unionism: Some Contrary U.S. Evidence. *Manchester Sch. Econ. Soc. Stud.*, December 1984, *52*(4), pp. 417–24. **[G: U.S.]**

Burton, John. The Economic Analysis of the Trade Union as a Political Institution. In *Rosa, J.-J., ed.*, 1984, pp. 123–54.

Caire, Guy. Recent Trends in Collective Bargaining in France. *Int. Lab. Rev.*, November–December 1984, *123*(6), pp. 723–41. **[G: France]**

Calmfors, Lars. Stabilization Policy and Wage Formation in Economies with Strong Trade Unions. In *Emerson, M., ed.*, 1984, pp. 89–121. **[G: Scandinavia; Belgium; Austria; Netherlands]**

Cameron, Samuel. The Stability of the Post-War Aggregate British Strike Function. *Scot. J. Polit. Econ.*, February 1984, *31*(1), pp. 28–43. **[G: U.K.]**

Carroll, Gene. How to Get Labor Involved. In *Gordon, S. and McFadden, D., eds.*, 1984, pp. 219–30. **[G: U.S.]**

Chaison, Gary N. A Note on the Limitations of Union Membership Data. *Ind. Relat.*, Winter 1984, *23*(1), pp. 113–18. **[G: U.S.]**

Chamberlain, John. Unions and Politics: A Journalist's View. *J. Lab. Res.*, Summer 1984, *5*(3), pp. 309–13. **[G: U.S.]**

Clark, Kim B. Unionization and Firm Performance: The Impact on Profits, Growth, and Productivity. *Amer. Econ. Rev.*, December 1984, *74*(5), pp. 893–919. **[G: U.S.]**

Córdova, Efrén. Labor Disputes: Their Nature and Settlement. In *Córdova, E., ed.*, 1984, pp. 169–88. **[G: Latin America]**

Córdova, Efrén. Other Features of Labor Relations at the Undertaking Level. In *Córdova, E., ed.*, 1984, pp. 129–46. **[G: Latin America]**

Córdova, Efrén. Workers' Participation in Management. In *Córdova, E., ed.*, 1984, pp. 109–27. **[G: Latin America]**

Dalton, Amy H. The Organization of State and Local Government Employees: Reply. *J. Lab. Res.*, Spring 1984, *5*(2), pp. 201–04. **[G: U.S.]**

Davies, Annette. Management-Union Participation during Microtechnological Change. In *Warner, M., ed.*, 1984, pp. 149–70. **[G: U.K.]**

Dickman, Howard. Exclusive Representation and American Industrial Democracy: An Historical Reappraisal. *J. Lab. Res.*, Fall 1984, *5*(4), pp. 325–50. **[G: U.S.]**

DiLorenzo, Thomas J. Exclusive Representation in Public Employment: A Public Choice Perspective. *J. Lab. Res.*, Fall 1984, *5*(4), pp. 371–89. **[G: U.S.]**

Doeringer, Peter B. Unions: Economic Performance and Labor Market Structure. In *Rosa, J.-J., ed.*, 1984, pp. 315–38. **[G: U.S.; OECD]**

Dow, M. Bradley. The Labour Movement and Trade Unionism: Summary Outline. In *Wood, W. D. and Kumar, P., eds.*, 1984, pp. 217–92. **[G: Canada]**

Doyon, Louise M. La organización del movimiento sindical peronista, 1946–1955. (With English summary.) *Desarrollo Econ.*, July–September 1984, *24*(94), pp. 203–34. **[G: Argentina]**

Evans, Judith; Hoeffel, Paul Heath and James, Daniel. Reflections on Argentine Auto Workers and Their Unions. In *Kronish, R. and Mericle, K. S., eds.*, 1984, pp. 133–59. **[G: Argentina]**

Farber, Henry S. Right-to-Work Laws and the Extent of Unionization. *J. Lab. Econ.*, July 1984, *2*(3), pp. 319–52. **[G: U.S.]**

Flanagan, Robert J. Wage Concessions and Long-Term Union Wage Flexibility. *Brookings Pap. Econ. Act.*, 1984, (1), pp. 183–216. **[G: U.S.]**

Fosu, Augustin Kwasi. Unions and Fringe Benefits: Additional Evidence. *J. Lab. Res.*, Summer 1984, *5*(3), pp. 247–54. **[G: U.S.]**

Fraser, Steve. From the "New Unionism" to the New Deal. *Labor Hist.*, Summer 1984, *25*(3), pp. 405–30. **[G: U.S.]**

Freeman, Richard B. Longitudinal Analyses of the Effects of Trade Unions. *J. Lab. Econ.*, January 1984, *2*(1), pp. 1–26. **[G: U.S.]**

Friedman, Samuel R. The Work Process and Worker Mobilization among Teamster Drivers. In *Zarembka, P., ed.*, 1984, pp. 161–83.

Fürstenberg, Friedrich. Recent Trends in Collective Bargaining in the Federal Republic of Germany. *Int. Lab. Rev.*, September–October 1984, *123*(5), pp. 615–30. **[G: W. Germany]**

Garbarino, Joseph W. Unionism without Unions: The New Industrial Relations? *Ind. Relat.*, Winter 1984, *23*(1), pp. 40–51. **[G: U.S.]**

Giannola, Giuseppina. Il "potere sindacale" ed i modelli di "inflazione salariale": un'analisi statistica dell'esperienza italiana per il periodo 1951–1977. (Trade-union Power and the Models of "Wage Inflation": A Statistical Analysis for Italy, 1951–1977. With English summary.) *Econ. Lavoro*, Apr.-June 1984, *18*(2), pp. 105–18. **[G: Italy]**

Giugni, Gino. Recent Trends in Collective Bargaining in Italy. *Int. Lab. Rev.*, September–October 1984, *123*(5), pp. 599–614.
[G: Italy]

Glavanis, Pandeli. State and Labour in Libya. In *Lawless, R. and Findlay, A., eds.*, 1984, pp. 120–49.
[G: Libya]

Goldfield, Michael. The Causes of U.S. Trade Union Decline and Their Future Prospects. In *Zarembka, P., ed.*, 1984, pp. 81–159.
[G: U.S.]

Goldthorpe, John H. The End of Convergence: Corporatist and Dualist Tendencies in Modern Western Societies. In *Goldthorpe, J. H., ed.*, 1984, pp. 315–43.

Gomez-Mejia, Luis R. and Balkin, David B. Union Impacts on Secretarial Earnings: A Public Sector Case. *Ind. Relat.*, Winter 1984, *23*(1), pp. 97–102.
[G: U.S.]

Gordon, Michael E.; Beauvais, Laura L. and Ladd, Robert T. The Job Satisfaction and Union Commitment of Unionized Engineers. *Ind. Lab. Relat. Rev.*, April 1984, *37*(3), pp. 359–70.
[G: U.S.]

Gourevitch, Peter, et al. Unions and Economic Crisis: Britain, West Germany, and Sweden: Introduction. In *Gourevitch, P., et al.*, 1984, pp. 1–11.
[G: W. Europe]

Green, Max. Labor's Bad Bargain: The AFL-CIO Lurches Left. *Policy Rev.*, Fall 1984, (30), pp. 14–19.
[G: U.S.]

Griffin, Tony. Technological Change and Craft Control in the Newspaper Industry: An International Comparison. *Cambridge J. Econ.*, March 1984, *8*(1), pp. 41–61. [G: U.S.; U.K.; Australia]

Grossman, Gene M. International Competition and the Unionized Sector. *Can. J. Econ.*, August 1984, *17*(3), pp. 541–56.

Gylfason, Thorvaldur and Lindbeck, Assar. Competing Wage Claims, Cost Inflation, and Capacity Utilization. *Europ. Econ. Rev.*, February 1984, *24*(1), pp. 1–21.

Gylfason, Thorvaldur and Lindbeck, Assar. Union Rivalry and Wages: An Oligopolistic Approach. *Economica*, May 1984, *51*(202), pp. 129–39.

Hanson, Charles and Rathkey, Paul. Industrial Democracy: A Post-Bullock Shopfloor View. *Brit. J. Ind. Relat.*, July 1984, *22*(2), pp. 154–68.
[G: U.K.]

Harper, Michael C. The Consumer's Emerging Right to Boycott: *NAACP v. Claiborne Hardware* and Its Implications for American Labor Law. *Yale Law J.*, January 1984, *93*(3), pp. 409–54.
[G: U.S.]

Hart-Landsberg, Martin and Lembcke, Jerry. Class Struggle and Economic Transformation. *Rev. Radical Polit. Econ.*, Winter 1984, *16*(4), pp. 14–31.

Haworth, Nigel. Proletarianisation in the World Order: The Peruvian Experience. In *Munslow, B. and Finch, H., eds.*, 1984, pp. 234–54.
[G: Peru]

Helburn, I. B. and Shearer, John C. Human Resources and Industrial Relations in China: A Time of Ferment. *Ind. Lab. Relat. Rev.*, October 1984, *38*(1), pp. 3–15.
[G: China]

Hendricks, Wallace E. and Kahn, Lawrence M. The Demand for Labor Market Structure: An Economic Approach. *J. Lab. Econ.*, July 1984, *2*(3), pp. 412–38.
[G: U.S.]

Hennart, Jean-François. The Determinants of Union Staff Salaries: A New Meaning to Business Unionism: Comment. In *Rosa, J.-J., ed.*, 1984, pp. 306–11.
[G: U.S.; France]

Hennart, Jean-François. The Relative Wage Effect of French Unions. In *Rosa, J.-J., ed.*, 1984, pp. 63–81.
[G: France]

Henschel, Rudolf. Ursachen der Beschäftigungskrise im Meinungsspektrum der Gewerkschaften. (The Spectrum of Opinions on the Causes of the Employment Crisis in the German Trade Union Movement. With English summary.) *Konjunkturpolitik*, 1984, *30*(2/3), pp. 73–92.
[G: W. Germany]

Hersoug, Tor. Union Wage Responses to Tax Changes. *Oxford Econ. Pap.*, March 1984, *36*(1), pp. 37–51.

Heshizer, Brian and Graham, Harry. Are Unions Facing a Crisis? Labor Officials Are Divided. *Mon. Lab. Rev.*, August 1984, *107*(8), pp. 23–25.
[G: U.S.]

Hill, John K. Union Wage Distortions and the Size and Efficiency of the Optimal Tariff. *Can. J. Econ.*, February 1984, *17*(1), pp. 146–55.
[G: U.S.]

Hine, William C. Black Organized Labor in Reconstructed Charleston. *Labor Hist.*, Fall 1984, *25*(4), pp. 504–17.
[G: U.S.]

Hingel, Anders J. A Promethean Change of Industrial Relations: A Comparative Study of Western European Unions and Technological Developments. In *Warner, M., ed.*, 1984, pp. 255–72.
[G: W. Europe]

Hirsch, Barry T. and Berger, Mark C. Union Membership Determination and Industry Characteristics. *Southern Econ. J.*, January 1984, *50*(3), pp. 665–79.
[G: U.S.]

Hirsch, Barry T. and Link, Albert N. Unions, Productivity, and Productivity Growth. *J. Lab. Res.*, Winter 1984, *5*(1), pp. 29–37.
[G: U.S.]

Hobsbawm, E. J. Artisan or Labour Aristocrat? *Econ. Hist. Rev.*, 2nd Ser., August 1984, *37*(3), pp. 355–72.
[G: U.K.]

Hojman, David E. Minimum Wages, Union Membership, and Differentials: The Phillips Curve and the Chilean Labour Market Revisited. *J. Econ. Stud.*, 1984, *11*(4), pp. 3–22.
[G: Chile]

Hopt, Klaus J. New Ways in Corporate Governance: European Experiments with Labor Representation on Corporate Boards. *Mich. Law Rev.*, April–May 1984, *82*(5 & 6), pp. 1338–63.
[G: W. Europe]

Horne, Jocelyn. Trying to Understand Stagflation: Comment. *Australian Econ. Rev.*, 3rd Quarter 1984, (67), pp. 57–58.
[G: Australia]

Horowitz, Joel. Ideologías sindicales y políticas estatales en la Argentina, 1930–1943. (With

English summary.) *Desarrollo Econ.*, July–September 1984, *24*(94), pp. 275–96.
[G: Argentina]

Hunnicutt, Benjamin Kline. The End of Shorter Hours. *Labor Hist.*, Summer 1984, *25*(3), pp. 373–404. **[G: U.S.]**

Ishikawa, Akihiro. Japanese Trade-Unionism in a Changing Environment. *Int. Soc. Sci. J.*, 1984, *36*(2), pp. 271–83. **[G: Japan]**

Izraeli, Dafna N. The Attitudinal Effects of Gender Mix in Union Committees. *Ind. Lab. Relat. Rev.*, January 1984, *37*(2), pp. 212–21.
[G: Israel]

Johnson, George E. Changes Over Time in the Union–Nonunion Wage Differential in the United States. In *Rosa, J.-J., ed.*, 1984, pp. 3–19. **[G: U.S.]**

Jones, J. C. H. and Walsh, W. D. Inter-Industry Strike Frequencies: Some Pooled Cross-Sectional Evidence from Canadian Secondary Manufacturing. *J. Lab. Res.*, Fall 1984, *5*(4), pp. 419–25. **[G: Canada]**

Kahn, Lawrence M. The Effect of Collective Bargaining on Production Technique: A Theoretical Analysis. *J. Lab. Res.*, Winter 1984, *5*(1), pp. 1–12.

Kalleberg, Arne L.; Wallace, Michael and Raffalovich, Lawrence E. Accounting for Labor's Share: Class and Income Distribution in the Printing Industry. *Ind. Lab. Relat. Rev.*, April 1984, *37*(3), pp. 386–402. **[G: U.S.]**

Kaufman, Bruce E. Determinants of Strikes: Reply [The Determinants of Strikes in the United States, 1900–1977]. *Ind. Lab. Relat. Rev.*, January 1984, *37*(2), pp. 269–72. **[G: U.S.]**

Kemp, Murray C. Craft Unions, Wages and Employment. *Kobe Econ. Bus. Rev.*, 1984, *30*, pp. 11–16.

Kenyon, Peter D. Trying to Understand Stagflation: Comment. *Australian Econ. Rev.*, 3rd Quarter 1984, (67), pp. 59–61. **[G: Australia]**

Kierzkowski, Henryk. Trade Unions, Wage Relativities and Employment. *Australian Econ. Pap.*, June 1984, *23*(42), pp. 91–104.

Kleiner, Morris M. Unionism and Employer Discrimination: Analysis of 8(a)(3) Violations. *Ind. Relat.*, Spring 1984, *23*(2), pp. 234–43.
[G: U.S.]

Kochan, Thomas A. and Cappelli, Peter. The Transformation of the Industrial Relations and Personnel Function. In *Osterman, P., ed.*, 1984, pp. 133–61.

Kolchin, Michael G. and Hyclak, Thomas. Participation of Union Activities: A Multivariate Analysis. *J. Lab. Res.*, Summer 1984, *5*(3), pp. 255–62. **[G: U.S.]**

Korn, Sarah. Property Rights and Job Security: Workplace Solicitation by Nonemployee Union Organizers. *Yale Law J.*, December 1984, *94*(2), pp. 374–93. **[G: U.S.]**

Kosters, Marvin H. Disinflation in the Labor Market. In *Fellner, W., ed.*, 1984, pp. 247–86.
[G: U.S.]

Kosters, Marvin H. Wage Concessions and Long-Term Union Wage Flexibility: Comments.

Brookings Pap. Econ. Act., 1984, (1), pp. 217–20. **[G: U.S.]**

Krahn, Harvey and Lowe, Graham S. Public Attitudes towards Unions: Some Canadian Evidence. *J. Lab. Res.*, Spring 1984, *5*(2), pp. 149–64. **[G: Canada]**

Kreye, Otto. Western Europe's Economic and Social Development and the Rationality and Reality of a New International Economic Order. In *Addo, H., ed.*, 1984, pp. 119–37.
[G: W. Europe]

LaJeunesse, Raymond J., Jr. Employees' Freedom from Ideological Conformity: A Right without a Remedy? *J. Lab. Res.*, Summer 1984, *5*(3), pp. 265–74. **[G: U.S.]**

Lane, A. T. American Trade Unions, Mass Immigration and the Literacy Test: 1900–1917. *Labor Hist.*, Winter 1984, *25*(1), pp. 5–25.
[G: U.S.]

Lang, Kevin. Unions, Firms, and the Return to Seniority. *J. Lab. Res.*, Winter 1984, *5*(1), pp. 81–92.

Lange, Peter. Unions, Workers and Wage Regulation: The Rational Bases of Consent. In *Goldthorpe, J. H., ed.*, 1984, pp. 98–123.

Lawler, John J. The Influence of Management Consultants on the Outcome of Union Certification Elections. *Ind. Lab. Relat. Rev.*, October 1984, *38*(1), pp. 38–51. **[G: U.S.]**

Lawler, John J. and Walker, J. Malcolm. Representation Elections in Higher Education: Occurrence and Outcomes. *J. Lab. Res.*, Winter 1984, *5*(1), pp. 63–80. **[G: U.S.]**

Lehmbruch, Gerhard. Concertation and the Structure of Corporatist Networks. In *Goldthorpe, J. H., ed.*, 1984, pp. 60–80.
[G: OECD]

Leigh, J. Paul. Do Union Members Receive Compensating Wages for Accepting Employment in Strike-Prone or Hazardous Industries? *Soc. Sci. Quart.*, March 1984, *65*(1), pp. 89–99.
[G: U.S.]

Leigh, J. Paul. Unionization and Absenteeism. *Appl. Econ.*, February 1984, *16*(1), pp. 147–57. **[G: U.S.]**

Lentz, Bernard. The Determinants of Union Staff Salaries: A New Meaning to Business Unionism. In *Rosa, J.-J., ed.*, 1984, pp. 277–305.
[G: U.S.]

MaCoy, Ramelle and Morand, Martin J. Short-Time Compensation: An Alternative to Layoff: A Labor Viewpoint. In *MaCoy, R. and Morand, M. J., eds.*, 1984, pp. 36–50. **[G: U.S.]**

Maier, Charles S. Preconditions for Corporatism. In *Goldthorpe, J. H., ed.*, 1984, pp. 39–59.

Marginson, Paul M. The Distinctive Effects of Plant and Company Size on Workplace Industrial Relations. *Brit. J. Ind. Relat.*, March 1984, *22*(1), pp. 1–14. **[G: U.K.]**

Markovits, Andrei S. and Allen, Christopher S. Trade Unions and the Economic Crisis: The West German Case. In *Gourevitch, P., et al.*, 1984, pp. 91–188. **[G: W. Germany; OECD]**

Martin, Andrew. Trade Unions in Sweden: Stra-

tegic Responses to Change and Crisis. In *Gourevitch, P., et al.*, 1984, pp. 191–359.
[G: Sweden]

Martin, Donald L. The Agency Problem in a Nonproprietary Theory of Union Behavior. In *Rosa, J.-J., ed.*, 1984, pp. 191–220.

Martin, Roderick. New Technology and Industrial Relations in Fleet Street: 'New Technology Will Make it Possible for Managers to Manage.' In *Warner, M., ed.*, 1984, pp. 240–52.
[G: U.K.]

Martin, Stephen and Rence, Cynthia. Vertical Spillovers, Market Concentration, Union Coverage, and Wages. *J. Lab. Res.*, Spring 1984, 5(2), pp. 177–89. [G: U.S.]

Masters, Marick F. and Delaney, John Thomas. Interunion Variation in Congressional Campaign Support. *Ind. Relat.*, Fall 1984, 23(3), pp. 410–16. [G: U.S.]

McCormick, Brian J. Personnel Management. In *Pickering, J. F. and Cockerill, T. A. J., eds.*, 1984, pp. 179–220. [G: U.S.; U.K.]

McDonald, Ian M. Trying to Understand Stagflation. *Australian Econ. Rev.*, 3rd Quarter 1984, (67), pp. 32–56. [G: Australia]

Miller, James C., III. Is Organized Labor Rational in Supporting OSHA? *Southern Econ. J.*, January 1984, 50(3), pp. 881–85. [G: U.S.]

Miller, Marcus H. Government, Unions and Stagflation in the UK. *Nat. Inst. Econ. Rev.*, August 1984, (109), pp. 68–72. [G: U.K.]

Montgomery, Edward. Aggregate Dynamics and Staggered Contracts: A Test of the Importance of Spillover Effects: A Note. *J. Money, Credit, Banking*, Part 1 November 1984, 16(4), pp. 505–14. [G: U.S.]

Morrissey, Charles T. Team Interviewing and the Merger of the AFL and CIO in 1955: Notes on Some Options in Oral History. *Labor Hist.*, Summer 1984, 25(3), pp. 448–55. [G: U.S.]

Moss, Bernard H. Workers and Communists in France. *Sci. Soc.*, Fall 1984, 48(3), pp. 350–57. [G: France]

Munck, Ronaldo. The Formation and Development of the Working Class in Argentina, 1857–1919. In *Munslow, B. and Finch, H., eds.*, 1984, pp. 255–71. [G: Argentina]

Munslow, Barry. Proletarianisation in Mozambique. In *Munslow, B. and Finch, H., eds.*, 1984, pp. 77–98. [G: Mozambique]

Muramatsu, Kuramitsu. The Effect of Trade Unions on Productivity in Japanese Manufacturing Industries. In *Aoki, M., ed.*, 1984, pp. 103–23. [G: Japan]

Neumann, George R. and Rissman, Ellen R. Where Have All the Union Members Gone? *J. Lab. Econ.*, April 1984, 2(2), pp. 175–92. [G: U.S.]

Newman, Richard. Vanguard of the Proletariat? Communists and Unions in Shanghai and Bombay, 1927–1929. In *Munslow, B. and Finch, H., eds.*, 1984, pp. 272–98. [G: China; India]

Northrup, Herbert R. The Rise and Demise of PATCO. *Ind. Lab. Relat. Rev.*, January 1984, 37(2), pp. 167–84. [G: U.S.]

Oestreicher, Richard. A Note on Knights of Labor

Membership Statistics. *Labor Hist.*, Winter 1984, 25(1), pp. 102–08. [G: U.S.]

Paldam, Martin and Pedersen, Peder J. Determinants of Strikes: Reply [The Macroeconomic Strike Model: A Study of Seventeen Countries, 1948–1975]. *Ind. Lab. Relat. Rev.*, 1984, 37(2), pp. 275–78. [G: OECD]

Paldam, Martin and Pedersen, Peder J. The Large Pattern of Industrial Conflict—A Comparative Study of 18 Countries, 1919–79. *Int. J. Soc. Econ.*, 1984, 11(5), pp. 3–28. [G: OECD]

Pencavel, John H. The Empirical Performance of a Model of Trade Union Behavior. In *Rosa, J.-J., ed.*, 1984, pp. 221–76. [G: U.S.]

Pencavel, John H. The Tradeoff between Wages and Employment in Trade Union Objectives. *Quart. J. Econ.*, May 1984, 99(2), pp. 215–31. [G: U.S.]

Pencavel, John H. Trade Unions and Restrictive Practices: Comment. In *Rosa, J.-J., ed.*, 1984, pp. 115–19. [G: U.S.]

Pencavel, John H. and Hartsog, Catherine E. A Reconsideration of the Effects of Unionism on Relative Wages and Employment in the United States, 1920–1980. *J. Lab. Econ.*, April 1984, 2(2), pp. 193–232. [G: U.S.]

Perlman, Mark. Collective Bargaining and Industrial Relations: The Past, the Present, and the Future. In *Fellner, W., ed.*, 1984, pp. 287–322. [G: U.S.]

Petridis, Anastasios. Trade Unions and the Theory of Competition. *Eastern Econ. J.*, July–September 1984, 10(3), pp. 295–314.

Pohjola, Matti. Union Rivalry and Economic Growth: A Differential Game Approach. *Scand. J. Econ.*, 1984, 86(3), pp. 365–70.

Poole, Michael. A Framework for Analysis and an Appraisal of Main Developments. In *Poole, M., et al.*, 1984, pp. 41–94. [G: U.K.]

von Potobsky, Geraldo. Industrial Relations in Latin America: Trade Unions. In *Córdova, E., ed.*, 1984, pp. 27–51. [G: Latin America]

Pugh, Cedric. Public Policy, Welfare and the Singaporean Economy. *Ann. Pub. Co-op. Econ.*, Oct.–Dec. 1984, 55(4), pp. 433–55. [G: Singapore]

Pulliam, Mark S. Legal Aspects of Exclusive Representation: Ruminations on the Private–Public Sector Analogy. *J. Lab. Res.*, Fall 1984, 5(4), pp. 351–70. [G: U.S.]

Quan, Nguyen T. Unionism and the Size Distribution of Earnings. *Ind. Relat.*, Spring 1984, 23(2), pp. 270–77. [G: U.S.]

Regini, Marino. The Conditions for Political Exchange: How Concertation Emerged and Collapsed in Italy and Great Britain. In *Goldthorpe, J. H., ed.*, 1984, pp. 124–42. [G: U.K.; Italy]

Reid, Joseph D., Jr. and Kurth, Michael M. The Contribution of Exclusive Representation to Union Strength. *J. Lab. Res.*, Fall 1984, 5(4), pp. 391–412. [G: U.S.]

Reid, Joseph D., Jr. and Kurth, Michael M. The Organization of State and Local Government

Employees: Comment. *J. Lab. Res.*, Spring 1984, 5(2), pp. 191–99. [G: U.S.]

Reynolds, Morgan O. Union Violence: A Review Article. *J. Lab. Res.*, Summer 1984, 5(3), pp. 237–46. [G: U.S.]

Robinson, Chris and Tomes, Nigel. Union Wage Differentials in the Public and Private Sectors: A Simultaneous Equations Specification. *J. Lab. Econ.*, January 1984, 2(1), pp. 106–27. [G: Canada]

Rosa, Jean-Jacques. Toward a Theory of the Union Firm. In *Rosa, J.-J., ed.*, 1984, pp. 157–86.

Ross, George and Gourevitch, Peter. Unions and Economic Crisis: Britain, West Germany, and Sweden: Conclusion. In *Gourevitch, P., et al.*, 1984, pp. 360–86. [G: U.K.; W. Germany; Sweden]

Roxborough, Ian. Labor in the Mexican Motor Vehicle Industry. In *Kronish, R. and Mericle, K. S., eds.*, 1984, pp. 161–94. [G: Mexico]

Ruback, Richard S. and Zimmerman, Martin B. Unionization and Profitability: Evidence from the Capital Market. *J. Polit. Econ.*, December 1984, 92(6), pp. 1134–57. [G: U.S.]

Rubery, Jill; Tarling, Roger and Wilkinson, Frank. Industrial Relations Issues in the 1980s: An Economic Analysis. In *Poole, M., et al.*, 1984, pp. 97–137. [G: U.K.]

Rush, Howard and Williams, Robin. Consultation and Change: New Technology and Manpower in the Electronics Industry. In *Warner, M., ed.*, 1984, pp. 171–88. [G: U.K.]

Salinger, Michael A. Tobin's *q*, Unionization, and the Concentration–Profits Relationship. *Rand J. Econ.*, Summer 1984, 15(2), pp. 159–70. [G: U.S.]

Sapsford, David. The Determinants of Trade Union Growth in the Republic of Ireland: An Econometric Investigation. *Econ. Soc. Rev.*, July 1984, 15(4), pp. 305–23. [G: U.K.]

Schäfer, Hermann. Italian Migrant Workers in Germany, 1890–1914. In *Engels, W. and Pohl, H., eds.*, 1984, pp. 77–94. [G: W. Germany]

Seifert, Roger V. Some Aspects of Factional Opposition: Rank and File and the National Union of Teachers, 1967–1982. *Brit. J. Ind. Relat.*, November 1984, 22(3), pp. 372–90. [G: U.K.]

Sengenberger, Werner. West German Employment Policy: Restoring Worker Competition. *Ind. Relat.*, Fall 1984, 23(3), pp. 323–43. [G: W. Germany]

Servais, Jean-Michel. ILO Standards on Freedom of Association and Their Implementation. *Int. Lab. Rev.*, November–December 1984, 123(6), pp. 765–81.

Shah, Anup R. Job Attributes and the Size of the Union/Non-union Wage Differential. *Economica*, November 1984, 51(204), pp. 437–46. [G: U.K.]

Sheflin, Neil. Transition Function Estimation of Structural Shifts in Models of American Trade Union Growth. *Appl. Econ.*, February 1984, 16(1), pp. 73–80. [G: U.S.]

Shimomura, Kazuo. A Simple General Equilib-rium Model Involving a Maximizing Labour Union. *Kobe Econ. Bus. Rev.*, 1984, 30, pp. 87–96.

Shulenburger, David; McLean, Robert A. and Rasch, Sara B. CISC Controls and the Union/Non-union Wage Ratio. *J. Behav. Econ.*, Summer 1984, 13(1), pp. 57–66. [G: U.S.]

Skeels, Jack W. Determinants of Strikes: Reply [The Economic and Organizational Basis of Early United States Strikes, 1900–1948]. *Ind. Lab. Relat. Rev.*, January 1984, 37(2), pp. 272–75. [G: U.S.]

Sloan, Frank A. and Adamache, Killard W. The Role of Unions in Hospital Cost Inflation. *Ind. Lab. Relat. Rev.*, January 1984, 37(2), pp. 252–62. [G: U.S.]

Smith, W. Rand. Dynamics of Plural Unionism in France: The CGT, CFDT and Industrial Conflict. *Brit. J. Ind. Relat.*, March 1984, 22(1), pp. 15–33. [G: France]

Soskice, David. Industrial Relations and the British Economy, 1979–1983. *Ind. Relat.*, Fall 1984, 23(3), pp. 306–22. [G: U.K.]

Southall, Roger J. Third World Trade Unionism: Equity and Democratization in the Changing International Division of Labour. *Can. J. Devel. Stud.*, 1984, 5(1), pp. 147–56.

Speziale, Valerio. Interventi legislativi e democrazia sindacale: il caso inglese. (The Recent English Legislation on Union Democracy. With English summary.) *Econ. Lavoro*, Jan.-Mar. 1984, 18(1), pp. 89–103. [G: U.K.]

Spizman, Lawrence and Cicarelli, James. Unions, Politicians, and the Public Interest: Retrenchment in the Public Sector. *J. Lab. Res.*, Fall 1984, 5(4), pp. 413–18. [G: U.S.]

Streeck, Wolfgang. Neo-Corporatist Industrial Relations and the Economic Crisis in West Germany. In *Goldthorpe, J. H., ed.*, 1984, pp. 291–314. [G: W. Germany]

Sullivan, James M. Unions in Politics: A Madisonian Faction in Our Federal System. *J. Lab. Res.*, Summer 1984, 5(3), pp. 275–85. [G: U.S.]

Süssekind, Arnaldo. The Influence of International Labour Standards on Brazilian Legislation. *Int. Lab. Rev.*, July–August 1984, 123(4), pp. 441–56. [G: Brazil]

Swabe, A. I. R. and Price, Patricia. Building a Permanent Association? The Development of Staff Associations in the Building Societies. *Brit. J. Ind. Relat.*, July 1984, 22(2), pp. 195–204. [G: U.K.]

Treble, John G. Does the Union/Non-Union Wage Differential Exist? *Manchester Sch. Econ. Soc. Stud.*, June 1984, 52(2), pp. 160–70. [G: U.K.]

Troy, Leo and Sheflin, Neil. Union Membership and Union Management: A Research Agenda for the 80s. In *Rosa, J.-J., ed.*, 1984, pp. 339–52. [G: U.S.]

Tullock, Gordon. Toward a Theory of the Union Firm: Comment. In *Rosa, J.-J., ed.*, 1984, pp. 187–89.

Turbin, Carole. Reconceptualizing Family, Work, and Labor Organizing: Working Women in Troy, 1860–1890. *Rev. Radical Polit. Econ.*, Spring 1984, *16*(1), pp. 1–16. [G: U.S.]

Ulman, Lloyd and Sorensen, Elaine. Exit, Voice, and Muscle: A Note. *Ind. Relat.*, Fall 1984, *23*(3), pp. 424–28. [G: U.S.]

Utrecht, Ernst. Labour and Trade Unions. In *Utrecht, E., ed.*, 1984, pp. 269–82. [G: Fiji]

Voos, Paula B. Trends in Union Organizing Expenditures, 1953–1977. *Ind. Lab. Relat. Rev.*, October 1984, *38*(1), pp. 52–63. [G: U.S.]

Vroman, Wayne. Wage Contract Settlements in U.S. Manufacturing. *Rev. Econ. Statist.*, November 1984, *66*(4), pp. 661–65. [G: U.S.]

Walsh, Vivien. The Post Office, the Unions and the New Technology. In *Warner, M., ed.*, 1984, pp. 210–23. [G: U.K.]

Wheeler, Hoyt N. Determinants of Strikes: Comment [The Determinants of Strikes in the United States, 1900–1977] [The Economic and Organizational Basis of Early United States Strikes, 1900–1948] [The Macroeconomic Strike Model: A Study of Seventeen Countries, 1948–1975]. *Ind. Lab. Relat. Rev.*, January 1984, *37*(2), pp. 263–69.

Willoughby, John. Economic Nationalism, the Left and the World Economy. *Rev. Radical Polit. Econ.*, Winter 1984, *16*(4), pp. 1–13.

Winpisinger, William W. Why Labor Unions Do Not Accept the New Economic Policy. In *Wachter, M. L. and Wachter, S. M., eds.*, 1984, pp. 28–33. [G: U.S.]

832 Collective Bargaining

8320 General

Addison, John T. Trade Unions and Restrictive Practices. In *Rosa, J.-J., ed.*, 1984, pp. 83–114. [G: U.S.]

Behrend, Hilde. Reflections on the Incidence of Strikes. In *Behrend, H.*, 1984, pp. 34–57. [G: U.K.]

Blair, Douglas H. and Crawford, David L. Labor Union Objectives and Collective Bargaining. *Quart. J. Econ.*, August 1984, *99*(3), pp. 547–66.

Blanpain, R. Recent Trends in Collective Bargaining in Belgium. *Int. Lab. Rev.*, May–June 1984, *123*(3), pp. 319–32. [G: Belgium]

Brown, William and Sisson, Keith. Current Trends and Future Possibilities. In *Poole, M., et al.*, 1984, pp. 13–38. [G: U.K.]

Buck, Andrew J. Modelling a Poisson Process: Strike Frequency in Great Britain. *Atlantic Econ. J.*, March 1984, *12*(1), pp. 60–64. [G: U.K.]

Burton, John. Strike Cost and Wage Rates: Cross-Industry Differences: Comment. In *Rosa, J.-J., ed.*, 1984, pp. 37–41. [G: U.S.]

Caire, Guy. Recent Trends in Collective Bargaining in France. *Int. Lab. Rev.*, November–December 1984, *123*(6), pp. 723–41. [G: France]

Cameron, Samuel. The Stability of the Post-War Aggregate British Strike Function. *Scot. J. Polit. Econ.*, February 1984, *31*(1), pp. 28–43. [G: U.K.]

Carroll, Gene. How to Get Labor Involved. In *Gordon, S. and McFadden, D., eds.*, 1984, pp. 219–30. [G: U.S.]

Chaloupek, Gunter. The Regulation of Inflation in Western Countries and the Degree of Neocorporatism: Comment. In *Cavaco Silva, A., ed.*, 1984, pp. 75–78. [G: OECD]

Chapman, Paul G. and Fisher, Malcolm R. Union Wage Policies: Comment [Wage Bargaining and Employment]. *Amer. Econ. Rev.*, September 1984, *74*(4), pp. 755–58.

Córdova, Efrén. Industrial Relations in Latin America: Labor Courts. In *Cérdova, E., ed.*, 1984, pp. 227–42. [G: Latin America]

Dabscheck, Braham and Niland, John. Recent Trends in Collective Bargaining in Australia. *Int. Lab. Rev.*, September–October 1984, *123*(5), pp. 631–46. [G: Australia]

Dickman, Howard. Exclusive Representation and American Industrial Democracy: An Historical Reappraisal. *J. Lab. Res.*, Fall 1984, *5*(4), pp. 325–50. [G: U.S.]

Dow, M. Bradley. The Labour Movement and Trade Unionism: Summary Outline. In *Wood, W. D. and Kumar, P., eds.*, 1984, pp. 217–92. [G: Canada]

Esping-Andersen, Gösta and Korpi, Walter. Social Policy as Class Politics in Post-war Capitalism: Scandinavia, Austria, and Germany. In *Goldthorpe, J. H., ed.*, 1984, pp. 179–208. [G: Scandinavia; Austria; Germany]

Faxén, Karl O. Risk Management. In *[Kozmetsky, G.]*, 1984, pp. 155–75. [G: U.S.; Sweden]

Fürstenberg, Friedrich. Recent Trends in Collective Bargaining in the Federal Republic of Germany. *Int. Lab. Rev.*, September–October 1984, *123*(5), pp. 615–30. [G: W. Germany]

Garbarino, Joseph W. Unionism without Unions: The New Industrial Relations? *Ind. Relat.*, Winter 1984, *23*(1), pp. 40–51. [G: U.S.]

Ghosh, B. N. Brain Migration from Third World: An Implicative Analysis. *Rivista Int. Sci. Econ. Com.*, April 1984, *31*(4), pp. 346–70. [G: LDCs]

Giugni, Gino. Recent Trends in Collective Bargaining in Italy. *Int. Lab. Rev.*, September–October 1984, *123*(5), pp. 599–614. [G: Italy]

Gordon, Michael E.; Schmitt, Neal and Schneider, Walter G. Laboratory Research on Bargaining and Negotiations: An Evaluation. *Ind. Relat.*, Spring 1984, *23*(2), pp. 218–33.

Gravelle, Hugh S. E. Bargaining and Efficiency in Public and Private Sector Firms. In *Marchand, M.; Pestieau, P. and Tulkens, H., eds.*, 1984, pp. 193–220.

Hartog, Joop. On the Efficiency of Labor Markets. *De Economist*, 1984, *132*(3), pp. 279–99. [G: Netherlands]

Howells, John M. Mediation in New Zealand: A Mild Case of Schizophrenia? *Int. Lab. Rev.*, November–December 1984, *123*(6), pp. 753–63. [G: New Zealand]

Hyde, Alan. Democracy in Collective Bargaining. *Yale Law J.*, April 1984, *93*(5), pp. 793–856.

Jaeger, Franz and Schips, Bernd. Teuerungsausgleich und funktionelle Einkommensvertei-lung. (Wage Indexation and Income Distribu-tion. With English summary.) *Schweiz. Z. Volkswirtsch. Statist.*, March 1984, *120*(1), pp. 43–63. **[G: Switzerland]**

Lévy-Garboua, Louis. Homo Economicus and the Labour Market: Comment. In *Wiles, P. and Routh, G., eds.*, 1984, pp. 154–58.

Maier, Charles S. Preconditions for Corporatism. In *Goldthorpe, J. H., ed.*, 1984, pp. 39–59.

Marsden, David. Homo Economicus and the La-bour Market. In *Wiles, P. and Routh, G., eds.*, 1984, pp. 121–53.

McDonald, Ian M. and Solow, Robert M. Union Wage Policies: Reply [Wage Bargaining and Employment]. *Amer. Econ. Rev.*, September 1984, *74*(4), pp. 759–61.

Mitchell, Daniel J. B. The Australian Labor Mar-ket. In *Caves, R. E. and Krause, L. B., eds.*, 1984, pp. 127–93. **[G: Australia]**

Naslund, Bertil. Uncertainty and the Need for Innovation in Management Techniques and Methods. In *[Kozmetsky, G.]*, 1984, pp. 177–80. **[G: Sweden]**

Paldam, Martin and Pedersen, Peder J. The Large Pattern of Industrial Conflict—A Com-parative Study of 18 Countries, 1919–79. *Int. J. Soc. Econ.*, 1984, *11*(5), pp. 3–28. **[G: OECD]**

Panayotopoulos, A. and Yannacopoulos, N. Bar-gaining and the Negotiation Set. *Rivista Int. Sci. Econ. Com.*, January 1984, *31*(1), pp. 40–48.

Pencavel, John H. The Tradeoff between Wages and Employment in Trade Union Objectives. *Quart. J. Econ.*, May 1984, *99*(2), pp. 215–31. **[G: U.S.]**

Pencavel, John H. Trade Unions and Restrictive Practices: Comment. In *Rosa, J.-J., ed.*, 1984, pp. 115–19. **[G: U.S.]**

Poole, Michael. A Framework for Analysis and an Appraisal of Main Developments. In *Poole, M., et al.*, 1984, pp. 41–94. **[G: U.K.]**

Pulliam, Mark S. Legal Aspects of Exclusive Rep-resentation: Ruminations on the Private–Public Sector Analogy. *J. Lab. Res.*, Fall 1984, *5*(4), pp. 351–70. **[G: U.S.]**

Reder, Melvin W. Strike Cost and Wage Rates: Cross-Industry Differences. In *Rosa, J.-J., ed.*, 1984, pp. 27–37. **[G: U.S.]**

Roberts, B. C. Recent Trends in Collective Bar-gaining in the United Kingdom. *Int. Lab. Rev.*, May–June 1984, *123*(3), pp. 287–306.
[G: U.K.]

Rubery, Jill; Tarling, Roger and Wilkinson, Frank. Industrial Relations Issues in the 1980s: An Economic Analysis. In *Poole, M., et al.*, 1984, pp. 97–137. **[G: U.K.]**

Schwerin, Don S. Historic Compromise and Plu-ralist Decline? Profits and Capital in the Nordic Countries. In *Goldthorpe, J. H., ed.*, 1984, pp. 231–56. **[G: OECD]**

Shirai, Taishiro. Recent Trends in Collective Bar-gaining in Japan. *Int. Lab. Rev.*, May–June 1984, *123*(3), pp. 307–18. **[G: Japan]**

Swint, John Michael. Collective Bargaining in

Not-For-Profit Hospitals: A Model amd Its Im-plications for the Likelihood of Strikes. *South-ern Econ. J.*, July 1984, *51*(1), pp. 24–40.

Tarantelli, Ezio. The Regulation of Inflation in Western Countries and the Degree of Neocor-poratism. In *Cavaco Silva, A. A., ed.*, 1984, pp. 27–66. **[G: OECD]**

Thore, Sten. Uncertainty and the Opportunities for Innovation and Investment. In *[Kozmetsky, G.]*, 1984, pp. 181–83. **[G: U.S.; Sweden]**

Utrecht, Ernst. Labour and Trade Unions. In *Utrecht, E., ed.*, 1984, pp. 269–82. **[G: Fiji]**

Wood, W. D., et al. Collective Bargaining: Sum-mary Outline. In *Wood, W. D. and Kumar, P., eds.*, 1984, pp. 295–426. **[G: Canada]**

8321 Collective Bargaining in the Private Sector

Adams, Walter and Brock, James W. Counter-vailing or Coalescing Power? The Problem of Labor/Management Coalitions. *J. Post Keynes-ian Econ.*, Winter 1983-84, *6*(2), pp. 180–97.
[G: U.S.]

Albert, Bill. The Creation of a Proletariat on Pe-ru's Coastal Sugar Plantations: 1880–1920. In *Munslow, B. and Finch, H., eds.*, 1984, pp. 99–120. **[G: Peru]**

Armstrong, E. G. A. Employers Associations in Great Britain. In *Windmuller, J. P. and Glad-stone, A., eds.*, 1984, pp. 44–78. **[G: U.K.]**

Banaji, Jairus. Accumulation and Exploitability: Wage Determination and Pay Conflict. In *Ngo, M., ed., vol. 1*, 1984, pp. 295–323.
[G: India]

Behrend, Hilde. A Fair Day's Work. In *Behrend, H.*, 1984, *1961*, pp. 145–63.

Blandy, Richard. The Future of Australia's Indus-trial Relations System: A Summary and Com-ment. *Australian Bull. Lab.*, Supplement Sep-tember 1984, *10*(5), pp. S1–S10.
[G: Australia]

Bohlander, George W. and Farris, Martin T. Collective Bargaining in Trucking—The Effects of Deregulation. *Logist. Transp. Rev.*, Sep-tember 1984, *20*(3), pp. 223–38. **[G: U.S.]**

Bronstein, Arturo S. Industrial Relations in Latin America: Employers' Organizations. In *Cér-dova, E., ed.*, 1984, pp. 53–67.
[G: Latin America]

Bronstein, Arturo S. and Córdova, Efrén. Indus-trial Relations in Latin America: Collective Bargaining. In *Cérdova, E., ed.*, 1984, pp. 87–108. **[G: Latin America]**

Bunel, Jean and Saglio, Jean. Employers Associa-tions in France. In *Windmuller, J. P. and Glad-stone, A., eds.*, 1984, pp. 232–63.
[G: France]

Bunn, Ronald F. Employers Association in the Federal Republic of Germany. In *Windmuller, J. P. and Gladstone, A., eds.*, 1984, pp. 169–201. **[G: W. Germany]**

Cappelli, Peter. What Do Unions Get in Return for Concessions? *Mon. Lab. Rev.*, May 1984, *107*(5), pp. 40–41. **[G: U.S.]**

Coffey, Joseph D. The California Agricultural La-bor Relations Act and National Agricultural Labor Relations Legislation: Discussion. In *Emerson, R. D., ed.*, 1984, pp. 370–75. **[G: U.S.]**

Córdova, Efrén. Industrial Relations in Latin America: Conciliation. In *Cérdova, E., ed.*, 1984, pp. 189–207. **[G: Latin America]**

Córdova, Efrén. Industrial Relations in Latin America: Arbitration. In *Cérdova, E., ed.*, 1984, pp. 209–26. **[G: Latin America]**

Córdova, Efrén. Industrial Relations in Latin America: Departments of Labor. In *Cérdova, E., ed.*, 1984, pp. 69–83. **[G: Latin America]**

Córdova, Efrén. Labor Disputes: Their Nature and Settlement. In *Cérdova, E., ed.*, 1984, pp. 169–88. **[G: Latin America]**

Córdova, Efrén. The Latin American Picture. In *Cérdova, E., ed.*, 1984, pp. 3–24. **[G: Latin America]**

Córdova, Efrén. Workers' Participation in Management. In *Cérdova, E., ed.*, 1984, pp. 109–27. **[G: Latin America]**

Córdova, Efrén and Morgado, Emilio. Industrial Relations in Latin America: Strikes and Lockouts. In *Cérdova, E., ed.*, 1984, pp. 243–67. **[G: Latin America]**

Crisp, Jeff. The Labour Question in the Gold Coast, 1870–1906. In *Munslow, B. and Finch, H., eds.*, 1984, pp. 18–41. **[G: Ghana]**

Derber, Milton. Employers Associations in the United States. In *Windmuller, J. P. and Gladstone, A., eds.*, 1984, pp. 79–114. **[G: U.S.]**

Downer, Alexander. The Future of Australian Industrial Relations. *Australian Bull. Lab.*, Supplement September 1984, *10*(5), pp. S11–S23. **[G: Australia]**

Dufty, Norman F. Employers Associations in Australia. In *Windmuller, J. P. and Gladstone, A., eds.*, 1984, pp. 115–48. **[G: Australia]**

Elliott, Ralph D. and Huffman, James R. The Impact of Right-to-Work Laws on Employer Unfair Labor Practice Charges. *J. Lab. Res.*, Spring 1984, *5*(2), pp. 165–76. **[G: U.S.]**

Elwell, Karen and Feuille, Peter. Arbitration Awards and *Gardner-Denver* Lawsuits: One Bite or Two? *Ind. Relat.*, Spring 1984, *23*(2), pp. 287–97. **[G: U.S.]**

Epstein, Edythe. Negotiating over Technological Change in Banking and Insurance. *Int. Lab. Rev.*, July–August 1984, *123*(4), pp. 405–22.

Evans, Judith; Hoeffel, Paul Heath and James, Daniel. Reflections on Argentine Auto Workers and Their Unions. In *Kronish, R. and Mericle, K. S., eds.*, 1984, pp. 133–59. **[G: Argentina]**

Fernández, Manuel A. British Nitrate Companies and the Emergence of Chile's Proletariat, 1880–1914. In *Munslow, B. and Finch, H., eds.*, 1984, pp. 42–76. **[G: Chile]**

Flanagan, Robert J. Wage Concessions and Long-Term Union Wage Flexibility. *Brookings Pap. Econ. Act.*, 1984, (1), pp. 183–216. **[G: U.S.]**

Friedman, Samuel R. The Work Process and Worker Mobilization among Teamster Drivers. In *Zarembka, P., ed.*, 1984, pp. 161–83.

Gay, Robert S. Union Settlements and Aggregate Wage Behavior in the 1980s. *Fed. Res. Bull.*, December 1984, *70*(12), pp. 843–56. **[G: U.S.]**

Gladstone, Alan. Employers Associations in Comparative Perspective: Functions and Activities. In *Windmuller, J. P. and Gladstone, A., eds.*, 1984, pp. 24–43. **[G: OECD]**

Harrison, Bennett and Bluestone, Barry. The Incidence and Regulation of Plant Closings. In *Sawers, L. and Tabb, W. K., eds.*, 1984, *1982*, pp. 368–402. **[G: U.S.]**

Hayes, Beth. Unions and Strikes with Asymmetric Information. *J. Lab. Econ.*, January 1984, *2*(1), pp. 57–83.

Hayes, Sue Eileen. The California Agricultural Labor Relations Act and National Agricultural Labor Relations Legislation. In *Emerson, R. D., ed.*, 1984, pp. 328–70. **[G: U.S.]**

Hendricks, Wallace E. and Kahn, Lawrence M. The Demand for Labor Market Structure: An Economic Approach. *J. Lab. Econ.*, July 1984, *2*(3), pp. 412–38. **[G: U.S.]**

Hettlage, Robert. Interest-Group Conflict, Consensus-building, and "Cooperative Bargaining": The Swiss Industrial Peace Agreement as a Model. *Z. ges. Staatswiss.*, September 1984, *140*(3), pp. 475–99. **[G: Switzerland]**

Holland, A. Steven. The Impact of Inflation Uncertainty on the Labor Market. *Fed. Res. Bank St. Louis Rev.*, August/September 1984, *66*(7), pp. 21–28. **[G: U.S.]**

Irving, John S., Jr. Plant Relocations and Transfers of Work: The NLRB's "Inherently Destructive" Approach. In *McKenzie, R. B., ed. (II)*, 1984, *1983*, pp. 233–52. **[G: U.S.]**

Jacoby, Sanford M. and Mitchell, Daniel J. B. Employer Preferences for Long-Term Union Contracts. *J. Lab. Res.*, Summer 1984, *5*(3), pp. 215–28. **[G: U.S.]**

Jones, J. C. H. and Walsh, W. D. Inter-Industry Strike Frequencies: Some Pooled Cross-Sectional Evidence from Canadian Secondary Manufacturing. *J. Lab. Res.*, Fall 1984, *5*(4), pp. 419–25. **[G: Canada]**

Joyce, Paul and Woods, Adrian. The Management of Conflict: A Quantitative Analysis. *Brit. J. Ind. Relat.*, March 1984, *22*(1), pp. 63–77. **[G: U.K.]**

Kain, Peter G. Reshaping Australia's Industrial Relations System for the Future. *Australian Bull. Lab.*, Supplement September 1984, *10*(5), pp. S24–S35. **[G: Australia]**

Katz, Harry C. The U.S. Automobile Collective Bargaining System in Transition. *Brit. J. Ind. Relat.*, July 1984, *22*(2), pp. 205–17. **[G: U.S.]**

Kaufman, Bruce E. Determinants of Strikes: Reply [The Determinants of Strikes in the United States, 1900–1977]. *Ind. Lab. Relat. Rev.*, January 1984, *37*(2), pp. 269–72. **[G: U.S.]**

Kaufman, Roger T. and Woglom, Geoffrey. The Effects of Expectations on Union Wages. *Amer. Econ. Rev.*, June 1984, *74*(3), pp. 418–32. **[G: U.S.]**

Kelly, James. Management Strategy and the Reform of Collective Bargaining: Cases from the

British Steel Corporation. *Brit. J. Ind. Relat.*, July 1984, 22(2), pp. 135–53. **[G: U.K.]**

Kochan, Thomas A.; McKersie, Robert B. and Cappelli, Peter. Strategic Choice and Industrial Relations Theory. *Ind. Relat.*, Winter 1984, 23(1), pp. 16–39. **[G: U.S.]**

Kosters, Marvin H. Disinflation in the Labor Market. In *Fellner, W., ed.*, 1984, pp. 247–86. **[G: U.S.]**

Kosters, Marvin H. Wage Concessions and Long-Term Union Wage Flexibility: Comments. *Brookings Pap. Econ. Act.*, 1984, (1), pp. 217–20. **[G: U.S.]**

Kübler, Friedrich. Dual Loyalty of Labor Representatives. In *Hopt, K. J. and Teubner, G., eds.*, 1984, pp. 429–44. **[G: W. Germany]**

Lacombe, John J., II and Conley, James R. Collective Bargaining Calendar Crowded Again in 1984. *Mon. Lab. Rev.*, January 1984, 107(1), pp. 19–32. **[G: U.S.]**

Lange, Peter. Unions, Workers and Wage Regulation: The Rational Bases of Consent. In *Goldthorpe, J. H., ed.*, 1984, pp. 98–123.

Lawrence, R. J. The Lognormal Distribution of the Duration of Strikes. *J. Roy. Statist. Soc.*, 1984, 147(3), pp. 464–83. **[G: U.K.]**

Leigh, J. Paul. A Bargaining Model and Empirical Analysis of Strike Activity across Industries. *J. Lab. Res.*, Spring 1984, 5(2), pp. 127–37. **[G: U.S.]**

Leigh, J. Paul. Do Union Members Receive Compensating Wages for Accepting Employment in Strike-Prone or Hazardous Industries? *Soc. Sci. Quart.*, March 1984, 65(1), pp. 89–99. **[G: U.S.]**

Levine, Solomon B. Employers Associations in Japan. In *Windmuller, J. P. and Gladstone, A., eds.*, 1984, pp. 318–56. **[G: Japan]**

Marginson, Paul M. The Distinctive Effects of Plant and Company Size on Workplace Industrial Relations. *Brit. J. Ind. Relat.*, March 1984, 22(1), pp. 1–14. **[G: U.K.]**

Martinelli, Alberto and Treu, Tiziano. Employers Associations in Italy. In *Windmuller, J. P. and Gladstone, A., eds.*, 1984, pp. 264–93. **[G: Italy]**

McCormick, Brian J. Personnel Management. In *Pickering, J. F. and Cockerill, T. A. J., eds.*, 1984, pp. 179–220. **[G: U.S.; U.K.]**

McLachlan, Ian. Principles for the Future of Australian Industrial Relations. *Australian Bull. Lab.*, Supplement September 1984, 10(5), pp. S62–S69. **[G: Australia]**

Miller, Ronald L. Arbitration in New Zealand: Mediation Plus Decision Making. *Ind. Relat.*, Winter 1984, 23(1), pp. 126–38. **[G: New Zealand]**

Munslow, Barry. Proletarianisation in Mozambique. In *Munslow, B. and Finch, H., eds.*, 1984, pp. 77–98. **[G: Mozambique]**

Neumann, George R. Cyclical Strike Activity and Mature Collective Bargaining: Evidence from Canadian Data: 1960–1976. In *Rosa, J.-J., ed.*, 1984, pp. 43–56. **[G: Canada]**

Neumann, George R. and Reder, Melvin W. Output and Strike Activity in U.S. Manufactur-

ing: How Large Are the Losses? *Ind. Lab. Relat. Rev.*, January 1984, 37(2), pp. 197–211. **[G: U.S.]**

Noakes, Bryan. The Future of Australian Industrial Relations Systems. *Australian Bull. Lab.*, Supplement September 1984, 10(5), pp. S49–S61. **[G: Australia]**

Nolan, Peter and Edwards, P. K. Homogenise, Divide and Rule: An Essay on *Segmented Work, Divided Workers:* Review Article. *Cambridge J. Econ.*, June 1984, 8(2), pp. 197–215. **[G: U.S.]**

O'Keefe, Edward P. and Tuohey, Seamus M. Economically Motivated Relocations of Work and an Employer's Duties under Section 8(d) of the National Labor Relations Act: A Three-Step Analysis. In *McKenzie, R. B., ed. (II)*, 1984, 1983, pp. 253–305. **[G: U.S.]**

Osborne, Martin J. Capitalist–Worker Conflict and Involuntary Unemployment. *Rev. Econ. Stud.*, January 1984, 51(1), pp. 111–27.

Paldam, Martin and Pedersen, Peder J. Determinants of Strikes: Reply [The Macroeconomic Strike Model: A Study of Seventeen Countries, 1948–1975]. *Ind. Lab. Relat. Rev.*, January 1984, 37(2), pp. 275–78. **[G: OECD]**

Perlman, Mark. Collective Bargaining and Industrial Relations: The Past, the Present, and the Future. In *Fellner, W., ed.*, 1984, pp. 287–322. **[G: U.S.]**

Roberts, Markley. A Labor Perspective on Technological Change. In *Collins, E. L. and Tanner, L. D., eds.*, 1984, pp. 183–205. **[G: U.S.]**

Roomkin, Myron J. and Harris, Dawn A. Interindustry Patterns in Unfair Labor Practice Cases. *J. Lab. Res.*, Spring 1984, 5(2), pp. 113–26. **[G: U.S.]**

Roxborough, Ian. Labor in the Mexican Motor Vehicle Industry. In *Kronish, R. and Mericle, K. S., eds.*, 1984, pp. 161–94. **[G: Mexico]**

Ruben, George. Developments in Industrial Relations. *Mon. Lab. Rev.*, April 1984, 107(4), pp. 48–51. **[G: U.S.]**

Shirom, Arie. Employers Associations in Israel. In *Windmuller, J. P. and Gladstone, A., eds.*, 1984, pp. 294–317. **[G: Israel]**

Skeels, Jack W. Determinants of Strikes: Reply [The Economic and Organizational Basis of Early United States Strikes, 1900–1948]. *Ind. Lab. Relat. Rev.*, January 1984, 37(2), pp. 272–75. **[G: U.S.]**

Skogh, Göran. Cyclical Strike Activity and Mature Collective Bargaining: Evidence from Canadian Data: 1960–1976: Comment. In *Rosa, J.-J., ed.*, 1984, pp. 56–62. **[G: Canada]**

Skogh, Göran. Employers Associations in Sweden. In *Windmuller, J. P. and Gladstone, A., eds.*, 1984, pp. 149–68. **[G: Sweden]**

Smith, W. Rand. Dynamics of Plural Unionism in France: The CGT, CFDT and Industrial Conflict. *Brit. J. Ind. Relat.*, March 1984, 22(1), pp. 15–33. **[G: France]**

Sockell, Donna. The Legality of Employee-Participation Programs in Unionized Firms. *Ind.*

Lab. Relat. Rev., July 1984, *37*(4), pp. 541–56. **[G: U.S.]**

Stieber, Jack. Most U.S. Workers Still May Be Fired under the Employment-at-Will Doctrine. *Mon. Lab. Rev.*, May 1984, *107*(5), pp. 34–38. **[G: U.S.]**

van Voorden, William. Employers Associations in the Netherlands. In *Windmuller, J. P. and Gladstone, A., eds.*, 1984, pp. 202–31. **[G: Netherlands]**

Vroman, Wayne. Wage Contract Settlements in U.S. Manufacturing. *Rev. Econ. Statist.*, November 1984, *66*(4), pp. 661–65. **[G: U.S.]**

Wheeler, Hoyt N. Determinants of Strikes: Comment [The Determinants of Strikes in the United States, 1900–1977] [The Economic and Organizational Basis of Early United States Strikes, 1900–1948] [The Macroeconomic Strike Model: A Study of Seventeen Countries, 1948–1975]. *Ind. Lab. Relat. Rev.*, January 1984, *37*(2), pp. 263–69.

Whiffin, R. A. The Future Course of Australian Industrial Relations. *Australian Bull. Lab.*, Supplement September 1984, *10*(5), pp. S36–S48. **[G: Australia]**

Winch, Graham, et al. Industrial Relations, New Technology and the BL Metro. In *Warner, M., ed.*, 1984, pp. 189–209. **[G: U.K.]**

8322 Collective Bargaining in the Public Sector

Ashenfelter, Orley C. and Bloom, David E. Models of Arbitrator Behavior: Theory and Evidence. *Amer. Econ. Rev.*, March 1984, *74*(1), pp. 111–24. **[G: U.S.]**

DiLorenzo, Thomas J. Exclusive Representation in Public Employment: A Public Choice Perspective. *J. Lab. Res.*, Fall 1984, *5*(4), pp. 371–89. **[G: U.S.]**

Eberts, Randall W. Union Effects on Teacher Productivity. *Ind. Lab. Relat. Rev.*, April 1984, *37*(3), pp. 346–58. **[G: U.S.]**

Horn, Robert N. and McGuire, William J. Determinants of Secondary School Teacher Salaries in a Large Urban School District. *Southern Econ. J.*, October 1984, *51*(2), pp. 481–94. **[G: U.S.]**

Hyman, Jeffrey and Schuller, Tom. Occupational Pension Schemes and Collective Bargaining. *Brit. J. Ind. Relat.*, November 1984, *22*(3), pp. 289–310. **[G: U.K.]**

Lacroix, Robert and Dussault, François. The Spillover Effect of Public-Sector Wage Contracts in Canada. *Rev. Econ. Statist.*, August 1984, *66*(3), pp. 509–12. **[G: Canada]**

Maier, Mark. Management Strategies in Public Sector Labor Law: A Case Study of New York City. In *Tabb, W. K. and Sawers, L., eds.*, 1984, pp. 346–63. **[G: U.S.]**

McCormick, Mary. Setting Municipal Priorities: Budgeting and Management: Labor Relations. In *Brecher, C. and Horton, R. D., eds.*, 1984, pp. 302–28. **[G: U.S.]**

Northrup, Herbert R. The Rise and Demise of PATCO. *Ind. Lab. Relat. Rev.*, January 1984, *37*(2), pp. 167–84. **[G: U.S.]**

Olson, Craig A. The Role of Rescheduled School Days in Teacher Strikes. *Ind. Lab. Relat. Rev.*, July 1984, *37*(4), pp. 515–28. **[G: U.S.]**

Taxell, Christoffer. Tankar om den economiska lagstiftningen. (Views on Economic Legislation. With English summary.) *Ekon. Samfundets Tidskr.*, 1984, *37*(4), pp. 237–44. **[G: Finland]**

Thompson, Mark and Ponak, Allen. Industrial Relations in Canadian Public Enterprises. *Int. Lab. Rev.*, September–October 1984, *123*(5), pp. 647–63. **[G: Canada]**

833 Labor–Management Relations

8330 General

Albin, Peter S. Job Design within Changing Patterns of Technical Development. In *Collins, E. L. and Tanner, L. D., eds.*, 1984, pp. 125–61. **[G: U.S.]**

Arai, Joji. U.S. and European Approaches to Improving Labor Productivity and the Quality of Work Life: Comments. In *Kendrick, J. W., ed.*, 1984, pp. 393–96. **[G: U.S.; W. Europe]**

Behrend, Hilde. Problems in the Field of Industrial Relations. In *Behrend, H.*, 1984, *1963*, pp. 7–21.

Behrend, Hilde. Problems of Labour and Inflation: Introduction. In *Behrend, H.*, 1984, pp. 1–6.

Behrend, Hilde. Why so much Fuss about Industrial Relations? In *Behrend, H.*, 1984, pp. 22–33.

Benello, C. George. Workplace Democracy in the United States: Present Trends and Counter-Trends. *Econ. Anal. Worker's Manage.*, 1984, *18*(4), pp. 385–97. **[G: U.S.]**

Briefs, Henry W. Solidarity within the Firm: Principles, Concepts and Reflections. *Rev. Soc. Econ.*, December 1984, *42*(3), pp. 295–317.

Chaudhuri, K. K. Participation in Indian Society. *Int. Soc. Sci. J.*, 1984, *36*(2), pp. 255–69. **[G: India]**

Child, John, et al. Microelectronics and the Quality of Employment in Services. In *Marstrand, P., ed.*, 1984, pp. 163–90. **[G: U.K.]**

Dickens, Linda, et al. The British Experience under a Statute Prohibiting Unfair Dismissal. *Ind. Lab. Relat. Rev.*, July 1984, *37*(4), pp. 497–514. **[G: U.K.]**

Donnison, David. The Progressive Potential of Privatisation. In *Le Grand, J. and Robinson, R., eds.*, 1984, pp. 45–57.

Dugger, William M. Human Liberation: Workplace Reform as the Next Step in Social Evolution. *Int. J. Soc. Econ.*, 1984, *11*(5), pp. 29–39.

Ellerman, David P. Theory of Legal Structure: Worker Cooperatives. *J. Econ. Issues*, September 1984, *18*(3), pp. 861–91. **[G: U.S.; Yugoslavia; Spain]**

Ellerman, David P. Workers' Cooperatives: The Question of Legal Structure. In *Jackall, R. and Levin, H. M., eds.*, 1984, pp. 257–74. **[G: U.S.]**

Elliott, John E. Recapitulation and Prospects: Worker Ownership and Self-Government. *Rev. Soc. Econ.*, December 1984, *42*(3), pp. 433–38.

Esterin, Saul. Self-Management and Capitalism Compared: A Review of M. R. Sertel's, *Workers and Incentives*. *Econ. Anal. Worker's Manage.*, 1984, *18*(1), pp. 103–07.

FitzRoy, Felix R. and Kraft, Kornelius. Mitarbeiterbeteiligung bei deutschen Industrieaktiengesellschaften—Ein Kommetar. (With English summary.) *Z. Betriebswirtshaft*, January 1984, *54*(1), pp. 79–83. [G: W. Germany]

Ford, G. W. The Democratization of Work in Australia. *Econ. Anal. Worker's Manage.*, 1984, *18*(1), pp. 77–102. [G: Australia]

Gamson, Zelda F. and Levin, Henry M. Obstacles to the Survival of Democratic Workplaces. In *Jackall, R. and Levin, H. M., eds.*, 1984, pp. 219–44. [G: U.S.]

Giannini, Mirella. Strategie aziendali e comportamento dei lavoratori nelle organizzazioni industriali: il caso Italsider–Taranto. (Managerial Strategies and Workers' Behaviour in Industrial Organization: The Case of Italsider–Taranto. With English summary.) *Econ. Lavoro*, Oct.-Dec. 1984, *18*(4), pp. 47–68. [G: Italy]

Gordon, Michael E.; Schmitt, Neal and Schneider, Walter G. Laboratory Research on Bargaining and Negotiations: An Evaluation. *Ind. Relat.*, Spring 1984, *23*(2), pp. 218–33.

Gruenberg, Gladys W. Prospects: Solidarity within the Firm. *Rev. Soc. Econ.*, December 1984, *42*(3), pp. 424–26.

Hart, Oliver. The Firm as a Collection of Human Resources: Comment. In *Wiles, P. and Routh, G., eds.*, 1984, pp. 207–10.

Helburn, I. B. and Shearer, John C. Human Resources and Industrial Relations in China: A Time of Ferment. *Ind. Lab. Relat. Rev.*, October 1984, *38*(1), pp. 3–15. [G: China]

Held, Thomas. Mitarbeiterbeteiligung bei deutschen Industrieaktiengesellschaften: Eine Entgegnung. (With English summary.) *Z. Betriebswirtshaft*, January 1984, *54*(1), pp. 84–88. [G: W. Germany]

Hentze, Joachim. Die Stellung des Menschen in der sozialistischen Arbeitsökonomie. (With English summary.) *Z. Betriebswirtshaft*, January 1984, *54*(1), pp. 63–77.

Hill, Lewis E. A Comment on Solidarity within the Firm [Solidarity within the Firm: Principles, Concepts and Reflections] [Industrial Justice in a Practical Sense]. *Rev. Soc. Econ.*, December 1984, *42*(3), pp. 328–29.

Horvat, Branko. Work and Power: The Prospects for the Disalienation of Work. *Econ. Anal. Worker's Manage.*, 1984, *18*(4), pp. 365–69.

Howells, John M. Mediation in New Zealand: A Mild Case of Schizophrenia? *Int. Lab. Rev.*, November–December 1984, *123*(6), pp. 753–63. [G: New Zealand]

Ireland, Norman J. Codetermination, Wage Bargaining and the Horizon Problem. *Z. Nationalökon.*, 1984, *44*(1), pp. 1–10.

Jackall, Robert and Levin, Henry M. The Prospects for Worker Cooperatives in the United States. In *Jackall, R. and Levin, H. M., eds.*, 1984, pp. 277–90. [G: U.S.]

Jacoby, Sanford M. The Development of Internal Labor Markets in American Manufacturing Firms. In *Osterman, P., ed.*, 1984, pp. 23–69. [G: U.S.]

Kozyr, M. I. New Features of Labour Relations in Soviet Agriculture. *Int. Soc. Sci. J.*, 1984, *36*(2), pp. 285–97. [G: U.S.S.R.]

Lenel, Hans Otto. Ein dritter Weg? Zu Ota Šiks "Hummaner Wirtschaftsdemokratie." (With English Summary.) In *Eucken, W. and Böhm, F., eds.*, 1984, pp. 179–230.

Levin, Henry M. Employment and Productivity of Producer Cooperatives. In *Jackall, R. and Levin, H. M., eds.*, 1984, pp. 16–31. [G: Spain]

Levine, Solomon B. Social Consequences of Industrialization in Japan. In *Sherman, M., ed.*, 1984, pp. 39–68. [G: Japan]

Lichtenstein, Peter M. Economic Democracy: The Rawls–Vanek–Sraffa Connection. *Rev. Soc. Econ.*, October 1984, *42*(2), pp. 170–81.

Linge, G. J. R. Industrialization and the Household. *Int. Soc. Sci. J.*, 1984, *36*(2), pp. 319–39.

Long, Richard J. Microelectronics and Quality of Working Life in the Office: A Canadian Perspective. In *Warner, M., ed.*, 1984, pp. 273–93. [G: Canada]

Milkovich, George. Personnel Strategy and Evaluation. *Ind. Relat.*, Spring 1984, *23*(2), pp. 151–55.

Mills, Ted. U.S. and European Approaches to Improving Labor Productivity and the Quality of Work Life. In *Kendrick, J. W., ed.*, 1984, pp. 361–91. [G: U.S.; W. Europe]

Miyazaki, Hajime. Work Norms and Involuntary Unemployment. *Quart. J. Econ.*, May 1984, *99*(2), pp. 297–311.

Odagiri, Hiroyuki. The Firm as a Collection of Human Resources. In *Wiles, P. and Routh, G., eds.*, 1984, pp. 190–206.

Osterman, Paul. Introduction: The Nature and Importance of Internal Labor Markets. In *Osterman, P., ed.*, 1984, pp. 1–22.

Pachter, Henry. The Right to be Lazy. In *Pachter, H.*, 1984, *1956*, pp. 3–15.

Poole, Michael. A Framework for Analysis and an Appraisal of Main Developments. In *Poole, M., et al.*, 1984, pp. 41–94. [G: U.K.]

Pulliam, Mark S. Legal Aspects of Exclusive Representation: Ruminations on the Private–Public Sector Analogy. *J. Lab. Res.*, Fall 1984, *5*(4), pp. 351–70. [G: U.S.]

Rosner, Menachem. Report from the International Workshop on Workplace Democracy and the Community of Tel-Aviv, 8–12 April, 1984. *Econ. Anal. Worker's Manage.*, 1984, *18*(4), pp. 399–403.

Rubery, Jill; Tarling, Roger and Wilkinson, Frank. Industrial Relations Issues in the 1980s: An Economic Analysis. In *Poole, M., et al.*, 1984, pp. 97–137. [G: U.K.]

Rürup, Bert and Struwe, Jochen. Arbeitszeitflexibilisierung als Instrument der Beschäftigungspolitik. (Flexibilisation of Working Times as an Instrument of Employment Policies. With English summary.) *Konjunkturpolitik*, 1984, *30*(1), pp. 1–22. **[G: W. Germany]**

Schneider, Benjamin. Industrial and Organizational Psychology Perspective. In *Brief, A. P., ed.*, 1984, pp. 174–206.

Shalev, Michael. Labor, State, and Crisis: An Israeli Case Study. *Ind. Relat.*, Fall 1984, *23*(3), pp. 362–86. **[G: Israel]**

Soskice, David. Industrial Relations and the British Economy, 1979–1983. *Ind. Relat.*, Fall 1984, *23*(3), pp. 306–22. **[G: U.K.]**

Svirchevskii, V. and Nikol'skii, D. Developing the Brigade Form of Organizing and Stimulating Industrial Labor. *Prob. Econ.*, September 1984, *27*(5), pp. 85–90. **[G: U.S.S.R.]**

Thanawala, Kishor. Solidarity: Reflections and Prospects. *Rev. Soc. Econ.*, December 1984, *42*(3), pp. 427–32.

Waters, William R. Development of Solidarist Economics in the U.S. *Int. J. Soc. Econ.*, 1984, *11*(1/2), pp. 100–116. **[G: U.S.]**

Wood, W. D., et al. Collective Bargaining: Summary Outline. In *Wood, W. D. and Kumar, P., eds.*, 1984, pp. 295–426. **[G: Canada]**

8331 Labor–Management Relations in Private Sector

Addison, John T. Trade Unions, Corporatism, and Inflation. *J. Lab. Res.*, Winter 1984, *5*(1), pp. 39–62.

Akerlof, George A. Labor Contracts as Partial Gift Exchange. In *Akerlof, G. A.*, 1984, *1982*, pp. 145–74. **[G: U.S.]**

Alexander, Kenneth O. The Promise and Perils of Worker Participation in Management. *Amer. J. Econ. Soc.*, April 1984, *43*(2), pp. 197–204. **[G: U.S.]**

Armstrong, E. G. A. Employers Associations in Great Britain. In *Windmuller, J. P. and Gladstone, A., eds.*, 1984, pp. 44–78. **[G: U.K.]**

Ashenfelter, Orley C. and Bloom, David E. Models of Arbitrator Behavior: Theory and Evidence. *Amer. Econ. Rev.*, March 1984, *74*(1), pp. 111–24. **[G: U.S.]**

Beatty, Bess. Textile Labor in the North Carolina Piedmont: Mill Owner Images and Mill Worker Response, 1830–1900. *Labor Hist.*, Fall 1984, *25*(4), pp. 485–503. **[G: U.S.]**

Behrend, Hilde. A Fair Day's Work. In *Behrend, H.*, 1984, *1961*, pp. 145–63.

Behrend, Hilde. Financial Incentives as the Expression of a System of Beliefs. In *Behrend, H.*, 1984, *1959*, pp. 132–44.

Behrend, Hilde. In-Company Criteria for Evaluating Absences. In *Behrend, H.*, 1984, pp. 90–109. **[G: U.K.]**

Behrend, Hilde. Problems of Labour and Inflation: Concluding Comments. In *Behrend, H.*, 1984, pp. 224–43.

Behrend, Hilde. Some Aspects of Company Wage Policy. In *Behrend, H.*, 1984, pp. 164–77.

Behrend, Hilde. The Effort Bargain. In *Behrend, H.*, 1984, *1957*, pp. 110–31.

Behrend, Hilde. Voluntary Absence from Work. In *Behrend, H.*, 1984, *1959*, pp. 58–89. **[G: U.K.]**

Bequele, Assefa. The Costs and Benefits of Protecting and Saving Lives at Work: Some Issues. *Int. Lab. Rev.*, January-February 1984, *123*(1), pp. 1–16.

Biles, Roger. Ed Crump versus the Unions: The Labor Movement in Memphis during the 1930s. *Labor Hist.*, Fall 1984, *25*(4), pp. 533–52. **[G: U.S.]**

Blandy, Richard. The Future of Australia's Industrial Relations System: A Summary and Comment. *Australian Bull. Lab.*, Supplement September 1984, *10*(5), pp. S1–S10. **[G: Australia]**

Blumenthal, Tuvia. Some Reflections on the Japanese Motivation System. In *Aoki, M., ed.*, 1984, pp. 413–16. **[G: Japan]**

Blyton, Paul. Some Old and New Problems in Employee Participation in Decision-making. *Int. Soc. Sci. J.*, 1984, *36*(2), pp. 217–32.

Bowles, Samuel; Gordon, David M. and Weisskopf, Thomas E. A Social Model for U.S. Productivity Growth. *Challenge*, March/April 1984, *27*(1), pp. 41–48. **[G: U.S.]**

Braun, Jerome S. Industrial Justice in a Practical Sense. *Rev. Soc. Econ.*, December 1984, *42*(3), pp. 318–27.

Bronstein, Arturo S. Industrial Relations in Latin America: Employers' Organizations. In *Córdova, E., ed.*, 1984, pp. 53–67. **[G: Latin America]**

Bunel, Jean and Saglio, Jean. Employers Associations in France. In *Windmuller, J. P. and Gladstone, A., eds.*, 1984, pp. 232–63. **[G: France]**

Bunn, Ronald F. Employers Association in the Federal Republic of Germany. In *Windmuller, J. P. and Gladstone, A., eds.*, 1984, pp. 169–201. **[G: W. Germany]**

Carter, Michael R. Resource Allocation and Use under Collective Rights and Labour Management in Peruvian Coastal Agriculture. *Econ. J.*, December 1984, *94*(376), pp. 826–46. **[G: Peru]**

Chang, Chien-Min and Chen, Kar-Nin Peter. Factors Affecting Industrial Relations in the Electronics Industry of Hong Kong—An Empirical Research Analysis. *Managerial Dec. Econ.*, June 1984, *5*(2), pp. 104–15. **[G: Hong Kong]**

Charnovitz, Steve. Caribbean Basin Initiative: Setting Labor Standards. *Mon. Lab. Rev.*, November 1984, *107*(11), pp. 54–56. **[G: Caribbean]**

Chomitz, Kenneth M. and Lave, Charles A. Part-Time Labour, Work Rules, and Urban Transit Costs. *J. Transp. Econ. Policy*, January 1984, *18*(1), pp. 63–73. **[G: U.S.]**

Clark, Gregory. Authority and Efficiency: The Labor Market and the Managerial Revolution of

the Late Nineteenth Century. *J. Econ. Hist.*, December 1984, *44*(4), pp. 1069–83.
[G: U.S.; U.K.]

Conard, Alfred F. The Supervision of Corporate Management: A Comparison of Developments in European Community and United States Law. *Mich. Law Rev.*, April–May 1984, *82*(5 & 6), pp. 1459–88. [G: U.S.; EEC]

Córdova, Efrén. Other Features of Labor Relations at the Undertaking Level. **In** *Córdova, E., ed.*, 1984, pp. 129–46.
[G: Latin America]

Córdova, Efrén. The Latin American Picture. **In** *Córdova, E., ed.*, 1984, pp. 3–24.
[G: Latin America]

Córdova, Efrén. Workers' Participation in Management. **In** *Córdova, E., ed.*, 1984, pp. 109–27. [G: Latin America]

Curtis, Fred. "Cheap" African Labor-Power and South African Capitalism: 1948–1978. **In** *Zarembka, P., ed.*, 1984, pp. 185–235.
[G: S. Africa]

Davies, Annette. Management-Union Participation during Microtechnological Change. **In** *Warner, M., ed.*, 1984, pp. 149–70.
[G: U.K.]

Derber, Milton. Employers Associations in the United States. **In** *Windmuller, J. P. and Gladstone, A., eds.*, 1984, pp. 79–114. [G: U.S.]

Downer, Alexander. The Future of Australian Industrial Relations. *Australian Bull. Lab.*, Supplement September 1984, *10*(5), pp. S11–S23.
[G: Australia]

Drago, Robert and McDonough, Terry. Capitalist Shopfloor Initiatives, Restructuring, and Organizing in the '80s. *Rev. Radical Polit. Econ.*, Winter 1984, *16*(4), pp. 52–71.

Dufty, Norman F. Employers Associations in Australia. **In** *Windmuller, J. P. and Gladstone, A., eds.*, 1984, pp. 115–48. [G: Australia]

Elliott, Ralph D. and Huffman, James R. The Impact of Right-to-Work Laws on Employer Unfair Labor Practice Charges. *J. Lab. Res.*, Spring 1984, *5*(2), pp. 165–76. [G: U.S.]

Elwell, Karen and Feuille, Peter. Arbitration Awards and *Gardner-Denver* Lawsuits: One Bite or Two? *Ind. Relat.*, Spring 1984, *23*(2), pp. 287–97. [G: U.S.]

Fadem, Joel A. Automation and Work Design in the U.S.: Case Studies of Quality of Working Life Impacts. **In** *Warner, M., ed.*, 1984, pp. 294–310. [G: U.S.]

Flanagan, Robert J. Wage Concessions and Long-Term Union Wage Flexibility. *Brookings Pap. Econ. Act.*, 1984, (1), pp. 183–216. [G: U.S.]

Ford, Bill. Technology, Women and Employment: The Australian Experience. **In** *Warner, M., ed.*, 1984, pp. 339–48. [G: Australia]

Foster, James C. Western Miners and Silicosis: "The Scourge of the Underground Toiler," 1890–1943. *Ind. Lab. Relat. Rev.*, April 1984, *37*(3), pp. 371–85. [G: U.S.]

Frease, Dean E. Workers' Rights and Freedoms. *Can. Public Policy*, June 1984, *10*(2), pp. 235–38. [G: Canada]

Friedman, Samuel R. The Work Process and Worker Mobilization among Teamster Drivers. **In** *Zarembka, P., ed.*, 1984, pp. 161–83.

Furubotn, Eirik G. and Wiggins, Steven N. Plant Closings, Worker Reallocation Costs and Efficiency Gains to Labor Representation on Boards of Directors. *Z. ges. Staatswiss.*, March 1984, *140*(1), pp. 176–92. [G: U.S.]

Gitelman, H. M. Being of Two Minds: American Employers Confront the Labor Problem, 1915–1919. *Labor Hist.*, Spring 1984, 25(2), pp. 189–216. [G: U.S.]

Gladstone, Alan. Employers Associations in Comparative Perspective: Functions and Activities. **In** *Windmuller, J. P. and Gladstone, A., eds.*, 1984, pp. 24–43. [G: OECD]

Glick, Henry A. and Feuer, Michael J. Employer-sponsored Training and the Governance of Specific Human Capital Investments. *Quart. Rev. Econ. Bus.*, Summer 1984, *24*(2), pp. 91–103.

Goldthorpe, John H. The End of Convergence: Corporatist and Dualist Tendencies in Modern Western Societies. **In** *Goldthorpe, J. H., ed.*, 1984, pp. 315–43.

Gordon, Michael E.; Beauvais, Laura L. and Ladd, Robert T. The Job Satisfaction and Union Commitment of Unionized Engineers. *Ind. Lab. Relat. Rev.*, April 1984, 37(3), pp. 359–70. [G: U.S.]

Greenberg, Edward S. Producer Cooperatives and Democratic Theory: The Case of the Plywood Firms. **In** *Jackall, R. and Levin, H. M., eds.*, 1984, pp. 171–214. [G: U.S.]

Griffin, Tony. Technological Change and Craft Control in the Newspaper Industry: An International Comparison. *Cambridge J. Econ.*, March 1984, *8*(1), pp. 41–61. [G: U.S.; U.K.; Australia]

Gunn, Christopher. Hoedads Co-op and Cooperation at Work. **In** *Jackall, R. and Levin, H. M., eds.*, 1984, pp. 141–70.
[G: U.S.]

Guzda, Henry P. Industrial Democracy: Made in the U.S.A. *Mon. Lab. Rev.*, May 1984, *107*(5), pp. 26–33. [G: U.S.]

Hanson, Charles and Rathkey, Paul. Industrial Democracy: A Post-Bullock Shopfloor View. *Brit. J. Ind. Relat.*, July 1984, *22*(2), pp. 154–68. [G: U.K.]

Harrison, Bennett. The International Movement for Prenotification of Plant Closures. *Ind. Relat.*, Fall 1984, 23(3), pp. 387–409.
[G: U.S.; Europe]

Heery, Edmund. Group Incentives and the Mining Supervisor: The Effects of a Payment System on First-Line Management. *Brit. J. Ind. Relat.*, November 1984, 22(3), pp. 333–45.
[G: U.K.]

Hettlage, Robert. Interest-Group Conflict, Consensus-building, and "Cooperative Bargaining": The Swiss Industrial Peace Agreement as a Model. *Z. ges. Staatswiss.*, September 1984, *140*(3), pp. 475–99. [G: Switzerland]

Hopt, Klaus J. New Ways in Corporate Governance: European Experiments with Labor Representation on Corporate Boards. *Mich.*

Law Rev., April–May 1984, *82*(5 & 6), pp. 1338–63. [G: W. Europe]

Humphrey, John. Labor in the Brazilian Motor Vehicle Industry. In *Kronish, R. and Mericle, K. S., eds.*, 1984, pp. 95–131. [G: Brazil]

Ishikawa, Akihiro. Japanese Trade-Unionism in a Changing Environment. *Int. Soc. Sci. J.*, 1984, *36*(2), pp. 271–83. [G: Japan]

Ishikawa, Akihiro. Microelectronics and Japanese Industrial Relations. In *Warner, M., ed.*, 1984, pp. 349–60. [G: Japan]

Jackall, Robert. Paradoxes of Collective Work: A Study of the Cheeseboard, Berkeley, California. In *Jackall, R. and Levin, H. M., eds.*, 1984, pp. 109–35. [G: U.S.]

Jackall, Robert and Crain, Joyce. The Shape of the Small Worker Cooperative Movement. In *Jackall, R. and Levin, H. M., eds.*, 1984, pp. 88–108. [G: U.S.]

Jackall, Robert and Levin, Henry M. Work in America and the Cooperative Movement. In *Jackall, R. and Levin, H. M., eds.*, 1984, pp. 3–15. [G: U.S.]

Jones, Derek C. American Producer Cooperatives and Employee-Owned Firms: A Historical Perspective. In *Jackall, R. and Levin, H. M., eds.*, 1984, pp. 37–56. [G: U.S.]

Joyce, Paul and Woods, Adrian. The Management of Conflict: A Quantitative Analysis. *Brit. J. Ind. Relat.*, March 1984, *22*(1), pp. 63–77. [G: U.K.]

Kain, Peter G. Reshaping Australia's Industrial Relations System for the Future. *Australian Bull. Lab.*, Supplement September 1984, *10*(5), pp. S24–S35. [G: Australia]

Kanter, Rosabeth Moss. Variations in Managerial Career Structures in High-Technology Firms: The Impact of Organizational Characteristics on Internal Labor Market Patterns. In *Osterman, P., ed.*, 1984, *1983*, pp. 109–31.

Kleiner, Morris M. Unionism and Employer Discrimination: Analysis of 8(a)(3) Violations. *Ind. Relat.*, Spring 1984, *23*(2), pp. 234–43. [G: U.S.]

Kochan, Thomas A. and Cappelli, Peter. The Transformation of the Industrial Relations and Personnel Function. In *Osterman, P., ed.*, 1984, pp. 133–61.

Kochan, Thomas A.; McKersie, Robert B. and Cappelli, Peter. Strategic Choice and Industrial Relations Theory. *Ind. Relat.*, Winter 1984, *23*(1), pp. 16–39. [G: U.S.]

Koike, Kazuo. Skill Formation Systems in the U.S. and Japan: A Comparative Study. In *Aoki, M., ed.*, 1984, pp. 47–75. [G: U.S.; Japan]

Kosters, Marvin H. Wage Concessions and Long-Term Union Wage Flexibility: Comments. *Brookings Pap. Econ. Act.*, 1984, (1), pp. 217–20. [G: U.S.]

Kübler, Friedrich. Dual Loyalty of Labor Representatives. In *Hopt, K. J. and Teubner, G., eds.*, 1984, pp. 429–44. [G: W. Germany]

Levin, Henry M. ESOPs and the Financing of Worker Cooperatives. In *Jackall, R. and Levin, H. M., eds.*, 1984, pp. 245–56. [G: U.S.]

Levine, Solomon B. Employers Associations in

Japan. In *Windmuller, J. P. and Gladstone, A., eds.*, 1984, pp. 318–56. [G: Japan]

Levitan, Sar A. and Werneke, Diane. Worker Participation and Productivity Change. *Mon. Lab. Rev.*, September 1984, *107*(9), pp. 28–33. [G: U.S.]

Lewchuk, Wayne A. The Role of the British Government in the Spread of Scientific Management and Fordism in the Interwar Years. *J. Econ. Hist.*, June 1984, *44*(2), pp. 355–61. [G: U.K.]

Lindner, Clausjohann. Demokratisierung von Organisationen und Leistungssteigerung. (Democratisation of Organisations and Performance. With English summary.) *Z. Wirtschaft. Sozialwissen.*, 1984, *104*(1), pp. 45–74.

Lindsay, Franklin A.; Rubin, Jerome S. and Cohen, Richard L. The Need for New Private and Public Policies. In *Wachter, M. L. and Wachter, S. M., eds.*, 1984, pp. 115–43. [G: U.S.]

Lohman, Jeff and Mayer, Henry C. Top Notch Is More than a Slogan. *Rev. Soc. Econ.*, December 1984, *42*(3), pp. 330–38. [G: U.S.]

Lundine, Stan. Motivation and New Technologies: Comment. In *Wachter, M. L. and Wachter, S. M., eds.*, 1984, pp. 179–82. [G: U.S.]

Maccoby, Michael. Helping Labor and Management Set Up a Quality-of-Worklife Program. *Mon. Lab. Rev.*, March 1984, *107*(3), pp. 28–32. [G: U.S.]

MaCoy, Ramelle and Morand, Martin J. STC and Labor–Management Cooperation. In *MaCoy, R. and Morand, M. J., eds.*, 1984, pp. 183–95. [G: U.S.]

Marginson, Paul M. The Distinctive Effects of Plant and Company Size on Workplace Industrial Relations. *Brit. J. Ind. Relat.*, March 1984, *22*(1), pp. 1–14. [G: U.K.]

Martin, Roderick. New Technology and Industrial Relations in Fleet Street: 'New Technology Will Make it Possible for Managers to Manage.' In *Warner, M., ed.*, 1984, pp. 240–52. [G: U.K.]

Martinelli, Alberto and Treu, Tiziano. Employers Associations in Italy. In *Windmuller, J. P. and Gladstone, A., eds.*, 1984, pp. 264–93. [G: Italy]

Maruo, Naomi. Productivity Improvement in Japan: An Econometric Analysis. In *Intn'l. Productivity Symp.*, 1984, pp. 219–65. [G: Japan]

Maurice, Marc; Sellier, François and Silvestre, Jean-Jacques. Rules, Contexts, and Actors' Observations Based on a Comparison between France and Germany. *Brit. J. Ind. Relat.*, November 1984, *22*(3), pp. 346–63. [G: France; Germany]

Maurice, Marc; Sellier, François and Silvestre, Jean-Jacques. The Search for a Societal Effect in the Production of Company Hierarchy: A Comparison of France and Germany. In *Osterman, P., ed.*, 1984, pp. 231–70. [G: W. Germany; France]

McCormick, Brian J. Personnel Management. In

Pickering, J. F. and Cockerill, T. A. J., eds., 1984, pp. 179–220.   **[G: U.S.; U.K.]**

McKenzie, Richard B. Summary Remarks. In McKenzie, R. B., ed. (II), 1984, pp. 309–13.   **[G: U.S.]**

McLachlan, Ian. Principles for the Future of Australian Industrial Relations. *Australian Bull. Lab.*, Supplement September 1984, *10*(5), pp. S62–S69.   **[G: Australia]**

McMurray, David. Labour Legislation and Policy: Summary Outline. In Wood, W. D. and Kumar, P., eds., 1984, pp. 93–216.   **[G: Canada]**

Miller, Ronald L. Arbitration in New Zealand: Mediation Plus Decision Making. *Ind. Relat.*, Winter 1984, *23*(1), pp. 126–38.   **[G: New Zealand]**

Mroczkowski, Tomasz. Is the American Labour–Management Relationship Changing? *Brit. J. Ind. Relat.*, March 1984, *22*(1), pp. 47–62.   **[G: Japan; U.S.; W. Europe]**

Murphy, John W. Organizational Issues in Worker Ownership: Problems of Organizational Order in Worker Control of Production in Plants Dropped as Obsolete. *Amer. J. Econ. Soc.*, July 1984, *43*(3), pp. 287–99.

Murrin, Thomas J. Motivation and New Technologies: Comment. In Wachter, M. L. and Wachter, S. M., eds., 1984, pp. 175–78.   **[G: U.S.]**

Nemirow, Martin. Work-Sharing Approaches: Past and Present. *Mon. Lab. Rev.*, September 1984, *107*(9), pp. 34–39.   **[G: U.S.; Germany]**

Noakes, Bryan. The Future of Australian Industrial Relations Systems. *Australian Bull. Lab.*, Supplement September 1984, *10*(5), pp. S49–S61.   **[G: Australia]**

Okuno, Masahiro. Corporate Loyalty and Bonus Payments: An Analysis of Work Incentives in Japan. In Aoki, M., ed., 1984, pp. 387–411.   **[G: Japan]**

Overbeck, Egon. "Co-Determination at Company Level." In Engels, W. and Pohl, H., eds., 1984, pp. 11–17.   **[G: W. Germany]**

Parpart, Jane L. The "Labor Aristocracy" Debate in Africa: The Copperbelt Case, 1924–1967. *African Econ. Hist.*, 1984, (13), pp. 171–91.   **[G: Africa]**

Reber, Robert A.; Wallen, Jerry A. and Chhokar, Jagdeep S. Reducing Industrial Accidents: A Behavioral Experiment. *Ind. Relat.*, Winter 1984, *23*(1), pp. 119–25.   **[G: U.S.]**

Regini, Marino. The Conditions for Political Exchange: How Concertation Emerged and Collapsed in Italy and Great Britain. In Goldthorpe, J. H., ed., 1984, pp. 124–42.   **[G: U.K.; Italy]**

Reynolds, Morgan O. Union Violence: A Review Article. *J. Lab. Res.*, Summer 1984, *5*(3), pp. 237–46.   **[G: U.S.]**

Roberts, Markley. A Labor Perspective on Technological Change. In Collins, E. L. and Tanner, L. D., eds., 1984, pp. 183–205.   **[G: U.S.]**

Rosen, Corey; Whyte, William Foote and Blasi, Joseph. Creating a More Participatory Econ-

omy. In Alperovitz, G. and Skurski, R., eds., 1984, pp. 141–66.

Rosner, David and Markowitz, Gerald. Safety and Health on the Job as a Class Issue: The Workers' Health Bureau of America in the 1920s. *Sci. Soc.*, Winter 1984-1985, *48*(4), pp. 464–82.   **[G: U.S.]**

Rothwell, Sheila G. Company Employment Policies and New Technology in Manufacturing and Service Sectors. In Warner, M., ed., 1984, pp. 111–33.   **[G: U.K.]**

Rush, Howard and Williams, Robin. Consultation and Change: New Technology and Manpower in the Electronics Industry. In Warner, M., ed., 1984, pp. 171–88.   **[G: U.K.]**

Ryan, Paul. Job Training, Employment Practices, and the Large Enterprise: The Case of Costly Transferable Skills. In Osterman, P., ed., 1984, pp. 191–229.   **[G: U.S.]**

Sakudō, Yōtarō. Labor Management Practices and Philosophy of a Spinning Company in the Early Showa Period—Riemon Uno and Toyobo Himeji Factory. (In Japanese. With English summary.) *Osaka Econ. Pap.*, December 1984, *34*(2–3), pp. 345–61.   **[G: Japan]**

Schlicht, Ekkehart. Plant Closings, Worker Reallocation Costs and Efficiency Gains to Labor Representation on Board of Directors: Comment. *Z. ges. Staatswiss.*, March 1984, *140*(1), pp. 193–94.

Schott, Kerry. Investment, Order and Conflict in a Simple Dynamic Model of Capitalism. In Goldthorpe, J. H., ed., 1984, pp. 81–97.

Shirom, Arie. Employers Associations in Israel. In Windmuller, J. P. and Gladstone, A., eds., 1984, pp. 294–317.   **[G: Israel]**

Skogh, Göran. Employers Associations in Sweden. In Windmuller, J. P. and Gladstone, A., eds., 1984, pp. 149–68.   **[G: Sweden]**

Sockell, Donna. The Legality of Employee-Participation Programs in Unionized Firms. *Ind. Lab. Relat. Rev.*, July 1984, *37*(4), pp. 541–56.   **[G: U.S.]**

Spinrad, William. Work Democracy: An Overview. *Int. Soc. Sci. J.*, 1984, *36*(2), pp. 195–215.

Spyropoulos, Georges. Working Conditions in the Industrial Nations: What Lies Ahead? *Int. Lab. Rev.*, July–August 1984, *123*(4), pp. 391–404.   **[G: OECD]**

Stieber, Jack. Most U.S. Workers Still May Be Fired under the Employment-at-Will Doctrine. *Mon. Lab. Rev.*, May 1984, *107*(5), pp. 34–38.   **[G: U.S.]**

Stollenwerk, James H. *Rexworks:* A Case Study of Applied Social Economic Justice. *Rev. Soc. Econ.*, December 1984, *42*(3), pp. 253–56.   **[G: U.S.]**

Streeck, Wolfgang. Neo-Corporatist Industrial Relations and the Economic Crisis in West Germany. In Goldthorpe, J. H., ed., 1984, pp. 291–314.   **[G: W. Germany]**

Taira, Koji. The Management of Employment Adjustment in Electric and Electronics Firms in the 1970s. *Rivista Int. Sci. Econ. Com.*, September 1984, *31*(9), pp. 833–43.   **[G: Japan]**

Thakur, C. P. Computers, Manpower and the Indian Labour Market: Some Experiences in a Labour-Surplus Economy. In *Warner, M., ed.*, 1984, pp. 325–38.   [G: India]

Treu, Tiziano. Nuove tecnologie e (vecchie) relazioni industriali. (New Technologies and [Old] Industrial Relations. With English summary.) *L'Impresa*, 1984, *26*(2), pp. 83–86. [G: Italy]

Vasche, Jon David. Unemployment Benefits for Work Sharing: A Further Consideration. *Bus. Econ.*, April 1984, *19*(3), pp. 59–61.
[G: U.S.]

van Voorden, William. Employers Associations in the Netherlands. In *Windmuller, J. P. and Gladstone, A., eds.*, 1984, pp. 202–31.
[G: Netherlands]

Wallace, Phyllis A. Motivation and New Technologies: Comment. In *Wachter, M. L. and Wachter, S. M., eds.*, 1984, pp. 171–75.
[G: U.S.]

Weber, Wolfgang. The Impact of Population Change on Enterprise Behavior. In *Steinmann, G., ed.*, 1984, pp. 404–15.

Whiffin, R. A. The Future Course of Australian Industrial Relations. *Australian Bull. Lab.*, Supplement September 1984, *10*(5), pp. S36–S48.   [G: Australia]

Willman, Paul and Cowan, Rowena. New Technology in Banking: The Impact of Autotellers on Staff Numbers. In *Warner, M., ed.*, 1984, pp. 224–39.   [G: U.K.]

Wilpert, Bernhard. Participation in Organizations: Evidence from International Comparative Research. *Int. Soc. Sci. J.*, 1984, *36*(2), pp. 355–66.   [G: W. Europe]

Windmuller, John P. Employers Associations in Comparative Perspective: Organization, Structure, Administration. In *Windmuller, J. P. and Gladstone, A., eds.*, 1984, pp. 1–23.
[G: OECD]

Yankelovich, Daniel and Immerwahr, John. The Work Ethic and Economic Vitality. In *Wachter, M. L. and Wachter, S. M., eds.*, 1984, pp. 144–70.   [G: U.S.]

Yudken, Joel S. Conversion in the Aerospace Industry: The McDonnell Douglas Project. In *Gordon, S. and McFadden, D., eds.*, 1984, pp. 130–43.   [G: U.S.]

8332 Labor–Management Relations in Public Sector

DiLorenzo, Thomas J. Exclusive Representation in Public Employment: A Public Choice Perspective. *J. Lab. Res.*, Fall 1984, *5*(4), pp. 371–89.   [G: U.S.]

Horvat, Branko. Two Widespread Ideological Deviations in Contemporary Yugoslav Society. *Eastern Europ. Econ.*, Fall 1984, *23*(1), pp. 45–57.   [G: Yugoslavia]

Jones, Derek C. and Schneider, Donald J. Self-Help Production Cooperatives: Government-Administered Cooperatives during the Depression. In *Jackall, R. and Levin, H. M., eds.*, 1984, pp. 57–84.   [G: U.S.]

Krawchenko, Bohdan. Workers and Bosses in the

USSR: Aspects of Their Relationship. In *Zarembka, P., ed.*, 1984, pp. 269–83.
[G: U.S.S.R.]

Reid, Joseph D., Jr. and Kurth, Michael M. The Contribution of Exclusive Representation to Union Strength. *J. Lab. Res.*, Fall 1984, *5*(4), pp. 391–412.   [G: U.S.]

840 DEMOGRAPHIC ECONOMICS

841 Demographic Economics

8410 Demographic Economics

Abercrombie, Keith and McCormack, Arthur. Population Growth and Food Supplies in Different Time Perspectives. In *Ghosh, P. K., ed., no. 6*, 1984, *1976*, pp. 18–39.   [G: Global]

Adelman, Carol. Baby Feat. *Policy Rev.*, Summer 1984, (29), pp. 80–82.   [G: Global]

Ahlburg, Dennis A. and Schapiro, Morton Owen. Socioeconomic Ramifications of Changing Cohort Size: An Analysis of U.S. Postwar Suicide Rates by Age and Sex. *Demography*, February 1984, *21*(1), pp. 97–108.   [G: U.S.]

Ainsworth, Martha. Population Policy: Country Experience. *Finance Develop.*, September 1984, *21*(3), pp. 18–20.   [G: Mexico; Indonesia; India]

Akin, John S.; Guilkey, David K. and Popkin, Barry M. Response to: "A Comment on J. Akin et al., 'Determinants of Breastfeeding in Sri Lanka.'" *Demography*, November 1984, *21*(4), pp. 687–88.   [G: Sri Lanka]

Alston, Lee J. and Schapiro, Morton Owen. Inheritance Laws across Colonies: Causes and Consequences. *J. Econ. Hist.*, June 1984, *44*(2), pp. 277–87.   [G: U.S.]

Altimir, Oscar. Poverty, Income Distribution and Child Welfare in Latin America: A Comparison of Pre- and Post-Recession Data. *World Devel.*, March 1984, *12*(3), pp. 261–82.   [G: Chile; Colombia; Costa Rica; Panama; Venezuela]

Altimir, Oscar. Poverty, Income Distribution and Child Welfare in Latin America: A Comparison of Pre- and Post-recession Data. In *Jolly, R. and Cornia, G. A., eds.*, 1984, pp. 91–112.
[G: Latin America]

Anderson, Otto. The Decline in Danish Mortality before 1850 and Its Economic and Social Background. In *Bengtsson, T.; Fridlizius, G. and Ohlsson, R., eds.*, 1984, pp. 115–26.
[G: Denmark]

Anker, Richard and Farooq, Ghazi M. Population and Socio-economic Development: The New Perspective. In *Ghosh, P. K., ed., no. 5*, 1984, *1978*, pp. 265–79.

Anselin, Luc. Specification Tests and Model Selection for Aggregate Spatial Interaction: An Empirical Comparison. *J. Reg. Sci.*, February 1984, *24*(1), pp. 1–15.   [G: Canada]

Arriaga, Eduardo E. Measuring and Explaining the Change in Life Expectancies. *Demography*, February 1984, *21*(1), pp. 83–96.
[G: U.S.]

Arthur, W. Brian. The Analysis of Linkages in

Demographic Theory. *Demography*, February 1984, *21*(1), pp. 109–28.

Ashton, Basil, et al. Famine in China, 1958–61. *Population Devel. Rev.*, December 1984, *10*(4), pp. 613–45. **[G: China]**

Atkinson, Anthony B. and Jenkins, S. P. The Steady-State Assumption and the Estimation of Distributional and Related Models. *J. Human Res.*, Summer 1984, *19*(3), pp. 358–76. **[G: U.S.]**

Auerbach, Alan J. and Kotlikoff, Laurence J. Social Security and the Economics of the Demographic Transition. In *Aaron, H. J. and Burtless, G., eds.*, 1984, pp. 255–76. **[G: U.S.]**

Azrael, Jeremy R. Emergent Nationality Problems in the USSR. In *Hoffmann, E. P. and Laird, R. F., eds.*, 1984, *1978*, pp. 607–31. **[G: U.S.S.R.]**

Bacci, Massimo Livi. Tendenze demografiche e fabbisogno di abitazioni. (Demographic Trends and Housing Requirements. With English summary.) *Bancaria*, July 1984, *40*(7), pp. 618–22. **[G: Italy]**

Bachu, Amara and O'Connell, Martin. Developing Current Fertility Indicators for Foreign-Born Women from the Current Population Survey. *Rev. Public Data Use*, October 1984, *12*(3), pp. 185–95. **[G: U.S.]**

Bailar, Barbara A. Nonresponse: What It Is and What We Do about It. *Statist. J.*, December 1984, *2*(4), pp. 381–92. **[G: U.S.]**

Banerjee, Biswajit. Rural-to-Urban Migration and Conjugal Separation: An Indian Case Study. *Econ. Develop. Cult. Change*, July 1984, *32*(4), pp. 767–80. **[G: India]**

Banister, Judith. An Analysis of Recent Data on the Population of China. *Population Devel. Rev.*, June 1984, *10*(2), pp. 241–71. **[G: China]**

Barnes, Roberta and Gillingham, Robert. Demographic Effects in Demand Analysis: Estimation of the Quadratic Expenditure System Using Microdata. *Rev. Econ. Statist.*, November 1984, *66*(4), pp. 591–601. **[G: U.S.]**

Bartlett, Robin L. and Callahan, Charles, III. Wage Determination and Marital Status: Another Look. *Ind. Relat.*, Winter 1984, *23*(1), pp. 90–96. **[G: U.S.]**

Bates, Timothy. Black Economic Well-Being Since the 1950s. *Rev. Black Polit. Econ.*, Spring 1984, *12*(4), pp. 5–39. **[G: U.S.]**

Bauer, P. T. and Yamey, B. S. The Economics of Post-war Immigration Policy in British West Africa. In *Bauer, P. T.*, 1984, pp. 128–39. **[G: Nigeria; Gold Coast]**

Bausell, Charles W., Jr. and Anders, Gary C. Impacts of Back to the Land Policies. *J. Devel. Econ.*, April 1984, *14*(3), pp. 429–39. **[G: LDCs]**

Bean, Frank D., et al. Generational Differences in Fertility among Mexican Americans: Implications for Assessing the Effects of Immigration. *Soc. Sci. Quart.*, June 1984, *65*(2), pp. 573–82. **[G: U.S.]**

Behrman, Jere R. and Wolfe, Barbara L. A More General Approach to Fertility Determination

in a Developing Country: The Importance of Biological Supply Considerations, Endogenous Tastes and Unperceived Jointness. *Economica*, August 1984, *51*(203), pp. 319–39. **[G: Nicaragua]**

Beier, George J. Can Third World Cities Cope? In *Ghosh, P. K., ed., no. 2*, 1984, *1976*, pp. 57–95. **[G: LDCs; MDCs]**

Bengtsson, Tommy. Harvest Fluctuations and Demographic Response: Southern Sweden 1751–1859. In *Bengtsson, T.; Fridlizius, G. and Ohlsson, R., eds.*, 1984, pp. 329–55. **[G: Sweden]**

Bennett, Neil G. and Horiuchi, Shiro. Mortality Estimation from Registered Deaths in Less Developed Countries. *Demography*, May 1984, *21*(2), pp. 217–33. **[G: Argentina]**

Berger, Mark C. Cohort Size and the Earnings Growth of Young Workers. *Ind. Lab. Relat. Rev.*, July 1984, *37*(4), pp. 582–91. **[G: U.S.]**

Berthold, Norbert and Roppel, Ulrich. Demographic Change and Old-Age Security. In *Steinmann, G., ed.*, 1984, pp. 218–37. **[G: W. Germany]**

Bhat, P. N. Mari and Kanbargi, R. Estimating the Incidence of Widow and Widower Re-Marriages in India from Census Data. *Population Stud.*, March 1984, *38*(1), pp. 89–103. **[G: India]**

Birdsall, Nancy. Analytical Approaches to the Relationship of Population Growth and Development. In *Ghosh, P. K., ed., no. 5*, 1984, *1977*, pp. 177–220.

Birdsall, Nancy. Health Planning and Population in Africa. In *Ghosh, P. K., ed., no. 6*, 1984, *1976*, pp. 352–69. **[G: Africa]**

Birdsall, Nancy. Population Growth. *Finance Develop.*, September 1984, *21*(3), pp. 10–15. **[G: Global]**

Birg, Herwig. Demographic Aspects of Labour Market Efficiency. In *Steinmann, G., ed.*, 1984, pp. 303–92. **[G: W. Germany]**

Blake, Judith. Catholicism and Fertility: On Attitudes of Young Americans. *Population Devel. Rev.*, June 1984, *10*(2), pp. 329–40. **[G: U.S.]**

Blau, Francine D. The Use of Transfer Payments by Immigrants. *Ind. Lab. Relat. Rev.*, January 1984, *37*(2), pp. 222–39. **[G: U.S.]**

Bloom, David E. and Trussell, James. What Are the Determinants of Delayed Childbearing and Permanent Childlessness in the United States? *Demography*, November 1984, *21*(4), pp. 591–611. **[G: U.S.]**

Blundell, Richard and Walker, Ian. A Household Production Specification of Demographic Variables in Demand Analysis. *Econ. J.*, 1984 Supplement, *94*, pp. 59–68. **[G: U.K.]**

Bojadziev, George. Population Modelling by Second Order Differential Systems. In *Avula, X. J. R., et al.*, 1984, pp. 939–41.

Böker, Fred. Über die Beschreibung von Wanderungsbewegungen mit Hilfe von Zählprozessen. (About the Description of Migrations Using Counting Processes. With English summary.) *Ifo-Studien*, 1984, *30*(4), pp. 307–15. **[G: W. Germany]**

Bongaarts, John. Implications of Future Fertility Trends for Contraceptive Practice. *Population Devel. Rev.*, June 1984, *10*(2), pp. 341–52. **[G: Global]**

Bongaarts, John; Frank, Odile and Lesthaeghe, Ron. The Proximate Determinants of Fertility in Sub-Saharan Africa. *Population Devel. Rev.*, September 1984, *10*(3), pp. 511–37. **[G: Africa]**

Booth, Heather. Transforming Gompertz's Function for Fertility Analysis: The Development of a Standard for the Relational Gompertz Function. *Population Stud.*, November 1984, *38*(3), pp. 495–506.

Boserup, Ester. Demographic Pressure, Growth and Productivity in an Historical Perspective. In *Amin, S., ed.*, 1984, pp. 20–32. **[G: OECD; U.S.S.R.; LDCs]**

Boserup, Ester. Technical Change and Human Fertility in Rural Areas of Developing Countries. In *Schutjer, W. A. and Stokes, C. S., eds.*, 1984, pp. 23–33. **[G: LDCs]**

Boskin, Michael J. Social Security and the Economics of the Demographic Transition: Comment. In *Aaron, H. J. and Burtless, G., eds.*, 1984, pp. 276–78. **[G: U.S.]**

Boswell, John Eastburn. *Expositio* and *Oblatio*: The Abandonment of Children and the Ancient and Medieval Family. *Amer. Hist. Rev.*, February 1984, *89*(1), pp. 10–33.

Boulding, Kenneth E. Sources of Reasonable Hope for the Future. *Amer. Econ. Rev.*, May 1984, *74*(2), pp. 221–25. **[G: Global]**

Boulier, Bryan L. and Rosenzweig, Mark R. Schooling, Search, and Spouse Selection: Testing Economic Theories of Marriage and Household Behavior. *J. Polit. Econ.*, August 1984, *92*(4), pp. 712–32. **[G: Philippines]**

von Braun, Joachim. Demographic-Economic Interaction in a Shrinking Agricultural Sector: Population and Labor Market Effects in the Federal Republic of Germany. In *Steinmann, G., ed.*, 1984, pp. 203–16. **[G: W. Germany]**

Breen, Richard. Population Trends in Late Nineteenth and Early Twentieth Century Ireland: A Local Study. *Econ. Soc. Rev.*, January 1984, *15*(2), pp. 95–108. **[G: Ireland]**

Bregger, John E. The Current Population Survey: A Historical Perspective and BLS' Role. *Mon. Lab. Rev.*, June 1984, *107*(6), pp. 8–14. **[G: U.S.]**

Brosnan, Peter. Australian Net Interstate Migration: 1911 to 1961. *Australian Econ. Hist. Rev.*, September 1984, *24*(2), pp. 150–72. **[G: Australia]**

Brouwer, Floor and Nijkamp, Peter. Linear Logit Models for Categorical Data in Spatial Mobility Analysis. *Econ. Geogr.*, April 1984, *60*(2), pp. 102–10. **[G: Netherlands]**

Brouwer, J.; Gordijn, H. E. and Heida, H. R. Toward Unravelling the Interdependency between Migration and Housing Stock Development: A Policy Model. In *ter Heide, H. and Willekens, F. J., eds.*, 1984, pp. 287–307. **[G: Netherlands]**

Brown, David L.; Heaton, Tim B. and Huffman, Benjamin L. Sociodemographic Pressures on Farmland Value in Nonmetropolitan America. *Soc. Sci. Quart.*, September 1984, *65*(3), pp. 789–802. **[G: U.S.]**

Brown, Lester R. The Urban Prospect: Reexamining the Basic Assumptions. In *Ghosh, P. K., ed., no. 2*, 1984, *1976*, pp. 96–108.

Bryceson, Deborah Fahy and Vuorela, Ulla. Outside the Domestic Labor Debate: Towards a Theory of Modes of Human Reproduction. *Rev. Radical Polit. Econ.*, Summer & Fall 1984, *16*(2&3), pp. 137–66. **[G: Global]**

Bubnys, Edward L. Ethnicity and Occupational Mobility: Chicago, 1870 and 1900. *Rev. Soc. Econ.*, April 1984, *42*(1), pp. 50–62. **[G: U.S.]**

Buhr, Walter. A Model of Regional Economic Growth Simulation Results for the Case of Population Decline. In *Steinmann, G., ed.*, 1984, pp. 147–66. **[G: W. Germany]**

Bulatao, Rodolfo A. Fertility Control at the Community Level: A Review of Research and Community Programs. In *Schutjer, W. A. and Stokes, C. S., eds.*, 1984, pp. 269–90. **[G: LDCs]**

Burgalassi, Silvano. La condizione anziana ad una svolta: oggetto o soggetto del proprio futuro? (Old Age at a Turning Point: Object or Subject of Its Future? With English summary.) *Giorn. Econ.*, Nov.-Dec. 1984, *43*(11–12), pp. 743–58.

Caldwell, John C. and Srinivasan, K. New Data on Nuptiality and Fertility in China. *Population Devel. Rev.*, March 1984, *10*(1), pp. 71–79. **[G: China]**

Carlson, Elwood D. Social Determinants of Low Birth Weight in a High-Risk Population. *Demography*, May 1984, *21*(2), pp. 207–15. **[G: U.S.]**

Chamberlin, John. Pension Plan Equity: The Debate Continued [Equity between the Sexes: The Pension Problem]. *J. Policy Anal. Manage.*, Fall 1984, *4*(1), pp. 121. **[G: U.S.]**

Choi, E. Kwan and Hicks, W. Whitney. Agricultural Mechanization Policy and Human Fertility. In *Schutjer, W. A. and Stokes, C. S., eds.*, 1984, pp. 252–68. **[G: LDCs]**

Cigno, Alessandro. Consumption vs. Procreation in Economic Growth. In *Steinmann, G., ed.*, 1984, pp. 2–28.

Cigno, Alessandro. Further Implications of Learning by Doing: The Effect of Population on Per-Capita Income. *Bull. Econ. Res.*, November 1984, *36*(2), pp. 97–108.

Cleland, J. G. and Sathar, Zeba Ayesha. The Effect of Birth Spacing on Childhood Mortality in Pakistan. *Population Stud.*, November 1984, *38*(3), pp. 401–18. **[G: Pakistan]**

Coale, Ansley J. Fertility in Prerevolutionary Rural China: In Defense of a Reassessment. *Population Devel. Rev.*, September 1984, *10*(3), pp. 471–80. **[G: China]**

Coale, Ansley J. The Demographic Transition. *Pakistan Devel. Rev.*, Winter 1984, *23*(4), pp. 531–52. **[G: OECD; LDCs]**

Cohn, Raymond L. Mortality on Immigrant Voyages to New York, 1836–1853. *J. Econ. Hist.*, June 1984, *44*(2), pp. 289–300. **[G: U.S.]**

Colombino, Ugo. An Econometric Investigation of the Condition of Children in Italy. *World Devel.*, March 1984, *12*(3), pp. 365–80. **[G: Italy]**

Colombino, Ugo. An Econometric Investigation of the Condition of Children in Italy. In *Jolly, R. and Cornia, G. A., eds.*, 1984, pp. 195–210. **[G: Italy]**

Conde, Julien. Rapid Population Growth in Developing Countries. In *Ghosh, P. K., ed., no. 5*, 1984, *1978*, pp. 102–25. **[G: Global]**

Condran, Gretchen A. An Evaluation of Estimates of Underenumeration in the Census and the Age Pattern of Mortality, Philadelphia, 1880. *Demography*, February 1984, *21*(1), pp. 53–69. **[G: U.S.]**

Cookingham, Mary E. Bluestockings, Spinsters and Pedagogues: Women College Graduates, 1865–1910. *Population Stud.*, November 1984, *38*(3), pp. 349–64. **[G: U.S.]**

Cornia, Giovanni Andrea. A Summary and Interpretation of the Evidence. *World Devel.*, March 1984, *12*(3), pp. 381–91. **[G: Global]**

Cornia, Giovanni Andrea. A Survey of Cross-sectional and Time-series Literature on Factors Affecting Child Welfare. In *Jolly, R. and Cornia, G. A., eds.*, 1984, pp. 17–32. **[G: LDCs]**

Cornia, Giovanni Andrea. The Impact of World Recession on Children: A Summary and Interpretation of the Evidence. In *Jolly, R. and Cornia, G. A., eds.*, 1984, pp. 211–21.

Cornia, Giovanni Andrea. The Impact of World Recession on Children: A Survey of Cross-Sectional and Time-Series Literature on Factors Affecting Child Welfare. *World Devel.*, March 1984, *12*(3), pp. 187–202. **[G: Global]**

Correa, H. A Quantitative Evaluation of the Impact of Population Laws on Fertility. In *Cohen, S. I., et al., eds.*, 1984, pp. 91–105. **[G: Latin America]**

Corsini, Carlo A. Structural Changes in Infant Mortality in Tuscany from the 18th to the 19th Century. In *Bengtsson, T.; Fridlizius, G. and Ohlsson, R., eds.*, 1984, pp. 127–50. **[G: Italy]**

Crafts, N. F. R. A Time Series Study of Fertility in England and Wales, 1877–1938. *J. Europ. Econ. Hist.*, September–December 1984, *13*(3), pp. 571–90. **[G: U.K.]**

Craig, John. Averaging Population Density. *Demography*, August 1984, *21*(3), pp. 405–12. **[G: U.K.]**

Crimmins, Eileen M., et al. New Perspectives on the Demographic Transition: A Theoretical and Empirical Analysis of an Indian State, 1951–1975. *Econ. Develop. Cult. Change*, January 1984, *32*(2), pp. 227–53. **[G: Taiwan; India]**

Cutright, Phillips and Hargens, Lowell. The Threshold Hypothesis: Evidence from Less

Developed Latin American Countries, 1950 to 1980. *Demography*, November 1984, *21*(4), pp. 459–73. **[G: Latin America]**

Dagodag, W. Tim. Illegal Mexican Aliens in Los Angeles: Locational Characteristics. In *Jones, R. C., ed.*, 1984, pp. 199–217. **[G: U.S.]**

Dagodag, W. Tim. Illegal Mexican Immigration to California from Western Mexico. In *Jones, R. C., ed.*, 1984, pp. 61–73. **[G: U.S.; Mexico]**

Danziger, Sheldon. Public Policy and the Condition of Black Family Life: Comments. *Rev. Black Polit. Econ.*, Summer–Fall 1984, *13*(1–2), pp. 188–93. **[G: U.S.]**

Darby, Michael R. The U.S. Productivity Slowdown: A Case of Statistical Myopia. *Amer. Econ. Rev.*, June 1984, *74*(3), pp. 301–22. **[G: U.S.]**

Darity, William A., Jr. and Myers, Samuel L., Jr. Public Policy and the Condition of Black Family Life. *Rev. Black Polit. Econ.*, Summer–Fall 1984, *13*(1–2), pp. 165–87. **[G: U.S.]**

Datta, Samar K. and Nugent, Jeffrey B. Are Old-Age Security and the Utility of Children in Rural India Really Unimportant? *Population Stud.*, November 1984, *38*(3), pp. 507–09. **[G: India]**

DaVanzo, Julie. A Household Survey of Child Mortality Determinants in Malaysia. *Population Devel. Rev.*, Supplement 1984, *10*, pp. 307–22. **[G: Malaysia]**

Davies, Richard B. and Crouchley, Robert. Calibrating Longitudinal Models of Residential Mobility and Migration: An Assessment of a Non-Parametric Marginal Likelihood Approach. *Reg. Sci. Urban Econ.*, May 1984, *14*(2), pp. 231–47. **[G: U.S.]**

Davis, Kingsley. Demographic Dilemmas in the Mid-1980s. In *Moore, J. H., ed.*, 1984, pp. 369–92. **[G: U.S.]**

Davis, Kingsley. Wives and Work: The Sex Role Revolution and Its Consequences. *Population Devel. Rev.*, September 1984, *10*(3), pp. 397–417. **[G: U.S.; U.K.; Sweden]**

De Cola, Lee. Statistical Determinants of the Population of a Nation's Largest City. *Econ. Develop. Cult. Change*, October 1984, *33*(1), pp. 71–98. **[G: Global]**

Demeny, Paul. A Perspective on Long-Term Population Growth. *Population Devel. Rev.*, March 1984, *10*(1), pp. 103–26. **[G: Global]**

Demeny, Paul. Population Policy: The Role of National Governments. In *Ghosh, P. K., ed., no. 5*, 1984, *1975*, pp. 280–93.

Demerath, Nicholas J. Paths to International Political Economy: World Politics and Population. In *Strange, S., ed.*, 1984, pp. 33–52. **[G: Global]**

Denslow, David A., Jr. and Tyler, William. Perspectives on Poverty and Income Inequality in Brazil. *World Devel.*, October 1984, *12*(10), pp. 1019–28. **[G: Brazil]**

Denton, Frank T. and Spencer, Byron G. The Time Path of the Economy as the Population Moves towards a Stationary State. In *Steinmann, G., ed.*, 1984, pp. 109–31.

Dhar, Sanjay. Interstate and Within-State Migration in India. In *Binswanger, H. P. and Rosenzweig, R., eds.*, 1984, pp. 280–304. [G: India]

Dholakia, Ruby Roy. Models-of-Man Approach to Family Planning. In *Kindra, G. S., ed.*, 1984, pp. 130–37. [G: LDCs]

Dinkel, Reiner H. Demographical Influences on Social Security Burden. In *Steinmann, G. ed.*, 1984, pp. 87–107. [G: W. Germany]

Dinkel, Reiner H. Haben die geburtenfördernden Massnahmen der DDR Erfolg? Eine vergleichende Darstellung der Fertilitätsentwicklung in beiden deutschen Staaten. (Have the Pronatalistic Policy Measures in the GDR Been Successful? A Comparison of Fertility Development in East and West Germany. With English summary.) *Ifo-Studien*, 1984, *30*(2), pp. 139–62. [G: E. Germany; W. Germany]

Donnithorne, Audrey. The Chinese Census of 1982: Preparations, Conduct and Evaluation. *Hong Kong Econ. Pap.*, 1984, (15), pp. 79–86. [G: China]

Eberstadt, Nick. On Infant Mortality in the Soviet Union: A Comment. *Population Devel. Rev.*, March 1984, *10*(1), pp. 91–98. [G: U.S.S.R.]

Eberstein, Isaac W. and Parker, Jan Reese. Racial Differences in Infant Mortality by Cause of Death: The Impact of Birth Weight and Maternal Age. *Demography*, August 1984, *21*(3), pp. 309–21. [G: U.S.]

Eckstein, Zvi; Schultz, T. Paul and Wolpin, Kenneth I. Short-run Fluctuations in Fertility and Mortality in Pre-industrial Sweden. *Europ. Econ. Rev.*, December 1984, *26*(3), pp. 295–317. [G: Sweden]

Eichperger, C. L. Regional Population Forecasts: Approaches and Issues. In *ter Heide, H. and Willekens, F. J., eds.*, 1984, pp. 235–52. [G: Netherlands]

Eldridge, Noel. Melbourne: Population Density; Distance; the Relationship. *J. Urban Econ.*, May 1984, *15*(3), pp. 310–16. [G: Australia]

Eltis, David. Mortality and Voyage Length in the Middle Passage: New Evidence from the Nineteenth Century. *J. Econ. Hist.*, June 1984, *44*(2), pp. 301–08. [G: Africa]

Emanuele, L.; Montagnana, M. and Prizzon, F. A Population Model Accounting for Household Dimensions. In *Avula, X. J. R., et al.*, 1984, pp. 988–92.

Encarnación, José, Jr. Becker on the Interaction between Quantity and Quality of Children. *Philippine Rev. Econ. Bus.*, Mar./June 1984, *21*(1/2), pp. 113–15.

Engels, Benno. Population Problems and North–South Cooperation. In *Ghosh, P. K., ed., no. 9*, 1984, *1976*, pp. 145–51.

Entwisle, Barbara and Winegarden, Calman R. Fertility and Pension Programs in LDCs: A Model of Mutual Reinforcement. *Econ. Develop. Cult. Change*, January 1984, *32*(2), pp. 331–54. [G: LDCs]

Entwisle, Barbara, et al. A Multilevel Model of Family Planning Availability and Contraceptive Use in Rural Thailand. *Demography*, November 1984, *21*(4), pp. 559–74. [G: Thailand]

van der Erf, R. F. Internal Migration in the Netherlands: Measurement and Main Characteristics. In *ter Heide, H. and Willekens, F. J., eds.*, 1984, pp. 47–68. [G: Netherlands]

Espenshade, Thomas J. Comment on Mitra's Generalization [Generalization of the Immigration and the Stable Population Model]. *Demography*, August 1984, *21*(3), pp. 431–32. [G: U.S.]

Falasco, Dee and Heer, David M. Economic and Fertility Differences between Legal and Undocumented Migrant Mexican Families: Possible Effects of Immigration Policy Changes. *Soc. Sci. Quart.*, June 1984, *65*(2), pp. 495–504. [G: U.S.]

Farber, Stephen C. and Lee, Bun Song. Fertility Adaptation of Rural-to-Urban Migrant Women: A Method of Estimation Applied to Korean Women. *Demography*, August 1984, *21*(3), pp. 339–45. [G: Korea]

Farooq, Ghazi M. Population, Human Resources and Development Planning: Towards an Integrated Approach. In *Ghosh, P. K., ed., no. 5*, 1984, *1981*, pp. 161–76.

Farooqui, M. Naseem Iqbal and Soomro, Ghulam Yasin. An Analysis of Fertility Change in Pakistan. *Pakistan Devel. Rev.*, Summer-Autumn 1984, *23*(2&3), pp. 225–35. [G: Pakistan]

Feeney, G. and Ross, J. A. Analysing Open Birth Interval Distributions. *Population Stud.*, November 1984, *38*(3), pp. 473–78.

Felderer, Bernhard. Population and Per-capita Income in Simulation Models. In *Steinmann, G., ed.*, 1984, pp. 132–46. [G: W. Germany]

Feshbach, Murray. A Different Crisis. In *Hoffmann, E. P. and Laird, R. F., eds.*, 1984, *1981*, pp. 895–902. [G: U.S.S.R.]

Feshbach, Murray. On Infant Mortality in the Soviet Union: A Comment. *Population Devel. Rev.*, March 1984, *10*(1), pp. 87–90. [G: U.S.S.R.]

Fethke, Carol C. An Economic Model of Asset Division in the Dissolution of Marriage. *Amer. Econ. Rev.*, May 1984, *74*(2), pp. 265–70.

Fischer, Nancy A. and Marcum, John P. Ethnic Integration, Socioeconomic Status, and Fertility among Mexican Americans. *Soc. Sci. Quart.*, June 1984, *65*(2), pp. 583–93. [G: U.S.]

Folbre, Nancy R. Household Production in the Philippines: A Non-neoclassical Approach. *Econ. Develop. Cult. Change*, January 1984, *32*(2), pp. 303–30. [G: Philippines]

Folbre, Nancy R. Market Opportunities, Genetic Endowments, and Intrafamily Resource Distribution: Comment. *Amer. Econ. Rev.*, June 1984, *74*(3), pp. 518–20. [G: India]

Folbre, Nancy R. The Pauperization of Motherhood: Patriarchy and Public Policy in the United States. *Rev. Radical Polit. Econ.*, Winter 1984, *16*(4), pp. 72–88. [G: U.S.]

Foot, David K. The Demographic Future of Fiscal Federalism in Canada. *Can. Public Policy*, December 1984, *10*(4), pp. 406–14.
[G: Canada]

Foot, David K. and Milne, William J. Net Migration Estimation in an Extended, Multiregional Gravity Model. *J. Reg. Sci.*, February 1984, *24*(1), pp. 119–33. [G: Canada]

Forbes, John F. and McGregor, Alan. Unemployment and Mortality in Post-war Scotland. *J. Health Econ.*, December 1984, *3*(3), pp. 239–57. [G: Scotland]

Foxley, Alejandro and Raczynski, Dagmar. Vulnerable Groups in Recessionary Situations: The Case of Children and the Young in Chile. *World Devel.*, March 1984, *12*(3), pp. 223–46.
[G: Chile]

Foxley, Alejandro and Raczynski, Dagmar. Vulnerable Groups in Recessionary Situations: The Case of Children and the Young in Chile. In *Jolly, R. and Cornia, G. A., eds.*, 1984, pp. 53–76. [G: Chile]

Frejka, Tomas. Long-term Prospects for World Population Growth. In *Ghosh, P. K., ed., no. 5*, 1984, *1981*, pp. 306–30. [G: Global]

Fridlizius, Gunnar. The Mortality Decline in the First Phase of the Demographic Transition: Swedish Experiences. In *Bengtsson, T.; Fridlizius, G. and Ohlsson, R., eds.*, 1984, pp. 71–114. [G: Sweden]

Fridlizius, Gunnar and Ohlsson, Rolf. Mortality Patterns in Sweden 1751–1802—A Regional Analysis. In *Bengtsson, T.; Fridlizius, G. and Ohlsson, R., eds.*, 1984, pp. 299–328.
[G: Sweden]

Friedlander, Dov. Erratum [Demographic Responses and Socioeconomic Structure: Population Processes in England and Wales in the Nineteenth Century]. *Demography*, May 1984, *21*(2), pp. 270. [G: U.K.]

Galster, George C. On the Measurement of Metropolitan Decentralization of Blacks and Whites. *Urban Stud.*, November 1984, *21*(4), pp. 465–70. [G: U.S.]

Ghosh, B. N. Brain Migration from Third World: An Implicative Analysis. *Rivista Int. Sci. Econ. Com.*, April 1984, *31*(4), pp. 346–70.
[G: LDCs]

Goldman, Noreen. Changes in Widowhood and Divorce and Expected Durations of Marriage. *Demography*, August 1984, *21*(3), pp. 297–307. [G: U.S.; Nepal; Colombia]

Goldman, Noreen; Pebley, Anne R. and Lord, Graham. Calculation of Life Tables from Survey Data: A Technical Note. *Demography*, November 1984, *21*(4), pp. 647–53.
[G: Colombia; Jordan; Panama; Sri Lanka]

Goldscheider, Calvin. Migration and Rural Fertility in Less Developed Countries. In *Schutjer, W. A. and Stokes, C. S., eds.*, 1984, pp. 34–48. [G: LDCs]

Gomes, Melba. Family Size and Education Attainment in Kenya. *Population Devel. Rev.*, December 1984, *10*(4), pp. 647–60.
[G: Kenya]

Gopal, K. Rani. Benefit-Cost Analysis of the In-

dian Family Welfare Programme. *Indian Econ. J.*, April–June 1984, *31*(4), pp. 45–52.
[G: India]

Gordijn, H. E.; Heida, H. R. and ter Heide, Henk. Monitoring Migration and Population Redistribution. In *ter Heide, H. and Willekens, F. J., eds.*, 1984, pp. 95–110.
[G: Netherlands]

Gordon, Ian. Lagged Response in Intra-urban Migration of Home Owners: A Comment. *Reg. Stud.*, December 1984, *18*(6), pp. 505–06.
[G: Israel]

Gosovic, Branislav. Population–Resources–Environment–Development Interrelationships in the United Nations: In Search of an Approach. *Cepal Rev.*, 1984, (23), pp. 135–54.
[G: Global]

Gottlieb, Rhonda. The Political Economy of Sexuality. *Rev. Radical Polit. Econ.*, Spring 1984, *16*(1), pp. 143–65.

Goubert, Jean-Pierre. Public Hygiene and Mortality Decline in France in the 19th Century. In *Bengtsson, T.; Fridlizius, G. and Ohlsson, R., eds.*, 1984, pp. 151–59. [G: France]

Gramlich, Edward M. and Laren, Deborah S. Migration and Income Redistribution Responsibilities. *J. Human Res.*, Fall 1984, *19*(4), pp. 489–511. [G: U.S.]

Gravelle, Hugh S. E. Time Series Analysis of Mortality and Unemployment [Unemployment and Mortality in Post-war Scotland]. *J. Health Econ.*, December 1984, *3*(3), pp. 297–305.

Graves, Philip E. and Knapp, Thomas A. A Theory of International Migration Flows: United States Immigration from Mexico. *Rev. Reg. Stud.*, Winter 1984, *14*(1), pp. 1–7.
[G: U.S.; Mexico]

Green, Reginald Herbold and Singer, Hans W. Sub-Saharan Africa in Depression: The Impact on the Welfare of Children. *World Devel.*, March 1984, *12*(3), pp. 283–95. [G: Nigeria; Zambia; Tanzania]

Greenwood, Michael J. and Hunt, Gary L. Econometrically Accounting for Identities and Restrictions in Models of Interregional Migration. *Reg. Sci. Urban Econ.*, February 1984, *14*(1), pp. 113–28. [G: U.S.]

Grossbard-Shechtman, Amyra. A Theory of Allocation of Time in Markets for Labour and Marriage. *Econ. J.*, December 1984, *94*(376), pp. 863–82.

Gunatilleke, Godfrey and Kurukulasuria, G. I. O. M. The Global Economic Crisis and the Impact on Children in Sri Lanka. In *Jolly, R. and Cornia, G. A., eds.*, 1984, pp. 139–58. [G: Sri Lanka]

Gunatilleke, Godfrey and Kurukulasuria, G. I. O. M. The Global Economic Crisis and the Impact on Children in Sri Lanka. *World Devel.*, March 1984, *12*(3), pp. 309–16.
[G: Sri Lanka]

Gutierrez Muniz, José A., et al. The Recent Worldwide Economic Crisis and the Welfare of Children: The Case of Cuba. *World Devel.*, March 1984, *12*(3), pp. 247–60. [G: Cuba]

Haberman, S. and Fox, A. J. Implications of Demographic Change for the Adult Population (20–59 years). In *Lopez, A. D. and Cliquet, R. L., eds.*, 1984, pp. 149–59. [G: Europe]

Happel, Stephen K.; Hill, John K. and Low, Stuart A. An Economic Analysis of the Timing of Childbirth. *Population Stud.*, July 1984, *38*(2), pp. 299–311. [G: U.S.]

Harper, A. E. Nutrition and Health in the Changing Environment. In *Simon, J. L. and Kahn, H., eds.*, 1984, pp. 490–527. [G: Global]

Harris, William G. Problems in the Use of Historical Data in Estimating Economic Loss in Wrongful Death and Injury Cases: Comment. *J. Risk Ins.*, March 1984, *51*(1), pp. 122–26. [G: U.S.]

Haskey, J. Social Class and Socio-economic Differentials in Divorce in England and Wales. *Population Stud.*, November 1984, *38*(3), pp. 419–38. [G: U.K.]

Heida, H. R. and Gordijn, H. E. Residential Preferences and Inclination to Move. In *ter Heide, H. and Willekens, F. J., eds.*, 1984, pp. 153–70. [G: Netherlands]

ter Heide, Henk. Demographic Research Questions Arising from Spatial Policy in the Netherlands. In *ter Heide, H. and Willekens, F. J., eds.*, 1984, pp. 3–20. [G: Netherlands]

ter Heide, Henk. The Use of Demographic Research in Physical Planning. In *ter Heide, H. and Willekens, F. J., eds.*, 1984, pp. 337–54. [G: Netherlands]

Heikkinen, E. Implications of Demographic Change for the Elderly Population (60 years and over). In *Lopez, A. D. and Cliquet, R. L., eds.*, 1984, pp. 161–75. [G: Europe]

Henin, Roushdi A. Alternative Population Projections for Kenya, 1969–89. In *Ominde, S. H., ed.*, 1984, pp. 78–90. [G: Kenya]

Henin, Roushdi A. Recent Demographic Trends in Kenya and their Implication for Economic and Social Development. In *Ominde, S. H., ed.*, 1984, pp. 40–53. [G: Kenya]

Herberger, L. Trends and Perspectives in Family Formation. In *Lopez, A. D. and Cliquet, R. L., eds.*, 1984, pp. 69–91. [G: Europe]

Hingstman, L. and Harts, J. J. Analysis of Migration Histories. In *ter Heide, H. and Willekens, F. J., eds.*, 1984, pp. 133–52 [G: Netherlands]

Hobcraft, J. N. and Little, R. J. A. Erratum [Fertility Exposure Analysis: A New Method for Assessing the Contribution of Proximate Determinants to Fertility Differentials]. *Population Stud.*, July 1984, *38*(2), pp. 191. [G: Dominican Republic]

Hobcraft, J. N. and Little, R. J. A. Fertility Exposure Analysis: A New Method for Assessing the Contribution of Proximate Determinants to Fertility Differentials. *Population Stud.*, March 1984, *38*(1), pp. 21–45. [G: Dominican Republic]

Hobcraft, J. N.; McDonald, J. W. and Rutstein, S. O. Socio-Economic Factors in Infant and Child Mortality: A Cross-National Comparison. *Population Stud.*, July 1984, *38*(2), pp. 193–223. [G: LDCs]

Hoem, Jan M. and Selmer, Randi. The Negligible Influence of Premarital Cohabitation on Marital Fertility in Current Danish Cohorts, 1975. *Demography*, May 1984, *21*(2), pp. 193–206. [G: Denmark]

Hoenack, Stephen A.; Peris, Jose Antonio and Weiler, William C. Can Economic Incentives Explain the Recent Population Movements to Nonmetropolitan Areas? *Ann. Reg. Sci.*, November 1984, *18*(3), pp. 81–93. [G: U.S.]

Hofferth, Sandra L. Long-Term Economic Consequences for Women of Delayed Childbearing and Reduced Family Size. *Demography*, May 1984, *21*(2), pp. 141–55. [G: U.S.]

Hogan, Timothy D. Evaluating the Demographic Impact of Societal Events through Intervention Analysis: The Brown vs. Board of Education Decision. *Demography*, November 1984, *21*(4), pp. 673–77. [G: U.S.]

Hollander, Samuel. Marx and Malthusianism: Marx's Secular Path of Wages. *Amer. Econ. Rev.*, March 1984, *74*(1), pp. 139–51.

Hosek, William R. Problems in the Use of Historical Data in Estimating Economic Loss in Wrongful Death and Injury Cases: Reply. *J. Risk Ins.*, March 1984, *51*(1), pp. 127–30. [G: U.S.]

Hoy, Don R. and Bélisle, François J. Environmental Protection and Economic Development in Guatemala's Western Highlands. *J. Devel. Areas*, January 1984, *18*(2), pp. 161–76. [G: Guatemala]

Hull, Terence H. and Hull, Valerie J. Population Change in Indonesia: Findings of the 1980 Census. *Bull. Indonesian Econ. Stud.*, December 1984, *20*(3), pp. 95–119. [G: Indonesia]

Humphries, Jane and Rubery, Jill. The Reconstitution of the Supply Side of the Labour Market: The Relative Autonomy of Social Reproduction. *Cambridge J. Econ.*, December 1984, *8*(4), pp. 331–46.

Hunt, Janet C. and Kiker, B. F. Parental Time Devoted to Children in Two- and One-Wage-Earner Families. *Econ. Educ. Rev.*, 1984, *3*(1), pp. 75–83. [G: U.S.]

Hunter, Kevin A. Marital Dissolution: An Economic Analysis. *Amer. Econ.*, Spring 1984, *28*(1), pp. 63–68. [G: U.S.]

Imhof, Arthur E. The Amazing Simultaneousness of the Big Differences and the Boom in the 19th Century—Some Facts and Hypotheses about Infant Mortality in Germany, 18th to 20th Century. In *Bengtsson, T.; Fridlizius, G. and Ohlsson, R., eds.*, 1984, pp. 191–222. [G: Germany]

Inoki, Takenori. Japanese Emigration to Hawaii and North America in 1890s. (In Japanese. With English summary.) *Osaka Econ. Pap.*, December 1984, *34*(2–3), pp. 239–47. [G: Japan; U.S.]

James, William and Roumasset, James. Migration and the Evolution of Tenure Contracts in Newly Settled Regions. *J. Devel. Econ.*, January–February 1984, *14*(1–2), pp. 147–62. [G: Philippines]

Jeshurun, Chandran. Refugee Flows and Other Destabilizing Factors: Recent Trends in Southeast Asia. In *Downen, R. L. and Dickson, B. J., eds.*, 1984, pp. 227–34.

Johnson, Nan E. Rural Development and the Value of Children: Implications for Human Fertility. In *Schutjer, W. A. and Stokes, C. S., eds.*, 1984, pp. 172–93. [G: LDCs]

Jolly, Richard and Cornia, Giovanni Andrea. The Impact of World Recession on Children: Editors' Introduction. In *Jolly, R. and Cornia, G. A., eds.*, 1984, pp. 1–6.

Jones, Ellen and Grupp, Fred W. On Infant Mortality in the Soviet Union: Rejoinder. *Population Devel. Rev.*, March 1984, *10*(1), pp. 98–102. [G: U.S.S.R.]

Jones, Richard C. Changing Patterns of Undocumented Mexican Migration to South Texas. *Soc. Sci. Quart.*, June 1984, *65*(2), pp. 465–81. [G: U.S.]

Jones, Richard C. Patterns of Undocumented Migration: Introduction. In *Jones, R. C., ed.*, 1984, pp. 1–12. [G: U.S.; Mexico]

Jonsson, Ulf. Population Growth and Agrarian Economic and Social Structure: Some Swedish Examples. In *Bengtsson, T.; Fridlizius, G. and Ohlsson, R., eds.*, 1984, pp. 223–34. [G: Sweden]

Jud, G. Donald. Public Schools in In-Migration in North Carolina Counties, 1975–80. *Amer. J. Econ. Soc.*, July 1984, *43*(3), pp. 313–22. [G: U.S.]

Juviler, Peter H. The Urban Family and the Soviet State: Emerging Contours of a Demographic Policy. In *Morton, H. W. and Stuart, R. C., eds.*, 1984, pp. 84–112. [G: U.S.S.R.]

Katz, Arnold; Teuter, Klaus and Sidel, Philip. Comparison of Alternative Ways of Deriving Panel Data from the Annual Demographic Files of the Current Population Survey. *Rev. Public Data Use*, March 1984, *12*(1), pp. 35–44. [G: U.S.]

Kaukiainen, Yrjö. Harvest Fluctuations and Mortality in Agrarian Finland (1810–1870). In *Bengtsson, T.; Fridlizius, G. and Ohlsson, R., eds.*, 1984, pp. 235–54. [G: Finland]

Kawanabe, Noboru. Urban Traditional Sector and Rural–Urban Migration in LDCs. (In Japanese. With English summary.) *Osaka Econ. Pap.*, December 1984, *34*(2–3), pp. 248–60. [G: LDCs]

Kelley, Allen C. and Williamson, Jeffrey G. Population Growth, Industrial Revolutions, and the Urban Transition. *Population Devel. Rev.*, September 1984, *10*(3), pp. 419–41. [G: LDCs]

Kemp, Murray C.; Leonard, Daniel and Long, Ngo Van. Three Pitfalls in the Construction of Family-based Models of Population Growth. *Europ. Econ. Rev.*, August 1984, *25*(3), pp. 345–54.

Kemper, Franz-Josef. Categorical Regression Models for Large Samples. In *Bahrenberg, G.; Fischer, M. M., and Nijkamp, P.*, 1984, pp. 303–16. [G: W. Germany]

Kendig, Hal L. Housing Careers, Life Cycle and Residential Mobility: Implications for the

Housing Market. *Urban Stud.*, August 1984, *21*(3), pp. 271–83. [G: U.S.]

Keyfitz, Nathan. Pension Plan Equity: The Debate Continued [Equity between the Sexes: The Pension Problem]. *J. Policy Anal. Manage.*, Fall 1984, *4*(1), pp. 120–21. [G: U.S.]

Khan, Akhtar Hasan. An Analysis of Fertility Change in Pakistan: Comment. *Pakistan Devel. Rev.*, Summer-Autumn 1984, *23*(2&3), pp. 237–38. [G: Pakistan]

Khan, M. Ali. Reproductive Behaviour in Pakistan: Insights from the Population, Labour Force, and Migration Survey, 1979–80: Comment. *Pakistan Devel. Rev.*, Summer-Autumn 1984, *23*(2&3), pp. 219–23. [G: Pakistan]

Khan, M. R. Economic Development and Population Policy in Bangladesh. *Bangladesh Devel. Stud.*, September 1984, *12*(3), pp. 1–18. [G: Bangladesh]

Kim, Young J. and Strobino, Donna M. Decomposition of the Difference between Two Rates with Hierarchical Factors. *Demography*, August 1984, *21*(3), pp. 361–72. [G: U.S.]

Kindra, G. S.; Dholakia, Ruby Roy and Pangotra, Prem. The Public Sector and the Marketing of Birth Control in LDCs. In *Kindra, G. S., ed.*, 1984, pp. 138–55. [G: India; LDCs]

Klinger, A. Trends and Perspectives in Fertility. In *Lopez, A. D. and Cliquet, R. L., eds.*, 1984, pp. 93–116. [G: Europe]

van der Knaap, G. A. and Sleegers, W. F. Structural Analysis of Interregional and Intraregional Migration Patterns. In *ter Heide, H. and Willekens, F. J., eds.*, 1984, pp. 113–31. [G: Netherlands]

Knodel, John; Havanon, Napaporn and Pramualratana, Anthony. Fertility Transition in Thailand: A Qualitative Analysis. *Population Devel. Rev.*, June 1984, *10*(2), pp. 297–328. [G: Thailand]

Kocher, James E. Income Distribution and Fertility. In *Schutjer, W. A. and Stokes, C. S., eds.*, 1984, pp. 216–34. [G: LDCs]

Koenig, M. A.; Simmons, G. B. and Misra, B. D. Husband–Wife Inconsistencies in Contraceptive Use Responses. *Population Stud.*, July 1984, *38*(2), pp. 281–98. [G: U.S.]

Kogut, Edy Luiz and Langoni, Carlos Geraldo. Population Growth, Income Distribution and Economic Development. In *Ghosh, P. K., ed.*, no. 5, 1984, *1975*, pp. 147–60. [G: Latin America; U.S.]

Koo, Helen P.; Suchindran, C. M. and Griffith, Janet D. The Effects of Children on Divorce and Re-marriage: A Multivariate Analysis of Life Table Probabilities. *Population Stud.*, November 1984, *38*(3), pp. 451–71.

Krämer, Walter and Neusser, Klaus. The Emergence of Countercyclical U.S. Fertility: Note. *Amer. Econ. Rev.*, March 1984, *74*(1), pp. 201–02. [G: U.S.]

Krumm, Ronald J. Household Tenure Choice and Migration. *J. Urban Econ.*, November 1984, *16*(3), pp. 259–71. [G: U.S.]

Kvasha, A. Theoretical Problems of Demographic

Policy in the USSR. *Prob. Econ.*, July 1984, 27(3), pp. 3–21. [G: U.S.S.R.]

Lam, D. The Variance of Population Characteristics in Stable Populations, with Applications to the Distribution of Income. *Population Stud.*, March 1984, 38(1), pp. 117–27.
[G: Brazil; U.S.]

Land, Kenneth C.; Hough, George C., Jr. and McMillan, Marilyn M. New Midyear Age–Sex–Color-Specific Estimates of the U.S. Population for the 1940s and 1950s: Including a Revision of Coverage Estimates for the 1940 and 1950 Censuses. *Demography*, November 1984, 21(4), pp. 623–45. [G: U.S.]

Latos, Charles J. Non-white Migration Patterns in Northern Metropolitan Areas, 1960–1970: The Interaction between Economic and Affinitive Factors. *Rev. Black Polit. Econ.*, Winter 1984–85, 13(3), pp. 5–19. [G: U.S.]

Lavely, W. R. The Rural Chinese Fertility Transition: A Report from Shifang Xian, Sichuan. *Population Stud.*, November 1984, 38(3), pp. 354–84. [G: China]

Lee, Bun Song and Farber, Stephen C. Fertility Adaptation by Rural–Urban Migrants in Developing Countries: The Case of Korea. *Population Stud.*, March 1984, 38(1), pp. 141–55.
[G: S. Korea]

Lee, Kye S. The Direction of Migration: A Dynamic General Equilibrium Model. *J. Reg. Sci.*, November 1984, 24(4), pp. 509–17.

Lee, W. Robert. Mortality Levels and Agrarian Reform in Early 19th Century Prussia: Some Regional Evidence. In *Bengtsson, T.; Fridlizius, G. and Ohlsson, R., eds.*, 1984, pp. 161–90. [G: Germany]

Leff, Nathaniel H. Dependency Rates and Savings: Another Look [Dependency Rates and Aggregate Savings: A New International Cross-Section Study]. *Amer. Econ. Rev.*, March 1984, 74(1), pp. 231–33. [G: LDCs; MCDs]

Lehrer, Evelyn. The Impact of Child Mortality on Spacing by Parity: A Cox-Regression Analysis. *Demography*, August 1984, 21(3), pp. 323–37. [G: Malaysia]

Leontief, Wassily. Population Growth and Economic Development: Illustrative Projections. In *Ghosh, P. K., ed., no. 5*, 1984, 1979, pp. 221–46. [G: Global]

Lewes, F. M. M. A Note on the Origin of the Net Reproduction Ratio. *Population Stud.*, July 1984, 38(2), pp. 321–24.

Lieberman, Samuel S. Accommodation and Control of Population Growth. In *Burki, S. J. and LaPorte, R., Jr., eds.*, 1984, pp. 139–200.
[G: Pakistan]

Linge, G. J. R. Industrialization and the Household. *Int. Soc. Sci. J.*, 1984, 36(2), pp. 319–39.

Lipfert, Frederick W. Air Pollution and Mortality: Specification Searches Using SMSA-Based Data. *J. Environ. Econ. Manage.*, September 1984, 11(3), pp. 208–43. [G: U.S.]

Lopez, A. D. Demographic Change in Europe and its Health and Social Implications: An Overview. In *Lopez, A. D. and Cliquet, R. L., eds.*, 1984, pp. 5–67. [G: Europe; Algeria; Morocco; Turkey]

Lubell, Harold. Third World Urbanization and International Assistance. *Urban Stud.*, February 1984, 21(1), pp. 1–13. [G: LDCs]

Lynch, Gerald J. and Hyclak, Thomas. Cyclical and Noncyclical Unemployment Differences among Demographic Groups. *Growth Change*, January 1984, 15(1), pp. 9–17. [G: U.S.]

Lynge, E. Trends and Perspectives in Mortality. In *Lopez, A. D. and Cliquet, R. L., eds.*, 1984, pp. 117–32. [G: Europe]

Macedo, Roberto. Brazilian Children and the Economic Crisis: Evidence from the State of São Paulo. In *Jolly, R. and Cornia, G. A., eds.*, 1984, pp. 33–51. [G: Brazil]

Macedo, Roberto. Brazilian Children and the Economic Crisis: Evidence from the State of São Paulo. *World Devel.*, March 1984, 12(3), pp. 203–21. [G: Brazil]

Mack, Ruth P. and Leigland, T. J. Elective Decisions to Move to New York City. In *[Ferber, R.]*, 1984, pp. 217–51. [G: U.S.]

Macura, M. and Popović, B. BACHUE—Yugoslavia: Background Structure and Utilisation. In *Cohen, S. I., et al., eds.*, 1984, pp. 107–38.

Maffenini, Walter and Rossi, Fiorenzo. Stima di fecondita' per eta' con dati italiani di censimento: problemi e prospettive. (Age-Specific Fertility Estimation from Italian Census Data: Problems and Perspectives. With English summary.) *Statistica*, July–September 1984, 44(3), pp. 423–41. [G: Italy]

Mahar, Dennis J. Population Distribution within LDCs. *Finance Develop.*, September 1984, 21(3), pp. 15–17. [G: LDCs]

Mahmud, Simeen and Becker, Stan. Error Patterns in Children's Age Reports in Retrospective Sample Surveys. *Bangladesh Devel. Stud.*, December 1984, 12(4), pp. 123–35.
[G: Bangladesh]

Massey, Douglas S. and Mullan, Brendan P. A Demonstration of the Effect of Seasonal Migration on Fertility. *Demography*, November 1984, 21(4), pp. 501–17. [G: U.S.]

Matossian, Mary Kilbourne. Mold Poisoning and Population Growth in England and France, 1750–1850. *J. Econ. Hist.*, September 1984, 44(3), pp. 669–86. [G: U.K.; France]

Mauskopf, Josephine and Wallace, T. Dudley. Fertility and Replacement: Some Alternative Stochastic Models and Results for Brazil. *Demography*, November 1984, 21(4), pp. 519–36. [G: Brazil]

McAvinchey, Ian D. Economic Factors and Mortality—Some Aspects of the Scottish Case, 1950–1978. *Scot. J. Polit. Econ.*, February 1984, 31(1), pp. 1–27. [G: U.K.]

McCutcheon, Laurie. Measuring Migrant Change: A Look at Housing in Bogota, Seoul, and Surabaya. *J. Devel. Areas*, April 1984, 18(3), pp. 357–72. [G: Colombia; Korea; Indonesia]

McDaniel, C. K. and Hammel, E. A. A Kin-Based

Measure of *r* and an Evaluation of Its Effectiveness. *Demography*, February 1984, *21*(1), pp. 41–51.

McHugh, Richard and Morgan, James N. The Determinants of Interstate Student Migration: A Place-to-Place Analysis. *Econ. Educ. Rev.*, 1984, *3*(4), pp. 269–78. **[G: U.S.]**

McNamara, Robert S. Time Bomb or Myth: The Population Problem. *Foreign Aff.*, Summer 1984, *62*(5), pp. 1107–31. **[G: Global]**

McNeill, William H. Human Migration in Historical Perspective. *Population Devel. Rev.*, March 1984, *10*(1), pp. 1–18. **[G: Global]**

McNicoll, Geoffrey. Consequences of Rapid Population Growth: An Overview and Assessment. *Population Devel. Rev.*, June 1984, *10*(2), pp. 177–240. **[G: Global]**

McNicoll, Geoffrey and Nag, Moni. Population Growth: Current Issues and Strategies. In *Ghosh, P. K., ed.*, no. 5, 1984, *1982*, pp. 126–46. **[G: Global]**

Meerman, Jacob and Cochrane, Susan Hill. Population Growth and Food Supply in Sub-Saharan Africa. In *Ghosh, P. K., ed.*, no. 5, 1984, *1982*, pp. 331–42. **[G: Sub-Saharan Africa]**

Meerman, Jacob and Cochrane, Susan Hill. Population Growth and Food Supply in Sub-Saharan Africa. In *Ghosh, P. K., ed.*, no. 6, 1984, *1982*, pp. 340–51. **[G: Sub-Saharan Africa]**

Merrick, Thomas W. Population, Development, and Planning in Brazil. In *Ghosh, P. K., ed.*, no. 5, 1984, *1976*, pp. 343–62. **[G: Brazil]**

Mielke, James H., et al. Historical Epidemiology of Smallpox in Åland, Finland: 1751–1890. *Demography*, August 1984, *21*(3), pp. 271–95. **[G: Finland]**

Miller, C. Arden and Coulter, Elizabeth J. The World Economic Crisis and the Children: A United States Case Study. *World Devel.*, March 1984, *12*(3), pp. 339–64. **[G: U.S.]**

Miller, C. Arden and Coulter, Elizabeth J. The World Economic Crisis and the Children: A United States Case Study. In *Jolly, R. and Cornia, G. A., eds.*, 1984, pp. 169–94. **[G: U.S.]**

Miller, Lawrence W.; Polinard, Jerry L. and Wrinkle, Robert D. Attitudes toward Undocumented Workers: The Mexican American Perspective. *Soc. Sci. Quart.*, June 1984, *65*(2), pp. 482–94. **[G: U.S.; Mexico]**

Mitra, S. Estimating the Expectation of Life at Older Ages. *Population Stud.*, July 1984, *38*(2), pp. 313–19. **[G: Selected Countries]**

Mitra, S. On Espenshade's Comments on Mitra's Generalization [Generalization of the Immigration and the Stable Population Model]. *Demography*, August 1984, *21*(3), pp. 433–34. **[G: U.S.]**

Moffitt, Robert. Profiles of Fertility, Labour Supply and Wages of Married Women: A Complete Life-Cycle Model. *Rev. Econ. Stud.*, April 1984, *51*(2), pp. 263–78. **[G: U.S.]**

Moffitt, Robert. The Estimation of Fertility Equations on Panel Data. *J. Human Res.*, Winter 1984, *19*(1), pp. 22–34. **[G: U.S.]**

Mohan, Rakesh. The Effect of Population Growth, the Pattern of Demand and of Technology on the Process of Urbanization. *J. Urban Econ.*, March 1984, *15*(2), pp. 125–56. **[G: India]**

Mokyr, Joel and Ó Gráda, Cormac. New Developments in Irish Population History, 1700–1850. *Econ. Hist. Rev., 2nd Ser.*, November 1984, *37*(4), pp. 473–88. **[G: Ireland; France; U.K.]**

Morgan, S. Philip and Rindfuss, Ronald R. Household Structure and the Tempo of Family Formation in Comparative Perspective. *Population Stud.*, March 1984, *38*(1), pp. 129–39. **[G: Malaysia; S. Korea]**

Morgan, S. Philip; Rindfuss, Ronald R. and Parnell, Allan. Modern Fertility Patterns: Contrasts between the United States and Japan. *Population Devel. Rev.*, March 1984, *10*(1), pp. 19–40. **[G: Japan; U.S.]**

Morgan, V. and MacAfee, W. Irish Population in the Pre-Famine Period: Evidence from County Antrim. *Econ. Hist. Rev., 2nd Ser.*, May 1984, *37*(2), pp. 182–96. **[G: Ireland]**

Morrissey, Michael P. A Rural–Urban Stratification of Jamaica for Sampling Procedures. *Soc. Econ. Stud.*, December 1984, *33*(4), pp. 101–23. **[G: Jamaica]**

Mosher, William D. and Hendershot, Gerry E. Religion and Fertility: A Replication. *Demography*, May 1984, *21*(2), pp. 185–91. **[G: U.S.]**

Moskoff, William. The Soviet Urban Labor Supply. In *Morton, H. W. and Stuart, R. C., eds.*, 1984, pp. 65–83. **[G: U.S.S.R.]**

Mosley, W. Henry and Chen, Lincoln C. An Analytical Framework for the Study of Child Survival in Developing Countries. *Population Devel. Rev.*, Supplement 1984, *10*, pp. 25–45. **[G: LDCs]**

Mueller, Eva. Income, Aspirations, and Fertility in Rural Areas of Less Developed Countries. In *Schutjer, W. A. and Stokes, C. S., eds.*, 1984, pp. 121–50. **[G: LDCs]**

Muller, Thomas. Public Sector Performance: A Demographic Perspective. In *Miller, T. C., ed.*, 1984, pp. 131–60. **[G: U.S.]**

Mundle, Sudipto. Recent Trends in the Condition of Children in India: A Statistical Profile. In *Jolly, R. and Cornia, G. A., eds.*, 1984, pp. 127–37. **[G: India]**

Mundle, Sudipto. Recent Trends in the Condition of Children in India: A Statistical Profile. *World Devel.*, March 1984, *12*(3), pp. 297–307. **[G: India]**

Muniz, José A. Gutierrez, et al. The Recent Worldwide Economic Crisis and the Welfare of Children: The Case of Cuba. In *Jolly, R. and Cornia, G. A., eds.*, 1984, pp. 77–90. **[G: Cuba]**

Murdock, Steve H., et al. An Assessment of the Accuracy of a Regional Economic–Demographic Projection Model. *Demography*, August 1984, *21*(3), pp. 383–404. **[G: U.S.]**

Nag, Moni and Kak, Neeraj. Demographic Transition in a Punjab Village. *Population Devel. Rev.*, December 1984, *10*(4), pp. 661–78. **[G: India]**

Narayana, D. L. Population Growth and Economic Growth. *Indian Econ. J.*, Oct.–Dec. 1984, *32*(2), pp. 1–40.

Neal, Larry. Slowing Population Growth and Investment Demand: The West German Case. In *Steinmann, G., ed.*, 1984, pp. 179–202.
[G: W. Germany]

Nerlove, Marc; Razin, Assaf and Sadka, Efraim. Bequests and the Size of Population When Population Is Endogenous. *J. Polit. Econ.*, June 1984, *92*(3), pp. 527–31.

Newman, John L. and McCulloch, Charles E. A Hazard Rate Approach to the Timing of Births. *Econometrica*, July 1984, *52*(4), pp. 939–61.
[G: Costa Rica]

Norrie, Kenneth H. and Percy, Michael B. Sustained Harvest Fluctuations and Economic Change: A General Equilibrium Analysis. In *Bengtsson, T.; Fridlizius, G. and Ohlsson, R., eds.*, 1984, pp. 391–418.

Nour, El-Sayed and Suchindran, C. M. Multistate Mortality by Cause of Death: A Life Table Analysis. *J. Roy. Statist. Soc.*, 1984, *147*(4), pp. 582–97.
[G: U.S.]

Nour, El-Sayed and Suchindran, C. M. The Construction of Multi-State Life Tables: Comments. *Population Stud.*, July 1984, *38*(2), pp. 325–28.
[G: Belgium]

Ó Gráda, Cormac. Malthus and the Pre-famine Economy. In *Murphy, A. E., ed.*, 1984, pp. 75–95.
[G: Ireland]

Ohlsson, Rolf and Bengtsson, Tommy. Population and Economic Fluctuations in Sweden 1749–1914. In *Bengtsson, T.; Fridlizius, G. and Ohlsson, R., eds.*, 1984, pp. 277–97.
[G: Sweden]

Ominde, S. H. General Background to the Population Situation in the World and Kenya. In *Ominde, S. H., ed.*, 1984, pp. 25–33.
[G: Global; Kenya]

Ominde, S. H. Population of Kenya. In *Ominde, S. H., ed.*, 1984, pp. 23–24.
[G: Kenya]

Ominde, S. H. Population Distribution and Urbanization. In *Ominde, S. H., ed.*, 1984, pp. 54–67.
[G: Kenya]

Ominde, S. H. Total Population of Kenya. In *Ominde, S. H., ed.*, 1984, pp. 34–39.
[G: Kenya]

Op 't Veld, A.; Bijlsma, E. and Starmans, J. Explanatory Analysis of Interregional Migration in the Nineteen-Seventies. In *ter Heide, H. and Willekens, F. J., eds.*, 1984, pp. 171–200.
[G: Netherlands]

Palloni, A. and Kominski, R. Estimation of Adult Mortality Using Forward and Backward Projections. *Population Stud.*, November 1984, *38*(3), pp. 479–93.
[G: Central America; Colombia]

Palloni, A.; Massagli, M. and Marcotte, J. Estimating Adult Mortality with Maternal Orphanhood Data: Analysis of Sensitivity of the Techniques. *Population Stud.*, July 1984, *38*(2), pp. 255–79.
[G: Peru]

Papagni, Erasmo. Stratificazione delle famiglie secondo la forza-lavoro e segmentazione in un mercato locale del lavoro. (The Distribution of Labour Force in the Economic Structure of the Families and Segmentation in a Local Labour Market. With English summary.) *Econ. Lavoro*, Jan.-Mar. 1984, *18*(1), pp. 77–87.
[G: Italy]

Parsons, Donald O. On the Economics of Intergenerational Control. *Population Devel. Rev.*, March 1984, *10*(1), pp. 41–54.

Pebley, Anne R. Intervention Projects and the Study of Socioeconomic Determinants of Mortality. *Population Devel. Rev.*, Supplement 1984, *10*, pp. 281–305.
[G: LDCs]

Perlman, Mark. The Role of Population Projections for the Year 2000. In *Simon, J. L. and Kahn, H., eds.*, 1984, pp. 50–66. [G: Global]

Perrenoud, Alfred. Mortality Decline in Its Secular Setting. In *Bengtsson, T.; Fridlizius, G. and Ohlsson, R., eds.*, 1984, pp. 41–69.
[G: France; Sweden; Norway; Switzerland]

Pestieau, Pierre. The Effects of Varying Family Size on the Transmission and Distribution of Wealth. *Oxford Econ. Pap.*, November 1984, *36*(3), pp. 400–417.

Pfaff, Martin and Huber, Walter. Disability Policy in the Federal Republic of Germany. In *Haveman, R. H.; Halberstadt, V. and Burkhauser, R. V.*, 1984, pp. 193–239.
[G: W. Germany]

Pinstrup-Andersen, Per and Kumar, Shubh K. Food Policy, Human Nutrition, and Fertility. In *Schutjer, W. A. and Stokes, C. S., eds.*, 1984, pp. 235–51.
[G: LDCs]

Piore, Michael J. Alien Workers in the American Economy: Economic Consequences and Alternative Policies. In *Ullrich, R. A., ed.*, 1984, pp. 41–58.
[G: U.S.]

Plane, David A. A Systemic Demographic Efficiency Analysis of U.S. Interstate Population Exchange, 1935–1980. *Econ. Geogr.*, October 1984, *60*(4), pp. 294–312.
[G: U.S.]

Pope, David. Some Factors Inhibiting Australian Immigration in the 1920s. *Australian Econ. Hist. Rev.*, March 1984, *24*(1), pp. 34–52.
[G: Australia]

Powell, Dorian. The Role of Women in the Caribbean. *Soc. Econ. Stud.*, June 1984, *33*(2), pp. 97–122.
[G: Caribbean]

Pressat, Roland. Les previsions de population urbaine: examen critique des methodes. (Population Forecasts for Cities: A Critical Analysis of Methods. With English summary.) *Giorn. Econ.*, July–August 1984, *43*(7–8), pp. 451–69.
[G: France]

Presser, Harriet B. Job Characteristics of Spouses and Their Work Shifts. *Demography*, November 1984, *21*(4), pp. 575–89. [G: U.S.]

Preston, Samuel H. Children and the Elderly: Divergent Paths for America's Dependents. *Demography*, November 1984, *21*(4), pp. 435–57.
[G: U.S.]

Preston, Samuel H. Health Programs and Population Growth. In *Ghosh, P. K., ed., no. 6*, 1984, *1975*, pp. 7–17.

Preston, Samuel H. Urban Growth in Developing Countries—A Demographic Appraisal. In *Ghosh, P. K., ed., no. 2*, 1984, *1979*, pp. 36–56.
[G: LDCs]

Preston, Samuel H. and Bhat, P. N. Mari. New Evidence on Fertility and Mortality Trends in India. *Population Devel. Rev.*, September 1984, *10*(3), pp. 481–503. [G: India]

Preston, Samuel H. and Haines, Michael R. New Estimates of Child Mortality in the United States at the Turn of the Century. *J. Amer. Statist. Assoc.*, June 1984, *79*(386), pp. 272–81. [G: U.S.]

Primeaux, Walter J., Jr.; Pursell, Donald E. and Bare, Charles L. Forecasting First Births. *J. Behav. Econ.*, Summer 1984, *13*(1), pp. 41–55. [G: U.S.]

Raj, K. N. The Causes and Consequences of World Recession. *World Devel.*, March 1984, *12*(3), pp. 177–85. [G: Global]

Raj, K. N. The Causes and Consequences of World Recession. In *Jolly, R. and Cornia, G. A., eds.*, 1984, pp. 7–15. [G: MDCs; LDCs]

Ram, Rati. Dependency Rates and Savings: Reply. *Amer. Econ. Rev.*, March 1984, *74*(1), pp. 234–37. [G: LDCs; MDCs]

Ram, Rati. Market Opportunities, Intrafamily Resource Allocation, and Sex-Specific Survival Rates: An Intercountry Extension. *Amer. Econ. Rev.*, December 1984, *74*(5), pp. 1080–86. [G: U.S.; OECD; LDCs]

Ramos, Joseph. Urbanization and the Labour Market. *Cepal Rev.*, 1984, (24), pp. 63–81. [G: Latin America]

Ravenholt, R. T. Addiction Mortality in the United States, 1980: Tobacco, Alcohol, and Other Substances. *Population Devel. Rev.*, December 1984, *10*(4), pp. 697–724. [G: U.S.; LDCs]

Reichert, Joshua S. and Massey, Douglas S. Patterns of U.S. Migration from a Mexican Town. In *Jones, R. C., ed.*, 1984, pp. 93–109. [G: Mexico; U.S.]

Reid, Clifford E. Are Blacks Making It in the Suburbs? A Correction. *J. Urban Econ.*, November 1984, *16*(3), pp. 357–59. [G: U.S.]

Retherford, Robert D.; Cho, Lee-Jay and Kim, Nam-Il. Census-derived Estimates of Fertility by Duration since First Marriage in the Republic of Korea. *Demography*, November 1984, *21*(4), pp. 537–58. [G: Korea]

Richards, Toni. Weather, Nutrition and the Economy: The Analysis of Short Run Fluctuations in Births, Deaths and Marriages, France 1740–1909. In *Bengtsson, T.; Fridlizius, G. and Ohlsson, R., eds.*, 1984, pp. 357–89. [G: France]

Robinson, Warren and Schutjer, Wayne A. Agricultural Development and Demographic Change: A Generalization of the Boserup Model. *Econ. Develop. Cult. Change*, January 1984, *32*(2), pp. 355–66. [G: LDCs]

Rogerson, Peter A. New Directions in the Modelling of Interregional Migration. *Econ. Geogr.*, April 1984, *60*(2), pp. 111–21.

Rosenzweig, Mark R. and Schultz, T. Paul. Market Opportunities, Genetic Endowments, and Intrafamily Resource Distribution: Reply.

Amer. Econ. Rev., June 1984, *74*(3), pp. 521–22. [G: India]

Rowland, D. T. Old Age and the Demographic Transition. *Population Stud.*, March 1984, *38*(1), pp. 73–87. [G: Australia]

Rykiel, Zbigniew. Intra-Metropolitan Migration in the Warsaw Agglomeration. *Econ. Geogr.*, January 1984, *60*(1), pp. 55–70. [G: Poland]

Sabagh, Georges. Fertility Expectations and Behavior among Mexican Americans in Los Angeles, 1973–82. *Soc. Sci. Quart.*, June 1984, *65*(2), pp. 594–608. [G: U.S.]

Santow, Gigi and Bracher, M. D. Child Death and Time to the Next Birth in Central Java. *Population Stud.*, July 1984, *38*(2), pp. 241–53. [G: Indonesia]

Sathar, Zeba Ayesha. Does Female Education Affect Fertility Behaviour in Pakistan? *Pakistan Devel. Rev.*, Winter 1984, *23*(4), pp. 573–90. [G: Pakistan]

Sathar, Zeba Ayesha and Irfan, Mohammad. Reproductive Behaviour in Pakistan: Insights from the Population, Labour Force, and Migration Survey, 1979–80. *Pakistan Devel. Rev.*, Summer-Autumn 1984, *23*(2&3), pp. 207–18. [G: Pakistan]

Scheurwater, Jan. Toward a Spatial Demographic Information System. In *ter Heide, H. and Willekens, F. J., eds.*, 1984, pp. 69–93. [G: Netherlands]

Schlottmann, Alan M. and Herzog, Henry W., Jr. Career and Geographic Mobility Interactions: Implications for the Age Selectivity of Migration. *J. Human Res.*, Winter 1984, *19*(1), pp. 72–86. [G: U.S.]

Schmidt, Rainer. Population Change, Labour Market and Unemployment—The Case of the German Domestic Labour Force from 1965–1982. In *Steinmann, G., ed.*, 1984, pp. 278–94. [G: W. Germany]

Schmitt-Rink, Gerhard. Population Growth and Income Distribution. In *Steinmann, G., ed.*, 1984, pp. 59–67.

Schoen, R. and Baj, J. Twentieth-Century Cohort Marriage and Divorce in England and Wales. *Population Stud.*, November 1984, *38*(3), pp. 439–49. [G: U.K.]

Schofield, Roger. Population Growth in the Century after 1750: The Role of Mortality Decline. In *Bengtsson, T.; Fridlizius, G. and Ohlsson, R., eds.*, 1984, pp. 17–39. [G: U.K.; Sweden; France]

Schultz, T. Paul. Studying the Impact of Household Economic and Community Variables on Child Mortality. *Population Devel. Rev.*, Supplement 1984, *10*, pp. 215–35. [G: U.S.]

Schutjer, Wayne A. and Stokes, C. Shannon. Rural Development and Human Fertility in Developing Nations. In *Schutjer, W. A. and Stokes, C. S., eds.*, 1984, pp. 1–22. [G: LDCs]

Schwartz, Saul; Danziger, Sheldon and Smolensky, Eugene. The Choice of Living Arrangements by the Elderly. In *Aaron, H. J. and Burtless, G., eds.*, 1984, pp. 229–50. [G: U.S.]

Seers, Dudley. Active Life Profiles for Different Social Groups. In *[Chenery, H. B.]*, 1984, pp. 515–42. **[G: Brazil; Malaysia; Hong Kong; U.K.]**

Seiver, Daniel A. and Cymrot, Donald J. A New Approach to Household Fertility Behavior. *Eastern Econ. J.*, January-March 1984, *10*(1), pp. 31–41. **[G: U.S.]**

Sen, Amartya. Economics and the Family. In *Sen, A.*, 1984, *1983*, pp. 369–85.

Serow, William J. The Impact of Population Change on Consumption. In *Steinmann, G.*, *ed.*, 1984, pp. 168–78.

Simmons, Ozzie G. Population Policy Analysis and Development Planning. *J. Devel. Areas*, July 1984, *18*(4), pp. 433–48. **[G: LDCs]**

Simmons, Ozzie G. Rural Development and Human Fertility: Conclusions and Policy Implications. In *Schutjer, W. A. and Stokes, C. S.*, *eds.*, 1984, pp. 291–308. **[G: LDCs]**

Simon, Julian L. Immigrants, Taxes, and Welfare in the United States. *Population Devel. Rev.*, March 1984, *10*(1), pp. 55–69. **[G: U.S.]**

Simon, Julian L. and Kahn, Herman. The Resourceful Earth: A Response to Global 2000: Introduction. In *Simon, J. L. and Kahn, H.*, *eds.*, 1984, pp. 1–49. **[G: Global]**

Simon, Julian L. and Steinmann, Gunter. The Economic Implications of Learning-by-Doing for Population Size and Growth. *Europ. Econ. Rev.*, October–November 1984, *26*(1–2), pp. 167–85.

Sinha, J. N. Development Strategy and Demographic Change. In *Singh, A. K.; Papola, T. S. and Mathur, R. S.*, *eds.*, 1984, pp. 66–88. **[G: India]**

Slater, Paul B. Origin and Destination Entropies of U.S. 1965–70: Age–Sex-Specific Intercounty Migration Flows. *Math. Soc. Sci.*, February 1984, *7*(1), pp. 21–32.

Sloane, Douglas M. and Lee, Che-Fu. Achieving Expected Parities: A Reanalysis of Freedman et al.'s Data, 1962–1977. *Demography*, August 1984, *21*(3), pp. 413–22. **[G: U.S.]**

Sly, David F. Lifetime Migration Patterns in Kenya, 1969. In *Ominde, S. H.*, *ed.*, 1984, pp. 68–77. **[G: Kenya]**

Sly, David F. Modern Economic-Sector Development and Population Change. In *Ominde, S. H.*, *ed.*, 1984, pp. 91–100. **[G: Kenya]**

Smith, David P. A Comment on J. Akin et al., "The Determinants of Breastfeeding in Sri Lanka." *Demography*, November 1984, *21*(4), pp. 683–86. **[G: Sri Lanka]**

Smith, David P. Robustness of $_5q_x$ Estimators under Nonstationarity. *Demography*, November 1984, *21*(4), pp. 613–22. **[G: U.S.]**

Smith, Lawrence B. Household Headship Rates, Household Formation, and Housing Demand in Canada. *Land Econ.*, May 1984, *60*(2), pp. 180–88. **[G: Canada]**

Smith, Lawrence B., et al. The Demand for Housing, Household Headship Rates, and Household Formation: An International Analysis. *Urban Stud.*, November 1984, *21*(4), pp. 407–14. **[G: U.S.; Canada; U.K.; France]**

Smith, Stanley K. and Mandell, Marylou. A Comparison of Population Estimation Methods: Housing Unit versus Component II, Ratio Correlation, and Administrative Records. *J. Amer. Statist. Assoc.*, June 1984, *79*(386), pp. 282–89. **[G: U.S.]**

Söderberg, Johan. Interrelationships between Short-term Economic and Demographic Fluctuations in a Period of Crisis: South-eastern Sweden 1866–1872. In *Bengtsson, T.; Fridlizius, G. and Ohlsson, R.*, *eds.*, 1984, pp. 255–76. **[G: Sweden]**

Sokal, Robert R. Spatial Analysis in Population Biology and Regional Science. In *Andersson, Å. E.; Isard, W. and Puu, T.*, *eds.*, 1984, pp. 241–66. **[G: U.S.]**

Srinivasan, K., et al. Factors Affecting Fertility Control in India: A Cross-Sectional Study. *Population Devel. Rev.*, June 1984, *10*(2), pp. 273–96. **[G: India]**

Srivastava, J. N. Education and Demographic Behaviour: Some Empirical Findings. In *Singh, A. K.; Papola, T. S. and Mathur, R. S.*, *eds.*, 1984, pp. 89–108. **[G: India]**

Stark, Oded. Bargaining, Altruism, and Demographic Phenomena. *Population Devel. Rev.*, December 1984, *10*(4), pp. 679–92.

Stark, Oded. Discontinuity and the Theory of International Migration. *Kyklos*, 1984, *37*(2), pp. 206–22. **[G: Taiwan; U.S.; U.K.]**

Stark, Oded. Rural-to-Urban Migration in LDCs: A Relative Deprivation Approach. *Econ. Develop. Cult. Change*, April 1984, *32*(3), pp. 475–86. **[G: LDCs]**

Stark, Oded. Rural-to-Urban Migration in LDCs: A Relative Deprivation Approach. *Econ. Develop. Cult. Change*, April 1984, *32*(3), pp. 475–86. **[G: LDCs]**

Stark, Oded. Rural-to-Urban Migration in LDCs: A Relative Deprivation Approach. *Econ. Develop. Cult. Change*, April 1984, *32*(3), pp. 475–86.

Staroverov, O. V. Markov Models of Mobility. *Matekon*, Spring 1984, *20*(3), pp. 3–21.

Steinmann, Gunter. A Model of the History of Demographic-Economic Growth. In *Steinmann, G.*, *ed.*, 1984, pp. 29–49.

Stephan, G. Edward and Stephan, Karen H. Population Redistribution and Changes in the Size-Density Slope. *Demography*, February 1984, *21*(1), pp. 35–40. **[G: U.S.; W. Europe]**

Stoddart, David R. and Pethick, John S. Environmental Hazard and Coastal Reclamation: Problems and Prospects in Bangladesh. In *[Farmer, B. H.]*, 1984, pp. 339–61. **[G: Bangladesh]**

Stokes, C. Shannon and Schutjer, Wayne A. Access to Land and Fertility in Developing Countries. In *Schutjer, W. A. and Stokes, C. S.*, *eds.*, 1984, pp. 195–215. **[G: LDCs]**

Stone, Leroy O. and Fletcher, Susan. Why We Should be Cautious in Accepting Forecasts of the Dependency Ratios in the 21st Century. In *Conklin, D. W.; Bennett, J. H. and Courchene, T. J.*, *eds.*, 1984, pp. 474–86. **[G: Canada]**

Stone, Richard [Sir]. Accounting Matrices in Economics and Demography. In *van der Ploeg, F., ed.*, 1984, pp. 9–36.

Straub, Martin and Wenig, Alois. Human Fertility and the Distribution of Wealth. In *Steinmann, G., ed.*, 1984, pp. 68–86.

Stuart, Robert C. The Sources of Soviet Urban Growth. In *Morton, H. W. and Stuart, R. C., eds.*, 1984, pp. 25–41. **[G: U.S.S.R.]**

Suh, Sang Mok. Effects of the Current World Recession on the Welfare of Children: The Case of Korea. *World Devel.*, March 1984, *12*(3), pp. 329–38. **[G: Korea]**

Sullivan, Teresa A. and Tienda, Marta. Integration of Multiple Data Sources in Immigrant Studies. *Rev. Public Data Use*, December 1984, *12*(4), pp. 233–44. **[G: U.S.]**

Sullivan, Teresa A., et al. Alternative Estimates of Mexican American Mortality in Texas, 1980. *Soc. Sci. Quart.*, June 1984, *65*(2), pp. 609–17. **[G: U.S.]**

Sun, Te-Hsiung. Urban-Industrial Development as a Force in Rural Fertility Change: The Case of Taiwan, Republic of China. In *Schutjer, W. A. and Stokes, C. S., eds.*, 1984, pp. 49–76. **[G: Taiwan]**

Swanson, David A. and Tedrow, Lucky M. Improving the Measurement of Temporal Change in Regression Models Used for County Population Estimates. *Demography*, August 1984, *21*(3), pp. 373–81. **[G: U.S.]**

de Sweemer, Cécile. The Influence of Child Spacing on Child Survival. *Population Stud.*, March 1984, *38*(1), pp. 47–72. **[G: India]**

Sweet, James A. Components of Change in the Number of Households: 1970–1980. *Demography*, May 1984, *21*(2), pp. 129–40. **[G: U.S.]**

Swicegood, C. Gray; Morgan, S. Philip and Rindfuss, Ronald R. Measurement and Replication: Evaluating the Consistency of Eight U.S. Fertility Surveys. *Demography*, February 1984, *21*(1), pp. 19–33. **[G: U.S.]**

Tabah, Léon. Preparations for the 1984 International Conference on Population. *Population Devel. Rev.*, March 1984, *10*(1), pp. 81–86. **[G: Global]**

Tabah, Léon. World Population Trends: A Stocktaking. In *Ghosh, P. K., ed., no. 5*, 1984, *1980*, pp. 35–71.

Tabard, Nicole. Mobilité sociale, fratrie et descendance. (Social Mobility, Size of Family of Origin and Descendance. With English summary.) *Consommation*, July–September 1984, *31*(3), pp. 19–50. **[G: France]**

Tabuchi, Takatoshi. The Systemic Variables and Elasticities in Alonso's General Theory of Movement. *Reg. Sci. Urban Econ.*, May 1984, *14*(2), pp. 249–64. **[G: U.S.; Japan; Canada]**

Tawiah, E. O. Determinants of Cumulative Fertility in Ghana. *Demography*, February 1984, *21*(1), pp. 1–8. **[G: Ghana]**

Taylor, Carl E. Nutrition and Population in Health Planning. In *Ghosh, P. K., ed., no. 6*, 1984, *1977*, pp. 249–66.

Tekçe, Belgin and Shorter, Frederic C. Determinants of Child Mortality: A Study of Squatter

Settlements in Jordan. *Population Devel. Rev.*, Supplement 1984, *10*, pp. 257–80. **[G: Jordan]**

Teper, S. and Backett, M. Implications of Demographic Change for the Young Population (0–19 years). In *Lopez, A. D. and Cliquet, R. L., eds.*, 1984, pp. 133–47. **[G: Europe; Algeria; Morocco; Turkey]**

Thatcher, A. R. Topic of Public Interest: The 1981 Census of Population in England and Wales. *J. Roy. Statist. Soc.*, 1984, *147*(2), pp. 222–32. **[G: U.K.]**

Thornton, Arland D.; Chang, Ming-Cheng and Sun, Te-Hsiung. Social and Economic Change, Intergenerational Relationships, and Family Formation in Taiwan. *Demography*, November 1984, *21*(4), pp. 475–99. **[G: Taiwan]**

Thornton, Arland D.; Freedman, Ronald and Freedman, Deborah S. Further Reflections on Changes in Fertility Expectations and Preferences. *Demography*, August 1984, *21*(3), pp. 423–29. **[G: U.S.]**

Tien, H. Yuan. Induced Fertility Transition: Impact of Population Planning and Socio-economic Change in the People's Republic of China. *Population Stud.*, November 1984, *38*(3), pp. 385–400. **[G: China]**

Tobier, Emanuel. Setting Municipal Priorities: The Setting: Population. In *Brecher, C. and Horton, R. D., eds.*, 1984, pp. 19–42. **[G: U.S.]**

Todaro, Michael P. Intergenerational Income–Fertility Linkages in Developing Countries: A Conceptual Framework. In *[Reynolds, L. G.]*, 1984, pp. 42–62. **[G: LDCs]**

Todaro, Michael P. Urbanization in Developing Nations: Trends, Prospects, and Policies. In *Ghosh, P. K., ed., no. 2*, 1984, pp. 7–26. **[G: LDCs]**

Tolnay, Stewart E. and Guest, Avery M. American Family Building Strategies in 1900: Stopping or Spacing. *Demography*, February 1984, *21*(1), pp. 9–18. **[G: U.S.]**

Toney, Michael B. and Swearengen, Roger. Migration Data: Prospects for Research Based on the Youth Cohort of the NLS. *Rev. Public Data Use*, October 1984, *12*(3), pp. 211–19. **[G: U.S.]**

Trager, Lillian. Migration and Remittances: Urban Income and Rural Households in the Philippines. *J. Devel. Areas*, April 1984, *18*(3), pp. 317–40. **[G: Philippines]**

Trebici, Vl.; Sora, V. and Hristache, I. Accelerated Demographic Growth—Reflected in the Directives of the XIIIth Congress of the Romanian Communist Party. *Econ. Computat. Cybern. Stud. Res.*, 1984, *19*(4), pp. 21–25. **[G: Romania]**

Tung, S. L. An Econometric Analysis of the Effects of Population Change on Economic Growth: A Study of Taiwan. *Appl. Econ.*, August 1984, *16*(4), pp. 523–38. **[G: Taiwan]**

Turchi, Boone A. Rural Development Policy and Fertility: A Framework for Analysis at the

Household Level. In *Schutjer, W. A. and Stokes, C. S., eds.*, 1984, pp. 97–120.
[G: LDCs]

Turner, John A. Population Age Structure and the Size of Social Security. *Southern Econ. J.*, April 1984, *50*(4), pp. 1131–46. [G: U.S.]

Urquidi, Victor L. Population and a New International Economic Order: A Missing Link. In *Ghosh, P. K., ed., no. 9*, 1984, *1979*, pp. 152–63.

Urquidi, Victor L. Population and a New International Order: A Missing Link? In *Ghosh, P. K., ed., no. 5*, 1984, *1979*, pp. 294–305.

Valdez, Avelardo and Jones, Richard C. Geographical Patterns of Undocumented Mexicans and Chicanos in San Antonio, Texas: 1970 and 1980. In *Jones, R. C., ed.*, 1984, pp. 218–35.
[G: U.S.]

Vining, Daniel R., Jr. Family Salaries and the East German Birth Rate: A Comment [The French Population Debate]. *Population Devel. Rev.*, December 1984, *10*(4), pp. 693–96.
[G: E. Germany; W. Germany]

Vinovskis, Maris A. Historical Perspectives on Rural Development and Human Fertility in Nineteenth-Century America. In *Schutjer, W. A. and Stokes, C. S., eds.*, 1984, pp. 77–96.
[G: U.S.]

Vlassoff, M. A Rejoinder to S. K. Datta and J. B. Nugent [Old Age Security and the Utility of Children in Rural India]. *Population Stud.*, November 1984, *38*(3), pp. 510–12.
[G: India]

Wachter, Michael L. and Wascher, William L. Leveling the Peaks and Troughs in the Demographic Cycle: An Application to School Enrollment Rates. *Rev. Econ. Statist.*, May 1984, *66*(2), pp. 208–15. [G: U.S.]

Wagner, Adolf. Aspects of Demographic Unemployment. In *Steinmann, G., ed.*, 1984, pp. 295–302. [G: W. Germany]

Wander, Hilde. What Does it Cost to Support the Young and the Old Generations? In *Steinmann, G., ed.*, 1984, pp. 238–57.
[G: W. Germany]

Ward, W. Peter and Ward, Patricia C. Infant Birth Weight and Nutrition in Industrializing Montreal. *Amer. Hist. Rev.*, April 1984, *89*(2), pp. 324–45. [G: Canada]

Ware, Helen. Effects of Maternal Education, Women's Roles, and Child Care on Child Mortality. *Population Devel. Rev.*, Supplement 1984, *10*, pp. 191–214. [G: LDCs]

Weber, Wolfgang. The Impact of Population Change on Enterprise Behavior. In *Steinmann, G., ed.*, 1984, pp. 404–15.

Weir, David R. Life under Pressure: France and England, 1670–1870. *J. Econ. Hist.*, March 1984, *44*(1), pp. 27–47. [G: U.K.; France]

ter Welle, F. Uncertainty and Policy Targets in Migration Projections. In *ter Heide, H. and Willekens, F. J., eds.*, 1984, pp. 271–85.
[G: Netherlands]

Weller, Robert H. The Gainful Employment of Females and Fertility—With Special Reference to Rural Areas of Developing Countries.

In *Schutjer, W. A. and Stokes, C. S., eds.*, 1984, pp. 151–71. [G: LDCs]

Wessman, James W. Sugar and Demography: Population Dynamics in the Spanish Antilles During the Nineteenth and Twentieth Centuries. In *Albert, B. and Graves, A., eds.*, 1984, pp. 95–108. [G: Cuba; Puerto Rico]

Willekens, F. J. Approaches and Innovations in Policy-Oriented Migration and Population Distribution Research. In *ter Heide, H. and Willekens, F. J., eds.*, 1984, pp. 21–43.
[G: Netherlands]

Willekens, F. J. Spatial Policy and Demographic Research Opportunities. In *ter Heide, H. and Willekens, F. J., eds.*, 1984, pp. 355–401.

Willekens, F. J. and Drewe, P. A Multiregional Model for Regional Demographic Projection. In *ter Heide, H. and Willekens, F. J., eds.*, 1984, pp. 309–34. [G: Netherlands]

Williamson, Jeffrey G. British Mortality and the Value of Life, 1781–1931 *Population Stud.*, March 1984, *38*(1), pp. 157–72. [G: U.K.]

Wilson, C. Natural Fertility in Pre-Industrial England, 1600–1799. *Population Stud.*, July 1984, *38*(2), pp. 225–40. [G: U.K.]

Winegarden, Calman R. Income Redistribution versus Accelerated Economic Growth: A Comparison of Demographic Effects. *Oxford Bull. Econ. Statist.*, August 1984, *46*(3), pp. 255–71. [G: LDCs]

Winegarden, Calman R. Women's Fertility, Market Work and Marital Status: A Test of the New Household Economics with International Data. *Economica*, November 1984, *51*(204), pp. 447–56. [G: W. Europe]

Wolf, Arthur P. Fertility in Prerevolutionary Rural China. *Population Devel. Rev.*, September 1984, *10*(3), pp. 443–70. [G: China]

Wolf, Douglas A. Changes in Household Size and Composition Due to Financial Incentives. *J. Human Res.*, Winter 1984, *19*(1), pp. 87–103.
[G: U.S.]

Wolf, Douglas A. The Choice of Living Arrangements by the Elderly: Comment. In *Aaron, H. J. and Burtless, G., eds.*, 1984, pp. 250–53. [G: U.S.]

Wolfe, Barbara L. and Behrman, Jere R. Who Is Schooled in Developing Countries? The Roles of Income, Parental Schooling, Sex, Residence, and Family Size. *Econ. Educ. Rev.*, 1984, *3*(3), pp. 231–45. [G: Nicaragua]

Wolpin, Kenneth I. An Estimable Dynamic Stochastic Model of Fertility and Child Mortality. *J. Polit. Econ.*, October 1984, *92*(5), pp. 852–74. [G: Malaysia]

Yotopoulos, Pan A. A Reinterpretation of Rural–Urban Fertility Differentials in Developing Countries. *METU*, 1984, *11*(1–2), pp. 207–23.
[G: LDCs; MDCs]

Zimmermann, Klaus F. The Dynamics of Women's Labor Force Participation and Fertility: A Simultaneous ARX-Model. In *Steinmann, G., ed.*, 1984, pp. 386–403.
[G: W. Germany]

851 Human Capital; Value of Human Life

8510 Human Capital; Value of Human Life

Adelman, Irma and Levy, Amnon. The Equalizing Role of Human Resource Intensive Growth Strategies: A Theoretical Model. *J. Policy Modeling*, May 1984, *6*(2), pp. 271–87.

Alexander, Elmore R., III and Frey, Donald E. An Econometric Estimate of the Demand for MBA Enrollment. *Econ. Educ. Rev.*, 1984, *3*(2), pp. 97–103. **[G: U.S.]**

Antonelli, Gilberto. Risorse umane e redditi da lavoro. Domanda di istruzione, offerta di lavoro e comparazioni tra settore privato e settore pubblico. (Human Resources and Labour Incomes. Demand for Education, Labour Supply and Comparison between Private and Public Sector. With English summary.) *Econ. Lavoro*, Jan.-Mar. 1984, *18*(1), pp. 17–41. **[G: Italy]**

Arnold, Wolfgang. Growth, Distribution and Motivation in LDCs. In *Ghosh, P. K., ed., no. 7, 1984, 1979*, pp. 204–15.

Atkinson, Anthony B. and Jenkins, S. P. The Steady-State Assumption and the Estimation of Distributional and Related Models. *J. Human Res.*, Summer 1984, *19*(3), pp. 358–76. **[G: U.S.]**

Barzel, Yoram and Yu, Ben T. The Effect of the Utilization Rate on the Division of Labor. *Econ. Inquiry*, January 1984, *22*(1), pp. 18–27.

Behrman, Jere R. and Wolfe, Barbara L. The Socioeconomic Impact of Schooling in a Developing Country. *Rev. Econ. Statist.*, May 1984, *66*(2), pp. 296–303. **[G: Nicaragua]**

Bell, Carolyn Shaw. Human Capital Formation and the Decision Makers. *J. Econ. Issues*, June 1984, *18*(2), pp. 429–37.

Bell, Edward B. Imperfect Capital Markets and Investment in Education. *Econ. Educ. Rev.*, 1984, *3*(2), pp. 105–10.

Bell, Martin. 'Learning' and the Accumulation of Industrial Technological Capacity in Developing Countries. In *Fransman, M. and King, K., eds., 1984*, pp. 187–209. **[G: LDCs]**

Berg, Ivar. Current Conceptions of Unemployment: Some Logical and Empirical Difficulties. In *Ullrich, R. A., ed., 1984*, pp. 95–126. **[G: U.S.]**

Berg, Ivar. Unemployment, Productivity, and Inflation: Misgivings About the Sapient Orthodoxy. In *Brief, A. P., ed., 1984*, pp. 71–89.

Berger, Mark C. Cohort Size and the Earnings Growth of Young Workers. *Ind. Lab. Relat. Rev.*, July 1984, *37*(4), pp. 582–91. **[G: U.S.]**

Birdsall, Nancy and Behrman, Jere R. Does Geographical Aggregation Cause Overestimates of the Returns to Schooling? *Oxford Bull. Econ. Statist.*, February 1984, *46*(1), pp. 55–72. **[G: Brazil]**

Blakemore, Arthur E. Human Capital Investment and the Reduction in the Unemployment Rate Consistent with Nonaccelerating Inflation. *Quart. J. Bus. Econ.*, Spring 1984, *23*(2), pp. 3–14. **[G: U.S.]**

Blakemore, Arthur E. and Low, Stuart A. Sex Differences in Occupational Selection: The Case of College Majors. *Rev. Econ. Statist.*, February 1984, *66*(1), pp. 157–63. **[G: U.S.]**

Blakemore, Arthur E. and Low, Stuart A. The High-School Dropout Decision and Its Wage Consequences. *Econ. Educ. Rev.*, 1984, *3*(2), pp. 111–19. **[G: U.S.]**

Blau, David M. Family Earnings and Wage Inequality Early in the Life Cycle. *Rev. Econ. Statist.*, May 1984, *66*(2), pp. 200–207. **[G: U.S.]**

Boulier, Bryan L. and Rosenzweig, Mark R. Schooling, Search, and Spouse Selection: Testing Economic Theories of Marriage and Household Behavior. *J. Polit. Econ.*, August 1984, *92*(4), pp. 712–32. **[G: Philippines]**

Butler, Richard J. The Effect of Education on Wages—Hedonic Makes Selectivity Bias (Sort of) Simpler. *Econ. Inquiry*, January 1984, *22*(1), pp. 109–20.

Caillods, Françoise. Education, Organisation of Work and Indigenous Technological Capacity. In *Fransman, M. and King, K., eds., 1984*, pp. 211–22. **[G: LDCs]**

Cassidy, George W. L. R. Dual Market and Human Capital Theories Revisited: The Role of Secondary Labor Market Intermediaries. *Rivista Int. Sci. Econ. Com.*, February 1984, *31*(2), pp. 109–25.

Chasse, John Dennis. Marshall, the Human Agent and Economic Growth: Wants and Activities Revisited. *Hist. Polit. Econ.*, Fall 1984, *16*(3), pp. 381–404.

Chaudhuri, T. Datta and Khan, M. Ali. Educated Unemployed, Educational Subsidies, and Growth. *Pakistan Devel. Rev.*, Summer-Autumn 1984, *23*(2&3), pp. 395–409.

Chillemi, Ottorino. Un modello per l'analisi della produzione di capitale umano specifico. (A Model for the Analysis of the Production of Specific Human Capital. With English summary.) *Rivista Int. Sci. Econ. Com.*, December 1984, *31*(12), pp. 1201–20.

Chiswick, Carmel U. The Impact of Education Policy on Economic Development: Quantity, Quality, and Earnings of Labor. *Econ. Educ. Rev.*, 1984, *3*(2), pp. 121–30.

Chizhova, L. Balancing Labor Resources with Economic Demands. *Prob. Econ.*, May 1984, *27*(1), pp. 63–78. **[G: U.S.S.R.]**

Christl, Josef. The Explanatory Power of the Human Capital Earnings Function. *Empirica*, 1984, *11*(1), pp. 47–57. **[G: Austria]**

Clogg, Clifford C. and Shockey, James W. Mismatch between Occupation and Schooling: A Prevalence Measure, Recent Trends and Demographic Analysis. *Demography*, May 1984, *21*(2), pp. 235–57. **[G: U.S.]**

Conlisk, John. Four Invalid Propositions about Equality, Efficiency, and Intergenerational Transfers through Schooling. *J. Human Res.*, Winter 1984, *19*(1), pp. 3–21.

Corman, Hope and Davidson, Patricia K. Economic Aspects of Post-secondary Schooling Decisions. *Econ. Educ. Rev.*, 1984, *3*(2), pp. 131–39. **[G: U.S.]**

Coyte, Peter C. Optimal Job Assignment and Investment in Specific Human Capital: An Application to Professional Teachers. *Appl. Econ.*, October 1984, *16*(5), pp. 703–15. **[G: Canada]**

Coyte, Peter C. Specific Human Capital and Sorting Mechanisms in Labor Markets. *Southern Econ. J.*, October 1984, *51*(2), pp. 469–80.

Datcher, Linda P. The Effect of Racial Differences in Background on Schooling: A Survey. In *Darity, W., Jr., ed.*, 1984, pp. 119–32. **[G: U.S.]**

Daymont, Thomas N. and Andrisani, Paul J. Job Preferences, College Major, and the Gender Gap in Earnings. *J. Human Res.*, Summer 1984, *19*(3), pp. 408–28. **[G: U.S.]**

Dean, Edwin. Education and Economic Productivity: Introduction. In *Dean, E., ed.*, 1984, pp. 1–17. **[G: U.S.]**

Donaldson, David and Eaton, B. Curtis. Person-Specific Costs of Production: Hours of Work, Rates of Pay, Labour Contracts. *Can. J. Econ.*, August 1984, *17*(3), pp. 441–49.

Dooley, Martin D. and Gottschalk, Peter. Earnings Inequality among Males in the United States: Trends and the Effect of Labor Force Growth. *J. Polit. Econ.*, February 1984, *92*(1), pp. 59–89. **[G: U.S.]**

Evans, E. W. and Wiseman, N. C. Education, Training and Economic Performance: British Economists' Views, 1868–1939. *J. Europ. Econ. Hist.*, Spring 1984, *13*(1), pp. 129–48. **[G: U.K.]**

Evans, Robert, Jr. 'Lifetime Earnings' in Japan for the Class of 1955. *Mon. Lab. Rev.*, April 1984, *107*(4), pp. 32–36. **[G: Japan]**

Fareed, A. E. and Riggs, G. D. The Human Wealth of American Men. *Amer. Econ.*, Spring 1984, *28*(1), pp. 27–33. **[G: U.S.]**

Forester, Thomas H.; McNown, Robert F. and Singell, Larry D. A Cost–Benefit Analysis of the 55 MPH Speed Limit. *Southern Econ. J.*, January 1984, *50*(3), pp. 631–41. **[G: U.S.]**

Fraser, Clive D. Optimal Compensation for Potential Fatality. *J. Public Econ.*, April 1984, *23*(3), pp. 307–32.

Friedman, Samuel R. Structure, Process, and the Labor Market. In *Darity, W., Jr., ed.*, 1984, pp. 175–217.

Garen, John. The Returns to Schooling: A Selectivity Bias Approach with a Continuous Choice Variable. *Econometrica*, September 1984, *52*(5), pp. 1199–1218. **[G: U.S.]**

Gates, John H. Human Capital Investment in Health: A Measurement Framework and Estimates for the United States, 1952–78. *Rev. Income Wealth*, March 1984, *30*(1), pp. 39–52. **[G: U.S.]**

Ghosh, B. N. Brain Migration from Third World: An Implicative Analysis. *Rivista Int. Sci. Econ. Com.*, April 1984, *31*(4), pp. 346–70. **[G: LDCs]**

Glick, Henry A. and Feuer, Michael J. Em-

ployer-sponsored Training and the Governance of Specific Human Capital Investments. *Quart. Rev. Econ. Bus.*, Summer 1984, *24*(2), pp. 91–103.

Guisinger, Stephen E.; Henderson, James W. and Scully, Gerald W. Earnings, Rates of Return to Education and the Earnings Distribution in Pakistan. *Econ. Educ. Rev.*, 1984, *3*(4), pp. 257–67. **[G: Pakistan]**

Gunning, J. Patrick. Marriage Law and Human Capital Investment: A Comment. *Southern Econ. J.*, October 1984, *51*(2), pp. 594–97.

Hart, Oliver. The Firm as a Collection of Human Resources: Comment. In *Wiles, P. and Routh, G., eds.*, 1984, pp. 207–10.

Hartog, Joop. On the Private Benefits of Subsidies to Education. *Econ. Educ. Rev.*, 1984, *3*(1), pp. 23–35. **[G: Netherlands]**

Haveman, Robert H. and Wolfe, Barbara L. Education, Productivity, and Well-Being: On Defining and Measuring the Economic Characteristics of Schooling. In *Dean, E., ed.*, 1984, pp. 19–55.

Haveman, Robert H. and Wolfe, Barbara L. Schooling and Economic Well-Being: The Role of Nonmarket Effects. *J. Human Res.*, Summer 1984, *19*(3), pp. 377–407.

Henze, Jürgen. Higher Education: The Tension between Quality and Equality. In *Hayhoe, R., ed.*, 1984, pp. 93–153. **[G: China]**

Hirsch, Barry T. Physical Capital, Human Capital and the Distribution of Earnings. *Econ. Educ. Rev.*, 1984, *3*(1), pp. 55–64. **[G: U.S.]**

Hoffman, Saul D. Black–White Differences in Returns to Higher Education: Evidence from the 1970s. *Econ. Educ. Rev.*, 1984, *3*(1), pp. 13–21. **[G: U.S.]**

Hoffman, Saul D. Comment [Discrimination Against Women: Theory and Evidence] [The Effect of Racial Differences in Background on Schooling: A Survey]. In *Darity, W., Jr., ed.*, 1984, pp. 241–55. **[G: U.S.]**

Holcombe, Randall G. and Holcombe, Lora P. The Return to the Federal Government from Investment in Higher Education. *Public Finance Quart.*, July 1984, *12*(3), pp. 365–71. **[G: U.S.]**

Hossain, Najmul and Downing, Paul B. The Economic Returns from U.S. Higher Education to Foreign Students. *J. Behav. Econ.*, Winter 1984, *13*(2), pp. 67–92. **[G: U.S.]**

Jeffries, John M. and Stanback, Howard. Employment and Training Policy for Black America: Beyond Placebo to Progressive Public Policy. *Rev. Black Polit. Econ.*, Summer–Fall 1984, *13*(1–2), pp. 119–37.

Johnson, George E. Subsidies for Higher Education. *J. Lab. Econ.*, July 1984, *2*(3), pp. 303–18. **[G: U.S.]**

Johnson, William G. and Heler, Edward. Compensation for Death from Asbestos. *Ind. Lab. Relat. Rev.*, July 1984, *37*(4), pp. 529–40.

Jorgenson, Dale W. The Contribution of Education to U.S. Economic Growth, 1948–73. In *Dean, E., ed.*, 1984, pp. 95–162. **[G: U.S.]**

Kalirajan, K. P. and Shand, R. T. Schooling,

Non-formal Education and Productivity. *Indian Econ. J.*, April–June 1984, *31*(4), pp. 35–44. [G: India]

Kaufman, Roger T. A Note on Richard Freeman's "Overinvestment in College Training." *J. Human Res.*, Spring 1984, *19*(2), pp. 278–79. [G: U.S.]

Kenyon, Daphne A. and McCandless, George T., Jr. A Note on the Required Compensation Test as the Theoretical Basis for Putting a Value on Human Life. *Southern Econ. J.*, July 1984, *51*(1), pp. 258–66.

Kiker, B. F. and Roberts, R. Blaine. A Note on the Effect of Schooling, Experience and Aging on Wage Growth. *Econ. Educ. Rev.*, 1984, *3*(2), pp. 155–58. [G: U.S.]

Kiker, B. F. and Roberts, R. Blaine. The Durability of Human Capital: Some New Evidence. *Econ. Inquiry*, April 1984, *22*(2), pp. 269–81. [G: U.S.]

Kleinhückelskoten, Hans-Dieter. Optimale Strategien unternehmerischer Humankapitalinvestitionen und deren Einfluss auf Lohnentwicklung und Lohnstruktur. (Optimal Strategies for the Firm's Investment in Human Capital and Their Influence on Wage Movements and Wage Structure. With English summary.) *Z. ges. Staatswiss.*, September 1984, *140*(3), pp. 510–27.

Kodde, David A. and Ritzen, Jozef M. M. Integrating Consumption and Investment Motives in a Neoclassical Model of Demand for Education. *Kyklos*, 1984, *37*(4), pp. 598–608. [G: Canada; U.S.]

Koike, Kazuo. Skill Formation Systems in the U.S. and Japan: A Comparative Study. In *Aoki, M.*, ed., 1984, pp. 47–75. [G: U.S.; Japan]

Landefeld, J. Steven. Measuring the Returns to Biomedical Research: Issues and Problems. In *Lindgren, B.*, ed., 1984, pp. 255–86. [G: U.S.]

Landskroner, Yoram and Paroush, Jacob. Human Capital and Financial Equilibrium. *J. Econ. Bus.*, December 1984, *36*(4), pp. 443–52. [G: U.S.]

Lehrer, Evelyn and Nerlove, Marc. A Life-Cycle Analysis of Family Income Distribution. *Econ. Inquiry*, July 1984, *22*(3), pp. 360–74. [G: U.S.]

Leigh, Duane E. Why Is There Mandatory Retirement? An Empirical Reexamination. *J. Human Res.*, Fall 1984, *19*(4), pp. 512–31. [G: U.S.]

Lemelin, Clément. Interprétations de la corrélation éducation-revenu. (Interpretations of the Education–Income Correlation. With English summary.) *L'Actual. Econ.*, June 1984, *60*(2), pp. 223–39.

Levine, Victor and Moock, Peter R. Labor Force Experience and Earnings: Women and Children. *Econ. Educ. Rev.*, 1984, *3*(3), pp. 183–93. [G: U.S.]

Little, Angela. Education, Earnings and Productivity—the Eternal Triangle. In *Oxenham, J.*, ed., 1984, pp. 87–110. [G: Selected LDCs]

Malveaux, Julianne. Employment and Training Policy for Black America: Beyond Placebo to Progressive Public Policy: Comments. *Rev. Black Polit. Econ.*, Summer–Fall 1984, *13*(1–2), pp. 138–44. [G: U.S.]

Marcus, Alan J. Efficient Risk Sharing, Non-marketable Labor Income and Fixed-Wage Contracts. *Europ. Econ. Rev.*, August 1984, *25*(3), pp. 373–85.

Mathur, Gautam. Employment and Manpower Generation. In *Amin, S.*, ed., 1984, pp. 67–93.

McMahon, Walter W. The Relation of Education and R&D to Productivity Growth. *Econ. Educ. Rev.*, 1984, *3*(4), pp. 299–313. [G: U.S.]

McMahon, Walter W. Why Families Invest in Education. In *[Ferber, R.]*, 1984, pp. 75–91. [G: U.S.]

Meng, Ronald and Sentance, Jim. Religion and the Determination of Earnings: Further Results. *Can. J. Econ.*, August 1984, *17*(3), pp. 481–88. [G: Canada]

Miller, Edward M. Can the Public's Desire for Future Benefits Be Deduced from Their Private Decisions? Returns from Human Capital and from Public Goods Investments Are Directly Analogous. *Amer. J. Econ. Soc.*, October 1984, *43*(4), pp. 443–49.

Miller, Paul W. The Causes and Consequences of Interruptions to Full-Time Education. *Australian Econ. Pap.*, June 1984, *23*(42), pp. 61–70. [G: Australia]

Miller, Paul W. and Volker, Paul A. The Screening Hypothesis: An Application of the Wiles Test. *Econ. Inquiry*, January 1984, *22*(1), pp. 121–27. [G: Australia]

Mincer, Jacob. Human Capital and Economic Growth. *Econ. Educ. Rev.*, 1984, *3*(3), pp. 195–205.

Myers, Samuel L., Jr. Labor Economics, Preferences, and the Rationality Assumption: A Comment on Blau, Dickens, and Malveaux. In *Darity, W., Jr.*, ed., 1984, pp. 257–68. [G: U.S.]

Neale, Walter C. Technology as Social Process: A Commentary on Knowledge and Human Capital. *J. Econ. Issues*, June 1984, *18*(2), pp. 573–80.

Nerlove, Marc; Razin, Assaf and Sadka, Efraim. Investment in Human and Nonhuman Capital, Transfers among Siblings, and the Role of Government. *Econometrica*, September 1984, *52*(5), pp. 1191–98.

Odagiri, Hiroyuki. The Firm as a Collection of Human Resources. In *Wiles, P. and Routh, G.*, eds., 1984, pp. 190–206.

Oxenham, John. Employers, Jobs and Qualifications. In *Oxenham, J.*, ed., 1984, pp. 41–86. [G: Tanzania; Kenya; Zambia; Sri Lanka; Mexico]

Palmer, Ransford W. The Impact of Emigration of Human Capital on the Jamaican Economy: An Empirical Assessment. In *Palmer, R. W.*, 1984, pp. 31–38. [G: Jamaica]

Patalinghug, Epictetus. Labor Quality and Growth Accounting: The Philippines. *Philippine Rev. Econ. Bus.*, Sept./Dec. 1984, *21*(3/4), pp. 201–17. [G: Philippines]

Paul, Jean-Jacques. Comportement en cours d'étude et emploi. (The Influence of Students' Behaviour Patterns on Their Subsequent Employment. With English summary.) *Consommation*, 1984, *31*(1), pp. 89–106. **[G: France]**

Perri, Timothy J. Health Status and Schooling Decisions of Young Men. *Econ. Educ. Rev.*, 1984, *3*(3), pp. 207–13. **[G: U.S.]**

Plant, Mark W. and Welch, Finis. Measuring the Impact of Education on Productivity. In *Dean, E., ed.*, 1984, pp. 163–93. **[G: U.S.]**

Psacharopoulos, George. The Contribution of Education to Economic Growth: International Comparisons. In *Kendrick, J. W., ed.*, 1984, pp. 335–55. **[G: Selected Countries]**

Psacharopoulos, George and Zabalza, Antonio. The Effect of Diversified Schools on Employment Status and Earnings in Colombia. *Econ. Educ. Rev.*, 1984, *3*(4), pp. 315–31. **[G: Colombia]**

Pujol, Michèle A. Gender and Class in Marshall's *Principles of Economics. Cambridge J. Econ.*, September 1984, *8*(3), pp. 217–34.

Qadir, Asghar. Educated Unemployed, Educational Subsidies, and Growth: Comment. *Pakistan Devel. Rev.*, Summer-Autumn 1984, *23*(2&3), pp. 411–12.

Rumberger, Russell W. The Changing Economic Benefits of College Graduates. *Econ. Educ. Rev.*, 1984, *3*(1), pp. 3–11. **[G: U.S.]**

Rumberger, Russell W. and Daymont, Thomas N. The Economic Value of Academic and Vocational Training Acquired in High School. In *Borus, M. E., ed.*, 1984, pp. 157–91. **[G: U.S.]**

Ryan, Paul. Job Training, Employment Practices, and the Large Enterprise: The Case of Costly Transferable Skills. In *Osterman, P., ed.*, 1984, pp. 191–229. **[G: U.S.]**

Sahota, Gian S. and Sahota, Chander K. A Theory of Human Investment in Physical Skills and Its Application to Achievement in Tennis. *Southern Econ. J.*, January 1984, *50*(3), pp. 642–64. **[G: U.S.]**

Sander, William. The Economics of Time and Community. *Rev. Soc. Econ.*, April 1984, *42*(1), pp. 44–49. **[G: U.S.]**

Schelling, Thomas C. The Life You Save May Be Your Own. In *Schelling, T. C.*, 1984, pp. 113–46.

Schultz, Theodore W. A Comment on Education and Economic Growth. In *Kendrick, J. W., ed.*, 1984, pp. 357–60. **[G: Selected Countries]**

Shaw, Kathryn L. A Formulation of the Earnings Function Using the Concept of Occupational Investment. *J. Human Res.*, Summer 1984, *19*(3), pp. 319–40. **[G: U.S.]**

Siow, Aloysius. Occupational Choice under Uncertainty. *Econometrica*, May 1984, *52*(3), pp. 631–45. **[G: U.S.]**

Smith, James P. Race and Human Capital. *Amer. Econ. Rev.*, September 1984, *74*(4), pp. 685–98. **[G: U.S.]**

Stewart, James B. and Hyclak, Thomas. An Analysis of the Earnings Profiles of Immigrants. *Rev. Econ. Statist.*, May 1984, *66*(2), pp. 292–96. **[G: U.S.]**

Tachibanaki, Toshiaki. Labor Mobility and Job Tenure. In *Aoki, M., ed.*, 1984, pp. 77–102. **[G: Japan; U.S.]**

Tomes, Nigel. The Effects of Religion and Denomination Earnings and the Returns to Human Capital. *J. Human Res.*, Fall 1984, *19*(4), pp. 472–88. **[G: Canada]**

Trost, Robert P. and Lee, Lung-Fei. Technical Training and Earnings: A Polychotomous Choice Model with Selectivity. *Rev. Econ. Statist.*, February 1984, *66*(1), pp. 151–56. **[G: U.S.]**

Turchi, Boone A. The Monetary Cost of a Child. In *Steinmann, G., ed.*, 1984, pp. 258–76. **[G: U.S.]**

Vrooman, John. Effect of Technology on the Distribution of Labor Income. In *Collins, E. L. and Tanner, L. D., eds.*, 1984, pp. 115–23. **[G: U.S.]**

Weiler, William C. Time Effects in Earnings of Faculty Members. *Econ. Educ. Rev.*, 1984, *3*(3), pp. 223–30. **[G: U.S.]**

Young, Anne McDougall and Hayghe, Howard. More U.S. Workers Are College Graduates. *Mon. Lab. Rev.*, March 1984, *107*(3), pp. 46–49. **[G: U.S.]**

900 Welfare Programs; Consumer Economics; Urban and Regional Economics

910 WELFARE, HEALTH, AND EDUCATION

9100 General

Brooks, Harvey. Seeking Equity and Efficiency: Public and Private Roles. In *Brooks, H.; Liebman, L. and Schelling, C. S., eds.*, 1984, pp. 3–29. **[G: U.S.]**

Clarkson, Kenneth W. The Safety Net from the Reagan Administration's Perspective. In *Weicher, J. C., ed.*, 1984, pp. 169–88. **[G: U.S.]**

Colombino, Ugo. An Econometric Investigation of the Condition of Children in Italy. *World Devel.*, March 1984, *12*(3), pp. 365–80. **[G: Italy]**

Cornia, Giovanni Andrea. A Summary and Interpretation of the Evidence. *World Devel.*, March 1984, *12*(3), pp. 381–91. **[G: Global]**

Doolittle, Fred C. State Legislatures and Federal Grants: An Overview. *Public Budg. Finance*, Summer 1984, *4*(2), pp. 7–23. **[G: U.S.]**

Doolittle, Fred C. State Legislatures and Federal Grants: Developments in the Reagan Years. *Public Budg. Finance*, Summer 1984, *4*(2), pp. 3–6. **[G: U.S.]**

Esping-Andersen, Gösta and Korpi, Walter. Social Policy as Class Politics in Post-war Capitalism: Scandinavia, Austria, and Germany. In *Goldthorpe, J. H., ed.*, 1984, pp. 179–208. **[G: Scandinavia; Austria; Germany]**

Foxley, Alejandro and Raczynski, Dagmar. Vulnerable Groups in Recessionary Situations: The Case of Children and the Young in Chile. *World Devel.*, March 1984, *12*(3), pp. 223–46.
[G: Chile]

Freeman, Katherine B. The Significance of Motivational Variables in International Public Welfare Expenditures. *Econ. Develop. Cult. Change*, July 1984, *32*(4), pp. 725–48.
[G: OECD]

Gustafsson, Björn. Macroeconomic Performance, Old Age Security and the Rate of Social Assistance Recipients in Sweden. *Europ. Econ. Rev.*, December 1984, *26*(3), pp. 319–38.
[G: Sweden]

Gutierrez Muniz, José A., et al. The Recent Worldwide Economic Crisis and the Welfare of Children: The Case of Cuba. *World Devel.*, March 1984, *12*(3), pp. 247–60. [G: Cuba]

Islam, Iyanatul. Socio-economic Progress in Indonesia under the New Order. In *Thambipillai, P., ed.*, 1984, pp. 137–50. [G: Indonesia]

Jayawardena, Kumari. The Plantation Sector in Sri Lanka: Recent Changes in the Welfare of Children and Women. *World Devel.*, March 1984, *12*(3), pp. 317–28. [G: Sri Lanka]

Joe, Tom. Shredding an Already Tattered Safety Net. In *Weicher, J. C., ed.*, 1984, pp. 189–202. [G: U.S.]

Macedo, Roberto. Brazilian Children and the Economic Crisis: Evidence from the State of São Paulo. *World Devel.*, March 1984, *12*(3), pp. 203–21. [G: Brazil]

Miller, C. Arden and Coulter, Elizabeth J. The World Economic Crisis and the Children: A United States Case Study. *World Devel.*, March 1984, *12*(3), pp. 339–64. [G: U.S.]

Richards, Peter J. Target Setting for Basic-Needs Services: Some Possible Approaches. In *Ghosh, P. K., ed., no. 13*, 1984, *1981*, pp. 173–87. [G: Madagascar; India; Sri Lanka]

Suh, Sang Mok. Effects of the Current World Recession on the Welfare of Children: The Case of Korea. *World Devel.*, March 1984, *12*(3), pp. 329–38. [G: Korea]

Szymanski, Al. Productivity Growth and Capitalist Stagnation. *Sci. Soc.*, Fall 1984, *48*(3), pp. 295–322. [G: U.S.; Japan; W. Europe]

Weicher, John C. The Safety Net after Three Years. In *Weicher, J. C., ed.*, 1984, pp. 1–19. [G: U.S.]

911 General Welfare Programs

9110 General Welfare Programs

Aaron, Henry J. Social Welfare in Australia. In *Caves, R. E. and Krause, L. B., eds.*, 1984, pp. 349–90. [G: Australia]

Aaron, Henry J. The Social Policy of the Reagan Administration: Comments. In *Bawden, D. L., ed.*, 1984, pp. 241–44. [G: U.S.]

Akerlof, George A. The Economics of "Tagging" as Applied to the Optimal Income Tax, Welfare Programs, and Manpower Planning. In *Akerlof, G. A.*, 1984, *1978*, pp. 45–68.

Alam, M. Shahid. Consumption and Employment Effects of Income Redistribution in Pakistan: Comment. *Pakistan Devel. Rev.*, Summer-Autumn 1984, *23*(2&3), pp. 361–63.
[G: Pakistan]

Anderson, Martin. The Objectives of the Reagan Administration's Social Welfare Policy. In *Bawden, D. L., ed.*, 1984, pp. 15–27.
[G: U.S.]

Ball, Joseph. Implementation of the Supported Work Program Model. In *Hollister, R. G., Jr.; Kemper, P. and Maynard, R. A., eds.*, 1984, pp. 50–89. [G: U.S.]

Barth, Michael C. Budget Cuts in the Reagan Administration: A Question of Fairness: Comments. In *Bawden, D. L., ed.*, 1984, pp. 65–67. [G: U.S.]

Bawden, D. Lee and Palmer, John L. Social Policy: Challenging the Welfare State. In *Palmer, J. L. and Sawhill, I. V., eds.*, 1984, pp. 177–215. [G: U.S.]

Bendick, Marc, Jr. Privatization of Public Services: Recent Experience. In *Brooks, H.; Liebman, L. and Schelling, C. S., eds.*, 1984, pp. 153–71. [G: U.S.]

Berkowitz, Edward D. Changing the Meaning of Welfare Reform. In *Weicher, J. C., ed.*, 1984, pp. 23–42. [G: U.S.]

Bernstein, Blanche. Welfare Dependency. In *Bawden, D. L., ed.*, 1984, pp. 125–52.
[G: U.S.]

Betson, David and Haveman, Robert H. The Role of Income Transfers in Reducing Inequality between and within Regions. In *Moon, M., ed.*, 1984, pp. 283–322. [G: U.S.]

Blau, Francine D. The Use of Transfer Payments by Immigrants. *Ind. Lab. Relat. Rev.*, January 1984, *37*(2), pp. 222–39. [G: U.S.]

Bosanquet, Nick. Is Privatisation Inevitable? In *Le Grand, J. and Robinson, R., eds.*, 1984, pp. 58–69.

Brown, Mark G. and Johnson, S. R. Equivalent Scales, Scale Economies, and Food Stamp Allotments: Estimates from the Nationwide Food Consumption Survey, 1977–78. *Amer. J. Agr. Econ.*, August 1984, *66*(3), pp. 286–93.
[G: U.S.]

Burtless, Gary and Haveman, Robert H. Policy Lessons from Three Labor Market Experiments. In *Robson, R. T., ed.*, 1984, pp. 105–33. [G: U.S.]

Cheema, Aftab Ahmad and Malik, Muhammad Hussain. Consumption and Employment Effects of Income Redistribution in Pakistan. *Pakistan Devel. Rev.*, Summer-Autumn 1984, *23*(2&3), pp. 347–59. [G: Pakistan]

Chiswick, Barry R. Welfare Dependency: Comments. In *Bawden, D. L., ed.*, 1984, pp. 153–56. [G: U.S.]

Clark, Robert M. Comments [Reforming Public Pensions in Canada: Issues and Options] [Tax-Transfer Benefits for the Elderly]. In *Conklin, D. W.; Bennett, J. H. and Courchene, T. J., eds.*, 1984, pp. 266–73. [G: Canada]

Colombino, Ugo. An Econometric Investigation of the Condition of Children in Italy. In *Jolly,*

R. and Cornia, G. A., eds., 1984, pp. 195–210. [G: Italy]

Disney, Richard. Public Expenditure Policy, 1984–85: Social Security. In Cockle, P., ed., 1984, pp. 149–71. [G: U.K.]

Dixon, John. The People's Republic of China: Politics and Social Welfare. In Groth, A. J. and Wade, L. L., eds., 1984, pp. 127–48. [G: China]

Dixon, William J. Trade Concentration, Economic Growth, and the Provision of Basic Human Needs. Soc. Sci. Quart., September 1984, 65(3), pp. 761–74. [G: LDCs]

Eizenstat, Stuart E. The Objectives of the Reagan Administration's Social Welfare Policy: Comments. In Bawden, D. L., ed., 1984, pp. 28–32. [G: U.S.]

Ellman, Michael. The Crisis of the Welfare State—The Dutch Experience. In Boulding, K. E., ed., 1984, pp. 191–211. [G: Netherlands; OECD]

Englander, Valerie and Englander, Fred. The Demand for General Assistance in New Jersey: A New Look at the Deterrence Effect. J. Behav. Econ., Winter 1984, 13(2), pp. 53–65. [G: U.S.]

Folbre, Nancy R. The Pauperization of Motherhood: Patriarchy and Public Policy in the United States. Rev. Radical Polit. Econ., Winter 1984, 16(4), pp. 72–88. [G: U.S.]

Foxley, Alejandro and Raczynski, Dagmar. Vulnerable Groups in Recessionary Situations: The Case of Children and the Young in Chile. In Jolly, R. and Cornia, G. A., eds., 1984, pp. 53–76. [G: Chile]

Ginzberg, Eli; Nathan, Richard P. and Solow, Robert M. The Lessons of the Supported Work Demonstration. In Hollister, R. G., Jr.; Kemper, P. and Maynard, R. A., eds., 1984, pp. 305–19. [G: U.S.]

Glazer, Nathan. The Social Policy of the Reagan Administration. In Bawden, D. L., ed., 1984, pp. 221–40. [G: U.S.]

Goodman, John C. Poverty and Welfare. In Moore, J. H., ed., 1984, pp. 137–52. [G: U.S.]

Gopal, K. Rani. Benefit-Cost Analysis of the Indian Family Welfare Programme. Indian Econ. J., April–June 1984, 31(4), pp. 45–52. [G: India]

Gorham, William. The Social Contract Revisited: Overview. In Bawden, D. L., ed., 1984, pp. 1–14. [G: U.S.]

Gottschalk, Peter. The Role of Income Transfers in Reducing Inequality between and within Regions: Comment. In Moon, M., ed., 1984, pp. 322–26. [G: U.S.]

Goudreau, Karen; Oberheu, Howard and Vaughan, Denton R. An Assessment of the Quality of Survey Reports of Income from the Aid to Families with Dependent Children (AFDC) Program. J. Bus. Econ. Statist., April 1984, 2(2), pp. 179–86. [G: U.S.]

Gramlich, Edward M. and Laren, Deborah S. Migration and Income Redistribution Respon-

sibilities. J. Human Res., Fall 1984, 19(4), pp. 489–511. [G: U.S.]

Green, Cynthia B. and Sanger, Mary Bryna. Setting Municipal Priorities: Service Delivery: Aiding the Poor. In Brecher, C. and Horton, R. D., eds., 1984, pp. 519–50. [G: U.S.]

Green, Reginald Herbold and Singer, Hans W. Sub-Saharan Africa in Depression: The Impact on the Welfare of Children. In Jolly, R. and Cornia, G. A., eds., 1984, pp. 113–25. [G: Sub-Saharan Africa]

Gregorio, David I. and Marshall, James R. Fine Tuning Well-being: Food Stamp Use and Nutritional Adequacy of Children's Diets. Soc. Sci. Quart., December 1984, 65(4), pp. 1137–46. [G: U.S.]

Grubb, W. Norton. The Price of Local Discretion: Inequalities in Welfare Spending within Texas. J. Policy Anal. Manage., Spring 1984, 3(3), pp. 359–72. [G: U.S.]

Gueron, Judith. Lessons from Managing the Supported Work Demonstration. In Hollister, R. G., Jr.; Kemper, P. and Maynard, R. A., eds., 1984, pp. 286–304. [G: U.S.]

Gustafsson, Siv. Equal Opportunity Policies in Sweden. In Schmid, G. and Weitzel, R., eds., 1984, pp. 132–54. [G: Sweden]

Halberstadt, Victor, et al. Inefficiencies in Public Transfer Policies in Western Industrialized Democracies. In Hanusch, H., ed., 1984, pp. 189–208. [G: OECD]

Hamilton, David. The Myth Is Not the Reality: Income Maintenance and Welfare. J. Econ. Issues, March 1984, 18(1), pp. 143–58. [G: U.S.]

Hannon, Joan Underhill. The Generosity of Antebellum Poor Relief. J. Econ. Hist., September 1984, 44(3), pp. 810–21. [G: U.S.]

Haveman, Robert H. How Much Have the Reagan Administration's Tax and Spending Policies Increased Work Effort? In Hulten, C. R. and Sawhill, I. V., eds., 1984, pp. 91–125. [G: U.S.]

Haveman, Robert H. and Wolfe, Barbara L. Disability Transfers and Early Retirement: A Causal Relationship? J. Public Econ., June 1984, 24(1), pp. 47–66. [G: W. Europe; U.S.]

Hill, Marianne T. and Udall, Alan T. An Econometric Analysis of the Effects of Reductions in Food Stamp Benefits and Cash-Out in Puerto Rico. Rev. Reg. Stud., Fall 1984, 14(3), pp. 25–33. [G: Puerto Rico]

Hoagland, G. William. Is the Safety Net Still Intact? Comments. In Bawden, D. L., ed., 1984, pp. 121–24. [G: U.S.]

Hoagland, G. William. Perception and Reality in Nutrition Programs. In Weicher, J. C., ed., 1984, pp. 43–71. [G: U.S.]

Hoffman, Emily P. The Deserving and the Nondeserving Poor. Eastern Econ. J., October–December 1984, 10(4), pp. 432–40. [G: U.S.]

Hollister, Robinson G., Jr. The Design and Implementation of the Supported Work Evaluation. In *Hollister, R. G., Jr.; Kemper, P. and Maynard, R. A., eds.*, 1984, pp. 12–49. [G: U.S.]

Hollister, Robinson G., Jr. The National Supported Work Demonstration: Introduction. In *Hollister, R. G., Jr.; Kemper, P. and Maynard, R. A., eds.*, 1984, pp. 3–11. [G: U.S.]

Hollister, Robinson G., Jr. and Maynard, Rebecca A. The Impacts of Supported Work on AFDC Recipients. In *Hollister, R. G., Jr.; Kemper, P. and Maynard, R. A., eds.*, 1984, pp. 90–135. [G: U.S.]

Hurl, Lorna F. Privatized Social Service Systems: Lessons from Ontario Children's Services. *Can. Public Policy*, December 1984, *10*(4), pp. 395–405. [G: Canada]

Jolly, Richard and Cornia, Giovanni Andrea. The Impact of World Recession on Children: Editors' Introduction. In *Jolly, R. and Cornia, G. A., eds.*, 1984, pp. 1–6.

Kemper, Peter; Long, David A. and Thornton, Craig. A Benefit–Cost Analysis of the Supported Work Experiment. In *Hollister, R. G., Jr.; Kemper, P. and Maynard, R. A., eds.*, 1984, pp. 239–85. [G: U.S.]

Kirwan, R. M. The Demise of Public Housing? In *Le Grand, J. and Robinson, R., eds.*, 1984, pp. 133–45. [G: U.K.]

Klein, Rudolf. Privatization and the Welfare State. *Lloyds Bank Rev.*, January 1984, (151), pp. 12–29. [G: U.K.]

Le Grand, Julian and Robinson, Ray. Privatisation and the Welfare State: An Introduction. In *Le Grand, J. and Robinson, R., eds.*, 1984, pp. 1–14. [G: U.K.]

Lewis, Gordon H. The Taichman–Young Knot Unravelled [The Day Care Tangle]. *J. Policy Anal. Manage.*, Fall 1984, *4*(1), pp. 119–20. [G: U.S.]

Lustig, Nora. Distribution of Income, Food Consumption, and Fiscal Cost of Alternative Policy Options. In *Aspe, P. and Sigmund, P. E., eds.*, 1984, pp. 439–79. [G: Mexico]

Maddison, Angus. Origins and Impact of the Welfare State, 1883–1983. *Banca Naz. Lavoro Quart. Rev.*, March 1984, (148), pp. 55–87. [G: Selected OECD]

Maguire, Maria. Components of Growth of Income Maintenance Expenditure in Ireland 1951–1979. *Econ. Soc. Rev.*, January 1984, *15*(2), pp. 75–85. [G: Ireland]

Makolo, Philomène. Reflections on Development Administration with Special Reference to Africa. *Can. J. Devel. Stud.*, 1984, *5*(1), pp. 79–112. [G: Africa]

Maynard, Rebecca A. The Impacts of Supported Work on Youth. In *Hollister, R. G., Jr.; Kemper, P. and Maynard, R. A., eds.*, 1984, pp. 205–38. [G: U.S.]

Meyer, Jack A. Budget Cuts in the Reagan Administration: A Question of Fairness. In *Bawden, D. L., ed.*, 1984, pp. 33–64. [G: U.S.]

Miller, C. Arden and Coulter, Elizabeth J. The World Economic Crisis and the Children: A United States Case Study. In *Jolly, R. and Cornia, G. A., eds.*, 1984, pp. 169–94. [G: U.S.]

Moffitt, Robert A. The Effects of Grants-in-Aid on State and Local Expenditures: The Case of AFDC. *J. Public Econ.*, April 1984, *23*(3), pp. 279–305. [G: U.S.]

Mundle, Sudipto. Recent Trends in the Condition of Children in India: A Statistical Profile. *World Devel.*, March 1984, *12*(3), pp. 297–307. [G: India]

Muniz, José A. Gutierrez, et al. The Recent Worldwide Economic Crisis and the Welfare of Children: The Case of Cuba. In *Jolly, R. and Cornia, G. A., eds.*, 1984, pp. 77–90. [G: Cuba]

Nathan, Richard P. and Doolittle, Fred C. The Budget Cuts: The Day After. *Challenge*, January/February 1984, *26*(6), pp. 29–36. [G: U.S.]

Onitsuka, Yusuke. Economic Growth and Social Welfare Policy in the 1980s. In *Miyawaki, N., ed.*, 1984, pp. 220–27.

Patterson, Orlando. The Realities of Intervention in Alienated Cultures: A Jamaican Case Study. In *Brooks, H.; Liebman, L. and Schelling, C. S., eds.*, 1984, pp. 131–52. [G: Jamaica]

Piliavin, Irving and Gartner, Rosemary. The Impacts of Supported Work on Ex-offenders. In *Hollister, R. G., Jr.; Kemper, P. and Maynard, R. A., eds.*, 1984, pp. 172–204. [G: U.S.]

Plant, Mark W. An Empirical Analysis of Welfare Dependence. *Amer. Econ. Rev.*, September 1984, *74*(4), pp. 673–84. [G: U.S.]

Plotnick, Robert. The Redistributive Impact of Cash Transfers. *Public Finance Quart.*, January 1984, *12*(1), pp. 27–50. [G: U.S.]

Prasad, Kamta. Scope and Functioning of the Public Distribution System in India. In *Singh, A. K.; Papola, T. S. and Mathur, R. S., eds.*, 1984, pp. 207–30. [G: India]

Robins, Philip K. The Labor Supply Response of Twenty-Year Families in the Denver Income Maintenance Experiment. *Rev. Econ. Statist.*, August 1984, *66*(3), pp. 491–95. [G: U.S.]

Sa-Aadu, Jarjisu. Alternative Estimates of Direct Tenant Benefit and Consumption Inefficiencies from the Section 8 New Construction Program. *Land Econ.*, May 1984, *60*(2), pp. 189–201. [G: U.S.]

Sayeed, Adil. Tax-Transfer Benefits for the Elderly. In *Conklin, D. W.; Bennett, J. H. and Courchene, T. J., eds.*, 1984, pp. 241–63. [G: Canada]

Simon, Julian L. Immigrants, Taxes, and Welfare in the United States. *Population Devel. Rev.*, March 1984, *10*(1), pp. 55–69. [G: U.S.]

Smeeding, Timothy M. Is the Safety Net Still Intact? In *Bawden, D. L., ed.*, 1984, pp. 69–120. [G: U.S.]

Stutzer, Michael J. Variable Rate Subsidies: The Inefficiency of In-Kind Transfers Revisited. *Public Finance Quart.*, January 1984, *12*(1), pp. 77–95. [G: U.S.]

Suh, Sang Mok. Effects of the Current World Recession on the Welfare of Children: The Case of Korea. In *Jolly, R. and Cornia, G. A., eds.*, 1984, pp. 159–68. [G: S. Korea]

Taichman, Ettie and Young, Dennis R. A Knot

in the Day Care Tangle. *J. Policy Anal. Manage.*, Fall 1984, *4*(1), pp. 117–19.   [G: U.S.]

Van Loo, M. Frances. Welfare Payments and Family Size: Implications for Public Policy and the Economic Theory of the Family. In *[Ferber, R.]*, 1984, pp. 267–87.   [G: U.S.]

Venti, Steven F. The Effects of Income Maintenance on Work, Schooling, and Non-Market Activities of Youth. *Rev. Econ. Statist.*, February 1984, *66*(1), pp. 16–25.

Walker, Alan. The Political Economy of Privatisation. In *Le Grand, J. and Robinson, R., eds.*, 1984, pp. 19–44.

Waugh, Frederick V. Programs for Using Agricultural Surpluses to Reduce Malnutrition and to Benefit Farmers. In *Waugh, F. V.*, 1984, *1940*, pp. 146–56.   [G: U.S.]

Weicher, John C. Halfway to a Housing Allowance? In *Weicher, J. C., ed.*, 1984, pp. 92–118.   [G: U.S.]

Wellington, Donald C. The English Poor Law: A Negative Income Tax. *Atlantic Econ. J.*, December 1984, *12*(4), pp. 46–50.   [G: U.K.]

Whitehead, Christine M. E. Privatisation and Housing. In *Le Grand, J. and Robinson, R., eds.*, 1984, pp. 116–32.   [G: U.K.]

Wolf, Douglas A. Changes in Household Size and Composition Due to Financial Incentives. *J. Human Res.*, Winter 1984, *19*(1), pp. 87–103.   [G: U.S.]

Wolfe, Barbara L., et al. Income Transfers and Work Effort: The Netherlands and the United States in the 1970s. *Kyklos*, 1984, *37*(4), pp. 609–37.   [G: Netherlands; U.S.]

912 Economics of Education

9120 Economics of Education

Alam, M. Shahid. An Assessment of the Priorities and Efficiency of Pakistan's Public Sector Educational Expenditure: Comment. *Pakistan Devel. Rev.*, Summer-Autumn 1984, *23*(2&3), pp. 425–27.   [G: Pakistan]

Alexander, Elmore R., III and Frey, Donald E. An Econometric Estimate of the Demand for MBA Enrollment. *Econ. Educ. Rev.*, 1984, *3*(2), pp. 97–103.   [G: U.S.]

Arrow, Kenneth J. Higher Education as a Filter. In *Arrow, K. J., vol. 4*, 1984, *1973*, pp. 115–35.

Aspe, Pedro and Beristain, Javier. Distribution of Education and Health Opportunities and Services. In *Aspe, P. and Sigmund, P. E., eds.*, 1984, pp. 265–326.   [G: Mexico]

Augenblick, John. Elementary and Secondary Education: Issues in Budgeting and Financial Management. *Public Budg. Finance*, Winter 1984, *4*(4), pp. 4–6.

Baksh, Ishmael J. Factors Influencing Occupational Expectations of Secondary School Students in Trinidad and Tobago. *Soc. Econ. Stud.*, September 1984, *33*(3), pp. 1–29.   [G: Trinidad and Tobago]

Baltz, Richard B. An Incentive Early Retirement Model for College and University Faculty. *J.*

Risk Ins., September 1984, *51*(3), pp. 477–97.

Baxter, J. L. and McCormick, Brian J. Seventy Per Cent of Our Future: The Education, Training and Employment of Young People. *Nat. Westminster Bank Quart. Rev.*, August 1984, pp. 36–44.

Behrman, Jere R. and Wolfe, Barbara L. The Socioeconomic Impact of Schooling in a Developing Country. *Rev. Econ. Statist.*, May 1984, *66*(2), pp. 296–303.   [G: Nicaragua]

Benson, Charles S. State Government Contributions to the Public Schools. *Public Budg. Finance*, Winter 1984, *4*(4), pp. 17–29.
[G: U.S.]

Blakemore, Arthur E. and Low, Stuart A. The High-School Dropout Decision and Its Wage Consequences. *Econ. Educ. Rev.*, 1984, *3*(2), pp. 111–19.   [G: U.S.]

Blaug, Mark. Education Vouchers—It All Depends on What You Mean. In *Le Grand, J. and Robinson, R., eds.*, 1984, pp. 160–76.

Borus, Michael E. and Carpenter, Susan A. Choices in Education. In *Borus, M. E., ed.*, 1984, pp. 81–110.   [G: U.S.]

Borus, Michael E. and Carpenter, Susan A. Factors Associated with College Attendance of High-School Seniors. *Econ. Educ. Rev.*, 1984, *3*(3), pp. 169–76.   [G: U.S.]

Bourdon, F.; Bourdon, J. and Hallak, J. The EDFOREM Model: A Case Study of Thailand. In *Cohen, S. I., et al., eds.*, 1984, pp. 139–59.   [G: Thailand]

Brooke, Nigel and Oxenham, John. The Influence of Certification and Selection on Teaching and Learning. In *Oxenham, J., ed.*, 1984, pp. 147–75.

Buckles, Stephen; Strom, Robert J. and Walstad, William B. An Evaluation of a State Consumer and Economic Education Program: Implications for Effective Program Delivery. *J. Econ. Educ.*, Spring 1984, *15*(2), pp. 101–10.
[G: U.S.]

Butler, Richard J. The Effect of Education on Wages—Hedonic Makes Selectivity Bias (Sort of) Simpler. *Econ. Inquiry*, January 1984, *22*(1), pp. 109–20.

Caillods, Françoise. Education, Organisation of Work and Indigenous Technological Capacity. In *Fransman, M. and King, K., eds.*, 1984, pp. 211–22.   [G: LDCs]

Carter, Susan B. and Savoca, Elizabeth. The Effect of Public Policy on Gender Differences in the Demand for Higher Education. *Eastern Econ. J.*, October-December 1984, *10*(4), pp. 402–08.   [G: U.S.]

Chambers, David I. Adult Education in Urban-Industrial China: Problems, Policies, and Prospects. In *Hayhoe, R., ed.*, 1984, pp. 178–204.
[G: China]

Chatterjee, Jay and Davidow, Carol. Schools and the Private Sector in Partnership. In *Porter, P. R. and Sweet, D. C., eds.*, 1984, pp. 93–110.   [G: U.S.]

Chaudhuri, T. Datta and Khan, M. Ali. Educated Unemployed, Educational Subsidies, and

Growth. *Pakistan Devel. Rev.*, Summer-Autumn 1984, *23*(2&3), pp. 395–409.

Chiswick, Carmel U. The Impact of Education Policy on Economic Development: Quantity, Quality, and Earnings of Labor. *Econ. Educ. Rev.*, 1984, *3*(2), pp. 121–30.

Chitnis, S. and Suvannathat, C. Schooling for the Children of the Urban Poor. In *Richards, P. J. and Thomson, A. M., eds.*, 1984, pp. 189–213. **[G: LDCs]**

Chizmar, John F., Jr. and McCarney, Bernard J. An Evaluation of a "Trade Offs" Implementation Using Canonical Estimation of Joint Educational Production Functions. *J. Econ. Educ.*, Winter 1984, *15*(1), pp. 11–20.

Chizmar, John F., Jr. and Zak, Thomas A. Canonical Estimation of Joint Educational Production Functions. *Econ. Educ. Rev.*, 1984, *3*(1), pp. 37–43. **[G: U.S.]**

Cicarelli, James and Spizman, Lawrence. The Production of Economic Knowledge. *Quart. Rev. Econ. Bus.*, Summer 1984, *24*(2), pp. 41–50. **[G: U.S.]**

Cohn, Elchanan. Equity Effects of the Educational Finance Act in South Carolina. *Econ. Educ. Rev.*, 1984, *3*(4), pp. 333–39.
[G: U.S.]

Colwell, Peter F. and Guntermann, Karl L. The Value of Neighborhood Schools. *Econ. Educ. Rev.*, 1984, *3*(3), pp. 177–82. **[G: U.S.]**

Conlisk, John. Four Invalid Propositions about Equality, Efficiency, and Intergenerational Transfers through Schooling. *J. Human Res.*, Winter 1984, *19*(1), pp. 3–21.

Cookingham, Mary E. Bluestockings, Spinsters and Pedagogues: Women College Graduates, 1865–1910. *Population Stud.*, November 1984, *38*(3), pp. 349–64. **[G: U.S.]**

Coughlin, Cletus C. and Erekson, O. Homer. An Examination of Contributions to Support Intercollegiate Athletics. *Southern Econ. J.*, July 1984, *51*(1), pp. 180–95. **[G: U.S.]**

Craven, B. M.; Dick, B. and Wood, B. The British Response of Higher Education to Changing Educational Perspectives. *Econ. Educ. Rev.*, 1984, *3*(4), pp. 279–88. **[G: U.K.]**

Crouse, James and Brams, Marvin. Benefits and Costs of the SAT for College Admissions Policies. *Atlantic Econ. J.*, July 1984, *12*(2), pp. 80.

D'Amico, Ronald. The Time-Use Behavior of Young Adults. In *Borus, M. E., ed.*, 1984, pp. 193–238. **[G: U.S.]**

Davies, Duncan. Actions to Strengthen University–Industry Cooperation. In *Fusfeld, H. I. and Haklisch, C. S., eds.*, 1984, pp. 161–67.

Dean, Edwin. Education and Economic Productivity: Introduction. In *Dean, E., ed.*, 1984, pp. 1–17. **[G: U.S.]**

Denielou, Guy. The Role of The University. In *Fusfeld, H. I. and Haklisch, C. S., eds.*, 1984, pp. 151–54.

Denzau, Arthur and Grier, Kevin. Determinants of Local School Spending: Some Consistent Estimates. *Public Choice*, 1984, *44*(2), pp. 375–83. **[G: U.S.]**

Dickson, Vaughan A. An Economic Model of Faculty Grading Practices. *J. Econ. Educ.*, Summer 1984, *15*(3), pp. 197–203. **[G: Canada]**

Dobson, Richard B. Soviet Education: Problems and Policies in the Urban Context. In *Morton, H. W. and Stuart, R. C., eds.*, 1984, pp. 156–79. **[G: U.S.S.R.]**

Dore, Ronald P. and Oxenham, John. Educational Reform and Selection for Employment—An Overview. In *Oxenham, J., ed.*, 1984, pp. 3–40.

Doyle, Denis P. and Hartle, Terry W. Ideology, Pragmatic Politics, and the Education Budget. In *Weicher, J. C., ed.*, 1984, pp. 119–53.
[G: U.S.]

Eberts, Randall W. Union Effects on Teacher Productivity. *Ind. Lab. Relat. Rev.*, April 1984, *37*(3), pp. 346–58. **[G: U.S.]**

Ehrenberg, Ronald G. and Sherman, Daniel R. Optimal Financial Aid Policies for a Selective University. *J. Human Res.*, Spring 1984, *19*(2), pp. 202–30. **[G: U.S.]**

Eisemon, Thomas Owen. Insular and Open Strategies for Enhancing Scientific and Technological Capacities: Indian Educational Expansion and its Implications for African Countries. In *Fransman, M. and King, K., eds.*, 1984, pp. 263–77. **[G: India]**

Evans, E. W. and Wiseman, N. C. Education, Training and Economic Performance: British Economists' Views, 1868–1939. *J. Europ. Econ. Hist.*, Spring 1984, *13*(1), pp. 129–48.
[G: U.K.]

Fairchild, Halford H. School Size, Per-Pupil Expenditures, and School Achievement. *Rev. Public Data Use*, October 1984, *12*(3), pp. 221–29. **[G: U.S.]**

Feldstein, Martin. Public Education: Reply [Wealth Neutrality and Local Choice in Public Education]. *Amer. Econ. Rev.*, September 1984, *74*(4), pp. 820–21. **[G: U.S.]**

Freeman, Roger A. Pursuit of Excellence? The Income and the Outcome of Education. In *Moore, J. H., ed.*, 1984, pp. 319–41.
[G: U.S.]

Fund, John H. Bill Honig's Balancing Act. *Policy Rev.*, Summer 1984, (29), pp. 77–79.
[G: U.S.]

Garen, John. The Returns to Schooling: A Selectivity Bias Approach with a Continuous Choice Variable. *Econometrica*, September 1984, *52*(5), pp. 1199–1218. **[G: U.S.]**

Ginzberg, Eli. Conference Summary: The Expanding Physician Supply: Policy Options. In *Ginzberg, E. and Ostow, M., eds.*, 1984, pp. 1–8. **[G: U.S.]**

Gold, Steven D. State Aid for Local Schools: Trends and Prospects. *Public Budg. Finance*, Winter 1984, *4*(4), pp. 30–40. **[G: U.S.]**

Goldwater, Carmel. Humanitarian Situation in Kampuchea. In *Thambipillai, P., ed.*, 1984, pp. 162–76. **[G: Cambodia]**

Gomes, Melba. Family Size and Education Attainment in Kenya. *Population Devel. Rev.*, December 1984, *10*(4), pp. 647–60.
[G: Kenya]

Goodman, Richard H. Providing Adequate Resources for Public Elementary and Secondary Schools. *Public Budg. Finance*, Winter 1984, *4*(4), pp. 41–52. [G: U.S.]

Greene, Kenneth V. Sequential Referenda and Bureaucratic Man. *Public Choice*, 1984, *43*(1), pp. 77–82. [G: U.S.]

Gunatilleke, Godfrey and Kurukulasuria, G. I. O. M. The Global Economic Crisis and the Impact on Children in Sri Lanka. In *Jolly, R. and Cornia, G. A., eds.*, 1984, pp. 139–58. [G: Sri Lanka]

Hansen, W. Lee. Economic Growth and Equal Opportunity: Conflicting or Complementary Goals in Higher Education? In *Dean, E., ed.*, 1984, pp. 57–93. [G: U.S.]

Hartog, Joop. On the Private Benefits of Subsidies to Education. *Econ. Educ. Rev.*, 1984, *3*(1), pp. 23–35. [G: Netherlands]

Haveman, Robert H. and Wolfe, Barbara L. Education, Productivity, and Well-Being: On Defining and Measuring the Economic Characteristics of Schooling. In *Dean, E., ed.*, 1984, pp. 19–55.

Haveman, Robert H. and Wolfe, Barbara L. Schooling and Economic Well-Being: The Role of Nonmarket Effects. *J. Human Res.*, Summer 1984, *19*(3), pp. 377–407.

Hayhoe, Ruth. Chinese-Western Scholarly Exchange: Implications for the Future of Chinese Education. In *Hayhoe, R., ed.*, 1984, pp. 205–29. [G: China]

Hayhoe, Ruth. The Evolution of Modern Chinese Educational Institutions. In *Hayhoe, R., ed.*, 1984, pp. 26–46. [G: China]

Heller, Peter S. and Cheasty, Adrienne. Sectoral Adjustment in Government Expenditure in the 1970s: The Educational Sector in Latin America. *World Devel.*, October 1984, *12*(10), pp. 1039–49. [G: Latin America]

Henze, Jürgen. Higher Education: The Tension between Quality and Equality. In *Hayhoe, R., ed.*, 1984, pp. 93–153. [G: China]

Hiestand, Dale L. Medical Residencies in a Period of Expanding Physician Supply. In *Ginzberg, E. and Ostow, M., eds.*, 1984, pp. 69–82. [G: U.S.]

Holcombe, Randall G. and Holcombe, Lora P. The Return to the Federal Government from Investment in Higher Education. *Public Finance Quart.*, July 1984, *12*(3), pp. 365–71. [G: U.S.]

Hollis, Meldon. Education, Economics, and Equity. *Rev. Black Polit. Econ.*, Summer–Fall 1984, *13*(1–2), pp. 145–61. [G: U.S.]

Holmes, Brian. A Comparativist's View of Chinese Education. In *Hayhoe, R., ed.*, 1984, pp. 7–25. [G: China]

Hunt, Janet C. and Kiker, B. F. Parental Time Devoted to Children in Two- and One-Wage-Earner Families. *Econ. Educ. Rev.*, 1984, *3*(1), pp. 75–83. [G: U.S.]

Jamison, Dean T. and Moock, Peter R. Farmer Education and Farm Efficiency in Nepal: The Role of Schooling, Extension Services, and Cognitive Skills. *World Devel.*, January 1984, *12*(1), pp. 67–86. [G: Nepal]

Johnson, George E. Subsidies for Higher Education. *J. Lab. Econ.*, July 1984, *2*(3), pp. 303–18. [G: U.S.]

Johnson, Michael S. The Impact of Property Tax Revaluation of Wealth-based State Aid to Schools—A Case Study of Tompkins County, New York. *Econ. Educ. Rev.*, 1984, *3*(1), pp. 45–54. [G: U.S.]

Jones, Gary L. Achieving Excellence in Education and Management. *J. Policy Anal. Manage.*, Winter 1984, *3*(2), pp. 248–54. [G: U.S.]

Jorgenson, Dale W. The Contribution of Education to U.S. Economic Growth, 1948–73. In *Dean, E., ed.*, 1984, pp. 95–162. [G: U.S.]

Jud, G. Donald. Public Schools in In-Migration in North Carolina Counties, 1975–80. *Amer. J. Econ. Soc.*, July 1984, *43*(3), pp. 313–22. [G: U.S.]

Katz, David A. and Tuckman, Howard P. Displacement of Full-Timers by Part-Timers—A Model for Projection. *Econ. Educ. Rev.*, 1984, *3*(1), pp. 85–90. [G: U.S.]

Kaun, David E. Faculty Advancement in a Non-traditional University Environment. *Ind. Lab. Relat. Rev.*, July 1984, *37*(4), pp. 592–606.

Khan, Shahrukh Rafi; Mahmood, Naushin and Siddiqui, Rehana. An Assessment of the Priorities and Efficiency of Pakistan's Public Sector Educational Expenditure. *Pakistan Devel. Rev.*, Summer-Autumn 1984, *23*(2&3), pp. 413–23. [G: Pakistan]

Kiesling, Herbert J. Assignment Practices and the Relationship of Instructional Time to the Reading Performance of Elementary School Children. *Econ. Educ. Rev.*, 1984, *3*(4), pp. 341–50. [G: U.S.]

King, Kenneth. Science, Technology and Education in the Development of Indigenous Technological Capability. In *Fransman, M. and King, K., eds.*, 1984, pp. 31–63. [G: LDCs]

Kirst, Michael W. The New Agenda for Education: A Perspective for Policymakers. *Public Budg. Finance*, Winter 1984, *4*(4), pp. 7–16. [G: U.S.]

Kodde, David A. and Ritzen, Jozef M. M. Integrating Consumption and Investment Motives in a Neoclassical Model of Demand for Education. *Kyklos*, 1984, *37*(4), pp. 598–608. [G: Canada; U.S.]

Krashinsky, Michael. Some Limitations on the Usefulness of Revenue Dependency: Why Governments Often Produce What They Subsidize. *Can. Public Policy*, March 1984, *10*(1), pp. 35–46.

Lawler, John J. and Walker, J. Malcolm. Representation Elections in Higher Education: Occurrence and Outcomes. *J. Lab. Res.*, Winter 1984, *5*(1), pp. 63–80. [G: U.S.]

Lee, Robert H. Subsidizing the Affluent: The Case of Medical Education. *J. Policy Anal. Manage.*, Winter 1984, *3*(2), pp. 276–84. [G: U.S.]

Lemelin, Clément. Interprétations de la corrélation éducation-revenu. (Interpretations of the Education–Income Correlation. With English summary.) *L'Actual. Econ.*, June 1984, *60*(2), pp. 223–39.

Leppel, Karen. The Academic Performance of Returning and Continuing College Students: An Economic Analysis. *J. Econ. Educ.*, Winter 1984, *15*(1), pp. 46–54.

Lerman, Donald L. The Economics of Public School Closings. *J. Urban Econ.*, November 1984, *16*(3), pp. 241–58. **[G: U.S.]**

Lethem, Francis J. Basic Education. In *Weiss, C. and Jéquier, N., eds.*, 1984, pp. 157–74.

Lewin, Keith. Selection and Curriculum Reform. In *Oxenham, J., ed.*, 1984, pp. 115–46. **[G: Sri Lanka; Malaysia]**

Little, Angela. Combating the Diploma Disease. In *Oxenham, J., ed.*, 1984, pp. 197–228.

Lo, Billie L. C. Primary Education in China: A Two-Track System for Dual Tasks. In *Hayhoe, R., ed.*, 1984, pp. 47–64. **[G: China]**

Lo, Billie L. C. Teacher Education in the Eighties. In *Hayhoe, R., ed.*, 1984, pp. 154–77. **[G: China]**

Long, Franklin A. Potential Contributions of Western Business to the Service Sector of LDCs. In *Brooks, H.; Liebman, L. and Schelling, C. S., eds.*, 1984, pp. 319–37. **[G: LDCs]**

Lumsden, Keith and Scott, Alex. How to Maximize Golden Opinions. *Appl. Econ.*, October 1984, *16*(5), pp. 647–54. **[G: U.K.]**

Lundeen, Robert W. Labor Productivity and Demographics: Comment. In *Wachter, M. L. and Wachter, S. M., eds.*, 1984, pp. 103–05. **[G: U.S.]**

Mace, John. Public Expenditure Policy, 1984–85: Education and Science. In *Cockle, P., ed.*, 1984, pp. 109–27. **[G: U.K.]**

Marais, M. A. The Allocation of Resources to Education in South Africa. *S. Afr. J. Econ.*, March 1984, *52*(1), pp. 75–89. **[G: S. Africa]**

Mason, Andrew; Koo, Sung-Yeal and Song, Wi-Sup. Labor Force and Industrial Development in the Pacific Basin. In *Benjamin, R. and Kudrle, R. T.*, 1984, pp. 163–89. **[G: Selected Countries]**

McConnell, Campbell R. and Sosin, Kim H. Some Determinants of Student Attitudes toward Large Classes. *J. Econ. Educ.*, Summer 1984, *15*(3), pp. 181–90. **[G: U.S.]**

McHugh, Richard and Morgan, James N. The Determinants of Interstate Student Migration: A Place-to-Place Analysis. *Econ. Educ. Rev.*, 1984, *3*(4), pp. 269–78. **[G: U.S.]**

Megdal, Sharon Bernstein. A Model of Local Demand for Education. *J. Urban Econ.*, July 1984, *16*(1), pp. 13–30. **[G: U.S.]**

Mincer, Jacob. Comment: Overeducation or Undereducation? In *Dean, E., ed.*, 1984, pp. 205–211.

Monk, David H. Interdependencies among Educational Inputs and Resource Allocations in Classrooms. *Econ. Educ. Rev.*, 1984, *3*(1), pp. 65–73. **[G: U.S.]**

Moore, Mary T. Cost Cutting without Goal Set-

ting: A Recipe for Failure. *J. Policy Anal. Manage.*, Winter 1984, *3*(2), pp. 255–63. **[G: U.S.]**

Morgan, William R. Quantity of Learning and Quality of Life for Public and Private High School Youth. In *Borus, M. E., ed.*, 1984, pp. 111–56. **[G: U.S.]**

Muller, Steven. Research Universities and Industrial Innovation in America. In *Coles, J. S., ed.*, 1984, pp. 8–29. **[G: U.S.]**

Mulligan, James G. A Classroom Production Function. *Econ. Inquiry*, April 1984, *22*(2), pp. 218–26. **[G: U.S.]**

Munley, Vincent G. Has the Median Voter Found a Ballot Box That He Can Control? *Econ. Inquiry*, July 1984, *22*(3), pp. 323–36. **[G: U.S.]**

Murnane, Richard J. A Review Essay—Comparisons of Public and Private Schools: Lessons from the Uproar. *J. Human Res.*, Spring 1984, *19*(2), pp. 263–77. **[G: U.S.]**

Murnane, Richard J. Comment: Alternative Views of the Quality of U.S. Education. In *Dean, E., ed.*, 1984, pp. 195–203. **[G: U.S.]**

Murnane, Richard J. Selection and Survival in the Teacher Labor Market. *Rev. Econ. Statist.*, August 1984, *66*(3), pp. 513–18. **[G: U.S.]**

Murnane, Richard J. and Nelson, Richard R. Production and Innovation When Techniques Are Tacit: The Case of Education. *J. Econ. Behav. Organ.*, September–December 1984, *5*(3–4), pp. 353–73. **[G: U.S.]**

Nawaz, Shuja. Mass Media in Development—An Overview. *Finance Develop.*, June 1984, *21*(2), pp. 44–46. **[G: Selected LDCs]**

Nelson, F. Howard. A Note on the Effects of Commercial and Industrial Property in School Spending Decisions. *Nat. Tax J.*, March 1984, *37*(1), pp. 121–25. **[G: U.S.]**

O'Boyle, Edward J. On the University Researcher as an Entrepreneur. *Int. J. Soc. Econ.*, 1984, *11*(3/4), pp. 114–23. **[G: U.S.]**

O'Hagan, John W. and Kelly, Morgan. Components of Growth in Current Public Expenditure on Education and Health. *Econ. Soc. Rev.*, January 1984, *15*(2), pp. 87–93. **[G: Ireland]**

O'Neill, David M. The Quiet Revolution in Educational Attainment. *Challenge*, September/October 1984, *27*(4), pp. 57–61. **[G: U.S.]**

Olson, Craig A. The Role of Rescheduled School Days in Teacher Strikes. *Ind. Lab. Relat. Rev.*, July 1984, *37*(4), pp. 515–28. **[G: U.S.]**

Oxenham, John. Employers, Jobs and Qualifications. In *Oxenham, J., ed.*, 1984, pp. 41–86. **[G: Tanzania; Kenya; Zambia; Sri Lanka; Mexico]**

Perkins, George M. Public Education: Comment [Wealth Neutrality and Local Choice in Public Education]. *Amer. Econ. Rev.*, September 1984, *74*(4), pp. 814–19. **[G: U.S.]**

Peston, Maurice. Privatisation of Education. In *Le Grand, J. and Robinson, R., eds.*, 1984, pp. 146–59. **[G: U.K.]**

Plant, Mark W. and Welch, Finis. Measuring the Impact of Education on Productivity. In *Dean, E., ed.*, 1984, pp. 163–93. **[G: U.S.]**

Polzin, Paul E. The Impact of Economic Trends on Higher Education Enrollment. *Growth Change*, April 1984, *15*(2), pp. 18–22.
[G: U.S.]

Psacharopoulos, George. The Contribution of Education to Economic Growth: International Comparisons. In *Kendrick, J. W., ed.*, 1984, pp. 335–55. [G: Selected Countries]

Psacharopoulos, George and Zabalza, Antonio. The Effect of Diversified Schools on Employment Status and Earnings in Colombia. *Econ. Educ. Rev.*, 1984, *3*(4), pp. 315–31.
[G: Colombia]

Qadir, Asghar. Educated Unemployed, Educational Subsidies, and Growth: Comment. *Pakistan Devel. Rev.*, Summer-Autumn 1984, *23*(2&3), pp. 411–12.

Rätzer, Ernst. Institutionelle Ursachen der geringen ökonomischen Forschungsaktivität im deutschsprachigen Raum. (Institutional Causes of the Low Economic Research Activity in German Speaking Countries. With English summary. *Kyklos*, 1984, *37*(2), pp. 223–46.
[G: Germany; Switzerland; Austria]

Reimers, Niels. The Government-Industry-University Interface: Improving the Innovative Process. In *Coles, J. S., ed.*, 1984, pp. 109–48. [G: U.S.]

Romer, Thomas; Rosenthal, Howard and Ladha, Krishna. If at First You Don't Succeed: Budgeting by a Sequence of Referenda. In *Hanusch, H., ed.*, 1984, pp. 87–108. [G: U.S.]

Rosen, Stanley. New Directions in Secondary Education. In *Hayhoe, R., ed.*, 1984, pp. 65–92.
[G: China]

Rumberger, Russell W. and Daymont, Thomas N. The Economic Value of Academic and Vocational Training Acquired in High School. In *Borus, M. E., ed.*, 1984, pp. 157–91.
[G: U.S.]

Sathar, Zeba Ayesha. Does Female Education Affect Fertility Behaviour in Pakistan? *Pakistan Devel. Rev.*, Winter 1984, *23*(4), pp. 573–90.
[G: Pakistan]

Schmidt, Henning. Die Finanzierung der Hochschulausbildung. Eine ökonomische Analyse. (The Financing of Higher Education—An Economic Analysis. With English summary.) *Z. Wirtschaft. Sozialwissen.*, 1984, *104*(2), pp. 151–75.

Schultz, Theodore W. A Comment on Education and Economic Growth. In *Kendrick, J. W., ed.*, 1984, pp. 357–60.
[G: Selected Countries]

Selby, Cecily Cannan. Current Trends in Mathematics, Science, and Technology Education: Implications for Technological Innovation. In *Coles, J. S., ed.*, 1984, pp. 149–82. [G: U.S.]

Simms, Margaret C. Education, Economics, and Equity: Comments. *Rev. Black Polit. Econ.*, Summer–Fall 1984, *13*(1–2), pp. 162–64.
[G: U.S.]

Srivastava, J. N. Education and Demographic Behaviour: Some Empirical Findings. In *Singh, A. K.; Papola, T. S. and Mathur, R. S., eds.*, 1984, pp. 89–108. [G: India]

Starnick, Jürgen and Allesch, Jürgen. Compatibility of University Integrity with Industrial Cooperation. In *Fusfeld, H. I. and Haklisch, C. S., eds.*, 1984, pp. 129–33.

Swanson, August G. Implications of the Expanding Physician Supply for Medical Schools and Medical Students. In *Ginzberg, E. and Ostow, M., eds.*, 1984, pp. 49–68. [G: U.S.]

Thiemann, Hugo. Overview of Policy Issues: Panel Report on Compatibility of University Integrity with Industrial Cooperation. In *Fusfeld, H. I. and Haklisch, C. S., eds.*, 1984, pp. 135–38.

Thompson, Frederick How to Stay within the Budget Using Per-Unit Subsidies. *J. Policy Anal. Manage.*, Winter 1984, *3*(2), pp. 285–88. [G: U.S.]

Tienda, Marta and Neidert, Lisa J. Language, Education, and the Socioeconomic Achievement of Hispanic Origin Men. *Soc. Sci. Quart.*, June 1984, *65*(2), pp. 519–36.
[G: U.S.]

Tilak, Jandhyala B. G. Urban Bias and Rural Neglect in Education: A Study on Rural–Urban Disparities in Education in Andhra Pradesh. *Margin*, October 1984, *17*(1), pp. 61–86.
[G: India]

Unger, Jonathan. Severing the Links between Education and Careers: The Sobering Experience of China's Urban Schools. In *Oxenham, J., ed.*, 1984, pp. 176–91. [G: China]

Useem, Elizabeth L. Education and High-Technology Industry: The Case of Silicon Valley. *Econ. Educ. Rev.*, 1984, *3*(3), pp. 215–21.
[G: U.S.]

Venti, Steven F. The Effects of Income Maintenance on Work, Schooling, and Non-Market Activities of Youth. *Rev. Econ. Statist.*, February 1984, *66*(1), pp. 16–25.

Wachter, Michael L. and Wascher, William L. Leveling the Peaks and Troughs in the Demographic Cycle: An Application to School Enrollment Rates. *Rev. Econ. Statist.*, May 1984, *66*(2), pp. 208–15. [G: U.S.]

Weiss, Janet A. and Gruber, Judith E. Deterring Discrimination with Data. *Policy Sci.*, May 1984, *17*(1), pp. 49–66. [G: U.S.]

Wentzler, Nancy A. Net Regional Impact of State Education Aid. *Growth Change*, July 1984, *15*(3), pp. 3–9. [G: U.S.]

Williams, Ross A. Interactions between Government and Private Outlays: Education in Australia, 1949–50 to 1981–82. *Econ. Rec.*, December 1984, *60*(171), pp. 317–25. [G: Australia]

Winkler, Donald R. The Fiscal Consequences of Foreign Students in Public Higher Education: A Case Study of California. *Econ. Educ. Rev.*, 1984, *3*(2), pp. 141–54. [G: U.S.]

Wolfe, Barbara L. and Behrman, Jere R. Who Is Schooled in Developing Countries? The Roles of Income, Parental Schooling, Sex, Residence, and Family Size. *Econ. Educ. Rev.*, 1984, *3*(3), pp. 231–45. [G: Nicaragua]

Woolcock, Joseph. Class Conflict and Class Reproduction: An Historical Analysis of the Jamaican Educational Reforms of 1957 and 1962.

Soc. Econ. Stud., December 1984, *33*(4), pp. 51–99. **[G: Jamaica]**

Wyatt, Joe B. Science, Technology, and Employment: The Reindustrialization of America. In *Ullrich, R. A., ed.*, 1984, pp. 59–80. **[G: U.S.]**

Wyckoff, James H. The Nonexcludable Publicness of Primary and Secondary Public Education. *J. Public Econ.*, August 1984, *24*(3), pp. 331–51. **[G: U.S.]**

913 Economics of Health (including medical subsidy programs)

9130 Economics of Health (including medical subsidy programs)

Aaron, Henry J. Health Care Financing and Pension Programs: Comment. In *Mills, G. B. and Palmer, J. L., eds.*, 1984, pp. 157–61. **[G: U.S.]**

Aaron, Henry J. Social Welfare in Australia. In *Caves, R. E. and Krause, L. B., eds.*, 1984, pp. 349–90. **[G: Australia]**

Ahlburg, Dennis A. and Schapiro, Morton Owen. Socioeconomic Ramifications of Changing Cohort Size: An Analysis of U.S. Postwar Suicide Rates by Age and Sex. *Demography*, February 1984, *21*(1), pp. 97–108. **[G: U.S.]**

Ahlburg, Dennis A. and Schapiro, Morton Owen. The Social Cost of Economic Decline: Some Earlier Evidence. *J. Post Keynesian Econ.*, Winter 1983-84, *6*(2), pp. 303–04. **[G: U.S.]**

Alexander, Jeffrey A.; Evashwick, Connie J. and Rundall, Thomas. Hospitals and the Provision of Care to the Aged: A Cluster Analysis. *Inquiry*, Winter 1984, *21*(4), pp. 303–14. **[G: U.S.]**

Alexander, Jeffrey A. and Lewis, Bonnie L. The Financial Characteristics of Hospitals under For-Profit and Nonprofit Contract Management. *Inquiry*, Fall 1984, *21*(3), pp. 230–42. **[G: U.S.]**

Alpert, Geraldine and McCarthy, Thomas R. Beyond *Goldfarb:* Applying Traditional Antitrust Analysis to Changing Health Markets. *Antitrust Bull.*, Summer 1984, *29*(2), pp. 165–204. **[G: U.S.]**

Altman, Stuart H. The Growing Physician Surplus: Will It Benefit or Bankrupt the U.S. Health System? In *Ginzberg, E. and Ostow, M., eds.*, 1984, pp. 9–36. **[G: U.S.]**

Anderson, Gerard and Knickman, James. Adverse Selection under a Voucher System: Grouping Medicare Recipients by Level of Expenditure. *Inquiry*, Summer 1984, *21*(2), pp. 135–43. **[G: U.S.]**

Angel, Ronald. The Costs of Disability for Hispanic Males. *Soc. Sci. Quart.*, June 1984, *65*(2), pp. 426–43. **[G: U.S.]**

Arnould, Richard J.; Debrock, Lawrence W. and Pollard, John W. Do HMOs Produce Specific Services More Efficiently? *Inquiry*, Fall 1984, *21*(3), pp. 243–53. **[G: U.S.]**

Arrow, Kenneth J. Optimal Insurance and Generalized Deductibles. In *Arrow, K. J., vol. 3,* 1984, *1974*, pp. 212–60.

Arrow, Kenneth J. Permanent and Transitory Substitution Effects in Health Insurance Experiments. *J. Lab. Econ.*, April 1984, *2*(2), pp. 259–67.

Arrow, Kenneth J. The Economics of Moral Hazard: Further Comment. In *Arrow, K. J., vol. 4,* 1984, *1968*, pp. 103–05.

Ashby, John L., Jr. The Impact of Hospital Regulatory Programs on Per Capita Costs, Utilization, and Capital Investment. *Inquiry*, Spring 1984, *21*(1), pp. 45–59. **[G: U.S.]**

Aspe, Pedro and Beristain, Javier. Distribution of Education and Health Opportunities and Services. In *Aspe, P. and Sigmund, P. E., eds.*, 1984, pp. 265–326. **[G: Mexico]**

Austin, James E. Institutional Dimensions of the Malnutrition Problem. In *Ghosh, P. K., ed., no. 6,* 1984, *1978*, pp. 125–52. **[G: Global]**

Banerji, Debabar. The Political Economy of Western Medicine in Third World Countries. In *McKinlay, J. B., ed.*, 1984, pp. 257–82.

Barer, Morris L.; Stark, Annette J. and Kinnis, Claire. Manpower Planning, Fiscal Restraint, and the "Demand" for Health Care Personnel. *Inquiry*, Fall 1984, *21*(3), pp. 254–65. **[G: Canada]**

Barnum, Howard N. and Barlow, Robin. Modeling Resource Allocation for Child Survival. *Population Devel. Rev.*, Supplement 1984, *10*, pp. 367–87. **[G: Colombia]**

Beazoglou, Tryfon J. Price Variation and Its Determinants across Dental Markets. *Eastern Econ. J.*, October-December 1984, *10*(4), pp. 353–66. **[G: U.S.]**

Behrman, Jere R. and Wolfe, Barbara L. More Evidence on Nutrition Demand: Income Seems Overrated and Women's Schooling Underemphasized. *J. Devel. Econ.*, January–February 1984, *14*(1–2), pp. 105–28. **[G: Nicaragua]**

Benyoussef, Amor. Monitoring and Servicing National Health. In *Ghosh, P. K., ed., no. 6,* 1984, *1977*, pp. 267–90. **[G: LDCs]**

Berger, Mark C. and Fleisher, Belton M. Husband's Health and Wife's Labor Supply. *J. Health Econ.*, April 1984, *3*(1), pp. 63–75. **[G: U.S.]**

Bevan, R. Gwyn. Organising the Finance of Hospitals by Simulated Markets. *Fisc. Stud.*, November 1984, *5*(4), pp. 44–63. **[G: U.K.; U.S.]**

Birdsall, Nancy. Health Planning and Population in Africa. In *Ghosh, P. K., ed., no. 6,* 1984, *1976*, pp. 352–69. **[G: Africa]**

Bissell, Thomas St.G.; Skadden, Donald H. and White, Frederic E. Social Security Contributions as a Fiscal Burden on Enterprises Engaged in International Activities: United States. In *Intn'l. Fisc. Assoc., vol. 69b,* 1984, pp. 317–37. **[G: U.S.]**

Black, Jennifer Ann. The Path to a "Sane Society," A Note. *Amer. Econ.*, Fall 1984, *28*(2), pp. 76–80.

Blackstone, Erwin A. and Fuhr, Joseph P., Jr. Antitrust and Exclusive Agreements: The Case of Hospital-based Physicians. *Antitrust Bull.*, Winter 1984, *29*(4), pp. 739–58.   [G: U.S.]

Blomqvist, Åke and Horn, Henrik. Public Health Insurance and Optimal Income Taxation. *J. Public Econ.*, August 1984, *24*(3), pp. 353–71.

Bodenheimer, Thomas S. The Transnational Pharmaceutical Industry and the Health of the World's People. In *McKinlay, J. B., ed.*, 1984, pp. 187–216.

Bolze, Ray S. and Pennak, Mark W. Reconciliation of the Sherman Act with Federal Health-planning Legislation: Implied Antitrust Immunity in the Health Care Field. *Antitrust Bull.*, Summer 1984, *29*(2), pp. 225–52.   [G: U.S.]

Bossert, Thomas John. Health-Policy Innovation and International Assistance in Central America. *Polit. Sci. Quart.*, Fall 1984, *99*(3), pp. 441–55.   [G: Guatemala; Honduras]

Brandeau, Margaret L. and Hopkins, David S. P. A Patient Mix Model for Hospital Financial Planning. *Inquiry*, Spring 1984, *21*(1), pp. 32–44.   [G: U.S.]

Brecher, Charles and Roswick, Diana. Setting Municipal Priorities: Service Delivery: The City's Role in Health Care. In *Brecher, C. and Horton, R. D., eds.*, 1984, pp. 482–518.   [G: U.S.]

Breyer, Friedrich. Anbieterinduzierte Nachfrage nach ärztlichen Leistungen und die Zieleinkommens-Hypothese. (Supplier-Induced Demand for Physicians' Services and the Target Income Hypothesis. With English summary.) *Jahr. Nationalökon. Statist.*, September 1984, *199*(5), pp. 415–32.

Breyer, Friedrich. Moral Hazard und der optimale Krankenversicherungsvertrag. Eine Übersicht. (Moral Hazard and the Optimal Health Insurance Contract: A Survey. With English summary.) *Z. ges. Staatswiss.*, June 1984, *140*(2), pp. 288–307.

Buchanan, Cathy and Prior, Elizabeth W. Bureaucrats and Babies: Government Regulation of the Supply of Genetic Material. *Econ. Rec.*, September 1984, *60*(170), pp. 222–30.

Buglione, Enrico and France, George. Skewed Fiscal Federalism in Italy: Implications for Public Expenditure Control. In *Premchand, A. and Burkhead, J., eds.*, 1984, pp. 69–89.   [G: Italy]

Busche, Kelly and Kennedy, Peter. On Economists' Belief in the Law of Small Numbers. *Econ. Inquiry*, October 1984, *22*(4), pp. 602–03.   [G: U.S.]

Carrin, Guy and Van Dael, Jaak. An Empirical Model of the Demand for Health Care in Belgium. *Appl. Econ.*, June 1984, *16*(3), pp. 317–34.   [G: Belgium]

Chaudhury, Rafiqul Huda. Determinants of Nutrient Adequacy for Lactating and Pregnant Mothers in a Rural Area of Bangladesh. *Bangladesh Devel. Stud.*, December 1984, *12*(4), pp. 107–22.   [G: Bangladesh]

Chester, T. E. and van Oss, M. G. M. Economic Priorities and Social Expenditure: A Comparison of Dutch and British Health Service Poli-

cies. *Nat. Westminster Bank Quart. Rev.*, February 1984, pp. 16–30.   [G: Netherlands; U.K.]

Child, John, et al. Microelectronics and the Quality of Employment in Services. In *Marstrand, P., ed.*, 1984, pp. 163–90.   [G: U.K.]

Chirikos, Thomas N. and Nestel, Gilbert. Economic Determinants and Consequences of Self-reported Work Disability. *J. Health Econ.*, August 1984, *3*(2), pp. 117–36.   [G: U.S.]

Cho, Dongsae. Rehabilitation for Workers' Compensation Loss Exposures. *J. Risk Ins.*, March 1984, *51*(1), pp. 80–98.   [G: U.S.]

Christianson, Jon B. Provider Participation in Competitive Bidding for Indigent Patients. *Inquiry*, Summer 1984, *21*(2), pp. 161–77.   [G: U.S.]

Cohen, Alvin. Review Article: The Macroeconomic versus the Microeconomic Approach to Development: The Futility of Development Efforts as a Function of Institutional Inertia. *Econ. Develop. Cult. Change*, January 1984, *32*(2), pp. 423–30.   [G: LDCs]

Cohen, David R. and Mooney, Gavin H. Prevention Goods and Hazard Goods: A Taxonomy. *Scot. J. Polit. Econ.*, February 1984, *31*(1), pp. 92–99.

Cook, Philip J. The Economics of Alcohol Consumption and Abuse. In *West, L. J., ed.*, 1984, pp. 56–77.   [G: U.S.]

Cornia, Giovanni Andrea. The Impact of World Recession on Children: A Survey of Cross-Sectional and Time-Series Literature on Factors Affecting Child Welfare. *World Devel.*, March 1984, *12*(3), pp. 187–202.   [G: Global]

Costilo, L. Barry and Kazon, Peter M. Preferred Provider Plans: Avoiding Problems of Horizontal Price-fixing. *Antitrust Bull.*, Summer 1984, *29*(2), pp. 403–22.   [G: U.S.]

Cox, Howard and Smith, Ronald P. Political Approaches to Smoking Control: A Comparative Analysis. *Appl. Econ.*, August 1984, *16*(4), pp. 569–82.   [G: OECD]

Crawford, Robert. A Cultural Account of "Health": Control, Release, and the Social Body. In *McKinlay, J. B., ed.*, 1984, pp. 60–103.

Crocker, Thomas D., et al. The Sixty-City Limit. In *Ahmad, Y. J.; Dasgupta, P. and Mäler, K.-G., eds.*, 1984, pp. 114–61.   [G: U.S.]

Cutler, Peter. The Measurement of Poverty: A Review of Attempts to Quantify the Poor, with Special Reference to India. *World Devel.*, November–December 1984, *12*(11–12), pp. 1119–30.   [G: India]

Danzon, Patricia M. Health Policy in 1984: The Crisis in Costs. In *Moore, J. H., ed.*, 1984, pp. 125–36.   [G: U.S.]

Danzon, Patricia M. The Frequency and Severity of Medical Malpractice Claims. *J. Law Econ.*, April 1984, *27*(1), pp. 115–48.   [G: U.S.]

DaVanzo, Julie. A Household Survey of Child Mortality Determinants in Malaysia. *Population Devel. Rev.*, Supplement 1984, *10*, pp. 307–22.   [G: Malaysia]

Davis, Karen. Physician Supply and Health Care Costs. In *Ginzberg, E. and Ostow, M., eds.,* 1984, pp. 37–48. **[G: U.S.]**

Derber, Charles. Physicians and Their Sponsors: The New Medical Relations of Production. In *McKinlay, J. B., ed.,* 1984, pp. 217–54.

Duan, Naihua, et al. Choosing between the Sample-Selection Model and the Multi-part Model. *J. Bus. Econ. Statist.,* July 1984, *2*(3), pp. 283–89. **[G: U.S.]**

Duffy, Sarah W. and Kraut, Alan G. Understanding and Influencing the Federal Budget for Psychological Research. In *Dusek, E. R., et al., eds.,* 1984, pp. 19–27. **[G: U.S.]**

Dunkelberg, John S.; Furst, Richard W. and Roenfeldt, Rodney L. Relationship between Hospital Capital Expenditures and Operating Costs. *J. Econ. Bus.,* December 1984, *36*(4), pp. 433–42. **[G: U.S.]**

Ebrahim, G. J. Health Care and The Urban Poor. In *Richards, P. J. and Thomson, A. M., eds.,* 1984, pp. 93–121. **[G: LDCs]**

Eyer, Joe. Capitalism, Health, and Illness. In *McKinlay, J. B., ed.,* 1984, pp. 23–59.

Feshbach, Murray. Soviet Health Problems. In *Hoffmann, E. P., ed.,* 1984, pp. 81–97. **[G: U.S.S.R.]**

Field, Mark G. Soviet Urban Health Services: Some Problems and Their Sources. In *Morton, H. W. and Stuart, R. C., eds.,* 1984, pp. 129–55. **[G: U.S.S.R.]**

Finot, Paul-Andre. Some Methods to Improve Nutrition in the Developing Countries. In *Ghosh, P. K., ed., no. 6, 1984, 1974,* pp. 199–212.

Finsinger, Jörg and Kraft, Kornelius. Marktordnung und Kostenstruktur in der Privaten Krankenversicherung. (The Private Health Insurance Market and the Cost Structure of the Insurance Firms. With English summary.) *Z. Wirtschaft. Sozialwissen.,* 1984, *104*(4), pp. 389–415. **[G: Germany]**

Finsinger, Jörg and Kraft, Kornelius. Markup Pricing and Firm Decisions. *Z. ges. Staatswiss.,* September 1984, *140*(3), pp. 500–509. **[G: Germany]**

Forbes, John F. and McGregor, Alan. Unemployment and Mortality in Post-war Scotland. *J. Health Econ.,* December 1984, *3*(3), pp. 239–57. **[G: Scotland]**

Fowler, David J. and Gordon, Myron J. The Effect of Public Policy Initiatives on Drug Prices in Canada. *Can. Public Policy,* March 1984, *10*(1), pp. 64–73. **[G: Canada; U.S.]**

Foxley, Alejandro and Raczynski, Dagmar. Vulnerable Groups in Recessionary Situations: The Case of Children and the Young in Chile. In *Jolly, R. and Cornia, G. A., eds.,* 1984, pp. 53–76. **[G: Chile]**

Freund, Deborah Anne. Equality of Opportunity and the Demand for Medical Care by Race. *Quart. Rev. Econ. Bus.,* Spring 1984, *24*(1), pp. 42–55. **[G: U.S.]**

Fridlizius, Gunnar. The Mortality Decline in the First Phase of the Demographic Transition: Swedish Experiences. In *Bengtsson, T.; Frid-*

lizius, G. and Ohlsson, R., eds., 1984, pp. 71–114. **[G: Sweden]**

Friedman, Bernard; Ross, Caroline and Misek, Glen. On the Surprisingly Low Cost of State Catastrophic Health Insurance Programs. *J. Risk Ins.,* March 1984, *51*(1), pp. 31–48. **[G: U.S.]**

Gabriel, Stuart A. and Wolch, Jennifer R. Spillover Effects of Human Service Facilities in a Racially Segmented Housing Market. *J. Urban Econ.,* November 1984, *16*(3), pp. 339–50. **[G: U.S.]**

Gadreau, Maryse and Poisson, Marie-Aude. L'hôpital de jour, une alternative à l'hospitalisation classique? L'exemple des Hospices Civils de Lyon. (Is Hospital Day Care an Alternative to Traditional Hospital Care? The Lyons Public Hospital System. With English summary.) *Consommation,* July–September 1984, *31*(3), pp. 75–91. **[G: France]**

Gafni, Amiram and Peled, Dan. The Effect of Labelling on Illness Related Absenteeism: An Economic Explanation for the Case of Hypertension. *J. Health Econ.,* August 1984, *3*(2), pp. 173–78. **[G: U.S.]**

Gates, John H. Human Capital Investment in Health: A Measurement Framework and Estimates for the United States, 1952–78. *Rev. Income Wealth,* March 1984, *30*(1), pp. 39–52. **[G: U.S.]**

Getzen, Thomas E. A "Brand Name Firm" Theory of Medical Group Practice. *J. Ind. Econ.,* December 1984, *33*(2), pp. 199–215. **[G: U.S.]**

Gheorghe, F. C. and Ştefănescu, St. Simulation Models for the Study of the Active Population Evolution and of the Health State of Entire Population. *Econ. Computat. Cybern. Stud. Res.,* 1984, *19*(4), pp. 37–46.

Gingrich, Newt. The Best Health Care for Everyone. *Policy Rev.,* Summer 1984, (29), pp. 66–70. **[G: U.S.]**

Ginsburg, Paul B. The Competition Debate Five Years Later [Corporate Benefit Policies and Health Insurance Costs]. *J. Health Econ.,* December 1984, *3*(3), pp. 307–11.

Ginzberg, Eli. Conference Summary: The Expanding Physician Supply: Policy Options. In *Ginzberg, E. and Ostow, M., eds.,* 1984, pp. 1–8. **[G: U.S.]**

Ginzberg, Eli. The Future Supply of Physicians: Directions for Policy. In *Ginzberg, E. and Ostow, M., eds.,* 1984, pp. 116–25. **[G: U.S.]**

Glaser, William A. Juggling Multiple Payers: American Problems and Foreign Solutions. *Inquiry,* Summer 1984, *21*(2), pp. 178–88. **[G: U.S.]**

Goddeeris, John H. Insurance and Incentives for Innovation in Medical Care. *Southern Econ. J.,* October 1984, *51*(2), pp. 530–39.

Goddeeris, John H. Medical Insurance, Technological Change, and Welfare. *Econ. Inquiry,* January 1984, *22*(1), pp. 56–67.

Goldwater, Carmel. Humanitarian Situation in Kampuchea. In *Thambipillai, P., ed.,* 1984, pp. 162–76. **[G: Cambodia]**

Golladay, Fredrick L. Community Health Care

in Developing Countries. In *Ghosh, P. K., ed., no. 6, 1984, 1980*, pp. 238–48.   [G: LDCs]

Gottinger, Hans W. Lower-Bound Benefits of Air Pollution Reductions in the Munich Metropolitan Area (MMA) In *[Beckmann, M. J.]*, 1984, pp. 243–55.   [G: W. Germany]

Goubert, Jean-Pierre. Public Hygiene and Mortality Decline in France in the 19th Century. In *Bengtsson, T.; Fridlizius, G. and Ohlsson, R., eds.*, 1984, pp. 151–59.   [G: France]

Gravelle, Hugh S. E. Time Series Analysis of Mortality and Unemployment [Unemployment and Mortality in Post-war Scotland]. *J. Health Econ.*, December 1984, *3*(3), pp. 297–305.

Greene, S. B. and Gunselman, D. L. The Conversion of Claims Files to an Episode Data Base: A Tool for Management and Research. *Inquiry*, Summer 1984, *21*(2), pp. 189–94.
    [G: U.S.]

Gregorio, David I. and Marshall, James R. Fine Tuning Well-being: Food Stamp Use and Nutritional Adequacy of Children's Diets. *Soc. Sci. Quart.*, December 1984, *65*(4), pp. 1137–46.   [G: U.S.]

Gunnerson, Charles G. Sanitation Systems for Developing Countries. In *Weiss, C. and Jéquier, N., eds.*, 1984, pp. 125–39.

Hamm, Walter. Programmierte Unfreiheit und Verschwendung: Zur überfällign Reform der Gesetzlichen Krankenversicherung. (With English Summary.) In *Eucken, W. and Böhm, F., eds.*, 1984, pp. 21–42. [G: W. Germany]

Hannan, Edward L. and O'Donnell, Joseph F. Adult Day Care Services in New York State: A Comparison with Other Long-Term Care Providers. *Inquiry*, Spring 1984, *21*(1), pp. 75–83.   [G: U.S.]

Hannan, Edward L. and O'Donnell, Joseph F. An Evaluation of Hospices in the New York State Hospice Demonstration Program. *Inquiry*, Winter 1984, *21*(4), pp. 338–48.
    [G: U.S.]

Harper, A. E. Nutrition and Health in the Changing Environment. In *Simon, J. L. and Kahn, H., eds.*, 1984, pp. 490–527.   [G: Global]

Hay, Joel W. Variation in U.S. Per Capita Pharmaceutical Expenditures: Are Drugs Health Care Complements or Substitutes? In *Lindgren, B., ed.*, 1984, pp. 21–35.   [G: U.S.]

Hay, Joel W. and Leahy, Michael J. Competition among Health Plans: Some Preliminary Evidence. *Southern Econ. J.*, January 1984, *50*(3), pp. 831–46.   [G: U.S.]

Hay, Joel W. and Olsen, Randall J. Let Them Eat Cake: A Note on Comparing Alternative Models of the Demand for Medical Care. *J. Bus. Econ. Statist.*, July 1984, *2*(3), pp. 279–82.   [G: U.S.]

Hemmer, Hans-Rimbert. Possible Consequences of Nutritional Improvements for the Economic Development. In *Ghosh, P. K., ed., no. 6, 1984, 1979*, pp. 213–21.   [G: LDCs]

Hersch, Philip L. Competition and the Performance of Hospital Markets. *Rev. Ind. Organ.*, Winter 1984, *1*(4), pp. 324–41.   [G: U.S.]

Hershey, John C., et al. Health Insurance under

Competition: Would People Choose What Is Expected? *Inquiry*, Winter 1984, *21*(4), pp. 349–60.   [G: U.S.]

Hiestand, Dale L. Medical Residencies in a Period of Expanding Physician Supply. In *Ginzberg, E. and Ostow, M., eds.*, 1984, pp. 69–82.   [G: U.S.]

Hochstein, Alan. A Cost Comparison in the Treatment of Long Stay Patients. *Can. Public Policy*, June 1984, *10*(2), pp. 177–84.   [G: Canada]

Holmer, Martin. Tax Policy and the Demand for Health Insurance. *J. Health Econ.*, December 1984, *3*(3), pp. 203–21.   [G: U.S.]

Holt, Virginia E. Federal Funding Trends for Research in Psychology. In *Dusek, E. R., et al., eds.*, 1984, pp. 29–39.   [G: U.S.]

Ippolito, Pauline M. and Ippolito, Richard A. Measuring the Value of Life Saving from Consumer Reactions to New Information. *J. Public Econ.*, November 1984, *25*(1/2), pp. 53–81.

Jacobs, Philip and Wilder, Ronald P. Pricing Behavior of Non-profit Agencies: The Case of Blood Products. *J. Health Econ.*, April 1984, *3*(1), pp. 49–61.   [G: U.S.]

Jensen, Gail; Feldman, Roger and Dowd, Bryan. Corporate Benefit Policies and Health Insurance Costs. *J. Health Econ.*, December 1984, *3*(3), pp. 275–96.   [G: U.S.]

Johnson, Allan N. and Appel, Gary L. DRGs and Hospital Case Records: Implications for Medicare Case Mix Accuracy. *Inquiry*, Summer 1984, *21*(2), pp. 128–34.   [G: U.S.]

Johnson, William G. and Heler, Edward. Compensation for Death from Asbestos. *Ind. Lab. Relat. Rev.*, July 1984, *37*(4), pp. 529–40.

Joseph, Hyman. Reimbursement Methods and Hospital Quality. *Eastern Econ. J.*, July-September 1984, *10*(3), pp. 285–93.   [G: U.S.]

Kass, David I. and Pautler, Paul A. On Economists' Belief in the Law of Small Numbers: A Reply [The Administration Costs of Non-profit Health Insurers]. *Econ. Inquiry*, October 1984, *22*(4), pp. 604–06.   [G: U.S.]

Keating, Barry. Cost Shifting: An Empirical Examination of Hospital Bureaucracy. *Appl. Econ.*, April 1984, *16*(2), pp. 279–89.
    [G: U.S.]

Keating, Barry. Direct and Indirect Impacts of the Matchbook Safety Standard of the Consumer Products Safety Commission. *Quart. Rev. Econ. Bus.*, Autumn 1984, *24*(3), pp. 29–36.   [G: U.S.]

Kenyon, Daphne A. and McCandless, George T., Jr. A Note on the Required Compensation Test as the Theoretical Basis for Putting a Value on Human Life. *Southern Econ. J.*, July 1984, *51*(1), pp. 258–66.

Khan, Qaiser M. The Impact of Household Endowment Constraints on Nutrition and Health: A Simultaneous Equation Test of Human Capital Divestment. *J. Devel. Econ.*, May–June–August 1984, *15*(1,2,3), pp. 313–28.
    [G: Bangladesh]

Kinzer, David M. Care of the Poor Revisited. *Inquiry*, Spring 1984, *21*(1), pp. 5–16.
    [G: U.S.]

Knowles, James C. Interactions between Malnutrition and Disease: A Simultaneous Equations Model Applied to Data from a Low-Income Area of Karachi. *Pakistan J. Appl. Econ.*, Winter 1984, *3*(2), pp. 107–38. **[G: Pakistan]**

Krashinsky, Michael. Some Limitations on the Usefulness of Revenue Dependency: Why Governments Often Produce What They Subsidize. *Can. Public Policy*, March 1984, *10*(1), pp. 35–46.

Landefeld, J. Steven. Measuring the Returns to Biomedical Research: Issues and Problems. In *Lindgren, B., ed.*, 1984, pp. 255–86.
[G: U.S.]

Lave, Judith R. Competitive Bidding and Public Insurance Programs. *J. Health Econ.*, August 1984, *3*(2), pp. 195–98. **[G: U.S.]**

Layton, Allan P. The Impact of Increased Penalties on Australian Drink/Driving Behavior—A Procedural Note. *Logist. Transp. Rev.*, June 1984, *20*(2), pp. 187–89. **[G: Australia]**

Lee, Maw Lin. Demographic Variables in Medical Care Demand Analysis. *Math. Soc. Sci.*, April 1984, *7*(2), pp. 167–75.

Lee, Robert H. Subsidizing the Affluent: The Case of Medical Education. *J. Policy Anal. Manage.*, Winter 1984, *3*(2), pp. 276–84.
[G: U.S.]

Leigh, J. Paul and Folsom, Roger N. Estimates of the Value of Accident Avoidance at the Job Depend on the Concavity of the Equalizing Differences Curve. *Quart. Rev. Econ. Bus.*, Spring 1984, *24*(1), pp. 56–66. **[G: U.S.]**

Lerner, Arthur N. Federal Trade Commission Antitrust Activities in the Health Care Services Field. *Antitrust Bull.*, Summer 1984, *29*(2), pp. 205–24. **[G: U.S.]**

Leu, Robert E. Anti-smoking Publicity, Taxation, and the Demand for Cigarettes. *J. Health Econ.*, August 1984, *3*(2), pp. 101–16.
[G: Switzerland]

Leu, Robert E. Medical Technology Assessment in Terms of Improved Life Quality. In *Lindgren, B., ed.*, 1984, pp. 97–121.
[G: Switzerland]

Leu, Robert E., et al. Externe Kosten der Energie am Beispiel von Mortalität und Morbidität. (External Costs of Energy: Effects on Mortality and Morbidity. With English summary.) *Schweiz. Z. Volkswirtsch. Statist.*, September 1984, *120*(3), pp. 383–408. **[G: Switzerland]**

Lindsay, Cotton M. and Feigenbaum, Bernard. Rationing by Waiting Lists. *Amer. Econ. Rev.*, June 1984, *74*(3), pp. 404–17. **[G: U.K.]**

Lindsay, Cotton M. and Zycher, Benjamin. Substitution in Public Spending: Who Pays for Canadian National Health Insurance? *Econ. Inquiry*, July 1984, *22*(3), pp. 337–59.
[G: Canada]

Long, Franklin A. Potential Contributions of Western Business to the Service Sector of LDCs. In *Brooks, H.; Liebman, L. and Schelling, C. S., eds.*, 1984, pp. 319–37.
[G: LDCs]

Long, Stephen H., et al. Medical Expenditures of Terminal Cancer Patients during the Last

Year of Life. *Inquiry*, Winter 1984, *21*(4), pp. 315–27. **[G: U.S.]**

Lopez, A. D. Demographic Change in Europe and its Health and Social Implications: An Overview. In *Lopez, A. D. and Cliquet, R. L., eds.*, 1984, pp. 5–67. **[G: Europe; Algeria; Morocco; Turkey]**

Lucas, Adetokunbo O. The Tropical Diseases Research Program. In *Weiss, C. and Jéquier, N., eds.*, 1984, pp. 283–94.

Lynge, E. Trends and Perspectives in Mortality. In *Lopez, A. D. and Cliquet, R. L., eds.*, 1984, pp. 117–32. **[G: Europe]**

Macedo, Roberto. Brazilian Children and the Economic Crisis: Evidence from the State of São Paulo. In *Jolly, R. and Cornia, G. A., eds.*, 1984, pp. 33–51. **[G: Brazil]**

Martin, Suzanne G.; Frick, Alexander P. and Shwartz, Michael. An Analysis of Hospital Case Mix, Cost, and Payment Differences for Medicare, Medicaid, and Blue Cross Plan Patients Using DRGs. *Inquiry*, Winter 1984, *21*(4), pp. 369–79. **[G: U.S.]**

Martinelli, Alberto. I sistemi sanitari delle società industriali avanzate. (Health Systems in Advanced Industrial Societies. With English summary.) *Giorn. Econ.*, Nov.-Dec. 1984, *43*(11–12), pp. 763–81. **[G: U.K.; U.S.; W. Germany]**

Maynard, Alan. Public Expenditure Policy, 1984–85: Health and Personal Social Services. In *Cockle, P., ed.*, 1984, pp. 128–48. **[G: U.K.]**

Maynard, Alan and Williams, Alan H. Privatisation and the National Health Service. In *Le Grand, J. and Robinson, R., eds.*, 1984, pp. 95–110. **[G: U.K.]**

McAvinchey, Ian D. Economic Factors and Mortality—Some Aspects of the Scottish Case, 1950–1978. *Scot. J. Polit. Econ.*, February 1984, *31*(1), pp. 1–27. **[G: U.K.]**

McClure, Walter. On the Research Status of Risk-adjusted Capitation Rates. *Inquiry*, Fall 1984, *21*(3), pp. 205–13. **[G: U.S.]**

McCombs, Jeffrey S. Physician Treatment Decisions in a Multiple Treatment Model: The Effects of Physician Supply. *J. Health Econ.*, August 1984, *3*(2), pp. 155–71.

McGuirk, Marjorie A. and Porell, Frank W. Spatial Patterns of Hospital Utilization: The Impact of Distance and Time. *Inquiry*, Spring 1984, *21*(1), pp. 84–95. **[G: U.S.]**

McKinlay, John B. Issues in the Political Economy of Health Care: Introduction. In *McKinlay, J. B., ed.*, 1984, pp. 1–19.

Mennemeyer, Stephen T. Effects of Competition on Medicare Administrative Costs. *J. Health Econ.*, August 1984, *3*(2), pp. 137–54.
[G: U.S.]

Meyer, Jack A. Health Care Financing and Pension Programs: Comment. In *Mills, G. B. and Palmer, J. L., eds.*, 1984, pp. 162–64.
[G: U.S.]

Meyer, Jack A. The Unfinished Agenda in Health Policy. In *Weicher, J. C., ed.*, 1984, pp. 72–91. **[G: U.S.]**

Mielke, James H., et al. Historical Epidemiology

of Smallpox in Åland, Finland: 1751–1890. *Demography*, August 1984, *21*(3), pp. 271–95. [G: Finland]

Miles, Ian. Work, Well-being and Unemployment: A Study of Men in Brighton. In *Marstrand, P., ed.*, 1984, pp. 93–102. [G: U.K.]

Miles, John J. Hospital Mergers and the Antitrust Laws: An Overview. *Antitrust Bull.*, Summer 1984, *29*(2), pp. 253–99. [G: U.S.]

Mitchell, Janet B. Why Do Women Physicians Work Fewer Hours than Men Physicians? *Inquiry*, Winter 1984, *21*(4), pp. 361–68. [G: U.S.]

Molina, Nelly. Automédication et perceptions a l'égard de la médecine. (Self-Medication and Perceptions of Medicine. With English summary.) *Consommation*, April–June 1984, *31*(2), pp. 23–64. [G: France]

Morgan, N. C. An Analysis of Selected Hospice Programs. *J. Risk Ins.*, March 1984, *51*(1), pp. 99–114. [G: U.S.]

Morrisey, Michael A., et al. Hospital Rate Review: A Theory and an Empirical Review. *J. Health Econ.*, April 1984, *3*(1), pp. 25–47.

Mosley, W. Henry. Child Survival: Research and Policy. *Population Devel. Rev.*, Supplement 1984, *10*, pp. 3–23. [G: Global]

Mosley, W. Henry and Chen, Lincoln C. An Analytical Framework for the Study of Child Survival in Developing Countries. *Population Devel. Rev.*, Supplement 1984, *10*, pp. 25–45. [G: LDCs]

Mullner, Ross and Hadley, Jack. Interstate Variations in the Growth of Chain-owned Proprietary Hospitals, 1973–1982. *Inquiry*, Summer 1984, *21*(2), pp. 144–51. [G: U.S.]

Mulstein, Suzanne. The Uninsured and the Financing of Uncompensated Care: Scope, Costs, and Policy Options. *Inquiry*, Fall 1984, *21*(3), pp. 214–29. [G: U.S.]

Muniz, José A. Gutierrez, et al. The Recent Worldwide Economic Crisis and the Welfare of Children: The Case of Cuba. In *Jolly, R. and Cornia, G. A., eds.*, 1984, pp. 77–90. [G: Cuba]

Navarro, Vicente. The Crisis of the International Capitalist Order and Its Implications on the Welfare State. In *McKinlay, J. B., ed.*, 1984, pp. 107–40. [G: U.S.]

Newhouse, Joseph P. Cream Skimming, Asymmetric Information, and a Competitive Insurance Market. *J. Health Econ.*, April 1984, *3*(1), pp. 97–100.

Nichol, W. The Medical Profession in New South Wales, 1788–1850. *Australian Econ. Hist. Rev.*, September 1984, *24*(2), pp. 115–31. [G: Australia]

Nicholson, Norman K. and Esseks, John D. The Politics of Food Scarcities in Developing Countries. In *Ghosh, P. K., ed., no. 6*, 1984, *1978*, pp. 153–98. [G: LDCs]

O'Hagan, John W. and Kelly, Morgan. Components of Growth in Current Public Expenditure on Education and Health. *Econ. Soc. Rev.*, January 1984, *15*(2), pp. 87–93. [G: Ireland]

Palmer, John L. and Torrey, Barbara Boyle.

Health Care Financing and Pension Programs. In *Mills, G. B. and Palmer, J. L., eds.*, 1984, pp. 121–56. [G: U.S.]

Paul, Chris. Physician Licensure Legislation and the Quality of Medical Care. *Atlantic Econ. J.*, December 1984, *12*(4), pp. 18–30. [G: U.S.]

Pauly, Mark V. Is Cream-skimming a Problem for the Competitive Medical Market? *J. Health Econ.*, April 1984, *3*(1), pp. 87–95.

Pebley, Anne R. Intervention Projects and the Study of Socioeconomic Determinants of Mortality. *Population Devel. Rev.*, Supplement 1984, *10*, pp. 281–305. [G: LDCs]

Pedroni, Gabriella. Drugs and Adverse Reactions: An Economic View of a Medical Problem. In *Lindgren, B., ed.*, 1984, pp. 67–95. [G: Selected Countries]

Perri, Timothy J. Health Status and Schooling Decisions of Young Men. *Econ. Educ. Rev.*, 1984, *3*(3), pp. 207–13. [G: U.S.]

Peskin, Janice. Approaches to Measuring and Valuing In-Kind Subsidies and the Distribution of Their Benefits: Comment. In *Moon, M., ed.*, 1984, pp. 171–76. [G: U.S.]

Peto, Richard. Why Cancer? In *Simon, J. L. and Kahn, H., eds.*, 1984, pp. 528–44. [G: Global]

Pinstrup-Andersen, Per and Kumar, Shubh K. Food Policy, Human Nutrition, and Fertility. In *Schutjer, W. A. and Stokes, C. S., eds.*, 1984, pp. 235–51. [G: LDCs]

Preston, Samuel H. Health Programs and Population Growth. In *Ghosh, P. K., ed., no. 6*, 1984, 1975, pp. 7–17.

Ravenholt, R. T. Addiction Mortality in the United States, 1980: Tobacco, Alcohol, and Other Substances. *Population Devel. Rev.*, December 1984, *10*(4), pp. 697–724. [G: U.S.; LDCs]

Reutlinger, Shlomo. Project Food Aid and Equitable Growth: Income–Transfer Efficiency First! *World Devel.*, September 1984, *12*(9), pp. 901–11. [G: Egypt; India; Pakistan]

Rohn, George. CMHA: Local Autonomy and Institutional Change [The Adjustment of a National Voluntary Association to Change in Its Environment: The Case of the Canadian Mental Health Association]. *Can. Public Policy*, March 1984, *10*(1), pp. 94–95. [G: Canada]

Romeo, Anthony A.; Wagner, Judith L. and Lee, Robert H. Prospective Reimbursement and the Diffusion of New Technologies in Hospitals. *J. Health Econ.*, April 1984, *3*(1), pp. 1–24. [G: U.S.]

Romero-Barceló, Carlos. Economic Challenges in Puerto Rico and the Caribbean Community. *Atlantic Econ. J.*, September 1984, *12*(3), pp. 1–3. [G: Puerto Rico]

Rosenthal, Marilynn M. and Frederick, Deborah. Physician Maldistribution in Cross-Cultural Perspectives: United States, United Kingdom, and Sweden. *Inquiry*, Spring 1984, *21*(1), pp. 60–74. [G: Sweden; U.K.; U.S.]

Rossiter, Louis F. and Wilensky, Gail R. Identifi-

cation of Physician-Induced Demand. *J. Human Res.*, Spring 1984, *19*(2), pp. 231–44.
[G: U.S.]

Roth, Alvin E. The Evolution of the Labor Market for Medical Interns and Residents: A Case Study in Game Theory.*'J. Polit. Econ.*, December 1984, *92*(6), pp. 991–1016. [G: U.S.]

Rubin, Jeffrey. Economic Incentives and Safety Regulation: An Analytical Framework: Comments. *Amer. Econ.*, Spring 1984, *28*(1), pp. 25–26.

Rushton, Gerard. Use of Location-Allocation Models for Improving the Geographical Accessibility of Rural Services in Developing Countries. *Int. Reg. Sci. Rev.*, December 1984, *9*(3), pp. 217–40. [G: LDCs]

Russell, Louise B. Prospective Reimbursement and New Hospital Services. *J. Health Econ.*, April 1984, *3*(1), pp. 77–81. [G: U.S.]

Sai, Fred T. The Priority of Nutrition in a Nation's Development. In *Ghosh, P. K., ed., no. 6,* 1984, *1974*, pp. 61–76. [G: Latin America]

Salmon, J. Warren. Organizing Medical Care for Profit. In *McKinlay, J. B., ed.*, 1984, pp. 143–86. [G: U.S.]

Schelling, Thomas C. Strategic Relationships in Dying. In *Schelling, T. C.*, 1984, pp. 147–57.

Schofield, Frank. Health Planning in Developing Countries. In *Ghosh, P. K., ed., no. 6,* 1984, *1974*, pp. 222–37.

Schultz, T. Paul. Studying the Impact of Household Economic and Community Variables on Child Mortality. *Population Devel. Rev.*, Supplement 1984, *10*, pp. 215–35. [G: U.S.]

Schulz, Rockwell I.; Greenley, James R. and Peterson, Robert W. Differences in the Direct Costs of Public and Private Acute Inpatient Psychiatric Services. *Inquiry*, Winter 1984, *21*(4), pp. 380–93. [G: U.S.]

Sen, Amartya. Family and Food: Sex Bias in Poverty. In *Sen, A.*, 1984, pp. 346–68.
[G: India; Bangladesh]

Sen, Amartya. Ingredients of Famine Analysis: Availability and Entitlements. In *Sen, A.*, 1984, *1981*, pp. 452–84. [G: India; Bangladesh]

Shammas, Carole. The Eighteenth-Century English Diet and Economic Change. *Exploration Econ. Hist.*, July 1984, *21*(3), pp. 254–69.
[G: U.K.]

Sharpston, Michael J. Health and the Human Environment. In *Ghosh, P. K., ed., no. 6,* 1984, *1976*, pp. 77–86.

Shavell, Steven. A Model of the Optimal Use of Liability and Safety Regulation. *Rand J. Econ.*, Summer 1984, *15*(2), pp. 271–80.

Sherman, H. David. Improving the Productivity of Service Businesses. *Sloan Manage. Rev.*, Spring 1984, *25*(3), pp. 11–23.

Sider, Hal. Economic Incentives and Safety Regulation: An Analytical Framework. *Amer. Econ.*, Spring 1984, *28*(1), pp. 18–24. [G: U.S.]

Sloan, Frank A. Hospital Rate Review: A Theory and an Empirical Review. *J. Health Econ.*, April 1984, *3*(1), pp. 83–86.

Sloan, Frank A. Physicians and Hospitals: Impli-

cations of an Expanding Physician Supply. In *Ginzberg, E. and Ostow, M., eds.*, 1984, pp. 99–115. [G: U.S.]

Sloan, Frank A. State Discretion in Federal Categorical Assistance Programs: The Case of Medicaid. *Public Finance Quart.*, July 1984, *12*(3), pp. 321–46. [G: U.S.]

Sloan, Frank A. and Adamache, Killard W. The Role of Unions in Hospital Cost Inflation. *Ind. Lab. Relat. Rev.*, January 1984, *37*(2), pp. 252–62. [G: U.S.]

Smallwood, David and Blaylock, James. Scaling Household Nutrient Data. *Agr. Econ. Res.*, January 1984, *36*(1), pp. 12–22. [G: U.S.]

Smeeding, Timothy M. Approaches to Measuring and Valuing In-Kind Subsidies and the Distribution of Their Benefits. In *Moon, M., ed.*, 1984, pp. 139–71. [G: U.S.]

South, Scott J. Racial Differences in Suicide: The Effect of Economic Convergence. *Soc. Sci. Quart.*, March 1984, *65*(1), pp. 172–80.
[G: U.S.]

Spector, William D. and Mor, Vincent. Utilization and Charges for Terminal Cancer Patients in Rhode Island. *Inquiry*, Winter 1984, *21*(4), pp. 328–37. [G: U.S.]

Stevens, Rosemary A. Defining and Certifying the Specialists. In *Ginzberg, E. and Ostow, M., eds.*, 1984, pp. 83–98. [G: U.S.]

Sudman, Seymour and Lannom, Linda Bean. Methods for Collecting Health Behavior and Expenditure Data. In *[Ferber, R.]*, 1984, pp. 329–54. [G: U.S.]

Sullivan, Teresa A., et al. Alternative Estimates of Mexican American Mortality in Texas, 1980. *Soc. Sci. Quart.*, June 1984, *65*(2), pp. 609–17. [G: U.S.]

Swanson, August G. Implications of the Expanding Physician Supply for Medical Schools and Medical Students. In *Ginzberg, E. and Ostow, M., eds.*, 1984, pp. 49–68. [G: U.S.]

Swint, John Michael. Collective Bargaining in Not-For-Profit Hospitals: A Model amd Its Implications for the Likelihood of Strikes. *Southern Econ. J.*, July 1984, *51*(1), pp. 24–40.

Taylor, Carl E. Nutrition and Population in Health Planning. In *Ghosh, P. K., ed., no. 6,* 1984, *1977*, pp. 249–66.

Tekçe, Belgin and Shorter, Frederic C. Determinants of Child Mortality: A Study of Squatter Settlements in Jordan. *Population Devel. Rev.*, Supplement 1984, *10*, pp. 257–80.
[G: Jordan]

Thalmann, Emilio Lozoya. Social Security, Health, and Social Solidarity in Mexico. In *Aspe, P. and Sigmund, P. E., eds.*, 1984, pp. 397–437. [G: Mexico]

Thaman, R. R. Food Dependency and Malnutrition: Deterioration of Traditional Pacific Food Systems. In *Utrecht, E., ed.*, 1984, pp. 69–117. [G: Pacific Islands]

Venanzoni, Giuseppe. I consumi sanitari privati in Italia 1973–1982. (Private Health Care Consumption in Italy, 1973–1982. With English summary.) *Statistica*, July–September 1984, *44*(3), pp. 473–99. [G: Italy]

Versztovsek, Radmila. The Effect of Price Increases on the Average Food Consumption and on the Nutrition Standards of Social Groups in Hungary. *Acta Oecon.*, 1984, *32*(1–2), pp. 163–74. **[G: Hungary]**

Viscusi, W. Kip. Regulating Uncertain Health Hazards When There Is Changing Risk Information. *J. Health Econ.*, December 1984, *3*(3), pp. 259–73.

Viscusi, W. Kip. The Lulling Effect: The Impact of Child-Resistant Packaging on Aspirin and Analgesic Ingestions. *Amer. Econ. Rev.*, May 1984, *74*(2), pp. 324–27. **[G: U.S.]**

Viscusi, W. Kip and O'Connor, Charles J. Adaptive Responses to Chemical Labeling: Are Workers Bayesian Decision Makers? *Amer. Econ. Rev.*, December 1984, *74*(5), pp. 942–56. **[G: U.S.]**

Vroman, Susan and Anderson, Gerard. The Effect of Income Taxation on the Demand for Employer–Provided Health Insurance. *Appl. Econ.*, February 1984, *16*(1), pp. 33–43. **[G: U.S.]**

Wang, Yungming Paul and Grimes, Richard M. The Health Planners Dilemma and the Problem of Aggregation Bias—An Irresolvable Conflict. *Rev. Public Data Use*, March 1984, *12*(1), pp. 69–82. **[G: U.S.]**

Ward, W. Peter and Ward, Patricia C. Infant Birth Weight and Nutrition in Industrializing Montreal. *Amer. Hist. Rev.*, April 1984, *89*(2), pp. 324–45. **[G: Canada]**

Ware, Helen. Effects of Maternal Education, Women's Roles, and Child Care on Child Mortality. *Population Devel. Rev.*, Supplement 1984, *10*, pp. 191–214. **[G: LDCs]**

Warner, Kenneth E. Publicity, Price, and Puffing: A Health Economics Contribution to Disease Prevention. *J. Health Econ.*, August 1984, *3*(2), pp. 179–86. **[G: Switzerland]**

Wassermann, Ursula. Traditional Medicine and the Law. *J. World Trade Law*, March–April 1984, *18*(2), pp. 155–63.

Watson, Roy E. L. Rejoinder [The Adjustment of a National Voluntary Association to Change in Its Environment: The Case of the Canadian Mental Health Association]. *Can. Public Policy*, March 1984, *10*(1), pp. 95. **[G: Canada]**

Waugh, Frederick V. Programs for Using Agricultural Surpluses to Reduce Malnutrition and to Benefit Farmers. In *Waugh, F. V.*, 1984, *1940*, pp. 146–56. **[G: U.S.]**

West, Peter A. Private Health Insurance. In *Le Grand, J. and Robinson, R.*, eds., 1984, pp. 111–15. **[G: U.K.]**

Williams, Sankey V., et al. Methodological Limitations in Case Mix Hospital Reimbursement, with a Proposal for Change. *Inquiry*, Spring 1984, *21*(1), pp. 17–31. **[G: U.S.]**

Wolfe, Barbara L. Measuring Disability and Health. *J. Health Econ.*, August 1984, *3*(2), pp. 187–93. **[G: U.S.]**

Wolfe, Barbara L. and Behrman, Jere R. Determinants of Women's Health Status and Health-Care Utilization in a Developing Country: A Latent Variable Approach. *Rev. Econ. Statist.*, November 1984, *66*(4), pp. 696–703. **[G: Nicaragua]**

Woodward, Robert S. and Warren-Boulton, Frederick. Considering the Effects of Financial Incentives and Professional Ethics on 'Appropriate' Medical Care. *J. Health Econ.*, December 1984, *3*(3), pp. 223–37.

Youle, Robert E. and Daw, Paul C. Preferred Provider Organizations: An Antitrust Perspective. *Antitrust Bull.*, Summer 1984, *29*(2), pp. 301–401. **[G: U.S.]**

Zweifel, Peter. Drugs as an Ambulatory Care Technology: Costs and Benefits to the Insurer. In *Lindgren, B., ed.*, 1984, pp. 37–65. **[G: Switzerland]**

Zweifel, Peter. Technological Change in Health Care: Why Are Opinions So Divided? *Managerial Dec. Econ.*, September 1984, *5*(3), pp. 177–82. **[G: U.S.]**

914 Economics of Poverty

9140 Economics of Poverty

Akin, John S.; Guilkey, David K. and Popkin, Barry M. The School Lunch Program and Nutrient Intake: A Switching Regression Analysis: Reply. *Amer. J. Agr. Econ.*, November 1984, *66*(4), pp. 513–14. **[G: U.S.]**

Altimir, Oscar. Poverty, Income Distribution and Child Welfare in Latin America: A Comparison of Pre- and Post-recession Data. In *Jolly, R. and Cornia, G. A., eds.*, 1984, pp. 91–112. **[G: Latin America]**

Altimir, Oscar. Poverty, Income Distribution and Child Welfare in Latin America: A Comparison of Pre- and Post-Recession Data. *World Devel.*, March 1984, *12*(3), pp. 261–82. **[G: Chile; Colombia; Costa Rica; Panama; Venezuela]**

Asimakopulos, Athanasios. Reforming Public Pensions in Canada: Issues and Options: Comments. In *Conklin, D. W.; Bennett, J. H. and Courchene, T. J., eds.*, 1984, pp. 274–82. **[G: Canada]**

Aspe, Pedro and Sigmund, Paul E. The Political Economy of Income Distribution in Mexico: Introduction. In *Aspe, P. and Sigmund, P. E., eds.*, 1984, pp. 3–13. **[G: Mexico]**

Bawden, D. Lee and Palmer, John L. Social Policy: Challenging the Welfare State. In *Palmer, J. L. and Sawhill, I. V., eds.*, 1984, pp. 177–215. **[G: U.S.]**

Bequele, Assefa and van der Hoeven, Rolf. Poverty and Inequality in Sub-Saharan Africa. In *Ghosh, P. K., ed., no. 13*, 1984, *1980*, pp. 232–44. **[G: Sub-Saharan Africa]**

Brambilla, Francesco. Povertà e ricchezza. (Poverty and Wealth. With English summary.) *Giorn. Econ.*, Nov.-Dec. 1984, *43*(11–12), pp. 801–50. **[G: Italy]**

Brown, Mark G. and Johnson, S. R. Equivalent Scales, Scale Economies, and Food Stamp Allotments: Estimates from the Nationwide Food Consumption Survey, 1977–78. *Amer. J. Agr. Econ.*, August 1984, *66*(3), pp. 286–93. **[G: U.S.]**

Chachere, Bernadette. Internally Directed Action for Black Community Development: The Next Frontier for "The Movement": Comments. *Rev. Black Polit. Econ.*, Summer–Fall 1984, *13*(1–2), pp. 47–49. [G: U.S.]

Chenery, Hollis B. Poverty and Progress— Choices for the Developing World. In *Ghosh, P. K., ed., no. 13*, 1984, *1980*, pp. 75–84.

Chenery, Hollis B. The Alleviation of Poverty. In *Trent, J. and Lamy, P., eds.*, 1984, pp. 99–111. [G: LDCs]

Chitnis, S. and Suvannathat, C. Schooling for the Children of the Urban Poor. In *Richards, P. J. and Thomson, A. M., eds.*, 1984, pp. 189–213. [G: LDCs]

Clark, Robert M. Comments [Reforming Public Pensions in Canada: Issues and Options] [Tax-Transfer Benefits for the Elderly]. In *Conklin, D. W.; Bennett, J. H. and Courchene, T. J., eds.*, 1984, pp. 266–73. [G: Canada]

Clarkson, Kenneth W. The Safety Net from the Reagan Administration's Perspective. In *Weicher, J. C., ed.*, 1984, pp. 169–88. [G: U.S.]

Colasanto, Diane; Kapteyn, Arie and van der Gaag, Jacques. Two Subjective Definitions of Poverty: Results from the Wisconsin Basic Needs Study. *J. Human Res.*, Winter 1984, *19*(1), pp. 127–38. [G: U.S.]

Colombino, Ugo. An Econometric Investigation of the Condition of Children in Italy. In *Jolly, R. and Cornia, G. A., eds.*, 1984, pp. 195–210. [G: Italy]

Cornuel, Didier. Pourquoi y a-t-il peu de pauves en H.L.M.? (Why Are There Few Poors in H.L.M. [French Public Housing]? With English summary.) *Consommation*, April–June 1984, *31*(2), pp. 65–85. [G: France]

Couriel, Alberto. Poverty and Underemployment in Latin America. *Cepal Rev.*, 1984, (24), pp. 39–62. [G: Latin America]

Cox, Robert W. The Alleviation of Poverty: Comment. In *Trent, J. and Lamy, P., eds.*, 1984, pp. 113–18. [G: LDCs]

Cutler, Peter. The Measurement of Poverty: A Review of Attempts to Quantify the Poor, with Special Reference to India. *World Devel.*, November–December 1984, *12*(11–12), pp. 1119–30. [G: India]

Danziger, Sheldon, et al. The Direct Measurement of Welfare Levels: How Much Does It Cost to Make Ends Meet? *Rev. Econ. Statist.*, August 1984, *66*(3), pp. 500–505. [G: U.S.]

Denslow, David A., Jr. and Tyler, William. Perspectives on Poverty and Income Inequality in Brazil. *World Devel.*, October 1984, *12*(10), pp. 1019–28. [G: Brazil]

Desai, Meghnad. A General Theory of Poverty? A Review Article. *Indian Econ. Rev.*, July–Dec. 1984, *19*(2), pp. 157–69. [G: India]

Ebrahim, G. J. Health Care and The Urban Poor. In *Richards, P. J. and Thomson, A. M., eds.*, 1984, pp. 93–121. [G: LDCs]

Foster, James E.; Greer, Joel and Thorbecke, Erik. A Class of Decomposable Poverty Mea-

sures. *Econometrica*, May 1984, *52*(3), pp. 761–66. [G: Kenya]

Frieburger, William. War Prosperity and Hunger: The New York Food Riots of 1917. *Labor Hist.*, Spring 1984, *25*(2), pp. 217–39. [G: U.S.]

Gilbert, Alan and Ward, Peter. Community Action by the Urban Poor: Democratic Involvement, Community Self-Help or a Means of Social Control? *World Devel.*, August 1984, *12*(8), pp. 769–82. [G: Colombia; Mexico; Venezuela]

Gilbert, Alan and Ward, Peter. Community Participation in Upgrading Irregular Settlements: The Community Response. *World Devel.*, September 1984, *12*(9), pp. 913–22. [G: Mexico; Venezuela; Colombia]

Goodman, John C. Poverty and Welfare. In *Moore, J. H., ed.*, 1984, pp. 137–52. [G: U.S.]

Gorham, William. The Social Contract Revisited: Overview. In *Bawden, D. L., ed.*, 1984, pp. 1–14. [G: U.S.]

Gotsch-Thomson, Susan. Correlates of Poverty: An Analysis of Demographic, Structural, and Individual Factors Related to Poverty in the Black-Belt Counties of Alabama. *Rev. Black Polit. Econ.*, Winter 1984–85, *13*(3), pp. 61–80. [G: U.S.]

Gottschalk, Peter and Danziger, Sheldon. Macroeconomic Conditions, Income Transfers, and the Trend in Poverty. In *Bawden, D. L., ed.*, 1984, pp. 185–215. [G: U.S.]

Graciarena, Jorge. The Basic Needs Strategy as an Option: Its Possibilities in the Latin American Context. In *Ghosh, P. K., ed., no. 13*, 1984, *1979*, pp. 245–66. [G: Latin America]

Green, Cynthia B. and Sanger, Mary Bryna. Setting Municipal Priorities: Service Delivery: Aiding the Poor. In *Brecher, C. and Horton, R. D., eds.*, 1984, pp. 519–50. [G: U.S.]

Haaland, Gunnar and Keddeman, Willem. Poverty Analysis: The Case of Rural Somalia. *Econ. Develop. Cult. Change*, July 1984, *32*(4), pp. 843–60. [G: Somalia]

Hamilton, Colleen and Whalley, John. Reforming Public Pensions in Canada: Issues and Options. In *Conklin, D. W.; Bennett, J. H. and Courchene, T. J., eds.*, 1984, pp. 62–137. [G: Canada]

Hamilton, David. The Myth Is Not the Reality: Income Maintenance and Welfare. *J. Econ. Issues*, March 1984, *18*(1), pp. 143–58. [G: U.S.]

Hannon, Joan Underhill. Poverty in the Antebellum Northeast: The View from New York State's Poor Relief Rolls. *J. Econ. Hist.*, December 1984, *44*(4), pp. 1007–32. [G: U.S.]

Hannon, Joan Underhill. The Generosity of Antebellum Poor Relief. *J. Econ. Hist.*, September 1984, *44*(3), pp. 810–21. [G: U.S.]

Hicks, Norman L. Is There a Tradeoff Between Growth and Basic Needs? In *Ghosh, P. K., ed., no. 13*, 1984, *1980*, pp. 216–25.

Hicks, Norman L. Is There a Tradeoff Between

Growth and Basic Needs? In *Seligson, M. A., ed., 1984, 1980*, pp. 338–47. [G: LDCs]

Hihn, Jairus M. and Lane, Sylvia. The School Lunch Program and Nutrient Intake: A Switching Regression Analysis: Comment. *Amer. J. Agr. Econ.*, November 1984, *66*(4), pp. 511–12. [G: U.S.]

Hoffman, Emily P. The Deserving and the Non-deserving Poor. *Eastern Econ. J.*, October-December 1984, *10*(4), pp. 432–40. [G: U.S.]

Joe, Tom. Shredding an Already Tattered Safety Net. In *Weicher, J. C., ed.*, 1984, pp. 189–202. [G: U.S.]

Joël, Marie-Ève. L'économie de l'assistance dans la période prérévolutionnaire. (The Economics of Assistance during the Prerevolutionary Period. With English summary.) *Écon. Soc.*, March 1984, *18*(3), pp. 199–231. [G: France]

Johnson, Paul. Self-Help versus State Help: Old Age Pensions and Personal Savings in Great Britain, 1906–1937. *Exploration Econ. Hist.*, October 1984, *21*(4), pp. 329–50. [G: U.K.]

Jones, Brian J. Toward a Constructive Theory for Anti-Poverty Policy. *Amer. J. Econ. Soc.*, April 1984, *43*(2), pp. 247–56.

Kanbur, S. M. Ravi. The Measurement and Decomposition of Inequality and Poverty. In *van der Ploeg, F., ed.*, 1984, pp. 403–32.

Kay, John A. The Effect of Increasing Tax Thresholds on the Poverty and Unemployment Traps. *Fisc. Stud.*, February 1984, *5*(1), pp. 32–34. [G: U.K.]

Kearns, Kevin C. Homelessness in Dublin: An Irish Urban Disorder. *Amer. J. Econ. Soc.*, April 1984, *43*(2), pp. 217–33. [G: Ireland]

Kinzer, David M. Care of the Poor Revisited. *Inquiry*, Spring 1984, *21*(1), pp. 5–16. [G: U.S.]

Korten, David C. and Carner, George. Reorienting Bureaucracies to Serve People: Two Experiences from the Philippines. *Can. J. Devel. Stud.*, 1984, *5*(1), pp. 7–24.

Loury, Glenn C. Internally Directed Action for Black Community Development: The Next Frontier for "The Movement": Rejoinder. *Rev. Black Polit. Econ.*, Summer–Fall 1984, *13*(1–2), pp. 49.

Loury, Glenn C. Internally Directed Action for Black Community Development: The Next Frontier for "The Movement." *Rev. Black Polit. Econ.*, Summer–Fall 1984, *13*(1–2), pp. 31–46. [G: U.S.]

Macedo, Roberto. Brazilian Children and the Economic Crisis: Evidence from the State of São Paulo. *World Devel.*, March 1984, *12*(3), pp. 203–21. [G: Brazil]

May, Martha. The "Good Managers": Married Working Class Women and Family Budget Studies, 1895–1915. *Labor Hist.*, Summer 1984, *25*(3), pp. 351–72. [G: U.S.]

Miller, C. Arden and Coulter, Elizabeth J. The World Economic Crisis and the Children: A United States Case Study. In *Jolly, R. and Cornia, G. A., eds.*, 1984, pp. 169–94. [G: U.S.]

Miller, C. Arden and Coulter, Elizabeth J. The World Economic Crisis and the Children: A United States Case Study. *World Devel.*, March 1984, *12*(3), pp. 339–64. [G: U.S.]

O'Keefe, Philip. Poverty, Proletarianisation and the Production of Uneven Development: A Kenyan Village. In *Munslow, B. and Finch, H., eds.*, 1984, pp. 148–63. [G: Kenya]

O'Neill, June A. Macroeconomic Conditions, Income Transfers, and the Trend in Poverty: Comments. In *Bawden, D. L., ed.*, 1984, pp. 216–19. [G: U.S.]

Papanek, Hanna. The Alleviation of Poverty: Comment. In *Trent, J. and Lamy, P., eds.*, 1984, pp. 119–29. [G: LDCs]

Parikh, Ashok and Shah, C. H. Poverty, Growth and Policy Options. *Can. J. Devel. Stud.*, 1984, *5*(2), pp. 257–72. [G: Kenya; Taiwan; Sri Lanka]

Plant, Mark W. An Empirical Analysis of Welfare Dependence. *Amer. Econ. Rev.*, September 1984, *74*(4), pp. 673–84. [G: U.S.]

Prasad, Kamta. Scope and Functioning of the Public Distribution System in India. In *Singh, A. K.; Papola, T. S. and Mathur, R. S., eds.*, 1984, pp. 207–30. [G: India]

Raj, K. N. The Causes and Consequences of World Recession. *World Devel.*, March 1984, *12*(3), pp. 177–85. [G: Global]

Rao, S. J. Some Reflections on Income Distribution and Poverty in Asia with Special Reference to India. In *Ghosh, P. K., ed., no. 18*, 1984, *1979*, pp. 239–66. [G: India; Asia]

Rao, V. G. and Chandrashekar, H. Inter-State Variations in Urban Poverty. *Margin*, April 1984, *16*(3), pp. 77–93. [G: India]

Richards, Peter J. Basic Needs and the Urban Poor: Conclusions. In *Richards, P. J. and Thomson, A. M., eds.*, 1984, pp. 243–55. [G: LDCs]

Richards, Peter J. Basic Needs and the Urban Poor: Introduction. In *Richards, P. J. and Thomson, A. M., eds.*, 1984, pp. 1–7. [G: LDCs]

Roth, G. Improving the Mobility of the Urban Poor. In *Richards, P. J. and Thomson, A. M., eds.*, 1984, pp. 215–42. [G: LDCs]

Sarvasy, Wendy and Van Allen, Judith. Fighting the Feminization of Poverty: Socialist–Feminist Analysis and Strategy. *Rev. Radical Polit. Econ.*, Winter 1984, *16*(4), pp. 89–110.

Saulter, Kenneth J. Home Energy Costs and the Housing of the Poor and the Elderly: Comment. In *Downs, A. and Bradbury, K. L., eds.*, 1984, pp. 78–84. [G: U.S.]

Sen, Amartya. Family and Food: Sex Bias in Poverty. In *Sen, A.*, 1984, pp. 346–68. [G: India; Bangladesh]

Sen, Amartya. Goods and People. In *Sen, A.*, 1984, *1983*, pp. 509–32.

Sen, Amartya. Poor, Relatively Speaking. In *Sen, A.*, 1984, pp. 325–45.

Söderberg, Johan. Interrelationships between Short-term Economic and Demographic Fluctuations in a Period of Crisis: South-eastern Sweden 1866–1872. In *Bengtsson, T.; Fridlizius, G. and Ohlsson, R., eds.*, 1984, pp. 255–76. [G: Sweden]

Spinanger, Dean. Free Enterprise Zones in Economic Development: Comment. In *Giersch, H., ed.*, 1984, pp. 236–41.   [G: LDCs]

Srinivasan, T. N. Development, Poverty, and Basic Human Needs: Some Issues. In *Ghosh, P. K., ed., no. 13*, 1984, *1977*, pp. 7–28.   [G: LDCs]

Streeten, Paul. Basic Needs: Some Unsettled Questions. *World Devel.*, September 1984, *12*(9), pp. 973–78.

Struyk, Raymond J. Home Energy Costs and the Housing of the Poor and the Elderly. In *Downs, A. and Bradbury, K. L., eds.*, 1984, pp. 35–78.   [G: U.S.]

Suh, Sang Mok. Effects of the Current World Recession on the Welfare of Children: The Case of Korea. *World Devel.*, March 1984, *12*(3), pp. 329–38.   [G: Korea]

Suh, Sang Mok. Effects of the Current World Recession on the Welfare of Children: The Case of Korea. In *Jolly, R. and Cornia, G. A., eds.*, 1984, pp. 159–68.   [G: S. Korea]

Thomson, A. M. Urban Poverty and Basic Needs: The Role of the Public Sector. In *Richards, P. J. and Thomson, A. M., eds.*, 1984, pp. 9–39.   [G: LDCs]

Venti, Steven F. The Effects of Income Maintenance on Work, Schooling, and Non-Market Activities of Youth. *Rev. Econ. Statist.*, February 1984, *66*(1), pp. 16–25.

Vidyarthi, Varun. Energy and the Poor in an Indian Village. *World Devel.*, August 1984, *12*(8), pp. 821–36.   [G: India]

Von Witzke, Harald. Poverty, Agriculture, and Economic Development: A Survey. *Europ. Rev. Agr. Econ.*, 1984, *11*(4), pp. 439–53.

Watanabe, Barbara and Mueller, Eva. A Poverty Profile for Rural Botswana. *World Devel.*, February 1984, *12*(2), pp. 115–27. [G: Botswana]

Yeh, S. Urban Low-income Housing in South-east Asia. In *Richards, P. J. and Thomson, A. M., eds.*, 1984, pp. 41–80.   [G: S. E. Asia]

915 Social Security

9150 Social Security

Aaron, Henry J. Health Care Financing and Pension Programs: Comment. In *Mills, G. B. and Palmer, J. L., eds.*, 1984, pp. 157–61.   [G: U.S.]

Arango Mejia, Alvaro. Social Security Contributions as a Fiscal Burden on Enterprises Engaged in International Activities: Colombia. *Intn'l. Fisc. Assoc., vol. 69b*, 1984, pp. 271–88.   [G: Colombia]

Ascah, Louis. Recent Pension Reports in Canada: A Survey. *Can. Public Policy*, December 1984, *10*(4), pp. 415–28.   [G: Canada]

Asher, Martin A. On the Estimation of Payroll Tax Incidence: Comment. *Southern Econ. J.*, April 1984, *50*(4), pp. 1224–30.   [G: U.S.]

Asimakopulos, Athanasios. Financing Canada's Public Pensions—Who Pays? *Can. Public Policy*, June 1984, *10*(2), pp. 156–66.   [G: Canada]

Asimakopulos, Athanasios. Reforming Public Pensions in Canada: Issues and Options: Comments. In *Conklin, D. W.; Bennett, J. H. and Courchene, T. J., eds.*, 1984, pp. 274–82.   [G: Canada]

Atkinson, Anthony B., et al. Unemployment Benefit, Duration and Incentives in Britain: How Robust Is the Evidence? *J. Public Econ.*, February/March 1984, *23*(1/2), pp. 3–26.   [G: U.K.]

Auerbach, Alan J. and Kotlikoff, Laurence J. Social Security and the Economics of the Demographic Transition. In *Aaron, H. J. and Burtless, G., eds.*, 1984, pp. 255–76.   [G: U.S.]

Balassa, Bela. The Economic Consequences of Social Policies in the Industrial Countries. *Weltwirtsch. Arch.*, 1984, *120*(2), pp. 213–27.   [G: U.S.; EEC]

Beach, Charles M. Who Will Pay for Proposed Public Pension Reforms? In *Conklin, D. W.; Bennett, J. H. and Courchene, T. J., eds.*, 1984, pp. 210–40.   [G: Canada]

Beach, Charles M.; Boadway, Robin and Gibbons, Jack O. Social Security and Aggregate Capital Accumulation Revisited: Dynamic Simultaneous Estimates in a Wealth-Generation Model. *Econ. Inquiry*, January 1984, *22*(1), pp. 68–79.   [G: U.S.]

Bell, Donald and Hill, Diane. How Social Security Payments Affect Private Pensions. *Mon. Lab. Rev.*, May 1984, *107*(5), pp. 15–20.   [G: U.S.]

Berthold, Norbert and Roppel, Ulrich. Demographic Change and Old-Age Security. In *Steinmann, G., ed.*, 1984, pp. 218–37.   [G: W. Germany]

Bischofberger, Peter. Die Sozialabgaben als Belastungsfaktor bei Unternehmen mit internationaler Tätigkeit: Schweiz. (Social Security Contributions as a Fiscal Burden on Enterprises Engaged in International Activities: Switzerland. With English summary.) In *Intn'l. Fisc. Assoc., vol. 69b*, 1984, pp. 497–526.   [G: Switzerland]

Bissell, Thomas St.G.; Skadden, Donald H. and White, Frederic E. Social Security Contributions as a Fiscal Burden on Enterprises Engaged in International Activities: United States. In *Intn'l. Fisc. Assoc., vol. 69b*, 1984, pp. 317–37.   [G: U.S.]

Boskin, Michael J. Social Security and the Economics of the Demographic Transition: Comment. In *Aaron, H. J. and Burtless, G., eds.*, 1984, pp. 276–78.   [G: U.S.]

Burbidge, John B. Who Will Pay for Proposed Public Pension Reforms? Comments. In *Conklin, D. W.; Bennett, J. H. and Courchene, T. J., eds.*, 1984, pp. 264–65.   [G: Canada]

Burkhauser, Richard V. Alternative Social-Security Responses to the Changing Roles of Women and Men. In *Campbell, C. D., ed.*, 1984, pp. 141–62.   [G: U.S.]

Burtless, Gary and Moffitt, Robert A. The Effect of Social Security Benefits on the Labor Supply of the Aged. In *Aaron, H. J. and Burtless, G., eds.*, 1984, pp. 135–71.   [G: U.S.]

Cagan, Phillip. The Consumer Price Index as an Escalator of Social-Security Benefits and Other Payments. In *Campbell, C. D., ed.*, 1984, pp. 207–32. [G: U.S.]

Campbell, Colin D. Controlling the Cost of Social Security: Introduction. In *Campbell, C. D., ed.*, 1984, pp. vii–xvii.

Clark, Robert M. Comments [Reforming Public Pensions in Canada: Issues and Options] [Tax-Transfer Benefits for the Elderly]. In *Conklin, D. W.; Bennett, J. H. and Courchene, T. J., eds.*, 1984, pp. 266–73. [G: Canada]

Conklin, David. Pensions, Today and Tomorrow: Background Studies: Introduction. In *Conklin, D. W.; Bennett, J. H. and Courchene, T. J., eds.*, 1984, pp. 3–16. [G: Canada]

Danziger, Sheldon, et al. Implications of the Relative Economic Status of the Elderly for Transfer Policy. In *Aaron, H. J. and Burtless, G., eds.*, 1984, pp. 175–93. [G: U.S.]

Dicks-Mireaux, Louis and King, Mervyn A. Pension Wealth and Household Savings: Tests of Robustness. *J. Public Econ.*, February/March 1984, *23*(1/2), pp. 115–39. [G: Canada]

Dinkel, Reiner H. Demographical Influences on Social Security Burden. In *Steinmann, G., ed.*, 1984, pp. 87–107. [G: W. Germany]

Disney, Richard. Public Expenditure Policy, 1984–85: Social Security. In *Cockle, P., ed.*, 1984, pp. 149–71. [G: U.K.]

Duggan, James E. The Labor-Force Participation of Older Workers. *Ind. Lab. Relat. Rev.*, April 1984, *37*(3), pp. 416–30. [G: U.S.]

Entwisle, Barbara and Winegarden, Calman R. Fertility and Pension Programs in LDCs: A Model of Mutual Reinforcement. *Econ. Develop. Cult. Change*, January 1984, *32*(2), pp. 331–54. [G: LDCs]

Faget Prati, Alberto A. and Papa Molina, Raúl. Social Security Contributions as a Fiscal Burden on Enterprises Engaged in International Activities: Uruguay. In *Intn'l. Fisc. Assoc., vol. 69b*, 1984, pp. 527–48. [G: Uruguay]

Fields, Gary S. and Mitchell, Olivia S. The Effects of Social Security Reforms on Retirement Ages and Retirement Incomes. *J. Public Econ.*, November 1984, *25*(1/2), pp. 143–59. [G: U.S.]

Fillenbaum, Gerda G. U.S. Social Security Administration Longitudinal Retirement History Survey: Data Set Report. *Rev. Public Data Use*, December 1984, *12*(4), pp. 325–47. [G: U.S.]

Grebler, Eduardo. Social Security Contributions as a Fiscal Burden on Enterprises Engaged in International Activities: Brazil. In *Intn'l. Fisc. Assoc., vol. 69b*, 1984, pp. 247–69. [G: Brazil]

Gruat, J. V. The Extension of Social Protection in the Gabonese Republic: Consolidating the Development Process. *Int. Lab. Rev.*, July–August 1984, *123*(4), pp. 457–71. [G: Gabon]

Halberstadt, Victor, et al. Inefficiencies in Public Transfer Policies in Western Industrialized Democracies. In *Hanusch, H., ed.*, 1984, pp. 189–208. [G: OECD]

Hamermesh, Daniel S. Life-Cycle Effects on Consumption and Retirement. *J. Lab. Econ.*, July 1984, *2*(3), pp. 353–70. [G: U.S.]

Hamermesh, Daniel S. On the Estimation of Payroll Tax Incidence: Reply. *Southern Econ. J.*, April 1984, *50*(4), pp. 1231. [G: U.S.]

Hamermesh, Daniel S. The Costs of Increased Life Expectancy. *Challenge*, September/October 1984, *27*(4), pp. 55–57. [G: U.S.]

Hamilton, Colleen and Whalley, John. Reforming Public Pensions in Canada: Issues and Options. In *Conklin, D. W.; Bennett, J. H. and Courchene, T. J., eds.*, 1984, pp. 62–137. [G: Canada]

Hanestad, Bjørn. Social Security Contributions as a Fiscal Burden on Enterprises Engaged in International Activities: Norway. In *Intn'l. Fisc. Assoc., vol. 69b*, 1984, pp. 411–25. [G: Norway]

Hauser, Richard. Probleme des Anrechnungsmodells in der Hinterbliebenensicherung—Ein Vergleich mit einer allgemeinen bedingten Hinterbliebenenrente und dem Teilhabemodell. (Problems of Means-tested Survivors' Pensions—A Comparison with Two Other Pension Reform Proposals: Conditional Survivors' Pensions and Participatory Pensions. With English summary.) *Ifo-Studien*, 1984, *30*(2), pp. 107–37. [G: Germany]

Haveman, Robert H.; Wolfe, Barbara L. and Warlick, Jennifer L. Disability Transfers, Early Retirement, and Retrenchment. In *Aaron, H. J. and Burtless, G., eds.*, 1984, pp. 65–93. [G: U.S.]

Hoagland, G. William. Is the Safety Net Still Intact? Comments. In *Bawden, D. L., ed.*, 1984, pp. 121–24. [G: U.S.]

Hurd, Michael D. and Boskin, Michael J. The Effect of Social Security on Retirement in the Early 1970s. *Quart. J. Econ.*, November 1984, *99*(4), pp. 767–90. [G: U.S.]

Ingberg, Mikael. Eläkkeet ja tulonjako. (Pensions and Redistribution. With English summary.) *Kansant. Aikak.*, 1984, *80*(2), pp. 141–62. [G: Finland]

Jafari-Samimi, Ahmad. Social Security and Private Savings: Empirical Analysis. *Public Finance*, 1984, *39*(2), pp. 226–45. [G: U.S.]

Kimura, Yoko. The Most Desirable Public Pension and Economic Welfare—The Full-funded System and the Pay-as-You-Go System. (In Japanese. With English summary.) *Econ. Stud. Quart.*, December 1984, *35*(3), pp. 245–52.

Kotlikoff, Laurence J. Reforming Social Security for the Young: A Framework for Consensus. In *Campbell, C. D., ed.*, 1984, pp. 83–109. [G: U.S.]

Kurz, Mordecai. Optimal Retirement Age. In *Campbell, C. D., ed.*, 1984, pp. 111–37. [G: U.S.]

Lampreave, D. José L. Les prélèvements sociaux, élément de la charge fiscale pesant sur les entreprises engagées dans des activités internationales: Espagne. (Social Security Contributions as a Fiscal Burden on Enterprises Engaged in International Activities: Spain.

With English summary.) In *Intn'l. Fisc. Assoc.*, *vol. 69b*, 1984, pp. 289–315. **[G: Spain]**

Lessu, Bernard. Les prélèvements sociaux, élément de la charge fiscale pesant sur les entreprises engagées dans des activités internationales: France. (Social Security Contributions as a Fiscal Burden on Enterprises Engaged in International Activities: France. With English summary.) In *Intn'l. Fisc. Assoc., vol. 69b*, 1984, pp. 345–82. **[G: France]**

Levy, Frank. Implications of the Relative Economic Status of the Elderly for Transfer Policy: Comment. In *Aaron, H. J. and Burtless, G., eds.*, 1984, pp. 193–96. **[G: U.S.]**

Levy, Mickey D. Achieving Financial Solvency in Social Security. In *Campbell, C. D., ed.*, 1984, pp. 3–58. **[G: U.S.]**

Lupo, Nancy Altman. Influencing Retirement Behavior: A Further Analysis. *J. Policy Anal. Manage.*, Spring 1984, *3*(3), pp. 439–46. **[G: U.S.]**

Macón, Jorge and Reig, Enrique J. Social Security Contributions as a Fiscal Burden on Enterprises Engaged in International Activities: General Report. In *Intn'l. Fisc. Assoc., vol. 69b*, 1984, pp. 97–134. **[G: Selected Countries]**

Maguire, Maria. Components of Growth of Income Maintenance Expenditure in Ireland 1951–1979. *Econ. Soc. Rev.*, January 1984, *15*(2), pp. 75–85. **[G: Ireland]**

Maisto, G. Social Security Contributions as a Fiscal Burden on Enterprises Engaged in International Activities: Italy. In *Intn'l. Fisc. Assoc., vol. 69b*, 1984, pp. 383–95. **[G: Italy]**

Manning, Ian G. Income Tests in the Australian Social Security System. *Australian Econ. Rev.*, 1st Quarter 1984, (65), pp. 34–46. **[G: Australia]**

Marshall, Adriana. El "salario social" en la Argentina. (With English summary.) *Desarrollo Econ.*, April–June 1984, *24*(93), pp. 41–70. **[G: Argentina]**

Merry, Robert W. The Social Security Hot Potato: Could Ronald Reagan Have Handled It Better? *Policy Rev.*, Spring 1984, (28), pp. 64–68. **[G: U.S.]**

Meyer, Jack A. Health Care Financing and Pension Programs: Comment. In *Mills, G. B. and Palmer, J. L., eds.*, 1984, pp. 162–64. **[G: U.S.]**

Moffitt, Robert A. Trends in Social Security Wealth by Cohort. In *Moon, M., ed.*, 1984, pp. 327–53. **[G: U.S.]**

Munnell, Alicia H. and Blais, Lynn E. Do We Want Large Social Security Surpluses? *New Eng. Econ. Rev.*, September–October 1984, pp. 5–21. **[G: U.S.]**

Neipp, Joachim. Stabilitätspolitische Auswirkungen einer Reduzierung der Lohnfortzahlung bei Arbeitsunfähigkeit. (Reducing Social Benefits in Case of Disability to Work: A Contribution to the Achievement of Stabilization Policy Goals? With English summary.) *Jahr. Nationalökon. Statist.*, September 1984, *199*(5), pp. 401–14. **[G: Germany]**

Nektarios, Milton. The Economic Foundations of Public Pensions. *Int. J. Soc. Econ.*, 1984, *11*(1/2), pp. 31–40.

Newhouse, Joseph P. Disability Transfers, Early Retirement, and Retrenchment: Comment. In *Aaron, H. J. and Burtless, G., eds.*, 1984, pp. 93–96. **[G: U.S.]**

Ochs, Jack and Merz, Thomas. On Testing the Hypothesis that Myopia Is a Cause of Municipal Pension Underfunding. *J. Urban Econ.*, May 1984, *15*(3), pp. 371–77. **[G: U.S.]**

Padilla, Javier Moreno. Social Security Contributions as a Fiscal Burden on Enterprises Engaged in International Activities: Mexico. In *Intn'l. Fisc. Assoc., vol. 69b*, 1984, pp. 397–410. **[G: Mexico]**

Palmer, John L. and Torrey, Barbara Boyle. Health Care Financing and Pension Programs. In *Mills, G. B. and Palmer, J. L., eds.*, 1984, pp. 121–56. **[G: U.S.]**

Perelman, S. and Pestieau, Pierre. The Effect of Social Security on Saving: The Case of Belgium with a Particular Emphasis on the Behavior of the Aged. *Empirical Econ.*, 1984, *9*(1), pp. 15–26. **[G: Belgium]**

Pesando, James E. Employee Evaluation of Pension Claims and the Impact of Indexing Initiatives. *Econ. Inquiry*, January 1984, *22*(1), pp. 1–17. **[G: U.S.; Canada]**

Pesando, James E. Valuing Pensions (Annuities) with Different Types of Inflation Protection in Total Compensation Comparisons. *Can. J. Econ.*, August 1984, *17*(3), pp. 569–87. **[G: Canada]**

Petersen, Jørn Henrik. The Political Economy of Financing Old-Age Pensions. *Z. ges. Staatswiss.*, September 1984, *140*(3), pp. 430–47.

Pilkey, Clifford G. Public Versus Private Pensions. In *Conklin, D. W.; Bennett, J. H. and Courchene, T. J., eds.*, 1984, pp. 432–38. **[G: Canada]**

Quinn, Joseph F. Trends in Social Security Wealth by Cohort: Comment. In *Moon, M., ed.*, 1984, pp. 353–58. **[G: U.S.]**

Rejda, George E. and Schmidt, James R. The Impact of Social Security and ERISA on Insured Private Pension Contributions. *J. Risk Ins.*, December 1984, *51*(4), pp. 640–51. **[G: U.S.]**

Ricardo-Campbell, Rita. Social Security Reform: A Mature System in an Aging Society. In *Moore, J. H., ed.*, 1984, pp. 91–123 **[G: U.S.]**

Rosen, Sherwin. Some Arithmetic of Social Security. In *Campbell, C. D., ed.*, 1984, pp. 233–55. **[G: U.S.]**

Rosen, Sherwin. The Effect of Social Security Benefits on the Labor Supply of the Aged: Comment. In *Aaron, H. J. and Burtless, G., eds.*, 1984, pp. 171–74. **[G: U.S.]**

Ryderberg, Ulf. Social Security Contributions as a Fiscal Burden on Enterprises Engaged in International Activities: Sweden. In *Intn'l. Fisc. Assoc., vol. 69b*, 1984, pp. 477–96. **[G: Sweden]**

Sabaíni, Juan C. Gómez and Iurcovich, Luis. Social Security Contributions as a Fiscal Burden on Enterprises Engaged in International Activities: Argentina. In *Intn'l. Fisc. Assoc., vol. 69b*, 1984, pp. 197–225. [G: Argentina]

Sayeed, Adil. A Survey of Pension Reform Recommendations. In *Conklin, D. W.; Bennett, J. H. and Courchene, T. J., eds.*, 1984, pp. 17–61. [G: Canada]

Sayeed, Adil. Public Pensions and Elderly Women. *Can. Public Policy*, December 1984, *10*(4), pp. 468–71.

Sayeed, Adil. Tax-Transfer Benefits for the Elderly. In *Conklin, D. W.; Bennett, J. H. and Courchene, T. J., eds.*, 1984, pp. 241–63.
[G: Canada]

Schieber, Sylvester J. Universal Social-Security Coverage and Alternatives: The Benefits and Costs. In *Campbell, C. D., ed.*, 1984, pp. 163–204. [G: U.S.]

Schmähl, Winfried. Überlegungen zur Veränderung des Anpassungsverfahrens für Renten in der Bundesrepublik Deutschland: Von der bruttolohn- zur nettolohnbezogenen Anpassung? (With English summary.) *Z. Wirtschaft. Sozialwissen.*, 1984, *104*(3), pp. 269–306.
[G: W. Germany]

Skurnik, L. Social Security Contributions as a Fiscal Burden on Enterprises Engaged in International Activities: Finland. In *Intn'l. Fisc. Assoc., vol. 69b*, 1984, pp. 339–43.
[G: Finland]

Slade, Frederic P. Older Men: Disability Insurance and the Incentive to Work. *Ind. Relat.*, Spring 1984, *23*(2), pp. 260–69. [G: U.S.]

Smeeding, Timothy M. Is the Safety Net Still Intact? In *Bawden, D. L., ed.*, 1984, pp. 69–120. [G: U.S.]

Spremann, Klaus. Intergenerational Contracts and Their Decomposition. *Z. Nationalökon.*, 1984, *44*(3), pp. 237–53.

Stein, Bruno. The New Social Security Legislation in the U.S. *Econ. Lavoro*, Jan.-Mar. 1984, *18*(1), pp. 129–34. [G: U.S.]

Stevens, Leo G. M. Social Security Contributions as a Fiscal Burden on Enterprises Engaged in International Activities: Netherlands. In *Intn'l. Fisc. Assoc., vol. 69b*, 1984, pp. 427–55. [G: Netherlands]

Tesfatsion, Leigh. Welfare Implications of Net Social Security Wealth. *J. Public Econ.*, June 1984, *24*(1), pp. 1–27.

Thalmann, Emilio Lozoya. Social Security, Health, and Social Solidarity in Mexico. In *Aspe, P. and Sigmund, P. E., eds.*, 1984, pp. 397–437. [G: Mexico]

Turner, John A. Financing Social Security. *Rev. Soc. Econ.*, October 1984, *42*(2), pp. 105–16.
[G: U.S.]

Turner, John A. Population Age Structure and the Size of Social Security. *Southern Econ. J.*, April 1984, *50*(4), pp. 1131–46. [G: U.S.]

Van de Water, Paul N. Social-Security Financing: An Overview of the Issues and Options. In *Campbell, C. D., ed.*, 1984, pp. 59–79.
[G: U.S.]

Warlick, Jennifer L. and Burkhauser, Richard

V. Raising the Normal Retirement Age under Social Security: A Life-Cycle Analysis. In *Moon, M., ed.*, 1984, pp. 359–79. [G: U.S.]

Willems, Christian. Les prélèvements sociaux, élément de la charge fiscale pesant sur les entreprises engagées dans des activités internationales: Belgique. (Social Security Contributions as a Fiscal Burden on Enterprises Engaged in International Activities: Belgium. With English summary.) In *Intn'l. Fisc. Assoc., vol. 69b*, 1984, pp. 227–45. [G: Belgium]

Williams, David W. Social Security Contributions as a Fiscal Burden on Enterprises Engaged in International Activities: United Kingdom. In *Intn'l. Fisc. Assoc., vol. 69b*, 1984, pp. 457–76. [G: U.K.]

Wolfe, Barbara L., et al. Income Transfers and Work Effort: The Netherlands and the United States in the 1970s. *Kyklos*, 1984, *37*(4), pp. 609–37. [G: Netherlands; U.S.]

Zschiegner, Hans. Die Sozialabgaben als Belastungsfaktor bei Unternehmen mit internationaler Tätigkeit: Deutschland. (Social Security Contributions as a Fiscal Burden on Enterprises Engaged in International Activities: Germany. With English summary.) In *Intn'l. Fisc. Assoc., vol. 69b*, 1984, pp. 179–95.
[G: W. Germany]

916 Economics of Law and Crime

9160 Economics of Law and Crime

Acharya, Shankar. The Underground Economy in the United States: Comment. *Int. Monet. Fund Staff Pap.*, December 1984, *31*(4), pp. 742–46. [G: U.S.]

de Albuquerque, Klaus. A Comparative Analysis of Violent Crime in the Caribbean. *Soc. Econ. Stud.*, September 1984, *33*(3), pp. 93–142.
[G: Selected Caribbean]

Alston, Lee J. and Schapiro, Morton Owen. Inheritance Laws across Colonies: Causes and Consequences. *J. Econ. Hist.*, June 1984, *44*(2), pp. 277–87. [G: U.S.]

Balkin, Steven and McDonald, John F. A Market Analysis for Handguns and Gun Control Issues. In *Kates, D. B., Jr., ed.*, 1984, pp. 259–93.
[G: U.S.]

Barron, John M. and Umbeck, John R. The Effects of Different Contractual Arrangements: The Case of Retail Gasoline Markets. *J. Law Econ.*, October 1984, *27*(2), pp. 313–28.
[G: U.S.]

Baxt, Robert. The Corporate Veil in Tax Law— The Legal Perception of Companies as Separate Entities. *Australian Tax Forum*, September 1984, *1*(3), pp. 239–52. [G: Australia]

Bebchuk, Lucian Arye. Litigation and Settlement under Imperfect Information. *Rand J. Econ.*, Autumn 1984, *15*(3), pp. 404–15.

Benson, Bruce L. Guns for Protection and Other Private Sector Responses to the Fear of Rising Crime. In *Kates, D. B., Jr., ed.*, 1984, pp. 329–56. [G: U.S.]

van den Berg, Kent T. Approval of Take-Out

Mergers by Minority Shareholders: From Substantive to Procedural Fairness. *Yale Law J.*, May 1984, *93*(6), pp. 1113–26.

Bhagat, Sanjai and Brickley, James A. Cumulative Voting: The Value of Minority Shareholder Voting Rights. *J. Law Econ.*, October 1984, *27*(2), pp. 339–65. **[G: U.S.]**

Bork, Robert H. A Lawyer's View of Constitutional Economics. In *McKenzie, R. B., ed. (I)*, 1984, pp. 227–34. **[G: U.S.]**

Boyle, Anthony J. The Private Law Enforcement of Directors' Duties. In *Hopt, K. J. and Teubner, G., eds.*, 1984, pp. 261–82.

Boyle, G. E. In Search of Ireland's Black Economy. *Irish Banking Rev.*, March 1984, pp. 32–42. **[G: Ireland]**

Braeutigam, Ronald R.; Owen, Bruce M. and Panzar, John. An Economic Analysis of Alternative Fee Shifting Systems. *Law Contemp. Probl.*, Winter 1984, *47*(1), pp. 173–85. **[G: U.S.]**

Braun, Rachel Eisenberg. Equal Opportunity and the Law in the United States. In *Schmid, G. and Weitzel, R., eds.*, 1984, pp. 92–106. **[G: U.S.]**

Brown, C. V., et al. Tax Evasion and Avoidance on Earned Income: Some Survey Evidence. *Fisc. Stud.*, August 1984, *5*(3), pp. 1–22. **[G: U.K.]**

Brunt, Maureen. The Economics of Law: Economic Imperialism in Negligence Law, No-Fault Insurance, Occupational Licensing and Criminology: Comment. *Australian Econ. Rev.*, 3rd Quarter 1984, (67), pp. 113–19. **[G: Australia; New Zealand]**

Burton, F. N. and Inoue, Hisashi. Expropriations of Foreign-owned Firms in Developing Countries: A Cross-National Analysis. *J. World Trade Law*, September–October 1984, *18*(5), pp. 396–414. **[G: LDCs]**

Carson, Carol S. The Underground Economy: An Introduction. *Surv. Curr. Bus.*, July 1984, *64*(7), pp. 106–18. **[G: U.S.]**

Carson, Carol S. The Underground Economy: An Introduction. *Surv. Curr. Bus.*, May 1984, *64*(5), pp. 21–37. **[G: OECD]**

Clark, Roger D. and Roche, John P. Functional Typologies of Metropolitan Areas: An Examination of Their Usefulness. *Urban Stud.*, February 1984, *21*(1), pp. 63–71. **[G: U.S.]**

Coleman, Jules L. The Foundations of Constitutional Economics. In *McKenzie, R. B., ed. (I)*, 1984, pp. 141–55.

Córdova, Efrén. Industrial Relations in Latin America: Labor Courts. In *Cérdova, E., ed.*, 1984, pp. 227–42. **[G: Latin America]**

Crowley, Joan E. Delinquency and Employment: Substitutions or Spurious Associations. In *Borus, M. E., ed.*, 1984, pp. 239–95. **[G: U.S.]**

Cullis, John G. Opportunity Cost and Choice. In *Sandford, C. and Bradbury, M., eds.*, 1984, pp. 27–41. **[G: U.K.]**

Danzon, Patricia M. The Frequency and Severity of Medical Malpractice Claims. *J. Law Econ.*, April 1984, *27*(1), pp. 115–48. **[G: U.S.]**

Deutsch, Joseph; Hakim, Simon and Weinblatt, J. Interjurisdictional Criminal Mobility: A Theoretical Perspective. *Urban Stud.*, November 1984, *21*(4), pp. 451–58.

Edwards, Linda N. and Edwards, Franklin R. A Legal and Economic Analysis of Manipulation in Futures Markets. *J. Futures Markets*, Fall 1984, *4*(3), pp. 333–66. **[G: U.S.]**

Ellerman, David P. Workers' Cooperatives: The Question of Legal Structure. In *Jackall, R. and Levin, H. M., eds.*, 1984, pp. 257–74. **[G: U.S.]**

Feige, Edgar L. Macroeconomics and the Unobserved Sector. In *Block, W. and Walker, M., eds.*, 1984, pp. 21–37. **[G: U.S.; U.K.]**

Frey, Bruno S. Schattenwirtschaft und Wirtschaftspolitik. (Shadow Economy and Economic Policy. With English summary.) *Kredit Kapital*, 1984, *17*(1), pp. 102–19. **[G: Selected OECD]**

Frey, Bruno S. and Pommerehne, Werner W. The Hidden Economy: State and Prospects for Measurement. *Rev. Income Wealth*, March 1984, *30*(1), pp. 1–23. **[G: OECD]**

Frey, Bruno S. and Weck-Hanneman, Hannelore. The Hidden Economy as an 'Unobserved' Variable. *Europ. Econ. Rev.*, October–November 1984, *26*(1–2), pp. 33–53. **[G: OECD]**

Gaudin, Jocelyne and Schiray, Michel. L'économie cachée en France: état du débat et bilan des travaux. (The Hidden Economy in France: A State of the Art Review. With English summary.) *Revue Écon.*, July 1984, *35*(4), pp. 691–731. **[G: France]**

Gilson, Ronald J. Value Creation by Business Lawyers: Legal Skills and Asset Pricing. *Yale Law J.*, December 1984, *94*(2), pp. 239–313.

Gomard, Bernhard. Board Members' Liability for Damages. In *Hopt, K. J. and Teubner, G., eds.*, 1984, pp. 208–60.

Grasmick, Harold G.; Finley, Nancy J. and Glaser, Deborah L. Labor Force Participation, Sex-Role Attitudes, and Female Crime. *Soc. Sci. Quart.*, September 1984, *65*(3), pp. 703–18. **[G: U.S.]**

Greenberg, Joseph. Avoiding Tax Avoidance: A (Repeated) Game-Theoretic Approach. *J. Econ. Theory*, February 1984, *32*(1), pp. 1–13.

Greffe, Xavier. Etat-providence et économie non officielle: liaisons possibles et impossibles. (The Relationship between Welfare State and Informal Economy. With English summary.) *Revue Écon.*, July 1984, *35*(4), pp. 667–89.

Gupta, Sanjeev. Unrecorded Trade at Black Exchange Rate: Analysis, Implications and Estimates. *Aussenwirtschaft*, May 1984, *39*(1/2), pp. 75–90. **[G: India; Pakistan; Turkey]**

Hakim, Simon; Spiegel, Uriel and Weinblatt, J. Substitution, Size Effects, and the Composition of Property Crime. *Soc. Sci. Quart.*, September 1984, *65*(3), pp. 719–34. **[G: U.S.]**

Hakim, Simon and Weinblatt, J. Towards a Theory of the Impact of Criminal Mobility Influences on Land Values. *Int. J. Soc. Econ.*, 1984, *11*(1/2), pp. 24–30.

Hannesson, Rögnvaldur. Fisheries Management and Uncertainty. *Marine Resource Econ.*, 1984, *1*(1), pp. 89–96.   **[G: Europe]**

Harries, Heinrich. Adaptation of Long-term Contracts. In *Pearce, D. W.; Siebert, H. and Walter, I.*, eds., 1984, pp. 165–68.

Harris, Robert G. and Jorde, Thomas M. Market Definition in the Merger Guidelines: Implications for Antitrust Enforcement. In *Fox, E. M. and Halverson, J. T.*, eds., 1984, pp. 225–51.   **[G: U.S.]**

von Hayek, Friedrich A. Reflections on Constitutional Economics. In *McKenzie, R. B.*, ed. (*I*), 1984, pp. 235–37.

Hersch, Philip L. and Netter, Jeffrey M. The Effects of Crime Rates on Time Served in Prison: An Empirical Analysis. *Public Finance*, 1984, *39*(3), pp. 314–20.   **[G: U.S.]**

Heyne, Paul. The Economics of Law: Economic Imperialism in Negligence Law, No-Fault Insurance, Occupational Licensing and Criminology: Comment. *Australian Econ. Rev.*, 3rd Quarter 1984, (67), pp. 109–12.
     [G: Australia; New Zealand]

Hillman, Arye L. and Katz, Eliakim. Excise Taxes, Import Restrictions, and the Allocation of Time to Illegal Income-earning Activity. *Int. Rev. Law Econ.*, December 1984, *4*(2), pp. 213–22.

Holland, Daniel M. Measuring and Combatting Income Tax Evasion. In *Hanusch, H.*, ed., 1984, pp. 329–48.   **[G: U.S.]**

Hopt, Klaus J. Self-dealing and Use of Corporate Opportunity and Information: Regulating Directors' Conflicts of Interest. In *Hopt, K. J. and Teubner, G.*, eds., 1984, pp. 285–326.

Howick, Wallace M. Purchase and Sale of Assets. In *Purden, C.*, ed., 1984, pp. 156–202.
     [G: Canada]

Hrezo, Margaret S. and Hrezo, William E. Judicial Regulation of the Environment under Posner's Economic Model of the Law. *J. Econ. Issues*, December 1984, *18*(4), pp. 1071–91.
     [G: U.S.]

Hurst, J. Willard. Public Power and Market Power. In *Sherman, M.*, ed., 1984, pp. 23–37.   **[G: U.S.]**

Hyde, Alan. Democracy in Collective Bargaining. *Yale Law J.*, April 1984, *93*(5), pp. 793–856.

Jackson, Nick. The Economic Explanation of Legal Phenomena. *Int. Rev. Law Econ.*, December 1984, *4*(2), pp. 163–83.

Jennings, William P., Jr. A Note on the Economics of Organized Crime. *Eastern Econ. J.*, July-September 1984, *10*(3), pp. 315–21.

Kellogg, Robert L. Accounting Activities, Security Prices, and Class Action Lawsuits. *J. Acc. Econ.*, December 1984, *6*(3), pp. 185–204.
     [G: U.S.]

Kellough, Howard J. Splitting Up the Business of a Private Corporation. In *Purden, C.*, ed., 1984, pp. 12–39.   **[G: Canada]**

Klevorick, Alvin K.; Rothschild, Michael and Winship, Christopher. Information Processing and Jury Decisionmaking. *J. Public Econ.*, April 1984, *23*(3), pp. 245–78.   **[G: U.S.]**

Kraakman, Reinier H. Corporate Liability Strategies and the Costs of Legal Controls. *Yale Law J.*, April 1984, *93*(5), pp. 857–98.

Kraakman, Reinier H. The Economic Functions of Corporate Liability. In *Hopt, K. J. and Teubner, G.*, eds., 1984, pp. 178–207.

Linttel, Stephen H. and McBride, Mark E. Enforcement Costs and Regulatory Reform: The Agency and Firm Response. *J. Environ. Econ. Manage.*, December 1984, *11*(4), pp. 327–46.

Long, Robert A., Jr. A Theory of Hypothetical Contract. *Yale Law J.*, December 1984, *94*(2), pp. 415–34.

Magaddino, Joseph P. and Medoff, Marshall H. An Empirical Analysis of Federal and State Firearm Control Laws. In *Kates, D. B., Jr.*, ed., 1984, pp. 225–58.   **[G: U.S.]**

Mann, H. Michael. Discussion of "Credible Commitments." *Antitrust Bull.*, Spring 1984, *29*(1), pp. 85–88.   **[G: U.S.]**

Martin, Lawrence W. and Panagariya, Arvind. Smuggling, Trade, and Price Disparity: A Crime-Theoretic Approach. *J. Int. Econ.*, November 1984, *17*(3/4), pp. 201–17.

Matthews, K. G. P. The GDP Residual Error and the Black Economy: A Note. *Appl. Econ.*, June 1984, *16*(3), pp. 443–48.   **[G: U.K.]**

McCormick, Robert E. and Tollison, Robert D. Crime on the Court. *J. Polit. Econ.*, April 1984, *92*(2), pp. 223–35.   **[G: U.S.]**

McDowall, David and Loftin, Colin. Conflict, Crime, and Budgetary Constraint: Police Strength in Detroit, 1927–1976. In *McDonald, T. J. and Ward, S. K.*, eds., 1984, pp. 101–24.   **[G: U.S.]**

McPheters, Lee R.; Mann, Robert and Schlagenhauf, Don E. Economic Response to a Crime Deterrence Program: Mandatory Sentencing for Robbery with a Firearm. *Econ. Inquiry*, October 1984, *22*(4), pp. 550–70.   **[G: U.S.]**

Mead, Arthur C. and Barnett, Harold C. Regional Crime Patterns: A Question of Stability? *Growth Change*, July 1984, *15*(3), pp. 10–14.
     [G: U.S.]

Mubyarto. Social and Economic Justice. *Bull. Indonesian Econ. Stud.*, December 1984, *20*(3), pp. 36–54.   **[G: Indonesia]**

Myers, Samuel L., Jr. Do Better Wages Reduce Crime? A Research Note. *Amer. J. Econ. Soc.*, April 1984, *43*(2), pp. 191–95.   **[G: U.S.]**

Myers, Samuel L., Jr. Race and Punishment: Directions for Economic Research. *Amer. Econ. Rev.*, May 1984, *74*(2), pp. 288–92.
     [G: U.S.]

Nobel, Peter. Internationalisierung der Tatbestände und nationalstaatliches Recht. (International Facts and National Law. With English summary.) *Aussenwirtschaft*, May 1984, *39*(1/2), pp. 91–118.   **[G: Global]**

Partee, J. Charles. Statement to the Commerce, Consumer, and Monetary Affairs Subcommittee of the U.S. House Committee on Government Operations, May 3, 1984. *Fed. Res. Bull.*, May 1984, *70*(5), pp. 423–26.   **[G: U.S.]**

Pattison, Joseph E. Extraterritorial Enforcement

of the Export Administration Act. In *Czinkota, M. R., ed.*, 1984, pp. 87–102.   [G: U.S.; Selected countries]

Phillips, Llad and Votey, Harold L., Jr. Black Women, Economic Disadvantage, and Incentives to Crime. *Amer. Econ. Rev.*, May 1984, 74(2), pp. 293–97.   [G: U.S.]

Picciotto, Sol. Political Economy and International Law. In *Strange, S., ed.*, 1984, pp. 164–82.   [G: Global]

Piliavin, Irving and Gartner, Rosemary. The Impacts of Supported Work on Ex-offenders. In *Hollister, R. G., Jr.; Kemper, P. and Maynard, R. A., eds.*, 1984, pp. 172–204.   [G: U.S.]

Polinsky, A. Mitchell and Shavell, Steven. The Optimal Use of Fines and Imprisonment. *J. Public Econ.*, June 1984, 24(1), pp. 89–99.

Posner, Richard A. Wealth Maximization and Judicial Decision-making. *Int. Rev. Law Econ.*, December 1984, 4(2), pp. 131–35. [G: U.S.]

Pryor, J. H. Commenda: The Operation of the Contract in Long Distance Commerce at Marseilles during the Thirteenth Century. *J. Europ. Econ. Hist.*, Fall 1984, 13(2), pp. 397–440.   [G: France]

Reid, Robert J. Tax Implications of a Change in Control. In *Purden, C., ed.*, 1984, pp. 84–113.   [G: Canada]

Reuter, Peter. The Economic Significance of Illegal Markets in the United States: Some Observations. *Econ. Lavoro*, Jan.-Mar. 1984, 18(1), pp. 135–42.   [G: U.S.]

Rogerson, William P. Efficient Reliance and Damage Measures for Breach of Contract. *Rand J. Econ.*, Spring 1984, 15(1), pp. 39–53.

Ryser, Walter. Exterritorialité et Droit Fiscal. (Extra-Territoriality and Fiscal Law. With English summary.) *Aussenwirtschaft*, May 1984, 39(1/2), pp. 119–36.   [G: OECD]

Samuels, Warren J. and Mercuro, Nicholas. Posnerian Law and Economics on the Bench. *Int. Rev. Law Econ.*, December 1984, 4(2), pp. 107–30.   [G: U.S.]

Schelling, Thomas C. Economics and Criminal Enterprise. In *Schelling, T. C.*, 1984, pp. 158–78.

Schelling, Thomas C. Thinking about Nuclear Terrorism. In *Schelling, T. C.*, 1984, pp. 309–27.

Schelling, Thomas C. What Is the Business of Organized Crime? In *Schelling, T. C.*, 1984, pp. 179–94.

Segelhorst, E. and Brady, M. A Theoretical Analysis of the Effect of Fear on the Location Decisions of Urban–Suburban Residents. *J. Urban Econ.*, March 1984, 15(2), pp. 157–71.   [G: U.S.]

Seidman, Louis Michael. Soldiers, Martyrs, and Criminals: Utilitarian Theory and the Problem of Crime Control. *Yale Law J.*, December 1984, 94(2), pp. 315–49.

Seldon, Arthur. Taxation in the United Kingdom: Reply. In *Block, W. and Walker, M., eds.*, 1984, pp. 217–21.   [G: U.K.]

Seldon, Arthur. Taxation in the United Kingdom. In *Block, W. and Walker, M., eds.*, 1984, pp. 157–213.   [G: U.K.; OECD]

Shafer, Joel. Divestiture and the Courts. In *Purden, C., ed.*, 1984, pp. 47–83.   [G: Canada; U.K.]

Shavell, Steven. A Model of the Optimal Use of Liability and Safety Regulation. *Rand J. Econ.*, Summer 1984, 15(2), pp. 271–80.

Shelley, Louise I. Urbanization and Crime: The Soviet Experience. In *Morton, H. W. and Stuart, R. C., eds.*, 1984, pp. 113–26.   [G: U.S.S.R.]

Shepard, Lawrence. Personal Failures and the Bankruptcy Reform Act of 1978. *J. Law Econ.*, October 1984, 27(2), pp. 419–37.

Smith, Dennis C. Setting Municipal Priorities: Service Delivery: Police. In *Brecher, C. and Horton, R. D., eds.*, 1984, pp. 380–414.   [G: U.S.]

Sommers, Paul M. The Effect of Gun Control Laws on Suicide Rates. *Atlantic Econ. J.*, March 1984, 12(1), pp. 67–69.

Stanbury, W. T. How Wide the Ocean? The Regulated Conduct Exemption in Canada. *Antitrust Bull.*, Fall 1984, 29(3), pp. 577–604.   [G: Canada]

Streit, Manfred E. The Shadow Economy: A Challenge to the Welfare State? In *Eucken, W. and Böhm, F., eds.*, 1984, pp. 109–19.

Sullivan, Lawrence A. The New Merger Guidelines: An Afterword. In *Fox, E. M. and Halverson, J. T., eds.*, 1984, pp. 319–35. [G: U.S.]

Summers, Robert S. The Foundations of Constitutional Economics: Comment. In *McKenzie, R. B., ed. (I)*, 1984, pp. 157–60.

Swan, Peter L. The Economics of Law: Economic Imperialism in Negligence Law, No-Fault Insurance, Occupational Licensing and Criminology? *Australian Econ. Rev.*, 3rd Quarter 1984, (67), pp. 92–108.   [G: Australia; New Zealand]

Sykes, Alan O. The Economics of Vicarious Liability. *Yale Law J.*, June 1984, 93(7), pp. 1231–280.

Tanzi, Vito. The Underground Economy in the United States: Comment. *Int. Monet. Fund Staff Pap.*, December 1984, 31(4), pp. 747–50.   [G: U.S.]

Templeman, Joseph. The Effect of Gun Control Laws on Suicide Rates: A Comment. *Atlantic Econ. J.*, December 1984, 12(4), pp. 71.

Trebilcock, Michael. Restrictive Covenants in the Sale of a Business: An Economic Perspective. *Int. Rev. Law Econ.*, December 1984, 4(2), pp. 137–61.   [G: U.K.; U.S.; Canada]

Ulen, Thomas S. The Efficiency of Specific Performance: Toward a Unified Theory of Contract Remedies. *Mich. Law Rev.*, November 1984, 83(2), pp. 341–403.   [G: U.S.]

Vanagunas, Stanley. Crime and Unemployment: Another Look. *J. Behav. Econ.*, Summer 1984, 13(1), pp. 101–12.   [G: U.S.]

Vieira, Edwin, Jr. The Constitutional Chaos of Industrial Policy. *Cato J.*, Fall 1984, 4(2), pp. 549–86.   [G: U.S.]

Weck, Hannelore and Frey, Bruno S. Tax Financing and the Shadow Economy. In *Hanusch, H., ed.,* 1984, pp. 313–27. **[G: OECD]**

Wedderburn, K. W. [Lord]. The Legal Development of Corporate Responsibility: For Who Will Corporate Managers Be Trustees? In *Hopt, K. J. and Teubner, G., eds.,* 1984, pp. 3–54. **[G: U.K.]**

Williamson, Oliver E. Credible Commitments: Further Remarks. *Amer. Econ. Rev.,* June 1984, *74*(3), pp. 488–90.

Williamson, Oliver E. Pretrial Uses of Economists: On the Use of "Incentive Logic" to Screen Predation. *Antitrust Bull.,* Fall 1984, *29*(3), pp. 475–500. **[G: U.S.]**

Withers, Glenn. Crime, Punishment and Deterrence in Australia: An Empirical Investigation. *Econ. Rec.,* June 1984, *60*(169), pp. 176–85. **[G: Australia]**

Wolfram, Charles W. The Second Set of Players: Lawyers, Fee Shifting, and the Limits of Professional Discipline. *Law Contemp. Probl.,* Winter 1984, *47*(1), pp. 293–320. **[G: U.S.]**

Zemans, Frances Kahn. Fee Shifting and the Implementation of Public Policy. *Law Contemp. Probl.,* Winter 1984, *47*(1), pp. 187–210. **[G: U.S.]**

917 Economics of Minorities; Economics of Discrimination

9170 Economics of Minorities; Economics of Discrimination

Abowd, John M. and Killingsworth, Mark R. Do Minority/White Unemployment Differences Really Exist? *J. Bus. Econ. Statist.,* January 1984, *2*(1), pp. 64–72. **[G: U.S.]**

Ahmad, Zubeida. Rural Women and Their Work: Dependence and Alternatives for Change. *Int. Lab. Rev.,* January-February 1984, *123*(1), pp. 71–86. **[G: LDCs]**

Akande, Jadesola O. Participation of Women in Rural Development (Nigeria). In *Intn'l. Lab. Office,* 1984, pp. 129–35. **[G: Nigeria]**

Akerlof, George A. The Economics of Caste and of the Rat Race and Other Woeful Tales. In *Akerlof, G. A.,* 1984, *1976,* pp. 23–44.

Aldrich, Howard; Jones, Trevor P. and McEvoy, David. Ethnic Advantage and Minority Business Development. In *Ward, R. and Jenkins, R., eds.,* 1984, pp. 189–210. **[G: U.K.]**

Alexis, Marcus. Politics and Economics. *Rev. Black Polit. Econ.,* Summer–Fall 1984, *13*(1–2), pp. 9–24. **[G: U.S.]**

Alexis, Marcus. Politics and Economics: Rejoinder. *Rev. Black Polit. Econ.,* Summer–Fall 1984, *13*(1–2), pp. 27–29. **[G: U.S.]**

Alexis, Marcus and Medoff, Marshall H. Becker's Utility Approach to Discrimination: A Review of the Issues. *Rev. Black Polit. Econ.,* Spring 1984, *12*(4), pp. 41–58.

Allaghi, Farida. Rural Women in a Resettlement Project: The Case of the Libyan Arab Jamahiriya. In *Intn'l. Lab. Office,* 1984, pp. 137–45. **[G: Libya]**

Almaguer, Tomás. Racial Domination and Class

Conflict in Capitalist Agriculture: The Oxnard Sugar Beet Workers' Strike of 1903. *Labor Hist.,* Summer 1984, *25*(3), pp. 325–50. **[G: U.S.]**

Alpers, Edward A. State, Merchant Capital, and Gender Relations in Southern Mozambique to the End of the Nineteenth Century: Some Tentative Hypotheses. *African Econ. Hist.,* 1984, (13), pp. 23–55. **[G: Mozambique]**

Angel, Ronald. The Costs of Disability for Hispanic Males. *Soc. Sci. Quart.,* June 1984, *65*(2), pp. 426–43. **[G: U.S.]**

Angel, Ronald and Cleary, Paul D. The Effects of Social Structure and Culture on Reported Health. *Soc. Sci. Quart.,* September 1984, *65*(3), pp. 814–28. **[G: U.S.]**

Asher, Martin A. and Popkin, Joel. The Effect of Gender and Race Differentials on Public–Private Wage Comparisons: A Study of Postal Workers. *Ind. Lab. Relat. Rev.,* October 1984, *38*(1), pp. 16–25. **[G: U.S.]**

Auster, Ellen and Aldrich, Howard. Small Business Vulnerability, Ethnic Enclaves and Ethnic Enterprise. In *Ward, R. and Jenkins, R., eds.,* 1984, pp. 39–54. **[G: U.S.]**

Babb, Florence E. Women in the Marketplace: Petty Commerce in Peru. *Rev. Radical Polit. Econ.,* Spring 1984, *16*(1), pp. 45–59. **[G: Peru]**

Baglini, Norman A. Towards a Comprehensive Compensation Programme. *Int. J. Soc. Econ.,* 1984, *11*(1/2), pp. 41–48. **[G: U.S.]**

Bardhan, Kalpana. Work Patterns and Social Differentiation: Rural Women of West Bengal. In *Binswanger, H. P. and Rosenzweig, R., eds.,* 1984, pp. 184–207. **[G: India]**

Bates, Timothy. Black Economic Well-Being Since the 1950s. *Rev. Black Polit. Econ.,* Spring 1984, *12*(4), pp. 5–39. **[G: U.S.]**

Bates, Timothy. Urban Economic Transformation and Minority Business Opportunities. *Rev. Black Polit. Econ.,* Winter 1984–85, *13*(3), pp. 21–36. **[G: U.S.]**

Bawden, D. Lee and Palmer, John L. Social Policy: Challenging the Welfare State. In *Palmer, J. L. and Sawhill, I. V., eds.,* 1984, pp. 177–215. **[G: U.S.]**

Bearse, Peter J. An Econometric Analysis of Black Entrepreneurship. *Rev. Black Polit. Econ.,* Spring 1984, *12*(4), pp. 111–34. **[G: U.S.]**

Behrman, Jere R. and Wolfe, Barbara L. Labor Force Participation and Earnings Determinants for Women in the Special Conditions of Developing Countries. *J. Devel. Econ.,* May–June–August 1984, *15*(1,2,3), pp. 259–88. **[G: Nicaragua]**

Berch, Bettina. 'The Sphinx in the Household': A New Look at the History of Household Workers. *Rev. Radical Polit. Econ.,* Spring 1984, *16*(1), pp. 105–20. **[G: U.S.]**

Bergmann, Barbara R. Feminism and Economics. *Challenge,* July/August 1984, *27*(3), pp. 46–49. **[G: U.S.]**

Betson, David and van der Gaag, Jacques. Working Married Women and the Distribution of

Income. *J. Human Res.*, Fall 1984, *19*(4), pp. 532–43. [G: U.S.]

Binswanger, Hans P., et al. Common Features and Contrasts in Labor Relations in the Semiarid Tropics of India. In *Binswanger, H. P. and Rosenzweig, R., eds.*, 1984, pp. 143–68. [G: India]

Bisset, Terry. Pensions and Divorce. In *Conklin, D. W.; Bennett, J. H. and Courchene, T. J., eds.*, 1984, pp. 426–31. [G: Canada]

Björklund, Anders. A Look at the Male–Female Unemployment Differentials in the Federal Republic of Germany, Sweden, United Kingdom, and the United States of America. In *Schmid, G. and Weitzel, R., eds.*, 1984, pp. 20–43. [G: Sweden; U.K.; U.S.; W. Germany]

Black, Harold. Politics and Economics: Comments. *Rev. Black Polit. Econ.*, Summer–Fall 1984, *13*(1–2), pp. 25–27. [G: U.S.]

Blau, Francine D. Discrimination Against Women: Theory and Evidence. In *Darity, W., Jr., ed.*, 1984, pp. 53–89. [G: U.S.]

Blumrosen, Ruth Gerber. Work Sharing, STC, and Affirmative Action. In *MaCoy, R. and Morand, M. J., eds.*, 1984, pp. 139–57. [G: U.S.]

Borjas, George J. Race, Turnover, and Male Earnings. *Ind. Relat.*, Winter 1984, *23*(1), pp. 73–89. [G: U.S.]

Boucher, Michel. Les Canadiens français dans la Ligue nationale de hockey: une analyse statistique. (French-Canadians in the National Hockey League: A Statistical Note. With English summary.) *L'Actual. Econ.*, September 1984, *60*(3), pp. 308–25. [G: Canada]

Braun, Rachel Eisenberg. Equal Opportunity and the Law in the United States. In *Schmid, G. and Weitzel, R., eds.*, 1984, pp. 92–106. [G: U.S.]

Brimmer, Andrew F. Long-Term Economic Growth and Black Employment Opportunities. *Rev. Black Polit. Econ.*, Summer–Fall 1984, *13*(1–2), pp. 61–73. [G: U.S.]

Brown, Charles. Black–White Earnings Ratios since the Civil Rights Act of 1964: The Importance of Labor Market Dropouts. *Quart. J. Econ.*, February 1984, *99*(1), pp. 31–44. [G: U.S.]

Brown, Lisa Jo. Neoclassical Economics and the Sexual Division of Labor. *Eastern Econ. J.*, October-December 1984, *10*(4), pp. 367–79.

Burggraf, Shirley P. Women, Youth, and Minorities and the Case of the Missing Productivity. *Amer. Econ. Rev.*, May 1984, *74*(2), pp. 254–59. [G: U.S.]

Burkhauser, Richard V. Pension Plan Equity: Second-Round Consequences. *J. Policy Anal. Manage.*, Summer 1984, *3*(4), pp. 613–18. [G: U.S.]

Cain, Glen. Estimating the Impact of Labor Market Policies on Women: A Discussion of the Four-Country Studies on the Employment of Women. In *Schmid, G. and Weitzel, R., eds.*, 1984, pp. 249–63. [G: Sweden; U.K.; U.S.; W. Germany]

Campbell, Everett J. Discrimination: Market or Societal? *Int. J. Soc. Econ.*, 1984, *11*(1/2), pp. 14–23.

Cannon, Lynn Weber. Trends in Class Identification among Black Americans from 1952–1978. *Soc. Sci. Quart.*, March 1984, *65*(1), pp. 112–26. [G: U.S.]

Carter, Susan B. and Savoca, Elizabeth. The Effect of Public Policy on Gender Differences in the Demand for Higher Education. *Eastern Econ. J.*, October-December 1984, *10*(4), pp. 402–08. [G: U.S.]

Cater, John. Acquiring Premises: A Case Study of Asians in Bradford. In *Ward, R. and Jenkins, R., eds.*, 1984, pp. 211–28. [G: U.K.]

Cavalli, Alessandro. Giovani, politica sociale e "Welfare State." (Young People, Social Policy and Welfare State. With English summary.) *Giorn. Econ.*, Nov.-Dec. 1984, *43*(11–12), pp. 861–66.

Chachere, Bernadette. Internally Directed Action for Black Community Development: The Next Frontier for "The Movement": Comments. *Rev. Black Polit. Econ.*, Summer–Fall 1984, *13*(1–2), pp. 47–49. [G: U.S.]

Chacon, Ramón D. Labor Unrest and Industrialized Agriculture in California: The Case of the 1933 San Joaquin Valley Cotton Strike. *Soc. Sci. Quart.*, June 1984, *65*(2), pp. 336–53. [G: U.S.]

Chapman, Bruce J. Affirmative Action for Women: Economic Issues. *Australian Bull. Lab.*, December 1984, *11*(1), pp. 30–42. [G: Australia]

Chen, Gavin M. Business Formation and Investment in the Minority Community. In *Bingham, R. D. and Blair, J. P., eds.*, 1984, pp. 79–98. [G: U.S.]

Chiswick, Barry R. and Chiswick, Carmel U. Race and Public Policy: The Statistical Connection. *Challenge*, September/October 1984, *27*(4), pp. 51–55. [G: U.S.]

Cloutier, Norman R. The Effect of Structural and Demographic Change on Urban Residential Segregation. *Rev. Soc. Econ.*, April 1984, *42*(1), pp. 32–43. [G: U.S.]

Cloutier, Norman R. The Measurement and Modeling of Segregation: A Survey of Recent Empirical Research. *Reg. Sci. Persp.*, 1984, *14*(2), pp. 15–32. [G: U.S.]

Conrad, Cecilia A. Industrial Policy: Minority Economic Interests and American Political Response: Comments. *Rev. Black Polit. Econ.*, Summer–Fall 1984, *13*(1–2), pp. 99–102.

Conway, Delores A. and Roberts, Harry V. Rejoinder to Comments on "Reverse Regression, Fairness, and Employment Discrimination." *J. Bus. Econ. Statist.*, April 1984, *2*(2), pp. 126–39. [G: U.S.]

Cooley, Richard A. Evolution of Alaska Land Policy. In *Morehouse, T. A., ed.*, 1984, pp. 13–49. [G: U.S.]

Cooper, J. H. Southern Africa and the Threat of Economic Sanctions. *S. Afr. J. Econ.*, September 1984, *52*(3), pp. 266–81. [G: Africa]

Corbett, Marie. The Impact of Pension Reforms

on Women: Employment Pension Plans. **In** *Conklin, D. W.; Bennett, J. H. and Courchene, T. J., eds.*, 1984, pp. 417–25. **[G: Canada]**

Cox, Donald. Panel Estimates of the Effects of Career Interruptions on the Earnings of Women. *Econ. Inquiry*, July 1984, *22*(3), pp. 386–403. **[G: U.S.]**

Curtis, Fred. "Cheap" African Labor-Power and South African Capitalism: 1948–1978. **In** *Zarembka, P., ed.*, 1984, pp. 185–235. **[G: S. Africa]**

Dalsimer, Marlyn and Nisonoff, Laurie. The New Economic Readjustment Policies: Implications for Chinese Urban Working Women. *Rev. Radical Polit. Econ.*, Spring 1984, *16*(1), pp. 17–43. **[G: China]**

Danziger, Sheldon. Public Policy and the Condition of Black Family Life: Comments. *Rev. Black Polit. Econ.*, Summer–Fall 1984, *13*(1–2), pp. 188–93. **[G: U.S.]**

Darity, William A., Jr. and Myers, Samuel L., Jr. Public Policy and the Condition of Black Family Life. *Rev. Black Polit. Econ.*, Summer–Fall 1984, *13*(1–2), pp. 165–87. **[G: U.S.]**

Datcher, Linda P. The Effect of Racial Differences in Background on Schooling: A Survey. **In** *Darity, W., Jr., ed.*, 1984, pp. 119–32. **[G: U.S.]**

Date-Bah, Eugenia. Rural Women, Their Activities and Technology in Ghana: An Overview. **In** *Intn'l. Lab. Office*, 1984, pp. 89–98. **[G: Ghana]**

Davila, Alberto E. Racial Earnings Differentials in Texas. *Fed. Res. Bank Dallas Econ. Rev.*, November 1984, pp. 13–23. **[G: U.S.]**

Daymont, Thomas N. and Andrisani, Paul J. Job Preferences, College Major, and the Gender Gap in Earnings. *J. Human Res.*, Summer 1984, *19*(3), pp. 408–28. **[G: U.S.]**

DeBoer, Larry and Seeborg, Michael C. The Female–Male Unemployment Differential: Effects of Changes in Industry Employment. *Mon. Lab. Rev.*, November 1984, *107*(11), pp. 8–15. **[G: U.S.]**

Dhamija, Jasleen. Income-Generating Activities for Rural Women in Africa: Some Successes and Failures. **In** *Intn'l. Lab. Office*, 1984, pp. 75–78. **[G: Africa]**

Dolton, Peter J. Testing for Sex Discrimination in Maximum Likelihood Models. *Appl. Econ.*, April 1984, *16*(2), pp. 225–35. **[G: U.K.]**

Dometrius, Nelson C. Minorities and Women among State Agency Leaders. *Soc. Sci. Quart.*, March 1984, *65*(1), pp. 127–37. **[G: U.S.]**

Fagnani, Jeanne. Marital Status and Occupational Structures in the Ile-de-France Region. *Urban Stud.*, May 1984, *21*(2), pp. 139–48. **[G: France]**

Fairbanks, Robert B. and Miller, Zane L. The Martial Metropolis: Housing, Planning, and Race in Cincinnati, 1940–55. **In** *Lotchin, R. W., ed.*, 1984, pp. 191–222. **[G: U.S.]**

Fareed, A. E. and Riggs, G. D. The Human Wealth of American Men. *Amer. Econ.*, Spring 1984, *28*(1), pp. 27–33. **[G: U.S.]**

Farley, John E. P* Segregation Indices: What Can They Tell Us about Housing Segregation in 1980? *Urban Stud.*, August 1984, *21*(3), pp. 331–36. **[G: U.S.]**

Felmlee, Diane H. A Dynamic Analysis of Women's Employment Exits. *Demography*, May 1984, *21*(2), pp. 171–83. **[G: U.S.]**

Ferber, Marianne A. Suggestions for Improving the Classroom Climate for Women in the Introductory Economics Course: A Review Article. *J. Econ. Educ.*, Spring 1984, *15*(2), pp. 160–68. **[G: U.S.]**

Ferber, Marianne A. and Green, Carole A. What Kind of Fairness Is Fair? A Comment [Reverse Regression, Fairness, and Employment Discrimination]. *J. Bus. Econ. Statist.*, April 1984, *2*(2), pp. 111–13. **[G: U.S.]**

Ferber, Marianne A. and Spaeth, Joe L. Work Characteristics and the Male–Female Earnings Gap. *Amer. Econ. Rev.*, May 1984, *74*(2), pp. 260–64. **[G: U.S.]**

Fischer, Nancy A. and Marcum, John P. Ethnic Integration, Socioeconomic Status, and Fertility among Mexican Americans. *Soc. Sci. Quart.*, June 1984, *65*(2), pp. 583–93. **[G: U.S.]**

Fishback, Price. Segregation in Job Hierarchies: West Virginia Coal Mining, 1906–1932. *J. Econ. Hist.*, September 1984, *44*(3), pp. 755–74. **[G: U.S.]**

Folbre, Nancy R. The Pauperization of Motherhood: Patriarchy and Public Policy in the United States. *Rev. Radical Polit. Econ.*, Winter 1984, *16*(4), pp. 72–88. **[G: U.S.]**

Ford, Bill. Technology, Women and Employment: The Australian Experience. **In** *Warner, M., ed.*, 1984, pp. 339–48. **[G: Australia]**

Fossett, Mark A. City Differences in Racial Occupational Differentiation: A Note on the Use of Odds Ratios. *Demography*, November 1984, *21*(4), pp. 655–66. **[G: U.S.]**

Freund, Deborah Anne. Equality of Opportunity and the Demand for Medical Care by Race. *Quart. Rev. Econ. Bus.*, Spring 1984, *24*(1), pp. 42–55. **[G: U.S.]**

Gardner, Mona J. Minority Owned Banks: A Managerial and Performance Analysis. *J. Bank Res.*, Spring 1984, *15*(1), pp. 26–34. **[G: U.S.]**

Gastwirth, Joseph L. Statistical Methods for Analyzing Claims of Employment Discrimination. *Ind. Lab. Relat. Rev.*, October 1984, *38*(1), pp. 75–86. **[G: U.S.]**

Gauthier, Anne. Les femmes et l'impôt sur le revenu. (Women and Income Tax. With English summary.) *L'Actual. Econ.*, March 1984, *60*(1), pp. 122–31. **[G: Canada]**

Gibbins, Roger and Ponting, J. Rick. The Paradoxical Nature of the Penner Report. *Can. Public Policy*, June 1984, *10*(2), pp. 221–24. **[G: Canada]**

Glazer, Nona Y. Servants to Capital: Unpaid Domestic Labor and Paid Work. *Rev. Radical Polit. Econ.*, Spring 1984, *16*(1), pp. 61–87. **[G: U.S.]**

Glucklich, Pauline. The Effects of Statutory Employment Policies on Women in the United

Kingdom Labour Market. In *Schmid, G. and Weitzel, R., eds.*, 1984, pp. 107–31.
[G: U.K.]

Goldberger, Arthur S. Redirecting Reverse Regression [Reverse Regression, Fairness, and Employment Discrimination]. *J. Bus. Econ. Statist.*, April 1984, 2(2), pp. 114–16.
[G: U.S.]

Goldberger, Arthur S. Reverse Regression and Salary Discrimination. *J. Human Res.*, Summer 1984, 19(3), pp. 293–318. [G: U.S.]

Goldin, Claudia. The Historical Evolution of Female Earnings Functions and Occupations. *Exploration Econ. Hist.*, January 1984, 21(1), pp. 1–27. [G: U.S.]

Gordon, Marc. The Black–White Income Differential over Time: Past Trends and Future Prospects. *Amer. Econ.*, Spring 1984, 28(1), pp. 57–62. [G: U.S.]

Gotsch-Thomson, Susan. Correlates of Poverty: An Analysis of Demographic, Structural, and Individual Factors Related to Poverty in the Black-Belt Counties of Alabama. *Rev. Black Polit. Econ.*, Winter 1984–85, 13(3), pp. 61–80. [G: U.S.]

Gottfried, Heidi and Fasenfest, David. Gender and Class Formation: Female Clerical Workers. *Rev. Radical Polit. Econ.*, Spring 1984, 16(1), pp. 89–103. [G: U.S.]

Gottlieb, Rhonda. The Political Economy of Sexuality. *Rev. Radical Polit. Econ.*, Spring 1984, 16(1), pp. 143–65.

Grasmick, Harold G.; Finley, Nancy J. and Glaser, Deborah L. Labor Force Participation, Sex-Role Attitudes, and Female Crime. *Soc. Sci. Quart.*, September 1984, 65(3), pp. 703–18. [G: U.S.]

Green, Carole A. and Ferber, Marianne A. Employment Discrimination: An Empirical Test of Forward versus Reverse Regression. *J. Human Res.*, Fall 1984, 19(4), pp. 557–69.
[G: U.S.]

Green, Louis C. Working in an Antagonistic Work Environment: A Note. *Econ. Forum*, Summer 1984, 15(1), pp. 139–44.

Greene, William H. Reverse Regression: The Algebra of Discrimination [Reverse Regression, Fairness, and Employment Discrimination]. *J. Bus. Econ. Statist.*, April 1984, 2(2), pp. 117–20. [G: U.S.]

Greenwood, Daphne. The Economic Significance of "Woman's Place" in Society: A New-Institutionalist View. *J. Econ. Issues*, September 1984, 18(3), pp. 663–80. [G: U.S.]

Greenwood, Daphne. The Institutional Inadequacy of the Market in Determining Comparable Worth: Implications for Value Theory. *J. Econ. Issues*, June 1984, 18(2), pp. 457–64.
[G: U.S.]

Grenier, Gilles. The Effects of Language Characteristics on the Wages of Hispanic-American Males. *J. Human Res.*, Winter 1984, 19(1), pp. 35–52. [G: U.S.]

Grenier, Gilles. Une analyse microéconomique des déterminants des transferts linguistiques des minorités hors-Québec en 1971. (A Micro-economic Analysis of the Determinants of Language Shifts by Minorities outside Quebec in 1971. With English summary.) *L'Actual. Econ.*, June 1984, 60(2), pp. 149–63.
[G: Canada]

Gustafsson, Siv. Equal Opportunity Policies in Sweden. In *Schmid, G. and Weitzel, R., eds.*, 1984, pp. 132–54. [G: Sweden]

Hamilton, Earl G. Long-Term Economic Growth and Black Employment Opportunities: Comments. *Rev. Black Polit. Econ.*, Summer–Fall 1984, 13(1–2), pp. 74–79. [G: U.S.]

Handy, John and Swinton, David H. The Determinants of the Rate of Growth of Black-Owned Businesses: A Preliminary Analysis. *Rev. Black Polit. Econ.*, Spring 1984, 12(4), pp. 85–110.
[G: U.S.]

Hane Ba, Fama, et al. The Impact of Territorial Administration Reform on the Situation of Women in Senegal. In *Intn'l. Lab. Office*, 1984, pp. 107–15. [G: Senegal]

Hansson, Göte and Lundahl, Mats. A Social Clause against Discrimination in the Labor Market. *J. Devel. Econ.*, April 1984, 14(3), pp. 395–405.

Harper, Michael C. The Consumer's Emerging Right to Boycott: *NAACP v. Claiborne Hardware* and Its Implications for American Labor Law. *Yale Law J.*, January 1984, 93(3), pp. 409–54. [G: U.S.]

Harris, Donald J. The Strategy of Macroeconomic Policy and Black Americans: Comments. *Rev. Black Polit. Econ.*, Summer–Fall 1984, 13(1–2), pp. 56–59. [G: U.S.]

Harrison, Bennett. Urban Policy and Economic Reform. *Rev. Black Polit. Econ.*, Summer–Fall 1984, 13(1–2), pp. 116–18. [G: U.S.]

Hein, Catherine. Jobs for the Girls: Export Manufacturing in Mauritius. *Int. Lab. Rev.*, March–April 1984, 123(2), pp. 251–65.
[G: Mauritius]

Henderson, Jeff and Karn, Valerie. Race, Class and the Allocation of Public Housing in Britain. *Urban Stud.*, May 1984, 21(2), pp. 115–28.
[G: U.K.]

Hill, James Richard and Spellman, William. Pay Discrimination in Baseball: Data from the Seventies. *Ind. Relat.*, Winter 1984, 23(1), pp. 103–12. [G: U.S.]

Hill, M. Anne. Female Labor Force Participation in Japan: An Aggregate Model. *J. Human Res.*, Spring 1984, 19(2), pp. 280–87. [G: Japan]

Himmelweit, Susan. The Real Dualism of Sex and Class. *Rev. Radical Polit. Econ.*, Spring 1984, 16(1), pp. 167–83.

Hofferth, Sandra L. Long-Term Economic Consequences for Women of Delayed Childbearing and Reduced Family Size. *Demography*, May 1984, 21(2), pp. 141–55. [G: U.S.]

Hoffman, Saul D. Black–White Differences in Returns to Higher Education: Evidence from the 1970s. *Econ. Educ. Rev.*, 1984, 3(1), pp. 13–21. [G: U.S.]

Hoffman, Saul D. Comment [Discrimination Against Women: Theory and Evidence] [The Effect of Racial Differences in Background on

Schooling: A Survey]. In *Darity, W., Jr., ed.*, 1984, pp. 241–55. [G: U.S.]

Hoffman, Saul D. and Link, Charles R. Selectivity Bias in Male Wage Equations: Black–White Comparisons. *Rev. Econ. Statist.*, May 1984, *66*(2), pp. 320–24. [G: U.S.]

Hollis, Meldon. Education, Economics, and Equity. *Rev. Black Polit. Econ.*, Summer–Fall 1984, *13*(1–2), pp. 145–61. [G: U.S.]

Hylton, Keith. Illusory Wage Differentials: Comment [The Narrowing of Black–White Wage Differentials Is Illusory]. *Amer. Econ. Rev.*, December 1984, *74*(5), pp. 1124–27. [G: U.S.]

Izraeli, Dafna N. The Attitudinal Effects of Gender Mix in Union Committees. *Ind. Lab. Relat. Rev.*, January 1984, *37*(2), pp. 212–21. [G: Israel]

Jackson, Christine. Policies and Implementation of Anti-discrimination Strategies. In *Schmid, G. and Weitzel, R., eds.*, 1984, pp. 191–201. [G: Sweden; U.K.; U.S.]

Jaussaud, Danielle P. Can Job Evaluation Systems Help Determine the Comparable Worth of Male and Female Occupations? *J. Econ. Issues*, June 1984, *18*(2), pp. 473–82. [G: U.S.]

Jayawardena, Kumari. The Plantation Sector in Sri Lanka: Recent Changes in the Welfare of Children and Women. *World Devel.*, March 1984, *12*(3), pp. 317–28. [G: Sri Lanka]

Jaynes, Gerald David. Urban Policy and Economic Reform. *Rev. Black Polit. Econ.*, Summer–Fall 1984, *13*(1–2), pp. 103–15. [G: U.S.]

Jeffries, John M. and Stanback, Howard. Employment and Training Policy for Black America: Beyond Placebo to Progressive Public Policy. *Rev. Black Polit. Econ.*, Summer–Fall 1984, *13*(1–2), pp. 119–37.

Jenkins, Richard. Acceptability, Suitability, and the Search for the Habituated Worker: How Ethnic Minorities and Women Lose Out. *Int. J. Soc. Econ.*, 1984, *11*(7), pp. 64–76. [G: U.K.]

Jenkins, Richard. Ethnic Minorities in Business: A Research Agenda. In *Ward, R. and Jenkins, R., eds.*, 1984, pp. 231–38.

Jenkins, Richard. Ethnicity and the Rise of Capitalism in Ulster. In *Ward, R. and Jenkins, R., eds.*, 1984, pp. 57–72. [G: U.K.]

Johnson, Ronald. The Strategy of Macroeconomic Policy and Black Americans. *Rev. Black Polit. Econ.*, Summer–Fall 1984, *13*(1–2), pp. 51–55. [G: U.S.]

Jonung, Christina. Patterns of Occupational Segregation by Sex in the Labor Market. In *Schmid, G. and Weitzel, R., eds.*, 1984, pp. 44–68. [G: Sweden]

Kausker, Karl. Encouraging Domesticity: A Closer Look. *J. Policy Anal. Manage.*, Summer 1984, *3*(4), pp. 603–07.

Kottis, Athena Petraki. Female–Male Earnings Differentials in the Founder Countries of the European Economic Community: An Econometric Investigation. *De Economist*, 1984, *132*(2), pp. 204–23. [G: Selected EEC]

Ladbury, Sarah. Choice, Chance or No Alternative? Turkish Cypriots in Business in London. In *Ward, R. and Jenkins, R., eds.*, 1984, pp. 105–24. [G: U.K.]

Landau, C. E. Recent Legislation and Case Law in the EEC on Sex Equality in Employment. *Int. Lab. Rev.*, January-February 1984, *123*(1), pp. 53–70. [G: EEC]

Latos, Charles J. Non-white Migration Patterns in Northern Metropolitan Areas, 1960–1970: The Interaction between Economic and Affinitive Factors. *Rev. Black Polit. Econ.*, Winter 1984–85, *13*(3), pp. 5–19. [G: U.S.]

Lazear, Edward P. Illusory Wage Differentials: Reply. *Amer. Econ. Rev.*, December 1984, *74*(5), pp. 1128.

Lee, Byung Sung. Analytical Comparisons of Internal, External and Differential Indices of Income Inequality between Black and White for 1964–1977. *Amer. Econ.*, Fall 1984, *28*(2), pp. 41–47. [G: U.S.]

Leonard, Jonathan S. Antidiscrimination or Reverse Discrimination: The Impact of Changing Demographics, Title VII, and Affirmative Action on Productivity. *J. Human Res.*, Spring 1984, *19*(2), pp. 145–74. [G: U.S.]

Leonard, Jonathan S. Employment and Occupational Advance under Affirmative Action. *Rev. Econ. Statist.*, August 1984, *66*(3), pp. 377–85. [G: U.S.]

Leonard, Jonathan S. The Impact of Affirmative Action on Employment. *J. Lab. Econ.*, October 1984, *2*(4), pp. 439–63. [G: U.S.]

Leuthold, Jane H. Income Splitting and Women's Labor-Force Participation. *Ind. Lab. Relat. Rev.*, October 1984, *38*(1), pp. 98–105. [G: U.S.]

Levine, Victor and Moock, Peter R. Labor Force Experience and Earnings: Women and Children. *Econ. Educ. Rev.*, 1984, *3*(3), pp. 183–93. [G: U.S.]

Lewis, Mary Agnes. The Black Matriarchy: Exercises in Culture and Ideology. *Econ. Forum*, Summer 1984, *15*(1), pp. 17–38. [G: U.S.]

Linder, Douglas O. Freedom of Association after *Roberts v. United States Jaycees*. *Mich. Law Rev.*, August 1984, *82*(8), pp. 1878–1903. [G: U.S.]

Lindley, James T.; Selby, Edward B., Jr. and Jackson, John D. Racial Discrimination in the Provision of Financial Services. *Amer. Econ. Rev.*, September 1984, *74*(4), pp. 735–41. [G: U.S.]

Lloyd, P. J. Mining Rights as a Component of Aboriginal Land Rights: An Economic Assessment. In *Lloyd, P. J., ed.*, 1984, pp. 138–56. [G: Australia]

Longhurst, Richard. Rural Development Planning and the Sexual Division of Labour: A Case Study of a Moslem Hausa Village in Northern Nigeria. In *Intn'l. Lab. Office*, 1984, pp. 117–22. [G: Nigeria]

Loury, Glenn C. Internally Directed Action for Black Community Development: The Next Frontier for "The Movement": Rejoinder. *Rev.*

Black Polit. Econ., Summer–Fall 1984, *13*(1–2), pp. 49.

Loury, Glenn C. Internally Directed Action for Black Community Development: The Next Frontier for "The Movement." *Rev. Black Polit. Econ.*, Summer–Fall 1984, *13*(1–2), pp. 31–46.   [G: U.S.]

Lundahl, Mats. Economic Effects of a Trade and Investment Boycott against South Africa. *Scand. J. Econ.*, 1984, *86*(1), pp. 68–83.
                    [G: S. Africa]

Lundahl, Mats. Employer Discrimination with and without Substitution: A Note on the Thurow Model. *Rivista Int. Sci. Econ. Com.*, June 1984, *31*(6), pp. 537–44.

MacLennan, Emma and Weitzel, Renate. Labour Market Policy in Four Countries: Are Women Adequately Represented? In *Schmid, G. and Weitzel, R., eds.*, 1984, pp. 202–48.
          [G: Sweden; U.K.; U.S.; W. Germany]

Macon, Janet. BLS' 1982 Survey of Work-Related Deaths. *Mon. Lab. Rev.*, March 1984, *107*(3), pp. 43–45.   [G: U.S.]

Malveaux, Julianne. Employment and Training Policy for Black America: Beyond Placebo to Progressive Public Policy: Comments. *Rev. Black Polit. Econ.*, Summer–Fall 1984, *13*(1–2), pp. 138–44.   [G: U.S.]

Malveaux, Julianne. Theoretical Explanations of the Persistence of Racial Unemployment Differentials. In *Darity, W., Jr., ed.*, 1984, pp. 91–118.   [G: U.S.]

Mandala, Elias. Capitalism, Kinship and Gender in the Lower Tchiri (Shire) Valley of Malawi, 1860–1960: An Alterntive Theoretical Framework. *African Econ. Hist.*, 1984, (13), pp. 137–69.

Margo, Robert A. "Teacher Salaries in Black and White": The South in 1910. *Exploration Econ. Hist.*, July 1984, *21*(3), pp. 306–26.
                    [G: U.S.]

Mars, Gerald and Ward, Robin. Ethnic Business Development in Britain: Opportunities and Resources. In *Ward, R. and Jenkins, R., eds.*, 1984, pp. 1–19.   [G: U.K.]

Marshall, Susan E. Politics and Female Status in North Africa: A Reconsideration of Development Theory. *Econ. Develop. Cult. Change*, April 1984, *32*(3), pp. 499–524.   [G: Tunisia; Egypt; Morocco; Libya; Algeria]

Mason, T. David. Individual Participation in Collective Racial Violence: A Rational Choice Synthesis. *Amer. Polit. Sci. Rev.*, December 1984, *78*(4), pp. 1040–56.

May, Martha. The "Good Managers": Married Working Class Women and Family Budget Studies, 1895–1915. *Labor Hist.*, Summer 1984, *25*(3), pp. 351–72.   [G: U.S.]

McDougall, Harold A. Land Reform and the Struggle for Black Liberation: From Reconstruction to Remote Claims. In *Geisler, C. C. and Popper, F. J., eds.*, 1984, pp. 172–87.
                    [G: U.S.]

McGahey, Richard. Industrial Policy: Minority Economic Interests and American Political Re-

sponse. *Rev. Black Polit. Econ.*, Summer–Fall 1984, *13*(1–2), pp. 81–98.   [G: U.S.]

Medoff, Marshall H. Christian Politics and the Economic Status of Women. *J. Behav. Econ.*, Summer 1984, *13*(1), pp. 23–40.   [G: U.S.]

Mellor, Earl F. Investigating the Differences in Weekly Earnings of Women and Men. *Mon. Lab. Rev.*, June 1984, *107*(6), pp. 17–28.
                    [G: U.S.]

Mernissi, Fatima. Capitalist Development and Perceptions of Women in Arab-Muslim Society: An Illustration of Peasant Women in Gharb, Morocco. In *Intn'l. Lab. Office*, 1984, pp. 123–28.   [G: Morocco]

Michelson, Stephan and Blattenberger, Gail. Reverse Regression and Employment Discrimination [Reverse Regression, Fairness, and Employment Discrimination]. *J. Bus. Econ. Statist.*, April 1984, *2*(2), pp. 121–22.
                    [G: U.S.]

Miller, C. Arden and Coulter, Elizabeth J. The World Economic Crisis and the Children: A United States Case Study. *World Devel.*, March 1984, *12*(3), pp. 339–64.   [G: U.S.]

Miller, John J. Some Observations, a Suggestion, and Some Comments on the Conway–Roberts Article [Reverse Regression, Fairness, and Employment Discrimination]. *J. Bus. Econ. Statist.*, April 1984, *2*(2), pp. 123–25.
                    [G: U.S.]

Miller, Michael V. and Valdez, Avelardo. Immigration and Perceptions of Economic Deprivation among Working-Class Mexican American Men. *Soc. Sci. Quart.*, June 1984, *65*(2), pp. 455–64.   [G: U.S.]

Mogull, Robert G. Racial Discrimination in Professional Basketball: A Retort. *Amer. Econ.*, Fall 1984, *28*(2), pp. 69–70.   [G: U.S.]

Molho, Ian and Elias, Peter. A Study of Regional Trends in the Labour Force Participation of Married Women in the UK, 1968–1977. *Appl. Econ.*, April 1984, *16*(2), pp. 163–73.
                    [G: U.K.]

Mundle, Sudipto. Recent Trends in the Condition of Children in India: A Statistical Profile. *World Devel.*, March 1984, *12*(3), pp. 297–307.
                    [G: India]

Myers, Samuel L., Jr. Labor Economics, Preferences, and the Rationality Assumption: A Comment on Blau, Dickens, and Malveaux. In *Darity, W., Jr., ed.*, 1984, pp. 257–68.
                    [G: U.S.]

Myers, Samuel L., Jr. Race and Punishment: Directions for Economic Research. *Amer. Econ. Rev.*, May 1984, *74*(2), pp. 288–92.
                    [G: U.S.]

Nene, Daphne Sbongile. A Survey of African Women Petty Traders and Self-employed in Town and Country in South Africa. In *Intn'l. Lab. Office*, 1984, pp. 147–54. [G: S. Africa]

Norton, Mary Beth. The Evolution of White Women's Experience in Early America. *Amer. Hist. Rev.*, June 1984, *89*(3), pp. 593–619.
                    [G: U.S.]

Nowikowski, Susan. Snakes and Ladders: Asian

Business in Britain. In *Ward, R. and Jenkins, R., eds.*, 1984, pp. 149–65. [G: U.K.]

O'Neill, June A. Earnings Differentials: Empirical Evidence and Causes. In *Schmid, G. and Weitzel, R., eds.*, 1984, pp. 69–91. [G: OECD]

Ortiz, Roxanne Dunbar. Land Reform and Indian Survival in the United States. In *Geisler, C. C. and Popper, F. J., eds.*, 1984, pp. 151–71. [G: U.S.]

Ortiz, Vilma and Cooney, Rosemary Santana. Sex-Role Attitudes and Labor Force Participation among Young Hispanic Females and Non-Hispanic White Females. *Soc. Sci. Quart.*, June 1984, *65*(2), pp. 392–400. [G: U.S.]

Palmer, Robin. The Rise of the Britalian Culture Entrepreneur. In *Ward, R. and Jenkins, R., eds.*, 1984, pp. 89–104. [G: U.K.]

Penley, Larry E.; Gould, Sam and de la Viña, Lynda Y. The Comparative Salary Position of Mexican American College Graduates in Business. *Soc. Sci. Quart.*, June 1984, *65*(2), pp. 444–54. [G: U.S.]

Pfarr, Heide M. and Eitel, Ludwig. Equal Opportunity Policies for Women in the Federal Republic of Germany. In *Schmid, G. and Weitzel, R., eds.*, 1984, pp. 155–90.
 [G: W. Germany]

Phillips, Llad and Votey, Harold L., Jr. Black Women, Economic Disadvantage, and Incentives to Crime. *Amer. Econ. Rev.*, May 1984, *74*(2), pp. 293–97. [G: U.S.]

Pittin, Renée. Documentation and Analysis of the Invisible Work of Invisible Women: A Nigerian Case-Study. *Int. Lab. Rev.*, July–August 1984, *123*(4), pp. 473–90. [G: Nigeria]

Pollard, Tom K. Changes over the 1970s in the Employment Patterns of Black and White Young Men. In *Borus, M. E., ed.*, 1984, pp. 57–79. [G: U.S.]

Pollins, Harold. The Development of Jewish Business in the United Kingdom. In *Ward, R. and Jenkins, R., eds.*, 1984, pp. 73–88. [G: U.K.]

Porter, Richard C. Apartheid, the Job Ladder, and the Evolutionary Hypothesis: Empirical Evidence from South African Manufacturing, 1960–1977. *Econ. Develop. Cult. Change*, October 1984, *33*(1), pp. 117–41. [G: S. Africa]

Powell, Dorian. The Role of Women in the Caribbean. *Soc. Econ. Stud.*, June 1984, *33*(2), pp. 97–122. [G: Caribbean]

Power, Marilyn. Unity and Division among Women: Feminist Theories of Gender and Class in Capitalist Society. *Econ. Forum*, Summer 1984, *15*(1), pp. 39–62. [G: U.S.]

Ram, Rati. Market Opportunities, Intrafamily Resource Allocation, and Sex-Specific Survival Rates: An Intercountry Extension. *Amer. Econ. Rev.*, December 1984, *74*(5), pp. 1080–86. [G: U.S.; OECD; LDCs]

Reese, Richard M. and Stanton, Wilbur W. Further Segmenting a Minority Bank's Customer Set. *J. Bank Res.*, Winter 1984, *14*(4), pp. 297–301. [G: U.S.]

Reeves, Frank and Ward, Robin. West Indian Business in Britain. In *Ward, R. and Jenkins, R., eds.*, 1984, pp. 125–46. [G: U.K.]

Reid, Clifford E. Are Blacks Making It in the Suburbs? A Correction. *J. Urban Econ.*, November 1984, *16*(3), pp. 357–59. [G: U.S.]

Reid, Clifford E. The Reliability of Fair Housing Audits to Detect Racial Discrimination in Rental Housing Markets. *Amer. Real Estate Urban Econ. Assoc. J.*, Spring 1984, *12*(1), pp. 86–96. [G: U.S.]

Reimers, Cordelia. The Wage Structure of Hispanic Men: Implications for Policy. *Soc. Sci. Quart.*, June 1984, *65*(2), pp. 401–16.
 [G: U.S.]

Remy, Dorothy and Sawers, Larry. Urban Industrial Decline and the Dynamics of Sexual and Racial Oppression. In *Sawers, L. and Tabb, W. K., eds.*, 1984, pp. 128–51.

Ricardo-Campbell, Rita. Social Security Reform: A Mature System in an Aging Society. In *Moore, J. H., ed.*, 1984, pp. 91–123.
 [G: U.S.]

Rich, Jonathan M. Municipal Boundaries in a Discriminatory Housing Market: An Example of Racial Leapfrogging. *Urban Stud.*, February 1984, *21*(1), pp. 31–40. [G: U.S.]

Rickman, Bill D. Faculty Salaries at a Small University: Does Sex Matter? *Quart. J. Bus. Econ.*, Spring 1984, *23*(2), pp. 47–57.
 [G: U.S.]

Ryker, Randy E.; Pol, Louis G. and Guy, Rebecca F. Racial Discrimination as a Determinant of Home Improvement Loans. *Urban Stud.*, May 1984, *21*(2), pp. 177–82.
 [G: U.S.]

Sarvasy, Wendy and Van Allen, Judith. Fighting the Feminization of Poverty: Socialist–Feminist Analysis and Strategy. *Rev. Radical Polit. Econ.*, Winter 1984, *16*(4), pp. 89–110.

Savané, Marie Angelique. The Employment of Women with Social Change and Freedom of Women: The Case of Africa. In *Amin, S., ed.*, 1984, pp. 52–66. [G: Africa]

Sayeed, Adil. Public Pensions and Elderly Women. *Can. Public Policy*, December 1984, *10*(4), pp. 468–71.

Schmid, Günther. The Political Economy of Labor Market Discrimination: A Theoretical and Comparative Analysis of Sex Discrimination. In *Schmid, G. and Weitzel, R., eds.*, 1984, pp. 264–308. [G: Sweden; U.K.; U.S.;
 W. Germany Managemt,]

Schuster, Michael and Miller, Christopher S. An Empirical Assessment of the Age Discrimination in Employment Act. *Ind. Lab. Relat. Rev.*, October 1984, *38*(1), pp. 64–74. [G: U.S.]

Semyonov, Moshe; Hoyt, Danny R. and Scott, Richard Ira. Place, Race and Differential Occupational Opportunities. *Demography*, May 1984, *21*(2), pp. 259–70. [G: U.S.]

Semyonov, Moshe; Hoyt, Danny R. and Scott, Richard Ira. The Place of Odds Ratios in the Study of Place, Race and Differential Occupational Opportunities. *Demography*, November 1984, *21*(4), pp. 667–71.

Sen, Amartya. Family and Food: Sex Bias in Poverty. In *Sen, A.*, 1984, pp. 346–68.
 [G: India; Bangladesh]

Shapiro, David. Wage Differentials among Black, Hispanic, and White Young Men. *Ind. Lab. Relat. Rev.*, July 1984, *37*(4), pp. 570–81. [G: U.S.]

Shorey, John. Employment Discrimination and the Employer Tastes Model. *Scot. J. Polit. Econ.*, June 1984, *31*(2), pp. 157–75.

Shulman, Steven. Competition and Racial Discrimination: The Employment Effects of Reagan's Labor Market Policies. *Rev. Radical Polit. Econ.*, Winter 1984, *16*(4), pp. 111–28. [G: U.S.]

Shulman, Steven. The Measurement and Interpretation of Black Wage and Occupational Gains: A Reevaluation. *Rev. Black Polit. Econ.*, Spring 1984, *12*(4), pp. 59–69. [G: U.S.]

Sieling, Mark S. Staffing Patterns Prominent in Female–Male Earnings Gap. *Mon. Lab. Rev.*, June 1984, *107*(6), pp. 29–33. [G: U.S.]

Simms, Margaret C. Education, Economics, and Equity: Comments. *Rev. Black Polit. Econ.*, Summer–Fall 1984, *13*(1–2), pp. 162–64. [G: U.S.]

Sly, David F. Modern Economic-Sector Development and Population Change. In *Ominde, S. H., ed.*, 1984, pp. 91–100. [G: Kenya]

Smith, James P. Race and Human Capital. *Amer. Econ. Rev.*, September 1984, *74*(4), pp. 685–98. [G: U.S.]

Smith, James P. and Welch, Finis. Affirmative Action and Labor Markets. *J. Lab. Econ.*, April 1984, *2*(2), pp. 269–301. [G: U.S.]

Sorensen, Elaine. Equal Pay for Comparable Worth: A Policy for Eliminating the Undervaluation of Women's Work. *J. Econ. Issues*, June 1984, *18*(2), pp. 465–72. [G: U.S.]

South, Scott J. Racial Differences in Suicide: The Effect of Economic Convergence. *Soc. Sci. Quart.*, March 1984, *65*(1), pp. 172–80. [G: U.S.]

Spitze, Glenna. The Effect of Family Migration on Wives' Employment: How Long Does It Last? *Soc. Sci. Quart.*, March 1984, *65*(1), pp. 21–36. [G: U.S.]

Squires, Gregory D. Capital Mobility versus Upward Mobility: The Racially Discriminatory Consequences of Plant Closings and Corporate Relocations. In *Sawers, L. and Tabb, W. K., eds.*, 1984, pp. 152–62.

Stevans, Lonnie K.; Register, Charles and Grimes, Paul. Civil Rights Legislation and Racial Employment Differentials. *Rev. Black Polit. Econ.*, Winter 1984–85, *13*(3), pp. 49–59. [G: U.S.]

Stevens, Richard L. Measuring Minority Business Formation and Failure. *Rev. Black Polit. Econ.*, Spring 1984, *12*(4), pp. 71–84. [G: U.S.]

Stevens, Yvette. Technologies for Rural Women's Activities: Problems and Prospects in Sierra Leone. In *Intn'l. Lab. Office*, 1984, pp. 79–88. [G: Sierra Leone]

Stewart, James B. Building a Cooperative Economy: Lessons from the Black Experience. *Rev. Soc. Econ.*, December 1984, *42*(3), pp. 360–68. [G: U.S.]

Stewart, James B. and Hyclak, Thomas. An Analysis of the Earnings Profiles of Immigrants. *Rev. Econ. Statist.*, May 1984, *66*(2), pp. 292–96. [G: U.S.]

Stolzenberg, Ross M. and Waite, Linda J. Local Labor Markets, Children and Labor Force Participation of Wives. *Demography*, May 1984, *21*(2), pp. 157–70. [G: U.S.]

Streker-Seeborg, Irmtraud; Seeborg, Michael C. and Zegeye, Abera. The Impact of Nontraditional Training on the Occupational Attainment of Women. *J. Human Res.*, Fall 1984, *19*(4), pp. 452–71. [G: U.S.]

Swords-Isherwood, N.; Zmroczek, C. and Henwood, F. Technical Change and its Effect on Employment Opportunities for Women. In *Marstrand, P., ed.*, 1984, pp. 191–213. [G: U.K.]

Tadesse, Zenebeworke. Studies on Rural Women in Africa: An Overview. In *Intn'l. Lab. Office*, 1984, pp. 65–73. [G: Africa]

Taylor, Patricia A. and Shields, Susan Walker. Mexican Americans and Employment Inequality in the Federal Civil Service. *Soc. Sci. Quart.*, June 1984, *65*(2), pp. 381–91. [G: U.S.]

Tennant, Paul. Indian Self-Government: Progress or Stalemate? *Can. Public Policy*, June 1984, *10*(2), pp. 211–15. [G: Canada]

Tienda, Marta and Neidert, Lisa J. Language, Education, and the Socioeconomic Achievement of Hispanic Origin Men. *Soc. Sci. Quart.*, June 1984, *65*(2), pp. 519–36. [G: U.S.]

Townson, Monica. Pension Reform for Women. In *Conklin, D. W.; Bennett, J. H. and Courchene, T. J., eds.*, 1984, pp. 412–16. [G: Canada]

Traoré, Aminata. Women's Access to Resources in the Ivory Coast: Women and Land in Adioukrou District. In *Intn'l. Lab. Office*, 1984, pp. 99–106. [G: Ivory Coast]

Turbin, Carole. Reconceptualizing Family, Work, and Labor Organizing: Working Women in Troy, 1860–1890. *Rev. Radical Polit. Econ.*, Spring 1984, *16*(1), pp. 1–16. [G: U.S.]

Tzannatos, P. Z. and Zabalza, Antonio. The Anatomy of the Rise of British Female Relative Wages in the 1970s: Evidence from the New Earnings Survey. *Brit. J. Ind. Relat.*, July 1984, *22*(2), pp. 177–94. [G: U.K.]

Vandell, Kerry D. and Zerbst, Robert H. Estimates of the Effect of School Desegregation Plans on Housing Values over Time. *Amer. Real Estate Urban Econ. Assoc. J.*, Summer 1984, *12*(2), pp. 109–35. [G: U.S.]

Verdugo, Naomi Turner and Verdugo, Richard R. Earnings Differentials among Mexican American, Black, and White Male Workers. *Soc. Sci. Quart.*, June 1984, *65*(2), pp. 417–25. [G: U.S.]

Warner, Harriet. EC Social Policy in Practice: Community Action on Behalf of Women and Its Impact in the Member States. *J. Common Market Stud.*, December 1984, *23*(2), pp. 141–67. [G: EEC]

Watts, Susan J. Rural Women as Food Processors and Traders: *Eko* Making in the Ilorin Area of Nigeria. *J. Devel. Areas*, October 1984, *19*(1), pp. 71–82. [G: Nigeria]

Weaver, Sally M. A Commentary on the Penner Report. *Can. Public Policy*, June 1984, *10*(2), pp. 215–21. [G: Canada]

Weiler, William C. Time Effects in Earnings of Faculty Members. *Econ. Educ. Rev.*, 1984, *3*(3), pp. 223–30. [G: U.S.]

Weiss, Janet A. and Gruber, Judith E. Deterring Discrimination with Data. *Policy Sci.*, May 1984, *17*(1), pp. 49–66. [G: U.S.]

Weller, Robert H. The Gainful Employment of Females and Fertility—With Special Reference to Rural Areas of Developing Countries. In *Schutjer, W. A. and Stokes, C. S., eds.*, 1984, pp. 151–71. [G: LDCs]

Werbner, Pnina. Business on Trust: Pakistani Entrepreneurship in the Manchester Garment Trade. In *Ward, R. and Jenkins, R., eds.*, 1984, pp. 166–88. [G: U.K.]

Wright, Sanford. Struggling against Apartheid: The Use of Economic Sanctions on South Africa. *Rev. Black Polit. Econ.*, Winter 1984–85, *13*(3), pp. 37–47. [G: S. Africa]

Zimmermann, Klaus F. The Dynamics of Women's Labor Force Participation and Fertility: A Simultaneous ARX-Model. In *Steinmann, G., ed.*, 1984, pp. 386–403. [G: W. Germany]

918 Economics of Aging

9180 Economics of Aging

Aaron, Henry J. Social Welfare in Australia. In *Caves, R. E. and Krause, L. B., eds.*, 1984, pp. 349–90. [G: Australia]

Aaron, Henry J. and Burtless, Gary. Retirement and Economic Behavior: Introduction and Summary. In *Aaron, H. J. and Burtless, G., eds.*, 1984, pp. 1–22. [G: U.S.]

Alexander, Jeffrey A.; Evashwick, Connie J. and Rundall, Thomas. Hospitals and the Provision of Care to the Aged: A Cluster Analysis. *Inquiry*, Winter 1984, *21*(4), pp. 303–14. [G: U.S.]

Allen, Steven G.; Clark, Robert L. and Sumner, Daniel A. A Comparison of Pension Benefit Increases and Inflation, 1973–79. *Mon. Lab. Rev.*, May 1984, *107*(5), pp. 42–46. [G: U.S.]

Ascah, Louis. Recent Pension Reports in Canada: A Survey. *Can. Public Policy*, December 1984, *10*(4), pp. 415–28. [G: Canada]

Asimakopulos, Athanasios. Reforming Public Pensions in Canada: Issues and Options: Comments. In *Conklin, D. W.; Bennett, J. H. and Courchene, T. J., eds.*, 1984, pp. 274–82. [G: Canada]

Baily, Martin Neil. The Retirement and Unemployment Behavior of Older Men: Comment. In *Aaron, H. J. and Burtless, G., eds.*, 1984, pp. 132–34. [G: U.S.]

Berthold, Norbert and Roppel, Ulrich. Demo-graphic Change and Old-Age Security. In *Steinmann, G., ed.*, 1984, pp. 218–37. [G: W. Germany]

Burgalassi, Silvano. La condizione anziana ad una svolta: oggetto o soggetto del proprio futuro? (Old Age at a Turning Point: Object or Subject of Its Future? With English summary.) *Giorn. Econ.*, Nov.-Dec. 1984, *43*(11–12), pp. 743–58.

Burtless, Gary and Moffitt, Robert A. The Effect of Social Security Benefits on the Labor Supply of the Aged. In *Aaron, H. J. and Burtless, G., eds.*, 1984, pp. 135–71. [G: U.S.]

Cavalieri, Ugo. Il contributo di Angelo Pagani alla gerontologia. (The Contribution of Angelo Pagani to Gerontology. With English summary.) *Giorn. Econ.*, Nov.-Dec. 1984, *43*(11–12), pp. 759–61.

Clark, Robert L.; Gohmann, Stephan F. and Sumner, Daniel A. Wages and Hours of Work of Elderly Men. *Atlantic Econ. J.*, December 1984, *12*(4), pp. 31–40. [G: U.S.]

Conklin, David. Pensions, Today and Tomorrow: Background Studies: Introduction. In *Conklin, D. W.; Bennett, J. H. and Courchene, T. J., eds.*, 1984, pp. 3–16. [G: Canada]

Coxe, Donald. A Look at the Pension Iceberg. In *Conklin, D. W.; Bennett, J. H. and Courchene, T. J., eds.*, 1984, pp. 439–44. [G: Canada]

Danziger, Sheldon, et al. Implications of the Relative Economic Status of the Elderly for Transfer Policy. In *Aaron, H. J. and Burtless, G., eds.*, 1984, pp. 175–93. [G: U.S.]

Danziger, Sheldon, et al. Income Transfers and the Economic Status of the Elderly. In *Moon, M., ed.*, 1984, pp. 239–76. [G: U.S.]

Diamond, Peter A. and Hausman, Jerry A. The Retirement and Unemployment Behavior of Older Men. In *Aaron, H. J. and Burtless, G., eds.*, 1984, pp. 97–132. [G: U.S.]

Duggan, James E. The Labor-Force Participation of Older Workers. *Ind. Lab. Relat. Rev.*, April 1984, *37*(3), pp. 416–30. [G: U.S.]

Fields, Gary S. and Mitchell, Olivia S. Economic Determinants of the Optimal Retirement Age: An Empirical Investigation. *J. Human Res.*, Spring 1984, *19*(2), pp. 245–62. [G: U.S.]

Fields, Gary S. and Mitchell, Olivia S. The Effects of Social Security Reforms on Retirement Ages and Retirement Incomes. *J. Public Econ.*, November 1984, *25*(1/2), pp. 143–59. [G: U.S.]

Fillenbaum, Gerda G. Development of Functional Status Scales for the Longitudinal Retirement History Survey. *Rev. Public Data Use*, October 1984, *12*(3), pp. 197–209. [G: U.S.]

Fillenbaum, Gerda G. U.S. Social Security Administration Longitudinal Retirement History Survey: Data Set Report. *Rev. Public Data Use*, December 1984, *12*(4), pp. 325–47. [G: U.S.]

Fillenbaum, Gerda G., et al. U.S. General Accounting Office Survey of the Well-Being of Older People in Cleveland, Ohio: Data Set Report. *Rev. Public Data Use*, December 1984, *12*(4), pp. 349–60. [G: U.S.]

Gustman, Alan L. and Steinmeier, Thomas L. Modeling the Retirement Process for Policy Evaluation and Research. *Mon. Lab. Rev.*, July 1984, *107*(7), pp. 26–33. [G: U.S.]

Gustman, Alan L. and Steinmeier, Thomas L. Partial Retirement and the Analysis of Retirement Behavior. *Ind. Lab. Relat. Rev.*, April 1984, *37*(3), pp. 403–15. [G: U.S.]

Hamermesh, Daniel S. Consumption during Retirement: The Missing Link in the Life Cycle. *Rev. Econ. Statist.*, February 1984, *66*(1), pp. 1–7. [G: U.S.]

Hamermesh, Daniel S. Life-Cycle Effects on Consumption and Retirement. *J. Lab. Econ.*, July 1984, *2*(3), pp. 353–70. [G: U.S.]

Hamermesh, Daniel S. The Costs of Increased Life Expectancy. *Challenge*, September/October 1984, *27*(4), pp. 55–57. [G: U.S.]

Hamilton, Colleen and Whalley, John. Reforming Public Pensions in Canada: Issues and Options. In *Conklin, D. W.; Bennett, J. H. and Courchene, T. J.*, eds., 1984, pp. 62–137. [G: Canada]

Heikkinen, E. Implications of Demographic Change for the Elderly Population (60 years and over). In *Lopez, A. D. and Cliquet, R. L.*, eds., 1984, pp. 161–75. [G: Europe]

Hoagland, G. William. Is the Safety Net Still Intact? Comments. In *Bawden, D. L.*, ed., 1984, pp. 121–24. [G: U.S.]

Hofferth, Sandra L. Long-Term Economic Consequences for Women of Delayed Childbearing and Reduced Family Size. *Demography*, May 1984, *21*(2), pp. 141–55. [G: U.S.]

Kurz, Mordecai. Optimal Retirement Age. In *Campbell, C. D.*, ed., 1984, pp. 111–37. [G: U.S.]

Ledolter, Johannes and Power, Mark L. A Study of ERISA's Impact on Private Retirement Plan Growth. *J. Risk Ins.*, June 1984, *51*(2), pp. 225–43. [G: U.S.]

Lee, Don. Pensions in Other Nations: The Implications for Reform in Canada. In *Conklin, D. W.; Bennett, J. H. and Courchene, T. J.*, eds., 1984, pp. 174–88. [G: Canada; U.S.; Sweden; U.K.]

Leigh, Duane E. Why Is There Mandatory Retirement? An Empirical Reexamination. *J. Human Res.*, Fall 1984, *19*(4), pp. 512–31. [G: U.S.]

Levy, Frank. Implications of the Relative Economic Status of the Elderly for Transfer Policy: Comment. In *Aaron, H. J. and Burtless, G.*, eds., 1984, pp. 193–96. [G: U.S.]

Lupo, Nancy Altman. Influencing Retirement Behavior: A Further Analysis. *J. Policy Anal. Manage.*, Spring 1984, *3*(3), pp. 439–46. [G: U.S.]

Maekawa, Kaichi. A Study on Public Policy for the Aged Workers. *Kyoto Univ. Econ. Rev.*, October 1984, *54*(2), pp. 1–12. [G: Japan]

Marchant, C. K. Registered Pension Accounts (RPAs) as an Instrument of Pension Reform. In *Conklin, D. W.; Bennett, J. H. and Courchene, T. J.*, eds., 1984, pp. 360–91. [G: Canada]

Merrill, Sally R. Home Equity and the Elderly. In *Aaron, H. J. and Burtless, G.*, eds., 1984, pp. 197–225. [G: U.S.]

Mitchell, Olivia S. and Fields, Gary S. The Economics of Retirement Behavior. *J. Lab. Econ.*, January 1984, *2*(1), pp. 84–105. [G: U.S.]

Moffitt, Robert A. Trends in Social Security Wealth by Cohort. In *Moon, M.*, ed., 1984, pp. 327–53. [G: U.S.]

Perelman, S. and Pestieau, Pierre. The Effect of Social Security on Saving: The Case of Belgium with a Particular Emphasis on the Behavior of the Aged. *Empirical Econ.*, 1984, *9*(1), pp. 15–26. [G: Belgium]

Preston, Samuel H. Children and the Elderly: Divergent Paths for America's Dependents. *Demography*, November 1984, *21*(4), pp. 435–57. [G: U.S.]

Quinn, Joseph F. Trends in Social Security Wealth by Cohort: Comment. In *Moon, M.*, ed., 1984, pp. 353–58. [G: U.S.]

Rosen, Sherwin. The Effect of Social Security Benefits on the Labor Supply of the Aged: Comment. In *Aaron, H. J. and Burtless, G.*, eds., 1984, pp. 171–74. [G: U.S.]

Rowland, D. T. Old Age and the Demographic Transition. *Population Stud.*, March 1984, *38*(1), pp. 73–87. [G: Australia]

Saulter, Kenneth J. Home Energy Costs and the Housing of the Poor and the Elderly: Comment. In *Downs, A. and Bradbury, K. L.*, eds., 1984, pp. 78–84. [G: U.S.]

Sayeed, Adil. A Survey of Pension Reform Recommendations. In *Conklin, D. W.; Bennett, J. H. and Courchene, T. J.*, eds., 1984, pp. 17–61. [G: Canada]

Sayeed, Adil. Public Pensions and Elderly Women. *Can. Public Policy*, December 1984, *10*(4), pp. 468–71.

Sayeed, Adil. Tax-Transfer Benefits for the Elderly. In *Conklin, D. W.; Bennett, J. H. and Courchene, T. J.*, eds., 1984, pp. 241–63. [G: Canada]

Schuster, Michael and Miller, Christopher S. An Empirical Assessment of the Age Discrimination in Employment Act. *Ind. Lab. Relat. Rev.*, October 1984, *38*(1), pp. 64–74. [G: U.S.]

Schwartz, Saul; Danziger, Sheldon and Smolensky, Eugene. The Choice of Living Arrangements by the Elderly. In *Aaron, H. J. and Burtless, G.*, eds., 1984, pp. 229–50. [G: U.S.]

Smeeding, Timothy M. Is the Safety Net Still Intact? In *Bawden, D. L.*, ed., 1984, pp. 69–120. [G: U.S.]

Stone, Leroy O. and Fletcher, Susan. Why We Should be Cautious in Accepting Forecasts of the Dependency Ratios in the 21st Century. In *Conklin, D. W.; Bennett, J. H. and Courchene, T. J.*, eds., 1984, pp. 474–86. [G: Canada]

Struyk, Raymond J. Home Energy Costs and the Housing of the Poor and the Elderly. In

Downs, A. and Bradbury, K. L., eds., 1984, pp. 35–78. **[G: U.S.]**

Struyk, Raymond J. Home Equity and the Elderly: Comment. In *Aaron, H. J. and Burtless, G., eds.*, 1984, pp. 225–27. **[G: U.S.]**

Torrey, Barbara Boyle. Income Transfers and the Economic Status of the Elderly: Comment. In *Moon, M., ed.*, 1984, pp. 276–82. **[G: U.S.]**

Wander, Hilde. What Does it Cost to Support the Young and the Old Generations? In *Steinmann, G., ed.*, 1984, pp. 238–57.

[G: W. Germany]

Warlick, Jennifer L. and Burkhauser, Richard V. Raising the Normal Retirement Age under Social Security: A Life-Cycle Analysis. In *Moon, M., ed.*, 1984, pp. 359–79. **[G: U.S.]**

Williamson, John B. Old Age Relief Policy Prior to 1900: The Trend Toward Restrictiveness. *Amer. J. Econ. Soc.*, July 1984, *43*(3), pp. 369–84. **[G: U.S.]**

Wolf, Douglas A. The Choice of Living Arrangements by the Elderly: Comment. In *Aaron, H. J. and Burtless, G., eds.*, 1984, pp. 250–53. **[G: U.S.]**

920 CONSUMER ECONOMICS

921 Consumer Economics; Levels and Standards of Living

9210 General

Adamowicz, W. L. and Phillips, W. E. A Comparison of Extra Market Benefit Evaluation Techniques: A Reply. *Can. J. Agr. Econ.*, November 1984, *32*(3), pp. 590–92. **[G: Canada]**

Afriat, S. N. The True Index. In *[Pearce, I. F.]*, 1984, pp. 37–56.

Alston, Lee J. and Schapiro, Morton Owen. Inheritance Laws across Colonies: Causes and Consequences. *J. Econ. Hist.*, June 1984, *44*(2), pp. 277–87. **[G: U.S.]**

Belk, Russell; Mayer, Robert and Driscoll, Amy. Children's Recognition of Consumption Symbolism in Children's Products. *J. Cons. Res.*, March 1984, *10*(4), pp. 386–97. **[G: U.S.]**

Capon, Noel and Davis, Roger. Basic Cognitive Ability Measures as Predictors of Consumer Information Processing Strategies. *J. Cons. Res.*, June 1984, *11*(1), pp. 551–63.

[G: U.S.]

Colasanto, Diane; Kapteyn, Arie and van der Gaag, Jacques. Two Subjective Definitions of Poverty: Results from the Wisconsin Basic Needs Study. *J. Human Res.*, Winter 1984, *19*(1), pp. 127–38. **[G: U.S.]**

Coughlin, Cletus C. and Erekson, O. Homer. An Examination of Contributions to Support Intercollegiate Athletics. *Southern Econ. J.*, July 1984, *51*(1), pp. 180–95. **[G: U.S.]**

Dobbs, Ian M. and Hill, Martyn B. Technical Innovation and the Demand for Goods. *Scot. J. Polit. Econ.*, June 1984, *31*(2), pp. 147–56.

Dominguez, Luis V. and Page, Albert L. Formulating a Strategic Portfolio of Profitable Retail Market Segments for Commercial Banks. *J. Econ. Bus.*, May 1984, *36*(2), pp. 189–206.

[G: U.S.]

Dwyer, F. Robert. Are Two Better than One? Bargaining Behavior and Outcomes in an Asymmetrical Power Relationship. *J. Cons. Res.*, September 1984, *11*(2), pp. 680–93.

Finney, Ben R. The Ocean and the Quality of Life. In *Gopalakrishnan, C., ed.*, 1984, pp. 187–92. **[G: U.S.]**

Folbre, Nancy R. Household Production in the Philippines: A Non-neoclassical Approach. *Econ. Develop. Cult. Change*, January 1984, *32*(2), pp. 303–30. **[G: Philippines]**

Folkes, Valerie S. Consumer Reactions to Product Failure: An Attributional Approach. *J. Cons. Res.*, March 1984, *10*(4), pp. 398–409.

[G: U.S.]

Franz, A. and Schwarzl, R. ICP 1980—A Brief Account from Austria. *Rev. Income Wealth*, June 1984, *30*(2), pp. 167–84. **[G: Austria]**

Fraser, Cynthia and Bradford, John W. Competitive Market Structure Analysis: A Reply [Competitive Market Structure Analysis: Principal Partitioning of Revealed Substitutabilities]. *J. Cons. Res.*, December 1984, *11*(3), pp. 842–47. **[G: U.S.]**

Gershuny, Jonathan I. Growth, Social Innovation and Time Use. In *Boulding, K. E., ed.*, 1984, pp. 36–57. **[G: OECD]**

van Ginneken, Wouter and Baron, Christopher. Appropriate Products, Employment and Technology: Conclusions and Policy Implications. In *van Ginneken, W. and Baron, C., eds.*, 1984, pp. 238–54.

Glazer, Rashi. Multiattribute Perceptual Bias as Revealing of Preference Structure. *J. Cons. Res.*, June 1984, *11*(1), pp. 510–21.

[G: U.S.]

Greenwald, Anthony G. and Leavitt, Clark. Audience Involvement in Advertising: Four Levels. *J. Cons. Res.*, June 1984, *11*(1), pp. 581–92. **[G: U.S.]**

Grether, David M. and Wilde, Louis. An Analysis of Conjunctive Choice: Theory and Experiments. *J. Cons. Res.*, March 1984, *10*(4), pp. 373–85.

Hagerty, Michael R. and Aaker, David A. A Normative Model of Consumer Information Processing. *Marketing Sci.*, Summer 1984, *3*(3), pp. 227–46.

Hannah, Darlene B. and Sternthal, Brian. Detecting and Explaining the Sleeper Effect. *J. Cons. Res.*, September 1984, *11*(2), pp. 632–42.

Harper, Michael C. The Consumer's Emerging Right to Boycott: *NAACP v. Claiborne Hardware* and Its Implications for American Labor Law. *Yale Law J.*, January 1984, *93*(3), pp. 409–54. **[G: U.S.]**

Harris, Sara. Making it on $400 a Month—Soviet Style. In *Shaffer, H. G., ed.*, 1984, *1978*, pp. 430–34. **[G: U.S.S.R.]**

Helgeson, James G., et al. Trends in Consumer Behavior Literature: A Content Analysis. *J. Cons. Res.*, March 1984, *10*(4), pp. 449–54.

Helmstädter, Ernst. Sättigung: Ein Phänomen und kein Begriff. (Saturation: A Phenomenon and Not a Concept. With English summary.) *Ifo-Studien*, 1984, *30*(3), pp. 243–47.

Hensher, David A. Achieving Representativeness of the Observable Component of the Indirect Utility Function in Logit Choice Models: An Empirical Revelation. *J. Bus.*, April 1984, *57*(2), pp. 265–80. [G: U.S.]

Hey, John D. Optimal Consumption When Income Follows a Markov Process. *Bull. Econ. Res.*, November 1984, *36*(2), pp. 109–18.

Hornik, Jacob. Subjective vs. Objective Time Measures: A Note on the Perception of Time in Consumer Behavior. *J. Cons. Res.*, June 1984, *11*(1), pp. 615–18. [G: U.S.]

Hunt, Janet C. and Kiker, B. F. Parental Time Devoted to Children in Two- and One-Wage-Earner Families. *Econ. Educ. Rev.*, 1984, *3*(1), pp. 75–83. [G: U.S.]

Ito, Shuntaro. Turning Points of Civilization and the Role of Japan Today. In *Miyawaki, N., ed.*, 1984, pp. 89–99. [G: Japan]

Jacoby, Jacob. Perspectives on Information Overload. *J. Cons. Res.*, March 1984, *10*(4), pp. 432–35.

Johnson, Eric J. and Meyer, Robert J. Compensatory Choice Models of Noncompensatory Processes: The Effect of Varying Context. *J. Cons. Res.*, June 1984, *11*(1), pp. 528–41. [G: U.S.]

Johnson, Eric J. and Russo, J. Edward. Product Familiarity and Learning New Information. *J. Cons. Res.*, June 1984, *11*(1), pp. 542–50. [G: U.S.]

Kehret-Ward, Trudy and Yalch, Richard F. To Take or Not to Take the Only One: Effects of Changing the Meaning of a Product Attribute on Choice Behavior. *J. Cons. Res.*, March 1984, *10*(4), pp. 410–16. [G: U.S.]

Kenyon, Daphne A. and McCandless, George T., Jr. A Note on the Required Compensation Test as the Theoretical Basis for Putting a Value on Human Life. *Southern Econ. J.*, July 1984, *51*(1), pp. 258–66.

Kirschen, E. S. La valeur horaire du temps. (With English summary.) *Cah. Écon. Bruxelles*, 2nd Trimester 1984, (102), pp. 243–78. [G: Belgium]

Linge, G. J. R. Industrialization and the Household. *Int. Soc. Sci. J.*, 1984, *36*(2), pp. 319–39.

Mahoney, Paul G. A Market Power Test for Noncommercial Boycotts. *Yale Law J.*, January 1984, *93*(3), pp. 523–40. [G: U.S.]

Malhotra, Naresh K. Reflections on the Information Overload Paradigm in Consumer Decision Making [Perspectives on Information Overload]. *J. Cons. Res.*, March 1984, *10*(4), pp. 436–40.

Marion, Donald R. and Grinnell, Gerald. Estimates of Consumer Loss Due to Monopoly in the U.S. Food Manufacturing Industries: Comment. *Amer. J. Agr. Econ.*, November 1984, *66*(4), pp. 520–23. [G: U.S.]

McKenzie, Joseph A. Who Holds Alternative Market-Yield Accounts? *J. Finan. Res.*, Summer 1984, *7*(2), pp. 175–83. [G: U.S.]

McSweeney, Frances K. and Bierley, Calvin. Recent Developments in Classical Conditioning. *J. Cons. Res.*, September 1984, *11*(2), pp. 619–31.

Midgley, David F. Parsimony or Explanation: On the Estimation of Systems Defined by Nonlinear Differential Equations [A Simple Mathematical Theory of Innovative Behavior]. *J. Cons. Res.*, March 1984, *10*(4), pp. 445–48.

Munger, Michael C. The Costs of Protectionism. *Challenge*, January/February 1984, *26*(6), pp. 54–58. [G: U.S.]

Nissel, Muriel. Indicators of Human Betterment. In *Boulding, K. E., ed.*, 1984, pp. 15–35. [G: U.K.]

Offe, Claus. Alternative Strategies in Consumer Policy. In *Offe, C.*, 1984, *1981*, pp. 220–38.

Ofir, Chezy and Lynch, John G., Jr. Context Effects on Judgment under Uncertainty. *J. Cons. Res.*, September 1984, *11*(2), pp. 668–79.

Orlov, Ia. The Demand of the Population and Tasks of Production and Trade. *Prob. Econ.*, June 1984, *27*(2), pp. 3–19. [G: U.S.S.R.]

Parker, Russell C. and Connor, John M. Estimates of Consumer Loss Due to Monopoly in the U.S. Food Manufacturing Industries: Second Reply. *Amer. J. Agr. Econ.*, November 1984, *66*(4), pp. 524–28. [G: U.S.]

Parsons, Donald O. On the Economics of Intergenerational Control. *Population Devel. Rev.*, March 1984, *10*(1), pp. 41–54.

Quizon, Jaime B.; Binswanger, Hans P. and Machina, Mark J. Attitudes toward Risk: Further Remarks. *Econ. J.*, March 1984, *94*(373), pp. 144–48. [G: India]

Sander, William. The Economics of Time and Community. *Rev. Soc. Econ.*, April 1984, *42*(1), pp. 44–49. [G: U.S.]

Schelling, Thomas C. Ethics, Law, and the Exercise of Self-Command. In *Schelling, T. C.*, 1984, pp. 83–112.

Schelling, Thomas C. Strategic Relationships in Dying. In *Schelling, T. C.*, 1984, pp. 147–57.

Schelling, Thomas C. The Intimate Contest for Self-Command. In *Schelling, T. C.*, 1984, pp. 57–82.

Schelling, Thomas C. The Life You Save May Be Your Own. In *Schelling, T. C.*, 1984, pp. 113–46.

Sen, Amartya. Goods and People. In *Sen, A.*, 1984, *1983*, pp. 509–32.

Seymour, Daniel and Lessne, Greg. Spousal Conflict Arousal: Scale Development. *J. Cons. Res.*, December 1984, *11*(3), pp. 810–21. [G: U.S.]

Shimp, Terence A. and Kavas, Alican. The Theory of Reasoned Action Applied to Coupon Usage. *J. Cons. Res.*, December 1984, *11*(3), pp. 795–809. [G: U.S.]

Shocker, Allan D.; Zahorik, Anthony J. and Stewart, David W. Competitive Market Structure Analysis: A Comment on Problems. [Competitive Market Structure Analysis: Principal Parti-

tioning of Revealed Substitutabilities]. *J. Cons. Res.*, December 1984, *11*(3), pp. 836–41.
[G: U.S.]

Silver, Steven D. A Simple Mathematical Theory of Innovative Behavior: Comment. *J. Cons. Res.*, March 1984, *10*(4), pp. 441–44.

Steinberg, Richard. A Comment on Motives Underlying Individual Contributions to Charity. *Atlantic Econ. J.*, July 1984, *12*(2), pp. 61–64.

Stoller, Michael A. The Economics of Collectible Goods. *J. Cult. Econ.*, June 1984, *8*(1), pp. 91–104. [G: Israel]

Strümpel, Burkhard. New Bases of Social and Institutional Conflict. In *Miyawaki, N., ed.*, 1984, pp. 80–88.

Sussman, Frances G. A Note on the Willingness to Pay Approach to the Valuation of Longevity. *J. Environ. Econ. Manage.*, March 1984, *11*(1), pp. 84–89.

Teeters, Nancy H. Statement to the U.S. Senate Subcommittee on Consumer Affairs, Committee on Banking, Housing, and Urban Affairs, February 7, 1984. *Fed. Res. Bull.*, February 1984, *70*(2), pp. 102–05. [G: U.S.]

Van Kooten, G. C. A Comparison of Extra Market Benefit Evaluation Techniques: Comment. *Can. J. Agr. Econ.*, November 1984, *32*(3), pp. 584–89.

Winett, Richard A. and Kagel, John H. Effects of Information Presentation Format on Resource Use in Field Studies. *J. Cons. Res.*, September 1984, *11*(2), pp. 655–67.

9211 Living Standards, Composition of Overall Expenditures, and Empirical Consumption and Savings Studies

Adulavidhaya, Kamphol, et al. The Comparative Statics of the Behavior of Agricultural Households in Thailand. *Singapore Econ. Rev.*, April 1984, *29*(1), pp. 67–96. [G: Thailand]

Afridi, Usman; Qadir, Asghar and Zaki, Javed. Effects of Dual Sector Inflation across Income Levels in Pakistan. *Pakistan Devel. Rev.*, Summer-Autumn 1984, *23*(2&3), pp. 381–90.
[G: Pakistan]

Akin, John S.; Guilkey, David K. and Popkin, Barry M. The School Lunch Program and Nutrient Intake: A Switching Regression Analysis: Reply. *Amer. J. Agr. Econ.*, November 1984, *66*(4), pp. 513–14. [G: U.S.]

Aleksandrova, E. and Fedorovskaia, E. The Formation and Heightening of Needs. *Prob. Econ.*, October 1984, *27*(6), pp. 54–70.
[G: U.S.S.R.]

Altimir, Oscar. Poverty, Income Distribution and Child Welfare in Latin America: A Comparison of Pre- and Post-Recession Data. *World Devel.*, March 1984, *12*(3), pp. 261–82. [G: Chile; Colombia; Costa Rica; Panama; Venezuela]

Altimir, Oscar. Poverty, Income Distribution and Child Welfare in Latin America: A Comparison of Pre- and Post-recession Data. In *Jolly, R. and Cornia, G. A., eds.*, 1984, pp. 91–112.
[G: Latin America]

Aspe, Pedro and Beristain, Javier. Toward a First

Estimate of the Evolution of Inequality in Mexico. In *Aspe, P. and Sigmund, P. E., eds.*, 1984, pp. 31–57. [G: Mexico]

Auerbach, Alan J. and Kotlikoff, Laurence J. Social Security and the Economics of the Demographic Transition. In *Aaron, H. J. and Burtless, G., eds.*, 1984, pp. 255–76. [G: U.S.]

Avery, Robert B.; Elliehausen, Gregory E. and Canner, Glenn B. Survey of Consumer Finances, 1983. *Fed. Res. Bull.*, September 1984, *70*(9), pp. 679–92. [G: U.S.]

Avery, Robert B., et al. Survey of Consumer Finances, 1983: A Second Report. *Fed. Res. Bull.*, December 1984, *70*(12), pp. 857–68.
[G: U.S.]

Balassa, Bela. The Policy Experience of Twelve Less Developed Countries, 1973–1979. In *[Reynolds, L. G.]*, 1984, pp. 96–123.
[G: Selected LDCs]

Beach, Charles M.; Boadway, Robin and Gibbons, Jack O. Social Security and Aggregate Capital Accumulation Revisited: Dynamic Simultaneous Estimates in a Wealth-Generation Model. *Econ. Inquiry*, January 1984, *22*(1), pp. 68–79. [G: U.S.]

Beeman, William J. How Bad Are the Large Deficits? Comment. In *Mills, G. B. and Palmer, J. L., eds.*, 1984, pp. 74–78. [G: U.S.]

Benoit, J. Pierre V. Artificially Low Interest Rates versus Realistic or Market Interest Rates. In *Kessler, D. and Ullmo, P.-A., eds.*, 1984, pp. 35–78. [G: LDCs; MDCs]

Blundell, Richard and Walker, Ian. A Household Production Specification of Demographic Variables in Demand Analysis. *Econ. J.*, 1984 Supplement, *94*, pp. 59–68. [G: U.K.]

Boskin, Michael J. Social Security and the Economics of the Demographic Transition: Comment. In *Aaron, H. J. and Burtless, G., eds.*, 1984, pp. 276–78. [G: U.S.]

Buchele, Robert. Reaganomics and the Fairness Issue. *Challenge*, September/October 1984, *27*(4), pp. 25–31. [G: U.S.]

Caceres, Luis René. Savings in a Global Context. In *Kessler, D. and Ullmo, P.-A., eds.*, 1984, pp. 323–49. [G: Latin America]

Cattin, Philippe and Punj, Girish N. Factors Influencing the Selection of Preference Model Form for Continuous Utility Functions in Conjoint Analysis. *Marketing Sci.*, Winter 1984, *3*(1), pp. 73–82.

Cebula, Richard J. Determinants of Geographic Living-Cost Differentials in the United States: Reply. *Land Econ.*, February 1984, *60*(1), pp. 120–21. [G: U.S.]

Christian, James W. and Wilson, Michael L. Capital Requirements for Housing in the 1980s. *Contemp. Policy Issue*, May 1984, (6), pp. 30–44. [G: U.S.]

Cornia, Giovanni Andrea. The Impact of World Recession on Children: A Survey of Cross-Sectional and Time-Series Literature on Factors Affecting Child Welfare. *World Devel.*, March 1984, *12*(3), pp. 187–202. [G: Global]

Courant, Paul N.; Gramlich, Edward M. and Laitner, John P. A Dynamic Microeconomic

Estimate of the Life-Cycle Model. In *Aaron, H. J. and Burtless, G., eds.*, 1984, pp. 279–309. [G: U.S.]

D'Amico, Ronald. The Time-Use Behavior of Young Adults. In *Borus, M. E., ed.*, 1984, pp. 193–238. [G: U.S.]

Daly, Michael J. and Naqib, Fadle. The Treatment of Registered Retirement Savings Plans at Maturity. *J. Econ. Dynam. Control*, September 1984, 7(3), pp. 233–40.

Danziger, Sheldon, et al. Implications of the Relative Economic Status of the Elderly for Transfer Policy. In *Aaron, H. J. and Burtless, G., eds.*, 1984, pp. 175–93. [G: U.S.]

Danziger, Sheldon, et al. Income Transfers and the Economic Status of the Elderly. In *Moon, M., ed.*, 1984, pp. 239–76. [G: U.S.]

Danziger, Sheldon, et al. The Direct Measurement of Welfare Levels: How Much Does It Cost to Make Ends Meet? *Rev. Econ. Statist.*, August 1984, 66(3), pp. 500–505. [G: U.S.]

David, Martin and Menchik, Paul L. Nonearned Income, Income Instability, and Inequality: A Life-Cycle Interpretation. In *[Ferber, R.]*, 1984, pp. 53–73. [G: U.S.]

Davis, E. P. The Consumption Function in Macroeconomic Models: A Comparative Study. *Appl. Econ.*, December 1984, 16(6), pp. 799–838. [G: U.K.]

Diamond, Peter A. and Hausman, Jerry A. Individual Retirement and Savings Behavior. *J. Public Econ.*, February/March 1984, 23(1/2), pp. 81–114. [G: U.S.]

Dicks-Mireaux, Louis and King, Mervyn A. Pension Wealth and Household Savings: Tests of Robustness. *J. Public Econ.*, February/March 1984, 23(1/2), pp. 115–39. [G: Canada]

Dorrance, G. Morris, Jr. Savings and Investment: Comment. In *Wachter, M. L. and Wachter, S. M., eds.*, 1984, pp. 251–54. [G: U.S.]

Downes, E. Beverly. Tanzania (1969) In *van Ginneken, W. and Park, J., eds.*, 1984, pp. 145–49. [G: Tanzania]

Duncan, Greg J.; Juster, F. Thomas and Morgan, James N. The Role of Panel Studies in a World of Scarce Research Resources. In *[Ferber, R.]*, 1984, pp. 301–28. [G: U.S.]

Ellman, Michael. *Odnowa* in Statistics. In *Ellman, M.*, 1984, 1982, pp. 242–49.
[G: Poland]

Evans, Owen J. Empirical Tests of the Life Cycle Hypothesis: Comment. *Amer. Econ. Rev.*, March 1984, 74(1), pp. 254–57. [G: U.S.]

Farkas, Katalin Z. and Pataki, Judit. Shortage of Commodities and Public Opinion in Hungary. *Acta Oecon.*, 1984, 32(3–4), pp. 287–301.
[G: Hungary]

Fellner, William. Monetary and Fiscal Policy in a Disinflationary Process: Justified and Unjustified Misgivings about Budget Deficits. In *Fellner, W., ed.*, 1984, pp. 55–86. [G: U.S.]

Ferris, Tom. Productivity and Living Standards—Some Further Comparisons. *Irish Banking Rev.*, June 1984, pp. 40–45. [G: Ireland]

Flaim, Paul O. Proposed Spendable Earnings Se-

ries Retains Basic Faults of Earlier One. *Mon. Lab. Rev.*, November 1984, 107(11), pp. 43–44. [G: U.S.]

Flinn, M. W. English Workers' Living Standards during the Industrial Revolution: A Comment. *Econ. Hist. Rev.*, 2nd Ser., February 1984, 37(1), pp. 88–92. [G: U.K.]

Gazioglou, Shaziye. Alternative Theories of the Consumption Function: The Case of Turkey. *Greek Econ. Rev.*, August 1984, 6(2), pp. 203–32. [G: Turkey]

Gershuny, Jonathan I. Growth, Social Innovation and Time Use. In *Boulding, K. E., ed.*, 1984, pp. 36–57. [G: OECD]

van Ginneken, Wouter. Denmark (1976) In *van Ginneken, W. and Park, J., eds.*, 1984, pp. 33–39. [G: Denmark]

Gourvez, Jean-Yves. Intermediation and Traditional Circuits. Conditions for Mobilizing Financial Savings. In *Kessler, D. and Ullmo, P.-A., eds.*, 1984, pp. 107–20.

Graham, John W. and Bradley, Michael G. Consumer Asset Composition in an Inflationary Environment. In *[Ferber, R.]*, 1984, pp. 39–52. [G: U.S.]

Gramlich, Edward M. How Bad Are the Large Deficits? In *Mills, G. B. and Palmer, J. L., eds.*, 1984, pp. 43–68. [G: U.S.]

Green, Francis. A Critique of the Neo-Fisherian Consumption Function. *Rev. Radical Polit. Econ.*, Summer & Fall 1984, 16(2&3), pp. 95–114. [G: U.S.]

Grubel, Herbert G. The Impact of the Tax System—Federal Republic of Germany: Comment. In *Block, W. and Walker, M., eds.*, 1984, pp. 320–23. [G: W. Germany]

Guillaume, Y., et al. Impact of Subsidies and of Tax Deductions on Consumer's Energy Savings—The Belgian Case. In *Avula, X. J. R., et al.*, 1984, pp. 815–21. [G: Belgium]

Gunatilleke, Godfrey and Kurukulasuria, G. I. O. M. The Global Economic Crisis and the Impact on Children in Sri Lanka. *World Devel.*, March 1984, 12(3), pp. 309–16.
[G: Sri Lanka]

Gupta, Kanhaya L. Financial Intermediation, Interest Rate and Structure of Savings: Evidence from Asia. *J. Econ. Devel.*, July 1984, 9(1), pp. 7–23. [G: Asia]

Hamermesh, Daniel S. Consumption during Retirement: The Missing Link in the Life Cycle. *Rev. Econ. Statist.*, February 1984, 66(1), pp. 1–7. [G: U.S.]

Hamermesh, Daniel S. Life-Cycle Effects on Consumption and Retirement. *J. Lab. Econ.*, July 1984, 2(3), pp. 353–70. [G: U.S.]

Hamermesh, Daniel S. The Role of Time in the Measurement of Transfers and Well-Being: Comment. In *Moon, M., ed.*, 1984, pp. 234–38. [G: U.S.]

Hansen, Gerd. Der Einfluss Zinsen und Preisen auf die Ersparnisse und die Nachfrage nach dauerhaften Gütern in der Bundesrepublik, 1961–1981. (With English summary.) *Z. Wirtschaft. Sozialwissen.*, 1984, 104(3), pp. 227–49. [G: W. Germany]

Haveman, Robert H. How Bad Are the Large Deficits? Comment. In *Mills, G. B. and Palmer, J. L., eds.*, 1984, pp. 69–73.
[G: U.S.]

Henry, Mark S. and Martin, Thomas L. Estimating Income Distribution Effects on Regional Input–Output Multipliers. *Reg. Sci. Persp.*, 1984, *14*(2), pp. 33–45. [G: U.S.]

Henry, Mark S. and Martin, Thomas L. Rural Area Consumer Demand and Regional Input–Output Analysis: Reply. *Amer. J. Agr. Econ.*, May 1984, *66*(2), pp. 176–79. [G: U.S.]

Hihn, Jairus M. and Lane, Sylvia. The School Lunch Program and Nutrient Intake: A Switching Regression Analysis: Comment. *Amer. J. Agr. Econ.*, November 1984, *66*(4), pp. 511–12. [G: U.S.]

Hill, Peter. Inflation, Holding Gains and Saving. *OECD Econ. Stud.*, Spring 1984, (2), pp. 151–64.

Hogan, Timothy D. Determinants of Geographic Living—Cost Differentials in the United States: Comment. *Land Econ.*, February 1984, *60*(1), pp. 115–19. [G: U.S.]

Hogan, Timothy D. and Rex, Tom R. Intercity Differences in Cost of Living: Results from a New Database. *Growth Change*, October 1984, *15*(4), pp. 16–23. [G: U.S.]

Horioka, Charles Yuji. The Applicability of the Life-Cycle Hypothesis of Saving to Japan. *Kyoto Univ. Econ. Rev.*, October 1984, *54*(2), pp. 31–56. [G: Japan]

Hubbard, R. Glenn. Do IRAs and Keoghs Increase Saving? *Nat. Tax J.*, March 1984, *37*(1), pp. 43–54. [G: U.S.]

Ippolito, Pauline M. and Ippolito, Richard A. Measuring the Value of Life Saving from Consumer Reactions to New Information. *J. Public Econ.*, November 1984, *25*(1/2), pp. 53–81.

Ishikawa, Tsuneo and Ueda, Kazuo. The Bonus Payment System and Japanese Personal Savings. In *Aoki, M., ed.*, 1984, pp. 133–92.
[G: Japan]

Jafari-Samimi, Ahmad. Social Security and Private Savings: Empirical Analysis. *Public Finance*, 1984, *39*(2), pp. 226–45. [G: U.S.]

Janssen, Jürgen. Strukturen der Ersparnisentwicklung im privatwirtschaftlichen Sektor der Bundesrepublik, 1962–1980. (Changes in the Structure of Private Sector Savings in the Federal Republic of Germany, 1962–1980. With English summary.) *Konjunkturpolitik*, 1984, *30*(5), pp. 304–16. [G: W. Germany]

Jayawardena, Kumari. The Plantation Sector in Sri Lanka: Recent Changes in the Welfare of Children and Women. *World Devel.*, March 1984, *12*(3), pp. 317–28. [G: Sri Lanka]

Johnson, Paul. Self-Help versus State Help: Old Age Pensions and Personal Savings in Great Britain, 1906–1937. *Exploration Econ. Hist.*, October 1984, *21*(4), pp. 329–50. [G: U.K.]

Johnson, Thomas G. and Capps, Oral, Jr. Rural Area Consumer Demand and Regional Input–Output Analysis: Comment. *Amer. J. Agr. Econ.*, May 1984, *66*(2), pp. 173–76.
[G: U.S.]

Jorgenson, Dale W. Econometric Methods for Applied General Equilibrium Analysis. In *Scarf, H. E. and Shoven, J. B., eds.*, 1984, pp. 139–203. [G: U.S.]

Jorgenson, Dale W. and Slesnick, Daniel T. Aggregate Consumer Behaviour and the Measurement of Inequality. *Rev. Econ. Stud.*, July 1984, *51*(3), pp. 369–92. [G: U.S.]

Jump, G. V. Financing Public Pensions: Some Capital Market Implications. In *Conklin, D. W.; Bennett, J. H. and Courchene, T. J., eds.*, 1984, pp. 295–326. [G: Canada]

Kao, Charles H. C. and Liu, Ben-chieh. Socioeconomic Advance in the Republic of China (Taiwan): An Intertemporal Analysis of Its Quality of Life Indicators. *Amer. J. Econ. Soc.*, October 1984, *43*(4), pp. 399–412. [G: Taiwan]

Kay, John A.; Keen, Michael J. and Morris, C. Nick. Estimating Consumption from Expenditure Data. *J. Public Econ.*, February/March 1984, *23*(1/2), pp. 169–81. [G: U.K.]

Kelly, William A., Jr. and Chambers, Donald R. Inflation, Taxes, and Savings "Incentives." *Financial Rev.*, May 1984, *19*(2), pp. 222–31.
[G: U.S.]

Khan, Qaiser M. The Impact of Household Endowment Constraints on Nutrition and Health: A Simultaneous Equation Test of Human Capital Divestment. *J. Devel. Econ.*, May–June–August 1984, *15*(1,2,3), pp. 313–28.
[G: Bangladesh]

Khan, Shahrukh Rafi. Effects of Dual Sector Inflation across Income Levels in Pakistan: Comment. *Pakistan Devel. Rev.*, Summer-Autumn 1984, *23*(2&3), pp. 391–92. [G: Pakistan]

Korayem, Karima. Egypt (1974–75) In *van Ginneken, W. and Park, J., eds.*, 1984, pp. 41–48. [G: Egypt]

Koskela, Erkki and Virén, Matti. Household Saving Out of Different Types of Income Revisited. *Appl. Econ.*, June 1984, *16*(3), pp. 379–96.
[G: OECD]

Koskela, Erkki and Virén, Matti. Hushållens sparande och penningmarknaderna i norden. (Household Saving and Credit Markets in the Nordic Countries. With English summary.) *Ekon. Samfundets Tidskr.*, 1984, *37*(4), pp. 245–65. [G: Finland; Norway; Sweden]

Kovács, Ilona. The Development of Living Standards in Hungary from 1975 to 1983. *Acta Oecon.*, 1984, *33*(1–2), pp. 155–66.
[G: Hungary]

Kula, Erhun. Derivation of Social Time Preference Rates for the United States and Canada. *Quart. J. Econ.*, November 1984, *99*(4), pp. 873–82. [G: U.S.; Canada]

Lau, Lawrence J. Numerical Specification of Applied General Equilibrium Models: Estimation, Calibration, and Data: Comments. In *Scarf, H. E. and Shoven, J. B., eds.*, 1984, pp. 127–37. [G: U.S.; U.K.]

de Leeuw, Frank. Conflicting Measures of Private Saving. *Surv. Curr. Bus.*, November 1984, *64*(11), pp. 17–23. [G: U.S.]

Leff, Nathaniel H. Dependency Rates and Savings: Another Look [Dependency Rates and

Aggregate Savings: A New International Cross-Section Study]. *Amer. Econ. Rev.*, March 1984, *74*(1), pp. 231–33.   [G: LDCs; MCDs]

Lehrer, Evelyn and Nerlove, Marc. A Life-Cycle Analysis of Family Income Distribution. *Econ. Inquiry*, July 1984, *22*(3), pp. 360–74.
[G: U.S.]

Levy, Frank. Implications of the Relative Economic Status of the Elderly for Transfer Policy: Comment. In *Aaron, H. J. and Burtless, G.*, eds., 1984, pp. 193–96.   [G: U.S.]

Ligeti, Sandor. Rural Savings and Agricultural Credits. In *Kessler, D. and Ullmo, P.-A.*, eds., 1984, pp. 87–106.

Lillard, Lee A. and Aigner, Dennis J. Time-of-Day Electricity Consumption Response to Temperature and the Ownership of Air Conditioning Appliances. *J. Bus. Econ. Statist.*, January 1984, *2*(1), pp. 40–53.   [G: U.S.]

Lindert, Peter H. and Williamson, Jeffrey G. Reply [English Workers' Living Standards during the Industrial Revolution: A New Look]. *Econ. Hist. Rev.*, 2nd Ser., February 1984, *37*(1), pp. 93–94.   [G: U.K.]

Lütkepohl, Helmut. Forecasting Contemporaneously Aggregated Vector ARMA Processes. *J. Bus. Econ. Statist.*, July 1984, *2*(3), pp. 201–14.   [G: U.S.]

MacKinnon, James G. Econometric Methods for Applied General Equilibrium Analysis: Comments. In *Scarf, H. E. and Shoven, J. B.*, eds., 1984, pp. 203–07.   [G: U.S.]

Mansur, Ahsan Habib and Whalley, John. Numerical Specification of Applied General Equilibrium Models: Estimation, Calibration, and Data. In *Scarf, H. E. and Shoven, J. B.*, eds., 1984, pp. 69–127.   [G: U.S.; U.K.]

Martynov, A. V. and Solov'ev, Iu. P. A Mathematical and Economic Analysis of the Time Path of Major Consumer Purchases and Household Savings. *Matekon*, Spring 1984, *20*(3), pp. 59–73.   [G: U.S.S.R.]

May, Martha. The "Good Managers": Married Working Class Women and Family Budget Studies, 1895–1915. *Labor Hist.*, Summer 1984, *25*(3), pp. 351–72.   [G: U.S.]

Maynes, E. Scott, et al. Informationally Imperfect Markets: Implications for Consumers. In *[Ferber, R.]*, 1984, pp. 185–97.   [G: U.S.]

McKenzie, George and Thomas, Stephen. The Econometric Modelling of Aggregate Consumer Behaviour. *Europ. Econ. Rev.*, August 1984, *25*(3), pp. 355–72.

Meganck, B. and Maes, G. Experience in Belgium with Business Surveys in Trade: Elements of Forecasting the Evolution of Private Consumption. In *Oppenländer, K. H. and Poser, G.*, eds., 1984, pp. 309–42.
[G: Belgium]

Mehran, F. Islamic Republic of Iran (1973–74) In *van Ginneken, W. and Park, J.*, eds., 1984, pp. 75–81.   [G: Iran]

Mellor, John W. Food Price Policy and Income Distribution in Low-Income Countries. In *Eicher, C. K. and Staatz, J. M.*, eds., 1984, 1978, pp. 147–67.   [G: India]

Menchik, Paul L. Is the Family Wealth Squandered? A Test of the Merry-Widow Model. *J. Econ. Hist.*, September 1984, *44*(3), pp. 835–38.   [G: U.S.]

Michel, Richard C., et al. Are We Better Off in 1984? *Challenge*, September/October 1984, *27*(4), pp. 10–17.   [G: U.S.]

Millar, James R. The Household Sector: The View from the Bottom. In *Hoffmann, E. P. and Laird, R. F.*, eds., 1984, 1981, pp. 529–61.   [G: U.S.S.R.]

Moon, Marilyn and Sawhill, Isabel V. Family Incomes: Gainers and Losers. In *Palmer, J. L. and Sawhill, I. V.*, eds., 1984, pp. 317–46.
[G: U.S.]

Morgan, James N. The Role of Time in the Measurement of Transfers and Well-Being. In *Moon, M.*, ed., 1984, pp. 199–234. [G: U.S.]

Mosley, Paul. The Behaviour of the Macro-economy. In *Sandford, C. and Bradbury, M.*, eds., 1984, pp. 145–63.   [G: U.K.]

Mueller, Eva. The Value and Allocation of Time in Rural Botswana. *J. Devel. Econ.*, May–June–August 1984, *15*(1,2,3), pp. 329–60.
[G: Botswana]

Nechemias, Carol and Bahry, Donna. The Soviet Union: Consumer Sector. In *Groth, A. J. and Wade, L. L.*, eds., 1984, pp. 101–26.
[G: U.S.S.R.]

Nerlove, Marc; Razin, Assaf and Sadka, Efraim. Bequests and the Size of Population When Population Is Endogenous. *J. Polit. Econ.*, June 1984, *92*(3), pp. 527–31.

Nolan, Peter and White, Gordon. Urban Bias, Rural Bias or State Bias? Urban–Rural Relations in Post-revolutionary China. In *Harriss, J. and Moore, M.*, eds., 1984, pp. 52–81.
[G: China]

Nordberg, Leif. Hushållsbudgetundersökningarna i ekonomisk analys. (Household Surveys in Economic Analysis. With English summary.) *Ekon. Samfundets Tidskr.*, 1984, *37*(3), pp. 191–203.   [G: Finland; Norway]

Öhlén, S. L. Plans and Attitudes from the Survey of Consumer Buying Expectations in Forecasting the Total Private Consumption. In *Oppenländer, K. H. and Poser, G.*, eds., 1984, pp. 243–79.   [G: Sweden]

Oswald, Rudolph A. Savings and Investment: Comment. In *Wachter, M. L. and Wachter, S. M.*, eds., 1984, pp. 254–57.   [G: U.S.]

Patterson, K. D. Some Properties of Consumption Functions with Integral Correction Mechanisms. *Manchester Sch. Econ. Soc. Stud.*, December 1984, *52*(4), pp. 347–62.
[G: U.K.]

Pearl, Robert B. and Frankel, Matilda. Composition of the Personal Wealth of American Households at the Start of the Eighties. In *[Ferber, R.]*, 1984, pp. 19–37.   [G: U.S.]

Perasso, Giancarlo. Sviluppo economico e qualità della vita: un confronto fra i paesi OPEC e altri paesi in via di sviluppo. (Economic Development and Quality of Life: A Comparison between OPEC Countries and Other Developing Countries. With English summary.) *Rivista*

Int. Sci. Econ. Com., June 1984, *31*(6), pp. 558–75. **[G: LDCs]**

Perelman, S. and Pestieau, Pierre. The Effect of Social Security on Saving: The Case of Belgium with a Particular Emphasis on the Behavior of the Aged. *Empirical Econ.*, 1984, *9*(1), pp. 15–26. **[G: Belgium]**

Pesaran, M. H. and Evans, Robert A. Inflation, Capital Gains and U.K. Personal Savings: 1953–1981. *Econ. J.*, June 1984, *94*(374), pp. 237–57. **[G: U.K.]**

Petersen, Hans-Georg. The Impact of the Tax System—Federal Republic of Germany. **In** *Block, W. and Walker, M., eds.*, 1984, pp. 283–319. **[G: W. Germany]**

Portes, Richard, et al. Estimation de la taille des erreurs de planification. (Estimation of the Possible Size of Plan Errors. With English summary.) *Ann. INSEE*, July–December 1984, (55/56), pp. 245–55. **[G: Poland]**

Praet, Peter and Vuchelen, Jozef. The Integration of Consumer Survey Results in the Modelling of Private Consumption in Italy. *Econ. Notes*, 1984, (3), pp. 74–85. **[G: Italy]**

Práger, László. The Impoverished Rich and the Well-to-Do Poor (Investigations Concerning Personal Income). *Eastern Europ. Econ.*, Winter 1984–85, *23*(2), pp. 3–28. **[G: Hungary]**

Pratschke, John L. Aspects of the Redistribution of Income in Urban and Rural Ireland, 1973–1980. *Irish J. Agr. Econ. Rural Soc.*, 1984, *10*(1), pp. 13–27. **[G: U.K.]**

Pratschke, John L. Expenditure Functions of Urban and Rural Households in Ireland, 1973. *Irish J. Agr. Econ. Rural Soc.*, 1984, *10*(1), pp. 43–63. **[G: U.K.]**

Pryor, Frederic L. A Quantitative Study of the Structure and Behavior of Consumption and Prices in Different Economic Systems. **In** *Bohnet, A., ed.*, 1984, pp. 213–46. **[G: Selected Countries]**

al-Qudsi, Sulayman S. An Empirical Evaluation of Consumption Behaviour in Oil Societies: The Case of Kuwait. *Pakistan Devel. Rev.*, Spring 1984, *23*(1), pp. 81–94. **[G: Kuwait]**

Ram, Rati. Dependency Rates and Savings: Reply. *Amer. Econ. Rev.*, March 1984, *74*(1), pp. 234–37. **[G: LDCs; MDCs]**

Rao, V. G. and Chandrashekar, H. Inter-State Variations in Urban Poverty. *Margin*, April 1984, *16*(3), pp. 77–93. **[G: India]**

Rodriguez, Justine Farr. Savings and Investment: Comment. **In** *Wachter, M. L. and Wachter, S. M., eds.*, 1984, pp. 257–60. **[G: U.S.]**

Rothchild, Donald. Middle Africa: Hegemonial Exchange and Resource Allocation. **In** *Groth, A. J. and Wade, L. L., eds.*, 1984, pp. 151–80. **[G: Africa]**

Sarma, I. R. K. Recent Trends in the Distribution of Personal Income. *Margin*, January 1984, *16*(2), pp. 86–94. **[G. India]**

Sen Amartya. The Living Standard. *Oxford Econ. Pap.*, Supplement November 1984, *36*, pp. 74–90.

Sen, Amartya. The Living Standard. **In** *Collard, D. A., et al., eds.*, 1984, pp. 74–90.

Shammas, Carole. The Eighteenth-Century English Diet and Economic Change. *Exploration Econ. Hist.*, July 1984, *21*(3), pp. 254–69. **[G: U.K.]**

Sheffrin, Steven M. The Dispersion Hypothesis in Macroeconomics. *Rev. Econ. Statist.*, August 1984, *66*(3), pp. 482–85. **[G: U.S.]**

Shoven, John B. A Dynamic Microeconomic Estimate of the Life-Cycle Model: Comment. **In** *Aaron, H. J. and Burtless, G., eds.*, 1984, pp. 310–13. **[G: U.S.]**

Shoven, John B. Saving in the U.S. Economy. **In** *Wachter, M. L. and Wachter, S. M., eds.*, 1984, pp. 187–223. **[G: U.S.]**

Stuart, Edward F. The PQLI as a Measure of Comparative Economic Performance. *ACES Bull.*, Winter 1984, *26*(4), pp. 43–53. **[G: Global]**

Stuart, O. D. J. The Role of Attitudes in Consumer Spending. **In** *Oppenländer, K. H. and Poser, G., eds.*, 1984, pp. 281–303. **[G: S. Africa]**

Sturgess, Brian T. and Wilson, Nicholas. Advertising Expenditure and Aggregate Consumption in Britain and West Germany: An Analysis of Causality. *Managerial Dec. Econ.*, December 1984, *5*(4), pp. 219–27. **[G: U.K.; W. Germany]**

Subralmanyam, Ganti. Market Imperfection and Life-Cycle Savings: An Empirical Note. *J. Econ. Devel.*, July 1984, *9*(1), pp. 67–75. **[G: U.S.]**

Summers, Lawrence H. The After-Tax Rate of Return Affects Private Savings. *Amer. Econ. Rev.*, May 1984, *74*(2), pp. 249–53. **[G: U.S.]**

Theil, Henri and Finke, Renate. The Decline of the Marginal Utility of the Guilder, 1952–1977. *De Economist*, 1984, *132*(4), pp. 497–502. **[G: Netherlands]**

Tickamyer, Ann R. and Duncan, Cynthia L. Economic Activity and the Quality of Life in Eastern Kentucky: A Distributional Model. *Growth Change*, October 1984, *15*(4), pp. 43–51. **[G: U.S.]**

Torrey, Barbara Boyle. Income Transfers and the Economic Status of the Elderly: Comment. **In** *Moon, M., ed.*, 1984, pp. 276–82. **[G: U.S.]**

Turchi, Boone A. The Monetary Cost of a Child. **In** *Steinmann, G., ed.*, 1984, pp. 258–76. **[G: U.S.]**

Virén, Matti. Inflation, Relative Prices and Household Saving Behavior. *Empirical Econ.*, 1984, *9*(3), pp. 183–97. **[G: OECD]**

Wander, Hilde. What Does it Cost to Support the Young and the Old Generations? **In** *Steinmann, G., ed.*, 1984, pp. 238–57. **[G: W. Germany]**

Warfel, George, Jr. Consumer Acceptance of Technology. **In** *Fed. Res. Bank Atlanta*, 1984, pp. 103–12. **[G: U.S.]**

Weisskopf, Thomas E. Use of Hourly Earnings Proposed to Revive Spendable Earnings Series. *Mon. Lab. Rev.*, November 1984, *107*(11), pp. 38–43. **[G: U.S.]**

White, Betsy Buttrill. Empirical Tests of the Life

Cycle Hypothesis: Reply. *Amer. Econ. Rev.*, March 1984, 74(1), pp. 258–59. [G: U.S.]

Williamson, Jeffrey G. British Mortality and the Value of Life, 1781–1931 *Population Stud.*, March 1984, 38(1), pp. 157–72. [G: U.K.]

Wright, J. F. Real Wage Resistance: Eighty Years of the British Cost of Living. In *Collard, D. A., et al., eds.*, 1984, pp. 152–67. [G: U.K.]

Wright, J. F. Real Wage Resistance: Eighty Years of the British Cost of Living. *Oxford Econ. Pap.*, Supplement November 1984, 36, pp. 152–67. [G: U.K.]

Wrigley, N. and Dunn, R. Diagnostics and Resistant Fits in Logit Choice Models. In *Pitfield, D. E., ed.*, 1984, pp. 44–66. [G: U.K.]

Yang, Shengming. Earnings, Prices, and Lives. *Chinese Econ. Stud.*, Winter 1983–84, 17(2), pp. 31–36. [G: China]

Yaprak, Attila and Parameswaran, Ravi. Reliability Measurement in Cross-National Survey Research: An Empirical Evaluation. In *Kaynak, E., ed.*, 1984, pp. 172–93. [G: Turkey; U.S.; W. Germany; Japan; Italy]

Zietz, Joachim. The Interest Elasticity of Savings: An Analysis Based on Explicit Priors. *Oxford Bull. Econ. Statist.*, November 1984, 46(4), pp. 311–27. [G: U.S.]

9212 Expenditure Patterns and Consumption of Specific Items

Aigner, Dennis J. The Welfare Econometrics of Peak-Load Pricing for Electricity: Editor's Introduction. *J. Econometrics*, September/October 1984, 26(1/2), pp. 1–15. [G: U.S.]

Aigner, Dennis J. and Leamer, Edward E. Estimation of Time-of-Use Pricing Response in the Absence of Experimental Data: An Application of the Methodology of Data Transferability. *J. Econometrics*, September/October 1984, 26(1/2), pp. 205–27. [G: U.S.]

Aigner, Dennis J.; Sorooshian, Cyrus and Kerwin, Pamela. Conditional Demand Analysis for Estimating Residential End-Use Load Profiles. *Energy J.*, July 1984, 5(3), pp. 81–97. [G: U.S.]

Alam, M. Shahid. Consumption and Employment Effects of Income Redistribution in Pakistan: Comment. *Pakistan Devel. Rev.*, Summer-Autumn 1984, 23(2&3), pp. 361–63. [G: Pakistan]

Anderson, Gordon J. and Blundell, Richard. Consumer Non-Durables in the U.K. A Dynamic Demand System. *Econ. J.*, 1984 Supplement, 94, pp. 35–44. [G: U.K.]

Andreasen, Alan R. Life Status Changes and Changes in Consumer Preferences and Satisfaction. *J. Cons. Res.*, December 1984, 11(3), pp. 784–94. [G: U.S.]

Andrikopoulos, Andreas A.; Brox, James A. and Carvalho, E. Substitution in Demand for Protein Commodities: The Canadian Experience, 1958 to 1981. *Can. J. Agr. Econ.*, March 1984, 32(1), pp. 141–50. [G: Canada]

Andrikopoulos, Andreas A.; Brox, James A. and

Gamaletsos, Theodore. Forecasting Canadian Consumption Using the Dynamic Generalized Linear Expenditure System (DGLES). *Appl. Econ.*, December 1984, 16(6), pp. 839–53. [G: Canada]

Anttila, Mai and Möller, Kristian. Conjoint Analysis Models in Explaining Consumer Price Utility Structures. *Liiketaloudellinen Aikak.*, 1984, 33(4), pp. 379–404. [G: Finland]

Aryee, George A. Income Distribution, Technology and Employment in the Footwear Industry in Ghana. In *van Ginneken, W. and Baron, C., eds.*, 1984, pp. 120–47. [G: Ghana]

Asplund, Rita. Hushållens efterfrågan på eluppvärmning: En empirisk undersökning för åren 1975–82. (Residential Demand of Electric Space Heating: An Empirical Investigation for 1975–82. With English summary.) *Ekon. Samfundets Tidskr.*, 1984, 37(3), pp. 163–79. [G: Finland]

Asplund, Rita. Kotitaloussähkön kysynnästä Suomessa. (Household Electricity Demand in Finland. With English summary.) *Kansant. Aikak.*, 1984, 80(1), pp. 66–75. [G: Finland]

Atkinson, Scott E. and Halvorsen, Robert. A New Hedonic Technique for Estimating Attribute Demand: An Application to the Demand for Automobile Fuel Efficiency. *Rev. Econ. Statist.*, August 1984, 66(3), pp. 417–26. [G: U.S.]

Baltagi, Badi H. and Griffin, James M. U.S. Gasoline Demand: What Next? *Energy J.*, January 1984, 5(1), pp. 129–40. [G: U.S.]

Barnes, Carolyn. The Historical Context of the Fuelwood Situation in Kisii District. In *Barnes, C.; Ensminger, J. and O'Keefe, P., eds.*, 1984, pp. 61–78. [G: Kenya]

Barnes, Carolyn; Ensminger, Jean and O'Keefe, Philip. Energy Environment and Development in Africa: Introduction. In *Barnes, C.; Ensminger, J. and O'Keefe, P., eds.*, 1984, pp. 1–13. [G: Kenya]

Barnes, Roberta and Gillingham, Robert. Demographic Effects in Demand Analysis: Estimation of the Quadratic Expenditure System Using Microdata. *Rev. Econ. Statist.*, November 1984, 66(4), pp. 591–601. [G: U.S.]

Barnett, William A. On the Flexibility of the Rotterdam Model: A First Empirical Look. *Europ. Econ. Rev.*, April 1984, 24(3), pp. 285–89.

Barthold, Thomas and Plotnick, Robert. Estate Taxation and Other Determinants of Charitable Bequests. *Nat. Tax J.*, June 1984, 37(2), pp. 225–37. [G: U.S.]

Barzelay, Michael and Iusem, Alfredo. Consumer Behavior and Energy Demand Forecasts for the United States: A Synthesis of Neoclassical and Behavioral Approaches Using the Stanford Pilot CESM. *J. Policy Modeling*, August 1984, 6(3), pp. 389–410. [G: U.S.]

Bass, Frank M., et al. An Investigation into the Order of the Brand Choice Process. *Marketing Sci.*, Fall 1984, 3(4), pp. 267–87. [G: U.S.]

Beggs, John J. The Value of Travel to Recreational

Facilities: The Uncertainty Issue. *Int. J. Transport Econ.*, April 1984, *11*(1), pp. 53–59. [G: Australia]

Bellante, Don and Foster, Ann C. Working Wives and Expenditure on Services. *J. Cons. Res.*, September 1984, *11*(2), pp. 700–707. [G: U.S.]

Bemmaor, Albert. Durée de vie des biens durables: modèles et tests. (Life Duration for Consumer Durables: Models and Tests. With English summary.) *Consommation*, July–September 1984, *31*(3), pp. 51–73.

Bera, Anil K.; Jarque, Carlos M. and Lee, Lung-Fei. Testing the Normality Assumption in Limited Dependent Variable Models. *Int. Econ. Rev.*, October 1984, *25*(3), pp. 563–78. [G: Mexico]

Berkowitz, Michael K. and Haines, George H., Jr. The Relationship between Relative Attributes, Relative Preferences, and Market Share: The Case of Solar Energy in Canada. *J. Cons. Res.*, December 1984, *11*(3), pp. 754–62. [G: Canada]

Bernanke, Ben S. Permanent Income, Liquidity, and Expenditure on Automobiles: Evidence from Panel Data. *Quart. J. Econ.*, August 1984, *99*(3), pp. 587–614. [G: U.S.]

Berndt, Ernst R. and Samaniego, Ricardo. Residential Electricity Demand in Mexico: A Model Distinguishing Access from Consumption. *Land Econ.*, August 1984, *60*(3), pp. 268–77. [G: Mexico]

Bhagavan, M. R. Angola. In *O'Keefe, P. and Munslow, B., eds., Part I*, 1984, pp. 5–63. [G: Angola]

Bharier, Julian. Energy Demand Management. In *Baum, V., et al.*, 1984, pp. 25–35. [G: LDCs]

Biehn, Gary Paul. Study on the Demand for New Automobiles: 1947–1979. *Amer. Econ.*, Spring 1984, *28*(1), pp. 74–79. [G: U.S.]

Binswanger, Hans P.; Quizon, Jaime B. and Swamy, Gurushri. The Demand for Food and Foodgrain Quality in India. *Indian Econ. J.*, April–June 1984, *31*(4), pp. 73–96. [G: India]

Blackburn, Joseph and Clancy, Kevin. An Empirical Comparison of Awareness Forecasting Models of New Product Introduction: Comment. *Marketing Sci.*, Summer 1984, *3*(3), pp. 198–201. [G: U.S.]

Blair, Roger D.; Kaserman, David L. and Tepel, Richard C. The Impact of Improved Mileage on Gasoline Consumption. *Econ. Inquiry*, April 1984, *22*(2), pp. 209–17. [G: U.S.]

Blandford, David. Changes in Food Consumption Patterns in the OECD Area. *Europ. Rev. Agr. Econ.*, 1984, *11*(1), pp. 43–64. [G: OECD]

Bloch, Harry and Wirth, Michael. The Demand for Pay Services on Cable Television. *Info. Econ. Policy*, 1984, *1*(4), pp. 311–32. [G: U.S.]

Blundell, Richard and Ray, Ranjan. Testing for Linear Engel Curves and Additively Separable Preferences Using a New Flexible Demand System. *Econ. J.*, December 1984, *94*(376), pp. 800–811. [G: U.K.]

Bockstael, Nancy E. Uncertainty about Consumption and Consumer Uncertainty. *Marine Resource Econ.*, 1984, *1*(1), pp. 67–76.

Bohn, Roger E.; Caramanis, Michael C. and Schweppe, Fred C. Optimal Pricing in Electrical Networks over Space and Time. *Rand J. Econ.*, Autumn 1984, *15*(3), pp. 360–76. [G: U.S.]

Bolyard, Joan E. International Travel and Passenger Fares, 1983. *Surv. Curr. Bus.*, May 1984, *64*(5), pp. 11–15. [G: U.S.]

Bond, Eric W. Test of the Lemons Model: Reply [A Direct Test of the 'Lemons' Model: The Market for Used Pickup Trucks]. *Amer. Econ. Rev.*, September 1984, *74*(4), pp. 801–04. [G: U.S.]

Bradbury, Malcolm. Supply and Demand. In *Sandford, C. and Bradbury, M., eds.*, 1984, pp. 1–26. [G: U.K.]

Brambilla, Francesco. Inchiesta sul mercato dell'antiquariato in Italia. Un modello interpretativo. (An Inquiry into the Antiques Market in Italy. An Interpretive Model. With English summary.) *Giorn. Econ.*, January–February 1984, *43*(1–2), pp. 3–35. [G: Italy]

Bresnahan, Timothy F. Comment on "Conjoint Analysis of Price Premiums for Hotel Amenities." *J. Bus.*, Part 2, January 1984, *57*(1), pp. S133–38.

Bronsard, Camille and Salvas-Bronsard, Lise. On Price Exogeneity in Complete Demand Systems. *J. Econometrics*, March 1984, *24*(3), pp. 235–47. [G: U.S.; Canada]

Brown, Gardner M., Jr. and Mendelsohn, Robert. The Hedonic Travel Cost Method. *Rev. Econ. Statist.*, August 1984, *66*(3), pp. 427–33. [G: U.S.]

Brown, Mark G. and Johnson, S. R. Equivalent Scales, Scale Economies, and Food Stamp Allotments: Estimates from the Nationwide Food Consumption Survey, 1977–78. *Amer. J. Agr. Econ.*, August 1984, *66*(3), pp. 286–93. [G: U.S.]

Burch, Susan W. and Gordon, Stephen E. The Michigan Surveys and the Demand for Consumers Durables. *Bus. Econ.*, October 1984, *19*(5), pp. 40–44. [G: U.S.]

Byron, R. P. On the Flexibility of the Rotterdam Model. *Europ. Econ. Rev.*, April 1984, *24*(3), pp. 273–83.

Capps, Oral, Jr. and Havlicek, Joseph, Jr. National and Regional Household Demand for Meat, Poultry and Seafood: A Complete Systems Approach. *Can. J. Agr. Econ.*, March 1984, *32*(1), pp. 93–108.

Carpenter, Edwin H. and Chester, S. Theodore, Jr. Are Federal Energy Tax Credits Effective? A Western United States Survey. *Energy J.*, April 1984, *5*(2), pp. 139–49. [G: U.S.]

Caves, Douglas W.; Christensen, Laurits R. and Herriges, Joseph A. Consistency of Residential Customer Response in Time-of-Use Electricity Pricing Experiments. *J. Econometrics*, September/October 1984, *26*(1/2), pp. 179–203. [G: U.S.]

Caves, Douglas W.; Christensen, Laurits R. and

Herriges, Joseph A. Modelling Alternative Residential Peak-Load Electricity Rate Structures. *J. Econometrics*, March 1984, *24*(3), pp. 249–68. [G: U.S.]

Caves, Douglas W., et al. A Comparison of Different Methodologies in a Case Study of Residential Time-of-Use Electricity Pricing: Cost–Benefit Analysis. *J. Econometrics*, September/October 1984, *26*(1/2), pp. 17–34. [G: U.S.]

Cha, Dong-deuck and Saklas, James G. Integration of Choice Set Reduction in Behavioral Choice Travel Demand Models. In *Avula, X. J. R., et al.*, 1984, pp. 853–59.

Charney, Alberta H. and Woodard, Gary C. A Test of Consumer Demand Response to Water Prices: Comment [Urban Residential Demand for Water in the United States: Further Discussion]. *Land Econ.*, November 1984, *60*(4), pp. 414–16. [G: U.S.]

Cheema, Aftab Ahmad and Malik, Muhammad Hussain. Consumption and Employment Effects of Income Redistribution in Pakistan. *Pakistan Devel. Rev.*, Summer-Autumn 1984, *23*(2&3), pp. 347–59. [G: Pakistan]

Chirarattananon, Surapong. Analysis of Rural Energy Development in Thailand. In *Islam, M. N.; Morse, R. and Soesastro, M. H., eds.*, 1984, pp. 169–240. [G: Thailand]

Claycamp, H. J.; Dodson, Joe A., Jr. and Doughty, N. An Empirical Comparison of Awareness Forecasting Models of New Product Introduction: Comment. *Marketing Sci.*, Summer 1984, *3*(3), pp. 201–02. [G: U.S.]

Collesano, Stephen; Greenwald, Mathew and Katosh, John P. Consumer Information Seeking in Purchasing Life Insurance. In *[Ferber, R.]*, 1984, pp. 199–216. [G: U.S.]

Conrad, Klaus. Konsumnachfrage, Folgekosten und Kostenpreise. (With English summary.) *Z. Wirtschaft. Sozialwissen.*, 1984, *104*(3), pp. 251–68. [G: W. Germany]

Cox, Howard and Smith, Ronald P. Political Approaches to Smoking Control: A Comparative Analysis. *Appl. Econ.*, August 1984, *16*(4), pp. 569–82. [G: OECD]

Crom, Richard. Effects of Simulated Changes in Consumer Preference on the Meat and Poultry Industries. *Agr. Econ. Res.*, Spring 1984, *36*(2), pp. 16–24. [G: U.S.]

Dahl, Carol A. Vertical Equity Effects and Total Consumer Losses for Emergency Allocation Schemes for the Gasoline Market. *Appl. Econ.*, February 1984, *16*(1), pp. 25–32. [G: U.S.]

Dalal, S. R.; Lee, J. C. and Sabavala, D. J. Prediction of Individual Buying Behavior: A Poisson–Bernoulli Model with Arbitrary Heterogeneity. *Marketing Sci.*, Fall 1984, *3*(4), pp. 352–67. [G: U.S.]

Darden, William R. and Lumpkin, James R. Psychographic and Demographic Profile of Convenience Food Store Users: Why People Convenience Shop. *Rev. Bus. Econ. Res.*, Spring 1984, *19*(2), pp. 68–80. [G: U.S.]

De Borger, Bruno L. Household Attributes and the Demand for Private Rental Housing: Com-

ment. *Economica*, August 1984, *51*(203), pp. 351–55. [G: U.K.]

Deaton, Angus and Irish, Margaret. Statistical Models for Zero Expenditures in Household Budgets. *J. Public Econ.*, February/March 1984, *23*(1/2), pp. 59–80. [G: U.K.]

Deb, Nibaran C. and Hossain, Mahabub. Demand for Rural Industries Products in Bangladesh. *Bangladesh Devel. Stud.*, March-June 1984, *12*(1–2), pp. 81–99. [G: Bangladesh]

Decaestecker, J. P. and Mouillart, M. Rationing and Aggregation in a Multi-level Model of Household Behaviour: The S.A.B.I.N.E. Model. In *Ancot, J. P., ed.*, 1984, pp. 63–86. [G: France]

Dodson, Joe A., Jr. An Empirical Comparison of Awareness Forecasting Models of New Product Introduction: Comment. *Marketing Sci.*, Summer 1984, *3*(3), pp. 202. [G: U.S.]

Donnelly, William A. Residential Electricity Demand Modeling in the Australian Capital Territory: Preliminary Results. *Energy J.*, April 1984, *5*(2), pp. 119–31. [G: Australia]

Donnelly, William A. and Saddler, H. D. W. The Retail Demand for Electricity in Tasmania. *Australian Econ. Pap.*, June 1984, *23*(42), pp. 52–60. [G: Tasmania]

Downs, Anthony and Bradbury, Katharine L. What Does It All Mean? In *Downs, A. and Bradbury, K. L., eds.*, 1984, pp. 1–34. [G: U.S.]

Doxsey, Lawrence B. Demand for Unlimited Use Transit Passes. *J. Transp. Econ. Policy*, January 1984, *18*(1), pp. 7–22. [G: U.S.]

Drollas, Leonidas P. The Demand for Gasoline: Further Evidence. *Energy Econ.*, January 1984, *6*(1), pp. 71–82. [G: U.S.; W. Europe]

Dubin, Jeffrey A. and McFadden, Daniel L. An Econometric Analysis of Residential Electric Appliance Holdings and Consumption. *Econometrica*, March 1984, *52*(2), pp. 345–62. [G: U.S.]

Dumnov, D. and Dmitrichev, I. From the History of Studying Family Budgets. *Prob. Econ.*, August 1984, *27*(4), pp. 78–85. [G: U.S.S.R.]

Einhorn, Michael. FEA Efficiency Standards and Energy Usage: Resolving Khazzoom versus Besen and Johnson [Economic Implications of Mandated Efficiency Standards for Household Appliances]. *Energy J.*, January 1984, *5*(1), pp. 173–76.

Ellis, James E., et al. Aspects of Energy Consumption in a Pastoral Ecosystem: Wood Use by the South Turkana. In *Barnes, C.; Ensminger, J. and O'Keefe, P., eds.*, 1984, pp. 164–87. [G: Kenya]

Ellman, Michael. Soviet Grain Imports and the Weather. In *Ellman, M.*, 1984, pp. 97–107. [G: U.S.S.R.]

Ensminger, Jean. Monetization of the Galole Orma Economy: Changes in the Use of Fuel and Woodstock. In *Barnes, C.; Ensminger, J. and O'Keefe, P., eds.*, 1984, pp. 124–40. [G: Kenya]

Erickson, Gary M.; Johansson, Johny K. and Chao, Paul. Image Variables in Multi-Attribute Product Evaluations: Country-of-Origin Effects. *J. Cons. Res.*, September 1984, *11*(2), pp. 694–99. [G: U.S.]

Fong, Chan Onn. Basic Needs and Appropriate Technology in the Malaysian Bicycle Industry. In *van Ginneken, W. and Baron, C., eds.*, 1984, pp. 54–83. [G: Malaysia]

Freund, Deborah Anne. Equality of Opportunity and the Demand for Medical Care by Race. *Quart. Rev. Econ. Bus.*, Spring 1984, *24*(1), pp. 42–55. [G: U.S.]

Fujii, Edwin T. and Mak, James. A Model of Household Electricity Conservation Behavior. *Land Econ.*, November 1984, *60*(4), pp. 340–51. [G: U.S.]

Furse, David H.; Punj, Girish N. and Stewart, David W. A Typology of Individual Search Strategies among Purchasers of New Automobiles. *J. Cons. Res.*, March 1984, *10*(4), pp. 417–31. [G: U.S.]

Gallant, A. Ronald and Koenker, Roger W. Costs and Benefits of Peak-Load Pricing of Electricity: A Continuous-Time Econometric Approach. *J. Econometrics*, September/October 1984, *26*(1/2), pp. 83–113. [G: U.S.]

Gallasch, H. Frederick, Jr. Price Elasticities of Demand at Retail and Wholesale Levels: An Automotive Example. *Bus. Econ.*, January 1984, *19*(1), pp. 61–62.

Garbacz, Christopher. A National Micro-Data Based Model of Residential Electricity Demand: New Evidence on Seasonal Variation. *Southern Econ. J.*, July 1984, *51*(1), pp. 235–49. [G: U.S.]

Garbacz, Christopher. Residential Electricity Demand: A Suggested Appliance Stock Equation. *Energy J.*, April 1984, *5*(2), pp. 151–54. [G: U.S.]

Gardini, Attilio. Modelli stocastici di analisi della domanda: un'applicazione ai consumi alimentari. (Stochastic Models of Demand Analysis: A Study of Food Consumption in Italy. With English summary.) *Statistica*, April–June 1984, *44*(2), pp. 249–70. [G: Italy]

Garen, John. The Returns to Schooling: A Selectivity Bias Approach with a Continuous Choice Variable. *Econometrica*, September 1984, *52*(5), pp. 1199–1218. [G: U.S.]

Gillingham, Robert and Hagemann, Robert P. Household Demand for Fuel Oil. *Appl. Econ.*, August 1984, *16*(4), pp. 475–82. [G: U.S.]

van Ginneken, Wouter. Ireland (1973) In *van Ginneken, W. and Park, J., eds.*, 1984, pp. 83–88. [G: Ireland]

van Ginneken, Wouter. Mexico (1968) In *van Ginneken, W. and Park, J., eds.*, 1984, pp. 95–99. [G: Mexico]

Givon, Moshe. Variety Seeking through Brand Switching. *Marketing Sci.*, Winter 1984, *3*(1), pp. 1–22. [G: U.S.]

Golanty, John L. Clarification of the Tracker Methodology and Limitations [An Empirical Comparison of Awareness Forecasting Models of New Product Introduction]. *Marketing Sci.*, Summer 1984, *3*(3), pp. 203. [G: U.S.]

Goldberg, Stephen M.; Green, Paul E. and

Wind, Yoram. Conjoint Analysis of Price Premiums for Hotel Amenities. *J. Bus.*, Part 2, January 1984, *57*(1), pp. S111–32.

Goodhardt, G. J.; Ehrenberg, A. S. C. and Chatfield, C. The Dirichlet: A Comprehensive Model of Buying Behaviour. *J. Roy. Statist. Soc.*, 1984, *147*(5), pp. 621–43. [G: U.K.]

Goodman, Allen C. and Kawai, Masahiro. Estimation and Policy Implications of Rental Housing Demand. *J. Urban Econ.*, July 1984, *16*(1), pp. 76–90. [G: U.S.]

Graham, John W. and Green, Carole A. Estimating the Parameters of a Household Production Function with Joint Products. *Rev. Econ. Statist.*, May 1984, *66*(2), pp. 277–82. [G: U.S.]

Greene, David L. and Roberts, Glenn F. Fuel Consumption for Road Transport in the USA— A Comment. *Energy Econ.*, April 1984, *6*(2), pp. 145–47. [G: U.S.]

Greenlees, John S. and Zieschang, Kimberly D. Grouping Tests for Misspecification: An Application to Housing Demand. *J. Bus. Econ. Statist.*, April 1984, *2*(2), pp. 159–69. [G: U.S.]

Guillaume, Y., et al. Etude des incitants financiers aux économies d'énergie dans le secteur domestique. Le cas de la Belgique. (Energy Saving Is One of the Major Economic Problems of This Period. Governments Try to Encourage It by Various Measures. With English summary.) *Cah. Écon. Bruxelles*, 1st Trimester 1984, (101), pp. 57–73. [G: Belgium]

Hansen, Gerd. Der Einfluss Zinsen und Preisen auf die Ersparnisse und die Nachfrage nach dauerhaften Gütern in der Bundesrepublik, 1961–1981. (With English summary.) *Z. Wirtschaft. Sozialwissen.*, 1984, *104*(3), pp. 227–49. [G: W. Germany]

Hartman, Raymond S. The Importance of Technology and Fuel Choice in the Analysis of Utility-sponsored Conservation Strategies for Residential Water Heating. *Energy J.*, July 1984, *5*(3), pp. 99–118. [G: U.S.]

Hassan, Zuhair A. and Johnson, S. R. Consumer Demand Analysis at Agriculture Canada—Past and Future. *Can. J. Agr. Econ.*, March 1984, *32*(1), pp. 125–40. [G: Canada]

Haugerud, Angelique. Economy, Ecology and the Unequal Impact of Woodfuel Scarcity in Embu, Kenya. In *Barnes, C.; Ensminger, J. and O'Keefe, P., eds.*, 1984, pp. 79–101. [G: Kenya]

Hauser, John R. and Gaskin, Steven P. Application of the "Defender" Consumer Model. *Marketing Sci.*, Fall 1984, *3*(4), pp. 327–51. [G: U.S.]

Hausman, Jerry A. and Trimble, John. Appliance Purchase and Usage Adaptation to a Permanent Time-of-Day Electricity Rate Schedule. *J. Econometrics*, September/October 1984, *26*(1/2), pp. 115–39. [G: U.S.]

Hay, Joel W. Variation in U.S. Per Capita Pharmaceutical Expenditures: Are Drugs Health Care Complements or Substitutes? In *Lindgren, B., ed.*, 1984, pp. 21–35. [G: U.S.]

Heckman, James J. and Singer, Burton. Econometric Duration Analysis. *J. Econometrics*, January/February 1984, *24*(1/2), pp. 63–132.

Hensher, David A. and Louviere, J. J. Towards an Approach to Forecasting Attendance at Unique Events Using a Discrete Choice Model and Experimental Design Data. In *Pitfield, D. E., ed.,* 1984, pp. 67–87. [G: Australia]

Henson, Steven E. Electricity Demand Estimates under Increasing-Block Rates. *Southern Econ. J.,* July 1984, *51*(1), pp. 147–56. [G: U.S.]

Hershey, John C., et al. Health Insurance under Competition: Would People Choose What Is Expected? *Inquiry,* Winter 1984, *21*(4), pp. 349–60. [G: U.S.]

Hjorth-Andersen, Christian. The Concept of Quality and the Efficiency of Markets for Consumer Products. *J. Cons. Res.,* September 1984, *11*(2), pp. 708–18. [G: U.S.]

Hoffer, George E. and Reilly, Robert J. Automobile Styling as a Shift Variable: An Investigation by Firm and by Industry. *Appl. Econ.,* April 1984, *16*(2), pp. 291–97. [G: U.S.]

Holbrook, Morris B., et al. Play as a Consumption Experience: The Roles of Emotions, Performance, and Personality in the Enjoyment of Games. *J. Cons. Res.,* September 1984, *11*(2), pp. 728–39.

Horsky, Dan. Comments on "Conjoint Analysis of Price Premiums for Hotel Amenities." *J. Bus.,* Part 2, January 1984, *57*(1), pp. S139–47.

Hosier, Richard. Domestic Energy Consumption in Rural Kenya: Results of a Nationwide Survey. In *Barnes, C.; Ensminger, J. and O'Keefe, P., eds.,* 1984, pp. 14–60. [G: Kenya]

Hosier, Richard. Zimbabwe. In *O'Keefe, P. and Munslow, B., eds., Part II,* 1984, pp. 171–210. [G: Zimbabwe]

House, William J. Product Choice and Employment in Furniture-making in Kenya. In *van Ginneken, W. and Baron, C., eds.,* 1984, pp. 148–67. [G: Kenya]

Howrey, E. Philip and Varian, Hal R. Estimating the Distributional Impact of Time-of-Day Pricing of Electricity. *J. Econometrics,* September/October 1984, *26*(1/2), pp. 65–82. [G: U.S.]

Hutton, Sandra. Domestic Fuel Expenditure: An Analysis of Three National Surveys. *Energy Econ.,* January 1984, *6*(1), pp. 52–58. [G: U.K.]

Ihlanfeldt, Keith R. Property Taxation and the Demand for Housing: An Econometric Analysis. *J. Urban Econ.,* September 1984, *16*(2), pp. 208–24. [G: U.S.]

Imhoff, Evert. Estimation of Demand Systems Using Both Time Series and Cross Section Data. *De Economist,* 1984, *132*(4), pp. 419–39. [G: Netherlands]

Iqbal, Mahmood. Residential Energy Demand: A Case Study of Pakistan. *J. Econ. Stud.,* 1984, *11*(1), pp. 40–48. [G: Pakistan]

Ironmonger, Duncan; Manning, Ian G. and Tran, Van Hoa. Longitudinal Working Models: Estimates of Household Energy Consumption in Australia. *Energy Econ.,* January 1984, *6*(1), pp. 41–46. [G: Australia]

Jackson, Laurence Fraser. Hierarchic Demand and the Engel Curve for Variety. *Rev. Econ. Statist.,* February 1984, *66*(1), pp. 8–15. [G: U.S.]

Jaffee, Dwight M. New Residential Construction and Energy Costs. In *Downs, A. and Bradbury, K. L., eds.,* 1984, pp. 143–84. [G: U.S.]

James, Jeffrey. Technology, Products and Income Distribution: The Soap Market in Barbados. In *van Ginneken, W. and Baron, C., eds.,* 1984, pp. 168–94. [G: Barbados]

Jensen, Cynthia L. Wood Use by the Amboseli Maasai. In *Barnes, C.; Ensminger, J. and O'Keefe, P., eds.,* 1984, pp. 188–204. [G: Kenya]

Jimenez, Emmanuel and Keare, Douglas H. Housing Consumption and Permanent Income in Developing Countries: Estimates from Panel Data in El Salvador. *J. Urban Econ.,* March 1984, *15*(2), pp. 172–94. [G: El Salvador]

Jones, C. Vaughan and Morris, John R. Instrumental Price Estimates and Residential Water Demand. *Water Resources Res.,* February 1984, *20*(2), pp. 197–202. [G: U.S.]

Kabir, M. and Ridler, N. B. The Demand for Atlantic Salmon in Canada. *Can. J. Agr. Econ.,* November 1984, *32*(3), pp. 560–68. [G: Canada]

Karp, Larry. Demand for Energy and Insulation. *Energy Econ.,* July 1984, *6*(3), pp. 208–10.

Kiefer, Nicholas M. Microeconometric Evidence on the Neoclassical Model of Demand. *J. Econometrics,* July 1984, *25*(3), pp. 285–302. [G: Belgium]

Kim, Kyoo H. Price Elasticity of Demand at Retail and Wholesale: A Comment. *Bus. Econ.,* October 1984, *19*(5), pp. 62.

Kohler, Daniel F. and Mitchell, Bridger M. Response to Residential Time-of-Use Electricity Rates: How Transferable Are the Findings? *J. Econometrics,* September/October 1984, *26*(1/2), pp. 141–77. [G: U.S.]

Kouris, George. Fuel Consumption for Road Transport in the USA—A Reply. *Energy Econ.,* April 1984, *6*(2), pp. 148. [G: U.S.]

Kuo, Shirley W. Y. Urbanization and Income Distribution: The Case of Taiwan, 1966–1980. In *[Chenery, H. B.],* 1984, pp. 217–34. [G: Taiwan]

Kurz, Mordecai. Capital Accumulation and the Characteristics of Private Inter-Generational Transfers. *Economica,* February 1984, *51*(201), pp. 1–22. [G: U.S.]

La Croix, Sumner J. Marketing, Price Discrimination, and Welfare: Reply. *Southern Econ. J.,* January 1984, *50*(3), pp. 900–901. [G: U.S.]

Lahiri, A. K. Non-luxurious Money, Secular Behaviour of Velocity and Implications for Development Planning. *Indian Econ. J.,* July–Sept. 1984, *32*(1), pp. 94–99.

Landgren-Gudina, Marie-Ann. Weaning Food and Low-income Consumers in Ethiopia. In *van Ginneken, W. and Baron, C., eds.,* 1984, pp. 195–210. [G: Ethiopia]

Lange, Mark D. and Luksetich, William A. Demand Elasticities for Symphony Orchestras. *J. Cult. Econ.*, June 1984, *8*(1), pp. 29–47.
[G: U.S.]

Larsen, Hans Kryger and Nilsson, Carl-Axel. Consumption and Production of Bicycles in Denmark, 1890–1980. *Scand. Econ. Hist. Rev.*, 1984, *32*(3), pp. 143–58. [G: Denmark]

Lerviks, Alf-Erik. The Predictive Accuracy of a Combined Segmentation-Diffusion Model for New Consumer Durables. *Liiketaloudellinen Aikak.*, 1984, *33*(1), pp. 3–22. [G: Finland]

Leu, Robert E. Anti-smoking Publicity, Taxation, and the Demand for Cigarettes. *J. Health Econ.*, August 1984, *3*(2), pp. 101–16.
[G: Switzerland]

Levedahl, J. William. Marketing, Price Discrimination, and Welfare: Comment. *Southern Econ. J.*, January 1984, *50*(3), pp. 886–91.
[G: U.S.]

Levin, Irwin P. and Johnson, Richard D. Estimating Price–Quality Tradeoffs Using Comparative Judgments. *J. Cons. Res.*, June 1984, *11*(1), pp. 593–600. [G: U.S.]

Lustig, Nora. Distribution of Income, Food Consumption, and Fiscal Cost of Alternative Policy Options. In *Aspe, P. and Sigmund, P. E., eds.*, 1984, pp. 439–79. [G: Mexico]

Mahajan, Vijay; Muller, Eitan and Sharma, Subhash. An Empirical Comparison of Awareness Forecasting Models of New Product Introduction. *Marketing Sci.*, Summer 1984, *3*(3), pp. 179–97. [G: U.S.]

Mahajan, Vijay; Muller, Eitan and Sharma, Subhash. Reflections on Awareness Forecasting Models of New Product Introduction: Rejoinder. *Marketing Sci.*, Summer 1984, *3*(3), pp. 205–06. [G: U.S.]

Martynov, A. V. and Solov'ev, Iu. P. A Mathematical and Economic Analysis of the Time Path of Major Consumer Purchases and Household Savings. *Matekon*, Spring 1984, *20*(3), pp. 59–73. [G: U.S.S.R.]

Mathur, Vijay K. Effectiveness of Building Energy Performance Standards to Curtail Household Energy Demand: A Theoretical Analysis. *Energy J.*, January 1984, *5*(1), pp. 99–114.

McCarthy, Patrick S. The Shared Vehicle Fleet: A Study of Its Impact upon Accessibility and Vehicle Ownership. *J. Transp. Econ. Policy*, January 1984, *18*(1), pp. 75–94. [G: U.S.]

McMahon, Walter W. Why Families Invest in Education. In *[Ferber, R.]*, 1984, pp. 75–91.
[G: U.S.]

Mehran, F. Islamic Republic of Iran (1973–74) In *van Ginneken, W. and Park, J., eds.*, 1984, pp. 75–81. [G: Iran]

Mellor, John W. and Johnston, Bruce F. The World Food Equation: Interrelations among Development, Employment, and Food Consumption. *J. Econ. Lit.*, June 1984, *22*(2), pp. 53–74. [G: Global]

Mendelsohn, Robert. Estimating the Structural Equations of Implicit Markets and Household Production Functions. *Rev. Econ. Statist.*, November 1984, *66*(4), pp. 673–77.

Metwally, Mokhtar M. and Tamaschke, H. U. The Effect of Inflation on the Patterns of Consumption. *Indian Econ. J.*, July–Sept. 1984, *32*(1), pp. 81–93. [G: Europe; Japan; U.S.]

Moe, R. J. and Adams, R. C. Residential Energy Use and Improved Building Thermal Efficiency: An Econometric Analysis. In *Lev, B., et al., eds.*, 1984, pp. 135–49. [G: U.S.]

Morey, Edward R. The Choice of Ski Areas: Estimation of a Generalized CES Preference Ordering with Characteristics. *Rev. Econ. Statist.*, November 1984, *66*(4), pp. 584–90.
[G: U.S.]

Morse, Richard, et al. Organizing Current Information for Rural Energy and Development Planning. In *Islam, M. N.; Morse, R. and Soesastro, M. H., eds.*, 1984, pp. 473–518.
[G: Asian LDCs]

Mubin, A. K. A. and Forsyth, David J. C. Technology, Employment and Income Distribution: The Soap Industry in Bangladesh. In *van Ginneken, W. and Baron, C., eds.*, 1984, pp. 14–53. [G: Bangladesh]

Mung'ala, Patrick Mutula and Openshaw, Keith. Estimation of Present and Future demand for Woodfuel in the Machakos District. In *Barnes, C.; Ensminger, J. and O'Keefe, P., eds.*, 1984, pp. 102–23. [G: Kenya]

Munslow, Barry. Swaziland. In *O'Keefe, P. and Munslow, B., eds., Part II*, 1984, pp. 49–85.
[G: Swaziland]

Murfin, Andy. Market Shares in the UK Passenger Car Market: Marketing, Expenditure and Price Effects, 1975–80. *Appl. Econ.*, August 1984, *16*(4), pp. 611–32. [G: U.K.]

Murray, Jane. Retail Demand for Meat in Australia: A Utility Theory Approach. *Econ. Rec.*, March 1984, *60*(168), pp. 45–56.
[G: Australia]

Narasimhan, Chakravarthi. A Price Discrimination Theory of Coupons. *Marketing Sci.*, Spring 1984, *3*(2), pp. 128–47. [G: U.S.]

Nguyen, The-Hiep. On Energy Coefficients and Ratios. *Energy Econ.*, April 1984, *6*(2), pp. 102–09. [G: OECD]

Olsen, Marvin E. and Cluett, Christopher. Public Willingness to Invest in Household Weatherization. *Energy J.*, January 1984, *5*(1), pp. 165–68.

Opaluch, James J. A Test of Consumer Demand Response to Water Prices: Reply [Urban Residential Demand for Water in the United States: Further Discussion]. *Land Econ.*, November 1984, *60*(4), pp. 417–21. [G: U.S.]

Openshaw, Keith. Tanzania. In *O'Keefe, P. and Munslow, B., eds., Part II*, 1984, pp. 87–132.
[G: Tanzania]

Oren, Shmuel S. and Rothkopf, Michael H. A Market Dynamics Model for New Industrial Products and Its Application. *Marketing Sci.*, Summer 1984, *3*(3), pp. 247–65.

Palmquist, Raymond B. Estimating the Demand for the Characteristics of Housing. *Rev. Econ. Statist.*, August 1984, *66*(3), pp. 394–404.
[G: U.S.]

Pandey, R. K. and Sarin, B. S. Estimation of

Demand for Foodgrains in Uttar Pradesh. *Margin*, April 1984, *16*(3), pp. 70–76. **[G: India]**

Papola, T. S. and Sinha, R. C. Metal Household Utensils and Basic Needs in India. In *van Ginneken, W. and Baron, C.*, eds., 1984, pp. 84–119. **[G: India]**

Parks, Richard W. and Weitzel, David. Measuring the Consumer Welfare Effects of Time-differentiated Electricity Prices. *J. Econometrics*, September/October 1984, *26*(1/2), pp. 35–64. **[G: U.S.]**

Partch, M. Megan. An Analysis of Household Expenditures on Durables in 1970 and 1977: The Effect of Selection Bias. *Appl. Econ.*, August 1984, *16*(4), pp. 497–506. **[G: U.S.]**

Perlov, Diane Catherine. Exploiting the Forest: Patterns and Perceptions in Highland Samburu. In *Barnes, C.; Ensminger, J. and O'Keefe, P.*, eds., 1984, pp. 141–63. **[G: Kenya]**

Phlips, Louis and Spinnewyn, Frans. True Indexes and Rational Habit Formation. *Europ. Econ. Rev.*, March 1984, *24*(2), pp. 209–23. **[G: U.S.]**

Pitts, Robert E. and Skelly, Gerald U. Economic Self-Interest and Other Motivational Factors Underlying Charitable Giving. *J. Behav. Econ.*, Winter 1984, *13*(2), pp. 93–109. **[G: U.S.]**

Planning Ser., Ministry of Energy, Philippines. Philippine Rural Energy Resource and Consumption Survey. In *Islam, M. N.; Morse, R. and Soesastro, M. H.*, eds., 1984, pp. 135–68. **[G: Philippines]**

Plaut, Steven E. Endogenous Mortgage Interest and the Consumption of Housing. *J. Urban Econ.*, July 1984, *16*(1), pp. 31–45.

Polasek, Wolfgang. Extreme Bound Analysis for Residential Load Curve Models: Empirical Evidence for a 16-Household Example. *Empirical Econ.*, 1984, *9*(3), pp. 165–81. **[G: U.S.]**

Polasek, Wolfgang. Multivariate Regression Systems. In *Kadane, J. B.*, ed., 1984, pp. 231–309. **[G: U.S.]**

Polzin, Paul E. The Specification of Price in Studies of Consumer Demand under Block Price Scheduling: Additional Empirical Evidence. *Land Econ.*, August 1984, *60*(3), pp. 306–09. **[G: U.S.]**

Pratt, Michael D. and Hoffer, George E. Test of the Lemons Model: Comment [A Direct Test of the 'Lemons' Model: The Market for Used Pickup Trucks]. *Amer. Econ. Rev.*, September 1984, *74*(4), pp. 798–800. **[G: U.S.]**

Pringle, Lewis G. An Audience Flow Model of Television Viewing Choice: A Comment. *Marketing Sci.*, Spring 1984, *3*(2), pp. 125–26. **[G: U.S.]**

Pringle, Lewis G.; Wilson, R. Dale and Brody, Edward I. Issues in Comparing the Awareness Component of New Product Models. *Marketing Sci.*, Summer 1984, *3*(3), pp. 203–05. **[G: U.S.]**

Quigley, John M. Residential Energy Standards and the Housing Market: A Regional Analysis.

Int. Reg. Sci. Rev., December 1984, *9*(3), pp. 201–16. **[G: U.S.]**

Quigley, John M. The Production of Housing Services and the Derived Demand for Residential Energy. *Rand J. Econ.*, Winter 1984, *15*(4), pp. 555–67. **[G: U.S.]**

Reinhard, Michael. Sättigung, privater Verbrauch und Konsumgüterinnovation—Das Beispiel der Informationstechnik. (Saturation, Private Consumption, and Consumer Good Innovation—The Example of Information Technology. With English summary.) *Ifo-Studien*, 1984, *30*(3), pp. 209–29. **[G: W. Germany]**

Ring, Raymond J., Jr. The Effect of Permanent Income on Retail Sales by Sales Category. *Quart. J. Bus. Econ.*, Autumn 1984, *23*(4), pp. 13–30. **[G: U.S.]**

Rossiter, Louis F. and Wilensky, Gail R. Identification of Physician-Induced Demand. *J. Human Res.*, Spring 1984, *19*(2), pp. 231–44. **[G: U.S.]**

Roy, C. R. Consumer Behaviour under Partial Rationing. *Margin*, July 1984, *16*(4), pp. 48–63. **[G: India]**

Rust, Roland T. and Alpert, Mark I. An Audience Flow Model of Television Viewing Choice. *Marketing Sci.*, Spring 1984, *3*(2), pp. 113–24. **[G: U.S.]**

Rust, Roland T. and Alpert, Mark I. On Establishing a Dialogue in Television Viewing Research. *Marketing Sci.*, Spring 1984, *3*(2), pp. 126–27. **[G: U.S.]**

Sa-Aadu, Jarjisu. Another Look at the Economics of Demand-Side versus Supply-Side Strategies in Low-Income Housing. *Amer. Real Estate Urban Econ. Assoc. J.*, Winter 1984, *12*(4), pp. 427–60. **[G: U.S.]**

Salvas-Bronsard, Lise and Bastien, Ernest. A Note on the Estimation of Complete Demand Systems from Canadian Household Budget Data. *Can. J. Econ.*, February 1984, *17*(1), pp. 48–61. **[G: Canada]**

Santerre, Michael T. Financial and Resource Analyses of Anaerobic Digestion (Biogas) Systems. In *Islam, M. N.; Morse, R. and Soesastro, M. H.*, eds., 1984, pp. 415–71. **[G: China; India; Asian LDCs]**

Sapounas, George. Household Expenditudre in Greece: The Case of Socioeconomic Groups. *Greek Econ. Rev.*, August 1984, *6*(2), pp. 233–48. **[G: Greece]**

Saros, Georg. A Model for Planning Energy Requirements for Residential Heating. *Energy Econ.*, July 1984, *6*(3), pp. 202–07. **[G: Sweden]**

Saulter, Kenneth J. Home Energy Costs and the Housing of the Poor and the Elderly: Comment. In *Downs, A. and Bradbury, K. L.*, eds., 1984, pp. 78–84. **[G: U.S.]**

Sav, G. Thomas. Micro Engineering Foundations of Energy–Capital Complementarity: Solar Domestic Water Heaters. *Rev. Econ. Statist.*, May 1984, *66*(2), pp. 334–38. **[G: U.S.]**

Schloss, Nathan. Use of Employment Data to Es-

timate Office Space Demand. *Mon. Lab. Rev.*, December 1984, *107*(12), pp. 40–44.
[G: U.S.]

Scobey, Richard. Malawi. In *O'Keefe, P. and Munslow, B., eds., Part I,* 1984, pp. 171–86.
[G: Malawi]

Secrest, T. J. Economic and Energy End-Use Assessment. In *Lev, B., et al., eds.,* 1984, pp. 185–200.
[G: U.S.]

Sheehan, Robert J. New Residential Construction and Energy Costs: Comment. In *Downs, A. and Bradbury, K. L., eds.,* 1984, pp. 184–87.
[G: U.S.]

Sherden, William A. An Analysis of the Determinants of the Demand for Automobile Insurance. *J. Risk Ins.*, March 1984, *51*(1), pp. 49–62.
[G: U.S.]

Shmueli, A. and Tapiero, Charles S. Adaptive Econometric Forecasting by an Approximate Filtering-Smoothing Algorithm: The Case of the Israeli Meat Sector. In *Hughes Hallet, A.J., ed.,* 1984, pp. 63–84.
[G: Israel]

Shonkwiler, J. S. and Taylor, Timothy G. The Implications of Estimating Market Demand Curves by Least Squares Regression. *Europ. Rev. Agr. Econ.*, 1984, *11*(1), pp. 107–18.
[G: U.S.]

Shore, Haim. Summer Time and Electricity Conservation: The Israeli Case. *Energy J.*, April 1984, *5*(2), pp. 53–70.
[G: Israel]

Skinner, Steven J. and Dubinsky, Alan J. Purchasing Insurance: Predictors of Family Decision-making Responsibility. *J. Risk Ins.*, September 1984, *51*(3), pp. 513–23.
[G: U.S.]

Smallwood, David and Blaylock, James. Scaling Household Nutrient Data. *Agr. Econ. Res.*, January 1984, *36*(1), pp. 12–22.
[G: U.S.]

Solís, Leopoldo. Food Marketing and Income Distribution. In *Aspe, P. and Sigmund, P. E., eds.,* 1984, pp. 481–522.
[G: Mexico]

Stapleton, David C. Errors-in-Variables in Demand Systems. *J. Econometrics*, December 1984, *26*(3), pp. 255–70.
[G: U.K.]

Strauss, John. Joint Determination of Food Consumption and Production in Rural Sierra Leone: Estimates of a Household-Firm Model. *J. Devel. Econ.*, January–February 1984, *14*(1–2), pp. 77–103.
[G: Sierra Leone]

Struyk, Raymond J. Home Energy Costs and the Housing of the Poor and the Elderly. In *Downs, A. and Bradbury, K. L., eds.,* 1984, pp. 35–78.
[G: U.S.]

Sudman, Seymour and Lannom, Linda Bean. Methods for Collecting Health Behavior and Expenditure Data. In *[Ferber, R.],* 1984, pp. 329–54.
[G: U.S.]

Susman, Paul. Zambia. In *O'Keefe, P. and Munslow, B., eds., Part II,* 1984, pp. 133–70.
[G: Zambia]

Sweeney, James L. The Response of Energy Demand to Higher Prices: What Have We Learned? *Amer. Econ. Rev.*, May 1984, *74*(2), pp. 31–37.
[G: U.S.]

Thobani, Mateen. Passenger Transport in Karachi. In *van Ginneken, W. and Baron, C., eds.,* 1984, pp. 211–37.
[G: Pakistan]

Thom, D. Rodney. The Demand for Alcohol in Ireland. *Econ. Soc. Rev.*, July 1984, *15*(4), pp. 325–36.
[G: U.K.]

Timmermans, H. J. P. Discrete Choice Models versus Decompositional Multiattribute Preference Models: A Comparative Analysis of Model Performance in the Context of Spatial Shopping-Behaviour. In *Pitfield, D. E., ed.,* 1984, pp. 88–101.
[G: Netherlands]

Tishler, Asher and Zilcha, Itzhak. A Model of the Household's Demand for Durables and Energy. *Scand. J. Econ.*, 1984, *86*(4), pp. 411–22.

Urban, Glen L.; Johnson, Philip L. and Hauser, John R. Testing Competitive Market Structures. *Marketing Sci.*, Spring 1984, *3*(2), pp. 83–112.
[G: U.S.]

Uri, Noel D. Interbeverage Substitution in the United States. *J. Behav. Econ.*, Winter 1984, *13*(2), pp. 135–54.
[G: U.S.]

Venanzoni, Giuseppe. I consumi sanitari privati in Italia 1973–1982. (Private Health Care Consumption in Italy, 1973–1982. With English summary.) *Statistica*, July–September 1984, *44*(3), pp. 473–99.
[G: Italy]

Venezia, Itzhak. Aspects of Optimal Automobile Insurance. *J. Risk Ins.*, March 1984, *51*(1), pp. 63–79.

Venti, Steven F. and Wise, David A. Moving and Housing Expenditure: Transaction Costs and Disequilibrium. *J. Public Econ.*, February/March 1984, *23*(1/2), pp. 207–43.
[G: U.S.]

Versztovsek, Radmila. The Effect of Price Increases on the Average Food Consumption and on the Nutrition Standards of Social Groups in Hungary. *Acta Oecon.*, 1984, *32*(1–2), pp. 163–74.
[G: Hungary]

Vickerman, R. W. and Barmby, T. A. The Structure of Shopping Travel: Some Developments of the Trip Generation Model. *J. Transp. Econ. Policy*, May 1984, *18*(2), pp. 109–21.
[G: U.S.]

Walsh, Richard G.; Loomis, John B. and Gillman, Richard A. Valuing Option, Existence, and Bequest Demands for Wilderness. *Land Econ.*, February 1984, *60*(1), pp. 14–29.
[G: U.S.]

Ward, Frank A. Specification Considerations for the Price Variable in Travel Cost Demand Models. *Land Econ.*, August 1984, *60*(3), pp. 301–05.

Warner, Kenneth E. Publicity, Price, and Puffing: A Health Economics Contribution to Disease Prevention. *J. Health Econ.*, August 1984, *3*(2), pp. 179–86.
[G: Switzerland]

Waugh, Frederick V. A Partial Indifference Surface for Beef and Pork. In *Waugh, F. V.,* 1984, *1956*, pp. 52–62.
[G: U.S.]

Waugh, Frederick V. Regressions between Sets of Variables. In *Waugh, F. V.,* 1984, *1942*, pp. 251–71.
[G: U.S.; Canada]

Waugh, Frederick V. The Marginal Utility of Money in the United States from 1917 to 1921 and from 1922 to 1932. In *Waugh, F. V.,* 1984, *1935*, pp. 3–26.
[G: U.S.]

Westley, Glenn D. Electricity Demand in a Developing Country. *Rev. Econ. Statist.*, August 1984, *66*(3), pp. 459–67.   [G: Paraguay]

Wiest, Raymond E. External Dependency and the Perpetuation of Temporary Migration to the United States. In *Jones, R. C., ed.*, 1984, pp. 110–35.   [G: U.S.; Mexico]

Winston, Clifford and Mannering, Fred. Consumer Demand for Automobile Safety. *Amer. Econ. Rev.*, May 1984, *74*(2), pp. 316–19.
                 [G: U.S.]

Winters, L. Alan. British Imports of Manufactures and the Common Market. *Oxford Econ. Pap.*, March 1984, *36*(1), pp. 103–18.   [G: U.K.; EEC]

Wisner, Ben. Botswana. In *O'Keefe, P. and Munslow, B., eds., Part I*, 1984, pp. 65–133.
                 [G: Botswana]

Woo, Chi-Keung. A Note on Measuring Household Welfare Effects of Time-of-Use (TOU) Pricing. *Energy J.*, July 1984, *5*(3), pp. 170–81.   [G: U.S.]

Yousefi, Mahmood and Abizadeh, Sohrab. An Analysis and Forecast of Demand for Food in Iran. *Econ. Anal. Worker's Manage.*, 1984, *18*(1), pp. 65–76.   [G: Iran]

Yucelt, Ugur and Kaynak, Erdener. A Study of Measuring Influence of Advertising and Forecasting Cigarette Sales. *Managerial Dec. Econ.*, December 1984, *5*(4), pp. 213–18.
                 [G: U.S.]

9213 Consumer Protection

Adler, Robert S. and Pittle, R. David. Cajolery or Command: Are Education Campaigns an Adequate Substitute for Regulation? *Yale J. Regul.*, 1984, *1*(2), pp. 159–93.   [G: U.S.]

Boyer, Marcel and Dionne, Georges. Sécurité routière: efficacité, subvention et réglementation. (Road Security: Efficiency, Subsidies, Regulation. With English summary.) *L'Actual. Econ.*, June 1984, *60*(2), pp. 200–222.

Cox, Howard and Smith, Ronald P. Political Approaches to Smoking Control: A Comparative Analysis. *Appl. Econ.*, August 1984, *16*(4), pp. 569–82.   [G: OECD]

Crandall, Robert W. and Graham, John D. Automobile Safety Regulation and Offsetting Behavior: Some New Empirical Estimates. *Amer. Econ. Rev.*, May 1984, *74*(2), pp. 328–31.
                 [G: U.S.]

Eckard, E. Woodrow. Regulatory Relief and the Automobile Industry: Comments. In *Eads, G. C. and Fix, M., eds.*, 1984, pp. 106–09.
                 [G: U.S.]

Einhorn, Michael. FEA Efficiency Standards and Energy Usage: Resolving Khazzoom versus Besen and Johnson [Economic Implications of Mandated Efficiency Standards for Household Appliances]. *Energy J.*, January 1984, *5*(1), pp. 173–76.

Fischel, Daniel R. and Grossman, Sanford J. Customer Protection in Futures and Securities Markets. *J. Futures Markets*, Fall 1984, *4*(3), pp. 273–95.   [G: U.S.]

Graham, John D. Technology, Behavior, and

Safety: An Empirical Study of Automobile Occupant-Protection Regulation. *Policy Sci.*, October 1984, *17*(2), pp. 141–51.   [G: U.S.]

Graham, John D. and Garber, Steven. Evaluating the Effects of Automobile Safety Regulation. *J. Policy Anal. Manage.*, Winter 1984, *3*(2), pp. 206–24.   [G: U.S.]

Horn, Ernst-Jürgen. Reassessing Consumer Safety Regulation: Comment. In *Giersch, H., ed.*, 1984, pp. 216–21.

Jones, Trefor T. Restrictive Practices in the Supply of Inclusive Tours. *Nat. Westminster Bank Quart. Rev.*, February 1984, pp. 31–40.
                 [G: U.K.]

Keating, Barry. Direct and Indirect Impacts of the Matchbook Safety Standard of the Consumer Products Safety Commission. *Quart. Rev. Econ. Bus.*, Autumn 1984, *24*(3), pp. 29–36.   [G: U.S.]

Lave, Lester B. Controlling Contradictions among Regulations. *Amer. Econ. Rev.*, June 1984, *74*(3), pp. 471–75.   [G: U.S.]

Leone, Robert A. Regulatory Relief and the Automobile Industry. In *Eads, G. C. and Fix, M., eds.*, 1984, pp. 87–105.   [G: U.S.]

Maynard, Alan and Hartley, Keith. The Regulation of the Pharmaceutical Industry. In *Lindgren, B., ed.*, 1984, pp. 123–37.   [G: U.K.]

Pedroni, Gabriella. Drugs and Adverse Reactions: An Economic View of a Medical Problem. In *Lindgren, B., ed.*, 1984, pp. 67–95.
                 [G: Selected Countries]

Peterson, Richard L. and Aoki, Kiyomi. Bankruptcy Filings before and after Implementation of the Bankruptcy Reform Law. *J. Econ. Bus.*, February 1984, *36*(1), pp. 95–105. [G: U.S.]

Shavell, Steven. A Model of the Optimal Use of Liability and Safety Regulation. *Rand J. Econ.*, Summer 1984, *15*(2), pp. 271–80.

Shepard, Lawrence. Personal Failures and the Bankruptcy Reform Act of 1978. *J. Law Econ.*, October 1984, *27*(2), pp. 419–37.

Streit, Manfred E. Reassessing Consumer Safety Regulation. In *Giersch, H., ed.*, 1984, pp. 190–215.   [G: W. Germany]

Viscusi, W. Kip. The Lulling Effect: The Impact of Child-Resistant Packaging on Aspirin and Analgesic Ingestions. *Amer. Econ. Rev.*, May 1984, *74*(2), pp. 324–27.   [G: U.S.]

Wiggins, Steven N. The Effect of U.S. Pharmaceutical Regulation on New Introductions. In *Lindgren, B., ed.*, 1984, pp. 191–205.
                 [G: U.S.]

Winston, Clifford and Mannering, Fred. Consumer Demand for Automobile Safety. *Amer. Econ. Rev.*, May 1984, *74*(2), pp. 316–19.
                 [G: U.S.]

930 URBAN ECONOMICS

9300 General

Ettlinger, Nancy. A Note on Rank-Size and Primacy: In Pursuit of a Parsimonious Explanation. *Urban Stud.*, May 1984, *21*(2), pp. 195–97.

Fakhraei, S. Hamid; Narayanan, Rangesan and Hughes, Trevor C. Price Rigidity and Quantity Rationing Rules under Stochastic Water Supply. *Water Resources Res.*, June 1984, *20*(6), pp. 664–70.

Findlay, Allan; Findlay, Anne M. and Paddison, Ronan. Maintaining the Status Quo: An Analysis of Social Space in Post-Colonial Rabat. *Urban Stud.*, February 1984, *21*(1), pp. 41–51. [G: Morocco]

Gilbert, Alan and Ward, Peter. Community Action by the Urban Poor: Democratic Involvement, Community Self-Help or a Means of Social Control? *World Devel.*, August 1984, *12*(8), pp. 769–82. [G: Colombia; Mexico; Venezuela]

Hughes, Helen. Industrialization, Employment, and Urbanization. In *Ghosh, P. K., ed., no. 2*, 1984, *1971*, pp. 149–59.

Johnson, Michael W. Mobility, Market Failure and Zoning Laws. *Atlantic Econ. J.*, July 1984, *12*(2), pp. 71.

Knight, Richard V. and Gappert, Gary. Cities and the Challengee of the Global Economy. In *Bingham, R. D. and Blair, J. P., eds.*, 1984, pp. 63–78.

Kunde, James E. Process Lessons from a Cities' Fair. In *Porter, P. R. and Sweet, D. C., eds.*, 1984, pp. 111–19. [G: U.S.]

Livesey, David. Aspects of the New Urban Economics. In *van der Ploeg, F., ed.*, 1984, pp. 479–517.

Vickerman, R. W. Urban and Regional Change, Migration and Commuting—The Dynamics of Workplace, Residence and Transport Choice. *Urban Stud.*, February 1984, *21*(1), pp. 15–29. [G: U.K.]

Witchard, Les. A Comparative Static Analysis of the Optimum Town. *J. Urban Econ.*, May 1984, *15*(3), pp. 259–69.

931 Urban Economics and Public Policy

9310 Urban Economics and Public Policy

Abbott, Carl. Planning for the Home Front in Seattle and Portland, 1940–45. In *Lotchin, R. W., ed.*, 1984, pp. 163–89. [G: U.S.]

de Albuquerque, Klaus; Van Riel, Wesley and Taylor, J. Mark. Uncontrolled Urbanization in the Developing World: A Jamaican Case Study. In *Ghosh, P. K., ed., no. 2*, 1984, *1980*, pp. 253–86. [G: Jamaica]

Alperovich, Gershon. The Size Distribution of Cities: On the Empirical Validity of the Rank-Size Rule. *J. Urban Econ.*, September 1984, *16*(2), pp. 232–39. [G: Selected MDCs; Selected LDCs]

Armstrong, John M. The Future of Urban Public Works: New Ways of Doing Business: Discussion. In *Hanson, R., ed.*, 1984, pp. 204–05. [G: U.S.]

Balydon, R.; Woods, Adrian and Zafiris, N. Inner City versus New Town: A Comparison of Manufacturing Performance. *Oxford Bull. Econ. Statist.*, February 1984, *46*(1), pp. 21–29. [G: U.K.]

Barth, Gunther. Urbanization in the American West—A Review Article. *Bus. Hist. Rev.*, Summer 1984, *58*(2), pp. 263–67. [G: U.S.]

Basu, D. N. and Sundaram, A. K. The Urban Informal Sector: a Search for the Processes and Appropriate Strategies. In *Amin, S., ed.*, 1984, pp. 243–64.

Bates, Timothy. Urban Economic Transformation and Minority Business Opportunities. *Rev. Black Polit. Econ.*, Winter 1984–85, *13*(3), pp. 21–36. [G: U.S.]

Batty, Michael. Urban Development as Exchange. In *Andersson, Å. E.; Isard, W. and Puu, T., eds.*, 1984, pp. 309–29. [G: U.K.]

Beier, George J. Can Third World Cities Cope? In *Ghosh, P. K., ed., no. 2*, 1984, *1976*, pp. 57–95. [G: LDCs; MDCs]

Benjamin, Robert L. Cook. From Waterways to Waterfronts: Public Investment for Cities, 1815–1980. In *Bingham, R. D. and Blair, J. P., eds.*, 1984, pp. 23–45. [G: U.S.]

Benton, J. Edwin and Gamble, Darwin. City/County Consolidation and Economies of Scale: Evidence from a Time-Series Analysis in Jacksonville, Florida. *Soc. Sci. Quart.*, March 1984, *65*(1), pp. 190–98. [G: U.S.]

Berkowitz, Bernard L. Economic Development Really Works: Baltimore, Maryland. In *Bingham, R. D. and Blair, J. P., eds.*, 1984, pp. 201–221. [G: U.S.]

Berliant, Marcus. A Characterization of the Demand for Land. *J. Econ. Theory*, August 1984, *33*(2), pp. 289–300.

Bertsch, Dale F. Non-profit Institutions and Urban Revitalization. In *Porter, P. R. and Sweet, D. C., eds.*, 1984, pp. 52–64. [G: U.S.]

Bienen, Henry. Urbanization and Third World Stability. *World Devel.*, July 1984, *12*(7), pp. 661–91. [G: LDCs]

Bingham, Richard D. and Blair, John P. Urban Economic Development. In *Bingham, R. D. and Blair, J. P., eds.*, 1984, pp. 11–19.

Blair, John P. and Wechsler, Barton. A Tale of Two Cities: A Case Study of Urban Competition for Jobs. In *Bingham, R. D. and Blair, J. P., eds.*, 1984, pp. 269–82. [G: U.S.]

Boehm, Thomas P. Inflation and Intra-Urban Residential Mobility. *Housing Finance Rev.*, January 1984, *3*(1), pp. 19–37. [G: U.S.]

Booth, Douglas E. and Fortis, Louis C. Building a Cooperative Economy: A Strategy for Community Based Economic Development. *Rev. Soc. Econ.*, December 1984, *42*(3), pp. 339–59.

Bradbury, Katharine L. Urban Decline and Distress: An Update. *New Eng. Econ. Rev.*, July–August 1984, pp. 39–55. [G: U.S.]

Braid, Ralph M. The Effects of Government Housing Policies in a Vintage Filtering Model. *J. Urban Econ.*, November 1984, *16*(3), pp. 272–96.

Brecher, Charles and Horton, Raymond D. Setting Municipal Priorities: Introduction. In *Brecher, C. and Horton, R. D., eds.*, 1984, pp. 1–12. [G: U.S.]

Brecher, Charles and Roswick, Diana. Setting

Municipal Priorities: Service Delivery: The City's Role in Health Care. In *Brecher, C. and Horton, R. D., eds.*, 1984, pp. 482–518. **[G: U.S.]**

Brooks, Harvey. Seeking Equity and Efficiency: Public and Private Roles. In *Brooks, H.; Liebman, L. and Schelling, C. S., eds.*, 1984, pp. 3–29. **[G: U.S.]**

Brown, Lester R. The Urban Prospect: Reexamining the Basic Assumptions. In *Ghosh, P. K., ed., no. 2*, 1984, *1976*, pp. 96–108.

Brown, M. Craig and Halaby, Charles N. Bosses, Reform, and the Socioeconomic Bases of Urban Expenditure, 1890–1940. In *McDonald, T. J. and Ward, S. K., eds.*, 1984, pp. 69–99. **[G: U.S.]**

Burnell, Barbara S. Metropolitan Fiscal Disparities and the Geographic Distribution of Income. *Urban Stud.*, August 1984, *21*(3), pp. 285–93. **[G: U.S.]**

Butler, Stuart M. Free Zones in the Inner City. In *Bingham, R. D. and Blair, J. P., eds.*, 1984, pp. 141–53. **[G: U.K.; U.S.]**

Büttler, Hans-Jürg. Ist eine negative Einkommensteuer auf städtischer Ebene möglich? (Is a Negative Local Income Tax Possible? With English summary.) *Z. Wirtschaft. Sozialwissen.*, 1984, *104*(5), pp. 477–88.

Cavaco, Carminda. A pequena horticultura doméstica de nao agricultores das periferias urbanas: o caso de Lisboa. (With English summary.) *Economia (Portugal)*, May 1984, *8*(2), pp. 395–423. **[G: Portugal]**

Chambers, David I. Adult Education in Urban-Industrial China: Problems, Policies, and Prospects. In *Hayhoe, R., ed.*, 1984, pp. 178–204. **[G: China]**

Charney, Alberta H. and Woodard, Gary C. A Test of Consumer Demand Response to Water Prices: Comment [Urban Residential Demand for Water in the United States: Further Discussion]. *Land Econ.*, November 1984, *60*(4), pp. 414–16. **[G: U.S.]**

Chatterjee, Jay and Davidow, Carol. Schools and the Private Sector in Partnership. In *Porter, P. R. and Sweet, D. C., eds.*, 1984, pp. 93–110. **[G: U.S.]**

Chen, Gavin M. Business Formation and Investment in the Minority Community. In *Bingham, R. D. and Blair, J. P., eds.*, 1984, pp. 79–98. **[G: U.S.]**

Chitnis, S. and Suvannathat, C. Schooling for the Children of the Urban Poor. In *Richards, P. J. and Thomson, A. M., eds.*, 1984, pp. 189–213. **[G: LDCs]**

Cloutier, Norman R. City Size Distribution as a Markov Process. *Atlantic Econ. J.*, December 1984, *12*(4), pp. 72. **[G: U.S.]**

Cochrane, Harold C. and Huszar, Paul C. Economics of Timing Storm Drainage Improvements. *Water Resources Res.*, October 1984, *20*(10), pp. 1331–36.

Cohen, Michael A. Cities in Developing Countries: 1975–2000. In *Ghosh, P. K., ed., no. 2*, 1984, *1976*, pp. 27–35. **[G: LDCs]**

Cohen, Michael A. Urban Policy and Develop-

ment Strategy. In *Zartman, I. W. and Delgado, C. L., eds.*, 1984, pp. 57–75. **[G: Ivory Coast]**

Crocker, Thomas D., et al. The Sixty-City Limit. In *Ahmad, Y. J.; Dasgupta, P. and Mäler, K.-G., eds.*, 1984, pp. 114–61. **[G: U.S.]**

Cummings, Scott and Snider, Edmond. Municipal Code Enforcement and Urban Redevelopment: Private Decisions and Public Policy in an American City. *Rev. Radical Polit. Econ.*, Winter 1984, *16*(4), pp. 129–50. **[G: U.S.]**

Cushing, Brian J. Capitalization of Interjurisdictional Fiscal Differentials: An Alternative Approach. *J. Urban Econ.*, May 1984, *15*(3), pp. 317–26. **[G: U.S.]**

Dagodag, W. Tim. Illegal Mexican Aliens in Los Angeles: Locational Characteristics. In *Jones, R. C., ed.*, 1984, pp. 199–217. **[G: U.S.]**

Davis, John Emmeus. Reallocating Equity: A Land Trust Model of Land Reform. In *Geisler, C. C. and Popper, F. J., eds.*, 1984, pp. 209–32. **[G: U.S.]**

Davis, Kingsley. Asia's Cities: Problems and Options. In *Ghosh, P. K., ed., no. 2*, 1984, *1975*, pp. 236–52. **[G: LDCs]**

De Cola, Lee. Statistical Determinants of the Population of a Nation's Largest City. *Econ. Develop. Cult. Change*, October 1984, *33*(1), pp. 71–98. **[G: Global]**

Dearborne, Philip. Politics and Urban Public Facilities: Discussion. In *Hanson, R., ed.*, 1984, pp. 169–71. **[G: U.S.]**

Deutsch, Joseph; Hakim, Simon and Weinblatt, J. Interjurisdictional Criminal Mobility: A Theoretical Perspective. *Urban Stud.*, November 1984, *21*(4), pp. 451–58.

Dobson, Richard B. Soviet Education: Problems and Policies in the Urban Context. In *Morton, H. W. and Stuart, R. C., eds.*, 1984, pp. 156–79. **[G: U.S.S.R.]**

Dommel, Paul R. Local Discretion: The CDBG Approach. In *Bingham, R. D. and Blair, J. P., eds.*, 1984, pp. 101–13. **[G: U.S.]**

Donnison, David. The Progressive Potential of Privatisation. In *Le Grand, J. and Robinson, R., eds.*, 1984, pp. 45–57.

Drennan, Matthew. Setting Municipal Priorities: The Setting: The Local Economy and Local Revenues. In *Brecher, C. and Horton, R. D., eds.*, 1984, pp. 43–68. **[G: U.S.]**

Ebrahim, G. J. Health Care and The Urban Poor. In *Richards, P. J. and Thomson, A. M., eds.*, 1984, pp. 93–121. **[G: LDCs]**

El-Hodiri, Mohamed Ali. Boom Towns: Queue Up or Bust: A Welfare Economy Analysis. In *Avula, X. J. R., et al.*, 1984, pp. 799–801.

Eldridge, Noel. Melbourne: Population Density; Distance; the Relationship. *J. Urban Econ.*, May 1984, *15*(3), pp. 310–16. **[G: Australia]**

Ellis, Frank. Relative Agricultural Prices and the Urban Bias Model: A Comparative Analysis of Tanzania and Fiji. In *Harriss, J. and Moore, M., eds.*, 1984, pp. 28–51. **[G: Tanzania; Fiji]**

Epple, Dennis and Zelenitz, Allan. Profit-Maximizing Communities and the Theory of Local

Public Expenditures: Comment. *J. Urban Econ.*, September 1984, *16*(2), pp. 149–57.

Evans, Jeremy. The Growth of Urban Centres in Java since 1961. *Bull. Indonesian Econ. Stud.*, April 1984, *20*(1), pp. 44–57. [G: Indonesia]

Fairbanks, Robert B. and Miller, Zane L. The Martial Metropolis: Housing, Planning, and Race in Cincinnati, 1940–55. In *Lotchin, R. W., ed.*, 1984, pp. 191–222. [G: U.S.]

Falchi, Paul and Mariano, Reynaldo. Calibration of Residential Location Models for a Multiplant Firm. *J. Reg. Sci.*, February 1984, *24*(1), pp. 93–104. [G: U.S.]

Feagin, Joe R. Sunbelt Metropolis and Development Capital: Houston in the Era of Late Capitalism. In *Sawers, L. and Tabb, W. K., eds.*, 1984, pp. 99–127. [G: U.S.]

Feeser, Larry J. The Future of Urban Public Works: New Ways of Doing Business: Discussion. In *Hanson, R., ed.*, 1984, pp. 205–07. [G: U.S.]

Felbinger, Claire L. Economic Development or Economic Disaster? Joliet, Illinois. In *Bingham, R. D. and Blair, J. P., eds.*, 1984, pp. 223–44. [G: U.S.]

Field, Mark G. Soviet Urban Health Services: Some Problems and Their Sources. In *Morton, H. W. and Stuart, R. C., eds.*, 1984, pp. 129–55. [G: U.S.S.R.]

Firestine, Robert E.; Weinstein, Bernard L. and Hayden, Shelley M. Intergovernmental Fiscal Cooperation in Growing Metropolitan Economies. In *Carr, J. H., ed.*, 1984, *1978*, pp. 221–29. [G: U.S.]

Fisher, Susan M. and Williams, Thomas L. The Economics of Incorporation: An Empirical Study of Lakeland, TN. *Amer. Econ.*, Fall 1984, *28*(2), pp. 64–68. [G: U.S.]

Florestano, Patricia S. and Gordon, Stephen B. A Survey of City and County Use of Private Contracting. In *Carr, J. H., ed.*, 1984, *1981*, pp. 252–63. [G: U.S.]

Fontenot, Gregory. Junction City–Fort Riley: A Case of Symbiosis. In *Lotchin, R. W., ed.*, 1984, pp. 35–60. [G: U.S.]

Friedland, Roger; Piven, Frances Fox and Alford, Robert R. Political Conflict, Urban Structure, and the Fiscal Crisis. In *Tabb, W. K. and Sawers, L., eds.*, 1984, *1978*, pp. 273–97. [G: U.S.]

Fujita, Masahisa. The Spatial Growth of Tokyo Metropolitan Area. In *Andersson, Å. E.; Isard, W. and Puu, T., eds.*, 1984, pp. 41–59. [G: Japan]

Galster, George C. On the Measurement of Metropolitan Decentralization of Blacks and Whites. *Urban Stud.*, November 1984, *21*(4), pp. 465–70. [G: U.S.]

Gardner, Henry. Politics and Urban Public Facilities: Discussion. In *Hanson, R., ed.*, 1984, pp. 173–75. [G: U.S.]

Garnick, Daniel H. Shifting Balances in U.S. Metropolitan and Nonmetropolitan Area Growth. *Int. Reg. Sci. Rev.*, December 1984, *9*(3), pp. 257–73. [G: U.S.]

Gatons, Paul K. and Brintnall, Michael. Competitive Grants: The UDAG Approach. In *Bingham, R. D. and Blair, J. P., eds.*, 1984, pp. 115–40. [G: U.S.]

Gilbert, Alan and Ward, Peter. Community Participation in Upgrading Irregular Settlements: The Community Response. *World Devel.*, September 1984, *12*(9), pp. 913–22. [G: Mexico; Venezuela; Colombia]

Gist, John R. and Hill, R. Carter. Political and Economic Influences on the Bureaucratic Allocation of Federal Funds: The Case of Urban Development Action Grants. *J. Urban Econ.*, September 1984, *16*(2), pp. 158–72. [G: U.S.]

Goetze, Rolf. Private Efforts to Initiate Neighborhood Recovery. In *Porter, P. R. and Sweet, D. C., eds.*, 1984, pp. 42–51. [G: U.S.]

Goldsmith, William W. Bringing the Third World Home: Enterprise Zones for America? In *Sawers, L. and Tabb, W. K., eds.*, 1984, *1982*, pp. 339–50. [G: U.S.]

Gordon, David M. Capitalist Development and the History of American Cities. In *Tabb, W. K. and Sawers, L., eds.*, 1984, pp. 21–53. [G: U.S.]

Gordon, Ian. Lagged Response in Intra-urban Migration of Home Owners: A Comment. *Reg. Stud.*, December 1984, *18*(6), pp. 505–06. [G: Israel]

Graves, Philip E. and Sexton, Robert Louis. Overurbanization and Its Relation to Economic Growth for Less Developed Countries. In *Ghosh, P. K., ed., no. 2*, 1984, *1979*, pp. 160–66.

Green, Cynthia B. and Sanger, Mary Bryna. Setting Municipal Priorities: Service Delivery: Aiding the Poor. In *Brecher, C. and Horton, R. D., eds.*, 1984, pp. 519–50. [G: U.S.]

Guldmann, Jean-Michel. A Further Note on the Structure of Gas Distribution Costs in Urban Areas. *Reg. Sci. Urban Econ.*, November 1984, *14*(4), pp. 583–88.

Haar, Charles M. The Joint Venture Approach to Urban Renewal: From Model Cities to Enterprise Zones. In *Brooks, H.; Liebman, L. and Schelling, C. S., eds.*, 1984, pp. 63–87. [G: U.S.]

Harrison, Bennett. Urban Policy and Economic Reform. *Rev. Black Polit. Econ.*, Summer–Fall 1984, *13*(1–2), pp. 116–18. [G: U.S.]

Harriss, Barbara and Harriss, John C. 'Generative' or 'Parasitic' Urbanism? Some Observations from the Recent History of a South Indian Market Town. In *Harriss, J. and Moore, M., eds.*, 1984, pp. 82–101. [G: India]

Hartman, James M. Setting Municipal Priorities: Service Delivery: Sanitation. In *Brecher, C. and Horton, R. D., eds.*, 1984, pp. 415–45. [G: U.S.]

Haurin, Donald R. The Effects of Output and Factor Subsidies or Taxes on an Urban Area. *Reg. Sci. Urban Econ.*, November 1984, *14*(4), pp. 533–46.

Hawkins, Benjamin M. The Impact of the Enterprise Zone on Urban Areas. *Growth Change*, January 1984, *15*(1), pp. 35–40.   [G: U.S.]

Heffley, Dennis R. Pricing in an Urban Spatial Monopoly: A Reply. *J. Reg. Sci.*, May 1984, *24*(2), pp. 291–93.

Henton, Douglas C. and Waldhorn, Steven A. The Future of Urban Public Works: New Ways of Doing Business. In *Hanson, R., ed.*, 1984, pp. 178–204.   [G: U.S.]

Hill, Richard Child. Economic Crisis and Political Response in the Motor City. In *Sawers, L. and Tabb, W. K., eds.*, 1984, pp. 313–38.   [G: U.S.]

Hill, Richard Child. Fiscal Crisis, Austerity Politics, and Alternative Urban Policies. In *Tabb, W. K. and Sawers, L., eds.*, 1984, pp. 298–322.   [G: U.S.]

Hoch, Charles. City Limits: Municipal Boundary Formation and Class Segregation. In *Tabb, W. K. and Sawers, L., eds.*, 1984, pp. 101–19.   [G: U.S.]

Holland, Robert C. The New Era in Public–Private Partnerships. In *Porter, P. R. and Sweet, D. C., eds.*, 1984, pp. 209–11.   [G: U.S.]

Hopkins, George W. From Naval Pauper to Naval Power: The Development of Charleston's Metropolitan-Military Complex. In *Lotchin, R. W., ed.*, 1984, pp. 1–34.   [G: U.S.]

Horton, Raymond D. and Smith, John Palmer. Setting Municipal Priorities: Service Delivery: Expenditures and Services. In *Brecher, C. and Horton, R. D., eds.*, 1984, pp. 337–79.   [G: U.S.]

House, William J. Nairobi's Informal Sector: Dynamic Entrepreneurs or Surplus Labor? *Econ. Develop. Cult. Change*, January 1984, *32*(2), pp. 277–302.   [G: Kenya]

Hulten, Charles R. and Peterson, George E. The Public Capital Stock: Needs, Trends, and Performance. *Amer. Econ. Rev.*, May 1984, *74*(2), pp. 166–73.   [G: U.S.]

Hunter, Albert. Suburban Autonomy/Dependency: Elite Perceptions. *Soc. Sci. Quart.*, March 1984, *65*(1), pp. 181–89.   [G: U.S.]

Ionescu, C. and Matei, I. The Development of Social Structures within the Local Communities Systems and the National Wealth Growth. *Econ. Computat. Cybern. Stud. Res.*, 1984, *19*(2), pp. 77–83.   [G: Romania]

Jackson, Kenneth T. The City Loses the Sword: The Decline of Major Military Activity in the New York Metropolitan Region. In *Lotchin, R. W., ed.*, 1984, pp. 151–62.   [G: U.S.]

James, Franklin J. Urban Economic Development: A Zero-Sum Game? In *Bingham, R. D. and Blair, J. P., eds.*, 1984, pp. 157–74.   [G: U.S.]

Jaynes, Gerald David. Urban Policy and Economic Reform. *Rev. Black Polit. Econ.*, Summer–Fall 1984, *13*(1–2), pp. 103–15.   [G: U.S.]

Jeffers, J. N. R. The Development of Models in Urban and Regional Planning. In *Richardson, J., ed.*, 1984, *1981*, pp. 87–99.

Johnson, David R. The Failed Experiment: Military Aviation and Urban Development in San Antonio, 1910–40. In *Lotchin, R. W., ed.*, 1984, pp. 89–108.   [G: U.S.]

Johnson, Scott. Politics and Urban Public Facilities: Discussion. In *Hanson, R., ed.*, 1984, pp. 171–72.   [G: U.S.]

Jones, Bryan D. and Bachelor, Lynn W. Local Policy Discretion and the Corporate Surplus. In *Bingham, R. D. and Blair, J. P., eds.*, 1984, pp. 245–67.   [G: U.S.]

Jones, Donald W. Regional Economic Adjustment Mechanisms: Theory and Evidence from United States Cities, 1918–1931. *J. Reg. Sci.*, August 1984, *24*(3), pp. 391–402.   [G: U.S.]

Jones, Gavin W. Links between Urbanization and Sectoral Shifts in Employment in Java. *Bull. Indonesian Econ. Stud.*, December 1984, *20*(3), pp. 120–57.   [G: Indonesia]

Joubert, M. J. An Extension of the Concept of Structural Sensitivity in an Urban Model. In *Avula, X. J. R., et al.*, 1984, pp. 139–42.

Juviler, Peter H. The Urban Family and the Soviet State: Emerging Contours of a Demographic Policy. In *Morton, H. W. and Stuart, R. C., eds.*, 1984, pp. 84–112. [G: U.S.S.R.]

Kau, James B. and Sirmans, C. F. Changes in Urban Land Values: 1836–1970. *J. Urban Econ.*, January 1984, *15*(1), pp. 18–25.   [G: U.S.]

Keane, Michael J. Accessibility and Urban Growth Rates: Evidence for the Irish Urban System. *Econ. Soc. Rev.*, January 1984, *15*(2), pp. 125–39.   [G: Ireland]

Kelley, Allen C. and Williamson, Jeffrey G. Population Growth, Industrial Revolutions, and the Urban Transition. *Population Devel. Rev.*, September 1984, *10*(3), pp. 419–41.   [G: LDCs]

Kennedy, Thomas E. and Nord, Stephen. The Effect of City Size on the Urban Income Distribution through Time: 1950–70. *Appl. Econ.*, October 1984, *16*(5), pp. 717–28.   [G: U.S.]

Khorev, B. Current Scientific and Practical Problems in Restricting the Growth of Large Cities in the USSR. *Prob. Econ.*, December 1984, *27*(8), pp. 3–19.   [G: U.S.S.R.]

Kipnis, Baruch A. Plant Size and Urban Growth. *Urban Stud.*, February 1984, *21*(1), pp. 53–61.   [G: Brazil]

Kirke, J. and Arthur, J. Water Supply Issues. In *Richards, P. J. and Thomson, A. M., eds.*, 1984, pp. 123–51.   [G: LDCs]

Kleniewski, Nancy. From Industrial to Corporate City: The Role of Urban Renewal. In *Tabb, W. K. and Sawers, L., eds.*, 1984, pp. 205–22.   [G: U.S.]

Kraemer, Kenneth L. The Politics of Model Implementation. In *Richardson, J., ed.*, 1984, *1981*, pp. 131–60.

Kraushaar, Robert. After Advocacy: The Transformation of Community in England. In *Sawers, L. and Tabb, W. K., eds.*, 1984, pp. 353–67.   [G: U.K.]

Krumholz, Norman. Recovery of Cities: An Alternate View. In *Porter, P. R. and Sweet, D. C., eds.*, 1984, pp. 173–90.   [G: U.S.]

Kuo, Shirley W. Y. Urbanization and Income Dis-

tribution: The Case of Taiwan, 1966–1980. In *[Chenery, H. B.]*, 1984, pp. 217–34.
[G: Taiwan]

Kwon, Won-Yong. An Examination of Residential Location Behavior in the Seoul Metropolitan Area. *Ann. Reg. Sci.*, November 1984, *18*(3), pp. 33–48. [G: S. Korea]

Lamonde, Pierre and Polèse, Mario. L'évolution de la structure économique de Montréal 1971–1981: désindustrialisation ou reconversion? (The Evolution of Montreal's Economic Structure, 1971–1981: Deindustrialization or Reconversion? With English summary.) *L'Actual. Econ.*, December 1984, *60*(4), pp. 471–94.
[G: Canada]

Lasater, Donald E. A Banker's View of Redevelopment. In *Porter, P. R. and Sweet, D. C., eds.*, 1984, pp. 33–41. [G: U.S.]

Latos, Charles J. Non-white Migration Patterns in Northern Metropolitan Areas, 1960–1970: The Interaction between Economic and Affinitive Factors. *Rev. Black Polit. Econ.*, Winter 1984–85, *13*(3), pp. 5–19. [G: U.S.]

Ledebur, Larry C. The Reagan Revolution and Beyond. In *Porter, P. R. and Sweet, D. C., eds.*, 1984, pp. 191–208. [G: U.S.]

Lerman, Donald L. The Economics of Public School Closings. *J. Urban Econ.*, November 1984, *16*(3), pp. 241–58. [G: U.S.]

Lerman, S. R. and Liu, T.-K. Microlevel Econometric Analysis of Retail CLosure. In *Pitfield, D. E., ed.*, 1984, pp. 181–201. [G: U.S.]

Lieske, Joel. The Salvation of American Cities. In *Porter, P. R. and Sweet, D. C., eds.*, 1984, pp. 71–92. [G: U.S.]

Lipton, Michael. Family, Fungibility and Formality: Rural Advantages of Informal Non-farm Enterprise versus the Urban-Formal State. In *Amin, S., ed.*, 1984, pp. 189–242.

Lissner, Will. A. R. Prest's Investigation of the Case for Site Value Taxation. *Amer. J. Econ. Soc.*, April 1984, *43*(2), pp. 163–66.
[G: U.K.; U.S.]

Littman, Daniel A. and Lee, Myung-Hoon. Plant Closings and Worker Dislocation. In *McKenzie, R. B., ed. (II)*, 1984, *1983*, pp. 127–54.
[G: U.S.]

Lotchin, Roger W. The Martial Metropolis: Conclusion. In *Lotchin, R. W., ed.*, 1984, pp. 223–32. [G: U.S.]

Lotchin, Roger W. The Martial Metropolis: Introduction. In *Lotchin, R. W., ed.*, 1984, pp. x–xiii. [G: U.S.]

Lubell, Harold. Third World Urbanization and International Assistance. *Urban Stud.*, February 1984, *21*(1), pp. 1–13. [G: LDCs]

Luger, Michael I. Federal Tax Incentives as Industrial and Urban Policy. In *Sawers, L. and Tabb, W. K., eds.*, 1984, pp. 201–34.
[G: U.S.]

Lund, Leonard. Factors in Corporate Locational Decisions. In *Carr, J. H., ed.*, 1984, *1979*, pp. 267–88. [G: U.S.]

Luria, Dan and Russell, Jack. Motor City Changeover. In *Sawers, L. and Tabb, W. K., eds.*, 1984, pp. 271–312. [G: U.S.]

Mack, Ruth P. and Leigland, T. J. Elective Decisions to Move to New York City. In *[Ferber, R.]*, 1984, pp. 217–51. [G: U.S.]

Maier, Mark. Management Strategies in Public Sector Labor Law: A Case Study of New York City. In *Tabb, W. K. and Sawers, L., eds.*, 1984, pp. 346–63. [G: U.S.]

Manson, Donald M.; Howland, Marie and Peterson, George E. The Effect of Business Cycles on Metropolitan Suburbanization. *Econ. Geogr.*, January 1984, *60*(1), pp. 71–80.
[G: U.S.]

Markusen, Ann R. Class and Urban Social Expenditure: A Marxist Theory of Metropolitan Government. In *Tabb, W. K. and Sawers, L., eds.*, 1984, pp. 82–100.

McDonald, Terrence J. San Francisco: Socioeconomic Change, Political Culture, and Fiscal Politics, 1870–1906. In *McDonald, T. J. and Ward, S. K., eds.*, 1984, pp. 39–67.
[G: U.S.]

McDonald, Terrence J. and Ward, Sally K. The Politics of Urban Fiscal Policy: Introduction. In *McDonald, T. J. and Ward, S. K., eds.*, 1984, pp. 13–37.

McDowall, David and Loftin, Colin. Conflict, Crime, and Budgetary Constraint: Police Strength in Detroit, 1927–1976. In *McDonald, T. J. and Ward, S. K., eds.*, 1984, pp. 101–24. [G: U.S.]

McKenzie, Richard B. The Case for Plant Closures. In *McKenzie, R. B., ed. (II)*, 1984, *1981*, pp. 205–19. [G: U.S.]

McTavish, D. Regional Policy, Urban Unemployment and the Development of Community Businesses in Scotland. *Reg. Stud.*, February 1984, *18*(1), pp. 81–84. [G: U.K.]

Mercer, John and Goldberg, Michael A. The Fiscal Condition of American and Canadian Cities. *Urban Stud.*, August 1984, *21*(3), pp. 233–43.
[G: U.S.; Canada]

Mier, Robert. Job Generation as a Road to Recovery. In *Porter, P. R. and Sweet, D. C., eds.*, 1984, pp. 160–72. [G: U.S.]

Mills, Edwin S. and Price, Richard G. Metropolitan Suburbanization and Central City Problems. *J. Urban Econ.*, January 1984, *15*(1), pp. 1–17. [G: U.S.]

Modell, John. The Politics of Urban Fiscal Policy: Afterword. In *McDonald, T. J. and Ward, S. K., eds.*, 1984, pp. 161–74.

Mohan, Rakesh. The Effect of Population Growth, the Pattern of Demand and of Technology on the Process of Urbanization. *J. Urban Econ.*, March 1984, *15*(2), pp. 125–56. [G: India]

Monaco, R. and Rabino, G. A. A Stochastic Treatment of a Dynamic Model for an Interacting Cities System. In *Avula, X. J. R., et al.*, 1984, pp. 326–30.

Monkkonen, Eric H. The Politics of Municipal Indebtedness and Default, 1850–1936. In *McDonald, T. J. and Ward, S. K., eds.*, 1984, pp. 125–59. [G: U.S.]

Moore, Mick. Categorising Space: Urban–Rural

or Core–Periphery in Sri Lanka. In *Harriss, J. and Moore, M., eds.*, 1984, pp. 102–22.
[G: Sri Lanka]

Moore, Richard J. Urbanization and Housing Policy in Mexico. In *Aspe, P. and Sigmund, P. E., eds.*, 1984, pp. 327–56. [G: Mexico]

Morrissey, Michael P. A Rural–Urban Stratification of Jamaica for Sampling Procedures. *Soc. Econ. Stud.*, December 1984, *33*(4), pp. 101–23. [G: Jamaica]

Morton, Henry W. The Contemporary Soviet City. In *Morton, H. W. and Stuart, R. C., eds.*, 1984, pp. 3–24. [G: U.S.S.R.]

Morton, Henry W. and Stuart, Robert C. The Contemporary Soviet City: Conclusion. In *Morton, H. W. and Stuart, R. C., eds.*, 1984, pp. 244–50. [G: U.S.S.R.]

Moskoff, William. The Soviet Urban Labor Supply. In *Morton, H. W. and Stuart, R. C., eds.*, 1984, pp. 65–83. [G: U.S.S.R.]

Muller, Thomas. Public Sector Performance: A Demographic Perspective. In *Miller, T. C., ed.*, 1984, pp. 131–60. [G: U.S.]

Nabi, Ijaz. Village-End Considerations in Rural–Urban Migration. *J. Devel. Econ.*, January–February 1984, *14*(1–2), pp. 129–45.
[G: Pakistan]

Neenan, William B. and Ethridge, Marcus E. Competition and Cooperation among Localities. In *Bingham, R. D. and Blair, J. P., eds.*, 1984, pp. 175–90.

Nolan, Peter and White, Gordon. Urban Bias, Rural Bias or State Bias? Urban–Rural Relations in Post-revolutionary China. In *Harriss, J. and Moore, M., eds.*, 1984, pp. 52–81.
[G: China]

Nord, Stephen. Urban Income Distribution, City Size, and Urban Growth: Some Further Evidence. *Urban Stud.*, August 1984, *21*(3), pp. 325–29. [G: U.S.]

O'Kelly, M. E. and Storbeck, J. E. Hierarchical Location Models with Probabilistic Allocation. *Reg. Stud.*, April 1984, *18*(2), pp. 121–29.

Oberai, A. S. and Singh, H. K. Manmohan. Migration, Employment and the Urban Labour Market: A Study in the Indian Punjab. *Int. Lab. Rev.*, July–August 1984, *123*(4), pp. 507–23. [G: India]

Ochitwa, Jerome M. Applicability and Efficiency in a Land Use Plan Design Model: An Input–Output Linear Programming Approach. *Urban Stud.*, May 1984, *21*(2), pp. 149–54.

Ohta, Hiroshi and Okamura, M. Pricing in an Urban Spatial Monopoly: A Comment. *J. Reg. Sci.*, May 1984, *24*(2), pp. 287–90.

Opaluch, James J. A Test of Consumer Demand Response to Water Prices: Reply [Urban Residential Demand for Water in the United States: Further Discussion]. *Land Econ.*, November 1984, *60*(4), pp. 417–21. [G: U.S.]

Owen, Wilfred. The Evolution of the Urban Infrastructure in the Nineteenth and Twentieth Centuries: Discussion. In *Hanson, R., ed.*, 1984, pp. 60–62. [G: U.S.]

Pedrao, Fernando. Problems of Urban Development and Regional Planning in Latin America.

In *Ghosh, P. K., ed., no. 2*, 1984, *1974*, pp. 312–42. [G: Latin America]

Peterson, George E. Financing the Nation's Infrastructure Requirements. In *Hanson, R., ed.*, 1984, pp. 110–30. [G: U.S.]

Pickford, J. Human Waste Disposal in Urban Areas. In *Richards, P. J. and Thomson, A. M., eds.*, 1984, pp. 153–87. [G: LDCs]

Pines, David and Sadka, Efraim. Gasoline Prices, Welfare and Congestion Tolls. *Scand. J. Econ.*, 1984, *86*(4), pp. 440–51.

Pinto, Aníbal. Metropolization and Tertiarization: Structural Distortions in Latin American Development. *Cepal Rev.*, 1984, (24), pp. 17–38.
[G: Latin America]

Pommerehne, Werner W. and Schneider, Friedrich. Identification of Individual Preferences for Government Activity from Voting Behavior. In *Hanusch, H., ed.*, 1984, pp. 109–26.
[G: Switzerland]

Porter, Paul R. A Few Who Made a Difference. In *Porter, P. R. and Sweet, D. C., eds.*, 1984, pp. 1–21. [G: U.S.]

Porter, Paul R. and Sweet, David C. Goals, Processes and Leadership. In *Porter, P. R. and Sweet, D. C., eds.*, 1984, pp. 212–29.
[G: U.S.]

Premus, Robert. Urban Growth and Technological Innovation. In *Bingham, R. D. and Blair, J. P., eds.*, 1984, pp. 47–61. [G: U.S.]

Pressat, Roland. Les previsions de population urbaine: examen critique des methodes. (Population Forecasts for Cities: A Critical Analysis of Methods. With English summary.) *Giorn. Econ.*, July–August 1984, *43*(7–8), pp. 451–69.
[G: France]

Preston, Samuel H. Urban Growth in Developing Countries—A Demographic Appraisal. In *Ghosh, P. K., ed., no. 2*, 1984, *1979*, pp. 36–56. [G: LDCs]

Raimondo, Henry J. and Stuart, Robert C. Financing Soviet Cities. In *Morton, H. W. and Stuart, R. C., eds.*, 1984, pp. 45–64.
[G: U.S.S.R.]

Raines, Franklin D. Financing the Nation's Infrastructure Requirements: Discussion. In *Hanson, R., ed.*, 1984, pp. 131–35. [G: U.S.]

Ramos, Joseph. Urbanization and the Labour Market. *Cepal Rev.*, 1984, (24), pp. 63–81.
[G: Latin America]

Rao, V. G. and Chandrashekar, H. Inter-State Variations in Urban Poverty. *Margin*, April 1984, *16*(3), pp. 77–93. [G: India]

Ravallion, Martin. The Social Appraisal of Local Public Spending Using Revealed Fiscal Preferences. *J. Urban Econ.*, July 1984, *16*(1), pp. 46–64. [G: Australia]

Redclift, M. R. 'Urban Bias' and Rural Poverty: A Latin American Perspective. In *Harriss, J. and Moore, M., eds.*, 1984, pp. 123–38.
[G: Latin America]

Reid, Clifford E. Are Blacks Making It in the Suburbs? A Correction. *J. Urban Econ.*, November 1984, *16*(3), pp. 357–59. [G: U.S.]

Remy, Dorothy and Sawers, Larry. Urban Industrial Decline and the Dynamics of Sexual and

Racial Oppression. In *Sawers, L. and Tabb, W. K., eds.*, 1984, pp. 128–51.

Richards, Peter J. Basic Needs and the Urban Poor: Introduction. In *Richards, P. J. and Thomson, A. M., eds.*, 1984, pp. 1–7.
[G: LDCs]

Richards, Peter J. Basic Needs and the Urban Poor: Conclusions. In *Richards, P. J. and Thomson, A. M., eds.*, 1984, pp. 243–55.
[G: LDCs]

Richardson, Harry W. An Urban Development Strategy for Kenya. In *Ghosh, P. K., ed., no. 2*, 1984, *1980*, pp. 287–311. [G: Kenya]

Richardson, Harry W. National Urban Development Strategies in Developing Countries. In *Ghosh, P. K., ed., no. 2*, 1984, *1981*, pp. 122–48.
[G: LDCs]

Riefler, Roger F. Development of the U.S. Urban System: A Review Article. *J. Econ. Hist.*, March 1984, *44*(1), pp. 179–84. [G: U.S.]

Rondinelli, Dennis A. Balanced Urbanization, Regional Integration and Development Planning in Asia. In *Ghosh, P. K., ed., no. 2*, 1984, *1980*, pp. 216–35. [G: LDCs]

Rouse, James W. The Case for Vision. In *Porter, P. R. and Sweet, D. C., eds.*, 1984, pp. 22–32. [G: U.S.]

Rykiel, Zbigniew. Intra-Metropolitan Migration in the Warsaw Agglomeration. *Econ. Geogr.*, January 1984, *60*(1), pp. 55–70. [G: Poland]

Sanders, Heywood T. Politics and Urban Public Facilities. In *Hanson, R., ed.*, 1984, pp. 143–69. [G: U.S.]

Savas, E. S. Alternative Institutional Models for the Delivery of Public Services. In *Carr, J. H., ed.*, 1984, *1981*, pp. 233–42. [G: U.S.]

Sawers, Larry. New Perspectives on the Urban Political Economy. In *Tabb, W. K. and Sawers, L., eds.*, 1984, pp. 3–17.

Schiesl, Martin J. Airplanes to Aerospace: Defense Spending and Economic Growth in the Los Angeles Region, 1945–60. In *Lotchin, R. W., ed.*, 1984, pp. 135–49. [G: U.S.]

Schloss, Nathan. Use of Employment Data to Estimate Office Space Demand. *Mon. Lab. Rev.*, December 1984, *107*(12), pp. 40–44.
[G: U.S.]

Schroeder, Gertrude E. Retail Trade and Personal Services in Soviet Cities. In *Morton, H. W. and Stuart, R. C., eds.*, 1984, pp. 203–20. [G: U.S.S.R.]

Schwartz, Seymour I.; Hansen, David E. and Green, Richard. The Effect of Growth Control on the Production of Moderate-Priced Housing. *Land Econ.*, February 1984, *60*(1), pp. 110–14. [G: U.S.]

Segelhorst, E. and Brady, M. A Theoretical Analysis of the Effect of Fear on the Location Decisions of Urban–Suburban Residents. *J. Urban Econ.*, March 1984, *15*(2), pp. 157–71.
[G: U.S.]

Shelley, Louise I. Urbanization and Crime: The Soviet Experience. In *Morton, H. W. and Stuart, R. C., eds.*, 1984, pp. 113–26.
[G: U.S.S.R.]

Silver, Christopher. Norfolk and the Navy: The

Evolution of City–Federal Relations, 1917–46. In *Lotchin, R. W., ed.*, 1984, pp. 109–33.
[G: U.S.]

Skinner, Reinhard. Searching for Urban Problems: Review Article. *J. Devel. Stud.*, January 1984, *20*(2), pp. 256–62. [G: LDCs]

Smith, Dennis C. Setting Municipal Priorities: Service Delivery: Police. In *Brecher, C. and Horton, R. D., eds.*, 1984, pp. 380–414.
[G: U.S.]

Smith, T. Michael. Becoming a Good and Competent Community. In *Porter, P. R. and Sweet, D. C., eds.*, 1984, pp. 123–42. [G: U.S.]

Soroka, Lewis A. City Size and Income Distributions: The Canadian Experience. *Urban Stud.*, November 1984, *21*(4), pp. 359–66.
[G: Canada]

Stewart, James B. Building a Cooperative Economy: Lessons from the Black Experience. *Rev. Soc. Econ.*, December 1984, *42*(3), pp. 360–68. [G: U.S.]

Stokes, Charles J. Is the New England Urban Tax Rate Too High? *Amer. J. Econ. Soc.*, January 1984, *43*(1), pp. 75–90. [G: U.S.]

Straszheim, Mahlon R. Urban Agglomeration Effects and Employment and Wage Gradients. *J. Urban Econ.*, September 1984, *16*(2), pp. 187–207.

Stuart, Robert C. The Sources of Soviet Urban Growth. In *Morton, H. W. and Stuart, R. C., eds.*, 1984, pp. 25–41. [G: U.S.S.R.]

Sullivan, Arthur M. Land Use and Zoning in the Central Business District. *Reg. Sci. Urban Econ.*, November 1984, *14*(4), pp. 521–32.

Sullivan, Arthur M. Large-Lot Zoning as Second-Best Policy. *J. Reg. Sci.*, November 1984, *24*(4), pp. 581–89. [G: U.S.]

Sullivan, Arthur M. The General Equilibrium Effects of the Industrial Property Tax: Incidence and Excess Burden. *Reg. Sci. Urban Econ.*, November 1984, *14*(4), pp. 547–63.

Sun, Te-Hsiung. Urban-Industrial Development as a Force in Rural Fertility Change: The Case of Taiwan, Republic of China. In *Schutjer, W. A. and Stokes, C. S., eds.*, 1984, pp. 49–76. [G: Taiwan]

Sundaram, K. V. and Prakasa Rao, V. L. S. Metropolitan Expansion in India: Spatial Dynamics and Rural Transformation. In *[Farmer, B. H.]*, 1984, pp. 280–95. [G: India]

Tabb, William K. A Pro-People Urban Policy. In *Tabb, W. K. and Sawers, L., eds.*, 1984, pp. 367–82. [G: U.S.]

Tabb, William K. The Failures of National Urban Policy. In *Tabb, W. K. and Sawers, L., eds.*, 1984, pp. 255–69. [G: U.S.]

Tabb, William K. The New York City Fiscal Crisis. In *Tabb, W. K. and Sawers, L., eds.*, 1984, pp. 323–45. [G: U.S.]

Tabb, William K. Urban Development and Regional Restructuring, an Overview. In *Sawers, L. and Tabb, W. K., eds.*, 1984, pp. 3–15.
[G: U.S.]

Takagi, Yasuoki. The Migration Function and the Todaro Parodox. *Reg. Sci. Urban Econ.*, May 1984, *14*(2), pp. 219–30.

Tarr, Joel A. The Evolution of the Urban Infrastructure in the Nineteenth and Twentieth Centuries. In *Hanson, R., ed.*, 1984, pp. 4–60. [G: U.S.]

Tauchen, Helen and Witte, Ann D. Socially Optimal and Equilibrium Distributions of Office Activity: Models with Exogenous and Endogenous Contacts. *J. Urban Econ.*, January 1984, *15*(1), pp. 66–86.

Thomas, June Manning. Redevelopment and Redistribution. In *Porter, P. R. and Sweet, D. C., eds.*, 1984, pp. 143–59. [G: U.S.]

Thomson, A. M. Urban Poverty and Basic Needs: The Role of the Public Sector. In *Richards, P. J. and Thomson, A. M., eds.*, 1984, pp. 9–39. [G: LDCs]

Tobier, Emanuel. Setting Municipal Priorities: The Setting: Population. In *Brecher, C. and Horton, R. D., eds.*, 1984, pp. 19–42. [G: U.S.]

Todaro, Michael P. Urbanization in Developing Nations: Trends, Prospects, and Policies. In *Ghosh, P. K., ed., no. 2*, 1984, pp. 7–26. [G: LDCs]

Urban Land Institute. Revitalizing Downtown Retailing: Trends and Opportunities. In *Carr, J. H., ed.*, 1984, *1983*, pp. 289–323. [G: U.S.]

Valdez, Avelardo and Jones, Richard C. Geographical Patterns of Undocumented Mexicans and Chicanos in San Antonio, Texas: 1970 and 1980. In *Jones, R. C., ed.*, 1984, pp. 218–35. [G: U.S.]

Varaiya, Pravin and Wiseman, Michael. Bifurcation Models of Urban Development. In *Andersson, Å. E.; Isard, W. and Puu, T., eds.*, 1984, pp. 61–88. [G: U.S.]

Vipond, Joan. The Intra-urban Unemployment Gradient: The Influence of Location on Unemployment. *Urban Stud.*, November 1984, *21*(4), pp. 377–88. [G: Australia]

Weimer, A. M. A Note on the Early History of Land Economics. *Amer. Real Estate Urban Econ. Assoc. J.*, Fall 1984, *12*(3), pp. 408–16. [G: U.S.]

Wijkander, Hans. Provision of Public Goods in Congested Cities. *J. Public Econ.*, November 1984, *25*(1/2), pp. 127–41.

Wiltshaw, D. G. Planning Gain: A Theoretical Note. *Urban Stud.*, May 1984, *21*(2), pp. 183–87. [G: U.K.]

Witsman, Forest. Financing the Nation's Infrastructure Requirements: Discussion. In *Hanson, R., ed.*, 1984, pp. 135–37. [G: U.S.]

Wolman, Abel. The Evolution of the Urban Infrastructure in the Nineteenth and Twentieth Centuries: Discussion. In *Hanson, R., ed.*, 1984, pp. 62–64. [G: U.S.]

Yeh, Anthony Gar-On and Xu, Xueqiang. Provincial Variation of Urbanization and Urban Primacy in China. *Ann. Reg. Sci.*, November 1984, *18*(3), pp. 1–20. [G: China]

Zodrow, George. The Incidence of Metropolitan Property Tax Base Sharing and Rate Equalization. *J. Urban Econ.*, March 1984, *15*(2), pp. 210–29. [G: U.S.]

932 Housing Economics

9320 Housing Economics (including nonurban housing)

Achour, Dominique and Brown, Robert L. Un marche d'options sur indice de prix fonciers: nouvel instrument d'une politique de l'habitition. (With English summary.) *Can. Public Policy*, September 1984, *10*(3), pp. 287–95. [G: Canada]

Agarwal, Vinod B. and Phillips, Richard A. Mortgage Rate Buydowns: Further Evidence. *Housing Finance Rev.*, April 1984, *3*(2), pp. 191–97. [G: U.S.]

Agarwal, Vinod B. and Phillips, Richard A. Mortgage Rate Buydowns: Implications for Housing Price Indexes. *Soc. Sci. Quart.*, September 1984, *65*(3), pp. 868–75. [G: U.S.]

Albon, Robert. The Appropriate Tax Treatment of Owner-Occupiers. *Australian Tax Forum*, December 1984, *1*(4), pp. 391–400. [G: Australia]

Albon, Robert; Findlay, Christopher and Piggott, John. The Welfare Costs of Owner–Occupier Housing Subsidies: Inflation, Tax Treatment, and Interest Rate Regulation. *Australian Econ. Pap.*, December 1984, *23*(43), pp. 206–18. [G: Australia]

Albouy, Michel. Plan d'épargne logement et théorie des options. (Housing Saving Plan and Option Theory. With English summary.) *Écon. Soc.*, November–December 1984, *18*(11–12), pp. 81–98. [G: France]

Alm, James and Follain, James R., Jr. Alternative Mortgage Instruments, the Tilt Problem, and Consumer Welfare. *J. Finan. Quant. Anal.*, March 1984, *19*(1), pp. 113–26.

Alperovich, Gershon. Intraurban Residential Location: A Simultaneous Equations Model. *Atlantic Econ. J.*, July 1984, *12*(2), pp. 32–40. [G: Israel]

Amis, Philip. Squatters or Tenants: The Commercialization of Unauthorized Housing in Nairobi. *World Devel.*, January 1984, *12*(1), pp. 87–96. [G: Kenya]

Anas, Alex and Chu, Chaushie. Discrete Choice Models and the Housing Price and Travel to Work Elasticities of Location Demand. *J. Urban Econ.*, January 1984, *15*(1), pp. 107–23. [G: U.S.]

Anas, Alex and Eum, Sung Jick. Hedonic Analysis of a Housing Market in Disequilibrium. *J. Urban Econ.*, January 1984, *15*(1), pp. 87–106. [G: U.S.]

Anderson, Gary S. Characteristics of Discrete Housing Market Model Equilibria. *J. Urban Econ.*, September 1984, *16*(2), pp. 125–48.

Andrikopoulos, Andreas A. and Brox, James A. The Urban Housing Market: A New Approach for Estimating Demand for Housing by Dwelling Type. *J. Urban Econ.*, March 1984, *15*(2), pp. 230–43. [G: Canada]

Annez, Philippe and Wheaton, William C. Economic Development and the Housing Sector:

A Cross-National Model. *Econ. Develop. Cult. Change*, July 1984, *32*(4), pp. 749–66. [G: Global]

Arnott, Richard; Davidson, Russell and Pines, David. Unanticipated Shocks and the Maintenance and Replacement of Durable Goods. *J. Econ. Dynam. Control*, October 1984, *8*(1), pp. 99–115.

Ashton, Patrick J. Urbanization and the Dynamics of Suburban Development under Capitalism. In *Tabb, W. K. and Sawers, L., eds.*, 1984, pp. 54–81.

Bacci, Massimo Livi. Tendenze demografiche e fabbisogno di abitazioni. (Demographic Trends and Housing Requirements. With English summary.) *Bancaria*, July 1984, *40*(7), pp. 618–22. [G: Italy]

Bajic, Vladimir. An Analysis of the Demand for Housing Attributes. *Appl. Econ.*, August 1984, *16*(4), pp. 597–610. [G: Canada]

Bandyopadhyay, Pradeep. The State, Private Capital and Housing in the Paris Region. *Sci. Soc.*, Summer 1984, *48*(2), pp. 161–91. [G: France]

Barrow, M. M. and O'Sullivan, A. J. The Empirical Determination of House Prices, Error Correction Mechanisms and the Correction of Errors: Comment. *Urban Stud.*, February 1984, *21*(1), pp. 89–91. [G: U.K.]

Bassin, Peter. Housing in Europe: Yugoslavia. In *Wynn, M., ed.*, 1984, pp. 155–77. [G: Yugoslavia]

Bjornstad, David J. and Vogt, David P. Some Comments Relating to Model Specification on "Effects of Nuclear Plants on Residential Property Values." *J. Reg. Sci.*, February 1984, *24*(1), pp. 135–36. [G: U.S.]

Blackwell, John. Housing Finance in Ireland in the 1980s. *Irish Banking Rev.*, December 1984, pp. 69–84. [G: Ireland]

Boehm, Thomas P. Inflation and Intra-Urban Residential Mobility. *Housing Finance Rev.*, January 1984, *3*(1), pp. 19–37. [G: U.S.]

Boleat, Mark. Alternative Housing Finance Systems. *Nat. Westminster Bank Quart. Rev.*, August 1984, pp. 2–12. [G: U.S.; U.K.; Germany]

Boleat, Mark. Housing Finance in Developing Countries. In *Kessler, D. and Ullmo, P.-A., eds.*, 1984, pp. 183–203. [G: LDCs; MDCs]

Braid, Ralph M. The Effects of Government Housing Policies in a Vintage Filtering Model. *J. Urban Econ.*, November 1984, *16*(3), pp. 272–96.

Brouwer, J.; Gordijn, H. E. and Heida, H. R. Toward Unravelling the Interdependency between Migration and Housing Stock Development: A Policy Model. In *ter Heide, H. and Willekens, F. J., eds.*, 1984, pp. 287–307. [G: Netherlands]

Brueckner, Jan K. Creative Financing and House Prices: A Theoretical Inquiry into the Capitalization Issue. *Amer. Real Estate Urban Econ. Assoc. J.*, Winter 1984, *12*(4), pp. 417–26.

Brueckner, Jan K. The Flexible Mortgage: Optimal Financing of a Consumer Durable. *Amer. Real Estate Urban Econ. Assoc. J.*, Summer 1984, *12*(2), pp. 136–52.

Carr, Jack L. and Smith, Lawrence B. Housing Finance Contracts and the Nonneutrality of Inflation. *Housing Finance Rev.*, January 1984, *3*(1), pp. 39–49. [G: U.S.]

Cebula, Richard J. The Urban Family Housing Budget in SMSAs. *Soc. Sci. Quart.*, December 1984, *65*(4), pp. 1157–59. [G: U.S.]

Checkoway, Barry. Large Builders, Federal Housing Programs, and Postwar Suburbanization. In *Tabb, W. K. and Sawers, L., eds.*, 1984, *1980*, pp. 152–73. [G: U.S.]

Christian, James W. and Wilson, Michael L. Capital Requirements for Housing in the 1980s. *Contemp. Policy Issue*, May 1984, (6), pp. 30–44. [G: U.S.]

Clapham, David and Kintrea, Keith. Allocation Systems and Housing Choice. *Urban Stud.*, August 1984, *21*(3), pp. 261–69. [G: U.K.]

Clemmer, Richard B. Measuring Welfare Effects of In-Kind Transfers. *J. Urban Econ.*, January 1984, *15*(1), pp. 46–65. [G: U.S.]

Cloutier, Norman R. The Effect of Structural and Demographic Change on Urban Residential Segregation. *Rev. Soc. Econ.*, April 1984, *42*(1), pp. 32–43. [G: U.S.]

Cloutier, Norman R. The Measurement and Modeling of Segregation: A Survey of Recent Empirical Research. *Reg. Sci. Persp.*, 1984, *14*(2), pp. 15–32. [G: U.S.]

Cobas, José A. Estimating Cost of Living in SMSAs: A Further Note. *Soc. Sci. Quart.*, December 1984, *65*(4), pp. 1160. [G: U.S.]

Cobb, Steven. The Impact of Site Characteristics on Housing Cost Estimates. *J. Urban Econ.*, January 1984, *15*(1), pp. 26–45. [G: U.S.]

Colwell, Peter F. and Guntermann, Karl L. The Value of Neighborhood Schools. *Econ. Educ. Rev.*, 1984, *3*(3), pp. 177–82. [G: U.S.]

Cook, D. B. Building Codes and Regulations in Low Income Settlements. In *Richards, P. J. and Thomson, A. M., eds.*, 1984, pp. 81–91. [G: LDCs]

Cooke, Timothy W. and Hamilton, Bruce W. Evolution of Urban Housing Stocks: A Model Applied to Baltimore and Houston. *J. Urban Econ.*, November 1984, *16*(3), pp. 317–38. [G: U.S.]

Cornuel, Didier. Pourquoi y a-t-il peu de pauvres en H.L.M.? (Why Are There Few Poors in H.L.M. [French Public Housing]? With English summary.) *Consommation*, April–June 1984, *31*(2), pp. 65–85. [G: France]

Cosciani, Cesare. Le distorsioni fiscali nel settore edilizio. (Fiscal Distortions in the Residential-Property Sector. With English summary.) *Bancaria*, July 1984, *40*(7), pp. 623–32. [G: Italy]

Cunningham, Donald F. and Hendershott, Patric H. Pricing FHA Mortgage Default Insurance. *Housing Finance Rev.*, October 1984, *3*(4), pp. 373–92. [G: U.S.]

Cushing, Brian J. Capitalization of Interjurisdictional Fiscal Differentials: An Alternative Approach. *J. Urban Econ.*, May 1984, *15*(3), pp. 317–26. [G: U.S.]

Dale-Johnson, David and Phillips, G. Michael. Housing Attributes Associated with Capital Gain. *Amer. Real Estate Urban Econ. Assoc. J.*, Summer 1984, *12*(2), pp. 162–75. [G: U.S.]

Dániel, Zsuzsa. A Model for Analyzing Desired and Realizable Changes in Housing. *Matekon*, Summer 1984, *20*(4), pp. 3–47. [G: Hungary]

De Borger, Bruno L. Household Attributes and the Demand for Private Rental Housing: Comment. *Economica*, August 1984, *51*(203), pp. 351–55. [G: U.K.]

DeGiovanni, Frank F. An Examination of Selected Consequences of Revitalization in Six U.S. Cities. *Urban Stud.*, August 1984, *21*(3), pp. 245–59. [G: U.S.]

Diamond, Douglas B., Jr. The Impact of Inflation on New House Prices. *Contemp. Policy Issue*, May 1984, (6), pp. 5–16. [G: U.S.]

Diskin, Barry A. and Tashchian, Armen. Application of Logit Analysis to the Determination of Tenant Absorption in Condominium Conversion. *Amer. Real Estate Urban Econ. Assoc. J.*, Summer 1984, *12*(2), pp. 191–205. [G: U.S.]

Doucet, Michael and Weaver, John. The North American Shelter Business, 1860–1920: A Study of a Canadian Real Estate and Property Management Agency. *Bus. Hist. Rev.*, Summer 1984, *58*(2), pp. 234–62. [G: Canada]

Drakakis-Smith, David. Housing in Asia: Review Article. *J. Devel. Stud.*, July 1984, *20*(4), pp. 339–42. [G: Asia]

Dreier, Peter. The Tenants' Movement. In *Tabb, W. K. and Sawers, L., eds.*, 1984, pp. 174–201. [G: U.S.]

Eckart, Wolfgang. A Welfare Analysis of the German Tenants' Protection Legislation. *Z. Nationalökon.*, 1984, *44*(1), pp. 39–56. [G: W. Germany]

Edgren, John A. and Hayworth, Steven C. The Implications of Land Contracts for Property Tax Assessment Practices. *Housing Finance Rev.*, April 1984, *3*(2), pp. 177–89. [G: U.S.]

Edmonds, Radcliffe G., Jr. A Theoretical Basis for Hedonic Regression: A Research Primer. *Amer. Real Estate Urban Econ. Assoc. J.*, Spring 1984, *12*(1), pp. 72–85.

Emanuele, L.; Montagnana, M. and Prizzon, F. A Population Model Accounting for Household Dimensions. In *Avula, X. J. R., et al.*, 1984, pp. 988–92.

Emmi, Philip C. Primal/Dual Relationships in a Pair of Multisectoral Housing Market Models. *J. Reg. Sci.*, February 1984, *24*(1), pp. 17–34.

Esaki, Howard and Wachtenheim, Judy A. Explaining the Recent Level of Single-Family Housing Starts. *Fed. Res. Bank New York Quart. Rev.*, Winter 1984–85, *9*(4), pp. 31–38. [G: U.S.]

Falchi, Paul and Mariano, Reynaldo. Calibration of Residential Location Models for a Multiplant

Firm. *J. Reg. Sci.*, February 1984, *24*(1), pp. 93–104. [G: U.S.]

Fallis, George and Smith, Lawrence B. Uncontrolled Prices in a Controlled Market: The Case of Rent Controls. *Amer. Econ. Rev.*, March 1984, *74*(1), pp. 193–200. [G: U.S.]

Färe, Rolf and Yoon, Bong Joon. Technological Change in Urban Housing Production. *J. Urban Econ.*, November 1984, *16*(3), pp. 351–56. [G: U.S.]

Farley, John E. P* Segregation Indices: What Can They Tell Us about Housing Segregation in 1980? *Urban Stud.*, August 1984, *21*(3), pp. 331–36. [G: U.S.]

Feigenbaum, Susan and Jenkinson, Thomas. Government Incentives for Historic Preservation. *Nat. Tax J.*, March 1984, *37*(1), pp. 113–19. [G: U.S.]

Ferreira, Eurico J. and Sirmans, G. Stacy. Assumable Loan Value in Creative Financing. *Housing Finance Rev.*, April 1984, *3*(2), pp. 139–47.

Fleming, Michael and Nellis, Joseph G. Housing Prices in the United Kingdom: The Problems of Measurement. *Nat. Westminster Bank Quart. Rev.*, November 1984, pp. 43–52. [G: U.K.]

Frankena, Frederick and Koebernick, Thomas. The Pattern of Recent Housing Growth in a Nonmetropolitan County: Effects of Environment and Location. *Growth Change*, October 1984, *15*(4), pp. 32–42. [G: U.S.]

Frech, H. E., III and Lafferty, Ronald N. The Effect of the California Coastal Commission on Housing Prices. *J. Urban Econ.*, July 1984, *16*(1), pp. 105–23. [G: U.S.]

French, Dan W. and Haney, Richard L., Jr. Pricing the Shared-Appreciation Mortgage in a Stochastic Environment. *Housing Finance Rev.*, October 1984, *3*(4), pp. 431–43.

Fry, Maxwell J. and Mak, James. Is Land Leasing a Solution to Unaffordable Housing? An Answer from Fee Simple versus Leasehold Property Price Differentials in Hawaii. *Econ. Inquiry*, October 1984, *22*(4), pp. 529–49. [G: U.S.]

Gabriel, Stuart A. A Note on Housing Market Segmentation in an Israeli Development Town. *Urban Stud.*, May 1984, *21*(2), pp. 189–94. [G: Israel]

Gabriel, Stuart A. and Wolch, Jennifer R. Spillover Effects of Human Service Facilities in a Racially Segmented Housing Market. *J. Urban Econ.*, November 1984, *16*(3), pp. 339–50. [G: U.S.]

Gahvari, Firouz. The Optimal Taxation of Housing. *Public Finance*, 1984, *39*(2), pp. 213–25.

Gainer, William J. Mortgage Revenue Bonds: Their Costs Outweigh Their Benefits to Homebuyers. *Housing Finance Rev.*, October 1984, *3*(4), pp. 457–65. [G: U.S.]

Gamble, Hays B. and Downing, Roger H. Some Comments Relating to Model Specification on "Effects of Nuclear Power Plants on Residential

Property Values": Reply. *J. Reg. Sci.*, February 1984, *24*(1), pp. 137–38. [G: U.S.]

Goodman, Allen C. and Kawai, Masahiro. Estimation and Policy Implications of Rental Housing Demand. *J. Urban Econ.*, July 1984, *16*(1), pp. 76–90. [G: U.S.]

Goodman, Allen C. and Kawai, Masahiro. Functional Form and Rental Housing Market Analysis. *Urban Stud.*, November 1984, *21*(4), pp. 367–76. [G: U.S.]

Goodman, Allen C. and Kawai, Masahiro. Replicative Evidence on the Demand for Owner-Occupied and Rental Housing. *Southern Econ. J.*, April 1984, *50*(4), pp. 1036–57. [G: U.S.]

Gordon, Ian. Lagged Response in Intra-urban Migration of Home Owners: A Comment. *Reg. Stud.*, December 1984, *18*(6), pp. 505–06. [G: Israel]

Green, Cynthia B. and Sanger, Mary Bryna. Setting Municipal Priorities: Service Delivery: Aiding the Poor. In *Brecher, C. and Horton, R. D., eds.*, 1984, pp. 519–50. [G: U.S.]

Greenlees, John S. and Zieschang, Kimberly D. Grouping Tests for Misspecification: An Application to Housing Demand. *J. Bus. Econ. Statist.*, April 1984, *2*(2), pp. 159–69. [G: U.S.]

Hakim, Simon and Weinblatt, J. Towards a Theory of the Impact of Criminal Mobility Influences on Land Values. *Int. J. Soc. Econ.*, 1984, *11*(1/2), pp. 24–30.

Hamnett, Chris. Housing the Two Nations: Socio-Tenurial Polarization in England and Wales, 1961–81. *Urban Stud.*, November 1984, *21*(4), pp. 389–405. [G: U.K.]

Hårsman, Björn. Operational Information Systems for the Housing Market. In *Nijkamp, P. and Rietveld, P., eds.*, 1984, pp. 177–92.

Hartman, Chester. The Right to Stay Put. In *Geisler, C. C. and Popper, F. J., eds.*, 1984, pp. 302–18. [G: U.S.]

Haywood, Ian. Housing in Europe: Denmark. In *Wynn, M., ed.*, 1984, pp. 178–219. [G: Denmark]

Henderson, Jeff and Karn, Valerie. Race, Class and the Allocation of Public Housing in Britain. *Urban Stud.*, May 1984, *21*(2), pp. 115–28. [G: U.K.]

Hendry, David F. Econometric Modelling of House Prices in the United Kingdom. In *Hendry, D. F. and Wallis, K. F., eds.*, 1984, pp. 211–52. [G: U.K.]

Hirsch, Werner Z. The Economics of Landlord–Tenant Relations Laws in Their Local–Federal Setting. In *[Ferber, R.]*, 1984, pp. 255–66. [G: U.S.]

Hogan, Timothy D. The Urban Family Housing Budget in SMSAs: Comment. *Soc. Sci. Quart.*, December 1984, *65*(4), pp. 1161. [G: U.S.]

Hutchens, Robert. The Effect of Different Measures of Benefit on Estimates of the Distributive Consequences of Government Programs: Comment. In *Moon, M., ed.*, 1984, pp. 195–98. [G: U.S.]

Ihlanfeldt, Keith R. Property Taxation and the Demand for Housing: An Econometric Analy-

sis. *J. Urban Econ.*, September 1984, *16*(2), pp. 208–24. [G: U.S.]

Jackson, Jerry R.; Johnson, Ruth C. and Kaserman, David L. The Measurement of Land Prices and the Elasticity of Substitution in Housing Production. *J. Urban Econ.*, July 1984, *16*(1), pp. 1–12. [G: U.S.]

Jaffee, Dwight M. House-Price Capitalization of Creative Finance: An Introduction. *Housing Finance Rev.*, April 1984, *3*(2), pp. 107–17.

Jaffee, Dwight M. New Residential Construction and Energy Costs. In *Downs, A. and Bradbury, K. L., eds.*, 1984, pp. 143–84. [G: U.S.]

Jimenez, Emmanuel. Tenure Security and Urban Squatting. *Rev. Econ. Statist.*, November 1984, *66*(4), pp. 556–67. [G: Philippines]

Jimenez, Emmanuel and Keare, Douglas H. Housing Consumption and Permanent Income in Developing Countries: Estimates from Panel Data in El Salvador. *J. Urban Econ.*, March 1984, *15*(2), pp. 172–94. [G: El Salvador]

Jones, Colin. The Future of Building Societies. *Nat. Westminster Bank Quart. Rev.*, May 1984, pp. 33–46. [G: U.K.]

Kearns, Kevin C. Homelessness in Dublin: An Irish Urban Disorder. *Amer. J. Econ. Soc.*, April 1984, *43*(2), pp. 217–33. [G: Ireland]

Kemeny, Jim. The Swedish Housing Model: A Commentary. *Urban Stud.*, February 1984, *21*(1), pp. 81–82. [G: Sweden]

Kendig, Hal L. Housing Careers, Life Cycle and Residential Mobility: Implications for the Housing Market. *Urban Stud.*, August 1984, *21*(3), pp. 271–83. [G: U.S.]

Kennedy, Declan. Housing in Europe: West Germany. In *Wynn, M., ed.*, 1984, pp. 55–74. [G: W. Germany]

Kent, Richard J. Housing Tenure Choice: Evidence from Time Series. *J. Urban Econ.*, March 1984, *15*(2), pp. 195–209. [G: U.S.]

Kersten, H. M. P. and Bethlehem, J. G. Exploring and Reducing the Nonresponse Bias by Asking the Basic Question. *Statist. J.*, December 1984, *2*(4), pp. 369–80. [G: Netherlands]

Kirwan, R. M. The Demise of Public Housing? In *Le Grand, J. and Robinson, R., eds.*, 1984, pp. 133–45. [G: U.K.]

Krumm, Ronald J. Household Tenure Choice and Migration. *J. Urban Econ.*, November 1984, *16*(3), pp. 259–71. [G: U.S.]

Kwon, Won-Yong. An Examination of Residential Location Behavior in the Seoul Metropolitan Area. *Ann. Reg. Sci.*, November 1984, *18*(3), pp. 33–48. [G: S. Korea]

Lapointe, Alain and Moisan, Hugues. Élasticité de la demande de logement au Canada: nouveaux résultats sur des données désagrégées. (Housing Demand Elasticities in Canada: New Results on Disaggregated Data. With English summary.) *L'Actual. Econ.*, March 1984, *60*(1), pp. 5–23. [G: Canada]

Lauber, Daniel. Condominium Conversions: A Reform in Need of Reform. In *Geisler, C. C. and Popper, F. J., eds.*, 1984, pp. 273–301. [G: U.S.]

Laumas, Prem S. and Williams, Martin. Urbanization and Economic Development. *Eastern Econ. J.*, July–September 1984, *10*(3), pp. 325–32. **[G: Global]**

Lee, Barrett A. and Hodge, David C. Spatial Differentials in Residential Displacement. *Urban Stud.*, August 1984, *21*(3), pp. 219–31. **[G: U.S.]**

LeGates, Richard T. and Murphy, Karen. Austerity, Shelter, and Social Conflict in the United States. In *Tabb, W. K. and Sawers, L., eds.*, 1984, pp. 123–51. **[G: U.S.]**

Lewis, J. R. and Williams, Allan M. Housing in Europe: Portugal. In *Wynn, M., ed.*, 1984, pp. 281–325. **[G: Portugal]**

van Lierop, Wal F. J. and Nijkamp, Peter. Perspectives of Disaggregate Choice Models on the Housing Market. In *Pitfield, D. E., ed.*, 1984, pp. 141–62. **[G: Netherlands]**

van Lierop, Wal F. J. and Rima, Annemarie. Residential Mobility and Probit Analysis. In *Bahrenberg, G.; Fischer, M. M., and Nijkamp, P.*, 1984, pp. 393–407. **[G: Netherlands]**

Lim, Gill-Chin; Follain, James R., Jr. and Renaud, Bertrand. Economics of Residential Crowding in Developing Countries. *J. Urban Econ.*, September 1984, *16*(2), pp. 173–86. **[G: Selected Countries]**

Longley, Paul A. Comparing Discrete Choice Models: Some Housing Market Examples. In *Pitfield, D. E., ed.*, 1984, pp. 163–80. **[G: U.K.]**

Longstreth, Molly; Coveney, Anne R. and Bowers, Jean S. Conservation Characteristics among Determinants of Residential Property Value. *J. Cons. Res.*, June 1984, *11*(1), pp. 564–71. **[G: U.S.]**

MacCannell, Dean and White, Jerry. The Social Costs of Large-Scale Agriculture: The Prospects of Land Reform in California. In *Geisler, C. C. and Popper, F. J., eds.*, 1984, pp. 35–54. **[G: U.S.]**

Mark, Jonathan H. and Goldberg, Michael A. Alternative Housing Price Indices: An Evaluation. *Amer. Real Estate Urban Econ. Assoc. J.*, Spring 1984, *12*(1), pp. 30–49. **[G: Canada]**

Marks, Denton. The Effect of Rent Control on the Price of Rental Housing: An Hedonic Approach. *Land Econ.*, February 1984, *60*(1), pp. 81–94. **[G: U.S.]**

Marks, Denton. The Effects of Partial-Coverage Rent Control on the Price and Quantity of Rental Housing. *J. Urban Econ.*, November 1984, *16*(3), pp. 360–69.

Massey, Pat. The Role of Building Societies in Irish Financial Markets. *Irish Banking Rev.*, March 1984, pp. 6–17. **[G: Ireland]**

Mattsson, Lars-Göran. Equivalence between Welfare and Entropy Approaches to Residential Location. *Reg. Sci. Urban Econ.*, May 1984, *14*(2), pp. 147–73. **[G: Sweden]**

McCutcheon, Laurie. Measuring Migrant Change: A Look at Housing in Bogota, Seoul, and Surabaya. *J. Devel. Areas*, April 1984, *18*(3), pp. 357–72. **[G: Colombia; Korea; Indonesia]**

Millar, James R. The Household Sector: The View from the Bottom. In *Hoffmann, E. P. and Laird, R. F., eds.*, 1984, 1981, pp. 529–61. **[G: U.S.S.R.]**

Moore, James S.; Reichert, Alan K. and Cho, Chien-Ching. Analyzing the Temporal Stability of Appraisal Model Coefficients: An Application of Ridge Regression Techniques. *Amer. Real Estate Urban Econ. Assoc. J.*, Spring 1984, *12*(1), pp. 50–71. **[G: U.S.]**

Moore, Richard J. Urbanization and Housing Policy in Mexico. In *Aspe, P. and Sigmund, P. E., eds.*, 1984, pp. 327–56. **[G: Mexico]**

Morgenstern, Richard D. Energy Prices and Urban Decentralization: Comment. In *Downs, A. and Bradbury, K. L., eds.*, 1984, pp. 104–09. **[G: U.S.]**

Morlan, Terry H. Energy and the Existing Stock of Housing: Comment. In *Downs, A. and Bradbury, K. L., eds.*, 1984, pp. 139–42. **[G: U.S.]**

Morton, Henry W. Housing in the Soviet Union. In *Hoffmann, E. P., ed.*, 1984, pp. 69–80. **[G: U.S.S.R.]**

Morton, Henry W. The Contemporary Soviet City. In *Morton, H. W. and Stuart, R. C., eds.*, 1984, pp. 3–24. **[G: U.S.S.R.]**

Muller, Thomas. Urban and Regional Change: The Federal Role and National Policy. In *Carr, J. H., ed.*, 1984, 1982, pp. 342–49. **[G: U.S.]**

Muth, Richard F. Energy Prices and Urban Decentralization. In *Downs, A. and Bradbury, K. L., eds.*, 1984, pp. 85–104. **[G: U.S.]**

Neels, Kevin and Murray, Michael P. Energy and the Existing Stock of Housing. In *Downs, A. and Bradbury, K. L., eds.*, 1984, pp. 110–39. **[G: U.S.]**

Nellis, Joseph G. The Empirical Determination of House Prices, Error Correction Mechanisms and the Correction of Errors: A Reply. *Urban Stud.*, February 1984, *21*(1), pp. 93–94. **[G: U.K.]**

Nelson, Robert H. Private Neighborhoods: A New Direction for the Neighborhood Movement. In *Geisler, C. C. and Popper, F. J., eds.*, 1984, pp. 319–38. **[G: U.S.]**

Netzer, Dick. On Modernizing Local Public Finance: Why Aren't Property Taxes in Urban Areas Being Reformed into Land Value Taxes? *Amer. J. Econ. Soc.*, October 1984, *43*(4), pp. 497–501. **[G: U.S.]**

Occhiuto, Antonino. I problemi dell'edilizia abitativa in Italia. (Residential-building Problems in Italy. With English summary.) *Bancaria*, July 1984, *40*(7), pp. 603–06. **[G: Italy]**

Olsen, Edgar O. and York, Kathy A. The Effect of Different Measures of Benefit on Estimates of the Distributive Consequences of Government Programs. In *Moon, M., ed.*, 1984, pp. 177–95. **[G: U.S.]**

Ozanne, Larry. The Financial Stakes in Due-on-Sale: The Case of California's State-chartered Savings and Loans. *Amer. Real Estate Urban*

Econ. Assoc. J., Winter 1984, *12*(4), pp. 473–94. **[G: U.S.]**

Padovani, Liliana. Housing in Europe: Italy. **In** *Wynn, M., ed.*, 1984, pp. 247–80. **[G: Italy]**

Palmquist, Raymond B. Estimating the Demand for the Characteristics of Housing. *Rev. Econ. Statist.*, August 1984, *66*(3), pp. 394–404.
[G: U.S.]

Patterson, Orlando. The Realities of Intervention in Alienated Cultures: A Jamaican Case Study. **In** *Brooks, H.; Liebman, L. and Schelling, C. S., eds.*, 1984, pp. 131–52. **[G: Jamaica]**

Pearsall, Jon. Housing in Europe: France. **In** *Wynn, M., ed.*, 1984, pp. 9–54. **[G: France]**

Peña, Daniel and Ruiz-Castillo, Javier. Distributional Aspects of Public Rental Housing and Rent Control Policies in Spain. *J. Urban Econ.*, May 1984, *15*(3), pp. 350–70. **[G: Spain]**

Peña, Daniel and Ruiz-Castillo, Javier. Robust Methods of Building Regression Models—An Application to the Housing Sector. *J. Bus. Econ. Statist.*, January 1984, *2*(1), pp. 10–20. **[G: Spain]**

Peskin, Janice. Approaches to Measuring and Valuing In-Kind Subsidies and the Distribution of Their Benefits: Comment. **In** *Moon, M., ed.*, 1984, pp. 171–76. **[G: U.S.]**

Piggott, John. The Value of Tenant Benefits from UK Council Housing Subsidies. *Econ. J.*, June 1984, *94*(374), pp. 384–89. **[G: U.K.]**

Plaut, Steven E. Endogenous Mortgage Interest and the Consumption of Housing. *J. Urban Econ.*, July 1984, *16*(1), pp. 31–45.

Poterba, James M. Tax Subsidies to Owner-occupied Housing: An Asset-Market Approach. *Quart. J. Econ.*, November 1984, *99*(4), pp. 729–52. **[G: U.S.]**

Prentice, Richard. Comparability and Incomparability in Housing Programmes in Wales; A Spatial Analysis for 1981. *Urban Stud.*, November 1984, *21*(4), pp. 427–38. **[G: U.K.]**

Quigley, John M. Residential Energy Standards and the Housing Market: A Regional Analysis. *Int. Reg. Sci. Rev.*, December 1984, *9*(3), pp. 201–16. **[G: U.S.]**

Quigley, John M. The Production of Housing Services and the Derived Demand for Residential Energy. *Rand J. Econ.*, Winter 1984, *15*(4), pp. 555–67. **[G: U.S.]**

Rabiega, William A.; Lin, Ta-Win and Robinson, Linda M. The Property Value Impacts of Public Housing Projects in Low and Moderate Density Residential Neighborhoods. *Land Econ.*, May 1984, *60*(2), pp. 174–79.
[G: U.S.]

Reece, B. F. The Price Adjustment Mechanism in Glasgow's Rental Housing Market, 1871–1913: The Claim of "Sticky" Rents Re-assessed. *Scot. J. Polit. Econ.*, November 1984, *31*(3), pp. 286–93. **[G: U.K.]**

Reid, Clifford E. The Reliability of Fair Housing Audits to Detect Racial Discrimination in Rental Housing Markets. *Amer. Real Estate Urban Econ. Assoc. J.*, Spring 1984, *12*(1), pp. 86–96. **[G: U.S.]**

Remolona, Eli M. A Simple Model of Squatters. *Philippine Rev. Econ. Bus.*, Mar./June 1984, *21*(1/2), pp. 101–11. **[G: Philippines]**

Rich, Jonathan M. Municipal Boundaries in a Discriminatory Housing Market: An Example of Racial Leapfrogging. *Urban Stud.*, February 1984, *21*(1), pp. 31–40. **[G: U.S.]**

Roistacher, Elizabeth and Tobier, Emanuel. Setting Municipal Priorities: Service Delivery: Housing Policy. **In** *Brecher, C. and Horton, R. D., eds.*, 1984, pp. 446–81. **[G: U.S.]**

Rosen, Harvey S.; Rosen, Kenneth T. and Holtz-Eakin, Douglas. Housing Tenure, Uncertainty, and Taxation. *Rev. Econ. Statist.*, August 1984, *66*(3), pp. 405–16. **[G: U.S.]**

Rosen, Kenneth T. Creative Financing and House Prices: A Study of Capitalization Effects. *Housing Finance Rev.*, April 1984, *3*(2), pp. 119–27. **[G: U.S.]**

Rosenthal, Leslie. Quarterly Owner-occupied House Price Indices for the U.K., 1975–81. *Manchester Sch. Econ. Soc. Stud.*, September 1984, *52*(3), pp. 272–83. **[G: U.K.]**

Rossano, Geoffrey. Suburbia Armed: Nassau County Development and the Rise of the Aerospace Industry, 1909–60. **In** *Lotchin, R. W., ed.*, 1984, pp. 61–87. **[G: U.S.]**

Rudel, Thomas K. and Neaigus, Alan. Inflation, New Homeowners and Downgrading in the 1970s. *Urban Stud.*, May 1984, *21*(2), pp. 129–38. **[G: U.S.]**

Ryker, Randy E.; Pol, Louis G. and Guy, Rebecca F. Racial Discrimination as a Determinant of Home Improvement Loans. *Urban Stud.*, May 1984, *21*(2), pp. 177–82.
[G: U.S.]

Sa-Aadu, Jarjisu. Alternative Estimates of Direct Tenant Benefit and Consumption Inefficiencies from the Section 8 New Construction Program. *Land Econ.*, May 1984, *60*(2), pp. 189–201.
[G: U.S.]

Sa-Aadu, Jarjisu. Another Look at the Economics of Demand-Side versus Supply-Side Strategies in Low-Income Housing. *Amer. Real Estate Urban Econ. Assoc. J.*, Winter 1984, *12*(4), pp. 427–60. **[G: U.S.]**

Saulter, Kenneth J. Home Energy Costs and the Housing of the Poor and the Elderly: Comment. **In** *Downs, A. and Bradbury, K. L., eds.*, 1984, pp. 78–84. **[G: U.S.]**

Savas, E. S. More Insights on Rental Vouchers and Housing Subsidies. *J. Policy Anal. Manage.*, Spring 1984, *3*(3), pp. 449–50.
[G: U.S.]

Scafuri, Allen J. Uncertainty and Equilibrium in a Housing Market. *Reg. Sci. Persp.*, 1984, *14*(2), pp. 81–93.

Scheurwater, Jan. Toward a Spatial Demographic Information System. **In** *ter Heide, H. and Willekens, F. J., eds.*, 1984, pp. 69–93.
[G: Netherlands]

Scholten, H. J. Residential Mobility and Log-Linear Modelling. **In** *Bahrenberg, G.; Fischer, M. M., and Nijkamp, P.*, 1984, pp. 271–87.
[G: Netherlands]

Schwartz, Arthur L., Jr. and Kapplin, Steven

D. Economic Implications of Alternative Home Financing. *Housing Finance Rev.*, April 1984, 3(2), pp. 165–75.   [G: U.S.]

Schwartz, Seymour I.; Hansen, David E. and Green, Richard. The Effect of Growth Control on the Production of Moderate-Priced Housing. *Land Econ.*, February 1984, 60(1), pp. 110–14.   [G: U.S.]

Sewel, J.; Twine, F. and Williams, N. The Sale of Council Houses: Some Empirical Evidence. *Urban Stud.*, November 1984, 21(4), pp. 439–50.   [G: U.K.]

Sheehan, Robert J. New Residential Construction and Energy Costs: Comment. In *Downs, A. and Bradbury, K. L., eds.*, 1984, pp. 184–87.   [G: U.S.]

Skjoldager, Arne. Housing Finance in Denmark. *Irish Banking Rev.*, June 1984, pp. 24–32.   [G: Denmark]

Smeeding, Timothy M. Approaches to Measuring and Valuing In-Kind Subsidies and the Distribution of Their Benefits. In *Moon, M., ed.*, 1984, pp. 139–71.   [G: U.S.]

Smith, Lawrence B. Household Headship Rates, Household Formation, and Housing Demand in Canada. *Land Econ.*, May 1984, 60(2), pp. 180–88.   [G: Canada]

Smith, Lawrence B., et al. The Demand for Housing, Household Headship Rates, and Household Formation: An International Analysis. *Urban Stud.*, November 1984, 21(4), pp. 407–14.   [G: U.S.; Canada; U.K.; France]

Smith, Roger. Housing in Europe: Great Britain. In *Wynn, M., ed.*, 1984, pp. 75–120.   [G: U.K.]

Smith, Stanley D. and Sirmans, G. Stacy. The Shifting of FHA Discount Points: Actual vs. Expectations. *Amer. Real Estate Urban Econ. Assoc. J.*, Summer 1984, 12(2), pp. 153–61.   [G: U.S.]

Smith, Stanley D.; Sirmans, G. Stacy and Sirmans, C. F. The Valuation of Creative Financing in Housing. *Housing Finance Rev.*, April 1984, 3(2), pp. 129–38.   [G: U.S.]

St. John, Craig and Clark, Frieda. Race and Social Class Differences in the Characteristics Desired in Residential Neighborhoods. *Soc. Sci. Quart.*, September 1984, 65(3), pp. 803–13.   [G: U.S.]

Staemmler, Gerlind. Housing in Europe: East Germany (The German Democratic Republic). In *Wynn, M., ed.*, 1984, pp. 220–46.   [G: E. Germany]

Strassmann, W. Paul. The Timing of Urban Infrastructure and Housing Improvements by Owner Occupants. *World Devel.*, July 1984, 12(7), pp. 743–53.   [G: Peru]

Strathman, James G.; DeLacy, P. Barton and Dueker, Kenneth J. Creative Financing "Concessions" in Residential Sales: Effects and Implications. *Housing Finance Rev.*, April 1984, 3(2), pp. 149–63.   [G: U.S.]

Struyk, Raymond J. Home Energy Costs and the Housing of the Poor and the Elderly. In *Downs, A. and Bradbury, K. L., eds.*, 1984, pp. 35–78.   [G: U.S.]

Sullivan, Arthur M. Large-Lot Zoning as Second-Best Policy. *J. Reg. Sci.*, November 1984, 24(4), pp. 581–89.   [G: U.S.]

Sundaram, K. V. and Prakasa Rao, V. L. S. Metropolitan Expansion in India: Spatial Dynamics and Rural Transformation. In *[Farmer, B. H.]*, 1984, pp. 280–95.   [G: India]

Swan, Craig. A Model of Rental and Owner-occupied Housing. *J. Urban Econ.*, November 1984, 16(3), pp. 297–316.

Taylor, William M.; Wichern, Dean W. and Stanley, Craig E. An Intertemporal Analysis of the Shifting of FHA Discount Points to Buyers. *Managerial Dec. Econ.*, December 1984, 5(4), pp. 242–50.   [G: U.S.]

Tuccillo, John A. Disinflation and Housing Investment: A Revisionist Analysis. *Contemp. Policy Issue*, May 1984, (6), pp. 17–29.   [G: U.S.]

Vandell, Kerry D. and Zerbst, Robert H. Estimates of the Effect of School Desegregation Plans on Housing Values over Time. *Amer. Real Estate Urban Econ. Assoc. J.*, Summer 1984, 12(2), pp. 109–35.   [G: U.S.]

Veldhuisen, K. J. An Application of a Linear Logit Regression Model to Residential Mobility. In *Bahrenberg, G.; Fischer, M. M., and Nijkamp, P.*, 1984, pp. 289–301.   [G: Netherlands]

Venti, Steven F. and Wise, David A. Moving and Housing Expenditure: Transaction Costs and Disequilibrium. *J. Public Econ.*, February/March 1984, 23(1/2), pp. 207–43.   [G: U.S.]

Wegner, Eckhard. Die Bedeutung der Einkommensverteilung für die Funktionsweise des Wohnungsmarktes. Eine Modellanalyse unter Einschluss der Betrachtung von Politikmöglichkeiten. (The Relevance of the Income Distribution for the Functioning Mode of the Housing Market. With English summary.) *Z. Wirtschaft. Sozialwissen.*, 1984, 104(2), pp. 177–94.

Weicher, John C. Disinflation in the Housing Market. In *Fellner, W., ed.*, 1984, pp. 155–204.   [G: U.S.]

Weicher, John C. Halfway to a Housing Allowance? In *Weicher, J. C., ed.*, 1984, pp. 92–118.   [G: U.S.]

Weicher, John C. Housing and Housing Finance in an Era of Inflation and Disinflation: Introduction. *Contemp. Policy Issue*, May 1984, (6), pp. 1–4.   [G: U.S.]

Weistroffer, H. Roland. Modelling the Demand for Construction. *J. Stud. Econ. Econometrics*, January 1984, (18), pp. 36–47. [G: S. Africa]

ter Welle, F. Uncertainty and Policy Targets in Migration Projections. In *ter Heide, H. and Willekens, F. J., eds.*, 1984, pp. 271–85.   [G: Netherlands]

Werlin, Herbert H. Urban Shelter and Community Development. In *Weiss, C. and Jéquier, N., eds.*, 1984, pp. 141–55.   [G: Selected Countries]

Whinihan, Michael J. Condominium Conversion and the Tax Reform Acts of 1969 and 1976. *Amer. Real Estate Urban Econ. Assoc. J.*, Winter 1984, 12(4), pp. 461–72.   [G: U.S.]

Whitehead, Christine M. E. Privatisation and

Housing. In *Le Grand, J. and Robinson, R.*, eds., 1984, pp. 116–32. **[G: U.K.]**

Wiesmeth, Hans. Contract Equilibria in Housing Markets. *Reg. Sci. Urban Econ.*, November 1984, *14*(4), pp. 505–19.

Williams, Ross A. An Australian Housing Model. *Econ. Rec.*, June 1984, *60*(169), pp. 143–55. **[G: Australia]**

Wynn, Martin. Housing in Europe: Introduction. In *Wynn, M., ed.*, 1984, pp. 1–8. **[G: W. Europe]**

Wynn, Martin. Housing in Europe: Spain. In *Wynn, M., ed.*, 1984, pp. 121–54. **[G: Spain]**

Yang, Chin-Wei and Dennis, Enid. Elasticities and Rent Control Revisited. *Atlantic Econ. J.*, December 1984, *12*(4), pp. 59–61.

Yeh, S. Urban Low-income Housing in South-east Asia. In *Richards, P. J. and Thomson, A. M.*, eds., 1984, pp. 41–80. **[G: S. E. Asia]**

933 Urban Transportation Economics

9330 Urban Transportation Economics

Anas, Alex and Chu, Chaushie. Discrete Choice Models and the Housing Price and Travel to Work Elasticities of Location Demand. *J. Urban Econ.*, January 1984, *15*(1), pp. 107–23. **[G: U.S.]**

Anas, Alex and Moses, Leon N. Qualitative Choice and the Blending of Discrete Alternatives. *Rev. Econ. Statist.*, November 1984, *66*(4), pp. 547–55. **[G: S. Korea]**

Bajic, Vladimir. Choice of Travel Mode for Work Trips: Some Findings for Metropolitan Toronto. *Int. J. Transport Econ.*, April 1984, *11*(1), pp. 79–96. **[G: Canada]**

Bee, C. K. and Sargious, M. A. Modeling Community Reactions to Transportation Impacts. In *Avula, X. J. R., et al.*, 1984, pp. 847–52. **[G: Canada]**

Berglas, Eitan; Fresko, David and Pines, David. Right of Way and Congestion Toll. *J. Transp. Econ. Policy*, May 1984, *18*(2), pp. 165–87. **[G: U.S.]**

Borins, Sandford F. The Economic Effects of Non-Optimal Pricing and Investment Policies for Substitutable Transport Facilities. *Can. J. Econ.*, February 1984, *17*(1), pp. 80–98. **[G: Canada]**

Brailovskii, N. O. Modeling Urban Transport Systems (Experience, Problems, and the Future). *Matekon*, Winter 1984–85, *21*(2), pp. 26–48. **[G: U.S.S.R.]**

Button, K. J. Subsidies and the Provision of Urban Public Transport. *Int. J. Transport Econ.*, Aug.-Dec. 1984, *11*(2–3), pp. 177–88. **[G: U.K.]**

Chomitz, Kenneth M. and Lave, Charles A. Part-Time Labour, Work Rules, and Urban Transit Costs. *J. Transp. Econ. Policy*, January 1984, *18*(1), pp. 63–73. **[G: U.S.]**

Crampton, Graham. Subsidies to Urban Public Transport and Privatisation. In *Le Grand, J. and Robinson, R., eds.*, 1984, pp. 201–11. **[G: U.K.]**

De Borger, Bruno L. Cost and Productivity in Regional Bus Transportation: The Belgian Case. *J. Ind. Econ.*, September 1984, *33*(1), pp. 37–54. **[G: Belgium]**

Doxsey, Lawrence B. Demand for Unlimited Use Transit Passes. *J. Transp. Econ. Policy*, January 1984, *18*(1), pp. 7–22. **[G: U.S.]**

Dunne, John Paul. Commuting Mode Choice in New Towns: A Case Study of Livingston. *Scot. J. Polit. Econ.*, February 1984, *31*(1), pp. 60–71. **[G: U.K.]**

Glaister, Stephen. The Allocation of Urban Public Transport Subsidy. In *Le Grand, J. and Robinson, R., eds.*, 1984, pp. 177–200. **[G: U.K.]**

Grava, Sigurd. Urban Transport in the Soviet Union. In *Morton, H. W. and Stuart, R. C., eds.*, 1984, pp. 180–201. **[G: U.S.S.R.]**

Heffley, Dennis R. Pricing in an Urban Spatial Monopoly: A Reply. *J. Reg. Sci.*, May 1984, *24*(2), pp. 291–93.

Hensher, David A. A Rejoinder [The Value of Commuter Travel Time Savings: Empirical Estimation Using an Alternative Valuation Model]. *J. Transp. Econ. Policy*, May 1984, *18*(2), pp. 201–03.

Kanemoto, Yoshitsugu. Pricing and Investment Policies in a System of Competitive Commuter Railways. *Rev. Econ. Stud.*, October 1984, *51*(4), pp. 665–81.

Layton, Allan P. The Value of Commuter Travel Time Savings: Some Clarifications. *J. Transp. Econ. Policy*, May 1984, *18*(2), pp. 199–201.

Lee, Li Way. The Economics of Carpools. *Econ. Inquiry*, January 1984, *22*(1), pp. 128–35.

Loeb, Peter D. and Gilad, Benjamin. The Efficacy and Cost-Effectiveness of Vehicle Inspection: A State Specific Analysis Using Time Series Data. *J. Transp. Econ. Policy*, May 1984, *18*(2), pp. 145–64. **[G: U.S.]**

McCarthy, Patrick S. Automobile Captive Choice Behavior—An Application of Nested Logit Analysis. *Logist. Transp. Rev.*, June 1984, *20*(2), pp. 127–48. **[G: U.S.]**

McGeehan, H. Forecasting the Demand for Inter-Urban Railway Travel in the Republic of Ireland. *J. Transp. Econ. Policy*, September 1984, *18*(3), pp. 275–92. **[G: Ireland]**

Morgenstern, Richard D. Energy Prices and Urban Decentralization: Comment. In *Downs, A. and Bradbury, K. L., eds.*, 1984, pp. 104–09. **[G: U.S.]**

Muth, Richard F. Energy Prices and Urban Decentralization. In *Downs, A. and Bradbury, K. L., eds.*, 1984, pp. 85–104. **[G: U.S.]**

Obeng, Kofi. The Economics of Bus Transit Operation. *Logist. Transp. Rev.*, March 1984, *20*(1), pp. 45–65. **[G: U.S.]**

Ohta, Hiroshi and Okamura, M. Pricing in an Urban Spatial Monopoly: A Comment. *J. Reg. Sci.*, May 1984, *24*(2), pp. 287–90.

Peiser, Richard B. Land Use versus Road Network Design in Community Transport Cost Evaluation. *Land Econ.*, February 1984, *60*(1), pp. 95–109.

Petretto, Alessandro and Viviani, Alessandro. An Econometric Model for Cross-Section Analysis of the Production of Urban Transport Service. *Econ. Notes*, 1984, (1), pp. 35–65. **[G: Italy]**

Pines, David and Sadka, Efraim. Gasoline Prices, Welfare and Congestion Tolls. *Scand. J. Econ.*, 1984, 86(4), pp. 440–51.

Roth, G. Improving the Mobility of the Urban Poor. In *Richards, P. J. and Thomson, A. M., eds.*, 1984, pp. 215–42. **[G: LDCs]**

Rothwell, Roy. Creating a Regional Innovation-oriented Infrastructure: The Role of Public Procurement. *Ann. Pub. Co-op. Econ.*, April–June 1984, 55(2), pp. 159–72. **[G: U.K.]**

Rüsch, Gerhard. Is the Crisis of Urban Transport (Also) a Crisis of Transport Planning? *Int. J. Transport Econ.*, April 1984, 11(1), pp. 7–21. **[G: Austria]**

Savage, Ian P. "Unnecessary and Wasteful" Competition in Bus Transport. *J. Transp. Econ. Policy*, September 1984, 18(3), pp. 303–09.

Sawers, Larry. The Political Economy of Urban Transportation: An Interpretive Essay. In *Tabb, W. K. and Sawers, L., eds.*, 1984, pp. 223–54. **[G: U.S.]**

Stephanedes, Y. J. and Kumar, V. Comparative Evaluation of Intercity Demand Models. In *Pitfield, D. E., ed.*, 1984, pp. 114–21. **[G: U.S.]**

Thobani, Mateen. A Nested Logit Model of Travel Mode to Work and Auto Ownership. *J. Urban Econ.*, May 1984, 15(3), pp. 287–301. **[G: Pakistan]**

Werlin, Herbert H. Urban Traffic Management. In *Weiss, C. and Jéquier, N., eds.*, 1984, pp. 69–84. **[G: Selected Countries]**

940 REGIONAL ECONOMICS

941 Regional Economics

9410 General

Bartels, Cornelis P. A. and Van Duijn, Jacob J. Implementing Regional Economic Policy: An Analysis of Economic and Political Influences in The Netherlands. *Reg. Stud.*, February 1984, 18(1), pp. 1–11. **[G: Netherlands]**

Batey, Peter W. J. Information for Long-Term Planning of Regional Development. In *Nijkamp, P. and Rietveld, P., eds.*, 1984, pp. 63–79. **[G: W. Germany]**

Booth, Douglas E. and Fortis, Louis C. Building a Cooperative Economy: A Strategy for Community Based Economic Development. *Rev. Soc. Econ.*, December 1984, 42(3), pp. 339–59.

Brown, Peter J. B. Monitoring and Regional Information Systems under Uncertainty. In *Nijkamp, P. and Rietveld, P., eds.*, 1984, pp. 81–100.

Cuthbert, J. R. Proportion Analysis on Cell Data: Distortions Due to Variations in Cell Sizes. *Urban Stud.*, February 1984, 21(1), pp. 83–88. **[G: U.K.]**

Damesick, Peter. The Future of Regional Planning and Policy in the UK: The Findings of the RSA Inquiry. *Reg. Stud.*, April 1984, 18(2), pp. 165–73. **[G: U.K.]**

Dendrinos, Dimitrios S. Regions, Antiregions, and Their Dynamic Stability: The U.S. Case (1929–1979). *J. Reg. Sci.*, February 1984, 24(1), pp. 65–83. **[G: U.S.]**

Drozd, Antonin. Information Systems for Integrated Regional Planning and Policy Making in Czechoslovakia. In *Nijkamp, P. and Rietveld, P., eds.*, 1984, pp. 375–87.

Dujnic, P.; Issaev, B. and Slimak, D. Regional Information Systems in Centrally Planned Economies. In *Nijkamp, P. and Rietveld, P., eds.*, 1984, pp. 121–38.

van Est, Jan; Scheurwater, Jan and Voogd, Henk. Information Systems for Integrated Regional Planning and Policy Making in the Netherlands. In *Nijkamp, P. and Rietveld, P., eds.*, 1984, pp. 353–73.

van Est, Jan and de Vroege, Frans. Disaggregate Spatial Information Systems: The Use of Geocoding in Regional Planning. In *Nijkamp, P. and Rietveld, P., eds.*, 1984, pp. 251–61.

Garnick, Daniel H. Information Systems for Integrated Regional Planning and Policy Making in the United States. In *Nijkamp, P. and Rietveld, P., eds.*, 1984, pp. 335–51.

Grubel, Herbert G. Free Enterprise Zones in Economic Development. In *Giersch, H., ed.*, 1984, pp. 222–35.

Guteland, G. and Nygren, O. Information Systems for Integrated Regional Planning and Policy Making in Sweden. In *Nijkamp, P. and Rietveld, P., eds.*, 1984, pp. 297–317.

Hinloopen, Edwin and Nijkamp, Peter. Information Systems and Uncertainty in Planning. In *Nijkamp, P. and Rietveld, P., eds.*, 1984, pp. 101–19.

Hoffmann, Lutz. Free Enterprise Zones in Economic Development: Comment. In *Giersch, H., ed.*, 1984, pp. 242–48.

Hope, Kempe Ronald. Unemployment, Labour Force Participation, and Urbanization in the Caribbean. *Rev. Reg. Stud.*, Fall 1984, 14(3), pp. 9–16. **[G: Caribbean]**

Janhunen, Olli. Information Systems for Integrated Regional Planning and Policy Making in Finland. In *Nijkamp, P. and Rietveld, P., eds.*, 1984, pp. 389–409.

Lakshmanan, T. R. Information Systems for Regional Development, with Special Emphasis on Developing Countries. In *Nijkamp, P. and Rietveld, P., eds.*, 1984, pp. 139–59. **[G: Sri Lanka; LDCs]**

McTavish, D. Regional Policy, Urban Unemployment and the Development of Community Businesses in Scotland. *Reg. Stud.*, February 1984, 18(1), pp. 81–84. **[G: U.K.]**

Muguet, Jean. Information Systems for Integrated Regional Planning and Policy Making in France. In *Nijkamp, P. and Rietveld, P., eds.*, 1984, pp. 319–33.

Nijkamp, Peter. Information Systems: A General Introduction. In *Nijkamp, P. and Rietveld, P., eds.*, 1984, pp. 3–33.

Nijkamp, Peter and Rietveld, Piet. A General Framework for Comparison of Regional Information Systems. In *Nijkamp, P. and Rietveld, P., eds.*, 1984, pp. 287–96.

Nijkamp, Peter and Rietveld, Piet. Information Systems: Retrospect and Prospect. In *Nijkamp, P. and Rietveld, P., eds.*, 1984, pp. 429–45.

Nijkamp, Peter and Rietveld, Piet. Spatially Oriented Information Systems. In *Nijkamp, P. and Rietveld, P., eds.*, 1984, pp. 35–54.

Pedrao, Fernando. Problems of Urban Development and Regional Planning in Latin America. In *Ghosh, P. K., ed., no. 2*, 1984, *1974*, pp. 312–42. **[G: Latin America]**

Peters, Aribert B. Political, Social, and Technical Bottlenecks in Computerized Spatial Information Systems. In *Nijkamp, P. and Rietveld, P., eds.*, 1984, pp. 55–60.

Peters, Aribert B. Technical Aspects of Computerized Spatial Information Systems. In *Nijkamp, P. and Rietveld, P., eds.*, 1984, pp. 263–69.

Rasmussen, David W.; Bendick, Marc, Jr. and Ledebur, Larry C. A Methodology for Selecting Economic Development Incentives. *Growth Change*, January 1984, *15*(1), pp. 18–25. **[G: U.S.]**

Rondinelli, Dennis A. Balanced Urbanization, Regional Integration and Development Planning in Asia. In *Ghosh, P. K., ed., no. 2*, 1984, *1980*, pp. 216–35. **[G: LDCs]**

Schweickart, David. Plant Relocations: A Philosophical Reflection. *Rev. Radical Polit. Econ.*, Winter 1984, *16*(4), pp. 32–51.

Tabb, William K. Economic Democracy and Regional Restructuring: An Internationalization Perspective. In *Sawers, L. and Tabb, W. K., eds.*, 1984, pp. 403–16. **[G: U.S.]**

Tabb, William K. Urban Development and Regional Restructuring, an Overview. In *Sawers, L. and Tabb, W. K., eds.*, 1984, pp. 3–15. **[G: U.S.]**

Udovenko, V. Location of the Productive Forces and the Effectiveness of Social Production. *Prob. Econ.*, June 1984, *27*(2), pp. 57–74. **[G: U.S.S.R.]**

Wannop, U. A. Strategic Planning and the Area Development Projects of the Scottish Development Agency. *Reg. Stud.*, February 1984, *18*(1), pp. 77–81. **[G: U.K.]**

Wigan, M. R. Information Technology and Integrated Regional Development. In *Nijkamp, P. and Rietveld, P., eds.*, 1984, pp. 271–83.

Wiltshaw, D. G. Planning Gain: A Theoretical Note. *Urban Stud.*, May 1984, *21*(2), pp. 183–87. **[G: U.K.]**

Yamaguchi, S. and Kuczek, E. The Social and Economic Impact of Large-Scale Energy Projects on the Local Community. *Int. Lab. Rev.*, March-April 1984, *123*(2), pp. 149–65. **[G: U.S.]**

9411 Theory of Regional Economics

Anselin, Luc. Specification Tests and Model Selection for Aggregate Spatial Interaction: An Empirical Comparison. *J. Reg. Sci.*, February 1984, *24*(1), pp. 1–15. **[G: Canada]**

Arcelus, Francisco J. An Extension of Shift-Share Analysis. *Growth Change*, January 1984, *15*(1), pp. 3–8.

Bahrenberg, G. Spatial Analysis: A Retrospective View. In *Bahrenberg, G.; Fischer, M. M., and Nijkamp, P.*, 1984, pp. 35–49.

Bahrenberg, G.; Fischer, M. M. and Nijkamp, Peter. Methodology, Measurement and Models in Spatial Analysis: Some Major Lines of Recent Developments. In *Bahrenberg, G.; Fischer, M. M., and Nijkamp, P.*, 1984, pp. 3–31.

Barnes, Trevor and Sheppard, Eric. Technical Choice and Reswitching in Space Economies. *Reg. Sci. Urban Econ.*, August 1984, *14*(3), pp. 345–62.

Beckmann, Martin J. Reflections on Palander's "Beiträge Zur Standortstheorie" In *Andersson, Å. E.; Isard, W. and Puu, T., eds.*, 1984, pp. 31–40.

Benson, Bruce L. On the Ability of Spatial Competitors to Price Discriminate. *J. Ind. Econ.*, December 1984, *33*(2), pp. 251–55.

Benson, Bruce L. Spatial Competition with Free Entry, Chamberlinian Tangencies, and Social Efficiency. *J. Urban Econ.*, May 1984, *15*(3), pp. 270–86.

Benson, Bruce L. The Level of Average Production Cost Chosen by a Multiplant Spatial Monopolist. *Reg. Sci. Urban Econ.*, February 1984, *14*(1), pp. 37–44.

Berliant, Marcus. A Characterization of the Demand for Land. *J. Econ. Theory*, August 1984, *33*(2), pp. 289–300.

Black, Philip A. The Regional Income Multiplier: A Comment [Injection Leakages, Trade Repercussions and the Regional Income Multiplier]. *Scot. J. Polit. Econ.*, June 1984, *31*(2), pp. 199–201. **[G: U.K.]**

Böker, Fred. Über die Beschreibung von Wanderungsbewegungen mit Hilfe von Zählprozessen. (About the Description of Migrations Using Counting Processes. With English summary.) *Ifo-Studien*, 1984, *30*(4), pp. 307–15. **[G: W. Germany]**

von Böventer, Edwin. The von Thünen-Hotelling Rule: On Johann Heinrich von Thünen's Model of General Economic Interdependence in Space and Time. In *[Beckmann, M. J.]*, 1984, pp. 137–49.

Bowes, Marianne. Profit-Maximizing vs. Optimal Behavior in a Spatial Setting: Summary and Extensions. *Southern Econ. J.*, January 1984, *50*(3), pp. 680–89.

Bröcker, Johannes. Die Attraktionsanalyse: Ein missglückter Versuch, die regionale Input–Output-Analyse zu verallgemeinern. (Attraction Analysis—A Failed Attempt to Generalise Regional Input–Output Analysis. With English summary.) *Z. Wirtschaft. Sozialwissen.*, 1984, *104*(1), pp. 29–43.

Casetti, Emilio. Peripheral Growth in Mature Economies. *Econ. Geogr.*, April 1984, *60*(2), pp. 122–31.

Chen, M.-L.; Francis, R. L. and Lowe, T. J.

P-Centers on Bitrees. *J. Reg. Sci.*, May 1984, *24*(2), pp. 203–17.

Church, Richard L. The Planar Maximal Covering Location Problem. *J. Reg. Sci.*, May 1984, *24*(2), pp. 185–201.

Clapp, John M. and Richardson, Harry W. Technological Change in Information-processing Industries and Regional Income Differentials in Developing Countries. *Int. Reg. Sci. Rev.*, December 1984, *9*(3), pp. 241–56.   **[G: LDCs]**

Clarke, Harry R. The Separability of Production and Location Decisions: Comment. *Amer. Econ. Rev.*, June 1984, *74*(3), pp. 528–30.

Current, John; ReVelle, Charles and Cohon, Jared. The Shortest Covering Path Problem: An Application of Locational Constraints to Network Design. *J. Reg. Sci.*, May 1984, *24*(2), pp. 161–83.

DeCanio, Stephen J. Delivered Pricing and Multiple Basing Point Equilibria: A Reevaluation. *Quart. J. Econ.*, May 1984, *99*(2), pp. 329–49.

Deloche, Régis. Aménagement infrastructurel du territoire et politique de concurrence. (With English summary.) *Revue Écon. Polit.*, January–February 1984, *94*(1), pp. 92–115.
    [G: France]

El-Hodiri, Mohamed Ali. Boom Towns: Queue Up or Bust: A Welfare Economy Analysis. In *Avula, X. J. R., et al.*, 1984, pp. 799–801.

Faini, Riccardo. Increasing Returns, Non-Traded Inputs and Regional Development. *Econ. J.*, June 1984, *94*(374), pp. 308–23.

Friesz, Terry L.; Harker, Patrick T. and Tobin, Roger L. Alternative Algorithms for the General Network Spatial Price Equilibrium Problem. *J. Reg. Sci.*, November 1984, *24*(4), pp. 475–507.

Fujita, Masahisa. The Spatial Growth of Tokyo Metropolitan Area. In *Andersson, Å. E.; Isard, W. and Puu, T., eds.*, 1984, pp. 41–59.
    [G: Japan]

Goldstein, Gerald S. and Gronberg, T. J. Economies of Scope and Economies of Agglomeration. *J. Urban Econ.*, July 1984, *16*(1), pp. 91–104.

Griffith, D. A. Measuring the Arrangement of Property of a System of Areal Units Generated by Partitioning a Planar Surface. In *Bahrenberg, G.; Fischer, M. M., and Nijkamp, P.*, 1984, pp. 191–99.

Grigg, Trevor. Parameters of the Retail Trade Model: A Utility Based Interpretation. *Urban Stud.*, February 1984, *21*(1), pp. 73–79.
    [G: U.S.]

Haining, Robert P. Testing a Spatial Interacting-Markets Hypothesis. *Rev. Econ. Statist.*, November 1984, *66*(4), pp. 576–83.   **[G: U.K.]**

Hanjoul, Pierre and Thisse, Jacques-François. The Location of a Firm on a Network. In *Hughes Hallet, A.J., ed.*, 1984, pp. 289–326.

Harris, Britton. Spatial Analysis: Some Working Principles. In *Andersson, Å. E.; Isard, W. and Puu, T., eds.*, 1984, pp. 89–107.

Hsu, Song-ken and Mai, Chao-cheng. Production Location and Random Input Price. *Reg. Sci.*

Urban Econ., February 1984, *14*(1), pp. 45–62.

Hurter, Arthur P., Jr.; Martinich, Joseph S. and Venta, Enrique R. The Separability of Production and Location Decisions: Reply. *Amer. Econ. Rev.*, June 1984, *74*(3), pp. 531–32.

Ionescu, C. and Matei, I. The Development of Social Structures within the Local Communities Systems and the National Wealth Growth. *Econ. Computat. Cybern. Stud. Res.*, 1984, *19*(2), pp. 77–83.   **[G: Romania]**

Johnston, R. J. Quantitative Ecological Analysis in Human Geography: An Evaluation of Four Problem Areas. In *Bahrenberg, G.; Fischer, M. M., and Nijkamp, P.*, 1984, pp. 131–41.

Jones, Donald W. Geographical Transmission of Economic Events. *Econ. Geogr.*, April 1984, *60*(2), pp. 132–49.

Karmann, Alexander J. Space–Time Economies under Free Mobility: Competitive Equilibria and Efficiency. *Reg. Sci. Urban Econ.*, August 1984, *14*(3), pp. 303–15.

Katz, Eliakim. The Optimal Location of the Competitive Firm under Price Uncertainty. *J. Urban Econ.*, July 1984, *16*(1), pp. 65–75.

Kuenne, Robert E. Economic Decision Making in a Poisson Demand Space. In *Andersson, Å. E.; Isard, W. and Puu, T., eds.*, 1984, pp. 331–46.

Kulikowski, Roman. Optimization of Regional Growth in the Presence of Scale Economies and Externalities. In *Andersson, Å. E.; Isard, W. and Puu, T., eds.*, 1984, pp. 369–81.
    [G: Poland]

Kusumoto, Sho-Ichiro. On a Foundation of the Economic Theory of Location—Transport Distance vs. Technological Substitution. *J. Reg. Sci.*, May 1984, *24*(2), pp. 249–70.

Lassudrie-Duchêne, Bernard. Les incidences régionales des échanges internationaux. (With English summary.) *Revue Écon. Polit.*, January–February 1984, *94*(1), pp. 26–48.
    [G: France]

Lee, Kye S. The Direction of Migration: A Dynamic General Equilibrium Model. *J. Reg. Sci.*, November 1984, *24*(4), pp. 509–17.

Leonardi, Giorgio and Tadei, Roberto. Random Utility Demand Models and Service Location. *Reg. Sci. Urban Econ.*, August 1984, *14*(3), pp. 399–431.

Livesey, David. Aspects of the New Urban Economics. In *van der Ploeg, F., ed.*, 1984, pp. 479–517.

Mai, Chao-cheng. Demand Function and Location Theory of the Firm under Price Uncertainty. *Urban Stud.*, November 1984, *21*(4), pp. 459–64.

Mai, Chao-cheng. Location and the Theory of the Imperfectly Competitive Firm under Demand Uncertainty. *Southern Econ. J.*, April 1984, *50*(4), pp. 1160–70.

Mai, Chao-cheng and Shieh, Yeung-Nan. Transport Rates Structure, Optimum Location, and Theory of Production: Reexamination. *J. Urban Econ.*, September 1984, *16*(2), pp. 225–31.

Mattsson, Lars-Göran. Equivalence between Welfare and Entropy Approaches to Residential Location. *Reg. Sci. Urban Econ.*, May 1984, *14*(2), pp. 147–73. **[G: Sweden]**

Mazzoleni, Piera and Montesano, Aldo. General Competitive Equilibrium of the Spatial Economy. *Reg. Sci. Urban Econ.*, August 1984, *14*(3), pp. 285–302.

Michel, Philippe; Pestieau, Pierre and Thisse, Jacques-François. A Propos de la répartition interrégionale des investissements. (With English summary.) *Revue Écon. Polit.*, January–February 1984, *94*(1), pp. 49–59.

Miglierina, Claudio. Dimensione, dominanza ed economie esterne nella teoria della localizzazione. (Size, Dominance, and External Economies in the Location Theory. With English summary.) *Giorn. Econ.*, January–February 1984, *43*(1–2), pp. 89–102.

Molho, Ian. Distance Deterrence Relationships in Multi-Stream Migration Models. *Manchester Sch. Econ. Soc. Stud.*, March 1984, *52*(1), pp. 49–69. **[G: U.K.]**

Moore, Craig L. and Jacobsen, Marilyn. Minimum Requirements and Regional Economics, 1980. *Econ. Geogr.*, July 1984, *60*(3), pp. 217–24. **[G: U.S.]**

Mosler, Karl Clemens. Location Theory of the Firm Facing Uncertain Prices and Transport Rates. In *[Beckmann, M. J.]*, 1984, pp. 163–74.

Mosler, Karl Clemens. Robust Comparisons of Spatial Patterns. *Reg. Sci. Urban Econ.*, August 1984, *14*(3), pp. 453–63.

Mulligan, Gordon F. Agglomeration and Central Place Theory: A Review of the Literature. *Int. Reg. Sci. Rev.*, September 1984, *9*(1), pp. 1–42.

Mulligan, Gordon F. and Gibson, Lay James. Regression Estimates of Economic Base Multipliers for Small Communities. *Econ. Geogr.*, July 1984, *60*(3), pp. 225–37. **[G: U.S.]**

Nadji, Mehrzad and Harris, Curtis C., Jr. Derivation of Regional Shadow Prices. *Reg. Sci. Urban Econ.*, November 1984, *14*(4), pp. 589–93.

Nijkamp, Peter. A Multidimensional Analysis of Regional Infrastructure and Economic Development. In *Andersson, Å. E.; Isard, W. and Puu, T., eds.*, 1984, pp. 267–93.

Nijkamp, Peter and Voogd, Henk. Multidimensional and Homogeneous Scaling in Spatial Analysis. In *Bahrenberg, G.; Fischer, M. M., and Nijkamp, P.*, 1984, pp. 201–14.

Ó hUallacháin, Breandán. Linkages and Foreign Direct Investment in the United States. *Econ. Geogr.*, July 1984, *60*(3), pp. 238–53. **[G: U.S.]**

O'Kelly, M. E. and Storbeck, J. E. Hierarchical Location Models with Probabilistic Allocation. *Reg. Stud.*, April 1984, *18*(2), pp. 121–29.

Ochitwa, Jerome M. Applicability and Efficiency in a Land Use Plan Design Model: An Input–Output Linear Programming Approach. *Urban Stud.*, May 1984, *21*(2), pp. 149–54.

Ohta, Hiroshi. Agglomeration and Competition.

Reg. Sci. Urban Econ., February 1984, *14*(1), pp. 1–17.

Ohta, Hiroshi. On the Neutrality of Freight in Monopoly Spatial Pricing. *J. Reg. Sci.*, August 1984, *24*(3), pp. 359–71.

Olson, Dennis O. The Interregional Incidence of Energy-Production Taxes. *Int. Reg. Sci. Rev.*, November 1984, *9*(2), pp. 109–24. **[G: U.S.]**

Pang, Jong-Shi. Solution of the General Multicommodity Spatial Equilibrium Problem by Variational and Complementarity Methods. *J. Reg. Sci.*, August 1984, *24*(3), pp. 403–14.

Persson, Håkan. A Way of Modelling Investment in a Multisectoral Model. *Reg. Sci. Urban Econ.*, August 1984, *14*(3), pp. 331–43.

Pickles, Andrew and Rogerson, Peter A. Wage Distributions and Spatial Preferences in Competitive Job Search and Migration. *Reg. Stud.*, April 1984, *18*(2), pp. 131–42.

Puu, Tönu. The Long-run Equilibrium of a Continuous Spatial Exchange Economy. In *Andersson, Å. E.; Isard, W. and Puu, T., eds.*, 1984, pp. 15–30.

ten Raa, Thijs. Spatial Interaction Analysis. *J. Reg. Sci.*, November 1984, *24*(4), pp. 535–39.

ten Raa, Thijs. The Distribution Approach to Spatial Economics. *J. Reg. Sci.*, February 1984, *24*(1), pp. 105–17.

Richardson, Harry W. National Urban Development Strategies in Developing Countries. In *Ghosh, P. K., ed., no. 2*, 1984, *1981*, pp. 122–48. **[G: LDCs]**

Roy, John R. and Johansson, Börje. On Planning and Forecasting the Location of Retail and Service Activity. *Reg. Sci. Urban Econ.*, August 1984, *14*(3), pp. 433–52.

Schweizer, Urs. Fiscal Decentralization under Free Mobility. *Reg. Sci. Urban Econ.*, August 1984, *14*(3), pp. 317–29.

Sheppard, Eric. Value and Exploitation in a Capitalist Space Economy. *Int. Reg. Sci. Rev.*, November 1984, *9*(2), pp. 97–107.

Shieh, Yeung-Nan and Mai, Chao-cheng. Location and the Theory of Production: Clarifications and Extensions. *Reg. Sci. Urban Econ.*, May 1984, *14*(2), pp. 199–218.

Spulber, Daniel F. Competition and Multiplant Monopoly with Spatial Nonlinear Pricing. *Int. Econ. Rev.*, June 1984, *25*(2), pp. 425–39.

Ståhl, Ingolf. Gaming for Game Theory Conflict Situations in Regional Planning. In *Andersson, Å. E.; Isard, W. and Puu, T., eds.*, 1984, pp. 347–67. **[G: Sweden]**

Storper, Michael and Walker, Richard. The Spatial Division of Labor: Labor and the Location of Industries. In *Sawers, L. and Tabb, W. K., eds.*, 1984, pp. 19–47.

Straszheim, Mahlon R. Urban Agglomeration Effects and Employment and Wage Gradients. *J. Urban Econ.*, September 1984, *16*(2), pp. 187–207.

Tabuchi, Takatoshi. The Systemic Variables and Elasticities in Alonso's General Theory of Movement. *Reg. Sci. Urban Econ.*, May 1984, *14*(2), pp. 249–64. **[G: U.S.; Japan; Canada]**

Takagi, Yasuoki. The Migration Function and the

Todaro Parodox. *Reg. Sci. Urban Econ.*, May 1984, *14*(2), pp. 219–30.

Takagi, Yasuoki. Urban Unemployment and Rural–Urban Migration in LDC's: A Survey. (In Japanese. With English summary.) *Econ. Stud. Quart.*, December 1984, *35*(3), pp. 216–29. **[G: LDCs]**

Tauchen, Helen and Witte, Ann D. Socially Optimal and Equilibrium Distributions of Office Activity: Models with Exogenous and Endogenous Contacts. *J. Urban Econ.*, January 1984, *15*(1), pp. 66–86.

Von Hohenbalken, Balder and West, Douglas S. Manhattan versus Euclid: Market Areas Computed and Compared. *Reg. Sci. Urban Econ.*, February 1984, *14*(1), pp. 19–35. **[G: Canada]**

Von Hohenbalken, Balder and West, Douglas S. Predation among Supermarkets: An Algorithmic Locational Analysis. *J. Urban Econ.*, March 1984, *15*(2), pp. 244–57. **[G: Canada]**

Wendell, Richard E. and Peterson, Elmor L. A Dual Approach for Obtaining Lower Bounds to the Weber Problem. *J. Reg. Sci.*, May 1984, *24*(2), pp. 219–28.

Wilson, John D. The Excise Tax Effects of the Property Tax. *J. Public Econ.*, August 1984, *24*(3), pp. 309–29.

9412 Regional Economic Studies

de Albuquerque, Klaus; Van Riel, Wesley and Taylor, J. Mark. Uncontrolled Urbanization in the Developing World: A Jamaican Case Study. In *Ghosh, P. K., ed., no. 2, 1984, 1980,* pp. 253–86. **[G: Jamaica]**

Allen, Larry and Price, Don. Variations in the Flow of Credit from Regional Financial Institutions as a Source of Cyclical Instability in the Regional Economy: An Application of Causal Analysis. *Reg. Sci. Persp.*, 1984, *14*(2), pp. 3–14. **[G: U.S.]**

Amirizadeh, Hossain and Todd, Richard M. More Growth Ahead for Ninth District States. *Fed. Res. Bank Minn. Rev.*, Fall 1984, *8*(4), pp. 8–17. **[G: U.S.]**

Andersson, Åke E. Regional Science and Policies in a Swedish Perspective. In *Andersson, Å. E.; Isard, W. and Puu, T., eds.,* 1984, pp. 1–14. **[G: Sweden]**

Auty, R. M. The Product Life-Cycle and the Location of the Global Petrochemical Industry after the Second Oil Shock. *Econ. Geogr.*, October 1984, *60*(4), pp. 325–38. **[G: OECD]**

Bain, Andrew D. and Reid, Richard G. The Finance Sector. In *Hood, N. and Young, S., eds.,* 1984, pp. 365–89. **[G: U.K.]**

Bain, John S. Transfer Payment Impacts on Rural Retail Markets: A Regression Analysis. *Reg. Sci. Persp.*, 1984, *14*(1), pp. 3–17. **[G: U.S.]**

Bajetti, Luisa. Note per un'analisi delle implicazioni del rapporto banca-territorio. (Considerations for an Analysis of the Implications of Banks' Support for Geographic Economic Development. With English summary.) *Bancaria*, March 1984, *40*(3), pp. 295–301. **[G: Italy]**

Balydon, R.; Woods, Adrian and Zafiris, N. Inner City versus New Town: A Comparison of Manufacturing Performance. *Oxford Bull. Econ. Statist.*, February 1984, *46*(1), pp. 21–29. **[G: U.K.]**

Bearse, Peter J. An Econometric Analysis of Black Entrepreneurship. *Rev. Black Polit. Econ.*, Spring 1984, *12*(4), pp. 111–34. **[G: U.S.]**

Begg, H. M. A Scottish Perspective on the RSA Inquiry into Regional Problems in the United Kingdom. *Reg. Stud.*, August 1984, *18*(4), pp. 345–48. **[G: U.K.]**

Bell, David. Trends in Scottish Industry. In *Hood, N. and Young, S., eds.,* 1984, pp. 1–27. **[G: U.K.]**

Berry, Sara S. Oil and the Disappearing Peasantry: Accumulation, Differentiation and Underdevelopment in Western Nigeria. *African Econ. Hist.*, 1984, (13), pp. 1–22. **[G: Nigeria]**

Betson, David and Haveman, Robert H. The Role of Income Transfers in Reducing Inequality between and within Regions. In *Moon, M., ed.,* 1984, pp. 283–322. **[G: U.S.]**

Bierbaum, C. B. Structural Change: The South Australian Experience. *Australian Econ. Pap.*, December 1984, *23*(43), pp. 281–90. **[G: Australia]**

Birch, David. The Contribution of Small Enterprise to Growth and Employment. In *Giersch, H., ed.,* 1984, pp. 1–17. **[G: U.S.]**

Blackley, Paul R. A Hedonic Approach to the Decentralization of Manufacturing Activity. *J. Reg. Sci.*, November 1984, *24*(4), pp. 541–57. **[G: U.S.]**

Bradbury, Katharine L. Urban Decline and Distress: An Update. *New Eng. Econ. Rev.*, July–August 1984, pp. 39–55. **[G: U.S.]**

Brewer, H. L. Regional Economic Stabilization: An Efficient Diversification Approach. *Rev. Reg. Stud.*, Winter 1984, *14*(1), pp. 8–21. **[G: U.S.]**

Brouwer, Floor and Nijkamp, Peter. Multiple Rank Correlation and Association Analysis. In *Bahrenberg, G.; Fischer, M. M., and Nijkamp, P.,* 1984, pp. 317–34. **[G: Netherlands]**

Browne, Lynn E. How Different Are Regional Wages? A Second Look. *New Eng. Econ. Rev.*, March–April 1984, pp. 40–47. **[G: U.S.]**

Bruch, Mathias. The Contribution of Small Enterprise to Growth and Employment: Comment. In *Giersch, H., ed.,* 1984, pp. 18–22. **[G: U.S.]**

Button, K. J. Regional Variations in the Irregular Economy: A Study of Possible Trends. *Reg. Stud.*, October 1984, *18*(5), pp. 385–91. **[G: U.K.]**

Cantarelli, Davide and Bressan, Franco. Diseguaglianze regionali e sviluppo economico: un'analisi econometrica "internazionale." (Regional Inequalities and Economic Development: An "International" Econometric Analysis. With English summary.) *Giorn. Econ.*, March–April 1984, *43*(3–4), pp. 161–89. **[G: Global]**

Carlton, Dennis W. Energy and the Location of

Industry: Comment. In *Downs, A. and Bradbury, K. L., eds.*, 1984, pp. 219–25.
[G: U.S.]

Casetti, Emilio. Manufacturing Productivity and Snowbelt–Sunbelt Shifts. *Econ. Geogr.*, October 1984, *60*(4), pp. 313–24. [G: U.S.]

Cebula, Richard J. Determinants of Geographic Living-Cost Differentials in the United States: Reply. *Land Econ.*, February 1984, *60*(1), pp. 120–21. [G: U.S.]

Chang, Semoon. Do Disaster Areas Benefit from Disasters? *Growth Change*, October 1984, *15*(4), pp. 24–31. [G: U.S.]

Chesire, William P. West Virginia's Rocky Road. *Policy Rev.*, Winter 1984, (27), pp. 64–66.
[G: U.S.]

Chisholm, M. Regional Policy for the Late Twentieth Century. *Reg. Stud.*, August 1984, *18*(4), pp. 348–52. [G: U.K.]

Clark, Gordon L. The Changing Composition of Regional Employment. *Econ. Geogr.*, April 1984, *60*(2), pp. 175–93. [G: U.S.]

Clark, Roger D. and Roche, John P. Functional Typologies of Metropolitan Areas: An Examination of Their Usefulness. *Urban Stud.*, February 1984, *21*(1), pp. 63–71. [G: U.S.]

Connaughton, John E. and Madsen, Ronald A. Explaining Differentials in State Unemployment Rates during Recessions. *Reg. Sci. Persp.*, 1984, *14*(1), pp. 18–24. [G: U.S.]

Cooke, Philip; Morgan, Kevin and Jackson, David. New Technology and Regional Development in Austerity Britain: The Case of the Semiconductor Industry. *Reg. Stud.*, August 1984, *18*(4), pp. 277–89. [G: U.K.]

Crichton, David. The Textile and Clothing Sectors. In *Hood, N. and Young, S., eds.*, 1984, pp. 213–48. [G: U.K.]

Crouchley, Robert. Some Corrections to Coelho and Wilson, 1976: The Optimum Location and Size of Shopping Centres. *Reg. Stud.*, October 1984, *18*(5), pp. 393–96. [G: U.S.]

Cullison, William E. Equalizing Regional Differences in Wages: A Study of Wages and Migration in the South and Other Regions. *Fed. Res. Bank Richmond Econ. Rev.*, May/June 1984, *70*(3), pp. 20–33. [G: U.S.]

Dagodag, W. Tim. Illegal Mexican Immigration to California from Western Mexico. In *Jones, R. C., ed.*, 1984, pp. 61–73. [G: U.S.; Mexico]

DaVanzo, Julie and Kusnic, Michael. Regional Income Differences and the Definition of Income: The Case of Malaysia. *Int. Reg. Sci. Rev.*, September 1984, *9*(1), pp. 59–73.
[G: Malaysia]

Davila, Alberto E.; Schmidt, Ronald H. and Ziegler, Gary M. Industrial Diversification, Exchange Rate Shocks, and the Texas–Mexico Border. *Fed. Res. Bank Dallas Econ. Rev.*, May 1984, pp. 1–9. [G: U.S.; Mexico]

van Delft, A. and Suyker, W. B. C. Interregional Migration in a Multiregional Labour Market Model for the Netherlands. In *ter Heide, H. and Willekens, F. J., eds.*, 1984, pp. 253–69.
[G: Netherlands]

Disney, Richard. The Regional Impact of Unemployment Insurance in the United Kingdom. *Oxford Bull. Econ. Statist.*, August 1984, *46*(3), pp. 241–54. [G: U.K.]

Eichengreen, Barry. Mortgage Interest Rates in the Populist Era. *Amer. Econ. Rev.*, December 1984, *74*(5), pp. 995–1015. [G: U.S.]

Eichperger, C. L. Regional Population Forecasts: Approaches and Issues. In *ter Heide, H. and Willekens, F. J., eds.*, 1984, pp. 235–52.
[G: Netherlands]

Eldridge, Noel. Melbourne: Population Density; Distance; the Relationship. *J. Urban Econ.*, May 1984, *15*(3), pp. 310–16. [G: Australia]

Ellman, Michael. Income Distribution in the USSR. In *Ellman, M.*, 1984, pp. 112–29.
[G: U.S.S.R.]

Ellson, Richard W.; Milliman, Jerome W. and Roberts, R. Blaine. Measuring the Regional Economic Effects of Earthquakes and Earthquake Predictions. *J. Reg. Sci.*, November 1984, *24*(4), pp. 559–79. [G: U.S.]

Ersenkal, Caryl R. and Dillman, B. L. The Product Cycle and Shifts in the Location of Manufacturing. *Reg. Sci. Persp.*, 1984, *14*(1), pp. 30–39. [G: U.S.]

Firn, John R. and Roberts, David. High-technology Industries. In *Hood, N. and Young, S., eds.*, 1984, pp. 288–325. [G: U.K.]

Fisch, Oscar. Regional Income Inequality and Economic Development. *Reg. Sci. Urban Econ.*, February 1984, *14*(1), pp. 89–111.
[G: U.S.]

Flynn, Patricia M. Lowell: A High Technology Success Story. *New Eng. Econ. Rev.*, September–October 1984, pp. 39–49. [G: U.S.]

Fothergill, Stephen, et al. Differences in the Profitability of the U.K. Manufacturing Sector between Conurbations and Other Areas. *Scot. J. Polit. Econ.*, February 1984, *31*(1), pp. 72–91. [G: U.K.]

Fox, William F. and Quindry, Kenneth E. State and Local Government Fiscal Constraints: Public Sector and Private Sector Effects. *Public Finance Quart.*, October 1984, *12*(4), pp. 425–56. [G: U.S.]

Fridlizius, Gunnar and Ohlsson, Rolf. Mortality Patterns in Sweden 1751–1802—A Regional Analysis. In *Bengtsson, T.; Fridlizius, G. and Ohlsson, R., eds.*, 1984, pp. 299–328.
[G: Sweden]

Funke, Ursula H. The Locational Behaviour of the Chemical Industry in the United States after World War II. In *[Beckmann, M. J.]*, 1984, pp. 151–61. [G: U.S.]

Gardini, Attilio. Indici settoriali per l'analisi territoriale delle tecniche e della produttivita'. Un'applicazione al confronto fra l'economia italiana e quella emiliano-romagnola. (Multisectoral Indices for the Spatial Analysis of the Techniques and of Productivity. An Application for the Comparison between the Economic Structure of Italy and of Emilia Romagna. With English summary.) *Statistica*, July–September 1984, *44*(3), pp. 443–62. [G: Italy]

Garnick, Daniel H. Shifting Balances in U.S.

Metropolitan and Nonmetropolitan Area Growth. *Int. Reg. Sci. Rev.*, December 1984, *9*(3), pp. 257–73. **[G: U.S.]**

Garofalo, Gasper A. and Malhotra, Devinder M. Input Substitution in the Manufacturing Sector during the 1970's: A Regional Analysis. *J. Reg. Sci.*, February 1984, *24*(1), pp. 51–63.
[G: U.S.]

Gertler, Meric S. The Dynamics of Regional Capital Accumulation. *Econ. Geogr.*, April 1984, *60*(2), pp. 150–74. **[G: U.S.]**

Giles, David E. A. and Hampton, Peter. Regional Production Relationships during the Industrialization of New Zealand, 1935–1948. *J. Reg. Sci.*, November 1984, *24*(4), pp. 519–33.
[G: New Zealand]

Goddard, J. B. and Thwaites, A. T. Unemployment in the North: Jobs in the South. In *Marstrand, P., ed.*, 1984, pp. 45–72. **[G: U.K.]**

Goldstein, Gerald S. and Pittman, Robert H. Transportation and the Commodity Composition of Interstate Trade. *Growth Change*, July 1984, *15*(3), pp. 15–24. **[G: U.S.]**

Goodman, Allen C. and Kawai, Masahiro. Functional Form and Rental Housing Market Analysis. *Urban Stud.*, November 1984, *21*(4), pp. 367–76. **[G: U.S.]**

Gordijn, H. E.; Heida, H. R. and ter Heide, Henk. Monitoring Migration and Population Redistribution. In *ter Heide, H. and Willekens, F. J., eds.*, 1984, pp. 95–110.
[G: Netherlands]

Gottschalk, Peter. The Role of Income Transfers in Reducing Inequality between and within Regions: Comment. In *Moon, M., ed.*, 1984, pp. 322–26. **[G: U.S.]**

Gouedard-Comte, Olivier. Formes et degrés d'insertion régionale des groupes: une comparaison entre groupes français et groupes étrangers. (Regional Insertions of Groups: A Comparison between French and Foreign Groups. With English summary.) *Revue Écon.*, March 1984, *35*(2), pp. 313–46. **[G: France]**

Gould, Andrew and Keeble, David. New Firms and Rural Industrialization in East Anglia. *Reg. Stud.*, June 1984, *18*(3), pp. 189–201.
[G: U.K.]

Green, Milford B. and Cromley, Robert G. Merger and Acquisition Fields for Large United States Cities, 1955–1970. *Reg. Stud.*, August 1984, *18*(4), pp. 291–301. **[G: U.S.]**

Greenhut, M. L.; Hwang, M. and Shwiff, S. Differences in Spatial Pricing in the United States: A Statistical Analysis and Case Studies. *Ann. Reg. Sci.*, November 1984, *18*(3), pp. 49–66.
[G: U.S.]

Greenwood, Michael J. and Hunt, Gary L. Econometrically Accounting for Identities and Restrictions in Models of Interregional Migration. *Reg. Sci. Urban Econ.*, February 1984, *14*(1), pp. 113–28. **[G: U.S.]**

Greenwood, Michael J. and Hunt, Gary L. Migration and Interregional Employment Redistribution in the United States. *Amer. Econ. Rev.*, December 1984, *74*(5), pp. 957–69.
[G: U.S.]

Greider, Thomas and Krannich, Richard S. Diffusion and Development in the Rocky Mountain Region, 1970–80. *Growth Change*, January 1984, *15*(1), pp. 41–49. **[G: U.S.]**

Gudgin, G. and Fothergill, Stephen. Geographical Variation in the Rate of Formation of New Manufacturing Firms. *Reg. Stud.*, June 1984, *18*(3), pp. 203–06. **[G: U.K.]**

Handy, John and Swinton, David H. The Determinants of the Rate of Growth of Black-Owned Businesses: A Preliminary Analysis. *Rev. Black Polit. Econ.*, Spring 1984, *12*(4), pp. 85–110.
[G: U.S.]

Harrison, Bennett. Regional Restructuring and "Good Business Climates": The Economic Transformation of New England since World War II. In *Sawers, L. and Tabb, W. K., eds.*, 1984, pp. 48–96. **[G: U.S.]**

Harrison, Bennett and Bluestone, Barry. The Incidence and Regulation of Plant Closings. In *Sawers, L. and Tabb, W. K., eds.*, 1984, *1982*, pp. 368–402. **[G: U.S.]**

Haug, Peter. Regional Policy Incentives in the Scottish Electronics Industry: Survey Evidence. *Scot. J. Polit. Econ.*, November 1984, *31*(3), pp. 274–83. **[G: U.K.]**

Healey, Michael and Clark, David. Industrial Decline and Government Response in the West Midlands: The Case of Coventry. *Reg. Stud.*, August 1984, *18*(4), pp. 303–18.
[G: U.K.]

Heida, H. R. and Gordijn, H. E. Residential Preferences and Inclination to Move. In *ter Heide, H. and Willekens, F. J., eds.*, 1984, pp. 153–70. **[G: Netherlands]**

Hekman, John S. and Strong, John S. Is There a Case for Plant-Closing Laws? In *McKenzie, R. B., ed. (II)*, 1984, *1980*, pp. 49–77.
[G: U.S.]

Henderson, David M. The Natural Resource-Based Sector. In *Hood, N. and Young, S., eds.*, 1984, pp. 249–87. **[G: U.K.]**

Henderson, Robert A. The Employment Performance of Established Manufacturing Industry in the Scottish New Towns. *Urban Stud.*, August 1984, *21*(3), pp. 295–315. **[G: U.K.]**

Henry, Mark S. and Martin, Thomas L. Estimating Income Distribution Effects on Regional Input–Output Multipliers. *Reg. Sci. Persp.*, 1984, *14*(2), pp. 33–45. **[G: U.S.]**

Hill, Raymond D. State Enterprise and Income Distribution in Mexico. In *Aspe, P. and Sigmund, P. E., eds.*, 1984, pp. 357–96.
[G: Mexico]

Hingstman, L. and Harts, J. J. Analysis of Migration Histories. In *ter Heide, H. and Willekens, F. J., eds.*, 1984, pp. 133–52.
[G: Netherlands]

Hinloopen, Edwin; Nijkamp, Peter and Rietveld, Piet. International Comparison of Regional Planning and Information Systems. In *Nijkamp, P. and Rietveld, P., eds.*, 1984, pp. 411–26. **[G: Europe; U.S.]**

Hobbs, Daryl. New Directions in Development-Cases of High, Medium and Low Technologies.

Rev. Reg. Stud., Spring 1984, *14*(2), pp. 13–19. [G: U.S.]

Hogan, Timothy D. Determinants of Geographic Living—Cost Differentials in the United States: Comment. *Land Econ.*, February 1984, *60*(1), pp. 115–19. [G: U.S.]

Hogan, Timothy D. and Rex, Tom R. Intercity Differences in Cost of Living: Results from a New Database. *Growth Change*, October 1984, *15*(4), pp. 16–23. [G: U.S.]

Hood, Neil. The Small-Firm Sector. In *Hood, N. and Young, S., eds.*, 1984, pp. 57–92. [G: U.K.; OECD]

Hood, Neil and Young, Stephen. Conclusions: The Way Ahead. In *Hood, N. and Young, S., eds.*, 1984, pp. 390–412. [G: U.K.]

Hopkins, Frank. Energy and Regional Development: Comment. In *Downs, A. and Bradbury, K. L., eds.*, 1984, pp. 283–86. [G: U.S.]

Howells, J. R. L. The Location of Research and Development: Some Observations and Evidence from Britain. *Reg. Stud.*, February 1984, *18*(1), pp. 13–29. [G: U.K.]

Howland, Marie. Age of Capital and Regional Business Cycles. *Growth Change*, April 1984, *15*(2), pp. 29–37. [G: U.S.]

Huddleston, Jack R. Tax Increment Financing as a State Development Policy. *Growth Change*, April 1984, *15*(2), pp. 11–17. [G: U.S.]

Hulten, Charles R. and Schwab, Robert M. Regional Productivity Growth in U.S. Manufacturing: 1951–78. *Amer. Econ. Rev.*, March 1984, *74*(1), pp. 152–62. [G: U.S.]

Irving, John S., Jr. Plant Relocations and Transfers of Work: The NLRB's "Inherently Destructive" Approach. In *McKenzie, R. B., ed. (II)*, 1984, 1983, pp. 233–52. [G: U.S.]

Izraeli, Oded and Lin, An-Loh. Recent Evidence on the Effect of Real Earnings on Net Migration. *Reg. Stud.*, April 1984, *18*(2), pp. 113–20. [G: U.S.]

Jackson, Randall W. An Evaluation of Alternative Measures of Regional Industrial Diversification. *Reg. Stud.*, April 1984, *18*(2), pp. 103–12. [G: U.S.]

Jacobson, Louis. A Tale of Employment Decline in Two Cities: How Bad Was the Worst of Times? *Ind. Lab. Relat. Rev.*, July 1984, *37*(4), pp. 557–69. [G: U.S.]

Jeanrenaud, Claude and Meyer, Daniel. L'incidence a moyen et long terme des commandes de materiel de telecommunication: deux etudes de cas. (The Medium- and Long-term Incidence of Orders of Telecommunication Material: Two Case Studies. With English summary.) *Ann. Pub. Co-op. Econ.*, April–June 1984, *55*(2), pp. 191–203. [G: Switzerland]

Johansson, Börje and Marksjö, Bertil. Interactive Systems for Regional Analysis of Industrial Sectors. In *Nijkamp, P. and Rietveld, P., eds.*, 1984, pp. 231–49. [G: Sweden]

Jones, Gavin W. Links between Urbanization and Sectoral Shifts in Employment in Java. *Bull. Indonesian Econ. Stud.*, December 1984, *20*(3), pp. 120–57. [G: Indonesia]

Joshi, M. D. Development of the Hill Region of Uttar Pradesh. In *Singh, A. K.; Papola, T. S. and Mathur, R. S., eds.*, 1984, pp. 292–308. [G: India]

Jusenius, Carol L. and Ledebur, Larry C. Where Have All the Firms Gone? An Analysis of the New England Economy. In *McKenzie, R. B., ed. (II)*, 1984, 1977, pp. 79–117. [G: U.S.]

Keane, Michael J. Accessibility and Urban Growth Rates: Evidence for the Irish Urban System. *Econ. Soc. Rev.*, January 1984, *15*(2), pp. 125–39. [G: Ireland]

Kelton, Christina M. L. Nonstationary Markov Modeling: An Application to Wage-influenced Industrial Relocation. *Int. Reg. Sci. Rev.*, September 1984, *9*(1), pp. 75–90. [G: U.S.]

Kemper, Franz-Josef. Categorical Regression Models for Large Samples. In *Bahrenberg, G.; Fischer, M. M., and Nijkamp, P.*, 1984, pp. 303–16. [G: W. Germany]

Kieschnick, Robert L., Jr. State Energy Modeling and Planning: The Current Texas Experience. In *Lev, B., et al., eds.*, 1984, pp. 311–16. [G: U.S.]

King, J. C. Assessment of Electric Power Conservation and Supply Resources in the Pacific Northwest: An Overview. In *Lev, B., et al., eds.*, 1984, pp. 95–108. [G: U.S.]

Kneese, Allen V. and Bower, Blair T. Regional Residuals Management Models and the Lower Delaware Valley Case Study. In *Ahmad, Y. J.; Dasgupta, P. and Mäler, K.-G., eds.*, 1984, pp. 222–301. [G: U.S.]

Krumm, Ronald J. Regional Wage Differentials, Labor Supply Responses, and Race. *J. Reg. Sci.*, August 1984, *24*(3), pp. 431–42. [G: U.S.]

Kumar, Pradeep. The Economy: Summary Outline. In *Wood, W. D. and Kumar, P., eds.*, 1984, pp. 3–37. [G: Canada; U.S.]

Lakshmanan, T. R.; Anderson, W. and Jourabchi, M. Regional Dimensions of Factor and Fuel Substitution in U.S. Manufacturing. *Reg. Sci. Urban Econ.*, August 1984, *14*(3), pp. 381–98. [G: U.S.]

Lamonde, Pierre and Polèse, Mario. L'évolution de la structure économique de Montréal 1971–1981: désindustrialisation ou reconversion? (The Evolution of Montreal's Economic Structure, 1971–1981: Deindustrialization or Reconversion? With English summary.) *L'Actual. Econ.*, December 1984, *60*(4), pp. 471–94. [G: Canada]

Langston, Vicky C. An Investment Model for the U.S. Gulf Coast Refining/Petrochemical Complex for Policy Analysis. In *Lev, B., et al., eds.*, 1984, pp. 355–71. [G: U.S.]

Lanhan, W. Joe. New Directions for Economic Development Strategies in the South. *Rev. Reg. Stud.*, Spring 1984, *14*(2), pp. 1–2. [G: U.S.]

Lassudrie-Duchêne, Bernard. Les incidences régionales des échanges internationaux. (With English summary.) *Revue Écon. Polit.*, January–February 1984, *94*(1), pp. 26–48. [G: France]

Laurent, Eugene A. and Miley, Harry W., Jr.

State Economic Development Policy and the Political Process. *Rev. Reg. Stud.*, Spring 1984, *14*(2), pp. 20–23. **[G: U.S.]**

Lipner, J. Kenneth and Dutt, Amitava Krishna. South Florida as a Gateway to U.S. Trade with Latin America. In *Salazar-Carrillo, J. and Tirado de Alonso, I., eds., no. 2,* 1984, pp. 1–12. **[G: U.S.; Latin America]**

Lipner, J. Kenneth and Dutt, Amitava Krishna. South Florida as a Gateway to U.S. Trade with Latin America. In *Jorge, A.; Salazar-Carrillo, J. and Sanchez, E. P.,* 1984, pp. 131–40. **[G: Latin America; U.S.]**

Lloyd, P. E. and Mason, C. M. Spatial Variations in New Firm Formation in the United Kingdom: Comparative Evidence from Merseyside, Greater Manchester and South Hampshire. *Reg. Stud.*, June 1984, *18*(3), pp. 207–20. **[G: U.K.]**

Luger, Michael I. Investment Incentives and the Demand for Labor in U.S. Regions. *Reg. Sci. Urban Econ.*, November 1984, *14*(4), pp. 481–503. **[G: U.S.]**

Lund, Leonard. Factors in Corporate Locational Decisions. In *Carr, J. H., ed.,* 1984, *1979,* pp. 267–88. **[G: U.S.]**

Mackay, Tony. The Oil and Oil-Related Sector. In *Hood, N. and Young, S., eds.,* 1984, pp. 326–64. **[G: U.K.]**

Manson, Donald M.; Howland, Marie and Peterson, George E. The Effect of Business Cycles on Metropolitan Suburbanization. *Econ. Geogr.*, January 1984, *60*(1), pp. 71–80. **[G: U.S.]**

Manuel, David P. Unemployment and Drilling Activity in Major Energy-producing States. *J. Energy Devel.*, Autumn 1984, *10*(1), pp. 44–62. **[G: U.S.]**

Marlin, Matthew R. Industrial Development Bonds: Reviewing the Evidence in the Norfolk–Virginia Beach SMSA. *Rev. Reg. Stud.*, Winter 1984, *14*(1), pp. 45–53. **[G: U.S.]**

Martin, Ronald L. Redundancies, Labour Turnover and Employment Contraction in the Recession: A Regional Analysis. *Reg. Stud.*, December 1984, *18*(6), pp. 445–58. **[G: U.K.]**

Mayer, Jean. Regional Employment Development: The Evolution of Theory and Practice. *Int. Lab. Rev.*, January-February 1984, *123*(1), pp. 17–34. **[G: Global]**

McCrostie, M. J. and Peacock, Alan. Disability Policy in the United Kingdom. In *Haveman, R. H.; Halberstadt, V. and Burkhauser, R. V.,* 1984, pp. 517–73. **[G: U.K.]**

McHugh, Richard and Widdows, Richard. The Age of Capital and State Unemployment Rates. *J. Reg. Sci.*, February 1984, *24*(1), pp. 85–92. **[G: U.S.]**

McKenzie, Richard B. Business Mobility: Economic Myths and Realities. In *McKenzie, R. B., ed. (II),* 1984, pp. 11–27. **[G: U.S.]**

McKenzie, Richard B. The Right to Close Up Shop. In *McKenzie, R. B., ed. (II),* 1984, pp. 3–8. **[G: U.S.]**

McMurray, David. Labour Legislation and Pol-

icy: Summary Outline. In *Wood, W. D. and Kumar, P., eds.,* 1984, pp. 93–216. **[G: Canada]**

Meager, Nigel. Job Loss and the Regions: How Important Is Redundancy? *Reg. Stud.*, December 1984, *18*(6), pp. 459–67. **[G: U.K.]**

Merrifield, John. Impact Mitigation in Western Energy Boomtowns. *Growth Change*, April 1984, *15*(2), pp. 23–28. **[G: U.S.]**

Miernyk, William H. Energy and Regional Development. In *Downs, A. and Bradbury, K. L., eds.,* 1984, pp. 226–83. **[G: U.S.]**

Miller, James P. Manufacturing Relocations in the United States, 1969–1975. In *McKenzie, R. B., ed. (II),* 1984, pp. 29–47. **[G: U.S.]**

Molho, Ian. A Dynamic Model of Interregional Migration Flows in Great Britain. *J. Reg. Sci.*, August 1984, *24*(3), pp. 317–37. **[G: U.K.]**

Molho, Ian and Elias, Peter. A Study of Regional Trends in the Labour Force Participation of Married Women in the UK, 1968–1977. *Appl. Econ.*, April 1984, *16*(2), pp. 163–73. **[G: U.K.]**

Mulkey, David. Changing Socio-economic Conditions and the Need for New Development Policies in the South. *Rev. Reg. Stud.*, Spring 1984, *14*(2), pp. 3–12. **[G: U.S.]**

Mulkey, David and Espinal, Juan Jose. Income Dimensions of Caribbean Development Problems: The Las Cuevas Region of the Dominican Republic. *Rev. Reg. Stud.*, Fall 1984, *14*(3), pp. 3–8. **[G: Dominican Republic]**

Muller, Thomas. Urban and Regional Change: The Federal Role and National Policy. In *Carr, J. H., ed.,* 1984, *1982,* pp. 342–49. **[G: U.S.]**

Mulligan, Gordon F. and Gibson, Lay James. A Note on Sectoral Multipliers in Small Communities. *Growth Change*, October 1984, *15*(4), pp. 3–7. **[G: U.S.]**

Murdock, Steve H., et al. An Assessment of the Accuracy of a Regional Economic–Demographic Projection Model. *Demography*, August 1984, *21*(3), pp. 383–404. **[G: U.S.]**

Murphy, Kevin J. and Hofler, Richard A. Determinants of Geographic Unemployment Rates: A Selectively Pooled–Simultaneous Model. *Rev. Econ. Statist.*, May 1984, *66*(2), pp. 216–23. **[G: U.S.]**

Nijkamp, Peter; Rietveld, Piet and Rima, Annemarie. Information Content of Data from Different Spatial Aggregation Levels. In *Nijkamp, P. and Rietveld, P., eds.,* 1984, pp. 215–28. **[G: Netherlands]**

Noone, A. A CBI Perspective on the Future of Regional Policy. *Reg. Stud.*, August 1984, *18*(4), pp. 357–59. **[G: U.K.]**

van den Noord, P. J. Relocation of State Services and Regional Unemployment in the Netherlands. *De Economist*, 1984, *132*(4), pp. 451–67. **[G: Netherlands]**

Nord, Stephen. An Economic Analysis of Changes in the Relative Shape of the Interstate Size Distribution of Family Income during the 1960's. *Amer. Econ.*, Fall 1984, *28*(2), pp. 18–25. **[G: U.S.]**

O'Farrell, P. N. and Crouchley, Robert. An Industrial and Spatial Analysis of New Firm Formation in Ireland. *Reg. Stud.*, June 1984, *18*(3), pp. 221–36.   [G: Ireland]

Ó hUalacháin, Breandán. Linkages and Foreign Direct Investment in the United States. *Econ. Geogr.*, July 1984, *60*(3), pp. 238–53.
[G: U.S.]

O'Keefe, Edward P. and Tuohey, Seamus M. Economically Motivated Relocations of Work and an Employer's Duties under Section 8(d) of the National Labor Relations Act: A Three-Step Analysis. In *McKenzie, R. B., ed. (II)*, 1984, *1983*, pp. 253–305.   [G: U.S.]

Oakey, Raymond P. Innovation and Regional Growth in Small High Technology Firms: Evidence from Britain and the USA. *Reg. Stud.*, June 1984, *18*(3), pp. 237–51.   [G: U.S.; U.K.]

Oksanen, E. H. and Williams, J. R. Industrial Location and Inter-industry Linkages. *Empirical Econ.*, 1984, *9*(3), pp. 139–50.
[G: Canada]

Op 't Veld, A.; Bijlsma, E. and Starmans, J. Explanatory Analysis of Interregional Migration in the Nineteen-Seventies. In *ter Heide, H. and Willekens, F. J., eds.*, 1984, pp. 171–200.
[G: Netherlands]

Owen, D. W.; Gillespie, A. E. and Coombes, M. G. 'Job Shortfalls' in British Local Labour Market Areas: A Classification of Labour Supply and Demand Trends, 1971–1981. *Reg. Stud.*, December 1984, *18*(6), pp. 469–88.
[G: U.K.]

Parsons, D. Employment Stimulation and the Local Labour Market: A Case Study of Airport Growth. *Reg. Stud.*, October 1984, *18*(5), pp. 423–28.   [G: U.K.]

Pautrat, Charles; Guérard, Agnès and Lafarge, Guy. La dimension régionale dans l'évolution des biens et services. Une nouvelle méthode d'analyse. (With English summary.) *Revue Écon. Polit.*, January–February 1984, *94*(1), pp. 60–91.   [G: France]

Peck, Francis and Townsend, Alan. Contrasting Experience of Recession and Spatial Restructuring: British Shipbuilders, Plessey and Metal Box. *Reg. Stud.*, August 1984, *18*(4), pp. 319–38.   [G: U.K.]

Perry, Charles S. Economic Activity and Social Indicators: A Rural–Urban Discontinuum? *Amer. J. Econ. Soc.*, January 1984, *43*(1), pp. 61–74.   [G: U.S.]

Plaut, Thomas R. A Supply-Side Model of Texas Manufacturing Growth. *J. Reg. Sci.*, August 1984, *24*(3), pp. 373–89.   [G: U.S.]

Ponsard, Claude and Tranqui, Phuoc. La régionalisation floue de l'économie européenne. (With English summary.) *Revue Écon. Polit.*, January–February 1984, *94*(1), pp. 1–25.
[G: EEC]

Porto, Manuel Carlos Lopes. Os países da Península Ibérica e a problemática regional no seio da CEE. (With English summary.) *Economia (Portugal)*, October 1984, *8*(3), pp. 471–507.
[G: Spain; Portugal; EEC]

Premus, Robert and Fichtenbaum, Rudy. Labor

Turnover and the Sunbelt/Frostbelt Controversy: An Empirical Test. In *McKenzie, R. B., ed. (II)*, 1984, *1977*, pp. 119–26.   [G: U.S.]

Prentice, Richard. Comparability and Incomparability in Housing Programmes in Wales; A Spatial Analysis for 1981. *Urban Stud.*, November 1984, *21*(4), pp. 427–38.   [C: U.K.]

Pulver, Glen C. The Application of Comprehensive Community Economic Analysis. *Rev. Reg. Stud.*, Spring 1984, *14*(2), pp. 24–28.
[G: U.S.]

Quigley, John M. Residential Energy Standards and the Housing Market: A Regional Analysis. *Int. Reg. Sci. Rev.*, December 1984, *9*(3), pp. 201–16.   [G: U.S.]

Raab, Raymond L. Statistical Determinants of Several Retail Activities for Various Homogeneous Regions in the State of Minnesota. *Reg. Sci. Persp.*, 1984, *14*(1), pp. 40–51.
[G: U.S.]

Reed, J. David and Hoag, John H. Regional Coalmining Employment in the United States from 1985 to 2000. *Growth Change*, July 1984, *15*(3), pp. 43–50.   [G: U.S.]

Richardson, Harry W. An Urban Development Strategy for Kenya. In *Ghosh, P. K., ed., no. 2*, 1984, *1980*, pp. 287–311.   [G: Kenya]

Riefler, Roger F. and Lamphear, F. Charles. Climate and Manufacturing Location. *Reg. Sci. Persp.*, 1984, *14*(2), pp. 46–59.   [G: U.S.]

Ringleb, Al. Sectoral Shifts and U.S. Regional Economic Growth, 1953–73. *Reg. Sci. Persp.*, 1984, *14*(2), pp. 60–80.   [G: U.S.]

Rosen, Richard J. Regional Variations in Employment and Unemployment during 1970–82. *Mon. Lab. Rev.*, February 1984, *107*(2), pp. 38–45.   [G: U.S.]

Rothwell, Roy. Creating a Regional Innovation-oriented Infrastructure: The Role of Public Procurement. *Ann. Pub. Co-op. Econ.*, April–June 1984, *55*(2), pp. 159–72.   [G: U.K.]

Salvatore, Dominick. An Econometric Model of Internal Migration and Development: Extensions and Tests. *Reg. Sci. Urban Econ.*, February 1984, *14*(1), pp. 77–87.   [G: Italy]

Saraceno, Pasquale. I divari interni al Mezzogiorno. (The Disequilibria within Southern Italy. With English summary.) *Bancaria*, September 1984, *40*(9), pp. 856–61.   [G: Italy]

Savoie, Donald J. The Toppling of DREE and Prospects for Regional Economic Development. *Can. Public Policy*, September 1984, *10*(3), pp. 328–37.   [G: Canada]

Saxenian, AnnaLee. The Urban Contradictions of Silicon Valley: Regional Growth and the Restructuring of the Semiconductor Industry. In *Sawers, L. and Tabb, W. K., eds.*, 1984, pp. 163–97.   [G: U.S.]

Schmenner, Roger W. Energy and the Location of Industry. In *Downs, A. and Bradbury, K. L., eds.*, 1984, pp. 188–219.   [G: U.S.]

Scott, A. J. Industrial Organization and the Logic of Intra-Metropolitan Location, III: A Case Study of the Women's Dress Industry in the Greater Los Angeles Region. *Econ. Geogr.*, January 1984, *60*(1), pp. 3–27.   [G: U.S.]

Short, John. Public Finance and Devolution: Money Flows between Government and Regions in the United Kingdom. *Scot. J. Polit. Econ.*, June 1984, *31*(2), pp. 114–30. [G: U.K.]

Small, Drummond B. and Smith, Lawrence D. The Food, Drink, and Tobacco Sectors. In *Hood, N. and Young, S.*, eds., 1984, pp. 174–212. [G: U.K.]

Smith, Edward K. South Florida as a Gateway to U.S. Trade with Latin America. In *Jorge, A.; Salazar-Carrillo, J. and Sanchez, E. P.*, 1984, pp. 141. [G: U.S.; Latin America]

Smith, Stephen M. Export Orientation of Nonmanufacturing Businesses in Nonmetropolitan Communities. *Amer. J. Agr. Econ.*, May 1984, *66*(2), pp. 145–55. [G: U.S.]

Söderberg, Johan. A Long-Term Perspective on Regional Economic Development in Sweden, Ca. 1550–1914. *Scand. Econ. Hist. Rev.*, 1984, *32*(1), pp. 1–16. [G: Sweden]

Söderberg, Johan. Interrelationships between Short-term Economic and Demographic Fluctuations in a Period of Crisis: South-eastern Sweden 1866–1872. In *Bengtsson, T.; Fridlizius, G. and Ohlsson, R.*, eds., 1984, pp. 255–76. [G: Sweden]

Sokal, Robert R. Spatial Analysis in Population Biology and Regional Science. In *Andersson, Å. E.; Isard, W. and Puu, T.*, eds., 1984, pp. 241–66. [G: U.S.]

Squires, Gregory D. Capital Mobility versus Upward Mobility: The Racially Discriminatory Consequences of Plant Closings and Corporate Relocations. In *Sawers, L. and Tabb, W. K.*, eds., 1984, pp. 152–62.

Stamas, George D. State and Regional Employment and Unemployment in 1983. *Mon. Lab. Rev.*, September 1984, *107*(9), pp. 9–15. [G: U.S.]

Steeley, G. C. A Local Authority Perspective on the RSA Inquiry into Regional Problems in the UK. *Reg. Stud.*, August 1984, *18*(4), pp. 352–57. [G: U.K.]

Steinnes, Donald N. Business Climate, Tax Incentives, and Regional Economic Development. *Growth Change*, April 1984, *15*(2), pp. 38–47. [G: U.S.]

Storper, Michael. Who Benefits from Industrial Decentralization? Social Power in the Labour Market, Income Distribution and Spatial Policy in Brazil. *Reg. Stud.*, April 1984, *18*(2), pp. 143–64. [G: Brazil]

Strickland, Donald and Aiken, Michael. Corporate Influence and the German Urban System: Headquarters Location of German Industrial Corporations, 1950–1982. *Econ. Geogr.*, January 1984, *60*(1), pp. 38–54. [G: Germany]

Syverson, William M. Identification of Regional Wage Leadership within a System of Labor Markets. *Reg. Sci. Persp.*, 1984, *14*(1), pp. 52–64. [G: U.S.]

Thomas, June Manning. Redevelopment and Redistribution. In *Porter, P. R. and Sweet, D. C.*, eds., 1984, pp. 143–59. [G: U.S.]

Thore, Sten; Kozmetsky, George and Burtis,

Michelle. Effects of Defense Spending on the Texas Economy: An Example of Concave Programming. *J. Policy Modeling*, November 1984, *6*(4), pp. 573–86. [G: U.S.]

Tickamyer, Ann R. and Duncan, Cynthia L. Economic Activity and the Quality of Life in Eastern Kentucky: A Distributional Model. *Growth Change*, October 1984, *15*(4), pp. 43–51. [G: U.S.]

Tiller, Richard B. Labor Market Efficiency and the Dynamic Behavior of Regional Unemployment Differentials. *Ann. Reg. Sci.*, November 1984, *18*(3), pp. 21–32. [G: U.S.]

Tödtling, Franz. Organizational Characteristics of Plants in Core and Peripheral Regions of Austria. *Reg. Stud.*, October 1984, *18*(5), pp. 397–411. [G: Austria]

Townroe, Peter M. and Hamer, Andrew M. Who Benefits from Industrial Decentralization? Response. *Reg. Stud.*, August 1984, *18*(4), pp. 339–44. [G: Brazil]

Townroe, Peter M. and Keen, David. Polarization Reversal in the State of São Paulo, Brazil. *Reg. Stud.*, February 1984, *18*(1), pp. 45–54. [G: Brazil]

Uri, Noel D. The Pricing and Allocation of Electrical Energy. *Energy Econ.*, April 1984, *6*(2), pp. 94–101. [G: U.S.]

Vaux, H. J., Jr. and Howitt, Richard E. Managing Water Scarcity: An Evaluation of Interregional Transfers. *Water Resources Res.*, July 1984, *20*(7), pp. 785–92. [G: U.S.]

Weinstein, Bernard L. and Rees, John. Sunbelt/Frostbelt Confrontation? In *McKenzie, R. B.*, ed. (II), 1984, *1980*, pp. 193–203. [G: U.S.]

Weiss, Frank D. The Contribution of Small Enterprise to Growth and Employment: Comment. In *Giersch, H.*, ed., 1984, pp. 23–28. [G: U.S.]

Whittington, R. C. Regional Bias in New Firm Formation in the UK. *Reg. Stud.*, June 1984, *18*(3), pp. 253–56. [G: U.K.]

Wigren, Rune. Measuring Regional Efficiency: A Method Tested on the Fabricated Metal Products Industry in Sweden, 1973–75. *Reg. Sci. Urban Econ.*, August 1984, *14*(3), pp. 363–79. [G: Sweden]

Wilmoth, David. Regional Economic Policy and the New Corporatism. In *Sawers, L. and Tabb, W. K.*, eds., 1984, pp. 235–58. [G: U.S.]

Wright, M.; Coyne, J. and Lockley, H. Regional Aspects of Management Buyouts: Some Evidence. *Reg. Stud.*, October 1984, *18*(5), pp. 428–31. [G: U.K.]

Yandle, Bruce. Environmental Control and Regional Growth. *Growth Change*, July 1984, *15*(3), pp. 39–42. [G: U.S.]

Young, Stephen. The Foreign-Owned Manufacturing Sector. In *Hood, N. and Young, S.*, eds., 1984, pp. 93–127. [G: U.K.]

Young, Stephen and Hood, Neil. Industrial Policy and the Scottish Economy. In *Hood, N. and Young, S.*, eds., 1984, pp. 28–56. [G: U.K.]

Young, Stephen and Reeves, Alan. The Engineering and Metals Sector. In *Hood, N. and Young, S.*, eds., 1984, pp. 128–73. [G: U.K.]

Zacchia, Carlo. Rural Industrialization in Italy. *J. World Trade Law*, March–April 1984, *18*(2), pp. 110–24. **[G: Italy]**

Zwicky, Heinrich. Eine Methode zur Schätzung der personellen Einkommensverteilung in den Schweizer Kantonen. (A Method of Estimating the Personal Distribution of Income in the Swiss Cantons. With English summary.) *Schweiz. Z. Volkswirtsch. Statist.*, June 1984, *120*(2), pp. 191–222. **[G: Switzerland]**

9413 Regional Economic Models and Forecasts

Bahrenberg, G.; Fischer, M. M. and Nijkamp, Peter. Methodology, Measurement and Models in Spatial Analysis: Some Major Lines of Recent Developments. In *Bahrenberg, G.; Fischer, M. M., and Nijkamp, P.*, 1984, pp. 3–31.

Batten, David F. Adaptive Learning and Multistage Compromises for Multilevel Decision Making in Macroeconomic Systems. In *Despontin, M.; Nijkamp, P. and Spronk, J., eds.*, 1984, pp. 23–53. **[G: Australia]**

Berzeg, Korhan. A Note on Statistical Approaches to Shift-Share Analysis. *J. Reg. Sci.*, May 1984, *24*(2), pp. 277–85.

Bianchi, Giuliano; Johansson, Börje and Snickars, Folke. Models as Integral Parts of Regional Information Systems: Experiences from Italy and Sweden. In *Nijkamp, P. and Rietveld, P., eds.*, 1984, pp. 203–14. **[G: Italy; Sweden]**

Black, Philip A. The Regional Income Multiplier: A Comment [Injection Leakages, Trade Repercussions and the Regional Income Multiplier]. *Scot. J. Polit. Econ.*, June 1984, *31*(2), pp. 199–201. **[G: U.K.]**

Boisvert, Richard N. Decomposing the Induced Income Changes in Inpug–Output Models. *Amer. J. Agr. Econ.*, February 1984, *66*(1), pp. 99–103.

Bon, Ranko. Comparative Stability Analysis of Multiregional Input–Output Models: Column, Row, and Leontief–Strout Gravity Coefficient Models. *Quart. J. Econ.*, November 1984, *99*(4), pp. 791–815.

Braschler, Curtis; Procter, Michael and Kuehn, John A. Comparison of Non-survey Input–Output Estimates Using Alternative Reduction Techniques. *Rev. Reg. Stud.*, Winter 1984, *14*(1), pp. 22–33. **[G: U.S.]**

Bröcker, Johannes. How Do International Trade Barriers Affect Interregional Trade? In *Andersson, Å. E.; Isard, W. and Puu, T., eds.*, 1984, pp. 219–39. **[G: EEC]**

Brouwer, J.; Gordijn, H. E. and Heida, H. R. Toward Unravelling the Interdependency between Migration and Housing Stock Development: A Policy Model. In *ter Heide, H. and Willekens, F. J., eds.*, 1984, pp. 287–307. **[G: Netherlands]**

Buhr, Walter. A Model of Regional Economic Growth Simulation Results for the Case of Population Decline. In *Steinmann, G., ed.*, 1984, pp. 147–66. **[G: W. Germany]**

Casetti, Emilio. Peripheral Growth in Mature Economies. *Econ. Geogr.*, April 1984, *60*(2), pp. 122–31.

Casetti, Emilio. Verdoorn Law and the Components of Manufacturing Productivity Growth: A Theoretical Model and an Analysis of U.S. Regional Data. In *Andersson, Å. E.; Isard, W. and Puu, T., eds.*, 1984, pp. 295–308. **[G: U.S.]**

Charles, M., et al. Un modèle de la région wallonne: outil de développement sectoriel et régional. (With English summary.) *Cah. Écon. Bruxelles*, 2nd Trimester 1984, (102), pp. 279–303. **[G: Belgium]**

Charney, Alberta H. and Taylor, Carol A. Decomposition of Ex Ante State Model Forecasting Errors. *J. Reg. Sci.*, May 1984, *24*(2), pp. 229–47. **[G: U.S.]**

Courbis, Raymond. Multiregional Modeling and Statistical Information. In *Nijkamp, P. and Rietveld, P., eds.*, 1984, pp. 193–201.

Cruz, Robert David. The Impact of Foreign Trade on the Economy of South Florida: An Econometric Model Forecast. In *Jorge, A.; Salazar-Carrillo, J. and Sanchez, E. P.*, 1984, pp. 143–54. **[G: U.S.; Latin America]**

Cruz, Robert David. The Impact of Foreign Trade on the Economy of South Florida: An Econometric Model Forecast. In *Salazar-Carrillo, J. and Tirado de Alonso, I., eds., no. 2*, 1984, pp. 1–13. **[G: U.S.; Latin America]**

Despontin, Marc. Interactive Economic Policy Formulation with Multiregional Econometric Models. In *Despontin, M.; Nijkamp, P. and Spronk, J., eds.*, 1984, pp. 205–20.

Fischer, M. M. Theory and Testing in Empirical Sciences. In *Bahrenberg, G.; Fischer, M. M., and Nijkamp, P.*, 1984, pp. 51–71.

Folmer, H. and Nijkamp, Peter. Linear Structural Equation Models with Latent Variables and Spatial Correlation. In *Bahrenberg, G.; Fischer, M. M., and Nijkamp, P.*, 1984, pp. 163–70.

Foot, David K. and Milne, William J. Net Migration Estimation in an Extended, Multiregional Gravity Model. *J. Reg. Sci.*, February 1984, *24*(1), pp. 119–33. **[G: Canada]**

Fortuna, Zenon and Krus, Lech. Simulation of an Interactive Method Supporting Collective Decision Making Using a Regional Development Model. In *Grauer, M. and Wierzbicki, A. P., eds.*, 1984, pp. 202–09.

Halperin, W. C. and Gale, N. Towards Behavioural Models of Spatial Choice: Some Recent Developments. In *Pitfield, D. E., ed.*, 1984, pp. 9–28.

Harrigan, Frank and Buchanan, Iain. A Quadratic Programming Approach to Input–Output Estimation and Simulation. *J. Reg. Sci.*, August 1984, *24*(3), pp. 339–58. **[G: U.K.; U.S.]**

Hauer, J. Towards Multilevel Analysis: General and Theoretical Considerations. In *Bahrenberg, G.; Fischer, M. M., and Nijkamp, P.*, 1984, pp. 117–30.

Henry, Mark S. and Martin, Thomas L. Rural Area Consumer Demand and Regional Input–

Output Analysis: Reply. *Amer. J. Agr. Econ.*, May 1984, *66*(2), pp. 176–79. **[G: U.S.]**

Hewings, G. J. D. Limited Information in Spatial Analysis and Development Planning. In *Bahrenberg, G.; Fischer, M. M., and Nijkamp, P.*, 1984, pp. 145–62. **[G: U.S.]**

Hobbs, Benjamin F. Regional Energy Facility Location Models for Power System Planning and Policy Analysis. In *Lev, B., et al., eds.*, 1984, pp. 53–66.

Hoehn, James G.; Gruben, William C. and Fomby, Thomas B. Time Series Forecasting Models of the Texas Economy: A Comparison. *Fed. Res. Bank Dallas Econ. Rev.*, May 1984, pp. 11–23. **[G: U.S.]**

Hubert, L. J., et al. Nonparametric Tests for Directional Data. In *Bahrenberg, G.; Fischer, M. M., and Nijkamp, P.*, 1984, pp. 171–89.

Isard, Walter and Smith, Christine. Incorporation of Conflict and Policy Analyses in an Integrated Multiregion Model. In *Andersson, Å. E.; Isard, W. and Puu, T., eds.*, 1984, pp. 109–31.

de Janvry, Alain. The Political Economy of Rural Development in Latin America: An Interpretation. In *Eicher, C. K. and Staatz, J. M., eds.*, 1984, *1975*, pp. 82–95. **[G: Latin America]**

Jeffers, J. N. R. The Development of Models in Urban and Regional Planning. In *Richardson, J., ed.*, 1984, *1981*, pp. 87–99.

Johnson, Thomas G. and Capps, Oral, Jr. Rural Area Consumer Demand and Regional Input–Output Analysis: Comment. *Amer. J. Agr. Econ.*, May 1984, *66*(2), pp. 173–76. **[G: U.S.]**

Jones, Donald W. Regional Economic Adjustment Mechanisms: Theory and Evidence from United States Cities, 1918–1931. *J. Reg. Sci.*, August 1984, *24*(3), pp. 391–402. **[G: U.S.]**

Jones, Donald W. and Morrow-Jones, Charles R. Local Taxation and the Consequences of Revenue Distribution Patterns. *Reg. Sci. Urban Econ.*, February 1984, *14*(1), pp. 63–76.

Jordan, Jeffrey L. and Brooks, Rusty. IO/EAM: An Input–Output Economic Assessment Model. *Southern J. Agr. Econ.*, December 1984, *16*(2), pp. 145–49.

Joubert, M. J. An Extension of the Concept of Structural Sensitivity in an Urban Model. In *Avula, X. J. R., et al.*, 1984, pp. 139–42.

Kimbell, Larry J. and Harrison, Glenn W. General Equilibrium Analysis of Regional Fiscal Incidence. In *Scarf, H. E. and Shoven, J. B., eds.*, 1984, pp. 275–313. **[G: U.S.]**

Kipnis, Baruch A. Input–Output Tables for Medium-Sized Cities: Survey Coefficients or Short-Cut Methods? A Case Study in Brazil. *J. Reg. Sci.*, August 1984, *24*(3), pp. 443–50. **[G: Brazil]**

Kuprianov, Anatoli and Lupoletti, William. The Economic Outlook for Fifth District States in 1984: Forecasts from Vector Autoregression Models. *Fed. Res. Bank Richmond Econ. Rev.*, Jan./Feb. 1984, *70*(1), pp. 12–23. **[G: U.S.]**

Lakshmanan, T. R. and Roy, Probir. Regional–National Linkages in Multiregional Models: Alternative Perspectives. In *Despontin, M.; Nijkamp, P. and Spronk, J., eds.*, 1984, pp. 183–203.

Levy, Mickey D. The Impact of Foreign Trade on the Economy of South Florida: An Econometric Model Forecast. In *Jorge, A.; Salazar-Carrillo, J. and Sanchez, E. P.*, 1984, pp. 155–56. **[G: U.S.; Latin America]**

Liew, Chong K. and Liew, Chung J. Measuring the Development Impact of a Proposed Transportation System. *Reg. Sci. Urban Econ.*, May 1984, *14*(2), pp. 175–98. **[G: U.S.]**

Liew, Chong K. and Liew, Chung J. Multi-Modal, Multi-Output, Multiregional Variable Input–Output Model. *Reg. Sci. Urban Econ.*, May 1984, *14*(2), pp. 265–81.

Liew, Chung J. Pollution-Related Variable Input–Output Model: The Tulsa SMSA as a Case Study. *J. Urban Econ.*, May 1984, *15*(3), pp. 327–49. **[G: U.S.]**

Liew, Leong H. "Tops-down" versus "Bottoms-up" Approaches to Regional Modeling. *J. Policy Modeling*, August 1984, *6*(3), pp. 351–67. **[G: Australia]**

Liew, Leong H. A Johansen Model for Regional Analysis. *Reg. Sci. Urban Econ.*, February 1984, *14*(1), pp. 129–46.

Longley, Paul A. Discrete Choice Modelling and Complex Spatial Choice: An Overview. In *Bahrenberg, G.; Fischer, M. M., and Nijkamp, P.*, 1984, pp. 375–91.

MacMillan, William D. Multiple Objective Economic Control Problems and Fuzzy Systems Analysis. In *Despontin, M.; Nijkamp, P. and Spronk, J., eds.*, 1984, pp. 239–62.

McHone, W. Warren. State Industrial Development Incentives and Employment Growth in Multistate SMSAs. *Growth Change*, October 1984, *15*(4), pp. 8–15. **[G: U.S.]**

McLure, Charles E., Jr. General Equilibrium Analysis of Regional Fiscal Incidence: Comments. In *Scarf, H. E. and Shoven, J. B., eds.*, 1984, pp. 313–17. **[G: U.S.]**

Moe, R. J.; Adams, R. C. and Scott, Michael J. Master: A Forecast Model of Regional Economic Activity. In *Lev, B., et al., eds.*, 1984, pp. 165–84. **[G: U.S.]**

Monaco, R. and Rabino, G. A. A Stochastic Treatment of a Dynamic Model for an Interacting Cities System. In *Avula, X. J. R., et al.*, 1984, pp. 326–30.

Nadji, Mehrzad and Harris, Curtis C., Jr. A Note on Regional Investment Functions. *J. Reg. Sci.*, May 1984, *24*(2), pp. 271–75.

Nijkamp, Peter; Rietveld, Piet and Snickars, Folke. A Survey of Multiregional Economic Models. In *Bahrenberg, G.; Fischer, M. M., and Nijkamp, P.*, 1984, pp. 93–115. **[G: Selected Countries]**

Nijkamp, Peter and Voogd, Henk. Multidimensional and Homogeneous Scaling in Spatial Analysis. In *Bahrenberg, G.; Fischer, M. M., and Nijkamp, P.*, 1984, pp. 201–14.

O'Brien, L. G. and Wrigley, N. A Generalised Linear Models Approach to Categorical Data Analysis: Theory and Applications in Geography and Regional Science. In *Bahrenberg, G.; Fischer, M. M., and Nijkamp, P.*, 1984, pp. 231–51.

Oosterhaven, Jan. A Family of Square and Rectangular Interregional Input–Output Tables and Models. *Reg. Sci. Urban Econ.*, November 1984, *14*(4), pp. 565–82.

Oppenheim, Norbert. Dynamic Models of Urban and Regional Systems: Some Conceptual and Methodological Issues. In *Avula, X. J. R., et al.*, 1984, pp. 172–77.

Pitfield, D. E. Discrete Choice Models in Regional Science: Introduction. In *Pitfield, D. E., ed.*, 1984, pp. 1–7.

Prasad, Pradhan H. Changing Class Relations in India's Agriculture: A Statistical Appraisal. In *Ngo, M., ed., vol. 2*, 1984, pp. 567–605. [G: India]

Rietveld, Piet. Information Systems for Regional Labor Markets. In *Nijkamp, P. and Rietveld, P., eds.*, 1984, pp. 163–76.

Ro, Young Key and Forster, D. Lynn. Regional Input–Output Analysis of an Environmental Regulation. *J. Econ. Devel.*, July 1984, *9*(1), pp. 167–88. [G: U.S.]

van Rompuy, Paul and de Bruyne, Guido. A General Framework for Analysing the Stability of Fiscal Federalism. In *Despontin, M.; Nijkamp, P. and Spronk, J., eds.*, 1984, pp. 141–53.

Rushton, Gerard. Use of Location-Allocation Models for Improving the Geographical Accessibility of Rural Services in Developing Countries. *Int. Reg. Sci. Rev.*, December 1984, *9*(3), pp. 217–40. [G: LDCs]

Sasaki, Komei and Shibata, Hiroo. Nonsurvey Methods for Projecting the Input–Output System at a Small-Region Level: Two Alternative Approaches. *J. Reg. Sci.*, February 1984, *24*(1), pp. 35–50. [G: Japan]

Scholten, H. J. Residential Mobility and Log-Linear Modelling. In *Bahrenberg, G.; Fischer, M. M., and Nijkamp, P.*, 1984, pp. 271–87. [G: Netherlands]

Sheppard, Eric. Value and Exploitation in a Capitalist Space Economy. *Int. Reg. Sci. Rev.*, November 1984, *9*(2), pp. 97–107.

Smith, Hilary H. Farmers and Economic Shocks: Ranking Texas Agricultural Production Regions. *Fed. Res. Bank Dallas Econ. Rev.*, July 1984, pp. 23–34. [G: U.S.]

Timmermans, H. J. P. Decision Models for Predicting Preferences among Multiattribute Choice Alternatives. In *Bahrenberg, G.; Fischer, M. M., and Nijkamp, P.*, 1984, pp. 337–54.

Verster, A. C. P. A Double Allocation Model for Interregional Residential and Job Mobility. In *ter Heide, H. and Willekens, F. J., eds.*, 1984, pp. 201–31. [G: Netherlands]

West, G. R.; Morison, J. B. and Jensen, R. C. A Method for the Estimation of Hybrid Interregional Input–Output Tables. *Reg. Stud.*, October 1984, *18*(5), pp. 413–21. [G: Australia]

Willekens, F. J. and Drewe, P. A Multiregional Model for Regional Demographic Projection. In *ter Heide, H. and Willekens, F. J., eds.*, 1984, pp. 309–34. [G: Netherlands]

Wolsky, Alan Martin. Disaggregating Input–Output Models. *Rev. Econ. Statist.*, May 1984, *66*(2), pp. 283–91.

**Topical Guide
To Classification Schedule**

TOPICAL GUIDE TO CLASSIFICATION SCHEDULE

This index refers to the subject index *group, category,* or *subcategory* in which the listed topic may be found. The subject index classifications include, in most cases, related topics as well. The term *category* generally indicates that the topic may be found in all of the *subcategories* of the 3-digit code; the term *group,* indicates that the topics may be found in all of the *subcategories* in the 2-digit code. The classification schedule (p. xxxiii) serves to refer the user to cross references.

ABSENTEEISM: 8240

ACCELERATOR: 0233

ACCOUNTING: firm, 5410; national income, 2210, 2212; social, 2250

ADMINISTERED PRICES: theory, 0226; empirical studies, 6110; industry, 6354

ADMINISTRATION: 513 category; business, 5131; and planning, programming, and budgeting: national, 5132, 3226, state and local, 3241; public, 5132

ADVERTISING: industry, 6354; and marketing, 5310

AFFLUENT SOCIETY: 0510, 0110

AGENT THEORY, 0228

AGING: economics of, 9180

AGGREGATION: 2118; in input-output analysis, 2220; from micro to macro, 0220, 0230

AGREEMENTS: collective, 832 category; commodity, 4220, 7130; international trade, 4220

AGRIBUSINESS: *see* CORPORATE AGRICULTURE

AGRICULTURAL: commodity exchanges, 3132, 7150; cooperatives, 7150; credit, 7140; research and innovation, 621 category; employment, 8131; marketing, 7150; outlook, 7120; productivity, 7110, 7160; situation, 7120; supply and demand analysis, 7110; surpluses, 7130

AGRICULTURE: 710 group; government programs and policy, 7130; and development, 7100, 1120

AIR TRANSPORTATION: 6150

AIRPORT: 6150, 9410

AIRCRAFT MANUFACTURING: 6314

ALLOCATION: welfare aspects, 0242; and general equilibrium, 0210

ALUMINUM INDUSTRY: 6312

ANCIENT ECONOMIC HISTORY: 043 category

ANCIENT ECONOMIC THOUGHT: 0311; individuals, 0322

ANTITRUST POLICY: 6120

APPLIANCE INDUSTRY: 6313

APPRENTICESHIP: 8110

ARBITRATION: labor, 832 category

ASSISTANCE: foreign, 4430

ATOMIC ENERGY: conservation and pollution, 7220; industries, 6352, 7230

AUCTION MARKETS: theory, 0227

AUSTRIAN SCHOOL: 0315; individuals, 0322

AUTOMATION: employment: empirical studies, 8243, theory, 8210

AUTOMOBILE MANUFACTURING: 6314

BALANCE OF PAYMENTS: 431 category; accounting, 4310; empirical studies, 4313; theory, 4312

BANK FOR INTERNATIONAL SETTLEMENTS: 4320

BANKS: central, 3116; commercial, 3120; investment, 3140; other, 3140; portfolios, 3120; savings and loan, 3140; savings, 3140; supervision and regulation of, 3120, 3140, 3116

BARGAINING: collective, 832 category; theory, 0262

BAYESIAN ANALYSIS: 2115

BENEFIT-COST ANALYSIS: theory 0242; applied, see individual fields

BEQUESTS: empirical, 9211; theoretical, 0243

BEVERAGE INDUSTRIES: 6318

BIBLIOGRAPHY: 0110; see also the GENERAL heading under each subject

BIOGRAPHY: businessmen, 040 group; history of thought, 0322

BOND MARKET: 3132

BOOK PUBLISHING: 6352

BOYCOTTS, LABOR: 833 category; 832 category

BRAIN DRAIN: 8230, 8410

BRAND PREFERENCE: 5310; and consumers, 9212

BREAK-EVEN ANALYSIS: 5120

BRETTON WOODS AGREEMENT: 4320

BUDGETS: consumers, 9211; governments: theory, 3212, national studies, 3226, state and local studies, 3241

BUILDING: construction industry, 6340; materials industry, 6317